W9-CHC-252

American Casebook Series
Hornbook Series and Basic Legal Texts
Black Letter Series and Nutshell Series

of

WEST PUBLISHING
P.O. Box 64526
St. Paul, Minnesota 55164–0526

Accounting

FARIS' ACCOUNTING AND LAW IN A NUTSHELL, 377 pages, 1984. Softcover. (Text)

FIFLIS' ACCOUNTING ISSUES FOR LAWYERS, TEACHING MATERIALS, Fourth Edition, 706 pages, 1991. Teacher's Manual available. (Casebook)

SIEGEL AND SIEGEL'S ACCOUNTING AND FINANCIAL DISCLOSURE: A GUIDE TO BASIC CONCEPTS, 259 pages, 1983. Softcover. (Text)

Administrative Law

AMAN AND MAYTON'S HORNBOOK ON ADMINISTRATIVE LAW, 917 pages, 1993. (Text)

BONFIELD AND ASIMOW'S STATE AND FEDERAL ADMINISTRATIVE LAW, 826 pages, 1989. Teacher's Manual available. (Casebook) 1993 Supplement.

GELLHORN AND LEVIN'S ADMINISTRATIVE LAW AND PROCESS IN A NUTSHELL, Third Edition, 479 pages, 1990. Softcover. (Text)

MASHAW, MERRILL, AND SHANE'S CASES AND MATERIALS ON ADMINISTRATIVE LAW—THE AMERICAN PUBLIC LAW SYSTEM, Third Edition, 1187 pages, 1992. Teacher's Manual available. (Casebook)

ROBINSON, GELLHORN AND BRUFF'S THE ADMINISTRATIVE PROCESS, Fourth Edition, approximately 1000 pages, 1993. (Casebook)

Admiralty

HEALY AND SHARPE'S CASES AND MATERIALS ON ADMIRALTY, Second Edition, 876 pages, 1986. (Casebook)

MARAIST'S ADMIRALTY IN A NUTSHELL, Second Edition, 379 pages, 1988. Softcover. (Text)

SCHOENBAUM'S HORNBOOK ON ADMIRALTY AND MARITIME LAW, Student Edition, 692 pages, 1987 with 1992 pocket part. (Text)

Agency—Partnership

DEMOTT'S FIDUCIARY OBLIGATION, AGENCY AND PARTNERSHIP: DUTIES IN ONGOING BUSINESS RELATIONSHIPS, 740 pages, 1991. Teacher's Manual available. (Casebook)

FESSLER'S ALTERNATIVES TO INCORPORATION FOR PERSONS IN QUEST OF PROFIT, Third Edition, 339 pages, 1991. Softcover. (Casebook)

HENN'S CASES AND MATERIALS ON AGENCY, PARTNERSHIP AND OTHER UNINCORPORATED BUSINESS ENTERPRISES, Second Edition, 733 pages, 1985. Teacher's Manual available. (Casebook)

REUSCHLEIN AND GREGORY'S HORNBOOK ON THE LAW OF AGENCY AND PARTNERSHIP, Second Edition, 683 pages, 1990. (Text)

SELECTED CORPORATION AND PARTNERSHIP STATUTES, RULES AND FORMS. 1993 Edition, approximately 975 pages. Softcover.

STEFFEN AND KERR'S CASES ON AGENCY-PARTNERSHIP, Fourth Edition, 859 pages, 1980. (Casebook)

STEFFEN'S AGENCY–PARTNERSHIP IN A NUTSHELL, 364 pages, 1977. Softcover. (Text)

Alternative Dispute Resolution

NOLAN–HALEY'S ALTERNATIVE DISPUTE RESOLUTION IN A NUTSHELL, 298 pages, 1992.

List current as of July, 1993

Alternative Dispute Resolution—Cont'd

Softcover. (Text)

RISKIN AND WESTBROOK'S DISPUTE RESOLUTION AND LAWYERS, 468 pages, 1987. Teacher's Manual available. (Casebook) 1993 Supplement.

RISKIN AND WESTBROOK'S DISPUTE RESOLUTION AND LAWYERS. Abridged Edition, 223 pages, 1987. Softcover. Teacher's Manual available. (Casebook) 1993 Supplement.

RISKIN'S DISPUTE RESOLUTION FOR LAWYERS VIDEO TAPES, 1992. (Available for purchase by schools and libraries.)

American Indian Law

CANBY'S AMERICAN INDIAN LAW IN A NUTSHELL, Second Edition, 336 pages, 1988. Softcover. (Text)

GETCHES, WILKINSON AND WILLIAMS' CASES AND MATERIALS ON FEDERAL INDIAN LAW, Third Edition, approximately 900 pages, 1993. Teacher's Manual expected. (Casebook)

Antitrust—see also Regulated Industries, Trade Regulation

BARNES AND STOUT'S ECONOMIC FOUNDATIONS OF REGULATION AND ANTITRUST LAW, 102 pages, 1992. Softcover. Teacher's Manual available. (Casebook)

FOX AND SULLIVAN'S CASES AND MATERIALS ON ANTITRUST, 935 pages, 1989. Teacher's Manual available. (Casebook) 1993 Supplement.

GELLHORN AND KOVACIC'S ANTITRUST LAW AND ECONOMICS IN A NUTSHELL, Fourth Edition, approximately 475 pages, 1993. Softcover. (Text)

HOVENKAMP'S BLACK LETTER ON ANTITRUST, Second Edition, 347 pages, 1993. Softcover. (Review)

HOVENKAMP'S HORNBOOK ON ECONOMICS AND FEDERAL ANTITRUST LAW, Student Edition, 414 pages, 1985. (Text)

POSNER AND EASTERBROOK'S CASES AND ECONOMIC NOTES ON ANTITRUST, Second Edition, 1077 pages, 1981. (Casebook) 1984–85 Supplement.

SULLIVAN'S HORNBOOK OF THE LAW OF ANTITRUST, 886 pages, 1977. (Text)

Appellate Advocacy—see Trial and Appellate Advocacy

Architecture and Engineering Law

SWEET'S LEGAL ASPECTS OF ARCHITECTURE, ENGINEERING AND THE CONSTRUCTION PROCESS, Fourth Edition, 889 pages, 1989. Teacher's Manual available. (Casebook)

Art Law

DUBOFF'S ART LAW IN A NUTSHELL, Second Edition, 350 pages, 1993. Softcover. (Text)

Banking Law

BANKING LAW: SELECTED STATUTES AND REGULATIONS. Softcover. 263 pages, 1991.

LOVETT'S BANKING AND FINANCIAL INSTITUTIONS LAW IN A NUTSHELL, Third Edition, 470 pages, 1992. Softcover. (Text)

SYMONS AND WHITE'S BANKING LAW: TEACHING MATERIALS, Third Edition, 818 pages, 1991. Teacher's Manual available. (Casebook)

Statutory Supplement. *See Banking Law: Selected Statutes*

Bankruptcy—see Creditors' Rights

Business Planning—see also Corporate Finance

PAINTER'S PROBLEMS AND MATERIALS IN BUSINESS PLANNING, Second Edition, 1008 pages, 1984. (Casebook) 1990 Supplement.

Statutory Supplement. *See Selected Corporation and Partnership*

Civil Procedure—see also Federal Jurisdiction and Procedure

AMERICAN BAR ASSOCIATION SECTION OF LITIGATION—READINGS ON ADVERSARIAL JUSTICE: THE AMERICAN APPROACH TO ADJUDICATION, 217 pages, 1988. Softcover. (Coursebook)

CLERMONT'S BLACK LETTER ON CIVIL PROCEDURE, Third Edition, 318 pages, 1993. Softcover. (Review)

COUND, FRIEDENTHAL, MILLER AND SEXTON'S CASES AND MATERIALS ON CIVIL PROCEDURE, Sixth Edition, approximately 1300 pages, 1993. Teacher's Manual available. (Casebook)

COUND, FRIEDENTHAL, MILLER AND SEXTON'S

Civil Procedure—Cont'd

CIVIL PROCEDURE SUPPLEMENT. Approximately 475 pages, 1993. Softcover. (Casebook Supplement)

FEDERAL RULES OF CIVIL PROCEDURE—1993–94 EDUCATIONAL EDITION. Softcover. Approximately 1200 pages, 1993.

FRIEDENTHAL, KANE AND MILLER'S HORNBOOK ON CIVIL PROCEDURE, Second Edition, approximately 1000 pages, 1993. (Text)

KANE AND LEVINE'S CIVIL PROCEDURE IN CALIFORNIA: STATE AND FEDERAL 1992 Edition, 551 pages. Softcover. (Casebook Supplement)

KANE'S CIVIL PROCEDURE IN A NUTSHELL, Third Edition, 303 pages, 1991. Softcover. (Text)

LEVINE, SLOMANSON AND WINGATE'S CALIFORNIA CIVIL PROCEDURE, CASES AND MATERIALS, 546 pages, 1991. Teacher's Manual available. (Casebook)

MARCUS, REDISH AND SHERMAN'S CIVIL PROCEDURE: A MODERN APPROACH, 1027 pages, 1989. Teacher's Manual available. (Casebook) 1991 Supplement.

MARCUS AND SHERMAN'S COMPLEX LITIGATION–CASES AND MATERIALS ON ADVANCED CIVIL PROCEDURE, Second Edition, 1035 pages, 1992. Teacher's Manual available. (Casebook)

PARK AND MCFARLAND'S COMPUTER-AIDED EXERCISES ON CIVIL PROCEDURE, Third Edition, 210 pages, 1991. Softcover. (Coursebook)

SIEGEL'S HORNBOOK ON NEW YORK PRACTICE, Second Edition, Student Edition, 1068 pages, 1991. Softcover. (Text) 1993–94 Supplement.

SLOMANSON AND WINGATE'S CALIFORNIA CIVIL PROCEDURE IN A NUTSHELL, 230 pages, 1992. Softcover. (Text)

Commercial Law

ALCES AND BENFIELD'S PAYMENT SYSTEMS: CASES, MATERIALS, AND PROBLEMS, 569 pages, 1993. Teacher's Manual available. (Casebook)

BAILEY AND HAGEDORN'S SECURED TRANSACTIONS IN A NUTSHELL, Third Edition, 390 pages, 1988. Softcover. (Text)

EPSTEIN, MARTIN, HENNING AND NICKLES' BASIC UNIFORM COMMERCIAL CODE TEACHING MATERIALS, Third Edition, 704 pages, 1988. Teacher's Manual available. (Casebook)

HENSON'S HORNBOOK ON SECURED TRANSACTIONS UNDER THE U.C.C., Second Edition, 504 pages, 1979, with 1979 pocket part. (Text)

MEYER AND SPEIDEL'S BLACK LETTER ON SALES AND LEASES OF GOODS, 317 pages, 1993. Softcover. (Review)

MURRAY AND FLECHTNER'S SALES AND LEASES: PROBLEMS AND MATERIALS ON NATIONAL AND INTERNATIONAL TRANSACTIONS, Approximately 650 pages, September, 1993 pub. Teacher's Manual available. (Casebook)

NICKLES' BLACK LETTER ON NEGOTIABLE INSTRUMENTS (AND OTHER RELATED COMMERCIAL PAPER), Second Edition, 574 pages, 1993. Softcover. (Review)

NICKLES, MATHESON AND DOLAN'S MATERIALS FOR UNDERSTANDING CREDIT AND PAYMENT SYSTEMS, 923 pages, 1987. Teacher's Manual available. (Casebook)

NORDSTROM, MURRAY AND CLOVIS' PROBLEMS AND MATERIALS ON SALES, 515 pages, 1982. (Casebook)

RUBIN AND COOTER'S THE PAYMENT SYSTEM: CASES, MATERIALS AND ISSUES, 885 pages, 1989. Teacher's Manual Available. (Casebook)

SELECTED COMMERCIAL STATUTES. Softcover. Approximately 1900 pages, 1993.

SPEIDEL AND NICKLES' NEGOTIABLE INSTRUMENTS AND CHECK COLLECTION IN A NUTSHELL, Fourth Edition, 544 pages, 1993. Softcover. (Text)

SPEIDEL, SUMMERS AND WHITE'S PAYMENT SYSTEMS: TEACHING MATERIALS, Fifth Edition, approximately 575 pages, 1993. Softcover. Teacher's Manual available. (Casebook)

SPEIDEL, SUMMERS AND WHITE'S SALES AND SECURED TRANSACTIONS: TEACHING MATERIALS, Fifth Edition, approximately 1150 pages, 1993. Teacher's Manual available. (Casebook)

SPEIDEL, SUMMERS AND WHITE'S SECURED TRANSACTIONS: TEACHING MATERIALS, Fifth

Commercial Law—Cont'd

Edition, approximately 500 pages, October, 1993 pub. Reprint from Speidel et al., Sales and Secured Transactions, Fifth Edition. Softcover. Teacher's Manual available. (Casebook)

STOCKTON AND MILLER'S SALES AND LEASES OF GOODS IN A NUTSHELL, Third Edition, 441 pages, 1992. Softcover. (Text)

STONE'S UNIFORM COMMERCIAL CODE IN A NUTSHELL, Third Edition, 580 pages, 1989. Softcover. (Text)

WHITE AND SUMMERS' HORNBOOK ON THE UNIFORM COMMERCIAL CODE, Third Edition, Student Edition, 1386 pages, 1988 with 1993 pocket part (covering Rev. Arts. 3, 4, new 2A, 4A). (Text)

Community Property

MENNELL AND BOYKOFF'S COMMUNITY PROPERTY IN A NUTSHELL, Second Edition, 432 pages, 1988. Softcover. (Text)

VERRALL AND BIRD'S CASES AND MATERIALS ON CALIFORNIA COMMUNITY PROPERTY, Fifth Edition, 604 pages, 1988. (Casebook)

Comparative Law

BARTON, GIBBS, LI AND MERRYMAN'S LAW IN RADICALLY DIFFERENT CULTURES, 960 pages, 1983. (Casebook)

GLENDON, GORDON AND OSAKWE'S COMPARATIVE LEGAL TRADITIONS: TEXT, MATERIALS AND CASES ON THE CIVIL LAW, COMMON LAW AND SOCIALIST LAW TRADITIONS, 1091 pages, 1985. (Casebook)

GLENDON, GORDON AND OSAKWE'S COMPARATIVE LEGAL TRADITIONS IN A NUTSHELL. 402 pages, 1982. Softcover. (Text)

Computers and Law

MAGGS, SOMA AND SPROWL'S COMPUTER LAW—CASES, COMMENTS, AND QUESTIONS, 731 pages, 1992. Teacher's Manual available. (Casebook)

MASON'S USING COMPUTERS IN THE LAW: AN INTRODUCTION AND PRACTICAL GUIDE, Second Edition, 288 pages, 1988. Softcover. (Coursebook)

Conflict of Laws

CRAMTON, CURRIE, KAY AND KRAMER'S CASES—COMMENTS—QUESTIONS ON CONFLICT OF LAWS, Fifth Edition, approximately 750 pages, 1993. (Casebook)

HAY'S BLACK LETTER ON CONFLICT OF LAWS, 330 pages, 1989. Softcover. (Review)

SCOLES AND HAY'S HORNBOOK ON CONFLICT OF LAWS, Student Edition, 1160 pages, 1992. (Text)

SIEGEL'S CONFLICTS IN A NUTSHELL, 470 pages, 1982. Softcover. (Text)

Constitutional Law—Civil Rights—see also First Amendment and Foreign Relations and National Security Law

ABERNATHY'S CIVIL RIGHTS AND CONSTITUTIONAL LITIGATION, CASES AND MATERIALS, Second Edition, 753 pages, 1992. (Casebook)

BARNES AND STOUT'S THE ECONOMICS OF CONSTITUTIONAL LAW AND PUBLIC CHOICE, 127 pages, 1992. Softcover. Teacher's Manual available. (Casebook)

BARRON AND DIENES' BLACK LETTER ON CONSTITUTIONAL LAW, Third Edition, 440 pages, 1991. Softcover. (Review)

BARRON AND DIENES' CONSTITUTIONAL LAW IN A NUTSHELL, Second Edition, 483 pages, 1991. Softcover. (Text)

ENGDAHL'S CONSTITUTIONAL FEDERALISM IN A NUTSHELL, Second Edition, 411 pages, 1987. Softcover. (Text)

FARBER, ESKRIDGE AND FRICKEY'S CONSTITUTIONAL LAW: THEMES FOR THE CONSTITUTION'S THIRD CENTURY, 1127 pages, 1993. Teacher's Manual available. (Casebook) 1993 Supplement.

FARBER AND SHERRY'S HISTORY OF THE AMERICAN CONSTITUTION, 458 pages, 1990. Softcover. Teacher's Manual available. (Text)

FISHER AND DEVINS' POLITICAL DYNAMICS OF CONSTITUTIONAL LAW, 333 pages, 1992. Softcover. (Casebook Supplement)

GARVEY AND ALEINIKOFF'S MODERN CONSTITUTIONAL THEORY: A READER, Second Edition, 559 pages, 1991. Softcover. (Reader)

LOCKHART, KAMISAR, CHOPER AND SHIFFRIN'S CONSTITUTIONAL LAW: CASES—COMMENTS—QUESTIONS, Seventh Edition, 1643 pages, 1991. (Casebook) 1993 Supplement.

LOCKHART, KAMISAR, CHOPER AND SHIFFRIN'S

Constitutional Law—Civil Rights—Cont'd

THE AMERICAN CONSTITUTION: CASES AND MATERIALS, Seventh Edition, 1255 pages, 1991. Abridged version of Lockhart, et al., Constitutional Law: Cases–Comments–Questions, Seventh Edition. (Casebook) 1993 Supplement.

LOCKHART, KAMISAR, CHOPER AND SHIFFRIN'S CONSTITUTIONAL RIGHTS AND LIBERTIES: CASES AND MATERIALS, Seventh Edition, 1333 pages, 1991. Reprint from Lockhart, et al., Constitutional Law: Cases–Comments–Questions, Seventh Edition. (Casebook) 1993 Supplement.

MARKS AND COOPER'S STATE CONSTITUTIONAL LAW IN A NUTSHELL, 329 pages, 1988. Softcover. (Text)

NOWAK AND ROTUNDA'S HORNBOOK ON CONSTITUTIONAL LAW, Fourth Edition, 1357 pages, 1991. (Text)

ROTUNDA'S MODERN CONSTITUTIONAL LAW: CASES AND NOTES, Fourth Edition, 1137 pages, 1993. (Casebook) 1993 Supplement.

VIEIRA'S CONSTITUTIONAL CIVIL RIGHTS IN A NUTSHELL, Second Edition, 322 pages, 1990. Softcover. (Text)

WILLIAMS' CONSTITUTIONAL ANALYSIS IN A NUTSHELL, 388 pages, 1979. Softcover. (Text)

Consumer Law—see also Commercial Law

EPSTEIN AND NICKLES' CONSUMER LAW IN A NUTSHELL, Second Edition, 418 pages, 1981. Softcover. (Text)

SELECTED COMMERCIAL STATUTES. Softcover. Approximately 1900 pages, 1993.

SPANOGLE, ROHNER, PRIDGEN AND RASOR'S CASES AND MATERIALS ON CONSUMER LAW, Second Edition, 916 pages, 1991. Teacher's Manual available. (Casebook)

Contracts

BARNES AND STOUT'S THE ECONOMICS OF CONTRACT LAW, 127 pages, 1992. Softcover. Teacher's Manual available. (Casebook)

CALAMARI AND PERILLO'S BLACK LETTER ON CONTRACTS, Second Edition, 462 pages, 1990. Softcover. (Review)

CALAMARI AND PERILLO'S HORNBOOK ON CONTRACTS, Third Edition, 1049 pages, 1987. (Text)

CALAMARI, PERILLO AND BENDER'S CASES AND PROBLEMS ON CONTRACTS, Second Edition, 905 pages, 1989. Teacher's Manual Available. (Casebook)

CORBIN'S TEXT ON CONTRACTS, One Volume Student Edition, 1224 pages, 1952. (Text)

FRIEDMAN'S CONTRACT REMEDIES IN A NUTSHELL, 323 pages, 1981. Softcover. (Text)

FULLER AND EISENBERG'S CASES ON BASIC CONTRACT LAW, Fifth Edition, 1037 pages, 1990. (Casebook)

HAMILTON, RAU AND WEINTRAUB'S CASES AND MATERIALS ON CONTRACTS, Second Edition, 916 pages, 1992. Teacher's Manual available. (Casebook)

KEYES' GOVERNMENT CONTRACTS IN A NUTSHELL, Second Edition, 557 pages, 1990. Softcover. (Text)

SCHABER AND ROHWER'S CONTRACTS IN A NUTSHELL, Third Edition, 457 pages, 1990. Softcover. (Text)

SUMMERS AND HILLMAN'S CONTRACT AND RELATED OBLIGATION: THEORY, DOCTRINE AND PRACTICE, Second Edition, 1037 pages, 1992. Teacher's Manual available. (Casebook)

Copyright—see Intellectual Property

Corporate Finance—see also Business Planning

HAMILTON'S CASES AND MATERIALS ON CORPORATION FINANCE, Second Edition, 1221 pages, 1989. (Casebook)

OESTERLE'S THE LAW OF MERGERS, ACQUISITIONS AND REORGANIZATIONS, 1096 pages, 1991. (Casebook) 1992 Supplement.

Corporations

HAMILTON'S BLACK LETTER ON CORPORATIONS, Third Edition, 732 pages, 1992. Softcover. (Review)

HAMILTON'S CASES AND MATERIALS ON CORPORATIONS—INCLUDING PARTNERSHIPS AND LIMITED PARTNERSHIPS, Fourth Edition, 1248 pages, 1990. Teacher's Manual available. (Casebook) 1990 Statutory Supplement.

HAMILTON'S THE LAW OF CORPORATIONS IN A NUTSHELL, Third Edition, 518 pages, 1991. Softcover. (Text)

Corporations—Cont'd

HENN AND ALEXANDER'S HORNBOOK ON LAWS OF CORPORATIONS, Third Edition, Student Edition, 1371 pages, 1983, with 1986 pocket part. (Text)

SELECTED CORPORATION AND PARTNERSHIP STATUTES, RULES AND FORMS. 1993 Edition, approximately 975 pages. Softcover.

SOLOMON, SCHWARTZ AND BAUMAN'S MATERIALS AND PROBLEMS ON CORPORATIONS: LAW AND POLICY, Second Edition, 1391 pages, 1988. Teacher's Manual available. (Casebook) 1992 Supplement.

Statutory Supplement. *See Selected Corporation and Partnership*

Corrections

KRANTZ' THE LAW OF CORRECTIONS AND PRISONERS' RIGHTS IN A NUTSHELL, Third Edition, 407 pages, 1988. Softcover. (Text)

KRANTZ AND BRANHAM'S CASES AND MATERIALS ON THE LAW OF SENTENCING, CORRECTIONS AND PRISONERS' RIGHTS, Fourth Edition, 619 pages, 1991. Teacher's Manual available. (Casebook) 1993 Supplement.

Creditors' Rights

BANKRUPTCY CODE, RULES AND OFFICIAL FORMS, LAW SCHOOL EDITION. Approximately 925 pages, 1993. Softcover.

EPSTEIN'S DEBTOR-CREDITOR LAW IN A NUTSHELL, Fourth Edition, 401 pages, 1991. Softcover. (Text)

EPSTEIN, LANDERS AND NICKLES' CASES AND MATERIALS ON DEBTORS AND CREDITORS, Third Edition, 1059 pages, 1987. Teacher's Manual available. (Casebook)

EPSTEIN, NICKLES AND WHITE'S HORNBOOK ON BANKRUPTCY, 1077 pages, 1992. (Text)

LOPUCKI'S PLAYER'S MANUAL FOR THE DEBTOR-CREDITOR GAME, 123 pages, 1985. Softcover. (Coursebook)

NICKLES AND EPSTEIN'S BLACK LETTER ON CREDITORS' RIGHTS AND BANKRUPTCY, 576 pages, 1989. (Review)

RIESENFELD'S CASES AND MATERIALS ON CREDITORS' REMEDIES AND DEBTORS' PROTECTION, Fourth Edition, 914 pages, 1987. (Casebook) 1990 Supplement.

WHITE AND NIMMER'S CASES AND MATERIALS ON BANKRUPTCY, Second Edition, 764 pages, 1992. Teacher's Manual available. (Casebook)

Criminal Law and Criminal Procedure—see also Corrections, Juvenile Justice

ABRAMS AND BEALE'S FEDERAL CRIMINAL LAW AND ITS ENFORCEMENT, Second Edition, approximately 990 pages, 1993. (Casebook)

BUCY'S WHITE COLLAR CRIME, CASES AND MATERIALS, 688 pages, 1992. Teacher's Manual available. (Casebook)

DIX AND SHARLOT'S CASES AND MATERIALS ON CRIMINAL LAW, Third Edition, 846 pages, 1987. (Casebook)

GRANO'S PROBLEMS IN CRIMINAL PROCEDURE, Second Edition, 176 pages, 1981. Teacher's Manual available. Softcover. (Coursebook)

HEYMANN AND KENETY'S THE MURDER TRIAL OF WILBUR JACKSON: A HOMICIDE IN THE FAMILY, Second Edition, 347 pages, 1985. (Coursebook)

ISRAEL, KAMISAR AND LAFAVE'S CRIMINAL PROCEDURE AND THE CONSTITUTION: LEADING SUPREME COURT CASES AND INTRODUCTORY TEXT. Approximately 825 pages, 1993 Edition. Softcover. (Casebook)

ISRAEL AND LAFAVE'S CRIMINAL PROCEDURE—CONSTITUTIONAL LIMITATIONS IN A NUTSHELL, Fifth Edition, 475 pages, 1993. Softcover. (Text)

JOHNSON'S CASES, MATERIALS AND TEXT ON CRIMINAL LAW, Fourth Edition, 759 pages, 1990. Teacher's Manual available. (Casebook)

JOHNSON'S CASES AND MATERIALS ON CRIMINAL PROCEDURE, 859 pages, 1988. (Casebook) 1993 Supplement.

KAMISAR, LAFAVE AND ISRAEL'S MODERN CRIMINAL PROCEDURE: CASES, COMMENTS AND QUESTIONS, Seventh Edition, 1593 pages, 1990. (Casebook) 1993 Supplement.

KAMISAR, LAFAVE AND ISRAEL'S BASIC CRIMINAL PROCEDURE: CASES, COMMENTS AND QUESTIONS, Seventh Edition, 792 pages, 1990. Softcover reprint from Kamisar, et al., Modern Criminal Procedure: Cases, Comments and Questions, Seventh Edition. (Casebook) 1993 Supplement.

Criminal Law and Criminal Procedure—Cont'd

LaFave's Modern Criminal Law: Cases, Comments and Questions, Second Edition, 903 pages, 1988. (Casebook)

LaFave and Israel's Hornbook on Criminal Procedure, Second Edition, 1309 pages, 1992 with 1992 pocket part. (Text)

LaFave and Scott's Hornbook on Criminal Law, Second Edition, 918 pages, 1986 with 1993 pocket part. (Text)

Loewy's Criminal Law in a Nutshell, Second Edition, 321 pages, 1987. Softcover. (Text)

Low's Black Letter on Criminal Law, Revised First Edition, 443 pages, 1990. Softcover. (Review)

Podgor's White Collar Crime in a Nutshell, Approximately 300 pages, 1993. Softcover. (Text)

Saltzburg and Capra's Cases and Commentary on American Criminal Procedure, Fourth Edition, 1341 pages, 1992. Teacher's Manual available. (Casebook) 1993 Supplement.

Subin, Mirsky and Weinstein's The Criminal Process: Prosecution and Defense Functions, 470 pages, 1993. Softcover. Teacher's Manual available. (Text)

Vorenberg's Cases on Criminal Law and Procedure, Second Edition, 1088 pages, 1981. Teacher's Manual available. (Casebook) 1993 Supplement.

Domestic Relations

Clark's Hornbook on Domestic Relations, Second Edition, Student Edition, 1050 pages, 1988. (Text)

Clark and Glowinsky's Cases and Problems on Domestic Relations, Fourth Edition. 1150 pages, 1990. Teacher's Manual available. (Casebook) 1992 Supplement.

Krause's Black Letter on Family Law, 314 pages, 1988. Softcover. (Review)

Krause's Cases, Comments and Questions on Family Law, Third Edition, 1433 pages, 1990. (Casebook) 1993 Supplement.

Krause's Family Law in a Nutshell, Second Edition, 444 pages, 1986. Softcover. (Text)

Economics, Law and—see also Antitrust, Regulated Industries

Barnes and Stout's Cases and Materials on Law and Economics, 538 pages, 1992. Teacher's Manual available. (Casebook)

Malloy's Law and Economics: A Comparative Approach to Theory and Practice, 166 pages, 1990. Softcover. (Text)

Education Law

Alexander and Alexander's The Law of Schools, Students and Teachers in a Nutshell, 409 pages, 1984. Softcover. (Text)

Yudof, Kirp and Levin's Educational Policy and the Law, Third Edition, 860 pages, 1992. (Casebook)

Employment Discrimination—see also Gender Discrimination

Estreicher and Harper's Cases and Materials on the Law Governing the Employment Relationship, Second Edition, 966 pages, 1992. (Casebook) 1992 Statutory Supplement.

Jones, Murphy and Belton's Cases and Materials on Discrimination in Employment, (The Labor Law Group). Fifth Edition, 1116 pages, 1987. (Casebook) 1990 Supplement.

Player's Federal Law of Employment Discrimination in a Nutshell, Third Edition, 338 pages, 1992. Softcover. (Text)

Player's Hornbook on Employment Discrimination Law, Student Edition, 708 pages, 1988. (Text)

Player, Shoben and Lieberwitz' Cases and Materials on Employment Discrimination Law, 827 pages, 1990. Teacher's Manual available. (Casebook) 1992 Supplement.

Energy and Natural Resources Law—see also Oil and Gas

Laitos' Cases and Materials on Natural Resources Law, 938 pages, 1985. Teacher's Manual available. (Casebook)

Laitos and Tomain's Energy and Natural Resources Law in a Nutshell, 554 pages, 1992. Softcover. (Text)

Selected Environmental Law Statutes—1993–94 Educational Edition. Softcover. Approximately 1300 pages, 1993.

Environmental Law—see also Energy and Natural Resources Law; Sea, Law of

CAMPBELL-MOHN, BREEN AND FUTRELL'S ENVIRONMENTAL LAW: FROM RESOURCES TO RECOVERY, (Environmental Law Institute) Approximately 975 pages, 1993. (Text)

BONINE AND MCGARITY'S THE LAW OF ENVIRONMENTAL PROTECTION: CASES—LEGISLATION—POLICIES, Second Edition, 1042 pages, 1992. (Casebook)

FINDLEY AND FARBER'S CASES AND MATERIALS ON ENVIRONMENTAL LAW, Third Edition, 763 pages, 1991. Teacher's Manual available. (Casebook) 1993 Supplement.

FINDLEY AND FARBER'S ENVIRONMENTAL LAW IN A NUTSHELL, Third Edition, 355 pages, 1992. Softcover. (Text)

PLATER, ABRAMS AND GOLDFARB'S ENVIRONMENTAL LAW AND POLICY: NATURE, LAW AND SOCIETY, 1039 pages, 1992. Teacher's Manual available. (Casebook)

RODGERS' HORNBOOK ON ENVIRONMENTAL LAW, 956 pages, 1977, with 1984 pocket part. (Text)

SELECTED ENVIRONMENTAL LAW STATUTES—1993-94 EDUCATIONAL EDITION. Softcover. Approximately 1300 pages, 1993.

Equity—see Remedies

Estate Planning—see also Trusts and Estates; Taxation—Estate and Gift

LYNN'S INTRODUCTION TO ESTATE PLANNING IN A NUTSHELL, Fourth Edition, 352 pages, 1992. Softcover. (Text)

Evidence

BERGMAN'S TRANSCRIPT EXERCISES FOR LEARNING EVIDENCE, 273 pages, 1992. Softcover. Teacher's Manual available. (Coursebook)

BROUN AND BLAKEY'S BLACK LETTER ON EVIDENCE, 269 pages, 1984. Softcover. (Review)

BROUN, MEISENHOLDER, STRONG AND MOSTELLER'S PROBLEMS IN EVIDENCE, Third Edition, 238 pages, 1988. Softcover. Teacher's Manual available. (Coursebook)

CLEARY, STRONG, BROUN AND MOSTELLER'S CASES AND MATERIALS ON EVIDENCE, Fourth Edition, 1060 pages, 1988. (Casebook)

FEDERAL RULES OF EVIDENCE FOR UNITED STATES COURTS. Softcover. Approximately 575 pages, 1993.

FRIEDMAN'S THE ELEMENTS OF EVIDENCE, 315 pages, 1991. Teacher's Manual available. (Coursebook)

GRAHAM'S FEDERAL RULES OF EVIDENCE IN A NUTSHELL, Third Edition, 486 pages, 1992. Softcover. (Text)

LEMPERT AND SALTZBURG'S A MODERN APPROACH TO EVIDENCE: TEXT, PROBLEMS, TRANSCRIPTS AND CASES, Second Edition, 1232 pages, 1983. Teacher's Manual available. (Casebook)

LILLY'S AN INTRODUCTION TO THE LAW OF EVIDENCE, Second Edition, 585 pages, 1987. (Text)

MCCORMICK, SUTTON AND WELLBORN'S CASES AND MATERIALS ON EVIDENCE, Seventh Edition, 932 pages, 1992. Teacher's Manual available. (Casebook)

MCCORMICK'S HORNBOOK ON EVIDENCE, Fourth Edition, Student Edition, 672 pages, 1992. (Text)

ROTHSTEIN'S EVIDENCE IN A NUTSHELL: STATE AND FEDERAL RULES, Second Edition, 514 pages, 1981. Softcover. (Text)

Federal Jurisdiction and Procedure

CURRIE'S CASES AND MATERIALS ON FEDERAL COURTS, Fourth Edition, 783 pages, 1990. (Casebook)

CURRIE'S FEDERAL JURISDICTION IN A NUTSHELL, Third Edition, 242 pages, 1990. Softcover. (Text)

FEDERAL RULES OF CIVIL PROCEDURE—1993-94 EDUCATIONAL EDITION. Softcover. Approximately 775 pages, 1993.

REDISH'S BLACK LETTER ON FEDERAL JURISDICTION, Second Edition, 234 pages, 1991. Softcover. (Review)

REDISH'S CASES, COMMENTS AND QUESTIONS ON FEDERAL COURTS, Second Edition, 1122 pages, 1989. (Casebook) 1992 Supplement.

WRIGHT'S HORNBOOK ON FEDERAL COURTS, Fourth Edition, Student Edition, 870 pages, 1983. (Text)

First Amendment

BARRON AND DIENES' FIRST AMENDMENT LAW IN A NUTSHELL, Approximately 450

First Amendment—Cont'd

pages, September, 1993 pub. Softcover. (Text)

GARVEY AND SCHAUER'S THE FIRST AMENDMENT: A READER, 527 pages, 1992. Softcover. (Reader)

SHIFFRIN AND CHOPER'S FIRST AMENDMENT, CASES—COMMENTS—QUESTIONS, 759 pages, 1991. Softcover. (Casebook) 1993 Supplement.

Foreign Relations and National Security Law

FRANCK AND GLENNON'S FOREIGN RELATIONS AND NATIONAL SECURITY LAW, Second Edition, approximately 1150 pages, 1993. (Casebook)

Future Interests—see Trusts and Estates

Gender Discrimination—see also Employment Discrimination

KAY'S TEXT, CASES AND MATERIALS ON SEX-BASED DISCRIMINATION, Third Edition, 1001 pages, 1988. (Casebook) 1992 Supplement.

THOMAS' SEX DISCRIMINATION IN A NUTSHELL, Second Edition, 395 pages, 1991. Softcover. (Text)

Health Law—see Medicine, Law and

Human Rights—see International Law

Immigration Law

ALEINIKOFF AND MARTIN'S IMMIGRATION: PROCESS AND POLICY, Second Edition, 1056 pages, 1991. (Casebook)

Statutory Supplement. *See Immigration and Nationality Laws*

IMMIGRATION AND NATIONALITY LAWS OF THE UNITED STATES: SELECTED STATUTES, REGULATIONS AND FORMS. Softcover. 519 pages, 1992.

WEISSBRODT'S IMMIGRATION LAW AND PROCEDURE IN A NUTSHELL, Third Edition, 497 pages, 1992. Softcover. (Text)

Indian Law—see American Indian Law

Insurance Law

DEVINE AND TERRY'S PROBLEMS IN INSURANCE LAW, 240 pages, 1989. Softcover. Teacher's Manual available. (Coursebook)

DOBBYN'S INSURANCE LAW IN A NUTSHELL, Second Edition, 316 pages, 1989. Softcover. (Text)

KEETON'S COMPUTER-AIDED AND WORKBOOK EXERCISES ON INSURANCE LAW, 255 pages, 1990. Softcover. (Coursebook)

KEETON AND WIDISS' INSURANCE LAW, Student Edition, 1359 pages, 1988. (Text)

WIDISS AND KEETON'S COURSE SUPPLEMENT TO KEETON AND WIDISS' INSURANCE LAW, 502 pages, 1988. Softcover. Teacher's Manual available. (Casebook)

WIDISS' INSURANCE: MATERIALS ON FUNDAMENTAL PRINCIPLES, LEGAL DOCTRINES AND REGULATORY ACTS, 1186 pages, 1989. Teacher's Manual available. (Casebook)

YORK AND WHELAN'S CASES, MATERIALS AND PROBLEMS ON GENERAL PRACTICE INSURANCE LAW, Second Edition, 787 pages, 1988. Teacher's Manual available. (Casebook)

Intellectual Property Law—see also Trade Regulation

CHOATE, FRANCIS AND COLLINS' CASES AND MATERIALS ON PATENT LAW, INCLUDING TRADE SECRETS, COPYRIGHTS, TRADEMARKS, Third Edition, 1009 pages, 1987. (Casebook)

HALPERN, SHIPLEY AND ABRAMS' CASES AND MATERIALS ON COPYRIGHT, 663 pages, 1992. (Casebook)

MILLER AND DAVIS' INTELLECTUAL PROPERTY—PATENTS, TRADEMARKS AND COPYRIGHT IN A NUTSHELL, Second Edition, 437 pages, 1990. Softcover. (Text)

NIMMER, MARCUS, MYERS AND NIMMER'S CASES AND MATERIALS ON COPYRIGHT AND OTHER ASPECTS OF ENTERTAINMENT LITIGATION—INCLUDING UNFAIR COMPETITION, DEFAMATION, PRIVACY, ILLUSTRATED, Fourth Edition, 1177 pages, 1991. (Casebook) Statutory Supplement. See *Selected Intellectual Property Statutes*

SELECTED INTELLECTUAL PROPERTY AND UNFAIR COMPETITION STATUTES, REGULATIONS AND TREATIES. Softcover.

International Law—see also Sea, Law of

BERMANN, DAVEY, FOX AND GOEBEL'S CASES AND MATERIALS ON EUROPEAN COMMUNITY LAW, 1218 pages, 1993. (Casebook) Statutory Supplement. *See European Economic Community: Selected Documents*

International Law—Cont'd

BUERGENTHAL'S INTERNATIONAL HUMAN RIGHTS IN A NUTSHELL, 283 pages, 1988. Softcover. (Text)

BUERGENTHAL AND MAIER'S PUBLIC INTERNATIONAL LAW IN A NUTSHELL, Second Edition, 275 pages, 1990. Softcover. (Text)

EUROPEAN COMMUNITY LAW: SELECTED DOCUMENTS. 687 pages, 1993. Softcover

FOLSOM'S EUROPEAN COMMUNITY LAW IN A NUTSHELL, 423 pages, 1992. Softcover. (Text)

FOLSOM, GORDON AND SPANOGLE'S INTERNATIONAL BUSINESS TRANSACTIONS—A PROBLEM-ORIENTED COURSEBOOK, Second Edition, 1237 pages, 1991. Teacher's Manual available. (Casebook) 1991 Documents Supplement.

FOLSOM, GORDON AND SPANOGLE'S INTERNATIONAL BUSINESS TRANSACTIONS IN A NUTSHELL, Fourth Edition, 548 pages, 1992. Softcover. (Text)

HENKIN, PUGH, SCHACHTER AND SMIT'S CASES AND MATERIALS ON INTERNATIONAL LAW, Third Edition, approximately 1500 pages, 1993. (Casebook) 1993 Documents Supplement.

INTERNATIONAL LITIGATION AND ARBITRATION: SELECTED TREATIES, STATUTES AND RULES. 277 pages, 1993. Softcover

INTERNATIONAL ORGANIZATIONS IN THEIR LEGAL SETTING: SELECTED DOCUMENTS. 371 pages, 1993. Softcover

JACKSON AND DAVEY'S CASES, MATERIALS AND TEXT ON LEGAL PROBLEMS OF INTERNATIONAL ECONOMIC RELATIONS, Second Edition, 1269 pages, 1986. (Casebook) 1989 Documents Supplement.

KIRGIS' INTERNATIONAL ORGANIZATIONS IN THEIR LEGAL SETTING, Second Edition, 1119 pages, 1993. Teacher's Manual available. (Casebook) Statutory Supplement.

LOWENFELD'S INTERNATIONAL LITIGATION AND ARBITRATION, 869 pages, 1993. Teacher's Manual available. (Casebook) Statutory Supplement. *See International Litigation: Selected Documents*

WESTON, FALK AND D'AMATO'S INTERNATIONAL LAW AND WORLD ORDER—A PROBLEM-ORIENTED COURSEBOOK, Second Edition, 1335 pages, 1990. Teacher's Manual available. (Casebook) 1990 Documents Supplement.

Interviewing and Counseling

BINDER AND PRICE'S LEGAL INTERVIEWING AND COUNSELING, 232 pages, 1977. Softcover. Teacher's Manual available. (Coursebook)

BINDER, BERGMAN AND PRICE'S LAWYERS AS COUNSELORS: A CLIENT-CENTERED APPROACH, 427 pages, 1991. Softcover. (Coursebook)

SHAFFER AND ELKINS' LEGAL INTERVIEWING AND COUNSELING IN A NUTSHELL, Second Edition, 487 pages, 1987. Softcover. (Text)

Introduction to Law—see Legal Method and Legal System

Introduction to Law Study

HEGLAND'S INTRODUCTION TO THE STUDY AND PRACTICE OF LAW IN A NUTSHELL, 418 pages, 1983. Softcover. (Text)

KINYON'S INTRODUCTION TO LAW STUDY AND LAW EXAMINATIONS IN A NUTSHELL, 389 pages, 1971. Softcover. (Text)

Judicial Process—see Legal Method and Legal System

Jurisprudence

CHRISTIE'S JURISPRUDENCE—TEXT AND READINGS ON THE PHILOSOPHY OF LAW, 1056 pages, 1973. (Casebook)

SINHA'S JURISPRUDENCE (LEGAL PHILOSOPHY) IN A NUTSHELL. 379 pages, 1993. Softcover. (Text)

Juvenile Justice

FOX'S JUVENILE COURTS IN A NUTSHELL, Third Edition, 291 pages, 1984. Softcover. (Text)

Labor and Employment Law—see also Employment Discrimination, Workers' Compensation

CONISON'S EMPLOYEE BENEFIT PLANS IN A NUTSHELL, Approximately 465 pages, 1993. Softcover. (Text)

FINKIN, GOLDMAN AND SUMMERS' LEGAL PROTECTION OF INDIVIDUAL EMPLOYEES, (The Labor Law Group). 1164 pages, 1989. (Case-

Labor and Employment Law—Cont'd

book)

GORMAN'S BASIC TEXT ON LABOR LAW—UNIONIZATION AND COLLECTIVE BARGAINING, 914 pages, 1976. (Text)

LESLIE'S LABOR LAW IN A NUTSHELL, Third Edition, 388 pages, 1992. Softcover. (Text)

NOLAN'S LABOR ARBITRATION LAW AND PRACTICE IN A NUTSHELL, 358 pages, 1979. Softcover. (Text)

OBERER, HANSLOWE, ANDERSEN AND HEINSZ' CASES AND MATERIALS ON LABOR LAW—COLLECTIVE BARGAINING IN A FREE SOCIETY, Third Edition, 1163 pages, 1986. Teacher's Manual available. (Casebook) 1986 Statutory Supplement. 1991 Case Supplement.

RABIN, SILVERSTEIN AND SCHATZKI'S LABOR AND EMPLOYMENT LAW: PROBLEMS, CASES AND MATERIALS IN THE LAW OF WORK, (The Labor Law Group). 1014 pages, 1988. Teacher's Manual available. (Casebook) 1988 Statutory Supplement.

WOLLETT, GRODIN AND WEISBERGER'S COLLECTIVE BARGAINING IN PUBLIC EMPLOYMENT, (The Labor Law Group). Fourth Edition, approximately 425 pages, 1993. (Casebook)

Land Finance—Property Security—see Real Estate Transactions

Land Use

CALLIES AND FREILICH'S CASES AND MATERIALS ON LAND USE, 1233 pages, 1986. (Casebook) 1991 Supplement.

HAGMAN AND JUERGENSMEYER'S HORNBOOK ON URBAN PLANNING AND LAND DEVELOPMENT CONTROL LAW, Second Edition, Student Edition, 680 pages, 1986. (Text)

WRIGHT AND GITELMAN'S CASES AND MATERIALS ON LAND USE, Fourth Edition, 1255 pages, 1991. Teacher's Manual available. (Casebook)

WRIGHT AND WRIGHT'S LAND USE IN A NUTSHELL, Second Edition, 356 pages, 1985. Softcover. (Text)

Legal History—see also Legal Method and Legal System

PRESSER AND ZAINALDIN'S CASES AND MATERIALS ON LAW AND JURISPRUDENCE IN AMERICAN HISTORY, Second Edition, 1092 pages, 1989. Teacher's Manual available. (Casebook)

Legal Method and Legal System—see also Legal Research, Legal Writing

BERCH, BERCH AND SPRITZER'S INTRODUCTION TO LEGAL METHOD AND PROCESS, Second Edition, 585 pages, 1992. Teacher's Manual available. (Casebook)

BODENHEIMER, OAKLEY AND LOVE'S READINGS AND CASES ON AN INTRODUCTION TO THE ANGLO-AMERICAN LEGAL SYSTEM, Second Edition, 166 pages, 1988. Softcover. (Casebook)

KEETON'S JUDGING, 842 pages, 1990. Softcover. (Coursebook)

KELSO AND KELSO'S STUDYING LAW: AN INTRODUCTION, 587 pages, 1984. (Coursebook)

KEMPIN'S HISTORICAL INTRODUCTION TO ANGLO-AMERICAN LAW IN A NUTSHELL, Third Edition, 323 pages, 1990. Softcover. (Text)

MEADOR'S AMERICAN COURTS, 113 pages, 1991. Softcover. (Text)

REYNOLDS' JUDICIAL PROCESS IN A NUTSHELL, Second Edition, 308 pages, 1991. Softcover. (Text)

Legal Research

COHEN AND OLSON'S LEGAL RESEARCH IN A NUTSHELL, Fifth Edition, 370 pages, 1992. Softcover. (Text)

COHEN, BERRING AND OLSON'S HORNBOOK ON HOW TO FIND THE LAW, Ninth Edition, 716 pages, 1989. (Text)

COHEN, BERRING AND OLSON'S FINDING THE LAW, 570 pages, 1989. Softcover reprint from Cohen, Berring and Olson's How to Find the Law, Ninth Edition. (Coursebook)

Legal Research Exercises, 4th Ed., for use with Cohen, Berring and Olson, 253 pages, 1992. Teacher's Manual available.

HAZELTON'S COMPUTER-ASSISTED LEGAL RESEARCH: THE BASICS, Approximately 70 pages, 1993. Softcover. (Coursebook)

ROMBAUER'S LEGAL PROBLEM SOLVING—ANALYSIS, RESEARCH AND WRITING, Fifth

Legal Research—Cont'd

Edition, 524 pages, 1991. Softcover. Teacher's Manual with problems available. (Coursebook)

TEPLY'S LEGAL RESEARCH AND CITATION, Fourth Edition, 436 pages, 1992. Softcover. (Coursebook)

Student Library Exercises, Fourth Edition, 276 pages, 1992. Answer Key available.

Legal Writing and Drafting

CHILD'S DRAFTING LEGAL DOCUMENTS: PRINCIPLES AND PRACTICES, Second Edition, 425 pages, 1992. Softcover. Teacher's Manual available. (Coursebook)

FELSENFELD AND SIEGEL'S WRITING CONTRACTS IN PLAIN ENGLISH, 290 pages, 1981. Softcover. (Text)

MARTINEAU'S DRAFTING LEGISLATION AND RULES IN PLAIN ENGLISH, 155 pages, 1991. Softcover. Teacher's Manual available. (Text)

MELLINKOFF'S DICTIONARY OF AMERICAN LEGAL USAGE, 703 pages, 1992. Softcover. (Text)

MELLINKOFF'S LEGAL WRITING—SENSE AND NONSENSE, 242 pages, 1982. Softcover. Teacher's Manual available. (Text)

PRATT'S LEGAL WRITING: A SYSTEMATIC APPROACH, Second Edition, 426 pages, 1993. Teacher's Manual available. (Coursebook)

RAY AND COX'S BEYOND THE BASICS: A TEXT FOR ADVANCED LEGAL WRITING, 427 pages, 1991. Softcover. Teacher's Manual available. (Text)

RAY AND RAMSFIELD'S LEGAL WRITING: GETTING IT RIGHT AND GETTING IT WRITTEN, Second Edition, approximately 350 pages, 1993. Softcover. (Text)

SQUIRES AND ROMBAUER'S LEGAL WRITING IN A NUTSHELL, 294 pages, 1982. Softcover. (Text)

STATSKY AND WERNET'S CASE ANALYSIS AND FUNDAMENTALS OF LEGAL WRITING, Third Edition, 424 pages, 1989. Teacher's Manual available. (Text)

TEPLY'S LEGAL WRITING, ANALYSIS AND ORAL ARGUMENT, 576 pages, 1990. Softcover. Teacher's Manual available. (Coursebook)

WEIHOFEN'S LEGAL WRITING STYLE, Second Edition, 332 pages, 1980. (Text)

Legislation—see also Legal Writing and Drafting

DAVIES' LEGISLATIVE LAW AND PROCESS IN A NUTSHELL, Second Edition, 346 pages, 1986. Softcover. (Text)

ESKRIDGE AND FRICKEY'S CASES AND MATERIALS ON LEGISLATION: STATUTES AND THE CREATION OF PUBLIC POLICY, 937 pages, 1988. Teacher's Manual available. (Casebook) 1992 Supplement.

STATSKY'S LEGISLATIVE ANALYSIS AND DRAFTING, Second Edition, 217 pages, 1984. Teacher's Manual available. (Text)

Local Government

FRUG'S CASES AND MATERIALS ON LOCAL GOVERNMENT LAW, 1005 pages, 1988. (Casebook) 1991 Supplement.

MCCARTHY'S LOCAL GOVERNMENT LAW IN A NUTSHELL, Third Edition, 435 pages, 1990. Softcover. (Text)

REYNOLDS' HORNBOOK ON LOCAL GOVERNMENT LAW, 860 pages, 1982 with 1993 pocket part. (Text)

VALENTE AND MCCARTHY'S CASES AND MATERIALS ON LOCAL GOVERNMENT LAW, Fourth Edition, 1158 pages, 1992. Teacher's Manual available. (Casebook)

Mass Communication Law

GILLMOR, BARRON, SIMON AND TERRY'S CASES AND COMMENT ON MASS COMMUNICATION LAW, Fifth Edition, 947 pages, 1990. (Casebook)

GINSBURG, BOTEIN AND DIRECTOR'S REGULATION OF THE ELECTRONIC MASS MEDIA: LAW AND POLICY FOR RADIO, TELEVISION, CABLE AND THE NEW VIDEO TECHNOLOGIES, Second Edition, 657 pages, 1991. (Casebook) 1991 Statutory Supplement.

ZUCKMAN, GAYNES, CARTER AND DEE'S MASS COMMUNICATIONS LAW IN A NUTSHELL, Third Edition, 538 pages, 1988. Softcover. (Text)

Medicine, Law and

FISCINA, BOUMIL, SHARPE AND HEAD'S MEDICAL LIABILITY, 487 pages, 1991. Teacher's

Medicine, Law and—Cont'd

Manual available. (Casebook)

FURROW, JOHNSON, JOST AND SCHWARTZ' HEALTH LAW: CASES, MATERIALS AND PROBLEMS, Second Edition, 1236 pages, 1991. Teacher's Manual available. (Casebook)

FURROW, JOHNSON, JOST AND SCHWARTZ' BIOETHICS: HEALTH CARE LAW AND ETHICS, Reprint from Furrow et al., Health Law, Second Edition. Softcover. Teacher's Manual available. (Casebook)

FURROW, JOHNSON, JOST AND SCHWARTZ' THE LAW OF HEALTH CARE ORGANIZATION AND FINANCE, Reprint from Furrow et al., Health Law, Second Edition. Softcover. Teacher's Manual available.

FURROW, JOHNSON, JOST AND SCHWARTZ' LIABILITY AND QUALITY ISSUES IN HEALTH CARE, Reprint from Furrow et al., Health Law, Second Edition. Softcover. Teacher's Manual available. (Casebook)

HALL AND ELLMAN'S HEALTH CARE LAW AND ETHICS IN A NUTSHELL, 401 pages, 1990. Softcover (Text)

JARVIS, CLOSEN, HERMANN AND LEONARD'S AIDS LAW IN A NUTSHELL, 349 pages, 1991. Softcover. (Text)

KING'S THE LAW OF MEDICAL MALPRACTICE IN A NUTSHELL, Second Edition, 342 pages, 1986. Softcover. (Text)

SHAPIRO AND SPECE'S CASES, MATERIALS AND PROBLEMS ON BIOETHICS AND LAW, 892 pages, 1981. (Casebook) 1991 Supplement.

Mining Law—see Energy and Natural Resources Law

Mortgages—see Real Estate Transactions

Natural Resources Law—see Energy and Natural Resources Law, Environmental Law

Negotiation

GIFFORD'S LEGAL NEGOTIATION: THEORY AND APPLICATIONS, 225 pages, 1989. Softcover. (Text)

TEPLY'S LEGAL NEGOTIATION IN A NUTSHELL, 282 pages, 1992. Softcover. (Text)

WILLIAMS' LEGAL NEGOTIATION AND SETTLEMENT, 207 pages, 1983. Softcover. Teacher's Manual available. (Coursebook)

Office Practice—see also Computers and Law, Interviewing and Counseling, Negotiation

MUNNEKE'S LAW PRACTICE MANAGEMENT: MATERIALS AND CASES, 634 pages, 1991. Teacher's Manual available. (Casebook)

Oil and Gas—see also Energy and Natural Resources Law

HEMINGWAY'S HORNBOOK ON THE LAW OF OIL AND GAS, Third Edition, Student Edition, 711 pages, 1992. (Text)

KUNTZ, LOWE, ANDERSON AND SMITH'S CASES AND MATERIALS ON OIL AND GAS LAW, Second Edition, approximately 1000 pages, 1993. (Casebook) 1993 Forms Manual.

LOWE'S OIL AND GAS LAW IN A NUTSHELL, Second Edition, 465 pages, 1988. Softcover. (Text)

Patents—see Intellectual Property

Partnership—see Agency—Partnership

Products Liability

FISCHER AND POWERS' CASES AND MATERIALS ON PRODUCTS LIABILITY, 685 pages, 1988. Teacher's Manual available. (Casebook)

PHILLIPS' PRODUCTS LIABILITY IN A NUTSHELL, Fourth Edition, approximately 325 pages, 1993. Softcover. (Text)

Professional Responsibility

ARONSON, DEVINE AND FISCH'S PROBLEMS, CASES AND MATERIALS IN PROFESSIONAL RESPONSIBILITY, 745 pages, 1985. Teacher's Manual available. (Casebook)

ARONSON AND WECKSTEIN'S PROFESSIONAL RESPONSIBILITY IN A NUTSHELL, Second Edition, 514 pages, 1991. Softcover. (Text)

DVORKIN, HIMMELSTEIN AND LESNICK'S BECOMING A LAWYER: A HUMANISTIC PERSPECTIVE ON LEGAL EDUCATION AND PROFESSIONALISM, 211 pages, 1981. Softcover. (Text)

LESNICK'S BEING A LAWYER: INDIVIDUAL CHOICE AND RESPONSIBILITY IN THE PRACTICE OF LAW, 422 pages, 1992. Softcover. Teacher's Manual available. (Coursebook)

MELLINKOFF'S THE CONSCIENCE OF A LAWYER, 304 pages, 1973. (Text)

MOLITERNO AND LEVY'S ETHICS OF THE LAWYER'S WORK, 305 pages, 1993. Softcover.

Professional Responsibility—Cont'd

Teacher's Manual available. (Coursebook)

PIRSIG AND KIRWIN'S CASES AND MATERIALS ON PROFESSIONAL RESPONSIBILITY, Fourth Edition, 603 pages, 1984. Teacher's Manual available. (Casebook)

ROTUNDA'S BLACK LETTER ON PROFESSIONAL RESPONSIBILITY, Third Edition, 492 pages, 1992. Softcover. (Review)

SCHWARTZ, WYDICK AND PERSCHBACHER'S PROBLEMS IN LEGAL ETHICS, Third Edition, 402 pages, 1993. (Coursebook)

SELECTED STATUTES, RULES AND STANDARDS ON THE LEGAL PROFESSION. Softcover. Approximately 950 pages, 1993.

SMITH AND MALLEN'S PREVENTING LEGAL MALPRACTICE, 264 pages, 1989. Reprint from Mallen and Smith's Legal Malpractice, Third Edition. (Text)

SUTTON AND DZIENKOWSKI'S CASES AND MATERIALS ON PROFESSIONAL RESPONSIBILITY FOR LAWYERS, 839 pages, 1989. Teacher's Manual available. (Casebook)

WOLFRAM'S HORNBOOK ON MODERN LEGAL ETHICS, Student Edition, 1120 pages, 1986. (Text)

WYDICK AND PERSCHBACHER'S CALIFORNIA LEGAL ETHICS, 439 pages, 1992. Softcover. (Coursebook)

Property—see also Real Estate Transactions, Land Use, Trusts and Estates

BARNES AND STOUT'S THE ECONOMICS OF PROPERTY RIGHTS AND NUISANCE LAW, 87 pages, 1992. Softcover. Teacher's Manual available. (Casebook)

BERNHARDT'S BLACK LETTER ON PROPERTY, Second Edition, 388 pages, 1991. Softcover. (Review)

BERNHARDT'S REAL PROPERTY IN A NUTSHELL, Third Edition, 475 pages, 1993. Softcover. (Text)

BOYER, HOVENKAMP AND KURTZ' THE LAW OF PROPERTY, AN INTRODUCTORY SURVEY, Fourth Edition, 696 pages, 1991. (Text)

BROWDER, CUNNINGHAM, NELSON, STOEBUCK AND WHITMAN'S CASES ON BASIC PROPERTY LAW, Fifth Edition, 1386 pages, 1989. Teacher's Manual available. (Casebook)

BRUCE, ELY AND BOSTICK'S CASES AND MATERIALS ON MODERN PROPERTY LAW, Second Edition, 953 pages, 1989. Teacher's Manual available. (Casebook)

BURKE'S PERSONAL PROPERTY IN A NUTSHELL, Second Edition, 399 pages, 1993. Softcover. (Text)

CUNNINGHAM, STOEBUCK AND WHITMAN'S HORNBOOK ON THE LAW OF PROPERTY, Second Edition, approximately 900 pages, 1993. (Text)

DONAHUE, KAUPER AND MARTIN'S CASES AND MATERIALS ON PROPERTY, AN INTRODUCTION TO THE CONCEPT AND THE INSTITUTION, Third Edition, 1189 pages, 1993. Teacher's Manual available. (Casebook)

HILL'S LANDLORD AND TENANT LAW IN A NUTSHELL, Second Edition, 311 pages, 1986. Softcover. (Text)

JOHNSON, JOST, SALSICH AND SHAFFER'S PROPERTY LAW, CASES, MATERIALS AND PROBLEMS, 908 pages, 1992. Teacher's Manual available. (Casebook)

KURTZ AND HOVENKAMP'S CASES AND MATERIALS ON AMERICAN PROPERTY LAW, Second Edition, 1232 pages, 1993. Teacher's Manual available. (Casebook)

MOYNIHAN'S INTRODUCTION TO REAL PROPERTY, Second Edition, 239 pages, 1988. (Text)

Psychiatry, Law and

REISNER AND SLOBOGIN'S LAW AND THE MENTAL HEALTH SYSTEM, CIVIL AND CRIMINAL ASPECTS, Second Edition, 1117 pages, 1990. Teacher's Manual available. (Casebook) 1992 Supplement.

Real Estate Transactions

BRUCE'S REAL ESTATE FINANCE IN A NUTSHELL, Third Edition, 287 pages, 1991. Softcover. (Text)

MAXWELL, RIESENFELD, HETLAND AND WARREN'S CASES ON CALIFORNIA SECURITY TRANSACTIONS IN LAND, Fourth Edition, 778 pages, 1992. Teacher's Manual available. (Casebook)

NELSON AND WHITMAN'S BLACK LETTER ON LAND TRANSACTIONS AND FINANCE, Second Edition, 466 pages, 1988. Softcover. (Review)

NELSON AND WHITMAN'S CASES AND MATERI-

Real Estate Transactions—Cont'd

ALS ON REAL ESTATE TRANSFER, FINANCE AND DEVELOPMENT, Fourth Edition, 1346 pages, 1992. (Casebook)

NELSON AND WHITMAN'S HORNBOOK ON REAL ESTATE FINANCE LAW, Second Edition, 941 pages, 1985 with 1989 pocket part. (Text)

Regulated Industries—see also Mass Communication Law, Banking Law

GELLHORN AND PIERCE'S REGULATED INDUSTRIES IN A NUTSHELL, Second Edition, 389 pages, 1987. Softcover. (Text)

MORGAN, HARRISON AND VERKUIL'S CASES AND MATERIALS ON ECONOMIC REGULATION OF BUSINESS, Second Edition, 666 pages, 1985. (Casebook)

Remedies

DOBBS' HORNBOOK ON REMEDIES, Second Edition, approximately 900 pages, 1993. (Text)

DOBBS AND KAVANAGH'S PROBLEMS IN REMEDIES, Second Edition, 218 pages, 1993. Softcover. Teacher's Manual available. (Coursebook)

DOBBYN'S INJUNCTIONS IN A NUTSHELL, 264 pages, 1974. Softcover. (Text)

FRIEDMAN'S CONTRACT REMEDIES IN A NUTSHELL, 323 pages, 1981. Softcover. (Text)

LEAVELL, LOVE AND NELSON'S CASES AND MATERIALS ON EQUITABLE REMEDIES, RESTITUTION AND DAMAGES, Fourth Edition, 1111 pages, 1986. Teacher's Manual available. (Casebook)

O'CONNELL'S REMEDIES IN A NUTSHELL, Second Edition, 320 pages, 1985. Softcover. (Text)

SCHOENBROD, MACBETH, LEVINE AND JUNG'S CASES AND MATERIALS ON REMEDIES: PUBLIC AND PRIVATE, 848 pages, 1990. Teacher's Manual available. (Casebook) 1992 Supplement.

YORK, BAUMAN AND RENDLEMAN'S CASES AND MATERIALS ON REMEDIES, Fifth Edition, 1270 pages, 1992. Teacher's Manual available. (Casebook)

Sea, Law of

SOHN AND GUSTAFSON'S THE LAW OF THE SEA IN A NUTSHELL, 264 pages, 1984. Softcover. (Text)

Securities Regulation

HAZEN'S HORNBOOK ON THE LAW OF SECURITIES REGULATION, Second Edition, Student Edition, 1082 pages, 1990. (Text)

RATNER'S SECURITIES REGULATION IN A NUTSHELL, Fourth Edition, 320 pages, 1992. Softcover. (Text)

RATNER AND HAZEN'S SECURITIES REGULATION: CASES AND MATERIALS, Fourth Edition, 1062 pages, 1991. Teacher's Manual available. (Casebook) 1991 Problems and Sample Documents Supplement.

Statutory Supplement. *See Securities Regulation, Selected Statutes*

SECURITIES REGULATION, SELECTED STATUTES, RULES, AND FORMS. Softcover. Approximately 1375 pages, 1993.

Sports Law

CHAMPION'S SPORTS LAW IN A NUTSHELL. 325 pages, 1993. Softcover. (Text)

SCHUBERT, SMITH AND TRENTADUE'S SPORTS LAW, 395 pages, 1986. (Text)

WEILER AND ROBERTS' CASES, MATERIALS, AND PROBLEMS ON THE LAW OF SPORTS, Approximately 765 pages, 1993. (Casebook) 1993 Statutory and Document Supplement.

Tax Policy

DODGE'S THE LOGIC OF TAX, 343 pages, 1989. Softcover. (Text)

UTZ' TAX POLICY: AN INTRODUCTION AND SURVEY OF THE PRINCIPAL DEBATES, 260 pages, 1993. Softcover. Teacher's Manual available. (Coursebook)

Tax Practice and Procedure

GARBIS, RUBIN AND MORGAN'S CASES AND MATERIALS ON TAX PROCEDURE AND TAX FRAUD, Third Edition, 921 pages, 1992. (Casebook)

MORGAN'S TAX PROCEDURE AND TAX FRAUD IN A NUTSHELL, 400 pages, 1990. Softcover. (Text)

Taxation—Corporate

KAHN AND GANN'S CORPORATE TAXATION, Third Edition, 980 pages, 1989. Teacher's Manual available. (Casebook) 1991 Supplement.

SCHWARZ AND LATHROPE'S BLACK LETTER ON

Taxation—Corporate—Cont'd

CORPORATE AND PARTNERSHIP TAXATION, 537 pages, 1991. Softcover. (Review)

WEIDENBRUCH AND BURKE'S FEDERAL INCOME TAXATION OF CORPORATIONS AND STOCKHOLDERS IN A NUTSHELL, Third Edition, 309 pages, 1989. Softcover. (Text)

Taxation—Estate & Gift—see also Estate Planning, Trusts and Estates

MCNULTY'S FEDERAL ESTATE AND GIFT TAXATION IN A NUTSHELL, Fourth Edition, 496 pages, 1989. Softcover. (Text)

PEAT AND WILLBANKS' FEDERAL ESTATE AND GIFT TAXATION: AN ANALYSIS AND CRITIQUE, 265 pages, 1991. Softcover. (Text)

PENNELL'S CASES AND MATERIALS ON INCOME TAXATION OF TRUSTS, ESTATES, GRANTORS AND BENEFICIARIES, 460 pages, 1987. Teacher's Manual available. (Casebook)

Taxation—Individual

GUNN AND WARD'S CASES, TEXT AND PROBLEMS ON FEDERAL INCOME TAXATION, Third Edition, 817 pages, 1992. Teacher's Manual available. (Casebook)

HUDSON AND LIND'S BLACK LETTER ON FEDERAL INCOME TAXATION, Fourth Edition, 410 pages, 1992. Softcover. (Review)

MCNULTY'S FEDERAL INCOME TAXATION OF INDIVIDUALS IN A NUTSHELL, Fourth Edition, 503 pages, 1988. Softcover. (Text)

POSIN'S FEDERAL INCOME TAXATION, Second Edition, approximately 550 pages, 1993. Softcover. (Text)

ROSE AND CHOMMIE'S HORNBOOK ON FEDERAL INCOME TAXATION, Third Edition, 923 pages, 1988, with 1991 pocket part. (Text)

SELECTED FEDERAL TAXATION STATUTES AND REGULATIONS. Softcover. Approximately 1700 pages, 1994.

Taxation—International

DOERNBERG'S INTERNATIONAL TAXATION IN A NUTSHELL, Second Edition, approximately 375 pages, 1993. Softcover. (Text)

KAPLAN'S FEDERAL TAXATION OF INTERNATIONAL TRANSACTIONS: PRINCIPLES, PLANNING AND POLICY, 635 pages, 1988. (Casebook)

Taxation—Partnership

BERGER AND WIEDENBECK'S CASES AND MATERIALS ON PARTNERSHIP TAXATION, 788 pages, 1989. Teacher's Manual available. (Casebook) 1991 Supplement.

BISHOP AND BROOKS' FEDERAL PARTNERSHIP TAXATION: A GUIDE TO THE LEADING CASES, STATUTES, AND REGULATIONS, 545 pages, 1990. Softcover. (Text)

BURKE'S FEDERAL INCOME TAXATION OF PARTNERSHIPS IN A NUTSHELL, 356 pages, 1992. Softcover. (Text)

SCHWARZ AND LATHROPE'S BLACK LETTER ON CORPORATE AND PARTNERSHIP TAXATION, 537 pages, 1991. Softcover. (Review)

Taxation—State & Local

GELFAND AND SALSICH'S STATE AND LOCAL TAXATION AND FINANCE IN A NUTSHELL, 309 pages, 1986. Softcover. (Text)

HELLERSTEIN AND HELLERSTEIN'S CASES AND MATERIALS ON STATE AND LOCAL TAXATION, Fifth Edition, 1071 pages, 1988. (Casebook)

Torts—see also Products Liability

BARNES AND STOUT'S THE ECONOMIC ANALYSIS OF TORT LAW, 161 pages, 1992. Softcover. Teacher's Manual available. (Casebook)

CHRISTIE AND MEEKS' CASES AND MATERIALS ON THE LAW OF TORTS, Second Edition, 1264 pages, 1990. (Casebook)

DOBBS' TORTS AND COMPENSATION—PERSONAL ACCOUNTABILITY AND SOCIAL RESPONSIBILITY FOR INJURY, Second Edition, approximately 1050 pages, 1993. Teacher's Manual available. (Casebook)

KEETON, KEETON, SARGENTICH AND STEINER'S CASES AND MATERIALS ON TORT AND ACCIDENT LAW, Second Edition, 1318 pages, 1989. (Casebook)

KIONKA'S BLACK LETTER ON TORTS, Second Edition, approximately 350 pages, 1993. Softcover. (Review)

KIONKA'S TORTS IN A NUTSHELL, Second Edition, 449 pages, 1992. Softcover. (Text)

PROSSER AND KEETON'S HORNBOOK ON TORTS, Fifth Edition, Student Edition, 1286 pages, 1984 with 1988 pocket part. (Text)

ROBERTSON, POWERS AND ANDERSON'S CASES

Torts—Cont'd

AND MATERIALS ON TORTS, 932 pages, 1989. Teacher's Manual available. (Casebook)

Trade Regulation—see also Antitrust, Regulated Industries

MCMANIS' UNFAIR TRADE PRACTICES IN A NUTSHELL, Third Edition, 471 pages, 1993. Softcover. (Text)

SCHECHTER'S BLACK LETTER ON UNFAIR TRADE PRACTICES AND INTELLECTUAL PROPERTY, Second Edition, approximately 300 pages, 1993. Softcover. (Review)

WESTON, MAGGS AND SCHECHTER'S UNFAIR TRADE PRACTICES AND CONSUMER PROTECTION, CASES AND COMMENTS, Fifth Edition, 957 pages, 1992. Teacher's Manual available. (Casebook)

Trial and Appellate Advocacy—see also Civil Procedure

APPELLATE ADVOCACY, HANDBOOK OF, Third Edition, 101 pages, 1993. Softcover. (Text)

BERGMAN'S TRIAL ADVOCACY IN A NUTSHELL, Second Edition, 354 pages, 1989. Softcover. (Text)

BINDER AND BERGMAN'S FACT INVESTIGATION: FROM HYPOTHESIS TO PROOF, 354 pages, 1984. Teacher's Manual available. (Coursebook)

CARLSON'S ADJUDICATION OF CRIMINAL JUSTICE: PROBLEMS AND REFERENCES, 130 pages, 1986. Softcover. (Casebook)

CARLSON AND IMWINKELRIED'S DYNAMICS OF TRIAL PRACTICE: PROBLEMS AND MATERIALS, 414 pages, 1989. Teacher's Manual available. (Coursebook) 1990 Supplement.

CLARY'S PRIMER ON THE ANALYSIS AND PRESENTATION OF LEGAL ARGUMENT, 106 pages, 1992. Softcover. (Text)

DESSEM'S PRETRIAL LITIGATION IN A NUTSHELL, 382 pages, 1992. Softcover. (Text)

DESSEM'S PRETRIAL LITIGATION: LAW, POLICY AND PRACTICE, 608 pages, 1991. Softcover. Teacher's Manual available. (Coursebook)

DEVINE'S NON-JURY CASE FILES FOR TRIAL ADVOCACY, 258 pages, 1991. (Coursebook)

GOLDBERG'S THE FIRST TRIAL (WHERE DO I SIT? WHAT DO I SAY?) IN A NUTSHELL, 396 pages, 1982. Softcover. (Text)

HAYDOCK, HERR, AND STEMPEL'S FUNDAMENTALS OF PRE-TRIAL LITIGATION, Second Edition, 786 pages, 1992. Softcover. Teacher's Manual available. (Coursebook)

HAYDOCK AND SONSTENG'S TRIAL: THEORIES, TACTICS, TECHNIQUES, 711 pages, 1991. Softcover. (Text)

HEGLAND'S TRIAL AND PRACTICE SKILLS IN A NUTSHELL, 346 pages, 1978. Softcover. (Text)

HORNSTEIN'S APPELLATE ADVOCACY IN A NUTSHELL, 325 pages, 1984. Softcover. (Text)

JEANS' TRIAL ADVOCACY, Second Edition, approximately 575 pages, 1993. Softcover. (Text)

LISNEK AND KAUFMAN'S DEPOSITIONS: PROCEDURE, STRATEGY AND TECHNIQUE, Law School and CLE Edition. 250 pages, 1990. Softcover. (Text)

MARTINEAU'S CASES AND MATERIALS ON APPELLATE PRACTICE AND PROCEDURE, 565 pages, 1987. (Casebook)

SONSTENG, HAYDOCK AND BOYD'S THE TRIALBOOK: A TOTAL SYSTEM FOR PREPARATION AND PRESENTATION OF A CASE, 404 pages, 1984. Softcover. (Coursebook)

WHARTON, HAYDOCK AND SONSTENG'S CALIFORNIA CIVIL TRIALBOOK, Law School and CLE Edition. 148 pages, 1990. Softcover. (Text)

Trusts and Estates

ATKINSON'S HORNBOOK ON WILLS, Second Edition, 975 pages, 1953. (Text)

AVERILL'S UNIFORM PROBATE CODE IN A NUTSHELL, Third Edition, approximately 450 pages, 1993. Softcover. (Text)

BOGERT'S HORNBOOK ON TRUSTS, Sixth Edition, Student Edition, 794 pages, 1987. (Text)

CLARK, LUSKY AND MURPHY'S CASES AND MATERIALS ON GRATUITOUS TRANSFERS, Third Edition, 970 pages, 1985. (Casebook)

DODGE'S WILLS, TRUSTS AND ESTATE PLANNING–LAW AND TAXATION, CASES AND MATERIALS, 665 pages, 1988. (Casebook)

MCGOVERN, KURTZ AND REIN'S HORNBOOK ON WILLS, TRUSTS AND ESTATES–INCLUDING

Trusts and Estates—Cont'd

TAXATION AND FUTURE INTERESTS, 996 pages, 1988. (Text)

MENNELL'S WILLS AND TRUSTS IN A NUTSHELL, 392 pages, 1979. Softcover. (Text)

SIMES' HORNBOOK ON FUTURE INTERESTS, Second Edition, 355 pages, 1966. (Text)

TURANO AND RADIGAN'S HORNBOOK ON NEW YORK ESTATE ADMINISTRATION, 676 pages, 1986 with 1991 pocket part. (Text)

UNIFORM PROBATE CODE, OFFICIAL TEXT WITH COMMENTS. 863 pages, 1991. Softcover.

WAGGONER'S FUTURE INTERESTS IN A NUTSHELL, 361 pages, 1981. Softcover. (Text)

Water Law—see also Energy and Natural Resources Law, Environmental Law

GETCHES' WATER LAW IN A NUTSHELL, Second Edition, 459 pages, 1990. Softcover. (Text)

SAX, ABRAMS AND THOMPSON'S LEGAL CONTROL OF WATER RESOURCES: CASES AND MATERIALS, Second Edition, 987 pages, 1991. Teacher's Manual available. (Casebook)

TRELEASE AND GOULD'S CASES AND MATERIALS ON WATER LAW, Fourth Edition, 816 pages, 1986. (Casebook) 1993 Supplement.

Wills—see Trusts and Estates

Workers' Compensation

HOOD, HARDY AND LEWIS' WORKERS' COMPENSATION AND EMPLOYEE PROTECTION LAWS IN A NUTSHELL, Second Edition, 361 pages, 1990. Softcover. (Text)

LITTLE, EATON AND SMITH'S CASES AND MATERIALS ON WORKERS' COMPENSATION, 537 pages, 1992. Teacher's Manual available. (Casebook)

WEST'S LAW SCHOOL ADVISORY BOARD

---

*

CASES AND MATERIALS ON
REMEDIES
Fifth Edition

By

Kenneth H. York
Professor of Law Emeritus, University of California, Los Angeles
Distinguished Professor of Law Emeritus, Pepperdine University School of Law

John A. Bauman
Professor of Law, University of California, Los Angeles

Doug Rendleman
Professor of Law, Washington & Lee University

AMERICAN CASEBOOK SERIES®

WEST PUBLISHING CO.
ST. PAUL, MINN., 1992

610 Opperman Drive
P.O. Box 64526
St. Paul, MN 55164-0526

Printed in the United States of America

Library of Congress Cataloging-in-Publication Data

York, Kenneth H.
Cases and materials on remedies / by Kenneth H. York, John A. Bauman, Doug Rendleman. — 5th ed.
p. cm. — (American casebook series)
Includes index.
ISBN 0-314-88137-9
1. Remedies (Law)—United States—Cases. I. Bauman, John A. II. Rendleman, Doug. III. Title. IV. Series.
KF9010.A7Y6 1991
347.73'77—dc20
[347.30777] 91-22873
CIP

ISBN 0-314-88137-9

(Y., B. & R.) Remedies, 5th Ed. ACB
1st Reprint—1993

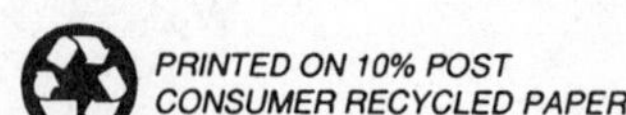

Preface to the Fifth Edition

The preface to the fourth edition begins, "As the number of editions increases, the length of prefaces should decrease." This is true.

K.H.Y.
J.A.B.
D.R.R.

Malibu, California
October, 1991

*

Summary of Contents

*

Table of Contents

PART III. REMEDIES IN CONTEXT—DISRUPTED TRANSACTIONS

Table of Cases

The principal cases are in bold type. Cases cited or discussed in the text are roman type. References are to pages. Cases cited in principal cases and within other quoted materials are not included.

CASES AND MATERIALS ON

REMEDIES

*

Part I

BASIC CHARACTERISTICS OF THE REMEDIAL SYSTEM

Chapter 1

REMEDIAL GOALS

A. INTRODUCTION

The study of pure substantive law leads to the interesting, but rather barren, conclusion that B is, or is not, liable to A—a conclusion of some concern to both A and B, and doubtless worthy of the mental involutions necessary to reach it.

Conversely the study of pure procedure—the mechanics of litigation, such as pleading, proof, and the enforcement of judgments—is equally bereft of significance pending complainant's decision of what and how much he or she wants (or may be likely to obtain) in consequence of the outrage done him or her.

The study of "Remedies" is intended to fit the important mid-range between pure substance and procedure. In the process of our study, a marked indifference to the substantive elements of the cases will be shown. A will be conceded his right against B without undue belaboring. The line of departure will be set by that unfinished classic of juridical righteousness, the statement that "For every wrong there is a remedy." We will attempt to complete the statement by determining how many truly effective remedies exist.

The basic remedial alternatives of any judicial system are relatively few and roughly classifiable. To begin with, the judgment in a case may in itself result in a declaration of rights or status that resolves the dispute without further implementation.

Beyond this, a dual categorization of a court's capabilities is necessary in terms of what it may do *for* the plaintiff and conversely what it can do *to* the defendant. These are not symmetrical, and no mirror image results.

First, what may a court do on behalf of the winning litigant?

It may:

1. Award specific relief.

If a contract is breached, defendant may be ordered to perform his promise. If property was taken, defendant may be ordered to restore it to plaintiff. If property was destroyed, defendant may be ordered to replace it. If defendant has engaged in tortious acts, he or she may be ordered to stop. Specific relief in our remedial scheme is restricted; indeed it is not allowed in a number of situations where it is a possible remedy.

2. Award substitutionary relief.

The court may award a sum of money as compensation or indemnity for the loss sustained. Compensation is the basic principle of common law remedies.

Second, what sanctions may a court impose on the losing party? The classification is much different. The court may (and there is obviously some overlapping here):

1. Punish corporeally (e.g., imprison).
2. Require the payment of money either to compensate or punish.
3. Require the transfer of title or possession of real or personal property.
4. Order the performance of certain acts.
5. Prohibit the performance of certain acts.

Refinement of this elementary classification leads to certain concepts of the judicial system operating against the person ("in personam") or his things ("in rem"), as well as "specific" as distinguished from "substitutional" relief. One jurisprudential system may emphasize one set of these refinements over the other; within our pluralistic system of common law, equity, and statutes, we will find that the common law segment has become associated with the terms "in rem" and "substitutional relief," whereas equity jurisprudence is associated with the expressions "in personam" and "specific relief." Statutory remedies may and do provide both types of relief. Generalizations here are, of course, rather untrustworthy, the result of emphasis, not rigid compartmentalization.

We now turn to the goals sought to be achieved. These are not the ineluctable result of any particular legal system, but are determined by the society that employs them. Remedial goals are affected by the views a social organization has about individual rights, property concepts, and the demands of commerce. Our jurisprudential system combines remedies developed over the centuries by statute and by the common law and equity courts; but these goals are seldom discussed or consciously articulated. One of the purposes of our study will be to isolate and examine possible remedial goals and evaluate our present remedial structure.

B. REMEDIAL GOALS IN CONTRACT CASES

1. *Fulfillment of the Aggrieved Party's Expectancy of Gain, had the Contract Been Carried Out:* to put the parties in the position they would have been in if the contract had been performed.[1]

Ideally this would consist of prevention of breach by compelling performance of the contract, but where this is not available money must fulfill the remedial goal, so far as money can.

2. *Protection of the Reliance Interest:* to compensate in money for the detriment incurred by the aggrieved party acting in reliance upon the promise to perform.

> "A contract-breaker can be charged with the amount of an expected gain that his breach has prevented, if when the contract was made he had reason to foresee that his breach would prevent it from accruing. He can be charged

1. See the landmark article, Fuller & Perdue, The Reliance Interest in Contract Damages, 46 Yale L.J. 52, 373 (1936), for this classification and analysis of the interests of the aggrieved party.

with an expenditure made in reliance on the contract if he had reason to foresee that it would be incurred and that his breach would make it futile. It is only such harms that his breach can be said to have caused. It is not enough to show that an expenditure was in reliance on the contract. It must be shown that but for his breach the expenditure would have been reimbursed by expected gains and that he had reason to know it."

A. Corbin, Contracts § 992 (1964).

3. *Protection of the Restitutionary Interest:* to restore the parties to their original positions prior to the transaction by returning benefits received in part performance.

4. *Punishment—Goal of Prevention.* The common law attains the goal of prevention by awarding the nonbreaching party's expectation; economists say that measure will prevent the breaches that the law should prevent. R. Posner, Economic Analysis of Law § 4.8 (1986). Punitive damages are normally not available for breach of contract.

5. *A Declaration of Rights or Duties (or termination thereof) under the Contract.*

> "A declaratory judgment or decree is one in which the court states or declares the existing legal relations between the parties, but does not give any order or direction to an administrative officer of the state for the enforcement of the judgment or decree. It is a remedy that may be granted either before or after a wrong has been committed. No doubt, its purpose is usually the prevention of a wrong; but it differs in form from a preventive injunction in that it commands nothing, and it authorizes no administrative officer to take action under it. By such a judgment, the court may declare the existence of legal relations other than rights and duties. It may declare the existence of privileges, powers, or immunities. These are legal relations that neither require nor permit immediate administrative enforcement."

A. Corbin, Contracts § 991 (1964).

C. REMEDIAL GOALS IN TORT CASES

1. *Specific Restoration of the Status Quo Ante.* One of the most obvious remedial goals in tort cases is to restore things as they were before the wrong. If property, real or personal, is wrongfully seized, one of the best and most satisfactory remedies is to require that the property be returned. While unavailable in many cases (e.g., personal injuries), restoration in specie is clearly a recognized and legitimate remedial goal in tort cases.

2. *Compensation in Money for the Detriment Proximately Caused by the Tortfeasor.* The indemnity principle is pervasive and dominant in the common law remedial scheme. If an injury is caused by defendant's tort, a sum of money may be awarded as compensation or indemnity for the loss.

Restatement (Second) of Torts,† § 901, General Principle *Comment a:* * * * While the law of contracts gives to a party to a contract as damages for its breach an amount equal to the benefit he would have received had the contract been performed (see Restatement, Second, Contracts, Chapter 16 (Tent. Draft)), the law of torts attempts primarily to put an injured person in a position as nearly as possible equivalent to his position prior to the tort. The law is able to do this only in varying degrees dependent upon the nature of the harm. Thus when the plaintiff has been harmed in body or mind, money damages are no equivalent but are given to compensate the plaintiff for the pain or distress or for the deterioration of the bodily structure. On the other hand, when land or chattels have been wrongfully taken from a person, he can be placed substantially in the position that he formerly occupied by giving him specific restoration of that which was taken from him, or by giving him its value, together with, in either case, compensation for the deprivation during the period of detention. In other situations, as when there has been harm to earning capacity, the law can indemnify the plaintiff for a pecuniary loss although the indemnity is not the exact equivalent, but one that approximates the pecuniary harm the injured person has suffered or is likely to suffer in the future. In determining the measure of compensation, indemnity or restitution, the law of torts ordinarily does not measure its recovery as do the rules based upon unjust enrichment, on the benefit received by the defendant. This first purpose of tort law leads to compensatory damages. (See §§ 903–906).

3. *Prevention.* The best remedy for threatened tortious interference with plaintiff's rights is a court order prohibiting such activity.

4. *A Declaration of Rights, Duties, or Status.* A judicial declaration of rights may resolve certain tort controversies, such as domestic relations, problems involving status, and threatened invasions of property rights.

Restatement (Second) of Torts § 901, *Comment b.* The second purpose of the law of torts, that is, to determine or to assert rights, results from the inability of the common law to settle controversies before some wrongful act has been done. The existence of other remedies for testing rights, such as equitable proceedings and declaratory judgments, does not displace the common law remedy of granting nominal damages. These damages are a frequent consequence of actions brought merely to determine or to assert rights. (See § 907).

5. *Punishment.* A money award or other penalty may be exacted as punishment for the wrongful act and to deter similar acts in the future.

Restatement (Second) of Torts § 901, *Comment c.* Finally, unlike the law of contracts or of restitution, the law of torts, which was once scarcely separable from the criminal law, has within it elements of punishment or deterrence. In certain types of cases punitive damages can be awarded (see §§ 908 and 909); and the measure of recovery against a conscious wrongdoer may be greater than that permitted against a tortfeasor who was not aware that his act was tortious. (See § 927, Comments *g* and *i*).

Originally the primary purpose of the law of torts was to induce the injured party and members of his family or clan to resort to the courts for relief, rather than taking the law into their own hands by attempting to wreak vengeance on the wrongdoer or by resorting to violent means of self-help. This purpose still has significance today, and both compensatory and punitive damages may be utilized to promote it.

In addition, for certain types of dignitary torts, the law serves the purpose of vindicating the injured party. Thus, in suits for defamation, invasion of privacy or interference with civil rights, the major purpose of the suit may be to obtain a public declaration that the plaintiff is right and was improperly treated. This is more than a simple determination of legal rights for which nominal damages may be sufficient, and will normally require compensatory or punitive damages.

D. REMEDIAL GOALS IN UNJUST ENRICHMENT CASES

1. *Restoration of the Benefits Unjustly Held by the Defendant, usually simply called "Restitution."*

2. *Punishment.*

3. *Prevention.*

Comment: "Unjust enrichment" describes a substantive law area as extensive as *either* tort or contract. Although the concept is primordial, a coherent body of doctrinal and remedial material has evolved only recently under the heading of "Restitution." Because "unjust enrichment" frequently arises as a result of tort or breach of contract, people understandably tend to consider restitution, restoration of the status quo ante, as a tort or contract remedy. In this sense, restitution is listed above as a remedial goal in both tort and contract situations. More realistically the substantive law giving rise to the remedial goal of restitution emerges from the enrichment of the defendant. Whether he has committed a tort or broken a contract is irrelevant except in determining whether the enrichment is unjust. In short, unjust enrichment is the substantive law, restitution is the remedy.

The subordinate goal of punishment (the sanction element) is served where the defendant is compelled to disgorge benefits in excess of the plaintiff's harm.

This book largely ignores the substantive law of contract and torts; however, we intend to include most of the material that would be covered in a separate course on "Restitution." Chapter 4 devotes special attention to Unjust Enrichment–Restitution both as a remedy and a substantive law doctrine.

E. THE HISTORICAL BACKGROUND OF MODERN REMEDIES

Introduction

Once we have stated the goal of contract, tort, and unjust enrichment remedies and determined the injured party's options, the choice of an appropriate remedy ought to be straightforward. Unfortunately, the choice is often difficult. Most state constitutions or statutes say that the common law of England is the rule of decision in state courts. These states inherited the English division between law and equity. This dual system of courts, each with its own peculiar remedies, complicates the injured party's choice of remedy. What might otherwise require the judge to ask a pragmatic question about which award best achieves the remedial goals in a particular substantive area is complicated by forcing him to inquire into the relationship between legal and equitable remedies.

Because this history has had a significant impact on modern remedies, we begin by describing the common law remedies and explaining why the overlapping and supplementary system of equity developed. These distinctions will remain important in the chapters that follow.

1. ACCOMMODATION OF REMEDIAL GOALS WITHIN THE COMMON LAW SYSTEM: A SUMMARY OF COMMON LAW ACTIONS

A. Tort Cases

1. *Specific Restitution of Property.* The common law with its origin in the feudal days always had a well-developed system to recover wrongfully withheld property. The old real actions such as writs of right and writs of entry, dating back to the Norman Conquest, provided for the specific recovery of real property. When procedural complexities destroyed the effectiveness of these remedies, they were supplanted by the writ of *ejectment.* Originally developed as a remedy to recover possession of a leasehold estate, *ejectment* was extended by a series of ingenious and elaborate fictions to provide also an expeditious procedure to try title to land.

Remedies for the specific recovery of personal property were more limited and less common. *Detinue,* one of the earliest of these remedies, developed from the writ of *debt* as a distinct form of action for the wrongful detention of specific chattels. Devised as a remedy against unfaithful bailees, it was extended to include chattels wrongfully withheld. In addition to other procedural disadvantages, the judgment in *detinue* gave the losing defendant the option of returning the chattel or paying value ascertained as of the time of trial. *Replevin,* the other action to recover personalty, originated as a remedy to test the lawfulness of a distraint. Although in form available for any wrongful taking of chattels, and, indeed, used in that way in America, *replevin* was to a large extent restricted to its original purpose in England.

Today, of course, the remedies of *replevin* and *ejectment* survive *eo nomine;* "*detinue*" may occasionally draw a blank expression. Both are largely governed by statute. These statutes afford the means of attaining this remedial goal without many of the limiting technicalities of the common law, though recent due process decisions make prejudgment recapture of chattels a less summary remedy.

2. *Compensatory Damages.* So well developed has the common law become in affording this remedy that, apart from the instances just mentioned, it is considered a "substitutional" system—money for harm. *Trespass* in its various forms had this goal for intentional injuries to the person (*vi et armis*), for taking chattels (*de bonis asportatis*), and for invasion of possession of realty (*quare clausum fregit*). *Trespass on the case* provided compensation for injuries ranging from indirect and negligent injuries to the person to nuisances and various business torts. The action of *trover* for conversion of chattels gave compensatory damages measured by the value of the chattel at the time of the conversion. While *trespass* and *trover,* and even *case,* are described in the past tense, it is erroneous to assume that these legal labels have altogether dropped out of current usage.

3. *Punishment.* From earliest times, the common law regarded punishment of the tortfeasor as a legitimate remedial objective. Damages, said Lord Mansfield, are designed not only to compensate the injured party but also as a punishment to deter future action and as proof of the jury's "detestation" of

the act itself. Originally an integral part of the remedy provided by the common law action of *trespass,* punitive or exemplary damages today are limited to conduct judged to be at some uncertain level of meanness, wantonness, or maliciousness.

4. *Prevention.* Inability to directly attain the goal of preventing harm in tort cases is a major deficiency of the common law system of substitutional money damages. Deterrence results indirectly, however, from the realization that liability for compensatory and possibly punitive damages is highly probable for tortious misconduct. An economist confirms the common law's insight. R. Posner, Economic Analysis of the Law §§ 6.1, 6.10, 6.15 (1986).

5. *Declaration of Rights, Obligations and Status.* The common law provided no remedy with a sole purpose of a judgment determining rights or status. The incidental effect of an action of *ejectment* adjudicates title; but the judgment itself orders restoration of possession. The common law approaches this remedial goal through nominal damages. Thus in actions of *trespass,* nominal damages are recoverable to vindicate plaintiff's right even though no actual injury is sustained. In cases of defamation, where the defamatory language is actionable per se, plaintiff may have his or her reputation sustained by recovering a few cents.

B. Contract Cases

The common law actions developed to meet the needs of commerce and the mercantile community in securing performance of consensual obligations. They were *account, covenant, debt* and *assumpsit.*

Account, dating from the thirteenth century, was a common law excursion into remedies for breach of obligations owed by fiduciaries. Originally it was directed toward bailiffs of manors. Under the nudge of statutes, it was extended to guardians, partners, and the like. It withered for essentially two reasons: (a) the weight of a cumbersome procedure that involved double litigation, and (b) the special claim of Chancery over fiduciaries.

Covenant is interesting because it was originally the only method to recover unliquidated damages for breach of what today would be termed executory contracts. By the end of the thirteenth century its focus was narrowed to instruments under seal; it did not lie where *debt* was applicable, where a sum certain was due until the end of the sixteenth century.

Debt is one of the oldest personal actions. *Debt* would lie to enforce a legal duty created by contract, custom, or record, so long as the duty so created was to pay a sum certain. In this context, contract meant either a specialty, an obligation under seal, or a simple contract where a quid pro quo had been exchanged for the promise to pay. *Debt* was also the proper remedy to recover statutory penalties (a duty created "by custom") and to enforce money judgments, the so-called "*debt on a record.*"

In the development of our present contractual remedies, *assumpsit* is the most important form of action; its history is by far the most complicated. *Assumpsit* derives from the amorphous writ of *trespass on the case* as shown by the original form of the action *case sur assumpsit.* Precise classification of rights as ex contractu or ex delicto was no more characteristic of fifteenth century English legal thought than it is today. Thus the breach of a contractual obligation could be conceived of as deception and hence tortious; this concept still affects the remedies which may be invoked for breach of warranty. While

England developed into a nation of traders and shopkeepers, *assumpsit* separated from the action *on the case* to become a distinct form of action for the enforcement of contractual obligations. It was first allowed for breach of express promises supported by consideration consisting of either detriment to the promisee or the exchange of mutual promises. The decision in Slade's Case in 1602 extended *assumpsit* to any action in which *debt* would lie on a simple contract. This was accomplished by implying a second promise to pay the debt upon which the action of *assumpsit* could be premised; it meant that *assumpsit* would lie where a party promised to pay a sum certain upon receipt of a benefit, the quid pro quo. This form of action became known as *indebitatus assumpsit* ("being indebted, he promised"). If defendant received a benefit in the form of either goods or services in a transaction where payment was anticipated by both parties but no fixed sum of money had been agreed upon, *indebitatus assumpsit* was not the proper action since *debt* would not lie. But once having discovered the ease with which a promise could be implied in Slade's Case, the common law courts experienced little difficulty in extending *assumpsit* by inferring a promise to pay reasonable value. This was achieved with the *quantum* counts which permitted a pleader to sue in *assumpsit* and recover either the reasonable value of services (*quantum meruit*) or the reasonable value of goods and materials (*quantum valebant*). The further development of *assumpsit* into the area of obligations imposed by law (quasi-contract) is adverted to briefly later in this Chapter and will be the subject matter of Chapter 4.

The action of *assumpsit* as thus developed assumed two forms:

a. *Special assumpsit* was an action on a simple express contract, supported by consideration, whether executory or partially executed. In strict common law pleading, if the contract was under seal it was a specialty, in common law terms, and *special assumpsit* would not lie; the proper action was either *debt* or *covenant.*

b. *General assumpsit* described actions of *assumpsit* where the pleader employed generalized formulations known as common counts. The common counts are nothing but simple, stylized forms of declarations in *indebitatus assumpsit;* with suitable deletions of excess verbiage, they are still commonplace today. The six usual varieties are: for *goods sold and delivered,* for *work done,* for *money lent,* for *money paid by the plaintiff to the use of the defendant,* for *money had and received,* and for *money due on an account stated.* The common count for *money had and received* was the vehicle seized upon by common law judges when at a later time they chose to extend the remedy of *assumpsit* into the area we now call quasi-contract.

Against this background, the attainment of the various remedial goals by the common law may be examined. Achievement of these goals has not been through disparate forms of action, but by particularizing the rules for measuring damages.

1. *Fulfillment of the Plaintiff's Expectancy Interest.* The dominant goal is to fulfill the plaintiff's expectancy interest; it is reflected in the normal "benefit of the bargain" measure of damages, the profit or gain that plaintiff would have enjoyed had the contract not broken. Should such damages be speculative and unprovable, as they frequently are, the primary goal must be abandoned. Indeed the plaintiff may elect to abandon this goal purely for reasons of his or her own.

2. *Protection of the Plaintiff's Restitutionary Interest.* The restitutionary remedial goal in contracts is to return the parties to a broken contract to their original positions. This is the antithesis of the usual aim of fulfilling the plaintiff's expectancy. The common law reaches it through disaffirmance of the contract, either rescission *in pais* or rescission at law, followed by a legal restitutionary action. It thereby subjects the whole proceeding to the limitation of those actions.

3. *Protection of the Plaintiff's Reliance Interest.* The alternate goal is compensatory in the conventional sense. The measure of damages is the plaintiff's expenditures, including work, in reliance upon the binding effect of the agreement. This rule of damages is often referred to as the "out of pocket" measure; it is subject to the proviso that the plaintiff not be engaged in an overall losing proposition where his losses would not be attributable to the defendant's breach, but to the unwisdom of the bargain.

4. *Punishment and Prevention.* As to attainment of this goal in contracts cases, the common law has defaulted. Punitive damages are virtually excluded. Any deterrent effect is derived from the litigation itself and the attainment of the other goals.

C. Unjust Enrichment Cases

1. *Restoration of Benefits.* The goal is simply to compel the defendant to return unjust gain. The possessory actions at common law, *ejectment, replevin,* and *detinue,* suffice to a point. Where it became necessary to value defendant's enrichment in money, the common law eventually utilized the common counts of *general assumpsit* to reach the goal of restitution. This odd development gave rise to a peculiar body of doctrine entitled "quasi-contract," together with the somewhat parallel development of restitutionary theory and practice. It warrants treatment, as has already been repeatedly promised, in a separate chapter.

2. *Punishment and Prevention.* Restitution is not always based on detriment to the plaintiff; but the additional goal of punishment by inflicting punitive monetary awards has been disclaimed. Where unjust enrichment derives from defendant's tortious conduct, however, the punitive factor may enter. Recently the instances of the outright imposition of punitive damages in addition to a restitution award have increased. Moreover, the common law developed no effective preventive remedy.

D. Status

A few instances have been mentioned whereby the common law achieved a declaration of rights, obligations, etc., without further remedial action, but no common law action for a declaratory judgment as such evolved. Nor, given the substitutionary characteristic of legal remedies, could it be expected. Besides, such status matters as marriage, divorce, etc. could be safely entrusted to ecclesiastical tribunals.

E. Conclusion

Even this barest sketch of the way the common law adopted its methods to attain remedial goals discloses glaring deficiencies. Most notable:

1. the lack of remedial devices to prevent harm; and

2. the lack of remedies to afford specific relief, except for the elementary possessory actions of *replevin, detinue,* and *ejectment.*

2. HISTORY AND DEVELOPMENT OF THE CHANCERY COURT

E. MORGAN, THE STUDY OF LAW

9–13 (2nd ed. 1948).

Reproduced with permission of Callaghan & Company.

Court of Chancery. It will be remembered that immediately after the Norman Conquest justice for the ordinary man in the usual case was administered in the local courts. The notion that royal tribunals should be made available for all men and all causes was not yet conceived. But the idea that the King and his Curia were the great reservoir of justice for the entire kingdom was implicit in the assumption that they could and would provide a remedy in the exceptional case, where for one reason or another the local courts could not function effectively. As time went on, royal justice became more and more common. The cases where the Curia, or its delegates, or the courts which evolved from it exercised jurisdiction, grew in number and variety.

The device by which actions were normally brought into the royal tribunals was a royal mandate or writ. By this writ issued in the name of the king the defendant was summoned before his justices, and they were authorized to hear and determine the controversy. Obviously neither the sovereign personally nor the Curia in assembly could handle the numerous applications for such writs. This business was committed to the Chancery, a department of government with the Chancellor at its head. And just as clearly, the Chancellor had to delegate the routine work to a body of subordinates. Set forms to fit the usual case were developed, and ordinarily the Chancellor's clerks had only to adapt them to the needs of the particular plaintiff. If no suitable form could be found, the Chancellor, in the first half of Henry III's reign, did not hesitate to manufacture a new one; and for a time it looked as if no litigant, able to pay the requisite fee, need be turned away from the courts of the crown. But in the latter half of the thirteenth century the Chancellor's power to frame new writs was greatly limited. Consequently, unless there was a formed writ which exactly or nearly fitted the applicant's case, he must generally take such inadequate relief as the inferior local courts offered, or go remediless.

But the source of royal justice was not dried up. The King and his Council could still grant relief in extraordinary cases. This was never denied. The general recognition of this power strikingly appears in the petitions made to justices on general eyre in the last years of the thirteenth century and the first part of the fourteenth. These justices were regarded as the direct representatives of the king. Litigants who could not afford to follow the regular procedure or whose adversaries were able to block the usual paths to relief, came before them in the most unconventional manner—came with petitions poorly written, badly phrased, wrongly spelled. Alice, after telling how Thomas had wronged her, said: "Alice can get no justice at all, seeing that she is poor and this Thomas is rich. Think of me, sir, for God's sake and for the Queen's soul's sake." In another prayer, she entreated: "For God's sake, Sir Justices, think of me, for I have none to help me save God and you." * * * John Feyrewyn addressed a justice thus: "Dear Sir, I cry mercy of you who are put in the place of our lord the king to do right to poor and to rich." After describing how his adversary had defrauded him, and praying a return of his money, he promised: "As soon, my lord, as I get my money, I will go to the Holy Land, and there I will pray for the King of England and for you especially, Sir John of Berewick, for I tell you that I have not a halfpenny to spend on a pleader; and so for this, dear Sir, be gracious unto me that I may get my money back." And the records show that the justices entertained these petitions and granted appropriate relief.

If mere delegates of the King and Council could thus disregard the restrictions of the formulary system, certainly the King and Council, acting directly, were beyond its limitations. Indeed, the very provisions which curbed the Chancellor expressly affirmed the power of the King and Council to grant extraordinary relief and to direct the manufacture of new writs. And the litigant who was remediless by ordinary process, was not slow to seek this source of redress. He petitioned the King or the King in Council, or the King in Parliament, because his case was unusual, or his opponent was too powerful, or the offense too heinous, or the subject matter too difficult, or the usual remedies inadequate. In handling such petitions, naturally the Chancellor's assistance and advice must be sought. His office, better than any other, must know what cases the ordinary courts could and would generally entertain. He more than any other official would be likely to have a sound judgment as to the proper remedy. And when the applications became too numerous for the King or the Council or Parliament to manage, he was the member of the official family best fitted to take them over, and his office the best equipped to care for them. And so in the reign of Edward III an ordinance directed all matters of grace to be referred to the Chancellor. Consequently suppliants began to address their prayers to the Chancellor instead of to the King or the Council. Like the poor petitioners to the justices in eyre, they prayed relief "for God and in way of charity." Like them they gave reasons why the ordinary courts could not furnish an adequate remedy. * * *

Frequently the Chancellor had but to direct the applicant to the proper court. But at times, though a common law tribunal was competent to handle the subject matter, the parties were too powerful. Again, in a case of unusual content the Chancellor might issue a new and special writ to an existing court, but the judges on motion were too likely to quash it as unwarranted. Thus it fell out that the Chancellor or his deputies often had to hear and determine cases. So in the fourteenth and fifteenth centuries the Chancellor was performing the functions of a court, and by the end of the 1400s he can be said to be the head of an independent court separate and apart from the Council.

The procedure which was developed in Chancery differed materially from that of the common law courts. The summons to the defendant directed him to appear under penalty of forfeiting a specified sum of money, and was called a subpoena. He was not advised of the details of the complaint against him, but was commanded to come in and answer before the Chancellor the complaints made by the plaintiff. When he appeared, he had to respond under oath to every charge made in plaintiff's bill. The Chancellor decided all questions both of law and fact. His court did not consider itself bound by precedent. It administered the "rules of equity and good conscience." Obviously these must have been rather elastic and indefinite; and they aroused the disapproval and contempt of the common lawyers. Selden called chancery "a roguish thing" because it had no measure more constant than the length of the Chancellor's foot. But gradually these rules lost their elasticity; decisions of the court were preserved and recorded, and they finally came to have the same effect in their proper sphere as the common law decisions in courts of common law.

As our cases * * * show, the Chancellor in the fourteenth century probably did not hesitate to take jurisdiction of a cause merely because its subject matter fell within the cognizance of the courts of common law. And he doubtless conceived of himself as applying the same rules which the common law would enforce in the same cases. His less costly and more effective procedure attracted litigants. But this fact aroused the opposition of the common law judges and lawyers and of Parliament, with the result that he was deprived of jurisdiction generally in those cases in which the common law courts could furnish a reasonable satisfactory remedy.

F. JAMES & G. HAZARD, CIVIL PROCEDURE

§ 1.5, at 14–16 (3d ed.1985).

The extensive jurisdiction of equity was not attained without a struggle. Opposition to the extension came from Parliament and later from the law courts. The struggle was fanned by equity's assertion of the right to implement its decisions by issuing injunctions restraining suitors at law from prosecuting their actions where the chancellor determined that successful prosecution of the lawsuit would result inequitably because of the existence of an equitable defense which the law court would not recognize. Matters came to a head during the reign of James I over equitable injunctions issued for similar reasons against enforcements of judgments already rendered at law. In this case the common law position was bolstered by two statutes: Praemunire, 1353, 27 Edw. III, c. 1, which denounced with severe penalties those "who * * * sue in any other court to defeat or impeach the judgment given in the King's Court," and Prohibition, 1402, 4 Hen. IV, c. 23, which provided that after judgment given in the king's courts "the parties * * * shall be thereof in peace until the judgment be undone by attaint or by error."

A typical situation in this struggle was presented by an action at law on a specialty (e.g., bond under seal) which had been obtained from the defendant by "fraud in the inducement," such as misrepresentation concerning the value or quality of something sold by plaintiff to defendant on credit where the bond in a large penal sum was given to secure payment of the purchase price. If the defendant had indeed executed the bond, knowing it was a bond, then the kind of fraud by which he was induced to execute it was not recognized in the law courts as a defense to an action on the bond. Equity, however, did recognize this kind of fraud and would entertain a suit by the debtor against the creditor (obligee on the bond) for a rescission of the bond. If the debtor succeeded in showing the fraud the chancellor would order the obligee to deliver the bond up for cancellation or to give a release of it under seal, on condition that the debtor restore to the creditor whatever benefit he had received in the course of the transaction. Equity would, in short, try to put the parties back into the position they occupied before the fraudulent transaction took place.

If the debtor discovered the fraud and brought his bill in equity before the creditor got his judgment at law, then the chancellor would enjoin the creditor from pursuing his action at law pending determination of the issue of fraud. If the chancellor found fraud, he would make this temporary injunction a permanent one as part of his final decree. If he found no fraud, he would dissolve the temporary injunction and the creditor would be free to continue prosecuting his action at law. If a judgment at law had already been obtained, effective equitable relief would necessarily involve interference with a law court's judgment.

This happened in Courtney v. Glanvil when Courtney, a young gentleman who had been defrauded in the sale of a jewel to him by Glanvil, found himself faced with a judgment on the bond he had given to secure the sale price. He exhibited his bill in chancery and the chancellor, finding fraud, decreed that Glanvil should take again his jewel and £100 (the value of other jewels sold) and give Courtney a satisfaction of the judgment at law, i.e., a written discharge of the judgment. Glanvil was imprisoned for not performing this decree and he sought a writ of habeas corpus from the King's Bench, which found that the decree violated the statute Praemunire and issued the writ.

Coke, who was then chief justice of the King's Bench and had given the judgment in Glanvil's case, and some colleagues persuaded creditors in similar cases to secure indictments against their opponents for attacking judgments of the king's courts. The chancellor, Lord Ellsmere, appealed to the king, who referred the question to a body of lawyers, with Bacon at its head. This commission found that the statutes invoked (Praemunire and Prohibition) were not leveled against the chancery but against foreign ecclesiastical courts. Moreover the report "adroitly inflated the wind-ball that has ever since gone bouncing down the ages, that the chancery '*does not assume to undo the judgment,* but *only to restrain the corrupt conscience of the party.*' " James' stamp of approval on this judgment decisively established the supremacy of equity in those situations where its rules and those of the common law came into practical conflict.

The dual system, with equity in the ascendancy, lasted for the next two and half centuries. There was some growth on each side and an increasing field of overlap. Equity, for one thing, came to develop remedies which were no longer dependent on coerced obedience but had a practical in rem effect of their own. On its part, the law developed remedies that depended upon equitable principles and let in defenses formerly cognizable only in equity.

Chapter 2

MODERN LAW OF DAMAGES

A. THE NATURE OF LEGAL DAMAGES

GAVCUS v. POTTS

United States Court of Appeals, Seventh Circuit, 1986.
808 F.2d 596.

FAIRCHILD, SENIOR CIRCUIT JUDGE. Constance Gavcus brought an action in district court against members of the Potts family for trespass and unlawful removal of silver coins from her home. The jury returned a special verdict finding an unauthorized removal of property and awarding Mrs. Gavcus the cost of installing new locks and an alarm, attorney's fees incurred in a prior action concerning the silver coins, and punitive damages. The district court set aside the jury's damage awards and entered judgment for Mrs. Gavcus for nominal damages of one dollar. Mrs. Gavcus appeals from that judgment.

Mr. Gavcus died in March of 1981. Lillian Potts was Mr. Gavcus' daughter by a prior marriage and was a residual beneficiary under her father's will. Lillian's family attended his funeral and left several days afterwards after staying with Mrs. Gavcus in her home. The Potts returned to Mrs. Gavcus' home the day after they left and, in her absence, removed a large quantity of silver coins valued at more than $150,000. The deputy who investigated the removal of the coins contacted Mrs. Potts, who later returned the coins to the sheriff's office. A couple of weeks later, Mrs. Gavcus hired an attorney to get the coins back for her. The attorney initiated a proceeding pursuant to § 968.20 of the Wisconsin Statutes for return of the coins. * * * The circuit court determined that the coins belonged to Mrs. Gavcus individually and ordered their return. * * * Mrs. Gavcus then brought the suit at bar for damages, including the attorney fees she incurred in the prior litigation.

Mrs. Gavcus did not claim any physical injury to the real property. The court did allow her to offer evidence of the cost of new locks and the burglar alarm she installed after the removal of the coins, and of the amount of attorney's fees incurred in the earlier litigation. Apparently the district court had some doubt as to the propriety of these items of damage and chose to admit the evidence and submit questions concerning those items in a special verdict, and to address the legal questions after the verdict was returned. The appeal arises from the court's determination that these items were not properly recoverable as damages. The jury had awarded by special verdict $3,126 for the cost of locks and a burglar alarm and $12,000 in attorney's fees.

Nominal compensatory damages can be awarded when no actual or substantial injury has been alleged or proved, since the law infers some damage from the unauthorized entry of land. Additionally, compensatory damages can be awarded for actual or substantial injury to realty. These latter damages are generally measured by the cost of restoring the property to its former condition or by the change in value before and after the trespass. Consequential damages can also be recovered for a trespass, since a trespasser is liable in damages for all injuries flowing from his trespass which are the natural and proximate result of it. One such compensable result of a trespass is personal injury to the owner of the land. If a trespass causes mental distress, the trespasser is liable in damages for the mental distress and any resulting illness or physical harm. [citations]

The installation of locks and a burglar alarm was not a repair of physical damage, and the cost was not recoverable as compensation for injury to property. Mrs. Gavcus' theory is that the trespass had caused an impairment of her sense of security and that the installation became reasonably necessary on account of that impairment.

We reject the theory, however, for two reasons. * * * [First,] there was a failure of proof as to the nature, extent, and causation of any emotional distress, or cost of required treatment.

Second, assuming that she could have proved that the trespass caused increased nervousness, uneasiness, and worry, she cites no authority, nor was any authority found, which shows that the cost of an improvement to property intended to alleviate distress of that type would be properly allowable as damages. * * *

In Wisconsin, attorney's fees incurred in a prior action are allowable as damages in a subsequent action only if the prior litigation was the natural and proximate result of the subsequent defendant's wrongful act and involved the plaintiff and a third party. [citations] Thus, to recover the $12,000 in attorney's fees which the jury awarded, Mrs. Gavcus must show that (1) because of the defendants' unlawful removal of the coins, (2) she became involved in litigation with a third party. We will first examine the requirement that the prior litigation involve a third party.

For a plaintiff to receive attorney's fees for prior litigation, the prior litigation must have been between the plaintiff and a third party; it cannot have been between the same parties that are involved in the subsequent lawsuit. [citations] In the above cited cases, the questions of whether third parties were involved in the prior litigation were relatively easily answered. The question is not quite so easily answered here.

Mrs. Gavcus asserts that the sheriff was the required third party. The sheriff, however, did not actively participate in the litigation, and seems to have been a mere stakeholder. By September of 1981, Mrs. Potts had appeared in the probate proceeding, seeking a determination of the title to the silver coins. Apparently, had the coins been the joint property of both Mr. and Mrs. Gavcus or an asset of the estate, Mrs. Potts' residual share would have been increased. Sometime between mid-March and December 1, 1981, the silver coins were transferred from the sheriff's possession to the possession of the personal representative. At the end of July, 1982, a trial was held on the issue of the ownership of the silver. The circuit court found that the coins were Mrs. Gavcus' individual property, obtained either through her own efforts or as gifts from Mr. Gavcus and ordered them returned to Mrs. Gavcus pursuant to her attorney's motion under § 968.20. The attorney's fees were incurred in this litigation over ownership of the coins. Whether the silver was owned jointly by Mr. and Mrs. Gavcus, was an asset of the estate, or was owned individually by Mrs. Gavcus was the essence of this entire dispute. The dispute was between Mrs. Potts and Mrs. Gavcus, both of whom were beneficiaries and both of whom are involved as parties in the case at bar. Since both the prior and present actions are between the same parties, attorney's fees are not recoverable.

There is some authority in Wisconsin which suggests that prior actions against third parties may be separated into those for which attorney's fees are available and those for which attorney's fees are not available. In *Baker v. Northwestern National Casualty Co.,* the plaintiff and his insurance company had been sued in an action in which the defendant was awarded damages beyond the plaintiff's policy amount. The plaintiff thereafter became involved in litigation concerning the garnishment of his wages, in the creation of a trust in favor of his mother, which required a divestment of some of his assets, and in obtaining legal advice about declaring bankruptcy. The plaintiff later sued his insurance company for the coverage and requested attorney's fees for the coverage suit. Although the supreme court ruled that attorney fees were not available for the coverage action itself, it suggested that fees might be obtained for some of the other actions in which the plaintiff had become involved. While in *Baker,* fees were not available for various other reasons, the court did suggest that where some portions of a plaintiff's prior litigation met all the requirements, fees could be awarded for those portions. * * *

Even if the litigation over ownership had involved a third party, Mrs. Gavcus did not fulfill the other requirement for recovery of attorney's fees—the requirement that the prior litigation was a natural and proximate result of a wrongful act by the defendant. To fulfill this requirement, Mrs. Gavcus must show that the defendants' unauthorized removal of the coins caused her to enter into the litigation. Analysis of the facts shows that the prior litigation was not proximately caused by the defendants' removal of the coins.

Mrs. Potts knew of the coins' existence prior to her removal of them from the Gavcus home. The litigation was caused by her claim that the coins were jointly owned by her father and Mrs. Gavcus or were the property of the estate, not by her resort to self-help to obtain possession of them. Since the prior litigation did not result from the taking of the silver, the second part of the test is not met and attorney's fees cannot be awarded.

Attorney's fees are not available because the prior action was not against a third party and was not naturally and proximately caused by the Potts' conduct. Both parties agree that the award of punitive damages could not be sustained unless compensatory damages had been awarded. [citation]

The judgment appealed from is AFFIRMED.

Note

Bowen v. Massachusetts, 487 U.S. 879, 893–95 (1988). Justice Stevens discussed basic distinctions between categories of damages: "Our cases have long recognized the distinction between an action at law for damages—which are intended to provide a victim with monetary compensation for an injury to his person, property, or reputation—and an equitable action for specific relief—which may include an order providing for the reinstatement of an employee with back pay, or for 'the recovery of specific property *or monies,* ejectment from land, or injunction either directing or restraining the defendant officer's actions.' Larson v. Domestic & Foreign Commerce Corp., 337 U.S. 682, 688 (1949) (emphasis added). The fact that a judicial remedy may require one party to pay money to another is not a sufficient reason to characterize the relief as 'money damages'. Thus, we have recognized that relief that orders a town to reimburse parents for educational costs that Congress intended the town to pay is not 'damages': * * *

> " 'In this Court, the Town repeatedly characterizes reimbursement as "damages," but that simply is not the case. Reimbursement merely requires the Town to belatedly pay expenses that it should have paid all along and would have borne in the first instance.' * * * School Committee of Burlington v. Department of Education of Massachusetts, 471 U.S. 359, 370–371 (1985).

"Judge Bork's explanation of the plain meaning of the critical language in this statute merits quotation in full. In his opinion for the Court of Appeals for the District of Columbia Circuit in Maryland Dept. of Human Resources v. Department of Health and Human Services, 246 U.S.App.D.C. 180, 763 F.2d 1441 (1985), he wrote:

> " 'We turn first to the question whether the relief Maryland seeks is equivalent to money damages. Maryland asked the district court for a declaratory judgment and for injunctive relief "enjoin[ing] defendants from reducing funds otherwise due to plaintiffs, or imposing any sanctions on such funds for alleged Title XX violations." * * * We are satisfied that the relief Maryland seeks here is not a claim for money damages, although it is a claim that would require the payment of money by the federal government.
>
> " 'We begin with the ordinary meaning of the words Congress employed. The term "money damages," 5 U.S.C. § 702, we think, normally refers to a sum of money used as compensatory relief. Damages are given to the plaintiff to *substitute* for a suffered loss, whereas specific remedies "are not substitute remedies at all, but attempt to give the plaintiff the very thing to which he was entitled." D. Dobbs, Handbook on the Law of Remedies 135 (1973). Thus, while in many instances an award of money is an award of damages, "[o]ccasionally a money award is also a specie remedy." Courts frequently describe equitable actions for monetary relief under a contract in exactly those terms. See, e.g., First National State Bank v. Commonwealth Federal Savings & Loan Association, 610 F.2d 164, 171 (3d Cir.1979) (specific performance of contract to borrow money); Crouch v. Crouch, 566 F.2d 486, 488 (5th Cir.1978) (contrasting lump-sum damages for breach of promise to pay monthly support payments with an order decreeing specific performance as to future installments); Joyce v. Davis, 539 F.2d 1262, 1265 (10th Cir.1976) (specific performance of a promise to pay money bonus under a royalty contract).' "

BOEING COMPANY v. AETNA CASUALTY AND SURETY COMPANY

Supreme Court of Washington, En Banc, 1990.
113 Wash.2d 869, 784 P.2d 507.

DORE, JUDGE. * * * In 1983, the United States Environmental Protection Agency designated the Western Processing hazardous waste facility at Kent, Washington, as one of 400 hazardous waste sites requiring cleanup. On February 25, 1983, the EPA filed a complaint against Western Processing and its owners in the United States District Court for the Western District of Washington. In May 1983, pursuant to the Comprehensive Environmental

Response, Compensation, and Liability Act of 1980 (CERCLA), 42 U.S.C. § 9601 *et seq.*, the EPA notified the appellants (hereinafter policyholders) that they were generators of hazardous waste at the Western Processing site and were responsible parties for the "response costs" at this site. * * * On April 13, 1987, the Court entered a "Consent Decree" between EPA and policyholders for the cleanup of hazardous waste contamination of the subsurface of the Western Processing site.

EPA, in its complaint, alleged that the policyholders generated or transported hazardous substances found at the site. Further, that the migration of such wastes has contaminated the groundwater, aquifer (water bearing geological zone), commercial and agricultural property adjoining the site, and nearby surface waters. It further alleged that the United States, in order to combat the effects of contaminated groundwater, aquifer and property adjoining the site, had incurred and was incurring "response costs" as defined by CERCLA for which policyholders were liable. CERCLA defines the costs of "response" to include costs of removal of hazardous substances from the environment and the costs of other remedial work. CERCLA provides that any person or business entity responsible for a release or threatened release of hazardous substances "shall be liable for * * * all costs of removal or remedial action incurred by the United States Government or a State. * * *" Pursuant to the action by EPA, the policyholders have paid and will continue to pay environmental response costs relating to the Western Processing hazardous waste facility.

During the period of time that the policyholders generated and transported hazardous wastes to Western Processing, they carried Comprehensive General Liability (CGL) insurance purchased from the respondents (hereinafter insurers). The operative coverage provision of four of the policies provide that the insurer " 'will pay on behalf of the insured all sums which the insured shall become obligated to pay *as damages* because of bodily injury or property damage to which this policy applies, caused by an occurrence * * *.' " * * * The policies do not specifically define "damages."

The policyholders sued the insurers for indemnification for the "response costs" they incurred relating to the Western Processing facility. In each case, motions for summary judgment were filed in the United States District Court. Since the motions raised a determinative question of state law, the question of whether "response costs" constitute "damages" within the CGL policies issued by insurers, this question was certified to this court. * * * In order for the policyholders to be indemnified, the plain meaning of the contract must provide coverage for the subject "response costs." [1] Alternatively, before the insurers can avoid indemnifying the policyholders, this court must be satisfied that the plain meaning of "damages," as it would be understood by the average lay person, unmistakably precludes coverage for response costs, and any ambiguity is to be construed against the insurer.

The insurers have attempted to meet this burden by drawing lines, increasingly limited, around the word "damages." First, insurers draw a bright line between law remedies and equity remedies under common law. They assert that the legal technical meaning of "damages" includes monetary

1. It is important to note the absence of public policy in the construction of insurance contracts. While this case implicitly presents a grave question of policy, namely who should bear the cost of polluting our environment, the task presently before this court only requires us to construe the terms of the policies under Washington law. Washington courts rarely invoke public policy to override express terms of an insurance policy. [citations]

compensation for injury but not monetary equitable remedies such as sums paid to comply with an injunction or restitution. The insurers conclude that costs incurred under CERCLA are like injunction and restitution costs; therefore, they are equitable rather than legal and they are not "damages" within the policy language because equity does not award damages. The linchpin to insurers' argument is that "damages" should be given its legal technical meaning. Next, they draw a line between law remedies, excluding restitution-type law damages, such as remedies like CERCLA. Finally, they draw a line through the available common law damages and exclude everything except the tort-type damages.

The court is not persuaded that, under the rules of insurance contract analysis in Washington, the words "as damages" communicate these restrictions. * * *

Undefined terms in an insurance contract must be given their "plain, ordinary, and popular" meaning. * * *

The plain, ordinary meaning of damages as defined by the dictionary defeats insurers' argument. Standard dictionaries uniformly define the word "damages" inclusively, without making any distinction between sums awarded on a "legal" or "equitable" claim. For example, Webster's Third New International Dictionary 571 (1971) defines "damages" as "the estimated reparation in money for detriment or injury sustained". See also The Random House Dictionary of the English Language 504 (2d ed. 1987) (cost or expense). Indeed, even the insurers' own dictionaries define "damages" in accordance with the ordinary, popular, lay understanding: "Damages. Legal. The amount required to pay for a loss." Merit, Glossary of Insurance Terms 47 (1980). Even a policyholder with an insurance dictionary at hand would not learn about the coverage-restricting connotation to "damages" that the insurers argue is obvious.

Numerous federal and sister-state decisions (counsel at oral argument stated over 56 judges across the country) agree that "damages" include cleanup costs. [citations] This persuasive authority includes federal district courts in California, Colorado, Michigan, Pennsylvania, New Jersey, Missouri, Massachusetts, New York, Texas, and Delaware and state appellate courts in Wyoming, New Jersey, North Carolina, Michigan and Wisconsin.

These cases have found that cleanup costs are essentially compensatory damages for injury to property, even though these costs may be characterized as seeking "equitable relief." [citations] Or put another way, "coverage does not hinge on the form of action taken or the nature of relief sought, but on an actual or threatened use of legal process to coerce payment or conduct by a policyholder." Fireman's Fund Ins. Cos. v. Ex–Cell–O Corp., 662 F.Supp. 71, 75 (E.D.Mich.1987). * * * According to * * * United States Aviex Co. v. Travelers Ins. Co., 125 Mich.App. 579, 589–90, 336 N.W.2d 838 (1983), the environmental cleanup costs are covered because they are equivalent to "damages" under state law:

> "If the state were to sue in court to recover in traditional 'damages,' including the state's costs incurred in cleaning up the contamination, for the injury to the ground water, defendant's obligation to defend against the lawsuit and to pay damages would be clear. It is merely fortuitous from the standpoint of either plaintiff or defendant that the state has chosen to have plaintiff remedy the contamination problem, rather than choosing to incur the costs of clean-up

itself and then suing plaintiff to recover those costs. The damage to the natural resources is simply measured in the cost to restore the water to its original state."

Courts consistently agree that the "common-sense" understanding of damages within the meaning of the policy "includes a claim which results in causing [the policyholder] to pay sums of money because his acts or omissions affected adversely the rights of third parties * * * [*i.e.,* the public.]" United States Fid. & Guar. Co. v. Thomas Solvent Co., 683 F.Supp. 1139, 1168 (W.D.Mich.1988). * * *

In contrast to the plain ordinary meaning accorded to damages by courts across the country, insurers insist upon an accepted technical and legal meaning of damages. Insurers rely * * * on * * * Continental Ins. Cos. v. Northeastern Pharmaceutical & Chem. Co., 842 F.2d 977 (8th Cir.1988), and Maryland Cas. Co. v. Armco, Inc., 822 F.2d 1348 (4th Cir.1987), cert. denied, 484 U.S. 1008 (1988).

The definition of damages used by *Armco* was taken from Aetna Cas. & Sur. Co. v. Hanna, 224 F.2d 499, 503 (5th Cir.1955) (damages include "only payments to third persons when those persons have a legal claim for damages."). As a very recent case stated "[i]t is not clear why the *Armco* court turned to a 30–year–old case for a definition of 'damages,' a definition which is essentially a tautology defining damages as payment to a person who has 'a legal claim for damages.'" *Aerojet–General Corp.* The *Armco* court did express the opinion that it is a "dangerous step" for courts to construe insurance policies to cover "essentially prophylactic" or "harm avoidance" costs. However, a construction of "damages" which includes equitable relief "is not a boundless universe—such 'damages' still must be 'because of' property damage. Thus *Armco's* conclusion that an insurer would be held liable for prophylactic safety measures, taken in advance of any damage to property, is not applicable to the policies under review." *Aerojet–General Corp.*

In *Northeastern Pharmaceutical,* the Eighth Circuit in a sharply divided en banc decision reached a similar result as in *Armco.* The majority relied primarily on the narrow, technical decision espoused in *Armco* and *Hanna.* As with the *Armco* court, the *Continental* majority was concerned that absent a limited definition of damages, "'all sums which the insured shall become legally obligated to pay *as damages*'" would be reduced to "'*all sums* which the insured shall become legally obligated to pay.'" *Northeastern Pharmaceutical.* However, both *Armco* and *Northeastern Pharmaceutical* effectively sever "damages" from the additional restrictive phrase "because of property damage." *Northeastern Pharmaceutical, Armco* and insurers are in effect trying to write out of the CGL policy a concept that is expressly stated—that damages paid as a consequence of property damage caused by an occurrence are covered by the policy—and to write into the policy a condition that is not there—that such sums are covered only if they have been imposed pursuant to a "legal", as opposed to an "equitable" basis for liability. * * *

[T]hese cases are not helpful to the insurers' position because they are inconsistent with Washington law. In this state, legal technical meanings have never trumped the common perception of the common man. "[T]he proper inquiry is not whether a learned judge or scholar can, with study, comprehend the meaning of an insurance contract" but instead "whether the insurance policy contract would be meaningful to the layman * * * " Dairyland Ins. Co. v. Ward, 83 Wash.2d 353, 358, 517 P.2d 966 (1974). * * *

Insurers * * * argue that when legal words are used in a document, this court applies their usual legal interpretations. [citation] However, before an insurance company can avail itself of a legal technical meaning of a word or words, it must be clear that *both* parties to the contract intended that the language have a legal technical meaning. [citations] * * *

Here, there is nothing about the language from the subject standard form policies that indicates the parties intended a legal meaning to apply to the disputed term. Therefore, the words "as damages" should be interpreted in accordance with its plain, ordinary meaning, as dictated by the well established rules of construction under Washington law.

Insurers also try to argue that this court, when it is dealing with corporations, analyzes the contract language and determines its meaning without reference to what the average lay person might understand. * * *

[O]n the facts of this case, it is questionable whether these standard rules of construction are no less applicable merely because the insured is itself a corporate giant. The critical fact remains that the policy in question is a standard form policy prepared by the company's experts, with language selected by the insurer. The specific language in question was not negotiated, therefore, it is irrelevant that some corporations have company counsel. Additionally, this standard form policy has been issued to big and small businesses throughout the state. Therefore it would be incongruous for the court to apply different rules of construction based on the policyholder because once the court construes the standard form coverage clause as a matter of law, the court's construction will bind policyholders throughout the state regardless of the size of their business. * * *

[T]he substance of the claim for response costs in the present case concerns compensation for restoration of contaminated water and real property. The cost of repairing and restoring property to its original condition has long been considered proper measure of damages for property damage. Consequently, the substance of the claim for response costs constitutes a claim for property damage and falls within the scope of coverage afforded by a CGL policy. * * *

The policy defines property damage as "physical injury to or destruction of tangible property, which occurs during the policy period. * * * " "Property damage" includes discharge of hazardous waste into the water. In Port of Portland v. Water Quality Ins. Syndicate, 796 F.2d 1188, 1196 (9th Cir.1986), the court held that the discharge of pollution into water caused "damage to tangible property," within the meaning of the policy defining property damage as physical injury to or destruction of tangible property. * * *

The issue of when costs are or are not incurred "because of" property damage is illustrated in *Aerojet* by the following hypothetical:

> "Petitioners have two underground storage tanks for toxic waste. Tank # 1 has leaked wastes into the soil which have migrated to the groundwater or otherwise polluted the environment. Tank # 2 has not leaked, but government inspectors discover that it does not comply with regulatory requirements, and could eventually leak unless corrective measures are taken. Response costs associated with Tank # 1 will be covered as damages, because pollution has occurred. Tank # 2 would not be covered. Likewise, the expense of

capital improvements to prevent pollution in an area of a facility where there is none, or improvements or safety paraphernalia required by government regulation and not causally related to property damage, would not be covered as 'damages.' "

Aerojet–General Corp. v. San Mateo Cy. Superior Court, 209 Cal.App.3d 973, 211 Cal.App.3d 216, 257 Cal.Rptr 621, 635 (1989). Thus, costs owing because of property damages are remedial measures taken after pollution has occurred, but preventive measures taken before pollution has occurred are not costs incurred because of property damage.

The occurrence of the hazardous wastes leaking into the ground contaminating the groundwater, aquifer and adjoining property constituted "property damage" and thus triggered the "damages" provision of the policies carried by the policyholders. The costs assessed against the policyholders by the underlying lawsuits are covered by the subject policies to the extent that these costs are because of property damage. This duty to pay money is no different from the legal obligation that burdens a party who has been held liable to restore property to the condition it was in prior to the occurrence of the tortfeasor's conduct or damages consisting of amounts necessary to restore property to its status quo.

Response costs in response to actual releases of hazardous wastes are "damages" within the meaning of CGL coverage clauses at issue. The term "damages" does not cover safety measures or other preventive costs taken in advance of any damage to property. Consequently, we concur with the great majority of judges across the country that response costs incurred under CERCLA are "damages" to the extent that these costs are incurred "because of" property damage within the meaning of the CGL coverage clauses at issue. * * *

CALLOW, CHIEF JUSTICE (dissenting). * * * The majority's contrary holding upsets settled rules of insurance construction, violates controlling precedent, and contravenes public policy.

Washington law defines damages as:

> [T]he sum of money which the law imposes or awards as compensation, or recompense, or in satisfaction for an injury done, or a wrong sustained as a consequence, *either* of a breach of a contractual obligation or a tortious act or omission.

Puget Constr. Co. v. Pierce Cy., 64 Wash.2d 453, 392 P.2d 227 (1964).

Damages for injury to property are measured in terms of the amount necessary to compensate for the injury to the property interest. D. Dobbs, Remedies § 5.1, at 311 (1973). Therefore, damages for injury to property are limited under Washington law to *the lesser of* diminution in value of the property or the cost to restore or replace the property. [citations] Damages compensate for the injured party's loss.

Restitution stands "in bold contrast" to damages, because it is based upon a benefited party's gain. D. Dobbs, Remedies § 3.1, at 137. Restitutionary recovery is appropriate when the defendant has received a benefit under circumstances which make it unjust for him to retain it.

> "A person confers a benefit upon another if he gives to the other possession of or some other interest in money, land, chattels, or choses in action, *performs services beneficial to or at the request of the other,* satisfies a debt or a duty of

the other, or in any way adds to the other's security or advantage. He confers a benefit not only where he adds to the property of another, *but also where he saves the other from expense or loss.* The word 'benefit,' therefore, denotes any form of advantage."

Restatement of Restitution, § 1(b), at 12 (1937). The measure of recovery is the reasonable value of the benefit received by the defendant. Unlike compensatory damages, the amount of a restitutionary recovery can therefore greatly exceed the value of any property harmed. Olwell v. Nye & Nissen Co., 26 Wash.2d 282, 285, 173 P.2d 652 (1946).

CERCLA authorizes the President, acting through the Environmental Protection Agency (EPA), to respond to the release or the substantial threat of a release of any hazardous substance or any pollutant or contaminant which may present an imminent and substantial danger to public health or welfare. The EPA has broad authority to take whatever response measures it deems necessary to remove or neutralize hazardous waste. Alternatively, the EPA may seek injunctive relief to compel "responsible parties" to take necessary response action. Private citizens also have standing to sue to force compliance with CERCLA.

CERCLA permits certain governmental bodies (but not private citizens) to recover "damages for injury to, destruction of, or loss of natural resources." CERCLA does *not* provide for compensation to private individuals for personal injury, property damages and economic losses resulting from releases of hazardous substances. * * *

Natural resource damages are essentially a compensatory remedy. The measure of natural resource damages is "*the lesser of:* restoration or replacement costs or diminution of use values". (Italics mine.) 43 C.F.R. § 11.35(b)(2). Natural resource damages must be based on actual injury or loss. They are available only to governmental bodies "act[ing] on behalf of the public as trustee" of the natural resources. Total liability is limited to the value of the injured property. 42 U.S.C. § 9651(c); 43 C.F.R. § 11.35(b)(2).

In addition to natural resource damages, CERCLA permits both the EPA and other parties to recover costs which they have incurred as a result of a response action from "responsible parties." Responsible parties include hazardous waste generators, hazardous waste transporters, and hazardous waste disposal facility owners and operators.

CERCLA defines the term "response" to mean "removal * * * and remedial action * * * includ[ing] enforcement activities related thereto." Among the many safety measures identified as potential response actions are monitoring, security fencing, dikes, on-site treatment or incineration, recycling, provision of alternative water supplies, and related enforcement activities.

CERCLA response cost liability is essentially restitutional:

"When a party, governmental or non-governmental, incurs response costs it is performing the duty of the responsible party. In seeking recovery of those costs, that party is asking for the return of money spent on behalf of the responsible party to safeguard public health. Thus, response cost recovery restores the status quo by returning to the plaintiff what rightfully belongs to it, rather than compensating the plaintiff for loss sustained to its interest as a result of the responsible parties' wrongful conduct, and is a classic example of equitable restitution."

(Footnotes omitted.) Brett, Insuring Against the Innovative Liabilities and Remedies Created by Superfund, 6 J.Envtl.L. 1, 35 (1986).

The contrast between natural resource damage liability and response cost liability further indicates that CERCLA response costs are a restitutionary remedy. First, a responsible party can be held liable for response costs even though there is no property damage to compensate, because no actual release has yet occurred. Second, parties without an economic interest in the affected property can maintain an action for response costs. Finally, liability for response costs can greatly exceed the economic value of the affected property. See Abraham, Environmental Liability and the Limits of Insurance, 88 Colum. L.Rev. 942, 969 (1988).

The contrast between response costs and natural resource damages makes clear that response costs are an equitable restitutionary remedy, not a compensatory damage remedy. Verlan, Ltd. v. John L. Armitage & Co., 695 F.Supp. 950 (N.D.Ill.1988). Every court that has examined the nature of Superfund response costs liability outside of the insurance context has held that such costs are a form of equitable restitution. [citations] In fact, this authority is so overwhelming that *even the policyholders admit that "the governmental remedy under CERCLA is equitable."* Brief of Policyholders, at 37. Therefore, this court must also hold that CERCLA response costs are a restitutionary remedy.

The insurance policies in this case provide that the insurer "will pay on behalf of the insured all sums which the insured shall become legally obligated to pay as damages * * * because of * * * property damage. * * *" This language unambiguously extends coverage only to compensatory "damages" liability, not claims for restitutionary CERCLA response cost liability.

The majority makes several arguments attempting to show that this language is ambiguous. * * *

[It] asserts that because standard dictionaries do not explicitly distinguish between "legal" and "equitable" claims, the "as damages" clause can reasonably be interpreted to provide coverage for CERCLA response costs. Standard dictionary definitions of "damages," *including the definition cited by the majority,*[1] in fact unambiguously distinguish damages from restitution. *"Damages" are compensatory*—reparation for detriment or injury sustained. *CERCLA response cost liability, in contrast, is restitutionary*—reimbursement of a benefit unjustly retained by a responsible party.

Of course, no dictionary explicitly defines damages as "not equitable relief." Dictionaries define what a word means, not everything a word does not mean. But standard dictionaries' definitions of "damages" do establish that the "plain, ordinary, and popular meaning" of "damages" *is* reparation for detriment or injury sustained. Because CERCLA response costs are not rep-

1. [Footnotes renumbered.] "Standard dictionaries uniformly define the word 'damages' inclusively, without making any distinction between sums awarded on a 'legal' or 'equitable' claim. For example, Webster's Third New International Dictionary 571 (1971) defines 'damages' as 'the estimated reparation in money for detriment or injury sustained'." [as cited by the Majority]

This dictionary's complete entry for "damages" is: "damages *pl:* the estimated reparation in money for detriment or injury sustained: compensation or satisfaction imposed by law for a wrong or injury caused by a violation of a legal right {bring a suit for s} {was awarded compensatory s of $4000}—compare damnum absque injuria; see compensatory damages, general damages, nominal damages, punitive damages, special damages 4: expense, cost, charge, syn see injury" Webster's Third New International Dictionary 571 (1981).

aration for detriment or injury sustained, they do not fall within the "plain, ordinary and popular meaning" of damages. * * *

Unlike the majority, the policyholders recognized that if the word "damages" is given this plain, ordinary meaning, the insurance policies will not cover their CERCLA response cost liabilities. They therefore vigorously advocate an alternative "cost or expense" interpretation of the word "damages."

The majority does cite *The Random House Dictionary of the English Language* in an attempt to show that damages can also mean "cost or expense." The majority neglects to mention that this dictionary labels the "cost or expense" definition informal. The entire definition reads:

> 2. damages, law. the estimated money equivalent for detriment or injury sustained. 3. Often, damages. *Informal.* cost; expense; charge: *What are the damages for the lubrication job on my car?*

The Random House Dictionary of the English Language 365 (1973).

This court should reject the "cost or expense" definition for several reasons. First, the phrase "legally obligated to pay as damages" lies at the heart of a legal document, insuring against legal liability. Every dictionary cited indicates that the "compensation" definition is appropriate to a legal context. In contract, every dictionary that evaluates usage describes "cost or expense" as informal, colloquial or slang.[2]

Second, the "compensation" definition gives meaning to the "as damages" clause while the "cost or expense" definition renders "as damages" redundant. The "as damages" clause qualifies the phrase "all sums which the insured shall become legally obligated to pay." Amounts payable in reparation for detriment or injury sustained constitute a subset of the amounts an insured is "legally obligated to pay." The "compensation" definition therefore makes the "as damages" clause meaningfully qualify its referent.

In contrast, if interpreted to mean "cost or expense" the "as damages" clause redundantly repeats its referent. Because all sums which an insured is "legally obligated to pay" already constitute a "cost or expense" to the insured, the "as damages" clause becomes "mere surplusage, because any obligation to pay would be covered." Maryland Cas. Co. v. Armco, Inc., 822 F.2d 1348, 1352 (4th Cir.1987), cert. denied 484 U.S. 1008 (1988). * * *

The majority next emphasizes that "56 judges" have held that "damages" can include CERCLA cleanup costs. While the judicial "head-count" is hardly dispositive, it is not nearly as one-sided as the majority implies. In addition to the three cases discussed by the majority, the following reported cases also hold that CERCLA response costs are not covered "as damages:" [citations] * * *

In addition, numerous cases from other jurisdictions hold that liability insurers need not indemnify their insured's restitutionary liabilities, even if payable in money. See, e.g., * * * Desrochers v. New York Cas. Co., 99 N.H. 129, 106 A.2d 196 (1954) [in which] the insureds had been enjoined to remove a culvert placed upon their land. In holding the insurer not liable for the cost of complying with the injunction, the court stated:

2. Only Webster's Third New International Dictionary and the related Webster's New Collegiate Dictionary do not identify the "cost or expense" definition of damages as informal, colloquial, or slang. These dictionaries do not specially identify such usages.

> "The cost of compliance with the mandatory injunction is not reasonably to be regarded as a sum payable 'as damages.' Damages are recompense for injuries sustained. Restatement, Torts, § 902. They are remedial rather than preventive, and in the usual sense are pecuniary in nature. 1 Sedgwick on Damages (9th ed.) §§ 2, 29. The expense of restoring the plaintiff's property to its former state will not remedy the injury previously done, nor will it be paid to the injured parties * * *
>
> "In short, the expense of complying with the order is neither a sum which the insured is obligated to pay as damages, nor is it in any real sense equivalent thereto. No equitable principle requires the [insurer] to pay it, and it is not within the scope of its undertaking as a reasonable man * * * would interpret it."

* * * The "as damages" clause in these policies unambiguously limits coverage to compensatory damage remedies, not restitutionary remedies like CERCLA response costs. However, even if the phrase "as damages" were ambiguous, this term should not automatically be construed against the insurer. The "average lay person" rule of insurance interpretation does not apply to corporate giants. * * *

The majority acknowledges that at least some of the policyholders in the present case are "corporate giant[s]". Because these insureds *do* possess the ability and expertise to negotiate the language of the policy, the "average lay person" rule applicable to the typical consumer insurance contract should not extend to this case. * * *

[Finally] the majority's interpretation of these insurance policies ignores the public policy expressed by the United States Congress in enacting CERCLA.

* * * Congress clearly recognized that corporate polluters have reaped enormous benefits from their past inadequate waste disposal practices. These practices created significant short-term savings for polluters, resulting in higher profits for them, but caused enormous long-term harm in the form of environmental degradation. CERCLA response cost liability forces these polluters to disgorge these profits.

The insurers from whom these polluters now seek indemnification, in contrast, did not charge a premium to cover response cost liability. See Note, CERCLA Cleanup Costs Under Comprehensive General Liability Insurance Policies: Property Damage or Economic Damage, 56 Fordham L.Rev. 1169, 1176 (1988). * * * By requiring these insurers to indemnify the corporate polluters for the cost of cleanup, the majority permits the polluters to both reap the benefits and avoid the costs attributable to their pollution. This directly violates the congressional intent that polluters internalize their pollution costs. See Brett, Insuring Against the Innovative Liabilities and Remedies Created by Superfund, 6 J.Envtl.L. 1, 52 (1986).

The majority holding also violates public policy because it requires insurers to insure liability which is fundamentally uninsurable. The innovative new features of CERCLA's liability scheme simply prevent insurers from calculating and charging premiums that bear any real relation to the risk of CERCLA liability.

CERCLA's liability provisions differ from ordinary tort liability in many important respects. First, CERCLA imposes an especially strict liability upon responsible parties. Liability attaches even to those who nonnegligently dispose of a hazardous substance using state of the art procedures.

Second, CERCLA liability is retroactive. Responsible parties who disposed of hazardous waste in a completely legal, non-actionable manner before the enactment of CERCLA are now potentially liable for response costs.

Third, CERCLA regularly makes individuals liable for harms they did not cause. CERCLA imposes joint and several liability upon every responsible party connected with a hazardous waste site. Therefore, both the government and private parties may recover response costs from a "responsible party" with virtually no showing of causation.

Fourth, private citizens without any proprietary interest in the property harmed have standing to sue to enforce CERCLA. To recover response costs, a private party need only show an outlay of costs and that the costs were incurred consistently with the National Contingency Plan promulgated by the EPA.

Fifth, CERCLA authorizes the initiation of response action in response to the *threat* of a hazardous waste release. For example CERCLA authorizes the government to recoup the costs of health assessment and health effects studies. Therefore, responsible parties may be held liable for CERCLA response costs even in the absence of any actual harm to persons or property.

Sixth, CERCLA response cost liability is inevitable. Every hazardous waste containment system eventually will leak. Because CERCLA imposes liability even if hazardous waste is disposed of in a state of the art manner, every responsible party should expect eventually to be subject to CERCLA response liability.

Seventh, CERCLA response cost liability is essentially boundless, both in amount and duration. The EPA has an almost unfettered discretion to incur and recoup whatever response cost it believes are necessary to clean up a site. Moreover, because the EPA currently refuses to grant settling parties releases from further litigation, a responsible party's liability exists indefinitely into the future regardless of how much it has paid to clean up a site.

CERCLA's broadly worded provisions mean that insurers have no way of predicting what insured conduct may lead to liability. * * *

A congressionally authorized study group report on the availability of private insurance for CERCLA liability recognizes that CERCLA's radically unique approach to the imposition of response costs renders the insured's potential liability so limitless that such liability cannot be assessed by prospective insurers seeking to set premium levels. * * * A Report in Compliance With Section 301(b) of P.L. 96–105, at 83–87 & 94–95 (June 1983). In fact, since the enactment of CERCLA, pollution insurance has become unavailable in any insurance market. * * *

Congress enacted CERCLA's innovative response cost liability provisions in order to properly address the threat posed by inadequate past hazardous waste disposal practices. CERCLA liability accordingly differs substantially from ordinary tort liability. Normal tort liability results in a compensatory "damages" remedy. CERCLA response cost liability, in contrast, results in a restitutionary remedy.

The insurance policies at issue in this case require the insurer to indemnify the insureds for "all sums which the insured shall be legally obligated to pay as damages. * * *" The plain, ordinary and popular meaning of damages, as recognized by the majority, is "reparation for detriment or injury sustained." Because CERCLA response costs do not constitute reparation for detriment or injury sustained, they do not constitute "damages" within the meaning of these policies. * * *

I respectfully dissent.

DOLLIVER, J., concurs.

Note

To reach the desired result, does the court redefine legal "damages" or merely manipulate the canons of insurance policy interpretation? For legal purposes, is "plain language" an oxymoron?

See also AIU Insurance Co. v. Superior Court, 51 Cal.3d 820, 274 Cal.Rptr. 820, 799 P.2d 1253 (1990).

B. THE REQUIREMENT OF CERTAINTY

1. PROOF OF THE EXISTENCE OF DAMAGES

Introduction

Uncertainty frequently intrudes in calculating damages. "Pecuniary damage" is a *substantive* element of most torts. No pecuniary damage, no cause of action. (Trespass and defamation are notable exceptions.) We first encounter uncertainty here.

POLLOCK v. JOHNS-MANVILLE SALES CORPORATION

United States District Court, District of New Jersey, 1988.
686 F.Supp. 489.

WOLIN, DISTRICT JUDGE. * * * In this action, plaintiff alleges that as a result of his exposure to asbestos and asbestos-containing products he is currently suffering from a disease which has manifested itself as a thickening of the lung tissue. Plaintiff, however, does not now suffer from any cancerous condition. Nevertheless, plaintiff seeks to present to the jury specific statistical evidence of his increased risk of developing cancer, and he is prepared to show, by way of expert testimony, that due to his exposure to asbestos he now has a 43 percent chance of developing cancer. Subsequently, defendants moved to exclude this issue of increased risk of cancer from trial.

In addressing this issue, the Court must begin with the axiom that tort law does not compensate for mere speculative injury. Thus, in order to recover damages for a prospective injury such as the increased risk of developing cancer, plaintiff must establish proof of "reasonable medical probability." Coll v. Sherry, 29 N.J. 166, 179, 148 A.2d 481 (1959). For example, in Lorenc v. Chemirad Corp., 37 N.J. 56, 179 A.2d 401 (1962), the Supreme Court of New Jersey allowed a plaintiff to offer expert medical testimony that as a result of spilling defendant's corrosive liquid on his hand, it was "medically probable" that a malignancy would develop. Furthermore, in Evers v. Dollinger, 95 N.J. 399, 471 A.2d 405 (1984), the New Jersey Supreme Court held that a plaintiff could present evidence of increased risk of cancer upon the actual *recurrence* of a malignancy—because at that point the risk has materialized as reality.

Clearly, the thrust of New Jersey tort law, as recently recognized by the State Supreme Court in Ayers v. Jackson Township, 106 N.J. 557, 598–599, 525 A.2d 287 (1987), is that a plaintiff may not recover for "unquantifiable future risks." Instead, a plaintiff must establish either: (1) medical probability, or (2) realization of the risk. * * *

Plaintiff, in asserting the validity his increased risk claim, contends that this case is clearly distinguishable from *Ayers* because, unlike the unquantifiable claims with which the *Ayers* Court was presented, plaintiff is prepared to establish that his risk of cancer is: (1) caused by a diagnosed medical injury, and (2) definable medically and scientifically as having a 43 percent statistical probability of occurring in the future.

It is this ability to precisely quantify the statistical probability of occurrence upon which plaintiff rests his argument. Moreover, it is this application of mathematical precision which, asserts plaintiff, delivers his claim from the nebulus realm of speculation to the firm ground of reasonable certainty such that it may properly be presented to the jury. Notwithstanding the fact that the relevant probability to which plaintiff's expert will testify is less than 50 percent, this Court notes the recent decision in this district by the Honorable Judge Thompson in *Wolozen v. Johns–Manville:*

> "Neither in *Coll* nor in any subsequent cases discussing the enhanced risk of disease has the New Jersey Supreme Court or any other New Jersey court stated that a reasonable probability must be over 50 percent."

Curiously, however, the *Wolozen* opinion makes only a passing reference to the reported case of Herber v. Johns–Manville, 785 F.2d 79 (3d Cir.1986). In *Herber,* the Third Circuit affirmed the district court's refusal to permit litigation on the increased risk of cancer element at trial because:

> "Mr. Herber has proffered no expert opinion or other evidence that would permit a factual finding that he will more likely than not experience cancer in the future. The district court held that New Jersey law does not provide compensation for an increased risk of a future injury that remains a possibility rather than a probability."

Moreover, the Third Circuit went on to note that plaintiff's expert "had no epidemiological data showing a class risk in excess of 50 percent and was not prepared to offer an opinion that [plaintiff], more likely than not, would experience cancer."

It appears that Judge Thompson based her opinion in *Wolozen* on a strict interpretation of the phrase "medical probability." The *Wolozen* opinion apparently turns on the assumption that that which is quantifiable is, by definition, appropriate for consideration by a jury. This Court, however, does not agree that a close reading of *Ayers* yields the conclusion that the mere transformation of an uncertain future event to a calculated mathematical probability automatically renders a claim amenable to decision by a jury.[1] * * * The *Ayers* Court * * * cited a string of cases which, when summarized, appear to stand for the proposition that reasonable certainty is that which is more probable than not. Issues of the inherent reliability of statistics aside, a

1. [Footnote renumbered.] In other words this Court finds that there exists a clear distinction between legal probability and mathematical probability.

43 percent risk factor, although tangible, is clearly not "more probable than not." * * *

Accordingly, even though plaintiff has been able to quantify the risk of cancer, because he is not able to show that such risk is more probable than not, this Court must now preclude plaintiff from litigating the issue of increased risk of cancer. * * *

[N]otwithstanding the present denial of plaintiff's enhanced risk claim this Court recognizes plaintiff's "right to sue in the future should the increased risk created by the exposure to asbestos come to fruition." * * *

This approach is a fair and sensible accommodation to the litigant whose risk of cancer claim does not meet the standard of "more likely than not," (i.e., not presently cognizable at law) since it provides the litigant his or her day in court if and when the disease or injury is actually suffered. * * *

Note

Mauro v. Raymark Industries, Inc., 116 N.J. 126, 132, 561 A.2d 257, 260 (1989): "It is important to recognize at the outset that the rule of law advocated by plaintiffs, i.e., that tort victims should have a present cause of action for a significant but unquantified enhanced risk of future injury, represents a significant departure from traditional, prevailing legal principles. The general rule is that set forth in the Restatement:

> 'When an injured person seeks to recover for harms that may result in the future, he is entitled to damages based upon the probability that harm of one sort or another will ensue and upon its probable seriousness if it should ensue. When a person has suffered physical harm that is more or less permanent in nature * * * he is entitled to recover damages not only for harm already suffered, but also for that which probably will result in the future.' [*Restatement (Second) of Torts* § 912 comment e (1979).]

"See also 3 Personal Injury: Actions, Defenses and Damages § 3.03 (L. Frumer & M. Friedman ed. 1984) ('Plaintiff is entitled to recover damages for those losses which are reasonably certain to occur in the future * * *. Like any other future loss, the permanent nature of the injury must be proved to a degree of reasonable certainty, or probability.'). * * *

"The long-standing rule in New Jersey is that prospective damages are not recoverable unless they are reasonably probable to occur. The rationale for adopting this standard was explained by Justice Francis, then sitting in the Appellate Division, in Budden v. Goldstein, 43 N.J.Super. 340, 346–47, 128 A.2d 730 (1957):

> 'In the admeasurement of damages, it is well known that no recovery can be allowed for *possible* future consequences of an injury inflicted by a wrongdoer. In order for suggested future results to be includible as an element of damage, it must appear that they are reasonably certain or reasonably probable to follow.'

"* * * [M]any of the authorities throughout the country use the expression 'reasonably certain' or 'reasonable certainty' as the test and consider 'reasonably probable' or 'reasonable probability' inadequate and erroneous; others accept the latter statement. Our cases do not seem to have dealt specifically with the question of whether the two have the same significance in relation to *quantum* of proof, and so may be used interchangeably. It seems to us that in a resolution of the conflicting interests involved, reasonable probability is the just yardstick to be applied. Basically, our view comes down to this: a consequence of an injury which is possible, which may possibly ensue, is a risk which the injured person must bear because the law cannot be administered so as to do reasonably efficient justice if conjecture and speculation are to be used as a measure of damages. On the other hand, a consequence which stands on the plane of reasonable probability, although it is not certain to occur, may be considered in the evaluation of the damage claim against the defendant. In this way, to the extent that men can achieve justice through general rules, a just balance of the warring interests is accomplished. [citations]."

YOUST v. LONGO

Supreme Court of California, 1987.
43 Cal.3d 64, 233 Cal.Rptr. 294, 729 P.2d 728.

LUCAS, JUSTICE. Is a racehorse owner entitled to tort damages when the harness driver of another horse negligently or intentionally interferes with the owner's horse during a race, thereby preventing the owner from the chance of winning a particular cash prize? It is a well-settled general tort principle that interference with the *chance* of winning a contest, such as the horserace at issue here, usually presents a situation too uncertain upon which to base tort liability. We agree that application of this principle should govern here. * * *

Plaintiff Harlan Youst entered his standardbred trotter horse, Bat Champ, in the eighth harness race at Hollywood Park in Inglewood, California. Also entered in the race was The Thilly Brudder, driven by defendant, Gerald Longo. During the race, defendant allegedly drove The Thilly Brudder into Bat Champ's path and struck Bat Champ with his whip, thereby causing the horse to break stride. Bat Champ finished sixth while The Thilly Brudder finished second. The Board reviewed the events of the race and disqualified The Thilly Brudder, which moved Bat Champ into fifth place, entitling plaintiff to a purse of only $5,000.[1]

Plaintiff filed a complaint for damages asserting [intentional interference with prospective economic advantage]. Plaintiff sought as compensatory damages the difference in prize money between Bat Champ's actual finish and the finish which allegedly would have occurred but for defendant's interference. Plaintiff requested compensatory damages in three alternative amounts, namely, the purse amount for either first, second or third place (less the fifth place prize of $5,000 which Bat Champ has already received). Ascertainment of the amount of actual damages apparently would require a finding as to the position in which Bat Champ would have finished but for defendant's interference. Punitive damages of $250,000 were also sought. * * *

Each of the three counts in the complaint purports to state a claim for loss of prospective economic advantage, rather than for physical personal injury or property damage. The torts of negligent or intentional interference with prospective economic advantage require proof of various elements as a prerequisite to recovery. However, as a matter of law, a threshold causation requirement exists for maintaining a cause of action for either tort, namely,

1. [Footnotes renumbered.] The purse for the race was $100,000 distributed as follows: the winner received $50,000; second place received $25,000; third place received $12,000; fourth place received $8,000, and fifth place received $5,000.

proof that it is reasonably *probable* that the lost economic advantage would have been realized but for the defendant's interference. * * *

Determining the probable expectancy of winning a *sporting* contest but for the defendant's interference seems impossible in most if not all cases, including the instant case. Sports generally involve the application of various unique or unpredictable skills and techniques, together with instances of luck or chance occurring at different times during the event, any one of which factors can drastically change the event's outcome. In fact, certain intentional acts of interference by various potential "defendant" players may, through imposition of penalties or increased motivation, actually allow the "victim" player or team to prevail. Usually, it is impossible to predict the outcome of most sporting events without awaiting the actual conclusion.

The Restatement Second of Torts specifically addresses the speculative nature of the outcome of a horse race. The relevant comment is contained in a "Special Note on Liability for Interference With Other Prospective Benefits of a Noncontractual Nature." The comment states that various possible situations may justify liability for interference with prospective economic benefits of a noncommercial character. Special mention is given to "[c]ases in which the plaintiff is wrongfully deprived of the expectancy of winning a race or a contest, when he has had *a substantial certainty or at least a high probability of success.* For example, the plaintiff is entered in a contest for a large cash prize to be awarded to the person who, during a given time limit, obtains the largest number of subscriptions to a magazine. At a time when the contest has one week more to run and the plaintiff is leading all other competitors by a margin of two to one, the defendant unjustifiably strikes the plaintiff out of the contest and rules him ineligible. In such a case there may be sufficient certainty established so that the plaintiff may successfully maintain an action for loss of the prospective benefits. *On the other hand, if the plaintiff has a horse entered in a race and the defendant wrongfully prevents him from running, there may well not be sufficient certainty to entitle the plaintiff to recover.* * * *" (Rest.2d Torts, § 774B, special note, pp. 59–60, italics added.)

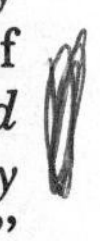

As indicated by the Restatement comment, certain contests may have a higher probability of ultimate success than others. To this end, the cases cited by the Court of Appeal here, awarding damages to competitors in contests, are distinguishable because in each case there was a high probability of winning.[2] In addition to the Restatement position, one older case has specifically held that the loss of a chance to win a prize purse at a trotting horse race was too speculative to support tort liability. (See Western Union Tel. Co. v. Crall (1888) 39 Kan. 580, 18 P. 719.)

Applying the foregoing analysis to the instant case, it seems clear that plaintiff's complaint fails adequately to allege facts showing interference with a *probable* economic gain, i.e., that Bat Champ would have won this horserace, or at least won a larger prize, if defendant had not interfered. Here, the

2. Nor are we persuaded by the Court of Appeal's argument that damages should be allowed for the value of the lost chance of benefit. (See Schaefer, Uncertainty and the Law of Damages (1978) 19 Wm. & Mary L.Rev. 719.) Under this approach, plaintiff would not recover the full value of the lost prize but that value discounted by the probability of winning in the absence of defendant's interference. We believe this calculation is incorporated in the basic analysis for interference with prospective economic advantage; the speculative nature of the chance of winning is examined in establishing the first element of the tort as opposed to determining specific damages after recognizing a cause of action. In the instant case, the potential economic advantage is simply too speculative to allow *any recovery.*

complaint only alleged in conclusory terms that defendant's wrongful interference resulted in a lost "opportunity" to finish higher in the money. The complaint merely indicated that defendant's maneuvers and whipping forced Bat Champ to break stride and fall out of contention.[3]

We conclude, as a matter of law, that the threshold element of probability for interference with prospective economic advantage was not met by the facts alleged. * * *

Note

Nothing or All? If the plaintiff in *Pollock* had established a 51% statistical probability that he would develop cancer, we assume he would have stated a cause of action. Similarly the plaintiff in *Youst* would not have struck out if he had convinced anybody that, if not interfered with, "Bat Champ" had a "high probability" of making it to the wire on the same day. The idea of a specific breaking point leads to the "all or nothing" approach, a methodology that denies any recovery for a less-than-even chance.

Academic writers favor allowing the plaintiff to recover the value of the lost chance regardless of the exact probabilities involved. The *Youst* court cites Professor Schaefer's thoughtful article in a footnote yet rejects its reasoning. In addition see King, Causation, Valuation, and Chance in Personal Injury Torts Involving Pre-existing Conditions and Future Consequences, 90 Yale L.J. 1353 (1981).

If a plaintiff could be compensated for the value of a lost chance according to the statistical probability value of that chance, the substantive requirement of "damages" for the *existence* of a cause of action would be virtually eliminated. Anything over 0% chance would keep the plaintiff in court. The prospect of increased litigation has less appeal to the judiciary than to statistically minded analysts.

The decisions that adopt the "value of the chance" approach to uncertainty issues have usually been breach of contract cases where the plaintiff lost a chance for a prize in a contest. The best known is Chaplin v. Hicks, 2 K.B. 786 (1911) where the plaintiff, one of 50 contestants for 12 prizes in a beauty contest, lost any chance of winning because she was not properly notified of appearance time. Another is Kansas City, Mexico & Orient Railway v. Bell, 197 S.W. 322 (Tex.Civ. App.1917). A railroad breached a contract to deliver hogs in time for a contest and the plaintiff received a second instead of a possible first prize. Mange v. Unicorn Press, 129 F.Supp. 727 (S.D.N.Y.1955) is a third. Plaintiff's answer to a puzzle contest was erroneously marked "wrong". If the answer had not disqualified him, he would have become one of a pool of 23,548 contestants to compete for 210 prizes including a $307,500 first prize. Figure the value of that chance. Finally McDonald v. John P. Scripps Newspaper, 210 Cal.App.3d 100, 257 Cal.Rptr. 473 (1989). A disappointed contestant in a spelling bee sued alleging that the contest officials allowed an ineligible candidate to compete. In dismissing the complaint, the trial

3. Presented in plaintiff's opposition to the demurrer were the following additional facts: "As the horses entered in the eighth race rounded the last turn, Bat Champ *began to make his move* to the lead of the group. As his move progressed, Defendant drove his horse into Bat Champ's path and thereafter whipped Bat Champ with his whip. Bat Champ's advance was halted, his stride broken and his *chances* at finishing 'in the money' ended." (Italics added.) Further, at oral argument, plaintiff asserted that the alleged interference took place 100 yards from the finish line. However, despite these asserted facts, Bat Champ's chance of placing higher in the purse money remained highly speculative.

judge stated, "I see a gigantic causation problem * * * common sense tells me this lawsuit is nonsense." See also D. Dobbs, Remedies § 3.3, at 156–157 (1973).

Fennell v. Southern Maryland Hospital Center, 320 Md. 776, 580 A.2d 206 (1990). Plaintiffs sued for wrongful death seeking full recovery for medical malpractice. At the time the alleged malpractice occurred, the decedent had a less than 50% chance of living. The trial court declined to allow a "loss of chance recovery either as a new cause of action by relaxing traditional rules of causation or in the alternative by establishing a new form of damages for loss of chance." Held, affirmed. Compare Perez v. Las Vegas Medical Center, 107 Nev. 1, 805 P.2d 589 (1991).

2. PROVING THE AMOUNT OF DAMAGES

a. *The Quantum of Proof*

Preliminary Note

Uncertainty plagues the calculation of damages as much as the rest of the law. Some tentative categorization of the usual types of uncertainty may help at the outset.

1. Most damages that have accrued by the time of trial are determinable with some confidence about their accuracy—e.g. lost wages (as distinguished from other forms of income), medical expenses, value of damaged property, reliance damages for breach of contract, etc. Uncertainty here, more likely than not, results from plaintiff's lack of vigor in preserving or accumulating evidence. For example, in Wenzler & Ward Plumbing & Heating Co. v. Sellen, 53 Wash.2d 96, 330 P.2d 1068 (1958), a prime contractor on a construction contract was compelled by a subcontractor's failure to furnish plans and essential preliminary work to perform these services not only for the particular subcontractor but others as well. Unfortunately, the prime contractor neglected to keep a separate cost record for each sub-contractor. The trial court, unable to find a proportionate sum chargeable to the sub-contractor or a reasonable cost basis, "immunized" the sub-contractor from all liability. The Supreme Court of Washington reversed, distinguishing between uncertainty of the fact of damage and the quantity. Under the circumstances, a remand to the trial court seems pointless because the absence of evidence remains. However, it makes the injured party the winner instead of loser for purposes of court costs and related considerations.

2. Pecuniary damages which will accrue in the future, impaired earning capacity and future medical expenses in personal injury cases, or lost future profits of a business, are much more intractable. Even determining the lost profits of a business prior to judgment has given much difficulty. Washington v. American Community Stores Corp., p. 38, deals with this problem.

3. Some supposedly compensatory damages are inherently uncertain. These include nonpecuniary damages, such as pain and suffering, mental anguish, or special damages from dignitary torts. All must nonetheless be translated into pecuniary form by the trier of fact under guidelines that can at best be described as "uncertain," as is illustrated by the typical jury instruction on p. 40. Ratner v. Arrington, infra p. 40, shows trial tactics to fix the amount of these "uncertain" damages in the minds of the jury.

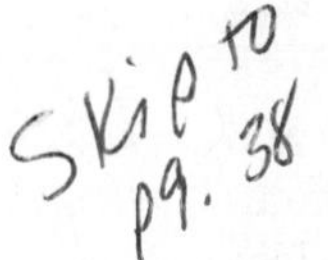

ATKIN WRIGHT & MILES v. MOUNTAIN STATES TELEPHONE AND TELEGRAPH CO.

Supreme Court of Utah, 1985.
709 P.2d 330.

STEWART, JUSTICE. This suit arose out of an error made by Mountain States Telephone & Telegraph Co. (Mountain Bell) in listing the same telephone number in the yellow-page directory for the law firm of Atkin, Wright and Miles (Atkin) and also for the law firm of Allen, Thompson and Hughes (Allen). A jury awarded general and punitive damages to Atkin, and Mountain Bell appeals the award. We reverse.

When Mountain Bell distributed its St. George yellow-page directory in October, 1980, the directory correctly listed the Atkin firm's telephone number as 673–4605 in both the white pages and the yellow pages of the directory. However, the same number was also erroneously listed in the yellow pages as the number for Michael D. Hughes, one attorney in the law firm of Allen, Thompson and Hughes. Thus, anyone who dialed the number listed for Mr. Hughes in the yellow pages reached the Atkin firm. To correct the problem, Mountain Bell changed Atkin's phone number and placed an intercept on Atkin's original number so that when it was dialed the caller heard the following:

> The number you have dialed, 673–4605, is no longer in service due to a directory listing error. If you are calling Atkin, Wright and Miles, the number is 629–2612 or if you are calling Allen, Thompson and Hughes, the number is 673–4892. This is a telephone company recording.

As soon as the intercept was installed, Atkin filed a complaint in district court for damages. * * *

[At] the trial of Atkin's claim for damages against Mountain Bell, [t]he jury was instructed on [the theory of] negligence by Mountain Bell in listing the Atkin phone number under both the Atkin and Allen firm names; and interference by Mountain Bell with Atkin's prospective business relationships. The jury found for the plaintiff, and awarded general damages of $25,000 and punitive damages of $30,000. * * *

Atkin's claims for negligence and for intentional interference with economic relations were subject to the district court's jurisdiction. Public utilities have no wholesale immunity from the duties imposed by tort law generally.

[The court held that Mountain Bell was not negligent in preparing the phone book.] However, Atkin did adduce evidence that Mountain Bell was negligent in the operation of the intercept. Since the tariffs do not purport to limit Mountain Bell's liability with respect to the operation of an intercept, Atkin could recover damages upon proof that the operation of the intercept was negligent, that Atkin was in fact damaged, and that the amount of the damages was reasonably ascertainable. Plaintiff adduced evidence that the intercept did not always work properly, and the jury returned a general verdict of $25,000 damages in favor of Atkin.

We accord Atkin the full benefit of the evidence that reasonably supports the verdict, even though controverted. To prove damages, the plaintiff must prove two points. First, it must prove the fact of damages. The evidence must do more than merely give rise to speculation that damages in fact occurred; it must give rise to a reasonable probability that the plaintiff suffered damage as result of a breach. Second, the plaintiff must prove the amount of damages. The level of persuasiveness required to establish the *fact* of loss is generally higher than that required to establish the *amount* of a loss. [citations] It is, after all, the wrongdoer, rather than the injured party, who should bear the burden of some uncertainty in the amount of damages. While the standard for determining the amount of damages is not so exacting as the standard for proving the fact of damages, there still must be evidence that rises above speculation and provides a reasonable, even though not necessarily precise, estimate of damages. [citations] The amount of damages may be based upon approximations, if the fact of damage is established, and the approximations are based upon reasonable assumptions or projections. [citations]

In this case, Atkin offered no proof whatsoever of lost net income. Proof of loss of gross income only is an insufficient foundation for proof of amount of damages. [citations]

Furthermore, Atkin did not prove that its reduction in gross income, (i.e., the fact of damage), was caused by the negligent operation of the intercept. The evidence did not raise more than a speculative possibility of the fact of damage or of the amount of damages incurred. Atkin's evidence showed only that the firm income declined for a three month period during only a small part of which the intercept was in place. Although the second intercept did not always function properly, the testimony indicated that clients were able to obtain Atkin's phone number. That Atkin's quarterly gross revenues decreased for a three month period does not establish that it was the occasionally malfunctioning intercept which caused the reduced revenues. To attribute a three-month decline in revenues to the short one-month intercept is only speculative. The incomes of law firms generally fluctuate from year to year and throughout the months of each year. Atkin's own witness confirmed that such fluctuations also occur within that firm. Atkin also conceded that one attorney in the firm could substantially affect the firm's income for a month or a quarter of the year by the manner in which he turned in his billable time and billed his clients. In addition, the members of the firm were devoting substantial periods of time to the firm's own litigation against Mountain Bell.

Mountain Bell's first intercept lasted only 36 hours. A client or potential client could reach the firm by calling information for the number. One witness testified that he was unable to reach the Atkin firm for legal advice, but that his legal problem was resolved before he was able to retain counsel. The specific type of service needed by that client and the amount usually charged for the type of service was not put into evidence. Another witness testified that she had difficulty reaching the Atkin firm when she wanted to have a will prepared but that she finally was able to contact the firm and one of the attorneys drafted the will. Two other witnesses testified that they had difficulty reaching the Atkin firm, but Atkin was not able to attribute any specific loss to that difficulty. Finally, one of the Atkin attorneys testified that he lost a client due to the malfunctioning intercept. However, there was no evidence as to what the value of the lost fees was.[1] * * *

1. [Footnote renumbered.] In Southwestern Bell Telephone Co. v. Reeves, Tex.Civ.App., 578 S.W.2d 795 (1979), the court sustained a $10,000 damage award to a lawyer who changed his phone number and arranged for an intercept to be placed on the old number. The suit arose

The award of punitive damages must be vacated since the plaintiff did not prove compensatory damages.

Note

Having passed the threshold and established a cause of action, the plaintiff has still not escaped uncertainty. He or she still must introduce *some* evidence of the amount of damages. This case is the first in the book where plaintiff seeks future lost business profit. Plaintiff may use various methods to calculate profit but still must meet a minimum evidentiary obligation. (Remember, for what it's worth, the plaintiff is technically a prevailing party.)

The court mentions a principle that assists many plaintiffs to recover uncertain damages: a defendant who is responsible for the uncertainty of proof of plaintiff's damages risks the worst case scenario. This principle began in the grand old case of Armory v. Delamirie, 93 Eng.Rep. 664 (1722) where the jeweler conned a poor little chimneysweep out of a "jewel" that the boy had found and the court awarded the sweep the value of a jewel "of the first water." It applies as well to large antitrust cases where the damages presumed against the defendant may be trebled. Bigelow v. RKO Radio Pictures, 327 U.S. 251 (1946).

WASHINGTON v. AMERICAN COMMUNITY STORES CORP.

Supreme Court of Nebraska, 1976.
196 Neb. 624, 244 N.W.2d 286.

WHITE, CHIEF JUSTICE. This is an appeal from a jury verdict and judgment in the sum of $76,000 arising out of a motor vehicle collision. The trial court directed a verdict against the defendant on the issue of liability. * * *

The accident took place April 11, 1972. The plaintiff was then 24 years old [life expectancy, 49.9 years] and had been actually employed by the state as an adult parole officer since he was graduated from college in December 1971. At the outset we point out that there is no dispute concerning the permanency of the plaintiff's injury nor the fact that the injury disabled the plaintiff from pursuing the wrestling sport. * * *

[T]he basic thrust of the defendant's contention in this appeal is that the court should not have submitted the plaintiff's loss of earning capacity to the jury. It is argued that the evidence is based upon speculation and conjecture, that evidence of contingent, uncertain future possibilities, and uncertain future happenings, is speculative and conjectural and therefore incompetent, and the verdict is excessive.

* * * The plaintiff had attended the University of Nebraska at Omaha and he has compiled an outstanding record as an intercollegiate wrestler. He won first place in his weight division in the NAIA wrestling tournament his sophomore and senior years, was second once, and placed third in his freshman year. His collegiate record was 103 wins and 4 losses. * * * Expert testimony on his behalf was that before his injury he was a prime candidate for the 1972 United States Olympic team and had the qualifications to become a great international wrestler and to win a medal. There was evidence that those who compete in the Olympics and win a medal have a much better opportunity to

because the phone company failed to install the intercept. A client of the lawyer testified that when he could not reach the plaintiff after several attempts, he contacted other lawyers and spent approximately $25,000 in legal fees during the year. In this case, Atkin made no similar showing.

secure employment in the coaching or professional wrestling fields. * * * At the time of the injury he was in excellent physical condition and had consistently demonstrated the training habits required to successfully compete in the Olympic trials. The plaintiff testified that prior to the accident he intended to try to make the United States Olympic team. The plaintiff offered no evidence of his earnings at the time of the injury or at the time of the trial that were derived from his wrestling skills. * * * There was evidence offered and rejected that supports a finding that as a coach he could have received earnings in the range of $16,000 to $20,000 per year. * * *

The defendant nevertheless argues that the evidence is insufficient and that the instructions submitting the issue are in error because there was no evidence of his earnings from the wrestling sport or profession at the time of the injury or at the time of trial. This argument has been rejected by this court ever since Bliss v. Beck, 80 Neb. 290, 114 N.W. 162, in which this court held that a married woman could recover for her diminished earning capacity, and that it was not necessary that she actually engaged in business on her own account, or intended to do so before her injury. It is settled law in Nebraska that loss of earning capacity, as distinct from loss of wages, salary, or earnings, is a separate element of damage. It is equally well settled that a loss of past earnings is an item of special damage and must be specifically pleaded and proved. Impairment of earning capacity is an item of general damage and proof may be had under general allegations of injury and damage. [citation] Proof of an actual loss of earnings or wages is not essential to recovery for loss of earning capacity. [citations] Recovery for loss or diminution of the power to earn in the future is based upon such factors as the plaintiff's age, life expectancy, health, habits, occupation, talents, skill, experience, training, and industry. From our quite detailed review of the facts, it is clear that there was ample evidence to sustain the findings of the jury as to the talents, skill, experience, training, and industry in the pursuit of the wrestling sport and preparation for professional occupation and career in this area. The other evidence as to plaintiff's age, life expectancy, health, and habits sustains the presence of all these elements required as to the proof of loss of earning capacity.

The defendant complains that the proof of prospective earnings of a coach or a professional wrestler fell short of adequacy and was insufficient to support the verdict. As we have pointed out such specific evidence is unnecessary for the plaintiff to recover under a general allegation of damage. But, more importantly, in this case the plaintiff offered evidence of the earning capacity of coaches and wrestlers. He specifically offered to prove that the average starting salary of a collegiate wrestling coach was approximately $20,000 per year, and that a good professional wrestler would average $500 to $1,000 per week. The defendant objected to this testimony and it was excluded by the court. The defendant is now in no position to complain of the insufficiency of the evidence. A party who objects to the evidence and causes it to be excluded, cannot obtain a reversal of the judgment as unsupported for want of the evidence so excluded. [citation] There is no merit to this contention. * * *

Affirmed.

Moran, District Judge. I respectfully dissent. There was no evidence of plaintiff's earnings from any source at the time of the injury or at the trial. I contend that the plaintiff had the duty to produce this evidence.

Notes

1. The plaintiff has established economic damages, the existence of some lost future income. Is uncertainty about the amount of damages to be resolved with a statistical valuation of the "lost chance"? If the plaintiff had one chance of five of making the Olympic team should he receive 20% of the anticipated benefit of Olympic participation? See note after Youst v. Longo, pp. 34–35 supra.

2. A typical jury instruction on non-pecuniary injuries: Damages—Emotional Distress

If, under the court's instructions, you find that plaintiff is entitled to a verdict against defendant, you must then award plaintiff damages in an amount that will reasonably compensate him for all loss or harm, provided that you find it was [or will be] suffered by him and proximately caused by the defendant's conduct. The amount of such award shall include:

Reasonable compensation for any pain, discomfort, fears, anxiety and other emotional distress suffered by the plaintiff [and for similar suffering reasonably certain to be experienced in the future from the same cause].

No definite standard [or method of calculation] is prescribed by law by which to fix reasonable compensation for pain and suffering. Nor is the opinion of any witness required as to the amount of such reasonable compensation. [Furthermore, the argument of counsel as to the amount of damages is not evidence of reasonable compensation.] In making an award for pain and suffering you shall exercise your authority with calm and reasonable judgment and the damages you fix shall be just and reasonable in the light of the evidence.

3. *Unit of Time Arguments.* Ratner v. Arrington, 111 So.2d 82, 88–89 (Fla. App.1959). "In recent years the question has received consideration in a number of jurisdictions. The weight of authority favors allowing use in argument of a mathematical formula such as suggesting amounts on a per diem basis when damages for pain and suffering are involved. * * *

"Authorities opposing per diem amount arguments as to damages for pain and suffering give varied reasons: (1) that there is no evidentiary basis for converting pain and suffering into monetary terms; (2) that it is improper for counsel to suggest a total amount for pain and suffering, and therefore wrong to suggest per diem amounts; (3) that to do so amounts to the attorney giving testimony, and expressing opinions and conclusions on matters not disclosed by the evidence; (4) that juries frequently are misled thereby into making excessive awards, and that admonitions of the court that the jury should not consider per diem arguments as evidence fail to erase all prejudicial effect; (5) that following such argument by plaintiff, a defendant is prejudiced by being placed in a position of attempting to rebut an argument having no basis in the evidence, with the result that if he does not answer plaintiff's argument in kind he suffers its effect on the jury, but if defendant does answer in kind he thereby implies approval of the per diem argument for damage determination for pain and suffering.

"Authorities approving such arguments give numerous reasons: (1) that it is necessary that the jury be guided by some reasonable and practical considerations; (2) that a trier of the facts should not be required to determine the matter in the abstract, and relegated to a blind guess; (3) that the very absence of a yardstick makes the contention that counsel's suggestions of amounts mislead the jury a questionable one; (4) the argument that the evidence fails to provide a foundation for per diem suggestion is unconvincing, because the jury must, by that or some other reasoning process, estimate and allow an amount appropriately tailored to the particular evidence in that case as to the pain and suffering or other such element of damages; (5) that a suggestion by counsel that the evidence as to pain and suffering justifies allowance of a certain amount, in total or by per diem figures, does no more than present one method of reasoning which the trier of the facts may employ to aid him in making a reasonable and sane estimate; (6) that such per diem arguments are not evidence, and are used only as illustration and suggestion; (7) that the claimed danger of such suggestion being mistaken for evidence is an exaggeration, and such danger, if present, can be dispelled by the court's charges; and (8) that when counsel for one side has made such argument the opposing counsel is equally free to suggest his own amounts as inferred by him from the evidence relating to the condition for which the damages are sought."

4. *How Much is Too Much?* Westbrook v. General Tire and Rubber Co., 754 F.2d 1233, 1239–40 (5th Cir.1985): "In reviewing the entire argument in context as we must, we also note that the jury appears to have adopted counsel's unit of time argument which urged the jury to evaluate a long period of pain and suffering, or loss, as a multiple of its smaller time equivalents. In arguing the damages due Kathy Westbrook for loss of consortium, counsel suggested a figure of $25 per week as reasonable to compensate her loss. Counsel then calculated her cumulative loss at $25 per week over the course of Charles Westbrook's stipulated life expectancy of 45.6 years to be $59,280. The jury awarded Kathy Westbrook $59,000.

"In a similar manner, counsel used $1.00 per waking hour as a sum which would adequately compensate Charles Westbrook for his future pain, suffering, and mental anguish. Again, counsel did his arithmetic and arrived at a figure of $298,711.20.[1] Similarly, counsel set $1.00 per waking hour as the worth attributable to Westbrook's loss of the capacity to enjoy life and reached a total of $298,711.20 over 45.6 years. Consequently, for pain, suffering, mental anguish, and restrictions on leisure activities caused by the accident, counsel calculated a damage figure of $597,000.

"Counsel then argued that lost earnings should be awarded by assuming Westbrook would experience 38 years of diminished earning capacity. By working at minimum wage over those 38 years, Westbrook would lose $328,000 in income he could have made as a truck driver. Counsel then calculated for the jury that $597,000 for pain, suffering, mental anguish and loss of life's enjoyment, plus $328,000 for lost earnings, totaled $925,000. It is the exact figure the jury awarded.

"It is difficult to evaluate whether awards for pain and suffering are excessive. Here, the jury was not asked to delineate the portion of damages awarded for lost earnings and the amount awarded for pain and suffering. However, because Westbrook's request was granted to the penny, we can safely assume that $597,000 represented damages for pain, suffering and diminished capacity to enjoy life, while $328,000 was intended to compensate for lost earnings. Looking at the lost earnings sum alone, we are drawn to notice the extreme generosity of this award.

"Lost future earnings provide the victim with a sum of money to replace the money he would have earned. The law requires and this jury was instructed to make a reasonable adjustment for the present value of this lump sum by taking into account the rate of return Westbrook could be expected to receive upon investing this money at the prevailing interest rate. Westbrook's award could be invested in a wide variety of securities which would yield varying rates. However, if we were to make a conservative assumption that Westbrook would invest this lump sum award in secure long-term bonds, at a currently available interest rate of 10%, he would receive an annual income of $32,800 for the rest of his life without ever touching the principal. A yearly income of $32,800 is more than double the

1. [Footnotes renumbered.] According to our calculations, counsel must have used 18 as the number of waking hours in a day to arrive at this figure.

$15,600 a year the proof showed Westbrook would have made as a truck driver for Pilot Point. When we add the $597,000 arrived at by using a unit of time formula, we can confidently state that the entire award of $925,000 is at or above the maximum permissible award. * * *

"Breaking down a large time span into its smaller parts of weeks, days or even hours holds a great appeal to a juror looking for a more understandable and manageable way to approach the task of fixing damages. However, this court has found such arguments impermissible because they tend to produce excessive verdicts. Baron Tube Co. v. Transport Insurance Co., 365 F.2d 858 (5th Cir.1966) (en banc). This tendency came to fruition in Charles Westbrook's case.

"In *Baron Tube,* this court stated:

> '[T]he [unit of time] argument cannot be supported by evidence because pain and suffering cannot be measured in dollars on a unit of time basis; that the amount of such damages must necessarily be left, without mathematical formula, to the sound discretion of the jury, because there is no mathematical rule by which the equivalent of such injuries in money can be legally determined; that such arguments create an illusion of certainty in the jury's mind which does not and cannot in fact exist; and that the whole argument is designed and framed to present an appeal to the jurors to put themselves in the plaintiff's shoes.'

"The court went on, however, to recognize that such arguments are 'not improper where accompanied by a suitable cautionary instruction' to protect against an excessive verdict. The en banc court further emphasized its holding by stating that while a trial judge has much discretion in the means employed to protect against excessive verdicts, a cautionary instruction should have been given to ameliorate the effects of a unit of time argument. 'We hasten to reiterate that these matters, *except for requiring a cautionary instruction,* are left to the discretion of the trial court.' (emphasis added).

"No cautionary instruction was given in this case. Furthermore, General Tire neither objected to the argument nor requested a cautionary instruction. Indeed, it has not raised this error in disputing the excessive verdict on this appeal. Nevertheless, the specific challenge to the amount of the award has directly led us to this error. That the jury awarded precisely the amount of money the formula produced is conclusive evidence that the jury adopted the unit of time formula. Thus, we are convinced that the size of this award is, in part, directly attributable to an uncorrected unit of time argument. This implicates the concerns expressed in *Baron Tube.*"[2]

5. *Proposals to Reduce the Uncertainty of Future Damages*

a. *An Economic Evaluation of Future Damages.* In a paper presented to the Remedies section of the Association of American Law Schools in 1979,[1] Professor E.J. Schaefer observed:

"When confronted with uncertainty [about future damages], courts have usually adopted one of two extreme approaches. Under the first approach, the plaintiff's loss of income may be characterized as so uncertain that to award damages would be speculative. Therefore, it is concluded, no damages at all should be awarded on the basis of lost income. This approach is associated in particular with the

2. We caution that we do not read *Baron Tube* to hold a unit of time argument reversible per se. Rather, such argument may be allowed when couched with proper safeguards or otherwise cured.

1. The paper became an article, Schaefer, Uncertainty and the Law of Damages, 19 Wm. & Mary L.Rev. 719 (1978).

certainty rule in contract law, which requires that a plaintiff seeking special damages prove any lost earnings with reasonable certainty. Under the second approach, the uncertainty is ignored, and the plaintiff's damages are calculated as though his lost income would otherwise have been a sure thing. This frequently happens in personal injury cases. The insistence on all or nothing has been criticized by influential commentators as requiring courts to select the less unfair of two unfair alternatives. It differs strikingly from the approach taken by economists and financial analysts to the valuation of risky opportunities to receive income. Use of the techniques of economic analysis in the law of damages would lead to more accurate valuation of a lost income opportunity. It would also permit a court to choose from a wider range of outcomes than simply the two extremes of all or nothing."

Schaefer suggests various techniques to factor in the uncertainty more precisely than leaving it to the factfinder's instinct. In commercial cases involving the future loss of uncertain profits, the "value of the chance" of actually making those profits could be considered, just as all businessmen, bankers and financial analysts do. The market evaluation of the opportunity (contract value of the chance) times the "probability" of the anticipated income being realized is susceptible of calculation according to recognized economic models.[2]

The process of determining loss of future income or impairment of earning capacity in personal injury or wrongful death cases (e.g., *Washington,* supra) might include a "deduction for the risk." This might lessen the overall uncertainty, particularly when the injured person is very young and has no "track record" of earnings; when plaintiff's projections involve a risky (from the standpoint of earnings) type of occupation, like entertainer, professional athlete, speculative investor, etc.; or when plaintiff predicts a change to a higher-earning occupation. Admittedly a market valuation for these future earnings is more difficult than lost profits of a business which can be capitalized, since it is unusual, but not impossible, to find a market for personal earning capacities.

Such a deduction might allow for the "vicissitudes of life" or for "contingencies," which has found some favor in English[3] and Canadian cases. Or the risk could be reflected by increasing the rate at which the lump sum will be discounted to present value.

Professor Schaefer refers to a number of American cases, primarily from New York,[4] that express the uncertainty by reducing a projected award, without utiliz-

2. The simplest form of the "value of the chance" calculation is where the breach of contract or tort cost the plaintiff an opportunity to win a contest. Kansas City, Mexico & Orient Railway v. Bell, 197 S.W. 322 (Tex.Civ.App. 1917); Chaplin v. Hicks [1911] 2 K.B. 786.

3. See Schaefer, supra note 1, at 754.

4. For example in Grayson v. Irvmar Realty Corp., 7 A.D.2d 436, 440, 184 N.Y.S.2d 33, 37 (1959), the plaintiff was a prospective opera singer whose voice was impaired as a result of the defendant's negligence. The court said:

> "In determining, therefore, the amount to be recovered, the jury may consider the gifts attributed to plaintiff; the training she has received; the training she is likely to receive; the opportunities and the recognition she already has had; the opportunities she is likely to have in the future; the fact that even though the opportunities may be many, that the full realization of those opportunities is limited to the very few; the fact that there are many other risks and contingencies, other than accidents, which may divert a would-be vocal artist from her career; and finally, that *it is assessing directly not so much future earning capacity as the opportunities for a practical chance at such future earning capacity.*" [emphasis added]

Zaninovich v. American Airlines, Inc., 26 A.D.2d 155, ___, 271 N.Y.S.2d 866 (1966), was a wrongful death case. The court said:

> "There is no doubt that the father's earning potentialities for the future are to be considered * * *. Nevertheless, those potentialities must be discounted, not only financially in determining the present value of future funds, *but practically in recognizing that potentialities are contingent and subject to unforeseen and unforeseeable vicissitudes* * * *. *This* * * * *the jury did not do.* * * *

ing the tools of economic analysis. A trial court that ventures to indulge in such refinements will not likely have its calculations disturbed on appeal because of the considerable discretion which is tolerated in awards affected by uncertainty.

b. *Structured Awards.* The uncertainty in lump sum damages for future damages can be removed by making them payable as the expenses accrue. This is practical for future medical expenses, but much less so for lost profits or future lost earnings. Many examples of voluntary *settlements* of personal injury cases on this basis exist, particularly where the defendant is an institution:

From TIME, Oct. 18, 1982,

FUTURE FUNDING†

A New Way to Treat Tragedy

Twice, a worried Charles Younger, 38, asked the staff in the Stanford University Hospital delivery room about his newborn's inactivity. He got only brisk reassurances. Finally, after 40 minutes, Younger pleaded: "How can I tell if my baby is alive?" Anna was alive, barely. She was suffering from oxygen deprivation, and the child today is a quadriplegic. But at least Anna will have few financial worries. The reason: an increasingly popular new way to settle malpractice lawsuits.

Last week Anna's parents received the first payment of an annual allowance that starts at $81,990 and will climb to $5.5 million if she lives to be 78, as her doctors say she could. Soon she and her parents will also collect $1.2 million, of which $650,000 will go to their lawyer. The $122 million package, agreed to by both sides, is known as a structured settlement, and it offers something for everyone. The plaintiff escapes the risk of mismanaging a lump-sum payment and owes no taxes on the annuities. The defendant, or his insurer, ends up paying relatively modest amounts if, as often happens, the plaintiff dies early. And such settlements sound so generous. Actually, Anna's potential $122 million is equivalent to a properly managed trust fund of just $8.1 million.

However, so far as periodic payment of *judgments* is concerned, lump sum damages have been so firmly imbedded in the common law that it apparently can only be changed by statute. Such statutes exist in the workers' compensation field. See, e.g. Valles v. Daniel Construction Co., 589 S.W.2d 911 (Tenn.1979). More than a dozen states have adopted some form of periodic payment statutes, usually for bodily injury damages in products liability cases. The California Supreme Court rejected due process and equal protection challenges to a California statute that provides for medical malpractice damages for "future damages" in the form of periodic payments. American Bank and Trust Co. v. Community Hospital of Los Gatos–Saratoga, Inc., 36 Cal.3d 359, 204 Cal.Rptr. 671, 683 P.2d 670 (1984).

c. The National Conference of Commissioners on Uniform State Laws in 1980 proffered a Model Periodic Payment of Judgments Act, 14 U.L.A. 20. Henderson, Designing a Responsible Periodic–Payment System for Tort Awards: Arizona Enacts a Prototype, 32 Ariz.L.Rev. 21 (1990). Among the benefits claimed for such legislation is that it protects the unsophisticated plaintiff from squandering a large judgment by improvident investments, while saving the plaintiff investment counselling fees. *Future* inflation is not a present concern, but it will be recognized by

[W]ith people as young as those who died here, at the start of their careers, the contingencies for the future become extremely great and require all but total discounting of the suggested expectations." [emphasis supplied]

An award of $50,000 was reduced to $20,000. See Schaefer, supra, note 1, at 741, for other citations.

adjustments of periodic payments as the future turns out; an inflation factor is not included in the discount to present value. Presumably this will benefit the plaintiff since the periodic payments will be tax free. A lump sum payment, although itself tax free, yields taxable investment income in the future. Also the plaintiff will benefit by not having to pay a large contingent fee off the top of a lump sum award, but will be able to spread the fees over the years as the periodic payments accrue.

In theory, defendants benefit by purchasing an annuity for a fixed sum to cover the judgment, while being able to terminate payments if the actual event calls for their cessation. In addition they do not have to guess the *future* inflation because that will result in adjustments to the actual rate; insurance companies may regard this as a potentially mixed blessing.

New York recently adopted a periodic payment system for damage awards for personal injury, injury to property or wrongful death that exceed $250,000. N.Y. Civ.Proc. & R. § 5041 (McKinney Supp.1990). The statute sets out a method for computing future payments and provides for an annuity contract. If the injured party dies, a portion of the annuity payment terminates. See Frey v. Chester E. Smith and Sons, Inc., 751 F.Supp. 1052 (N.D.N.Y.1990).

b. Reducing Uncertainty by Agreement: Liquidated Damages

Brecher v. Laikin, 430 F.Supp. 103, 106 (S.D.N.Y.1977): "Liquidated damage provisions have had a checkered history. While the freedom of parties to structure their agreement is universally acknowledged to be at the heart of the law of contract, 1 Corbin, Contracts § 1 (1963), the limited enforcement of clauses where parties have agreed to specified measures of damages is a judicial check on the freedom of contract based on public policy notions of the courts of equity. 5 Corbin, Contracts § 1055 (1964). As a general test, if a contested clause providing for definite preagreed damages is intended by the parties to operate in lieu of performance, it will be deemed a liquidated damages clause and may be enforced by the courts. If such a clause is intended to operate as a means to compel performance, it will be deemed a penalty and will not be enforced. 5 Williston, Contracts § 776 (3d Ed.1961). If a contract with many terms of varying degrees of importance provides that the liquidated damages clause will be enforceable for any breach of the contract, serious or trivial, the liquidated damages clause will be viewed as a penalty and, as such, be unenforceable as to any breach. On the other hand, if a liquidated damages clause is general in a contract with several clauses of varying importance, the clause will be held applicable only to material breaches and enforceable only as to such breaches. Where the court has sustained a liquidated damages clause the measure of damages for a breach will be the sum in the clause, no more, no less. If the clause is rejected as being a penalty, the recovery is limited to actual damages proven.

"New York law permits the use of liquidated damages clauses in contracts. See, e.g., N.Y.U.C.C. § 2–718 (McKinney's 1964); 14 N.Y.Jur., Damages § 155. A party seeking to enforce a liquidated damages clause must meet two tests. First, at the time the contract was entered into, the anticipated damages in the event of a breach must be incapable of, or very difficult of, accurate estimation. Second, the amount of the damages specified in the liquidated damages clause must not be disproportionate to the damage reasonably anticipated for the breach as of the time the contract was made."

Skip to 50

UNITED STATES v. CONWAY, M.D.

United States District Court, Eastern District of Louisiana, 1988.
686 F.Supp. 571.

[Under the National Health Service Corps Scholarship Program eligible students receive scholarships and agree to serve in a designated health manpower shortage area. The agreement provides that if the student defaults on the promise to serve, he or she will be liable for liquidated damages of three times the scholarship plus interest.]

PATRICK E. CARR, DISTRICT JUDGE. * * * On June 7, 1979, the defendant, Dr. Marianne Denise Conway, who had already been accepted as a medical student applicant at the University of Health Services Chicago Medical College, applied for a scholarship award through the National Health Service Corps (NHSC) Scholarship Program. The Scholarship Program was established by Section 751 *et seq.* of the Public Service Health Act.

Also, on June 7, 1979, Dr. Conway executed a NHSC Scholarship Program contract in which she agreed, *inter alia,* to serve one year of obligated service for each year the scholarship award was provided, with a minimum obligation of two years. Prior to applying for this scholarship, the defendant received an Applicant Information Bulletin dated December, 1978 which contained information concerning the consequences of breach of the obligation to serve.

Dr. Conway subsequently applied for and received a continuation of the NHSC scholarship for the academic years of July 1, 1980 through June 30, 1981, July 1, 1981 through June 30, 1982, and July 1, 1982 through June 30, 1983. In accordance with the scholarship contract and the extension and amendment contracts, scholarship awards were made by the NHSC Scholarship Program totalling $79,567.09. Under the terms of the scholarship contract, Dr. Conway was obligated to serve four (4) years either in the National Health Service Corps or through other enumerated methods following completion of her academic training. However, Dr. Conway could request a deferment of her service obligation in order to pursue advanced clinical training. In accordance with the applicable statutes and regulations, the NHSC Scholarship Program was required to approve all requests from physician scholars for a deferment of up to three years in order to complete advanced clinical training. Deferment requests of greater than three years may be approved by the NHSC Scholarship Program if the request is consistent with the needs of the NHSC, in accordance with the applicable law.

On October 15, 1982, Dr. Conway contacted the NHSC Scholarship Program about a four year deferment of her service obligation to NHSC in order to pursue a a residency program in ophthalmology. She was orally advised that the NHSC Scholarship Program would not defer service obligations for physicians seeking residencies in ophthalmology. On April 12, 1982, the NHSC Scholarship Program had sent Dr. Conway written notification of the training programs for which deferments would be granted.

Dr. Conway graduated from medical school in June, 1983. On May 17, 1873 [sic], prior to her graduation, Dr. Conway requested a deferment to complete a one year flexible internship. The NHSC approved her request and the commencement of Dr. Conway's service obligation was deferred until July 1, 1984. On June 20, 1983, the NHSC sent Dr. Conway a packet of information outlining the policies and procedures applicable to the placement of scholarship recipients scheduled to begin service in July, 1984. This placement package included a Site Selection Questionaire (SSQ) to be completed and returned to the NHSC by July 15, 1983. Dr. Conway elected not to submit a completed SSQ and consequently the NHSC notified her on November 1, 1983 that upon completion of her one year internship she would be assigned to the Indian Health Service (IHS) for fulfillment of her NHSC obligation commencing in July, 1984. The deadline for confirming was April 15, 1984.

On December 9, 1983, Dr. Conway contacted the Scholarship Program personnel about extending her deferment. The NHSC Scholarship Program verbally advised the defendant that the deadline for requesting a deferment had passed and that she would have to send in a written request. On February 28, 1984, Dr. Conway was notified by letter that her continued deferment would be considered if she informed the NHSC of the type of training which she wished to pursue and the letter re-confirmed that deferment for ophthalmological training would not be approved.

On March 27, 1984, Dr. Conway was contacted again by the IHS about finalizing a placement with the IHS and was reminded of the April 15, 1984 deadline for doing so. Dr. Conway failed to confirm placement with the IHS or obtain an approved deferment resulting in notice to the defendant on May 18, 1984 of the IHS's intent to recommend that Dr. Conway be placed in default of her scholarship awards. Dr. Conway did not correspond with the NHSC or reply to notices or demands by them after the December 11, 1983 correspondence.

On July 3, 1984, Dr. Conway was declared to be in breach of her NHSC Scholarship contract as a result of her failure to begin her service obligation on July 1, 1984. She was advised that due to her default, she would be required to pay three times the amount of all NHSC scholarship funds paid to her for her medical education plus interest. By letter dated June 7, 1985, Dr. Conway was informed by the NHSC that she owed $400,408.39 consisting of principal in the amount of $238,701.27 and interest in the amount of $161,707.12, with interest accruing thereafter at the rate of 17.395 percent per annum. Dr. Conway was requested to pay this amount by June 30, 1985.

By letter of May 6, 1987, Dr. Conway offered to perform ophthalmologic health care services in a designated Health Manpower Shortage Area (HMSA) to be agreed upon between the NHSC and Dr. Conway, conditioned upon her being allowed to complete her residency in ophthalmology. Dr. Conway's request to fulfill her service obligations by working at Charity Hospital, in New Orleans, Louisiana was denied on November 3, 1987 due to the fact that by NHSC criteria New Orleans is not a "need" area for ophthalmology. Counsel for plaintiff, the United States of America, at that time also advised counsel for Dr. Conway that as of July, 1988, that there was a vacancy in ophthalmology with the Indian Health Service (IHS) in Gallup, New Mexico. Dr. Conway was given until November 30, 1987 to make a decision regarding whether she wished to arrange a site visit and accept that position. By agreement of counsel, the position was held open through February 15, 1988. Some two and a half months later, the defendant finally inquired about the position at Gallup, New Mexico, but the IHS had hired someone else to fill the position due to the defendant's tardiness in making the necessary arrangements for a site visit.

As of today's date, Dr. Conway has failed to accept any assignment for completion of her service obligation in lieu of repayment and has made no payment towards the debt.

She has repeatedly failed to serve out her obligatory service as requested by the Secretary through the NHSC. Dr. Conway has agreed to serve out her four year commitment only at Charity Hospital and requests that it be deemed a health manpower shortage area.

This Court finds that to permit a recipient of scholarship funds to make an agreement with NHSC for such funds and then to permit the recipient to decide what service will be rendered and where it would be rendered would result in absolute chaos in any such program. Such actions would be intolerable and would most certainly destroy any such program. * * *

Due to the default of the NHSC Scholarship contract, Dr. Conway owes to the United States of America the sum of $520,993.86 through May 25, 1988 with interest accruing thereafter at the rate of 17.395 percent per annum or $113.76 per day.

This Court holds that the defendant, Dr. Marianne Denise Conway has breached her contract with the government in failing to perform her period of obligated service and that the government's motion for summary judgment will be granted and the defendant's motion will be denied. Judgment shall be rendered accordingly.

Notes

1. United States v. Redovan, 656 F.Supp. 121, 127–29 (E.D.Pa.1986). Dr. Redovan also declined an assignment to the Indian Health Service: "The third contention of the defendant is that the treble damage provision contained in the statute and his agreement with NHSC is void and unenforceable because it is a penalty. The United States takes the position that the clause is a valid stipulation of liquidated damages. All cases addressing the enforceability of this provision of which I am aware have agreed that the clause is indeed enforceable. United States v. Bills, 639 F.Supp. 825 (D.N.J.1986); United States v. Hayes, 633 F.Supp. 1183 (M.D.N.C.1986); United States v. Swanson, 618 F.Supp. 1231 (D.Mich.1985). I have made my own independent assessment of the question in light of the facts before me and the cases reported and conclude that the provision is an enforceable damage provision.

"In construing liquidated damages provisions in United States contracts, the court must apply principles of general federal contract law. [citations] And generally, it is permissible to allow the enforcement of liquidated damages provisions where the actual damages are uncertain in amount but demonstrable, as is often the case with government contracts. * * *

"I conclude that the damage provision contained in the contract and the statute is a valid and enforceable provision, because I simply am unable to find that it is disproportionate to the injury inflicted on the United States by Redovan's failure to perform. First and most obviously, the government has lost and must recover the money provided to Redovan for his education, costs and living expenses. That aspect of damage is simple to ascertain. However, the other costs imposed on the United States are decidedly less easy to measure.

"By defaulting on his service obligation, Redovan has deprived the United States of the services of a physician in a critically underserved location. As Judge Thompson observed in *Bills,*

'One cannot readily estimate the damages occasioned by the * * * loss of a doctor's services in an area determined to be medically underserved.'

'A physician * * * is not a fungible handyman.' *Swanson.*

"Redovan's selfish conduct results in additional burdens on those already overburdened doctors providing medical care in the health manpower shortage area to which he was assigned. It requires citizens in that area to continue to suffer for the lack of adequate numbers of trained medical professionals. And in addition, his refusal to live up to his obligation subverts the lauditory goal of curing the maldistribution of medical care in the nation. For all of these reasons, I am unable to conclude that the liquidated damage provision is unreasonable or disproportionate to the harm suffered because of Redovan's breach.

"Further, I should also consider the likely expense of hiring a similarly trained physician to serve for three years in the location to which Redovan was assigned. Viewed in that light, I find the liquidated damages provision to be a reasonable estimate of the harm caused by defendant's breach.

"Defendant contends that the damage provision is intended to ensure performance and not to compensate reasonably for the harm caused. Because I conclude that the damage provision is indeed a reasonable prior estimate of harm caused, the fact that it also encourages performance of the service obligation does not defeat the provision.

"Defendant's final contention in opposing the suit is that the damage provision of the NHSC statute and contract violates the thirteenth amendment's prohibition of involuntary servitude. Section one of the Thirteenth Amendment provides as follows:

'Section 1. Neither slavery nor involuntary servitude, except as a punishment for crime whereof the party shall have been duly convicted, shall exist within the United States, or any place subject to their jurisdiction.'

"Subsequent federal legislation enacted to enforce the Thirteenth Amendment prohibited the practice of 'peonage', which is defined as 'compulsory service in payment of a debt. A peon is one who is compelled to work for his creditor until his debt is paid.' Bailey v. Alabama, 219 U.S. 219, 242 (1911). As the Supreme Court observed in Clyatt v. United States, 197 U.S. 207, 215–16 (1905):

'A clear distinction exists between peonage and voluntary performance of labor or rendering of services in payment of a debt. In the latter case the debtor, though contracting to pay his indebtedness by labor or service, and subject, like any other contractor, to an action for breach of that contract, can elect at any time to break it, and no law or force compels performance or a continuance of the service.'

"In the case before me, it is abundantly clear that Redovan has not been compelled to perform or continue any service whatever. Instead, he has chosen not to perform any service whatever. He has remained in Philadelphia and not reported to his assigned place of service. Because the Government has not sought to compel service—and Redovan may choose to have a civil money judgment entered against him in lieu of service—the enforcement of the government's rights in this lawsuit does not constitute peonage or some other form of involuntary servitude.

"Indeed, the rights the government seeks to enforce in this action are for a money judgment. Peonage, or the coerced service of labor in payment of a debt, is not implicated. Rather, this case presents the converse, that of payment of a debt in the place of an agreed upon service obligation.

"The peonage cases cited by the defendant are readily distinguishable. From Clyatt v. United States in 1905, and Bailey v. Alabama, in 1911, to United States v. Mussry, 726 F.2d 1448 (9th Cir.1984), the touchstone of involuntary servitude has been 'law or force compel[ling] * * * service.' *Bailey* and the line of similar cases involve the use of criminal sanctions which employ presumptions to convert breach of a contract into a criminal offense, with the purpose of compelling labor. * * * All of the cases cited by the defendant involved unfortunate individuals, some of whom were illiterate and even unable to communicate in English, who were ill equipped to understand the scope of the obligation they entered into until the die was cast. Redovan can hardly claim to be in a similar position. He understood the nature of the obligation before he entered into it as an educated professional.

"Further, as I concluded earlier, the damage provision is a reasonable estimation of the harm caused by defendant's default. Because defendant is required to make recompense for the harm, and he is unable financially to do so, he claims that the damage provision coerces his involuntary servitude. It is clear, however, that in assessing damages for breach of a contract, the court is not required to consider the breaching party's ability to pay, in order to stay within constitutional bounds. The fact that the consequences of a large money judgment may encourage Redovan to perform a service obligation does not convert him into a peon.

"For all of these reasons, the defense of involuntary servitude fails, and judgment will be entered for the United States."

2. Schwartz, The Myth That Promisees Prefer Supracompensatory Remedies: An Analysis of Contracting for Damage Measures, 100 Yale L.J. 369 (1990).

C. GENERAL AND SPECIAL DAMAGES

COHN v. J.C. PENNEY CO., INC.

Supreme Court of Utah, 1975.

537 P.2d 306.

ELLETT, JUSTICE. The plaintiff fell on premises occupied by defendants and claimed damages. * * *

The case was tried to a jury and submitted thereto on a special verdict. * * * It found damages as follows:

Medical expenses	$352.25
Loss of income	656.00
General Damages	0

Judgment was entered in accordance with the answers contained in the special verdict. The plaintiff duly moved for a new trial, claiming inadequacy of general damages. The trial court overruled the motion, apparently thinking that lost wages were an element of general damages. He instructed the jury regarding damages for the injury which plaintiff claimed she sustained and specifically mentioned suffering, both mental and physical, and the extent which she had been prevented from pursuing the ordinary affairs of life, and the disability or *loss of earning capacity* resulting from the injury. He also instructed that the jury could not allow more than $656 for lost earnings. He further instructed in regard to special damages to include, inter alia, expenses paid for doctors, medicines, nurses, and x-rays, in the amount of $352.25.

His Honor noticed the inconsistency of the answers to the interrogatories in that hospital and doctor bills and lost wages were awarded but nothing was found for pain or suffering. A bench conference was called, and the court indicated to counsel that he thought the verdict was proper since lost wages were a part of general damages. He undoubtedly would not have accepted the verdict had he thought that lost wages were special damages.

There should be a consensus of opinion amongst the bench and bar of this state as to the distinction between various categories of general and special damages. We, therefore, set forth what we consider to be the proper distinction between the two. The difference between the two types of damages is of importance because special damages must ordinarily be pleaded in order to be recovered.

General damages are those which naturally and necessarily result from the harm done. They are damages which everybody knows are likely to result from the harm described and so are said to be implied in law. Special damages are those which occur as a natural consequence of the harm done but are not so certain to flow therefrom as to be implied in law. One claiming them must plead them so as to let his adversary know what will be involved. An illustration will show the difference:

Plaintiff sues defendant for blowing up his dam in the river and claims damages in the amount of $5,000. His proof shows the cost of repairs to the dam to be $1,000. He offers evidence to the effect that he had a water mill which had to be shut down for two months during the rebuilding of the dam and that he lost profits in the amount of $4,000 as a result thereof. The rebuilding of the dam is an item of general damages, but the loss of profits due to inoperation of the mill is an item of special damage because it is peculiar to his case. Another man might have his dam blown up and might not even own a mill, or it might not be operative. Still another man might have special damages because he could not irrigate his farm as a result of the destruction of the dam which he owned and the lowering of the water below the bottom of his lateral ditch. Each dam owner would need to set forth his particular special damages because such special damages do not of necessity follow as a result of the tort. * * *

The distinctions between general and special damages are principally important with regard to the pleadings in damage actions. General damages, which necessarily result from the injury complained of, may be recovered under a general allegation of damage, whereas special damages must be specially pleaded. * * *

McCormick on Damages (Hornbook Series) makes the following statement at pages 37 and 38:

> "In personal injury suits, the following are usually treated as matters to be specially pleaded: Loss of time and earnings; impairment of future earning capacity; expenses of drugs, nursing, and medical care; aggravation by the injury of a pre-existing disease; and insanity resulting from the injury. Almost any of these, however, might be results so usually accompanying the particular injury alleged as that they would be regarded as sufficiently pleaded by the statement of the injury. * * *
>
> "Where the injuries alleged are of such a character as to give notice to all the world of the damages which would of necessity follow, then, of course, items usually classified as special damages could be proved without pleading them. A typist or a pianist who alleges the loss of a hand should be able to prove loss

of earning capacity without specially alleging it because all the world knows that two hands are necessary to either occupation. * * * "

In Pauly v. McCarthy, 109 Utah 431, 184 P.2d 123 (1947), this court in speaking on the question of whether recovery for permanent disability could be proved without specially pleading it set out three lines of decision, the first two of which are summarized and the third of which is quoted:

"(1) Recovery can be had under a general allegation for damages.

"(2) Not recoverable under a general allegation of damages, without specially pleading the fact of permanency. (A theory that permanent injury is in the nature of special damages, which must be specifically pleaded to allow recovery therefor.)

"(3) A third line of authorities holds that unless facts from which the permanency of the injury will necessarily be implied are alleged, there must be a special averment that the injuries are permanent, in order to let in proof to that effect. This is really a qualification of the second rule. Under this rule the fact that permanency may possibly or even probably follow from the nature of the injury is not sufficient to allow recovery therefor, in the absence of a specific allegation of permanency."

It thus seems clear that the loss of earnings to date of trial and impairment of earning capacity are both items of special damages, and yet they may be proved under an allegation of general damages where the description of the injuries is such that everyone must know that of necessity there would be a loss of earnings and an impairment of earning capacity.

In Utah there does not seem to be an inflexible rule regarding the pleading of special damages. It is a question of whether or not the pleadings contain such information as will apprise the defendant of such damages as must of necessity flow from that which is alleged.

In the instant matter there was not merely an inadequate award of general damages—there was no award at all. The verdict was deficient in form, and counsel had an opportunity to have the jury sent back for further deliberations. This he did not do, perhaps fearing that the jury might either award some nominal amount or even change the verdict and award nothing to the plaintiff. It would be a smart trial tactic if he could have had a new trial on damages only before a jury which would not be acquainted with the weakness of plaintiff's cause of action. The judgment is, therefore, affirmed.

Note

Applied Data Processing, Inc. v. Burroughs Corp., 394 F.Supp. 504, 508–10 (D.Conn.1975). An equipment lessee sued for breach of warranty. The lessor asserted that the contract excluded liability for "indirect or consequential damages." The court comments about the meaning of this exclusionary clause:

"Although the Michigan Supreme Court has on at least one occasion enforced a contract provision similar to paragraph 8, neither in Michigan nor elsewhere does the term 'consequential damages' have a clearly established meaning.

"In the absence of a settled rule, it is not surprising that the parties urge widely divergent construction of the term. Burroughs maintains that in this action 'direct' (and therefore recoverable) damages are measured by the difference between the value of the data-processing equipment had it been as warranted, and its value as actually delivered, and that all damages that followed the breach are consequential. ADP agrees that consequential damages follow or flow from a breach, but, relying on cases decided under the Uniform Commercial Code, suggests that only those post-breach damages whose valuation is somewhat speculative, such as lost profits, are properly called 'consequential.'

"* * * The only firm starting point to be derived from the case law is that the commercial context in which a contract is made is of substantial importance in determining whether particular damages flowing from its breach are direct or consequential. It may also be said at the outset that no rule limits direct damages to the difference between the value of the equipment as warranted and its value as delivered.

"In Ruggles v. Buffalo Foundry, 27 F.2d 234 (6th Cir.1928) the Court explained the distinction between 'general' and 'special' damages while construing a clause that prohibited recovery of 'any special, indirect, or consequential damages * * *.' That Court appears to have equated consequential and special damages, an equation endorsed by Corbin, Contracts, § 1011 and one to which this Court will adhere.

"The distinction between general and special damages is not that one is and the other is not the direct and proximate consequence of the breach complained of, but that general damages are such as naturally and ordinarily follow the breach, whereas special damages are those that ensue, not necessarily or ordinarily, but because of special circumstances.

"The Court's first task in the present case is thus to decide whether the damages claimed by ADP on the contract counts (in excess of the reliance damages) were, in an objective sense, foreseeable. The Court must then inquire, with regard to those damages found to be foreseeable, whether they are in that category because such damages ordinarily follow the breach of a contract such as the lease agreement entered into by ADP and Burroughs, or only because Burroughs had knowledge of special circumstances. Those damages in the latter class are not recoverable because of the consequential damages exclusion clause of the lease."

D. THE PROBLEM OF VALUATION

HEWLETT v. BARGE BERTIE

United States Court of Appeals, Fourth Circuit, 1969.
418 F.2d 654, cert. denied 397 U.S. 1021 (1970).

Albert V. Bryan, Circuit Judge. Computation of pecuniary damages recoverable for a [barge's] injury in a maritime collision centers this cause. The minim of the injury here, however, obscures and tempts neglect of the importance of the issue.

* * * [T]he respondents confessed negligence at trial and relied exclusively on absence of injury. The admiralty court only allowed the libelant "the sum of $1.00 by way of nominal damages" with costs. He appeals.

The basis of the decision was that as the [barge] BA–1401 had been declared a constructive loss two years before, the District Court was of the opinion that a subsequent injury could not sustain a claim. The declaration followed upon her misfortune on November 11, 1958, when she foundered in Chesapeake Bay. * * * Raised and refloated by the present libelant as contractor-salvor in June 1959, the repair and recovery cost of the barge was estimated to exceed both her 1958 purchase price of $40,000.00 and current insurance of $45,000.00. In these circumstances she was released to Hewlett in satisfaction of his claim for services. After $1305.76 was expended upon her in temporary repairs, such as leak stoppages, she was brought to Norfolk.

The barge was used or useable for carrying pilings or logs—weather-proof cargo. She was engaged on one occasion as a pontoon or caisson in lifting a steamer from the river bottom. * * *

Admittedly, the barge had no market value as an instrument of navigation and could be sold only for scrap. The skin of the barge was not pierced in the collision, and the only mark of impact was a dent in her starboard side. It produced no harmful effect upon the barge's seaworthiness or carrying capacity.

Our concern is the acceptance by the instance court of the respondent's defense to the damage claim, i.e. "the barge was a constructive total loss and that no real or actual damages have been shown, thus restricting the recovery to nominal damages." The decree on review purports to fix "nominal damages," but this is in reality a dismissal of the libel, for admiralty does not recognize nominal damages. * * * Presently the Court stated, "We find no precedent for allowing damages where a vessel, deemed a constructive total loss, suffers still further damage." Apparently, the award of $1.00 was the product of this proposition. It is, we think, an untenable postulate; if accepted, it could result in unjust deprivations.

Actually, the case does not commence with the barge as a constructive loss, as the admiralty judge believed. True, that was her status more than a year previous, but only as between the owner and the salvor. Even this, however, was not a decree of outlawry. She was not a derelict, to be jostled about with impunity. Indeed, as a sheer-hulk she had a demonstrated utility for the libelant. Slightly more than a year previous to repeat, $1305.76 had been expended in restoration. The accused tugboat and tow cannot escape liability by recall of the past ill luck of the BA–1401. Nor are they relieved by showing that she has not suffered in utility value or in market value.

To illustrate, although an automobile through age or misfortune may have no value in the market save for scrap, and although still another nick in its paint or shape may not appreciably reduce the usefulness or dollar-value of the car, nevertheless its checkered career and disreputable appearance do not assure absolution to one who negligently further scars the vehicle. The owner is entitled to have the automobile free of even that dent. De minimis non curat lex does not, semble, apply to damages but only to injury.

"Restitutio in integrum" is the precept in fixing damages, and "where repairs are practicable the general rule followed by the admiralty courts in such cases is that the damages assessed against the respondent shall be sufficient to restore the injured vessel to the condition in which she was at the time the collision occurred." The Baltimore, 8 Wall. 377, 75 U.S. 377, 385 (1869).

The workable guides to this end, generally stated, are these. If the ship sinks and is beyond recovery, the damages are her value just before she sank, plus interest thereon until payment. If she is not a complete loss and repossession or repairs are both physically and economically feasible, then the reasonable cost of recovery, including repairs and an allowance for deprivation of use, is the measure. But if the reclamation expense including repairs exceeds the ship's just value at the time of the casualty, or if repairs are not both physically and economically practicable, then it is a constructive total loss, and the limit of compensation is the value plus interest. * * *

The case at bar comes closer to the second category—the loss was not complete, repairs were physically practicable, but the question remains whether they were economically so. The answer depends on whether the repair cost was more than the value of the barge. Libelant has shown a fair estimate for the repairs to be between $2895.00 and $3000.00. If this expense was beyond the fair and reasonable monetary value of the vessel to the owner, then the recovery is limited to such value.

When, as here, the tortfeasors assert that the value is less than the cost of repairs, they have the burden to establish that fact. The respondents have failed to do so. Consequently, the case stands on the proof of the repair cost, and the libelant is entitled to a decree in that amount.

The District Court made no finding of value. It merely found that the BA–1401 had no value save for sale as scrap, but this is not the equivalent of fixing a figure of value. Moreover, it is erroneous. It is refuted by the other uncontested findings of her continuing utility.

Apparently, the chief factor influencing the District Judge in this determination was the absence of any market for the sale of the barge. That problem, however, cannot justify withholding all value from libelant's vessel. The special value to the owner is a consideration of substance. * * *

Even if the cost of repairs be limited to the *diminution* in value of the ship rather than to her entire value, our decision would for at least two reasons, not be different. The first point of our conclusion here is that no such values were proved. Beyond that, however, the second point is that in admiralty, the cost of repairs is the equivalent of value-diminution. "Damage less than total loss is compensated by reference to cost of repairs. * * * " Gilmore & Black, Admiralty 436; Pan–American Petroleum & Transport Co. v. United States, 27 F.2d 684, 685 (2 Cir.1928):

> "Strictly the measure of damages in collision is the difference in value between the ship before and after the collision, but the cost of the necessary repairs and the loss of earnings while they are being made have long been regarded as its equivalent."

Furthermore, the cost of repairs is considered an accurate measure. Diminution in value is always dependent upon an opinion, while repairs are not quite so speculative. * * *

The order on appeal will be vacated, and the cause remanded with request to the District Court to enter a decree awarding the appellant Hewlett damages of $2895.00, with interest at 6% per annum from the date of the collision until paid, together with costs in the trial and appellate courts.

Reversed and remanded for entry of judgment.

HAYNSWORTH, CHIEF JUDGE (dissenting): * * * The barge in her then condition had a market value of $5,616. This was her scrap value, but it was a ready market value, and it seems to me to be a mistake to approach the case as if there were no market value when everyone agrees there was.

Everyone agrees, too, that the market value of $5,616 was not affected in the slightest by the additional dent inflicted in her side when the Barge Bertie collided with her. The already battered Barge 1401 had a scrap value after the additional dent of $5,616, just as she had before.

* * * She was as useful as a pontoon after she sustained this dent as she was before, and whatever potential she had for use in carrying deck cargo was not impaired in the slightest.

Under these circumstances, of course, the owner did not attempt to effect the repair of the barge for the repairs were estimated to cost $2,895, and that expenditure would not enhance the value of the barge or its usefulness to the libelant, or to anyone else in the slightest. No one claims that any such repairs would ever be attempted. * * *

I think the damages are to be measured by the economic loss sustained by the libelant and that no different rule can be found in admiralty by looking at isolated statements lifted from their context.

[In] Williamson v. Barrett, 54 U.S. (13 How.) 101, 110, the Court stated what until today never seems to have been doubted: "The general rule in regulating damages in cases of collision is to allow the injured party an indemnity to the extent of the loss sustained." The loss sustained, of course, is the difference in the value of the vessel before and after the collision, together with a sum to compensate for the loss of her service during the completion of repairs, if she is reparable. The particular question in *Williamson* related to the latter assessment. When repairs are economically feasible, however, the assessment of the first item of damage may not depend upon generalized appraisals of the value of the vessel before and after the collision, for the difference in fact is measured by the cost of repair. This was clearly stated in The Schooner Catharine v. Dickinson, 58 U.S. (17 How.) 170. The Catharine sank as a result of a collision just off the New Jersey coast and her owners sold her where she lay for $140. They claimed the difference between the appraised value of the vessel before the collision and $140. The fact, however, was that the schooner had been raised, repaired and returned to service. The Supreme Court held that the actual cost of raising the vessel, repairing her and returning her to service was a more accurate measure of the diminution in value than could be gotten by use of the owner's sales price before she was raised or by the general opinions of inexpert witnesses that the vessel was worth no more than the owner's appraisal before she was refloated.

Since the Supreme Court's decision in *The Catharine* one frequently encounters the expression that the cost of repairs is the equivalent of the diminution in value. This is factually true whenever repairs are economically feasible, for whatever the appraisal of the vessel's value before the collision, all practical men know that the diminution in value is measured by the reasonable cost of necessary repairs to substantially return the vessel to its former condition. That is a more accurate measure of the diminution than a comparison of appraisals by some of the precollision value with general appraisals by others of the post-collision value, as was held in *The Catharine.* * * *

There is not factual equivalency between diminution in value and the cost of repair when the cost of repair is greater than the precollision value of the vessel. In such a case, the measure of damages is clearly the precollision value of the vessel. That this truism is sometimes expressed as a limitation upon the right to recover cost of repairs does not obscure the absence of factual equivalency between diminution in value and cost of repair and the irrelevance of the cost of repair in such a situation. Cost of repair is not the measure of damages simply because in that situation it is not the factual equivalent of diminution in value.

In this case there is no factual equivalency between diminution in value and cost of repair.

If my brothers are right, the libelant is unduly enriched. He must hope greatly that another errant navigator will hit his battered barge again, and still another yet again, so that each time he may happily pocket the estimated cost of theoretical repairs which neither he nor anyone else will ever dream of undertaking while retaining all along a barge as seaworthy and useful to him and of undiminished worth if he chooses to sell it.

E. THE DIVERGENCE BETWEEN TORT AND CONTRACT IN LIMITING DAMAGES

1. THE TRADITIONAL DOCTRINE

FREUND v. WASHINGTON SQUARE PRESS, INC.

Court of Appeals of New York, 1974.
34 N.Y.2d 379, 357 N.Y.S.2d 857, 314 N.E.2d 419.

SAMUEL RABIN, JUDGE. * * * In 1965, plaintiff, an author and a college teacher, and defendant, Washington Square Press, Inc., entered into a written agreement which, in relevant part, provided as follows. Plaintiff ("author") granted defendant ("publisher") exclusive rights to publish and sell in book form plaintiff's work on modern drama. Upon plaintiff's delivery of the manuscript, defendant agreed to complete payment of a nonreturnable $2,000 "advance." Thereafter, if defendant deemed the manuscript not "suitable for publication," it had the right to terminate the agreement by written notice within 60 days of delivery. Unless so terminated, defendant agreed to publish the work in hardbound edition within 18 months and afterwards in paperbound edition. The contract further provided that defendant would pay royalties to plaintiff, based upon specified percentages of sales. (For example, plaintiff was to receive 10% of the retail price of the first 10,000 copies sold in the continental United States.) If defendant failed to publish within 18 months, the contract provided that "this agreement shall terminate and the rights herein granted to the Publisher shall revert to the Author. In such event all payments theretofore made to the Author shall belong to the Author without prejudice to any other remedies which the Author may have." * * *

Plaintiff performed by delivering his manuscript to defendant and was paid his $2,000 advance. Defendant thereafter merged with another publisher and ceased publishing in hardbound. Although defendant did not exercise its 60–day right to terminate, it has refused to publish the manuscript in any form.

Plaintiff * * * initially sought specific performance of the contract. The Trial Term Justice denied specific performance but, finding a valid contract and a breach by defendant, set the matter down for trial on the issue of monetary damages, if any, sustained by the plaintiff. At trial, plaintiff sought to prove: (1) delay of his academic promotion; (2) loss of royalties which would have been earned; and (3) the cost of publication if plaintiff had made his own arrangements to publish. The trial court found that plaintiff had been promoted despite defendant's failure to publish, and that there was no evidence that the breach had caused any delay. Recovery of lost royalties was denied without discussion. The court found, however, that the cost of hardcover publication to plaintiff was the natural and probable consequence of the breach and, based upon expert testimony, awarded $10,000, to cover this cost. It denied recovery of the expenses of paperbound publication on the ground that plaintiff's proof was conjectural.

The Appellate Division (3 to 2) affirmed, finding that the cost of publication was the proper measure of damages. In support of its conclusion, the majority analogized to the construction contract situation where the cost of completion may be the proper measure of damages for a builder's failure to complete a house or for use of wrong materials. The dissent concluded that the cost of publication is not an appropriate measure of damages and consequently, that plaintiff may recover nominal damages only. We agree with the dissent. In so concluding, we look to the basic purpose of damage recovery * * *.

It is axiomatic that * * * the law awards damages for breach of contract to compensate for injury caused by the breach—injury which was foreseeable, i.e., reasonably within the contemplation of the parties, at the time the contract was entered into. [citation] Money damages are substitutional relief designed in theory "to put the injured party in as good a position as he would have been put by full performance of the contract, at the least cost to the defendant and without charging him with harms that he had no sufficient reason to foresee when he made the contract." (5 Corbin, Contracts, § 1002, pp. 31–32.) In other words, so far as possible, the law attempts to secure to the injured party the benefit of his bargain, subject to the limitations that the injury—whether it be losses suffered or gains prevented—was foreseeable, and that the amount of damages claimed be measurable with a reasonable degree of certainty and, of course, adequately proven. [citations] But it is equally fundamental that the injured party should not recover more from the breach than he would have gained had the contract been fully performed. (Baker v. Drake, 53 N.Y. 211, 217; see, generally, Dobbs, Law of Remedies, p. 810.)

Measurement of damages in this case according to the cost of publication to the plaintiff would confer greater advantage than performance of the contract would have entailed to plaintiff and would place him in a far better position than he would have occupied had the defendant fully performed. Such measurement bears no relation to compensation for plaintiff's actual loss or anticipated profit. Far beyond compensating plaintiff for the interests he had in the defendant's performance of the contract—whether restitution, reliance or expectation (see Fuller & Perdue, Reliance Interest in Contract Damages, 46 Yale L.J. 52, 53–56) an award of the cost of publication would enrich plaintiff at defendant's expense.

Pursuant to the contract, plaintiff delivered his manuscript to the defendant. In doing so, he conferred a value on the defendant which, upon defendant's breach, was required to be restored to him. Special Term, in addition to ordering a trial on the issue of damages, ordered defendant to return the manuscript to plaintiff and plaintiff's restitution interest in the contract was thereby protected.

At the trial on the issue of damages, plaintiff alleged no reliance losses suffered in performing the contract or in making necessary preparations to perform. Had such losses, if foreseeable and ascertainable, been incurred, plaintiff would have been entitled to compensation for them.

As for plaintiff's expectation interest in the contract, it was basically twofold—the "advance" and the royalties. (To be sure, plaintiff may have expected to enjoy whatever notoriety, prestige or other benefits that might have attended publication, but even if these expectations were compensable, plaintiff did not attempt at trial to place a monetary value on them.) There is no dispute that plaintiff's expectancy in the "advance" was fulfilled—he has received his $2,000. His expectancy interest in the royalties—the profit he stood to gain from sale of the published book—while theoretically compensable, was speculative. Although this work is not plaintiff's first, at trial he provided no stable foundation for a reasonable estimate of royalties he would have earned had defendant not breached its promise to publish. In these circumstances, his claim for royalties falls for uncertainty.

Since the damages which would have compensated plaintiff for anticipated royalties were not proved with the required certainty, we agree with the dissent in the Appellate Division that nominal damages alone are recoverable. Though these are damages in name only and not at all compensatory, they are nevertheless awarded as a formal vindication of plaintiff's legal right to compensation which has not been given a sufficiently certain monetary valuation.

In our view, the analogy by the majority in the Appellate Division to the construction contract situation was inapposite. In the typical construction contract, the owner agrees to pay money or other consideration to a builder and expects, under the contract, to receive a completed building in return. The value of the promised performance to the owner is the properly constructed building. In this case, unlike the typical construction contract, the value to plaintiff of the promised performance—publication—was a percentage of sales of the books published and not the books themselves. Had the plaintiff contracted for the printing, binding and delivery of a number of hardbound copies of his manuscript, to be sold or disposed of as he wished, then perhaps the construction analogy, and measurement of damages by the cost of replacement or completion, would have some application.

Here, however, the specific value to plaintiff of the promised publication was the royalties he stood to receive from defendant's sales of the published book. Essentially, publication represented what it would have cost the defendant to confer that value upon the plaintiff, and, by its breach, defendant saved that cost. The error by the courts below was in measuring damages not by the value to plaintiff of the promised performance but by the cost of that performance to defendant. Damages are not measured, however, by what the defaulting party saved by the breach, but by the natural and probable consequences of the breach *to the plaintiff.* In this case, the consequence to plaintiff of defendant's failure to publish is that he is prevented from realizing the gains promised by the contract—the royalties. But, as we have stated, the amount of royalties plaintiff would have realized was not ascertained with adequate certainty and, as a consequence, plaintiff may recover nominal damages only.

Accordingly, the order of the Appellate Division should be modified to the extent of reducing the damage award of $10,000 for the cost of publication to six cents, but with costs and disbursements to the plaintiff.

WARTZMAN v. HIGHTOWER PRODUCTIONS, LTD.

Court of Special Appeals of Maryland, 1983.
53 Md.App. 656, 456 A.2d 82.

James S. Getty, Judge. (Specially Assigned). Woody Hightower did not succeed in breaking the Guinness World Record for flagpole sitting; his failure to accomplish this seemingly nebulous feat, however, did generate protracted litigation. We are concerned here with whether Judge Robert L. Karwacki, presiding in the Superior Court of Baltimore City, correctly permitted a jury to consider the issue of "reliance damages" sustained by the appellees. * * *

Hightower Productions, Ltd. came into being in 1974 as a promotional venture conceived by Ira Adler, Frank Billitz and J. Daniel Quinn. The principals intended to employ a singer-entertainer who would live in a specially constructed mobile flagpole perch from April 1, 1975, until New Year's Eve at which time he would descend in Times Square in New York before a nationwide television audience, having established a new world record for flagpole sitting.

The young man selected to perform this feat was to be known as "Woody Hightower." The venture was to be publicized by radio and television exposure, by adopting a theme song and by having the uncrowned champion make appearances from his perch throughout the country at concerts, state fairs and shopping centers.

In November, 1974, the three principals approached Michael Kaminkow of the law firm of Wartzman, Rombro, Rudd and Omansky, P.A., for the specific purpose of incorporating their venture. Mr. Kaminkow, a trial attorney, referred them to his partner, Paul Wartzman.

The three principals met with Mr. Wartzman at his home and reviewed the promotional scheme with him. They indicated that they needed to sell stock to the public in order to raise the $250,000 necessary to finance the project. Shortly thereafter, the law firm prepared and filed the articles of incorporation and Hightower Productions, Ltd. came into existence on November 6, 1974. The Articles of Incorporation authorized the issuance of one million shares of stock of the par value of 10¢ per share, or a total of $100,000.00.

Following incorporation, the three principals began developing the project. With an initial investment of $20,000, they opened a corporate account at Maryland National Bank and an office in the Pikesville Plaza Building. Then began the search for "Woody Hightower." After numerous interviews, twenty-three year old John Jordan emerged as "Woody Hightower."

After selecting the flagpole tenant, the corporation then sought and obtained a company to construct the premises to house him. This consisted of a seven foot wide perch that was to include a bed, toilet, water, refrigerator and heat. The accommodations were atop an hydraulic lift system mounted upon a flat bed tractor trailer.

Hightower employed two public relations specialists to coordinate press and public relations efforts and to obtain major corporate backers. "Woody" received a proclamation from the Mayor and City Council of Baltimore and after a press breakfast at the Hilton Hotel on "All Fools Day" ascended to his home in the sky.

Within ten days, Hightower obtained a live appearance for "Woody" on the Mike Douglas Show, and a commitment for an appearance on the Wonderama television program. The principals anticipated a "snow-balling" effect from commercial enterprises as the project progressed with no substantial monetary commitments for approximately six months.

Hightower raised $43,000.00 by selling stock in the corporation. Within two weeks of "Woody's" ascension, another stockholders' meeting was scheduled, because the corporation was low on funds. At that time, Mr. Wartzman informed the principals that no further stock could be sold, because the corporation was "structured wrong," and it would be necessary to obtain the services of a securities attorney to correct the problem. Mr. Wartzman had acquired this information in a casual conversation with a friend who recommended that the corporation should consult with a securities specialist.

The problem was that the law firm had failed to prepare an offering memorandum and failed to assure that the corporation had made the required disclosures to prospective investors in accordance with the provisions of the Maryland Securities Act. Mr. Wartzman advised Hightower that the cost of the specialist would be between $10,000.00 and $15,000.00. Hightower asked the firm to pay for the required services and the request was rejected.

Hightower then employed substitute counsel and scheduled a shareholders' meeting on April 28, 1975. At that meeting, the stockholders were advised that Hightower was not in compliance with the securities laws; that $43,000.00, the amount investors had paid for issued stock, had to be covered by the promoters and placed in escrow; that the fee of a securities specialist would be $10,000.00 to $15,000.00 and that the additional work would require between six and eight weeks. In the interim, additional stock could not be sold, nor could "Woody" be exhibited across state lines. Faced with these problems, the shareholders decided to discontinue the entire project.

On October 8, 1975, Hightower filed suit alleging breach of contract and negligence for the law firm's failure to have created a corporation authorized to raise the capital necessary to fund the venture. At the trial, Hightower introduced into evidence its obligations and expenditures incurred in reliance on the defendant law firm's creation of a corporation authorized to raise the $250,000.00 necessary to fund the project. The development costs incurred included corporate obligations amounting to $155,339 including: initial investments by Adler and Billitz, $20,000; shareholders, excluding the three promoters, $43,010; outstanding liabilities exclusive of salaries, $58,929; liability to talent consultants, $25,000; and accrued salaries to employees, $8,400.

* * * The only claim submitted for the jury's consideration was the claim of the corporation, Hightower, against the defendant law firm.

The jury returned a verdict in favor of Hightower in the amount of $170,508.43. Wartzman, Rombro, Rudd, and Omansky, P.A., appealed to this Court. * * *

The appellants raise [these] issues for our consideration:

1. The trial court erred in permitting Hightower to recover "reliance damages" or "development costs."

2. If "reliance damages" were recoverable, the trial court failed to properly instruct the jury on the law concerning their recovery.

3. The trial court erred in refusing to instruct the jury on the duty to mitigate damages. * * *

The appellants first contend that the jury verdict included all of Hightower's expenditures and obligations incurred during its existence resulting in the law firm being absolute surety for all costs incurred in a highly speculative venture. While they do not suggest the analogy, the appellants would no doubt equate the verdict as tantamount to holding the blacksmith liable for the value of the kingdom where the smith left out a nail in shoeing the king's horse, because of which the shoe was lost, the horse was lost, the king was lost and the kingdom was lost. Appellants contend that there is a lack of nexus or causation between the alleged failure of Mr. Wartzman to discharge his duties as an attorney and the loss claimed by Hightower. Stated differently, an unjust result will obtain where a person performing a collateral service for a new venture will, upon failure to fully perform the service, be liable as full guarantor for all costs incurred by the enterprise.

Ordinarily, profits lost due to a breach of contract are recoverable. Where anticipated profits are too speculative to be determined, monies spent in part performance, in preparation for or in reliance on the contract are recoverable. Dialist Co. v. Pulford, 42 Md.App. 173, 399 A.2d 1374 (1979).

In *Dialist,* supra, a distributor, Pulford, brought suit for breach of an exclusive contract that he had with Dialist. Pulford paid $2500.00 for the distributorship, terminated his employment with another company and expended funds in order to begin developing the area where the product was to be sold. When Pulford learned that another distributor was also given part of his territory he terminated his services.

This Court upheld the award of development costs to Pulford which included out of pocket expenses, telephone installation, office furniture, two months of forfeited salary and the value of medical insurance lost. The Court determined that the expenditures were not in preparation for or part performance of a contract, but in reliance upon it. "Such expenditures are not brought about by reason of the breach. They are induced by reliance on the contract itself and rendered worthless by its breach."

Recovery based upon reliance interest is not without limitation. If it can be shown that full performance would have resulted in a net loss, the plaintiff cannot escape the consequences of a bad bargain by falling back on his reliance interest. Where the breach has prevented an anticipated gain and made proof of loss difficult to ascertain, the injured party has a right to damages based upon his reliance interest, including expenditures made in preparation for performance, or in performance, less any loss that the party in breach can prove with reasonable certainty the injured party would have suffered had the contract been performed. Restatement, Second, Contracts, Sec. 349.

The appellants' contention that permitting the jury to consider reliance damages in this case rendered the appellants insurers of the venture is without merit. Section 349 of the Restatement, cited above, expressly authorizes the breaching party to prove any loss that the injured party would have suffered had the contract been performed. Such proof would avoid making the breaching party a guarantor of the success of the venture. * * *

In the present case the appellants knew, or should have known, that the success of the venture rested upon the ability of Hightower to sell stock and secure advertising as public interest in the adventure accelerated. Appellant's contention that their failure to properly incorporate Hightower was collateral and lacked the necessary nexus to permit consideration of reliance damages is not persuasive. The very life blood of the project depended on the corporation's ability to sell stock to fund the promotion. This is the reason for the employment of the appellants. In reliance thereon, Hightower sold stock and incurred substantial obligations. When it could no longer sell its stock, the entire project failed. No greater nexus need be established. Aside from questioning the expertise of the promoters based upon their previous employment, the appellants were unable to establish that the stunt was doomed to fail. The inability to establish that financial chaos was inevitable does not make the appellants insurers and does not preclude Hightower from recovering reliance damages. The issue was properly submitted to the jury.

Appellants contend that the appellees should be limited to the recovery of damages under traditional contract and negligence concepts * * * that a contracting party is expected to take account of only those risks that are foreseeable at the time he makes the contract and is not liable in the event of breach for loss that he did not at the time of contracting have reason to foresee as a probable result of such a breach. This limitation is set forth in Restatement, Contracts, (2d), Sec. 351.

Exceptional perception is not relevant to the test of foreseeability when applied to an attorney who is relied upon by a layman to protect his investment from pitfalls which are not readily apparent to those in foreign fields of endeavor. * * *

The appellants are aggrieved by the amount of the verdict which they consider to be excessive. According to the docket entries, the appellants did not seek any modification of the verdict. * * * We note that in answer to interrogatories filed in October, 1981, corporate damages were stated to be $155,339.00. This figure included shareholders' investments and accrued salaries amounting to $51,410. The court's instructions precluded inclusion of these items as recoverable damages. It would appear, therefore, that the verdict may well have exceeded the guidelines set forth by the trial court. That issue is not before us, however. * * *

The Court instructed the jury that in order to find liability that the plaintiff must prove three things:

> "First, the employment of the defendants in behalf of the Plaintiff and the extent of the duties for which the Defendants were employed; secondly, that the Defendants neglected the duties undertaken in the employment and, thirdly, that such negligence resulted in and was the proximate cause of loss by the Plaintiff, that is that the Plaintiff was deprived of any right or parted with anything of value in reliance upon the negligence of the Defendants."

The instruction given fairly apprised the jury of the Plaintiffs' burden and adequately covered the reliance damage concept. Additionally, the court instructed the jury that they could not consider unpaid salaries due its officers or employees or amounts invested by stockholders as recoverable damages. * * *

We find no error in the instructions.

Appellants further except to the trial court's refusal to grant any instruction on the issue of Hightower's obligation to mitigate its damages. The instruction offered by appellants is a correct statement of the law. Correctness alone, however, is insufficient to require the court to grant the prayer; there must be evidence to support the proposition to which it relates.

The evidence in this case establishes that Hightower did not have the $43,000.00 to place in escrow covering stock sold, did not have the $10,000.00 or $15,000.00 to employ a securities specialist and could not continue stock sales or exhibitions to obtain the necessary funds. Mr. Wartzman's offer to set up an appointment for Hightower with an expert in security transactions at Hightower's expense can hardly be construed as a mitigating device that Hightower was obligated to accept. The party who is in default may not mitigate his damages by showing that the other party could have reduced those damages by expending large amounts of money or incurring substantial obligations. Since such risks arose because of the breach, they are to be borne by the defaulting party.

The doctrine of avoidable consequences, moreover, does not apply where both parties have an equal opportunity to mitigate damages. Appellants had the same opportunity to employ and pay a securities specialist as they contend Hightower should have done. They refused. Having rejected Hightower's request to assume the costs of an additional attorney, they are estopped from asserting a failure by Hightower to reduce its loss.

There is no evidence in this case that the additional funds necessary to continue the operation pending a restructuring of the corporation were within the financial capabilities of Hightower. The Court properly declined to instruct the jury on the issue of mitigation. * * *

Judgment Affirmed.

Notes

1. The opinion analyzes "reliance" damages for breach of contract; but the court-approved jury instruction mentions only the negligence tort. Are contract "reliance" damages the same as those proximately caused by negligence? Do we ever rely upon someone else's negligence to our injury? The differences between tort and contract damages are the subject of much of the material in this Chapter.

2. The plaintiff has a judgment larger than the reliance damages claimed. Moreover the court approved instructions to the jury to exclude from damages the amounts the shareholders invested and the unpaid salaries due officers and employees. Why aren't these items reliance damages?

BYROM, DO DAMAGES DEPEND ON THE SAME PRINCIPLES THROUGHOUT THE LAW OF TORT AND CONTRACT?

6 U.Queensland L.J. 118, 120–122 (1968).

In both tort and contract, the wrongdoer is to be held responsible for the consequences of his wrongful acts, but as Fleming says,[1] "As a matter of practical politics, some limitation must be placed upon legal responsibility, because the consequences of an act theoretically stretch to infinity. * * * Legal

1. Fleming, The Law of Torts 176 (3rd ed. 1965).

policy and accepted value judgments must be the final arbiter of what balance to strike between the claim to full reparation for the loss suffered by an innocent victim of another's culpable activity and the grievous burden that would be imposed on human activity if a wrongdoer were held to answer for all the consequences of his default." * * *

Thus far the policies in tort and contract are the same. They differ in the formulation of the claim of the wrongdoer not to be held responsible for all the consequences of his default, no matter how widespread or bizarre those consequences may be.

In tort, the duty is imposed by law. The person under that tortious duty has no choice as to whether he will shoulder it or not. So his claim to relief cannot be formulated in terms of what he can expect at the time when he undertakes his duty. Rather it is relevant to consider the time at which he commits the act which is alleged to be the breach of duty. It is here that the limits are imposed. * * *

In contract, on the other hand, the limits are employed at a different stage. The contractual duty is accepted voluntarily, presumably after an assessment of how onerous the duty will be, compared with the value of the consideration to be furnished in return. Once the duty is accepted, i.e., once the contract is made, the duty is strict. No amount of care will excuse a breach of that duty.

The limits are not invoked by enquiring as to the consequences which ought to be guarded against at the time when the purported breach occurs. The answer to any such enquiry would be simply that a party to a contract must guard against everything he has expressly or impliedly promised to guard against. We are taken back in time to the formation of the contract. We must ask how onerous the duty was which the party alleged to be in breach undertook. The exact limits of that duty may be expressly prescribed in the contract. The provision of a genuine estimate of liquidated damages or of a valid exclusion clause covering the alleged breach are examples of this. In such cases there is no need for other limits, and none are introduced. On the other hand, in the great majority of cases, no such express limits to the duty will be found in the contract. Then the extent of the duty must be gleaned from the surrounding circumstances when the duty was accepted. As in tort the limits to the duty are employed to protect the wrongdoer at the expense of the injured party, but in contract, unlike tort, the law makes demands of the injured party, and if those demands are not met, his interests will then be ignored with far more freedom than is ever possible in tort.

As has been said, the contractual duty is undertaken after a comparison of the value of the consideration and of how onerous the duty will prove. This latter factor has three facets, the difficulty of discharging the duty, the likelihood of failing to discharge the duty, and the consequences of that failure which will amount to the quantum of the compensation he will have to pay. Only if he thinks the value of the consideration outweighs this threefold combination will a party undertake the contractual duty. The first two facets are things of which he must judge alone, but the final one, the consequences of a breach of duty, may well be beyond his knowledge, and yet within the knowledge of the other party. Here it is that the law makes its demand of the injured party. If he knows of factors which may take the consequences of breach of contract beyond what is to be expected and hence make the quantum of compensation greater than normal, the law demands that he disclose those factors to the other party in time for that party to consider them as he assesses whether or not it is worth his while to undertake the duty. The price of non-disclosure is that recovery will be limited. This then is a policy for establishing additional limits to recovery for breaches of contract which has no analogy in the policies underlying the rules of tort. * * *

As has been stated, the principles upon which damages depend, in both tort and contract, are aimed at striking a balance between the claim to full reparation by the innocent party on the one hand and the need to limit the wrongdoer's obligation to compensate for consequences which are unacceptably widespread or bizarre.

* * * Of course, only those consequences which were directly caused by the default can possibly be the subjects of compensation. It is not suggested that the principles of causation are in any way different in tort and contract, nor could it be expected that they would be, in view of the fact that the policy of attempting full reparation is identical in both fields.

When it comes to the problem of applying limits to full reparation, however, just as there are differences in the policies underlying tort and contract, so there are differences in the principles by which damages are to be determined. * * *

In tort there is no doubt that, in general, if the consequences of a default can be reasonably foreseen, damages are recoverable. Conversely, if no injury is foreseeable, no damages are recoverable. * * *

[I]t has never been suggested that it would be in the slightest degree relevant to enquire if the amount of compensation which will have to be paid is greater or less than the amount which can reasonably be foreseen. * * * The cases of the eggshell skull in personal injury and of Lord Justice Scrutton's "shabby millionaire" in the field of pecuniary loss resulting from personal injury are too well known to allow such an argument. They are representative, as Fleming says,[2] "of the truism that a tortfeasor cannot invoke the plea that he had no reason to expect his casualty to be so expensive." In tort, then, damages are recoverable in full or not at all. Recovery is not limited by reference to reasonable quantum.

In contract, no one doubts that Hadley v. Baxendale is the source of the general rule for computing damages. No court would entertain any suggested formulation which ran contrary to the famous test formulated by Alderson B. in that case.

It has been asserted there are two differences between the rules discussed as applicable to tort and this rule. They will be examined in turn.

The first difference is in the degree of foresight demanded if liability is to follow. In contract, following Baron Alderson's test, the consequence must either be reasonably considered as following naturally from the breach, or be within the reasonable contemplation of the parties as the probable result of the breach. How unusual may a consequence be without falling outside the ambit of compensation? Could there be a consequence which is "reasonably foreseeable," as that is understood in tort, and yet which is not "within the reasonable contemplation of the parties as the probable result of the breach," as that is

2. Fleming, The Law of Torts 188 (3rd ed. 1965).

understood in contract? If so, this clearly points to a difference between the rules of contract and tort.

The second alleged difference between the rules of tort and contract is that in tort the rule of foresight is applied to the kind of damage, not its quantum, whereas in contract the main use of the contemplation rule is to limit quantum. As has been said, in tort, for each separate item, damages are recovered in full or not at all. A consideration of the policy discussed above leads one to expect a different result in contract. In tort, the way the default occurs may be all important, but in contract, it is the extent of the duty shouldered at the time of contract which is vital. The extent of this duty is measured at least as much by the amount to be paid in compensation as by the way in which the compensation becomes payable. * * *

At this stage it is proposed to examine the results of these differences as the rules of contract and tort are applied to various hypothetical fact situations in each of which an injured party claims compensation for loss of earnings resulting from a personal injury.

If an average man is injured through careless driving and as a result must spend ten days off work, it is clear he can recover from the driver any loss of earnings he may suffer during those ten days.

If an average man engages a surgeon to perform a minor operation, but due to the surgeon's admitted carelessness, he has to spend ten days longer off work than would normally be the case, it is reasonably clear that he too can recover his loss of earnings, if he brought his action upon his contract with the surgeon. That is a consequence which the surgeon should contemplate as a not unlikely result of his breach of contract in failing to take proper care in the conduct of the operation.

If a pop-singer with a gigantic earning power were injured as a result of careless driving and was unable to appear for ten days, he too could recover his actual loss of earnings from the driver. The fact that the quantum of loss is unforeseeable is irrelevant.

Suppose such a pop-singer were to engage a surgeon as in the earlier example. If he uses his real name, rather than his stage name, and does not disclose his true identity to the surgeon, how much will he recover from the surgeon if he brings his claim in contract? The surgeon could not reasonably contemplate the actual loss of earnings, although he ought to contemplate some lesser amount. It is submitted that the singer would recover no more than the maximum loss of earnings which could normally be expected to result from ten days' incapacity, however such figure may be assessed.

If the singer brought an action against the surgeon in tort, how could the position be distinguished from the similar action against the driver in the earlier example? In tort, it is submitted, he would recover the full extent of his loss.

Here is a serious anomaly. That two different amounts should be recovered in contract and tort is unfortunate.

EVRA CORP. v. SWISS BANK CORP.

United States Court of Appeals, Seventh Circuit, 1982.
673 F.2d 951.

[Hyman–Michaels, a scrap metal dealer, lost a valuable charter contract with Pandora Shipping because Swiss Bank failed to effect a telex deposit in Pandora's Paris account. Hyman–Michaels sued Swiss Bank to recover the expenses of an arbitration with the other party to the charter contract and the profits it lost because of the cancellation of the charter.

The trial judge awarded Hyman–Michaels $2.1 million, $16,000 for the arbitration, the rest lost profit. The parts of the opinion that deal with the remoteness issue are reproduced.]

POSNER, CIRCUIT JUDGE. * * * When a bank fails to make a requested transfer of funds, this can cause two kinds of loss. First, the funds themselves or interest on them may be lost, and of course the fee paid for the transfer, having bought nothing, becomes a loss item. These are "direct" (sometimes called "general") damages. Hyman–Michaels is not seeking any direct damages in this case and apparently sustained none. It did not lose any part of the $27,000; although its account with Continental Bank was debited by this amount prematurely, it was not an interest-bearing account so Hyman–Michaels lost no interest; and Hyman–Michaels paid no fee either to Continental or to Swiss Bank for the aborted transfer. A second type of loss, which either the payor or the payee may suffer, is a dislocation in one's business triggered by the failure to pay. Swiss Bank's failure to transfer funds to the Banque de Paris when requested to do so by Continental Bank set off a chain reaction which resulted in an arbitration proceeding that was costly to Hyman–Michaels and in the cancellation of a highly profitable contract. It is those costs and lost profits—"consequential" or, as they are sometimes called, "special" damages—that Hyman–Michaels seeks in this lawsuit, and recovered below. It is conceded that if Hyman–Michaels was entitled to consequential damages, the district court measured them correctly. The only issue is whether it was entitled to consequential damages. * * *

The rule of Hadley v. Baxendale—that consequential damages will not be awarded unless the defendant was put on notice of the special circumstances giving rise to them—has been applied in many Illinois cases, and *Hadley* cited approvingly. In *Siegel* [v. Western Union Tel. Co., 312 Ill.App. 86, 37 N.E.2d 868 (1941)], the plaintiff had delivered $200 to Western Union with instructions to transmit it to a friend of the plaintiff's. The money was to be bet (legally) on a horse, but this was not disclosed in the instructions. Western Union misdirected the money order and it did not reach the friend until several hours after the race had taken place. The horse that the plaintiff had intended to bet on won and would have paid $1650 on the plaintiff's $200 bet if the bet had been placed. He sued Western Union for his $1450 lost profit, but the court held that under the rule of Hadley v. Baxendale Western Union was not liable, because it "had no notice or knowledge of the purpose for which the money was being transmitted."

The present case is similar, though Swiss Bank knew more than Western Union knew in *Siegel;* it knew or should have known, from Continental Bank's previous telexes, that Hyman–Michaels was paying the Pandora Shipping

Company for the hire of a motor vessel named *Pandora.* But it did not know when payment was due, what the terms of the charter were, or that they had turned out to be extremely favorable to Hyman–Michaels. And it did not know that Hyman–Michaels knew the *Pandora's* owner would try to cancel the charter, and probably would succeed, if Hyman–Michaels was ever again late in making payment, or that despite this peril Hyman–Michaels would not try to pay until the last possible moment and in the event of a delay in transmission would not do everything in its power to minimize the consequences of the delay. Electronic funds transfers are not so unusual as to automatically place a bank on notice of extraordinary consequences if such a transfer goes awry. Swiss Bank did not have enough information to infer that if it lost a $27,000 payment order it would face a liability in excess of $2 million.

It is true that in both *Hadley* and *Siegel* there was a contract between the parties and here there was none. * * * We must therefore ask what difference it should make whether the parties are or are not bound to each other by a contract. On the one hand, it seems odd that the absence of a contract would enlarge rather than limit the extent of liability. After all, under Swiss law the absence of a contract would be devastating to Hyman–Michaels' claim. Privity is not a wholly artificial concept. It is one thing to imply a duty to one with whom one has a contract and another to imply it to the entire world.

On the other hand, contract liability is strict. A breach of contract does not connote wrongdoing; it may have been caused by circumstances beyond the promisor's control—a strike, a fire, the failure of a supplier to deliver an essential input. And while such contract doctrines as impossibility, impracticability, and frustration relieve promisors from liability for some failures to perform that are beyond their control, many other such failures are actionable although they could not have been prevented by the exercise of due care. The district judge found that Swiss Bank had been negligent in losing Continental Bank's telex message and it can be argued that Swiss Bank should therefore be liable for a broader set of consequences than if it had only broken a contract. But *Siegel* implicitly rejects this distinction. Western Union had not merely broken its contract to deliver the plaintiff's money order; it had "negligently misdirected" the money order. "The company's negligence is conceded." Yet it was not liable for the consequences.

Siegel, we conclude, is authority for holding that Swiss Bank is not liable for the consequences of negligently failing to transfer Hyman–Michaels' funds to Banque de Paris; reason for such a holding is found in the animating principle of Hadley v. Baxendale, which is that the costs of the untoward consequence of a course of dealings should be borne by that party who was able to avert the consequence at least cost and failed to do so. In *Hadley* the untoward consequence was the shutting down of the mill. The carrier could have avoided it by delivering the engine shaft on time. But the mill owners, as the court noted, could have avoided it simply by having a spare shaft. Prudence required that they have a spare shaft anyway, since a replacement could not be obtained at once even if there was no undue delay in carting the broken shaft to and the replacement shaft from the manufacturer. The court refused to imply a duty on the part of the carrier to guarantee the mill owners against the consequences of their own lack of prudence, though of course if the parties had stipulated for such a guarantee the court would have enforced it. The notice requirement of Hadley v. Baxendale is designed to assure that such an improbable guarantee really is intended.

This case is much the same, though it arises in a tort rather than a contract setting. Hyman–Michaels showed a lack of prudence throughout. It was imprudent for it to mail in Chicago a letter that unless received the next day in Geneva would put Hyman–Michaels in breach of a contract that was very profitable to it and that the other party to the contract had every interest in canceling. It was imprudent thereafter for Hyman–Michaels, having narrowly avoided cancellation and having (in the words of its appeal brief in this court) been "put * * * on notice that the payment provision of the Charter would be strictly enforced thereafter," to wait till arguably the last day before payment was due to instruct its bank to transfer the necessary funds overseas. And it was imprudent in the last degree for Hyman–Michaels, when it received notice of cancellation on the last possible day payment was due, to fail to pull out all the stops to get payment to the Banque de Paris on that day * * *.

This is not to condone the sloppy handling of incoming telex messages in Swiss Bank's foreign department. But Hyman–Michaels is a sophisticated business enterprise. It knew or should have known that even the Swiss are not infallible.

We are not the first to remark the affinity between the rule of Hadley v. Baxendale and the doctrine, which is one of tort as well as contract law and is a settled part of the common law of Illinois, of avoidable consequences. See Dobbs, Handbook on the Law of Remedies 831 (1973). If you are hurt in an automobile accident and unreasonably fail to seek medical treatment, the injurer, even if negligent, will not be held liable for the aggravation of the injury due to your own unreasonable behavior after the accident. If in addition you failed to fasten your seat belt, you may be barred from collecting the tort damages that would have been prevented if you had done so. See, e.g., Mount v. McClellan, 91 Ill.App.2d 1, 5, 234 N.E.2d 329, 331 (1968). Hyman–Michaels' behavior in steering close to the wind prior to April 27 was like not fastening one's seat belt; its failure on April 27 to wire a duplicate payment immediately after disaster struck was like refusing to seek medical attention after a serious accident. The seat-belt cases show that the doctrine of avoidable consequences applies whether the tort victim acts imprudently before or after the tort is committed. Hyman–Michaels did both.

The rule of Hadley v. Baxendale links up with tort concepts in another way. The rule is sometimes stated in the form that only foreseeable damages are recoverable in a breach of contract action. E.g., Restatement (Second) of Contracts § 351 (1979). So expressed, it corresponds to the tort principle that limits liability to the foreseeable consequence of the defendant's carelessness. See, e.g., Neering v. Illinois Cent. R.R. Co., 383 Ill. 366, 380, 50 N.E.2d 497, 503 (1943). The amount of care that a person ought to take is a function of the probability and magnitude of the harm that may occur if he does not take care. See, e.g., United States v. Carroll Towing Co., 159 F.2d 169, 173 (2d Cir.1947). If he does not know what that probability and magnitude are, he cannot determine how much care to take. That would be Swiss Bank's dilemma if it were liable for consequential damages from failing to carry out payment orders in timely fashion. To estimate the extent of its probable liability in order to know how many and how elaborate fail-safe features to install in its telex rooms or how much insurance to buy against the inevitable failures, Swiss Bank would have to collect reams of information about firms that are not even its regular customers. It had no banking relationship with Hyman–Michaels. It did not know or have reason to know how at once precious and fragile

Hyman–Michaels' contract with the *Pandora's* owner was. These were circumstances too remote from Swiss Bank's practical range of knowledge to have affected its decisions as to who should man the telex machines in the foreign department or whether it should have more intelligent machines or should install more machines in the cable department, any more than the falling of a platform scale because a conductor jostled a passenger who was carrying fireworks was a prospect that could have influenced the amount of care taken by the Long Island Railroad. See Palsgraf v. Long Island R.R., 248 N.Y. 339, 162 N.E. 99 (1928).

In short, Swiss Bank was not required in the absence of a contractual undertaking to take precautions or insure against a harm that it could not measure but that was known with precision to Hyman–Michaels, which could by the exercise of common prudence have averted it completely. As Chief Judge Cardozo (the author of *Palsgraf*) remarked in discussing the application of Hadley v. Baxendale to the liability of telegraph companies for errors in transmission, "The sender can protect himself by insurance in one form or another if the risk of non-delivery or error appears to be too great. * * * The company, if it takes out insurance for itself, can do no more than guess at the loss to be avoided." Kerr S.S. Co. v. Radio Corp. of America, 245 N.Y. 284, 291–92, 157 N.E. 140, 142 (1927). * * *

The undisputed facts, recited in this opinion, show as a matter of law that Hyman–Michaels is not entitled to recover consequential damages from Swiss Bank.

2. WHERE THE REMEDIAL GOAL OF TORT DAMAGES ENDS

Although the announced remedial goal of tort damages is to compensate, cutoffs are inevitable. Proximate causes, whatever they may be, eventually become too attenuated to justify damages. A more definite cutoff that may or may not be explicable in terms of proximate cause affects "economic loss" in negligence cases.

LOCAL JOINT EXECUTIVE BOARD, CULINARY WORKERS UNION, LOCAL NO. 226 v. STERN

Supreme Court of Nevada, 1982.
98 Nev. 409, 651 P.2d 637.

Per Curiam. This lawsuit arises from the November 1980 fire at the MGM Grand Hotel in Las Vegas, Nevada. The individual appellants were employees at the time of the fire, and brought this class action to recover lost salaries and employment benefits for the period they were unemployed as a result of the fire. The unions also sued to recover union dues lost because of the fire. Respondents were involved in the design or construction of the hotel. Appellants sought recovery under both negligence and strict liability theories. The district court granted respondents' motions to dismiss, on the ground that appellants had not stated a cause of action to recover economic loss. This appeal followed.

The well established common law rule is that absent privity of contract or an injury to person or property, a plaintiff may not recover in negligence for economic loss. Robins Dry Dock & Repair Co. v. Flint, 275 U.S. 303 (1927);

Kingston Shipping Co., Inc. v. Roberts, 667 F.2d 34 (11th Cir.1982); Restatement (Second) of Torts § 766C (1979). Purely economic loss is recoverable in actions for tortious interference with contractual relations or prospective economic advantage, but the interference must be intentional. Straube v. Larson, 287 Or. 357, 600 P.2d 371 (1979); Chanay v. Chittenden, 115 Ariz. 32, 563 P.2d 287 (1977). The primary purpose of the rule is to shield a defendant from unlimited liability for all of the economic consequences of a negligent act, particularly in a commercial or professional setting, and thus to keep the risk of liability reasonably calculable.

A small minority of jurisdictions do permit recovery for negligent interference with economic expectancies under certain limited circumstances. See, e.g., J'Aire Corp. v. Gregory, 24 Cal.3d 799, 157 Cal.Rptr. 407, 598 P.2d 60 (1979). However, we believe the tests that have been developed to determine who should recover for negligent interference with contract or prospective economic advantage are presently inadequate to guide trial courts to consistent, predictable, and fair results. The foreseeability of economic loss, even when modified by other factors, is a standard that sweeps too broadly in a professional or commercial context, portending liability that is socially harmful in its potential scope and uncertainty. We therefore decline to adopt the minority view allowing such recovery.

Notes

1. The court cuts short recovery of economic losses by all those whose persons or property have not been affected by the negligence of a tortfeasor (but whose pocketbook certainly has). The doctrine is customarily traced through maritime cases back to the United States Supreme Court's decision in *Robins Dry Dock and Repair*—the lead citation in the opinion above. Justice Holmes said: "The law does not spread its protection so far."

A typical maritime case is In re Kinsman Transit Co. (Kinsman No. 2), 388 F.2d 821 (2d Cir.1968). The combined negligence of ship and bridge owners blocked the Buffalo river so that the plaintiff company could not reach its grain elevators; it therefore lost considerable sums in meeting its contractual commitments to supply grain. Recovery of these losses was denied. See also Kingston Shipping Co., Inc. v. Roberts, cited in *Local No. 226.*

Something of an exception has developed in recent marine cases involving toxic spillages. In Louisiana ex rel. Guste v. M/V TEST–BANK, 524 F.Supp. 1170 (E.D.La.1981), a negligent collision between two vessels dumped 12 tons of toxic PCP in the lower Mississippi. The Coast Guard closed the waters to commercial fishing. The court recognized that fishermen, clammers, and oystermen have no individual property rights to aquatic life harmed by the defendant's negligence; but it held that they could sue for the tortious invasion of a *public* right because they suffered damages in a greater degree than the general public. See also Union Oil Co. v. Oppen, 501 F.2d 558 (9th Cir.1974), where the court considers specifically lost profits by fishermen, but not others, from the Santa Barbara Channel oil spill.

Outside of admiralty, unsuccessful attempts to change the rule have usually involved precisely the same situation as *Local No. 226*—employees' lost wages from plant closures—or employer's lost income when an important employee is put out of action by a negligent tort feasor, e.g. Snow v. West, 250 Or. 114, 440 P.2d 864 (1968); Phoenix Professional Hockey Club, Inc. v. Hirmer, 108 Ariz. 482, 502 P.2d 164 (1972).

2. *The Rationale for the Rule Limiting Economic Damages.* Some explanation for the rule is in order. Many have been attempted—ranging from the assertion that there is no substantive tort at all, to the idea that a simple remedies problem concerns the certainty rather than the existence of damages. The issue has been stated: "While it may seem that there should be a remedy for every wrong, this is an ideal limited perforce by the realities of this world. Every injury has ramifying consequences like the ripplings of the waters without end. The problem for the law is to limit the legal consequences of wrongs to a controllable degree." Tobin v. Grossman, 24 N.Y.2d 609, 619, 301 N.Y.S.2d 544, 559, 249 N.E.2d 419, 424 (1969).

a. *"Non proximately caused—too remote and speculative."* In the words of Judge Kaufman in *In re Kinsman Transit Co.,* supra, "we conclude that recovery was properly denied because the injuries to [plaintiffs] were too 'remote' or 'indirect' a consequence of defendant's negligence." The court expressly assumes that a tort has been committed, but that the remedy is lacking. Common experience makes this explanation, by itself, unsatisfactory. Any lawyer tied up in a traffic jam caused by negligent drivers impacted across the highway ahead and losing clients by the minute will readily understand. Are these lost billings significantly more remote than the economic losses of the owner of one of the *directly* involved vehicles? Are the resort owner's economic losses from the negligent destruction of an access bridge more remote than those of the bridge owner? etc., etc. A shade of the time-worn "privity" requirement seems to be cast here, for the parasite must be privy to a host.

News Item (1980): **THE NEW YORK YANKEES'** $4.5 million suit against Cessna Aircraft Co. and Flight Safety International Inc. in the death of all-star catcher Thurman Munson has been dismissed by U.S. District Judge Leroy Contie Jr. In a 16 page opinion, the judge said the baseball club is not entitled to damages from the loss of Munson's services. Munson, who lived in nearby Canton, died Aug. 2, 1979, when his Cessna twin-engine jet crashed and burned at Akron–Canton Airport. Contie ruled that the Yankees' "loss is merely a remote and indirect consequence of the defendants' negligence and not the proximate cause [sic] of such negligence."

b. "*Economic damages in these circumstances are not foreseeable.*" The word "foreseeable" in this matrix is unfortunately confusing. "Foreseeable" is acceptable in determining breach of contract damages, as we have just seen. "Foreseeability" of injury is acceptable and necessary in order to render conduct negligent, but this is a matter of substantive law of torts rather than damages. If "negligence" has been established, then the defendant is, we are told, liable for all damages proximately caused. Surely it should not be necessary to run through a *Palsgraf* (if a citation is required, the student should stop and reapply for admission) routine on the issue of existence of a duty, and again on the issue of the quantum of damages. As Judge Friendly more elegantly summarized it:

"The oft encountered argument that failure to limit liability to foreseeable consequences may subject the defendant to a loss wholly out of proportion to his fault seems scarcely consistent with the universally accepted rule that the defendant takes the plaintiff as he finds him and will be responsible for the full extent of the injury even though a latent susceptibility of the plaintiff renders this far more serious than could reasonably have been anticipated. * * *

"The weight of authority in this country rejects the limitation of damages to consequences foreseeable at the time of the negligent conduct, when the consequences are 'direct' and the damages, although other and greater than expectable, is of the same general sort as was risked." In re Kinsman Transit Co., 338 F.2d 708 (2dCir.1964), cert. denied, 380 U.S. 944 (1965).

Nevertheless it is admittedly difficult to disassociate "foreseeability" from the calculation of damages for the tort of negligence. After all, the *existence* of damages is a necessary substantive component of the negligence tort, unlike intentional torts like trespass. And even the quote from Judge Friendly, above, does not close the door.

c. *Persons suffering purely economic damages from another's negligence comprise a class outside of those to whom a duty is owed.* This "rationale" is abrupt—no tort, no damages. It allows the assertion that here is admittedly a wrong proximately causing nonspeculative damages for which there is no remedy. See, for example, Phoenix Professional Hockey Club, Inc. v. Hirmer, supra p. 72. The hockey club sought damages for the cost of a substitute goalie while their regular one was incapacitated by an auto accident negligently caused by the defendant. The court conceded the claim was not speculative; but it denied recovery because employers are outside the "class of people" to whom the tortfeasor owes a duty. (Note the difference in rationale between a hockey player and Thurman Munson.)

The current trend has been to expand a duty of care to groups of indirectly affected individuals previously excluded: to wives and perhaps children and live-in companions for loss of consortium; to parents and even nonrelatives who are emotionally shocked and psychologically, but not physically, injured when they witness negligent physical harm, Restatement (Second) of Torts § 313 (1965); Kately v. Wilkinson, 148 Cal.App.3d 576, 195 Cal.Rptr. 902 (1983); to fetuses for personal injuries, etc. Pursuing this tendency, an enlargement of the scope of "duty" would remove the barrier to damages remedy leaving only the question of uncertainty.

d. *A policy approach—Pandora's Box, floodgate, slippery slopes, etc.* In Stevenson v. East Ohio Gas Co., 73 N.E.2d 200, 203–04 (Ohio App.1946), a worker's unsuccessful claim for wages much like the main case, the fears are elaborated: "While the reason usually given for the refusal to permit recovery in this class of cases is that the damages are 'indirect' or are 'too remote' it is our opinion that the principal reason that has motivated the courts in denying recovery in this class of cases is that to permit recovery of damages in such cases would open the door to a mass of litigation which might very well overwhelm the courts so that in the long run while injustice might result in special cases, the ends of justice are conserved by laying down and enforcing the general rule as is so well stated by Mr. Justice Holmes in Robins Dry Dock & Repair Co. v. Flint, supra.

"If one who by his negligence is legally responsible for an explosion or a conflagration should be required to respond in damages not only to those who have sustained personal injuries or physical property damage but also to every one who has suffered an economic loss, by reason of the explosion or conflagration, we might well be appalled by the results that would follow. * * *

"Cases might well occur where a manufacturer would be obliged to close down his factory because of the inability of his supplier due to a fire loss to make prompt deliveries; the power company with a contract to supply a factory with electricity would be deprived of the profit which it would have made if the operation of the factory had not been interrupted by reason of fire damage; a man who had a contract to paint a building may not be able to proceed with his work; a salesman who would have sold the products of the factory may be deprived of his commissions; the neighborhood restaurant which relies on the trade of the factory employees may suffer a substantial loss. The claims of workmen for loss of wages who were employed in such a factory and cannot continue to work there because of a fire, represent only a small fraction of the claims which would arise if recovery is allowed in this class of cases.

"It is our opinion that the courts generally have reached a wise result in limiting claims for damages in this class of cases to who may have sustained personal injuries or physical property damage and in refusing to open their doors in such cases to claims of loss of wages and other economic loss based on contract."

J'AIRE CORP. v. GREGORY

Supreme Court of California, 1979.
24 Cal.3d 799, 157 Cal.Rptr. 407, 598 P.2d 60.

BIRD, CHIEF JUSTICE. * * * Appellant, J'Aire Corporation, operates a restaurant at the Sonoma County Airport in premises leased from the County of Sonoma. Under the terms of the lease the county was to provide heat and air conditioning. In 1975 the county entered into a contract with respondent for improvements to the restaurant premises, including renovation of the heating and air conditioning systems and installation of insulation.

* * * The work was not completed within a reasonable time. Because the restaurant could not operate during part of the construction and was without heat and air conditioning for a longer period, appellant suffered loss of business and resulting loss of profits.

* * * The second cause of action sounded in tort and was based upon negligence in not completing the work within a reasonable time. Damages of $50,000 were claimed.

* * * On appeal the sustaining of the demurrer to the cause of action is challenged. * * *

This court has held that a plaintiff's interest in prospective economic advantage may be protected against injury occasioned by negligent as well as intentional conduct. For example, economic losses such as lost earnings or profits are recoverable as part of general damages in a suit for personal injury based on negligence. [citations] Where negligent conduct causes injury to real or personal property, the plaintiff may recover damages for profits lost during the time necessary to repair or replace the property.

Even when only injury to prospective economic advantage is claimed, recovery is not foreclosed. Where a special relationship exists between the parties, a plaintiff may recover for loss of expected economic advantage through the negligent performance of a contract although the parties were not in contractual privity.[1]

It is evident that a duty was owed by respondent to appellant in the present case. (1) The contract entered into between respondent and the county was for the renovation of the premises in which appellant maintained its business. The contract could not have been performed without impinging on

1. Countervailing public policies may preclude recovery for injury to prospective economic advantage in some cases, such as the strong public policy favoring organized activity by workers. Accordingly, interference with the prospective economic advantage of an employer or business has traditionally not been considered tortious when it results from union activity, including picketing, striking, primary and secondary boycotts or similar activity, that is otherwise lawful and reasonably related to labor conditions. The present case does not alter this principle.

that business. Thus respondent's performance was intended to, and did, directly affect appellant. (2) Accordingly, it was clearly foreseeable that any significant delay in completing the construction would adversely affect appellant's business beyond the normal disruption associated with such construction. Appellant alleges this fact was repeatedly drawn to respondent's attention. (3) Further, appellant's complaint leaves no doubt that appellant suffered harm since it was unable to operate its business for one month and suffered additional loss of business while the premises were without heat and air conditioning. (4) Appellant has also alleged that delays occasioned by the respondent's conduct were closely connected to, indeed directly caused its injury. (5) In addition, respondent's lack of diligence in the present case was particularly blameworthy since it continued after the probability of damage was drawn directly to respondent's attention. (6) Finally, public policy supports finding a duty of care in the present case. The wilful failure or refusal of a contractor to prosecute a construction project with diligence, where another is injured as a result, has been made grounds for disciplining a licensed contractor. * * *

As appellant points out, injury to a tenant's business can often result in greater hardship than damage to a tenant's person or property. Where the risk of harm is foreseeable, as it was in the present case, an injury to the plaintiff's economic interests should not go uncompensated merely because it was unaccompanied by any injury to his person or property.

To hold under these facts that a cause of action has been stated for negligent interference with prospective economic advantage is consistent with the recent trend in tort cases. This court has repeatedly eschewed overly rigid common law formulations of duty in favor of allowing compensation for foreseeable injuries caused by a defendant's want of ordinary care. [citations] Rather than traditional notions of duty, this court has focused on foreseeability as the key component necessary to establish liability: * * * Respondent is liable if his lack of ordinary care caused foreseeable injury to the economic interests of appellant. * * *

Respondent cites Fifield Manor v. Finston (1960) 54 Cal.2d 632, 7 Cal.Rptr. 377, 354 P.2d 1073 for the proposition that recovery may not be had for negligent loss of prospective economic advantage. *Fifield* concerned the parallel tort of interference with contractual relations. There a non-profit retirement home that had contracted with Ross to provide him with lifetime medical care sued a driver who negligently struck and killed Ross. The plaintiff argued it had become liable under the contract for Ross' medical bills and sought recovery from the driver, on both a theory of direct liability and one of subrogation. Recovery was denied.

The critical factor of foreseeability distinguishes *Fifield* from the present case. Although it was reasonably foreseeable that defendant's negligence might cause injury to Ross, it was less foreseeable that it would injure the retirement home's economic interest. Defendant had not entered into any relationship or undertaken any activity where negligence on his part was reasonably likely to affect plaintiff adversely. * * *

Respondent also relies on Adams v. Southern Pac. Transportation Co. (1975) 50 Cal.App.3d 37, 123 Cal.Rptr. 216. In *Adams* plaintiff employees were held unable to sue the railroad whose cargo of bombs exploded, destroying the factory where they worked. It should be noted that the Court of Appeal in

Adams clearly believed that plaintiffs should be permitted to maintain an action for negligent interference with prospective economic interests. It reluctantly held they could not only under the belief that *Fifield* precluded such recovery. Adhering to the *Fifield* rule, the Court of Appeal in *Adams* did not determine whether the railroad owed plaintiffs a duty of care. In the present case, plaintiff's injury stemmed directly from conduct intended to affect plaintiff and was more readily foreseeable than the damage to the employer's property in *Adams.* To the extent that *Adams* holds that there can be no recovery for negligent interference with prospective economic advantage, it is disapproved.

The chief dangers which have been cited [above] in allowing recovery for negligent interference with prospective economic advantage are the possibility of excessive liability, the creation of an undue burden on freedom of action, the possibility of fraudulent or collusive claims and the often speculative nature of damages. * * * Central to these fears is the possibility that liability will be imposed for remote consequences, out of proportion to the magnitude of the defendant's wrongful conduct.

However, the factors enumerated * * * [above] place a limit on recovery by focusing judicial attention on the foreseeability of the injury and the nexus between the defendant's conduct and the plaintiff's injury. These factors and ordinary principles of tort law such as proximate cause are fully adequate to limit recovery without the drastic consequence of an absolute rule which bars recovery in all such cases. (See Dillon v. Legg, supra, 68 Cal.2d at p. 746, 69 Cal.Rptr. 72, 441 P.2d 912.) Following these principles, recovery for negligent interference with prospective economic advantage will be limited to instances where the risk of harm is foreseeable and is closely connected with the defendant's conduct, where damages are not wholly speculative and the injury is not part of the plaintiff's ordinary business risk. * * *

The judgment of dismissal is reversed.

Note

Compare: Nebraska Innkeepers, Inc. v. Pittsburgh–Des Moines Corp., 345 N.W.2d 124 (Iowa 1984). The defendant contractor negligently built a bridge which had to be shut down for repairs. It was held that the affected hotel operators and local businesses could not recover their economic losses.

RARDIN v. T & D MACHINE HANDLING, INC.

United States Court of Appeals, Seventh Circuit, 1989.
890 F.2d 24.

Posner, Circuit Judge. Jack Rardin, the plaintiff, bought for use in his printing business a used printing press from Whitacre–Sunbelt, Inc. for $47,700. The price included an allowance of $1,200 to cover the cost of dismantling the press for shipment and loading it on a truck at Whitacre's premises in Georgia for transportation to Rardin in Illinois. The contract of sale provided that the press was to be "Sold As Is, Where Is," that payment was to be made before the removal of the press from Whitacre's premises, and that Whitacre was to be responsible only for such damage to the press as might be "incurred by reason of the fault or negligence of [Whitacre's] employees, agents, contractors or representatives." To dismantle and load the press,

Whitacre hired T & D Machine Handling, Inc., which performed these tasks carelessly; as a result the press was damaged. Not only did Rardin incur costs to repair the press; he also lost profits in his printing business during the time it took to put the press into operating order. He brought this suit against Whitacre, T & D, and others; settled with Whitacre; dismissed all the other defendants except T & D; and now appeals from the dismissal of his case against T & D for failure to state a claim. (The facts we recited are all taken from the complaint.) The only issue is whether Rardin stated a claim against T & D under Illinois law, which the parties agree controls this diversity suit.

The contract indemnified Rardin against physical damage to the press caused by the negligence of Whitacre's contractor, T & D, and the settlement with Whitacre extinguished Rardin's claim for the cost of repairing the damage. The damages that Rardin seeks from T & D are the profits that he lost as a result of the delay in putting the press into operation in his business, a delay caused by T & D's negligence in damaging the press. Rardin could not have sought these damages from Whitacre under the warranty, because consequential damages (of which a loss of profits that is due to delay is the classic example) are not recoverable in a breach of contract suit, with exceptions not applicable here. Rardin had no contract with T & D, and his claim against T & D is a tort claim; consequential damages are the norm in tort law.

We agree with the district judge that Illinois law does not provide a tort remedy in a case such as this. We may put a simpler version of the case, as follows: A takes his watch to a retail store, B, for repair. B sends it out to a watchmaker, C. Through negligence, C damages the watch, and when it is returned to A via B it does not tell time accurately. As a result, A misses an important meeting with his creditors. They petition him into bankruptcy. He loses everything. Can he obtain damages from C, the watchmaker, for the consequences of C's negligence? There is no issue of causation in our hypothetical case; there is none in Rardin's. We may assume that but for C's negligence A would have made the meeting and averted the bankruptcy, just as but for T & D's negligence the press would have arrived in working condition. The issue is not causation; it is duty.

The basic reason why no court (we believe) would impose liability on C in a suit by A is that C could not estimate the consequences of his carelessness, ignorant as he was of the circumstances of A, who is B's customer. In principle, it is true, merely to conclude that C was negligent is to affirm that the costs of care to him were less than the costs of his carelessness to all who might be hurt by it; that, essentially, is what negligence means, in Illinois as elsewhere. See McCarty v. Pheasant Run, Inc., 826 F.2d 1554, 1556–57 (7th Cir.1987). So in a perfect world of rational actors and complete information, and with damages set equal to the plaintiff's injury, there would be no negligence: the costs of negligence would be greater to the defendant than the costs of care and therefore it would never pay to be negligent. And if there were no negligence, the scope of liability for negligence would have no practical significance. But all this is a matter of abstract principle, and it is not realistic to assume that *every* responsible citizen can and will avoid *ever* being negligent. In fact, all that taking care does is make it less likely that one will commit a careless act. In deciding how much effort to expend on being careful—and therefore how far to reduce the probability of a careless accident—the potential injurer must have at least a rough idea of the extent of liability. C in our example could not form such an idea. He does not know the circumstances of the myriad owners of watches sent him to repair. He cannot know what costs he will impose if through momentary inattention he negligently damages one of the watches in his charge.

Two further points argue against liability. The first is that A could by his contract with B have protected himself against the consequences of C's negligence. He could have insisted that B guarantee him against all untoward consequences, however remote or difficult to foresee, of a failure to redeliver the watch in working order. The fact that B would in all likelihood refuse to give such a guaranty for a consideration acceptable to A is evidence that liability for all the consequences of every negligent act is not in fact optimal. Second, A could have protected himself not through guarantees but simply by reducing his dependence on his watch. Knowing how important the meeting was he could have left himself a margin for error or consulted another timepiece. Why impose liability for a harm that the victim could easily have prevented himself?

The present case is essentially the same as our hypothetical example. T & D is in the business of dismantling and loading printing presses. It is not privy to the circumstances of the owners of those presses. It did not deal directly with the owner, that is, with Rardin. It knew nothing about his business and could not without an inquiry that Rardin would have considered intrusive (indeed bizarre) have determined the financial consequences to Rardin if the press arrived in damaged condition.

The spirit of Hadley v. Baxendale, 9 Ex. 341, 156 Eng.Rep. 145 (1854), still the leading case on the nonrecoverability of consequential damages in breach of contract suits, broods over this case although not cited by either party or by the district court and although the present case is a tort case rather than a contract case. The plaintiffs in *Hadley v. Baxendale* owned a mill, and the defendants were in business as a common carrier. The defendants agreed to carry the plaintiffs' broken mill shaft to its original manufacturer, who was to make a new shaft using the broken one as a model. The defendants failed to deliver the broken shaft within the time required by the contract. Meanwhile, the plaintiffs, having no spare shaft, had been forced to shut down the mill. The plaintiffs sued the defendants for the profits lost during the additional period the mill remained closed as a result of the defendants' delay in delivering the shaft to the manufacturer. The plaintiffs lost the case. The defendants were not privy to the mill's finances and hence could not form an accurate estimate of how costly delay would be and therefore how much care to take to prevent it. The plaintiffs, however, as the court noted, could have protected themselves from the consequences of a delay by keeping a spare shaft on hand. Indeed, simple prudence dictated such a precaution, both because a replacement shaft could not be obtained immediately in any event (it had to be manufactured), and because conditions beyond the defendants' control could easily cause delay in the delivery of a broken shaft to the manufacturer should the shaft ever break. See also *EVRA Corp. v. Swiss Bank Corp.* Rardin, too, could have taken measures to protect himself against the financial consequences of unexpected delay. He could have arranged in advance to contract out some of his printing work, he could have bought business insurance, or he could have negotiated for a liquidated-damages clause in his contract with Whitacre that would have compensated him for delay in putting the press into working condition after it arrived.

As we noted in *EVRA Corp. v. Swiss Bank Corp.,* Illinois follows *Hadley v. Baxendale.* So if this were a contract case, Rardin would lose—and this regardless of whether the breach of contract were involuntary or, as he alleges, due to the promisor's negligence. It is a tort case, but so was *EVRA,* where, applying Illinois law, we concluded that the plaintiff could not recover consequential damages. The plaintiff had instructed its bank to deposit a payment in the bank account of a firm with which the plaintiff had a contract. The bank telexed its correspondent bank in Geneva—which happened to be Swiss Bank Corporation—to make the transaction. As a result of negligence by Swiss Bank, the transaction was not completed, whereupon the plaintiff lost its contract because the other party to it declared a default. The plaintiff sued Swiss Bank for the lost contract profits, and lost. We held that the principle of *Hadley v. Baxendale* is not limited to cases in which there is privity of contract between the plaintiff and the defendant. Swiss Bank could not have estimated the consequences of its negligence and the plaintiff, like the plaintiffs in *Hadley,* could have averted disaster by simple precautions. This case differs from both *Hadley* and *EVRA* in that there is no suggestion that Rardin was imprudent in failing to take precautions against damage or delay. But as in those cases the defendant was not in a position to assess the consequences of its negligence. In this respect the present case and *EVRA* are actually stronger for defendants even though these are tort rather than contract cases since neither case involves a defendant who is dealing face-to-face with the plaintiff. While it is generally true that consequential damages are recoverable in tort law although not in contract law, *EVRA* shows that the classification of a case as a tort case or a contract case is not decisive on this question.

We are reinforced in our conclusion that T & D is not liable to Rardin by a series of cases—beginning with Moorman Mfg. Co. v. National Tank Co., 91 Ill.2d 69, 61 Ill.Dec. 746, 435 N.E.2d 443 (1982) (decided only a few weeks before *EVRA*, and not cited to or by us in that case), continuing in cases like Redarowicz v. Ohlendorf, 92 Ill.2d 171, 65 Ill.Dec. 411, 441 N.E.2d 324 (1982), and discussed by this court in Chicago Heights Venture v. Dynamit Nobel of America, Inc., 782 F.2d 723, 726–29 (7th Cir.1986), and Dundee Cement Co. v. Chemical Laboratories, Inc., 712 F.2d 1166 (7th Cir.1983)—in which the Supreme Court of Illinois has held that damages for "purely economic loss" cannot be recovered in tort cases. The doctrine is not unique to Illinois. Originating in Chief Justice Traynor's opinion in Seely v. White Motor Co., 63 Cal.2d 9, 45 Cal.Rptr. 17, 403 P.2d 145 (1965), it has become the majority rule. [citations] We need not consider the outer boundaries of the doctrine; it is enough that it bars liability in a suit for lost profits resulting from negligence in carrying out a commercial undertaking.

The doctrine (called in Illinois the *Moorman* doctrine) rests on the insight, which is consistent with the analysis in *EVRA,* that contractual-type limitations on liability may make sense in many tort cases that are not contract cases only because there is no privity of contract between the parties. The contractual linkage between Rardin and T & D was indirect but unmistakable, and Rardin could as we have said have protected himself through his contractual arrangements with Whitacre, while there was little that T & D could do to shield itself from liability to Whitacre's customer except be more careful—and we have explained why a finding of negligence alone should not expose a defendant to unlimited liability.

The *Moorman* doctrine goes further than is necessary to resolve this case. Once a case is held to fall within it, the plaintiff has no tort remedy. In our hypothetical case about the watch, the plaintiff could not sue the repairer even for property damage. *Moorman* itself was a case in which there was a contract between the parties, so there was no reason to allow a tort remedy. The present case, like *Anderson,* is one where, although there is no contract, the policies that animate the principle which denies recovery of consequential damages in contract cases apply fully and forbid a tort end-run around that principle.

The "economic loss" doctrine of *Moorman* and of its counterpart cases in other jurisdictions is not the only tort doctrine that limits for-want-of-a-nail-the-kingdom-was-lost liability. It is closely related to the doctrine, thoroughly discussed in Barber Lines A/S v. M/V Donau Maru, 764 F.2d 50 (1st Cir.1985), that bars recovery for economic loss even if the loss does not arise from a commercial relationship between the parties—even if for example a negligent accident in the Holland Tunnel backs up traffic for hours, imposing cumulatively enormous and readily monetizable costs of delay. Admittedly these doctrines are in tension with other doctrines of tort law that appear to expose the tortfeasor to unlimited liability. One is the principle that allows recovery of full tort damages in a personal-injury suit for injury resulting from a defective or unreasonably dangerous product—a form of legal action that arises in a contractual setting and indeed originated in suits for breach of warranty. Another is the principle, also of personal-injury law, that the injurer takes his victim as he finds him and is therefore liable for the full extent of the injury even if unforeseeable—even if the person he runs down is Henry Ford and sustains a huge earnings loss, or because of a preexisting injury sustains a much greater loss than the average victim would have done. Both are doctrines of personal-injury law, however, and there are at least three differences between the personal-injury case and the economic-loss case, whether in a stranger or in a contractual setting. The first difference is that the potential variance in liability is larger when the victim of a tort is a business, because businesses vary in their financial magnitude more than individuals do; more precisely, physical capital is more variable than human capital. The second is that many business losses are offset elsewhere in the system: Rardin's competitors undoubtedly picked up much or all of the business he lost as a result of the delay in putting the press into operation, so that his loss overstates the social loss caused by T & D's negligence. Third, tort law is a field largely shaped by the special considerations involved in personal-injury cases, as contract law is not. Tort doctrines are, therefore, prima facie more suitable for the governance of such cases than contract doctrines are.

True, the "thin skull" principle illustrated by *Stoleson* is sometimes invoked to allow recovery of lost profits in cases where there is physical damage to property. See, e.g., Consolidated Aluminum Corp. v. C.F. Bean Corp., 772 F.2d 1217, 1222–24 (5th Cir.1985). The thinking here seems to be that the requirement of physical damage at least limits the number of plaintiffs. Rardin could appeal to that principle here—since title had passed to him before T & D began dismantling and loading the press—were it not that the *Moorman* line rejects it, as we explained in *Chicago Heights Venture,* a case in which there was some property damage. There is also liability (under an exception discussed in *Chicago Heights Venture*) when the injury is the consequence of a sudden, calamitous accident as distinct from a mere failure to perform up to commercial expectations. *Consolidated Aluminum* illustrates this exception, which is related to the principle that allows consumers injured by a defective product to sue the supplier in tort whether or not the consumer has a contract with him. There are other exceptions. The largest perhaps is the familiar principle that allows a suit for fraud against a person with whom the plaintiff has a contract, while the closest to the present case is the principle that allows a suit against an attorney or accountant for professional malpractice or negligent misrepresentation that causes business losses to the plaintiff. [citations] These cases are distinguishable, however, as ones in which the role of the defendant is, precisely, to guarantee the performance of the other party to the plaintiff's contract, usually a seller. The guaranty would be worth little without a remedy, necessarily in tort (or in an expansive interpretation of the doctrine of third-party beneficiaries) against the guarantor.

Although cases barring the recovery, whether under tort or contract law, of consequential damages in contractual settings ordinarily involve smaller potential losses than pure stranger cases do, this is not always so. In our watch hypothetical, in *EVRA,* and for all we know in *Hadley* and in the present case, the financial consequences of a seemingly trivial slip might be enormous. And it is in contractual settings that the potential victim ordinarily is best able to work out alternative protective arrangements and need not rely on tort law. Our conclusion that there is no tort liability in this case does not, therefore, leave buyers in the plaintiff's position remediless. Rardin could have sought guarantees from Whitacre (at a price, of course), but what he could not do was require the tort system to compensate him for business losses occasioned by negligent damage to his property.

A final example will nail the point down. The defendant in H.R. Moch Co. v. Rensselaer Water Co., 247 N.Y. 160, 159 N.E. 896 (1928), had agreed to supply the City of Rensselaer with water of specified pressure for the city's mains. There was a fire, the company was notified but failed to keep up the pressure, and as a result the fire department could not extinguish the fire, which destroyed the plaintiff's building. In a famous opinion denying liability, Chief Judge Cardozo stated that even if the failure of pressure was due to negligence on the defendant's part, the plaintiff could not obtain damages. The city was acting as the agent of its residents in negotiating with the water company, and the water company was entitled to assume that, if it was to be the fire insurer for the city's property, the city would compensate it accordingly. Similarly, in dealing with T & D, Whitacre was acting in effect as Rardin's agent, and T & D was entitled to assume that, if it was to be an insurer of Rardin's business losses, Whitacre on behalf of Rardin would compensate it accordingly. Rardin in short could protect itself against T & D's negligence by negotiating appropriate terms with Whitacre.

The protracted analysis that we have thought necessary to address the parties' contentions underscores the desirability—perhaps urgency—of harmonizing the entire complex and confusing pattern of liability and nonliability for tortious conduct in contractual settings. But that is a task for the Supreme Court of Illinois rather than for us in this diversity case governed by Illinois law. It is enough for us that Illinois law does not permit a tort suit for profits lost as the result of the failure to complete a commercial undertaking.

Affirmed.

3. DO REMEDIES AFFECT THE CHOICE OF SUBSTANTIVE THEORY?

This book is not intended to draw theoretical distinctions between tort and contract or to say when alternative substantive rights may in theory arise from a given set of facts. Such matters have been thoroughly discussed in G. Gilmore, The Death of Contract (1974); O'Connell, The Interlocking Death and Rebirth of Contract and Tort, 75 Mich.L.Rev. 659 (1977); Considine, Some Implications from Recent Cases on the Differences Between Contract and Tort, 12 U.Br.Col.L.Rev. 85 (1978); Note, Contractual Recovery for Negligent Injury, 29 Ala.L.Rev. 519 (1978).

We cannot ignore the dramatic development of a "tort" cause of action based upon the breach of the covenant of good faith and fair dealing implied, it is said, in every contract. See Restatement (Second) of Contracts § 205 (1981). This cause of action originated in third party (i.e. liability) insurance cases where the insurance company improperly failed to settle its insured's liability within the policy limits. Crisci v. Security Insurance Co., 66 Cal.2d 425, 58 Cal.Rptr. 13, 426 P.2d 173 (1967), is the leading case. The theory overcame redoubtable resistance (with some ramparts still held) and spread into first party insurance cases, initially in refusal to pay medical disability claims and later to property damage or even title insurance claims. See K. York and J. Whelan, Insurance Law 56 (1982).

Courts have limited the tort action for breach of the covenant of good faith and fair dealing to contracts that involve a special relationship. They have resisted pressure to extend the tort to ordinary commercial transactions, probably because the law of contracts would indeed soon be dead if the trend continued unabated. See Seaman's Direct Buying Service, Inc. v. Standard Oil Co., 36 Cal.3d 752, 206 Cal.Rptr. 354, 686 P.2d 1158 (1984); Martin v. U–Haul Co., 204 Cal.App.3d 396, 251 Cal.Rptr. 17 (1988).

In an important 1988 decision, Foley v. Interactive Data Corp., p. 1151 infra, the California Supreme Court rejected an attempt to extend the tort to employment contracts. "We believe that focus on available contract remedies offers the most appropriate method of expanding available relief for wrongful terminations. The expansion of tort remedies in the employment context has potentially enormous consequences for the stability of the business community."

Similarly Judge Robert Keeton, in declining to find a tort theory to support Vanessa Redgrave's claim that the Boston Symphony Orchestra terminated a contract for a series of concerts because of her political views, stated:

"Rights are not to be determined by playing a game of labels. If the relationship of the parties is such as to support a cause of action in tort that cause of action is not to be denied because the parties happen also to have made a contract. Conversely a breach of contract is not, standing alone, a tort as well. And it cannot be converted into a tort merely by attaching to the contract, or to the breach, new labels that sound in tort. Calling a breach of contract a tortious repudiation of contract is no more helpful in identifying a ground of tort liability than would be an argument that every breach of contract—or perhaps every willful breach is a tort." Redgrave v. Boston Symphony Orchestra, Inc., 557 F.Supp. 230, 238 (D.Mass.1983). Redgrave v.

Boston Symphony Orchestra, Inc., 855 F.2d 888 (1st Cir.1988), affirmed plaintiff's damage verdict for breach of contract.

However the potential rewards of successful probings along the frontiers of this theory make it certain that they will continue.

A legal wrong that can be translated into either a contract or a tort presents a claimant with both procedural and remedial opportunities. In a real and practical sense, when an opportunity arises, remedial considerations totally dictate the course of action the plaintiff should pursue.

A sketchy list of remedial or procedural considerations may explain the otherwise puzzling choice of substantive law in many of the cases throughout this book:

1. The amount of compensatory damages plaintiff may recover under the divergent rules of tort and contract damages. This was illustrated above.

2. The possibility of punitive damages—a most potent motivation to frame a cause of action in tort.

3. The possibility of prejudgment interest on the awards. On balance, this consideration may militate against a tort approach.

4. The length of the statute of limitations. Tort statutes of limitations tend to be shorter than those for breach of contract. In medical malpractice, in particular circumstances, a delay may leave the plaintiff with only a breach of contract possibility.

5. The Statute of Frauds may bar breach of contract actions, but not torts.

6. The possible defense of contributory or comparative negligence. Obviously a reason to incline toward breach of contract.

7. Governmental agencies' immunity from suit. Immunity from breach of contract actions has yielded; to a large extent the same is true of tort liability under the Federal Tort Claims Act and its state equivalents. Some holdouts exist: a county-owned hospital contracts to care for the plaintiff during child birth and does so negligently. See Paul v. Escambia County Hospital Board, 283 Ala. 488, 218 So.2d 817 (1969).

8. The availability of provisional remedies. For example, prejudgment attachment may not be permitted in tort cases. Cal.Civ.Proc.Code § 483.010 (1970).

9. The assignability or survivability of the cause of action. These considerations militate against the tort approach, but they have been drastically modified in recent years.

10. Whether a claim will be discharged in defendant's bankruptcy.

11. Recovery of attorneys' fees.

12. Are there others?

F. LIMITATIONS ON RECOVERY

1. AVOIDABLE CONSEQUENCES

The expression "mitigation of damages" properly describes the ways a defendant may lessen his or her damages. The same expression is frequently used to describe what more correctly is termed avoidable consequences, the measures plaintiff should take to prevent damages from mounting.

MUNN v. ALGEE

United States Court of Appeals, Fifth Circuit, 1991.

924 F.2d 568.

Jerry E. Smith, Circuit Judge: Plaintiff Ray James Munn asserts that his and his deceased wife's adherence to the Jehovah's Witnesses faith was used improperly to impair his ability to recover compensation for their injuries. Finding no reversible error, we affirm. * * *

On Christmas morning 1986, vehicles driven by Munn and defendant Trudy Algee collided in Tunica County, Mississippi. Elaine Munn, Munn's wife and a passenger in his car, was transported to the Regional Medical Center in Memphis, Tennessee, arriving approximately three hours after the accident. Doctors identified a variety of injuries, including multiple rib and pelvic fractures, a lacerated chest artery, and a retroperitoneal hematoma.

Upon arrival at the hospital, Mrs. Munn informed doctors that she was a Jehovah's Witness and thus would not accept blood transfusions. Responding to her deteriorating condition, doctors unsuccessfully sought Munn's permission later in the day to perform a blood transfusion on his wife. Munn also refused to allow doctors to transfuse Mrs. Munn's own blood back into her.

Mrs. Munn died on the operating table from a loss of blood. Elaine and Ray James Munn incurred medical expenses in the amounts of $10,411.67 and $241.44, respectively. * * *

Munn brought suit against Algee in three separate capacities: (1) individually for his own injuries; (2) as administrator of his deceased spouse's estate; and (3) on behalf of his children, who, along with Mr. Munn, are the wrongful death beneficiaries under the Mississippi wrongful death statute. The district court granted Algee's motion for partial summary judgment, thereby precluding Munn from establishing what his wife's damages would have been had she consented to the blood transfusions and survived. The court granted a directed verdict in favor of plaintiffs on the question of liability.

After a trial, the jury awarded Munn $241.44 for his own medical expenses. It also returned a verdict for Munn in the amount of $20,411.67 to compensate Mrs. Munn's estate for her medical bills ($10,411.67) and her pain and suffering ($10,000.00). With respect to the wrongful death claim, the jury concluded that Mrs. Munn would not have died had she accepted blood transfusions and thus awarded the wrongful death beneficiaries no damages.

Munn moved for a new trial, asserting that the court erred in (1) admitting evidence of Jehovah's Witnesses' beliefs; (2) allowing Algee to invoke the avoidable consequences doctrine; (3) refusing to allow Munn to show what his wife's damages would have been had she accepted blood and lived; (4) refusing to apply the eggshell skull doctrine; (5) entering judgment on allegedly inconsistent answers to jury interrogatories; and (6) its instructions to the jury. Munn also argued that the verdict was against the great weight of the evidence and that the damage award was inadequate. The court denied the motion for new trial and Munn now appeals. * * *

Over Munn's objection, the district court allowed Algee's counsel to question him about many aspects of the Jehovah's Witnesses faith, including, *inter alia*, the following beliefs and practices: (1) Christ's physical return to earth in 1914; (2) the eternal damnation of all those not adhering to the faith; (3) the non-existence of hell; (4) the non-existence of souls; (5) refusal to "do service to their country"; and (6) refusal to salute the flag. Algee's counsel further questioned Munn about his and his wife's adherence *vel non* to the faith's prohibition on premarital cohabitation.

The admission of this evidence raises two questions: (1) whether the district court abused its discretion in admitting Munn's testimony, and (2) assuming the court abused its discretion, whether this error affected any substantial right of Munn's, see Fed.R.Evid. 103(a).

* * * Because we are unable to discern a fact of consequence of which this testimony is probative, we hold that the court erred in allowing the questions and that the error constitutes an abuse of discretion. * * *

After reviewing the record, we conclude—although it is a close question—that the admission of Munn's testimony did not adversely influence the jury. Munn failed to articulate any substantial right affected by this evidence's admission, and no prejudice is reflected in the jury's verdict.

First, Munn cannot plausibly argue that the amount of damages for pain and suffering awarded to Elaine Munn's estate demonstrates prejudice. For approximately eight hours of pain and suffering, the jury awarded $10,000.00, an amount not so small as to arouse suspicion as to the jury's motives.

Second, the jury's failure to award Munn any damages for his own pain and suffering most likely reflects the relatively minor nature of his injuries. He incurred only $241.44 in medical expenses and by his own admission suffered only "bruises and contusions."

The jury's failure to award any wrongful death damages is the most plausible expression of any prejudice caused by the erroneous admission of this evidence. However, the jury most likely refused to compensate the wrongful death beneficiaries because it believed that Mrs. Munn would have lived had she taken blood transfusions. A number of doctors testified as to whether blood transfusions would have saved Mrs. Munn's life, and although their testimony was conflicting, the evidence was such that in deciding the cause of Mrs. Munn's death, there is no indication that the jury was using her refusal to take blood as a pretext for expressing its possible distaste for Jehovah's Witnesses. * * *

In an effort to avoid liability for Mrs. Munn's death, Algee argued that Mrs. Munn's refusal to accept blood transfusions was unreasonable and thus that the doctrine of avoidable consequences[1] precluded any recovery. Munn now asserts that application of this doctrine violated the first amendment's free

1. [Footnotes renumbered.] Under Mississippi law, an injured plaintiff may not recover for damages that he did not take reasonable efforts to avoid. Courts frequently use the phrases "avoidance of consequences" and "mitigation of damages" interchangeably.

exercise and establishment clauses, arguing that the rule burdened his wife's exercise of the Jehovah's Witnesses faith and invited the jury to consider the reasonableness of that religion.

Munn cites a published article to support his argument that application of this doctrine violates the first amendment. See Comment, *Medical Care, Freedom of Religion and Mitigation of Damages,* 87 Yale L.J. 1466 (1978). The comment writer accurately identifies two judicial approaches to religiously motivated refusals to mitigate tort damages. The first, labelled the "objective" approach, holds that religion may not justify an otherwise unreasonable failure to mitigate. The second, termed the "case-by-case" approach, attempts to accommodate religious beliefs by allowing the jury to consider the plaintiff's religious beliefs in determining whether his or her failure to mitigate was reasonable.

The author concludes that the objective approach violates the free exercise clause, while the case-by-case approach violates the establishment clause. In the instant case, the court applied the case-by-case approach, attempting to accommodate Mrs. Munn's religious beliefs.[2]

Without identifying the court's approach, Munn argues that its application of the avoidable consequences doctrine violated both first amendment clauses. He accordingly desires, as did the comment author, that we recognize a special exemption from the doctrine's application for religiously motivated failures to mitigate damages. We decline to do so, as we conclude that proper application of the avoidable consequences doctrine does not violate the first amendment. * * *

Munn contends that applying the mitigation of damages principle to this case violates the first amendment because it incidentally affects Mrs. Munn's exercise of her religion. This argument is foreclosed by Supreme Court cases holding that generally applicable rules imposing incidental burdens on particular religions do not violate the free exercise clause. See McGowan v. Maryland, 366 U.S. 420 (1961) (Sunday closing laws do not violate free exercise rights of Saturday sabbatarians); Braunfeld v. Brown, 366 U.S. 599 (1961) (same); see also Employment Div., Dept. of Human Resources v. Smith ___ U.S. ___, 110 S.Ct. 1595 (1990) (free exercise clause does not prohibit application of Oregon drug laws to ceremonial ingestion of peyote). Accordingly, we hold that the application of the mitigation of damages doctrine, under either of the two approaches, does not violate the free exercise clause of the first amendment. Accord Corlett v. Caserta, 204 Ill.App.3d 403, 149 Ill.Dec. 793, 562 N.E.2d 257 (1st Dist.1990) (involving Jehovah's Witness). * * *

The more compelling problem with the application of the doctrine in this case is that it potentially invited the jury to judge the reasonableness of the Jehovah's Witnesses' religion. See Hernandez v. Commissioner, 490 U.S. 680 (1989); United States v. Ballard, 322 U.S. 78, 87 (1944). We conclude that in an appropriate case, application of the case-by-case approach to religiously motivated refusals to mitigate damages can involve weighing the reasonableness of religious beliefs and thus arguably would violate the establishment clause.

2. The court stated that "[t]he jury is going to be called upon to determine the reasonableness of their beliefs considering their religion as one of the factors." Later in the proceedings the court similarly declared that "[o]ne of the issues for the jury to decide is the reasonableness of the deceased, presumably Mr. Munn's decision, based on their belief in the Jehovah's Witness doctrine."

However, because here the court's application of this approach was designed to *assist* Munn in circumventing the avoidable consequences doctrine, we need not address squarely the constitutionality of the case-by-case approach, for in any event Munn is entitled to no relief.

Application of the case-by-case approach allows a jury to consider the religious nature of a plaintiff's refusal to avoid the consequences of a defendant's negligence. Accordingly, otherwise unreasonable conduct may be deemed reasonable. However, the question of whether a jury decides to label such conduct as reasonable may depend upon its view of the the religious tenet that motivated the plaintiff's failure to mitigate damages.

If the jury finds the religion plausible, it will more likely deem the conduct reasonable; on the other hand, if the particular faith strikes the jury as strange or bizarre, the jury will probably conclude that the plaintiff's failure to mitigate was unreasonable. Because the plaintiff's religion is the only basis upon which otherwise unreasonable conduct can be deemed reasonable, the jury undoubtedly assesses the plaintiff's religion in reaching its conclusion. A strong case can be made that the first amendment forbids such an assessment.

However, simply because the case-by-case approach might involve impermissible assessment of a religion's reasonableness does not mean that Munn is entitled to a new trial. Munn himself interjected religion into the case, seeking to explain his wife's conduct. Had he been prohibited from doing so, the jury undoubtedly would have deemed her decision unreasonable. In short, the jury's assessment of Elaine Munn's religion did not harm Munn's case. Consequently, we find the court's application of the case-by-case approach to be, at most, harmless error.[3] * * *

In granting Algee's motion for partial summary judgment, the district court precluded Munn from establishing what Mrs. Munn's damages would have been had she accepted the blood transfusions and lived. Munn unsuccessfully challenged this decision in his motion for a new trial and now appeals that denial. * * *

We nonetheless agree with the court's determination that Munn should not be compensated for these hypothetical damages, as Mrs. Munn did not actually suffer the harm from which the damages are sought. Mississippi law compels this conclusion. In Entex, Inc. v. Rasberry, 355 So.2d 1102 (Miss.1978), the court stated that "[t]he general rule is that where it is established that future consequences from an injury to a person will ensue, recovery therefor may be had, but such future consequences must be established in terms of reasonable probabilities." It is not "reasonably probable" that the described injuries to Mrs. Munn will occur; in fact, because she did not survive the accident, it is certain that they will *not* occur. We thus affirm the denial of Munn's new trial motion insofar as it related to proof of damages.[4] * * *

3. However, we urge the district courts to apply the "objective" approach to religiously motivated refusals to mitigate damages, for that approach plainly violates neither the free exercise clause nor the establishment clause.

4. The combined effect of this conclusion and the avoidable consequences doctrine is at least superficially harsh: Mrs. Munn's estate and her husband and children are unable to recover either the damages she would have suffered or wrongful death damages. The district

Munn argues that the "eggshell skull" doctrine, which requires a defendant to compensate a plaintiff for unforeseeable injury flowing from some pre-existing condition, entitles him to compensation for his wife's wrongful death. Munn attempts to extend the doctrine's application to situations in which the plaintiff's pre-existing condition is "mental" rather than physical.

However, the principle has been applied only to pre-existing *physical* injuries. [citations] We decline the invitation to extend its scope, absent substantial indication that the state courts of Mississippi would do so. Accordingly, the court did not err in refusing to apply the eggshell skull doctrine to the instant case, and its denial of Munn's new trial motion in this respect is affirmed.[5] * * *

The following interrogatory was submitted to the jury:

> 4. Do you find that the original injuries sustained by Elaine Munn combined with her unreasonable refusal of blood to cause her death?
>
> Answer: ______
>
> Enter "Yes" or "No"
>
> If your answer to this interrogatory is "Yes," what percentage did Elaine Munn's unreasonable refusal of blood contribute to her death? ___ percent (%)

The jury answered "yes" to the first part and "100%" to the second. Munn contends that these answers are inconsistent and consequently that the court erred in denying his motion for a new trial. More specifically, Munn argues that because his wife's original injuries "combined" with her refusal of blood to cause her death (according to the jury's answer to the first part of the question), her refusal to take blood could not possibly constitute 100% of the cause of her death.

When a litigant claims that the jury's answers to interrogatories are inconsistent, the seventh amendment compels the district court to seek a "view of the case which makes the jury's answers consistent." Griffin v. Matherne, 471 F.2d 911, 915, (5th Cir.1973). The court properly applied this test, holding that the jury's answers were consistent with one another and with the applicable instruction.[6]

court, perceiving unfairness, crafted a jury instruction that allowed the jury to award wrongful death damages even if it found that Mrs. Munn's refusal to accept blood was unreasonable and that she would have lived had she accepted the blood. We reject this approach.

5. Even if we were inclined to extend application of the doctrine to pre-existing "mental" conditions (as Munn characterizes his wife's religious beliefs), the situation in this case is distinguishable from one in which the defendant's negligence aggravates some pre-existing psychological defect (e.g., where a car accident makes an already paranoid plaintiff even more so). Algee's negligence did not aggravate some pre-existing mental illness; rather it put Mrs. Munn in a situation in which she felt obliged to follow one of her beliefs.

6. The court instructed the jury to "determine the percentage of wrongful death damages attributable to Elaine Munn's refusal to accept the transfusions," allowing it "to place this percentage at 0%, 100%, or any percentage in between." In its opinion denying Munn's motion for a new trial, the court noted that it instructed the jury "that even if it found that Mrs. Munn's death was avoidable and that her refusal of the blood transfusion was unreasonable, it could still award the plaintiff wrongful death damages, if it further found that the defendant's negligence was a contributing cause of Mrs. Munn's death." The interrogatory challenged in this appeal corresponds to this instruction.

We reject this approach. Apportioning wrongful death damages is inconsistent with the mitigation of damages doctrine. If a jury finds that a certain consequence of the defendant's negligence could reasonably have been avoided by the plaintiff, the plaintiff cannot recover for that consequence. The bar on recovery is total; retreating to notions of causation is inappropriate in light of the purposes of the doctrine, which are to encourage plaintiffs to reduce the societal costs of their injuries and to ensure fair treatment of defendants. That the defendant's negligence may have caused the avoidable injury is irrelevant. [citations]

We agree with the court's conclusion. These answers do not conflict; instead, they reflect the entirely plausible view that although both the injury and the refusal were causal factors in Mrs. Munn's death, she would have survived had she taken the blood. * * *

Although the court did admit potentially prejudicial testimony into evidence the jury's award is not so inadequate as to shock the judicial conscience. That the jury was not improperly biased against the Munns is evident in its award of $10,000.00 for Mrs. Munn's eight hours of pain and suffering. Furthermore, its decision to deny the wrongful death beneficiaries any compensation reflects a reasoned application of the avoidable consequences doctrine. In addition, the jury's refusal to award Munn any pain and suffering damages mirrors the relatively minor nature of his injuries. * * *

Munn asserts that the court erroneously instructed the jury in two ways: (1) by directing the jury to judge the reasonableness of Mrs. Munn's decision to refuse blood against an objective standard; and (2) by refusing to inform the jury of the identity of the potential wrongful death beneficiaries. The court's instructions were appropriate in both regards, and we therefore affirm.

During the jury instruction conference, Munn's counsel urged the court to direct the jury to ask what a reasonable Jehovah's Witness would have done in Mrs. Munn's situation. The court refused to adopt this instruction, instead instructing the jury in a way that defies easy categorization as "objective" or "subjective":

> In determining whether or not Elaine Munn's decision to refuse the blood transfusion was unreasonable, you may consider that the blood transfusions were medically recommended. But, you may also consider her religious beliefs and related teachings, together with the known risks of blood transfusions, if you find that to be a factor in her decision.

Contra Corlett v. Caserta (where "the patient exercises his fundamental and religious right to refuse a reasonable life-saving medical procedure and subsequently dies, the patient's estate should bear a proportionate share of tort liability for the patient's wrongful death to the extent that the patient's death was proximately caused by the patient's refusal of the reasonable life-saving treatment").

The mitigation doctrine is designed to operate in precisely this kind of situation, i.e., where the defendant's negligence concededly *caused* all of the plaintiff's injuries, some of which might reasonably have been avoided by the injured plaintiff. There is no need for a doctrine that precludes recovery only where "the defendant's negligence was [not] a contributing cause" of damages that might reasonably have been avoided by the plaintiff; causation principles prevent imposition of liability on the defendant therefor.

Although we understand the district court's desire to prevent the arguable unfairness of the result, we note that Munn's inability to recover neither wrongful death damages nor hypothetical damages flows from Mrs. Munn's own behavior, which was deemed unreasonable by the jury. If she had acted reasonably, she would have survived (according to the jury), and thus wrongful death would not have been an issue in the case. (Had she acted reasonably and *not* survived, her wrongful death beneficiaries *would* have been able to recover, since death would not have been an *avoidable* consequence.) Had she acted reasonably and lived, she would have been able to recover for pain, suffering, medical expenses, and lost wages.

Both parties blithely conclude that this language reflects an "objective" standard of reasonableness. However, this standard is not purely objective; it does not ask the jury whether reasonable people would have done what Mrs. Munn did. It contains a subjective component, allowing the jury to "consider her religious beliefs and related teachings."

In any event, the proper characterization of this instruction is not the issue at hand; instead, the question is whether the instruction was wrong as a matter of Mississippi law. This instruction does not incorrectly state Mississippi law. * * * North Am. Accident Ins. Co. v. Henderson, 180 Miss. 395, 177 So. 528 (1937). * * *

Some cases do apply a standard of reasonableness that is "subjective" in the sense that the nature of the plaintiff is taken into account. In *Henderson,* the plaintiff sought damages for his continuing physical disability, even though surgery would have enabled him to return to work and thus mitigate his damages. The plaintiff argued that he was unable to pay for the operation, and the defendant responded by asserting that the plaintiff's financial condition was not relevant to the reasonableness of his failure to mitigate damages.

The Mississippi Supreme Court rejected this position, stating that the mitigation of damages rule is "one of reason, and, if the injured person be powerless to take the needed step, reasonableness has become exhausted and the applicability of the rule is at an end."[7] Although *Henderson* effectively jettisons the notion that Mississippi has a purely objective standard of reasonableness,[8] it does not render erroneous the district court's instruction, which did not contain a purely objective standard. The instruction allowed the jury to consider factors unique to the decedent, such as "her religious beliefs and related teachings." Hence, because the instruction comported with Mississippi law, the district court's judgment in this regard is affirmed.[9]

The judgment of the district court is in all respects affirmed. * * *

ALVIN B. RUBIN, CIRCUIT JUDGE, dissenting: The personal-injury and wrongful-death claims of two black Jehovah's Witnesses from Tennessee were being tried before a predominantly white jury in Clarksdale, Mississippi. Judge Smith correctly finds that the trial court erred in admitting irrelevant evidence that was calculated to evoke the jury's prejudices, but concludes that this inflammatory effort by counsel and error by the trial court did not affect a substantial right of the plaintiffs. In my opinion, this * * * minimizes the potential consequences of the deliberate appeal to religious prejudice and to chauvinism permitted by the trial court. * * *

7. Incidentally, Munn could argue that Mrs. Munn was "powerless" to mitigate her damages. However, she was not "powerless" to accept blood transfusions in the sense that the plaintiff in *Henderson* was "powerless" to pay for the operation. There is a difference between hard choices and physical impossibility.

8. At the same time, however, neither *Henderson* nor any other Mississippi case mandates a purely subjective approach to reasonableness.

9. That Mississippi law allows a court to permit a jury to consider personal attributes in determining reasonableness does not in any way undermine our observation that jury consideration of religious beliefs may violate the establishment clause.

Ms. Algee had admitted her liability. The jury was called upon to decide only the damages due Mr. Munn and his wife's children. In doing so, the jurors were asked to make four necessarily subjective determinations: (1) Whether Ms. Munn's refusal to take blood was reasonable; (2) What portion of Mrs. Munn's damages were attributable to her unreasonable refusal to take blood; (3) What amount of damages would compensate Ms. Munn's estate for her pain and suffering; and (4) What amount of damages would compensate Mr. Munn for his pain and suffering. The jury's sympathy for or antipathy to the Munns might substantially affect their decision on each of these issues. * * *

Apparently, neither of my brothers accepts the view that any lawyer who has tried personal injury cases considers fundamental: the sympathy or disaffection the jury has for the victim affects the amount of damages. * * *

* * * Anecdote has it that the late Sammy Davis Jr., when about to play golf, was asked, "What is your handicap?" He replied, "I'm black, one-eyed and Jewish, and you still want to know my handicap?!" The Munns were quadruply handicapped—black nonresidents adhering to an unpopular faith, some of whose members were unpatriotic, trying a case before a north Mississippi jury, five of whose six members were white.

Judge Smith concludes that inducing this predominantly white Mississippi jury to believe or at least to infer that the Munns believed that Christ returned to earth in 1914 and has invisibly ruled since that time, that there will not be a resurrection but that the jury (like all others ever on earth save Jehovah's Witnesses) will be eternally damned, that Munn believes man has no soul, that Munn is a conscientious objector who will not expose himself to the dangers inherent in military service even when the nation is threatened, that the Munns even refuse to salute the flag, and that they lived together in adultery prior to their marriage all likely had no effect on the Munns' substantial rights. * * * This to me, with all respect to both of my brethren, is contrary to the universal knowledge and experience of trial lawyers and judges, and to the human disposition to favor those we like and to discountenance those we disfavor. Algee's lawyer deliberately threw the proverbial skunk of inadmissible evidence into the jury box. No amount of conjecture that the jury *might* not have smelled the stink can undo the odor that, even now, permeates the record. I therefore respectfully dissent.

Notes

1. The distinction between avoidable consequences to reduce damages and the substantive doctrines of contributory negligence, assumption of risk, and last clear chance is not always maintained. EVRA Corp. v. Swiss Bank Corp., p. 68.

2. Numerous decisions discuss whether, if an automobile accident victim has failed to buckle available seat and shoulder belts, the evidence of nonuse should be excluded or whether the jury should consider it under the head of contributory negligence, comparative negligence, or avoidable consequences. Note, Caveat Viator: Safety is No Longer the Only Good Reason for Oregonians to "Buckle Up," 67 Or.L.Rev. 901, 904 (1988), surveys the legislation and decisions and quotes the Earl of Andrews's statement in 1683 before His Majesty's Order of Scribes: "Quoth what

fool darest upon the highways of this realm without properly strapping his ass to his cart."

URICO v. PARNELL OIL CO.

United States Court of Appeals, First Circuit, 1983.
708 F.2d 852.

TAURO, DISTRICT JUDGE. The appellant (Parnell) seeks relief from a jury award to the appellees (Uricos) for the loss of use to them of their truck, following its collision with another truck driven by a Parnell employee. * * *

The underlying facts are novel and require somewhat detailed exposition. On April 11, 1977, a truck driven by a Parnell employee struck the rear of one owned by the Uricos. The Uricos' truck had been leased by them to Richard Lester. Without permission from the Uricos, Lester had turned the truck over to Harold Windsor who was its operator at the time of the accident.

Shortly after the accident, Parnell's insurer, Bankers and Shippers Insurance Co. (B & S), contacted Windsor, arrived at a settlement, and issued checks in the amount of $15,102.05 for repairs and $3,500 for loss of use of the truck. B & S later stopped payment on the repair check when it learned that Windsor failed to retrieve the repaired vehicle.

The Uricos did not learn of the accident until June of 1977. They then informed B & S that Windsor lacked authority to reach a settlement on their behalf. Later, in August of 1977, they made a demand on B & S of $19,490.13 for property damage and $1,000.00 a week for loss of use. B & S took the position that it had already settled the claim with Windsor, but would be willing to pay the Uricos $15,102.05 for repairs if they, in turn, would waive their loss of use claim. The Uricos rejected this offer.

The truck had been repaired by the end of August, 1977, but the Uricos were unable to pay for the repairs and so could not take possession of it. The truck remained at the repair garage until September of 1979 when, by order of the district court, B & S issued a check to the Uricos in the amount of $15,102.05.

At trial, the Uricos sought damages for the loss of the truck's use from the time of the accident until B & S made payment for the repairs under court order. The Uricos' theory at trial was that B & S's wrongful refusal to make a reasonable settlement offer prevented them from mitigating their damages during the post-repair period. The jury found in favor of the Uricos, awarding $11,400.00 for loss of use during the repair period, and $51,100.00 for loss of use following repair. * * *

The Uricos had a clear duty to take all reasonable steps to mitigate damages. They introduced evidence as to the course of settlement negotiations in order to excuse their failure to mitigate. Their evidentiary theory at trial was that 1) their truck was damaged and could not be used by them in business, 2) the circumstance of their truck being rear ended while parked in a breakdown lane forecast the substantial likelihood of a liability finding should the issue of fault be litigated, 3) they were unable to pay for the repairs, and so could not get the truck back on the road in furtherance of their business, 4) B & S was aware that the Uricos did not have the financial means to retrieve the truck from the repairer, and 5) even though aware of these facts, B & S refused to pay for the repairs unless the Uricos waived their other claims. In short, the Uricos attempted to show that B & S unreasonably held their truck hostage in an effort to reach a total and advantageous settlement. Such evidence was clearly relevant to the factual issue of whether actions taken by B & S on behalf of Parnell unreasonably prevented the Uricos from mitigating damage to them due to loss of use. * * *

Ordinarily, recovery for loss of use of a damaged vehicle is limited to that period of time reasonably necessary to complete repairs. [citations] Here, the jury found that the Uricos were entitled to additional loss of use damages beyond the repair period, because of B & S's unreasonably dilatory settlement tactics.

The extension of loss of use damages beyond the repair period raises difficulty policy questions. Limiting loss of use damages to a reasonable repair period recompenses the plaintiff for a finite period in which the vehicle is simply unavailable for use. An award of loss of use damages after the vehicle had been repaired, however, is potentially boundless. Anticipation of such an award could conceivably reduce any incentive that a plaintiff might have to mitigate losses. The evidence here, however, relieves us of these theoretical concerns. The Uricos, despite their good faith best efforts, could not mitigate their losses without possession of the repaired truck. B & S knew this. Nonetheless, B & S refused to issue payment for the repairs, despite the fact that they had previously done so to an unauthorized party.

Arbitrary conduct by an insurer, which serves to prolong rather than contain the interval of loss, is an appropriate circumstance for awarding damages beyond the traditional reasonable repair period. In Valencia v. Shell Oil Co., 23 Cal.2d 840, 147 P.2d 558 (1944), defendant initially promised to pay for repairs to a truck damaged in a collision with plaintiff. Repairs were undertaken in reliance on this promise. After the repairs were completed, defendant refused to pay unless plaintiff agreed to waive all other claims. In *Valencia,* the Supreme Court of California held that where plaintiff was financially incapable of paying for the repairs, and defendant's refusal to pay caused additional losses, plaintiff could recover loss of use damages for an extended period. The application of that theory in no way diminishes the traditional requirement that plaintiffs may not recover for damages which could have been avoided by their reasonable efforts to mitigate.

Affirmed.

Notes

1. *Avoidable Consequences: Property Damages Cases.*

a. City & County of Denver v. Noble, 124 Colo. 392, 237 P.2d 637 (1951). Plaintiff recovered damages for loss of crops from the wrongful destruction of an irrigation ditch. In reversing the judgment for error in jury instructions, the court stated:

"It was the duty of plaintiff to mitigate her damages, if she could reasonably do so, by constructing another ditch or lateral to convey water to her land * * *. Plaintiff made no claim that she could not do this. She took no steps toward that end. However, she complainingly, if not stubbornly, sat by over a period of years, allowed the new ditch as constructed by defendant to become filled with weeds, debris and other obstructions, and sought $24,000 damages on the theory that she could not raise crops because she did not have water for her land. According to the record she did nothing to remedy the condition of which she complained.

"There was no evidence before the jury that plaintiff's irrigation system could not be made as efficient as it was prior to the construction of the road. Witness Prouty testified that a certain culvert would have to be slightly lowered in order to accomplish this result, but he was quite positive that plaintiff could obtain the use of her water by conveying it through a gate north of the highway. He further testified that the expense would be about $200, which would be nominal when compared to the $9,000 damages awarded by the jury."

b. Green v. Smith, 261 Cal.App.2d 392, 67 Cal.Rptr. 796 (1968). Plaintiff recovered $17,000 for loss of nursery trees although the consequences could have been avoided by an expenditure of $600.

c. Lourence v. West Side Irrigation District, 233 Cal.App.2d 532, 43 Cal.Rptr. 889, 894 (1965):

"The court instructed the jury as follows:

> 'A person whose property had been damaged by the wrongful act of another is bound to exercise reasonable care and diligence to avoid loss and to minimize the damages, and he may not recover for losses which could have been prevented by reasonable efforts on his part or by expenditures that he might reasonably have made.'

"Plaintiff assails this instruction on the grounds that it compels a land owner to take reasonable precautions to prevent the adjoining canals from seeping water onto his property. Plaintiff relies on Kleinclaus v. Marin Realty Co. (1949), 94 Cal.App.2d 733, 211 P.2d 582. In that case water seeped through an embankment, built to create a pond, and resulted in the flooding of the plaintiff's field. The plaintiffs had a drainage ditch running through their field which if it had not been stopped up would have allowed the seeping water to run off his land thereby causing him no harm. In regard to the issue of plaintiff's blocking their ditch and thereby allegedly contributively causing their own injury, the court said:

" 'We are satisfied to hold that plaintiffs were not obliged to anticipate the negligent flooding of their land by defendants and that their permitting the drainage ditch to become clogged before the flooding started cannot constitute contributory negligence. If they had chosen to fill up the drainage ditch deliberately before the danger from flooding by defendants' negligence occurred they would only have been exercising the rights of an owner to use his land in any lawful fashion.'

"This rule of the *Kleinclaus* case is not applicable to an instruction on the issue of mitigation of damages. In fact the rule pertains only to contributory negligence. The instruction complained of refers to mitigation of damages. Actually *Kleinclaus,* supra, supports the court in giving the instruction on mitigation of damages. There the court, after holding that the plaintiff was not guilty of contributory negligence in clogging a ditch on his own land before defendant negligently flooded plaintiff's land, said: 'The most that can be said is that when plaintiffs discovered that the culvert was clogged they may have been under a duty to clear it out to mitigate their damages. Their land was then already invaded by the water negligently cast upon it by defendants, but the duty to mitigate damages exists alike in cases of breach of contract and tort, wilful as well as negligent.' Plaintiff, while under no obligation to assume that seepage water would come on his land or to protect against such happening, was obligated to use reasonable care and diligence to mitigate damage caused by defendant's unwarranted acts, if there were any. The instruction given is (B.A.J.I. 179–A).

"There was no error in the instruction given."

The court vacated the judgment for other reasons; but it adhered to its discussion of the quoted instructions. The instruction "deals only with the duty of a property owner to use reasonable care and diligence to mitigate damage due to another's unwarranted acts after those acts have caused damage to his property. Perhaps it would be advisable to make it more clearly appear that the duty referred to does not require anticipation of damage."

2. *Avoidable Consequences and Overhead Costs.* United States v. Denver & Rio Grande Western Railroad Co., 547 F.2d 1101 (10th Cir.1977). A fire, negligently started by a railroad, burned over U.S. government lands. The plaintiff was held entitled to fire suppression costs; but not the general expense of maintaining an Emergency Fire Center.

2. COLLATERAL SOURCE RULE AND CREDIT FOR BENEFIT

HELFEND v. SOUTHERN CALIFORNIA RAPID TRANSIT DISTRICT

Supreme Court of California, 1970.

2 Cal.3d 1, 84 Cal.Rptr. 173, 465 P.2d 61.

TOBRINER, JUSTICE. [Plaintiff was injured in a bus-auto collision.]

Plaintiff filed a tort action against the Southern California Rapid Transit District, a public entity, and Mitchell, an employee of the transit district. At trial plaintiff claimed slightly more than $2,700 in special damages, including $921 in doctor's bills, a $336.99 hospital bill, and about $45 for medicines. Defendant requested permission to show that about 80 percent of the plaintiff's hospital bill had been paid by plaintiff's Blue Cross insurance carrier and that some of his other medical expenses may have been paid by other insurance. * * *

After the jury verdict in favor of plaintiff in the sum of $16,300, defendants appealed, raising only two contentions: (1) The trial court committed prejudicial error in refusing to allow the introduction of evidence to the effect that a portion of the plaintiff's medical bills had been paid from a collateral source. (2) The trial court erred in denying defendant the opportunity to determine if plaintiff had been compensated from more than one collateral source for damages sustained in the accident.

We must decide whether the collateral source rule applies to tort actions involving public entities and public employees in which the plaintiff has received benefits from his medical insurance coverage. * * *

The Supreme Court of California has long adhered to the doctrine that if an injured party receives some compensation for his injuries from a source wholly independent of the tortfeasor, such payment should not be deducted from the damages which the plaintiff would otherwise collect from the tortfeasor. * * *

Although the collateral source rule remains generally accepted in the

United States, nevertheless many other jurisdictions[1] have restricted[2] or repealed it. In this country most commentators have criticized the rule and called for its early demise. * * *

The collateral source rule as applied here embodies the venerable concept that a person who has invested years of insurance premiums to assure his medical care should receive the benefits of his thrift. The tortfeasor should not garner the benefits of his victim's providence.

The collateral source rule expresses a policy judgment in favor of encouraging citizens to purchase and maintain insurance for personal injuries and for other eventualities. Courts consider insurance a form of investment, the benefits of which become payable without respect to any other possible source of funds. If we were to permit a tortfeasor to mitigate damages with payments from plaintiff's insurance, plaintiff would be in a position inferior to that of having bought no insurance, because his payment of premiums would have earned no benefit. Defendant should not be able to avoid payment of full compensation for the injury inflicted merely because the victim has had the foresight to provide himself with insurance.

Some commentators object that the above approach to the collateral source rule provides plaintiff with a "double recovery," rewards him for the injury, and defeats the principle that damages should compensate the victim but not punish the tortfeasor. We agree with Professor Fleming's observation, however, that "double recovery is justified only in the face of some exceptional, supervening reason, as in the case of accident or life insurance, where it is felt unjust that the tortfeasor should take advantage of the thrift and prescience of the victim in having paid the premiums." (Fleming, Introduction to the Law of Torts (1967) p. 131.) * * * [R]ecovery in a wrongful death action is not defeated by the payment of the benefit on a life insurance policy.

Furthermore, insurance policies increasingly provide for either subrogation or refund of benefits upon a tort recovery, and such refund is indeed called for in the present case. * * * Hence, the plaintiff receives no double recovery; the collateral source rule simply serves as a means of bypassing the antiquated doctrine of nonassignment of tortious actions and permits a proper transfer of risk from the plaintiff's insurer to the tortfeasor by way of the victim's tort recovery. The double shift from the tortfeasor to the victim and then from the victim to his insurance carrier can normally occur with little cost in that the

1. [Footnotes renumbered.] After a period in which it appeared that the courts of the United Kingdom, the country of the rule's origin, would disavow it [citations], the House of Lords in Parry v. Cleaver (1969) 2 W.L.R. 821, has recently reaffirmed the rule and applied it to a case of a tort victim who, following the automobile accident in which he was disabled, received a pension. [citations] Most other western European nations have repudiated the rule.

2. The New York Court of Appeals has, for example, quite reasonably held that an injured physician may not recover from a tortfeasor for the value of medical and nursing care rendered gratuitously as a matter of professional courtesy. (See Coyne v. Campbell (1962) 11 N.Y.2d 372, 230 N.Y.S.2d 1, 183 N.E.2d 891). The doctor owed at least a moral obligation to render gratuitous services in return, if ever required: but he had neither paid premiums for the services under some form of insurance coverage nor manifested any indication that he would endeavor to repay those who had given him assistance. Thus this situation differs from that in which friends and relatives render assistance to the injured plaintiff with the expectation of repayment out of any tort recovery; in that case, the rule has been applied. [citations] On the other hand, New York has joined most states in holding that a tortfeasor may not mitigate damages by showing that an injured plaintiff would receive a disability pension. [citations] In these cases the plaintiff had actually or constructively paid for the pension by having received lower wages or by having contributed directly to the pension plan.

insurance carrier is often intimately involved in the initial litigation and quite automatically receives its part of the tort settlement or verdict.[3]

Even in cases in which the contract or the law precludes subrogation or refund of benefits,[4] or in situations in which the collateral source waives such subrogation or refund, the rule performs entirely necessary functions in the computation of damages. For example, the cost of medical care often provides both attorneys and juries in tort cases with an important measure for assessing the plaintiff's general damages. * * * To permit the defendant to tell the jury that the plaintiff has been recompensed by a collateral source for his medical costs might irretrievably upset the complex, delicate, and somewhat indefinable calculations which result in the normal jury verdict. * * *

We also note that generally the jury is not informed that plaintiff's attorney will receive a large portion of the plaintiff's recovery in contingent fees or that personal injury damages are not taxable to the plaintiff and are normally deductible by the defendant. Hence, the plaintiff rarely actually receives full compensation for his injuries as computed by the jury. The collateral source rule partially serves to compensate for the attorney's share and does not actually render "double recovery" for the plaintiff. Indeed, many jurisdictions that have abolished or limited the collateral source rule have also established a means for assessing the plaintiff's costs for counsel directly against the defendant rather than imposing the contingent fee system. In sum, the plaintiff's recovery for his medical expenses from both the tortfeasor and his medical insurance program will not usually give him "double recovery," but partially provides a somewhat closer approximation to full compensation for his injuries.[5]

If we consider the collateral source rule as applied here in the context of the entire American approach to the law of torts and damages, we find that the rule presently performs a number of legitimate and even indispensible functions. Without a thorough revolution in the American approach to torts and the consequent damages, the rule at least with respect to medical insurance benefits has become so integrated within our present system that its precipitous judicial nullification would work hardship. * * *

We therefore reaffirm our adherence to the collateral source rule in tort cases in which the plaintiff has been compensated by an independent collateral source—such as insurance, pension, continued wages, or disability payments—for which he had actually or constructively paid or in cases in which the

3. In personal injury cases in which the tort victim is unwilling to sue, subrogation subjects the tort victim to additional trouble and incurs further cost. A provision for refund of benefits, such as in the present case, avoids these difficulties by permitting the tort victim to decide whether to undertake litigation against the tortfeasor.

4. Certain insurance benefits are regarded as the proceeds of an investment rather than as an indemnity for damages. Thus it has been held that the proceeds of a life insurance contract made for a fixed sum rather than for the damages caused by the death of the insured are proceeds of an investment and can be received independently of the claim for damages against the person who caused the death of the insured. The same rule has been held applicable to accident insurance contracts.

5. Of course, only in cases in which the tort victim has received payments or services from a collateral source will he be able to mitigate attorney's fees by means of the collateral source rule. Thus the rule provides at best only an incomplete and haphazard solution to providing all tort victims with full compensation. Depriving some tort victims of the salutary protections of the collateral source rule will, short of a thorough reform of our tort system, only decrease the available compensation for injuries. * * *

collateral source would be recompensed from the tort recovery through subrogation, refund of benefits, or some other arrangement. * * *

Defendants would have this court create a special form of sovereign immunity as a novel exception to the collateral source rule for tortfeasors who are public entities or public employees. * * * We see no justification for such special treatment. In the present case the nullification of the collateral source rule would simply frustrate the transfer of the medical costs from the medical insurance carrier, Blue Cross, to the public entity. The public entity or its insurance carrier is in at least as advantageous a position to spread the risk of loss as is the plaintiff's medical insurance carrier. To deprive Blue Cross of repayment for its expenditures on plaintiff's behalf merely because he was injured by a public entity rather than a private individual would constitute an unwarranted and arbitrary discrimination. * * *

The judgment is affirmed.

Notes

1. *Joint Tortfeasors and the Collateral Source Rule.* The collateral source rule does not apply to payments either to the plaintiff by the defendant himself or by someone who is identified with him. D. Dobbs, Remedies 583 (1973). A joint tortfeasor falls in the latter category, so that any settlement payments or any insurance proceeds paid on behalf of one tortfeasor will be credited against the damage liability of the "defendant-tort feasor." Grynbal v. Grynbal, 32 A.D.2d 427, 302 N.Y.S.2d 912 (1969). Cf. Sweep v. Lear Jet Corp., 412 F.2d 457 (5th Cir.1969).

2. Benefits conferred on an injured person through government sponsored social insurance such as Medicare, Social Security or one of the various retirement acts present difficult problems when a government agency is sued under the Federal Tort Claims Act. Application of the collateral source rule usually turns upon whether the benefit is funded at least in part by the injured party or whether it is derived solely from general government resources. Seiverson v. United States, infra p. 676.

A related problem arises in lawsuits based on violations of the Federal Employers' Liability Act when payments to the injured party are made pursuant to an insurance policy funded entirely by the employer. In Perry v. Metro–North Commuter Railroad, 716 F.Supp. 61, 62 (D.Conn.1989), the court stated the distinction as follows: "The problem that has troubled the courts has been whether to treat the insurance as a fringe benefit in part compensation for the employee's work. If it is viewed as the product of the employee's labors, it is deemed to come from a source collateral to the employer/tortfeasor rather than from the employer/tortfeasor itself. Set off would permit avoidance of FELA liability, and such avoidance is prohibited by [§ 55]. If, on the other hand, the insurance is viewed as a contribution by the employer intended to fulfill FELA obligations, it would appear to fall within the proviso [of § 55] and set off would be permitted."

MACON–BIBB COUNTY WATER AND SEWERAGE AUTHORITY v. TUTTLE/WHITE CONSTRUCTORS, INC.

United States District Court, District of Georgia, 1981.
530 F.Supp. 1048.

[The plaintiff, Authority, was confronted with the problem of disposing of waste sludge by incineration. It solicited bids on the basis of the current state of the art; and the defendant, TWC, submitted the lowest bid of $8,694,000.

The next lowest bid was $9,883,700, $1,189,760 more. However, when a subcontractor, Zurn, withdrew its bid, TWC notified the Authority that it could not perform. A prolonged dispute resulted in litigation. The court held, for present purposes, that TWC was in breach of contract. In the interim, Georgia Kraft Company advised the Authority that a new type of boiler could facilitate the incineration at a savings over the TWC plan of $1,220,000 in capital expenditures and $155,375 in annual costs. Naturally the Authority adopted the Georgia Kraft plan. The report below concerns the amount of damages that TWC should pay for breach of contract.]

OWENS, CHIEF JUDGE. * * * In the present case, the plaintiff is claiming, *inter alia,* that to be made whole the court must consider the defendant's bid for the Rocky Creek Project and that of the next lowest bidder. In other words, the correct measure of damages in a case of this nature is the difference between the lowest bid and the next lowest bid.

The court does not agree with this assessment of the Authority's damages. General damage rules such as the one relied on by the plaintiff do not exist in a vacuum. They are to be utilized in light of the particular circumstances of each case, and are to be subject to certain limiting exceptions. One of these limiting rules is that an abstract measure of damages should not exceed the *actual* damages suffered. Stolz v. Kapp, 156 Ga.App. 169, 274 S.E.2d 142 (1980). In *Stolz* for example, appellant entered a contract with appellee to purchase a lot and have appellee construct a home for $58,500.00. In the course of construction, the appellant requested and got changes made in the structure, but before the house was completed appellant became dissatisfied, repudiated the contract and sued for his earnest money. The appellee countered by demanding $1,060.00 which it cost him to reverse the modifications which he had made at appellant's request. The court of appeals refused to award these expenses, explaining that "the record does not show that appellee incurred any damages because of the changes it made after appellant repudiated the contract; *the house was sold to a third party by appellee for $62,000.00 one week after construction was completed.*" (emphasis added). In essence, the $3,500.00 that appellee gained by being able to sell the house to someone other than appellant was used to offset the expenses he incurred in reversing the modifications.

This method of offsetting the damages suffered from a breach or tortious conduct by the benefits in savings or profits from that breach is appropriately called the theory of offsetting benefits. It is advanced by the defendants in the instant case as a necessary ingredient in determining the Authority's actual damages.

Basically, where the defendant's tortious misconduct or breach of contract causes damages, but also operates directly to confer some benefit upon the plaintiff, the plaintiff's claim for damages may be diminished by the amount of the benefit received. The offset theory can only be utilized "when the benefits accruing to the plaintiff are sufficiently proximate to the contract to warrant reducing the plaintiff's damages and the failure to do so would permit the plaintiff to obtain unreasonable damages." Louisiana Sulphur Carriers, Inc. v. Gulf Resources and Chemical Corp., 53 F.R.D. 458, 462 (D.Del.1971). When the offset theory is available, it involves two basic situations. First, the means necessary for the plaintiff to have obtained the profit or savings from the subsequent contract would have been unavailable if the original contract had been performed. Second, the breach resulted in a direct and immediate savings to the plaintiff, i.e., savings on the cost of performance.

This theory is clearly applicable in the present case. * * * The Authority could not have obtained this savings if TWC had performed its obligations on the original contract.

Neither is the court persuaded by the plaintiff's argument that the offsetting benefits rule is inapplicable in the present case because the benefits it received from the Georgia Kraft plan were from a "collateral source."

* * * The Authority contends that the collateral source rule applies in this case because there is "no connection, relationship or bearing between the breaches of contract by TWC and Zurn and the tortious conduct of Zurn, on the one hand, and the contract between the Authority and Georgia Kraft Company * * * on the other hand."

It is true that the collateral source rule has been used many times in Georgia to bar the defendant from offsetting benefits the plaintiff received as a result of defendant's breach or tortious conduct. Cincinnati, New Orleans and Texas Pacific Railway Co. v. Hilley, 121 Ga.App. 196, 173 S.E.2d 242, 246, n. 2 (1970). However, in each of these cases the benefits received were the result of the plaintiff's forethought (for instance, in purchasing insurance) or a gift or benefit from a "distinct" third party (as in the payment of lost wages by relatives).

In contrast, Georgia Kraft in the instant case is not such a sufficiently distinct third party. The contract with TWC concerning the Rocky Creek Project was made in furtherance of an overall plan between the Authority and Georgia Kraft dating from 1970 and concerning the construction and operation of the plant and concerning additions and betterments to the plant. Furthermore, it is evident from the record that the Authority needed and wanted only one system for disposal of the sewage sludge, and that there was never an intention to construct two projects. Both the original project and the Georgia Kraft plan were designed to burn the same sludge; and the Georgia Kraft project will occupy the same piece of land intended for the original project. In short, the two construction projects are mutually exclusive, and but for the defendants' presumed breach and tortious interference, the Authority would not have turned to the Georgia Kraft plan. Therefore, it is obvious that the subsequent contract with Georgia Kraft was *not* an independent collateral transaction with no relation to the defendants' breached contracts.

As stated above, the purpose of compensatory damages is to compensate the plaintiff for injury actually sustained. When the benefits which plaintiff received (over $1,220,000.00) as a proximate result of the defendants' presumed breaches are taken into consideration, it is evident that the plaintiff is not entitled to the $1,189,700.00 difference between the TWC bid and the next lowest bid.

Notes

1. *"Offset of Benefits" in Breach of Contracts.*

Section 2–713 Uniform Commercial Code.

(a) * * * The measure of damages for non-delivery or repudiation by the seller is the difference between the market price at the time when the buyer learned of the breach and the contract price together with any incidental or consequential damages * * * but less expenses saved in consequence of the seller's breach.

2. Consider offsetting benefits and avoidable consequences when damages are awarded for a negligently performed sterilization that results in the birth of a normal child. When the parents receive damages for the expense of rearing the child, the courts differ about whether to offset the parents' benefit from the youngster's comfort, society, and aid. Should the judge instruct the jury to consider whether plaintiffs failed to avoid the consequences by not securing an abortion or placing the child for adoption? Jones v. Malinowski, 299 Md. 257, 473 A.2d 429 (1984). See Sherlock v. Stillwater Clinic, 260 N.W.2d 169 (Minn.1977); Note, Judicial Limitations on Damages for Wrongful Birth of a Healthy Infant, 68 Va.L.Rev. 1311 (1982).

3. In Green v. General Petroleum Corp., 205 Cal. 328, 334–38, 270 P. 952, 955–56 (1928), the plaintiff was driven from his residence when the defendant brought in a gusher nearby.

"In the matter of the injury to the realty, the court specially found, by specific items, what it would cost to restore the premises to their original condition, and allowed the aggregate amount as damages. Appellant does not dispute the accuracy of the court's figures, but contends that the discovery of oil in its well gave a new value to the property of the respondents—a value as oil property, greatly in excess of its previous value as residential property—and that the restoration of the property to its original condition will add nothing to its value for its new use. Wherefore, the value being greater after the 'blowout' than it was before, appellant argues, the respondents suffered no loss by reason of the injury to the realty. We are not impressed with appellant's argument on this point."

4. Suppose defendant kidnaps plaintiff. Plaintiff writes a best-seller recounting the experience. Is defendant entitled to offset the revenue from the book against his civil damages? See Restatement (Second) of Torts § 920, illustration 6 (1979).

5. Investors purchased limited partnership shares in a motel; they deducted the partnership's large losses from their income tax. After the motel failed, the investors sued the seller under the federal securities statutes arguing misrepresentations and omissions. Should the court award them the purchase price plus interest or that amount minus the tax benefits they received? In Randall v. Loftsgaarden, 478 U.S. 647 (1986), the Supreme Court declined to offset the plaintiffs' tax benefits; the offset, the Court emphasized, would undercut the securities law's goal of deterring misrepresentation.

Holding that tax consequences could not be offset against damages. Billings Clinic v. Peat Marwick Main & Co., 244 Mont. 324, 797 P.2d 899 (1990); DePalma v. Westland Software House, 225 Cal.App.3d 1534, 276 Cal.Rptr. 214 (1990).

6. See Gits v. Norwest Bank Minneapolis, 390 N.W.2d 835, 837 (Minn.App. 1986): "The benefits rule provides that if a defendant's tortious conduct confers a benefit, as well as a harm, upon the plaintiff, the jury may weigh the value of the benefit against the claimed harm."

Query: Should the jury "value" the "benefit" as the plaintiff subjectively does or should it assign a reasonable person's "value"?

G. ENHANCEMENT AND ADJUSTMENT OF THE AWARD

1. PRE–JUDGMENT INTEREST

PETERSON v. CROWN FINANCIAL CORP.

United States Court of Appeals, Third Circuit, 1981.
661 F.2d 287.

[The plaintiff, Peterson, a Nebraska farmer and rancher, borrowed money from the defendant finance company and executed a series of promissory notes (escalating in amounts) bearing interest 2½% above the prime rate. At the time the fifth note for $4,500,000 was executed, the defendant cancelled and returned the fourth note to the plaintiff. However, when the fifth note became due the defendant demanded $1,899,312.05 in interest including $363,875.62 "arrearages" on the fourth note. The plaintiff paid this latter amount under protest and he seeks to recover this overpayment. The court held that the renewal note (fifth) indeed operated to cancel the prior note and that the lender was not entitled to collect the balance of interest on the prior note when the interest was not explicitly carried over to the new note. The court also held that plaintiff's payment was not voluntary and that he was entitled to restitution. Whether he was entitled to restitution on the ground of economic coercion or mistake is not important here.]

ADAMS, CIRCUIT JUDGE. * * * We turn now to the issue of prejudgment interest.[1] Neither party disputes the district court's holding that Peterson was entitled to prejudgment interest on the sum he unwillingly paid to Crown. The question on appeal is rather the *rate* of interest properly chargeable to Crown under Pennsylvania law.

The district court conceded that "[t]here is considerable logic in plaintiff's contention that 2½ points above prime would be a singularly equitable measure of prejudgment interest in this case." Nonetheless, the court concluded that it did not believe that it had discretion to award prejudgment interest at a rate greater than six percent, the legal rate in Pennsylvania. 41 P.S.A. § 202 (Purdons Supp.1981). The court determined that six percent was "the applicable interest rate in contract-related claims," and noted that, even if Peterson's claim could fairly be characterized as an equitable claim for restitution, "six percent remains the appropriate measure."

We agree with the district court that, under Pennsylvania law, prejudgment interest in the ordinary suit for contract damages is limited to the six percent legal rate. But because Peterson's claim sounds in restitution, it calls for the exercise of the court's broader equitable powers. Under our reading of the relevant Pennsylvania precedents, the trial judge does have discretion in such cases to award damages in the nature of prejudgment interest in an amount greater than six percent.

The law of Pennsylvania with respect to the rate of prejudgment interest is far from perspicuous. It is clear, however, that in contract actions, the

1. [Footnotes renumbered.] As will be discussed infra, prejudgment "interest" *as such* in Pennsylvania is conceptually distinguishable from detention damages *in the nature* of interest. For simplicity's sake we will use the term "prejudgment interest" throughout this opinion to refer generically to both types of awards: we will make specific reference to "interest as such" or "damages in the nature of interest" when necessary.

prejudgment interest award properly is measured by the legal rate. Thus, in Miller v. City of Reading, 369 Pa. 471, 87 A.2d 223 (1952), the Pennsylvania Supreme Court held that, in an action of assumpsit to recover the principal and interest on a municipal bond, the bondholder was entitled to interest at the legal rate of six percent rather than at the five percent rate specified in the bond. * * * This legal principle is reflected in § 337(a) of the Restatement of Contracts. * * * That section states:

> "If the parties have not by contract determined otherwise, *simple interest at the statutory legal rate is recoverable as damages for breach of contract* as follows:
>
> '(a) Where the defendant commits a breach of a contract to pay a definite sum of money, or to render a performance the value of which in money is stated in the contract or is ascertainable by mathematical calculations from a standard fixed in the contract or from established market prices of the subject matter, interest is allowed on the amount of the debt or money value from the time performance was due, after making all the deductions to which the defendant may be entitled.' "

The court is thus obligated to award "simple interest at the statutory legal rate" only in those circumstances in which the plaintiff proves that the defendant breached a promise to pay "a definite sum of money," or render a performance the value of which is ascertainable with exactitude. In such a case, the plaintiff is entitled to interest at the six percent legal rate as a matter of law. [citations]

In tort cases, prejudgment interest is not allowable as a matter of law. The Pennsylvania courts have instead awarded "compensation for delay" or "detention damages" at the prejudgment stage. The contours of this remedy were first delineated in Citizens' Natural Gas Co. v. Richards, 130 Pa. 37, 18 A. 600 (1889), in which the Court explained:

> "Interest, as such, is recoverable only where there is a failure to pay a liquidated sum, due at a fixed day, and the debtor is in absolute default. It cannot, therefore, be recovered in actions of tort, or in actions of any kind where the damages are not in their nature capable of exact computation, both as to time and amount. In such cases, the party chargeable cannot pay or make tender until both the time and the amount have been ascertained, and his default is not, therefore, of that absolute nature that necessarily involves interest for the delay. But there are cases sounding in tort, and cases of unliquidated damages, where not only the principle on which the recovery is to be had is compensation, but where, also, the compensation can be measured by market value or other definite standard. Such are cases of the unintentional conversion or destruction of property, etc. Into these cases the element of time may enter as an important factor, *and the plaintiff will not be fully compensated unless he receive not only the value of his property, but receive it, as nearly as may be, as of the date of his loss.* Hence it is that the jury may allow additional damages in the nature of interest for the lapse of time. It is never interest as such, nor as a matter of right, but compensation for the delay, *of which the rate of interest affords the fair legal measure.* (emphasis added)."

The distinction between interest, as such, and compensation for delay, has continued to trouble the courts. See, e.g., Hussey Metals Division v. Lectromelt Furnace Division, 417 F.Supp. 964 (W.D.Pa.1976) at 967 ("Logic does not inherently require separate rules where the loss of use of property or detention of damages results not from tort but from breach of contract." Indeed, it has played a significant role in the present appeal. Peterson, sensing greater flexibility in the tort remedy, contends that Crown committed the tort of business coercion when it "forced" him to pay the $363,875.62 overcharge. He thus argues that he is entitled, not to "interest," but to detention damages; and further, that the amount of such damages is not governed by the six percent legal rate established at 41 P.S.A. § 202.[2] Crown, on the other hand, stresses the contractual nature of Peterson's cause of action. Crown maintains that because Peterson seeks a "definite sum" of money, he is entitled, under § 337(a) of the Restatement of Contracts as adopted by the Pennsylvania courts, to interest at the six percent legal rate—no more, and no less.

We decline to accept Crown's contention that the case at bar falls under the § 337(a) rubric. That section, as adopted and applied in Pennsylvania, addresses only the situation in which the defendant "commits a breach of a contract to pay a definite sum of money" and the plaintiff sues for contract damages. Without exception, the case law reflects this precise scenario. [citations] In the case at bar, however, Crown did not breach a promise to pay Peterson the $363,875.62 in dispute. It made no promises; as the district court found, it simply extracted the money from Peterson, forcing Peterson to sue, under a restitution theory, for its return. There is nothing in either the language of § 337(a) or the relevant Pennsylvania precedents to suggest that a plaintiff can recover only "simple interest at the statutory legal rate * * * as *damages for breach of contract*" in a case such as this.

We agree with Peterson that—in this situation—the district court has discretion to award damages in the nature of prejudgment interest at a rate higher than the statutory six percent rate. Our holding is based not on our characterization of the underlying substantive dispute, but rather on the equitable nature of the remedy the plaintiff seeks—restitution of money unjustly received. We thus find it unnecessary to decide whether, as Peterson urges, Crown's conduct constituted the tort of business coercion.

That Peterson's claim rests upon equitable considerations is not disputed. The district court held that Peterson is entitled to "restitution of an undeserved benefit" from Crown. Under Pennsylvania law, "when a person receives a benefit from another, and it would be unconscionable for the recipient to retain that benefit, the doctrine of unjust enrichment requires the recipient to make restitution. * * * This *equitable doctrine* imposes on the recipient an obligation in the nature of quasi-contract." Myers–Macomber Engineers v. M.L.W. Construction Corp., 271 Pa.Super. 484, 414 A.2d 357 (1979) (emphasis added).

In resolving Peterson's equitable claim, we are guided by the mandate of the Pennsylvania Supreme Court in Murray Hill Estates, Inc. v. Bastin, 442 Pa. 405, 276 A.2d 542 (1971). There, the Court stated that, in equity cases,

> "The decided trend of courts of law and courts of equity has been 'to break away from hard and fast rules and charge and allow interest in accordance with principles of equity, in order to accomplish justice in each particular case.' * * * Unless a case can be found, which is a conclusive precedent, the safest and at the same time the fairest way for a court is to decide questions

2. The question of the applicable interest rate has been raised infrequently in the tort context. Those courts that have addressed the issue have apparently adhered to the six percent legal rate. See, e.g., *Hussey Metals Division*.

pertaining to interest according to a plain and single consideration of justice and fair dealing."

The flexible approach advocated in *Murray Hills Estates* has been followed by the Pennsylvania Supreme Court on several occasions. In In re Kenin's Estate, 343 Pa. 549, 23 A.2d 837 (1942), for example, which involved the wrongful investment by a trustee of the proceeds of insurance policies, the Court concluded that the trustee was liable for "interest as damages for detention." Stating that "[t]here is no statutory requirement that damages for the detention of funds be measured by the legal rate of interest for the period of the detention," the Court added:

> "The Act of May 28, 1858 [the predecessor to 41 P.S.A. § 201] * * * fixing at 6% the lawful rate of interest for the loan or use of money, in all cases where no express contract shall have been made for a less rate does not rule the question of 'damages for detention.' The word 'use' when referring to money is often employed as a synonym for 'loan.' Money is not 'used' within the meaning of this act when it is detained under the circumstances here present."

Finding that, if safely invested, the proceeds could not have yielded more than two-and-one-half percent per year, the Court reduced the interest rate for detention damages from six percent to two-and-one-half percent for the six-year period during which the trustee had improperly collected and distributed the funds.

The district court here read *Kenin's Estate* as according the courts discretion to set prejudgment interest at a rate *lower* than six percent when the prevailing rate of return is below the legal rate. * * * We believe, however, that the principles upon which *Kenin's Estate* relied are broad enough to permit the courts discretion to adjust rates upwards or downwards as economic realities and fairness require. * * *

The recent case of Sack v. Feinman, 489 Pa. 152, 413 A.2d 1059 (1980), supports our conclusion. In *Sack,* an equity action, one sister alleged that an older sister had fraudulently converted savings bonds, placed by the mother in a trust for the younger sister, to the older sister's account. The Chancellor found that the older sister had abused a confidential relationship between herself and her mother, and consequently imposed a constructive trust for the benefit of the younger sister. * * * The Pennsylvania Supreme Court engaged in a substantial discussion of the wide scope of its theory on the applicability of pre-verdict interest. As the Court explained, the underlying principle was the prevention of unjust enrichment:

> "Hence, any claim based upon unjust enrichment or restitution, rather than upon compensation or damages, not only permits pre-judgment interest, but also permits an award of compound interest.
>
> "Because all of this was most obvious in fiduciary cases, and because those cases were decided in equity courts, the generalization often made was that interest *would be permitted in equity,* as a matter *of the chancellor's discretion,* even where not permitted at law because the claim was unliquidated. The principle behind this, however, is clearly broader than the scope of purely equitable actions: it is a principle based upon unjust enrichment notions. For that reason it should be stated, not as a rule about equity, but as a rule about restitution. Whenever the defendant holds money or property that belongs in good conscience to the plaintiff, and the objective of the court is to force disgorgement of his unjust enrichment, interest upon the funds or property so

held may be necessary to force complete restitution. This may be true in law as well as in equity."

* * * The language and the logic of the case *Sack v. Feinman*—and the lack of conclusive precedent to the contrary—compel the holding that, in the restitution context at least, the court has discretion to award damages in the nature of prejudgment interest at a rate higher than the six percent legal rate. Our conclusion is buttressed by the fact that in *Sack* the Court sanctioned the award of *compound* interest. This in itself is considerably more generous than the "simple interest" allowable in a contract action.[3]

We concede, too, that it is difficult to draw a logical distinction between the present case—a wrongful demand and acceptance of a sum paid under protest—and the refusal to pay funds due under a contract. It may be inequitable to require debtors to pay only six percent under present Pennsylvania law yet force creditors who have made wrongful demands to disgorge at money-market rates. As to the former situation, however, Pennsylvania has provided clear—if questionable—precedent to which a federal court sitting in diversity is bound. In the present case, to the contrary, we find support in the Pennsylvania case law for the proposition that prejudgment interest in restitution awards can be set at the trial court's discretion, and find no conclusive precedent to the contrary. Mindful of "those considerations of basic fairness and equity which suggest a more flexible rule * * *, [and] not unmindful of the fact that at the currently high money-market rates [a contrary] ruling appears to create a built-in incentive to withhold sums due, and indeed, to prolong litigation," we will remand the case for a redetermination by the district court of the damages for delay, which may be set at a rate greater than Pennsylvania's legal rate of interest.

Affirmed in part, vacated in part, and remanded.

Notes

1. Gorenstein Enterprises, Inc. v. Quality Care–USA, Inc., 874 F.2d 431, 435–37, 438–39 (7th Cir.1989): "So weak are the Gorensteins' arguments regarding their infringement of Quality Care's trademark, and so deliberate the infringement, that it might have been an abuse of discretion for the district judge *not* to have

3. Our holding is not without precedent in other jurisdictions. See, e.g., Davis Cattle Co. v. Great Western Sugar Co., 544 F.2d 436, 441 (10th Cir.1976) (11.5% award upheld; "The true measure of monetary interest is the *benefit* to the wrongdoer, and * * * the statutory rate should be used only in the absence of proof as to the benefit accruing to the wrongdoer as the result of his wrongful detention"), cert. denied, 429 U.S. 1094 (1977); E.I. DuPont de Nemours & Co. v. Lyles & Lang Construction Co., 219 F.2d 328, 342 (4th Cir.1955) ("the interest should be computed not at the legal rate fixed by statute but at the rate the plaintiff would have had to pay upon a loan of a similar amount, considering the state of the money market and the rate charged by banks for the use of money"), cert. denied, 349 U.S. 956 (1955); Employer–Teamsters Joint Council No. 84 v. Weatherall Concrete, Inc., 468 F.Supp. 1167 (S.D.W.Va.1979) (8% award, citing *DuPont,* supra); Lynch v. Vickers Energy Corp., 429 A.2d 497 (Del.1981) (7% award); First City National Bank of Paris v. Haynes, 614 S.W.2d 605, 610 (Tex.Civ.App.1981) (10% award; "In prejudgment interest cases the trend is to hold its award to be a matter within the sound discretion of the trial judge"); Rollins Environmental Services, Inc. v. WSMW Industries, 426 A.2d 1363, 1366 (Del.Super.1980) ("allowance of interest in cases following within equity jurisdiction has been held to be within the discretion of the Chancellor * * * and in the exercise of that discretion the interest rate has not been considered to be a fixed 'legal rate,' but has varied according to a showing of the rate which a prudent investor could have obtained."). But cf. Wooten v. McClendon, 272 Ark. 61, 612 S.W.2d 105 (Ark.1981) (prejudgment interest rate limited to legal rate in property damage action).

awarded Quality Care treble damages, attorney's fees, and prejudgment interest [The court quotes the trademark act.] * * *

"While the statute makes no reference to prejudgment interest, the Gorensteins do not question that federal common law authorizes the award of such interest in appropriate cases to victims of violations of federal law. [citations] The areas in which such interest is allowed, illustrated by the cases just cited, are diverse. The time has come, we think, to generalize, and to announce a rule that prejudgment interest should be presumptively available to victims of federal law violations. Without it, compensation of the plaintiff is incomplete and the defendant has an incentive to delay.

"The award of prejudgment interest is particularly appropriate in a case such as this where the violation was intentional, and indeed outrageous. For although the Gorensteins argue that in continuing to use Quality Care's trademark they were just following their first lawyer's advice, and hence acting in good faith, the judge found, not clearly erroneously, that the lawyer gave the Gorensteins this advice only because they had given him a false statement of the facts. The advice could not rise above its tainted source. You do not show good faith that will defeat a finding of willful violation of law by acting on legal advice based on your own misrepresentations.

"There is no federal statutory interest rate on prejudgment interest. But as the 9 percent figure used by the district judge was well below the average interest rate for 'securities' comparable in riskiness to Quality Care's cause of action for trademark infringement against the Gorensteins, he can hardly be criticized for setting too high a rate. Surely the rate was too low; there were times while this suit was pending when the prime rate exceeded 20 percent. For the future, we suggest that district judges use the prime rate for fixing prejudgment interest where there is no statutory interest rate. That is a readily ascertainable figure which provides a reasonable although rough estimate of the interest rate necessary to compensate plaintiffs not only for the loss of the use of their money but also for the risk of default. The defendant who has violated the plaintiff's rights is in effect a debtor of the plaintiff until the judgment is entered and paid or otherwise collected. At any time before actual payment or collection of the judgment the defendant may default and the plaintiff come up empty-handed. The plaintiff is an unsecured, uninsured creditor, and the risk of default must be considered in deciding what a compensatory rate of interest would be.

"A federal statute, 28 U.S.C. § 1961, fixes the *post* judgment interest rate for federal cases as the rate on 52–week Treasury bills at the last auction of those bills before the judgment was entered. This rate is too low, because there is no default risk with Treasury bills. Of course the courts are bound by that rate so far as postjudgment interest is concerned. But prejudgment interest is governed by federal common law, and the courts are free to adopt a more discriminating approach. [citation] We have chosen the prime rate for convenience; a more precise estimate would be the interest rate paid by the defendant for unsecured loans. We do not want to straitjacket the district judges but we do want to caution them against the danger of setting prejudgment interest rates too low by neglecting the risk, often nontrivial, of default.

"We also reject the Gorensteins' argument that the judge should not have awarded *compound* prejudgment interest. Their dilatory tactics denied Quality Care the use of its money, including the opportunity to obtain interest on interest. * * * In Dynamics Corp. of America v. United States, 766 F.2d 518 (Fed.Cir.1985), the district court's *refusal* to compound prejudgment interest was reversed as an abuse of discretion. * * *

"RIPPLE, CIRCUIT JUDGE, concurring. I join the judgment of the court and am also pleased to join the essential reasoning of the majority's thoughtful and comprehensive opinion. I write separately only to emphasize that I do not understand the majority's rather expansive treatment of the prejudgment interest issue as constituting a departure from the settled law of the circuit that 'the decision to award prejudgment interest rests in the sound discretion of the adjudicatory tribunal and involves a balancing of the equities between the parties under the circumstances of the particular case.' Myron v. Chicoine, 678 F.2d 727, 734 (7th Cir.1982). In exercising that discretion, the district court must give its prime attention to the intent of Congress in enacting the substantive statutory provision at issue. Therefore, prejudgment interest usually will be 'necessary to carry out the federal policies of compensation and deterrence.' Williamson v. Handy Button Mach. Co., 817 F.2d 1290, 1297 (7th Cir.1987). On the other hand, ' "[o]rdinary" does not imply inevitable,' and, as the Supreme Court pointed out in General Motors Corp. v. Devex Corp., 461 U.S. 648, 656–57 (1983), prejudgment interest might be inappropriate at some times. * * * As our court pointed out in *Williamson*, '[s]ubstantial, unexplained delay in filing suit might be * * * a reason [making prejudgment interest inappropriate], because delay shifts the investment risk to the defendant, allowing the plaintiff to recover interest without bearing the corresponding risk.' A jury verdict that already compensates the plaintiff for the lost time value of money would also be an appropriate exception.

"The majority 'suggest[s]' that district courts use the prime rate for fixing prejudgment interest where there is no statutory interest rate. Use of the prime interest rate, at least as a starting point, is a sensible approach. 'Courts have increasingly looked to the prevailing interest rate * * * as [an] indicator of just compensation.' Central Rivers Towing, Inc. v. City of Beardstown, 750 F.2d 565, 574 (7th Cir.1985). However, in this matter as well, we have recognized that the determination is 'within the trial court's discretion.'

"In short, today's decision sets forth useful guidelines to assist the district court in the exercise of its discretion on the matter of prejudgment interest. As the majority also emphasizes, I trust that today's guidelines will not become a rigid litmus test when a district court determines that fulfillment of the congressional intent requires another approach. In such an instance, we have a right, of course, to expect that the district court will provide us with reasoned elaboration for its departure in order that our review may be meaningful.

"The majority also addresses the adequacy of the measure of postjudgment interest provided by 28 U.S.C. § 1961. This congressional determination is not at issue in this case. Accordingly, I respectfully decline to express a view on this matter."

2. Cal.Civ.Code, provides:

§ 3287. Interest on Damages; Right to Recover; Time From Which Interest Runs

(a) Every person who is entitled to recover damages certain, or capable of being made certain by calculation, and the right to recover which is vested in him upon a particular day, is entitled also to recover interest thereon from that day, except during such time as the debtor is prevented by law, or by the act of the creditor from paying the debt. * * *

(b) Every person who is entitled under any judgment to receive damages based upon a cause of action in contract where the claim was unliquidated, may also recover interest thereon from a date prior to the entry of judgment as the court may, in its discretion, fix, but in no event earlier than the date the action was filed.

§ 3288. Interest on Damages; Noncontractual Obligation; Discretion of Jury

In an action for the breach of an obligation not arising from contract, and in every case of oppression, fraud, or malice, interest may be given, in the discretion of the jury.

The California legislature added this next section in 1982. How will it affect trial tactics?

§ 3291. In any action brought to recover damages for personal injury sustained by any person resulting from or occasioned by the tort of any other person, corporation, association, or partnership, whether by negligence or by willful intent of the other person, corporation, association, or partnership, and whether the injury was fatal or otherwise, it is lawful for the plaintiff in the complaint to claim interest on the damages alleged as provided in this section.

If the plaintiff makes an offer * * * which the defendant does not accept prior to trial or within 30 days, whichever occurs first, and the plaintiff obtains a more favorable judgment, the judgment shall bear interest at the legal rate of 10 percent per annum calculated from the date of the plaintiff's first offer * * * which is exceeded by the judgment, and interest shall accrue until the satisfaction of judgment.

3. State v. Phillips, 470 P.2d 266, 272 (Alaska 1970):

"The following hypothetical case illustrates the injustice of denying prejudgment interest. Suppose A inflicts precisely the same amount of damage of any type on B and C at the same moment, evaluated by juries as $1,000 each. If C wins his judgment a year later than B and does not get prejudgment interest for the year, C recovers less than B for the same injury; C has been deprived of the use value of $1,000 for one year while B has enjoyed the use value. Interest is the market, or in the case of the legal rate the legislative evaluation of the use value of money. B obviously has not gotten too much for he had a right to be made whole immediately upon being injured, and B and C should get the same amount for the same injury, so C must have gotten too little. Only by awarding prejudgment interest from the time the cause of action accrues, when a plaintiff is entitled to be made whole, can the sort of injustice which happened to C in the hypothetical case be avoided. We are also influenced by the policy consideration that failure to award prejudgment interest creates a substantial financial incentive for defendants to litigate even where liability is so clear and the jury award so predictable that they should settle."

4. Restatement (Second) of Restitution § 28 (Tent.Draft No. 1, 1983): †

§ 28. Interest Charged to Defendant

A judgment or order for restitution will, at the claimant's instance, include an award of an amount as interest required to prevent unjust enrichment of the defendant. Such an award will be limited or denied to the extent that

(a) it would duplicate an award of use value or of other benefit to the defendant,

(b) it depends on circumstances in which he cannot justly be charged for failure to make restitution, or

(c) the court cannot determine with reasonable certainty the extent of his unjust enrichment.

5. Prejudgment interest is allowable only on the primary or actual damage portion of an award and not on the punitive or enhanced portion. Leinoff v. Louis Milona & Sons, Inc., 726 F.2d 734 (Fed.Cir.1984) (a patent case). Should prejudgment interest be allowed on a statutory treble damage award? See Trans World Airlines Inc. v. Hughes, 308 F.Supp. 679 (S.D.N.Y.1969). How about allowing postjudgment interest on accrued prejudgment interest? See Rudd Construction Equipment Co. v. Clark Equipment Co., 735 F.2d 974 (6th Cir.1984).

6. See generally Note, Prejudgment Interest: Survey and Suggestion, 77 Nw.U.L.Rev. 192 (1982).

7. *Adjustment for Inflation.* Anchorage Asphalt Paving Co. v. Lewis, 629 P.2d 65 (Alaska 1981). In 1970 Anchorage Asphalt breached a contract to pave roads. When damages were finally tried in 1979, the trial judge awarded Lewis the cost to complete the roads in 1979 and prejudgment interest from 1970: "As a general rule in contract actions, the date of breach affords the most appropriate time for valuing damages. [citations] However, this is not a rule to be applied inflexibly when it undermines the remedial goals of a damage award.

"A case such as the one at bar, where litigation has been protracted over the length of a decade and the appropriate remedy is the cost of repair, presents a situation where limiting the plaintiff to the time of breach cost or repair has the potential of subverting the remedial purposes of the damage award. Simply put, where inflation has eroded the time of breach monetary valuation of an injury to a fraction of what is required to remedy the plaintiff's injury, then the time of breach rule may be regarded as inappropriate. Because the circumstances of individual cases differ drastically, it is impractical to adopt a definite point in time to value damages. It has been found preferable to leave the question to the trial court's discretion. Fairway Builders, Inc. v. Malouf, 124 Ariz. 242, 603 P.2d 513, 526 (Ariz.App.1979).

"In this case, in view of the substantial inflation which took place between 1972, when the full extent of the breakdown of the streets became apparent, and the time of the trial in 1979, we cannot say that the court abused its discretion using 1979 as the date of damage valuation. * * *

"Anchorage Asphalt urges that the award of prejudgment interest from April 9, 1970, to the date of judgment in the damage award is improper. We agree and reverse the trial court on this point.

"One purpose of prejudgment interest is to compensate the plaintiff for the loss of use of money from the date of injury until the date of judgment. A corollary purpose is to deprive the defendant of unjust enrichment resulting from the use of the money from the date of injury, thereby encouraging settlement. But prejudgment interest should not be awarded where it would work an injustice. * * *

"The award of damages at 1979 values suffices, in our view, to give Lewis what he initially bargained for, an acceptable paved road system. Ordinarily his award would be his cost of repair at or near the time of the breach, plus prejudgment interest up to the time of trial. Here, for the reasons previously explained, the court was justified in deviating from this standard method. However, to calculate the cost of repair at 1979 values and award prejudgment interest on that from 1970 strikes us as an unwarranted and unjustifiable compounding of damages."

8. Southern Pacific Transportation Co. v. San Antonio, Texas, 748 F.2d 266, 275–76 (5th Cir.1984). Railroads successfully sued the city of San Antonio to collect underpayments on several coal shipments for the city: "The railroads contend that since there were several payments, each due on a different date during the period June 1980–May 1981, we should apply a different rate (of prejudgment interest) to

each. We should use the Treasury Bill rate in effect as of the date each payment was due. The railroads argue that this method would correct for fluctuations in the rate during the period and, therefore, better approximate the inflationary effects at that time." However, the court rejected the argument. "We hold that where a *carrier* is suing to recover for a series of underpayments, one interest rate applies as of the date the first payment is due. This approach may not result in a perfect measure of inflation, but * * * it is somewhat simpler than the railroads' shifting rate approach. Above all, our approach helps produce a uniform, coherent practice in the area of railroad rates."

2. DISCOUNTING FUTURE DAMAGES TO PRESENT VALUE—ADJUSTMENTS FOR INFLATION

JONES & LAUGHLIN STEEL CORP. v. PFEIFER

Supreme Court of the United States, 1983.
462 U.S. 523.

STEVENS, JUSTICE. Respondent was injured in the course of his employment as a loading helper on a coal barge. As his employer, petitioner was required to compensate him for his injury under § 4 of the Longshoremen's and Harbor Workers' Compensation Act (the Act). 44 Stat. 1426, 33 U.S.C. § 904. As the owner *pro hac vice* of the barge, petitioner may also be liable for negligence under § 5 of the Act. 86 Stat. 1263, 33 U.S.C. § 905. We granted certiorari to * * * consider whether the Court of Appeals correctly upheld the trial court's computation of respondent's damages. * * *

The District Court's calculation of damages was predicated on a few undisputed facts. At the time of his injury respondent was earning an annual wage of $26,065. He had a remaining work expectancy of 12½ years. On the date of trial (October 1, 1980), respondent had received compensation payments of $33,079.14. If he had obtained light work and earned the legal minimum hourly wage from July 1, 1979 until his 65th birthday, he would have earned $66350.

The District Court arrived at its final award by taking 12½ years of earnings at respondent's wage at the time of injury ($325,312.50), subtracting his projected hypothetical earnings at the minimum wage ($66,352) and the compensation payments he had received and adding $50,000 for pain and suffering. The Court did not increase the award to take inflation into account, and it did not discount the award to reflect the present value of the future stream of income. The Court instead decided to follow a decision of the Supreme Court of Pennsylvania, which had held "as a matter of law that future inflation shall be presumed equal to future interest rates with these factors offsetting." Kaczkowski v. Bolubasz, 491 Pa. 561, 583, 421 A.2d 1027, 1038–1039 (1980). Thus, although the District Court did not dispute that respondent could be expected to receive regular cost-of-living wage increases from the date of his injury until his presumed date of retirement, the Court refused to include such increases in its calculation, explaining that they would provide respondent "a double consideration for inflation." For comparable reasons, the Court disregarded changes in the legal minimum wage in computing the amount of mitigation attributable to respondent's ability to perform light work.

It does not appear that either party offered any expert testimony concerning predicted future rates of inflation, the interest rate that could be appropriately used to discount future earnings to present value, or the possible connection between inflation rates and interest rates. Respondent did, however, offer an estimate of how his own wages would have increased over time, based upon recent increases in the company's hourly wage scale.

The Court of Appeals affirmed. * * * On the damages issue, the Court of Appeals first noted that even though the District Court had relied on a Pennsylvania case, federal law controlled. The Court of Appeals next held that in defining the content of that law, inflation must be taken into account:

> "Full compensation for lost prospective earnings is most difficult, if not impossible, to attain if the court is blind to the realities of the consumer price index and the recent historical decline of purchasing power. Thus if we recognize, as we must, that the injured worker is entitled to reimbursement for his loss of future earnings, an honest and accurate calculation must consider the stark reality of inflationary conditions."

The Court understood, however, that the task of predicting future rates of inflation is quite speculative. It concluded that such speculation could properly be avoided in the manner chosen by the District Court—by adopting Pennsylvania's "total offset method" of computing damages. The Court of Appeals approved of the way the total offset method respects the twin goals of considering future inflation and discounting to present value, while eliminating the need to make any calculations about either, "because the inflation and discount rates are legally presumed to be equal and cancel one another." Accordingly, it affirmed the District Court's judgment. * * *

The District Court found that respondent was permanently disabled as a result of petitioner's negligence. He therefore was entitled to an award of damages to compensate him for his probable pecuniary loss over the duration of his career, reduced to its present value. It is useful at the outset to review the way in which damages should be measured in a hypothetical inflation-free economy. We shall then consider how price inflation alters the analysis. Finally, we shall decide whether the District Court committed reversible error in this case.

In calculating damages, it is assumed that if the injured party had not been disabled, he would have continued to work, and to receive wages at periodic intervals until retirement, disability, or death. An award for impaired earning capacity is intended to compensate the worker for the diminution in that stream of income.[1] The award could in theory take the form of periodic payments, but in this country it has traditionally taken the form of a lump sum, paid at the conclusion of the litigation. The appropriate lump sum cannot be computed without first examining the stream of income it purports to replace.

The lost stream's length cannot be known with certainty; the worker could have been disabled or even killed in a different, non-work-related accident at any time. The probability that he would still be working at a given date is

1. [Footnotes renumbered.] See generally D. Dobbs, Handbook of the Law of Remedies § 8.1 (1973). It should be noted that in a personal injury action such as this one, damages for impaired earning capacity are awarded to compensate the injured person for his loss. In a wrongful death action, a similar but not identical item of damages is awarded for the manner in which diminished earning capacity harms either the worker's survivors or his estate. See generally S. Speiser, Recovery for Wrongful Death 2d, ch. 3 (1975). Since the problem of incorporating inflation into the award is the same in both types of action, we shall make occasional reference to wrongful death actions in this opinion.

constantly diminishing.[2] Given the complexity of trying to make an exact calculation, litigants frequently follow the relatively simple course of assuming that the worker would have continued to work up until a specific date certain. In this case, for example, both parties agreed that the petitioner [sic] would have continued to work until age 65 (12½ more years) if he had not been injured.

Each annual installment[3] in the lost stream comprises several elements. The most significant is, of course, the actual wage. In addition, the worker may have enjoyed certain fringe benefits, which should be included in an ideal evaluation of the worker's loss but are frequently excluded for simplicity's sake.[4] On the other hand, the injured workers' lost wages would have been diminished by state and federal income taxes. Since the damages award is tax-free, the relevant stream is ideally of *after-tax* wages and benefits. See Norfolk & Western R. Co. v. Liepelt, 444 U.S. 490 (1980). Moreover, workers often incur unreimbursed costs, such as transportation to work and uniforms, that the injured worker will not incur. These costs should also be deducted in estimating the lost stream.

In this case the parties appear to have agreed to simplify the litigation, and to presume that in each installment all the elements in the stream would offset each other, except for gross wages. However, in attempting to estimate even such a stylized stream of annual installments of gross wages, a trier of fact faces a complex task. The most obvious and most appropriate place to begin is with the worker's annual wage at the time of injury. Yet the "estimate of loss from lessened earnings capacity in the future need not be based solely upon the wages which the plaintiff was earning at the time of his injury." C. McCormick, Damages § 86 (1935). Even in an inflation-free economy—that is to say one in which the prices of consumer goods remain stable—a worker's wages tend to "inflate." This "real" wage inflation reflects a number of factors, some linked to the specific individual and some linked to broader societal forces.[5]

With the passage of time, an individual worker often becomes more valuable to his employer. His personal work experiences increase his hourly contributions to firm profits. To reflect that heightened value, he will often receive "seniority" or "experience" raises, "merit" raises, or even promotions.[6] Although it may be difficult to prove when, and whether, a particular injured worker might have received such wage increases, see Feldman v. Allegheny Air Lines, 524 F.2d 384, 392–393 (CA2 1975) (Friendly, J., concurring *dubitante*), they may be reliably demonstrated for some workers.

Furthermore, the wages of workers as a class may increase over time. [citations] Through more efficient interaction among labor, capital, and tech-

2. For examples of calculations that take this diminishing probability into account, and assume that it would fall to zero when the worker reached age 65 [citations].

3. Obviously, another distorting simplification is being made here. Although workers generally receive their wages in weekly or biweekly installments, virtually all calculations of lost earnings, including the one made in this case, pretend that the stream would have flowed in large spurts, taking the form of annual installments.

4. These might include insurance coverage, pension and retirement plans, profit sharing, and in-kind services.

5. As will become apparent, in speaking of "societal" forces we are primarily concerned with those macroeconomic forces that influence wages in the worker's particular industry. The term will be used to encompass all forces that tend to inflate a worker's wage without regard to the worker's individual characteristics.

6. It is also possible that a worker could be expected to change occupations completely. See, e.g., Stearns Coal & Lumber Co. v. Williams, 164 Ky. 618, 176 S.W. 15 (1915).

nology, industrial productivity may increase, and workers' wages may enjoy a share of that growth. Such productivity increases—reflected in real increases in the gross national product per worker hour—have been a permanent feature of the national economy since the conclusion of World War II. Moreover, through collective bargaining, workers may be able to negotiate increases in their "share" of revenues, at the cost of reducing shareholders' rate of return on their investments. Either of these forces could affect the lost stream of income in an inflation-free economy. * * *

Of course, even in an inflation-free economy the award of damages to replace the lost stream of income cannot be computed simply by totaling up the sum of the periodic payments. For the damages award is paid in a lump sum at the conclusion of the litigation, and when it—or even a part of it—is invested, it will earn additional money. It has been settled since our decision in Chesapeake & Ohio R. Co. v. Kelly, 241 U.S. 485 (1916) that "in all cases where it is reasonable to suppose that interest may safely be earned upon the amount that is awarded, the ascertained future benefits ought to be discounted in the making up of the award." [7]

The discount rate should be based on the rate of interest that would be earned on "the best and safest investments." Once it is assumed that the injured worker would definitely have worked for a specific term of years, he is entitled to a risk-free stream of future income to replace his lost wages; therefore, the discount rate should not reflect the market's premium for investors who are willing to accept some risk of default. Moreover, since under *Liepelt,* supra, the lost stream of income should be estimated in after-tax terms, the discount rate should also represent the after-tax rate of return to the injured worker.[8]

Thus, although the notion of a damage award representing the present value of a lost stream of earnings in an inflation-free economy rests on some fairly sophisticated economic concepts, the two elements that determine its calculation can be stated fairly easily. They are: (1) the amount that the employee would have earned during each year that he could have been expected to work after the injury; and (2) the appropriate discount rate, reflecting the safest available investment. The trier of fact should apply the discount rate to each of the estimated installments in the lost stream of income, and then add up the discounted installments to determine the total award.

Unfortunately for triers of fact, ours is not an inflation-free economy. Inflation has been a permanent fixture in our economy for many decades, and there can be no doubt that it ideally should affect both stages of the calculation described in the previous section. * * *

The first stage of the calculation required an estimate of the shape of the lost stream of future income. For many workers, including respondent, a

7. Although this rule could be seen as a way of ensuring that the lump-sum award accurately represents the pecuniary injury as of the time of trial, it was explained by reference to the duty to mitigate damages.

8. The arithmetic necessary for discounting can be simplified through the use of a so-called "present value table," such as those found in R. Wixon, Accountants' Handbook, at 29.58–29.59 (1956 ed.), or S. Speiser, Recovery for Wrongful Death 2d § 8:4, at 713–718 (1975). These tables are based on the proposition that if i is the discount rate, then "the present value of $1 due in n periods must be $1/(1 + i)^n$." Wixon, supra, at 29.57. In this context, the relevant "periods" are years; accordingly, if "i" is a market interest rate, it should be the effective annual yield.

contractual "cost-of-living adjustment" automatically increases wages each year by the percentage change during the previous year in the consumer price index calculated by the Bureau of Labor Statistics. Such a contract provides a basis for taking into account an additional societal factor—price inflation—in estimating the worker's lost future earnings.

The second stage of the calculation requires the selection of an appropriate discount rate. Price inflation—or more precisely, anticipated price inflation—certainly affects market rates of return. If a lender knows that his loan is to be repaid a year later with dollars that are less valuable than those he has advanced, he will charge an interest rate that is high enough both to compensate him for the temporary use of the loan proceeds and also to make up for their shrinkage in value.[9]

At one time many courts incorporated inflation into only one stage of the calculation of the award for lost earnings. [citations] In estimating the lost stream of future earnings, they accepted evidence of both individual and societal factors that would tend to lead to wage increases even in an inflation-free economy, but required the plaintiff to prove that those factors were not influenced by predictions of future price inflation. [citation] No increase was allowed for price inflation, on the theory that such predictions were unreliably speculative. In discounting the estimated lost stream of future income to present value, however, they applied the market interest rate.

The effect of these holdings was to deny the plaintiff the benefit of the impact of inflation on his future earnings, while giving the defendant the benefit of inflation's impact on the interest rate that is used to discount those earnings to present value. Although the plaintiff in such a situation could invest the proceeds of the litigation at an "inflated" rate of interest, the stream of income that he received provided him with only enough dollars to maintain his existing *nominal* income; it did not provide him with a stream comparable to what his lost wages would have been in an inflationary economy.[10] This

9. The effect of price inflation on the discount rate may be less speculative than its effect on the lost stream of future income. The latter effect always requires a prediction of the future, for the existence of a contractual cost-of-living adjustment gives no guidance about how big that adjustment will be in some future year. However, whether the discount rate also turns on predictions of the future depends on how it is assumed that the worker will invest his award.

On the one hand, it might be assumed that at the time of the award the worker will invest in a mixture of safe short-term, medium-term, and long-term bonds, with one scheduled to mature each year of his expected worklife. In that event, by purchasing bonds immediately after judgment, the worker can be ensured whatever future stream of nominal income is predicted. Since all relevant effects of inflation on the market interest rate will have occurred at that time, future changes in the rate of price inflation will have no effect on the stream of income he receives. [citations] On the other hand, it might be assumed that the worker will invest exclusively in safe short-term notes, reinvesting them at the new market rate whenever they mature. Future market rates would be quite important to such a worker. Predictions of what they will be would therefore also be relevant to the choice of an appropriate discount rate, in much the same way that they are always relevant to the first stage of the calculation. For a commentary choosing a discount rate on the basis of this assumption, see Sherman, Projection of Economic Loss: Inflation v. Present Value, 14 Creighton L.Rev. 723 (1981) [hereafter Sherman]. We perceive no intrinsic reason to prefer one assumption over the other, but most "offset" analyses seem to adopt the latter.

10. As Judge Posner has explained it.

"But if there is inflation it will affect wages as well as prices. Therefore to give Mrs. O'Shea $2318 today because that is the present value of $7200 10 years hence, computed at a discount rate—12 percent—that consists mainly of an allowance for anticipated inflation, is in fact to give her less than she would have been earning then if she was earning $7200 on the date of the accident, even if the only wage increases she would have received would have been those necessary to keep pace with inflation." O'Shea v. Riverway Towing Co., 677 F.2d 1194, 1199 (CA7 1982).

inequity was assumed to have been minimal because of the relatively low rates of inflation.

In recent years, of course, inflation rates have not remained low. There is now a consensus among courts that the prior inequity can no longer be tolerated. See, e.g., United States v. English, 521 F.2d 63, 75 (CA9 1975) ("While the administrative convenience of ignoring inflation has some appeal when inflation rates are low, to ignore inflation when the rates are high is to ignore economic reality"). There is no consensus at all, however, regarding what form an appropriate response should take.

Our sister common law nations generally continue to adhere to the position that inflation is too speculative to be considered in estimating the lost stream of future earnings; they have sought to counteract the danger of systematically undercompensating plaintiffs by applying a discount rate that is below the current market rate. Nevertheless, they have each chosen different rates, applying slightly different economic theories. In England, Lord Diplock has suggested that it would be appropriate to allow for future inflation "in a rough and ready way" by discounting at a rate of 4¾%. Cookson v. Knowles, [1979] A.C. 565–573. He accepted that rate as roughly equivalent to the rates available "[i]n times of stable currency." The Supreme Court of Canada has recommended discounting at a rate of seven percent, a rate equal to market rates on long-term investments minus a government expert's prediction of the long-term rate of price inflation. Andrews v. Grand & Toy Alberta Ltd., [1978] 2 S.C.R. 229, 83 D.L.R. (3d) 452, 474. And in Australia, the High Court has adopted a 2% rate, on the theory that it represents a good approximation of the long-term "real interest rate." See Pennant Hills Restaurants Pty. Ltd. v. Barrell Insurances Pty. Ltd., 55 A.L.J.R. 258 (1981).

In this country, some courts have taken the same "real interest rate" approach as Australia. See Feldman v. Allegheny Airlines, 524 F.2d 384, 388 (CA2 1975), affirming 382 F.Supp. 1271 (1974) (1.5%); Doca v. Marina Mercante Nicaraguense, S.A., 634 F.2d 30, 39–40 (CA2 1980) (2%, unless litigants prove otherwise). They have endorsed the economic theory suggesting that market interest rates include two components—an estimate of anticipated inflation, and a desired "real" rate of return on investment—and that the latter component is essentially constant over time.[11] They have concluded that the inflationary increase in the estimated lost stream of future earnings will therefore be perfectly "offset" by all but the "real" component of the market interest rate.[12]

11. In his dissenting opinion in Pennant Hills Restaurant Pty. Ltd. v. Barrell Insurances Pty. Ltd., 55 A.L.J.R. 258, 266–267 (1981), Justice Stephen explained the real interest rate approach to discounting future earnings, in part, as follows:

"It rests upon the assumption that interest rates have two principal components: the market's own estimation of likely rates of inflation during the term of a particular fixed interest investment, and a 'real interest' component, being the rate of return which, in the absence of all inflation, a lender will demand and a borrower will be prepared to pay for the use of borrowed funds. It also relies upon the alleged economic fact that this 'real interest' rate, of about two per cent, will always be much the same and that fluctuations in nominal rates of interest are due to the other main component of interest rates, the inflationary expectation."

12. What is meant by the "real interest rate" depends on how one expects the plaintiff to invest the award. If one assumes that the injured worker will immediately invest in bonds having a variety of maturity dates, in order to ensure a particular stream of future payments, then the relevant "real interest rate" must be the difference between (1) an average of short-term, medium-term, and long-term market interest rates in a given year and (2) the average rate of price inflation in subsequent years (i.e., during the terms of the investments). * * *

Still other courts have preferred to continue relying on market interest rates. To avoid undercompensation, they have shown at least tentative willingness to permit evidence of what future price inflation will be in estimating the lost stream of future income. [citations]

Within the past year, two federal Courts of Appeals have decided to allow litigants a choice of methods. Sitting *en banc,* the Court of Appeals for the Fifth Circuit has overruled its prior decision in *Penrod,* supra, and held it acceptable either to exclude evidence of future price inflation and discount by a "real" interest rate, or to attempt to predict the effects of future price inflation on future wages and then discount by the market interest rate. Culver v. Slater Boat Co., 688 F.2d 280, 308–310 (CA5 1982) (en banc). A panel of the Court of Appeals for the Seventh Circuit has taken a substantially similar position. O'Shea v. Riverway Towing Co., 677 F.2d 1194, 1200 (CA7 1982).

Finally, some courts have applied a number of techniques that have loosely been termed "total offset" methods. What these methods have in common is that they presume that the ideal discount rate—the after-tax market interest rate on a safe investment—is (to a legally tolerable degree of precision) completely offset by certain elements in the ideal computation of the estimated lost stream of future income. They all assume that the effects of future price inflation on wages are part of what offsets the market interest rate. The methods differ, however, in their assumptions regarding which if any other elements in the first stage of the damages calculation contribute to the offset.

Beaulieu v. Elliott, 434 P.2d 655 (Alaska 1967), is regarded as the seminal "total offset" case. The Supreme Court of Alaska ruled that in calculating an appropriate award for an injured worker's lost wages, no discount was to be applied. It held that the market interest rate was fully offset by two factors: price inflation and real wage inflation. * * *

In State v. Guinn, 555 P.2d 530 (Alaska 1976), the *Beaulieu* approach was refined slightly. In that case, the plaintiff had offered evidence of "small, automatic increases in the wage rate keyed to the employee's length of service with the company," and the trial court had included those increases in the estimated lost stream of future income but had not discounted. It held that this type of "certain and predictable" individual raise was not the type of wage increase that offsets the failure to discount to present value. Thus, the market interest rate was deemed to be offset by price inflation, societal sources of wage inflation, and individual sources of wage inflation that are not "certain and predictable." [citations]

Kaczkowski v. Bolubasz, 491 Pa. 561, 421 A.2d 1027 (1980), took still a third approach. The Pennsylvania Supreme Court followed the approach of the District Court in *Feldman,* supra, and the Court of Appeals for the Fifth Circuit in Higginbotham v. Mobil Oil Corp., 545 F.2d 422 (CA5 1977), in concluding that the plaintiff could introduce all manner of evidence bearing on likely sources—both individual and societal—of future wage growth, except for predictions of price inflation. However, it rejected those courts' conclusion that the resulting estimated lost stream of future income should be discounted by a

It appears more common for "real interest rate" approaches to rest on the assumption that the worker will invest in low-risk short-term securities and will reinvest frequently. E.g., O'Shea v. Riverway Towing Co., 677 F.2d 1194, 1199 (CA7 1982). Under that assumption, the relevant real interest rate is the difference between the short-term market interest rate in a given year and the average rate of price inflation during that same year. Several studies appear to have been done to measure this difference. * * *

"real interest rate." Rather, it deemed the market interest rate to be offset by future price inflation. [citations]

The litigants and the amici in this case urge us to select one of the many rules that have been proposed and establish it for all time as the exclusive method in all federal trials for calculating an award for lost earnings in an inflationary economy. We are not persuaded, however, that such an approach is warranted. For our review of the foregoing cases leads us to draw three conclusions. First, by its very nature the calculation of an award for lost earnings must be a rough approximation. Because the lost stream can never be predicted with complete confidence, any lump sum represents only a "rough and ready" effort to put the plaintiff in the position he would have been in had he not been injured. Second, sustained price inflation can make the award substantially less precise. Inflation's current magnitude and unpredictability create a substantial risk that the damage award will prove to have little relation to the lost wages it purports to replace. Third, the question of lost earnings can arise in many different contexts. In some sectors of the economy, it is far easier to assemble evidence of an individual's most likely career path than in others.

These conclusions all counsel hesitation. Having surveyed the multitude of options available, we will do no more than is necessary to resolve the case before us. * * * The Court of Appeals correctly noted that respondent's cause of action "is rooted in federal maritime law." [citations] The fact that Pennsylvania has adopted the total offset rule for all negligence cases in that forum is therefore not of controlling importance in this case. * * *

In calculating an award for a longshoreman's lost earnings caused by the negligence of a vessel, the discount rate should be chosen on the basis of the factors that are used to estimate the lost stream of future earnings. If the trier of fact relies on a specific forecast of the future rate of price inflation, and if the estimated lost-stream of future earnings is calculated to include price inflation along with individual factors and other societal factors, then the proper discount rate would be the after-tax market interest rate. But since specific forecasts of future price inflation remain too unreliable to be useful in many cases, it will normally be a costly and ultimately unproductive waste of longshoremen's resources to make such forecasts the centerpiece of litigation under § 5(b). As Judge Newman has warned, "The average accident trial should not be converted into a graduate seminar on economic forecasting." Doca v. Marina Mercante Nicaraguense, S.A. 634 F.2d 30, 39 (CA2 1980). For that reason, both plaintiffs and trial courts should be discouraged from pursuing that approach.

On the other hand, if forecasts of future price inflation are not used, it is necessary to choose an appropriate below-market discount rate. As long as inflation continues, one must ask how much should be "offset" against the market rate. Once again, that amount should be chosen on the basis of the same factors that are used to estimate the lost stream of future earnings. If full account is taken of the individual and societal factors (excepting price inflation) that can be expected to have resulted in wage increases, then all that should be set off against the market interest rate is an estimate of future price inflation. This would result in one of the "real interest rate" approaches described above. Although we find the economic evidence distinctly inconclusive regarding an essential premise of those approaches,[13] we do not believe a trial court adopting such an approach in a suit under § 5(b) should be reversed if it adopts a rate between one and three percent and explains its choice.

There may be a sound economic argument for even further set-offs. In 1976, Professor Carlson of the Purdue University economics department wrote an article in the American Bar Association Journal contending that in the long run the societal factors excepting price inflation—largely productivity gains—match (or even slightly exceed) the "real interest rate." Carlson, Economic Analysis v. Courtroom Controversy, 62 ABAJ 628 (1976). He thus recommended that the estimated lost stream of future wages be calculated without considering either price inflation or societal productivity gains. All that would be considered would be individual seniority and promotion gains. If this were done, he concluded that the entire market interest rate, including both inflation and the real interest rate, would be more than adequately offset.

Although such an approach has the virtue of simplicity and may even be economically precise,[14] we cannot at this time agree with the Court of Appeals for the Third Circuit that its use is mandatory in the federal courts. Naturally, Congress could require it if it chose to do so. And nothing prevents parties interested in keeping litigation costs under control from stipulating to its use before trial.[15] But we are not prepared to impose it on unwilling litigants, for we have not been given sufficient data to judge how closely the national patterns of wage growth are likely to reflect the patterns within any given industry. The legislative branch of the federal government is far better

13. The key premise is that the real interest rate is stable over time. It is obviously not perfectly stable, but whether it is even relatively stable is hotly disputed among economists. In his classic work, Irving Fisher argued that the rate is not stable because changes in expectations of inflation (the factor that influences market interest rates) lag behind changes in inflation itself. I. Fisher, The Theory of Interest 43 (1930). He noted that the "real rate of interest in the United States from March to April, 1917, fell below minus 70 percent!"

14. We note that a substantial body of literature suggests that the Carlson rule might even undercompensate some plaintiffs. See S. Speiser, Recovery for Wrongful Death, Economic Handbook, 36–37 (1970) (average interest rate 1% below average rate of wage growth); Formuzis & O'Donnell, Inflation and the Valuation of Future Economic Losses, 38 Mont.L.Rev. 297, 299 (1977) (interest rate 1.4% below rate of wage growth); Franz, Simplifying Future Lost Earnings, Trial 34 (Aug. 1977) (rate of wage growth exceeds interest rate by over 1% on average); Coyne, Present Value of Future Earnings: A Sensible Alternative to Simplistic Methodologies, 49 Ins.Couns.J. 25, 26 (1982) (noting that Carlson's own data suggest that rate of wage growth exceeds interest rate by over 1.6%, and recommending a more individualized approach). See generally Note, 57 St. John's L.Rev. 316, 342–345 (1983). But see Comment, 49 U.Chi.L.Rev. 1003, 1023, and n. 87 (1982) (noting "apparent congruence" between government projections of 2% average annual productivity growth and real interest rate, and concluding that total offset is accurate).

It is also interesting that in O'Shea v. Riverway Towing Co., 677 F.2d 1194 (CA7 1982), Judge Posner stated that the real interest rate varies between one and three percent, and that "it would not be outlandish to assume that even if there were no inflation, Mrs. O'Shea's wages would have risen by three percent a year." Depending on how much of Judge Posner's estimated wage inflation for Mrs. O'Shea was due to individual factors (excluded from a total offset computation), his comments suggest that a total offset approach in that case could have meant over-discounting by as much as two percent.

15. If parties agree in advance to use the Carlson method, all that would be needed would be a table of the after-tax values of present salaries and fringe benefits for different positions and levels of seniority ("steps") within an industry. Presumably this would be a matter for stipulation before trial, as well. The trier of fact would be instructed to determine how many years the injured worker would have spent at each step. It would multiply the number of years the worker would spend at each step by the current net value of each step (as shown on the table) and then add up the results. The trier of fact would be spared the need to cope with inflation estimates, productivity trends, and present value tables.

equipped than we are to perform a comprehensive economic analysis and to fashion the proper general rule.

As a result, the judgment below must be set aside. In performing its damages calculation, the trial court applied the theory of *Kaczkowski,* supra, as a mandatory federal rule of decision. * * *

On remand, the decision on whether to reopen the record should be left to the sound discretion of the trial court. * * *

Note

See Culver v. Slater Boat Co., 722 F.2d 114 (5th Cir.1983).

3. PUNITIVE DAMAGES

TUTTLE v. RAYMOND, III.

Supreme Judicial Court of Maine, 1985.
494 A.2d 1353.

VIOLETTE, JUSTICE. * * * On July 6, 1977, the plaintiff, Hattie Tuttle, was seriously injured when a Lincoln driven by the defendant, Ralph Raymond, III, struck the Plymouth in which she was a passenger. The force of the impact sheared the Plymouth in half. Based on the evidence presented at trial, the jury could have found that the defendant was driving at an excessive speed in a 25 mile per hour zone when he struck the Plymouth, and that the defendant went through a red light just before the impact.

The defendant conceded liability at trial and focused instead on the amount of damages the jury should properly award. From the outset of the litigation, the defendant asserted both that punitive damages should not be recognized under the law of Maine and that, in any event, the facts of this case did not generate the issue of punitive damages. Nevertheless, the trial court submitted this issue to the jury, and refused to disturb the jury's decision to award [$50,000 compensatory damages and] $22,000 in exemplary damages.

Vigorous criticism of the doctrine of punitive damages is hardly a recent development in the field of jurisprudence. Arguments against the availability of such awards have been circulating for one hundred years and longer. [citations] During those hundred years, commentators have exhaustively analyzed the doctrine. [citations] Nonetheless, a substantial majority of jurisdictions today allow common law punitive damages in appropriate cases as a recovery beyond the amount necessary to compensate the plaintiff, for the purpose of deterrence or punishment or both. [citations]

The law of Maine on this issue is in accord with the position of this substantial majority. Since adopting the doctrine of punitive damages in Pike v. Dilling, 48 Me. 539 (1861), this Court has frequently and consistently reaffirmed the availability of such awards at common law under the appropriate circumstances. [citations] "It would be simplistic to characterize [this position] as mere blind adherence to an outmoded principle. Rather, the doctrine of punitive damages survives because it continues to serve the useful purposes of expressing society's disapproval of intolerable conduct and deterring such conduct where no other remedy would suffice." Mallor and Roberts, [Punitive Damages: Toward a Principled Approach, 31 Hastings L.J. 639, 641 (1980)].

The defendant in the case at bar contends that we should nevertheless abandon the judicially created rule of punitive damages in this state. In support of this position, the defendant proffers several arguments, which we consider seriatim. After careful consideration, we conclude that the doctrine of punitive damages retains its viability, and we refuse to abrogate the availability of exemplary awards at common law in Maine.

One objection raised by the defendant is that the civil law is ill-suited to accomplish the goals that purportedly justify the doctrine of punitive damages. The defendant contends that the proper function of the civil tort law is to make plaintiffs whole, and that grave problems arise when it is used to extract from defendants something beyond full compensation for the victim. The defendant asserts that the primary purpose allegedly served by the doctrine of punitive damages, deterrence through punishment, is more properly left to the criminal law with its attendant procedural safeguards.

The bright line that the defendant attempts to interpose between the civil and the criminal law is in fact artificial. The courts of this country historically have not restricted the civil law to a compensatory function. In 1851, the United States Supreme Court, relying on over a century of judicial precedent, observed: "By the common as well as by statute law, men are often punished for aggravated misconduct or lawless acts, by means of a civil action, and the damages, inflicted by way of a penalty or punishment, given to the party injured." Day v. Woodworth, 54 U.S. (13 How.) 363, 371 (1851). Use of the civil law to shape social behavior is both logical and desirable. There are many instances where the criminal law alone is inadequate to achieve the desired deterrent effect. For instance, even when the defendant's conduct violates a criminal statute, it may be a crime that is rarely prosecuted, or the maximum applicable penalty may not correspond to the actual outrageousness of the conduct and the defendant's ability to pay. Of course, where a criminal sanction does constitute an adequate deterrent in a given case, there is no justification for adding a civil penalty in the form of punitive damages. This potential problem, however, does not require the wholesale abrogation of the doctrine of punitive damages. A more sensible solution is to allow the fact finder to consider evidence of any criminal punishment imposed for the conduct in question as a mitigating factor on the issue of punitive damages,[1] a step already taken by this Court. See Hanover Insurance Co. v. Hayward, 464 A.2d 156, 159 (Me.1983).

Furthermore, the lack of certain procedural safeguards, which are required in criminal prosecutions,[2] does not render the civil law unfit to serve this

1. [Footnotes renumbered.] We note that, despite our decision in Hanover Insurance Co. v. Hayward, 464 A.2d 156 (Me.1983), the trial court in this case excluded evidence of the fact that the defendant was convicted and punished criminally for the same conduct that gave rise to this civil litigation. A defendant is entitled to have the jury consider such evidence when it decides whether to assess punitive damages and, if so, in what amount. Because of our disposition of this case, however, we need not decide whether the trial court's exclusion of this evidence constitutes reversible error.

2. As stated by one commentator, who was obviously uncomfortable with the notion of punitive damages:

> Again, when assessed exemplary damages, the accused [sic] is really punished for a criminal offense without the safeguards of a criminal trial. He is summoned into court to make compensation for a purely private injury, with no issue upon a criminal charge presented; punishment by fine is inflicted without indictment or sworn information; the rules of evidence as to criminal trials are rejected; the doctrine of reasonable doubt is replaced by the rule of preponderance of evidence; the defendant is compelled to testify against himself; and, though in criminal offenses the law fixes a maximum penalty which is imposed by the court, the jury is entirely free to assess exemplary damages, subject only to the power of the court, unwillingly exercised, to set aside the verdict. The procedure and principles of criminal law are disregarded. * * * Willis, Measure of Damages When Property Is Wrongfully Taken by a Private Individual, 22 Harv.L.Rev. 419, 421 (1909).

deterrent function. The statute books provide many examples where penalties, in the form of multiple damages payable to a private party, are imposed in civil actions for the purpose of discouraging undesirable conduct.[3] The absence of these procedural safeguards presents no constitutional bar to the imposition of punitive damages in a civil action. [citations] The reason for requiring such safeguards in the criminal arena, the threat to the defendant of incarceration or other substantial stigma, does not justify their application in actions for punitive damages.

In a related argument, the defendant criticizes the doctrine of punitive damages because it permits a person to be punished twice for the same offense. The defendant observes that in the case at bar he was *both* convicted and fined in a criminal proceeding *and* assessed with punitive damages in a subsequent civil proceeding based upon the same conduct. The defendant contends that the assessment of an exemplary award in addition to criminal punishment for the same conduct offends the constitutional prohibition against placing a defendant twice in jeopardy. * * *

"In the constitutional sense," jeopardy is a technical term that encompasses only the risk inherent in proceedings that are "essentially criminal." [citation] Accordingly, a civil action for punitive damages cannot infringe on a defendant's constitutional right to be free from double jeopardy. [citations] A claim for punitive damages is based upon a *private* wrong, and is clearly distinguishable from a criminal prosecution, which is brought solely on the behalf of the public. [citations] The state and federal constitutional prohibitions against double jeopardy present no bar to actions for punitive damages. * * *

Another objection to punitive damages raised by the defendant is that they bestow a windfall upon the plaintiff. As the defendant observes, such damages are awarded in Maine in excess of any amount necessary to compensate the plaintiff. [citation] The defendant contends that a plaintiff injured by a tort is entitled to be made whole, and not to be put in a better position than if the tort had never occurred. [citations]

We find, however, that the extra recovery afforded to plaintiffs by punitive damages, rather than constituting a "windfall," serves a useful purpose. The potential for recovering an exemplary award provides an incentive for private civil enforcement of society's rules against serious misconduct.[4] As noted earlier, the civil law effectively augments the criminal law in deterring intolerable conduct. The doctrine of punitive damages encourages the use of civil actions by private parties in response to such conduct, especially when the

3. See e.g., 10 M.R.S.A. § 1322 (1980) (providing for treble damages, attorney's fees, and costs for willful violation of Fair Credit Reporting Act); 14 M.R.S.A. § 6034 (1980) (providing for double damages, attorney's fees, and costs for willful retention of security deposit in violation of law); 15 U.S.C. § 15 (1976) (providing for treble damages, attorney's fees, and costs for violation of antitrust laws); 15 U.S.C. § 72 (1976) (providing for treble damages, attorney's fees, and costs for unfair competition in importing trade).

4. The defendant contends that this incentive is in fact a drawback because plaintiffs will attempt to maximize their recoveries without any regard as to what amount of punitive damages would serve as a just and sufficient deterrent. This, however, is not so much a problem inherent in the doctrine of punitive damages as it is a byproduct of our chosen adversary system of justice. We use this system because potential excesses, such as the one raised by the defendant, are hopefully cured by an equally zealous and competent advocate on the opposing side, an impartial jury as a fact finder, and a wise and wary judge overseeing the entire proceeding.

prospective compensatory recovery is low or the expected cost of litigation is high.[5]

The defendant next argues that the doctrine of punitive damages invites abuse because there is no objective standard by which to determine the amount of a proper award. According to the defendant, the jury is left to speculate concerning the appropriate amount of punitive damages in a given case, with the result of arbitrary and excessive awards. The defendant contends that this is a flaw in the doctrine that outweighs any justification for allowing exemplary awards.

In fact, however, the lack of any precise formula by which punitive damages can be calculated is one of the important assets of the doctrine. "Punitive damages * * * can be individualized to provide a deterrent that will be adequate for each case." Mallor and Roberts, at 657. Such flexibility can ensure a sufficient award in the case of a rich defendant and avoid an overburdensome one where the defendant is not as wealthy. Flexibility is also necessary to avoid situations where the potential benefits of wrongdoing could outweigh a known maximum liability. In short, "[a]lthough a quantitative formula would be comforting, it would be undesirable." Mallor and Roberts, at 666.

We, of course, do not advocate the availability of punitive damages on a completely open-ended basis. The trial court must reject a claim for punitive damages as a matter of law unless the plaintiff presents adequate proof that the defendant acted in a sufficiently culpable manner. Further, even after the plaintiff has satisfied his prima facie burden on the issue of exemplary damages, the fact finder must weigh "all relevant aggravating and mitigating factors" presented by the parties, including the egregiousness of the defendant's conduct, the ability of the defendant to pay such an award, and any criminal punishment imposed for the conduct in question. After such consideration, an exemplary award is "within the *sound* discretion of the fact finder." *Hanover Insurance Co.* (emphasis added). If the fact finder awards punitive damages that are excessive in light of the relevant factors, the trial court or this Court can intervene. [citations]

We also observe that the lack of precision in measuring appropriate exemplary awards is not a trait unique to the doctrine of punitive damages. Compensatory awards for intangible harm, such as pain and suffering, and emotional distress, are likewise not subject to any exact standard for determining an appropriate amount.

In conclusion, we are not persuaded that we should abolish common law

5. In Wangen v. Ford Motor Co., 97 Wis.2d 260, 294 N.W.2d 437 (1980), the defendant argued that, in order to avoid giving the plaintiff a windfall, the court should award any punitive damages to the public. After noting that this argument had "a certain equitable ring" to it, the Wisconsin Supreme Court ultimately rejected it. The court stated:

"The 'windfall criterion' overlooks that the payment of punitive damages to the injured party is justifiable as a practical matter, because such damages do serve to compensate the injured party for uncompensated expenses, e.g., attorneys' fees and litigation expenses, and that the windfall motivates reluctant plaintiffs to go forward with their claims. If punitive damages were paid to the public treasury, fewer wrongdoers would be punished because the injured would have no inducement to spend the extra time and expense to prove a claim for punitive damages once an action had been brought."

A Maine author has suggested that punitive damages could be split between plaintiffs and the state pursuant to legislative action. [citation] punitive damages in Maine.[6] It may well be, as the defendant argues, that the doctrine of punitive damages no longer serves any purpose for which it was originally intended.[7]

> "This argument, however, fails to account for the fact that many legal doctrines serve purposes that differ from those for which they originally were developed. * * * So long as a doctrine continues to serve a necessary policy goal, the fact that it has diverged from its original function does not provide a basis for abolishing the doctrine. *The pertinent question is whether punitive damages continue to serve a rational policy.*"

Mallor & Roberts, at 644 (emphasis added). We conclude that they do.

Although we reject the defendant's contention that we should abolish common law punitive damages in Maine, we perceive cogent reasons for avoiding an overbroad application of the doctrine. Notions of fairness and efficiency weigh against allowing exemplary awards where the stated goal of deterring reprehensible conduct would be furthered only marginally or not at all. Rather, punitive damages should be available based only upon a limited class of misconduct where deterrence is both paramount and likely to be achieved. With this in mind, we turn to a re-examination of the type of tortious conduct that can justify an exemplary award in Maine.

It is generally accepted that mere negligence cannot support an award of punitive damages. Beyond that, however, there has been some variation in describing the quality of tortious conduct necessary to support an exemplary award. Recent decisions of this Court have indicated that Maine law recognizes the availability of punitive damages based upon "wanton, malicious, reckless or grossly negligent conduct." [citations]

Such a standard is overbroad. Whatever qualitative difference exists between mere negligence and "gross" negligence, it is insufficient to justify allowing punitive damages based upon the latter class of conduct. "Gross" negligence simply covers too broad and too vague an area of behavior, resulting in an unfair and inefficient use of the doctrine of punitive damages. A similar problem exists with allowing punitive damages based merely upon "reckless" conduct. "To sanction punitive damages solely upon the basis of conduct characterized as 'heedless disregard of the consequences' would be to allow virtually limitless imposition of punitive damages." [citation] A standard that allows exemplary awards based upon gross negligence or mere reckless disregard of the circumstances overextends the availability of punitive damages,

6. We note that, although our opinion today provides a careful evaluation of a longstanding doctrine, many issues concerning the availability of punitive damages, which are not raised by this case, remain for future consideration and resolution. These issues include, inter alia, whether one can insure against the assessment of punitive damages, whether one can be vicariously liable for punitive damages, and the application of punitive damages in products liability and multiple plaintiff litigation. It should be clear that our decision not to abandon the doctrine of punitive damages does not eliminate the need for future definition and modification of it.

7. Some theorize that punitive damages initially compensated plaintiffs for intangible harms, which were not cognizable under the existing common law. [citation] Of course, modern tort law now allows compensatory damages for such intangible injuries, eliminating that particular basis for punitive damages. It has also been suggested that punitive damages first arose in cases involving "affronts to the honor of the victims," as a means of satisfying insulted plaintiffs and preventing them from resorting to violent forms of self-help, such as dueling. [citation] It is not so clear that this function of the doctrine of punitive damages has become obsolete. In any event, it is not the primary justification given for exemplary awards today.

and dulls the potentially keen edge of the doctrine as an effective deterrent of truly reprehensible conduct.

We therefore determine that a new standard is needed in Maine. "If one were to select a single word or term to describe [the] essence [of conduct warranting punitive damages], it would be 'malice.'" [citations] Indeed, the *malicious* commission of a tort is a common thread running through many of the decisions in which this Court has upheld an award of punitive damages. [citations] We therefore hold that punitive damages are available based upon tortious conduct only if the defendant acted with malice.

This requirement of malice will be most obviously satisfied by a showing of "express" or "actual" malice. Such malice exists where the defendant's tortious conduct is motivated by ill will toward the plaintiff. [citations] Punitive damages will also be available, however, where deliberate conduct by the defendant, although motivated by something other than ill will toward any particular party, is so outrageous that malice toward a person injured as a result of that conduct can be implied. We emphasize that, for the purpose of assessing punitive damages, such "implied" or "legal" malice will not be established by the defendant's mere reckless disregard of the circumstances.

We recognize that in some other jurisdictions the malice necessary to support an award of punitive damages can be implied from a mere reckless disregard of the circumstances. [citations] We adopt a narrower view in order to reduce the vagueness and uncertainty surrounding the concept of implied malice in this context. As we indicated earlier, by allowing punitive damages based only upon this more certain and more culpable class of conduct, the efficiency and the fairness of the doctrine as a deterrent is increased.

In the case at bar, the evidence shows that the plaintiff was seriously injured by the defendant's reckless operation of an automobile. The plaintiff contends that such conduct on the part of the defendant is sufficient to support an award of punitive damages. Under the standard we announce today, it clearly is not. We certainly do not condone the defendant's conduct; nor do we fail to appreciate the tragic injuries imposed upon the plaintiff as a result of that conduct. We have determined, however, that deterrence—recognized by this Court as "*the* proper justification" for punitive damages [citations]—cannot justify imposing an exemplary award in addition to compensatory damages and possibly criminal sanctions based solely upon a defendant's reckless disregard of the circumstances. Because the defendant's conduct was not accompanied by malice, either express or implied, we vacate the award of punitive damages.

Our stated goal of avoiding an overbroad application of the doctrine of punitive damages leads us to consider another issue raised by the defendant, namely, the standard of proof that should govern a claim for an exemplary award. Presently in Maine, a plaintiff must prove his case for punitive damages by a preponderance of the evidence. See McKinnon v. Tibbetts, 440 A.2d 1028, 1031 (Me.1982). The defendant urges us to abandon that rule, and to impose instead the more stringent proof requirement of clear and convincing evidence upon a plaintiff seeking an exemplary award. * * *

This Court recently noted that "although the preponderance [of the evidence] standard normally prevails in a civil case, appellate courts in a large number of categories of litigation have found compelling reasons for requiring a higher form of proof." Taylor v. Commissioner of Mental Health, 481 A.2d 139, 150 (Me.1984). In *Taylor,* we listed a wide variety of cases where the

United States Supreme Court, the Law Court, or a court of some other jurisdiction has imposed the requirement of clear and convincing evidence upon the party bearing the burden of proof. Under this standard of proof, we observed, "the party with the burden of persuasion may prevail only if he can 'place in the ultimate factfinder an abiding conviction that the truth of [his] factual contentions are "highly probable".' "

We conclude that such a higher standard of proof is appropriate for a claim for punitive damages. It should be obvious from our discussion that, although punitive damages serve an important function in our legal system, they can be onerous when loosely assessed. The potential consequences of a punitive damages claim warrant a requirement that the plaintiff present proof greater than a mere preponderance of the evidence. Therefore, we hold that a plaintiff may recover exemplary damages based upon tortious conduct only if he can prove by clear and convincing evidence that the defendant acted with malice. * * *

Judgment amended by vacating award of punitive damages; as so amended, judgment affirmed.

All concurring.

The Arguments

In an Appendix to Woolstrum v. Mailloux, 114 Cal.App.3d Supp. 1, 190 Cal.Rptr. 129 (1983), the court summarized the arguments against and for punitive damages:

1. Inflames the cupidity of plaintiffs.

2. Adds a grossly intangible element to a negligence case grievously interfering with rational settlement negotiations.

3. Leads to lengthy and rancorous discovery process and disputes.

4. Places before the jury inflammatory evidence affecting their dispassionate judgment as to negligence (often, this is its principal purpose) and compensatory damages.

5. Moreover, if the plaintiff can inject the issue of punitive damages in a case, he can show the wealth of the defendant. This results in the trial of a negligence case becoming a *field day* with the issue of the defendant's wealth.

6. Places upon the defendants the risk of vast, unforseeable damages for which usually no insurance protection is available (thus thwarting the policy of the law of spreading the risk and the cost thereof).

7. Places a social policy decision in the hands of a jury without giving them access to the huge and broad array of facts necessary to reach an intelligent and useful decision.

8. Outrageously gives a windfall to a few plaintiffs who are fortunate enough to be injured by a millionaire (or a billionaire corporation).

9. Imposes punishment for conduct (rather than reimbursement for loss), a decision usually, and better, left to the criminal law and the decision for the legislative, judicial or administrative representatives of the people, not a small group of haphazardly selected citizens.

10. Jury punitive damage awards of an unpredictable nature and appalling inconsistency continue to proliferate. Neither the Legislature nor the

appellate courts have been able to formulate coherent, reasonable guidelines and limitations for the remedy. Perhaps the quest is utopian and unrealizable.

In practice, it lacks any semblance of consistency between defendants, or even the same defendant, in cases tried by different juries.

Because the Legislature has not prescribed guidelines for punitive damages, they may be awarded by juries at whim.

11. The extreme unpredictability of punitive damages and the occasional crushing amount set by a vindictive jury approaches a due process violation because, in a practical sense, the defendant *lacks notice* of the extent his conduct may result in loss of his entire assets.

12. To the extent that the defendant has been, or will be, punished for his conduct by the criminal process, the imposition of punitive damages constitutes double punishment.

13. If the punitive damage issue is injected into accident cases, the jury must be informed as to whether the compensatory award will come out of the defendant's pocket or be paid by an insurance carrier, for otherwise damages cannot be sensibly assessed. This has the evil of injecting the issue of insurance coverage in the case in violation of statutory policy.

14. Punitive damages awarded as a result of a fortuitous or accidental result rather than an intended result will have no deterrent effect, for the negligent actor just assumes they will not occur.

15. Because insurance carriers do not have to pay for injuries resulting from conduct that merits punitive damages, plaintiffs will only ask for punitive damages in negligence cases where defendant is uninsured or the defendant is wealthy. This will reduce the deterrent effect of permitting punitive damages in negligence cases.

16. The "punishment" of punitive damages is assessed without the constitutional safeguards of criminal punishment.

The punishment is imposed by only a preponderance of the evidence.

Although the remedy is quasi-criminal, the defendant does not have the protections of a criminal defendant, such as freedom from self-incrimination, prohibition of excessive fines, etc.

17. The doctrine developed in the common law to provide *full* compensation to the plaintiff. But now that the scope of damages has increased markedly in negligence cases to include compensation for various *intangible* injuries (including negligent infliction of emotional distress without proof of physical injury), the extra remedy is no longer necessary.

18. Because compensatory damages include recovery for such intangibles as shock, loss of comfort and society, loss of enjoyment of life, etc., they probably often contain an element of retribution.

19. A closely related argument is that civil juries are inexperienced and ill-equipped to mete out punishment that would be in the best interests of society.

The most frequently stated benefits of permitting punitive damage awards are:

1. To provide a plaintiff who has suffered only nominal damages with an incentive to litigate,

2. To punish the defendant for the transgression, and

3. To deter the defendant and others from committing similar acts in the future.

It is obvious that the first rationale does not apply to negligence cases, and the second and third should not apply to ordinary negligence cases, but only those with an element of outrageous conduct.

Moreover, the second rationale (punishment) infringes on the sphere of the criminal law and the third (deterrence) is wholly unsupported by any objective or scientific proof that it is effective.

Notes

1. Browning-Ferris Industries v. Kelco Disposal, Inc., 492 U.S. 257 (1989). The eighth amendment to the United States Constitution forbids "excessive fines." A defendant that had been mulcted $6,000,000 punitive damages in addition to $51,146 compensatory damages sought relief. The Supreme Court decided that a jury's civil punitive damages award to a private plaintiff is not limited by the excessive fines clause; but the Court's opinions suggested that the fourteenth amendment's due process clause might provide a source that limits excessive awards of punitive damages.

2. As this edition went to the publishers, the Supreme Court decided Pacific Mutual Life Insurance Co. v. Haslip, 111 S.Ct. 1032 (1991). Rejecting Pacific Mutual's argument that an $840,000 punitive damages award was the "product of unbridled jury discretion and violative of its due process rights," the Court upheld the award. Alabama's punitive damages satisfied the requirements of due process because of the instructions to the jury and review by both the trial judge and the state supreme court. Justice O'Connor dissented: the punitive damage scheme was void for vagueness, and due process compelled a better method of controlling the jury's freedom to award punitive damages.

Do *Browning-Ferris* and *Haslip* mean that tort reformers' quest to curb punitive damages must move from the federal courts to state courts and legislatures?

3. Smith v. Wade, 461 U.S. 30, 41, 46–49, 56 (1983). In a prison inmate's suit against a guard, the jury awarded the plaintiff $5000 punitive damages.

"The rule in a large majority of jurisdictions was that punitive damages (also called exemplary damages, vindictive damages, or smart money) could be awarded without a showing of actual ill will, spite, or intent to injure. * * *

"The same rule applies today. The Restatement (Second) of Torts (1979), for example, states: 'Punitive damages may be awarded for conduct that is outrageous, because of the defendant's evil motive *or his reckless indifference to the rights of others.*' § 908(2) (emphasis added). Most cases under state common law, although varying in their precise terminology, have adopted more or less the same rule, recognizing that punitive damages in tort cases may be awarded not only for actual intent to injure or evil motive, but also for recklessness, serious indifference to or disregard for the rights of others, or even gross negligence. * * *

"Smith's argument, which he offers in several forms, is that an actual-intent standard is preferable to a recklessness standard because it is less vague. He points out that punitive damages, by their very nature, are not awarded to compensate the injured party. [citations] He concedes, of course, that deterrence of future egregious conduct is a primary purpose of both § 1983, [citations] and of punitive damages. [citations] But deterrence, he contends, cannot be achieved unless the standard of conduct sought to be deterred is stated with sufficient clarity to enable potential defendants to conform to the law and to avoid the proposed sanction. Recklessness or callous indifference, he argues, is too uncertain a standard to achieve deterrence rationally and fairly. A prison guard, for example, can be expected to know whether he is acting with actual ill will or intent to injure, but not whether he is being reckless or callously indifferent.

"Smith's argument, if valid, would apply to ordinary tort cases as easily as to § 1983 suits; hence, it hardly presents an argument for adopting a different rule under § 1983. In any event, the argument is unpersuasive. While, *arguendo,* an intent standard may be easier to understand and apply to particular situations than a recklessness standard, we are not persuaded that a recklessness standard is too vague to be fair or useful. * * *

"We hold that a jury may be permitted to assess punitive damages in an action under § 1983 when the defendant's conduct is shown to be motivated by evil motive or intent, or when it involves reckless or callous indifference to the federally protected rights of others. We further hold that this threshold applies even when the underlying standard of liability for compensatory damages is one of recklessness. Because the jury instructions in this case are in accord with this rule, the judgment of the Court of Appeals is affirmed."

In the § 1983 civil rights action, defendant Wade was entitled to a qualified privilege that protected him from liability for even compensatory damages unless his misconduct was "reckless." The Court allowed the same verbal threshold for compensatory damages and punitive damages because punitive damages are discretionary with the factfinder, not "a matter of right, no matter how egregious the defendant's conduct."

Also a successful plaintiff in an action under § 1983, the civil rights act, recovers attorney fees pursuant to 42 U.S.C. § 1988.

Compare Masaki v. General Motors Corp., 71 Hawaii 1, 7, 780 P.2d 566, 571 (1989) where the court, quoting McCormick on Damages, stated that "a positive element of conscious wrongdoing is always required" to justify the award of punitive damages.

4. O'Gilvie v. International Playtex, Inc., 821 F.2d 1438, 1440–41, 1448–49 (10th Cir.1987), cert. denied, 486 U.S. 1032 (1988). The jury found that decedent died because of Playtex's failure to warn her of the fatal risk of toxic shock syndrome from its tampons and awarded $1,525,000 actual damages and $10,000,000 punitive damages. "After the entry of judgment and apparently in response to the trial court's suggestion, Playtex represented that it was discontinuing the sale of some of its products, instituting a program of alerting the public to the dangers of toxic shock syndrome, and modifying its product warning. The trial court thereupon ordered the punitive damage award reduced to $1,350,000." * * *

"Under both federal and Kansas law, remittitur is not proper unless the amount of damages awarded is so excessive that it shocks the judicial conscience. [citations] * * *

"In this case, the judge reviewed his notes on the evidence supporting the award of punitive damages at the post-trial hearing and stated that he was 'satisfied there was sufficient evidence there' and 'that the jury's answers were intelligently drawn, they were not drawn out of passion or prejudice, they understood this evidence.' The judge also stated that 'the amount of the verdict does not bother me, nor shock my conscience, and in light of the findings this jury made I'm not surprised with it.' He then declared that had O'Gilvie been allowed to seek punitive damages of $20,000,000, an award for that amount would not have been a surprise to him and would not have been remitted.

"Notwithstanding the court's ruling that the punitive damages verdict was supported by the evidence, was not excessive, and did not shock its conscience, it assured counsel for Playtex that substantial modification or complete remittitur would be forthcoming if Playtex should decide to remove its super-absorbent tampons from the market. In so doing, the court stated its view that this verdict was only the beginning, and that other cases would follow.

"We find no authority in either the relevant federal or state law that would permit a trial court to remit a punitive damage award under the circumstances of this case."

5. *Punitive Damages in Contracts.* In General Motors Corp. v. Piskor, 281 Md. 627, 638–39, 381 A.2d 16, 22 (1977), the court said:

"However valid these [punitive] policy objectives might be in respect to pure torts involving conduct of an extraordinary and outrageous character, they have little relevance in the area of contract law, where breaches of contract do not ordinarily engender as much resentment or mental or physical discomfort as do torts of the former variety. Hence, the rule has developed that punitive damages may never be recovered in pure breach of contract suits [citations] on the theory that it is sufficient to provide pecuniary compensation to the aggrieved party without the necessity of assuaging his feelings or allaying community outrage by means of exemplary damages. * * * A further reason for prohibiting recovery for punitive damages in pure contract cases is that the mere availability of such a remedy would seriously jeopardize the stability and predictability of commercial transactions, so vital to the smooth and efficient operation of the modern American economy." The plaintiff must present an independent tort to base punitive damages on.

The recent erosion of the prohibition has resulted largely from an undermining of the distinction between tort and contract actions. Occasional opinions openly award punitive damages in contract. Davis v. Gage, 106 Idaho 735, 682 P.2d 1282 (App.1984), involved breach of a covenant not to compete. Although the defendant's egregious conduct might be considered unfair competition, the court chose to base punitive damages solely on breach of a covenant.

6. *Punitive Damages in Equity.* The traditional rule has been that a court of equity has neither the power nor "equitable jurisdiction" to award punitive damages. Where law and equity are merged, it can easily be argued that any civil court therefore has the "power" to impose punitive damages. I.H.P. Corp. v. 210 Central Park South Corp., infra, p. 231. See also Charles v. Epperson & Co., 258 Iowa 409, 137 N.W.2d 605 (1965). Courts have concluded that punitive damages where only equitable remedies are involved is "incompatible with equitable principles"—i.e., want of equitable jurisdiction. See Anno., 48 A.L.R.2d 947 (1956). This may reflect an idealized view of the function of equity or it may reflect a concern that judicial awards of punitive damages contradict the right to a trial by jury. See, Rexnord, Inc. v. Ferris, 294 Or. 392, 657 P.2d 673 (1983).

In Mississippi, where separate chancery courts are maintained, the Supreme Court, abandoning a well-established rule to the contrary, has confirmed the power of the courts to award punitive damages in cases within their subject matter jurisdiction. Tideway Oil Programs, Inc. v. Serio, 431 So.2d 454, 461–62 (Miss. 1983): "We have here a case where the core charge made by Plaintiff Serio in his complaint is 'collusive, deceitful and fraudulent conduct.' Complete relief, Serio charges, requires temporary and permanent injunctive relief, and accounting, actual and punitive damages. Our chancery courts delight to do complete justice and not by halves. * * * There is no sensible reason why all relief to which he may be entitled should not be afforded by * * * a chancery court." The dissent raised the jury trial question.

Oakley v. Simmons, 799 S.W.2d 669 (Tenn.App.1990). If plaintiff was entitled to an injunction, the court may uphold an award of punitive damages without any compensatory damages.

7. *Punitive Damages in Restitution.* Restitution remedies are nominally disassociated from punitive damages. The first Restatement of Restitution does not refer to punitive awards at all. Perhaps this is because even when "legal," restitution is governed by "equitable" principles. But, as suggested in note 6, the distinctions that allow punitive damages in law but not in equity are not wholly stable.

Restitution and punitive damages are not necessarily incompatible. Where restitution is an alternative remedy for tortious acts, why not tack on punitive damages? Should waiver of the tort to sue in assumpsit justify denying punitives as has been assumed in traditional quasi-contract cases? On the other hand should a defendant compelled to disgorge profits on restitutionary principles also be hit with a punitive award?

8. *Insurance Against Punitive Damages.* A number of insurance companies were surprised to learn that the customary promise in their liability policies, "to pay on behalf of the insured all sums which the latter shall become legally obligated to pay as damages because of bodily injury or property damage," could include punitive damages. See Dayton Hudson Corp. v. American Mutual Liability Insurance Co., 621 P.2d 1155 (Okl.1980), where the "policy promised to pay damages because of false arrest committed in the conduct of the insured's business." As might be expected the industry's response was to adopt policy forms expressly excluding coverage of punitive damages. See Current Damages Decisions, 19 F.T.D. 13 (Jan.1978).

The problem is a matter of public policy: whether to permit an insurance company that is prepared to calculate and assume risks to insure against punitive damages. This is a point of much contention and difference of opinion. In general, decisions seem to oppose insurance for punitive damages, Northwestern National Casualty Co. v. McNulty, 307 F.2d 432 (5th Cir.1962), particularly where "actual malice" is demanded before punitive damages can be imposed. But the moral sense implicit in public policy is diminished where the punitive damages are connected with purely vicarious liability, where the tort is unintentional, or even where public officials commit intentional torts such as false arrest and malicious prosecution. Some decisions reveal no overriding policy objections to insurance coverage. See First Bank (N.A.)—Billings v. Transamerica Insurance Co., 209 Mont. 93, 679 P.2d 1217 (1984). Anno., 16 A.L.R. 4th 11 (1982).

Query: Should the prison guards in Smith v. Wade be allowed to insure against their potential damage liability? Should these guards, through union bargaining, have the government pay for liability coverage as a fringe benefit?

9. *Vicarious Liability for Punitive Damages.* In Agarwal v. Johnson, 25 Cal.3d 932, 943 160 Cal.Rptr. 141, 152, 603 P.2d 58, 69 (1979), the California Supreme Court adopted language from several lower court cases that "while an employer may be liable for an employee's tort under the doctrine of *respondeat superior,* he is not responsible for punitive damages where he neither directed nor ratified the act. California follows the rule laid down in the Restatement of Torts, sec. 909; it provides that punitive damages can properly be awarded against a principal because of the act by an agent, if but only if, '(a) the principal authorized the doing and the manner of the act, or (b) the agent was unfit and the principal

was reckless in employing him, or (c) the agent was employed in a managerial capacity and was acting in the scope of employment, or, (d) the employer or manager of the employer ratified or approved the act.'" Accord, Loughry v. Lincoln First Bank, 67 N.Y.2d 369, 502 N.Y.S.2d 965, 494 N.E.2d 70 (1986).

Thus a defendant-principal, when doubt exists about the agent's managerial status, must request separate instructions on the principal's vicarious liability for compensatory and punitive damages. In Egan v. Mutual of Omaha Ins. Co., 24 Cal.3d 809, 157 Cal.Rptr. 482, 598 P.2d 452 (1979), the court rejected a narrow construction of the Restatement rules in determining whether employees were employed in a managerial capacity. "The determination whether employees act in a managerial capacity, however, does not necessarily hinge on their level in the corporate hierarchy. Rather the critical inquiry is the degree of discretion the employees possess in making decisions that will ultimately determine corporate policy." Insurance company claims agents were held to be managerial employees.

Compare, Stroud v. Denny's Restaurant, Inc., 271 Or. 430, 532 P.2d 790 (1975). Defendant's cook made a citizens' arrest of plaintiff for his refusal to pay for an order of toast because it came with a pat of butter rather than melted butter as the menu indicated. The court upheld an award of punitive damages. It ruled that a corporation is liable for punitive damages, regardless of whether the employee is classified as "menial" rather than "managerial," so long as the employee acts within the scope of employment.

Punitive damages imposed on corporations are borne by shareholders who are personally without malice or callousness, and who do not manage the corporation. One of the multitude of personal injury and wrongful death actions against manufacturers of asbestos products, Moran v. Johns–Manville Sales Corp., 691 F.2d 811, 817 (6th Cir.1982) states:

"We are not dissuaded from allowing punitive damages because this cost will ultimately be borne by 'innocent' shareholders. Punitive damage awards are a risk that accompanies investment. Shiman v. Frank, 625 F.2d 80 (6th Cir.1980) did not establish a contrary rule. In that case we reduced, but did not eliminate, an award of punitive damages against a union; we noted that 'the ones who will end up paying for the punitive damages award are the union members. For this reason, courts should be slow to award huge punitive damages awards against unions.' The case of a union member and shareholder are, however, not wholly analogous. Individual workers only seldom can choose which union to belong to; a group of workers cannot change bargaining agents overnight. Investors may typically place their money where they choose and withdraw it when they wish. The prospect of ultimate liability for punitive damages may encourage investors to entrust their capital to the most responsible concerns.

"JM urges with particular force that punitive damages should not be awarded against a company that faces a multitude of product liability actions. If punitive damages are awarded in many of these actions, JM argues that it will not be punished, but destroyed. We have read Judge Friendly's interesting essay on such a prospect, and its implications for the law, in Roginsky v. Richardson–Merrell, 378 F.2d 832, 838–41 (2d Cir.1967). However eloquent the essay, it is confessed dictum."

[Parenthetically, Manville Corp. (nee Johns–Manville) filed for bankruptcy.]

Government entities are not vicariously liable for punitive damages. Why not? If punitive damages are assessed against a *mutual* life insurance company for breach of a covenant of good faith and fair dealing, who ultimately must bear the burden?

10. *Vindictiveness as Basis for Punitive Damages.* Despite cautionary statements (e.g. Behrens v. Raleigh Hills Hospital, Inc., 675 P.2d 1179 (Utah 1983), some courts do allow "vindictiveness" as a basis for punitive damages in particularly inflammatory cases. "Juries may be allowed to give damages that express indignation at defendant's wrong rather than a value set on plaintiffs loss." Gostkowski v. Roman Catholic Church of the Sacred Hearts, 262 N.Y. 320, 325, 186 N.E. 798, 800 (1933). "The public benefit and a display of ethical indignation are among the ends of policy to grant punitive damages," stated the Civil Court of the City of New York approving a punitive award of $1,000 against a landlord who withheld services and repairs. Davis v. Williams, 92 Misc.2d 1051, 1054, 402 N.Y.S.2d 92, 94 (1977).

The court in Malandris v. Merrill Lynch, 447 F.Supp. 543, 547 (D.Colo.1977), cited "a sense of outrage and indignation about the callous and cavalier conduct of the defendants' agent" as a reason for a $3,000,000 punitive damage award against the brokerage firm. The firm's account executive was found to have caused plaintiff's wife to suffer severe emotional injury by the way he handled trades in stock options in connection with a $30,000 loss, half of the couple's life savings. The court of appeals reduced the punitive damages to $1,000,000. 703 F.2d 1152 (10th Cir.1981). Consider also Filartiga v. Pena–Irala, 577 F.Supp. 860 (E.D.N.Y. 1984), where an award of $5,000,000 was regarded as "appropriate to reflect adherence to the world community's proscription of torture."

Query: Should a juror ever be given free license to be vindictive in a civil action?

11. *Should Criminal Liability Bar or Mitigate Punitive Damages for the Same Act?* At least for assault and battery, an overwhelming majority considers that exemplary damages in a civil case are not barred by either the potential or actual criminal punishment of the defendant. Tuttle v. Raymond supra, p. 121. The court in Husted v. McCloud, 436 N.E.2d 341 (Ind.App.1982), stated a contrary general rule, but indicated that a defendant who negotiated immunity from criminal prosecution would still be open to punitive damages in a civil suit or that a corporation or partnership which might not be criminally liable itself could be subject to punitive damages for acts of its employees or partners.

12. *Wealth of the Defendant—Net Worth v. Net Earnings.* "The wealth of the defendant is also relevant, since the purposes of exemplary damages are to punish for a past event and to prevent future offenses, and the degree of punishment or deterrence resulting from a judgment is to some extent in proportion to the means of the guilty person." Restatement (Second) of Torts, § 908 comment e (1979). Smith v. Lightning Bolt Productions, 861 F.2d 363 (2d Cir.1988).

Cf. Fopay v. Noveroske, 31 Ill.App.3d 182, 334 N.E.2d 79 (1975). The court, in excluding evidence of "net earnings," ruled that "net worth" was the proper measure of defendant's wealth. In a products liability case the court said that punitive damages "of necessity" should relate to the wealth of the wrongdoer. Thiry v. Armstrong World Industries, 661 P.2d 515 (Okl.1983).

It has been strongly urged that, in the interest of fairness, evidence of defendant's net worth should be withheld from the jury until a judgment for plaintiff on liability has been returned. See Rupert v. Sellers, 48 A.D.2d 265, 368 N.Y.S.2d 904 (1975), for a recommended procedure. The case is noted in 44 Alb.L.Rev. 422 (1980). Hall, Pretrial Discovery of Net Worth in Punitive Damages, 54 S.Cal.L.Rev. 1141 (1981).

Why not ask the jury to assess punitive damages as a percentage of defendant's net worth without disclosing what it is?

13. *Excessive Verdicts.* The only limit on punitive damages is whether the judge's conscience is shocked. Courts frequently compare the size of the verdict to net worth. For example, $5,000,000 punitive damages was shocking and patently excessive when a corporation had a net worth of $3,500,000 and annual net income of $1,750,000. Herman v. Hess Oil Virgin Island Corp., 379 F.Supp. 1268 (D.V.I. 1974). The "net worth" calculation may make punitive damages appear miniscule for large corporate defendants: $1,000,000 is only 1/20 of 1% of Prudential Insurance Company's net worth. Pistorious v. Prudential Life Insurance Co., 123 Cal.App.3d 541, 176 Cal.Rptr. 660 (1981).

Many courts require some relationship between punitive and compensatory damages, although they reject precise ratios. For example, $10,000,000 punitive vs. $158,000 actual damages for fraud—a ratio of 63 to 1—was held excessive in Rosener v. Sears, Roebuck & Co., 110 Cal.App.3d 740, 168 Cal.Rptr. 237 (1980). Also, $40,000 punitive vs. $100 actual damages in defamation case—a 400 to 1 ratio—was held excessive in Gray v. Allison Division, General Motors Corp., 52 Ohio App.2d 348, 370 N.E.2d 747 (1977).

14. *Multiple Punitive Damages in Mass Tort Actions.* The ultimate sum of punitive damages separately awarded to individual victims of mass torts may reach menacing proportions as jury verdicts continue to come in. The potential of "punitive overkill" has encountered the charge of unconstitutional double jeopardy and lack of due process. In Palmer v. A.H. Robins Co., 684 P.2d 187 (Colo.1984), the court upheld $600,000 actual and $6,800,000 punitive damages in a single products liability case against the manufacturer of the Dalkon Shield. The court remarked that the record was devoid of a showing of past punitive damages verdicts that would make this award oppressive enough to raise a colorable due process claim. It suggested that where an adequate showing is made the trial court could simply instruct the jury, at defendant's request, to consider the amount of past punitive verdicts imposed on the defendant. *Query:* Is defense counsel likely to request this?

When Johns–Manville filed for Chapter 11 reorganization in August 1982, it pointed out that in 1981 and the first half of 1982, asbestosis litigation had resulted in ten punitive damages verdicts against it at an average of $616,000. This, of course, was still early in the unfolding scenario. The fifth circuit in Hansen v. Johns–Manville Products Corp., 734 F.2d 1036 (5th Cir.1984), after noting the foregoing data, nevertheless held that Texas law did not preclude adding another $300,000 (reduced from $1,000,000) in punitive damages in the wrongful death case before it.

Question: Is it procedurely possible, without legislation, to establish the total punitive damage liability of a products liability defendant to be parceled out amongst the individual successful plaintiffs?

15. *New Vistas in Punitive Damages.* Claiming the same power to increase punitive damages that exists for compensatory damages, a court granted plaintiffs a new trial solely on punitive damages unless the defendant agreed to an award of $5,000 punitive damages for each student-victim of a teacher's sexual abuse. Micari v. Mann, 126 Misc.2d 422, 481 N.Y.S.2d 967 (Sup.Ct.1984).

16. Most damages for negligent torts and breach of contract are discharged in the defendant's bankruptcy. Exceptions to discharge include those for debts:

(4) for fraud or defalcation while acting in a fiduciary capacity, embezzlement, or larceny; * * *

(6) for willful and malicious injury by the debtor to another entity or to the property of another entity; * * *

11 U.S.C. § 523(a).

The required degree of malice and intent as well as the effect, of state court decisions in bankruptcy court are subject to pulling and hauling. Punitive damages, however, should survive the defendant's bankruptcy.

17. Dobbs, Ending Punishment in "Punitive" Damages: Deterrence Measured Remedies, 40 Ala.L.Rev. 831 (1989).

4. ATTORNEY FEES

In the United States, under the "American Rule," litigants bear their own expenses including attorney fees. The principal exceptions to the American Rule are found in statutes, judicial doctrines and contracts. These exceptions tell whether one party will pay the other's attorney fees and, if so, the amount. Congress has created more than 100 exceptions in statutes ranging from the Civil Rights Act, 42 U.S.C. § 1988, to the Copyright Act, 17 U.S.C. § 116; each issue of Attorney Fee Awards Reporter lists all federal statutes. State legislatures have been equally active.

Major judicial doctrines are the "common fund" and the bad-faith litigation exceptions; other exceptions call for attorney fees when defendant's breach of contract or tort leads plaintiff into litigation with a third party, Peters v. Lyons, 168 N.W.2d 759 (Iowa 1969); Gavcus v. Potts, p. 15 supra, or as an item of damages when suing for malicious prosecution.

When contracts call for the breaching party to pay the nonbreaching party's attorney fees, as many form contracts do, courts routinely award attorney fees to the nonbreaching party.

SALA v. NATIONAL RAILROAD PASSENGER CORPORATION

United States District Court, Eastern District of Pennsylvania, 1989.
721 F.Supp. 80.

RAYMOND J. BRODERICK, DISTRICT JUDGE. In this class action in mass tort, plaintiffs' legal counsel, Fine, Kaplan and Black of Philadelphia and Williams & Connolly of Washington, D.C., have produced a settlement valued approximately at $1.79 million, including accrued interest. Counsel now moves jointly for an award of attorneys' fees amounting to one-third of the settlement fund, in addition to costs of $97,538.56.

The underlying litigation arose out of a collision between Amtrak Train No. 66 (The Night Owl) and a 17-ton piece of track equipment during the early morning hours of January 29, 1988. * * * Upon impact, The Night Owl's two engines and eight cars derailed, injuring an estimated forty to fifty passengers. Fortunately, no one was killed. * * *

Although some passengers on The Night Owl suffered concussions and one lost several teeth, most of those who eventually became class members sustained "soft tissue" injuries, such as bruises, strains, and stiffness. Twenty-one class members received medical attention, and eleven missed some work. Plaintiffs also later reported either temporary or enduring emotional injury and various degrees of pain and suffering. The most common psychological malady experienced was a fear of travel, which has hampered a few class members from properly fulfilling job responsibilities.

Marta Sala commenced this action against Amtrak on February 25, 1988. Her complaint, filed on behalf of herself and all other passengers injured in the accident, sought compensatory and punitive damages against Amtrak for alleged negligence and willful misconduct. This Court granted class certification pursuant to Federal Rules of Civil Procedure 23(a) and (b)(3) on April 29, 1988. Seeking dismissal of plaintiffs' punitive damages claims, Amtrak then filed a motion for partial summary judgment, which the Court denied on June 14, 1989. The parties submitted a detailed pre-trial order on June 19, and plaintiffs filed six motions *in limine.* On the last business day before trial, scheduled for June 26, the parties agreed to a settlement, which the Court later approved.

The Supreme Court has recognized that a "litigant who recovers a common fund for the benefit of persons other than himself or his client is entitled to a reasonable attorney's fee from the fund as a whole." *Boeing Co. v. Van Gemert,* 444 U.S. 472, 478 (1980). This common fund doctrine rests on the perception that individuals who profit from a lawsuit "without contributing to its costs are unjustly enriched at the successful litigant's expense." *Boeing Co.* To prevent this inequitable result, a court may assess fees against the entire fund and thereby spread litigation costs proportionately among those whom the suit benefits. Similarly, the Third Circuit has noted that in the class action context, attorneys who create a settlement fund are entitled to recover fees against that fund. "The award of fees under the equitable fund doctrine is analogous to an action in quantum meruit; the individual seeking compensation has, by his actions, benefited another and seeks payment for the value of the service performed." Lindy Bros. Builders v. American Radiator & Standard Sanitary Corp. (Lindy I), 487 F.2d 161, 165 (3d Cir.1973).

Although it is well established that attorneys' fees may be drawn from a fund in court, there is some controversy regarding the proper method by which the amount of compensation should be calculated. Until 1973, the size of the fee award in both common fund cases and statutory fee shifting cases was left to the court's discretion. "Awards often reflected what the court believed was a 'reasonable percentage' of the amount recovered." Court Awarded Attorney Fees: Report of the Third Circuit Task Force (1985), reprinted in 108 F.R.D. 237, 242. Although judges at that time utilized a multitude of factors in establishing amounts for fee awards, they relied most heavily on "the size of the fund or the amount of benefit produced for the class." Yet, given the open-ended and contextual nature of the reasonable percentage standard, it often was maligned as investing unlimited discretion in trial judges, producing inconsistent results, and authorizing the collection of windfall profits by attorneys.

Responding to these criticisms, the Third Circuit, in *Lindy I* and *Lindy II,* developed the lodestar method of setting fees. This approach is composed of two steps. First, to determine the "lodestar," the court multiplies the hours spent on the case by a reasonable hourly rate of compensation for each attorney involved. Second, the court adjusts that figure to reflect the contingent nature of the litigation and the quality of the attorney's work. The Supreme Court, however, reasoning that the latter step is largely subsumed within the former, has curtailed the availability of contingency and quality enhancements to the lodestar. See Pennsylvania v. Delaware Valley Citizens' Council for Clean Air (Delaware Valley II), 483 U.S. 711 (1987).

With the advent of *Lindy,* courts soon began applying the lodestar formulation to both equitable fund and statutory fee cases "without any real analysis of the propriety of doing so," and even though the "public policy considerations in the two situations are not obviously identical." In particular, "rather than being based on the equitable notion that those who have benefited from litigation should share its costs," fee shifting provisions were intended to encourage the private enforcement of those substantive rights that " 'Congress considered of the highest importance.' " But because civil rights claims often produce only nominal damages or else declarations of rights, which do not translate easily into pecuniary terms, Carey v. Piphus, 435 U.S. 247, 266 (1978), fee awards reflecting the reasonable number of hours expended, instead of the amount of money recovered, were thought necessary to induce competent counsel to undertake representation of civil rights plaintiffs. See e.g., City of Riverside v. Rivera, 477 U.S. 561, 577 (1986) (plurality opinion) ("[T]he contingent fee arrangements that make legal services available to many victims of personal injuries would often not encourage lawyers to accept civil rights cases, which frequently involve substantial expenditures of time and effort but produce only small monetary recoveries.") In contrast, the minimum compensation guaranteed to prevailing plaintiffs' attorneys by the *Lindy* approach is not needed "in the traditional fund case or in those statutory fee cases likely to produce a sizeable fund from which counsel fees could be paid." Of course, this Court does not presume to criticize *Lindy* and its progeny. Rather, like the Task Force, it perceives merely that applying variant fee recovery methods to these two categories of actions will best achieve the differing policy objectives each was designed to further.

Moreover, the Supreme Court not only has distinguished between fund-in-court and statutory fee cases, it also has recognized the propriety of employing the percentage of recovery method in the common fund context. "Unlike the calculation of attorney's fees under the 'common fund doctrine,' where a reasonable fee is based on a percentage of the fund bestowed on the class, a reasonable fee under [fee shifting statutes] reflects the amount of attorney time reasonably expended on the litigation." Blum v. Stenson, 465 U.S. 886, 901 n. 16 (1984). In the wake of *Blum,* several courts have held that the percentage of recovery method is an acceptable basis upon which to calculate fee awards. [citations] The Court therefore concludes that in equitable fund situations it typically should employ a percentage of recovery approach in setting attorneys' fees. As there are no circumstances suggesting its application would be unjust, the Court will employ the percentage method in this case.

Because the instant suit involves a straightforward common fund, certain principles guide our disposition of plaintiffs' motion. First, the district court retains discretion to calculate the fee. *Task Force Report,* 108 F.R.D. at 256. Courts have allowed attorney compensation ranging from 19 to 45% of the settlement fund created. [citations] In general, the percentage of recovery fee should "decrease as the size of the fund increases." Second, because of "the potential for conflict of interest between the attorneys seeking compensation and the clients" in the equitable fund context, "the trial court has an independent duty to scrutinize fee applications." [citations] The Court does note, however, that no class members have registered exceptions to counsel's request for fees comprising one-third of the settlement fund or to the proposed reimbursement for expenses.

The Court has examined both the fee petition submitted by plaintiffs' counsel and the entire record of this litigation. Based on that review, we conclude that the class was well served by experienced counsel who effectively prosecuted a case that presented vexing factual, legal, and logistical difficulties, but who nonetheless obtained a highly favorable recovery.

Petitioners also brought this action to a close only sixteen months after filing the complaint, despite the problems with which they contended. This is precisely the sort of result that the percentage of recovery fee method is intended to foster and stands as a counterexample to complaints about the slow pace of complex litigation. Moreover, plaintiffs' counsel terminated this controversy by settlement and thereby avoided burdening the federal judicial system with a trial and appeals. Because "a prompt and efficient attorney who achieves a fair settlement without litigation serves both his client and the interests of justice," McKenzie Constr. Co. v. Maynard, 758 F.2d 97, 101–02 (3d Cir.1985), courts and legal commentators sensibly have rejected the view that early settlement necessarily should reduce the amount of the fee award. [citations] Indeed, this Court has stated that "it would be the height of folly to penalize an efficient attorney for settling a case on the ground that less total hours were expended in the litigation."

The Court also finds, however, that the percentage of recovery fee should decrease as the size of the common fund increases. The employment of a sliding scale * * * was recommended by the Third Circuit Task Force. For example, in situations involving funds comparable in magnitude to the one extracted here, courts have awarded percentage of recovery fees comprising 25 to 30% of the fund. [citations] Recognition of this general inverse relationship between fund and fee—in conjunction with a healthy acknowledgment that the setting of attorney compensation will never be an exact science and that the percentage of recovery fee approach is extremely particularistic—assists in explaining the facially disparate award percentages that some critics have identified in equitable fund cases.

In light of the foregoing, the Court will grant to the applicants jointly attorneys' fees in the amount of $570,333.00, which constitutes 33% of the first million dollars in settlement plus 30% of the remainder between one and two million dollars, or slightly less than 32% of the total fund of $1,790,000.

We note [that Professor Coffee] has suggested that in order to avoid allowing the kind of windfall fee awards which depressed support for the percentage of recovery method in the first place, courts should compare the level of compensation to be granted under the percentage approach with that which the lodestar time formula would produce. [citation] In this case, either approach yields substantially the same award. Counsel for the class documented a collective expenditure of over 3500 attorney and paralegal hours during the course of this action. According to their petition and affidavits, application of the *Lindy* method would produce an unenhanced attorneys' fee of $545,224.58. * * * Even a modest delay enhancement would render the lodestar product essentially identical in size to the one permitted today under the reasonable percentage approach. * * *

IT IS ORDERED that plaintiffs' counsel are jointly awarded $570,333.00 in attorneys' fees and $97,538.56 in costs, for a total award of $667,871.56, to be paid from the common fund established pursuant to the Settlement Agreement approved by this Court on September 27, 1989.

Notes

1. Skelton v. General Motors Corp., 860 F.2d 250 (7th Cir.1988), cert. denied, 110 S.Ct. 53 (1988), was brought under a fee shifting statute, the Magnuson–Moss Act, and produced a $17,000,000 "common fund" to divide among beneficiaries. Plaintiffs' attorneys had agreed to take their fee from the fund and to calculate it on an hourly basis; but they sought a 75% multiplier to enhance fees because they had taken a risk of losing. The court of appeals found that the Act's language that fees will be "based on actual time expended" did not bar a risk multiplier and remanded to the trial judge to determine whether 75% was a proper multiplier.

2. A.G. Ship Maintenance Corp. v. Lezak, 69 N.Y.2d 1, 3–6, 511 N.Y.S.2d 216, 217–19, 503 N.E.2d 681, 682–84 (1986), discussed "whether a court may, in the absence of legislation authorizing it to do so, impose a sanction upon an attorney or litigant appearing before it who asserts frivolous claims or pursues frivolous pretrial proceedings." * * *

"For purposes of this appeal, we accept respondent's contention that petitioner instituted these proceedings without any legal or factual justification and that the courts below would be warranted in granting him attorneys' fees and disbursements if they had the power to do so. Moreover, we recognize that frivolous court proceedings present a growing problem which must be deterred. Indeed, the problem is larger than the difficulties highlighted by the facts of this case, extending beyond the institution of vexatious litigation or the assertion of meritless defenses or counterclaims and including baseless procedures pursued to gain tactical advantage in a lawsuit or to exhaust an opponent. Such practices not only injure and debilitate the honest litigant, but they also waste judicial resources. Existing remedies for such conduct, such as disciplinary proceedings for attorneys, contempt or possibly criminal proceedings if perjury is involved, or seeking redress in a separate action for damages on theories of malicious prosecution or abuse of process have not proved effective to deter frivolous litigation in the past. Thus, the assessment of attorneys' fees and disbursements has become the single most important device suggested to deter such misconduct. [citations] We are asked to approve such awards either as a sanction authorized under the exercise of the court's inherent powers or to create a new remedy or cause of action which may be asserted within the action itself to provide a prompt remedy to an aggrieved party.

"Under the general rule, attorneys' fees and disbursements are incidents of litigation and the prevailing party may not collect them from the loser unless an award is authorized by agreement between the parties or by statute or court rule. [citations] The rule is based upon the high priority accorded free access to the courts and a desire to avoid placing barriers in the way of those desiring judicial redress of wrongs. The preferred remedy for deterring malicious or vexatious litigation has been the use of separate, plenary actions after the challenged proceedings have concluded. * * *

"Under the State Constitution the authority to regulate practice and procedure in the courts is delegated primarily to the Legislature (N.Y.Const., art. VI, § 30). There are some matters which are not subject to legislative control because they deal with the inherent nature of the judicial function. [citation] Generally, however, the Legislature has the power to prescribe rules of practice governing court proceedings, and any rules the courts adopt must be consistent with existing legislation and may be subsequently abrogated by statute. [citation] In addition, court rules must be adopted in accordance with procedures prescribed by the Constitution and statute. [citation]

"The Legislature has not been indifferent to the problems suggested by this case. [Examples omitted.] It has not addressed the problem generally, however. Thus because frivolous litigation is so serious a problem affecting the proper administration of justice, the courts may proscribe such conduct and impose sanctions in this exercise of their rule-making powers, in the absence of legislation to the contrary (see, N.Y.Const., art. VI, § 30; Judiciary Law § 211[1][b]).

"It is not necessary to determine whether the power of the courts to impose sanctions for frivolous proceedings is inherent to the judicial function or is merely delegable by the Legislature under our Constitution. The fact is that the most practicable means for establishing appropriate standards and procedures which will provide an effective tool for dealing with this problem is by plenary rule rather than by ad hoc judicial decisions.

"Thus in the case now before us sanctions cannot be imposed because at the time the petitioner instituted the proceeding, there was neither a statute nor a court rule authorizing the imposition of sanctions for frivolous actions."

In June 1991, differing from the *Lezak* court above, the United States Supreme Court held in Chambers v. Nasco, Inc., 111 S.Ct. 2123 (1991), that, under the bad faith exception to the American rule, a federal district judge had inherent power to sanction abusive, bad-faith misconduct related to litigation by requiring the party to pay his opponent's attorney fees.

3. Under existing procedural rules, judges may assess attorney fees against counsel who abuse the judicial process. Fed.R.Civ.P. 11, 16, 26, and 37.

4. In Alyeska Pipeline Service Co. v. Wilderness Society, 421 U.S. 240 (1975), the Supreme Court rejected the argument that an equitable exception to the American Rule existed for "private attorney generals" who create significant public benefits through litigation. Following this decision Congress enacted the Civil Rights Attorney's Fees Act of 1976, 42 U.S.C. § 1988 to allow attorney fees under the federal civil rights act.

The California Supreme Court authorized attorney fees on the private attorney general theory where litigants vindicated a public policy based on a constitutional theory. Serrano v. Priest, 20 Cal.3d 25, 141 Cal.Rptr. 315, 569 P.2d 1303 (1977), aff'd, Serrano v. Unruh, 32 Cal.3d 621, 186 Cal.Rptr. 754, 652 P.2d 985 (1982). The California legislature passed a statute that allows attorney fees where litigation results in a significant pecuniary or nonpecuniary benefit to the public. Cal.Civ. Proc.Code § 1021.5.

5. Litigation over the amount of statutory attorney fees, particularly under the Civil Rights Act, is one of the nation's most popular indoor sports.

Grendel's Den, Inc. v. Larkin, 749 F.2d 945, 949, 952–57 (1st Cir.1984), may be somewhat atypical except for the judicial attention to examining the minute details concerning the number of hours, the proper hourly charge, and the reasonableness of expenses.

Having prevailed in civil rights action in the Supreme Court in Larkin v. Grendel's Den, 459 U.S. 116 (1982), the successful attorneys applied for fees. Some of the issues the court examined were: whether professors must support requests for attorney fees with contemporaneous time records; whether Professor Tribe spent too much time reading opponents' briefs, writing briefs and preparing for oral argument; whether Professor Tribe's "relevant community" for fee rate was that of "nationally prominent constitutional law scholars" or "the Boston Market" and his prior charges; and the proper amount to charge for hotel board and room for the argument before the Supreme Court.

6. In Evans v. Jeff D., 475 U.S. 717 (1986), plaintiffs brought a § 1983 class action claiming that the state had provided deficient health and education services. The state agreed to a settlement conditioned upon a fee waiver. The Supreme Court ruled that it was not an abuse of discretion for the district judge to approve a settlement which included a complete fee waiver. What are the implications of this decision for Civil Rights lawyers?

Chapter 3

INTRODUCTION TO EQUITABLE REMEDIES

A. EQUITABLE JURISDICTION

1. POWER OF A COURT DISTINGUISHED FROM EQUITABLE JURISDICTION

CHAFEE, SOME PROBLEMS OF EQUITY

(The Thomas M. Cooley Lectures) 301–306 (1950).

"JURISDICTION" AND "EQUITY JURISDICTION"

"Jurisdiction" is one of those words which keeps jumping around. In equity cases it is used in at least four different senses:

(1) *Jurisdiction considered internationally—does the sovereign have power to deal with this matter and these persons?* This can be taken for granted in all the situations discussed in this chapter.

(2) *Has the sovereign entrusted the decision of the particular case to this court?* Here we have to look at constitutions and statutes. They usually deal with two aspects of jurisdiction:

(a) *Jurisdiction over the person.* Unless certain conditions are fulfilled as to service of process, the court has no power to adjudicate the rights and duties of the parties. Any order it makes is void by the "due process" clauses and is not entitled to "full faith and credit" in another court. This chapter will assume that jurisdiction over all the parties has been properly obtained.

(b) *Jurisdiction over the subject matter.* By this, says Mr. Justice Miller, "is meant the nature of the cause of action and of the relief sought." Some courts have powers limited to specified kinds of crimes or controversies, such as police courts, probate courts, etc. Some tribunals can take only civil suits involving less than $100 or $500, or some other maximum. Still, we are chiefly interested in courts of general jurisdiction which, in almost every state today, deal with what used to be actions at law and suits in equity. Their jurisdiction over the subject matter is rarely limited at all, except that certain types of disputes, e.g., over workmen's compensation, are frequently given by statutes to administrative boards and not to judges. So far as state courts go, we can usually be sure that if the court can entertain suits in equity at all, then it does have jurisdiction over the subject matter of any dispute which is brought before it of the sort I am going to discuss. We cannot take this for granted as to the United States district courts, because the Constitution and Congress have imposed certain special requisites such as a federal question or diversity of citizenship, an amount in controversy over [$50,000], etc., which are commonly thought to be limitations on the power of the federal judges. However, it is not necessary to go into that problem now. If these requisites are satisfied, as we shall assume in the present chapter, we can say that a federal district court almost always has jurisdiction over the subject matter. Yet we do have to consider the possibility of further Congressional limitations on federal judicial power, particularly the effect of the Norris–LaGuardia Act (to be examined in the next chapter). But aside from such special situations, if the decrees I am going to discuss (either state or federal) are indeed void and capable of being disobeyed with impunity, it will not be for want of power in the court over either the parties or the subject matter. The jurisdictional defect must be found elsewhere.

(3) *Equity jurisdiction—is there a proper basis for coming into equity?* This third meaning is obviously the heart of our problems, and I shall return to it in a moment.

(4) Finally, courts sometimes speak of having "jurisdiction" or not, when they are really deciding *whether they ought to exercise equitable jurisdiction.* When the word is employed in this unfortunate and confusing sense, it is wholly disconnected with the existence of power. Of course, the court possesses the power in such cases, but power alone is not enough to justify relief.

"O, it is excellent

To have a giant's strength; but it is tyrannous,

To use it like a giant."

One of the chief troubles with the frequent preoccupation of judges with questions of power is that it makes them slide over much more important questions of wisdom and fairness which ought to receive careful attention. For example, the whole field of injunctions to protect interests of personality has been messed up because of too much talk about jurisdiction and too little talk about whether an injunction will do any good. Still, important as exercise of jurisdiction surely is, it is simply a bundle of sound principles of decision, delimiting the judge's duty but not his power. Everybody agrees that a decree which is mistaken exercise of jurisdiction must be obeyed so long as it is in force.

Now, come back to "equity jurisdiction." The basic problem of most of this chapter is this: Is equity jurisdiction really jurisdictional? That is the traditional view. Even though jurisdiction is present in the first two senses, the court still lacks power to grant equitable relief unless in addition the plaintiff has a reason for coming into equity.

The opposite view, which I shall advocate as desirable, is that today, with law and equity merged in a single court, "equity jurisdiction" like exercise of jurisdiction is simply a bundle of sound principles of decision concerning particular kinds of relief. Only the first two senses of "jurisdiction" are elements of power, and both the third and fourth senses concern right action. "If the court has jurisdiction of the subject matter and of the parties nothing further is required" to make the decree an order which must be obeyed until modified. If the court gives specific relief contrary to all the precedents, that is merely reversible error and not absence of power. What Mr. Justice Stone said with regard to "equitable jurisdiction" in the federal courts is equally desirable in the state courts:

> "Whether a suitor is entitled to equitable relief * * * other jurisdictional requirements being satisfied, is strictly not a question of jurisdiction in the sense of the power of a * * * court to act. It is a question only of the merits; whether the case is one for the peculiar type of relief which a court of equity is competent to give."

In other words, when a suit for some kind of specific relief is brought in a regular trial court and the parties are properly served or appear voluntarily (or it is a case of jurisdiction over a res within the court's control), then in my opinion the judge has power to decide, rightly or wrongly, whether to give the relief sought or a different kind of relief or no relief at all. The legislature and settled judge-made rules have placed at his disposal several kinds of remedies—damages, ouster from possession of land, specific performance, injunction, etc. If he gives a remedy which used to be issued in a separate court of chancery before David Dudley Field and the Judicature Act of 1873 when he ought to choose damages instead, he should of course be reversed, but he has the power to choose wrongly and his decree must be obeyed until reversed or stayed. The appellate court may declare equity jurisdiction wanting, but this is merely equivalent to saying that he has disregarded sound principles of decision and made a wrong choice. In the witty words of Mr. Sabel, "Equity jurisdiction has as little to do with jurisdiction as quasi-contracts has to do with contracts."

Before going any further, I hope it is clear that equity jurisdiction is something entirely different from jurisdiction over the subject matter. Perhaps they coincided to some extent when equity was administered in a separate court of chancery, for then, unless the bill averred some reason for coming into equity, that court had no business at all to do anything about the case. For example, it can be said that the chancellor had no jurisdiction over the subject matter of a suit seeking damages for negligent injuries to the person. But the separate court of chancery is as extinct as the separate estate of a married woman. Nowadays, so far as regular trial courts administering both law and equity are concerned, jurisdiction over the subject matter exists when the constitution or the legislature or the unwritten law has told *this court* to do *something* about *this kind of dispute.*

MOORE v. McALLISTER

Supreme Court of Maryland, 1958.
216 Md. 497, 141 A.2d 176.

HORNEY, JUDGE. This appeal presents a technical question of jurisdiction. * * *

(The Moores) filed a bill in the Circuit Court for Dorchester County complaining that * * * (McAllister) was encroaching upon, and interfering with the lawful use of, a 50 foot strip of land situated between the respective tracts of the opposing parties, and extending from the Sharptown–Eldorado state highway approximately 3,000 feet to the northwest fork of the Nanticoke River. The Moores contend (i) that they own the strip of land, (ii) that for more than twenty years they have used a single track roadway which has always existed within the limits of the strip, and (iii) that McAllister has plowed, planted, and tilled crops on the strip as if it were his own. In addition to alleging irreparable damage, the Moores further claim that the roadway is the only access to their tract, and that the destruction thereof had caused them great distress and hardship. The bill sought a permanent injunction and further relief. McAllister, by his answer, admits that his property is bounded by a 50 foot strip of land, but denies that the roadway described in the bill lies within the strip referred to in the deeds. He contends that the roadway which he has plowed, and otherwise tilled, lies either wholly or partly within the lines of his own property. * * * The chancellor passed an order for a hearing, but before the hearing was commenced, he dismissed the bill by a final decree for the reason that he was satisfied that the court was without jurisdiction to determine the issues raised by the pleadings. From the decree of dismissal, the Moores appealed.

Although the appeal presents other minor points or questions of law, the only *real* question for us to decide is whether the chancellor under the circumstances in this case could raise, on his own motion, the lack of jurisdiction to hear and determine a title dispute on the theory that there was an adequate remedy at law.

There is no doubt that in the early decisions, an injunction would not be granted to restrain a trespass where title was in dispute between the parties until the question of title had been settled by an action at law. It was axiomatic that equity would not determine a controversy involving the *legal* title to land. There is, however, no clear exposition in the decisions of the reason for the rule.[1] The cases simply state the rule without explaining its origin. It certainly could not rest upon the question-begging maxim that "equity will not determine *legal* rights," for quite often equity would determine controversies involving the construction of purely legal rights and questions of fact. In specific performance cases, for example, equity did not hesitate to construe the law and determine the facts as to whether a valid legal contract existed or not.

Great respect for the rule was engendered in 1801 when Lord Eldon in Pillsworth v. Hopton, 6 Ves. 51, refused an injunction against a defendant in possession, it appearing that the plaintiff had failed in an action of ejectment. He said:

> "I remember perfectly being told from the bench very early in my life, that if the plaintiff filed a bill for an account, and an injunction to restrain waste, stating that the defendant claimed by a title adverse to his, he stated himself out of the Court as to the injunction."

Gradually, however, the judiciary in both England and the United States began to realize that there was no longer any good reason for the rule. Exception after exception have whittled away the rule from time to time to such an extent that by 1952 Judge Markell in Lichtenberg v. Sachs, 1952, 200 Md. 145, 88 A.2d 450, 455 was able to say:

1. [Footnote renumbered.] Legal historians suggest that the reasons for the rule were: (i) the practical difficulty of settling questions of title before the Chancellor, sitting only at Westminster, by requiring litigants to appear there from all parts of England, while from the beginning, through judges of assize and their successors, questions of title were tried locally at common law; and (ii) the method of trial by deposition in equity was not as satisfactory as trial by oral testimony in open court at law.

"Whether or not in the course of a century the rule that equity ordinarily has not jurisdiction to enjoin trespasses or interference with easements until after title has been established at law has become an exception and the exceptions to the rule have become the rule is a speculation we need not pursue." * * *

The trend away from the stricter rule in cases seeking an injunction to restrain a trespass where the title was in dispute began with White v. Flannigain, [1 Md. 525] decided in 1852, when this Court declared that "a court of equity will not, as a general rule, interfere by injunction, to restrain a mere trespass, * * * to land; but that it *will* so interfere under certain circumstances, * * * [to] prevent irreparable mischief or ruin."

When there is a *real* dispute as to the legal title to land—sufficient to constitute substantial doubt as to who is the owner thereof—and a question of the jurisdiction of equity to try the issue has been properly and seasonably raised, then the question of ownership must be determined in a court of law. The proper procedure in such an event was laid down in 1887 by this Court in Clayton v. Shoemaker, 67 Md. at page 221, 9 A. at page 637:

"There should be a temporary injunction prohibiting the [defendant] from proceeding with the erection of his building until the title has been decided in a court of law * * *. The plaintiffs below should be required to immediately institute an action at law, with a view to have their title determined; and if they fail to do so, or, having done so, are unsuccessful in maintaining their title, the injunction should be dissolved. But, if the decision of a court of law is adverse to the claim of title set up by the defendant below, the injunction should be made perpetual." * * *

But when there is no *real* dispute over the title, or when there has been a waiver of jurisdiction, a court of equity has full and complete jurisdiction to try and determine the question of title.

When there is no real dispute over the legal title sought to be protected, or when such title is not in doubt, there is no reason to require the parties to resort to a court of law to determine the title issue * * *.

Likewise, when a defendant to a bill in equity files an answer, and does not think it proper or omits to make objection by the pleadings to the jurisdiction of equity to try and determine the question of title, he is deemed to have waived jurisdiction, and the equity court should proceed to try the issue * * *.

Whether the chancellor had a right to raise the lack of jurisdiction requires a limited inquiry into the meaning of that equivocal word "jurisdiction." Juridically, jurisdiction refers to two quite distinct concepts: (i) the *power* of a court to render a valid decree, and (ii) the *propriety* of granting the relief sought. To ascertain whether a court has power, it is necessary to consult the Constitution of the State and the applicable statutes. * * * If jurisdiction is lacking in this sense, a decree rendered by the court would be void. This is so because in such cases there are no circumstances whatever which could give the court jurisdiction. * * * Stated otherwise, there is a fundamental lack of jurisdiction over the parties or the subject matter, or both. * * * Under such circumstances, before a decree is even rendered, there is no doubt that the court may—indeed it should—dismiss the action on its own motion. Furthermore, where the court lacks power to decide a case, such fundamental jurisdiction cannot be conferred by waiver or consent of the parties. * * * For instance, the parties to an automobile accident could not confer jurisdiction by consent on a court of equity.

Originally the term "equity jurisdiction" referred to the category of controversies that a court of equity was authorized to decide. So long as the principles of equity were administered by separate courts, questions of equity jurisdiction were often considered to be jurisdictional in the strict sense, i.e., if the cause of action was not of a kind that fell within the province of the chancellor, a court of equity had no power to decide the case. However, in those states where law and equity have been merged, equity jurisdiction is something entirely different from jurisdiction over the subject matter. See Chafee, Some Problems of Equity (1950) 305–6. Thus, in those states which have a single system of courts administering principles of both law and equity, the lack of equity jurisdiction does not necessarily mean that the court lacks power to adjudicate the controversy, but only means that under the historic principles of equity the party seeking relief is not entitled to it. There the concept of equity jurisdiction is one that relates to the question of the merits of a controversy rather than to the basic power of the court to decide the case. As Mr. Justice Holmes stated in Massachusetts State Grange v. Benton, 1926, 272 U.S. 525:

> "Courts sometimes say that there is no jurisdiction in equity when they mean only that equity ought not to give the relief asked. In a strict sense the Court in this case had jurisdiction. It had power to grant an injunction, and if it had granted one its decree, although wrong, would not have been void."

Some law writers think that in states where there are still separate equity courts, equity jurisdiction is a fundamental question of power. However, the late Professor Chafee of Harvard pointed out the fallacy of this point of view. It is unsound, he said, to suppose that a chancellor has no power to deal with a suit for equitable relief if he was wrong in deciding that the remedy at law was inadequate without having evidence to support such conclusion. Chafee, supra, 327–32. As Lord Sumner said in the Privy Council in Rex v. Nat Bell Liquors, Ltd., 2 L.R. [1922] A.C. 128:

> "How a magistrate, who has acted within his jurisdiction up to the point at which the missing evidence should have been, but was not, given, can, thereafter, be said, by a kind of relation back, to have had no jurisdiction over the charge at all, it is hard to see."

Maryland has adopted the theory that equity jurisdiction does not relate to the *power* of the chancellor. In Fooks' Executors v. Ghingher, 1937, 172 Md. 612, 192 A. 782, there is an elaborate discussion on the meanings of and differences between "jurisdiction" and "equity jurisdiction." This was an equity suit to enforce the liability of a stockholder in an insolvent bank which should have been brought on the law side of the court since the assessment sought was for the full par value of the stock. There was no appeal from the decree entered against the stockholder. Two years later he attempted to obtain relief from the decree, alleging that it was void for lack of jurisdiction. We stated that if equity jurisdiction were a question of power, the decree would have been void. However, since the lack of equity jurisdiction only rendered the decree voidable, the issue could not be raised after the time for appeal had expired. * * *

In a case such as the one now before us, where the objection to equity jurisdiction is the existence of an adequate remedy at law, and the objection goes merely to the *propriety* rather than the *power* to act, the courts have generally held that the chancellor has the *discretionary* power to decide whether to dismiss the case on his own motion. The disposition that a court can make of a case, i.e., whether it must dismiss the bill or may simply transfer it to the law court, might very well affect the exercise of its discretion.

In a jurisdiction, unlike Maryland, where a case improperly brought in equity may not be transferred to a court of law, the chancellor has only two alternatives: either retain the bill, or dismiss it, and thereby compel the complaining party to commence anew. * * *

In a jurisdiction, like Maryland, which has a statute or rule of court, such as Maryland Rule 515, permitting the transfer of actions from equity to law or vice versa, it is generally erroneous to dismiss the suit absolutely, either on motion of the defendant or on the chancellor's own motion, merely because the remedy at law is adequate, the usual procedure being to transfer the action to the law side. However, although the chancellor should not *dismiss* the bill on his own motion, he can raise the question himself and then transfer the action. * * *

[Reversed.]

Note

For the present state of Maryland law, see Bourne & Lynch, Merger of Law and Equity Under the Revised Maryland Rules: Does It Threaten Trial By Jury?, 14 U.Balt.L.Rev. 1 (1984).

2. EQUITY ACTS IN PERSONAM

a. Introduction

GLENN AND REDDEN, EQUITY: A VISIT TO THE FOUNDING FATHERS

31 Va.L.Rev. 753, 770–773 (1945).

(Reprinted with permission of the Virginia Law Review Association).

In an artificial period, say from the middle nineteenth century backwards into the seventeenth, our judges were fond of quoting so called "maxims of equity." Some of these made sense, others did not; but they owe their place to "a bouquet of highsounding maxims" which the Chancellors obtained from the canon law where Roman law had found a second home. Thus, it was natural for early Chancellors, being churchmen, to draw upon this treasury to point up their deliverances, although they did not intend to "Romanize the law of England." One of the "maxims of equity," however, has no such definite lineage; and yet, in describing the action of the court, it is, as the late Dean Keener of Columbia used to say, "the only maxim of equity that is really true." Such then, is the rule to which chapters of old treatises used to be devoted, or sections at least, that "Equity acts against the person."

Now this is important in any study of equitable jurisdiction. Of course the exigencies of later years forced statutory aids that are now commonplace; and sometimes the action of an equity court may seem to be *in rem,* although in the last analysis it will be plain that the court was really acting upon the person. Many arguments have been intended to show that equity does not necessarily act *in personam.* Sometimes latter day courts will voice the same doubt; but, taking it by and large, one will find that the ancient idea has never been impaired. In any event, the reader will learn that this principle is his best working tool if, indeed, it is not his key to the workshop.

How this principle worked is shown by a case for which we are indebted to Dean Ames, who took the Year Book version (it was also later reported in Jenkin's Century Cases, but in digest form), translated it into our own English, and included it within his Cases on Equity. It is J.R. v. M.P., decided by the Common Pleas in 1457. [37 Hen. VI fol. 13, pl. 3 (1459)] There the Chancellor had directed a man to surrender a bond to the chancery clerk for cancellation. That was because the bond lacked a valid consideration, but the point could not be raised in an action at law, inasmuch as by the common law ideas of that day neither lack of consideration, nor the illegality of such consideration as had been given, was available as a defense at law. It was equally clear, on the other hand, that if the holder of the bond should be unable to "make profert" of it, or produce it upon the trial of his action at law, then he could not recover. Hence, to require him to surrender the bond to a chancery clerk for purposes of destruction, would be the relief *in personam* that would precisely fit the case of the debtor upon such an obligation. But if this direction is not obeyed, and the bond, intact, is triumphantly produced upon the trial at law, then what happens?

Well, the answer to that question will be found in a study of J.R. v. M.P., and cases of a far later date as well. It will also be observed that in J.R. v. M.P. the recalcitrant creditor who disobeyed the Chancellor's direction to turn in his bond for cancellation, was languishing in the Fleet, a famous prison which still flourished in Dickens's time. Does the reader remember the "Chancery prisoner" whom Mr. Pickwick met in the Fleet? But in J.R. v. M.P., the Chancery prisoner had managed to get the bond into the hands of his attorney, and it was the latter who attended the trial of the action that was brought upon the bond and produced it in court as evidence. In later days that attorney might have found himself in trouble with the Chancellor because modern injunctions run not only against the party, but also "his attorneys, agents, and servants", but that is a minor point. The things here to be observed are that (a) the Chancellor's ruling, "this bond is bad," did not make it bad, and so we have an illustration of the point that equity does not act *in rem;* but (b) if the ruling had been obeyed, it would have resulted in no bond at all, and thus the ends of equity would have been fulfilled; hence (c) the jurisdiction of equity is accomplished, not by pronouncements, but by the coercion of action on the part of the defendant. Therein the Chancery differs from a court of law, which acts *in rem,* and necessarily must.

POMEROY, EQUITY JURISPRUDENCE

Volume I, Section 428, page 469 (1881).

In the infancy of the court of chancery, while the chancellors were developing their system in the face of a strong opposition, in order to avoid a direct collision with the law and with the judgments of law courts, they adopted the principle that their own remedies and decrees should operate *in personam* upon defendants and not *in rem.* The meaning of this simply is, that a decree of a court of equity, while declaring the equitable estate, interest, or right of the plaintiff to exist, did not operate by its own intrinsic force to vest the plaintiff with the legal estate, interest, or right to which he was pronounced entitled; it was not itself a legal title, nor could it either directly or indirectly transfer the title from the defendant to the plaintiff. A decree of chancery spoke in terms of personal command to the defendant, but its directions could only be carried into effect by his personal act. It declared, for example, that the plaintiff was equitable owner of certain land, the legal title of which was held by the defendant, and ordered the defendant to execute a conveyance of the estate; his own voluntary act was necessary to carry the decree into execution; if he refused to convey, the court could endeavor to compel his obedience by fine and imprisonment. The decree never stood as a title in the place of an actual conveyance by the defendant; nor was it ever carried into effect by any officer acting in the defendant's name.

H. HANBURY & D. YARDLEY, ENGLISH COURTS OF LAW

95–96 (5th ed., 1979).

Reproduced with permission of Oxford University Press, London.

In what did equitable procedure differ from the procedure of the common law courts? * * *

In case of contumacy, the Chancellor would order the arrest of the defendant, and his imprisonment for contempt. The rule that "Equity acts in personam" is the lantern that guides us through the entire labyrinth of equity jurisprudence. A common law court's only resource was to order the payment of damages, followed, in case of nonpayment, by a writ of *fieri facias,* or of *elegit,* addressed to the sheriff, empowering him to seize and sell sufficient of the defendant's goods in the one case, and land in the other, to satisfy the judgement. But the courses open to the Chancellor were less monotonous. He could grant specific performance, that is to say, order the defendant to perform a contract according to its terms, or injunction, that is to say, order him to desist from conduct prejudicial to the plaintiff; and, like a skillful fisherman, would never let him go, once hooked, but could always jerk him back to obedience by the threat or fact of personal constraint.

b. Decrees Prohibiting Foreign Lawsuits

TABOR & CO. v. McNALL

Appellate Court of Illinois, Fourth District, 1975.

30 Ill.App.3d 593, 333 N.E.2d 562.

CRAVEN, JUSTICE. Tabor & Company, a Nevada corporation authorized to do business in Illinois, contracted with * * * McNall Bros. Grain Service, for the purchase and delivery of a large amount of grain. McNall is a Wisconsin corporation, but the grain was to be delivered to the buyer Tabor in LaSalle, Illinois. The contracts for this delivery, seven in all, were negotiated by phone between the Wisconsin office of McNall Bros. and the Illinois office of Tabor, and confirmed in writings sent from Tabor to McNall.

McNall performed partially, then defaulted. On June 4, 1974, Tabor filed a complaint on the contract in the circuit court of Macon County, Illinois. On June 18, 1974, McNall filed a suit in the circuit court of Rock County, Wisconsin, admitting default on the contract and seeking to limit its damages. McNall thereafter filed a limited appearance in the Illinois court, contesting that court's jurisdiction on the grounds that McNall had insufficient business contacts with Illinois to support such jurisdiction. The accompanying motion to quash service of process was denied August 2, 1974.

On August 27, 1974, Tabor petitioned the Illinois court to enjoin McNall from proceeding further with the suit in Wisconsin. At the same time, Tabor filed a petition for writ of prohibition in the Supreme Court of Wisconsin in an attempt to arrest the progress of the circuit court action there. On September 10, 1974, the Supreme Court of Wisconsin denied the request for a writ of prohibition.

Finally, on October 11, 1974, the Illinois court issued a writ of temporary injunction restraining McNall from proceeding further with the action in Rock County, Wisconsin. The order noted that there was no just reason for denying its enforcement or appeal. The McNalls nevertheless proceeded with their action in the Wisconsin court which proceeded to a verdict on October 16, 1974. On November 8, Tabor filed a petition for rule to show cause why McNall should not be held in contempt of court for violating the temporary injunction. The McNalls then appealed the order enjoining them from proceeding in Wisconsin, contending [*inter alia*] that the trial court was in error in enjoining them from pursuing the Wisconsin action. * * *

The McNalls' third and final contention is that the trial court judge issued the temporary injunction solely to protect the earlier acquired jurisdiction of the Illinois court, and that such is an insufficient justification for enjoining a foreign court proceeding. The trial court made no finding that the Wisconsin proceeding would be likely to result in fraud or oppression, or that any equity appeared to require intervention. On the contrary, the trial court specifically found that the McNalls had filed suit in Wisconsin to protect themselves, not to harass Tabor.

The only reason for intervention suggested by the trial court is a fear that Wisconsin law might not afford the Illinois defendant the protection he deserves:

> "THE COURT: We are all aware, and we are getting more firsthand knowledge all the time, apparently as a result of the—I hesitate to use the word, but the socialistic background of the State of Wisconsin, the Farmers' Labor Party and the LaFollettes and all the rest, they do have some pretty strange laws up there that I sometimes fail to comprehend, as witness this law suit where a plaintiff can come in and state under oath that he has breached his contract but I want my damages mitigated, it seems a little foreign to our experience here."

Such reasoning does not constitute sufficient basis for enjoining prosecution of a foreign suit:

> "It is not enough that there may be reason to anticipate a difference of opinion between the two courts, and that the courts of a foreign state would arrive at a judgment different from the decisions of the courts in the state of the residence of the parties. [citation] It is not inequitable for a party to prosecute a legal demand against another in any forum that will take legal jurisdiction of the case, merely because that forum will afford him a better remedy than that of his domicile. To justify equitable interposition it must be made to appear that an equitable right will otherwise be denied the party seeking relief. [citation]" (Royal League v. Kavanagh, 233 Ill. 175, 183, 84 N.E. 178, 181.)

Nor is it sufficient that the suit in Illinois was instituted before the suit in Wisconsin:

> "A party has the legal right to bring his action in any court which has jurisdiction of the subject-matter and which can obtain jurisdiction of the

parties. Should he begin two suits within the same jurisdiction, the pendency of the suit first brought may be pleaded in abatement of the later proceeding. This is not true of suits brought in different jurisdictions upon the same cause of action. The mere pendency of a suit in a sister state or in a court of the United States cannot be pleaded in abatement of a proceeding in a state court. * * * [I]t is only where it clearly appears that the prosecution of an action in a foreign state will result in a fraud, gross wrong, or oppression, that a court of equity will interfere with the general right of a party to press his action in any jurisdiction in which he may see fit and in as many of them as he chooses and restrain him from the prosecution of such a suit." (Illinois Life Insurance Co. v. Prentiss, 277 Ill. 383, 387, 115 N.E. 554, 556.)

The trial judge did not cite, nor does the record disclose, any facts to show why an injunction is necessary to avert "fraud, gross wrong or oppression." Consequently, it was error to enjoin the McNalls from proceeding in a foreign court.

Finally, Tabor contends that McNalls, by violating the injunction of the circuit court of Illinois, deprived themselves of the "clean hands" required from one who seeks equity. We have been advised of no authority which would bar them from seeking reversal of the order they disobeyed. The rule to show cause why they should not be cited for contempt is not before this court.

The circuit court erred in the issuance of the injunction.

Reversed.

Notes

1. Injunctions against foreign suits may be granted to prevent evasion of the laws of the forum state (e.g. divorce or debtor exemption laws) or to avoid harassment, oppression or inconvenience to the litigant in the foreign state. See Brown v. Brown, 120 R.I. 340, 387 A.2d 1051 (1978); American Re–Insurance Co. v. MGIC Investment Corp., 73 Ill.App.3d 316, 391 N.E.2d 532 (1979).

2. In Wells v. Wells, 36 Ill.App.3d 91, 93, 343 N.E.2d 215, 217 (1976), the court stated that the power to enjoin a foreign suit by a court of equity "is a matter of great delicacy invoked with great restraint in order to avoid distressing conflicts and reciprocal interference with jurisdiction." The court referred to the well known case of James v. Grand Trunk Western Railroad Co., 14 Ill.2d 356, 152 N.E.2d 858 (1958), cert. denied, 358 U.S. 915 (1959), where the Illinois court issued an injunction prohibiting enforcement of a Michigan decree enjoining the prosecution of a wrongful death action in Illinois for an accident in Michigan. Does this result in the ultimate absurdity of making all parties subject to contempt for pursuing a remedy in court? Compare China Trade and Development Corp. v. M.V. Choong Yong, 837 F.2d 33, 36 (2d Cir.1987), where the court, in denying an injunction against a foreign suit, stated that injunctions should be "used sparingly" and "only with care and great restraint."

3. It has generally been thought that full faith and credit need not be given to injunctions. See Lowe v. Norfolk & Western Railway Co., 96 Ill.App.3d 637, 421 N.E.2d 971 (1981); cf. Fuhrman v. United America Insurors, 269 N.W.2d 842, 847 (Minn.1978) (recognition of an injunction "is granted strictly as a matter of comity."); but see Smith v. Walter E. Heller & Co., 82 Cal.App.3d 259, 147 Cal.Rptr. 1 (1978) (court may not allow the enjoined action to be maintained); Vanneck v. Vanneck, 49 N.Y.2d 602, 427 N.Y.S.2d 735, 404 N.E.2d 1278 (1980) (interpretation of the Uniform Child Custody Jurisdiction Act); Restatement (Second) of Conflict of Laws § 103 (1971).

4. Full faith and credit is not relevant to injunctions issued by courts of other nations. In Laker Airways Ltd. v. Sabena, Belgian World Airlines, 731 F.2d 909, 933–34 (2d Cir.1984), the court upheld a counter injunction in antitrust litigation:

"The district court's injunction was within its discretion even though the United Kingdom courts have issued in personam injunctions stopping Laker from proceeding against British Airways and British Caledonian. Long experience derived from this country's federal system teaches that a forum state may, but need not, stay its own proceedings in response to an antisuit injunction against a party before the court. * * * In suits involving states, even the Full Faith and Credit Clause does not compel recognition of an antisuit injunction. * * * The same result is reached here *a fortiori,* since the mandatory policies of the [clause] do not apply to international assertions of exclusive jurisdiction. The antisuit injunction was a necessary and proper vehicle to protect the [district court's] jurisdiction and prevent the evasion by KLM and Sabena of important domestic laws governing the conduct of business within the United States * * *. KLM and Sabena do not dispute the power of the United States District Court to issue the injunction. They contend rather that [it] abused its discretion."

The court also rejected the argument of paramount sovereignty, that Laker Airways' nationality required deference to the courts of the United Kingdom.

5. Federal courts are prohibited from enjoining state court proceedings by 28 U.S.C. § 2283 (1976). Even if the case falls within a statutory exception of the Act, injunctive relief may still be refused because of the abstention doctrines set out in Younger v. Harris, discussed infra. See generally, C. Wright, Federal Courts §§ 47, 52, 52A (4th ed. 1983). Similarly a state court is prohibited from enjoining federal proceedings except where necessary to protect property under its control. See General Atomic Co. v. Felter, 434 U.S. 12 (1977); Arnold, State Power to Enjoin Federal Court Proceedings, 51 Va.L.Rev. 59 (1965); Comment, State Injunction of Proceedings in Federal Courts, 75 Yale L.J. 150 (1965). Some states reinforce this policy by statutory prohibition. See Cal.Civ.Code § 3423.

6. Injunctions prohibiting a litigant from initiating abusive and harassing litigation present a different problem. See Colorado ex rel. Colorado Judicial Department v. Fleming, 726 F.Supp. 1216 (D.Colo.1989).

Historically, vexatious litigation took the form of multiple ejectment suits. An injunction to prohibit this harassment illustrates the classic equitable bill of peace. For a modern example, see Nuttelman v. Julch, 228 Neb. 750, 424 N.W.2d 333 (1988), cert. denied, 489 U.S. 1031 (1989).

c. *Decrees With Extra-Territorial Effect*

CONNELL v. ALGONQUIN GAS TRANSMISSION CO.

United States District Court, District of Rhode Island, 1959.
174 F.Supp. 453.

DAY, DISTRICT JUDGE. This is an action brought by James J. Connell and Agnes Connell, his wife, both citizens of the State of Rhode Island, against Algonquin Gas Transmission Company, a Delaware corporation, duly qualified to do business in the State of Rhode Island and having a regular place of business in said state.

* * * In Count I, the plaintiffs allege that the plaintiff James J. Connell was on or about July 14, 1952 the owner of a tract of land in the Town of

Seekonk, County of Bristol, in the Commonwealth of Massachusetts; that on or about July 10, 1952 the defendant was granted an order from the Department of Public Utilities of said Commonwealth under which the defendant is claiming an easement on, over, through and under said land to lay, construct, maintain and alter a natural gas transmission pipe line; that the defendant has filed certain documents in the Registry of Deeds of said Bristol County, thereby claiming said alleged easement; that by the defendant's entry on said land and the laying out of said pipe line, the plaintiffs have sustained irreparable damages; that said actions of the defendant were allegedly taken pursuant to Chapters 79 and 164 of the General Laws of Massachusetts, as amended, which require the defendant to pay a landowner, whose land has been so damaged by its actions, a reasonable sum for the damages sustained to said land; and that no damages have been paid to the plaintiffs despite their requests for payment. Count I concludes with a request that this Court "assess damages against the defendant in the sum of Thirty Thousand Dollars" with interest, costs and expenses of this action.

In Count II, the plaintiffs repeat the same allegations and further allege that the defendant took said easement without complying with the provisions of said Chapters 79 and 164 and that said taking was therefore invalid and arbitrary. Count II concludes with a prayer that this Court decree said taking was invalid; order the defendant to remove its equipment and effects from said land and to remove the cloud on plaintiffs' title now existing in said Registry of Deeds by reason of its actions; and award the plaintiffs damages in said sum of thirty thousand dollars with interest, costs and the expenses of this action. * * *

The defendant has moved to dismiss on the following grounds (1) because the causes of action alleged in the complaint arise out of Massachusetts condemnation proceedings involving land located in Seekonk, Bristol County, Massachusetts, as appears from the complaint, and (2) because the Court lacks jurisdiction of the subject matter.

With respect to Count I, the defendant contends that the action alleged therein is a local action and hence not within the jurisdiction of this Court. Plaintiffs assert with equal vigor that it is transitory and that, since this Court has jurisdiction over the parties, it is properly maintainable here. It is clear that Count I is in essence a petition for the assessment of damages for the taking by the defendant of an easement in land situated in the Commonwealth of Massachusetts, and brought pursuant to the provisions of the General Laws of that Commonwealth. The General Laws of Massachusetts provide that a petition for the assessment of damages is the proper mode for enforcing a landowner's right to compensation where his land (or any interest therein) is taken pursuant to the eminent domain laws of said Commonwealth. Mass. Gen.L. (Ter.Ed.1932), c. 79 § 7. Said chapter provides that such a petition shall be heard only by the Superior Court for the county in which the land is located. Id. § 14. In addition, said chapter makes provision for trial by jury, and a jury view of the land taken. Id. § 22. And the remedies afforded by said chapter are expressly stated to be exclusive. Id. § 45.

It is well settled that where the legislature of a state authorizes the taking of land or rights therein for public use, and the taking is in accordance with the statute, and a plain and adequate remedy is provided for compensation—that remedy is exclusive.

Plaintiff contends that Count I may be regarded as an action upon an implied contract imposed by law upon the defendant to pay damages to the plaintiffs for the taking of their lands; and that it is hence a transitory action over which this Court has jurisdiction. The contention is without merit.

In this count, the plaintiffs seek to recover damages for injury to their land. By the great weight of authority an action to recover damages for injury to land is local and can be maintained only in the courts of the state where the land is situated.

Since the claim alleged in Count I is local, it is not within the jurisdiction of the United States District Court for the District of Rhode Island to hear and determine. The defendant's motion to dismiss said count must therefore be granted. * * *

In Count II the plaintiffs seek not only an award of damages for injury to their land but also equitable relief by way of mandatory injunctions against the defendant. They contend that since this Court has jurisdiction over the defendant, it has jurisdiction to grant the relief sought even though land situated in the Commonwealth of Massachusetts may be affected by the granting thereof.

The limitations which restrict the actions of a court of equity in controversies involving real estate situated beyond the territorial jurisdiction of such a court are not entirely clear. In the landmark case of Massie v. Watts, 1810, 6 Cranch 148, at page 159, Chief Justice Marshall said:

> "Upon the authority of these cases and others which are to be found in the books, as well as upon general principles, this court is of opinion that, in a case of fraud, or trust, or of contract, the jurisdiction of a court of chancery is sustainable, wherever the person be found, although lands not within the jurisdiction of that court may be affected by the decree.
>
> "The inquiry, therefore, will be, whether this be an unmixed question of title, or a case of fraud, trust or contract?"

This statement of the rule may, as suggested by Judge Learned Hand, be too narrow. [citations] Be that as it may, it appears to be well settled that where the defendant is under no personal obligation which a court may enforce, such as to convey land to the plaintiff or to hold land for his benefit, the court will abstain from exercising jurisdiction in cases involving realty situated in another state. * * *

In Count II, the plaintiffs do not allege the existence of, nor do they seek to enforce, any personal obligation owed to them by the defendant arising out of contract, trust or fraud. On the contrary, the plaintiffs' right to equitable relief under this count depends directly on the validity of the defendant's easement. Their primary objective is not to require the defendant to perform a contract, to carry out a trust or to undo the effects of a fraud, but rather to determine the title and incidental right to possession of land. This is a local question which should be decided only by the courts within whose territorial jurisdiction such land is located.

In my judgment Count II falls within the rule laid down in Northern Indiana R. Co. v. Michigan Central R. Co. [56 U.S. (15 How.) 233 (1853)] where similar equitable relief was sought in a federal court not having territorial jurisdiction over the land. In affirming the lower court's dismissal of the bill on jurisdictional grounds, the Supreme Court said:

"It will readily be admitted, that no action at law could be sustained in the district of Michigan, on such ground, for injuries done in Indiana. No action of ejectment, or for trespass on real property, could have a more decidedly local character than the appropriate remedy for the injuries complained of. And is this character changed by a bill in chancery? By such a procedure, we acquire jurisdiction of the defendants, but the subject-matter being local, it cannot be reached by a chancery jurisdiction, exercised in the State of Michigan. A State court of Michigan, having chancery powers, may take the same jurisdiction, in relation to this matter, which belongs to the Circuit Court of the United States, sitting in the district of Michigan. And it is supposed that no court in that state, could assume such a jurisdiction."

Since the cause of action alleged in Count II is likewise local, this Court is without jurisdiction to hear and determine it. Accordingly, the defendant's motion to dismiss that count is granted.

In conclusion, the defendant's motion to dismiss the entire complaint for want of jurisdiction is granted.

Notes

1. The classification of a trespass to land action as "local" is a historical anomaly, explainable only by the intricacies of laying venue under the common law system of pleading. See A. Scott, Fundamentals of Procedure in Actions of Law 18–23 (1922). The local action rule means that even though a plaintiff seeks a personal judgment for compensatory damages against a party over whom personal jurisdiction has been obtained, a court will refuse to proceed if the land is in another state. This unjust rule has been rejected by judicial decision in several states and by legislation in others. See R. Leflar, American Conflicts Law § 44 (4th ed. 1986).

2. In *Connell,* the court had primary jurisdiction to decide an in personam case between the parties; but it declined because the dispute arose out of a trespass to lands in another state rather than out of "fraud, trust or contract." The impulse to avoid a decision that affects foreign lands is strong. Equity literature abounds with statements that an equity court lacks "power" to grant relief. This may foster the thought that were the equity court to enjoin a trespass to foreign land, the decree would be void.

Another approach is to concede the court's primary jurisdiction, but to insist that for strong policy reasons the court should practically never act.

3. Cf. Laslie v. Gragg Lumber Co., 184 Ga. 794, 796–798, 193 S.E. 763, 765 (1937). In denying injunctive relief against trespass to timber land located in Florida, the Georgia court followed much the same reasoning as that of the court in the principal case. In addition, the court ruled that a Georgia statute authorizing injunctive relief "although property not within the jurisdiction may be affected" did not apply because the case did not involve "fraud, trust, or contract." The dissenting opinion argued that since the action was in personam, only a court in Georgia where defendant resided could grant the relief to which the plaintiff was entitled. Although the court thus ruled that injunctive relief was not available, it also decided that a good cause of action was stated for damages, the plaintiff having amended the complaint from a trespass to a conversion theory.

4. Ramirez de Arellano v. Weinburger, 745 F.2d 1500, 1529, 1531–32 (D.C.Cir. 1984). Plaintiff, a U.S. citizen, owned a cattle ranch in Honduras. Plaintiff sued the Secretaries of State and Defense to enjoin the operation of a facility on the

property for training Salvadoran soldiers. Declaratory and injunctive relief granted (6–4 opinion). On the issue of equitable jurisdiction the court said:

"The location of plaintiffs' land in a foreign country does not prevent the district court from granting relief. * * * Where, as here, the court adjudicating the controversy has personal jurisdiction over the defendants, the extraterritorial nature of the property * * * is no bar to equitable relief. * * * The local action rule of common law as applied to complaints seeking money damages for trespass to land has no bearing on this case.

"[C]ourts are specially willing to grant equitable relief involving property outside the court's jurisdiction when the law of the court's jurisdiction governs the controversy instead of the law of the situs. Here the plaintiffs' causes of action against the United States officials * * * arise under United States laws and the United States Constitution. * * * The occasional deference in equity to the courts of the situs state in actions involving trespass brought under the situs state's law is inapposite here. * * *

"The suggestion that the enforcement of any equitable decree would present insurmountable problems of compliance and judicial monitoring rests entirely on wild speculation. It must be presumed that the defendants * * * will obey an order of the district court. * * * Courts do not monitor compliance with decrees by personal, on-site inspections. * * * If a dispute arises * * * the parties can introduce evidence in the district court to establish whether a violation in fact has occurred. * * * (I)t is a method universally used no matter where any acts occur or property is located."

UNITED STATES v. McNULTY

United States District Court.
Northern District of California, 1978.
446 F.Supp. 90.

ZIRPOLI, DISTRICT JUDGE. On or about March 24, 1973, the defendant, Franklin L. McNulty, won the Irish Hospitals Sweepstakes. He collected 50,000 Irish pounds, or $128,410 at the prevailing rate of exchange. Defendant soon learned, however, that he had a silent partner which would claim its share of the prize. That partner was the Internal Revenue Service, whose interest defendant sought to defeat by collecting his winnings in Ireland and depositing them in a secret bank account on the Island of Jersey, which is located between the United Kingdom and France.

In a narrow sense, defendant has been successful in his efforts to avoid sharing his winnings with the government, for the money apparently remains on the Island of Jersey. Defendant himself, however, having been convicted of income tax evasion, remains in federal prison. On January 23, 1978, moreover, the government prevailed in a civil action for collection of taxes, and defendant was found liable in the amount of $67,791, representing taxes, penalty and interest. The government, though successful in its action, is unlikely to collect its money unless defendant transfers his assets from the Island of Jersey, for he has no other known funds with which to satisfy the judgment.

The government has therefore moved for an order directing defendant to repatriate his assets from the Island of Jersey and deposit them with the clerk of the court. Although no memorandum of points and authorities was submitted with the motion, the Assistant United States Attorney indicated in court that 26 U.S.C. section 7402 provides the authority for the issuance of such an order:

> "The district courts of the United States at the instance of the United States shall have such jurisdiction to make and issue in civil actions, writs and orders of injunction, and of *ne exeat republica,* orders appointing receivers, and such other orders and processes, and to render such judgments and decrees as may be necessary or appropriate for the enforcement of the internal revenue laws. The remedies hereby provided are in addition to and not exclusive of any and all other remedies of the United States in such courts or otherwise to enforce such laws."

While this court has found no case specifically invoking that section of the Internal Revenue Code for the type of order sought herein, it is relatively well established that this court may issue such an order. In United States v. Ross, 302 F.2d 831 (2d Cir.1962), an action had been brought to subject defendant's property to jeopardy assessments for unpaid income taxes. The district court had issued a series of interlocutory orders, one of which directed defendant to surrender to a receiver stock located in the Bahamas. Defendant contended that such an order was in excess of the court's jurisdiction, but the court of appeals disagreed:

> "The District Court's order to Ross to turn over his stock certificates to the receiver was not in excess of the court's statutory authorization. The court had personal jurisdiction over Ross, acquired by personal service of summons on his authorized agent. Personal jurisdiction gave the court power to order Ross to transfer property whether that property was within or without the limits of the court's territorial jurisdiction."

In United States v. First National City Bank, 379 U.S. 378 (1965), the Commissioner of Internal Revenue had made jeopardy assessments of some $19 million against a Uruguayan corporation. Although the district court lacked personal jurisdiction over the corporation, it did have jurisdiction over the bank in whose Montevideo branch the corporation maintained a deposit. The court issued an injunction under 26 U.S.C. section 7402(a) "freezing" the corporation's account in the foreign branch of the New York bank. The Supreme Court sustained the order. Implying that once personal jurisdiction over the corporation was acquired the district court could order payment of the foreign assets, the Court observed:

> "The temporary injunction issued by the district Court seems to us to be eminently appropriate to prevent further dissipation of assets. [citation] If such relief were beyond the authority of the District Court, foreign taxpayers facing jeopardy assessments might either transfer assets abroad or dissipate those in foreign accounts under control of American institutions before personal service on the foreign taxpayer could be made. * * * [T]here is here property which would be 'the subject of the provisions of any final decree in the cause.' [citation] We conclude that this temporary injunction is 'a reasonable measure to preserve the status quo' [citation] pending service of process on [the corporation] and an adjudication of the merits."

While the Ninth Circuit has not, as far as this court has been able to determine, confronted this particular question in the area of taxes, it would apparently approve such an order. In Securities and Exchange Commission v. Minas De Artemisa, S.A., 150 F.2d 215 (9th Cir.1945), the court ordered a corporation, which was subject to the personal jurisdiction of the court, to produce corporate books located in Mexico in connection with an SEC investigation. As was done in *First National City Bank* and *Ross,* the court observed that such an order must be framed so as not to conflict with the internal law of the foreign state in which the act was to be performed. There has been no indication, however, that the instant order will violate the banking laws of the Island of Jersey.

It is clear, then, that this court, by virtue of its jurisdiction over the defendant, has the power to order him to repatriate the assets located in the foreign bank. Moreover, there appears to be little hesitation on the part of courts to issue such orders. The view was expressed most directly by the district court in *Ross:*

> "Only for the most compelling reasons should a court refuse relief to the Government where a citizen of the United States keeps most of his assets in a foreign country and claims that they are immune from application to his income tax liability because of their situs in a foreign country."

Accordingly, plaintiff's motion is granted, and the defendant is ordered to repatriate assets sufficient to satisfy the judgment entered against him by this court from the Island of Jersey and to deposit said assets with the Clerk of this Court within sixty (60) days of the entry of this order.

Notes

1. The criminal conviction failed to produce the money. The government could not itself collect the civil judgment for taxes in the Island of Jersey. In October, 1978, Frank McNulty was found in contempt for failing to obey the preceding order to repatriate; and he was committed to the custody of the United States marshall. After five months in custody failed to coerce McNulty to repatriate the funds, Judge Zirpoli concluded that "further incarceration would cease to serve the coercive objective of civil contempt and would become punitive." McNulty was discharged on March 16, 1979. He promised to send Judge Zirpoli an Irish Sweepstakes ticket: "If he wins, God bless him, I hope he goes to Ireland and does the same thing I did." (News Item)

See Rendleman, Disobedience and Coercive Contempt Confinement: The Terminally Stubborn Contemnor, 48 Wash. & Lee L.Rev. 185 (1991).

2. Probably the best known litigation involving extra-territorial decrees is The Salton Sea Cases, 172 Fed. 792 (9th Cir.1909). The court ruled that it had "jurisdiction" to restrain diversion of water from the Colorado River even though compliance with the decree compelled the defendant to perform acts in Mexico. It illustrates the technique employed by the courts in these situations. The decree did not order the defendant to take corrective action in Mexico. Rather, the court prohibited a diversion of water injurious to plaintiff's lands in California, leaving it up to the defendant to determine how to accomplish this.

3. An early case illustrating *McNulty*'s direct approach is Madden v. Rosseter, 114 Misc. 416, 187 N.Y.S. 462 (1921). The New York court ordered a defendant to deliver a race horse from California to the plaintiff in Kentucky and appointed a receiver to see that the decree was carried out. It was. Suppose, however, that the receiver was arrested in California as a horse thief.

4. In Hertz System, Inc. v. McIllree, 26 Ill.App.2d 390, 168 N.E.2d 468 (1960), the defendant, an Australian citizen, ran a car rental business in Australia. He had registered for himself the names "Hertz," "Hertz Rent-a-Car," etc. in conjunction with his business. By letter he had contracted to transfer the registration to the plaintiff but failed to do so. Defendant was personally served in Chicago while on a business trip. He was represented by counsel during the initial stage of the

proceedings; but he returned to Australia and ordered the attorneys to withdraw. A default decree ordering defendant to transfer his right to the business name was affirmed:

"The decree merely orders the transfer, and although it provides the form to be used for transfer by a Commissioner should defendant refuse to transfer, there is no attempt to anticipate what an Australian court will do should plaintiff seek enforcement in Australia. For this reason we see no offense against comity between Australia and the United States. * * * [T]he decree does not encroach upon the sovereign power of Australia nor offend fundamental policy of British Courts against [sic] enforcement of foreign judgments violating fundamental notions of justice."

5. White, Enforcement of Foreign Judgments in Equity, 9 Sidney L.Rev. 630 (1982).

MATARESE v. CALISE

Supreme Court of Rhode Island, 1973.
111 R.I. 551, 305 A.2d 112.

PAOLINO, JUSTICE. This case is before us on the defendant's appeal from a judgment entered in the Superior Court ordering the defendant to convey to the plaintiff certain real estate located in Forio, Ischia, Italy. * * *

The plaintiff was a businessman in the town of Forio on the island of Ischia which is located off the coast of Naples. The defendant was born in Italy but was an American citizen. * * * He came to this country from Forio in 1955. * * *

The property involved in this case was formerly owned by one Anna Coppa DiMaio, who was born in this country and had never been to Italy. Her brother, Philip Coppa, who owned an unimproved parcel of land adjacent to that of his sister, occupied a residence located on Anna's land. In 1954 plaintiff purchased the unimproved parcel from Philip. * * * Around 1965 plaintiff made plans to erect a large building on the land he bought from Philip, and, in 1966, started construction. The plaintiff needed Anna's property because his building encroached on a portion thereof, and he decided to attempt to purchase it. At the time plaintiff did not know where Anna resided in the United States. * * *

In March, 1966, defendant was again visiting in Forio, Italy. * * * At the hearing in the Superior Court plaintiff testified that in March, 1966, defendant went to plaintiff's store in Forio and that a conversation took place between them about the purchase of Anna's land. [T]he conversation between plaintiff and defendant was in substance as follows:

"Plaintiff asked defendant, when he returned to the United States, to try to see Anna Coppa DiMaio and to purchase the property for him at any cost since he had started construction of his building and a portion of the foundation was on that property. Plaintiff further stated that he would send defendant money when requested to make a down payment and later would send defendant a power of attorney so that a deed could be transferred to plaintiff and defendant could act fully on plaintiff's behalf. Plaintiff also stated that if defendant would secure the property for him, he would give defendant the entire top floor of the building on the Anna Coppa DiMaio property in which Philip Coppa was then living. Defendant stated that he had learned where Mrs. DiMaio lived and he would do his best to convince her to sell the property and make a contract with her for plaintiff."

The defendant contacted Anna in New York and in September, 1968, in New York, secured a deed to her property but placed the property in his own name. After the defendant purchased the property, he sent a telegram to his mother in Italy stating that the property had been bought for $22,000 and asking that $3,000 be sent to him. The defendant's mother showed the telegram to plaintiff who, thinking that defendant was purchasing the property for him, sent $3,000 to defendant in North Providence. The trial justice found that no more than $3,000 was paid for the property. The defendant claimed at the trial that the figure $22,000 in the telegram was a mistake by the telegraph company. The trial justice said that this statement was a deliberate fabrication and that it was clear to him that "* * * defendant by sending the telegram, was attempting to set plaintiff up for a $22,000 demand for the property because he knew plaintiff was keeping in touch with the situation through his mother." The defendant's father recorded the deed in Italy on October 22, 1968, the date of the last check sent to defendant by plaintiff. * * * The trial justice said that defendant had worked his scheme to perfection, noting that defendant "* * * not only had record title to the property which he knew plaintiff wanted very desperately, but he also had plaintiff's $3,000.00 in hand and he was out of pocket no money in making the purchase."

* * * At the time this action was commenced against him, defendant was a resident of this state, residing at North Providence. He went back to Italy in August, 1969. * * *

[The trial judge] concluded that defendant had perpetrated a fraud upon plaintiff and, therefore, held the property in question as a constructive trustee for the benefit of plaintiff; that since the constructive trustee had no duties to perform other than conveying the property to the rightful owner, it was appropriate that defendant be ordered to convey the subject property to plaintiff; and that although the property was in Italy the Rhode Island court had jurisdiction over the person of defendant and, thus, had power to order a conveyance of the land, which was situated outside its territorial limits.

The trial justice ordered defendant to convey the property in question "by deed in form appropriate for recording in Italy," but he allowed defendant to reserve to himself a fee simple interest in the top floor of the building located on said premises. He also allowed defendant 60 days within which to make the conveyance and stated that if defendant did not abide by the court's order, plaintiff could apply to the court for the appointment of a commissioner to make the conveyance in the name of defendant. The trial justice continued in effect an injunction enjoining defendant from transferring the property to anyone except plaintiff. * * *

[D]efendant raises the question of whether the courts of this state have jurisdiction to compel an action relating to real property by a person no longer in this state. The defendant concedes that as a general principle of law, a court of equity may, under proper circumstances, order an individual over whom it has personal jurisdiction to execute a deed conveying an interest in real property situated outside the jurisdiction of the court. However, defendant argues that the aforesaid rule is of no effect in the present action because the trial justice found as a fact that "[d]efendant moved back to Italy in August

1969" and such situation having occurred, the Superior Court was without power to effect a conveyance of the land in question by defendant. * * *

We agree with the trial justice's conclusion that the court had jurisdiction over the person of defendant and, therefore, had power to order a conveyance even though the land was situated outside the territorial limits of this state. See Fall v. Eastin, 215 U.S. 1 (1909), cited by defendant, where the court said:

> "But this legislation does not affect the doctrine which we have expressed, which rests, as we have said, on the well-recognized principle that when the subject-matter of a suit in a court of equity is within another state or country, but the parties within the jurisdiction of the court, the suit may be maintained and remedies granted which may directly affect and operate upon the person of the defendant, and not upon the subject-matter, although the subject-matter is referred to in the decree, and the defendant is ordered to do or refrain from certain acts toward it, and it is thus ultimately but *indirectly* affected by the relief granted. In such case the decree is not of itself legal title, nor does it transfer the legal title. It must be executed by the party, and obedience is compelled by proceedings in the nature of contempt, attachment or sequestration. On the other hand, where the suit is strictly local, the subject-matter is specific property, and the relief, when granted is such that it *must* act directly upon the subject-matter, and not upon the person of the defendant, the jurisdiction must be exercised in the state where the subject-matter is situated." * * *

[Judgment affirmed.]

Notes

1. Mills v. Mills, 147 Cal.App.2d 107, 115, 305 P.2d 61, 67 (1956). Plaintiff sought to declare resident defendants constructive trustees of land located in Illinois. In upholding the complaint, the court stated: "Equity acts in personam, not in rem. After the court has obtained jurisdiction of the parties it may, by decree operating in personam against them, control their actions with respect to property situated without its jurisdiction whenever such action is necessary for it to effect a complete disposition of the controversy." The court stated that the decree "does not of itself affect title of the realty in [the state of the situs.]"

In *Mills,* the court also ruled that plaintiff was entitled to a decree establishing an equitable lien on the Illinois property. In Matarese v. Calise, the decree rendered by the trial court provided that if defendant failed to comply, plaintiff "could apply to the court for the appointment of a commissioner to make the conveyance in the name of the defendant." Are these decrees appropriate exercises of in personam jurisdiction? Are such decrees jurisdictionally valid? McKay v. Palmer, 170 Mich.App. 288, 427 N.W.2d 620 (1988).

2. In Duke v. Andler, 4 D.L.R. 529 (1932), the Supreme Court of Canada dealt with a California decretal transfer of land in British Columbia. Duke, the buyer, had agreed to secure payment of British Columbia land with a mortgage on land in California, but he was unable to perform that agreement because the California land was already encumbered. Duke fraudulently conveyed the British Columbia property to his wife. In an action brought by the seller in California, the court ordered reconveyance of the property and failing compliance, a Clerk's conveyance. The Clerk executed the conveyance.

The British Columbia courts held that the plaintiffs owned the land by reason of the California judgment and conveyance. On appeal, however, the Canadian Supreme Court refused to enforce the California judgment on the ground that the law and the courts of the situs determine rights in land. Neither the Clerk's conveyance nor the judgment could affect the title. Since the California judgment operates in personam, the Canadian courts should not lend it an in rem effect by vesting title in plaintiff.

3. California courts have continued to assert power to authorize a clerk to execute a deed to land in a foreign jurisdiction. In the most recent case, Phelps v. Kozakar, 146 Cal.App.3d 1078, 194 Cal.Rptr. 872 (1983), the only limitation the court was willing to recognize was lack of jurisdiction over the property owners.

4. If the defendant leaves the forum state, what practical value has a decree ordering defendant to execute a deed to land in another state? When the controversy involves sister states, the full faith and credit clause provides a solution. Restatement (Second) of Conflicts of Law § 102 (1971): "A valid judgment that orders the doing of an act other than the payment of money or enjoins the doing of an act, may be enforced, or be the subject of remedies in other states." Orders to convey land fall within this section (see comment d), and are routinely enforced by courts of the state where the land is located as a matter of full faith and credit under the federal constitution or simply as a matter of comity. In re Wiswall's Estate, 11 Ariz.App. 314, 464 P.2d 634 (1970), reh'g denied, 12 Ariz.App. 26, 467 P.2d 250 (1970); Currie, Full Faith and Credit to Foreign Land Decrees, 21 U.Chi.L.Rev. 620 (1954). This solves the problem of the disappearing defendant in Mills v. Mills. But what of defendant in *Calise* who left Rhode Island for Italy?

5. Plaintiffs may also use in personam jurisdiction to enjoin extra-territorial misconduct. Calvin Klein Industries, Inc. v. BFK Hong Kong, Ltd., 714 F.Supp. 78, 78–80 (S.D.N.Y.1989): "In this trademark case, Calvin Klein Industries, Inc. seeks a preliminary injunction restraining the distribution or sale of sportswear bearing the Calvin Klein label. Calvin Klein entered into a manufacturing contract with defendants BFK Hong Kong, Ltd. and its director, James Langford, but after several delays in delivery, Calvin Klein refused to accept the merchandise, citing tardiness and deviation from other manufacturing requirements. As a result, the garments remain in Pakistan, and Calvin Klein seeks an injunction prohibiting defendants from trying to sell them independently. * * *

"The only remaining issue, therefore, pertains to the necessary scope of the injunction, specifically, whether, having found plaintiff entitled to a preliminary injunction on sales in the United States, this court also may enjoin sale of these garments abroad. The Lanham Act ordinarily supports injunctions only against sales in the United States, where the trademark is registered. However, the law may reach abroad, and apply extraterritorially, under certain circumstances. Steele v. Bulova Watch Co., Inc., 344 U.S. 280, 289 (1952). In *Bulova,* the Supreme Court applied the Lanham Act to bar the defendant from selling infringing watches in Mexico, because the sales had an effect on United States commerce and because certain acts relating to the manufacture of the watches had occurred in the United States. Finding that Congress intended to make the Lanham Act's reach coextensive with the Commerce Clause, *Bulova* holds that under the statute 'a United States District Court has jurisdiction to award relief to an American corporation against acts of infringement and unfair competition consummated in a foreign country by a citizen and resident of the United States.'

"In determining whether such relief is appropriate, however, the following factors are to be considered: 1) whether defendant's conduct has a substantial effect on United States commerce; 2) whether the defendant is a United States citizen; and 3) whether extraterritorial enforcement of the trademark will encroach upon foreign trademark rights. * * *

"Consideration of the relevant factors supports the issuance of an extraterritorial injunction in this case. There is no dispute that defendant possesses no rights under foreign law with which an injunction against it might conflict. Although defendant Langford is not a United States citizen, the evidence indicates that he resides in New York, and is the controlling force behind BFK, a New York corporation. Therefore, both Langford and BFK may be treated as United States citizens for the purpose of this discussion. * * *

"The final factor for consideration—the effect of foreign, infringing sales on United States commerce—also supports Calvin Klein's application for a preliminary injunction. Effects on domestic commerce may include certain harms to plaintiff, as a domestic corporation, such as diversion of sales, [citation] or harm to licensees. [citation] In addition, a substantial effect on commerce may be found where the defendant's activities are supported by or related to conduct in United States commerce. In *Bulova,* for example, diversion of sales to consumers, who could find cheap, imitation watches just over the Mexican border, as well as the defendant's purchase of component parts in the United States, constituted sufficient effects on commerce.

"Calvin Klein is entitled to injunctive relief against infringing sales where such sales would divert Calvin Klein's sales, or would harm licensees. Because the garments at issue were manufactured under a contract made in New York, for delivery to New York, the remedies for breach of that contract necessarily have some effect on commerce. Calvin Klein claims that, because of its worldwide advertising and use of authorized licensees, any sale of the garments will irreparably damage Calvin Klein directly, by undermining Calvin Klein's good will and reputation for quality manufacture, or indirectly, by depriving Calvin Klein licensees of their exclusive rights. Such injuries would have a substantial effect on United States commerce, and, therefore, are enjoinable under the Lanham Act.

"Accordingly, defendants are preliminarily enjoined from selling the infringing goods in the United States, and in such other markets as Calvin Klein may demonstrate that it has established its presence, through either direct sales or licensees. Additionally, defendants must make reasonable efforts to ensure that those to whom they sell the goods do not resell or otherwise introduce the goods into territories in which Calvin Klein has a presence, as described above."

See also Reebok International Ltd. v. Marnatech Enterprises, Inc., 737 F.Supp. 1515 (S.D.Cal.1989). The court enjoined the sale of counterfeit shoes in Mexico.

6. See R. Leflar, American Conflicts Law §§ 82, 173, 174 (4th ed. 1986); E. Scoles & P. Hay, Conflict of Laws §§ 19.8, 24.10 (1982); White, Enforcement of Foreign Judgments in Equity, 9 Sydney L.Rev. 630 (1982); Note, U.S. Recognition and Enforcement of Foreign Country Injunctive and Specific Performance Decrees, 20 Cal.W.Int'l L.J. 91 (1989–90).

d. Transformation of Some Equity Suits Into In Rem Proceedings

CLEM v. GIVEN'S EX'R

Supreme Court of Virginia, 1906.
106 Va. 145, 55 S.E. 567.

WHITTLE, J. The bill in this case was filed by the appellant, W.J. Clem, against J.E. Givens, executor of W.C. Givens, deceased, and the widow and children of the testator, five of the latter being infants, for specific performance of a written contract of sale between the executor and the appellant, of real estate situated in Augusta county, Va.

By his will * * * the testator empowered the executor to sell and convey his real estate at any time during the minority of his youngest child, and to distribute the proceeds among his children. * * * The widow and children are residents of the county of Augusta, but the bill alleges that the executor is a nonresident of the state, and he was proceeded against by publication. [Editors: The executor demurred to the bill for want of jurisdiction. The circuit court sustained the demurrer.] * * *

It may be conceded in the outset that a personal judgment against a nonresident upon substituted process is void, under the due process clause of the fourteenth amendment of the Constitution of the United States, even in the state where rendered. This was distinctly held in the leading case on the subject of Pennoyer v. Neff, 95 U.S. 714. * * *

> "Jurisdiction is acquired in one of two modes: First, as against the person of the defendant, by the service of process; or, second, by a procedure against the property of the defendant within the jurisdiction of the court. In the latter case, the defendant is not personally bound by the judgment, beyond the property in question. And it is immaterial whether the proceeding against the property be by an attachment or bill in chancery. It must be substantially a proceeding in rem. The bill for the specific execution of a contract to convey real estate is not strictly a proceeding in rem, in ordinary cases: but where such a procedure is authorized by statute, on publication, without personal service of process, it is substantially of that character." Boswell's Lessee v. Otis, 50 U.S. (9 How.) 336.

Arndt v. Griggs, 134 U.S. 316, is authority for the proposition, that "a state may provide by statute that the title to real estate within its limits shall be settled and determined by a suit in which a defendant, being a nonresident, is brought into court by publication."

That was an action to recover possession of land, and to quiet title. Mr. Justice Brewer, in response to the suggestion that an action to quiet title is a suit in equity, and that equity acts upon the person, observes:

> "While these propositions are doubtless correct as statements of the general rules respecting bills to quiet title, and proceedings in courts of equity, they are not applicable or controlling here. The question is not what a court of equity, by virtue of its general powers and in the absence of a statute, might do, but it is: What jurisdiction has a state over titles to real estate within its limits, and what jurisdiction may it give by statute to its own courts, to determine the validity and extent of the claims of nonresidents to such real estate?
>
> "If a state has no power to bring a nonresident into its courts for any purposes by publication, it is impotent to perfect the titles of real estate within its limits held by its own citizens. And a cloud cast upon such title by a claim of nonresident will remain for all time a cloud, unless such nonresident shall voluntarily come into its courts for the purpose of having it adjudicated. But no such imperfections attend the sovereignty of the state. It has control over property within its limits, and the condition of ownership of real estate therein, whether the owner be stranger or citizen, is subject to its rules concerning the holding, the transfer, liability to obligations, private and public, and the modes of establishing titles thereto. It cannot bring the person of a nonresident within its limits—its process goes not beyond its borders—but it may determine the extent of his title to real estate within its limits, and for the purpose of such determination may provide any reasonable methods of imparting notice."

This is an instructive case, and reviews the authorities bearing on the subject under discussion, and it leaves no room to doubt the power of the states to provide substituted process in all proceedings relating to or affecting the titles to lands within their respective limits.

The subject is also interestingly treated in 5 Pomeroy's Eq.Jur. (Pom.Eq. Remedies, vol. 1) §§ 12, 13, 14, and 15. At section 15, the author says: "As a result of statute, it is held in many states that a decree removing a cloud from or quieting title to land within the jurisdiction may be based upon publication of summons. Likewise a decree for specific performance, acting upon the land itself, may issue upon such service."

In a note to section 14, reference is made to the statutes of the various states, including section 3418, Va.Code 1904. That section provides: "A court of equity, in a suit wherein it is proper to decree or order the execution of any deed or writing, may appoint a commissioner to execute the same; and the execution thereof shall be as valid to pass, release, or extinguish the right, title, and interest of the party on whose behalf it is executed, as if such party had been at the time capable in law of executing the same, and had executed it."

It has been held that a deed made by a special commissioner appointed and empowered to convey land under that section passes the legal title of all parties to the suit. Hurt v. Jones, 75 Va. 341.

Va.Code 1904, §§ 3230, 3231, 3232, provide for process by publication; and section 3232 declares that "upon any trial or hearing under this section, such judgment, decree, or order, shall be entered, as may appear just." While the language of these sections is general, we are of opinion that it comprehends quasi proceedings in rem, the object of which is to reach and dispose of property within the state.

This construction of the statute is sanctioned by the decision of the Supreme Court of the United States in the case of Roller v. Holly, 176 U.S. 398, a proceeding against a nonresident of Texas to foreclose a vendor's lien upon land in that state. In the course of his opinion, Mr. Justice Brown, remarks:

> "It is true there is no statute of Texas specially authorizing a suit against a nonresident to enforce an equitable lien for purchase money, but article 1230 of the Code of Texas * * * contains a general provision for the institution of suits against absent and nonresident defendants, and lays down a method of procedure applicable to all such cases. * * *
>
> "When the statute specifies certain classes of cases which may be brought against nonresidents, such specification doubtless operates as a restriction and limitation upon the power of the court; but where, as in article 1230 of the Texas Code, the power is a general one, we know of no principle upon which we can say that it applies to one class of cases and not to another. Unless we are to hold it to be wholly inoperative, it would seem that suits to foreclose mortgages or other liens were obviously within its contemplation."

Upon the authority of the foregoing decisions, we conclude that it is clearly within the competency of the state of Virginia "to provide by statute that the title to real estate within its limits shall be settled and determined by a suit in which the defendant, being a nonresident, is brought into court only by publication,"—and we are of opinion that the sections of Va.Code 1904, referred to, though general in their character, offered authority for such procedure.

A fortiori should this be true in the present case, where the nonresident defendant stands in the relation of trustee merely to the property, and is impleaded along with the beneficial owners, who are residents of the state and are before the court on personal service of process.

In the precise form in which it is now presented, the question involved is of first impression in this court. * * * The case of McGavock v. Clark, 93 Va. 810, 22 S.E. 864, was also a suit for specific performance of a contract of sale of real estate. The bill was filed by a resident vendor against nonresident vendees, and prayed for a personal decree against them, as additional security to the land itself, for the purchase money due upon it. But the court denied the prayer, for the obvious reason that the nonresident defendants had been proceeded against by publication, and had never appeared. The distinction between that case and the one under review is, however, quite apparent. The object of this suit is to acquire title to the land merely, and no relief is sought against the nonresident personally.

[Reversed.]

Notes

1. The result in *Clem* has been generally reached throughout the United States. *Clem* combines a so called "appointive" statute with one providing for substituted service in "in rem" proceedings to effectuate specific performance of a contract for the sale of forum land. A variant device is to combine a so-called "vesting" statute (making the decree self-executing as a conveyance) and one for substituted service. E.g., Associated Truck Lines, Inc. v. Baer, 346 Mich. 106, 77 N.W.2d 384 (1956). As indicated in the opinion, the desired result has also been obtained in Texas with the substituted service statute alone. In California the practice of appointing a "commissioner" to execute the conveyance is well-established, but the origin of the practice is obscure and is not based on a typical "appointive" statute. See Seculovich v. Morton, 101 Cal. 673, 36 P. 387 (1894).

2. The Federal Rules of Civil Procedure authorize either type of procedure:

Rule 70. Judgment for Specific Acts; Vesting Title. If a judgment directs a party to execute a conveyance of land or to deliver deeds or other documents or to perform any other specific act and the party fails to comply within the time specified, the court may direct the act to be done at the cost of the disobedient party by some other person appointed by the court and the act when so done has like effect as if done by the party. On application of the party entitled to performance, the clerk shall issue a writ of attachment or sequestration against the property of the disobedient party to compel obedience to the judgment. The court may also in proper cases adjudge the party in contempt. If real or personal property is within the district, the court in lieu of directing a conveyance thereof may enter a judgment divesting the title of any party and vesting it in others and such judgment has the effect of a conveyance executed in due form of law. When any order or judgment is for the delivery of possession, the party in whose favor it is entered is entitled to a writ of execution or assistance upon application to the clerk.

3. Mendrochowicz v. Wolfe, 139 Conn. 506, 95 A.2d 260 (1953). Plaintiff sued to set aside a deed to property within the forum state fraudulently obtained by nonresident defendants. In overruling the defendant's plea to the jurisdiction, the Supreme Court of Errors ruled that the equity court is authorized by statute to act in rem and hence personal jurisdiction over defendants was unnecessary. "The basis of the jurisdiction of the Court of Equity is that title to the real estate is within its control."

4. The decision in McGavock v. Clark (last paragraph of *Clem*) is standard insofar as it goes. The seller, however, may still be entitled to a modicum of relief. Prudential Insurance Co. v. Berry, 153 S.C. 496, 498–499, 151 S.E. 63, 64 (1930): "The buyer in a contract for the sale of land has an equity in the land, which as long as it may continue and be enforceable, is an encumbrance upon the owner's title * * *. To that extent, the seller would be entitled, considering his action as one in rem, to a decree declaring that such equity had expired." The decree operates as a strict foreclosure of the nonresident's equity. The extent of this equity, whether effectuated by specific performance or restitution, will be dealt with later.

5. Long arm statutes authorizing in personam jurisdiction to the full extent constitutionally permissible cast doubt on the proposition in *McGavock* that a valid judgment or decree cannot be entered against a nonresident buyer. For example, in Filsam Corp. v. Dyer, 422 F.Supp. 1126 (E.D.Pa.1976), the court held the nonresident purchaser had "sufficient contacts" with the forum state where the land was located. An action at law for damages for breach of the contract to buy would lie. Does in personam jurisdiction exist to decree specific performance?

6. The *Clem* principle applies where the absentee defendant does not assume personal obligations. If the contract imposes personal duties on the defendant plus an obligation to convey land, a court will refuse to proceed without obtaining personal jurisdiction over the defendant. Otis Oil & Gas Corp. v. Maier, 74 Wyo. 137, 284 P.2d 653 (1955).

7. Even though difficulties in acquiring personal jurisdiction over nonresidents have now been minimized by long arm statutes, enforceability problems unique to equitable remedies remain. The removal of primary jurisdiction or power obstacles through long arm statutes facilitates in personam legal actions for damages; but it does little for effective equitable relief. It does deprive the court of the lack of *power* rationale to justify declining to grant a probably ineffective decree.

McGee v. International Life Insurance Co., 355 U.S. 220 (1957), held that a plaintiff may proceed to a money judgment against a foreign insurance corporation conducting its business in the forum by mail solicitation. It is quite another thing to enjoin a corporation from soliciting business by mail only in the forum state. Travelers Health Association v. Commonwealth of Virginia, 339 U.S. 643, 651 (1950). In upholding in personam jurisdiction in *Travelers Health Association,* the majority found "no occasion" to discuss "methods by which the state might attempt to enforce [the decree]."

8. Mennonite Board of Missions v. Adams, 462 U.S. 791, 800 (1983). An Indiana tax sale statute allowed the sale of property for unpaid taxes with no notice to mortgage creditors except notice posted in the courthouse and published for three weeks. The Supreme Court held that the statute violated the creditor's right to due process: "Notice by mail or other means as certain to ensure actual notice is a minimum constitutional precondition to a proceeding which will adversely affect the liberty or property interests of any party, whether unlettered or well versed in commercial practice, if its name and address are reasonably ascertainable."

How does that holding affect the procedure in *Clem*?

3. EQUITABLE JURISDICTION: EXISTENCE AND EXERCISE

a. The Requirement of an Inadequate Legal or Other Remedy

(1) Traditional Views

"Few legal rubrics can vie in frequency of use with the maxim that equity will not grant specific relief—injunction or specific performance of contracts—

when there exists any adequate remedy at law. Under this doctrine, injunctions have been denied on the ground that damages, extraordinary legal remedies, detinue and replevin, criminal sanctions, and statutory civil, criminal, and administrative procedures were adequate to deal with the plaintiff's problem. Using analogous language, courts have referred injunction plaintiffs to the political process, the police or self-help.

"The adequate remedy rule well reflected Chancery's subordinate position as it developed in medieval England against the background of the established courts of law. Equity was a 'gloss' on the law; its sole justification for assuming jurisdiction was that traditional legal remedies and procedures could not offer the plaintiff satisfactory relief. Chancery waxed powerful during the Elizabethan and Stuart periods, and maintained its broadened jurisdiction during the eighteenth and nineteenth centuries notwithstanding improvements in the common law. Yet, held in check by the notion of adequacy, equitable remedies remained essentially supplementary. The adequacy doctrine was carried over to the Colonies, where it was fixed upon the federal courts by the Judiciary Act of 1789, and incorporated into the statutes or decisions of almost every American jurisdiction.

"The adequate remedy test has been expounded in forms that differ as to what burden the plaintiff must meet: it must be shown 'that he has exhausted his remedies at law'; that 'the refusal of a court of equity to interpose would, from the insufficiency of the legal relief, or the imperfection of the legal procedure, work a substantial injustice to the litigant party under all the facts of the case'; or merely that the remedy at law is not 'as practical and as efficient to the ends of justice and its prompt administration, as the remedy in equity.'

"The merger of law and equity, by bringing to a close the long competition between the two courts and committing the choice of remedies to a single set of judges, might be thought to have ended the traditional preference for nonequitable remedies and procedures. But at least in form, the adequacy test remains on the books and appears in the case law." Developments in the Law—Injunctions, 78 Harv.L.Rev. 994, 997–998 (1965) [citations deleted].

(2) The Inadequacy Test's Obituary.

"I conclude that the irreparable injury rule is dead. It does not describe what the cases do, and it cannot account for the results. Injunctions are routine, and damages are never adequate unless the court wants them to be. Courts can freely turn to the precedents granting injunctions or the precedents denying injunctions, depending on whether they want to hold the legal remedy adequate or inadequate. Whether they want to hold the legal remedy adequate depends on whether they have some other reason to deny the equitable remedy, and it is these other reasons that drive the decisions.

"Instead of one general principle for choosing among remedies—legal remedies are preferred where adequate—we have many narrower rules. There is a rule about fungible goods in orderly markets, a rule about preliminary relief, a rule about undue hardship, and so on. These rules are often stated in the cases. But when courts invoke these rules, they often go on to invoke the irreparable injury rule as well. Sometimes they rely solely or principally on the irreparable injury rule, and leave the application of some more specific rule merely implicit in their statement of the case. Analysis would be both simpler and clearer if we abandoned the rhetoric of irreparable injury and spoke solely and directly of the real reasons for choosing remedies. * * *

"I seek to complete the assimilation of equity, and to eliminate the last remnant of the conception that equity is subordinate, extraordinary, or unusual. Except where a statute or constitution requires it, I would not ask whether a remedy is legal or equitable. Instead, I would ask functional questions: is the remedy specific or substitutionary, is it a personal command or an impersonal judgment, is it preliminary or permanent? On the facts of each case, does plaintiff's preferred remedy impose unnecessary costs, or undermine substantive or procedural policies?" Laycock, The Death of the Irreparable Injury Rule, 103 Harv.L.Rev. 687, 692–93 (1990).

For a different but equally critical view of the irreparable injury doctrine, see Wasserman, Equity Transformed: Preliminary Injunctions to Require the Payment of Money, 70 B.U.L.Rev. 623 (1990).

More precise rules that articulate the real reasons will emerge from the crucible of the existing doctrine. Readers of this chapter will learn the language of irreparability and the habits of thought it created.

One attempt to sort out what contemporary judges mean by the phrases inadequate remedy and irreparable injury is Rendleman, The Inadequate Remedy at Law Prerequisite for an Injunction, 33 U.Fla.L.Rev. 346 (1981).

(3) In Perspective—Comment

Recently we have been apprised of the death of God, of Contract, and now the Irreparable Injury Requirement for equitable jurisdiction. Such obits would be more convincing if the designated decedents were to behave in the conventional and appropriate manner of the genuinely dead. Inconveniently they have not.

The irreparable injury requirement (demoted to lower case) has been the subject of penetrating and accurate academic criticism. No doubt an immutable "hierarchy of judicial remedies" is an unacceptable encumbrance to protecting and cleaning up the environment and to ending unconstitutional institutional practices in education, penology, and health care.

In civil litigation between private parties, our primary concern here, we can criticize courts for applying the irreparable injury loosely and using it to disguise results reached for other reasons.

Nevertheless, because of habit or conviction, the rule continues to appear in practice as well as print in civil litigation. Recurring scenarios have led to standard treatments that are unlikely to change much. Breach of contracts for sale of ordinary goods: adequate legal remedies. Breach of contracts for the sale of land: inadequate legal remedies. If other remedies are indisputably adequate for any particular dispute, does plaintiff have a real reason to seek equitable jurisdiction? The burden placed upon a plaintiff to establish the inadequacy of other remedies is not a heavy one.

Finally, the irreparable injury rule plays a major role in applications for temporary injunctions, probably the numerical bulk of occasions to put the rule into play. This subject will receive attention shortly. The importance attached to the irreparable injury requirement appears in this sample. The terminal debility of the rule is nowhere detectable.

(4) Iavarone v. Raymond Keyes Associates, 733 F.Supp. 727 (S.D.N.Y.1990)

Plaintiff, a former president and current stockholder of RKA brought suit against the Corporation and its current board of directors to postpone the holding of a shareholders' meeting relative to a tender offer being planned by the board. Plaintiff alleged (and the Court agreed) that the defendants have violated the Williams Act (§ 14(e) of the Securities Exchange Act, 15 U.S.C. § 78n(e)) by making false statements and withholding material information in the notice of the proposed takeover attempt.

Plaintiff claimed that equitable relief is necessary to forestall violations of federal law. Defendants argued in response that even if plaintiff establishes a violation of the federal law and that harm will be caused the Corporation by the takeover the plaintiff still has failed to show the inadequacy of monetary relief. Defendants pointed out that the individual defendant, Keyes, is worth $5,000,000 and that even if the Corporation is so financially weakened by the takeover that it cannot compensate plaintiff for damages at law, Keyes could cover any liability.

The Court *denied* the injunction at the same time holding that the defendants violated the Statute. Some of the quotes dealing with the irreparable injury requirement follow:

"A violation of the Williams Act will not trigger *per se* the right to equitable relief; rather, the movant must demonstrate that he will be irreparably harmed by defendants' conduct if not enjoined. See Rondeau v. Mosinee Paper Corp., 422 U.S. 49, 60–61 (1975)."

"[T]he [Supreme] Court made clear that traditional principles of equity applied, and that the Williams Act was not a prophylactic measure which could be used to enjoin all offending transactions."

"This Court agrees * * * that [Jackson Dairy Inc. v. H.P. Hood & Sons, 596 F.2d 70 (2d Cir.1979)] created an unmistakably clear requirement in this Circuit that movants for equitable relief must show irreparable harm, noncompensable in money damages, in all circumstances in which an injunction is requested."

"The requirement of irreparable harm has been consistently maintained by the Second Circuit to date."

Iavarone, however, is a private cause of action arising out of a violation of Federal Securities Regulations. These regulations are notoriously silent about which remedies are available to private parties.

Where the S.E.C. seeks to enforce the regulation, a different analysis applies. United States v. Schmitt, 734 F.Supp. 1035, 1049 (E.D.N.Y.1990): "Where Congress expressly provides for Government enforcement of a statute by way of injunction, and the Government has satisfied the statutory conditions of the statute, irreparable harm to the public is presumed. For example, in Securities Exchange Commission v. Management Dynamics, Inc., 515 F.2d 801 (2d Cir.1975) [an action to enjoin violations of the Securities Act of 1933 and the Securities and Exchange Act of 1934] the court held: 'Unlike private actions, which are rooted wholly in the equity jurisdiction of the federal court, SEC suits for injunctions are "creatures of statute." "[P]roof of irreparable injury or the inadequacy of other remedies as in the usual suit for injunction" ' is not required."

The *Schmitt* court concludes nevertheless, that if the Government sues to enjoin a violation of an act of Congress for which no injunctive remedy was specified, Clean Water Act, 33 U.S.C. § 1344(S)(3), "the Government must demonstrate the element of irreparable harm with regard to this claim." United States v. Schmitt, 734 F.Supp. at 1053.

Integrated Information Service, Inc. v. Mountain States Telephone and Telegraph Co., 739 F.Supp. 488 (D.Neb.1990); Hodge Business Computer Systems v. U.S.A. Mobile Communications, Inc., II, 910 F.2d 367, 369 (6th Cir.1990) (harm "must be irreparable, not merely substantial.").

b. Equitable Jurisdiction: Traditional Inclusions and Exclusions

Certain matters have historically been considered by their very nature to be within the jurisdiction of the Chancery Courts. Typically, these include guardianships, trusts and fiduciary relationships, probate, enforcement of liens, and quiet title.

The automatic classification as "equitable" derives from law courts' original lack of subject matter jurisdiction rather than of adequacy of remedy.

The indadequacy test and other equitable limitations operate where matters are subject to either law or equity. Plaintiff triggers the analysis by seeking an equitable remedy: an injunction, a constructive or resulting trust, an equitable lien, subrogation, an accounting for profits, specific performance, reformation, or some kinds of rescission.

(1) Equity Lacks Jurisdiction to Protect Personal, Political, or Religious Rights

Equitable jurisdiction traditionally included situations where either the rights or interests sought to be vindicated were equitable and there was no remedy at law or where the interests were legal but the remedy at law was not adequate.

Equitable jurisdiction may also be defined negatively by noting those controversies that were excluded because they were thought to be beyond its scope. Thus earlier courts often stated that equity would not protect personal rights but only rights of property. See Kenyon v. City of Chicopee, 320 Mass. 528, 70 N.E.2d 241 (1946); Hawks v. Yancey, 265 S.W. 233 (Tex.Civ.App.1924).

In *Kenyon,* the government argued that, while equity would protect the Jehovah's Witnesses' property rights to conduct a business, the chancellor could not grant an injunction to protect their personal rights to free speech and free exercise of religion. "We are impressed," the court responded, "by the plaintiffs' suggestion that if equity would safeguard their right to sell bananas it ought to be at least equally solicitous of their personal liberties guaranteed by the Constitution." Kenyon v. City of Chicopee, 320 Mass. 528, 533, 70 N.E.2d 241, 244 (1946).

Today not many judges will disclaim the ability to protect "personal" rights. Courts find other ways to limit injunctive legerdemain. Another restriction, stated almost in terms of a maxim, was that equity would not resolve disputes of a "peculiarly political nature." Colegrove v. Green, 328 U.S. 49 (1946). Such controversies were to be resolved by legislative or executive action. Judicial resolution was thought to be impractical as well as dangerously infringing upon the separation of powers doctrine.

The word "politics" however, has different levels of meanings ranging from "grass roots" (in the urban context the word "gutter" may be more meaningful) politicking, on through the election process up to the realm of national and foreign policy matters. At the lowest level the restriction still holds. For example, in Porter County Democratic Party Precinct Review Committee v. Spinks, 551 N.E.2d 457, 459 (Ind.App.1990), county precinct committeemen sought an injunction against their removal by the County Central Committee. In denying the injunction the court observed: "Courts of equity have no jurisdiction * * * with respect to matters * * * of a political nature unless civil property rights are involved * * *. A court of equity will not supervise the acts and management of a political party. * * * [A] member of a political party when denied certain rights as such member must look to some other source for redress."

On a higher level the rule of nonintervention in political disputes has been subject to a considerable erosion, as any reader of the newspapers can attest. Thus the precise question raised by Colegrove v. Green, the apportionment of Congressional districts, was held to be justiciable in Baker v. Carr, 369 U.S. 186 (1962). Since that decision, the entire spectrum of possible disputes over the election process has been presented for judicial review. Since our present study is concerned primarily with private disputes, the results reached by the courts need not detain us. The interested student is referred to a comprehensive note, Developments in the Law—Elections, 88 Harv.L.Rev. 1111 (1975).

In December of 1990 members of Congress sought a preliminary injunction to prevent the president from offensive military action against Iraq without a declaration of war. Relief was not barred because the issue was a "political question"; members of Congress are threatened with enough injury to possess "standing" to sue; but, absent some signal from a majority in Congress, the doctrine of "ripeness" prevented the preliminary injunction. Dellums v. Bush, 752 F.Supp. 1141 (D.D.C.1990). In early 1991 Congress's signal was a green light for the invasion.

Just as courts traditionally have been loath to enter the "political thicket," so also have religious controversies been held beyond the scope of judicial power. For obvious reasons, courts have felt incompetent to resolve ecclesiastical questions or to determine the true religion. See Pfeifer v. Christian Science Committee on Publications, 31 Ill.App.3d 845, 334 N.E.2d 876 (1975); Brown v. Mt. Olive Baptist Church, 225 Iowa 857, 124 N.W.2d 445 (1963). Disputes over property rights may be resolved, but only on the basis of "neutral principles of law, developed for use in all property disputes." Presbyterian Church v. Mary Elizabeth Blue Hull Memorial Presbyterian Church, 393 U.S. 440, 449 (1969). No consideration of doctrinal matters, "whether the ritual or liturgy of worship or the tenets of faith" is permissible. Maryland and Virginia Eldership of Churches of God v. Church of God, 396 U.S. 367 (1970). It has been held, however, that where the church structure is congregational, "* * * the First Amendment does not bar a civil court from giving effect to an authoritative resolution by the governing church body of a church property or related dispute as long as the governing body followed its own rules in reaching that resolution." Antioch Temple, Inc. v. Parekh, 383 Mass. 854, 860, 422 N.E.2d 1337, 1341 (1981).

(2) Equity Lacks Jurisdiction to Enjoin a Criminal Prosecution

NORCISA v. BOARD OF SELECTMEN

Supreme Judicial Court of Massachusetts, 1975.
368 Mass. 161, 330 N.E.2d 830.

QUIRICO, JUSTICE. This is an appeal by the defendants, the board of selectmen of Provincetown (selectmen) and their agent, from a decree * * * declaring that the plaintiff and her retail clothing business in the town of Provincetown (town) are not within the scope of G.L. c. 101, §§ 1–12, the Transient Vendor Statute, and ordering that the town and its agents, servants, and employees "are hereby restrained and permanently enjoined from enforcing * * * any of the provisions of Mass.G.L. c. 101, §§ 1–12, against the Petitioner or the retail business she operates." * * * Prior to the commencement of this suit in equity, a criminal complaint had issued * * * charging the plaintiff with violating G.L. c. 101, §§ 6, 8. This criminal complaint was still pending when the decree appealed from issued. The obvious purpose and effect of the decree was to enjoin the pending criminal prosecution. We reverse.

* * * It appears * * * that sometime late in 1973 the plaintiff, who was a resident of Provincetown, opened a retail clothing business in that town under the name of The Town Crier Wearhouse. At the time she opened her business, the plaintiff was informed by the agent for the selectmen "that she would not be able to open and operate her business unless she paid to Provincetown a license fee of two hundred dollars ($200.00), furnish a bond of five hundred dollars ($500.00), to the Commonwealth, and applied for both a state and town Transient Vendor's License, all of the above pursuant to and authorized by G.L. c. 101, § 3."

The plaintiff's position * * * is that she was not a transient vendor at the time the selectmen sought to categorize her as one, that she had not been a transient vendor in the past, and that she would not be a transient vendor in the future. She further asserted that she had performed no acts which could be construed as classifying her as anything except a retailer of clothes, that she intended to conduct her business as a full time retail clothing shop, and that she would take no action inconsistent with these assertions. * * *

At one time, it was common for courts to express the view that an equity court had no "jurisdiction" to enjoin a criminal prosecution. In In re Sawyer, 124 U.S. 200 (1888), the court said, "The office and jurisdiction of a court of equity, unless enlarged by express statute, are limited to the protection of rights of property. It has no jurisdiction over the prosecution, the punishment, or the pardon of crimes or misdemeanors * * *. To assume such a jurisdiction, or to sustain a bill in equity to restrain or relieve against proceedings for the punishment of offences, * * * is to invade the domain of the courts of common law, or of the executive and administrative department of the government."

In this Commonwealth, however, it was clearly established that courts with general equity powers have the power to restrain criminal prosecutions. In Shuman v. Gilbert, 229 Mass. 225, 118 N.E. 254 (1918), for example, this court recognized the "general rule" that criminal prosecutions are not to be enjoined, but pointed out, "[T]here is an exception to this comprehensive statement.

Jurisdiction in equity to restrain the institution of prosecutions under unconstitutional or void statutes or local ordinances has been upheld by this court when property rights would be injured irreparably, and when other elements necessary to support cognizance by equity are present."

As pointed out in the *Shuman* case, the occasions when an equity court may properly enjoin a criminal prosecution remain the exception to the "general rule" of nonintervention. Some of the basic policy reasons underlying the rule of nonintervention were well-expressed by the Supreme Court of Hawaii: "Courts of equity are not constituted to deal with crimes and criminal proceedings. They have no power to punish admitted offenders of a challenged penal statute after holding it to be valid, or to compensate those injured by the violations thereof while the hands of the officers of the law have been stayed by injunction. To that extent such courts are incapable of affording a complete remedy. Equity, therefore, takes no part in the administration of the criminal law. It neither aids, restrains, nor obstructs criminal courts in the exercise of their jurisdiction. Ordinarily a court of equity deals only with civil cases involving property rights where it can afford a complete remedy by injunctive relief. Hence it does not interfere in the enforcement of penal statutes even though invalid unless there be exceptional circumstances and a clear showing that an injunction is urgently necessary to afford adequate protection to rights of property so as to circumvent great and irreparable injury until the validity of the particular penal statute is sustained." Liu v. Farr, 39 Hawaii 23, 35–36 (1950).

Both the *Shuman* and *Liu* cases quoted above indicated that equity would act only to protect "property rights" from irreparable damage by criminal prosecution. In the leading case of Kenyon v. Chicopee, 320 Mass. 528, 70 N.E.2d 241 (1946), however, we largely rejected the personal rights-property rights distinction as a factor in considering whether an injunction should issue. We considered this question and said: "We believe the true rule to be that equity will protect personal rights by injunction upon the same conditions upon which it will protect property rights by injunction. In general, these conditions are, (1) that unless relief is granted a substantial right of the plaintiff will be impaired to a material degree; (2) that the remedy at law is inadequate; and (3) that injunctive relief can be applied with practical success and without imposing an impossible burden on the court or bringing its processes into disrepute." This, then, is the test which the probate judge should have applied in considering the request for an injunction, and it is the test which we now apply to the facts before us. In so doing, we assume without deciding that parts (1) and (3) of the *Kenyon* test are satisfied and concentrate on part (2), that is, whether the remedy at law would be adequate in this case.

The plaintiff variously claims that G.L. c. 101, §§ 1–12, is either unconstitutional on its face or as applied, or that the statute, properly construed, does not apply to her at all. In accordance with these claims, she asserts that she cannot be prosecuted for failure to comply with the statute. If we assume, again without deciding the question, that the plaintiff indeed cannot properly be prosecuted under this statute, the issue resolves itself simply to whether the available defenses to the District Court criminal complaint amount to an adequate remedy at law. In the circumstances of this case, we think they plainly do.

In both the *Shuman* and *Kenyon* cases, the question was considered whether, in the circumstances of those cases, the defense to the criminal prosecution provided an adequate remedy at law. Since the injunction was denied in the former case and granted in the latter, it is instructive to compare them.

In the *Shuman* case, six merchants alleged that the defendant chief of police of Northampton threatened to prosecute them for conducting a business without a license, which they claimed they were not obligated to obtain. The plaintiff's bill sought to make out a case of irreparable damage and inadequacy of legal remedy by alleging, inter alia, that it would take several months to obtain a decision on the case from an appellate court and that in the intervening period the loss of profits and advantageous business relations would cause the plaintiffs great and irreparable damage. To these averments, a demurrer was sustained. This court upheld the sustaining of the demurrer. After noting that in the event of multiple, oppressive, and wrongful prosecutions, an injunction might properly issue, we said: "A possibility that complaints may be lodged against six persons is not enough under these circumstances to make out a case of multiplicity. The allegations as to repeated complaints are not sufficient to warrant the inference that the courts of this commonwealth will countenance continued and oppressive prosecutions when once a genuine test case open to fair question has been presented and is on its way to final decision." We further rejected any notion that our courts of criminal jurisdiction could not protect the rights in question: "[The bill] assumes that one innocent of any infraction of the law will be found guilty by the district court and by the superior court, a presumption which as matter of law cannot be indulged, at least upon such general allegations. The allegations as to property damage are nothing more than the ordinary averments which might be made by anybody engaged in business, undertaking a branch of commercial adventure believed by the officers charged with enforcing the law to be in contravention of some penal statute confessedly valid in itself. Simply that one is in business and may be injured in respect of his business by prosecution for an alleged crime, is no sufficient reason for asking a court of equity to ascertain in advance whether the business as conducted is in violation of a penal statute."

In the *Kenyon* case, by contrast, we reversed interlocutory decrees sustaining demurrers where the bill alleged that members of Jehovah's Witnesses had been repeatedly, on different dates, arrested, prosecuted, and convicted under an unconstitutional ordinance, prohibiting distribution of handbills, that on at least two occasions a defendant judge had convicted some of the plaintiffs despite being shown United States Supreme Court decisions holding such an ordinance unconstitutional, that the defendants well knew that the ordinances were unconstitutional and void, that the plaintiffs' means of paying bail fees and of posting bail and appeal bonds were exhausted, and that the defendants had threatened to and would continue to make false arrests, all to the irreparable damage of the plaintiffs' attempts to exercise their constitutional rights. In these circumstances, we held that an injunction against further prosecutions could properly issue if the allegations were ultimately proved. We observed: "The plaintiffs' rights are of the most fundamental character. According to the bill they have been violated repeatedly. It is plain that the legal remedies by defending against repeated complaints and bringing successive actions for malicious prosecution or false arrest are not adequate."

In the present case, the plaintiff is the subject of a complaint charging a single violation of the statute. She avers that the statute is either unconstitutional on its face or as applied, or that, properly construed, it is inapplicable to her. These averments, of course, would, if established, each constitute a complete defense to the violation charged. We repeat here a passage from a United States Supreme Court case which applies equally to the matter before us: "It is a familiar rule that courts of equity do not ordinarily restrain criminal prosecutions. No person is immune from prosecution in good faith for his alleged criminal acts. Its imminence, even though alleged to be in violation of constitutional guarantees, is not a ground for equity relief since the lawfulness or constitutionality of the statute or ordinance on which the prosecution is based may be determined as readily in the criminal case as in a suit for injunction. * * * It does not appear from the record that petitioners have been threatened with any injury other than that incidental to every criminal proceeding brought lawfully and in good faith, or that a * * * court of equity by withdrawing the determination of guilt from the * * * [criminal] courts could rightly afford petitioners any protection which they could not secure by prompt trial and appeal pursued to this Court." Douglas v. Jeannette, 319 U.S. 157, 163–164 (1943).

In general, we believe the Federal policy of ordinarily refusing to enjoin pending State criminal prosecutions is sound. This policy, based partly on principles of Federal–State comity and partly on the general equitable principles we have summarized in this opinion, Younger v. Harris, 401 U.S. 37, 43–44 (1971), prohibits equitable interference with criminal prosecutions absent "very special circumstances." "Very special circumstances" may be merely a shorthand way of requiring a stricter application of general equitable principles, for example, that no injunction will issue unless the plaintiff will suffer irreparable and immediate injury without it. But however the concept is phrased, the necessity of defending a single criminal prosecution rarely, if ever, justifies issuance of the injunction.

Our decision would not be different if we were considering only those portions of the proceedings below which involved a request for and grant of declaratory relief under G.L. c. 231A, §§ 2. The fundamental jurisprudential considerations underlying the general prohibition against enjoining a pending criminal prosecution apply with full force to support a prohibition against issuing declaratory decrees concerning a pending criminal prosecution. To conclude otherwise would encourage fragmentation and proliferation of litigation and disrupt the orderly administration of the criminal law.

The rule we adopt today in regard to the issuance of declaratory judgments when criminal litigation is pending is merely a logical extension of our rules which generally proscribe the issuance of such a judgment when an appropriate administrative proceeding is in progress, East Chop Tennis Club v. Massachusetts Commn. Against Discrimination, 364 Mass. 444, 305 N.E.2d 507 (1973), or when a civil proceeding in which the same issue is or can be raised is already pending between the parties. Jacoby v. Babcock Artificial Kidney Center, Inc., 364 Mass. 561, 307 N.E.2d 2 (1974). In the latter case we said: "Generally, '[a] court cannot declare rights as to matters involved in a prior pending action.' Anderson, Actions for Declaratory Judgments (2d ed.) § 209 (1951). While declarations of rights may be appropriate in exceptional cases even when other proceedings are in progress, there is an ordinary presumption against such relief. * * * In the *East Chop* case we stated that 'the existence of * * * [a] dispute alone is insufficient reason to disrupt the ordinary administrative process.' * * * This applies a fortiori to pending court proceedings. The declaratory relief procedure was not intended to permit the same claim to be adjudicated in multiple suits." In applying these principles in the criminal prosecution context, we follow the Federal rule, Samuels v. Mackell, 401 U.S. 66, 69–73 (1971); and the rule adopted in most States which have considered the issue. Cases in which declaratory relief was granted where no criminal prosecution was actually pending are, of course, readily distinguishable. Steffel v. Thompson, 415 U.S. 452, 457 (1974). [citations]

For the reasons given above, the injunction and declaratory relief should not have been granted.

Notes

1. See denying injunctive relief prohibiting the enforcement of valid penal statutes and ordinances. Sullivan v. San Francisco Gas and Electric Co., 148 Cal. 368, 83 P. 156 (1905) (statute prohibiting interference with electrical transmission wires); Holt v. City of San Antonio, 547 S.W.2d 715 (Tex.Civ.App.1977) (regulation of massage parlors); Chevron Oil Co. v. City of El Paso, 537 S.W.2d 472 (Tex.Civ.App.1976) (ordinance regulating the transportation of flammable liquids); City of Dallas v. Dallas County Housemovers Association, 555 S.W.2d 212 (Tex.Civ.App.1977) (ordinance regulating housemovers).

In denying an injunction against the confiscation of the plaintiff's poker machines pursuant to a gaming statute, the Ohio Supreme Court in Garono v. State, 37 Ohio St.3d 171, 173, 524 N.E.2d 496, 499 (1988), stated: "A court should exercise great caution regarding the granting of an injunction which would interfere with another branch of government and especially with the ability of the executive branch to enforce the law. * * * Unless the police seek to enforce an unconstitutional or void law, we will not inhibit their efforts to enforce the law."

A limited injunction was granted for machines that were picked up despite the absence of any proof they were being used for profit.

2. As the court in *Norcisa* suggests, injunctive relief may be granted prohibiting the enforcement of a penal statute found to be unconstitutional. See Stoner McCray System v. Des Moines, 247 Iowa 1313, 1324, 78 N.W.2d 843, 850–51 (1956): A "court of equity may enjoin the attempted enforcement of an unconstitutional statute * * * to prevent irreparable injury to the business and property of the plaintiff and to avoid a multiplicity of suits." See also Bojangles, Inc. v. City of Elmhurst, 39 Ill.App.3d 19, 25–26, 349 N.E.2d 478, 483–84 (1976). In Andrews v. Waste Control, Inc., 409 So.2d 707 (Miss.1982), the court approved an injunction against enforcement of a void county resolution regulating the weight loads of trucks on a county road necessarily used by plaintiff in his waste disposal business.

3. Relief may be granted because of the inapplicability of a concededly valid statute to a particular factual situation. See Huntworth v. Tanner, 87 Wash. 670, 152 P. 523 (1915) (injunction prohibiting the enforcement of an act regulating employment agencies). Plaintiff sought to invoke this line of cases in *Norcisa.* While the attempt was unsuccessful, it suggests that the imprecision and lack of fixed content in terms like "material injury" or "irreparable harm" give courts considerable flexibility and make predictions of success hazardous.

4. Younger v. Harris, cited by the court, involves the propriety of a federal court enjoining a state criminal prosecution. The resolution of this question does include consideration of "general equitable principles," as the court states; but the problem is complex because it also involves the relationship between federal and

state courts. When *Younger* was decided, Dombrowski v. Pfister, 380 U.S. 479 (1965), was thought by many to authorize federal courts to enjoin state prosecutions under void or overbroad state statutes having a "chilling effect" on First Amendment rights. This expansive reading of the decision was rejected by *Younger;* it held that a federal court should not enjoin a state prosecution except upon a "showing of bad faith, harassment, or any other unusual circumstance that would call for equitable relief." Justification for this result was based on the Court's view of "our federalism" that requires accommodation of "the legitimate interests of both State and National Governments." Numerous decisions since *Younger* have sought to explain and apply this doctrine. The result, along with citations of law review comments, may be found in C. Wright, Federal Courts § 52A (4th ed. 1983); Developments in the Law—Section 1983 and Federalism, 90 Harv.L.Rev. 1133, 1274–1330 (1977); Laycock, Federal Interference with State Prosecutions: The Need For Prospective Relief, 1977 Sup.Ct.Rev. 193; Sedler, Younger and Its Progeny: A Variation on the Theme of Equity, Comity and Federalism, 9 U.Tol.L. Rev. 681 (1978).

5. Where no criminal prosecution has been instituted, declaratory judgment procedure is frequently utilized to determine whether a statute is unconstitutional or whether it is applicable to an undisputed set of facts. See Abbott v. City of Los Angeles, 53 Cal.2d 674, 3 Cal.Rptr. 158, 349 P.2d 974 (1960); New York Foreign Trade Zone Operators, Inc. v. State Liquor Authority, 285 N.Y. 272, 34 N.E.2d 316 (1941); Bunis v. Conway, 17 A.D.2d 207, 234 N.Y.S.2d 435 (1962). The Supreme Court ruled that federal courts may grant declaratory relief to determine the validity of state statutes without satisfying the *Younger* tests. Steffel v. Thompson, 415 U.S. 452 (1974). Once a criminal prosecution has commenced, however, declaratory relief is not available as the court in *Norcisa* noted. The date the federal declaratory action is commenced does not control; *Younger*'s principles govern if the state begins criminal proceedings "after the federal complaint is filed but before any proceedings of substance have taken place in the federal court." Hicks v. Miranda, 422 U.S. 332, 349 (1975). See also, Doran v. Salem Inn, Inc., 422 U.S. 922 (1975).

6. How far *Younger* applies to preclude injunctions against state civil actions has not been resolved. To date, the Court has found *Younger* applicable to a federal suit to enjoin the enforcement of a state court judgment finding a theatre exhibiting obscene films a nuisance, Huffman v. Pursue, Ltd., 420 U.S. 592 (1975); to an injunction prohibiting enforcement of a contempt citation in supplemental proceedings brought by judgment creditors, Juidice v. Vail, 430 U.S. 327 (1977); to an injunction against the utilization of the Illinois attachment procedure by a state agency, Trainor v. Hernandez, 431 U.S. 434 (1977); to a child custody proceeding, Moore v. Sims, 442 U.S. 415 (1979); to a proceeding to discipline an attorney, Middlesex County Ethics Committee v. Garden State Bar Association, 457 U.S. 423 (1982); to a state administrative procedure where a religious school argued a first amendment right to be free from the agency's jurisdiction, Ohio Civil Rights Commission v. Dayton Christian Schools, Inc., 477 U.S. 619 (1986); and to a request to enjoin collection of the Texas civil judgment in the Texaco–Pennzoil lawsuit, p. 529 infra, while the appeal was pending, Pennzoil Co. v. Texaco, Inc., 481 U.S. 1 (1987).

Courses in Constitutional Law and Federal Courts explore these issues in depth.

(3) Equity Lacks Jurisdiction to Enjoin a Crime

Introductory Note

Courts and writers have frequently asserted that equity lacks jurisdiction to enjoin crimes. Pomeroy thought the doctrine so obvious that he reduced it to a brief footnote: "Injunction never granted to restrain criminal acts." Pomeroy, Equity Jurisprudence § 1347, at 1347 n. 1 (1883). A more cautious statement may be found in Halsbury: "The court has no jurisdiction to prevent the commission of acts which are merely criminal or illegal, and do not affect any rights of property." 18 H. Halsbury, The Laws of England, § 16 (2d ed. 1935).

Thus, the denial of jurisdiction has been less than complete. Where property rights are involved, the court may grant equitable relief if the activity, though criminal, could be classified as a public nuisance. The subsequent expansion of equitable jurisdiction occurred through the manipulation of this concept.

PEOPLE v. LIM

Supreme Court of California, 1941.
18 Cal.2d 872, 118 P.2d 472.

GIBSON, C.J. The District Attorney of Monterey County commenced this action on behalf of the People of the State of California to restrain defendants from continuing the operation of a gambling establishment in the city of Monterey. The complaint set forth the manner in which the various games were played and alleged that the operation of this gambling house constituted a public nuisance by encouraging idle and dissolute habits, by disturbing the public peace and by corrupting the public morals. It was further alleged that previous attempts to eradicate this evil by prosecutions under the penal laws had proven ineffective and that the aid of equity was necessary to accomplish its suppression. A preliminary injunction was asked to restrain defendants from conducting and operating gambling games pending a trial of the action. Defendants interposed both general and special demurrers. The trial court sustained the demurrers and denied plaintiff's motion for a temporary injunction. After plaintiff's refusal to amend the complaint, the court entered its judgment in favor of defendants.

Upon this appeal it is contended in behalf of the people that the complaint states a proper cause of action and that it was error on the part of the trial court to sustain the general demurrer. The authority of a district attorney to bring such an action is found in the Code of Civil Procedure, section 731, which provides: "A civil action may be brought in the name of the people of the State of California to abate a public nuisance, as the same is defined in section thirty-four hundred and eighty of the Civil Code, by the district attorney of any county in which such nuisance exists * * *." Civil Code, section 3480 provides: "A public nuisance is one which affects at the same time an entire community or neighborhood, or any considerable number of persons, although the extent of the annoyance or damage inflicted upon individuals may be unequal." The definition of "nuisance," as the term is used in section 3480, is found in the provisions of the preceding section, Civil Code, section 3479: "Anything which is injurious to health, or is indecent or offensive to the senses, or an obstruction to the free use of property, so as to interfere with the comfortable enjoyment of life or property * * * is a nuisance." It is stated in the allegations of the complaint that the action was instituted under statutory provisions. Thus, it is alleged that the gambling house operated by defendants constitutes a public nuisance "for the reason that it tends to and does in fact debauch and corrupt the public morals, encourage idle and dissolute habits, draws together great numbers of disorderly persons, disturbs the public peace, brings together idle persons and cultivates dissolute habits among them, creates traffic and fire hazards, and is thereby injurious to health, indecent and offensive to the senses and impairs the free enjoyment of life and property."

Although this proceeding purports to have been brought under the code provisions governing such actions, the plaintiff upon this appeal relies rather upon the theory that the statutory definition of "public nuisance" is not intended to be exclusive and that gaming houses, which were recognized as public nuisances at common law, are inherently public nuisances apart from the provisions of our statute. Plaintiff cites those statutes which provide that the common law must be given effect as the rule of decision where not repugnant to or inconsistent with the Constitution or laws of the state. Thus, it is said, a gambling house constitutes an inherent public nuisance in this state and equity will enjoin such a public nuisance in an action brought on behalf of the people. Defendants argue, however, that the authority conferred upon a district attorney to bring such an action in equity extends only to those nuisances specified by statute and that their activities are not within the terms of our statute.

It must be conceded that the cases cited by plaintiff, as well as many others, demonstrate that a gambling house constituted a public nuisance at common law for the purposes of a criminal prosecution. [citations] While these cases indicate that gambling houses were recognized as public nuisances in criminal prosecutions, they do not hold that an equity action on behalf of the state might be maintained at common law to enjoin the operation of a gambling house. On the contrary, it is clear that the jurisdiction of equity was very sparingly exercised on behalf of the sovereign to enjoin public nuisances. The attitude of the early English cases is expressed by Chancellor Kent in a leading case: "I know that the Court is in the practice of restraining private nuisances to property, and of quieting persons in the enjoyment of private right; but it is an extremely rare case, and may be considered, if it ever happened, as an anomaly, for a Court of equity to interfere at all, and much less preliminarily, by injunction, to put down a *public* nuisance which did not violate the rights of property, but only contravened the general policy." (Attorney–General v. Utica Insurance Co., 2 Johns. Ch. (N.Y.) 371, 380.) The authorities support the conclusion that this statement accurately represents the attitude of the earlier courts of equity where the sovereign sought injunctions against public nuisances. The common law recognized various types of wrongful activity as indictable public nuisances, including such miscellaneous acts as eavesdropping, being a common scold and maintaining for hire a place of amusement which served no useful purpose. (See 1 Wood, Nuisances, pp. 37, 60, 68, 72.) The kinds of public nuisance at common law, however, where injunctions were granted on behalf of the sovereign included only those cases of public nuisance in which the sovereign's rights were given the same protection that would have been given to the rights of a private person. An action on behalf of the state, therefore, to enjoin activity which violates general concepts of public policy finds no basis in the doctrines of the common law.

It has been recognized that the tendency to utilize the equity injunction as a means of enforcing public policy is a relatively recent development in the law. (Mack, "Revival of Criminal Equity," (1903) 16 Harv.L.Rev. 389, 392.) Courts have held that public and social interests, as well as the rights of property, are entitled to the protection of equity. [citations] This development has resulted in a continuous expansion of the field of public nuisances in which equitable relief is available at the request of the state. It has been held, for example, that the legislature may properly define the term "public nuisance" for the purposes of an equity injunction so as to include activity which was not a nuisance at common law or activity which offends concepts of public policy even though no rights of property are involved. [citations] Where a particular activity, such as gambling or horse-racing, has been held to come within the language of a statute defining the term "public nuisance" for the purposes of equity jurisdiction on behalf of the state, courts have granted injunctions, or indicated that they would grant them, even though the acts were also criminal. [citations] Upon at least two occasions the legislature of this state has passed statutes authorizing an action in equity to enjoin particular activity contrary to the public policy as a "public nuisance." Thus, houses of prostitution and houses where narcotics are illegally sold may be enjoined in an action brought by the district attorney of the county in which they are located. [citations]

It must be admitted, however, that the authorities are divided as to whether the expansion of the field of public nuisances in which equity will grant injunctions must be accomplished by an act of the legislature. Some courts have attempted by judicial action alone to define "public nuisance" very broadly in order to grant injunctions on behalf of the state. Thus, it has been said that any place where a public statute is continuously flouted constitutes a public nuisance which may be enjoined by the state. (State ex rel. Vance v. Crawford, 28 Kan. 726, 733.) Other courts have flatly stated that a particular form of activity, such as bullfighting, is so objectionable as to constitute a public nuisance for the purposes of an equity injunction without the aid of a statute. (State ex rel. Atty.-Gen. v. Canty, 207 Mo. 439 [105 S.W. 1078]. The courts of this state, however, have refused to sanction the granting of injunctions on behalf of the state merely by a judicial extension of the definition of "public nuisance." The case of In re Wood, 194 Cal. 49 [227 P. 908], which has been severely criticized (see, Chafee, Free Speech in the United States (1941), p. 336, et seq.), held only that the injunction granted was not void even though conceivably erroneous. This was so because the conspiracy there involved could be considered a public nuisance as a threatened impairment of the free use of property of the citizens of the state. Similarly, in Weis v. Superior Court, 30 Cal.App. 730 [159 P. 464], it was held that the District Attorney of San Diego County was authorized, under Code of Civil Procedure, section 731, to enjoin the performance of a public exhibition which was shown to have been indecent, and thus within the statutory definition of public nuisance in Civil Code, section 3479. In People v. Seccombe, 103 Cal.App. 306 [284 P. 725], however, the court refused to permit the maintenance of a suit in equity on behalf of the state to restrain defendant's continued practice of usury. It was held that, though reprehensible, the practice of usury could not be brought within any of the sections of the statute defining public nuisances. The courts have thus refused to grant injunctions on behalf of the state except where the objectionable activity can be brought within the terms of the statutory definition of public nuisance. Where the legislature has felt that the summary power of equity was required to control activity contrary to public policy, it has enacted statutes specifying that such activity constitutes a public nuisance which may be enjoined in an action brought on behalf of the state. We think the proper rule, therefore, and the one to which this state is committed is expressed in the following language from State v. Ehrlick, [65 W.Va. 700,] 64

S.E. 935 (1909): "It is also competent for the Legislature, within the constitutional limits of its powers, to declare any act criminal and make the repetition or continuance thereof a public nuisance * * * or to vest in courts of equity the power to abate them by injunction; but it is not the province of the courts to ordain such jurisdiction for themselves."

In addition to the historical precedents which we have considered, compelling reasons of policy require that the responsibility for establishing those standards of public morality, the violations of which are to constitute public nuisances within equity's jurisdiction, should be left with the legislature. "Nuisance" is a term which does not have a fixed content either at common law or at the present time. Blackstone defined it so broadly as to include almost all types of actionable wrong, that is, "any thing that worketh hurt, inconvenience or damage." (2 Cooley's Blackstone (4th ed. 1899), p. 1012.) We have already referred to those modern definitions which seek to make of equity an additional remedy for the enforcement of the criminal law by defining "public nuisance" for the purposes of an injunction as any repeated and continuous violation of the law. In a field where the meaning of terms is so vague and uncertain it is a proper function of the legislature to define those breaches of public policy which are to be considered public nuisances within the control of equity. Activity which in one period constitutes a public nuisance, such as the sale of liquor or the holding of prize fights, might not be objectionable in another. Such declarations of policy should be left for the legislature.

Conduct against which injunctions are sought in behalf of the public is frequently criminal in nature. While this alone will not prevent the intervention of equity where a clear case justifying equitable relief is present [citations] it is apparent that the equitable remedy has the collateral effect of depriving a defendant of the jury trial to which he would be entitled in a criminal prosecution for violating exactly the same standards of public policy. The defendant also loses the protection of the higher burden of proof required in criminal prosecutions and, after imprisonment and fine for violation of the equity injunction, may be subjected under the criminal law to similar punishment for the same acts. For these reasons equity is loath to interfere where the standards of public policy can be enforced by resort to the criminal law, and in the absence of a legislative declaration to that effect, the courts should not broaden the field in which injunctions against criminal activity will be granted. Thus, for the reasons set forth, the basis for an action such as this must be found in our statutes rather than by reference to the common law definitions of public nuisance.

* * * In support of the court's ruling on the general demurrer, defendants argue that the allegations of the complaint are insufficient because no facts are alleged from which the court could conclude that a nuisance existed under the provisions of Civil Code, sections 3479, 3480, and Code of Civil Procedure section 731. It is contended that the allegations of the complaint present merely conclusions of the pleader, framed in the language of the statute. * * *

Although the defendant's contention that particular allegations of fact are required is correct, we think that the allegations of the present complaint are adequate as against a general demurrer. The complaint alleges that the gambling house operated by defendants "draws together great numbers of disorderly persons, disturbs the public peace, brings together idle persons and cultivates dissolute habits among them, creates traffic and fire hazards, and is thereby injurious to health, indecent and offensive to the senses and impairs the free enjoyment of life and property." Crowds of disorderly people who disturb the peace and obstruct the traffic may well impair the free enjoyment of life and property and give rise to the hazards designated in the statute. * * * It follows that the trial court was in error in sustaining the general demurrer. * * *

The judgment is reversed.

Notes

1. Courts continue to shape the malleable public nuisance concept to deal with contemporary issues.

"Crack": Kellner v. Cappellini, 135 Misc.2d 759, 516 N.Y.S.2d 827 (Civ.Ct.1986). (Neighboring owners brought the action.)

AIDS: City of New York v. New Saint Mark's Baths, 130 Misc.2d 911, 497 N.Y.S.2d 979 (Sup.Ct.1986).

Antiabortion protests: Town of West Hartford v. Operation Rescue, 726 F.Supp. 371 (D.Conn.1989).

Love Canal hazardous waste site: United States v. Hooker Chemicals & Plastics Corp., 722 F.Supp. 960 (W.D.N.Y.1989).

2. The public nuisance approach to controlling obscenity in books and live shows has met with indifferent success and created much confusion.

The defendants' constitutional right to free expression may prevent the authorities from closing an "adult" business to curtail customers' illegal activity. The United States Supreme Court held that the federal First Amendment would not bar an injunction that closed the bookstore. Arcara v. Cloud Books, Inc., 478 U.S. 697 (1986). But on remand the New York Court of Appeals found that the state constitution afforded more breathing space than the "minimal standards" in the first amendment. The authorities had not shown that an injunction closing the store was the narrowest course to accomplish its goals. The authorities were left with criminal prosecutions of the customers and narrower injunctions. People ex rel. Arcara v. Cloud Books, Inc., 68 N.Y.2d 553, 510 N.Y.S.2d 844, 503 N.E.2d 492 (1986), rev'd, 478 U.S. 697 (1986).

In People v. Sequoia Books, Inc., 127 Ill.2d 271, 288–91, 537 N.E.2d 302, 310–12 (1989), cert. denied, 110 S.Ct. 835 (1990), the only crime that defendants had committed was the sale of obscene material. The authorities argued for an injunction closing the bookstore with a provision that it could post a bond and remain open. The Illinois Supreme Court held the closure and bond provisions unconstitutional:

"Insofar as the remedy of nuisance abatement is intended as simply another weapon in the State's antiobscenity arsenal, it is too blunt an instrument. Under the ordinary penal law relating to obscenity, punishment is fairly well calibrated to the nature and gravity of the crime. Each discrete act of selling obscene material is subject to penal sanction. Someone who sells 100 obscene books is, theoretically at least, subject to more severe punishment than someone who sells only a single volume. Under the nuisance statute, on the other hand, the owner of property from which a single obscene work is sold stands in the same danger of losing, for one year, the entire value of his investment, as does the owner of a property from which are sold obscene works in the hundreds or thousands.

"This blunderbuss approach to the regulation of obscenity is inconsistent with our traditional insistence that the regulation of any form of expression, even of obscenity, be carefully drawn so as not to impact unduly upon protected speech. * * * Moreover, obscenity, unlike the other criminal acts which may trigger a nuisance abatement, is unique—because it is so closely related to, and so hard to distinguish from, protected speech. For this reason, nuisance abatements tend to single out owners of bookstores for harsher treatment than the owners of other kinds of commercial property, and may also be unconstitutional on that ground as well. * * *

"Lastly, we consider the State's interest in controlling the environmental or secondary effects of the sale of obscenity. This interest may be what the State is talking about when it says that 'the property focus of the instant legislation is what distinguishes this case from those which involve the licensing or banning of the communicative activity itself.' However, the State has at its disposal far less draconian, and far more narrowly focused, means of combatting pornography's environmental effects. Zoning restrictions, which may either disperse sale of sexually explicit materials to widely separated locations (Young v. American Mini Theatres, Inc., 427 U.S. 50 (1976)), or confine it to a relatively small, nonresidential zone (County of Cook v. Renaissance Arcade and Bookstore, 122 Ill.2d 123, 522 N.E.2d 73 (1988)), have been repeatedly upheld. The State can also abate as nuisances establishments which tolerate or promote sexual and other crimes on their premises. (Arcara v. Cloud Books, Inc., 478 U.S. 697 (1986)). Given the existence of these alternatives, the State has no need to combat obscenity's environmental effects by abating, as nuisances, particular properties upon which obscene works have been sold."

3. In abatement suits, courts often ignore the inadequacy of the remedy at law. Some courts, however, deny injunctions if plaintiff fails to prove that a criminal prosecution will be ineffective. In United States v. Menominee Indian Tribe, 694 F.Supp. 1373 (E.D.Wis.1988) and United States v. Bay Mills Indian Community, 692 F.Supp. 777 (W.D.Mich.1988), injunctions to forbid gambling on Indian reservations were denied because the remedy of criminal law was adequate. In Pizza v. Sunset Fireworks Co., 25 Ohio St.3d 1, 494 N.E.2d 1115 (1986), the court granted an injunction against illegal sale of fireworks because criminal prosecution was ineffectual. In Airlines Reporting Corp. v. Barry, 825 F.2d 1220 (8th Cir.1987), an injunction was necessary to prevent future acts of fraud. See also City of Kansas City v. Mary Don Co., 606 S.W.2d 411 (Mo.App.1980), where 103 citations and repeated fines failed to secure compliance with building maintenance ordinances.

4. Not all jurisdictions agree with the California ruling that the practice of usury does not constitute a public nuisance. Consider State v. J.C. Penney Co., 48 Wis.2d 125, 179 N.W.2d 641 (1970). The court enjoined as a public nuisance a revolving charge account system with usurious interest charges. See also State ex rel. Goff v. O'Neil, 205 Minn. 366, 286 N.W. 316 (1939).

5. State v. Red Owl Stores, Inc., 253 Minn. 236, 92 N.W.2d 103 (1958), aff'd in part, rev'd in part, 262 Minn. 31, 43, 115 N.W.2d 643, 651 (1962). Defendant, operator of a large chain of retail food stores, sold such products as Anacin, Alka–Seltzer, Ex–Lax, etc. allegedly in violation of a statute that prohibited the sale of drugs and medicines except in a pharmacy. The state sought to enjoin the sale of such products by asserting that defendant's violation of the statute constituted a continuing public nuisance. In affirming a judgment denying the injunction, the supreme court held that the sale of these drugs by the defendant "did not

constitute a nuisance nor did such sales affect or endanger the public health to the point where injunctive relief is required."

6. The public nuisance approach is frequently employed to enjoin the unlicensed practice of a profession. See Arizona State Board of Dental Examiners v. Hyder, 114 Ariz. 544, 562 P.2d 717 (1977) (unauthorized practice of dentistry); Florida Bar v. Borges–Caignet, 321 So.2d 550 (Fla.1975) (unauthorized practice of law); People ex rel. Bennett v. Laman, 277 N.Y. 368, 14 N.E.2d 439 (1938) (practicing medicine without a license). For a contrary result see Massachusetts Society of Optometrists v. Waddick, 340 Mass. 581, 165 N.E.2d 394 (1960). Cf. State ex rel. State Board of Examiners in Optometry v. Kuhwald, 372 A.2d 214 (Del.Ch. 1977) (construing the Delaware Optometry Act).

In Kelley v. State Board of Medical Examiners, 467 S.W.2d 539, 546 (Tex.Civ. App.1971), the court prohibited a dentist from practicing medicine (the treatment of cancer), and enjoined the publication and distribution of a book, "One Answer to Cancer." In response to defendant's contention that such an injunction violated his constitutional right of free speech, the court ruled that "The constitutional guarantee of freedom of expression must yield in the case at bar to afford reasonable protection to the public."

7. In People ex rel. Bennett v. Laman, 277 N.Y. 368, ___, 14 N.E.2d 439, 443 (1938), the state, under pressure from the medical profession, obtained an injunction against the defendant, whose post-high school education consisted of 22 months of chiropractic study, from practicing medicine. The opinion notes that nuisance is an elastic concept and says that while "invasion of property rights or pecuniary interests is emphasized in some of the earlier cases as a basis for equitable interference, there appeared later a recognition that public health, morals, safety and welfare of the community equally required protection from irreparable injury."

Under that definition is every crime also a public nuisance? If so, what limits the exercise of equitable jurisdiction?

8. *Injunctions By Businesses to Enjoin Crimes That Constitute Unfair Competition.* The step from a rule that a public nuisance may be enjoined even though a crime to one that unfair competition violating a criminal ordinance may also be enjoined is not a large one in light of the obvious protection afforded the practitioners of medicine, dentistry and the law.

Western Supply Co. v. T.V. Appliance Mart, Inc., 146 Wis.2d 216, ___, 430 N.W.2d 720, 722 (App.1988), involved a Transient Vendor Statute (or "Greenriver Ordinance") of the type discussed in *Norcisa,* p. 174. The court held that a local merchant was not preempted by the statute from suing a transient merchant and that the criminal character of defendant's proposed sales is not an obstacle to injunctive relief if all legal criteria for that relief are satisfied. "[T]he court exercises its powers to prevent injury to protected private interest and ignores the 'public' or penal features of the act. The remedy remains preventative, not punitive."

Is this consistent with the language in the preceding note?

c. *How Legislation May Affect the Existence and Exercise of Equitable Jurisdiction*

WEINBERGER v. ROMERO–BARCELO

Supreme Court of the United States, 1982.

456 U.S. 305.

WHITE, JUSTICE. The issue in this case is whether the Federal Water Pollution Control Act (FWPCA or the Act) 33 U.S.C. § 1251 et seq. (1976 ed.

and Supp. III), requires a district court to enjoin immediately all discharges of pollutants that do not comply with the Act's permit requirements or whether the district court retains discretion to order other relief to achieve compliance. * * *

For many years, the Navy has used Vieques Island, a small island off the Puerto Rico coast, for weapons training. Currently all Atlantic Fleet vessels assigned to the Mediterranean and the Indian Ocean are required to complete their training at Vieques because it permits a full range of exercises under conditions similar to combat. During air-to-ground training, however, pilots sometimes miss land-based targets, and ordnance falls into the sea. That is, accidental bombings of the navigable waters and, occasionally, intentional bombings of water targets occur. The District Court found that these discharges have not harmed the quality of the water.

In 1978, respondents, who include the Governor of Puerto Rico and residents of the island, sued to enjoin the Navy's operations on the island. * * *

Under the FWPCA, the "discharge of any pollutant" requires a National Pollutant Discharge Elimination System (NPDES) permit. 33 U.S.C. § 1311(a), § 1323(a) (1976 ed. and Supp. III). * * * As the District Court construed the FWPCA, the release of ordnance from aircraft or from ships into navigable waters is a discharge of pollutants. * * *

Recognizing that violations of the Act "must be cured," the District Court ordered the Navy to apply for a NPDES permit. It refused, however, to enjoin Navy operations pending consideration of the permit application. It explained that the Navy's "technical violations" were not causing any "appreciable harm" to the environment. "Moreover, because of the importance of the island as a training center, the granting of the injunctive relief sought would cause grievous, and perhaps irreparable harm, not only to Defendant Navy, but to the general welfare of this Nation."[1] The District Court concluded that an injunction was not necessary to ensure suitably prompt compliance by the Navy. To support this conclusion, it emphasized an equity court's traditionally broad discretion in deciding appropriate relief and quoted from the classic description of injunctive relief in Hecht v. Bowles, 321 U.S. 321, 329–330 (1944): "The historic injunctive process was designed to deter, not to punish."

The Court of Appeals for the First Circuit vacated the District Court's order and remanded with instructions that the court order the Navy to cease the violation until it obtained a permit. Relying on TVA v. Hill, 437 U.S. 153 (1978), in which this Court held that an imminent violation of the Endangered Species Act required injunctive relief, the Court of Appeals concluded that the District Court erred in undertaking a traditional balancing of the parties' competing interests. "Whether or not the Navy's activities in fact harm the coastal waters, it has an absolute statutory obligation to stop any discharges of pollutant until the permit procedure has been followed and the Administrator of the Environmental Protection Agency, upon review of the evidence, has granted a permit." The court suggested that "if the order would interfere significantly with military preparedness, the Navy should request that the

1. [Footnotes renumbered.] The District Court also took into consideration the delay by plaintiffs asserting their claims. It concluded that although laches should not totally bar the claims, it did strongly militate against the granting of injunctive relief.

President grant it an exemption from the requirements in the interest of national security." [2]

It goes without saying that an injunction is an equitable remedy. It "is not a remedy which issues as of course," Harrisonville v. U.S. Dickey Clay Mfg. Co., 289 U.S. 334, 338 (1933), or "to restrain an act the injurious consequences of which are merely trifling." [citations] The Court has repeatedly held that the basis for injunctive relief in the federal courts has always been irreparable injury and the inadequacy of legal remedies. [citations]

Where plaintiff and defendant present competing claims of injury, the traditional function of equity has been to arrive at a "nice adjustment and reconciliation" between the competing claims, Hecht Co. v. Bowles, supra. In such cases, the court "balances the conveniences of the parties and possible injuries to them according as they may be affected by the granting or withholding of the injunction." Yakus v. United States, 321 U.S. 414, 440 (1944). "The essence of equity has been the power of the chancellor to do equity and to mold each decree to the necessities of the particular case. Flexibility rather than rigidity has distinguished it." Hecht Co. v. Bowles.

In exercising their sound discretion, courts of equity should pay particular regard for the public consequences in employing the extraordinary remedy of injunction. Railroad Comm'n. v. Pullman Co., 312 U.S. 496, 500 (1941). Thus, the Court has noted that "the award of an interlocutory injunction by courts of equity has never been regarded as strictly a matter of right, even though irreparable injury may otherwise result to the plaintiff," and that "where an injunction is asked which will adversely affect a public interest for whose impairment, even temporarily, an injunction bond cannot compensate, the court may in the public interest withhold relief until a final determination of the rights of the parties, though postponement may be burdensome to the plaintiff." Yakus v. United States, supra, (footnote omitted). The grant of jurisdiction to insure compliance with a statute hardly suggests an absolute duty to do so under any and all circumstances, and a federal judge sitting as chancellor is not mechanically obligated to grant an injunction for every violation of law. TVA v. Hill; Hecht Co. v. Bowles.

These commonplace considerations applicable to cases in which injunctions are sought in the federal courts reflect a "practice with a background of several hundred years of history," Hecht Co. v. Bowles, a practice of which Congress is assuredly well aware. Of course, Congress may intervene and guide or control the exercise of the courts' discretion, but we do not lightly assume that Congress has intended to depart from established principles. Hecht Co. v. Bowles. As the Court said in Porter v. Warner Holding Co., 328 U.S. 395, 398 (1946):

> "Moreover, the comprehensiveness of this equitable jurisdiction is not to be denied or limited in the absence of a clear and valid legislative command. Unless a statute in as many words, or by a necessary and inescapable inference, restricts the court's jurisdiction in equity, the full scope of that jurisdiction is to be recognized and applied. 'The great principles of the equity,

2. 33 U.S.C. § 1323(a) (Supp. III 1976) provides, in relevant part:

The President may exempt any affluent source of any department, agency, or instrumentality in the executive branch from compliance with any such a requirement if he determines it to be in the paramount interest of the United States to do so. * * *

securing complete justice, should not be yielded to light inferences, or doubtful construction.' Brown v. Swann, 10 Pet. 497, 503."

In TVA v. Hill, we held that Congress had foreclosed the exercise of the usual discretion possessed by a court of equity. There, we thought that "one would be hard pressed to find a statutory provision whose terms were any plainer" than that before us. The statute involved, the Endangered Species Act, required the district court to enjoin completion of the Tellico Dam in order to preserve the snail darter, a species of perch. The purpose and language of the statute under consideration in *Hill,* not the bare fact of a statutory violation, compelled that conclusion. Section 1536 of the Act requires federal agencies to "insure that actions authorized, funded, or carried out by them do not jeopardize the continued existence of [any] endangered species * * * or result in the destruction or habitat of such species which is determined * * * to be critical." The statute thus contains a flat ban on the destruction of critical habitats.

It was conceded in *Hill* that completion of the dam would eliminate an endangered species by destroying its critical habitat. Refusal to enjoin the action would have ignored the "explicit provisions of the Endangered Species Act." Congress, it appeared to us, had chosen the snail darter over the dam. The purpose and language of the statute limited the remedies available to the district court; only an injunction could vindicate the objectives of the Act.

That is not the case here. An injunction is not the only means of ensuring compliance. The FWPCA itself, for example, provides for fines and criminal penalties. 33 U.S.C. § 1319(c) and (d). Respondents suggest that failure to enjoin the Navy will undermine the integrity of the permit process by allowing the statutory violation to continue. The integrity of the nation's waters, however, not the permit process, is the purpose of the FWPCA.[3] As Congress explained, the objective of the FWPCA is to "restore and maintain the chemical, physical and biological integrity of the Nation's waters." 33 U.S.C. § 1251(a).

This purpose is to be achieved by compliance with the Act, including compliance with the permit requirements. Here, however, the discharge of ordnance had not polluted the waters, and, although the District Court declined to enjoin the discharges, it neither ignored the statutory violation nor undercut the purpose and function of the permit system. The court ordered the Navy to apply for a permit.[4] It temporarily, not permanently, allowed the Navy to continue its activities without a permit.

3. The objective of this statute is in some respects similar to that sought in nuisance suits, where courts have fully exercised their equitable discretion and ingenuity in ordering remedies. E.g., Spur Ind. Inc. v. Del E. Webb Development Co., 108 Ariz. 178, 494 P.2d 700 (1972); Boomer v. Atlantic Cement Co., 26 N.Y.2d 219, 309 N.Y.S.2d 312, 257 N.E.2d 870 (1970).

4. The Navy applied for an NPDES permit in December, 1979. In May, 1981, the EPA issued a draft NPDES permit and a notice of intent to issue that permit. The FWPCA requires a certification of compliance with state water quality standards before the EPA may issue an NPDES permit. 33 U.S.C. § 134(a). The Environmental Quality Board of the Commonwealth of Puerto Rico denied the Navy a water quality certificate in connection with this application for an NPDES in June, 1981. In February, 1982, the Environmental Quality Board denied the Navy's reconsideration request and announced it was adhering to its original ruling. In a letter dated April 9, 1982, the Solicitor General informed the Clerk of the Court that the Navy has filed an action challenging the denial of the water quality certificate. United States of America v. Commonwealth of Puerto Rico, No. 82–0726 (D.P.R.).

Other aspects of the statutory scheme also suggest that Congress did not intend to deny courts the discretion to rely on remedies other than an immediate prohibitory injunction. Although the ultimate objective of the FWPCA is to eliminate all discharges of pollutants into the navigable waters by 1985, the statute sets forth a scheme of phased compliance. As enacted, it called for the achievement of the "best practicable control technology currently available" by July 1, 1977 and the "best available technology economically achievable" by July 1, 1983. 33 U.S.C. § 1311(b) (Supp. IV 1970). This scheme of phased compliance further suggests that this is a statute in which Congress envisioned, rather than curtailed, the exercise of discretion.

The FWPCA directs the Administrator of the EPA to seek an injunction to restrain immediately discharges of pollutants he finds to be presenting "an imminent and substantial endangerment of the health of persons or to the welfare of persons." 33 U.S.C. § 1364(a). This rule of immediate cessation, however, is limited to the indicated class of violations. For other kinds of violations, the FWPCA authorizes the Administrator of the EPA "to commence a civil action for appropriate relief, including a permanent or temporary injunction, for any violation for which he is authorized to issue a compliance order. * * * " 33 U.S.C. 1319(b).[5] The provision makes clear that Congress did not anticipate that all discharges would be immediately enjoined. Consistent with this view, the administrative practice has not been to request immediate cessation orders. "Rather, enforcement actions typically result, by consent or otherwise, in a remedial order setting out a detailed schedule of compliance designed to cure the identified violation of the Act." Brief for United States 17. Here, again, the statutory scheme contemplates equitable consideration.

This Court explained in Hecht v. Bowles, that a major departure from the long tradition of equity practice should not be lightly implied. As we did there, we construe the statute at issue "in favor of that interpretation which affords a full opportunity for equity courts to treat enforcement proceedings * * * in accordance with their traditional practices, as conditioned by the necessities of the public interest which Congress has sought to protect." We do not read the FWPCA as foreclosing completely the exercise of the court's discretion. Rather than requiring a District Court to issue an injunction for any and all statutory violations, the FWPCA permits the District Court to order that relief it considers necessary to secure prompt compliance with the Act. That relief can include, but is not limited to, an order of immediate cessation.

The exercise of equitable discretion, which must include the ability to deny as well as grant injunctive relief, can fully protect the range of public interests at issue at this stage in the proceedings. The District Court did not face a situation in which a permit would very likely not issue and the requirements and objective of the statute could therefore not be vindicated if discharges were permitted to continue. Should it become clear that no permit will be issued

5. The statute at issue in Hecht v. Bowles, contained language very similar to that in § 1319(b). It directed the Administrator to seek "a permanent or temporary injunction, restraining order, or other order" to halt violations. The Court determined that such statutory language did not require the court to issue an injunction even when the Administrator had sued for injunctive relief. In *Hecht,* the court's equitable discretion overrode that of the Administrator. If a court can properly refuse an injunction in the circumstances of *Hecht,* the exercise of its discretion seems clearly appropriate in a case such as this, where the EPA Administrator was not a party and had not yet expressed his judgment. The action of the district court permitted it to obtain the benefit of the EPA's recommendation before deciding to enjoin the discharge.

and that compliance with the FWPCA will not be forthcoming, the statutory scheme and purpose would require the court to reconsider the balance it has struck.

Because Congress, in enacting the FWPCA, has not foreclosed the exercise of equitable discretion, the proper standard for appellate review is whether the district court abused its discretion in denying an immediate cessation order while the Navy applied for a permit. We reverse and remand to Court of Appeals for proceedings consistent with this opinion.

It is so ordered.

STEVENS, JUSTICE, dissenting. * * * Our cases concerning equitable remedies have repeatedly identified two critical distinctions that the Court simply ignores today. The first is the distinction between cases in which only private interests are involved and those in which a requested injunction will implicate a public interest. Second, within the category of public interest cases, those cases in which there is no danger that a past violation of law will recur have always been treated differently from those in which an existing violation is certain to continue.

Yakus v. United States, 321 U.S. 414, 441, illustrates the first distinction. The Court there held that Congress constitutionally could preclude a private party from obtaining an injunction against enforcement of federal price control regulations pending an adjudication of their validity. In that case, the public interest, reflected in an act of Congress, was in opposition to the availability of injunctive relief. The Court stated, however, that the public interest factor would have the same special weight if it favored the granting of an injunction. * * *

Hecht Co. v. Bowles, which the Court repeatedly cites, did involve an attempt to obtain an injunction against future violations of a federal statute. That case fell into the category of cases in which a past violation of law had been found and the question was whether an injunction should issue to prevent future violations. [citations] Because the record established that the past violations were inadvertent, that they had been promptly terminated, and that the defendant had taken vigorous and adequate steps to prevent any recurrence, the Court held that the District Court had discretion to deny injunctive relief. But in reaching that conclusion, the Court made it clear that judicial discretion "must be exercised in light of the large objectives of the Act. For the standards of the public interest, not the requirements of private litigation, measure the propriety and need for injunctive relief in these cases." Indeed, the Court emphasized that any exercise of discretion "should reflect an acute awareness of the congressional admonition" in the statute at issue.

In contrast to the decision in *Hecht,* today the Court pays mere lip service to the statutory mandate and attaches no weight to the fact that the Navy's violation of law has not been corrected.[1] The Court cites no precedent for its holding that an ongoing deliberate violation of a federal statute should be treated like any garden-variety private nuisance action in which the chancellor has the widest discretion in fashioning relief.[2] * * *

1. The Navy has been in continuous violation of the statute during the entire decade since its enactment.

2. Indeed, I am unaware of any case in which the Court has permitted a statutory violation to continue.

The Court distinguishes TVA v. Hill, on the ground that the Endangered Species Act contained a "flat ban" on the destruction of critical habitats. But the statute involved in this case also contains a flat ban against discharges of pollutants into coastal waters without a permit. Surely the congressional directive to protect the Nation's waters from gradual but possibly irreversible contamination is no less clear than the command to protect the snail darter. To assume that Congress has placed a greater value on the protection of vanishing forms of animal life than on the protection of our water resources is to ignore the text, the legislative history,[3] and the previously consistent interpretation of this statute.

It is true that in TVA v. Hill there was no room for compromise between the federal project and the statutory objective to preserve an endangered species; either the snail darter or the completion of the Tellico Dam had to be sacrificed. In the FWPCA, the Court tells us, the congressional objective is to protect the integrity of the Nation's waters, not to protect the integrity of the permit process. Therefore, the Court continues, a federal court may compromise the process chosen by Congress to protect our waters as long as the court is content that the waters are not actually being harmed by the particular discharge of pollutants.

On analysis, however, this reasoning does not distinguish the two cases. Courts are in no better position to decide whether the permit process is necessary to achieve the objectives of the FWPCA than they are to decide whether the destruction of the snail darter is an acceptable cost of completing the Tellico Dam. Congress has made both decisions, and there is nothing in the respective statutes or legislative histories to suggest that Congress invited the federal courts to second-guess the former decision any more than the latter. * * *

The Court's sophistry is premised on a gross misunderstanding of the statutory scheme. Naturally, in 1972 Congress did not expect dischargers to end pollution immediately. Rather, it entrusted to expert administrative agencies the task of establishing timetables by which dischargers could reach that ultimate goal. These timetables are determined by the agencies and included in the NPDES permits; the conditions in the permits constitute the terms by which compliance with the statute is measured. Quite obviously, then, the requirement that each discharger subject itself to the permit process is crucial to the operation of the "scheme of phased compliance." By requiring each discharger to obtain a permit *before* continuing its discharges of pollutants, Congress demonstrated an intolerance for delay in compliance with the statute. It is also obvious that the "exercise of discretion and balancing of equities" were tasks delegated by Congress to expert agencies, not to federal courts, yet the Court simply ignores the difference. * * *

The decision in TVA v. Hill did not depend on any peculiar or unique statutory language. Nor did it rest on any special interest in snail darters. The decision reflected a profound respect for the law and the proper allocation of lawmaking responsibilities in our government.[4] There we refused to sit as a

3. The Senate Report emphasized that "if the timetables established throughout the Act are to be met, the threat of sanction must be real, and enforcement provisions must be swift and direct." S.Rep. No. 91–414, 92d Cong., 1st Sess., 65 (1971).

4. Our individual appraisal of the wisdom or unwisdom of a particular course consciously selected by the Congress is to be put aside in the process of interpreting a statute. Once the meaning of an enactment is discerned and its

committee of review. Today the Court authorizes free thinking federal judges to do just that. Instead of requiring adherence to carefully integrated statutory procedures that assign to nonjudicial decisionmakers the responsibilities for evaluating potential harm to our water supply as well as potential harm to our national security, the Court unnecessarily and casually substitutes the chancellor's clumsy foot for the rule of law.

I respectfully dissent.

Notes

1. Did the Court ignore the legislative branch of government? Both the majority and the dissent rely heavily on equity tradition. Which is the more "liberal" and which the more "conservative" opinion? If the Court feels that Congress has failed to vote sufficient money for environmental protection, does it have the power to increase the appropriation? Can a legislature write a statute that will limit judicial discretion? Does the holding turn on whether the defendant violated the statute or on whether the judge had discretion to excuse an admitted violation? Does the Court merely order defendants to comply as promptly as is feasible? See Plater, Statutory Violations and Equitable Discretion, 70 Calif.L.Rev. 524 (1982).

2. Legislatures can pass statutes that: a. confer or take away subject matter jurisdiction of a court; b. affect "equitable jurisdiction"; or c. purport to control the nature and characteristics of equitable remedies themselves. These statutes are ambiguous; they open opportunities to debate legislative intent as well as to raise separation of powers.

3. *Statutes That Expand Equitable Jurisdiction.* Example: Professor Laycock proposes a statute to remove the barrier of the irreparable injury prerequisite for equitable remedies: "Suppose Congress and each state enacted the following statute: 'The existence of another adequate remedy does not preclude a final judgment of injunction, specific performance, or other equitable relief, in cases where such relief is appropriate.'" Laycock, The Death of the Irreparable Injury Rule, 103 Harv.L.Rev. 687, 771 (1990).

This is a clear, succinct statutory extension of equitable jurisdiction by any measure. But suppose a federal district judge denies an application for an injunction for the express reason that an adequate remedy at law exists. An abuse of discretion? Reversible error? What possible directive could an appellate court issue?

Example: The statute defining the wrong provides for an injunction as *the* remedy. See discussion pp. 171–72 supra. Under some authority this automatically confers equitable jurisdiction dispensing with proof of irreparable injury. See Carroll v. El Dorado Estates Division Number Two Association, 680 P.2d 1158 (Alaska 1984).

constitutionality determined, the judicial process comes to an end. We do not sit as a committee of review, nor are we vested with the power of veto. The lines ascribed to Sir Thomas More by Robert Bolt are not without relevance here: "The law, Roper, the law. I know what's legal, not what's right. And I'll stick to what's legal. * * * I'm *not* God. The currents and eddies of right and wrong, which you find such plain-sailing, I can't navigate, I'm no voyager. But in the thickets of the law, oh there I'm a forester. * * * What would you do? Cut a great road through the law to get after the Devil? * * * And when the last law was down, and the Devil turned around on you—where would you hide, Roper, the laws all being flat? * * * This country's planted thick with laws from coast to coast—Man's laws, not God's—and if you cut them down * * * d'you really think you could stand upright in the winds that would blow them? * * * Yes, I'd give the Devil benefit of law, for my own safety's sake." R. Bolt, A Man for All Seasons, Act I, p. 147 (Three Plays, Heinemann ed. 1967)." Tennessee Valley Authority v. Hill, 437 U.S. 153, 194–195 (1978).

4. *Statutes That Create a Cause of Action But Provide Only Legal Remedies.*

a. Hill v. Nationwide Insurance Co., 391 Pa.Super. 184, 186–92, 199, 570 A.2d 574, 575–78, 581 (1990). The plaintiff held a policy of automobile insurance issued by the defendant providing coverage for first party benefits. Injuries occurred, but no compensation was paid. The applicable statute is the Pennsylvania Motor Vehicle Financial Responsibility Law which provides that if benefits due have not been paid within 30 days, they shall bear interest at the rate of 12% per annum, and if the denial is unreasonable, attorney's fees may be recovered. The plaintiff sued for specific performance, past and future medical benefits, which were granted, *as well as the interest and attorney's fees.* The appellate court affirmed.

The majority opinion: "This appeal raises the question of whether the [MVFRL] provides an adequate and complete statutory remedy that precludes equity jurisdiction in [this] action * * *. 'Generally, where the legislature provides a statutory remedy which is mandatory and exclusive, equity is without power to act, and a jurisdictional question is presented.' However, it has also been recognized that a 'court of equity has the power to afford relief despite the existence of a legal remedy when, from the nature and complications of a given case, justice can best be reached by means of equity's flexible machinery.' This proposition is equally true where the legal remedy is provided by statute. * * * [S]uch a remedy is clearly not adequate and complete where [as here], because of the continuing nature of the plaintiff's injury, the plaintiff would be required to bring a succession of legal actions. * * * To interpret the MVFRL as precluding this remedy would clearly contravene the policies underlying the statute."

The dissent, of course, disagreed: "These provisions contemplate an action at law for money damages. * * * The statute does not envision and the courts should not create a remedy which requires courts of equity to supervise insurance companies in the performance of their duties under MVFRL. * * * The majority, although conceding that an action at law is an adequate remedy to recover money damages, allows an action in equity for specific performance because Nationwide *may* refuse to make future payments, in which event Hill will be required to institute multiple actions to enforce his rights. I do not find this argument persuasive."

Question? Should the plaintiff give up a jury trial?

b. Orloff v. Los Angeles Turf Club, 30 Cal.2d 110, ___, 180 P.2d 321, 323 (1947), rev'd, 36 Cal.2d 734, 227 P.2d 449 (1951). An early version of a civil rights statute, Cal.Civ.Code § 52, designed to afford non-discriminatory access to public places of amusement provided only money as a remedy: actual damages plus $100. The plaintiff, having been twice thrown out of the race track, sued for an injunction. The California Supreme Court reversed the trial court's dismissal. It stated: "A recovery of compensatory damages and $100 is plainly inadequate relief in a case of this character. Compensable damages would be extremely difficult if not impossible to measure and prove. * * * If the objects of the Civil Code [§ 52] are to be effectuated, and justice promoted * * * certainly specific relief should be available."

c. Fletcher v. Coney Island, 165 Ohio St. 150, 134 N.E.2d 371 (1956). Essentially the same as *Orloff* above except that the violation of the statute was also made a misdemeanor. By a split decision the court denied the request for an injunction.

There was another difference. Fletcher was excluded because of race, Orloff because of gambling associations. The California statute was later amended to remove persons of Orloff's category from the coverage of the act.

5. *Statutes That Limit Equitable Jurisdiction.* For various reasons Congress and state legislatures enact statutes that curtail equitable remedies. The motives range from protection of the public fisc to the postponement of constitutional challenges to the legislation itself. Interpretive questions arise concerning whether legislatures intend anti-injunction statutes to deprive the courts of subject matter jurisdiction thereby making any injunction in violation void or only to restrict equitable jurisdiction thereby making the issuance of an injunction erroneous and subject to reversal upon appeal. Or perhaps the statute was intended to be admonitory only.

a. Mathes v. United States, 901 F.2d 1031, 1033 (11th Cir.1990), refers to 26 U.S.C. § 7421(a) which provides: "no suit for the purpose of restraining the assessment or collection of any tax shall be maintained in any court by any person * * *" [specific exceptions are allowed]. Here the government issued a notice of deficiency including $230,000 from alleged drug sales although it had no independent basis for the assertion. The taxpayer filed a petition for redetermination (one of the exceptions stated above) but the petition was rejected because of late filing. The appellate court affirmed dismissal of the suit: "[F]ederal courts may enjoin the collection of taxes if it can be shown that (1) under no circumstances could the government ultimately prevail on its tax claim and (2) equity jurisdiction otherwise exists; either ground being conclusive. Enochs v. Williams Packing & Nav. Co., 370 U.S. 1, 6–7 (1962). Therefore, the general rule is that, except in very rare and compelling circumstances, federal courts will not entertain actions to enjoin the collection of taxes. This case does not present one of those [circumstances] * * *. Our conclusion is based solely on the taxpayer's failure to meet the traditional equity test of having no adequate remedy of law. * * * Equitable jurisdiction is not present because the taxpayer had an adequate remedy at law available to him [by] a petition [to] the Tax Court for a redetermination of the deficiency. * * * [H]is petition * * * was untimely and denied by the Tax Court. * * * Therefore the prerequisite equitable jurisdiction necessary * * * is not present."

Query: The Anti–Injunction Act certainly assures prompt collection of taxes and in the past virtually forced the taxpayer to pay and then sue for a refund. Of course, a forced payment may push a small business over the edge into insolvency and ruin even though its cause was just. Is this irreparable injury? Not according to the *Enochs* case.

b. *The Norris–LaGuardia Act and State Variations.* In Publishers' Association v. New York Newspaper Printing Pressman's Union No. 2, 246 F.Supp. 293, 295 (S.D.N.Y.1965), the court said:

"29 U.S.C. § 104 (Section 4 of the Norris–LaGuardia Act) provides: 'No court of the United States shall have *jurisdiction* to issue any restraining order or temporary or permanent injunction in any case involving or growing out of any labor dispute.' (Emphasis added) Admittedly, the instant case involves a 'labor dispute' within the meaning of 29 U.S.C. § 113(c) so that the Norris–LaGuardia Act is applicable.

"On the face of 29 U.S.C. § 104 it would seem that the federal district court does not have original jurisdiction where an injunction alone is sought in a Section 185(a) case. However, we must consider the meaning of the statute. To say the least, the courts and the commentators are split. Some say that the word 'jurisdiction' in 29 U.S.C. § 104 means the authority to take cognizance of the suit and argue that a federal district court cannot entertain the suit at all. [citations] On the contrary, others say that jurisdiction in Section 104 refers only to the authority to grant an injunction *after* entertaining the suit. [citations] I am inclined to agree with the latter view. * * *

"It is unreasonable to argue that a court without authority to take cognizance of a suit does have the power to make findings of fact and to hold a hearing in accordance with the provisions of 29 U.S.C. § 107 (Section 7 of the Norris–LaGuardia Act). The preferable view would seem to be that federal courts do have original jurisdiction over Section 185(a) suits in which injunctions, even injunctions alone, are sought, but simply cannot grant injunctive relief in certain instances."

Professor Chafee thought that injunctions in violation of the Norris–LaGuardia Act were erroneous but not void. The distinction is important because a defendant may disobey a void injunction and assert its invalidity in defending against contempt proceedings while a merely erroneous injunction is insulated from collateral attack. Z. Chafee, Some Problems of Equity 374, 376 (1950).

In Boys Markets, Inc. v. Retail Clerk's Local 770, 398 U.S. 235 (1970), the Court recognized an "exception" to the "policy" of the Norris–LaGuardia Act; the court permitted district judges to enjoin a strike that involves an arbitrable dispute in violation of a contract that calls for binding arbitration.

Violation of a properly issued *Boys Market* injunction subjects the union to contempt. Consolidation Coal Co. v. Local 1702, U.M.W., 683 F.2d 827 (4th Cir.1982).

Several states modeled legislation on the Norris–LaGuardia Act. In New York the statute read: "No injunctive relief shall be granted (in labor dispute) to any plaintiff, etc." In Minnesota the statute provided: "No court of the state shall have jurisdiction to issue [an] injunction in a case * * * growing out of a labor dispute, etc." Assume an injunction is in fact issued against a strike under each statute. Assume that defendant violates the injunction, is charged with contempt, and defends by asserting that the injunction is void. What decision? Compare People ex rel. Sandnes v. Sheriff of Kings County, 164 Misc. 355, 299 N.Y.S. 9 (1937) with Reid v. Independent Union, 200 Minn. 599, 275 N.W. 300 (1937).

c. *Miscellaneous Statutes*

28 U.S.C. § 2283 reads: "A Court of the United States may not grant an injunction to stay proceedings in a State Court except as expressly authorized by Act of Congress, or where necessary in aid of its jurisdiction, or to protect or effectuate its judgments.

Cal.Civ.Code § 3390: "The following obligations cannot be specifically enforced: (1) An obligation to render personal service, * * * (5) An agreement, the terms of which are not sufficiently certain to make the precise act which is to be done clearly ascertainable."

Cal.Civ.Code § 3423: "An injunction cannot be granted * * * Second—To stay proceedings in a court of the United States."

6. *Limits on Equitable Discretion?* Matter of Freligh, 894 F.2d 881, 887 (7th Cir.1989), examines limits on equitable discretion. "A modern federal equity judge does not have the limitless discretion of a medieval Lord Chancellor to grant or withhold a remedy. * * * Modern equity has rules and standards, just like law. * * * And although the ratio of rules to standards is lower in equity than in law, in cases where the plaintiff has an established entitlement to an equitable remedy the judge cannot refuse the remedy because it offends his personal sense of justice."

d. Modern Equitable Remedies

(1) Characteristics—Discretion and Flexibility

Preliminary Note

The legacy of the English Chancery Courts to the American judicial system has been generous. A merged procedure has welcomed and embraced the terms and forms of chancery practice, interpleader, depositions, interrogatories, subpoenas, declaratory relief, injunctions, receivers, appeals, complaints, answers, decrees, petitioners, civil contempt, and more.

On a different level, the English Chancery decisions have served as a conduit for certain essential components of a working jurisprudence: a. the recognition that a law otherwise irreproachable and necessary may sometimes need an ethical override; and b. a mechanism for obtaining this override without collapsing the structure of laws and regulations into an ad hoc or ad hominem vacuum.

Our inherited equitable remedies carry with them certain well-known characteristics. Freed by equitable jurisdiction from a prescribed set of legal rules, the remedies of equity become discretionary and therefore flexible—a combination which has proved an irresistible attraction to judicial activists and social engineers and an anathema to those who think that the function of judges is to judge. Hence the remedial arena is another one where tactical maneuvering between liberals and conservatives occurs.

NAVAJO ACADEMY, INC. v. NAVAJO UNITED METHODIST MISSION SCHOOL, INC.

Supreme Court of New Mexico, 1990.
109 N.M. 324, 785 P.2d 235.

MONTGOMERY, JUSTICE. This appeal challenges the propriety of a district court order which, while it has the effect of terminating a tenancy as to real property, allows the tenant to remain in possession of the property for an extended period after termination. * * * We hold that, given the trial court's findings and the unusual circumstances of this case, the court did not abuse its equitable discretion as a court of equity in permitting the tenant to remain on the property for three years following termination of the lease, and accordingly we affirm.

The Navajo Academy, Inc. (the Academy), is a New Mexico corporation organized by the Navajo Tribe to operate a preparatory school for Navajo college-bound youth. Originally located in Ganado, Arizona, it moved its campus to Farmington, New Mexico, in 1978 at the invitation of the Navajo United Methodist Mission School, Inc. (the Mission School). The Mission School is a New Mexico corporation operated in conjunction with the United Methodist Church to conduct a school in Farmington. Its facilities were deteriorating and its student enrollment declining when it invited the Academy to move to the Farmington campus and commence operations there.

The terms and conditions of this move were not written. There was an understanding, however, between the Academy's headmaster and the Mission School's superintendent that the Academy could occupy as much of the campus, including dormitories, classrooms and support buildings, as it needed to house its program, rent-free. There was a tacit understanding that the Academy could stay on the campus for as long as it provided a quality educational program for Navajo children.

In the 1978–79 school year, the Academy's enrollment was about twenty-five students. Because of the quality of its program and the fact that it charged no tuition, whereas the Mission School did make such a charge, the Academy's enrollment climbed steadily and the Mission School's enrollment declined. Within a few years the Mission School had lost all of its students, who were not enrolled in the Academy, and by the 1986–87 school year the Academy's enrollment had grown to approximately 250 students.

The one hundred-acre Farmington campus is owned by the Women's Division of the Board of Global Ministries of the United Methodist Church (the Women's Division). Over the years, the Women's Division had leased the campus to the Mission School in a series of four-year leases which were continually renewed. By 1982 the Academy had come to occupy virtually the entire campus. The original understanding remained unwritten but became even more clearly understood to encompass a long-term relationship of indefinite duration. At about the same time, it also became clear that something had to be done about the deteriorating condition of the campus. The Academy and the Mission School agreed on a course of action: The Academy would make application to the Bureau of Indian Affairs (BIA) for substantial sums of money to repair and renovate the facilities, and the Mission School would support this application with a commitment that the Academy would have the use of the campus for a long term. Pursuant to this arrangement, the Mission School delivered to the Academy an executed copy of a resolution by the Mission School's board authorizing and directing the development of a long-term lease with an indefinite term of no less than twenty-five years. The trial court found that this resolution constituted a promise to provide a long-term lease so that the BIA would embark on a multi-year program of providing substantial sums to the Academy for facilities repair and renovation.

In the same year, 1982, the parties began entering into what was to be a series of short-term subleases, under which the Academy leased the campus from the Mission School for each succeeding school year from 1982–83 to 1986–87. (In 1983–84 there was a direct lease between the Women's Division and the Academy.) Neither the subleases nor the 1983–84 direct lease required that any rent, other than a token amount, be paid. The only consideration for these leases was performance by the Academy of its commitment to provide a quality educational program for Navajo youth and to carry out ordinary maintenance of the facilities. The trial court found that the sub-leases were not intended to replace the understanding between the Academy and the Mission School relating to the Academy's continued, indefinite occupancy of the campus.

The Mission School's promise to provide a long-term lease was not kept. For one thing, the Women's Division had a strict policy against leasing its property for periods longer than four years, and despite the efforts of the Academy and the Mission School that policy could not be changed. However, according to the trial court's findings, the Women's Division condoned the relationship between the Academy and the Mission School and placed representatives of the Mission School in positions of apparent authority to act for and bind the Women's Division. * * *

In 1987 the relationship between the two organizations began quickly to deteriorate. The Mission School requested that, for the next ensuing school year (1987–88), substantial rent ($220,000.00) be paid by the Academy. The Mission School proposed other changes in the sublease relationship and eventually delivered an ultimatum to the Academy requiring it to vacate the property if the Mission School's new sublease was not signed by a stipulated date. * * * It had become clear that the relationship had broken down and that the Academy's occupancy of the campus would have to end.

The Mission School thereupon brought an action in magistrate court for forcible entry and detainer, seeking to evict the Academy. The Academy responded by bringing this action in the District Court for San Juan County to prohibit the magistrate court from entertaining the eviction action and to obtain various other forms of relief. Among the items of relief sought in the Academy's complaint were a declaration that it was entitled to continued occupancy of the property under a "constructive" long-term lease, damages of $1,800,000 for conversion as a result of its expenditures in improving the campus, declaratory and injunctive relief on behalf of the students and compensatory and punitive damages for interference with contractual relations. After a five-day bench trial, the court entered findings of fact and conclusions of law generally favorable to the Academy but awarding none of the relief requested except for the order permitting the Academy to remain on the campus for three years after the date of the trial court's judgment. * * *

The trial court found that the Mission School promised to give a twenty-five-year lease in exchange for the making of certain expenditures by the Academy. It is undisputed that the Academy did make those expenditures (even though the funds for the expenditures were derived from the BIA), and our review of the evidence convinces us that the Mission School did indeed promise to enter into a long-term lease in exchange for these expenditures. It is similarly undisputed that the Mission School never tendered a long-term lease. Therefore, it breached the agreement which the trial court found, and that breach had nothing to do with the Academy's own disavowal of any future involvement by the Mission School in its educational program. * * *

[D]espite the assumption underlying most or all of the appellants' arguments, the trial court did not specifically enforce the Mission School's promise to give a twenty-five-year lease. Rather, the trial court determined, in effect, that the Academy's leasehold interest had terminated—or was, as appellants argue, "terminable at will"—but nevertheless considered the practical effect of an order evicting the Academy from the premises. The trial court further considered the equities in the case before it and found that the Academy had come before the court with clean hands. Under the circumstances, therefore, the trial court decided that the most equitable remedy, while making clear that the Academy would be required to vacate the premises at the end of three years at most, would be to grant it that long a period in which to locate a new campus and move its 250 students to another location. As indicated previously, we do not believe that the fashioning of this equitable remedy, in a suit invoking the equitable powers of the court, was an abuse of discretion.

At bottom, this suit was originated by the Mission School when it applied to the magistrate for relief from forcible entry and detainer. When the Academy sought to prohibit the magistrate court from entertaining this action, it requested equitable relief in the form of a declaration that it held under a "constructive" long-term lease. Though the original action was to prevent relief by way of forcible entry and detainer, which has its origins at law, and to enforce a long-term lease, it is anything but new for this Court to validate an equitable solution to a problem such as the one before us when a party asks for justice and a "legal" remedy is inadequate; "equity frequently interferes." * * * See also Hilburn v. Brodhead, 79 N.M. 460, 464, 444 P.2d 971, 975 (1968) ("[A] court of equity has power to meet the problem presented, and to fashion a proper remedy to accomplish a just and proper result."); 1 J. Pomeroy, Equity Jurisprudence § 109 (5th ed. 1941)

> "Equitable remedies * * * are distinguished by their flexibility, their unlimited variety, their adaptability to circumstances, and the natural rules which govern their use. There is in fact no limit to their variety and application; the court of equity has the power of devising its remedy and shaping it so as to fit the changing circumstances of every case and the complex relations of all the parties."

In the case at bar, the trial court devised a remedy that permits the Academy to continue functioning as a school as it searches for a new home. * * *

We believe that this remedy did not "exceed the bounds of reason," since, in addition to all the other factors, the numerous and costly improvements the Academy bestowed upon the Mission School campus can be viewed as the equivalent of several years' rent. We conclude that the trial court's order permitting the Academy to remain on the campus for a period of time not to exceed three years from the date of the judgment was not an abuse of discretion, and the judgment is affirmed.

Note

This decision fits the classical pattern. The Academy is subject to eviction under summary unlawful detainer procedures, a provisional statutory legal remedy in which equitable considerations are barred, usually, anyway. What is the Academy to do? Is there equitable jurisdiction? Are there viable legal alternatives? Assuming equitable jurisdiction, consider the exceedingly wide range of possible solutions. Where is the appellate court likely to draw the line? Can it act de novo?

(2) Can a Practically Effective Decree Be Drafted?

One general consideration that affects the judge's decision to exercise equitable jurisdiction is whether she can draft a practically effective decree. Several traditional considerations overlap and eventually coalesce in a decision to compose a decree.

First, will the decree create or perpetuate an inherently unstable relationship between the parties? Characteristically these issues arise out of troubled personal relationships in a family or neighborhood or business or fiduciary relationships that are not entirely at arm's length.

Second, will the decree necessitate continuous supervision over an extended period of time thereby consuming the judge's time and taxing both her competence and patience?

Furthermore can the judge enforce the contemplated decree with the means at her disposal? We will be taking that up shortly.

LYNCH v. UHLENHOPP

Supreme Court of Iowa, 1956.
248 Iowa 68, 78 N.W.2d 491.

THOMPSON, CHIEF JUSTICE. * * * A divorce was granted to the petitioner * * * on April 9, 1953. * * * On April 8, the parties entered into a stipulation, the material part of which provided: "Item I. That the care, custody and control of Richard R. Lynch shall be awarded to the Plaintiff (Gladys M. Lynch) and it is provided that the said child shall be reared in the Roman Catholic Religion and that the Defendant (Francis L. Lynch) shall have the right of visitation at all reasonable hours and that the Defendant shall pay monthly support money of $40.00 per month commencing with the date of decree." * * * the provisions of the stipulation were incorporated in the decree. Richard was about five years old at this time, and was in his seventh year when the contempt proceedings were instituted.

The record shows that the petitioner was at the time of the divorce, and apparently still is, a Protestant, while Francis L. Lynch has at all material times been a Roman Catholic. On June 17, 1955, Francis L. Lynch filed his "Information for Contempt" setting out Item I of the stipulation, as made a part of the decree, and alleging that prior to the divorce Richard had been baptized in the Roman Catholic church and reared as a member of that church. Violation of the decree [is alleged]. * * *

It appears without contradiction that the petitioner, since the divorce, has not taken Richard to a Roman Catholic church, but that he has been attending a Congregational church Sunday school, and has attended Bible school summer camp, apparently conducted by the same church, for about two weeks in the summers of 1953 and 1955. Mrs. Lynch did not take him to Sunday school, but sent him with "her former sister-in-law"; she "saw that he got there." The father's right of visitation was not denied him, and twice he took the boy to the Roman Catholic church. * * *

It is well settled that a judgment may be so indefinite and uncertain as to be wholly void. * * * In 49 C.J.S., Judgments, § 72, pp. 191, 192, it is said:

> "A judgment must be definite and certain in itself, or capable of being made so by proper construction. It must fix clearly the rights and liabilities of the respective parties to the cause, *and be such as defendant may readily understand* and be capable of performing * * *. Where the record entry is wholly uncertain * * * the judgment is at least erroneous, and it may be void." (Italics added.)

This is particularly true in contempt proceedings, where the alleged contemnor is in danger of drastic punishment if the judgment does not clearly inform him what is required. The contempt proceeding is so near in its nature to criminal prosecutions that the well-known rule which commands that one cannot be convicted of a crime unless the statute is clear and definite so that he may know what he can and what he cannot do, is at least analogous. * * *

A sound expression of the rule is found in Seastrunk Rendering Co. v. Hollingsworth, Tex.Civ.App., 177 S.W.2d 1014, 1016, 1017:

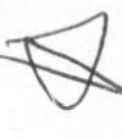

> "To warrant a decree of injunction, enforceable through contempt proceedings, the acts commanded or restrained must be described in the decree with sufficient definiteness for the defendant to know in advance what he must or

must not do in order to abide by the decree and escape the penalties attaching to its infringement. The vice in the decree lies in the fact that it enjoins, not specific acts or omissions, but results, evidence of the existence vel non of which must of necessity be determined by the opinion evidence of witnesses, which could not be forecast or anticipated."

The language is appropriate in the case at bar, since we think it would at least require expert opinion to determine what steps must be taken to rear the boy in the specified religion. * * *

Applying the foregoing well-established principles to the instant case, and keeping in mind that we have before us a contempt proceeding in which the punishment will in all probability be a fine or imprisonment of unknown but real severity, we can only conclude that that part of the decree involved should be held void for uncertainty and indefiniteness. The pertinent language is this: "It is provided the said child shall be reared in the Roman Catholic Religion * * *." Is this language so clear, specific and unequivocal that it can be readily understood? Are the steps which must be taken so certainly pointed out that a judgment of contempt and substantial punishment should follow if the required things are not done? The decree must meet these tests, or it is void and unenforceable.

A negative answer to the question posed is clearly indicated. How are we to determine what must be done to rear a child in any given religion? Religion itself is a term difficult to define. * * *

Both Funk & Wagnall's New Standard Dictionary and Webster's New International Dictionary give somewhat long, involved and alternative definitions of religion. But the word "religion" is often confused in terms with cultus or form of worship of the different denominations. * * * So we think the parties and the court here confounded the terms. They referred to the "Roman Catholic Religion" when they meant the cultus or forms of worship of that church; perhaps what was really intended was that the child should be reared in the Christian religion in conformity to the forms, discipline, organization and dogma of the Roman Catholic Church. If nothing more than the Christian religion was intended, rearing in any Christian church would satisfy the requirements of the decree; but obviously more than this was meant. * * * The decree itself does not specify who shall rear the child in the stated religion. * * * The petitioner says her understanding of the decree was that the question should be left open until the boy reached an age where he would be capable of deciding for himself. It may be argued that since the petitioner was given the custody of the child, the major duty of complying with the portion of the decree in controversy, if it could be complied with, was upon her. The controversy at this juncture merely points up the indefiniteness and uncertainty of the controversial portion of the decree. There is some force to the petitioner's contention that she, not being a communicant of the Roman Catholic church, would find it inconvenient to attend its services, and difficult to train the boy in its forms and beliefs. The decree itself is silent as to whose duty it was to do these things.

It may seem at first impression that the decree tells the petitioner sufficiently what she must do. But this impression, if indeed it be held at all, will not bear analysis. What constitutes "rearing" a child in the religion or cultus of this church, or of any church? Must he be taken to church once a week, or once in two weeks, on Sunday? If mid-week services are held, must he be taken to them? Is it required that he attend catechism class? Must he attend a parochial school if the particular denomination in question maintains such schools? What fast days must be observed, what Lenten observances followed? [The court mentioned several similar problems.]

Again, the matter of rearing a child in any religion is commonly, and we believe properly, thought to be a matter of cooperation between church and home. In order to avoid a conviction for contempt here, must the petitioner endeavor to supplement the teachings of the church, of which she is not a member, in her home? Without this cooperation, church attendance might well result in lip service only, to the faith taught there.

The fact that the exact duties required of the petitioner are vague and uncertain is somewhat pointed up by her own testimony of what she understood she was to do. The trial court, after finding her guilty of contempt, continued the hearing for some weeks, with the provision that if by a specified date the petitioner filed her affidavit that she was raising the boy "in the Catholic faith" she should stand purged of contempt. There is still no indication of what specific action she should take. The court apparently left it to her to determine what was meant; but she had already told her version of the meaning of the doubtful clause in the decree and found it unacceptable. * * *

[T]he judgment of the trial court [could not] be upheld here if petitioner had at no time raised the question of uncertainty. * * * Generally points not raised in the trial court, or not argued in this court, cannot be made the basis for reversal. But a different rule prevails where there is no jurisdiction. "Strictly speaking, lack of jurisdiction means lack of judicial power to act in the premises * * *." 21 C.J.S., Courts, § 15b, p. 32. And it is the duty of a court to take notice of a lack of jurisdiction on its own motion, even though the question is not raised by the contending parties. * * * Likewise, it seems self-evident that a court attempting to enforce a void decree by contempt proceedings is acting illegally and without jurisdiction. * * *

[Editors: The discussion of the first and fourteenth amendments is omitted.]

[By a vote of 5–4 the court ordered dismissal of the information charging contempt.]

Notes

1. Could an enforceable decree be written to embody what were clearly the wishes of the parties? Was the decree, in fact, too specific?

2. Are there some agreements that cannot be reduced to language but can be specifically enforced?

3. Was the child raised as a Catholic?

4. Federal Rule of Civil Procedure 65(d): "Every order granting an injunction and every restraining order shall set forth the reasons for its issuance; shall be specific in terms; shall describe in reasonable detail" the act or acts sought to be restrained.

5. Carrico v. Blevins, ___ Va.App. ___, 402 S.E.2d 235 (1991). A divorce decree awarded custody of the child to the father and visitation rights to the mother; the judge ordered the mother either to take the child to church during her visitation period or to allow the father to do so. Citing the Virginia Constitutional provision that "no man shall be compelled to frequent or support any religious worship," the

court of appeals reversed the trial judge's order. Could a trial judge forbid a parent from taking the child to "church"? Would this order be unenforceable?

TRAVELLERS INTERNATIONAL AG v. TRANS WORLD AIRLINES, INC.

United States District Court, Southern District of New York, 1989.
722 F.Supp. 1087.

Travellers, a Swiss corporation with its principal place of business in London, England, is wholly owned by Windsor, a Missouri corporation with its principal place of business in St. Louis County, Missouri. Barney Ebsworth ("Ebsworth") is the sole shareholder of Windsor. TWA is a Delaware corporation with its principal place of business in New York. Carl Icahn ("Icahn"), who acquired control of TWA in the fall of 1985, is Chairman of its Board of Directors and its Chief Executive Officer.

The relationship between Travellers and TWA began more than twenty (20) years ago, when both corporations were controlled by different owners. Travellers is in the vacation tour business. It contracts with hotels and other service providers in order to develop and operate tours in various countries. TWA is an international airline. In the early 1970's, TWA commenced its "Getaway Tours" to Europe. TWA, through the Getaway Tours, offered air transportation to passengers purchasing land tour packages. TWA owns the Getaway mark and the Getaway Tours are proprietary to it.

Beginning in 1972, Travellers sold tours to TWA, which TWA marketed as Getaway Tours. Pursuant to a written agreement between the two companies, Travellers was responsible for developing and operating the land tour packages of the Getaway Tours (the "Tours"). In 1974, Travellers and TWA entered into a Land Agreement and a Brochure Agreement, each dated April 25, 1974 (the "1974 Agreements"). The 1974 Agreements were the first in a series of successive long term contracts under which TWA was to provide air transportation for the Tours, market the Tours, wholesale the Tours to independent travel agents, and accept reservations directly for the Tours, while Travellers was to continue to develop and operate the land arrangements and to produce promotional brochures for the Tours. The brochures were to be used as selling tools by travel agents and TWA. * * *

Providing the tours and the brochures as required under the Contract demanded substantial advance preparation by both parties. It had been the practice of Travellers and TWA to hold an annual planning meeting early each year to discuss the number and content of the Tours to be offered during the next calendar year, as well as the format, content, design, and number of brochures to be produced. Paragraph A.3 of the Contract provides that the final retail price for the land component of the Tours was to be agreed upon by Travellers and TWA by September 1 of the year prior to when the Tours would be offered to the public.

The prices paid by a Getaway Tour vacationer included both the cost of the Tour and the airfare to the tour destination. Travellers and TWA shared in the revenue generated by the Tours, but not the airfare, which TWA collected alone. In the past, the retail price for the land based component of a Getaway Tour was disbursed by TWA as follows: approximately fourteen percent (14%) was paid to the travel agent responsible for booking the Tour, six percent (6%)

was retained by TWA as its own margin, and the balance of eighty percent (80%) was remitted to Travellers. From the percentage of the retail land tour price Travellers received, it paid the costs of operating the Tours. In addition to the 6% margin on the land-based tour aspect of the Getaway Program, TWA earned substantial revenue from the airfares it collected from Tour passengers. An internal TWA memorandum indicated that, in 1985, the Getaway Program provided incremental revenue which TWA would not have received absent its participation in the Program of over forty-nine million dollars ($49,000,000.00).

World events in 1985 and 1986, including the hijacking of a TWA jet, highly publicized acts of terrorism, the 1986 raid on Libya by the United States and the Chernobyl nuclear disaster, as well as the TWA flight attendants' strike, combined to reduce significantly the demand for the Getaway Tours covered by the Contract.

In late 1985, Icahn acquired control of TWA. He became Chairman of the Board of TWA in January 1986. In late 1986 or early 1987, TWA began to reexamine the economics of the Getaway Tours and the Contract. In late March or early April 1987, Craig Pavlus ("Pavlus"), a vice president of TWA, was put in charge of the Getaway Program.

In early 1986, Gerald Herrod ("Herrod"), the founder, chairman and sole owner of Travellers at the time of the Contract, sought to sell Travellers. He had been the moving force behind Travellers from its inception, although since 1980 he had begun to devote more and more time to his new venture, Ocean Cruise Lines. Herrod approached TWA and suggested that TWA acquire Travellers. Peter McHugh, a senior vice president of TWA, recommended the purchase to Morton Ehrlich, an Executive Vice President of TWA, and Icahn. According to McHugh's testimony at the preliminary injunction hearing, Icahn rejected this proposal because he was unsure if TWA should expand its involvement in the international field, in part because of the recent rise in terrorism.

Subsequently, Herrod reached an understanding with Ebsworth to purchase Travellers. Prior to consummating the purchase, Ebsworth sought and obtained TWA's written consent to the acquisition. * * *

Unfortunately, the change in control of the two companies foreshadowed a change in the harmonious relationship the two companies had enjoyed for over a decade. The spring and summer of 1987 saw a series of confrontational meetings between representatives of Travellers and TWA escalate into a battle between Ebsworth and Icahn, culminating in a heated exchange between the two men at a dinner meeting on August 5, 1987. For a specific recounting of the details of these meetings, including the accusations hurled by each party at the other and the positions taken with respect to continued performance under the Contract, the reader is referred to Judge Sweet's opinion, Travellers International AG v. Trans World Airlines. Suffice it to say that TWA, believing the Contract unduly benefitted Travellers at its expense, sought to alter certain of the past practices between the parties.

Accordingly, in May 1987, TWA successfully renegotiated a reduction in the price paid to Travellers under the Contract for preparing the 1988 brochures, and reduced the number of brochures to be produced by Travellers. In June 1987, TWA proposed to increase its margin for the land-based tour. After stormy negotiations throughout the summer, TWA's margin was increased from six percent (6%) to ten percent (10%) of the retail land tour price.

Furthermore, in August 1987, Icahn had a change of heart regarding the propriety of TWA expanding into the international tour business. He offered to purchase Travellers from Ebsworth for the same price Ebsworth had paid a year earlier. When this offer was rejected by Ebsworth as inequitable, TWA began looking into developing its own in-house tour capacity. * * *

On September 16, 1987, Pavlus sent Travellers a letter purporting to terminate the Contract. The letter, which was also copied to both Ehrlich and Icahn, stated that the termination would be "effective December 31, 1988 with respect to Tours and as of December 31, 1987 with respect to Tour Brochures" and set forth six grounds justifying the termination. [The court rejected all six.] * * *

Travellers seeks a permanent injunction requiring TWA to specifically perform the Contract. Specific performance of a contract is appropriate when (1) the contract is valid, (2) plaintiff has substantially performed under the contract and is willing and able to perform its remaining obligations, (3) defendant is able to perform its obligations, and (4) plaintiff has no adequate remedy at law. [citations]

The evidence established that the Contract was valid and that Travellers had substantially performed its obligations. Travellers demonstrated that it will not be able to continue as a going concern at this time if the Contract, representing 90–95% of its business, is terminated. The destruction of a business has long been held to constitute the type of irreparable injury for which there is no adequate monetary remedy. [citation]

In addition, the balance of equities tips markedly in favor of Travellers. Termination of the Contract will put Travellers out of business, while continued performance under the Contract is likely to also continue to be profitable for TWA. Regardless of the profitability of the Tours to TWA, its dealings with Travellers represent only a small fraction of its overall business, and the continuation of the Contract in no way threatens TWA's ability to remain in business.

TWA's final argument against the imposition of a permanent injunction is that compliance with the injunction would require constant judicial intervention in the business activities of the parties. [citation] This argument, like the many that came before it, is inapposite. While Travellers and TWA are required to work together in order to agree on pricing and the substantive content of the Tours and brochures, the long history of their relationship indicates they can do just that without constant judicial intervention. In fact, the evidence indicated that the representatives of TWA involved in actually planning the Getaway Tours have had much less trouble dealing with their counterparts at Travellers than do the leaders of the respective organizations.

While there have been certain disputes regarding continued performance under the preliminary injunction and an inordinate amount of petty complaints by both sides, the parties have been able to offer Getaway Tours to the public during 1989. A continuation of the requirement that disputes under the Contract be resolved with reference to the past practices of the parties provides more than adequate direction to enable them to operate the Getaway Tours in the future without continual judicial involvement.[1] In addition, the planning

1. [Footnote renumbered.] Plaintiffs argue that TWA has acted in bad faith in its efforts to perform the Contract as required by the preliminary injunction. They rely largely on TWA's

meeting for the 1990 Tours, held during the recess in the trial, was reported to have been successful, and the Court is unaware of any recent conflicts that would make continued performance under the Contract an especially onerous burden on TWA.

Plaintiffs have demonstrated that they adequately performed their obligations under the Contract and therefore that TWA's termination was unjustified. They have also proven that they will be irreparably harmed absent TWA's continued performance under the Contract. Accordingly, plaintiffs' request for a permanent injunction preventing TWA from terminating the Contract is granted.

Note

For a less benign view of the problem of judicial supervision, see New Park Forest Associates II v. Rogers Enterprises, Inc., 195 Ill.App.3d 757, 765, 552 N.E.2d 1215, 1220 (1990). The court refused to enjoin the breach of a ten year shopping mall lease, remarking that the court did not want to find itself "in the business of managing a shopping center." Both the majority and the dissent rely heavily on equity tradition.

e. Maxims of Equity

For a starting maxim we may say that "Equity is Fond of Maxims." Professor Pomeroy in Volume II § 363 of the 5th edition of his work on Equity Jurisprudence (1941) lists:

1. Equity regards as done which ought to be done.
2. Equity looks to the intent rather than to the form.
3. He who seeks equity must do equity.
4. He who comes into equity must come with clean hands.
5. Equality is equity.
6. Where there are equal equities, the first in time shall prevail.
7. Where there is equal equity, the law must prevail.
8. Equity aids the vigilant, not those who slumber on their rights.
9. Equity imputes an intention to fulfill an obligation.
10. Equity will not suffer a wrong without a remedy.
11. Equity follows the law.

There are numerous other aphorisms such as "equity abhors forfeitures," "he who trusts most loses most," "equity acts in personam," "equity delights in doing justice and not by halves," and (in half jest perhaps) "equity does everything by fifths."

business with other tour operators, its reduction in the number of brochures and an internal sales force target of sixty-four thousand (64,000) Getaway Tour passengers. It is worth emphasizing that the duty of good faith and fair dealing still applies to the efforts of both parties to perform the Contract and comply with the injunction. More specifically, the target figure of one hundred thousand (100,000) Tour passengers per year, provided for in paragraph A.5, implies that both parties will exercise good faith efforts to reach that desired volume of Tour passengers. The evidence adduced to this point has not sufficiently demonstrated bad faith on the part of TWA, however, TWA's future compliance with the injunction will be measured by the extent of its efforts to fulfill its contractual obligations.

Most of these have nothing to do with equitable jurisdiction, but are principles to be applied once equitable jurisdiction is assumed. Some of the maxims can be used as pretext to expand equitable jurisdiction—notably "equity will not suffer a wrong without a remedy."

At least two of the maxims do constrain equitable jurisdiction: the "clean hands" maxim and that concerning laches: "equity aids the vigilant".

(1) Clean Hands

GREEN v. HIGGINS

Supreme Court of Kansas, 1975.
217 Kan. 217, 535 P.2d 446.

PRAGER, JUSTICE. This is an action for specific performance of a contract for the sale of real estate. The facts are not in dispute and are essentially as follows: On May 7, 1969, the defendants-appellees, Damon W. Higgins and Cleo D. Higgins, sold a tract of land to Robert E. Brown and Mark S. Gilman. At the time of this transaction and as a part of the consideration therefor, the Higgins agreed that Brown and Gilman should have a right of first refusal to purchase adjoining land from the Higgins should they desire to sell it. In addition, as a result of this same sale, a real estate agent, Lienna McCulley, obtained an agreement with the Higgins which gave Miss McCulley the right to handle any subsequent sale of the adjoining tract if the contracting or sale occurred prior to June 1, 1971. In April of 1971 the Higgins desired to sell the adjoining tract of land which was subject to the contractual rights just mentioned. The plaintiffs-appellants, Philip A. Green and Barbara A. Green, desired to purchase the adjoining tract of land from the Higgins at a proposed purchase price of $30,000. A contract for the purchase of the property for the proposed price was executed by the Greens and the Higgins on April 21, 1971. Prior to the time the contract was prepared and executed the Higgins advised the Greens that Lienna McCulley would be entitled to a commission on the sale if the contracting or sale occurred prior to June 1, 1971. The contract was dated June 2, 1971, in order to defeat Lienna McCulley's right to handle the sale of the property and to cheat her out of her real estate commission.

Plaintiff, Philip A. Green, testified in his deposition that after this contract was signed Higgins advised him that the property was subject to the right of first refusal held by Brown and Gilman pursuant to the contract of May 7, 1969. Green and Higgins apparently decided that something had to be done to avoid Higgins's obligation to give the first right of refusal to Brown and Gilman. Green testified in substance that he suggested to Higgins that a fictitious contract be prepared and delivered to Brown and Gilman with a letter giving them the opportunity to enter into a contract for the same price or otherwise the right of first refusal would be waived. The fictitious contract was dictated by Mr. Green and typed by Mrs. Green. In this fictitious contract the purchase price was stated to be $40,000 and the designated purchaser of the property was Medallion Investment Properties, Inc., a corporation of which Mr. Green was the president. It is undisputed that this fictitious contract with an inflated purchase price in the amount of $40,000 was prepared and delivered to Brown and Gilman to discourage them from exercising their right of first refusal, since the indicated purchase price of $40,000 was an excessive price for the property. This gambit was apparently successful since Brown and Gilman did not exercise their right of first refusal to purchase the property under the terms stated in the fictitious contract.

Thereafter the Higgins decided that they did not want to carry out their contract with the Greens and so advised the Greens. At that point the only money which had changed hands was the $100 given to Higgins by Green at the time the contract was executed. The Higgins offered to return this in August or September of 1971. In January of 1972 Green tendered the balance of the purchase price, $29,900 and requested a warranty deed from Higgins which Higgins refused to provide. On March 28, 1972, the Greens filed this action for specific performance of the contract. The Higgins counterclaimed for damages based upon an alleged clouding of their title and further prayed that their title to the land be quieted against the Greens. * * *

In denying relief to both parties the district court found * * * that the conduct of both the plaintiffs Green and the defendants Higgins had been willful, fraudulent, illegal, and unconscionable, that neither party had come into court with clean hands, and thus neither should be granted any relief by the court. The plaintiffs Green have appealed to this court from the judgment of the district court dismissing their petition and denying them specific performance. * * *

In this case the clean hands doctrine had been specifically raised as an affirmative defense in the defendants' answer. That defense was the basis of the defendants' motion to dismiss. * * * The clean hands doctrine in substance provides that no person can obtain affirmative relief in equity with respect to a transaction in which he has, himself, been guilty of inequitable conduct. It is difficult to formulate a general statement as to what will amount to unclean hands other than to state it is conduct which the court regards as inequitable. Like other doctrines of equity, the clean hands maxim is not a binding rule, but is to be applied in the sound discretion of the court. The clean hands doctrine has been recognized in many Kansas cases. The application of the clean hands doctrine is subject to certain limitations. Conduct which will render a party's hands unclean so as to deny him access to a court of equity must be willful conduct which is fraudulent, illegal or unconscionable. Furthermore the objectionable misconduct must bear an immediate relation to the subject-matter of the suit and in some measure affect the equitable relations subsisting between the parties to the litigation and arising out of the transaction. Stated in another way the misconduct which may justify a denial of equitable relief must be *related* misconduct rather than *collateral* misconduct arising outside the specific transaction which is the subject-matter of the litigation before the court.

It should also be emphasized that in applying the clean hands maxim, courts are concerned primarily with their own integrity. The doctrine of unclean hands is derived from the unwillingness of a court to give its peculiar relief to a suitor who in the very controversy has so conducted himself as to shock the moral sensibilities of the judge. It has nothing to do with the rights or liabilities of the parties. In applying the unclean hands doctrine, courts act for their own protection, and not as a matter of "defense" to the defendant.

The plaintiffs Green on this appeal argue that a defendant cannot invoke the protection of the clean hands maxim unless he has suffered from the misconduct of the plaintiff. They argue that here the defendants Higgins participated in the claimed misconduct and that any injury suffered would be to third parties and not to the defendants themselves. [citations] In our judgment such an interpretation of the clean hands doctrine does not accord with its principal purpose. A court may refuse its relief to the plaintiff though the defendant himself participated in the misconduct, not because it is a privilege of such a defendant, but because the court refuses to lend its aid to either party to such a transaction. The best-reasoned cases hold that the maxim applies, even though the misconduct of the plaintiff has not injured anyone and even though the defendant himself was a participant in the misconduct. [citations]

With these basic principles in mind we turn now to the undisputed facts in this case to determine whether or not the district court abused its discretion in denying relief to both the plaintiffs and the defendants. Here all parties have conceded that the following facts are true: That the contract entered into between the parties on April 21, 1971 was dated June 2, 1971, in order to deprive Lienna McCulley of her right to a sales commission which she had previously obtained through contract; that a fictitious contract was prepared by which it appeared the Higgins agreed to sell the real estate to Medallion Investment Properties, Inc. for $40,000; that the fraudulent contract was prepared at the suggestion of the plaintiff, Philip A. Green, and was submitted by Higgins to Brown and Gilman in order to deprive them of their right of first refusal to purchase the property at a proposed price. It simply cannot be denied that the plaintiffs Green actively and willfully participated in fraudulent and unconscionable activities to obtain title to the land and to defeat various legal rights held by third parties. The misconduct involved here was directly related to the subject-matter of the litigation and must be classified as related misconduct, not collateral misconduct. Under all the facts and circumstances we cannot say that the trial court abused its discretion in denying relief to both the plaintiffs and defendants by reason of the clean hands doctrine.

The judgment of the trial court is affirmed.

Note

Compare Judge Posner's description of the doctrine in Shondel v. McDermott, 775 F.2d 859, 867–68 (7th Cir.1985):

"The maxim that 'he who comes into equity must come with clean hands,' although comparatively recent as equity maxims go, see Chafee, Coming Into Equity With Clean Hands [I], 47 Mich.L.Rev. 877, 880 (1949), captures very nicely the moralistic, rule-less, natural-law character of the equity jurisprudence created by the Lord Chancellors of England when the office was filled by clerics. The moralistic language in which the principles of equity continue to be couched is a legacy of the time when a common lawyer could, without sounding too silly, denounce equity as 'a Roguish thing' because 'Equity is according to the Conscience of him that is Chancellor, and as that is larger or narrower, so is equity.' The Table–Talk of John Selden 64 (Singer ed. 1847 [1689]). But the time itself is long past, and the proposition that equitable relief is 'discretionary' cannot be maintained today without careful qualification. A modern judge, English or American, state or federal, bears very little resemblance to a Becket or a Wolsey or a More, but instead administers a system of rules which bind him whether they have their origin in law or in equity and whether they are enforced by damages or by injunctions. To tell a plaintiff that although his legally protected rights have been invaded and he has no adequate remedy at law (i.e., damages) the judge has decided to withhold equitable relief as a matter of discretion just would not wash today.

Even when the plaintiff is asking for the extraordinary remedy of a preliminary injunction—extraordinary because it is often a very costly remedy to the defendant, yet is ordered on the basis of only a summary inquiry into the merits of the plaintiff's suit—the request is evaluated according to definite standards, rather than committed to a free-wheeling ethical discretion.

"Today, 'unclean hands' really just means that in equity as in law the plaintiff's fault, like the defendant's, may be relevant to the question of what if any remedy the plaintiff is entitled to. See Chafee, Coming Into Equity With Unclean Hands [II], 47 Mich.L.Rev. 1065, 1092 (1949). An obviously sensible application of this principle is to withhold an equitable remedy that would encourage, or reward (and thereby encourage), illegal activity, as where the injunction would aid in consummating a crime, the issue in Johnson v. Yellow Cab Transit Co., 321 U.S. 383 (1944)."

In Byron v. Clay, 867 F.2d 1049, 1051 (7th Cir.1989), Judge Posner gave further evidence of his skepticism about relying on undefined ethical considerations in applying the clean hands doctrine. He stated that the doctrine "functionally rather than moralistically conceived, gives recognition to the fact that equitable decrees may have effects on third parties—persons who are not parties to a lawsuit, including taxpayers and members of the law-abiding public—and so should not be entered without consideration of those effects."

McKINLEY v. WEIDNER

Court of Appeals of Oregon, 1985.
73 Or.App. 396, 698 P.2d 983.

GILLETTE, PRESIDING JUDGE. Plaintiff brought this action to recover damages resulting from the alleged negligence of defendant, an attorney. The complaint alleged that, following defendant's advice, plaintiff tendered and subsequently dishonored a check in a ploy to recover possession of a boat from a third party. Ultimately, the third party was granted summary judgment in a separate proceeding for amounts due, plus costs and interest, and foreclosed on the boat to satisfy the judgment. Plaintiff's action was dismissed by the trial court on a motion alleging that he had "unclean hands" as a result of his having tendered a check with the intent to dishonor it. On appeal, he assigns as error the trial court's use of the "clean hands" doctrine as a bar to his action for money damages. We reverse.

Generally, the "clean hands" doctrine is referred to as an equitable maxim. In Rise v. Steckel, 59 Or.App. 675, 681, 652 P.2d 364 (1982), this court described it as a maxim that:

> "' "*is based on conscience and good faith. It is not strictly or primarily a matter of defense, but is invoked on grounds of public policy and for the protection of the integrity of the court.*" ' " Quoting Taylor et ux v. Grant et al, 204 Or. 10, 24, 279 P.2d 479, 279 P.2d 1037, 281 P.2d 704 (1955).

Our decision in *Rise* relied, *inter alia,* on our earlier decision in Gratreak v. North Pacific Lumber Co., 45 Or.App. 571, 609 P.2d 375, rev. den. 289 Or. 373 (1980). In *Gratreak,* the plaintiff, a former employe of the defendant, brought an action for malicious interference with the plaintiff's contractual relations with his new employer. In addition to a general denial, the defendant alleged three affirmative defenses. By way of reply, the plaintiff asserted that enforcement of any of the three defenses should be barred "because of defendant's *unclean hands.*" We said:

"The plaintiff by his reply seeks to deny the defendants equitable relief because they do not have clean hands. The trouble is that the defendants are not requesting the intervention of a court of equity. The plaintiff chose the forum—the complaint alleges an action at law. The defendants' answer pleads a legal defense * * *.

"The plaintiff acknowledges that the complaint and the answer are on the law side of the court, but contends that the clean hands doctrine is an 'equitable defense' and therefore can be pleaded as a defense to a law action * * *.

"Clean hands in the context of this case is not an equitable defense. Rather, it is a doctrine, maxim or principle of equity which may be invoked to deny the opposing party the right to come into a court of equity. 2 Pomeroy's Equity Jurisprudence § 359 at 5 (5th ed. 1941) * * *.

"In this case the plaintiff by its reply could not invoke the doctrine of clean hands to prevent the defendants from pleading and claiming under a legal defense * * *."

All of the foregoing would have been fine, had this court not then decided Kirkland v. Mannis, 55 Or.App. 613, 639 P.2d 671, *rev. den.* 292 Or. 863, 648 P.2d 850 (1982). In *Kirkland,* the plaintiff, a prisoner, brought a malpractice action against the defendant, an attorney, alleging, *inter alia,* that the defendant

"unethically, wantonly and with the intent to defraud the plaintiff and the court * * * manufactured a story for the plaintiff's defense to [criminal charges] * * *."

The trial court had granted the defendant judgment as to the foregoing allegation. We affirmed, stating:

"[W]e agree with the trial judge that no cause of action is stated. The essence of this paragraph is that plaintiff and defendant cooperatively presented a perjurious tale at plaintiff's criminal trial, and the tale did not sell. *Because of his acknowledged perjury, plaintiff brings his complaint with unclean hands and may not recover.*"

The emphasized statement in *Kirkland* was wrong. The claim was a legal one; the equitable doctrine did not apply, as we had earlier explained in *Gratreak.* The only argument that would conceivably square *Gratreak* and *Kirkland* is that the adoption of the Oregon Rules of Civil Procedure abolished many of the distinctions between law and equity and should, therefore, be deemed impliedly to extend the availability of the clean hands doctrine to law actions.

We do not think that view can be sustained. ORCP 2 removed only procedural distinctions between law and equity, not substantive differences. Under code pleading systems that have eliminated distinctions between law and equity, one authority has noted that such an elimination of procedural distinctions has not

"obliterated the essential and inherent distinctions between law and equity as two separate sciences. What was an action at law before the code, is still an action founded on legal principles; and what was a bill in equity before the code, is still a civil action founded on principles of equity." 1 Sutherland *Code Pleading,* § 87 at 71 (1910).

We conclude that *Kirkland's* substantive application of the equitable doctrine of clean hands to an action at law was technically incorrect.

While technically incorrect, however, the public policy considerations in *Kirkland,* are certainly of importance to actions at law as well as proceedings in equity. As defendant puts it in his brief, "[w]hether we give plaintiff's conduct the nomenclature of 'clean hands,' contributory negligence as a matter of law, or simply a violation of public policy, the courts should not entertain claims based upon such antisocial conduct."

Kirkland was right in substance. The proper nomenclature, however, is that the parties were *in pari delicto, i.e.,* "[i]n equal fault; in a similar offense or crime; equal in guilt or in legal fault." *Black's Law Dictionary* 1270 (4th Ed.Rev.1968). That the parties are *in pari delicto* is often asserted in contract disputes and claims for indemnity. It has also been applied in negligence actions. See McGhee's Admir. v. Elcomb Coal, 288 Ky. 540, 156 S.W.2d 868 (1941).

In pari delicto has been referred to as a "companion principle" to the equitable maxim of clean hands, to be applied in actions at law where equitable doctrines are irrelevant. Furman v. Furman, et al., 178 Misc. 582, 34 N.Y.S.2d 699 (1941) ("[T]he doctrine of 'clean hands' is closely akin to the maxim *in pari delicto,* and the two are sometimes discussed as though involving substantially the same principle"), quoting Heflinger v. Heflinger, 136 Va. 289, 291, 118 S.E. 316, 318 (1923). The *Tarasi* court held that, when parties are *in pari delicto,* recovery may be barred if a litigant's "losses are substantially caused by activities the law forbade him to engage in."

Oregon has recognized the public policy orientation of the doctrine. In McElwee v. McElwee, 171 Or. 462, 138 P.2d 208 (1943), the court said:

> "The maxim being one founded on public policy, public policy may require its relaxation. Even when the parties have been found to be *in pari delicto,* relief has at times been awarded on the ground that in the particular case public policy has been found to be best conserved by that course." Quoting Condit v. Condit, 115 Or. 481, 482–83, 237 P. 360 (1925).

We understand from the foregoing that the rule is this: The doctrine of *in pari delicto* may—but need not—be applied to prevent recovery in a law action, when the party against whom it is to be applied is as culpable as, or more culpable than, his opponent. The question then becomes whether, on the state of the record the trial court had before it in this case, it could be established that plaintiff was equally culpable with, or more culpable than, defendant.

We think not. As the allegation now stands, plaintiff claims that he undertook a particular course of conduct relying on the expertise of defendant. His allegation shows that he acted wrongfully, but it does not establish a parity of fault. Defendant is an attorney—a presumed expert in the law; plaintiff is not. Evidence could be presented under this complaint to show that defendant was in the superior position to appreciate the wrongfulness of plaintiff's actions and that his culpability is, therefore, greater. The policy reasons behind the doctrine of *in pari delicto* do not justify dismissal of plaintiff's complaint.

Reversed and remanded.

Notes

1. Does this holding affect public policy?

2. Byron v. Clay, 867 F.2d 1049, 1051 (7th Cir.1989): "But with the merger of law and equity, it is difficult to see why equitable defenses should be limited to equitable suits any more; and of course many are not so limited [citation], and

perhaps unclean hands should be one of these. Even before the merger there was a counterpart legal doctrine to unclean hands—*in pari delicto*—which forbid a plaintiff to recover damages if his fault was equal to the defendant's. [citation] We need not worry about the precise scope of the doctrine. [citation] It is enough to observe that a highwayman who decided to sue his partner for common law damages as well as for an equitable accounting for profits would surely have gotten no further with his 'legal' claim than with his 'equitable' one."

More on "the precise scope of the doctrine" of *in pari delicto* is in the final chapter, infra, p. 1239.

Blain v. The Doctor's Co., 222 Cal.App.3d 1048, 272 Cal.Rptr. 250 (1990). Unclean hands was held to bar a doctor's claim against a lawyer for damages for emotional distress resulting from alleged legal malpractice.

3. *The Parties' Unclean Hands and the Public Interest.* Alpo Petfoods, Inc. v. Ralston Purina Co., 720 F.Supp. 194, 197, 214 (D.D.C.1989). Ralston made a false advertising claim about its Puppy Chow; Alpo also advertised its puppy food falsely. In the lawsuit that followed, each claimed the other had violated § 43(a) of the federal Lanham Act and both sought injunctions. If defendant's false advertising deceives the public, a competitor is entitled to an injunction. The district judge said:

"[B]oth parties have made false, deceptive, and misleading claims which are actionable. * * * [B]oth parties are entitled to relief * * *." The unclean hands defense is available against Lanham Act remedies. To be unclean hands, the misconduct must relate to the matter in controversy. Both parties had misbehaved concerning the same product, puppy food. Each claimed the other's hands are unclean, and each argued against any injunctions:

"[T]he court must take into account the public and the competitors' interests in preventing the proliferation of false and deceptive advertising. [citations] The defenses may be rejected where, as is the case here, failure to grant an injunction would only increase the damage inflicted on the buying public. Given that the worst effects of Alpo's and Ralston's conduct have been visited on the buying public, this court believes that the equitable defenses raised cannot bar relief which is necessary and in the public interest."

Alpo Petfoods Inc. v. Ralston Purina Co., aff'd in part, rev'd in part, 913 F.2d 958, 970 (D.C.Cir.1990). The dog food fight continued in the appellate court, but neither party appealed the trial judge's decision to reject both parties' unclean hands defenses.

Edwards v. Academy Publishing Corp., 562 N.E.2d 60 (Ind.App.1990). A publisher sued employees who had misappropriated its list of customers; but the court refused to grant injunctive relief to the publisher, for it was found to have defrauded the public and to have unclean hands.

(2) Laches

STONE v. WILLIAMS

United States Court of Appeals, Second Circuit, 1989.
873 F.2d 620.

CARDAMONE, CIRCUIT JUDGE. Cathy Yvonne Stone brought this action * * * for her purported share of copyright renewal rights to songs composed by Hank Williams, Sr., her natural father. The defendants in this action are Hank Williams, Jr., the son of Hank Williams and stepson of Billie Jean Williams

Berlin, who was married to Hank Williams at the time of his death, and a number of music companies * * *. The sole issue presented is whether the district court abused its discretion when it granted defendants' motion for summary judgment and dismissed appellant's complaint on the grounds of laches. Even granting to Ms. Stone's situation the fullest stretch of sympathy, her own delay and procrastination in the end bars her suit. The district court's judgment, therefore, is affirmed.

The dispute arises over copyright renewal proceeds for 60 published and copyrighted songs written or performed by country and western singer Hank Williams (Williams, Sr.) who died intestate on January 1, 1953 at the age of 29. During his lifetime the well-known singer and composer wrote such popular hits as "Your Cheatin' Heart" and "Hey Good Lookin'." We set forth the facts briefly in chronological order.

Appellant Stone was born on January 6, 1953 in Alabama, five days after Williams, Sr. died. While Ms. Stone's biological mother, Bobbie Jett, was pregnant with her in October of 1952, she and Williams, Sr. executed an agreement under which he acknowledged that he might be the father of appellant, but specifically did not admit paternity. The agreement further provided that Williams, Sr. pay Bobbie Jett for Ms. Stone's support, and placed the infant's custody until age 2 in Lillian Williams Stone, mother of Williams, Sr., who was present at the drafting and the execution of the agreement together with the two principals. Pursuant to its terms, Lillian Stone adopted plaintiff, and Bobbie Jett left for California. Until her death in 1955 Mrs. Stone cared for appellant. At that point, Williams, Sr.'s sister, Irene Smith, reneged on her promise to care for Cathy Stone if anything happened to Lillian Stone. As a result, appellant became a ward of the State of Alabama, and at age three in 1956 a foster child of the Deupree family. The Deuprees adopted her in 1959.

Williams, Sr. had a son, Hank Williams, Jr. The assignment of Hank Williams, Jr.'s copyright interests in his father's music generated litigation in 1967 and 1968 in the Circuit Court of Montgomery County, Alabama. That court appointed a guardian *ad litem,* attorney Drayton Hamilton, to ascertain any unknown potential heirs to the Williams' estate and to represent their interests. After investigating, Hamilton concluded that the only such person was appellant Stone. Unbeknownst to Ms. Stone, her adoptive family, the Deuprees, had asked Hamilton to leave her out of the 1967 proceedings, because they thought it unlikely that she would win and were worried that their then 14–year–old daughter would be subjected to embarrassing publicity because of her status as the illegitimate child of a famous country western singer. Nonetheless, Hamilton zealously litigated Ms. Stone's interests, but to no avail. The Alabama court determined that Hank Williams, Jr. was the sole heir of his father, and further held that appellant, as a natural child who had been adopted by another family, had no rights in any proceeds from the Williams, Sr.'s songs or their renewal rights. * * *

After the disruptive first few years of her life, Ms. Stone appears to have enjoyed an ordinary childhood, and developed a closely bonded relationship with the Deuprees, with no knowledge of her natural parents. Then, in late 1973, shortly before appellant's 21st birthday, Mrs. Deupree told her of the rumors regarding the identity of her natural father, but added that everything had been decided against her. This disclosure was necessary because, upon turning age 21, Ms. Stone was entitled to a small inheritance from Williams, Sr.'s mother, Lillian Stone. The Deuprees were concerned that appellant might encounter reporters while claiming the inheritance and wanted to arm her with knowledge. After picking up the inheritance check (about $3,800) at the Mobile County Courthouse, Ms. Stone went to a library and read a biography on Williams, Sr., entitled *Sing a Sad Song,* written by Roger Williams. This book mentioned the possibility that Williams, Sr. had fathered an illegitimate daughter, and the author speculated on the child's entitlement to a renewal interest in his songs. Ms. Stone surmised that she might be that daughter.

In the following years, appellant asked the Deuprees about her background and talked to some attorney acquaintances, but did little else to ascertain her connection to Williams. She recalls that the Deuprees told her that there was nothing more to do. In 1979, she met with personnel from the state agency responsible for adoptions—the Alabama Department of Pensions and Securities—but states that she no longer remembers the substance of the conversation. The record, including appellant's deposition, suggests that her feelings about Williams' parentage were ambivalent.

Her attitude crystallized in 1980 when she received a telephone call from her adoptive father, George Deupree. Evidently alluding to his decision not to pursue Ms. Stone's rights in the 1967–68 lawsuits, Deupree told her that he had undergone a change of heart after seeing Hank Williams, Jr. on a television show. Deupree has since died, but appellant related the conversation in her deposition: "I want to ask you if you would like to find out if Hank Williams is your father. He said think about it. And he said I will help you in any way that I can. And he said I think I was wrong in withholding information from you and not discussing it. And I will do everything I can to help you."

Following this call, Ms. Stone stepped up her efforts to learn about her relationship to Williams, Sr. She looked up newspaper articles about him, and sought out his relatives and those of her natural mother, Bobbie Jett, who had also since died. She met with attorney Hamilton, her former guardian *ad litem,* and discussed with him the 1952 custody and support agreement between Bobbie Jett and Williams, Sr., and obtained the records from the 1967 and 1968 Circuit Court proceedings. But Ms. Stone did not examine those documents until after she met attorney Keith Adkinson (who later became her husband) in 1984.

Appellant filed the original declaratory judgment complaint in this action on September 12, 1985 which, as amended to include all of the above-named defendants, contains two claims. The first claim against all the defendants arises under the Copyright Acts of 1909 and 1976 and seeks a number of declarations, including that Ms. Stone is the natural daughter of Williams, Sr., and as such is entitled to a proportionate share of the renewal rights from his songs. The second claim alleges that certain of the defendants committed a conspiracy to defraud her.

In addition to this federal action, Hank Williams, Jr. and Ms. Stone sued each other in Alabama state court in 1985, each seeking a declaratory judgment on appellant's status vis-à-vis Hank Williams, Sr. That court held that even though Ms. Stone was the natural child of Williams, Sr., she was not his heir under Alabama law. Thus, it gave preclusive effect to the prior 1967 and 1968 Alabama Circuit Court state ruling.

* * * The district court, in granting defendants' motion for summary judgment and dismissing her complaint, relied on the doctrine of laches and did not reach the other issues.

Historically laches developed as an equitable defense based on the Latin maxim *vigilantibus non dormientibus aequitas subvenit* (equity aids the vigilant, not those who sleep on their rights). [citation] In contrast to a statute of limitations that provides a time bar within which suit must be instituted, laches asks whether the plaintiff in asserting her rights was guilty of unreasonable delay that prejudiced the defendants. [citations] The answers to these questions are to be drawn from the equitable circumstances peculiar to each case.

A ruling on the applicability of laches is overturned only when it can be said to constitute an abuse of discretion. * * *

Although laches promotes many of the same goals as a statute of limitations, the doctrine is more flexible and requires an assessment of the facts of each case—it is the reasonableness of the delay rather than the number of years that elapse which is the focus of inquiry. [citations] In holding that Ms. Stone unreasonably delayed in bringing this action to have her rights declared, the district court focused on the years 1974–85, beginning with Mrs. Deupree's conversation with appellant regarding the inheritance, and ending with the filing of the complaint that initiated the instant case.

In our view, the delay for the period from 1974 to 1980 may well have been entirely excusable under the circumstances. First, her relationship with the Deuprees is by all indications the paradigm of a successful adoption. Thus, it is not surprising that loyalty and gratitude to Mr. and Mrs. Deupree, whom she considered her real parents, gave her pause at doing anything that might hurt their feelings. For this reason, George Deupree's telephone call to Ms. Stone is significant. Only after he called in 1980 could appellant be sure that investigating her natural parentage would not damage the only family bonds she knew. Second, Ms. Stone's embarrassment at asserting her relationship to Williams, Sr. is also understandable, because his notoriety would have made publicity almost impossible for her to avoid. This is substantiated by the extensive press coverage of the 1967 and 1968 court proceedings.

Third, only in recent years have courts and the general public come to recognize that children born of unmarried parents should not be penalized by being accorded a status for which they are not to blame. In the 1967 and 1968 proceedings, attorney Hamilton argued on Ms. Stone's behalf that discriminating against illegitimate children violated the Federal Constitution. Unfortunately for appellant, Hamilton was before his time; the case that would remove much of the stigma associated with illegitimacy was then pending before the Supreme Court, but not decided until after appellant's rights had been adjudicated. See Levy v. Louisiana, 391 U.S. 68 (1968) (holding unconstitutional state statute that discriminated against illegitimates to discourage births out of wedlock).

But even though Ms. Stone might arguably be excused for the reasons just stated from filing suit until 1980, there is simply no plausible explanation for delay in filing the instant complaint until September 1985, after five more years had passed. Appellant's filial loyalty is admirable, and one can sympathize with her feelings of embarrassment and trepidation attendant upon widespread personal publicity. But these reasons for delay cannot last forever for purposes of laches. A point arrives when a plaintiff must either assert her rights or lose them. Here Ms. Stone's procrastination and delay, which silently allowed time to slip away, remain as the only reason for her failure to bring suit earlier.

Where plaintiff has not slept on her rights, but has been prevented from asserting them based, for example, on justified ignorance of the facts constituting a cause of action, personal disability, or because of ongoing settlement negotiations, the delay is reasonable and the equitable defense of laches will not bar an action. There is no such reasonable excuse, or any issue of fact presented in the instant case that would permit a jury to excuse appellant's delay for the five years beginning in 1980 and ending in September 1985.

Laches is not imposed as a bar to suit simply because a plaintiff's delay is found unexcused; it must also be determined whether the defendants have been prejudiced as a result of that delay. [citation] Although an evaluation of prejudice is another subject of focus in laches analysis, it is integrally related to the inquiry regarding delay. Where there is no excuse for delay, as here, defendants need show little prejudice; a weak excuse for delay may, on the other hand, suffice to defeat a laches defense if no prejudice has been shown. [citation] Defendants may be prejudiced in several different ways. [citation] One form of prejudice is the decreased ability of the defendants to vindicate themselves that results from the death of witnesses or on account of fading memories or stale evidence. Another type of prejudice operates on the principle that it would be inequitable in light of some change in defendant's position to permit plaintiff's claim to be enforced. Defendants here were prejudiced in both ways.

As the district court noted, some of the key people having knowledge of the events preceding Ms. Stone's birth have died since 1974—George Deupree, Bobbie Jett and Audrey Mae Williams. All of their deaths are not equally prejudicial. For example, Bobbie Jett died in 1974, so absence of her testimony cannot be found to prejudice defendants because she would not have been alive to testify even if appellant had filed suit immediately. Nevertheless, the circumstances giving rise to this appeal have already spanned over two decades and the additional five years of Ms. Stone's unexcused delay doubtless would hamper the defense further—appellant's deposition reveals that even her memory has faded significantly in the interim. We conclude that the defendants were prejudiced to some degree by evidence that was lost by death or weakened during the delay. Because the defendants were injured in other ways by the delay, we need not hold that a finding of this kind of prejudice is alone sufficient to support the laches defense.

Prejudice may also be found if, during the period of delay, the circumstances or relationships between the parties have changed so that it would be unfair to let the suit go forward. The defendants have entered into numerous transactions involving Williams, Sr.'s songs. Ms. Stone responds that these transactions need not be unravelled—she could simply share in the profits. But that argument ignores the fact that the transactions were premised on the apparent certainty of the ownership of the songs' renewal rights—attributable to appellant's delay. This procrastination prejudiced defendants by lulling them into a false sense of security that the renewal rights were as they appeared and that she would not contest the 1967 and 1968 court rulings. [citations]

We cannot be sure that defendants would have struck the bargains they did had they anticipated the dimunition in their profits that Ms. Stone seeks. This result is logically not altered by whether the defendants made actual expenditures or whether they simply incurred the opportunity costs implicated in foregoing other ventures. As Judge Learned Hand wrote as a district court judge in a copyright case in which the plaintiff delayed for 16 years before filing suit, it would be unfair for a plaintiff "to stand inactive while the proposed infringer spends large sums of money in its exploitation, and to intervene only when his speculation has proved a success. Delay under such circumstances allows the owner to speculate without risk with the other's money, he cannot possibly lose, and he may win." Haas v. Leo Feist, Inc., 234 F. 105, 108 (S.D.N.Y.1916). We therefore agree with the district court that the change in relationships and circumstances that occurred while Ms. Stone delayed would prejudice the defendants if the case were allowed to proceed at this late date.

Finally, we note that the underlying value of the laches doctrine, as with statutes of limitations, is that of repose. Even assuming that appellant's claims are meritorious, the availability of the laches defense represents a conclusion that the societal interest in a correct decision can be outweighed by the disruption its tardy filing would cause. Thus, courts, parties and witnesses "ought to be relieved of the burden of trying stale claims when a plaintiff has slept on his rights." See Burnett v. New York Central R.R. Co., 380 U.S. 424, 428 (1965).

[Affirmed.]

Note

Stone v. Williams, 891 F.2d 401, 403 (2d Cir.1989). Plaintiff Stone filed a petition for rehearing. The court granted the petition and reversed the preceding opinion, Judge Cardamone again writing for the court. After the preceding opinion was argued but before it was decided, the Alabama Supreme Court had decided Stone's appeal in separate litigation where she was seeking to reopen her father's estate and to obtain her share of the estate. The Alabama court "reversed the trial court's award of summary judgment to defendants finding that they had intentionally, willfully and fraudulently concealed plaintiff's identity, existence, claim and rights as a natural child of Hank Williams, Sr." Because of fraud and errors of law, the Alabama court had also set aside the Montgomery Circuit Court decrees that Stone was not an heir to the estate. The Alabama court also held that laches did not bar plaintiff's claim because her delay was excusable. Although the parties and applicable law differed, the court of appeals reconsidered on two related theories:

"However, recited evidence in the Alabama court makes clear that the present defendants were aware of plaintiff's rights to the copyright renewals long before plaintiff. Irene Smith, who was instrumental in concealing from plaintiff evidence of who her father was, acted as Hank Williams, Jr.'s guardian during the 1967–68 proceedings. Similarly, Smith, as administratrix, and Stewart, as attorney, of Hank Williams' estate, conspired to conceal from Cathy Stone her potential rights, and took pains to cut off those rights. These actions of his guardian benefited Hank Williams, Jr. Hank Williams, Jr.'s counsel was further advised by Stewart that a portion of the estate income was being withheld for appellant. Williams, Jr. never disavowed Stewart's actions, or mentioned any of these facts in prior court proceedings in Alabama in 1985 or in the district court proceeding we earlier reviewed and to which he and plaintiff were parties.

"The prejudice to defendants we identified in our prior opinion, would not have existed but for the failure of the present defendants to reveal the facts of which they had knowledge. Defendants could have sought a court declaration of their rights vis-a-vis plaintiff. Instead they chose to remain silent. They should not now be allowed to claim that they are prejudiced by plaintiff's present assertion of her rights when they were aware of them all along.

"Consequently, in reassessing the equitable circumstances peculiar to this case, the equities fall on plaintiff's side. The present litigation is a contest, after all, between Hank Williams' heirs over copyright renewal rights. To allow defendants to bar plaintiff from claiming her rights when the availability of the laches defense was obtained by them in such an unworthy manner would not only grant defendants a windfall in this suit to which they are not entitled, but would also encourage a party to deliberately mislead a court. Courts of equity exist to relieve a party from the defense of laches under such circumstances. [citation]

"Consequently, the evidence of fraud, which the Alabama Supreme Court found persuasive, makes summary judgment dismissing plaintiff's claim on the grounds of laches inappropriate. The figure representing justice is blindfolded so that the scales are held even, but justice is not blind to reality."

WHITFIELD v. ANHEUSER-BUSCH, INC.

United States Court of Appeals, Eighth Circuit, 1987.
820 F.2d 243.

McMillian, Circuit Judge. Sidney B. Whitfield appeals from a final order entered in the District Court * * * based on the equitable doctrine of laches. For reversal, Whitfield argues the district court improperly granted summary judgment because there are issues of material fact regarding whether laches should apply in the circumstances of this case. Whitfield contends specifically that (1) he was not guilty of unreasonable and unexcused delay in filing this suit and (2) Anheuser-Busch was not prejudiced as a result of this delay. For the reasons discussed below, we affirm the judgment of the district court.

Whitfield, a black man, was employed as a research assistant in the Corn Products Division of Anheuser-Busch from May 1968 to January 1973. In late 1972, Dr. James Teng, supervisor of the Corn Products Division, was notified by his superior, Dr. Barry Scallet, that a personnel reduction was necessary. Dr. Teng determined that Whitfield would be laid-off and notified Whitfield that his employment would end January 30, 1973.

On January 17, 1973, Whitfield filed a charge of discrimination with the Equal Employment Opportunity Commission (EEOC) alleging he was chosen for termination on the basis of race, while white employees with less seniority retained their jobs. The EEOC investigated the charge and in October 1974 held a hearing. The case then remained dormant for almost ten years, until, in July 1983, the EEOC issued Whitfield a Notice of Right to Sue.

Whitfield filed suit in district court on October 4, 1983, within the statutory time following issuance of the Notice of Right to Sue. The parties began discovery and Dr. Teng and Dr. Scallet were deposed by Whitfield's counsel. At the deposition, both men testified that they could no longer accurately recall the events leading up to the decision to terminate Whitfield. Based on the depositions of these two key witnesses, Anheuser-Busch filed a motion for summary judgment based on the doctrine of laches.

The district court granted Anheuser–Busch's motion for summary judgment, ruling that Whitfield's action was barred by the doctrine of laches. The district court concluded that Whitfield's ten-year delay in filing suit was unreasonable and unexcused and that Anheuser–Busch had been prejudiced by the delay because the impaired recollection of the employer's two key witnesses would harm its defense. Whitfield now appeals.

The equitable doctrine of laches is a proper defense in a Title VII action and a court may use laches to reach "a just result." [citations] Laches may be used to bar a lawsuit when the plaintiff is guilty of (1) unreasonable and unexcused delay, (2) resulting in prejudice to the defendant. [citations] Laches is an affirmative defense and the burden of persuasion generally rests with the defendant.[1] In this circuit, laches may apply either when the delay in bringing suit was caused by a private plaintiff or when the delay is the fault of an administrative agency.[2] * * *

In examining the "unreasonable and unexcused delay" prong of the laches standard, we consider both the length of the delay and the plaintiff's reasons for the delay. Whitfield filed an EEOC charge promptly upon his termination in 1973 by Anheuser–Busch. Yet for ten years after the EEOC investigation and hearing, Whitfield made no attempts to check on the status of his charge. Whitfield has not provided any meaningful explanation for his long silence or denied that he knew he could request the Notice of Right to Sue from the EEOC within 180 days after first filing his charge of discrimination. See 29 C.F.R. § 1601.28 (1978). We agree with the district court's finding that Whitfield's ten-year delay in filing this suit was unexcused.

In the circumstances of this case, we also agree with the district court's finding that the length of delay was unreasonable. Each case must be considered on its own facts in determining the reasonableness of the delay; laches is an equitable, hence flexible, doctrine, and no length of time is considered per se unreasonable. The district court compared the facts of the present case with the facts underlying other decisions of this court and determined that ten years was an unreasonable delay. * * *

The second prong of the laches standard requires Anheuser–Busch to show that it was prejudiced by the delay. In support of its motion for summary judgment, Anheuser–Busch submitted the depositions of the two employees responsible for terminating Whitfield in 1973. Both employees testified that they could no longer accurately recall the events leading to the decision to lay-off Whitfield. The district court found that the hampered recollection of these two key witnesses would hinder Anheuser–Busch's defense and therefore ruled that Anheuser–Busch had been prejudiced by Whitfield's delay in filing suit.

Not all prejudice to a defendant will be recognized as supporting a defense of laches. The prejudice that will support a defense of laches includes loss of

1. [Footnotes renumbered.] In Goodman v. McDonnell Douglas Corp., 606 F.2d 800 (8th Cir.1979), however, this court observed that in assigning the burden of proof of laches, a court may take into account which party can best provide proof of a particular aspect of the case. "Thus," we noted, "a defendant may better be able to establish that it has been prejudiced because of delay, while the plaintiff will generally have greater knowledge of the reasons for the delay and any excuse therefor."

2. But see, e.g., Cleveland Newspaper Guild v. The Plain Dealer Publishing Co., 813 F.2d 101 (6th Cir.1987) (reliance on EEOC's administrative process, even resulting in ten-year delay in filing suit, does not constitute inexcusable delay for laches purposes in Title VII case).

evidence in support of the defendant's position or the unavailability of witnesses. Whitfield contends that Anheuser–Busch's claim that its two key witnesses are unavailable by reason of impaired recollection is contrived and self-serving. Whitfield has presented no evidence to support this allegation, however. Further, Whitfield's counsel was present when both witnesses were deposed and had ample opportunity to cross-examine them to expose any lack of credibility. The witnesses' claim of limited recollection is persuasive in light of the fact that the events involved were a part of everyday business life that occurred some ten years ago and not some momentous occasion. Based on the impaired recollection of Anheuser–Busch's two key witnesses, we agree with the district court's finding that Anheuser–Busch was prejudiced by the delay in bringing this action. * * *

[Affirmed.]

Notes

1. *Effect of the Statute of Limitations.* Goodman v. McDonnell Douglas Corp., 606 F.2d 800, 804–805 (8th Cir.1979): "In applying the doctrine of laches, an important consideration is the appropriate role of an analogous statute of limitation. Appellants argue that the District Court abused its discretion by mechanically applying the analogous statute of limitation in Missouri for contract actions. * * *

"The lower federal courts have ascribed varying degrees of importance to analogous statutes of limitation. Some courts have held that the running of an analogous statute of limitation creates a rebuttable presumption of unreasonable delay and prejudice flowing therefrom. [citation] Other courts have completely disregarded statutes of limitation in considering a defense of laches, [citations], or treated them as merely one element in the congeries of factors to be considered in determining whether the length of delay was unreasonable and whether the potential for prejudice was great. [citations] We find that the last approach accords most favorably with the purpose of the doctrine of laches and congressional intent regarding the doctrine's application to claims pursuant to 38 U.S.C. § 2021 et seq., to protect veteran's reemployment rights.

"In Holmberg v. Armbrecht, 327 U.S. 392, 396 (1946) the Supreme Court stated:

> 'Traditionally and for good reasons, statutes of limitation are not controlling measures of equitable relief. Such statutes have been drawn upon by equity solely for the light they may shed in determining that which is decisive for the chancellor's intervention, namely, whether the plaintiff has inexcusably slept on his rights so as to make a decree against the defendant unfair.' "

2. *Laches in Legal Actions.* Bauer v. P.A. Cutri Co., 434 Pa. 305, 310, 253 A.2d 252, 255 (1969), was an action by the seller of an insurance agency against a sub-purchaser to declare a covenant not to compete void and for sum due on the original sale:

"It is clear at the outset that appellee's claim for money damage is one normally cognizable at law. Of course since appellee asked to have the covenant-not-to-compete declared null and void, this action was properly in equity, and having granted the equitable relief prayed for, the chancellor was also free to resolve other questions raised in the litigation. This does not mean, however, that appellant can use equitable defenses to defeat appellee's legal claim for money damages. These equitable defenses are designed only to prevent an 'undeserving' plaintiff from obtaining by an appeal to the chancellor's 'conscience' the kind of *extraordinary* remedies available in equity, but they in no way prejudice his rights at law. Therefore it has long been the rule in this Commonwealth that in dealing with legal rights, a court of equity follows and is bound by rules of law, and does not use equitable considerations to deprive a party of his rights at law. Thus even assuming arguendo that we could find—as the chancellor apparently did not—that appellee was guilty of laches, appellant could not prevail. Appellee was only required to bring his claim for money damages within the six year period established in the statute of limitations, and this he clearly did."

In accord: M. Lowenstein & Sons v. Austin, 430 F.Supp. 844, 846 (S.D.N.Y. 1977). "The answer short and simple is that laches is a defense only to actions in equity, and is not a defense to an action at law. The relevant statute of limitations provides the only barrier to stale actions at law. Reviewing the complaint, it is apparent that this is an action for breach of contract and that no equitable relief is sought. Accordingly, this defense is not available to defendant."

3. Congress in 1990 passed a new federal catch-all statute of limitations for federal legislation enacted after 1990. 28 U.S.C. § 1658.

B. PROVISIONAL EQUITABLE REMEDIES: TRO AND PRELIMINARY INJUNCTION

Introductory Note

Pretrial injunctions and temporary restraining orders maintain the status quo and preserve the controversy for a meaningful decision after full trial. The intractable problem is how to accomplish this while protecting the defendant from the severity and harshness of an order granted after less than a full hearing.

The terminology used in designating these decrees is varied and confusing. The federal system uses the terms injunction or permanent injunction, preliminary injunction, and temporary restraining order, frequently referred to as TRO. Injunctions and permanent injunctions are granted only after a full trial. Preliminary or interlocutory injunctions are granted after a hearing and adversary proceeding. See Federal Rule of Civil Procedure 65 below. A temporary restraining order may be issued with no adversary hearing at all; such orders are called ex parte decrees. In addition to these terms, state practice rules and statutes may refer to interlocutory decrees as provisional, pendente lite, or temporary. Refer to the appropriate sources in your jurisdiction for full understanding of this material.

Federal Rule of Civil Procedure 65:

(a) Preliminary Injunction

(1) *Notice.* No preliminary injunction shall be issued without notice to the adverse party.

(2) *Consolidation of Hearing With Trial on Merits.* Before or after the commencement of the hearing of an application for a preliminary injunction, the court may order the trial of the action on the merits to be advanced and consolidated with the hearing of the application. Even when this consolidation is not ordered, any evidence received upon an application for preliminary injunction which would be admissible upon the trial on the merits becomes part of the record on the trial and need not be repeated upon the trial. This

subdivision (a)(2) shall be so construed and applied as to save to the parties any rights they may have to trial by jury.

WILLIAMS v. STATE UNIVERSITY

United States District Court, Eastern District of New York, 1986.
635 F.Supp. 1243, 1250.

[Plaintiff was discharged from her position as associate director of nursing at the State University of New York Downstate Medical Center. A Costa Rican born black Hispanic woman, she sued the hospital alleging that she was discharged because of intentional discrimination based on color, sex, and national origin. She applied for a preliminary injunction. The judge was "unable to conclude that plaintiff has evinced a likelihood of success on the merits," but was "more willing to acknowledge that plaintiff's papers may [have] pose[d] sufficiently serious questions going to the merits." The parts of the opinion that deal with irreparable harm and the balance of hardship follow.]

PLATT, DISTRICT JUDGE. The law in the Second Circuit governing the granting of a preliminary injunction is now well settled. Since 1976 to successfully seek a preliminary injunction in this Circuit a moving party must show (1) irreparable harm *and* (2) either (a) a likelihood of success on the merits or (b) sufficiently serious questions going to the merits and a balance of hardships tipping in movant's favor. See Power Test Petroleum Distributors v. Calcu Gas, 754 F.2d 91, 95 (2d Cir.1985). * * *

Irreparable Harm. Satisfying this test is critical to plaintiff's application and consequently warrants clear and careful scrutiny by the Court. In her affidavit plaintiff sets forth her reasons why she will suffer irreparable harm if she is not reinstated. She states that (1) her career will be destroyed because no one will hire her for a *comparable position* after being discharged and suing her employer; (2) her employment position was *unique* in view of all her responsibilities; and (3) she is a self-supporting widow with mortgage payments and a daughter's college education to finance.

Little doubt exists in the mind of this Court that Williams may indeed suffer some anguish and some economic hardship during the course of this litigation. Nevertheless, sympathy for plaintiffs has no place in the application of the Second Circuit's standard to the facts of a case. The sole issue confronting this Court and requiring its decision is whether the plaintiff's circumstances are such that a refusal to issue a preliminary injunction in her favor will wreak irreparable harm upon her.

In an employment discharge case "the requisite irreparable harm is not established * * * by financial distress or inability to find other employment, unless truly extraordinary circumstances are shown." [citations] "'Mere injuries, however substantial, in terms of money, time and energy necessarily expended in the absence of a stay, are not enough' to justify injunctive relief." [citation] Nor will damage to reputation and self esteem, or hardship imposed on a plaintiff's family alone or in combination merit a preliminary injunction. In all cases where a plaintiff, if successful in obtaining a permanent injunction, could calculate the interim damages with sufficient accuracy to make damages an adequate substitute, no preliminary injunction ought to issue. [citations]

Culling the factors from cases on point which have been deemed to constitute "extraordinary circumstances," this Court concludes that a discharged plaintiff must show that she (1) has very little chance of securing further employment; (2) has no personal or family resources at her disposal; (3) lacks private unemployment insurance; (4) is unable to obtain a privately financed loan; (5) is ineligible for any type of public support or relief, and (6) any other compelling circumstances which weigh heavily in favor of granting interim equitable relief. In essence the plaintiff must quite literally find herself being forced into the streets or facing the spectre of bankruptcy before a court can enter a finding of irreparable harm.

In the instant action plaintiff has failed to document her efforts to find interim employment beyond a passing reference in her supplemental affidavit. ("It will be impossible for me to find a comparable hospital managerial position. * * * I have not met with any fortune in this respect so far.") The Court notes that plaintiff may have to seek any employment for which she is qualified, *i.e.,* as a registered nurse, rather than an identical position to the one she lost. Nor, to the Court's knowledge, has she tried to collect either private or public unemployment insurance. Furthermore, plaintiff has presented no evidence of any attempts to obtain an extension of her mortgage payments, nor of her daughter's efforts to apply for emergency financial aid or a summer job. Consequently, this Court may not in good conscience find the extraordinary circumstances necessary to a determination of irreparable harm. * * *

[The court held that there was little likelihood that plaintiff would succeed on the merits, but that she raised a serious question going to the merits.]

The Balance of Hardships. Each side argues vigorously that an adverse decision will weigh more heavily against it. Plaintiff reiterates those reasons listed in her claim of irreparable harm. Defendants assert that allowing reinstatement would (1) unequivocally change the *status quo* and provide plaintiff with relief beyond the extent contemplated by Fed.R.Civ.P. 65; (2) undermine the decision-making capacity of the administrators at the Hospital; (3) destroy confidence in the administration and the rules and regulations that guide personnel, and (4) would give rise to a flood of litigation by any and all parties discharged by the defendants.

This Court does not believe that the hardships resulting to either party from an adverse decision would be intolerable. Nevertheless, the Court maintains its position enunciated over a decade ago, that "of all fields which the federal courts should hesitate to invade and take over, education and faculty appointments at a University level are probably the least suited for federal intervention." Moore v. Kibbee, 381 F.Supp. 834, 839 (E.D.N.Y.1974) (citation omitted). Plaintiff's former position as associate director of nursing in the State University system is within the parameters of this principle.

The plaintiff has failed to establish to this Court's satisfaction either irreparable harm—a prerequisite to preliminary injunctive relief—or likelihood of success on the merits. Although plaintiff's papers do suggest the existence of a cognizable claim * * *, this Court is also unable to conclude that the balance of hardships tips decidedly in her favor. For the reasons fully elaborated herein, the Court hereby denies plaintiff's application for injunctive relief.

Notes

1. The idea that courts use injunctions to prevent irreparable injury will remain part of equity's traditional lexicon. The irreparable injury analysis interacts with other factors in preliminary injunction tests. While the flexible approach is encumbered by the inflexible word "irreparable," the inflexibility may be more appropriate here than before a final injunction. For when courts use the term irreparable injury to state the standard for a preliminary injunction, it has more teeth than it does when used to state the prerequisite for final injunctions. The procedure used to protect plaintiff's right to preventive relief may increase the risk of error that may injure the defendant.

2. Triebwasser & Katz v. American Telephone & Telegraph Co., 535 F.2d 1356, 1359 (2d Cir.1976). Defendants declined to publish plaintiff's advertisement in the Queens County Yellow Pages; plaintiffs sued under the antitrust statutes. The trial judge granted a preliminary injunction in part because damages to plaintiffs' "fledgling business" would be "quite difficult to compute." "While the difficulty of ascertaining damages with certainty is a proper test of irreparable harm, we have also pointed out that in antitrust cases the courts have allowed the plaintiff a broad latitude in establishing proof of damages. Hence we cannot agree that plaintiffs will not be able to establish their monetary damages with a reasonable degree of certainty.

"Moreover, it is apparent that the plaintiffs have an obligation to mitigate their damages. The Yellow Pages are not the only advertising media available to Katz. While the court below accepted the Katz testimony that similar coverage would entail prohibitive costs (the Katz affidavit estimates the cost of alternative advertising at $2,400,000 per annum), there is no indication that the defendants are financially unable to respond in damages in the event judgment is eventually entered against them. We do not suggest of course that such an estimate is reasonable. We simply indicate that whatever reasonable costs are undertaken to secure comparable advertising in media not adverse to accepting the advertisement rejected here are obviously capable of proof and are therefore reparable.

"Finally, we should note that the normal function of the preliminary injunction is to maintain the status quo pending a full hearing on the merits. The injunction granted below would in effect give the plaintiffs substantially the ultimate relief they seek, the publication of the debugging advertisement in the Yellow Pages, before there has been any trial of the issues and where the district court has not found that there has been a showing of probable success on the merits. Thus the preliminary injunction would give Katz an advantage not presently accorded to its competition."

3. DiDomenico v. Employers Cooperative Industry Trust, 676 F.Supp. 903, 906–07, 908 (N.D.Ind.1987). Plaintiff, diagnosed as having cirrhosis of the liver but an "ideal candidate" for a liver transplant, was scheduled for an operation as soon as a donor became available. He sued to prevent defendant from denying coverage under his group insurance plan. A hearing on plaintiff's request for a preliminary injunction was held the day after he filed suit; the opinion bears the date of the hearing.

"[P]laintiff filed suit in this court alleging that absent coverage under the defendant's Plan, he will be unable to afford the expenses incurred [$125,000] in a liver transplant operation. Because of the threat to plaintiff's life it is his position that he has no adequate remedy at law absent a preliminary injunction.

"The Seventh Circuit outlined the non-discretionary actions that a district judge must take when considering a motion for preliminary injunction. Darryl v. Gregory Coler, 801 F.2d 893 (7th Cir.1986).

1. He must evaluate the traditional factors enumerated in the case law: whether there is an adequate remedy at law, the danger of irreparable harm, some likelihood of success on the merits. See Roland Machinery Co. v. Dresser Industries, Inc., 749 F.2d 380, 386–88 (7th Cir.1984).

2. He must make factual determinations on the basis of a fair interpretation of the evidence before the court.

3. He must draw legal conclusions in accord with the principled application of the law.'

"The court went on to state that 'the district court must somehow balance the nature and degree of the plaintiff's injury, the likelihood of prevailing at trial, the possible injury to the defendant if the injunction is granted, and the wild card that is the public interest.'

"In Lawson Products, Inc. v. Avnet, Inc., 782 F.2d 1429, 1432–35 (7th Cir.1986), the Seventh Circuit reviewed two of its prior opinions on the law of preliminary injunctions. See Roland Machinery Co. v. Dresser Industries, Inc., 749 F.2d 380 (7th Cir.1984) and American Hospital Supply Corp. v. Hospital Products Limited, 780 F.2d 589 (7th Cir.1986). The court in *Lawson,* noted that both *Roland* and *American Hospital* make it clear that while preliminary injunctions are an equitable form of relief, they are an exercise of far-reaching power. This court recognizes that preliminary injunctive relief invokes a far-reaching power:

'The idea underlying these equivalent approaches is that the task for the district judge in deciding whether to grant or deny a motion for preliminary injunction is to minimize errors: the error of denying an injunction to one who will in fact (though no one can know this for sure) go on to win the case on the merits, and the error of granting an injunction to one who will go on to lose. The judge must try to avoid the error that is more costly in the circumstances.'

"*Roland.* Thus, this court must choose the course of action that will minimize the costs of being mistaken.

"*Lawson, Roland,* and *American Hospital* all adopted a 'sliding scale' approach where the possibility of mistake would be minimized by weighing the costs of injunctive relief against the benefits. This principle was stated in mathematical terms, in *American Hospital. The preliminary injunction should be granted if, but only if:*

$$P \times Hp > (1 - P) \times Hd$$

"The left hand of the equation is the magnitude of erroneously denying the injunction, arrived at by multiplying the probability that plaintiff will prevail at trial (P) by the harm to the plaintiff caused by the denial of the injunction (Hp). The right hand represents the magnitude of an erroneously granted injunction measured by multiplying the probability that the defendant will prevail at trial (1 − P, the inverse of the plaintiff's probability of success) by the harm to the defendant caused by the granting of the motion (Hd). [citations] Obviously, this formula is not a substitute for, but an aid to, judgment. A figure representing the probability of success, for example, can only be arrived at through subjective estimate by the court. Nevertheless, the 'sliding scale' approach is helpful and will be considered in determining whether or not plaintiff is entitled to a preliminary injunction.

"It is well established in the Seventh Circuit that the plaintiff has the burden of proving each of the factors enumerated in *Coler,* above. [citations] A close examination of plaintiff's claims, reveals that plaintiff has carried his burden of proof.

"To prevail, plaintiff must prove that he has no adequate remedy at law or that he will suffer irreparable harm if the injunction is denied. 'The requirement of irreparable harm is needed to take care of the case where although the ultimate relief that the plaintiff is seeking is equitable, implying that he has no adequate remedy at law, he can easily wait until the end of trial to get that relief.' *Roland.* In the present matter, it is clear beyond peradventure of doubt that plaintiff has established that he will suffer irreparable harm absent preliminary relief. This is not a case where plaintiff can wait until after trial for a remedy. Simply put, absent some form of preliminary relief plaintiff runs the real risk of dying and in such circumstances money damages would be wholly useless to plaintiff.

"Aside from irreparable harm, plaintiff has also established a likelihood of success on the merits. Plaintiff's burden is to show that his likelihood of success is more than negligible. *Roland.*

"The language of the Plan relating to organ transplants is, to engage in understatement, ambiguous. At one point the Plan provides that organ transplants are covered while at another point the Plan provides that organ transplants which are 'experimental' are not covered. * * *

"In addition to the foregoing, a court in ruling on a motion for a preliminary injunction should also consider the public interest in the granting or denying of an injunction. With respect to public interest, it suffices to state that the interest in the sanctity and quality of life is paramount.

"As indicated, the Seventh Circuit has adopted a 'sliding scale formula' whereby the possibility of mistake is minimized by weighing the cost of injunctive relief against the benefits. *American Hospital.* As also indicated, 'a district judge asked to decide whether to grant or deny a preliminary injunction must choose the course of action that will minimize the cost of being mistaken.' In the present matter it is altogether clear that in order to minimize the cost of being mistaken plaintiff's request must be granted. If this court denies the request and plaintiff dies, it will have made the ultimate mistake as far as plaintiff is concerned. If, on the other hand, the court grants the request and it is mistaken, the only loss will be of a monetary nature."

Assume that DiDomenico's transplant operation occurred promptly after this decision. If so, did the order preserve the status quo? Would it be better, instead of referring to the order as a preliminary injunction, to call it a final injunction?

4. The Ninth Circuit test was reformulated in People of Village of Gambel v. Hodel, 774 F.2d 1414, 1419 (9th Cir.1985):

"This court has recognized two sets of standards for evaluating a claim for injunctive relief. We refer to one as the 'traditional' test and the other as the 'alternative' test. American Motorcyclist Ass'n v. Watt, 714 F.2d 962, 965 (9th Cir.1983). In *American Motorcyclist Ass'n* we described the traditional test as follows: 'The traditional equitable criteria for determining whether an injunction should issue are (1) Have the movants established a strong likelihood of success on the merits; (2) does the balance of irreparable harm favor the movants; (3) does the public interest favor granting the injunction?'

" 'The "alternative" test permits the moving party to meet its burden by demonstrating either a combination of probable success and the possibility of irreparable injury or that serious questions are raised and the balance of hardships tips sharply in its favor.'

"We have concluded, however, that the traditional and the alternative tests are 'not really two entirely separate tests, but that they are merely extremes of a single continuum.'

"We have also noted that '[t]he difference between the two formulations is insignificant. Therefore, we accept either as satisfactory.' "

5. Vaughn, A Need for Clarity: Toward a New Standard for Preliminary Injunctions, 68 Or.L.Rev. 839 (1989).

6. *Preserving the Status Quo.* The purpose of the preliminary injunction is to preserve the status quo. Court's aversion to temporary orders altering the status quo arises from a natural unwillingness to create exceptions to rules, and from a sense that a self-destructive inconsistency may be involved. An example is Martin v. International Olympic Committee, 740 F.2d 670 (9th Cir.1984), where the court refused to approve a preliminary mandatory injunction requiring the Olympic Committee to include certain track events for women. Moreover, if the defendant wins on the merits, there is a certain embarrassment at having to undo an act compelled by the court itself. This aversion is not immutable; but the instances are rare, and the burden on the plaintiff to make a strong case from the other factors is "very demanding." Flood v. Kuhn, 309 F.Supp. 793 (S.D.N.Y.1970).

Unfortunately the analysis of whether the status quo will be altered has too often been cast in terms of whether the order is "mandatory" or "prohibitory." A typical statement is "that courts are more reluctant to grant a [preliminary] mandatory injunction than a prohibitory one and that generally an injunction will not lie except in prohibitory form." [1] Or "Every lawyer is aware of the hoary maxim that mandatory injunctive relief, particularly where it changes the *status quo* is the rarest form of relief prior to final adjudication, * * * [and] issuance of such a drastic order as here sought would be an abuse of discretion." [2] Such statements may be misinterpreted as overemphasizing the importance of the form of the preliminary injunction.[3] More and more courts openly recognize that the "last uncontested status preceding the pending controversy" may be a state of action as well as one of passivity. To fulfill the purpose of the preliminary injunction may require an order mandatory in effect. Considerations of feasibility of supervision may militate against an injunction; but it is doubtful if the mandatory or prohibitory form, standing alone, should increase the plaintiff's burden. Typical examples of mandatory decrees maintaining the status quo as a state of continuing action include orders compelling the delivery of greyhounds for

1. Clune v. Publishers' Association, 214 F.Supp. 520, 531 (S.D.N.Y.1936).

2. Dino Dlaurentiis Cinematografica S.A. v. D150, Inc., 258 F.Supp. 459, 463 (S.D.N.Y.1966). The trial judge's prognosis proved faulty. The second circuit reversed and directed the issuance of an injunction upon the filing of sufficient bond. 366 F.2d 373, 377 (1966).

3. A mechanical application of the mandatory-prohibitory distinction occasionally leads to strange results. In some jurisdictions mandatory injunctions are automatically stayed on appeal while prohibitory ones are not. The California Department of Employment stopped referring workers to the plaintiff who obtained a preliminary order directing the Department to continue to do so. In Bowers v. Department of Employment, 183 Cal.App.2d 686, 7 Cal.Rptr. 14 (1960), the court held that the injunction was "mandatory" and therefore automatically stayed on appeal. This left the employer with his decree but no laborers during the harvest season that happened to coincide with the appellate proceedings. By analogy, had the water company shut off the plaintiff's irrigation ditches during harvest, the plaintiff might obtain his injunction (but no water) if the company appealed. Fortunately the California courts have usually taken a more pragmatic approach. See Paramount Pictures Corp. v. Davis, 228 Cal. App.2d 827, 39 Cal.Rptr. 791 (1964). Moreover the appellate court may on its own, issue mandatory orders which maintain the status quo pending appeal. Agriculture Labor Relations Board v. Superior Court, 149 Cal.App.3d 709, 196 Cal.Rptr. 920 (1983).

a racing meet,[4] the maintenance of a franchise relationship,[5] the reinstatement of a college instructor,[6] reinstatement of air traffic controllers,[7] the restoration of a water supply to a pet cemetery,[8] the resumption of money payments representing licensing fees for use of music by a TV network,[9] and even the restoration of terminated Social Security disability benefit payments.[10]

A category remains where a preliminary injunction, regardless of how phrased, would clearly alter the status quo. Here courts often cast a heavy burden upon the plaintiff to produce a strong showing for equitable relief based on the factors outlined above. Obviously many plaintiffs' cases founder on this additional burden.

Where the question of what the status quo ante actually was is peculiarly difficult, the emphasis on whether it is changed by the preliminary order may be muted. The court may view the purpose of the injunction as creating "a common sense modus vivendi to keep peace between the * * * parties, and avoid unnecessary economic waste until the case is adjudicated." Unicon Management Corp. v. Koppers Co., 366 F.2d 199, 204 (2d Cir.1966).

See also Shodeen v. Chicago Title and Trust Co., 162 Ill.App.3d 667, 515 N.E.2d 1339 (1987); Norris v. Harbin, 541 So.2d 486 (Ala.1989).

7. *The Injunction Bond.* Many jurisdictions have statutes or rules that require a plaintiff to post security as a prerequisite for a TRO or preliminary injunction.

Fed.R.Civ.P. 65(c) provides: "No restraining order or preliminary injunction shall issue except upon the giving of security by the applicant, in such sum as the court deems proper, for the payment of such costs and damages as may be incurred or suffered by any party who is found to have been wrongfully enjoined or restrained." See Cal.Civ.Proc.Code § 529; N.Y.Civ.Prac.L. & R. 6312(b) (1980).

In private litigation the amount of the bond may stagger. For example, $2,500,000 in Philadelphia World Hockey Club v. Philadelphia Hockey Club, 351 F.Supp. 462 (E.D.Pa.1972).

Two developments appreciably diminish the impact of apparently mandatory bonds. Some courts have dispensed with the bond where plaintiff asserts constitutional rights. Smith v. Board of Election Commissioners, 591 F.Supp. 70 (N.D.Ill. 1984) appeal dismissed sub nom. Gjertsen v. Board of Election Commissioners, 751 F.2d 199 (7th Cir.1984). In Burns v. Montgomery, 299 F.Supp. 1002 (N.D.Cal.1968), aff'd, 394 U.S. 848 (1969), the court enjoined the state from enforcing residence qualifications for welfare recipients apparently without any bond. Davis v. East St. Louis & Interurban Water Co., 133 Ill.App.2d 801, 270 N.E.2d 424 (1971).

Other courts have decided that under Rule 65(c)'s language, the amount of the bond is within the judge's discretion. Judges set nominal bonds. For example $100 for an injunction against a timber sale, Wilderness Society v. Tyrrel, 701 F.Supp. 1473, 1492 (E.D.Cal.1988). In Friends of the Earth, Inc. v. Brinegar, 518 F.2d 322

4. Wilson v. Sandstrom, 317 So.2d 732 (Fla. 1975); Dyer v. Weedon, 769 S.W.2d 711 (Tex. App.1989).

5. Auburn News Co. v. Providence Journal Co., 504 F.Supp. 292 (D.R.I.1980); Zurn Constructors, Inc. v. B.F. Goodrich Co., 685 F.Supp. 1172 (D.Kan.1988) (supply contract); Wilson v. United Farm Workers, 774 S.W.2d 760 (Tex. App.1989) (enforcement of state health regulations for farm workers).

6. Lafferty v. Carter, 310 F.Supp. 465 (W.D. Wis.1970).

7. United States v. Moore, 427 F.2d 1020 (10th Cir.1970).

8. Memory Gardens v. Pet Ponderosa Memorial Gardens, 88 Nev. 1, 492 P.2d 123 (1972).

9. Columbia Broadcasting System v. American Society of Composers, Authors and Publishers, 320 F.Supp. 389 (S.D.N.Y.1970). Cf. Fretz v. Burke, 247 Cal.App.2d 741, 55 Cal.Rptr. 879 (1967).

10. Tustin v. Heckler, 591 F.Supp. 1049 (D.N.J.1984).

(9th Cir.1975), the court said that a $1000 bond was reasonable security for an injunction prohibiting the expansion of the San Francisco airport. In Environmental Defense Fund, Inc. v. Corps of Engineers, 324 F.Supp. 878 (D.D.C.1971), the judge granted a preliminary injunction that prohibited the construction of a barge canal across Florida and required a bond of one dollar. Would substantial bonds in environmental litigation undermine mechanisms for private enforcement?

"[D]eparture from the bond requirement is justified only when the plaintiff is indigent or sues as a 'private attorney general' to protect the public interest. In all other cases, courts should require a plaintiff to post a bond equal to the amount of costs and damages that the court estimates will result from the injunction." Note, Recovery for Wrongful Interlocutory Injunctions Under Rule 65(c), 99 Harv.L.Rev. 828, 829 (1986).

Should the judge waive a bond where plaintiff shows an extraordinarily high likelihood of success on the merits? In Maine Association of Interdependent Neighborhoods v. Petit, 647 F.Supp. 1312, 1319 (D.Me.1986), the court said yes.

8. *Recovery on the Injunction Bond.* If the TRO or preliminary injunction turns out to have been incorrect, plaintiff and surety are liable to defendant for losses the order caused. Fed.R.Civ.P. 65.1.

The usual rule is: No bond, no damages. Defendant may recover only if plaintiff posted a bond, and the amount of the bond limits defendant's recovery. "A party injured by the issuance of an injunction later determined to be erroneous has no action for damages in the absence of a bond." W.R. Grace and Co. v. Local Union 759, 461 U.S. 757, 770 n. 14 (1983) (dicta). In re Ladner, 799 F.2d 1023 (5th Cir.1986); Coyne–Delany Co. v. Capitol Development Board, 717 F.2d 385 (7th Cir.1983); Stevenson v. North Carolina Department of Insurance, 45 N.C.App. 53, 262 S.E.2d 378 (1980).

Defendant may pursue an action for malicious prosecution and recover more than the amount of the bond. Buddy Systems v. Exer–Genie, Inc., 545 F.2d 1164, 1167–68 (9th Cir.1976), cert. denied, 431 U.S. 903 (1977). See also, Monroe Division Litton Business Systems v. De Bari, 562 F.2d 30 (10th Cir.1977), where the court of appeals said defendant could recover damages if the trial judge dispensed with bond because of plaintiff's financial strength.

9. *Measure of Recovery.* In an action on the bond, defendant may recover losses directly attributable to the TRO or preliminary injunction. Atomic Oil Co. v. Bardahl Oil Co., 419 F.2d 1097 (10th Cir.1969), cert. denied, 397 U.S. 1063 (1970). Attorney fees may not be part of "costs and damages." Fireman's Fund Insurance Co. v. S.E.K. Construction Company, 436 F.2d 1345, 1351 (10th Cir.1971). But defendant may recover attorney fees if a statute authorizes. United States Steel Corp. v. United Mine Workers, 456 F.2d 483 (3d Cir.1972). State decisions may differ.

Courts have said that they retain discretion to deny defendant recovery on the bond because plaintiff sued in good faith. Zenith Radio Corp. v. United States, 643 F.Supp. 1133 (CIT 1986); H & R Block, Inc. v. McCaslin, 541 F.2d 1098, 1099–1100 (5th Cir.1976) (per curiam), cert. denied, 430 U.S. 946 (1977). Should courts deny defendants reimbursement for damages inflicted upon them? Is a negative answer consistent with allowing judges to dispense with bonds or set them in a nominal amount?

"[C]ourts should allow a defendant to recover on an injunction bond only if the injunction deprived him of the right to engage in an activity in which he was legally entitled to engage—an activity that a court after determining the merits of the plaintiff's original claim would hold was within the defendant's rights." Note,

Recovery for Wrongful Interlocutory Injunctions Under Rule 65(c), 99 Harv.L.Rev. 828, 836 (1986).

10. *Calendar Preference for Preliminary Injunctions.* Although an application for a preliminary injunction will be set down for an early hearing, once the judge grants or denies relief, the winner has a diminished sense of urgency to proceed to a plenary trial on the merits. Victory or defeat at this stage is significant because of the trial backlog in most jurisdictions and the absence of any further right to step to the head of the trial line.

The losing party may appeal. Interlocutory appeals are permitted in the federal courts from orders "granting, continuing, modifying, refusing or dissolving injunctions." 28 U.S.C. § 1292(a)(1). There are similar state provisions. See, e.g., Minn.Stat.Ann. § 103.03(b), N.Y.Civ.Prac.L. & R. 5701(a)(2). This exception to the final judgment rule is justified because if an immediate appeal is denied, an incorrect preliminary injunction may injure important rights irreparably. See C. Wright, Federal Courts, § 101–102 (4th ed. 1983).

Avoiding irreparable harm is a noble goal; but an interlocutory appeal further delays the final decision on the merits. Semmes Motors, Inc. v. Ford Motor Co., 429 F.2d 1197, 1204 (2d Cir.1970): "The issues presented by Semmes' motion for a temporary injunction were difficult and complex, and a great deal of time and energy has been spent by Judge Ryan in deciding them and by us in reviewing his action. We see no reason for further expenditure of judicial time on this interlocutory issue when the important thing is to get on with the final hearing."

C. MERGER OF LAW AND EQUITY—THE RESIDUALS

1. HOW FAR?

I.H.P. CORP. v. 210 CENTRAL PARK SOUTH CORP.

Court of Appeals of New York, 1963.
12 N.Y.2d 329, 239 N.Y.S.2d 547, 189 N.E.2d 812.

BURKE, JUDGE. The principal law question on these cross appeals is whether the Supreme Court committed reversible error in awarding [$4,817.00] exemplary damages as incidental to injunctive relief.

* * * The facts alleged were that plaintiff was the lessee in possession of the street level floor in the building of one of the defendants; that all of the defendants caused the premises to be broken into at night on two occasions during which certain damage was done to the leasehold; that each time barriers were placed on the means of access to bar plaintiff from the premises all with the purpose of harassing plaintiff into surrendering its valuable lease; that similar acts will occur in the future unless restrained by the court. The relief requested was an injunction and treble damages. The note of issue repeated the request for injunction, and "$5,000 plus exemplary damages besides injunction."

Defendants challenge the propriety of the award, not as a matter of the law of damages but rather on the procedural ground that "the function of a court of equity goes no further than to award compensatory damages as incidental to injunctive relief: it may not assess exemplary damages." Defendants' position, aside from the right to a jury trial, which we think is waived here, is based on an erroneous concept of the court system of this State. We have one court of general jurisdiction which administers *all* of New York law, be that law of legal or equitable origin. Therefore, defendants are mistaken

when they suggest that a Justice of the Supreme Court of the State of New York cannot apply a particular principle of New York law to a case before him for decision where that principle is properly applicable to the facts as determined. The court in Dunkel v. McDonald (272 A.D. 267, 70 N.Y.S.2d 653, affd. on other issues, 298 N.Y. 586, 81 N.E.2d 323), which the Appellate Division overruled in reaching its conclusion in this case, mistook the issue in stating that "The court has no power in an action in equity to award exemplary or punitive damages. * * * The function of a court of equity goes no further than to award as incidental to other relief, or in lieu thereof, compensatory damages; it may not assess exemplary damages." This, as we have said, presupposes a court intrinsically limited to granting remedies solely equitable in historical origin. There is no such court in this State.

No amount of authority in other States should persuade us that Judge Cardozo was wrong when he said in Susquehanna S.S. Co. v. Anderson & Co. (239 N.Y. 285, 294, 146 N.E. 381, 384): "The whole body of principles, whether of law or of equity, bearing on the case, becomes the reservoir to be drawn upon by the court in enlightening its judgment." Maitland expressed the same view when he predicted that "The day will come when lawyers will cease to inquire whether a given rule be a rule of equity or a rule of common law; suffice it that it is a well-established rule administered by the High Court of Justice." (Maitland, Equity [1909], p. 20.) Needless to say, we have accepted Maitland's and Judge Cardozo's understanding of the consequences of the merger.

Of course, we are obliged to preserve inviolate "Trial by jury in all cases in which it has heretofore been guaranteed by constitutional provision" (N.Y. Const., art. I, § 2). [The court held] that the failure to move to separately state and number the causes of action or to demand a jury trial constituted a waiver of any such right.

* * * The judgment should therefore, be affirmed, without costs.

Notes

1. White v. Ruditys, 117 Wis.2d 130, ___, 343 N.W.2d 421, 426 (App.1983) also followed *I.H.P.* A union member obtained a permanent injunction against the union forbidding the union from calling him a "scab" and finding him in bad standing. The court sanctioned punitive damages within the trial judge's discretion: "[P]unitive damages is not a jury issue."

2. Jones v. Wittenberg, 330 F.Supp. 707, 721 (N.D.Ohio 1971), was a civil rights suit brought by a prisoner in a county jail. No statute was involved. A mandatory injunction to correct conditions in the jail was granted. The court concluded the opinion:

"The complaint includes a prayer for damages, and the law seems to contemplate that damages are presumed to result from the proof of a deprivation of civil rights, without the necessity of any showing of actual damages. This concept, however, in such an action as this one, presents a basic, and perhaps irreconcilable conflict in legal principles. It is clear that civil rights actions are basically equitable. Damages may, of course, be awarded in equitable actions, but the Court of Appeals for this Circuit has held very explicitly in the case of National Union Electric Corp. v. Wilson, 434 F.2d 986 (6th Cir.), that punitive damages may only be fixed by a jury, in an action at law, and may not be allowed by a chancellor. It seems to this Court that damages awarded merely because of violation of rights, other than nominal damages, can only be considered as punitive damages, which this Court has been held without power to allow."

Superior Construction Co. v. Elmo, 204 Md. 1, 102 A.2d 739, 104 A.2d 581 (1954), also analyzes the problem in terms of want of power of an equity court. Other opinions have concluded that punitive damages are "incompatible with equitable principles."

In Kohler v. Fletcher, 442 N.W.2d 169 (Minn.App.1989), the beneficiary of an express trust (together with her husband) sued for breach of the trustees' fiduciary duty. She asked for damages for loss of consortium (the beneficiary was quite distraught) and punitive damages. The court held that under the Restatement (Second) of Trusts §§ 197 and 198, the beneficiary's remedies for breach of an express trust, were exclusively equitable. Recovery of emotional distress damages, lost consortium or punitive damages was precluded. See Seal v. Hart, 755 P.2d 462 (Colo.App.1988).

3. The procedural merger of law and equity has proceeded apace with every revision of civil practice statutes and rules of civil procedure. Only a handful of states retain separate courts of law and equity; and we may find the judges doubling as Chancellors. In a few others, separate procedures may exist. Court rules requiring the labelling of complaints as legal or equitable are common.

Little more can be said in a course on Remedies, except the admonition, "beware" of conscious retentions of procedural distinctions between law and equity.

4. Substantively, the distinction between law and equity persists in the concept of "equitable jurisdiction" to which this work has devoted so much space. The Court of Appeals in New York may expand equitable jurisdiction by appending punitive damages to an injunction, but does a procedural merger of law and equity automatically modify principles of equitable jurisdiction? Does the court miss the thrust of what it is doing?

2. SUBJECT MATTER JURISDICTION

CASTELLINI v. MUNICIPAL COURT OF SAN FRANCISCO

Court of Appeal of California, First District, 1970.
7 Cal.App.3d 174, 86 Cal.Rptr. 698.

ELKINGTON, ASSOCIATE JUSTICE. Anderson & Perkins, Inc., as assignee for collection, commenced an action in the San Francisco Municipal Court against Edgar A. Castellini, Columbia Electric Co., a corporation, and others for money owed. The parties and the municipal court interpreted the complaint as alleging that Columbia Electric Company had contracted the indebtedness, but that Castellini was also liable, since the corporation was the instrumentality through which he for convenience transacted his business. Castellini demurred generally, contending: "An action which seeks to hold an individual defendant liable for the debts of a corporation on the alter ego theory is of an equitable nature, and jurisdiction is to be determined accordingly." * * * We find ourselves in agreement.

The municipal court is not a court of general jurisdiction; its jurisdiction is limited by the Constitution to that prescribed by the Legislature. * * * The Constitution, article VI, section 5, and its implementing statute, Code of Civil Procedure section 89, make it clear that the court's jurisdiction is exclusive; it does not have any concurrent jurisdiction with the superior court. * * *

The doctrine authorizing disregard of the fiction of separate corporate existence, when necessary to circumvent fraud or to protect the rights of third persons, *is essentially equitable in nature.* * * *

No sound policy reason occurs as to why in a case otherwise within municipal court jurisdiction, equitable principles should not be generally applicable. Such a rule would tend to obviate the frequent and understandable misapprehension of litigants as to just where jurisdiction lies. It would prevent time consuming delays, such as here, which must at times result in denial of justice. But the state Constitution, article VI, section 5, casts the power to make such a determination on the Legislature, not the courts. Confronted with a somewhat similar legislative denial of equitable jurisdiction to the municipal court, the Court of Appeal in Strachan v. American Ins. Co., 260 Cal.App.2d 113, 119, 66 Cal.Rptr. 742, 746, said: "While the matter could be well handled by the municipal court, it is not within our power to enlarge the legislative grant of jurisdiction to the municipal court. The respondent must be left to his remedy by independent action in equity in the superior court."

The judgment is reversed; the superior court will issue the writ of prohibition as prayed.

Notes

1. If the action were now brought in the Superior Court, would there be a right to a jury trial?

2. Larionoff v. United States, 533 F.2d 1167, 1181 (D.C.Cir.1976), aff'd, 431 U.S. 864 (1977): "Rescission is an equitable remedy, and we must keep in mind that courts exercising Tucker Act jurisdiction generally do not have jurisdiction over suits for equitable relief against the United States. The Act authorizes jurisdiction only over actions for money judgments. There nevertheless seems to be a narrow 'exception' to this limitation on Tucker Act jurisdiction, in that '[w]here the relief is monetary, [courts exercising Tucker Act jurisdiction] can call upon such equitable concepts as rescission and reformation to help * * * reach the right result.' "

3. JURY TRIAL

DAIRY QUEEN, INC. v. WOOD

United States Supreme Court, 1962.
369 U.S. 469.

[Respondents had sued petitioner for breach of a licensing agreement covering the trade-mark "Dairy Queen" seeking injunctive relief and an accounting for profits arising out of the alleged infringement of the mark. Mandamus to compel the federal district judge to vacate an order striking petitioner's demand for a jury trial.]

JUSTICE BLACK. * * * Petitioner's contention, * * * is that insofar as the complaint requests a money judgment it presents a claim which is unquestionably legal. We agree with that contention. The most natural construction of the respondents' claim for a money judgment would seem to be that it is a claim that they are entitled to recover whatever was owed them under the contract as of the date of its purported termination plus damages for infringement of their trade-mark since that date. * * * As an action on a debt allegedly due under a contract, it would be difficult to conceive of an action of a more traditionally legal character. And as an action for damages based upon a charge of trade-mark infringement, it would be no less subject to cognizance by a court of law.

The respondents' contention that this money claim is "purely equitable" is based primarily upon the fact that their complaint is cast in terms of an "accounting," rather than in terms of an action for "debt" or "damages." But the constitutional right to trial by jury cannot be made to depend upon the choice of words used in the pleadings. The necessary prerequisite to the right to maintain a suit for an equitable accounting, like all other equitable remedies, is, as we pointed out in *Beacon Theatres,* the absence of an adequate remedy at law. [citations] Consequently, in order to maintain such a suit on a cause of action cognizable at law, as this one is, the plaintiff must be able to show that the "accounts between the parties" are of such a "complicated nature" that only a court of equity can satisfactorily unravel them. In view of the powers given to District Courts by Federal Rule of Civil Procedure, 53(b) to appoint masters to assist the jury in those exceptional cases where the legal issues are too complicated for the jury adequately to handle alone,[1] the burden of such a showing is considerably increased and it will indeed be a rare case in which it can be met.[2] But be that as it may, this is certainly not such a case. A jury, under proper instructions from the court, could readily determine the recovery, if any, to be had here, whether the theory finally settled upon is that of breach of contract, that of trademark infringement, or any combination of the two. The legal remedy cannot be characterized as inadequate merely because the measure of damages may necessitate a look into petitioner's business records.

Notes

1. *Dairy Queen* shifts the jury trial test from the historical law-equity classification toward a simpler criterion of whether the claim asks (at least in part) some form of monetary redress. But compare Atlas Roofing Co. v. Occupational Safety and Health Review Committee, 430 U.S. 442, 459–60 (1977): "The Seventh Amendment was declaratory of the existing law, for it required only that jury trial in suits at common law was to be 'preserved.' It thus did not purport to require a jury trial where none was required before. Moreover, it did not seek to change the factfinding mode in equity or admiralty nor to freeze equity jurisdiction as it existed in 1789, preventing it from developing new remedies where those available in courts of law were inadequate."

2. Dealing with a shareholders' derivative suit, which is considered equitable, the Court upheld the right to a jury trial if the underlying corporate claim for breaches of directors' fiduciary duty was for money. Ross v. Bernhard, 396 U.S. 531 (1970). In Kalish v. Franklin Advisers, Inc., 928 F.2d 590 (2d Cir.1991), the court held that, if the monetary claim was "restitutionary," no jury trial right existed.

3. Carrington, The Seventh Amendment: Some Bicentennial Reflections, 1990 U.Chi.Leg.F. 33.

1. [Footnotes renumbered.] Even this limited inroad upon the right to trial by jury "'should seldom be made, and if at all only when unusual circumstances exist.'" La Buy v. Howes Leather Co., 352 U.S. 249, 258.

2. It was settled in *Beacon Theatres* that procedural changes which remove the inadequacy of a remedy at law may sharply diminish the scope of traditional equitable remedies by making them unnecessary in many cases. "Thus, the justification for equity's deciding legal issues once it obtains jurisdiction, and refusing to dismiss a case, merely because subsequently a legal remedy becomes available, must be reevaluated in the light of the liberal joinder provisions of the Federal Rules which allow legal and equitable causes to be brought and resolved in one civil action. Similarly the need for, and therefore, the availability of such equitable remedies as Bills of Peace, *Quia Timet* and Injunction must be reconsidered in view of the existence of the Declaratory Judgment Act as well as the liberal joinder provision of the Rules."

C & K ENGINEERING CONTRACTORS v. AMBER STEEL CO.

Supreme Court of California, 1978.
23 Cal.3d 1, 151 Cal.Rptr. 323, 587 P.2d 1136.

Skip to 241

RICHARDSON, JUSTICE. The issue posed by this case is whether or not defendant was improperly denied its constitutional right to a jury trial. (Cal. Const., art. I, § 16.) We will conclude that because plaintiff's suit for damages for breach of contract was based entirely upon the equitable doctrine of promissory estoppel, the gist of the action must be deemed equitable in nature and, under well established principles, neither party was entitled to a jury trial as a matter of right.

Plaintiff, a general contractor, solicited bids from defendant and other subcontractors for the installation of reinforcing steel in the construction of a waste water treatment plant in Fresno County. Plaintiff included defendant's bid in its master bid, which was ultimately accepted by the public sanitation district, the proposed owner of the plant. After defendant refused to perform in accordance with its bid on the subcontract, plaintiff brought the present action to recover $102,660 in damages for defendant's alleged breach of contract. * * *

The allegations of plaintiff's first cause of action may be summarized: defendant submitted a written bid of $139,511 for the work; defendant gave a subsequent "verbal promise" that the work would be performed for the bid price; plaintiff "reasonably relied" on defendant's bid and promise in submitting its master bid; defendant knew or should have known that plaintiff would submit a master bid based upon defendant's bid; defendant refused to perform in accordance with its bid; plaintiff was required to expend $242,171 to perform the reinforcing steel work; as a result plaintiff was damaged in the amount of $102,660; and "Injustice can be avoided only by enforcement of defendant's promise to perform. * * *"

Defendant's answer to the complaint alleged its bid was the result of an "honest mistake" in calculation; plaintiff knew of the mistake but failed to notify defendant or permit it to revise its bid as is customary in the industry; and plaintiff's conduct in this regard should bar it from recovering damages.

Defendant demanded a jury trial. The trial court, deeming the case to be essentially in equity, denied the request but empaneled an advisory jury to consider the sole issue of plaintiff's reasonable reliance on defendant's promise. The jury found that plaintiff reasonably relied to its detriment on defendant's bid. The trial court adopted this finding and entered judgment in plaintiff's favor for $102,610, the approximate amount of its prayer, together with interest and costs. Defendant appeals.

Defendant's primary contention is that it was improperly denied a jury trial of plaintiff's action for damages. In resolving this contention we first review the nature and derivation of the doctrine of promissory estoppel. Thereafter, we discuss certain authorities governing the right to jury trial in this state. As will appear, we have concluded that by reason of the essentially equitable nature of the doctrine and plaintiff's exclusive reliance upon it in the present action, the case was properly triable by the court with an advisory jury. * * *

The elements of the doctrine of promissory estoppel, as described concisely in section 90 of the Restatement of Contracts, are as follows: "A promise which the promisor should reasonably expect to induce action or forbearance of a definite and substantial character on the part of the promisee and which does induce such action or forbearance is binding if injustice can be avoided only by enforcement of the promise." The foregoing rule has been judicially adopted in California and it applies to actions, such as the present case, to enforce a subcontractor's bid. [citations] It is undisputed that plaintiff's complaint in the matter before us relies exclusively upon the doctrine to enforce defendant's alleged promise to perform its bid. In fact, the language of the complaint, summarized above, paraphrases that of section 90 in asserting that "Injustice can be avoided only by enforcement of defendant's promise to perform." * * *

We have recently characterized promissory estoppel as "a doctrine which employs *equitable* principles to satisfy the requirement that consideration must be given in exchange for the promise sought to be enforced. [citations]" * * *

Treatise writers and commentators have confirmed the generally *equitable* nature of promissory estoppel in enforcing a promise which otherwise would be unenforceable. [citations] As expressed by Professor Henderson, "[P]romissory estoppel is a *peculiarly equitable doctrine* designed to deal with situations which, in total impact, necessarily call into play discretionary powers * * *." One distinguished commentator has observed that promissory estoppel derives from both "the decisions of the courts of common law from the very beginnings of the action of assumpsit [as well as] the decrees of courts of equity making a very flexible use of the doctrine of 'estoppel,' * * * " (1A Corbin, Contracts (1963) § 194, at p. 193, fn. omitted; see also id., § 195.)

The equitable character of promissory estoppel is confirmed by a close scrutiny of the purpose of the doctrine, namely, that "*injustice* can be avoided only by enforcement of the promise." (Rest., Contracts, supra, § 90, italics added.) As expressed by us in a similar subcontractor bid case, once the prerequisites of the doctrine are met, " * * * *it is only fair* that plaintiff should have at least an opportunity to accept defendant's bid after the general contract has been awarded to him." [citations] * * *

We conclude, accordingly, that the doctrine of promissory estoppel is essentially equitable in nature, developed to provide a remedy (namely, enforcement of a gratuitous promise) which was not generally available in courts of law prior to 1850. We now move to an examination of the authorities on the subject of the right to a jury trial, to determine whether the equitable nature of plaintiff's action precluded a jury trial as a matter of right.

The right to a jury trial is guaranteed by our Constitution. (Cal. Const., art. I, § 16.) We have long acknowledged that the right so guaranteed, however, is the right as it existed at common law in 1850, when the Constitution was first adopted, "and what that right is, is a purely historical question, a fact which is to be ascertained like any other social, political or legal fact." [citations] As a general proposition, "The jury trial is a matter of right in a civil action at law, but not in equity." [citations]

As we stated, "If the action has to deal with ordinary common-law rights cognizable in courts of law, it is to that extent an action at law. In determining whether the action was one triable by a jury at common law, the court is not bound by the form of the action but rather by the nature of the rights involved and the facts of the particular case—the *gist* of the action. A jury trial must be granted where the *gist* of the action is legal, where the action is in reality cognizable at law." On the other hand, if the action is essentially one in equity and the relief sought "depends upon the application of equitable doctrines," the parties are not entitled to a jury trial. (E.g., Hartman v. Burford (1966) 242 Cal.App.2d 268, 270, 51 Cal.Rptr. 309, 311 [enforcement of promise to make a will]; Tibbetts v. Fife (1958) 162 Cal.App.2d 568, 572, 328 P.2d 212 [establishment of constructive trust].) Although we have said that "the legal or equitable nature of a cause of action ordinarily is determined by the mode of relief to be afforded" (Raedeke v. Gibraltar Sav. & Loan Assn., 10 Cal.3d 665, 672, 111 Cal.Rptr. 693, 696, 517 P.2d 1157, 1160), the prayer for relief in a particular case is not conclusive [citations]. Thus, "The fact that damages is one of a full range of possible remedies does not guarantee * * * the right to a jury * * *." [citations]

In the present case, the complaint purports to seek recovery of damages for breach of contract, in form an action at law in which a right to jury trial ordinarily would exist. [citations] As we have seen, however, the complaint seeks relief which was available only in equity, namely, the enforcement of defendant's gratuitous promise to perform its bid through application of the equitable doctrine of promissory estoppel. Although there is no direct authority on point, several cases have held that actions based upon the analogous principle of equitable estoppel may be tried by the court without a jury. (Jaffe v. Albertson Co. (1966) 243 Cal.App.2d 592, 607–608, 53 Cal.Rptr. 25 [estoppel to bar reliance on statute of frauds]; Moss v. Bluemm (1964) 229 Cal.App.2d 70, 72–73, 40 Cal.Rptr. 50 [estoppel to bar statute of limitations defense]; Richard v. Degan & Brody, Inc. (1960) 181 Cal.App.2d 289, 295, 5 Cal.Rptr. 263 [estoppel as defense to unlawful detainer action]; [citations]

Defendant responds by relying primarily upon certain dictum in *Raedeke,* which also concerned an action based on promissory estoppel. The *Raedeke* complaint alleged *dual* theories of traditional breach of contract and promissory estoppel. We stressed that the "resolution of the instant case did not depend entirely upon the application of equitable principles; the doctrine of promissory estoppel was only one of two alternative theories of recovery." Accordingly, we held in *Raedeke* that plaintiffs were entitled to a jury trial, and that the trial court erred in treating the jury's findings and verdict as advisory only. In a footnote, however, we added the following dictum: "Moreover, even as to plaintiff's reliance upon promissory estoppel, there is some basis for holding that the action remained one at law. 'The fact that equitable principles are applied in the action does not necessarily identify the resultant relief as equitable. [citations] Equitable principles are a guide to courts of law as well as of equity. [citations] Furthermore, the incidental adoption of equitable sounding measures to effect the application of equitable principles in an action at law, such as for damages, does not change the character of that action. [citations]' "

The foregoing general principles do not alter our conclusion that the present action is, essentially, one recognized only in courts of equity and, despite plaintiff's request for damages, is not an "action at law" involving, to use the *Raedeke* language, the "incidental adoption of equitable sounding measures." Defendant before us has argued that because plaintiff sought to recover damages rather than to compel defendant to perform its bid, plaintiff requested relief which is available at common law. Yet, as we have seen, damages at law were unavailable in actions for breach of a gratuitous promise.

The only manner in which damages have been recognized in such cases of gratuitous promises is by application of the equitable doctrine of promissory estoppel which renders such promises legally binding. Without the employment of this doctrine, essentially equitable, there was no remedy at all. As illustrated by the express language of section 90 of the Restatement of Contracts, promissory estoppel is used to avoid injustice "by *enforcement* of the promise." (Italics added.)

Furthermore, the addition, in such cases, of a prayer for damages does not convert what is essentially an equitable action into a legal one for which a jury trial would be available. This was demonstrated in a recent case, Southern Pac. Transportation Co. v. Superior Court, supra, 58 Cal.App.3d 433, 129 Cal.Rptr. 912, wherein plaintiff sought damages as a good faith improver of land owned by another person. (See Code Civ.Proc., § 871.1 et seq.) The appellate court rejected the contention that plaintiff's request for damages necessarily identified the action as one at law. The court first noted that since the good faith improver statute had no counterpart in English common law, "classification of the action as either legal or equitable depends upon characterization of the nature of the relief sought."

The *Southern Pac. Transportation* court properly observed that under the statute, the trial court must "effect such an adjustment of the rights, equities, and interests" of the parties as was consistent with substantial justice. (Code Civ.Proc., § 871.5.) Thus, the action was essentially one calling for the exercise of equitable principles. The court added, "The fact that damages is one of a full range of possible remedies does not guarantee real parties the right to a jury," since "there is no possibility of severing the legal from the equitable."

We conclude that the trial court properly treated the action as equitable in nature, to be tried by the court with or without an advisory jury as the court elected. * * *

The judgment is affirmed.

NEWMAN, JUSTICE, dissenting. I dissent. The Chancery Court in England sometimes created rights, sometimes remedies. When California courts decide whether a jury trial should be assured, I believe that they should focus not on rights but on remedies. A plaintiff who seeks damages should be entitled to a jury. One who seeks specific performance or an injunction or quiet title, etc. (plus supplementary damages or "damages in lieu" that would have been allowed in Chancery) is not entitled to a jury.

The majority opinion here discusses "promissory estoppel," "equitable estoppel," "equitable principles," "equitable doctrine," "equitable nature," and even "injustice." To pretend that words like those enable us to isolate "ordinary common-law rights cognizable in courts of law" or that "the *gist* of the action" governs seems to me to be uninstructive fictionalizing. We are told that courts deal with "a purely historical question, a fact which is to be ascertained like any other social, political or legal fact." Yet how often, I wonder, do (or should) California judges instead decide whether the wisdom of a Corbin, in 1963, outweighs comments by Ames, Seavey, Shattuck, and Williston written during the period from 1888 to 1957?

In fact, most rights that are now enforced via a jury were created not by courts but by legislatures. We look at the *remedy* sought, not at the judicial or legislative history of the *right,* to decide whether the trial is to be "legal" or "equitable." There are troubling borderlines, but the basic rule should be that no jury is required when plaintiff seeks equitable relief rather than "legal" damages. That approach requires no complex, historical research regarding when and by whom certain rights were created. It also requires less reliance on the anomalies of England's unique juridical history. Courts thus may focus on a basic policy concern; that is, the typically more continuing and more personalized involvement of the trial judge in specific performance and injunctive decrees than in mere judgments for damages.

The doctrine of promissory estoppel was not, I suggest, "developed to provide a remedy (namely, enforcement of a gratuitous promise)" as the majority here contend. What it really did was to help create a new right (just as statutes help create new rights) that apparently, but only if we reject what seems to have been Corbin's view, was enforced as of 1850 in Chancery but not at common law.

Plaintiff in this case sought damages for an alleged breach of contract. He did not seek equitable relief. Thus defendant should have been granted the jury trial he requested.

Notes

1. California courts have generally adhered to the historical test in determining the right to jury trial. Thus in Wyle v. Alioto, 191 Cal.App.3d 1128, 236 Cal.Rptr. 849, 851 (1987), the court held that only a court of equity can pierce the corporate veil. "There is no right to jury trial of the alter ego issue." Other state courts agree with the dissenting opinion that the remedy claimant seeks determines the right to jury trial.

Thus in ECCO Limited v. Balimoy Manufacturing Co., 179 Mich.App. 748, 446 N.W.2d 546 (1989), the court agreed that promissory estoppel is a traditional equity doctrine, but held a jury trial was required because the remedy sought was damages rather than traditional equitable relief. See also Strickler v. Sussex Life Care Associates, 541 A.2d 587 (Del.Super.1987), holding that the jurisdiction of the Chancery Court depends upon the remedy the plaintiff "truly" seeks.

2. How would a federal court, bound by Dairy Queen v. Wood, supra p. 235 decide *C & K Engineering*?

3. *Advisory Juries in Equity.* Hargrove v. American Central Insurance Co., 125 F.2d 225, 228 (10th Cir.1942), was under the Federal Declaratory Judgments Act: "If the issues tendered are purely equitable, the court has the indisputable right under the rules of civil procedure to call a jury in an advisory capacity of its own initiative and to submit to them such issues of fact as he sees fit, and to accept or disregard its verdict thereon in his discretion. Or the court with the consent of both parties, may order a trial with a jury whose verdict has the same effect as if trial by jury had been a matter of right. Rule 39(c) (Federal Rules of Civil Procedure)."

4. EQUITABLE CLEANUP

ZIEBARTH v. KALENZE

Supreme Court of North Dakota, 1976.
238 N.W.2d 261.

VOGEL, JUSTICE. * * * The plaintiff-appellee, Silver Ziebarth, a cattle buyer, sought specific performance of a contract for the sale of cattle from the defendant-appellant, Leroy Kalenze, a rancher in the business of selling cattle.

The district court, without a jury, found for Ziebarth. The court awarded damages in the sum of $4,589 plus costs in lieu of specific performance. Kalenze moved at the end of the plaintiff's case, for dismissal of the action on the ground that the pleadings asked for specific performance of the contract, whereas the subject matter of the contract, the cattle, was no longer available, making specific performance impossible. The district court denied the motion. Kalenze appeals * * * from the order of the district court denying his motion to dismiss, and asserts that he was deprived of a jury trial on the issue of damages because of the denial of the motion. He never filed a demand for a jury in the trial court. * * *

On June 16, 1971, Ziebarth and Kalenze entered into a written contract. Ziebarth agreed to purchase all of the Simmental heifer calves produced from Kalenze's cows which were to be artificially inseminated with Simmental semen furnished by Ziebarth.

* * * Ziebarth claims that Kalenze breached the contract when he sold the calves to another party for $450 per head. * * *

The first issue to be decided in this appeal is whether the trial judge erred in denying the defendant's motion to dismiss when it became apparent that the specific relief prayed for in the plaintiff's complaint was impossible to grant as a remedy.

The plaintiff Zeibarth brought this case in equity, demanding specific performance of the contract at the agreed price pursuant to the remedies available to a buyer under the Uniform Commercial Code (UCC § 2–716). This section provides, in part:

"1. Specific performance may be decreed where the goods are unique or in other proper circumstances.

"2. The decree for specific performance may include such terms and conditions as to payment of the price, *damages,* or other relief as the court may deem just." [Emphasis supplied.]

The Code clearly allows the court to grant damages in an action by a buyer for specific performance, *in the court's decree* for specific performance. It is not clear, however, whether the Code allows damages to be awarded *in lieu of a decree* in equity. This case presents the unusual circumstance of a case brought in equity in which specific performance was not possible: The subject matter of the contract had been sold to a third party prior to commencement of the suit. It is not apparent from the pleadings or the testimony whether the plaintiff in this case knew that specific performance was impossible at the time he pled his case in equity.

Of course, the defendant knew when he was served with process that specific performance was impossible, but he did not mention that fact in his answer. If the plaintiff had known that damages, and not specific performance, was the proper remedy—in fact, the only remedy available in this case—and had made the appropriate motion to amend, then the trial court should have allowed the plaintiff to amend his pleadings to conform to his remedy at law or dismissed the suit in equity. * * *

The case law on the issue of the court's jurisdiction to grant damages in lieu of the equitable relief prayed for is conflicting. Some courts recognize the doctrine of substituted legal relief in equity. Historically, where the ground for equitable relief failed, the bill in equity was dismissed and the parties were left to seek in the common-law courts whatever legal remedies remained. But in 1786, an equity court did not dismiss the bill, but retained jurisdiction for granting legal relief where specific performance failed only because of the defendant's wrongful conduct after the suit was begun. This became the basis for granting substituted legal relief in equity. James, Right to Jury Trial in Civil Actions, 72 Yale L.J. 655, 659 (1962). In order for the doctrine to be applied in a particular case, however, the plaintiff must first establish his right to equitable relief, to which damages might then be incidental or subsidiary. [citation] In Raasch v. Goulet, 57 N.D. 674, 223 N.W. 808 (1929), this court held that the right to recover damages under the doctrine of substituted legal relief (or equity's "clean up" jurisdiction, as it is sometimes referred to) depends on the right to specific performance and is not available until the latter is established.

It is thus the rule in some jurisdictions, and the traditional view, that the court cannot give judgment for damages in an action brought in equity unless the plaintiff first proves his right to equitable relief. [citations] There is language in Raasch v. Goulet to support this rule of "substituted legal relief." But we decline to follow this rule of the common law, and to the extent that *Raasch* indicates acceptance of it, we overrule it. In our view, the fusion of law and equity, which has been the law of North Dakota since Statehood, and the law of the Territory of Dakota from the time of its adoption of the Field Code of Civil Procedure at the first legislative session in 1862, puts the authority to grant equitable or legal relief in courts of general jurisdiction, regardless of technicalities such as the rule of "substituted legal relief." Early judges, trained in common-law pleading, were perhaps unwilling to accept the fusion of law and equity at face value. More recently, however, we have at least followed the "clean up jurisdiction" theory and we have held that the existence of a remedy at law does not prelude equitable relief if the equitable remedy is better adapted to render more perfect and complete justice than the remedy at law. We believe that a legal remedy should be granted where equity fails. It would involve needless waste of time and money to send the case back for repleading and retrial to accomplish the same result we have now before us.

The holding of the two preceding paragraphs, of course, is limited to cases where the rules stated in them do not operate to deprive a litigant of a right to a jury trial. The distinction between law and equity is still of primary importance in determining the right to a jury trial. But a jury trial can be waived by failing to demand it.

In the present case, it is apparent that the defendant knew that specific performance was impossible when the complaint was served on him. He therefore must have known that the only possible remedy, if the plaintiff prevailed, would be damages. If so, he knew he had a right to a jury trial. The right to a jury trial, if demanded under the facts of this case, would be absolute. The defendant could have demanded a jury trial, even though the complaint on its face showed grounds for equitable relief only. [citations] At a hearing on a motion based on the demand for a jury, the defendant could have shown his right to a jury trial and the trial court would have erred if it had refused to order the jury trial. But in the absence of a demand, there was no error. The trial court decides which cases are triable by a jury by examining the complaint. [citations] * * * We hold today that the right to a jury trial is likewise waived if not demanded in a case where the complaint demands equitable relief but the defendant is aware that only legal relief could be granted if the plaintiff should prevail. Or, as Professor James puts it,

> "waiver of jury trial under statute or rule will not be relieved against because of the emergence of legal claims based on facts which were pleaded at the time of the waiver. In the usual case plaintiff claims specific performance of a contract which he claims was breached; defendant denies the contract, or the breach or both and claims specific performance is inappropriate anyhow. In this situation it is perfectly foreseeable to defendant that if the court should agree with his own claim about the inappropriateness of specific performance, the pleaded facts present a legal issue. Armed with this chance for foresight, defendant should not be allowed to withhold his jury claim without waiver." [citations]

[Reversed and remanded on other grounds.]

Notes

1. *Equitable Jurisdiction to Substitute Damages When Equitable Relief is Precluded by Circumstances Prior to or Subsequent to the Filing of the Bill of Complaint.* This problem is less acute where law and equity have been merged. It was typically presented in Walker v. Mackey, 197 Or. 197, 253 P.2d 280 (1953). The vendee under an executory land sale contract sued to compel conveyance of the entire tract although apparently aware that the Highway Commission had, as a bona fide purchaser, acquired title to a slice of the parcel for a non-access highway. The court quoted J. Pomeroy, Equity Jurisprudence § 237f (5th ed.):

"In suits for a specific performance the following rules have been established by American decisions: If through a failure of the vendor's title, or any other cause, *a specific performance is really impossible,* and the vendee is aware of the true condition of affairs before and at the time he brings his suit, the court, being of necessity obliged to refuse the remedy of specific performance, will not, in general, retain the suit and award compensatory damages, because, as has been said, the court never acquired a jurisdiction over the cause for any purpose.

"A second rule is, that if the remedy of specific performance is possible at the commencement of a suit by the vendee, and while the action is pending the vendor renders this remedy impracticable by conveying the subject-matter to a *bona fide* purchaser for value, the court will not compel the plaintiff to bring a second action at law, but, having acquired jurisdiction, will do full justice by decreeing a recovery of damages.

"The third rule is as follows: If a specific performance was originally possible, but *before the commencement of the suit* the vendor *makes it impossible* by a conveyance to a third person; or if the disability existed at the very time of entering into the contract on account of a defect in the vendor's title, or other similar reason,—in either of these cases, if the vendee brings his suit in good faith, without a knowledge of the existing disability, supposing, and having reason to suppose, himself entitled to the equitable remedy of a specific performance, and the *impossibility* is first disclosed by the defendant's answer or in the course of the hearing, then, although the court cannot grant a specific performance, it will retain the cause, assess the plaintiff's damages, and decree a pecuniary judgment in place of the purely equitable relief originally demanded. This rule is settled by an overwhelming preponderance of American authorities." [Second and third italics by the court]

"Another rule has been suggested, as follows: 'Even though the court should deny a specific performance of the contract in the exercise of that judicial discretion which it has in all cases asking that particular relief, yet, if the facts be such that the plaintiff might fairly and reasonably have expected the court to grant the equitable relief of specific performance, there would be such a show of equitable cognizance and doubtful remedy and probable cause as would save the plaintiff from the penalty of a dismissal of the bill for want of jurisdiction because of a plain, adequate and complete remedy at law.' "

Although plaintiff did not ask for specific performance with abatement in his complaint, the court pointed out that such equitable relief was at all times possible, if not practicable, and that equitable jurisdiction to grant substitutional relief as it saw fit was well within the rules outlined by Pomeroy.

2. *Other Residuals.* Classification of a claim as legal or equitable may have other important effects. a. The provisional remedy of *attachment* may not be authorized for suits in equity. See Jennings v. McCall Corp., 224 F.Supp. 919 (W.D.Mo.1963). A careful examination of the applicable attachment statute is required to make this determination. b. *Prejudgment interest* may be affected by labeling. See, e.g., N.Y.Civ.Prac.L. & R. 5001(a). c. There is an equity exception to the general rule denying recovery of *attorneys' fees.*

Finally, the classification is important in the appellate process. d. It may determine the *appealability* of certain interlocutory orders in the federal courts. See Pepper v. Miani, 734 F.2d 1420 (10th Cir.1984); C. Wright, Federal Courts § 102 (4th ed. 1983). e. And it may affect the *scope of review.* In many jurisdictions appellate review in equity is de novo. An appellate court in equity is not bound by the trial court's findings of fact; it may review both facts and law. Harris v. Turner, 329 F.2d 918 (10th Cir.1964); Bartlett v. Kloepping, 195 Neb. 755, 240 N.W.2d 592 (1976); Mitchell v. Mitchell, 527 P.2d 1359 (Utah 1974).

D. TRADITIONAL METHODS OF ENFORCEMENT

1. CONTEMPT

Introductory Note

An equity suit does not end with an injunction any more than an action at law ends with a money judgment. The defendant must still be made to pay the judgment or obey the injunction. In the usual equity case, enforcement takes the form of contempt proceedings. Orderly analysis of this complicated procedure will be advanced if certain distinctions are made at the outset. A firm grasp of the differences in classification between direct and indirect, civil and criminal, and prospective and retrospective contempt will greatly assist understanding the cases that follow.

The simplest distinction, that between direct and indirect contempt, turns on geography. Direct contempt is recalcitrant or unseemly conduct that occurs in the courtroom or within the judge's presence; overly zealous lawyers or obstreperous parties provide the usual examples. Most contempts, however, consist of disobedience of personal orders outside the courtroom, and our primary concern is with these indirect contempts. The major consequence of this classification is procedural. A judge may punish the direct contemnor on the spot. Parties guilty of indirect contempt, on the other hand, are entitled to notice and hearing.

The second and more important classification is between civil and criminal contempt. That distinction turns on the remedy imposed. The criminal contempt sanction has as its purpose punishment and deterrence; whereas civil contempt is intended to secure for a party the benefits of the decree. Civil contempt in most jurisdictions may take the form of compensation, forcing the contemnor to indemnify the plaintiff for any loss caused by the violation. McDonald's Corp. v. Victory Investments, 727 F.2d 82 (3d Cir.1984). It may also be coercive with the goal of securing for the plaintiff the benefits awarded by the injunction. A coercive contempt order is a revocable, indeterminate threat to imprison or fine for continued disobedience, and resembles a second injunction with the penalty for breach specified. If the contemnor complies with the order, it is never in fact applied at all. Thus Judge Zirpoli told Frank McNulty, "you have the key to the jail door yourself."

Because their purpose is to benefit the plaintiff, these compensatory and coercive procedures are classified as civil contempt. The procedure employed is therefore civil with two refinements: there is no jury and the burden of proof requires clear and convincing evidence. The criminal contemnor, on the other hand, may claim almost complete criminal procedural protections. The rule that a judge may not impose "criminal" contempt except after following criminal procedure has been a fertile source of error and appellate reversals beginning with Gompers v. Buck's Stove & Range Co., 221 U.S. 418 (1911).

A third and final way of classifying contempt is retrospective-prospective. Retrospective contempt confesses failure; defendant breached the injunction and the judge no longer can secure for plaintiff the conduct to which she is entitled. The judge must therefore substitute money compensation or punishment of the wrongdoer. Since the conduct mandated by the injunction cannot be attained, compensatory contempt includes an additional irony: the judge must employ the backward-looking money remedy notwithstanding a prior decision that money is an inadequate remedy to protect plaintiff's interest. Coercive contempt, on the other hand, is a prospective remedy devised by the judge to compel future conduct from the defendant. As stated above, the devices normally relied on are threats to fine or imprison. As we have already learned, coercive contempt sometimes fails. When coercive imprisonment failed to coerce deeds in specific performance of land sale contract cases, legislatures provided for decretal transfers to provide plaintiffs with marketable title. See p. 167 supra. Coercive imprisonment of Frank McNulty only stiffened his resistance; Judge Zirpoli released him after five months. pp. 157–59 supra.

For further discussion, see Dobbs, Contempt of Court: A Survey, 56 Cornell L.Rev. 183 (1971); Martineau, Contempt of Court: Eliminating the Confusion Between Civil and Criminal Contempt, 50 U.Cin.L.Rev. 677 (1981); Rendleman, Compensatory Contempt: Plaintiff's Remedy When a Defendant Violates an Injunction, 1980 U.Ill.L.F. 971; Rendleman, How to Enforce an Injunction, Litigation, Fall 1983, at 23.

H.K. PORTER CO. v. NATIONAL FRICTION PRODUCTS

United States Court of Appeals, Seventh Circuit, 1977.
568 F.2d 24.

WYZANSKI, SENIOR DISTRICT JUDGE. Plaintiff appeals from the March 4, 1977 order of the District Court for the Northern District of Indiana, South Bend Division, dismissing plaintiff's August 28, 1975 "Motion for issuance of order to show cause and for contempt judgment." * * *

October 3, 1967 plaintiff filed a complaint alleging that the corporate and individual defendants infringed plaintiff's rights in trade secrets and confidential information. March 25, 1968 plaintiff and defendants entered into a four-page Settlement Agreement. Paragraph 2 provided:

> "That National and Figert agree that they will not sell any of said two compounds previously submitted by National to Frigidaire Division of General Motors Corporation for use in making of an air conditioner pulley in competition with the molding compound presently supplied by Porter to said Frigidaire Division of General Motors Corporation and, particularly, that National will not submit any compound to Frigidaire Division of General Motors Corporation for use in making an air conditioner pulley in which the formula of such compound is taken directly from plaintiff's formula and Compound No. 7580–1C, as contained in plaintiff's deposition exhibits one (1) through four (4) inclusive, as aforesaid."

April 15, 1968, in response to a motion made by all the parties, the district court entered an order which included the following: * * *

> The Court further orders * * * that the said Settlement Agreement is hereby adopted and made a part of the decree by reference as the judgment herein.

August 28, 1975 plaintiff filed its "Motion for issuance of order to show cause and for contempt judgment." Therein it was alleged:

> 4. National Friction Products Corporation and its President and General Manager, Edward J. Sydor, individually, have failed and refused to comply with and have disobeyed and disregarded the provisions of said Court order and consent decree. * * *

Plaintiff prayed that the corporate defendant and its president (who is not a defendant) should be adjudged in contempt of the district court for having violated the terms of the April 15, 1968 court order and that the court order the corporate defendant and its president to "purge themselves of said contempt by payment to the plaintiff of the sum of Three Hundred Thousand and No/100 Dollars ($300,000.00) in compensatory damages and One Million and No/100 Dollars ($1,000,000.00) in punitive damages, together with all costs of this proceeding, including reasonable attorneys' fees." * * *

Our view is that contempt proceedings were improper because the April 15, 1968 order of the District Court failed to comply with Fed.Civ.Proc. Rule 65(d).

We begin by noting that we are dealing exclusively with the power of the district court with respect to civil contempts. * * *

What we are faced with is plaintiff's prayer for both compensatory and coercive remedies for a civil contempt. [citation] $300,000 is sought to reimburse plaintiff for $200,000 in already-sustained losses in expected profits and defined additional losses and expenses incurred because the corporate defendant and its president, allegedly, did not comply with the Settlement Agreement "made part of the [April 15, 1968] decree [of the district court] by reference." A further $1,000,000 is sought to coerce the corporate defendant and its president into compliance.

Before either the compensatory or coercive aspects of a court's civil contempt power can be brought into play first, there must have been disobedience of "an operative command capable of 'enforcement.'" International Longshoremen's Association, Local 1291 v. Philadelphia Marine Trade Assoc., 389 U.S. 64, 74 (1967), and second, that command, if it is in substance an injunction, must comply with Rule 65(d) of the Federal Rules of Civil Procedure.

We turn to the question whether the district court's April 15, 1968 order met the first of these conditions precedent. Of course, a party may incur a legal duty by entering into a settlement agreement, and a court may, pursuant to that agreement, incorporate the terms of the party's obligation in its judgment; but to furnish support for a contempt order the judgment must set forth in specific detail an unequivocal command. Here the district court on April 15, 1968 did not go beyond entering a judgment approving of the obligations incurred under the Settlement Agreement. Its judgment did not use language which turned a contractual duty into an obligation to obey an operative command. This case thus resembles one where a court issues a declaratory judgment as to obligations under a contract. In that situation, a party who departed from the judgment so declared would not be in contempt of court because there was no command, although there was a judgment of specific obligation.

Even if we could construe the April 15, 1968 order of the district court as embodying an operative command, it would be unenforceable by contempt proceedings because it would then have to be regarded as an injunctive order required to conform to Fed.Rule of Civ.Proc. 65(d).

It is beyond cavil that when it merely incorporated by reference the Settlement Agreement, the April 15, 1968 order ignored that rule's mandatory requirement that an injunction "shall describe in reasonable detail, and not by reference to the complaint or other document, the act or acts sought to be restrained." The error in the April 15, 1968 order was "serious and decisive" and precluded the plaintiff from successfully invoking the district court's contempt powers.

Rule 65(d) is no mere extract from a manual of procedural practice. It is a page from the book of liberty.

Equitable decrees, unlike mere money judgments issuing from a common law court, do not depend upon execution by the sheriff but are direct orders to a party. They trace their historical origin to the royal command addressed to a defeated litigant, directing him, under peril of imprisonment, to obey the chancellor's direction. [citation] Because of the risks of contempt proceedings, civil or criminal, paramount interests of liberty and due process make it indispensable for the chancellor or his surrogate to speak clearly, explicitly, and specifically if violation of his direction is to subject a litigant—(not to mention, as in the case at bar, a third person who is not a party of record but merely an officer of a party)—to coercive or penal measures, as well as to payment of damages.

The failure of the equity court to spell out in a decree's text the specific obligations resting upon the defeated litigant is fatal to any contempt proceeding unless we are to disregard the teachings of the masters of our law (see Swift and Co. v. United States, 196 U.S. 375, 401 (1905), where Justice Holmes, in oft-quoted language, said that "The defendants ought to be informed as accurately as the case permits what they are forbidden to do,") and the political struggles to limit the powers of the federal judiciary.

When the question of contempt is raised, just as it is inadequate if the decree has merely referred to a statute, even though the statute clearly created the legal obligation which warranted the decree, so it is not enough for enforcement by contempt proceedings if the decree merely referred to a contract, even though the contract clearly created the legal obligation which warranted the decree.

Judgment is affirmed.

Notes

1. In Professional Association of College Educators v. El Paso County Community College District, 730 F.2d 258, 273 (5th Cir.1984), the court held an injunction prohibiting retaliation or discrimination by the District against employees because of membership in the plaintiff or similar associations was sufficiently specific and not overly broad.

"The standards requiring specificity in injunctions are fully met here. These rules do not require 'unwieldly' specificity, but only that the injunction, 'be framed so that those enjoined will know what conduct the court has prohibited.' Meyer v. Brown & Root Construction Co., 661 F.2d 369 (5th Cir.1981). * * * "It is difficult to imagine how the injunction could be more specific without attempting to catalogue every conceivable means by which an employer might retaliate or discriminate against an employee."

2. Compare Hall v. Wood, 443 So.2d 834, 841–42 (Miss.1983). Lakeside property owners were the victims of pollution caused by the erosion of stripped upper lands near a lake. The lower court issued a mandatory injunction. The Supreme Court of Mississippi said:

"On the matter of the content of the specific injunction issued, we applaud the wisdom of the chancellor's recognition that no court under such circumstances should 'try * * * to spell out exactly what should be done to stop the erosion.' We emphasize that his failure in this regard in no way runs afoul of our long established rule that mandatory injunctions must be clear and explicit on their face so that the party enjoined will be distinctly informed as to what he is enjoined from doing or is commanded to do. [citations] Nor did the chancellor depart from our current rule found in rule 65(d)(2) Miss.R.Civ.P. [essentially the same as the rule in H.K. Porter].

"When ordering the achievement of ends necessarily reached only through the employment of scientific or engineering techniques, courts of equity should be particularly cautious. An overly precise specification of *means* will generally be beyond judicial competence in fact or in law. What should and ought be done is the very clear specification of the *end* to be achieved. The party enjoined should then be directed to proceed with reasonable dispatch."

Question: What should a lawyer tell a client who is handed a murky or possibly incomplete injunction?

a. nothing and invite contempt proceedings?

b. attempt to comply as best as possible pending clarification?

c. move to modify?

3. Davis v. City and County of San Francisco, 890 F.2d 1438, 1450 (9th Cir.1989): "The Union argues that the incorporation by the district court of sections of the SFFD General Order into its 1988 injunction violated Rule 65(d) and was an abuse of discretion which requires reversal.

"The law of this circuit is that '[o]rdinarily, an injunction should not incorporate by reference another document.' [citation] The Union cites language in the opinions of other circuits which appears to read the incorporation requirement very strictly. [citation to *H.K. Porter*] * * *

"The primary purpose of Rule 65(d) is to assure adequate notice to parties faced with the possibility of contempt. [citations] Here, the document incorporated into the 1988 injunction consisted of fire department rules already binding upon the officers of the SFFD. It is unlikely the officers could argue they were unaware of these rules.

"We conclude that the district court's failure to cause a copy of the SFFD General Order to be stapled to the 1988 injunction does not require reversal of the court's grant of the injunction."

LATROBE STEEL CO. v. UNITED STEELWORKERS OF AMERICA

United States Court of Appeals, Third Circuit, 1976.
545 F.2d 1336.

ADAMS, CIRCUIT JUDGE. This appeal presents two principal issues. First, we must decide whether the district court had jurisdiction to enjoin the appellant union from refusing to cross a "stranger picket line."[1] Then, if that question is answered in the negative, we must determine whether a coercive civil contempt decree, based on a violation of the injunction, can survive the invalidation of the underlying order.

United Steelworkers of America and its Local Union No. 1537 have for many years represented the production and maintenance employees of the Latrobe Steel Company. Local 1537 and Latrobe Steel were signatories to a collective bargaining agreement that contained a broad no-strike clause and an expansive grievance-arbitration provision.

* * * After efforts to negotiate a collective bargaining agreement between the office workers local and Latrobe Steel proved unsuccessful, the office employees established a picket line outside of the Latrobe facility at about 11:00 P.M. on September 4, 1975. As a result of the picket line, the production workers on the midnight shift refused to enter the plant.

Early the next morning, September 5th, Latrobe Steel brought an action in the district court under section 301 of the Labor Management Relations Act of 1947, seeking a temporary restraining order against the refusal of the production employees to cross the picket line. [A] hearing was held on the afternoon of September 5th. At its conclusion, Judge Ralph Scalera issued a preliminary injunction prohibiting the union and its members from engaging in any work stoppage and directing the parties to the suit to utilize the grievance and arbitration mechanism to resolve any disputes.

After the entry of the preliminary injunction, the officers of Local 1537 proceeded to inform their members that a meeting would be held on September 7th, and urged them to return to work. It appears from the record that the production workers complied with the injunction on September 6th and 7th. However, mass picketing by the office workers prevented members of Local 1537 from entering the plant on September 8th and 9th. But even after Latrobe Steel had obtained a state court injunction against the striking office workers and the mass picketing had ceased, the production employees continued to stay off the job and did not return to work until September 18, 1975.

1. [Footnotes renumbered.] A "stranger picket line" is a picket line established by a union other than the one against which the injunction is sought.

When the production workers did not report for work on September 10th, Latrobe Steel moved the district court to hold Local 1537 and certain of its officers and members in "civil contempt." Following a full hearing the district court ruled that the union was "adjudged in civil contempt." Judge Scalera did not rely on the events of September 8 and 9, noting that it may have been impossible for the union to comply on those days. Instead, he grounded his holding on the refusal of the workers to report on September 11th and 12th, after the mass picketing had terminated and there was no question of the ability of the production workers union to comply with the preliminary injunction.

The district court's contempt order levied a two-part fine on the union. An assessment of $10,000 was imposed, payable to the United States, if the production employees did not report for work at the next shift beginning midnight, September 12th. The court's adjudication also provided that the union would have to pay an additional $10,000, again to the United States, for each subsequent day the union failed to comply with the preliminary injunction. On October 3, 1975, the district court entered an order staying all proceedings to enforce the contempt judgment until disposition of a motion to vacate the preliminary injunction and any appeals from such disposition.

In an opinion filed on December 10, 1975, the district court denied the union's motion to vacate the preliminary injunction. The present appeal followed. * * *

After a careful review of the facts and the authorities, we conclude that the preliminary injunction as well as the contempt judgment in this case must be vacated.

The opinion of the Supreme Court in Buffalo Forge Co. v. United Steelworkers of America,[2] entered after the appeal in this case was filed, significantly altered the backdrop against which the question of the district court's power to enter a preliminary injunction must be considered.

Buffalo Forge presented a factual pattern closely analogous to that in the case at hand. A production and maintenance union was a party to a collective bargaining agreement that contained broad no-strike and grievance-arbitration provisions. Office, clerical and technical workers at the plant, after failing to negotiate a satisfactory collective bargaining agreement, established a picket line which the production and maintenance employees refused to cross. The employer then sought an injunction in the district court. Relief was denied, the district court stated, because section 4 of the Norris–LaGuardia Act deprived it of jurisdiction. The Second Circuit affirmed. On appeal, the Supreme Court held that district courts are not empowered to enjoin a "sympathy" strike pending an arbitrator's decision as to whether the strike was forbidden by a no-strike clause of a collective bargaining agreement. * * * Since the work stoppage in this case, as was true in *Buffalo Forge*, was not over an arbitrable dispute, the prohibition of section 4 of the Norris–LaGuardia Act is applicable, and the district court was without jurisdiction to enter a preliminary injunction.

We now turn to the question whether the district court's order of contempt survives the invalidation of the underlying injunction.

2. 428 U.S. 397 (1976).

The general rule is that whether a contempt judgment survives the avoidance of an underlying order depends on the nature of the contempt decree. If the contempt is criminal it stands; if it is civil it falls.[3]

Although Judge Scalera denominated the contempt order as "civil contempt," the cases admonish us to ascertain independently the nature of the decree instead of treating the district court's mere characterization or label as dispositive. It is well established that the nature of the defendant's conduct is not the primary differentiating factor in determining the nature of the contempt. This is so since a single act of contempt may give rise to both criminal and civil sanctions.[4] Rather, the most significant variables are the purpose and character of the sanctions that are imposed against the contemnor.

The purpose of criminal contempt is to vindicate the authority of the court. Criminal contempt seeks to punish past acts of disobedience and may be maintained only with the court's approval. Its proceedings are separate from the actions which spawned them. If a criminal contempt action develops from a civil proceeding, it bears a separate caption apart from the civil suit. And the penalties arising out of adjudications of criminal contempt are generally an absolute fine of a specific amount or a determinate period of confinement.

On the other hand, the objective of a civil contempt decree is to benefit the complainant. Civil contempt proceedings are instituted primarily on the motion of the plaintiff and are part of the underlying action.

While the *Gompers* case speaks in terms of a dichotomy between criminal and civil contempt, civil contempt itself may be divisible into two sub-categories which benefit the aggrieved party in distinctive ways. Remedial or compensatory actions are essentially backward looking, seeking to compensate the complainant through the payment of money for damages caused by past acts of disobedience. Coercive sanctions, in contrast, look to the future and are designed to aid the plaintiff by bringing a defiant party into compliance with the court order or by assuring that a potentially contumacious party adheres to an injunction by setting forth in advance the penalties the court will impose if the party deviates from the path of obedience.

Trial judges have a variety of weapons with which they can achieve these ends. They may impose an indeterminate period of confinement which may be brought to an end only by the contemnor's ultimate adherence to the court order. Alternatively, the court may levy a fine of a specified amount for past refusal to conform to the injunction, conditioned, however, on the defendant's continued failure to obey. The court may also specify that a disobedient party will be fined a certain amount for each day of non-compliance. Indeed, the methods that may be employed to coerce a recalcitrant party into compliance with an injunction are many and varied.

3. United States v. United Mine Workers, 330 U.S. 258, 289–95 (1947).

4. See, e.g., United States v. United Mine Workers, 330 U.S. 258, 289–99 (1947); Gompers v. Buck Stove & Range Co., 221 U.S. 418, 441 (1911).

The Supreme Court in *Gompers* suggested that one test which might generally reveal the nature of contempt penalties was whether the contemptuous conduct was "refusing to do an act commanded" or "doing an act prohibited." The former would be civil contempts, the latter criminal contempts. We agree, however, with the Seventh Circuit's statements in *Shakman* that this was not intended to be a dispositive test, and that it is a less than adequate yardstick. Indeed, the present case provides an excellent example of how those categories could be manipulated, since Local 1537's action could be classified as either the refusal to perform a commanded act, i.e., return to work, or as the commission of proscribed conduct, i.e., continuing to strike.

After reviewing the elements of Judge Scalera's order, we conclude that it was in the nature of a coercive civil contempt. While there are some indications that the district judge may have been seeking to vindicate the authority and dignity of the court, and although the fines ultimately imposed were to be paid to the United States, a factor which frequently denotes a criminal contempt, the principal thrust of the decree was to benefit Latrobe Steel by providing disincentives for the union to continue its defiance of the court order.

Specifically, although the first $10,000 fine was predicated on past acts of contempt—the failure of the production employees to report to work on September 10th and 11th—the order provided that the fine would not be executed if the union immediately expurgated itself of the contempt. Thus, the principal beneficiary of the union's compliance would be Latrobe Steel and not the court or the government. The second aspect of the judgment is even more clearly coercive in nature, since the additional fine of $10,000 per day could be triggered only by future intransigence on the part of the union. Such intransigence would harm Latrobe, and the prospects of a fine of $10,000 per day would chill the chance of disobedience and thus redound to the benefit of Latrobe.

Our conclusion that the contempt here was not criminal in nature but rather civil and coercive, is buttressed by the fact that the order and the proceedings below display other badges of civil rather than criminal contempt. The contempt order was bottomed on the motion of Latrobe Steel, not on the motion of the court, and was closely related to the underlying civil lawsuit. Also, it was captioned "Latrobe Steel Co. v. United Steelworkers of America, et. al.," not "In re United States Steelworkers of America, et al." or "United States v. United Steelworkers of America." The latter citation would have been utilized for a criminal contempt action.

The remaining issue, whether a civil contempt order that is coercive in nature falls with the underlying injunction, is one which has received scant judicial consideration. The paucity of analysis of this problem, which is critical to the disposition of the present case, is particularly surprising, given the wealth of precedent on the effect generally of the invalidation of a prior injunction on subsequent criminal and compensatory civil contempts.

With regard to criminal contempt, the Supreme Court's opinions in Walker v. Birmingham [5] and United States v. United Mine Workers [6] clearly hold that a criminal contempt judgment does survive the voiding of an injunction.[7] *United Mine Workers* also teaches that a compensatory civil contempt judgment cannot withstand the reversal of an injunction.[8]

Although the cases do not fully explicate the reasoning behind the general principle that compensatory civil contempt does not survive the abrogation of the underlying decree, the precept is, in our opinion, a sound one. A compensatory contempt proceeding is similar in several particulars to an ordinary damage action, since it is in essence an action between private parties, with rights created by the injunctive order rather than by a statute or the common law. The invalidation of an injunction in such a setting is equivalent to a holding that the plaintiff never had a legally cognizable interest which the

5. 388 U.S. 307 (1967).

6. 330 U.S. 258 (1947).

7. The *United Mine Workers* court expressly stated that "violations of an order are punishable as criminal contempt even though the order is set aside on appeal."

8. 330 U.S. at 294–95 ("The right to remedial relief falls with an injunction which events prove was erroneously issued.")

defendant was obliged to respect, a conclusion which should be distinguished from the nearly unconditional duty of obedience owed by a defendant to a court. The *United Mine Workers'* doctrine thus recognizes that a private party should not profit as a result of an order to which a court determines, in retrospect, he was never entitled.

Dicta in *Bangor and Aroostook Railroad* and *Inland Steel,*[9] however, suggest that a coercive fine, as distinguished from a compensatory award, straddles to some degree the line between criminal and compensatory civil contempts. Several factors would appear to support the thesis of these two courts. In the case of a coercive fine, no money passes to the complainant as damages, as contrasted with the situation in remedial civil contempt; instead, it is paid into the court or the public treasury. And at the exaction stage of coercive contempt—the point where the total fine is tallied and executed—the proceeding does resemble criminal contempt, since at that juncture the court is ordering a definite sum to be paid into the public fisc on account of past contumacy. Compelling payment of this fine would thus, in some measure, vindicate the integrity of the judicial process.

Despite these arguments, it would appear that the analysis inherent in the dicta in *Bangor and Aroostook Railroad* and in *Inland Steel* is questionable. While coercive fines have some tendency to vindicate the court's authority, as well as to assist the plaintiff, *Gompers* noted that all contempt sanctions are to some degree double edged, assisting the plaintiff to some extent but also vindicating the court. Moreover, the logic supporting the principle enunciated in *United Mine Workers* and *Salkeld,* that a civil contempt is akin to a private action for damages, appears to be equally applicable in the context of coercive contempt. This would seem to be the case since coercive contempt proceedings are brought by litigants and are essentially private disputes between the parties, and not between the court and an individual, as is the case with criminal contempts.

Given this analysis, the reasoning implicit in *United Mine Workers* requires that coercive contempt be treated in the same fashion as compensatory contempt.[10] In coercive contempt, as with remedial contempt, the reversal of the underlying injunction indicates that the complainant never had a valid

9. Inland Steel Co. v. Local Union No. 1545, 505 F.2d 293, 296–97 (7th Cir.1974) and Brotherhood of Locomotive Engineers and Firemen v. Bangor & Aroostook RR., 127 U.S.App.D.C. 23, 380 U.S. 327 (1967).

10. We agree with the statements in the concurring opinion that the discussions in *United Mine Workers* and *Salkeld* of the viability of contempt decrees in the face of the avoidance of an underlying injunction, as well as the cases they rely upon, explicitly address only compensatory civil contempt. Our suggestion, however, is not that *United Mine Workers* directly disposes of the question before us, but that its conceptual underpinnings would appear to be equally applicable in the present context. We also note the assertion in the concurring opinion that *United Mine Workers* distinguished between "contempt orders which are designed to safeguard the public interest," and those which are "entered to assist or recompense a private litigant." There appears to be no textual foundation in the Supreme Court's opinion to support this proposition. At no point in the Court's discussion of the effect of the invalidation of an injunction upon an adjudication of contempt does the Court make reference to civil contempts designed to protect the public interest. All of its references are to "criminal contempt."

It should also be mentioned that the Supreme Court's use of the term "remedial" in describing those contempts which cannot survive the invalidation of an underlying order, do [sic] not necessarily exclude coercive civil contempts. Several cases refer to coercive sanctions as "remedial in nature." For example, the *Gompers* case, the seminal opinion on the distinctions between criminal and civil contempts, stated that coercive imprisonments are "intended to be *remedial* by coercing the defendant to do what he had refused to do." It is not suggested, however, that this is at all dispositive of the problem before us.

right which was enforceable against the defendant. Just as a person is not entitled to reap a monetary benefit in such circumstances, so too, should he be unable to insist upon the exaction of coercive sanctions to finalize a process initiated by himself for his own benefit.[11]

We are aware that some might maintain that when a person willfully violates a court order, any court order, the invalidation of the decree should not disturb the imposition of contempt sanctions upon a disobedient party. Respect for the law, the argument goes, demands no less. But it is also true that one of the fundamental postulates of our legal system is that a decree of a court without jurisdiction is void, and that it might well be anomalous to hold a party accountable for violation of such a void order.

These are both weighty considerations, but there does not appear to be a need, at least in a situation such as that presented here, to express an absolute preference for one over the other. Thus, our task, as often the case in litigation, is to reconcile two legal principles, in order to prevent either from destroying the other. Here, the importance of each of the principles can be acknowledged by recognizing that a court may uphold respect for law through the utilization of the criminal contempt process, while preventing litigants from benefitting from void court orders through the medium of either remedial or coercive civil contempt.

Furthermore, it must be kept in mind that the survival of even a criminal contempt sanction, despite the invalidation of an underlying order, is an exception to the fundamental rule that when a court has no jurisdiction its orders and decrees have no effect. To expand the exception applicable to criminal contempts to encompass a civil contempt order, even when such order is coercive in nature would create a further inroad into the basic precept regarding jurisdiction. Since a court may, at its election, provide for the survival of a contempt by affording the party the protections surrounding a criminal contempt, there would appear to be no sound justification for such an extension, at least in the context of this case. * * *

Even if we were to conclude that the contempt order sought was criminal in nature, the judgment of the district court would have to be vacated nonetheless. This is so since it does not appear that the union was afforded any of the procedures required in criminal contempt situations by the applicable rules and statutes, or by the constitutional safeguards mandated by *Gompers* and *Bloom.*[12] Accordingly, the injunction and the order of contempt will be vacated and the cause remanded for proceedings consistent with this opinion.

GARTH, CIRCUIT JUDGE (concurring). * * * I am severely troubled by the doctrine enunciated by the majority that every coercive civil contempt order must fall if the underlying order upon which it is predicated is subsequently determined to be invalid. * * *

11. We note that we are not presented with a case in which the coercive fine has been paid to the Clerk of the Court and deposited in the United States Treasury. In such an instance the controversy regarding the payment of such sum may become moot because the only method to obtain a refund of the executed fine would be through an Act of Congress.

12. In Duncan v. Louisiana, 391 U.S. 145, 161–62 (1968), the Supreme Court indicated that a criminal defendant had a right to a jury trial when the government sought to impose upon him a fine in excess of $500. Insofar as the fine inflicted upon Local 1537 exceeded this sum, it was entitled to a jury trial under the principles of *Duncan* and Bloom v. Illinois, 391 U.S. 194 (1968).

I see no reason why, if a criminal contempt can survive an invalid underlying order, the same effect should not be given to a coercive civil contempt order. I would opt for the following principle: In those cases in which a district court judge has made an express finding that the action compelled was required in the public interest, a coercive civil contempt fine should survive the subsequent invalidation of the underlying order. Indeed, as I read the majority opinion, it leaves open the possibility that this principle may some day become the law in this Circuit. Thus, the majority's holding does not reach cases in which the district court predicated the civil contempt on the presence of "an overarching public interest." In my view, the appropriate disposition of this case would require a remand to the district court with instructions to determine the presence of an "overarching public interest." Such an inquiry might require the record to be supplemented by additional testimony and evidence, inasmuch as the district court * * * had no reason to consider the concepts discussed here.

No reason has been given in either *Spectro Foods* or *Latrobe* as to why we should deprive the district courts of the complete and effective utilization of a perfectly valid and necessary sanction. Criminal contempts, which are limited in the case of a natural person to a fine of $1,000 and imprisonment for six months (18 U.S.C.A. § 402), can not compel compliance and, in certain circumstances where the public interest is predominant, just cannot supply the required remedy. While I am obliged to bow to this Court's expression of the law as found in *Spectro Foods* and now *Latrobe,* I do so with the fear that the cutback in civil contempt effectiveness as now reflected in the holdings in these cases will cause untold difficulties in situations in which vital public interests require immediate protection.

Notes on Criminal Contempt

1. The label "criminal" on contempt should remove the matter, for most purposes, from private equity remedies. The private litigant ostensibly takes no more than vicarious enjoyment from a criminal contempt order against his opponent, since it is not designed to aid him enforce his rights. Realistically, however, the threat of punitive measures increases the possibility that the equitable decree will be obeyed. The private equity litigant may derive more than a subjective pleasure from criminal contempt, while maintaining the pretense that only the integrity of the judicial process is at stake.

Observe the distinction between civil and criminal contempt carefully. Criminal and civil contempt follow different procedures, and a court cannot follow civil procedure and impose a punitive or criminal sanction.

2. *Procedural Considerations.* In general, summary procedures are approved for direct contempt, i.e., contumacious or obstructive behavior in the presence of the court. A plenary trial is considered to be unnecessary to apprise the court that what it saw happen really happened. Some restraints are imposed to prevent the abuse of the direct contempt power; but these are of slight relevance to the enforcement of equity decrees.

Some protective notice and hearing procedures are required for criminal contempt. In different jurisdictions these vary, ranging from supplementary proceedings in the civil action all the way to a separate full-scale criminal case. Occasionally a court observes that the contempt process is *sui generis.* Some aspects of criminal contempt procedure are sketched out in *Latrobe.* The variances in practice suggest reference to local statutes and decisions for the technical framework in which indirect contempt is tried.

Principles of criminal law administration permeate the criminal contempt process. The violation of an equity decree poses the possibility of citations for indirect criminal contempt and civil contempt or both; the hearing may be compatible with either. It becomes important to segregate the elements and to avoid the confusion and obscurity that invite an expensive appeal. Professor Dobbs summarizes the effect of a decision that a contempt hearing is criminal:

"The burden of proof is on the prosecution, the party charged cannot be required to testify against himself, cannot be put in double jeopardy, and cannot be tried without appropriate notice of the charge. Inferentially at least, he is entitled to counsel and to compulsory process for bringing in his witnesses. He is now entitled to a jury trial if the criminal sentence is a potentially serious one. As with other crimes, intent is an element of criminal contempt, and it must be proven before criminal punishment can be inflicted, though intent to violate the court's order is not an issue in a civil contempt proceeding. * * * The classification of a contempt hearing as a criminal one may also affect the right of appeal or the route that an appeal takes. At least in some criminal contempt cases, the state should be a party to any appeal proceedings. The criminal classification will also invoke the pardoning power of the state, which, of course, would not exist in civil cases.

"There are disadvantages for the party charged if his contempt case is classified as a criminal one. Any fine levied is not dischargeable in bankruptcy. Moreover, he may be held in criminal contempt for violating an order that is later reversed since it may be important to vindicate judicial power even when it is erroneously exercised. * * *

"Civil contempt cases are not altogether different, of course. Even in civil cases, apart from the summary contempts in open court, some sort of hearing and notice is ordinarily required, though the form of hearings may be somewhat less significant here. But proof beyond a reasonable doubt is not required as it is in criminal cases, and, though no doubt res judicata rules will apply to civil contempt cases, the double jeopardy provisions will not." [1]

For an exhaustive review of the procedural differences between the two kinds of contempt, see In re Marriage of Betts, 200 Ill.App.3d 26, 558 N.E.2d 404 (1990).

3. *Improper Elements in Contempt.* A determinate jail sentence for disobedience of an injunction is an improper punitive sanction in civil contempt. In Baker v. Baker, 473 A.2d 1325 (Md.App.1984), husband was sentenced to 89 days in jail for violating an injunction against harassing his wife. On appeal he was held to have been improperly convicted of criminal contempt in civil proceedings.

In Mechanic v. Gruenfelder, 461 S.W.2d 298, 303, 305 (Mo.Ct.App.1970), Washington University at St. Louis obtained a TRO, forbidding certain persons from "molesting, converting, abusing or otherwise physically disturbing any personal or real property of plaintiff." The campus R.O.T.C. building was burned down. Seven persons were cited for criminal contempt and given sentences of from three months in jail and $150 fine to six months and $500. In addition, civil contempt sentences of from 10 to 30 days in jail were imposed. The *civil* contempt sentences were reversed: "Contempt proceedings could not restore the building, recall the rocks and firecrackers thrown or unbreak the windows. No enforcement of the order for the benefit of the University could be accomplished by civil contempt proceedings

1. Dobbs, Contempt of Court: A Survey, 56 Cornell L.Rev. 183, 242–43 (1971). © 1971 by Dan B. Dobbs. The author's footnote citations are omitted.

resulting in imprisonment nor could the petitioners purge their completed contempt."

Occasionally the judge includes a suspended determinate jail sentence in the original injunction decree, to be activated if the injunction is violated. E.g., Jencks v. Goforth, 57 N.M. 627, 261 P.2d 655 (1953). This practice has been criticized, see Dobbs, 56 Cornell L.Rev. at 244 (1971), despite the argument that it is a coercive device and the defendant may avoid confinement by the simple expedient of compliance. The New Mexico Supreme Court later repeated its approval with a half-hearted apology that "we did not intend to indicate that this was the best method of handling a civil contempt." Local 890 v. New Jersey Zinc Co., 58 N.M. 416, 419, 272 P.2d 322, 324 (1954).

The "in terrorem" fine as a coercive measure is a variation of this technique with a fixed money penalty rather than a fixed jail sentence. Would a "fine" exceeding compensatory damages caused by a past act of contempt be vulnerable?

4. Perhaps the best way to avoid reversal of civil contempt as embodying penal elements is to observe criminal contempt procedural requirements. As the Court said in United States v. United Mine Workers, 330 U.S. 258, 298–99 (1947):

"If the defendants were thus accorded all the rights and privileges owing to defendants in criminal contempt cases, they are put in no better position to complain because their trial included a proceeding in civil contempt and was carried on in the main equity suit. Common sense would recognize that conduct can amount to both civil and criminal contempt. The same acts may justify a court in resorting to coercive and to punitive measures. Disposing of both aspects of the contempt in a single proceeding would seem at least a convenient practice."

5. *Confusion in the Coalfields.* Union members violated separate federal and state injunctions; the federal and state courts found the union in contempt; each court imposed fines triggered by future violations; the members' violations continued; and the parties settled the controversy. What effect did the settlement have on the union's liability for the accumulated contempt fines? The federal judge declined to vacate $280,000 in fines. Clark v. International Union, United Mine Workers of America, 752 F.Supp. 1291 (W.D.Va.1990). The state court of appeals held, however, that fines which exceeded $20,000,000 were moot and due to be vacated. International Union, United Mine Workers of America v. Clinchfield Coal Co., ___ Va.App. ___, 402 S.E.2d 899 (1991).

In a related appeal the state court decided that triggered contempt fines were criminal and had to follow criminal procedure. This failed to clarify the distinction. The rehearing en banc that the court scheduled while this book was in press may clear the air. International Union, United Mine Workers of America v. Covenant Coal Corp., ___ Va.App. ___, 402 S.E.2d 906 (1991).

EX PARTE PURVIS

Supreme Court of Alabama, 1980.
382 So.2d 512.

EMBRY, JUSTICE. This petition for writ of habeas corpus arises out of a strike against The Water Works Board of the City of Birmingham by hourly employees of that Board. The petition was filed on behalf of James R. Purvis after he was incarcerated under a sentence of criminal contempt by the Circuit Court of Jefferson County. The contempt sentence was based on Purvis' violation of a temporary restraining order enjoining the strike and all picketing activities against the Board. Purvis was sentenced to an aggregate of fifteen days in jail for three separate instances of contempt. This court granted a stay of execution of the sentence after Purvis had served eight days of the sentence.

We deny the petition.

The dispositive issue in this proceeding is whether Purvis can challenge, by petition for the writ of habeas corpus, the constitutional validity of the trial court's temporary restraining order when Purvis failed to try to have the order dissolved or modified before violating it?

In July of 1979, Purvis requested the Board to recognize his union as the exclusive bargaining representative for the hourly-paid employees of the Board. * * * On 31 July 1979 Purvis advised the Board its employees would commence a strike against it and all of its facilities unless the union's demands were met. Upon the Board's refusal, the strike and picketing of the Board's facilities were commenced at approximately 6:00 a.m. on Thursday, 2 August 1979. That same morning the Board petitioned the Jefferson County Circuit Court for a temporary restraining order alleging, *inter alia,* the strike was illegal, striking employees were harassing and interfering with customers entering and leaving its buildings and property, and it, and the City of Birmingham would suffer irreparable injury if the order was not issued before notice could be served on the defendants.

At 1:40 on Thursday, 2 August 1979, a temporary restraining order was issued which contained, among other things, the following:

> "A. The defendants, separately and severally, their officers, agents, and members, and all persons acting in concert or combination with them, who have actual notice of this temporary restraining order by personal service or otherwise be and they are hereby restrained, pending the final determination of this action, from:
>
> "1. causing, inducing, engaging in or encouraging a strike, work stoppage, or concerted refusal to work at The Board or any of its facilities for the purpose of requiring The Board to agree to defendants' demands that the plaintiff recognize, bargain with or enter into agreements with the defendant Union. * * *"

At 4:08 p.m. on Thursday, 2 August 1979, Purvis was served with a copy of the temporary restraining order by a deputy sheriff. The evidence at the contempt hearing discloses that Purvis told the deputy "* * * he would stay out, even if he had to go to jail." Consistent with this declaration Purvis continued to picket the Board's Shades Mountain facility the rest of Thursday afternoon and the morning of Friday, 3 August 1979. The evidence further discloses that Purvis ignored and violated the order by threatening a supervisor that drove through the picket line.

On Friday, 3 August 1979, the Board filed a petition to show cause why Purvis should not be held in contempt of court. Purvis was served that same day at 1:55 p.m. Purvis then filed a motion to dissolve or modify the temporary restraining order. The court ordered Purvis to appear before the court on Monday morning, 6 August 1979, to show cause why he should not be held in contempt and, further, denied Purvis' motion to dissolve or modify the temporary restraining order.

On Saturday morning, 4 August 1979, the Board amended its petition to show cause. On Monday, 6 August 1979, after a hearing, the trial court found Purvis had violated the temporary restraining order after having received proper notice by: (1) continuing to picket Thursday afternoon; (2) threatening to assault a supervisor; and (3) his picketing activities on Friday morning. Three separate judgments of criminal contempt were entered against Purvis and he was sentenced to three consecutive five day sentences for each offense as well as being fined $100 for each offense. Thereafter, this petition was filed.

Purvis contends the trial court's temporary restraining order was transparently invalid, unconstitutional and required the irretrievable surrender of his important constitutional rights; therefore, there can be no valid finding of contempt because adequate and effective appellate procedures did not exist to challenge the order's validity. We cannot agree with this contention.

It has long been the rule of law that an order issued by a court with jurisdiction over the subject matter must be obeyed by the parties subject to the order until it is reversed by orderly and proper proceedings even though the order may be constitutionally defective or invalid. Walker v. City of Birmingham, 279 Ala. 53, 181 So.2d 493 (1966), affirmed, 388 U.S. 307 (1967); United States v. United Mine Workers of America, 330 U.S. 258 (1947). Purvis acknowledges this established principle of law but asserts the order had such a chilling effect on his First Amendment rights that the order was void on its face, therefore, he was entitled to disregard the order because there was insufficient time to appeal from it. We cannot agree that the order was transparently invalid or that such exigent circumstances existed as to allow Purvis to disregard it.

We recognize that court orders may be disregarded in certain rare cases where compliance with the court order would cause irreparable injury and appellate vindication would not have its ordinary consequences of totally repairing the error. However, such cases generally involve orders issued during criminal trials. We further recognize that if an injunction is transparently invalid, or only has a frivolous pretense to validity, its validity may be challenged in a contempt proceeding. Walker v. City of Birmingham, 388 U.S. 307 (1967). In this case, however, Purvis was not justified in refusing to obey the temporary restraining order. See United States v. United Mine Workers of America, supra.

The United States Supreme Court has consistently recognized that the state has a strong interest in regulating the use of its streets and other public places; and when protest takes the form of mass demonstration, parades, or picketing on public streets and sidewalks, the state has a legitimate concern in preventing public disorder and violence and promoting the free passage of traffic. *Walker,* supra. Moreover, the First and Fourteenth Amendments to the United States Constitution, although they do protect, do not afford the same kind of freedom to those who communicate ideas by conduct, such as picketing on streets and highways, as the amendments afford those who communicate ideas by mere speech. Shuttlesworth v. City of Birmingham, 394 U.S. 147 (1969); *Walker,* supra. Since violence erupted during the strike and picketing, and the City of Birmingham's water service was in danger of being shut down, the trial court's temporary restraining order was not transparently invalid or frivolous. Also, a hearing was scheduled within five days, and Purvis could easily have sought modification or dissolution of the order before disobeying it.

In reaching our decision we must emphasize that we are not encouraging the issuance of temporary restraining orders against peaceful picketing. It is very clear that peaceful picketing is protected by the First Amendment. *Shuttlesworth,* supra; Thornhill v. State of Alabama, 310 U.S. 88 (1940). First Amendment rights should only be enjoined in extreme situations. *Temporary restraining orders should only be issued without a prior hearing when it is clear from specific facts alleged by affidavit or by verified complaint that immediate and irreparable injury, loss, or damage, will result if the temporary restraining order is not issued prior to allowing the opposing party an opportunity to be heard.* Rule 65(b)(1), ARCP. When a temporary restraining order is to be issued without hearing, curtailing First Amendment rights, even closer scrutiny of the existing circumstances under which it is sought should be exercised by the trial court.

The sole basis for our decision in this case is the need to maintain the integrity of court orders. In reaching this decision we make no finding respecting the constitutional validity of the temporary restraining order. It is clear in this case that Purvis was fully cognizant that he risked jail confinement if he deliberately defied the court order; yet he chose to do so. We fully agree with the statement of Justice Stewart in Walker v. City of Birmingham:

> "The rule of law that Alabama followed in this case reflects a belief that in the fair administration of justice no man can be judge in his own case, however exalted his station, however righteous his motives, and irrespective of his race, color, politics, or religion. This Court cannot hold that the petitioners were constitutionally free to ignore all the procedures of the law and carry their battle to the streets. One may sympathize with the petitioners' impatient commitment to their cause. But respect for judicial process is a small price to pay for the civilizing hand of law, which alone can give abiding meaning to constitutional freedom." * * *

[T]he petition for writ of habeas corpus is denied and the stay of execution of the remainder of the sentences vacated.

Notes

1. United States v. United Mine Workers, 330 U.S. 258 (1947). During the late 1940s, coal mines were in possession of the federal government, being run under an agreement concerning the terms and conditions of employment. Whether the agreement could be unilaterally terminated by John L. Lewis and the United Mine Workers was the subject of litigation. Pending determination of whether the Norris–LaGuardia Act applied, the federal district court issued a temporary restraining order which was admittedly disobeyed. Fines were imposed: Ch. J. Vinson held:

"The District Court had the power to preserve existing conditions while it was determining its own authority to grant injunctive relief. The defendants, in making their private determination of the law, acted at their peril. * * *

"Assuming, * * * that the Norris–LaGuardia Act applied to this case * * * we would set aside the preliminary injunction * * * and the judgment for civil contempt: but we would, subject to any infirmities in the contempt proceedings or fines imposed, affirm the judgment for criminal contempt as validly punishing violations of an order then outstanding and unreversed."

In a sense the remarks are dicta because the Court decided that the Norris–LaGuardia Act did not apply to the United States government.

2. In re Providence Journal Co., 820 F.2d 1342, 1344, 1347–48, 1352–53, 1355 (1st Cir.1986), modified, 820 F.2d 1354 (1987), presented "an apparent conflict between two fundamental legal principles: the hallowed First Amendment princi-

ple that the press shall not be subjected to prior restraints; the other, the sine qua non of orderly government, that, until modified or vacated, a court order must be obeyed." The trial judge granted a TRO forbidding the Journal from publishing material about a deceased man who was reputed to have been involved with organized crime; but the paper published the material two days later. The trial judge imposed criminal contempt sanctions on the paper and its editor.

The court of appeals panel decision thought the TRO was a prior restraint of speech and reversed the contempt under the "exception to the collateral bar rule for transparently invalid court orders. Requiring a party subject to such an order to obey or face contempt would give the courts powers far in excess of any authorized by the Constitution or Congress. Recognizing an exception to the collateral bar rule for transparently invalid orders does not violate the principle that 'no man can be judge in his own case' anymore than does recognizing such an exception for jurisdictional defects. The key to both exceptions is the notion that although a court order—even an arguably incorrect court order—demands respect, so does the right of the citizen to be free of clearly improper exercises of judicial authority.

"Although an exception to the collateral bar rule is appropriate for transparently void orders, it is inappropriate for arguably proper orders. This distinction is necessary both to protect the authority of the courts when they address close questions and to create a strong incentive for parties to follow the orderly process of law. No such protection or incentive is needed when the order is transparently invalid because in that instance the court is acting so far in excess of its authority that it has no right to expect compliance and no interest is protected by requiring compliance.

"The line between a transparently invalid order and one that is merely invalid is, of course, not always distinct. As a general rule, if the court reviewing the order finds the order to have had any pretence to validity at the time it was issued, the reviewing court should enforce the collateral bar rule. Such a heavy presumption in favor of validity is necessary to protect the rightful power of the courts. Nonetheless, there are instances where an order will be so patently unconstitutional that it will be excepted from the collateral bar rule."

The panel opinion and the whole court of appeals, en banc, differed on the other exception to the collateral bar rule.

The panel: "When, as here, the court order is a transparently invalid prior restraint on pure speech, the delay and expense of an appeal is unnecessary. Indeed, the delay caused by an appellate review requirement could, in the case of a prior restraint involving news concerning an imminent event, cause the restrained information to lose its value. The absence of such a requirement will not, however, lead to wide-spread disregard of court orders. Rarely will a party be subject to a transparently invalid court order. Prior restraints on pure speech represent an unusual class of orders because they are presumptively unconstitutional. And even when a party believes it is subject to a transparently invalid order, seeking review in an appellate court is a far safer means of testing the order. For if the party chooses to violate the order and the order turns out not to be transparently invalid, the party must suffer the consequences of a contempt citation."

Five months later the whole court issued an en banc opinion "as an addendum to, and modification of, said panel opinion."

"Nevertheless it seems to us that some finer tuning is available to minimize the disharmony between respect for court orders and respect for free speech.

"It is not asking much, beyond some additional expense and time, to require a publisher, even when it thinks it is the subject of a transparently unconstitutional order of prior restraint, to make a good faith effort to seek emergency relief from the appellate court. If timely access to the appellate court is not available or if timely decision is not forthcoming, the publisher may then proceed to publish and challenge the constitutionality of the order in the contempt proceedings. In such event whatever added expense and time are involved, such a price does not seem disproportionate to the respect owing court processes; and there is no prolongation of any prior restraint. On the other hand, should the appellate court grant the requested relief, the conflict between principles has been resolved and the expense and time involved have vastly been offset by aborting any contempt proceedings.

"We realize that our ruling means that a publisher seeking to challenge an order it deems transparently unconstitutional must concern itself with establishing a record of its good faith effort. But that is a price we should pay for the preference of court over party determination of invalidity. * * * [We] would deem it unfair to subject the publisher to the very substantial sanctions imposed by the district court because of its failure to follow the procedure we have just announced. We recognize that our announcement is technically dictum, but are confident that its stature as a deliberate position taken by us in this en banc consideration will serve its purpose."

3. In re Berry, 68 Cal.2d 137, 146, 65 Cal.Rptr. 273, 282, 436 P.2d 273, 282 (1968). At the instance of Sacramento County a TRO was issued ex parte to prohibit a threatened strike by the Social Workers' Union. No attempt was made to modify the decree; defendants fully aware of its existence deliberately disobeyed it. Arrests were made. The defendants were charged, not under the contempt provision of the Code of Civil Procedure, but instead under an unusual and seldom used provision of the Penal Code (§ 166 subsection 4) that makes certain conduct in contempt of court a misdemeanor. A writ of habeas corpus, a collateral attack on the decree, was sought. The California Supreme Court did not deny that the specific acts of disobedience charged could have been properly inhibited, but it held that the order as a whole was too vague to pass the constitutional standards required when first amendment rights were affected. Wilful disobedience was therefore not punishable by criminal contempt. With reference to Walker v. Birmingham the court said:

"The County herein relies heavily upon the *Walker* case in an effort to sustain its position that petitioners must be precluded from raising constitutional objections to the subject order because they did not seek its modification or vacation prior to their willful disobedience of it. It is apparent, however, that the *holding* of the *Walker* case, as distinguished from its language, is only that the rule of law followed by the State of Alabama did not, in the particular circumstances of that case, constitute an intrusion upon First Amendment freedoms. In California, as we have shown above, the rule followed is considerably more consistent with the exercise of First Amendment freedoms than that adopted in Alabama, and it is therefore difficult to perceive how the *Walker* decision is of relevance herein. Further, it is notable that the majority in *Walker* indicated that the Alabama rule might be constitutionally impermissible in a case wherein the order or ordinance involved was unconstitutional on its face, or was 'transparently invalid or had only a frivolous pretense to validity.' Thus it appears that the *Walker* decision is consistent with the California rule that an order void upon its face cannot support a contempt judgment."

2. WHO MUST OBEY?

EX PARTE DAVIS

Supreme Court of Texas, 1971.
470 S.W.2d 647.

PER CURIAM. The relator, J. Boyd Davis, pastor of the Bible Baptist Church of Beaumont, seeks a writ of habeas corpus releasing him from restraint of a contempt order of the 58th District Court of Jefferson County. Relator was held in contempt on May 10, 1971, for violating a temporary injunction issued May 16, 1962 "pending final hearing and determination of this case" enjoining Roy D. Brite and wife from making use of certain tracts of land which they owned in the Lakeview Terrace Addition to the City of Beaumont for the purpose of an animal clinic or for any purpose other than residential use. There was no subsequent hearing on the merits or issuance of a permanent injunction. There is no evidence that Mr. or Mrs. Brite ever violated the terms of the temporary injunction or caused others to do so.

On August 16, 1965, the Brites conveyed the property to the Bible Baptist Church, whose pastor is relator here. After learning of the conveyance, the plaintiffs in the original suit, through their attorney, wrote a letter to Bible Baptist Church, attention Rev. J. Boyd Davis, reciting certain residential restrictions recorded in the Jefferson County deed records, enclosing a copy of the temporary injunction against the Brites, and stating that "our clients would be forced to file injunction proceedings against you to enforce such restrictions" if a church structure were placed upon the property. On April 28, 1971, the Bible Baptist Church moved a structure to be used as a church building onto the property. It is this act and Mr. Davis' refusal to remove the structure which caused him to be held in contempt of the temporary injunction issued May 16, 1962, fined and ordered to jail until he removed the church building.

Rule 683, Texas Rules of Civil Procedure states that an injunction is "binding only upon the parties to the action, their officers, agents, servants, employees, and attorneys, and upon those persons in active concert or participation with them [who receive actual notice of the order by personal service or otherwise.]"

* * * The question here is whether a non-party to the original injunction proceeding was in active concert or participation with the Brites. This court in Ex Parte Foster, 144 Tex. 65, 188 S.W.2d 382 (1945) said that while a person not named as a party is not ordinarily bound by the terms of injunction decree and therefore cannot be punished for violating its terms, he is "in active concert or participation" with the named party if he participated in the original proceeding and was a real party in interest when the decree was rendered. There are other Texas cases dealing with "active concert or participation," but they all contain some evidence of involvement with the named enjoined party or involvement in the original injunctive proceeding. [citations]

The United States Supreme Court in interpreting Rule 65(d) F.R.C.P., from which Texas Rule 683 is taken, said in Regal Knitwear Co. v. Board, 324 U.S. 9, 14 (1944), that the inclusion of those in "active concert or participation with them" is so that "defendants may not nullify a decree by carrying out prohibited acts through aiders and abettors, although they were not parties to the original proceeding." If a non-party does an act prohibited by the injunction he must be in active concert or participation with the named party in order to be in contempt for violation of the injunction.

No fact presented here establishes that relator was a party at interest in the original proceeding as in *Foster,* or that there was any relationship between him and the Brites other than the subsequent grantor-grantee relationship of his church.

Respondents insist that, as grantee of the Brites, Bible Baptist Church and its pastor were "privy" to them. For some purposes this may be true, but standing alone it is not the type of relationship which brings them within the class of persons bound by a temporary injunction under the terms of Rule 683 and punishable for violation thereof. The remedy of injunction generally acts, not in rem, but in personam. [citations] The temporary injunction here was against the Brites only. It did not attempt to include their successors in ownership of the property. In *Regal,* it was held that even when the injunction is worded to include "successors and assigns," it is not effective as to non-party successors because the "enforcement order of course may not enlarge its scope beyond that defined by the Federal Rules of Civil Procedure." * * *

Accordingly, it is ordered that relator be discharged and released.

Notes

1. Restatement (Second) of Judgments § 43 (1982): † Effect of Judgment Determining Interests in Property on Successors to the Property. A judgment in an action that determines interests in real or personal property: (1) With respect to the property involved in the action: (a) Conclusively determines the claims of the parties to the action regarding their interests; and (b) Has preclusive effects upon a person who succeeds to the interest of a party to the same extent as upon the party himself. (2) With respect to other property held by a party to the action, does not preclude a person who is a successor in interest thereof from subsequently litigating issues determined in the action.

2. *Davis* raises an issue of due process. The initial question is whether a person who is not served with process and who did not participate in the lawsuit may validly be held in contempt. A further question is, did the nonparty receive adequate notice of the order he is charged with violating?

Considering the question of notice, first, due process requires that a person cited for contempt had knowledge of the court order, either actual or by service of process. Megantz v. Ash, 412 F.2d 804 (1st Cir.1969). Where personal service of the decree was not accomplished, knowledge of the order may be shown by proof of publication in a newspaper or by radio broadcast. United Packing House Workers v. Boynton, 240 Iowa 212, 35 N.W.2d 881 (1949). More informal notice may suffice. Evidence that an announcement was made by bullhorn or that notice was in general circulation in the affected group may be adequate to establish actual knowledge. See Megantz v. Ash, supra.

3. Holding a nonparty in contempt of an order issued in a lawsuit presents a serious due process issue. The underlying proposition was forcefully stated by Judge Learned Hand in Alemite Manufacturing Corp. v. Staff, 42 F.2d 832, 833 (2d Cir.1930). In reversing contempt, Judge Hand stated: "[N]o court can make a decree which will bind anyone but a party; a court of equity is as much limited as a

court of law; it cannot lawfully enjoin the world at large, no matter how broadly it words its decree. If it assumes to do so, the decree is pro tanto brutum fulmen, and the persons enjoined are free to ignore it." Thus a non-party, acting independently in furtherance of his own interest, is free to ignore an injunction. Heyman v. Kline, 444 F.2d 65 (2d Cir.1971); Kean v. Hurley, 179 F.2d 888 (8th Cir.1950).

4. If the original action is a representative or class action, are all members of the class bound as parties? See United Packing House Workers v. Boynton, supra.

In addition, as Federal Rule of Civil Procedure 65(d) and state equivalents indicate, agents and servants of parties, once having notice of the decree, can be held in contempt for disobeying it. See Petersen v. Fee International, Ltd., 435 F.Supp. 938 (W.D.Okl.1975); Stavros v. Karkomi, 28 Ill.App.3d 996, 329 N.E.2d 563 (1975). Beyond that, persons who are not agents may be held in contempt for violation if they aid and abet or act in concert with the named parties to the lawsuit. Securities and Exchange Commission v. Barraco, 438 F.2d 97 (10th Cir.1971); Lance v. Plummer, 353 F.2d 585 (5th Cir.1965), cert. denied 384 U.S. 929 (1966).

A crucial question is whether the non-parties did aid and abet the named party or acted independently in furtherance of their own interests. This question cannot be avoided by drafting the decree to include large groups of nonparties, e.g. "all persons who are residents of Colquitt County, Georgia." Harrington v. Colquitt County Board of Education, 449 F.2d 161 (5th Cir.1971). Or by charging the defendant as the "John Doe" or "unknown party" described in the decree. State v. Gross, 117 N.H. 853, 379 A.2d 804 (1977). Rather, proof must be presented showing that the non-parties actively participated with the named party in violating the decree. The difficulties are apparent.

State University v. Denton, 35 A.D.2d 176, 316 N.Y.S.2d 297, 299 (1970). An injunction prohibited students "and all other persons" from acting within or adjacent to plaintiff's buildings in "such unlawful manner as to disrupt or interfere with plaintiff's lawful and normal operations." Faculty members, sympathetic with the students but not parties, entered the President's office and refused to leave. The court ruled that they had acted independently and not in concert with the students—who had obeyed the injunction. Evidence that the faculty members agreed with the general purpose of the strike was not sufficient to establish that their conduct was in concert with named defendants.

On the other hand, in United States v. Hall, 472 F.2d 261, 265 (5th Cir.1972), the court dealt with racial unrest in paired high schools by an order providing that "no person shall enter" the school premises other than teachers and students. In violation of that order, Hall, a nonparty, went on the school grounds where he was arrested. Hall was subsequently convicted of contempt. In rejecting the argument that Hall was a nonparty who acted in pursuance of his independent interests, the court ruled that Hall had "imperiled the court's fundamental power to make a binding adjudication between the parties properly before it." The judge had inherent power to punish Hall for contempt in order to protect the court's ability to render judgment.

Planned Parenthood Association of Cincinnati, Inc. v. Project Jericho, 52 Ohio St.2d 56, 66 n.9, 556 N.E.2d 157, 168 n.9 (1990). An injunction which controlled anti-abortion protest at an abortion clinic ran against a defendant class of "all persons picketing" that location. The court found several contemnors in active concert with named defendants. While declining to disapprove the class, the court noted "it is difficult to see, as a practical matter, how the decision to certify a defendant class added to the reach of the trial court's powers under Civ.R. 65(D)."

The court did not consider the possibility that pro-abortion protestors in dissonance instead of concert with named defendants might act contrary to the injunction.

5. In considering the impact of the "aider and abettor rule," reflect on the ruling of the court in Waffenschmidt v. MacKay, 763 F.2d 711, 714 (5th Cir.1985): "Nonparties who reside outside the territorial jurisdiction of a district court may be subject to that court's jurisdiction if, with actual notice of the court's order, they actively aid and abet a party in violating that order. This is so despite the absence of other contacts with the forum."

See also Charles Milne Associates v. Toponce, 770 P.2d 1313 (Colo.App.1988).

6. General discussions of the problem of enforcing a decree against nonparties may be found in Dobbs, Contempt of Court: A Survey, 56 Cornell L.Rev. 183, 249–261 (1971); Dobbyn, Contempt Power of the Equity Court Over Outside Agitators, 8 St. Mary's L.J. 1 (1976); Rendleman, Beyond Contempt: Obligors to Injunctions, 53 Tex.L.Rev. 873 (1975); and Note, Binding Nonparties to Injunction Decrees, 49 Minn.L.Rev. 719 (1965).

STATE v. TERRY

Supreme Court of Washington, 1917.
99 Wash. 1, 168 P. 513.

ELLIS, C.J. Defendants were charged with contempt in violating, with knowledge and notice thereof, a permanent injunction issued from the superior court of King county on November 2, 1915, in a red light abatement case. Defendants Colanzelo were the owners of the property involved; defendant Terry their tenant. The proceedings were by information, attachment, arrest, and trial before the court without a jury upon oral testimony pursuant to Rem.Code, § 946—4. The cause was dismissed as to defendant Rosa Colanzelo. The other defendants were adjudged guilty. Defendant Guiseppe Colanzelo was fined $200. On a showing which the trial court deemed sufficient his fine was afterward remitted. Defendant Terry was fined $300 and sentenced to serve three months in the county jail. She moved for a new trial. The motion was overruled. She appeals.

The decree in the original abatement case so far as here material, was as follows:

"Now, therefore, it is hereby considered, ordered, adjudged and decreed that defendants * * * and each of them, and their agents, servants, and all other persons acting by, through or under them, and all other persons whatsoever, be, and they hereby are perpetually restrained and enjoined from causing, participating in, or permitting, directly or indirectly, any act of lewdness, assignation, or prostitution in, about, or upon the property hereinafter described; and that the land, and buildings thereon, and its contents, all hereinafter described, be, and the same hereby are, declared a nuisance and forever enjoined as such; and that any and all acts of lewdness, assignation, or prostitution, or practice thereof and the resort thereto, in, about, and upon said property, be, and the same hereby are, prohibited and enjoined at any and all times."

Appellant was not a party to that suit, and it is admitted that she was never served with a copy of the final decree rendered therein. She contends that she was not properly subject to summary punishment for contempt: * * *

It may be stated as a general rule that one not a party to the injunction suit cannot be charged with contempt in violating the injunction in the absence of service upon him of the injunctional order or a showing that he had actual knowledge thereof. * * * To this general rule there is, however, an exception resting in sound reasons and supported by authority. Where the decree of injunction is not only in personam against the defendant in the injunction suit, but also operates in rem against specific property, or rather against a given illegal use of such property, the decree is a limitation upon the use of the property of which all subsequent owners, lessees, or occupants must take notice. In such a case the decree, if broad enough in its terms to enjoin all persons, is sufficient as a public record to impart constructive notice to all persons. The following cases so holding are based upon statutes declaring premises used for the unlawful sale of intoxicating liquors to be nuisances and authorizing perpetual injunctions to be entered against the use of such places for such purposes. The only essential difference between the statutes involved in our red light law is in the character of the use prohibited. [citations]

Appellant cites and relies upon the more recent Iowa case of Harris v. Hutchinson, 160 Iowa 149, 140 N.W. 830 urging that it limits the earlier Iowa decisions to cases in which the filing of a complaint affecting real estate operates under a general statute of that state as a notice of lis pendens, and therefrom argues that an injunctional decree binding real estate in this state cannot be effective as against third parties unless lis pendens was filed when the injunction suit was commenced. * * *

The sum of the decision in Harris v. Hutchinson is that a person employed as a bartender by the occupant of premises which had been enjoined from use for saloon purposes is not affected with constructive notice of the decree so as to be subject to a charge of contempt for violating it, and this simply because he is not a person dealing with the property itself, either as a purchaser or lessee or occupant. * * *

The exception to the rule requiring notice of the injunction in order to bind third persons is not peculiar to injunctions against liquor nuisances. Where the injunction is in rem affecting specific property, it binds, not only the parties to the suit, but persons in privity with such parties as subsequent purchasers and lessees. * * *

But we find it unnecessary to rest our decision entirely upon the constructive notice imposed by the decree itself. * * * We are satisfied, as was the trial court, that appellant had actual knowledge of the injunction prior to the commission of the acts which led to her arrest. An assistant prosecuting attorney testified that soon after her arrest he asked her if she did not know that the place had been red-lighted and the injunction issued, and that she answered, "Yes, I know the place was closed up and red-lighted last year." * * * Though appellant was not a party to the decree and was never served with a copy of it, her actual knowledge of the injunction renders her liable to punishment for contempt in violating it. * * *

The judgment is affirmed.

Note

Dobbs, Contempt of Court: A Survey, 56 Cornell L.Rev. 183, 257–258 (1971): "It seems undesirable to regulate conduct—as distinct from title—without having the parties whose conduct is regulated before the court. * * * The in rem theory would permit enforcement of the injunction by the contempt power even against persons who had no notice of the decree, since the res theory is that the whole world is bound by the court's control of the property. * * * Presumably, cases taking this extreme view would raise serious due process issues."

3. CONTEMPT AND MONEY

MALJAK v. MURPHY

Court of Appeals of Michigan, 1970.
22 Mich.App. 380, 177 N.W.2d 228.

DANHOF, JUDGE. * * * In 1958 Nicholas Begovich was arrested and charged with the crime of murder. While in custody he retained the services of defendant, Neil F. Murphy, an attorney licensed to practice in the State of Michigan. Defendant agreed to represent Nicholas Begovich for a fee of $10,000. Defendant initially received $2,500 and subsequently another $4000 making a $6500 advance on the fee. Prior to the trial Nicholas Begovich committed suicide.

* * * [His] administrator contended that the $6500 advance by Nicholas Begovich had not been earned and sought recovery in the amount of $4000. On March 10, 1959 [the] administrator commenced a common law action in assumpsit against the defendant in the Wayne county circuit court for $4000. This action was dismissed on motion by the trial court, the trial judge finding that the deceased had entered into a definite contract to pay the defendant $10,000 to represent him in the murder trial. Thus, by committing suicide the deceased had breached his express contract, and therefore, the administrator was barred from recovery. Plaintiff appealed. * * * [The Michigan] Supreme Court found that the lower court record did not support the finding of an express contract, but rather that plaintiff's declaration sought repayment of funds advanced on an implied contract. Thus, the matter was reversed and remanded for trial. On February 1, 1963 trial resulted in a verdict for the plaintiff, administrator, in the amount of $4000 plus costs.

On October 9, 1963 plaintiff, administrator, instituted supplementary proceedings in Wayne county circuit court seeking discovery of defendant's assets and to enjoin defendant from transferring or disposing of any property. On December 24, 1963, the circuit judge ordered the defendant to set up and maintain a set of books and accounts and granted the injunction.

[Various delaying procedural maneuvers are omitted.]

On September 26, 1967 an order was entered under GCR 1963, 908 compelling defendant to pay plaintiffs the sum of $4000 payable at the rate of $200 per month. * * * On February 7, 1969 a petition to show cause why the defendant should not be held in contempt of court was filed in circuit court, and on February 18, 1969 a hearing on this petition was held at which the defendant was found to be in contempt of court for failure to obey the order of September 26, 1967, and was ordered committed to the Wayne county jail for a period of 90 days.

Ordinarily the contempt powers of the court * * * may not be used to collect sums of money unless they cannot be collected by execution. But this defendant being an attorney is not an ordinary debtor. GCR 1963, 908 states as follows:

"Attorneys and counselors are officers of the courts of this State and as such are subject to the summary jurisdiction of such courts. The circuit court of the county in which an attorney resides or has an office has jurisdiction, on verified written complaint of any client, either in person or by attorney and after reasonable notice and hearing, to *make any order for the payment of money or for the performance of any act by the attorney which law and justice may require.* All courts of record have a like jurisdiction as to all such complaints regarding matters arising in suits or proceedings in such courts." (emphasis supplied)

As an attorney defendant bears a special responsibility which is placed upon him by reason of being licensed to practice law. Having received the money by reason of an attorney-client relationship, it having been found that he was unjustly enriched to the extent of $4000 and having failed to complete an appeal from the order of the court entered on September 26, 1967 he cannot now be heard to complain of punishment for having failed to comply with that order. * * *

While it is true that at the time that the September 26, 1967 order was entered the defendant had filed for bankruptcy and the trial court may have felt that execution was unavailable we do not deem this to be of importance, even though the bankruptcy proceedings were subsequently abandoned.

The defendant having been found to be in violation of a direct order of the circuit court, the court had power to punish the willful disobedience of this order by ordering the imprisonment of the defendant.

Affirmed with costs to the plaintiffs.

[Editors: This judgment was affirmed on appeal, 385 Mich. 210, 188 N.W.2d 539 (1971). In dissenting, Swainson, J., stated:]

We have here a contract dispute between two individuals. We are no longer dealing with the attorney and his client, or even the attorney and his client's administrator. The plaintiffs in this cause are successors in interest to the administrator of Mr. Begovich. The majority fails to state why this action should be treated differently from any other contract action. An attorney, merely because of his license to practice law, should not be treated differently from any other judgment debtor. His assets are clearly subject to attachment and execution, the same as any other judgment debtor. If the plaintiffs had attempted to use attachment and execution, and for some reason this was not possible, then a question might arise as to whether GCR 1963, 908, was applicable. But, that is not the situation we are faced with here. The plaintiffs have made absolutely no attempt to use the normal method of securing execution on a judgment.

Despite the assertions of the majority, defendant is being jailed for failure to pay a debt.

Notes

1. In the principal case, defendant unsuccessfully sought to take advantage of the rule that contempt cannot be used to enforce money decrees. This restriction is based on constitutional and statutory prohibitions against imprisonment for civil debt. In this context, "debt" is generally construed to mean a contractual obligation. As thus defined, decrees for the payment of alimony or child support and obligations owed by fiduciaries are not within the prohibition. Dobbs, Contempt of Court: A Survey, 56 Cornell L.Rev. 183, 270–72 (1971); Burdick & Richardson, Body

Attachment and Body Execution: Forgotten But Not Gone, 17 Wm. & Mary L.Rev. 543 (1976).

2. State law governing imprisonment for debt is followed in the federal court. See 28 U.S.C. § 2007; Fed.R.Civ.P. 64.

3. Although as indicated in Note 1, certain money decrees are enforceable by contempt because not debts, imprisonment is nevertheless permissible only for contumacious behavior. Inability to pay is a valid defense that contemnor may assert in the contempt proceeding. Shillitani v. United States, 384 U.S. 364, 371 (1966): "[T]he justification for coercive imprisonment as applied to civil contempt depends upon the ability of the contemnor to comply with the court's order."

The allocations of the burden of proving inability to comply may depend upon the classification of the contempt as civil or criminal. In Hicks v. Feiock, 485 U.S. 624, 637–38 (1988), a father was served with an order to show cause why he should not be held in contempt for failure to make court ordered child support payments. He was adjudged in contempt and sentenced to five days in jail on a total of five counts, but his jail sentence was suspended and he was placed on probation for three years; one of the conditions of probation was payment of the accumulated arrearages. On appeal, he contended that a state statute making proof of nonpayment prima facie evidence of contempt violated his constitutional right to due process by shifting the burden of proof of inability to pay to defendant. The California Court of Appeals annulled the contempt order.

The United States Supreme Court held that if the statutory presumption was applied to a criminal contempt "such a statute would violate the Due Process Clause because it would undercut the State's burden to prove guilt beyond a reasonable doubt. If applied in a civil proceeding, however, this particular statute would be constitutionally valid." The case was remanded for a determination of whether payment of arrearages would purge the defendant of past violation. If so, the contempt was classified as civil and the statutory presumption would not violate due process.

Compare King v. Department of Social and Health Services, 110 Wash.2d 793, 756 P.2d 1303, 1310 (1988), where defendant was imprisoned for refusing to bring his son to a dependency hearing. The court ruled that in a civil contempt, "the law presumes that one is capable of performing those actions required by the court. Thus, inability to comply is an affirmative defense. A contemnor has both the burden of production of inability to comply, as well as the burden of persuasion."

4. In Maljak v. Murphy, the court bases authority to enter the decree and enforce it by contempt on a Michigan statute applicable to attorneys. Other statutes authorize judgment creditors to institute proceedings in aid of execution. These statutes permit a creditor to conduct discovery proceedings against his debtor, to set aside fraudulent conveyances, to reach assets not subject to execution, and in some jurisdictions, to impose a continuing lien on wages. See 1 G. Glenn, Fraudulent Conveyances and Preferences, §§ 26–36 (1940). Since orders are entered only after a hearing to determine the debtor's ability to perform, they may be enforced by contempt even though the order requires the payment of money. Failure to comply is regarded as contumacious conduct. See Reeves v. Crownshield, 274 N.Y. 74, 8 N.E.2d 283 (1937); and Glenn, supra, § 35.

4. OTHER METHODS OF ENFORCEMENT

Where a defendant imprisoned in contempt proceedings remained obdurate, the court traditionally had available as additional enforcement devices writs of assistance and sequestration. The former directed a sheriff to put plaintiff into possession of property that was the subject of the dispute. The latter directed sequestrators to take possession of defendant's chattels and the rents and profits of his land. Where money decrees were involved, it became the practice to sell the chattels and apply the proceeds and the accrued rents to the satisfaction of the judgment.

Modern statutes authorizing the enforcement of judgments have largely supplanted these traditional equitable remedies. They continue to be recognized, however. A good example is Fed.R.Civ.P. 70. P. 167 supra. They are occasionally found useful in enforcing a court decree. The writ of assistance was authorized as the enforcement device used in the bitter and lengthy dispute over tribal lands between the Hopi and Navajo Indian tribes. See Hamilton v. Nakai, 453 F.2d 152 (9th Cir.1971). Writs of sequestration appear from time to time, usually in the dissolution of a marriage. See Hellwig v. Hellwig, 100 Ill.App.3d 452, 426 N.E.2d 1087 (1981). But the writ has also been found useful as a kind of receivership. See Hirko v. Hirko, 166 N.J.Super. 111, 398 A.2d 1353 (1979).

The writ of ne exeat is a kind of provisional civil arrest that is intended to prevent the defendant's threatened departure from the jurisdiction. Because the enforcement of equitable decrees was formerly personal, defendant could defeat and frustrate the plaintiff's claims by departing from the jurisdiction. Ne exeat insured the continued physical presence of the defendant until the suit was satisfactorily resolved.

Equitable decrees are now enforceable by execution and imprisonment for debt is abolished; but ne exeat is still recognized by the federal courts and by some states. Courts use it to collect support and alimony and federal taxes. See United States v. Shaheen, 445 F.2d 6 (7th Cir.1971); United States v. Union National Bank, 371 F.Supp. 763 (W.D.Pa.1974); United States v. Robbins, 235 F.Supp. 353 (E.D.Ark.1964); Beveridge v. Beveridge, 7 Conn.App. 11, 507 A.2d 502 (1986); Maudsley v. Navarro, 510 So.2d 1079 (Fla.App.1987); Gredone v. Gredone, 361 A.2d 176 (D.C.App.1976). Since ne exeat restrains liberty, the moving party has the burden of establishing that it is necessary to protect plaintiff's claim.

Courts of equity developed a number of procedural devices to aid parties whose claims or defenses were purely legal. Thus where a party might sustain severe hardship because of the necessity of asserting or defending numerous legal actions, the equity court granted relief by a bill of peace. Multiplicity was avoided by having the entire dispute over legal rights resolved in a single equity suit. Today the bill of peace has been largely supplanted by liberal joinder provisions and by the class action procedure in ordinary civil suits. However, *Norsica*, supra p. 174 and *Lim*, supra p. 180 afford lively examples of injunctions used as bills of peace to confine criminal litigation.

To aid a party confronted with conflicting claims to a single obligation, the equity courts developed a bill of interpleader. This procedure permitted a debtor to avoid litigation by turning the disputed property over to the court. The claimants were then required to litigate the right to the res among themselves. The classical bill of interpleader was hedged by a series of technical requirements that had little to do with the basic problem of overlapping claims to one obligation. Accordingly it has been largely superceded today by a simplified interpleader procedure. See Fed.R.Civ.P. 22; 28 U.S.C. § 1335; C. Wright, Federal Courts § 75 (4th ed. 1983).

The masters and commissioners traditionally employed by the Chancery Court in making its decrees effective persist in modern practice, though their appointment and authority is now governed by rule or statute. See Fed.R. Civ.P. 53. Masters are particularly useful in complex litigation involving extensive discovery or complicated accounting and in structural injunctions. In the litigation over the Texas prison system, the document defining the master's power covers more than five pages of the report. See Ruiz v. Estelle, 679 F.2d 1115, 1168–1172 (5th Cir.1982). Use of masters has its drawbacks, however. Unlike courts, they must be compensated by the parties themselves. See New York State Association for Retarded Children v. Carey, 631 F.2d 162 (2d Cir.1980). More importantly, not being Article III judges, the precise extent of their powers is a matter of doubt. See Pacemaker Diagnostic Clinic of America v. Instromedix, Inc., 712 F.2d 1305 (9th Cir.1983), reh'g granted, opinion withdrawn, 718 F.2d 971 (1983).

5. SPECIAL ENFORCEMENT PROBLEMS: THE ENFORCEMENT OF PUBLIC LAW THROUGH STRUCTURAL INJUNCTIONS

While our present study focuses on the remedies available in civil disputes between private citizens, the existence of the vast body of law dealing with the enforcement of public (i.e. constitutional) rights by injunctions should not be ignored. Beginning with school desegregation in the 1950s, the protection of the constitutional rights of citizens has been accomplished almost exclusively with injunctions. Indeed, damage verdicts for the victims of officially sanctioned school desegregation or malapportioned legislatures have not even been seriously suggested. Almost without discussion, the injunction has become the remedy of choice to protect constitutional rights. Elrod v. Burns, 427 U.S. 347, 373 (1976); Rendleman, The Inadequate Remedy at Law Prerequisite for an Injunction, 33 U.Fla.L.Rev. 346, 352–3 (1981). An intensive study of this litigation cannot be undertaken in this course, but we will provide a brief overview of the way courts use injunctions to redress oppressive and unconstitutional action by government agencies.

Some idea of how far we have traveled can be seen by remembering that a generation ago a leading casebook on Equity limited the entire reference to this subject to one decision. Dayton v. Hunter, 176 F.2d 108 (10th Cir.1949). That was a suit to restrain the warden of the federal penitentiary at Leavenworth from opening a prisoner's romantic letters to a young lady. The opinion was short and to the point: "But the control of federal penitentiaries is entrusted to the Attorney General of the United States and the Bureau of Prisons. A court of equity does not have power in a case of this kind to supervise through injunctive processes the conduct of a federal penitentiary or its discipline."

Today such a statement sounds hopelessly archaic. Courts discovered that prisoners possess certain constitutional rights that could be protected from infringement. As a result, today prisons and jails in more than half the states operate under judges' watchful eyes. Mercer v. Mitchell, 908 F.2d 763 (11th Cir.1990) (county jail). Judicial regulation has been continually expanded so that it now includes schools, mental institutions, and even police departments. Because these judicially mandated orders protect constitutional rights by "restructuring" governmental bureaucracies, they have been named "structural injunctions" by Professor Owen Fiss. The injunctions both prohibit specific acts and, more importantly, direct and manage the entire administrative operation of the affected institution.

Structural injunctions uniquely strain the legal process. The rules of procedure were designed for two party litigation aimed at resolving defined issues. Structural litigation, on the other hand, is unfocused, amorphous, and oriented toward the future. Moreover, such litigation raises questions about the legitimacy of such intrusive regulation by the judiciary. Underlying this extensive litigation is the issue of whether the judges in their eagerness to secure a more just society have usurped legislative, executive and state functions.

Even accepting structural injunctions as a legitimate exercise of judicial authority, their use raises a number of problems. Can a judge issue directions to the executive or the legislature? Can a judge insist on increased expenditures to maintain public institutions? Missouri v. Jenkins, 110 S.Ct. 1651, 1665 (1990): "[A] court order directing a local government body to levy its own taxes is plainly a judicial act within the power of a federal court." How can these orders be enforced? Given the parameters of our federalism, should a federal judge tell state and local officials how to run their institutions?

United States v. City of Yonkers, 856 F.2d 444 (2d Cir.1988), rev'd sub nom. Spallone v. United States, 493 U.S. 265 (1990). To combat discrimination in public housing, the federal judge imposed coercive fines on individual councilmembers. Under the doctrine of using the least possible contempt power to achieve obedience, the Supreme Court said the judge "should have proceeded with such contempt sanctions first against the city alone in order to secure compliance."

Benjamin v. Sielaff, 752 F.Supp. 140 (S.D.N.Y.1990). The city department of corrections failed to comply with an order regulating the housing of inmates. The judge imposed a sanction: a fine to be paid to each individual confined in a non-housing area.

Further complications result from the protracted nature of this litigation. Decades may pass, since structural change takes time. Vast administrative details are to be managed, necessitating masters, receivers, and monitors. Judges have neither the time nor the inclination to become involved in the tedious work of running a large institution.

A good place to begin thinking about the problems of the structural injunction is Ruiz v. Estelle, 679 F.2d 1115 (5th Cir.1982). This lengthy opinion considers Judge Justice's structural orders against the Texas Department of Corrections. It includes as Appendix A the Consent Decree and as Appendix B the Order of Reference appointing a Special Master. Judge Justice said on remand that "well over $1,000,000,000 will be required to repair the constitutional deficiencies demonstrated by measures that were not reversed on appeal." Ruiz v. Estelle, 553 F.Supp. 567, 593 (S.D.Tex.1982).

Structural injunctions are the subject of a large secondary literature. O. Fiss, The Civil Rights Injunction (1978), is the best place to begin. Chapter 9 of O. Fiss and D. Rendleman, Injunctions (1983), treats the Arkansas prison litigation extensively and contains a bibliography.

E. EQUITY TRIUMPHANT

SUBRIN, HOW EQUITY CONQUERED COMMON LAW: THE FEDERAL RULES OF CIVIL PROCEDURE IN HISTORICAL PERSPECTIVE

135 U.Pa.L.Rev. 909, 1000–02 (1987).

The major change in American civil procedure over the centuries is that equity procedures have swallowed those of common law. Common law procedure represented, among other things, an attempt to confine and define disputes so that the law could be applied to relatively few issues by lay juries. Field and the Code Commissioners, in the mid-nineteenth century, moved in the direction of equity practice, but continually emphasized the restrictions of procedure. Judicial discretion was an anathema.

The movement toward equity procedures reached fruition in the Federal Rules of Civil Procedure and structural change cases that take advantage of a procedural mentality based in equity. The Field Code was born in the political, social, and economic climates of the nineteenth century. It was grounded first in liberalism and then in laissez faire economics and Social Darwinism. Similarly, the Federal Rules represented a conservative impulse to empower judges as a bulwark against progressive attacks, which was joined later by a legal realist, anti-formalist, pro-regulatory, New Deal mentality. Commentators as divergent as Roscoe Pound, Thomas Shelton, and Charles Clark had overlapping procedural agendas and visions.

The idea of law application and rights vindication lost prominence for a number of reasons. Legal formalism and procedures necessary for rigorous law application obtained a bad name, particularly because the federal courts from about 1890 to 1935 used a formalized view of law to thwart social change. The legal realists raised doubts whether facts can ever be found, or whether law can ever be applied in a predictable manner. Much of the attack was against a formalistic, oracular view of law that allegedly used deductive logic to decide who had what rights and whether the government could constitutionally intervene. Legal realism, however, became skepticism about any type of legal categories and definitions. The answer of proceduralists such as Pound and Clark was to rely on expertise and judicial discretion. Give judges all the facts and a litigation package that includes every possible theory and every possibly interested party, and the judges—largely on an ad hoc basis—will figure out what the law and remedy should be.

As Dickens and others had known for centuries, equity procedure is slow and cumbersome, and has a high potential for arbitrariness. Over the years, those who have both stressed individual rights and liberties, and distrusted centralized power, have also criticized unbridled equity power. One has to be very careful here, for equity also had the admirable ability to act with a conscience and to create new rights. Such new rights, over time, tended to become defined and part of the more rigorous common law. Maitland and others warned that although equity and law worked well complementing each other, equity without common law had the capacity to be unwieldy or chaotic.

The modern procedural experience bears out this prophecy. Common law procedure, of course, had its own burdens. It is also obvious that many factors other than procedure have contributed to unwieldy litigation and undefined law. The point is that equity practice standing alone also has extreme burdens, and many of the complaints about modern law and contemporary court processes are related to equity's engorgement of common law practice.

Our infatuation with equity has helped us to forget the historic purpose of adjudication. Courts exist not only to resolve disputes, but to resolve them in a way that takes law seriously by trying to apply legal principles to the events that brought the parties to court. The total victory of equity process has caused us to forget the essence of civil adjudication: enabling citizens to have their legitimate expectancies and rights fulfilled. We are good at using equity process and thought to create new legal rights. We have, however, largely failed at defining rights and providing methods for their efficient vindication. The effort to defeat formalism so that society could move forward toward new ideas of social justice neglected the benefits of formalism once new rights had been created. The momentum toward case management, settlement, and alternative dispute resolution represents, for the most part, a continued failure to use predefined procedures in a manner that will try, however imperfectly, to deliver predefined law and rights.

We need judges who judge as well as judges who manage. We need oral testimony, oral argument, and juries to balance documents, judges, and magistrates. This is not a plea for arid formalism that over-emphasizes the value of form. Nor is it a plea for uncontrolled juries. This is a reminder that there is another rich tradition to draw upon, that the common law virtues of form and focus are necessary to help us develop methods that can realize our rights. It is a reminder that law and equity developed as companions, and that equity set adrift without the common law may in fact be Maitland's 'castle in the air.' The cure for our uncontrolled system does not require the elimination of equity. It does require that we revisit our common law heritage.

Chapter 4

UNJUST ENRICHMENT AND RESTITUTIONARY REMEDIES

A. GENERAL PRINCIPLES

KOSSIAN v. AMERICAN NATIONAL INSURANCE CO.

Court of Appeal of California, Fifth District, 1967.
254 Cal.App.2d 647, 62 Cal.Rptr. 225.

STONE, ASSOCIATE JUSTICE. On February 19, 1964, fire destroyed a portion of the Bakersfield Inn, owned by one Reichert. At the time, the property was subject to a first deed of trust in which defendant was the beneficiary. Pursuant to the requirements of the deed of trust, defendant's interest in the property was protected by policies of fire insurance. On March 16, 1964, Reichert, as owner in possession, entered into a written contract with plaintiff whereby plaintiff agreed to clean up and remove the debris from the fire damaged portion of the Inn for the sum of $18,900. Defendant had no knowledge of the execution of the agreement between plaintiff and Reichert.

Plaintiff commenced work in the middle of March 1964, and completed it in early April. During the entire time work was in progress Reichert was in possession of the premises as owner, although defendant caused a notice of Reichert's default under the deed of trust to be filed four days after the contract for demolition was entered into between plaintiff and Reichert. The record does not reflect that plaintiff had actual knowledge of the notice of default until after the work was completed.

Some time after plaintiff had fully performed the contract, Reichert filed a petition in bankruptcy. The trustee in bankruptcy abandoned the premises comprising the Bakersfield Inn, together with any interest in the four fire insurance policies up to the amount of $424,000. Each policy contained a provision insuring against the cost of cleaning up and removing debris caused by fire damage.

Following abandonment of the policies by the trustee in bankruptcy, Reichert and his wife assigned their interest in them to defendant in accordance with the terms of the deed of trust. Defendant submitted proofs of loss, claiming a total of $160,000, including the sum of $18,000 as the estimated cost for recovering and cleaning up debris. These claims were rejected by the carriers; negotiations followed; the compromise figure of $135,620 was agreed upon and this amount paid to defendant. We do not have an itemization of the adjusted claims of loss upon which the compromised loss settlement was made, so that the record is not clear as to what part of the $18,900 cost of debris removal defendant received. It is clear, however, that the insurance payment included at least a part of the cost of debris removal and demolition.

Defendant demonstrates, by a careful analysis of the facts, that there was no direct relationship between plaintiff and defendant in regard to either the work performed on the property after the fire or in relation to the fire insurance policies. The contract for debris removal was between plaintiff and Reichert, and defendant did not induce plaintiff, directly or indirectly, to enter into that contract. Plaintiff had no lien against the property resulting from his work, and if he had such a lien it would have been wiped out by defendant's foreclosure of its first deed of trust.

Had the circumstances been simply that defendant, by foreclosure, took the property improved by plaintiff's debris removal, there would be a benefit conferred upon defendant by plaintiff, but no unjust enrichment. It is the additional fact that defendant made a claim to the insurance carriers for the value of work done by plaintiff that is the nub of the case.

Defendant argues that plaintiff was not a party to the insurance contracts, while defendant had a contract right to collect indemnity for losses resulting from the fire, including the debris removal cost. This contract right was embodied in the insurance policies. Defendant relies upon Russell v. Williams, 58 Cal.2d 487, 490, 24 Cal.Rptr. 859, 861, 374 P.2d 827, 829 where it is said:

"It is a principle of long standing that a policy of fire insurance does not insure the property covered thereby, but is a personal contract indemnifying the insured against loss resulting from the destruction of or damage to his interest in that property. [citations] This principle gives rise to the supplemental rule that, in the absence of a special contract, the proceeds of a fire insurance policy are not a substitute for the property the loss of which is the subject of indemnity."

Defendant says it made no agreement, express or implied, with plaintiff that it would pay for the debris removal or that any part of the insurance proceeds would be applied for that purpose. Therefore, concludes defendant, there being no privity of relationship between it and plaintiff, and no fraud or deceit alleged or proved, defendant has the right to the property benefitted by plaintiff's work and labor expended in removing the debris and to the insurance payments as well.

Plaintiff makes no claim to the insurance "fund" upon the ground he relied thereon similar to the reliance of a mechanic or materialman that forms the basis of an equitable claim to a building fund. He relies upon the basic premise that defendant should not be allowed to have the fruits of plaintiff's labor and also the money value of that labor. This, of course, is a simplified

pronouncement of the doctrine of unjust enrichment, a theory which can, in some instances, have validity without privity of relationship. The most prevalent implied-in-fact contract recognized under the doctrine of unjust enrichment is predicated upon a relationship between the parties from which the court infers an intent. However, the doctrine also recognizes an obligation *imposed* by law regardless of the intent of the parties. In these instances there need be no relationship that gives substance to an implied intent basic to the "contract" concept, rather the obligation is imposed because good conscience dictates that under the circumstances the person benefitted should make reimbursement. * * *

Plaintiff's claim does not rest upon a quasi-contract implied in fact, but upon an equitable obligation imposed by law. It is true that defendant's right to the insurance payment was a contract right embodied in the policies of insurance; nevertheless the indemnity payment was based in part upon a claim of loss that did not exist because plaintiff had already remedied the loss by his work for which he was not paid.

We are cited no California cases that are close aboard, and independent research reveals none. Lack of precedent applicable to the facts peculiar to this case is not surprising, however, as the authors of the Restatement recognize that the essential nature of equity cases concerned with problems of restitution makes definitive precedent unlikely. We are guided by the "Underlying Principles" delineated in the Restatement on Restitution:

> "The rules stated in the Restatement of this Subject depend for their validity upon certain basic assumptions in regard to what is required by justice in the various situations. In this Topic, these are stated in the form of principles. They cannot be stated as rules since either they are too indefinite to be of value in a specific case or, for historical or other reasons, they are not universally applied. They are distinguished from rules in that they are intended only as general guides for the conduct of the courts * * *."

The governing principle is expressed in the opening sentence of the Restatement on Restitution, as follows:

> "The Restatement of this Subject deals with situations in which one person is accountable to another on the ground that otherwise he would unjustly benefit or the other would unjustly suffer loss."

The question, simply stated, is whether in a jurisdiction that recognizes the equitable doctrine of unjust enrichment one party should be indemnified twice for the same loss, once in labor and materials and again in money, to the detriment (forfeiture) of the party who furnished the labor and materials. We conclude that the doctrine of unjust enrichment is applicable to the facts of this case, and that plaintiff is entitled to reimbursement out of the insurance proceeds paid defendant for work done by plaintiff.

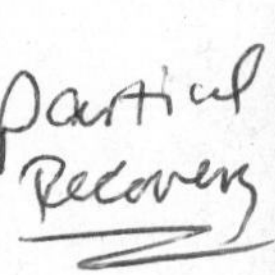

[I]t is clear that defendant, in addition to taking over the property which plaintiff cleared of debris, also received indemnity insurance payments covering at least part of the cost for clearing that property of debris. The amount can be made certain by a trial on the merits, and if it develops that defendant recovered only a part of the cost for debris removal, this fact does not preclude a partial recovery by plaintiff. We learn from the Restatement.

> "Where a person is entitled to restitution from another because the other, without tortious conduct, has received a benefit, the measure of recovery for the benefit thus received is the value of what was received * * *."

Thus, to the extent defendant received insurance for debris removal performed by plaintiff, plaintiff should recover. If defendant received less than the value of plaintiff's work, as defendant seems to contend, then plaintiff should recover *pro tanto.*

The judgment is reversed.

Notes

A Preliminary Note: The Substantive Basis for Restitution.

1. *Enrichment.* Before being held liable to make restitution defendant must have received a "benefit." What will qualify as a benefit for restitution is a technical remedial determination. The benefit may not exist in a form that a banker would think constitutes good collateral for a loan. In fact, the defendant may find himself "enriched" by a "benefit" he may personally regard as neutral or even somewhat detrimental. Plaintiff may dig a hole in defendant's ground or discharge an obligation that defendant never intended to pay.

2. *Origin of Benefit.* The defendant's benefit may be plaintiff's direct loss. Sometimes however, defendant's benefit may originate with a third party. When this happens a fundamental divergence in the substantive basis of unjust enrichment may appear. One approach seems to have emerged from the quasi-contract actions developed in the common law courts; it tends to insist that defendant's "benefit" (the plus) be acquired at plaintiff's expense (the minus). The older, more rigid, decisions might even require an equivalence of the plus and minus.

The other approach is characteristic of the equity courts. It concentrates primarily on defendant's "enrichment" and de-emphasizes the idea that the defendant's enrichment must have originated with the plaintiff. If defendant acquired a benefit from a third party that would have gone to plaintiff had it not been diverted, this enrichment may be characterized as at plaintiff's expense.

But consider again the events in the principal case. The alleged enrichment appears to be a portion of some fire insurance proceeds. Were the proceeds diverted from the plaintiff? What is the insurance company's position? Could it be argued that the defendant was "enriched" at *its* expense since the insured had already been indemnified?

The Louisiana courts approach unjust enrichment differently. Following French law, Louisiana law requires an enrichment, an impoverishment, and a connection between the enrichment and the impoverishment. See Barton Land Co. v. Dutton, 541 So.2d 382 (La.App.1989), cert. denied, 543 So.2d 23 (La.1989). "Impoverishment" has been imported from the civil law into restitution in common law states. D.C. Trautman Co. v. Fargo Excavating Co., 380 N.W.2d 644 (N.D.1986).

3. *Enrichment Must Be Unjust: Donors and Officious Intermeddlers.* Enrichment by itself will not trigger restitution. It must be unjust. To make headway here, we set aside philosophical conundrums beclouding that word and leave to later the fraud, breach of contract, coercion, mistake, change of position, etc. that tip the scales.

Two kinds of restitution plaintiffs will be disqualified at the outset, for they confer enrichment that is not considered to be "unjust."

a. Plaintiff may have conferred the benefit as a gift. Courts deny the genuine "Good Samaritan" restitution not merely because he acted voluntarily, but specifically because crass commercial purposes will not be ascribed to detract from the high moral quality of his conduct.

Turner v. Unification Church, 473 F.Supp. 367, 378 (D.R.I.1978). Plaintiff sought recovery on a quantum meruit theory for services rendered for the Unification Church. The court denied restitution because it found that plaintiff performed the services "without expecting any reward other than the creation of a better world."

b. The plaintiff, despite otherwise good reasons for conferring a benefit, must not have acted officiously.

4. Laycock, The Scope and Significance of Restitution, 67 Tex.L.Rev. 1277 (1989).

KNAUS v. DENNLER

Appellate Court of Illinois, Fifth District, 1988.
170 Ill.App.3d 746, 525 N.E.2d 207.

JUSTICE WELCH delivered the opinion of the court. Plaintiffs appeal from a judgment of the circuit court of St. Clair County dismissing their complaint seeking proportionate sharing of expenses between owners of adjoining lakefront properties for the repair of the dam which retains the lake around which the properties are situated.

In March 1982, plaintiffs purchased real property known as Lot 1 of the Fifth Addition to Lakewood Place. The lot purchased by plaintiffs abutted a lake, and included approximately one-half to two-thirds of the earthen dam which retained the lake. The remaining portion of the dam was situated on the lakefront property adjoining plaintiffs' property immediately to the south.

In June 1982, plaintiffs discovered one or two small holes developing in the portion of the dam situated on their property. Plaintiffs were aware at the time of purchase that their lot included a portion of the earthen dam, but, according to the record, plaintiffs made no inquiry as to the condition of the dam; nor did the previous owner disclose at any time prior to the closing of the sale that the dam had required repairs for leakage during the seller's ownership.

Prompted by interest in repairing the leaking dam, plaintiffs contacted the United States Department of Agricultural Soil Conservation and an independent excavating contractor. At plaintiffs' request, the excavating contractor visited plaintiffs' property in July 1982 and inspected the dam. Later in July or early in August of 1982, a heavy rain resulted in an enlarging of the holes in the dam. Again the excavating contractor inspected the dam at plaintiffs' request. On August 9 or 12, 1982, plaintiffs arranged a meeting with other owners of property abutting the lake so that a decision could be made as to what procedures should be taken to repair the dam. Although the record is replete with conflicting testimony pertaining to what transpired at the meeting and whether a unanimous decision among lakefront property owners was attained, repairs began at plaintiffs' request on August 18, 1982. A second property owners meeting followed on August 19, 1982, at which, according to the record, differences of opinion resulted in the meeting becoming "heated."

At the second meeting, the excavator recommended that the entire dam be reconstructed so as to comply with the accepted standards for dam construction and maintenance. The Smedleys, owners of the portion of the dam not owned by the Knauses, objected to their portion of the dam being reconstructed, and advised the excavator to stay off their property. The excavating work, reconstructing only the portion of the dam situated on the Knaus' property, was completed on September 11, 1982. The total cost for the excavating was $11,920.51. An additional $1,360 was expended for landscaping and repairs necessary to cosmetically finish the reconstructed portion of the dam and restore the asphalt driveway and surrounding area which had suffered superficial damages resulting from the traverse of large trucks transporting excavating equipment to and from the job site.

The underlying law suit was filed originally on June 6, 1983, seeking to recover from the named defendants proportionate shares of the expenses incurred in reconstructing the dam. While some lakefront property owners had contributed money to help cover the costs, the defendants had refused to do so. * * * On April 11, 1985, the court dismissed counts one, two, and three of plaintiffs' second amended complaint, and entered judgment in favor of defendants. * * *

Counts two and three of plaintiffs' complaint claim that the defendants breached an implied contract. In count two, the alleged implied contract arose out of the common law riparian rights of property owners. Under common law, riparian rights of property owners abutting the same body of water are equal, and no such property owner may exercise its riparian rights in such a manner so as to prevent the exercise of the same rights by other similarly situated property owners. Therefore, according to plaintiffs, there existed an implied contract in law between the plaintiffs and defendants to maintain the lake, including the dam, so that all lakefront property owners could continue exercising their riparian rights.

Count three alleged that an implied contract arose out of language contained in the plat depicting the lakefront property situated around the lake here in issue. The plat states, *inter alia,* "[t]hat the purchaser of any lot in this subdivision shall acquire the fee simple title to the entire area of the lot. However, the right to use that part of the area of said lot comprising the lake area (*i.e.* within the "Water Line"), shall be reserved for the joint use of all the present or future owners of lots in this subdivision." Therefore, according to plaintiffs, there existed an implied contract between plaintiffs and defendants to maintain the dam of the lake and be mutually responsible for costs incurred for any necessary repairs. We find neither count two nor count three sufficient to state a cause of action, and therefore the trial court's dismissal of these counts was proper.

Illinois courts recognize an action derived from the doctrine referred to as quasi contract, contract implied in law, or *quantum meruit,* the obligations of which may be enforced independent of any agreement between the parties or of their personal intentions. An implied contract is one which reason and justice dictate, and is founded on the equitable doctrine of unjust enrichment. Recovery under an unjust enrichment theory requires a showing that the defendant has voluntarily accepted a benefit which it would be inequitable for him to retain without payment since the law implies a promise to pay compensation when value of services are knowingly accepted. [citation]

In the present case, the record indicates that plaintiffs attempted to enter into a written agreement with the defendants binding defendants to pay a portion of the cost of repairing the dam. Defendants refused to enter such an agreement, and trial testimony indicates that defendants Smedley informed plaintiffs prior to the initiation of repairs that defendants Smedley did not consider themselves responsible for the cost of repairs performed on plaintiffs' property. Defendants Dennler refused to sign any agreement proposed by the plaintiffs, and became upset with the extensiveness of repairs once undertaken. Defendant Woolard did not express objection to the repairs, but did not sign the agreement offered by plaintiffs, and stated that she was not in a position financially to contribute to the cost of repairs.

Because plaintiffs instructed that repairs be commenced notwithstanding defendants' opposition and lack of willingness to enter the agreement proposed by plaintiffs, we are unable to find that defendants voluntarily accepted a benefit, as required to establish unjust enrichment under Premier Electrical Construction Company v. LaSalle National Bank (1984), 132 Ill.App.3d 485, 87 Ill.Dec. 721, 477 N.E.2d 1249. Instead, because the benefit was conferred in the face of opposition and disinterest, it appears to fall into the category of "officiously" or "gratuitously" conferred benefit for which quasi-contractual relief is not available in Illinois. * * *

Finally, plaintiffs contend that the trial court's judgment in favor of defendants Smedley in the amount of $130 against the plaintiffs for trespass was against the manifest weight of the evidence. Trespass is the invasion of exclusive possession and physical condition of land. (Colwell Systems, Inc. v. Henson (1983), 117 Ill.App.3d 113, 116, 72 Ill.Dec. 636, 639, 452 N.E.2d 889, 892.) In the present case, plaintiffs hired the excavator to repair the dam, and in repairing the dam the excavator's machinery invaded the physical condition of defendants Smedley's property. Plaintiffs' defense based on consent is of no merit as plaintiff Diane Knaus testified that shortly after the excavation began defendant Frank Smedley stated that he did not want the excavator on the Smedley property. * * * Therefore, we find that the trial court's finding in favor of defendants Smedley on their counterclaim for trespass damages is not against the manifest weight of the evidence and will stand.

For the foregoing reasons, the judgment of the circuit court of St. Clair County is hereby affirmed.

Affirmed.

Notes

1. Numerous opinions deny restitution to someone who makes repairs or improvements that benefit the defendant's property where defendant refused to pay or participate in the project. Ranquist v. Donahue, 710 F.Supp. 1160 (N.D.Ill.1989); Schmeckpeper v. Koertje, 222 Neb. 800, 388 N.W.2d 51 (1986); Board of Directors v. Western National Bank, 139 Ill.App.3d 542, 487 N.E.2d 974 (1985).

2. In Norton v. Haggett, 117 Vt. 130, 132–33, 85 A.2d 571, 573–74 (1952), a bank held the defendant's note secured by a mortgage. Plaintiff had had some personal disagreements with the defendants and was ill disposed toward them. Apparently intending to purchase the note, the plaintiff walked into the bank and gave a check for the amount of the note. The bank stamped the note paid with the comment "You junk men must be making plenty of money in order to be paying someone else's mortgage." The court denied plaintiff's request for restitution: "His good faith was apparently questionable. He had no motive of self-interest; he was not protecting any interest which he had or thought he had; nor was he discharging any duty which he owed or thought he owed. * * * No protection is deserved by one who intermeddles by paying another's debt either without reason or to secure right against the debtor without the consent of the creditor."

See also, Bank of Nova Scotia v. Bloch, 533 F.Supp. 1356 (D.V.I.1982) (officious payment on a mortgage debt, restitution denied).

3. In Martin v. Little, Brown and Co., 304 Pa.Super. 424, 450 A.2d 984 (1981), plaintiff had volunteered information about plagiarism of a book published by defendant. The information ultimately resulted in a successful action for copyright infringement. Plaintiff then sought one-third of the award. Finding that plaintiff was "purely a volunteer," the court dismissed.

See also Mehl v. Norton, 201 Minn. 203, 275 N.W. 843 (1937). Tenant holding over despite efforts to evict him, planted a crop which eventually the landlord harvested. Restitution was denied.

For the overeager workman, see Zaleski v. Congregation of Sacred Hearts, 256 A.2d 424 (D.C.App.1969).

4. For a general discussion see Dawson, The Self–Serving Intermeddler, 87 Harv.L.Rev. 1409 (1974); McCamus, The Self–Serving Intermeddler and the Law of Restitution, 16 Osgoode Hall L.J. 515 (1978).

5. *Benefits Incidentally Conferred.* A homeowner may make extensive improvements and increase the market value of neighbors' properties. A mineowner may, at considerable expense, drain flooded shafts, coincidentally lowering the water level in the adjacent mines. Neither may have had charitable motives in conferring benefits, but neither has a restitutionary remedy.

The ill-starred Bakersfield Inn produced another legal action before burning down. Griffith Co. v. Hofues, 201 Cal.App.2d 502, 19 Cal.Rptr. 900, 903–04 (1962). In 1959, the hotel was in probate. The probate court approved a sale to the Nelson–Smith Hotel Company. An escrow was opened, conditioned upon performance by the buyer. Shortly thereafter the buyer entered into possession and contracted with the plaintiff to repave the driveways and parking lots. Plaintiff performed, but did not perfect a mechanic's or materialman's lien. The buyer defaulted against both the plaintiff and the seller of the hotel; the probate court set aside the decree of confirmation; and the estate had to retake possession. Plaintiff sued the administrator:

"The only theory upon which the recovery is sought to be sustained is unjust enrichment.

"No California case has been cited by either plaintiff or defendant in which the factual situation is similar to that here involved. Our research has not developed a case of this state which is closely parallel. * * *

"It is contended that the defendant acquiesced to, and had knowledge of, and accepted the benefit of, the services, and it is therefore claimed that he should be compelled to pay for them, whether they were authorized or whether he wanted them or not. We do not think this proposition is sound. The work, itself, was done after Nelson took possession of the inn on August 17, 1959. It was done by his authority. Nelson was in as purchaser and defendant could not then reasonably foresee that the total purchase price would not be paid and he would be compelled to regain possession. He was therefore not in a position to forbid the work going on. He was not called upon to forbid or otherwise restrain it. * * *

"We are of the opinion that plaintiff does not have a cause of action against this defendant. It saw fit to accept employment from the Nelson–Smith Hotel Company, which was admittedly without authority from this defendant. It dealt with Smith, Nelson's representative, without ascertaining his authority to bind the owners of the inn, and it is fundamental that one so dealing does so at his peril. He is bound to inquire and to know if the authority exists. This the plaintiff failed to do. * * * It went ahead with the work relying on an express written contract with Nelson–Smith Hotel Company, expecting that its services would be paid for by that company. It must now look to that company for payment.

"Under the circumstances here, plaintiff may not recover from this defendant, and the judgment must, therefore, be reversed.

"Although our conclusion may seem harsh to this plaintiff, it must be remembered that one situated as was the plaintiff in this case is amply protected by the law. It has its remedy against the Nelson–Smith Hotel Company. Further, it was protected by appropriate sections of the Code of Civil Procedure applicable to liens of mechanics and materialmen. Apparently plaintiff did not choose to file and perfect a lien against the land, but elected to seek a recovery on the theory of unjust enrichment which would be enforceable against the general assets of defendant. Plaintiff chose its weapons in the court below and is now bound by the result of its choice."

6. As a condition of County approval for a new subdivision, a developer was required to construct an access road to an adjoining landowner's property. The developer sought restitution from the adjoining landowner for part of the construction cost; it claimed the defendant-landowner was unjustly enriched. In denying relief, the court ruled that defendant was simply the incidental beneficiary of the developer's plan to develop its own land. Dinosaur Development, Inc. v. White, 216 Cal.App.3d 1310, 265 Cal.Rptr. 525 (1989).

A lawyer tried to collect a fee from a hospital that benefited from the lawyer's successful effort to compel an insurance company to pay its insured's hospital bills. The lawyer met a fate similar to the developer above. Lynch v. Deaconess Medical Center, 113 Wash.2d 162, 776 P.2d 681 (1989).

7. Coffee Pot Plaza Partnership v. Arrow Air Conditioning, 412 So.2d 883 (Fla.Dist.Ct.App.1982). A tenant contracted with plaintiff to repair equipment located in a leased store. The lease was terminated for failure to pay rent. A mechanics lien was not available, and plaintiff was unable to assert a possessory lien because of the size of the equipment. The court denied plaintiff's action against the landlord to recover for unjust enrichment.

8. Green Quarries, Inc. v. Raasch, 676 S.W.2d 261 (Mo.Ct.App.1984). A general contractor failed to pay a subcontractor and became bankrupt. The subcontractor, who could not satisfactorily establish a statutory mechanics' lien, sued the owner of the property in quasi-contract for the value of the improvements. He did not allege that the owner had not paid the general contractor. The owner prevailed because the complaint omitted an essential element of unjust enrichment.

BAILEY v. WEST

Supreme Court of Rhode Island, 1969.

105 R.I. 61, 249 A.2d 414.

PAOLINO, JUSTICE. This is a civil action wherein the plaintiff alleges that the defendant is indebted to him for the reasonable value of his services rendered in connection with the feeding, care and maintenance of a certain race horse named "Bascom's Folly" from May 3, 1962 through July 3, 1966. The case was tried before a justice of the superior court sitting without a jury and resulted in a decision for the plaintiff for his cost of boarding the horse for the five months immediately subsequent to May 3, 1962, and for certain expenses incurred by him in trimming its hoofs. [Defendant appeals.]

In late April 1962, defendant, accompanied by his horse trainer, went to Belmont Park in New York to buy race horses. On April 27, 1962, defendant purchased "Bascom's Folly" from a Dr. Strauss and arranged to have the horse shipped to Suffolk Downs in East Boston, Massachusetts. Upon its arrival defendant's trainer discovered that the horse was lame, and so notified defendant, who ordered him to reship the horse by van to the seller at Belmont Park. The seller refused to accept delivery at Belmont on May 3, 1962, and thereupon, the van driver, one Kelly, called defendant's trainer and asked for further instructions. Although the trial testimony is in conflict as to what the trainer told him, it is not disputed that on the same day Kelly brought "Bascom's Folly" to plaintiff's farm where the horse remained until July 3, 1966, when it was sold by plaintiff to a third party.

While "Bascom's Folly" was residing at his horse farm, plaintiff sent bills for its feed and board to defendant at regular intervals. According to testimony elicited from defendant at the trial, the first such bill was received by him some two or three months after "Bascom's Folly" was placed on plaintiff's farm. He also stated that he immediately returned the bill to plaintiff with the notation that he was not the owner of the horse nor was it sent to plaintiff's farm at his request. * * *

We hold that there was no mutual agreement and "intent to promise" between the plaintiff and defendant so as to establish a contract "implied in fact" for defendant to pay plaintiff for the maintenance of this horse. From the time Kelly delivered the horse to him plaintiff knew there was a dispute as to its ownership, and his subsequent actions indicated he did not know with whom, if anyone, he had a contract. After he had accepted the horse, he made inquiries as to its ownership and, initially, and for sometime thereafter, sent his bills to both defendant and Dr. Strauss, the original seller.[1] * * *

The defendant's second contention is that, even assuming the trial justice was in essence predicating defendant's liability upon a quasi-contractual theory, his decision is still unsupported by competent evidence and is clearly erroneous. * * *

The key question raised by this appeal with respect to the establishment of a quasi-contract is whether or not plaintiff was acting as a "volunteer" at the time he accepted the horse for boarding at his farm. There is a long line of authority which has clearly enunciated the general rule that "* * * if a performance is rendered by one person without any request by another, it is very unlikely that this person will be under a legal duty to pay compensation." 1 A Corbin, Contracts § 234.

The Restatement of Restitution, § 2 (1937) provides: "A person who officiously confers a benefit upon another is not entitled to restitution therefor." Comment *a* in the above-mentioned section states in part as follows:

> "Policy ordinarily requires that a person who has conferred a benefit * * * by way of giving another services * * * should not be permitted to require the other to pay therefor, unless the one conferring the benefit had a valid reason for so doing. A person is not required to deal with another unless he so desires and, ordinarily, a person should not be required to become an obligor unless he so desires."

Applying those principles to the facts in the case at bar it is clear that plaintiff cannot recover. * * * The defendant's attorney asked plaintiff if he had any conversation with Kelly at that time, and plaintiff answered in substance that he had noticed that the horse was very lame and that Kelly had told him: "That's why they wouldn't accept him at Belmont Track." The plaintiff also testified that he had inquired of Kelly as to the ownership of "Bascom's Folly," and had been told that "Dr. Strauss made a deal and that's all I know." It further appears from the record that plaintiff acknowledged

1. [Editors' footnote.] The defendant was held liable to Dr. Strauss for the purchase price of the horse. Strauss v. West, 100 R.I. 388, 216 A.2d 366 (1966).

receipt of the horse by signing a uniform livestock bill of lading, which clearly indicated on its face that the horse in question had been consigned by defendant's trainer not to plaintiff, but to Dr. Strauss's trainer at Belmont Park. Knowing at the time he accepted the horse for boarding that a controversy surrounded its ownership, plaintiff could not reasonably expect remuneration from defendant, nor can it be said that defendant acquiesced in the conferment of a benefit upon him. * * *

It is our judgment that the plaintiff was a mere volunteer who boarded and maintained "Bascom's Folly" at his own risk and with full knowledge that he might not be reimbursed for expenses he incurred incident thereto.

Judgment for the defendant.

Notes

1. *Exceptions to the Rule Disallowing Restitution to a Volunteer.* For policy reasons arising from a sensible concern to preserve life, health, and property, the volunteer is not entirely discouraged. If she is not officious and is not acting gratuitously, the volunteer is allowed restitution for necessaries furnished minors, destitutes, the mentally disabled, and similar examples. The right of restitution exists despite defendant's direct refusal to assume contract liability to the plaintiff before she acts. Restatement of Restitution § 113 (1937). Restitution is allowed for services necessary to protect life or health in emergencies, when the person legally liable cannot be located quickly. Recovery under the emergency exception is limited to the bare essentials. Moreover the requirement of an intent to charge restricts recovery for medical services to licensed practitioners. Restatement of Restitution § 114.

Restitution for the reasonable value of medical services directly performed on a patient has been allowed, Restatement of Restitution § 116; but the conditions are restrictive. An emergency must exist. The patient must perforce be unconscious, or at least be mentally distraught, otherwise the substantive basis of recovery will rest on contract; the plaintiff must intend to charge and have no reason to believe that the patient would decline the services.

Finally, a volunteer may under certain circumstances obtain restitution for services and expenditures in caring for another's property. Restatement of Restitution § 117. To obviate officiousness, the possession of the property must be lawfully the plaintiff's. This limits recovery to persons like bailees who receive goods from non-owners for shipment or custody, finders, and persons caring for property following the death of the owner. Restitution is limited to expenditures incurred before contact with the owner, and to amounts essential to preserve and not to improve. The plaintiff must believe that the benefit will be acceptable, and the owner must actually accept the benefit. In Bailey v. West the agister's claim for the care of "Bascom's Folly" may have faltered at this stage.

2. Good Samaritans' quasi-contract claims for compensation for emergency services have received kindly treatment.

Peninsular & Oriental Steam Navigation Co. v. Overseas Oil Carriers, 553 F.2d 830 (2d Cir.1977). The court rejected a long standing admiralty rule that rescuing lives at sea ("pure life salvage") merited moral approbation, but no pecuniary award. Instead it allowed reimbursement to the owner of a vessel that altered its course to aid a stricken seaman aboard a ship without a medical staff. The court concluded that the reasonable value of the services, measured by the expenses incurred in changing the ship's course, was a proper amount to recover regardless of the actual benefit conferred. The claim was against the ship owner, not the seaman who fortunately recovered. What was the actual benefit?

Tipper v. Great Lakes Chemical Co., 281 So.2d 10, 14 (Fla.1973). The defendant's truck carrying dangerous chemicals was wrecked on the road far from the company's headquarters. The local authorities immediately called in the claimant, a qualified expert. He responded successfully to the emergency call, but incurred chemical burns. He applied for workers' compensation; but the State Commission turned him down because he was not employed by the company and had not even been contacted by it. The Supreme Court of Florida reversed, finding that there was an "implied in law" employment contract, citing the Restatement of Restitution § 112, by analogy. "This man, whose praiseworthy conduct resulted in personal injuries to him * * * is entitled to more, under Florida law, than a pat on the back and the label: 'Admirable Volunteer.' "

Florida Power & Light v. Allis–Chalmers Corp., 752 F.Supp. 434 (S.D.Fla.1990), aff'd, 893 F.2d 1313 (11th Cir.1990). Plaintiff sought restitution of costs incurred in clearing up a hazardous waste site. The court denied relief. Unlike defendant in *Tipper,* this defendant had not created and was not responsible for the contamination, and it was not benefited by plaintiff's efforts.

B. THE COMMON LAW REMEDIES TO PREVENT UNJUST ENRICHMENT: QUASI–CONTRACTS

Introductory Note

Restitution may be accomplished either by returning the benefit in specie or by awarding an equivalent monetary value. Remedies of the former type include replevin, ejectment, and, in equity, the mandatory injunction. Specific restitution remedies will be examined in later chapters of this book. Remedies of the latter type are both legal and equitable. In equity, substitutionary relief is afforded by the constructive trust, equitable lien, and subrogation. For the moment we are concerned with monetary restitution in the law courts, and our attention is focused on indebitatus assumpsit.

By default, historical accident, and a judicial *tour de force,* indebitatus assumpsit became the medium of monetary restitution at common law. The critical decision is Lord Mansfield's in Moses v. MacFerlan which truly merits the cliché, a "landmark of the law."

MOSES v. MACFERLAN (or MACPHERLAN)

Kings Bench, 1760.
1 W.Bl. 219, 96 Eng.Rep. 120.
2 Burr 1005, 97 Eng.Rep. 676.

[FROM THE BLACKSTONE REPORT] Moses had four notes of one Chapman Jacob, dated 11th July, 1757, value 30s. each. Macpherlan, 7th November, 1758, prevailed upon Moses to indorse these notes to him, upon an express written agreement to indemnify Moses against all consequences of such indorsement, and that no suit should be brought against Moses the indorser, but only against Jacob the drawer. Notwithstanding which, Macpherlan brought four actions in the Court of Conscience[1] upon these very notes against Moses;

1. [Courts of Conscience were local law courts of limited jurisdiction over small claims. They were supplanted in 1846 by the county courts. Editors.]

and, upon trial of the first, the commissioners refused to go into any evidence of this agreement; whereupon the plaintiff recovered, and the defendant paid in the whole 6£. And now Moses brought *indebitatus assumpsit* against Macpherlan for money had and received to his use, and obtained a verdict for 6£., subject to the opinion of this Court.

On the argument, Mansfield, C.J., doubted if the action would lie, after a judgment in the Court of Conscience; but wished to extend this remedial action as far as might be: To which Dennison, J., agreed, and inclined strongly that the action would lie. Foster, J., was afraid of the consequences of overhauling the judgment of a court of a competent jurisdiction. Wilmot, J., was clear that the action would not lie; because this action always arises from a contract of repayment, implied by law; and it would be absurd, if the law were to raise an implication in one Court, contrary to its own express judgment in another Court.

LORD MANSFIELD, C.J., delivered the opinion of the Court—It has been objected to this action: 1st, That debt will not lie upon this ground of complaint; therefore *indebitatus assumpsit* will not lie. But there is no foundation for this argument. It is held, indeed, in Slade's Case, 4 Rep. 93, that where debt will lie, *assumpsit* will also lie; but the negative doctrine, *e converso,* is not any where held; it is rather a general rule, that where debt will not lie, *indebitatus assumpsit* will. 2dly, That in this case no implied contract can arise, whereupon to ground an *assumpsit.* But surely, if a man is *bona fide* obliged to refund whatever money he has unlawfully received, an implied debt is thereby raised, *quasi ex contractu.* 3dly, That where money is recovered in a Court having a competent jurisdiction, it cannot be overhauled in another Court, but by writ of error or false judgment. But the verdict given in this cause is consistent with the determination of the Court of Conscience. The commissioners determined merely upon the indorsement, and refused to go into the collateral matter of the agreement; in which they did right; else, upon such a matter as a note of 30s., they might go into a large and extensive account; and might settle the balance of a series of mercantile transactions, much superior to their conusance. And yet, though the judgment was right, the iniquity of keeping the money so adjudged to be paid may appear in another Court. Suppose an insurer is condemned to pay money on the death of a person who afterwards appears to be alive; would not a new action lie for him, against the person who recovered upon the former judgment? The admission that an action will lie upon the express agreement, is conclusive upon this case. For the great benefit of this action (upon an implied contract) is, that the plaintiff need not set out the particular circumstances, on which, *ex aequo et bono,* he demands a satisfaction; but may declare generally for money had and received to his use, and may give the special matter in evidence. And it is equally beneficial to defendant, who may give in evidence any equitable matter, in order to discharge himself. Therefore, if it stood merely upon principles, there is no reason why the plaintiff should be confined to his action on the special agreement, and be debarred his remedy on the *assumpsit* implied by law.

[FROM BURROUGHS' REPORT]

For here [fraud] is express. The indorsement, which enabled the defendant to recover, was got by fraud and falsehood, for one purpose, and abused to another.

This kind of equitable action, to recover back money, which ought not in justice to be kept, is very beneficial, and therefore much encouraged. It lies only for money which, ex aequo et bono, the defendant ought to refund: it does not lie for money paid by the plaintiff, which is claimed of him as payable in point of honor and honesty, although it could not have been recovered from him by any course of law; as in payment of a debt barred by the Statute of Limitations, or contracted during his infancy, or to the extent of principal and legal interest upon an usurious contract, or, for money fairly lost at play: because in all these cases, the defendant may retain it with a safe conscience, though by positive law he was barred from recovering. But it lies for money paid by mistake; or upon a consideration which happens to fail; or for money got through imposition, (express, or implied;) or extortion; or oppression; or an undue advantage taken of the plaintiff's situation, contrary to laws made for the protection of persons under those circumstances.

[BACK TO BLACKSTONE'S REPORT] Therefore we are all of opinion, that the defendant ought in justice to refund this money thus mala fide recovered; and though an action on the agreement would also have indemnified him for his costs in the Court below, yet he may waive this advantage and pursue the present remedy.

The postea must be delivered to the plaintiff.

Notes

1. Both the attorneys as well as the judges conceded that Moses had a cause of action for special assumpsit on the agreement to idemnify him against the consequences of his agreement. Had this action been pursued, a reliance interest would have been present. Consider this in light of the penultimate paragraph of the report.

2. *A suggestion.* Slade's Case reduced the "assumpsit" to a fiction. Moses v. MacFerlan performed a similar service for the "indebitatus." Reading the decisions below against this background of unreality, attempt to state the meaning, meaningfulness, and comparative nuances of the following expressions:

a. a quasi-contract

b. a quasi-contract action

c. a quasi-contractual obligation

d. an obligation to make restitution imposed by law enforced by a form of action traditionally ex contractu.

Professor Arthur L. Corbin devoted considerable time and talent to this exercise. He concluded a book review in 55 Yale L.J. 848 (1946): "But nothing will be gained by fighting for a particular definition of the term 'quasi contract.'"

3. The central issue in Moses v. MacFerlan was the substantive basis for restitution. That also promptly came under attack in England. The notes to the Blackstone report call attention to the attitude of Lord Alvanley, C.J., in Johnson v. Johnson, 3 Bos. & Pul. 162 (1802):

"In the case of Moses v. MacFerlan, some principles were laid down which are certainly too large and which I do not mean to rely on, such as that, wherever one man has money which another ought to have, an action for money had and received may be maintained; or that whenever a man has an equitable claim he has also a legal action. I agree with the opinion of my Lord Chancellor in the case of Cooth v. Jackson, 6 Ves.Jun. 39, where he expresses his doubts as to whether courts of law have not gone too far in the discussion of equitable rights, since they cannot administer equity in the same way courts of equity do."

This quotation probably reflects the reservations many of the English judiciary entertained toward the vague generalization, "ties of natural justice and equity," as the substantive basis for the principal legal restitutionary remedy. Instead, the focus was directed to the "fictitious contract" as the basis of the action. The diversion from Lord Mansfield's views perhaps reached the widest point in 1914 in Sinclair v. Brougham, [1914] A.C. 398. Viscount Haldane, L.C., stated the prevailing opinion and the unavoidable result:

"When it [the English common law] speaks of actions arising ex contractu, it refers merely to a class of action in theory based on a contract which is imputed to the defendant by a fiction of law. The fiction can only be set up with effect if such a contract would have been valid if it really existed. * * *

"My Lords, notwithstanding the wide scope of the remedy so described, I think it must be taken to have been given only, as I have already said, where the law could consistently impute to the defendant at least the fiction of a promise."

In Sinclair v. Brougham the fictitious contract which the court would have had to impute to the corporate defendant would have been an ultra vires one; thus plaintiff's action for money had and received failed. Equitable restitution was eventually effected, thus demonstrating that immunity to the appeals of equity and good conscience was not total.

Evaluation and re-evaluation of the English position has been the subject of a voluminous literature. See R. Goff & G. Jones, The Law of Restitution (1986).

COMMENT, RESTITUTION: CONCEPT AND TERMS

19 Hastings L.J. 1167, 1182–86 (1968)

Reprinted with permission

Of the terms used in connection with the subject of restitution, "assumpsit" is one of the oldest and also perhaps one of the most troublesome. Although a great deal of restitutional law developed under the wing of indebitatus assumpsit, the term has long since lost its potency, at least in relation to restitution. One cannot help but wonder how much more lucid our law would be today, and how many problems in the area of restitution could have been avoided, had the term been jettisoned years ago. There are two major objections to the term "assumpsit."

First, the word has been used to encompass a huge area of the law and was developed more to facilitate the requirements of common law pleading and jurisdiction than to serve as a subcategory of the law. That is, in order to allow new actions based on unjust enrichment, assumpsit was expanded to extend the jurisdiction of the common law courts. Today such devices are unnecessary, and the word, "assumpsit," should be either eliminated or restricted to pure contract actions. "Assumpsit" means to assume or undertake; thus "indebitatus assumpsit" means literally an assumed indebtedness—a meaning which does not seem appropriate to an unjust enrichment action.

Second, assumpsit and indebitatus assumpsit tend to perpetuate the fallacious connection between contract situations and those dealing with unjust enrichment, a connection which was the result of considering both implied in fact contracts and the so-called implied in law contracts or quasi-contracts under general assumpsit. Even those states that have abolished the common law forms of action continue, for the most part, to treat restitution actions as though they were actions on a contract with respect to the statute of limitations, counterclaims or set-offs, assignments of rights of action, joinder, attachments and survival. Considering the basic difference between contract actions and restitution actions, where the former concern an obligation voluntarily assumed, while the latter concern an obligation imposed by law, the procedural treatment of restitution actions as contract actions is questionable at best. It is suggested that, along with dropping the restitutionary application of the terms "assumpsit" and "indebitatus assumpsit," new procedural rules should be formulated for the restitution actions, divorcing them from contract rules. In accordance with this view, it is also thought that it would be beneficial if legal digests and encyclopedias would index and classify the subject under the unified heading of restitution, rather than under the present diversity of titles.

A second undesirable term is "implied contract." There is little logical or practical justification for its usage in connection with the subject of restitution. The term originally referred to implied in fact contracts. Its latter application to unjust enrichment situations was achieved through the use of a fictional promise allowing the new action to be brought under the writ of assumpsit. The notion that there is an implied contract in unjust enrichment situations has had a profound effect on the development of this area of the law. Although perhaps a necessary concept in the beginning, it has caused considerable confusion between contract and restitution and should no longer be retained.

A third term that deserves mention is "money had and received." The term designates a form of action in assumpsit based on a quasi-contractual obligation but is restricted to situations where a person has been unjustly enriched by the retention of money or its equivalent. The difficulty is that there has been an unfortunate tendency by the courts to use the terms quasi-contract, implied contract and indebitatus assumpsit, in addition to money had and received in discussing the same type of fact situation. This duplication is unnecessary and confusing. In light of the need for a modern terminology of restitution, use of the term "money had and received" should be reconsidered.

A more difficult task is clarifying the meaning and usage of the terms "quasi-contract," "unjust enrichment," and "restitution." There is considerable disagreement as to what the terms themselves mean, and what, if any, distinctions exist between them.

The most modern manifestation of this confusion has been the statement in a handful of cases since the Restatement of Restitution to the effect that the terms "restitution" and "unjust enrichment" are the modern designation for the older doctrine of "quasi-contract." While it might be argued that unjust enrichment is synonymous with restitution, there seems to be little basis for considering quasi-contract the same as the other two. Specifically, quasi-contract, since its inception, has been limited to actions at law, while restitution and unjust enrichment have, at least since the Restatement of Restitution, included both legal and equitable remedies.

Notes

1. *Pleading quasi-contract claims.*

a. Restatement, Restitution (1937) † § 5. Forms of Action:

The appropriate proceeding in an action at law for the payment of money by way of restitution is:

(a) in States retaining common law forms of action, an action of general assumpsit;

(b) in States distinguishing actions of contract from actions of tort, an action of contract;

(c) in States which have statutes providing for the abolition of the distinctions between forms of action, an action in which the facts entitling the plaintiff to restitution are set forth.

b. Federal Rules of Civil Procedure

Rule 84. Forms

The forms contained in the Appendix of Forms are sufficient under the rules and are intended to indicate the simplicity and brevity of statement which the rules contemplate.

Form 5. *Complaint for Goods Sold and Delivered*

1. Allegation of jurisdiction.

2. Defendant owes plaintiff ______ dollars for goods sold and delivered by plaintiff to defendant between June 1, 1936 and December 1, 1936.

Wherefore (etc.)

Form 7. *Complaint for Money Paid by Mistake*

1. Allegation of jurisdiction.

2. Defendant owes plaintiff ______ dollars for money paid by plaintiff to defendant by mistake on June 1, 1936, under the following circumstances: [here state the circumstances with particularity—see Rule 9(b)].

Wherefore (etc.).

Form 8. *Complaint for Money Had and Received*

1. Allegation of jurisdiction.

2. Defendant owes plaintiff ______ dollars for money had and received from one G.H. on June 1, 1936, to be paid by defendant to plaintiff.

Wherefore (etc.).

2. For a discussion of quasi- and implied contracts, see Morrison, I Imply What You Infer Unless You Are a Court: Reporter's Notes to Restatement (Second) of Contracts § 19 (1980), 35 Okla.L.Rev. 707 (1982).

C. MEASURING THE DEFENDANT'S BENEFIT—SERVICES

Introductory Note

Frequently a person assuming a contract obligation will confer a benefit. The assumption may be erroneous for a variety of reasons. For example, the contract may fail because of a misunderstanding. Or the plaintiff may believe wrongly that he or she was dealing with an authorized agent, whose "principal" winds up with the benefit. Restitution obviously affords the sole remedy here because no contract exists and no tort intrudes. In a somewhat analogous situation the person conferring the benefit may find the bargain to exist but to be unenforceable for example, because of the statute of frauds. Here restitution is the primary remedy. Difficult questions arise: whether the recipient (equally mixed up) should be liable at all; and if so, how to calculate her "enrichment."

Consider the plight of the worker who has performed services under the mistaken belief that an enforceable claim exists. Curbside equity suggests splitting the difference to solve this classic dilemma of contriving a remedy between innocent parties. But the rules may cast the entire loss on the person performing the services. This outcome may be harsh, but as stated in the Restatement of Restitution § 41 comment a, "it could be still more harsh to require a recipient to pay for services which he did not want or for which he could not afford to pay although he may be glad to have them." Courts may be astute to blame, however slightly, the recipient and to shift the entire burden on to him or her. This is easy if the worker performed the work in reliance on an unenforceable bargain, since the recipient has at least broken his or her word.

As you apply Restatement of Restitution §§ 40 and 41 to services conferred in misreliance upon a supposed contract, the following questions may influence your decision to allow or disallow restitution:

a. Did the recipient expect someone to pay for the services?

b. Although perhaps the recipient did not expect to pay, did he or she request the services?

c. Was the recipient aware that services were being rendered?

If your answers justify telling the recipient to pay for the services, the next question is how much. Where the defendant's benefit is capable of specific restitution, tangibles or money paid, there is no difficulty in measuring it. Restatement of Restitution § 39 (1937). But when the plaintiff's mistaken performance improves property or is services generally, questions arise about how to value defendant's benefit.

a. Should the court measure the value from the standpoint of the plaintiff or the defendant? Literal application of unjust enrichment doctrine might limit plaintiff's recovery to the defendant's actual benefit; this may be slight, even less than nothing. On the other hand awarding the plaintiff market value may resemble contract damages in the guise of restitution. The plaintiff may recover the same amount on a contract implied in law as on one implied in fact. This anomoly does little to diminish confusion between the two.

b. No contract may exist because of misunderstandings, but the recipient may have mentioned a rate of pay. Or an oral agreement at an explicit rate of compensation may be unenforceable under the statute of frauds. Should the stipulated compensation measure the defendant's actual benefit? Note that this may award the plaintiff contract "expectancy" damages in the guise of restitution.

c. The final question: why not drop the pretense and develop other theories to allow one who performs services at another's request to recover "damages" in a more straightforward fashion, without distorting unjust enrichment principles.

CAMPBELL v. TENNESSEE VALLEY AUTHORITY

United States Court of Appeals, Fifth Circuit, 1969.
421 F.2d 293.

LEWIS R. MORGAN, CIRCUIT JUDGE. This is an action in *quantum meruit* brought by Raymond Campbell against the Tennessee Valley Authority (hereafter TVA) to recover $30,240 for the microfilming of certain technical trade journals which were a part of TVA's technical library located at Muscle Shoals, Alabama. The District Court entered a judgment upon a verdict for Campbell in the amount of $30,240. We affirm.

Campbell entered into an oral agreement with Earl Daniel, Director of the TVA Technical Library, to reproduce 13 sets of technical trade journals on 16 mm. microfilm at a price of $90 per roll. Mr. Daniel had no authority to make such a purchase for TVA and entered into the agreement with Campbell without the knowledge of his superiors. Campbell photographed, developed and processed 336 rolls of 16 mm. film containing the journals in question, placed the film in cartridges and delivered them to the TVA Technical Library at Muscle Shoals. Under the terms of the oral agreement, the charge for this work was to have been $30,240. The cartridges were placed on the shelves of the library and were available to its patrons for approximately two months.[1] The microfilm cartridges were then returned to Campbell by registered mail along with a letter from Daniel stating that there was no contract for their reproduction, that he had no authority to enter into such a contract, and that the price of the film was excessive. Campbell refused to accept the film and it was returned to the library, where it has since been stored. TVA has refused to pay for the film. The journals reproduced by Campbell were destroyed upon instruction by Daniel.

Campbell's original complaint relied on an express contract with TVA. TVA's motion for summary judgment on the ground that there could be no express contract since its employee Daniel had no authority to enter such a contract was granted. Campbell then amended his complaint to set out a claim for recovery based on *quantum meruit* or a contract implied in law. * * *

The principal contention made by appellant TVA is that the District Court committed error in instructing the jury that the measure of damages in this case was "the fair market value of the microfilm that benefitted TVA."[2] It is

1. [Footnotes renumbered.] There is evidence in the record that in this two-month period three of the cartridges were each used once.

2. The portions of the District Court's instructions to the jury dealing with the question of the measure of damages are as follows:

"Another authority has said 'The obligee shall be compensated, not for any loss or damage suffered by him, but for the benefit which he has conferred upon the obligor.' * * *

"In valuing the benefits or loss to TVA, you must use fair market value. In other words, you must use the values that the same or similar microfilm and the journals would sell for on the open market.

"* * * If the TVA had agreed to purchase, we will say, a typewriter—they used the expression bulldozer—and they used the typewriter and sent it back, under the authorities the plaintiff would be entitled to recover only the value of the use of the typewriter, because the typewriter could be sold to somebody else. * * * There would be a market value for the typewriter. * * * But if something is designed for a person to use for a particular thing, and they accept it, and it has no market value other than that particular use, you could see that it would be a complete loss. Those are the two

TVA's contention that it "is obligated to pay not for the film itself, but only for the 'benefit,' or unjust enrichment, if any, which it received by reason of the *use* it made of the film while it was in the library." The first question thus presented to this Court is whether a person who is entitled to recover from an agency of the federal government under a theory of *quantum meruit* is entitled to the reasonable, or fair market, value of the goods or services so provided, or to the reasonable value of the benefit so realized by the Government. In other words, is the measure of recovery to be determined by the amount of money that would be necessary to acquire on the open market the goods or services from which the benefit is derived, or is the measure of recovery how much the benefit has been worth to the person upon whom it was conferred? * * *

In re Moyer, W.D. Virginia 1960, 190 F.Supp. 867, 873, held that "the measure of recovery * * * on the principle of *quantum meruit* * * * is the reasonable value of the work performed, less the amount of compensation, whether in money or otherwise, already received." Evans v. Mason, 82 Ariz. 40, 308 P.2d 245, 65 A.L.R.2d 936 (1957), an action in *quantum meruit* to recover for services rendered to decedent pursuant to a parol contract barred by the Statute of Frauds held that the measure of damages is the actual value of the services rendered to the decedent. On the other hand, Hill v. Waxberg (9 Cir.1956) 237 F.2d 936, 16 Alaska 477, an action by a contractor to recover for services and expenditures made in contemplation of a proposed building contract, held the "restitution is properly limited to the value of the benefit which was acquired."

This confusion in the cases is clarified by a statement made in a footnote of the court's decision in Martin v. Campanaro (2 Cir., 1946), 156 F.2d 127, 130 n. 5, cert. den. 329 U.S. 759:

> "The claimants are entitled to recover on a quantum meruit basis. But 'quantum meruit' is ambiguous; it may mean (1) that there is a contract 'implied in fact' to pay the reasonable value of the services, or (2) that, to prevent unjust enrichment, the claimant may recover on a quasi-contract (an 'as if' contract) for that reasonable value. It has been suggested that the latter is a rule-of-thumb measure of damages adopted in quasi contract cases where the actual unjust enrichment or benefit to the defendant is too difficult to prove."

In the present situation the District Court was correct in using the "rule of thumb" measure of damages and in instructing the jury that the measure of damages was "the fair market value of the microfilm that benefited TVA," instead of instructing that the measure of damages was the reasonable value of the benefit realized by TVA from the microfilm, since the actual benefit to TVA would not have been susceptible of proof. The value realized by a library in having a particular reference work available to its patrons cannot be adequately expressed in dollars and cents. The real benefit is realized, not so much by the library itself, as by those who depend upon the library in their research activities, and the benefit is not so much that the books, technical journals and other research sources are actually *used,* on a regular basis, but that they are conveniently *available for use.* If use, rather than availability, were the only test of the benefit conferred by a book in a library, a good

extremes that you might visualize. You have here certain microfilm that were (sic) made. What would be the value of these microfilm if they could be sold to somebody else? * * *"

university library could be many times smaller than the present day standard and still retain its effectiveness as a center for research.

Furthermore, in view of the fact that the microfilmed technical journals furnished by Campbell had no readily marketable value to anyone except the TVA because of their unique character and the special circumstances[3] of this case, the District Court properly instructed the jury that the measure of recovery was the fair market value, even though the microfilm was available on the library's shelves for only two months. * * *

TVA argues that if the jury could find that the "fair market value of the microfilm that benefited TVA" could be the contract price between the parties, it could not exceed the lowest contract price that would have been obtainable had competitive bidding taken place on the microfilming under 16 U.S.C.A. § 831h(b)(1964), and that the evidence is uncontradicted that University Microfilming, a division of Xerox Corporation, would have done the microfilming for $10,000. Thus, TVA contends that Campbell could recover no more than $10,000 and that his recovery of $30,240 was contrary to the law and the evidence.

While there is authority for the proposition that the upper limit of recovery in an action of this nature is the amount agreed to by the parties in the unenforceable contract, Hill v. Waxberg, 237 F.2d at 940, n. 6, the testimony of Holladay, the representative from the University Microfilm division of Xerox, that his company would have done the microfilming here in question for $10,000 did not constitute a bid under 16 U.S.C.A. § 831h(b), and thus can in no way be considered an upper limit on Campbell's recovery. It is also hornbook law that the jury is in no way bound by the testimony of experts. * * *

The judgment of the District Court is Affirmed.

RIVES, CIRCUIT JUDGE (dissenting). With deference, I submit that the district judge inadvertently imported into the claimed quasi contract, "implied in law," too much of the actual agreement between the appellee Campbell and Daniel, the *unauthorized* agent of TVA. Campbell concedes, as he must, that only a quasi contract is now involved. * * *

This litigation began with the filing of a complaint which alleged that Earl Daniel, as agent of the TVA, acting within the line and scope of his authority, agreed with Campbell for him to produce and deliver microfilm of certain trade journals for which Campbell was to be paid $90.00 per roll; that TVA ordered 336 rolls, all of which were delivered; but that TVA refused to pay to Campbell the agreed amount of the contract, $30,240.00. The district court granted TVA's motion for summary judgment as to that claim.

Campbell then amended his complaint by filing counts in general assumpsit seeking to recover a quantum meruit.[4]

3. The journals which had been reproduced had been destroyed, making the microfilm copies the only ones available. Moreover, there was evidence that the journals in question were a necessary part of a technical library. Likewise, it does not appear the microfilm copies had value to anyone other than to the library.

4. "Amendment

"Comes now the plaintiff in the above captioned cause and amends his complaint by adding the following:

Second Cause of Action Count 2

"The Plaintiff expressly adopts the allegations of Paragraph 1 of Count 1.

"The plaintiff claims of the defendant $30,240.00 due from it for merchandise, goods and

While the amended complaint is broad enough to sustain recovery on a contract implied *in fact,* as well as on one implied *in law,* I repeat that the sole claim is on a contract implied *in law.* Judge Grooms correctly so charged the jury:

"Members of the jury, this case began as a contract case, but it was determined at the outset that Mr. Earl Daniel had no authority to make a contract; the contract was void for that reason, and the contract aspect went out and then the complaint was amended to claim for work and labor and for goods and chattels, merchandise, goods, and chattels sold to the defendant, T.V.A. on the theory of what we know as a quantum meruit. That is an old form of action, and it literally means as much as he deserves. Quantum means quantity, merit [sic], as much as he deserves. The case has proceeded since then on the theory of quantum meruit. * * *

"As I stated to you the words quantum meruit, liberally [sic] translated, means as much as he deserves. The basis of a recovery under a quantum meruit is that the defendant has received a benefit from the plaintiff which it is unjust for him to retain without paying for it. Quantum meruit is a devise [sic] to prevent unjust enrichment by requiring a recipient of work or services to pay the party furnishing such work and services as much as he reasonably deserves for this work."

The jury verdict of $30,240.00 is in the exact amount the plaintiff Campbell claimed that Daniel promised for TVA to pay for the film (336 rolls at $90.00 per roll). A reading of the record makes obvious, I submit, that the unauthorized express contract has simply been enforced under the guise of a quasi contract or quantum meruit. * * *

[W]hen goods or services are furnished to the federal government pursuant to an unenforceable or invalid contract, the courts will, in certain limited fact situations, grant relief of a quasi-contractual nature. Such relief is appropriate only when it serves to prevent the government from being unjustly enriched at the expense of another. * * *

[In] Crocker v. United States, 240 U.S. 74, 81–82, Mr. Justice Van Devanter, speaking for the Court, said:

"It [the corrupt arrangement] was made by Lorenz and Crawford while endeavoring to secure the contract for the company and was a means to that end. They were the company's agents and were securing the contract at its request. It accepted the fruits of their efforts and thereby sanctioned what they did, and made their knowledge its own. * * *

"It results that no recovery could be had upon the contract with the Postmaster General, because it was tainted with fraud and rescinded by him on that ground. But this was not an obstacle to a recovery upon a *quantum valebat.*"

* * * Continuing, the Court held that no recovery could be had upon a quantum valebat because there was lacking the requisite proof of the value of

chattel sold by the plaintiff to the defendant from the first day of January, 1967 through the 13th day of February, 1967, which sum of money with the interest thereon is still unpaid.

Count 3

"The Plaintiff claims of the defendant $30,240.00 due from it for work and labor done for the defendant by the plaintiff from the first day of January, 1967 through the 13th day of February, 1967, which sum of money with the interest thereon is still unpaid. Plaintiff expressly adopts the allegations of paragraph 1 of Count 1 of the bill of complaint."

the letter carriers' satchels so furnished and retained. The claimant's insistence in *Crocker,* was remarkably similar to that of Campbell in the present case. As stated by Mr. Justice Van Devanter for the Court:

> "He [the claimant] insists, however, that the findings show the price at which the government contracted to take the satchels with the shoulder straps, and also what it cost the government to supply the straps, and that the difference should be regarded, in the absence of other evidence, as representing the value of the satchels as furnished,—that is, without the straps. The insistence proceeds upon the theory that the contract price was in the nature of an admission by the government of the value of the satchels with the straps. However this might be in other circumstances, it is wholly inadmissible here, for the fraud with which the contract was tainted completely discredited the contract price, and prevented it from being treated as an admission of the value by the government. It therefore was incumbent upon the claimant to show the value by other evidence, and, as this was not done, no recovery could be had upon a *quantum valebat.*"

Thus, it would seem that the *possible* basis for recovery considered in *Crocker* was a contract implied *in fact,* rather than *in law,* because the Government actually accepted and permanently retained the satchels and, hence, was contractually liable for their value. In the present case, as has been shown, no TVA employee with proper authority accepted the microfilm, and TVA made every reasonable effort to return the rolls to Campbell. Upon Campbell's refusal to accept delivery of the film, it was stored and its use forbidden.[5]

In Prestex, Inc. v. United States, 1963, 320 F.2d 367, the government contracting officer advertised for bids on white duck cloth of certain specifications to be used in making summer uniforms for the cadets of the United States Military Academy. Prestex submitted its bid with an attached sample which appeared to meet the specifications, but which, as a later laboratory test showed, was in material variance. Prestex was awarded the contract and had the 25,000 yards of cloth manufactured. The government, after testing a sample of the finished cloth, refused to accept delivery. The Court of Claims held that the award was illegal and granted the government's motion for summary judgment. Clearly, that decision does not support the majority ruling. The opinion does, however, contain an admirable statement of the principles of equity and justice which call for "relief of a quasi-contractual nature * * * *in certain limited fact situations.*" (Emphasis supplied.)

> "Even though a contract be unenforceable against the Government, because not properly advertised, not authorized, or for some other reason, it is only fair and just that the Government pay for goods delivered or services rendered and accepted under it. In certain limited fact situations, therefore, the courts will grant relief of a quasi-contractual nature when the Government elects to rescind an invalid contract. No one would deny that ordinary principles of equity and justice preclude the United States from retaining the services, materials, and benefits and at the same time refusing to pay for them

5. In forbidding use of the film, TVA may have gone further than law and equity required in view of the fact that Campbell had destroyed TVA's original journals.

It should be noted that in *Crocker* the contract price of the satchels was inadmissible to prove value because the contract was tainted with fraud. While there was no fraud in the present case, there was a complete absence of competitive bidding necessary to establish a valid contract price. Let me divert to express my opinion that the price agreed on between Daniel and Campbell is wholly inadmissible to prove the value of the film.

on the ground that the contracting officer's promise was unauthorized, or unenforceable for some other reason. However, the basic fact of legal significance charging the Government with liability in these situations is its retention of benefits in the form of goods or services." (Footnotes omitted.)

In Williams v. United States, 1955, 127 F.Supp. 617, it was held that the contracting officer had ratified the agreement in question and that the government had received the benefits of its performance. The *Williams* case involved a contract implied *in fact.* Indeed it has been held that the Court of Claims has no jurisdiction of an action against the United States in those cases where, if the transaction were between private parties, recovery could be had upon a contract implied *in law.*

The underlying principle is that of forbidding unjust enrichment. "A person who has been unjustly enriched at the expense of another is required to make restitution to the other." A.L.I. Restatement, Restitution § 1, p. 12.

Chapter 2 of that text "states the conditions under which there is a right to restitution because of a mistake in the conferring of a benefit." A.L.I. Restatement, Restitution Introductory Note, p. 26. Such a right may arise in the case of a person who has paid money (Id. § 16) or transferred property (Id. § 39), or rendered services (Id. § 40) to another which have inured to the latter's benefit, in the mistaken belief that he is performing a valid contract with the other, although the contract is later avoided. A right to restitution, however, does not arise in such cases unless the recipient of the property or services is *unjustly enriched.*

> "Even where a person has received a benefit from another, he is liable to pay therefor only if the circumstances of its receipt or retention are such that, as between the two persons, it is unjust for him to retain it. The mere fact that a person benefits another is not of itself sufficient to require the other to make restitution therefore."

A.L.I. Restatement, Restitution p. 13.

Under the facts and circumstances of this case, it is doubtful whether TVA was *enriched* or *harmed* by Campbell's services when consideration is given to the fact that Campbell destroyed TVA's original journals.

Assuming arguendo that TVA was benefitted by Campbell's services, it was not *unjustly* enriched: It has been demonstrated that no authorized agent of TVA accepted delivery of the rolls of microfilm; that TVA has not wrongfully retained the microfilm, but has made every reasonable effort to return it to Campbell, and that upon Campbell's refusal to accept the film, TVA has stored it and forbidden its use. The only possible benefit retained by TVA is in the two-month period that the microfilm remained in its Technical Library. In that two months, three of the rolls were each used once. There was no evidence that the person making such limited use of the film knew or had reason to know that he was using film which did not belong to TVA or that he was in any way obligating TVA to pay for the film. Such knowledge is, I submit, necessary for this limited user to impose upon TVA a duty of restitution. See A.L.I. Restatement, Restitution §§ 40 and 41. Further, a precedent should not be laid for the public policy requirement of competitive bidding to be frustrated by the application of some principle of restitution or quasi contract. For all of the foregoing reasons, I am firmly of the opinion that TVA is not liable to Campbell in any amount.

[Even] *If* Liable, What Is the Extent of TVA's Liability.

It is incomprehensible to me that Campbell should be rewarded for *his* destruction of TVA's original trade journals. Perhaps the best precedent is the classic case of the son who murdered his father and mother, but was granted mercy because he was an orphan.

The majority holding measures the extent of TVA's liability by Campbell's loss. That overlooks the fundamental reason for granting restitution or quantum meruit relief, *viz.*, to avoid unjust enrichment. Ordinarily in such cases the benefit to the one and the loss to the other are co-extensive. However, when the benefit is less than the loss, the recovery is limited to the benefit. * * *

I respectfully dissent.

Notes

1. Is the "contract" price evidence of the amount of "benefit" Campbell conferred on TVA? Does Campbell's recovery of the "contract" price undermine the statutory policy of requiring competitive bids? Is Campbell's recovery justified because TVA knew that he expected to be paid? What evidence of TVA's "actual benefit" should it have presented? D. Dobbs, Remedies § 4.5 (1973).

2. Vortt Exploration Co. v. Chevron U.S.A., Inc., 787 S.W.2d 942, 944 (Tex. 1990): "To recover under quantum meruit a claimant must prove that: 1. valuable services were rendered or materials furnished; 2. for the person sought to be charged; 3. which services and materials were accepted by the person sought to be charged, used and enjoyed by him; 4. under such circumstances as reasonably notified the person sought to be charged that the plaintiff in performing such services was expecting to be paid by the person sought to be charged."

3. Westerhold v. Mullenix Corp., 777 S.W.2d 257, 262–63 (Mo.App.1989). The court explained ambiguity of quantum meruit:

"To address these arguments, we need no extended discussion of the historical antecedents of an action in quantum meruit. [citations] Suffice it to say that an action in quantum meruit was and is a remedy of restitution. 'The form of action at common law that was used to obtain the remedy of restitution was Assumpsit * * *.' 5 Corbin, *Contracts,* § 1102, p. 549 (1964). Assumpsit is now reflected in some legal relations we now characterize as 'contractual', and the restitutionary remedy of quantum meruit has followed those relations. But, to state the obvious, the remedy of quantum meruit varies with the particular 'contractual' relations in issue.

"Contracts are created by promissory expression. The expression of the promise may be verbal or by conduct. When the parties express their promises in explicit oral or written words, the contract is labeled: express. When they manifest their promises by language or conduct which is not explicit, the contract is labeled: implied in fact. The only difference in the two is the manner of manifesting mutual assent. In either case, the essential question is the degree of effectiveness of the expression used.

"On the other hand, a contract 'implied in law' or 'quasi-contract' 'is not a contract at all but an obligation to do justice even though it is clear that no promise was ever made or intended.' Calamari and Perillo, *Contracts,* § 1–12 (2d ed. 1977). This non-contractual obligation is treated procedurally as if it were a contract, but its principal function is to prevent unjust enrichment. * * *

"[T]he remedy of quantum meruit may be pursued for breach of an express contract. In this situation, the plaintiff provides his work and material pursuant to a written contract. The plaintiff's right to the reasonable value of his work and material prior to his complete performance is created only by a substantial breach of the express contract by the defendant. Without this breach, plaintiff is not entitled to the reasonable value of his work and material."

4. See Rover International v. Cannon Film Sales (No 3), [1989] 3 All E.R. 423, 425 (C.A.1988): "When assessing a quantum meruit which arose solely due to the invalidity of a supposedly valid contract, it was wrong in principle to place a ceiling on the quantum meruit by applying the provisions of the void contract. Instead, the proper basis for assessing the quantum meruit was equitable restitution as between the parties regardless of what their respective positions would have been had the contract been valid. Accordingly, the quantum meruit to which R was entitled was to be assessed on the basis that the contract of 5 December 1985 had been void ab initio without regard to the parties' position had the contract been valid and been lawfully terminated by C for R's breach on 13 October 1986."

5. See Vickery v. Ritchie, 202 Mass. 247, 88 N.E. 835 (1909). An architect fraudulently substituted documents. Defendant, a homeowner, believed he was to pay $23,200 for a Turkish bath house; plaintiff, a contractor, thought he was to be paid $33,721 to build it. The contractor's actual cost was $32,950; but the project increased the property's market value only $22,000. Defendant refused to pay more than $23,200, the contract price represented to him. Plaintiff sued seeking additional compensation for labor and materials. Should plaintiff recover $10,521? $9,750? Nothing? Or should the parties split the difference between $23,200 and $33,721? See Seavey, Embezzlement by Agents of Two Principals: Contribution?, 64 Harv.L.Rev. 431 (1951).

6. *United States Immunity From Quasi-Contractual Claims.* One reason to study "quasi-contract" is that, while the United States has yielded sovereign immunity for actual contracts and torts, it has not as yet done so for restitution. Wall and Childres, The Law of Restitution and the Federal Government, 66 Nw.U.L.Rev. 587 (1971). This, no doubt, reflects a general caution about exposing the treasury to claims of unjust enrichment that arise out of neither breach of contract nor tort. See Mass Transit Administration v. Granite Construction Co., 57 Md.App. 766, 471 A.2d 1121 (1984). For a decision holding that a state had waived governmental immunity for claims of unjust enrichment, see Hydro Conduit Corp. v. Kemble, 110 N.M. 173, 793 P.2d 855 (1990).

7. In measuring plaintiff's restitution for services, a large difference may exist between a benefit that adds to the defendant's actual wealth and one comprised of plaintiff's performance under the misfired agreement. G. Palmer, The Law of Restitution § 4.2 (1978).

If plaintiff may recover for the performance bargained for, several questions emerge. May this way of measuring restitution validate a noncontract as a contract? Does it lead restitution away from preventing unjust enrichment? Does it award reliance losses disguised as restitution? Does this kind of restitution undermine the reason to deny contract recovery?

Does the substantive occasion for restitution affect the answer? Should courts measure restitution by performance when defendant has breached? When the statute of frauds bars contract remedies? When the doctrines of mistake, impossibility, impracticability, or frustration discharge the contract?

FARASH v. SYKES DATATRONICS, INC.

Court of Appeals of New York, 1983.
59 N.Y.2d 500, 465 N.Y.S.2d 917, 452 N.E.2d 1245.

COOKE, CHIEF JUDGE. Plaintiff claims that he and defendant entered an agreement whereby defendant would lease a building owned by plaintiff, who was to complete its renovation and make certain modifications on an expedited basis. Defendant, however, never signed any contract and never occupied the building. Plaintiff commenced this litigation, and defendant unsuccessfully moved to dismiss for failure to state a cause of action. * * *

Plaintiff pleaded three causes of action in his complaint. The first was to enforce an oral lease for a term longer than one year. This is clearly barred by the Statute of Frauds (General Obligations Law, § 5–703, subd. 2). The third cause of action is premised on the theory that the parties contracted by exchanging promises that plaintiff would perform certain work in his building and defendant would enter into a lease for a term longer than one year. This is nothing more than a contract to enter into a lease; it is also subject to the Statute of Frauds. Hence, the third cause of action was properly dismissed.

Plaintiff's second cause of action, however, is not barred by the Statute of Frauds. It merely seeks to recover for the value of the work performed by plaintiff in reliance on statements by and at the request of defendant. This is not an attempt to enforce an oral lease or an oral agreement to enter a lease, but is in disaffirmance of the void contract and so may be maintained. [citation] That defendant did not benefit from plaintiff's efforts does not require dismissal; plaintiff may recover for those efforts that were to his detriment and that thereby placed him in a worse position. [citations] "The contract being void and incapable of enforcement in a court of law, the party * * * rendering the services in pursuance thereof, may treat it as a nullity, and recover * * * the value of the services" (Erben v. Lorillard, 19 N.Y. 299, 302).

The dissent's primary argument is that the second cause of action is equivalent to the third, and so is also barred by the Statute of Frauds. It is true that plaintiff attempts to take the contract outside the statute's scope and render it enforceable by arguing that the work done was unequivocally referable to the oral agreement. This should not operate to prevent recovery under a theory of quasi contract as a contract implied by law, which "is not a contract at all but an obligation imposed by law to do justice even though it is clear that no promise was ever made or intended" (Calamari and Perillo, Contracts [2d ed.], § 1–12, p. 19). Obviously, the party who seeks both to enforce the contract that is unenforceable by virtue of the Statute of Frauds and to recover under a contract implied in law will present contradictory characterizations. This, however, is proper in our courts where pleading alternative theories of relief is accepted. Moreover, the existence of any real promise is unnecessary; plaintiff's attempt to make his acts directly referable to the unenforceable contract simply is irrelevant.

The authorities all recognize that a promisee should be able to recover in the present situation. "[I]f the improvements made by the plaintiff are on land that is not owned by the defendant and in no respect add to his wealth, the plaintiff will not be given judgment for restitution of their value, even though he may have made such improvements in reliance upon the contract that the defendant has broken. For such expenditures as these in reliance on a contract, the plaintiff can get judgment only in the form of damages for consequential injury" (5 Corbin, Contracts, p. 578 [n. omitted]). Thus, plaintiff may recover for those expenditures he made in reliance on defendant's representations and that he otherwise would not have made. The Restatement provides that an injured party who has not conferred a benefit may not obtain restitution, but he or she may "have an action for damages, including one for recovery based on * * * reliance" (Restatement, Contracts 2d, § 370, Comment a). "[T]he injured party has a right to damages based on his reliance interest, including expenditures made in preparation for performance or in performance, less any loss that the party in breach can prove with reasonable certainty the injured party would have suffered had the contract been performed" (Restatement, Contracts 2d, § 349). The Restatement recognizes an action such as is involved here (see Restatement, Contracts 2d, §§ 139, 349, Comment b).

The dissent relies on Bradkin v. Leverton, 26 N.Y.2d 192, 309 N.Y.S.2d 192, 257 N.E.2d 643 and Miller v. Schloss, 218 N.Y. 400, 113 N.E. 337 for the proposition that plaintiff can recover only if there is an actual benefit to the defendant. Those cases do not state that there can be no recovery for work performed in the absence of any real benefit to defendant. As stated by Professor Williston (12 Williston, Contracts [3d ed.], pp. 282–284, 286–287 [nn. omitted]):

> "Again, even though the defendant's liability is imposed by law irrespective of the agreement of the parties, and may, therefore, be called quasi contractual, where the defendant is a wrongdoer the plaintiff may well be preferred, and if a complete restoration of the *status quo* or its equivalent is impossible the plaintiff should at least be replaced in as good a position as he originally was in, although the defendant is thereby compelled to pay more than the amount which the plaintiff's performance has benefitted him. * * *
>
> "That is, the law should impose on the wrongdoing defendant a duty to restore the plaintiff's former status, not merely to surrender any enrichment or benefit that he may unjustly hold or have received; although if the market value or, in the absence of a market value, the benefit to the defendant of what has been furnished exceeds the cost or value to the plaintiff, there is no reason why recovery of this excess should not be allowed.
>
> "These different possible situations, as has been said, have often been confused with one another, because the form of action in each of them was identical at common law—general assumpsit on a *quantum meruit* or *quantum valebat* count; and this tended to induce courts and others to inquire what is the rule of damages under such counts—a question not susceptible of a single answer."

A lesson in this area can be taken from Professors Calamari and Perillo: "The basic aim of restitution is to place the plaintiff in the same economic position as he enjoyed prior to contracting. Thus, unless specific restitution is obtained in Equity, the plaintiff's recovery is for the reasonable value of services rendered, goods delivered, or property conveyed less the reasonable value of any counter performance received by him. The plaintiff recovers the reasonable value of his performance whether or not the defendant in any economic sense benefitted from the performance. The quasi-contractual concept of benefit continues to be recognized by the rule that the defendant must have received the plaintiff's performance; acts merely preparatory to performance will not justify an action for restitution. 'Receipt,' however, is a legal concept rather than a description of physical fact. If what the plaintiff has done is part of the agreed exchange, it is deemed to be 'received' by the defendant." (Calamari and Perillo, Contracts [2d ed.], § 15–4, p. 574 [nn. omitted].

We should not be distracted by the manner in which a theory of recovery is titled. On careful consideration, it becomes clear that the commentators do not disagree in result, but only in nomenclature. Whether denominated "acting in reliance" or "restitution," all concur that a promisee who partially performs (e.g., by doing work in a building or at an accelerated pace) at a promisor's request should be allowed to recover the fair and reasonable value of the performance rendered, regardless of the enforceability of the original agreement.

Accordingly, the order of the Appellate Division should be modified, * * * by reinstating plaintiff's second cause of action and, as so modified, affirmed.

JASEN, JUDGE (dissenting). * * * The majority fails to specify the theory of recovery upon which it bases its conclusion that "plaintiff may recover for those efforts that were to his detriment and that thereby placed him in a worse position." Insofar as this conclusion is based upon quasi contract, it is incorrect for the well-established rule in this State is that in order for a plaintiff to recover under such a cause of action, he must demonstrate that the defendant was unjustly enriched by his efforts. The rule has been clearly set forth by this court and consistently followed: " '[a] *quasi* or constructive contract rests upon the equitable principle that a person shall not be allowed to enrich himself unjustly at the expense of another. In truth it is not a contract or promise at all. It is an obligation which the law creates, in the absence of any agreement, when and because the acts of the parties or others have placed in the possession of one person money, or its equivalent, under such circumstances that in equity and good conscience he ought not to retain it, and which *ex aequo et bono* belongs to another.' " [citations] Since, as the majority correctly points out, defendant did not benefit from plaintiff's efforts, no recovery under quasi contract may be had.

The "lesson" provided by Professors Calamari and Perillo, cited by the majority, is inapposite to the case before us because section 15–4 of their text deals exclusively with actions based on breach while plaintiff does not allege in his second cause of action that defendant breached any agreement. Additionally, I note that insofar as this statement would allow recovery by the plaintiff under a theory of restitution, even though the defendant has not been benefitted by any of plaintiff's efforts, such is not the law in New York. The majority itself concedes this point in stating, "an injured party who has not conferred a benefit may not obtain restitution." Moreover, assuming *arguendo* the accuracy of the legal principle stated by Calamari and Perillo, this principle does not accord relief to the plaintiff in the instant appeal. As the two professors correctly note, "the defendant must have received the plaintiff's performance; acts merely preparatory to performance will not justify an action for restitution." First, defendant received nothing from the plaintiff, as the majority accurately points out. Second, plaintiff's acts in renovating his building were "merely preparatory to performance" of the alleged oral contract whereby plaintiff and defendant agreed to enter into a two-year lease. Thus, even if section 15–4 were applicable, plaintiff would not be entitled to the relief which the majority is offering. * * *

It appears that the majority, in holding that plaintiff can recover the value of his efforts expended in reliance on defendant's alleged statements, is recognizing a cause of action sounding in promissory estoppel. * * *

While the doctrine of promissory estoppel has been recognized and applied in certain cases, to do so here, where the issue has not been pleaded or addressed in the parties' affidavits and has neither been argued nor briefed, is ill-advised. Moreover, it is difficult to understand why the majority, in discussing plaintiff's reliance damages, ignores the fact made abundantly clear by plaintiff's own affidavits and his conduct during the early stages of his litigation, that plaintiff has merely alleged, in all three causes of action, that he is entitled to monetary damages from defendant because he relied on defendant's alleged promise to enter into a two-year lease—a promise unenforceable under the Statute of Frauds. This is all the more puzzling because we are not presented here with an inexperienced or unsophisticated plaintiff who is unable to protect his own financial interests. To the contrary, Max Farash is a "prominent and successful [real estate] developer" who owns thousands of residential housing units in Monroe County and at least eight commercial buildings in downtown Rochester. In light of this, it is incredible that the majority would construe plaintiff's complaint and affidavits in a way that even the plaintiff never intended and then adopt a novel legal doctrine solely for the purpose of extending equitable relief to the plaintiff where it would previously have been unavailable. Surely a sophisticated businessman such as Max Farash knew that he could have easily insured that defendant would pay for the extensive renovation work plaintiff performed on his own building merely by obtaining defendant's promise to that effect. Plaintiff's failure to obtain such a promise leads inevitably to the conclusion that defendant never intended to pay for such renovation and, thus, never agreed to do so. Nevertheless, the majority unnecessarily provides plaintiff with an opportunity to go before a jury and request that the defendant, who received nothing from the plaintiff, be ordered to pay for the improvements made on plaintiff's own building. Nothing in logic or existing law supports such a result. * * *

EARHART v. WILLIAM LOW CO.

Supreme Court of California, 1979.

25 Cal.3d 503, 158 Cal.Rptr. 887, 600 P.2d 1344.

[The facts are taken from the concurring and dissenting opinion of Clark, Justice.] Defendant William Low Company owning 17 acres of property acquired a contract right to purchase the adjoining 17 acres (the Pillow property) intending to construct a mobile home park on the 34 acres. A special use permit allowing construction of a mobile home park on the Pillow property was to expire on 29 May 1971. After more than two months of negotiations between plaintiff, a building contractor, and defendant William Low, president of defendant company, agreement was reached for plaintiff to build the park for $892,557.86. On 16 April 1971 counsel for Low and the company sent to plaintiff's counsel a letter of intent to accept plaintiff's bid. The letter stated that acceptance was subject to defendants' obtaining requisite financing and plaintiff furnishing a construction bond. Neither condition was met.

The letter concluded: "It is my client's further understanding that in return for this letter of intent and in order to keep a conditional use permit effective, your client will commence immediate framing of a proposed laundry room on the subject property and move some equipment on said premises by Monday, April 19, 1971."

Subsequently, defendant Low on several occasions requested plaintiff to commence work to preserve the permits. Defendants never made an independent, express promise to pay for such work.

Late in May plaintiff commenced work on both parcels. He claimed that about a week later he learned defendants had not obtained the requisite financing. Plaintiff stopped work and commenced this action 14 June 1971.

The complaint states four causes of action: breach of contract, quantum meruit, fraud, and negligent misrepresentation. When the matter came on for trial on 17 May 1976, the trial court granted judgment on the pleadings on all causes of action except the quantum meruit count.

The trial court awarded recovery against defendant company in quantum meruit for the work done on its property. The court denied any recovery for the work done on the Pillow property. The court also denied any recovery against defendant Low.

TOBRINER, JUSTICE. In this case we must determine whether a party who expends funds and performs services at the request of another, under the reasonable belief that the requesting party will compensate him for such services, may recover in quantum meruit although the expenditures and services do not directly benefit property owned by the requesting party. * * *

As we shall explain, plaintiff is entitled to prove defendant's liability for the reasonable value of plaintiff's services rendered on both parcels of land. The trial court in the instant case apparently felt constrained to limit plaintiff's recovery because of this court's decision in Rotea v. Izuel (1939) 14 Cal.2d 605, 95 P.2d 927. In that case the court denied quasi-contractual recovery on the ground that the only "benefit" received by the defendant was the "incidental benefit" which he may have found in the satisfaction of obtaining compliance with his request. * * *

To understand the trial court's seemingly arbitrary refusal to grant complete recovery on the basis of quantum meruit, we must first examine this court's decision in Rotea v. Izuel, supra. Briefly to summarize the facts in that case: plaintiff's wife died, leaving five minor children in plaintiff's care. Plaintiff's sister-in-law Eugenia subsequently moved into plaintiff's home to assist in taking charge of the children. Although Eugenia later became ill, she nonetheless continued to care for the children.

Antonio Izuel, Eugenia's brother, also lived in plaintiff's home. Antonio helped support the family and, over the years, along with plaintiff and plaintiff's children, took care of Eugenia during her illness. On Antonio's death, plaintiff brought suit to recover from Antonio's estate the reasonable value of services rendered by plaintiff in caring for Eugenia. In support of plaintiff's claim, plaintiff's children testified that Antonio "promised to pay [their] father out of his estate for Eugenia's care."

Preliminarily this court stated that plaintiff could not recover upon his claimed oral agreement, since it violated the statute of frauds, and that plaintiff's cause of action, "if any, was one for the reasonable value of the services performed." The court distinguished cases that admitted proof of an oral agreement to show that the parties did not intend any services to be gratuitous, on the ground that there "the services were performed with respect to and for the direct benefit of the deceased person and under such circumstances as to create an original obligation implied in law to pay the reasonable value of such services, which obligations arose independently of the terms of the invalid oral agreement."

The court declined to extend the rule of those decisions to permit quasi-contractual recovery from Antonio's estate. As the court remarked, "The reason for the rule seems to be that the parties should ordinarily be required to rely upon their agreement and that in the absence of a valid agreement between the parties, the law will not imply an obligation unless the failure to imply such obligation will result in the unjust enrichment of the defendant." Tracing the principle of unjust enrichment in this context to the ancient action for money had and received, the court refused to assess liability without first finding receipt of a "*direct benefit.*" (Emphasis added.) Since the only "benefit" received by Antonio was the "incidental benefit which he may [have found] in the satisfaction of obtaining compliance with his request," the court denied recovery.

While the result which the court reached in *Rotea* is understandable in light of the mutual exchange of familial support which the record indicates, the court's statement that the satisfaction of obtaining compliance with one's request will not support quantum meruit recovery has ever since its rendition been criticized for its harshness. Commentators have attacked the requirement of a "direct benefit" to the defendant as "purely an historical one." [citations] * * *

To avoid the harshness of the reasoning in *Rotea* the courts of appeal have subsequently drawn frequent exceptions to the requirement of "direct benefit." In cases involving services, these courts have often implied an obligation to pay based upon the theory that performance at another's request may itself constitute a benefit. * * *

Indeed, the issue whether we should broaden the basis of quasi-contractual recovery so as to prevent any unconscionable injury to the plaintiff, is not a novel one for our court. In his dissenting opinion in Coleman Engineering Co. v. North American Aviation, Inc. (1966) 65 Cal.2d 396, 55 Cal.Rptr. 1, 420 P.2d 713, Chief Justice Traynor cogently urged that we abandon the unconscionable requirement of "benefit" to the defendant and allow recovery in quantum meruit whenever a party acts to his detriment in reliance on another's representation that he will give compensation for the detriment suffered.

Thus Chief Justice Traynor would have awarded plaintiff recovery notwithstanding defendant's lack of "benefit." As the Chief Justice concluded, "the one rendering performance and incurring expenses at the request of the other should receive reasonable compensation therefor without regard to benefit conferred upon the other. Such a rule places the loss where it belongs—on the party whose requests induced performance in justifiable reliance on the belief that the requested performance would be paid for." [1]

1. [Footnotes renumbered.] Courts in other jurisdictions have granted recovery in quantum meruit for one party's detrimental reliance on another's request for performance. In Abrams v. Financial Service Co. (1962) 13 Utah 2d 343, 374 P.2d 309, the court held that a prospective vendor could recover for work and material expended on his own property in reliance on a

The determination to protect "justifiable reliance" forms not only the inspiration for Chief Justice Traynor's application of a quasi-contractual remedy in *Coleman,* but also provides the basis for several parallel contractual doctrines as well. The first of these doctrines rests on the theory that "part performance" of an otherwise invalid contract may satisfy the purposes of the statute of frauds. Thus a court may award damages based on an unenforceable contract if unconscionable injury would result from denying enforcement after one party has been induced to make a serious change of position. [citations] Closely allied to the doctrine of part performance is the notion that reliance by one party on an oral contract may "estop" the other from setting up a defense based upon the statute of frauds. [citations]

Finally, section 90 of the Restatement of Contracts—the so-called "promissory estoppel" section—provides that reasonably expected reliance may under some circumstances make binding a promise for which nothing has been given or promised in exchange.[2] In Raedeke v. Gibraltar Savings & Loan Assn. (1974) 10 Cal.3d 665, 111 Cal.Rptr. 693, 517 P.2d 1157 we explained that a court may invoke the doctrine of promissory estoppel embodied in section 90 to bind a promisor " 'when he should reasonably expect a substantial change of position, either by act or forbearance, in reliance on his promise, if injustice can be avoided only by its enforcement.' "[3]

In view of the equitable considerations lying at the foundation of these several doctrines, and reflected in the opinion in *Coleman,* we conclude that compensation for a party's performance should be paid by the person whose request induced the performance.[4] In light of this conclusion, the portion of

void or unenforceable contract for its sale. As the court stated: "The basis for the recovery is the prospective vendee's request that the property be suited to his needs. Although the vendees here received no benefit from the expenditure and are relieved from performances of the contract, they are not relieved of their promise, which the law implies, to reimburse defendant for the expenditures made in preparing the property for plaintiffs' use."

See also Kearns v. Andree (1928) 107 Conn. 181, 187, 139 A. 695, 697, in which the court reached the same conclusion on similar facts, stating: "The basis of that [implied promise] is that the services have been requested and have been performed by the plaintiff in the known expectation that he would receive compensation, and neither the extent nor the presence of benefit to the defendant from their performance is of controlling significance."

2. Section 90 provides, "A promise which the promisor should reasonably expect to induce action or forbearance of a definite and substantial character on the part of the promisee and which does induce such action or forbearance is binding if injustice can be avoided only by enforcement of the promise." (Rest., Contracts (1932) p. 110.)

3. As Professor Gilmore states, "As we might expect, the refusal to give protection in the 'benefit conferred' cases has been gradually suffering a reversal. The difficulty which the courts have had with such cases is, perhaps, reflected in the variety of explanations which have been offered to justify the plaintiff's recovery. The old variant of the common law action of assumpsit known as indebitatus assumpsit has been a useful crutch to explain why plaintiff recovers, not, of course, strictly in contract, but in quantum meruit. More adventurous courts have turned to the idea of a 'contract implied in law,' a 'quasi-contract'—not really a contract, a legal fiction necessary to promote the ends of justice and, in particular, to prevent 'unjust enrichment.' Rules of 'substantial performance' were developed to protect plaintiffs who had almost, but not quite, completed performance. And reputable courts have even suggested that plaintiffs, conceded to be in willful and substantial default, should nevertheless recover the value of whatever it is they have conferred on the defendant. The rejection of classical theory has thus been preceeding, albeit in a confused and sprawling pattern, on the benefit side." (Gilmore, The Death of Contract (1974) pp. 73–74.)

4. Compare Palmer v. Gregg (1967) 65 Cal.2d 657, 56 Cal.Rptr. 97, 422 P.2d 985, in which plaintiff sought to recover both the reasonable value of nursing services which she rendered to a third party at defendant's request and reimbursement for the loss of necessary gardening services performed at her house during her absence. While plaintiff recovered the former at trial, on appeal we denied recovery for plaintiff's personal gardening expenses: "The rule espoused in the dissenting opinion of Chief Justice Traynor in *[Coleman;]* is inapplicable be-the judgment denying plaintiff recovery with respect to the Pillow property must be reversed. As we have explained, plaintiff's evidence indicated that he had performed services and furnished materials in work on the Pillow property at the urgent request of defendant. Moreover, according to plaintiff, the work was performed under circumstances in which plaintiff reasonably relied upon the belief that defendant would pay for it.

In denying plaintiff recovery for such work, the trial court rested solely on the broad implications of our *Rotea* decision. Since we have disapproved those implications, we reverse the trial court's ruling. On remand, the trial court should determine, under the principles set out in this opinion, whether plaintiff is entitled to recover under quantum meruit with respect to the Pillow property and, if so, the extent of the award.

The judgment is reversed and the case is remanded to the trial court for further proceedings consistent with this opinion.

D. EQUITABLE RESTITUTIONARY REMEDIES

COMMENT, RESTITUTION: CONCEPT AND TERMS

19 Hastings L.J. 1167, 1168 (1968).
Reprinted with Permission.

In Moses v. Macferlan, decided in 1760, Lord Mansfield established "unjust enrichment" as the basis of the action of indebitatus assumpsit, or quasi-contract as it was later termed, and marked it as a separate and distinct common law obligation. The chancery courts, however, were reluctant to relinquish jurisdiction once gained, and concurrent remedies in equity remained available to a person who had been deprived of his property by fraud, mistake or duress, as well as for breach of a fiduciary duty. These alternative equitable remedies were by no means ignored, due partly to the icy reception of Moses v. Macferlan by many English lawyers who were not quite ready for so vague a concept as unjust enrichment.

1. THE CONSTRUCTIVE TRUST

While the law was busily constructing "contracts" to create a remedy for unjust enrichment, equity was constructing "trusts." The relation between a "constructive trust" and an express trust is essentially the same as between a quasi-contract and a contract. The resulting trust created by inference from the conduct of the parties is the practical equivalent of the contract implied in fact.

ROGERS v. ROGERS

Court of Appeals of New York, 1984.
63 N.Y.2d 502, 483 N.Y.S.2d 976, 473 N.E.2d 226.

KAYE, JUDGE. In a separation agreement, the decedent promised his first wife to maintain his life insurance policy, which designated her and their children (plaintiffs in this action) as beneficiaries. He breached that agree-

cause, in contrast to the present case, the expenditures in *Coleman* were made *at the request of* the obligor." (Emphasis in original.)

ment when he allowed the policy to lapse and obtained another policy naming a subsequent wife as beneficiary. We hold that under Simonds v. Simonds, 45 N.Y.2d 233, 408 N.Y.S.2d 359, 380 N.E.2d 189, a constructive trust may be impressed on the proceeds in favor of plaintiffs.

In 1968, decedent Jerome Rogers and plaintiff Susan Rogers entered into a separation agreement which provided for the continuation of decedent's life insurance policy as follows: "ninth: The Husband promises and agrees to continue in full force and effect his present life insurance policy in the face amount of approximately $15,000.00 with the wife and children as NAMED EQUAL irrevocable beneficiaries." The agreement was subsequently incorporated into a divorce decree. At the time, decedent's life was insured for $15,000 through a Travelers Insurance Company group policy issued to Grumman Aerospace Company, decedent's employer. This coverage terminated in 1970 when decedent left Grumman. He married defendant Judith Rogers in June 1974. From 1970 to 1976, decedent held a number of jobs but there is no indication that his life was insured during this period. In 1976, decedent obtained employment with Technical Data Specialists, Inc., and, by virtue of this employment, his life was insured for $15,000 through a group policy issued by defendant Phoenix Mutual Life Insurance Company. He designated Judith Rogers beneficiary. Jerome Rogers died on April 1, 1980.

Judith Rogers and plaintiffs both notified Phoenix of their intent to claim benefits. Phoenix informed the parties of the dispute on October 17, 1980 and said that it would file an interpleader action if it did not hear from them within 30 days. Subsequently, however, Phoenix communicated with Judith Rogers' attorney and satisfied itself that the proceeds should be paid to her. On January 9, 1981, it informed plaintiffs' attorney that it would disburse the benefits to Judith unless within 15 days it was prohibited from doing so by court order. Since no court order was obtained, Phoenix made payment to Judith on February 4, 1981.

Plaintiffs commenced this action to impress a constructive trust on the insurance proceeds. Judith Rogers moved to dismiss the complaint or for summary judgment and Phoenix also moved for summary judgment. Plaintiffs cross-moved for summary judgment against both defendants. Special Term granted defendants' motions and dismissed the complaint, reasoning that plaintiffs were not entitled to the proceeds because the separation agreement did not address the decedent's duties in the event of cancellation or lapse of the first insurance policy. The Appellate Division affirmed and this court granted plaintiffs' motion for leave to appeal. The appeal against Phoenix has been withdrawn.

A constructive trust may be imposed in favor of one who transfers property in reliance on a promise originating in a confidential relationship where the transfer results in the unjust enrichment of the holder (Sharp v. Kosmalski, 40 N.Y.2d 119, 386 N.Y.S.2d 72, 351 N.E.2d 721). Accordingly, one who possesses equity in an asset is entitled to restitution of the asset by a subsequent title holder who paid no value even if the latter had no knowledge of the predecessor's equitable interest. [citations] In general, it is necessary to trace one's equitable interest to identifiable property in the hands of the purported constructive trustee. [citations] But in view of equity's goal of softening where appropriate the harsh consequences of legal formalisms, in limited situations the tracing requirement may be relaxed.

In Simonds v. Simonds, decedent and his first wife entered into a separation agreement which provided: " 'The husband agrees that he will keep all of the policies of Insurance now in full force and effect on his life. Said policies now being in the sum of $21,000.00 and the Husband further agrees that the Wife shall be the beneficiary of said policies in an amount not less than $7,000.00 and the Husband further agrees that he shall pay any and all premiums necessary to maintain such policies of Insurance and if for any reason any of the now existing policies shall be cancelled or be caused to lapse. He shall procure additional insurance in an amount equal to the face value of the policies having been cancelled or caused to lapse.' " After the divorce, the husband remarried and permitted his insurance policies to lapse. However, he acquired three other policies, totaling more than $55,000, which named as beneficiaries his second wife and their daughter. On the husband's death, and faced with his insolvent estate, the first wife brought an action against the second wife to impose a constructive trust on the insurance proceeds to the extent of $7,000. The court affirmed the grant of summary judgment in favor of the first wife.

As the court noted, a promise in a separation agreement to maintain an insurance policy designating a spouse as beneficiary vests in the spouse an equitable interest in the policy specified, and that spouse will prevail over a person in whose favor the decedent executed a gratuitous change in beneficiary. [citations] The first spouse's superior right to the insurance proceeds will not necessarily be defeated simply because the insured changes policies or insurance companies instead of beneficiaries. The court explained that "inability to trace plaintiff's equitable rights precisely should not require that they not be recognized." Simonds v. Simonds. [citations] The need to relax the tracing requirement in exceptional circumstances has been acknowledged in a tentative draft of the Restatement of Restitution, Second: "If the holder of property has acquired it as a replacement for another asset of known value, and owes restitution to a claimant who could have enforced against the holder an agreement to preserve or replace that asset, a constructive trust or an equitable lien will be imposed on the holder's interest according to § 30 and clause (e) of § 32" (Restatement, Restitution 2d, Tent.Draft No. 2, § 33, subd. 2; see, also, Comment c thereto).

Defendant Rogers argues that *Simonds* is distinguishable because the separation agreement there obligated the husband to procure additional insurance in the event of lapse—an obligation not explicitly set forth in the agreement here. But the existence of such a provision was not the articulated basis of the *Simonds* decision. The "additional insurance" language in the agreement in *Simonds* did not and could not identify a specific *res* as subject to the first wife's superior right. It simply made the persistence of the equitable interest "all the more evident." The survival of the equitable interest is also evident here. No less than in *Simonds,* what was certainly the contemplation of the parties, embodied in paragraph ninth of their separation agreement, was the promise that decedent would maintain or replace a $15,000 life insurance policy, and not a promise that would persist only so long as he remained an employee of Grumman. Both life insurance policies were obtained by virtue of decedent's employment, both were in the amount of $15,000, and there is no indication that decedent maintained any other life insurance during the respective terms of the policies. He maintained one $15,000 life insurance policy while an employee of Grumman and, after that had lapsed, maintained a later $15,000 life insurance policy while an employee of Technical Data Services. Thus, despite the time period between the lapse of the Travelers policy and the issuance of the Phoenix policy, the latter may properly be considered a fulfillment of decedent's implied promise to replace the former. To find that decedent had escaped the obligation imposed upon him by the separation agreement simply because of the absence from the agreement of words specifically addressing the cancellation of the first policy, when the intendment is plain, would be to erect a legal formalism and defeat an essential purpose of equity.

The *Simonds* decision itself evinced the court's rejection of defendant's position by its criticism of Rindels v. Prudential Life Ins. Co., 83 N.M. 181, 489 P.2d 1179, a case conceded by defendant at Special Term to be "almost identical" to the situation here. In *Rindels*, the husband agreed to "maintain his present life insurance policy and/or policies setting out the minor children as beneficiaries thereunder." The husband was then insured under a group policy through his employer. However, the husband changed jobs and became insured under a new group policy issued by a different carrier. The *Rindels* court refused to impress a constructive trust on the proceeds and emphasized that the case involved not a mere change of beneficiary or substitution of policies but a completely new policy which arose from a change of employment. *Simonds* criticized *Rindels* because it relied "heavily on formalism and too little on basic equitable principles." Notably, this court did not distinguish *Rindels* because there had been no express provision in the agreement for future insurance policies.

In opposing plaintiffs' request for summary judgment, defendant in this court relies exclusively on the absence from the separation agreement of specific provision governing after-acquired policies. Accordingly, the order of the Appellate Division should be reversed, with costs, defendant Judith Rogers' summary judgment motion denied, and plaintiffs' cross motion for summary judgment granted.

COOKE, C.J., and JASEN, JONES, WACHTLER, MEYER and SIMONS, JJ., concur.

Order reversed, etc.

Notes

1. Restatement of Restitution (1937) †

§ 160. Constructive Trust: Where a person holding title to property is subject to an equitable duty to convey it to another on the ground that he would be unjustly enriched if he were permitted to retain it, a constructive trust arises.

Comment: a. Constructive trust and express trust.

The term "constructive trust" is not altogether a felicitous one. It might be thought to suggest the idea that it is a fiduciary relation similar to an express trust, whereas it is in fact something quite different from an express trust. An express trust and a constructive trust are not divisions of the same fundamental concept. They are not species of the same genus. They are distinct concepts. A constructive trust does not, like an express trust, arise because of a manifestation of an intention to create it, but it is imposed as a remedy to prevent unjust enrichment. A constructive trust, unlike an express trust, is not a fiduciary relation, although

the circumstances which give rise to a constructive trust may or may not involve a fiduciary relation.

It is true that both in the case of an express trust and in that of a constructive trust one person holds the title to property subject to an equitable duty to hold the property for or to convey it to another, and the latter has in each case some kind of an equitable interest in the property. In other respects, however, there is little resemblance between the two relationships.

2. See Papazian v. American Steel & Wire Co., 155 F.Supp. 111, 118–19 (N.D.Ohio 1957): "Constructive trust is not a title. As was said in International Refugee Organization v. Maryland Dry Dock Co., 4 Cir., 179 F.2d 284, 287:

" 'A constructive trust is not a title to or lien upon property but a mere remedy to which equity resorts in granting relief against fraud; and it does not exist so as to affect the property held by a wrongdoer until it is declared by a court of equity as a means of affording relief. See Restatement of Restitution § 160; * * * Edwards v. Culbertson, 111 N.C. 342, 16 S.E. 233, 234. As said in the case last cited: "The trusts of which we are speaking are not what is known as 'technical trusts,' and the ground of relief in such cases is, strictly speaking, fraud, and not trust. Equity declares the trust in order that it may lay its hand upon the thing and wrest it from the possession of the wrongdoer." ' "

"It is not without significance that in the Restatement, the subject of Constructive Trusts is treated in the Restatement of Restitution rather than in the Restatement of the Law of Trusts."

Compare Burch & Cracchiolo, P.A. v. Pugliani, 144 Ariz. 281, 286, 697 P.2d 674, 679 (1985). The court refused to impose a constructive trust on a party who had disbursed trust funds. "A prerequisite to the imposition of a constructive trust is the identification of a specific property belonging to the claimant. * * * A general claim for money damages will not give rise to a constructive trust."

3. Republic of Philippines v. Marcos, 806 F.2d 344 (2d Cir.1986). The Republic of the Philippines, in its effort to recover money allegedly wrongfully taken by ex-President Marcos, was granted a preliminary injunction to prevent the transfer of property that it claimed to be held under a constructive trust.

Lis pendens may serve a similar function if the alleged constructive trust property is realty. MDO Development Corp. v. Kelly, 726 F.Supp. 79, 86–87 (S.D.N.Y.1989).

4. In light of the principal case and the commentary, consider the validity of the following statements:

a. Elliott v. Elliott, 231 Cal.App.2d 205, 211, 41 Cal.Rptr. 686, 689 (1964), presented the question of whether defendant could be declared the constructive trustee of a promissory note made unenforceable by the statute of limitations. In reviewing a decree imposing a constructive trust, the California Court of Appeals made the following pronouncement: "To charge a constructive trustee with an unconscionable loss he has caused the beneficiary is simply the converse of charging him with profits rightly belonging to the beneficiary; the loss is equally real to the beneficiary in either case and in each case it results from wrongful acts of the trustee. To apply the constructive trust doctrine in both instances lends congruity to the law."

For a critique, see Note, The Necessity for Unjust Enrichment in a Constructive Trust in California: Elliott v. Elliott, 19 Hastings L.J. 1268, 1279 (1968).

b. Harris v. Sentry Title Co., 715 F.2d 941, 947 (5th Cir.1983), involved the imposition of a constructive trust on proceeds from a complicated land acquisition scheme. Summarizing Texas law, Judge Williams found two "general prerequisites" for a constructive trust: "The first is a prior, unrelated history of close and trusted dealings of the same general nature or scope as the subject transactions. The second is a finding that unjust enrichment would result if the remedy of constructive trust were not imposed."

The court, in a subsequent proceeding in the case, reemphasized the necessity of a confidential relationship in the absence of fraud. 727 F.2d 1368 (5th Cir.1984).

Compare the reporter's comment in Tentative Draft No. 2, Restatement (Second) of Restitution, at 28 (1984), "Sometimes it is said that a constructive trust can be predicated only on a fiduciary relationship or actual fraud. Such expressions are to be rejected as stating the grounds for the remedy too narrowly."

5. The time when a constructive trust arises may be crucial in determining the rights of the parties. In Palmland Villas I Condominium v. Taylor, 390 So.2d 123, 124 (Fla.App.1980), the court resolved the issue as follows: "The result in this case turns upon the answer to the question, when does a constructive trust come into existence. We determine that a constructive trust comes into existence on the date of the order or judgment of a court of competent jurisdiction declaring that a series of events has given rise to a constructive trust."

2. THE EQUITABLE LIEN

FRAMBACH v. DUNIHUE

District Court of Appeal of Florida, Fifth District, 1982.
419 So.2d 1115.

FRANK D. UPCHURCH, JR., JUDGE. The Frambachs appeal from a judgment awarding Dunihue an undivided one-half interest in their property. * * *

Dunihue was a widower with seven children to raise ranging in age from three to eleven. The Frambachs lived nearby with their four children. Contact between the parties started when Mrs. Frambach, a devoted churchwoman, asked if she could take the Dunihue children to church. She later became a babysitter and took care of the Dunihue children sometimes at their home and sometimes at hers for which she was paid $25.00 per week.

This arrangement continued for a few months. In September, 1960, the Frambachs and the Dunihues waited out a hurricane in the Frambachs' home. The Frambachs' house was small (a bedroom, living room and kitchen, 600 square feet in all) and had no inside plumbing. As fate would have it, the relationships which developed as the storm howled proved so interesting and the two families so congenial that the Frambachs and Dunihues decided to see if the two families could live together.

Dunihue set out to enlarge the house. A bedroom and bath were added and various improvements made. As the years passed, Mrs. Frambach had another child and for a time, until the Dunihue children began to move out, fifteen people (three adults and twelve children) lived in the house. Mrs. Frambach ran the household, did the cooking, and saw that the children cleaned, helped with the washing, and did such chores as were required and within their capabilities.

Improvements in the home continued to be made. Dunihue's contributions to these improvements undoubtedly were the most valuable although everyone assisted. At the time of this litigation, the value of the home had appreciated to approximately $65,000. The court received considerable testimony of Dunihue's contributions to the improvements, but very little evidence was adduced as to the value of the services received by Dunihue and his family.

This arrangement lasted for nineteen years until the last of the Dunihue children were grown and gone. The relationship was suddenly terminated when Mrs. Frambach called Dunihue at work and told him to come get his things and get out. He was given thirty minutes to comply. The reason for the sudden end to the friendship was not clear.

After being ejected from the Frambachs' home, Dunihue brought suit to impose an equitable lien on the property. Dunihue claimed that the Frambachs had promised him a place to live for the rest of his life in exchange for his work. He further alleged that he had relied on this promise and that the Frambachs will be unjustly enriched at his expense if he is not compensated for his work. The Frambachs denied that they had made any such promise to Dunihue claiming that without the improvements it would have been impossible to house that many people.

The trial court determined that the two families had operated as a single family * * * and that it would award Dunihue an equitable lien in the home. Regarding the amount of the lien, the court stated the following:

> "They did start out with a thousand-dollar equity, the [Frambachs]. But in effect because of the way they treated everything through the years, they really are just as though this was a divorce. And we are dividing up the property between a wife that had two husbands, so to speak. That's why I think the only fair thing to do is to make them tenants in common right down the middle. So that's my judgment."

As a general rule, a court of equity may give restitution to a plaintiff and prevent the unjust enrichment of a defendant by imposing a constructive trust or by imposing an equitable lien upon the property in favor of the plaintiff. However, where the plaintiff makes improvements upon the land of another under circumstances which entitle him to restitution, he is entitled only to an equitable lien upon the land and he cannot charge the owner of the land as constructive trustee and compel the owner to transfer the land to him. Restatement of Restitution § 161, Comment a. Neither a constructive trust nor a resulting trust arises in favor of a person who pays no part of the purchase price even though he pays for improvements on the property. 5 Scott, The Law of Trusts §§ 455.7, 472 (3d ed. 1967.) The person does not become, in whole or in part, a beneficial owner of the property although he may be entitled to reimbursement.

In the present case, the court, in effect, determined that the Frambachs held an undivided one-half interest in the property in trust for Dunihue. However, there was no evidence of a promise or agreement to deed a portion of the Frambach's property to Dunihue in return for the improvements. Nor has Dunihue alleged that he actually paid a part of the purchase price. In these circumstances, Dunihue was not entitled to have a constructive trust imposed on the property. We therefore reverse the award to Dunihue of a tenancy in common and remand the cause for further consideration.

Upon remand, the trial court should determine the value of the respective contributions of Dunihue and the Frambachs. This can be accomplished by calculating the fair market value of the improvements attributable to Dunihue and the fair market value of the services rendered by the Frambachs to him during the nineteen years the parties lived together. In the alternative, the court could determine the cost to Dunihue for his labor, services and material in making the improvements as compared to the cost to the Frambachs of providing services to Dunihue. We suspect that, under either measure, the contributions of the parties will be equal. However, if the court finds that Dunihue's contributions exceed the value of the benefits received by him from the Frambachs, an equitable lien in this amount should be imposed to prevent the unjust enrichment of the Frambachs.

Reversed and Remanded.

Notes

1. Restatement (Second) of Restitution (Tentative Draft No. 2, 1984) †

§ 30, Comment a: Constructive trust and equitable lien compared. A principal use of constructive trust is to award to a claimant a gain produced by an investment of property that was acquired from him by wrongdoing such as fraud; another is to charge a fiduciary for gain he acquired by a breach of loyalty to the claimant. Imposing a constructive trust is also a means of requiring specific restitution to the claimant. In contrast, imposing an equitable lien on an asset does not vest ownership in the claimant and does not afford him specific restitution. The lien assures the claimant that the asset will be devoted to satisfying his right to restitution in preference to the claims of ordinary creditors of the person owing restitution. When a sum of money has been acquired from the claimant by fraud and partly dissipated, the claimant has a right to restitution greater in amount than the money remaining in the wrongdoer's control. That is a proper case for an equitable lien. The claimant can get a judgment for the amount acquired by the wrongdoer (with interest as appropriate) and an order that the money remaining with the wrongdoer be applied to the judgment. The claimant can get comparable relief if the wrongdoer has made a losing investment of the money he acquired by fraud: property acquired by the wrongdoer through the investment will be subjected to an equitable lien. If the claimant wants specific restitution of that property, and the requirements of § 10 are satisfied, a constructive trust is an appropriate form of relief. (See, however, § 9.) As Comment a to that section states, specific restitution of money may be denied when relief in another form would be equally effective. An equitable lien on money—or other property—will not be denied, as a constructive trust may be, on the ground that other relief would be adequate, since the purpose of the lien is to reduce the risk that a restitution claim will prove to be uncollectible.

In general, a claimant whose property has been misappropriated and exchanged for other property of less value will be best served by enforcing an equitable lien on the latter and preserving, as a deficiency claim, any unsatisfied part of his right to restitution. Asserting a constructive trust on property of a wrongdoer (or of a successor in interest) will give the claimant more complete relief only when the value of the property includes a gain by investment, appreciation, or natural increase.

2. In considering the extent of an equitable lien imposed on property, the Illinois Appellate Court stated in Robinson v. Robinson, 100 Ill.App.3d 437, 446–47, 429 N.E.2d 183, 190 (1981):

"One scholar has suggested that when one builds a house on another's land, there are at least two feasible objective measures of restitution and one subjective measure. They are (1) the objective value of the labor and materials which went into the house; (2) the increased value of the land resulting from the addition of the house to it; and (3) the personal value to the defendant landowner for his particular purposes. D. Dobbs, Remedies, § 4.5 at 261 (1973). We have been supplied no case which has adopted the latter approach perhaps because of the almost impossibility of determining the subjective approach.

"The Illinois cases have variously given an equitable lien for (1) the cost of the improvements or (2) the enhanced value of the premises, or (3) a right to purchase the premises if the owner elects to sell."

3. Rotary Club v. Chaprales Ramos de Pena, 160 Ariz. 362, 365–66, 773 P.2d 467, 470–71 (App.1989). Plaintiff, the specific devisee of property, alleged that defendants wrongfully sold the property and used the proceeds of the sale to purchase a home.

"The trial court imposed both a constructive trust and an equitable lien on the home. There is a difference between these two remedies. Under a constructive trust the appellants hold the title to the townhouse for appellees. Appellees have a judgment for $42,699.98. If the townhouse is worth $150,000 appellees will make a profit of $107,300.02.

"There are different results from an equitable lien. Appellees can foreclose this lien and any proceeds from the sale in excess of their judgment goes to the appellants. If the proceeds are insufficient, appellees can obtain a personal judgment against appellants for the balance.

"Appellants used the majority of the proceeds they received from the Palm Tree Drive property to pay off an outstanding overdue mortgage on the townhouse which was also part of the Chaprales estate. They contend that they acted in a good faith belief pursuant to what they thought was a valid Mexican judgment. Appellees do not dispute the fact that appellants acted in such good faith belief. The Restatement of Restitution, § 203 (1937) states:

> 'Where a person converts the property of another without notice of the facts which make him a converter and being still without such notice exchanges it for other property, the other is entitled to an equitable lien upon the property received in exchange to secure his claim for restitution, but is not entitled to enforce a constructive trust of the property.'

"The reason for the Restatement rule is set forth in Comment *a:*

> 'Where the converter is a conscious wrongdoer, he can be compelled to surrender any profit which he makes by a disposition of the claimant's property, and not merely to restore to the claimant the value of his property, since if he were permitted to keep the profit there would be an incentive to wrongdoing, and compelling him to surrender the profit operates as a deterrent upon the wrongful disposition of the property of others. * * * This reason is not applicable to persons who are not conscious wrongdoers. A person who innocently converts the property of another is liable to the other for the value of the property converted, and if through the disposition of this property he acquires other property, the other can enforce an equitable lien upon the property so acquired as security for his claim against the converter for the value of the property converted, and if the property so acquired is of less value than the property converted, the other can hold the converter personally liable for the balance of his claim. If the property so acquired is of greater value than the property converted, the other cannot reach the profit by enforcing a constructive trust of the property so acquired. The owner of the property converted is entitled to be made whole but not to reach the profit.'

"The trial court erred in declaring a constructive trust but did not err in declaring an equitable lien on the townhouse."

3. SUBROGATION

WILSON v. TODD

Supreme Court of Indiana, 1940.
217 Ind. 183, 26 N.E.2d 1003.

SHAKE, CHIEF JUSTICE. The appellant's complaint alleged and the trial court found that during the year 1930 the appellee Roy W. Todd perpetrated an actionable fraud upon the appellant, Charles Wilson, by means of which more than $12,000 in money was extorted from said appellant. The money so obtained was deposited by said Roy W. Todd to his account in a bank. Thereafter, he used $774.38 thereof to pay and discharge a mortgage held by one Henry N. Wilson on a 33-acre tract of land. The further sum of $3,548.16 was withdrawn from said bank by said appellee and applied to the payment of a mortgage held by the Fletcher Joint Stock Land Bank on a 160-acre farm. Title to both pieces of real estate was held by the appellees, who are husband and wife, as tenants by the entireties, and they were both personally liable for the payment of the debts secured by said mortgages. On September 21, 1934, the appellant obtained a tort judgment against Roy W. Todd for the sum of $12,000, for the money that had been obtained by him as aforesaid. This judgment has never been satisfied. The appellee Ruth A. Todd had no knowledge of the fraudulent acts of her husband at the time said acts were committed, but did have knowledge thereof at the time of commencement of this action.

The present action was begun on April 24, 1935. The complaint was drawn upon the theory of subrogation. The prayer was that the satisfaction of the aforesaid mortgage liens be set aside and vacated; that there be an adjudication that said liens stand for appellant's use and benefit; and that said mortgages be foreclosed, said real estate sold, and the proceeds applied on the appellant's claim. On the facts found the trial court pronounced conclusions of law to the effect that the law was with the appellant on the issues joined as to his right of subrogation to the mortgage on the 33-acre tract of land, which was discharged by the payment of $774.38; that the law was with the appellee Ruth A. Todd as to the appellant's right of subrogation with respect to the mortgage on the 160-acre farm, which was discharged by the payment of $3,548.16; and that the appellant was entitled to recover from the appellee Roy W. Todd the sum of $12,000, less any amount recovered from the foreclosure of the mortgage on the 33-acre tract of land. * * *

The appellees contend that the conclusion denying subrogation to the mortgage on the 160-acre farm was proper because the findings and the evidence failed to disclose certain essential facts, namely: (1) Knowledge on the part of Ruth A. Todd of the fraud practiced by her husband or of the judgment rendered against him therefor; (2) that the mortgage debts were paid with money belonging to the appellant; (3) that in discharging the mortgage liens Roy W. Todd acted for Ruth A. Todd; and (4) that demand was made on Ruth A. Todd prior to the bringing of this action.

Subrogation is the substitution of another person in the place of a creditor, so that the person in whose favor it is exercised succeeds to the right of the

creditor in relation to the debt. So, one whose property is applied by others to the satisfaction of a debt or incumbrance is subrogated to the rights of the creditor or incumbrancer; and subrogation may also be allowed where funds to which one is equitably entitled have been applied to the payment of the debts of another, in which case the former is subrogated to the position of the latter. If it be conceded that the appellant Ruth A. Todd had no knowledge of the fraud perpetrated by her husband, by means of which he obtained the funds out of which he discharged the mortgage debts, and that in paying said debts the husband acted for himself and not as her agent, we do not think this would preclude appellant's right to recover. After being charged with full knowledge of the facts, Ruth A. Todd failed to disavow the acts of her husband, retained the benefits thereof, and resisted the appellant's efforts to obtain redress. She thereby ratified all that had been done by her husband and placed herself in a position to be estopped from denying knowledge of the transaction and the authority of her husband to act for her. And if there was no ratification or no estoppel, we do not think the contention of the appellee Ruth A. Todd could be sustained. According to her own theory she occupies the position of a third party so far as the relation of her husband and the appellant is concerned. She parted with nothing, and will suffer no disadvantages on account of the appellant being subrogated to the rights of the mortgagees.

It cannot be seriously contended that the mortgage debts were not discharged with money that belonged to the appellant. The funds that were fraudulently taken from him were directly traced into the bank account of Roy W. Todd and paid to the mortgagees by checks drawn by him on said account. The court's special findings set out in detail the means by which this was accomplished. There was no such commingling of funds as would require a holding that they could not be identified or followed. * * *

The judgment is reversed, with directions to the trial court to restate its third and fourth conclusions of law in conformity with this opinion, and to enter judgment in favor of the appellant.

Notes

1. Restatement of Restitution (1937) † § 162, *Comment a:* The right to subrogation.

A court of equity may give restitution to the plaintiff and prevent the unjust enrichment of the defendant, where the plaintiff's property has been used in discharging an obligation owed by the defendant or a lien upon the property of the defendant, by creating in the plaintiff rights similar to those which the obligee or lien-holder had before the obligation or lien was discharged. In such a case the procedure is called subrogation, and the plaintiff is said to be subrogated to the position of the obligee or lien-holder. Although the obligation or lien has been discharged, the plaintiff can maintain a proceeding in equity to revive it for his benefit; in such a proceeding the court will create for the benefit of the plaintiff an equitable obligation or lien similar to that which was discharged.

2. The advantages of qualifying as a subrogee are several. Most frequently the subrogee seeks the benefit of the security interest covering the debt that has been discharged. Where no security interest exists, the subrogee may benefit from substitution into the position of a preferred creditor. Hardaway v. National Surety

Co., 211 U.S. 552 (1909): Records v. McKim, 115 Md. 299, 80 A. 968 (1911); United States Fidelity & Guaranty Co. v. Bramwell, 108 Or. 261, 217 P. 332 (1923).

Even where the discharged creditor lacked secured or preferred position, subrogation may have advantages. When a debtor filed bankruptcy, the court let a surety that had paid the debtor's taxes subrogate to the state's exception from discharging unpaid taxes. Matter of Fields, 926 F.2d 501 (5th Cir.1991). If a person is fraudulently induced to discharge the promissory note of another or discharges the note by mistake, subrogation to the note holder's position could entitle the subrogee to a longer statute of limitations. Cf. Zuellig v. Hemerlie, 60 Ohio St. 27, 53 N.E. 447 (1899).

A person who is entitled to restitution for discharging a tax lien on another's land is entitled to subrogation, in a general sense, to the claims of the state, insofar as security, priority, etc., but not to the taxing power's plenary measures to collect. If the tax lien is perpetual, the subrogee may have a claim free from the statute of limitations. Swingley v. Reichoff, 112 Mont. 59, 112 P.2d 1075 (1941); Childs v. Smith, 51 Wash. 457, 99 P. 304 (1909). In other cases the subrogee's claim has been held subject to the statute of limitations applicable to "implied contract claims not in writing." Brookfield v. Rock Island Improvement Co., 205 Ark. 573, 160 S.W.2d 662 (1943).

3. *Problem:* X embezzled $10,000 from her employer. An indemnity company having issued a fidelity bond to the employer paid the employer $10,000, and thereby became entitled to subrogation. X purchased Blackacre with the embezzled funds. Blackacre is now worth $15,000. What are the indemnity company's remedial rights? See Haskel Engineering Co. v. Hartford Indemnity Co., 78 Cal.App.3d 371, 144 Cal.Rptr. 189 (1978).

4. *Subrogation distinguished from indemnity.* Phoenix Insurance Co. v. United States Fire Insurance Co., 189 Cal.App.3d 1511, 1525–26, 235 Cal.Rptr. 185, 192–93 (1987). In an excess insurer's declaratory judgment action against the primary insurer seeking reimbursement of the amount expended in settling a lawsuit, the court compared subrogation with indemnity:

"That there is a distinction between subrogation and indemnification needs little discussion. Subrogation is '[t]he substitution of one person in the place of another with reference to a lawful claim, demand or right, so that he who is substituted succeeds to the rights of the other in relation to the debt or claim, and its rights, remedies, or securities. [citations]' Black's Law Dictionary 1279 (5th ed. 1979).

"Indemnity, however, has been defined as the obligation resting on one party to make good a loss or damage which another party has incurred. The obligation may arise from either of two general sources: 'First, it may arise by virtue of express contractual language establishing a duty in one party to save another harmless upon the occurrence of specified circumstances. Second, it may find its source in equitable considerations brought into play either by contractual language not specifically dealing with indemnification or *by the equities of the particular case.* [citations]'

"As we stated in Aetna Life & Cas. Co. v. Ford Motor Co. (1975) 50 Cal.App.3d 49, 52–53, 122 Cal.Rptr. 852: '[Equitable indemnification] applies in cases in which one party pays a debt for which another is primarily liable and which in equity and good conscience should have been paid by the latter party. Equitable indemnity * * * is not available to a volunteer. It extends to those who pay in performance of a legal duty in order to protect their own rights or interests. [citation] However, one acting in good faith in making payment under a reasonable belief that it is necessary to his protection is entitled to indemnity * * * even though it develops that he in fact had no interest to protect. [citation]' "

5. *Equitable Accounting.* Historically the bill of accounting was brought against express trustees, over whom the chancery court exercised exclusive jurisdiction, to compel them to account to the beneficiaries of the trust for their management of trust assets. The remedy was later extended by ordering an accounting incidental to another equitable remedy like an injunction or specific performance. After law and equity were merged, it was suggested that an accounting should be allowed where a wrongdoer profits from the unlawful use of plaintiff's property even though a traditional basis of equity jurisdiction is absent. See Eichengrun, Remedying the Remedy of Accounting, 60 Ind.L.J. 463 (1985); G. Palmer, The Law of Restitution § 2.12, at 165 (1978). We shall consider this again with Fur & Wool Trading Co. v. George I. Fox, Inc., infra p. 402.

Merger of law and equity and liberal rules of civil procedure may well resolve jurisdictional problems about the availability of an accounting; but at this point in our study we focus on the nature of the relief it provides. We can state firmly that an accounting is a restitutional remedy and that its function is to wrest from the wrongdoer the profits he unlawfully obtained from the victim's property. The United States Supreme Court recognized the restitutional character of the accounting remedy in Hamilton–Brown Shoe Co. v. Wolf Brothers & Co., 240 U.S. 251, 258 (1916). The plaintiff sought an injunction and an accounting for profits for an unlawful infringement of a trademark. In commenting on the right to an accounting, the Court said:

"Having reached the conclusion that complainant is entitled to the use of the words 'The American Girl' as a trademark, it results that it is entitled to the profits acquired by the defendant from the manifestly infringing sales under the label 'American Lady,'—at least to the extent that such profits are awarded in the decree under review. The right to use a trademark is recognized as a kind of property, of which the owner is entitled to the exclusive enjoyment to the extent that it has been actually used. [citation] The infringer is required in equity to account for and yield up his gains to the true owner, upon a principle analogous to that which charges a trustee with the profits acquired by wrongful use of the property of the *cestui que trust.* Not that equity assumes jurisdiction upon the ground that a trust exists. As pointed out in Root v. Lake Shore & M.S.R. Co., 105 U.S. 189, 214; and Tilghman v. Proctor, 125 U.S. 136, 148 (patent cases), the jurisdiction must be rested upon some other equitable ground,—in ordinary cases, as in the present, the right to an injunction—but the court of equity, having acquired jurisdiction upon such a ground, retains it for the purpose of administering complete relief, rather than send the injured party to a court of law for his damages. And profits are then allowed as an equitable measure of compensation, on the theory of a trust *ex maleficio.*"

6. *Problem.* Accounting for profits is easy to order but hard to figure. Here is a deceptively simple example from Rasmussen v. Van Riel, 708 P.2d 471, 472–73 (Colo.App.1985).

"The parties owned the house in question in joint tenancy during their marriage. A decree of dissolution of marriage was granted on August 29, 1980, and matters of custody, maintenance and property division were reserved for a later hearing. Before this hearing, however, the holder of a second mortgage foreclosed on the house because of failure to make the required monthly payments.

"In July 1981, the parties entered into a stipulation as to custody, maintenance, child support, and property division. As part of the stipulation, the parties agreed to divide the proceeds of the sale of the house, if they were able to redeem it 'prior to the issuance of a Public Trustee's Deed.'

"There was testimony at trial that husband had found a buyer for the house whose offer of $90,000 was sufficient to redeem the property and leave the parties with a small return of their equity. Wife refused to agree to the sale, however, and on September 23 a deed was issued to the secured party. Two days later, the secured party sold the house to wife for an amount substantially equivalent to the amount which had been secured by the mortgage, and wife in turn conveyed the property to two purchasers for $110,000. There was evidence that wife had negotiated this transaction prior to the expiration of the redemption period.

"Husband brought this suit seeking an accounting, imposition of a constructive trust, and damages. * * * Under these circumstances, an equitable duty existed, and thus, a constructive trust was properly imposed.

"Wife's contention that the constructive trust should extend only to the profits which husband would have received under the contract that wife refused is without merit. A restitutionary remedy for unjust enrichment extends to all benefits received as a result of a violation of an equitable duty to the injured party even if those benefits exceed the injured party's loss. See 1 G. Palmer, The Law of Restitution § 2.10 (1978)."

Note that two figures are not given with precision: a. the amount of the mortgage and b. the dollar amount of the "all benefits received." Assume that figure a. is $80,000, what is figure b.?

7. Combining an equitable accounting for profits with a constructive trust creates a potent remedy. The court uses the wrongdoer's gain to measure unjust enrichment whenever it exceeds the plaintiff's damages. The remedy's "punitive" nature is an important consideration in choosing among the remedies outlined in Part I, now completed, when placed in the assorted contexts which make up Parts II and III, the balance of this book. Its impact will become particularly apparent in the next few pages.

*

Part II

REMEDIES IN CONTEXT—TORTIOUS WRONGS

Chapter 5

REMEDIES FOR INJURIES TO TANGIBLE PROPERTY INTERESTS INCLUDING MONEY

A. MISAPPROPRIATION OF MONEY

1. LEGAL REMEDIES INCLUDING DAMAGES AND RESTITUTION

SHAHOOD v. CAVIN

District Court of Appeal of California, Second District, 1957.
154 Cal.App.2d 745, 316 P.2d 700.

ASHBURN, J. Appeal from judgment for plaintiff for $3,410.15 and costs. Appellant's first point is that the court erred in overruling a demurrer to the first amended complaint. Appellant argues that that complaint, labeled conversion, does not state a cause of action because the subject matter is money and mere money is not susceptible of conversion. We agree that the complaint does not allege a conversion but hold that the demurrer was properly overruled, disregarding in the process the faulty conclusion of the pleader.

The complaint in summary alleges the following. Plaintiff Debee K. Shahood is and was the owner of real property * * * in the city of Torrance. She gave a written power of attorney to her son, George N. Shahood, authorizing him to manage or sell the property for plaintiff's benefit. He conveyed it to defendant Cavin on January 9, 1955, as security for a personal loan of $1,500, defendant agreeing to reconvey upon repayment of the loan within six months. Defendant knew at all times that the loan was not to be used for the benefit of plaintiff or her property, and that the son George had no authority to convey except for the benefit of plaintiff. Thereafter, on May 1, 1955, George and Cavin made a superseding agreement to the effect that Cavin should sell the property to John Ard, deduct the amount of his loan from the proceeds and pay over the balance to George or Debee Shahood; the property was sold and conveyed to Ard for $11,200. Plaintiff had never authorized any sale or conveyance other than one for her own personal benefit and therefore the conveyances to Cavin and to Ard were unlawful; "[h]owever, Debee Shahood herewith ratifies the sale to the Ards." Cavin withholds the proceeds of the Ard sale from plaintiff "and has converted them to his own use and benefit, all to plaintiff's damage in the amount of $11,200.00;" * * *

Appellant cites Haigler v. Donnelly, 18 Cal.2d 674, 117 P.2d 331, and Olschewski v. Hudson, 87 Cal.App. 282, 262 P. 43, to the point that conversion does not lie for alleged misappropriation of money derived from the sale of an interest in land because that action applies to money "only where there is an obligation to keep intact or deliver the specific money in question and where such money can be identified." The authorities support this general proposition. Haigler v. Donnelly says: "While it is true that money cannot be the subject of an action for conversion unless a specific sum capable of identification is involved it is not necessary that each coin or bill be earmarked. When an agent is required to turn over to his principal a definite sum received by him on his principal's account, the remedy of conversion is proper." (To the same effect, see Anderson Elec. Car Co. v. Savings Trust Co., 212 Mo.App. 400, 212 S.W. 60.) "[T]rover lies only for specific chattels wrongfully converted, and not for money had and received for payment of debts, money being the subject of conversion only when it can be described or identified as a specific chattel."

The complaint says the price paid was $11,200 and that defendant withholds the proceeds of sale from plaintiff and has converted same to his own use, to plaintiff's damage in the amount of $11,200. This is susceptible of the interpretation that the property was sold for cash and the entire price paid to defendant. If so, that money might be the subject of conversion within the doctrine of the *Haigler* and other cases above cited; we do not decide the specific point. But plaintiff destroyed her claim of conversion by alleging that she "herewith ratifies the sale to the Ards." This was a definite waiver of the tort and an election to stand upon the resulting implied contract. * * *

Having waived the tort she was no longer entitled to damages, but was limited to recovery on the basis of unjust enrichment.

Appellant correctly argues that there was error in awarding judgment for $3,410.15 because defendant had sold the property to Ard on contract, with no down payment, installments being payable at $114.50 a month (of which $64.50 went to pay plaintiff's obligation to January Company, the seller named in the contract which she had purchased) and that defendant had received but 17 such payments, making a present obligation to plaintiff of $850. Defendant sold the equity to Ard on June 1, 1955. At the time of rendition of judgment in January, 1957, 19 payments had accrued and the court found the aggregate to be $950 as of January 1, 1957. Those are the moneys found to have been received by defendant and withheld from plaintiff. The findings show that the trial judge awarded to plaintiff not only the $950 found to have been collected by defendant from Ard, but also the present value of the balance due on the contract. As the award must proceed upon the basis of implied contract growing out of unjust enrichment this latter phase of the computation, anticipatory recovery of moneys to become due in the future, was erroneous. * * * While defendant becomes liable for each payment as received by him, he cannot be subjected to a judgment covering any installment prior to receipt of same by him. * * *

Because of the excessive amount of the award the judgment must be and is reversed and the cause remanded to the lower court for further proceedings not inconsistent with the views herein expressed.

Notes

1. Refusing to permit recovery for conversion of money, the court in Belford Trucking Co. v. Zagar, 243 So.2d 646, 648 (Fla.Dist.Ct.App.1970), stated: "To be a proper subject of conversion each coin or bill need not be earmarked, but there

must be an obligation to keep intact or deliver the specific money, so that such money can be identified * * *. The requirement that the money be identified as a specific chattel does not permit as a subject of conversion an indebtedness which may be discharged by the payment of money generally." See also Houston National Bank v. Bibes, 613 S.W.2d 771 (Tex.Civ.App.—Houston [14th Dist.] 1981); Cf. Bob White Chevrolet v. Hayles, 44 Ala.App. 411, 413, 211 So.2d 157, 159 (1968), holding that identification in an action of detinue is stricter, and requires "the description * * * to specifically identify the exact coins or currency in question."

Reason v. Payne, 793 S.W.2d 471 (Mo.App.1990). Specific and identifiable funds deposited in a savings account can be the subject of a conversion.

2. Courts may award punitive damages where defendant's conduct is "sufficiently aggravated." See Allen v. Allen, 275 Or. 471, 551 P.2d 459 (1976).

3. Suppose that defendant accepts converted funds in good faith to satisfy a valid pre-existing obligation owed by a converter. Defendant then has a good defense to an action for conversion brought by the injured party. "It is a rule of law that title to currency passes with delivery to the person who receives it in good faith and for valuable consideration." In Transamerica Insurance Co. v. Long, 318 F.Supp. 156, 160 (W.D.Pa.1970), a bank robber used the stolen money to pay his federal income tax; and the United States had a good defense to an action for conversion.

4. *Quasi-contract as an alternative legal remedy—advantages and disadvantages.* In Bertone v. City and County of San Francisco, 11 Cal.App.2d 579, 245 P.2d 29 (1952), plaintiff was allowed to recover money misappropriated by defendant in an action for money had and received although a "claim for damages" was barred for failure to comply with a sixty-day notice of claim provision in defendant's charter. In Crouch v. Mountain States Mixed Feed Co., 140 Colo. 213, 343 P.2d 1052 (1959), two defendants jointly defrauded plaintiff of a sum of money. Plaintiff waived the tort and sued for money had and received. The court ruled that a judgment could not be entered jointly against both defendants for the full amount misappropriated but was limited to the extent each defendant was unjustly enriched by the actual receipt of the money.

5. *Restitution (and maybe more) Through Criminal Procedure.* Although this book deals with civil remedies, criminal law mechanisms may compel restitution more cheaply and effectively through the growing practice of moderating criminal penalties if the criminal reimburses the victim. See Colson and Benson, Restitution as an Alternative to Imprisonment, 1980 Det.C.L.Rev. 523.

Statutory authority exists for ordering restitution in addition to a criminal sentence. See Sentencing Reform Act of 1984, 18 U.S.C. §§ 3551, 3556; Victim and Witness Protection Act of 1982, 18 U.S.C. §§ 3579, 3580. The court may assess restitution even though the defendant is at present indigent. United States v. Ryan, 874 F.2d 1052 (5th Cir.1989), but see United States v. Mitchell, 893 F.2d 935 (8th Cir.1990).

The decisions themselves reflect ambivalence about the purpose of restitution as a condition of probation. United States v. Hix, 545 F.2d 1247, 1247 (9th Cir.1976): "Although a fine is inherently punitive, restitution is not. So long as repayment is made to the victim * * * restitution is essentially rehabilitative, and hence consistent with the purpose of the Youth Corrections Act."

On the other hand when a criminal was ordered to repay a bank $25,000 for a fraudulently obtained loan, which had been discharged in bankruptcy, the court said the order was intended to punish the borrower and deter future fraud, not to repay the victim. United States v. Vetter, 895 F.2d 456 (8th Cir.1990).

Usually the order is for true restitution: it forces the defendant to return to the victim the amount the crime unjustly enriched him or her. In the federal courts the loss caused by the specific conduct that constitutes the offense defendant is convicted of limits the restitutionary award. Hughey v. United States, 110 S.Ct. 1979 (1990).

However, as might be anticipated, other criminal courts confuse the term restitution with compensatory damages and condition probation on payments by the criminal even though he did not benefit financially from the crime. See People v. Goss, 109 Cal.App.3d 443, 167 Cal.Rptr. 224 (1980) (payment of $150 as a condition for probation for *attempted* burglary), and Commonwealth v. Fuqua, 267 Pa.Super. 504, 407 A.2d 24 (1979) (convicted drunken driver must make "restitution for damage" to a house). In 1983 a California ballot proposition known as the "Victims Bill of Rights Act" made the victim's right of reimbursement through criminal procedure a constitutional one. Cal. Penal Code § 1203.04 (1990), enacted as a result, uses an expansive definition of "restitution" specifically to cover victim's damages apart from the criminal's gain. See People v. Ryan, 203 Cal. App.3d 189, 249 Cal.Rptr. 750 (1988). There need be no express finding of ability to pay at the time of sentencing, but the matter may be determinative at later probation hearings.

In applying the statute, the California courts have insisted it serve a valid rehabilitative purpose and not merely address civil liability.

People v. Hernandez, 226 Cal.App.3d 1374, 277 Cal.Rptr. 444 (1991). Co-defendants in a false bomb reporting case may be jointly and severally liable as a civil matter; but criminal court order of "restitution" of $4,000 to victim making defendants jointly and severally liable for that amount as condition of probation is void for vagueness. "Defendants enters probation not knowing the parameters of his probationary conditions." The criminal court invaded the "forbidden area of determining civil liability."

Other state statutes attempt to coordinate criminal "restitution" with civil remedies. For example, the Arizona statute requires a local court to impose restitution for "economic loss" as part of defendant's sentencing (A.R.S. § 13–603(C)). State v. Wideman, 165 Ariz. 364, 798 P.2d 1373 (App.1990). The defendant was sentenced for murder and grand theft and ordered to pay restitution. The victim's family claimed compensation for travel expenses to attend trial and for mental health counseling for the family. The appellate court denied "restitution" for the first expense, but approved $8,601 for the latter item. How does this mesh with wrongful death statutes?

The existence of an order of restitution by a criminal court does not preclude recovery in a civil case. Teachers Insurance and Annuity Association v. Green, 636 F.Supp. 415 (S.D.N.Y.1986). An additional advantage of criminal restitution is that the defendant may be banned from discharging it in bankruptcy proceedings. Kelly v. Robinson, 479 U.S. 36 (1986).

2. EQUITABLE REMEDIES AND TRACING

Preliminary Note

One advantage of equitable remedies for the misappropriation of money is the possibility of "tracing" the funds to a substituted "res" which may have even increased in value, or in establishing a preferred position over other claims through an equitable lien or equitable subrogation.

Supervision of trustees and fiduciaries, together with the correlative principle of protecting the cestui que trust, make up an ancient and well-guarded branch of equitable jurisdiction. The rules are strict. In the course of developing the "constructive" trust, the courts used language and concepts from the law of express trusts. This influenced (as well as beclouded) the development of the remedy. (Much the same thing occurred when the law developed "quasi-contract" remedies using the forms and language associated with express contracts.)

A frequent description is that the defendant is a "trustee ex maleficio." Applied to an express trustee, who has consciously and perhaps for hire, assumed the high obligations of the post and then misused the funds, the expression adds nothing to the liabilities and remedies. The Restatement (Second) of Trusts § 202 (1957), however, transforms the express trustee who wrongfully disposes of trust property and acquires other property into a "constructive" trustee. Unfortunately this may create classes of "constructive" trustees: 1) those express trustees who have been guilty of malfeasance, and 2) others with no or only a limited previous fiduciary relationship to the plaintiff who have acquired property to which he or she is equitably entitled. Most of the principal cases that follow involve embezzlements by employees. Equitable jurisdiction exists because of the confidence reposed, but it is difficult to conceive of the defendants as possessing a res (funds) under the same terms as an express trustee under a trust indenture. Does policy require the same equitable protection of employers as beneficiaries of express trusts, particularly when third party claimants might be adversely affected by a plaintiff's preferred status?

The conceptual difficulties become more acute when theft rather than embezzlement occurs. As long as the thief has ample funds, the legal remedies are adequate. But, if he is short, the principles of equitable tracing obtain a preferred position for the victim. What gives the theft victim a superior equity over the thief's other creditors?

When an express trustee purchases something with the trust funds in violation of his trust, the item can be treated as a substituted trust res. On the other hand, when a thief buys something with the stolen funds he, of course, has legal title, which precludes the legal possessory remedy of replevin. To say that he holds the item as trustee suggests that the original moneys were, at the time of theft, a trust res. Factually, of course, nothing could be further from the truth. The charade can be useful if the fancies are not taken too seriously. Certainly some authority supports the proposition that a thief may be treated as a trustee for purposes of impressing a constructive trust on the product of stolen funds. See Anno., 38 A.L.R.3d 1354 (1971).

MARCUS v. OTIS

United States Court of Appeals, Second Circuit, 1948.
168 F.2d 649.

[The defendants in this shareholders' derivative suit were directors of Automatic Products Corporation. They wrongfully used corporate monies (which were restored) to acquire for themselves "Majestic" stock from a third corporation. Because of the way the transaction was handled it was possible that Automatic may have technically acquired title to the shares; arguably the litigation could be framed as conversion of Automatic's stock instead of misappropriation of Automatic's money; the conversion-of-stock theory was the basis of the lower court's decision; and, as Judge L. Hand states it received "tentative approval" in a former appeal. Therefore, some discussion of the measure of damages for conversion of stock remains in this edited report. Further attention is paid to this matter below.

[This decision is easier to understand on the constructive assumption that defendants bought Majestic at $1.20, Majestic peaked at $5; and defendants sold Majestic at $1.50.]

L. HAND, CIRCUIT JUDGE. * * * Plainly the defendants violated their duty as directors, when they converted the company's funds to buy their shares, and, like any other fiduciaries, they made themselves liable for all profits. That is so fundamental a doctrine as to fiduciaries of all sorts, that it is somewhat surprising to find it questioned. We do not hold them for stepping in ahead of the company, and seizing for themselves a promising bargain available to them only because they were directors, for we accept the judge's finding that the purchase of the "Majestic" shares was not a "business opportunity" which the defendants should have allowed "Automatic" to take for itself. The wrong is much simpler and more fundamental—the misappropriation of funds—and it is neither an excuse that they later repaid what they had taken, nor that they allowed "Automatic" to buy 25,000 shares at 57 cents. The bargain was voidable from the outset, no matter how favorable the terms might be, and "Automatic" can follow and reclaim the abstracted funds in any form they may take, however enhanced in value. * * *

The remaining questions are as to the measure of the recovery against the defendants as constructive trustees. That they must pay at least the actual profits which they made upon the sale of the shares goes without saying but the plaintiffs argue that their liability goes further, and that they are liable for profits based upon the highest price which the shares attained from April 26, 1943, until a reasonable time after "Automatic" came into the control of the new board of directors. Their argument is as follows. Since the law treats such purchases as though the misappropriating directors had bought the shares on behalf of their company, they are chargeable with the same duty as directors to sell at the best price available. While they were in control, the company had no opportunity to make a disinterested decision when to sell, because they were holding in their own interest. They must prove when under disinterested control the company would have sold, because of the general doctrine that "the wrongdoer shall bear the risk of uncertainty which his own wrong has created."[1] Since they have not shown when the company would have sold, and since that might have been at the highest price within the period we have mentioned, they are chargeable with that price. This argument the plaintiffs made upon the former appeal as to the measure of damages in conversion, and we gave it a tentative approval. Nor was our ruling in conflict with the ordinary measure of damages for the conversion of shares of stock; that is, the highest value of the shares over only a reasonable period after the customer gets notice of the conversion. That situation is different from a conversion by directors who have control over a corporation. If a customer, who does not know that the broker has converted his shares, but supposes that he retains the power of selling them, does not order a sale throughout a given period, it is conclusive evidence that he did not wish to sell at any intermediate price; and he ought not to be allowed to charge the broker

1. [Footnotes renumbered.] Bigelow v. R.K.O. Radio Pictures, 327 U.S. 251, 265.

on the assumption that he might have; while, if a corporation is under the control of directors who have converted property, it is impossible to say that a disinterested board might have not sold the property at some intermediate price. Conceivably therefore in such a case the ordinary measure of damages will not apply; and at any rate that was what we were discussing on the first appeal, for on that record the wrong then appeared to be a conversion of the shares. The argument does not of course apply to the conversion of funds, because money does not fluctuate in value.

We all agree that the defendants, as "constructive trustees," are not subject to the same measure of damages as though they had converted the shares; and my brothers hold that their liability does not go beyond the actual profits which they have made. They regard "Automatic's" right to follow the converted funds into the shares as a remedy for the conversion no different because the wrongdoers were also fiduciaries. They think that, although the victim may trace his money into any substitute into which the wrongdoer may have changed it, and reclaim it as though it had remained in specie, the law does not in addition impose upon him, even though he be a fiduciary, any of those duties as to the substitute which he would have been under, had the substitute been part of the trust res. It follows that the liability of the defendants at bar must be limited to their actual profits; and, in the case of those who may not have sold the shares, to a return of these and any dividends received, upon payment of $1.20 a share.

I am personally not in accord with this measure of recovery; and I trust that it is permissible for me to state my reasons. I agree that, when the wrongdoer is not a fiduciary, there is no ground for imposing upon him any duties touching the substituted property; but it seems to me that when he is, he should be subject to those duties towards the substitute which he had accepted towards the res. This would mean that a fiduciary, who misappropriates trust funds and turns them into other property, should be treated as though the substitute had been a part of the res, when he became a fiduciary. It seems to me incongruous with the beneficiary's conceded power to treat the substitute as a part of the res, to relieve the fiduciary of those duties regarding it to which he would have been subject, if it had been so in fact. By hypothesis he has committed the gravest dereliction possible—pro tanto a complete repudiation of the trust he expressly assumed—yet that will excuse him from a duty which would have rested upon him, had the substitute innocently come within his control as trustee. True, so far as I can find, the case has never come up in any court, but I submit that it is a corollary of well settled principles.

Therefore, I would impose upon the defendants the same duties towards the shares that they would have been under had they found them in "Automatic's" portfolio when they became directors. The record is full of testimony from them themselves that they never thought the shares a proper addition to "Automatic's" existing investments; and, if so, it would have been incumbent upon them to dispose of them as soon as they reasonably could. They need not, and indeed they ought not, have thrown them overboard; they had a reasonable time within which to sell; but they are chargeable with any loss if they failed to do so. I would not accept as the end of that period the dates of the actual sales made by them, because, not only did they sell at different times, but the dates they chose were not the result of that collective and unbiased judgment to which "Automatic" was entitled. Obviously what is a reasonable time within which to dispose of shares, selling upon a market, varies with the shares to be sold and with the number to be disposed of * * *. The proper course would be to send the case to a master to determine within what period the defendants ought to have disposed of 100,000 shares, considering the available market.

What price should be selected from among those which prevailed during the period is another matter. In the only case in which the suggestion has come up that it should be the highest intermediate value,[2] the Seventh Circuit refused to impose so severe a standard, following Professor Scott who says that that "would seem * * * clearly not chargeable." Whether or not that is always true, at least it was true in the particular circumstances at bar; for plainly over 100,000 shares could not have been sold at the highest price which obtained on any day within any putative period. Presumably the most profitable way to dispose of so many shares would have been to feed them upon the market gradually, and the best approximation to what would have been so realized, would be to take the average over the whole period. * * * Here, the defendants would have been at fault, had they waited till the end of the period; and, the nearest realization of what they should have done, would be to take the average. However, all this is beside the mark, for my view is not to prevail, and the recovery will be limited to the actual gains, as I have said above.

AUGUSTUS N. HAND, CIRCUIT JUDGE. I agree with the holding announced in the opinion of Judge L. Hand and with the view expressed that there was no conversion of corporate securities but that there was a misappropriation of corporate funds. I only differ with his personal view as to the amount of recovery and add this memorandum to state why Judge Chase and I hold that in case of such a breach the liability should be limited to profits. The breach that is the basis for granting any recovery in this case was the use of corporate funds for the directors' personal benefit. These funds have been repaid with interest so there has been no damage to the corporation, but the wrongdoers should also pay over all profits so that they will not be permitted to benefit in any manner by their wrong. It is to be noted that in the decisions where fiduciaries have been held liable for converting funds none has been found which has required them to do more than to repay the moneys with interest and in addition to turn over any profits received, including any property still retained in which the funds have been invested. We see no reason for extending the purpose of a constructive trust so as to impose a greater liability upon a fiduciary for misappropriating funds than upon any other person who commits the same wrong. The creation of such a trust is only to afford a remedy to reach the avails of property unlawfully appropriated. The directors did not intend to hold these securities for Automatic nor did the latter ever invest in the securities on its own account but, on the contrary, objected to acquiring them. Nor can we see any policy which justifies the imposition of a serious liability which we think would employ a fiction to superimpose upon a constructive trust an obligation of an express trust to sell trust property which has no basis in the actual facts of the case at bar and is unnecessary either to restore the corporation to the position it would have been in had its corporate funds not been converted or to prevent profits from being realized by unfaithful directors. Where damages for a breach of a duty to sell corporate assets have been awarded, they were to recompense the corporation for an actual loss

2. Paul v. Girard Trust Co., 7 Cir., 124 F.2d 809.

sustained and directly caused by the fiduciary's breach. The corporation in the case at bar has lost no such sum as it would recover if a theoretical duty to sell were imposed upon the directors; nor have the defendants received any such gain. If the corporation had owned this property, the directors would be liable for damages if they failed to act as prudent managers; but this was not the case here and we therefore do not believe that they were under such obligations. As constructive trustees we think their responsibility stopped with accountability for the principal sum, interest, and any actual profits realized.

G & M MOTOR CO. v. THOMPSON

Supreme Court of Oklahoma, 1977.
567 P.2d 80.

BERRY, JUSTICE. [M]ay a trial court impress a constructive trust upon proceeds of life insurance policies where a portion of the premiums were paid with wrongfully obtained funds? We hold sound reason and interest of justice require an affirmative answer.

The facts, for the purpose of deciding this question, are simple. A. Wayne Thompson was an accountant for G & M Motor Company [motor company] from January 1, 1968, until his death on August 2, 1970. During this period decedent embezzled $78,856.45 from motor company; a portion of which was used to pay premiums on various insurance policies insuring the life of decedent: [Editors' note: Assume for purposes of understanding that Thompson spent all but $250, and used that $250 to buy a $100,000 life insurance policy.] The trial court impressed a constructive trust upon various items of real and personal property and the insurance proceeds in possession of decedent's surviving wife, Shirley Thompson, and child.

Court of Appeals, Division 1, upon wife's appeal, affirmed trial court's impressment of a constructive trust on the real and personal property, but modified the trust on insurance proceeds. The court, relying on American National Bank of Okmulgee v. King, 158 Okl. 278, 13 P.2d 164, said "only that part of the funds that the trial court found was used to pay for the payments of the policies while deceased was employed for appellee * * * together with interest at the rate of 10% per annum from date of judgment * * * until paid" are subject to a constructive trust in favor of motor company.

The proper basis for impressing a constructive trust is to prevent unjust enrichment. The Restatement of Restitution foresaw that a wrongdoer may exchange misappropriated property for other property; thus, § 202 provides:

"Where a person wrongfully disposes of property of another knowing that the disposition is wrongful and acquires in exchange other property, the other is entitled * * * to enforce * * * a constructive trust of the property so acquired."

The drafters explained § 202 as follows:

> "Where a person by the consciously wrongful disposition of the property of another acquires other property, the person whose property is so used is * * * entitled * * * to the property so acquired. If the property so acquired is or becomes more valuable than the property used in acquiring it, the profit thus made by the wrongdoer cannot be retained by him; the person whose property was used in making the profit is entitled to it. The result, it is true, is that the claimant obtains more than the amount of which he was deprived, more than

restitution for his loss; he is put in a better position than that in which he would have been if no wrong had been done to him. Nevertheless, since the profit is made from his property, it is just that he should have the profit rather than that the wrongdoer should keep it. It is true that if there had been a loss instead of a profit, the wrongdoer would have had to bear the loss, since the wrongdoer would be personally liable to the claimant for the value of the claimant's property wrongfully used by the wrongdoer. If, however, the wrongdoer were permitted to keep the profit, there would be an incentive to wrongdoing, which is removed if he is compelled to surrender the profit. The rule which compels the wrongdoer to bear any losses and to surrender any profits operates as a deterrent upon the wrongful disposition of the property of others. Accordingly, the person whose property is wrongfully used in acquiring other property can by a proceeding in equity reach the other property and compel the wrongdoer to convey it to him. The wrongdoer holds the property so acquired upon a constructive trust for the claimant."

Thus, it is not necessary for a plaintiff to have suffered any loss or suffer a loss as great as the benefit of defendant.

Where the wrongdoer mingles wrongfully and rightfully acquired funds, owner of wrongfully acquired funds is entitled to share proportionately in acquired property to the extent of his involuntary contributions. This principle is specifically applicable to life insurance proceeds where a portion of the premiums were paid with wrongfully acquired money. The drafters said:

"Just as the claimant is entitled to enforce a constructive trust upon property which is wholly the product of his property, so he is entitled to enforce a constructive trust upon property which is the product in part of his own property and in part of the property of the wrongdoer. The difference is that where the property is the product of his property only in part, he is not entitled by enforcing a constructive trust to recover the whole of the property, but only a share in such proportion as the value of his property bore to the value of the mingled fund."

Having carefully considered the matter, we adopt the Restatement view. However, Motor Company has sought no more than the embezzled monies, interest and costs. Further, the surviving wife is an innocent beneficiary. * * * We hold Motor Company is entitled to * * * insurance proceeds, but not to exceed the total amount of embezzled monies, interest and costs.

Note

A court may impose a constructive trust on property defendant purchased with embezzled funds even though the property is exempt from defendant's creditors under the homestead exemption. Cox v. Waudby, 433 N.W.2d 716 (Iowa 1988). While neither an equitable lien nor a constructive trust is available against a person who acquires the property as a bona fide purchaser for value, a person who is given property the donor acquired with embezzled funds takes the property subject to the claims of the victim of the embezzlement. In re Marriage of Allen, 724 P.2d 651 (Colo.1986).

SLATER v. ORIENTAL MILLS

Supreme Court of Rhode Island, 1893.

18 R.I. 352, 27 A. 443.

STINESS, J. The question raised by the demurrer to the bill is whether the Forestdale Manufacturing Company, of which the complainants are stockholders, has a preferred claim upon the respondent assignee of the Oriental Mills, an insolvent corporation, for funds wrongfully taken from the former company and used to pay liabilities of the latter company, and otherwise, by persons who were officers in control of both companies. The rule is clear that one has an equitable right to follow and reclaim his property, which has been wrongfully appropriated by another, so long as he can find the property, or its substantial equivalent if its form has been changed, upon the ground that such property, in whatever form, is impressed with a trust in favor of the owner. If the trustee has mingled it with his own, he will be deemed to have used his own, rather than another's, and so to leave the remainder under the trust; and this is a sufficient identification for the owner. But in this case we are asked to go further, and to hold that, where one's property has been wrongfully applied and dissipated by another, a charge remains upon the estate of the latter for the amount thus wrongfully taken, upon the ground that his estate is thereby so much larger, and that the trust property is really and clearly there, in a substituted form, although it cannot be directly traced. This view is pressed with much skill and some authority, but we are unable to adopt it. While one who has been wronged may follow and take his own property, or its visible product, it is quite a different thing to say that he may take the property of somebody else. The general property of an insolvent debtor belongs to his creditors, as much as particular trust property belongs to a cestui que trust. Creditors have no right to share in that which is shown not to belong to the debtor, and, conversely, a claimant has no right to take from creditors that which he cannot show to be equitably his own. But right here comes the argument that it is equitably his own because the debtor has taken the claimant's money and mingled it with his estate, whereby it is swelled just so much. But, as applicable to all cases, the argument is not sound. Where the property or its substantial equivalent remains, we concede its force; but, where it is dissipated and gone, the appropriation of some other property in its stead simply takes from creditors that which clearly belongs to them. In the former case, as in Pennell v. Deffell, 4 De Gex, M. & G. 372, and In re Hallett's Estate, (Knatchbull v. Hallett,) 13 Ch.Div. 696, the illustration may be used of a debtor mingling trust funds with his own in a chest or bag. Though the particular money cannot be identified, the amount is swelled just so much, and the amount added belongs to the cestui que trust. But in the latter case there is no swelling of the estate, for the money is spent and gone; or, as respondent's counsel pertinently suggests, "Knight Bruce's chest—Jessel's bag—is empty." Shall we therefore order a like amount to be taken out of some other chest or bag, or out of the debtor's general estate? * * *

In examining the question upon authority we think it is equally clear that there can be no equitable relief except in cases where the fund claimed is in some way apparent in the debtor's estate. Of the cases cited by the complainants, only four go to the extent of holding that a cestui que trust is entitled to a lien for reimbursement on the general estate of the trustee where the trust fund does not, in some form, so appear. These are Plow Co. v. Lamp, 80 Iowa 722, 45 N.W.Rep. 1049; Francis v. Evans, 69 Wis. 115, 33 N.W.Rep. 93. In the first of these cases the court lost sight of the distinction, which we desire to make clear, between funds remaining in the estate, which go to swell the assets, and funds which, having been dissipated or used in the payment of debts, do not remain in the estate, and so do not swell the estate. Upon the former fact, as we have stated above, we concede the right to relief. But the court in the Iowa case seems to ignore this very important distinction, and in so doing overthrows the foundation on which its decision is based, for it says: "The creditors, if permitted to enforce their claims as against the trust, would secure the payment of their claims out of trust moneys." Now, how can this be so if the trust moneys, or their substantial equivalent, are not there? The court assumes that the payment of debts is the same thing as an increase of assets or perhaps that it works the same result to a creditor by increasing his dividends. But this is not so. How the satisfaction of a debt by incurring another of equal amount either decreases one's liabilities or increases his assets can only be comprehended by the philosophic mind of a Micawber. If a debtor is solvent, it is all right either way, because he will have enough to pay everything he owes; but, if he is insolvent, the injustice of the doctrine of the Iowa court is made almost painfully plain by the following illustration from the dissenting opinion of Taylor and Cassoday, JJ., in Francis v. Evans "Suppose that an insolvent debtor, D., has only $1,000 of property, but is indebted to the amount of $2,000, one-half of which is due to A., and the other half to B. In this condition of things D.'s property can only pay fifty per cent of his debts. By such distribution A. and B. would each be equitably entitled to $500. Now, suppose D. while in that condition, collects $1,000 for F., but instead of remitting the money, as he should, he uses it in paying his debt in full to A. By so doing, D., has not increased his assets a penny, nor diminished his aggregate indebtedness a penny. The only difference is that he now owes $1,000 each to B. and F., whereas he previously owed $1,000 each to A. and B. Now if F. is to have preference over B., then his claim will absorb the entire amount of D.'s property, leaving nothing whatever for B. In other words, the $500 to which B. was equitably entitled from his insolvent debtor, upon a fair distribution of the estate, has, without any fault of his, been paid to another, merely in consequence of the wrongful act of the debtor." It is impossible to state the case more clearly. The illustration demonstrates that the mere fact that a trustee has used the money does not show that it has gone into his estate. If used to pay debts, he has simply turned it over to a creditor, thereby giving him a preference, while his own estate and indebtedness remains exactly as before. Suppose he had stolen the money, and turned it over to somebody from whom it could not be reclaimed. Can any one say the owner should have an equitable lien upon the thief's insolvent estate in preference to his creditors? They and the owner are equally innocent, and each must bear his own misfortune.

[The demurrer was overruled on a different point.]

Notes

The Mechanics of Tracing. Peirce v. Sheldon Petroleum Co., 589 S.W.2d 849, 853 (Tex.Civ.App. 1979). "Unless the tracing requirement is observed with reasonable strictness, any suit on a debt or obligation could be used to impress a constructive trust on the assets of the defendant."

The court also outlined elementary rules of tracing: "When the beneficiary can point to the specific property that was purchased or inherited, or to its mutation, the tracing burden is met. When, however, tracing to specific property is impossible because the trustee has commingled the property, the right is not defeated if the beneficiary can trace to the commingled fund. If the commingling was wrongful, the burden is on the trustee to establish which property is rightfully the trustee's. If the trustee is unable to do so, the entire commingled property is subject to the trust. If the commingling is not wrongful, the beneficiary has the burden of establishing the nature and extent of the beneficial interest in the commingled fund."

Tracing itself is simply investigative detective work to obtain the evidence. See United States v. Garcia, 532 F.Supp. 325 (D.P.R.1981). The government traced payments fraudulently obtained from the Veterans Administration as tuition for students in a privately-run school into a 99.55% interest in an apartment house. If the tracing process runs out of an identifiable res or into a bona fide purchaser, the equitable remedies cease. Some long-established presumptions help the tracing process, however, in the special circumstance of commingled funds.

McCONVILLE, TRACING AND THE RULE IN CLAYTON'S CASE

79 Law Quarterly Review 388 (1963).

[Editors: this closely reasoned article is much abridged.]

A consideration of the proprietary remedies available to a beneficiary for the recovery of trust property inevitably leads in particular to the problems of mixed money and bank accounts. Here three basic situations are recognized:

(a) A trustee or fiduciary pays trust money into his bank account where it is mixed with his own private money;

(b) a trustee or fiduciary pays money of two or more trusts into his bank account where they become mixed; and

(c) an innocent donee of trust money pays it into his bank account where it is mixed with money of his own.

In the event of a subsequent depletion of the account, it is often important, as where the trustee, fiduciary or donee is insolvent, to determine how much of the depletion is to be borne by the trust and how much by the other money. In this connection the courts have had to consider the possible application of the rule in *Clayton's* Case, whereby first withdrawals from an account are deemed to be made out of first payments in. It is widely accepted that the rule does not apply in situation (a), but that it does apply in situations (b) and (c). The view is respectfully put forward, however, that *Clayton's* Case does not apply to any of the three situations and is, indeed, totally irrelevant to the law of tracing. This conclusion is reached by recognizing a distinction in the position of a bank account depending on whether the relationship of banker and customer or that of trustee and beneficiary is involved. * * *

Banker and Customer

Devaynes v. Noble, *Clayton's* Case[1] concerned a specialized aspect of the relationship of debtor and creditor. A banking firm of five partners held an account for a customer Clayton. This account was a current one and from time to time Clayton made deposits and withdrawals. In November 1809 one of the partners died. At that time the account stood at £1,713 in credit. The remaining four partners carried on the banking business and Clayton continued making deposits and withdrawals as before, withdrawals to the total

1. [Footnotes renumbered.] (1816) 1 Mer. 572, esp. p. 585 et seq. There were seven other representative claims against the estate of the deceased partner, in respect of bank accounts and wrongful sale of clients' exchequer bills and bonds by the partners both before and after his death.

amount of £1,717 and deposits to an amount exceeding this. In July 1810 the four partners became insolvent and Clayton sought to claim against the deceased partner's estate (which was solvent) for the £1,713 owed to him at the date of the partner's death, which he alleged had not been discharged or affected by his subsequent dealings with the four remaining partners in making deposits and withdrawals from his account.

His argument was that if a debtor owed several debts and made a general payment without indicating (expressly or by implication) which debt he intended to discharge, then the creditor could at any time elect to which debt he would allocate the payment. A bank account was for this purpose to be considered as a series of debts owed by the banker to the customer in respect of each deposit made by the customer. Hence when making a withdrawal, the customer was in the same position as a creditor receiving a general payment from a debtor; Clayton was therefore entitled to say that any money he had drawn out of the account was to be applied in discharging other items of deposit than the particular ones represented by the £1,713. The £1,717 he had drawn out since the death of the partner he could attribute to deposits made since then which in amount exceeded this sum.

Sir William Grant M.R. admitted the general rules as to appropriation of debts but in the instant case laid down a new rule that applied in the case of a bank account. Here the parties were at liberty to appropriate particular payments to particular deposits, but in the absence of such an arrangement, the law presumed that deposits were discharged in order of their creation by subsequent withdrawals. First payments in were cancelled by the first payments out. Thus the £1,713 which Clayton claimed must be taken to have been repaid by the subsequent withdrawals before any subsequent deposits were taken to be repaid. As these withdrawals came to £1,717, they completely discharged the amount claimed. The deceased partner's estate was freed from liability and the claim therefore failed. * * *

TRUSTEE AND BENEFICIARY

The situation where a trustee pays trust money into his private account, where it is mixed with his own money, first appears to have arisen in Pennell v. Deffell.[2] In this case, one Green, an official assignee of the Court of Bankruptcy, had paid money received by him in his official capacity into two accounts kept in his own name. On his death, it was found that one of these accounts was composed entirely of such money and the other substantially so. His successor sought to charge both these accounts for the total amount of such money, and the Master's report was in favour of granting him this relief. On further directions, however, Lord Romilly M.R. held that there could be no following of such money into the bank accounts and that these formed part of the general estate of Green. This decision was reversed by the Court of Appeal in Chancery * * * where the right of following money held in a fiduciary capacity into a bank account was recognised, even if there was other money in the account. Knight Bruce L.J. reached this result by drawing on the analogy of a chest or repository in which trust money had been mixed with other money, and held that a claim would lie against a bank account in just the same way as on the mixture in such a chest or repository.

2. (1853) 4 De G.M. & G. 372.

Here, however, some withdrawals had been made from the accounts and the point arose whether these reduced the trust fund or the other money with which it had become mixed in the accounts. The Master's report proceeded on the footing that money should be treated in the same way as shares that had no distinguishing mark. If a trustee held some such shares on trust and some in his own right and having confused the two, disposed of some, it had already been established that the beneficiary was entitled to treat those as being a disposal of the trustee's own shares and thus claim the full number of trust shares from the remaining mixtures. [citations] By analogy the full amount of trust money could be claimed from the mixed fund in the account despite the subsequent withdrawals. The fact that the mixed money was in an account rather than in a chest or repository did not make any difference. But in the Court of Appeal in Chancery, both Lords Justices thought that withdrawals from the account must be deemed to be of earlier deposits, according to the rule in *Clayton's* Case. If these had been trust money, then it must be taken that they were no longer in the account and therefore could not be recovered from it. In the instant case some of the earlier deposits had in fact been trust money and it was held the later withdrawals had the effect of destroying the claim to a small extent. Turner L.J. thought to apply the same principles as were applied to shares having no distinguishing mark would be attended "with the greatest inconvenience" and that it would mean debts extinguished at law would be revived in equity.

It seems a little strange that the court should first allow the claim to trace into the account on the analogy of a box or repository of notes and coins, in other words, treat the account as a piece of property, and then regard it as a series of debts in order to determine how withdrawals might reduce the amount of trust money recoverable from the account.

But the application of the rule in *Clayton's* Case clearly created an arbitrary hazard to tracing actions, for they depended for their success on the accident of how the trustee kept his accounts with the banker. If by some good fortune there was enough in the trustee's account before the deposit of trust money to cover the amount of later withdrawals, the equitable claim was secure on the mixed account, but not otherwise. The courts were not long in discovering reasons why such an inconvenient result could be avoided.

In re Hallett's Estate,[4] a solicitor had improperly sold two sets of bonds he held for a client, one for £341, the other for £1,804, and a further set, which represented a trust fund in which he was interested, for £770. He paid the £341 into his private bank account on November 3 and the other two sums on November 14, 1877. There they were mixed with his own private money to form a total of £4,370 on the latter date. Subsequently, withdrawals were made amounting to £2,662 and deposits amounting to £1,320. In a creditor's action for administration of the solicitor's estate, both the client and the trustee of the trust fund claimed against the account. Thus, not only did the rights of the two claimants against the solicitor (and the creditor claiming through him) fail to be decided, but also their rights *inter se* in respect of the bank account. Fry J. applied *Clayton's* Case to resolve both these questions. Thus the client's claim would fail as to the £341 and that of the £1,804 would be reduced to £1,708. The claim of the trustee of the trust fund would fail altogether.

4. Re Hallett's Estate, Knatchbull v. Hallett (1880) 13 Ch.D. 696.

The Court of Appeal, by a majority, reversed this decision. Thesiger L.J. in a dissenting judgment agreed with Fry J. and was of opinion that Pennell v. Deffell concluded the point. However, the other members of the court (Sir George Jessel M.R. and Baggallay L.J.) held that the solicitor, in making the later withdrawals of £2,662, ought to be taken to have drawn on his own money. This was so because an honest intention ought to be attributed to him as far as possible. Here such an intention might be recognized by the fact that he had at all times left enough in his account to satisfy the amounts of both claimants in full. As a fiduciary, he could not be heard to say that, in making withdrawals, he was intending to deplete the trust funds before touching his own money, since this would be allowing a person to set up his own wrong where what he had done could have been done rightfully. As there was enough in the account to satisfy each of the claims, both succeeded, and the Court of Appeal did not have to consider the rights of the claimants *inter se* in a deficiency.

But instead of this reasoning of a "presumed honest intention," the court might have reached the same decision on the simple ground that the rule in *Clayton's* Case was irrelevant to the issue in hand. Such a result was achieved for all practical purposes in Re Oatway.[5] Here a trustee paid trust money into his private account where it was mixed with his own money. With his first withdrawals he purchased some Oceana shares, but later withdrawals were dissipated and exhausted the account. The trustee having become insolvent, the beneficiary claimed a charge on the shares for the amount of trust money originally paid into the trustee's account, and out of which the purchase money for the shares was found. It was suggested by counsel that on the basis of the decision in re Hallett's Estate the trustee in making withdrawals from the account must be deemed to draw on his own money first. Hence the first withdrawals having been used to buy the shares, these would be the trustee's own property not that of the trust fund. Joyce J., however, allowed the claim. In his judgment the basic problem was confusion of identical property. The person who had brought about the mixing was "entitled to claim his proper quantity, but subject to the quantity of the other proprietor being first made good out of the whole mass." Thus, where withdrawals had been made from the account, "in order to determine to whom any remaining balance or any investment that may have been paid for out of the account ought to be deemed to belong, the trustee must be debited with all the sums that have been withdrawn and applied to his own use so as to be no longer recoverable, and the trust money in like manner be debited with any sums taken out and duly invested in the names of the proper trustees. The order of priority in which the various withdrawals and investments may have been respectively made is wholly immaterial."

This decision is authority for the view that the beneficiary can assert his equitable title on any part of the amalgam, whether it is in the account or has been changed into an investment or in any other identifiable form, or it is submitted, where it exists partly in one and partly in the other. Joyce J. in this case recognized the true proprietary basis of a tracing claim. * * *

Where two or more trust funds are mixed together [and also where a volunteer's money is mixed with trust money], the same principles should apply. For example, nine trust funds each of £5 may be mixed with £5 of

5. Re Oatway, Hertslet v. Oatway [1903] 2 Ch. 356.

volunteer's money in the latter's bank account. Subsequently, the volunteer deposits a further £50 of his own money and then withdraws £30 which he uses in purchasing stock, £45 for a dinner party and the remainder he transfers to a Post Office Savings Account where he has £175 already. How the respective rights of the parties are resolved is a fairly simple task, remembering the original mixing was of the nine trust funds with one part of the volunteer's money all of which amounted to a total of £50. At the moment of mixing there were therefore ten equal charges of £5 each existing against the account and the subsequent increase in its amount by reason of the deposit of £50 made no difference, there were now ten charges of £5 each on the £100. When the £30 was withdrawn and invested in the stock, all of these charges could be asserted either against the stock or the balance remaining in the account or partly against one and partly against the other. In fact this would be the most preferable course since there is not enough in the stock to satisfy all the claims in full but only to the extent of three-fifths of each one. But then the bank account is reduced again by a withdrawal of £45 which is spent on a dinner and so dissipated. The ten charges, however, remain on the £25 left in the account (though of course they all abate by half in amount). Hence when this £25 is withdrawn and mixed with £175 in the second account, the charges extend over the whole resulting £200, but only to the extent of £25, and this is divided up *pari passu* amongst the ten. Thus the original nine trust funds can be traced into the Post Office Savings Account and into the stock, and a charge placed on both to recover either the full or some lesser amount of trust money. The volunteer has a charge also on these to the amount of his money which was originally mixed with the money of the trust funds, and if there is not enough to pay every claim in full, all will abate rateably.

Notes

1. Restatement of Restitution § 211 (1937) †

(1) Where a person wrongfully mingles money of another with money of his own and subsequently makes withdrawals from the mingled fund, the other is entitled to an equitable lien upon the part which remains and the part which is withdrawn or upon their product, except as stated in Subsection (3).

(2) If the wrongdoer knew that he was acting wrongfully, the other is entitled at his option to a proportionate share both of the part which remains and of the part which is withdrawn or of their product, except as stated in Subsection (3).

(3) Where the wrongdoer has effectively separated the money of the other from his own money, the other is entitled to, and only to, his own money or its product.

2. Professor Palmer devotes an entire section to the "inadequate" Restatement formula. G. Palmer, The Law of Restitution § 2.17 (1978).

3. *Problems:* Wrongdoer embezzles $5000 of Victim's money and commingles it with $5000 in Wrongdoer's own bank account. Under the rules of the Restatement of Restitution should the Victim seek a constructive trust or an equitable lien, if:

a. Wrongdoer withdraws the $10,000 to acquire property now having a market value of $12,000?

b. Wrongdoer withdraws $5000 and uses the money to purchase property which now has a market value of $3000?

c. Wrongdoer withdraws $5000 and dissipates the money buying lottery tickets?

REPUBLIC SUPPLY CO. v. RICHFIELD OIL CO.

United States Court of Appeals, Ninth Circuit, 1935.
79 F.2d 375.

[Richfield Oil was in equitable receivership. It had wrongfully acquired access to $1,625,000 in cash of Universal Consolidated Oil Co. and had gradually drained off the cash, which it commingled in its general checking account. Interspersed with the gradual misappropriations were daily deposits and withdrawals by Richfield in its general operations. Certain of the funds were traced into specific assets now in the hands of Richfield's receivers. The present case concerns the balance in the bank account, also in the hands of the receiver, and more specifically the determination of the lowest intermediate balance upon which Universal claimed a lien.

St. Sure, District Judge. In attaching the liens, the master had three alternatives or theories before him for computing the amounts thereof:

1. The daily closing balance, after crediting the opening balance and all deposits during the day and charging all withdrawals for the day, without regard to the order in point of time in which deposits and withdrawals were made.

2. The balance shown during the day as a result of periodical posting of deposits and withdrawals, after crediting the opening balance, with or without regard to the order in point of time of the transactions, observing or neglecting to observe the true balance, according to the arbitrary inclination of the posting clerk.

3. The balance shown by deducting all withdrawals posted during the day from the opening balance without crediting deposits for the day; disregarding the true order of transactions and assuming an order in point of time which would produce the lowest possible balance during the day.

The third alternative was used.

It is urged by Universal that the method followed limits its recovery to the lowest possible figure, and that the daily closing balances should have been the basis of recovery; if not that, at least the lowest daily intermediate posted balances. * * *

If the lowest intermediate balance between the misappropriations and the purchases is to be taken literally, that is to say at any moment of any day, it is obvious that the order in which deposits and withdrawals were made would be indispensable to proof. None of the three alternatives pretend to show sequence of transactions. It is a matter of common knowledge and, indeed, of record, that the volume and complexity of business and banking practice do not permit of keeping an accurate momentary balance current with deposits and withdrawals in large commercial accounts, for the reason that banks have various departments and many tellers, and the credit and debit transactions react upon one another in rapid succession.

The evidence in this case establishes that the daily intermediate posted balances are merely working balances in the bank; that they do not necessarily represent the actual balance resulting from all transactions in the account up to the time of posting. They represent only the balance of the deposits and withdrawals actually posted, and whether all transactions up to the time of posting shall be included in the intermediate balance is left to the arbitrary inclination of the posting clerk. * * *

We are not persuaded, however, that the method adopted by the master and the District Court is any more applicable, for it assumes an order of transactions which is wholly unsupported by evidence or reason, and disregards entirely a most essential element of any bank account, namely credits. The adoption of this method was based upon the premise that the order in point of time of deposits and withdrawals was essential to proof and that the burden was upon claimant; and upon the reasoning that claimant must fail unless there is a minimum situation which "assumes an order of deposits and withdrawals which, at the worst, must have occurred." We are not in accord with that view.

The evidence discloses that the bank itself, which handles both deposits and withdrawals, and the bookkeeping of the account, cannot, in ordinary cases (and in this case did not), prove accurately the chronology of transactions in large commercial accounts. Why, then, should that insuperable burden penalize the cestui que trust whose funds have been wrongfully taken from it?

Notwithstanding the established doctrine that subsequent deposits in a commingled account such as the one herein does not restore a trust fund once exhausted [citation], the burden of proof is upon claimant to show that its funds purchased the property upon which it is sought to fasten a lien, [citation] under the facts in this case we are disinclined to follow either rule to the extent of defeating recovery, or even limiting recovery to the lowest possible figure, upon an unwarranted assumption of the chronology of transactions and a disregard of the credit side of the bank account. The facts disclosed by the record prompt the observation that if any assumption is to be indulged in, it should not favor Richfield or its creditors, for the reason that Universal's funds were surreptitiously abstracted and deposited in Richfield's account, out of which, the evidence shows, all of the properties involved were wholly or in part paid for, and the account was completely exhausted prior to receivership. From this it is apparent that Universal's claim is superior in right and in time to the creditors of Richfield. Under these circumstances, we know of no equitable principle which would entitle the creditors to equal or greater consideration than is due Universal.

No citation of authority is necessary to support the statement that the daily closing balance is the one which reflects the actual state of the ordinary commercial bank account, and is the only one accepted and used by both bank and customer in ordinary business transactions. For obvious reasons, heretofore adverted to, it disregards the chronological order of deposits and withdrawals. It does not, however, disregard any transaction on either side of the ledger.

It seems perfectly clear to us that under the prevailing system of bookkeeping in the bank the essential elements for determining the lowest intermediate balances are not ascertainable with accuracy until the close of the banking day, when all transactions for that day are posted. If in the interim between daily closing balances there was a transgression of the rule with reference to subsequent deposits not restoring trust funds once exhausted, and the balance did in fact fall below the amount of the trust funds then in the account, the burden was upon defendants to show that fact with accuracy.

Notes

1. In Church v. Bailey, 90 Cal.App.2d 501, 203 P.2d 547 (1949), the court, relying on a case involving an express trust account, ruled that a subsequent deposit of personal funds in any depleted commingled account was presumed to be a restoration pro tanto of the funds belonging to plaintiff. Consider the effect this decision would have on the award in *Richfield Oil Co.*

2. Restatement (Second) of Restitution (Tent. Draft No. 2, 1984): †

§ 38. Effect on Fund of Withdrawals

(1) Upon a withdrawal from a fund that is subject to a right to restitution, the right to restitution from that fund is limited in amount to the balance of the fund immediately following the withdrawal. In determining the balance affected by a series of withdrawals and deposits rapidly recorded, a court will use the most exact method of accounting that is just and practicable in the circumstances.

(2) Except as provided in subsection (1), a right to restitution from a fund continues, unchanged in amount, following a withdrawal from the fund.

3. Compare United States Department of Energy v. Seneca Oil Co. (In re Seneca Oil Co.), 906 F.2d 1445 (10th Cir.1990), where the court relied on a bankrupt's general ledger rather than the daily closing balance to determine the lowest balance in a commingled account.

4. United States v. Banco Cafetero Panama, 797 F.2d 1154, 1159 (2d Cir.1986). Pursuant to a federal statute, the United States sought to forfeit bank deposits traced to drug sales. The problem was complicated, however, because the bank accounts were active and included non-drug related funds. In analyzing the resulting problem, the court found three approaches to the tracing problem:

"If $100 from a drug sale is deposited into an active account, one approach is to consider the account to be 'traceable proceeds' to the extent of $100 as long as the account balance never falls below that sum. This might be called a 'drugs-in, last-out' rule. This approach, more properly called the 'lowest intermediate balance' rule, is used to determine the rights of a trust beneficiary to a trustee's bank account in which trust funds and the trustee's personal funds have been commingled. See Restatement (Second) of Trusts § 202(1) comment j (1959). This method is also used in the area of secured transactions to trace proceeds of the sale of collateral in commingled funds in the hands of a debtor or to a debtor's transferee not in the ordinary course of business. [citation] A second approach is to consider 'traceable proceeds' to be a pro rata share of any withdrawal from the account or of any asset purchased with such withdrawal, the share determined by the ratio of the $100 tainted deposit to the funds in the account immediately after the deposit. This option of an 'averaging' rule, as an alternative to the 'lowest intermediate balance' rule, is used to resolve tracing problems where withdrawals are made from an account in which trust and personal funds have been commingled. See Restatement (Second) of Trusts, supra, § 202(1) comment i. A third approach is to consider 'traceable proceeds' to be any one withdrawal, or any asset purchased with such withdrawal, to the extent of $100. This might be called a 'drugs-in, first-out' rule.

The Government contends that it is entitled to the benefit, at its option, of either the first or third approach.

"We conclude that the Government's position is sufficiently correct to enable it to prevail on this appeal."

5. For a different view of the problem, see Finkelstein and Robbins, A Probabilistic Approach to Tracing Presumptions in the Law of Restitution, 24 Jurimetrics J. 65 (1983).

IN RE WALTER J. SCHMIDT CO.

United States District Court, Southern District of New York, 1923.
298 Fed. 314.

LEARNED HAND, DISTRICT JUDGE. For various reasons not necessary to state the petitioners all have claims against the bank deposit in the Lincoln Trust Company, which the receiver recognizes as entitling them collectively to the whole of it as a trust fund. The only question is how it shall be divided between them.

* * * The rule in Clayton's Case is to allocate the payments upon an account. Some rule had to be adopted, and though any presumption of intent was a fiction, priority in time was the most natural basis of allocation. It has no relevancy whatever to a case like this. Here two people are jointly interested in a fund held for them by a common trustee. There is no reason in law or justice why his depredations upon the fund should not be borne equally between them. To throw all the loss upon one, through the mere chance of his being earlier in time, is irrational and arbitrary, and is equally a fiction as the rule in Clayton's Case, supra. When the law adopts a fiction, it is, or at least it should be, for some purpose of justice. To adopt it here is to apportion a common misfortune through a test which has no relation whatever to the justice of the case.

It does not follow, however, that the claimants should divide the fund in the proportions of their original deposits. An illustration will perhaps be clearest. Suppose three claimants, A., B., and C., for $5,000 each, whose money was deposited at intervals of a month, January, February, and March. Suppose that the fund had been reduced on some day in January to $3,000. A. has lost $2,000, which he cannot throw on B. Hence, when B.'s money is deposited on February 1st, A. and B. will share $8,000 in the proportion of 3 to 5. Suppose that during February the account gets as low as $4,000. A. and B. cannot throw this loss on C., and when C.'s money is deposited they will share the $9,000 in the proportion of 3, 5, and 10. But any subsequent depletion below $9,000 they must bear in that proportion, just as A. and B. bore theirs in February. At least, to me it would be a parody of justice if, out of a remainder, for example, of $7,000, C. should get $5,000, B. $2,000, and A. get nothing at all. Such a result, I submit with the utmost respect, can only come from a mechanical adherence to a rule which has no intelligible relation to the situation. * * *

SUPPLEMENTAL OPINION

Since filing my opinion of November 12, 1923, counsel have called to my attention the case of In re Bolognesi & Co., 254 Fed. 770, 166 C.C.A. 216, to which I referred. The end of that case, which I regret to say I did not observe at the time, distributed the funds in accordance with the rule of Knatchbull v.

Hallett, L.R. 13 Ch.Div. 696, and Empire, etc., Co. v. Carroll County, 194 Fed. 593, 114 C.C.A. 435. Of course, it constitutes authority absolutely binding upon me and I must therefore modify my directions to the referee so as to accord with the law which controls in this circuit, regardless of my own opinion on the question. The referee will therefore in dividing the trust fund follow the principle that the last depositor shall be paid in full and so on until the fund is exhausted. This is the only modification necessary.

Notes

1. Restatement (Second) of Restitution (Tent. Draft No. 2, 1984):†

§ 42. Apportioning an Insufficient Fund

Except as provided in § [ ] (Conflicting Rights to Restitution), if a right to restitution from a fund cannot be satisfied without infringing a similar right, and there is no just cause for a different disposition, the fund will be apportioned pro rata among all those having similar rights.

2. Cunningham v. Brown, 265 U.S. 1 (1924), involved a controversy over funds obtained from a number of victims of the famous Ponzi swindle. Rejecting the presumption of Knatchbull v. Hallett, the Court ruled that between equally innocent victims of the fraud equality is equity. See also Re British Red Cross Balkan Fund, [1914] 2 Ch. 419.

3. Constructive trusts in bankruptcy present special problems. If the claimant is granted a constructive trust on property in a bankruptcy estate, that claimant will recover a larger proportion of the debt than the bankrupt's general creditors. For a comprehensive discussion see Sherwin, Constructive Trusts in Bankruptcy, 1989 U.Ill.L.Rev. 297.

4. Uniform Commercial Code provisions govern a debtor's commingled bank account that contains funds subject to a security interest. Weinberg, The Malformed Mouse Meets the LIBR: Secured and Restitutionary Claims to Commingled Funds, 8 Ann.Rev. of Banking Law 269 (1989) discusses the complications.

B. INJURIES TO PERSONAL PROPERTY

1. PARTIAL OR COMPLETE DESTRUCTION

HEWLETT v. BARGE BERTIE

Supra p. 53.

Notes

1. *Question:* Suppose that the damaged chattel has been repaired so that functionally it is as good as new. Is plaintiff then limited to recovering the cost of the repairs? See Kirkhof Electric Co. v. Wolverine Express, 269 F.2d 147 (6th Cir.1959).

2. Rosenfield v. Choberka, 140 Misc.2d 9, 529 N.Y.S.2d 455 (1988). A personal automobile substantially damaged in an accident suffers a loss in market or trade-in value even though the physical defects have been repaired. The owner may recover that decline from the tortfeasor.

3. Spreader Specialists, Inc. v. Monroc, Inc., 114 Idaho 15, 752 P.2d 617 (App.1987). Defendant's vehicle negligently struck an oil spreader truck. The owner repaired the truck. The court ruled that where owner repairs a commercial vehicle with the aim of reducing business losses, it may recover the cost of repairs plus any diminution in the repaired vehicle's value, even though that sum exceeded the difference between the market value of the vehicle before and immediately after the injury.

KUWAIT AIRWAYS CORP. v. OGDEN ALLIED AVIATION SERVICES

United States District Court, Eastern District of New York, 1989.
726 F.Supp. 1389.

DEARIE, DISTRICT JUDGE. This case arises out of a fender bender between two rather extraordinary fenders: one attached to a truck of the type used to hoist meals onto aircraft, the other on a Boeing 747. * * *

On May 29, 1984, a Boeing 747 aircraft owned and operated by plaintiff was, while parked at John F. Kennedy International Airport, struck by a truck owned and operated by defendant. Defendant has admitted liability for the accident and stipulated to the amount of damages for actual costs of repairing plaintiff's aircraft and accommodating plaintiff's passengers who were inconvenienced by the accident. The only dispute remaining between the parties is whether plaintiff is entitled to any damages for temporary loss of use of the aircraft and, if so, what the measure of those damages should be.

There is no question that the damaged aircraft was out of service for several days while repairs were being made. Plaintiff argues that this fact, coupled with defendant's admission of liability, entitles plaintiff to an award of damages for loss of use of the aircraft. Plaintiff moves for partial summary judgment establishing that the measure of its loss of use damages is the reasonable rental value of a replacement 747 for the time during which plaintiff's 747 was out of service.

Plaintiff concedes, however, that it did not actually rent a replacement 747. In fact, it appears that plaintiff was able to service all of the grounded plane's flights by using an A300 Airbus that was in plaintiff's fleet and was not otherwise engaged. Defendant submits evidence that, because no flights were cancelled and the Airbus had sufficient capacity to seat all passengers who would have flown on the grounded 747, plaintiff suffered no lost profits—and may indeed have benefitted financially—as a result of the 747's grounding. Absent an actual pecuniary loss resulting from the accident, defendant contends, there can be no recovery of damages for loss of use of the jumbo jet.

The present motion thus requires the Court to decide whether proof of actual pecuniary loss is required in order to recover for loss of use of a damaged chattel, and whether the reasonable cost of securing a replacement for the damaged chattel may be recovered even if no substitute is actually rented.[1] There are undoubtedly disputed, material issues of fact regarding the *amount*

1. These two questions, although closely linked, are not necessarily one and the same. If a substitute is rented to replace a damaged chattel, the rental fee represents the total pecuniary effect of loss of use *only* if the net operating profit (or loss) of the substitute is identical to that of the original. Were the substitute more (or less) profitable to operate than the original, the actual pecuniary damage attributable to loss of use of the original chattel would be smaller (or larger) than the rental fee.

of loss of use damages suffered by plaintiff in this case—for example, the number of days the plane was out of service, the appropriate rental fee, and the relative net operating profit of the Airbus as compared to that of the 747. However, the appropriate *measure* of those damages—in effect, the decision whether the rental fee and operating profit are even relevant to determining damages in the factual context of this case—is purely a question of law that is appropriately addressed on a motion for summary judgment. * * *

Given this state of authority, the positions taken by the parties in the case at bar are unsurprising. Plaintiff contends that *Storms* and *K.L.M.* [Mountain View Coach Lines, Inc. v. Storms, 102 A.D.2d 663, 476 N.Y.S.2d 918 (1984); Koninklijke Luchtvaart Maatschaapij, N.V. (K.L.M. Royal Dutch Airlines) v. United Technologies Corp., 610 F.2d 1052 (2d Cir.1979)] correctly state New York law, and that it may therefore recover, as a matter of law, "the reasonable rental value of a substitute aircraft," even if plaintiff submits no proof of actual pecuniary loss, or indeed even in the face of evidence tending to negate the proposition that plaintiff suffered actual pecuniary loss. Defendant, predictably, counters that plaintiff is not entitled to summary judgment of entitlement to loss of use damages, because defendant has offered proof that at least raises a material issue of fact as to whether the collision caused plaintiff any loss of profits. Defendant argues that its showing either entirely precludes loss of use damages, or, at least, shifts the burden to the plaintiff to prove actual, rather than presumed, financial damages arising from the loss of use of the 747. Defendant relies on *CTI, Hartnett* and *Gehr* [CTI International, Inc. v. Lloyds Underwriters, 735 F.2d 679 (2d Cir.1984); Mountain View Coach Lines, Inc. v. Hartnett, 99 Misc.2d 271, 415 N.Y.S.2d 918 (1978), leave to appeal denied, 47 N.Y.2d 710, 419 N.Y.S.2d 1026 (1979); Mountain View Coach Lines, Inc. v. Gehr, 80 A.D.2d 949, 439 N.Y.S.2d 632 (1981)] as accurate statements of New York law.[2]

Sitting in diversity and bound to apply New York law, this Court must choose—in the absence of an applicable decision of the New York Court of Appeals—between directly conflicting doctrines followed by different Departments of this State's intermediate appellate court. * * *

This Court is convinced that the New York Court of Appeals, were it called upon to decide the issue, would adopt the *KLM–Storms* approach and reject *Gehr–Hartnett–CTI.* The approach of *Storms* and *KLM* represents sounder reasoning than the contrary decisions and are more consistent with settled principles of tort doctrine and, as discussed in *KLM,* with earlier, somewhat analogous cases.

As Judge Gurfein observed in *KLM,* loss of use damages exist to compensate for the deprivation of the owner's right to use its chattel as the owner sees fit. This right has a value, and its deprivation necessarily entails what economists call "opportunity cost." *Any* particular allocation of a resource necessarily costs the owner the opportunity to put that resource to other, competing uses. When a tortfeasor by its negligence forces a thing's owner to allocate that chattel to the singularly unsatisfying use of sitting in a repair

2. Defendant attempts to distinguish *Storms* based on that opinion's statement that "the parties stipulated * * * that the damages sustained for loss of use were $3,000," whereas in this case, defendant denies that *any* loss of use damages were in fact sustained. As explained [below] this distinction is illusory.

shop for a while, that tortfeasor forecloses the owner's opportunity to put the chattel to some productive use.

The opportunity cost exists irrespective of the normal use to which the owner allocates the damaged item. For example, in the case of a vehicle that is used only for pleasure—say, a privately owned, high-powered sports car—the loss of the car's use deprives the owner of the opportunity to drive the car for pleasure during the repair period. Again invoking the economist's language, one could say that the owner has lost "utility." The value of that utility is measurable by the amount the owner is willing or required to spend to obtain it. There is no controversy, as a matter of tort doctrine, that the sports car owner so deprived is entitled to replace the lost utility directly, by renting an equivalent automobile and recovering the rental cost from the tortfeasor. No sound reason exists for denying that same recovery for the value of lost utility even if the owner does not rent a substitute car.

The result is no different in the case of a driver who owns a second, identical sports car that is kept in reserve for just such contingencies. The reserve sports car might enable the owner to do the same amount of pleasure driving after the tort as before, but the tort still carries with it an opportunity cost. The owner has lost the opportunity to lend the second sports car to a friend, or to keep one car brand-new while using the other, or simply to drive home in one car while smugly knowing that there is another in the garage. This lost opportunity also has a compensable value.

Shifting from a pleasure vehicle, maintained only to enhance its owner's utility, to a commercial vehicle that is maintained to provide a return on investment, has no effect whatever on the analysis.[3] To an airline, ownership of a 747 represents a bundle of valuable opportunities. Those opportunities range from the chance to use the plane to entertain the board of directors and important shareholders, through flying the plane on regularly-scheduled routes, through leasing it to another airline, through holding it in reserve for use as a replacement in case another aircraft must be taken out of service. Those opportunities are all temporarily lost when a tortfeasor renders the aircraft unserviceable for a period of time. That opportunity cost *cannot* be valueless; it *must* be worth something. The difficulty sometimes encountered, of course, is choosing the appropriate method by which to measure that value.

In some cases, the best way to approximate that value will be perfectly obvious. If a replacement plane were actually rented, the rental fee would be an appropriate choice. Or, if, as was the case in *KLM,* the damaged plane were itself leased rather than owned by the victim of the tort, the prorated portion of the lease payments would approximate the value of the use of the plane for the time during which it was out of service.

The foregoing examples are the easy ones, because the proxy used to measure the airline's opportunity cost is in each case an actual out-of-pocket sum spent by the airline. Almost as easy is the case in which an airline, having no substitute plane available and choosing not to rent one, cancels the damaged airliner's flights. In such a case, the ready measure of the airline's

3. The sharp distinction between pleasure and profit-making vehicles is somewhat artificial. A classic sports car may be a valuable investment as well as being fun to drive. And the decision to use the car only for pleasure in fact represents a resource allocation that carries its own opportunity cost. By giving up some hours of pleasure driving, and therefore some utility, the owner might be able to make money renting the car for hour-long joyrides.

loss would be the lost revenue from the cancelled flights, less operating costs saved by not flying.

Suppose, however, that an airline with no spare planes did not cancel any flights but instead met its schedules by stretching its regular fleet (minus the damaged plane) just enough to cover its needs. This is the *Brooklyn Terminal* case, and here the actual measure of damages is still more difficult to prove. Yet even in this case, the damages still exist. As Justice Cardozo pointed out, had the tugboat operator in *Brooklyn Terminal* been able to document overtime wages or "extra wear and tear" on the undamaged tugs, those damages would have been recoverable.

Finally, consider the case in which an airline maintains one or more airplanes that are normally held in reserve. When a front-line plane is damaged, the airline presses the reserves into service. As Justice Cardozo observed, that "result is all one" whether the replacement plane is rented from a lessor or moved from reserve status into active duty. The "spare boat doctrine" reasoning was adopted by *Storms*.

The concept of opportunity cost makes it easy to see how the airline using a spare plane suffers a genuine loss even though it does not spend money to rent an aircraft. Any prudent airline that is obligated to fly, say, 100 planes to meet its daily schedule, will own more than 100 airliners in recognition of the actuarial inevitability that some planes will be out of service on some days. The airline might determine, for example, that to be reasonably secure from the risk of flight cancellation, it would need to own 110 planes to cover a 100–plane daily need. The need for a 10–plane reserve arises from several sources: lost service days for regular inspection and maintenance, unforseen breakdowns, accidents caused by the airline's own carelessness—*and* accidents caused by the negligence of others. If an airline could be certain that its planes would never be damaged by the fault of tortfeasors, it would be able to get by with a smaller reserve fleet. As a practical matter, it is probably impossible to know whether one, two, or more of the spare planes must be maintained solely as insurance against negligence of others. But it is possible, after a particular accident has occurred, and the airline has utilized a particular spare airplane, to estimate the lifetime cost of owning and maintaining that spare airplane. It is also possible to calculate the percentage of the spare plane's lifetime represented by the number of days the accident causes the airline to use the spare plane. That percentage, multiplied by the lifetime cost of the plane, represents the fraction of the airline's reserve fleet costs that are directly attributable to a particular tortfeasor, and approximates the economic injury to the airline that results from loss of use of the damaged front-line plane.[4]

Tort doctrine requires full compensation for tortiously-inflicted damage. The position taken by defendant in this lawsuit would restrict parties in the position of the plaintiff in this case (and in *Gehr, Harnett,* and *Storms*) to

4. There might be other costs as well—for example, the incremental depreciation of the spare plane that results from its being flown instead of standing idle, or profits lost from a charter that had to be foregone because the spare plane was needed to fly scheduled routes—but they are not of analytical importance. The point is not to show that prorated lifetime cost of the spare is an exclusive measure of loss of use damages in a case such as this, but rather to demonstrate that such damages exist even absent out-of-pocket expense. For the same reason, this section does not consider the possible offsetting economic benefits to the airline.

recovery of out-of-pocket payments made to replace a damaged vehicle, or to profits lost as a result of trip cancellations. As the discussion *supra* reveals, however, a real economic loss may be incurred, and approximately measured, even in the absence of apparent pecuniary losses. Thus the doctrine of *Storms* is sound, and this Court predicts that the New York Court of Appeals, were it to decide the question, would hold that damages for loss of use of a vehicle may be recovered even absent a showing that profitable vehicle trips were cancelled or that a substitute vehicle was rented.

The story, however, cannot quite end there, because the conclusion just reached does not imply that the plaintiff is entitled to the partial summary judgment. Quite the contrary is the case.

The Court agrees with plaintiff that loss of use damages *may* be proven and recovered even though no substitute plane was actually rented. The plaintiff asks for more, however, than a determination that it is entitled to recover loss of use damages. Plaintiff also seeks a ruling "that these damages are to be measured by the reasonable rental value of a substitute aircraft." To this second requested ruling plaintiff is not entitled.

In *Storms,* the Appellate Division directed entry of judgment in the plaintiff's favor for $3,200, the stipulated rental value of a replacement for the damaged bus. Because the parties had stipulated how the loss of use damages were to be measured if recovery for loss of use were allowed, the *Storms* court had no need to consider the method of measuring damages; the Court had only to determine that the plaintiff's failure to rent a substitute bus did not bar recovery of the stipulated damages.

The present case is quite different. It is undisputed that there is no market for rental of Boeing 747's to commercial passenger airlines for six-day periods. The "reasonable rental cost" urged by plaintiff as a measure of damages is apparently the output of an economic model devised by plaintiff or by plaintiff's retained expert. The evidence presented by defendant on this motion is sufficient to raise a material issue of fact as to the reliability and suitability of plaintiff's analysis. Defendant is entitled to attempt to prove at trial that the "reasonable rental cost" proferred by plaintiff is nothing more than speculation and as such insufficient to support a recovery. See *Brooklyn Terminal.*

While it is appropriate at this time for the Court to determine that plaintiff may recover a reasonable measure of loss of use damages, it would be premature for the Court to hold that any particular measure of damages is the one to be applied.[5]

Finally, defendant in this case has also raised a material issue of fact as to the effect that using the Airbus had on the profitability of the route the Airbus flew in the damaged 747's stead. Defendant is wrong when it argues that if the Airbus' lower operating costs resulted in higher profits, plaintiff *necessarily* suffered no loss of use damages. However, under settled principles of tort law in New York and elsewhere, increased operating profits could partially or entirely offset the damages for loss of use (no matter how loss of use damages

5. Reasonable replacement rental cost might turn out to be the best available estimation, but other approximations are possible. The prorated lifetime cost of the spare plane, is a conceivable alternative measure, and there are doubtless others.

are calculated).[6] "Damages are to restore injured parties, not to reward them." *Hartnett.* Even if this Court agreed with plaintiff that "reasonable replacement rental value" represented the appropriate gross measure of loss of use damages, the Court could not grant the requested summary judgment in the face of a material issue of fact directly affecting the net amount of such recovery. Plaintiff is entitled to a reasonable measure of loss of use damages even absent any out-of-pocket expenditures, but those damages must be reduced to the extent, if any, that they were recouped by operating efficiencies that are proven to have resulted from the accident.[7]

For the reasons stated above, plaintiff's motion for partial summary judgment is denied. At trial, the recoverable damages for loss of use of plaintiff's 747, if any, shall be determined in accordance with the principles set forth, supra.

SO ORDERED.

Notes

1. Brownstein, What's the Use? A Doctrinal and Policy Critique of the Measurement of Loss of Use Damages, 37 Rutgers L.Rev. 433 (1985).

2. Owner may recover damages for lost use of an automobile maintained for personal pleasure even though she does not rent a substitute vehicle. Many jurisdictions measure the loss by the cost of renting a substitute vehicle; but a New Jersey court held that the proper standard is the extent of the owner's personal inconvenience which will vary depending upon the individual circumstances of the injured party. Camaraza v. Bellavia Buick Corp., 216 N.J.Super. 263, 523 A.2d 669 (App.Div.1987).

6. This conclusion is not inconsistent with the analysis [above. It] implicitly assumed that all the planes in the airline's primary and reserve fleets were absolutely interchangeable. In the real world, fungibility would be the exception rather than the rule. For instance, one might normally expect a reserve fleet to be populated with older, relatively inefficient aircraft. The extra fuel costs resulting from use of the older plane would then be *added* to the loss of use damages as measured by rental value or other method. Similarly, because an Airbus is smaller than a 747, in times of peak demand the use of an Airbus would likely reduce flight revenues and hence profits. The lost profits would be added to the loss of use damages. These additions make perfect sense: had the airline actually needed to rent a replacement plane, that turned out to be less profitable to fly, the damages would clearly include both the rental fee and the lost profits. So with the use of a spare plane. But with the good plaintiff must take the bad: if the replacement plane turns out to be more profitable to use than the damaged plane, the increased profits must be subtracted from the recovery.

7. In *KLM,* the Second Circuit noted that "saved operating costs and depreciation are normally deducted from rental value to arrive at damages for loss of use of an automobile" in cases where no replacement car was actually rented. The theory behind this rule is quite simple: the owner who chooses to do without the car for a time does lose all the benefits of driving it, but he also avoids the costs of filling it with gasoline, wearing down the tire tread, etc.; it is only fair that these foregone costs be deducted from the recovery. The rule of "automatically" offsetting saved operating costs should not be applied to commercial aircraft because "there is always the possibility that any operating costs and depreciation saved by loss of use of the vehicle would have been offset by revenues generated if the vehicle had been available * * *."

KLM's reasoning is sound but in this respect its facts are distinguishable from those of the case at bar. In KLM there was no replacement plane. The plane that was out of service neither cost the airline money to operate nor generated any ticket revenues for the airline. Any prediction by the Court of the net effect of lost revenues and saved expenses would have been guesswork, which the court quite properly refused to indulge. In the case before this Court, by contrast, a reserve plane was used, and the defendant has offered to prove that use of the reserve plane reduced operating costs while having no effect on revenues. If defendant can establish those facts, the recovery must be reduced by the proven amount of increased profits.

3. In American Telephone & Telegraph Co. v. Connecticut Light & Power Co., 470 F.Supp. 105, 107 (D.Conn.1979), the court made the following findings of fact:

1. On the afternoon of March 2, 1979, the AT&T Hartford–New Haven underground "B" telephone cable was damaged by a CL & P work crew.
2. The cable was out of service for less than twelve hours.
3. The cable contained 225 active circuits.
4. 2239.03 circuit hours were lost.
5. The cost to AT&T to repair the cable was $4,797.11.
6. During March, 1970, AT&T offered circuits on the cable for rent at the rate of $121.00 per month.
7. No evidence was offered from which a court could conclude that AT & T actually lost any operating revenue as a result of the cable being out of service.

What are AT&T's damages?

BOND v. A.H. BELO CORP.

Court of Civil Appeals of Texas, Dallas, 1980.
602 S.W.2d 105.

CARVER, JUSTICE. Becky J. Bond appeals from a judgment awarding her only the actual value of certain family papers and photographs lost while in the possession of A.H. Belo Corporation and its employee Dottie Griffith. Bond's complaint on appeal is that the trial court refused to apply the correct measure of damages under which Bond would be entitled to recover the *reasonable special value of such articles to their owner taking into consideration the feelings of the owner for such property.* We agree and accordingly reverse and remand.

In August 1976, Griffith wrote a story on unwanted children which Belo published in its newspaper "The Dallas Morning News." Bond read the story and contacted Griffith. This led to an interview at Bond's home. Bond told Griffith that she (Bond) was an adopted child who had some interesting experiences in trying to locate her biological parents and brothers. Bond exhibited a legal size envelope crammed with "pictures and birth records and newspaper clippings, copies of newspaper stories" accumulated during her search. By mutual agreement, Griffith took the envelope with her to help in writing another story. The envelope and its contents disappeared, apparently during an office shuffle at the newspaper, and the parties concede that they are irretrievable. Bond sued for damages. * * *

[T]he parties stipulated that the actual value of the lost papers was $2,500.00 but that the "sentimental value and the special value and feelings of Becky Bond for such articles" was *greater* than the actual value. The court discharged the jury, and judgment was entered for Bond for the $2,500.00 *actual value* lost.

* * * Belo and Griffith urge here, and apparently took the position in the trial court, that the correct measure of damages is to be found in Crisp v. Security National Insurance Co., 369 S.W.2d 326 (Tex.1963), which held:

> "It is a matter of common knowledge and of usual acceptation by the courts that used household goods, clothing and personal effects have no market

value in the ordinary meaning of that term. They may be sold but only at considerable sacrifice which by no means represents the value of the articles to the owner. We find no recognized authority which would hold the insured to a recovery based solely on the proceeds obtainable on a secondhand market. Likewise, replacement costs do not afford a fair test. In some instances on account of obsolescence, change in style and fashion, this measure might represent an economic gain to the insured quite aside from the difficulty of application and proof. The measure of damage that should be applied in case of destruction of this kind of property is the actual worth or value of the articles to the owner for use in the condition in which they were at the time of the fire excluding any fanciful or sentimental considerations." [citations]

We disagree. *Crisp* was a suit to recover for fire insurance and dealt only with "used household goods, clothing, and personal effects," none of which were shown to have any "sentimental" value. Bond urges that the correct measure of damages is provided by Brown v. Frontier Theatres, Inc., 369 S.W.2d 299 (Tex.1963). In *Brown* * * * the court addressed the appropriate damages for the loss of a variety of personal property. As to such personal property as may have its "primary value in sentiment" the court held:

"As a general rule recovery for sentimental value for personal property cannot be had in a suit for the loss of property for personal use such as wearing apparel and household goods. This rule has been applied in Texas so as to deny the recovery for sentimental value in a suit for the loss of heirlooms. However, in our opinion such is not the rule to be applied in a suit to recover for the loss or destruction of items which have their primary value in sentiment.

"It is a matter of common knowledge that items such as these generally have no market value which would adequately compensate their owner for their loss or destruction. Such property is not susceptible of supply and reproduction in kind, and their greater value is in sentiment and not in the market place. In such cases the most fundamental rule of damages that every wrongful injury or loss to persons or property should be adequately and reasonably compensated requires the allowance of damages in compensation for the reasonable special value of such articles to their owner taking into consideration the feelings of the owner for such property. * * * Where such special value is greater than the market value, it becomes the only criterion for the assessment of damages." [citations.]

In *Brown* the court also described some of the personal property reflected by the record stating:

"The law recognizes that articles of small market value of which their owner is despoiled may have a special value to him as heirlooms, and there is evidence in the record that with the exception of the coin collection and the land patent the primary value of these items to Mrs. Brown was their sentimental value. For example: the wedding veil, one of the emerald rings, the shoes and the point lace collar belonged to her grandmother; the pistol belonged to her grandfather; the watch belonged to her great grandmother; and the two slumber spreads were made by hand by her great, great, great grandmothers."

We hold that under the record, including the stipulations of the parties, the correct measure of damages is supplied by *Brown,* that is "the reasonable special value of such articles to their owner taking into consideration the feelings of the owner for such property." * * *

Reversed and remanded with costs assessed to Belo and Griffith.

Notes

1. Defendant landlord ordered all of plaintiff's possessions removed from his apartment and deposited in the trash. Plaintiff burst into tears when he discovered that a garbage truck had driven away with all his belongings. Plaintiff sued to recover for conversion of his property. May he recover damages for emotional distress? See Parker v. Stein, 557 A.2d 1319 (D.C.App.1989).

2. Whether plaintiff should be allowed to testify to the value of his or her property is a matter of dispute. Should courts distinguish between household effects and items of only sentimental value? See Campins v. Capels, 461 N.E.2d 712 (Ind.App.1984).

3. *Valuation of Chattels—Unusual Examples.*

a. A school board threw out the file cabinet of a high school coach containing his personal coaching library consisting of notes compiled over thirteen years of playing football and seventeen years of coaching. The files occupied two and a half file drawers approximately three feet long. What is their value? See Williams v. Board of Education, 52 Ill.App.3d 328, 367 N.E.2d 549 (1977).

b. Plaintiff filed a personal injury action against a trucking company and settled for $300,000. He then sued defendant for conversion of a tire on the vehicle in which he had sustained his injuries. He claimed that the tire would have been valuable evidence in the personal injury action and that without it he had to settle for far less. His claim is for $1,000,000.00. What decision? See Villarreal v. Brown Express Co., 529 F.2d 1219 (5th Cir.1976).

c. Defendant negligently destroyed one roadside utility pole in an integrated system of transmission lines. How should the pole be valued? See Pacific Gas & Electric v. Mounteer, 66 Cal.App.3d 809, 136 Cal.Rptr. 280 (1977), construing Cal.Pub. Util. Code § 7952.

4. Criminal cases raise problems about valuation of chattels.

a. A jacket is stolen from a retail store. The wholesale value is $80; the retail $110 at this store. Anything valued over $100 is grand theft. Some other stores were selling the same jacket at $101. What is the correct value in a civil action for destruction or conversion? See People v. Pena, 68 Cal.App.3d 100, 135 Cal.Rptr. 602 (1977).

b. A credit card is stolen. It cannot lawfully be sold. What is its value? Cf. Miller v. People, 193 Colo. 415, 566 P.2d 1059 (1977).

c. Twenty-five stolen unissued airline tickets were transported in interstate commerce. Stolen blank tickets are worth between $20 and $27 on the black market. Yet airlines lose between $379 and $1000 on each stolen ticket exchanged for travel or refund. Could the court affirm defendant's conviction for transporting stolen goods worth more than $5000 in interstate commerce? United States v. Wallace, 800 F.2d 1509, 1511–12 (9th Cir.1986), cert. denied, 481 U.S. 1019 (1987).

ACME DELIVERY SERVICE, INC. v. SAMSONITE CORP.

Supreme Court of Colorado, 1983.
663 P.2d 621.

Rovira, Justice. The facts are not in dispute. In February of 1979, Acme Delivery Service, Inc. (carrier or petitioner), received from Samsonite Corporation (shipper or respondent) 715 pieces of luggage to be transported to the warehouse of the consignee, May D & F Company. The luggage was taken instead to a dump, where it was discarded. Of the 715 pieces of luggage, 637 were "lost or destroyed," and the remaining 78 were returned to Samsonite.

The invoice price—the amount to be paid by May D & F to Samsonite—was $15,364.90. The cost of manufacturing the 637 pieces of luggage was $8,603.23. Samsonite provided replacement luggage to May D & F for the luggage lost or destroyed by Acme.

Samsonite then brought an action for breach of contract against Acme, seeking as damages the invoice price of the luggage together with interest from the date of loss. Acme admitted liability but argued that the correct measure of damages was the cost of manufacturing the luggage. * * *

The court of appeals determined that the trial court erred in using the cost of manufacture instead of the invoice price as the * * * measure of damages. * * *

It is undisputed that the standard for assessing damages is that the carrier is liable for the "full actual loss." See Sutherland v. Ringsby Truck Lines, Inc., 37 Colo.App. 333, 549 P.2d 784 (1976); Chicago, Milwaukee & St. Paul Ry. Co. v. McCaull–Dinsmore Co., 253 U.S. 97 (1920); Polaroid Corp. v. Schuster's Express, Inc., 484 F.2d 349 (1st Cir.1973); Gore Products, Inc. v. Texas & N.O.R. Co., 34 So.2d 418 (La.App.1948); Meletio Sea Food Co. v. Gordons Transports, 191 S.W.2d 983 (Mo.App.1946).

Samsonite argues that the fair measure of compensation is the invoice price, because when Samsonite manufactured the 637 suitcases that were lost, it did so with the expectation that it would earn its normal profit on each one. It did earn its normal profit on the replacement group of 637 suitcases, but, viewed as a whole, it earned profit on only 637 of 1,274 pieces of luggage. Therefore, Samsonite argues, it has lost its expected profit on 637 pieces of luggage, and that lost profit should be considered part of the "full actual loss."

Acme, on the other hand, argues that Samsonite would be compensated for its full actual loss by recovery of the cost of manufacture, that is, the replacement cost. If Samsonite is allowed to recover its invoice cost, it would be granted a double profit and would be in a better position than if the loss had never occurred.

The court of appeals held that its opinion in Sutherland v. Ringsby Truck Lines, Inc., supra, was dispositive of the damages issue. In *Sutherland*, a shipper sought recovery from a carrier for loss of a shipment of equipment. The equipment had been purchased by the shipper at auction in Utah for $15 and was to be shipped to its place of business in Denver. The replacement cost of the goods in Denver was $22,678.30. Both parties agreed that the standard to be applied was "full actual loss." The trial court held that the shipper was entitled to recover the $15 cost of the goods, as that figure reflected its out-of-pocket loss. The court of appeals reversed, holding that replacement cost (less expenses saved) was the proper measure of damages. The court noted that if the contract had been performed, the shipper would have had the equipment available at his place of business in Denver, and that use of a cost figure would deprive the shipper of the benefit of the bargain he struck in Utah.

The reasoning of *Sutherland* is not controlling here. First, the replacement cost was far higher than the original cost. Here, it was stipulated that the replacement cost and the original cost of manufacture were the same. Second, the shipper would have been worse off after the loss of the shipment if he were awarded only $15. There was no way for the shipper to duplicate the bargain he made in Utah, and, consequently, only the replacement cost (as measured by the value of the goods at destination) would compensate for the full actual loss.

Other courts have reached differing results when considering the question of what constitutes "full actual loss." Much of the conflict is more apparent than real, however, as the results are often dictated by the peculiar facts of the cases.

In Polaroid Corp. v. Schuster's Express, Inc., the court held that the shipper was entitled to recover its price to its dealer rather than merely its costs of manufacture to compensate for the hijacking of a shipment of photographic equipment. Although questioning the idea that an award of replacement cost would ever adequately compensate for the loss of a shipment, the court held that, in any event, special circumstances of the case militated against an award of only replacement cost. There was strong reason to believe that the hijacked goods would ultimately compete with the manufacturer and that sales would therefore be lost.[1]

Meletio Sea Food Co. v. Gordons Transports, presented facts similar to those in the case at hand. The carrier was transporting a mixture to be used for breading fish and meats when part of the shipment was contaminated by turpentine and rendered unfit for human consumption. The question was whether the shipper could recover its cost or the invoice price. In rejecting a mechanistic use of the invoice price as the measure of damages, the court stated:

> "It is to be noted, however, that the test of market value, whether considered independently or in its relation to a contract price, is at best but a convenient means of determining the extent of the loss; and it may therefore be discarded, and other more accurate means resorted to, if, for special reasons, or under the circumstances of the particular case, it is not exact, or is otherwise inapplicable. As already pointed out, the federal act gives only a right of recovery for actual loss, and in that respect conforms to the basic principle of the law of damages, which contemplates that the remedy provided in a given case shall only afford compensation for whatever injury is actually sustained."

It also said that by awarding the cost price, "the matter stands precisely as though there had been no damage to the original shipment."

On similar facts, the court in Gore Products, Inc. v. Texas & N.O.R. Co., reached the opposite result. The carrier broke a container of medicine, which was replaced from inventory by the shipper. The court rejected the carrier's reliance upon *Meletio,* stating that there were no "special circumstances" to warrant use of the cost of manufacture rather than the invoice price as the measure of damages. The court raised the question of what would happen if a second, third, or fourth container had been destroyed, and asked, "Could plaintiff be required to continue to manufacture goods for the defendant at

1. [Footnotes renumbered.] Samsonite argues that it comes within the rule of *Polaroid,* because there is a possibility that the goods that were "lost or destroyed" will ultimately compete with its sales. However, there is nothing in the record to create the inference that such competition will in fact occur.

cost?" It is not clear why the court felt compelled to raise hypothetical situations when it had already implied that "special circumstances" might be considered.

Samsonite raises a similar argument, quoting the following passage from a treatise on the subject:

> "If the [*Meletio*] decision is accepted in its literal sense, a manufacturer could be forced to operate its plants for months without profit whatever in order to replace at cost goods lost or damaged by a carrier, and conceivably the manufacturer could be forced into bankruptcy while operating its facilities for the benefit of carriers. The law certainly never contemplated a result of this nature and the aforementioned decision is contrary to the general law on this subject."

Miller, Freight Loss and Damage Claims 300 (4th ed. 1974).

Little attention need be directed to this argument. It is certainly an argument against a requirement that the cost of goods always be used as the measure of damages, but it is hardly a justification for a rule that cost never be used.[2] It is highly unlikely that the manufacturer would have to operate its plant for months to replace a lost shipment without being able to demonstrate that other sales were lost as a consequence or that the cost of replacement was higher than the original cost of manufacture. If the manufacturer can establish that it was unable to fill orders because its plant had been given over to replacing lost goods, it would have established the loss of profits. Its ability to do so will depend upon the circumstances. A manufacturer whose production capacity is less than or equal to the demand for its product (that is, it can sell all it can make) can easily show the loss of profits. On the other hand, a manufacturer whose production capacity exceeds the demand for its products would not ordinarily be able to establish loss of profits.

The question is not whether a shipper can recover lost profits, for certainly lost profits are part of the shipper's loss. See *Sutherland. Instead, the question is whether the shipper can recover profits in the absence of a showing that it did in fact lose profits. Samsonite would have us adopt a rule that no such showing is required. We decline to do so.*

In a breach of contract action, the burden of proving damages rests upon the wronged party. Samsonite has not established any damage above and beyond the cost of replacing the goods, but has instead argued that as a matter of law it is not required to.[3]

In many instances, an award of damages based on the invoice price would constitute overcompensation to the shipper, contrary to the rule that a plaintiff in a breach of contract action is not entitled to be placed in a position more favorable than the position he contracted for. The effect of an award of invoice price in this case would be as if May D & F had ordered twice as much luggage from Samsonite as it had, thus increasing Samsonite's total sales and total profits. It is fair to say that most manufacturers desire, and would benefit

2. Because the cost figure in this case was stipulated, it is unnecessary for us to determine how the cost of manufacture should be determined.

3. Samsonite also argues that it should be allowed to recover invoice price because if May D & F had sued that is the amount it would have recovered. However, the measure of damages recoverable is the loss suffered by the plaintiff and not the loss suffered by someone else. Moreover, under Samsonite's reasoning, May D & F should be permitted to recover retail price, as it expected to profit from every suitcase it ordered.

from, an increase in sales and profits. In such a case, a manufacturer receives more than it "would have had if the contract had been performed." Chicago, Milwaukee & St. Paul Railway v. McCaull–Dinsmore Co.

In the absence of any evidence showing lost profits, we believe the court of appeals erred in using the invoice price as the measure of damages.

Notes

1. Restatement (Second) of Torts § 911 comment d (1977):†

Wholesale or retail value. From the time when a chattel is manufactured to the time of its actual use, there may be many markets in which it is sold. Thus, different prices are paid by the wholesaler, the retail dealer and the consumer. Since the measure of recovery is determined by the harm done, the market which determines the measure of recovery by a person whose goods have been taken, destroyed or detained is that to which he would have to resort in order to replace the subject matter. Thus the consumer can recover the retail price; the retail dealer, the wholesale price. The manufacturer, who does not buy in a market, receives his selling price. Damages for the profits which the wholesale dealer or the retail dealer would normally anticipate from a sale are not ordinarily allowed. However, if such a dealer has made a contract to sell certain goods which another has destroyed, taken or detained and he has been unable to obtain similar goods for delivery to the purchaser, he is entitled to recover damages for the loss of profits thus caused, if he can satisfy the requirement of certainty (see § 912). Likewise, a consumer or user may recover for the harm done through the loss of use of the chattel until he can obtain a substitute; the dealer or manufacturer is entitled to damages for any harm done to his business through his inability to obtain substitutes and thus satisfy his customers (see § 927).

2. Tozzi v. Testa, 97 Ill.App.3d 832, 423 N.E.2d 948, 951–52 (1981): "At first blush the 'wholesale replacement cost' appears to be the correct valuation for such property since this amount would be what the plaintiff actually paid for the various items of furniture and furnishings. In short, the plaintiff would be reimbursed for the out of pocket cash loss which he suffered as the result of the destruction of the various pieces of personal property. However, the 'wholesale replacement cost' valuation does not stand the test when closely examined. The plaintiff in this case is a merchant engaged in the selling of home furnishings, i.e., tables, chairs, carpeting, draperies, etc. To apply the 'wholesale replacement cost' fails to take into account damages sustained by reason of the absence of such articles while awaiting replacement. It ignores delivery charges and certainly this court should judicially notice that for a number of years our nation's economy has experienced crippling inflation. The 'wholesale cost' paid by a merchant one month with few exceptions is substantially increased each month thereafter."

3. Farer v. Benton, 740 S.W.2d 676 (Mo.App.1987). Plaintiff, the owner of a shoe store, was limited to the replacement cost of a stock of shoes damaged by defendant's failure to repair a roof properly.

4. Stark Bro's Nurseries & Orchards Co. v. Wayne Daniel Truck, Inc., 718 S.W.2d 204, 206 (Mo.App.1986). After a nursery recovered for nursery stock on its way to be sold to buyers, the carrier challenged use of retail value to measure "full actual loss."

"Defendant contends that because the trees here, which were received in January, were not to be delivered until spring they constituted stock of the plaintiff and purchase price plus shipping is the proper measure of damages. We do not agree. The testimony supports a finding that the destroyed trees had already been sold and that refunds and pro rata delivery to customers who had ordered them was necessary. Because of their nature trees are harvested only while in their dormant state (winter) and are delivered for planting in the spring. Plaintiff's business requires it to receive the trees several months before making delivery to its customers. But that delay in delivery does not make the trees a part of the 'stock' of plaintiff. The trees were already sold and were warehoused on plaintiff's premises until the appropriate delivery date during the planting season.

"Nor do we find the trees subject to replacement as defendant contends. These trees were grown on a particular root stock giving them certain advantages for orchards. They included a variety of species which are not interchangeable. * * * The evidence clearly established that plaintiff lost trees which it had already sold and which it could not replace. Retail price was the proper measure of damages."

5. Pelletier v. Eisenberg, 177 Cal.App.3d 558, 566–67, 223 Cal.Rptr. 84, 89–90 (1986). An artist's pictures on consignment at a gallery were destroyed and the artist sued the gallery for damages.

The trial judge instructed the jury: "An art gallery consignee is not entitled to a commission if the artwork consigned is destroyed and not sold. The artist is entitled to recover 100% of the fair market value, whether that is less or more than any consignment contract, in the event of the art's destruction or loss. A commission agreed upon for the sale of artwork is not binding if the item is destroyed as compared to being sold."

The trial judge concluded that the artist should receive wholesale value instead of fair market value and granted a motion for a limited new trial. The artist appealed.

"It is well established that under section 3333, the measure of damages for the loss or destruction of personal property is generally determined by the value of the property at the time of such loss or destruction. [citation]

"We see no reason to depart from the standard fair market value measure of damages for the destruction of Pelletier's paintings. The parties agreed to a commission if the paintings were sold, not if they were destroyed, and thus the Eisenbergs have not earned their commission. Since the paintings cannot be sold, Pelletier has lost all benefits emanating from a potential sale (i.e., enhancement of his reputation). Even payment of the full fair market value cannot compensate Pelletier for the intangible aspects of a work of art which are forever lost when the property is destroyed. * * * Pelletier would not be compensated for his losses if he had to pay for something which he never acquired (i.e., benefits from the sale of his paintings), and which the Eisenbergs never earned (i.e., the commission for the sale of the paintings). We conclude that the fair market value of the paintings is the most accurate measure of damages to compensate Pelletier for his losses."

NEWBERY ALASKA, INC. v. ALASKA CONSTRUCTORS, INC.

Supreme Court of Alaska, 1982.

644 P.2d 224.

RABINOWITZ, JUSICE. Rogers Electric, Inc. ["Rogers"] operated a warehouse and an electrical subcontracting and supply business on the North Slope of Alaska. Newbery Alaska, Inc. ["Newbery"] is Rogers' successor in interest.

Rogers leased its warehouse and office facilities at the Crazyhorse camp from Alaska Constructors, Inc. ["ACI"].

As a result of a fire on March 12, 1978, virtually all of Rogers' inventory at the camp was destroyed. At trial, ACI was found to be responsible for the fire, and as a result, Newbery was awarded damages totaling $55,500.40, plus interest, costs, and attorney's fees.

Newbery appeals, asserting that the superior court erred by not including in the damages awarded the cost of transporting the destroyed property from Anchorage, the nearest market, to Crazyhorse. ACI argues that transportation costs are not mandated given that Rogers' operations were at a standstill at the time of the fire and were actually shut down thereafter and that some items had no associated transportation expense. * * *

In the case of destroyed chattels, the property owner is ordinarily entitled to the cost of transporting the goods to the place where the destruction occurred. See generally D. Dobbs, Handbook on the Law of Remedies 375 (1973); C. McCormick, Handbook on the Law of Damages 181–82 (1935).

The general rule does not apply, however, where the circumstances are such that the cost of transportation to the place of destruction is not a loss to the owner. Professor Dobbs illustrates the point nicely:

> "If there is no market at the place where the chattel is destroyed, some other market, normally the 'nearest,' is said to furnish the guide, and when a market at some distant point is involved, cost of transporting the chattel to that point must be adjusted. Adjustments may either deduct the cost of transportation or add it, depending on circumstances. If an automobile is totally destroyed in a collision in a desert and the nearest reasonable market is Los Angeles, the owner intending to sell the automobile intended to transport it to Los Angeles and to pay the cost of so doing. This transportation cost was a cost he would pay even had there been no destruction of the car. Accordingly it is not a loss caused by the destruction and he cannot recover it. His measure of damages is thus the price of the Los Angeles market, less the transportation cost he would have expended in getting the car to that market. On the other hand, if the owner of the car is a prospector living in the desert where the car is destroyed and using it there, the principle of full reparation calls for an award that will allow him the monetary equivalent of a replacement. The monetary equivalent is the Los Angeles market *plus* the reasonable cost of transporting the car to the desert."

D. Dobbs, supra, at 375 (footnotes omitted) (emphasis in original).

After the fire, Rogers closed down its Crazyhorse operation as unprofitable. This means, in effect, that there was no longer a market for the property at the point of loss. ACI's position is that the loss of a Crazyhorse market through the closure of the Crazyhorse facility puts Rogers in the position of Professor Dobbs' hypothetical car owner whose car, which the owner intended to sell in Los Angeles, is destroyed in the desert. ACI argues that if Rogers uses the proceeds of its judgment to obtain similar property to that destroyed, the property will be obtained and used to be resold in Anchorage, making it a windfall to give Rogers any award for transportation to Crazyhorse.

If it were true that Rogers' decision to close down its Crazyhorse operation was not prompted by the fire, ACI's argument would make sense; the fire in that case would have saved the additional expense of transporting the materials back to Anchorage. But if the fire and the closure were substantially related, to deny the cost of transportation from Anchorage to Crazyhorse would impose a distinct loss on Rogers, since by the loss of the business in Crazyhorse Rogers has been deprived of a means of recouping the transportation costs already incurred.

On remand, the superior court should determine whether the fire was the proximate cause of Rogers' decision to close its Crazyhorse operation. If it was, the superior court should include in the award of the damages actual transportation costs to the extent that they have been proven.

The award of damages is Reversed, and the case Remanded.

Note

Total Destruction of Chattel—Loss of Use Damages. The traditional rule has been that "when a chattel has been totally destroyed, no additional recovery for loss of use is allowed." Pickett v. J.J. Willis Trucking Co., 624 S.W.2d 664, 668 (Tex.App.1981). There has been a noticeable trend away from this position. Long v. McAllister, 319 N.W.2d 256 (Iowa 1982); DTS Tank Service v. Vanderveen, 683 P.2d 1345 (Okl.1984); Lenz Construction Co. v. Cameron, 207 Mont. 506, 674 P.2d 1101 (1984) (damages for a reasonable time to replace). The Restatement of Torts (Second) § 927 (1965), permits recovery of prejudgment interest from the date the value is fixed plus loss of use not otherwise compensated.

2. WRONGFUL TAKING, RETENTION OR USE

a. *Specific Restitution*

Preliminary Note

If a wrongdoer takes and retains someone's personal property, the owner may obtain specific restitution in replevin at law or a suit in equity where necessary, unless barred by the doctrine of accession, the statute of limitations or laches. The doctrine of accession means that the owner has lost "ownership" for purposes of a possessory action. The running of the statute of limitations or laches means that the owner is barred from court-ordered redress, leaving a conceptual problem—who is the "owner?"

CAPITOL CHEVROLET CO. v. EARHEART and CRASS v. BENNETT v. SARTIN v. HORN v. PACK

Court of Appeals of Tennessee, 1981.

627 S.W.2d 369.

LEWIS, JUDGE. On May 1, 1975, a 1965 Chevrolet Corvette was stolen from William T. Revis of Indianapolis, Indiana. Subsequently, it was stripped and the stripped-down hull was bought by James Billy Pack from Howard's Used Cars. Pack then sold the stripped-down hull to Doug Horn, who sold it to W.A. Sartin on August 23, 1976, for the sum of $200.

Sartin used the stripped-down hull to build a functioning Corvette automobile with his own labor and materials and sold it to Randy Bennett for $4,750. Bennett then sold it to Robert Earheart for $4,775. Earheart then traded the car to Capitol Chevrolet on May 7, 1979, for a 1979 Corvette. Capitol allowed $6,052 on the trade-in and Earheart paid the balance by check.

On May 9, 1979, Capitol Chevrolet sold the rebuilt 1965 Corvette to Dave Crass.

It was stolen from Crass in Atlanta on June 12, 1979, and was recovered by the Atlanta police, who returned it to the original owner Revis on July 4, 1979. Revis had identified the car by the serial number remaining on the original hull of the car that had been stolen from him in 1975.

Crass has never paid anything to Capitol Chevrolet on the car, alleging he owed nothing because the car was stolen merchandise when sold to him. Capitol sued both Crass, its vendee, and Earheart, its vendor. Third-party suits have been entered back up the chain of title as far as Pack. Crass filed a counter-complaint against Capitol for selling him a stolen car.

The Chancellor, after a bench trial, found that all defendants were innocent purchasers acting in good faith. The Chancellor further found that Sartin acquired title by accession when he rebuilt the car, stating as follows:

> "When Sartin acquired the hull salvage, it was no longer an automobile. No part was intact. By making the improvement he acquired good title which he conveyed to Bennett and the others in the chain of title.
>
> "Any liability would be only to the true owner of the misappropriated property and limited to the value of the property innocently used which would be the scrap value of the hull.
>
> "Capitol Chevrolet conveyed good title to Crass and is entitled to a judgment against him for $7,257.00, plus $2,400.00 attorney's fee and the costs."

Capitol, in this Court, contends (1) that the Corvette did not become the property of Sartin by reason of Sartin's improvements, (2) that all purchasers in the chain of title were not innocent good faith purchasers, (3) that Earheart breached an implied warranty of title under T.C.A. § 47–2–312 when he sold the car to Capitol, and (4) that Capitol is entitled to a security interest in the successor vehicle to the one it sold Earheart.

As to the first issue, all appellees rely on Ochoa v. Rogers, 234 S.W. 693 (Tex.Civ.App.1921). In that case a car had been stolen from Ochoa and subsequently purchased from the United States Government by Rogers. At the time it was purchased by Rogers, no part of the car was intact. It had no top, except part of the frame, no steering wheel, no tires, wheels, cushions, or batteries. The motor and radiator were present but removed from the car and the car overall was "a pile of broken and dismantled * * * 'junk.'" Rogers paid $85 for it. Subsequently, Rogers used the parts to construct a delivery truck worth about $1000. Ochoa happened to see the truck, recognized the hood and radiator, and confirmed his identification by checking the serial numbers. He then brought suit for possession.

The Court held that title to the new vehicle was in Rogers, but that Ochoa was entitled to $85, the value of the scrap at the time Rogers purchased it.

> "It is * * * the general rule that, where it can be shown that the labor and materials of an innocent trespasser contributed more to the value of the present chattel than those materials which he took without intending a wrong, he is entitled to keep the chattel as his own, making, however, due compensation to the owner of the materials for what he took."

If, of course, Sartin himself had not been an innocent purchaser he would have acquired no title to the car no matter how much he improved it.

We approve the following:

"(3) Relative Values * * *

"Where the appropriation of the property was unintentional and labor or material has been expended or added which greatly enhances its value, and the value of the original article is insignificant in comparison with the value of the new product, the title to the property in its converted form will pass to the person who has thus expended or added his labor and materials, compensating the owner for the value of the original article or materials. Where the value of improvements placed upon a car by one innocent of the invalidity of his title thereto is substantially less than the car's value at the time he obtained it, the true owner may reclaim his property; but if the improvements approach or exceed the value of the car, title passes to the purchaser who is liable to the owner for the market value of the car as it was when he obtained it.

"* * * When it is remembered that what the law aims at is the accomplishment of substantial equity, it will be readily perceived that the fact that the value of the materials has been considerably increased is of more importance than any chemical change or mechanical transformation, which, however radical, is not expensive or does not materially add to the value. It is not the excess of the artificial over the natural value, but the degree of such excess that is the controlling principle.

"* * * Where the identity of the original article is susceptible of being traced, the idea of a change in property is never admitted, unless the value of that which has been expended upon it is sufficiently great, as compared with the original value, to render the injustice of permitting its appropriation by the original owner so gross and palpable as to be apparent at the first blush."

1 C.J.S. Accession § 5 (1936).

The above rule hinges on the good faith of the innocent trespasser and is unavailable to a thief or to one who obtains possession knowing the property is stolen or fails to exercise due care to ascertain that it is stolen.

We next consider Capitol's second contention: That the members of the chain of title were not innocent purchasers acting in good faith.

As stated by Capitol, this argument reduces to a contention that Sartin should have obliterated the vehicle identification number and secured a new one from the Tennessee Motor Vehicle Registration and Title Division. * * *

We fail to see how failure to alter or obliterate the vehicle identification number is in anywise indicative of bad faith on the part of Sartin. If anything, it is probative of good faith and innocence. The course of action urged by Capitol is what would be probative of bad faith.

Our review of this record sustains the Chancellor's finding that Sartin acquired title to the car by accession and that all defendants herein acted in good faith. Earheart conveyed good title to Capitol Chevrolet, which conveyed the same to Crass. Crass is the owner of the car less any claim held by the original owner Revis to an amount corresponding to the value of the unimproved stripped-down hull purchased by Sartin. * * *

The judgment of the Chancellor is affirmed with costs to appellant Capitol Chevrolet.

TODD, PRESIDING JUDGE, concurring. I respectfully differ with the statement in Ochoa v. Rogers, Tex.Civ.App.1921, 234 S.W. 693, that one who incorporates an identifiable stolen part into a reconstructed vehicle thereby acquires title to the stolen part by accession so as to defeat the claim of the true owner of the part for possession. The award of the value of the stolen part does not necessarily make him whole, for the judgment awarded may be uncollectible. Theft cannot deprive an owner of title to his property, and requiring him to substitute a money claim for his property is an unconstitutional taking of private property for a private use. * * *

The doctrine of accession has been discussed and applied in a number of cases, but is not universal in scope. It definitely should not be applied in cases of stolen property which is clearly identifiable.

It is true that the present case presents a situation in which the payment of the value of the stolen part to the owner would be far more practical than to dismantle the vehicle to restore the stolen part to the owner. However, the principle of rights in property is more important than avoiding the practical difficulty of applying the principle in a given case. * * *

The owner of the stolen part is not a party to this case, hence his rights may not be determined herein.

Notes

1. Each of the following extracts is quoted in Succession of Onorato, 219 La. 1, 51 So.2d 804 (1951): 10 Scott, The Digest of Justinian at 268: "Where anyone steals a silver ingot belonging to me, and makes cups out of it, I can either bring suit for the theft of the ingot, or a personal one for the recovery of the property."

Pirtle v. Price, 31 La.Ann. 357 (1879): "In New York a majority of the judges of the Court of Appeals held 'that it is an elementary principle in the law of all civilized communities, that no man can be deprived of his property, except by his own voluntary act, or by operation of law; that a wilful wrongdoer acquires no property in the goods of another, either by the wrongful taking or by any change wrought in them by his labor or skill, however great that change may be.'

"The same principle is to be found in the Digest of Justinian. 'If anyone shall make wine with my grapes, oil with my olives, or garments with my wool, knowing that they are not his own, he shall be compelled by action to produce the said wine, oil or garments.'

"In his Commentaries, the late Chancellor Kent declared that the English law will not allow a man to give a title to the property of another upon the principle of accession, if he took the other's property wilfully as a trespasser; and that it was settled as early as the time of the Year Book, that *whatever alterations* of form any property had undergone, the owner might seize it in its new shape, if he could prove the identity of the original materials.

"Relying on those authorities, the New York court decided, with but two dissenting opinions, that where a quantity of corn was taken from the owner by a wilful trespasser and converted by him into whiskey, the whiskey belonged to the owner of the corn."

2. The element of "wilfulness" may be overemphasized, since the owner of a chattel may retake it from an innocent converter without offset for the value of mistaken improvements. The same is true where a replevin action for repossession is undertaken. See the discussion in Grays Harbor County v. Bay City Lumber Co., infra p. 381. Ameliorating statutes similar to "Occupying Claimants Acts" available to good faith improvers of land would change the common law rule. Some protection of the innocent improver of chattels is possible in jurisdictions which allow the specific recovery in a replevin action to be defeated by the posting of a

bond, thereby changing the action to one essentially in trover with the same measure of damage recovery. See Restatement of Restitution § 42 comment d (1937). And if specific restitution by an equitable decree is sought, presumably the maxim of "he who seeks equity, etc." permits a discretionary allowance for good faith improvements as a condition for entry of the decree.

3. Storms v. Reid, 691 S.W.2d 73, 75 (Tex.App.1985). The court refused to allow the plaintiff to recover an improved chattel, a house, innocently converted by defendant. Specific recovery would have resulted in a large gain to plaintiff since defendant had substantially improved the house. In conversion cases, a trial court has discretion "to fashion an equitable remedy"!

4. *Election to Take Damages Instead of Return of Property—Statutes.* Several states permit the plaintiff in a possessory action to elect to recover the value of the withheld property *at the time of trial* instead of specific restitution. E.g. Hallmark v. Stillings, 620 S.W.2d 436 (Mo.App.1981). Elaborate statutory provisions are set forth in Flickinger v. Mark IV Apartments Association, infra at p. 370. Note that the statute allows the plaintiff to elect the most advantageous damage elements of both replevin and conversion and that it builds in possible recovery for inflation.

5. *The Statute of Limitations and Adverse Possession.* Stolen art works and other collectibles that have passed into the hands of honest collectors have led to litigation in which the statute of limitations or laches has been a critical factor.

a. [Georgia] O'Keeffe v. Snyder, 83 N.J. 478, 416 A.2d 862 (1980). The victimized artist encountered difficulties with the limitations period and the court's intrusion of "equitable considerations" into its operation.

b. DeWeerth v. Baldinger, 658 F.Supp. 688 (S.D.N.Y.1987), cert. denied, 486 U.S. 1056 (1988). The West German owner of a Monet painting succeeded in recovering it from an innocent purchaser. The court ruled that the three-year New York statute of limitations did not commence running until a demand is made for the return of the property and the demand is refused.

c. Autocephalous Greek–Orthodox Church v. Goldberg & Feldman Fine Arts, 917 F.2d 278 (7th Cir.1990). In awarding recovery of stolen mosaics to the plaintiff, the court held that the statute of limitations did not begin to run until the chattels were discovered to be in defendant's possession.

d. State v. West, 293 N.C. 18, 235 S.E.2d 150 (1977). The court held that the state of North Carolina owned two Colonial Court bills of indictment in the hands of collectors despite the passage of 200 years. The statute of limitations, the court said, does not run against the state.

The conceptual problem is stated in R. Brown, Personal Property § 4.1 (3d ed. 1975): "While in form these statutes [of limitations] merely limit the right of the owner to bring legal proceedings to repossess his property, * * * all but universally in the United States the expiration of the statutory period has the effect not only of barring the legal remedy, but also extinguishing the owner's title and of transferring it to the adverse possessor." Quoted in Gee v. CBS, Inc., 471 F.Supp. 600, 653 (E.D.Pa.1979).

FUENTES v. SHEVIN

Supreme Court of the United States, 1972.
407 U.S. 67.

[Plaintiff sued for declaratory and injunctive relief to prevent the continued enforcement of the Florida prejudgment replevin procedures on the ground that the state statutes violated the due process clause of the fourteenth amendment.]

JUSTICE STEWART delivered the opinion of the Court. * * * Under the Florida statute challenged here, "[a]ny person whose goods or chattels are wrongfully detained by any other person * * * may have a writ of replevin to recover them * * *." Fla.Stats. § 78.01, F.S.A. There is no requirement that the applicant make a convincing showing before the seizure that the goods are, in fact, "wrongfully detained." Rather, Florida law automatically relies on the bare assertion of the party seeking the writ that he is entitled to one and allows a court clerk to issue the writ summarily. It requires only that the applicant file a complaint, initiating a court action for repossession and reciting in conclusory fashion that he is "lawfully entitled to the possession" of the property, and that he file a security bond.

> "In at least double the value of the property to be replevied conditioned that plaintiff will prosecute his action to effect and without delay and that if defendant recovers judgment against him in the action, he will return the property, if return thereof is adjudged, and will pay defendant all sums of money recovered against plaintiff by defendant in the action." Fla.Stats. § 78.07, F.S.A.

On the sole basis of the complaint and bond, a writ is issued "command[ing] the officer to whom it may be directed to replevy the goods and chattels in possession of defendant * * * and to summon the defendant to answer the complaint." Fla.Stats. § 78.08. If the goods are "in any dwelling house or other building or enclosure," the officer is required to demand their delivery; but if they are not delivered, "he shall cause such house, building or enclosure to be broken open and shall make replevin according to the writ * * *." Fla.Stats. § 78.10, F.S.A.

Thus, at the same moment that the defendant receives the complaint seeking repossession of property through court action, the property is seized from him. He is provided no prior notice and allowed no opportunity whatever to challenge the issuance of the writ. *After* the property has been seized, he will eventually have an opportunity for a hearing, as the defendant in the trial of the court action for repossession, which the plaintiff is required to pursue. And he is also not wholly without recourse in the meantime. For under the Florida statute, the officer who seizes the property must keep it for three days, and during that period the defendant may reclaim possession of the property by posting his own security bond in double its value. But if he does not post such a bond, the property is transferred to the party who sought the writ, pending a final judgment in the underlying action for repossession. Fla.Stats. § 78.13, F.S.A. * * *

Although these prejudgment replevin statutes are descended from the common law replevin action of six centuries ago, they bear very little resemblance to it. Replevin at common law was an action for the return of specific goods wrongfully taken or "distrained." Typically, it was used after a landlord (the "distrainor") had seized possessions from a tenant (the "distrainee") to satisfy a debt allegedly owed. If the tenant then instituted a replevin action and posted security the landlord could be ordered to return the property at once, pending a final judgment in the underlying action. However, this prejudgment replevin of goods at common law did *not* follow from an entirely *ex parte* process of pleading by the distrainee. For "[t]he distrainor could always stop the action of replevin by claiming to be the owner of the goods; and as this claim was often made merely to delay the proceedings, the writ *de proprietate probanda* was devised early in the fourteenth century which enabled the sheriff to determine summarily the question of ownership. If the question of ownership was determined against the distrainor the goods were delivered back to the distrainee [pending final judgment]." 3 Holdsworth, History of English Law 284 (1927).

Prejudgment replevin statutes like those of Florida * * * are derived from this ancient possessory action in that they authorize the seizure of property before a final judgment. But the similarity ends there. As in the present cases, such statutes are most commonly used by creditors to seize goods allegedly wrongfully detained—not wrongfully taken—by debtors. At common law, if a creditor wished to invoke state power to recover goods wrongfully detained, he had to proceed through the action of debt or detinue. These actions, however, did not provide for a return of property before final judgment.[1] And, more importantly, on the occasions when the common law did allow prejudgment seizure by state power, it provided some kind of notice and opportunity to be heard to the party then in possession of the property, and a state official made at least a summary determination of the relative rights of the disputing parties before stepping into the dispute and taking goods from one of them.

For more than a century the central meaning of procedural due process has been clear: "Parties whose rights are to be affected are entitled to be heard; and in order that they may enjoy that right they must be notified." Baldwin v. Hale, 68 U.S. 223. * * * It is equally fundamental that the right to notice and an opportunity to be heard "must be granted at a meaningful time and in a meaningful manner." Armstrong v. Manzo, 380 U.S. 545, 552.

The primary question in the present cases is whether these state statutes are constitutionally defective in failing to provide for hearings "at a meaningful time." * * *

We hold that the Florida * * * prejudgment replevin provisions work a deprivation of property without due process of law insofar as they deny the right to a prior opportunity to be heard before chattels are taken from their possessor. Our holding, however, is a narrow one. We do not question the power of a State to seize goods before a final judgment in order to protect the security interests of creditors so long as those creditors have tested their claim to the goods through the process of a fair prior hearing. The nature and form of such prior hearings, moreover, are legitimately open to many potential variations and are a subject, at this point, for legislation—not adjudication. Since the essential reason for the requirement of a prior hearing is to prevent unfair and mistaken deprivations of property, however, it is axiomatic that the hearing must provide a real test. "[D]ue process is afforded only by the kinds of 'notice' and 'hearing' which are aimed at establishing the validity, or at least the probable validity, of the underlying claim against the alleged debtor *before* he can be deprived of his property * * *." Sniadach v. Family Finance Corp., 395 U.S. at 343 (Harlan, J., concurring).

JUSTICE WHITE, dissenting. * * * Third: The Court's rhetoric is seductive, but in end analysis, the result it reaches will have little impact and represents no more than ideological tinkering with state law. It would appear that creditors could withstand attack under today's opinion simply by making clear in the controlling credit instruments that they may retake possession without a

1. [Footnotes renumbered.] The creditor could, of course, proceed without the use of state power, through self-help, by "distraining" the property before a judgment.

hearing, or, for that matter, without resort to judicial process at all. Alternatively, they need only give a few days' notice of a hearing, take possession if hearing is waived or if there is default; and if hearing is necessary merely establish probable cause for asserting that default has occurred. It is very doubtful in my mind that such a hearing would in fact result in protections for the debtor substantially different from those the present law provides. On the contrary, the availability of credit may well be diminished or, in any event, the expense of securing it increased.

None of this seems worth the candle to me. The procedure which the Court strikes down is not some barbaric hangover from bygone days. The respective rights of the parties in secured transactions have undergone the most intensive analysis in recent years. The Uniform Commercial Code, which now so pervasively governs the subject matter with which it deals, provides in Art. 9, § 9–503, that:

> "Unless otherwise agreed a secured party has on default the right to take possession of the collateral. In taking possession a secured party may proceed without judicial process if this can be done without breach of peace or may proceed by action * * *."

I am content to rest on the judgment of those who have wrestled with these problems so long and often and upon the judgment of the legislatures that have considered and so recently adopted provisions that contemplate precisely what has happened in these cases.

Notes

1. See in accord, Blair v. Pitchess, 5 Cal.3d 258, 96 Cal.Rptr. 42, 486 P.2d 1242 (1971) (California claim and delivery statute); Laprease v. Raymours Furniture Co., 315 F.Supp. 716 (N.D.N.Y.1970) (New York statute); Hamrick v. Ashland Finance Co., 423 F.Supp. 1033 (S.D.W.Va.1976) (West Virginia detinue statute). The California Code was revised to comply with the requirements of notice and hearing prescribed by *Pitchess.* See Cal.Civ.Proc.Code § 512.020b. Excepted from these requirements are actions of claim and delivery to recover stolen property, credit cards, and property about to be destroyed or removed from the state. But ex parte writs of possession are still disfavored except in the most exigent circumstances. Sea Rail Truckloads, Inc. v. Pullman, Inc., 131 Cal.App.3d 511, 182 Cal.Rptr. 560 (1982).

2. Later refinements of the procedural issues raised by *Fuentes* may be found in Connecticut v. Doehr, 111 S.Ct. 2105 (1991); Mitchell v. W.T. Grant Co., 416 U.S. 600 (1974); North Georgia Finishing Inc. v. Di-Chem Inc., 419 U.S. 601 (1975); First National Bank v. Southwest Yacht & Marine Supply Corp., 101 N.M. 431, 684 P.2d 517 (1984). See Rendleman, Analyzing the Debtor's Due Process Interest, 17 Wm. & Mary L.Rev. 35 (1975).

FLICKINGER v. MARK IV APARTMENTS, ASSOCIATION

Supreme Court of Iowa, 1982.
315 N.W.2d 794.

SCHULTZ, JUSTICE. On September 4, 1976, Flickinger was delinquent on her rental obligation to Mark IV [apartment association]. She returned to her apartment at approximately 9:00 p.m. but was unable to gain entrance because Mark IV had installed a new lock. Mark IV had previously utilized such a "lock-out" as a means of collecting rent from Flickinger. On this occasion, however, Flickinger did not contact Mark IV with respect to either access to the apartment or payment of the overdue rent. She left Iowa City and within a few days was arrested in Hardin County, where she was incarcerated until November 10, 1976.

Flickinger's parents, Pennsylvania residents, came to Iowa and took custody of her children. Before returning to Pennsylvania, the parents apprised Mark IV of Flickinger's situation and were allowed to remove the children's clothing and toys from the apartment. Mark IV then moved the contents of Flickinger's apartment to a locked storage facility. When she was released from jail, Flickinger made no attempt to contact Mark IV to recover her property.

In January 1977, at which time Flickinger resided in Eldora, Iowa, Mark IV obtained a default judgment against her in the Johnson District Small Claims Court in the amount of $500 for the delinquent rent. Subsequently, Flickinger moved to Pennsylvania to be with her children and parents. Telephonic and written communications followed.

During a telephone conversation in August 1977, Mark IV advised Flickinger that her property had been stored and that she could settle the default judgment for $200. On January 20, 1978, Flickinger's attorney, a staff member of Hawkeye Legal Services Society, informed her that Mark IV wanted her property removed by February 15. On February 16 Mark IV gave Flickinger written notice to remove her possessions by March 13 or to give it written permission to dispose of the property. Flickinger responded by requesting that the property be allowed to remain in storage until May, and Mark IV assented. Flickinger then sent Mark IV three checks for $20 each, to be applied toward the settlement for the delinquent rent. Flickinger did not remove her furniture in May, however, and in September Mark IV notified Flickinger that if she did not remove her property it would be given to Goodwill Industries.

The evidence concerning the disposition of Flickinger's property is conflicting. Flickinger testified that she returned to Iowa City in the fall of 1978 and removed items of her property from the storage facility on three occasions. * * * Flickinger testified that she received some, but not all, of her property. She stated that during her last telephone conversation with Mark IV she was informed that her remaining property was in the process of being disposed of and would not be there when she came to claim it. * * *

Flickinger introduced into evidence a schedule of the items of personal property she allegedly did not recover from Mark IV. The trial court found as a matter of fact that all of the items on the schedule, with the exception of baby clothes, had been wrongfully detained by Mark IV. The court ordered Mark IV to return the property to Flickinger or, if it were unable to do so, to pay her damages of $2471, the value assigned to the property by the court. * * * [Both parties appeal] Flickinger assigns error to the trial court's failure to award her damages for loss of use of the property during the period of detention.

General Principles. Replevin is an action to recover specific personal property that has been wrongfully taken or wrongfully detained, with an incidental right to damages caused by reason of such detention. In Iowa the action is statutory, ch. 643, The Code; it combines the features of the common-law actions of replevin and detinue. The pleading requirements are contained in section 643.1, The Code. The petition must state, *inter alia:* facts showing the plaintiff's right to possession of the property; that the property was neither

taken pursuant to court order or judgment nor attachment or execution, or, if so, that it was exempt from seizure by such process; and the alleged cause of the detention of the property. § 643.1(3)–(5), The Code.

The gist of a replevin action is enforcement of the plaintiff's right to immediate possession of the property wrongfully taken or detained. [citations] A wrongful taking need not be by forcible dispossession; any unlawful interference with, or assertion of control over, the property is sufficient. A wrongful detention occurs when the defendant wrongfully withholds or retains possession of the property sought to be recovered.

Replevin is an action at law. § 643.2, The Code. * * *

Wrongful detention. * * * Mark IV contends that the court seems to have found a wrongful taking rather than a wrongful detention. It concedes that the "lock-out" constituted a wrongful taking, since it thereby obtained control over Flickinger's property. However, it claims that, unless followed by a wrongful detention, a wrongful taking will not sustain an action in replevin.

Mark IV's assertion that the fact that Flickinger was at all times free to recover her property changed the nature of its possession from wrongful to rightful is without merit. Once there has been a wrongful taking or detention, possession does not become rightful until some form of redelivery occurs. Wrongful possession of property does not become rightful merely by agreeing to allow recovery by the party entitled to possession.

When the plaintiff in a replevin action satisfies the burden of proving a wrongful taking of property, the burden shifts to the defendant to show that he or she no longer has possession; if the defendant fails to do so, it is presumed that possession continues. * * *

Damages for loss of use. In Universal C.I.T. Credit Corp. v. Jones, 227 N.W.2d 473, 478 (Iowa 1975), this court summarized the law of damages in a replevin action as follows:

"(1) The injured party may demand the return of his property plus damages for its wrongful detention.

(2) He may seek judgment for the money value of the property, treating the conversion as complete either at the time it was taken or at the time of trial.

(3) If the former, he may have interest on the value as determined by the trier of fact from the date of the seizure until the date of judgment and nothing more. The judgment itself, of course, bears interest thereafter.

(4) If he elects under (2) above to rely on a conversion as of the time of trial, he may have the money value of the property as of that date, plus damages for loss of use from the time it was seized until the time of trial."

Flickinger maintains that since she elected to treat the conversion as occurring at the time of trial she is entitled to loss-of-use damages from the time of the lock-out until the time of trial.

The trial court concluded that Flickinger was not entitled to damages for loss of use. The court found that she was in no position to use the property during the two-month period following the lock-out and that Mark IV did not prevent her from recovering the use of her property. Relying on *Universal* and Barry v. State Surety Co., 261 Iowa 222, 154 N.W.2d 97 (1967), however,

Flickinger contends that she was not required to show that she would have used the property as a prerequisite to recovering damages for loss of use.

In *Barry* an implement company had obtained immediate possession of a tractor in a replevin action by filing a replevin bond. Judgment was later entered determining the replevin was wrongful and ordering the tractor to be returned to the plaintiffs. The plaintiffs then brought an action against the surety on the bond for wrongful seizure and detention of the tractor. The defendant surety company contended that the plaintiffs were not entitled to damages for loss of use because the evidence did not disclose any actual loss. This court stated:

> "The fact, if it be a fact, that plaintiffs here did not hire equipment to replace theirs and that they would not have used this equipment anyway, even if it had been in their possession, does not appeal to us. It was their equipment. They were entitled to its possession and to its use, and defendant's interference with that possession entitles plaintiffs to damages."

The rule authorizing recovery for loss of use when the property could not or would not have been used, is not applicable when use of the property is not prevented by the party that wrongfully seized the property, however. [citations] In *Barry* the plaintiffs' use was prevented by the implement company's replevy of the tractor pursuant to legal process; the plaintiffs could not have recovered the tractor during the pendency of the replevin action. In the present case the trial court found that Mark IV did not prevent Flickinger from recovering the use of her property. * * * We therefore hold that the court correctly denied Flickinger damages for loss of use. * * *

Affirmed.

Notes

1. France v. Nelson, 292 Ark. 219, 222–25, 729 S.W.2d 161, 164–65 (1987). Justice Newbern concurring:

"My primary objection to the majority opinion is that it leaves the impression that this court fails to understand that conversion damages and incidental damages accompanying replevin are wholly inconsistent remedies. The distinguishing feature of an action for *conversion* is an interference with property so serious as to justify a forced judicial sale to the wrongdoer. See W. Prosser and W. Keeton, Law of Torts, § 15 (5th ed. 1984). The property owner is compensated by an award for value of the property at the time and place of the conversion.

"On the other hand, the primary object of a replevin action is the actual *recovery of possession* of the property. The owner cannot be required to accept the value of the item in lieu of return of possession. [citation] By statute, the property owner may, in addition to return of the item, recover damages for loss of use while it was out of his possession. Ark.Stat.Ann. § 34–2116 (Repl.1962).

"It is generally recognized that the *value of the use* of the property converted is not recoverable in a conversion action. Ford Motor Credit Co. v. Herring, 267 Ark. 201, 589 S.W.2d 584 (1979) (measure of damages for conversion is the market value at the time and place of conversion, not the purchase, rental, or replacement cost); Hardin v. Marshall, 176 Ark. 977, 5 S.W.2d 325 (1928) (instruction allowing jury to assess as damages rental value of property converted in addition to value of property was error in a conversion cause of action)."

2. Where a favorable judgment is entered for plaintiff in a replevin action, defendant does not have the option of satisfying that judgment by paying value.

Plaintiff may insist on return of the chattel and is entitled to recover damages for the detention. S.T. Enterprises v. Brunswick Corp., 57 Ill.2d 461, 315 N.E.2d 1 (1974); Brook v. Cullimore & Co., 436 P.2d 32 (Okl.1967). If defendant retained the chattel during the litigation under a redelivery bond, plaintiff may recover damages in a subsequent action against the surety. Commercial Credit Corp. v. McAdams, 241 S.C. 532, 129 S.E.2d 429 (1963). Where the plaintiff regains possession of the chattel at the commencement of the action by prejudgment replevin, on the other hand, he must recover detention damages in the main action. A subsequent action for damages is barred by the judgment. McCallister v. M-A-C Finance Co., 332 F.2d 633 (10th Cir.1964); McFaddin v. H.S. Crocker Co., 219 Cal.App.2d 585, 33 Cal.Rptr. 389 (1963).

Where plaintiff succeeds in obtaining possession of the chattel by prejudgment replevin but fails in the main action, judgment for the defendant requires plaintiff to return the chattel or its value at defendant's option. Godfrey v. Gilsdorf, 86 Nev. 714, 476 P.2d 3 (1970). In addition plaintiff is liable for lost use and any depreciation in value during the period of his possession. Crosswhite v. American Insurance Co., 61 Cal.2d 300, 38 Cal.Rptr. 412, 392 P.2d 5 (1964); Larson v. Mobile Home Finance Co., 83 Ill.App.2d 210, 226 N.E.2d 882 (1967).

3. When chattels are held for sale rather than use, detention damages are measured by the depreciation in the value of the chattels from the time of wrongful possession until the time of return. Gicinto v. Credithrift of America, 219 Kan. 766, 549 P.2d 870 (1976).

FRAN-WELL HEATER CO. v. ROBINSON

Court of Appeal of California, Second District, 1960.
182 Cal.App.2d 125, 5 Cal.Rptr. 900.

FOX, PRESIDING JUSTICE. Plaintiff brought this action to recover possession of certain personal property, or the value thereof, together with damages for its wrongful detention. Defendant Robinson has appealed from an adverse judgment. * * *

The court rendered judgment in plaintiff's favor and against Robinson for the possession of said equipment and upon the failure to deliver same within 10 days, then for its value in the sum of $1,679.26, and damages for detention from October 1, 1955, to date of trial, April 24, 1958, at the rate of $200 per month, a total of $5,160. * * *

Robinson further contends that no valid judgment "in claim and delivery" could be rendered against him since the pleadings and evidence clearly establish that he was not in possession of the heaters at the time the suit was filed. This contention states what is undoubtedly the general rule. However, there is an exception to this general rule. This exception is stated and explained in Faulkner v. First National Bank, 130 Cal. 258, 62 P. 463. * * *

The court pointed out that the cause of action was based on a "contract of bailment"; that the original possession was lawful but the detention was wrongful. The court then stated: "Now, that is just the kind of wrong for which at common law the action of detinue was especially appropriate, and the averments in the complaint in the case at bar are substantially those required in such action. [citations] While we have no forms of action here, yet when the averments of facts in a complaint show the case to be one for which a particular form of action would have been a proper one at common law, then the general principles of pleading and practice apply to it which apply to the special form of common law action. Now, it was no defense to the action of detinue to plead that the defendant, before the commencement of the action, had wrongfully disposed of the property, and therefore was not in possession of it." * * *

In New Liverpool Salt Co. v. Western etc. Co., 151 Cal. 479, 91 P. 152, these principles were again reiterated and applied. It appeared there that defendant was in possession of a quantity of salt as bailee; that prior to the commencement of the action plaintiff had become entitled to possession upon demand which was made by plaintiff and delivery of possession was refused by defendant. Suit was then brought to recover possession of the property or, in the alternative, its value. Defendant in the meantime had parted with possession of the salt. The court, however, held: "The fact that the defendant had, before the demand, or before the action was begun, parted with the possession of the salt, was no defense." The court further stated, "If a bailee wrongfully deliver the goods to another, he will continue liable in detinue for the goods or their value, that it does not lie in his mouth to set up his wrongful act in answer to such action, or to say that he is unable to comply with the demand for possession because of his own breach of duty, and that the burden is on him to show any excuse, such as that his possession ceased before suit brought, by accident, or some means beyond his control and without his fault."

Applying these principles to the factual situation at bar it is clear there is no merit in Robinson's contention. He came into possession of the heaters through his lease-rental agreement with plaintiff. As a result of that agreement he was under certain contractual duties (the nature of which need not here be discussed) to plaintiff. When Robinson sold the oil lease and delivered possession of the wells to Spur Oil Company the heaters were in the bottom of the oil wells and were turned over to Spur as an integral part of the wells. By the terms of the stipulation, plaintiff was still the owner of the heaters and entitled to their possession at the time of trial. * * *

Robinson urges that the trial court applied an erroneous theory in fixing the measure of damages for wrongful detention, and also that the damages awarded are excessive as a matter of law. Robinson is correct in these contentions.

The trial court fixed the damages for wrongful detention at $200 per month for the period from October, 1955, to date of trial (April 24, 1958). This allowance was commensurate with the usual rental charge made by Fran-Well and also represented the monthly rentals paid by Robinson prior to October, 1955. However, assessment of damages for wrongful detention at a flat rate based solely upon the gross rental value of a chattel is erroneous as a matter of law. As stated in Mutch v. Long Beach Improvement Co., 47 Cal.App. 267: "* * * one thus deprived of the use of an automobile cannot recover the gross rental value of a fully equipped and maintained car, free from all expense of maintenance, repairs, and natural wear and tear, such as a rented car would naturally be subject to." * * * The correct measure of damages under these circumstances is stated in Guerin v. Kirst, 33 Cal.2d 402, 414, 202 P.2d 10, 17: "in computing such damages it is only the 'net usable value less the expense of keeping up the property' which can be recovered by the aggrieved party." [citations] The "net usable value" is determined by "appropriate allowance * * * for the decline in rental value * * * over the years—perhaps to the vanishing point—consistent with the normal deterioration of a piece of machin-

ery [as] the measure of its condition for the continued performance of effective work."

No pleading or proof of these considerations was made or offered by Fran–Well. The only evidence in the record is Sanchez' testimony that $200 was reasonable monthly rental and that Fran–Well maintains and services the equipment it leases, this latter factor being an element in the total rental charge. No attempt was made to fix the "net usable value" of the heaters. It therefore appears that there was no proper evidence to support the judgment for damages for wrongful detention. * * *

Furthermore, the award of damages for wrongful detention is excessive as a matter of law. The total value of the property was stipulated to be $1,679.26, yet the judgment awards Fran–Well $2,400 for each year of detention, so that the total allowance for damages is more than three times the value of the equipment. The case of Guerin v. Kirst, supra, is apposite. There the damage claim (value of chattel was $6,600 and claim was for $9,900 per year) was in nearly the same proportion as in this case. The rental value of the chattel was stipulated to by the defendant. Nevertheless, the Supreme Court held: "Obviously such damage claim is grossly excessive and disproportionate when correlated with the value of the tractor * * *. The mere recital of plaintiffs' exorbitant demand demonstrates their position to be one wholly irreconcilable with the question of 'reasonableness' as an essential condition which enters into 'all cases' of damage recovery—and the impropriety of such excessive relief need not be further discussed." * * *

The judgment is reversed.

Notes

1. See Rozen v. Redco Corp., 362 P.2d 1095, 1096–97 (Okl.1961): "If the defendant came into possession of usable pipe and equipment, and the jury found that such was the case, then defendant's possession of the usable property was in its inception wrongful and remained wrongful. Accordingly, the fact that defendant was not in possession of the usable property sought to be replevined at the time this action was filed is not fatal and does not bar plaintiff's action as a matter of law, but such case comes within the exception to the general rule relied on by the defendant.

"The rule as stated in 46 Am.Jur., Replevin, Sec. 35 is as follows: 'In a number of jurisdictions, however, the rule has been established that an action of replevin is not defeated by the fact that the defendant has parted with the possession of the property sought to be recovered, where such transfer was made in bad faith, with the intention of resisting or defeating its recovery. In defense of the rule it has been pointed out that permitting the defendant to set up as a defense to the action the fact that he has parted with the possession of the property, when this was done wrongfully, would be allowing him to take advantage of his own wrong. It would enable one who had wrongfully taken or detained property from the owner to refuse to deliver, and hold to the last moment before the writ, and then evade a suit by a transfer of possession. His successor might do the same; and his after him; and so on, until the cost of successive writs would exceed the value of the property.' "

First National Bank v. Rickel, Inc., 229 Neb. 478, 478, 427 N.W.2d 777, 777 (1988): "Replevin will not lie against one who is not detaining the property when the writ is sued out."

2. Will of Rothko, 56 A.D.2d 499, 504, 392 N.Y.S.2d 870, 874 (1977). The children of a deceased painter sought restitution of 798 paintings from the executors. In computing the award for paintings that could not be returned, the court ruled: "However, where the property involved is unique and irreplacable, such as the works of art in the case at bar, then failure to return the property must result in the wrongdoer's responding in damages to the extent of the value of the item at the time of trial."

3. For recovery of possession of chattels under U.C.C. § 9—503, see Honeywell Information Systems, Inc. v. Demographic Systems, Inc., 396 F.Supp. 273 (S.D.N.Y. 1975); Schmitt and Peck, Self Help Repossession—The Recurring Problems of Section 9—503 of the U.C.C., 80 Com.L.J. 223 (1975).

4. *Loss of Use Damages in Replevin Actions Against Bailees.* Later California replevin decisions have consciously taken a different attitude toward "excessive" loss of use claims than *Fran–Well Heater.* Harris v. Dixon Cadillac Co., 132 Cal.App.3d 485, 183 Cal.Rptr. 299 (1982), involved a car wrongfully detained because of nonpayment for unauthorized repairs. The owner received the return of a car valued at $2,500, plus $7,500 general damages for loss of use and $45,000 punitive damages. Note, however, that the court in *Fran–Well Heater* permits the possessory action although the property can *never* be recovered. The loss of use damages could be projected to infinity unless the "net useable value" with appropriate allowance for depreciation formula is employed. Morfeld v. Bernstrauch, 216 Neb. 234, 343 N.W.2d 880 (1984). Loss of use damages of $9570 (calculated at $10 per day) were awarded to the owner of a personal automobile wrongfully towed to defendant's storage yard.

5. *Query:* Should the avoidable consequences rule apply to loss of use damages in replevin? See Culligan Rock River Water Conditioning Co. v. Gearhart, 111 Ill.App.3d 254, 443 N.E.2d 1065 (1982).

6. Curiously all the old standard texts on Replevin, Cobbey, 1900, Shinn, 1899, and Wells, 1907, say that a replevin plaintiff must show he could use the property and would have used it had it not been detained. These authorities were cited to deny loss of use damages for wrongfully detained construction equipment. Korb v. Schroedel, 93 Wis.2d 207, 286 N.W.2d 589 (1980); International Harvester Credit Corp. v. Helland, 151 Ill.App.3d 848, 503 N.E.2d 548 (1986).

7. *Query:* Should a court take a different attitude toward loss of use damages when an owner's truck is wrongfully detained than when it is damaged and being repaired?

8. Loss of profits instead of loss of use damages were allowed in a replevin action against a mechanic who wrongfully withheld a flying service's airplane. Rocky Mountain Turbines, Inc. v. 660 Syndicate, 623 P.2d 758 (Wyo.1981).

CHARLES SIMKIN & SONS v. MASSIAH

United States Court of Appeals, Third Circuit, 1961.
289 F.2d 26.

McLaughlin, Circuit Judge. * * * In April 1959, plaintiff entered into a contract with the City of Trenton, New Jersey for the construction of a Sewage Treatment Plant at Duck Island, Trenton. * * *

Plaintiff, by written agreement, subcontracted the concrete work to the defendant. During the course of performance of the subcontract, various disputes arose between the parties, and on June 10, 1960, the plaintiff gave notice of termination for the alleged default of the defendant. * * * On July

13, 1960, the plaintiff took possession of defendant's tools and equipment and assumed performance of the concrete work.

Ten days later, plaintiff instituted an action in the Superior Court of New Jersey. * * * Upon the requisite showing, the defendant removed the case to the Federal District Court. Defendant filed an answer and counterclaimed for sums allegedly due under the contract, breach of contract, conversion of the tools and equipment and injunctive relief against the plaintiff's continued use and possession of them. * * *

The district court denied defendant's petition for an injunction against plaintiff's continued possession and use of defendant's equipment and tools. We agree with the district court's conclusion.

The relief sought by the defendant is in the nature of equitable replevin. The basis for invoking this type of relief is well-settled.

> "A court of equity may compel the delivery of a specific chattel wrongfully withheld, notwithstanding replevin or trover may lie therefor, but only in cases where damages would be an inadequate redress for the injury, for instance, as in the case of heirlooms, and other articles incapable of being replaced, which are prized for their associations rather than for intrinsic value. Burr v. Bloomsburg, 101 N.J.Eq. 615 [138 A. 876]."

To support the assertion that the tools and equipment are a proper subject for equitable relief, the defendant has cited several cases. In no way do they support his position. In all of them the chattels involved were "unique" and could not be replaced by purchase on the open market. E.g., Coven v. First Savings and Loan Ass'n, Ch.1947, 141 N.J.Eq. 1, 55 A.2d 244 (an attorney's title plant); Redmond v. New Jersey Historical Society, E. & A. 1942, 132 N.J.Eq. 464, 28 A.2d 189 (Stuart's portrait of Captain Lawrence); Burr v. Bloomsburg, Ch.1927, 101 N.J.Eq. 615, 138 A. 876 (a family heirloom).

In this appeal, the tools and equipment are not "unique" but are standard-made and readily available on the open market. Items such as electric fans, electric drills, shovels, boots, wheelbarrows, rakes, scrapers, wire cutters, etc., are not within the category of personalty which affords a proper basis to invoke the remedy of equitable replevin.[1] * * *

Therefore on the defendant's appeal, the judgment of the district court will be affirmed.

Notes

1. See Kunstsammlungen Zu Weimar v. Elicofon, 536 F.Supp. 829, 859 (E.D.N.Y.1981): "Because the Duerers are unique chattels the court may exercise its equitable jurisdiction to enter a judgment directing Elicofon to deliver the paintings to the Kunstsammlungen. N.Y.—McKinney's C.P.L.R. § 7109. * * * The con-

1. [Footnote renumbered.] In his brief the defendant argues: "But * * * [defendant's] remedy may not be measured by the loss of wheelbarrows and concrete mixers. It is the sum total of what was taken, embracing as it did the defendant's entire working tools and equipment, that lends significance and invokes the remedy."

This misconceives the theory that invokes equitable remedies in the case of chattels. *It is not a quantitative evaluation.* The reason for the granting of equitable relief is the inadequacy of the remedy at law. "Such a case is established, where a chattel * * * is unique, or not purchasable in the market." Williston on Contracts § 1419, p. 3954 (Rev. ed. 1937). "The equitable jurisdiction in these cases really rests upon the fact that the only relief which the plaintiff can have is possession of the *identical* thing, and this remedy cannot *with certainty* be obtained by any common-law action." Pomeroy, Equity Jurisprudence § 185, pp. 265–66 (5th ed. 1941).

tempt remedy is provided in N.Y.—McKinney's C.P.L.R. § 7109(b) to compel delivery after judgment. Thus an alternative provision for recovery of the value of the chattel need not be included in the judgment where the chattel is unique."

2. Equitable jurisdiction to issue a mandatory injunction ordering the return of nonunique chattels may rest on the sheer impracticability of the legal remedy. For example, in Board of Commissioners v. Faircloth, 237 Ga. 136, 227 S.E.2d 35 (1976), the defendant was the sheriff wrongfully withholding one of the county's cars.

3. Equitable jurisdiction may also be exercised to preserve the status quo by prohibiting the removal of chattels. This is a common feature of replevin statutes amended to meet *Fuentes*'s due process requirements. See Cal.Civ.Code § 513–010.

b. *Monetary Recovery: Damages or Restitution*

(1) Damages

BARAM v. FARUGIA

United States Court of Appeals, Third Circuit, 1979.
606 F.2d 42.

ALDISERT, CIRCUIT JUDGE. In this age of space travel and computer technology, a horse named Foxey Toni requires us to return to a more tranquil era and examine elements of trover and conversion under Pennsylvania common law. * * *

Dr. Joseph Baram, appellee, acquired legal title to Foxey Toni, a bay filly race horse, for $3,000 in a claiming race at the Keystone Race Track, Bucks County, Pennsylvania. Dennis Fredella became the trainer for Foxey Toni and was given authority to enter her in races in Dr. Baram's name. Foxey Toni raced under Dr. Baram's name on October 11, October 17, and November 8, 1975. Thereafter, a Certificate of Foal Registration for the horse, issued by the Jockey Club of America, came into Fredella's possession at a time when he was indebted to appellant Robert Farugia. Without the knowledge or consent of Dr. Baram, Farugia obtained possession of the horse from Fredella and was given the foal certificate bearing the forged signature of Dr. Baram. The district court found that both Fredella and Farugia knew or should have known that the signature on the foal certificate had been forged and that Fredella had no authority to transfer Foxey Toni.

Farugia first dated the certificate, transferring the horse to himself, and then transferred her to appellant Glenn Hackett and himself. Foxey Toni was subsequently raced in Canada by the putative new owners without the knowledge or consent of Dr. Baram. After Dr. Baram learned of these events, he met with Farugia and demanded the return of Foxey Toni. Farugia refused to return the horse or pay her value of $3,000 but offered instead a modest cash settlement. Dr. Baram rejected the settlement offer and initiated litigation.

Dr. Baram filed a complaint sounding in "Trespass for Conversion," in the district court against Farugia, Hackett, and Fredella. A default judgment for failure to appear was entered against Fredella. Dr. Baram acknowledged at trial that, as a result of previous criminal proceedings against Fredella in state court, he had been paid $3,000 by Fredella covering Dr. Baram's claim "for the value of the horse, Foxey Toni," and that he "agreed to accept that." This case then proceeded as a bench trial for compensatory and punitive damages for conversion against Farugia and Hackett. The court awarded compensatory damages of $3,000 against both defendants for the value of Foxey Toni and assessed punitive damages of $5,000 against Farugia. The court dismissed the complaint against Fredella with prejudice. This appeal by Farugia and Hackett followed.

Appellants argue that the judgment must be reversed because the $3,000 payment by the converter Fredella for the value of the horse extinguished any further claim in conversion by Dr. Baram. We agree with appellants' argument. * * *

The modern law remedy for conversion has emerged from the common law action of trover, which was premised on the theory that the defendant had appropriated the plaintiff's chattel, for which he must pay. * * * A plaintiff who proved conversion in a common law trover action was entitled to damages equal to the full value of the chattel at the time and place of conversion. [citation] According to Professor Prosser,

> "[w]hen the defendant satisfied the judgment in trover, the title to the chattel passed to him, and the plaintiff had nothing more to do with it. The effect was that the defendant was compelled, because of his wrongful appropriation, to buy the chattel at a forced sale, of which the action of trover was the judicial instrument. [citation]"

Pennsylvania courts have long recognized the forced sale aspect of conversion actions.

The title-passing and forced-sale concepts distinguished trover from the common law action of trespass, which was premised on the theory that the plaintiff remained the owner of the chattel and was entitled only to the damages he had sustained through loss of possession, and from the action of replevin, which also left title in the plaintiff and returned the chattel to his possession. The modern day tort of conversion retains the conceptual underpinnings of trover and is generally applicable only to cases such as this one in which there has been a major or serious interference with a chattel or with the plaintiff's right in it. It is the seriousness of the interference that justifies the forced judicial sale to the defendant, described by Prosser as "the distinguishing feature of the action." The Restatement (Second) of Torts preserves this conceptual basis:

> "When the defendant satisfies the judgment in the action for conversion, title to the chattel passes to him, so that he is in effect required to buy it at a forced judicial sale. Conversion is therefore properly limited, and has been limited by the courts, to those serious, major, and important interferences with the right to control the chattel which justify requiring the defendant to pay its full value."

§ 222A, Comment c (1965). Although Pennsylvania law is unclear about whether title passes on entry of judgment against the converter or only when the converter satisfies the judgment, the rule recognized in most states is that title to the chattel passes only when the judgment against the converter is satisfied. We need not venture our opinion on how the Pennsylvania courts would resolve this question, however, because in this case both the judicial order that Fredella pay the value as a condition of his probation and actual payment of $3,000 to Dr. Baram, events related to the first conversion, preceded judgment on the second claim. * * *

On receipt by Dr. Baram of the $3,000 from Fredella, and acknowledgement that this sum reflected the true value of the horse, a common law forced sale was effected, passing title from the legal owner to the converter at the time and place of the original conversion. Had the converter made no offer of an amount reflecting the horse's value, and had Dr. Baram not received full value, he could have made out a conversion action against Farugia and Hackett. But the acceptance by Dr. Baram of the horse's true market value with the resultant passage of title in the nature of "a forced judicial sale" had the effect of vesting title in Fredella retroactively from November 29, 1975, the date of the conversion. [citation] With title so vested, Fredella therefore had the right to transfer Foxey Toni on November 29, 1975, and Farugia, by the same reasoning, then took possession of the horse from a person legally entitled to possess and transfer. Dr. Baram retroactively lost his right to possession of Foxey Toni, and without a right of possession at the time of the alleged conversion could not maintain an action for conversion against Farugia and Hackett. [citation] Thus, although successive and independent actionable conversions of the same chattel are possible, satisfaction of the earlier conversion by payment in full of the value of the chattel acts as a complete bar to subsequent recoveries. * * *

Accordingly, the judgment of the district court will be reversed * * *.

Note

Since conversion is defined as a forced sale of personal property, the plaintiff has the initial burden of establishing a right to the thing allegedly converted. Plaintiff failed to surmount this fundamental hurdle in Moore v. Regents of University of California, 51 Cal.3d 120, 271 Cal.Rptr. 146, 793 P.2d 479 (1990). Plaintiff asserted that defendants wrongfully converted his cells to use in medical research. But the California Supreme Court refused to find property in excised cell tissue; it reasoned that other legal theories protect a patient seeking medical assistance.

GRAYS HARBOR COUNTY v. BAY CITY LUMBER CO.

Supreme Court of Washington, 1955.
47 Wash.2d 879, 289 P.2d 975.

[A group of loggers inadvertently cut timber on plaintiff's land and sold it to the defendant lumber company which was unaware of any wrong. The timber had a stumpage value of $8 per thousand board feet at the time and place of the original conversion and $35 per thousand board feet at the time and place of conversion by the lumber company—the difference was the value added by cutting and transporting the logs to the lumber company's place of business. Plaintiff sued the lumber company for conversion claiming the enhanced value as damages; the lumber company brought in the loggers as cross-defendants. The trial court held the lumber company liable for the enhanced value of the logs; the supreme court, however, held that stumpage was the proper measure of damages.]

ROSELLINI, JUSTICE. If the original conversion was in *mala fides,* then damages in an action against a subsequent converter should be based upon the market value of the property as of the time and place the defendant first exercised control and dominion over it, and this rule applies even though the subsequent converter is an innocent purchaser for value. E.E. Bolles Wooden-Ware Co. v. United States, 106 U.S. 432. * * *

[However, concluded the court, the original trespass here was not wilful.]

This court early committed itself to the view that the doctrine of exemplary or punitive damages is unsound in principle and that such damages cannot be recovered except when explicitly allowed by statute. * * * However, we have adopted the punitive measure of damages where a trespass or conversion is willful or in bad faith. * * *

It was recognized in the early case of Bailey v. Hayden, 65 Wash. 57, 117 P. 720, 721, an action brought under the treble-damage statute (now RCW 64.-12.-030, 040), that the wrongdoer is punished and the owner more than compensated when no allowance is made for the value added by the former's labor and expenditures. We held in that case that the measure of damages to be trebled was the stumpage, not the market value after cutting and removal. In discussing the common-law rule allowing recovery of the higher value where the trespass is wilful, we stated that such damages are punitive, not merely compensatory, and quoted from Beede v. Lamprey, 64 N.H. 510, 15 A. 133, 10 Am.St.Rep. 426, as follows:

> "In cases of conversion by willful act or fraud, the value added by the wrongdoer after the conversion is sometimes given as exemplary or vindictive damages, or because the defendant is precluded from showing an increase in value by his own wrong, and from claiming a corresponding reduction of damages."

In commenting on the quoted portion of the New Hampshire case, we said:

> "But whether the larger damages be frankly called vindictive damages, or are allowed on the last-mentioned ground without any express name, their nature is the same. It is obvious that the increased measure is allowed, not as compensation to the person wronged, but as punishment to the wrongdoer. It is not a mere question of terms, but of the inherent quality of the thing. The increased measure is punitive in its very nature, in that it exceeds the true measure of compensation. It is plain that the person whose trees are cut suffers exactly the same injury where the trespass is involuntary as where it is willful. In each case he suffers the loss of his trees."

It is argued that since the owner may replevy his property wherever he may find it, he should be able to recover its value at whatever time and place he is entitled to replevy it. But this argument is equally valid in the case where the conversion was inadvertent, and yet under such circumstances the wrongdoer is not liable in damages for the increased value. The theory under which replevin is allowed bears no consistent relation to the various measures of damage allowed when the latter remedy is elected. For example, the innocent purchaser from a wilful converter is liable in damages only for the value of the goods at the time and place of his own conversion and cannot be held for any value which he may add to them by his own labors. Yet, if the owner finds the goods in the hands of an innocent purchaser after he has enhanced their value, they may be replevied, provided, of course, that the enhancement in value has not become so great as to divest the original owner of title. Meyers v. Gerhart, 54 Wash. 657, 103 P. 1114. In view of these considerations, the mere fact that the goods can be replevied does not justify the imposition of punitive damages.

Notes

1. Montana's statute provided that damage for conversion should be: "(1) the value at the time of conversion with interest from that time; or (2) where the

action has been prosecuted with reasonable diligence, the highest market value of the property at any time between the conversion and the verdict, without interest, at the option of the injured party." Thus a lumber company that negligently but not wilfully trespassed and cut timber was held liable under the second alternative for the market value of lumber at its mill without interest. Rickl v. Brand S. Lumber Co., 171 Mont. 528, 559 P.2d 1182 (1977).

2. An unknowing purchaser from a wilful converter is liable as an innocent converter, but the courts in the timber cases continue to be divided about the measure of that liability. Mineral Resources, Inc. v. Mahnomen Construction Co., 289 Minn. 412, 184 N.W.2d 780 (1971), held that an unknowing purchaser from a wilful converter is liable only for the value of the property at the time of the original taking—i.e. stumpage. But Masonite Corp. v. Williamson, 404 So.2d 565 (Miss.1981), held that he is liable for the delivered value.

3. After successfully proceeding to judgment against C, could A subsequently seek recovery from B for converting the logs? See Bauman, Multiple Liability, Multiple Remedies, and the Federal Rules of Civil Procedure, 46 Minn.L.Rev. 729, 737 (1962):

"A further question arises as to the effect to be given to a favorable judgment in the first action in subsequent actions brought against the other wrongdoers. Here the position taken is that not judgment alone, but only judgment and satisfaction bars further actions. Moreover, 'no matter how many judgments may be obtained for the same trespass, or what the varying amounts of those judgments, the acceptance of satisfaction of any one of them by the plaintiff is a satisfaction of all the others. * * *' The theory is that satisfaction of the judgment transfers title to the wrongdoers, such title relating back to the date of the conversion."

4. Traditionally, conversion is limited to tangible personal property including commercial paper. Thus a wrongdoer who misappropriates a promissory note can be held liable in conversion for the face value of the note. Where the maker of the note is not personally liable for the obligation, however, a different measure of damages is employed: the owner's loss is measured by the value of the property given to secure the obligation. Knudsen v. Hill, 227 Cal.App.2d 639, 38 Cal.Rptr. 859 (1964).

5. *Prejudgment Interest in Conversion Cases.* Interest from the date of conversion is traditionally part of the damage remedy. This modifies the rule denying prejudgment interest in torts cases; no doubt it has deterred many plaintiffs from waiving the tort to sue in quasi-contract.

Prejudgment interest is virtually mandated by statutes as in the principal case, and by judicial opinions such as Imperial Sugar Co., Inc. v. Torrans, 604 S.W.2d 73 (Tex.1980). On the other hand, Illinois allows prejudgment interest in conversion actions only upon proof of an unreasonable or vexatious delay of payment. In Arkansas, interest runs from the date of a wilful conversion, but for an innocent conversion, only from the date of plaintiff's demand. Auston v. Loyd, 533 F.Supp. 737 (W.D.Ark.1982).

6. *Lost Use or Profits, and Other Damages.* Recovery for loss of use of a converted chattel has not been common, probably because it is theoretically inconsistent with the theory of a "forced sale" dating back to the time of conversion, and because of the availability of prejudgment interest. However, the Restatement (Second) of Torts § 927 (1965) expressly sanctions lost use damage if "not otherwise compensated."

Section 927 does not specifically address damages for lost profits but does provide generally for "[t]he amount of any further pecuniary loss of which the deprivation has been a legal cause." In effect this reiterates the general measure of tort damages and affords a large loophole to escape from the standard crystallized measure of damages for conversion. See e.g., Myers v. Stephens, 233 Cal. App.2d 104, 43 Cal.Rptr. 420 (1965), which applied Cal.Civ.Code § 3336 to permit plaintiff to recover lost profits caused by the wrongful conversion of a house that plaintiff had contracted to move.

Lost profit from the prospective sale of sand that defendants converted was allowed in Martin Marietta Corp. v. New Jersey National Bank, 505 F.Supp. 946 (D.N.J.1981). The defendant asserted that the plaintiff could have avoided the lost profits by "covering," citing the U.C.C.; but the court rejected this argument because the "cover" provisions of the U.C.C. did not apply to a tort.

Query: Apart from the U.C.C., should an owner who seeks lost profits from a conversion still have an obligation to avoid the consequences?

See Lance Productions, Inc. v. Commerce Union Bank, 764 S.W.2d 207 (Tenn. App.1988), requiring proof that a substitute vehicle was not available.

Occasional conversion cases allow special damages for such items as inconvenience, shock, and mental anguish. E.g. Guidry v. Rubin, 425 So.2d 366 (La.App. 1982), where the defendants were attorneys who improperly retained funds from a wrongful death settlement.

7. Punitive damages are common in conversion cases. E.g. Matter of Barney's Boats, 616 F.2d 164 (5th Cir.1980) (Bankruptcy Court awarded $50,000 in punitive damages against creditor for conversion of bankrupt's property); Fahrenberg v. Tengel, 96 Wis.2d 211, 291 N.W.2d 516 (1980) ($200,000 reduced to $125,000 for converting $20,000 in coins).

8. May a converter mitigate damages by tendering back the converted chattel? In Magic City Steel & Metal Corp. v. Mitchell, 265 P.2d 473 (Okl.1953), the Oklahoma Supreme Court noted that while some courts had liberalized the early case law unequivocally denying defendant the right to escape liability or reduce damages by tender back of the converted property, the strict rule still applied where the physical condition of the property tendered back was impaired. The Restatement (Second) of Torts § 922 (1965) permits damages to be reduced where the conversion is innocent and the value of the chattel is substantially unimpaired, if a prompt tender is made by the converter and kept open.

If the owner regains possession of the converted chattel, damages must be reduced accordingly. The accepted practice for taking account of this factor is explained by the court in National Motor Service Co. v. Walters, 85 Idaho 349, 361, 379 P.2d 643, 651 (1963): "[D]amages recoverable by the owner are based on the value at the time of the conversion, but in mitigation, the wrongdoer is entitled to credit for the value of the property at the time of return, though he is chargeable with the value of its use, of which the owner has been deprived, during the period of wrongful detention."

Welch v. Kosasky, 24 Mass.App.Ct. 402, 509 N.E.2d 919 (1987).

If the chattel is recovered as the result of the plaintiff's own efforts, he may recover the expenses of procuring its return as well as cost of repairs and damages for loss of use. Beetson v. Hollywood Athletic Club, 109 Cal.App. 715, 293 P. 821 (1930). In Gladstone v. Hillel, 203 Cal.App.3d 977, 250 Cal.Rptr. 372 (1988) [certified for partial publication], a plaintiff spent 1088 hours in attempting to recover molds, jewelry and other property wrongfully converted by defendants. The court, after reducing the amount sought, allowed recovery even though part of the time and expense had some connection with preparation for litigation. What if the expense incurred by plaintiff was a ransom paid to thieves to recover his property? Cf. Kraut v. Morgan & Brothers Manhattan Storage Co., 38 N.Y.2d 445, 381 N.Y.S.2d 25, 343 N.E.2d 744 (1976).

TRANSCONTINENTAL OIL CORP. v. TRENTON PRODUCTS CO.

United States Court of Appeals, Second Circuit, 1977.
560 F.2d 94.

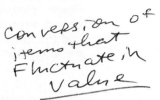

MARKEY, CHIEF JUDGE. [Transcontinental Oil (Trans) sued a former president of the corporation for conversion of the corporation's stock.]

Under well settled legal principles, the appropriate measure of damages for the conversion of items of fluctuating value, such as stock certificates, is the replacement value—the highest market price—reached within a reasonable period after the discovery of the conversion. [citations] * * *

On the basis of the record now before the Court, the best evidence of the market value of Trans stock during the applicable period is the bid and asked prices for that stock as reported by the National Quotation Bureau (the NQB), a standard reference used by dealers in securities to determine the prices quoted, on a given date, by dealers who are "making the market" in a particular stock. In fact, during the applicable period, the NQB provided the only record of bid and asked prices for over-the-counter stock.

Concededly, these quotations do not represent actual transactions, nor do they include retail markup, markdown or commission. However, they do represent a willingness—indeed, a commitment to the extent of 100 shares—on the part of the listed market makers to entertain contractual bids and offerings at or around the stated prices.

During the applicable period, eleven market makers in Trans stock reported "bid" prices ranging from thirty-five to forty-three cents per share and "asked" prices ranging from forty to forty-four cents per share. Applying the so-called "highest market value" rule outlined above, in the absence of any persuasive contrary proof of market value, I find that the replacement value of the converted stock was forty-four cents per share. Incidentally, I have not attempted to determine the premium, if any, which Trans might have had to pay for the acquisition of such a large block of stock in a rather "thin" market, because there was no evidence thereon, and because Trans could have spaced its purchases to minimize their effect on the market price, there being no apparent reason for haste in replacing treasury shares which had been improperly issued years before.

In addition, Trans may recover the amount of any proceeds received by Fein upon his sale of the Desilets stock to the extent such proceeds exceed forty-four cents per share.

Notes

1. Compare the measure of damages applied in the principal case with that Judge L. Hand suggested as appropriate for conversion by a fiduciary in Marcus v. Otis, supra, p. 330.

2. See Schultz v. Commodity Futures Trading Commission, 716 F.2d 136, 140 (2d Cir.1983): "[W]hat constitutes a reasonable period between the act complained of and the time when reentry into the market would be both warranted and possible will vary from case to case, but the injured party is not actually required to

reenter the market in order to determine when he might have done so. Practical reasons dictate this. The value of lost securities may rise dramatically the day after a wrongful conversion and then embark on a prolonged downward spiral. Had the owner of such securities not been wrongfully parted with them, he might well have been prompted to sell them within a few days, as their value began to plummet. To require him actually to reenter the market and repurchase the same securities as a predicate for a damage claim, when steadily falling prices render such an investment imprudent, would frustrate the rule which seeks to make an investor whole. Rather than mitigating damages, as this example illustrates, a requirement that there be an actual repurchase could result in an increase in damages."

3. In Kaplan v. Cavicchia, 107 N.J.Super. 201, 257 A.2d 739, 742 (App.Div. 1969), the court stated: "Upon the conversion of securities the injured party has an election of remedies. He may sue at law in replevin and obtain his securities, if defendant still has them, plus damages for the wrongful detention. He may also sue at law for money damages in trover for the wrongful conversion. In such case, the damages recoverable would be the highest intermediate value of the securities between the date of the conversion and the date of judgment. Then, too, he may sue in equity for a judgment declaring the wrongdoer a constructive trustee of the securities, or of any money or property derived from their disposition. He may obtain an accounting. There may also be injunctive relief where the facts warrant it."

4. Trahan v. First National Bank, 690 F.2d 466 (5th Cir.1982), approved under Louisiana law an order that required the converter to "procure and deliver" the number of shares that it had converted. The court rejected both the time and place of conversion measure and the highest value between conversion and judgment.

5. Brown v. Campbell, 536 So.2d 920, 921 (Ala.1988). Plaintiff may recover the value of the stock at the date of conversion "or its value at any time subsequent to conversion and before trial, whichever is greater."

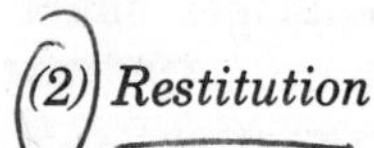

(2) *Restitution*

FELDER v. REETH

United States Court of Appeals, Ninth Circuit, 1929.
34 F.2d 744.

WILBUR, CIRCUIT JUDGE. Appellants brought an action in the District Court for the territory of Alaska to recover $5,402.65 for goods, wares, and merchandise sold to the appellee and for appellee's checks cashed by appellant. The appellee admitted the obligations sued upon, and by second amended answer and counterclaim alleged that he was engaged in placer mining upon 1,200 acres of placer mining ground, and that to carry on said mining operations he purchased a certain hydraulic mining plant in San Francisco, and transported the same to a point 40 miles below his placer mining camp, for the reason that because of low water in the stream he could not transport the machinery to the mining camp; that it remained at that point during the seasons of 1919, 1920, and 1921 by reason of low water in the river; that the freight charge for transportation of this plant from San Francisco was $1,045; that during the summer of 1921 the appellants wrongfully took possession of the hydraulic plant, transported the same down the river to Bethel, and converted same to their own use and sold a part thereof. It is further alleged:

> "That under the conditions then existing at said Golden Gate Falls and 'Supply Camp' the said mining machinery and equipment was reasonably worth to defendant and were of the value to him of $10,000.00.

"That defendant elects to waive the tort involved in the said unlawful taking and conversion of said property and to rely upon an implied contract upon the part of the plaintiffs, created by the law, to pay him the said sum of $10,000.00 for said machinery and equipment, the same being the reasonable value therefor by the time it reached the 'Supply Camp'; that the said plaintiffs, by reason of the premises, impliedly agreed, and in law did agree, to pay him the said sum of $10,000.00 for the said machinery and equipment."

Under the Alaska Code, a counterclaim to an action arising out of contract must be either one arising out of the transaction sued upon by the plaintiff, or, "In an action arising on contract, any other cause of action arising also on contract, and existing at the commencement of the action." Comp.Laws Alaska 1913, § 896.

The purpose of the form of pleading adopted by the appellee waiving, or attempting to waive, the tort, and suing upon the implied obligation of the appellant, was to bring his counterclaim within the purview of the statute, authorizing the setting up of a counterclaim. * * *

The appellant demurred to the counterclaim on the ground that the court had no jurisdiction of the subject-matter set up in the amended answer and counterclaim, and the counterclaim did not state facts sufficient to constitute a defense to the plaintiff's complaint. The demurrer was overruled, and appellants replied, denying that the sum of $10,000 was or is a reasonable and fair value of the hydraulic mining equipment, or that it was worth more than $550. Appellants admitted taking the property, and alleged that it was taken to avoid a total loss of thereof by flood waters of the Riglugalic river, on whose banks it had been placed. Appellants alleged that the property was in an abandoned condition until the fall of 1921; that they took possession of the property, and transported it to Bethel, and notified the defendant; that appellee ignored the entire matter; that they retained possession of the hydraulic plant until 1923, when for the first time they had an opportunity to dispose of the same; and that they sold it for the sum of $550, and that that sum was all the property was worth in Kuskokwin Precinct.

The case was tried at Bethel, and by stipulation neither of the attorneys appeared at the trial. * * * Thereupon the case was transferred to Fairbanks, and counsel argued the case before the judge, who, by reason of written stipulation waving the jury, determined the facts. The court found that the appellee was indebted to the appellant in the sum of $8,690.21, and that the appellants were indebted to the appellees in the sum of $8,000, with 8 per cent. interest from September 1, 1921, aggregating $12,480, and rendered judgment in favor of appellees for the difference, $3,789.79. With reference to the value of the hydraulic plant, the court found:

"That under the circumstances and conditions as they existed at that time and by reason of the fact that there was no market value for said machinery at that time and place, and by reason of the use that the defendant could have put it to, the said machinery was worth to him the sum of $8,000 and he is entitled to counterclaim that amount with interest thereon at eight per cent. per annum from September 1, 1921, aggregating $12,480 as against the debt owing by him to the plaintiffs.

"That the action of the plaintiffs in taking the said machinery and disposing of it was without the knowledge or consent of the defendant, was unlawful, unjustifiable and oppressive and resulted in compelling the defendant to abandon his mining enterprise at Golden Gate Falls."

Before the findings were signed, appellant proposed amendments to the defendant's proposed findings of fact and conclusions of law to the effect that appellees were indebted to appellants in the sum of $550 on account of the hydraulic plant, and that that amount had already been credited in their accounts.

There seems to be no doubt that appellees can assert their claim against the appellants in this action by a counterclaim in the event and because of the fact that they waived the tortious conversion and counted in assumpsit as for goods sold and delivered. * * *

The most serious question in this case is the measure of damages for breach of the implied contract sued upon. At common law, under the older rule, the result of waiving the tort in a case of conversion and sale was a right to recover the amount received upon the sale, as for money had and received, but later cases hold that the action can be maintained as for goods sold and delivered without awaiting sale, or even after sale, and the measure of recovery is the market value of the property. Terry v. Munger, 121 N.Y. 161, 24 N.E. 272. In a case where the owner waives the tort if he accepts the tort-feasor as his agent both in the taking and in the sale, he would necessarily be limited in his recovery to the money received by the agent. There seems, however, to be no good reason why the owner cannot waive the tortious taking and ignore the subsequent sale and recover the reasonable value of the property taken as for goods sold and delivered. This was done by the appellee, who ignored the sale of his property made by the appellants, and sought to recover as upon an implied agreement to pay the value of the hydraulic plant. The complaint, construed more strongly against the pleader, does not allege the market value or reasonable value of the property taken by the appellants. The allegation is of the reasonable value "to him." * * *

This is made clearer by the findings of the court above quoted, where the court held that "the unlawful and oppressive conversion" resulted in compelling the abandonment of the appellees' mining operations, and that "the value to him was $8,000 because of the use to which he could have put it." Assuming that this is a proper measure of damages in a suit for conversion under the peculiar circumstances found by the court, it does not follow that the appellee is entitled to recover that amount upon his counterclaim in which he waived the tort. It must be evident that, by consenting to the taking of his property and treating the taking as a sale by him, he cannot in justice or in law count upon the special value to him of the use of property which he thus declares he no longer intends to use. * * *

The significance of the allegation of the counterclaim and the finding of the court as to the value to the appellee of said hydraulic plant is manifest, in that it appears that $5,000 was or may have been added by the court to the cost of said property because of the special value of the property to the plaintiff [defendant?] under the circumstances. * * * The primary question presented by the record is the sufficiency of the counterclaim to state a cause of action against the appellant. The demurrer raising this point was overruled. It should have been sustained for lack of an allegation as to the value of the property impliedly sold by the appellee to the appellant. * * * For this error in overruling the demurrer, and for the further reason that the findings do not follow the pleadings, in that the trial court ignores the waiver of the tort and gives damages as for a tort, the judgment must be reversed. In view of the fact that this case must be tried again, it should be stated that, as the appellee by his counterclaim seeks to recover the value of the property as upon an implied sale, he should be permitted to amend his counterclaim and allege that value.

"If the wrong-doer has not sold the property, but still retains it, the plaintiff has the right to waive the tort, and proceed upon an implied contract of sale to the wrong-doer himself, and in such event he is not charged as for money had and received by him to the use of the plaintiff. The contract implied is one to pay the value of the property as if it had been sold to the wrong-doer by the owner. If the transaction is thus held by the plaintiff as a sale, of course the title to the property passes to the wrong-doer, when the plaintiff elects to so treat it." * * * Terry v. Munger. If on the trial it appears that there is no market at the point of conversion or implied sale, as from the findings appears to be the case, the value must be determined at the nearest market less the costs of transportation thereto, * * * for in case of a waiver of a tort in conversion the action ex contractu is sustained rather on the theory of benefit derived by the taker than of damage to the owner, Keener, Quasi Contracts 200; Woodward on the Law of Quasi Contracts, § 292. * * *

Interest should be allowed from the date of the taking as the plaintiff's election relates back thereto.

Judgment reversed.

Notes

1. On remand, defendant amended the counterclaim to state a cause of action in tort. On plaintiff's objection, the counterclaim was struck as improper, without prejudice to defendant's right to maintain a separate action for conversion. Felder v. Reeth, 62 F.2d 730 (9th Cir.1933).

2. In most jurisdictions, where the wrongdoer has sold converted chattels, the owner electing restitution may choose either the common count for goods sold and delivered or the count for money had and received. The amount of recovery depends upon the theory adopted. A plaintiff proceding on the money count is limited to the proceeds the converter realized from the sale. On the other hand, if plaintiff chooses sale of goods, recovery is measured by the value of the converted property. See Canepa v. Sun Pacific, Inc., 126 Cal.App.2d 706, 272 P.2d 860 (1954).

3. *Misuse of the Election of Remedies Doctrine.* The notion that waiving the tort ratifies a "sale and delivery" to the converter shows courts confusing reality with fiction. By itself this is a harmless indulgence. However, some courts have acted upon this fiction to hold that a party had elected an improvident remedy. Consider the following extracts:

Korns v. Thomson & McKinnon, 22 F.Supp. 442, 450 (D.Minn.1938): "One whose property has been converted by others may maintain an action in tort against the wrongdoer, or he may waive the tort and sue upon an implied contract to recover the value of his property, but he cannot maintain an action upon an implied contract as against some of the wrongdoers, and then an action in tort against other wrongdoers." Perez v. Boatmen's National Bank, 788 S.W.2d 296, 299 (Mo.App.1990): "In general, where a plaintiff can choose to proceed in tort or contract on a course of conduct involving two possible defendants and he chooses to proceed to a final judgment against one defendant in contract, he may not later attempt to pursue a tort action against the second defendant; the initial waiver of tort waived tort for all purposes."

Consider these decisions in light of the House of Lords opinions below. Compare also the plaintiff's express ratification in Shahood v. Cavin, supra, p. 326.

United Australia, Ltd. v. Barclays Bank, Ltd., [1941] A.C. 1.

Lord Atkins (p. 29): "If I find that a thief has stolen my securities and is in possession of the proceeds, when I sue him for them I am not excusing him. I am protesting violently that he is a thief and because of his theft I am suing him: indeed he may be in prison upon my prosecution. Similarly with the blackmailer: in such a case I do not understand what can be said to be waived. The man has my money which I have not delivered to him with any real intention of passing to him the property. I sue him because he has the actual property taken; and I suggest that it can make no difference if he extorted a chattel which he afterwards sold. I protest that a man cannot waive a wrong unless he either has a real intention to waive it, or can fairly have imputed to him such an intention, and in the cases which we have been considering there can be no such intention either actual or imputed. These fantastic resemblances of contracts invented in order to meet requirements of the law as to forms of action which have now disappeared should not in these days be allowed to affect actual rights. When these ghosts of the past stand in the path of justice clanking their mediaeval chains the proper course for the judge is to pass through them undeterred.

"Concurrently with the decisions as to waiver of tort there is to be found a supposed application of election; and the allegation is sometimes to be found that the plaintiff elected to waive the tort. It seems to me that in this respect it is essential to bear in mind the distinction between choosing one of two alternative remedies, and choosing one of two inconsistent rights. As far as remedies were concerned, from the oldest time the only restriction was on the choice between real and personal actions. If you chose the one you could not claim on the other. Real actions have long disappeared; and, subject to the difficulty of including two causes of action in one writ which has also now disappeared, there has not been and there certainly is not now any compulsion to choose between alternative remedies. You may put them in the same writ; or you may put one in first, and then amend and add or substitute another."

Lord Romer (p. 34): "A person whose goods have been wrongfully converted by another has the choice of two remedies against the wrongdoer. He may sue for the proceeds of the conversion as money had and received to his use, or he may sue for the damages that he has sustained by the conversion. If he obtains judgment for the proceeds, it is certain that he is precluded from thereafter claiming damages for the conversion. But, in my opinion, this is not due to his having waived the tort but to his having finally elected to pursue one of his two alternative remedies. The phrase 'waive the tort' is a picturesque one. It has a pleasing sound. Perhaps it was for these reasons that it was regarded with so much affection by the old Common Lawyers, one of whom, indeed, was moved to break into verse upon the subject. But with all respect to their memories, I firmly believe that the phrase was an inaccurate one if and so far as it meant that the tortious act was affirmed. What was waived by the judgment was not the tort, but the right to recover damages for the tort."

4. Waiver of tort is not the only way courts have used election of remedies to arrive at questionable conclusions. The misguided learning surrounding that doctrine has also been applied to find an inconsistency between replevin and conversion. Hence the choice of one of these remedies has been held to constitute a binding election precluding resort to the other. See Equitable Trust Co. v. Connecticut Brass & Manufacturing Corp., 290 Fed. 712, 725 (2d Cir.1923); Satterwhite v. Harriman National Bank & Trust Co., 13 F.Supp. 493, 500 (S.D.N.Y.1935). *Satter-*

white involved misappropriated stock. The court said: "If a plaintiff can sue in replevin and then sue in conversion, and then sue in replevin again, he can substantially reinstate the discarded rule of [highest market value between conversion and trial] and throw all of the risk of market fluctuations on the defendant."

5. *Indebitatus Assumpsit as a "Sale" Under the U.C.C. The Fictions Still Live.* A longer statute of limitation continues to be a major reason for plaintiff to waive conversion and sue in assumpsit. In Taylor's Fire Prevention Service v. Coca Cola Bottling Co., 99 Cal.App.3d 711, 160 Cal.Rptr. 411 (1979), the plaintiff under an oral agreement delivered CO_2 in cylinders to the defendant. The defendant failed to return the cylinders. The tort statute of limitations had run, as had the California two year statute of limitations on "an action upon a contract, obligation or liability not founded upon an instrument in writing." Cal.Civ.Proc.Code § 339 (a section which has been frequently applied to quasi-contractual actions). Only the four-year statute of limitations of U.C.C. § 2–725(1) remained. It reads: "An action for breach of any contract for sale must be commenced within four years after the cause of action has accrued."

The court affirmed the trial court's holding that the plaintiff could recover in quasi-contract: "The trial court found that Coca–Cola's failure to return the cylinders was conversion. Nonetheless, the court ruled that Taylor had waived the tort after demanding return of the chattels and had *elected to treat the transaction as a sale of the cylinders.* This ruling appears to comport with California law, which allows a bailor in Taylor's position to treat a conversion as a *fictional or implied by law contract of sale* * * *. Since indebitatus assumpsit is a common count, we are of the opinion that it is an action for 'price due the seller' and thereby cognizable under the Commercial Code."

OLWELL v. NYE & NISSEN CO.

Supreme Court of Washington, 1946.
26 Wash.2d 282, 173 P.2d 652.

MALLERY, JUSTICE. On May 6, 1940, plaintiff, E.L. Olwell, sold and transferred to the defendant corporation his one-half interest in Puget Sound Egg Packers, a Washington corporation having its principal place of business in Tacoma. By the terms of the agreement, the plaintiff was to retain full ownership in an "Eggsact" egg-washing machine, formerly used by Puget Sound Egg Packers. The defendant promised to make it available for delivery to the plaintiff on or before June 15, 1940. It appears that the plaintiff arranged for and had the machine stored in a space adjacent to the premises occupied by the defendant but not covered by its lease. Due to the scarcity of labor immediately after the outbreak of the war, defendant's treasurer, without the knowledge or consent of the plaintiff, ordered the egg washer taken out of storage. The machine was put into operation by defendant on May 31, 1941, and thereafter for a period of three years was used approximately one day a week in the regular course of the defendant's business. Plaintiff first discovered this use in January or February of 1945 when he happened to be at the plant on business and heard the machine operating. Thereupon plaintiff offered to sell the machine to defendant for $600 or half of its original cost in 1929. A counter offer of $50 was refused and approximately one month later this action was commenced to recover the reasonable value of defendant's use of the machine, and praying for $25 per month from the commencement of the unauthorized use until the time of trial. * * * The court entered judgment for plaintiff in the amount of $10 per week for the period of 156 weeks covered by the statute of limitations, or $1,560, and gave the plaintiff his costs.

Defendant has appealed to this court assigning error upon the judgment, upon the trial of the cause on the theory of unjust enrichment, upon the amount of damages, and upon the court's refusal to make a finding as to the value of the machine and in refusing to consider such value in measuring damages.

The theory of the respondent was that the tort of conversion could be "waived" and suit brought in quasi-contract, upon a contract implied in law, to recover, as restitution, the profits which inured to appellant as a result of its wrongful use of the machine. With this the trial court agreed and in its findings of facts found that the use of the machine "resulted in a benefit to the users, in that said use saves the users approximately $1.43 per hour of use as against the expense which would be incurred were eggs to be washed by hand; that said machine was used by Puget Sound Egg Packers and defendant, on an average of one day per week from May of 1941, until February of 1945 at an average saving of $10.00 per each day of use."

In substance, the argument presented by the assignments of error is that the principle of unjust enrichment, or quasi-contract, is not of universal application, but is imposed only in exceptional cases because of special facts and circumstances and in favor of particular persons; that respondent had an adequate remedy in an action at law for replevin or claim and delivery; that any damages awarded to the plaintiff should be based upon the use or rental value of the machine and should bear some reasonable relation to its market value. Appellant therefore contends that the amount of the judgment is excessive.

It is uniformly held that in cases where the defendant *tort feasor* has benefited by his wrong, the plaintiff may elect to "waive the tort" and bring an action in assumpsit for restitution. Such an action arises out of a duty imposed by law devolving upon the defendant to repay an unjust and unmerited enrichment.

It is clear that the saving in labor cost which appellant derived from its use of respondent's machine constituted a benefit.

According to the Restatement of Restitution, § 1(b), p. 12.

> "A person confers a benefit upon another if he gives to the other possession of or some other interest in money, land, chattels or choses in action, performs services beneficial to or at the request of the other, satisfies a debt or a duty of the other, or in any way adds to the other's security or advantage. *He confers a benefit not only where he adds to the property of another, but also where he* saves the other from expense or loss. The word 'benefit,' therefore denotes any form of advantage." (Italics ours)

It is also necessary to show that while appellant benefited from its use of the egg-washing machine, respondent thereby incurred a loss. It was argued by appellant that since the machine was put into storage by respondent, who had no present use for it, and for a period of almost three years did not know that appellant was operating it and since it was not injured by its operation and the appellant never adversely claimed any title to it, nor contested respondent's right of repossession upon the latter's discovery of the wrongful operation, that the respondent was not damaged because he is as well off as if the machine had not been used by appellant.

The very essence of the nature of property is the right to its exclusive use. Without it, no beneficial right remains. However plausible, the appellant cannot be heard to say that his wrongful invasion of the respondent's property right to exclusive use is not a loss compensable in law. To hold otherwise would be subversive of all property rights since his use was admittedly wrongful and without claim of right. The theory of unjust enrichment is applicable in such a case.

We agree with appellant that respondent could have elected a "common garden variety of action," as he calls it, for the recovery of damages. It is also true that except where provided for by statute, punitive damages are not allowed, the basic measure for the recovery of damages in this state being compensation. If, then, respondent had been *limited* to redress *in tort* for damages, as appellant contends, the court below would be in error in refusing to make a finding as to the value of the machine. In such case the award of damages must bear a reasonable relation to the value of the property. * * *

But respondent here had an election. He chose rather to waive his right of action *in tort* and to sue *in assumpsit* on the implied contract. Having so elected, he is entitled to the measure of restoration which accompanies the remedy.

> "Actions for restitution have for their primary purpose taking from the defendant and restoring to the plaintiff something to which the plaintiff is entitled, or if this is not done, causing the defendant to pay the plaintiff an amount which will restore the plaintiff to the position in which he was before the defendant received the benefit. If the value of what was received and what was lost were always equal, there would be no substantial problem as to the amount of recovery, since actions of restitution are not punitive. In fact, however, the plaintiff frequently has lost more than the defendant has gained, and sometimes the defendant has gained more than the plaintiff has lost.
>
> "In such cases the measure of restitution is determined with reference to the tortiousness of the defendant's conduct or the negligence or other fault of one or both of the parties in creating the situation giving rise to the right to restitution. If the defendant was tortious in his acquisition of the benefit he is required to pay for what the other has lost although that is more than the recipient benefited. *If he was consciously tortious in acquiring the benefit, he is also deprived of any profit derived from his subsequent dealing with it.* If he was no more at fault than the claimant, he is not required to pay for losses in excess of benefit received by him and he is permitted to retain gains which result from his dealing with the property." (Italics ours) Restatement of Restitution, pp. 595, 596.

Respondent may recover the profit derived by the appellant from the use of the machine.

Respondent has prayed "on his first cause of action for the sum of $25.00 per month from the time defendant first commenced to use said machine subsequent to May 1940 (1941) until present time."

In computing judgment, the court below computed recovery on the basis of $10 per week. This makes the judgment excessive since it cannot exceed the amount prayed for.

We therefore direct the trial court to reduce the judgment, based upon the prayer of the complaint, to $25 per month for thirty-six months, or $900.

The judgment as modified is affirmed.

Note

Compare Woodward, Quasi–Contract § 292 (1916): "Since the obligation is to make restitution, not to account, profits, as such, are not recoverable. Thus, if A owns a vehicle for the carriage of passengers which he lets for fifteen dollars per day, and B wrongfully takes and uses the vehicle for five days, thereby making an actual profit of one hundred dollars, A should be allowed to recover, not one hundred dollars, the profit realized by the wrongdoer, but seventy-five dollars, the value of that which was taken from the party injured. However, if B, instead of using the vehicle himself, lets it to C for five days at twenty dollars per day, and receives from C the sum of one hundred dollars, A would probably be allowed, in a count for money had and received, to recover the amount received by B from C."

SCHLOSSER v. WELK

Appellate Court of Illinois, Third District, 1990.
193 Ill.App.3d 448, 550 N.E.2d 241.

JUSTICE WOMBACHER delivered the opinion of the court. The defendant, Rhonda Welk, appeals from a $549 judgment entered in favor of the plaintiff, Marianne Schlosser, d/b/a Select–A–Video. The record shows that the defendant was an employee of Select–A–Video until her termination on October 5, 1987. As a general policy, employees were allowed to take video tapes home for their personal use without checking the tapes out or paying a rental fee. On the day the defendant was terminated, she had placed eight video tapes in her car. At the end of the work day, the defendant was told that she was being terminated. The defendant took the tapes home and during a conversation with her husband placed them in a storage closet. She testified that a number of weeks later she discovered the tapes while cleaning. She also testified that the tapes were never viewed by her or her family while they were in her possession. She returned the video tapes to the plaintiff's store on December 10, 1987.

At the conclusion of the bench trial, the court found that an implied contract existed between the parties. The court then ruled that the plaintiff was entitled to $549, which was the amount the defendant would have owed if she had rented the tapes for the two months she kept them.

On appeal, the defendant contends that the trial court erred in granting judgment for the plaintiff, because the plaintiff failed to show that the defendant had watched the video tapes. According to the defendant, the plaintiff therefore failed to show that the defendant derived any benefit from her possession of the tapes. She claims that because the plaintiff failed to show a benefit to the defendant, the plaintiff failed to prove an essential element necessary for recovery on its unjust enrichment claim.

The theory of unjust enrichment is based upon a finding of a contract implied in law. The essential element of a contract implied in law is the receipt of benefits by one party, which it would be inequitable for him to retain without payment; it is predicated on the principle that no one should unjustly enrich himself at another's expense.

From the record, it is clear that the defendant derived a benefit from her possession of the plaintiff's video tapes and that therefore an implied contract existed between herself and the plaintiff. The tapes were available for her use. Under any other circumstances she would have had to buy or rent the tapes in order to view them. In sum, by showing that the defendant had possession of the tapes for her private use, the plaintiff proved that the defendant had derived a benefit.

The defendant next argues that the trial court erred in determining the amount of the plaintiff's recovery.

The plaintiff's recovery is limited to the reasonable amount by which the trial court finds the defendant was unjustly enriched at the expense of the plaintiff. * * *

On review of the record, we find the evidence insufficient to support the full amount of the instant award. The unrebutted evidence showed that the defendant and her family never watched the video tapes. There was no evidence that the defendant intentionally withheld the tapes from the plaintiff. Further, the plaintiff presented no evidence that it lost money because it was unable to rent the tapes to a paying customer. Under the circumstances of this case, we find it unreasonable to treat the tapes as having been rented on a day-by-day basis for the entire time the defendant had them. The inequity in such an award is at least as great as allowing the defendant to retain the tapes without paying any rental fee. A more reasonable approach is to hold that the defendant was enriched to the extent of one day's rental fee for each of the tapes in her possession. The evidence showed that the six children's tapes held by the defendant each rented for $1 a day and the two adult tapes together rented for $3 a day during the week. Therefore, the defendant was enriched to the extent of $9, and the trial court should have entered judgment for the plaintiff in that amount. Accordingly, having found the trial court's decision contrary to the manifest weight of the evidence, we modify the judgment in favor of the plaintiff, reducing the award from $549 to $9.

The judgment of the circuit court of Peoria County is affirmed as modified.

Affirmed as modified.

JUSTICE HEIPLE, concurring in part; dissenting in part. * * * The trial court found an implied contract had arisen which entitled the store to an award of $549 for lost rentals. While the majority order affirms the principle of implied contract, it reduces the damages to $9 on the grounds that there was no evidence that the defendant viewed the tapes more than once or that the plaintiff actually suffered a loss from lost rentals. I respectfully disagree with that portion of the order.

The evidence showed a daily rental rate of $1 for the six children's tapes that were taken plus $1.50 a day for each of the two adult tapes. Hence, the majority arrived at a reduced figure of $9 which assumes a single viewing of each of the eight tapes during the course of one day's rental.

The error here is that the question of whether the tapes were viewed or not and how many times they were viewed is wholly irrelevant. The fact is that the tapes were unlawfully in the possession of the defendant and available for viewing for a period of two months whether viewed in fact or not. Likewise, the plaintiff was deprived of the tapes for two months and thereby the possibility of renting them for that period of time. The benefit conferred on the defendant is the possession of the tapes for two months. Whether she viewed them once, not at all, or used them to prop up a short leg on her dining room table is really quite beside the point. She took them, kept them, had them in her possession for such use as she chose to make of them and, in fact, deprived the lawful owner of their use and potential rental for a period of two months. Therein lies the benefit and the detriment.

PEARSON v. DODD

United States Court of Appeals, District of Columbia Circuit, 1969.
410 F.2d 701.

J. Skelly Wright, Circuit Judge. This case arises out of the exposure of the alleged misdeeds of Senator Thomas Dodd of Connecticut by newspaper columnists Drew Pearson and Jack Anderson. The District Court has granted partial summary judgment to Senator Dodd, appellee here, finding liability on a theory of conversion. At the same time, the court denied partial summary judgment on the theory of invasion of privacy. Both branches of the court's judgment are before us on interlocutory appeal. We affirm the District Court's denial of summary judgment for invasion of privacy [Editors: that discussion is omitted] and reverse its grant of summary judgment for conversion.

The undisputed facts in the case were stated by the District Court as follows:

> "[O]n several occasions in June and July, 1965, two former employees of the plaintiff, at times with the assistance of two members of the plaintiff's staff, entered the plaintiff's office without authority and unbeknownst to him, removed numerous documents from his files, made copies of them, replaced the originals, and turned over the copies to the defendant Anderson, who was aware of the manner in which the copies had been obtained. The defendants Pearson and Anderson thereafter published articles containing information gleaned from these documents." * * *

We conclude that appellants are not guilty of conversion on the facts shown. * * *

The most distinctive feature of conversion is its measure of damages, which is the value of the goods converted. * * *

Because of this stringent measure of damages, it has long been recognized that not every wrongful interference with the personal property of another is a conversion. Where the intermeddling falls short of the complete or very substantial deprivation of possessory rights in the property, the tort committed is not conversion, but the lesser wrong of trespass to chattels.

The Second Restatement of Torts has marked the distinction by defining conversion as:

> "[A]n intentional exercise of dominion or control over a chattel which so seriously interferes with the right of another to control it that the actor may justly be required to pay the other the full value of the chattel." [1]

Less serious interferences fall under the Restatement's definition of trespass.[2]

1. [Footnotes renumbered.] Restatement (Second) of Torts § 222A(1) (1965).

2. Id., § 217: "A trespass to a chattel may be committed by intentionally (a) dispossessing another of the chattel, or (b) using or intermeddling with a chattel in the possession of another."

The difference is more than a semantic one. The measure of damages in trespass is not the whole value of the property interfered with, but rather the actual diminution in its value caused by the interference. More important for this case, a judgment for conversion can be obtained with only nominal damages, whereas liability for trespass to chattels exists only on a showing of actual damage to the property interfered with.[3] Here the District Court granted partial summary judgment on the issue of liability alone, while conceding that possibly no more than nominal damages might be awarded on subsequent trial. Partial summary judgment for liability could not have been granted on a theory of trespass to chattels without an undisputed showing of actual damages to the property in question.

It is clear that on the agreed facts appellants committed no conversion of the physical documents taken from appellee's files. Those documents were removed from the files at night, photocopied, and returned to the files undamaged before office operations resumed in the morning. Insofar as the documents' value to appellee resided in their usefulness as records of the business of his office, appellee was clearly not substantially deprived of his use of them.

This of course is not an end of the matter. It has long been recognized that documents often have value above and beyond that springing from their physical possession.[4] They may embody information or ideas whose economic value depends in part or in whole upon being kept secret. The question then arises whether the information taken by means of copying appellee's office files is of the type which the law of conversion protects. The general rule has been that ideas or information are not subject to legal protection,[5] but the law has developed exceptions to this rule. Where information is gathered and arranged at some cost and sold as a commodity on the market, it is properly protected as property. Where ideas are formulated with labor and inventive genius, as in the case of literary works[6] or scientific researches,[7] they are protected. Where they constitute instruments of fair and effective commercial competition, those who develop them may gather their fruits under the protection of the law.

The question here is not whether appellee had a right to keep his files from prying eyes, but whether the information taken from those files falls under the

3. "To support an action of trespass to a chattel where the invasion of interests does not result in its destruction or in a dispossession thereof, it was early held there must be some physical harm to the chattel or to its possessor. Unlike the action of trespass quare clasum fregit in the case of land, no action could be maintained for a mere harmless intermeddling with goods. The possessor's proprietary interest in the inviolability of his personal property did not receive that protection which the similar interest in the possession of land or the dignitary interest in the inviolability of the person receives."

F. Harper & F. James, The Law of Torts § 2.3. (Footnotes omitted.)

4. United States v. Bottone, 2 Cir., 365 F.2d 389, cert. denied, 385 U.S. 974 (1966).

5. See International News Service v. Associated Press, 248 U.S. 215, 246 (1918) (opinion of Mr. Justice Holmes).

The traditional rule has been that conversion will lie only for the taking of tangible property, or rights embodied in a tangible token necessary for the enforcement of those rights. This overly restrictive rule has recently been relaxed in favor of the reasonable proposition that any intangible generally protected as personal property may be the subject matter of a suit for conversion. [citation]

6. This protection is developed by the branch of the law known as common-law copyright, which reserves to an author the right of first publication of his work.

7. See, e.g., United States v. Bottone, supra Note 4 (employees who sold photocopies of documents describing drug company's methods of manufacturing convicted of transporting stolen goods across state lines).

protection of the law of property, enforceable by a suit for conversion. In our view, it does not. The information included the contents of letters to appellee from supplicants, and office records of other kinds, the nature of which is not fully revealed by the record. Insofar as we can tell, none of it amounts to literary property, to scientific invention, or to secret plans formulated by appellee for the conduct of commerce. Nor does it appear to be information held in any way for sale by appellee, analogous to the fresh news copy produced by a wire service.[8]

Appellee complains, not of the misappropriation of property bought or created by him, but of the exposure of information either (1) injurious to his reputation or (2) revelatory of matters which he believes he has a right to keep to himself. Injuries of this type are redressed at law by suit for libel and invasion of privacy respectively, where defendants' liability for those torts can be established under the limitations created by common law and by the Constitution.[9]

Because no conversion of the physical contents of appellee's files took place, and because the information copied from the documents in those files has not been shown to be property subject to protection by suit for conversion, the District Court's ruling that appellants are guilty of conversion must be reversed.

So ordered.

TAMM, CIRCUIT JUDGE (concurring). Some legal scholars will see in the majority opinion—as distinguished from its actual holding—an ironic aspect. Conduct for which a law enforcement officer would be soundly castigated is, by the phraseology of the majority opinion, found tolerable; conduct which, if engaged in by government agents would lead to the suppression of evidence obtained by these means, is approved when used for the profit of the press. There is an anomaly lurking in this situation: the news media regard themselves as quasi-public institutions yet they demand immunity from the restraints which they vigorously demand be placed on government. That which is regarded as a mortal taint on information secured by any illegal conduct of government would appear from the majority opinion to be permissible as a technique or modus operandi for the journalist. Some will find this confusing, but I am not free to act on my own views under the doctrine of stare decisis which I consider binding upon me.

Note

Question: Is restitution an alternate remedy?

MATTSON v. COMMERCIAL CREDIT BUSINESS LOANS, INC.

Supreme Court of Oregon, In Banc, 1986.
301 Or. 407, 723 P.2d 996.

CAMPBELL, JUSTICE. This case involves conversion of lumber and the payment to defendant of the proceeds from the converted lumber. Plaintiffs,

8. See International News Service v. Associated Press, supra Note 5.

9. We have held that appellee is not entitled to summary judgment for invasion of privacy. Appellee originally sued appellants for libel, but has dropped this claim during the course of the litigation.

owners of the converted lumber, sought recovery of the proceeds from the sale of the lumber from the defendant creditor of the converter based on two claims for relief. The first was labeled money had and received, pursuant to which plaintiffs requested actual and punitive damages. The second, which was labeled unjust enrichment, requested a constructive trust.

Plaintiffs and West Coast Lumber Sales, which is not a party to this action, had a contract whereby West Coast would cut plaintiffs' logs at plaintiffs' site for orders pre-sold by West Coast and approved by plaintiffs. In May 1980, West Coast removed 285,000 board feet of lumber from plaintiffs' site without plaintiffs' approval. In September 1980, plaintiffs sued West Coast seeking only money damages for conversion of the lumber. Plaintiffs did not seek replevin, or an injunction to prevent the sale of the lumber, or a constructive trust on the proceeds.

In February 1981, while the litigation between plaintiffs and West Coast was pending, Commercial Credit, defendant in this action, opened a line of credit for West Coast which was secured by inventory and accounts. West Coast's attorney advised defendant of the pending litigation between plaintiffs and West Coast, but the attorney advised defendant that the existence of the litigation did not prevent defendant from making a loan to West Coast so long as plaintiffs were making no claim to the collateral on which defendant was relying in making the loan. In June 1982, plaintiffs won a judgment for $192,011.17 against West Coast for conversion. Shortly thereafter, West Coast filed a petition for bankruptcy.

Under the terms of the accounts receivable contract between West Coast and defendant, all money received by West Coast was turned over to defendant; defendant would then make fresh advances. During the one and one-half years that the contract was in operation, defendant loaned West Coast approximately $2,000,000 more than it received back. Defendant declared West Coast in default in July 1982.

During the pendency of the bankruptcy proceeding, plaintiffs learned that defendant claimed a security interest in all of West Coast's inventory, including the converted lumber and the money generated from the sales of the converted lumber. In March 1983, plaintiffs filed this action asserting a claim against the proceeds West Coast received from the sale of the converted lumber which, plaintiffs asserted, defendant received as part of the revolving credit arrangement with West Coast.

Defendant moved for summary judgment and the trial court granted the motion. The Court of Appeals affirmed without opinion. We reverse and remand. * * *

Plaintiffs claim that summary judgment could have been based on one of two arguments which defendant presented to the trial court. First, plaintiffs were not entitled to the money generated by the sale of the converted lumber because defendant had a security interest in those proceeds under its accounts receivable financing arrangement with West Coast. Second, even in the absence of a valid security interest, plaintiffs could not recover proceeds from the sale of converted property from third parties; plaintiffs were limited either to recovering the converted lumber from third parties to whom it had been sold, or to recovering the proceeds from such sales from the converter. Plaintiffs contend that the granting of summary judgment on either of these bases was error.

[The court ruled that] defendant had no security interest which could prevail over plaintiffs' claimed rights to proceeds from the sale of the converted lumber.

The trial court may also have granted summary judgment on the basis that, even in the absence of a valid security interest, plaintiffs could not recover proceeds from the sale of the converted property from third parties. Plaintiffs assert that they are entitled to recover identifiable proceeds based on the theories of tracing rights and unjust enrichment.

In moving for summary judgment, defendant argued that such tracing and recovery of proceeds are not permitted at common law. Although we have found no cases involving the precise fact situation involved here, there are cases which have permitted tracing and recovery from third parties. As one writer has noted:

> "As far back as 1705, courts have held that the victim of conversion could recover the proceeds from the sale of the converted property by the wrongdoer. The early cases justified the result through a fiction that the plaintiff could 'suppose the sale made by his consent, and bring an action for the money [so obtained], as money received to his use.' Lamine v. Dorrell, 2 Ld Raym. 1216, 92 Eng Rep 303 (1705). Modern cases base recovery of the sale proceeds on the principle of unjust enrichment."

Oesterle, Deficiencies of the Restitutionary Right to Trace Misappropriated Property in Equity and in UCC § 9–306, 68 Cornell L.Rev. 172, 219 (1983).

In addition, tracing doctrine operates against innocent transferees who receive no legal title and transferees who are not bona fide purchasers and receive legal but not equitable title. If either type of transferee exchanges the acquired property for other property, or receives income from the acquired property, tracing may apply.

As Professor Palmer notes, "There is no theoretical limit on the number of transactions or changes in form through which the claimant will be allowed to trace." 1 Palmer, Law of Restitution 178 (1978). For example,

> "In a decision of the Third Circuit the president of the plaintiff corporation misappropriated $170,000 of its funds, bought bonds with the money, and transferred the bonds to the two defendant corporations which he organized and controlled. The proceeds from the sale of these bonds were used in part by the defendants to develop and perfect inventions and patents; in addition, the remaining assets of the defendant corporations were found to be the product of the bonds. The court ordered specific restitution of the patents, inventions, and all other assets of the defendant corporations. [Flannery v. Flannery Bolt Co., 108 F2d 531 (3d Cir 1939)]."

Professor Goode notes that under English law an owner may follow proceeds from the disposition of converted property into the hands of a third party. Goode, The Right to Trace and Its Impact in Commercial Transactions —I, 92 L.Q.Rev. 360, 376 (1978). Goode also provides the following example with facts similar to those involved in this case:

> "Suppose, for example, that B, holding goods as O's bailee, wrongfully sells them to T1 and passes the proceeds to T2, who takes as a volunteer or with notice of B's breach of duty. Here there are infringements of no less than four different rights vested in O; a right to possession of the original goods against B; a like right against T1; a right to require B to account for the proceeds; and a like right against T2. Possible remedies open to O are (i) against B, a claim

for damages for conversion of the goods, a personal claim at common law to the proceeds as money had and received, and a personal claim in equity to account for the proceeds as a constructive trustee; (ii) against T1, a claim for damages for conversion, or a claim for delivery up of the goods and damages for their detention; (iii) *against T2, a personal claim at common law for money had and received and a proprietary claim in equity by way of a tracing order.*

Goode, The Right to Trace and Its Impact in Commercial Transactions—II, 92 L.Q.Rev. 528, 541 (1978). (Emphasis added.) Defendant's position in this case is analogous to "T2."

Defendant argues that the tracing of proceeds of converted goods in the hands of third party transferees should not be permitted because "the parties liable would increase like an inverted pyramid ever upward and outward" making such tracing commercially impracticable. Defendant asserts that under plaintiffs' theory if West Coast had used the proceeds from the sale of the converted lumber to pay its employees, its employees would be liable to plaintiffs. Similarly, each lumber company that bought plaintiffs' lumber presumably later resold it and used those proceeds to pay its bills. Defendant argues that under plaintiffs' theory the creditors of subsequent converters who are paid with those proceeds are also liable.

Defendant's commercial impracticability argument ignores the reality that tracing of proceeds into the hands of third, fourth, fifth, etc. party transferees is permitted under the Uniform Commercial Code. [§ 9–306(2)] indicates that tracing proceeds into the hands of remote transferees is considered commercially practicable. [§ 9–306(2)] provides:

"(2) Except where * * * otherwise provide[d], a security interest continues in collateral notwithstanding sale, exchange or other disposition thereof unless the disposition was authorized by the secured party in the security agreement or otherwise, and also continues in any identifiable proceeds including collections received by the debtor."

Tracing proceeds into the hands of third party transferees is routinely sanctioned in a variety of UCC contexts. See, e.g., In Re Guaranteed Muffler Supply Co., Inc., 1 B.R. 324, 27 UCC Rep. 1217 (Bankr.N.D.Ga.1979) (permitting secured creditor to trace proceeds from sale of debtor's inventory and accounts into hands of third-party transferee); Baker Prod. Credit v. Long Cr. Meat, 266 Or. 643, 513 P.2d 1129 (1973) (allowing creditor with security interest in farm products to recover proceeds from sale of products from third-party transferees).

Defendant's argument also ignores the fact that a bona fide purchaser would cut off plaintiffs' tracing rights. See Lane County Escrow v. Smith, Coe, 277 Or. 273, 285, 560 P.2d 608 (1977). Section 208(1) of the Restatement on Restitution provides:

"(1) Where a person wrongfully disposes of property of another knowing that the disposition is wrongful and in exchange therefore other property is transferred to a third person, the other can enforce a constructive trust or an equitable lien upon the property, unless the third person is a bona fide purchaser."

The creditors or employees of the companies that bought the lumber are analogous to purchasers in that they are exchanging their services for money. If they "purchased" in good faith without knowledge that the money they received was proceeds from stolen property, they would be like bona fide purchasers and thus would also cut off plaintiffs' tracing rights.

Whether defendant is a bona fide purchaser cutting off plaintiffs' tracing rights is a question of material fact which precludes summary judgment. An innocent purchaser is one who has no reasonable grounds to suspect that the person from whom he buys an article did not have good title. As this court noted long ago, whether one is a purchaser in good faith is an issue of fact that must be determined from many circumstances, including actual and constructive notice and suspicious circumstances. The facts surrounding the transaction, including any unusual or peculiar business methods of the vendor that were known to the purchaser, may properly be submitted to the jury to be considered on the ultimate question of good or bad faith. * * *

In addition, plaintiffs' right to recover under a tracing theory is limited by their ability to trace the proceeds from the converted lumber. If they cannot trace the proceeds to defendant then they cannot recover under this theory. Plaintiffs submitted evidentiary materials to the trial court describing how such tracing could be established. Defendant claims that the proceeds from the sale of the converted lumber have long since passed through its hands to undetermined third parties. Plaintiffs' ability to identify and trace proceeds from the sale of the converted lumber is evidentiary, a matter of proof. It is not an appropriate basis for summary judgment. * * *

In light of these genuine issues of material fact, the grant of summary judgment to defendant was error. The decision of the Court of Appeals is reversed. The case is remanded to the trial court for further proceedings.

FUR & WOOL TRADING CO. v. GEORGE I. FOX, INC.

Court of Appeals of New York, 1927.
245 N.Y. 215, 156 N.E. 670.

ANDREWS, J. The complaint alleges that goods belonging to the plaintiff were taken from its possession by force. The defendant, receiving them with knowledge of the facts, sold them at a large profit but at a price unknown to the plaintiff. It has refused a demand to account for the sums received. The plaintiff, consequently, brings an action in equity to compel the defendant to disclose what amounts were so received by it, to repay the proceeds of such sale, and it asks for general equitable relief. This it has been held may not be done. The only redress is such as the law may give. Therefore, upon motion, the complaint has been dismissed.

Some remedy at law there certainly is. The plaintiff might sue for conversion. If successful, it would, as a general rule, recover a personal judgement for the value of the goods at the time and place of the conversion. Or if the goods had remained in the hands of the wrongdoer, an action in replevin would have afforded a complete remedy for their recovery. Or, again, if they have been sold, there is an action for money had and received, resulting in a personal judgment for the proceeds. If the plaintiff has no information as to this sum it may acquire it, should it be necessary to enable it to frame a complaint, by an examination of the defendant. Even though this be so, is the plaintiff entitled to still other relief in excess of what a court of law is competent to give? Or is his case one where, under historic rules, equity has been wont to assume jurisdiction?

At the outset we should say that the action may not be sustained as a bill of discovery, brought as such a bill was, not as an end in itself but as an aid to an independent proceeding. A complete remedy of this character being otherwise provided, such an action no longer survives. Civ.Prac.Act § 345. But in certain cases equity will entertain a suit for an accounting. This is so where such a relation exists between the parties as under established principles entitles the one to demand it of the other. A trustee in possession of trust funds may in a proper case be called to account to his cestui que trust, and this rule is enforced as well where the trust is implied as where it is express.

Clearly a thief, having sold stolen goods, may be treated as a trustee of the proceeds and also of any property into which they have been transformed, so long as either may be identified. Under such circumstances broader relief may be obtained in equity than at law. Where necessary, an accounting may be had. A lien may be declared. A surrender of the trust property may be decreed. Newton v. Porter, 69 N.Y. 133, American Sugar Ref. Co. v. Fancher, 145 N.Y. 522, 40 N.E. 206. The added reason that the defendant is insolvent is not essential.

Where, however, the specific proceeds, in their original or in their transformed shape, may not be traced then no lien may be obtained. No identification—no lien. The complaint will not be dismissed, however, if ultimately it is determined that such proceeds are not found in possession of the defendant. Because a trustee has mingled them with his general funds, the right to a resort to equity is not ended. The same rule exists as to a trustee ex maleficio. If equity has properly obtained jurisdiction, it may retain it so as to afford proper relief—personal judgment in such a case against the wrongdoer.

At least such jurisdiction is obtained where the trust fund has come into the hands of the trustee, where the cestui que trust is ignorant of its amount and of its subsequent fate, and where the trustee refuses to account. Such either by express statement or by fair inference is the complaint we consider. We so held in Lightfoot v. Davis, 198 N.Y. 261, 91 N.E. 582. Bonds are stolen and sold. Years thereafter the estate of the thief was required to account for the proceeds and repay that amount to the true owner from its general assets. The only relief prayed for, we said, was that the administrator "may account and pay over the amount of said bonds, and the income thereof if it can be traced, and, if it cannot be traced," that the plaintiff have judgment for the sum of $16,000, and we added: "The method by which equity proceeds in all these cases is to turn the wrongdoer into a trustee. If it may do so for the purpose of subjecting identified funds to the claim of the defrauded party, I do not see why it should not pursue the same method wherever it is necessary to protect the rights of the original owner. In the case of an actual trustee the cestui que trust may not only reclaim the trust property if he is able to trace it, but, failing to trace it, he is entitled to an accounting and personal judgment against the trustee."

* * * The judgment * * * should be reversed and the motion for judgment dismissing the complaint denied, with costs in all courts.

Lehman, J., dissents.

Notes

1. Equity has usually hesitated to hold that a thief is a "trustee." The excuse is usually that plaintiff's legal remedy is adequate. United States v. Bitter Root

Development Co., 200 U.S. 451, 472 (1906). Defendant allegedly trespassed on government lands and cut approximately $2,000,000 of timber. The principal wrongdoer, Daly, passed the moneys realized through various corporations, eventually leaving a personal estate of $12,000,000. The United States sought an accounting and to impose a trust on the estate. The Court stated:

"The principal ground upon which it is claimed that the remedy at law [for trover or trespass—the Court did not mention quasi-contract] is inadequate is really nothing more than a difficulty of proving the case against the defendants. The bill shows that whatever was done in the way of cutting timber and carrying it away was done by the defendants as tort feasors, and the various devices alleged to have been resorted to by the deceased, Daly, by way of organizing different corporations, in order to, as alleged, 'cover up his tracks and to render it more difficult for the complainant to make proof of his action,' does not in the least tend to give a court of equity jurisdiction on that account. It is simply a question of evidence to show who did the wrong and upon that point the fact could be ascertained as readily at law as in equity.

"The complainant is entitled in an action at law to an inspection of the books and records of these various corporations, and it has the same power to obtain the facts therefrom in that action as it would in a suit in equity."

The Court's real reluctance to extend the constructive trust doctrine to thieves has some roots in the unwillingness to extend equitable *accounting* where there was no fiduciary relationship between the parties. "Bills for account" in equity have been regarded as limited in scope. See Lile, Bills for Account, 8 Va.L.Rev. 181 (1922). But the same necessity that has rendered complicated financial transactions unsuitable for jury trials in the past, may exist in cases like United States v. Bitter Root Development Co., supra note 1. On the other hand, where the exact amount of property converted is unknown even by the owner, the bill in equity for a trust, accounting and discovery may shift the proof of a tort (and perhaps crimes) to the converter.

2. Lamb v. Rooney, 72 Neb. 322, 100 N.W. 410 (1904). Defendant bought stolen cattle, resold them, and purchased other cattle with the proceeds. A "resulting" trust was imposed on the new herd to the extent of the funds traced to it.

3. In Darlagiannis v. Darlagiannis, 48 A.D.2d 875, 369 N.Y.S.2d 475 (1975), plaintiff sought an equitable accounting of her share of wedding gifts. *Held:* Plaintiff is not precluded from equitable relief predicated upon a fiduciary relation, even though a legal remedy may be available, citing *Fur & Wool Trading Co.*

4. Eichengrun, Remedying the Remedy of Accounting, 60 Ind.L.J. 463 (1985), argues that the remedy of accounting should be available to recover the profit made by a tortfeasor from the conversion of another's property.

C. REAL PROPERTY

1. GENERAL RULES OF DAMAGES

ORNDORFF v. CHRISTIANA COMMUNITY BUILDERS

Court of Appeal, Fourth District, Division 1, 1990.
217 Cal.App.3d 683, 266 Cal.Rptr. 193.

BENKE, ACTING PRESIDING JUSTICE. Plaintiffs have lived in their home since 1977. They have no plans to leave it. Unfortunately their home was built on defectively compacted soil. * * *

The Orndorffs presented evidence that further settlement was likely and that, in light of future settlement, a pier or caisson and beam system was necessary to repair their house. The Orndorffs' expert estimated it would cost $221,792.68 to install such a system. In addition to the cost of repair, the Orndorffs presented evidence they would be required to incur $21,747 in additional engineering costs, permit fees and relocation expenses while the repairs were completed. * * *

[The trial judge] found the measure of damages for construction defects was either the diminution in value or the likely repair costs and that in this case an award of repair costs, plus relocation expenses, was appropriate. He found fill settlement was likely to continue and that a pier or caisson and grade system was the most efficient method of repair. Thus he awarded the Orndorffs the $243,539.95 needed to install a pier and grade system and pay the Orndorffs' relocation expenses while the repairs were performed. * * *

On appeal the defendants argue the measure of damages in construction defect cases is the lesser of the diminution in value caused by the defect or the cost of repair. Since the Orndorffs' appraiser testified their home was worth $67,500 without repair and would be worth $238,500 following repairs, the defendants claim the trial court had no power to award more than the $171,000 diminution in value established by the Orndorffs' appraiser.

In their reply brief the defendants also argue the trial court erred because it gave the Orndorffs an amount needed to repair the defect, rather than an amount needed to repair the damage caused by the defect.

We do not find the law as rigid as the defendants suggest. Where, as here, the plaintiffs have a personal reason to repair and the costs of repair are not unreasonable in light of the damage to the property and the value after repair, costs of repair which exceed the diminution in value may be awarded. (See Heninger v. Dunn (1980) 101 Cal.App.3d 858, 863–866, 162 Cal.Rptr. 104 (*Heninger*).) In *Heninger* the defendants bulldozed a road over the plaintiffs' land. The road damaged or killed 225 of plaintiffs' trees and destroyed much vegetative undergrowth. However because of improved access the trial court found the road actually increased the value of the land from $179,000 to $184,000. The trial court also found it would cost $221,647 to replace the dead or dying trees and that the undergrowth could be restored for $19,610. Because the value of the property had been increased, the trial court denied the plaintiffs any award of damages.

The Court of Appeal reversed and remanded. In rejecting the trial court's rigid approach to damage calculation, the Court of Appeal stated: "The rule precluding recovery of restoration costs in excess of diminution in value is, however, not of invariable application. Restoration costs may be awarded even though they exceed the decrease in market value if 'there is a reason personal to the owner for restoring the original condition' (Rest.2d Torts, § 929, com. b, at pp. 545–546), or 'where there is reason to believe that the plaintiff will, in fact, make the repairs' (22 Am.Jur.2d, Damages, § 132, at p. 192)." *Heninger.* * * *

In *Heninger* the court also discussed a number of cases from other jurisdictions which allowed similar recoveries in cases involving destruction of shade or ornamental trees which were of personal value to their owners. "Where such trees or shrubbery are destroyed by a trespasser, '[s]ound principle and persuasive authority support the allowance to an aggrieved landowner of the fair cost of restoring his land to a reasonable approximation of its former condition, without necessary limitation to the diminution in the market value of the land * * *.' [citations] If restoration of the land to a reasonable approximation of its former condition is impossible or impracticable, the landowner may recover the value of the trees or shrubbery, either as timber or for their aesthetic qualities, again without regard to the diminution in the value of the land. [citations] The overall principles by which the courts are to be guided are 'flexibility of approach and full compensation to the owner, within the overall limitation of reasonableness.' [citation]" Thus the Court of Appeal in *Heninger* held that "If the trial court determined that appellants had personal reasons for restoring their land to its original condition, and that such a restoration could be achieved at a cost that was not unreasonable in relation to the damage inflicted and the value of the land prior to the trespass, the court should have exercised its discretion to award such restoration costs."

Although the Court of Appeal in *Heninger* found that it would not be reasonable to award the plaintiffs the $221,647 needed to entirely restore the land, "On retrial, the court's determination whether a reasonable restoration is possible should focus on the question whether an award of the cost of restoring the vegetative undergrowth (or some other method of covering the scar on the land and preventing further erosion) would achieve compensation within the overall limits of what the court determines to be just and reasonable."

Here the "personal reason" exception adopted in *Heninger* supports the trial court's award. Contrary to the defendants' argument, the "personal reason" exception does not require that the Orndorffs own a "unique" home. Rather all that is required is some personal use by them and a bona fide desire to repair or restore. For instance in *Heninger* the court relied on the plaintiff's simple statement that " 'I think the land is beautiful, the natural forest beautiful, and I would like to see it that way.' " According to the commentators to the Restatement, "if a building such as homestead *is used for a purpose personal to the owner,* the damages ordinarily include an amount for repairs, even though this might be greater than the entire value of the building. So, when a garden has been maintained in a city in connection with a dwelling house, the owner is entitled to recover the expense of putting the garden in its original condition even though the market value of the premises has not been decreased by the defendant's invasion." (Rest.2d., Torts § 929, com. b, p. 546, italics added.) * * *

We also find untenable the defendants' argument that by allowing recovery in excess of diminution in value we will somehow distort the loss distribution goals which the doctrine of strict liability in tort was designed to foster. * * *

By requiring that repair costs bear a reasonable relationship to value before harm and to the level of harm actually suffered, the *Heninger* case prevents the unusual or bizarre results the defendants in this case contend would occur should we stray in any manner from a diminution in value measure of damages. Contrary to the defendants' argument, application of the personal reason exception does not permit a plaintiff to insist on reconstruction of a unique product where the cost of repair will far exceed either the value of the product or the damage the defendant has caused. As we interpret *Heninger,* the owner of a unique home or automobile cannot insist on its reconstruction where the cost to do so far exceeds the value of the home or automobile.

Nor are repair costs appropriate where only slight damage has occurred and the cost of repair is far in excess of the loss in value.

Here the damages awarded are well within the limitations imposed by *Heninger.* The record establishes that the Orndorffs' home was worth $238,500 in an undamaged condition. A total award—$243,539.95—which is 2.5 percent greater than the undamaged value of the realty, is in our view, well within reason.

However, it bears emphasis that even where the repair costs are reasonable in relation to the value of the property, those costs must also be reasonable in relation to the harm caused. Here the trial court's finding that fill settlement was likely to continue and the Orndorffs' appraiser's opinion the home was worth only $67,500 in its present condition, suggest the damage sustained was indeed significant. Plainly this is not a case where the tortfeasors' conduct improved the value of the real property or only diminished it slightly. Rather we believe where, as here, the damage to a home has deprived it of most of its value, an award of substantial repair costs is appropriate.

Without citation to any case which has articulated the distinction, the defendants argue the trial court had no power to award the amount needed to cure the defect as opposed to the amount needed to repair the damage caused by the defect. In particular defendants contend the damage the Orndorffs' house has suffered could be remedied by installation of the less expensive reinforced mat.

While there may be cases where repairing damage rather than curing a defect would be appropriate, this is not one of them. As we have seen the trial court found that further settlement is likely. The Orndorffs presented evidence that in light of future settlement the only way of preventing future damage was installation of the more costly pier and grade system. In giving the Orndorffs the amount needed to install such a system it is plain the trial court accepted the Orndorffs' evidence. Thus the record demonstrates the amount needed to repair all the damage caused by the defect is the amount needed to install a pier and grade system.

Judgment affirmed.

Notes

1. *Repair v. Diminution in Value for Real Property Cases.* Essentially the same debate about damages occurs when a building is damaged as when the barge was damaged in Hewlett v. Barge Bertie, supra p. 53. "L" Investments, Ltd. v. Lynch, 212 Neb. 319, 322 N.W.2d 651 (1982): Defendant's truck pushed in an 8′ × 4′ portion of the wall of plaintiff's 100′ × 100′ building and damaged some windows. Repair estimates were $2,640; but plaintiff introduced no evidence of diminished value. The court said:

"Dobbs, in his Handbook on the Law of Remedies, observes: 'Most courts follow the rule that repair costs, when used as a measure, may not exceed the diminution in value of the property. Several courts have varied this formula by allowing repair or restoration cost to exceed the diminution in the value of the property but limiting such cost to the total pretort value of the property * * *. A few courts have allowed recovery for cost of restoration that exceeds the diminished value of the property, or have at least stated that cost of restoration is the measure without any ceiling.' § 5.1 at 317–18 (1973).

"An examination of just some of the cases reported discloses that there may in fact be as many as four or five different rules. [citations from 22 states]

"An examination of our own cases discloses that the confusion which has occurred elsewhere may also be found in Nebraska. * * *

"We now declare that the proper measure of damages for injury to an improvement upon real estate which can be repaired is as follows: Except as otherwise hereinafter limited, where an improvement upon realty is damaged without damage to the realty itself and where the nature of the thing damaged is such that it is capable of being repaired or restored and the cost of doing so is capable of reasonable ascertainment, the measure of damages for its negligent damage is the reasonable cost of repairing or restoring the property in like kind and quality. This would be in addition to any other consequential damages which the injured party may establish by proper proof.

"While certain of the writers, and perhaps some courts, argue that right of recovery should be without limitation, we believe the award for such damage should not exceed the market value of the property immediately preceding the damage to the property. It seems that one ought not to be able to recover a greater amount for partial destruction than one could recover for total destruction."

2. We return to the cost-value issue in breaches of contract. Hourihan v. Grossman Holdings Ltd—Grossman Holdings Ltd v. Hourihan, supra, pp. 1126–31.

3. Suppose that the damaged building is a special purpose building such as a church or boy's club where no active market exists. How should damages be measured? In Gramercy Boys' Club Association v. City of New York, 74 N.Y.2d 678, 543 N.Y.S.2d 372, 541 N.E.2d 401 (1989), replacement cost less depreciation was held to be the proper measure.

Where this measure is used, a test of reasonableness is imposed. Trinity Church v. John Hancock Mutual Life Insurance Co., 399 Mass. 43, 50, 502 N.E.2d 532, 536 (1987) involved damage to Trinity Church, a national historical landmark, during the construction of the John Hancock Tower in Boston. "Not only must the cost of replacement or reconstruction be reasonable, the replacement or reconstruction itself must be reasonably necessary in light of the damage inflicted by a particular defendant."

4. *Profits lost, or delayed.* Short v. Wise, 239 Kan. 171, 175–77, 718 P.2d 604, 607–08 (1986): "Short next claims he was entitled to the profits from oil production he lost when Wise's actions caused him to cease production. Finding that Wise had either breached the terms of the grant or trespassed on Short's rights and thus wrongfully caused Short to shut down production on the Chambers lease from May 23, 1980, to October 16, 1980, the court awarded Short $22,792 as lost profits during the shutdown. * * *

"An oil producer who suffers a delay in production suffers no loss of his oil reserve because the reserve is still available to the producer. A delay in production of oil may cause damages because of a market loss sustained by the producer. Unlike Mai, Short actually sustained damages because he was unable to produce the oil during a period when oil prices dropped.

"Exhibits presented at trial indicated that Short lost 5 barrels a day for 146 days.

"From 5/23/80—10/15/80

Income from oil from producing Chambers wells 5bb per day for 146 days:		$27,625.00
Ave. daily production '75–'79	=	4.97bb
Ave. daily production '81–'82	=	5.11 bb
05/24/80–07/31/80 69 days × 5bb × $39	=	13,455.00
08/01/80–08/31/80 31 days × 5bb × $38	=	5,890.00
09/01/80–10/16/80 46 days × 5bb × $36	=	8,280.00
		$27,625.00"

Examination of this exhibit indicates that the price of crude declined roughly three dollars a barrel between May 24, 1980, and October 16, 1980.

5/24/80–7/31/80	69 days × 5 bb × $3	=	1,035.00
8/1/80–8/31/80	31 days × 5 bb × $2	=	310.00
			$1,345.00

"The $1,345.00 figure represents the loss in market value of plaintiff's reserves occasioned by the five-month delay in production. The trial judge's award to Short for lost profits due to Wise's action is reduced to the loss in the market value of the oil."

Has the court overlooked the credit-for-benefit rule?

5. For more about the "personal reason" exception, see McKinney v. Christiana Community Builders, 229 Cal.App.3d 611, 280 Cal.Rptr. 242 (1991).

UNITED STATES v. EDEN MEMORIAL PARK ASSOCIATION

United States Court of Appeals, Ninth Circuit, 1965.
350 F.2d 933.

CRAIG, DISTRICT JUDGE. This is a suit in condemnation wherein the United States seeks to condemn 11.14 acres in fee and a .60 acre slope easement from the Appellee and Cross–Appellant, Eden Memorial Park Association, for use in the construction of the San Diego Freeway, a part of the Federal Interstate Highway System.

At the time of the taking, Eden owned 60.51 acres, 53.96 acres of which were zoned for cemetery purposes, and 6.5 acres were not so zoned. Of the 11.74 acres taken, approximately 5.2 acres were zoned for cemetery purposes and 6.5 acres were not so zoned. * * *

At the time of the acquisition of the instant property by Eden in 1953, the California State Highway Department had already planned a highway to traverse a portion of the Eden property. Apparently because of this fact, the Los Angeles City Planning Commission withheld a conditional use permit or zone variance for the 6.5 acres then contemplated to be used for highway purposes. * * *

The first question raised by Appellant is whether the trial court erred in admitting evidence of the land owner directed to capitalization of future income. The American Institute of Real Estate Appraisers in its work "The Appraisal of Real Estate" (1964) states:

"Appraisers commonly think of value in three ways:

1. The current cost of reproducing a property less depreciation from all sources, that is, deterioration and functional and economic obsolescence.

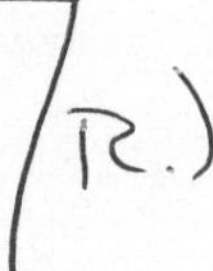

2. The value which the property's net earning power will support, based upon a capitalization of net income.

3. The value indicated by recent sales of comparable properties in the market.

"The three approaches—Cost, income, and market data—are based on these three facets of value. In the majority of his assignments, the appraiser utilizes all three approaches. On occasion he may believe the value indication from one approach will be more significant than from the other two, yet he will use all three as a check against each and to test his own judgment. Obviously there are appraisal problems in which they cannot all be applied. A value indication for vacant land cannot be obtained through the use of the cost approach, nor one for a specialized property such as municipal garden by the market data approach, nor but rarely for an owner-occupied home by the income approach. The use of all three approaches is pertinent in the solution of most appraisal problems; their application is well established in appraisal technique and held to be part of the fundamental procedure."

We conclude the Court properly admitted the evidence as to capitalization of income to establish the value of the property taken.

The second question raised by Appellant is whether the trial court erred in the rejection of certain evidence offered by Appellant as to "comparable sales." Evidence of comparable sales is an appropriate method to the determination of value in condemnation cases. * * *

Whether or not a sale constitutes a "comparable sale" so as to constitute evidence of value is within the sound discretion of the trial court. * * * [T]he record in this case does not disclose an abuse of discretion by the trial court. * * *

The final question for us to determine is Cross–Appellant's assertion that the 6.5 acres not zoned for cemetery purposes should have been valued as though the land had been zoned for cemetery purposes.

At the trial of this case, the Court allowed the jury to consider evidence as to the probability of a change in the zoning of the 6.5 acres to cemetery use. It is obvious from the jury's verdict that it considered the possibility of such a change as an extremely remote one, if in fact there was any possibility at all.

In a condemnation proceeding the land taken must be valued as it exists at the time of taking and subject to the then applicable zoning regulations. * * *

The record in this case discloses that at the time the land owner acquired the property it was contemplated by state and local authorities that some portion of the property would ultimately be required for highway purposes. At the time the land owner sought a zoning classification for cemetery purposes it was aware of the possible future use for highway purposes.

It was not an abuse of the trial court's discretion in rejecting Cross–Appellant's request to value the 6.5 acres as though zoned for cemetery purposes.

Judgment is affirmed.

Notes

1. *Valuation of Property in Terms of Use.* The problem of determining the value of realty is not restricted to indemnity for damage. Valuation is also required to assess taxes, to compensate in eminent domain cases (like *Eden Memorial Park*), and to perform contracts. In valuing real property courts seem to devote more attention to the so-called "use value" than in the cases of physical damage to the property. Owners argue that courts should value the property in

terms of higher potential uses rather than the value in terms of its present use. Methods for taking account of potential uses vary. Some courts permit juries to consider value based on a hypothetical "best use" while others state that value must be determined on the basis of "all available uses." 1 Orgel, Valuation Under the Law of Eminent Domain § 30 (2d ed. 1953) gives the example of land that would sell for $5,000 as a farm, $10,000 as a residence, $15,000 as an office building, and $20,000 if it were good for nothing but oil land. The "best use" rule has been rejected because of the fear that it leads to over-valuation based on hindsight. Sacramento Southern Railroad v. Heilbron, 156 Cal. 408, 412, 104 P. 979, 981 (1909) stated the rule:

"It is seen, therefore, that this court by its latest utterances has definitively aligned itself with the great majority of the courts in holding that damages must be measured by the market value of the land at the time it is taken, that the test is not the value for a special purpose, but the fair market value of the land in view of all the purposes to which it is naturally adapted; that therefore while evidence that it is 'valuable' for this or that or another purpose may always be given and should be freely received, the value in terms of money, the price, which one or another witness may think the land would bring for this or that or the other specific purposes is not admissible as an element in determining that market value. For such evidence opens wide the door to unlimited vagaries and speculations concerning problematical prices which might under possible contingencies be paid for the land, and distracts the mind of the jury from the single question—that of market value—the highest sum which the property is worth to persons generally, purchasing in the open market in consideration of the land's adaptability for any proven use."

2. Suppose that the evidence shows that the condemned property is dedicated for cemetery use and has a potential for 155,900 gravesites. Based on the projected rate of sales, the property has an estimated life of 760 years. Should the appraised value of the land for cemetery purposes of between $817,000 to $3 million be accepted? The court, in Department of Transportation v. James Co., 183 Ga.App. 798, 802, 360 S.E.2d 56, 59 (1987), ruled that these appraisals were speculative and ordered that compensation should be determined on the basis of the "highest and best use for other than cemetery purposes."

3. *The Broad Evidence Rule.* The recognition of only a few basic tests for determining "value" cuts down on litigation time. A number of jurisdictions have sanctioned a more expansive approach described in Miller, Property Losses and the Broad Evidence Rule, 4 Forum 229 (1970):

"In the most general sense, this Rule can be said to mean that the court will consider *any* evidence which logically tends to allow the most accurate estimate of the value of damaged or destroyed property. A New Jersey Court [1] has recently stated what might well be a key note in this area:

> 'Value is a matter of opinion. The adoption of an invariable test of value would only serve to shackle sound opinion in a situation where other factors may overcome or qualify its influence. This cannot be done in the name of Speedy Simple Administration.' * * *

"The Broad Evidence Rule, it must be noted, does not replace either market value or reproduction/replacement, less physical depreciation value. Rather,

1. [Footnotes renumbered.] Messing v. Reliance Ins. Co., 77 N.J.Super. 531, 187 A.2d 49, 51–52 (1962).

courts using the Rule look upon these more traditional measures as mere guides in making a determination of value. * * *

"The Broad Evidence Rule has been recognized either explicitly by name or implicitly by the court's holding in 21 states.

"Many interesting cases have involved the process of determining the actual cash value of buildings under the Broad Evidence Rule. The goal of the Rule is to place '* * * all facts and circumstances which would logically enable the trier of such facts to determine a correct estimate of the loss * * *' of property as it stood on the day of the fire. The jury should be aided by such information as the size and dimensions of the building, the kind and quality of the materials from which it was constructed, its age, the amount of wear and tear to which it has been subjected, its state of repair, and even, unless too remote, the original cost of the building. The area in which a building is located and the obsolescence of its decoration may also be legitimate considerations.

"In the famous case of McAnarney v. Newark Fire Insurance Co.,[2] the basic case from which the Broad Evidence Rule can be traced, the New York Court stated simply that in finding the actual cash value of a building, which could have no real market value, the court must find a value expressed in terms of money."

[Editors' Insert: *McAnarney* involved the destruction of a brewery that had been idled during Prohibition. Under the circumstances market value was irrelevant. Replacement less deterioration was determinable and would have yielded a substantial figure. "Obsolescence," however, reduced the figure. "Obsolescence" is automatically considered when market value is used. It is questionable whether "obsolescence" can ever be justifiable for purely residential realty.]

"One rather interesting New York case, Eshan Realty Corp. v. Stuyvesant Insurance Co.,[3] has even suggested that an older apartment building, abandoned approximately one week prior to the damaging fire, was not necessarily obsolete. Indeed, by conversion and renovation it could be a very useful property. To this New York Court, then, actual cash value was to be figured even on the basis of possible renovation.

"The length to which the New York Courts have gone, in the application of the Broad Evidence Rule, can perhaps best be seen in Girard Insurance Co. v. Taylor.[4] Here, the insured owned a building standing on the land of another person and, within a six month period, if the insured did not remove the building, it would no longer be his. The court held that actual cash value is not relative value, but is real value at the time of the fire, and not a value looking to the time of possible removal."

4. A striking illustration of the liberality of courts in admitting evidence bearing on value is the decision in San Diego Gas & Electric Co. v. Daley, 205 Cal.App.3d 1334, 253 Cal.Rptr. 144 (1988). The court allowed the owner of the condemned property to introduce evidence showing that the use of the condemned land for overhead transmission wires resulted in a depreciation in the market value of the remaining land because of the public's "irrational fear" of electromagnetic radiation from the wires.

2. 247 N.Y. 176, 159 N.E. 902 (1928).

3. 25 Misc.2d 828, 202 N.Y.S.2d 899 (1960), modified on other grounds, 12 A.D.2d 818, 210 N.Y.S.2d 256 (1961).

4. 6 A.D.2d 359, 177 N.Y.S.2d 42 (1958).

a. Value of Cost of Repair

FREEPORT SULPHUR CO. v. THE S/S HERMOSA

United States Court of Appeals, Fifth Circuit, 1976.
526 F.2d 300.

WISDOM, CIRCUIT JUDGE. During the early morning hours of March 21, 1971, the S.S. Hermosa, while attempting to moor at a dock owned by the Freeport Sulphur Company (Freeport), struck the upstream end of the dock, causing severe damage to the structure. The district court held the shipowner, Pansuiza Compania de Navigacion, S.A. (Pansuiza), liable. Pansuiza does not contest its liability per se; the dispute in this case relates to the district court's calculation of damages.

First, of the $84,141.20 Freeport is alleged to have paid for the reconstruction of the dock, it claims about $16,000 as the cost of engineering work performed by its employees. Pansuiza argues that this is an inflated figure and that inhouse services cannot properly be included as an element of damages.

Second, the district court found that the value of the dock was enhanced by its reconstruction, because the repairs extended the useful life of the dock. In deducting the cost of this improvement from Freeport's compensation for its repair expenses, the district court rejected the straight-line depreciation formula commonly used in calculating the costs attributable to the extension of useful life and instead relied on a formula based on the "percentage of useful life extension." Pansuiza contests the court's adoption of this "novel," "unsupported and unsupportable" theory and asserts, moreover, that the court improperly applied its own formula.

Third, Pansuiza objects to the compensation that was awarded to Freeport because, as a result of the collision, Freeport paid for the useful life extension much earlier than such an expenditure would otherwise have been necessary.

Pansuiza's objections to the inclusion of the labor and overhead costs of Freeport's engineering department in the damages award are twofold. First, it asserts that Freeport's use of its own salaried engineers and draftsmen did not involve any additional cost or expense. Second, it argues that the claim for engineering expenses was an inflated figure.

Freeport has arranged with an independent engineering concern to be furnished supplemental personnel when its own salaried engineering staff is overworked. Because Freeport found it unnecessary to tap this outside during the period of the engineering work on the dock, Pansuiza contends that, were it not for the dock work, Freeport's engineers would have been idle or engaged in essentially nonproductive work. Pansuiza argues, therefore, that the engineering work was performed without any additional expense or overhead. We reject this argument as being wholly based on speculation. It is at least as plausible that there were other Freeport projects that would have been worked on by Freeport's internal engineers, but were not of such an emergency nature that they required the immediate employment of the outside firm. * * *

The cost of repairs performed internally by the injured party, including overhead, are recoverable in a negligence action.

The purpose of compensatory damages in tort cases is to place the injured person as nearly as possible in the condition he would have occupied if the wrong had not occurred. When there is a tortious injury to property and the market value of that property is unknown, the amount of damages must be determined by the cost of repairs to the property. These two principles are in apparent conflict when the repairs that are necessary to correct damage caused by negligence enhance the pretort value of the plaintiff's property. In such a case, the increase in value is deducted from the plaintiff's recovery for the cost of repairs.[1] A major issue in the present case is the method of computing the increase in the value in Freeport's dock that was caused by its reconstruction following the collision.

The only betterment to Freeport's dock that was proved is the extension of its remaining useful life. The district court found, as a matter of fact, that the precollision remaining useful life of the dock was 25 years, but that the repairs had extended its useful life to 35 years. This extension of 10 years in its remaining useful life is a benefit to Freeport that should be deducted from its award.[2]

Pansuiza argues that the "correct, long established, and fair" method of accounting for betterment is to compensate the plaintiff only for those repairs that replace the portion of its property that was undepreciated at the time of the tort. At the time of the collision, the old dock was 16 years old and had a remaining useful life of 25 years. It was thus 16/41 or 39 percent depreciated. Pansuiza contends, therefore, that 39 percent of Freeport's repair costs of $84,481.20 should be deducted from its recovery. In support of its argument that the straight-line depreciation method of calculating betterment is the "long established" method applied by the courts in cases where the damaged or destroyed property had a definite life span that had partially elapsed at the time of the accident, Pansuiza cites numerous cases that have applied the formula. [citations]

We stated in Canal Barge Co., Inc. v. Griffith, 5 Cir.1973, 480 F.2d 11, 27, that depreciation is often "a handy tool to reduce the recovery for repair costs to the level necessary to return the injured party to the economic position in which he was found." The underlying issues, however, are whether the repairs extended the useful life of the property and, if so, what portion of the repair costs is attributable to the useful life extension. In Allied Chemical Corp. v. Edmundson Towing Co. [320 F.Supp. 448 (E.D.La.1970)] prior depreciation was a "handy tool" for measuring the nonrecoverable portion of repair costs. The defendant's tugboat had negligently collided with the piling cluster at the plaintiff's dock, causing the cluster's complete destruction. The cost of its replacement was $3500. When new, both the old and the replaced clusters had life expectancies of 20 years; the old cluster was 3½ years old at the time of the collision. The court awarded the plaintiff damages in the amount of 16½/20 of

1. [Footnotes renumbered.] See Restatement of Torts § 928 (Tent.Draft No. 19, 1973): D. Dobbs, Law of Remedies 392 (1973). In The Baltimore, 1869, 75 U.S. 18 Wall. 377, 385–86, dicta indicate that, in negligence cases, there should not be any deduction for new materials furnished in place of the old. This dicta has not generally been followed, as the cases cited throughout of this opinion indicate. Two other cases that denied deductions for new replacements and contain equally broad dicta are distinguishable from the present case. In Paxson Co. v. Board of Chosen Freeholders of Cumberland County, 3 Cir.1912, 201 F. 656, 663, the replacement structure was made of materials inferior to that of the old structure, and it was uncertain whether the new structure was more valuable than the old. And in United States v. Ebinger, 2 Cir.1967, 386 F.2d 557, 561, the damaged property was an integral part of a larger unit, whose realizable value was probably not enhanced by the replacement.

2. When other types of betterment have been proven, their value has been offset against the plaintiff's award. See, e.g., United States v. Ebinger, 386 F.2d 561 (credit for maintenance expenses saved by new structure): Patterson Terminals, Inc. v. S.S. Johannes Frans, E.D.Pa. 1962, 209 F.Supp. 705, 711 (credit for enlargement of caisson).

the replacement cost. Because the damaged piling cluster was completely replaced by a cluster that had a useful life identical with that of the destroyed cluster when it was new, the portion of the destroyed property that had depreciated before the collision accurately measured the extent to which the replacement of the property extended its useful life.

In many of the other cases in which the straight-line depreciation formula has been applied, the court either assumed or explicitly found that the repaired or replaced property had a useful life identical with the old property when it was purchased by the plaintiff. In many cases, however, courts have improperly reduced the plaintiff's recovery by the percentage of depreciation without giving any indication of the expected useful life of the repaired property.

Courts are increasingly recognizing that the "handy tool" of straight-line depreciation should not be used for all occasions. In Oregon v. Tug Go–Getter, 9 Cir.1972, 468 F.2d 1270, for example, the defendant's barge collided with and caused severe damage to the south pier of the plaintiff's bridge. Although the pier was twelve years old and, according to the district court, had a precollision useful life expectancy of eighteen years, the Court of Appeals awarded the plaintiff the full cost of repairs. The court reasoned that the repairs did not add to the life expectancy of the pier because it was an integral part of the bridge, and, regardless of its condition, would have to be replaced when the bridge required replacement. * * *

Thus, where the expected useful life of the property after repairs is the same as it was at the time of its acquisition by the plaintiff, the straight-line depreciation formula should be applied. But where the repairs do not extend the useful life of the property as it existed just before the collision, there should be no deduction for depreciation. In the remaining cases, of which the instant case is an example, the repairs extend the useful life of the property, but to a different degree from the expected useful life of the property at the time of its acquisition by the plaintiff.

The district judge's solution to these cases—in which we concur—requires the calculation of the percentage of the repair expenses representing the cost of the useful life extension. This he termed the "percentage of useful life extension." This percentage is the portion of the total useful life of the repaired property that the useful life extension constitutes. The allocable cost of the useful life extension may then be derived by multiplying this percentage by the total repair expenses. If this allocable cost is then deducted from the total cost of repairs, the resulting damages award will precisely compensate the plaintiff for the cost of restoring his property to its precollision condition.

In the present case the precollision useful life of the dock was 25 years. As a result of the repairs this expected useful life was increased by 10 years. The percentage of useful life extension is thus 10/35, or 28.6 percent. The district court erred in applying the fraction 10/25, or 40 percent, to the cost of repairs. This fraction represents the useful life extension as a percentage of the precollision remaining useful life of the property. As indicated above, however, the proper ratio is that which the useful life extension bears to the remaining useful life of the property after repairs. Because the total cost of the repairs, $84,141.20, was the cost of obtaining a dock with a useful life of 35 years, the numerator of 10 years should be applied to the denominator of the total number of years of useful life purchased by the $84,141.20 to derive that portion of the total repair costs that is the cost of the 10 year useful life extension.

The cost of repairs that is allocable to the useful life extension is thus 28.6 percent of $84,141.20, or $24,064.38. Deducting this from the total repair costs leaves $60,076.82 as the repair costs recoverable by Freeport.

III [†]

The district court held:

> "To the extent that depreciation is allowed against the amount of damages, the owner must expend funds for replacement and repair of the dock long before it would have been required to do so in the normal course of business. To reimburse it for capital before it would normally be required to divert funds from operation, it should be allowed interest on the amounts so expended for the remainder of the useful life of the original dock."

The district court reasoned that, were it not for the collision, Freeport would not have had to spend the amount allocable to the useful life extension until 1996, the date at which the useful life of the old dock would have expired. The court therefore awarded Freeport, in addition to other recoveries, the difference between the amount of repairs allocable to the useful life extension and the present worth of that sum of money paid 25 years hence.[3]

To the extent that the district court attempts a new measure of damages as a principle of law, reversal is required because the general principle that has been rather universally applied in other jurisdictions, as well as in this Circuit, denies the plaintiff recovery for expenditures that enhance the value of his property.

As a factual matter, the district court based its decision on a finding that the dockowner has suffered damage by being required to expend funds for capital improvements before the time that such funds would have been expended in the normal course of business, but for the accident. * * *

In this case, however, we have been unable to find in the record any evidence as to what damage, if any, may have accrued because of the repair costs attributable to the enhancement of the dock's useful life. There is nothing in the record to show: whether the dock might be rebuilt long before it crumbles into the water at the end of its estimated useful life; the extent to which a reasonable return may be obtained on the cost of the enhanced value as on other capital expenditures; the possible savings in the cost of extended useful life construction now as opposed to the possible future cost; the extent to which sinking fund commitments may be reduced by the extended life of the dock and the possible reduction of maintenance costs on the new structure, both of which would tend to lessen the diversion of funds from the operation; the effect on possible loss to the dockowner of the many other considerations

† Part III was written by Judge Roney.

3. As indicated [above] the district court deducted 40 percent ($33,656.48) from Freeport's repair expenses for the useful life extension of the dock. After determining that the present value of $1 paid 25 years hence is $.18, the court added 82 percent of $33,656.48, or $27,598.31, back to Freeport's award. The net effect was a deduction of 18 percent of $33,656.48, or $6,058.17, for the improvement of the dock. In accordance with our holding, this amount must be recomputed to accurately state the result of the district court's holding. Given a 7 percent rate of interest, the present value of $1 paid 25 years hence is $.18. S. Selby, Standard Mathematics Tables 646 (1970). We concluded that repair costs allocable to the useful life extension were $24,064.38. The present value of that sum paid 25 years hence is thus 18 percent of $24,064.38, or $4,331.58.

that might be relevant to whether the dockowner will suffer any real damage from the early expenditure of funds. It may well be that full evaluation of the damage question would demonstrate no actual damage or that some of the considerations would be so speculative as to be incapable of the reasonable ascertainment required to sustain a damage award. In any event, the dockowner offered no proof on this item of damage and there is no support in the record for the conclusion that loss occurred as a result of premature extension costs. In view of the absence of factual support, a court should apply the general rule that a plaintiff is denied consideration for expenditure of repair costs beyond that necessary to restore its property to the condition it was in before the accident.

The extended useful life of the dock may well increase the dock's present value in the amount of the attributable repair cost, so that to follow the district judge's analysis would permit a plaintiff to turn a ready profit from the accident by selling the damaged property immediately after reconstruction and payment of the award. See General Outdoor Advertising Co. v. LaSalle Realty Corp., Ind.App.1966, 218 N.E.2d 141; compare Restatement of Torts § 929, Comment b (1939) (suggesting a distinction in damage computation depending on whether damaged property is put to a personal or commercial use).

The award concerning the present value computation of the extended useful life component of the cost of repairs should be eliminated. * * *

[Judge Wisdom concurred in the result in part III which eliminated the present value computation of the extended life component of the cost of repairs. Judge Wisdom reached the same conclusion by a different route. He recognized that this component constitutes lump sum damages accruing in a future frought with inflation. Up to this time the fifth circuit had refused to consider an inflation factor relating to such damages and required reduction to present value of future damages calculated in terms of present dollars (Johnson v. Penrod Drilling Co.). Judge Wisdom recommended instead the "Alaska rule" of total offset, Beaulieu v. Elliott, 434 P.2d 665 (Alaska 1967). Under this rule the future damages are not discounted to present value—in other words, the same result as in the majority opinion.]

[After this decision, the fifth circuit adopted a position that considers inflation in calculating future damage awards. See Culver v. Slater Boat Co., 688 F.2d 280 (5th Cir.1982). It rejected the "Alaska rule" of total offset urged by Judge Wisdom in this case. See again the full discussion in Jones & Laughlin Steel Corp. v. Pfiefer, supra, p. 112.]

Note

Inflation and Repair Costs. Where repair cost measures damages to realty, should the costs be figured at the time of the injury or the time of judgment? In Tortolano v. DiFilippo, 115 R.I. 496, 503, 349 A.2d 48, 52 (1975) the Supreme Court of Rhode Island held that the cost is computed as of the date of damage; "the trial justice erred in adding the sum of $1000 to account for the inflationary trends in the cost of restoring plaintiffs' land." A contrary decision is Rovetti v. City and County of San Francisco, 131 Cal.App.3d 973, 183 Cal.Rptr. 1 (1982). Cost of repairs at time of damage in 1972 (found to be $40,000) had risen to $58,479 at time of trial in 1978. The latter amount was awarded. See also Anchorage Asphalt Paving Co. v. Lewis, supra p. 111. Where do prejudgment interest, loss of use damages, and the avoidable consequences doctrine fit in?

b. *Value of Trees and Crops*

BRERETON v. DIXON

Supreme Court of Utah, 1967.
20 Utah 2d 64, 433 P.2d 3.

CROCKETT, CHIEF JUSTICE. Plaintiff, Rulon Brereton, sued the defendant, Ralph Dixon, alleging that the latter negligently permitted a fire in which he was burning rubbish in connection with a construction project to escape and destroy the usefulness of 111 peach and pear trees, being about one-third of plaintiff's three-acre orchard adjacent to his home in North Provo, Utah. A jury found the issues for the plaintiff and awarded damage of $5,700.

On appeal defendant concedes that the jury verdict on disputed evidence concludes the issue of defendant's negligence, but assails the damage as excessive and based on improper evidence and instructions to the jury.

The basic proposition urged by the defendant is that, inasmuch as the fruit trees are part of the realty, the only proper measure of damages is the difference in the value of the land before and after the destruction of the trees. We are aware that in appropriate circumstances this method of assessing damages has been approved in numerous cases. [citation] But we do not agree that it should be the sole and exclusive method of assessing such damages in all circumstances. * * * In some situations destruction or removal of part of the property might actually enhance the value of the remaining property by conditioning it for some other use; for example, for residential or industrial purposes not desired by the owner. In such a case application of the rule of value of the realty before and after the injury would penalize the owner * * *. In addition, there are other, sometimes far greater, difficulties encountered in appraising the before and after values of extensive and varied tracts of lands than in determining the value of a comparatively small damage which can be separately ascertained.

In order to obviate the inequity and the difficulties just discussed, and to get more simply and directly at the valuation of the specific damage caused, in proper cases the courts have applied another rule: if that which is destroyed, even though part of the realty, has a value which can be ascertained separate from the land, recovery is allowed for the value of the thing destroyed or damaged, rather than for the difference in the value of the land before and after the injury. The significant point here is that this latter rule has heretofore been approved by this court.

In comparing the relative merits of the two rules above set forth, we deem it appropriate to observe that in some instances the latter "separate value" rule may also result in inequity. There are some situations in which trees, for example, have some separate value, but because of landscaping, erosion control, or for other reasons, have a substantially greater value on the land than if separated from it. In these circumstances it would be unfair to compel the owner to take the value of the damaged property separated from the land, which would likewise give him less than his true damage and confer an unjustified advantage on the wrongdoer * * *.

Because of the fact that any attempt at unvarying uniformity in applying either of the foregoing rules results in the inequities above discussed, a third rule, which we believe to be the better considered and more practical one, has been applied. It gives the injured party the benefit of whichever of the two rules will best serve the objective hereinabove stated of giving him reasonable and adequate compensation for his actual loss as related to his use of his property. This more flexible approach avoids a rigid application of either rule where it would result in conferring a favor on the wrong-doer at the expense of the victim; and it allows the owner of property which has been damaged the privilege which should be his of having the decision as to how he desires to use his property, by giving him the amount of damage he suffers on the basis of that use. If he wants to maintain a fruit orchard, a wood lot, or even a primitive area, though his property may be more valuable if turned to an industrial or residential purpose, that should be his prerogative; and if it is wrongfully destroyed or damaged, the wrongdoer should pay for the actual damage he caused.

Upon our survey of the total situation disclosed by this record it appears to us that the trial court correctly analyzed the situation and allowed the presentation of the issue of damages to the jury in harmony with what we have said above. * * *

A further point raised by the defendant is that the testimony of plaintiff's experts as to value of the fruit trees was incompetent because it was based on their future income. This evidence was adduced through two witnesses: Vern A. Stratton and Clarence D. Ashton. Both had graduate degrees in horticulture, had taught the subject at universities, had operated substantial fruit farms, and had inspected the plaintiff's orchard after the fire. After showing their qualifications as experts they were allowed, over the defendant's objection, to give their judgment as to the value of the trees. This was as to the value the trees had in and of themselves, separate from the land. It properly and necessarily entailed consideration of their ability to produce fruit over their productive life. We are entirely in accord with the idea that the value could not properly be arrived at simply by a calculation based upon anticipated profits from the production of fruit. The reason for this is that there are so many uncertain factors involved in the making of profits that this is not a sound foundation upon which to calculate value. But this does not mean that the facts concerning the capacity of the trees for production of fruit and making income is not one of the facts to be considered in the overall picture in appraising their value.

The testimony of these men, including the cross-examination, indicates that their appraisal was not based solely upon anticipated profits. They had taken into consideration numerous other factors, including the planting and maturation, the amount and duration of productivity, the contingencies of frost, blight, variations in market, availability of labor, and indeed appear to have covered the total picture about as fully as any reasonable person could expect. The argument made leads one to suspect that the real difficulty with their testimony from the defendant's point of view is that their appraisals exceeded his idea of the value of the orchard. * * *

Affirmed.

TUCKETT, JUSTICE (dissenting). I dissent. It appears that the majority opinion adopts a special rule of damages in the case of fruit trees which is followed by a minority of the jurisdictions in this country. The majority of the cases hold that the proper measure of damages for the destruction of or injury to fruit and other productive trees is the difference in the value of the land with the trees before and after the act complained of. It appears to the writer that this rule is more easily understood and is more easily applied than the one we have adopted in this case.

The plaintiff in this case established the value of the trees destroyed and his damages by the testimony of witnesses who based their estimates of the value of the trees destroyed upon the factors of the longevity of the trees; the estimated productiveness of the trees; the price of the fruit on the market; less the costs of production. It is my opinion that damages based upon these factors are highly speculative and that a verdict based upon this type of speculation should not be approved.

Notes

1. Replacement Value: Ornamental Trees. If the cost to replace is reasonable and practicable, courts commonly allow it for ornamental trees where there are personal reasons for wanting restoration. See, e.g., Bowman v. McFarlin, 1 Ark.App. 235, 615 S.W.2d 383 (1981); Farny v. Bestfield Builders, Inc., 391 A.2d 212 (Del.1978); Heninger v. Dunn, 101 Cal.App.3d 858, 162 Cal.Rptr. 104 (1980). This rule's availability depends upon the existence of a retail market for ornamental and exotic trees.

Some state statutes allow recovery of double, triple or even five times the "value" of a destroyed ornamental tree. In Woodburn v. Chapman, 117 N.H. 906, 379 A.2d 1038 (1977), the court added $577 to the damages award because the tree was also a boundary marker.

2. *Aesthetic Damages.* Replacement value will ordinarily compensate injuries to aesthetic sensibilities, but it may be unrealistic. Sums are now frequently awarded for purely "aesthetic" injuries in guesswork fashion. In Kroulik v. Knuppel, 634 P.2d 1027, 1030 (Colo.App.1981), a 73–year–old, 50–foot high tree on a promontory overlooking the Animas river was destroyed. "No other trees of that size were visible in that locale. Several witnesses testified with respect to the particular grace, majesty and beauty of this isolated tree in that setting." The only specific testimony of value, however, was an expert who valued the tree at $8.40 for lumber and $229.63 (!) for aesthetic value. A trial court judgment for $1500 was reduced to $229.63.

Non-fatal injuries to ornamental trees have been compensated in terms of the loss per year of the aesthetic value until the victim has healed. Williams v. Hanover Insurance Co., 351 So.2d 858 (La.App.1977); Anno., 95 A.L.R.3d 508 (1979). The court perceived that the aesthetic depreciation in the later years of the healing process would not be as great as in the earlier ones. Oil spills pose extraordinarily difficult questions of valuing harmful effects on fauna and flora. See Commonwealth v. S.S. Zoe Colocotroni, 628 F.2d 652 (1st Cir.1980), cert. denied, 450 U.S. 912 (1981).

3. *Avoidable Consequences.* The court may reduce plaintiff's recovery for damages to trees or crops if plaintiff fails to avoid the consequences, see pp. 84–96 supra in general. Delay in replanting an orchard precludes recovery of net production loss for destroyed trees. Elwood v. Bolte, 119 N.H. 508, 403 A.2d 869 (1979). Does the avoidable consequences rule apply the same way when plaintiff seeks the diminution of value measure of damages?

4. *Collateral Source Rule.* Defendant negligently damaged plaintiff's cotton crop with a commercial aerial application of 2–4–D in violation of State Plant Board regulations. Plaintiff received a disaster payment from the state. Should

the court deduct this from plaintiff's tort recovery? See J.L. Wilson Farms, Inc. v. Wallace, 267 Ark. 643, 590 S.W.2d 42 (1979).

FARM BUREAU LUMBER CORP. v. McMILLAN

Supreme Court of Arkansas, 1947.
211 Ark. 951, 203 S.W.2d 398.

McFADDIN, J. The landowner, McMillan (appellee), brought action against the Farm Bureau Lumber Corporation (appellant), for damages for the alleged destruction of a "20–acre meadow * * * which could have been harvested at a profit of $20 per ton." Damages for $400 were claimed. The jury verdict was for $300. McMillan claimed that his meadow had been planted to lespedeza in 1945, and that the lespedeza reseeded itself in 1945, and would have produced a crop of hay, except that, in late April or early May of 1946, cattle (trespassing because of appellant's alleged negligence) consumed and otherwise destroyed the growing hay crop. He testified that the fair cash market value of the crop at the time the hay was destroyed was $400. Other witnesses testified how much the hay crop would have been, except for the destruction thereof by the cattle. The trial court gave plaintiff's instruction No. 4, which reads, in part: "If you find from a preponderance of the evidence that the hay meadow was destroyed as alleged in plaintiff's complaint the measure of damages would be the actual cash value of such hay meadow at the time of its destruction. * * *"

Defendant (appellant) offered a general objection to the above instruction; and the giving of this instruction No. 4 is the only point argued on appeal. * * *

Under the facts in this case we hold that the instruction given by the trial court was not erroneous, since: (1) there was no proof of injury to the land, but only proof as to the injury to the hay crop, and (2) witnesses testified as to the fair cash market value of the hay at the time of its destruction, and (3) it was shown that the hay crop was then actually growing and had a value. What Mr. Justice Butler said in Missouri Pac. R. Co. v. Benham [192 Ark. 35, 89 S.W.2d 930] is apropos: "From our own cases and the great weight of authority, the correct rule for the measurement of damages in ordinary cases for the destruction of grass or other perennial plants used on lands for meadow or pasture seems to be this: The damage recoverable is the value of the grass or crop at the time of its destruction where no permanent injury is suffered to the soil by the destruction of the roots of the grass or plants. * * *

The case of St. Louis, I.M. & S. Ry. Co. v. Saunders [85 Ark. 111, 107 S.W. 194] most strongly relied on by appellant inferentially points out the distinction between the "annual rental value of the land" and the "fair cash market value of the crop:" if the total destruction of the crop was at a time when the crop was too young to have a market value and when it was too late to plant another crop, then the "rental value of the land" is the rule that governs; but if the destruction of the crop was at a time when the market value could be determined, then the "market value of the crop" is the rule to govern * * *. In the case at bar there was proof that the hay was growing and had a market value, so the giving of instruction No. 4 was not erroneous.

On the assignment argued, we affirm the judgment of the Circuit Court.

Notes

1. Compare Black v. Ellithorp, 382 P.2d 23, 27 (Okl.1963). The court ruled that in an action "for the destruction of a perennial crop with its roots, such as alfalfa, the rental value of the land for such time as is reasonably necessary to restore the crop is a proper element of damages."

2. In Crow v. Davidson, 186 Okl. 84, 86–87, 96 P.2d 70, 71 (1939), defendant argued that there was insufficient evidence of the value of crops totally destroyed. The Supreme Court of Oklahoma agreed:

"The questions put to this witness, who was an expert, read: 'do you know about what the fair cash value from an acre or per acre of watermelons in the year 1937, if they were properly tended?' and, 'About what would watermelons make per acre if they were properly tended in the year 1937?' To these he answered, over objections: 'About $40.00 an acre.' Under the decisions of this court these questions did not contain the elements essential to establish the value of growing crops as of the time they were destroyed. * * * The test is the value of the crops at the time of destruction, established by deducting from their value as matured salable crops certain elements of expense relating to their planting, cultivation, harvesting and sale. The particular questions asked did not express or imply these elements, and the answer did not purport to consider them. There is considerable evidence respecting the extent of the crops planted, the manner in which plaintiff cultivated them and there are some estimates as to the expected yield; but, except for the previous estimated value of the melons, there is no competent evidence of the loss sustained by the destruction of the crops."

3. An annotation to the principal case, states that the "most widely accepted" method for ascertaining the value of totally destroyed crops is: "first, to estimate the probable yield had the crop not been destroyed; second, calculate the value of that yield in the market; and, third, deduct the value and amount of labor and expense which subsequently to the destruction and but for it would have been required to mature, care for, and market the crop." Anno., 175 A.L.R. 159, 174 (1948). See Cutler Cranberry Co. v. Oakdale Electric Cooperative, 78 Wis.2d 222, 254 N.W.2d 234 (1977).

4. Should a court, in calculating the value of a totally destroyed crop, take into account actual subsequent events that would affect probable yield? In St. Louis, Iron Mountain & Southern Railway v. Yarborough, 56 Ark. 612, ___, 20 S.W. 515, 517 (1892), plaintiff's crops were destroyed by an overflow of water caused by a railroad embankment defendant constructed. A few days later, a general overflow of the river bordering on plaintiff's farm caused water to flow directly over the entire field. The court stated that "the destruction of the crops by the general overflow was impending, if not inevitable, at the time the water was backed upon them;" and that this factor had to be considered by the jury in estimating damages.

Should the result in *Yarborough* depend upon whether the formula for measuring damages is that stated in *McMillan* rather than that suggested by the A.L.R. annotation in Note 3?

2. WASTE

DORSEY v. SPEELMAN

Court of Appeals of Washington, 1969.
1 Wash.App. 85, 459 P.2d 416.

JAMES, CHIEF JUDGE. Defendants (appellants) leased an 80–acre dairy farm from the plaintiffs (respondents) for a period of five years. After the expiration of the lease, plaintiffs brought this action for damages to the real property, alleging waste committed thereon. For a number of the items, plaintiffs sought treble damages under RCW 64.12.020, which provides in part:

> "If a * * * tenant * * * of real property commit[s] waste thereon, any person injured thereby may maintain an action at law for damages therefor against such * * * tenant * * * in which action, if the plaintiff prevails, there shall be judgment for treble damages * * *."

The trial was without a jury. The trial judge found that the defendants had both "committed" and "permitted" waste. Finding of fact No. 4 describes 10 items of damage; five are categorized as commissive waste. For these items the judge awarded treble damages.

The only error urged by defendants is the award of treble damages. Their argument is that exemplary or punitive damages are not favored in the law and that a statute which permits them must be strictly construed. Defendants find support for this contention in DeLano v. Tennent, 138 Wash. 39, 47, 244 P. 273, 276, (1926) wherein it is stated:

> "This court, early in its history, announced the doctrine that the rule allowing recovery of exemplary and punitive damages was unsound in principle, and held that such damages were not recoverable in this jurisdiction unless expressly so provided by statute. * * * [T]he statute permits recovery in treble damages only where the waste is willful and wanton. * * * "

Waste may be either voluntary or permissive. Voluntary waste, sometimes spoken of as commissive waste, consists of the commission of some deliberate or voluntary destructive act, such as pulling down a house, or removing things fixed to and constituting a material part of the freehold. Permissive waste implies negligence or omission to do that which will prevent injury, as, for instance, to suffer a house to go to decay for want of repair or to deteriorate from neglect.

It is defendants' contention that the evidence upon which the trial judge based his finding that the defendants "committed" rather than "permitted" waste does not satisfy the standard of strict statutory construction. The largest separate item for which there was an award of treble damages involved a small cabin near the farm house occupied by the defendants. * * *

Except for one witness who testified that he saw a relative of defendants throw materials out of a broken window of the small house, there was no direct evidence as to the identity of the person or persons who actually perpetrated the destruction found by the trial judge to constitute commissive waste. But the trial judge found that the circumstantial evidence strongly suggested that the destruction in each case was either the act of the defendants or was committed with their knowledge and approval. With reference to the small house, the trial judge made his observation in his oral opinion:

> "I cannot believe that sort of damage was caused by a windstorm. * * * [T]he type of damage that appears in * * * is just plain malicious damage. * * *
>
> "While I do not believe that Speelman is [defendants are] responsible for windstorm damage to the roof, it is a little hard to believe that a windstorm took out all of the windows and window sashes. It just doesn't ring true. I can't believe that a water tank could be ripped out, or cupboards torn off the walls by anything other than a person deliberately doing it."

* * * Defendants argue that the damage could have been done by third persons without defendants' knowledge. * * *

It is not logical to assume the defendants did not know of the destruction going on. It was too extensive and of such a nature that a person who was in the vicinity for 365 days a year would be compelled to know, unless they intentionally sought to ignore what was going on.

In each instance in which the trial judge awarded treble damages, he found that the damage was the result of something more than neglect. The concept of "commissive" waste does not require proof of a solitary personal performance by the tenant in possession. A perpetrator of waste can act through an agent or participate as an aider and abettor. The judge's finding that the waste was "committed" either by the defendants or with their knowledge, encouragement or consent, is supported by substantial evidence. It will not be disturbed.

Notes

1. Tenants may be liable in damages for either permissive or voluntary waste. See Anno., 82 A.L.R.2d 1106 (1962); Lipton Realty, Inc. v. St. Louis Housing Authority, 705 S.W.2d 565 (Mo.App.1986); Regan v. Moyle Petroleum Co., 344 N.W.2d 695 (S.D.1984).

Duckett v. Whorton, 312 N.W.2d 561, 562 (Iowa 1981). "We believe the proper measure of damages for waste, when it occurs where the owner is aware of the injury, is the same as the ordinary measure for injuries to realty. * * * It makes no difference whether the building could or could not be repaired. Either way [i.e. repair or diminution of value] damages are to be measured as of the time of the injury. It is apparent that replacement cost, *computed here as of the time the lease terminated was erroneous.*" [Emphasis added] Why was this computation erroneous? The different results of the usual standards for measuring value are, of course, magnified by the statutes trebling damages.

2. The statute in *Dorsey* is a typical variant of the Statutes of Marlbridge and Gloucester. A detailed examination of these statutes may be found in 5 American Law of Property § 20.18 (1952). Statutes in some jurisdictions also provide that the tenant forfeits the estate. Reams v. Henney, 88 Ohio App. 409, 97 N.E.2d 37 (1950). The court in Worthington Motors v. Crouse, 80 Nev. 147, 390 P.2d 229 (1964), held that forfeiture is not available as part of the common law but only when explicitly provided by statute.

3. Moore v. Phillips, 6 Kan.App.2d 94, 97, 627 P.2d 831, 835 (1981): "Where the right of action of the remainderman is based upon permissive waste, it is generally held that the injury is continuing in nature and the statute of limitations does not commence to run until the expiration of the tenancy [by death of life tenant]. Under certain state statutes * * * the period of limitations commences at the time the waste is committed."

4. In Winans v. Valentine, 152 Or. 462, 54 P.2d 106 (1936), where treble damages were assessed, subtenants converted a dwelling house into a night club, a chicken house into a cockpit, and a garage into bedrooms for the accommodation of guests. The defendant was aware of these developments. Compare a lessee who removes ordinary fixtures, e.g., sinks, cabinets, etc., easily replaceable. A damage cause of action, of course, arises, but the action is not "waste." The point is relevant because then treble damages are not allowable. See Kane v. Timm, 11 Wash.App. 910, 527 P.2d 480 (1974).

GLEASON v. GLEASON

Appellate Court of Indiana, 1909.
43 Ind.App. 426, 87 N.E. 689.

HADLEY, J. As stated in appellant's brief, under head of "Nature of the Action": "This action was brought by Jerome A. Gleason, the owner of the fee of the lands described in the complaint, against Elizabeth Gleason, seeking to compel her to keep in repair said property and to prevent her from allowing permissive waste, and to compel her to make such repairs as were then required." Appellee is the owner of a life estate in said real estate. The proceeding is in the nature of a mandatory injunction. A demurrer was sustained to the complaint, and, appellant refusing to plead further, judgment was rendered against him.

The waste complained of was in permitting the buildings to become and remain out of repair, failing to paint, permitting the roof to sag and leak, etc. The complaint does not show that appellee is insolvent. It does not show any damage that may not be repaired. It does not show that appellee will not make the necessary repairs in the future, or before the termination of her estate. It does not show any damages that may not be fully compensated. In order to establish his right to a mandatory injunction, plaintiff must show an unlawful invasion of his rights, irreparable and continuing in its nature, that there is no adequate remedy at law, and that he cannot be compensated in damages. * * * The complaint does not bring this case within the rule. * * *

Judgement affirmed.

Notes

1. Compare the principal case with Cannon v. Barry, 59 Miss. 289, 303 (1881): "He has been guilty of permissive waste in suffering the mansion to go to decay, and also perhaps with respect to the orchard, but courts of equity take no jurisdiction of permissive waste by a life tenant. Their constant interference in such matters would render the enjoyment of the life estate impossible."

The reluctance of equity to enter a mandatory injunction ordering repairs finds its counterpart in the refusal to specifically enforce contracts to repair.

2. Suppose that the waste committed by a life tenant consists of a failure to pay real estate taxes. What remedy is available to the vested remaindermen? In Chapman v. Chapman, 526 So.2d 131 (Fla.Dist.Ct.App.1988), the court held that a receiver should be appointed to collect rents, pay taxes, and account to the remaindermen.

3. Watson v. Wolff–Goldman Realty Co., 95 Ark. 18, 23–25, 128 S.W. 581, 583 (1910): "The most serious question in the case is whether a contingent remainderman may seek relief in equity for waste already committed. The courts of this country have held that a contingent remainderman cannot maintain an action at law to recover damages for waste already committed. The reason a contingent remainderman has no standing in a court of law is that it cannot be known in advance of the happening of the contingency whether he would suffer damage or loss by the waste, and, if the estate never became vested in him, he would be paid for that which he had not lost. On the other hand, it is a rule of universal application that a contingent remainderman may obtain relief in equity by injunction to prevent waste, and this remedy is given him on the theory that he is entitled to prevent the loss or destruction of that which may become his at the

termination of the life estate. If a contingent remainderman has right to appeal to a court of equity for the preservation and security of the property to the end that it may be forthcoming at the termination of the life estate with like reason, he should have some remedy for waste already committed. Neither the life tenant nor his grantee have the right to commit waste, and it necessarily follows that they should not be entitled to, or enjoy, the fruits of their wrongdoing. As we have already seen, the contingent remainderman has no remedy at law in such cases, and it is obvious that, if he cannot obtain relief in equity, he must suffer irreparable injury. * * * We are of the opinion that it is in accord with the principles of equity for the chancellor in cases like this to take an account of the amount of the damage suffered and impound the same and invest the proceeds for the benefit of the one to whom the estate tail would first pass according to the course of the common law by virtue of the deed in question, in which interest the plaintiffs have an expectancy." Accord, Sermon v. Sullivan, 640 S.W.2d 486 (Mo.App.1982).

Compare Pedro v. January, 261 Or. 582, 494 P.2d 868 (1972), where the court held that if the contingency is fairly certain, damages may be awarded and impounded by the court to await the outcome of the contingencies.

4. *Remedies for Ameliorating Waste.*

Yardley, Ameliorating Waste in England and the United States, 19 Mod.L.Rev. 150 (1956): "Let us pose a problem. A tenant has leased for a term of twenty years a farm which included a windmill pumping water for the farm, and he has covenanted, among other things, to repair the windmill and to insure it against destruction by lightning. After the lease has run for eighteen years the windmill is badly damaged by lightning, and the tenant pulls down what remains of it, constructing in its place a new shed containing an engine, which is more powerful and capable of producing more water than the old windmill. Does the action of the tenant amount to ameliorating waste, or is he guilty of ordinary voluntary waste? Has the property inevitably increased in value, or is it open to the landlord to insist that the tenant should have repaired the windmill and not replaced it by any other building or engine, however more efficient the new structure may be?

"In seventeenth-century England a landlord similarly placed (given the possibility of some engine other than a windmill existing) would have been able to call the tune. Any change in the character or nature of the land or property was waste, whether the actual value of the property had been thereby improved or not."

D. Dobbs, Remedies, 119–120 (1973): "A problem of both substance and remedy arises where the act of waste adds to the value of the land, so that the remaindermen or reversioners when they come into possession will have land more, rather than less, valuable. One view is that in such a case of 'ameliorating waste,' there is really no waste at all. If this is the substantive law, then no damages problem arises since there is no valid claim at all. But such a view is probably too rigid and it probably oversimplifies the cases too much. Certainly there is authority that protects the remainderman not merely from a loss in the capital value of the land, but from an unreasonable change in the basic character of the land's use or an unreasonable increase in the expense of operating the land, even where the capital value itself has risen. This, of course, does not mean that every improvement in the land's value is waste any more than it means the contrary. What acts constitute waste is determined by substantive law with a view to affording reasonable use to the tenant and reasonable protection to the reversioner or remainderman. The increase in the value of the land may be one factor in determining whether waste is committed, but it is not conclusive. Once waste is found to exist, the fact that the value of the land on the market is increased presents problems in assessing damages. It may be reasonable to hold the wasting tenant liable for increased taxes or insurance imposed on his property by reason of the improvements in some cases. If the value of the land is increased by the tenant's changes, but taxes and insurance are not substantially increased thereby, presumably a finding of waste would justify recovery of the cost of replacing the land in its earlier condition, at least if the remainderman intends to occupy rather than sell the land."

CAMDEN TRUST CO. v. HANDLE

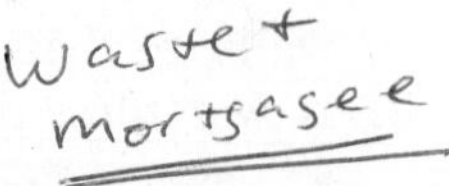

Court of Errors and Appeals of New Jersey, 1942.
132 N.J.Eq. 97, 26 A.2d 865.

[The statement of facts is from the opinions of Berry V.C., in the Court of Chancery, 130 N.J.Eq. 125, 21 A.2d 354 (1941). A portion of Vice Chancellor Berry's opinion is also set forth.]

Berry, Vice Chancellor. The bill of complaint filed herein sought the foreclosure of a real estate and chattel mortgage for $125,000, given by the defendant Morris Handle and his wife to the Camden Safe Deposit and Trust Company, the complainant's predecessor trustee. The mortgage was dated February 20, 1930, covered premises located on Broadway, Camden, New Jersey, known as the Towers Theatre. Drawn in two counts, it prays, first, for the foreclosure of the mortgage and second, for a decree for damages for waste alleged to have been committed or suffered by the defendant Warner Brothers Theatres, Inc., which corporation purchased the Towers Theatre from the mortgagor in May, 1930. The defaults in the mortgage as alleged in the bill were not denied. * * *

Subsequent proceedings resulted in a decree of foreclosure dated May 4, 1939, adjudging the sum of $101,391.32, plus interest and costs, to be due on complainant's mortgage. Pursuant to that decree, the mortgaged real estate was sold by the Sheriff of Camden County on June 30, 1939, for the sum of $64,000, subject to delinquent taxes amounting to $7,458.04, the purchaser being a stranger to these proceedings. The admitted deficiency as of the date of the sheriff's sale was $40,893.31. Subsequently, the complainant filed another bill in this court to recover that deficiency from the defendant Warner Brothers, Inc., but, on motion to strike, the bill was dismissed by Vice Chancellor Sooy on the ground that since this defendant had not assumed the mortgage debt when it purchased the mortgaged premises, it could not be held liable for the resulting deficiency * * *.

The waste for which complainant seeks to hold Warner Brothers Theatres, Inc., hereinafter referred to as the "defendant," liable, is charged in substance in the bill as follows:

a. By closing the theatre shortly after it bought it and keeping it closed, thereby preventing its being used as a theatre, and destroying the value of the land and the rentals, income, profits, etc., of the mortgaged premises.

b. By removal of the marquee and the fire escapes, and by neglect and refusal to repair the buildings, as a result of which plaster fell from the walls and water came in through the roof ruining all the interior decorations, carpets, draperies, floorings, etc., and caused all the metal work to become rusted, and all the woodwork, especially the balcony and roof supports, to become rotten.

c. By removing from the theatre certain personal property covered by the chattel mortgage and permitting the remainder to become ruined by water and dampness.

d. By failing to pay taxes as they accrued and by permitting an accumulation of such taxes in the sum of $4,368.80 at the date of the filing of the bill.

e. By neglecting and refusing to repair the building, the roof and the walls, so that the entire building, its equipment and fixtures, became completely worthless and of no value as security for the mortgage. * * *

The defendant admits that its exercise of the rights of ownership of the mortgaged premises was subject to a limitation that it refrain from doing those acts which would impair the complainant's mortgage security and render it insufficient, but urges that this limitation is confined to voluntary or active waste, and does not apply to acts of omission, or permissive waste. Defendant further contends that the only voluntary or active waste charged is the removal of the marquee and the fire escapes for which it is not liable because their removal was due to their hazardous and dangerous condition; and that all other waste charged is permissive waste for which defendant as mortgagor is not liable. However, an analysis of the law of waste as recognized in this state will, I think, indicate that the point is not well taken. * * *

The measure of damages for waste is the diminution in the value of the mortgage security; that is, the difference between the value of the premises after the commission of the waste and the value in the absence of such waste. * * * The damage is the amount the mortgaged premises would have sold for at foreclosure sale, had the waste not been suffered or committed, in excess of what they actually sold for.

[Applying this measure of damages, a decree for $40,000 was entered. This amount represented the difference between the highest bid of $64,000 and $104,000, the price for which the property could have been sold had the waste not been suffered.]

HEHER, JUSTICE. * * * Voluntary or active waste impairing the sufficiency of the security is remediable. Tate v. Field, 57 N.J.Eq. 632, 42 A. 742. Such is actionable as a positive, affirmative wrong injurious to the mortgagee's property; and it is variously held to give rise to a right of action in trespass or in case * * *. It is generally recognized that the primary distinction between waste and trespass is that in the former case the injury is done by one rightfully in possession. It would seem that there cannot be waste unless there is privity of estate or title. * * *

But damages for permissive waste are not recoverable by the mortgagee. As respects mere acts of omission, the mortgagor and his assigns are not liable for waste otherwise than upon their covenant. * * * If the party in possession (whether mortgagor or mortgagee, or their respective assigns) "does anything in respect to the mortgaged property which constitutes waste, and as such essentially impairs the value of the inheritance," he is responsible in damages to the party injured, but a mortgagor "is not guilty of waste, on account of acts of omission. In the absence of an express covenant to repair, he is not guilty of waste, as against the mortgagee, if he fails to keep the premises in repair." Tiedeman on Real Property, sec. 265. * * *

[I]n Tate v. Field, 57 N.J.Eq. 632, 42 A. 743, Chief Justice Gummere for this court declared: "The position of a mortgagor, in possession of the mortgaged estate, bears no analogy to that of tenant for life. The mortgagor in possession is in equity, the owner of the estate, and may exercise all acts of ownership, even to the committing of waste, provided he does not diminish the security, and render it insufficient. * * * And not only is there no analogy between the position of a mortgagor in possession and that of a tenant for life with reference to waste committed, but the rule for the admeasurement of damages is different. In the case of the former the measure of damages is the diminution in the value of the mortgage security." * * *

The case in hand is not one of the "special cases," referred to by Chancellor Kent, in which indemnity may be had through the exercise of "the enlarged discretion of a court of equity." "Equitable waste" is a nebulous term—a doctrine of obscure limitations. It is such as is cognizable only in a court of equity. It is said that it has reference to cases where, by the terms of the will, deed settlement or lease, the tenant holds the land without impeachment of waste. Pomeroy's Equity Jurisprudence, 5th Ed., sec. 1348. * * * [A]n eminent authority on equity jurisprudence defines equitable waste as "such acts as at law would not be esteemed to be waste under the circumstances of the case, but which in the view of a Court of Equity are so esteemed from their manifest injury to the inheritance, although they are not inconsistent with the legal rights of the party committing them." Story's Equity Jurisprudence, 14th Ed., sec. 1242. He gives as instances of this class the felling of timber on the mortgaged premises to such an extent as to render the security insufficient, and the pulling down of houses by a tenant for life without impeachment for waste, or the commission of other waste wantonly and maliciously; and he cites holdings that "a Court of Equity ought to moderate the exercise of such a power, and pro bono publico restrain extravagant humorous waste." Pointing out that "tenants for life without impeachment for waste, and tenants in tail, after possibility of issue extinct, have been restrained not only from acts of waste to the destruction of the estate, but also from cutting down trees planted for the ornament or shelter of the premises," he continues: "In all such cases the party is deemed guilty of a wanton and unconscientious abuse of his rights, ruinous to the interests of other parties." * * *

Thus it is that equitable jurisdiction in this behalf seems to have been confined to wanton, malicious and unconscientious acts of the particular tenant injurious to the inheritance, in contravention of the presumed will of the creator of the limited estate. It is largely upon this ground that equity has afforded a remedy where the acts denominated waste were not inconsistent with the legal rights of the holder of the partial estate. But the particular tenant is not so punishable for merely permissive waste grounded on the omission of repairs that are not commanded either by statute or the contract. Such is not included within this equitable jurisdiction. * * *

The decree is reversed, with costs; and the cause is remanded with direction to assess the damages for voluntary waste only and to enter a decree accordingly.

Notes

1. Prudential Insurance Co. v. Spencer's Kenosha Bowl Inc., 137 Wis.2d 313, 404 N.W.2d 109 (App.1987). The court rejected the distinction between permissive and voluntary waste. It found a nonassuming grantee of the mortgagor liable for conduct that results in either active or passive waste. The grantee's liability was limited, however, to the amount of the deficiency judgment entered in the fore-

closure action. See generally, Leipziger, The Mortgagee's Remedies for Waste, 64 Cal.L.Rev. 1086 (1976).

2. Jaffe–Splindler Co. v. Genesco, Inc., 747 F.2d 253, 257–58 (4th Cir.1984):

"Under South Carolina law a mortgagee is deemed to have only a lien on real property as opposed to actual title * * *. Lien states generally only allow a mortgagee to recover [damages] for waste if the value of the collateral goes below the amount of the outstanding indebtedness * * *. Title states, on the other hand, allow a mortgagee to recover for any diminution in the value of security given for a debt. The differing results come because any diminution in value injures the mortgagee's property in a title state. In a lien state the mortgagee has no property interest which can be injured."

The agreement restricted the mortgagee's security interest to the value of the collateral. The court said: "[G]iven the special facts, the district court was correct in [applying] the rule which usually governs in title states * * * [that] any diminution in the value of the premises greatly prejudiced [mortgagee's] security interest."

3. A mortgagee or other lien holder may enjoin active waste by the debtor in possession "if the security is being impaired." When is that? Assume property worth $200,000 is encumbered by a $100,000 mortgage. The mortgagor commits acts of waste which if continued will reduce the value to $50,000. Is the security impaired when the waste begins? When the property value reaches $100,000? When it reaches $50,000? Or at some other point? Genesco Inc. v. Monumental Life Insurance Co., 577 F.Supp. 72 (D.S.C.1983). See Frio Investments, Inc. v. 4M–IRC/Rohde, 705 S.W.2d 784 (Tex.App.1986). Removal of improvements leaving property worth one million dollars to secure debts of $300,000 did not constitute waste.

3. TRESPASS

a. Trespass With Ouster

DEAKYNE v. LEWES ANGLERS, INC.

United States District Court, District of Delaware, 1962.
204 F.Supp. 415.

LEAHY, SENIOR DISTRICT JUDGE. An action in ejectment was brought by Ethel C. Deakyne, a Pennsylvania resident, against Lewes Anglers, Inc., a Delaware corporation. Plaintiff avers the defendant corporation is in wrongful possession of her land and seeks to recover possession as well as mesne profits in the amount of $24,000.

[The court ruled that plaintiff had title to the property which she bought in 1960.]

After a recovery in ejectment, a plaintiff may recover mesne profits for the three year period preceding the commencement of the action. 10 Del.Code, § 8109. In the present case, expert testimony has been adduced that the fair rental value of the property for the three year period was $10,000. Defendants have offered no evidence as to rental value.

Defendant argues that as plaintiff Deakyne only obtained her rights to the property in question in March 1960, her right to recover profits should be limited to the period after that date. But plaintiff purchased all rights that [her predecessor] had to the property, one of which was to bring action for such rents as were owed. "A plaintiff in ejectment may recover damages or mesne profits for lands unlawfully detained by defendant prior to his acquiring title, if the right of action therefor is transferred to him by his grantor." Lord v. Dearing, 24 Minn. 110.

In an action at ejectment the value of improvements made upon the premises by defendant may be recouped or recovered by him analogously to a set-off against the demand of plaintiff. Here defendants made improvements to the property of such value that Harry M. Grieves testifying for plaintiffs as to value of the property, initially declared that if the boat slips built by defendants were not present, the property would be "valueless." Defendant claims that where such improvements are made by defendants, plaintiff must either place a fair rental valuation on the property without the improvements or fail in its efforts to prove damages. But this confuses plaintiff's obligation to prove damages with defendant's obligation to bring to the Court's attention matters that might result in their mitigation or reduction. Recoupment is not a right of defendant to be assumed until disproved by plaintiff. Evidence submitted by defendant as to improvements placed upon the land is limited to uncontradicted statements of Irven S. Maull, presently treasurer of Lewes Anglers, Inc. Mr. Maull testified the Anglers had borrowed $4200 from the Lewes Trust Company in 1937 (repaid a total of $4500 to the bank, including interest) and spent it on improvements of the property. $600 was given to the Anglers by the Town Commissioners; $300 by the Chamber of Commerce; $150 by merchants in Lewes; and a total of from $210 to $240 was contributed by members on dues at the founding of the Anglers. The above was, according to Maull, used to finance improvements. He further testified that in the last year $1900 had been spent for dredging the boat slips and repairing docks. Other testimony of Mr. Maull as to amounts spent on improvements fails of sufficient clarity to enable the Court to determine what further amounts may have been spent.

Accepting the $10,000 figure suggested by Mr. Grieves to be the fair rental value of the property, and subtracting: (a) $4500 repaid to the Lewes Trust Company by 1942 for the loan spent on improvements; (b) $1260 contributed by miscellaneous sources at the inception of the Anglers, spent on improvements; (c) $1900 spent in the last year for improvements, the figure of $2360 remains. An additional matter must be considered. Defendant apparently claims that as seven docks, renting for $80 apiece, were not rented last year, the figure of $560 should be deducted from fair rental value. While it would not be wholly equitable to penalize plaintiff title-holder for failure of defendant to rent seven docks, under all the equities of the case it is concluded that upon the analogous doctrine of divided damages, the figure should be halved and $280 deducted from the total figure. Even the remaining amount cannot be left without further consideration. For "fair rental value" need not be the same as a fair statement of mesne profits. Evidence presented to this Court on the issue of damages by both sides has been so scanty and inconclusive that the Court is forced, on the basis of an examination of the record as a whole, to decide whether the figure of $2080 is either insufficient or excessive. Taking into account the small amounts of rent paid on this property in the past (totalling $100 per year by the Anglers) and the small bank account remaining at the end of the last three years of operation of the Anglers, the Court reduces the figure of $2080 by $1000 (the total amount paid by the Anglers as rent for a ten year period) and orders:

(1) The Anglers to restore to plaintiff the possession of the property herein discussed.

(2) The Anglers to pay mesne profits in the sum of $1080.

Notes

1. Compare Sabourin v. Woish, 117 Vt. 94, 99, 85 A.2d 493, 497 (1952):

"Mesne profits at common law were the pecuniary gains and benefits received by the disseizor during his unlawful occupancy, and the term is commonly used to denote the damages recoverable in ejectment. These may be measured by the rental value of the premises, or they may be more. When the rental value, alone, compensates the plaintiff, it governs the award of damages; when that value falls short of such compensation, it does not. Compensation being the basis of the recovery, the wrongdoer must respond for gains prevented as well as for losses sustained, so far as the same are sufficiently alleged and proved. The plaintiff could also, if specially alleged, have recovered in ejectment such consequential damages as had resulted from the acts of the defendant, Chester A. Woish, while in wrongful occupation of the premises."

In Van Ruymbeke v. Patapsco Industrial Park, 261 Md. 470, 276 A.2d 61 (1971), the court ruled that the best test of mesne damages is rental value. It refused to allow recovery of defendant's profits.

2. Contrary to *Deakyne* is an Oregon statute that limits mesne damages for withholding property to the rental value of the property excluding the value of permanent improvements made by defendant. Beaver v. Davis, 275 Or. 209, 550 P.2d 428 (1976).

3. Suppose a farmer is receiving payments for idling land under federal law and has been deprived of possession by a trespasser. Would the trespasser be liable for mesne profits? Cf. Horton v. Boatright, 242 Miss. 153, 133 So.2d 725 (1961).

4. Salesian Society v. Village of Ellenville, 121 A.D.2d 823, 505 N.Y.S.2d 197 (1986). The trespasser, the telephone company, condemned the land it wrongfully occupied; but it was required to pay to the owner the rental value of the property during the wrongful occupation.

JAMES v. BAILEY

United States District Court, District of Virgin Islands, 1974.
370 F.Supp. 469.

WARREN H. YOUNG, DISTRICT JUDGE. This is an appeal from a judgment of the Municipal Court granting plaintiff compensation for improvements constructed by mistake on land belonging to defendant. The Court below found that defendant had no actual notice that the improvement (a cistern) was being constructed by plaintiff and attempted to stop the construction when he learned of it. Based on these facts, the Court entered judgment for plaintiff in the amount of $1,800 "as equitable relief."

The issue presented by this appeal is quite narrow. Simply stated, it is whether a person who, by mistake, makes improvements on another's land can maintain an independent action to obtain compensation for their value when the true owner had no notice of the construction. The rule of law to which I must refer as a guide to my decision is stated in Section 42(1) of the Restatement of Restitution:

"Improvements upon Land or Chattels

"(1) Except to the extent that the rule is changed by statute, a person who, in the mistaken belief that he or a third person on whose account he acts is the owner, has caused improvements to be made upon the land of another, is not thereby entitled to restitution from the owner for the value of such improvements."

Appellee's brief correctly points out that the harshness of this rule is relaxed by various qualifications, most often observed in "equitable" actions. These qualifications, then, render the rule when "taken out of context" somewhat misleading. However, it is my view that none of the generally recognized relaxations of the rule, and none of the qualifications expressly noted in the Restatement apply in this case.

The general rule of the Restatement reflects the notion at common law that one who improved property did so at his own risk. If it later developed that his title to the improved land was defective or that through some error he had built on property he did not own, the true owner had no legal obligation to compensate him. The rule was "founded upon the idea that the owner should not pay an intruder, or disseisor, or occupant, for improvements which he never authorized. It is supposed to be founded in good policy, inasmuch as it induces diligence in the examination of titles, and prevents intrusion upon and appropriation of the property of others." Parsons v. Moses, 16 Iowa 440 (1864). The Restatement Reporters further note in Comment (a) to Section 42 that the reason for the harsh rule "is that in many cases it would be still more harsh to require the one receiving the benefits to pay therefor." After making this observation, however, the Reporters do acknowledge that the rule is "not wholly consistent with the principles of restitution for mistake" and that its harshness has been substantially relieved either by statute or by equity. I will now turn to an examination of these two possible methods for avoiding application of the general rule in this case.

The first possibility can be quickly dismissed. It is true that many jurisdictions have enacted statutes protecting the investment of a person who improves land which he later discovers is not his own. Such an occupying claimants act or betterment statute, if enacted in the Virgin Islands, would constitute a "local law to the contrary" within the meaning of 1 V.I.C. § 4 justifying departure from the Restatement's general rule. However, no such statute has been enacted.

The second possible technique for avoiding the general common law rule is to apply principles of equity to mitigate its harshness in particular cases. As I stated at the outset, I feel that the generally recognized equitable exceptions to the rule do not apply to the facts of this case. I will review briefly these qualifications of the no compensation rule.

First it should be noted that the widely accepted doctrines providing relief from the rule are all defensive. That is, they do not authorize an independent action by the improver but rather allow him a counterclaim or setoff in an action commenced by the true owner. Two of these exceptions are included in the Restatement of Restitution and require restitution to the improver (provided his mistake was reasonable) "to the extent that the land has been increased in value" whenever: (1) the true owner obtains a judgment in an equitable proceeding (perhaps clearing his title), or (2) the true owner commences an action of trespass or other action for mesne profits.[1]

It is puzzling why the right to compensation should turn on the question whether the true owner commences an action seeking some relief for himself from the improver's occupancy of the land. The origin of the rule would seem to lie in the notion that one who seeks the aid of the court in equity must, in turn, "do equity." But it is hard to see why the injustice of allowing an owner of land to retain the benefit of improvements constructed by another should receive judicial recognition only when the party benefited is seeking some further relief. To a certain extent, the cases in other jurisdictions have attempted to deal with this inconsistency of treatment.

One group of cases in which most courts, and the Restatement,[2] would allow the improver to maintain an independent action to recover the value of his improvement is that in which the owner has been guilty of some inequitable conduct. For example, if an owner stands silently by while another, acting in good faith, constructs valuable improvements on his property, the improver may recover the value of those improvements. In such cases where the owner is guilty of fraud or acquiescence with knowledge, the law of unjust enrichment is invoked to grant the improver compensation for his work. In this case, no such inequitable conduct was found. Indeed, the court below made specific findings that the defendant had no actual notice that the improvement was being constructed and attempted to stop the construction when it came to his attention. The question for decision, then, is whether, absent the negligence, bad faith or acquiescence of the owner, an independent action for compensation can be permitted in this jurisdiction.

* * * I cannot ignore the fact that the Restatement was written in 1937 and should not be applied without some consideration of more recent developments. Still, I cannot hold that an improver is always entitled to compensation when he builds by mistake and without the knowledge of the true owner. Even the most far-reaching decisions in this area require a finding that the improver acted in good faith and that his mistake could not have been discovered with ordinary diligence. Equitable relief should not be granted to one who acts recklessly and upon a belief of ownership which is completely without foundation. As the court below made no finding on this issue, I must reverse and remand. * * *

Notes

1. The spectrum of remedies (if any) available to good faith trespassers remains wide. Dickinson, Mistaken Improvers of Real Estate, 64 N.C.L.Rev. 37 (1985).

In Hughey v. Bennett, 264 Ark. 64, 568 S.W.2d 46 (1978), the court held that if the plaintiff in an ejectment action does not seek mesne profits or the removal of the improvement, the defendant is not entitled to a set off unless a betterment statute is affirmatively asserted. However, several recent decisions have granted affirmative relief to a good faith mistaken improver. See Duncan v. Akers, 147 Ind.App. 511, 262 N.E.2d 402 (1970) (improver entitled to equitable relief); Sugarman v. Olsen, 254 Or. 385, 459 P.2d 545 (1969) (judgment for value of improve-

1. [Footnotes renumbered.] In most jurisdictions, compensation for the value of improvements is achieved by permitting a setoff against the amount recoverable by the owner in actions for rents, profits and damages as well.

2. See Restatement of Restitution § 42, comment (b).

ments); Comer v. Roberts, 252 Or. 189, 448 P.2d 543 (1968) (owner compelled to convey for value); Somerville v. Jacobs, 153 W.Va. 613, 170 S.E.2d 805 (1969) (alternative judgment for value of improvement or conveyance of land for value).

2. *Betterment Statutes:* Various statutory schemes have been adopted to aid the mistaken improver. The most common are those allowing the mistaken improver to set off when the owner sues to recover mesne damages. Even this limited remedy may not be available unless the mistaken party can show that the improvements were made in good faith and under "color of title." Uhlhorn v. Keltner, 723 S.W.2d 131 (Tenn.App.1986).

Much less common is the expansive remedy provided by the California code. It allows the improver to bring an action based on his improvements; and it directs the court to "effect such an adjustment of the rights, equities, and interest of the good faith improver, the owner of the land, and other interested parties * * * as is consistent with substantial justice to the parties under the circumstances of the particular case." Cal.Civ.Proc.Code, §§ 871.1–871.7. See also Southern Pacific Transportation Co. v. Superior Court, 58 Cal.App.3d 433, 129 Cal.Rptr. 912 (1976).

NEW YORK v. WHITE

United States Court of Appeals, Second Circuit, 1975.
528 F.2d 336.

LUMBARD, CIRCUIT JUDGE. * * * The genesis of the present controversy lies in events far in the past. Following the victory of the American colonies in the Revolutionary War, the Mohawk Indian Nation, which had sided with the British, migrated from New York to the more hospitable soil of Canada in an endeavor to avoid possible reprisals. Having received a grant from the King of England of 12,000 square miles in Canada in which to settle, the Mohawks entered into a treaty with the State of New York on April 27, 1798, by which they did

> "cede and release to the people of the State of New York forever all the right or title of the said nation to lands within the said State; and the claim of the said nation to lands within the said State is hereby wholly and finally extinguished."

Included within the lands thus acquired by New York were the 612.7 acres in Herkimer County which, on August 27, 1798, the State patented to Alexander Macomb. As detailed in the plaintiff's complaint, the chain of title then passed through a succession of private owners until August 7, 1973 when the property was conveyed to the State by the Nature Conservancy for incorporation within the New York State Forest Preserve.

The State's plans for the land were, however, seriously disrupted when forty-two members of the Mohawk Nation, defendants herein, seized possession of the property and the buildings thereon in May 1974, thus dramatically ending 175 years of silent acquiescence in non-Indian ownership. Proclaiming what they believed to be the Mohawk's aboriginal rights, defendants and others issued the so-called Ganienkeh Manifesto attacking the validity of the 1798 treaty from which the State ultimately derives its title.

These actions prompted the State to institute the instant lawsuit, basing jurisdiction on 28 U.S.C.A. § 1331 and seeking declaratory relief pursuant to 28 U.S.C.A. §§ 2201 and 2202. In its prayer for relief, New York requested the district court to: "grant plaintiff's judgment removing, as a cloud on plaintiff's title, the effect of defendant's contention that they are rightfully in possession of the hereinbefore described premises and declaring that plaintiff is the owner in fee of said premises and restoring possession of the premises to plaintiff and that the defendants be barred from reentering possession of the same."

Construing the State's claim as basically one for ejectment, Judge Port concluded that the "well-pleaded complaint" need only establish the plaintiff's right to possession and that this was adequately done by pleading the 1973 deed. He held that the State's extended references to the 1798 treaty were unnecessary surplusage included only to blunt the defense which the Ganienkeh Manifesto had led it to expect. * * *

At the outset, we must therefore deal with the plaintiff's contention that the district court erred in rejecting the State's self-serving characterization of its complaint as an action to remove a cloud on title rather than one for ejectment. The flaw in plaintiff's argument is its fallacious assumption that the pleader operates free of constraints in choosing between these two related causes of action. A bill to remove a cloud on title is traditionally a suit in equity, and, as such, available only when there is no adequate remedy at law. Despite the merger of law and equity in 1938, this basic principle of federal jurisprudence retains its viability as a safeguard for the right to a jury trial guaranteed by the Seventh Amendment. Possession is the critical determinant. Since the State is concededly not in possession of the land in Herkimer County, it was obliged first to pursue the legal remedy of ejectment. Judge Port was correct in construing the State's complaint consonant with this obligation.

In an action for ejectment, plaintiff need only allege that he is the owner in fee and that he has been wrongfully ousted from possession by the action of the defendants. Neither of these elements required the State to plead, as it did, the validity of the treaty of 1798. Stripped of this assertion, New York's complaint is bereft of any allusion to federal law.

It is doubtless true, as the State contends, that the Ganienkeh Manifesto gave it strong reason to believe that the defendants would attempt to justify their conduct by challenging the treaty executed by their ancestors. But the jurisdiction of the federal courts cannot be made to hinge upon such expectations. * * *

Thus, we would ordinarily have little difficulty in affirming the district court's decision to dismiss New York's complaint for lack of jurisdiction. As the Supreme Court has just recently reiterated, "for the most part, matters of local property law [are] to be vindicated in local courts," Oneida Indian Nation v. County of Oneida, 414 U.S. 661, 676 (1974). However, during oral argument we were informed by the State that the Ganienkeh Manifesto promulgated by the defendants represents a cloud on title not only to the 612.7 acres in Herkimer County but to all of northeastern New York and parts of neighboring states. As to land so challenged and still within the State's control, a suit to remove a cloud on title would properly lie. Moreover, in contrast to an action for ejectment, a bill to remove a cloud on title may, as the State's complaint does, introduce a question of federal law in its description of the cloud which plaintiff seeks to remove. Under these circumstances, we believe the proper course is to allow New York the opportunity to amend its complaint. * * *

Affirmed, as modified.

Notes

1. Evidently neither the New York officials nor the federal courts had much taste for removing the Mohawks from the Herkimer County land. New York tried to pass the job to the federal courts by using the equitable quiet title suit, but the tender was declined—ejectment is the appropriate remedy.

2. Republic Financial Corp. v. Mize, 682 P.2d 207 (Okl.1983), reiterated the rule that equity will not quiet title in favor of a plaintiff who is out of possession; but the court did not apply the rule to plaintiff, a remainderman, who lacked a present right to possess and could not sue for ejectment.

Another exception governs "wild lands" where nobody is in possession, Vaughan v. Vaughan, 253 Ga. 76, 317 S.E.2d 201 (1984).

3. Assume a successful statutory quiet title suit by a legal owner whose property is occupied by others. What has the owner gained as far as recovering possession? The statute that follows is typical of many that remove the requirement that plaintiff be in possession to maintain suit. Statutory suits are governed by equitable principles; but their use to substitute for ejectment is somewhat negated by the requirement of a jury trial where ejectment is also available.

4. Cal.Civ.Proc.Code § 738: An action may be brought by any person against another who claims an estate or interest in real or personal property, adverse to him, for the purpose of determining such adverse claim; * * * provided, however, that nothing herein contained shall be construed to deprive a party of the right to a jury trial in any case where by the law such right is now given.

FLORO v. PARKER

District Court of Appeal of Florida, Second District, 1968.
205 So.2d 363.

PIERCE, JUDGE. This is an appeal by Grace M. Floro, plaintiff below, from an adverse summary final judgment entered by the DeSoto County Circuit Court in an unlawful entry and detainer proceeding. * * *

Plaintiff filed her complaint in statutory form, F.S. Sec. 82.06 F.S.A., alleging that defendants had "unlawfully turned her out of, and unlawfully and without her consent withheld from her possession," certain described real estate. The complaint prayed for "restitution of possession and her damages."

Defendants Parker answered that, as owners of the "record fee simple title" to the property, they had the right of possession, asserting that "the ultimate question to be determined * * * is whether the defendants are the owners of said land" and that "the substantial question involved * * * is one of title." * * *

The parties filed reciprocal motions for summary judgment, with supporting proofs. Plaintiff's motion was denied. Defendants' motion was granted and the cause dismissed, the Court holding there was "no genuine issue of any material fact." Plaintiff has appealed. The question here is whether there was any disputed fact engendered by the proofs submitted that raised a genuine issue bearing upon the determination of the case. We think there was and therefore reverse. * * *

The action of forcible entry and unlawful detainer is one of the most misunderstood—or more accurately, one of the least understood—proceedings in the field of remedial law. This is perhaps due, in large part, to the fact that the embryo lawyer, when first exposed to this type action in law school, is told that unlawful entry and detainer may be brought "to regain possession of real property," but is told in the next breath that "title is not involved" and cannot be inquired into. He begins to wonder why, if *possession* is the issue, *title* is of no consequence; reflecting in his *naiveté* that he always understood that possession is *dependent* upon title.

But he usually remains quiet and asks no questions for fear of "displaying his ignorance." And unfortunately, the mystery is seldom cleared up for him. So he usually goes through his career of "lawyering" without ever really understanding the basic theory of the proceeding. The saving grace is that he will not perhaps have over one or two such cases during his entire practice, and he will invariably try to "settle" these without having to come to grips in Court.

Actually the explanation is very simple. The issues in a suit for forcible entry and detainer as here, are (1) whether the plaintiff was in peaceful possession of the premises, and (2) whether the defendant forcibly took and retained such possession from him. And the reason title does not come into the case is because it is immaterial whether plaintiff had the *legal right of possession* or not. He may have been devoid of any muniments of title or even be a trespasser. So long as he had peaceful prior possession and had been forcibly put out of that possession by defendant, the action would lie.

The action was not a common law remedy; in fact, it was in derogation of the common law. It is, and always has been, a statutory remedy. It had its genesis in the English statute of 5 Rich. II, c. 8, a strictly criminal statute, which denounced as a crime the practice of subverting actual possession by the employment of force, even though the possession of the one forcibly displaced was itself wrongful. The reason for the original statute, as well as the later English statutes, was to prevent breaches of the peace which arose when one person would enter upon the land of another and, frequently by sheer physical power, oust the other from peaceful, albeit wrongful possession. This was unusually prevalent in cases where the relationship of landlord and tenant prevailed and the tenant would merely continue to retain the premises after his lawful occupancy.

It was to allay such public disturbances that the early English statutes were passed. Others were the statute of 5 Rich. II, c. 2, providing for a summary conviction, for a forcible entry, by a justice of the peace merely upon a view, "the justice being authorized to go upon the premises, remove the force, and convict, fine and imprison the wrongdoer;" the statute of 8 Hen. VI, c. 9, which enlarged the remedy to cases where there was both a forcible entry and a detainer, and also where there was a peaceful entry followed by a forcible detainer; and the statutes of 31 Eliz. c. 11 and 21 Jac. 1, c. 15, which provided for restitution of possession to the injured party. * * *

Our present Florida statutes, F.S. Sec. 82.01 F.S.A. et seq. are almost identical with the early English statutes. F.S. Sec. 82.03 F.S.A. reads as follows:

> "82.03 Remedy declared for unlawful entry and forcible entry.
>
> "If any person shall enter * * * into lands * * * where entry is not given by law, * * * the party turned out or deprived of possession * * * by such forcible entry, by whatever right or title he held such possession * * * shall at

any time within three years thereafter be entitled to the summary remedy herein provided."

Then follow F.S. Secs. 82.06, F.S.A. et seq., which provide a single summary remedy, including a statutory form of complaint, for either forcible entry or unlawful detainer or a combination of the two. This statutory form was followed in this case.

And while F.S. Sec. 82.05 F.S.A. says that "no question of title, but only a right of possession and of damages, shall be involved in the action," the Supreme Court has construed the language "right of possession" therein to mean "the *present* right of possession, and not the *ultimate* right. It has reference to the right of possession to be determined under the issues made by the pleadings prescribed by the statute and not the *ultimate* right of possession as might be determined by a suit in ejectment," or in the nature of a "trespass to try title to land." (Emphasis supplied). Florida Athletic and Health Club v. Royce, 1948, 160 Fla. 27, 33 So.2d 222. Such *ultimate* right of possession, so determinable in a separate proceeding at law, would not be prejudiced by any judgment rendered in the unlawful entry or detainer action, under F.S. Sec. 82.17 F.S.A., which provides:

> "No judgment rendered [in an entry and detainer action] either for plaintiff or defendant shall bar any action of trespass for injury to the property, or ejectment, between the same parties respecting the same property in question; nor shall any verdict be held conclusive of the facts therein found, in any action of trespass or ejectment."

The entry and detainer action is designed to compel the party out of actual possession, whether the real owner and as such entitled to the *ultimate* right of possession, or not, to respect the actual *present* possession of another, wrongful though it might be, by requiring him, in order to obtain the possession he claims to be his, to resort to legal channels, such as a suit for ejectment, or trespass to try title, or removal of tenant proceedings under Sec. 83.20 et seq. * * *

In the *Florida Athletic & Health Club* case, supra, the essential ingredients of the forcible entry and detainer proceeding are set forth as follows:

> "The elements of plaintiffs' actions are: (1) The plaintiffs must have been in possession; (2) must be ousted of possession; (3) the defendants withhold possession from the plaintiffs and without their consent; (4) the plaintiffs were deprived of possession within three years of the filing of the suit."

So much for the legal principles governing the instant action. We revert now to the facts before the Circuit Judge when defendants Parker moved for summary judgment. The plaintiff had occupied the disputed tract openly, peaceably, and notoriously since 1952. Her predecessors in title had likewise occupied it for ten years immediately before that time. During all these years plaintiff and her predecessors had maintained, fertilized, and cultivated an orange grove thereon and received the profits therefrom. * * *

The whole defense of the Parkers was obviously predicated upon the claim of *ownership* of the disputed tract, derived from the deed from Joshua Creek Corporation just twelve days before they put up the fence and took over possession. But the crucial elements were *present possession* of the disputed strip by Mrs. Floro and the *ouster* of such possession by erection of the fence.

* * * [P]laintiff went forward and proved affirmatively that a genuine issue of a material fact did exist. In such state of the case, summary judgment should not have been entered upon either of the motions. It was a typical case for trial by jury.

The judgment appealed from is reversed.

Notes

1. *Unlawful Detainer in Landlord–Tenant Cases.* In unlawful detainer actions just as in the forcible entry action in *Floro,* only the right to possession is at issue. Thus, the landlord should be able to recover possession much more quickly than in an ordinary ejectment action because the issues that the tenant may raise are limited. Enlarging these issues can curtail the expeditious nature of the provisional remedy. V.F.W. Post No. 7222 v. Summersville Saddle Club, 788 S.W.2d 796 (Mo.App.1990).

In California the tenant is permitted to raise the issue of "retaliatory eviction," S.P. Growers Association v. Rodriguez, 17 Cal.3d 719, 131 Cal.Rptr. 761, 552 P.2d 721 (1976), and the landlord's breach of an implied warranty of habitability, Green v. Superior Court, 10 Cal.3d 616, 111 Cal.Rptr. 704, 517 P.2d 1168 (1974). This warranty has been held to include failure to provide adequate security guards as "directly relevant to the issue of possession." Secretary of Housing and Urban Development v. Layfield, 88 Cal.App.3d Supp. 28, 152 Cal.Rptr. 342 (1978).

2. A defendant in an unlawful detainer action who wishes to claim title to the property must file a separate action to assert that right. The unlawful detainer action can then be stayed until the ownership of the property is determined. Sternaman v. Hall, 411 N.W.2d 18 (Minn.App.1987).

3. The summary aspects of the remedy may be influenced by Pernell v. Southall Realty, 416 U.S. 363 (1974). The Court held that a jury trial is required in the District of Columbia in all actions to recover possession of real property even in summary proceedings under the local statute.

The summary aspects have been subjected to constitutional attack. Thornton v. Butler, 728 F.Supp. 679 (M.D.Ala.1990), held that an Alabama statute providing for service of unlawful detainer notice by leaving it at the tenant's "usual place of abode" violated the tenant's right to due process. In Harrington v. Harrington, 269 A.2d 310 (Me.1970), the court held that a statute requiring a defendant to file security for payment of costs and rent as a condition to pleading a defense of title is an unconstitutional denial of equal protection where applied to an impoverished person unable to provide the bond.

The United States Supreme Court, in Lindsey v. Normet, 405 U.S. 56 (1972), found the "double bond" prerequisite to appeal in the Oregon Forcible Entry and Wrongful Detainer Statute unconstitutional; but it held that summary procedure did not violate the due process clause.

Advice: Check the files of the nearest legal aid office for a realistic appraisal of how "speedy" unlawful detainer proceedings actually are.

4. While the purpose of the remedy is to restore the landlord to possession, the court may award damages; if plaintiff shows malice and wilfulness, these damages may be trebled. See Erbe Corp. v. W & B Realty Co., 255 Cal.App.2d 773, 63 Cal.Rptr. 462 (1967).

5. *Self help.* Summary remedies for recovering possession of land were instituted to curtail self help. The history of these remedies is traced in Daluiso v. Boone, 71 Cal.2d 484, 78 Cal.Rptr. 707, 455 P.2d 811 (1969). The court held that a

party in peaceable possession of land, "may recover *in tort* for all damages for injuries to his person or goods which are the natural and proximate result of a forcible entry by another irrespective of whether the entering party has title or the right to possession." Self help is available where possession can be regained without breach of the peace.

WARLIER v. WILLIAMS

Supreme Court of Nebraska, 1897.
53 Neb. 143, 73 N.W. 539.

[Plaintiffs alleged that: defendants were squatters on bottomlands along the Missouri River belonging to plaintiff; they were cultivating crops; all were insolvent; and that title by adverse possession could be claimed after ten years. The court sustained defendant's demurrer. Plaintiffs appealed.]

This proceeding is, in effect, an application to a court of equity for a mandatory injunction to remove the defendants in error from the real estate of the plaintiff in error, upon which they have forcibly and wrongfully entered, and are wrongfully occupying.

* * * A litigant cannot successfully invoke the extraordinary remedy of injunction to enforce a legal right unless the facts and circumstances in the case are such that his ordinary legal remedies are inadequate; * * * Now, the facts stated in the petition of the plaintiff in error show simply this: That the defendants in error have forcibly entered upon, and are occupying, his real estate. The plaintiff in error has the legal title, and is in possession of this real estate. He might then institute against these defendants in error an action of forcible entry and detainer, under chapter 10 of the Code of Civil Procedure, section 1020 of which expressly provides that such an action may be brought against a defendant who is a settler or occupier of lands, without color of title, and to which the complainant in the forcible detainer suit has the right of possession. Here, then, is a plain statutory remedy for the wrong of which the plaintiff in error complains in this action. Is this remedy an adequate one? The statute provides that this action of forcible entry and detainer may be brought before a justice of the peace, after giving the parties in possession of the land three days' notice to quit; that no continuance for more than eight days shall be granted in the case, unless the party made defendant shall give bond for the payment of rent; and, if the judgment shall be entered in favor of the plaintiff, a writ of restitution shall be awarded in his favor, unless appellate proceedings are taken by defendants, in which case they shall give a bond to pay a reasonable rent for the premises while they wrongfully detain the same. This remedy is not only an adequate one, but it is a summary and a speedy one. The relief demanded by the plaintiff in error in this injunction proceeding is the ousting of the defendants in error from his real estate, so that he may have the exclusive possession of it. A judgment and a writ of restitution in a forcible entry and detainer suit would afford him the same and a more speedy redress than a proceeding by injunction. But it is said by the plaintiff in error that he is entitled to pursue the injunction remedy, because of the insolvency of the defendants in error. This argument, as applied to this case, is untenable. If the defendants in error are insolvent, then the plaintiff in error has no redress for the costs and expenses that he may incur in prosecuting either an injunction suit, or a forcible entry and detainer suit. Another argument is that the proceeding by injunction will avoid a multiplicity

of suits. This argument we also think untenable. We do not understand the mere fact that there exists divers causes of action, which may be the foundation for as many different suits between the parties is a ground upon which equity may be called upon to assume jurisdiction, and settle all such matters in one suit. * * *

Affirmed.

Note

Restatement of Restitution (1937) †

§ 129. Dispossession of and Trespass to Land (1): A person who tortiously has taken possession of another's land without the other's consent is not thereby under a duty of restitution to the other for its value or use, except a person who, having the power to take the land by eminent domain for a particular purpose, has taken possession of it for such purpose but does not take the required proceedings.

Illustration: 1. A disseises B of Blackacre and opens a store thereon, making thereby a profit of $10,000. The reasonable rental value of the land is $1000 for the period occupied by A. In addition to regaining the land, B is entitled only to $1000 in an action of tort. B is not entitled to maintain an action of assumpsit.

b. Trespass by Encroachment: Partial Ouster

Introductory Note

The practical obstacles to enforcing an ejectment judgment against encroaching structures have long been recognized. The comment below was written in 1917; but the force of the observations has hardly been diminished by modern technological advances.

Comment, 27 Yale L.J. 265, 266–7 (1917):

"From the standpoint of practical application to actual conditions, the disadvantage of ejectment as a remedy in cases of encroachment lies not so much in the difficulty of determining what constitutes ouster, as in the obstacles which may confront the sheriff in the execution of the judgment. The order to remove encroaching overhead wires may be carried out easily enough when the wires in question are merely telephone wires; but the sheriff well might hesitate to remove wires carrying a powerful current of electricity. The removal of encroaching underground waterpipes would probably be a task of no considerable magnitude provided the pipes were empty; but if water under pressure were being forced through them, the difficulties of the sheriff who should attempt to remove them would be almost insurmountable. Nor should the sheriff be expected to carry out an order of removal when by so doing he would be forced to enter upon the defendant's land or injure his building, and thus render himself liable to an action of trespass. It has been recognized that even in such a seemingly simple operation as cutting off projecting cornices, the sheriff ought to be protected against the danger of taking more than his 'pound of flesh.' And on what basis shall the sheriff execute a writ commanding the removal of two feet of an encroaching foundation wall, when it is found that the remaining portion of the wall would not be sufficient to support the building?"

L'ENFANT PLAZA EAST INC. v. JOHN McSHAIN, INC.

Court of Appeals, District of Columbia, 1976.
359 A.2d 5.

NEBEKER, ASSOCIATE JUDGE. Appellant L'Enfant Plaza East, Inc. (L'Enfant) complains of the trial court's order granting summary judgment against it in its suit seeking damages against appellee John McShain, Inc. (McShain) for trespass and delay in a construction project. The judgment was based upon McShain's motion for summary judgment on the ground that the suit was untimely filed under the applicable statute of limitations.[1] We find error and reverse.

In the late 1960's McShain, a general contractor, constructed a building for the Department of Housing and Urban Development (HUD). The western boundary of the HUD building adjoined the property leased to L'Enfant. During construction of the HUD building, a portion of the footings extended beyond HUD's boundary line and into L'Enfant's property. This encroachment, consisting of concrete with steel reinforcing bars, ran along the common boundary line for approximately 240 feet. It extended 1½ to 3½ feet into L'Enfant's property. The encroaching structure was approximately 3 feet thick and was buried 23 feet below the surface.

L'Enfant, through a contractor, commenced development of its property on May 11, 1971. On June 11, 1971, during excavation for the construction of its building, the encroachment was discovered. After demand, McShain contracted for the removal of the encroachment during the month of July 1971. Construction resumed following such removal and L'Enfant's building was completed on June 25, 1973. The complaint was filed on June 21, 1974.

Our research, and that of the parties, reveals that this is a case of first impression in this jurisdiction. A cause of action for trespass usually accrues at the time of the original encroachment. We note a similarity to this general rule for permanent structural encroachments. In such cases, the cause of action accrues at the time the trespass occurs; however, we believe that a continuing unknown encroachment is another matter.

McShain argues, pursuant to the general rule, that the encroachment occurred and was discovered more than three years before L'Enfant filed its complaint for damages and therefore the cause of action is barred. We agree that D.C.Code 1973, § 12–301(3), is the controlling statutory provision. The encroachment, however, was unlike that in most cases regarding permanent structures. First, we are not persuaded that the encroachment was permanent in nature simply because it was an injury to real property. Moreover, it is significant that the encroachment was not vital to or supportive of the HUD building since it was easily removed without affecting the stability of that building. It was not included in the HUD construction plans and was promptly

1. [Footnotes renumbered] D.C.Code 1973, § 12–301(3) provides in pertinent part:

[A]ctions for the following purposes may not be brought after the expiration of the period specified below from the time the right to maintain the action accrues:

* * *

(3) for the recovery of damages for an injury to real * * * property—3 years[.]

removed at a reasonable expense. Three factors for determining permanency are articulated in D. Dobbs, Remedies § 5.4 at 338 (1973):

> "(1) is the source of the invasion physically permanent, i.e., is it likely, in the nature of things, to remain indefinitely? (2) is the source of the invasion the kind of thing an equity court would refuse to abate by injunction because of its value to the community or because of relations between the parties? (3) which party seeks the permanent or prospective measure of damages?"

Once this encroachment was discovered, it was removed without undue difficulty. Therefore, "in the nature of things" it was not likely to remain indefinitely. Second, this case reveals a concealed subterranean encroachment buried at least 23 feet below the surface. Such a trespass is unlike that in Sustrik v. Jones & Laughlin Steel Corp., 413 Pa. 324, 197 A.2d 44, 46 (1964). There, a pipe was installed "more than forty years before the * * * action was instituted. While constructed underground, [the pipe] was clearly visible in certain sections of plaintiffs' property." The claim for damages based upon what was viewed as a readily apparent trespass was properly barred by the statute of limitations.

After an extensive survey of the case law, we conclude that the instant subterranean encroachment was a continuing trespass. 509 Sixth Ave. Corp. v. New York City Transit Authority, 15 N.Y.2d 48, 255 N.Y.S.2d 89, 92, 203 N.E.2d 486, 488 (1964). "[A]lthough the nature of the structure may be permanent, the nature of the trespass is continuous." L'Enfant's knowledge of the trespass for more than three years prior to filing a complaint does not necessarily bar its cause of action. The cause of action accrued on the date of the trespass and continued until three years after the encroachment had been removed. We further note that L'Enfant's recovery is limited to damages resulting from the trespass during "the [three-year] statutory period preceding the filing of the suit." Underwater Storage, Inc. v. United States Rubber Co., 125 U.S.App.D.C. 297, 300, 371 F.2d 950, 953 (1966).[2] This calculation will allow L'Enfant to recover damages for delay which occurred after June 21, 1971. However, damages experienced prior to June 21, 1971, are barred by the statute of limitations.

We hold that the instant subterranean encroaching structure was a continuing trespass which gave rise to successive causes of action until its removal. Accordingly, the trial court's ruling on the motion for summary judgment is reversed and the case is remanded for further proceedings.

WILLIAMS v. SOUTH & SOUTH RENTALS, INC.

Court of Appeals of North Carolina, 1986.
82 N.C.App. 378, 346 S.E.2d 665.

On 1 March 1984, plaintiff filed his complaint in this action alleging (i) that he owned property contiguous on the east to property owned by defendant (ii) that defendant had constructed a two-story brick and frame apartment building, the northwest corner of which encroaches upon plaintiff's property, (iii) that this trespass is a continuing trespass and (iv) that he has demanded

2. Since the "trespass is * * * 'continuous,' a new cause of action arises day by day * * * with the result that the plaintiff in such a case can always recover for such damages as have accrued within the statutory period immediately prior to suit." D. Dobbs, Remedies, supra at 343.

that defendant remove that portion of the building which encroaches upon plaintiff's property. In his prayer for relief, plaintiff prayed for a mandatory injunction ordering removal of the encroachment.

Defendant's answer, filed 30 March 1984, set forth several affirmative and equitable defenses including the statute of limitations, laches, the equitable burden test and unclean hands. In opposition to plaintiff's motion for summary judgment, defendant filed the affidavit of John B. South, who stated *inter alia* that he and his father are corporate officers of defendant, that they neither were aware of any alleged encroachment until 1984, that upon learning of the alleged encroachment, they informed plaintiff that they wanted no problems with the title, that plaintiff responded that defendant could purchase his adjoining property for a sum in excess of $45,000.00, and that plaintiff's land has never been used for any purpose, is oddly shaped, is located substantially in a creek bed, is practically unusable and consists of one-fourth to one-third of an acre.

On 31 March 1985, the Honorable Joseph A. Pachnowski entered the following judgment: * * *

1. The encroachment of Defendant's building is, alleged in the Complaint, a continuing trespass.

2. North Carolina General Statute 1–52(3) is therefore applicable and requires that an action for a continuing trespass "shall be commenced within three years from the original trespass and not thereafter."

3. The Complaint having been filed approximately nine years after the original trespass, Plaintiff's claim for relief is barred by North Carolina General Statute 1–52(3).

IT IS THEREFORE ORDERED, ADJUDGED AND DECREED that Plaintiff's claim be and the same is hereby dismissed, that he take nothing by this action and that he pay the costs of this action, the same to be taxed against him by the Clerk. * * * From the entry of this judgment, plaintiff appealed.

PARKER, JUDGE. In his first assignment of error, plaintiff contends that the trial judge erred in finding that the encroachment was a continuing trespass, and in his second assignment of error, plaintiff asserts that the trial judge erred in concluding as a matter of law that G.S. 1–52(3) barred plaintiff's claim for relief.

The relationship between application of G.S. 1–52(3), the statute of limitations for a continuing trespass to real property, and G.S. 1–40, the limitations period for adverse possession, was addressed many years ago by our Supreme Court in Teeter v. Telegraph Co., 172 N.C. 784, 90 S.E. 941 (1916). In *Teeter,* defendant had moved its telegraph poles onto plaintiff's property in 1909; the action was commenced in either December 1914 or January 1915; not long before the action was instituted, defendant had repaired a portion of its line and caused further damage and injury to plaintiff's land. Defendant contended on appeal that the action was barred by the three-year statute of limitations, present G.S. 1–52(3). Hoke, J., wrote for the court as follows:

> "Speaking to this section in Sample v. Lumber Co., 150 N.C. [165], pp. 165–166, [63 S.E. 731] action for wrongful entry and cutting timber on another's land, the Court said: 'True, the statute declares that actions for trespass on real estate shall be barred in three years, and when the trespass is a continuing one such action shall be commenced within three years from the original

trespass, and not thereafter; but this term, "continuing trespass," was no doubt used in reference to wrongful trespass upon real property, caused by structures permanent in their nature and made by companies in the exercise of some *quasi*-public franchise. Apart from this, the term could only refer to cases where a wrongful act, being entire and complete, causes continuing damage, and was never intended to apply when every successive act amounted to a distinct and separate renewal of wrong.' "

"Referring to the language of the section and the interpretation of it suggested in that decision, the Court is inclined to the opinion that this is a continuing trespass within the meaning of the law, and for damages incident to the original wrong, and for that alone, no recovery could be sustained. But this is a suit for permanent damages, and on recovery and payment, so far as plaintiff is concerned, confers on the defendant the right to maintain its line on plaintiff's land for an indefinite period and to enter on the same whenever reasonably required for the 'planting, repairing, and preservation of its poles and other property.' Caviness v. R.R., ante, 305. It is a suit to recover for the value of the easement, which can pass to defendant only by grant or by proceedings to condemn the property pursuant to the statute, Revisal, secs. 1572–1573, or by adverse and continuous user for the period of twenty years."

By analogy, in the case *sub judice,* an apartment building encroaches approximately one square foot on plaintiff's land, hence the encroachment is permanent in nature; since the structure is permanent, the physical trespass is continuous; and the building was built in 1975 more than three years before institution of the action. Therefore, we conclude that this is a continuing trespass and for damages incident to the original wrong, *i.e.,* the construction of the building itself, and for that alone, no recovery can be had. However, like in *Teeter,* supra, this action is for something more than damages to the land caused by the construction. The action is to redress defendant's unauthorized taking of the land. While the action sounds in trespass because there is no dispute over title or location of the boundary line, plaintiff seeks a permanent remedy and is subject to the twenty-year statute of limitations for adverse possession.

As noted in Bishop v. Reinhold, 66 N.C.App. 379, 311 S.E.2d 298, disc. rev. denied, 310 N.C. 748, 315 S.E.2d 700 (1984), an action similar on its facts to the case at bar, "[t]o deny plaintiffs a right of action * * * would be to allow the defendants a right of eminent domain as private persons (and without the payment of just compensation) or grant defendants a permanent prescriptive easement to use the plaintiffs' land. This the law will not do, as the defendants have not been in possession for twenty years from 1973, the date the house was constructed." We agree with plaintiff that the action for permanent redress is not barred by the statute of limitations.

In his third assignment of error, plaintiff contends that the trial judge erred by failing to enter judgment directing defendant to remove the encroachment. * * *

North Carolina is among those jurisdictions requiring that damages for a continuing trespass be brought in one action. In other words, North Carolina does not recognize successive causes of action for continuing trespass. However, on the theory that an award of monetary damages for a permanent encroachment is tantamount to condemnation by a private citizen without the right of eminent domain, our courts have permitted permanent monetary damages only in those situations involving quasi-public entities, for example, the telegraph company in *Teeter*. Hence the usual remedy for a continuing trespass is a permanent injunction which in this case would be a mandatory injunction for removal of the encroachment.

We recognize that in today's economic environment with multi-investor ownership of properties having substantial improvements, there may be situations, other than the traditional quasi-public franchise, where sufficient public interest exists to make the right of abatement at the instance of an individual improper, and defendant should be permitted to demand that permanent damages be awarded. D. Dobbs, Trespass to Land, 47 N.C.Law Rev. 31 (1968). Where the encroachment is minimal and the cost of removing the encroachment is most likely substantial, two competing factors must be considered in fashioning a remedy. On the one hand, without court intervention, a defendant may well be forced to buy plaintiff's land at a price many times its worth rather than destroy the building that encroaches. On the other hand, without the threat of a mandatory injunction, builders may view the legal remedy as a license to engage in private eminent domain. The process of balancing the hardships and the equities is designed to eliminate either extreme. Factors to be considered are whether the owner acted in good faith or intentionally built on the adjacent land and whether the hardship incurred in removing the structure is disproportionate to the harm caused by the encroachment. Mere inconvenience and expense are not sufficient to withhold injunctive relief. The relative hardship must be disproportionate.

Notwithstanding the foregoing discussion, we are compelled by this Court's prior holding in Bishop v. Reinhold, to hold that since the encroachment and continuing trespass have been established, and since defendant is not a quasi-public entity, plaintiff is entitled as a matter of law to the relief prayed for, namely removal of the encroachment.

Accordingly, we remand this case to the Superior Court for entry of a mandatory injunction ordering defendant to remove that part of its apartment building that sits upon plaintiff's land as shown on the plat contained in the record.

Reversed and remanded.

WEBB, J., dissenting. I dissent. I do not agree with the statement of the majority that "since defendant is not a quasi-public entity, plaintiff is entitled as a matter of law to the relief prayed for, namely removal of the encroachment." I believe that the rule stated in Clark v. Asheville Contracting Co., Inc., 316 N.C. 475, 342 S.E.2d 832 (1986) governs. In determining whether to grant an injunction, the court must consider the relative convenience-inconvenience and the comparative injuries to the parties.

Notes

1. Compare Morrison v. Jones, 58 Tenn.App. 333, 430 S.W.2d 668 (1968). Injunctive relief was refused although the encroaching building extended over the boundary line 88 inches and the trial judge found that defendant was either wilful or reckless. Ordinarily the doctrine of relative hardship does not apply to wilful encroachers. See Welton v. 40 East Oak Street Building. Corp., 70 F.2d 377 (7th Cir.1934), cert. denied, 293 U.S. 590 (1934); Brown Derby Hollywood Corp. v. Hatton, 61 Cal.2d 855, 40 Cal.Rptr. 848, 395 P.2d 896 (1964); Missouri Power & Light Co. v. Barnett, 354 S.W.2d 873 (Mo.1962) (order for removal of $16,000 home from power company's easement); Papanikolas Brothers Enterprises v. Sugarhouse

Shopping Center Associates, 535 P.2d 1256 (Utah 1975); Keeton and Morris, Notes on "Balancing the Equities," 18 Tex.L.Rev. 412 (1940); Note, Injunction Negotiations: An Economic, Moral, and Legal Analysis, 27 Stan.L.Rev. 1563 (1975).

2. Calhoon v. Communications Systems Construction, Inc., 140 Ill.App.3d 1012, 1016–17, 489 N.E.2d 23, 26–27 (1986). CSC suspended a cable television line from utility poles across plaintiffs' farms. The utility had an easement; it permitted CSC to use the poles. But neither plaintiff had granted CSC permission to construct the line. The trial judge awarded plaintiffs $528 and $507:

"Should CSC have been required to remove its equipment from plaintiffs' property? CSC argues that what plaintiffs seek is essentially injunctive relief, which should be granted only on plaintiffs' showing of necessity and the inadequacy of any remedy at law, i.e. damages in this case. CSC relies on the proposition familiar to cases where one landowner's construction encroaches upon the land of an adjoining landowner, that courts will refuse injunctive relief (i.e. tearing down the construction) and leave the complaining party to his remedy at law (i.e. damages), provided that the encroachment is slight and unintentional, the cost of removing it great, and the corresponding benefit to the adjoining owner of removal small. * * *

"We cannot agree. CSC does not claim it had any right to be on plaintiffs' land. Mr. Calhoon protested early on in the construction, yet CSC persisted in completing the very structure it now claims is too expensive to move. On these facts there is no reason to stray from the principles established in cases involving encroachments by adjacent landowners: One who knows of a claim to land which he proposes to use as his own, proceeds at his peril if he goes forward in the face of protest from the claimant and places structures upon the land. [citations] Mere belief in one's right, no matter how honestly and reasonably entertained, is no justification for preventing removal of the offending structure, nor is great expense of removal, when there has been a deliberate invasion of a plaintiffs' title to real estate, and protest, followed by resort to the courts to ascertain the legal rights of the parties. The encroachment will be deemed deliberate if made after due warning. * * *

"CSC suggests that it should be protected from the expense of moving the cable line in question because of the disastrous effect such an order would have on the providing of cable television service in the affected area. CSC suggests that it is entitled to protection because of the nature of the service it provides. It has been said that the court will generally stay its hand in the public interest where it appears the private right will not suffer by the refusal of injunctive relief, where the damage to the complainant from denying the injunction will be slight, where the right invaded is insubstantial, or where the injury is compensable in damages, whereas issuing the order may or would occasion public inconvenience. However, 'the convenience of the public should not be allowed to influence the court to disregard the complainant's clear legal right * * *. The public interest is that property rights, as guaranteed by constitutional and statutory law, be preserved against inroads, and injunctive relief against illegal appropriation of property cannot be defeated by any claim that the public interest requires it.' 42 Am.Jur.2d Injunctions § 59 (1969).

"In sum, we conclude that the trial court had no discretion on these facts but to order that CSC's cable and equipment be removed from plaintiffs' property. This cause is reversed and remanded so that the court may enter an order to that effect."

3. In Frustuck v. City of Fairfax, 212 Cal.App.2d 345, 370–72, 28 Cal.Rptr. 357, 372–73 (1963), the tort was committed by a municipality. The significance of this

in determining plaintiff's remedies emerges from the court's denial of plaintiff's prayer for an injunction. The court summarized the California law:

"In addition to her action in inverse condemnation and for trespass the plaintiff sought an injunction to restrain the City from continuing to do the acts she claimed constituted a trespass and inverse condemnation. The general rule is that where a taking of private property for public use *is attempted* under the power of eminent domain without any provision having been made for compensation, an injunction will lie. If the property *has been taken* for a public use without any provision being made for compensation, an unqualified injunction may be refused if a public use has intervened. Accordingly, it has been held that when a public use *has attached* a prohibitory injunction should be granted only in the event no other relief is adequate. The appropriate course to pursue when such a use has attached is to sue for damages in inverse condemnation, and unless the plaintiff can show good reason why such remedy would not be adequate, he is not entitled to an injunction where a public use has intervened. Moreover, where a property owner permits the completion by a public agency of the work which results in the taking of private property for a public use he will be denied the right to enjoin the agency. His only remedy under such circumstances is a proceeding in inverse condemnation to recover damages."

4. Inverse condemnation has been defined as "an eminent domain proceeding initiated by the property owner rather than the condemner." See Breidert v. Southern Pacific Co., 61 Cal.2d 659, 663, 39 Cal.Rptr. 903, 905, 394 P.2d 719, 721 (1964).

5. Professor M.T. Van Hecke studied whether mandatory injunctions against encroachment were effective and whether they had led to extortionate settlements. He contacted 44 lawyers in 29 cases and received replies from 31 lawyers concerning 25 injunctions. He concluded that 75% of the injunctions were effective and that little evidence existed that the injunctions had been used to coerce settlements. Attorneys who participated in "extortionate" settlements may not have responded to the survey. Van Hecke, Injunction to Remove or Remodel Structures Erected in Violation of Building Restrictions, 32 Tex.L.Rev. 521 (1954).

c. *Trespass Involving Severance From Freehold—Damages*

Preliminary Note

Removal of timber or minerals from land leads to several substantive theories: a. conversion of the severed chattels; b. trespass de bonis asportatis; and c. trespass for the harm done to the land itself. The landowner's suit for damages for conversion of timber has been treated supra at pp. 381–85. Although distinguishable in theory, the rules for calculating the basic damages are essentially the same under any theory. The landowner may choose to pursue conversion of the chattels rather than trespass to the realty for procedural reasons or because of relevant statutes. For example in Britt v. Georgia–Pacific Corp., 46 N.C.App. 107, 109–10, 264 S.E.2d 395, 397–98 (1980), the owner sued a lumber company for damages to real property *and also* for the value of merchantable timber removed. The trial court had awarded a total of $5010: $10 nominal damages, $2000 for "incidental" damages, and $3000 representing double the value of the timber removed. In reducing the judgment to $3000, the court said:

"Last, defendant contends the court erred in awarding plaintiffs 'incidental damages' in addition to damages for timber cut. Where plaintiff sues for the unlawful cutting or removal of timber, there are two alternative measures of damages available. One gives the landowner the difference in the value of his property immediately before and immediately after the cutting. The other gives plaintiff the value of the timber itself. This latter value is then doubled by reason of N.C.G.S. 1–539.1(a) which allows plaintiff to recover double the value of timber cut or removed. This statute not only doubles the value of the timber cut but imposes strict liability as well.

"Here plaintiffs seek to recover both their statutory damages and damages for the diminution in value of their property. The loss of value for the timber cut is inextricably involved in the damages for diminution in value of the real property. Plaintiffs cannot recover both. We hold that plaintiffs made an election to recover their statutory damages when they proceeded upon that theory at trial and recovered damages thereunder, albeit the court erroneously awarded them 'incidental damages.'

"Our holding today is in effect a continuation of the election of remedies a landowner had at common law to sue in *trespass de bonis asportatis* for the value of the trees (now doubled by reason of the statute) or in *trespass quare clausum fregit* for injury to the freehold."

The owner may choose the trespass action rather than conversion because the statute of limitations may be longer.

In timber trespasses, courts measure the diminution in the value of land by stumpage value. Stumpage value is the uncut timber's market value: what a purchaser would pay the property owner for the right to cut and remove the standing timber. Gerdes v. Bohemia, Inc., 88 Or.App. 62, 744 P.2d 275 (1987).

UNITED STATES v. MARIN ROCK & ASPHALT CO.

United States District Court, Central District of California, 1969.
296 F.Supp. 1213.

IRVING HILL, DISTRICT JUDGE. * * * In the action the government sues as landowner for damages for trespass on its land. It seeks damages against each Defendant in the amount of $7,162.50 plus interest and costs. The alleged damages result from the removal of sand and gravel from the land in question. The Fosters (and others to whose interest they eventually succeeded) were locators, i.e. purported owners, of mining claims on government land located in Imperial County, California. As a result of litigation tried in this court before another judge, their mining claims were held to be invalid. * * * Before that judgment was entered, the Fosters spent money in making the land ready for the extraction of sand and gravel. Most of this money was spent on neighboring lands to procure and to pipe water for the extraction operations on the land in question. Whether any of the money was spent on the land in question is not clear. But as will be discussed infra that question is not important. It can be assumed *arguendo* that the money was spent on the very land in issue.

* * * In 1960 the Fosters entered a lease with Marin. The lease permitted Marin to remove sand and gravel from the land in question upon payment to the Fosters of a royalty of 2½¢ per ton, which Marin agreed to pay. In addition, Marin agreed to improve the said water well and water piping facilities. Pursuant to the lease, Marin removed 286,500 tons of sand and gravel from the land in question. At the royalty rate of 2½¢ per ton, this equals $7,162.50, the amount of the damages sought herein. Marin admits that it owes the sum of $7,162.50 under its lease with the Fosters and that it has not paid the Fosters that sum. In lieu of paying the Fosters, by agreement between the Defendants, that sum has been deposited in trust for the benefit of

the government and the Fosters as their interests may be determined in this action.

It is assumed for the purposes of this opinion that both Defendants were good faith trespassers.

Defendants allege that the "direct expenses" of mining the sand and gravel and the cost of producing water for the purpose, exceeded the value of the sand and gravel extracted and were "substantially" in excess of $7,162.50, [and also that] "development expenses" and the cost of sinking a well and producing water for the mining operations were "substantially" in excess of the value of the minerals removed and in excess of $7,162.50.

* * * Defendants are in essence asserting that under the law governing the measure of damages in such cases, they are permitted to prove amounts expended by them in extracting the sand and gravel to diminish the Plaintiff's recovery. And where the amounts so expended exceed the amount of damages demanded, Defendants contend that the government as Plaintiff is entitled to nothing. * * *

If a reasonable royalty rate is a correct measure of damages for good faith trespass of this type under California law, how then can one reconcile with such a measure of damages the result in Whittaker v. Otto, [248 Cal.App.2d 666, 56 Cal.Rptr. 836] in which the plaintiff was allowed to recover the value of the minerals extracted less the cost of extraction? The answer to this question is provided in National Lead Co. v. Magnet Cove Barium Corp., 231 F.Supp. 208 (W.D.Ark.1964). In that opinion, which involves a good faith trespasser who extracted minerals, the court concludes that the plaintiff may elect between two different damage formulae, i.e. a royalty rate *or* the value of the extracted minerals less costs of production. The court goes on to analyze the purpose and advantages of the two formulae. As the court says:

> "There are two general measures of damage for trespass to minerals which are described as the 'mild' and the 'harsh' rules. The 'mild' rule applies where the trespass is inadvertent, innocent or not in bad faith, and fixes the damages as the value of the minerals in situ. The so-called 'harsh' rule, applied when the trespass is wilful, intentional, or in bad faith, allows the injured party the enhanced value of the product at the time of conversion.
>
> "*Within the framework of the mild measure, there are two different guidelines to determine the in-place value of ore:* first, the royalty value whereby the injured party is allowed as damages an amount equivalent to the value of the privilege of mining and removing the minerals; second, another application of the mild rule allows the injured party to recover the value of the minerals after extraction less a credit to the trespasser of its production costs. The effect of allowing the royalty method as damages is not to punish the nonwilful trespasser, but to compensate the injured party for being deprived of the possibility of extracting the minerals. Alternatively, allowing the injured party to recover the enhanced value of the converted minerals with a deduction in favor of the trespasser for the cost of mining them will also compensate for being deprived of the right of mining the minerals and developing them, while preventing the trespasser from profiting from his wrongdoing. *When the royalty method is used in applying the in-place measure of damages, the question of allowance to the trespasser of credit for his expenses in producing the minerals is not reached.*" [Emphasis added.]

The royalty formula obviously is a simpler one to apply. It does not involve the parties or the court in any complicated accounting. It provides damages to the aggrieved party even where the trespasser's operations have proved unprofitable. The other formula, as stated in the above quotation from *National Lead,* prevents the trespasser from profiting from his wrongdoing and requires him to account to the aggrieved party for all of his net profits. Surely fairness would dictate that the Plaintiff in this type of a case have such an election of remedies and I hold that such an election exists under California law. In the instant case the government has elected to claim under the royalty formula.

For the reasons stated, the government is entitled to a judgment under the royalty formula for the full amount of $7,162.50 against both Defendants. Neither Defendant may minimize or defeat this liability by deducting or offsetting therefrom any amount that either may have spent by way of production or land improvement costs.

As to Marin, there is still another ground which would support a judgment in the full amount of $7,162.50. Marin, by contract, has agreed to pay that amount as a royalty for the privilege of removing the sand and gravel. Marin owes that amount under the contract, without reference to any expenses it may have incurred and without reference to whether its operation was profitable or not. Surely the government, as the true owner of the land, is subrogated to the rights of the Fosters under their contract with Marin. Among the true owner's rights is the right to affirm such a contract made by a trespasser and claim its profits. Shahood v. Cavin, 154 Cal.App.2d 745, 748, 316 P.2d 700 (1957).

It follows from what has been said up to this point, that the government is entitled to a summary judgment against each Defendant for the amount claimed.

Notes

1. Daly v. Smith, 220 Cal.App.2d 592, 603, 33 Cal.Rptr. 920, 926 (1963). The converter sought to defeat an action for conversion and sale of 9,326,000 pounds of gypsite by showing that extraction and marketing costs equalled the selling price. In reversing the judgment for the converter, the court said: [I]t shocks the conscience of lawyer and layman alike that trespassers may convert [the gypsite] without being liable in substantial damages."

2. The measure of damages against even innocent trespassers may be affected by collateral factors, such as operative mines on the property or even the prospect of commercial exploitation of the mineral deposit by the landowner. Bowman v. Hibbard, 257 S.W.2d 550, 552 (Ky.1952):

"In fixing the measure of damages where the trespass is not willful this Court has recognized alternative measures of recovery. Originally, the rule in this state was that the measure of liability as applied to innocent trespassers was the usual and customary royalty paid for the right of mining the substance taken. [citations] * * *

"In these cases the value of the coal taken as it lay in place in the mine was held to be synonymous with the reasonable and customary royalty paid for the right of mining it. In the later case of Hughett v. Caldwell County, 313 Ky. 85, 230 S.W.2d 92, the rule was modified. It was there recognized that an invariable application of reasonable royalty as the measure of damage for an innocent trespass did not always afford full compensation to the owner. It was pointed out that limiting recovery to the royalty was in effect compelling the landowner by operation of law to execute a retroactive lease to the trespasser. A distinction was, therefore, recognized, and two separate classifications of landowners were defined for application of alternative measures of recovery. With respect to a landowner who could not himself extract the minerals in a practical or feasible way or who was merely holding the property for development in the unforeseeable future, the measure of recovery was fixed at the value of the mineral as it lay in the ground, the customary and reasonable royalty being the best proof of that value. In cases where the owner was in a position to mine his own minerals and thus derive any profits which might be realized from their production and sale, the measure of damages was fixed at the net market value of the mineral after it was mined, which is the value of the mineral after its taking, less the reasonable cost of mining."

3. In Thompson v. United States, 308 F.2d 628, 633 (9th Cir.1962), the court, in rejecting defendant's claim for a setoff of the reasonable value of his personal services in a case of wilful trespass, stated:

"We find no case, and appellant has cited none, which permits a recovery on quantum meruit where the person performing the service did so against the wishes of the person against whom the claim was made. By permitting such a recovery, the court would be placing a premium on the commission of a wrongful act and would thus encourage, rather than discourage, similar transgressions. When the circumstances of a case clearly repel the idea that the services were performed with the expectation of payment being either made or received a promise to pay will not be implied and the common law action will not lie."

ST. LOUIS SMELTING & REFINING CO. v. HOBAN

Supreme Court of Missouri, 1948.

357 Mo. 436, 209 S.W.2d 119.

DALTON, COMMISSIONER. * * * On November 30, 1940, the respondent and appellants entered into a written agreement. The licensor (respondent), in consideration of certain "royalty payments" and the covenants of the licensees (appellants) as therein set out, did "license and let unto licensees so much of the surface of" 51 acres, more or less, of described real estate in Madison County, Illinois, as might be required by licensees, for the purpose of the agreement. All subsurface and surface rights not expressly granted were reserved. The license was to continue for five years "from the date of the agreement." Licensees were "to have and to hold such premises for the purpose of crushing, sizing and otherwise preparing for market, and removing from the licensed premises, blast furnace slag on the surface of said property." * * * It was further provided that "upon expiration of this license * * * this license shall be at an end, and licensees shall surrender peaceful possession of the licensed premises."

Appellants entered upon the described premises and removed some 200,000 tons of slag and paid the royalty thereon. Prior to the expiration of the agreement, the appellants consulted respondent's manager concerning an extension of time. According to appellants' evidence, they were led to believe that an extension might be granted subject to a change in rate, but respondent's manager advised that, in the event of an unforeseen change in plans, he could guarantee them at least 90 days notice before terminating the agreement.

On November 13, 1945, respondent's manager advised appellants in writing, as follows: "This will advise you that our lease agreement covering the shipment of slag from the Collinsville Dump expires on November 30th of this year. As indicated to you some time back, I am now advising that you will be permitted to continue for a period of sixty days beyond November 30, 1945. At this time it does not appear that renewal of the lease will be in order."

Thereafter, on November 29, 1945, appellants advised respondent in writing, in part as follows: "We have not as yet been able to remove all of the slag upon which you gave us a purchase option at ten (10¢) cents per ton. * * * Under existing conditions the removal of the remainder can be accomplished within a reasonable time, approximately three to five years depending upon the amount involved. * * * Therefore, we hand you herewith fifty thousand ($50,000.00) dollars in cash in payment of the remaining slag. * * * "

Appellants' proposition and the tender were promptly rejected. Appellants continued their operations and, thereafter, in January 1946, paid to respondent royalties in the sum of $319.42 on slag shipped in December 1945. On February 6, 1946, appellants forwarded a statement and check to cover royalties on shipments made in January 1946, but the statement included three cars of slag shipped subsequent to January 29, 1946. Respondent refused the check, returned it to appellants and advised them that the removal of slag from the premises, after January 29, 1946, constituted a conversion of respondent's property.

Thereafter, appellants continued to dig and ship the slag from respondent's premises over respondent's protest. On February 9, 1946, respondent notified appellants' customers that appellants' right to remove slag from respondent's premises had terminated on January 29, 1946; that appellants had no title to any slag shipped after that date; and that respondent would hold the purchasers responsible.

On February 12, 1946, respondent instituted the present action seeking to enjoin the appellants from continuing to trespass on the described real estate, from continuing to remove slag therefrom "to the damage of the hereditaments of the same," and from continuing the appropriation and conversion of respondent's slag to appellants' use and purposes. Respondent further prayed an accounting for the value of slag wrongfully removed.

* * * Appellants continued operations until stopped by a temporary injunction issued by the court on May 13, 1946. Other facts will be stated in the course of the opinion. * * *

The trial court found that appellants' prior right to remove slag from respondent's premises had terminated on January 29, 1946; that, thereafter, appellants had no right whatsoever to remove any slag from said premises; * * * that no title to real estate was involved; and that appellants were indebted to respondent for the full value of the slag so appropriated and converted by them in the sum of $16,184.27, for which sum judgment was entered against appellants.

In support of the decree the respondent insists that "equity will enjoin the wilful and deliberate action of a continuous trespasser, who, without shadow of right, spoliates real estate by repeatedly carrying away part and parcel of the land itself to the injury of the hereditaments, and converts these severed portions to his own use." Echelkamp v. Schrader, 45 Mo. 505, 508; Heman v. Wade, 74 Mo.App. 339 (quarrying rock after termination of lease); Graham v. Womack, 82 Mo.App. 618 (mining lead and zinc ore after forfeiture of lease); Bryant v. West, Mo.Sup., 219 S.W. 355 (landing ferry after license had terminated). Respondent further insists that equity acts in personam and jurisdiction of the parties gives the court jurisdiction to render an appropriate decree no matter where the subject matter may be situated. * * * We do not understand appellants to question these general rules of law, but they rely on exceptions thereto.

Appellants contend that the subject matter of respondent's action was personal property physically located on real estate in Madison County, Illinois; that none of the subject matter of the action was alleged to be located in this state or within the jurisdiction of the trial court; and that the court lacked jurisdiction over the subject matter and was without authority to enter the injunction decree or determine the amount of damages. * * *

Was the blast furnace slag real or personal property? Did respondent have an adequate remedy at law in replevin or for conversion? Appellants say that one action for conversion or replevin of the entire pile of slag would afford an adequate remedy; and that "there is no suggestion in either the pleadings or in the evidence as to why legal damages and replevin are not an adequate remedy."

The evidence shows that a blast furnace or smelter for the production of pig lead and refined lead had once been located upon the described real estate; and that a biproduct known as slag was produced. "Slag is a composition of lime iron silica essentially, with lesser quantities of zinc and a small quantity of lead." It was a refuse of the smelting operations and was poured into slag pots while hot, and was transported out to the slag pile, where it was poured out. It cooled and corroded into a hard substance. When operations ceased, the slag pile extended for some distance east, north and south of the furnace location. Various gulches, low spots and irregularities in the natural surfaces of the land had been filled with slag. The area built up covered some six or eight acres and presented a relatively level surface on top. The only way to remove the slag was by blasting it out with dynamite. * * *

The trial court heard the evidence and found that the slag was real property and applied the law respecting the severance and removal of timber, clay, etc. In view of the evidence we must hold that the slag was real property; and that the parties have not treated the unsevered slag other than as real property. * * * The law respecting real estate, therefore, applies. The mining, taking and carrying away of the slag from the premises, if wrongful, must be regarded as an irreparable injury for which an action for damages is an inadequate remedy. Respondent had no adequate remedy at law in replevin or for conversion on the theory that the entire slag pile was personal property.

Did the trial court have jurisdiction to issue an injunction to prevent appellants from digging and carrying respondent's real property, slag, to the injury and destruction of the inheritance? Appellants rely upon an alleged exception to the general rule which upholds the jurisdiction of a court of equity when the parties are personally within the jurisdiction and before the court and when effective relief to prevent an injury to land may be granted by a decree in personam, the exception being that the court of one state or country will not assume jurisdiction of a suit that in its essentials involves merely the title or possession of land in another, and presents no ground for equitable intervention. The weight of authority seems to support the exception. The reason for the exception is that, if the action in its essence involves merely the legal title or right of possession of the land, it is essentially a local, and not a transitory action. * * *

In this state equitable relief by injunction will not be denied in a proper case, where title or the right to possession is only incidentally and collaterally involved. * * * Further, the general rule is that "a right or title to property may be protected by injunction without its prior establishment at law where such right or title is admitted or where, notwithstanding a formal denial, it is clear from the facts." Carpenter v. Grisham, 59 Mo. 247, 250. Whether the court had jurisdiction to issue the injunction must be determined from the particular facts of this case.

Appellants urge that "an injunction will not issue to prevent a trespass on foreign real estate, nor to eject a holdover tenant from the possession of land." We have pointed out that appellants made no affirmative plea of title or the right to possession of the described real estate. They now contend that, under the general denials in their answers, they showed a right to possession as respondent's holdover tenants. Title is not involved here, since appellants recognize respondent's title, but the claim of right to possession as holdover tenants requires an examination of the evidence and the law of Illinois on the mentioned issue. We assume, without deciding, that the agreement gave possession, rather than a mere license.

[The court ruled that holding over after the expiration of the original lease did not create a year-to-year tenancy.]

In view of our conclusions * * * that the record otherwise presents facts and circumstances clearly cognizable in equity because of irreparable damage to the land and for the purpose of avoiding a multiplicity of suits; and that equity, acting in personam, can give full and complete relief, it follows that the court did not err, on the grounds assigned, when issuing the injunction. * * * Since equity had jurisdiction, appellants were not entitled to a jury trial on the issue of damages.

[After modifying the award of damages, the court affirmed judgment for plaintiff.]

Notes

1. A party seeking to enjoin a continuing trespass usually seeks an interlocutory injunction pending trial. In determining whether to grant an interlocutory decree, what effect should the court give to whether the plaintiff is or is not in possession of the disputed property? Compare Erhardt v. Boaro, 113 U.S. 537 (1885), with Gause v. Perkins, 56 N.C. 177 (1857).

2. What would have happened in *Hoban* if defendant had claimed title to the Illinois property? See Moore v. McAllister, supra, p. 144. Would the merger of law and equity solve this problem?

3. If no issue of title is raised, equity readily grants injunctive relief against the wrongful removal and cutting of timber. See 4 J. Pomeroy, Equity Jurisprudence § 1357 (5th ed.1941). For an interesting case granting relief where a tree stood directly on the boundary line, see Weisel v. Hobbs, 138 Neb. 656, 294 N.W. 448 (1940).

4. The remedies to effect the duty of restitution are considered under Injuries to Personal Property Interests, supra, pp. 386–404. Restitution arises from the conversion of the severed chattels rather than from the injury to the land.

d. *Other Acts Constituting Trespass*

(1) Dumping

Skip to

DON v. TROJAN CONSTRUCTION CO.

District Court of Appeal of California.
First District, 1960.
178 Cal.App.2d 135, 2 Cal.Rptr. 626.

DEVINE, J., PRO TEM. Plaintiffs appeal from a judgment which was rendered in their favor, on the ground of inadequacy of the award. * * *

On February 21, 1957, plaintiffs, husband and wife, bought a commercially zoned lot in the city of Campbell. They intended to build a supermarket on the lot, and placed a sign on it announcing their intention to do so, but conditions on the stock market, in which they had holdings, were not favorable to them at the time, so they postponed construction of the market. They did not intend to rent the lot to anyone, and Mr. Don testified that he would not have accepted a proposal to rent although he might have allowed a brief use of the lot without charge had he been asked for it.

The land had been owned by the Trojan Construction Company, one of the defendants, but was sold on February 21, 1957, to Ad–Mor Enterprises, Inc., a corporation. That grantee immediately, and by the next deed of record conveyed the lot to plaintiffs.

On or about June 1, 1957, Trojan Construction Company was building a subdivision near the Don lot. Streets had to be built, and there was dirt to be taken away and stored somewhere. The general manager of Trojan Construction Company, Mr. Burchfield, testified that he asked a Mr. James of Ad–Mor for permission to store the dirt on the lot, but there is no fixing of the date of the conversation. Mr. Burchfield testified that Mr. James gave Ad–Mor's consent. He testified that he did not know about Mr. Don or his ownership of the property until the suit was brought.

Mr. Burchfield instructed Kebble Construction Company, which was Trojan's subcontractor for putting in the streets, to store the dirt on the lot. During June and July, 1957, dirt was being put on the land and taken off. In August, 1957, Trojan decided it did not need any of the dirt, and advertised that free dirt was available. The public began to remove the dirt. It was stipulated that in March, 1958, there was still "substantial dirt on it," but by the end of March, 1958, there was no dirt on the property. * * *

On November 26, 1957, plaintiffs filed the action, alleging that defendants Trojan and Keeble placed large quantities of dirt on plaintiffs' land, without their permission. They alleged the rental value of the land to be $750 per month, and they prayed damages in the amount of $750 per month until all the dirt should have been removed.

They alleged that the land had been rendered unusable in its state at that time for the building of the intended supermarket, and they prayed damages in the sum of $10,000 for prevention of the use of plaintiffs' property. * * *

The evidence as to rental value of the land was: (1) The testimony of plaintiff Don that he estimated the rental value to be $650 per month; (2) Testimony (it was not actually given, but defendants stipulated it would be given if the witnesses took the stand) of two real estate brokers; one, Harry

Walters estimated the rental value at $550 per month, and the other, Glenn Hannard at $450 per month.

Don's reasoning was that the average value of the land during the time of the occupation was, in his estimation, $65,000, and that he thought one per cent per month was a fair rental. Walters reasoned that there was no other vacant land in the vicinity and that the highest rental use was for storing heavy equipment. Hannard reasoned that it is difficult to find a tenant for unimproved land, that an investor in unimproved commercial property should get two-thirds of one per cent plus cost. He estimated the value at $60,000 and the rental value at two-thirds of one per cent at $400, and he added $50 per month as taxes.

The court found that the value of the lot was neither greater nor less by reason of the use of the land by defendants; that the average rental value during the period when the land was used by defendants was $550 per month, and the total $5,500. However, the court found that plaintiffs would not have made any use of the land during that time, nor did they intend to rent it out for any purpose, and would not have rented it had an offer been made. The court found that the only damages "are nominal damages sustained by reason of the technical invasion of their possessory rights in the land." The court awarded damages against both defendants in the total amount of $200, and no costs to plaintiffs.

The judgment cannot be sustained. Section 3334 of the Civil Code provides that the detriment caused by the wrongful occupation of real property (except in certain cases of wilful holding over wherein the damages are higher), "is deemed to be the value of the use of the property for the time of such occupation * * *." The court found that the rental value was $5,500, but awarded $200 and stated that this amount was merely nominal damages. It is plain that the measure explicitly required by the code was not used.

The argument made by respondents throughout the trial was that the owners had lost nothing because they did not intend to rent the land out anyway. If this subject were open to be debated upon, it could be pointed out that if only nominal damages are awarded, the appropriators of the use of land could gain a virtually expense free use of property for profitable purposes on the single condition that the owner did not presently intend to lease the land or to use it himself. However, the Civil Code in section 3334 has fixed the measure of damages, and has made no exception in cases where the plaintiff did not intend to use the land or to rent it out so that the court can do no other than apply that measure, namely, the "value of the use." That the owners did not intend to make any use of the land themselves does not deprive them of their proper award. * * *

A point relative to the nature of the action is made by respondents. It is necessary, they say, for owners who wish to claim damages according to the measure established in section 3334 of the Civil Code to waive the tort and to sue in assumpsit on an implied contract. They cite the cases of Samuels v. Singer, 1 Cal.App.2d 545 [36 P.2d 1098, 37 P.2d 1050], and Herond v. Bonsall, 60 Cal.App.2d 152 [140 P.2d 121]. In both of those cases, the action had been essentially in assumpsit, so we have no more than the statement therein that one may waive the tort and sue for the damages described in section 3334 of the Civil Code, which the landowners did, and successfully, in those two cases. * * *

The court having found that $5,500 was the fair rental value of the property for the whole period of the wrongful occupation, judgment should be entered by the court in that amount. * * *

DANDOY v. OSWALD BROTHERS PAVING

District Court of Appeal of California, Second District, 1931.
113 Cal.App. 570, 298 P. 1030.

CONREY, P.J. The plaintiff was the owner of * * * a little over one acre of land. The defendant, while performing a street work contract on a street not far from the plaintiff's premises, dumped upon plaintiff's land and spread out over said land a large quantity of materials which accumulated in the course of performance of the street work. * * *

The evidence leaves no doubt that defendant, without knowledge or consent of the plaintiff, entered upon plaintiff's land and placed thereon a large quantity of material * * *. The only questions of fact relate to the quality and description of the material, and amount, if any, of the resulting damage. There was evidence sufficient to justify the court in finding that the materials deposited did not include macadam, crushed rock, or oil, and that the value of the land was not diminished by the deposit on the land of the earth and soil (probably not less than one thousand cubic yards), placed thereon by appellant. [sic.] [The trial court, in fact, found the value increased.]

Appellant contends, however, that the measure of damages in such a case as this is to be determined by the cost of removing the obnoxious materials and restoring the property to its original condition. The evidence of the cost of removal of the materials, according to the varying opinions of the witnesses, varied from $1 to 50 cents per cubic yard. The court in its decision ignored this evidence. * * *

In the case at bar the evidence shows, without conflict, that the materials deposited by defendant on plaintiff's land can be removed, at a cost less than the value of the land. To hold that appellant is without remedy merely because the value of the land has not been diminished, would be to decide that by the wrongful act of another, an owner of land may be compelled to accept a change in the physical condition of his property, or else perform the work of restoration at his own expense. This would be a denial of the principle that there is no wrong without a remedy. The reasonable cost of restoration may be recovered, without regard to the fact that the plaintiff has not yet removed said materials from his land. The cost, as determined by the court, will be, in effect, the amount of diminution in value of the land, resulting from the wrong committed by defendant.

The judgment is reversed.

Notes

1. Cain v. Fontana, 423 S.W.2d 134 (Tex.Civ.App.1967). Defendant dumped concrete blocks, debris, and junk on the parking lot adjacent to plaintiff's restaurant. Plaintiff's damages included the actual cost for removing debris, the expense of resurfacing the parking lot, loss of profits, and exemplary damages. Also adopting the repair measure of damages for dumping is Myers v. Arnold, 83 Ill.App.3d 1, 403 N.E.2d 316 (1980).

WHEELOCK v. NOONAN

Court of Appeals of New York, 1888.
108 N.Y. 179, 15 N.E. 67.

FINCH, J. The findings of the trial court establish that the defendant, who was a total stranger to the plaintiff, obtained from the latter a license to place upon his unoccupied lots, in the upper part of the city of New York, a few rocks, for a short time, the indefiniteness of the period having been rendered definite by the defendant's assurance that he would remove them in the spring. Nothing was paid or asked for this permission, and it was not a contract in any just sense of the term, but merely a license which by its terms expired in the next spring. During the winter, and in the absence and without the knowledge of plaintiff, the defendant covered six of the lots of plaintiff with "huge quantities of rock," some of them 10 or fifteen feet long, and piled to the height of 14 to 18 feet. This conduct was a clear abuse of the license, and in excess of its terms, and so much so that if permission had been sought upon a truthful statement of the intention it would undoubtedly have been refused. In the spring the plaintiff, discovering the abuse of his permission, complained bitterly of defendant's conduct, and ordered him to remove the rocks to some other locality. The defendant promised to do so, but did not, and in the face of repeated demands has neglected and omitted to remove the rocks from the land. The court found as matter of law from these facts that the original permission given did not justify what was done either, as it respected the quantity of rock or the time allowed; that after the withdrawal of the permission in the spring, and the demand for the removal of the rock, the defendant was a trespasser, and the trespass was a continuing one which entitled plaintiff to equitable relief; and awarded judgment requiring defendant to remove the rocks before March 15, 1886, unless for good cause shown the time for such removal should be extended by the court.

The sole question upon this appeal is whether the relief granted was within the power of the court, and the contention of the defendant is mainly based upon the proposition that the equitable relief was improper since there was an adequate remedy at law. * * *

It is now said that the remedy was at law, that the owner could have removed the stone and then recovered of the defendant for the expense incurred. But to what locality could the owner remove them? He could not put them in the street; the defendant presumably had no vacant lands of his own on which to throw the burden; and it would follow that the owner would be obliged to hire some vacant lot or place of deposit, become responsible for the rent, and advance the cost of men and machinery to effect the removal. If any adjudication can be found throwing such burden upon the owner, compelling him to do in advance for the trespasser what the latter is bound to do, I should very much doubt its authority. On the contrary, the law is the other way. Beach v. Crain, 2 N.Y. 97. And all the cases which give to the injured party successive actions for the continuance of the wrong are inconsistent with the idea that the injured party must once for all remove it. Such is neither an adequate remedy nor one which the plaintiff was bound to adopt.

But it is further said that he could sue at law for trespass. That is undoubtedly true. The case of Uline v. Railroad Co., 101 N.Y. 98, 4 N.E.Rep. 536, demonstrates upon abundant authority that in such action only the damages to its date could be recovered, and for the subsequent continuance of the trespass new actions following on in succession would have to be maintained. But in a case like the present, would that be an adequate remedy? In each action the damages could not easily be anything more than the fair rental of the lot. It is difficult to see what other damages could be allowed, not because they would not exist, but because they would be quite uncertain in amount and possibly somewhat speculative in their character. The defendant, therefore, might pay those damages, and continue his occupation, and if there were no other adequate remedy, defiantly continue such occupation, and in spite of his wrong make of himself in effect a tenant who could not be dispossessed. The wrong in every such case is a continued unlawful occupation, and any remedy which does not or may not end it is not adequate to redress the injury or restore the injured party to his rights. On the other hand, such remedy in a case like the present might result to the wrongdoer in something nearly akin to persecution. He is liable to be sued every day, *die de diem,* for the renewed damages following from the continuance of the trespass; and while, ordinarily, there is no sympathy to be wasted on a trespasser, yet such multiplicity of suits should be avoided, and especially under circumstances like those before us. The rocks could not be immediately removed. The courts have observed that peculiarity of the case, and shaped their judgment to give time. It may take a long time, and during the whole of it the defendant would be liable to daily actions. For reasons of this character it has very often been held that while, ordinarily, courts of equity will not wield their power merely to redress a trespass, yet they will interfere under peculiar circumstances, and have often done so where the trespass was a continuing one, and a multiplicity of suits at law was involved in the legal remedy. * * *

These views of the case enable us to support the judgment rendered. It should be affirmed, with costs.

Notes

1. Belinsky v. Belinsky, 5 Conn.App. 133, 497 A.2d 84 (1985): "This is an appeal by the plaintiffs claiming that the trial court erred in finding that they had failed to sustain their burden of proving by a fair preponderance of credible evidence that irreparable harm had been done to them sufficient to warrant the issuance of a mandatory injunction.

"The defendant, Lewis P. Belinsky, the owner of an undivided one-quarter interest in a tract of land co-owned by the plaintiffs, joined with the defendant, Stephen Hornak, Jr., in a business venture to collect, store and sell used automobile tires. The defendants stored thousands of tires on the land and many tires still remain, even though the business is no longer in existence. The plaintiffs want the defendants to remove all the tires. * * *

"The plaintiffs presented evidence that the presence of the tires reduces the value of the land and thereby thwarts their efforts to sell the property at a reasonable price, that the presence of the tires creates a continuing zoning violation, and that the tires create a fire hazard and a condition of attractive nuisance. The plaintiffs also presented evidence that there were facilities which would take the tires, including one located in New Haven. The defendants, Lewis Belinsky and Stephen Hornak, Jr., allege in their pleadings that they had removed all the tires which they deposited on the plaintiffs' property.

"A mandatory injunction will not issue where the plaintiffs have an adequate remedy at law. [citations] Testimony disclosed that the tires could be removed and that certain facilities would accept those tires. Although this may be a costly procedure for the plaintiffs, it does not deprive them of an adequate remedy at law since a suit for damages for the cost of the removal could be brought. We, therefore, do not find that the trial court erred."

2. In evaluating the adequacy of the damages remedy, consider Markstrom v. United States Steel Corp., 182 Mich.App. 570, 452 N.W.2d 820 (1989). The defendant dumped 44,000 cubic yards of rock onto eight-tenths of an acre of plaintiff's land. The court reversed a judgment giving plaintiff the cost of removing the rock. The cost of repair, it held, may not exceed the market value of the affected land.

(2) Digging

HUMBLE OIL & REFINING CO. v. KISHI

Commission of Appeals of Texas, 1925.
276 S.W. 190.

K. Kishi, the owner of all the surface and three-fourths undivided interest in the oil and mineral rights, and Isaac Lang, the owner of the remaining one-fourth interest in the oil and mineral rights of 50 acres of land in Orange County, Tex., executed to the Humble Oil & Refining Company a lease granting to it the exclusive right to enter upon said land and drill oil wells and take therefrom the oil. * * * No drilling was begun within the time provided, and the lease expired. After the expiration of this lease, in January, 1923, oil was found on an adjoining tract of land in a well drilled near this 50 acres. On January 23, 1923, the Humble Oil & Refining Company entered upon this 50 acres of land, and began drilling an oil well thereon, claiming the exclusive right to the leasehold interest therein. It claimed that the leases had not expired, and that under its terms it did not expire until three years after it was signed and acknowledged by Lang and delivered. Kishi protested against this entry, and advised the Humble Oil & Refining Company that he would hold it responsible for any damages that might accrue to him. Lang, however, consented to the entry under the claim made.

The Humble Oil & Refining Company remained in possession under this entry until it completed the drilling of the well, which resulted in the failure to find oil, and it relinquished possession on May 10, 1923. As a result of the discovery of oil on the adjoining tract of land, the leasehold interest in the 50–acre tract was of the market value of $1,000 per acre. At the time the Humble Oil & Refining Company relinquished possession, and thereafter the leasehold interest had no value by reason of the failure to find oil on this tract.

In suit by Kishi against the Humble Oil & Refining Company for damages sustained by him, the district court awarded him nominal damages in the sum of $1 only, holding that the amount of damages sustained by him was uncertain and not susceptible of proof. On appeal from this judgment the Court of Civil Appeals held that he was under the facts entitled to recover the actual damages occasioned by reason of the wrongful entry and ouster which was the value to him of his three-fourths undivided leasehold interest, but that proof of the market value of the entire leasehold interest was not in law sufficient upon which to base the amount of his recovery.

Oil in place under the land is real estate. The exclusive right to enter upon the land, drill wells thereon, and remove therefrom the oil to exhaustion, paying therefor a portion of the oil when extracted or the equivalent of such portion, is a property right which the law protects. The Humble Oil & Refining Company, wrongfully claiming to own this right over the protest of Kishi, and excluding him therefrom, entered upon his 50 acres of land for the purpose of drilling the well. This was clearly a trespass and ouster. This right had a market value of $50,000, being $1,000 per acre. Had Lang not consented, and had he and Kishi joined in a suit to recover their damages for the wrongful entry, the measure of their damages would have been the market value of the leasehold interest which is here shown to be $1,000 per acre. Lang would have been entitled to one-fourth and Kishi to three-fourths of the amount recovered. We can conceive of no reason why Kishi should be permitted to recover either a larger or smaller amount, because it is shown that Lang consented to the entry.

The Humble Oil & Refining Company insists that it should not be required to pay as damages Kishi's proportionate share of the market value of this leasehold interest, because it entered upon the land in good faith, believing that its lease had not expired. Though it did so in good faith, without any intention to injure Kishi, it asserted a right it did not have. This right, at the time it was wrongfully asserted, had a market value. Had the oil company acquired this right by purchase before its entry, the presumption of law is that it would have been required to pay the market value therefor. Had it done so, Kishi would have been entitled to receive three-fourths of the market value of the leasehold interest. * * *

[On rehearing, 291 S.W. 538, the court reaffirmed that: "The value of Kishi's three-fourths undivided interest in the leasehold estate was the amount he was entitled to recover. * * *" The court also decided that: "A three-fourths undivided interest in the leasehold estate may or may not be three-fourths of $1,000 per acre. The fact that it was an undivided interest may have affected its value." The court set aside the prior judgment that reformed the damage award and remanded to ascertain the amount of damages.]

PHILLIPS PETROLEUM CO. v. COWDEN

United States Court of Appeals, Fifth Circuit, 1957.
241 F.2d 586.

TUTTLE, CIRCUIT JUDGE. * * * Plaintiffs below are the owners of the mineral estate in the lands in question, 2682 acres of land in Ector County, Texas, in which county defendant Phillips has important oil interests * * *.

In August, September, and October of 1953, appellant Phillips, through the employment of appellant Geophysical, caused a seismic survey by the reflection method to be made in the vicinity of the Harper Field, Ector County, Texas. Appellants' entry and activity at six locations ranging east-west across Sections 31 and 32, Block 43, form the basis of the District Court's findings and award for appellees. Appellants made no physical entry upon any of the other tracts comprising the 2682 acres in which appellees owned the minerals. * * *

The mineral estate * * * was owned * * * by appellees. * * * The surface estate in Sections 31 and 32 upon which entry was made * * * was owned by Paul Moss.

On August 20, 1953, and prior to commencement of the survey, appellant Phillips obtained the verbal permission of Paul Moss to use the land owned by him for conducting the survey in consideration of damage payments of $50.00 for each single hole shot and $100.00 for each pattern hole shot. Moss did not purport to act for the mineral owners insofar as their rights might be affected. * * *

It was shown by uncontradicted testimony that the purpose of the survey as a whole was to evaluate the deeper horizons underlying the Harper Pool area located generally in the central part of Block 44, not the lands in dispute. The specific purpose of the six locations in Block 43 was to project a single line or profile eastward into Sections 31 and 32, the land in dispute, in order to identify the detailed work in Block 44 with the known depth of a well known as the "Stanolind 1–E Cowden" located in the Southeast Quarter (SE/4) of Section 32, which was referred to in the testimony as an attempt to obtain "well control" for the survey.

The physical and mechanical features of the survey appeared also without dispute. The seismograph crew and equipment consisted of 16 men, 14 trucks, 3 trailers and other equipment. * * * In the entire survey there were 47 shot point locations, 6 of which were on appellees' tracts in Block 43, the remaining 41 locations being on lands in Block 44. At the six locations in Sections 31 and 32, Block 43, the crew made 15 seismic shootings, one of such shots being a single shot and the other 14 being pattern shots; when these shots were made, vibrations traveled in all directions from each shot point and the vibrations traveling downward through the earth were reflected by various geological formations back to the surface and the impulses were received on recording instruments called geophones or seismometers.

Appellants contend that the actual area "occupied" by the vibrations to the extent that they were theoretically or probably reflected and received in the recording devices to produce a single reading at intervals along the east-west line of the shots was restricted to a calculated 81.8 acres of the total 2682, but the court apparently accepted appellees' contention that the data from these shots could be correlated with geological information from other sources so as to permit interpretations as to the entire property. * * *

The district court found that * * * the market value of the right to conduct said seismograph explorations and also the reasonable value to appellants of exercising such right was the sum of $53,640.00. * * *

[The court concluded that the owner of the mineral estate had the right to explore for oil.]

Having thus established that appellants invaded some legally protected rights of the appellees it now remains to determine to what damages the latter are entitled. It appears well established that in Texas the mineral owner may sue the "geophysical trespasser" only in trespass and not for conversion of either the information or of the right to obtain it.

Appellants now contend that since in the present instance appellees are unable to establish any damage to their property measured by decrease in market value proximately due to the trespass, no information detrimental to value of appellees' mineral rights having been revealed,[1] they may recover only nominal damages. It appears, however, that Texas belongs to the minority of states that permit a landowner to waive the trespass and sue in assumpsit for the reasonable value of the use and occupation. * * *

1. [Footnote renumbered.] Cf. Humble Oil & Refining Co. v. Kishi, Tex.Com.App., 276 S.W. 190.

In the *Vahlsing* case [248 S.W.2d 762 (Tex.Civ.App.1952)], it is stated that the measure of damages "for use and occupancy of real property or a right of way could be measured by a market rental value if such can be established upon either a tort or assumpsit theory, for when one occupied a way having an ascertainable market value, the owner thereof is deprived of this rental. It is damage to *him* and not necessarily dependent upon the assumpsit theory." In the instant case it might thus be said that the desire of the appellants to make the survey and their willingness to pay for the privilege constituted an increment to the market value of appellees' property which disappeared when appellants, by means of their trespass, obtained the information without making any payment to the mineral owners. The expectation that a neighboring oil company wishes to make such an exploration might well be taken into account in establishing the price at which a mineral estate is sold.

In any case it is necessary to establish the reasonable market value of the use appellants made of appellees' property, and this value is independent of the benefit that appellants *actually* received from that use. * * * The trial court has found that the reasonable market value of the right to conduct the exploration was $53,640.00, which figure was evidently arrived at by multiplying a per acre price of $20 by the 2,682 acres of land on which appellees owned the mineral rights and to which the court found appellants' exploration extended.

* * * It appears that the trial court's determination that appellees' recovery should be figured on the entire 2,682 acres for which they owned the mineral rights was based on an erroneous interpretation of the measure by which the recovery is to be calculated. From the record it appears that uncontradicted testimony was introduced by appellants that the information directly obtained from the several shots set off on the land in controversy related to 81.8 acres—i.e. the vibrations that were actually detected by the instruments were echoed from that large an area, though the explosions may actually have resulted in spreading vibrations still more extensively, for which, however, no detecting instruments were provided. Appellees assert and the trial court evidently found that from the information thus directly obtained it was possible by projection and extrapolation and by correlation with other known geological data about the region, to evaluate to a certain extent the mineral potentials of the entire 2,682 acres owned by appellees (as well as that of other contiguous tracts not owned by them).

Upon this evidence appellees may not recover compensation for trespass to all their property, for the mere obtaining of information by extrapolation of data relating to one site does not constitute an invasion of other sites. * * * If appellees had owned merely the sites of the actual shots and instruments they could not now claim compensation based on the entire acreage as to which information was revealed, any more than they do not now claim compensation based on property not owned by them that is considerably closer to the site of the test blasts than the further reaches of their own irregularly shaped holdings. Nor could they claim any compensation at all if they owned all the property except that "occupied" by the exploration. Appellees may properly be compensated only for the use of that part of their property that was "occupied" by the exploration, and, since this recovery is in effect in assumpsit, it must be irrelevant whether they or others owned contiguous property as to which information was also revealed if no trespass was committed as to it.

On the other hand appellants may not restrict their liability to merely the narrow perimeter around each hole as to which direct information was obtained—which is apparently the basis of the claim of the "occupancy" of only 81.8 acres—since the recovery in assumpsit is based on an implied promise whose assumed terms should conform fairly closely to the sort of agreement that might actually have been reached by reasonable parties, and it is unreasonable to suppose that appellants could have obtained an exploration agreement obligating them to pay compensation only for the exactly circumscribed areas on which their instruments were placed for each explosion. We recognize that in the absence of any formula for dividing the value of information obtained about an extended territory from a test made at a particular site (analogous to the division of the flow from a well drawing from an extensive pool) it may in general be a difficult task to establish exactly what area was "occupied" by a series of small scattered explosion sites—though the problem is made somewhat manageable by the fact that there usually is a certain pattern to the exploration which may help to delimit a series of contiguous areas that are included in the scope of the survey from others that are not.

The trial court must establish what areas might reasonably be included in an agreement regarding such an exploration, considering that just as the trespasser may be held to pay only a reasonable per acre price for the rights he had invaded, regardless of how much the mineral owner claims he would have charged, so compensation need be paid only for the area reasonably regarded as "occupied" by the survey (including, but not restricted to, the areas from which vibration echoes were actually received), regardless of how many acres the mineral owner would have insisted on including in an agreement had one actually been bargained for. For this purpose evidence might be received as to the size and shape of the areas for which appellants would have had to obtain licenses in order to carry out the actual operation as they did, taking into account the particular geographic pattern of mineral ownership shown to exist here.

The judgment of the trial court must be reversed and the case remanded for a determination of the number of acres occupied by the trespass and the compensation that should be allowed therefor.

(3) Simple And Not So Simple Acts of Trespass

KRUVANT v. 12–22 WOODLAND AVENUE CORP.

Superior Court of New Jersey, 1975.
138 N.J.Super. 1, 350 A.2d 102.

DWYER, J.S.C. While sipping a drink and chatting with an attorney at a party about plans to develop what is labeled as Lot 1445–B in Block 152–X on the tax maps of Town of West Orange (Lot B), one of the owners was startled to hear the attorney tell him that those who had been riding horses across Lot B from the nearby stable might have acquired an easement across it because the activity had been going on for as long as the attorney could remember. Shortly thereafter the owners of Lot B demanded for the first time that the stable either pay rent or stop using Lot B. The stable refused both demands. The owners then commenced this action.

[P]laintiffs Philip Kruvant, Charles Kruvant and Bobcar Corporation are the record owners of Lot B. 12–22 Woodland Avenue Corporation, trading as

Suburban Essex Riding Club (club) operates a boarding stable for approximately 100 horses, and a riding academy on premises which the club owns on the north side of Nicholas Avenue, a paper street, and which premises face Lot B located on the opposite, or south, side of Nicholas Avenue.

The matters at issue are: (1) the right of plaintiffs to terminate the club's use of the bridle trail which extends approximately 800 feet diagonally across Lot B to an oversize culvert constructed in 1939 by Essex County to permit horses to pass from that bridle trail under Prospect Street and into Eagle Rock Reservation (Reservation) where there are several miles of bridle trails, the right to terminate the club's use of certain other areas of Lot B [called the "meadow" or "dressage" area] and the right of plaintiffs to collect money damages from 1973 based on use and occupancy, and (2) the right of the club, asserted by counterclaim, to have the court declare that it has either title to said bridle trail and said certain other areas under the doctrine of adverse possession, or a prescriptive easement for the bridle trail and those other areas. * * *

The court concludes that the club has established a prescriptive easement for the bridle trail. [T]he acts of those associated with the club were sufficiently open, notorious, continuous and limited to a fixed area to put the owners of Lot B on notice to take action. This they did not do for over 20 years. The court finds that the meadow area, or dressage field, was not used until after the area was bulldozed by plaintiffs in 1959 or 1960. * * * The court concludes that the club has not established a prescriptive easement in the meadow area. * * *

This leaves the question of what damages, if any, should be awarded to plaintiffs for the meadow area and what remedy should be granted to the club.

Where a party proves that another has trespassed on his lands, he is entitled to nominal damages even if there is no proof of injury or damage to the lands.

Plaintiffs have not established that the club and its predecessors damaged the lands, other than trampling some grass and enriching the area with horse manure. Plaintiffs, therefore, are not entitled to damages. They have not proved that they were denied the use of the lands for any activity they had planned.

However, plaintiffs have borne all the carrying costs for Lot B. Without permission, the club has used the meadow area in connection with its profit-making activities.

Although counsel for plaintiffs cited no authority for the proposition that plaintiffs were entitled to recover damages on the basis of rental value or use and occupancy, plaintiffs have asserted such a claim [and] were allowed to make an offer of proof as to what a reasonable rent or charge for use and occupancy would be.

Lasser [a real estate broker] testified that the real estate taxes were $12,000 annually. In his opinion Lot B was worth $250,000. It is zoned for office/research and civic center development. The zoning ordinance calls for 5 A minimum lots with a front setback of 100 feet, side and rear-yard setbacks of 75 feet, and permits buildings to occupy 20% of the lot.

On direct examination Lasser testified that in his opinion one-sixth of the carrying charges, allowing a 10% return on the land value, would be a reasonable rent or charge for use and occupancy of the bridle trail and meadow area. On his calculations this is $500 a month. On cross-examination he admitted that he had not measured the area of the bridle trail or meadow. He said that considering the activity and the carrying charges it was his opinion that an allocation of one-sixth of the carrying charges was fair and reasonable.

The court has found no New Jersey case as to whether a landowner is entitled to recover on the basis of rent, or use and occupancy, from a trespasser who has used the property for profit-making activity.

Comment b to § 931 of Restatement, Torts (1939), states:

> "The owner of the subject matter is entitled to recover as damages for the loss of the value of the use, at the rental value of the * * * land during the period of deprivation. This is true even though the owner in fact has suffered no harm through the deprivation, as where he was not using the subject matter at the time."

See also Baltimore & O. R. Co. v. Boyd, 67 Md. 32, 10 A. 315 (Ct.App.1887) (rental value of right of way for a railroad track across unimproved, unenclosed, vacant land held proper measure of damages for period of entry without permission and before condemnation).

The court concludes that where a person uses the land of another to carry on profit-making activities, without permission, the landowner should be able to recover a reasonable rent.

Plaintiffs have offered proof of taxes and that a 10% return on capital would be a fair means of calculating such a charge. They did not measure the meadow area although it is identified on a scaled map prepared for Essex County, as is the bridle trail. This map is in evidence. The club did not offer any contradictory evidence as to value because its objection was sustained. The court notes that there are tax stamps affixed to the deed in 1955 from Mayfair for Lot B. Lasser's opinion of value is substantially higher than the value reflected by the tax stamps. The court directs that parties calculate the meadow area; it will permit the club to submit evidence as to assessment value, or other value, of Lot B, and such comment by memoranda or a hearing (if it desires) as to value upon which return should be allowed. The period for which demand has been made by plaintiffs starts in July 1973 and money damages will be allowed only from that date.

Notes

1. *Equitable Jurisdiction to Enjoin Simple Trespasses.* Restatement (Second) of Torts § 944 comment g (1977).† In some situations repeated or continuing torts may, if maintained long enough, give the wrongdoer an easement by prescription. This is not, ordinarily, an additional factor in favor of injunction, because a series of damage actions, each seasonably brought, would not only give the plaintiff compensation but would also prevent prescription. However, a peculiar problem may arise in the case of a continuing or repeated tort which causes little if any immediate harm—for example, where the defendant has laid a water pipe across the plaintiff's waste land. So far as compensation is concerned, a damage action would not be worth its cost. Yet, if the plaintiff is not to suffer the acquisition of an easement he must either sue for damages or by some other means toll the

prescription. Here the easement factor is material. The case does not, however, present a simple dilemma of repeated actions or injunction against the tort. Prescription may be prevented by a decree which merely enjoins the defendant from asserting an easement, or one which requires him to accept a license. This form of relief might be the most appropriate if an injunction against the tort would cause grave hardship—for example, if the water pipe in the case suggested above were necessary to the operation of the defendant's mine.

2. *Injunctions Against Simple Trespasses.* Champie v. Castle Hot Springs Co., 27 Ariz. 463, 233 P. 1107 (1925) (hitching horses from a livery stable in front of plaintiff's hotel); Baker v. Howard County Hunt, 171 Md. 159, 188 A. 223 (1936) (a periodic fox hunt across plaintiff's property); Parkinson v. Winniman, 75 Nev. 405, 344 P.2d 677 (1959) (continuous use of a private road, nominal and exemplary damages also awarded).

FENTON v. QUABOAG COUNTRY CLUB

Supreme Judicial Court of Massachusetts, 1968.

353 Mass. 534, 233 N.E.2d 216.

Reardon, Justice. This appeal has to do with the game of golf and in particular with the abilities of certain golfers in the county of Hampden whose alleged transgressions gave rise to a suit. The plaintiffs * * * seek an injunction designed to terminate the operation of one of the holes in the defendant's nine-hole course, together with damages for injuries to person and property. * * *

A master to whom the case was referred filed a report which illuminates the deep antagonisms which spring to life when home and family are threatened by devotees of the great outdoors. We refer to his findings.

In 1952 the plaintiffs, John F. and Miriam E. Fenton, "not familiar with the details of the game of golf," bought their house, garage and land from one Lussier and his wife. * * * The Lussiers had purchased the land from the defendant in 1944 and had, as one may gather from the report, coexisted happily with the golf club, a state of affairs no doubt enhanced by the fact that during their tenure Lussier and his family had sold soft drinks and sandwiches to golfers on the course and thus found no fault when errant golf balls descended upon their property. The club itself had a lengthy history. It opened in 1900 * * *.

Into this posture, fraught with potential trouble which only a golfer could fully appreciate, came the plaintiffs "not familiar with the details of the game of golf." Any deficiency in their knowledge was soon remedied as they immediately came under the assault of balls "hit onto and over their property." "Except for a few isolated occasions, these balls were not intentionally directed" at the Fenton estate. However, the master has provided us with some chilling statistics which cast grave doubt on the proficiency of the golfers of Hampden County, at least those who were playing the defendant's course. From 1952 an annual average number of 250 balls "were left" on the land of the plaintiffs, save for the year 1960 when a grand total of 320 such deposits were made. Over the years sixteen panes of glass in the plaintiffs' house were broken, for six of which fractures the plaintiffs have received reimbursement. The cost of such replacements apparently defied inflation and remained constant throughout the years at $3.85 for each new pane. Affairs worsened in 1961 when the defendant added a sand trap "to the northwest corner of the ninth green." Since golfers intent on achieving the green drove from the tee in a southerly direction, they were faced with alternatives. They might aim somewhat to the west and face the sand trap, or they might veer more to the east and face the Fentons. The master inclined to the belief that they were prone to make the latter choice although, as he found, this was not without hazard, for the plaintiff John F. Fenton collected "all the balls he found on his land and sold them periodically." Continued unbridled hooking and slicing caused further aggravation. Some years back the Fentons were possessed of a German Shepherd dog which developed apprehension at the approach of golfers to the point that they were forced to dispense with his companionship. In his place they acquired a Doberman evidently made of sterner stuff. The dog is still with them notwithstanding that he has been struck by a flying golf ball. On one occasion the male plaintiff himself stopped an airborne ball supposedly directed to the ninth green but winging its way off course. At another time a Fenton family steak cookout was interrupted by a misdirected ball which came to rest "just under the grill." There were additional serious evidences of mutual annoyance. In an episode "after dark, a ball was driven from the * * * [defendant's] fairway directly against the * * * [plaintiffs'] house." In another, a battered ball bearing the greeting "Hi, Johnnie" descended upon the plaintiffs' close. Hostile incidents occurred. One player venturing on the plaintiffs' property to retrieve a ball swung his club first at the Fentons' dog, then raised it at John Fenton, following which, according to the master's report, he "withdrew."

It need not be emphasized that from the year 1952 the plaintiffs were not silent in their suffering, and there was some talk about a fence. After the commencement of this suit the defendant constructed on its land a fence twenty-four feet high and three feet in from part of the boundary lines on the northern and western sides of the plaintiffs' land. The master states that while this fence has substantially, it has not entirely, abated the problem caused by the rain of golf balls. We are told that the erection of the fence in 1965 was followed by the flight of some eighty-one balls in that year onto the plaintiffs' territory. This somewhat minimized invasion the master terms "a continuing nuisance and trespass." For all of these depredations he assessed damages at $38.50 for those broken panes as yet unreimbursed, and $2,250 "for loss in the fair market value of * * * [the] property" because of the trespasses as well because the fence "seriously diminishes the value of the property aesthetically." He also found damages at $2,600 for disturbance of the plaintiffs' "peace and comfort" for the thirteen years prior to the erection of the unaesthetic fence. He placed a value on the loss of the plaintiffs' peace and comfort since the fence went up at $50.

Following confirmation of the master's report the court entered a final decree enjoining the defendant from so operating its course "as to damage the property of the Plaintiffs, or to cause golf balls to be cast upon or propelled upon or against the property of the Plaintiffs." The failure to employ the technical language peculiar to the game of golf in the decree in no sense muddies its meaning. The damages assessed by the master were awarded in the interlocutory and final decrees.

We have the case on appeals from the decrees.

We have no doubts about the propriety of the injunction. The plaintiffs are clearly entitled to an abatement of the trespasses. Stevens v. Rockport

Granite Co., 216 Mass. 486, 489, 104 N.E. 371. We paraphrase the apt expression of Chief Justice Rugg in the *Stevens* case: "The pertinent inquiry is whether the noise [the invasion of golf balls] materially interferes with the physical comfort of existence, not according to exceptionally refined, uncommon, or luxurious habits of living [e.g. golf addiction], but according to the simple tastes and unaffected notions generally prevailing among plain people [nongolfers]. The standard is what ordinary people [again those who eschew golf], acting reasonably, have a right to demand in the way of health and comfort under all the circumstances." Were it not that this court cannot assume the function of a Robert Trent Jones we should make a judicial suggestion that the defendant's burden under the injunction will be considerably eased by shifting the location of the trap to the northeasterly corner of the green on the assumption, and on this the record is silent, that none exists there now.

On the damages awarded, the plaintiffs are entitled to the sum of $38.50 for the cost of replacing the glass, and also for the sum of $2,650 awarded them for their distress and discomfort over fourteen years. The master took testimony on the effect on the plaintiffs of their discomfort which was sufficient to enable him to make the award which he did. * * *

There was error, however, in the award of damages based on loss in the fair market value of the property due to what the master found to be a continuing trespass. This was a trespass of such a nature that it might be terminated by appropriate action, which is what the injunction in fact seeks to do. As such the true measure of damages is the loss in rental value of the property while injury continues. In the assessment of damages the defendant's erection of the fence on its own property can play no part. The interlocutory and final decrees are reversed. The case is remanded to the Superior Court for further proceedings consistent with this opinion.

So ordered.

Notes

1. According to the January 3, 1988 New York Times, the dispute between the Fentons and the golf club continued for twenty-two years and was not resolved until the club agreed to shorten its ninth hole.

2. Compare the injunction issued in *Fenton* with the one issued in Sierra Screw Products v. Azusa Greens, Inc., 88 Cal.App.3d 358, 364, 151 Cal.Rptr. 799, 802 (1979). Plaintiff alleged nuisance, trespass and negligence: "Plaintiffs are entitled to the issuance of a mandatory injunction * * * directing the defendants * * * to redesign and reconstruct the third and fourth holes of the existing golf course in such a manner as to minimize the intrusion of golf balls onto the plaintiff's adjoining property and upon completion thereof to file with the court a copy of the revised design together with evidence of the completion thereof." Why not "assume the function of a Robert Trent Jones"?

3. The "golf course" cases may be pleaded as either trespass or nuisance (or both); but the players commit the trespass whereas the golf course commits the nuisance. Patton v. Westwood County Club Co., 18 Ohio App.2d 137, 247 N.E.2d 761 (1969), analyzes the wandering-golf-balls nuisance from the point of view of the later purchaser. Notice that a similar situation exists in Edwards v. Lee's Adm'r below. Bearing in mind the in personam nature of equitable relief and the necessity of framing enforceable decrees, which tort theory is more suitable?

4. Protesters at abortion clinics have frequently trespassed and interfered with potential patients. Judicial relief has taken the form of injunctions prohibiting anti-abortion activists from blocking access to the clinics. Roe v. Operation Rescue, 919 F.2d 857 (3d Cir.1990); Town of West Hartford v. Operation Rescue, 726 F.Supp. 371 (D.Conn.1989); Northeast Women's Center, Inc. v. McMonagle, 689 F.Supp. 465 (E.D.Pa.1988), modified, 868 F.2d 1342 (3d Cir.1989); Right to Life Advocates, Inc. v. Aaron Women's Clinic, 737 S.W.2d 564 (Tex.App.1987), cert. denied, 488 U.S. 824 (1988).

5. Lloyd Corporation, Ltd. v. Whiffen, 307 Or. 674, 773 P.2d 1294 (1989). The owners of a shopping mall sought to enjoin defendants from entering the mall to obtain signatures on initiative petitions. The court held that the mall could not totally exclude the solicitors; but that reasonable restrictions on the time, place, and manner might be imposed.

EDWARDS v. LEE'S ADM'R

Court of Appeals of Kentucky, 1936.
265 Ky. 418, 96 S.W.2d 1028.

STITES, JUSTICE. About twenty years ago L.P. Edwards discovered a cave under land belonging to him and his wife, Sally Edwards. The entrance to the cave is on the Edwards land. Edwards named it the "Great Onyx Cave." This cave is located in the cavernous area of Kentucky, and is only about three miles distant from the world-famous Mammoth Cave. Its proximity to Mammoth Cave, which for many years has had an international reputation as an underground wonder, as well as its beautiful formations, led Edwards to embark upon a program of advertising and exploitation for the purpose of bringing visitors to his cave. Circulars were printed and distributed, signs were erected along the roads, persons were employed and stationed along the highways to solicit the patronage of passing travelers, and thus the fame of the Great Onyx Cave spread from year to year, until eventually, and before the beginning of the present litigation, it was a well-known and well-patronized cave. Edwards built a hotel near the mouth of the cave to care for travelers. He improved and widened the footpaths and avenues in the cave, and ultimately secured a stream of tourists who paid entrance fees sufficient not only to cover the cost of operation, but also to yield a substantial revenue in additional thereto. The authorities in charge of the development of the Mammoth Cave area as a national park undertook to secure the Great Onyx Cave through condemnation proceedings, and in that suit the value of the cave was fixed by a jury at $396,000. In April, 1928, F.P. Lee, an adjoining landowner, filed this suit against Edwards and the heirs of Sally Edwards, claiming that a portion of the cave was under his land, and praying for damages for an accounting of the profits which resulted from the operation of the cave, and for an injunction prohibiting Edwards and his associates from further trespassing upon or exhibiting any part of the cave under Lee's land.

* * * An injunction was granted prohibiting Edwards and his associates from further trespassing on the lands of Lee. On final hearing the chancellor stated separately his findings of law and of fact in the following language:

> "The Court finds as a matter of law the plaintiff is entitled to recover of defendants the proportionate part of the net proceeds defendants received from exhibiting Great Onyx Cave from the years 1923 to 1930, inclusive, as the footage of said cave under Lee's land bears to the entire footage of the cave

exhibited to the public for fees during the years 1923 to 1930, inclusive, with 6% interest on plaintiff's proportionate part of said fund for each year from the first day of the following year as set out in the memorandum opinion.

* * * "2. The Court finds as a matter of fact there was 6,449.88 feet of said cave exhibited to the public during 1923 to 1930, inclusive, and that 2,048.60 feet of said footage was under Lee's lands making plaintiff entitled to

$\frac{2048.60}{6449.88}$ or ⅓ of the proceeds." * * *

Appellants, in their attack here on the measure of damages and its application to the facts adduced, urge: (1) That the appellees had simply a hole in the ground, about 360 feet below the surface, which they could not use and which they could not even enter except by going through the mouth of the cave on Edwards' property; (2) the cave was of no practical use to appellees without an entrance, and there was no one except the appellants on whom they might confer a right of beneficial use; (3) Lee's portion of the cave had no rental value; (4) appellees were not ousted of the physical occupation or use of the property because they did not and could not occupy it; (5) the property has not in any way been injured by the use to which it has been put by appellants, and since this is fundamentally an action for damages arising from trespass, the recovery must be limited to the damages suffered by appellees (in other words, nominal damages) and cannot properly be measured by the benefits accruing to the trespasser from his wrongful use of the property; (6) as a result of the injunction, appellees have their cave in exactly the condition it has always been, handicapped by no greater degree of uselessness than it was before appellants trespassed upon it.

Appellees, on the other hand, argue that this was admittedly a case of willful trespass; that it is not analogous to a situation where a trespasser simply walks across the land of another for here the trespasser actually used the property of Lee to make a profit for himself; that even if nothing tangible was taken or disturbed in the various trips through Lee's portion of the cave, nevertheless there was a taking of esthetic enjoyment which, under ordinary circumstances, would justify a recovery of the reasonable rental value for the use of the cave; that there being no basis for arriving at reasonable rental values, the chancellor took the only course open to him under the circumstances and properly assessed the damages on the basis of the profits realized from the use of Lee's portion of the cave. Appellees have taken a cross-appeal, however, on the theory that, since the trespass was willful, their damages should be measured by the gross profits realized from the operation of the cave rather than from its net profits.

As the foregoing statement of the facts and the contentions of the parties will demonstrate, the case is sui generis, and counsel have been unable to give us much assistance in the way of previous decisions of this or other courts. We are left to fundamental principles and analogies.

We may begin our consideration of the proper measure of damages to be applied with the postulate that appellees held legal title to a definite segment of the cave and that they were possessed, therefore, of a right which it is the policy of the law to protect. We may assume that the appellants were guilty of repeated trespasses upon the property of appellees. * * * The proof likewise clearly indicates that the trespasses were willful, and not innocent.

Appellees brought this suit in equity, and seek an accounting of the profits realized from the operation of the cave, as well as an injunction against future trespass. In substance, therefore, their action is ex contractu and not, as appellants contend, simply an action for damages arising from a tort. Ordinarily, the measure of recovery in assumpsit for the taking and selling of personal property is the value received by the wrongdoer. On the other hand, where the action is based upon a trespass to land, the recovery has almost invariably been measured by the reasonable rental value of the property. Strictly speaking, a count for "use and occupation" does not fit the facts before us because, while there has been a recurring use, there has been no continuous occupation of the cave such as might arise from the planting of a crop or the tenancy of a house. Each trespass was a distinct usurpation of the appellees' title and interruption of their right to undisturbed possession. But, even if we apply the analogy of the crop cases or the wayleave cases, it is apparent that rental value has been adopted, either consciously or unconsciously, as a convenient yardstick by which to measure the proportion of profit derived by the trespasser directly from the use of the land itself [9 R.C.L. 942]. In other words, rental value ordinarily indicates the amount of profit realized directly from the land, as land, aside from all collateral contracts.

That profits rather than rent form the basis of recovery is illustrated by the cases involving the question of when an action of this character survives against the personal representative of a wrongdoer. If rent alone were the basis of recovery, we would expect to find that the action would survive against the estate of the trespasser. It would certainly be reasonable to assume that a simple action for debt would lie and that this would survive. The rule, however, has been established to the contrary. In considering what actions survive against an estate, Lord Mansfield, in Hambly v. Trott, 1 Cowp. 371, said:

> "If it is a sort of injury by which the offender acquires no gain to himself, at the expense of the sufferer, as beating or imprisoning a man, & c., there, the person injured, has only a reparation for the delictum in damages to be assessed by a jury. But where, besides the crime, property is acquired which benefits the testator, there an action for the value of the property shall survive against the executor. As for instance, the executor shall not be chargeable for the injury done by his testator in cutting down another man's trees, but for the benefit arising to his testator for the value or sale of the trees he shall.
>
> "So far as the tort itself goes, an executor shall not be liable; and therefore it is, that all public and all public crimes die with the offender, and the executor is not chargeable; but so far as the act of the offender is beneficial, his assets ought to be answerable; and his executor therefore shall be charged."

In the leading case of Phillips v. Homfray, 24 Ch.Div. 439, the plaintiffs were the owners of a farm, and the defendants had for some time past been working the minerals underlying lands adjoining plaintiffs' farm. Plaintiffs discovered that the defendants were not only getting minerals from under their farm, but were using roads and passages made by them through the plaintiffs' minerals for the conveyance of minerals gotten by the defendants from their own mines. An action was brought to recover for the minerals taken from under the plaintiffs' property, and also for damages to be paid as wayleave for the use of the roads and passages in transporting the minerals of the defendants across the property. One of the defendants having died, the question was presented as to whether either of these causes of action survived against his estate. The court held that this defendant's estate was liable in the action for the minerals taken because it had, to that extent, been enriched by the defendant's wrong. As to the recovery for wayleave, the court held that the action did not survive because nothing had been added to the defendant's estate through the use of the roads and passages under plaintiffs' land. The defendant had been saved expense in thus using the passages, but it was pointed out that this did not constitute an enrichment and that the action did not, therefore, survive. * * * Clearly, the unjust enrichment of the wrongdoer is the gist of the right to bring an action ex contractu. Rental value is merely the most convenient and logical means for ascertaining what proportion of the benefits received may be attributed to the use of the real estate. In the final analysis, therefore, the distinction made between assumpsit concerning real and personal property thus disappears. * * *

Similarly, in illumination of this conclusion, there is a line of cases holding that the plaintiff may at common law bring an action against a trespasser for the recovery of "mesne profits" following the successful termination of an action of ejectment. Here again, the real basis of recovery is the profits received, rather than rent. In Worthington v. Hiss, 70 Md. 172, 16 A. 534, 536, 17 A. 1026, the court said:

> "It is well settled that in an action to recover mesne profits, the plaintiff must show in the best way he can what those profits are, and there are two modes of doing so, to either of which he may resort,—he may either prove the profits actually received, or the annual rental value of the land. * * * The latter is the mode usually adopted. Where there is occupation of a farm or land used only for agricultural purposes, and the income and profits are of necessity the produce of the soil, the owner may have an account of the proceeds of the crops and other products sold or raised thereon, deducting the expense of cultivation. These are necessarily rents and profits in such cases, but even there it is more usual to arrive at the same result by charging the occupier, as tenant, with a fair annual money rent. But the proprietor of city lots, with improvements upon them, can only derive therefrom, as owner, a fair occupation rent for the purposes for which the premises are adapted. This constitutes the rents and profits, in the legal sense of the terms, of such property, and is all the owner can justly claim in this shape from the occupier."

Finally, in the current proposed final draft of the Restatement of Restitution and Unjust Enrichment (March 4, 1936), Part I, § 136, it is stated:

> "A person who tortiously uses a trade name, trade secret, profit a prendre, or other similar interest of another, is under a duty of restitution for the value of the benefit thereby received."

The analogy between the right to protection which the law gives a trade-name or trade secret and the right of the appellees here to protection of their legal rights in the cave seems to us to be very close. In all of the mineral and timber cases, there is an actual physical loss suffered by the plaintiff, as well as a benefit received by the defendant. In other words, there is both a plus and a minus quantity. In the trade-name and similar cases, as in the case at bar, there may be no tangible loss other than the violation of a right. The law, in seeking an adequate remedy for the wrong, has been forced to adopt profits received, rather than damages sustained, as a basis of recovery. In commenting on the section of the Restatement quoted above, the reporter says:

"Persons who tortiously use trade names, trade secrets, water rights, and other similar interests of others, are ordinarily liable in an action of tort for the harm which they have done. In some cases, however, no harm is done and in those cases if the sole remedy were by an action of tort the wrongdoer would be allowed to profit at little or no expense. In cases where the damage is more extensive, proof as to its extent may be so difficult that justice can be accomplished only by requiring payment of the amount of profits. Where definite damage is caused and is susceptible of proof, the injured person, as in other tort cases, can elect between an action for damages and an action for the value of that which was improperly received. The usual method of seeking restitution is by a bill in equity, with a request for an accounting for any profits which have been received, but the existence of a right to bring such a bill does not necessarily prevent an action at law for the value of the use. In the case of tortious interference with patents, under existing statutes there is a right to restitution only in connection with an injunction."

Whether we consider the similarity of the case at bar to (1) the ordinary actions in assumpsit to recover for the use and occupation of real estate, or (2) the common-law action for mesne profits, or (3) the action to recover for the tortious use of a trade-name or other similar right, we are led inevitably to the conclusion that the measure of recovery in this case must be the benefits, or net profits, received by the appellants from the use of the property of the appellees. The philosophy of all these decisions is that a wrongdoer shall not be permitted to make a profit from his own wrong. Our conclusion that a proper measure of recovery is net profits, of course, disposes of the cross-appeal. Appellees are not entitled to recover gross profits. They are limited to the benefits accruing to the appellants.

* * * In determining the profits which might fairly be said to arise directly from the use of appellees' segment of the cave, the chancellor considered not only the footage exhibited, but the relative value of the particular points of interest featured in advertising the cave, and their possible appeal in drawing visitors. Of thirty-one scenes or objects in the cave advertised by appellants, twelve were shown to be on appellees' property. Several witnesses say that the underground Lucikovah river, which is under the appellees' land for almost its entire exhibited length, is one of the most attractive features of the cave, if not its leading attraction. Other similar attractions are shown to be located on appellees' property. The chancellor excluded profits received by the appellants from the operation of their hotel, and we think the conclusion that one-third of the net profits received alone from the exhibition of the cave is a fair determination of the direct benefits accruing to the appellants from the use of the appellees' property.

* * * The judgment is affirmed [with adjustments].

Notes

1. Restatement of Restitution § 129 (1937).† Disposition of and Trespass to Land. (2) A person who has trespassed upon the land of another is not thereby under a duty of restitution to the other for the value of its use.

Illustration: A uses a road across B's land without B's knowledge for a period of two years in the transportation of materials, doing so without harm to the land.

A saves $2,000 thereby. A reasonable charge for the use of the road would be $200 per year. B is not entitled to recover for the use of the land in an action of assumpsit: in an action of tort he is entitled to recover only $200.

2. Compare the proposed replacement for this section. Work on this revision has been suspended. But would the new section apply to encroachments?

Restatement (Second) of Restitution § 46 (Tent. Draft No. 2, 1984)[††]. Restitution for Wrongful Use of Real Property (1) A person who, as a trespasser, makes use of another's real property, other than an occasional intrusion for the trespasser's personal convenience, owes restitution to the owner, measured according to § [ ], for any benefit resulting from that use. A person does not owe restitution under this section as a result of conduct that is wrongful only as a violation of an agreement.

RAVEN RED ASH COAL CO. v. BALL

Supreme Court of Appeals of Virginia, 1946.
185 Va. 534, 39 S.E.2d 231.

HUDGINS, JUSTICE. Plaintiff, Estil Ball, stated, in his notice of motion, that he was entitled to recover $5,000 from the defendant for the use and occupation of an easement across his land. Defendant denied any liability. The trial court entered judgment for plaintiff in the sum of $500 on the verdict returned by the jury. From that judgment, defendant obtained this writ of error.

There is no substantial conflict in the evidence. Plaintiff proved that he is the present owner of approximately 100 acres of land lying in Russell County which was a part of a 265-acre tract formerly owned by Reuben Sparks and that Reuben Sparks and his wife, by deed dated November 19, 1887, conveyed the coal and mineral rights on the 265-acre tract to Joseph I. Doran and William A. Dick. * * *

[The deed gave Doran and Dick an easement over what is now plaintiff's (Ball's) 100 acres to haul out the coal from their mines on adjacent land totalling 3000 acres. About 2000 feet of roadway was built over Ball's 100 acres to utilize the easement. Raven Red Ash Coal bought Doran and Dick's mining interests on their original 3000 acres, and acquired the mining rights on five more small tracts (about 80 acres total) besides. The easement does not grant any right to haul coal dug from these five tracts.]

The testimony reveals that, during the past five years, defendant transported 49,016 tons of coal mined from the five small tracts over the tramway erected across plaintiff's land and transported 950,000 tons of coal mined from lands formerly owned by Doran and Dick. There remains to be mined approximately 8,000,000 tons of coal on the tracts formerly owned by Doran and Dick and 180,000 tons of coal on the other small tracts.

Defendant's six assignments of error present two questions: (1) Whether the facts entitle plaintiff to maintain an action of trespass on the case in assumpsit; and (2) the measure of damages.

Ball concedes that defendant exercised its right in transporting across plaintiff's land the 950,000 tons of coal, but contends that it violated the property rights of plaintiff in transporting the 49,016 tons of coal across plaintiff's land to defendant's tipple. This principle was settled by this court in Clayborn v. Camilla, etc., Coal Co., 128 Va. 383, 105 S.E. 117. * * *

This case holds that every use of an easement not necessarily included in the grant is a trespass to realty and renders the owner of the dominant tenement liable in a tort action to the owner of the servient tenement for all damages proven to have resulted therefrom, and, in the absence of proof of special damage, the owner of the servient tenement may recover nominal damages only.

Plaintiff did not prove any specific damage to the realty by the illegal use of the easement, and admitted that he suffered "no more damage other than the exclusion of use during that moment and that's the reason we have sued for use and occupancy."

It thus appears that plaintiff bases his sole ground of recovery on the right to maintain assumpsit for use and occupation. * * *

Assumpsit is classified as an action ex contractu as distinguished from an action ex delicto. Hence, in order to sustain the action, it is necessary for the plaintiff to establish an express contract or facts and circumstances from which the law will raise an implication of a promise to pay. In such a case, a plaintiff may waive the tort and institute his action in assumpsit for money had and received.

Where a naked trespass is committed, whether upon the person or property, assumpsit will not lie. If one commits an assault and battery upon another, it is absurd to imply a promise by the defendant to pay the victim a reasonable compensation. There is no basis for an implication of a contract where cattle inadvertently invade a neighbor's premises and trample down and destroy his crops. In each instance, a wrong and nothing more and nothing less has been committed. On the other hand, if a trespasser invades the premises of his neighbor, cuts and removes timber or severs minerals from the land and converts them to his own use, the owner may waive the tort and sue in assumpsit for the value of the materials converted. * * * Such a person has depleted the value of the owner's property and materially enhanced his own possessions.

The general rule stated in the majority of cases we have found is that, in an action for use and occupation, or for damages to realty, based on assumpsit, the plaintiff must prove that the defendant occupied the premises with his permission, either express or implied, or that the trespasser obtained something from the soil, such as growing crops, timber or ore, and appropriated the same to his own use. If the trespasser simply used the property of another to save himself inconvenience or even expenditure of money, the owner cannot maintain an action of debt or assumpsit. [The court cited Restatement of Restitution § 129 and many cases.]

The precise question has never been decided in this jurisdiction. If the rule in force in the majority of States is followed, the landowner will be placed in this position: If he maintains an action for tort, he will be limited to nominal damages only. He may obtain an injunction and restrain the defendant from the further unlawful use of the easement, and thus indirectly, perhaps force him to agree to pay for future additional burdens imposed on the easement. Such proceedings would not give the owner compensation for past illegal use of his property, although the wrongdoer had received and retained substantial benefits by reason of his own wrongs. [The court reviewed material above: Edwards v. Lee's Adm'r, Phillips v. Homfrey, cited in *Edwards,* and the Reporter's notes to the first Restatement.]

The illegal transportation of the coal in question across plaintiff's land was intentional, deliberate and repeated from time to time for a period of years. Defendant had no moral or legal right to enrich itself by this illegal use of plaintiff's property. To limit plaintiff to the recovery of nominal damages for the repeated trespasses will enable defendant, as a trespasser, to obtain a more favorable position than a party contracting for the same right. Natural justice plainly requires the law to imply a promise to pay a fair value of the benefits received. Defendant's estate has been enhanced by just this much. * * *

While plaintiff offered no evidence to establish the value of the illegal use of the easement, we, as reasonable men, know that the transportation of 49,016 tons of coal over the tramroad across the plaintiff's land was a benefit to defendant. However, in the absence of proof of the value of the benefit, the court could enter no judgment for plaintiff. This proof is supplied by the testimony of the general manager on his cross-examination. The substance of his testimony on this point is that the prevailing rate of payment, or purchase of a right of way for transportation of coal across another's land, is one cent per ton, and that this purchase includes the right to construct and maintain a tramway for distances varying up to 2½ miles; but that, where the owner of the easement has already entered upon the land, and has constructed and is maintaining a tramroad for the transportation of coal from certain specified tracts, the purchase price should be much less—a small fraction of a cent per ton. The jury were instructed that they should fix the amount of damages, if any, at such as would fairly compensate plaintiff for the use and occupation of this strip of land in the hauling and transportation of 49,016 tons of coal over the same.

While the evidence on the value of the benefits retained by defendant is not as clear and full as it could be, and perhaps should have been, the jury had all the facts and circumstances before it and evidently concluded that the value of the benefit to the defendant for the illegal use of the easement should be computed at one cent per ton. Viewing the case as a whole, we find no reversible error, and the judgment of the trial court is affirmed.

Affirmed.

Notes

1. *Question:* Suppose that a commercial trucking company simply parks trucks on plaintiff's vacant lot. What are plaintiff's remedial possibilities? What would you recommend? See Marder v. Realty Construction Co., 43 N.J. 508, 205 A.2d 744 (1964); Pearl v. Pic Walsh Freight Co., 112 Ohio App. 11, 168 N.E.2d 571 (1960).

2. Brown v. Voss, 38 Wash.App. 777, 783, 689 P.2d 1111, 1114 (1984), rev'd, 105 Wash.2d 366, 715 P.2d 514 (1986). Brown, owner of an easement appurtenant to cross the Vosses' property to reach parcel B, used the easement to transport construction material to parcel C. The trial judge declined to grant the Vosses' request to stop misuse of the easement on the ground that "the Vosses would suffer no appreciable hardship or damages if the court denied their request for an injunction."

The appellate court reversed. "Where a continuing condition, such as the Browns' planned location for their residence, would result in frequent trespasses, an award of damages is not a sufficient remedy. Injunctive relief is far superior to a remedy at law under the circumstances."

But the Washington Supreme Court was "persuaded that the trial court acted within its discretion."

3. Payne v. Consolidation Coal Co., 607 F.Supp. 378, 382 n. 2 (W.D.Va.1985). The coal company had removed coal to construct a subterranean drainway through plaintiff's property. Plaintiffs sued for trespass for the coal and the use of the drainway:

"The plaintiffs have asserted the right to recover damages for the use of the drainway based upon the financial advantage which accrued to the defendant. If the plaintiffs had brought this action to recover on a theory of implied contract, the measure of damages would have been the value of the benefit received by the defendant. [Editors: The court cited and discussed *Raven Red Ash.*]

"The plaintiffs here, having chosen to bring an action for trespass, may recover only trespass damages. They may prove any damages which resulted from the use of the drainway. Absent such proof, they may recover nominal damages only.

"The court would further note that if the suit had been brought in contract the plaintiffs could not recover punitive damages. Punitive damages are not permitted in Virginia for breach of contract unless there is a separate independent tort. [citation] Here there is no separate independent tort. Since this suit is brought in tort the court is permitting the issue of punitive damages to go to the jury."

4. Sharpe & Waddams, Damages for Lost Opportunity to Bargain, 2 Oxford J. Legal Stud. 290 (1982).

e. Disturbance of Easements and Other Incorporeal Rights

LUCKY AUTO SUPPLY v. TURNER

Court of Appeal of California, Second District, 1966.
244 Cal.App.2d 872, 53 Cal.Rptr. 628.

Frampton, Justice Pro Tem. * * * Plaintiff, a California corporation, for more than 20 years last past, has been engaged in the business of selling automobile supplies, accessories and other merchandise some of which is heavy, and some of which is bulky such as automobile engines, tires, batteries, bicycles and large toy wagons. It operates 24 stores at different locations in southern and central California. On April 27, 1954, the defendants * * * owned * * * a one-story building divided into four separate storerooms and situated on the northwest corner of Pico Boulevard and Westwood Boulevard. The stores fronted on Pico Boulevard. The building was occupied by four tenants including the plaintiff. The corner storeroom had a width of approximately 25 feet and the storeroom occupied by the plaintiff had a width of approximately 40 feet and adjoined the corner storeroom immediately to the west thereof.

On April 27, 1954, the then owners of the property leased to the plaintiff the 40 foot storeroom * * * for the term of 10 years commencing July 1, 1954, at a rental of 3 per cent of the gross receipts with a minimum rental of $400 per month for the operation of a store for the sale of automobile supplies, accessories, and similar merchandise sold in automobile accessory stores then operated by the plaintiff.

The lease further provided in paragraph 28 thereof, as follows: "It is specifically agreed between the parties hereto that the parking lot having a frontage of approximately 50 feet on Westwood Boulevard and being across the alley from the rear of the building, of which the demised premises are a part, is owned by the Lessor and that said parking lot shall be available for the use of the Lessee and the other tenants in the building as a parking lot for the customers of various tenants in said building." * * *

The plaintiff maintained a service and installation department in the rear portion of the storeroom. This department and the rear entrance to the storeroom were located directly across the alley from the parking lot. * * * There were 25 stalls for automobile parking on the parking lot prior to the construction of the building thereon.

The employees of the plaintiff were able to observe the customers' automobiles which were parked directly across the alley from the service entrance for the purpose of identifying the parts needed for the various automobiles in accordance with the type, year and model of the automobile without being required to leave the service entrance or the store premises. The employees, together with the customers of the plaintiff who had purchased heavy or bulky types of merchandise, were able to carry the same across the alley to their parked cars on the parking lot. The parking lot was strategically located for the convenience of the plaintiff and its customers and was necessary for a more profitable operation of its business. * * *

During the month of July, 1955, the defendants requested permission from the plaintiff to construct a building on the parking lot and the plaintiff refused to grant such permission. On September 1, 1958, the defendants erected barricades and a fence around the boundary line of the parking lot, deposited building material on the lot and proceeded to construct a building thereon. During the construction of the building there was not sufficient space on the parking lot to park four automobiles. Since September 1, 1958, the plaintiff has not had the use of the parking lot either for itself or for its customers. Other parking facilities were furnished by the defendants after the erection of the building. These parking facilities were to be used by 13 tenants of the defendants and were not the parking facilities described in the plaintiff's lease.

[On October 14, 1958 the plaintiff sued for a mandatory injunction to compel the defendants to remove the building from the parking lot. An injunction was denied. The plaintiff, on June 9, 1961, sued for damages for trespass.]

The case went to trial upon [two counts]. The first count * * * alleged that by reason of the conduct of the defendants in willfully and wrongfully taking possession of the parking lot and depriving the plaintiff and its customers of the use thereof the plaintiff has suffered damages and loss of business profits and good will in the sum of $25,000. The second count incorporated substantially all of the allegations contained in the first count. * * * The plaintiff seeks damages under this count for the deprivation of the use of the property since September, 1958 in the sum of $17,000 plus $500 per month until the premises are restored or the lease expires. The sixth count seeks reasonable attorneys' fees allowable under the provisions of the lease.

The court rendered judgment for the plaintiff and against the defendants in the sum of $100 per month for loss of profits and good will from September 1, 1958, to June 30, 1964, the date of termination of the lease, in the total sum of $7,000. The court also awarded the sum of $500 as exemplary damages and $2,500 as reasonable attorneys' fees. * * *

The defendants' assertion that the plaintiff was not entitled to recover any damages is predicated upon the fact that after the construction of the building upon the parking lot area the profit and loss statements of the plaintiff disclosed that it had made some profit from the operation of its business notwithstanding the fact that it and its customers had been deprived of the use of the parking lot facilities. The plaintiff contends that had the facilities of the parking lot remained available to it and its customers it would have made a greater profit than was shown on its financial statements.

To sustain the plaintiff's claim of loss of profits it introduced evidence to show that the sales of the Pico store (the store involved under the lease) did not increase at the same average rate as did the sales of five of its comparable stores after the defendants had deprived the plaintiff and its customers of the use of the parking lot facilities.

In this connection one Maurice Getz testified that he was the secretary and vice president of the plaintiff and had been an officer of the corporation for about 26 years. * * * He testified that the books and records showed that there was a 48 per cent average increase in business in five comparable stores between the years 1958 and 1962, whereas there was only a 26 per cent increase in business in the Pico store. Getz produced summaries prepared from the books and records of five comparable stores and the Pico store showing the comparative sales made both before and after the plaintiff had been deprived of the use of the parking lot. These summaries, without going into great detail here as to their content, demonstrated a loss of sales at the Pico store for the years 1959 through 1962 in the sum of $35,000, and showed further that if such loss of sales figures were projected for the years 1963 and 1964 they would show an additional loss of sales in the sum of $35,000. Getz testified further that the plaintiff's net profit on the sales thus shown to have been lost would be the sum of $23,000.

A qualified expert real estate appraiser was called as a witness on behalf of the plaintiff and he testified that in his opinion the reasonable rental value of the demised property as it existed prior to September, 1958 was $600 per month, whereas the reasonable rental value of the property without access to automobile parking on the parking lot was $400 per month. * * *

It has been said that "Because a licensee has no interest in the land he cannot maintain an action in trespass or ejectment. At the most, he may maintain an action to enjoin or to redress a violation of his right to exercise the license. The principle is thus stated in Bell Tel. Co. [of Pennsylvania] v. Baltimore & O.R. Co., 155 Pa.Super. 286, 38 A.2d 732, 733: 'It is true that a license does not confer a right of possession sufficient to support an action in trespass quare clausum fregit or an action of ejectment. But a licensee may maintain an action of trespass in the nature of common-law case for any invasion or disturbance of the terms of the license whether by the licensor or by third parties.' " * * *

It is well established in California, moreover, that [tort] damages may include loss of anticipated profits where an established business has been injured. * * * Concomitant with this principle is the rule that the award for damages for loss of profits depends upon whether there is a satisfactory basis for estimating what the probable earnings would have been had there been no tort.

* * * If no such basis exists, it may be necessary to deny such recovery, but if, however, there has been an operating experience sufficient to permit a reasonable estimate of probable income and expense, damages for loss of profits are awarded. * * *

While the courts have often noted the difficulty of proving the amount of loss of profit, they have also recognized that a defendant cannot complain if the probable profits are of necessity estimated, the rationale being that it was the defendant himself who prevented the plaintiff from realizing profits.

[The court held that plaintiff's evidence was sufficient to sustain a damage award for lost profits.]

The plaintiff contends that it was not only entitled to damages measured by its loss of profits and good will but in addition thereto it was entitled to damages for the depreciation in the value of its leasehold. The trial court denied the latter upon the grounds that to allow damages for the depreciation in the value of the leasehold in addition to damages for the loss of profits and good will would constitute a double recovery.

The plaintiff continued in possession of the demised premises and operated its business thereon until the expiration of the term of the lease. The plaintiff was not evicted from the demised premises. Plaintiff's damages under these circumstances consisted of its loss of profits and good will resulting from the tortious act of the defendants in depriving the plaintiff of the parking privileges herein referred to. It was the continued use of the demised premises and the conduct of plaintiff's business thereon that brought about the loss in profits and good will. The depreciation in the value of plaintiff's leasehold under these circumstances is absorbed by and reflected in the damages for loss of profits and good will. Plaintiff, no doubt, could have sought damages upon the theory of depreciation in the value of its leasehold, however, under the circumstances here shown it may not recover damages for both its loss of profits and good will and for depreciation in the value of its leasehold for this would amount to a double recovery.

The plaintiff contends that the trial court committed error in sustaining the demurrer to the third count in the second amended complaint. This count sought recovery from the defendants of the rentals received by them from the tenants who occupied the building which the defendants had constructed upon the parking lot. Plaintiff based its right to recovery under this count upon the theory of restitution and unjust enrichment. * * *

The rentals received by the defendants from tenants who occupied the building constructed upon the parking lot are attributable to the defendants' ownership of and investment in the land and the building constructed thereon. The plaintiff had no right in the corpus which produced the rentals. The plaintiff's right was that of a license to use the parking lot in common with other tenants who occupied portions of the demised premises. The plaintiff having been deprived of this license by the wrongful act of the defendants nevertheless has been adequately compensated for such wrong in the way of damages for its loss of profits and good will occasioned by such wrongful act. Under the circumstances there is no foundation either in law or in equity upon which the plaintiff may claim the right to the rentals received by the defendants from tenants who occupied the building which was constructed upon the parking lot. We find no error in the trial court's ruling on the demurrer to the third count in the second amended complaint.

The judgment is affirmed. The plaintiff to recover its costs on appeal.

Notes

1. In Haywood v. Massie, 188 Va. 176, 49 S.E.2d 281 (1948), the plaintiff sought an injunction plus damages because defendant blocked a road over which plaintiff had an easement. Plaintiff claimed damages for a lost crop because the necessary farm machinery could not be brought in. The court decreed an injunction, but it denied the damages because plaintiff had other means of access; thus the court applied the rule of avoidable consequences.

2. Market valuation of a lost easement appurtenant would be impossible because of lack of buyers. How should a court measure damages for a total loss?

3. Hatfield v. Jefferson Standard Life Insurance Co., 85 N.C.App. 438, 445, 355 S.E.2d 199, 203, cert. denied, 320 N.C. 512, 358 S.E.2d 519 (1987). Both parties had an easement in an alley; defendant blocked the alley; defendant argued that plaintiff had an adequate remedy at law:

"[D]efendant's counsel argued to the court that while the defendant did not have the right of eminent domain, the plaintiffs should not be entitled to equitable relief because the impediments constructed by defendant, when viewed with the new alley constructed by defendant, did not decrease the value of plaintiffs' property. He argued to the trial court, and he argues here, that plaintiffs are not entitled to enforce their rights because defendant's plans constitute a better use of the property without reducing the value of plaintiffs' property. Our research has found no authority for the proposition that a private property owner must give up his interests in an easement because a second property owner wants to pay him damages for taking away that easement so that a more economical use of the second owner's property can be pursued."

KITZMAN v. NEWMAN

Court of Appeal of California, Second District, 1964.
230 Cal.App.2d 715, 41 Cal.Rptr. 182.

FORD, JUSTICE. This is an appeal by the defendants from a judgment awarding damages to the plaintiffs. The defendants' building was on land adjoining that of the plaintiffs' on Ventura Boulevard in the Encino section of the City of Los Angeles. The defendants extended their building across a sidewalk theretofore used by the public and thereby obstructed the view of the front of plaintiffs' building by persons proceeding along Ventura Boulevard in an easterly direction. * * *

The trial court found that, as to the area upon which the defendants constructed a sidewalk in front of their original building, it was the intention of the defendants to dedicate that strip of land to the public as an easement for street purposes; that use by the public of the sidewalk was not permissive; and that "the said easement was accepted by the public by open, public and adverse use by the public with the knowledge of the Defendants" for a period of approximately six and one-half years. The court further found that the building erected over that strip of land constituted a nuisance and that as a direct and proximate result of the defendants' acts, the plaintiffs' "easement of light, air, ingress and egress and view to and from the street appurtenant to their property was destroyed and the fair market value of Plaintiffs' property was decreased by $5,500.00." * * *

In Klaber v. Lakenan, 8 Cir., 64 F.2d 86, injunctive relief was sought against the maintenance of a sidewalk canopy and signs in front of a theatre adjoining the plaintiff's property. The complaint was that the canopy and signs obstructed a view of the plaintiff's store building from the street. While it was held that the denial of the relief sought was warranted under the facts of that case, Circuit Judge Kenyon stated: "The decided weight of authority as well as sound reason is in favor of the proposition that an abutting owner of property on a public highway has the easement, not only of light, air, and access, but of a reasonable view of his property from such public street." [citations] In the *Kelbro* case, the court stated: "An important right of this nature is the abutter's right of view to and from the property, from and to the highway; that is, his right to see and to be seen. This right of reasonable view has been generally recognized by the weight of authority and has been protected in numerous cases where encroachments on streets or sidewalks obscured the visibility of signs, window displays or show cases."

* * * The right of the plaintiffs to recover damages from the defendants remains for consideration. * * *

Dr. Kitzman, one of the plaintiffs, testified that prior to the extension of the defendants' building, the signs and windows in his building were easily viewed by persons in automobiles and by pedestrians traveling along Ventura Boulevard in an easterly direction from a point as far as eight hundred or nine hundred feet westerly of his property. After the construction of the defendants' new building, such view of the plaintiffs' premises did not arise until a person reached a point approximately due north of the west wall of his building. With respect to his property, Dr. Kitzman also testified as to vacancies and reduced rentals. In his opinion, the fair market value of the plaintiffs' property immediately prior to the extension of the defendants' building was $75,000, but the fair market value immediately after such construction was $48,000.

A real estate appraiser testified that, in his opinion, the plaintiffs' property had a fair market value of $55,000 prior to the extension of the defendants' building and a fair market value of $36,000 thereafter. He expressed the further opinion that the cause of the decrease in value was the construction of the addition to the defendants' building which blocked the view from the west of the store signs and window displays on the plaintiffs' property.

The real estate agent who had been employed to obtain tenants for the plaintiff's vacant stores testified that, in his opinion, the reason for the decrease in rental value was the loss of view of the tenants' stores, windows, displays, and signs because of the defendants' new building. He stated that a person could not see the stores until he was "right on top of them."

The trial court determined the amount of damages suffered by the plaintiffs because of the defendants' acts to be in the amount of $5,500. A review of the evidence shows that the finding of the trial court on the issue of damages was amply justified. * * *

The judgment is affirmed.

Notes

1. Interference with access may be accomplished in various ways. In Tushbant v. Greenfield's Inc., 308 Mich. 626, 14 N.W.2d 520 (1944), a queue of customers

on the public sidewalk awaiting admission to defendant's restaurant blocked the entry to plaintiff's store at certain times. Injunctive relief was granted. Accord, Shamhart v. Morrison Cafeteria Co., 159 Fla. 629, 32 So.2d 727 (1947). How should the injunction be framed? Would the decree entered in Fenton v. Quaboag Country Club, supra, p. 469, be an appropriate model?

2. Hutcherson v. Alexander, 264 Cal.App.2d 126, 70 Cal.Rptr. 366 (1968). The court enjoined the erection or placing of structures, particularly a "menu board," intended to obscure the view of and directions to plaintiff's drive-in business establishment.

3. The "clean hands" defense is available in suits to enjoin obstruction of an easement. Keller v. Devine, 550 S.W.2d 634 (Mo.App.1977). Is it possible that the result may be an impasse on the roadway?

4. The relative hardship doctrine applies and can result in the denial of equitable relief in favor of damages. Donnell v. Bisso Brothers, 10 Cal.App.3d 38, 88 Cal.Rptr. 645 (1970).

But compare Mid–America Pipeline Co. v. Wietharn, 246 Kan. 238, 787 P.2d 716 (1990). Defendant constructed buildings for a hog operation over a pipeline easement. The pipeline company sued to enjoin interference with its easement. The trial court ordered the removal and relocation of the pipeline with defendant to bear 40% of the costs. The Kansas Supreme Court reversed and granted a mandatory injunction ordering defendant to remove the buildings.

5. In Herzog v. Grosso, 41 Cal.2d 219, 259 P.2d 429 (1953), defendant interfered with access to plaintiffs' home (husband and wife) by dumping rocks, gravel, dirt and asphalt on the roadway. Plaintiffs were awarded $7,000 for permanent depreciation in the value of their home, $1500 each for mental distress and worry about the safety of themselves and others obliged to use the road, $521.80 for miscellaneous expenses, $2000 each for interference with the comfortable use and enjoyment of the home, and $2000 each exemplary damages. In addition, the court affirmed a mandatory injunction requiring defendant to restore one part of the easement to its original condition.

6. In the United States a property owner may or may not be entitled to an easement for light and air, "ancient lights," in the absence of protective ordinances or restrictive covenants. On Miami Beach when the neighboring Fontainebleau Hotel began a 14–story addition that cut off all the Florida Sunshine from patrons of the Eden Roc's outdoor swimming pool, the Eden Roc Hotel was not, the court held, entitled to an injunction. Fontainebleau Hotel Corp. v. Forty–Five Twenty–Five, Inc., 114 So.2d 357 (Fla.App.1959), cert. denied, 117 So.2d 842 (Fla.1960). In Collinson v. John L. Scott, Inc., 55 Wash.App. 481, 778 P.2d 534 (1989), the court refused to enjoin the construction of a condominium obstructing the view from plaintiff's home.

A Wisconsin court, on the other hand, held that, even though no ordinance was violated, a neighbor who proposed to obstruct sunlight from plaintiff's solar panels would commit a private nuisance. Prah v. Maretti, 108 Wis.2d 223, 321 N.W.2d 182 (1982).

Tenn v. 889 Associates, Ltd., 127 N.H. 321, 500 A.2d 366 (1985). The New Hampshire court accepted the Wisconsin court's nuisance approach; but it found that the construction of a building blocking windows in plaintiff's building did not constitute a nuisance under the circumstances.

If a property owner can successfully establish a right to a view, the court will generally protect the property against encroachment or obstruction with a mandatory injunction ordering defendant to remove the offending structure. Leonard v. Stoebling, 102 Nev. 543, 728 P.2d 1358 (1986).

f. *Private Nuisances*

Introductory Note

Nuisance has always defied simple definition. Imprecision in defining the tort has resulted in confusion about the interest it is designed to protect. This confusion, in turn, has generated problems in determining who is a proper plaintiff.

ARMORY PARK NEIGHBORHOOD ASSOCIATION v. EPISCOPAL COMMUNITY SERVICES IN ARIZONA

Supreme Court of Arizona, In Banc, 1985.

148 Ariz. 1, 712 P.2d 914.

FELDMAN, JUSTICE. On December 11, 1982, defendant Episcopal Community Services in Arizona (ECS) opened the St. Martin's Center (Center) in Tucson. The Center's only purpose is to provide one free meal a day to indigent persons. Plaintiff Armory Park Neighborhood Association (APNA) is a non-profit corporation organized for the purpose of "improving, maintaining and insuring the quality of the neighborhood known as Armory Park Historical Residential District." The Center is located on Arizona Avenue, the western boundary of the Armory Park district. On January 10, 1984, APNA filed a complaint in Pima County Superior Court, seeking to enjoin ECS from operating its free food distribution program. The complaint alleged that the Center's activities constituted a public nuisance and that the Armory Park residents had sustained injuries from transient persons attracted to their neighborhood by the Center.

The superior court held a hearing on APNA's application for preliminary injunction on March 6 and 7, 1984. * * * The residents * * * testified about the changes the Center had brought to their neighborhood. Before the Center opened, the area had been primarily residential with a few small businesses. When the Center began operating in December 1982, many transients crossed the area daily on their way to and from the Center. Although the Center was only open from 5:00 to 6:00 p.m., patrons lined up well before this hour and often lingered in the neighborhood long after finishing their meal. The Center rented an adjacent fenced lot for a waiting area and organized neighborhood cleaning projects, but the trial judge apparently felt these efforts were inadequate to control the activity stemming from the Center. Transients frequently trespassed onto residents' yards, sometimes urinating, defecating, drinking and littering on the residents' property. A few broke into storage areas and unoccupied homes, and some asked residents for handouts. The number of arrests in the area increased dramatically. Many residents were frightened or annoyed by the transients and altered their lifestyles to avoid them.

Following the hearing, ECS filed a motion to dismiss the complaint based on three grounds: 1) that compliance with all applicable zoning and health laws constituted a complete defense to a claim of public nuisance; 2) that there had been no allegation or evidence of a violation of a criminal statute or ordinance, which it argues is a prerequisite to a finding of public nuisance; and 3) that APNA lacked standing to bring an action to abate a public nuisance because it had neither pled nor proved any special injury differing in kind and degree from that suffered by the public generally.

Based on the hearing testimony, the trial court granted the preliminary injunction and denied ECS' motion to dismiss. * * *

A divided court of appeals reversed the trial court's order. * * * We granted review in this case because of the importance of the following questions:

(1) When does a voluntary association have standing to bring an action for public nuisance on behalf of its members?

(2) May a lawful business be enjoined for acts committed off its premises by clients who are not under its control or direction?

(3) Is it necessary to plead and prove a zoning or criminal violation by the defendant, or may a lawful activity be enjoined because the manner in which it is conducted is unreasonable and therefore constitutes a public nuisance?

Now considered a tort, a public nuisance action originated in criminal law. Early scholars defined public nuisance as "an act or omission 'which obstructs or causes inconvenience or damage to the public in the exercise of rights common to all her Majesty's subjects.'" Prosser, W. and W.P. Keeton, Handbook on the Law of Torts, § 90, at 643 (5th ed. 1984), quoting Stephen, General View of the Criminal Law in England 105 (1890). The sole remedy was criminal prosecution.

Historically, the remedy for a private nuisance was an action "upon the case," as it was an injury consequential to the act done and found its roots in civil law. Pearce, E. and D. Meston, Handbook on the Law Relating to Nuisances 2 (1926). A private nuisance is strictly limited to an interference with a person's interest in the enjoyment of real property. The Restatement defines a private nuisance as "a nontrespassory invasion of another's interest in the private use and enjoyment of land." Restatement (Second) of Torts § 821D. A public nuisance, to the contrary, is not limited to an interference with the use and enjoyment of the plaintiff's land. It encompasses any unreasonable interference with a right common to the general public. Restatement, supra, § 821B.

We have previously distinguished public and private nuisances. In City of Phoenix v. Johnson, 51 Ariz. 115, 75 P.2d 30 (1938), we noted that a nuisance is public when it affects rights of "citizens as a part of the public, while a private nuisance is one which affects a single individual or a definite number of persons in the enjoyment of some private right which is not common to the public." A public nuisance must also affect a considerable number of people. * * *

The defendant contends that the trial court erred in finding both public and private nuisances when the plaintiff had not asserted a private nuisance claim. * * * While we acknowledge that public and private nuisances implicate different interests, we recognize also that the same facts may support claims of both public and private nuisance. * * * However, both because plaintiff did not seek relief under the theory of private nuisance and because that theory might raise standing issues not addressed by the parties, we believe plaintiff's claim must stand or fall on the public nuisance theory alone. * * *

Defendant argues that the Association has no standing to sue and that, therefore, the action should be dismissed. The trial court disagreed and defendant claims it erred in so doing. Two standing questions are before us. The first pertains to the right of a private person, as distinguished from a public official, to bring a suit to enjoin the maintenance of a public nuisance. The original rule at common law was that a citizen had no standing to sue for abatement or suppression of a public nuisance since

> "such inconvenient or troublesome offences [sic], as annoy the whole community in general, and not merely some particular persons; and therefore are indictable only, and not actionable; as it would be unreasonable to multiply suits, by giving every man a separate right of action, by what damnifies him in common only with the rest of his fellow subjects."

IV Blackstone Commentaries 167 (1966). It was later held that a private individual might have a tort action to recover personal damages arising from the invasion of the public right. Y.B. 27 Hen. VIII, Mich, pl. 10, cited in Restatement, supra, § 821C comment a. However, the individual bringing the action was required to show that his damage was different in kind or quality from that suffered by the public in common. Prosser, supra, § 90, at 646.

The rationale behind this limitation was two-fold. First, it was meant to relieve defendants and the courts of the multiple actions that might follow if every member of the public were allowed to sue for a common wrong. Second, it was believed that a harm which affected all members of the public equally should be handled by public officials. Restatement, supra, § 821C comment a.

* * *

We hold, therefore, that because the acts allegedly committed by the patrons of the neighborhood center affected the residents' use and enjoyment of their real property, a damage special in nature and different in kind from that experienced by the residents of the city in general, the residents of the neighborhood could bring an action to recover damages for or enjoin the maintenance of a public nuisance.

Defendant claims that its business should not be held responsible for acts committed by its patrons off the premises of the Center. It argues that since it has no control over the patrons when they are not on the Center's premises, it cannot be enjoined because of their acts. We do not believe this position is supported either by precedent or theory.

In Shamhart v. Morrison Cafeteria Co., 159 Fla. 629, 32 So.2d 727 (1947), the defendant operated a well frequented cafeteria. Each day customers waiting to enter the business would line up on the sidewalk, blocking the entrances to the neighboring establishments. The dissenting justices argued that the defendant had not actually caused the lines to form and that the duty to prevent the harm to the plaintiffs should be left to the police through regulation of the public streets. The majority of the court rejected this argument, and remanded the case for a determination of the damages. See, also, Reid v. Brodsky, 397 Pa. 463, 156 A.2d 334 (1959) (operation of a bar enjoined because its patrons were often noisy and intoxicated; they frequently used the neighboring properties for toilet purposes and sexual misconduct); Barrett v. Lopez, 57 N.M. 697, 262 P.2d 981, 983 (1953) (operation of a dance hall enjoined, the court finding that "mere possibility of relief from another source [police] does not relieve the courts of their responsibilities"); Wade v. Fuller, 12 Utah 2d 299, 365 P.2d 802 (1961) (operation of drive-in cafe enjoined where patrons created disturbances to nearby residents); McQuade v. Tucson Tiller Apartments, 25 Ariz.App. 312, 543 P.2d 150 (1975) (music concerts at mall designed to attract customers enjoined because of increased crowds and noise in residential area).

Under general tort law, liability for nuisance may be imposed upon one who sets in motion the forces which eventually cause the tortious act; liability will arise for a public nuisance when "one person's acts set in motion a force or chain of events resulting in the invasion." Restatement, supra, § 824 comment b. We hold, therefore, that defendant's activity may be enjoined upon the showing of a causal connection between that activity and harm to another.

The testimony at the hearing establishes that it was the Center's act of offering free meals which "set in motion" the forces resulting in the injuries to the Armory Park residents. * * *

Since the rules of a civilized society require us to tolerate our neighbors, the law requires our neighbors to keep their activities within the limits of what is tolerable by a reasonable person. However, what is reasonably tolerable must be tolerated; not all interferences with public rights are public nuisances. As Dean Prosser explains, "[t]he law does not concern itself with trifles, or seek to remedy all of the petty annoyances and disturbances of everyday life in a civilized community even from conduct committed with knowledge that annoyance and inconvenience will result." Prosser, supra, § 88, at 626. Thus, to constitute a nuisance, the complained-of interference must be substantial, intentional and unreasonable under the circumstances. Restatement, supra, § 826 comment c and § 821F. Our courts have generally used a balancing test in deciding the reasonableness of an interference. The trial court should look at the utility and reasonableness of the conduct and balance these factors against the extent of harm inflicted and the nature of the affected neighborhood. We noted in the early case of MacDonald v. Perry:

> "What might amount to a serious nuisance in one locality by reason of the density of the population, or character of the neighborhood affected, may in another place and under different surroundings be deemed proper and unobjectionable. What amount of annoyance or inconvenience caused by others in the lawful use of their property will constitute a nuisance depends upon varying circumstances and cannot be precisely defined."

32 Ariz. 39, 50, 255 P. 494 (1927).

The trial judge did not ignore the balancing test and was well aware of the social utility of defendant's operation. His words are illuminating:

> "It is distressing to this Court that an activity such as defendants [sic] should be restrained. Providing for the poor and the homeless is certainly a worthwhile, praisworthy [sic] activity. It is particularly distressing to this Court because it [defendant] has no control over those who are attracted to the kitchen while they are either coming or leaving the premises. However, the right to the comfortable enjoyment of one's property is something that another's activities should not affect, the harm being suffered by the Armory Park Neighborhood and the residents therein is irreparable and substantial, for which they have no adequate legal remedy."

We believe that a determination made by weighing and balancing conflicting interests or principles is truly one which lies within the discretion of the trial judge. [citation] We defer to that discretion here. The evidence of the multiple trespasses upon and defacement of the residents' property supports the trial court's conclusion that the interference caused by defendant's operation was unreasonable despite its charitable cause.

The common law has long recognized that the usefulness of a particular activity may outweigh the inconveniences, discomforts and changes it causes some persons to suffer. We, too, acknowledge the social value of the Center. Its charitable purpose, that of feeding the hungry, is entitled to greater deference than pursuits of lesser intrinsic value. It appears from the record that ECS purposes in operating the Center were entirely admirable. However, even admirable ventures may cause unreasonable interferences. We do not believe that the law allows the costs of a charitable enterprise to be visited in their entirety upon the residents of a single neighborhood. The problems of dealing with the unemployed, the homeless and the mentally ill are also matters of community or governmental responsibility. * * *

ECS argued that there is no criminal violation and that a tort claim for nuisance must be based on such a violation. * * * We are squarely faced, therefore, with the issue of whether a public nuisance may be found in the absence of a statute making specific conduct a crime.

In *MacDonald v. Perry,* we indicated that the inquiry in a nuisance claim is not whether the activity allegedly constituting the nuisance is lawful but whether it is reasonable under the circumstances. The Restatement states that a criminal violation is only one factor among others to be used in determining reasonableness. That section reads:

> "(1) A public nuisance is an unreasonable interference with a right common to the general public.
>
> (2) Circumstances that may sustain a holding that an interference with a public right is unreasonable include the following:
>
> (a) Whether the conduct involves a significant interference with the public health, the public safety, the public peace, the public comfort or the public convenience, *or*
>
> (b) whether the conduct is proscribed by a statute, ordinance or administrative regulation, *or*
>
> (c) whether the conduct is of a continuing nature or has produced a permanent or long-lasting effect, and, as the actor knows or has reason to know, has a significant effect upon the public right."
>
> (*Emphasis supplied.*)

Restatement, supra, § 821B. Comment d to that section explains:

> "It has been stated with some frequency that a public nuisance is always a criminal offense. This statement is susceptible of two interpretations. The first is that in order to be treated as a public nuisance, conduct must have been already proscribed by the state as criminal. This is too restrictive. * * * [T]here is clear recognition that a defendant need not be subject to criminal responsibility. Restatement, supra, § 821B comment d, at 89.

Our earlier decisions indicate that a business which is lawful may nevertheless be a public nuisance. * * *

We hold, therefore, that conduct which unreasonably and significantly interferes with the public health, safety, peace, comfort or convenience is a public nuisance within the concept of tort law, even if that conduct is not specifically prohibited by the criminal law. * * *

The trial court's order granting the preliminary injunction is affirmed. By affirming the trial court's preliminary orders, we do not require that he close the center permanently. It is of course, within the equitable discretion of the trial court to fashion a less severe remedy, if possible.

Notes

1. As the principal case states, for a private person to have standing to sue to enjoin a public nuisance, the general common law rule required proof of some special injury to property. Thus in Pennsylvania Society for Prevention of Cruelty to Animals v. Brovo Enterprises, 428 Pa. 350, 237 A.2d 342 (1968), the SPCA was not permitted to enjoin bull baiting since no invasion of individual rights could be established. The public nuisance doctrine is also treated above, pages 180–86.

2. Mich.Comp.Laws Ann. § 691.1202 [Action in circuit court; granting of relief.] Sec. 2.(1) The attorney general, any political subdivision of the state, any instrumentality, or agency of the state or of a political subdivision thereof, any person, partnership, corporation, association, organization or other legal entity may maintain an action in the circuit court having jurisdiction where the alleged violation occurred or is likely to occur for declaratory and equitable relief against the state, any political subdivision thereof, any instrumentality or agency of the state or of a political subdivision thereof, any person, partnership, corporation, association, organization or other legal entity for the protection of the air, water and other natural resources and the public trust therein from pollution, impairment or destruction.

(2) In granting relief provided by subsection (1) where there is involved a standard for pollution or for an anti-pollution device or procedure, fixed by rule or otherwise, by an instrumentality or agency of the state or a political subdivision thereof, the court may:

(a) Determine the validity, applicability and reasonableness of the standard.

(b) When a court finds a standard to be deficient, direct the adoption of a standard approved and specified by the court.

§ 691.1202a [Posting of bond or cash.] Sec. 2a. If the court has reasonable ground to doubt the solvency of the plaintiff or the plaintiff's ability to pay any cost or judgment which might be rendered against him in an action brought under this act the court may order the plaintiff to post a surety bond or cash not to exceed $500.00.

3. See Comment, Equity and the Eco System: Can Injunctions Clear the Air, 68 Mich.L.Rev. 1254 (1970).

RIBLET v. SPOKANE–PORTLAND CEMENT CO.

Supreme Court of Washington, 1954.
45 Wash.2d 346, 274 P.2d 574.

HILL, JUSTICE. This appeal concerns the amount of damages to which the appellants, Royal N. Riblet and Mildred Riblet, are entitled as the result of cement dust emanating from the plant of the respondent, Spokane–Portland Cement Company. For detailed factual background, see Riblet v. Spokane–Portland Cement Co., 1952, 41 Wash.2d 249, 248 P.2d 380. We there held that the operation of the cement plant constituted an actionable nuisance but, since the two-year statute of limitations applied, the Riblets were entitled to recover damages only for the two-year period immediately preceding the institution of their action. Upon remand to the superior court and after consideration of the evidence taken both before and after the remand upon the issue of damages, judgment was entered for $970.

The Riblets again appeal, contending that the damages allowed are grossly inadequate and that the trial court erred in refusing to allow damages for personal discomfort and annoyance.

The trial court found that the depreciation of rental value by reason of falling cement dust was $30 a month, or $720 for a two-year period. Appellants, while claiming that these damages are grossly insufficient and inadequate, assign error, not to the propriety of measuring the damages in terms of the lessened use value or of employing the decrease in rental value as evidence of the decrease in use value, but on the theory that the trial court misunderstood the estimates of the expert witnesses and did not take into consideration all the evidence in making its determination. [The appellate court refused to disturb these findings however.]

There is abundant testimony in the record concerning the various facilities on the Riblet property and the amount of loose dust which collected thereon. Appellants' witness, Orville Hubbell, estimated the cost of cleaning up the loose dust at $10,000. No other testimony relative to the cost of removal of this item was offered by either side. The trial court found that the cost of removal of the loose dust which had accumulated on the premises over the two-year period would be $250. * * *

Hubbell testified that it would take two men two weeks to clear off eight hundred feet of three-foot sidewalk. His estimate for cleaning the swimming pool was that it would take two men a week. Mr. Riblet testified that he cleaned it every year himself and that it took him half a day to clean it and three quarters of a day to paint it, and that he had to have help to carry out a washtubful of sludge in buckets.

Appellants in their brief do not attempt to justify more than $3,360 of the Hubbell estimate. Even so they figure on two men to work on the swimming pool for seven days, to do what Riblet testified took him half a day, with help to carry out the sludge. * * *

[W]e will assume for the moment that appellants are correct in their contention that there is not "a scintilla of evidence" to sustain the finding that the cost of cleaning up the loose dust would be $250. Except for the testimony of Hubbell, which neither the trial court nor this court is willing to accept, there is then no evidence to substantiate any other figure for that item. Under such circumstances, they have no ground for complaint, the award of damages being more than nominal. * * *

Appellants also urge that the trial court erred in failing to find that they are entitled to recover $25,000 as the cost of removal of the cement dust which had become permanently encrusted on their property during the two-year period. Their theory is that the total cost of removing the encrustation, which developed during an eleven-year period, would have been $75,000 in 1951 (as testified to by Hubbell, whose credibility has heretofore been discussed), and that, consequently, they are entitled to at least two elevenths of that amount, or $13,635, for the two years in question. However, they increase this figure to $25,000 because much more dust fell during the last five than during the first five or six years of the eleven-year period. * * *

In the instant case, the evidence is that the additional encrustation which occurred during the two-year period in no way changed the appearance or the usability of the property. The condition was the same on May 22, 1950, as on

May 22, 1948, except that the encrustation was thicker. There is no evidence that the cost of removing the encrustation would have been any more at the end of the two-year period than at the beginning. On this phase of the case, the appellants failed to establish either the *amount* of the damage to their property during the two-year period in question or the *fact of any measurable additional damage* during that period.

Appellants further assign error to the trial court's finding that:

> "To award to plaintiffs [appellants] any damage for discomfort and annoyance resulting from the fall of cement dust over such two-year period in addition to awarding plaintiffs damage for the depreciation in the usable or rental value of their premises over such period would be to grant to plaintiffs, an award of double damages. In any event, there is no sufficient evidence in the record upon which the Court could base an award of damage on such items unless the Court were to engage in guess-work and speculation."

This assignment of error presents first a question of law as to whether the appellants are entitled to damages for discomfort and annoyance in addition to damages for depreciation in the use or rental value of the premises and, if that question is answered in appellants' favor, then a question of fact as to the extent of the damages proved. * * *

The annotator [in 142 A.L.R.] states the majority rule (p. 1322):

> "The question whether an occupant of real estate (whether owner or not) may recover damages for discomfort, annoyance, etc., personally resulting to him from a nuisance, in addition to, or separate from, any sort of property damages, is most distinctly presented in cases where the claim for the personal damages is accompanied by a claim for depreciation in rental or use value of premises. In most jurisdictions the rule is that the personal damages are recoverable in addition to, or separate from, damages for diminution in rental or use value. This rule seems clearly to involve the idea that the law will not presume that one responsible for a temporary nuisance will continue it, and will not require the occupant of premises to abandon them to avoid consequences to his person." * * *

In the instant case, the cement dust was the cause of both the depreciation in the use or rental value of the property and the personal discomfort and annoyance suffered by the occupants. As stated in Millett v. Minnesota Crushed Stone Co., 1920, 145 Minn. 475, 477, 478, 177 N.W. 641, 179 N.W. 682:

> "We think, too, it is something additional to diminished value of the use, as that term is ordinarily understood. The value of the use is the value not to particular persons, who may be of peculiar susceptibility to injury, or who may be subject to peculiar conditions or situations, but its general value to ordinary persons for the legitimate uses to which it may be adapted, including in this case use as a homestead. That value is determined by taking into account the various facts and circumstances which make the use more or less desirable, and in determining the extent to which a nuisance may have diminished such value, facts that naturally or reasonably tend to cause discomfort, annoyance, or illness may be taken into account. [citations] But the actual discomfort, annoyance, or illness which has resulted in damage or injury to the particular occupant involved is another and distinct element of damage. This distinction is not clearly brought out in the decided cases but we think it is recognized and it seems to us logical and just."

We are also convinced that the trial court erred in finding that there was insufficient evidence on which an award for damages for personal discomfort and annoyance could be based. Although the fall of cement dust usually was imperceptible, not being detected by sight, smell, or sound, as is usually the case when nuisance involves dust, gas, smoke, noise, etc., its effects soon became apparent to the physical senses. One cause of discomfort was the need to keep the windows of the sleeping rooms closed because the sleepers' "nostrils would be kind of filled up in the morning," and, as Mr. Riblet testified, "We just had a feeling that our nostrils were breathing dust." We think, too, that it can be inferred even if not testified to in explicit terms, that cement dust on tables, chairs, automobiles, etc., was an annoyance. Sludge on the bottom of the swimming pool, which caused Mr. Riblet to slip and slide and made it impossible to walk in the pool on the rare occasions when he used it in 1948 and 1949, created both a discomfort and an annoyance. The testimony reveals that drawings in Mr. Riblet's drafting room were constantly covered with cement dust; and when he was inking a drawing, dust would collect on the pen and blur the drawing, which clearly constituted an annoyance.

Admittedly, no one testified to damages in consequence of personal discomfort and annoyance in terms of dollars and cents, but the fact that no one has placed a monetary value on personal discomfort and annoyance does not make the damage speculative or conjectural. * * *

Because of the expressed view of the trial court that there is no evidence to sustain any judgment for personal discomfort and annoyance, it would serve no good purpose to remand the case for further consideration of those elements of damage. In our judgment, appellants are entitled to $1,000 as damages for personal discomfort and annoyance suffered during the two-year period, and we tentatively dispose of this issue by directing that the judgment be modified by increasing the damages in that amount. * * *

Notes

1. *The Applicability of the Avoidable Consequences Rule to Nuisance.* In S.C. Loveland, Inc. v. East West Towing, Inc., 608 F.2d 160, 67–69 (5th Cir.1979), a barge, adrift by reason of the owner's negligence, crashed into the Sunshine Skyway Bridge, owned by the state of Florida. Bridge employees were alerted when the barge was drifting dangerously close, and they watched it through binoculars, but took no action:

"The term nuisance is notoriously difficult to define, but it is at least possible that the drifting barge constituted a nuisance. If so, did or could the state's acts or omissions constitute either contributory negligence or a failure to avoid damages?

"In a nuisance setting it is often difficult to distinguish a plaintiff's contributory negligence from his failure reasonably to avoid foreseeable consequences. In fact some courts and commentators discuss the two together while noting that the former bars a plaintiff's claim while the latter only reduces his damage award. In principle one is required to avoid or mitigate damages only after the defendant has committed a tort but in a nuisance context the threat itself can be viewed as the tort. In the present case the result of finding that the state was contributorily negligent or that it failed to avoid foreseeable consequences is precisely the same—reduction of damages.

"Some courts and commentators have flatly stated that contributory negligence is not a defense to nuisance liability. Others including the authors of the Restatement of Torts have stated that contributory negligence is a defense to a nuisance resulting from negligent conduct of the defendant.[1]

"Some courts have declared that a plaintiff need not abate a nuisance or take affirmative steps on his premises to ward off a nuisance. Others have found plaintiff's claim barred when, without committing a trespass, he could have abated a nuisance caused by defendant's negligence. Specifically, courts have found plaintiffs contributorily negligent for failing to bury an animal decomposing on adjacent land, Central of Georgia Railway v. Steverson, 3 Ala.App. 313, 57 So. 494 (1911), and failing to avoid flood damage by building a levee, Mobile & Ohio Railroad v. Red Feather Coal Co., 218 Ala. 582, 119 So. 606 (1928), or by plowing a furrow, Louisville & N.R. Co. v. Moore, 31 Ky.L.Rptr. 141, 101 S.W. 934 (1907) (proof of failure to plow requires the trial court to instruct the jury on remand that no damages avoidable by plaintiff's exercise of ordinary care be awarded). * * *

"The more recent commentaries have argued persuasively that contributory negligence does and should operate in the nuisance area just as in other areas of tort law, and some courts have found plaintiffs contributorily negligent for failing reasonably to abate nuisance or avoid its consequences (although a 'trend' is less clear in case law than in commentaries). A finding of contributory negligence might well be incorrect as a matter of law in a case where the defendant acted willfully or recklessly or where a plaintiff could protect himself only by committing a trespass. Here, however, those responsible for the barge acted only negligently and the state or a tugboat company could have secured or removed the barge without committing a trespass. Noting these aspects of this case and the fact that contributory negligence does not act as a bar in admiralty we support the district court's finding of contributory negligence even if the drifting barge constituted a nuisance.

"A plaintiff is not entitled to recover damages for any harm that he could have avoided by the use of reasonable effort or expenditure after the commission of a tort. The reasonableness of a plaintiff's act or omission depends on 'the extent of threatened injury, as compared with the expense of remedying the situation, and the practical certainty of success in preventive effort.' Mobile & O.R. Co. v. Red Feather Coal Co., 218 Ala. 582, 119 So. 606 (1928).

"In the present case the district court found that the possibility of a collision was foreseeable to agents of the state and noted that ascertaining and notifying the barge's owner or calling a local towing service would have required either 'some' or no expenses. The collision caused the bridge to sustain damages of $123,025.47 and required closing two lanes of traffic. Any expenses in summoning aid pale in comparison.

"We therefore reject the state's argument that its fault could not be based on failure to act in these circumstances, whether such omission be described as contributory negligence or failure to avoid damages.

"We agree with the district court's conclusion that the doctrine of last clear chance is inapplicable in this case. As the district court's canvass of authority indicates, the doctrine of last clear chance is rarely applied in admiralty collision cases and then only where there is a definite line of cleavage between the final

1. [Footnote renumbered.] See, e.g., McFarlane v. Niagara Falls, 247 N.Y. 340, 160 N.E. 391 (1928) (Judge Cardozo disavowed any holding by implication that would apply to a situation where a defendant's conduct went beyond negligence): Restatement (Second) of Torts § 840B (1965) and comment d, which states that "many nuisances are * * * the result of mere negligence in failing to take proper precautions to prevent the invasion of the right. When this is the case the contributory negligence of the plaintiff is available as a defense as fully and under the same rules and conditions as in the case of any other action founded upon negligence."

fault and the preceding acts of negligence. We find a lack of cleavage on these facts for purposes of applying the last clear chance doctrine."

2. The California court held that comparative negligence is available in a nuisance action alleging damage to real property where the nuisance resulted from defendant's negligent conduct. Tint v. Sanborn, 211 Cal.App.3d 1225, 259 Cal.Rptr. 902 (1989).

3. *Statute of limitations.* Classification of a nuisance as permanent or temporary-continuing is crucial in assessing the way the statute of limitations affects the plaintiff's claim for relief. If the nuisance is classified as permanent, plaintiff must file the action within the statutory period and may recover all damages, past, present and prospective. If, on the other hand, the nuisance is temporary-continuing, a new cause of action accrues each day and plaintiff may recover for injuries sustained within the statutory period as the court allowed in *Riblet.*

In a later Washington case, particles falling on the plaintiff's property were classified as a trespass since they were found to have invaded his right to exclusive possession of the premises. The court applied the three-year trespass statute of limitations; but, as in *Riblet,* the plaintiff was allowed to recover for any damage sustained in the three-year period preceding the suit. Bradley v. American Smelting and Refining Co., 104 Wash.2d 677, 709 P.2d 782 (1985).

Miller v. Cudahy Co., 858 F.2d 1449 (10th Cir.1988), cert. denied, 492 U.S. 926 (1989). The court rejected the defendant's argument that salt pollution of a freshwater aquifer constituted a permanent nuisance. The court regarded a condition that may last for 200 years to be temporary. It did not apply the normal diminution-in-rental-value measure of damages. The court instead allowed the plaintiff to recover the difference between the net value of lost corn production and the net value of the wheat and milo crops actually grown.

4. Where the nuisance results from wilful, wanton, or malicious misconduct, punitive damages are recoverable. See Anno., 31 A.L.R.3d 1346 (1970). But a statute allowing treble damages for wilfully injuring or severing trees has been held to apply only to trespass and not to trees damaged by air pollution. Meyer v. Harvey Aluminum, 263 Or. 487, 501 P.2d 795 (1972).

KORNOFF v. KINGSBURG COTTON OIL CO.

Supreme Court of California, 1955.
45 Cal.2d 265, 288 P.2d 507.

CARTER, JUSTICE. * * * Defendant owns and operates a cotton gin on land adjacent to plaintiffs' property which is used for residential purposes and the operation of a planing mill. The area in question was zoned for business and commercial purposes. Defendant is engaged in the business of ginning lint cotton and processing cotton seed, which lasts approximately six months of each year. During the ginning season, plaintiffs alleged that large quantities of fumes, vapors, dust, dirt, sediment, lint and waste materials were emitted into the atmosphere and penetrated into the house and shop covering them with an offensive, injurious and adhesive coating of dust, lint and ginning waste and causing injury to their house, furniture, and persons. * * *

[O]n the sole issue of damages, the jury was instructed as follows:

"If, under the Court's instructions, you should find that plaintiffs are entitled to a verdict for a sum greater than merely nominal damages, then you shall determine the items of claimed detriment which I am now about to mention, provided you find each of such items to have been suffered by plaintiffs, and provided further that you find each of such items to have been suffered by plaintiffs as the proximate result of the act or acts of trespass complained of:

"1. Such sum as will reasonably compensate the said plaintiffs for the damage of their real property. That sum is equal to the difference in the fair market value of the real property immediately before and after the injury; provided, however, that if the injury has been repaired, or be capable of repair, so as to restore the fair market value of plaintiffs' real property as it existed immediately before the injury, at an expense less than such difference in value, then the measure of damage is the expense of such repair, rather than such difference in value.

"2. Such sum as will reasonably compensate plaintiffs as the owner-occupants of the land, including members of their household, *for discomfort and annoyance to them, if any,* proximately caused by the act or acts of trespass complained of. The amount of damages to be awarded for this element of the injury, if any, is left to the sound judgment and discretion of the jury based upon the evidence, and without the necessity of any witness having given his opinion with respect to the amount of such damages, if any." (Emphasis added.) * * *

At the trial, plaintiffs' attorney argued that plaintiffs were seeking past, present and future damages for the injury to their real property. Defendant contends that where a continuing trespass is involved, as distinguished from a permanent trespass, future damages are not recoverable. * * *

The parties apparently treated the trespass as permanent because of its recurrent character, rather than as a continuous trespass. The defendant's requested instructions, which were given, gave as the measure of damages that for a permanent trespass, although during the second trial, defendant's counsel argued that future damages were not recoverable.

The general rule appears to be that where a trespass to land is of a permanent nature, all damages, past and prospective, are recoverable in one action, but where the trespass is temporary in character, only those damages may be recovered which have accrued up to the time of the commencement of the action, since it is not to be presumed that the trespass will continue. * * * In Slater v. Shell Oil Co., 58 Cal.App.2d 864, 870, 137 P.2d 713, 715 an action for ejectment to enforce the removal of defendant's pipe line from the property of plaintiff, and for damages for the use and occupation of the land was involved. The court said: "Though the right to sue for ejectment and damages may be exercised in the same action by reason of section 427, subd. 2 of the Code of Civil Procedure they are nevertheless independent and inconsistent causes of action based upon the same invasion of the same right. Where, therefore, a party elects to sue for damages past and prospective he is deemed to have waived the invasion and consented to the continued occupancy of the land. Such is the rule of the majority of the cases. [citations]"

* * * In Thompson v. Illinois Cent. R.R. Co., 191 Iowa 35, 179 N.W. 191, plaintiff recovered and collected a judgment for damages for the market value of his land caused by defendant's construction and maintenance of a railway embankment. He sued again for additional damages. It was held that he was bound by his election because, in the first suit, he treated the invasions as a permanent injury to his land, recovered damages based upon a substantial

reduction in the market value of his land, and proceeded upon the theory that he should be treated as having cheaper land because the permanent and wrongful construction would injure his land at future times as it had in the past. In Spaulding v. Cameron, 38 Cal.2d 265, 267 et seq., 239 P.2d 625, 627, which involved a nuisance, this court said:

> "The remedy for a continuing nuisance was either a suit for injunctive relief or successive actions for damages as new injuries occurred. Situations arose, however, where injunctive relief was not appropriate or where successive actions were undesirable either to the plaintiff or the defendant or both. Accordingly, it was recognized that some types of nuisances should be considered permanent, and in such cases recovery of past and anticipated future damages were allowed in one action. * * *
>
> "The clearest case of a permanent nuisance or trespass is the one where the offending structure or condition is maintained as a necessary part of the operations of a public utility. Since such conditions are ordinarily of indefinite duration and since the utility by making compensation is entitled to continue them, it is appropriate that only one action should be allowed to recover for all the damages inflicted. It would be unfair to the utility to subject it to successive suits and unfair to the injured party if he were not allowed to recover all of his probable damages at once.
>
> "A more difficult problem is presented, however, if the defendant is not privileged to continue the nuisance or trespass but its abatement is impractical or the plaintiff is willing that it continue if he can secure full compensation for both past and anticipated future injuries. To attempt categorically to classify such a nuisance as either permanent or not may lead to serious injustice to one or the other of the parties. Thus, if the plaintiff assumes it is not permanent and sues only for past damages, he may be met with the plea of res judicata in a later action for additional injury if the court then decides the nuisance was permanent in character from its inception. * * * Similarly, if the initial injury is slight and plaintiff delays suit until he has suffered substantial damage and the court then determines that the nuisance was permanent, the defendant may be able to raise the defense that the statute of limitations ran from the time of the initial injury. * * * On the other hand, if the defendant is willing and able to abate the nuisance, it is unfair to award damages on the theory that it will continue. * * *
>
> "Because of these difficulties it has been recognized that in doubtful cases the plaintiff should have an election to treat the nuisance as either permanent or not. [citations] If the defendant is not privileged to continue the nuisance and is able to abate it, he cannot complain if the plaintiff elects to bring successive actions as damages accrue until abatement takes place. * * * On the other hand, if it appears improbable as a practical matter that the nuisance can or will be abated, the plaintiff should not be left to the troublesome remedy of successive actions."

In the present case, defendant's ginning mill is lawfully operated in a location properly zoned therefor and need not, or may not, Code Civ.Proc. § 731a, [set out p. 511, infra] be abated. If plaintiffs are not permitted to sue for all damages, past, present and future, then they must bring successive actions each year at the close of each ginning season with the attendant risk that the court may determine that the trespass occurring the previous year was a permanent one for which plaintiffs had been theretofore adequately compensated.

It appears that here plaintiffs elected to sue for all damages past, present and future and that such damages are recoverable under the rule heretofore set forth.

Defendant argues that damages for discomfort and annoyance are erroneously awarded in the absence of personal injury. This argument centers around the heretofore quoted instruction and upon the ground that plaintiffs did not allege such discomfort and annoyance. Plaintiffs' amended complaint shows that the "comfort and enjoyment of the plaintiffs and their family of their said home have been diminished to the extent that they have been unable to live normally and peacefully and follow ordinary pursuits, that the use of said shop has been seriously curtailed due to the said dust and cotton lint particles and plaintiffs have been deprived of the full value of same." It was also alleged that they had suffered severe nervous distress and mental anguish. The pleading would seem to be sufficient to permit damages for discomfort and annoyance if such damages are otherwise proper.

It appears to us that the discomfort and annoyance suffered by plaintiffs is an injury directly and proximately caused by defendant's invasion of their property and that such damages would naturally result from such an invasion. It also appears to us that discomfort and annoyance may be suffered where there is no physical injury suffered. * * *

While defendant's trespass here is not of the type to cause fright or shock or even physical illness (as found by the jury), it obviously is of the type to cause plaintiffs much annoyance and discomfort. * * *

Section 929 of the Restatement of Torts sets forth the rule as follows: "Where a person is entitled to a judgment for harm to land resulting from a past invasion and not amounting to a total destruction in value, the damages include compensation for * * * (c) *discomfort and annoyance,* in an action brought by the occupant." (Emphasis added.) "*Comment on Clause (c): g. Discomfort and other bodily and mental harms.* Discomfort and annoyance to an occupant of the land and to the members of his household are distinct grounds of compensation for which in ordinary cases the person in possession is allowed to recover in addition to the harm to his proprietary interest. He is also allowed to recover for his own serious sickness or other substantial bodily harm but is not allowed to recover for such serious harm to other members of the household, except so far as he maintains an action as a husband, parent or child, under the rules stated in §§ 693 and 703, vol. III. The owner of land who is not an occupant is not entitled to recover for such harms except as they may have affected the rental value of his land." * * *

In Judson v. Los Angeles Suburban Gas Co., 157 Cal. 168, 172, 106 P. 581, an action for damages for operating a nuisance in the form of a gasworks was involved. The court there said:

> "There is no proof that plaintiff's land has depreciated; that its rental value has been impaired; nor that the health of Mr. Judson or that of any member of his family has been injuriously affected by the operation of defendants' gas works. He did assert, however, that the smoke, odor, and noise produced by the manufacture of gas at defendants' works interfered with his comfortable enjoyment of his property.
>
> "In order that a judgment of this character may be upheld, it is not necessary that the health of plaintiff or of members of his household should

have been impaired. It is sufficient if the odors, sounds, and smoke were offensive to the senses." * * *

[Affirmed.]

Notes

1. Baker v. Burbank–Glendale–Pasadena Airport Authority, 39 Cal.3d 862, 218 Cal.Rptr. 293, 705 P.2d 866 (1985), cert. denied, 475 U.S. 1017 (1986). The California Supreme Court permitted a plaintiff to elect to treat the operation of an airport as a continuing nuisance (and hence avoid the bar of the statute of limitations) even though the nuisance could not be abated because of federal preemption of the regulation of commercial air transportation.

2. In Wilson v. Interlake Steel Co., 32 Cal.3d 229, 185 Cal.Rptr. 280, 649 P.2d 922 (1982), a property owner claimed the noise from a steel factory was a nuisance and sued to enjoin. Because the steel mill was in a properly zoned area, the plaintiffs came up against the bar of the anti-injunction statute (Cal.Civ.Proc.Code § 731a). The plaintiffs dropped the nuisance action and sued for damages for trespass. The court held that noise alone is not a trespass, and left plaintiffs to attempt to recover damages for a nuisance.

Compare Tamalunis v. City of Georgetown, 185 Ill.App.3d 173, 542 N.E.2d 402, appeal denied, 128 Ill.2d 672, 548 N.E.2d 1079 (1989). The court ruled that although the city had operated a disposal plant continuously for 70 years, the discharge of raw sewage from the plant was a temporary nuisance. An injunction was denied, the damage award was found to provide an adequate remedy.

3. *Question:* Suppose a sewer disposal plant is built near plaintiff's home. Some time after construction was completed, it begins to emit noxious odors. Plaintiff sues for damages for a permanent nuisance. The trial court instructs the jury that the damages are the difference between the market value of the residence before the plant was built and after the noxious odors were emitted. Is the instruction correct? See Varjabedian v. City of Madera, 20 Cal.3d 285, 142 Cal.Rptr. 429, 572 P.2d 43 (1977).

ANTUN INVESTMENTS CORP. v. ERGAS

District Court of Appeal of Florida, 1989.
549 So.2d 706.

Baskin, Judge. Antun Investments Corporation [Antun] appeals an adverse final judgment entered in an action to abate a nuisance and to recover damages. After considering the merits of the parties' contentions, we affirm in part and reverse in part.

Appellees Martin Ergas, and other owners of the Royal Palm Hotel [Ergas] instituted an action in which they alleged that Antun, owner of the adjacent Poinciana Hotel, created and maintained a nuisance that caused them to lose business and incur expenses to abate the nuisance. Seeking injunctive relief and damages, they asserted that the Poinciana Hotel was vacant, infested with mice, a repository for trash, and inhabited by vagrants. At the conclusion of a non-jury trial, the court granted the requested relief. The trial court awarded Ergas $156,868 for profits lost during the existence of the nuisance; $37,436 for out-of-pocket expenditures to rectify problems caused by the nuisance; $345,-000 to enable the Royal Palm Hotel to regain its reputation in the industry; and $18,000 for the prospective loss of business during the Passover holiday. Antun's appeal ensued. * * *

Antun also challenges the damage awards. We address each award in turn.

We find competent evidence to support the award of out-of-pocket costs incurred in restoring the property, and therefore affirm the $37,436 portion of the judgment attributed to this element.

Antun argues that Ergas failed to prove that the condition of the Poinciana Hotel was the proximate cause of Ergas' loss of profits. Antun contends that in the absence of such proof, damages are speculative. Although an improperly maintained vacant building may constitute a nuisance warranting recovery of damages, e.g., Puritan Holding Co., Inc. v. Holloschitz, 372 N.Y.S.2d 500, 82 Misc.2d 905 (1975), to recover lost prospective business profits Ergas was compelled to prove that "1) the defendant's action caused the damage and 2) there is some standard by which the amount of damages can be adequately determined." [citations] We have examined the record to determine whether it contains adequate proof.

Our review of the evidence discloses that Ergas proved that the nuisance maintained at the Poinciana Hotel caused the losses at the Royal Palm Hotel: witnesses testified that the Royal Palm Hotel guests refused to tolerate mice infestation, vagrants in the pool area, and security problems; guests checked out of the Royal Palm Hotel after observing conditions at the Poinciana Hotel; travel agents and tour operators refused to place customers at the Royal Palm Hotel after hearing of complaints; and witnesses confirmed that the source of these problems was the Poinciana Hotel. Expert testimony demonstrated that proper security at the Poinciana Hotel would have reduced crime and that pest control would have decreased the number of rodents at the Poinciana Hotel. * * *

Although Antun submitted some evidence in support of its contention, we find no basis for relieving Antun of liability. The question of causation is an issue of fact to be determined by the trier of fact. [citations] Although the evidence concerning causation is conflicting, there is record evidence which tends to prove that Antun caused Ergas' damages. [citations] The evidence was sufficient to be submitted to the trier of fact. Additionally, "the fact that other sources besides the nuisance created by the defendant may have contributed to the injury complained of does not relieve [defendant] from liability or defeat plaintiff's right to enjoin [defendant] from maintaining such nuisance." For example, in W. W. Gay Mechanical Contractor, Inc. v. Wharfside Two, Ltd., 545 So.2d 1348 (Fla.1989), the owner of a new hotel filed an action against the company that constructed the hotel's water system. The hotel owner attempted to prove that defendant installed a defective water system which created an odor problem, causing a reduction in occupancy at the hotel. The court held that "[t]here was competent and substantial evidence that the odor was *a* cause of reduced occupancy." Thus, Ergas' claim for damages was not foreclosed where Ergas demonstrated that the nuisance was *a* cause of its damages.

Because competent substantial evidence supports the lost profits award, affirmance is mandated. * * *

We find no basis, however, for the award of projected advertising expenses totaling $345,000 to enable the Royal Palm Hotel to regain its reputation in the industry, and for $18,000 representing anticipated lost profits from the Passover holiday. Recovery of past and future damages is appropriate where a nuisance is permanent; [citations]; the assessment of damages for future harm is inappropriate where the nuisance is merely temporary. A & P Food Stores, Inc. v. Kornstein, 121 So.2d 701, 704 (Fla. 3d DCA 1960); "Future harm * * * is nullified by the abatement of the nuisance through the injunctive processes of the court." *Kornstein.* Because the court found that the nuisance was remediable and issued a permanent injunction abating the nuisance, Ergas is not entitled to damages for future harm.

In summary, we affirm the award of $37,436 for out-of-pocket expenses incurred in mitigating problems caused by the nuisance, and the award of $156,868 for lost profits. We reverse the awards of $345,000 for prospective costs and $18,000 for the Passover holiday.

Affirmed in part; reversed in part.

WILMONT HOMES v. WEILER

Supreme Court of Delaware, 1964.
202 A.2d 576.

WOLCOTT, JUSTICE. * * * The plaintiffs are five families, each of which purchased a house and lot in Colonial Woods, a housing development of defendant, Wilmont Homes, Inc. * * *

An impasse having been reached, this action was filed for the abatement of a nuisance, viz., the continued flowing and collecting of large amounts of surface water upon plaintiffs' land caused by the defendant's negligent grading of the adjacent land.

* * * [T]he Vice Chancellor's order [directed] the defendant to abate the nuisance in accordance with an engineering plan submitted by the plaintiffs. The judgment ordered defendant within thirty days to commence the work and authorized plaintiffs, in the event defendant did not perform, to contract with a designated contractor, at defendant's expense, to have the work done. Defendant appeals.

Basically, defendant admits liability for the cost of getting rid of the excessive surface water collected on plaintiffs' land, but argues that plaintiffs have no standing in a Court of Chancery for the reason that by doing the necessary work themselves, they can establish their damages and sue for them at law. The argument is based upon the fundamental proposition that equity has jurisdiction only when there is no adequate remedy at law.

This action, however, is for the abatement of a nuisance, a subject matter over which equity has always had jurisdiction. * * * Indeed, there is more than a suggestion in the record to show that only defendant can abate this nuisance since its abatement probably requires going on the land of others, which defendant may do by reason of a reserved easement for that purpose, but which plaintiffs may not.

* * * It seems to us moreover that the plan approved by the Vice Chancellor is sufficiently precise and definite to permit an easy determination of ultimate compliance.

* * * Indeed, it is difficult to imagine what other form the relief could have taken.

Defendant, however, argues that the judgment in effect is a money judgment against the defendant, thus clearly demonstrating that plaintiffs had an adequate remedy at law. As we have pointed out, however, this suit falls within a field of original equity jurisdiction, the abatement of a nuisance. This being the case, it is settled law that when equity obtains jurisdiction over some portion of the controversy it will decide the whole controversy and give complete and final relief, even though that involves the grant of a purely law remedy such as a money judgment. * * *

The scheme evolved by the Vice Chancellor is a practical approach in the formulation of the relief to which plaintiffs are entitled. Furthermore, it is to be noted that defendant has the election to perform the work itself.

* * * For the foregoing reasons the judgment below is affirmed.

Notes

1. In Vane v. Lord Barnard, Chancery, 2 Vernon 738 (1716), the chancellor ordered the defendant to pay the expense of repair to damaged property. A life tenant committed waste, a commission was issued to ascertain what was to be done, and a master appointed to see that it was—although it is uncertain whether the decree was ever effectuated. The relative rarity of this form of decree is discussed in Langdell, A Brief Survey of Equitable Jurisdiction 37 (1905).

2. In *Wilmont Homes,* should the defendant be entitled to a jury trial on any of the issues? The problem, much mooted in early cases, of whether a nuisance will be enjoined before its existence has been established in an action at law is discussed in H. McClintock, Equity § 142 (2d ed. 1948), together with the implications on the right to jury trial.

Courts have ruled that, where the relief sought is abatement, there is no right to jury trial to determine the existence of a nuisance. Packett v. Herbert, 237 Va. 422, 377 S.E.2d 438 (1989); Wolford v. Thomas, 190 Cal.App.3d 347, 235 Cal.Rptr. 422 (1987).

3. Where a nuisance is only threatened, an injunction is possible but difficult to obtain. The threatened irreparable injury from defendant's proposed actions must be not merely probable but certain to result. See Ryan v. Pitkin Iron Corp., 444 F.2d 717 (10th Cir.1971); McCord v. Green, 555 So.2d 743 (Ala.1989); Freedman v. Briarcroft Property Owners, Inc., 776 S.W.2d 212 (Tex.App.1989).

HARRISON v. INDIANA AUTO SHREDDERS CO.

United States Court of Appeals, Seventh Circuit, 1976.
528 F.2d 1107.

CLARK, ASSOCIATE JUSTICE. This is an appeal from a judgment of the United States District Court for the Southern District of Indiana in a nuisance action, permanently enjoining appellant-Indiana Auto Shredders Company from operating its shredding plant for the recycling of automobiles in the Irish Hill section of Indianapolis, Indiana, and awarding $176,956 in compensatory and $353,912 in punitive damages to plaintiffs and intervenors. The suit was filed by appellee-Russell Harrison and some 33 other "claimants" who reside or work in the Irish Hill section, alleging: (1) that the dust, vibration, and noise generated by the company's shredding plant constituted a common law and statutory nuisance under Indiana law by damaging property and endangering the health and safety of residents and workers in the area; and (2) that the company's shredding plant violated various local air pollution regulations.

* * * For reasons stated below, we reverse the judgment of the district court.

* * * The concept of salvaging discarded automobiles and other metals by shredding them and recovering the ferrous metal was developed * * * in the early 1960's. Typically, a shredding machine is composed of massive rotary teeth (called "hammers") that rip off pieces of the automobile as it passes a cutting edge and then spits fist-sized chunks of metal and other matter across a series of "cascades," blowers, and magnets, which separate the ferrous metals from the non-ferrous metals and debris. A series of conveyors then carries the product and waste to storage. A "hammermill" such as the one in this case weighs 220 tons and measures approximately ten feet in width, fourteen feet in length, and nine feet in height. * * *

Most of the witnesses for the claimants were themselves residents or employers in the Irish Hill section, and they described first-hand the vibration, noise, and air pollution they had experienced. They testified that these conditions damaged their property and seriously affected their ability to live and work comfortably in the area. In presenting its defense, on the other hand, the company did not attempt to rebut this subjective evidence, but instead focused on its efforts to ameliorate the difficulties in "starting up" the shredder operation and upon its compliance with all of the applicable ordinances and regulations. In contrast to the "ordinary citizens" who testified for the claimants, most of the company's witnesses were experts and specialists in environmental, industrial, or real estate affairs.

To bolster the testimony they had given, the claimants presented various dignitaries and prominent citizens of Indianapolis who had become involved in the shredder dispute; radio and television publicity had apparently made the affair into something of a *cause celebre.* One by one, various members of the Indianapolis community testified for the claimants and corroborated their testimony about the noise, vibrations, and air pollution caused by the shredder. The Deputy Mayor of Indianapolis, the Corporation Counsel for the City of Indianapolis, a local school board member, the director of mayor's Office of Neighborhood Services, the medical community's representative to the Indianapolis Air Pollution Control Board, a local manufacturer's representative for heavy industrial equipment, and an aide to United States Senator Birch Bayh all testified to their personal observations of the shredder and the problems it caused to the Irish Hill section.

Although this testimony gave support to the claimants' characterization of the shredder as troublesome and annoying, none of it was competent to prove that the shredder constituted a threat or hazard to the health and life of the community. * * *

This case is representative of the new breed of lawsuit spawned by the growing concern for cleaner air and water. The birth and burgeoning growth of environmental litigation have forced the courts into difficult situations where modern hybrids of the traditional concepts of nuisance law and equity must be fashioned. Nuisance has always been a difficult area for the courts; the conflict of precedents and the confusing theoretical foundations of nuisance, led Prosser to tag the area a "legal garbage can."[1] In any case, environmental consciousness may be the saving prescript for our age. Thus the right of environmentally-aggrieved parties to obtain redress in the courts

1. [Footnote renumbered.] Prosser, "Nuisance Without Fault," 20 Tex.L.Rev. 399, 410 (1942).

serves as a necessary and valuable supplement to legislative efforts to restore the natural ecology of our cities and countryside.

Judicial involvement in solving environmental problems does, however, bring its own hazards. Balancing the interests of a modern urban community like Indianapolis may be very difficult. Weighing the desire for economic and industrial strength against the need for clean and livable surroundings is not easily done, especially because of the gradations in quality as well as quantity that are involved. There is the danger that environmental problems will be inadequately treated by the piecemeal methods of litigation. It is possible that courtroom battles may be used to slow down effective policymaking for the environment. Litigation often fails to provide sufficient opportunities for the expert analysis and broad perspective that such policymaking often requires.

As difficult as environmental balancing may be, however, some forum for aggrieved parties must be made available. If necessary, the courts are qualified to perform the task. The courts are skilled at "balancing the equities," a technique that traditionally has been one of the judicial functions. Courts are insulated from the lobbying that gives strong advantages to industrial polluters when they face administrative or legislative review of their operations. The local state or federal court, because of its proximity to the individual problem, is often in a better position to judge the effect of a pollution nuisance upon a locality. For all of these reasons, the balancing in this case, although difficult, was nonetheless a proper function for the court below to perform. All other forums for obtaining relief were cut-off from the claimants and they understandably turned to the courts for relief.

The problem of balancing the equities in this case, however, was compounded by the fact that the company was not the ordinary industrial polluter. Usually, industrial polluters bring only their proprietary rights to be balanced on the scale opposite the community interests in a cleaner environment. The polluter asks the court to give due weight to the contributions that the business enterprise makes to the community by its economic achievements: payroll, taxes, investment of profits. [The court noted that in order for defendant to comply with the injunction "it had to lay-off forty employees and it will have to expend an additional million dollars to move the shredder to some other location."] Although when contrasted with the direct damage caused by uncontrolled pollution, such contributions may seem indirect, they are nonetheless entitled to serious consideration. No court could lightly decide to shut down a business that was the sole or principal livelihood of a community's citizens. Economic and property interests are entitled to significant weight. But here, the Indiana Auto Shredders Company makes more than only those economic contributions to the Indianapolis community; it is making a direct contribution toward improving the environment and conserving its natural resources by the recycling of abandoned automobiles. In curtailing the company's operations, the court below chose a very serious course of action. It is our view that such a course of action must be based upon conspicuous facts and reasonable standards of law.

* * * At the outset, one notes that environmental litigation of this type, whether based upon the Indiana nuisance statute or the common law of nuisance, logically will involve two stages of adjudication. First, the court or trier of fact will determine whether the facts alleged actually constitute a nuisance and a nuisance of what type. Second, having determined the nature

of the alleged nuisance, the court will fashion relief appropriate to the equities of the case. Each of these two stages implicate their own legal standards.

Some activities, occupations, or structures are so offensive at all times and under all circumstances, regardless of location or surroundings, that they constitute "nuisance per se." Activities that imminently and dangerously threaten the public health fall into this category. It is more often the case, however, that the activities challenged by suitors in a nuisance case fall short of this standard of imminent and dangerous harm. Such activities as cause more remote harm to people or are the source of inconvenience, annoyance and minor damage to property are labeled "nuisance in fact" or "nuisance per accidens." These latter activities are nuisances primarily because of the circumstances or the location and surrounding of the activities, rather than the nature of the activities themselves. Most air and water pollution, when their effects are only minimally or remotely harmful to the public health, will be nuisances of this second type. Obviously, it is this second type that more frequently occurs. Very often this second type will present the offensive activities of an otherwise lawful business, activities that are being conducted in such a manner so as to become a nuisance.

When there is an imminent and dangerous threat of harm from particular business activities, the determination of nuisance per se can easily be made. The second class of nuisance, on the other hand, depends for its definition on the facts and circumstances of each case. Not every instance of inconvenience or interference will constitute a nuisance. Nevertheless property owners have a right to require that an adjoining business be properly managed and conducted so as to avoid any unnecessary inconvenience or annoyance to them. Although it is only unnecessary and substantial annoyance that the law reaches out to prevent, whenever annoyances of this type exist, the sufferers are entitled to have their suffering alleviated. * * * Even when the pollution does not present imminent health hazards, those suffering the pollution ought to be allowed to show how the quality of their lives is diminished, despite any scientific expert's statement that the pollution is harmless.

Thus, in this first stage in the adjudication of environmental nuisance suits, it is for the court trier of fact to determine whether the facts of the particular case of pollution bring the activities of the polluter within the reaches of nuisance law.

If a pollution nuisance has been found to exist, the court must then decide what relief to grant to those suffering the nuisance. In this second stage in the adjudication of environmental nuisance suits, balancing the equities becomes all important. The court must decide whether injunctive relief, damages, or some combination of the two best satisfies the particular demands of the case before it. This is the difficult but necessary work the court must perform.

Of course, where the pollution from a mill or factory creates hazards that imminently and dangerously affect the public health, the appropriate relief is a permanent injunction against the continuation of the polluting activities. It would be unreasonable to allow a private interest in the profits and product of such a polluting menace to outweigh the community's interests in the health of its citizens. However, a permanent injunction that shuts down a mill or factory without consideration of the extent of the harm that its pollution caused would be equally unreasonable. Pollution nuisance cases present no special features that should exempt them from the equitable requirements for injunctive relief, including proof of irreparable harm and inadequate remedy at law. * * * Ordinarily a permanent injunction will not lie unless (1) either the polluter seriously and imminently threatens the public health or (2) he causes non-health injuries that are substantial and the business cannot be operated to avoid the injuries apprehended. Thus the particular situation facts of each pollution nuisance case will determine whether a permanent injunction should be issued. When a business' offensive activities fall short of that standard, only the combination of both reckless disregard of substantial annoyances caused to adjoining property owners plus the impossibility of mitigating the offensive characteristics of the business will justify the granting of permanent injunctive relief.

Turning then to the instant case, the decision to permanently close the Indiana Auto Shredders Company was made in error. Although the record indicates that industrial wastes are generated beyond the confines of the property, such facts are not supportive of permanent injunctive action unless injury to health, safety, or welfare is shown. All of the testimony as to appellant's violation of the regulations of the Division of Public Health and Hospital Corporation of Marion County, Indiana, and the Indiana State Board of Health has been negative. The testimony of the authorities and scientific experts was that no violation of state or local health and safety regulations has occurred. Even the claimants' own scientific tests show compliance. Thus the findings of the district court as to violations of the zoning ordinance regarding the emission of particulate matter, earth, vibrations, sound, and odorous matter in such quantities as to endanger the public health and safety are clearly erroneous. Under these circumstances and in the absence of any proof of the substantiality of the damage or the incorrigibility of the shredder's operation, the permanent injunction must be ordered withdrawn. We turn then to the specific findings made by the district court.

The evidence showed that the residences in the Irish Hill section were for the most part about one hundred years old—none being less than 50 years, and that present law prevents residential construction in the future. It showed that the area was near an interstate highway, a main line railroad and a community dumping ground. Previously a railroad roundhouse was occupying the spot where the shredder was located. The area had been zoned for industrial use for over half a century, and the rezoning of the company site for shredder use was three years before appellant began construction. The I–5–U zoning category specifically permits use of the property for metal operations.

Most significant was the fact that not a single expert or governmental official charged with enforcement duties testified to a single significant violation by appellant of any relevant zoning standard. Indeed, all of the testimony showed that the shredding operation was well within standards and that appellant obtained all governmental certificates and permits required of it. * * *

We can well appreciate and fully sympathize with the unhappiness of the appellees over their situation. However, the problem of zoning is a local one, governed by local law; it must be solved in local perspective. The appropriate local authority has zoned the property specifically for shredder use; and appellant has been issued a permit to so use the property. After careful and continued tests by reputable experts as well as public officials, appellant's operation has met all the required standards. Under these circumstances and in the absence of an imminent hazard to health or welfare—none of which was established or found present here, the appellant cannot be prevented from continuing to engage in the operation of its shredding. See Reserve Mining Co. v. United States, 514 F.2d 492 (8th Cir.1975). The national environmental policy, as announced by Congress, allows offending industries a reasonable period of time to make adjustments to conform to standards. See, e.g., Clean Air Act, 42 U.S.C.A. §§ 1857c–5 to 8 (1970); National Environmental Policy Act, 42 U.S.C.A. § 4331 (1970). Appellant is a new undertaking in Irish Hill; it too is entitled to a reasonable period of time to correct any defects not of imminent or substantial harm. If there is damage to property, of course, it is recoverable here as in any other case.

The trial court based its action on the existence of a common nuisance but even if such were present, the drastic remedy of closing down the operation without endeavoring to launder its objectionable features would be impermissible under our law. In applying the test of the cases, we find no ground on which to base a permanent injunction here.

This is not to say that those features of the appellant's operation that are found to be offensive should not be remedied. We only say that the offender shall have time to correct the evil. If the appellant does not correct the infractions presently existing within a reasonable period, the district court may take action that will require the appellant so to do. * * *

It follows that the damage awards must fall. In this connection we believe effective administration requires that we express our opinion that the permanent damage award made here was not permissible in the light of the granting of injunctive relief. The measure of damages in Indiana in private non-permanent nuisances is loss of use and it is measured in rental value.

Nor do we believe that punitive damages, as of this date, are recoverable. Our reading of the record indicates that the appellant cooperated with all government agencies. It did its best to improve the operation of its shredder so as to alleviate damage, discomfort, and inconvenience. Indeed, the district court permitted it to continue in business for 40 days after its death sentence was pronounced. On balance, we do not find grounds for punitive damages.

The judgment is reversed, the permanent injunction is dissolved, and the case is remanded for further proceedings in accordance herewith. * * *

Notes

1. Courts are reluctant to enter permanent injunctions prohibiting useful enterprises. Sometimes the problem can be solved by permitting the defendant to continue operation after adopting the latest scientific devices for minimizing the nuisance. The classic illustration is Georgia v. Tennessee Copper Co., 206 U.S. 230 (1906); 237 U.S. 474 (1915); 240 U.S. 650 (1916). Learned Hand's able opinion in Smith v. Staso Milling Co., 18 F.2d 736 (2d Cir.1927), demonstrates this method of accommodating the conflicting interests of land owner and manufacturer.

2. *Judicial or Statutory Techniques to Balance Interests.* Consider and evaluate the "solutions" to a nuisance problem employed in the following examples:

a. Kutner v. Delaware Tool Steel Corp., 209 F.Supp. 326 (D.Del.1962). Plaintiff, a used car dealer, sought to enjoin the operation of an adjoining tool manufacturing plant, alleging excessive noise. Held, injunction denied. Since the noise does not interfere unreasonably with the conduct of plaintiff's business, there is no nuisance. What are the implications of this decision?

b. Steele v. Queen City Broadcasting Co., 54 Wash.2d 402, 411–13, 341 P.2d 499, 504–05 (1959). Plaintiff, a home owner, sought to enjoin a television tower on adjoining property. The court found that the tower constituted a nuisance, but denied injunctive relief conditioned on the payment of damages measured by the diminution in the value of the property. The court reasoned as follows:

"Whether or not an injunction will issue must be determined by balancing the equities of the parties. No one factor is controlling. In Restatement Torts § 936, it is stated: 'The appropriateness of injunction against tort depends upon a comparative appraisal of all of the factors in the case, including the following primary factors:

'(a) the character of the interest to be protected,

'(b) the relative adequacy to the plaintiff of injunction and of the other remedies available,

'(c) plaintiff's delay in bringing suit,

'(d) plaintiff's misconduct,

'(e) the relative hardship likely to result to defendant if injunction is granted and to plaintiff if it is denied,

'(f) the interests of third persons and of the public, and

'(g) the practicability of framing and enforcing the order of judgment.'

"While the plaintiffs could have taken legal action before the building permit was issued, the court found that they were not guilty of laches and there was no question that they were guilty of any misconduct. The interests of both parties were property interests, but the hardship to the defendant, the court found, would be much greater if it were required to remove the tower than would be the hardship to the plaintiff if injunctive relief were denied. The court also found that damages would adequately compensate the plaintiffs. This finding was justified by their evidence, since they were mainly concerned with the loss in value of their properties. While the homes in which they lived had many qualities which they found desirable, they did not contend that these qualities could not be found elsewhere for a comparable price.

"Particularly, the court considered the fact that the presence of two other towers, only a few blocks away, had already blighted the neighborhood, and the additional tower added little to the damage already done except as it affected those, such as the plaintiffs, living in close proximity. Consequently, it would be unfair to require the defendant to remove its tower, occasioning it great financial loss and probable loss of its right to broadcast over the channel, when the removal of the tower would not restore the value of any of the surrounding properties other than those immediately adjacent.

"The interest of the public in the functioning of this television station was not mentioned by the court; but it would seem that if an equity exists in this regard, it exists in behalf of the defendant."

In Baldwin v. McClendon, 292 Ala. 43, 288 So.2d 761 (1974), the court denied an injunction against a hog farm upon payment of $3000 damages.

c. Guttinger v. Calaveras Cement Co., 105 Cal.App.2d 382, 233 P.2d 914 (1951). Plaintiff, a rancher, sought to enjoin defendant, a cement company, from operating its factory in such a way as to cause cement dust to settle on grazing land. A decree was entered awarding damages and an injunction prohibiting more than 13% of all flue dust to be discharged from the defendant's kiln. The trial court determined that such a decree would be effective to abate the nuisance, since 13%

of flue dust was found to be non-injurious. What are the implications of this decision in a later suit for damages sustained after this decree? See Guttinger v. Calaveras Cement Co., 160 Cal.App.2d 460, 325 P.2d 145 (1958). Compare the opinion in Anderson v. Souza, 38 Cal.2d 825, 243 P.2d 497 (1952), where the court sought to fashion a decree that would permit the continued operation of an airport.

d. Cal.Civ.Proc.Code § 731a:

Whenever any city, city and county, or county shall have established zones or districts under authority of law wherein certain manufacturing or commercial uses or airport are expressly permitted, except in an action to abate a public nuisance brought in the name of the people of the State of California, no person or persons, firm or corporation shall be enjoined or restrained by the injunctive process from the reasonable and necessary operation in any such industrial or commercial zone or airport of any use expressly permitted therein, nor shall such use be deemed a nuisance without evidence of the employment of unnecessary and injurious methods of operation. Nothing in this act shall be deemed to apply to the regulation and working hours of canneries, fertilizing plants, refineries and other similar establishments whose operation produce offensive odors.

e. An Indiana statute protects industry by providing that no nuisance shall be found if the operation has been conducted continuously for one year, there has been no significant change in the hours or type of activity, and the enterprise would not have been classified as a nuisance at the time it began in that locality. See Erbrich Products Co. v. Wills, 509 N.E.2d 850 (Ind.App.1987). This solution to the problem of the plaintiff who "comes to the nuisance" may be compared to the result reached in Spur Industries v. Del E. Webb Development Co., 108 Ariz. 178, 494 P.2d 700 (1972) cited next.

f. Spur Industries v. Del E. Webb Development Co., 108 Ariz. 178, 494 P.2d 700 (1972). The Del Webb Corporation built Sun City catering to retired people in a sparsely populated area in Arizona next to defendant's cattle feeding operation. Although the plaintiffs "moved to the nuisance," they were entitled to an injunction; but the developer was required to pay the expenses of shutting and moving the offending operation. See Lewin, Compensated Injunctions and the Evolution of Nuisance Law, 71 Iowa L.Rev. 775 (1986).

3. Although the typical nuisance involves injuries from commercial enterprise, neighborhood squabbles occur:

a. Boudinot v. State, 340 P.2d 268, 269 (Okl.1959). The state sued to enjoin defendant from keeping a large number of cats. In her answer, defendant alleged that she kept no more than forty cats "in a perfect state of health" and "in an extremely sanitary manner." The court, finding a public nuisance, enjoined defendant from keeping or maintaining in excess of four cats on her premises.

b. Schork v. Epperson, 74 Wyo. 286, 294–95, 287 P.2d 467, 470 (1955). Defendant constructed a slab board fence nine feet high and 106 feet long, the full length of the lot adjoining plaintiff's home. He placed a red flag on top of the fence. Plaintiff, alleging that the fence was constructed solely to harass, sought injunctive relief. An injunction was granted compelling defendants to lower the fence to the height of the window sills on plaintiff's home. Applying the tests of the Restatement of Torts §§ 826, 829, the court found that the injury to the plaintiff outweighed any benefit to the defendant. Quoting from other authorities, the court noted that on the subject of "spite fences," it may be better to follow "the pandects of the heathen Romans" than "the principles of the common law as expounded by some Christian courts and text writers."

c. Rodrigue v. Copeland, 475 So.2d 1071, 1080 (La.1985), cert. denied, 475 U.S. 1046 (1986). Defendant's elaborate home Christmas lighting display attracted numerous sightseers into his residential neighborhood every evening during December. Neighbors sued for an injunction claiming several kinds of injury: traffic congestion that created difficulty in reaching and leaving their homes and finding parking, disruption from the display's amplified music as well as noisy and abusive visitors who deposited trash and worse on streets and lawns, and obstructions to obtaining emergency services. After protracted litigation and wide publicity, the Louisiana Supreme Court held that the neighbors' damage and irreparable injury could be prevented by enjoining defendant from maintaining a Christmas exhibition that attracts "bumper to bumper traffic and extremely large numbers of visitors to * * * [the] neighborhood."

The court rejected defendant's argument that time, place and manner limits infringed on his right to express his religious beliefs. The court specifically banned oversized, lighted snowmen and reindeer, but, in deference to defendant's religion, not "the Star of Bethlehem, nativity scene, religious tapestry and oversized lighted angels."

Questions: Was it a mistake to focus on the nuisance's effect rather than the nuisance itself? Should the court have limited the display more specifically?

4. Other interesting decisions that balance the competing interests of landowners include:

a. Sherk v. Indiana Waste Systems, 495 N.E.2d 815 (Ind.App.1986). The court ruled that the noise emanating from a landfill constituted a nuisance to plaintiff's hog breeding farm.

b. Hendricks v. Stalnaker, ___ W.Va. ___, 380 S.E.2d 198 (1989). Defendant drilled a well which precluded plaintiffs from developing a septic system on their property; but the court held no nuisance.

c. Pasulka v. Koob, 170 Ill.App.3d 191, 524 N.E.2d 1227, cert. denied, 122 Ill.2d 579, 530 N.E.2d 250 (1988). Defendant's operation of a sand and gravel pit did not constitute a nuisance as to plaintiff homeowner, who complained about noise, dust and odors.

d. Harford Penn–Cann Service, Inc. v. Zymblosky, 378 Pa.Super. 578, 549 A.2d 208 (1988). An injunction was modified to permit the defendant's truck stop to reduce dust pollution and to continue operations.

BOOMER v. ATLANTIC CEMENT CO.

Court of Appeals of New York, 1970.
26 N.Y.2d 219, 309 N.Y.S.2d 312, 257 N.E.2d 870.

BERGAN, JUDGE. Defendant operates a large cement plant near Albany. These are actions for injunction and damages by neighboring land owners alleging injury to property from dirt, smoke and vibration emanating from the plant. A nuisance has been found after trial, temporary damages have been allowed; but an injunction has been denied. * * * Cement plants are obvious sources of air pollution in the neighborhoods where they operate.

* * * The threshold question raised by the division of view on this appeal is whether the court should resolve the litigation between the parties now before it as equitably as seems possible; or whether, seeking promotion of the general public welfare, it should channel private litigation into broad public objectives.

A court performs its essential function when it decides the rights of parties before it. Its decision of private controversies may sometimes greatly affect public issues. Large questions of law are often resolved by the manner in which private litigation is decided. But this is normally an incident to the court's main function to settle controversy. It is a rare exercise of judicial power to use a decision in private litigation as a purposeful mechanism to achieve direct public objectives greatly beyond the rights and interests before the court.

Effective control of air pollution is a problem presently far from solution even with the full public and financial powers of government.

It seems apparent that the amelioration of air pollution will depend on technical research in great depth; on a carefully balanced consideration of the economic impact of close regulation; and of the actual effect on public health. It is likely to require massive public expenditure and to demand more than any local community can accomplish and to depend on regional and interstate controls.

A court should not try to do this on its own as a by-product of private litigation and it seems manifest that the judicial establishment is neither equipped in the limited nature of any judgment it can pronounce nor prepared to lay down and implement an effective policy for the elimination of air pollution. This is an area beyond the circumference of one private lawsuit. It is a direct responsibility for government and should not thus be undertaken as an incident to solving a dispute between property owners and a single cement plant—one of many—in the Hudson River valley.

The ground for the denial of injunction, notwithstanding the finding both that there is a nuisance and that plaintiffs have been damaged substantially, is the large disparity in economic consequences of the nuisance and of the injunction. This theory cannot, however, be sustained without overruling a doctrine which has been consistently reaffirmed in several leading cases in this court and which has never been disavowed here, namely that where a nuisance has been found and where there has been any substantial damage shown by the party complaining an injunction will be granted.

The rule in New York has been that such a nuisance will be enjoined although marked disparity be shown in economic consequence between the effect of the injunction and the effect of the nuisance.

The problem of disparity in economic consequence was sharply in focus in Whalen v. Union Bag & Paper Co., 208 N.Y. 1, 101 N.E. 805. A pulp mill entailing an investment of more than a million dollars polluted a stream in which plaintiff, who owned a farm, was "a lower riparian owner." The economic loss to plaintiff from this pollution was small. This court, reversing the Appellate Division, reinstated the injunction granted by the Special Term against the argument of the mill owner that in view of "the slight advantage to plaintiff and the great loss that will be inflicted on defendant" an injunction should not be granted. * * * "Such a balancing of injuries cannot be justified by the circumstances of this case," Judge Werner noted. He continued: "Although the damage to the plaintiff may be slight as compared with the defendant's expense of abating the condition, that is not a good reason for refusing an injunction."

Thus the unconditional injunction granted at Special Term was reinstated. The rule laid down in that case, then, is that whenever the damage resulting from a nuisance is found not "unsubstantial," viz., $100 a year, injunction would follow. This states a rule that had been followed in this court with marked consistency. [citations]

There are cases where injunction has been denied. McCann v. Chasm Power Co., 211 N.Y. 301, 105 N.E. 416 is one of them. There, however, the damage shown by plaintiffs was not only unsubstantial, it was non-existent. Plaintiffs owned a rocky bank of the stream in which defendant had raised the level of the water. This had no economic or other adverse consequence to plaintiffs, and thus injunctive relief was denied.

Thus if, within Whalen v. Union Bag & Paper Co., which authoritatively states the rule in New York, the damage to plaintiffs in these present cases from defendant's cement plant is "not unsubstantial," an injunction should follow.

Although the court at Special Term and the Appellate Division held that injunction should be denied, it was found that plaintiffs had been damaged in various specific amounts up to the time of the trial and damages to the respective plaintiffs were awarded for those amounts. The effect of this was, injunction having been denied, plaintiffs could maintain successive actions at law for damages thereafter as further damage was incurred.

The court at Special Term also found the amount of permanent damage attributable to each plaintiff, for the guidance of the parties in the event both sides stipulated to the payment and acceptance of such permanent damage as a settlement of all the controversies among the parties. The total of permanent damages to all plaintiffs thus found was $185,000. This basis of adjustment has not resulted in any stipulation by the parties.

This result at Special Term and at the Appellate Division is a departure from a rule that has become settled; but to follow the rule literally in these cases would be to close down the plant at once. This court is fully agreed to avoid that immediately drastic remedy; the difference in view is how best to avoid it.[1]

One alternative is to grant the injunction but postpone its effect to a specified future date to give opportunity for technical advances to permit defendant to eliminate the nuisance; another is to grant the injunction conditioned on the payment of permanent damages to plaintiffs which would compensate them for the total economic loss to their property present and future caused by defendant's operations. For reasons which will be developed the court chooses the latter alternative.

If the injunction were to be granted unless within a short period—e.g., 18 months—the nuisance be abated by improved methods, there would be no assurance that any significant technical improvement would occur.

The parties could settle this private litigation at any time if defendant paid enough money and the imminent threat of closing the plant would build up the pressure on defendant. If there were no improved techniques found, there

1. Respondent's investment in the plant is in excess of $45,000,000. There are over 300 people employed there.

would inevitably be applications to the court at Special Term for extensions of time to perform on showing of good faith efforts to find such techniques.

Moreover, techniques to eliminate dust and other annoying by-products of cement making are unlikely to be developed by any research the defendant can undertake within any short period, but will depend on the total resources of the cement industry nationwide and throughout the world. The problem is universal wherever cement is made.

For obvious reasons the rate of the research is beyond control of defendant. If at the end of 18 months the whole industry has not found a technical solution a court would be hard put to close down this one cement plant if due regard be given to equitable principles.

On the other hand, to grant the injunction unless defendant pays plaintiffs such permanent damages as may be fixed by the court seems to do justice between the contending parties. All of the attributions of economic loss to the properties on which plaintiffs' complaints are based will have been redressed.

The nuisance complained of by these plaintiffs may have other public or private consequences, but these particular parties are the only ones who have sought remedies and the judgment proposed will fully redress them. The limitation of relief granted is a limitation only within the four corners of these actions and does not foreclose public health or other public agencies from seeking proper relief in a proper court.

It seems reasonable to think that the risk of being required to pay permanent damages to injured property owners by cement plant owners would itself be a reasonable effective spur to research for improved techniques to minimize nuisance.

The power of the court to condition on equitable grounds the continuance of an injunction on the payment of permanent damages seems undoubted. * * *

It has been said that permanent damages are allowed where the loss recoverable would obviously be small as compared with the cost of removal of the nuisance (Kentucky–Ohio Gas Co. v. Bowling, 264 Ky. 470, 477, 95 S.W.2d 1).

The present cases and the remedy here proposed are in a number of other respects rather similar to Northern Indiana Public Service Co. v. W.J. & M.S. Vesey, 210 Ind. 338, 200 N.E. 620 decided by the Supreme Court of Indiana. The gases, odors, ammonia and smoke from the Northern Indiana company's gas plant damaged the nearby Vesey greenhouse operation. An injunction and damages were sought, but an injunction was denied and the relief granted was limited to permanent damages "present, past, and future."

Denial of injunction was grounded on a public interest in the operation of the gas plant and on the court's conclusion "that less injury would be occasioned by requiring the appellant [Public Service] to pay the appellee [Vesey] all damages suffered by it * * * than by enjoining the operation of the gas plant; and that the maintenance and operation of the gas plant should not be enjoined."

The Indiana Supreme Court opinion continued: "When the trial court refused injunctive relief to the appellee upon the ground of public interest in the continuance of the gas plant, it properly retained jurisdiction of the case and awarded full compensation to the appellee. This is upon the general equitable principle that equity will give full relief in one action and prevent a multiplicity of suits."

It was held that in this type of continuing and recurrent nuisance permanent damages were appropriate. See, also, City of Amarillo v. Ware, 120 Tex. 456, 40 S.W.2d 57 where recurring overflows from a system of storm sewers were treated as the kind of nuisance for which permanent depreciation of value of affected property would be recoverable.

There is some parallel to the conditioning of an injunction on the payment of permanent damages in the noted "elevated railway cases" (Pappenheim v. Metropolitan El. Ry. Co., 128 N.Y. 436, 28 N.E. 518 and others which followed.) Decisions in these cases were based on the finding that the railways created a nuisance as to adjacent property owners, but in lieu of enjoining their operation, the court allowed permanent damages.

Thus it seems fair to both sides to grant permanent damages to plaintiffs which will terminate this private litigation. The theory of damage is the "servitude on land" of plaintiffs imposed by defendant's nuisance. (See United States v. Causby, 328 U.S. 256, 261, 262, 267, where the term "servitude" addressed to the land was used by Justice Douglas relating to the effect of airplane noise on property near an airport.)

The judgment, by allowance of permanent damages imposing a servitude on land, which is the basis of the actions, would preclude future recovery by plaintiffs or their grantees.

This should be placed beyond debate by a provision of the judgment that the payment by defendant and the acceptance by plaintiffs of permanent damages found by the court shall be in compensation for a servitude on the land.

Although the Trial Term has found permanent damages as a possible basis of settlement of the litigation, on remission the court should be entirely free to reexamine this subject. It may again find the permanent damage already found; or make new findings.

The orders should be reversed, without costs, and the cases remitted to Supreme Court, Albany County to grant an injunction which shall be vacated upon payment by defendant of such amounts of permanent damage to the respective plaintiffs as shall for this purpose be determined by the court. * * *

JASEN, JUDGE (dissenting). * * * I see grave dangers in overruling our long-established rule of granting an injunction where a nuisance results in substantial continuing damage. In permitting the injunction to become inoperative upon the payment of permanent damages, the majority is, in effect, licensing a continuing wrong. It is the same as saying to the cement company, you may continue to do harm to your neighbor so long as you pay a fee for it. Furthermore, once such permanent damages are assessed and paid, the incentive to alleviate the wrong would be eliminated, thereby continuing air pollution of an area without abatement. * * *

This kind of inverse condemnation * * * may not be invoked by a private person or corporation for private gain or advantage. Inverse condemnation should only be permitted when the public is primarily served in the taking or impairment of property. [citations] The promotion of the interests of the polluting cement company has, in my opinion, no public use or benefit.

Nor is it constitutionally permissible to impose servitude on land, without consent of the owner, by payment of permanent damages where the continuing impairment of the land is for a private use. [citations] This is made clear by the State Constitution (art. I, § 7, subd. [a]) which provides that "[p]rivate property shall not be taken for *public use* without just compensation" (emphasis added). It is, of course, significant that the section makes no mention of taking for a *private* use. * * *

I would enjoin the defendant cement company from continuing the discharge of dust particles upon its neighbors' properties unless, within 18 months, the cement company abated this nuisance.

Notes

1. Damages were computed on remand. Boomer v. Atlantic Cement Co., 72 Misc.2d 834, 340 N.Y.S.2d 97 (1972), aff'd, Kinley v. Atlantic Cement Co., 42 A.D.2d 496, 349 N.Y.S.2d 199 (1973). Insurance coverage was litigated. Atlantic Cement Co. v. Fidelity and Casualty Company, 63 N.Y.2d 798, 481 N.Y.S.2d 329, 471 N.E.2d 142 (1984).

Farber, Reassessing *Boomer:* Justice, Efficiency, and Nuisance Law, Property Law and Legal Education: Essays in Honor of John E. Cribbett 7, 17 (P. Hay & M. Hoeflich eds. 1988), discusses the decision's background and impact. Professor Farber argues that judges should enjoin "egregious nuisances" like the one in *Boomer* except "where the balance tilts very strongly against plaintiffs" and an injunction is "infeasible." If the judge denies an injunction, damages should be measured by market value for buffer rights instead of the traditional value before less value after calculation.

2. Later decisions construe *Boomer* narrowly. Injunction granted when: (a) defendant's activity also violated zoning ordinance, Little Joseph Realty, Inc. v. Town of Babylon, 41 N.Y.2d 738, 395 N.Y.S.2d 428, 363 N.E.2d 1163 (1977); (b) defendant's activity violated pollution permit, Flacke v. Bio–Tech Mills, Inc., 95 A.D.2d 916, 463 N.Y.S.2d 899 (1983); (c) less than "vast" economic disparity between plaintiff and defendant, State v. Waterloo Stock Car Raceway, Inc., 96 Misc.2d 350, 409 N.Y.S.2d 40 (1978).

3. See Halper, Nuisance, Courts and Markets in the New York Court of Appeals, 1850–1915, 54 Alb.L.Rev. 301 (1990) (part of a symposium on *Boomer*); McLaren, The Common Law Nuisance Actions and the Environmental Battle—Well–Tempered Swords or Broken Reeds?, 10 Osgoode Hall L.J. 505 (1972); Polinsky, Resolving Nuisance Disputes: The Simple Economics of Injunctive and Damage Remedies, 32 Stan.L.Rev. 1075 (1980); Rabin, Nuisance Law: Rethinking Fundamental Assumptions, 63 Va.L.Rev. 1299 (1977); Wade, Environmental Protection, The Common Law of Nuisance and the Restatement of Torts, 8 The Forum 165 (1972); Comment, Internalizing Externalities: Nuisance Law and Economic Efficiency, 53 N.Y.U.L.Rev. 219 (1978).

4. *Question:* Why, at the close of this section on remedies for nuisance, are there no cases on restitutionary remedies or accounting for profits comparable to Olwell v. Nye & Nissen, supra, p. 391, or Edwards v. Lee's Adm'r., supra, p. 472 or Raven Red Ash Coal Co. v. Ball, supra, p. 477? May plaintiff waive a nuisance and seek restitution? See 1 G. Palmer, The Law of Restitution 137 (1978); Friedmann, Restitution of Benefits Obtained Through the Appropriation of Property or the Commission of a Wrong, 80 Colum.L.Rev. 504, 509 (1980).

5. In Zahn v. International Paper Co., 414 U.S. 291 (1973), the defendant was accused of polluting Lake Champlain. A class action for damages by four people on behalf of two hundred other people who owned or rented property along shore failed in the federal courts because individual claims did not exceed the $10,000

jurisdictional amount for damages, although cumulatively they did. An article argued that if plaintiffs had waived the tort of nuisance and brought the class action to compel International Paper to disgorge its profits, these procedural difficulties could have been avoided. Denbaux, Restitution and Mass Actions, 10 Seton Hall L.Rev. 273 (1979). The question of how to allocate the restitutionary award would, of course, remain.

Chapter 6

REMEDIES FOR INJURIES TO ECONOMIC INTERESTS

A. DIRECT INVASION OF BUSINESS INTERESTS

1. DAMAGES FOR TOTAL DESTRUCTION OF A BUSINESS

All the material in this chapter except this brief section relates to business entities, corporations, partnerships, sole proprietorships, that have been the victims of, or threatened with, economic damages and yet survived. Many, of course, do not. By analogy to total destruction of tangible property the accepted legal methods of calculating damages would be replacement less depreciation, market value determined by similar sales, or capitalization of income. United States v. Eden Memorial Park Association, supra p. 409. Replacement seems singularly inappropriate for a defunct entity. Market value determined by similar sales depends upon infrequent or improbable scenarios requiring that the business be either relatively small and marketable like a franchise operation or a larger business which, in the language of the takeover specialists, has been recently put in play. Capitalization of income is discussed in the following Note on the value of a business destroyed by a rival's antitrust violations. The possibility of treble damages adds zest to antitrust litigation.

Notes

1. Note, Private Treble Damage Antitrust Suits: Measure of Damages for Destruction of All or Part of a Business, 80 Harv.L.Rev. 1566, 1577 (1967):

"When an antitrust violation puts the plaintiff completely out of business, it deprives him of the profits that would have been forthcoming over the remaining life of his firm. A claim for future profits characteristically presents the major problem of the increasingly great unreliability of predicted profit levels as they are projected farther into the future. In private antitrust cases, the mandatory trebling provision magnifies the seriousness of this uncertainty. A counterbalancing factor is the necessity to discount future profits to present value. Even a moderate discount rate reduces sharply the amount of the award representing profits in the distant future, and reduces the effects of the increasing uncertainty of prediction to the same degree. Moreover, the discount rate applied should vary according to the amount of confidence the trier of fact has in the likelihood that the earnings level he has predicted actually would have been maintained: a low rate to produce a higher award where the business had a stable profit capacity; a high rate to minimize the damages where the firm was less likely to produce a continuing return.

"It has been suggested that profits cannot reliably be forecast for any business beyond a ten year period, and that consequently this is the maximum for which they should be awarded. But the span of time for which profits can be predicted varies from business to business according to a great many factors; this makes any standard less flexible than a 'reasonable' time seem unwise. Relevant factors in making the very difficult determination of the stability of a business would include its profit record in the past, the experience and ability of its management, and the quality and goodwill of its product. * * *

"An antitrust violation that puts the plaintiff's firm out of business may free for other profitable uses the time or assets which he would have employed to earn the firm's profits had it survived. The familiar contract principle requiring a plaintiff to mitigate his damages should be applied in the antitrust context to reduce a lost profits award by the amount which is in fact earned, or which reasonably should have been earned, by reinvesting these resources. An argument could be made that the private antitrust suit's enforcement goals of inducing suits and deterring violations require that the courts refuse to entertain the mitigation defense since it can defeat recovery entirely. For example, a retailer might earn meager profits selling the defendant manufacturer's merchandise; after an illegal refusal to deal he might immediately begin to make increased profits on sales of another brand. Here perhaps damages ought to be measured by the profits cut off at the moment of the violation, and the law should refuse to inquire into later events. But this seems a strained and artificial reading of the statutory command that it is the 'damages * * * sustained' which the courts are to treble. The mitigation defense would eliminate recovery only where a preponderance of the evidence shows that the plaintiff is no worse off than he would have been absent the violation. An economically unharmed plaintiff should not be given a 'damage' award which is essentially a prize for apprehending a violator. * * *

"In response to the difficulties that arise in measuring lost profits, a proposal has been made to measure damages for destruction of a business by the loss in its market value caused by the violation. In economic theory, of course, the current market value of a company is the discounted present value of the estimated flow of future earnings. Although market value reflects future profits indirectly and inexactly, it admits of more definite practical proof as a matter of expert appraisal by the business community than does the projection of future earnings that underlies it. Furthermore, the market value measure avoids problems of mitigation." [Copyright, 1967, The Harvard Law Review Association]

2. The plaintiff in a lawsuit for destruction of a business will be the owner(s) or successor(s), not the now non-existent business.

3. In Aetna Life & Casualty Co. v. Little, 384 So.2d 213, 216 (Fla.App.1980) the insurance company's bad faith wiped out an insured's business. A compensatory damage award of $386,000 was reduced by the amount allocated to lost profits: "Testimony placed the market value of the business destroyed at $250,193 and loss of profits up to trial time of $134,530. The jury verdict appears to be fairly close to an addition of the two, however we cannot be absolutely sure. Lost profits and loss of use may be a proper item of damages if the property or business is not completely destroyed. However, when the property or business is totally destroyed we hold the proper total measure of damages to be the market value on the date of loss."

Query: Based on the court's figures, was the owner of the business undercompensated? We are not told how much time elapsed between the destruction of the business and the trial.

2. BUSINESS DISPARAGEMENT

a. *Damages*

TESTING SYSTEMS, INC. v. MAGNAFLUX CORP.

United States District Court, Eastern District of Pennsylvania, 1966.
251 F.Supp. 286.

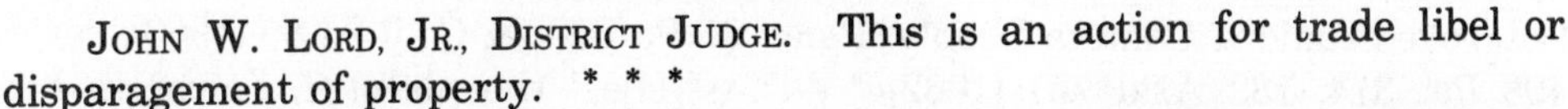

JOHN W. LORD, JR., DISTRICT JUDGE. This is an action for trade libel or disparagement of property. * * *

It appears further from the complaint that on or about May 23, 1965, while in attendance at a manufacturer's convention in Philadelphia, defendant's agent, in the presence of plaintiff's current and prospective customers, "did in a loud voice state that * * * [plaintiff's] * * * stuff is no good," and that "the government is throwing them out."

For the purposes of this motion, defendant admits the truth of the allegations, but asserts that the action must nevertheless be dismissed because * * * even assuming that the statements were actionable, plaintiff has failed to allege his damages with the required specificity. * * *

[The court held that the defendant's remarks were actionable product defamation.]

In his complaint, plaintiff states merely that as a result of the defendant's disparagement, he has suffered a loss of customers, current and prospective. No attempt is made to specify which customers, nor is there any effort to even approximate their value to him. * * *

After careful examination of the authorities on the question, it is apparent that plaintiff has failed to set forth his damages with the required particularity. The necessity of pleading and proving special damages has been an integral part of the action of disparagement of property since it first developed as an extension of slander of title. It arose as a result of the friction between the ecclesiastical and common law courts of England when the common law courts sought to assume jurisdiction over actions for defamation. "Since slander of any kind was a sin, church courts alone could punish unless temporal damage could be shown to have resulted from the defamatory words."

Until the 19th Century the requirement did not impose any untoward burden on the litigant. The early business community was devoid of the complexities that characterize the modern market place, and it was the rule, rather than the exception, that tradesmen knew their customers well. It was not too difficult, therefore, to determine just when and why one's customers began to favor a competitor.

As is so often the case, however, the rule respecting special damages continued in force long after its *raison d'etre* had passed. Today, in the vast majority of States, including Pennsylvania, a plaintiff in a disparagement of property action must both plead and prove special damages. The inflexibility of most courts in demanding strict compliance with the rule has hampered the effectiveness of the action and contributed to its unpopularity. One can appreciate the plight of the small metropolitan retailer whose patrons are, for the most part, unknown to him by name. Here, however, we are not dealing with small retailers. Both the defendant and the plaintiff in this action are business organizations of some substance who are well aware of their present and potential sources of business. The rule requiring some showing of damage, while perhaps harsh in some cases, is entirely reasonable under the circumstances as presented here.

But even if this were not so, this Court is not at liberty to disregard the law of the State and to substitute therefor its own conception of what the law ought to be. The Pennsylvania cases in this area, although few in number, leave little doubt as to how the State courts would receive plaintiff's claim. * * * Cosgrove Studio & Camera Shop v. Pane, 21 Pa.Dist. & Co.R.2d 89 (1960), rev'd 408 Pa. 314, 182 A.2d 751 (1962) * * *. "[H]e," the plaintiff, "must in his complaint set out the names of his lost customers and show by figures how much he has lost financially." * * *

Thus to avoid the necessity of specially pleading his damages, the plaintiff must show that the defendant's statements constituted libel *per se.* Although some argument to this effect appears in plaintiff's brief, it clearly falls short of the mark. It is possible in most disparagement cases to infer some criticism of the tradesman personally. However, where the comments fail to directly or by reasonable inference impugn the personal character or business conduct of the plaintiff, courts will not extend the range of judicial inventiveness to find libel *per se* where obviously none exists. * * *

Finally, even if the more liberal federal rules of pleading are applied [Fed.R.Civ.P. 9(g)], plaintiff's allegation of damages still fails to satisfy our requirements. Although, in general, all that is required is that the defendant be put on notice as to the general nature of the claim, the facts and information must be sufficient to form the basis of reasonably fruitful discovery proceedings. The defendant has called to the attention of this Court a case that appears to be peculiarly applicable here. In Fowler v. Curtis Publishing Co., 86 U.S.App.D.C. 349, 182 F.2d 377 (1950), the plaintiffs sought damages for personal defamation and trade libel. The following quotation appears in the opinion of the Circuit Court which affirmed the District Court's dismissal of the action.

> " '[I]t was * * * necessary for the plaintiff to allege either the loss of particular customers by name, or a general diminution in its business, and extrinsic facts showing that such special damages were the natural and direct result of the false publication. If the plaintiff desired to predicate its right to recover damages upon general loss of custom, it should have alleged facts showing an established business, the amount of sales for a substantial period preceding the publication, the amount of sales subsequent to the publication, facts showing that such loss in sales were the natural and probable result of such publication, and facts showing the plaintiff could not allege the names of particular customers who withdrew or withheld their custom.' "

The complaint in this action was filed almost immediately after the disparagement occurred. Nine months have expired since the cause of action arose. It may now be possible for plaintiff to plead over with the requisite degree of specificity. For this reason, the complaint will not be dismissed unless the plaintiff fails to so plead within the period specified below. [30 days]

Notes

1. *Product Disparagement and Personal Defamation—Differences in Pleading and Proof.* Harwood Pharmacal Co. v. National Broadcasting Co., 9 N.Y.2d 460, 463–64, 214 N.Y.S.2d 725, 727, 174 N.E.2d 602, 603–04 (1961).

A TV performer displayed to his audience a package of "plaintiff's" product called "Snooze" and remarked, " 'Snooze,' the new aid for sleep. Snooze is full of all kinds of habit-forming drugs. Nothing short of a hospital cure will make you stop taking 'Snooze.' You'll feel like a run-down hound dog and lose weight." Plaintiff's complaint for libel demanded a large amount of general damages, but no special damages were pleaded. The trial court dismissed the complaint for insufficiency, but the New York Court of Appeals decided otherwise:

"This allegedly telecast language could be readily understood by the television audience as charging the manufacturer of 'Snooze' with fraud and deceit in putting on the market an unwholesome and dangerous product [as distinguished from mere disparagement of quality, design and performance] * * * It is not of importance that the television actor did not mention plaintiff by name. The theory of action is that the manufacturer was directly defamed and that plaintiff was the manufacturer."

2. The distinction between trade and personal defamation is also important in determining the survival of the cause of action. "Business disparagement" will survive. See Menefee v. Columbia Broadcasting Systems, 458 Pa. 46, 329 A.2d 216 (1974). See also Note, Corporate Defamation and Product Disparagement: Narrowing the Analogy to Personal Defamation, 75 Colum.L.Rev. 963 (1975).

3. *Product Disparagement Distinguished From Defamation of a Business.* "Product" disparagement (as in the principal case) differs from other defamatory statements about a business, for example that it has engaged in fraudulent trade practices. In defamation the plaintiff's business is treated as any other victim of defamation; it may recover lost profits upon its general record of profitability rather than proof of loss of particular customers. See Golden Bear Distributing Sytems Inc. v. Chase Revel, Inc., 708 F.2d 944 (5th Cir.1983); Zerpol Corp. v. DMP Corp., 561 F.Supp. 404 (E.D.Pa.1983).

4. *Pleading and Proving Lost Customers in Trade Libel Cases.* Even if the plaintiff survives the pleading stage, it may founder on the evidentiary requirement for recovery of disparagement damage. A processor of Brazil nuts, whose product was disparaged, lost at the pleading stage in the district court, but the court of appeals reversed. At trial, plaintiff obtained a jury verdict of $212,000 actual and $212,000 punitive damages; but the trial court entered a judgment for the defendant n.o.v. Again plaintiff appealed; but this time it lost on the evidence point. The last decision, Continental Nut Co. v. Robert L. Berner Co., 393 F.2d 283, 284–86 (7th Cir.1968), indicates a somewhat different interpretation of the pleading requirements under the Federal Rules for trade libel than the principal case, but clearly emphasizes that plaintiff's difficulties are by no means over. The court uses the term "libel per quod" as the equivalent of "trade disparagement"; this may be ignored except by devotees of the substantive law of libel.

"In our opinion in the previous appeal we declined to follow the rigid rule of Erick Bowman Remedy Co. v. Jensen Salsbery Laboratories, Inc., 17 F.2d 255 (8th Cir.), that generally a complaint seeking special damages in a libel *per quod* case should specifically allege by name the customers claimed to have been lost. We observed that *Erick Bowman* antedated the liberalized pleading requirements of the Federal Rules of Civil Procedure. We found that the plaintiff's allegations of the specific figures of its gross sales before and after the publication coupled with the averment that the decrease was the natural and proximate result of the letter involved were sufficient from the pleading standpoint to state a claim in libel *per quod.* But we were not there concerned with the nature or quantum of the proof requisite to recovery upon such a claim. We recognized only that 'notice' pleading dispensed with any requirement that the complaint set forth with particularity the name of each customer allegedly lost. * * *

"[W]e are convinced that under the theory of the Illinois *per quod* decisions that in a libel *per quod* action based on loss of customers, where, such as in the case here, the plaintiff knows the identity of the customers it claims to have lost and has a record of the previous purchases of each, special damages in the form of profits lost because of the withdrawal of patronage by such customers, to be recoverable, must be proved with that specificity which shows the loss of profit attributable to patronage withheld by the particular customer and that such withholding was the result of the publication. This the plaintiff failed to do.

"As the trial judge so aptly pointed out, the striking fact about the record in this case is that plaintiff has not produced the testimony of a single customer or former customer on these questions. Nor has it shown the dollar value of lost sales to specific customers. And there is no evidence that more than seven or eight of these customers even knew of the publication referring to plaintiff as an importer of 'green' Brazil nuts. No customer, although all were known to plaintiff, was asked the questions; the jury was left to speculate.

"Plaintiff argues that for it to have interrogated its previous customers on the subject would have resulted only in aggravating the damage by alienating such customers. We do not find such argument to be persuasive."

But see, Charles Atlas, Ltd. v. Time–Life Books, Inc., 570 F.Supp. 150, 156 (S.D.N.Y.1983):

"[A]dopting such a rule would be grossly unfair in this case. The plaintiff sells only through mail orders. It is, therefore, virtually impossible to identify those who did not order the plaintiff's product because of the article in *Exercising for Fitness.* In all likelihood, such people would simply have failed to order, thus leaving no record of their identity.

"As Dean Prosser noted, [Handbook of the Law of Torts § 124, 4th ed. 1971] starting with a few cases involving goods offered for sale at an auction, and extending to others in which there has been obvious impossibility of any identification of the lost customers, a more liberal rule has been applied, requiring the plaintiff to be particular only where it is reasonable to expect him to do so."

5. *Product Disparagement—Avoidable Consequence Expenses.* Plaintiff Corporation supplied the government with cylinders manufactured to specification. The defendant, a former president of the plaintiff, publicly accused the plaintiff of defrauding the government. After holding the defendant liable for product disparagement and trade libel the trial court awarded: (a) $40,000 for the cost of retesting the cylinders to prove they were not faulty, and (b) the value of the time, measured by billable hours, the plaintiff's executive vice-president and the marketing manager spent attempting to mitigate the damage to its reputation in the government contracting community.

Appealed. Are these damages justifiable? See Comdyne I, Inc. v. Corbin, 908 F.2d 1142 (3d Cir.1990).

6. *False Advertising (with defamatory elements). Damages under § 35 Lanham Act* (15 U.S.C.A. 1125).

U–Haul International Inc. v. Jartran Inc., 522 F.Supp. 1238 (D.Ariz.1981), aff'd, 681 F.2d 1159 (9th Cir.1982). Jartran entered the move-it-yourself industry, dominated for years by U–Haul. Jartran's vigorous ad campaign falsely represented that its trucks and trailers were larger, safer, more stable, and better designed than U–Haul's. U–Haul proved a decline in gross revenues of $50 million in 1981. The court awarded U–Haul $20 million "additional damages" pursuant to § 35 of the Lanham Act as well as attorney's fees.

b. *Injunctions*

HAJEK v. BILL MOWBRAY MOTORS, INC.

Court of Appeals of Texas, Corpus Christi, 1982.
645 S.W.2d 827.

GONZALEZ, JUSTICE. This is an appeal from an order granting a temporary injunction, enjoining appellant-defendant James Hajek, from publishing and circulating defamatory statements which were painted on a vehicle appellant purchased from appellee-plaintiff Bill Mowbray Motors, Inc.

The issue is whether the temporary injunction constitutes an impermissible restraint on appellant's First Amendment rights. We affirm.

In early 1981, appellant special ordered a new 1981 Dodge Maxi van. Appellant explained to salesman, Jerry Roberts, that he wanted something economical but still capable of carrying small items. Shortly after taking delivery, appellant returned to the dealer and complained that the van was underpowered. * * * Roberts accompanied appellant on a test drive and concluded that although underpowered in certain situations, the van performed in accordance with factory specifications.

On April 11, 1981, appellant wrote Chrysler Corporation, complaining of poor performance and inquired about a 30–day money back guarantee which Chrysler had previously used to promote sales. Chrysler informed appellee of this letter. Appellee, contacted appellant and offered to exchange the van for a different one, but Hajek rejected the offer because of appellee's insistence on a depreciation allowance.

Appellant then painted the complained of statements on his van. The statements were painted in bright yellow, with approximately foot-high letters, on appellant's brown van:

(1) On the left side:

"Jerry Roberts sold this (representation of a lemon) Disaster (representation of a lemon) At Bill Mowbray Motors Inc. Help! It's a Dog!"

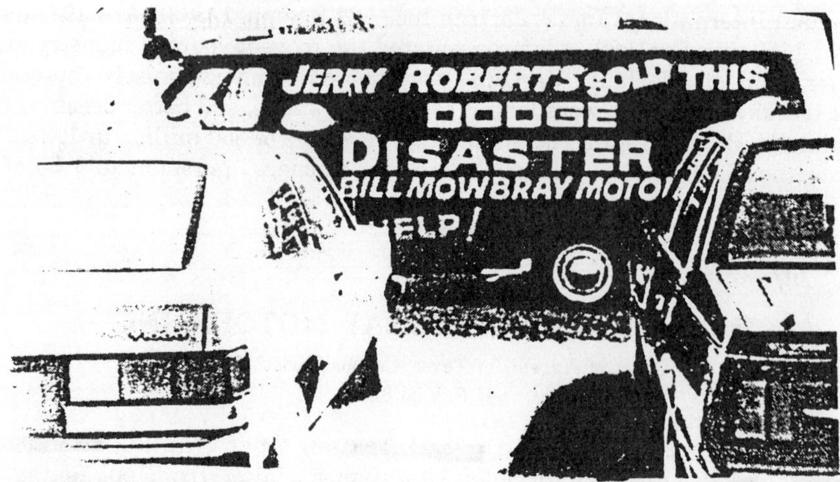

(2) On the rear:

"Help Bill Mowbray Motors Inc. Sold this (representation of a lemon)"

(3) On the right side:

"I bought this (representation of a lemon) At Bill Mowbray Motors Inc. Unhappiness! Help! (two representations of single lemons)"

(4) On the front:

"Disaster!"

On February 17, 1982, appellee again conducted a test drive. The van exceeded 55 miles per hour both with and against the wind, although it was underpowered in fourth gear going up over an overpass. Appellee was of the opinion that the van performed adequately for its size engine and transmission. With the matter unresolved and appellant's van moving conspicuously in the vicinity of the dealer and around the city, and people asking about "the story," appellee sued for a temporary injunction and in the alternative damages.

At the hearing, appellant complained of poor performance and said that the van got better gas mileage in third gear than in fourth. This was the sum total of appellant's evidence. * * *

[A]ny prior restraint on speech and publication, whether the speech was intended to have a coercive impact or not, is heavily presumed to be constitutionally invalid. [citations]

In his first point of error, appellant contends that the trial court erred in finding the complained of statements false and defamatory. Appellant points to the undisputed fact that he purchased the van from Jerry Roberts at Bill Mowbray Motors, Inc., as painted on the van. He then argues that "Disaster," "Help," "It's a Dog," "Unhappiness," and the illustrated lemons refer to the vehicle, not the appellee, and that in order to impute impropriety to appellee, one would have to extend the meaning of the language beyond that clearly stated. We disagree. * * *

[The court said that defendant's signs and lemon symbols falsely "imputed certain business improprieties" to plaintiff and were defamatory.]

[A]ppellant contends the temporary injunction abridges his right of free speech under the First and Fourteenth Amendments to the United States Constitution. Appellant characterizes his statements as "opinion" and argues that freedom of speech is absolute; that no matter how bizarre or offensive his statements might be, they should not be suppressed because society benefits from the competition of ideas and opinions.

Appellant, however, overstates the constitutional protection afforded one's right to speak. Until the Supreme Court's decision in New York Times v. Sullivan, 376 U.S. 254 (1964), the First Amendment did not protect defamation at all.

We find nothing to indicate that the major changes in the standards applicable to defamation brought about by the Supreme Court since New York Times Co. v. Sullivan, require dissolution of the temporary injunction. In fact, we find the rationale to support the contrary. * * *

In 1974, Justice Powell, writing for the court, noted that the "Court has struggled for nearly a decade to define the proper accommodation between the law of defamation and the freedoms of speech and press protected by the First Amendment." Gertz v. Robert Welch, Inc., 418 U.S. 323 (1974). The Court then went on to say that "there is no constitutional value in false statements of fact." Neither the intentional lie nor the careless error materially advances society's interest in "uninhibited, robust, and wide-open" debate on public issues. According to the Court, that category of utterances which "are no essential part of any exposition of ideas, and are of slight social value as a step to the truth that any benefit that may be derived from them is clearly outweighed by the social interest in order and morality." Nonetheless, the court emphasized that the First Amendment requires that some falsehoods be protected in order to "protect speech that matters."

Since 1964, the Supreme Court has followed a staggered path in extending constitutional protection to defamatory utterances, at times providing wide protection at other times retrenching. [citations] The court has given great constitutional protection to statements made in connection with *public affairs* and *public concerns.* Appellant's statements do not deal with public affairs or concerns. Therefore, in balancing the public's interest in free and full exchange of ideas and the public's interest in freedom from destructive invasions of reputation, in the context of the facts of this case, we do not think that the U.S. Supreme Court's rationale requires us to constitutionally protect appellant's statements defamatory of appellee's business reputation.

Appellant cites Stansbury v. Beckstrom, 491 S.W.2d 947 (Tex.Civ.App.—Eastland 1973, no writ) as authority for the proposition that the court erred in granting this temporary injunction. This was a case where a mother was dissatisfied with the charges a doctor had made in setting a broken finger in her son's hand. She and some of her friends picketed the doctor's office with signs indicating that the charge was outrageous. The doctor alleged that signs were false and libelous and obtained an injunction. The appellate court dissolved a temporary injunction, citing Better Austin v. Keefe, as controlling. *Keefe* was a case where a real estate broker in Chicago obtained an injunction against a racially integrated community organization from distributing leaflets describing the broker's activities as "panic peddling" and "blockbusting." The U.S. Supreme Court dissolved the injunction based on the First Amendment right to free speech.

We do not disagree with the *Keefe* decision. However, the complained of words there were *neither defamatory nor false, and they did not impute professional or business misconduct,* unlike those in our case.

We find support for our decision in a number of cases. In Carter v. Knapp Motor Co., 243 Ala. 600, 11 So.2d 383 (1943), injunctive relief was granted a dealer to prevent an unhappy customer from exhibiting a car on which he had painted large white elephants. The court noted that an injunction would not be issued against "a mere libel or slander" but would be granted in cases where business relationships are threatened. The court said:

> "Our decisions are to the effect that the right to conduct one's business without the wrongful interference of others is a valuable property right which will be protected, if necessary, by injunctive process. * * * And the enjoyment of the good name and good will of a business is likewise a valuable property right subject to like protection. * * * One's employment, trade or calling is likewise a property right, and the wrongful interference therewith is an actionable wrong" * * *

In his fourth point of error, appellant contends that there was no evidence to support a conclusion that his action was taken with a coercive intent. We disagree. Salesman Roberts testified that Hajek wanted Mowbray to replace the van's engine with a larger one. Although Hajek denied that his actions were motivated by a desire to force Mowbray to do anything, Roberts' testimony is sufficient to support the trial court's findings. We also note that Hajek himself said that without his actions, "they" would have let him talk until his tongue fell out. This certainly implies that he wanted to do more than merely talk or express his dissatisfaction. Appellant's fourth point of error is overruled.

The judgment of the trial court is affirmed.[1]

Notes

1. The Supreme Court of Texas accepted Hajek's appeal, and citing the Texas constitution, reversed the preceding decision without oral argument: "The temporary injunction granted by the trial court constitutes a prior restraint on free speech. * * * The language enjoined here evoked no threat of danger to anyone and, therefore, may not be subject to the prior restraint of a temporary injunction. Defamation alone is not a sufficient justification for restraining an individual's right to speak freely. [citation]" Hajek v. Bill Mowbray Motors, Inc., 647 S.W.2d 253, 255 (Tex.1983).

Question: Was it as easy as the Texas supreme court thought?

2. A considerable body of authority refuses to grant an injunction against trade libel except when it is accompanied by a separate enjoinable tort like unfair competition or conspiracy. See Fashion Two Twenty, Inc. v. Steinberg, 339 F.Supp. 836 (E.D.N.Y.1971). This, as a practical matter, limited injunctions to commercial rivalry.

1. We strongly recommend that the trial court give this case a preferential setting on a trial of the merits.

3. A plaintiff may obtain an injunction against a competitor's disparaging advertising under the Lanham Act, 15 U.S.C. § 1125(a), Alpo Petfoods, Inc. v. Ralston Purina Co., infra, p. 601 as well as under state law.

4. Many states have adopted deceptive trade practices acts that forbid false or misleading "commercial speech." These acts have survived constitutional attacks. Advance Training Systems, Inc. v. Caswell Equipment Co., 352 N.W.2d 1 (Minn. 1984).

5. *Along the Periphery.* Martin v. Reynolds Metals Co., 224 F.Supp. 978 (D.Or.1963), aff'd, 337 F.2d 780 (9th Cir.1964). An Oregon rancher sued a nearby alumina reduction plant for trespass damages allegedly caused by the escape of fluorides. He also erected a highway sign: "THIS RANCH IS CONTAMINATED 831 Cattle Killed in past six years FLUORIDE POISON from REYNOLDS METAL CO. kills our cattle * * * endangers human health CONTROLS MUST BE ENFORCED. THIS STATEMENT PAID FOR BY PAUL R. MARTIN." The defendant counterclaimed for libel, injurious falsehood, and interference with business relations. The court issued an injunction to take down the sign until the claim had been appropriately adjudicated.

3. INTERFERENCE WITH CONTRACTUAL RELATIONSHIPS

a. Damages

TEXACO, INC. v. PENNZOIL, CO.

Texas Court of Civil Appeals, 1987.
729 S.W.2d 768.

[Pennzoil reached an "agreement in principle" for a stock purchase-merger with Getty Oil Co. Under the arrangement Pennzoil would acquire 3/7ths of the Getty stock. At this point Texaco stepped in with a higher bid, and a merger between Getty Oil and Texaco was announced. Spectacular litigation ensued, Pennzoil charging Texaco with tortious interference with contract relations. The portion relating to damages in the key decision holding Texaco liable follows.]

WARREN, JUSTICE. * * * In its 57th through 69th points of error, Texaco claims that the evidence was legally and factually insufficient to support the jury's compensatory and punitive damage awards.

Texaco attacks Pennzoil's use of a replacement cost model to prove its compensatory damages. It urges that: (1) the court should have instructed the jury that the correct measure of Pennzoil's compensatory damages was the difference between the market price and contract price of Getty stock at the time of the breach; (2) the punitive damages award is contrary to New York law and public policy; (3) the punitive and compensatory damages are excessive; (4) and prejudgment interest should not have been allowed.

In a cause involving a tortious interference with an existing contract, New York courts allow a plaintiff to recover the full pecuniary loss of the benefits it would have been entitled to under the contract. Guard-Life Corp. v. S. Parker Hardware Manufacturing Corp., 50 N.Y.2d 183, 428 N.Y.S.2d 628, 406 N.E.2d 445 (1980). The plaintiff is not limited to the damages recoverable in a contract action, but instead is entitled to the damages allowable under the more liberal rules recognized in tort actions.

New York courts have cited and relied extensively on the Restatement (Second) of Torts in deciding damages issues, compensatory as well as punitive.

Section 774A of the Restatement (Second) of Torts (1977), reads in pertinent part:

(1) One who is liable to another for interference with a contract * * * is liable for damages for

(a) the pecuniary loss of the benefits of the contract * * *; [and]

(b) consequential losses for which the interference is a legal cause. * * *

Comment (a) under the above section provides that since the tort is an intentional one, punitive damages are recoverable in these actions under appropriate circumstances. * * *

Pennzoil relied on two witnesses to prove the amount of its damages: Dr. Thomas Barrow and Dr. Ronald Lewis. * * *

Texaco presented no witnesses to refute the testimony of Dr. Barrow or Dr. Lewis.

Dr. Barrow prepared three damages models, as follows:

(1) a replacement cost model,

(2) a discounted cash flow model, and

(3) a cost acquisition model.

Because the jury based its award of damages on the replacement cost model, the other two models will not be discussed. By Dr. Barrow's testimony, Pennzoil showed that because of Texaco's interference with its Getty contract, it was deprived of its right to acquire 3/7th's of Getty's proven reserves, amounting to 1.008 billion barrels of oil equivalent (B.O.E.), at a cost of $3.40 a barrel. Pennzoil's evidence further showed that its cost to find equivalent reserves (based on its last five years of exploration costs) was $10.87 per barrel. Therefore, Pennzoil contended that it suffered damages equal to 1.008 billion B.O.E. times $7.47 (the difference between $10.87, the cost of finding equivalent reserves, and $3.40, the cost of acquiring Getty's reserves) or $7.53 billion. The jury agreed.

Texaco first alleges that the trial judge should have instructed the jury that the measure of Pennzoil's damages was the difference between the market value of Getty Oil stock and its contract price at the time of the breach. We reject this contention. The Getty/Pennzoil agreement contemplated something more than a simple buy-sell stock transaction. Pennzoil's cause of action against Texaco was in tort, not in contract, and Pennzoil's measure of damages was the pecuniary loss of the benefits it would have been entitled to under the contract. [citation] There was ample evidence that the reason Pennzoil (and later, Texaco) wanted to buy Getty was to acquire control of Getty Oil's reserves, and not for any anticipated profit from the later sale of Getty stock. There was evidence that such fluctuations in market price are primarily of interest to holders of small, minority share positions.

The court in Special Issue No. 3 correctly instructed the jury that the measure of damages was the amount necessary to put Pennzoil in as good a position as it would have been in if its agreement, if any, with the Getty entities had been performed. If the measure of damages suggested by Texaco was correct, then there would have been no necessity to submit an issue at all, because no issue of fact would have existed, there being no dispute about the market value of the stock or the contract price of the stock at the time of the breach.

Texaco next contends that the replacement cost theory is based on the speculative and remote contention that Pennzoil would have gained direct access to Getty's assets. Texaco strongly urges that Pennzoil had a "good faith" obligation under its alleged contract to attempt to reorganize and restructure Getty Oil rather than to divide its assets. We agree. Under New York law, a duty of fair dealing and good faith is implied in every contract. [citations] But a duty of good faith and fair dealing does not require that Pennzoil completely subordinate its financial well-being to the proposition of reorganization or restructuring.

The directors of Pennzoil would have had a duty to the company's shareholders to obtain the greatest benefit from the merger assets, by either restructuring, reorganizing, or taking the assets in kind. If taking the assets in kind would be the most advantageous to Pennzoil, its directors would, in the absence of a great detriment to Getty, have a duty to take in kind. So the acquisition of a pro rata share of Getty Oil's reserves would be more than a mere possibility, unless the restructuring or reorganization of Getty would be just as profitable to Pennzoil as taking the assets in kind.

Next, Texaco urges that the jury's use of the replacement cost model resulted in a gross overstatement of Pennzoil's loss because:

(a) Pennzoil sought to replace Getty's low value reserves with reserves of a much higher value;

(b) Pennzoil based its replacement cost on its costs to find oil only during the period from 1980 to 1984, rather than over a longer period;

(c) Pennzoil improperly included future development costs in its exploration costs;

(d) Pennzoil used pre-tax rather than post-tax figures; and

(e) Pennzoil failed to make a present value adjustment of its claim for future expenses.

Our problem in reviewing the validity of these Texaco claims is that Pennzoil necessarily used expert testimony to prove its losses by using three damages models. In the highly specialized field of oil and gas, expert testimony that is free of conjecture and speculation is proper and necessary to determine and estimate damages. [citations] Texaco presented no expert testimony to refute the claims but relied on its cross-examination of Pennzoil's experts to attempt to show that the damages model used by the jury was flawed. Dr. Barrow testified that each of his three models would constitute an accepted method of proving Pennzoil's damages. It is inevitable that there will be some degree of inexactness when an expert is attempting to make an educated estimate of the damages in a case such as this one. Prices and costs vary, depending on the locale, and the type of crude found. The law recognizes that a plaintiff may not be able to prove its damages to a certainty. But this uncertainty is tolerated when the difficulty in calculating damages is attributable to the defendant's conduct. [citation]

In his replacement cost model, Dr. Barrow estimated the cost to replace 1.008 billion barrels of oil equivalent that Pennzoil had lost. Dr. Barrow admitted that some of Getty's reserves consisted of heavy crude, which was less valuable than lighter crude, and that he had made no attempt to determine whether there was an equivalency between the lost Getty barrels and the barrels used to calculate Pennzoil's exploration costs. Dr. Barrow also testified that there was no way to determine what grade of reserves Pennzoil would find in its future exploration; they could be better or worse than the Getty reserves. Finally Dr. Barrow testified that in spite of his not determining the value equivalency, the replacement cost model was an accepted method of figuring Pennzoil's loss. Dr. Lewis testified that with improved refining technology, the difference in value between light and heavy crude was becoming less significant.

Texaco next urges that Pennzoil should have calculated replacement cost by using a longer time period and industry wide figures rather than using only its own exploration costs, over a five year period. Dr. Lewis admitted that it might have been more accurate to use a longer period of time to estimate exploration costs, but he and Dr. Barrow both testified that exploration costs had been consistently rising each year and that the development cost estimates were conservative. Dr. Barrow testified that in his opinion, Pennzoil would, in the future, have to spend a great deal more than $10.87 a barrel to find crude. Dr. Lewis testified that industry wide exploration costs were higher than Pennzoil's, and those figures would result in a higher cost estimate than the $10.87 per barrel used by Pennzoil.

Next, Texaco claims that Pennzoil inflated its exploration costs by $1.86 per barrel by including "future development cost" in its historical exploration costs. Both Dr. Lewis' and Dr. Barrow's testimony refuted that contention. Texaco neither offered evidence to refute their testimony, nor did its cross-examination reveal that this was an unwarranted cost.

Texaco also claims that Pennzoil should have used post-tax rather than pre-tax figures in figuring its loss calculations. First, it contends that there are large tax incentives for exploration and development that are not applicable to acquisition of reserves. Second, it contends that there was a $2 billion tax penalty attached to the Pennzoil/Getty agreement, and Pennzoil's $900 million share of that penalty would have increased its $3.40 pre-tax acquisition cost by nearly a dollar.

Dr. Barrow testified that the fact that Pennzoil included $997 million as recapture tax in its costs of acquiring the Getty reserves, made the pre-tax comparison between the $3.40 per barrel to acquire Getty reserves and the $10.87 per barrel for Pennzoil to find new oil, "apples and apples"; in other words, the $997 million tax adjustment compensated for the tax benefits reaped when discovering, as compared with purchasing, reserves. Further, there was no conclusive proof that the Internal Revenue Service would have assessed a $2 billion penalty to Getty's purchase of the Museum's shares under the Pennzoil/Getty agreement, as alleged by Texaco. Several witnesses, familiar with tax law, testified that it was unlikely that such a tax would be imposed; therefore it was for the jury to decide when assessing damages, whether Pennzoil's pro rata share of the speculative tax penalty should reduce the amount of its damages.

Texaco's contention that Pennzoil's cost replacement model should be discounted to present value ignores the fact that Pennzoil's suit is not for future damages but for those already sustained. Pennzoil would have had an interest in the Getty reserves immediately if the agreement had been consummated, and it did not seek damages for reserves to be recovered in the future. The cases cited by Texaco are inapposite here because all involve damages that the plaintiff would incur in the future, such as lost wages or future yearly payments. * * *

In its 69th point of error, Texaco claims that the court erroneously applied New York Law when it allowed prejudgment interest, because most of the damages are to compensate for expenses to be incurred over the next 25 years. We have previously considered and rejected Texaco's contention that Pennzoil's recovery, or any part thereof, was for future damages.

Under New York law, a plaintiff in an action for inducing a breach of contract is entitled as a matter of right to interest on the amount of recovery, measured from the date of the accrual of the cause of action. [citation]

Texaco alleges five legal reasons why punitive damages were not available to Pennzoil in this case.

First, Texaco incorrectly claims that punitive damages are not available to a plaintiff in an inducement of breach of contract cause, where the alleged tortfeasor acted for its own economic benefit rather than gratuitously to injure the defendant, citing Guard–Life Corp., 67 A.D.2d 658, 412 N.Y.S.2d 623 (App.Div.1979). The *Guard–Life Corp.* court disallowed punitive damages because there was no evidence of malice, ill will, or a wrongful act done willfully or maliciously. The court there noted that the defendant's motive was to secure an economic advantage and merely contrasted that fact with the absence of evidence of malice or ill will. On appeal, New York's highest court stated that the defendant's status as a competitor would not protect it from the consequences of interfering with an existing contract, though it might excuse him from interfering with a prospective contract or a contract terminable at will.

Second, Texaco says that New York law prohibits punitive damages where the defendant was acting pursuant to the advice of counsel and believed its actions were proper. * * *

We agree that a good faith reliance on the advice of counsel is an important factor in determining whether a defendant's conduct is willful, wanton, or reckless, but we are of the opinion that such reliance would not necessarily preclude an award of punitive damages under New York law. * * *

Third, Texaco claims that New York law precludes an award of punitive damages absent a showing that Texaco's conduct constituted morally culpable conduct aimed at the public. * * * Even if there were such a requirement, Texaco's conduct, as found by the jury, could be considered conduct aimed at the public that punitive damages are designed to deter.

Fourth [omitted.]

Texaco's fifth contention is that the amount of punitive damages awarded is unreasonable. * * *

The amount of exemplary or punitive damages to be awarded depends on the facts of the case and rests largely within the sound discretion of the jury. [citations] Under Texas law, exemplary damages must be reasonably proportioned to actual damages. [citation] Factors to be considered in determining whether an award of exemplary damages is reasonable include: (1) the nature of the wrong, (2) the character of the conduct involved, (3) the degree of culpability of the wrongdoer, (4) the situation and sensibilities of the parties concerned, and (5) the extent to which such conduct offends a public sense of justice and propriety.

The proportion of punitive damages to actual damages presents no problem. The punitive damages awarded only amount to approximately 40% of actual damages, which in itself is not excessive. Under New York law, punitive damages need bear no ratio to compensatory damages. * * *

Considering the type of action, the conduct involved, and the need for deterrence, we are of the opinion that the punitive damages are excessive and that the trial court abused its discretion in not suggesting a remittitur. Though our Texas guidelines are similar to those of New York, New York courts have adopted a more conservative stance on punitive damages. There is a point where punitive damages may overstate their purpose and serve to confiscate rather than to deter or punish. In this case, punitive damages of one billion dollars are sufficient to satisfy any reason for their being awarded, whether it be punishment, deterrence, or encouragement of the victim to bring legal action. We conclude that the award of punitive damages is excessive by two billion dollars.

If within 30 days from the date of this opinion, Pennzoil files in this Court a remittitur of two billion dollars, the judgment of the trial court will be reformed, and the award of one billion dollars punitive damages will be affirmed; otherwise, the cause will be reversed and remanded. * * *

If within thirty days from the date of this judgment, Pennzoil files in this Court a remittitur of two billion dollars, as suggested above, the judgment will be reformed and affirmed as to the award of $7.53 billion in compensatory damages and $1 billion in exemplary damages; otherwise the judgment will be reversed and remanded.

Notes

1. Laycock, The Remedies Issues: Compensatory Damages, Specific Performance, Punitive Damages, Supersedeas Bonds, and Abstention, 9 Rev. of Litg. 473, 474, 499 (1990), is part of a symposium on the principal case.

a. *Compensation?* "[T]he compensatory part of the verdict might indeed have been correct. The rule by which damages were measured was entirely conventional, and the calculation of damages under this rule was a question for the jury. Astonishing as the jury's award may seem, there was no basis on which a reviewing court could set it aside. Any serious argument for remittitur would have required evidence that Texaco had not presented, and it would have required an argument fundamentally inconsistent with the argument Texaco actually made. * * *

b. *Punishment?* "[T]he traditional notion that punitive damages should be proportionate to compensatory damages is absurd. Where the compensatory damages are large enough to punish or deter, punitive damages are unnecessary. Thus, once the jury awarded $7.5 billion in compensatory damages, it did not need to award punitive damages to deter, or to punish. All these goals had been accomplished."

2. Satisfaction of a judgment against the contract breaker does not bar plaintiff from also recovering damages in tort against the party who induced the breach of contract. See Brotherhood of Locomotive Firemen and Enginemen v. Hammett, 273 Ala. 629, 144 So.2d 58 (1962); Bauman, Multiple Liability, Multiple

Remedies, and the Federal Rules of Civil Procedure, 46 Minn.L.Rev. 729, 743–745 (1962). For procedures to avoid double recovery see Ross v. Holton, 640 S.W.2d 166 (Mo.App.1982).

3. Restatement (Second) of Torts § 912 Illustrations (1979):† A has a contract with B by the terms of which A is to arrange for a boxing match between B and C. D tortiously causes B to break his contract before A has incurred any expenses with reference to it. A is entitled to compensatory damages from D only if he proves that it is more probable than not that the match would have been made by him and would have been a financial success, and if his proof offers a reasonable basis for estimating the profits.

4. Where the defendant has damaged a business by inducing the employees to break their contracts, the measure of damages may be calculated in terms of the cost of training new employees. Frederick Chusid & Co. v. Marshall Leeman & Co., 326 F.Supp. 1043 (S.D.N.Y.1971).

5. *Inducing Breach of Unenforceable Agreements.* Courts generally recognize a tort for inducing the breach of a legally unenforceable agreement. Harris v. Perl, 41 N.J. 455, ___, 197 A.2d 359, 363 (1964): "[O]ne who unjustifiably interferes with the contract of another is guilty of a wrong. And since men usually honor their promises no matter what flaws a lawyer can find, the offender should not be heard to say the contract he meddled with cannot be enforced."

But conceding the liability does not resolve the question of how to measure damages. How should damages, if any, be measured?

A dissenting judge in Northern Plumbing & Heating, Inc. v. Henderson Brothers, 83 Mich.App. 84, 98, 268 N.W.2d 296, 301 (1978) states the dilemma: "If a person does not suffer recoverable damages from the nonperformance of an enforceable contract, or from an agreement between the other party and the stranger not to perform a nonenforceable contract, likewise he should not recover any damages from the nonperformance of a nonenforceable contract which is induced by a stranger."

The same issue occurs in all torts broadly termed "interference with advantageous relationships."

b. Injunctions

NEW ENGLAND PATRIOTS FOOTBALL CLUB, INC. v. UNIVERSITY OF COLORADO

United States Court of Appeals, First Circuit, 1979.
592 F.2d 1196.

ALDRICH, SENIOR CIRCUIT JUDGE. In 1973 one Charles L. Fairbanks contracted with plaintiff New England Patriots Football Club, a professional football organization and member of the National Football League, to act as its manager and head coach. By later agreement the employment was to continue until January, 1983. The contract contained a provision that Fairbanks was not to provide services connected with football to any entity other than plaintiff, or to perform services of any kind for anyone, without plaintiff's permission, during the period of employment. In November, 1978 Fairbanks was approached by various persons, defendants herein, some of whom were officially, and some sentimentally, attached to the University of Colorado. Defendants' objective was to persuade Fairbanks to quit the Patriots and become head football coach at the University. Their successful initiation of this endeavor, at first behind the Patriots' back, and, later, over its vigorous opposition, resulted in the present action where, following a hearing, the district court entered a preliminary injunction enjoining defendant regents, defendant president, defendant athletic director, and defendant Vickers, a Colorado football fan and angel, from causing the University to employ Fairbanks as the University's coach. Fairbanks is not a party to the suit, and has not been enjoined. * * * We also acceded to Fairbanks' request, tendered through counsel for defendants, to file an amicus brief.[1] * * * Because in 1973 the Patriots allegedly had lured Fairbanks from the University of Oklahoma, inducing him to break his contract there, defendants conclude that the Patriots are barred from relief by the doctrine of unclean hands. We disagree. Both parties may have done the University of Oklahoma dirt, but that does not mean unclean hands with respect to "the controversy in issue." The precedential effect of a court's extending this doctrine to commercial transactions such as this staggers the imagination. * * * If ascertainable money damages could fully compensate the Patriots, under familiar principles there would be no basis for injunctive relief. The district court, however, found that ascertainment would be difficult. It further found that Fairbanks' services were unique, and that, accordingly, the loss of his services would occasion the Patriots irreparable harm.

Fairbanks was insufficiently modest to dispute this last. However, the cause was taken up by the defendants. They dispute both findings, offering reasons which, to put the matter in its kindest light, we may be too unsophisticated to understand. Then, in a turnabout for which, perhaps apprehending our shortcomings, no reasons are even offered, defendants state, "In contrast, the continuation of the preliminary injunction which prevents Fairbanks from signing with Colorado does irreparably harm the University."

While we are attempting to reconcile these conclusions, there comes the final drive. "Fairbanks' departure may have no effect or, even possibly a beneficial effect, on the Patriots' performance and attendance in the future." The injunction is an ungracious, even an ungrateful, act.

Somehow it seems as if there were an extra man on the field. * * *

[D]efendants are reduced to three claims: that they are protected from suit by the Eleventh Amendment of the Constitution, that the court lacks jurisdiction because Fairbanks, who was not joined, is an indispensable party, and that the injunction should not be granted, both because it is an indirect way of avoiding the rule that a personal service contract cannot be specifically enforced, and in any event, because Fairbanks, by employment at the college level, would not be engaging in competition with the Patriots. Because the injunctive issue flows naturally as part of the factual recitation we have just interrupted, we will treat it first.

1. [Footnote renumbered.] In granting permission we had assumed, wrongly, it proved, that counsel knew what an amicus is, namely, one who, "not as parties, * * * but, just as any stranger might," Martin v. Tapley, 1875, 119 Mass. 116, 120, "for the assistance of the court gives information of some matter of law in regard to which the court is doubtful or mistaken." 1 Bouvier's Law Dictionary 188 (3rd ed. 1914), rather than one who gives a highly partisan, ("eloquent," according to defendants) account of the facts.

At the hearing Fairbanks testified that although the contract read "services directly connected with football * * * [or for] another entity not connected with football," this meant, simply, activities competitively connected with the Patriots. Apparently he has no more regard for the parol evidence rule forbidding the contradiction of unambiguous language than for other rules foisted upon him by legalisms. Parenthetically, having in mind, as sometimes helpless dial-spinners, that professional and prominent college football teams compete for TV viewers, and hence, presumably, for the advertising dollar, we may wonder whether we have to accept at face value the protestation of no competitive activity here. In any event, there is ample authority contradicting both aspects of defendants' legal position. Indeed, some courts have gone even further, and have enjoined the defaulting athlete himself from noncompetitive sport. We would not distinguish between an athlete and a coach. To enjoin tortious interference by a third party, whether or not competitive, would seem a lesser step. * * *

We comment briefly on the self-serving statement in Fairbanks' amicus brief that he is "through with professional football." There is no such finding in the record, and even though that may now be the conventional wisdom, neither the Patriots nor the court are bound to accept it. At this stage Fairbanks could be expected to say no less. * * *

[As to] defendants' claim that Fairbanks is an indispensable party, F.R. Civ.P. 19(a) and (b), [i]t is to be borne in mind that any issue of fairness is only fairness to Fairbanks; defendants can suggest no unfairness to themselves resulting from his absence. They do say that it would be unfair to Fairbanks if, due to possibly divergent interests, they omitted points he might have made. Having been exposed, through his amicus brief, to the points that Fairbanks might personally make here, it might be difficult to be moved by this contention even if, in the abstract, it were a valid one. More important, on the single issue in this case, we perceive no different interests. On the broader questions, general rights of Fairbanks and the Patriots under the contract, the decision will have no effect because Fairbanks is not a party, and for the further reason that it could not seemingly affect them even if he were. * * *

We reject the claim that Fairbanks is an indispensable party.

Finally, although normally jurisdictional issues receive first treatment, because it requires an overview of the facts we have left to the last defendants' claim of the bar of the Eleventh Amendment to the Constitution. Briefly, defendants say that because the University is a state institution—part of the state—they share the state's Eleventh Amendment immunity from suit.

We accept, for this purpose, the University's identification with the state. It does not follow that everything its agents do falls under the constitutional umbrella. * * * In the present case, this is a very narrow issue. We may assume that if a contract had been entered into between Fairbanks and the University, suit would not lie to undo it. We do not, however, equate that with restraining the agents, while they are engaged in seeking a contract, from acting in an unlawful and tortious manner. The latter is not barred by the Eleventh Amendment. * * *

Affirmed.

Note

Postscript: A financial settlement was reached between the Patriots and the supporters of the University. Fairbanks coached at the University for three years and compiled a record of 7 wins and 26 losses. He later coached the New Jersey Generals in the United States Football League.

c. *Restitution*

FEDERAL SUGAR REFINING CO. v. UNITED STATES SUGAR EQUALIZATION BOARD

United States District Court, Southern District of New York, 1920.
268 Fed. 575.

[The circumstances that gave rise to this decision may be deduced from the following extract from a related opinion. The Gloria, 286 F. 188, 191 (S.D.N.Y. 1923):

"The complaint may be briefly summarized: The Kingdom of Norway had, through its Food Commission, contracted with the defendant, the Federal Sugar Refining company, to purchase 4,500 tons of refined sugar at $6.60 per hundredweight. Although the plaintiff was in great need of sugar to feed its people, it was prevented from receiving sugar under its contract, by reason of the embargo placed on the export of sugar by the United States government. On account of this embargo it was agreed between the plaintiff and the defendant that the time for the performance of their contract should be extended, and that the price should equal that fixed by the government for the market at the time delivery was actually made. It is alleged that the United States Sugar Equalization Board, Inc., a corporation organized and controlled by the Food Administration of the United States, which owned and held all the capital stock thereof, procured the government of the United States to refuse to license the export of sugar under the plaintiff's contract with the defendant, and that in the meantime the market price as fixed by the government rose to $8.12 per hundredweight. The United States Sugar Equalization Board is alleged to have taken advantage of the necessities of the plaintiff, and to have sold the plaintiff 4,500 tons of refined sugar at $11 per hundredweight, an extortionate price, $2.88 per hundredweight above the price fixed by the government. It is stated that the defendant herein, the Federal Sugar Refining Company, brought suit against the United States Sugar Equalization Board for tortious interference with its contract with the kingdom of Norway."

A demurrer was interposed to the answer. Only that part of the opinion relating to the complaint is set out below.]

MAYER, DISTRICT JUDGE. It is, of course, elementary that a demurrer searches the complaint, and therefore it becomes necessary at the outset to determine whether the complaint states one or more causes of action. So far as language goes, it is plain that the complaint is framed upon the theory that the facts set forth causes of action upon an implied promise upon the count for money had and received, which in equity and good conscience defendant should not retain and should pay to plaintiff. It will be unnecessary to determine whether the allegations of the complaint set forth causes of action upon any other theory, if the implied promise theory is sound. * * *

The law of quasi contracts, so called, has as one of its vital features the aim of the courts to apply a suitable remedy for the results flowing from certain kinds of wrongs. Thus it is that an action, in some circumstances, will be regarded as ex contractu, even though there has not been agreement between the parties. * * *

The implied promise springs up by virtue of or follows the commission of a wrong. In each of the causes of action here a wrong is alleged. * * *

A further contention of defendant, earnestly urged, is based on the expressions of Keener and Woodward in their works on Quasi Contracts. Woodward, Quasi Contracts, § 274, referring in part to Keener, says:

> "Perhaps it was arguable at one time that the obligation of a tort-feasor in assumpsit is analogous to that of a constructive trustee, and that he should be held accountable for any profits derived by him from his wrongful act. It seems to be now taken for granted, however, that the obligation is not to account for profits but to make restitution. It follows that it is not enough that the defendant has been enriched by his wrong; it must further appear that the benefit received by defendant has been taken from the plaintiff. As Prof. Keener puts it, there must be 'not only a plus but a minus quantity.' "

* * * [T]he principle announced is illogical in its limitations. The point is not whether a definite something was taken away from plaintiff and added to the treasury of defendant. The point is whether defendant unjustly enriched itself by doing a wrong to plaintiff in such manner and in such circumstances that in equity and good conscience defendant should not be permitted to retain that by which it has been enriched.

The whole trend of the law points to the aspiration of the courts to find an adequate and orderly remedy for wrongs as to which redress was elusive until this theory of quasi contracts was developed. Mr. Justice Brewer, early in the *Angle* Case, [151 U.S. 1, 12 (1894)] said: "Surely it would seem the recital of these facts would carry with it an assurance that there was some remedy, * * * and that such remedy would reach to the party * * * by whose acts these losses were caused." * * *

The correct principle, as it seems to me, is well stated in a recent note in the Columbia Law Review of May, 1920, at page 602:

> "The most that can be said is that ordinarily, and apart from some rule of policy which dictates the contrary result, recovery should be allowed where there has been actual enrichment at the plaintiff's expense."

In the case at bar it might further be contended, not without merit, that the case comes even within the limitations stated by Keener and Woodward; but I prefer to rest my conclusion on the broader ground.

It is further urged that, unless plaintiff has been actually damaged, it has no grievance, and that the complaint should have alleged ability profitably to perform plaintiff's contract with the Norwegian Commission. This position misconceives the nature of an action for money had and received as framed in this complaint. Whether inability to perform is a defense need not now be determined. The action is not for damages for breach of contract, but for the profit which defendant is alleged to have made as the result of its alleged wrongful acts. Ability to perform, in such circumstances, is no part of plaintiff's case. Angle Case, 151 U.S. 1.

In any event, at any time prior to October 1, 1918, the date to which the performance of plaintiff's contract had been extended, the necessary license might have been obtained. It was within Rolph's [Head of the Sugar Division of the Food Administration] power to grant the license before October 1st; but prior thereto (i.e., on September 20th) the Norwegian Commission notified plaintiff that it would not take the sugar from plaintiff, because defendant had filled its requirements. In other words, defendants' alleged tort having been committed prior to October 1st (i.e., prior to September 20th), ability of plaintiff to perform after September 20th becomes immaterial as a necessary requirement of plaintiff's causes of action. * * *

For the reasons thus outlined, I am of opinion that the complaint is not demurrable.

Notes

1. The case was settled for $165,000 before trial. See The Gloria, 286 Fed. 188, 191 (S.D.N.Y.1923).

2. Restatement of Restitution, § 133 (1937).† Property Tortiously Acquired From Third Person at Another's Expense. (1) A person who has committed a tort against another by obtaining property through fraud, duress or undue influence upon the transferor, thereby knowingly preventing the other from acquiring the property, is under a duty of restitution to the other.

Caveat: The institute takes no position as to a person's duty of restitution to another where the first person has made a profit by tortiously causing a third person to break his contract with the other.

Comment to Caveat: The situations included within this Caveat are those where the person causing the breach of contract used tortious means towards the contract breaker and also where no such tortious means were used with respect to him but where the interference with the contract was tortious with respect to the other party to it.

Illustration to Caveat: A, a singer, contracts with B to sing exclusively over B's radio network for a period of a year on such occasions, not exceeding thirty, as B shall designate. With knowledge of this contract, C unjustifiably causes A to sing over C's network and not to sing over B's network. C makes a profit of $30,000 from A's singing. The Institute takes no position as to B's right to restitution from C.

3. *Question:* Following *Federal Sugar Refining,* when should the statute of limitations begin to run on restitution? This question is suggested by Ross v. Stanley, 346 F.2d 645 (5th Cir.1965), cert. denied, 382 U.S. 1026 (1966).

ZIPPERTUBING CO. v. TELEFLEX INC.

United States Court of Appeals, Third Circuit, 1985.
757 F.2d 1401.

[Nab Construction had the contract for reinsulating the New York City Transit system. Zippertubing was a designer and supplier of closeable insulation to wrap around wires and cables. A supplier only, Zippertubing did not do its own fabrication. Zippertubing agreed to work with Nab on the design and supply phase, and contacted a prospective subcontractor for the fabrication. This subcontractor was short on capacity, and Teleflex entered the picture. Nab insisted on inspecting Teleflex's facilities; during that inspection Teleflex became aware of Zippertubing's previously confidential arrangements with Nab. Teleflex then arranged a deal with Nab, cutting out Zippertubing, and in effect appropriating Zippertubing's client Nab].

It is undoubtedly so that in most instances in which a New Jersey plaintiff has established liability for interference with a prospective advantage the judgment has been for the plaintiff's lost profits. Probably that is because in most instances the amount of plaintiff's loss and defendant's gain is the same. In the one case dealing with the question in New Jersey, however, the Court of Errors and Appeals held that an accounting for profits is an appropriate remedy for interference with a prospective advantage. Schechter v. Friedman, 141 N.J.Eq. 318, 57 A.2d 251 (1948). That holding is consistent with the New Jersey law respecting the analogous business tort of misappropriation of a business name, L. Martin Co. v. L. Martin & Wilckes Co., 75 N.J.Eq. 257, 72 A. 294 (1909), and that of misuse of trade secrets. A. Hollander & Son, Inc. v. Imperial Fur Blending, 2 N.J. 235, 66 A.2d 319 (1949). Teleflex points out that these accounting for profits cases were suits in equity, and urges that such a remedy is unavailable in an action at law. That simply is not the case. In a diversity suit the distinction between cases at law or in equity is significant only with regard to the respective roles of judge and jury. Fed.R.Civ.P. 1. The equitable or legal nature of the relief does not relieve the federal forum of the obligation to afford the same relief which a state court would afford with respect to state law claims. Guaranty Trust Co. v. York, 326 U.S. 99, 105 (1945). Moreover the plaintiff in Schecter v. Friedman, proceeded in equity because he sought injunctive relief as well as money damages. No New Jersey case has been called to our attention suggesting that if the victim of a tort who has suffered actual damages cannot or does not elect to seek injunctive relief he may not seek an accounting for profits. Certainly Red Devil Tools v. Tip Top Brush Co., Inc., 92 N.J.Super. 570, 224 A.2d 336 (App.Div.1966), on which Teleflex relies is not such a case. In *Red Devil* the owner of a common law trademark, who neither made nor sold paint brushes, successfully enjoined the use of the trademark for paint brushes. An accounting for profits was denied, not because profits of a tortfeasor cannot be recovered at law, but because the trademark owner, not in the brush business, lost no prospective business advantage of its own. Here, plainly, the plaintiffs lost a prospective advantage.

The remedy applied in Schecter v. Friedman, is consistent with constructive trust principles, and "it is possible to think of the accounting for profits in this kind of case as simply a special form of constructive trust." D. Dobbs, Remedies 253 (1973). The constructive trust is, of course a familiar remedy in the New Jersey Courts. The Schecter v. Friedman remedy is, moreover consistent with the election of remedies available in New Jersey to the victim of a conversion of personal property. Kaplan v. Cavicchia, 107 N.J.Super. 201, 257 A.2d 739 (App.Div.1969). All of these closely related damage rules are consistent with the policy of discouraging tortious conduct by depriving the tortfeasor of the opportunity to profit from wrongdoing. Consistent with that policy, the trial court properly permitted the plaintiffs to prove as damages the amount of Teleflex's profits. The court charged:

> "The law says that when one has unlawfully deprived another of a contract or a business opportunity and has made that opportunity his own, he is not to be permitted to retain any of the profits, any of the benefits of his unlawful conduct.

"Therefore, if you were to find that the plaintiff has met its burden of proof as I have defined it to you on each and every one of the elements of the case, it would be your job to award such damages as would deprive the defendant of any unlawful benefit of its unlawful conduct."

This charge was correct, and the jury's verdict, consistent with it, must stand.

As to the calculation of profits which might be recovered the court charged:

"In determining the amount of Teleflex's profits, I instruct you that profits equal the total amount of money that Teleflex earned as a result of the Nab contract, less any direct expenses that were incurred with respect to this particular conduct [contract]. Thus, any direct costs of this project should be subtracted from Teleflex's gross receipts in computing Teleflex's profits.

"You should not deduct from their gross receipts any expenses of running the business which they would have had anyway."

Teleflex objects that this charge precluded the jury from deducting its indirect costs in calculating its profits. The rule which the trial court charged is that generally applied in New Jersey in actions seeking lost profits for breach of contract. Applying New Jersey law in such a case Judge Seitz observed:

"We agree with the view that where the plaintiff's overhead or fixed expenses are not affected by the defendant's breach, no deduction should be made in calculating the profits which the plaintiff would have made had it not been for the breach. It is obvious that fixed expenses are an essential element in determining the net profits of any business and must, for accounting purposes, be allocated among each of the businesses' sales activities. Nevertheless, as we stated in Vitex Manufacturing Corp. v. Caribtex Corp., 377 F.2d 795 (3d Cir.1967), it does not follow that a proportionate share of fixed expenses should be considered a cost factor in the computation of lost profits:

'The point is that while these items all are paid from the proceeds of the business, they do not necessarily bear such a direct relationship to any individual transaction to be considered a cost in ascertaining lost profits.'

"Furthermore, it is apparent that the fixed expenses of a business must be paid from the profits remaining after all direct costs have been paid. Unless damages restore the latter amount to plaintiff, it will not be fully compensated for the breach."

Buono Sales, Inc. v. Chrysler Motors Corporation, 449 F.2d 715, 719–20 (3d Cir.1971). No authority has been cited to us casting any doubt upon the accuracy of this prediction as to the rule a New Jersey court would apply. We hold that the same rule should be applied when a wrongdoer is asked to disgorge profits. The wrongdoer should not be permitted, by misappropriating another's opportunity, to use that opportunity in order to help absorb fixed expenses of its own business.

Teleflex points out that its negotiations with Zippertubing involved extrusion of five specific diameters of closeable insulation. It later contracted with Nab not only to supply closeable insulation, but also to furnish some seamless insulation, and tie-wraps for the closeable insulation. Teleflex urges that the profits derived from the sale of these products should not have been included in the damage award. The measure of damages in tort cases includes those reasonably foreseeable at the time of the commission of the tortious act or omission. It was certainly reasonably foreseeable that in procuring insulation Nab would elect to deal with a single source of supply, and that, but for the tort, that source would have been Zippertubing. The jury could have so concluded based on inferences drawn from Simpson's testimony regarding Nab's customary practices in dealing with contractors, and from evidence that Nab did, in fact, purchase the seamless insulation and tie-wraps from its closeable insulation supplier. Thus, it was not error to permit the jury to base its award on the entire Teleflex–Nab transaction. * * *

Teleflex next contends on appeal that the court erred in submitting the plaintiffs' claim for punitive damages to the jury. Teleflex points out that it has been punished as a wrongdoer by being forced to disgorge its profits, and that the award of punitive damages is duplicative and an excessive punishment. The problem with this argument, of course, is that it is equally applicable to any case in which both compensatory and punitive damages may be awarded. It is conceivable, for example, that a business-tort plaintiff seeking its own lost profits rather than those gained by the wrongdoer, might prove and recover more than the wrongdoer gained from the transaction. Such a defendant would undoubtedly also feel "doubly punished" if assessed with punitive damages. The fact that a disgorgement of profits or unjust enrichment measure was applied with respect to compensatory damages cannot be dispositive.

B. MORE OR LESS INDIRECT INJURIES TO ECONOMIC INTERESTS

1. DIVERSION BY FIDUCIARIES

a. Competition by Associates or Employees

NICHOLS–MORRIS CORP. v. MORRIS

United States District Court, 1959.
Southern District of New York.
174 F.Supp. 691.

WEINFELD, DISTRICT JUDGE. This is an action by the plaintiff, a New York corporation, against its former President and Director, charging him with breach of fiduciary duty. The basic charge is that the defendant, while still an officer of the plaintiff, induced the cancellation of a profitable sales distributorship enjoyed by plaintiff for thirteen years, which thereupon was awarded to a corporation controlled by the defendant.

Plaintiff was organized in April 1943 by the defendant, Robert E. Morris, and his then close friend, Max J. Bloch, to act as sales representative for manufacturers of factory equipment. Each purchased 50 per cent of the corporation's capital stock for $15,000.

The plaintiff, upon its formation, was designated by the W.H. Nichols Company as its sole distributor, on a national and world-wide basis, of milling machines manufactured by it and known in the trade as "Nichols Millers." For some years previously, the defendant had acted as the New England sales representative of W.H. Nichols Company, and it was largely because of the esteem in which he was held by officials of the latter company that plaintiff corporation was designated. As national sales representative, plaintiff served as the sales and credit department of the W.H. Nichols Company; appointed retail dealers throughout the United States; passed upon the credit to be extended to them; furnished them with technical assistance; carried on promotional and advertising campaigns; and generally did whatever was required to promote the sale of the machines.

Plaintiff continued to act in this capacity without interruption until May 4, 1956 when the Nichols Company terminated plaintiff's appointment as its national distributor. The Robert E. Morris Company, a corporation of which the defendant was President and controlling stockholder, was named as plaintiff's successor. The plaintiff charges that the loss of the national distributorship of "Nichols Millers" was induced by the defendant in breach of his duty to it and in violation of its rights. * * *

We next turn to the question of damages. The plaintiff urges that it is entitled to the capitalized value of the national distributorship of "Nichols Millers" on November 1, 1956, the date of its termination. The claim is based not only on the fact that since 1950 the distributorship yielded annual net profits but also upon the prospect of its continuance for an indefinite period. Plaintiff's expert witness gave it as his opinion, based upon a five-year average annual net profit, after taxes, of $27,000 attributable to the distributorship, that the capitalized value of the distributorship as of November 1, 1956, was more than $250,000. Plaintiff asks that this sum be awarded to it as damages for the loss of the account.

The claim is utterly unrealistic and bears no reasonable relationship to the damages suffered by plaintiff nor to the factual situation touching upon the distributorship. * * *

Several factors compel rejection of the plaintiff's extravagant estimate of damages. First, the plaintiff's expert, in giving his opinion as to the value of the distributorship, applied a capitalization rate of ten times the average net earnings derived from the distributorship. Thus, the validity of his conclusion rests upon the correctness of the earnings base (assuming arguendo that the capitalization method normally used to determine the good will value of a going business is applicable in this instance). The domestic "Nichols Miller" agency was but one of a number of plaintiff's accounts. Plaintiff was also the foreign distributor for that product; in addition it was the exclusive sales agency for other and unrelated products. It did not keep separate books of account for its multiple activities and no breakdown of income and expense according to the separate activities was reflected upon its records. * * *

[The court rejected the allocation of income and expenses prepared by plaintiff's accountant.]

* * * [O]ther factors compel rejection of the plaintiff's estimate of its damages. It is recognized that it is entitled to recover as damages the amount of loss sustained by it including the opportunity for profit on the account which was diverted from it by defendant's conduct. The extent of this deprivation must be determined. In assessing the damages, the nature and character of the particular business and all the circumstances must be taken into account.

The distributorship was not for a fixed term of years. It was cancellable by the Nichols Company upon notice. There was no assurance of its continuity. It is true that until the occurrence of the events already described, W.H.

Nichols Company appeared likely to continue the plaintiff as its national distributor of "Nichols Millers." It is equally true that this prospect of continuance—the corporate opportunity—would remain only as long as the Nichols Company was of the view that the plaintiff had the capacity to perform as it had in the past. This was a matter which rested in the sole judgment of the Nichols Company. The record demonstrates that in the judgment of its officials the plaintiff's ability to perform to their satisfaction was conditioned upon the continued association with plaintiff of Morris and Bloch; that as between the two, Morris was regarded as the more effective and essential in the representation of the Nichols interests.

Morris was under no contractual obligation to continue with the plaintiff. He was free to resign as its officer and director. Once he properly severed his relationship with the plaintiff, he was not restricted from entering into a competitive situation, so long as he did not breach his fiduciary obligation.

The Nichols Company was entirely free to make an independent decision in its own interests. When the break came between the two associates, it had the choice of continuing with the plaintiff, appointing the defendant in its place, or naming a new designee. But Morris, as we have seen, was barred from interfering with plaintiff's rights with respect to the distributorship, because he occupied a position of trust and confidence toward it which continued at least until May 11, 1956, the date of his resignation. However, the restraints upon him were not perpetual. Had Morris bided his time after he and Bloch came to the parting of the ways, resigned, and acted within permissible legal limits, the record justifies a finding that upon, or soon after, his disaffiliation from the plaintiff, the Nichols Company would have cancelled the distributorship and awarded it to Morris, or to a company with which he was associated, as best qualified to serve the Nichols' interests. * * *

To accept plaintiff's claim, which finds no support in the facts, in effect would overcapitalize a cancellable distributorship, one that in the normal hazards of business plaintiff would not have continued to enjoy once the defendant withdrew from it.

The Court is fully persuaded that even without the defendant's inducement the Nichols Company, following his resignation, in its own interests and acting upon its own independent judgment, would have cancelled the distributorship and awarded it to the defendant. The inference is warranted that this action would have occurred within a year of the defendant's resignation. Under these circumstances, one year's loss of profits (realistically evaluated), represents just and adequate compensation.

Note

Frederick Chusid & Co. v. Marshall Leeman & Co., 326 F.Supp. 1043, 1061 (S.D.N.Y.1971): "Under New York law, a disloyal employee forfeits his right to compensation for services 'and if he is paid without knowledge of his disloyalty he may be compelled to return what he has improperly received [citations].' In the cited case, the date from which forfeiture for disloyalty was decreed was the date on which the certificate of incorporation of the competing business was filed."

b. *Diversion or Misappropriation of Business Opportunities: Including Bribery and Kickbacks*

Skip

ALVEST INC. v. SUPERIOR OIL CORP.

Supreme Court of Alaska, 1965.
398 P.2d 213.

DIMOND, JUSTICE. Appellant was awarded first priority for an oil and gas lease at a non-competitive lease drawing conducted by the state Division of Lands. Appellee was given second priority. Later the Division of Lands cancelled the award to appellant and gave it to appellee for the reason that two of appellant's officers and directors, White and Mueller, had filed applications for themselves in the same drawing. The Division of Lands held that this action on the part of White and Mueller gave appellant more than one chance at the drawing in violation of an administrative regulation which provided: "Each drawing shall be conducted in such a manner as the Director shall determine and each applicant shall have only one chance in any one drawing." The superior court affirmed the decision of the Division of Lands and this appeal followed.

A corporate officer or director stands in a fiduciary relationship to his corporation. Out of this relationship arises the duty of reasonably protecting the interests of the corporation. It is inconsistent with and a breach of such duty for an officer or director to take advantage of a business opportunity for his own personal profit when, applying ethical standards of what is fair and equitable in a particular situation, the opportunity should belong to the corporation. Where a business opportunity is one in which the corporation has a legitimate interest, the officer or director may not take the opportunity for himself. If he does, he will hold all resulting benefit and profit in his fiduciary capacity for the use and benefit of the corporation.

Whether a business opportunity is a corporate one or one within the legitimate scope of the individual interests of the officer or director depends upon the facts and circumstances of each case. Here appellant's chance to be the successful applicant at the lease drawing was a business opportunity in which appellant had expressed a definite interest. That interest was a legitimate one because appellant had made similar applications in previous drawings, and the leasing of oil and gas lands was within the scope of appellant's corporate activities. This was a corporate opportunity which appellant's officers and directors, White and Mueller, had no right to seek for themselves. If either had been the successful applicant at the drawing he would have held the lease in a fiduciary capacity for the use and benefit of appellant. This means that appellant did not have only one chance at the drawing, but three—its own, represented by the corporate application filed on its behalf, plus two additional chances, represented by White's and Mueller's individual applications. Since appellant had more than one chance in the drawing, it was not a qualified applicant under * * * the administrative regulations. The Division of Lands was correct in holding that appellant was not entitled to the lease. * * *

Appellant contends that it could not have claimed the benefits of the lease had it been awarded to White or Mueller, because a full disclosure of their actions in filing their individual applications had been made to the corporation, and because the filing of applications by appellant's officers and directors was consistent with corporate policy. There was evidence that the members of appellant's board of directors had generally approved the appropriateness of officers and directors filing on the same land that the corporation had filed on, although it was not established that this in fact had ever been done prior to the filings in this case. But there was no evidence that the shareholders of the corporation had consented to such a policy generally, or that in this particular instance they had approved White's and Mueller's actions in filing in competition with appellant. In the absence of such approval by the shareholders, the business opportunity in this case was not within the legitimate scope of the individual interests of appellant's officers and directors.

Appellant states that White and Mueller had at all times been open and above board and had acted in good faith in all their dealings here. That is apparently true. But it has no bearing on the decision of the issues in this case. A showing of bad faith is not essential to establish a duty on the part of officers or directors in connection with business opportunities which they wish to acquire for themselves. * * *

The judgment is affirmed.

Notes

1. Borden v. Sinskey, 530 F.2d 478, 489 (3d Cir.1976): "Briefly stated, the doctrine of 'corporate opportunity' precludes a corporate fiduciary from acquiring for himself a business opportunity that his 'corporation is financially able to undertake, and which, by its nature, falls into the line of the corporation's business and is of practical advantage to it, or it is an opportunity in which the corporation has an actual or expectant interest.'

"Equity Corp. v. Milton, 221 A.2d 494, 497 (Del.1966). Whether or not a given opportunity meets these requisites is largely a question of fact to be determined from the objective facts and surrounding circumstances existing at the time the opportunity arises. If these elements are found to be present, the opportunity is treated as a corporate asset and the corporate officer's or director's illicit diversion of it to his own use constitutes a violation of his fiduciary duty."

2. Diversion of a "corporate opportunity" is customarily considered in more detail in courses in Business Associations, as is diversion of benefits by majority shareholders from minority shareholders in conjunction with the sale of a controlling interest in the corporation. Given the fiduciary obligation between majority and minority shareholders, the principles of equitable restitution may be invoked. Difficult questions exist about whether the remedies are enforceable through derivative or individual actions.

SNEPP v. UNITED STATES

United States Supreme Court, 1980.
444 U.S. 507.

PER CURIAM. * * * Based on his experiences as a CIA agent, Snepp published a book about certain CIA activities in South Vietnam. Snepp published the account without submitting it to the Agency for prepublication review. As an express condition of his employment with the CIA in 1968, however, Snepp had executed an agreement promising that he would "not * * * publish * * * any information or material relating to the Agency, its activities or intelligence activities generally, either during or after the term of [his] employment * * * without specific prior approval by the Agency." The promise was an integral part of Snepp's concurrent undertaking "not to disclose any classified information relating to the Agency without proper authorization." Thus, Snepp had pledged not to divulge *classified* information and not to publish *any* information without prepublication clearance. The Government brought this suit to enforce Snepp's agreement. It sought a declaration that Snepp had breached the contract, an injunction requiring Snepp to submit future writings for prepublication review, and an order imposing a constructive trust for the Government's benefit on all profits that Snepp might earn from publishing the book in violation of his fiduciary obligations to the Agency.[1]

The District Court found that Snepp had "willfully, deliberately and surreptitiously breached his position of trust with the CIA and the [1968] secrecy agreement" by publishing his book without submitting it for prepublication review. * * * Finally, the court determined as a fact that publication of the book had "caused the United States irreparable harm and loss." The District Court therefore enjoined future breaches of Snepp's agreement and imposed a constructive trust on Snepp's profits.

The Court of Appeals accepted the findings of the District Court and agreed that Snepp had breached a valid contract. * * * The court, however, concluded that the record did not support imposition of a constructive trust. The conclusion rested on the court's perception that Snepp had a First Amendment right to publish unclassified information and the Government's concession—for the purposes of this litigation—that Snepp's book divulged no classified intelligence. In other words, the court thought that Snepp's fiduciary obligation extended only to preserving the confidentiality of classified material. It therefore limited recovery to nominal damages and to the possibility of punitive damages if the Government—in a jury trial—could prove tortious conduct. * * *

Snepp's employment with the CIA involved an extremely high degree of trust. In the opening sentence of the agreement that he signed, Snepp explicitly recognized that he was entering a trust relationship. The trust agreement specifically imposed the obligation not to publish *any* information relating to the Agency without submitting the information for clearance. Snepp stipulated at trial that—after undertaking this obligation—he had been "assigned to various positions of trust" and that he had been granted "frequent access to classified information, including information regarding intelligence sources and methods." Snepp published his book about CIA activities on the basis of this background and exposure. He deliberately and surreptitiously violated his obligation to submit all material for prepublication review. Thus, he exposed the classified information with which he had been entrusted to the risk of disclosure.

Whether Snepp violated his trust does not depend upon whether his book actually contained classified information. The Government does not deny—as a general principle—Snepp's right to publish unclassified information. Nor does it contend—at this stage of the litigation—that Snepp's book contains classified material. * * *

1. [Footnote renumbered.] At the time of suit, Snepp already had received about $60,000 in advance payments. His contract with his publisher provides for royalties and other potential profits.

Both the District Court and the Court of Appeals found that a former intelligence agent's publication of unreviewed material relating to intelligence activities can be detrimental to vital national interests even if the published information is unclassified. When a former agent relies on his own judgment about what information is detrimental, he may reveal information that the CIA—with its broader understanding of what may expose classified information and confidential sources—could have identified as harmful. In addition to receiving intelligence from domestically based or controlled sources, the CIA obtains information from the intelligence services of friendly nations and from agents operating in foreign countries. The continued availability of these foreign sources depends upon the CIA's ability to guarantee the security of information that might compromise them and even endanger the personal safety of foreign agents. * * *

The decision of the Court of Appeals denies the Government the most appropriate remedy for Snepp's acknowledged wrong. Indeed, as a practical matter, the decision may well leave the Government with no reliable deterrent against similar breaches of security. No one disputes that the actual damages attributable to a publication such as Snepp's generally are unquantifiable. Nominal damages are a hollow alternative, certain to deter no one. The punitive damages recoverable after a jury trial are speculative and unusual. Even if recovered, they may bear no relation to either the Government's irreparable loss or Snepp's unjust gain.

The Government could not pursue the only remedy that the Court of Appeals left it without losing the benefit of the bargain it seeks to enforce. Proof of the tortious conduct necessary to sustain an award of punitive damages might force the Government to disclose some of the very confidences that Snepp promised to protect. * * * When the Government cannot secure its remedy without unacceptable risks, it has no remedy at all.

A constructive trust, on the other hand, protects both the Government and the former agent from unwarranted risks. This remedy is the natural and customary consequence of a breach of trust. It deals fairly with both parties by conforming relief to the dimensions of the wrong. If the agent secures prepublication clearance, he can publish with no fear of liability. If the agent publishes unreviewed material in violation of his fiduciary and contractual obligation, the trust remedy simply requires him to disgorge the benefits of his faithlessness. Since the remedy is swift and sure, it is tailored to deter those who would place sensitive information at risk. And since the remedy reaches only funds attributable to the breach, it cannot saddle the former agent with exemplary damages out of all proportion to his gain. * * * We therefore reverse the judgment of the Court of Appeals insofar as it refused to impose a constructive trust on Snepp's profits, and we remand the cases to the Court of Appeals for reinstatement of the full judgment of the District Court.

So ordered.

JUSTICE STEVENS, with whom JUSTICE BRENNAN and JUSTICE MARSHALL join dissenting. * * * Plainly this is not a typical trust situation in which a settlor has conveyed legal title to certain assets to a trustee for the use and benefit of designated beneficiaries. Rather, it is an employment relationship in which the employee possesses fiduciary obligations arising out of his duty of loyalty to his employer. One of those obligations long recognized by the common law even in the absence of a written employment agreement, is the duty to protect confidential or "classified" information. If Snepp had breached that obligation, the common law would support the implication of a constructive trust upon the benefits derived from his misuse of confidential information.

But Snepp did not breach his duty to protect confidential information. Rather, he breached a contractual duty, imposed in aid of the basic duty to maintain confidentiality, to obtain prepublication clearance. In order to justify the imposition of a constructive trust, the majority attempts to equate this contractual duty with Snepp's duty not to disclose, labeling them both as "fiduciary." I find nothing in the common law to support such an approach.

The Court has not persuaded me that a rule of reason analysis should not be applied to Snepp's covenant to submit to prepublication review. * * * When the Government seeks to enforce a harsh restriction on the employee's freedom, despite its admission that the interest the agreement was designed to protect—the confidentiality of classified information—has not been compromised, an equity court might well be persuaded that the case is not one in which the covenant should be enforced.

But even assuming that Snepp's covenant to submit to prepublication review should be enforced, the constructive trust imposed by the Court is not an appropriate remedy. If an employee has used his employer's confidential information for his own personal profit, a constructive trust over those profits is obviously an appropriate remedy because the profits are the direct result of the breach. But Snepp admittedly did not use confidential information in his book; nor were the profits from his book in any sense a product of his failure to submit the book for prepublication review. For, even if Snepp had submitted the book to the Agency for prepublication review, the Government's censorship authority would surely have been limited to the excision of classified material. In this case, then, it would have been obliged to clear the book for publication in precisely the same form as it now stands. Thus, Snepp has not gained any profits as a result of his breach; the Government, rather than Snepp, will be unjustly enriched if he is required to disgorge profits attributable entirely to his own legitimate activity.

Despite the fact that Snepp has not caused the Government the type of harm that would ordinarily be remedied by the imposition of a constructive trust, the Court attempts to justify a constructive trust remedy on the ground that the Government has suffered *some* harm. The Court states that publication of "unreviewed material" by a former CIA agent "can be detrimental to vital national interests even if the published information is unclassified." It then seems to suggest that the injury in such cases stems from the Agency's inability to catch "harmful" but unclassified information before it is published.

* * * [I]t is difficult to believe that the publication of a book like Snepp's, which does not reveal classified information, has significantly weakened the Agency's position. Nor does it explain whether the unidentified foreign agencies who have stopped cooperating with the CIA have done so because of a legitimate fear that secrets will be revealed or because they merely disagree with our Government's classification policies.

In any event, to the extent that the Government seeks to punish Snepp for the generalized harm he has caused by failing to submit to prepublication review and to deter others from following in his footsteps, punitive damages is, as the Court of Appeals held, clearly the preferable remedy "since a constructive trust depends on the concept of unjust enrichment rather than deterrence and punishment." * * *

The uninhibited character of today's exercise in lawmaking is highlighted by the Court's disregard of two venerable principles that favor a more conservative approach to this case.

First, for centuries the English-speaking judiciary refused to grant equitable relief unless the plaintiff could show that his remedy at law was inadequate. Without waiting for an opportunity to appraise the adequacy of the punitive damages remedy in this case, the Court has jumped to the conclusion that equitable relief is necessary.

Second, and of greater importance, the Court seems unaware of the fact that its drastic new remedy has been fashioned to enforce a species of prior restraint on a citizen's right to criticize his government. Inherent in this prior restraint is the risk that the reviewing agency will misuse its authority to delay the publication of a critical work or to persuade an author to modify the contents of his work beyond the demands of secrecy. * * *

I respectfully dissent.

Notes

1. An obvious conflict of interest arises where a fiduciary accepts gifts, undisclosed commissions, or bribes. If a fiduciary breaches a trust relationship and benefits, she may not retain those benefits but must account to the principal. In United States v. Drisko, 303 F.Supp. 858 (E.D.Va.1969), defendant, an employee of the Department of Agriculture, accepted two automobiles and a deep freezer as gifts from one De Angelis, a participant in programs the department administered. Despite claims that Mr. De Angelis was just a friend and "a kind and generous man," judgment for these benefits was entered for the government.

2. County of Cook v. Barrett, 36 Ill.App.3d 623, 626–27, 344 N.E.2d 540, 544 (1975). The county sued Barrett, a former county clerk, for an accounting for bribes received:

"Barrett has suggested numerous reasons why the County cannot recover from him. He contends that the County is entitled only to fees and allowances which are legally collected, that to allow recovery by a public body of bribes or kickbacks paid to its officers would be against public policy; that the County alleged no damage and suffered none, that no money moved from the County to him, that if any money was paid it was paid by Shoup and Gallagher not by the County, and that since no money moved out of the County treasury it could not have been depleted; that the complaint did not allege that he had been unjustly enriched at the expense of the County or that in the absence of bribery the County would have paid less for voting machines or insurance. Attacking the equitable jurisdiction generally, he suggests that the facts alleged in the amended complaint did not warrant the grant of equitable relief and that there was an adequate remedy at law. Attacking the constructive trust doctrine specifically he contends that its application to one in his position would be unwarranted and unprecedented."

[The holding was against Barrett on this contention.]

3. *Employer's Remedy When Employee Bribed.* In Continental Management, Inc. v. United States, 527 F.2d 613, 619 (Ct.Cl.1975), the court held that the government had a common law action against a company whose former president had bribed federal employees to obtain mortgage insurance business with the government. The government was unable to prove any specific pecuniary damages

since it must be assumed that the company performed the contracts well and for the same consideration the government would have had to pay anyway:

"It is an old maxim of the law that, where the fact of injury is adequately shown, the court should not cavil at the absence of specific or detailed proof of the damages. Here, the plaintiffs engaged in wrongful conduct that clearly hurt the Government. Significant elements of that harm, such as the injury to the impartial administration of governmental programs, are not susceptible to an accurate monetary gauge. We should not deny the Government relief because Sirote managed to cause injury not readily traceable or measurable. Similarly, the Government's inability to attach an exact and provable dollar figure to the harm it sustained should not result in the effective exculpation of the plaintiffs. * * * As between the briber and the bribee's employer, the risks of damage determination should fall on the former.

"On this premise the amount of the bribe provides a reasonable measure of damage, in the absence of a more precise yardstick. That is, after all, the value the plaintiffs placed on their corruption of the defendant's employees; the other side of the coin is that the plaintiffs hoped and expected to benefit by more than the sum of the bribes. It is therefore fair to use that total as the measure of an injury which is probable in its impact but uncertain in its mathematical calculation. [citations] Of course, the Government cannot recover the bribes twice—once from the briber and again from the corrupted employee. But it is entitled to one such recovery."

Query: Considering the reasons given for compelling the bribee to disgorge, why should the government be limited to one recovery?

Dorsett Carpet Mills, Inc. v. Whitt Tile and Marble Distributing Co., 734 S.W.2d 322, 323–26 (Tenn.1987). In litigation involving an employer's claims against a bribing seller and an employee who had received kickbacks, the trial judge entered judgment against the seller for procuring breach of contract and measured the employer's recovery by the amount of the employee's salary "during the period of his duplicitous conduct." "The trial court also rendered a judgment against both [the bribing seller and the corrupt employee] for the amount of secret commissions." The seller appealed.

The Tennessee supreme court thought the salary was an appropriate recovery against the employee, but "an inappropriate element of damage to charge against the procurer of the breach." The secret kickbacks the seller paid the employee were the employer's proper damages. "[H]ad [the bribing seller] not paid this money to [plaintiff's employee], it may be presumed that these funds would have inured to the benefit of [the employer] in the form of lower prices or greater commissions." Recovery was trebled under a Tennessee statute.

The court quoted the Restatement (Second) of Torts § 774A(2) (1982): "any damages in fact paid by the third person will reduce the damages actually recoverable" for interference with contract. The question of whether the employer could collect judgments from both the seller and the employee without receiving duplicated damages was not, however, raised.

MDO Development Corp. v. Kelly, 726 F.Supp. 79, 86 (S.D.N.Y.1989). An employer sued an embezzling employee under the federal Racketeer Influenced Corrupt Organizations Act. The court imposed a constructive trust on a house defendant had purchased with the embezzlements and trebled the RICO damage judgment.

Moreover: "Mr. Kelly's claims for back salary and expense reimbursement are dismissed as not recoverable because of his disloyalty to his employer during the period for which he is making those claims."

Eden Hannon & Co. v. Sumitomo Trust & Banking Co., 914 F.2d 556 (4th Cir.1990). Defendant breached a noncircumvention and nondisclosure agreement with plaintiff investment analyst by bidding for a lease portfolio. Noting the difficulty plaintiff would have in trying to prove a loss, the court ordered a constructive trust imposed on the profits defendant made from the breach.

4. Two officers of a corporation learned inside information that would cause the corporation stock to fall in value and sold their personal holdings on the open market. They saved themselves several hundred thousand dollars because the market declined when the information became public. The *corporation* was allowed to recover these savings. Diamond v. Oreamuno, 24 N.Y.2d 494, 301 N.Y.S.2d 78, 248 N.E.2d 910 (1969).

Was a benefit that would have otherwise gone to the corporation diverted by a fiduciary? Attempts by *corporations* to recover "benefits" accruing to persons using "inside information" to trade in the corporation's stock on the open market beyond the limits of *Oreamuno* have not been successful—e.g., attempts to recover profits made by tippees from genuine insiders. Frigitemp Corp. v. Financial Dynamics Fund, 524 F.2d 275 (2d Cir.1975) emphasizes that *Oreamuno* is based on a breach of fiduciary duty. Schein v. Chasen, 313 So.2d 739 (Fla.1975) expressed reservations about whether *Oreamuno* itself had gone too far.

5. News Item: Damage Suit Filed for Manson Victim's Son: A $5 million damage suit was filed in U.S. District Court Wednesday on behalf of the 12-year-old son of Voityck Frykowski, one of the seven Tate–La Bianca murder victims.

The action for Bartek Frykowski named the New American Library, Twenty Pimlico, Inc., Lawrence Schiller, Beverly Hills National Bank and [two] attorneys.

The suit, prepared by attorney Nathaniel J. Friedman, accused the defendants of being unjustly enriched by monies which should have gone to young Frykowski.

New American Library published a book called "The Killing of Sharon Tate" after the blonde actress and four others, including Frykowski, were killed at her Benedict Canyon home Aug. 9, 1969.

The suit reiterated how Susan Denise Atkins, 22, one of the defendants in the case, was taken from jail to offices [of defendant attorneys] to give a first-person account of the Tate killings.

Thereafter, about Dec. 8, 1969, according to the action, Schiller, his Twenty Pimlico, Inc., the two attorneys, New American Library and the Beverly Hills bank entered into agreements to sell Miss Atkins' story.

As a result, the suit said, the defendants profited by about $90,000 in worldwide sales when all should have known that Miss Atkins and her co-conspirators were liable for damage claims from Frykowski's heirs.

The suit sought $5 million in punitive damages and an accounting of the money made through the sale of Miss Atkins' story.

Friedman won a $500,000 judgment [wrongful death] against Miss Atkins and her fellow Manson "family" defendants on young Frykowski's behalf last August in U.S. District Court.

6. N.Y. Exec. Law § 632–a, Crime Victims Compensation:

§ 632–a. Distribution of Moneys Received as a Result of the Commission of Crime. 1. Every person, firm, corporation, partnership, association or other legal entity contracting with any person or the representative or assignee of any person, accused of a crime in this state, with respect to the reenactment of such crime, by way of a movie, book, magazine article, radio or television presentation, live entertainment of any kind, or from the expression of such person's thoughts, feelings, opinions or emotions regarding such crime, shall pay over to the board any moneys which would otherwise, by terms of such contract, be owing to the person so convicted or his representatives. The board shall deposit such moneys in an escrow account for the benefit of and payable to any victim of crimes committed by such person, provided that such person is eventually convicted of the crime and provided further that such victim, within five years of the date of the crime, brings a civil action in a court of competent jurisdiction and recovers a money judgment against such person or his representatives.

2. The board, at least once every six months for five years from the date it receives such moneys, shall cause to have published a legal notice in newspapers of general circulation in each county of the state advising such victims that such escrow moneys are available to satisfy money judgments pursuant to this section.

The act has been called the "Son of Sam" Act.

2. BY OTHERS

Preliminary Note

Restitution for benefits diverted from the plaintiff by nonfiduciaries has long been recognized. In 1677 (83 years before Moses v. MacFerlan) Arris v. Stukely, Excheq. 2 Mod. 260, held that indebitatus assumpsit would lie in favor of a de jure officer to recover the emoluments of office collected by a de facto usurper. The familiar "want of privity" argument was raised and rejected, as were the points that plaintiff had other remedies such as an assize for his office and an action on the case for disturbing him in his office. The court relied upon the even more ancient analogy that "indebitatus assumpsit will lie for rent received by one who pretends a title; for in such case an account will lie. Wherever the plaintiff may have an account, an indebitatus will lie."

In such actions, the defendant may deduct expenses, but not the reasonable value of his services. See Woodward, Quasi Contracts § 287 (1913), and Restatement of Restitution § 137 (1937).

CHAMBERS v. KANE

Court of Chancery of Delaware, New Castle County, 1980.
424 A.2d 311.

BROWN, VICE CHANCELLOR. * * * Plaintiff asserts a personal claim against her brother for interference with her prospective right to inherit from their mother. Plaintiff seeks an accounting, a surcharge against the defendant for loss and diminishment of their mother's assets which plaintiff alleges have been brought about by the improper conduct of her brother, the imposition of a constructive trust as to all assets of their mother held or administered by him, and an injunction prohibiting the defendant from any further dealing in the assets of their mother. * * *

The complaint alleges that John W. Kane, the father of the parties, died in 1965. Under his Will he created two trusts. One was a marital trust for the benefit of his widow, Sally H. Kane. The other was a residual trust. The income from both trusts goes to Sally H. Kane for life. Upon her death, the residual trust is to be divided between the plaintiff, the defendant, and any grandchildren of John W. Kane. Principal from the marital trust can be invaded for the benefit of Sally Kane during her lifetime, and she is given the power by her Will to appoint any remaining principal of the marital trust. The challenged Paragraph 4 alleges that in 1978 Sally Kane executed a Will by means of which she created a trust of her residual estate. By such Will she has purported to exercise her power of appointment under the marital trust of her husband in favor of the plaintiff and defendant as equal income beneficiaries of her residual trust, with power to appoint their respective shares of the trust principal.

In the second count of the complaint, plaintiff alleges that Sally Kane is 75 years of age, is in poor health, and is unable to manage her assets or to independently evaluate the conduct of the defendant. It is alleged that since 1971 Sally Kane has relied upon and been dependent upon the defendant for advice and assistance in the management of all her assets, including the assets of the marital trust. It is alleged that * * * by virtue of his complete control over her financial affairs, he has benefitted personally by obtaining gifts of money from her, by having her pay his personal and business obligations out of her funds, by purchasing substantial amounts of stock from her at a price far less than its true worth, and by causing her to invest in highly speculative and improper investments. It is alleged that as a result of these and other violations of the fiduciary obligation he owes to his mother, defendant has caused the estate of Sally Kane to be reduced in value from in excess of $1.5 million to less than $700,000. * * *

[A]s a direct result plaintiff now stands to inherit considerably less from her mother upon her mother's death than she would have expected to inherit but for the wrongful and self-dealing conduct of her brother. * * *

[Defendant] argues that there is no cause of action in the plaintiff in her own right to seek relief for alleged undue influence practiced by him upon their mother, at least not during the mother's lifetime, based on the premise that it constitutes an intentional interference with her expectancy of inheritance.

It is conceded by the parties that there is no Delaware authority either recognizing or refusing to recognize the tort of intentional interference with an expectancy of inheritance. However, defendant cites numerous decisions from other jurisdictions which uniformly hold that the rights of an heir-apparent in the property of his ancestor do not vest until the death of the ancestor, and that as a consequence an heir has no enforceable interest, legal or equitable, in such property until his ancestor's demise.

Plaintiff concedes the existence of this line of authority. She says, however, that the defendant is missing the thrust of her claim. She says that she is not suing in an effort to enforce her interests in her mother's property. Rather, she is suing her brother for the injury done to her own interest—namely, her right that in the absence of wrongful interference by another she has a reasonable basis to expect that she will inherit from her natural parent upon the latter's death. In setting forth her position, plaintiff relies upon three things.

First, the Restatement (Second) of Torts specifically recognizes such a cause of action. Section 774B states as follows:

"One who by fraud, duress or other tortious means intentionally prevents another from receiving from a third person an inheritance or gift that he would otherwise have received is subject to liability to the other for loss of the inheritance or gift."

Secondly, in this jurisdiction it has been recognized that a cause of action will lie for tortious interference with a business or commercial expectancy. As a recommended extension of this principle of commercial law, it is stated as follows in Prosser, Law of Torts (4th Ed.1971) § 130:

"There is no essential reason for refusing to protect such noncommercial expectancies (interference with an expected gift or legacy under a will), at least where there is a strong probability that they would have been realized." * * *

Thirdly, plaintiff places heavy reliance on the recent decision of the Supreme Judicial Court of Maine in Harmon v. Harmon, Me.Supr., 404 A.2d 1020 (1979). In that case, which the Court characterized as being "[s]omewhere near the frontier of the expanding field of law relating to tortious interference with an advantageous relationship," a factual situation was presented which was strikingly similar to the situation presented here.

In *Harmon* one brother sued another, charging that by fraud and undue influence practiced upon their 87 year old mother who was in a poor state of health, the defendant had caused the mother to convey to him property which, under the terms of her Will, was to be devised to both brothers equally. The mother was still living and the defendant moved to dismiss, both for failure to state claim and because his brother lacked standing to proceed against him in his own right. On appeal, the dismissal of the action on these grounds was reversed. Making reference to early cases which recognized a cause of action in tort for interference with an existing employment relationship, and for interference with the rights of a person as a beneficiary under a contract of life insurance, the Court * * * summarized as follows:

"We conclude that where a person can prove that, but for the tortious interference of another, he would in all likelihood have received a gift or a specific profit from a transaction, he is entitled to recover the damages thereby done to him. [citation] We apply this rule to the case before us where allegedly the Defendant son and his wife have tortiously interfered with the Plaintiff son's expectation that under his mother's will he would receive a substantial portion of her estate."

In reaching this decision, the *Harmon* Court relied heavily on Dean Prosser and on the Restatement, noting that "the claim of the Plaintiff son is to a loss of his expectancy, not to a loss of the actual property of his mother."

As a consequence of the foregoing, it clearly appears that the plaintiff here is asking that the *Harmon* rationale be adopted as the law of Delaware. * * * However, I find it unnecessary to reach a decision on this point. I say this because even under the plaintiff's authorities, as I read them, the [complaint] must be dismissed. I reach this conclusion for two reasons.

First, plaintiff's authorities recognize a cause of action where one has been prevented from receiving an inheritance. Under the facts alleged here, plaintiff has not been disinherited or deprived of an expected right to any specific devise, bequest or legacy that she would have otherwise received from her mother. Rather, her complaint goes to the reduction in the amount that she feels she should be entitled to receive. And, as I read them, her authorities do not go that far. In other words, plaintiff has not been disinherited as the plaintiff was held to be in *Harmon.* Along with her brother, she still stands to receive one-half of the income from her mother's residual trust estate upon her mother's death, with a power of appointment over one-half of the trust principal. Her complaint now is that because of her brother's conduct her one-half will not be as large as she had a right to expect. But the right on which she seeks to rely is an expectation that she will receive what her mother had previously intended for her, and that is, essentially, one-half of her remaining estate at death. Any wrongful conduct of the defendant has not eliminated that expectancy. It has only reduced the size of the expectancy, and I do not interpret plaintiff's authorities to mean that a cause of action in tort lies because one may ultimately receive less than the full amount that he was counting on receiving under a general bequest of a percentage or a portion of a person's estate. Perhaps that is still a bit beyond the frontier.

But even independent of this, there is another reason which requires that the plaintiff's individual cause of action against her brother be dismissed. Plaintiff's authorities indicate that the cause of action on which she relies is one in tort. The usual remedy for a tort action is money damages. Here, presumably, such monetary damage would be the loss that the plaintiff could establish that she will suffer upon her mother's death as a result of the dissipation of her mother's estate brought about by the alleged wrongful conduct of the defendant. However, plaintiff is not seeking money damages against her brother here. Rather, she is seeking an accounting, a surcharge, and the imposition of a constructive trust against him. In other words, she is seeking equitable relief.

The difficulty I have with this is that the mother, Sally Kane, is still living. With this in mind, it must be remembered that the basis for the plaintiff's cause of action is the alleged undue influence practiced upon Sally Kane by the defendant together with his alleged wrongful exploitation of the confidential relationship existing between him and his mother. It is through this means that plaintiff charges that the defendant has taken advantage of his mother for his own personal benefit and to the detriment of the plaintiff's otherwise reasonable expectation that she would eventually inherit a larger amount under her mother's will. Thus, the basis for the plaintiff's claim for relief in her own right lies in the wrongs allegedly perpetrated by the defendant upon their mother. Thus, I guess, plaintiff is saying that any such wrongs committed against her mother also constitute a wrong against the plaintiff's personal right to reasonably expect to inherit from her mother.

Aside from getting a trifle far out as the justification for a present cause of action in tort, this theory has the following potential consequence when viewed in light of the equitable relief that plaintiff is seeking. It means that plaintiff is asking this Court of equity to preserve for her, and to require the defendant to presently account to her for, her fair share of that which the defendant has wrongfully taken from their still-living mother. No redress is sought on behalf of Sally Kane, the supposed victim of the defendant's alleged deceit. Rather, the plaintiff is asking the Court to marshal and impound in advance of her mother's death that portion of plaintiff's anticipated inheritance which she can prove at trial that her brother has obtained by improper means from their mother, and to enjoin him further from dealing with the assets of Sally Kane during the balance of the latter's lifetime. I do not feel this to be the type of relief as to which equity should lend its powers.

If Sally Kane were not living, it would be another matter. It has long been recognized that heirs or testamentary beneficiaries of a person deceased can maintain a suit in equity to set aside a transaction accomplished during the decedent's lifetime where it is contended that it was the product of undue influence or that it came about as the result of a violation for a confidential relationship, and where the effect has been to disinherit an heir or legatee. McKnatt v. McKnatt, Del.Ch., 93 A. 367 (1915).

But where a person has been caused to part with his property under such circumstances, and that person is still living, it is he * * * who has the cause of action to get it back, and the necessary corollary of that right is that the person who has obtained the property through undue influence * * * has no right to retain it. Swain v. Moore, Del.Ch., 71 A.2d 264 (1950). It would seem to follow that if the person who thus wrongfully acquired such property has no right to retain it against the party thus victimized, then there should be no equitable right in a third person to seek an accounting, a surcharge, or the imposition of a constructive trust against the wrongdoer for a claimed share of that which the wrongdoer has no right to retain. * * *

[I]t is the duty of a court of equity to protect an aged, infirm or dependent person from imposition. * * * To grant to the plaintiff the equitable relief that she is seeking here would run contrary to that duty since it would be to ignore the rights of the party who, in theory, is in need of the Court's protection.

Accordingly, as alleged, I hold that the complaint alleges no cause of action in the plaintiff against the defendant as to which such equitable relief can be granted during the lifetime of Sally Kane.

I pass no judgment on whether or not plaintiff may have a present cause of action, in tort, for the recovery of money damages against her brother for his alleged tortious interference with her expectation of receiving an inheritance from her mother. * * *

Notes

1. Plaintiff appealed to the Supreme Court of Delaware. Chambers v. Kane, 437 A.2d 163, 164–65 (Del.1981):

"First, to the extent that plaintiff seeks an independent or personal judgment against her brother on the basis of the allegations in the complaint, we are satisfied that the Vice Chancellor made the correct ruling and, to that extent, the judgment will be affirmed.

"Second, to the extent that plaintiff seeks relief for the benefit of Sally Kane (who is now a party) or the residuary trust created under John Kane's will, tested by the familiar rule governing notice pleadings, Klein v. Sunbeam Corp., Del.Supr., 94 A.2d 385, 391 (1952), the judgment will be reversed. In our view, the allegations that Mrs. Kane is seventy-five years of age, that she is in poor physical health, that she is partially paralyzed by a stroke, that she is unable to manage her assets and that defendant has wasted her assets for his own benefit, brings the complaint within the provisions of 12 Del.C. § 3914(a) [guardianship statute]. This aspect of the second count of the complaint, that is, any attempt to recover for the benefit of the residuary trust for Mrs. Kane or for her estate, depends initially, of course, on whether she is and has been competent and able to manage her own affairs during the period in issue. If she has been competent, that may end this phase of the lawsuit. And if the litigation continues, it seems to us that that should be the first inquiry made by the Trial Court.

"Affirmed in part, reversed in part and remanded for proceedings consistent herewith."

2. A "beneficiary" who wrongfully induces an intestate to make a will clearly diverts the estate from the person who would otherwise have received it. A constructive trust is routinely imposed. See Restatement (Second) of Torts § 774B (1979); Restatement of Restitution § 184 (1937).

3. If a will naming the defendant as beneficiary exists, and the defendant by coercion or otherwise prevents testator from revoking the will *and naming the plaintiff as the beneficiary,* the diversion is less clear. Is it certain that if the will had been revoked, the testator (now dead) would have (1) executed a new will that (2) named the plaintiff as beneficiary? The testator had no legal obligation to do so. Nevertheless the cases uniformly hold the named beneficiary a constructive trustee for the supposedly intended devisee or legatee. See § 184 comment i of the Restatement of Restitution (1937) and Latham v. Father Divine, 299 N.Y. 22, 26, 85 N.E.2d 168, 169 (1949), reh'g denied, 299 N.Y. 599, 86 N.E.2d 114 (1949).

Suppose the decedent had named plaintiff as beneficiary, but the heir wrongfully induced the revocation of the will so that the decedent dies intestate? Cf. Nemeth v. Banhalmi, 99 Ill.App.3d 493, 425 N.E.2d 1187 (1981).

4. *Damage Actions for Intentional Interference with Expected Inheritances or Bequests.* Suppose a defendant who is not an heir, devisee, or legatee prevents a testator from adding a codicil to a will which would have left $500,000 to the plaintiff. Does plaintiff have a cause of action at all? Lowe Foundation v. Northern Trust Co., 342 Ill.App. 379, 96 N.E.2d 831, 834 (1951), indicates a conflict of decisions. Sections 774B and 912 comment f, Restatement (Second) of Torts (1977), suggest that the one prevented from receiving an inheritance or gift does have a cause of action for damages.

Skip

BELL v. SMITH

Supreme Court of Florida, 1947.
159 Fla. 817, 32 So.2d 829.

BUFORD, JUSTICE. * * * [A tax authority assigned unpaid tax certificates to Kurtz, a trustee for bondholders.]

Thereupon Kurtz formulated a practice and policy of permitting the land owners in the district, owing delinquent taxes, to redeem their respective lands at a greatly reduced amount below the face value of the certificates and subsequent taxes, but would not let or permit any other person to purchase or redeem such delinquent certificates and taxes below the full face value thereof. In furtherance of this policy and to speedily liquidate such delinquent taxes, Kurtz made it well known to such delinquent land owners that he had adopted said policy. * * * [T]he bill of complaint sets forth the history of the dealing of Kurtz with the defendants, Walter Ashton Smith and Fort Myers Land Company * * * and alleges that defendants

> "did then and there fraudulently and with the intention of deceiving the said Kurtz and to circumvent and avoid said policy and practice, and with fraudulent intention to deprive the complainant of her interest in said land and her right to redeem said taxes under said policy and practice, did represent to said Kurtz that he, the defendant Walter Ashton Smith, was the owner of said land, or the owner of a part of the stock in Haviland Investment Company,

the title holder thereof, and that * * * the said Kurtz not knowing that the said Walter Ashton Smith did not own any interest in said lands and was not a stockholder in Haviland Investment Company and did not represent the owners of said land * * * did then and there sell, assign and transfer said certificates and subsequent taxes to the defendant, Fort Myers Land Company, as he was so instructed by the defendant Walter Ashton Smith, in a strict accordance with said policy and practice, in regard to owners of lands, at and for the sum of $210.00, which was about ten per cent of the face amount of said certificates and subsequent taxes."

The complainant, by her bill of complaint, offered to pay to the defendants such amount as may be found due them on an accounting being had by the court. The bill of complaint further, in effect, alleges that the defendants Walter Ashton Smith and Fort Myers Land Company made applications to the defendant D.T. Farabee, as Clerk of the Circuit Court of Lee County, Florida, for a tax deed based on the tax certificate issued on August 2, 1926, and that a tax sale would be held by the said Clerk on September 2, 1946, unless said defendant Clerk be enjoined from making such sale; that said certificate is more than 20 years old and barred by the statutes of limitation of the State of Florida; that the issuance of a tax deed thereon would make a cloud on the title of the complainant; and that the certificates and taxes purchased by the defendants as aforesaid cast a cloud on the title of the complainant unless the same are redeemed, all of which the complainant is willing to do under the terms of said policy of the purchase by land owners.

The bill of complaint prayed that the defendants Walter Ashton Smith and Fort Myers Land Company be decreed to hold the tax certificates and subsequent taxes as trustees in trust for the complainant; that an accounting be had to determine the amount owing the defendants by the complainant on such accounting and upon the payment of such amount that the certificates and taxes be cancelled and the title to the lands be quieted in the complainant. * * *

The defendants, Walter Ashton Smith and Fort Myers Land Company, filed a motion to dismiss the bill of complaint and for grounds said that the bill contained no grounds for equitable relief * * * and that no fraud is shown to have been committed on the complainant, the court or any officer of the court.

The court sustained the motion to dismiss the bill of complaint as amended; the complainant refusing to amend further the order of court dismissed the bill of complaint as amended.

From which ruling dismissing the bill of complaint the complainant appealed and assigned such ruling as error.

Therefore, we see that the question for our determination is: Where one falsely represents to a third party that he is the owner or represents the owner, of the land on which such third party holds tax sale certificates, and thereby procures an assignment of such tax certificates to himself at a price which would be accepted from only the owner of the lands and when owner of the lands learns of the transaction she tenders to the assignee of the certificates the amount which he paid for same, does such assignee thereafter hold the certificates in trust for the benefit of the true owner of the land?

The answer is, yes!

It is a well recognized legal maxim that for every wrong there is a remedy, and it therefore follows that where one by fraud and deception has procured property or a thing of value, equity and good conscience require that he who commits such fraud shall be required to account to the person or persons whom his wrong had injured and that he may not hold the property so acquired and be enriched thereby to the detriment of those who have been deprived of a substantial right as a result of his fraudulent act or misrepresentation. Under such conditions a constructive trust may be imposed on the fraudulent actor in favor of the person or persons who have thereby been deprived of the advantage which but for his act would have accrued to them. Especially is this true where, as in this case, the person suffering from the result of the wrongful act, upon the learning of the perpetration of such act in good faith offers to repay to the fraudulent actor such money or value which he has expended in the transaction. * * *

Scott on Trusts, 3rd Vol. Sec. 471, Wrong by Transferee to Third Person:

> "Where a person acquires property from another by fraud and thereby prevents the other from transferring the property to a third person as he would have done but for the fraud, a constructive trust may be imposed upon the fraudulent person in favor of the third person."

In Sec. 471.2 of 3 Scott on Trusts:

> "There are other situations in which it has been held that where the intention of the owner of property to make a gift to one person has been frustrated by the fraud or other wrongful conduct of another, the fraudulent person is chargeable as a constructive trustee for the intended donee. Thus it has been held that where the defendant, discovering a defect in the plaintiff's title to land, obtained a conveyance of the land for a small sum from the plaintiff's grantor by fraudulently representing that he was acting in behalf of the plaintiff and that his purpose was to cure the defect in the title, the defendant is chargeable as constructive trustee for the plaintiff of the interest so acquired. Rollins v. Mitchell, 52 Minn. 41, 53 N.W. 1020. * * * The underlying principle in all these cases is that where a person acquires property by fraud he can be compelled to surrender the property to the person who would have had it but for the fraud."

A search yielded no Florida cases on this point, but cases outside of the jurisdiction, on facts somewhat similar, indicate that a constructive trust will arise under the circumstances of the proposition before us.

> "Where a complaint states that the holder of a sheriff's certificate of sale of real estate by fraud and false promises prevented the owner from redeeming within the statutory period, and, in violation of his oral agreement to extend the period of redemption, took a sheriff's deed, such facts entitle the aggrieved party to relief in equity." Prondzinski v. Garbutt, 8 N.D. 191, 77 N.W. 1012.

Further, in the syllabus of this case, it was said:

> "A grantee obtained a conveyance in his own name by falsely representing to the grantor that the conveyance was made for the benefit of a third person, who was in possession of the premises, and the grantor was induced to make the conveyance because of his belief that he was thereby curing defects in former conveyances to the third person. The grantee paid the purchase money out of his own funds. Held, that the grantee was a trustee ex maleficio for the benefit of the third person." Virginia Pocahontas Coal Co. v. Lambert, 107 Va. 368, 58 S.E. 561.

The last cited case seems to constitute sufficient ground on which to hold a constructive trust here. In this last cited case a constructive trust was allowed even though the court would not hold that the conveyance belonged to the third person on theory of ratification of self-appointed agent's act.

So the order dismissing amended bill of complaint is reversed.

Notes

1. Saunders v. Kline, 55 A.D.2d 887, 391 N.Y.S.2d 1 (1977). Defendant received the Albert Lasker Foundation Award, including a $10,000 honorarium, for discovery of a drug useful in treating severe depression. Plaintiff sued for unjust enrichment claiming he first discovered the potential and developed the use of the drug, and that the award to the defendant was the result of misrepresentation. The trial court dismissed. The appellate court reversed, holding that a jury issue had been submitted. A jury later returned a verdict for the plaintiff of $3,333.33.

2. Remedies, particularly damages, for interference with expectancies other than those arising out of contracts, prospective inheritances, or prospective gifts are obviously somewhat murky. Comfort, if not enlightenment, may be found in the Comments to § 774B Restatement (Second) of Torts (1977): "In these noncommercial cases, the possibilities of the different fact situations are so varied and the rules so difficult to state, and the case authority so meager, particularly with respect to the degree of certainty required to show that the plaintiff would have received the benefits in question, that no attempt has been made to cover them."

HARPER v. ADAMETZ

Supreme Court of Errors of Connecticut, 1955.

142 Conn. 218, 113 A.2d 136.

Baldwin, Associate Justice. * * * Joseph B. Tesar was conservator of the estate of his father, William Tesar, an incompetent, who owned eighty acres of land and the buildings thereon in the town of Haddam. The defendant Jere Adametz, a real estate agent, hereinafter referred to as Jere, was acting as agent for the sale of Tesar's property. Jere advertised a portion of it, consisting of five acres and an old colonial house, for $6200, and the advertisement, in a New Haven newspaper, came to the attention of the plaintiff. On December 6, 1948, the plaintiff wrote to Jere expressing an interest in the property advertised. Jere acknowledged this letter on December 8. On December 12, Jere showed the plaintiff the eighty-acre farm and told him that the seller was asking $8500 for it but that the buildings and a smaller acreage could be bought for less. The plaintiff made no offer but showed an interest in purchasing the smaller acreage. On the following day, December 13, Jere wrote to Joseph Tesar, the conservator, stating that he had a client who had offered $6500 cash for the farm (meaning eighty acres) and asked for an immediate reply. On December 15, the attorney for Tesar wrote to Jere stating that Tesar would accept the offer for the entire farm subject to the approval of the Probate Court and asking that a written offer with at least a 10 per cent deposit be sent to him.

The plaintiff visited the property on December 19 and 26, and on one of those dates he made an offer to Jere of $7000 for the entire farm. Jere promised to convey this offer to Tesar, but he did not do so. Instead, he sent his own check for $500 to Tesar on December 29 as a deposit on the purported offer of $6500.

Jere told Fred Mazanek, a relative of the Tesars, that the plaintiff wanted to purchase only a small portion of the acreage and that he, Jere, would like to obtain the rest for his son but that he did not want to lose his commission. He prevailed upon Mazanek and John Hibbard, a friend of the family, to act as a medium for the passing of title to the farm. On or about January 2, 1949, Jere told the plaintiff that his offer had been rejected because Tesar desired to keep a major portion of the farm in the family and that certain relatives of the Tesars wished to buy most of the acreage, but that he, Jere, could arrange for the plaintiff to buy the buildings and part of the land. The plaintiff then made an offer of $6000 for seventeen acres, including the buildings, and Jere accepted the offer. The plaintiff was satisfied with his purchase.

On January 4, Joseph Tesar signed a contract to sell the entire farm of eighty acres to Mazanek and Hibbard for $6500. The sale was approved by the Probate Court, and a conservator's deed dated January 26 was delivered on February 8 to Mazanek and Hibbard. At the same time, on February 8, they executed and delivered a deed for seventeen acres, including the buildings, to the plaintiff, who paid $6000. On March 11, Mazanek and Hibbard conveyed sixty-three acres, the balance of the farm, to the defendant Walter Adametz, Jere's son. Mazanek and Hibbard were mere "go betweens" who paid nothing when they "bought" the farm and received nothing when they "sold" it to the plaintiff and Walter. Walter paid nothing for the sixty-three acres he acquired. Tesar did not know of the plaintiff's offer of $7000 for the entire farm, and the plaintiff did not know that this offer had not been transmitted to Tesar. The representation by Jere to Tesar on December 13 that he had a $6500 offer for the farm was false. At the time he sent his own check for $500 to Tesar on the purported offer of $6500, the only offer he had was the plaintiff's offer of $7000. Jere engineered the transactions herein related to obtain sixty-three acres of the farm for himself and Walter at the price of $500 and at the same time collect a commission of $325 for the sale.

On these facts, the court concluded that Jere was the agent for Tesar and not for the plaintiff, that there was no contract between Tesar and the plaintiff for the purchase of any property other than the buildings and seventeen acres of land, that the plaintiff sustained no loss by reason of any misrepresentation made by Jere, and that therefore the plaintiff had failed to prove actionable fraud.

It is the general rule that in an action at law for fraud the plaintiff, to recover, must prove that he has been injured. * * * In the ordinary case, this means that the plaintiff must sustain a substantial pecuniary loss. [citations] The plaintiff in this action did receive what he paid for. * * * He did not, however, because of Jere's fraud, obtain what he was seeking. While acting as an agent for Tesar but with the intent of making a secret profit for himself, Jere told his principal that he had a cash offer of $6500 for the entire farm. This statement was false, and in making it Jere violated his trust. His conduct was a fraud upon Tesar. * * *

Jere was not the agent of the plaintiff. Nevertheless, he could not deliberately deceive him. It was Jere's advertisement in the newspaper which had aroused the interest of the plaintiff in the property and had brought him to Haddam to inspect it. Jere told the plaintiff at that time that the entire farm was for sale for $8500. When the plaintiff later made an offer of $7000 for it, Jere said nothing about having submitted a bogus offer of $6500, and he promised to submit the plaintiff's offer to Tesar. He failed to do so and later lied to the plaintiff by telling him that Tesar had rejected it. It was not until after this that the plaintiff offered $6000 for seventeen acres and the buildings. It can be claimed that when the plaintiff made his $7000 offer Tesar had already signified his willingness to accept the purported offer of $6500 made by Jere in behalf of a fictitious client and that the plaintiff's offer came too late. But the $6500 offer was a fraud and Tesar was not bound to accept it. He could have revoked Jere's authority. * * * Thereafter, he could have sold the property to the plaintiff. Jere's false statements, his concealment of the facts, his promise to submit the plaintiff's offer to Tesar when everything indicates that he had no intention of doing so, worked a fraud upon the plaintiff. * * * As a result, the plaintiff has been denied the right to have his bona fide offer of $7000 submitted to Tesar. In short, the plaintiff has been deprived of his bargain. Jere and Walter, by their fraud, have acquired sixty-three acres of land for $175.

This is an action in equity as well as at law. Equity is a system of positive jurisprudence founded upon established principles which can be adapted to new circumstances where a court of law is powerless to give relief. [citations] In equity as in law, misrepresentation, to constitute fraud, must be material. [citations] That is to say, the representation must prejudice the party relying upon it. He must suffer some injury of pecuniary loss. Some courts have held that the pecuniary loss need be only slight. [citations] Others have held that mere lack of pecuniary injury or loss does not prevent the granting of relief by way of rescission and restitution. [citations] In Brett v. Cooney, 75 Conn. 338, 53 A. 729, the plaintiffs were induced by a series of false statements to sell their property to a person who in turn conveyed to another whom the plaintiffs had previously rejected as an undesirable purchaser. The plaintiffs suffered no financial loss. However, after citing Barnes v. Starr, 64 Conn. 136, 150, 28 A. 980, which states that proof of injury is a prerequisite to recovery for fraud, the court said: "But in measuring injury equity does not concern itself merely with money losses. If it finds that a clear right has been invaded, and that redress can be secured by putting the parties back in their original position, it will seldom refuse its aid because the plaintiff can show no substantial damage to his pecuniary interests." * * *

The plaintiff had a clear right to have his offer for the farm transmitted to Tesar. Having been invited by Jere's advertisement to bid for the property, he had a right to assume that Jere would deal honestly with him and be faithful to his principal. Instead, Jere withheld the offer, later lied to the plaintiff about it and, by using the plaintiff's willingness to accept seventeen acres, acquired the farm for himself for less than the plaintiff had offered for it. He induced the plaintiff to make an offer and then used that offer, and the plaintiff's money to make a secret profit. By his fraudulent misrepresentations, he deprived the plaintiff of his bargain and obtained for himself some of the land which the plaintiff had offered to buy. "If one acquires property by means of a fraudulent misrepresentation of a material fact, equity will assist the defrauded person by fastening a constructive trust on the property." It is true that this rule is most often applied in situations where the relationship between the plaintiff and the defendant is one which equity clearly recognizes as fiduciary. But equity has carefully refrained from defining a fiduciary relationship in precise detail and in such a manner as to exclude new situations. It has left the bars down for situations in which there is a justifiable trust confided on one side and a resulting superiority and influence on the other. * * *

Equity will not permit these defendants to keep a benefit which came to them by reason of Jere's fraudulent conduct. It is true that Tesar has not acted to right the wrong done to him. Had he done so, it is probable that the plaintiff could have had the farm. This should not prevent the plaintiff, in his own right, from having a remedy for the wrong done to him. The plaintiff has proffered $1000, which represents the balance of the amount of his original offer over and above the purchase price he paid for the seventeen acres. Upon the payment of this sum into court, to await further order, an order should enter directing the defendant Walter to convey the sixty-three acres to the plaintiff.

There is error, the judgment is set aside and the case is remanded to the Superior Court for proceedings in accordance with this opinion.

O'SULLIVAN, ASSOCIATE JUSTICE (dissenting). The case suggests two possible theories for claiming actionable fraud on the part of Jere Adametz, hereinafter called the defendant. The first is based on his failure to disclose to the plaintiff that he had bought the Tesar farm, and the second on certain fraudulent representations made by him to the plaintiff. In other words, the one rests on his silence, the other on what he said. Neither theory, it seems to me has any merit.

As indicated, the first theory is based on the fact that, while holding himself out as Tesar's agent, the defendant purchased the farm and thereafter sold to the plaintiff, through two dummies, seventeen of the eighty acres without revealing to the plaintiff the true nature of the entire transaction and the furtive steps which he, the defendant, had taken in acquiring the land for his son. Our law is clear that, under the circumstances found by the court to have prevailed, no duty was imposed upon the defendant to refrain from buying the farm himself or to disclose that he had done so, as long as he was not acting at the time as agent for, or did not occupy a confidential relationship towards, the plaintiff. Kurtz v. Farrington, 104 Conn. 257, 265, 132 A. 540, 48 A.L.R. 259. Since the plaintiff concedes that the defendant was not his agent and since the facts do not admit of the existence of any confidential relationship between the parties, neither the defendant's conduct nor his silence about it presents an instance of actionable fraud.

The second theory is grounded on certain representations, fraudulently made by the defendant, to the effect that he had submitted to Tesar the plaintiff's offer to pay $7,000 for the entire farm and that Tesar, while rejecting that offer, had authorized the defendant to sell to the plaintiff for $6,000 the seventeen acres upon which stood the house and the other buildings. To recover on the basis of these obviously false representations, the plaintiff had to establish (1) that they were made as statements of fact, (2) that they were untrue and known by the defendant to be untrue, (3) that they were made for the purpose of inducing the plaintiff to act upon them, (4) that the plaintiff was in fact induced to act upon them and (5) that in so acting he was legally injured. * * * All the foregoing essentials must be proven, and the absence of any one of them is fatal to recovery. * * *

It is to be noted that the plaintiff, as a result of the representations, took no positive act respecting the remaining sixty-three acres. It is, of course, true that fraudulent representations may be actionable even in the absence of a positive act, since fraud inducing inaction can be as culpable as fraud which prompts action. * * * Thus, recovery was permitted where the representations caused the plaintiff to refrain from perfecting an inchoate lien, or from rescinding a contract, or from selling his property, or from putting his merchandise on the market. Cases such as those cited, however, give no comfort to the plaintiff since his failure to act did not affect any property interest owned by him. The law does not appear to subject a defendant to legal culpability for fraudulent representations in those instances where the person, induced to inaction, sustains no damage to his property interests or rights. Such instances would be those of injuria absque damno. * * *

But even if the law were otherwise, the plaintiff would not be advantaged. * * * Since the finding does not disclose that the sixty-three acres are worth over $1,000, the plaintiff has failed to establish any pecuniary loss whatsoever.

For the reasons stated above, I must disagree with my colleagues.

Note

Blake Construction Co. v. American Vocational Association, Inc., 419 F.2d 308, 310–11, 313 (D.C.Cir.1969). "In 1964, Blake entered into a contract with the United States, acting through GSA, for the construction of two buildings in the District of Columbia. * * * During the course of excavating, AVA complained that defects were developing in its building, which was located on land adjacent to the construction site. GSA investigated and found extensive damage to AVA's building and to an adjoining building owned by Riggs. GSA concluded that the damage resulted from improper performance of the construction contract and gave notice to that effect to Blake. So great was the damage to AVA's building that it had to be razed, and the common wall between it and Riggs' building had to be replaced.

"After lengthy negotiations, GSA reached agreements with AVA and Riggs to settle their damage claims for $485,539.89 and $71,687.65, respectively. GSA paid these sums and withheld the aggregate as an offset against payments otherwise due Blake under the construction contract. Blake has long challenged GSA's authority to unilaterally settle and set off these claims, arguing that AVA and Riggs could not legally have asserted them against either GSA or Blake.

"Blake then brought its action against AVA and Riggs, omitting both GSA and the United States as parties. As to AVA and Riggs, the complaint sought a declaratory judgment determining the rights and liabilities of the parties, and the imposition of a trust on the settlement funds. * * *

[Judgment for defendant affirmed.]

"The monies GSA paid to AVA and Riggs came, not from Blake, but from the United States. If, as Blake charges, GSA made the payments without lawful authority to do so, or under a misapprehension as to Blake's responsibility for the property damage, the United States, and not Blake, would be entitled to restitution. By the same token, AVA and Riggs would be constructive trustees, not for Blake, but rather for the United States. * * *

"Blake has available its remedy by suit in the Court of Claims for vindication of its contractual rights against the United States."

3. PATENT INFRINGEMENT

Introductory Note

"Commercial piracy" is an apt expression. Operating on the illimitable sea of trade is a recognizable type of predator whose method of operation includes sailing under false colors, surreptitious boardings, casting nets in someone else's waters, and filching a free tow behind someone else's ship. The nautical metaphor need be stretched no further.

This section examines tortious trade practices consisting basically of infringement and imitation. The substantive nature of the wrong is not uniformly agreed upon, and the remedial possibilities are thereby directly affected. In one sense the defendant has simply damaged the plaintiff's business; in another he has misappropriated an intangible value—"property," if you will—created by the plaintiff's labor; in still another he has diverted customers who otherwise would have patronized the plaintiff. The statutory "awards" for infringement of patents and copyrights reflect these variant views as to the nature of the wrong. Where the patentee or copyright holder is actively exploiting his statutory monopoly, the infringer is clearly diverting trade; the appropriate remedy is an equitable accounting for the benefits received. But a patentee, in particular, may hold a patented product off the market for various reasons, such as to protect a heavy investment in an earlier generation of the same model. Infringement here may indicate compensatory damages.

Finally, however, it is difficult to escape the notion that a patent or copyright is a "property" right. We say that it is "owned," that it may be "sold." Yet it cannot be "converted" or "stolen." At best the infringer may be regarded as having misappropriated the plaintiff's exclusive right of use. "Misappropriation" is enough, however, to suggest a quasi-contractual measure of recovery as an appropriate alternative.

Cases concerning patents and copyrights are therefore included for two reasons: (1) to analyze the elements of the award in terms of damages and legal or equitable restitution, and (2) because the nonstatutory cases involving protection of trade secrets, ideas, trade marks, names, etc., fashion remedies by open analogy to the patent and copyright statute.

Note

THE PATENT ACT, 35 U.S.C.

§ 283. Injunction. The several courts having jurisdiction of cases under this title may grant injunctions in accordance with the principles of equity to prevent the violation of any right secured by patent, on such terms as the court deems reasonable.

§ 284. Damages. Upon finding for the claimant the court shall award the claimant damages adequate to compensate for the infringement, but in no event less than a reasonable royalty for the use made of the invention by the infringer, together with interest and costs as fixed by the court.

When the damages are not found by a jury, the court shall assess them. In either event the court may increase the damages up to three times the amount found or assessed.

The court may receive expert testimony as an aid to the determination of damages or of what royalty would be reasonable under the circumstances.

a. Damages

DEL MAR AVIONICS, INC. v. QUINTON INSTRUMENT CO.

United States Court of Appeals, Federal Circuit 1987.
836 F.2d 1320.

PAULINE NEWMAN, CIRCUIT JUDGE. Quinton Instrument Company ("Quinton") appeals the judgment of the United States District Court for the Western District of Washington * * * [T]he court held that Quinton had infringed U.S. Patent No. 3,267,934 entitled "Electrocardiac Computer", invented by William Thornton (the " '934 patent") and owned by Del Mar Avionics ("Del Mar"). A 5% royalty, which was doubled based on the court's finding of willful infringement, was awarded to Del Mar as damages. Prejudgment interest and attorney fees were also awarded.

Del Mar cross-appeals on the measure of damages.

We affirm the judgment in all respects except for the measure of damages. The damage award is vacated, and remanded for reassessment.

[Editors' Note: Plaintiff manufactured equipment for the electronic detection of heart abnormalities by processing ECG signals picked up by wiring the patient to a machine. The ECG signal includes pulses known as the "QRS complex." The special virtue of the Thornton invention lies in its ability to detect what is called the "ST segment" of the QRS complex of pulses. The infringement has been established in prior litigation.

[Lest this attempted editorial summary place an undue stress on the reader's own cardiovascular system, let us emphasize the point: the infringement pertains to but one part of a system to detect heart stress. As the court states, "The ST segment computer was sold by [plaintiff] as an option that could only be used in the [plaintiff's] stress test equipment that was built to hold it."]

* * * The district court stated that it was unable to determine Del Mar's lost profits:

> "Although there can be no doubt that plaintiff lost sales of its own ST segment computer because defendant was offering and selling its competing device, the Court is unable to determine by a preponderance of the evidence either the number of sales which were probably lost by plaintiff by reason of defendant's infringing sales or the loss in net profits suffered by plaintiff by reason of those lost sales. Both the loss in sales and the loss of net profits depend upon so many variables and so many indeterminate factors that the Court finds that it is unable to award damages to plaintiff based upon the net profits allegedly lost by it."

Therefore, the court concluded, "the most appropriate basis for the award of damages" was a royalty at the rate of 5% of the gross selling price of Quinton's infringing ST segment computer.

The court set the royalty at that which it concluded would have been acceptable to a prudent and willing licensor and licensee, although the court found that Del Mar was not a willing licensor:

> "Plaintiff was not in the practice of licensing its ST segment computer to anyone else and would not voluntarily have licensed. Its desire and intent was to be the exclusive producer and seller of the ST segment computer. Given a

choice it would have greatly preferred to retain its patent monopoly on its ST segment computer."

Del Mar asserts that the district court erred in not awarding damages measured by its lost profits, which Del Mar argues had been demonstrated adequately and accurately.

The statutory instruction for awarding damages for patent infringement is that the award must be "adequate to compensate for the infringement." 35 U.S.C. § 284. The Supreme Court discussed compliance with this standard in Aro Manufacturing Co. v. Convertible Top Co., 377 U.S. 476, 507 (1964):

> "The question to be asked in determining damages is 'how much had the Patent Holder and Licensee suffered by the infringement. And that question [is] primarily: had the Infringer not infringed, what would Patent Holder–Licensee have made?' "

The general rule for determining the actual damages to a patentee that is itself producing the patented item, is to determine the sales and profits lost to the patentee because of the infringement. Although the statute states that the damage award shall not be "less than a reasonable royalty," 35 U.S.C. § 284, the purpose of this alternative is not to provide a simple accounting method, but to set a floor below which the courts are not authorized to go. [citation]

In order to recover lost profits a patentee must show a reasonable probability that, but for the infringement, it would have made the sales that were made by the infringer. Del Mar presented evidence, generally uncontroverted, showing the demand for the product, the absence of acceptable noninfringing substitutes, and its ability to meet the demand. The patentee is not obliged to negate every possibility that a purchaser might not have bought the patentee's product instead of the infringing one, or might have foregone the purchase altogether. Paper Converting Machine Co. v. Magna–Graphics Corp., 745 F.2d 11, 21 (Fed.Cir.1984). The patent owner's burden of proof is not an absolute one, Lam, Inc. v. Johns–Manville Corp., 718 F.2d 1056, 1065 (Fed.Cir.1983), although liability does not extend to speculative profits. [citations]

When the patent owner and infringers were the only suppliers of the patented product, it is reasonable to infer that the patent owner would have made the sales made by the infringers. *Lam, Inc.* In its brief, Del Mar estimates its pro rata share of Quinton's sales based on the one or two (depending on the year) other suppliers who were also accused infringers. When the amount of the damages is not ascertainable with precision, reasonable doubt is appropriately resolved against the infringer.

The requirement to determine actual damages is not diminished by difficulty of determination. Although some calculations in some cases might present undue obstacles, we agree with Del Mar that such is not here the case. For example, the district court's Finding 42 as to the number and selling price of the accused models is not challenged by Quinton:

> 42. The following number of units of the Type A and B circuits were manufactured by defendant in the year indicated:

Year	Model 730	Model 740	Model 741
1971	36	19	—
1975	59	46	—
1976	66	50	—

Year	Model 730	Model 740	Model 741
1977	50	21	35
1978	55	8	101

The determination of a damage award is not an exact science, King Instrument Corp. v. Otari Corp., 767 F.2d 853, 863 (Fed.Cir.1985), cert. denied, 475 U.S. 1016 (1986), and "the amount need not be proven with unerring precision." *Bio-Rad Laboratories Inc. v. Nicolet Instrument Corp.*, 739 F.2d 604, 616 (Fed.Cir.1984). The trial court is required to approximate, if necessary, the amount to which the patent owner is entitled. "In such case, while the damages may not be determined by mere speculation or guess, it will be enough if the evidence show the extent of the damages as a matter of just and reasonable inference, although the result be only approximate." Story Parchment Co. v. Paterson Parchment Paper Co., 282 U.S. 555, 563 (1931).

Del Mar argues that computation of its lost profits should be based on the entire market value of the stress test machine, explaining that the ST segment computer was sold by it as an option that could only be used in the Del Mar stress test equipment that was built to hold it. Del Mar thus argues that it also lost sales (and profits) on its stress test line. We have held that in appropriate circumstances the patentee may prove the extent of its lost profits by the "entire market value rule," *Paper Converting Machine Co.*, based on a showing that the patentee could reasonably anticipate the sale of the unpatented components together with the patented components. * * * Other factors, such as development costs and business risks, may be taken into account if the circumstances warrant. Bendix Corp. v. United States, 676 F.2d 606, 615, 230 Ct.Cl. 247 (1982). Del Mar also offered a computation of its lost profits using an incremental income analysis such as was recognized in *Paper Converting Machine Co.* Although it appears that Quinton presented opposing evidence and argument on these points, the district court made no express findings thereon. Upon remand, it will be appropriate for the court to consider all factors reasonably pertinent to a determination of damages that bear a reasonable relationship to the damages actually suffered by the patent owner.

Del Mar states that the 5% royalty is not only an inappropriate measure of actual damages, but that if damages are to be measured by a royalty, a higher rate is required. Del Mar states that it presented evidence of an actual royalty of $400 per unit, paid for a similar optional component, between a willing licensor and licensee; this figure, substantially higher than that adopted by the court, appears to have been the only evidence of royalty practices in the industry.

The approach taken by the district court is suited to circumstances where there is an established royalty or licensing program, or if the patentee is not itself in the business, or if profits are too speculative to estimate. [citation] None of those situations here prevailed.

The principle underlying damage measurement is unchanged even when there is an established royalty, for it is reasonable to assume that this royalty is a fair measure of the actual damage to a patentee who has authorized others to practice the patented invention. In this case, we have been directed to no evidence of record in support of the 5% royalty here assessed. It was not an established royalty, and was not found by the district court or shown by Quinton to be an approximation of the damages actually sustained. Its imposition on a patent owner who would not have licensed his invention for this royalty is a form of compulsory license, against the will and interest of the person wronged, in favor of the wrongdoer. See Albemarle Paper Co. v. Moody, 422 U.S. 405, 418–19 (1975) (quoting Wicker v. Hoppock, 73 U.S. (6 Wall.) 94, 99 (1867)):

> [t]he general rule is, that when a wrong has been done, and the law gives a remedy, the compensation shall be equal to the injury. The latter is the standard by which the former is to be measured. The injured party is to be placed, as near as may be, in the situation he would have occupied if the wrong had not been committed.

We conclude that the district court erred in assessing damages, in the circumstances here shown, because, as the court stated, it gave controlling weight to the difficulty of the calculation, and in so doing adopted a measure of damages that was not designed to make whole the injured party.

We vacate the damages measured as a 5% royalty, and remand for determination of damages based on the patentee's lost profits.

The district court found that from Del Mar's first notice of infringement to its third notice letter more than five months later, Quinton did not consult an attorney regarding the charge. The court found that before Del Mar's suit Quinton did not procure a patent search, and that Quinton continued to manufacture and sell infringing devices even after commencement of suit. The court held that Quinton had "acted in wilful and conscious disregard of [Del Mar's] rights", and doubled the damages.

Del Mar contends that the district court insufficiently multiplied damages as authorized in 35 U.S.C. § 284, and that anything less than a trebled damage award constitutes an abuse of the court's discretion in view of Quinton's actions. Quinton argues that the district court was clearly in error in even doubling the damage award because "Quinton was advised by the patent counsel that the claims of the patent were either invalid and/or not infringed" after suit was filed, and because the presidents of Del Mar and Quinton met prior to the filing of suit in an attempt to resolve the issue.

In *Kori Corp.,* 761 F.2d at 656–57, the finding of willful infringement was based on the defendant's failure to establish good faith reliance on an authoritative opinion of invalidity before starting to manufacture the infringing units. This court saw no abuse of discretion in the doubling of that damage award. As we discussed in Rite–Hite Corp. v. Kelley Co., Inc., 819 F.2d 1120, 1125 (Fed.Cir.1987), "[t]he weight that may fairly be placed on the presence or absence of an exculpatory opinion of counsel has varied with the circumstances of each case, and has not been amenable to development of a rigorous rule."

Neither Quinton nor Del Mar has shown that the district court abused its discretion in doubling the damage award. A trial court's exercise of discretion in such circumstances is "informed by the court's familiarity with the matter in litigation and the interest of justice." S.C. Johnson & Son, Inc. v. Carter–Wallace, Inc., 781 F.2d 198, 201 (Fed.Cir.1986).

No clear error in the finding of willful infringement has been shown. The doubling of damages, and the refusal to triple them, are not unreasonable in the circumstances shown, and are sustained.

Holding that this was an exceptional case in terms of 35 U.S.C. § 285, the court awarded attorney fees and costs to Del Mar.

The finding of willful infringement is legally sufficient to meet the criterion of "exceptional case," and in such case it is within the court's discretionary authority to award attorney fees. That discretion has not been shown to have been abused, and accordingly the award is affirmed. * * *

Affirmed in part, vacated in part and remanded.

Notes

1. *Reasonable Royalty.* Fromson v. Western Litho Plate and Supply Co., 853 F.2d 1568, 1574–76 (Fed.Cir.1988):

"The statute, 35 U.S.C. § 284, mandates that damages shall be 'adequate to compensate' the patent owner for the infringement. * * * The patent owner bears the burden of proof on damages. When the evidence is inadequate to establish actual or nearly actual damages, a court may under Section 284 employ a 'reasonable royalty' as the floor below which a damage award may not fall. As used in Section 284, 'reasonable royalty' is handy shorthand for damages. As the statute provides, the royalty is 'for the use made of the invention by the infringer.' Thus the calculation is not a mere academic exercise in setting some percentage figure as a 'royalty.' The determination remains one of *damages* to the injured party.

"Determining a fair and reasonable royalty is often, as it was here, a difficult judicial chore, seeming often to involve more the talents of a conjurer than those of a judge. Lacking adequate evidence of an established royalty, the court was left with the judge-created methodology described as 'hypothetical negotiations between willing licensor and willing licensee.'

"Historically, the methodology has been problematic as a mechanism for doing justice to individual, non-manufacturing patentees. Because courts routinely denied injunctions to such patentees, infringers could perceive nothing to fear but the possibility of a compulsory license at a reasonable royalty, resulting in some quarters in a lowered respect for the rights of such patentees and a failure to recognize the innovation-encouraging social purpose of the patent system.

"Thus a cold, 'bottom line' logic would dictate to some a total disregard of the individual inventor's patent because: (1) ill-financed, he probably would not sue; (2) cost of counsel's opinion could await suit; (3) the patent may well be held invalid on one of many possible bases; (4) infringement may not be proven; (5) if the case be lost, a license can be compelled, probably at the same royalty that would have been paid if the patentee's rights had been respected at the outset. Though the methodology must on occasion be used for want of a better, it must be carefully applied to achieve a truly reasonable royalty, for the methodology risks creation of the perception that blatant, blind appropriation of inventions patented by individual, non-manufacturing inventors is the profitable, can't-lose course.

"The patent system encourages inventors to invent and disclose. Corporations don't invent; people do. Yet, the patent system also encourages corporations and investors to risk investment in research, development, and marketing without which the public could not gain the full benefit of the patent system. The right to exclude conferred by a valid patent thus deserves the same respect when that right is in the hands of an individual as when it is in the hands of a corporation. In applying the methodology, emphasis on an individual inventor's lack of money and manufacturing capacity can tend to distinguish the respect due the patent rights of impecunious individual inventors from that due the patent rights of well-funded, well-lawyered, large manufacturing corporations. Any such distinction should be rejected as the disservice it is to the public interest in technological advancement.

That 'survival of the fittest' jungle mentality was intended to be replaced, not served, by the law.

"Like all methodologies based on a hypothetical, there will be an element of uncertainty; yet, a court is not at liberty, in conducting the methodology, to abandon entirely the statutory standard of damages 'adequate to compensate' for the infringement. The royalty arrived at must be 'reasonable' under all the circumstances; i.e., it must be at least a close approximation of what would be 'adequate to compensate' for the 'use made of the invention by the infringer.' 35 U.S.C. § 284.

"The methodology encompasses fantasy and flexibility; fantasy because it requires a court to imagine what warring parties would have agreed to as willing negotiators; flexibility because it speaks of negotiations as of the time infringement began, yet permits and often requires a court to look to events and facts that occurred thereafter and that could not have been known to or predicted by the hypothesized negotiators. * * *

"As has been said by the Supreme Court: 'An imaginary bid by an imaginary buyer, acting upon the information available at the moment of the breach, is not the limit of recovery where the subject of the bargain is an undeveloped patent. Information at such a time might be so scanty and imperfect that the offer would be nominal. The promisee of the patent has less than fair compensation if the criterion of value is the price that he would have received if he had disposed of it at once, irrespective of the value that would have uncovered if he had kept it as his own. Formulas of measurement declared *alio intuitu* may be misleading if wrested from their setting and applied to new conditions.' Sinclair Ref. Co. v. Jenkins Petroleum Co., 289 U.S. 689, 698–99 (1933)."

"Forced to erect a hypothetical, it is easy to forget a basic reality—a license is fundamentally an agreement by the patent owner not to sue the licensee. In a normal negotiation, the potential licensee has three basic choices: forego all use of the invention; pay an agreed royalty; infringe the patent and risk litigation. The methodology presumes that the licensee has made the second choice, when in fact it made the third. Thus Western must be viewed as negotiating for the right to exclude competitors or to compete only with licensed competitors, a landscape far different from that created, post May 1965, by the infringement of Western and others.

"Whatever royalty may result from employment of the methodology, the law is not without means for recognizing that an infringer is unlike a true 'willing' licensee; nor is the law without means for placing the injured patentee 'in the situation he would have occupied if the wrong had not been committed.' Albemarle Paper Co., 422 U.S. 405, 418–19 (1975). Increased damages under § 284 for willfulness is one such means. Attorney fees in 'exceptional' cases under § 285 is another. * * * Prejudgment interest is a third such means."

2. *Interest.* In General Motors Corp. v. Devex Corp., 461 U.S. 648, 656 (1983), the Supreme Court held that interest on patent infringement damages of the reasonable royalty sort should "ordinarily" be calculated to begin on the date(s) defendant infringed. The Court sought to compensate the patentee fully and to prevent a windfall to the infringer because of protracted litigation. The Court also said, however, that trial courts could withhold or limit prejudgment interest, for example "where the patent owner has been responsible for undue delay in prosecuting the lawsuit."

Would denial of prejudgment interest treat an infringer better than a company that had obtained a license to make or use the patent and paid a royalty to the patentee?

3. *"Entire Market Value" Rule of Damages for Patent Infringement.* Paper Converting Machine Co. v. FMC Corp., 432 F.Supp. 907, 913 (E.D.Wis.1977), aff'd, 588 F.2d 832 (7th Cir.1978).

Plaintiff held a patent on a device for perforating toilet paper which was marketed by it in combination with a rewinding machine of its own manufacture:

"The master relied on the long-standing 'entire market value' rule which allows recovery based on the value of an entire mechanism containing several features, even though only one feature is patented, where substantially the entire marketable value of the total mechanism is attributable to the patented feature. [citations]. * * *

"The defendant's legal contention is that the 'patent misuse' doctrine which was developed subsequently to the entire market value rule, and which prohibits a patentee from extending its patent monopoly to unpatented elements, as for example, through a tie-in license, has done away with entire market value rule. [citations] I am unpersuaded that these cases have overturned the entire market value rule; I believe that the defendant has misconstrued the nature and purpose of that rule.

"The entire market value rule does not allow a patentee to over-extend its patent monopoly, but merely permits a recognition of the actual economic value of the patent under the unusual circumstances in which market conditions themselves would prevent an unlicensed and noninfringing seller from making sales in the market for the entire machine, even though only one or more elements are patented. The master's finding that inclusion of the plaintiff's patented perforator in rewinders was a prerequisite to their marketability simply reflects the market conditions that made the value of the entire rewinder properly attributable to the perforator alone."

b. Injunctions

ATLAS POWDER CO. v. IRECO CHEMICALS

United States Court of Appeals, Federal Circuit, 1985.
773 F.2d 1230.

RICH, CIRCUIT JUDGE. [Plaintiff holds a patent on a blasting compound. In a separate lawsuit plaintiff sued E.I. duPont de Nemours & Co.; that court upheld the validity of plaintiff's patent and found infringement. The instant suit was pending in a federal district court awaiting the outcome of the *duPont* appeal. When *duPont* was decided, the trial court issued a preliminary injunction and defendant appealed.]

Ireco argues that the district court's decision granting the preliminary injunction should be reversed because Atlas failed to meet the necessary requirements for a preliminary injunction. More specifically, Ireco argues that the injunction: (1) does not maintain the status quo; (2) is causing devastating, irreparable injury to Ireco; and (3) is based on a misapplication of the alleged "presumption" of irreparable harm. Ireco further argues that Atlas has not established likelihood of success on the merits concerning validity, infringement, and enforceability of the Bluhm patent in suit.

Ireco argues:

"In Litton Industries [Systems], Inc. v. Sundstrand, Inc. [sic, Corp.], 750 F.2d 952, 961 (Fed.Cir.1984), this court stated that the purpose of a preliminary injunction is to preserve 'that state of affairs existing immediately before the filing of the litigation, the last uncontested status which preceded the pending controversy.'

"Here the injunction does not preserve the state of affairs existing in early 1984, [Complaint filed January 1984] before the filing of the litigation, but returns the state of affairs to that existing in 1979, [when Ireco commenced manufacturing water-in-oil emulsion explosives] over *four years prior* to the filing of the litigation. The status quo is not preserved; it is completely changed, and that is error."

Ireco would have us maintain the status quo by allowing it to continue the alleged infringements at the rate they occurred when the suit was filed, even though the assessment of likelihood of success had shown that such acts would probably be held unlawful. Such a proposition is its own refutation and no other is necessary. The argument, for which no relevant authority is cited, is a prime example of the misuse of short quotations taken out of context to establish law in different contexts. * * * [A]uthorizing the wrongdoer to continue the wrong, only not at an increased rate, is in no realistic sense maintaining the status quo. * * *

The district court in its conclusions of law held:

"22. When a holder of a patent has clearly established validity and continuing infringement, irreparable injury will be presumed. [Smith International, Inc. v. Hughes Tool Co., 718 F.2d 1573, 1581 (Fed.Cir.1983).]

"23. * * * Plaintiff has also shown irreparable injury by continued infringement and the resultant loss of business opportunity based on the characteristics of the patented product, substantial loss of profits, inequity to present licensees, and encouragement of infringement by others. A preliminary injunction is also appropriate here because the patent will expire in less than two years."

Ireco argues that the district court improperly applied the presumption of irreparable harm as set forth in *Smith,* in which case the patent-in-suit had previously been adjudged valid in a litigation *between the same parties* and infringement had been admitted. Ireco attempts to distinguish *Smith,* arguing that this court held the patent valid in litigation involving a *different defendant,* DuPont, and that that previous adjudication is insufficient to support Atlas' burden of proof on likelihood of success. Ireco also argues that infringement has not been conceded or proven, and that the patent is unenforceable.

We agree with Ireco that it is not *bound* by the prior adjudication, as under the doctrine of res judicata. But that is not the use made of the prior adjudication. Rather, Atlas is using the prior adjudication as *evidence* supporting its burden of proving a likelihood of success on the merits. * * *

Ireco attempts to further distinguish *Smith* by arguing that the presumption of irreparable injury is not warranted "where there has been no final, binding adjudication of validity." * * * In essence, Ireco is arguing for a rule, said to be followed by various other circuits, that Atlas must prove validity and infringement "beyond question," in order to meet its burden of proof on irreparable harm. [citations]

The burden upon the movant should be no different in a patent case than for other kinds of intellectual property, where, generally, only a "clear showing" is required. [citations] Requiring a "final adjudication," "full trial," or proof "beyond question" would support the issuance of a permanent injunction and nothing would remain to establish the liability of the accused infringer. That is not the situation before us. We are dealing with a provisional remedy which provides equitable *preliminary* relief. Thus, when a patentee "clearly shows" that his patent is valid and infringed, a court may, after a balance of all of the competing equities, preliminarily enjoin another from violating the rights secured by the patent. * * *

Ireco also argues that since all of Atlas's possible damages are compensable in money, there is no irreparable harm to justify a preliminary injunction.

Ireco's arguments that infringement and related damages are fully compensible in money downplay the nature of the statutory right to exclude others from making, using, or selling the patented invention throughout the United States. While monetary relief is often the sole remedy for past infringement, it does not follow that a money award is also the sole remedy against future infringement. The patent statute further provides injunctive relief to preserve the legal interests of the parties *against future infringement* which may have market effects never fully compensable in money. If monetary relief were the sole relief afforded by the patent statute then injunctions would be unnecessary and infringers could become compulsory licensees for as long as the litigation lasts. * * *

Ireco argues that the injunction should not issue because it, as well as the mining industry it serves, will suffer irreparable injury. Ireco alleges that at the time the district court ordered the preliminary injunction its allegedly infringing products accounted for 66% of its total sales. Ireco also claims that it would have to lay off approximately 200 employees, and that all this is unnecessary since the patent expires in June 1986.

Balancing the equities is within the discretion of the district court. It found, on the basis of Atlas's strong showing of validity and infringement, that the injury to Ireco was not sufficient to outweigh the injury to Atlas's patent rights. We are unpersuaded that the district court abused its discretion in this respect.

The fact that the patent has only one year to run is not a factor in favor of Ireco in the balance of equities. Patent rights do not peter out as the end of the patent term, usually 17 years, is approached. * * *

[T]he district court's Order issuing the preliminary injunction is affirmed.

Affirmed.

Note

Henkel Corp. v. Coral, Inc., 754 F.Supp. 1280, 1321 (N.D.Ill.1991): "This presumption of irreparable harm derives in part from the finite term of the patent grant, for patent expiration is not suspended during litigation * * *. The opportunity to practice an invention during the notoriously lengthy course of patent litigation may itself tempt infringers."

4. COPYRIGHT INFRINGEMENT

COPYRIGHT ACT 17 U.S.C. §§ 502, 503, 504, 505, 506

§ 502. Remedies for Infringement: Injunctions

(a) Any court having jurisdiction of a civil action arising under this title may, * * * grant temporary and final injunctions on such terms as it may deem reasonable to prevent or restrain infringement of a copyright. * * *

§ 503. Remedies for Infringement: Impounding and Disposition of Infringing Articles

(a) At any time while an action under this title is pending, the court may order the impounding, on such terms as it may deem reasonable, of all copies or phonorecords claimed to have been made or used in violation of the copyright owner's exclusive rights, and of all * * * articles by means of which such copies or phonorecords may be reproduced.

(b) As part of a final judgment or decree, the court may order the destruction or other reasonable disposition of all [such items listed above].

§ 504. Remedies for Infringement: Damages and Profits

(a) In General. Except as otherwise provided by this title, an infringer of copyright is liable for either:

(1) the copyright owner's actual damages and any additional profits of the infringer, as provided by subsection (b); or

(2) statutory damages, as provided by subsection (c).

(b) Actual Damages and Profits. The copyright owner is entitled to recover the actual damages suffered by him or her as a result of the infringement, and any profits of the infringer that are attributable to the infringement and are not taken into account in computing the actual damages. In establishing the infringer's profits, the copyright owner is required to present proof only of the infringer's gross revenue, and the infringer is required to prove his or her deductible expenses and the elements of profit attributable to factors other than the copyrighted work.

(c) Statutory Damages. (1) Except as provided by clause (2) of this subsection, the copyright owner may elect, at any time before final judgment is rendered, to recover, instead of actual damages and profits, an award of statutory damages for all infringements involved in the action, with respect to any one work, for which any one infringer is liable individually, or for which any two or more infringers are liable jointly and severally, in a sum of not less than $250 or more than $10,000 as the court considers just. * * *

(2) In a case where the copyright owner sustains the burden of proving, and the court finds, that infringement was committed willfully, the court in its discretion may increase the award of statutory damages to a sum of not more than $50,000. In a case where the infringer sustains the burden of proving, and the court finds, that the infringer was not aware and had no reason to believe that his or her acts constituted an infringement of copyright, the court in its discretion may reduce the award of statutory damages to a sum of not less than $100 * * *.

§ 505. Remedies for Infringement: Costs and Attorney's Fees

In any civil action under this title, the court in its discretion may allow the recovery of full costs by or against any party other than the United States or an officer thereof. Except as otherwise provided by this title, the court may also award a reasonable attorney's fee to the prevailing party as part of the costs.

§ 506. Criminal Offenses

(a) Criminal Infringement. Any person who infringes a copyright willfully and for purposes of commercial advantage or private financial gain shall be fined not more than $2,500 or imprisoned not more than one year, or both, for the first such offense, and shall be fined not more than $10,000 or imprisoned not more than three years, or both, for any subsequent offense * * *.

WALT DISNEY CO. v. POWELL

United States Court of Appeals, District of Columbia Circuit, 1990.
897 F.2d 565.

WALD, CHIEF JUDGE. Carl Powell appeals from all three parts of a decision of the district court in a copyright infringement suit instituted against Powell, trading as J & L Distributors, by the Walt Disney Company ("Disney"). Pursuant to 17 U.S.C. § 504(c)(2), the district court awarded Disney statutory damages in the amount of $15,000 for each of six copyright infringements it found Powell had committed. It also awarded Disney $20,000 in attorneys' fees pursuant to 17 U.S.C. § 505. Finally, pursuant to 17 U.S.C. § 502, the court permanently enjoined Powell from infringing Disney's copyrights on the characters in suit—Mickey Mouse and Minnie Mouse—and all other Disney cartoon characters, including but not limited to, the copyrights in the characters Donald Duck, Huey, Duey, Louie, Pluto, Goofy and Roger Rabbit. We affirm both the district court's award of attorneys' fees and its issuance of a permanent injunction. Because, however, we hold that only two works were infringed, we vacate the district court's judgment finding Powell guilty of six infringements and ordering him to pay Disney $15,000 for each, and remand to the district court for a redetermination of damages.

At the time this suit arose, appellant conducted a wholesale souvenir business, selling items to local tourists through street vendors. Included in his inventory were shirts with mouse faces printed on them that resembled Mickey and Minnie Mouse. Since, as the district court found, Powell "did not keep normal business records," it is not possible to determine how many of these shirts he sold and how much profit he accrued from selling them. * * *

At trial, appellant admitted liability, but contested the propriety of relief beyond token damages. Much of his argument focused on his good faith, including his voluntary cessation of infringement, about which the district judge said the following:

> "Powell's counsel makes much of Powell's 'cooperation' and reformation. The Court has serious doubt that the defendant's professed reformation is more than skin deep. Powell's 'cooperation' in large part was simply a recognition of the strength of Disney's ability to show that its marks and trade dress were blatantly infringed. The investigator's reports and testimony establish Powell's continuing ambivalence *regarding possible future operations in copyright infringement,* operations which had been lucrative to him in the past. His

voluntary cessation did not occur even after some of his goods were seized on a federal warrant by another party, the Hard Rock Cafe, whose mark Powell was also exploiting * * *. Also Pepsi, Playboy and Georgetown University each complained about infringements of their marks. As the illegality of his affairs faced increasing exposure, Powell suddenly reformed."

The district judge also found that Powell's infringements were willful. Relying on the six copyrights of Mickey and Minnie Mouse entered into the record by Disney, the district judge found Powell guilty of six infringements and awarded Disney $15,000 per infringement. He also awarded Disney $20,000 in attorneys' fees and permanently enjoined Powell from infringing Disney's copyrights on the characters in suit and all other Disney cartoon characters.

Powell argues that the district judge abused his discretion in granting the permanent injunction, awarding attorneys' fees and awarding $90,000 in statutory damages. We will address each of his claims in turn.

Powell's claim that the district court abused its discretion in permanently enjoining him from future infringements of the characters in suit and all other Disney cartoon characters is without merit.

When a copyright plaintiff has established a threat of continuing infringement, he is *entitled* to an injunction. [citations]

Powell argues that since he voluntarily ceased infringing Disney's copyrights, there is no basis to assume that he will infringe them again in the future. The judge disagreed. He interpreted appellant's decision to cease infringing in a more Machiavellian light. The judge concluded that like Boris and Natasha, Snidely Whiplash and Bluto, Powell simply took the action that best suited him at the time; he was caught red-handed, thus "as the illegality of his affairs faced increasing exposure, Powell suddenly reformed." Consequently, the judge found it not unlikely that Powell would attempt to infringe Disney's copyrights in the future. Since there is nothing in the record contradicting the judge's finding, we conclude that he acted within his discretion in granting the injunction.

Powell argues alternatively that even if the injunction against future infringements of Mickey and Minnie was appropriate, the district court abused its discretion by extending it to Disney characters not in suit, the aforementioned Huey, Duey, Louie, *et al.* Powell is wrong. Where, as here, liability has been determined adversely to the infringer, there has been a history of continuing infringement and a significant threat of future infringement remains, it is appropriate to permanently enjoin the future infringement of works owned by the plaintiff but not in suit. [citations]

Powell's claim that the district court abused its discretion in awarding Disney attorneys' fees requires only brief discussion.

In *Reader's Digest,* 821 F.2d 800, 808 (D.C.Cir.1987), without taking sides, we noted that some courts have required a finding of deliberate infringement as a precondition to an award of fees [citation], while others have permitted such awards even when the infringement was not deliberate. [citation] Since the district court found that Powell's infringement was deliberate, that Powell acted "recklessly, willfully and knowingly," the award of $20,000 in fees was clearly within the district court's discretion even under the more stringent standard.

A copyright owner may elect an award of statutory damages "instead of actual damages and profits." 17 U.S.C. § 504(c)(1). Statutory damages in this action could have ranged from a minimum of $250 to a maximum $10,000 for infringement of "*any one work.*" *Id.* (emphasis added). If the infringement were willful, however, the maximum could be increased to $50,000 per infringed work. 17 U.S.C. § 504(c)(2).

Here, finding that Powell willfully infringed Disney's copyrights, the district judge elected to award $15,000 for each infringement he found. In explaining his decision on damages, the district judge said:

Six different *infringements* were proven by a preponderance of the evidence. * * * It is unnecessary to consider the precise application of the copyright to each of these examples. They all, without any doubt * * * definitely infringe [Disney's] copyright. * * * These violations are not overlapping. * * * Each of these is subject to damages to be assessed pursuant to 17 U.S.C. § 504(c)(2). The Court assesses $15,000 for each violation, or $90,000, plus interest from the date of judgment.

The district court erred in assessing damages based upon six "violations," mistakenly focusing on the number of infringements rather than on the number of works infringed. Both the text of the Copyright Act and its legislative history make clear that statutory damages are to be calculated according to the number of works infringed, not the number of infringements. * * *

While Mickey and Minnie are certainly distinct, viable works with separate economic value and copyright lives of their own, we cannot say the same is true for all six of the Disney copyrights of Mickey and Minnie in various poses which the district court found to be infringed in this case. Mickey is still Mickey whether he is smiling or frowning, running or walking, waving his left hand or his right. Thus, we find that Powell's mouse-face shirts infringed only two of Disney's works. * * *

We remand to the district court for a redetermination of damages based upon our holding that it is the number of works, not the number of infringements, that counts.

So ordered.

Notes

1. *Damages Plus Profits.* Dolori Fabrics, Inc. v. Limited, Inc., 662 F.Supp. 1347, 1355 (S.D.N.Y.1987):

"Section 504(b) of the Copyright Act entitles the owner of a copyright 'to recover the actual damages suffered by him or her as a result of the infringement, and any profits of the infringer that are attributable to the infringement and *are not taken into account in computing actual damages.*' 17 U.S.C. § 504(b) (emphasis added). Kenly contends that the italicized language precludes this court from awarding Dolori both actual damages and Kenly's profits. The court disagrees. In Abeshouse v. Ultragraphics, Inc., 754 F.2d 467, 471 (2d Cir.1985), Chief Judge Feinberg concluded that forcing a distributor to disgorge the profits from its sales in addition to reimbursing the plaintiff manufacturer for the profits it would have earned 'contain[ed] no element of double-counting.' The manufacturer 'could not have made the [sales which the distributor had made] and therefore cannot claim any lost profits on them.'

"Similarly, Dolori did not compete for, and therefore could not have made, the same sales as either Kenly or Brylane. Dolori may therefore recover from Kenly and Brylane both its actual damages and their profits due to the infringement. [citations] *Abeshouse* also answers Kenly's contention that this court may not order it to disgorge its profits to Dolori because the two companies compete in different markets."

FRANK MUSIC CORP. v. METRO-GOLDWYN-MAYER INC.

United States Court of Appeals, Ninth Circuit, 1989.
886 F.2d 1545.

FLETCHER, CIRCUIT JUDGE. * * * Plaintiffs are the copyright owners and authors of *Kismet,* a dramatico-musical work. MGM, Inc. under license produced a musical motion picture version of *Kismet.* Beginning April 26, 1974, MGM Grand presented a musical revue entitled *Hallelujah Hollywood* in the hotel's Ziegfeld Theatre. *Hallelujah Hollywood* was largely created by an employee of MGM Grand, Donn Arden, who also staged, produced and directed the show. The show comprised ten acts, four billed as "tributes" to MGM motion pictures. Act IV was entitled "Kismet," and was a tribute to the MGM movie of that name. It was based almost entirely on music from *Kismet,* and used characters and settings from that musical. Act IV "Kismet" was performed approximately 1700 times, until July 16, 1976, when, under pressure resulting from this litigation, MGM Grand substituted a new Act IV. * * *

In *Frank Music I,* we upheld the district court's conclusion that the plaintiffs failed to prove actual damages arising from the infringement, but vacated the district court's award of $22,000 in apportioned profits as "grossly inadequate," and remanded to the district court for reconsideration.

On remand, the district court calculated MGM Grand's net profit from *Hallelujah Hollywood* at $6,131,606, by deducting from its gross revenues the direct costs MGM Grand proved it had incurred. Neither party challenges this calculation.

In apportioning the profits between Act IV and the other acts in the show, the district court made the following finding:

> "Act IV of 'Hallelujah Hollywood' was one of ten acts, approximately a ten minute segment of a 100 minute revue. On this basis, the Court concludes that ten percent of the profits of 'Hallelujah Hollywood' are attributable to Act IV."

Plaintiffs assert that this finding is in error in several respects. First, they point out that on Saturdays *Hallelujah Hollywood* contained only eight acts, not ten, and that on Saturdays the show ran only 75 minutes, not 100. Second, Act IV was approximately eleven and a half minutes long, not ten. Because the show was performed three times on Saturdays, and twice a night on the other evenings of the week, the district court substantially underestimated the running time of Act IV in relation to the rest of the show.

If the district court relied exclusively on a quantitative comparison and failed to consider the relative quality or drawing power of the show's various component parts, it erred. [citations] However, the district court's apportionment based on comparative durations would be appropriate if the district court implicitly concluded that all the acts of the show were of roughly equal value. While a more precise statement of the district court's reasons would have been desirable, we find support in the record for the conclusion that all the acts in the show were of substantially equal value.

The district court went on to apportion the parties' relative contributions to Act IV itself:

> "The infringing musical material was only one of several elements contributing to the segment. A portion of the profits attributable to Act IV must be allocated to other elements, including the creative talent of the producer and director, the talents of performers, composers, choreographers, costume designers and others who participated in creating Act IV, and the attraction of the unique Ziegfeld Theatre with its elaborate stage effects. * * * While no precise mathematical formula can be applied, the Court concludes that * * * a fair approximation of the value of the infringing work to Act IV is twenty-five percent."

The district court was correct in probing into the parties' relative contributions to Act IV. Where a defendant alters infringing material to suit its own unique purposes, those alterations and the creativity behind them should be taken into account in apportioning the profits of the infringing work. [citations] However, the district court appears to have ignored its finding in its previous decision that defendants used not only the plaintiffs' music, but also their lyrics, characters, settings, and costume designs, recreating to a substantial extent the look and sound of the licensed movie version of *Kismet.*

While it was not inappropriate to consider the creativity of producers, performers and others involved in staging and adapting excerpts from *Kismet* for use in *Hallelujah Hollywood,* the district court erred in weighing these contributions so heavily. In performing the apportionment, the benefit of the doubt must always be given to the plaintiff, not the defendant. And while the apportionment may take into account the role of uncopyrightable elements of a work in generating that work's profits, the apportionment should not place too high a value on the defendants' staging of the work, at the expense of undervaluing the plaintiffs' more substantive creative contributions. Production contributions involving expensive costumes and lavish sets will largely be taken into account when deducting the defendants' costs. Indeed, defendants concede that had they produced *Kismet in toto,* it would have been proper for the district court to award 100% of their profits, despite their own creative efforts in staging such a production.

The district court found that defendants' staging of the *Kismet* excerpts was highly significant to Act IV's success. While we believe that a defendant's efforts in staging an infringing production will generally not support more than a *de minimis* deduction from the plaintiff's share of the profits, we cannot say the district court's conclusion that the defendants' contributions were substantial in this case is clearly erroneous. We recognize that there will be shows in which the attraction of the costumes, scenery or performers outweighs the attraction of the music or dialogue. On the other hand, a producer's ability to stage a lavish presentation, or a performer's ability to fill a hall from the drawing power of her name alone, is not a license to use freely the copyrighted works of others.

We conclude that apportioning 75% of Act IV to the defendants grossly undervalues the importance of the plaintiffs' contributions. Act IV was essentially *Kismet,* with contributions by the defendants, it was not essentially a new work incidentally plagiarizing elements of *Kismet.* A fairer apportionment, giving due regard to the district court's findings, attributes 75% of Act IV to elements taken from the plaintiffs and 25% to the defendants' contributions.[1]

In *Frank Music I,* we held that the plaintiffs were entitled to recover, in addition to direct profits, a proportion of ascertainable indirect profits from defendants' hotel and gaming operations attributable to the promotional value of *Hallelujah Hollywood.* The district court considered the relative contributions of *Hallelujah Hollywood* and other factors contributing to the hotel's profits, including the hotel's guest accommodations, restaurants, cocktail lounges, star entertainment in the "Celebrity" room, the movie theater, Jai Alai, the casino itself, convention and banquet facilities, tennis courts, swimming pools, gym and sauna, and also the role of advertising and general promotional activities in bringing customers to the hotel. The district court concluded that two percent of MGM Grand's indirect profit [$699,963.10] was attributable to *Hallelujah Hollywood.* In light of the general promotion and the wide variety of attractions available at MGM Grand, this conclusion is not clearly erroneous.

Notes

Copyright Injunctions and Free Speech. Courts have excused copyright proprietors from establishing irreparable injury as a prerequisite for an injunction. Indeed "an injunction will issue when there is a 'substantial likelihood of further infringement of plaintiffs' copyrights.'" Ocasek v. Hegglund, 116 F.R.D. 154, 160 (D.Wyo.1987).

The "writings" protected by copyright may, even under the defendant's alleged infringement, be speech and expression protected under the first amendment to the constitution.

Salinger v. Random House, Inc., 811 F.2d 90 (2d Cir.), cert. denied, 484 U.S. 890 (1987), grappled with whether a publisher may quote unpublished letters in a book. New Era Publications International v. Henry Holt & Co., 873 F.2d 576, petition for reh'g en banc denied, 884 F.2d 659 (2d Cir.1989), cert. denied, 110 S.Ct. 1168 (1990), created the impression that the publisher's fair use defense might not avail and the plaintiff might obtain an injunction that barred publication of a book. Legislation was introduced to correct or clarify the decisions.

Mr. Floyd Abrams addressed the proposed legislation in a July 11, 1990 statement to a joint Congressional hearing:

"There is an additional disturbing element of this jurisprudence that I would like to address: the rather promiscuous way in which courts issue injunctions for violations of the copyright laws. In the context of unpublished expression, my concerns are even stronger.

"In *Salinger,* Judge Newman concluded that if a biographer 'copies more than minimal amounts of [unpublished] expressive content, he deserved to be enjoined.'[1] Based upon Judge Newman's language, the majority opinion in *New Era* declared that '[s]ince the copying of "more than minimal amounts" of unpublished expressive material calls for an injunction barring unauthorized use * * * the consequences of the district court's finding [that a small, but more than negligible,

1. [Footnote renumbered.] Based on this allocation, plaintiffs are entitled to $551,844.54 as direct profits from the infringement.

1. [Footnotes renumbered.] Judge Newman later explained in his dissent from the decision not to rehear the *New Era* case, the "sentence from *Salinger* was concerned with the issue of infringement, not the choice of remedy."

amount was unfairly used] seem obvious.' Explaining his views in his response to the motion for rehearing, Judge Miner made plain that 'under ordinary circumstances' use of more than minimal amounts requires an injunction.

"In my view, both the language of the *Salinger* and the *New Era* rulings are consistent with the law that has generally existed in this area. It is perfectly accurate for Judge Miner to conclude that at least under 'ordinary circumstances' injunctions routinely follow findings of copyright liability. So they have. But should they?

"I start with the proposition, not unknown in First Amendment law, that injunctions on books are generally anathema to a free society. Prior restraints are generally viewed 'as the most serious and least tolerable infringement on First Amendment rights.' Nebraska Press Association v. Stuart, 427 U.S. 539, 559 (1976). We do not permit prior restraints in libel cases, no matter how persuasively a plaintiff demonstrates harm caused by the intended speech. The Supreme Court, to this date, has never held constitutional any prior restraints on publication by a newspaper. Why, then, are we quite so willing to interpret copyright law to require even the near-automatic issuance of an injunction against the publication of a book which includes in it some infringing material? If the First Amendment prevented a court from enjoining the entire Pentagon Papers, notwithstanding the national security concerns cited by the government which were explicitly accepted by a majority of the Court, why should selective unpublished quotations used in a significant piece of history or scholarly criticism routinely be subjected to the literary equivalent of capital punishment known as an injunction?

"I suggest no more than that, at the least, courts should weigh carefully what remedy should be awarded even after a finding of infringement. Enjoining publication of a book is serious, and ritualistic incantation of the availability of injunctions in copyright cases makes it no less so.[2] I thus agree with the views of Chief Judge Oakes in his opinion in *New Era*, in which he said that 'a non-injunctive remedy [often] provides the best balance between the copyright interests and the First Amendment interests at stake' in any given case.

"On one level, enacting this bill into law should go a long way toward reducing the number of nearly automatic injunctions by reducing the number of infringement claims against publishers and authors who make selective use of unpublished expression. But the injunction issue cuts deeper. I join other commentators in urging Congress formally to request the Copyright Office to evaluate how frequently and with what justification courts issue injunctions against publishers and authors in infringement cases. The Copyright Office should submit to Congress the results of its findings and Congress should review those findings, reflecting carefully on the profound implications for the First Amendment they may suggest."

5. MISAPPROPRIATION OF TRADE SECRETS

UNIVERSITY COMPUTING CO. v. LYKES–YOUNGSTOWN CORP.

United States Court of Appeals, Fifth Circuit, 1974.
504 F.2d 518.

[Action for misappropriation of a trade secret consisting in a computer software system called AIMES III (an acronym for Automated Inventory

2. Not insignificantly, the Copyright Act implicitly repudiates the automatic issuance of any injunction. It provides simply that "any Court * * * may * * * grant temporary and final injunction." (emphasis supplied)

Management Evaluation System) useful for retail inventory control. Georgia law controlled in this diversity action.]

TUTTLE, CIRCUIT JUDGE. * * * The defendants admit that LYCSC [Lykes-Youngstown Computer Services Corp., one of the defendants] paid one Ron Clinton, an employee of Leonard's Department Store in Fort Worth, Texas, $2500 to induce him to steal Leonard's copy of the AIMES III system and deliver the tapes and documents comprising that system to an LYCSC employee. The defendants do not now claim that this conduct was lawful or even defensible. * * *

A trade secret is protected against illegal appropriation and commercial use by a competitor. * * *

Under the Restatement formulation, a trade secret is defined as: "Any formula, pattern, device or compilation of information which is used on one's business and which gives him an opportunity to obtain an advantage over competitors who do not know or use it." * * *

Unlike a patent which is totally protected for the period of time for which it is granted, the protection afforded a trade secret is limited—for it is protected only so long as competitors fail to duplicate it by legitimate, independent research. * * *

Once having determined that the jury finding that AIMES III was a trade secret wrongfully appropriated by the defendants was proper, the problem remains as to what is the appropriate measure of damages. It seems generally accepted that "the proper measure of damages in the case of a trade secret appropriation is to be determined by reference to the analogous line of cases involving patent infringement, just as patent infringement cases are used by analogy to determine the damages for copyright infringement." International Industries, Inc. v. Warren Petroleum Corp., 248 F.2d 696, 699 (3d Cir.1957). The case law is thus plentiful, but the standard for measuring damages which emerges is very flexible.

In some instances courts have attempted to measure the loss suffered by the plaintiff. While as a conceptual matter this seems to be a proper approach, in most cases the defendant has utilized the secret to his advantage with no obvious effect on the plaintiff save for the relative differences in their subsequent competitive positions. Largely as a result of this practical dilemma, normally the value of the secret to the plaintiff is an appropriate measure of damages only when the defendant has in some way destroyed the value of the secret. The most obvious way this is done is through publication, so that no secret remains. [citation] Where the plaintiff retains the use of the secret, as here, and where there has been no effective disclosure of the secret through publication the total value of the secret to the plaintiff is an inappropriate measure.

Further, unless some specific injury to the plaintiff can be established—such as lost sales—the loss to the plaintiff is not a particularly helpful approach in assessing damages.

The second approach is to measure the value of the secret to the defendant. This is usually the accepted approach where the secret has not been destroyed and where the plaintiff is unable to prove specific injury.

Normally only the defendant's actual profits can be used as a measure of damages in cases where profits can be proved, and the defendant is normally not assessed damages on wholly speculative expectations of profits. Had the defendants here been able to sell the AIMES III system at a profit, our task would be simplified. Because the defendants failed in their marketing efforts, no actual profits exist by which to value the worth to the defendants of what they misappropriated. However, the Supreme Court has held in a patent case that the lack of actual profits does not insulate the defendants from being obliged to pay for what they have wrongfully obtained in the mistaken belief their theft would benefit them. In re Cawood Patent, 94 U.S. 695 (1877).

The rationale for this seems clearly to be that the risk of defendants' venture, using the misappropriated secret, should not be placed on the injured plaintiff, but rather the defendants must bear the risk of failure themselves. Accordingly the law looks to the time at which the misappropriation occurred to determine what the value of the misappropriated secret would be to a defendant who believes he can utilize it to his advantage, provided he does in fact put the idea to a commercial use.

This second technique frequently entails using what is called the "reasonable royalty" standard. * * *

As the term is presently understood, the "reasonable royalty" measure of damages is taken to mean more than simply a percentage of actual profits. The measure now, very simply, means "[t]he actual value of what has been appropriated." Vitro Corporation of America v. Hall Chemical Co., 292 F.2d 678, 683 (6th Cir.1961). When this is not subject to exact measurement, a reasonable estimate of value is used. * * *

> "As pointed out in many cases * * * in a case where no established royalty is shown it is for the Court to determine a reasonable royalty which represents the value of that which has been wrongfully taken by the infringer * * * it is sufficient to point out that in making such determination many factors were taken into consideration * * *. In fact, the reasonable royalty was based upon the advantages which would have accrued to (the infringer) had it negotiated a license * * *."

Union Carbide Corp. v. Graver Tank and Manufacturing Co., 282 F.2d 653, 674–675 (7th Cir.1960).

One other important variation on this "reasonable royalty" standard is the standard of comparison method, which also attempts to measure the value to the defendant of what he appropriated. * * *

Occasionally this has been taken to mean the difference in costs to the defendant of developing the trade secret on his own, using the actual development costs of the plaintiff as the complete measure of damages. [citation] This measure of damages simply uses the plaintiff's actual costs, and in our view is frequently inadequate in that it fails to take into account the commercial context in which the misappropriation occurred.

In certain cases, where the trade secret was used by the defendant in a limited number of situations, where the plaintiff was not in direct competition with the defendant, where the development of the secret did not require substantial improvements in existing trade practices but rather merely refined the existing practices, and where the defendant's use of the plaintiff's trade secret has ceased, such a limited measure might be appropriate. In the type of case which we now consider, when the parties were potentially in direct competition and the course of conduct of the defendant extended over a period of time and included a number of different uses of the plaintiff's trade secret, and where the process of developing a computer system was very difficult and required substantial technical and theoretical advances, we believe a broader measure of damages is needed.

This broader measure should take into consideration development costs, but as only one of a number of different factors.

Certain standards emerge from the cases. The defendant must have actually put the trade secret to some commercial use. The law governing protection of trade secrets essentially is designed to regulate unfair business competition, and is not a substitute for criminal laws against theft or other civil remedies for conversion. If the defendant enjoyed actual profits, a type of restitutionary remedy can be afforded the plaintiff—either recovering the full total of defendant's profits or some apportioned amount designed to correspond to the actual contribution the plaintiff's trade secret made to the defendant's commercial success. Because the primary concern in most cases is to measure the value to the defendant of what he actually obtained from the plaintiff, the proper measure is to calculate what the parties would have agreed to as a fair price for licensing the defendant to put the trade secret to the use the defendant intended at the time the misappropriation took place.

In calculating what a fair licensing price would have been had the parties agreed, the trier of fact should consider such factors as the resulting and foreseeable changes in the parties' competitive posture; the prices past purchasers or licensees may have paid; the total value of the secret to the plaintiff, including the plaintiff's development costs and the importance of the secret to the plaintiff's business; the nature and extent of the use the defendant intended for the secret; and finally whatever other unique factors in the particular case which might have affected the parties' agreement, such as the ready availability of alternative processes. [citation]

The district court charged the jury that the following factors should be considered by them in arriving at the proper damages for the defendants' misappropriation of AIMES III: (1) the development costs incurred by the plaintiff; (2) the fees paid by customers of the plaintiff who utilized the system on a service bureau basis; (3) the prices at which the system was leased or sold by the plaintiff for restrictive use; (4) the sale price placed on the system by the defendants; and (5) expert testimony as to what would constitute a reasonable royalty for the rights to unrestricted use of the system. We believe that these factors were proper to be considered by the jury. * * *

Notes

1. The Uniform Trade Secrets Act provides several remedies for misappropriation of trade secrets. a) Alternative measures of compensatory "damages": plaintiff's actual loss as well as the infringer's unjust enrichment "not taken into account" in calculating damages, or the "reasonable royalty." b) Exemplary damages of up to twice the amount of actual damages for wilful and malicious misappropriations. c) Injunctions for actual or threatened infringements. In exceptional circumstances an injunction may condition future use on payment of a royalty. Injunctions may be dissolved when trade secrets cease to exist. d. Attorney fees. Uniform Trade Secrets Act §§ 2–4, 14 U.L.A. 449–461 (1990).

2. The Uniform Act expressly displaces conflicting tort, restitutionary and other state law for misappropriation of trade secrets; but it does not affect claims

for breach of contract or breach of confidence. Boeing Co. v. Sierracin Corp., 108 Wash.2d 38, 738 P.2d 665 (1987).

3. *Injunctions Under the Uniform Act.* The statute simply states that "an actual or theoretical misappropriation may be enjoined." The following gloss was placed on this language in Boeing Co. v. Sierracin Corp., 108 Wash.2d 38, 62–63, 738 P.2d 665, 681 (1987):

"Sierracin argues that a finding of irreparable harm must be entered in order to support the trial court's injunction. We disagree. Neither the Uniform Trade Secrets Act nor the civil rules about injunctions require such a finding. To allow Sierracin in this case to continue to manufacture cockpit windows after deciding that it had misappropriated the information from Boeing would permit Sierracin to profit from its own wrongful conduct. The trial judge found that an injunction would not be unreasonable (finding of fact 10), and we agree. No finding of irreparable harm need be found to support this decision."

4. *Problem:* Assume that defendant, through breach of confidence, misappropriates a trade secret for a drug. Plaintiff immediately sues for an injunction and damages. Three months later the trade secret becomes available to the public. During the trial, the judge finds that it would have taken the wrongdoer six months to have replicated the research and develop the formula. a) Should a six-months lead-time injunction issue against the wrongdoer? b) If so, when should the lead-time period begin? A.L. Laboratories, Inc. v. Philips Roxane, Inc., 803 F.2d 378 (8th Cir.1986), cert. denied, 481 U.S. 1007 (1987).

5. Allis–Chalmers Manufacturing Co. v. Continental Aviation & Engineering Corp., 255 F.Supp. 645, 654–55 (E.D.Mich.1966), demonstrates the acute problem of attempting to control the disclosure of trade secrets by highly trained research scientists whose services are in great demand by corporations for their technical abilities as well as their special knowledge of a competitor's research results. Wolff was a skilled mechanical engineer in charge of Allis–Chalmers' fuel injection laboratory when he was hired away by Continental Aviation. The court acknowledged:

"The virtual impossibility of Mr. Wolff performing all of his prospective duties for Continental to the best of his ability, without in effect giving it the benefit of Allis–Chalmers' confidential information, makes a simple injunction against disclosure and use of this information inadequate.

"This court has attempted to formulate an order which will strike a proper balance between the public policy of Michigan, as declared in Mich.Stat.Ann. 28.61 of protecting and encouraging the right of the individual to pursue his livelihood in the vocation he chooses, including the right to migrate from one job to another, and the rights of an employer to its accumulated body of trade secrets obtained by the expenditure of great amounts of time and money.

"Thus, the injunction granted is as restricted as possible to protect the secrets involved without undue restraint on Mr. Wolff's right to pursue his chosen vocation, only prohibiting work in the design and development of distributor type pumps. Mr. Wolff is able to work at Continental in application engineering without limitation as to the field of activity, and to engage in design and development in all kinds of fuel injection systems and pumps except a distributor type pump. Furthermore, the injunction granted is limited in time. Being a preliminary injunction it will last in any event only until final hearing in the action, and it may terminate earlier by its own terms, if the confidential information comes into the possession of Continental by legitimate means."

6. Temporary injunctions as in *Allis–Chalmers Manufacturing Co.* are especially vulnerable to being set aside for violating Fed.R.Civ.P. 65, see supra, 246–50. Even more so when the alleged trade secret is purportedly shared distributively by numerous former employees. See, E.W. Bliss Co. v. Struthers–Dunn, Inc., 408 F.2d 1108 (8th Cir.1969), holding each single portion of a five section injunction invalid for "vagueness."

Henry Hope X–Ray Products, Inc. v. Marron Carrel, Inc., 674 F.2d 1336, 1343 (9th Cir.1982): "Ordinarily an injunction should not incorporate by reference another document. This is not a technical requirement, but is designed to insure adequate notice to defendants of the acts prohibited. * * * In this case the district court set out the acts prohibited in a sealed appendix which was to be transmitted only to the parties to ensure that Hope's trade secrets were not divulged in the injunction. The district court did not err in resorting to this eminently sensible expedient."

7. Footnote to Atlantic Wool Combing Co. v. Norfolk Mills, Inc., 357 F.2d 866, 871 n. 9 (1st Cir.1966): "It has been suggested that the fact, if such be the fact, that a reasonably skilled mechanic could devise a machine equivalent to the plaintiff's without using the plaintiff's secret information may justify limiting relief to money damages."

8. *Duration of Injunctive Relief: Elimination of "Lead Time."* Disclosure of a trade secret obviously ends its judicial protectability. Consider the person who wrongfully acquired the secret before it entered the public domain. Can he be enjoined from using what anyone else can lawfully use? If so, for how long? Winston Research Corp. v. Minnesota Mining & Manufacturing Co., 350 F.2d 134, 141–42 (4th Cir.1965):

"[T]he district court enjoined disclosure or use of the specifications of Mincom's machine for a period of two years from the date of judgment. Mincom argues that the injunction should have been permanent, or at least for a substantially longer period. Winston contends that no injunctive relief was appropriate.

"Mincom was, of course, entitled to protection of its trade secrets for as long as they remained secret. The district court's decision to limit the duration of injunctive relief was necessarily premised upon a determination that Mincom's trade secrets would shortly be fully disclosed, through no fault of Winston, as a result of public announcements, demonstrations, and sales and deliveries of Mincom machines. * * *

"Mincom argues that notwithstanding public disclosure subsequent to its former employees' breach of faith, Mincom was entitled to a permanent injunction under the *Shellmar* rule. Winston responds that under the competing *Conmar* rule public disclosure of Mincom's trade secrets would end the obligation of Mincom's former employees to maintain the information in confidence, and that neither the employees nor their privies may be enjoined beyond the date of disclosure.[1]

"Thus, Winston's argument would bar any injunction at all once there was public disclosure, and Mincom's argument would require an injunction in perpetuity without regard to public disclosure. The district court rejected both extremes and granted an injunction for the period which it concluded would be sufficient both to deny Winston unjust enrichment and to protect Mincom from injury from

1. [Footnotes renumbered.] The two rules take their names from Shellmar Products Co. v. Allen–Qualley Co., 87 F.2d 104 (7th Cir.1936), and Conmar Products Corp. v. Universal Slide Fastener Co., 172 F.2d 150 (2d Cir.1949). These decisions and their respective progeny are exhaustively considered in Turner, Law of Trade Secrets 427–58 (1962).

the wrongful disclosure and use of Mincom's trade secrets by its former employees prior to public disclosure.

"We think the district court's approach was sound. A permanent injunction would subvert the public's interest in allowing technical employees to make full use of their knowledge and skill and in fostering research and development. On the other hand, denial of any injunction at all would leave the faithless employee unpunished where, as here, no damages were awarded; and he and his new employer would retain the benefit of a headstart over legitimate competitors who did not have access to the trade secrets until they were publicly disclosed. By enjoining use of the trade secrets for the approximate period it would require a legitimate Mincom competitor to develop a successful machine after public disclosure of the secret information,[2] the district court denied the employees any advantage from their faithlessness, placed Mincom in the position it would have occupied if the breach of confidence had not occurred prior to the public disclosure, and imposed the minimum restraint consistent with the realization of these objectives upon the utilization of the employees' skills."

Sperry Rand Corporation v. A-T-O, Inc., 447 F.2d 1387, 1392 (4th Cir.1971): "Our view is that the district judge fashioned appropriate relief. He required the return of the misappropriated material, and he restrained the manufacture or sale of a slotted array type antenna for a period of two years. An order to return stolen property cannot be faulted. There was evidence that a small firm would require a period of four or five years to develop the misappropriated data and this evidence, together with evidence of the time consumed by Sperry Rand in developing the misappropriated data, shows that the two year restriction on the manufacture and sale of a slotted array type antenna was not unreasonable or did not constitute an abuse of discretion in fashioning equitable relief."

The trial judge also reserved the power to modify, enlarge or vacate this aspect of the remedy during the two year period.

9. Warner-Lambert Pharmaceutical Co. v. John J. Reynolds, Inc., 178 F.Supp. 655, 665–66 (S.D.N.Y.1959), aff'd without opinion, 280 F.2d 197 (2d Cir.1960). Plaintiff's predecessor bought the "Listerine" formula from defendant's predecessor in 1881 and agreed to make periodic payments based on the quantity of Listerine sold. Over a 75-year period payments totalled $22,000,000 and payments were now in excess of $1,500,000 annually [they have since risen].

Plaintiff sued for a declaratory judgment that it was no longer obligated to make the payments because the Listerine formula had ceased to be a secret since at least 1931. In denying relief the court said:

"A secret formula or trade secret may remain secret almost indefinitely. It may be discovered by someone else almost immediately after the agreement is entered into. Whoever discovers it for himself by legitimate means is entitled to its use. * * * But that does not mean that one who acquires a secret formula or a trade secret through a valid and binding contract is then enabled to escape from an obligation to which he bound himself simply because the secret is discovered by a third party or by the general public.

2. Compare Engelhard Indus., Inc. v. Research Instrumental Corp., 324 F.2d 347 (9th Cir.1963), where the argument advanced against a claim of misappropriation was that the accused's device was not built until after public disclosure. In answer, this court stated:

"Nevertheless, simply because the accused's [device] was not *built* until after the time the information was released to the public domain does not mean that the trade secrets were not wrongfully *used* before that time. [Court's emphasis] * * * *Such use would give rise to a claim for damages based upon the profits resulting from the acceleration of the date when production was possible.*" [Emphasis added.]

* * * "The inventor makes no representation that the secret is non-discoverable."

6. IMITATION OF TRADEMARKS, TRADE NAMES AND NON-FUNCTIONAL FEATURES OF ANOTHER'S PRODUCT

THE LANHAM ACT

§ 1116. Injunctive relief

(a) Jurisdiction; service. The several courts vested with jurisdiction of civil actions arising under this chapter shall have power to grant injunctions, according to the principles of equity and upon such terms as the court may deem reasonable, to prevent the violation of any right of the registrant of a mark registered in the Patent and Trademark Office or to prevent a violation under section 1125(a) of this title. * * *

§ 1117. Recovery for violation of rights

(a) Profits; damages and costs; attorney fees. When a violation of any right of the registrant of a mark registered in the Patent and Trademark Office, or a violation under section 1125(a) of this title, shall have been established in any civil action arising under this chapter, the plaintiff shall be entitled, subject to the provisions of sections 1111 and 1114 of this title, and subject to the principles of equity, to recover (1) defendant's profits, (2) any damages sustained by the plaintiff, and (3) the costs of the action. The court shall assess such profits and damages or cause the same to be assessed under its direction. In assessing profits the plaintiff shall be required to prove defendant's sales only; defendant must prove all elements of cost or deduction claimed. In assessing damages the court may enter judgment, according to the circumstances of the case, for any sum above the amount found as actual damages, not exceeding three times such amount. If the court shall find that the amount of the recovery based on profits is either inadequate or excessive the court may in its discretion enter judgment for such sum as the court shall find to be just, according to the circumstances of the case. Such sum in either of the above circumstances shall constitute compensation and not a penalty. The court in exceptional cases may award reasonable attorney fees to the prevailing party.

(b) Treble damages for use of counterfeit mark. In assessing damages under subsection (a) of this section, the court shall, unless the court finds extenuating circumstances, enter judgment for three times such profits or damages, whichever is greater, together with a reasonable attorney's fee, in the case of any violation of section 1114(1)(A) of this title or section 380 of Title 36 that consists of intentionally using a mark or designation, knowing such mark or designation is a counterfeit mark (as defined in section 1116(d) of this title), in connection with the sale, offering for sale, or distribution of goods or services. In such cases, the court may in its discretion award prejudgment interest on such amount at an annual interest rate established under section 6621 of Title 26, commencing on the date of the service of the claimant's pleadings setting forth the claim for such entry and ending on the date such entry is made, or for such shorter time as the court deems appropriate.

§ 1118. Destruction of infringing articles

In any action arising under this chapter, in which a violation of any right of the registrant of a mark registered in the Patent and Trademark Office, or a violation under section 1125(a) of this title, shall have been established, the court may order that all labels, signs, prints, packages, wrappers, receptacles, and advertisements in the possession of the defendant, bearing the registered mark or, in the case of a violation of section 1125(a) of this title, the word, term, name, symbol, device, combination thereof, designation, description, or representation that is the subject of the violation, or any reproduction, counterfeit, copy, or colorable imitation thereof, and all plates, molds, matrices, and other means of making the same, shall be delivered up and destroyed. * * *

The Rationale for Trademark Protection

Protection of trademarks, trade names, service marks, symbols, etc. (the distinction concerns registration procedures as much as anything else) arises under common law principles of unfair competition, state registration statutes, and the federal trademark act of 1946 (the Lanham Act), 15 U.S.C. §§ 1051–1127 (1988). Unlike the Patent and Copyright Acts, the Lanham Act does not preempt state common law actions or statutes protecting trademarks. There are some practical advantages in seeking coverage and remedies under the Lanham Act. Registration is constructive notice throughout the entire country rather than a single state. The registrant may sue in the federal courts without jurisdictional amount or diversity of citizenship. The use of a federally registered mark for a five-year period creates a prima facie case for protection that might be more difficult to achieve under common law unfair competition. The Lanham Act does not protect a mark from being "diluted" by the defendant, so that broader relief may be obtained under state enactments or perhaps state common law joined as pendant to a Lanham Act suit.

The Lanham Act provides typical civil remedies and treble damages. On the other hand punitive damages may be had in a common law action. State registration acts have varied remedies; many tend to treat infringement as quasi-criminal or criminal and to emphasize severe sanctions rather than civil remedies.

There is no need here to analyze, and certainly not to supplement, the huge amount of literature on the rationale for the protection against trademark infringement and unfair competition. The matter may be reduced to a few basic approaches, which, however, produce different goals to be attained through different combinations of remedies.

1. *Diversion of Trade.* This rationale is the "palming off" theory of trademark protection—i.e., forbidding defendant from presenting its product as that of the plaintiff. Perhaps the original basis for the equitable intervention, it remains the most widely recognized rationale.

Diversion of trade requires market competition between dealers in the same product. When the protectibility of a trade symbol rests solely on the "palming off" doctrine, the injunctive remedy should protect the symbol only in the market area where plaintiff has established priority—perhaps extending protection into geographical areas where the plaintiff has a strong possibility of projecting operations.

Injunctive relief may also fall short of an outright ban. When the defendant's motives are relatively innocent, the decree may be limited to requiring adjectives or disclaimers.

Damages, if any, are based on lost patronage. Plaintiff will normally seek the alternative, restitution of defendant's profits, if profits exceed provable damage. Borrowing from the statutory remedies of patent and copyright infringement is apparent.

2. *A "Property" Right in the Mark, Name or Product Appearance.* The conceptualization of intangibles as "property" should be viewed with reservations, and, in the following pages, with apprehension. More clearly even than in patent, copyright or trade secret, the alleged "property" in a trademark inheres not in the nominal subject but in the goodwill values of the affected business.

Boston Professional Hockey Association v. Dallas Cap & Emblem Manufacturing, 510 F.2d 1004 (5th Cir.), cert. denied, 423 U.S. 868 (1975), protects the reproduction and sale of the symbol itself. It relies on a "property" interest in a mark—perhaps because, under the circumstances, no other rationale seems convincing. The decision is important to, among others, the many universities that sell sweatshirts and beer mugs with the Alma Mater emblem to students and loyal alums.

The notion of intangibles as "property" is also fostered by the traditional requirement of property for equitable jurisdiction, and by the necessity of bookkeepers to come up with an asset to create the coveted surplus on the balance sheet.

The *misappropriation* doctrine of unfair competition has been built upon this foundation. Implications extend beyond the specific branch of trademarks.

Misappropriation remedies may extend equitable protection of the symbol beyond the boundaries of direct market competition. Without direct competition, however, the appropriateness of damages for lost profits or an accounting for defendants' profits may be challenged.

"Misappropriation" naturally suggests placing a dollar value on the intangible good will inherent in the symbol, dependent upon whether it is "strong" or "weak," to measure tort damage for its destruction or quasi-contract for its use. Trademark "misappropriation" may indeed lend itself to a quasi-contractual remedy, such as the reasonable royalty approach under a patent analogy.

Some decisions say that trademark law actually fosters competition. Observe, however, that the judicial protection of a "property" interest in trade symbols invariably tends to strengthen and broaden a monopolistic trade advantage.

3. *Consumer Confusion About the Source or Sponsorship of the Product.* With the aid of the language of the Lanham Act, this is usually the rationale for trademark protection. It thus embraces the "palming off" doctrine, as well as some elements of the property concept—notably when the confusion relates to the sponsorship of the product.

James Burrough Ltd. v. Sign of the Beefeater, Inc., 540 F.2d 266, 274 (7th Cir.1976), rev'd, 572 F.2d 574 (1978):

" '[T]he test under the statute, 15 U.S.C.A. § 1114(1), is likelihood of confusion.' Illinois law mandates application of the same test. In the consideration of evidence relating to trademark infringement, therefore, a court must expand the more frequent, one-on-one, contest-between-two-sides, approach. A third party, the consuming public, is present and its interests are paramount. Hence infringement is found when the evidence indicates a likelihood of confusion, deception or mistake on the part of the consuming public. Infringement does not exist, though the marks be identical and the goods very similar, when the evidence indicates no such likelihood. When equitable considerations impel the continuation of otherwise confusing trademark uses, courts will fashion appropriate relief, often requiring notices designed to limit or defeat confusion of the public.

"As has been said, 'people do not confuse trademarks—trademarks confuse people.' In re West Point–Pepperrell, Inc., 468 F.2d 200 (C.C.P.A.1972). * * *

"A 'trademark' is not that which is infringed. What is infringed is the right of the public to be free of confusion and the synonymous right of a trademark owner to control his product's reputation."

The consumer's interest in the accuracy of "brand" labelling is hardly primary to the real function of trademark protection; to entrust any form of consumer protection to the manufacturer may seem a bit awry. Nevertheless, a consumer's interest in not being confused or deceived by product misbranding may be more vigorously protected through "unfair competition" than in administrative proceedings or class actions. The consumer interest can be protected by injunctions drafted to prevent confusion—either requiring cessation, distinctive words or designs, or statements of disclaimer, as in the "palming off" situations. Compensatory awards because of customer confusion should be measured by injury to the actual plaintiff. But what about punitive damages or an accounting for defendant's profits?

4. *Dilution of the Trademark or Name.* The federal trademark act requires a likelihood of confusion for liability for infringement. State dilution statutes dispense with likelihood of confusion and create liability for defendant's use of a mark in ways that injure plaintiff's business reputation or dilute the distinctiveness of plaintiff's mark. The statutes limit remedies to injunctions and do not provide for money remedies.

Massachusetts passed the first anti-dilution statute in 1947. Some 20 states now have one. The Lanham Act is not an anti-dilution statute. "Trademark dilution, however, is exclusively a creature of state statute, and there is no [anti-dilution] provision in the Lanham Act." Anheuser–Busch, Inc. v. Florists Association, 603 F.Supp. 35, 39 (N.D.Ohio 1984). At first "dilution" appeared as ancillary to more traditional grounds particularly in federal cases where state theories were joined under pendent jurisdiction. More attention is now being paid to "dilution" as an independent ground for trademark protection.

Oregon's statute, Or.Rev.Stat. § 647.107 (1989) is typical: "Likelihood of injury to business reputation or of dilution of the distinctive quality of a mark registered under ORS 647.015, or a mark valid at common law, or a trade name valid at common law, shall be a ground for injunctive relief notwithstanding the absence of competition between the parties or the absence of confusion as to the source of goods or services."

Wedgwood Homes, Inc. v. Lund, 294 Or. 493, 498–503, 659 P.2d 377, 380–83 (1983). The plaintiff had been building and selling residential properties in one county in Oregon for 25 years. It sought an injunction against defendant's use of "Wedgwood" in connection with two retirement complexes in the county. Plaintiff asserted common law unfair competition and dilution under the statute. The trial court found there was no unfair competition because there was no likelihood of customer confusion; but it sustained the dilution claim and issued an injunction. The Supreme Court affirmed, emphasizing that dilution does not require customer confusion, or that plaintiff's mark be an inherently strong nationally recognized mark—only that it have acquired a secondary meaning in its trade area. The court continued:

"The antidilution statutes developed out of the growing recognition that trademarks now surpass the traditional identity role. * * * A mark may possess independent protectible value to the extent that it acquires advertising and selling power.

"In the context of dilution, the protectible quality of a mark has been defined as the mark's power to evoke images of the product, that is, its favorable associational value in the minds of consumers. This attribute may be developed in a variety of ways: long use, consistent superior quality instilling consumer satisfaction, extensive advertising. * * *

"We are aware of instances of judicial reluctance to apply antidilution statutes literally. Some courts refuse to issue injunctive relief because likelihood of confusion is not present, despite statutory language to the contrary. [citations] Other courts have refused to apply the statute where confusion exists, [citations] or where competition exists [citations]. We are persuaded, however, in light of the interest sought to be protected by the law and the very language of the statute, that ORS 647.107 protects this plaintiff's tradename.

"Allied Maintenance Corporation v. Allied Mechanical Trades, Inc., 42 N.Y.2d 538, 542, 399 N.Y.S.2d 628, 630, 369 N.E.2d 1162, 1164 (1977), * * * distinguished the rationale for the dilution statute from the common law actions of trademark infringement and unfair competition:

" 'The evil which the Legislature sought to remedy was not public confusion caused by similar products or services sold by competitors, but a cancer-like growth of dissimilar products or services which feeds upon the business reputation of an established distinctive trademark or name. * * * The harm that [the New York antidilution statute] is designed to prevent is the gradual whittling away of a firm's distinctive trademark or name.' * * *

"In Augusta National, Inc. v. Northwestern Mutual Life Ins. Co., 193 U.S.P.Q. 210 (S.D.Ga.1976), the court explained how dilution would occur if defendant were permitted to use 'Masters' in its golf tournament 'Ladies Masters at Moss Creek Plantation.' 'If the suspect name is used there is reasonable certainty that the value of plaintiff's mark will be eroded; a little now, more later, until the 'magic' of the Masters [Golf Tournament] will be mortally dissipated if not completely dispelled.' * * *

"To a significant percentage of the consuming public of eastern Washington County, Wedgwood connotes homes. Defendant's use of the name in connection with retirement apartments expands the associations consumers are likely to connect with the name and thereby reduces the name's effectiveness * * *. On these facts plaintiff has adequately demonstrated dilution of the distinctive quality of its name."

"Dilution" requires neither competition, actual destruction of the value of the mark, nor loss of goodwill. Damages are therefore unlikely. Injunctions, the remedy provided in the Oregon statute, may be extensive and unqualified. The *Wedgwood Homes* court rejected defendant's contention that a disclaimer of affiliation, a common decree in instances of "palming off" or confusion of source, would provide adequate relief. It said "In light of the detrimental impact any second use could have on the advertising value of plaintiff's name, injunction is the appropriate remedy."

A Problem: Advertising slogans may be protected in the same fashion as trademarks or names. Anheuser–Busch adopted the slogan "Where there's life there's Bud" in connection with Budweiser beer. A manufacturer of a floor wax containing an insecticide advertised its products under the slogan "Where there's life there's bugs." An injunction was granted. Chemical Corp. of America v. Anheuser–Busch, Inc., 306 F.2d 433 (5th Cir.1962), cert. denied, 372 U.S. 965 (1963). Which, if any, of the theories of trademark protection justifies this injunction?

The same brewer later used the slogan "This Bud's for you." A florist's association's promotional campaign for rosebuds used the identical slogan. The judge declined to grant a preliminary injunction. There was no competition between the parties; consumers were not likely to be confused; the state lacked a trademark dilution statute; and, unlike the "bugs" slogan, a rosebud "cannot be said to disparage A–B's slogan or its product." Anheuser–Busch, Inc. v. Florists Association, 603 F.Supp. 35 (N.D.Ohio 1984).

POLO FASHIONS, INC. v. DICK BRUHN, INC.

United States Court of Appeals, Ninth Circuit, 1986.
793 F.2d 1132.

SNEED, CIRCUIT JUDGE. This is a trademark infringement action. The plaintiff, Polo Fashions, Inc. (Polo), prevailed in the district court and received approximately $6,000, the amount of profits the defendants earned from sales of counterfeit Polo shirts. Polo argues that the district court did not award an adequate remedy. We agree in part. Therefore, we affirm in part, reverse in part, and remand.

Polo manufactures a popular line of quality menswear. It goes to great efforts to ensure that its products are of excellent quality and are sold only in suitable establishments. In January 1982, Larry Pickens, one of the defendants, began purchasing Polo shirts under unusual circumstances from Ladowitz & Sergio, a firm not party to this appeal. Pickens sold these shirts to Dick Bruhn, Inc. (Bruhn), a California retail clothing chain, the other defendant in the case. Bruhn sold a number of shirts to customers at a profit. The district court found, and the parties do not dispute, that the questionable nature of the supply arrangements, and the low quality of the shirts, put Pickens and Bruhn on notice that the shirts were not manufactured by Polo.

Polo soon learned that Bruhn was selling counterfeit shirts. On March 9, 1982, Polo sent an express mail letter demanding that Bruhn cease selling the shirts. After consultation with his attorney, Bruhn decided to continue selling the shirts. On March 16, Polo filed suit. Bruhn continued selling the shirts to retail customers and also, on March 22, shipped a number of the shirts at cost to another retailer. Bruhn's representations to Polo during this period nonetheless led Polo to believe that Bruhn had ceased selling and shipping the shirts. In fact, Bruhn did not cease disposing of the shirts until March 26, ten days after suit was filed.

The district court found for Polo. It characterized the defendants' actions as "callous disregard for the rights of the mark holder and a willful infringement." The parties do not contest the district court's finding of liability. The district court, however, refused to award any remedy other than a recovery of Pickens's and Bruhn's profits.

On appeal, Polo seeks three additional remedies: (1) attorneys' fees under 15 U.S.C. § 1117; (2) the receipts on the sales of shirts at cost to other retailers; and (3) a permanent injunction. * * *

Section 1117 provides that "[t]he court in exceptional cases may award reasonable attorney fees to the prevailing party." * * * The Senate Report described the breadth of the remedy as follows:

> "Effective enforcement of trademark rights is left to the trademark owners and they should, in the interest of preventing purchaser confusion, be encouraged to enforce trademark rights. It would be unconscionable not to provide a complete remedy including attorney fees for acts which courts have characterized as malicious, fraudulent, deliberate, and willful. The proposed amendment would limit attorney fees to 'exceptional cases' and the award of attorney fees would be within the discretion of the court."

S.Rep. No. 1400, 93d Cong., 2d Sess.

The text of section 1117 places a heavy burden on an attorney arguing that the district court abused its discretion in refusing to award attorneys' fees. First, the remedy is available only in "exceptional cases." Second, the statute provides that the court "may" award fees; it does not require them. Finally, the Senate Report expressly commends this decision to the discretion of the court.

Polo's argument that the district court abused its discretion rests squarely on Playboy Enterprises, Inc. v. Baccarat Clothing Co., 692 F.2d 1272 (9th Cir.1982). There we reversed a district court's refusal to award attorneys' fees under section 1117. We noted that the defendants premeditatedly manufactured counterfeit insignias and sold them for several years at a substantial profit. The defendants' conduct in this case is less blameworthy. Although Pickens and Bruhn must have known that the shirts were not genuine Polos, they did not invest the effort and time to manufacture them; they simply took advantage of a profitable business opportunity presented to them.

Moreover, the defendants in *Playboy* obstructed discovery during the lawsuit to prevent the plaintiffs from locating the counterfeit goods. The district judge in this case was clearly aware that he had the power to award fees; he just as clearly exercised his discretion not to award them. On the facts of this case, we decline to interfere in his performance of the function Congress assigned to him when it enacted section 1117.[1] * * *

1. We acknowledge that, since the institution of this action, the Lanham Act has been amended to provide for criminal penalties for trafficking in counterfeit goods. The statute also provides for attorneys' fees awards as the norm in cases of this sort. See Trademark Counterfeiting Act of 1984, Pub.L. No. 98–473, § 1502, 98 Stat. 1837, 2178 (providing for criminal penalties) (to be codified at 18 U.S.C. § 2320); id. § 1503(2), 98 Stat. 1837, 2182 (amending section 1117). The parties do not contend that these provisions apply to this case; obviously these amendments to the Lanham Act

Section 1117 provides that a successful plaintiff in a trademark infringement action is

> "entitled * * * to recover * * * defendant's profits. * * * In assessing profits the plaintiff shall be required to prove defendant's sales only; defendant must prove all elements of cost or deduction claimed. * * * If the court shall find that the amount of the recovery based on profits is either inadequate or excessive the court may in its discretion enter judgment for such sum as the court shall find to be just, according to the circumstances of the case."

After Bruhn realized that the shirts it had purchased from Pickens were not genuine Polo shirts, it sold some of the shirts to other retailers at cost. The district court refused to award Polo damages for the sale of these shirts, because Bruhn did not make a profit on the sale. Polo argues that the district court should have awarded the entire receipts from the sales as "profits." If Bruhn had not disposed of these shirts, Polo argues, they would have been confiscated by Polo, and Bruhn would have received no money for the shirts, losing its entire investment. Accordingly, the receipts on these shipments should be characterized as "profits."

While we reject the "profits" characterization of these receipts, we do agree that the court did not impose an adequate remedy for the "at cost" sales. As we noted in *Playboy,* the purpose of section 1117 is to "take all the economic incentive out of trademark infringement." Remedies that do not remove the economic incentive "would encourage a counterfeiter to merely switch from one infringing scheme to another as soon as the infringed owner became aware of the fabrication."

The district court's remedy in this case did not remove all of Bruhn's economic incentive to buy and sell counterfeit Polo shirts. Bruhn was charged exactly the same penalty it would have been charged if it had behaved legally, that is, if it had destroyed the counterfeits. See Lanham Act, 15 U.S.C. § 1118. Despite Bruhn's having acted unlawfully in selling the counterfeits, the district court's remedy left Bruhn $8,820 richer than it would have been had it acted lawfully. The mythic future infringer, well-versed in the precedents of this circuit and not unwilling to violate federal law, would ship the shirts just as Bruhn did. To remove this incentive, we hold that the recovery based on profits is inadequate. Bruhn must pay Polo the receipts from the sales of those shirts, $8,820; any lesser remedy would not remove the incentive for Bruhn to ship the shirts after discovering that they were counterfeit.

A district court's denial of an injunction is reviewed for an abuse of discretion. SEC v. Arthur Young & Co., 590 F.2d 785, 787 (9th Cir.1979). The legal standards it applied, however, are subject to de novo review.

The district court's judgment on this point stated that "[t]he facts and circumstances of this case also do not indicate that permanent injunctive relief is necessary. Polo has provided no evidence suggesting that defendants intend to, or are likely to, engage in future sales or distribution of counterfeit Polo merchandise."

The district court erred. As the Supreme Court has noted in this area, a trademark plaintiff

> "entitled to relief, is entitled to effective relief; and any doubt in respect of the extent thereof must be resolved in its favor as the innocent producer and

are not probative of the intent Congress had when it drafted section 1117 in 1975.

against the [defendant], which has shown by its conduct that it is not to be trusted."

William R. Warner & Co. v. Eli Lilly & Co., 265 U.S. 526, 532 (1924). In this case, the district court refused to grant an injunction because the plaintiffs had not introduced any specific evidence to demonstrate that the defendants would infringe in the future. * * * The defendants had willfully violated Polo's trademark rights. The defendants refused to stop violating those rights until Polo brought suit in federal district court. We should not require Polo also to introduce concrete evidence that the defendants are likely to infringe again. If the defendants sincerely intend not to infringe, the injunction harms them little; if they do, it gives Polo substantial protection of its trademark. Accordingly, we reverse the district court's refusal to grant permanent injunctive relief. We remand this case to the district court to provide the relief that this opinion require[s].

Affirmed in part, reversed in part, and remanded.

Notes

1. *Special Damages: Costs of Removing Confusion by Equivalent Advertising.* Big O Tire Dealers, Inc. v. Goodyear Tire & Rubber Co., 408 F.Supp. 1219 (D.Colo.1976), affirmed 561 F.2d 1365 (10th Cir.1977). The defendant, Goodyear, was held to have infringed plaintiff's trademark "Bigfoot." Plaintiff was a smaller corporation providing advertising concepts and other aids to independent tire dealers. Special damages of $2,800,000 were measured by the plaintiff's cost to counteract the effect of Goodyear's gigantic promotion of "Bigfoot" tires had on its business. The court said:

"There is direct precedent for an award of damages resulting from false advertising based upon the time and effort spent by the plaintiff in counteracting the effects of defamation. [citation] * * *

"The Tenth Circuit has recognized a similar measure of damages in Ira M. Petersime & Son v. Robbins, 81 F.2d 295 (10th Cir.1936). More significantly, in that case the court recognized that expenses of counteracting business disparagement qualified as special damages. * * *

"The only difference between those damages and this case is that Big O did not spend $2,800,000 in advertising to counteract the Goodyear advertising. It is clear that Big O did not have the economic resources to conduct such a campaign. * * * Should the law apply differently to those who have the economic power to help themselves compared to those who must seek redress through the courts? * * * In my view the answer must assuredly be no."

The Tenth Circuit affirmed this element of damages, but reduced it to $678,302.

2. *Injunction Without Damages?* a. Mutual of Omaha Insurance Co. v. Novak, 648 F.Supp. 905, 912 (D.Neb.1986), aff'd, 836 F.2d 397 (8th Cir.1987), cert. denied, 488 U.S. 933 (1988). Novak, an antinuclear activist, was marketing T-shirts and coffee mugs bearing the words "Mutant of Omaha" and a logo that resembled Mutual's. The reverse side of one of the shirts read, "When the world's in ashes, we'll have you covered." Finding Mutual's registered trademark infringed, the court enjoined defendant from employing the "Mutant" designations and said, "Because the parties sell noncompeting goods, and because the Court is satisfied that the injunction will satisfy the equities of the case, no further award shall be made."

b. El Greco Leather Products Co. v. Shoe World, Inc., 726 F.Supp. 25, 29 (E.D.N.Y.1989). Shoe World sold shoes that carried plaintiff's trademark but, unbeknownst to Shoe World, were from canceled lots. The court discussed authority that supported recovery of profits to prevent unjust enrichment or to deter and contrary authority that limits remedies to an injunction where an infringer lacked knowledge of intent to infringe:

"The Lanham Act makes any award of damages subject to the principles of equity. Equity requires that this court do what is fair and just. Shoe World which, acting in good faith, innocently infringed El Greco's trademark, should not be required to pay monetary damages where an injunction is in place which fully protects plaintiff from future harm."

c. General Electric Co. v. Speicher, 877 F.2d 531, 535–37 (7th Cir.1989):

"Without even considering whether General Electric had sustained any damages, Judge Sharp found that 'the equities of this case preclude a monetary award. Speicher was an innocent infringer who acted in good faith. Speicher is a reputable businessman who has always enjoyed a spotless business record. The infringement was confined to one particular job. Speicher's profit [$1,500] and G.E.'s alleged loss [roughly $25,000] are relatively small.' Naturally the judge also declined to award attorney's fees to GE.

"Section 1117(a) does provide that any monetary award under it shall be 'subject to the principles of equity,' and courts sometimes speak in broad terms about 'the award for damages' under the statute being ' "subject to the principles of equity," ' Carl Zeiss Stiftung v. VEB Carl Zeiss Jena, 433 F.2d 686, 706 (2d Cir.1970), or about 'all monetary recovery under § 35 be[ing] "subject to the principles of equity." ' Getty Petroleum Corp. v. Bartco Petroleum Corp., 858 F.2d 103, 111 (2d Cir.1988). In these and all the other cases we have found, however, including the leader of the pack, Champion Spark Plug Co. v. Sanders, 331 U.S. 125 (1947), the issue was whether to award the plaintiff the defendant's profits from the infringement (or in *Getty,* punitive damages), rather than whether merely to make good the plaintiff's losses. [citations] If the defendant is a more efficient producer than the plaintiff, his profits will exceed the plaintiff's losses, so an automatic award of profits in a trademark infringement case could confer a windfall on the plaintiff. This is fine if the defendant is a deliberate infringer, but questionable if he is an innocent one. (An intermediate case will be considered later.) Yet even if he is an innocent infringer he ought at least reimburse the plaintiff's losses. As between plaintiff and defendant, the defendant has violated the law and the plaintiff not, so it is hard to see how the defendant's equities could ever be superior to the plaintiff's if all the plaintiff were seeking was his actual losses. We have found no authority * * * for cutting down the plaintiff's recovery on equitable grounds in such a case, and, * * * we doubt that such a reduction would ever be justified. * * *

"The judge's ruling on damages was further flawed by his unexamined and erroneous premise that even compensatory damages are improper if the defendant infringed the plaintiff's trademark in good faith. Apart from what we said earlier on this score, notice that all that good faith means in this context is that the infringer didn't *know* he was infringing someone's trademark. This means rather little. Suppose that the infringer, although acting in good faith, was also acting negligently—a reasonable person in his position would have realized he was infringing, though he, being unreasonable, did not. * * *

"General Electric is entitled to a new trial on damages. That new trial will encompass its claim under 15 U.S.C. § 1117(b) for treble damages. Added in 1984, this subsection provides that in assessing damages 'the court shall, unless the court finds extenuating circumstances, enter judgment for three times such profits or damages, whichever is greater, together with a reasonable attorney's fee, in the case of any violation of section 1114(1)(A) * * * that consists of intentionally using a mark or designation, knowing such mark or designation is a counterfeit mark.' Judge Sharp refused to invoke this provision because he had just refused to award General Electric any damages under section 1117(a), so there was nothing to treble; but on reconsideration he added that he didn't think Speicher had been guilty of intentional misconduct. Whether Speicher's counterfeiting was intentional within the meaning of section 1117(b) is not foreclosed by the district judge's inadequate analysis of the issue of Speicher's good faith. This, together with the question whether there were any extenuating circumstances for his conduct, is a matter to be determined in the new trial that we are ordering on remand."

ALPO PETFOODS, INC. v. RALSTON PURINA CO.

United States District Court, District of Columbia, 1989.
720 F.Supp. 194.

SPORKIN, DISTRICT JUDGE. * * * On October 3, 1986, plaintiff ALPO filed suit alleging that Ralston violated the Lanham Act and engaged in unfair competition. ALPO claims that Ralston advertisements and promotions, which state that Puppy Chow puppy foods contain a formula that reduces hip joint laxity, promotes proper hip joint development and lessens the severity of canine hip dysplasia and degenerative joint disease ("CHD claims"), are false, misleading and deceptive in violation of § 43(a) of the Lanham Act and the common law. ALPO has also put in issue Ralston's claims that its Puppy food has superior digestibility compared to its competitors' brands. * * *

The court finds that ALPO was damaged by Ralston's misconduct. Dog owners would certainly be remiss in caring for their dogs if they did not feed them a chow that would substantially lessen the possibility of their pet contracting CHD. Based on the materiality of Ralston's CHD claims and the economic analysis by both parties of the success of the CHD campaign, the court finds that ALPO Puppy Food lost sales to Puppy Chow on account of the CHD claims.

The court finds that ALPO spent a substantial amount of money in advertising expenditures in order to counter the CHD campaign, an amount over and above its planned advertising costs for ALPO Puppy Food. Moreover, the court finds that plaintiff had to postpone the introduction of its new puppy food on a nationwide basis, and finds the delay was due in part to ALPO's difficulty in overcoming the extravagant and false claims made by Ralston.

A particularly effective way to measure the damages sustained would be to look to the sums Ralston expended in its CHD advertising campaign. That amount was 5.2 million dollars.

During the 1986 fiscal year, the approximate period in which Ralston made its CHD claims, Ralston earned 171.6 million dollars in sales from Puppy Chow products. When this figure is reduced by the appropriate production and sales costs, Ralston's profits (pre-tax) come to 50.1 million dollars for the period. The amount of Ralston's profits corresponding to ALPO's share (22 percent) of the non-Ralston puppy food market is 11 million dollars.

Ralston has maintained the validity of its CHD claims and unless enjoined would renew making them once this case has been concluded. It is also clear the CHD claims have made a lasting impression on the audiences to which they were directed. Thus, there is evidence of continuing injury to competitors, veterinarians, breeders, and dog owners who were exposed to the CHD claims.

The court does not find that Ralston is entitled to an award of damages based on ALPO's misconduct. Ralston, as a competitor, and the consuming public are in need of protection from ALPO's false and misleading advertisements of its puppy food. The court believes that such protection can best be accomplished by enjoining ALPO from engaging in false and deceptive advertising of its puppy food.

Section 43(a) of Lanham Act provides in relevant part:

> "Any person who shall affix, apply, or annex * * * any false description or representation, including words or other symbols tending falsely to describe or * * * represent the same, and shall cause such goods to enter into commerce * * * shall be liable to a civil action by any person * * * who believes that he is or is likely to be damaged by the use of any such false description or representation."

15 U.S.C. § 1125(a). The act creates a cause of action for representations and statements that are (1) facially false, (2) affirmatively misleading, (3) untrue due to a failure to disclose information, and (4) partially correct and literally true but convey a false impression. [citations]

While the Act is not directly available to consumers, it is nevertheless designed to protect consumers, by giving the cause of action to competitors who are prepared to vindicate the injury caused to consumers [citations] * * *

The literal message consistently communicated to the public by the Ralston advertisements and promotional materials was that Ralston Puppy Chow products help reduce hip joint laxity or help puppies develop a snugger hip joint fit, which can reduce the severity of CHD. Simply put, Ralston's claims lacked any reasonable basis in fact. Not only have such claims perpetrated a cruel hoax on dog owners, but also have severely disadvantaged Ralston's competitors who were attempting to sell their existing products and to introduce new products in the puppy food market.

The record establishes that with the exception of Ralston's own faulty research, there is no valid scientific support for the proposition that the nutritional balance in a dog's diet can affect hip joint formation, hip joint laxity, or the severity or occurrence of CHD. The overwhelming weight of scientific research indicates that hip joint laxity and CHD are hereditary in nature and are unaffected by the nutritional balance of a dog's diet. Against this background, and in view of the factual finding that Ralston's research lends no support to its claims, it is clear that they are false on their face.

Once a challenged claim has been found "actually false, relief can be granted on the court's own findings without reference to the reaction of the buyer or consumer of the product." PBX Enterprises v. Audiofidelity Enterprises, 818 F.2d 266, 272 (2nd Cir.1987).

Since this court has found that Ralston's CHD claims are actually false, their materiality thus may be presumed. This bolsters the court's earlier finding that Ralston's claims were material in fact.

A party is entitled to injunctive relief under the Lanham Act if it demonstrates a "likelihood of deception or confusion on the part of the buying public" caused by a product's false or misleading description or representation.

A permanent injunction may be granted where it is shown that the plaintiff and defendant are competitors in the relevant market, and the false claims were likely to injure the plaintiff.

ALPO and Ralston are direct competitors in the puppy food market. Further, the claims made by Ralston were false and deceptive, and the credible evidence shows that consumers were deceived by those claims. * * *

Based on the above, injunctive relief against Ralston is clearly warranted. But there is more. Ralston still maintains its position with respect to the viability of its CHD claims and has only halted its continued advertisement of the claims pending this court's decision. Thus, there is the real likelihood that Ralston will renew its CHD advertising campaign once this litigation is over. Ralston's persistence in its claims clearly evidences the likelihood of repeated future false claims and unless restrained Ralston will continue to violate the Lanham Act with its attendant adverse impact on the buying public and ALPO's business.

The court has also found that Ralston's CHD claims have left a lingering impression on veterinarians, breeders, and dog owners. As part of this court's injunctive relief Ralston shall be ordered to prepare and disseminate to those who received information concerning its CHD claims a corrective release in terms and in form to be approved by this court.

The Lanham Act permits the assessment of damages and the award of profits where the facts warrant. The measure of damages and profits may be assessed on a number of different bases where necessary to effectuate the purposes of the Act, which also permits the assessment of costs and allowance of attorneys' fees in appropriate circumstances. The Act allows the award of damages in an amount up to three times the actual damages proven. After considering the various measures of damages, the court finds the most appropriate measure would be one that is based on Ralston's advertising expenditures as they pertain to the dissemination of its deceptive message. This form of relief has support in the case law and would appear to be particularly appropriate here. See U–Haul Intern. v. Jartran, Inc., 793 F.2d 1034, 1037 (9th Cir.1986). Ralston's offending advertisements directly injured the public and adversely affected ALPO's business both in cutting into its existing business and depriving it of the opportunity to fully introduce and develop its new puppy food on a nationwide basis.

According to the evidence presented to this court, Ralston spent approximately 5.2 million dollars on its deceptive CHD advertising program. Since this figure does not measure the full impact caused by Ralston's impermissible conduct, the court finds this would be an appropriate case to double the damage award. Accordingly, the award of damages to ALPO is in the sum of 5.2 million dollars doubled to 10.4 million dollars. This amount is close to the 11 million dollar adjusted net profits Ralston earned from the sales of its Puppy Chow products during the period of its CHD advertising program. This sum is obtained by applying to Ralston's nationwide net profits of 50.1 million dollars ALPO's 22 percent share of the non-Ralston puppy food sales.

The court is also awarding ALPO its attorney's fees limited to its prosecution of its case in chief against Ralston, along with its related costs for this phase of the proceeding.

Notes

1. *False Advertising Under the Lanham Act.* Section 43(a) of the Lanham Act provides remedies when a business competitor falsely advertises a product. Remedial problems grow out of two features: (a) the consumers who purchased the product are the principal victims of false advertising, but they lack standing under the act, and (b) except in limited markets, a competitor will be hard put to prove that false advertising actually diverted sales from it.

2. *Query:* Was the district judge's bite worse than the statute's bark?

The dog-food fight continued in the court of appeals, but only Ralston appealed. Alpo Petfoods, Inc. v. Ralston Purina Co., 720 F.Supp. 194, 197, 212–15 (D.D.C.1989), aff'd in part, rev'd in part, 913 F.2d 958, 965–73 (D.C.Cir.1990).

The court of appeals dealt with several remedial issues: wilfulness; recovery of profits; ALPO's damages; multiple damages; attorney fees; and the injunction.

a. *Wilfulness.* The court of appeals found that the trial judge's implicit finding that Ralston had acted wilfully or in bad faith was clearly erroneous.

b. *Recovery of Profits.* Lacking proof of Ralston's wilfulness or bad faith, ALPO could not recover Ralston's profits. Deterrence without more cannot, the court said, justify an award of defendant's profits.

c. *Damages:* "We do not mean, however, to deny ALPO all monetary relief for Ralston's false advertising. Because the district court has so far focused on awarding Ralston's profits, it has not yet decided what actual damages ALPO has proved. On remand, the court should award ALPO its actual damages, bearing in mind the requirement that any amount awarded have support in the record, as well as the following points about the governing law.

"In a false-advertising case such as this one, actual damages under section [1117(a)] can include:

—profits lost by the plaintiff on sales actually diverted to the false advertiser [citation];

—profits lost by the plaintiff on sales made at prices reduced as a demonstrated result of the false advertising [citation];

—the costs of any completed advertising that actually and reasonably responds to the defendant's offending ads [citation]; and

—quantifiable harm to the plaintiff's good will, to the extent that completed corrective advertising has not repaired that harm [citation].

"When assessing these actual damages the district court may take into account the difficulty of proving an exact amount of damages from false advertising, as well as the maxim that 'the wrongdoer shall bear the risk of the uncertainty which his own wrong has created.' Otis Clapp & Son v. Filmore Vitamin Co., 754 F.2d 738, 745 (7th Cir.1985) (quoting Bigelow v. RKO Radio Pictures, Inc., 327 U.S. 251, 265 (1946). At the same time, the court must ensure that the record adequately supports all items of damages claimed and establishes a causal link between the damages and the defendant's conduct, lest the award become speculative or violate section 35(a)'s prohibition against punishment."

d. *Multiple damages.* If, on remand, the trial judge decides to enhance ALPO's damages under § 1117(a), he must explain "why the enhanced award is compensatory and not punitive."

e. *Attorney fees.* ALPO could recover its attorney fees only if it proved that Ralston had acted wilfully or in bad faith. Reversed.

f. *Injunction:* "The injunction at issue permanently bars Ralston and its associates 'from making any advertising or other related claims that are false, misleading, deceptive or made without substantiation in fact concerning the effects of Ralston dog food products on hip joint formation, hip joint laxity, Canine Hip Dysplasia, Degenerative Joint Disease and similar conditions.' The court also ordered Ralston and ALPO to adopt procedures for ensuring compliance with the injunction. Ralston and ALPO have complied, and an October 11, 1989 district court order formalizes the procedures, which are themselves a subject of appeal. The relevant section of these procedures subjects 'any advertising or other related claim concerning the effects of Ralston dog or puppy food products or low anion gap diets on hip joint formation, hip joint laxity, canine hip dysplasia, degenerative joint disease, and similar conditions' to a pre-clearance process. * * *

"The law requires that courts closely tailor injunctions to the harm that they address. [citation] * * * In enjoining Ralston, the district court identified the harm redressed by the injunctions as deception of puppy food buyers and erosion of ALPO's business. Yet the prohibitory injunction, both as entered and, particularly, as implemented, suppresses more speech than protecting these interests requires. ALPO's false-advertising claim against Ralston involves a dispute over whether Ralston may commercially claim that Puppy Chow confers certain unproved health benefits. Redressing the harm that these claims have caused in the puppy food market does not require that a court supervise all future debate on the anion gap theory. Moreover, we see little prospect that readers of a veterinary magazine who encounter a report on the false-advertising judgment against Ralston will conclude, simply because Ralston has had an opportunity to proclaim its innocence, that Puppy Chow actually ameliorates CHD. Especially given the prior restraint involved in the procedures described above, we think it important that the injunction and procedures cover only the speech most likely to deceive consumers and harm ALPO in the ways described in the district court's opinion: CHD-related *advertising.*

"We remand the prohibitory injunction against Ralston for removal of the words 'or other related,' and remand the October 11, 1989 order for removal of the words 'or other related' and the words 'or related.' These changes, which limit the injunction and procedures to advertising, will tailor the injunction to the harms attacked by ALPO's section 43(a) claim."

g. *Finally.* On remand Ralston could prove that *it* was damaged.

7. MISAPPROPRIATION OF IDEAS

The "Misappropriation" Doctrine of Unfair Competition—Superseded (in part) by Statute. During the middle years of the twentieth century, before the Lanham Act and the revisions of the Copyright Act, an elaborate body of substantive law developed; it provided the base for remedies for commercial piracy consisting of misappropriation of ideas, work products, and performances, that represented valuable intangibles but were not protected by statutory patents or copyrights.

International News Service v. Associated Press, 248 U.S. 215 (1918), began this doctrine. Briefly summarized, the plaintiff wire service obtained its product, news of World War I, by sending correspondents into the field. The defendant wire service obtained its news by sending someone to read the bulletins plaintiff posted in New York. "News" qua news was and still is not copyrightable, but defendant's conduct was clearly intolerable. Defendant's appropriation was enjoined. Teeth were given to the admonition not to reap where one has not sown.

Although *International News Service* may not actually be the first to have faced the general problem, it was the first decision to create a "quasi-property" in news to supply a legal rationale to the doctrine. The law seems more comfortable in protecting "property" than ephemeral values. Only a minor adjustment was thereafter needed to create the whole area of "literary property" or "common law copyright" as one description has it.

We need not dwell on the flowering and decline of "Misappropriation." One of its substantive requirements is that the idea, to be protectable, has been expressed in some elementary tangible form. Thus the doctrine has always been within reach of copyright protection, and the necessary coverage was extended in 1976 by copyright revision (17 U.S.C. § 301). The preemptive provision is § 301:

"Preemption with respect to other laws

"(a) On and after January 1, 1978, all legal or equitable rights that are equivalent to any of the exclusive rights within the general scope of copyright as specified by section 106 in works of authorship that are fixed in a tangible medium of expression and come within the subject matter of copyright as specified by sections 102 and 103, whether created before or after that date, whether published or unpublished, are governed exclusively by this title. Thereafter, no person is entitled to any such right or equivalent right in any such work under the common law statutes of any State.

"(b) Nothing in this title annuls or limits any rights or remedies under the common law or statutes of any State with respect to—

"(1) subject matter that does not come within the subject matter of copyright as specified by sections 102 and 103, including works of authorship not fixed in any tangible medium of expression; or

"(2) any cause of action arising from undertakings commenced before January 1, 1978; or

"(3) activities violating legal or equitable rights that are not equivalent to any of the exclusive rights within the general scope of copyright as specified by section 106."

Nash v. CBS, Inc., 704 F.Supp. 823, 834–35 (N.D.Ill.1989), aff'd, 899 F.2d 1537 (7th Cir.1990), discusses the extent of preemption. Nash alleged that a CBS TV series infringed his copyrighted story about John Dillinger; he appended a count for "common law misappropriation":

"The 'goal' underlying copyright law is the same as that driving the tort of misappropriation: balancing the need to provide economic incentives for authorship against the preservation of the freedom to imitate. Given the identical goals of the tort of misappropriation and the Copyright Act, we would be inclined to hold that § 301 always preempts the tort of misappropriation.

"We hesitate to go so far, though, because Congress clearly intended to preserve some form of the tort of misappropriation. The House Judiciary Committee Report on the 1976 Amendments to the Copyright Act states as follows:

'Misappropriation' is not necessarily synonymous with copyright infringement and thus a cause of action labeled as 'misappropriation' is not preempted if it is in fact based neither on a right within the general scope of copyright as specified by section 106 nor on a right equivalent thereto. For example, state law should have the flexibility to afford a remedy (under traditional principles of equity) against a consistent pattern of unauthorized appropriation by a competitor of the facts (i.e., not the literary expression) constituting 'hot' news, whether in the traditional mold of International News Service v. Associated Press, or in the newer form of data updates from scientific, business, or financial data bases. Likewise, a person having no trust or other relationship with the proprietor of a computerized data base should not be immunized from sanctions against electronically or cryptographically breaching the proprietor's security arrangements and accessing the proprietor's data. The unauthorized data access which should be remediable might also be achieved by the intentional interception of data transmissions by wire, microwave or laser transmissions, or by the common unintentional means of 'crossed' telephone lines occasioned by errors in switching.

"The proprietor of data displayed on the cathode ray tube of a computer terminal should be afforded protection against unauthorized printouts by third parties (with or without improper access), even if the data are not copyrightable. For example, the data may not be copyrighted because they are not fixed in a tangible medium of expression. * * *"

H. Report No. 1476, reprinted at 17 U.S.C.A. § 301.

"We do not believe the House report reflects Congress's intent to preserve all misappropriation actions. If all misappropriation claims escaped § 301 preemption, a plaintiff could always challenge the use of his copyrighted material under both federal copyright law and the state law tort of misappropriation. This, in turn, would emasculate § 301. Congress considered § 301 as 'one of the bedrock provisions' of the 1976 amendments to the Copyright Act and enacted § 301 in order to 'establish a single system of federal statutory copyright.' If we interpreted the House Report to preclude preemption of all misappropriation claims, we would assure that pendent claims could be asserted in almost all infringement actions. We do not believe that Congress intended this, and, therefore, we hold that all misappropriation claims, except those similar to the examples cited in the House Report, are preempted. Here, Count III does not involve the 'systematic' appropriation of 'hot news' or valuable stored information. Nor does it allege a special relationship between the parties. Therefore, we hold that § 301 preempts Count III of Nash's complaint."

Finally, the Lanham Act has also shared in the dispersion of the "Misappropriation" theory. See Note pp. 592–96 supra. Even where remnants of the common law misappropriation action can be found, there seems little incentive, apart from venue considerations, to pursue them, since the statutory remedies are more extensive than the non-statutory.

C. THE RIGHT OF PUBLICITY

NEW YORK CIVIL RIGHTS LAW

§ 50. Right of Privacy. A person, firm or corporation that uses for advertising purposes, or for the purposes of trade, the name, portrait or picture of any living person without having first obtained the written consent of such person, or if a minor of his or her parent or guardian, is guilty of a misdemeanor.

§ 51. Action for Injunction and for Damages. Any person whose name, portrait or picture is used within this state for advertising purposes or for the purpose of trade without the written consent first obtained as above provided may maintain an equitable action in the supreme court of this state against the person, firm or corporation so using his name, portrait or picture, to prevent and restrain the use thereof; and may also sue and recover damages for any injuries sustained by reason of such use and if the defendant shall have knowingly used such person's name, portrait or picture in such manner as is forbidden or declared to be unlawful by the last section, the jury, in its discretion, may award exemplary damages. But nothing contained in this act shall be so construed as to prevent any person, firm or corporation, practicing the profession of photography, from exhibiting in or about his or its establishment specimens of the work of such establishment, unless the same is continued by such person, firm or corporation after written notice objecting thereto has been given by the person portrayed; and nothing contained in this act shall be so construed as to prevent any person, firm or corporation from using the name, portrait or picture of any manufacturer or dealer in connection with the goods, wares and merchandise manufactured, produced or dealt in by him which he has sold or disposed of with such name, portrait or picture used in connection therewith; or from using the name, portrait or picture of any author, composer or artist in connection with his literary, musical or artistic productions which he has sold or disposed of with such name, portrait or picture used in connection therewith. * * *

Notes

1. Uhlaender v. Henricksen, 316 F.Supp. 1277, 1283 (D.Minn.1970) explains the New York Civil Rights Law:

"New York has a statute which creates penal and civil liability for the unauthorized use of anyone's name or likeness 'for advertising purposes or for the purposes of trade.' [citations] This is a *privacy* statute, damages under which are measured by injury to feelings, not by loss of the commercial value of that which has been appropriated. [citations] It would seem to the court, contrary to the suggestions of the defendant, that the effect of the New York privacy statute upon the law of that state is irrelevant to the entirely independent area of misappropriation of name or likeness. The fact that the statute creates a right in public figures to sue *for breach of privacy* does not determine that the common law does or does not allow suit for misappropriation."

2. Stephano v. News Group Publications, Inc., 64 N.Y.2d 174, 183, 485 N.Y. S.2d 220, 224, 474 N.E.2d 580, 584 (1984), seems to have settled the question of whether New York recognized a non-statutory right of publicity: "Since the 'right of publicity' is encompassed under the Civil Rights Law as an aspect of the right of privacy, which * * * is exclusively statutory in this state, the plaintiff cannot claim an independent common-law right of publicity."

See also Pirone v. MacMillan, Inc., 894 F.2d 579 (2d Cir.1990).

CARSON v. HERE'S JOHNNY PORTABLE TOILETS, INC.

United States Court of Appeals, Sixth Circuit, 1983.
698 F.2d 831.

BAILEY BROWN, SENIOR CIRCUIT JUDGE. * * * Appellant, John W. Carson (Carson), is the host and star of "The Tonight Show," a well-known television program broadcast five nights a week by the National Broadcasting Company. Carson also appears as an entertainer in night clubs and theaters around the country. From the time he began hosting "The Tonight Show" in 1962, he has been introduced on the show each night with the phrase "Here's Johnny." This method of introduction was first used for Carson in 1957 when he hosted a daily television program for the American Broadcasting Company. The phrase "Here's Johnny" is generally associated with Carson by a substantial segment of the television viewing public. In 1967, Carson first authorized use of this phrase by an outside business venture, permitting it to be used by a chain of restaurants called "Here's Johnny Restaurants."

Appellant Johnny Carson Apparel, Inc. (Apparel), formed in 1970, manufactures and markets men's clothing to retail stores. Carson, the president of Apparel and owner of 20% of its stock, has licensed Apparel to use his name and picture, which appear on virtually all of Apparel's products and promotional material. Apparel has also used, with Carson's consent, the phrase "Here's Johnny" on labels for clothing and in advertising campaigns. In 1977, Apparel granted a license to Marcy Laboratories to use "Here's Johnny" as the name of a line of men's toiletries. The phrase "Here's Johnny" has never been registered by appellants as a trademark or service mark.

Appellee, Here's Johnny Portable Toilets, Inc., is a Michigan corporation engaged in the business of renting and selling "Here's Johnny" portable toilets. Appellee's founder was aware at the time he formed the corporation that "Here's Johnny" was the introductory slogan for Carson on "The Tonight Show." He indicated that he coupled the phrase with a second one, "The World's Foremost Commodian," to make "a good play on a phrase."

Shortly after appellee went into business in 1976, appellants brought this action alleging unfair competition, trademark infringement under federal and state law, and invasion of privacy and publicity rights. They sought damages and an injunction prohibiting appellee's further use of the phrase "Here's Johnny" as a corporate name or in connection with the sale or rental of its portable toilets.

After a bench trial, the district court * * * ordered the dismissal of the appellants' complaint. On the unfair competition claim, the court concluded that the appellants had failed to satisfy the "likelihood of confusion" test. On the right of privacy and right of publicity theories, the court held that these rights extend only to a "name or likeness," and "Here's Johnny" did not qualify.

Appellants' first claim alleges unfair competition from appellee's business activities in violation of § 43(a) of the Lanham Act, 15 U.S.C. § 1125(a) (1976), and of Michigan common law. The district court correctly noted that the test for equitable relief under both § 43(a) and Michigan common law is the "likelihood of confusion" standard. * * *

[W]e agree with the district court that the appellants have failed to establish a likelihood of confusion. The general concept underlying the likelihood of confusion is that the public believe that "the mark's owner *sponsored or otherwise approved* the use of the trademark." Warner Bros., Inc. v. Gay Toys, Inc., 658 F.2d 76, 79 (2d Cir.1981) (emphasis added) (quoting Dallas Cowboys Cheerleaders, Inc. v. Pussycat Cinema, Ltd., 604 F.2d 200, 205 (2d Cir.1979)).

The facts as found by the district court do not implicate such likelihood of confusion, and we affirm the district court on this issue.

The appellants also claim that the appellee's use of the phrase "Here's Johnny" violates the common law right of privacy and right of publicity.[1] The confusion in this area of the law requires a brief analysis of the relationship between these two rights.

In an influential article, Dean Prosser delineated four distinct types of the right of privacy: (1) intrusion upon one's seclusion or solitude, (2) public disclosure of embarrassing private facts, (3) publicity which places one in a false light, and (4) appropriation of one's name or likeness for the defendant's advantage. Prosser, Privacy, 48 Calif.L.Rev. 383, 389 (1960). This fourth type has become known as the "right of publicity." [citations] Henceforth we will refer to Prosser's last, or fourth, category as the "right of publicity."

Dean Prosser's analysis has been a source of some confusion in the law. His first three types of the right of privacy generally protect the right "to be let alone," while the right of publicity protects the celebrity's pecuniary interest in the commercial exploitation of his identity. Thus, the right of privacy and the right of publicity protect fundamentally different interests and must be analyzed separately.

We do not believe that Carson's claim that his right of privacy has been invaded is supported by the law or the facts. Apparently, the gist of this claim is that Carson is embarrassed by and considers it odious to be associated with the appellee's product. Clearly, the association does not appeal to Carson's sense of humor. But the facts here presented do not, it appears to us, amount to an invasion of any of the interests protected by the right of privacy. In any event, our disposition of the claim of an invasion of the right of publicity makes it unnecessary for us to accept or reject the claim of an invasion of the right of privacy.

The right of publicity has developed to protect the commercial interest of celebrities in their identities. The theory of the right is that a celebrity's identity can be valuable in the promotion of products, and the celebrity has an interest that may be protected from the unauthorized commercial exploitation of that identity. * * *

The district court dismissed appellants' claim based on the right of publicity because appellee does not use Carson's name or likeness. It held that it "would not be prudent to allow recovery for a right of publicity claim which does not more specifically identify Johnny Carson." We believe that, on the contrary, the district court's conception of the right of publicity is too narrow. The right of publicity, as we have stated, is that a celebrity has a protected pecuniary interest in the commercial exploitation of his identity. If the celebrity's identity is commercially exploited, there has been an invasion of his right whether or not his "name or likeness" is used. Carson's identity may be exploited even if his name, John W. Carson, or his picture is not used. * * *

We therefore conclude that, applying the correct legal standards, appellants are entitled to judgment. The proof showed without question that appellee had appropriated Carson's identity in connection with its corporate name and its product. * * *

1. Michigan law, which governs these claims, has not yet clearly addressed the right of publicity. But the general recognition of the right, suggests to us that the Michigan courts would adopt the right. Michigan has recognized a right of privacy. Beaumont v. Brown, 401 Mich. 80, 257 N.W.2d 522 (1977).

The judgment of the district court is vacated and the case remanded for further proceedings consistent with this opinion.

Cornelia G. Kennedy, Circuit Judge, dissenting. * * * While I agree that an individual's identity may be impermissibly exploited, I do not believe that the common law right of publicity may be extended beyond an individual's name, likeness, achievements, identifying characteristics or actual performances, to include phrases or other things which are merely associated with the individual, as is the phrase "Here's Johnny." The majority's extension of the right of publicity to include phrases or other things which are merely associated with the individual permits a popular entertainer or public figure, by associating himself or herself with a common phrase, to remove those words from the public domain. * * *

The common law right of publicity has been held to protect various aspects of an individual's identity from commercial exploitation [citations]: name [citations], likeness [citations], achievements [citations], identifying characteristics [citations], actual performances [citations], and fictitious characters created, by a performer. [citations] Research reveals no case which has extended the right of publicity to phrases and other things which are merely associated with an individual. * * * I would affirm the judgment of the District Court.

CARSON v. HERE'S JOHNNY PORTABLE TOILETS, INC.

United States Court of Appeals, Sixth Circuit, 1987.
810 F.2d 104.

Per Curiam. In an earlier published opinion, Carson v. Here's Johnny Portable Toilets, Inc., 698 F.2d 831 (6th Cir.1983), this court held that under Michigan law Johnny Carson, one of the plaintiffs herein, has a "right of publicity" in the phrase "Here's Johnny." This case was remanded to the district court, for a determination of appropriate relief, the defendant having improperly exploited the phrase to its own advantage and to the plaintiff's detriment. Upon remand the district court enjoined the defendant from using the phrase anywhere in the country and awarded $31,661.96 in damages, measured by the defendant's profits, plus costs. On appeal the defendant challenges the damage award and asks that we limit the geographical scope of the injunction to the State of Michigan.

One cannot be sure how most jurisdictions other than Michigan would have ruled on the merits of this case. Many states have never considered whether a right of publicity exists, and even fewer have considered whether that right protects not only an entertainer's name or picture but also a phrase or nickname or other symbol associated with the entertainer. At least one of Michigan's neighbors has indicated that it recognizes a right of publicity no less broad than that recognized here: see Hirsch v. S.C. Johnson & Son, Inc., 90 Wis.2d 379, 280 N.W.2d 129 (1979), where Wisconsin extended protection to a famous football player's nickname, "Crazylegs." In Motschenbacher v. R.J. Reynolds Tobacco Co., 498 F.2d 821 (9th Cir.1974), similarly, it was held that the unauthorized depiction in a television commercial of a professional race car driver's distinctive automobile violated the driver's right of publicity under the law of California.

Because there are indications that other states would hold as we have predicted Michigan would, and because the defendant is uncertain, at this point, whether it wants to use the phrase "Here's Johnny" in any state where the substantive law arguably differs from Michigan's, we see no harm in letting the injunction stand in its present form for the time being, at least. If the defendant should hereafter decide that it wants to use the phrase in a state (other than Michigan) where it believes such use would be legal but for the injunction, it will be free to seek a modification of the injunction from the district court at that time. As we see the equities, in the light of the parties' conduct to date and the probable trend of the law nationally, it would be fairer to require the defendant to take the litigation initiative in such a situation than to require the plaintiffs to do so.

The defendant further contends that the plaintiffs waived their right to recover damages in the amount of the defendant's profits. The waiver allegedly occurred when the plaintiffs' counsel told the trial court in closing argument that the profits might or might not be great enough to justify the expense of an accounting, suggesting that the court could simply award $10,000 as damages if it chose not to order an accounting. We see no waiver in this.

The judgment of the district court is AFFIRMED, without prejudice to the defendant's right to seek future modification of the injunction in the event of changed conditions that might make modification appropriate.

Notes

1. *Copyright Preemptions of Privacy Actions.* Shipley, Publicity Never Dies; It Just Fades Away: The Right of Publicity and Federal Preemption, 66 Cornell L.Rev. 673, 736–37 (1981): †

"The effects of federal intellectual property policy and section 301 of the Copyright Act of 1976 on the right of publicity is problematic. The conduct that gives rise to a claim based on an invasion of this right is often nothing more than the unauthorized copying, reproduction, distribution, or display of one or more of the several publicity interests it protects. Thus, a right of publicity action often vindicates rights that are 'equivalent' to the exclusive rights within the general scope of copyright. However, these 'equivalent' rights do not necessarily inhere in 'works of authorship that are fixed in a tangible medium of expression and come within the subject matter of copyright.' Such intangible interests as names, likenesses, distinctive styles, attributes of personality, acts or performances, and other elements of one's 'persona' have been the bases of viable right of publicity claims. Because these interests are not all writings or fixed works of authorship, section 301 may not require preemption of some right of publicity actions.

"When one of these interests amounts to a work of authorship and is fixed in a tangible medium of expression, however, it falls within the subject matter of copyright. If the fixed expression is subsequently copied, reproduced, and distributed, forceful arguments support federal preemption of a state-created right of publicity aimed at redressing the appropriation of interests in the form of fixed expressions. The perpetual nature of the doctrine strengthens the argument for preemption. Otherwise, the right of publicity would conflict with the federal scheme of copyright and perhaps stifle the creative efforts of some individuals.

"No blanket generalizations can resolve the questions concerning the continued vitality of the right of publicity. Like misappropriation, some right of publicity actions may be preempted. Others may survive either because of the subject matter of the plaintiff's claim, or because the particular right being vindicated is not equivalent to copyright. Future defendants should assert the federal statutory preemption defense against state right of publicity claims under the 1976 Copyright

Act. In view of the variety of interests protected by this right, some of which can be classified as copyrightable subject matter, and the several rights that have been vindicated by publicity actions, the preemptive effects of federal law on right of publicity claims must be determined on a case by case basis."

2. The protection of a celebrity's "persona," as demonstrated above, may rest on one or more substantive law bases, violation of copyright, the Lanham Act, state statutes, including New York's Civil Rights Act, or a non-statutory right of publicity. The plaintiff's choice of substantive theory and the facts selected to establish the cause of action are affected by the remedy sought. Here is an opportunity to review the scope of remedies within these categories.

3. Does the right of publicity survive the death of the celebrity? The common law "right of publicity" has a mixed ancestry—in part an offshoot of the right of privacy, in part a derivation of the "quasi-property" theory created in International News Service v. Associated Press, 248 U.S. 215 (1918) to protect the commercial value of the work of creative people.

Courts have uniformly held that a living celebrity can assign publicity rights. This reflects the "quasi-property" characteristics of the right. Logically, it follows that "property" would pass to the heir upon the death of the "owner."

But a number of courts balked. The California Supreme Court in Lugosi v. Universal Pictures, 25 Cal.3d 813, 160 Cal.Rptr. 323, 603 P.2d 425 (1979), drove the stake through the heart of Dracula by declaring that the rights expired on Lugosi's death. Likewise, the sixth circuit held in 1980 that Elvis Presley's publicity rights terminated at his death (judicial confirmation that Elvis has not really been sighted) even though they had been vigorously exercised during his lifetime. Memphis Development Foundation v. Factors Etc., Inc., 616 F.2d 956 (6th Cir.), cert. denied, 449 U.S. 953 (1980). Obviously in this line of cases, the right of privacy characteristics dominate the "quasi-property" genes in the right of publicity. And of course no rights claimed under the New York Civil Rights Law §§ 50, 51 can survive. Pirone v. MacMillan, Inc., 894 F.2d 579 (2d Cir.1990).

Other decisions support survivability. Price v. Hal Roach Studios, Inc., 400 F.Supp. 836 (S.D.N.Y.1975) decided that the publicity rights of Laurel and Hardy survived their deaths. Some decisions have qualified survivability by requiring the celebrity, Agatha Christie, to have exploited the publicity rights commercially during her lifetime, Hicks v. Casablanca Records, 464 F.Supp. 426 (S.D.N.Y.1978). This requirement was rejected for Martin Luther King who had not attempted to exploit his extraordinary persona commercially during his lifetime. Martin Luther King Jr. Center for Social Change v. American Heritage Products, Inc., 250 Ga. 135, 296 S.E.2d 697 (1982), adopted and reprinted, 694 F.2d 674 (11th Cir.1983). This holding adds substance to the "property" nature of the right and extends future non-statutory remedies to descendants. Is the right of publicity includable in a celebrity's gross estate for federal estate tax purposes?

Chapter 7

REMEDIES FOR INJURIES TO PERSONAL DIGNITY OR STATUS

A. DEFAMATION

1. DAMAGES

CRUMP v. P & C FOOD MARKETS, INC.

Supreme Court of Vermont, 1990.
154 Vt. 284, 576 A.2d 441.

ALLEN, CHIEF JUSTICE. * * * The present action arose after defendant dismissed plaintiff as an employee in August 1983. Plaintiff had been employed by defendant for eighteen years and held the position of head receiver for dry goods at defendant's Vermont distribution center at the time of his dismissal. Plaintiff's dismissal followed an incident in which he placed some rejected merchandise on an outgoing truck, intending to pick it up later for his personal use. * * *

At trial, plaintiff argued that once the merchandise was rejected and returned to the independent trucker, it became the trucker's property who in turn could give it to him. Therefore, plaintiff's later removal of it from defendant's premises was not theft. Defendant contended that it did not allow employees to remove merchandise delivered to its facility in that manner, or to receive gratuities from customers or distributors, and that even if defendant never paid for the merchandise, any such removal constituted theft.

Defendant's evidence showed, and plaintiff admitted, that he had failed to follow defendant's prescribed procedures for such rejected merchandise. * * * Plaintiff argued that because the trucker gave the rejected merchandise to the plaintiff, his acceptance and removal of it without following the prescribed company procedures could not have constituted theft.

Plaintiff's evidence showed that he was called a thief at a meeting held at the distribution center a few days after the incident, and that in two written reports prepared subsequent to that meeting, he was characterized as a problem employee and his actions were referred to as employee theft. * * * Plaintiff also presented evidence on the effect of the incident on his social life, his health, his personal and family life, and his reputation in the community. * * *

Plaintiff brought the present action seeking damages for defamation, intentional infliction of emotional distress, unlawful employment practices and breach of contract. * * * The jury returned a verdict for the plaintiff on the defamation and intentional infliction of emotional distress claims and awarded him $19,000 in compensatory and $25,000 in punitive damages for each claim. Defendant moved for judgment notwithstanding the verdict and, in the alternative, for a new trial. The court denied defendant's motions and the present appeal followed. * * *

Defendant challenges the trial court's denial of its motion for judgment notwithstanding the verdict on the defamation count, claiming there was insufficient proof at trial of the elements of the tort. Defendant argues that there was insufficient evidence that the defamatory statements were false, that defendant acted with the malice necessary to overcome the conditional privilege, that the statements were made in a negligent fashion, and that the defamatory statements were the proximate cause of plaintiff's injuries.

As we have recently noted, Ryan v. Herald Association, Inc., 152 Vt. 275, 277, 566 A.2d 1316, 1317–18 (1989), the elements of a defamation action in Vermont are:

> (1) a false and defamatory statement concerning another; (2) some negligence, or greater fault, in publishing the statement; (3) publication to at least one third person; (4) lack of privilege in the publication; (5) special damages, unless actionable per se; and (6) some actual harm so as to warrant compensatory damages.

Because the common-law privileges have not necessarily been adequate to protect First Amendment values, federal constitutional jurisprudence has modified the elements of defamation, at least in cases in which the plaintiff is in some way a "public figure," see, e.g., New York Times Co. v. Sullivan, 376 U.S. 254 (1964), or the material published is "of public concern," Gertz v. Robert Welch, Inc., 418 U.S. 323 (1974), Ryan v. Herald Association, Inc., 152 Vt. at 280 n. 2, 566 A.2d at 1319 n. 2; or, possibly, if the defendant is engaged in the dissemination of information to subscribers or the general public, Dun & Bradstreet, Inc. v. Greenmoss Builders, Inc., 472 U.S. 749 (1985). *Gertz* struck one balance between the competing concerns of protecting First Amendment values and compensating defamed individuals. But as we noted in *Ryan v. Herald Association, Inc.,* where the defamatory statements are made by private individuals to private individuals, "the First Amendment interest in protecting the defendant's speech is arguably less pressing, and the resulting accommodation might be different." Unlike *Ryan,* which involved a matter of public concern and a defendant belonging to the "institutional media," the case at hand involves statements made privately in the employment context about an employee to agents of the employer and several other persons. However, we need not establish whether plaintiff must prove merely "some negligence" or a greater degree of fault in a "private" defamation case after *Greenmoss Builders, Inc.,* because here, defendant concededly enjoys a conditional privilege for intracorporate communications to protect its legitimate business interests. To prevail, plaintiff must show malice or abuse of the privilege sufficient to defeat it. [citations]

In reviewing the denial of motions for judgment notwithstanding the verdict, we must assess the elements of defamation by viewing the evidence in the light most favorable to the prevailing party, excluding the effect of any modifying evidence. * * * Viewed in that light, we discuss in turn each element of defamation put in issue by the parties.

With regard to the first element, plaintiff presented evidence sufficient to support the jury verdict that the statements were false and defamatory. A review of the record shows evidence that plaintiff's actions, while violating defendant's procedures, could fairly and reasonably be interpreted by the jury as not constituting theft, and that plaintiff's past employment record did not warrant his being called a "problem employee."

With respect to the second, third, and fourth elements, the trial court found as a matter of law that defendant enjoyed a conditional privilege for the protection of its legitimate business interests. See, e.g., Lent v. Huntoon, 143 Vt. 539, 548–49, 470 A.2d 1162, 1169 (1983) (holding conditional privilege applicable in Vermont). Plaintiff presented evidence that defendant acted with malice or abused its conditional privilege sufficient for the jury to find that the privilege had been overcome. The jury was properly instructed that plaintiff had to prove malice to defeat the privilege by clear and convincing evidence.

Under Vermont law, a plaintiff must show one of two types of malice in order to overcome the conditional privilege protecting legitimate business interests. *Lent v. Huntoon.* For the purposes of clarity in this discussion,[1] we will use the following full-phrase definitions for each type: "knowledge of the statement's falsity or with reckless disregard of its truth," or "conduct manifesting personal ill will, reckless or wanton disregard of plaintiff's rights, or carried out under circumstances evidencing insult or oppression." The first type of malice may be inferred.

Plaintiff presented evidence showing both types of malice. The jury could have found that the merchandise did not belong to defendant and therefore that defendant's characterization of the incident as theft evidenced a reckless disregard both for the truth and for plaintiff's rights. [citations] The jury could also have interpreted the circumstances of the meeting as "conduct evidencing oppression." Moreover, plaintiff's showing that the statements went to people in the trucking company, outside defendant's organization, who were therefore not proper persons to receive the communications, is evidence from which the jury could have found abuse of the privilege. [citations]

Defendant next argues that plaintiff did not present sufficient evidence on the fifth and sixth elements to warrant compensatory damages by failing to show actual harm proximately caused by the defamatory statements. We agree that plaintiff failed to prove that the defamation, rather than his discharge from employment, caused his inability to obtain new employment, or caused the changed attitudes shown towards him by his former friends, associates and members of the community. Plaintiff counters both that false accusation of theft is actionable per se, and that he presented sufficient evidence of injury caused by the defamation.

1. We note that much confusion has arisen over the terminology applied to the malice requirement in its various contexts: courts have used the term "actual malice" in reference to both types of malice. Compare New York Times Co. v. Sullivan (" 'actual malice'—that is, with knowledge that it was false or with reckless disregard of whether it was false or not") with ("punitive damages may be awarded on a showing of actual malice * * * shown by conduct manifesting personal ill will or * * * circumstances evidencing insult or oppression, or even by conduct showing a reckless or wanton disregard of one's rights"); see also Ryan v. Herald Ass'n, 152 Vt. at 281 n. 5, 566 A.2d at 1320 n. 5.

Courts have also termed the first type of malice as "constitutional" malice. See Gertz v. Robert Welch, Inc., Ryan v. Herald Ass'n. Moreover, the terms "simple malice" and "common-law malice," Ryan v. Herald Ass'n, as well as "express malice," Calero v. Del Chemical Corp., 68 Wis.2d 487, 499–500, 228 N.W.2d 737, 748 (1975), are used interchangeably in reference to the second type of malice.

False accusation of theft is actionable per se. As the Court noted in *Lent v. Huntoon,* the law of defamation in Vermont, with a few exceptions, "must be gleaned from nineteenth century case law." The plurality decision in *Greenmoss Builders, Inc.,* has been characterized as "restor[ing] the common law of defamation where the defamatory statement concerns a private issue, at least as far as presumed and punitive damages are concerned." Comment, American Defamation Law: From Sullivan, Through Greenmoss, and Beyond, 48 Ohio St.L.J. 513, 532 (1987).

Lent v. Huntoon confirmed the continuing validity of "slander per se" in Vermont. Under this doctrine, certain types of false statements, including false accusation of theft, constitute slander without requiring proof of special damages. Plaintiff bore the burden of introducing evidence of actual harm resulting from being called a thief, and he did put forth sufficient evidence of actual harm to himself for the case to go to the jury on the issue of damages for defamation. In addition to the emotional harm he suffered during the incident, plaintiff showed that he had problems sleeping, experienced a loss of appetite, developed a temporary drinking problem, and that his relationship with his wife and his children deteriorated. Such cases may go to the jury, as did this case, on broad jury instructions.

We conclude that plaintiff produced sufficient evidence at trial to go to the jury on each element of defamation, and that the trial court did not abuse its discretion by denying defendant's motion for judgment notwithstanding the verdict. * * *

Defendant argues that the trial court erred by failing to grant its motion for judgment notwithstanding the verdict on the jury's award of punitive damages, claiming that there was insufficient proof that defendant's conduct manifested personal ill will, evidenced insult or oppression, or showed a reckless or wanton disregard of plaintiff's rights. * * *

The same evidence of malice—i.e., conduct manifesting personal ill will, evidencing insult or oppression, or showing a reckless or wanton disregard of plaintiff's rights—which supported the jury verdicts on both counts was also sufficient to allow the jury to impose punitive or exemplary damages on both counts. [citations] The jury could have fairly and reasonably concluded that the conduct of defendant's representatives manifested personal ill will, was carried out under circumstances of insult or oppression, or manifested a reckless and wanton disregard for plaintiff's rights. [citations] Once evidence was presented which could support that finding by the jury, the imposition of punitive damages was within the discretion of the jury. [citations]

Affirmed.

Notes

1. *Constitutional Overlay.* Beginning in 1964 with New York Times Co. v. Sullivan, 376 U.S. 254 (1964), the Supreme Court developed first amendment refinements on the state common law defamation theme. Professor Anderson summarized these:

"The rule that public officials cannot recover unless they can show 'actual malice' is often perceived as the primary constitutional limit on libel law, but in fact that rule has become merely the keystone in a massive wall designed to protect defamatory speech. Whether the evidence is sufficient to identify the plaintiff as the target of the defamation, and whether the statement can be reasonably understood to be defamatory, are also issues of constitutional dimension, at least in some contexts.[1] The constitution also imposes procedural restraints; actual malice must be shown with convincing clarity (a burden a plaintiff in a federal court must meet merely to survive summary judgment),[2] and a finding of actual malice must be independently reviewed by all appellate courts.[3] Proof of malice in any of the usual senses does not meet the 'actual malice' requirement; there must be proof that the defendant actually had serious doubt as to the truth of the defamatory statement.[4]

"The actual malice test must be met not only by public officials, but by any 'public figure' as well—a category that includes people who have done nothing to invite media attention except excel in their vocations or avocations.[5] The public figure category includes not only national celebrities, but also those who are prominent in one controversy, industry, or community.[6] It may even include some who are involuntarily drawn into public view by events beyond their control.[7]

"Even those who are neither public officials nor public figures must meet the actual malice requirement if they hope to recover presumed or punitive damages for defamatory statements made in connection with matters of public concern.[8] Since few plaintiffs can prove enough actual, pecuniary loss to make litigation against media defendants feasible, actual malice has become a crucial issue in virtually all media libel cases. Private plaintiffs who are willing to forego presumed and punitive damages need not show actual malice, but still must show at least negligence on the part of the defendant.

"These restraints are the most familiar of the constitutional limitations on defamation, but they are supplemented by many other constitutional barriers. Truth is no longer a defensive matter; the plaintiff must prove falsity, at least in all cases except those involving purely private defamation.[9] * * * Some courts hold that the first amendment protects a 'neutral report' of defamatory statements by a third party even if the publisher knows the allegation is false.[10]

"The constitutional defamation rules are designed to achieve a tolerable accommodation between two well established and universally shared values—protecting reputation and encouraging robust debate on public issues. The rules are criticized for inadequately serving both of those values. They require enormous sacrifice by victims of defamatory falsehoods—by private persons who cannot show enough pecuniary loss to make litigating worthwhile, by public figures and public officials who cannot prove actual malice, and even by victims who can prove actual malice but run afoul of other constitutional rules that absolutely bar recovery. They exact a social cost by diminishing the effectiveness of defamation law as a deterrent of calumny in public discourse.

1. [Footnotes renumbered.] See Greenbelt Cooperative Publishing Association v. Bresler, 398 U.S. 6 (1970).

2. Anderson v. Liberty Lobby, Inc., 477 U.S. 242 (1986).

3. Bose Corp. v. Consumers Union, 466 U.S. 485 (1984).

4. St. Amant v. Thompson, 390 U.S. 727 (1968).

5. See, e.g., Curtis Publishing Co. v. Butts, 388 U.S. 130 (1967) (football coach); Chuy v. Philadelphia Eagles Football Club, 595 F.2d 1265 (3d Cir.1979) (en banc) (professional football player); Newton v. National Broadcasting Co., 677 F.Supp. 1066 (D.Nev.1987) (entertainer); James v. Gannett Co., 40 N.Y.2d 415, 386 N.Y.S.2d 871, 353 N.E.2d 834 (1976) (belly dancer).

6. See, e.g., Waldbaum v. Fairchild Publications, Inc., 627 F.2d 1287 (D.C.Cir.), cert. denied, 449 U.S. 898 (1980).

7. See, e.g., Dameron v. Washington Magazine, Inc., 779 F.2d 736 (D.C.Cir.1985), cert. denied, 476 U.S. 1141 (1986).

8. Gertz v. Robert Welch, Inc., 418 U.S. 323 (1974).

9. Philadelphia Newspapers, Inc. v. Hepps, 475 U.S. 767 (1986).

10. See, e.g., Edwards v. National Audubon Society, 556 F.2d 113 (2d Cir.), cert. denied, 434 U.S. 1002 (1977).

"On the other hand, the constitutional defamation rules are an expensive form of protection for the press and other speakers. They appear to have increased rather than diminished the cost of defending libel suits. Their emphasis on fault tends to shift the focus of litigation from the question of harm to the plaintiff's reputation to questions about the defendant's journalistic policies and practices. Consequently, in those instances where the jury is satisfied that the defendant's conduct is sufficiently egregious to meet the constitutional standards, damage awards are often very large." Anderson, Tortious Speech, 47 Wash. & Lee L.Rev. 71, 77–79 (1990).

2. *General Presumed Damages.* Courts had to modify common law defamation to take into account Gertz v. Robert Welch, Inc., 418 U.S. 323 (1974) and Dun & Bradstreet, Inc. v. Greenmoss Builders, Inc., 472 U.S. 749 (1985). One limitation these decisions imposed involved the degree of fault needed to establish a claim for defamation, the subject of the preceding note.

Gertz and *Greenmoss Builders* also affected the common law doctrine of presumed damages. At common law all libel and certain categories of slander are considered actionable per se, that is, without proof of any injury. Defamatory publications that did not fall within these categories were not actionable without proof of special damages, that is, evidence that proved actual injury. At early common law, only a pecuniary loss could satisfy this requirement. Thus the classification of the defamatory statement determined whether or not damages could be presumed. The United States Supreme Court rejected this doctrine in *Gertz* and required proof of actual loss in any matter of public concern. The rejection of presumed damages in *Gertz* raised questions about the viability of the doctrine in other situations.

Greenmoss answered at least some of these questions. It validated state law that allowed plaintiffs like Crump who were private parties to recover presumed damages where the defamatory publication did not involve matters of public concern. There, for the moment, the matter rests.

See Becker v. Alloy Hardfacing & Engineering Co., 401 N.W.2d 655, 661 (Minn.1987). Rejecting the argument that a libel claimant should be required to introduce evidence of harm to reputation before recovering damages, the Minnesota court reaffirmed "the rule that where a defendant's statements are defamatory per se, general damages are presumed."

Professor Anderson's proposal to reform defamation damages argues that presumed general damages should be eliminated completely. Plaintiff could recover for an injured reputation or emotional harm only if he proved an actual loss. Anderson, Reputation, Compensation and Proof, 25 Wm. & Mary L.Rev. 747 (1984).

3. *Damages for Emotional Distress.* The *Crump* court allowed evidence of emotional distress and mental suffering. There is a division of opinion; some courts permit recovery of reputational damage only. Compare Kassel v. Gannett Co., 875 F.2d 935 (1st Cir.1989) (denying recovery of damages for emotional distress), with Owens v. CBS, Inc., 173 Ill.App.3d 977, 527 N.E.2d 1296 (1988) (permitting proof of mental distress).

4. *Punitive Damages.* In purely private libel actions, the federal constitution does not bar punitive damages or presumed damages. Dun & Bradstreet, Inc. v. Greenmoss Builders, Inc., 472 U.S. 749 (1985).

But a state constitution may. Wheeler v. Green, 286 Or. 99, 593 P.2d 777 (1979). So may a state statute. See Brantley v. Zantop International Airlines, Inc., 617 F.Supp. 1032 (E.D.Mich.1985).

The debate about punitive damages for defamation continues. Arguing that the threat of punitive damages has so much of a chilling effect on expression that they should be abolished is Van Alstyne, First Amendment Limitations on Recovery from the Press, 25 Wm. & Mary L.Rev. 793, 805–09 (1984). Responding that the possibility of punitive damages empowers the "individual plaintiff to transform himself from David to Goliath" is Barron, Punitive Damages in Libel Cases—First Amendment Equalizer?, 47 Wash. & Lee L.Rev. 105, 122 (1990).

In DiSalle v. P.G. Publishing Co., 375 Pa.Super. 510, 544 A.2d 1345 (1988), app. denied, 521 Pa. 620, 557 A.2d 724, cert. denied, 492 U.S. 906 (1989), a $2,000,000 punitive damage verdict survived an appeal. The judgment was paid together with $561,000 interest. New York Times, July 12, 1989, p. 13:7.

When malice must be established to permit recovery of compensatory damages, does an award of punitive damages constitute an impermissible double recovery? See Winters v. Greeley, 189 Ill.App.3d 590, 545 N.E.2d 422, cert. denied, 128 Ill.2d 673, 548 N.E.2d 1079 (1989).

5. *Declaratory Judgments.* The *Sullivan* apparatus converts the trial from an examination of truth or falsity into an inquiry into the media's editorial process. Few plaintiffs recover anything, with most lawsuits hinging on *Sullivan* malice. Research showed that libel plaintiffs wanted to clear the record and restore a damaged reputation. R. Bezanson, G. Cranberg, & J. Soloski, Libel Law and the Press: Myth and Reality (1987). Some reform proposals eliminate money damages completely.

Judge Leval's emphasis reminds us that *Sullivan* says, "We hold today that the Constitution delimits a State's power to award *damages* for libel." New York Times Co. v. Sullivan, 376 U.S. 254, 283 (1964). Judge Leval suggests a libel action for a declaratory judgment of falsity without examining *Sullivan* malice and without awarding damages. Leval, The No–Money, No–Fault Libel Suit: Keeping *Sullivan* in Its Proper Place, 101 Harv.L.Rev. 1287 (1988).

Professor Smolla's work with the Annenberg Washington Program's Libel Reform Project led to a comprehensive reform proposal. First the defamation victim must demand a retraction; a retraction or opportunity to reply precludes suit. Second if a defamation suit is filed, either party can convert it into a no-fault declaratory judgment action of falsity or not. No money damages are permitted except attorney fees; the declaratory judgment will be tried promptly. Third if neither party chooses a declaratory judgment, the plaintiff's damage recovery will be limited to economic loss, harm to reputation and personal suffering and anguish, excluding recovery of presumed general damages or punitive damages.

Dienes, Libel Reform: An Appraisal, 23 U.Mich.J.L.Ref. 1, 16–17 (1989). "[C]laims notwithstanding, many libel plaintiffs *do* want money. Indeed, for a number of libel plaintiffs who suffer actual damage to reputation, particularly provable economic loss, from a libelous publication, money provides vital compensation. And yet, under the Annenberg proposal, no matter how much injury to reputation and economic damage the plaintiff suffers, no matter how wrongful the conduct of the defendant, the plaintiff can be barred from a damages action. Intentional libel resulting in provable economic harm could be redressed only by a declaration of falsity."

Halpern, Values and Value: An Essay on Libel Reform, 47 Wash. & Lee L.Rev. 227, 237 (1990). "The assumption that widely circulated publications or broadcasts, be they Time magazine or The National Enquirer or Sixty Minutes, would be significantly impressed by a non-monetary judgment declaring the defamatory falsity of a purported news item confuses professional pride with powerful arrogance. In short, recent experience indicates that, from defendant's point of view, a declaration of falsity would not mean very much."

6. *Retraction.* A compelled retraction, an injunction ordering defendant to recant, probably violates the first amendment. Miami–Herald Publishing Co. v. Tornillo, 418 U.S. 241 (1974). Most present retraction statutes provide that a retraction limits plaintiff's damages.

Do retractions undo the damage or restore a reputation? Halpern, Values and Value: An Essay on Libel Reform, 47 Wash. & Lee L.Rev. 227, 241 (1990).

7. *Special Verdicts.* In Sharon v. Time, Inc., 599 F.Supp. 538 (S.D.N.Y.1984), Ariel Sharon's suit against Time magazine, the trial judge instructed the jury to return separate special verdicts on the questions of falsity, defamation, and *Sullivan* malice. The jury found the magazine's statements were false and defamatory but insulated it from damages because *Sullivan* malice was lacking. Plaintiff Sharon felt that the widely publicized verdict of falsity meant that he had won a moral victory. Time issued a statement that the suit should never have been in court and that "Time has won it." R. Smolla, Suing the Press 80–100 (1986).

8. Cf. Restatement (Second) of Torts § 569 comment b (1976). "Some courts have taken the position that a libelous publication is actionable per se only if its defamatory meaning is apparent on its face without reference to extrinsic facts; otherwise proof of harm is required. The principal justification urged for this minority position * * * has now been eliminated by the current rule that the plaintiff must show fault on the part of the defendant regarding the defamatory character of the communication."

9. Defamatory publications in an election campaign present difficult remedial problems for the defamed candidate. For some suggested solutions, see Albert, The Remedies Available to Candidates Who Are Defamed by Television or Radio Commercials of Opponents, 11 Vt.L.Rev. 33 (1986).

10. Cal.Civ.Code § 45a. * * * A libel which is defamatory of the plaintiff without the necessity of explanatory matter, such as an inducement, innuendo or other extrinsic fact, is said to be a libel on its face. Defamatory language not libelous on its face is not actionable unless the plaintiff alleges and proves that he has suffered special damage as a proximate result thereof. Special damage is defined in Section 48a of this code.

§ 46. * * * Slander is a false and unprivileged publication, orally uttered, and also communications by radio or any mechanical or other means which:

1. Charges any person with crime, or with having been indicted, convicted, or punished for crime;

2. Imputes in him the present existence of an infectious, contagious, or loathsome disease;

3. Tends directly to injure him in respect to his office, profession, trade or business either by imputing to him general disqualification in those respects which the office or other occupation peculiarly requires, or by imputing something with reference to his office, profession, trade or business that has a natural tendency to lessen its profits;

4. Imputes to him impotence or want of chastity; or

5. Which, by natural consequence, causes actual damage.

§ 48a. * * *

4. As used herein, the terms "general damages," "special damages," "exemplary damages" and "actual malice," are defined as follows:

(a) "General damages" are damages for loss of reputation, shame, mortification and hurt feelings;

(b) "Special damages" are all damages which plaintiff alleges and proves that he has suffered in respect to his property, business, trade, profession or occupation, including such amounts of money as the plaintiff alleges and proves he has expended as a result of the alleged libel, and no other;

(c) "Exemplary damages" are damages which may in the discretion of the court or jury be recovered in addition to general and special damages for the sake of example and by way of punishing a defendant who has made the publication or broadcast with actual malice;

(d) "Actual malice" is that state of mind arising from hatred or ill will toward the plaintiff; provided, however, that such a state of mind occasioned by a good faith belief on the part of the defendant in the truth of the libelous publication or broadcast at the time it is published or broadcast shall not constitute actual malice.

2. INJUNCTIONS

WILLING v. MAZZOCONE

Supreme Court of Pennsylvania. 1978.
482 Pa. 377, 393 A.2d 1155.

MANDERINO, JUSTICE. On Monday, September 29, and Wednesday, October 1, 1975, appellant, Helen Willing, demonstrated in the pedestrian plaza between building number two and building number three, Penn Center Plaza, downtown Philadelphia, Pennsylvania. * * * While engaged in this activity, which lasted for several hours each day, appellant wore a "sandwich-board" sign around her neck. On the sign she had hand lettered the following:

LAW—FIRM
OF QUINN—MAZZOCONE
STOLE MONEY FROM ME—AND SOLD-ME-OUT-
TO-THE
INSURANCE COMPANY

As she marched back and forth, appellant also pushed a shopping cart on which she had placed an American flag. She continuously rang a cow bell and blew on a whistle to further attract attention.

Appellees in this case are two members of the legal profession, Carl M. Mazzocone and Charles F. Quinn, who are associated in the two member law firm of Mazzocone and Quinn, p.c. When appellant refused appellees' efforts to amicably dissuade her from further activity such as that described above, appellees filed a suit in equity in the Court of Common Pleas of Philadelphia County seeking to enjoin her from further demonstration. Three hearings were held, at which the following factual history emerged.

In 1968, appellees, who have specialized in the trial of workmen's compensation matters for several years, represented appellant in such a case. Pursuant to appellee's representation, appellant was awarded permanent/partial disability benefits which she collected for a number of years. At the time of the initial settlement distribution with appellant, appellees deducted the sum of $150.00 as costs of the case. This sum, according to appellees' evidence, was paid in full to Robert DeSilverio, M.D., a treating psychiatrist who testified on appellant's behalf in the Workmen's Compensation matter. Appellees presented copies of their records covering the transaction with Dr. DeSilverio. A cancelled check for the amount of the payment, and the testimony of Dr. DeSilverio himself, confirmed appellees' account of the transaction. Appellant offered no evidence other than her testimony that the cause of her antagonism towards appellees was not any dissatisfaction with the settlement, but rather, her belief that appellees had wrongfully diverted to themselves $25.00 of the $150.00 that was supposed to have been paid to Dr. DeSilverio.

Based on this evidence, the equity court concluded that appellant was "a woman firmly on the thrall of the belief that [appellees] defrauded her, an *idee fixe* which, either by reason of eccentricity or an even more serious mental instability, refuses to be dislodged by the most convincing proof to the contrary." The Court then enjoined appellant from

> "further unlawful demonstration, picketing, carrying placards which contain defamatory and libelous statements and or uttering, publishing and declaring defamatory statements against the [appellees] herein."

On appeal, the Superior Court modified the trial court's order to read,

> "Helen R. Willing, be and is permanently enjoined from further demonstrating against and/or picketing Mazzocone and Quinn, Attorneys-at-Law, by uttering or publishing statements to the effect that Mazzocone and Quinn, Attorneys-at-Law stole money from her and sold her out to the insurance company."

We granted appellant's petition for allowance of appeal, and now reverse.

* * * We believe the orders issued by the Superior Court and by the trial court in the instant case are clearly prohibited by Article I, Section 7 of the Pennsylvania Constitution and by Goldman Theatres v. Dana, 405 Pa. 83, 173 A.2d 59, cert. denied, 368 U.S. 897 (1961). In *Goldman Theatres* we held that Article I, Section 7 prohibits prior restraint on the exercise of an individual's right to freely communicate thoughts and opinions, * * *.

Our conclusion that the equity court violated appellant's state constitutional right to freely speak her opinion—regardless of whether that opinion is based on fact or fantasy—regarding appellees' professional integrity obviates the need for any discussion here of federal law.

Our resolution should also render unnecessary any discussion of the Superior Court's proposed exception to the so-called traditional view that equity lacks the power to enjoin the publication of defamatory matter. We do believe, however, that the Superior Court's observation that "in the present case an action for damages would be a pointless gesture since [appellant] is indigent," requires specific comment. We cannot accept the Superior Court's conclusion that the exercise of the constitutional right to freely express one's opinion should be conditioned upon the economic status of the individual asserting that right. * * *

Notes

1. The sharp division in Pennsylvania's appellate judiciary in *Willing* indicates some discomfort with the result. Were this a "trade" libel, the court might find a reason to enjoin. Should the practice of a profession fall automatically into this category? Apparently not according to the cases cited by the dissenting judge in the intermediate appellate court. Mazzocone v. Willing, 246 Pa.Super. 98, 113, 369 A.2d 829, 836 (1976), rev'd, 482 Pa. 377, 393 A.2d 1155 (1978):

"Gariepy v. Springer, 318 Ill.App. 523, 48 N.E.2d 572 (1943) (defendant circulating letters to plaintiff attorney's clients, defaming him); Greenberg v. DeSalvo, 254 La. 1019, 229 So.2d 83 (1969), cert. denied, 397 U.S. 1075 (1970) (defendant calling attorney 'crook,' 'crooked attorney,' etc.); Stansbury v. Beckstrom, 491 S.W.2d 947 (Tex.Ct.App.1973) (defendant parading, standing, sitting or lying in front of physician's office displaying libelous and false signs); Kwass v. Kersey, 139 W.Va. 497, 81 S.E.2d 237 (1954) (defendant widely circulating letters charging that plaintiff attorney was a 'shyster' who had betrayed the interests of his client)." In a recent case, Franklin Chalfont Associates v. Kalikow, 392 Pa.Super. 452, 573 A.2d 550 (1990), the Pennsylvania court reaffirmed its policy against prior restraints on speech, vacating an injunction prohibiting homeowners in a housing development from posting signs critical of the plaintiff's business practices.

2. If the lawyers obtained a judgment for nominal damages for libel, would equity then have jurisdiction to enjoin repetitions of the same defamatory material? A Special Note On Remedies for Defamation Other Than Damages, Restatement (Second) of Torts § 623 (1976), suggests that injunctive relief "might meet the need" of cases like Mazzocone v. Willing.

Lothschuetz v. Carpenter, 898 F.2d 1200, 1203, 1208 (6th Cir.1990). Plaintiffs' lawyers, were "embroiled in various judicial and administrative proceedings directly or indirectly involving" defendant Carpenter. Carpenter "developed a great deal of animosity" some of which he vented in numerous charges of unethical conflicts of interest. The trial judge entered a damage award of $1, nominal damages for defamation and declined an injunction "as an unwarranted prior restraint on freedom of speech."

Judge Wellford concurring and dissenting, joined by Judge Hull in "the opinion of the court on this issue: " "[I]n view of Carpenter's frequent and continuing defamatory statements, an injunction is necessary to prevent future injury to Carolyn Hill's personal reputation and business relations." The injunction forbids only "the statements which have been found in this and prior proceedings to be false and libelous."

3. RESTITUTION

HART v. E.P. DUTTON & CO.

Supreme Court of New York, 1949.

197 Misc. 274, 93 N.Y.S.2d 871.

MALPASS, JUSTICE. The complaint sets forth two separate causes of action based upon alleged libellous statements claimed by the plaintiff to have been contained in a book entitled "Under Cover" which, according to the complaint was published by the defendant on or about July 18, 1943. It is alleged in the complaint that the book contained statements which were libellous and defamatory of the plaintiff and numerous other persons, the names and identities of some of whom are unknown to the plaintiff. The plaintiff has brought the action "on behalf of himself and all other persons falsely and unjustly held out to the public as traitors to America in time of war, and/or agents of the Axis enemy, in time of war, in the book 'Under Cover,' similarly situated." In the first cause of action set forth in the complaint the plaintiff alleges "that solely by reason of the aforesaid libellous publication, the plaintiff and those similarly situated, have suffered great humiliation and loss of reputation; have been held out to great hatred and contempt; have been exposed to mob hysteria; and have been placed in great fear for the safety of themselves and their families; and in other respects have suffered damage." It is further alleged in the first cause of action that the defendant sold a large number of copies of the book and has received in sales from the book, royalties, etc., proceeds which amount to the sum of $2,450,000.00, "which money defendant had and received to the use of the plaintiff, and those similarly situated; and further, that five years have elapsed, between the receipt of said monies and the commencement of this action," and "that on or about March 15th, 1949, the plaintiff demanded of the defendant that it pay the said proceeds of the book 'Under Cover,' to the plaintiff for himself and for those similarly situated, but the defendant neglected and refused, and still neglects and refuses to pay the said proceeds, or any part thereof." The second cause of action is a repetition of the allegations contained in the first cause of action and in addition alleges that "the defendant maliciously contrived to convey to the public the idea that the plaintiff and those similarly situated were enemies of, or traitors to the United States of America in time of war; that he was understood as meaning that they were traitors, and/or agents of the enemy, by those who read the book; and further, that the defendant intended to profit through the sale and circulation of this libelous matter, and did so profit, to the extent already set forth." The prayer of the complaint is for judgment in favor of the plaintiff and those similarly situated for the sum of two million, four hundred and fifty thousand dollars ($2,450,000.00), the amount alleged to have been received by the defendant together with interest from March 15, 1944, which it may be assumed, is the date when the plaintiff claims the defendant received the profits derived from the publication of the book.

The defendant urges that the complaint fails to allege facts sufficient to constitute any cause of action except one to recover damages for libel and that such an action is barred by the statute of limitations. Section 51 of the Civil Practice Act provides that an action to recover damages for "libel or slander" must be brought within one year after the cause of action has accrued. A cause of action for libellous statements contained in a book accrues when the book is released by the publisher for sale in accord with trade practice. The complaint states "That on or about the 18th day of July, 1943, while America was at war with Germany and Japan, the defendant published, distributed, advertised, and circulated a book entitled 'Under Cover.'" The action was begun in March, 1949. Beyond doubt, if plaintiff's action is deemed to be one to recover damages for libel, the action is barred by the statute.

The plaintiff contends that the action is not an action to recover damages for libel but is an action for money had and received and that section 48, subdivision 1 of the Civil Practice Act is the applicable statute of limitation. This section provides that "an action upon a contract obligation or liability express or implied," must be commenced within six years after the cause of action has accrued. The plaintiff contends that the plaintiff has the right to waive his action for the tort and sue the defendant, in assumpsit, for the monies which the defendant realized from the sale of the book and certain rights in connection therewith, on the theory that the law implies a contract on the part of a tort feasor to account to the party injured by the tort for any monies acquired by the tort feasor in the commission of the tort. The plaintiff contends that the law forbids that any person shall profit by reason of a wrongful act against another and that to permit the defendant to retain the proceeds derived from the publication of the book containing the libellous statements would result in the unjust enrichment of the defendant and the law will imply a contract on the part of the defendant to pay to the plaintiff and those persons similarly situated the monies so received.

The question is squarely presented as to whether one who claims to have been damaged by the publication of a libel, under the circumstances alleged in this complaint, may waive the tort and maintain an action in assumpsit to recover the proceeds or profits derived from the publication of the libel. This seems to be a novel proposition. * * *

There are certain cases in which a person injured by a tort may waive the tort and sue for breach of what has been termed implied or quasi-contract. Such right is not allowed in all cases. "The torts which it has been held can be waived are usually, conversion, trespass to land or goods, deceit and the action for extorting money by threats." Salmond on the Law of Torts, 8th Edition, page 194. It is noteworthy that in all of those cases the tort involved an injury to property. Sec. 37–a of the General Construction provides that libel is a personal injury. * * *

An action based upon invasion of one's right of privacy may be said to resemble, in many respects, an action based upon libel. In Street on Foundations of Legal Liability, Volume 1, page 319, it is stated:

> "It is supposed that if such a right is to be born it must come in some way from the law of libel. Those who contend for a right of personal security broad enough to include a general right 'to be let alone' would not perhaps admit this, but unquestionably the law of libel furnishes a nearer approach to the indicated goal than any other branch of tort."

It would seem, therefore, that any adjudications where damages for invasion of one's right of privacy is involved might well be of assistance in determining the instant motion. In Bunnell v. Keystone Varnish Co., 254 A.D. 885, 5 N.Y.S.2d 415, the Court said:

> "*The plaintiff has no cause of action on quasi-contract.* An action under section 51 of the Civil Rights Law is the plaintiff's sole remedy for the unauthorized use of her name [citation] *and the alleged unjust enrichment of the defendant is a part of that cause of action.*" *(Italic ours)*

In Cason v. Baskin, 155 Fla. 198, 20 So.2d 243, 254, the Supreme Court of Florida said:

> "The demurrer to the fourth count was also properly sustained by the trial court. *That count in effect claimed that the plaintiff was entitled to share in the profits received by the defendant for the publication and sale of her book* to the extent of one hundred thousand dollars. * * * That many copies of the book were purchased and paid for by persons of Alachua County and throughout the United States and *that thereby the defendant had received great financial profit, and had thus become unjustly enriched at the expense of and to the damage of plaintiff,* to the extent of one hundred thousand dollars. * * * In our opinion this count states no cause of action."

These are the only cases to which my attention has been directed where an attempt has been made to recover the profits or proceeds derived from the invasion of a person's right of privacy. The theory of the plaintiff in each of these cases was substantially the same as is plaintiff's in the instant action. In each case the Court held that the plaintiff could not recover profits on the basis of a quasi-contract. The reasons which support this rule in regard to right of privacy are applicable to actions based upon libel.

As was stated in Miller v. Schloss, [218 N.Y. 400], "A quasi or constructive contract rests upon the equitable principle that a person shall not be allowed to enrich himself unjustly at the expense of another" and is created when "because [of] the acts of the parties" a person is possessed of money or property which in equity or good conscience he should not retain. The application of this rule requires inquiry, not only into the acts of the defendant, but also the acts of the plaintiff. One who publishes a libel, especially if done maliciously, as charged in this complaint, is guilty of conduct which makes him liable for damages. An action for damages affords the plaintiff full compensation for any injuries which he has suffered. In addition to compensatory damages he may recover punitive damages if proper foundation is established by the proof. The law requires that a plaintiff must bring his action to recover such damages within one year. It would seem that it is not equitable and just to permit a person, who has been the subject of a libellous article published in a book, to acquiesce in or permit the sale and distribution of such book to continue for a period of nearly six years without taking any steps whatsoever to protest or stop the sale and distribution of the book and then to maintain an action for the profits derived from the sale and distribution of the book. The publication of a book entails great expense and effort on the part of the publisher and the profits derived therefrom are due in large measure to elements outside of the printed matter contained therein. To permit such an action as the plaintiff has brought, under the circumstances alleged in the complaint, would have the effect of making the publisher for a period of years, the servant of the plaintiff, who, despite his failure to avail himself of a complete legal remedy, may now assert a right to the fruits of the defendant's labor and investment even beyond that which may flow from the alleged libel. Such a situation would be inequitable and would result in the unjust enrichment of the plaintiff. Under such circumstances no contract should be "implied in law" requiring the defendant to account to the plaintiff for profits derived from the publication of the book. * * *

The plaintiff asserts that the one year statute of limitations is not applicable for the reason that his action is not for damages but is in assumpsit for moneys had and received and is based upon an implied contract and the six year statute applies. In his brief, plaintiff's counsel states: "To call this an action for 'damages' for libel, ignores basic facts. To reiterate, we are waiving these damages, and suing for money 'had and received.' *We are undertaking to prove additional facts never before pleaded in a libel suit;* namely, that the defendant 'had and received' money by virtue of the publication of his libellous publication." Whatever the plaintiff may call the action, it is based upon the tort of libel and in the absence of any statute or common law authority, it must be considered as an action for damages for libel within the meaning of Section 51 of the Civil Practice Act. In applying the statute of limitations the Court should look for the reality and the essence of the action and not its mere name. * * * In Gregoire v. G.P. Putnam's Sons, 298 N.Y. 119, 124, 81 N.E.2d 45, 48, Judge Lewis said:

> "If, as the complaint alleges, the book 'Total Espionage' contained statements by which the plaintiff was defamed, a right of action for libel accrued to him. That right, however, was burdened with the *statutory limitation that unless he commenced an action to recover damages for the alleged libel within one year after such an action accrued his right thereafter to recover would be completely and forever barred for lapse of time.* Civ.Prac.Act, § 51. (Italics

ours.) Although we may not concern ourselves with the wisdom of the Statute of Limitation last cited above, * * * *our duty is to give to that statute its intended effect as a statute of repose.* * * * *The statute (Civ.Prac.Act, Sec. 51, subd. 3) which is controlling here is a declaration of public policy governing the right to litigate; it came into our law by way of the Legislature, not through the judicial process.* 'At times, it may bar the assertion of a just claim. Then its application causes hardship. The Legislature has found that such occasional hardship is outweighed by the advantage of outlawing stale claims.'"

The plaintiff should not be permitted to avoid the effect of the statute of limitations by attempting to plead a cause of action for which there is no authority in law.

Libel has been a field of much litigation both in England and this country and during the course of the years many judicial decisions have been handed down in libel actions. It is significant that in none of these cases has an action such as is brought by the plaintiff in this case been instituted. The plaintiff recognizes this fact and states: "We are undertaking to prove additional facts never before pleaded in a libel suit, namely, that the defendant had and received money by virtue of his libellous publication." The absence of attempts to bring an action similar to the instant one is evidence of the recognition by the legal profession and the courts that such an action would not lie under the common law. In Near v. State of Minnesota, 283 U.S. 697, 718, the Court said:

> "The fact that for approximately one hundred and fifty years there has been almost an entire absence of attempts to impose previous restraints upon publications relating to the malfeasance of public officers is significant of the deep-seated conviction that such restraints would violate constitutional right."
> * * *

It is evident that the right to recover based upon libel has been limited to the recovery of damages under the common law and statutes applicable thereto. It would seem, therefore, that the law is so well established that an innovation such as the plaintiff seeks in this action would impose new and unnecessary hazards upon publishers and would be contrary to the policy of our law. The reason for such conclusion can no better be expressed than in the language of the Court of Appeals in Roberson v. Rochester Folding Box Co., 171 N.Y. 538–556, 64 N.E. 442, 447.

> "An examination of the authorities leads us to the conclusion that the so-called 'right of privacy' has not as yet found an abiding place in our jurisprudence, and, as we view it, the doctrine cannot now be incorporated without doing violence to settled principles of law by which the profession and the public have long been guided."

In my opinion the complaint herein fails to state any cause of action other than a cause of action to recover damages for libel and such cause of action is barred by the statute of limitations. * * *

An order may be entered herein dismissing the complaint herein with ten dollars ($10.00) costs to the defendant.

Note

Compare G. Palmer, Restitution § 2.9 (1978) with York, Extension of Restitutional Remedies in the Tort Field, 4 U.C.L.A.L.Rev. 499 (1957). See also, R. Goff & G. Jones, Restitution 612–14 (1986).

B. INVASION OF PRIVACY

BIRNBAUM v. UNITED STATES

United States District Court, Eastern District of New York, 1977.
436 F.Supp. 967.

WEINSTEIN, DISTRICT JUDGE. In each of these three cases consolidated for trial the plaintiff complains that first-class mail was intercepted by the Central Intelligence Agency (CIA), opened without warrant and copied. Birnbaum and MacMillen each sent a letter abroad; Avery received one here. All the letters were resealed after copying and promptly returned to the mails. Plaintiffs, individually and as a class, seek to recover damages under the Federal Tort Claims Act. 28 U.S.C.A. § 1346(b). * * *

[T]he parties have stipulated that the substantive tort law of New York is applicable.

Most states recognize invasions of privacy as actionable torts.

In this context, the general rubric "right of privacy" encompasses four concepts. As described by the Restatement (Second) of Torts, they are:

(a) Intrusion upon the seclusion of another, * * * or

(b) Appropriation of the other's name or likeness, * * * or

(c) Publicity given to the other's private life [of a sort which is offensive and not of legitimate public concern], * * * or

(d) Publicity which places the other in a false light before the public. * * *

3 Restatement (Second) of Torts, § 625A (1977). Intrusion upon the seclusion of these plaintiffs is the branch of privacy involved in these cases. Comments to the Restatement make it plain that the tort is committed whenever an intrusive act is committed, even if the tortfeasor never reveals either the fact of the invasion or any information about the plaintiff to third persons. * * *

3 Restatement (Second) of Torts, § 652B, Comment a at 378 (1977). This common law right extends beyond the plaintiff's immediate physical environment and is infringed by examinations of bank accounts or of personal records under false pretenses, or by opening of mail.

* * * It is apparent, therefore, that, in the majority of states, case law would provide a right to recovery on the facts of these cases. * * *

The evidence is overwhelming that New York would recognize the common law right of privacy sufficiently to compensate for the kind of intrusion by the government into private mails represented by the instant case.

[Editors: The district judge found that, under New York law, the facts stated would also support a cause of action for infringement of a common law copyright and for invasion of plaintiff's property interest in private papers. In addition the district judge held that defendants had violated plaintiffs' constitutional rights giving rise to a tort action. The court of appeals, however, disagreed and decided that the plaintiffs' sole cause of action was for invasion of privacy. Birnbaum v. United States, supra.]

Recovery under the Federal Tort Claims Act is limited to compensatory damages. "The United States shall not be liable for * * * punitive damages." 28 U.S.C.A. § 2674.

Neither may the award take into account injuries inflicted upon the structure of American democracy. * * *

The plaintiffs in these cases suffered none of the tangible indicia of harm for which a dollar value may easily be assigned. They experienced no financial losses. Their jobs, their reputations and prestige in their communities did not suffer. They were not subjected to intrusive or humiliating investigations by the government. Their homes were not broken into. They were not assaulted or detained. They lost no time from work and incurred no medical expenses. Plaintiff MacMillen did testify that she broke out in hives and suffered some respiratory difficulties shortly after she learned of the CIA action, but even she did not claim damages for physical injury or medical bills.

The lack of objective harm is, however, no bar to recovery. The law generally recognizes that where a person suffers an invasion of the right to privacy, awards are appropriate for general damages covering the injury of invasion itself, as well as for the resulting mental distress. The Restatement (Second) of Torts, § 652H, summarizes the rule in privacy cases:

> "One who has established a cause of action for unreasonable invasion of his privacy is entitled to recover damages for
>
> (a) the harm to his interest in privacy resulting from the invasion;
>
> (b) his mental distress proved to have been suffered if it is of a kind which normally results from such an invasion; and
>
> (c) special damage of which the invasion is a legal cause."

The court credits the testimony of the plaintiffs in these cases that they suffered actual mental pain, outrage and shock when they learned that government agents had interfered with their privacy by opening and reading their mail. They are entitled, therefore, to recovery for that injury under any of the three tort theories supporting liability.

The parties are entitled to recover for the invasion of their rights, without respect to the consequences. The Restatement (Second) of Torts suggests that a deprivation of common law privacy is an independent injury for which damages are appropriate. The comment to the damages section of the Restatement notes:

> "A cause of action for invasion of privacy, in any of its four forms, entitles the plaintiff to recover damages for the harm to the particular element of his privacy which is invaded. Thus one who suffers an intrusion upon his solitude or seclusion * * * may recover damages for the deprivation of his seclusion. One to whose private life publicity is given * * * may recover for the harm resulting to his reputation from such publicity. One who is publicly placed in a false light * * * may recover damages for the harm to his reputation from the position in which he is so placed. One whose name, likeness or identity is appropriated to the use of another * * * may recover for the loss of the exclusive use of the value so appropriated."

3 Restatement (Second) of Torts, § 652H, Comment at 401–02 (1977).

Valuation of intangibles is difficult, but not impossible. In ordinary tort suits, judges and juries commonly draw upon the evidence and their shared experience to assess the dollar worth of such imponderables as future pain and suffering. Over time, a range of awards appropriate for certain kinds of losses is established, enabling courts to decide whether a given recovery is reasonable.

In this case, however, no precedents are available. For this reason the court decided to seek the assistance of an advisory jury.

While trial by jury is specifically prohibited in Federal Tort Claims Act cases, 28 U.S.C. § 2402, use of an advisory jury is permitted. The verdict of such an advisory panel is only part of the data taken into consideration in arriving at the court's independent conclusion.

It was, nevertheless, instructive that this panel of average citizens—representing a broad range of economic, education, social and political experience—uniformly found that the damages suffered by the plaintiffs in this case were substantial. Although the jurors were instructed that they could recommend nominal damages of one dollar if they found that the wrong done resulted only in slight harm, none chose this alternative. Three suggested that plaintiffs be awarded $10,000 each for their mental distress and for the encroachment upon their personal liberty; one suggested $2500; and the other eight jurors all agreed that $5000 was the compensation needed to make these plaintiffs whole.

In addition, the verdict of the advisory panel served to affirm the opinion of the court that the emotional distress these plaintiffs suffered was the sort that would be experienced by reasonable people under the almost unprecedented circumstances of these cases. Since normal principles of tort recovery in privacy do not permit compensation for unusual sensitivity, the consensus of the jurors on this point was particularly useful. * * *

The jurors' damage recommendations were somewhat high. Awards of the magnitude suggested by the advisory verdict have been found only where plaintiffs have suffered objective, observable injuries as a result of interferences with their civil liberties. See, e.g., Donovan v. Reinbold, 433 F.2d 738 (9th Cir.1970) ($5000 for loss of job because of the exercise of First Amendment rights); Manfredonia v. Barry, 401 F.Supp. 762 (E.D.N.Y.1975) ($3500 damages upon a finding that rights under the Fourth and First Amendments had been violated; plaintiff spent the night in jail, and was exposed to extensive notoriety in the press and her community); Zarcone v. Perry, 75–C–1619 (E.D.N.Y. July 20, 1977) (damage award of $141,000 for false arrest and imprisonment with handcuffing of the plaintiff, public humiliation and proof of substantial medical expenses and economic loss and substantial punitive damages). Cf. Dellums v. Powell, 561 F.2d 242 (D.C.Cir.1977) ($7500 excessive for First Amendment violations).

In the instant case it is possible to ameliorate the harm by the government's writing a letter of apology, a possibility raised by the jury. Assurance by the government that it regrets the injury to plaintiffs will serve to soothe their wounded faith in our democratic institutions, give assurances of nonrecurrence in the future, and restore some confidence in our government. In analogous defamation cases, New York law recognizes that an apology will mitigate damages, or at least that a failure to apologize will enhance them. It is appropriate to apply these precedents to the special facts of this case.

In arriving at an appropriate figure some guidance is found in the amount declared by Congress as proper compensation in a similar context. Under the Omnibus Crime Control and Safe Streets Act of 1968, P.L. 90–351, Congress created a right to civil recovery for individuals whose telephone or oral conversations were intercepted without legal sanction by wire-taps or eavesdropping. The basic damage figure was set at $100 a day, or $1000, whichever is larger; special damages, punitive damages and attorney's fees are also recoverable. 18 U.S.C.A. § 2520. Since the interests sought to be vindicated in these CIA cases and by the Omnibus Crime Control Act provisions are similar, comparability in the size of the non-punitive awards seems reasonable, even though it is the state rather than the federal law of damages that is being applied.

These considerations, * * * lead to a conclusion that plaintiffs should recover * * * the sum of $1000 each, provided the government furnishes a suitable letter of regret and assurance of non-recurrence. Of the $1000, twenty-five per cent is to be paid to the counsel for these plaintiffs as attorney's fees. While this legal fee clearly does not compensate the plaintiffs' talented lawyers for the time devoted to these cases, it is the maximum permitted by statute. 28 U.S.C.A. § 2678.

BIRNBAUM v. UNITED STATES

United States Court of Appeals, Second Circuit, 1978.

588 F.2d 319.

GURFEIN, CIRCUIT JUDGE. * * * Having determined that the United States is liable to these plaintiffs for harm caused by mail openings, we must review the District Court's award of $1000 in compensatory damages and of an apology to each plaintiff.

Although damages under the Act are governed by state law, the Act limits recovery to compensatory damages and provides that the United States shall not be liable for punitive damages, 28 U.S.C. § 2674. In New York, as we have seen, freedom from mental disturbance is a protected interest, but there must be a " 'guarantee of genuineness in the circumstances of the case.' " Ferrara v. Galluchio, 5 N.Y.2d at 21, 176 N.Y.S.2d at 999–1000, 152 N.E.2d at 252 (quoting Prosser). The question is whether the testimony of the plaintiffs sustains a finding of mental anguish under New York law, in which event the judgment for $1,000 each would not be excessive, or whether there was no actual damage, in which case only nominal damages of one dollar would have been proper. Cf. Carey v. Piphus, 435 U.S. 247 (1978) (construing § 1983).

The answer is not easy. There was no finding of physical injury and no loss of employment. There also was no mental injury in the sense of "permanent symptoms of anxiety." *Ferrara*, supra.

The question whether a finding of mental anguish is sustainable is further complicated by two unusual features of these cases. First, the plaintiffs deliberately sought to find out under the Freedom of Information Act whether their mail had been tampered with. In direct response to their curiosity, they received the information which resulted in the purported injury. Thus, in a strict sense, "but for" the plaintiffs' acts in uncovering the openings, they might never have been made to suffer anguish over the Government's wrongs. Second, the letters interfered with were being transported to or from the Soviet Union, a closed society in which, as most people are aware, mail may be opened by secret police without "constitutional" restraint. Only the naive would be emotionally unprepared for the possibility that a letter might be opened in the Soviet Union. Under those circumstances, it is somewhat difficult to credit the proposition that a reasonable person would be shocked by the mere fact that a letter going to or coming from the U.S.S.R. had been opened at *some point*.

Although, in a sense, the plaintiffs brought their feelings of outrage upon themselves by seeking information, we do not believe, upon reflection, that this is a meaningful break in the chain of causation that links the mail openings to any anguish suffered. The mail opening was an intentional tort and it may be deemed to have been foreseeable that anguish might ensue if there were discovery.

More troublesome is the fact that plaintiffs should have been aware that their mail *might* be opened by the Soviet officials (particularly in the case of Ms. MacMillen, who was writing to a well-known dissident). That could have convinced the trier of fact that there was no compensable damage. Indeed, the testimony of the plaintiffs with regard to their subjective feelings was both weak and meager. The nub of their testimony was that each felt "disappointment" that their own government could do such a thing. Such anguish is political rather than emotional, much as a member of a Senate investigating committee might feel toward the same revelation. The "injury" was principally to "their wounded faith in our democratic institutions," a loss of faith probably shared by many Americans who do not expect compensation for such intellectual injuries.

The issue comes down to whether each plaintiff suffered any mental injury whatever from the knowledge that a single letter had been opened. As the District Judge properly charged the advisory jury (and we assume charged himself), the plaintiffs could not recover money damages as a vindication of the rights of the American people. Nor do we think that they may recover simply to deter future action, for this particular statute prohibits punitive damages—the traditional "smart money" remedy used to discourage repetitive conduct.

The District Court did find, however, that "the emotional distress these plaintiffs suffered was the sort that would be experienced by reasonable people under the almost unprecedented circumstances of these cases." Though we could view this finding as one merely of damage presumed from the circumstances, worth only the nominal sum of one dollar, we interpret the finding more generously as determining that these plaintiffs, whose demeanor the trial judge observed, actually suffered personal anguish. We give "due regard * * * to the opportunity of the trial court to judge of the credibility of the witnesses." Fed.R.Civ.P. 52(a). Though the question of damages is close, we affirm the money judgments for $1,000 each, with the feeling that they represent the upper limit of allowable compensation in these cases.

With regard to the Judge's order that the Government send a letter of apology to each plaintiff, though such letters might some day achieve monetary value as collectors' items, we do not view them as "money damages," the only form of relief provided in the Act. 28 U.S.C. § 1346(b).

We accordingly reverse that part of the judgment ordering that letters of apology be sent.

Notes

1. *Remedies For Intrusion Upon the Seclusion of Another.*

a. *Injunctions.* There has been a marked retreat from the position taken in 1896 in Chappell v. Stewart, 82 Md. 323, 33 A. 542, that equity lacked jurisdiction to enjoin activities which are personally annoying or harassing such as employing detectives to shadow the plaintiff. The retreat has been in all directions. Chappell v. Stewart itself suggested criminal sanctions, and there are indeed "Peeping Tom" criminal statutes in some states. (e.g. Souder v. Pendleton Detectives, 88 So.2d 716 (La.App.1956). Open acts of surveillance—"rough shadowing"—may subject the plaintiff to public disrepute so as to constitute "the analogue to libel" with a concomitant damage remedy) (see Schultz v. Frankfort Marine Accident & Plate Glass Ins. Co., 152 Wis. 537, 139 N.W. 386 (1913). The pretext of a property interest is readily found where there is interference with business or professional interests, or even in some sort of a contract, as in Reed v. Carter, 268 Ky. 1, 103 S.W.2d 663 (1937).

Recent cases have flatly repudiated this supposed limitation on equity jurisdiction. Injunctions have been granted against vituperative letters, unreasonable telephone calls, and incessant harassment by jilted lovers. See Webber v. Gray, 228 Ark. 289, 307 S.W.2d 80 (1957); Kramer v. Downey, 680 S.W.2d 524 (Tex.App. 1984); Miller v. Linden, 172 Ill.App.3d 594, 527 N.E.2d 47 (1988). Relief has also been granted against noisy and quarrelsome neighbors. Daniels v. Griffin, 769 S.W.2d 199 (Mo.App.1989); Elster v. Friedman, 211 Cal.App.3d 1439, 260 Cal.Rptr. 148 (1989). Several states have enacted legislation that specifically authorizes injunctive relief against harassment. See Schraer v. Berkeley Property Owners' Association, 207 Cal.App.3d 719, 255 Cal.Rptr. 453 (1989); Bachowski v. Salamone, 139 Wis.2d 397, 407 N.W.2d 533 (1987).

Even public officials may enjoin harassing phone calls. Brookline v. Goldstein, 388 Mass. 443, 447 N.E.2d 641 (1983). Is there a First Amendment problem? See Mabe v. City of Galveston, 687 S.W.2d 769, 772 (Tex.App.1985). A beachfront business owner was enjoined from distributing pamphlets. The pamphlet contained city council members' phone numbers; the business distributed them to patrons who might call to register a protest on a matter of "public interest, i.e., the lack of public restroom facilities on the Seawall." The appellate court thought the "injunctive order constituted an unwarranted prior restraint on the exercise of Mabe's first amendment right of freedom of speech."

b. *Damages.* Given the possibility of recovering both compensatory and punitive damages, the legal remedy may provide effective relief against invasion of the right to privacy. In Donnel v. Lara, 703 S.W.2d 257 (Tex.App.1985), which involved telephone harassment, the plaintiff recovered only two dollars compensatory but $4500 in punitive damages. In LeFlore v. Reflections of Tulsa, Inc., 708 P.2d 1068 (Okl.1985), where the plaintiff's name was misappropriated, plaintiff recovered $6,136 compensatory and $12,500 in punitive damages. Even more striking is the recovery in Black v. United States, 389 F.Supp. 529 (D.D.C.1975), rev'd, 564 F.2d 531 (D.C.Cir.1977), where the government was held liable for $903,232 damages arising out of approximately ten weeks of electronic surveillance of the plaintiff by the F.B.I. Damages were held to include loss of name, reputation, friends and business associates; mental pain and suffering, embarrassment, and humiliation; plus loss of employment, livelihood and ability to obtain employment.

c. As is usual when the courts have removed long-standing barriers to the exercise of equitable jurisdiction, problems in drafting and enforcing the injunctive decrees have emerged. Generally, the problem is how to draft an order that protects the wronged plaintiff satisfactorily while at the same time not unduly (or even unconstitutionally) limiting the defendant's activities. For example, injunctive relief was granted to Mrs. Onassis, widow of President Kennedy, against obtrusive and continuous surveillance and harassment by Ron Galella, a photographer who described himself as the "world's only American paparazzi." Finding an invasion of her right of privacy, the court granted a permanent injunction prohibiting Galella from "approaching within 100 yards of the home of [Mrs.

Onassis] and her children, * * * at all other places and times 75 yards from the children and 50 yards from [Mrs. Onassis]; from performing surveillance of [Mrs. Onassis] or her children; from commercially appropriating [Mrs. Onassis's] photograph for advertising or trade purposes." Galella v. Onassis, 353 F.Supp. 196, 216 (S.D.N.Y.1972), modified, 487 F.2d 986, 993 (2d Cir.1973). The 40–page opinion was based on a six week trial and a 4,714 page record.

A majority of the second circuit concluded that the "injunction * * * is broader than is required to protect [Mrs. Onassis]." It removed restrictions on Galella's approach to the Onassis home; reduced the distance that Galella was to keep from 50 yards to 25 feet (but not to touch her) and the distance he was to keep from the children from 75 yards to 30 feet. Galella v. Onassis, 487 F.2d 986 (2d Cir.1973).

Galella continued his activities. He was cited for contempt. Galella v. Onassis, 533 F.Supp. 1076 (S.D.N.Y.1982) (a 22–page opinion). Does this inordinate amount of judicial time and paper demonstrate that injunctions are unsuitable devices to control harassment?

See also Valenzuela v. Aquino, 763 S.W.2d 43 (Tex.App.1988).

2. *The Appropriation of Another's Name or Likeness.* Manville v. Borg–Warner Corp., 418 F.2d 434, 437 (10th Cir.1969). A verdict of $2,500 actual and $7,500 punitive damages for the unauthorized use of plaintiff's picture in an advertisement of Norge coin operated laundries was set aside for lack of proof of *general* damages. "It is too much to say that general damages in privacy suits arise by inferences of law and need not be proved because that is the rule for libel per se * * *. The ordinary damage rules apply in this respect and without showing of some general damages Manville is entitled to recover only nominal damages."

In Monroe v. Darr, 221 Kan. 281, 281, 559 P.2d 322, 324 (1977), the court explained that *Manville* only required "some evidence to show [plaintiff] suffered anxiety, embarrassment, or some form of mental anguish."

Compare Leavy v. Cooney, 214 Cal.App.2d 496, 29 Cal.Rptr. 580 (1963). The prosecuting attorney in the notorious *Chessman* case was awarded $7,500 compensatory and $7,500 punitive damages for the unauthorized use of his picture and voice in a motion picture about the trial.

Recovery may also be based on the value of the interest appropriated, an approach that resembles restitution for unjust enrichment. Grant v. Esquire, Inc., 367 F.Supp. 876 (S.D.N.Y.1973).

New York Civil Rights Law §§ 50 and 51, pp. 607–08 supra, is a *privacy* statute.

3. *Personal Letters.* The traditional common law rule gave the sender of a personal letter a property right in the composition and the recipient a property right in the document; it originated in Lord Eldon's decision in Gee v. Pritchard, 2 Swanst. 402 (Ch. 1818). Lord Eldon protected the writer of personal letters against publication by third parties. No right of privacy existed. Lord Eldon found a property right on which to base equitable jurisdiction. Lord Eldon's oft quoted but elusive dictum restricting equitable relief to property interests is habitually attributed to his decision in Gee v. Pritchard.

This common law protection to authors of personal letters is not possible following the Copyright Act of 1976 (17 U.S.C. §§ 101 et seq.). Under the Act, letters are copyrightable within the provisions of the Copyright Act. State law is preempted; whatever protection an author may have is restricted to that provided by the Copyright Act. A claim that the letter itself was wrongfully taken from the possession of the writer or recipient is still possible, however, since the tort of conversion is outside the purview of the Copyright Act. Maheu v. CBS, Inc., 201 Cal.App.3d 662, 247 Cal.Rptr. 304 (1988).

4. *False Light.* Time, Inc. v. Hill, 385 U.S. 374, 388 (1967). The Supreme Court held that in a "false light" case, constitutional protections of free speech required proof "that the defendant published the report with knowledge of its falsity or in reckless disregard of the truth." Following *Gertz,* supra pp. 617–19, whether this strict standard must still be met is questionable. The issue was not resolved in Cantrell v. Forest City Publishing Co., 419 U.S. 245 (1974), since that publication was made with reckless disregard of the truth. In Cox Broadcasting Corp. v. Cohn, 420 U.S. 469, 499 (1975), no invasion of a right of privacy was found, but Justice Powell, in a concurring opinion questioned "the conceptual basis of Time, Inc. v. Hill." He pointed out that the Supreme Court had not been "called upon to determine whether a State may constitutionally apply a more relaxed standard of liability" to false light cases. As a result of this opinion, the Restatement (Second) of Torts, § 652E (1976), takes no position as to whether recovery in false light cases can be had for publications that are merely negligent. See Hill, Defamation and Privacy Under the First Amendment, 76 Colum.L.Rev. 1205 (1976).

A recent California decision, Fellows v. National Enquirer, Inc., 42 Cal.3d 234, 228 Cal.Rptr. 215, 721 P.2d 97 (1986), held that constitutional restrictions on defamation applied equally to false light. Thus whenever a claim for false light invasion of privacy is based on language that is defamatory, pleading and proof of special damages were required. Quoting from an article by the late Dean Prosser, the court suggested that if this were not done, all the restrictions on defamation actions to protect freedom of the press and freedom of speech could be swallowed up in the new tort of false light invasion of privacy.

Renwick v. News and Observer Publishing Co., 310 N.C. 312, 326, 329, 312 S.E.2d 405, 413, 415 (1984) went one step further. An Associate Dean filed an action for libel and false light invasion of privacy. The court declined to recognize the false light tort. It thought that the tort was "inherently constitutionally suspect" because it created liability for truthful, nondefamatory publication.

The court also dealt with the duplication issue: "[T]he recognition of claims for relief for false light invasions of privacy would reduce judicial efficiency by requiring our courts to consider two claims for the same relief which, if not identical, would not differ significantly."

Dissenting Justice Meyer: "A cause of action for both false light invasion of privacy and libel may be joined in the same action. [citation] However, there can be but one recovery for any particular publication. Restatement (Second) of Torts § 652E, Comment b."

See Zuckman, Invasion of Privacy—Some Communicative Torts Whose Time Has Gone, 47 Wash. & Lee L.Rev. 253 (1990).

5. *Privacy (False Light) Distinguished from Defamation.* Brink v. Griffith, 65 Wash.2d 253, 258, 396 P.2d 793, 796 (1964). Plaintiff, a police officer, recovered $10,000 on a claim for libel and $5,000 on a claim for invasion of privacy arising out of defendant's false assertion at a town meeting that plaintiff was a convicted criminal. The trial court set aside the privacy verdict. Held, affirmed:

"Theoretically, the difference between the torts of defamation and invasion of privacy is that a defamation action is primarily concerned with compensating the injured party for damage to reputation, while an invasion of privacy action is primarily concerned with compensation for injured feelings or mental suffering. Defamation and the Right of Privacy, 15 Vand.L.Rev. 1093 (1962). A problem arises, however, from the fact that for either defamation or invasion of privacy the damages recoverable are not limited to the theoretical bases of the respective torts. In defamation actions, the injured party is allowed to recover for emotional distress as well as injury to reputation, and vice versa in some actions for invasion of privacy, 15 Vand.L.Rev. 1112.

"In the instant case, the wrong complained of involves but one transaction, the import of which was to cast the plaintiff in a false light; the complaint alleges two claims for relief based thereon and indiscriminately prays for general damages upon each claim; the instructions to the jury indiscriminately permit recovery of damages for wounded feelings and injury to reputation; and the verdict awards damages upon each claim for relief. The conclusion appears inescapable that a duplication of damages has occurred.

"The problem thus presented is characterized and the solution suggested by Dean John W. Wade, in his article Defamation and the Right of Privacy:

> " 'Since the very first privacy case, it has often been held that an action can be maintained successfully for both defamation and invasion of the right of privacy, usually by separate counts in one civil action. The cases do not indicate how much attention is given to the prevention of duplication of damages. If the action in defamation can be maintained, plaintiff is entitled to damages for mental distress; and, if the privacy action can be maintained for being publicly placed in a false position, it could appear that plaintiff can recover damages for the harm to his reputation from the position in which he is so placed. A better position is taken by the New York cases which indicate that there is only a single action for the one transaction with complete damages being given for it.' "

6. *Class Actions for Invasion of Privacy.* Is a class action available to vindicate the right of privacy? Stilson v. Reader's Digest Association, 28 Cal. App.3d 270, 104 Cal.Rptr. 581 (1972), cert. denied, 411 U.S. 952 (1973). Plaintiffs sought damages and injunctive relief for themselves "and others similarly situated" against the Reader's Digest. They claimed that defendant's use of plaintiffs' and others' names to promote the "Lucky Number Sweepstakes" constituted an invasion of privacy. Mailings were made to approximately 21,300,000 persons in the first drawing and to 29,000,000 persons in the second. Defendant moved to strike the allegations relating to persons other than the named plaintiffs. The motion to strike was granted, and, on appeal, that order was affirmed. The class action was properly barred because "the court would be required to examine the mental and subjective state of each of the millions of plaintiffs, since in each case such individual appraisal is of the essence of the claim for damages and, indeed, of the cause of action." Such an assessment of individual sensitivity "would impose an unjustified and intolerable burden upon the court and the parties." Injunctive relief by class action was also held improper since it assumed "that each of the millions in the class objects to such use of his name, and injunction would hardly be granted absent some desire for it by each supposed beneficiary."

C. STATUS

1. FAMILIAL STATUS

a. Damages

ANTONELLI v. XENAKIS

Supreme Court of Pennsylvania, 1949.

363 Pa. 375, 69 A.2d 102.

JONES, JUSTICE. The plaintiff sued in trespass to recover damages from the defendant for the latter's alleged criminal conversation with the plaintiff's wife. The defendant filed preliminary objections which questioned the court's jurisdiction on the grounds that the cause of action, as pleaded by the plaintiff, was for alienation of affections and that the Act of June 22, 1935, P.L. 450, Sec. 1, as amended by the Act of June 25, 1937, P.L. 2317, Sec. 1, 48 P.S. § 170, abolished such actions save in certain instances not presently material. The learned court below held that the gravamen of the complaint was criminal conversation and that a right of action therefor was not abolished by the Act of 1935, cit. supra. * * *

The common law has long furnished an aggrieved husband with a right of action against his wife's adulterer for criminal conversation. Blackstone's Commentaries (Lewis' Ed.), Book 3, p. 139, lists "adultery, or criminal conversation" as one of the three principal "Injuries that may be offered to a person, considered as a husband, * * *" and goes on to state that "Adultery, or criminal conversation with a man's wife, though it is, as a public crime, left by our laws to the coercion of the spiritual courts; yet, considered as a civil injury, (and surely there can be no greater,) the law gives a satisfaction to the husband for it by action of trespass vi et armis against the adulterer. * * *"

Section 685 of the Restatement, Torts, specifically affirms the existence of a cause of action for criminal conversation as distinguished from an action for alienation of affections, which is treated with in § 683. The fact that both of such causes may be joined in one suit is merely a matter of procedural permission. Restatement, Torts, § 683, Comment c. And, while the liability in the two actions is, in general, the same, viz., "for the harm thereby caused to any of [the husband's] legally protected marital interests" (compare § 683 and § 685 of the Restatement, Torts), the causes represent nonetheless two distinct torts, "one may exist without the other." See 42 Corpus Juris Secundum, § 668, where it is also pointed out that "The lack of necessity for a physical debauchment distinguishes alienation of affections from criminal conversation." And, a single act of adultery is sufficient to entitle the husband of the woman to damages in an action against the adulterer for criminal conversation even though the husband sustains no further loss. See § 683, Comment c. and § 685, Comment b. of the Restatement, Torts. On the other hand, sexual intercourse between the wife and an alienator of her affections is not a requisite to an action for damages for the husband's consequent loss. Restatement, Torts, § 683, Comment c. Knowledge or belief that a woman is married is essential to liability for alienation of her affections while such knowledge is not necessary to liability for criminal conversation with her. A man who has sexual relations with a woman, not his wife, assumes the risk that she is married. Even her misrepresentation that she is single affords the offender no defense to liability for criminal conversation. Restatement, Torts, § 685, Comment d. We think there can be no doubt that alienation of affections and criminal conversation are two separate and distinct torts and that, for each, the common law affords a right of action unless, of course, the same has been statutorily abolished.

The Act of 1935, supra, did not abolish rights of action for criminal conversation. Nowhere therein is that cause mentioned or referred to. Nor may it be read into the statute by implication. * * * [The Court held the complaint stated a cause of action for criminal conversation.]

And, while it is true, as we have hereinbefore noted, that the elements of damage for which recovery can be had are, broadly speaking, the same for both alienation of affections and criminal conversation, the injuries averred in the instant complaint are such as are peculiarly associated with an action for criminal conversation, e.g., injury to the husband's social position, irreparable disgrace in the community where he lived and was engaged in business and dishonor to himself and his family.

Order affirmed.

Notes

1. The elements considered in determining compensatory damages include loss of support, injury to health, loss of consortium, mental anguish and humiliation. See Gray v. Hoover, 94 N.C.App. 724, 381 S.E.2d 472, review denied, 325 N.C. 545, 385 S.E.2d 498 (1989) (upholding a verdict of $30,000 compensatory and $10,000 punitive damages); Jennings v. Jessen, 93 N.C.App. 731, 379 S.E.2d 53 (1989), rev'd, 326 N.C. 43, 387 S.E.2d 167 (1990) (wife awarded judgment against other woman in the amount of $200,000 compensatory and $300,000 punitive damages).

The reasonableness of the damages is affected by the stability of the marital relationship prior to defendant's conduct. Roach v. Keane, 73 Wis.2d 524, 538, 243 N.W.2d 508, 516 (1976): "What was in the store before it was burglarized at least sets a limit to what could have been burglarized."

2. Common law actions for damages for alienation of affection, criminal conversation, and seduction—as well as for breach of promise to marry—have been variously affected by "heart balm" statutes, which must be consulted to ascertain local remedial possibilities. In addition, some states have abolished the actions by judicial decision. See Wyman v. Wallace, 94 Wash.2d 99, 615 P.2d 452 (1980); O'Neil v. Schuckardt, 112 Idaho 472, 733 P.2d 693 (1986). Where the actions for criminal conversation and alienation of affection have been abolished either by statute or judicial decision, attempts have been made to avoid the prohibition by recasting the action as one for intentional infliction of mental suffering. For a decision rejecting this approach to reviving the old actions, see Strock v. Pressnell, 38 Ohio St.3d 207, 527 N.E.2d 1235 (1988), overruling on this point Slusher v. Oeder, 16 Ohio App.3d 432, 476 N.E.2d 714 (1984). In O'Neil v. Schuckardt, 112 Idaho 472, 733 P.2d 693 (1986), supra, the Idaho court, in rejecting a claim based on alienation of affection did find evidence to support an action for invasion of privacy.

3. Why these actions have fallen into disfavor may be seen from Wilson v. Aylward, 207 Kan. 254, 258, 484 P.2d 1003, 1006 (1971). Defendant had engaged in illicit relations with plaintiff's wife and had paid her $65,000 to avoid a threatened disclosure. When defendant refused to pay more, the husband sued for alienation of affections. A judgment for $50,000 was reversed on appeal. In conclusion, the court stated: "Regardless of the label given to this bizarre affair—and whether it be denominated as blackmail, extortion or just a pure-and-simple 'shakedown'—the situation presented is a good illustration of what this court may have had in mind in 1936 when * * * it classified actions for alienation of affections as being obnoxious to the public welfare."

b. Equitable Relief

LYON v. IZEN

Appellate Court of Illinois, 1971.
131 Ill.App.2d 594, 268 N.E.2d 436.

[Plaintiff alleged that she and her husband were engaged in the practice of medicine, that they hired defendant as a laboratory technician, that defendant began a steady course of conduct toward the husband with the deliberate intent of alienating his affections, and that as a result plaintiff and her husband have separated. A temporary injunction was issued prohibiting defendant from "seeing, visiting, writing or talking" to plaintiff's husband. Defendant appeals, contending that the trial court erred in entering the temporary injunction.]

DRUCKER, JUSTICE. * * * The courts of our state have long recognized a distinction between property or pecuniary rights and personal rights in applying equity jurisdiction. Injury to property, whether actual or prospective, is the foundation upon which the jurisdiction of a court of equity rests. * * * Plaintiff's complaint does not allege any pecuniary loss but claims that the defendant, by her behavior has alienated the affection of plaintiff's husband and has thereby deprived plaintiff of her consortium, society and marital services. In Siegall v. Solomon, 19 Ill.2d 145, 149, 166 N.E.2d 5, 7, the court stated: "It is, however, the modern view that rights of a husband in his wife's affections and society are not property within the due process clause. * * * " Therefore, the rights of the plaintiff to her husband's affection and society, which are alleged to have been violated by the defendant in the instant case, are not property rights which can be governed by injunction, and the injunction must therefore be reversed.

Defendant also argues that the temporary injunction is too broad in scope and that the injunctive relief cannot be applied with any practical success by the trial court. * * *

In Snedaker v. King, 111 Ohio St. 225, 145 N.E. 15, the plaintiff-wife also sought an injunction to restrain defendant from seeing, speaking, communicating or associating with plaintiff's husband at plaintiff's home or elsewhere, so as to prevent plaintiff's husband from giving to plaintiff his love, affection, companionship, conjugal relation or support. The trial court ordered that an injunction issue against the defendant. However, on appeal the court held that the injunction decree should have been denied. As the court stated:

> "The decree in this case is an extreme instance of government by injunction. It attempts to govern, control, and direct personal relations and domestic affairs. Among other restrictions placed upon the defendant by this decree is that of remaining away from any place where plaintiff's husband may be, and from interfering with plaintiff's efforts to communicate with her husband, and with her efforts to regain his love, esteem, support and conjugal relation. * * *
>
> "Such extension of the jurisdiction of equity to regulate and control domestic relations, in addition to the legal and statutory remedies already provided, in our opinion is not supported by authority, warranted by sound reason, or in the interest of good morals or public policy. The opening of such a wide field for injunctive process, enforceable only by contempt proceedings, the difficulty if not impossibility of such enforcement, and the very doubtful beneficial results to be obtained thereby, warrant the denial of such a decree in this case, and require a modification of the judgment in that respect."

In a separate concurring opinion in *Snedaker,* supra, Justice Allen stated:

> "First. While it is true that any injunction is enforceable only through contempt proceedings, it is also true that this particular order is usually difficult of enforcement. * * * Proof of the violation of this particular order will depend, at least largely, upon the testimony, not of indifferent third parties but of these particular two people. Under these circumstances it is

difficult to see how the court can enforce the injunction granted herein without attaching a probation officer permanently to both Miss Snedaker and King.

"Second. The order passes all bounds in its lack of limitation. Under this order, what is Miss Snedaker to do if she passes King upon the street? Must she cross the street in order not to go 'near him * * * at * * * any * * * place where said Homer King may be,' or may she stay upon the same side of the street and pass him? Under such circumstances may she say 'good morning' to him, or in so doing will she be violating the order that she is not to communicate with King 'by word?' "

In the instant case we believe that the temporary injunction order is too broad in scope and that enforcement of this injunction by the court would be extremely difficult and impractical.

Reversed and remanded with directions.

Notes

1. The decisions on whether to grant an injunction to protect the love nest from intruders are split. Henley v. Rockett, 243 Ala. 172, 8 So.2d 852 (1942), is a representative decision approving an injunction.

2. Injunctions banning domestic violence are partial solutions to the problem of spouse abuse. Courts may base these injunctions on the common law, but special statutes are common. Taub, Equitable Relief in Cases of Adult Domestic Violence, 6 Women's Rts.L.Rep. 237 (1980). Divorce decrees may include enforceable orders against abuse of former spouse. Goodell v. Goodell, 421 So.2d 736 (Fla.App.1982); Cipolla v. Cipolla, 264 Pa.Super. 53, 398 A.2d 1053 (1979).

Does *Lyon* convince you that there is a kernel of truth to limiting injunctions to property rights? Can a family be held together by injunctions?

Consider Rosenbaum v. Rosenbaum, 184 Ill.App.3d 987, 989, 992, 541 N.E.2d 872, 874, 876 (1989), cert. denied, 110 S.Ct. 1297 (1990) where a trial judge ordered a son to telephone his mother "no less than once every three months." In reversing, the Illinois Appellate Court noted that "it takes more than a mere secular tribunal to command filial devotion."

3. Nowhere has the issue of the limits on equitable intervention been presented more dramatically than in disputes arising from surrogate parenting agreements. The social, ethical, and legal issues are meticulously examined in the opinions of the Superior Court and Supreme Court in the case of In re Baby "M," 217 N.J.Super. 313, 525 A.2d 1128 (1987), modified, 109 N.J. 396, 537 A.2d 1227 (1988).

2. ASSOCIATIONAL STATUS

TRAUTWEIN v. HARBOURT

Superior Court of New Jersey, 1956.
40 N.J.Super. 247, 123 A.2d 30.

[Action for compensatory and punitive damages. Plaintiffs, many of whom were members of other chapters, formed a new chapter seeking admission in the Order of the Eastern Star. The new chapter functioned under a temporary dispensation pending a grant of a permanent charter, which was denied, allegedly because of the wilful and concerted actions of the defendants actuated by malice.]

CONFORD, J.A.D. The gravamen of plaintiffs' argument is that defendants' activities caused them to be expelled from and made "outcasts" of a fraternal order in which they were members. Defendants, on the other hand, contend there was but a denial of membership in a voluntary, private, fraternal organization. The resolution of this issue is our first concern, since the law accords important rights and status to members of voluntary organizations not extended to mere aspirants to membership therein. One wrongfully expelled from such an organization may be restored to membership by mandamus. Or he may bring an action for damages. For a discussion of criteria of a lawful expulsion, see Chafee, "Internal Affairs of Associations not for Profit," 43 Harv.L.Rev. 993, 1014–1020 (1930). On the other hand, there is no "abstract right to be admitted" to membership in a voluntary association, and a court will not compel the admission of a person to membership in such an organization who has not been elected according to its rules and by-laws. The general rule is that there is no legal remedy for exclusion of such an individual from admission into a voluntary association, no matter how arbitrary or unjust the exclusion. * * * The authorities cited by plaintiffs are almost entirely expulsion cases. As we shall see, there are no adjudicated cases which can be regarded as square holdings as to the existence of a right of action for damages for wrongful exclusion from a purely social or fraternal organization, and our consideration of that subject must perforce be based upon principle and the analogies of related torts. [The court then held the situation to be one of exclusion rather than expulsion.]

We thus return to the crux of the case. Should the members of a strictly social or fraternal organization be held responsible in damages on the basis of the motives which actuate their concerted activity, within the confines of the organization, to exclude from membership those whom for any reason they deem objectionable? It is not without a search of conscience as well as for legal authorities that we have arrived at a negative conclusion upon the proposition posed. * * * We distinguish cases involving organizations, membership in which is an economic necessity; or those which are repositories of civic, civil or political rights.

Plaintiffs stress the high value which the courts have attached to membership in fraternal societies, clubs, and organizations, as evidenced by their readiness to redress unwarranted expulsion; and they imply that there should be equal readiness to protect against unwarranted interference with the opportunity for membership therein, just as against unjustified interference with prospective economic advantage. * * * There can be no doubt as to the conspicuous place of social and fraternal organizations in American society * * * nor as to the cachet attributed by almost every individual to membership in one or more particular voluntary associations, societies or groups. Professor Chafee has said that in comparison with "such emotional deprivations" as loss of membership in club, union, school or church, "mere losses of property often appear trivial." There is evidence that unwarranted obstruction of or interference with normal opportunities for social intercourse may be actionable. In Deon v. Kirby Lumber Co., 162 La. 671, 111 So. 55 (Sup.Ct.1926), it was held that the order of an employer to his employees not to patronize or visit the family of a local storekeeper gave rise to an action for damages. The charge in the complaint encompassed the malicious injury by the defendant of plaintiff's "social standing and character" and the effectuation of his ostracism. * * *

The only decided case we have found approaching the precise question here involved—liability in damages for malicious exclusion from membership in a fraternal organization—is Grand Lodge Order Hermann's Sons of Texas v.

Schuetze, [36 Tex.Civ.App. 539, 83 S.W. 241 (1904).] In that case a local lodge of a fraternal organization was dissolved by the grand lodge at the request of the local because of what was regarded as an inexcusable false charge of theft by one of the members against another, and a new lodge was formed consisting of the same membership but excluding the offending member. The latter sued the grand lodge for conspiracy with its officers to deprive her of her membership. The case seems to us clearly to have been one, in effect, of expulsion rather than exclusion. But the appellate court reversed a judgment for plaintiff. After declaring that the dissolution was "legal" and that "when a legal right exists the law does not award damages on account of the motive which prompts its exercise," the court went on to say:

> "It [grand lodge] had the legal right to sanction the disorganization of that lodge [subordinate lodge], and cannot be held liable for damages because its officers may have acted upon improper motives in accepting the dissolution of the local lodge * * *. It was the legal right of the members composing that body [new lodge], and of the grand lodge and its officers, not to invite her to its membership, regardless of the motives by which they were actuated; and the exercise of that right, upon whatever motive, did not fix legal liability for damages against the grand lodge or any one else."

The apparent absence of any other reported cases dealing with claims for damages for exclusion, as contrasted with the large number of cases involving damages for wrongful expulsion, is itself cogent evidence that such an action as is here laid is not generally deemed available, as the number of disappointed applicants for membership in fraternities, societies and private clubs of every kind, from town and eating clubs to country clubs, must be legion, and the range of motivation for exclusion kaleidoscopic.

We hold that what the defendants here did, in the aspect challenged by plaintiffs, was in the exercise of a primary right of the defendants; a right to act, individually and jointly, for the exclusion from the order of the proposed chapter for any reasons which they deemed warranted such action; and that in exercising such right their motives were immaterial.

Notes

1. *Exclusion from Membership.* Litigation in this area ranges all the way from suits to compel officials to permit children to join athletic teams, Brown v. Wells, 288 Minn. 468, 181 N.W.2d 708 (1970) (exclusion of a high school athlete, injunction refused), to petitions to compel admission to the state bar, In re Peterson, 459 P.2d 703 (Alaska 1969) (admission denied).

In general, equitable intervention occurs where membership in an association has serious economic or professional effects. Thus in Falcone v. Middlesex County Medical Society, 34 N.J. 582, 170 A.2d 791 (1961), an osteopath was successful in gaining admission to an unincorporated county medical association where the society had a virtual monopoly of local hospital facilities. Similarly, a proper case for equitable intervention was established by proof that exclusion from membership in a professional association precluded certification in orthodontics and thus deprived plaintiff of substantial economic advantages. Pinsker v. Pacific Coast Society of Orthodontists, 1 Cal.3d 160, 81 Cal.Rptr. 623, 460 P.2d 495 (1969). Even where a proper basis for relief is established, judicial review is limited to whether the exclusion is arbitrary or capricious. Reasonable rules governing admission to membership are enforceable. Grempler v. Multiple Listing Bureau, 258 Md. 419,

266 A.2d 1 (1970) (office requirement for admission to membership in the Bureau held to be reasonable).

2. *Expulsion from Membership.* Kronen v. Pacific Coast Society of Orthodontists, 237 Cal.App.2d 289, 46 Cal.Rptr. 808, 817 (1965), cert. denied, 384 U.S. 905 (1966): "However, the cases have emphasized a distinction between situations involving the expulsion of a member and those involving a refusal to admit him in the first place. In instances of *expulsion,* as distinguished from *exclusion,* the courts have been inclined to grant at least a limited review and, where the expulsion has been wrongfully or arbitrarily brought about, to compel the reinstatement of the member. The principles governing judicial review in such situations were stated as follows: 'In any proper case involving the expulsion of a member from a voluntary unincorporated association, the only function which the courts may perform is to determine whether the association has acted within its powers in good faith, in accordance with its laws and the law of the land.' [citations] It has been said 'that courts are reluctant to interfere in the internal affairs of private voluntary associations * * * [and] rarely grant relief to a person expelled or excluded from a voluntary association.' "

Compare Salkin v. California Dental Association, 176 Cal.App.3d 1118, 224 Cal.Rptr. 352 (1986) (applying the same requirement of a fair hearing where plaintiff was disciplined rather than expelled).

3. Discriminatory practices by private clubs have been vigorously attacked in recent years. See New York State Club Association v. City of New York, 487 U.S. 1 (1988).

Plaintiff wife was awarded membership in a country club in a divorce proceeding. When the club learned of the divorce, her membership was terminated because club rules provided that family membership could be issued only to an adult male. Plaintiff, claiming sex discrimination, filed a suit seeking injunctive relief prohibiting the termination of her membership. On appeal, the court held that a cause of action was stated for violation of plaintiff's civil rights. Warfield v. Peninsula Golf and Country Club, 214 Cal.App.3d 646, 262 Cal.Rptr. 890 (1989).

4. In Berrien v. Pollitzer, 165 F.2d 21, 23 (D.C.Cir.1947), plaintiff was excluded from the National Women's Party, a non-stock, nonprofit corporation, organized for the purpose of securing complete equality for women. In reversing the district court, which had dismissed a complaint seeking injunctive relief, the court of appeals flatly rejected any requirement of a property interest as a necessary element for equitable jurisdiction: "It is obviously immaterial that the National Women's Party is called a party and not a club or church. * * * The District Court has jurisdiction to grant an injunction. It should proceed to determine whether it should exercise this jurisdiction." The possible political overtones were not discussed.

Rejection of a property right as a prerequisite to equitable relief is, of course, commonplace today. Courts have nevertheless exercised considerable ingenuity in finding that membership in a voluntary association is a protectable contract or property right. An example is Willowbrook Country Club, Inc. v. Ferrell, 286 Ala. 281, 239 So.2d 298 (1970), where life membership in a country club was found to be a property right protectable in equity. How about a bridge club? See Aspell v. American Contract Bridge League, 122 Ariz. 399, 595 P.2d 191 (App.1979).

5. The plaintiff, though failing to secure an injunction may obtain essentially what she desires. The decree may amount to a declaratory judgment that the expulsion was morally unjustified although accomplished within the legal framework of the association's bylaws or regulations.

6. See Note, Developments in the Law—Judicial Control of Private Associations, 76 Harv.L.Rev. 983 (1963); Note, Judicial Protection of Membership in Private Associations, 11 W.Res.L.Rev. 346 (1963).

3. ACADEMIC STATUS

SUSAN M. v. NEW YORK LAW SCHOOL

Court of Appeals of New York, 1990.

76 N.Y.2d 241, 557 N.Y.S.2d 297, 556 N.E.2d 1104.

ALEXANDER, JUDGE. In this article 78 proceeding, petitioner challenges her dismissal for academic deficiency from respondent law school. Because her allegations are directed at the pedagogical evaluation of her test grades, a determination best left to educators rather than the courts, we conclude that her petition does not state a judicially cognizable claim. Accordingly, we modify the order of the Appellate Division to dismiss the petition in its entirety.

Petitioner enrolled at respondent law school in the fall of 1985. In accordance with respondent's published rules, petitioner was automatically placed on academic probation at the end of her first year for having failed to achieve a 2.0, or "C" cumulative average. The law school rules further provided that a student on probation who thereafter fails to achieve both a semester and a cumulative average of 2.0 is subject to academic dismissal at the discretion of the law school's Academic Status Committee (Committee). Such a student, however, has the right to present written and oral statements to the Committee explaining his or her failure to meet the school's academic standards.

Although petitioner earned a cumulative average of 2.001 at the end of her third semester, in her fourth semester her average dropped to 1.546, lowering her cumulative average to 1.89. Consequently she was notified that the Academic Status Committee would be considering whether she would be permitted to continue her studies. She submitted a written statement to the Committee, describing factors that she claimed affected her performance. In this written statement, petitioner blamed her less than "C" average on the grades she received in two of her fourth semester courses, namely, Constitutional Law II, in which she received a "C–," and Corporations, in which she received a "D." She argued that these grades did not fairly and accurately reflect the knowledge she had demonstrated on the exams in those courses. Petitioner also appeared before the Committee to state her case orally. She contends that when she attempted to raise the subject of the two grades, she was immediately interrupted by the Committee chairperson who told her that the Committee would not consider them. Petitioner then gave other reasons for her below average performance. They were unavailing and the Committee voted unanimously to dismiss her for failure to meet the law school's academic standards. Petitioner requested reconsideration of her case, and submitted an additional statement offering still further reasons for her substandard academic performance. The Committee accepted the new submission, but declined to reconsider its decision.

In this article 78 proceeding seeking a judgment directing respondent to reinstate her, petitioner alleges that the Committee's decision to dismiss her was arbitrary and capricious and that her poor performance in her fourth semester was directly attributable to the irrational testing and grading procedures of three of her four professors. She challenged the grades she received in Constitutional Law II, Corporations, and Lawyers and Systems of Justice, alleging that her Constitutional Law exam was unfairly graded and that the professor in Lawyers and Systems of Justice was "a complete incompetent". She also contends, *inter alia,* that the Committee failed to give sufficient weight to a variety of personal factors; and that she was dismissed in retaliation for complaining about her professors.

Petitioner also alleges that when she met with the Corporations professor to discuss her grade, the professor told her that she was given zero credit on an essay question worth 30% of the exam because she analyzed the problem under both Delaware law and New York law when only Delaware law was called for, that her answer did correctly analyze the problem under Delaware law and that she would have received full credit on this question had she only refrained from mentioning New York law. Notwithstanding petitioner's claim that she only mentioned New York law to get extra credit, the professor allegedly insisted that petitioner gave two answers to the question, thereby indicating that she did not know which one was correct, and was therefore not entitled to any credit. Petitioner also alleges that the professor advised her that points were deducted from the Corporations exam because she had misused the term "oppressive conduct" and because the exam was written in the style of a first-year student.

The responding affidavits of respondent's Dean of Academic Affairs and the Corporations professor asserted that the grading of the exam was purely a matter of academic discretion and that the exam grade was based upon the over-all quality of petitioner's answer and not on any narrow, formalistic concerns.

Supreme Court dismissed the petition, concluding that petitioner had not demonstrated that her dismissal was arbitrary, capricious or ordered in bad faith. The Appellate Division rejected most of petitioner's claims, but reversed Supreme Court and granted the petition to the extent of remanding the matter to respondent for further consideration of the Corporations grade to determine whether the grade given on the exam, including the disputed essay, was a rational exercise of discretion. * * *

On this appeal, respondent argues that the Appellate Division erred in concluding that petitioner's allegations as to her Corporations grade state a judicially cognizable claim. We agree.

Strong policy considerations militate against the intervention of courts in controversies relating to an educational institution's judgment of a student's academic performance. [citations] See also, Board of Curators, University of Missouri v. Horowitz, 435 U.S. 78, 89–90. Unlike disciplinary actions taken against a student, institutional assessments of a student's academic performance, whether in the form of particular grades received or actions taken because a student has been judged to be scholastically deficient, necessarily involve academic determinations requiring the special expertise of educators (*Board of Curators v. Horowitz*). These determinations play a legitimate and important role in the academic setting since it is by determining that a student's academic performance satisfies the standards set by the institution, and ultimately, by conferring a diploma upon a student who satisfies the institution's course of study, that the institution, in effect, certifies to society that the student possesses the knowledge and skills required by the chosen discipline [citations]. Thus, to preserve the integrity of the credentials conferred by educational institutions, the courts have long been reluctant to intervene in controversies involving purely academic determinations [citation].

Accordingly, although we have emphasized that the determinations of educational institutions as to the academic performance of their students are not completely beyond the scope of judicial review [citations], that review is limited to the question of whether the challenged determination was arbitrary and capricious, irrational, made in bad faith or contrary to Constitution or statute. [citation] This standard has rarely been satisfied in the context of challenges to academic determinations because the courts have repeatedly refused to become involved in the pedagogical evaluation of academic performance. Thus, we have declined, in the absence of bad faith, to compel a university to award a diploma where a student alleged that he had failed a final comprehensive exam because of his reliance on the professor's misstatement as to how the exam would be graded [citation], or to compel a medical school to permit a student who had failed a number of courses to repeat a year [citations], and we have concluded that a college did not act arbitrarily in refusing to "round off" a senior's grade so that she might graduate [citations].

As a general rule, judicial review of grading disputes would inappropriately involve the courts in the very core of academic and educational decision making. Moreover, to so involve the courts in assessing the propriety of particular grades would promote litigation by countless unsuccessful students and thus undermine the credibility of the academic determinations of educational institutions. We conclude, therefore, that, in the absence of demonstrated bad faith, arbitrariness, capriciousness, irrationality or a constitutional or statutory violation, a student's challenge to a particular grade or other academic determination relating to a genuine substantive evaluation of the student's academic capabilities, is beyond the scope of judicial review (see, Regents of University of Michigan v. Ewing, 474 U.S. 214, 225).

Petitioner's allegations do not meet this standard; rather, they go to the heart of the professor's substantive evaluation of the petitioner's academic performance and as such, are beyond judicial review. The claim that this Corporations grade resulted in petitioner's arbitrary dismissal from the law school was properly dismissed by Supreme Court. * * *

Notes

1. *Dismissal for Scholastic Deficiency.* The distinction made between the hearings required by due process for disciplinary and for academic matters was validated by the United States Supreme Court in Board of Curators of the University of Missouri v. Horowitz, 435 U.S. 78 (1978). A medical student, dismissed for inadequate clinical performance, was found not to be entitled to a formal hearing on her dismissal. This reluctance to become involved in academic evaluation is shared generally by the courts which have considered the question. See Jansen v. Emory University, 440 F.Supp. 1060 (N.D.Ga.1977), aff'd, 579 F.2d 45 (5th Cir.1978) (dental student); Paulsen v. Golden Gate University, 25 Cal.3d 803, 159 Cal.Rptr. 858, 602 P.2d 778 (1979); Johnson v. Sullivan, 174 Mont. 491, 571 P.2d 798 (1977) (law student).

2. *Judicial Review of Administrative Rules.* Where the dispute does not involve evaluation of academic performance, courts are much more willing to grant relief. Thus graduation of a high school student was mandated where the denial of

the diploma was based on the student's improper sequencing of required courses, Clark v. Board of Education, 51 Ohio Misc. 71, 367 N.E.2d 69 (1977), and where the student, for religious scruples, refused to take a required R.O.T.C. course, Spence v. Bailey, 325 F.Supp. 601 (W.D.Tenn.1971), aff'd, 465 F.2d 797 (6th Cir.1972). On the other hand, a law student graduating in the upper 10% of his class was refused an injunction directing his election to the Order of the Coif because the court found that restricting eligibility to members of the law review was not arbitrary or unreasonable. Blatt v. University of Southern California, 5 Cal.App.3d 935, 85 Cal.Rptr. 601 (1970). Rules governing eligibility for athletic programs have been almost routinely reviewed. See Kentucky High School Athletic Association v. Hopkins County Board of Education, 552 S.W.2d 685 (Ky.App.1977) (residency rules); Bednar v. Nebraska School Activities Association, 531 F.2d 922 (8th Cir. 1976) (female student); Indiana High School Athletic Association v. Raike, 164 Ind.App. 169, 329 N.E.2d 66 (1975) (married student); Ruman v. Eskew, 168 Ind.App. 428, 343 N.E.2d 806 (1976) (female student).

3. *Expulsion for Non-academic Reasons.* If the controversy involves a disciplinary rather than a scholastic problem, a much different situation is presented. The notion of the University standing in loco parentis has fallen into disfavor. Goldberg v. Regents of the University of California, 248 Cal.App.2d 867, 57 Cal.Rptr. 463 (1967). For the right of an educational institution to impose sanctions for violating codes of student conduct, see Boehm v. University of Pennsylvania School of Veterinary Medicine, 392 Pa.Super. 502, 573 A.2d 575 (1990); Haskell, Judicial Review of School Discipline, 21 Case W.Res.L.Rev. 211 (1970). The principle that has evolved is that students are entitled to notice and hearing prior to the imposition of sanctions. Hall v. Medical College of Ohio, 742 F.2d 299 (6th Cir.1984); Tedeschi v. Wagner College, 49 N.Y.2d 652, 427 N.Y.S.2d 760, 404 N.E.2d 1302 (1980). Once assured that procedural due process is satisfied, courts are unwilling to assume "plenary judicial oversight of the administration of tax supported educational institutions" or to interfere with the exercise of discretion by the appropriate administrative authority. Brown v. Greer, 296 F.Supp. 595, 602 (S.D.Miss.1969.) The court "will not act as a super school board to second guess the Board of Trustees." This view was reaffirmed by the United States Supreme Court. Wood v. Strickland, 420 U.S. 308, 326 (1975): "It is not the role of the federal courts to set aside decisions of school administrators which the court may view as lacking a basis in wisdom or compassion." The rules of conduct being enforced by the institution must, of course, be reasonable, and a student may not be dismissed for the exercise of rights protected by the first amendment. Papish v. Board of Curators of University of Missouri, 410 U.S. 667 (1973).

D. CIVIL RIGHTS

MEMPHIS COMMUNITY SCHOOL DISTRICT v. STACHURA

Supreme Court of the United States, 1986.
477 U.S. 299.

Justice Powell. This case requires us to decide whether 42 U.S.C. § 1983 authorizes an award of compensatory damages based on the factfinder's assessment of the value or importance of a substantive constitutional right.

Respondent Edward Stachura is a tenured teacher in the Memphis, Michigan, public schools. When the events that led to this case occurred, respondent taught seventh-grade life science, using a textbook that had been approved by the school board. The textbook included a chapter on human reproduction. During the 1978–1979 school year, respondent spent six weeks on this chapter.

As part of their instruction, students were shown pictures of respondent's wife during her pregnancy. Respondent also showed the students two films concerning human growth and sexuality. These films were provided by the county health department, and the principal of respondent's school had approved their use. Both films had been shown in past school years without incident.

After the showing of the pictures and the films, a number of parents complained to school officials about respondent's teaching methods. These complaints, which appear to have been based largely on inaccurate rumors about the allegedly sexually explicit nature of the pictures and films, were discussed at an open school board meeting held on April 23, 1979. Following the advice of the school superintendent, respondent did not attend the meeting, during which a number of parents expressed the view that respondent should not be allowed to teach in the Memphis school system.[1] The day after the meeting, respondent was suspended with pay. The school board later confirmed the suspension, and notified respondent that an "administration evaluation" of his teaching methods was underway. No such evaluation was ever made. Respondent was reinstated the next fall, after filing this lawsuit.

Respondent sued the school district, the board of education, various board members and school administrators, and two parents who had participated in the April 23 school board meeting. The complaint alleged that respondent's suspension deprived him of both liberty and property without due process of law and violated his First Amendment right to academic freedom. Respondent sought compensatory and punitive damages under 42 U.S.C. § 1983 for these constitutional violations.

At the close of trial on these claims, the District Court instructed the jury as to the law governing the asserted bases for liability. Turning to damages, the court instructed the jury that on finding liability it should award a sufficient amount to compensate respondent for the injury caused by petitioners' unlawful actions:

> "You should consider in this regard any lost earnings; loss of earning capacity; out-of-pocket expenses; and any mental anguish or emotional distress that you find the Plaintiff to have suffered as a result of conduct by the Defendants depriving him of his civil rights."

In addition to this instruction on the standard elements of compensatory damages, the court explained that punitive damages could be awarded, and described the standards governing punitive awards. Finally, at respondent's request and over petitioners' objection, the court charged that damages also could be awarded based on the value or importance of the constitutional rights that were violated:

> "If you find that the Plaintiff has been deprived of a Constitutional right, you may award damages to compensate him for the deprivation. Damages for this type of injury are more difficult to measure than damages for a physical injury or injury to one's property. There are no medical bills or other expenses by which you can judge how much compensation is appropriate. In one sense,

1. [Footnotes Renumbered.] One member of the school board described the meeting as follows:

"At this time, the public was in a total uproar and completely out of control. * * * People were hollering and shouting and the statement was made from the public that if Mr. Stachura was allowed to return in the morning, they would be there to picket the school.

"At this point of total panic, [the school superintendent] stated in order to maintain peace in our school district, we would suspend Mr. Stachura with full pay and get this mess straightened out."

no monetary value we place upon Constitutional rights can measure their importance in our society or compensate a citizen adequately for their deprivation. However, just because these rights are not capable of precise evaluation does not mean that an appropriate monetary amount should not be awarded.

"The precise value you place upon any Constitutional right which you find was denied to Plaintiff is within your discretion. You may wish to consider the importance of the right in our system of government, the role which this right has played in the history of our republic, [and] the significance of the right in the context of the activities which the Plaintiff was engaged in at the time of the violation of the right."

The jury found petitioners liable, and awarded a total of $275,000 in compensatory damages and $46,000 in punitive damages. The District Court entered judgment notwithstanding the verdict as to one of the defendants, reducing the total award to $266,750 in compensatory damages and $36,000 in punitive damages. * * *

The Court of Appeals for the Sixth Circuit affirmed, holding that respondent's suspension had violated both procedural due process and the First Amendment. Responding to petitioners' contention that the District Court improperly authorized damages based solely on the value of constitutional rights, the court noted only that "there was ample proof of actual injury to plaintiff Stachura both in his effective discharge * * * and by the damage to his reputation and to his professional career as a teacher. Contrary to the situation in Carey v. Piphus, 435 U.S. 247 (1978) * * * there was proof from which the jury could have found, as it did, actual and important damages."

We granted certiorari limited to the question whether the Court of Appeals erred in affirming the damages award in the light of the District Court's instructions that authorized not only compensatory and punitive damages, but also damages for the deprivation of "any constitutional right." [2] We reverse, and remand for a new trial limited to the issue of compensatory damages.

Petitioners challenge the jury instructions authorizing damages for violation of constitutional rights on the ground that those instructions permitted the jury to award damages based on its own unguided estimation of the value of such rights. Respondent disagrees with this characterization of the jury instructions, contending that the compensatory damages instructions taken as a whole focused solely on respondent's injury and not on the abstract value of the rights he asserted.

We believe petitioners more accurately characterize the instructions. The damages instructions were divided into three distinct segments: (i) compensatory damages for harm to respondent, (ii) punitive damages, and (iii) additional "compensat[ory]" damages for violations of constitutional rights. No sensible juror could read the third of these segments to modify the first. On the contrary, the damages instructions plainly authorized—in addition to punitive damages—two distinct types of "compensatory" damages: one based on respondent's actual injury according to ordinary tort law standards, and another based on the "value" of certain rights. We therefore consider whether the latter category of damages was properly before the jury.

2. Since our decision in *Carey v. Piphus*, several of the Courts of Appeals have concluded that damages awards based on the abstract value of constitutional rights are proper, at least as long as the right in question is substantive. [citations] Other courts have determined that our reasoning in *Carey* forecloses such awards. [citations]

We have repeatedly noted that 42 U.S.C. § 1983 [3] creates " 'a species of tort liability' in favor of persons who are deprived of 'rights, privileges, or immunities secured' to them by the Constitution." *Carey v. Piphus.* Accordingly, when § 1983 plaintiffs seek damages for violations of constitutional rights, the level of damages is ordinarily determined according to principles derived from the common law of torts. [citations]

Punitive damages aside, damages in tort cases are designed to provide "*compensation* for the injury caused to plaintiff by defendant's breach of duty." [citations] To that end, compensatory damages may include not only out-of-pocket loss and other monetary harms, but also such injuries as "impairment of reputation * * *, personal humiliation, and mental anguish and suffering." Gertz v. Robert Welch, Inc., 418 U.S. 323, 350 (1974). See also *Carey v. Piphus,* (mental and emotional distress constitute compensable injury in § 1983 cases). Deterrence is also an important purpose of this system, but it operates through the mechanism of damages that are *compensatory*—damages grounded in determinations of plaintiffs' actual losses. Congress adopted this common-law system of recovery when it established liability for "constitutional torts." Consequently, "the basic purpose" of § 1983 damages is "to *compensate persons for injuries* that are caused by the deprivation of constitutional rights." *Carey v. Piphus.*

Carey v. Piphus represents a straight-forward application of these principles. *Carey* involved a suit by a high school student suspended for smoking marijuana; the student claimed that he was denied procedural due process because he was suspended without an opportunity to respond to the charges against him. The Court of Appeals for the Seventh Circuit held that even if the suspension was justified, the student could recover substantial compensatory damages simply because of the insufficient procedures used to suspend him from school. We reversed, and held that the student could recover compensatory damages only if he proved actual injury caused by the denial of his constitutional rights. We noted that "[r]ights, constitutional and otherwise, do not exist in a vacuum. Their purpose is to protect persons from injuries to particular interests." Where no injury was present, no "compensatory" damages could be awarded.

The instructions at issue here cannot be squared with *Carey,* or with the principles of tort damages on which *Carey* and § 1983 are grounded. The jurors in this case were told that, in determining how much was necessary to "compensate [respondent] for the deprivation" of his constitutional rights, they should place a money value on the "rights" themselves by considering such factors as the particular right's "importance * * * in our system of government," its role in American history, and its "significance * * * in the context of the activities" in which respondent was engaged. These factors focus, not on compensation for provable injury, but on the jury's subjective perception of the importance of constitutional rights as an abstract matter. *Carey* establishes that such an approach is impermissible. The constitutional right transgressed in *Carey*—the right to due process of law—is central to our system of ordered

3. Section 1983 reads:

"Every person who, under color of any statute, ordinance, regulation, custom, or usage, of any State or Territory or the District of Columbia, subjects, or causes to be subjected, any citizen of the United States or other person within the jurisdiction thereof to the deprivation of any rights, privileges, or immunities secured by the Constitution and laws, shall be liable to the party injured in an action at law, suit in equity, or other proper proceeding for redress."

liberty. [citation] We nevertheless held that *no* compensatory damages could be awarded for violation of that right absent proof of actual injury. *Carey* thus makes clear that the abstract value of a constitutional right may not form the basis for § 1983 damages.[4]

Respondent nevertheless argues that *Carey* does not control here, because in this case a *substantive* constitutional right—respondent's First Amendment right to academic freedom—was infringed. The argument misperceives our analysis in *Carey.* That case does not establish a two-tiered system of constitutional rights, with substantive rights afforded greater protection than "mere" procedural safeguards. We did acknowledge in *Carey* that "the elements and prerequisites for recovery of damages" might vary depending on the interests protected by the constitutional right at issue. But we emphasized that, whatever the constitutional basis for § 1983 liability, such damages must always be designed "to *compensate injuries* caused by the [constitutional] deprivation."[5] That conclusion simply leaves no room for non-compensatory damages measured by the jury's perception of the abstract "importance" of a constitutional right.

Nor do we find such damages necessary to vindicate the constitutional rights that § 1983 protects. Section 1983 presupposes that damages that compensate for actual harm ordinarily suffice to deter constitutional violations. *Carey.* Moreover, damages based on the "value" of constitutional rights are an unwieldy tool for ensuring compliance with the Constitution. History and tradition do not afford any sound guidance concerning the precise value that juries should place on constitutional protections. Accordingly, were such damages available, juries would be free to award arbitrary amounts without any evidentiary basis, or to use their unbounded discretion to punish unpopular defendants. Such damages would be too uncertain to be of any great value to plaintiffs, and would inject caprice into determinations of damages in § 1983 cases. We therefore hold that damages based on the abstract "value" or "importance" of constitutional rights are not a permissible element of compensatory damages in such cases.

Respondent further argues that the challenged instructions authorized a form of "presumed" damages—a remedy that is both compensatory in nature and traditionally part of the range of tort law remedies. * * *

4. We did approve an award of nominal damages for the deprivation of due process in *Carey.* Our discussion of that issue makes clear that nominal damages, and not damages based on some undefinable "value" of infringed rights, are the appropriate means of "vindicating" rights whose deprivation has not caused actual, provable injury:

"Common-law courts traditionally have vindicated deprivations of certain 'absolute' rights that are not shown to have caused actual injury through the award of a nominal sum of money. By making the deprivation of such rights actionable for nominal damages without proof of actual injury, the law recognizes the importance to organized society that those rights be scrupulously observed; but at the same time, it remains true to the principle that substantial damages should be awarded only to compensate actual injury or, in the case of exemplary or punitive damages, to deter or punish malicious deprivations of rights."

5. *Carey* recognized that "the task * * * of adapting common-law rules of damages to provide fair compensation for injuries caused by the deprivation of a constitutional right" is one "of some delicacy." We also noted that "the elements and prerequisites for recovery of damages appropriate to compensate injuries caused by the deprivation of one constitutional right are not necessarily appropriate to compensate injuries caused by the deprivation of another." This "delicate" task need not be undertaken here. None of the parties challenges the portion of the jury instructions that permitted recovery for actual harm to respondent, and the instructions that *are* challenged simply do not authorize compensation for injury. We therefore hold only that damages based on the "value" or "importance" of constitutional rights are not authorized by § 1983, because they are not truly compensatory.

Presumed damages are a *substitute* for ordinary compensatory damages, not a *supplement* for an award that fully compensates the alleged injury. When a plaintiff seeks compensation for an injury that is likely to have occurred but difficult to establish, some form of presumed damages may possibly be appropriate. [citations] In those circumstances, presumed damages may roughly approximate the harm that the plaintiff suffered and thereby compensate for harms that may be impossible to measure. As we earlier explained, the instructions at issue in this case did not serve this purpose, but instead called on the jury to measure damages based on a subjective evaluation of the importance of particular constitutional values. Since such damages are wholly divorced from any compensatory purpose, they cannot be justified as presumed damages.[6] Moreover, no rough substitute for compensatory damages was required in this case, since the jury was fully authorized to compensate respondent for both monetary and non-monetary harms caused by petitioners' conduct. * * *

The judgment of the Court of Appeals is reversed, and the case is remanded for further proceedings consistent with this opinion.

It is so ordered.

JUSTICE BRENNAN and JUSTICE STEVENS join the opinion of the Court and also join JUSTICE MARSHALL'S opinion concurring in the judgment.

JUSTICE MARSHALL, with whom JUSTICE BRENNAN, JUSTICE BLACKMUN, and JUSTICE STEVENS join, concurring in the judgment. * * *

When a plaintiff is deprived, for example, of the opportunity to engage in a demonstration to express his political views, "[i]t is facile to suggest that no damage is done." Dellums v. Powell, 566 F.2d 167, 195 (1977). Loss of such an opportunity constitutes loss of First Amendment rights " 'in their most pristine and classic form,' " quoting Edwards v. South Carolina, 372 U.S. 229, 235 (1963). There is no reason why such an injury should not be compensable in damages. At the same time, however, the award must be proportional to the actual loss sustained.

The instructions given the jury in this case were improper because they did not require the jury to focus on the loss actually sustained by respondent. Rather, they invited the jury to base its award on speculation about "the importance of the right in our system of government" and "the role which this right has played in the history of our republic," guided only by the admonition that "[i]n one sense, no monetary value we place on Constitutional rights can measure their importance in our society or compensate a citizen adequately for

6. For the same reason, Nixon v. Herndon, 273 U.S. 536 (1927), and similar cases do not support the challenged instructions. In *Nixon,* the Court held that a plaintiff who was illegally prevented from voting in a state primary election suffered compensable injury. This holding did not rest on the "value" of the right to vote as an abstract matter; rather, the Court recognized that the plaintiff had suffered a particular injury—his inability to vote in a particular election—that might be compensated through substantial money damages.

Nixon followed a long line of cases, going back to Lord Holt's decision in *Ashby v. White,* 2 Ld.Raym. 938, 92 Eng.Rep. 126 (1703), authorizing substantial money damages as compensation for persons deprived of their right to vote in particular elections. [citations] Although these decisions sometimes speak of damages for the value of the right to vote, their analysis shows that they involve nothing more than an award of presumed damages for a non-monetary harm that cannot easily be quantified:

"In the eyes of the law th[e] right [to vote] is so valuable that damages are presumed from the wrongful deprivation of it without evidence of actual loss of money, property, or any other valuable thing, and the amount of the damages is a question peculiarly appropriate for the determination of the jury, because each member of the jury has personal knowledge of the value of the right."

their deprivation." These instructions invited the jury to speculate on matters wholly detached from the real injury occasioned respondent by the deprivation of the right. Further, the instructions might have led the jury to grant respondent damages based on the "abstract value" of the right to procedural due process—a course directly barred by our decision in *Carey.*

The Court therefore properly remands for a new trial on damages. I do not understand the Court, however, to hold that deprivations of constitutional rights can never themselves constitute compensable injuries. Such a rule would be inconsistent with the logic of *Carey,* and would defeat the purpose of § 1983 by denying compensation for genuine injuries caused by the deprivation of constitutional rights.

Notes

1. How do the majority and concurring opinions differ? Can presumed general damages for the inherent value of a constitutional right be distinguished from presumed general damages for a non-monetary harm that cannot be easily quantified? Should compensatory damages hinge on defendant's state of mind? Will the jury measure damages by dignitary harm or by emotional distress? How will plaintiff prove damages: expert witnesses, lay witnesses, direct evidence, circumstantial evidence?

2. Jacobs v. Meister, 108 N.M. 488, 495–501, 775 P.2d 254, 261–67 (App.1989). Jacobs recovered damages for emotional distress after termination of his employment as an assistant professor was held to have violated his constitutional rights to free speech and due process.

"As required by *Carey* and *Stachura,* New Mexico courts have placed the burden of proving the existence of injury and resulting damages with reasonable certainty on the plaintiff who is seeking compensatory damages. [citation] An award of damages must be based upon the evidence adduced at trial. [citation] Where plaintiff is claiming emotional distress, this court has not required that proof of the injury be by expert testimony, as argued by defendants. * * *

"Defendants have conceded Jacobs testified he was unable to obtain another permanent teaching position after leaving the university due to the circumstances surrounding defendants' refusal to rehire him. Injury to his self-image as a professional teacher and to his ability to retain other gainful employment may be inferred from his testimony. It is also clear that the extent of the injury was affected by the fact, later proved at trial, that he was terminated for having exercised his first amendment rights. Additionally, Jacobs testified his eventual divorce from his wife and the resulting separation from his family were caused by his inability to support his family, which, in turn, resulted from the manner in which he lost his job with the university. I find this evidence sufficient to support the trial court's finding on damages for emotional distress caused by defendants' wrongful conduct. * * *

"Even though Jacobs' testimony on emotional distress may be weak and thus fall at the low end of the scale of proof required to support a finding that such injury should be compensated in damages, I nonetheless conclude that the record supports the finding on damages. * * *

"It is reasonable to conclude that the involuntary loss of a job would cause emotional distress, and that the distress would be greater in circumstances such as this, where Jacobs devoted several years to a career that was terminated on pretextual grounds." * * *

BIVINS, CHIEF JUDGE (concurring in part and dissenting in part). * * *

"I disagree that substantial evidence exists to support an award of damages for emotional distress.

"I disagree with the characterization of defendants' argument as asserting 'there was insufficient evidence to support this finding ["plaintiff has incurred damages for emotional distress in the amount of $60,000.00"] *solely* because Jacobs did not produce medical expert or other evidence to support the award of damages for emotional distress.' (Emphasis mine.) Defendants' argument relating to damages is broken down into four parts: first, the trial court's finding is not supported by any evidence of emotional distress; second, damages for emotional distress cannot be presumed to flow from the deprivation of constitutional rights, citing *Carey v. Piphus;* third, even if plaintiff suffered emotional distress, there was no medical evidence to support the damage award; and fourth, even if plaintiff proved emotional distress, it was not caused by deprivation of his constitutional rights. * * *

"The problem in the case before us is that there was no evidence of emotional distress or evidence of facts and circumstances from which it could be inferred. One member of the panel noted that plaintiff's testimony on emotional distress may be weak and thus fall at the low end of the scale of proof required to support a finding. I submit that it does not exist. The thrust of plaintiff's damages was an economic loss. Not only did plaintiff offer no evidence of emotional distress, the subject did not come up. Nor did he bring other witnesses to describe any changes in his behavior following the termination.

"Citation to plaintiff's inability, after leaving the university, to obtain another permanent teaching position due to the circumstances surrounding his termination has been offered as evidence of emotional distress. Based on such, it is said that injury to plaintiff's self-image as a professional teacher and to his ability to retain other gainful employment may be inferred. I disagree for two reasons. First, this conclusion runs counter to the holdings of *Carey* and *Stachura* that damages for violation of constitutional rights may not be presumed and that actual damages must be established. Second, the record shows that plaintiff obtained another job teaching at Fisk University beginning in September 1976, and left that job after a few months for reasons unrelated to any actions by defendants. Plaintiff was simply unable to get along with the Fisk University administration.

"Testimony by plaintiff that his eventual divorce from his wife and the resulting separation from his family were caused by his inability to support his family, which, in turn, resulted from the manner in which he lost his job with the university, also fails to establish emotional distress. I agree with defendants that neither plaintiff's divorce, nor any inferred emotional distress associated with that event, can reasonably be considered a consequence of the employment termination. First, the divorce took place in 1980, nearly six years after plaintiff left the university (four years after leaving Fisk University). Second, by his own testimony plaintiff attributed the divorce not to the circumstances surrounding the termination, but rather to his financial condition. When asked on direct examination why he was divorced in 1980 and whether it was related to his termination from the university in 1975, plaintiff responded, 'Well, my lack of ability to support my family and the intense pressure that this put my family under and living in poverty the way we did. I think it has affected me, yes * * * has affected that.' Plaintiff is talking about the effects of his lost income. The trial court, by refusing to adopt plaintiff's finding on lost income, found against him on that issue.

"I do not believe that this testimony meets the requirements of *Carey* and *Stachura* that there must be proof of actual injury."

3. Courts grant injunctions freely to protect constitutional rights like free speech, right to due process, voting rights, religious liberty, establishment of religion, and unreasonable search and seizure. Constitutional rights are not "a series of propositions assuring the payment of money to the victims," O. Fiss, The Civil Rights Injunction 75 (1978). In Steele v. Van Buren Public School District, 845 F.2d 1492 (8th Cir.1988), the court enjoined school prayers without discussing alternate remedies. Rendleman, The Inadequate Remedy at Law Prerequisite for an Injunction, 33 U.Fla.L.Rev. 346 (1981); Laycock, The Death of the Irreparable Injury Rule, 103 Harv.L.Rev. 687, 707–09 (1990).

Is the Supreme Court's approach to damages consistent with this alacrity to enjoin?

Will specific and prospective injunctions define the hazy invasion of civil rights "tort" more promptly and clearly than damage actions tried to countless juries?

4. Punitive damages are available for constitutional violations. Newport v. Fact Concerts, Inc., 453 U.S. 247 (1981). Smith v. Wade, supra pp. 129–30.

5. Plaintiff may recover attorney fees in a § 1983 action, 42 U.S.C. § 1988.

6. Are damages necessary to create an incentive to sue to protect constitutional rights? Deter violations of constitutional rights? See Love, Damages: A Remedy for the Violation of Constitutional Rights, 67 Calif.L.Rev. 1242, 1281–85 (1979). An earlier survey is, Rendleman, The New Due Process: Rights and Remedies, 63 Ky.L.J. 531, 666–68 (1975). This article concludes that the damage remedy "is too often an aspiration rather than a policy." It suggests a minimum damage schedule for constitutional violations like the schedules in the copyright act, 17 U.S.C. § 504(c), supra, p. 577, and the wiretap act, 18 U.S.C. § 2520. See *Birnbaum*, pp. 629, 632.

JONES v. REAGAN

United States Court of Appeals, Seventh Circuit, 1983.
696 F.2d 551.

Posner, Circuit Judge. This is an appeal from the dismissal * * * of a complaint alleging that the plaintiffs, black noncommissioned officers in the United States Army Reserve, were transferred from the unit to which they belonged in a Chicago suburb to other units in the Chicago area solely because they are black and the officer commanding the unit wanted it to be all white. The defendants are this officer and his superiors in the chain of command up to and including the President of the United States. Their conduct is alleged to violate the due process clause of the Fifth Amendment. They are being sued in their individual rather than official capacities, and damages are sought; at oral argument, the plaintiffs' counsel indicated that the plaintiffs were abandoning any claim for injunctive relief. * * * The defendants defend the dismissal on the ground that the Fifth Amendment does not give rise to an action for damages in a case of this sort.

* * * No statute creates a remedy applicable to this case and the Fifth Amendment does not indicate what remedies the federal courts should provide for violations of due process of law. However, in Davis v. Passman, 442 U.S. 228 (1979), the Supreme Court held that at least some violations of the Fifth Amendment's due process clause may be redressed by damages actions in federal courts; we have to consider whether the violation alleged in this case is one of them.

The Court spoke of "implying" a right of action in damages from the Fifth Amendment, but the task is not really one of teasing out the implications of the Fifth Amendment; it is the more creative one of deciding whether a damages remedy is a good way of enforcing the Fifth Amendment, and, if the court decides it is, of creating that remedy as a matter of federal common law. The Court thought it a good method of enforcement in the circumstances of the *Davis* case. Miss Davis had been a deputy administrative assistant to a Congressman. He had fired her, allegedly because she was a woman. The Court said that "relief in damages would be judicially manageable, for the case presents a focused remedial issue without difficult questions of valuation or causation," and that "since respondent is no longer a Congressman * * * equitable relief in the form of reinstatement would be unavailing. And there are available no other forms of judicial relief." Thus, the Court compared a damages suit with other methods of enforcing Miss Davis's rights under the Fifth Amendment and found that the damage remedy was the best, and indeed only, remedy for the violation that she had alleged. In a later decision the Supreme Court created in effect a presumption in favor of implied rights of action under the Constitution, but a presumption that could be rebutted by a showing of " 'special factors counselling hesitation in the absence of affirmative action by Congress.' " Carlson v. Green, 446 U.S. 14, 18 (1980). * * * Presumably one such "special factor" would be that a damages remedy was inappropriate in the particular circumstances of the case.

A suit for damages is a natural remedy for conduct that causes an injury on which a judge or jury can put a price tag. Miss Davis lost her job. The termination of an employment contract is a familiar source of damages in breach of contract suits. * * * But the conduct complained of in this case is not the firing of anyone but simply a transfer of reservists from one unit in the Chicago area to other units in the same area. No one suffered demotion, or a reduction in pay, benefits, or work amenities, or even an adverse notation entered on his personnel records. No one was discharged, called to active duty, shipped overseas, or even transferred to another city or state. The plaintiffs' counsel acknowledged at the oral argument that these purely local, purely lateral transfers had not even caused his clients any inconvenience. And since he described the suit as one purely for punitive damages, the plaintiffs must not have suffered any emotional distress either, notwithstanding the alleged racial motivation for the transfers; for proof of humiliation or other emotional distress would justify awarding compensatory damages under tort principles. * * *

[I]t is true that tort law, including the law of constitutional torts, has a deterrent as well as a compensatory function. Indeed, it has long been one view that deterrence, accomplished through the setting of standards of conduct and the punishment by means of damage awards, compensatory and punitive, of those who deviate from them, is the main function of tort law. * * * Even if the plaintiffs in this case have not been injured, not measurably anyway, allowing them to bring actions for punitive damages would deter violations of the Constitution; and it can be argued that there is a social interest in such deterrence even if the particular violations do not give rise to damages that a court could measure.

This thinking has never carried the day in conventional tort law; the requirement of proving actual injury as a predicate for seeking punitive damages has been adhered to steadfastly. Maybe a different approach is warranted in constitutional cases, though it is noteworthy that the Supreme Court has been unwilling to allow "general" damages, that is, damages not based on a proven injury, to be awarded in damage actions under 42 U.S.C. § 1983 alleging violations of procedural rights under the due process clause of the Fourteenth Amendment. Carey v. Piphus. But in any event, if considerations of deterrence are to be brought to center stage, the potential for overdeterrence must also be considered, and it seems to be significant in the present case. Except for the President, the defendants are military officers, active or reserve. Few if any of them can be wealthy yet they are being sued in their individual capacities, which means that although the government will pay for their legal expenses they will be personally liable for any damages assessed against them. We are told that the government will not indemnify them and that no liability insurance policy is offered that would cover suits of this sort. The plaintiffs are asking for damages in excess of $400,000, and if the traditional common law rule of no contribution among tortfeasors were followed (an undecided question, so far as we are able to determine), the plaintiffs (if they won) could levy execution of the entire judgment against one defendant.

We must consider the probable impact of making a military officer liable in damages in these circumstances if he is found to have transferred a subordinate in violation of the due process clause of the Fifth Amendment. Of course it will make officers less likely to make racially discriminatory transfers. But it will also make them less likely to transfer on nonracial grounds anyone who is of a different race from their own. Such a transfer might give rise to a lawsuit which the officer might lose even though he was not in fact guilty of discrimination. The courts are not infallible, and they do not give defendants in civil suits the same protections against erroneous judgments that they give criminal defendants.

* * * The compensatory purpose of damage liability is not served when there are no actual damages and the deterrent purpose is ill served when damages actions are likely to overdeter—to make a military commander timid about transferring a subordinate who happens not to be of the same race.

There is no need for us to canvass the larger issues raised by cases such as Wallace v. Chappell, 661 F.2d 729 (9th Cir.1981), in which the Supreme Court has granted certiorari, ___ U.S. ___ (1982). In *Wallace,* a damage suit by several navy enlisted men against their superiors, the alleged racial discrimination took the form of punishing the plaintiffs with unusual severity for minor infractions, and in this and other ways retarding their military careers. Such injuries are measurable by the usual tort methods. There is still a problem of overdeterrence and it may lead the Supreme Court to decide that there should be no damage liability even in such cases, or, what amounts to virtually the same thing, that the defendants should have absolute immunity from suit. But we need not go that far in this case. It is enough for us to hold that damage remedies for constitutional torts are not appropriate and hence not available, unless expressly authorized by Congress, if no monetizable injury is alleged. * * * This does not mean that the military is "above the Constitution." It just means that in the circumstances of this case these plaintiffs have no damages remedy in federal court against their military superiors.

Affirmed.

Notes

1. Assume this is a civil action for intrusion upon the plaintiff's privacy against an individual rather than the federal government. In this type of invasion of privacy, the plaintiff is intensely interested in anonymity. While damages are primarily grounded upon the embarrassment from the exposure, the action itself increases the exposure. Should this affect the amount of damages?

2. Claims filed under Section 1983 (42 U.S.C. § 1983) asserting the violation of constitutional rights differ remedially from those brought under Title VII or the Age Discrimination in Employment Act (29 U.S.C. § 633a) asserting proscribed discrimination. Section 1983 claims may be tried to a jury on proper demand. Successful Section 1983 claims like *Stachura, Meister,* and *Reagan* award compensatory and punitive damages. Hunter v. Allis–Chalmers Corp., Engine Division, 797 F.2d 1417 (7th Cir.1986); Wulf v. City of Wichita, 883 F.2d 842 (10th Cir.1989); Smith v. Barton, 914 F.2d 1330 (9th Cir.1990).

Title VII claims, on the other hand, are limited to equitable monetary relief. There is, courts generally hold, no right to jury trial. See Walton v. Cowin Equipment Co., 733 F.Supp. 327 (N.D.Ala.1990); Simmons v. Sports Training Institute, 692 F.Supp. 181 (S.D.N.Y.1988). The successful litigant's award potentially includes back pay, front pay, prejudgment interest and attorneys fees, and reinstatement.

Back pay may include compensation based on the employee's career path. Brown v. Marsh, 713 F.Supp. 20 (D.D.C.1989). The collateral source rule applies to back pay awards. Hunter v. Allis–Chalmers Corp., Engine Division, 797 F.2d 1417 (7th Cir.1986) (supra). Recovery is conditioned upon reasonable diligence in searching for comparable employment. Sellers v. Delgado College, 902 F.2d 1189 (5th Cir.1990); Hansard v. Pepsi–Cola Metropolitan Bottling Co., 865 F.2d 1461 (5th Cir.), cert. denied, 110 S.Ct. 129 (1989).

Prejudgment interest is ordinarily granted. See Loeffler v. Frank, 486 U.S. 549 (1988); Hunter v. Allis–Chalmers, Engine Division, 797 F.2d 1417 (7th Cir.1986) (supra); Williamson v. Handy Button Machine Co., 817 F.2d 1290 (7th Cir.1987).

Reinstatement may be the wronged employee's preferred remedy. But if reinstatement seems inappropriate, particularly where the employment relationship has deteriorated to the point of hostility, animosity or fear, the court may award a lump sum for "front pay" instead. Sowers v. Kemira, Inc., 701 F.Supp. 809 (S.D.Ga.1988); Flores Cruz v. Avon Products, Inc., 693 F.Supp. 1314 (D.P.R.1988). If reinstating plaintiff means "bumping" or demoting an otherwise innocent employee, courts are reluctant to reinstate; they may prefer a lump sum for front pay. Walsdorf v. Board of Commissioners, 857 F.2d 1047 (5th Cir.1988). Nevertheless a court may order plaintiff reinstated even though someone else is demoted. Lander v. Lujan, 888 F.2d 153 (D.C.Cir.1989).

Chapter 8

REMEDIES FOR INJURIES TO PERSONS, INCLUDING DEATH

A. PERSONAL INJURIES

1. COMPENSATORY DAMAGES

a. Pecuniary Elements of Award: Lost Income and Medical Expenses

For the items of a personal injury award classified as "general" or "special" damages, see Cohn v. J.C. Penney Co., Inc., supra p. 50.

EARL v. BOUCHARD TRANSPORTATION CO., INC.

United States District Court, Eastern District of New York, 1990.
735 F.Supp. 1167.

WEINSTEIN, DISTRICT JUDGE. Plaintiff James Earl, a 66 year-old former tugboat deck hand, brings an action against his employer under the Jones Act, 46 U.S.C.App. § 688, and general maritime law for injuries suffered as a result of two separate accidents in 1984. As a consequence of his injuries he claims he was forced to retire on May 16, 1985, approximately a month before turning 62. He claims damages for, *inter alia,* loss of future earnings on the grounds that, absent injury, he would have continued to work at least an additional three years and five weeks—that is, until his 65th birthday, if not longer.

After a three day trial, the jury found for plaintiff and awarded him a total of $855,000 in damages, of which $425,000 was attributed to lost earnings suffered as a result of the second accident. Defendant moves for a new trial or remittitur. * * *

Theoretically the human working machine can last (with some decreases in effectiveness through illness and decrepitude)—and thus has economic value—almost to the point of death. As a matter of law, then, an award taking into account any loss of value due to injury or death caused by a tortfeasor, can take into account even this residual and declining loss of value up to the time of predicted death. Indeed, there is a considerable effort in a shrinking labor market to keep older people employed beyond the usual date of retirement. See Lewin, Too Much Retirement Time? A Move is Afoot to Change It, N.Y. Times, Apr. 22, 1990, § 1, at 1, col. 1. In fact, realities of the labor market in an industrial-commercial world make it unlikely that the last lurching mile of the rusted-out worker would ever be purchased by an employer. Moreover, as age increases, the probability that the worker may claim total disability, using the injury as justification for not pushing himself or herself to work probably increases.

These subtle nuances between loss of full work-capital value at one end of the spectrum and malingering at the other are generally best left to the judgment of the community as reflected in the jury's verdict. In computing the full value of a tort victim's depleted work-capital the jury may consider a variety of factors that differ from plaintiff to plaintiff, such as past earnings, the marketplace value of an individual's skills, the availability of suitable employment, and average work-life expectancy as projected by government statistical tables. This value may be affected as a result of particularized evidence bearing on a plaintiff's pre-accident intentions and proclivities. For example, if the jury credited evidence that before being injured a plaintiff had intended to retire early, a reduction of the full value of an award would be justified under the doctrine of mitigation, which requires tort victims to find alternative employment whenever possible. The award may be increased to the full or close to full value if, on the other hand, the jurors believed that a plaintiff was likely to work beyond that age at which the statistical tables or their common sense experience would normally predict retirement.

Where a jury verdict seems lopsidedly to favor one side or the other, the court has the obligation to require some equalization. This is such a case. * * *

Earl claimed that he injured his right elbow in an August 29, 1984 accident and that he injured his ankle and reinjured his elbow in a second accident on December 13, 1984. * * * Plaintiff contended, and the jury found, that both accidents occurred as a result of the employer's negligence and the unseaworthiness of the tugboat.

As a consequence of the first accident, Earl claimed he was unable to work for two weeks. It was undisputed that he was unable to work for 11 days after the second accident. He returned to work approximately a month later, in early 1985, but claimed that his injuries eventually forced him to retire on May 16, 1985—three years and five weeks before his planned retirement at age 65.

Evidence adduced by defendants at trial indicated that plaintiff's intention prior to the accidents had been to retire in June of 1985 when he turned 62 years of age. Captain Kenneth Bekkelund of the Marion C. Bouchard testified that it had been common knowledge prior to Earl's December 1984 accident that he "was looking forward to retiring and talked of it frequently." * * *

Plaintiff testified that he "would probably have retired * * * at 65." * * *

As an aid to interpreting the liabilities and rights created by the federal admiralty and maritime compensation law, courts have frequently referred to the same general principles that underlie state tort law. * * *

"An injury that reduces the period of work-life expectancy deprives the worker of the value of work-capital." In re Joint Eastern and Southern Dist. Asbestos Litigation (Rummo v. Celotex Corp.), 726 F.Supp. 426, 427 (E.D.N.Y. 1989). Unlike the plaintiff in *Rummo,* the life-expectancy of the plaintiff in the case at bar was not shortened. His work expectancy was, the jury found, reduced. While fortunately not terminal, James Earl's injuries were nonetheless permanently and fully disabling and, according to the jury, prevented him from working.

Regardless of whether or not a plaintiff would have exercised the choice to work as long as he could have, he or she is entitled to damages "measured by the extent to which [plaintiff's] capacity for earnings has been reduced." Restatement (Second) of Torts § 924 comment c. * * *

There is no requirement that an injured plaintiff even be employed at the time of the accident in order to recover for impairment of earning capacity. [citations]

Earning capacity is determined by what a plaintiff "*could* have earned even if he or she never worked to that capacity in the past." 2 M. Minzer, J. Nates, C. Kimball, D. Axelrod & R. Goldstein, Damages in Tort Actions § 10.22[3][a] (citations omitted). * * *

This principle is most clearly illustrated by cases involving injured students, homemakers, and infants. See, e.g., Feldman v. Allegheny Airlines, Inc., 524 F.2d 384, 388 (2d Cir.1975) (in determining future earnings of college-educated 25 year old woman who was unemployed when killed in plane crash, fact finder properly considered fact that she had been capable of working full-time for forty years until she was 65, had planned to attend law school and would have continued to work part-time for an estimated eight years while raising children); Pucino v. Crete, No. 89–644, 1990 WL 21303 (N.D.N.Y. Feb. 28, 1990) (LEXIS, Genfed library, Dist. file) (future earnings of aviation student killed while in last year of college are to be determined by wages he could have been expected to make as pilot over course of his pre-accident work-life expectancy); Kavanaugh v. Nussbaum, 129 A.D.2d 559, 514 N.Y.S.2d 55 (2d Dep't 1987) (injured infant's future earning capacity calculated using work-life expectancy of person having normal statistical life and work-life expectancies), aff'd as modified on other grounds, 71 N.Y.2d 535, 528 N.Y.S.2d 8, 523 N.E.2d 284 (1988); Ward v. La. & Ark. Railway, 451 So.2d 597, 608 (La.App.2d Cir.1984) (injured high school student entitled to recover for loss of earning capacity even though she had not as yet entered work force); Grimes v. Haslett, 641 P.2d 813, 818 n. 3 (Ala.1982) ("The right of an injured homemaker to recover for impaired earning capacity regardless of whether she was employed before the injury exemplifies the distinction between an award for lost earnings and an award for lost earning capacity.").

At most, some courts have required that the plaintiff have been *employable* or *potentially* employable, rather than actually employed at the time of the accident. For example, in Espana v. United States, 616 F.2d 41 (2d Cir.1980), the court of appeals observed that tort victims such as housewives or students who, prior to injury, have not earned as much as they could in the marketplace, are entitled to recover damages for loss of full-time earning capacity. In contrast, the court found that a plaintiff who had attempted and was unable before his accident to find full-time employment was not entitled to full-time compensation.

The conceptual difference between the loss of earning capacity and the loss of actual wages is also illustrated by cases holding that the injured party is not barred from recovering for loss of earning capacity even if he or she earns as much as or more than before the injury. Bochar v. J.B. Martin Motors, Inc., 374 Pa. 240, 244, 97 A.2d 813, 815 (1953) (tortfeasor not entitled to reduction in financial responsibility because, through fortuitous circumstance or unusual application on part of plaintiff, plaintiff's wages are as high or even higher than before accident). The rationale behind this seemingly paradoxical result is consistent with the concept of lost earning capacity, for, "[b]y having one less trade at his disposal the injured Plaintiff has a reduction in future employability." Draisma v. United States, 492 F.Supp. 1317, 1325 (W.D.Mich.1980).

Nor does the ability to recover for impaired earning capacity even where there is no actual wage loss necessarily undermine the doctrine of mitigation of damages. Under this doctrine, a Jones Act claimant, like other tort victims, has an obligation to mitigate damages where possible by finding other employment. Nonetheless, the plaintiff who does so may still recover a reduced award provided the diminution of his or her work-capital is reflected in the smaller number of employment options available to that person as a result of injury. But see Alferoff v. Casagrande, 122 A.D.2d 183, 504 N.Y.S.2d 719, 721 (2d Dep't 1986) (student may not recover for diminution of earning capacity in intended profession as cosmetologist since post-injury job as receptionist paid higher salary).

In the case at bar, plaintiff's announced plan, as testified to by defense witnesses, to retire at age 62, if it had been credited, would have been strong evidence of malingering. It could have shown that in fact he had not lost any of his work capital—e.g., the ability to earn money in the marketplace—and that he had refused or otherwise failed to mitigate his damages. It is clear, however, that the jury believed plaintiff to be completely disabled as a result of his accident, and thus exempt from the obligation to mitigate damages by continuing to work as a deck hand or by seeking other employment.

Courts have varied in their approaches to calculating work-life expectancy. * * *

In general "[t]he admissibility of evidence regarding future earning capacity is within the wide discretion of the trial judge." Oliveri v. Delta S.S. Lines, Inc., 849 F.2d 742, 745 (2d Cir.1988) (Jones Act). For example, trial courts have considered the likelihood that economic downturns in a particular industry would have resulted in lower wages in future years, as well as the likelihood that a given plaintiff would have been impervious to such economic vicissitudes. See, e.g., Pretre v. United States, 531 F.Supp. 931, 935 (E.D.Mo.1981) (although defendant established that plaintiff would have been laid off due to his seniority ranking four years after being injured, court found he would have sought similar work and ordered him compensated for loss of earning capacity, "not merely for the loss of income from any particular job"). Compare, e.g., Masinter v. Tenneco Oil Co., 867 F.2d 892, 899 (5th Cir.1989) (based on evidence of subsequent reduction in work force and in absence of evidence showing that longshoreman plaintiff would have been retained, it was not clearly erroneous for trial court to decide that plaintiff in future would have earned only 75% of his past earnings) with Connecticut National Bank v. Omi Corp., 733 F.Supp. 14 (S.D.N.Y.1990) (awarding full compensation for future loss of earnings despite showing that there was a general loss of seamen's jobs after seaman's death where widow claimed that she and decedent would have moved to area where shipping industry was healthiest).

In the absence of a mandatory retirement policy, a wide range of evidence bearing on retirement is admissible in the discretion of the trial court. Evidence regarding the pre-accident intentions of the plaintiff is often highly probative. See, e.g., O'Shea v. Riverway Towing Co., 677 F.2d 1194, 1198 (7th

Cir.1982) (court credits 57 year-old former ship cook's testimony that she had intended to work until age 70); Eich v. Metro–North Commuter R.R., No. 88–1720, 1989 WL 146792 (S.D.N.Y., Nov. 30, 1989) (upholding jury award of $1,166,274.00 in lost future earnings to "energetic" 45 year-old railroad engineer on grounds that evidence entitled jury to find that, but for injury, plaintiff would have worked until age 70); McGowan v. McGowan, 136 Misc.2d 225, 518 N.Y.S.2d 346, 351 (Sup.Ct.1987) (in projecting date of retirement for purposes of calculating pension benefits, trier of fact should take into consideration factors such as party's future intentions and mental disposition toward working until a later age), aff'd and modified, 142 A.D.2d 355, 535 N.Y.S.2d 990 (2d Dep't 1988); Gault v. Monongahela Power Co., 159 W.Va. 318, 223 S.E.2d 421, 426–27 (W.Va.1976) (crediting retired plaintiff's claim that he had intended to return to work as pipefitter).

The weight given such testimony of a desire and ability to work long beyond the average is, of course, left to the trier of fact. See, e.g., Kaylor v. Amerada Hess Corp., 141 A.D.2d 331, 528 N.Y.S.2d 845, 846 (1st Dep't 1988) (seaman not entitled to recover for future impairment of earning capacity despite stated intention to return to higher paying seagoing job when he currently held shore job and in recent years had worked primarily in shore jobs); Rosenbaum v. Lefrak Corp., 80 A.D.2d 337, 438 N.Y.S.2d 794, 799 (1st Dep't 1981) (rejecting plaintiff's claim that he would not have retired at age 62, but would have continued to work as carpenter until age 72 as a dubious and unsupported assumption).

In circumstances where there is no particularized information regarding a plaintiff's pre-accident intentions or other relevant characteristics, there appear to be no established rules in this circuit. Compare, e.g., Zavattoni v. Interstate Express, Inc., No. 88–4718, 1989 WL 156296 (S.D.N.Y. Dec. 18, 1989) (negligence case in which court found 61 year old victim of automobile accident to have one year work expectancy since he would have been eligible to retire at age 62) with Andrulonis v. United States, 724 F.Supp. 1421, 1517 (N.D.N.Y. 1989) ("Absent a reliable statistical basis for [either party's opinion as to work-life expectancy], the court assumes that [plaintiff] would have worked until age 65 if not for his tragic accident.") (FTCA case). See also Yodice v. Koninklijke Nederlandsche Stoomboot Maatschappij, 443 F.2d 76, 77–78 (2d Cir.1971) (in absence of other evidence bearing on work-life expectancy, defendant's request to charge jury that work-life expectancy of longshoreman could not reasonably be found to be in excess of 65 years was appropriate), appeal after remand, 471 F.2d 705 (2d Cir.1972), cert. denied, 411 U.S. 933 (1973).

Statistical charts, such as the mortality tables and work-life expectancy tables prepared by the United States Department of Labor, compile averages and are often deemed authoritative, particularly in the absence of contradictory particularized evidence. * * *

These tables are not binding on the fact finder. See Espana v. United States, 616 F.2d 41, 44 (2d Cir.1980) (mortality tables do not constitute absolute guides, but are data to be taken into account in calculating basis for damages award in light of all the evidence; court was not clearly erroneous in concluding that, absent accident, plaintiff's work life would have ended early at age 60 due to preexisting degenerative back condition); McWeeney v. New York, New Haven, & Hartford R.R., 282 F.2d 34, 35–36 (2d Cir.) (a refined computation of damages for loss of earning capacity would take into account not only life expectancy tables, but also "conditions unconnected with the accident that might have reduced plaintiff's expectancy below the normal term"), cert. denied, 364 U.S. 870 (1960); McDonald v. United States, 555 F.Supp. 935, 968 (M.D.Pa.1983) (where female plaintiff did not have children and, as result of illness probably could not have any, shortened work-life expectancy projected by U.S. Dept. of Labor table and based on assumption that women leave workforce to bear children, is not applicable); 1 New York Pattern Jury Instructions—Civil 2:290 (1974 & Supp.1989). Moreover, the statistical charts are updated on average every 10 years and therefore exhibit a lag in reflecting changing work and mortality patterns.

In the instant case the issue of plaintiff's retirement intentions was fully litigated. The jury obviously credited Earl's testimony. Unfortunately, it went far beyond that which could reasonably be inferred from the evidence. Even when viewed in the light most favorable to the plaintiff, the record does not support an award based upon a projected pre-accident work-life expectancy of 70 or more years—an assumption required by the jury award. Plaintiff's own testimony contradicts his claim that a statistical work-life expectancy of a 62 year old man—that is, a work-life expectancy of age 67—should be accepted. A retirement age of 65, on the other hand, has some support in the record and appears to be fair in view of all of the circumstances. It stretches the record as far as possible to favor the plaintiff and the jury's award.

Once the injured victim proves that he or she could have been gainfully employed, it is necessary to show with sufficient certainty the amount of damages. More is involved in computing the value of the diminution of work-capital " 'than comparing the amount earned before and after the injury.' " Burke v. United States, 605 F.Supp. 981, 999 (D.Md.1985) (citation omitted). It has long been the practice in New York, for example, to allow juries to consider the possibility that an injured victim would have advanced through promotions and thus be entitled to a recovery higher than that indicated by an average of his past earnings. * * * Atlantic and Pacific Tea Company, 30 Misc.2d 258, 215 N.Y.S.2d 175, 181 (Sup.Ct.1961) (permanent substitute school teacher had legal right to become permanent teacher and, despite lack of intent to do so, was entitled to recover higher amount). * * * Nonetheless, the trier of fact must not be left to speculate and to unreasonably inflate an award.

In determining damages for the diminution in the plaintiff's earning capacity, courts have normally utilized an "oversimplified formula * * * which seeks to determine what the [plaintiff's] earnings would have been had he survived in good health, multiplied by [plaintiff's] work life expectancy with the resultant dollar figure arrived at, then discounted to the present value." Connecticut National Bank v. Omi Corp., 733 F.Supp. 14 (S.D.N.Y.1990) (Carter, J.) In cases such as that at bar, past earnings—in the absence of unusual proven circumstances—serve as a dependable and adequate guide to future loss.

Earl was employed full-time before the accidents and there was no indication that he would or could have "retooled" at the age of 62 to go into a higher paying field. Any speculation that he might have been the beneficiary of an increase in wages is in effect cancelled out by the non-insubstantial possibility that he had never intended to work past age 62.

The reduced award was computed as follows, giving plaintiff every benefit of the doubt:

1) $105,000 was allowed for lost wages, based upon an average of $37,468.72 for five previous years, with a 25% agreed upon tax rate, making net loss of earnings $87,006.15. Fringe benefits were agreed on as $5,784.00 per year, or $17,908.15 for the three years and five weeks. The total is $104,914.30, rounded off to $105,000.00. There was no proof of increases in future wage rates. No allowance for discount was made because the judgment was entered after the probable date of retirement. No interest was sought for delayed payment, except as indicated in 3), below.

2) Pain and suffering and lost pleasure awards were exaggerated. An award of $100,000 for five years past is allowed. Assuming a possible additional life expectancy of 14 years an additional amount of $280,000 is permitted. The total is $380,000.

3) Maintenance and cure and interest factors were computed without objection at a rate most favorable to plaintiff in the sum of $40,000. This amount included past and future medical expenses.

The total award that could possibly be justified is $525,000.00. This sum seems excessive, but it allows maximum effect to the jury's exceptionally sympathetic verdict for the plaintiff.

Unless plaintiff agrees to a remittitur to $525,000.00, a new trial is granted.

Postcript: Earl v. Bouchard Transportation Co., 917 F.2d 1320 (2d Cir. 1990). The court of appeals affirmed this decision except for the maintenance and cure component which it held to be an impermissible additur.

WASHINGTON v. AMERICAN COMMUNITY STORES CORP.

Supreme Court of Nebraska, 1976.
196 Neb. 624, 244 N.W.2d 286.

Supra, p. ___.

Notes

1. Waldorf v. Shuta, 896 F.2d 723, 726, 742–43 (3d Cir.1990). Plaintiff "was rendered quadriplegic in a motor vehicle accident." The jury's verdict was for $8,400,000.

"The Borough and Officer Rego both appealed the district court's admission of evidence regarding Waldorf's future earnings as an attorney. During the trial, Waldorf was allowed to introduce testimony, over their objections, that he would have become an attorney but for his accident and evidence as to what his earnings as an attorney would have been. * * *

"In order to award damages for lost earnings from future employment in a particular field, the plaintiff must provide the factfinder with credible evidence of the 'prerequisites for employment' in that field, and evidence that the plaintiff had the ability and possessed the needed qualifications for employment in that field. Rodriquez v. U.S., 823 F.2d 735, 747, 749 (3d Cir.1987).

"In *Rodriquez,* the district court allowed a 25% enhancement of damages to represent plaintiff's loss of earnings as a commercial pilot. Rodriquez, at the time of his death, had both a private and a commercial pilot's license and was a certified flight instructor. It was his ambition to become a full-time commercial pilot, and he was trying to build up his flying hours, as he believed that this would help him to get such a position. Based on the evidence, the district court concluded that there was 'a good likelihood that he would someday seek and obtain * * * employment * * * [as a commercial pilot] and that he had the capacity to do so.' This court overturned the damages enhancement, holding that the trial court's conclusion was 'without evidential foundation.'

"By the standard of *Rodriquez,* Waldorf failed to provide the evidentiary foundation, the 'prerequisites for employment,' for the jury to consider his future earnings as an attorney. He was a 24–year old high school drop-out who had obtained his high school equivalency diploma in the military. He had worked as a paralegal in the military, but had been unable to find employment as a paralegal in civilian life; he had entered and dropped out of the New York Police Academy; he had been refused admission to a four-year degree program and had completed one year of a two-year Associate Degree Program at the College of Staten Island. At the time of the accident, he was taking six courses, three of which were photography, tennis and acting. While there is no reason to doubt Waldorf's aspiration to become a lawyer, no credible evidence had been presented that he had the ability to become a lawyer. At the time of the accident, he did not possess the qualifications, and it is not at all certain that he would have been admitted to law school. * * *

"The district court noted several cases in which awards of future earnings were upheld, though professional training had not been completed. In two cases, awards for future earnings were given in the death of young people who had shown truly exceptional promise. In Kopko v. New York Live Poultry Trucking Co., 3 N.J.Misc. 498, 128 A. 870 (Cty.Ct.1925), a damages award based on projected earnings as a violinist was supported by evidence that the decedent, a boy of twelve, had unusual aptitude, ability and promise as a musician; his violin teacher had testified that he would, because of his talent, become a great musician. Similarly, in Gluckauf v. Pine Lake Beach Club, Inc., 78 N.J.Super. 8, 187 A.2d 357 (App.Div.1963), the court upheld a jury award based on projected earnings as a biochemist where the fifteen year old decedent, who was in the top 1% of his class of 600 in a very competitive high school for gifted students, had an I.Q. of 157, excelled in biology and chemistry, and had the ambition of becoming a biochemist. The court also noted Bohrman v. Pennsylvania RR Co., 23 N.J.Super. 399, 93 A.2d 190 (App.Div.1952), cert. denied, 11 N.J. 496, 95 A.2d 35 (1953), a case in which a jury award based on projected earnings as a beautician was upheld where the deceased, an 18–year old girl, had almost finished her training and worked in her father's beauty shop. What is missing in the instant case is the exceptional talent shown by the young decedents in *Kopko* and *Gluckauf* or the near completion of training and virtual assurance of employment in the chosen field in *Bohrman.*

"In the instant case, the district court found that 'it is more probable than not that [Waldorf] would have pursued an education *leading toward* law school.' But that is not the same thing as being admitted to law school and completing it. * * *

"There was no credible evidence as to Waldorf's ability and qualifications as an attorney, and the district court erred in allowing the jury to consider whether to grant him future earnings as an attorney. Such consideration was unduly speculative."

2. Various evidentiary factors that may lessen the inherent guesswork about lost future earnings are discussed in several other cases and notes in this book. See Frankel v. United States, infra, p. 670; Flannery for Flannery v. United States, infra, p. 688; Jones & Laughlin Steel Corp. v. Pfeifer, supra, p. 112. In addition, for the factors to calculate the impaired future economic value of an injured homemaker see Note, pp. 724–25. For infants, the speculative nature of future lost earnings is in inverse ratio to the age of the injured party.

Individually tailored awards become more difficult in the absence of a "track" record: how much would this fetus have earned over a lifetime? Proof is still necessary for special damages; it must rest almost entirely on the broadest of statistical averages. The literature on the subject is voluminous, as are economic models. Refinements are now being developed for computer programs.

3. *Question:* Can an injured person who concededly has fully recovered from his injuries recover for impairment of future earning capacity? Held yes. Gooch v. Lake, 327 S.W.2d 132 (Mo.1959), where a former University of Missouri quarterback missed his senior year because of injuries in an auto accident.

4. *Question:* A Mexican national is killed or injured while working in the United States. Should U.S. or Mexican wage scales be used to calculate future lost income? Cf. Levinge Corp. v. Ledezma, 752 S.W.2d 641 (Tex.App.1988) and Hernandez v. M/V Rajaan, 841 F.2d 582 (5th Cir.), cert. denied, 488 U.S. 981 (1988).

SERHAN v. BESTEDER

Superior Court of Pennsylvania, 1985.
347 Pa.Super. 11, 500 A.2d 130.

ANDERSON, JUDGE. * * * During the early morning hours of November 13, 1977, twenty-six year old Sandra Marie Serhan was involved in an automobile accident. She suffered a compression fraction of thoracic 8 and 9 vertebrae which in turn has caused her to have neurogenic bladder disease. She has lost sensation and muscle control of her bladder and cannot urinate unless she takes a toxic medication. Her orthopedic and bladder problems had persisted to the time of trial, five years after the accident.

At the time of the accident, the plaintiff was the sole proprietor of Sara Sheen Draperies. She functioned as an interior decorator, visiting prospective clients in their homes to provide design ideas and to solicit work. In addition she maintained nine sewing machines in the basement of her home and made the draperies herself. She employed independent contractors to install the draperies and do slipcover work.

Prior to starting her own business in August, 1976, the plaintiff had been employed as an interior decorating consultant in a department store from 1973 to 1976. * * *

[The] evidence was more than sufficient to prove that the plaintiff sustained losses as a result of her injuries. The question then remained, how the plaintiff was to prove the amount of those losses.

To that end, the plaintiff testified about the conduct of her business; her capital investment in machinery, equipment and supplies; and her gross receipts and profits during 1977 from Schedule C of her income tax return. She detailed how the latter amount was calculated. Based on the above testimony, the plaintiff attempted to introduce Schedule C of her federal tax returns for 1977 through 1981. The trial court denied the motion, and refused to instruct the jury on lost earnings to the time of trial.

The reason set forth in the opinion below for these rulings is that the net earnings of the business was not an accurate measure of the value of plaintiff's services to the business. We do not agree. * * *

In Bell v. Yellow Cab Co., 399 Pa. 332, 160 A.2d 437 (1960), the Pennsylvania Supreme Court held:

> "Ordinarily, earnings which represent the result of combined capital and personal services is not capable of establishing the earning power of the

servitor. Where, however, the business is small and the income which it produces is principally due to the personal services and attention of the owner, the earnings of the business may afford a reliable criterion of the owner's earning power. * * * Each case must depend on the nature and extent of the business, the amount of personal direction and labor of the party engaged in connection therewith, as well as the amount of capital invested and the labor employed.' " [citations] Thus, for example, in Faber v. Gimbel Brothers, 264 Pa. 1, 107 A. 222 (1919), our Supreme Court held that evidence of earnings from a partnership of which plaintiff was a member both before and after the accident was admissible to show decreased earning power as a result of the injury. The Court in *Faber* considered the fact that both partners devoted their entire time to the business and the nominal capital investment in the auto repair enterprise as factors relevant to its decision. * * *

In explaining the trial court's ruling the opinion below states:

"* * * Plaintiff's income from her business after 1976 would not have properly shown loss of earning power, since the profits from her business were derived from the labor and skills of several individuals. The true test was the value of her services to the business, not her earnings. James v. Ferguson, 401 Pa. 92, 95 [162 A.2d 690] (1960)."

Specifically, the opinion cites the fact that "Plaintiff stated she must 'sublet' her work when she 'cannot fulfill' her obligations."

We find that the nature of the plaintiff's business clearly falls within the parameters of Bell v. Yellow Cab Co., supra, and the cases decided thereafter.

Miss Serhan's business was very small in scope. In 1977 she grossed only $11,805.00. Her profit was $4,237.00. Her capital investment involved principally the purchase and installation of sewing machines in her basement. Virtually, the entire business was based on her labors. She acted as an interior decorator and visited customers in their homes to solicit contracts, and before the accident she made all the drapes herself. She used independent contractors for installation and slipcover work only. The fact that she had the expense of subletting drapery work after the accident was a clear measure of a portion of her damages and proof of the value of her services to the business, not a reason to deny her a recovery. Under those circumstances, the tax records were admissible to prove the amount of the loss. An appropriate instruction regarding lost earnings should have been given.

With respect to impairment of earning capacity, the law requires only proof that the injured person's economic horizons have been shortened as a result of the tortfeasor's negligence. * * *

Miss Serhan's chronic orthopedic problems coupled with her bladder dysfunction caused disruptions to her business up to the time of trial, which was five years after the accident. The medical testimony was that her condition is permanent. There is no reason to conclude that her medical problems will not cause the same type of business disruptions in the future as they did in the past.

The opinion of the court below states: "we have no testimony indicating Plaintiff's injuries affect her ability to perform her occupation." This finding is clearly erroneous. An instruction on impairment of earning capacity should have been given.

Counsel for plaintiff requested that, in addition to Miss Serhan's income tax returns for the years 1977 through 1981, those for the three previous years when she worked at a department store as an interior decorator be admitted into evidence as proof of earning capacity. The court denied that request. Since impairment of earning capacity had been established, the earlier tax returns, as well as plaintiff's business returns, were admissible to prove her earning power.

In the case *sub judice,* the jury awarded plaintiff $15,000.00. Because substantial trial errors resulted in this shockingly low verdict, a new trial on the issue of damages is necessary.

FRANKEL v. UNITED STATES

United States District Court, Eastern District of Pennsylvania, 1970.
321 F.Supp. 1331.

SHERIDAN, CHIEF JUDGE (M.D.Pa., sitting by special designation). On April 30, 1966, a car driven by Mary Heym in which her daughter, Marilyn Heym, was a passenger collided with a car [negligently] driven by Ronald Glasser, an employee of the Department of the Army [acting within the scope of his employment]. * * *

Marilyn was severely injured. She was taken by ambulance to the Emergency Room of the Haverford Hospital. She was unconscious, in severe shock and appeared to be near death. * * *

At the present time, aside from her obvious physical injuries, her principal disabilities stem from the brain damage which affects her mentally, emotionally and her motor control. She is obsessed with food; her weight has increased from 130 pounds to 180 pounds; she has tremendous strength but cannot stand without help and support; she walks with a broad ataxic gait; her behavior is erratic; she frequently laughs or cries for no apparent reason and has problems described as emotional lability; her mental capacity is superficial and simple; her memory is inferior to 98 percent of the population; she is mentally about 5.13 years of age, with preservation and obsessive compulsive behavior; she is psychotic; men in general are targets of her emotional outbursts and stubbornness. Psychological tests show that she is so greatly disturbed that a complete examination could not be made. There is no hope of recovery or improvement.

The hospital and medical bills to the time of trial totaled $17,325.69. These expenses were fair, reasonable and necessary for the treatment of her injuries. Under Pennslyvania law, her father is entitled to recover for the expenses incurred before she reached the age of 21.

* * * At the time of the accident, Marilyn, born November 6, 1946, was 19 years of age, had completed two years of a four year course in commercial art at the Academy of Fine Arts in Philadelphia and intended and was expected to continue to graduation, after which she intended to enter upon a career as a commercial artist. She did generally well in school, and excelled in art. * * *

Plaintiff claims past loss of earning capacity from shortly after the time Marilyn would have completed school, or July 1, 1968, to the time of the award. She would have been 21 years of age in July of 1968. The evidence showed that she would have completed school and embarked on a career as a commercial artist. Her progress in school, her family background and her paintings indicated that she was making excellent progress. The evidence convincingly demonstrated that she would have earned an average of $5,000.00 a year commencing July 1, 1968. The sum of $12,500.00 will be awarded for past loss of earning capacity.

On the claim for future loss of earning capacity the question is to what extent has the economic horizon of Marilyn been shortened because of the injuries. She is now 24 years of age. At the time of trial she had a life expectancy, according to the tables, of 54.7 years. In addition to training, background, health and habits prior to the accident, consideration must be given to other factors such as the likelihood of marriage and motherhood and the effect of earning capacity. * * * Marilyn's life of 19½ years, prior to her devastating injuries, presents a clear picture of prospects for marriage. She was attractive, healthy, talented, well-adjusted, and intelligent. From the age of six she was interested in horses and became a proficient rider, winning many awards. She attended and participated in many horse shows. These and school and other activities brought her in contact with the opposite sex. She enjoyed male companionship. She enjoyed teaching others to ride and engaged in hunts with others 15 years of age and above. There was a likelihood of marriage and motherhood in her future. Marriage probably would have interrupted her career, but with her training she could have resumed her career, if it had become necessary or desirable during or after marriage. Her earning capacity, as interrupted, to age 65 is $125,000.00 which when reduced to present worth at 6% simple interest under the Pennsylvania rule is $62,000.00, which will be awarded for this item.

Other items of damage are physical and mental pain and suffering, loss of enjoyment of life's pleasures, inconvenience, disfigurement, and permanent injuries. The Government argues that a large part of Marilyn's pain and suffering was not conscious because she was in a coma or semi-coma. Even while in a coma she responded to painful stimuli. For many weeks when she was in a semi-coma she recognized members of her family but could not communicate with them. During this time she undoubtedly appreciated pain. In the future she will experience pain from her arm, the use of the prosthesis and from the therapy that she must undergo for the rest of her life. She frequently falls "with a thud," making no attempt to break her fall. She is suffering and will continue to suffer mentally. She knows that she is a girl and attempts to appear attractive. Her hostility toward men stems from an awareness that she is a girl but that she will never enjoy a normal relationship with men. She realizes that her sudden and uncontrollable outbursts are wrong and she feels badly that she cannot explain her actions and apologizes for them. In addition, she has lost the ability to engage in those activities which normally contribute to the enjoyment of life. The possibility of marriage and motherhood are gone. She cannot continue in the art career that she so enjoyed, or engage in horseback riding. She has lost peace of mind and well-being. She will never be able to dance, or engage in recreational or normal family activities. In short, she has lost almost every enjoyment that life can offer. An award of $650,000.00 will be made for these items.

A final item of damage is what plaintiff has characterized as future hospitalization and related medical and incidental expense. Plaintiff contends that: Marilyn is reasonably expected to live out her life expectancy of 54.7 years; she will need constant care for life, both physical and psychiatric; this care cannot be provided at home; only one private institution, Fairmount Farm, near Marilyn's residence, is prepared to accept her and to render this care; and at the present rate of $75.00 a day and taking into account projected increases, an award of at least $8,046,379.00 should be made for this item. A much larger amount is requested if any part is taxable.[1]

* * * Plaintiff's claim for private institutional care [at $75 per day] is a proper item of damage.

The Government suggests that the traditional lump-sum award should not be made because of the uncertainties in forecasting the cost of long-term institutional care, and the large amount of money necessary to pay for this care; it suggests that the court order the Government to establish a $500,000.00 trust fund under the control of a fiduciary which would pay all the institutional costs, and that the court retain jurisdiction to resolve any questions of administration of the trust and order the Government to replenish the corpus if the occasion should arise. Upon Marilyn's death, the balance in the fund would revert to the United States.

The common law provides for a single lump-sum judgment. There can be no judgment for an indefinite amount, or a judgment payable in installments. The single lump-sum judgment as it relates to future damages has been criticized.[2] On the other hand, if the single recovery rule were discarded, final disposition of cases could be delayed for years, and the courts would have to assume the added burden of supervision of their awards. In ordinary cases involving private parties there are practical considerations of insurance policy limits and the ability of defendants to pay. Frequently, cases are settled or disposed of for less than they are worth because of these. In Federal Tort Claims Act actions the ability of the Government to pay is never in question. An amendment to the Federal Tort Claims Act to provide for periodic payments when future, long range damages are significant seems desirable. If such an amendment were passed, the Government would pay more in some cases and less in others, than it would under a single recovery. In all cases justice through just compensation, no more—no less, would be achieved. Such drastic changes must come from the Congress, however, and not from the courts. The Government's suggestion is rejected.

What is the life expectancy of Marilyn after her injury? * * *

1. [Footnotes renumbered.] Plaintiff states in his brief: "These figures are subject to the qualification that medical costs are not taxable but income to cover nonmedical costs are taxable as income. How much of the room and board or other items may ultimately hold to be taxable cannot be predicted. One thing is certain in this area of uncertainty: if any part of the needed amount is taxable, the already huge figure will have to be increased substantially to satisfy the requirement of an adequate award for these expenses. It is not unreasonable to urge a figure of $10,000,000.00 for this item alone."

2. Schreiber. Damages in Personal Injury and Wrongful Death Cases (Practicing Law Institute, 1965) at page 21:

"There are two important practical consequences of the single recovery rule. For one thing it means that all damages, future as well as past, must be taken account of at the time of trial. This in turn faces the tribunal with the difficult and uncertain task of prophecy with no chance for second-guessing where the prophecy turns out to be mistaken or where the parties have failed to present all items of their claims.

"Another important aspect of a single recovery is the burden it casts on the successful plaintiff of wise investment and of providence whenever the recovery must be relied on to take care of future needs. * * *

"These features mean that the single recovery rule is often both capricious and inflexible in its operation so that damages in accident cases, even where they are awarded and actually paid, often fail to do the job they should if accident law is to perform its function of administering accident losses efficiently in the public interest."

[After reviewing the medical testimony, the court concluded that as a result of her injuries Marilyn's life expectancy had been shortened from 54.7 to 30 years.]

Plaintiff presented evidence that institutionalization costs have been increasing, and that the cost of mental institutional care in the Philadelphia area has increased about 5¼ percent each year over the past ten years. Thus, plaintiff's original request for damages of $1,497,412.50 ($75.00 a day × 365 days = $27,375.00 per year × life expectancy of 54.7 years = $1,497,412.50) becomes $8,046,071.00 with the application of a factor for future cost increases. Inflationary considerations have most commonly been used in the justification of awards. In many instances the consideration has been an evaluation of an award considering present inflationary trends as compared to awards *in the past.* * * *

The projected inflationary trend is speculation. Plaintiff has used the decade of the 1960's, one of the more inflationary times in the history of our country, as the basis for a projection of over fifty years. It is common knowledge that our Government is and has been attempting to control inflation, even to the point of considering wage and price controls. Economists differ on their predictions. Moreover, plaintiff will have money that can be invested and if inflation continues, the return on the money will be greater, and this would have an offsetting effect. Increased costs for institutional care will not be considered.

The Government urges that an award for private institutional care must be reduced to present worth. Plaintiff relies on Yost v. West Penn Railways Co., 1939, 336 Pa. 407, 9 A.2d 368, for the proposition that present worth does not apply to future medical expenses, and that the institutionalization required for Marilyn falls into this category. Many of the costs which make up the daily rate of care and maintenance are not future medical expenses but rather are custodial in nature. The Pennsylvania rule that future medical expenses are not to be reduced to present worth is based on the theory as expressed in *Yost* that:

> "Future medical attention presupposes an out-of-pocket expenditure by the plaintiff. She was entitled to have defendant presently place in her hands the money necessary to meet her future medical expenses, as estimated by the jury based upon the testimony heard, so that she will have it ready to lay out when the service is rendered."

Yost expresses a sound general rule, although the kind of medical attention to be rendered does not appear from the facts. In the usual case, future medical expenses are sought to remedy a specific malady. If an accident victim will be required to undergo surgery, he should have the money to pay for the service if it is rendered shortly after the verdict. To apply the present worth rule to future medical expenses in most instances would necessitate the resolution of many collateral, variable and imponderable factors such as whether the victim intended to have medical attention immediately or whether his health would permit immediate treatment and if not, when it would permit it. Clearly, there would be no workable way in which to apply the present worth rule.

Here, the expenses of institutionalization will recur periodically in the same manner as future earnings are payable periodically. If the rule of *Yost* were applied and the sum not reduced to present worth, plaintiff would have the money to "lay out" *far before* "the service is rendered." Moreover, the return on any non-reduced sum, properly invested, would exceed the cost of the institutional care. Thus, Marilyn would not only be compensated for her institutionalization but would reap a windfall. Damages means compensation for a legal injury sustained. * * * The general rule of *Yost,* as in the case with many general rules, must yield to exceptional circumstances. The award for institutionalization will be reduced to present worth. The amount so computed is $461,084.00 ($75.00 a day × 365 days = $27,375.00 per year × 30 years = $821,250.00 reduced to present worth = $461,084.00).

Finally, plaintiff argues that the court should add to the verdict an amount to cover income taxes on income derived from investment of the amount awarded for institutionalization because of the possibility that some of the income expended for care may be considered a non-medical cost and hence not deductible. In the usual case, it is the defendant who urges that income taxes be taken into account to reduce an award of future loss of earning capacity. The great weight of authority has refused to consider income taxes in fixing damages in personal injury and death cases. Pennsylvania adheres to this rule. * * *

To summarize, the damages to be awarded for the injuries suffered by Marilyn are $1,202,909.69:

To Alvin H. Frankel, Guardian of Marilyn Heym, an incompetent:	
Past medical and related expenses	$1,414.00
Loss of earning capacity, past and future	74,500.00
Pain, suffering, inconvenience, disfigurement and loss of life's pleasures	650,000.00
Future institutionalization expense	461,084.00
	$1,186,998.00
To Herbert Heym, her father:	
Medical and other expenses incurred during Marilyn's minority	$15,911.69

Notes

1. Reilly v. United States, 863 F.2d 149, 152–154, 167 (1st Cir.1988). Because of a government physician's negligence, Heather Reilly was born with "severe, apparently irremediable, brain damage" and "will never be able to walk, talk, feed, or take care of herself in any way." In a Federal Tort Claims Act suit for damage, the judge awarded $11,037,964 damages.

Included was $1,104,641 for lost earning capacity based on a working life of 48 years. The trial judge had declined to rely on tables which "showed that a person of Heather's age, sex, and assumed education level would, on average, work for only 28 years." The court of appeals affirmed: "In an environment where more and more women work in more and more responsible positions, and where signs of the changing times are all around us, it can no longer automatically be assumed that women will absent themselves from the work force for prolonged intervals during their child-bearing/child-rearing years."

2. The *Reilly* court, citing the court of appeals decision in *Frankel,* rejected the government's argument that the judgment should be satisfied through periodic

payments as the future expenses were incurred instead of all at once in a lump sum. The parties, the court said, could have agreed to a "structured settlement" to pay over time. Moreover the trial judge could (and did) order the lump sum for future damages placed in trust for the rest of Heather's life and provided for judicial approval of the trust and trustees. 863 F.2d 149, 168–70.

3. American Bank & Trust Co. v. Community Hospital, 36 Cal.3d 359, 204 Cal.Rptr. 671, 683 P.2d 670 (1984). The Supreme Court of California rejected constitutional attacks on a statute that set up periodic payments for future medical malpractice damages.

4. *Proof of Medical Expenses.* Stanley v. State, 197 N.W.2d 599, 606 (Iowa 1972):

"The last issue before us concerns medical and hospital expense, both past and future, for which recovery was allowed in the amount of $6000.00.

"Before there can be an award for such items the evidence must show they were made necessary by the negligent act of defendant and that the amounts charged represent the reasonable fair value of the services.

"Reasonableness may be shown by the direct testimony of one qualified to express an opinion on the subject; but such formal proof is not a requirement. Reasonableness may also be established by evidence of *payment* of the bill submitted. The amount charged, without payment, is not evidence of the propriety of the charges. While a few states have relaxed this rule [citation], it is still adhered to by most jurisdictions and we have not departed from it.

"In the case now under consideration, the only evidence of the reasonableness for past services was the admission without objection of an unpaid medical bill for $681.53 and an unpaid hospital bill for $1527.95. That is all. If an unpaid bill is no evidence of reasonableness, we cannot see how, as plaintiff claims, its admission without objection gives it greater effect.

"The situation is different, however, as to future medical expenses. One of the exhibits introduced without objection was a letter from Dr. Glenn S. Rost, who stated plaintiff would need prosthetic revisions annually until adulthood and a completely new prosthesis 'every two or three years.' These were minimum estimates. He further stated the 'conservative' cost would be from $50.00 to $75.00 for each revision and from $350.00 to $375.00 for each new appliance. The need for future medical attention was fixed with certainty and the reasonable cost established. Taking Dr. Rost's estimates in their most favorable light for plaintiff, we believe there is sufficient proof to allow recovery for future medical and prosthetic expense in the sum of $2700.00."

5. Pretrial medical expenses, like pretrial lost earnings, are items of special damage subject to pleading and proof. Most, if not all, courts will accept evidence of actual payment of medical bills as prima facie evidence of reasonableness. From the standpoint of trial tactics, the defendant's attorney may be well advised not to be overly insistent upon proof of the reasonableness of the various specific items of medical expense. Professor Dobbs points out that plaintiff's attorney may welcome the opportunity to have qualified specialists minutely detail to the jury the nature and extent of plaintiff's injuries as well as the expensive measures necessary to treat them. D. Dobbs, Remedies § 8.1 (1973).

b. Avoidable Consequences

MUNN v. SOUTHERN HEALTH PLAN INC.

United States District Court, Northern District of Mississippi, 1989.
719 F.Supp. 525, 528.

Supra, p. 85.

c. Mitigation—Collateral Source Rule

HELFEND v. SOUTHERN CALIFORNIA RAPID TRANSIT DISTRICT

Supreme Court of California, 1970.
2 Cal.3d 1, 84 Cal.Rptr. 173, 465 P.2d 61.

Supra, p. 96.

SIVERSON v. UNITED STATES

United States Court of Appeals, Ninth Circuit, 1983.
710 F.2d 557.

SKOPIL, CIRCUIT JUDGE. Siverson sued under the Federal Tort Claims Act (FTCA), alleging medical malpractice by the Veterans Administration Hospital in Tucson. The government conceded liability and a court trial was held on damages. The court awarded $869,000 in special damages, offset by Siverson's VA disability benefits, for an adjusted total of $464,730. The court also awarded $1 million in general compensatory damages for pain and suffering.

Siverson is a World War II veteran who suffers from ankylosing spondylitis, an arthritic spinal condition that caused his early retirement. In 1971, he applied for and received disability benefits from the Social Security Administration. He was also eligible for Medicare benefits. At that time Siverson was capable of and enjoyed many activities of daily living.

On June 25, 1978, Siverson fell and sustained a nondisplaced fracture of the cervical spine between the 6th and 7th vertebral level. X-rays were taken at the VA hospital in Phoenix. On June 29, 1978, he was transferred to the VA hospital in Tucson. The following day, under the direction and supervision of the VA hospital, a "halo" brace and vest was put on Siverson's head and neck. During this procedure Siverson experienced an "electric shock" through his body and extremities that ultimately developed into a complete paralysis.

1. Does the collateral source rule preclude a set-off for Medicare benefits?
2. Does an award of $1 million for pain and suffering constitute excessive damages?

In Overton v. United States, 619 F.2d 1299 (8th Cir.1980), the Eighth Circuit held that Medicare payments received by a widow had to be deducted from the widow's "swine flu" damage award. *Overton* is distinguishable, however, because unlike Overton, Siverson showed that he contributed to the Medicare fund through Social Security payments during employment. Moreover, the *Overton* court described Medicare and other social security benefits as a form of social insurance, and "if an FTCA plaintiff can show his benefits would be in the nature of insurance as to him, the collateral source rule would justify a 'double recovery' notwithstanding the connection between the social security fund in question and the government's general revenues."

Courts distinguish between those benefits that come from unfunded general revenues of the United States (deductible) and those that come from "a special fund supplied *in part* by the beneficiary or a relative upon whom the beneficiary is dependent" (nondeductible). United States v. Harue Hayashi, 282 F.2d 599, 603 (9th Cir.1960) (social security insurance benefits not deductible). In *Harue Hayashi,* we gave examples of unfunded general tax sources (hospital expenses paid by the Veterans Administration, disability benefits paid under the Veterans Act) and special funds (the National Service Life Insurance Policy, the Civil Service Retirement Act).

In Titchnell v. United States, 681 F.2d 165 (3d Cir.1982), the Third Circuit summarized the rationale that benefits paid out of a "special fund" need not be deducted. The government was held liable under the FTCA for negligent administration of a swine flu inoculation. The evidence established that plaintiff contributed to Medicare, resulting in the court's conclusion that such payments are from a collateral source under Pennsylvania law. See also Smith v. United States, 587 F.2d 1013 (3d Cir.1978) (Social Security Survivor benefits paid a widow and children not deducted from widow's damage award from government under FTCA); United States v. Price, 288 F.2d 448 (4th Cir.1961) (Civil Service Retirement benefits not deductible); and United States v. Brooks, 176 F.2d 482 (4th Cir.1949) (National Service Life Insurance Policy benefits not deductible from FTCA damage award). But see Steckler v. United States, 549 F.2d 1372 (10th Cir.1977) (burden on claimant to trace contributions to the Social Security fund in order to determine the percentage contributed to the fund by the government and ultimately the amount of Social Security payments that could be considered nondeductible).

Here, the district court held that "the United States of America has not sustained its burden of proof, as to any Medicare benefits which the plaintiff may receive, or be entitled to receive, in the future." We agree. The record here shows that the United States failed to sustain that burden as to either its contributions or the amount of benefits that Siverson would be expected to receive in the future. Under these circumstances, the district court did not err in refusing to deduct Medicare expenses from the damage award.

Section 2674 of the FTCA, 28 U.S.C. § 2674, describes the liability of the United States in tort claims cases to be "in the same manner and to the same extent as a private individual under like circumstances, but [the United States] shall not be liable for punitive damages."

The government contends to not deduct Medicare expenses from Siverson's award constitutes punitive damages because the effect is a windfall double recovery for Siverson. The government's rationale would essentially always find recovery from a collateral source to be "punitive" and ignores the collateral source doctrine's purpose of preventing a windfall to the defendant.

Notes

1. *Medicaid as a Collateral Source.* Bennett v. Haley, 132 Ga.App. 512, 522, 208 S.E.2d 302, 310 (1974):

"It should be noted that Medicaid differs from Medicare. Both were created under the Social Security Act. Medicare is a form of social insurance for the elderly with premiums being paid by those participating under the Social Security Act. The Medicaid Program provides free care in the form of public assistance to those whose indigency qualifies them for the receipt of such benefits.

"Should the collateral source rule apply to Medicaid Payments?" In answer the court said: "The Medicaid program is social legislation, it is the equivalent of health insurance for the needy; and just as any other insurance form, it is an acceptable collateral source."

In District of Columbia v. Jackson, 451 A.2d 867, 873 (D.C.App.1982), the defendant tortfeasor was the District of Columbia. It was allowed to deduct Medicaid payments received by the injured plaintiff. "[T]he source of Medicaid benefit was not 'wholly independent' of the wrongdoer, the District of Columbia. The District itself 'brought into being' the Medicaid program in this jurisdiction. * * * The District submitted a Medicaid plan to the federal government in 1968. When the plan was approved the District qualified for matching federal funds. The federal government pays 50% of the cost. * * * The District, however, is solely responsible for administering the program. On these facts, we conclude that the District was the source of Medicare payments."

2. *The Collateral Source Rule And Damage Claims By Government Employees Under The Federal Tort Claims Act.* Joyce v. United States, 329 F.Supp. 1242, 1248 (W.D.Pa.1971):

"Plaintiff, a postal employee en route to work, was hit on the head by a bar of soap that came from the window of a U.S. Courthouse. He sued under the Federal Tort Claims Act and established liability.

"The Government contends that it should be credited for having paid Mr. Joyce his wages while he was absent from work. This position cannot be legally sustained. Although the plaintiff continued to receive his 'wage' while absent from work due to the injuries herein involved, he was able to do this only by depleting his accumulated sick leave. The Government, as an employer, should not be entitled to claim the benefit of this accrued sick leave fund since the employee would receive the amount credited to his record upon his retirement. Six Hundred Forty-three (643) hours have been used up which are directly related to the injuries sustained; in other words, but for the accident herein complained of, the plaintiff would have had the benefit of those hours at retirement.

"The doctrine known as the collateral source rule, cited by the Government, precludes a tortfeasor from benefiting from wages paid from a source independent of the wrongdoer. The rule does not mean where an employer fortuitously is also tortfeasor that it should get credit under circumstances for the wages paid. * * *

"The plaintiff certainly has lost something because his accrued sick leave account has been reduced by the number of hours he was absent from work due to the injuries he sustained."

3. In A.H. Bull Steamship Co. v. Ligon, 285 F.2d 936 (5th Cir.1960), plaintiff introduced evidence of impaired earning capacity. The defendant sought to minimize these damages by showing that plaintiff was receiving social security payments or a veteran's pension that would be cut off if his earnings ever exceeded $1200 per year. Held: evidence inadmissible.

4. Evidence of disability pensions is inadmissible to reduce damages. May a defendant introduce this proof? In 8 ATLA Newsletter No. 3 at 98 (April 1965), the editors claim that defense attorneys employ this tactic: "We are offering the pension payments not to prejudice plaintiff by having the jury apply the payments

as a set-off against lost earnings, but simply to show plaintiff's motives for malingering. We only want to show that his motive for living in a wheelchair and rocker is that he is a low-life faker, a sham and a supersham slummocker who would rather rock than work and who prefers cushioned pension payments to the strenuous life."

Needless to say, the publishers of that particular newsletter took a dim view of such "maladroit maneuvers," commenting that this "would fool no one but a lawyer."

See Hannah v. Haskins, 612 F.2d 373 (8th Cir.1980), for comments on the admissibility into evidence of payments from a collateral source.

5. *Problem:* On the issue of the amount of damages for impairment of earning capacity, the defendant offers evidence that the plaintiff, a school teacher, has voluntarily taken early retirement and receives a pension. The plaintiff objects on ground the evidence would violate the collateral source rule. What ruling? See Kish v. Board of Education of New York, 76 N.Y.2d 379, 559 N.Y.S.2d 687, 558 N.E.2d 1159 (1990).

d. Nonpecuniary Elements of Award

(1) Pain and Suffering

Notes

1. Notes 2., 3., 4. following Washington v. American Community Stores pp. 40–42 supra.

2. *Closing Argument.* Waldorf v. Shuta, 896 F.2d 723, 743–44 (3d Cir.1990). Plaintiff "was rendered quadriplegic in a motor vehicle accident." The jury's verdict was for $8,400,000.

"Lt. Rego and the Borough of Kenilworth claim that they are entitled to a new trial because of improper references by plaintiff's counsel in his closing statement to a specific minimum amount to be awarded for pain and suffering. In his closing statement, Waldorf's counsel referred to testimony that if Waldorf had become an attorney, his lifetime earnings would have been approximately $3.8 million. He than went on to say:

> 'You heard the testimony. You saw the man. * * * And if you find that, you find the final figure, his loss of *$3,799,000* will make it whole. It doesn't make him whole. You want to know the truth: That's peanuts. *That's peanuts for the price that should be paid for what this man went through.* * * *
>
> 'So you take the $3 million. That's just the beginning. That's peanuts, because the real loss is not monetary, * * * what kind of money can pay him back? *$3,799,000? That's peanuts. That's a small part of what he should be paid for the kind of injuries that he's received, for the pain and suffering.* * * *

"Does the above scenario represent an argument by plaintiff's counsel for a specific amount of damages for pain and suffering? We think it does. It constitutes a plea for, at a minimum, an award of $3,799,000 for the elements of pain and suffering. As to the intended impact of counsel's proposed mere 'peanuts' multiplier factor, it is unclear how high a multiplier he was suggesting. But any jury would have to think that counsel was urging that the $3,799,000 should be doubled, tripled, quadrupled or enhanced even more.

"This court has been reluctant to decide the issue whether plaintiff's counsel should be permitted in closing arguments to a jury to make reference to specific lump sum damages for pain and suffering, or references to an ad damnum clause. * * *

"The question whether plaintiff's counsel may request a specific dollar amount for pain and suffering in his closing remarks is a matter governed by federal law, and we now hold that he may not make such a request. We note that effective advocacy can occur without employing the overly dramatic approach that plaintiff's counsel used in this case. In the final analysis, a jury trial should be an appeal to the rational instincts of a jury rather than a masked attempt to 'import into the trial elements of sheer speculation on a matter which by universal understanding is not susceptible to evaluation on any such basis.' Botta v. Brunner, 26 N.J. 82, 100, 138 A.2d 713, 723 (1958).

"We hold that the references by plaintiff's counsel in his closing remarks to a minimum dollar amount that plaintiff should be awarded for his pain and suffering could have irrationally inflated the damages award and, under the facts of this case, constituted reversible error."

3. In Stratis v. Eastern Air Lines, 682 F.2d 406 (2d Cir.1982), an award to plaintiff of $11,000 pain and suffering for eight or nine hours at hospital A was held not excessive. But an amount of $1,200,000 for his later stay at hospital B representing $29,000 pain and suffering for each day of the stay was excessive because the plaintiff became a quadriplegic after the fourth day and could thereafter feel no pain.

4. Precopio v. Detroit Department of Transportation, 415 Mich. 457, 330 N.W.2d 802 (1982), demonstrates judicial control over pain and suffering damages by cataloging *all* awards for the type of injury sustained. Computers should facilitate this technique.

5. *Whether to discount an award for future pain and suffering to present value.* Oliveri v. Delta Steamship Lines, Inc., 849 F.2d 742, 749, 751–52 (2d Cir.1988):

"Whether an award for future pain and suffering should be discounted to present value is not as clear as with an award for lost future earnings. The latter is the jury's estimate from specific evidence of the actual amounts that would have been received by the plaintiff over the course of his working years. Since those dollars will be received now, rather than in the years they would have been earned absent the injury, it makes sense to discount them to present value. And since the interest rate used to discount to present value is a function of lenders' estimates of future inflation, it makes sense to reflect the likely inflation rate in the discounting process, either by adjusting the wages upward to reflect inflation or adjusting the interest rate downward to arrive at an inflation-adjusted discount rate.

"With pain and suffering, however, as with other nonpecuniary losses (such as loss of consortium), the jury is not determining the precise amount of dollars the plaintiff would have received in future years. On the contrary, the jury is invited to select some general sum that the plaintiff should receive now as compensation for the pain and suffering he will endure in future years. Normally, that sum is a round number, determined without any precise calculation. It is rather artificial to take such a number, whether $50,000 in this case or $1,000,000 in another case, and then refine it with precision to present value by an inflation-adjusted discount rate. On the other hand, the sum to be awarded is compensation for the pain and suffering to be incurred in future years and, since the money received now can be invested, it makes sense to give some recognition to the time value of money in determining the sum the plaintiff should have available now and during the future years throughout which his disability will continue. * * *"

[The court discussed the majority rule "that awards for future non-pecuniary losses should not be discounted to present value" and its own decisions that supported discounting.] "We have concluded that the appropriate course is to accept the concept of discounting awards for non-pecuniary losses, but to forgo the precision appropriate for discounting future earnings. Since an award for a non-pecuniary loss is not a payment in lieu of a series of annual installments, as is the case with future wages, it is artificial to expect the fact-finder to divide non-pecuniary damages into yearly installments, discount each to present value, and aggregate the resulting figures. Even though the trial judge could, by stipulation, do the discounting from tables once the jury has selected a lump sum for non-pecuniary losses, use of such tables is appropriate only for awards, like earnings, that replace annual payments. In making an award for future pain and suffering, the fact-finder is not determining the aggregate of payments that would have been made to the plaintiff over the duration of the disability. Rather, the fact-finder is determining the sum that the plaintiff should have now as compensation for the pain and suffering he will endure. No doubt many juries intuitively make some sort of rough present value discount in determining awards for non-pecuniary losses, recognizing that their awards may be invested.

"As we noted all that is required for awards of non-pecuniary future damages is that the time value of money be 'take[n] into account.' That should be done by the same fact-finder that determines the amount of the award, without any precise mathematical adjustments. The time value of such an award is sufficiently recognized by permitting defendant's counsel to argue that awards for future non-pecuniary losses are being received now, rather than in the future, and may be somewhat reduced to reflect the opportunity to invest such awards, and to permit the plaintiff's counsel to point out that any such reduction may be tempered by the likelihood that inflation will reduce the purchasing power of any sum awarded. If requested to do so, the trial judge can bring these general considerations to the jury's attention but should make it clear that the precise method appropriate for discounting awards for pecuniary losses need not be followed. This form of generalized consideration of discounting awards for non-pecuniary losses will be appropriate both for cases in which the discounting of awards for pecuniary losses is done by the jury, aided by experts' calculations, and in cases where, as we have suggested, the parties stipulate to have the judge discount awards for pecuniary losses, using a 2% rate (if the parties agree), or whatever other rate the parties agree upon. Use of this generalized approach to discounting future non-pecuniary losses should, in practice, minimize the significance of our difference with other circuits on this issue."

6. Bovbjerg, Sloan, and Blumstein, Valuing Life and Limb in Tort: Scheduling "Pain and Suffering", 83 Nw.U.L.Rev. 980 (1989), propose a system of quantitative "scheduling" for non-pecuniary damages.

7. Why not adopt a "hedonic loss" theory for non-pecuniary damages? Read on.

(2) Loss of Enjoyment of Life—Hedonic Damages

McDOUGALD v. GARBER

Court of Appeals of New York, 1989.
73 N.Y.2d 246, 538 N.Y.S.2d 937, 536 N.E.2d 372.

WACHTLER, CHIEF JUDGE. * * * On September 7, 1978, plaintiff Emma McDougald, then 31 years old, underwent a Caesarean section and tubal ligation at New York Infirmary. Defendant Garber performed the surgery;

defendants Armengol and Kulkarni provided anesthesia. During the surgery, Mrs. McDougald suffered oxygen deprivation which resulted in severe brain damage and left her in a permanent comatose condition. * * *

A jury found all defendants liable and awarded Emma McDougald a total of $9,650,102 in damages, including $1,000,000 for conscious pain and suffering and a separate award of $3,500,000 for loss of the pleasures and pursuits of life. The balance of the damages awarded to her were for pecuniary damages—lost earnings and the cost of custodial and nursing care. Her husband was awarded $1,500,000 on his derivative claim for the loss of his wife's services. On defendants' posttrial motions, the Trial Judge reduced the total award to Emma McDougald to $4,796,728 by striking the entire award for future nursing care ($2,353,374) and by reducing the separate awards for conscious pain and suffering and loss of the pleasures and pursuits of life to a single award of $2,000,000. * * *

Also unchallenged are the awards in the amount of $770,978 for loss of earnings and $2,025,750 for future custodial care—that is, the pecuniary damage awards that survived defendants' posttrial motions.

What remains in dispute, primarily, is the award to Emma McDougald for nonpecuniary damages. At trial, defendants sought to show that Mrs. McDougald's injuries were so severe that she was incapable of either experiencing pain or appreciating her condition. Plaintiffs, on the other hand, introduced proof that Mrs. McDougald responded to certain stimuli to a sufficient extent to indicate that she was aware of her circumstances. Thus, the extent of Mrs. McDougald's cognitive abilities, if any, was sharply disputed.

The parties and the trial court agreed that Mrs. McDougald could not recover for pain and suffering unless she were conscious of the pain. Defendants maintained that such consciousness was also required to support an award for loss of enjoyment of life. The court, however, accepted plaintiffs' view that loss of enjoyment of life was compensable without regard to whether the plaintiff was aware of the loss. Accordingly, because the level of Mrs. McDougald's cognitive abilities was in dispute, the court instructed the jury to consider loss of enjoyment of life as an element of nonpecuniary damages separate from pain and suffering. The court's charge to the jury on these points was as follows:

> "If you conclude that Emma McDougald is so neurologically impaired that she is totally incapable of experiencing any unpleasant or painful sensation, then, obviously, she cannot be awarded damages for conscious pain * * *.
>
> "It is for you to determine the level of Emma McDougald's perception and awareness. Suffering relates primarily to the emotional reaction of the injured person to the injury. Thus, for an injured person to experience suffering, there, again, must be some level of awareness. If Emma McDougald is totally unaware of her condition or totally incapable of any emotional reaction, then you cannot award her damages for suffering. If, however, you conclude that there is some level of perception or that she is capable of an emotional response at some level, then damages for pain and suffering should be awarded * * *.
>
> "Damages for the loss of the pleasures and pursuits of life, however, require no awareness of the loss on the part of the injured person. Quite obviously, Emma McDougald is unable to engage in any of the activities which constitute a normal life, the activities she engaged in prior to her injury * * * Loss of the enjoyment of life may, of course, accompany the physical sensation

and emotional responses that we refer to as pain and suffering, and in most cases it does. It is possible, however, for an injured person to lose the enjoyment of life without experiencing any conscious pain and suffering. Damages for this item of injury relate not to what Emma McDougald is aware of, but rather to what she has lost. What her life was prior to her injury and what it has been since September 7, 1978 and what it will be for as long as she lives."

We conclude that the court erred, both in instructing the jury that Mrs. McDougald's awareness was irrelevant to their consideration of damages for loss of enjoyment of life and in directing the jury to consider that aspect of damages separately from pain and suffering. * * *

Damages for nonpecuniary losses are, of course, among those that can be awarded as compensation to the victim. This aspect of damages, however, stands on less certain ground than does an award for pecuniary damages. An economic loss can be compensated in kind by an economic gain; but recovery for noneconomic losses such as pain and suffering and loss of enjoyment of life rests on "the legal fiction that money damages can compensate for a victim's injury" (Howard v. Lecher, 42 N.Y.2d 109, 111, 397 N.Y.S.2d 363, 366 N.E.2d 64). We accept this fiction, knowing that although money will neither ease the pain nor restore the victim's abilities, this device is as close as the law can come in its effort to right the wrong. We have no hope of evaluating what has been lost, but a monetary award may provide a measure of solace for the condition created.

Our willingness to indulge this fiction comes to an end, however, when it ceases to serve the compensatory goals of tort recovery. When that limit is met, further indulgence can only result in assessing damages that are punitive. The question posed by this case, then, is whether an award of damages for loss of enjoyment of life to a person whose injuries preclude any awareness of the loss serves a compensatory purpose. We conclude that it does not.

Simply put, an award of money damages in such circumstances has no meaning or utility to the injured person. An award for the loss of enjoyment of life "cannot provide [such a victim] with any consolation or ease any burden resting on him * * * He cannot spend it upon necessities or pleasures. He cannot experience the pleasure of giving it away" (Flannery v. United States, 4th Cir., 718 F.2d 108, 111, cert. denied 467 U.S. 1226).

We recognize that, as the trial court noted, requiring some cognitive awareness as a prerequisite to recovery for loss of enjoyment of life will result in some cases "in the paradoxical situation that the greater the degree of brain injury inflicted by a negligent defendant, the smaller the award the plaintiff can recover in general damages." The force of this argument, however—the temptation to achieve a balance between injury and damages—has nothing to do with meaningful compensation for the victim. Instead, the temptation is rooted in a desire to punish the defendant in proportion to the harm inflicted. However relevant such retributive symmetry may be in the criminal law, it has no place in the law of civil damages, at least in the absence of culpability beyond mere negligence.

Accordingly, we conclude that cognitive awareness is a prerequisite to recovery for loss of enjoyment of life. We do not go so far, however, as to require the fact finder to sort out varying degrees of cognition and determine at what level a particular deprivation can be fully appreciated. With respect to pain and suffering, the trial court charged simply that there must be "some level of awareness" in order for plaintiff to recover. We think that this is an appropriate standard for all aspects of nonpecuniary loss. No doubt the standard ignores analytically relevant levels of cognition, but we resist the desire for analytical purity in favor of simplicity. A more complex instruction might give the appearance of greater precision but, given the limits of our understanding of the human mind, it would in reality lead only to greater speculation.

We turn next to the question whether loss of enjoyment of life should be considered a category of damages separate from pain and suffering.

There is no dispute here that the fact finder may, in assessing nonpecuniary damages, consider the effect of the injuries on the plaintiff's capacity to lead a normal life. Traditionally, in this State and elsewhere, this aspect of suffering has not been treated as a separate category of damages; instead, the plaintiff's inability to enjoy life to its fullest has been considered one type of suffering to be factored into a general award for nonpecuniary damages, commonly known as pain and suffering.

Recently, however, there has been an attempt to segregate the suffering associated with physical pain from the mental anguish that stems from the inability to engage in certain activities, and to have juries provide a separate award for each [citations].

Some courts have resisted the effort, primarily on the ground that duplicative and therefore excessive awards would result (see, e.g., Huff v. Tracy, 57 Cal.App.3d 939, 944, 129 Cal.Rptr. 551, 553). Other courts have allowed separate awards, noting that the types of suffering involved are analytically distinguishable [citations]. Still other courts have questioned the propriety of the practice but held that, in the particular case, separate awards did not constitute reversible error [citations].

We do not dispute that distinctions can be found or created between the concepts of pain and suffering and loss of enjoyment of life. If the term "suffering" is limited to the emotional response to the sensation of pain, then the emotional response caused by the limitation of life's activities may be considered qualitatively different. But suffering need not be so limited—it can easily encompass the frustration and anguish caused by the inability to participate in activities that once brought pleasure. Traditionally, by treating loss of enjoyment of life as a permissible factor in assessing pain and suffering, courts have given the term this broad meaning.

If we are to depart from this traditional approach and approve a separate award for loss of enjoyment of life, it must be on the basis that such an approach will yield a more accurate evaluation of the compensation due to the plaintiff. We have no doubt that, in general, the total award for nonpecuniary damages would increase if we adopted the rule. That separate awards are advocated by plaintiffs and resisted by defendants is sufficient evidence that larger awards are at stake here. But a larger award does not by itself indicate that the goal of compensation has been better served.

The advocates of separate awards contend that because pain and suffering and loss of enjoyment of life can be distinguished, they must be treated separately if the plaintiff is to be compensated fully for each distinct injury suffered. We disagree. Such an analytical approach may have its place when the subject is pecuniary damages, which can be calculated with some precision. But the estimation of nonpecuniary damages is not amenable to such analytical precision and may, in fact, suffer from its application. Translating human suffering into dollars and cents involves no mathematical formula; it rests, as we have said, on a legal fiction. The figure that emerges is unavoidably distorted by the translation. Application of this murky process to the component parts of nonpecuniary injuries (however analytically distinguishable they may be) cannot make it more accurate. If anything, the distortion will be amplified by repetition.

Thus, we are not persuaded that any salutary purpose would be served by having the jury make separate awards for pain and suffering and loss of enjoyment of life. We are confident, furthermore, that the trial advocate's art is a sufficient guarantee that none of the plaintiff's losses will be ignored by the jury.

The errors in the instructions given to the jury require a new trial on the issue of nonpecuniary damages to be awarded to plaintiff Emma McDougald. * * *

TITONE, JUDGE (dissenting). The majority's holding represents a compromise position that neither comports with the fundamental principles of tort compensation nor furnishes a satisfactory, logically consistent framework for compensating nonpecuniary loss. Because I conclude that loss of enjoyment of life is an objective damage item, conceptually distinct from conscious pain and suffering, I can find no fault with the trial court's instruction authorizing separate awards and permitting an award for "loss of enjoyment of life" even in the absence of any awareness of that loss on the part of the injured plaintiff. Accordingly, I dissent. * * *

The capacity to enjoy life—by watching one's children grow, participating in recreational activities, and drinking in the many other pleasures that life has to offer—is unquestionably an attribute of an ordinary healthy individual. The loss of that capacity as a result of another's negligent act is at least as serious an impairment as the permanent destruction of a physical function, which has always been treated as a compensable item under traditional tort principles (e.g., Simpson v. Foundation Co., 201 N.Y. 479, 95 N.E. 10 [loss of sexual potency]). Indeed, I can imagine no physical loss that is more central to the quality of a tort victim's continuing life than the destruction of the capacity to enjoy that life to the fullest.

Unquestionably, recovery of a damage item such as "pain and suffering" requires a showing of some degree of cognitive capacity. Such a requirement exists for the simple reason that pain and suffering are wholly subjective concepts and cannot exist separate and apart from the human consciousness that experiences them. In contrast, the destruction of an individual's capacity to enjoy life as a result of a crippling injury is an objective fact that does not differ in principle from the permanent loss of an eye or limb. * * *

Significantly, this equation does not suggest a need to establish the injured's awareness of the loss. The victim's ability to comprehend the degree to which his or her life has been impaired is irrelevant, since, unlike "conscious pain and suffering," the impairment exists independent of the victim's ability to apprehend it. Indeed, the majority reaches the conclusion that a degree of awareness must be shown only after injecting a new element into the equation. Under the majority's formulation, the victim must be aware of the loss because, in addition to being compensatory, the award must have "meaning or utility to the injured person." This additional requirement, however, has no real foundation in law or logic. "Meaning" and "utility" are subjective value judgments that have no place in the law of tort recovery, where the primary goal is to find ways of quantifying, to the extent possible, the worth of various forms of human tragedy.

Moreover, the compensatory nature of a monetary award for loss of enjoyment of life is not altered or rendered punitive by the fact that the unaware injured plaintiff cannot experience the pleasure of having it. The fundamental distinction between punitive and compensatory damages is that the former exceed the amount necessary to replace what the plaintiff lost [citation]. As the Court of Appeals for the Second Circuit has observed, "[t]he fact that the compensation [for loss of enjoyment of life] may inure as a practical matter to third parties in a given case does not transform the nature of the damages" (Rufino v. United States, 2nd Cir., 829 F.2d 354, 362).

Ironically, the majority's expressed goal of limiting recovery for nonpecuniary loss to compensation that the injured plaintiff has the capacity to appreciate is directly undercut by the majority's ultimate holding, adopted in the interest of "simplicity," that recovery for loss of enjoyment of life may be had as long as the injured plaintiff has " 'some level of awareness' ", however slight. Manifestly, there are many different forms and levels of awareness, particularly in cases involving brain injury. Further, the type and degree of cognitive functioning necessary to experience "pain and suffering" is certainly of a lower order than that needed to apprehend the loss of the ability to enjoy life in all of its subtleties. Accordingly, the existence of "some level of awareness" on the part of the injured plaintiff says nothing about that plaintiff's ability to derive some comfort from the award or even to appreciate its significance. Hence, that standard does not assure that loss of enjoyment of life damages will be awarded only when they serve "a compensatory purpose," as that term is defined by the majority.*

In the final analysis, the rule that the majority has chosen is an arbitrary one, in that it denies or allows recovery on the basis of a criterion that is not truly related to its stated goal. In my view, it is fundamentally unsound, as well as grossly unfair, to deny recovery to those who are completely without cognitive capacity while permitting it for those with a mere spark of awareness, regardless of the latter's ability to appreciate either the loss sustained or the benefits of the monetary award offered in compensation. In both instances, the injured plaintiff is in essentially the same position, and an award that is

* Another problem with the majority's analysis is the absence of any discussion about the time frame to be used in measuring the award of damages for plaintiff's loss of enjoyment of life. Damages for "pain and suffering" are directly correlated to the plaintiff's experience of "pain and suffering" and thus are routinely awarded only for that period of time during which the injured had sufficient cognitive powers to have that experience. Damages for loss of enjoyment of life, in contrast, are awarded as a monetary replacement for the plaintiff's diminished ability to participate in the pleasures and pursuits of healthy living during the remainder of his or her natural life span. Thus, a legitimate question exists as to whether the plaintiff is entitled to recover an award representing his entire lifetime's loss notwithstanding that he was conscious of the loss for only a few moments before lapsing into cognitive oblivion. Furthermore, in view of the majority's conclusion that an award is not truly compensatory if it cannot be enjoyed by the injured party, an additional question arises as to whether the cognitive capacity of the plaintiff must be measured at the time when the award is to be given rather than at some earlier point before the commencement of trial.

punitive as to one is equally punitive as to the other. Of course, since I do not subscribe to the majority's conclusion that an award to an unaware plaintiff is punitive, I would have no difficulty permitting recovery to both classes of plaintiffs.

Having concluded that the injured plaintiff's awareness should not be a necessary precondition to recovery for loss of enjoyment of life, I also have no difficulty going on to conclude that loss of enjoyment of life is a distinct damage item which is recoverable separate and apart from the award for conscious pain and suffering. The majority has rejected separate recovery, in part because it apparently perceives some overlap between the two damage categories and in part because it believes that the goal of enhancing the precision of jury awards for nonpecuniary loss would not be advanced. However, the overlap the majority perceives exists only if one assumes, as the majority evidently has, that the "loss of enjoyment" category of damages is designed to compensate only for "*the emotional response* caused by the limitation of life's activities" and "*the frustration and anguish caused by* the inability to participate in activities that once brought pleasure" (emphasis added), both of which are highly *subjective* concepts.

In fact, while "pain and suffering compensates the victim for the physical and mental discomfort caused by the injury; * * * loss of enjoyment of life compensates the victim for the limitations on the person's life created by the injury", a distinctly *objective* loss (Thompson v. National R.R. Passenger Corp., supra, at 824). In other words, while the victim's "emotional response" and "frustration and anguish" are elements of the award for pain and suffering, the "limitation of life's activities" and the "inability to participate in activities" that the majority identifies are recoverable under the "loss of enjoyment of life" rubric. Thus, there is no real overlap, and no real basis for concern about potentially duplicative awards where, as here, there is a properly instructed jury.

Finally, given the clear distinction between the two categories of nonpecuniary damages, I cannot help but assume that permitting separate awards for conscious pain and suffering and loss of enjoyment of life would contribute to accuracy and precision in thought in the jury's deliberations on the issue of damages. Indeed, the view that itemized awards enhance accuracy by facilitating appellate review has already been expressed by the Legislature in enacting CPLR 4111(d) and (f) (see, 4 Weinstein–Korn–Miller, N.Y.Civ.Prac. ¶ 4111.13, at 41–205). In light of the concrete benefit to be gained by compelling the jury to differentiate between the specific objective and subjective elements of the plaintiff's nonpecuniary loss, I find unpersuasive the majority's reliance on vague concerns about potential distortion owing to the inherently difficult task of computing the value of intangible loss. My belief in the jury system, and in the collective wisdom of the deliberating jury, leads me to conclude that we may safely leave that task in the jurors' hands.

For all of these reasons, I approve of the approach that the trial court adopted in its charge to the jury. Accordingly, I would affirm the order below affirming the judgment.

FLANNERY FOR FLANNERY v. UNITED STATES

United States Court of Appeals, Fourth Circuit, 1983.
718 F.2d 108.

HAYNSWORTH, SENIOR CIRCUIT JUDGE. The plaintiff, a twenty-two year old young man, became permanently comatose as a result of extensive brain damage suffered in an automobile accident later determined to have been caused by the negligence of the driver of the other vehicle who was a federal employee on official business. After a trial of this action, brought under the Federal Tort Claims Act, the court awarded damages of approximately $2,200,-000 consisting of $48,174.80 for medical expenses incurred before trial, $316,-984 for future medical expenses, $535,855 for impairment of earning capacity, and $1,300,000 for "loss of the ability to enjoy life."

On appeal, the United States does not question the determination of its substantive liability. It does question the calculation of damages.

When the case first came before us, we perceived the questions presented as principally to be determined as a matter of state law. We certified the two principal questions to the Supreme Court of Appeals of West Virginia without appreciating at the time that federal questions lurked in the case. The West Virginia Supreme Court of Appeals gave us a prompt response, holding that, as a matter of state law, the damages for loss of capacity to enjoy life were properly allowed notwithstanding the fact that the plaintiff has no awareness of his loss, and that no deduction of federal income taxes should be made in calculating the amount of loss of future earnings.

We should have first addressed the federal questions lurking in the case. We would have done so except, at the time, we failed to appreciate their presence.

Under 28 U.S.C. § 2674 of the Tort Claims Act, damages generally are determinable under state law, for the United States is to be held liable "to the same extent as a private individual under like circumstances." But there is a qualification, the relevance and importance of which is now clearly apparent. Punitive damages are not allowable. The Federal Tort Claims Act is a waiver of immunity from suit of the United States, and conditions attached to the waiver must be strictly enforced. The government's immunity is waived insofar as compensatory damages may be determined and awarded. The door for the assertion of private tort claims in federal courts is opened that far, but then the question arises about the allowability of damages treated and labeled under state law as "compensatory" which are in excess of those necessary to provide compensation for injuries and losses actually sustained.

The question of the allowance of such damages is one of federal law. What is compensatory and what is punitive, within the meaning of the statute, is related directly to the extent of the waiver of sovereign immunity. How widely the Congress intended to open the door is not a matter to be resolved under the widely varying laws of the fifty states, but under a uniform standard. Thus, as was said in D'Ambra v. United States, 481 F.2d 14 (1st Cir.1973), a state's statutory measure of damages "must be judged not by its language or the state's characterization, but by its consequences."

D'Ambra was a wrongful death action for the death of a child in Rhode Island. The Rhode Island statute provided an award to the decedent's parents of an amount computed in terms of the economic loss to the decedent. That bore no relation to the actual loss suffered by the parents. Since damages under the Rhode Island statute were not to be determined by an assessment of the loss suffered by the survivors, a damage award under the statute was held to be punitive and impermissible under the FTCA.

Similarly, it has now been repeatedly held that federal income taxes must be deducted in computing lost future earnings, notwithstanding the fact that such deductions are not permitted under state law. Felder v. United States, 543 F.2d 657 (9th Cir.1976). A living person, with earnings subject to federal taxation, may spend only his net income after taxes, and an award to a plaintiff for lost future earnings based upon lost gross earnings gives the plaintiff more than is truly compensatory. As the court pointed out in *Felder,* the punitive nature of the award based upon a computation of lost gross earnings is particularly apparent when the defendant is the taxing authority.

The FTCA's proscription of awards of punitive damages authorizes only those awards that compensate or reimburse, or provide recompense or redress for injuries suffered by the claimant. To the extent that an award gives more than the actual loss suffered by the claimant, it is "punitive" whether or not it carries with it the deterrent and punishing attributes typically associated with the word "punitive."

There is no doubt that Flannery has lost "his capacity to enjoy life." He is conscious of nothing and incapable of enjoying anything. In his condition, he is quite susceptible to infections, but with proper care he may have a life expectancy of as much as thirty years from the date of his injury. There is no likelihood whatever that he will ever become aware of anything.

The Supreme Court of Appeals of West Virginia held that, as a matter of state law, damages for the loss of the capacity to enjoy life were assessable upon an objective basis, and it did not matter that this particular plaintiff is unaware of his loss. It is perfectly clear, however, that an award of $1,300,000 for the loss of enjoyment of life cannot provide him with any consolation or ease any burden resting upon him. The award of the cost of future medical care provides for his maintenance as well as his nursing and professional care. It provides all of the money needed for the plaintiff's care, should he live out his life expectancy. He cannot use the $1,300,000. He cannot spend it upon necessities or pleasures. He cannot experience the pleasure of giving it away. If paid, the money would be invested and the income accumulated until Flannery's death, when it would be distributed to those surviving relatives of his entitled to inherit from him. If it is compensatory in part to any one, it is compensatory to those relatives who will survive him.

Since the award of $1,300,000 can provide Flannery with no direct benefit, the award is punitive and not allowable under the FTCA. * * *

The question has not been raised by the United States, but we feel compelled to reduce the award for lost earnings because, in part, it duplicates the award of future medical expenses.

An award of lost earnings is made to an incapacitated plaintiff so that he may provide for himself and his dependents those necessities, comforts and niceties he would have provided out of his earned income had he not been injured. In an FTCA wrongful death action, the survivors are entitled to an award based upon lost future earnings of the decedent only after a deduction of the decedent's estimated living expenses, for the survivors are entitled to no greater benefit than they would have enjoyed had the decedent lived and continued working. A successful plaintiff is entitled to be made as financially secure as he would have been had there been no injury or death, but no more.

In the usual case, a living plaintiff must pay his own living expenses, though an award for lost earnings may be the source of his funds. In this case, however, the plaintiff will be required to pay nothing, for the award of future medical expenses includes all of the personal expense that the plaintiff will incur. Indeed, the testimony was that, in the future, he will need little skilled medical care. His personal expenses will be to provide himself with housing, food, and nursing and custodial care of the kind provided in a nursing home. That is the expense covered by the award for future medical expense. The label should not be permitted to mislead us, for, in truth, the judgment requires the United States to pay the plaintiff's personal living expenses twice. Thus, the award for lost earnings, as finally determined, should be reduced by the amount of the award for future medical expenses.

Vacated and remanded.

K.K. HALL, CIRCUIT JUDGE, dissenting. Addressing first the issue of Flannery's entitlement to damages for loss of enjoyment of life, I note that the majority's view of "punitive" prevents Flannery from recovering a component of damages to which he is clearly and unequivocally entitled under West Virginia law. The majority has thus succeeded in creating two conflicting standards for damages awards in West Virginia. In the future, a victim, such as Flannery, who is injured by a private party, will be entitled to recover damages for loss of enjoyment of life, while that same person, if injured at the hands of the government will receive nothing. This I submit, is in direct conflict with the clear meaning and intent of the provisions of 28 U.S.C. §§ 2674 and 1346(b), which state that the government shall be liable *in the same manner and to the same extent* as a private party and in accordance with the laws of the place where the negligence occurred.

The majority premises its holding that an award to Flannery for loss of enjoyment of life is punitive on the ground that it is of no direct benefit to him. At least one federal appeals court has refused to follow the view that any award of damages over and above a plaintiff's actual loss is "punitive." In Kalavity v. United States, 584 F.2d 809 (6th Cir.1978), the Sixth Circuit held that under Ohio law an award of damages in a wrongful death action in favor of decedent's spouse could not be reduced on the ground that the spouse had remarried and received support from her new husband. The court rejected as "farfetched" the government's contention that this award did not compensate the plaintiff for any direct or actually-suffered loss. The Court then went on to note that the purpose of ordinary tort damages, as distinguished from "punitive" damages, is both to compensate and to deter. Tort law mixes these two purposes, compensation and deterrence, when it awards ordinary damages. Tort law may award as customary damages something more than simply out-of-pocket loss, something for deterrence, without spilling over into "punitive" damages awarded solely for the purpose of punishment. * * * In excluding "punitive" damages from the coverage of the Tort Claims Act, we believe that Congress simply prohibited use of a retributive theory of punishment against the government, not a theory of damages which would exclude all customary damages awarded under traditional tort law principles which mix theories of compensation and deterrence together.

I completely agree with this common-sense approach to the meaning of "punitive" under the FTCA and would, accordingly, find the damages awarded to Flannery for loss of enjoyment of life entirely outside the scope of the FTCA's prohibition of punitive damages.

Notes

1. The ninth circuit disagrees with the fourth circuit about whether damages for "loss of enjoyment of life," are punitive and prohibited under the FTCA. Shaw v. United States, 741 F.2d 1202 (9th Cir.1984); Lewin, The Tail Wags the Dog: Judicial Misinterpretation of the Punitive Damages Ban in the Federal Tort Claims Act, 27 Wm. & Mary L.Rev. 245 (1986).

2. Reilly v. United States, 863 F.2d 149, 165 (1st Cir.1988), addresses *Flannery*'s second question:

"Every time that a tort claimant is hospitalized for treatment of injuries, she 'saves' on certain personal expenditures. Her meals are provided by the hospital, thus reducing her food budget; she spends her time in a hospital gown, thus reducing her dry cleaning expense; utilities come with the accommodations, thus minimizing the costs of heat, light, and power at her residence. Despite this 'duplication,' it has never been suggested that the tortfeasor should be allowed to insist that his victim account for these savings and deduct them from the amount of the hospital bill when proving her damages.

"The reasons why such offsets are not accepted practice, we suggest, have both pragmatic and equitable roots. From a practical standpoint, the difficulties in attempting to prove such offsets are enormous. Unless we are prepared to say that damages must now be proved with sliderule precision—an approach which this court has never adopted, see, e.g., Knightsbridge Marketing Services, Inc. v. Promociones y Proyectos, S.A., 728 F.2d 572, 575 (1st Cir.1984) (disavowing 'mathematical accuracy' as a prerequisite to upholding damage computations)—it makes very little sense to devote the overtaxed resources of court, jury, and litigants to a search designed to sanitize every penny of consequential expense and certify it as altogether free from the taint of duplication. Once that rationale is accepted, equity comes into play. As a matter of simple justice, it is far fairer to give the injured plaintiff the benefit of what small duplication may inevitably occur than to confer the trouvaille upon the wrongdoer.[1]

"In view of these concerns, we find *Flannery* to rest on very shaky underpinnings and decline to adopt it as a model for this circuit."

3. Mental anguish engendered by fear that the injury may result in the development of another ailment, for example, cancer or insanity, may be compensable. See Ferrara v. Galluchio, 5 N.Y.2d 16, 17 N.Y.S.2d 966, 152 N.E.2d 249 (1958); Anno., 71 A.L.R.2d 331 (1960).

1. [Footnote Renumbered.] The collateral source doctrine illustrates much the same principle. That doctrine, still widely in force, generally allows recovery against a wrongdoer for the full amount of damages even though the injured party is also compensated for some or all of the same damages from a different source independent of the tortfeasor (and whose payment, therefore, is "collateral" to him). A principal justification for the rule is that "the wrongdoer does not deserve to benefit from the fortuity that the plaintiff has received or will receive compensation from a[n] [independent] source." Overton v. United States, 619 F.2d 1299, 1306 (8th Cir.1980). Since one party or the other will receive a windfall in such a situation, it is intuitively more just that the windfall accrue to the injured person as opposed to the wrongdoer.

Thomas v. United States, 327 F.2d 379, 380 (7th Cir.1964), presented a "unique" issue: "Whether the district court erred in allowing only nominal damages for the element of pain and suffering on the ground that plaintiff, because of her mental illness aroused by the injury, received a 'certain gratification.' We think the district court erred."

4. *Shortened Life Expectancy as a Separate Item of Damage.* This proposition is generally rejected in the United States. E.g., Paladino v. Campos, 145 N.J.Super. 555, 368 A.2d 429 (1976).

In Downie v. United States Lines Co., 359 F.2d 344 (3d Cir. 1966), cert. denied, 385 U.S. 897 (1966), the court expressed the opinion that "curtailment of life expectancy" could be considered as an *element* in overall calculation of the damages for plaintiff's permanent disability much the same as an amputation of a limb, disfigurement, or a brain disorder. However it disapproved of submitting the issue of diminution of life expectancy to a jury on a "per se theory."

Chief Judge Kalodner dissented:

"I disagree with the majority's view that the wrongful shortening of one's life expectancy is not a separate element of damages in a Jones Act case.

"I am of the opinion that the law accords a right to life and its enjoyment, and that the invasion of this right is properly compensable as a separate element of damages.

"As one text writer has graphically epitomized it, 'the shortening of life through injury involves an amputation of life substance and so an absolute and irremediable loss.'

"The English courts have long allowed recovery for shortening of life expectancy as a separate and distinct element of damages. Rose v. Ford, A.C. 826, 3 All E.R. 359 (1937).

"The English rule was succinctly stated by Lord Atkin, in Rose v. Ford, supra, as follows:

> 'It does not seem to me necessary to say that a man has a *personal* right of the nature of property in his life, so that when it is diminished he loses something in the nature of valuable property. * * * I am satisfied that the injured person is damnified by having cut short the period during which he had a normal expectation of enjoying life: and that the loss, damnum, is capable of being estimated in terms of money: and that the calculation should be made. * * *
>
> 'I am of opinion therefore that a living person can claim damages for loss of expectation of life.' "

B. PRE-NATAL INJURIES—WRONGFUL BIRTH, WRONGFUL LIFE, WRONGFUL CONCEPTION

SMITH v. COTE

Supreme Court of New Hampshire, 1986.
128 N.H. 231, 513 A.2d 341.

BATCHELDER, JUSTICE. * * * On January 1, 1980 [Linda J. Smith, a plaintiff] gave birth to a daughter, Heather B. Smith, who is also a plaintiff in this action. Heather was born a victim of congenital rubella syndrome. Today, at age six, Heather suffers from bilateral cataracts, multiple congenital heart defects, motor retardation, and a significant hearing impairment. She is legally blind, and has undergone surgery for her cataracts and heart condition.

In March 1984 the plaintiffs began this negligence action. They allege that Linda contracted rubella early in her pregnancy and that, while she was under the defendants' care, the defendants negligently failed to test for and discover in a timely manner her exposure to the disease. The plaintiffs further contend that the defendants negligently failed to advise Linda of the potential for birth defects in a fetus exposed to rubella, thereby depriving her of the knowledge necessary to an informed decision as to whether to give birth to a potentially impaired child. * * *

The plaintiffs do not allege that the defendants caused Linda to conceive her child or to contract rubella, or that the defendants could have prevented the effects of the disease on the fetus. Rather, the plaintiffs contend that if Linda had known of the risks involved she would have obtained an eugenic abortion.

The action comprises three counts, only two of which are relevant here. In Count I, Linda seeks damages for her emotional distress, for the extraordinary maternal care that she must provide Heather because of Heather's birth defects, and for the extraordinary medical and educational costs she has sustained and will sustain in rearing her daughter. * * * In Count III, Heather seeks damages for her birth with defects, for the extraordinary medical and educational costs she will sustain, and for the impairment of her childhood attributable to her mother's diminished capacity to nurture her and cope with her problems.

The defendants moved to dismiss all three counts. * * * Without ruling on the motion, the Superior Court transferred to us the following questions of law:

"A. Will New Hampshire Law recognize a wrongful birth cause of action by the mother of a wilfully conceived baby suffering from birth defects, against a physician on the grounds that the physician negligently failed to test for and discover that the mother had rubella, failed to advise the mother as to the risks of potential birth defects in a fetus exposed to rubella, and thereby deprived the mother of the information on which she would have had an abortion to prevent the birth of her deformed child, where the physician did not cause the baby's conception, and did not cause the deformities in the unborn fetus?

"B. If the answer to question A is in the affirmative, will New Hampshire law allow recovery in such a cause of action for damages for emotional distress, extraordinary maternal child care, and the extraordinary medical, institutional and other special rearing expenses necessary to treat the child's impairments?

"C. Will New Hampshire law recognize a cause of action for wrongful life brought by a minor child suffering from birth defects against a physician on the grounds that the physician negligently failed to test for, discover, and advise the child's mother as to the mother's having rubella and as to information concerning the potential effects of rubella on her unborn fetus, which failure allegedly caused the mother not to abort the fetus, thereby causing the plaintiff child to live and exist with mental and physical deformities?

"D. If the answer to question C is in the affirmative, what general and specific damages may the child recover in such an action?"

At the outset we emphasize that in deciding this case we express no opinion as to whether the plaintiffs ultimately should prevail in this action.

We recognize that the termination of pregnancy involves controversial and divisive social issues. Nonetheless, the Supreme Court of the United States has held that a woman has a constitutionally secured right to terminate a pregnancy. Roe v. Wade, 410 U.S. 113 (1973). * * * Today we decide only whether, given the existence of the right of choice recognized in *Roe,* our common law should allow the development of a duty to exercise care in providing information that bears on that choice.

For the sake of terminological clarity, we make some preliminary distinctions. A wrongful birth claim is a claim brought by the parents of a child born with severe defects against a physician who negligently fails to inform them, in a timely fashion, of an increased possibility that the mother will give birth to such a child, thereby precluding an informed decision as to whether to have the child. See Phillips v. United States, 508 F.Supp. 544, 545 n. 1 (D.S.C.1981). The parents typically claim damages for their emotional distress and for some or all of the costs of raising the child. We regard Count I of the plaintiffs' writ as alleging a claim for wrongful birth.

A wrongful life claim, on the other hand, is brought not by the parents of a child born with birth defects, but by or on behalf of the child. The child contends that the defendant physician negligently failed to inform the child's parents of the risk of bearing a defective infant, and hence prevented the parents from choosing to avoid the child's birth. The child typically claims damages for the extraordinary medical, educational, and institutional costs that it will sustain. We regard Count III of the plaintiffs' writ as a claim for wrongful life.

We first must decide whether New Hampshire law recognizes a cause of action for wrongful birth. Although we have never expressly recognized this cause of action, we have considered a similar claim, one for "wrongful conception." In Kingsbury v. Smith, 122 N.H. 237, 442 A.2d 1003 (1982), the plaintiffs, a married couple, had had three children and wanted no more. In an attempt to prevent the conception of additional offspring, Mrs. Kingsbury underwent a tubal ligation. The operation failed, however, and Mrs. Kingsbury later gave birth to a fourth child, a normal, healthy infant. * * *

We held that the common law of New Hampshire permitted a claim for wrongful conception, an action "for damages arising from the birth of a child to which a negligently performed sterilization procedure or a negligently filled birth control prescription which fails to prevent conception was a contributing factor." We reasoned that failure to recognize a cause of action for wrongful conception would leave "a void in the area of recovery for medical malpractice" that would dilute the standard of professional conduct in the area of family planning. * * *

The defendants argue that tort principles cannot be extended so as to accommodate wrongful birth, asserting that they did not cause the injury alleged here, and that in any case damages cannot be fairly and accurately ascertained.

The action for wrongful birth occupies a relatively recent place in the history of tort law. Gleitman v. Cosgrove, 49 N.J. 22, 227 A.2d 689 (1967), is the "fountainhead" for debate in cases of this type. Like the instant case, *Gleitman* involved claims for wrongful birth and wrongful life arising out of the birth of a child suffering from congenital rubella syndrome. * * *

The trial judge dismissed both the wrongful life and the wrongful birth complaints, and the Supreme Court of New Jersey affirmed. The court first disposed of the child's wrongful life claim, holding that the conduct complained of did not give rise to damages cognizable at law. The court explained that it was legally impossible to weigh "the value of life with impairments against the nonexistence of life itself." Turning to the parents' wrongful birth claim, the court emphasized the analytical difficulty posed by the dual character of the consequences of the defendants' alleged negligence. On the one hand, the defendants arguably had caused the plaintiffs to incur child rearing costs and to undergo emotional distress. On the other, the birth of the child had conferred the intangible benefits of parenthood on the plaintiffs. The court found that this difficulty made it impossible to determine compensatory damages.

The *Gleitman* court also was troubled by the policy implications of recognizing a cause of action for wrongful birth. According to the court, the parents' complaint sought damages for "the denial of the opportunity to take an embryonic life." The court reasoned that to allow such a claim would be to deny the "sanctity of the single human life," and that the child's right to live exceeded and precluded the parents' right not to endure financial and emotional injury. The court concluded that the wrongful birth complaint was not actionable because the defendants' conduct did not give rise to damages cognizable at law, and that, even if such damages were cognizable, the "countervailing public policy supporting the preciousness of human life" precluded the claim.

Gleitman's influence in wrongful birth cases has considerably diminished during the past two decades. The highest courts of Texas [citation], and Wisconsin [citation], recognized wrongful birth causes of action in 1975, and three years later the Court of Appeals of New York followed suit. [citation]. In 1979 the Supreme Court of New Jersey overruled *Gleitman* on the issue of wrongful birth. See Berman v. Allan, 80 N.J. 421, 404 A.2d 8 (1979). Today there is "quite general agreement" that some recovery should be permitted in wrongful birth cases. [citations] Of the jurisdictions that have considered the issue, only North Carolina refuses to allow recovery. * * *

We hold that New Hampshire recognizes a cause of action for wrongful birth. Notwithstanding the disparate views within society on the controversial practice of abortion, we are bound by the law that protects a woman's right to choose to terminate her pregnancy. Our holding today neither encourages nor discourages this practice, nor does it rest upon a judgment that, in some absolute sense, Heather Smith should never have been born. We cannot (and need not, for purposes of this action) make such a judgment. We must, however, do our best to effectuate the first principles of our law of negligence: to deter negligent conduct, and to compensate the victims of those who act unreasonably. * * *

In the present case, if the defendants' failure to advise Linda of the risks of birth defects amounted to negligence, then the reasonably foreseeable result of that negligence was that Linda would incur the expenses involved in raising her daughter. According to the usual rule of damages, then, Linda should recover the entire cost of raising Heather, including both ordinary child-rearing costs and the extraordinary costs attributable to Heather's condition.

However, "few if any jurisdictions appear ready to apply this traditional rule of damages with full vigor in wrongful birth cases." Azzolino v. Dingfelder, 315 N.C. 103, 337 S.E.2d 528, 534 (1985). Although at least one court has ruled that all child-rearing costs should be recoverable [citation], most courts are reluctant to impose liability to this extent. A special rule of damages has emerged; in most jurisdictions the parents may recover only the extraordinary medical and educational costs attributable to the birth defects. [citation] In the present case, in accordance with the rule prevailing elsewhere, Linda seeks to recover, as tangible losses, only her extraordinary costs.

The logic of the "extraordinary costs" rule has been criticized. See Becker v. Schwartz, 46 N.Y.2d 401, 421–22, 386 N.E.2d 807, 818, 413 N.Y.S.2d 895, 907 (1978) (Wachtler, J., dissenting in part). The rule in effect divides a plaintiff's pecuniary losses into two categories, ordinary costs and extraordinary costs, and treats the latter category as compensable while ignoring the former category. At first glance, this bifurcation seems difficult to justify.

The disparity is explained, however, by reference to the rule requiring mitigation of tort damages. The "avoidable consequences" rule, Restatement (Second) of Torts § 918 (1979), specifies that a plaintiff may not recover damages for "any harm that he could have avoided by the use of reasonable effort or expenditure" after the occurrence of the tort. Rigidly applied, this rule would appear to require wrongful birth plaintiffs to place their children for adoption. [citation] Because of our profound respect for the sanctity of the family [citation], we are loathe to sanction the application of the rule in these circumstances. If the rule is not applied, however, wrongful birth plaintiffs may receive windfalls. Hence, a special rule limiting recovery of damages is warranted.

Although the extraordinary costs rule departs from traditional principles of tort damages, it is neither illogical nor unprecedented. The rule represents an application in a tort context of the expectancy rule of damages employed in breach of contracts cases. Wrongful birth plaintiffs typically desire a child (and plan to support it) from the outset. It is the defendants' duty to help them achieve this goal. When the plaintiffs' expectations are frustrated by the defendants' negligence, the extraordinary costs rule "merely attempts to put plaintiffs in the position they *expected* to be in with defendant's help."

Under this view of the problem, ordinary child-rearing costs are analogous to a price the plaintiffs were willing to pay in order to achieve an expected result. According to contract principles, plaintiffs "may not have a return in damages of the price and also receive what was to be obtained for the price." McQuaid v. Michou, 85 N.H. 299, 303, 157 A. 881, 883 (1932). See Hawkins v. McGee, 84 N.H. 114, 146 A. 641 (1929). We note that expectancy damages are recoverable in other kinds of tort cases, see Wilson v. Came, 116 N.H. 628, 630, 366 A.2d 474, 475 (1976) (negligent misrepresentation), and that contract principles are hardly unknown in medical malpractice litigation, which has roots in contract as well as in tort. [citations] In light of the difficulty posed by tort damages principles in these circumstances, we see no obstacle—logical or otherwise—to use of the extraordinary costs rule.

The extraordinary costs rule ensures that the parents of a deformed child will recover the medical and educational costs attributable to the child's impairment. At the same time it establishes a necessary and clearly defined boundary to liability in this area. [citation] Accordingly, we hold that a plaintiff in a wrongful birth case may recover the extraordinary medical and educational costs attributable to the child's deformities, but may not recover ordinary child-raising costs.

Three points stand in need of clarification. First, parents may recover extraordinary costs incurred both before and after their child attains majority. Some courts do not permit recovery of post-majority expenses, on the theory that the parents' obligation of support terminates when the child reaches twenty-one. E.g., Bani–Esraili v. Wald, 127 Misc.2d 202, 485 N.Y.S.2d 708 (Sup.Ct.1985). In New Hampshire, however, parents are required to support their disabled adult offspring. [citations]

Second, recovery should include compensation for the extraordinary maternal care that has been and will be provided to the child. Linda alleges that her parental obligations and duties, which include feeding, bathing, and exercising Heather, substantially exceed those of parents of a normal child. One court has ruled that parents "cannot recover for services that they have rendered or will render personally to their own child without incurring financial expense." Schroeder v. Perkel, 87 N.J. 53, 69, 432 A.2d 834, 841 (1981). We see no reason, however, to treat as noncompensable the burdens imposed on a parent who must devote extraordinary time and effort to caring for a child with birth defects. Cf. Ernshaw v. Roberge, 86 N.H. 451, 456, 170 A. 7, 9–10 (1934) (father of injured child may recover value of care provided by mother); Connell v. Putnam, 58 N.H. 534 (1879) (father of injured child may recover value of nursing and care he provides). Avoiding these burdens is often among the primary motivations of one who chooses not to bear a child likely to suffer from birth defects. We hold that a parent may recover for his or her ministrations to his or her child to the extent that such ministrations:

(1) are made necessary by the child's condition;

(2) clearly exceed those ordinarily rendered by parents of a normal child; and

(3) are reasonably susceptible of valuation.

The trial judge should not allow the jury to consider such a claim unless there is concrete evidence indicating the probable nature and extent of the extra services that will be required. If the issue is submitted to the jury, the trial judge must instruct that damages for this purpose are not to be awarded as an expression of sympathy.

Third, to the extent that the parent's alleged emotional distress results in tangible pecuniary losses, such as medical expenses or counseling fees, such losses are recoverable. [citations]

Existing damages principles do not resolve the issue whether recovery for emotional distress should be permitted in wrongful birth cases. Emotional distress damages are not uniformly recoverable once a protected interest is shown to have been invaded. Compare Holyoke v. Grand Trunk Ry., 48 N.H. 541, 545 (1869) (plaintiff may recover for actual mental suffering in personal injury case) with Crowley v. Global Realty, Inc., 124 N.H. 814, 818, 474 A.2d 1056, 1058 (1984) (plaintiffs cannot recover for emotional distress in claim for negligent misrepresentation).

We look primarily to two analogous cases for guidance. In Prescott v. Robinson, 74 N.H. 460, 69 A. 522 (1908), a pregnant woman was injured in an automobile accident caused by the defendant's negligence. Her child was subsequently born permanently deformed. The woman brought an action for personal injuries in which she sought to recover for the mental distress she had suffered and would continue to suffer on account of her child's condition. We held that she could not recover for her post-natal emotional distress.

In Siciliano v. Capitol City Shows, Inc., 124 N.H. 719, 475 A.2d 19 (1984), an amusement ride accident resulted in the death of one child and cerebral injuries to another. The parents of the children sued, claiming damages for the loss of the society of their respective children. We held that the plaintiffs failed to state a cause of action.

Prescott and *Siciliano* illustrate our reluctance to permit parents of children injured or killed as a result of negligent conduct to recover for their consequent emotional distress. *See* Restatement (Second) of Torts § 703, comment h (1977). * * * *Prescott* and *Siciliano* were founded * * * on a practical consideration: the need to establish a clearly defined limit to the scope of negligence liability in this area. * * *

This case arises from a child's birth, not a child's injury or death. Nonetheless, we are struck by the parallels between the claims for emotional distress in *Prescott* and *Siciliano* and the claim before us. Moreover, we are mindful of the anomaly that would result were we to treat parental emotional distress as compensable. The negligent conduct at issue in *Prescott* and *Robinson* was the direct cause of injuries to or the death of otherwise healthy children. By contrast, in wrongful birth cases the defendant's conduct results, not in injuries or death, but in the birth of an unavoidably impaired child. It would be curious, to say the least, to impose liability for parental distress in the latter but not the former cases.

We also harbor concerns of proportionality. "[T]he unfairness of denying recovery to a plaintiff on grounds that are arbitrary in terms of principle may be outweighed by the perceived unfairness of imposing a burden on defendant that seems much greater than his fault would justify." We already have held that a wrongful birth defendant is liable for the pecuniary losses incurred by the parents. Were we additionally to impose liability for parents' emotional distress, we would run the risk of penalizing and overdeterring merely negligent conduct.

We hold that damages for emotional distress are not recoverable in wrongful birth actions. [citations]

The theory of Heather's wrongful life action is as follows: during Linda's pregnancy the defendants owed a duty of care to both Linda and Heather. The defendants breached this duty when they failed to discover Linda's exposure to rubella and failed to advise her of the possible effects of that exposure on her child's health. Had Linda been properly informed, she would have undergone an abortion, and Heather would not have been born. Because Linda was not so informed, Heather must bear the burden of her afflictions for the rest of her life. The defendant's conduct is thus the proximate cause of injury to Heather.

This theory presents a crucial problem, however: the question of injury. It is axiomatic that there is no cause of action for negligence unless and until there has been an injury. In the present case Heather claims to have had an interest in avoiding "the lifetime of suffering inflicted on [her] by [her] condition." In order to recognize Heather's wrongful life action, then, we must determine that the fetal Heather had an interest in avoiding her own birth, that it would have been best *for Heather* if she had not been born.

This premise of the wrongful life action—that the plaintiff's own birth and suffering constitute legal injury—has caused many courts to decline to recognize the claim. [citation] According to the Supreme Court of Texas, the perplexities involved in comparing the relative benefits of life and nonexistence render it "impossible" to decide the question of injury. Nelson v. Krusen, 678 S.W.2d 918, 925 (Tex.1984). The notion that nonexistence may be preferable to life with severe birth defects appears to contravene the policy favoring "the preciousness and sanctity of human life." Phillips v. United States, 508 F.Supp. 537, 543 (D.S.C.1980). As one court has written,

> "[w]hether it is better never to have been born at all than to have been born with even gross deficiencies is a mystery more properly to be left to the philosophers and the theologians. Surely the law can assert no competence to resolve the issue, particularly in view of the very nearly uniform high value which the law and mankind has placed on human life, rather than its absence."

Becker v. Schwartz, 46 N.Y.2d 401, 411, 386 N.E.2d 807, 812, 413 N.Y.S.2d 895, 900 (1978). * * *

The high courts of three states have adopted a special approach in wrongful life cases. See Turpin v. Sortini, 31 Cal.3d 220, 643 P.2d 954, 182 Cal.Rptr. 337 (1982); Procanik v. Cillo, 97 N.J. 339, 478 A.2d 755 (1984); Harbeson v. Parke–Davis, Inc., 98 Wash.2d 460, 656 P.2d 483 (1983). In *Turpin* a child suffering from hereditary deafness sued to recover (1) general damages for the deprivation of her right "to be born as a whole, functional human being without total deafness" and (2) special damages for extraordinary expenses for specialized training, teaching and hearing equipment that she would incur during her lifetime. The court denied the claim for general damages, concluding that it was impossible to determine whether the child had been injured, or to assess general damages in a fair, nonspeculative manner.

The court allowed recovery of the claimed special damages, however. It reasoned that "it would be illogical and anomalous to permit only parents, and not the child, to recover for the cost of the child's own medical care." The court noted that if the parents alone were allowed a right of action, recovery of medical expenses for the child "might well depend on the wholly fortuitous circumstance of whether the parents are available to sue and recover such damages or whether the medical expenses are incurred at a time when the parents remain legally responsible for providing such care." The court cited several other reasons for permitting recovery of special damages:

(1) the defendants' negligence placed a medical burden on the whole family unit, not just the parents;

(2) the claimed special damages were certain and readily measurable; and

(3) recovery of such damages would be vital to the child's survival.

We recognize that this approach represents a sincere and sympathetic judicial response to the plight of children whose frightfully burdened lives might have been prevented. Legal niceties aside, the reality of the situation in wrongful life cases is that a child both "*exists* and *suffers,* due to the negligence of others." Curlender v. Bio–Science Laboratories, 106 Cal.App.3d 811, 829, 165 Cal.Rptr. 477, 488 (1980). The essence of the *Turpin* rule is that logic should not defeat the claim of a severely impaired child in need of help.

Moreover, we are mindful that controversy regarding the *Turpin* rule may have little practical significance when recovery for wrongful *birth* is permitted. The same extraordinary expenses *Turpin* would allow in wrongful life actions are covered by our rule allowing parental recovery of post-majority expenses. Because such expenses cannot be recovered by both parent and child, the net effect is the same. Recognition of the wrongful life action would make a substantial difference only in limited circumstances, as when the statute of limitations bars the parental but not the filial claim (as in *Procanik*) or when the parents are unavailable to sue.

Even if adoption of the *Turpin* rule would have no practical consequences in the majority of cases, however, the doctrinal and symbolic implications of the rule are significant. Its primary deficiency is that it imposes liability even if the defendant has caused no harm. If the child cannot prove injury,

> "it is unfair and unjust to charge the doctors with the infant's medical expenses. The position that the child may recover special damages despite the failure of his underlying theory of wrongful life violates the moral code underlying our system of justice from which the fundamental principles of tort law are derived."

Procanik v. Cillo, 97 N.J. 339, 370, 478 A.2d 755, 772 (1984) (Schreiber, J., dissenting in part). Were we to permit a waiver of the injury requirement in this negligence action, it would be "difficult to envision any principled basis for refusing to extend the reasoning to other elements and other situations." Nelson v. Krusen, 678 S.W.2d 918, 931 (Tex.1984) (Robertson, J., concurring).

Unlike the *Turpin, Procanik,* and *Harbeson* courts, we perceive no anomaly in permitting the parents but not the child to recover the medical and educational expenses attributable to the child's impairments. This result obtains because the loss at issue is the parents', not the child's. A parent is liable for a minor's medical expenses when the minor is living with or supported by the parents. Hence the parent, and not the child, may recover the medical expenses of a minor child injured by another. If the parent has sustained an ascertainable injury, the right of recovery is properly hers. In permitting a child to recover for her parents' injury, the *Turpin* rule contravenes the principle that "negligence as a legal source of liability gives rise only to an obligation to compensate the person immediately injured." Norwest v. Presbyterian Intercommunity Hospital, 293 Or. 543, 569, 652 P.2d 318, 333 (1982).

We recognize that our rejection of the *Turpin* rule is not without cost. In the future recovery of an impaired child's necessary medical expenses may well depend on whether the child's parents are available to assert a claim for wrongful birth. But this cost is the price of our paramount regard for the value of human life, and of our adherence to fundamental principles of justice. We will not recognize a right not to be born, and we will not permit a person to recover damages from one who has done him no harm.

We decline to recognize a cause of action for wrongful life. * * *

Remanded.

SOUTER, J., concurred specially. I concur in the majority opinion and add this further word, not because that opinion fails to respond to the questions transferred to us, but because those questions fail to raise a significant issue in the area of malpractice litigation that we address today. The trial court did not ask whether, or how, a physician with conscientious scruples against abortion, and the testing and counselling that may inform an abortion decision, can discharge his professional obligation without engaging in procedures that his religious or moral principles condemn. To say nothing about this issue could lead to misunderstanding.

In response to the questions transferred, the court holds that a sphere of medical practice necessarily permitted under Roe v. Wade, 410 U.S. 113 (1973), is not exempt from standards of reasonable medical competence. Consequently we hold that the plaintiff alleges a violation of the physician's duty when she claims, in the circumstances of the case, that prevailing standards of medical practice called for testing and advice, which the defendants failed to provide.

It does not follow, however, and I do not understand the court to hold, that a physician can discharge the obligation of due care in such circumstances only by personally ordering such tests and rendering such advice. The court does not hold that some or all physicians must make a choice between rendering services that they morally condemn and leaving their profession in order to escape malpractice exposure. The defensive significance, for example, of timely disclosure of professional limits based on religious or moral scruples, combined with timely referral to other physicians who are not so constrained, is a question open for consideration in any case in which it may be raised.

Note

Arche v. United States Department of the Army, 247 Kan. 276, 290–91, 798 P.2d 477, 486–87 (1990), follows Smith v. Cote and 20 other states' courts to recognize a cause of action for wrongful birth. It differs from Smith v. Cote by holding that damages cannot extend beyond the child's life expectancy or age of majority, whichever is shorter. Despite this limitation, the court noted, the plaintiff claimed damages of $10,000,000. The court expressed concern that a lump sum would tempt the plaintiffs, mentioned one instance of the child being offered up for adoption, and recommended that if the trial court awards any damages, the damages be placed in a reversionary trust with payments made from corpus as required. A concurring opinion would have made the reversionary trust mandatory.

C. INTERRELATIONSHIP BETWEEN PERSONAL INJURY AND WRONGFUL DEATH ACTIONS—SURVIVAL STATUTES

Note

Cal.Prob.Code § 573: Except as provided in this section no cause of action shall be lost by reason of the death of any person but may be maintained by or against his executor or administrator.

"In an action brought under this section against an executor or administrator all damages may be awarded which might have been recovered against the decedent had he lived except damages awardable under Section 3294 of the Civil Code or other damages imposed primarily for the sake of example and by way of punishing the defendant.

"When a person having a cause of action dies before judgment, the damages recoverable by his executor or administrator are limited to such loss or damage as the decedent sustained or incurred prior to his death, including any penalties or punitive or exemplary damages that the decedent would have been entitled to recover had he lived, and shall not include damages for pain, suffering or disfigurement.

"This section is applicable where a loss or damage occurs simultaneously with or after the death of a person who would have been liable therefore if his death had not preceded or occurred simultaneously with the loss or damage."

D. WRONGFUL DEATH DAMAGES

Wiggins v. Lane & Co., 298 F.Supp. 194, 195 (E.D.La.1969): "The history of the enactment of state and federal wrongful death and survivorship statutes is thoroughly traced in two articles by Professor Wex S. Malone, American Fatal Accident Statutes—Part I: The Legislative Birth Pains, 1965 Duke L.J. 673, and The Genesis of Wrongful Death, 17 Stanford L.Rev. 1043 (1965). The Common law doctrine stemmed from the rule adopted by English courts that 'in a civil court the death of a human being could not be complained of as an injury.' Baker v. Bolton, 1808, 1 Camp. 493, 170 Eng.Rep. 1033. This opinion, rendered by Lord Ellenborough, 'whose forte,' Professor Prosser says, 'was never common sense,' was accepted in the United States with the result that it was cheaper for the defendant to kill a person than to tweak his nose. The rule was changed in England by the Fatal Accidents Act of 1846, otherwise known as Lord Campbell's Act. This created a cause of action for the death in favor of the decedent's personal representatives, for the benefit of designated persons.

"Each of the United States has adopted a statute changing the rule of Baker v. Bolton. A majority follow the pattern of Lord Campbell's Act; some merely preserve the cause of action vested in the decedent at the moment of his death and enlarge it to include the damages resulting from his death."

TYPES OF STATUTES †

§ 3:1. Loss to Survivors; Pecuniary Loss. Lord Campbell's Act of 1846 allowed the jury to award to the surviving beneficiaries "such damages as they may think proportioned to the injury." Shortly thereafter, in a case in which a judgment awarding a widow damages for wounded feelings was reversed, this general language was interpreted to restrict recovery to pecuniary losses suffered by the decedent's survivors. Consequently, although the Act, by its terms, does not expressly limit such death damages to pecuniary damages, it was so interpreted by the courts.

A number of American jurisdictions modeled their death statutes after Lord Campbell's Act, allowing the jury to award "damages," "damages proportioned to the injury," or "such damages as are deemed fair and just," with their courts interpreting these general terms as incorporating the loss to survivors theory. But many of the wrongful death statutes expressly provide that damages are to be assessed in accordance with the loss to the decedent's survivors. A majority of these jurisdictions have hence adopted the pecuniary loss requirement brought about by the early construction of Lord Campbell's Act, either by express provision within the statute or by judicial construction of general language. * * *

† Reprinted, with permission, from Recovery for Wrongful Death (2d ed.) Stuart S. Speiser, © 1975 by the Lawyers Cooperative Publishing Co. The original text is fully annotated to all statutes and most cases. Pocket parts provide current supplementary data.

Under statutes of the "loss-to-survivors" types, damages are awarded for the present value of probable contributions which the deceased would have made to the survivors had he lived, and for the pecuniary value of the services decedent would have rendered to the survivors, which, in many states, includes the value of a parent's training, guidance, nurture and education. In addition, a number of courts allow recovery of medical expenses, funeral expenses, and the amount of the probable inheritance the deceased would have left to the survivors, by either will or intestate succession, had he lived out his normal life span.

In some states, administration expenses and attorney's fees may be recovered. And a few jurisdictions, although bound by the pecuniary loss rule, permit recovery of the "pecuniary value" of the decedent's society, companionship, counsel, protection and attention.

In a number of other states, either by express statutory provision or by judicial construction of general statutory terms, non-pecuniary damages, such as mental anguish or the sentimental value of decedent's society, companionship and affection, may be recovered in addition to the other elements of damage already mentioned. * * *

Damages in actions under the Federal Tort Claims Act are assessed in accordance with the law of the state within which the cause of action arose, except that no punitive damages may be recovered in such actions. Thus, damages for non-pecuniary loss may be awarded in a F.T.C.A. action when such recovery is permitted by the applicable state law. [1] * * *

§ 3:2. Loss to the Estate; Theories of Measuring Damages. There are basically four different types of statutes under which damages for wrongful death are measured by the loss to decedent's estate, in whole or in part, rather than by loss to survivors: (a) the enlarged survival-death statute under which damages for both the fatal injury and the death may be recovered in a single action; (b) the wrongful death statute which, by judicial construction, measures recovery by loss to estate; (c) the wrongful death statute which authorizes decedent's personal representative to recover either all losses or certain losses to the estate in cases where the decedent is not survived by any statutory beneficiary; (d) the wrongful death statute which measures damages by loss to the survivors but, in addition, allows decedent's personal representative to recover certain specified losses to the estate.

While most survival-death statutes employ the loss to estate measure of damages, some of them specifically require that the recovery be distributed directly to the statutory beneficiaries. Thus it is clear that the various survival-death acts differ sharply from the pattern of the "true" survival statute (as well as differing greatly from one another). * * *

The enlarged survival-death action is essentially the ordinary or "true" survival action for decedent's lifetime personal injuries, enlarged by statute to include damages for wrongful death. Since the action is technically a survival

1. [Editors' footnote] Yowell v. Piper Aircraft Corp., 703 S.W.2d 630, 633 (Tex.1986): "We define the loss of inheritance damages in Texas as the present value that the deceased, in reasonable probability, would have added to the estate and left at natural death to the statutory wrongful death beneficiaries but for the wrongful act causing premature death. True, not every wrongful death beneficiary sustains loss of inheritance damages. If the decedent would have earned no more than he and his family would have used for support, or if the decedent would have outlived the wrongful death beneficiary, loss of inheritance damages would properly be denied. This is for the jury to decide."

to the estate of decedent's cause of action, with death damages added, damages should be measured by loss to the estate and should be recovered for the benefit of the estate. * * *

Several "true" wrongful death statutes (under which a new cause of action in favor of the survivors arises upon death) have been construed to measure damages in certain specified situations by loss to decedent's estate, or in all instances by such loss to the estate, although the damages, once recovered, are distributed directly to the statutory beneficiaries.

Several other "true" death acts measure damages by loss to survivors, but provide that if decedent is not survived by any statutory beneficiaries, the action may be maintained for the benefit of decedent's estate to recover either the loss to the estate in general, or certain specifically enumerated expenses to the estate. * * *

There are also a few death statutes which, although they measure damages by loss to survivors, in addition authorize decedent's personal representative to recover certain items of loss or expense to the estate.

Three different theories of measuring damages are utilized under the loss to estate type of statute. The first, and most prevalent, theory is that the damages should represent the present value of the decedent's probable future net earnings. In other words, the recovery should equal the decedent's probable future earnings, diminished by the amount he would have spent for his own living expenses had he survived, and reduced to present value. * * *

The second theory of recovery measures damages by the present worth of decedent's probable future accumulations. Under this theory, the recovery equals the amount which decedent would have earned (by his own efforts) and saved (from the time of his death to the time he probably would have died had he not been wrongfully killed) and left at his death as part of his estate, reduced to present value. * * *

The third theory of recovery measures damages by the present worth of decedent's probable gross earnings. According to this theory, the recovery consists of the total probable future earnings of the decedent with no deduction made for the amount decedent would have expended for his own expenses had he lived.

Although, in an action for the death of a minor child in jurisdictions which measure recovery by the loss to the parents, damages are frequently restricted to those accruing during the period of the decedent's minority, damages for the death of a minor child in jurisdictions which measure recovery by loss to the estate are not so restricted and, in several loss to the estate jurisdictions, such damages are calculated only for the period after the decedent would have reached his majority or become emancipated.

Notes

The state schemes differ widely in language and interpretation as summarized above. Beware of variants like the Federal Employers Liability Act, the Death on the High Seas Act, the Jones Act, Longshoremen and Harbor Workers' Compensation Act, and, occasionally, Structural Works Acts (Scaffolding Acts), Death to Minors Acts, Dram Shop Acts, or even provisions that the slayer of another person in a duel shall be liable for all the decedent's debts. Cal.Civ.Code § 3348. Furthermore, Workers' Compensation Acts may provide financial benefits to dependents of employees killed while acting within the scope of their employment.

The various statutory schemes include startlingly different calculations of the amount of possible damages for death or injury in favor of different classes of possible claimants. These combine with the increasing mobility to produce considerable forum shopping—as well as much legal learning about choice of law. E.g., Gordon v. Eastern Air Lines, 391 F.Supp. 31 (S.D.N.Y.1975).

No concise compilation can cover the considerations that enter into computation of damages, in whose favor, and the procedures to pursue. The decisions that follow present a sample. However, the attorney dealing with these matters cannot be content with mere local learning, but must be prepared to determine the details of several statutory schemes potentially applicable to the client's cause.

Questions When Evaluating a Potentially Applicable Wrongful Death Statute:

1. Who are the beneficiaries of the action: The estate? The heirs? The next of kin? Others?
2. What procedures govern the action? Parties? Statute of Limitations? Is the action single (unitary) or multiple?
3. Does the wrongful death cause of action mesh with a survival action? How?
4. Does the wrongful death action survive the death of the beneficiary?
5. Does beneficiary's contributory negligence bear on the action?
6. Can an action in contract be brought under the act?
7. Is the award limited by statute? If so, does the limitation apply to the wrongful act or to each claimant? A decided trend to eliminate statutory maximum limitations on wrongful death damages is discernable. Speiser reports that all states have eliminated their maxima on wrongful death recovery. S. Speiser, Recovery for Wrongful Death § 7.2 (2d ed. 1975 Supp.).
8. How will the award be apportioned among several beneficiaries?
9. Does the statute restrict recovery to "pecuniary damages?" Does it allow damages that are "just?" If limited to "pecuniary damages," are they defined?
10. Are punitive damages allowed?
11. Are pre-death damages for the pain and suffering allowed?
12. Can pre-judgment interest be recovered?
13. Are income taxes a factor in the award?
14. Will any part of the award be subject to estate taxes or the claims of the deceased's creditors?
15. Will the portion of the award for prospective losses be discounted to present value? If so, what guides the discount rate?
16. Are funeral expenses recoverable?
17. Do "aggravating circumstances" affect the award?

SEA-LAND SERVICES, INC. v. GAUDET

United States Supreme Court, 1974.

414 U.S. 573.

JUSTICE BRENNAN delivered the opinion of the Court. Moragne v. State Marine Lines, 398 U.S. 375 (1970), overruling The Harrisburg, 119 U.S. 199, (1886), held that an action for wrongful death based on unseaworthiness is maintainable under federal maritime law, but left the shaping of the new nonstatutory action to future cases. The question in this case is whether the widow of a longshoreman may maintain such an action for the wrongful death of her husband—alleged to have resulted from injuries suffered by him while aboard a vessel in navigable waters—after the decedent recovered damages in his lifetime for his injuries.

Respondent's husband suffered severe injuries while working as a longshoreman aboard petitioner's vessel, the S.S. Claiborne, in Louisiana navigable waters. He recovered $140,000 for his permanent disability, physical agony, and loss of earnings in an action based on unseaworthiness, but died shortly after the action was terminated. Respondent brought this wrongful death action in the District Court for the Eastern District of Louisiana for damages suffered by her. Based on her husband's recovery, the District Court dismissed the widow's suit on grounds of *res judicata* and failure to state a claim. The Court of Appeals for the Fifth Circuit reversed, holding that *Moragne* gave "Mrs. Gaudet * * * a compensable cause of action for Mr. Gaudet's death, wholly apart from and not extinguished by the latter's recovery for his personal injuries. * * *"

The harshness of the *Harrisburg* rule that in the absence of a statute, there is no maritime action for wrongful death, was only partially relieved by enactment of federal and state wrongful death statutes.[1] The Death on the High Seas Act, 46 U.S.C.A. §§ 761–768, created a wrongful death action for death outside the three-mile limit. The Jones Act, 46 U.S.C.A. § 688, incorporating the Federal Employees' Liability Act, 45 U.S.C.A. §§ 51–60, established such an action based on negligence for the wrongful death of a seaman regardless of the situs of the wrong; but otherwise, wrongful death actions for deaths occurring on navigable waters within the three-mile territorial waters of a State depended upon whether the State had enacted a wrongful death statute and, if so, whether the statute permitted recovery. * * *

In overruling *The Harrisburg, Moragne* ended these anomalies by the creation of a uniform federal cause of action for maritime death, designed to extend to the dependents of maritime wrongful death victims admiralty's "special solicitude for the welfare of those men who under[take] to venture upon hazardous and unpredictable sea voyages."

* * * Thus, *Moragne* created a true wrongful death remedy—founded upon the death itself and independent of any action the decedent may have had for his own personal injuries. Because the respondent's suit involves a different cause of action, it is not precluded by *res judicata*. * * *

To be sure, a majority of courts interpreting state and federal wrongful death statutes have held that an action for wrongful death is barred by the decedent's recovery for injuries during his lifetime. But the bar does not appear to rest in those cases so much upon principles of *res judicata* or public policy as upon statutory limitations on the wrongful death action. As one

1. [Footnotes renumbered.] Wrongful death statutes are to be distinguished from survival statutes. The latter have been separately enacted to abrogate the common law rule that an action for tort abated at the death of either the injured person or the tort-feasor. Survival statutes permit the deceased's estate to prosecute any claims for personal injury the *deceased* would have had, but for his death. They do not permit recovery for harms suffered by the deceased's family as a result of his death. Survival statutes, in one form or another, have been enacted in over one-half the States and supplement the state wrongful death statutes [citation], though in a small number of States the survival statute provides the only death remedy available, [citation]. The Federal Employers' Liability Act, 45 U.S.C.A. § 59, and the Jones Act, 46 U.S.C.A. § 688, but not the Death on High Seas Act, 46 U.S.C.A. § 761, contain survival provisions.

authority has noted, "[t]he fact that all civil remedies for wrongful death derive from statute has important consequences. Since the right was unknown to common law, the legislatures which created the right were free to impose restrictions upon it." 2 F. Harper & F. James, The Law of Torts § 24.2, p. 1285 (1956). Thus, England's Lord Campbell's Act, the first wrongful death statute, permits recovery "whensoever the death of a person shall be caused by wrongful act * * * of another and the act * * * is such as would (if death had not ensued) have entitled the party injured to maintain an action and recover damages in respect thereof. * * *" Early English cases interpreting the Act held that this language conditioned wrongful death recovery upon the existence of an actionable cause of the decedent at his death, if the deceased had reduced his claim to judgment, settled with or released his tort-feasor, and therefore could not maintain an action for his injuries at his death, his dependents could have no cause of action for his wrongful death. Since Lord Campbell's Act became the prototype of American wrongful death statutes, most state statutes contained nearly identical language and have been similarly interpreted by state courts.[2] Though the federal wrongful death statutes do not contain the same controversial language, the FELA, at least, has been held to be "essentially identical with" Lord Campbell's Act, Michigan C.R. Co. v. Vreeland, 227 U.S. 59, 69 (1913), and therefore similar restrictions have been placed on FELA wrongful death recovery.

Moragne, on the other hand, requires that the shape of the new maritime wrongful death remedy (not a statutory creation but judge-made) be guided by the principle of maritime law that "certainly it better becomes the humane and liberal character of proceedings in admiralty to give than to withhold the remedy, when not required to withhold it by established and inflexible rules." Since the policy underlying the remedy is to insure compensation of the dependents for *their* losses resulting from the decedent's death, the remedy should not be precluded merely because the decedent, during his lifetime, is able to obtain a judgment for his own personal injuries. No statutory language or "established and inflexible rules" of maritime law require a contrary conclusion.

Sea–Land argues that, if dependents are not prevented from bringing a separate cause of action for wrongful death in cases where the decedent has already received a judgment for his personal injuries, then necessarily it will be subject to double liability. In order to evaluate this argument it is necessary first to identify the particular harms suffered by the dependents, for which the maritime wrongful death remedy permits recovery of damages. In identifying these compensable harms, we are not without useful guides; for in *Moragne* we

2. See, e.g., Legg v. Britton, 64 Vt. 652, 24 A. 1016 (1892); Melitch v. United R. & E. Co., 121 Md. 457, 88 A. 229 (1913). This interpretation has been by no means universal. A number of courts interpreting Lord Campbell's Act-type state wrongful death statutes have held that a wrongful death action could be prosecuted even though at the time of his death the decedent could not bring a cause of action for his personal injuries because he had already recovered a judgment, settled or released his claims. A classic statement of this view is that of the South Dakota Supreme Court in Rowe v. Richards, 35 S.D. 201, 215–216, 151 N.W. 1001, 1006 (1915):

"We must confess our inability to grasp the logic of any so called reasoning through which the conclusion is drawn that the husband, simply because he may live to suffer from a physical injury and thus become vested with a cause of action for the violation of his own personal right has an implied power to release a cause of action—one which has not then accrued; one which may never accrue; and one which from its very nature cannot accrue until his death; and one which if it ever does accrue, will accrue in favor of his wife and be based upon the violation of a right vested solely in his wife."

recognized that with respect to "particular questions of the measure of damages, the courts will not be without persuasive analogy for guidance. Both the Death on the High Seas Act and the numerous state wrongful-death acts have been implemented with success for decades. The experience thus built up counsels that a suit for wrongful death raises no problems unlike those that have long been grist for the judicial mill." Our review of those authorities, and the policies of maritime law, persuade us that, under the maritime wrongful death remedy, the members of the decedent's dependents may recover damages for their loss of support, services, and society, as well as funeral expenses.

Recovery for loss of support has been universally recognized, and includes all the financial contributions that the decedent would have made to his dependents had he lived. Similarly, the overwhelming majority of state wrongful death acts and courts interpreting the Death on the High Seas Act have permitted recovery for the monetary value of services the decedent provided and would have continued to provide but for his wrongful death. Such services include, for example, the nurture, training, education and guidance that a child would have received had not the parent been wrongfully killed. Services the decedent performed at home or for his spouse are also compensable.

Compensation for loss of society, however, presents a closer question. The term "society" embraces a broad range of mutual benefits each family member received from the others' continued existence, including love, affection, care, attention, companionship, comfort and protection.[3] Unquestionably, the deprivation of these benefits by wrongful death is a grave loss to the decedent's dependents. Despite this fact, a number of early wrongful death statutes were interpreted by courts to preclude recovery for these losses on the ground that the statutes were intended to provide compensation only for "pecuniary loss," and that the loss of society is not such an economic loss.[4] Other wrongful death statutes contain express language limiting recovery to pecuniary losses; for example, the Death on the High Seas Act limits recovery to "a fair and just compensation for the *pecuniary* loss sustained by the persons for whose benefit the suit is brought * * *," 46 U.S.C.A. § 762 (emphasis added), and consequently has been construed to exclude recovery for the loss of society.

A clear majority of States, on the other hand, have rejected such a narrow view of damages, and, either by express statutory provision or by judicial

3. Loss of society must not be confused with mental anguish or grief, which are not compensable under the maritime wrongful death remedy. The former entails the loss of positive benefits, while the latter represents an emotional response to the wrongful death. The difference between the two is well expressed as follows:

"When we speak of recovery for the beneficiaries' mental anguish, we are primarily concerned, not with the benefits they have lost, but with the issue of compensating them for their harrowing experience resulting from the death of a loved one. This requires a somewhat negative approach. The fundamental question in this area of damages is what deleterious effect has the death, as such, had upon the claimants: In other areas of damage, we focus on more positive aspects of the injury such as what would the decedent, had he lived, have *contributed* in terms of support, assistance, training, comfort, consortium, etc. * * * The great majority of jurisdictions, including several which do allow damages for other types of nonpecuniary loss, hold that the grief, bereavement, anxiety, distress, or mental pain and suffering of the beneficiaries may not be regarded as elements of damage in a wrongful death action," S. Speiser, Recovery for Wrongful Death § 3.45, p. 223.

4. Lord Campbell's Act, which, by its terms, allows the jury to award "such damages as they may think proportional to the injury," was interpreted to permit recovery only for "pecuniary losses," Blake v. Midland R. Co., 18 Q.B. 93 (1852). Most American courts, interpreting similar wrongful death statutes, followed suit. [citations]

construction, permit recovery for loss of society. This expansion of damages recoverable under wrongful death statutes to include loss of society has led one commentator to observe that "[w]hether such damages are classified as 'pecuniary' or recognized and allowed as nonpecuniary, the recent trend is unmistakably in favor of permitting such recovery." S. Speiser, Recovery for Wrongful Death 218 (1966). Thus, our decision to permit recovery for loss of society aligns the maritime wrongful death remedy with a majority of state wrongful death statutes.[5] But in any event, our decision is compelled if we are to shape the remedy to comport with the humanitarian policy of the maritime law. * * *

Objection to permitting recovery for loss of society often centers upon the fear that such damages are somewhat speculative and that fact finders will return excessive verdicts. We are not unaware of this objection in *Moragne*, where we said,

> "[O]ther courts have recognized that calculation of the loss sustained by dependents or by the estate of the deceased, which is required under most wrongful-death statutes * * * does not present difficulties more insurmountable than assessment of damages for many nonfatal personal injuries."

For example, juries are often called upon to measure damages for pain and suffering, mental anguish in disfigurement cases, or intentional infliction of emotional harm. In fact, since the 17th century, juries have assessed damages for loss of consortium—which encompasses loss of society—in civil actions brought by husbands whose wives have been negligently injured. More recently, juries have been asked to measure loss of consortium suffered by wives whose husbands have been negligently harmed. * * *

As in all damage awards for tortious injury, "[i]nsistence on mathematical precision would be illusory and the judge or juror must be allowed a fair latitude to make reasonable approximations guided by judgment and practical experience," Whitaker v. Blidberg Rothchild Co., 296 F.2d 554, 555 (D.C.1961). Moreover, appellate tribunals have amply demonstrated their ability to control excessive awards.

Finally, in addition to recovery for loss of support, services, and society, damages for funeral expenses may be awarded under the maritime wrongful death remedy in circumstances where the decedent's dependents have either paid for the funeral or are liable for its payment. A majority of States provided for such recovery under their wrongful death statutes. Furthermore, although there is a conflict over whether funeral expenses are compensable under the Death on the High Seas Act, it is clear that funeral expenses were permitted under the general maritime law prior to *The Harrisburg*. We therefore find no persuasive reason for not following the earlier admiralty rule and thus hold that funeral expenses are compensable.

Turning now to Sea–Land's double liability argument, we note that, in contrast to the elements of damages which we today hold may be recovered in a maritime wrongful death action, the decedent recovered damages only for his loss of past and future wages, pain and suffering, and medical and incidental expenses. Obviously, the decedent's recovery did not include damages for the

5. We recognize, of course, that our decision permits recovery of damages not generally available under the Death on the High Seas Act. Traditionally, however, "Congress has largely left to this Court the responsibility for fashioning the controlling rules of admiralty law." Fitzgerald v. United States Lines Co., 374 U.S. 16, 20 (1963).

dependents' loss of services, society, and funeral expenses. Indeed, these losses—unique to the decedent's dependents—could not accrue until the decedent's death. Thus, recovery of damages for these losses in the maritime wrongful death action will not subject Sea-Land to double liability or provide the dependents with a windfall.

There is, however, an apparent overlap between the decedent's recovery for loss of future wages and the dependents' subsequent claim for support. In most instances, the dependents' support will derive, at least in part, from the decedent's wages. But, when a tort-feasor has already fully compensated the decedent, during his lifetime, for his loss of future wages, the tort-feasor should not be required to make further compensation in a subsequent wrongful death suit for any portion of previously paid wages. Any potential for such double liability can be eliminated by the application of familiar principles of collateral estoppel to preclude a decedent's dependents from attempting to relitigate the issue of the support due from decedent's future wages.[6] * * *

Under the prevailing American rule, a tort victim suing for damages for permanent injuries is permitted to base his recovery "on his prospective earnings for the balance of his life expectancy at the time of his injury *undiminished by any shortening of that expectancy as a result of the injury.*" 2 F. Harper & F. James, The Law of Torts § 24.6, pp. 1293–1294 (1956) (emphasis in original).[7] Thus, when a decedent brings his own personal injury action during his lifetime and recovers damages for his lost wages he acts in a fiduciary capacity to the extent that he represents his dependents' interest in that portion of his prospective earnings which, but for his wrongful death, they had a reasonable expectation of his providing for their support. Since the decedent's recovery of any future wages will normally be dependent upon his fully litigating that issue, we need not fear that applying principles of collateral estoppel to preclude the decedent's dependents' claim for a portion of those future wages will deprive the dependents of their day in court.

Affirmed.

JUSTICE POWELL, with whom THE CHIEF JUSTICE, JUSTICE STEWART, and JUSTICE REHNQUIST join, dissenting. * * * In holding that a wrongful death action may be brought although the decedent has previously recovered in his own suit based on the same wrongful act, the Court disregards a major body of maritime and state law. The majority opinion also opens up an area of sentimental damages that has not been allowed under traditional admiralty doctrine. It hopes to prevent double recovery through a novel application of collateral estoppel principles, which rests in turn on the unprecedented concept that a

6. If the dependents' total support received from the decedent exceeds the future wages paid to the decedent by the tort-feasor, the dependents will have an actionable cause for support against the tort-feasor for the difference. In that circumstance, if a special verdict was not rendered in the decedent's action specifying the amount of damages awarded for future wages, it may become necessary in the dependents' action to determine what portion of the decedent's lump sum recovery for his injuries was attributable to future wages. This in no way conflicts with our holding that the dependents will be estopped from relitigating the amount of future wages; it is merely an acknowledgement that the amount of the wage recovery in the first action may have to be clarified in the second.

7. This rule appears to have been rejected in England in favor of compensating a personal injury victim on the basis of his life expectancy *after* the accident. See Oliver v. Ashman, 3 Weekly L.R. 699 (CA 1961); Fleming, The Lost Years: A Problem in the Computation and Distribution of Damages, 50 Calif.L.Rev. 598, 600 (1962). Under the English rule, the accident victim is not permitted to recover lost wages for the difference in years between his preaccident and postaccident life expectancy.

seriously injured person acts as a fiduciary for an undefined class of potential beneficiaries with regard to his *own* recovery in his *own* personal injury action. Given the sweep of the majority's approach, the upshot in many areas will be a nearly total nullification of the congressional enactments previously governing maritime wrongful death. Except for a technical joinder of counts to obtain a jury and thus to maximize the benefits promised by the Court's opinion no one entitled to rely on the admiralty doctrine of unseaworthiness will, after today, seek relief under the federal maritime wrongful death statutes. Several limitations built into those congressional enactments have been swept aside by the majority's decision.

Notes

1. Miles v. Apex Marine Corp., 111 S.Ct. 317, 324–28 (1990). Torregano, the deceased seaman, was survived only by non-dependent parents. Two specific questions were posed:

a. When neither spouse nor child survives, may the seaman's nondependent parents recover for loss of his society?

No. Recovery is limited to pecuniary loss; recovery for nonpecuniary loss like loss of society is cut off.

b. May the decedent's estate recover the victim's lost future income?

No. In most states this loss is not recoverable in survival actions since it duplicates the dependent's recovery in wrongful death. Federal statutes limit "recovery to losses suffered during the decedent's lifetime."

2. The *Gaudet–Moragne* approach led state courts to experiment with the elements of wrongful death claims; the reader will observe the citations in the decisions that follow. Is the Supreme Court's period of judicial "creativity" over?

Probably: "Maritime tort law is now dominated by federal statute, and we are not free to expand remedies at will simply because it might work to the benefit of seamen and those dependent upon them. Congress has placed limits on recovery in survival actions that we cannot exceed." Miles v. Apex Marine Corp., 111 S.Ct. 317, 327–28 (1990).

The line is drawn. At the federal level at least.

ALFONE v. SARNO

Supreme Court of New Jersey, 1981.
87 N.J. 99, 432 A.2d 857.

[Departing from 80 years of precedent dictating that maintaining a wrongful death action depends upon the decedent's right to sue for his own injuries at the time of his death, the Supreme Court of New Jersey joined the "minority" of states mentioned in footnote 2 to Sea–Land Services, Inc. v. Gaudet. As in *Sea–Land* a wrongful death action is permitted even though the decedent had obtained a judgment for personal injuries during his lifetime. The court now confronts the possibility of a double recovery.]

PASHMAN, J. In attempting to preserve the beneficiaries' rights under a wrongful death statute, some courts have either ignored or brushed aside the double liability problem. [citations] * * * Other courts have allowed this problem so to confound the statutory rights of wrongful death beneficiaries as to wipe them out completely. In order to avoid double liability, these courts have viewed the wrongful death claim as totally derivative of the decedent's right to sue and therefore barred whenever the decedent either settled or pursued to judgment his own personal injury claim.

In Sea–Land Services v. Gaudet, the United States Supreme Court attempted to resolve the double liability problem. * * * The Court believed that "application of familiar principles of collateral estoppel" would eliminate the potential for double liability. Writing for the Court, Justice Brennan reasoned that collateral estoppel was appropriate because in recovering for his injuries the decedent acted in a fiduciary capacity for those who later brought the wrongful death action.

We do not agree with the formal notion of trusteeship suggested by *Gaudet.* "[A]s trustee the plaintiff in the personal injury action would have to assert not only his own claim but that of his prospective beneficiaries, on penalty of precluding the latter if he did not." Restatement (Second) of Judgments § 92.1, Reporter's Note at 57 (Tent. Draft No. 3, 1976). The question of what duties the injured party as trustee would have towards the potential wrongful death beneficiaries demonstrates that this concept causes more problems than it resolves.

We find none of the approaches taken in the cases described here satisfactory. * * * The troublesome problem of devising a method to avoid potential duplicate damages should not cause this Court to shy away from preserving the rights created by the statute. * * *

The general rule for maintenance of the wrongful death action must be that no elements of damages may be sought or recovered that were or could have been claimed in the earlier personal injury action. * * *

Of course, there are elements of damages recoverable in the wrongful death action that present no danger of double liability. The obvious example is funeral expenses. Another non-duplicative element of damages may be lost advice and guidance, such as that of a parent to a child. We need not decide today precisely which other elements present no danger of double liability; that decision can await future cases.

However, strict application of this rule would inject a different kind of unfairness in many cases where the decedent could not have sought certain elements of damages in his own action simply because those damages were not discoverable at that time. Considerations of fairness toward the survivors, who have suffered a loss at the hands of a wrongdoer, and the desire to fulfill the beneficent purposes of the wrongful death statute impel us to temper the severity of our general rule with an exception. Where the extent of injuries causing death was not reasonably discoverable at the time of the decedent's suit, the wrongful death plaintiff may pursue elements of damages that technically could have been but in fact were not recovered in the earlier action.

In many wrongful death actions, the major element of recovery for the survivors is the lost benefits that would have come out of the decedent's prospective earnings. It is this element that poses the greatest risk of duplication of recovery. Consequently, our rule limiting the wrongful death recovery to damages that were clearly not awarded in the personal injury action will usually require that this portion of the survivors' recovery be restricted to the lowest amount that the proofs in the earlier action show decedent would have earned between the date of his actual death and the end of his life expectancy.

That amount is subtracted by the personal injury jury in arriving at its damages award. Therefore, assuming due diligence by the decedent in investigating his injuries, the availability of that amount to the survivors poses no risk of double liability. It was "clearly not awarded" and "not reasonably discoverable" in the personal injury action.

An examination of the record in the personal injury action will enable the trial court in the wrongful death action to ascertain with a high degree of probability the lowest amount that could have constituted these post-injury (and post-death) earnings. The trial judge should determine the lowest amount admitted into evidence by either party in the personal injury action as decedent's likely post-injury earnings. Absent unusual circumstances or the failure of the decedent to have investigated his injuries diligently, the portion of that figure which represents decedent's post-injury earnings cut off by his premature death should be the amount the wrongful death plaintiffs may seek as the major source of their pecuniary losses allowed by the wrongful death statute.

In many cases payment by the defendant of even this limited amount will be unfair in the sense that the defendant may already have paid excessive future pain and suffering and medical expenses. We believe that fairness to the survivors requires us to disregard this inequity. It does not constitute double liability but is merely an unavoidable consequence of our tort system's policy of repose, which prevents us from correcting a verdict based upon events that occur thereafter.

The trial judge need not attempt to decipher what specific elements of compensation comprised the earlier jury award. Since the award usually takes the form of a single figure in dollars, such a task would often be no more than speculation and conjecture. Instead, the focus of the trial court's inquiry at the hearing will be what the decedent, assuming the exercise of due diligence, could reasonably have claimed in the earlier personal injury action.

The easier cases will be those where the discoverable injuries at the time of the earlier action were either very mild or very serious. If the decedent could have reasonably sought only minor damages previously because the injury seemed slight, the wrongful death plaintiff should be able to claim further damages normally available in a wrongful death action. If the decedent's original injuries were known to be extremely serious, however, the wrongful death plaintiff should be barred from claiming damages that the decedent could have sought himself. The difficult cases will be those in the middle, where it is not obvious what damages the decedent could have reasonably sought because the original injuries were neither slight nor extreme.

To conduct the hearing, plaintiff ordinarily must make available to the judge a transcript of the personal injury trial, including jury instructions and counsel's arguments. Within his discretion, the judge may decide whether the transcript, other documentary evidence or affidavits or certifications are sufficiently informative to make the determinations required. If not, he may require that further proofs, including the testimony of witnesses, be presented at the hearing. These proofs should show what damages the decedent could not reasonably have claimed in the earlier action because the injuries causing such damages were not discoverable. In making his decision, the primary concern of the judge must be fairness to both parties—avoiding the potential for double liability by the defendant and providing a means of redress to the plaintiff where it was not practically available through the earlier action.

The same procedures must be followed where the personal injury claim did not proceed to judgment but was settled or released. Because a trial transcript will not be available, the trial judge must examine the settlement agreement or release itself. We anticipate that settlement agreements in the future will clearly indicate what elements of damages the injured person is recovering and from what elements defendant has been released. A valid written settlement agreement specifically reciting what losses were compensated will be binding on the wrongful death parties on the issue of what damages can be claimed subsequently.[1] General recitals in a settlement agreement will be given such weight as the circumstances suggest they should be given; they will not be conclusive and will be binding on the parties only to the extent they reflect losses actually compensated pursuant to the agreement and discoverable claims actually relinquished in consideration of the settlement.

We recognize that our decision today may prevent insurance carriers from obtaining complete releases from all possible wrongful death claims, except perhaps by the inclusion in any such agreement of all persons who subsequently are determined to be wrongful death beneficiaries under N.J.S.A. 2A:31–4. The policy favoring settlement and finality of claims, cannot defeat statutory rights created for the protection of survivors of one wrongfully killed. In any event, insurance carriers will be able to obtain releases from a substantial part of their potential liability. Thus we see no insurmountable conflict between the policy favoring settlement and our decision today.

As a final note it might be prudent to add that we are well aware that the rules and procedures we have established today are not the final answer to the difficulties presented by these issues.

Notes

1. The two preceding decisions reject the majority rule that the decedent's right, at the time of death, to maintain an action is an essential prerequisite for a wrongful death action. Weinberg v. Johns–Manville Sales Corp., 299 Md. 225, 473 A.2d 22 (1984), restates the majority rule.

Problem: Suppose the jury in a wrongful death case finds that deceased was 50% negligent. Should the beneficiaries be barred from recovering anything in a state with the contributory negligence rule? What would be the effect in a state with the comparative negligence rule? Cf. Bevan v. Vassar Farms, 117 Idaho 1038, 793 P.2d 711 (1990).

2. *Special Features of Wrongful Death Damages*

a. *Pain and Suffering.* Most survival or combination survival-wrongful death statutes allow for the pain and suffering in the interval between accident and death. S. Speiser, Recovery for Wrongful Death § 14.5 (2d ed. 1975). Instantaneous death presumably excludes such damages, but the time period may be remarkably short. See, e.g., Wiggins v. Lane & Co., 298 F.Supp. 194 (E.D. La.1969) where a jury returned a verdict for $10,000 for pain and suffering for 1.76 seconds, but the parties settled before a motion for remittitur was acted upon. The opinion reviews

1. [Footnote renumbered.] For example, if the terms of a settlement recite that plaintiff has received from defendant $10,000, which figure represents a compromise, for 20% loss of earnings over the next five years, the wrongful death survivors are precluded from recovering those damages.

other awards for short periods of pain and suffering and questions the concept if instantaneous death, referring to suggestions of death "as process rather than an event." In passing, the opinion also intimates contrary to the usual holdings that consciousness must accompany the pain and suffering.

In Solomon v. Warren, 540 F.2d 777 (5th Cir.1976), reh'g denied, 545 F.2d 1298 (1977), cert. dismissed, 434 U.S. 801 (1977), $10,000 was allowed for the deceased's pain and suffering during the time *before* the impact that caused instantaneous death. It was permissible to infer that the four people aboard the airplane were aware of impending death because the pilot radioed plans to ditch it at sea.

Shatkin v. McDonnell Douglas Corp., 727 F.2d 202 (2d Cir.1984), cautions that even if pre-impact pain and suffering is allowed, it must be supported by reasonable evidence that it existed. The decedent in *Shatkin* was on the right side of the plane, and the problem began with an engine on the left; there was no evidence from which a jury could infer that the deceased knew the plane was in trouble. In another case from the same crash, Dr. Lin was sitting over the left wing where he no doubt saw the left engine fall off. His administrator recovered $10,000 for the three seconds of pre-impact conscious pain and suffering that the jury could infer Dr. Lin experienced. Shu–Tao Lin v. McDonnell Douglas Corp., 742 F.2d 45 (2d Cir.1984).

Question: Is it permissible to infer that a motorcyclist sustained pre-impact fear and apprehension during the five-second interval between the time the brakes locked and death? See, Nelson v. Dolan, 230 Neb. 848, 434 N.W.2d 25 (1989).

b. *Funeral Expenses.* Most jurisdictions allow reasonable funeral expenses in wrongful death actions, with or without express statutory authorization. A minority accepts the argument that funeral expenses would have been incurred eventually anyway and that the tortfeasor accelerated the inevitable. S. Speiser, Recovery for Wrongful Death § 3.58 (2d ed. 1975) questions the defense tactic of vigorously opposing this item.

c. *Allocation of Settlement Awards Among Beneficiaries.* The problem of allocating the judgment among multiple beneficiaries is present under statutes effecting unitary awards. Where lump sum *settlements* have been reached between the personal representative and the tortfeasor, litigation over the division may still result. For a court-evolved allocation of proceeds see Horsford v. Estate of Horsford, 561 P.2d 722 (Alaska 1977).

d. *Death of Beneficiary Before Trial.* In jurisdictions where the wrongful death act is of the "loss to beneficiaries" type, the prospective contributions a beneficiary may receive are of course, limited to the life expectancy of the beneficiary or the decedent whichever happens to be shorter.

Suppose the beneficiary, a widow with a life expectancy of 40 years, sues for the death of her husband who had an equal life expectancy. Unfortunately she dies before trial. Should the award to her estate include the contributions she would have received from her spouse over her projected life expectancy—or should it be limited to the actual period of her survival?

In Schneider v. Baisch, 256 N.W.2d 370 (N.D.1977), the court limited the award to the *actual length* of survival. The dissent posed an hypothetical based on the assumption that the beneficiary is survived by a child. Had the beneficiary lived beyond the completion of the wrongful death trial, the child would have inherited her estate including loss of benefits over her lifetime. Her unprovidential death a few days earlier would leave the child with a minimal inheritance. "Why should the defendant have [the] windfall [or 'undue profit']?" Is there an answer to this question?

Is *Schneider* consistent with the general rule that evidence of the beneficiary's remarriage is inadmissable?

e. *Punitive Damages.* Punitive damages depend upon the wrongful death statute. The disparity among the states emerges most graphically after airplane disasters when determinations of the applicable law put enormous sums at risk. In re Air Crash Disaster Near Chicago, 644 F.2d 594 (7th Cir.), cert. denied, 454 U.S. 878 (1981), is an example. Potential choices of law included: Illinois, no punitives; California, no punitives; Oklahoma, punitives; New York, no punitives; Texas, punitives; Missouri, allowed in certain circumstances; Puerto Rico, no punitives; and Hawaii, no punitives. The court chose Illinois law.

Actions under survival statutes are more likely to result in punitive damages; but many statutes expressly deny them. E.g., Cal.Prob.Code § 573; N.Y. Est. Powers & Trust Law § 11–3.2 (McKinney's 1986). Punitive damages have been awarded under the survival features of *general* maritime law. Complaint of Merry Shipping, Inc., 650 F.2d 622 (5th Cir.1981).

Courts have rejected arguments that the denial of punitive damages for wrongful death while permitting them in personal injury actions violates the equal protection clauses of the federal and state constitutions. In re Paris Air Crash, 622 F.2d 1315 (9th Cir.1980), cert. denied, 449 U.S. 976 (1980).

f. *Prejudgment Interest.* The disparate practices concerning prejudgment (moratory) interest on damage awards in wrongful death cases are reviewed in S. Speiser, Recovery for Wrongful Death § 8.6 (2d ed. 1975). Most jurisdictions continue to follow the common law rule and disallow interest on "unliquidated" tort claims; but a sizable number have modified their position. In the latter jurisdictions, pay attention to whether the interest is required or discretionary and to whether the court or the jury includes it. Because wrongful death actions are statutory, authority to add prejudgment interest must rest on express provisions or inferences drawn from related legislative enactments.

The size of verdicts and the delay in obtaining final judgments in major catastrophes emphasize the importance of prejudgment interest and choice of law. In Berner v. British Commonwealth Pacific Airlines, Ltd., 230 F.Supp. 240 (S.D.N.Y.1964), the date of death was Oct. 29, 1953; a jury verdict of $924,396 damages was awarded approximately ten years later. The question whether New York law (mandatory prejudgment interest) or California law (no prejudgment interest) applied; it was resolved in favor (?) of the California rule. Consider the sum involved. Now forget it because the verdict was later reversed on the issue of liability. Berner v. British Commonwealth Pacific Airlines, Ltd., 346 F.2d 532 (2d Cir.1965).

Shu–Tao Lin v. McDonnell Douglas Corp., 742 F.2d 45, 52 (2d Cir.1984). The question was whether to allow prejudgment interest on the portion of a wrongful death award for lost future income—discounted to present value: "Were prejudgment interest applied to the component of the award intended to compensate plaintiff for post-judgment losses, plaintiffs would effectively receive a double recovery. Finding no basis for such double recovery, we hold prejudgment interest is limited under New York law to losses suffered between the date of death and the entry of judgment."

g. The majority rule excludes evidence of possible or actual remarriage of the surviving plaintiff in death actions. Is this simply an application of the collateral source rule? Avoidable consequences rule? Might the practice amount to "punitive" damages if the Federal Tort Claims Act applies? See *Flannery,* supra, p. 688. Many courts frown on the defense tactic of asking the present name of the widow-plaintiff. This maneuver may have a lessened impact anyway because of the changing style in female surnames. Wood v. Detroit Edison, 409 Mich. 279, 294 N.W.2d 571 (1980).

NORFOLK and WESTERN RAILWAY v. LIEPELT

United States Supreme Court, 1980.
444 U.S. 490.

JUSTICE STEVENS delivered the opinion of the Court. In 1973, a fireman employed by petitioner suffered fatal injuries in a collision caused by petitioner's negligence. Respondent, as administratrix of the fireman's estate, brought suit under the FELA to recover the damages that his survivors suffered as a result of his death. In 1976, after a full trial in the Circuit Court of Cook County, the jury awarded respondent $775,000. On appeal, the Appellate Court of Illinois held that it was "not error to refuse to instruct a jury as to the nontaxability of an award" and also that it "[was] not error to exclude evidence of the effect of income taxes on future earnings of the decedent." The Illinois Supreme Court denied leave to appeal.

The evidence supporting the damages award included biographical data about the decedent and his family and the expert testimony of an economist. The decedent, a 37-year-old man, was living with his second wife and two young children and was contributing to the support of two older children by his first marriage. His gross earnings in the 11 months prior to his death on November 22, 1973, amounted to $11,988. Assuming continued employment, those earnings would have amounted to $16,828.26 in 1977.

The expert estimated that the decedent's earnings would have increased at a rate of approximately five percent per year, which would have amounted to $51,600 in the year 2000, the year of his expected retirement. The gross amount of those earnings, plus the value of the services he would have performed for his family, less the amounts the decedent would have spent upon himself, produced a total which, when discounted to present value at the time of trial, amounted to $302,000.

Petitioner objected to the use of gross earnings, without any deduction for income taxes, in respondent's expert's testimony and offered to prove through the testimony of its own expert, an actuary, that decedent's federal income taxes during the years 1973 through 2000 would have amounted to about $57,000. Taking that figure into account, and making different assumptions about the rate of future increases in salary and the calculation of the present value of future earnings, petitioner's expert computed the net pecuniary loss at $138,327. As already noted, the jury returned a verdict of $775,000.

Petitioner argues that the jury must have assumed that its award was subject to federal income taxation; otherwise, it is argued, the verdict would not have exceeded respondent's expert's opinion by such a large amount.[1] For that reason, petitioner contends that it was prejudiced by the trial judge's refusal to instruct the jury that "your award will not be subject to any income taxes, and you should not consider such taxes in fixing the amount of your award."

1. [Footnotes renumbered.] Respondent argues that the excess is adequately explained by the jury's estimate of the pecuniary value of the guidance, instruction, and training that the decedent would have provided to his children.

Whether it was error to refuse that instruction, as well as the question whether evidence concerning the federal taxes on the decedent's earnings was properly excluded, is a matter governed by federal law. It has long been settled that questions concerning the measure of damages in an FELA action are federal in character.

* * * The amount of money that a wage earner is able to contribute to the support of his family is unquestionably affected by the amount of the tax he must pay to the Federal Government. It is his after-tax income, rather than his gross income before taxes, that provides the only realistic measure of his ability to support his family. It follows inexorably that the wage earner's income tax is a relevant factor in calculating the monetary loss suffered by his dependents when he dies.

Although federal courts have consistently received evidence of the amount of the decedent's personal expenditures, [citations] and have required that the estimate of future earnings be reduced by "taking account of the earning power of the money that is presently to be awarded," Chesapeake & Ohio R. Co. v. Kelly, supra, 241 U.S., at 489, they have generally not considered the payment of income taxes as tantamount to a personal expenditure and have regarded the future prediction of tax consequences as too speculative and complex for a jury's deliberations. [citations]

Admittedly there are many variables that may affect the amount of a wage earner's future income-tax liability. The law may change, his family may increase or decrease in size, his spouse's earnings may affect his tax bracket, and extra income or unforeseen deductions may become available. But future employment itself, future health, future personal expenditures, future interest rates, and future inflation are also matters of estimate and prediction. Any one of these issues might provide the basis for protracted expert testimony and debate. But the practical wisdom of the trial bar and the trial bench has developed effective methods of presenting the essential elements of an expert calculation in a form that is understandable by juries that are increasingly familiar with the complexities of modern life. We therefore reject the notion that the introduction of evidence describing a decedent's estimated after-tax earnings is too speculative or complex for a jury.[2]

Respondent argues that if this door is opened, other equally relevant evidence must also be received. For example, she points out that in discounting the estimate of future earnings to its present value, the tax on the income to be earned by the damages award is now omitted. Logically, it would certainly seem correct that this amount, like future wages, should be estimated on an after-tax basis. But the fact that such an after-tax estimate, if offered in proper form, would also be admissible does not persuade us that it is wrong to use after-tax figures instead of gross earnings in projecting what the decedent's financial contributions to his survivors would have been had this tragic accident not occurred.

Section 104(a)(2) of the Internal Revenue Code, provides that the amount of any damages received on account of personal injuries is not taxable income.

2. This is not to say, however, that introduction of such evidence must be permitted in every case. If the impact of future income tax in calculating the award would be *de minimis,* introduction of the evidence may cause more confusion than it is worth. Cf. Fed.Rule Evid. 403.

The section is construed to apply to wrongful-death awards; they are not taxable income to the recipient.

Although the law is perfectly clear, it is entirely possible that the members of the jury may assume that a plaintiff's recovery in a case of this kind will be subject to federal taxation, and that the award should be increased substantially in order to be sure that the injured party is fully compensated. Judge Aldisert, writing for the Third Circuit, agreed:

> "We take judicial notice of the 'tax consciousness' of the American public. Yet, we also recognize, as did the court in Dempsey v. Thompson, 363 Mo. 339, 251 S.W.2d 42 (1952), that few members of the general public are aware of the special statutory exception for personal injury awards contained in the Internal Revenue Code.
>
> " '[T]here is always danger that today's tax-conscious juries may assume (mistakenly of course) that the judgment will be taxable and therefore make their verdict big enough so that plaintiff would get what they think he deserves after the imaginary tax is taken out of it.' II Harper & James, The Law of Torts § 25.12, at 1327–28 (1956)."

Domeracki v. Humble Oil & Refining Co., 443 F.2d 1245, 1251 (1971), cert. denied, 404 U.S. 883.

In this case the respondent's expert witness computed the amount of pecuniary loss at $302,000, plus the value of the care and training that decedent would have provided to his young children; the jury awarded damages of $775,000. It is surely not fanciful to suppose that the jury erroneously believed that a large portion of the award would be payable to the Federal Government in taxes, and that therefore it improperly inflated the recovery. Whether or not this speculation is accurate, we agree with petitioner that, as Judge Ely wrote for the Ninth Circuit,

> "[to] put the matter simply, giving the instruction can do no harm, and it can certainly help by preventing the jury from inflating the award and thus overcompensating the plaintiff on the basis of an erroneous assumption that the judgment will be taxable."

Burlington Northern, Inc. v. Boxberger, 529 F.2d 284, 297 (1975).

We hold that it was error to refuse the requested instruction in this case. * * *

The judgment is reversed, and the case is remanded to the Appellate Court of Illinois.

JUSTICE BLACKMUN, with whom JUSTICE MARSHALL joins, dissenting. * * * In my view, by mandating adjustment of the award by way of reduction for federal income taxes that would have been paid by the decedent on his earnings, the Court appropriates for the tortfeasor a benefit intended to be conferred on the victim or his survivors. And in requiring that the jury be instructed that a wrongful-death award is not subject to federal income tax, the Court opens the door for a variety of admonitions to the jury not to "misbehave," and unnecessarily interjects what is now to be federal law into the administration of a trial in a state court.

In this day of substantial income taxes, one is sorely tempted, in jury litigation, to accept the propriety of admitting evidence as to a tort victim's earnings *net* after estimated income taxes, and of instructing the jury that an award will be tax-free. This, it could be urged, is only common sense and a recognition of financial realities.

Ordinarily, however, the effect of an income tax upon the recipient of a payment is of no real or ultimate concern to the payer. Apart from required withholding, it just is not the payer's responsibility or, indeed, "any of his business." The concept of "net after taxes" and the omnipresence of the tax collector, to be sure, are present facts of life and are within the constant awareness of both recipient and payer. But these factors do not change the basic character of an award for damages, whether that award be one to compensate the surviving victim for his injury, or one to compensate the deceased victim's survivors, by way of statutory wrongful-death benefit, for their loss. The income tax effect should flow and be retained in its own channel. Surely, it should not operate to assist the tortfeasor by way of a benefit, perhaps even a windfall. * * *

The Court concludes that, as a matter of federal law, the jury in a FELA case must be instructed, on request, that the damages award is not taxable. This instruction is mandated, it is said, because "it is entirely possible that the members of the jury may assume that a plaintiff's recovery * * * will be subject to federal taxation, and that the award should be increased substantially in order to be sure that the injured party is fully compensated." * * *

It also is "entirely possible" that the jury "may" increase its damages award in the belief that the defendant is insured, or that the plaintiff will be obligated for substantial attorney's fees, or that the award is subject to state (as well as federal) income tax, or on the basis of any number of other extraneous factors. Charging the jury about every conceivable matter as to which it should not misbehave or miscalculate would be burdensome and could be confusing. Yet the Court's decision today opens the door to that possibility. * * *

Notes

1. *Liepelt* governs wrongful death actions arising under federal law. In diversity cases, however, the federal courts must follow state substantive rules. State law is sharply divided. New York, for example, dictates that in wrongful death cases neither social security nor income taxes should be considered in determining lost future income. In other words the sum is gross rather than net after taxes. Woodling v. Garrett Corp., 813 F.2d 543 (2d Cir.1987). Other states adopt, or a federal court assumes would adopt, the Restatement (Second) of Torts § 914A (1977).

Lux v. McDonnell Douglas Corp. (In re Air Crash Disaster Near Chicago, Illinois, on May 25, 1979), 803 F.2d 304, 310–11 (7th Cir.1986): "Divining in the absence of any relevant authority how a state's highest court would rule ordinarily would be as exact as foretelling the future from the flight of birds; however, in this case we have been spared such an exercise. The Arizona Supreme Court has repeatedly reaffirmed that, in the absence of a controlling statute or precedent, it will follow the Restatement of the Law whenever it is applicable. * * *

"The Restatement's position on the admissibility of evidence of income taxes in wrongful death suits is clear. In its comment to the section entitled Effect of Taxation on tort awards, the Restatement provides that:

" 'When the injured party dies and action is brought under a wrongful death statute, the problem before the court [concerning whether to admit evidence of income taxes] is not the same [as it is in personal injury cases]. In the majority of states, the recovery of the statutory beneficiaries is measured by the contributions that the deceased would have made to them if he had lived. * * * This amount obviously could not be equivalent to his gross earnings, as he could not have given them funds that he spent on himself or paid in taxes or used for other purposes; and an appropriate percentage of his expected earnings, taking into consideration these various types of expenditures, is proper.' Restatement (Second) of Torts § 914A comment b.

"The Restatement thus would allow evidence of the decedent's income taxes to reduce the survivors' pecuniary damages whenever a state's wrongful death statute measures damages by the amount that the decedent would have contributed to the survivors."

The *Liepelt* Court also considered whether the jury should be instructed that damages are not taxable. State law again varies. But giving or withholding an instruction may be "procedural" rather than substantive; the federal court in a diversity case may be free from state court rulings. Lux v. McDonnell Douglas Corp. (In re Air Crash Disaster Near Chicago, Illinois, on May 25, 1979), 803 F.2d 304, 315 (7th Cir.1986).

2. Hollinger v. United States, 651 F.2d 636 (9th Cir.1981), interprets *Liepelt* to entitle a prevailing FTCA plaintiff to recover, in addition to the lump-sum award, an amount sufficient to compensate for taxes on the income that would be earned by investing the award.

"The interest that Hollinger will earn on the discounted principal in a safe investment, however, will also be taxable. The effective interest rate for an investor is equal to the stated interest rate reduced by the product of the stated interest rate and the investor's tax rate. The principal amount necessary to produce a given after tax yield per month is the principal amount that would be necessary to produce that amount if there were no tax divided by the percentage of his income that the investor retains after taxes. Thus an award of $600,000, not taking the tax on interest into effect, would be increased to $1,000,000 for a 40% tax bracket recipient. Clearly, then, the possible adjustments involved in taking this aspect of taxes into account are significant."

KROUSE v. GRAHAM

Supreme Court of California, 1977.
19 Cal.3d 59, 137 Cal.Rptr. 863, 562 P.2d 1022.

[Elizabeth Krouse was killed as a result of defendant's negligence. Her husband and five children sued for wrongful death. The trial court awarded $300,000 to be divided amongst them.]

RICHARDSON, JUSTICE. The Krouse plaintiffs introduced extensive evidence showing that Elizabeth was a warm and devoted mother. At the time of her death she was 56 years old, had been healthy, and was an active homemaker who had recently retired as a legal secretary in order to care for her husband, Benjamin, whose condition of emphysema, in turn, caused him to retire and necessitated considerable nursing services. Elizabeth had the primary responsibility for maintaining the family home and garden and for attending to a minor son who resided at home. Trial testimony indicated that the minor son was totally dependent upon Elizabeth for the comforts and conveniences usually afforded by a mother to a youth of his age. The evidence also disclosed a high degree of family socializing, including Elizabeth's care of her grandchildren.

(a) *Award of "Nonpecuniary" Damages to Benjamin.* The jury was instructed that Benjamin could recover "reasonable compensation" for the loss of his wife's "love, companionship, comfort, affection, society, solace or moral support, any loss of enjoyment of sexual relations, or any loss of her physical assistance in the operation or maintenance of the home." Subsequent instructions, not challenged on appeal by defendant, further advised the jury that the Krouse plaintiffs could recover "just compensation for the pecuniary loss" each of them suffered by reason of Elizabeth's death, including "the pecuniary value of the society, comfort, protection, and right to receive support, if any," which plaintiffs may have lost by reason of her death.

Defendant asserts that the initial instruction improperly allowed Benjamin to recover damages for "nonpecuniary" losses. As we explain below, however, for the past century California courts have uniformly allowed wrongful death recovery for loss of the society, comfort, care and protection afforded by the decedent, despite the courts' insistence that only "pecuniary" losses are compensable. Accordingly, the challenged instruction listing comparable nonpecuniary losses was not erroneous.

The statutory cause of action for wrongful death, created in California in 1862, provided that "pecuniary or exemplary" damages were to be awarded by the jury in the amount found "just" under all the circumstances. Ten years after its enactment, the statute was amended to remove the words "pecuniary or exemplary," retaining the language that "damages may be given as under all the circumstances of the case, may be just. * * * " (Code Civ.Proc., § 377.) Nonetheless, in subsequent decisional law a theory developed that damages for wrongful death were recoverable only for the "pecuniary" losses suffered by the decedent's heirs.

California case law, however, has not restricted wrongful death recovery only to those elements with an ascertainable economic value, such as loss of household services or earning capacity. On the contrary, as early as 1911, we held that damages could be recovered for the loss of a decedent's "society, comfort, and protection" [citation] though only the "pecuniary value" of these losses was held to be a proper element of recovery. Other cases have held admissible such evidence as the closeness of the family unit [citation], the warmth of feeling between family members and the character of the deceased as "kind and attentive" or "kind and loving" [citation]. Not only was wrongful death compensation awarded historically to heirs who had been financially dependent upon their deceased relatives, but adult children received substantial awards for the wrongful death of retired, elderly parents and parents received compensatory damages for the death of young children [citation]. These cases suggest a realization that if damages truly were limited to "pecuniary" loss, recovery frequently would be barred by the heirs' inability to prove such loss. The services of children, elderly parents, or nonworking spouses often do not result in measurable net income to the family unit, yet unquestionably the death of such a person represents a substantial "injury" to the family for which just compensation should be paid.

Two earlier opinions discussing the loss of society, comfort, care and protection, disclose the rationale underlying the "pecuniary value" limitation. In Bond v. United Railroads, 159 Cal. 270, 113 P. 366, we explained: "The rule that allowance may be made for pecuniary loss from deprivation of society, comfort, and protection of a son is apparently settled and cannot now be disturbed. It is evident to us, however, from the cases that have come before us, that it often leads to extravagant verdicts in which the jury, in fact, allow a supposed compensation *for sad emotions and injured feelings,* instead of confining their verdict to the actual pecuniary loss. * * * Juries should be insistently cautioned not to allow compensation for the sorrow and distress which always ensues from such a death, * * * " A similar concern was echoed in Ure v. Maggio Bros. Co., Inc., 24 Cal.App.2d 490, 75 P.2d 534, in which the court in these words warned that juries may be awarding damages for grief and sorrow instead of limiting recovery to the properly compensable elements of support, society, comfort, care and protection: " 'But while loss of society and comfort, and protection may be an element of the injury sustained by the statutory beneficiaries, it is only the pecuniary, and not the sentimental, value of such loss which may be taken into consideration in the assessment of damages. Nothing can be recovered as a solatium for wounded feelings. * * *' "

While the cases uniformly have held that a wrongful death recovery may not include such elements as the grief or sorrow attendant upon the death of a loved one, it is both unnecessary and unwise to require a pecuniary loss instruction for the sole purpose of excluding these elements from jury consideration. To direct the jury, on the one hand, to limit plaintiff's recovery to pecuniary losses alone while also compensating the plaintiff for loss of such nonpecuniary factors as the society, comfort, care and protection of a decedent is calculated to mislead and invite confusion. Instead, a simple instruction excluding considerations of grief and sorrow in wrongful death actions will normally suffice.

We think it significant that the United States Supreme Court (announcing the rule under maritime law) permits recovery in a wrongful death action for the loss of such elements as comfort, love or affection without any accompanying requirement that such loss be deemed to be pecuniary in nature. (Sea-Land Services, Inc. v. Gaudet).

* * * It is greatly persuasive with us that in doing so the Supreme Court interpreted the term "society" as including "a broad range of mutual benefits each family member received from the others' continued existence, including love, affection, care, attention, companionship, comfort, and protection."

We note that in California those elements of recovery sought by Benjamin Krouse herein clearly would be available to him as "consortium" damages in the usual personal injury action for his wife's injuries. (See Rodriguez v. Bethlehem Steel Corp. (1974) 12 Cal.3d 382, 115 Cal.Rptr. 765, 525 P.2d 669.) As we explained in *Rodriguez,* " 'The concept of consortium includes not only loss of support or services, * * * [but also] such elements as love, companionship, affection, society, sexual relations, solace and more.' " * * *

[Reversed because of errors in unrelated jury instructions.]

Notes

1. *Standard California Jury Instruction.* BAJI 14.50 (1986 Revision) Measure of Damages—Death of Adult:

The plaintiff[s] [is] [are] the heirs of ______, deceased, [and] are [the real parties in interest in this action; they are] ______, the widow, [and ______, the child[ren]] of the deceased.

If, you find that plaintiff[s] [is] [are] entitled to recover against the defendant[s], you will award as damages [, economic and non-economic,] such sum as, under all the circumstances of the case, will be just compensation for the loss which each heir has suffered by reason of the death of ______, deceased.

In determining such loss, you may consider the financial support, if any, which each of said heirs would have received from the deceased except for his death, and the right to receive support, if any, which each of said heirs has lost by reason of his death. [This is economic damage.]

[The right of one person to receive support from another is not destroyed by the fact that the former does not need the support, nor by the fact that the latter has not provided it.]

You may also consider:

1. The age of the deceased and of each heir;

2. The health of the deceased and each heir immediately prior to death;

3. The respective life expectancy of the deceased and of each heir;

4. Whether the deceased was kindly, affectionate or otherwise;

5. The disposition of the deceased to contribute financially to support the heirs;

6. The earning capacity of the deceased;

7. His habits of industry and thrift; and

8. Any other facts shown by the evidence indicating what benefits each heir might reasonably have been expected to receive from the deceased had he lived.

With respect to life expectancies, you will only be concerned with the shorter of two, that of an heir or that of the decedent, as one can derive a benefit from the life of another only so long as both are alive.

Also you will award reasonable compensation for the loss of love, companionship, comfort, affection, society, solace or moral support, [any loss of the enjoyment of sexual relations], [any loss of the physical assistance to a spouse in the operation or maintenance of the home]. [This is non-economic damage.]

In determining the loss which each heir has suffered, you are not to consider:

1. Any pain or suffering of the decedent;

2. Any grief or sorrow of his heirs; or

3. The poverty or wealth of any heir.

[Also, you shall include in your award an amount that will compensate for whatever reasonable expense was paid out or incurred for funeral services in memory of the decedent and [or] for burial [disposition] of the body. In determining that amount, you shall consider the decedent's station in life and the financial condition of his estate, as these circumstances have been shown by the evidence.] [This is economic damage.]

2. One way to value the contributions of a parent-spouse who is not employed outside the home is to consider the economic value of the decedent's activity. Haddigan v. Harkins, 441 F.2d 844, 851–52 (3d Cir.1970):

"Mr. Haddigan testified on direct examination that the decedent's services for her family included services each week as a cook, 17½ hours; as a dishwasher, 14 hours; as a dietician, 2 hours; as a baker, 3 hours; as a practical nurse, 1 hour; as a chambermaid, 7 hours; as a manager, 10 hours; as a seamstress, 5 hours; as a hostess, 2 hours; as a housekeeper, 16 hours; as a governess, 20 hours; as a recreation worker, 5 hours; as a handyman, 8 hours; as a laundress, 10 hours; and as a waitress, 5 hours. (This left her 42½ hours a week, or six hours a day for all her other activities including sleeping.) Plaintiff then produced a witness, Rosner, an employment agency proprietor who specializes in placement of domestics, dishwashers, cooks, etc. Rosner was asked, without objection, to give the hourly rates of pay commanded by each of the above mentioned employment categories as of 1963 and as of 1967. Then, totaling the hours and the wages, he valued decedent's services in 1963 at $178.25 a week, and in 1967 at $236.72 a week.

"Expert opinion evidence as to the monetary value of lost services in a wrongful death action has been approved in the federal courts. * * * Preferably admission of such testimony should be followed by a charge that the expert's opinion is only advisory, and that the jury should make its own determination of the economic value of decedent's lost services.

"But, say the defendants, assuming there was evidence, properly admitted, to establish the value of decedent's services, the plaintiff offered little or no evidence of the cost which would have been incurred to maintain her while she performed those services. As one might expect, the attorney for plaintiff was considerably more enthusiastic in establishing the extent and value of the lost services than in establishing the cost of maintenance of decedent. There is, however, ample proof in the record from which the jury could make a fair determination."

3. Another method is to project the earning capacity of the deceased on the open job market. Kirby, The Housewife and the Economist, 11 Trial 63 (1975):

"Households are a production as well as a consumption unit and family consumption may be viewed as a production process. * * * The family that decides the female is to be employed full time in the production of home services has revealed by their preferences they place a higher value upon her home services than her value in the marketplace. * * * A court award for pecuniary damages incurred by a household for the injury or death of a full time housewife that is less than she would receive had she been a full time labor force participant is inconsistent with the revealed preferences of the family and economic reasoning."

See R. Posner, Economic Analysis of Law § 6.11 (1986).

4. *Lost Consortium in Wrongful Death.* This award presumably depends *solely* on the interpretation of the particular wrongful death statute. Some states continue to reject this element of damages. E.g., Liff v. Schildkrout, 49 N.Y.2d 622, 427 N.Y.S.2d 746, 404 N.E.2d 1288 (1980). But, as in this principal case, lost consortium or its essential equivalent is more and more commonly extracted from the general language of the statute. And some courts, witness the next case, apparently disregard the traditional wrongful death act.

Statutory rewrites of the applicable wrongful death act may allow siblings to recover loss of consortium damages. E.g., Crystal v. Hubbard, 414 Mich. 297, 324 N.W.2d 869 (1982). But Clark v. Jones, 658 P.2d 1147 (Okl.1983), held that a 1979 amendment to the Oklahoma wrongful death act, although extending the loss of consortium recovery to the parent-child relationship, did not encompass siblings.

5. *You're the Judge.* During a wrongful death trial, defense counsel rises to cross-examine the plaintiff, the widow of the decedent:

Question: Madam Plaintiff, your counsel in opening statement said that one million dollars would be fair compensation to you for the loss of society and companionship caused by the death of your husband. Would you please tell the court and the jury in what way you would have used, or what way you would use, all or any part of a million dollars, as a *means* to compensate you for your loss?

Plaintiff's Counsel: Objection. Irrelevant!

You're the judge. How do you rule?

Kaufman, Money Damages for Personal Injuries, What's It All About, For the Defense, Oct. 1983, at 28.

DAWSON v. HILL & HILL TRUCK LINES

Supreme Court of Montana, 1983.
206 Mont. 325, 671 P.2d 589.

MORRISON, JUSTICE. By declaratory relief, petitioners request this Court to answer the following question certified by the United States District Court for the District of Montana, Great Falls Division: "Are damages for the sorrow, mental distress or grief of the parents of a deceased minor recoverable in a wrongful death action brought pursuant to section 27–1–512, MCA, 1979?"

This is a wrongful death action arising out of a five-vehicle crash. * * * As a result of the accident, the Dawson's seventeen-year-old son was killed and a daughter was injured.

The deceased was the petitioner's only son. Petitioners allege he was an outstanding individual and student who would have been the valedictorian of his graduating high school class had he lived another four months.

The statute provides: "In every action [for wrongful death], such damages may be given as under all the circumstances of the case may be just."

Montana has not allowed wrongful death awards to be unrestricted. Rather, we have followed the pecuniary loss rule, although recovery is permitted for loss of society and companionship to the extent such loss has a pecuniary value.

The majority of jurisdictions has consistently refused to permit recovery for mental anguish in a wrongful death action. In so doing, these jurisdictions have followed the English decision rendered in Blake v. Midland Railway Co. (Q.B.1852), 118 Eng.Rep. 35. * * *

John Blake was killed when two of the defendant's trains collided. Liability was admitted and the case proceeded to trial on damages. The trial judge instructed the jury that the jury might, in addition to awarding loss of support, also compensate the widow for her emotional pain. The appellate court reversed the plaintiff's judgment, holding that the jury had been improperly instructed on damages. The court stated: "The title of this Act [Lord Campbell's Act] may be some guide to its meaning: and it is 'An Act for Compensating the Families of Persons Killed'; not for solacing their wounded feelings. * * *" The court seemed to feel that a more expansive rule would be impossible for the jury to apply.

The English rule has been followed by most American jurisdictions. See 1 S. Speiser, Recovery for Wrongful Death, (2d Ed.1975), § 3:1.

Blake must be read and understood in its historical context. The social policies existent in 1852 England and which may have influenced the court were traced by the Supreme Court of Michigan in Wycko v. Gnodtke (1960), 361 Mich. 331, 105 N.W.2d 118:

> "The rulings reflect the philosophy of the times, its ideals, and its social conditions. It was the generation of the debtor's prisons, of some 200 or more capital offenses, and of the public flogging of women. It was an era when ample work could be found for the agile bodies and nimble fingers of small children. * * *

"This, then, was the day from which our precedents come, a day when employment of children of tender years was the accepted practice and ther (sic) pecuniary contributions to the family both substantial and provable. * * *

"That this barbarous concept of the pecuniary loss to a parent from the death of his child should control our decisions today is a reproach to justice. We are still turning, actually, for guidance in decision, to 'one of the darkest chapters in the history of childhood.' Yet in other areas of the law the legal and social standards of 1846 are as dead as the coachman and his postilions who guided the coaches of its society through the dark and muddy streets, past the gibbets where still hung the toll of the day's executions."

The English court in *Blake* articulated the rule's rationale to be the certainty of loss estimation. The underpinnings of the rule were discussed by a Federal District judge in In Re Sincere Navigation Corp. (E.D.La.1971), 329 F.Supp. 652:

"Human experience, as well as the literature of psychiatry and psychology bear abundant evidence of the debilitating effect of grief and the resultant depression. It is certainly no less real, and no more difficult to appraise, than the 'mental and physical pain and suffering' attendant upon personal injury that is awarded those who survive, or the pain and suffering prior to death that is recoverable as part of the death action here." (citations omitted).

Montana, unlike many jurisdictions, allows recovery in a wrongful death action for loss of care, comfort, society and companionship, holding that the speculative nature of such awards is no objection. In Davis v. Smith (1968), 152 Mont. 170, 448 P.2d 133, this Court said:

"As to the third item, loss of society, comfort, care and protection * * * no extensive proof was made except that the son was a normal child. It is obvious that to put a monetary value on this is something solely within the province of the jury."

Although Montana has consistently adhered to the requirement that the loss of society and companionship be susceptible of "pecuniary loss" translation, this Court has refused to require a yardstick for measurement. If a jury can evaluate the intangible loss suffered from not having the decedent's care, comfort and companionship, surely that same jury can be trusted to ascribe damages to grief.

The remaining argument advanced for denying expansion of the rule lies embedded in stare decisis. * * *

The Supreme Court of Texas has overruled all prior decisions and decreed that damages for mental anguish will be permitted in a wrongful death action instituted by a parent for the death of a minor child. Sanchez v. Schindler (Tex.1983), 651 S.W.2d 249.

The Texas court addressed the question of whether the judiciary should await legislative action. The court said:

"The legislature has attempted to amend the Texas Wrongful Death Act to allow damages for loss of society and mental anguish; however, none of the bills have passed. This court should not be bound by the prior legislative inaction in an area like tort law which has traditionally been developed primarily through the judicial process. Green, Protection of the Family under Tort Law, 10 Hastings L.J. 237, 245 (1959). In his article, Dean Green stated that because the difficulties in reducing the refinements of tort law doctrines into statutory form often result in legislation which is either underinclusive or overbroad and which is frequently couched in ambiguous terms which the court must interpret, judicial decision is the best way to develop tort law. Inaction of the legislature cannot be interpreted as prohibiting judicial reappraisal of the judicially created pecuniary loss rule."

An English court in the 1852 *Blake* case judicially restricted a legislatively granted remedy. The courts which followed that lead should, one-hundred thirty-one years later, be free to apply a more fitting interpretation. Montana allows the estate of a decedent to recover damages for the decedent's pain suffered prior to death. Surely a jury which can lawfully weigh such intangible damage can be trusted to fairly compensate for the grief suffered by the survivors.

The same day that this opinion is being released another opinion from this Court is being released answering a certified question from the United States District Court in a case entitled Versland v. Caron Transport, Mont., 671 P.2d 583. In the *Versland* case, this Court, for the first time, recognized a cause of action for negligent infliction of mental and emotional distress. The opinion in this case, for the first time, allows recovery for mental distress damages in a wrongful death action. The two are not to be confused. A negligent infliction action, such as the one recognized in *Versland,* compensates for mental distress from having *witnessed* an accident. The mental distress for which recovery can be sought under the rationale of *Dawson,* is limited to mental anguish, sorrow or grief resulting from the death. The two actions are distinct and separate. If the two actions are joined in one case then damages for the negligent infliction of mental and emotional distress must be limited to those damages caused by the witnessing of the accident. Damages awarded for mental distress as the result of wrongful death must be limited to the damages which are caused by the loss of the decedent's life.

We hold that damages for the sorrow, mental distress or grief of the parents of a deceased minor are recoverable in a wrongful death action brought pursuant to section 27–1–512, MCA. Any previous Montana decisions, to the extent they conflict with this holding are expressly overruled.

WEBER, JUSTICE, respectfully dissents as follows. * * * The Texas case of *Sanchez* is discussed at length by the majority. One of the problems of using that case as authority is best stated by Chief Justice Pope, who noted in his dissent in *Sanchez* that the majority failed to:

> "cite a single case in which a court has authorized damages for mental anguish by overruling a longstanding statutory construction that has been ratified by legislative reenactment."

The Montana Legislature has met a number of times since the 1877 enactment of what today is section 27–1–323, MCA. The Legislature has not seen fit to modify this Court's interpretation of that statute by amendment or otherwise. In *Sanchez,* Chief Justice Pope noted that aside from the Supreme Court of Texas, only eleven states have permitted recovery for mental anguish of survivors in wrongful death cases. Ten of those eleven states have allowed recovery by legislative action. This is a strong argument for leaving to the Montana Legislature the decision which the majority is making here.

The trend to allow recovery for grief, sorrow and mental distress in wrongful death cases appears to be legislative, rather than judicial. I note that in the Pacific Reporter region, nine states including Montana have statutes allowing such damages as are just. Alaska Stat. § 09.55.580 (fair and just); Cal.Civ.Proc.Code § 377(a) (just); Hawaii Rev.Stat. § 663–3 (fair and just); Idaho Code § 5–311 (just); section 27–1–323, MCA (just); N.M.Stat.Ann. § 41–2–3 (fair and just); Utah Code Ann. § 78–11–7 (just); Wash.Rev.Code § 4.20–020 (just). Washington has, by statutory amendment, allowed recovery for injury to or destruction of the parent-child relationship. Wash.Rev.Code § 4.24.010. This statute has been judicially interpreted to include recovery for grief. Kansas, Nevada and Oklahoma statutory law specifically permit such recovery. Kan.Stat.Ann. § 60–1904 (mental anguish, suffering or bereavement); Nev.Rev.Stat. § 41–085 (grief or sorrow); Okl.Stat.Ann. title 12 § 1053 (grief). California, from which Montana adopted its wrongful death statute, has not amended its statute and has refused to allow recovery for grief and sorrow by judicial decision. Krouse v. Graham * * *

The majority opinion does not state if it is modifying or abandoning the pecuniary loss rule in Montana, as was done in *Sanchez* by the Texas Court. If the rule has not been abandoned, will substantial evidence of the pecuniary value of the loss of companionship and society still be required in Montana? Will a different standard be applied to measure damages recoverable for loss of companionship and damages recoverable for grief and sorrow?

I am unable to distinguish between mental or emotional distress recoverable in a wrongful death case (*Dawson*) and mental or emotional distress recoverable in a negligent infliction of emotional distress case (Versland v. Caron Transport). Our *Versland* decision is based upon the California case of Dillon v. Legg (1968), 68 Cal.2d 728, 441 P.2d 912, 69 Cal.Rptr. 72. In *Dillon,* the California Supreme Court allowed recovery for emotional distress suffered by a mother who witnessed her daughter being struck and killed by a motorist. That case is factually comparable to *Versland,* where the wife watched the collision in which her husband was killed. *Dillon* and subsequent California cases have allowed recovery by bystanders for emotional distress suffered as a result of witnessing or hearing the accident with damages including mental and emotional distress suffered after the victim's death. Note that California does not, however, allow recovery for grief, sorrow, or mental distress in a case like *Dillon.*

In seeking to analyze *Versland* in relation to *Dawson,* the majority points out that if the action for mental distress from having witnessed the accident is combined with a wrongful death action for mental anguish, sorrow and grief, then the recovery under *Versland* is limited to the damages caused by witnessing the accident but does not include the mental distress resulting from the death. That concept suggests that there is a line between the emotional distress suffered from witnessing an accident that results in the instantaneous death of a loved one, and the emotional distress suffered from sorrow and grief that follows the death. I do not understand that distinction and would be unable to explain it to a jury.

Notes

1. Texas has extended mental anguish damages to the parents of a deceased *adult* child. Moore v. Lillebo, 722 S.W.2d 683 (Tex.1986). The parents no longer have to prove mental anguish by physical manifestation.

On the other hand, the Nebraska Supreme Court, after reviewing the principal case's precedents, declined the invitation to follow them. Nelson v. Dolan, 230 Neb. 848, 434 N.W.2d 25 (1989).

May the parents of a deceased unborn child recover for mental anguish? Yes. Seef v. Sutkus, 205 Ill.App.3d 312, 150 Ill.Dec. 76, 562 N.E.2d 606 (1990).

2. Wycko v. Gnodtke, 361 Mich. 331, 105 N.W.2d 118 (1960), measured the parents' recovery by the value of their investment in the child. *Wycko* measured damages by "the expense of birth, of food, of clothing, of medicines, of instruction, of nurture and shelter."

Should the parents recover for the time they spent rearing the child? If so should it be measured by the cost of procuring a substitute or by alternative prices for their services? R. Posner, Economic Analysis of Law 183 (1986).

3. If parents recover the loss of the child's "society" disguised as "pecuniary" damages, then should their anticipated child-rearing expenses be deducted? If the parents' loss is characterized as "non-pecuniary," then would the costs of raising the child be offset? Cf. Bullard v. Barnes, 102 Ill.3d 505, 468 N.E.2d 1228 (1984).

4. Roberts v. Stevens Clinic Hospital, ___ W.Va. ___, 345 S.E.2d 791, 796–97 (W.Va.1986). The jury awarded $10,000,000 to the parents and siblings of a deceased two-and-one-half-year-old child. In the course of a decision leading to a remittitur of $7,000,000, the court discussed a videotape.

"At trial the plaintiff introduced into evidence a professionally prepared, twenty minute, videotape that combined "home movie" video recordings of Michael taken by a neighbor with a series of still, colored, photographs of Michael and the family. The audio background for this video presentation consisted of tape recordings of the child's voice as well as Joyces' voice singing and talking to the child. It is the defendant's contention that this film was a "theatrical" presentation that artistically highlighted certain aspects of Michael's life and Joyce's relationship to Michael in an inaccurate way.

"We have reviewed the tape in its entirety and we find nothing inflammatory or prejudicial about it. *W.Va.Code,* 55–7–6 [1982], our wrongful death statute, provides in section (c)(1):

> 'The verdict of the jury shall include, but may not be limited to, damages for the following: (A) Sorrow, mental anguish, and solace which may include society, companionship, comfort, guidance, kindly offices and advice of the decedent; * * *' "

The purpose of the videotape was to demonstrate that Michael was a healthy, intelligent, enthusiastic, and well loved child. So as a preliminary matter, the videotape was relevant. In our review of the tape, we find no artistic highlighting that emphasizes some scenes or photographs more than others, and we find no merit in the defendant's assertion that because the mother's voice went on several seconds after the screen turned black, an unduly sentimental atmosphere was evoked that would have prejudiced the jury.

"This Court has not previously addressed the admissibility of videotape "Day-in-the-Life" films. The same evidentiary rules that govern the admissibility of recordings and photographs govern the admissibility of videotape evidence. [citation] The general rule is that pictures or photographs that are relevant to any issue in a case are admissible. * * *

"We are not unmindful of the potential dangers inherent in such presentations. As one court has explained:

'Almost always an edited tape necessarily raises issues as to every sequence portrayed of whether the event shown is fairly representative of fact, after the editing process, and whether it is unduly prejudicial because of the manner of presentation.' "

Bolstridge v. Central Maine Power Co., 621 F.Supp. 1202 (D.C.Me.1985) (Plaintiff's "Day-in-the-Life" videotape excluded when open court testimony could demonstrate similar evidence, and admission of videotape would create risk of distracting jury and unfairly prejudicing defendant). A videotape's tone and editing, as well as the availability of similar evidence through in-court testimony, are all factors a trial court should consider in deciding whether to admit a videotape. But, we shall not reverse a trial court's decision in these matters unless the record shows a clear abuse of discretion."

E. CIVIL RIGHTS ACTIONS FOR WRONGFUL DEATH

1. A FEDERAL SURVIVAL ACTION

BERRY v. CITY OF MUSKOGEE, OKLAHOMA

United States Court of Appeals, Tenth Circuit, 1990.
900 F.2d 1489.

LOGAN, CIRCUIT JUDGE. Defendant City of Muskogee (the City) appeals from a jury verdict in favor of plaintiff Linnie Kay Berry (Berry) in this 42 U.S.C. § 1983 suit. * * *

Berry brought this suit on behalf of herself and her children and as the personal representative of the estate of Mark Berry, her deceased husband and father of the children. Mark Berry was murdered by fellow prisoners at the Muskogee City–Federal Jail, while in the custody and control of the City * * *. Her complaint alleged that these violations were caused by the City's deliberate indifference to her husband's safety. She sought damages for her husband's pain and suffering and expected loss of earnings, her grief and loss of consortium, and her children's grief and loss of companionship. The case was submitted to the jury under the Due Process Clause of the Fourteenth Amendment. The jury returned a verdict in favor of Berry and awarded $100,000 in damages. We vacate the judgment and remand for a new trial. * * *

Berry is the duly appointed administratrix of the Estate of Mark A. Berry, deceased. The complaint clearly asserts a survival action on behalf of the estate under Okla.Stat.Ann. tit. 12 § 1051, and a wrongful death claim under Okla.Stat.Ann. tit. 12 § 1053, an option permissible under Oklahoma law. [citations]

The difficult question we face here is whether damages in a § 1983 action in which death occurs are limited to those recoverable under the Oklahoma survival action alone, or to those recoverable by such a survival action and an Oklahoma wrongful death suit, or whether damages are determined by some federal standard either as a survival or wrongful death-type action not defined or limited by state law.

Section 1983, which is derived from § 1 of the Civil Rights Act of 1871, creates a cause of action in favor of "the party injured" against "[e]very person who, under color of any statute, ordinance, regulation, custom, or usage, of any State * * *, subjects, or causes to be subjected, any * * * person * * * to the deprivation of any rights * * * secured by the Constitution and laws." 42

U.S.C. § 1983. Although § 1983's "unique remedy make[s] it appropriate to accord the statute 'a sweep as broad as its language,'" its lack of detail leaves little to construe. [citations] The task of courts attempting to give content to § 1983's protection is, therefore, correspondingly difficult. * * *

Although Congress clearly envisioned § 1983 to serve as a remedy for wrongful killings that resulted from the proscribed conduct, the statute itself does not provide a mechanism to implement such a remedy. [citations] For instance, when the constitutional violation has resulted in death, § 1983 does not specify whether the cause of action it creates survives the death, who are the injured parties, the nature of the claims that may be pursued or who may pursue them, or the types of damages recoverable.

We are not left totally without guidance, however, in that 42 U.S.C. § 1988 authorizes federal courts to undertake a three-step process to determine whether to borrow law from another source to aid their enforcement of federal civil rights statutes. Section 1988 first directs that courts look to federal law "so far as such laws are suitable to carry [the civil and criminal civil rights statutes] into effect." Second, if federal law is "not adapted to the object" or is "deficient in the provisions necessary to furnish suitable remedies and punish offenses," courts must consider borrowing the law of the forum state.[1] Third, the federal court must reject the application of state law if it is "inconsistent with the Constitution and laws of the United States." * * *

Applying the principles set out in § 1988 for borrowing law from another source, we are satisfied that the Oklahoma survival action alone does not meet the stated criteria. As applied to the instant case, it would provide extraordinarily limited recovery, possibly only damages to property loss, of which there were none, and loss of decedent's earnings between the time of injury and death, of which there also were none. Thus, the Oklahoma survival action is clearly deficient in both its remedy and its deterrent effect.

The more difficult question is whether the Oklahoma law on survival actions, as supplemented by Oklahoma's wrongful death statute, sufficiently meets the § 1988 criteria to satisfy the test for borrowing state law. * * *

One problem with looking to the wrongful death statute is that traditionally these statutes have been viewed as creating a new cause of action for the benefit of survivors. * * *

We believe a strong argument can be made that borrowing state wrongful death statutes simply provides remedial assistance "to effectuate well-established primary rules of behavior" that are enforceable under § 1983. Moragne v. States Marine Lines, Inc., 398 U.S. 375, 403 (1970) (creating common law wrongful death action in admiralty). When the alleged constitutional violation results in death, Congress, through § 1988, has authorized resort to state law to assist the broad remedial policies of § 1983. * * *

On the other hand, if we were to define § 1983 remedies in terms of the state survival action, supplemented by the state wrongful death act, we place into the hands of the state the decision as to allocation of the recovery in a

1. [Footnotes renumbered.] Section 1988 does not specify when federal law is deficient or what federal law courts must look to before making a deficiency finding. [citations] Nor has the Supreme Court helped us, thus far, in construing the deficiency clause. We are confident, however, that federal law, whatever its scope may be, is deficient here because the Supreme Court in Robertson v. Wegmann, 436 U.S. 584 (1978), found it deficient in the analogous area of survival of § 1983 actions.

§ 1983 case, and, indeed, whether there can be any recovery at all. In an Oklahoma wrongful death action nearly all recoverable damages are expressly funneled to the decedent's surviving spouse and children to the exclusion of decedent's creditors or the beneficiaries of the decedent's will, if he or she has one. See Okla.Stat.Ann.tit. 12, § 1053(B). The statute also permits recovery for loss of consortium and grief of the surviving spouse, grief and loss of companionship of the children and parents, items decedent could not have recovered had he lived to sue for himself.

Allowing the state determinations to prevail also permits the state to define the scope and extent of recovery. For instance, some states may preclude, or limit, recovery for pain and suffering or for punitive damages. In addition, some state laws may deny all recovery in particular circumstances, as when wrongful death actions must be for dependents and there are none.

In Smith v. Wade, 461 U.S. 30 (1983), the Supreme Court ruled that punitive damages are recoverable in § 1983 cases. In reaching this conclusion the Court relied on the common law of torts, but not the common or statutory law of any one particular state. The rule announced in *Smith* is a general one, not one specific to Missouri (the forum state) based on state law remedies. There is no stated exception for § 1983 actions brought in states that do not permit punitive damage awards in other tort cases. Similarly, in Memphis Community School District v. Stachura, 477 U.S. 299 (1986), the Court looked to the common law of torts to hold that the abstract value of constitutional rights is not a permissible element of compensatory damages in § 1983 cases. But it did not make the rule different for suits brought in states that might have a different notion. The Court did not rely on borrowing the law of the forum state, but instead laid down a uniform rule. In Wilson v. Garcia, 471 U.S. 261 (1985), the Supreme Court looked to state law for statutes of limitations, but it did not permit the state law to define the cause of action. These cases suggest that the Supreme Court is fashioning a federal common law of remedies for § 1983 violations.

In the case before us the recovery permitted under the Oklahoma wrongful death act duplicates, in many respects, the recovery Mark Berry might have obtained had he lived to sue for his injuries. But, as we have noted, the act permits recovery of the loss of consortium and grief of the surviving spouse, children, and parents, which Mark Berry could not have recovered had he lived. Okla.Stat.Ann. tit. 12 § 1053(B). In considering whether the purposes of § 1983 are satisfied by adoption of state survival and wrongful death actions, we must consider that different states will define them differently, thus requiring individual analyses of each state's law. We might have to find that a state's law works satisfactorily in some instances, as when there are surviving dependents, but not in other cases, as when there is no one with a right to sue.

Weighing these concerns, and considering the Supreme Court's approach in *Smith, Memphis Community School District,* and *Garcia,* we conclude that supplementing a state survival action with a state wrongful death action does not satisfy the criteria of § 1988 for borrowing state law. The laws are not suitable to carry out the full effects intended for § 1983 cases ending in death of the victim; they are deficient in some respects to punish the offenses. Application of state law, at least in some instances, will be inconsistent with the predominance of the federal interest.

We therefore conclude, as did the Sixth Circuit in Jaco [v. Bloechle, 739 F.2d 239 (6th Cir.1984)], that the federal courts must fashion a federal remedy to be applied to § 1983 death cases. The remedy should be a survival action, brought by the estate of the deceased victim, in accord with § 1983's express statement that the liability is "to the party injured." 42 U.S.C. § 1983. It must make available to plaintiffs sufficient damages to serve the deterrent function central to the purpose of § 1983. In accord with *Smith,* punitive damages may be recovered in appropriate cases. * * * We believe appropriate compensatory damages would include medical and burial expenses, pain and suffering before death, loss of earnings based upon the probable duration of the victim's life had not the injury occurred, the victim's loss of consortium, and other damages recognized in common law tort actions.

The state wrongful death actions are not foreclosed by this approach; they remain as pendent state claims. But, of course, there can be no duplication of recovery.

Because the court's instructions to the jury were those for a wrongful death action, the court erred in instructing the jury. * * *

The judgment of the district court is VACATED and the cause is REMANDED for a new trial. [other opinions omitted.]

2. DAMAGES FOR THE LOSS OF ONE'S OWN LIFE

SHERROD v. BERRY

United States District Court, Northern District of Illinois, 1985.
629 F.Supp. 159.

[Lucien Sherrod, individually and in his capacity as administrator of the estate of his son Ronald Sherrod, sued the city of Joliet, Illinois, its police chief, and a police officer for violating Ronald's civil rights by wrongfully causing his death.]

LEIGHTON, DISTRICT JUDGE. A § 1983 action is a suit for tort damages, even though the duty a defendant is alleged to have breached is created by the Constitution or federal law. * * *

In this case, Ronald Sherrod's death was caused by the constitutional deprivation for which compensation was sought. Section 1983, and the applicable provisions of the Fourteenth Amendment, protect life. It is well established in this and other circuits that on the facts alleged, and on the evidence the jury heard, the estate of Ronald Sherrod could sue and recover damages for the loss of his life. [citations]

At the trial, in order to prove the damages he suffered from the death of his son, Lucien Sherrod called as an expert witness, Stanley Smith, an economist, holder of a master's degree in economics from the University of Chicago. Defendants did not question Smith's qualifications; instead, they filed a motion *in limine* asking that his testimony concerning the hedonic value of life be excluded from the jury on the ground that it was speculative. The motion was denied, this court ruling that such testimony was not speculative; that it was relevant and material and would aid the jury in determining the proper amount of damages in the event it found in favor of the plaintiff.

Accordingly, Smith, after explaining what he did and the information he used, testified to the amount of loss Lucien Sherrod suffered when he was deprived of his son's association and companionship. Smith described and explained how he had calculated the economic loss which Ronald Sherrod's estate incurred from his death. Smith told the jury the basis of his opinions, and the economic theories which supported his conclusions.

Apart from his testimony concerning the economic value of life, he gave the jury some "insight into the guidelines that economists use in looking at how society values what we call the hedonic aspect, the hedonic value of life, separate from economic productive value of an individual." He said there had been studies by economists which "indicate that a human life has value separate from the economic productive value that a human being would have." Of course, Smith said, the economic aspect of life valuation presents what may appear to be imponderable difficulties in those cases when the individual, because of infancy, old age, or physical incapacity, has no measurable economic productivity. These difficulties, however, did not apply to the case before the jury because Ronald Sherrod was gainfully employed up to the day he was killed by Berry.

Smith told the jury that in the last 10 years economic literature showed some 15 studies "with respect to the value of life." There "was a study by Blomquist here in Illinois" which in turn considered all the other studies and found that there was a relationship somewhere in the dimension of three times up to 30 times their economic productive income. Smith expressed agreement with Blomquist's conclusions, considering him an authoritative source of knowledge on the subject of the hedonic value of life. At the end of Smith's testimony, which included extensive direct and intensive cross-examination, this court asked Smith to define for the jury the word "hedonic" as it is used in the expression "the hedonic value of life." Smith said:

> "It derives from the word pleasing or pleasure. I believe it is a Greek word. It is distinct from the word economic. So it refers to the larger value of life, the life at the pleasure of society, if you will, the life—the value including economic, including moral, including philosophical, including all the value with which you might hold life, is the meaning of the expression 'hedonic value'. * * * "

"Life," Blackstone has reminded us, "is the immediate gift of God, a right inherent by nature in every individual. * * *" 1 W. Blackstone, Commentaries *129; Evans v. The People, 1 Cow.Cr.R. 494, 501 (N.Y.1872) (Grover, J., dissenting). The deprivation of life that is prohibited by the Fourteenth Amendment includes "not only of life [itself], but of whatever God has given to everyone with life for its growth and enjoyment. * * * " Munn v. Illinois, 4 Otto 113, 142, 94 U.S. 113, 142 (1876) (Field, J., dissenting). In other words, the loss of life means more than being deprived of the right to exist, or of the ability to earn a living; it includes deprivation of the pleasures of life.

This is the point that Smith discussed with the jury when he told them about "the hedonic value of life." As he explained to them, "hedonic" refers "to the larger value of life. * * * " This includes the pleasure of living which is destroyed by the blow that is lethal; in this case, the fatal pistol shot that Berry fired into the temple of Ronald Sherrod, a mere youth; and thus taking from him what all the wealth in the world could never purchase. Smith's expert testimony enabled the jury to consider this important aspect of injury which the estate of Ronald Sherrod suffered, an aspect they should have considered in the event they determined that Lucien Sherrod, as administrator, was entitled to a judgment against the defendants.

All competent evidence tending to establish a legitimate item of damage is, under proper pleadings, relevant and admissible. * * * The fact that the hedonic value of a human life is difficult to measure did not make either Smith's testimony or the damages speculative. Damages are speculative when the probability that a circumstance as an element of compensation is conjectural. The rule against recovery of "speculative damages" is generally directed against uncertainty as to cause rather than uncertainty as to measure or extent. * * *

Contrary to what may be the popular view, the idea that an estate can recover for the hedonic value of the life of the person killed is not new in Anglo–American law. In England, for example, hedonic damage awards have been allowed since 1976. Section 1 of the Law Reform (Miscellaneous Provisions) Act of 1934 has been construed by English judges so that the estate of a person killed can recover for "loss of expectation of life." Prichard, Personal Injury Litigation, 137–142 (London 1976); see also McCann v. Sheppard, 1 W.L.R. 540 (Ct. of App.Eng.1973). In this country, legal scholars, economists, and social scientists have grappled with the task of formulating a method by which the value of a human life can be measured in terms understood by a jury. [citations] Therefore, the concept, although novel, is not unknown. The testimony of Stanley Smith as an expert in economics enabled the jury to perform its function in determining the proper measure of damages in this case.

Notes

1. Appeals from Sherrod v. Berry are at 827 F.2d 195 (7th Cir.1987), affirming; 835 F.2d 1222 (7th Cir.1988), vacating and granting rehearing en banc; and 856 F.2d 802 (7th Cir.1988), reversing and remanding for a new trial. The court of appeals en banc reversed because of evidence rulings related to liability; the court of appeals's three decisions gave the damage award cursory attention.

2. As we might expect, *Sherrod* has provoked a storm of controversy. Awarding damages to the deceased's estate based on the value of his own life is uncertainty carried to the ultimate. Yet experts have emerged. The current quarrel concerns whether to admit their evidence.

Among the methods experts have proposed to quantify an award are: (a) the implied value individuals place on their lives based on what they are willing to pay for safety devices; (b) a study of life and accidental death insurance premium statistics; (c) wage premiums employees demand for hazardous duties; and d. OSHA studies on the cost of life-saving regulations. An article by P. Barrett, Wall Street Journal, Dec. 12, 1988, at A1, quotes Stanley Smith, the expert in *Sherrod,* "As a society, we clearly haven't come up with a single value that everyone recognizes" * * * "[Given a range, jurors] can apply their own philosophical, moral and religious beliefs about how much living is worth beyond earning power."

F. DAMAGES FOR OTHERS' PERSONAL INJURIES

BORER v. AMERICAN AIRLINES

Supreme Court of California, 1977.
19 Cal.3d 441, 138 Cal.Rptr. 302, 563 P.2d 858.

TOBRINER, ACTING CHIEF JUSTICE. In Rodriguez v. Bethlehem Steel Corp. (1974) 12 Cal.3d 382, 115 Cal.Rptr. 765, 525 P.2d 669 we held that a married person whose spouse had been injured by the negligence of a third party may maintain a cause of action for loss of "consortium." We defined loss of "consortium" as the "loss of conjugal fellowship and sexual relations," but ruled that the term included the loss of love, companionship, society, sexual relations, and household services. Our decision carefully avoided resolution of the question whether anyone other than the spouse of a negligently injured person, such as a child or a parent, could maintain a cause of action analogous to that upheld in *Rodriguez.* We face that issue today: the present case presents a claim by nine children for the loss of the services, companionship, affection and guidance of their mother. * * *

Rodriguez does not compel the conclusion that foreseeable injury to a legally recognized relationship necessarily postulates a cause of action; instead it clearly warns that social policy must at some point intervene to delimit liability. Patricia Borer, for example, foreseeably has not only a husband (who has a cause of action under *Rodriguez*) and the children who sue here, but also parents whose right of action depends upon our decision in the companion case of Baxter v. Superior Court; foreseeably, likewise, she has brothers, sisters, cousins, inlaws, friends, colleagues, and other acquaintances who will be deprived of her companionship. No one suggests that all such persons possess a right of action for loss of Patricia's consortium; all agree that somewhere a line must be drawn. As stated by Judge Breitel in Tobin v. Grossman (1969) 24 N.Y.2d 609, 619, 301 N.Y.S.2d 554, 561, 249 N.E.2d 419, 424; "Every injury has ramifying consequences, like the ripplings of the waters, without end. The problem for the law is to limit the legal consequences of wrongs to a controllable degree."

[S]trong policy reasons argue against extension of liability to loss of consortium of the parent-child relationship. Loss of consortium is an intangible, nonpecuniary loss; monetary compensation will not enable plaintiffs to regain the companionship and guidance of a mother; it will simply establish a fund so that upon reaching adulthood, when plaintiffs will be less in need of maternal guidance, they will be unusually wealthy men and women. To say that plaintiffs have been "compensated" for their loss is superficial; in reality they have suffered a loss for which they can never be compensated; they have obtained, instead, a future benefit essentially unrelated to that loss.

We cannot ignore the social burden of providing damages for loss of parental consortium merely because the money to pay such awards comes initially from the "negligent" defendant or his insurer. Realistically the burden of payment of awards for loss of consortium must be borne by the public generally in increased insurance premiums or, otherwise, in the enhanced danger that accrues from the greater number of people who may choose to go without any insurance. We must also take into account the cost of administration of a system to determine and pay consortium awards; since virtually every serious injury to a parent would engender a claim for loss of consortium on behalf of each of his or her children, the expense of settling or litigating such claims would be sizable. * * *

A second reason for rejecting a cause of action for loss of parental consortium is that, because of its intangible character, damages for such a loss are very difficult to measure. Plaintiffs here have prayed for $100,000 each; yet by what standard could we determine that an award of $10,000 was inadequate, or one of $500,000 excessive? Difficulty in defining and quantifying damages leads in turn to risk of double recovery: to ask the jury, even under carefully drafted instructions, to distinguish the loss to the mother from her inability to care for her children from the loss to the children from the mother's inability to care for them may be asking too much. Thus as observed by the New Jersey Supreme Court in Russell v. Salem Transportation Co. (1972) 61 N.J. 502, 507, 295, A.2d 862, 864: "The asserted social need for the disputed cause of action [a child's action for loss of parental consortium] may well be qualified, at least in terms of the family as an economic unit by the practical consideration recognized by many of the cases on the point that reflection of the consequential disadvantages to children of injured parents is frequently found in jury awards to the parents on their own claims under existing law and practice."

* * * Plaintiffs contend, however that no adequate ground exists to distinguish a cause of action for loss of spousal consortium from one for loss of parental consortium. We reject the contention for three reasons.

First, as *Rodriguez* pointed out, the spousal action for loss of consortium rests in large part on the "impairment or destruction of the sexual life of the couple." No similar element of damage appears in a child's suit for loss of consortium.

Second, actions by children for loss of parental consortium create problems of multiplication of actions and damages not present in the spousal context. As pointed out by the New Jersey Supreme Court in Russell v. Salem Transportation Co.:

> "If the claim were allowed there would be a substantial accretion of liability against the tortfeasor arising out of a single transaction (typically the negligent operation of an automobile). Whereas the assertion of a spouse's demand for loss of consortium involves the joining of only a single companion claim in the action with that of the injured person, the right here debated would entail adding as many companion claims as the injured parent had minor children, each such claim entitled to separate appraisal and award. The defendant's burden would be further enlarged if the claims were founded upon injuries to both parents. Magnification of damage awards to a single family derived from a single accident might well become a serious problem to a particular defendant as well as in terms of the total cost of such enhanced awards to the insured community as a whole."

The instant case illustrates the point. Patricia Borer has nine children, each of whom would possess his own independent right of action for loss of consortium. Even in the context of a consolidated action, the assertion of nine independent causes of action for the children in addition to the father's claim for loss of consortium and the mother's suit for ordinary tort damages, demonstrates the extent to which recognition of plaintiffs' asserted cause of action will multiply the tort liability of the defendant.

Finally, the proposition that a spouse has a cause of action for loss of consortium, but that a child does not, finds overwhelming approval in the decisions of other jurisdictions. Over 30 states, a clear majority of those who have decided the question, now permit a spousal suit for loss of consortium.[1] *No* state permits a child to sue for loss of parental consortium. That claim has

1. [Footnotes renumbered.] See listing in Love, Tortious Interference with the Parent–Child Relationship: Loss of an Injured Person's Society and Companionship (1976) 51 Ind.L.J. 590, 596, fn. 20.

been presented, at latest count, to 18 jurisdictions, and rejected by all of them. * * *

We therefore conclude that we should not recognize a cause of action by a child for loss of parental consortium. Plaintiffs contend, however, that such a conclusion would distinguish between the rights of the child in the present context and the rights afforded him in a wrongful death action, without any rational basis for the distinction in contravention of the equal protection of the laws.

Plaintiffs point out that section 377 of the Code of Civil Procedure authorizes an action for wrongful death by the heirs of the victim; judicial decisions interpreting this section permit recovery by children of the value of the deceased's affection and society. Plaintiffs contend that no rational basis supports a ruling that permits the children of a deceased parent to recover the value of lost affection and companionship, but denies the children of a seriously disabled parent a similar cause of action. * * *

We perceive two significant distinctions between the child whose parent is killed and one whose parent is disabled, both of which flow from the fact that in the latter case the living victim retains his or her own cause of action. The first distinction relates to the historical purpose of the wrongful death statutes. By 1846, the date of the enactment of the first wrongful death statute, the common law courts had settled that the heirs of a deceased victim could not bring a cause of action against the tortfeasor. This loophole in the law curtailed the deterrent function of tort recovery, providing to tortfeasors a substantial incentive to finish off their victims. The wrongful death statutes thus met an obvious logical and social need.

Similar policy reasons led the courts to permit the bereaved to recover for the loss of the affection and society of the deceased. As stated in Krouse v. Graham, "if damages truly were limited to 'pecuniary' loss, recovery frequently would be barred by the heirs' inability to prove such loss. The services of children, elderly parents, or non-working spouses often do not result in measurable net income to the family unit, yet unquestionably the death of such a person represents a substantial 'injury' to the family." Recovery for loss of affection and society in a wrongful death action thus fulfills a deeply felt social belief that a tortfeasor who negligently kills someone should not escape liability completely, no matter how unproductive his victim.

A suit for loss of consortium of a disabled parent presents a wholly different picture. Here the tortfeasor cannot escape with impunity, for the immediate victim of his tort retains a cause of action for the injuries inflicted. The claim by the child in this setting is not essential to prevent the tortfeasor from totally escaping liability.

Secondly, the wrongful death action serves as the only means by which the family unit can recover compensation for the loss of parental care and services in the case of the wrongful death of the parent. While the parent lives, however, "the tangible aspects of the child's loss can be compensated in the parent's own cause of action."

We conclude that the distinction between the award of damages for loss of affection and society to a child whose parent has been tortiously killed, and the denial of such damages to a child whose parent has been disabled, rests upon a rational basis. Plaintiffs' constitutional argument therefore fails.

Note

Other courts have adopted *Borer* and *Baxter*'s overall negative attitude about extending recovery between children and parents except for wrongful death. See e.g., Lewis v. Rowland, 287 Ark. 474, 701 S.W.2d 122 (1985); Gaver v. Harrant, 316 Md. 17, 557 A.2d 210 (1989); Vaughn v. Clarkson, 324 N.C. 108, 376 S.E.2d 236 (1989); and, Dearborn Fabricating & Engineering Corp. v. Wickham, 551 N.E.2d 1135 (Ind.1990). The facade is no longer monolithic; fissures and fractures, both simple and compound have appeared.

Some defecting jurisdictions recognize loss of parents' consortium but not loss of child's consortium. Norman v. Massachusetts Bay Transportation Authority, 403 Mass. 303, 529 N.E.2d 139 (1988). Whereas other jurisdictions seem to reverse that pattern. Dearborn Fabricating and Engineering Corp. v. Wickham, 551 N.E.2d 1135 (Ind.1990).

No doubt in the past non-economic injury has been surreptitiously included in awards for loss of an injured parent's (or child's) services or support which have a nominally quantifiable base. Open judicial approval of damages for loss of parental consortium or child consortium is recent. *Dearborn Fabricating,* supra, states that eight jurisdictions have recognized a child's claim for loss of parental consortium since 1980, while thirty-five still do not. In the relatively few jurisdictions that support the child's claim (or the comparable parent's claim), the courts must confront the hypothetical remedial problems presented in the main cases. Courts have commonly imposed severe restrictions. Villareal v. State, Department of Transportation, 160 Ariz. 474, 480, 774 P.2d 213, 219 (1989) is illustrative:

"A proper plaintiff is a child whose parent has been injured. We limit our definition of parent to include biological and adoptive parents. Injuries to siblings, grandparents, other relatives, or friends do not qualify as an injury to a parent for purposes of this claim.

"Not all injuries to parents will result in a child's claim for loss of consortium. We limit our holding to allow loss of consortium claims only when the parent suffers serious, permanent, disabling injuries rendering the parent unable to provide love, care, companionship, and guidance to the child. The parent's mental or physical impairment must be so overwhelming and severe that the parent-child relationship is destroyed or nearly destroyed."

The court appears to virtually eliminate the necessity of a sliding scale of damages that hinges on the extent the parent is incapacitated.

Another common qualification on recognizing the child's claim as an independent one is to compel it to be joined with the parent's underlying tort action "unless the child can show why joinder [is] not feasible." Ueland v. Reynolds Metals Co., 103 Wash.2d 131, 691 P.2d 190, 195 (1984).

A damage award for multiple children remains intractable. On the one hand their claims are independent. On the other hand how much consortium does a mother of nine have to distribute? How about requiring all children in the qualified class to join in a class action (in turn joined with the injured parent's personal injury suit). The damages, if any, for loss of parental consortium will then be distributed as determined by the judge or jury. A practical solution?

BAXTER v. SUPERIOR COURT

Supreme Court of California, 1977.
19 Cal.3d 461, 138 Cal.Rptr. 315, 563 P.2d 871.

TOBRINER, ACTING CHIEF JUSTICE. * * * Our opinion in Borer v. American Airlines, explains the policy considerations which impelled us to conclude that a child should not have a cause of action for loss of parental consortium. Those reasons for the most part apply fully to the present issue of a parental claim for loss of filial consortium. The intangible character of the loss, which can never really be compensated by money damages; the difficulty of measuring damages; the dangers of double recovery of multiple claims and of extensive liability—all these considerations apply similarly to both cases. To be sure, the risk of multiple claims and disproprotionate awards is slightly less in the present context, since an injured child has only two parents who can sue for loss of consortium, while an injured parent may have many children. That minor difference between the cases, however, plainly does not suffice to justify allowing a parental cause of action while denying a child's claim. Petitioners do not argue to the contrary.

Petitioners contend, however, that the decisions of other jurisdictions recognize a distinction between the right of the parent and that of the child. Although as we observed in Borer v. American Airlines, no jurisdiction allows a child to recover for loss of parental consortium, the states are divided on the question whether a parent can recover for loss of a child's consortium. [citations] Yet none of the decisions upholding a parental cause of action address the question whether the parent's claim can reasonably be distinguished from a child's claim. The majority of decisions that sustain the parental cause of action do so merely by citing the common law right of a parent to recover for loss of a child's services and by treating the child's affection and companionship as among the "services" to which the parent is entitled. The absence of any comparable right of action for the child at common law presumably accounts for the dearth of decisions permitting the child to recover for loss of parental affection and society.

The existence of a common law right to recover for the loss of a child's earnings and services does not, we believe, furnish a sufficient basis to distinguish a parent's suit for loss of consortium from the child's claim denied in Borer v. American Airlines. The common law right in question derives from the right of a master to recover for the loss of his servant's services and dates from the period when the labor of the child in his parent's business, or his earnings outside the home, served as an important economic resource of the family (see 1 Harper & James, Torts (1956) § 8.8).[1] With rare exceptions the parent's right to a child's earnings and services today is of little economic value; it exists less as a significant legal right than as a historical curiosity. While that historical atavism may explain why some jurisdictions permit a parent to recover for loss of his child's consortium yet deny the corresponding right of the child, it does not justify that distinction, and does not supply us with any reason to follow those decisions.

Although the parent's right to their child's earnings and services is established by statute in California (see Civ.Code, § 197), the few decisions enforcing that right grant recovery only for loss of earnings or services of economic value. Expansion of recovery to include damages for loss of affection and society encounters the same arguments invoked in *Borer* in denial of a child's claim for loss of parental consortium. We therefore conclude that a

1. [Footnote renumbered.] By common law tradition and by statute in California (see Civ. Code, § 197) the parent's cause of action is limited to cases in which the parent has an enforceable right to the child's services and earnings; thus no cause of action can be asserted when the child has reached majority or been emancipated. [citation]

parent has no cause of action in negligence to recover damages for loss of filial consortium.

Notes

1. Shockley v. Prier, 66 Wis.2d 394, 225 N.W.2d 495 (1975), is the leading decision contrary to *Baxter*. How severe must the injury to the child (in this case) be to trigger a claim for damages? In Pierce v. Casas Adobes Baptist Church, 162 Ariz. 269, 273, 782 P.2d 1162 (1989), the court explained:

"Not all injuries to a child will result in a parent's claim for loss of consortium. We hold that parents may maintain a cause of action for loss of their child's consortium when the child suffers a severe, permanent and disabling injury rendering the child unable to exchange love, affection, care, comfort, companionship and society in a normally gratifying way. Once the threshold of a significant interference with the normal relationship between parent and child is established, it is a question of fact whether, and to what extent, the child's injury justifies recovery."

Compare the test the same court laid down for lost parental consortium quoted in Villareal v. State Department of Transportation in Note 1, p. 740. Does this test reintroduce all the uncertainties of a sliding scale of damages depending upon the severity of the child's injury? Would the disabilities actually sustained by the child in *Pierce* cross the initial threshold? Spinal injuries that interfere with walking, bowel and bladder incontinence, frequent catheterization, sexual dysfunction, depression, and prospective intermittent hospitalization. Yet he is not confined to bed or wheelchair; he finished community college, lives with a fiancee, and works as a video technician.

Question: Assuming this passes the threshold test, of how much love, affection, and comfort have the parents been deprived—determined in dollar damages?

2. *Lost "Spousal" Consortium in Personal Injury Cases—The Relationship Required.*

a. The lengthy battle to establish co-equal spousal rights to loss of consortium has ended in total victory to the wives. Operations have now been opened on the new front of non-marital relationships. In Lieding v. Commercial Diving Center, 143 Cal.App.3d 72, 191 Cal.Rptr. 559 (1983), a wife was denied loss of consortium for injuries to her husband incurred while they were engaged but before the marriage which had to be postponed because of the accident.

New Jersey has denied the right to consortium in the absence of a legal marriage. Leonardis v. Morton Chemical Co., 184 N.J.Super. 10, 445 A.2d 45 (1982);

Live-In Companions. The California Supreme Court has settled a division in that state's intermediate appellate courts. It required an actual marital relationship. Elden v. Sheldon, 46 Cal.3d 267, 250 Cal.Rptr. 254, 758 P.2d 582 (1988). One of the intermediate appeals decisions, Butcher v. Superior Court, 139 Cal.App.3d 58, 71, 188 Cal.Rptr. 503, 512 (1983) created quite a ripple outside the state by holding that loss of consortium could be claimed upon a "showing that the nonmarital relationship is both stable and significant." The *Elden* decision reviews the spread and subsidence of the ripple.

b. Common law recognition of the right of spousal consortium is well established. It may not exist, however, when the cause of action is based upon special statutory enactments. Thus loss of consortium has been denied on a claim arising under 42 U.S.C. § 1983, Walters v. Oak Lawn, 548 F.Supp. 417 (N.D.Ill.1982); on claims arising under the F.E.L.A., 45 U.S.C. §§ 51–60, Kelsaw v. Union Pacific

Railroad, 686 F.2d 819 (9th Cir.1982); and under the Illinois Structural Work Act, Martin v. Kiendl Construction Co., 108 Ill.App.3d 468, 438 N.E.2d 1187 (1982).

3. *Punitive Damages to Spouses.* In Hammond v. North American Asbestos Corp., 105 Ill.App.3d 1033, 435 N.E.2d 540, 547 (1982), aff'd, 97 Ill.2d 195, 454 N.E.2d 210 (1983), the wife of a 54–year–old husband in declining health because of asbestiosis, was awarded $125,000 in compensatory damages, and $375,000 in punitive damages. The appellate court set aside the punitive award: "Allowing recovery of punitive damages in actions for loss of consortium would involve important considerations of public policy and such extension should be made by the Supreme Court."

When husband lost a hand, wife was allowed $50,000 because she "has had to perform and will continue to perform the most basic tasks for [husband]. Their married life, which was a happy, close, and highly traditional one, sharply altered for the worse." Feyers v. United States, 561 F.Supp. 362, 370 (E.D.Mich.1983). Is this lost consortium duplicative of elements in the husband's recovery?

4. Husband's claim allowed for travel expenses to visit his wife during her prolonged hospitalization as result of injuries caused by defendant. Hall v. Burkert, 117 Ohio App. 527, 193 N.E.2d 167 (1962).

In New Jersey, however, the wife recovers the value of the husband's services in caring for her instead of hiring a trained nurse. Byrne v. Pilgrim Medical Group, Inc., 187 N.J.Super. 386, 454 A.2d 920 (1982).

5. A parent is allowed to recover the value of services to nurse a child defendant negligently injured. Should the measure be the time the parent lost from regular employment or the market value of the nursing services? See Thompson v. United Railways, 203 Mo.App. 356, 218 S.W. 343 (1920). A choice of remedial theories may be indicated.

G. PREVENTIVE RELIEF AGAINST THREATENED PERSONAL INJURIES

STATE v. WELLER

Supreme Court of Vermont, 1989.
152 Vt. 8, 563 A.2d 1318.

DOOLEY, JUSTICE. * * * On May 4, 1989, defendant was arraigned on charges of reckless endangerment and simple assault, and the trial court found probable cause. The court found that a risk of flight existed and imposed a cash bail requirement of $2,500 to ensure defendant's appearance at trial. Further, the court imposed a peace bond "to insure that the defendant will keep the peace." The peace bond amount was set at $5,000, "cash or solvent sureties." * * *

The factual basis for the orders is generally undisputed. The State's allegation is that defendant has engaged in domestic violence on his wife. This violence led to a criminal conviction for which defendant was placed on probation. At some point, defendant was convicted of violating conditions of probation for the third time and was ordered to serve time as sentenced on the underlying charges. The conviction was appealed and the sentence was stayed. Because of the stay, defendant remained on probation under the preexisting conditions. He again violated those conditions, but again the underlying sentence was not imposed because of the stay. The State alleges that following the hearing on the second violation, defendant went directly to the victim's house and committed the underlying offenses for which he was arraigned on May 4, 1989. * * * While we agree that a peace bond was improperly required in this case, we reach this conclusion on different grounds than those argued by defendant. Because of our disposition, we do not reach the constitutional questions raised by defendant.

The peace bond statute, 13 V.S.A. § 7573, states:

> "A district court may order a person who is arrested for a criminal offense, to find sureties that he will keep the peace, when it is necessary, and may commit him to jail until he complies."

This statute is nearly as old as the state, and its roots run as deep as any concept in Anglo-American common law. By statute of 1360 it became the law in England. * * * 34 Edw. III, c. 1. * * * Virtually every state adopted some variation on the English peace bond statute. See Note, Peace Bond—A Questionable Procedure for a Legitimate State Interest, 74 W.Va.L.Rev. 326, 326 n. 4 (1972) (compendium of state statutes). Many of the state peace bond statutes are quite elaborate and detailed. See, e.g., Mass.Gen.Laws Ann. ch. 275, §§ 1–17. Our statute is probably the sparest implementation of the concept.

Peace bond statutes are measures intended to prevent future acts of violence rather than to punish past acts. Despite this preventive, rather than punitive, orientation, the statutes have been criticized by commentators because the preventive theory results in the punitive sanction of imprisonment when the defendant cannot raise the bail amount. The Alabama Court of Criminal Appeals described the peace bond as follows:

> "Like many common law doctrines the peace bond has become a nonheroic Don Quixote of the law which now masquerades aimlessly through the reports, still vigorous, still viable, but, as in this case, equally dangerous."

Ex parte James, 53 Ala.App. 632, 640, 303 So.2d 133, 140 (1974). Based on this sentiment, a number of courts have found constitutional violations in the use of peace bonds. See *James* (impermissible discrimination based on wealth, violation of equal protection of laws); Kolvek v. Napple, 158 W.Va. 568, 575, 212 S.E.2d 614, 619 (1975) (same; unconstitutional as applied to indigent defendants); Santos v. Nahiwa, 53 Haw. 40, 44, 487 P.2d 283, 285 (1971) (denial of due process of law unless bond imposition is based on proof beyond a reasonable doubt). But see Commonwealth v. Miller, 452 Pa. 35, 38–41, 305 A.2d 346, 348–49 (1973) (over two strong dissents, held that neither a jury trial nor proof beyond a reasonable doubt is constitutionally required). Apparently because of this criticism and the holdings from courts that have analyzed peace bond statutes, it has fallen into disuse virtually everywhere. There have been almost no cases dealing with peace bonds in the last fifteen years.

Although the use of the peace bond in Vermont goes back to at least the early nineteenth century, we have never had occasion to interpret our statute. Indeed, peace bonds were dormant in this state until recently, when trial courts began to use peace bonds as additional or alternative conditions of release in criminal cases. * * *

Based * * * on the review of statutes from other states, we conclude that the peace bond statute is not, as the trial court necessarily construed it, a pretrial bail statute, but is instead an independent proceeding. After one is "arrested for a criminal offense," 13 V.S.A. § 7573, an action may be brought against the defendant seeking a peace bond. This action can be initiated by the court, sua sponte, by the State, or by a third party with cause.[1] It is administered in that fashion in virtually all states although it is usually related to criminal proceedings.

In this state, it is triggered by the fact that the person from whom the bond is sought is "arrested for a criminal offense." 13 V.S.A. § 7573. Other states have more typically triggered the authorization to require a peace bond by the complaint of the victim of a threatened crime, see Mass.Gen.Laws Ann. ch. 275, § 2, or the conviction of a crime, see 15 Me.Rev.Stat.Ann. tit. 15, § 1706. In analyzing the statute, it is helpful to separate out this "trigger" from the operation of the proceeding.

This separate proceeding demands an independent burden of proof. Some courts have held that the burden of proof is the normal civil burden of preponderance of the evidence. [citation] Others have held that the burden is to prove the operative facts beyond a reasonable doubt. [citation] In any event, it must be satisfied by evidence and specific findings based on the evidence. [citation] The defendant must have an opportunity to oppose the bond in a "full hearing and investigation of the facts." Commonwealth v. Miller.

The purpose of the peace bond proceeding is to determine whether a bond is necessary to prevent specific acts in the future. It is important that defendant have notice of the specific facts in issue and that any conduct to be covered by a peace bond obligation be described specifically.

We note that the peace bond statute does not authorize a requirement that the defendant post cash, nor does it specify what type of surety is acceptable. The trial courts should use the surety requirement liberally to ensure a peace bond requirement is used for prevention rather than for detention.

Finally, we note that the statute is silent on the duration of any order to post a peace bond or of any incarceration for failure to post a peace bond. The peace bond is unrelated to the triggering criminal case and, in the absence of a time limit, will go on indefinitely. The better practice is to impose a time limit on the bond requirement or to provide for automatic review after a specified period of time.

The peace bond was imposed in this case with little of the protective process discussed above. Apparently, no notice was given that a peace bond requirement was under consideration, nor was there any specification of the factual issues involved. No evidence was taken and no findings were made. The conduct to be covered by the peace bond is not specifically described. Although the defendant is apparently indigent, there is no indication that the court considered alternative sureties. There is no indication of any limit on the duration of the peace bond.

The peace bond requirement in the case at bar appears to be set as a form of bail for preventive incarceration, which our statutes do not authorize. * * *

Affirmed as to appearance bond; reversed and remanded * * * as to the peace bond.

1. [Footnotes renumbered.] We refuse to classify this action as "civil," "criminal," or "quasi-criminal," as our sister states have done. [citations]

Notes

1. *Injunctions.* Historically courts could enjoin battery but seldom did. See H. McClintock, Equity § 158 (2d ed. 1948). The tort of battery amounts to a crime more serious than the personal harassment referred to in Chapter 7. The remedy at law, particularly as enhanced by the possible availability of peace bonds may be adequate. No property interests are involved.

Contemporary state statutes that deal with spouse abuse allow the court to enjoin an abusing spouse. Judges grant restraining orders and injunctions routinely. What does an injunction add to a criminal statute?

2. *Contempt.* Defendants who violate injunctions against abusing spouses are subject to contempt. May enforcement through contempt interfere with the usual criminal process?

Consider Williams v. State, 775 S.W.2d 812, 813 (Tex.App.1989):

"In a civil lawsuit Thomas Williams was enjoined in March of 1987 from 'causing or threatening to cause physical contact or bodily injury to the Defendants [Robert and Robbie Buffington].' On June 18, 1987, Williams shot both Buffingtons with a shotgun, and on November 24, 1987 he was held in contempt of court for causing bodily injury in violation of the March 1987 order. The district attorney's office became aware of the contempt proceedings after the judge had ruled from the bench on November 24 but before he signed a written order of contempt and commitment on January 25, 1988, sentencing Williams to 30 days' confinement, which he has served. On January 6, 1988, Williams was indicted on two counts of attempted capital murder of the Buffingtons based upon the shooting incident.

"Williams sought a writ of habeas corpus in district court, asking that the indictment be dismissed because the contempt adjudication and sentence should bar the criminal prosecution under double jeopardy principles."

What should the decision be?

Part III

REMEDIES IN CONTEXT—DISRUPTED TRANSACTIONS

Chapter 9

THE DECISION TO AFFIRM OR DISAFFIRM

Introduction

At this point in Remedies a major transition from tort to contract occurs. The second part of the book has been concerned with remedies for direct harms to persons, property, or economic interests. The third part concentrates on remedies arising out of disrupted consensual arrangements.

The aggrieved party has an ineluctable choice of substantive rights. One choice is to rescind, avoid the transaction; and if it is partially executed, to seek restitution. Often, for example, for bargains entered into by mistake, rescission may afford the sole method of obtaining relief. The other choice is to stand upon the transaction and to seek remedies compatible with that election, like tort damages for deceit or contract damages for breach.

Modern procedure has altered the starkness of plaintiff's choice. Plaintiff may seek alternative, even inconsistent, remedies, for example restitution and damages. He may amend the complaint freely. The federal rules tell judges to "grant the relief to which the party in whose favor it is rendered is entitled, even if the party has not demanded such relief in his pleadings." Fed.R.Civ.P. 54(c). After the plaintiff has been allowed a full opportunity to develop the whole case, a judgment precludes the plaintiff from pursuing remedies not sought in the first action. See Restatement (Second) of Judgments §§ 24–26 (1982). But plaintiff cannot escape the decision about substantive rights. Indecision itself is a decision.

A. THE ELECTION

1. PRESUIT ELECTION

GANNETT CO. v. REGISTER PUBLISHING CO.

United States District Court, District of Connecticut, 1977.
428 F.Supp. 818.

NEWMAN, DISTRICT JUDGE. On October 20, 1976, the Hartford Times ceased publication. Its obituary notice stated that the paper had been "strangled by litigation." The controversy has not ended with its demise. The issue now pending concerns whether Gannett Co., Inc. ("Gannett") or The Register Publishing Company ("the Register") owns what remains of the paper. In

lawyer's language, the question is whether the Register is entitled to rescind the contract by which it agreed to purchase from Gannett more than 99% of the shares of The Hartford Times, Inc.

* * * After negotiations culminating in a closing on October 10, 1973, Gannett entered into a Purchase Agreement [which] provided that Gannett would sell its shares of the common stock of The Hartford Times, Inc. together with all outstanding stock of Community Offset, Inc. to the Register for an aggregate purchase price of $7,000,000, with appropriate adjustments in the purchase price to be made based on the difference between current assets and liabilities as reflected on the consolidated balance sheet to be prepared for the Times.

Shortly after the closing the Register became aware of discrepancies in the circulation statistics and financial statements of the Times as provided by Gannett. It learned of overvaluation of assets and of a series of devices that had been used for several years to conceal the reporting of inflated circulation figures. Consequently the Register decided not to pay Gannett the amount due under the net current asset adjustment provisions of the Purchase Agreement. Audits conducted over the next several weeks confirmed the Register's suspicions that the information supplied to it by Gannett prior to the execution of the Purchase Agreement had been false and misleading in many respects. When [settlement negotiations] fell through, Gannett filed this federal court action against the Register on April 15, 1974, for failure to pay the amount due under the net current asset adjustment provision. On June 12, 1974, the Register filed its counterclaim, alleging breach of contract, common law fraud, and securities law violations. In its counterclaim the Register sought compensatory and exemplary damages, or in the alternative, rescission of the Purchase Agreement and restitution of all benefits conferred by it on Gannett.

* * * After full and careful consideration, it is the conclusion of the Court that rescission is unavailable.

New York law, like the law of most states, gives an injured party the option to rescind a contract induced by fraud. But the right does not persist indefinitely. New York law is very clear, that the right to rescind for fraud must be exercised within a reasonable time after the injured party learns of the wrong. If the injured party neglects to notify the other party promptly of his intention to rescind, or if he accepts benefits under the contract and thereby affirms it, he loses his right to rescind. * * * In determining whether the injured party has lost the power to avoid the contract by delaying unreasonably in manifesting to the other party his intention to avoid the transaction, the speculative character of the contract is an influential factor. Restatement, Contracts, § 483. Comment (a) to this section of the Restatement states:

> "But the injured party delays giving information of his intention at his peril. He cannot lie by and delay choosing whether avoidance or affirmance will be more profitable, especially if the contract relates to a speculative transaction."

It is somewhat misleading to think of the choice an injured party has to make between avoiding and affirming a contract in "election of remedies" terms. The Register argues that under Rule 8 of the Federal Rules of Civil Procedure it is permitted to use alternative pleadings, and that there is nothing improper about its prayer in the alternative for damages or rescission in the counterclaim.[1] As a matter of pleading, this is true. But the real issue is not one of pleading but of substantive contract law. Professor Moore has distinguished "election of inconsistent remedies" from "instances where a choice, afforded by substantive law, terminated rights upon which the remedy invoked was dependent":

> "One fraudulently induced into a contract, for instance, may, as a matter of substantive law, either affirm or disaffirm the agreement. An election of the substantive right to affirm *extinguishes* the substantive right to disaffirm. And so an attempt to invoke the remedy of rescission after an action on the contract may fail, not because of election of inconsistent remedies, *but because the plaintiff no longer has the substantive right to disaffirm.*" [Emphasis added].

1B Moore's Federal Practice ¶ 0.405[7]. It is the substantive law of contracts that extinguishes the right, and not any doctrine of pleading.

Similarly, the use of "waiver" terminology only obscures whether affirmance or avoidance has taken place. The Register argues that unless it "waived" its rescission remedy in writing, rescission is available as a matter of law by virtue of § 15(d) of the Purchase Agreement, which reads:

> "No waiver of any provision of this Agreement shall be effective unless in writing and similarly signed, nor shall any failure of any party to enforce any right or remedy hereunder be deemed a waiver of such right or remedy for the future in the same or any situation."

But if the Register affirmed the contract, then its right to rescind terminated by operation of law, regardless of whether it "waived" the right in writing.[2]

> "The right to terminate in the face of a breach is only an option to declare the contract at an end; if the contract is continued, the party doing so has not, strictly speaking, 'waived' his right but has executed it in favor of continued contractual relations."

Apex Pool Equipment Corp. v. Lee, 419 F.2d 556, 562 (2d Cir.1969).

For similar reasons the "laches" language used by the parties tends to obscure the real issue. When the Register argues that the doctrine of laches is inapplicable because the action is one at law rather than in equity, its attack on the use of a technical word may be abstractly correct; but when it implies that the remedy of rescission continues to be available as long as suit is filed within the statute of limitations, it is simply in error.[3] The right itself, and not just the remedy, is extinguished unless the injured party perfects the right by promptly taking the affirmative steps required by the law of contracts. In the

1. [Footnotes renumbered.] See also N.Y.C. P.L.R. § 3002(e), and Uniform Commercial Code, § 2–721, providing that claims for damages and rescission are not inconsistent.

2. Perhaps if the facts showed that the Register did promptly and unequivocally notify Gannett, thereby demonstrably preserving its rescission remedy, then the waiver provision of the Agreement might come into play if Gannett tried to claim that some offhand remark short of a written waiver and not constituting an affirmance of the contract was a relinquishment of the remedy.

3. In many cases one and two-month periods have been held to constitute excessive delay. See, e.g., Sy–Jo Luncheonette, Inc. v. Marsav Distributors, Inc., 279 A.D. 715, 108 N.Y.S.2d 349 (1st Dept.1951).

While Comment a to § 490 of the Restatement of Contracts states that the power of avoidance continues "indefinitely" and may be set up as a defense if the injured party waits to be sued, it adds the important qualification "unless he affirms the transaction, *or fails to give information of his intention to exercise his power of avoidance* when the circumstances are such as to require information." [emphasis added].

language of § 480 of the Restatement of Contracts, the power to avoid the transaction is *conditional* on an offer made promptly after acquiring knowledge of the fraud. Sections 483 and 484 provide that *the power of avoidance is lost* if the injured party unreasonably delays manifesting his intention to avoid to the other party, or if he manifests an intention to affirm, or if he exercises dominion over the object of the contract. The emphasized words are substantive and not procedural concepts.

Exercise of acts of ownership over the subject matter of the contract will validate the transaction and terminate the power of avoidance, regardless of whether the other party has suffered any prejudice. Restatement, Contracts, §§ 482, 484. The injured party must offer to restore the *status quo ante* by tendering what he has received in substantially as good condition as when it was transferred to him. Restatement, Contracts §§ 349, 480. But the *status quo ante* requirement is not inflexible. Mere depreciation in market value will not prevent rescission, and other factors may make the equitable remedy of rescission available even though the property cannot be returned in the same condition. Restatement, Contracts, § 349, comment (b). If the wrongful acts of the defrauding party are what make restoration of the *status quo* impossible, rescission is not foreclosed. Restatement, Contracts, § 349(2)(b).

Of course, the factual issues in determining whether an injured party has exercised acts of ownership over the property and whether changes in the property render rescission inequitable are substantially more difficult where the property is a multi-million dollar business rather than a car or a cow or a country estate. The newspaper business poses particularly intractable problems since someone—whether plaintiff or defendant—must make daily decisions to keep the paper running in order to preserve subscription and advertising revenues which are highly sensitive to a variety of circumstances. The cases that have dealt with rescission of a contract for the sale of a business have evolved a rule that the injured party need not ignore the business and allow it to fail if the other party refuses to take it back upon a timely demand for rescission.[4] Rather, as long as the injured party's actions can be fairly viewed as necessary steps to preserve the value of the business for the one ultimately determined to be the owner, rescission is still available.

A few cases illustrate the foregoing principles, in the context of relatively clearcut factual situations. In Caruso v. Moy, 164 Neb. 68, 81 N.W.2d 826 (1957), the plaintiff bought a prosperous Chinese–American restaurant, changed the bill of fare to Italian–American, and tried to rescind the contract of sale on the ground of fraud when business fell off. The court found that he had continued to operate the business for too long a period of time after learning of the fraud before seeking rescission and that he had thereby made the business his own. He changed the restaurant substantially so that business fell off to less than half what it had been previously, possibly due in part to his own mismanagement.[5] On these facts, he was not entitled to rescission.

In Sy–Jo Luncheonette, Inc. v. Marsav Distributors, Inc., 279 A.D. 715, 108 N.Y.S.2d 349 (1st Dept.1951), the plaintiffs discovered the alleged fraud within the first week after the purchase of the business. Yet they continued to

4. However, he may close the business upon proper notification to the other party. [citation]

5. Even the best management will not preserve the rescission right, however, where the pattern of facts shows an intent to affirm the contract.

operate the business for more than two months before sending a notice of election to rescind. Further, they inaugurated new pricing policies and changed the method of operating the business, causing a decline in gross receipts. Rescission was held to be unavailable.

But other cases have granted rescission even though the injured party has continued to operate the business. Especially where the property may depreciate materially if abandoned, as where a large part of its value stems from the fact that it is a going concern, the injured party may take such steps as are reasonably necessary to conserve the value of the business for the one ultimately determined to be the owner. The duty of care of a defrauded party who continues to operate a business for the benefit of the other party after sending a timely rescission notice and tendering the property back is that of a gratuitous bailee. * * *

In light of the foregoing legal standards, the pertinent factual inquiries are the following:

1. When did the Register discover the fraud?

2. Did the Register promptly notify Gannett of its intention to rescind and offer to return the property?

3. Did the Register affirm the contract after knowledge of the fraud by exercising acts of ownership over the Times? Or did its conduct in continuing to operate the Times constitute a justifiable attempt by a gratuitous bailee to conserve the property for the benefit of the ultimate owner?

4. If the Register has otherwise preserved its rights, is rescission nonetheless inequitable due to changed conditions and inability to restore the *status quo ante?*

The Register was on notice of the possibility of fraud on October 11, 1973, the day after the closing. On that day Raymond Dumont, the Controller of the Times, talked with Richard Harris, Vice President and Director of the Register and new Assistant Publisher of the Times, and told him that there were discrepancies in the circulation statistics of the Times. In meetings over the next few days Dumont disclosed the possible overvaluation of certain assets on the balance sheets of the Times as appended to the Purchase Agreement, and described a series of devices used for several years at the Times to conceal the reporting of inflated circulation figures to both Gannett and the Audit Bureau of Circulations, a nationally recognized organization that collects and publishes the circulation statistics of member newspapers.

A number of cases have held that the reasonable time period within which rescission must be demanded starts the moment the injured party is on notice of the fraud. Whether notice means actual knowledge or only facts reasonably prompting further inquiry need not be resolved here, since in this case actual knowledge followed closely on the heels of the date the Register was put on notice of the possibility of fraud. * * * Exhibits introduced by Gannett document that during the months of October and November most of the frauds came to light.

Further, the Register took a number of actions in the months of October and November indicating its awareness of the frauds and its apprehension that the frauds were of sufficient materiality to have breached the contract. On the advice of Curtiss Thompson, counsel to the Register, the payments due to Gannett under the net current asset adjustment provision of the Purchase

Agreement were withheld. This action was confirmed by a resolution of the Register's Board of Directors on October 25, 1973. * * * As of that date, John Fassett, who was a lawyer on the Register's board of directors, and possibly Thompson as well, were of the opinion that the Register had the option of rescinding the contract. * * *

I find, therefore, that full knowledge of the fraud may well have occurred at some point between October 11, 1973, and November 30, 1973, but that the very latest date for charging the Register with the responsibility of notifying Gannett within a reasonable time of its intention to rescind was November 30, 1973. * * *

The Register filed its counterclaim with a prayer for rescission on June 12, 1974. That date is therefore the latest date that the necessary rescission notice or demand took place. Whether any of the Register's earlier actions constituted notice of intent to rescind or otherwise preserved the right to rescind is the principal factual dispute between the parties. The difficulty in resolving this dispute stems in large part from the fact that during virtually the entire period between November 30, 1973, and June 12, 1974, the parties were engaged in serious settlement discussions. * * *

One claim is that the pendency of the settlement negotiations tolled the running of the promptness clock and that the Register was under no obligation to notify Gannett of intent to rescind until the negotiations had irrevocably fallen through. This approach, which would tend to further the general policy of the law to encourage settlement of disputes short of litigation, finds some support in the case law of rescission. As one court has stated of delay in seeking rescission:

> "Time alone is of slight significance, and, when it appears, as it does here, that the delay was occasioned by efforts to reach an amicable adjustment with offers and counter offers, the time so taken and the efforts so made cannot be counted as a time of sleeping on rights or an intention to forego remedy."

Plate v. Detroit Fidelity & Surety Co., 229 Mich. 482, 201 N.W. 457, 458 (1924). The appeal of this approach is that it favors the innocent party who has been trying in good faith to resolve the controversy amicably and puts the risk of uncertainty on the perpetrator of the fraud.

For several reasons, however, I am unwilling to accept an approach that would totally preclude any inquiry into what happened during the period of settlement negotiations. If the settlement period continues for any significant length of time, the buyer has the opportunity to indulge in just the sort of speculation the promptness rule was designed to prevent. Two sorts of essentially speculative delay could unreasonably prolong the period of settlement negotiations: delay for the purpose of speculation on the value of the property involved, and delay for the purpose of negotiating a favorable monetary settlement of the dispute. The latter is, in essence, speculation on the value of a potential lawsuit. While the amount of damages that might be acceptable in a settlement is not the item courts usually have in mind when they deny a rescinding buyer the right to "speculate," this amount bears a close relationship to the current value of the property being sold. The relationship is nonetheless close for being inverse: the buyer who sees the value of the property he bought declining will normally increase his damage demand so that an acceptable damage figure is inevitably a function of the subsequent value of the property. To let a rescinding buyer extend the time period in which he must demand rescission until the possibility of a monetary settlement has been pursued to an unsuccessful conclusion would have the undesirable feature of permitting the buyer to keep one eye on the fluctuating value of the property while he adjusts his negotiating demands. A complete tolling of the running of the reasonable time period during settlement negotiations could thus allow a buyer to prolong his opportunity for speculation, at least until the seller decided to call a halt by breaking off the discussions or by making his own unequivocal rescission offer, refusal of which would waive the buyer's rescission option or estop him from later asserting it. Furthermore, a party that wants rescission, even though the victim of a fraud, is not being disadvantaged at all by being required to make up his mind within a reasonable period after knowledge of the fraud and to give notice that he wants to return the property. At least with respect to functioning businesses, such an obligation promotes needed certainty in the marketplace. Moreover, it is a principle easily understood by parties seeking rescission and easily followed. Further, any inquiry into whether the period was prolonged for *bona fide* settlement purposes rather than with a speculative motive would require some examination of the reasonableness of the terms and figures demanded by the rescinder, in direct conflict with the settlement privilege and the policies behind it.

Counting the settlement period either entirely "in" or entirely "out" in determining the reasonable promptness of a rescission demand would each have undesirable risk allocation consequences. The first puts all the risk on the innocent buyer and deters the amicable resolution of disputes. The second places the entire risk of speculation on the seller, who may not even know until the unsuccessful end of damage negotiations that rescission has been in the buyer's mind all along.

The better approach, appropriate to a remedy as drastic as rescission, takes into account all the facts and circumstances that bear on reasonableness, with due regard for the sensitive nature of settlement negotiations and the policy reasons for protecting them. Though discussions may continue over months or even years, the acts and omissions of the parties must retain their normal legal significance. Exercise of acts of ownership over the property evidencing an intent to affirm the contract, will extinguish the right to disaffirm regardless of the pendency of negotiations, as will disposal of the property with knowledge of the fraud or any other act or omission that is clearly inconsistent with a later claim for rescission. Time no more stands still during settlement negotiations culminating with a rescission demand than it does when the statute of limitations runs during settlement. The fact that the parties agree, as they apparently did at the commencement of negotiations in this case, that settlement talks will be "without prejudice" and understand that participation in the negotiations will not *of itself* lessen their substantive rights does not always relieve the would-be rescinder of his duty to take the steps the law requires to preserve his rescission remedy. Legally significant acts and omissions can operate of their own force to terminate the right to rescission. The pendency of settlement discussions is simply one circumstance, albeit an important one, in determining the reasonableness of what the rescinding party did or failed to do.

There may well be situations in which the absence of a rescission demand would be reasonable under all the circumstances, as where the value and condition of the property remained constant during the negotiations so that no element of prejudice to the seller came into play, or where the seller's assurances of a favorable monetary settlement dissuaded the buyer from making an early demand. Or a slight delay in making a rescission demand, which would not preserve the remedy in the absence of settlement efforts, might well be reasonably timely if made unequivocally early in such discussions. Similarly if a buyer, once alerted to his right to rescind, promptly demands rescission, he should not lose the remedy because he negotiates with the seller, even for an extended time, to see if the rescission can be handled amicably without resort to litigation. I do not hold that the passage of time precludes rescission regardless of the circumstances. Rather I find that under the circumstances of this particular case rescission is unavailable. The absence of a rescission demand takes on special significance in this case, where the evidence is persuasive that even apart from the Register's omissions, its acts evidenced an intent to affirm the contract.

At no time during the relevant period did the Register's Board of Directors resolve to present a rescission offer to Gannett, although the subject of rescission was discussed at several board meetings. At the meeting on October 25, 1973, the possibility of rescission was discussed, but the operating officers of the Times reaffirmed their view that the purchase was desirable.

* * * It was not until February 25, 1975, that the Board of Directors specifically approved a rescission proposal to be submitted to Gannett. * * *

Several aspects of the testimony show convincingly that the Register wished to affirm the purchase contract and keep the Times rather than rescind. The first is Lionel Jackson's testimony in Court. The statements of Jackson, as Publisher and Chief Executive Officer of the Register and member of the negotiating committee appointed by the Board of Directors, are probably the most probative evidence of the corporate opinion of the Register during the time period in question. In response to questioning by the Court, Jackson testified:

> "I can say, your Honor, that the rest of the board—I can't speak for, I can only say for myself—that it was very, very distasteful for me to have to think about rescission because, after all, we didn't get into all this thing. We hoped to have a very successful joint newspaper situation in Hartford and New Haven, and we bought it with a purpose in mind, and it was—it certainly didn't help our reputation to have The Hartford Times turn out to be what it was, and rescission would have made it even worse.

Further, the Register had been engaged in defending the purchase of the Times in a lawsuit in the state court. The majority of the outstanding shares of the Register Publishing Company are owned by the John Day Jackson trust. When Jackson and Henry J. Conland, two of the three trustees of that trust, announced their intention to cause the Register to acquire the Times from Gannett, several beneficiaries of the trust instituted an action in the Superior Court in New Haven County in May of 1973 to enjoin the purchase. After injunctive relief was denied and the purchase consummated, the plaintiffs filed a substituted complaint alleging breach of fiduciary duty and seeking, *inter alia,* rescission of the sale. During the entire period in question the Register was defending the purchase of the Times in state court as a prudent investment. A decision to rescind the contract might well have been an admission that the beneficiaries were right. In a highly significant letter dated June 5, 1974, and sent by Lionel Jackson and Henry Conland to Rose Sheppard,

Jackson's sister and a plaintiff in the state court action, Jackson and Conland stated:

> "We don't know where you got the impression that The Register Publishing Company is seeking rescission, but it is obviously the result of misconstrued information which has caused the destruction of the family relationship."

This passage drastically undercuts the Register's claim that it was actively seeking to preserve the rescission remedy. * * *

On the basis of all the evidence I find that no notification of intent to rescind was given to Gannett within a reasonable time after the Register had discovered the frauds.

Wholly apart from the reasonableness of the delay in demanding rescission, the Register's conduct clearly evidences an intent to affirm the contract for the purchase of the Times. The evidence is persuasive that during the period after discovery of the frauds the Register exercised dominion over the Times by treating it as its own property and did not operate it as a gratuitous bailee for the benefit of the ultimate owner. * * *

If the Register had truly intended to hold the Times for Gannett's benefit in the event rescission was ultimately effected, one would have expected at least some sort of notice to Gannett of major changes to be made in the management of the Times to allow Gannett an opportunity to agree to voluntary rescission before irrevocable steps were taken. Probably the most important action taken was the decision to go to cold type from hot metal, a step that apparently most newspapers around the country are gradually taking, but one that requires substantial capital outlays. The testimony showed that the conversion to cold type was estimated to require an investment in the neighborhood of $500,000 to result in substantial savings over the long run after an initial period of increased expense during the transition period. I am willing to agree with the Register that the decision to go to cold type was a prudent one that would result in long-range savings. But this kind of major investment without consultation with or even notification to Gannett is inconsistent with the theory that the Register considered itself the bailee rather than the owner of the Times. * * *

Other substantial changes include a price increase of the Sunday paper from 15 cents to 25 cents and of the daily and Saturday papers from 10 cents to 15 cents, which had the effect of causing a significant drop in circulation not all of which could have been recouped even by a later price reduction after rescission; the cessation of distribution in outlying geographical areas; the discontinuation of 16 syndicated features and the addition of 48 others; and a shift in editorial policy. This catalogue is not exhaustive but illustrative. In short, many of the characteristics that give a newspaper its identity—editorial policy, features, price, and market, among others—were all significantly changed by the Register either before the rescission demand was made or while the claim was pending. The point is not that it would be impossible to reverse the changes, but rather that the pattern of the changes indicates the Register's intention to treat the Times as its own.

Equally supportive of the conclusion that the Register fully considered the Times to be its own property is the highly significant pattern of steps to integrate the operation of the Times with the operation of the New Haven Register and the New Haven Journal-Courier, the two New Haven papers published by the Register. Gannett has extensively catalogued the integration moves, and again not all of them need be discussed. Illustrative are the tying in of the cold type printing system to the Register's computer system in New Haven, the removal of a Univac Computer from the Times to New Haven to render computer services for the Times in New Haven, performance of bookkeeping functions for the Times by Register personnel in New Haven, the elimination of personnel from the Times staff and the absorption of their functions by Register staff, and others. I accept the Register's explanation that these moves were made to effect economies by eliminating duplication of equipment and personnel.[6] But as these steps were taken, it inevitably became more and more difficult to view the Times as a separate entity. After these changes neither Gannett nor any potential owner other than the Register would have been able to step in and operate the paper without substantial outlays and hiring to fill in for the functions then being performed in New Haven.

Under these circumstances, the Register must be deemed to have affirmed the contract and lost its right to rescission.

* * * Furthermore, to force return of the shares of The Hartford Times, Inc. upon Gannett at this stage would clearly be inequitable. The Times is no longer a going concern. Its value lies primarily in the tangible assets plus whatever highly speculative good will is still in existence that would to some extent help to reestablish circulation if publication were resumed.

While I have ruled against the Register on the availability of rescission, nothing in this memorandum should be taken as reflecting any view on the amount of damages that could eventually be awarded. This is entirely an open question at this point, and if the frauds as alleged and the damages as claimed can be proven, a substantial recovery of compensatory and exemplary damages may be possible.

Notes

1. Wynfield Inns v. Edward LeRoux Group, Inc., 896 F.2d 483, 488 (11th Cir.1990): "The doctrine of election of remedies is an 'application of the doctrine of estoppel' * * *. The purpose of the doctrine is to prevent duplicative recovery for the same wrong by requiring a party to elect between legally coexistent and inconsistent remedies."

2. Where the insured's misrepresentation is on an application for life insurance, the insurance company must refund the premiums the insured paid, with

6. The Register supports its "gratuitous bailee" characterization of its actions by pointing out that all the changes made were either necessary or desirable cost-cutting measures. This may well be true, but the fact that a significant change effects economies does not prove that rescission is still available. If the Register's argument were accepted, the rule of law requiring a rescinding party to refrain from acts of ownership over the property would shrink in scope to cover mismanagement or wastefulness only. The cases dealing with rescission of a going concern have never permitted substantive changes in the nature of the business, regardless of the effect on costs. See Gargotto v. Sherman, 297 Ky. 597, 180 S.W.2d 565 (1944) (removal of amusement machines and victrola from restaurant); Fryer v. Campbell, 48 Wyo. 122, 43 P.2d 994 (1935) (continued operation of motion picture theater causing deterioration in machinery and furniture); Meyers v. Hoops, 140 N.E.2d 65 (Ct.App.Ohio 1955) (changes in personnel equipment, and stock); Caruso v. Moy, 164 Neb. 68, 81 N.W.2d 826 (1957) (change in bill of fare of restaurant from Chinese–American to Italian–American); Sy–Jo Luncheonette, Inc. v. Marsav Distributors, Inc., 279 A.D. 715, 108 N.Y.S.2d 349 (1st Dept.1951) (new pricing policies). Charges of mismanagement were made in the latter two cases, but the rule of law on acts of ownership applies even where the rescinder's management is beyond reproach.

interest, as a condition for rescission or a declaration of invalidity. See Monarch Life Insurance Co. v. Donahue, 708 F.Supp. 674 (E.D.Pa.1989). What sanction is imposed on the insured for the fraudulent misrepresentation?

3. *Rescission Remedy Unavailable When Third Parties Would be Adversely Affected.* An automobile liability insurance company may attempt to cancel or rescind for fraud *after* the insured has caused injury. Indeed, a company may develop a practice of not checking the applicant's statements—particularly about prior arrest records or driving convictions—until the insured makes a claim. Thus if the insured has no accidents during the policy period, the insurer keeps the premiums; if he does, the insurer has a defense. The injured third party is, of course, seriously affected by this. Barrera v. State Farm Mutual Automobile Insurance Co., 71 Cal.2d 659, 79 Cal.Rptr. 106, 456 P.2d 674 (1969), imposes a duty on an automobile liability insurer to conduct a reasonable investigation of insurability even after issuing the policy: "Factors to be taken into account in assessing the reasonableness of the [insurers'] course of conduct in failing to investigate [the insured's] driving record are, inter alia, the cost of obtaining this information from the Department of Motor Vehicles, the availability of the information from the Department or elsewhere * * * and the general administrative burden of making the investigation." A breach of this duty precludes rescission ab initio of the policy, but the insurer has a cause of action for damages for deceit against the insured. Editors: The collectibility of damages may be imagined.

Barrera was followed in Fireman's Fund American Insurance Co. v. Escobedo, 80 Cal.App.3d 610, 145 Cal.Rptr. 785 (1978), even though the insurer was taking an "assigned" risk. Cf. Union Insurance Exchange, Inc. v. Gaul, 393 F.2d 151 (7th Cir.1968). Both *Escobedo* and *Gaul* suggest that knowledge imputed under agency principles may negate "justifiable reliance."

4. *Waiver of Right to Rescission.* Either an unreasonable delay in giving notice of rescission or conduct indicating an intention to enforce the contract defeats plaintiff's right to rescind. Whether delay is "unreasonable" or conduct is inconsistent with rescission are fact questions. There can be considerable disagreement. See Griffin v. Axsom, 525 N.E.2d 346 (Ind.App.1988) (a five year delay before giving notice of rescission because of a known title defect held to be unreasonable). Consider also Coggins v. New England Patriots Football Club, Inc., 397 Mass. 525, 492 N.E.2d 1112 (1986). The passage of time made it impossible to unscramble a merger which served no corporate purpose. Garcia v. Schell, 239 Mont. 475, 781 P.2d 274 (1989). Sale of personal property and execution of trust deed on realty held inconsistent with rescission.

ESTATE COUNSELING SERVICE v. MERRILL LYNCH, PIERCE, FENNER & SMITH, INC.

United States Court of Appeals, Tenth Circuit, 1962.
303 F.2d 527.

Skip

HILL, CIRCUIT JUDGE. This action was brought in the court below by appellant, as plaintiff, to recover damages for alleged fraud, breach of fiduciary duties in violation of Section 10(b) of the Securities Exchange Act of 1934 and Rule X–10B–5 promulgated thereunder. The suit resulted from a transaction involving the purchase of corporate common stock by the plaintiff, through the defendant as a broker. The appellee, defendant and third-party plaintiff below, answered, denying fraud or breach of fiduciary relationship in the transaction, raised certain affirmative defenses and counterclaimed against the plaintiff for the amount of $21,217.13, the amount of the loss it occasioned by the stock transactions. As third-party plaintiff it named William A. Lang and John R. Coombs as third-party defendants, and sought to recover from them also for its financial loss in the stock purchase and sale. Plaintiff, and the third-party defendants, as part of their defense to defendant's counterclaim against them, alleged, affirmatively, the rescission of the contract to purchase the stock.

After the issues were joined and an extensive pre-trial conference had, the Motion for Summary Judgment, on behalf of defendant, appellee here, was sustained. That order of the trial court is challenged by this appeal. * * *

On September 26, 1959, Jack R. Coombs, as President of appellant corporation, observed that common stock of Studebaker–Packard Corporation, whether traded under "regular way" or "when issued" contracts on the New York Stock Exchange was one of the ten most active stocks. He visited appellee's Salt Lake City branch office and obtained two bulletins relating to the stock. He thereafter talked with his friend and frequent business associate, William A. Lang, about the stock. Both had prior extensive dealings in securities as associates of brokerage firms. After this discussion, Lang talked on the telephone with Walter A. Roche, appellee's branch office manager in Salt Lake City, about the stock and was advised by Roche that Studebaker–Packard common stock "when issued" was a good speculation. Later the same day, Lang met and discussed with Kenneth Aitken, registered representative of defendant in the same city, the stock purchase. Lang indicated he was interested in buying 10,000 or 20,000 shares, and, if he bought, the purchase would be made in the name of appellant because of its tax loss carry forward. At this time all of the outstanding stock in plaintiff corporation was owned by Coombs and members of his family, the corporation was actually insolvent, had no regular office except the Coombs home and had no employees.

On September 29, 1959 * * * the purchase order was given to defendant to buy on the New York Stock Exchange in plaintiff's name 20,000 shares of common stock on a "when issued" basis at a price not to exceed $15.00 or $15.50 per share. The order was relayed to defendant's New York office on September 30, by Roche, and on that day Coombs was advised by Aitken that the stock had been purchased. Later that day Aitken personally delivered to Coombs and Lang confirmations of the purchases and asked payment for the margin deposit but was not paid. On October 5 Roche advised Lang and Coombs that the margin deposit of between $85,000 and $90,000 on the transaction would have to be paid. In the meantime the stock had declined in price. Lang told Roche that an alternative to paying the margin deposit was the liquidation and cancellation of the account, and as far as he was concerned the account could be cancelled. Roche refused to consent to such a cancellation. Again on October 6 demands were made on Lang and Coombs for paying of the margin deposit and refused.

On October 5 Lang and Coombs consulted with and retained Gordon I. Hyde to represent plaintiff and them in the controversy. On October 7 Hyde sent a letter to the chairman of the board of defendant corporation. The letter was composed in collaboration with Lang and Coombs and detailed charges of misrepresentation and misconduct on the part of defendant's local representatives. This letter reiterated Lang's proposal to cancel the transaction.

Thereafter, and on October 8 * * * counsel for Coombs, Lang and plaintiff sent another letter to the chairman of the board of defendant corporation as a follow-up of the Hyde letter, and in part, stated as follows:

> "This letter is written at the request of Mr. Hyde's clients and, in the absence of Mr. Hyde from Salt Lake City, as a follow-up to his letter of October 7, 1959, and to make clear that the aforesaid letter should be considered as a formal demand that the subject order and transaction, insofar as it concerns your firm of Estate Counseling Services, Inc., and persons interested therein, be rescinded on the basis of the material misrepresentations, omissions, and breaches of fiduciary obligation by your firm stated or referred to in the aforesaid letter, and in particular, on the following grounds."

This letter set forth seven grounds why the contracts should be rescinded.

By telegram, dated October 15, defendant rejected this last demand, and advised that unless the margin deposit was received it would sell out the stock at the opening of New York Stock Exchange at 7:00 o'clock A.M. Mountain Standard Time on October 16. The margin deposit was not paid and the stock was sold by defendant. A deficiency in the account of plaintiff with defendant in the amount of $21,217.13 resulted.

The granting of the Summary Judgment was based upon the legal theory that plaintiff, appellant here, had abandoned its right to seek damages by reason of its choice of the alternative of rescission, and under Utah law an action for damages and a rescission are inconsistent and mutually exclusive. [Merrill Lynch consented to summary judgment against it on its claims against Estate Counseling, and Coombs and Lang.] An appeal was taken only from the portion of the order granting defendant a Summary Judgment.

In our approach to the legal question before us, we must as the lower court did, assume for the purpose of the motion, that plaintiff was induced by fraud and breach of fiduciary duties, to place the order to purchase the stock.

The whole doctrine of election of remedies is equitable and in applying the doctrine the court should be sensitive to equitable principles. In Minneapolis National Bank of Minneapolis, Kansas v. Liberty Natl. Bank of Kansas City, 10 Cir., 72 F.2d 434, the court pointed out that the doctrine of election of remedy is disfavored in equity and should not be unduly extended. This Court, in Bernstein v. United States, 10 Cir., 256 F.2d 697, rejected the doctrine on a procedural ground. In diversity cases, we have acknowledged the doctrine as binding following the state substantive law. * * *

A fruitless attempt to recover on an unavailing remedy does not constitute an election which will deprive a person of rights which are availing by a different and appropriate remedy; the remedy must at least be to some extent efficacious in order to constitute an election. * * *

For the act to be effective as an election of remedies it must be decisive and unequivocal. Such election can be accomplished by legal proceedings or by "some other decisive act." Kuhl v. Hayes, 10 Cir., 212 F.2d 37; Cook v. Covey–Ballard Motor Co., 69 Utah 161, 253 P. 196, 199. * * *

The "formal demand for rescission," sent on behalf of the plaintiff * * * was an unequivocal, clear and unconditional statement. * * *

If there was any doubt as to whether the appellant intended to terminate its contractual relations with the appellee when the letter was sent, this doubt was resolved prior to the filing of the suit when the appellant consistently refused to meet the margin payment for the stocks purchased.

We agree with the findings of the trial court that the contention that there is an issue of fact with respect to the intent of the parties is wholly without merit. To submit to a jury the question of whether the letters manifested an intention to rescind the contract would be unthinkable. Such intention is manifested by the language of the letter so clearly that no room is left for doubt.

Furthermore, the equities of the situation do not justify departure from established principles, nor an extenuation of them. The appellee has not retained anything belonging to the appellant since nothing was ever paid to the appellee, even though frequent and repeated demands for the margin payment were made upon the appellant.

In view of the speculative nature of the transaction and with a fluctuating market, the law required the appellant to act promptly or waive its right to rescind. Where parties have the right to rescind, they cannot delay the exercise of that right to determine whether avoidance or affirmance will be more profitable to them. This is particularly true where the transaction is one of a speculative nature. * * * In the transaction herein involved it would doubtlessly have been more advantageous for the appellant to have had the benefit of claiming a rescission of the contract if a loss was imminent, and to disclaim the rescission if a profit was apparent. It is for this very reason, under the facts in this case, that the trial court was correct in granting the motion for summary judgment.

We, therefore, hold that the letters of October 7 and 8, 1959, manifested the intention of the appellant to rescind the contract and was the acceptance by it of the choice between contract and no contract, a choice between substantive right or no right. The letters, therefore, constituted a final election to rescind, and thereafter, precluded plaintiff from maintaining an action to recover damages for breach.

The defendant, in support of the lower court's ruling, also urges that plaintiff's causes of action must fail because the plaintiff suffered no damages as a result of the stock transaction. Likewise, there is merit to that contention.

The record is clear: That plaintiff was purchasing the stock on a "seven day in and out transaction" or "a seven day deal," and it was intended that the stock purchased would be sold within seven days after the purchase; that at the end of the seven days the stock was selling below the purchase price; plaintiff, in the transaction, had parted with nothing of value; and had the purchase and resale of the stock by the plaintiff, been carried out as intended, a loss and not a profit to the plaintiff would have resulted.

The law of Utah is well settled as to the necessary elements of a common law action for fraud and deceit. * * * Actions for fraud have failed because of lack of proof of damages. * * * The measure of damages in such actions is the difference between the value of what is purchased and the value of what he would have had if the alleged misrepresentations by the defendant had been true. * * *

The failure to show actual damages is also a fatal defect in the cause of action based on the Securities Exchange Act of 1934, 15 U.S.C.A. § 78a et seq. That Act permits recovery of "his actual damages on account of the act complained of." "Actual damages," under the Federal rule of damages for fraud is the "out of pocket rule." In the Federal courts the measure of damages recoverable by one who through fraud or misrepresentation has been induced to purchase bonds or corporate stock, is the difference between the contract price, or the price paid, and the real or actual value at the date of the sale, together with such outlays as are attributable to the defendant's conduct. Or in other words, the difference between the amount parted with and the value of the thing received. * * *

According to this theory, the question is not what the plaintiff might have gained, but what he has lost by being deceived into the purchase; the defendant is liable to respond in such damages as naturally and proximately result from the fraud; he is bound to make good the loss sustained—such moneys as the plaintiff has paid out, with interest, and any other outlay legitimately attributable to the defendant's fraudulent conduct—but this liability does not include the expectant fruits of an unrealized speculation. * * *

The undisputed facts, as shown by the record, disclose plaintiff to have paid out nothing, therefore, it suffered no actual damages under either cause of action.

The judgment of the lower court sustaining defendant's Motion For Summary Judgment is affirmed.

Notes

1. Threats to rescind, unless sincerely meant, should not be loosely tossed about under the assumption that remedial options will remain open. By sending a letter of intent to rescind or by filing suit asking for rescission (even in the alternative) the aggrieved party may find that if the other party simply accepts the offer, a binding election has occurred. A mutual rescission by consent has resulted. In Paularena v. Superior Court, 231 Cal.App.2d 906, 42 Cal.Rptr. 366 (1965), purchasers of land on executory land sale contracts sued a subdivider on various grounds including one cause of action seeking rescission. The subdivider promptly sent a letter of acceptance. Consider the consequences if, as might be inferred, a sudden economic turnaround occurs and creates a shortage of inexpensive housing.

2. In Doctor v. Lakeridge Construction Co., 252 Cal.App.2d 715, 60 Cal.Rptr. 824 (1967), the plaintiff, a land developer, bought a vacant lot and claimed that a misrepresentation of land conditions affected building possibilities. Plaintiff sued for damages in July, 1963, but did not mention rescission until the pretrial statement in February, 1966. The fraud claim failed for want of proof of substantive elements of deceit, that might not have been required for rescission. But by waiting too long and not acting promptly to rescind, the plaintiff had elected to affirm and was remedially bound by the choice.

2. ELECTION BY SUIT

SCHLOTTHAUER v. KRENZELOK

Supreme Court of Wisconsin, 1956.
274 Wis. 1, 79 N.W.2d 76.

Action * * * to recover damages in an action for fraud and deceit.

The complaint herein alleged that in October, 1952, the sellers were the owners of a farm and certain farm personalty located thereon, including a herd of dairy cattle; that prior to and on the 16th day of October, 1952, the sellers represented and warranted to the buyers that said herd of cattle was sound, healthy and free from infectious disease, * * * that after the date of purchase the buyers discovered that the herd was infected with brucellosis and it was necessary to dispose of said herd and to sell the farm, to their damage.

The answer admitted the ownership and sale of the farm and farm personalty but denied the other material allegations of the complaint. As a separate defense the answer alleged that on or about April 2, 1953, the buyers commenced an action against the sellers in the circuit court for Washington county for rescission, and said action was pending when the farm and farm personalty were sold. Because of the sale, the circuit court entered an order on October 7, 1954, dismissing the complaint. * * *

The present action was commenced on October 24, 1954, in the county court of Washington county. The sellers, in their answer, further pleaded as a separate defense that the buyers had made an election of remedies by commencing the former action for rescission, which precluded them from prosecuting the instant action. By an order entered October 14, 1955, the county court dismissed this action on the ground that there had been a binding election of remedies by the buyers. * * *

BROADFOOT, JUSTICE. In an annotation on the subject of Election of Remedies, appearing in 6 A.L.R.2d 15, it is stated:

> "The authorities are in conflict as to whether, as a general proposition, a conclusive election of remedies is effected on the one hand by the mere commencement of a suit or on the other hand, only where the suit has been prosecuted to judgment or where elements of estoppel in pais, other than the mere commencement of the suit, are present."

Such annotation cites the cases of Hildebrand v. Tarbell, 97 Wis. 446, 73 N.W. 53, and Carroll v. Fethers, 102 Wis. 436, 437, 78 N.W. 604, as holding that in Wisconsin a binding election is made at the time of commencement of suit. However, later decisions by this court would indicate that Wisconsin no longer adheres to such a harsh and arbitrary rule. The cases of Fuller–Warren Co. v. Harter, 110 Wis. 80, 85 N.W. 698 and Rowell v. Smith, 123 Wis. 510, 102 N.W. 1, lay down the principle that if the plaintiff has mistaken his remedy then there has been no binding election by the commencement of suit that precludes him from thereafter pursuing the proper remedy to judgment. The more recent cases of Bischoff v. Hustisford State Bank, 195 Wis. 312, 218 N.W. 353, and Beers v. Atlas Assurance Co., 231 Wis. 361, 285 N.W. 794, 795, raise grave doubt as to whether Wisconsin has not completely abandoned the holding of the earlier cases that conclusive election of remedies is made as of the time of the commencement of the action.

In Bischoff v. Hustisford State Bank, plaintiff first stated a cause of action for rescission of contract because of fraud, and then pleaded in the alternative a second cause of action to recover damages for fraud. This court held that the doctrine of election of remedies did not apply and that the complaint was proper. In the opinion by Mr. Justice Rosenberry it was stated:

> "If the plaintiff had set forth in his complaint the first cause of action, and had gone to trial thereon, and had been defeated, he would not thereby have been barred from suing on the contract for breach. The second action would not have been an attempt to relitigate the issues presented in the first cause of action. He would have sought recovery in the second cause of action upon an entirely different ground than the recovery sought in the first cause of action. * * * While the causes of action joined in this case would, as already pointed out, rest upon an inconsistent state of facts, the remedy sought in one is no substitute for the remedy sought in the other. *A suit in the first instance upon the contract for damages for breach would no doubt be an affirmance of it,*

which would preclude an action for rescission, but the reverse is not true." (Emphasis supplied.)

* * * We deem such italicized sentence is decisive of the issue before us on this appeal. The reason why a suit at law to recover damages for fraud bars a subsequent suit for rescission is not because there has been an election of inconsistent remedies, but rather that the act of instituting an action at law for damages recognizes the existence of the contract and affirms it. Once having been so affirmed, the right to rescind is forever lost. Such act is no different than any other act indicating an affirmance of the contract, such as proceeding with the performance of the contract after discovery of the fraud, or disposing of some of the property acquired under the contract, thus putting it beyond the power of the defrauded party to rescind and place the parties in *status quo*. As the author of the annotation in 6 A.L.R.2d 15, points out, one of the reasons for the conflict of the authorities on the subject of election of remedies "is the fact that the courts frequently fail to distinguish between a choice of inconsistent substantive rights afforded by law, with the result that the assertion of one, by suit or otherwise, results in the loss of the other, and a choice of inconsistent 'remedies' in the narrower sense, as to which the mere commencement of a suit pursuing one remedy should not, of itself, result in the loss of the other." The commencement of a suit for rescission for fraud involves merely a choice of procedural remedy and effects no change of substantive rights which should preclude the injured party from thereafter abandoning such remedy and affirming the contract by seeking damages for the fraud, unless something has occurred in the nature of an estoppel in pais which would make it inequitable from the standpoint of the defendant for the plaintiff to do so. There is no such element of estoppel present in the instant case.

The New Hampshire supreme court in Ricker v. Mathews, 94 N.H. 313, 53 A.2d 196, 199, recently had occasion to review the subject of election of remedies and we quote with approval from the opinion in that case as follows:

> "The doctrine of election of remedies has been the subject of much adverse criticism by courts and commentators because of the substantial injustice which frequently results from its application. * * * Although it is doubtful if the doctrine is obsolete, the trend of the decisions has been to limit it to avoid injustice. *To accomplish this purpose the formal doctrine of election of remedies should be confined to cases where the plaintiff may be unjustly enriched or the defendant has actually been misled by the plaintiff's conduct or the result is otherwise inequitable or res judicata can be applied.*" * * *

In view of our conclusion that plaintiffs' cause of action for fraud and deceit is not barred by the prior action in equity for rescission, the order and judgment appealed from must be reversed and the cause remanded for further proceedings.

Notes

1. *Pleading "Inconsistent" Counts.*

a. In Melby v. Hawkins Pontiac, Inc., 13 Wash.App. 745, 748–51, 537 P.2d 807, 810–11 (1975), plaintiff bought a new Maserati for $22,750. After using the automobile for six days, plaintiff returned it to defendant for repairs of indefinite duration. Three months later, plaintiff filed a complaint for "damages" arising from breach of warranty. Judgment was entered granting rescission and return of the money paid on the contract. In affirming, Pearson, J., stated:

"Defendant's second assignment of error on appeal is that rescission was not a proper remedy in this case because plaintiff elected his remedy by asking for damages only.

"[R]ecent Washington decisions have looked askance at the sometimes harsh application of the election of remedies doctrine. A liberal treatment is desirable for two reasons: First, because the doctrine was created solely to prevent a plaintiff from having a double recovery, a harsh application is often not necessary for the furtherance of this purpose; and second, the doctrine as sometimes applied is inconsistent with modern rules of pleading, such as CR 8(a) (which allows demands for alternative relief) and CR 15(b) (which allows amendments to the pleadings to conform to the evidence). However, the doctrine should not be ignored when the defendant has relied to his detriment on plaintiff's prayer for relief or has been otherwise prejudiced by plaintiff's actions.

"The instant case involves the sale of goods, and therefore is governed by the provisions of the Uniform Commercial Code, 2–703 (seller's remedies) states:

> 'This Article rejects any doctrine of election of remedy as a fundamental policy and thus the remedies are essentially cumulative in nature and include all of the available remedies for breach. Whether the pursuit of one remedy bars another depends entirely on the facts of the individual case.' "

RCW 62A.2–711 allows the buyer to cancel, and whether or not he had done so he may recover amounts paid and obtain damages.

"In view of the above analysis of the election of remedies doctrine and the official commentary to the Uniform Commercial Code, we hold that in cases involving the sale of goods, the election of remedies doctrine is no bar to the pursuit of alternate remedies so long as the plaintiff would not have a double recovery and the defendant is not seriously prejudiced thereby.

"We do not believe that the defendant could have been misled by plaintiff's complaint. The prayer for relief requested damages in the amount of $22,750—in other words, it requested restitution of the purchase price of the automobile and, a fortiori, rescission. Further, we have not seen any other evidence indicating defendant was prejudiced by a judgment of rescission as opposed to damages. Hence, we conclude that the judgment of rescission and restitution was proper."

b. Pleading fraud in alternative counts seeking restitution or damages now seems universally approved though some procedural anomalies remain. See Bancroft v. Woodward, 183 Cal. 99, 190 P. 445 (1920); Walraven v. Martin, 123 Mich.App. 342, 333 N.W.2d 569 (1983). This useful pleading technique does not eliminate the election of remedies problem. Since the remedies sought are alternative, an election between them must be made at some point. The plaintiff seeks to postpone that decision for as long as possible. Defendant, on the other hand, pushes for an early resolution. The point in the proceedings when the election will be compelled has received conflicting answers, not infrequently in the same court. Some federal courts have ruled that the election must be made "either at the pre-trial conference or at the trial." Paxton v. Desch Building Block Co., 146 F.Supp. 32, 37 (E.D.Pa.1956). Others say "during the trial." Venn–Severin Machine Co. v. John Kiss Sons Textile Mills, Inc., 2 F.R.D. 4, 5 (D.N.J.1941). Other federal courts have said that no election need be made but that all counts supported by proof may be submitted. Bernstein v. United States, 256 F.2d 697, 706 (10th Cir.1958), cert. dismissed 358 U.S. 924 (1959); North American Graphite Corp. v. Allan, 184 F.2d 387, 389 (D.C.Cir.1950).

Similar diversity exists in California decisions. Some indicate that no election is required before submission to judge or jury. One of the strongest statements is found in Williams v. Marshall, 37 Cal.2d 445, 457, 235 P.2d 372, 379 (1951):

"At various stages of the trial, the Marshalls [defendants] unsuccessfully moved the trial court to compel an election between the alternative remedies of rescission and damages. They argue that as a result of these erroneous rulings, they were compelled to defend both theories. A defrauded vendee may, in the same action, seek rescission or damages in the event rescission cannot be obtained. * * * There is no good reason why the plaintiff in such an action should be compelled to make an election between those remedies during the course of the trial, and such a rule would be contrary to fundamental principles of law."

Since the remedies sought are alternative, "it is for the court to say" after all the evidence is introduced, "to which remedy, if any, plaintiff is entitled." Buck v. Cardwell, 161 Cal.App.2d 830, 834, 327 P.2d 223, 225 (1958); Tanforan v. Tanforan, 173 Cal. 270, 274, 159 P. 709, 711 (1916) (election is "a matter for judge or jury").

A classic statement of the contrary approach, based on "the inexorable logic of the formulary system," may be found in Jozovich v. Central California Berry Growers Association, 183 Cal.App.2d 216, 228–9, 6 Cal.Rptr. 617, 626 (1960): "The cases have recognized the common-sense rule that an aggrieved party may not simultaneously pursue inconsistent procedures for relief."

c. The Restatement (Second) of Contracts, § 378 comment a (1981), states that commencing an action seeking one remedy does not in itself preclude a party from seeking another remedy so long as there is no change of position by the defendant. Election of remedies doctrine is thus based on an estoppel principle. One of the clearest illustrations is where a plaintiff commences an action seeking rescission and avails himself of the provisional remedy of attachment. Having secured this advantage over the defendant, plaintiff is held to have made a binding election to disaffirm the contract. Roam v. Koop, 41 Cal.App.2d 1035, 116 Cal.Rptr. 539 (1974); Steiner v. Rowley, 35 Cal.2d 713, 221 P.2d 9 (1950).

d. May v. Watt, 822 F.2d 896, 900–01, 902 (9th Cir.1987): "May has not waived his right to seek quantum meruit recovery by electing to submit a contract damage theory to the jury. 'The doctrine of election, as applied to a choice of remedies, either offensive or defensive, which precludes a party from claiming repugnant rights, is but an extension of the general principles of equitable estoppel, and proceeds upon a like theory that the inconsistent attitude of the party will put his adversary to some disadvantage.' McDanels v. General Insurance Co., 1 Cal.App.2d 454, 461, 36 P.2d 829 (1934). Here, May was not given any opportunity to make an election since the Court refused to instruct the jury on his quantum meruit claim. In any event, he was not required to make an election between the relevant contract theories he advocated (breach of contract and rescission) prior to a jury verdict. * * *

"[W]e remand for a new trial only on the question whether the defendants' breach was such as to warrant a rescission of the contract and, if so, applying quantum meruit principles, what the amount of any additional recovery should be.

"We also note that Watt and Ring Brothers have requested that if we reverse on the quantum meruit claim, we direct that the question of breach of contract be resubmitted to a jury. We are aware of no reason for doing so. The fact of breach has been established, as has the appropriate amount of damages for that breach. If a new trial is held on rescission, and the quantum meruit damages are greater than those already awarded for breach of contract, May will be entitled to the additional amount. If the award in quantum meruit is less, the verdict will be of academic interest only."

e. Compare West Pinal Family Health Center, Inc. v. McBryde, 162 Ariz. 546, 548, 785 P.2d 66, 68 (App.1989): "Any one or more of these remedies [rescission, specific performance or damages] may be sought in the complaint, and the party may wait until trial before electing the remedy to pursue."

2. Prosecution of one alternative remedy to judgment with full knowledge of the facts may constitute a binding election. Roberts v. Sears, Roebuck & Co., 617 F.2d 460, 461 (7th Cir.1980): "The plaintiff inventor sued the defendant retail store chain for breach of confidential relation, fraud, and negligent misrepresentation. The plaintiff prayed for rescission of the agreement assigning the patent rights to the defendant, an injunction against further use by the defendant, imposition of a constructive trust upon the defendant, an equitable accounting by the defendant and 'such further equitable relief as may be appropriate.' Included among these equitable prayers was a plea 'that damages be awarded to plaintiff.' " Unfortunately plaintiff persisted in pursuing his claims for money damages before a jury to a final judgment of $1,000,000. Although this might seem satisfactory, the court of appeals held that he was now barred from asserting the alternative equitable restitutionary theories that might have yielded over $40,000,000. See, Oesterle, Restitution and Reform, 79 Mich.L.Rev. 336, 343–50 (1980).

See also Najjar Industries, Inc. v. City of New York (Greenpoint Incinerator), 68 N.Y.2d 943, 510 N.Y.S.2d 82, 502 N.E.2d 997 (1986). Plaintiff sought rescission for breach of a construction contract and was awarded a judgment. Because of errors in the computation of the award, the judgment was reversed and the case was remanded for retrial of the issue of damages only. The court refused to permit plaintiff to assert a claim for contract damages at the second trial.

Compare Wedgewood Diner, Inc. v. Good, 368 Pa.Super. 480, 534 A.2d 537 (1987), where the plaintiff first recovered a judgment for damages against an agent and then sought to rescind the same contract in an action brought against the principal. The court held that the latter action was barred by plaintiff's election to affirm the contract and recover damages from the agent.

3. As the court in *Estate Counseling Service* noted, plaintiff's attempt to obtain a non-existent remedy is not an election. Thus a plaintiff who sought to recover damages for an alleged but non-existent fraudulent misrepresentation was not precluded by the election doctrine from later suing to reform the contract. Fina Supply, Inc. v. Abilene National Bank, 726 S.W.2d 537 (Tex.1987). What about the doctrine of res judicata? Has plaintiff split a cause of action?

4. *Federal Jurisdictional Amount and Choice of Remedy.* A defrauded plaintiff, who otherwise has access to the federal courts, may, of course, have more difficulty in meeting the minimum jurisdictional amount if the applicable state rule of damages is "out of pocket" rather than "benefit of the bargain."

On the other hand if plaintiff chooses rescission and asks less than $50,000, a state rule disallowing punitive damages where restitution is sought will preclude including this claim for purposes of diversity jurisdiction. Moreover, having under the circumstances effected rescission, he may have lost his right to sue in fraud for deceit, and his federal action may be dismissed for want of jurisdiction. See Ringsby Truck Lines, Inc. v. Beardsley, 331 F.2d 14 (8th Cir.1964). Cf. Deming v. Buckley's Art Gallery, 196 F.Supp. 246 (W.D.Ark.1961).

B. THE MECHANICS OF REESTABLISHING THE STATUS QUO

1. THE DISTINCTION BETWEEN LEGAL AND EQUITABLE RESCISSION

KNAEBEL v. HEINER

Supreme Court of Alaska, 1983.
663 P.2d 551.

[Knaebel, Heiner and Chipp founded Resources Associates of Alaska, a close corporation, to conduct mineral explorations. Tensions arose. The parties agreed to break up. As part of the process, Knaebel was to form a "Type D" (to minimize taxes) reorganization. The assets of RAA were divided pursuant to the agreement. Knaebel received cash and properties and agreed to serve as consultant. He also resigned as chief officer of the corporation. Disputes arose concerning the reorganization plan when counsel advised Knaebel that it contained many defects. Knaebel, considering himself the victim of a corporate squeeze-out, sought to rescind the reorganization agreement. The trial court denied rescission.]

CONNOR, JUSTICE. * * * Appellees contend that Knaebel is not entitled to seek equitable rescission because: (1) Knaebel has an adequate remedy at law, and * * * (3) Knaebel did not, before seeking rescission, return to RAA the proceeds he received pursuant to the reorganization agreement.

* * * The trial court shall decide on remand whether the facts of Knaebel's case indicate that damages would be an inadequate remedy.

* * * [W]e address the appellees' contention that Knaebel must return the proceeds he received pursuant to the reorganization agreement before he may seek equitable rescission.

Rescission *at law* is a suit based upon rescission already accomplished. At law the court has nothing to do with the rescission itself; it is only involved if a subsequent suit is brought by plaintiff to recover what he gave to defendant pursuant to the rescinded transaction. D. Dobbs, Remedies § 4.8, at 292–93.

"Restoration or tender [of the benefits received under the transaction being rescinded] before suit is a necessary element in legal rescission, but is wholly superfluous as a prerequisite to the commencement of a suit in equity for rescission or cancellation." Lightner v. Karnatz, 258 Mich. 74, 241 N.W. 841, 842 (Mich.1932).

Equitable rescission differs from rescission at law in that it is not conditioned upon restoration of benefits, nor does it require an offer of restoration.

> "Since rescission is not accomplished 'in equity' until the court so decrees, *the plaintiff has no obligation before suit to make restitution* of goods or money he received from the defendant. * * * [Since the court has the] capacity to protect the defendant by its decree and to condition rescission upon full restoration.
>
> This does not mean that the plaintiff is entitled to get back what he gave and keep what he got, too. It means only that *he need not make formal tender before suit.*"

D. Dobbs, Remedies § 4.8, at 294 (emphasis added).

Because Knaebel seeks equitable rescission rather than legal rescission, we hold, as a matter of law, that neither restoration nor tender is required by Knaebel before suit.

[Reversed and remanded]

Notes

1. Legal rescission is variously described as "out of court rescission," "rescission in pais," "rescission by an act of the parties," or "unilateral rescission." The theory is that giving notice and restoring or offering to restore disaffirms effectively. Thereafter a legal restitutionary action may be maintained. A buyer of goods, having accomplished legal rescission, may recover the price paid in a quasi-contractual action, in the meantime holding what are now the seller's goods in a custodial capacity. Conversely, a seller of a bicycle, by giving notice and tendering back the price received in theory revests himself with the legal title and may maintain a possessory action for the bicycle. Moreover, if the purchaser does not return the bicycle promptly upon the original demand, he becomes a tortfeasor; and seller may sue for conversion or in the alternative for goods sold and delivered. Crown Cycle v. Brown, 39 Or. 285, 64 P. 451 (1901).

Would these remedies be adequate in *Knaebel?* Whenever documentary legal title is transferred—e.g., deeds to realty—only an in personam equity decree to execute a reconveyance will effect rescission. Will an equity decree to rescind put Research Associates of Alaska back together?

2. The distinction between legal and equitable rescission is not always easy to understand and maintain. In Lithocraft, Inc. v. Rocky Mountain Marketing, Inc., 108 Idaho 247, 248, 697 P.2d 1261, 1262 (App.1985), the court stated that rescission was an equitable remedy and that he who seeks equity must do equity. One seeking equitable rescission must "first tender or offer to tender that which he has received." The Nebraska court, however, in Kracl v. Loseke, 236 Neb. 290, 461 N.W.2d 67 (1990), ruled that since the plaintiffs sought equitable rescission, they need not tender back benefits they had received from the defendant.

3. The right to jury trial in rescission is an equally vexing problem. The California court ruled that the "gist" of vendor's action to rescind a land sale contract was equitable and that there was no right to jury trial. Fowler v. Ross, 142 Cal.App.3d 472, 191 Cal.Rptr. 183, 187 (1983). On the other hand, in a vendee's action to rescind the sale of a home, the court ruled that the action was for money and that there was a right to jury trial. Paularena v. Superior Court, 231 Cal.App.2d 906, 42 Cal.Rptr. 366 (1965). See also, Philpott v. Superior Court, 1 Cal.2d 512, 36 P.2d 635 (1934). A cautious federal judge ruled that an action to rescind the sale of a newspaper was equitable, but he empaneled an advisory jury just to be on the safe side. McKinney v. Gannett Co., 660 F.Supp. 984 (D.N.M. 1981), appeal dismissed, 694 F.2d 1240 (10th Cir.1982).

4. In some jurisdictions, the decision of whether rescission is legal or equitable may affect subject matter jurisdiction. Coran v. Keller, 295 Ark. 308, 748 S.W.2d 349 (1988).

RUNYAN v. PACIFIC AIR INDUSTRIES, INC.

Supreme Court of California, 1970.

2 Cal.3d 304, 85 Cal.Rptr. 138, 466 P.2d 682.

SULLIVAN, JUSTICE. * * * Defendant Pacific Air Industries, Inc. (Pacific) is a corporation engaged in the business of aerial surveying and photogrammetric services with headquarters in Long Beach. In 1965 plaintiff was, and for several years prior thereto had been, a geologist and engineer employed by Tidewater Oil Company (Tidewater). In October of that year he responded to an advertisement placed by Pacific in the Wall Street Journal announcing the availability of Pacific franchise territories in various areas of California. A number of conferences with Pacific followed. Eventually on March 9, 1966, plaintiff and Pacific entered into a written area service contract whereby, in consideration of the payment by plaintiff of $25,000, he was awarded an exclusive photogrammetric franchise for the Counties of Inyo, Kern, Kings and Tulare. In the meantime, on February 18, 1966, he had resigned his position with Tidewater Oil Company. * * *

Pacific's performance in supplying and maintaining the local office did not comply with its obligations under the contract. * * *

Despite Pacific's failure to fully perform its promises plaintiff initially made no complaint. In late summer, however, he became concerned that his franchise was being treated by Pacific merely as a commission arrangement. He complained that Pacific was making charges for "first order instrument" work at arbitrary rates. Finally, on October 7, 1966, plaintiff gave Pacific written notice of rescission of the contract of March 9, 1966, based upon failure of consideration and fraud.

Shortly thereafter plaintiff brought the instant action for restitution and consequential damages. His complaint set forth four counts: the first based on rescission for failure of consideration; the second and third based on rescission for fraud; and the fourth a common count for money lent apparently grounded on a theory of rescission. Plaintiff sought recovery not only of the consideration paid by him but also of consequential damages consisting of office expenses, training expenses and loss of salary for the period during which he had attempted to operate under the franchise.

The trial court found in favor of plaintiff on the first count but against plaintiff on the remaining three counts. The court concluded that plaintiff had rescinded the area service contract on October 7, 1966, and was entitled to recover the $25,000 franchise fee and his "net consequential damages" in the sum of $5,273.25.[1] Judgment was entered accordingly. This appeal followed. * * *

We now take up Pacific's principal contention that the court erred in awarding consequential damages. Actually Pacific does not challenge the entire award of consequential damages. It raises no issue as to the item of $1,082 for training and office expense. It objects only to the item of "loss of income" in the sum of $7,256.25 upon the ground that there is no evidence that it had guaranteed to plaintiff a profit from the franchise equal to or greater than his former salary with Tidewater. In essence Pacific argues that plaintiff "assumed the risk" of loss which is inherent in an entrepreneurial activity. We are thus called upon to inquire into plaintiff's entitlement not only to the

1. [Footnotes renumbered.] The findings clearly indicate that the court's award of consequential damages in the net sum of $5,273.25 was arrived at as follows:

Loss of income from 3/9/66 to 9/30/66	$7,256.25
Training expense	550.00
Office expense	532.00
	$8,338.25
Less plaintiff's gross income from activities relating to franchise	3,065.00
	$5,273.25

restitution of the $25,000 franchise fee but also to consequential damages because of the loss of his salary income.

The positions of the parties may be briefly summarized thusly: Pacific argues that damages cannot be recovered in the event of rescission since the two remedies are mutually inconsistent, a claim for damages being based upon an affirmance of the contract while rescission is predicated upon its disaffirmance. Plaintiff in response maintains that although prior to 1961 an award of damages in cases of rescission "might have been subject to serious question," nevertheless Civil Code section 1692 enacted in that year not only authorized but probably requires an award of consequential damages where relief is sought based upon a rescission.

Section 1692 which provides for relief based upon rescission was added to the Civil Code in 1961 upon the recommendation of the California Law Revision Commission. * * * We set forth section 1692 in full in the footnote.[2]

At the start it would appear that the statute compels the rejection of Pacific's argument that damages cannot be recovered in an action for relief based on a rescission since the section expressly and unequivocally states that a "claim for damages is not inconsistent with a claim for relief based upon rescission" and that the aggrieved party "shall be awarded complete relief, including restitution of benefits, if any, * * * and any consequential damages to which he is entitled; * * * but * * * not * * * duplicate or inconsistent items of recovery." Our more proper inquiry then is whether the relief awarded in the instant case is that intended by the Legislature. Since the enactment of section 1692 was not an isolated event we must examine the section in the light of the historical background of rescission procedures and the purpose of the statutory changes enacted in 1961.

In California prior to 1961 there were two methods provided for in the Civil Code by which a party entitled to rescind could obtain rescissionary relief. The first, found in sections 1688–1691, specified certain instances in which a party to a contract might rescind it and provided that such rescission could be accomplished by the rescinding party by giving notice of the rescission and offering to restore everything of value which he had received. This method contemplated a rescission "by the individual act of one of the parties to the contract" and has been referred to as a unilateral rescission. McCall v. Superior Court (1934) 1 Cal.2d 527, 536, 36 P.2d 642, 646.) Having rescinded the contract by his own act, the rescinding party then brought an action to enforce the out-of-court rescission. (Philpott v. Superior Court (1934) 1 Cal.2d

2. Section 1692 provides: "When a contract has been rescinded in whole or in part, any party to the contract may seek relief based upon such rescission by (a) bringing an action to recover any money or thing owing to him by any other party to the contract as a consequence of such rescission or for any other relief to which he may be entitled under the circumstances or (b) asserting such rescission by way of defense, counterclaim or cross-complaint.

"If in an action or proceeding a party seeks relief based upon rescission and the court determines that the contract has not been rescinded, the court may grant any party to the action any other relief to which he may be entitled under the circumstances.

"A claim for damages is not inconsistent with a claim for relief based upon rescission. The aggrieved party shall be awarded complete relief, including restitution of benefits, if any, conferred by him as a result of the transaction and any consequential damages to which he is entitled; but such relief shall not include duplicate or inconsistent items of recovery.

"If in an action or proceeding a party seeks relief based upon rescission, the court may require the party to whom such relief is granted to make any compensation to the other which justice may require and may otherwise in its judgment adjust the equities between the parties."

512, 524, 36 P.2d 635.) Such action was considered to be one at law brought on the implied promise on the part of the nonrescinding party to repay or return the consideration received. "In reality, it is an action in which the law, in order to prevent the unjust enrichment of defendants from the property of plaintiff, itself implies a promise to repay the sum demanded. In other words, it is an action in *assumpsit* upon a promise implied by law."

The second method by which a party could obtain rescissionary relief was the action for a judicial rescission. * * * Unlike the method of unilateral rescission, however, this method was viewed as an action for specific judicial relief for the wrong giving rise to the right of rescission, and was deemed equitable in nature. * * * Significant substantive and procedural differences existed between these two methods for obtaining rescissionary relief. The right to a jury trial, the applicable statute of limitations, the availability of the provisional remedy of attachment and the possibility of joinder of other claims all depended upon which of these two methods the plaintiff elected to use in seeking rescissionary relief. The result was a body of law which was "unnecessarily complex and confusing to both courts and attorneys, to say nothing of laymen." 3 Cal.Law Revision Com.Rep. (1961).

As previously mentioned the Legislature made several changes in these procedures in 1961. Prominent among these was the addition of section 1692 and the repeal of sections 3406–3408. "This legislation, in effect, abolished the action to obtain court rescission and left only an action to obtain relief based upon a party effected rescission." (Paularena v. Superior Court (1965) 231 Cal.App.2d 906, 913, 42 Cal.Rptr. 366, 370.) * * *

We perceive in this fusing of the two former rescission procedures no intention on the part of the Legislature to disturb, much less eradicate, substantive differences theretofore underlying such procedures. Indeed the Law Revision Report which was the genesis of these statutory changes included among its specific recommendations the following: "The rescission statutes should make plain that, after rescinding a contract, a party may seek any form of relief warranted under the circumstances, whether legal or equitable. As all such actions will be to *enforce* a rescission, the right of the parties to a jury and the court in which the action must be brought will be determined by the nature of the substantive relief requested and not by the form of the complaint. For example, if a bare money judgment is sought, a justice court will have jurisdiction in appropriate cases, and the plaintiff may not convert the action into an equity action and thus deprive the justice court of jurisdiction merely by a prayer for rescission. The statute should also make plain that the court may grant any other relief that is appropriate under the circumstances if it develops at the trial that the plaintiff has mistaken his remedy and the purported rescission was not effective." * * *

Under the new statutory scheme, when a contract has been rescinded in accordance with the statutory procedure (§ 1691)[3] "any party to the contract

3. Section 1691 provides: "Subject to Section 1693, to effect a rescission a party to the contract must, promptly upon discovering the facts which entitle him to rescind if he is free from duress, menace, undue influence or disability and is aware of his right to rescind:

(a) Give notice of rescission to the party as to whom he rescinds; and

(b) Restore to the other party everything of value which he has received from him under the contract or offer to restore the same upon condition that the other party do likewise, unless the latter is unable or positively refuses to do so.

may seek relief based upon such rescission * * *." This is accomplished by bringing an action "to recover any money or thing owing to him" and "for any other relief" to which he may be entitled. Whatever may have been the rule under former decisional law dealing with "legal" rescission, the statute now expressly provides that a "claim for damages is not inconsistent with a claim for relief based upon rescission" and that the aggrieved party "shall be awarded complete relief" including restitution and consequential damages, if any. (All quotations are from section 1692.)

Under pre–1961 law, however, an action at law to enforce an out-of-court rescission was, by its very nature, invariably restricted to the recovery of the consideration given by the rescinding party. As we have explained, it was an action in *assumpsit* upon a promise implied by law. The scope of relief was therefore limited by the promise raised by implication of law on which the action was based—namely to return the consideration;[4] there was no implied "promise" to pay damages. The decisions were replete with statements that the remedies of rescission and damages were inconsistent. * * *

However, under pre–1961 law in actions in equity to obtain a judicial rescission, monetary awards including those of consequential damages, given in conjunction with restitution, have been sustained in a variety of contexts. Thus, it was settled that a vendee of real property who rescinded a land sale contract because of the vendor's fraud could recover the purchase money paid by him and the reasonable value of improvements less the reasonable rental value of the land while in the vendee's possession. * * * An award for the value of improvements was also available in some cases where the vendee rescinded because of failure of consideration. * * * Similarly, the rescinding vendee was entitled to monetary compensation for any payments by him to reduce the amount of a mortgage imposed upon the property by the vendor. Where the vendor rescinded, the vendee was liable for the rental value of the land while he had possession. When a contract for the sale of personal property was rescinded, a rescinding vendor was also entitled to an award for the reasonable value of the use of the property by the vendee, or for its cost of replacement where the specific property could not be returned. * * *

Some of these cases refer to such monetary awards given in an action for rescission as "damages" or "consequential damages." * * * For example, we said in Hines v. Brode (1914) 168 Cal. 507, 511–512, 143 P. 729, 731, that "[T]he vendee may rescind, and, in addition to the recovery of the consideration with which he has parted, obtain recoupment for *any other special damage* to which he has been subjected by the vendor's fraud." (Italics added.) * * *[5]

"When notice of rescission has not otherwise been given or an offer to restore the benefits received under the contract has not otherwise been made, the service of a pleading in an action or proceeding that seeks relief based on rescission shall be deemed to be such notice or offer or both."

4. Speaking of the action to enforce a unilateral rescission, the court in *Philpott* said: "[I]t is a case where the plaintiff has not elected to sue for damages, general or special or both, which he may have suffered from the tort inflicted upon him by defendants; likewise it is not a case where the plaintiff is seeking the application of equitable remedies to redress his grievances. All these elements, which may have been shown by appropriate allegations for such relief, are conspicuously absent. Plaintiff apparently *is content to merely seek a return from defendants of money given them,* with interest, *forgetting and foregoing all other elements of injury.* Is it not plain, therefore, that he has waived the tort of defendants and has come into court relying solely upon the promise created by law to return to him the consideration paid upon the contract?" (Italics added.) Philpott v. Superior Court.

5. In Lobdell v. Miller, 114 Cal.App.2d 328, 250 P.2d 357 which involved rescission for fraud, the court observed: "The remedy of re-

The fundamental principle underlying these decisions and the awards which they upheld is that "in such actions the court should do complete equity between the parties" and to that end "may grant any monetary relief necessary" to do so. (Stewart v. Crowley, supra, 213 Cal. 694, 701, 3 P.2d 562, 565.) * * *

As the cases already cited by us illustrate, California courts applying general principles of equity have recognized that the restoration to the rescinding party of the consideration with which he originally parted does not necessarily in all instances restore him to his former position and bring about substantial justice. The rescinding vendee of land who in reliance upon the contract has placed improvements on the property must invariably be compensated for them if he is to be afforded "complete relief." In instances such an adjustment may be compelled so as to forestall unjust enrichment of the nonrescinding party through whose fault the grounds of rescission have arisen.

This prompts us to point out that restitutionary damages have not been awarded the rescinding party in every case of rescission. Such damages may be awarded in conjunction with restitution where rescission has been sought for the nonrescinding party's fraud * * * misrepresentations, * * * and, in some cases, failure of consideration * * *. We have not found nor has our attention been directed to any reported California decisions in which the courts have awarded consequential damages when rescission has been sought merely upon the grounds of illegality or mistake * * *. It appears, therefore, that California decisions, in determining when restitutionary damages should be awarded, have differentiated between actions for rescission based upon a ground involving some fault on the part of the nonrescinding party, and actions based upon a ground not involving such fault. Only in the former category have courts of equity required the nonrescinding party to pay to the other restitutionary damages, for the obvious reason that otherwise he would be unjustly enriched. * * *

These traditional and deep-rooted principles of courts of equity can now be invoked through the simple procedure furnished by section 1692. * * *

Mindful of these principles and of the purpose of the statutory changes enacted in 1961, we turn to the case before us. Essentially the question we confront is whether the trial court, presumably responsive to the mandate that the aggrieved party be awarded complete relief, acted reasonably and equitably in making an award of consequential damages for plaintiff's "loss of income."

scission necessarily involves a repudiation of the contract. The remedy afforded by an action for the recovery of damages suffered by reason of fraud, * * * involves an affirmance of the contract. The measure of damages recoverable in an action for rescission is essentially different from that in a simple action for damages * * *. In the rescission action a plaintiff is entitled to recover the consideration he gave on restoration or offer of restoration of that which he received. He is also entitled to recover compensation for whatever consequential damages he may have suffered by reason of having entered into the contract."

Thus the damages available under each remedy are different. The award given in an action for damages compensates the party not in default for the loss of his "expectational interest" —the benefit of his bargain which full performance would have brought. (Fuller and Perdue, The Reliance Interest in Contract Damages: 1(1936) 46 Yale L.J. 52, 54.) Relief given in rescission cases—restitution and in some cases consequential damages—puts the rescinding party in the *status quo ante,* returning him to his economic position before he entered the contract.

The trial court gave plaintiff relief on the first count[6] of his complaint which sought rescissionary relief based upon failure of consideration. * * * The trial court found that plaintiff had in good faith substantially performed his part of the contract, that there had been a material failure of consideration because of specified acts of Pacific, that plaintiff gave Pacific notice of rescission based on such failure of consideration, that "*In reliance* upon said contract plaintiff necessarily incurred" (italics added) certain expenses including the "loss of income" here in question, and that while the franchise was in effect plaintiff had certain gross income from his franchise activities.

As we have pointed out, the trial court awarded plaintiff the sum of $7,256.25 to compensate him for his loss of income for the period from the execution of the area service contract to the giving of the notice of rescission, this loss being measured by the salary he would have received had he remained at Tidewater. We cannot find this award unreasonable or inequitable particularly since, as the court expressly found, plaintiff relied upon the contract in severing his relationship with Tidewater. * * *

The judgment is affirmed.

Notes

1. *Does the Reason for Rescission Affect Damages? Runyan* establishes that a rescinding party *may* recover special, consequential, or incidental damages, as distinguished from what the court persists in calling "restitutionary" damages. A word of caution will be interpolated. In later Chapters we will discover that courts may grant rescission for reasons that range from defendant's tortious conduct or breach to plaintiff's innocent mistake. While restitution normally follows rescission, the court may limit the rescinding party's damages. In transactions rescinded because of plaintiff's mistake, for example, defendant cannot be charged any damages, consequential or otherwise.

Even when damages accompany restitution, the reason for rescission may affect the way they are measured. Runyan originally charged defendant with fraud. If the court had granted rescission for fraud, Runyan, under tort damages measures, could have recovered "proximately caused" consequential damages.

But eventually rescission was granted for breach of contract; the court rescinded the contract because of failure of consideration. Runyan may recover consequential damages, reliance variety; but under contract damage doctrine, defendant may invoke Hadley v. Baxendale. Has Runyan established that the "consequential" damages were within the parties' contemplation when the contract was made?

2. *Special and Reliance Damages.* Suppose that the parties order their affairs assuming that a contract was formed; then the court finds that no contract exists. In Dursteler v. Dursteler, 108 Idaho 230, 697 P.2d 1244 (App.1985), aff'd, 112 Idaho 594, 733 P.2d 815 (App.1987), the sale of a mink ranch collapsed because the agreement failed to specify the parties' obligations. The seller, in reliance on the supposed contract, had purchased a home in a nearby town and moved off the ranch. In unscrambling this aborted sale, is the seller entitled to recover house-purchase expenses as reliance or consequential damages? The court held that since no contract had been formed, the seller's only remedy was restitution which required proof that the buyer had received a benefit. In Hollywood Dairy, Inc. v. Timmer, 411 N.W.2d 258 (Minn.App.1987), the sellers of a dairy canceled the sale

6. It will be recalled that the court found that the allegations of the remaining three counts were not true.

because of nonpayment. The court held that because the contract was canceled, the buyer was limited to quasi-contractual recovery for unjust enrichment.

3. *Punitive damages.* Whether the court may award punitive damages to the rescinding party apparently depends upon the reason for rescission. When defendants committed fraud in the transactions, several courts have allowed punitive damages in addition to granting restitution. See Thomas Auto Co. v. Craft, 297 Ark. 492, 763 S.W.2d 651 (1989); Michaels v. Morris, 174 Cal.App.3d 222, 220 Cal.Rptr. 22 (1985); Indiana & Michigan Electric Co. v. Harlan, 504 N.E.2d 301 (Ind.App.1987). In Roberts v. Estate of Barbagallo, 366 Pa.Super. 559, 531 A.2d 1125 (1987), the court said, however, that since the rescinding party cannot recover compensatory damages, there can be no punitive damages either. Where rescission was based on breach of contract, the court disallowed punitive damages in McKinney v. Gannett Co., 660 F.Supp. 984 (D.N.M.1981), appeal dismissed, 694 F.2d 1240 (10th Cir.1982).

4. Separate procedural systems for rescinding contracts in law or equity are natural targets for reform. According to the Recommendations and Study of the California Law Revision Commission, 1960, the California "unitary" system eliminates the former suit in equity to rescind. Retained are the legal prerequisites of notice of intent to rescind and offer of restoration (although these may be excused), leaving a quasi-contractual action for restoration designated as "action based on rescission." Anomalously, however, the Law Revision report recommended abandonment of the legal common counts for pleading in this action. Nevertheless, Klein v. Benaron, 247 Cal.App.2d 607, 56 Cal.Rptr. 5 (1967), accepted these pleadings. The reporter also recommended jury trials in all rescission cases and a single statute of limitation, subject to the underlying requirement of "promptness" in effecting a rescission. Porter v. Superior Court, 73 Cal.App.3d 793, 798–99, 141 Cal.Rptr. 59, 62 (1977), however, rejected a jury trial where no money claim was involved: "The [plaintiff] has confused the right to bring an action at law to recover the consideration paid or damages and the equitable action to cancel a deed."

Like other mergers of law and equity, certain rough spots remain, since an "action based on rescission" cannot completely obliterate the equitable jurisdiction and remedies that originally led to the equitable suit to rescind.

2. ADJUSTMENTS IN REAL ESTATE TRANSACTIONS

RENNER v. KEHL

Supreme Court of Arizona, En Banc, 1986.
150 Ariz. 94, 722 P.2d 262.

GORDON, VICE CHIEF JUSTICE. * * * In 1981 the petitioners, defendants below, acquired from the State of Arizona agricultural development leases covering 2,262 acres of unimproved desert land near Yuma. The petitioners made no attempt to develop the property themselves, but instead decided to sell their interest in the land. The respondents, plaintiffs below, were residents of the state of Washington interested in the large scale commercial cultivation of jojoba. The respondents and their agent, who was familiar with commercial jojoba development, were shown the petitioners' property and became interested in purchasing it. The property appeared to be ideal for the respondents' purposes; the soil and climate were good and both parties were of the opinion that sufficient water was available beneath the land to sustain jojoba production. The respondents made it clear that they were interested in the property only for jojoba production and required adequate water supplies.

The respondents decided to buy the leases and on June 5, 1981, executed a Real Estate Purchase Contract to that effect. Respondents agreed to pay $222,200 for the leases, and paid petitioners $80,200 as a down payment, the remainder to be paid in annual installments. In November of 1981 respondents began development of the property for jojoba production. As part of the development process the respondents had five test wells drilled, none of which produced water of sufficient quantity or quality for commercial jojoba cultivation. After spending approximately $229,000 developing the land respondents determined that the aquifer underlying the property was inadequate for commercial development of jojoba. At this point the project was abandoned and the respondents sued to rescind the purchase contract. The petitioners counterclaimed for the balance of payments due under the contract. * * * The court found that the respondents were entitled to rescission based on mutual mistake of fact and failure of consideration, and ordered the respondents to reassign the lease to the petitioners. The petitioners were ordered to pay the respondents $309,849.84 ($80,200 representing the down payment and $229,649.48 representing the cost of developing the property) together with costs and attorney's fees.

The petitioners appealed to the court of appeals, which affirmed. The petitioners raise the same arguments before this Court, *viz.*, that rescission was not justified, or if rescission was appropriate petitioners are not liable for consequential damages.

Mutual mistake of fact is an accepted basis for rescission. [citations] * * * The trial court found that the sole purpose of the contract was to enable respondents to grow jojoba, which depends upon an adequate water supply. The trial court specifically found that "There would have been no sale if both sellers and buyers had not believed it was possible to grow jojoba commercially on the leased acres. * * *" and that "[b]ased upon the factual data available, all parties were of the opinion that there would be sufficient good quality water for commercial jojoba production, and that it would be close enough to the surface that it would be economically feasible to pump it for irrigation of large acreages." Consequently, the trial court concluded that "[p]laintiffs are entitled to rescind the purchase agreement because of the mutual mistake of fact and because there was a total failure of consideration."

The belief of the parties that adequate water supplies existed beneath the property was "a basic assumption on which both parties made the contract," Restatement (Second) of Contracts § 152 comment b, and their mutual mistake "ha[d] such a material effect on the agreed exchange of performances as to upset the very bases of the contract." Id. comment a. The contract was therefore voidable and the respondents were entitled to rescission.

The trial court also ordered that petitioners pay the respondents $309,849.84 together with costs and attorney's fees. Of the $309,849.84 awarded to the respondents, $229,649.84 represents reimbursement of the costs borne by the respondents in developing the property for jojoba production. The petitioners challenge the $229,649.84 awarded as an improper grant of "consequential damages." [1]

1. [Footnotes renumbered.] Consequential or "incidental" damages represent a plaintiff's expenses incurred in reliance upon the contract. See Fousel v. Ted Walker Mobile Homes, Inc., 124 Ariz. 126, 602 P.2d 507 (App.1979). In *Fousel* these expenses included the cost of custom-made awnings, skirting and steps purchased for their mobile home, *see* discussion,

The court of appeals upheld the full award "[b]ecause the plaintiffs have not received a double recovery in the award of rescission and consequential damages. * * * The appeals court relied upon Fousel v. Ted Walker Mobile Homes, Inc., 124 Ariz. 126, 602 P.2d 507 (App.1979), for the proposition that rescission can support an award of consequential damages.

In *Fousel* the plaintiffs purchased a mobile home from the defendants, who engaged in a series of misrepresentations which cost the plaintiffs considerable inconvenience and expense. The plaintiffs prevailed upon their claim for fraud and breach of contract and were awarded $2,705.26 in consequential damages and $10,000 in punitive damages. The sole issue on appeal was whether any damages could be awarded where the plaintiffs elected to sue for rescission. The court of appeals held that the doctrine of election of remedies does not necessarily bar an award of consequential or punitive damages, only "benefit of the bargain" damages. However, *Fousel* was predicated upon proof of breach of contract for fraud. The court stated that a party who has rescinded a contract may recover "any incidental or consequential damages resulting from *a breach of the contract*" (emphasis added). The court quoted from Jennings v. Lee, supra, wherein we stated that "[t]here is ample authority that a *defrauded* party may not only receive back the consideration he gave, but also may recover any sums that are necessary to restore him to his position prior to the making of the contract."

In this case there was no breach of contract for fraud. We are dealing with a rescission based upon mutual mistake, which implies freedom from fault on the part of both parties. See Restatement (Second) of Contracts § 152. There was no determination that fraud or misrepresentation occurred; indeed, the trial court concluded that "[t]here was no fraud or misrepresentation on the part of the defendants or their agents. * * * " The reliance of the court of appeals upon *Fousel* was misplaced; we hold that absent proof of breach for fraud or misrepresentation a party who rescinds a contract may not recover consequential damages. Accordingly, we reverse that portion of the trial court's order awarding consequential damages and vacate that portion of the court of appeals' decision which affirms the award of consequential damages.

This does not mean, however, that the respondents are entitled only to recover their down payment. When a party rescinds a contract on the ground of mutual mistake he is entitled to restitution for any benefit that he has conferred on the other party by way of part performance or reliance. Restatement (Second) of Contracts § 376. Restitutionary recoveries are not designed to be compensatory; their justification lies in the avoidance of unjust enrichment on the part of the defendant. Thus the defendant is generally liable for restitution of a benefit that would be unjust for him to keep, even though he gained it honestly. Id.; Restatement (Second) of Contracts § 376 comment a. The issue we must now address is the proper measure of the restitutionary interest.

The first step determining the proper measure of restitution requires that the rescinding party return or offer to return, conditional on restitution, any interest in property that he has received in the bargain. Restatement (Second) of Contracts § 384(1)(a). In Arizona this includes reimbursement for the fair market value of the use of the property. With respect to land contracts we have noted that "[i]t is of course essential to justify the rescinding of a contract

infra; in this case they would represent the cost of developing the land for jojoba production.

that the rescinding party offer to place the other in status quo, and this includes the offer to credit the vendors with a reasonable rental value for the time during which the land was occupied." Mortensen v. Berzell Investment Company, 102 Ariz. at 351, 429 P.2d at 948. Earlier we stated that "[t]he offer to surrender possession of property received under the contract need not be unqualified, but may be made conditional upon the vendor's restitution of amounts paid on the contract, less proper allowances in respect of vendee's use of the premises." Mahurin v. Schmeck, 95 Ariz. 333, 341, 390 P.2d 576, 581 (1964). Thus the respondents were obliged to return the land to the petitioners in exchange for their down payment, and in addition to pay the petitioners the fair rental value of the land for the duration of their occupancy.

However, to avoid unjust enrichment the petitioners must pay the respondents a sum equal to the amount by which their property has been enhanced in value by the respondents' efforts. The Restatement (Second) of Contracts § 376 provides that "[i]f [a party] has received and must return land * * * he may have made improvements on the land in reliance on the contract and he is entitled to recover the reasonable value of those improvements. * * * The rule stated in this section applies to avoidance on any ground, including * * * mistake." comment a. The reasonable value of any improvements is measured by "the extent to which the other party's property has been increased in value or his other interests advanced." Restatement (Second) of Contracts § 371(b). Thus the petitioners must pay to the respondents that amount of money which represents the enhanced value of the land due to the respondents' development efforts. In short, the respondents are entitled to their down payment, plus the amount by which their efforts increased the value of the petitioners' property, minus an amount which represents the fair rental value of the land during their occupancy. They are not entitled to the $229,648.84 expended upon development, because that would shift the entire risk of mistake onto the petitioners, which is incompatible with equitable rescission.

Notes

1. When the court rescinds a contract because of mutual mistake, it generally only protects the parties' restitutionary interest. If the rescinding vendee's improvement does not benefit the vendor, the vendee cannot recover the amount expended. See Carter v. Matthews, 288 Ark. 37, 701 S.W.2d 374 (1986). Where vendee rescinded because of the vendor's breach, however, the vendee recovered the reasonable market value of the work done, not limited to the enhanced value of the property if that would be less. See Whitson v. Lende, 442 N.W.2d 267 (S.D.1989); MCC Investments v. Crystal Properties, 451 N.W.2d 243 (Minn.App.1990).

Although the court in the principal case does not mention it, a rescinding vendee recovers the price paid plus interest from the date of the payment. See Brunner v. LaCasse, 234 Mont. 368, 763 P.2d 662 (1988), aff'd, 241 Mont. 102, 785 P.2d 210 (1989); Miller v. Sears, 636 P.2d 1183 (Alaska 1981); Wall v. Foster Petroleum Corp., 791 P.2d 1148 (Colo.App.1989), allowed prejudgment interest from the date the complaint was filed.

The court may offset the vendee's claim for interest on the price against the vendor's claim for the reasonable value of using the premises. Dugan v. Jones, 724 P.2d 955 (Utah 1986).

2. *The Equitable Vendee's Lien.* The restitutionary claim of the vendee upon rescission of a land sale contract may be secured by a vendee's lien on the property. See generally 3 H. Black, Rescission and Cancellation §§ 561, 695 (2d ed. 1929);

Anno., 33 A.L.R.2d 1384 (1954); Anno., 82 A.L.R.3d 1040 (1978). A typical equitable lien falls within § 161 of the Restatement of Restitution. It is distinguished from the so-called vendor's lien (infra, p. 1041) which is essentially a contract-enforcing lien rather than one to secure restitution.

Mihranian v. Padula, 134 N.J.Super. 557, 563–64, 342 A.2d 523, 526–27 (1975):

"The vendee's lien is of ancient origin and it has been recognized and enforced in this State since at least 1830. * * * It is frequently referred to as the counterpart to the vendor's lien and, although courts elsewhere are not in entire accord as to the sources and reasons for its existence, it is enforced in most other jurisdictions in this country. * * * When the vendee pays a portion of the purchase money, the vendor becomes a trustee for him and the vendee acquires a lien just as if the vendor had executed a mortgage to him of his estate to the extent of the payment received. Plainfield Courier News Co. v. Hollander, 93 N.J.Super. 442, 226 A.2d 51 (1967). As stated in the latter case, quoting with approval from 3 American Law of Property, § 1178 at 195–196:

'Such lien, in England and in most American jurisdictions, is bestowed upon the purchaser even in the absence of any special equities in his favor, such as possession or improvements made by him, on the theory that with each payment the purchaser performs *pro tanto* and is thereby equitably vested with a ratable portion of the estate. If the vendor cannot convey, the purchaser, as equitable owner, *pro tanto,* may assert his rights in a court of equity to recover any payments made. If the vendor is not the absolute owner, the purchaser's lien attaches only to the extent of the vendor's interest, which may be converted into money by judicial sale—a remedy which is, in effect, the same as the foreclosure of an equitable mortgage.' "

The vendee's lien includes the purchaser's payments on the price, taxes, and expenditures for improvements. Iota Management Corp. v. Boulevard Investment Co., 731 S.W.2d 399 (Mo.App.1987); Comment, The Vendee's Lien on Land and Chattels, 33 Mich.L.Rev. 108, 112 (1934). Should it include the vendee's costs and attorney's fees? Warner v. Peterson, 234 Mont. 319, 762 P.2d 872 (1988) (held, no). What about reliance expenses like the title search and fire insurance?

Normally courts use a vendee's lien when rescission is based on the vendor's fraud or breach of contract. If the court rescinds for mistake, should a vendee's lien be imposed? Is there an analogy to restitution for a mistaken improver? Pp. 432–35, supra.

Question: Suppose an equity suit to rescind a land sale contract where the purchaser has been defrauded. May the purchaser attach the vendor's *other* property before judgment to secure at least his restitutionary claim? Consider that he already has the security of the vendee's lien. See McCall v. Superior Court, 1 Cal.2d 527, 36 P.2d 642 (1934).

In *Iota Management,* supra Note 2, the vendor had resold the property after the litigation was commenced. The court ruled that the equitable lien attached to the proceeds of the resale.

3. *Rescission of Land Sale Contract for Buyer's Fraud.* Upon recovery of the premises the vendor may also claim the rental value of the land while the buyer was in possession plus out-of-pocket expenses. Which of these are restitution and which damages? The confusing use of these terms continues. Head & Seemann, Inc. v. Gregg, 107 Wis.2d 126, 318 N.W.2d 381 (1982).

3. ADJUSTMENTS IN THE SALE OF A BUSINESS

WIDMER v. LEFFELMAN

Supreme Court of Oregon, 1952.
196 Or. 401, 249 P.2d 476.

TOOZE, JUSTICE. * * * [T]he trial court, upon the first trial, in its decree canceled the written agreement of conditional sale by defendant to the plaintiffs of the appliances, furniture, and fixtures of the KoZee Cafe, effective as of December 7, 1946, and awarded plaintiffs judgment against defendant for $4,000, with interest thereon at 6 per cent per annum from December 7, 1946, until March 23, 1948 (that being the date of the decree), amounting to $310, less $1,217.50 for rental for the cafe from November 16, 1946, until March 23, 1948, at the rate of $75 per month, the net amount of such judgment being $3,092.50. From that decree the defendant appealed to this court.

We affirmed the trial court's finding of fraud and its decree of rescission. However, we were of the opinion that the profits realized by plaintiffs in their operation of the cafe after December 7, 1946, rather than the reasonable value of the use of the property, should be considered as the yardstick for measuring the amount of money to be credited to defendant against the said sum of $4,000, and we remanded the case for an accounting to determine the amount of such profits. * * *

The record of the second hearing discloses that plaintiffs made a full and complete accounting of the operation of the business between December 7, 1946, and the closing thereof on January 3, 1948. The books and records kept by them in connection with such operation lack much of perfection, but they were sufficient to disclose a net operating loss, rather than a profit, in the sum of $584.37. This does not take into account a payment of $300 made by them after January 3, 1948, on account of rental of the premises, nor any compensation for plaintiffs' services. * * *

On the hearing, defendant offered evidence to establish the fact that in December, 1947, plaintiffs renewed the beer license for the KoZee Cafe for the year 1948, and that this license was surrendered to the Oregon Liquor Control Commission by plaintiffs in April, 1948, a short time after the first trial of this case. Defendant also offered to show that a Mrs. Kirkham, who operated a restaurant known as Sandy Crest Restaurant, which was located across the street from the KoZee Cafe, had, upon several occasions prior to the spring of 1948, attempted to procure a beer license from the Liquor Control Commission. Her applications had been denied. Defendant further offered to prove that, after plaintiffs had surrendered the 1948 license, a license was then issued to Mrs. Kirkham. The policy established by the Oregon Liquor Control Commission did not permit more than one beer license to be issued for use in the vicinity of these two restaurants. Defendant urged upon the trial, and renews his contention in this court, that surrender of this beer license by plaintiffs renders it impossible for plaintiffs to place defendant in statu quo, and, therefore, they are not entitled to a rescission.

In passing, we might say that defendant had the right to take back the property at any time after its tender by plaintiffs in December, 1946, and protect his own interests in a beer license, if he so desired. Plaintiffs were under no obligations whatever to defendant to continue such license in 1948, after the cafe was closed.

The principles of law applicable to this case are fully stated in our former opinion. By reason of fraud on the part of defendant, plaintiffs had the right to rescind the contract of sale and purchase in December, 1946, as they did, but, upon such rescission, they were not required to continue the operation of the business for the benefit of defendant. Upon defendant's refusal at that time to accept the return of the property, plaintiffs could have abandoned it and brought their action to recover the consideration they had paid on the contract. On the other hand, they were not required to abandon the property in order to preserve their right of rescission. They had the right to continue the operation of the restaurant for the benefit of the defendant, taking such steps as were reasonably necessary to conserve the value of the business. But their duty in this respect was to operate for defendant's benefit, not to his detriment. They had no right to continue such operation at a loss and then charge defendant with the amount thereof. The reasonable value of plaintiffs' services, performed in connection with the operation, stood upon the same footing as other expenses incident to conducting the business, was a part thereof, and might properly have been paid out of the income of the venture. However, if the income fell short of being enough to pay all such expenses, it follows, of course, that a loss was inevitable. When it appeared to plaintiffs that the business could not be operated at a profit, they had a right to close it as a matter of self-protection. Therefore, continued operation at a loss was at plaintiffs' own risk.

What we said in our former opinion respecting the reasonable value of plaintiffs' services applied only if, upon the accounting, it developed that there were profits from the operation of the business by plaintiffs, out of which such value could be paid, and credit for which would be allowed plaintiffs before defendant was credited with any part thereof against the original payment of $4,000 made on the purchase price by plaintiffs.

The limit of plaintiffs' recovery, under the facts of this case is the sum of $4,000, with interest. * * * In the absence of any profits in the conduct of such business by plaintiffs, defendant is entitled to no credit against said sums.

Notes

1. West v. McCoy, 70 Cal.App.3d 295, 302–03, 138 Cal.Rptr. 660, 664 (1977):

"We believe that the Restatement of Restitution properly articulates the principle to be applied where, as here, the subject matter of the rescission is a business enterprise ostensibly existing for the purpose of making a profit and the vendor is more at fault than the vendee. Although the guilty vendor is not fully restored to his original economic position unless compensation is made for the use of the subject matter for the period during which the innocent vendee was in possession, nevertheless, when compensating the guilty vendor for such use of the subject matter the innocent vendee is entitled to pay either the reasonable rental value thereof or the profits, if any, which he has made from the subject matter, whichever is less. (Rest., Restitution, § 157, com. a, at 622.) In this way the guilty vendor, the one more at fault, bears the loss, if any, resulting from a failure to use the subject matter profitably. (See Rest., Restitution, § 157, com. e, at 628. See also Civ.Code, § 3517.)" Puskar v. Hughes, 179 Ill.App.3d 522, 533 N.E.2d 962 (1989). Rescinding vendee must pay the reasonable rental value of the land.

2. Rescission of the sale of a corporation can involve a complicated accounting problem. Below is a brief excerpt from the accounting in McKinney v. Gannett Co., 660 F.Supp. 984, 1023 (D.N.M.1981), appeal dismissed, 694 F.2d 1240 (10th Cir. 1982):

"The Accounting. McKinney was ordered to return all shares of Gannett stock he received in the merger and to account for all dividends received on that stock. Because McKinney has sold and given away some of the stock, he must buy it back on the open market and account for dividends as if he had continued to own all the shares. Gannett was ordered to account for all amounts taken out of The New Mexican. From that figure Gannett was told to deduct for business expenses reasonably incurred in managing the property. Through correspondence, telephone conferences, informal meetings and formal hearings, all contested items in the accounting were identified and ruled on. The parties agreed on some of the items, and they were able to stipulate to some of the figures themselves because disclosure was afforded to McKinney by Gannett."

3. For the adjustments after rescinding a sale of securities under § 10b of the Securities Exchange Act of 1934, see Randall v. Loftsgaarden, 478 U.S. 647 (1986).

Chapter 10

REMEDIES FOR DECEPTION

A. AFFIRMED TRANSACTIONS

1. COMMON LAW DECEIT: THE MEASURE OF DAMAGES

SELMAN v. SHIRLEY

Supreme Court of Oregon, 1939.
161 Or. 582, 91 P.2d 312.

On July 1, 1933, S.W. Selman and his wife Nona entered into a written contract to purchase for $2,000 a 160–acre ranch in Benton county, Oregon, from H.E. Shirley and his wife. Payments were to be made in the following manner: $500 upon execution of the contract; $200 on or before October 1, 1934, and a like sum of $200 on or before the 1st day of October annually thereafter until the full purchase price was paid. Selman and his wife paid $550 upon execution of the contract, took possession of the premises and have retained the same ever since. $200 was paid on October 1, 1934, but the Selmans failed to make the annual payment due on October 1, 1935. On October 22, 1935, the Shirleys commenced an action in ejectment.

Soon after the action in ejectment was commenced, the Selmans instituted the instant suit * * * to recover damages for fraud and deceit alleged to have been practiced upon them in the transaction. * * *

Plaintiffs, in their amended complaint, charge that they were induced to buy the 160–acre tract of land on account of the following representations:

(1) "that said premises had growing thereon at least Four Thousand (4000) cords of merchantable fire wood;

(2) "that there was sufficient water in the stream running through said premises to irrigate at least ten acres of land thereon in the driest season of the year; * * * and,

(3) "that there was available, adjacent to the road leading to said premises from the Philomath–Alsea Highway, sufficient gravel to gravel said road and that said gravel could be had for the hauling, that said gravel belonged to Benton County, Oregon."

Plaintiffs allege that the above representations were false and fraudulent in that:

(1) "in truth and in fact there was no merchantable fire wood growing upon said premises;

(2) "that there was not sufficient water to irrigate ten acres or any other amount in excess of One–Eighth of an acre; and * * *,

(3) "that the gravel * * * was privately owned and was not available for graveling said road."

Plaintiffs inspected the premises before entering into the contract of purchase, but assert that they were strangers in Benton county and "had no knowledge or experience in judging timber or timber lands" and that they relied wholly upon the representations made to them. On trial they testified that on account of rain and the muddy ground they were unable to inspect the timber.

The trial court entered findings of fact: * * *

"IV. That the defendant H.E. Shirley knowingly and falsely represented to plaintiff that there was at least four thousand cords of wood on said premises; that said representation was false and was made by defendant H.E. Shirley with the intention of inducing plaintiffs to purchase said premises; that the plaintiffs in purchasing said premises relied upon said representation.

"V. That said premises so purchased by plaintiffs from defendants H.E. Shirley and Ruth Shirley were of the fair market value of $2000.00 at the time said contract was entered into, to-wit, July 1, 1933; that plaintiffs have suffered no damage, having agreed to pay $2000.00 for said premises."

The decree * * * dismissed the suit against the defendants based on the charge of fraud. From this decree, the plaintiffs appealed.

[Editors' Note: The statement of facts is from the dissenting opinion of Belt, J. The majority opinion held that plaintiffs were entitled to recover damages based on the benefit of the bargain rule.]

ROSSMAN, JUSTICE. [On Rehearing.] The brief accompanying the respondents' (defendants') petition for a rehearing contends that we erred when we applied in this suit the benefit-of-the-bargain rule. * * *

We are likely to become so engrossed in efforts to formulate a rule of damages capable of precise application in all future cases and incapable of misapplication in any, that we may lose sight of our real duty in the present case * * *. [T]he ascertainment of what, if any, damages were the proximate result of the wrong is the only problem before us.

Regardless of whether the out-of-pocket-loss rule or the benefit-of-the-bargain rule is the correct one, the fundamental rule, universally employed, is the one just indicated: The victims of fraud are entitled to compensation for every wrong which was the natural and proximate result of the fraud. * * *

In order to indicate the manner in which one writer, at least, has applied this simple formula in instances like the present we quote the following statement made in Sutherland on Damages, 4th ed., § 1171: "The party guilty of the fraud is to be charged with such damages as have naturally and proximately resulted therefrom. He is to make good his representations as though he had given a warranty to that effect. He is to make compensation for the difference between the real state of the case and what it was represented to be. Thus, in cases involving sales, leases or other like contracts, where it appears that there is a fraudulently false representation of quantity, quality, price, or title the measure of damages is the difference in value between that which is actual and that which was represented to exist."

To facilitate its application the proximate result rule is often subdivided into four auxiliary rules: (1) A defrauded party is entitled to all out-of-pocket losses; (2) he is entitled to the benefit of his bargain; (3) if the property was falsely represented as improved with or containing some items which are not there, he is entitled to the cost of installing them; and (4) he is entitled to all consequential damages. These are merely subdivisions of the main rule, and are employed by the courts according to the facts and demands of the various cases. * * *

This place was not a farm; it was not a wood lot; it was merely a tract of logged-off land no different in kind from thousands of other tracts in the Coast Range. But the plaintiffs had no thought of buying a piece of logged-off land. Logged-off land was never mentioned in the negotiations. The plaintiffs wanted a wood lot where they could cut wood and sell it. * * * It is evident that they wanted not only land, but also standing timber capable of being cut into cordwood. In fact, they depended upon the wood and a truckman indebted to them who had promised to cut the trees into cordwood as a means of paying for their purchase. The defendants, in order to make the deal more alluring, represented that the land contained an irrigating stream and that a gravel bed nearby would yield sufficient material, free of cost to make the road leading into this place passable. As a matter of fact, all of the representations were false, and the plaintiffs found themselves with a piece of logged-off land not substantially different from innumerable other tracts in this state which the owners permitted to revert to the tax-levying bodies after the removal of the timber. * * *

We shall now review a few facts concerning value. Selman testified that he would not have accepted the place even as a gift had he not been deceived into the belief that timber was growing upon it and that an irrigating stream flowed through it. Charles Franklin, a farmer who had lived in the vicinity of this property for sixty-five years, and who had logged it off, swore concerning it: "Not much value in any of it now. The principal value was in the timber, but the condition it is in now, it is run down so, that it would take a heck of a lot to get it in a prosperous condition again." * * * This tract is a mile off the main highway and the road leading to it is impassable most of the year. * * * The tract, according to one witness, is "hill land, ferns, fern land mostly." Two of the corners are covered with second-growth fir which has sprung up among the stumps. The first-growth fir, amounting to 200 cords, is unmerchantable. In one small area the Selmans found an abandoned strawberry patch which has proved to be non-productive. Another patch consisting of several acres was at one time planted in oats. Upon two sides of the property is a dilapidated fence. The improvements consist of a four-room house, twenty years old, which Franklin, who built it, described as "just a common box house, very common. * * * We just built it as cheap as we possibly could." Selman testified that the roof leaked like a sieve, and Blakely said, "It isn't a house I would care to live in." The barn, 30 by 50 feet in size, was built forty-six years ago. It was never painted and has a leaky roof. Shirley acquired the property in 1927 and during his ownership never lived upon it, although in the season of 1931–1932 he permitted it to be occupied by an individual named Hofstetter who sowed several acres in rye grass and planted the strawberry patch; otherwise the property remained unoccupied during Shirley's six-year ownership. * * *

The fact that the defendants represented that the property was served by a good irrigating stream and held a growth of timber capable of yielding 4000 cords worth 50 cents per cord, when they asked $2,000 for the property, is an admission that the bare ground, studded with stumps and without a supply of water, was not worth $2,000. The opinion evidence was insufficient to overcome the effect of this admission.

This is an instance, therefore, in which the proof of fraud is clear; in fact, virtually admitted. But, disregarding value for the time being, we shall consider for a moment the results which will follow if the plaintiffs are entitled to nothing, and if judgment must be entered against them for costs. To make the matter entirely clear, let us assume that the land is worth $2,000 and that we are committed to the out-of-pocket-loss rule which assumes that the proximate result of the vendor's fraud is his receipt of something worth more than that with which he parted. That rule does not concern itself with the fact that the fraudulent statements induced the innocent vendee to expect something which he did not receive. It views proximate result from the contemplations of the cozening vendor at the time he induced the vendee to make the purchase, and in this manner restricts recovery to the out-of-pocket-loss. Therefore, assuming that the land was worth $2,000, (1) the plaintiffs would not be entitled to judgment; (2) the action of ejectment would not be stayed; and (3) the plaintiffs would be evicted from the land. If that result occurs the fraudulent representations will have cost Shirley nothing, and upon regaining possession of the property he will be in a position to repeat the fraudulent representations to another prospective buyer, knowing beforehand that if the truth is discovered the worst that can happen to him is that he will again possess the property. But, in the event that the defrauded buyer pays the purchase price, Shirley will receive $2,000 for the land alone although his representations will have induced the buyer to expect not only land, but also timber, a stream and gravel. Thus, the benefit-of-the-bargain principle will operate, but it will operate in reverse—the fraudulent vendor, and not the innocent victim, will get the benefit of the bargain. Next, if the plaintiffs are awarded no damages we will have virtually remade the contract between the parties, for it is now admitted that for the purchase money the plaintiffs were entitled not merely to the land, but also to the wood, etc. Hence, if the law of damages leaves the plaintiffs empty handed, and they are compelled to pay $2,000 for the land in order to save themselves from eviction, they will receive only a fraction of that which the defendants' written words told them they would receive. Finally, if the contract had followed the preceding negotiations, as it should have done, it would have made some mention of the timber, and in that event the plaintiffs could have maintained an action for breach of contract. * * * In other words, the plaintiffs would have been entitled to damages for the Shirleys' failure to provide the timber. Are they now to fare worse because they were deceived into a belief that they would receive the timber as well as the land, and therefore neglected to see to it that the contract contained a warranty concerning the timber? If that is true, the defendants have improved their own condition by multiplying their misdeeds, and we have the paradox that it is less culpable—and cheaper too—to commit fraud (always legally and morally wrong) than merely to breach a contract which, although legally wrong, may in instances be morally excusable. But why should more be obtainable in one form of action than in the other? We abolished the forms of action in order to obviate that absurdity and to make it possible to award adequate relief to the victim of the wrong regardless of the form of the action. Generally, more is obtainable in tort actions than in those based upon a contract because in the former the damages include everything which was the proximate result of the wrong, including compensation for all injuries which were in the contemplation of the parties at the time the contract was effected, while in the latter the damages are limited to those which were in contemplation when the contract was entered into. * * *

The defendants, in seeking to ward off the plaintiffs' claim for damages, rely largely upon the reasoning set forth in Smith v. Bolles, 132 U.S. 125, and Sigafus v. Porter, 179 U.S. 116. In the former, the plaintiff, who claimed that he had been deceived by the defendant into the purchase of some shares of stock in a gold mining corporation, sought the recovery of damages under the benefit-of-the-bargain rule. In the second case the circumstances were the same except that the subject matter of the false representation was a gold mine. In each instance, the federal supreme court held that the damages were out-of-pocket losses. Concerning the first of these two decisions, Professor McCormick, in his treatise on Damages, states in a footnote on page 450: "Court bases result on view that wrongdoer is liable only for consequences which he might reasonably have contemplated—a proposition dubious in its soundness and in its application." We concur in that criticism. Because the out-of-pocket-loss rule determines the proximate result from the expectations of the fraudulent vendor rather than those of the innocent vendee, the vast majority of the jurisdictions have refused to embrace that rule; and apparently for the same reason Texas, in 1919, by legislative enactment (Art. 4004, Tex.Rev.Civ.Stat. 1925; 4 Tex.Law Rev. 386) substituted for it the benefit-of-the-bargain rule. The second decision, from which two of the judges dissented, was based largely upon the first. At the times when those two decisions were written the federal courts refused to employ the rule of damages embraced by local practice. * * * The so-called federal common law has disappeared and the federal courts now employ the common law as locally interpreted. * * *

Thus it is almost certain that neither of these cases would employ the out-of-pocket-loss rule were they to be decided by the same court today unless the court believed that the speculative losses which the plaintiffs sought were too conjectural to be recoverable. Therefore, the federal rule which has been the backbone of the out-of-pocket-loss rule is gone.

* * * Lichtenthaler v. Clow, 109 Or. 381, 220 P. 567, Purdy v. Underwood, 87 Or. 56, 169 P. 536, and Cawston v. Sturgis, 29 Or. 331, 43 P. 656, all of which are reviewed in our previous decision, likewise arose out of the purchase of real property for money. In each of those cases the buyer, in determining whether to make the purchase, contemplated the property, not in the abstract, but as a tract of a given size; and the seller, knowing that fact, represented that it contained the desired area. In each instance when it developed that the representation was false, the vendor was held liable for damages equal to the value of the missing area. In other words, the buyer was entitled, not merely to a part, but to all that he paid for, regardless of whether or not the amount he actually received was worth the sum he paid. * * * The rule is thus stated in Purdy v. Underwood: "When, however, as in the case at bar, a specified sum of money is paid for each integral part of property expected to be received, a failure to transfer a portion thereof at such ratable price, constitutes the measure of damages sustained." The situation is the same in the present case. Shirley represented that 4000 cords of timber, worth 50 cents per cord, stood

upon the property. As a matter of fact, only 200 cords were there. Standing trees are, of course, deemed part and parcel of the land. Had he represented that 170 acres were in the tract when actually it consisted of only 160, all would agree that he would be compelled to respond in damages. In the absence of homogeneity of value we would have divided the purchase price by the number of acres and in this manner have ascertained the value per acre. We would then have multiplied the value per acre by the number of missing acres and thus have arrived at the damages. We know that Shirley represented that the stumpage value of the timber was 50 cents per cord, and we also know that he represented that the property held 4000 cords. * * *

Suppose the defendants had conveyed to the plaintiffs the timber only, all would agree that damages equal in amount to the value of the land would be recoverable. The reverse must be true, and since the plaintiffs received only the land they must be entitled to damages equal to the value of the timber.

We shall now show by the decisions of the other courts that the mere fact that the missing item is not land but is something else, does not deny relief to the plaintiffs. In Nunn v. Howard, 216 Ky. 685, 288 S.W. 678, 679, the plaintiff had sold to the defendant a house and lot, falsely representing in so doing that an unfailing well was upon the premises. The defendant spent $158 in providing a well of the represented kind. The decision, after stating these facts, continued: "that being true, it follows that appellee is liable in damages for the representations so made, and that in the circumstances the most accurate measure of damages is the reasonable cost of drilling the new well. It follows that the item of $158 should have been allowed." In Okoomian v. Brandt, 101 Conn. 427, 126 A. 332, the defendant, who had sold the plaintiff an improved lot under a false representation that the three tenants were each paying $35 per month rental, was held liable in the amount of $325.50 damages, that being the sum which the plaintiff expended in the installation of permanent electrical equipment in order to bring the income of the property up to the represented amount. In Shane v. Jacobson, 136 Minn. 386, 162 N.W. 472, 473, the plaintiff had been induced to buy a farm under a false representation that 80 acres of it was tiled. The Minnesota court adheres to the out-of-pocket-loss rule. * * * In measuring the plaintiff's damages under that rule, the court held that the plaintiff was entitled to recover the cost of installing the tiling, together with the rental value of the land while the work was in progress. We quote from the decision the following: "In other words, the damages in contemplation of the parties as naturally flowing from a misrepresentation in respect to this tiling would be the cost thereof, to which, perhaps, should be added the depreciation of rental value of the land affected while the tiling was being done. The rule is that a defrauded party is entitled to such damages as naturally and proximately result from the fraud. * * * Suppose, in this case, that plaintiff had bought the farm when he met defendant in Iowa, without seeing it, upon defendant's representations as to soil, lay of the land, and improvements, and all the representations had been true, except that a granary of certain dimensions and material, represented to be one of the buildings, was not there, a structure which could be erected for say $200; could it be justly claimed that the natural and proximate loss to plaintiff for this one false representation could then have been more than the cost of placing such a granary as represented upon the farm? * * * Therefore the actual cost of placing tiling thereon, and the extent to which such improvement would increase the value of the farm was proper and very material evidence bearing upon the amount of recovery, and without which an intelligent answer could not be given as to the natural and proximate loss to plaintiff."

From all of the above it is seen, not only that the plaintiffs were damaged, for convincing evidence shows that the property is worth less than $2,000, but that we have an approved means of measuring the damages, which are the proximate result of the false statements made by the defendants. If the latter had represented that there was upon the property a pile of wood containing 4000 cords, the damages to which the plaintiffs would have been entitled would have been the value of that amount of wood. The same result ought to follow when, as in this case, the defendant represented that there was standing timber upon the property capable of yielding 4000 cords worth 50 cents per cord upon the stump. * * *

Of course, if one adheres rigorously to the out-of-pocket-loss rule or to the benefit-of-the-bargain rule certainty will be achieved, but it will be achieved in many instances at the expense of justice.

In our previous decision we cited authorities indicating that neither rule has been uniformly applied, and in preceding paragraphs of this decision have amplified them. We know of no difficulty which has resulted from flexibility. An examination of the decisions in the states employing flexibility discloses that they are not large in number, nor do they afford any indication that flexibility has created uncertainty. It is inevitable that ordinarily only out-of-pocket losses will be recoverable, for ordinarily that is the only loss which is incurred or which can be proved with sufficient certainty. Consequential damages are universally recoverable. If the representation can be made good by the expenditure of a sum less than that which is the difference between the actual value and the represented value, the cost of the installation is the sum which is recoverable. Professor McCormick recommends that the loss-of-the-bargain rule should also be employed where a false representation was made with moral culpability, as distinguished from one made by a person who is ignorant of the facts. But since punitive damages are recoverable in this state, there exists no occasion for a departure from the out-of-pocket-loss rule in cases of that kind. * * *

Since the petition for a rehearing has disclosed no error in our previous decision, we adhere to that opinion. * * *

BELT, JUSTICE (dissenting). On original hearing the court held, with the writer dissenting, that plaintiffs had been defrauded and were entitled to damages "upon the basis of 50 cents per cord for the difference between the represented 4,000 cords and the actual 200 cords," which amounted to $1,900. There was a balance of $1,250, together with interest due, on the purchase price, as $750 had been paid thereon. Therefore, this court's decree enabled plaintiffs to acquire this 160–acre ranch for $100. In reaching this conclusion, the majority of the court held that plaintiffs were entitled to the "benefit of the bargain" rule asserted by defendants. Had the "benefit of the bargain" rule been also applied so as to compensate plaintiffs for the failure of water to irrigate the 10–acre tract and the loss of gravel, we would have the anomalous situation of the vendors being deprived of their property without compensation and being mulcted in damages besides.

In the lower court, evidence was received on behalf of the defendant vendors that, at the time the contract was entered into, the land had a market value of $2,000. Since the contract price, or $2,000, was the market value of the land, the defendants contend that no damages are recoverable in an action of this kind. Plaintiffs introduced no evidence concerning the market value of the land. It was their contention that the "out of pocket" rule had no application to the facts and they relied on the benefit of their bargain in the assessment of damages.

It should be borne in mind that there was no misrepresentation concerning the quantity of land or the boundaries thereof. It is not a case of shortage in acreage as in Lichtenhaler v. Clow, 109 Or. 381, 220 P. 567. * * * The issue on this appeal is clearly and definitely defined. What is the proper measure of damages to be applied to the facts in this case? Are plaintiffs entitled to the benefit of their bargain, namely, the difference between the value of 4000 cords of wood and 200 cords of wood? Or is the proper measure the difference between the contract price of the land and its market value? * * *

What is the proper measure of damages in tort actions wherein fraud has induced the sale or exchange of property? This has long been a controversial question among judges, lawyers, professors, and text writers. As stated in a well-considered article entitled "The Measure of Damages in Tort for Deceit," 18 Boston U.L.Rev. 681: "Upon this subject American courts are divided; text-writers present a broken front; a left wing wars with a right; academicians cannot agree; the Law Institute advisers dissent from the reporters; precedent neutralizes precedent; abstract reasoning carries no persuasion; arguments have no other effect than to engender counter-arguments; one practical consideration clashes with another practical consideration; nothing is settled as the just law or general rule." * * *

No well-considered case holds that a hard and fast rule should be applied in all cases. Objections have been made to both rules. However, the American Law Institute, after a thorough consideration of the subject, reached the conclusion that the better-reasoned cases support the "out-of-pocket" rule. Hence, we find in the Restatement of the Law on Torts, § 549: "The measure of damages which the recipient of a fraudulent misrepresentation is entitled to recover from its maker as damages under the rule stated in § 525 is the pecuniary loss which results from the falsity of the matter represented, including * * *." The "comment" in reference to the above clause is so clear-cut and pertinent to the facts in this case that we quote it in full: "Under the rule stated in this Clause the recipient of a fraudulent misrepresentation is entitled to recover from its maker only the actual loss which because of its falsity he sustains by his action or inaction in reliance upon it. If notwithstanding the falsity of the representation the thing which a vendee acquires is of equal or greater value than the price paid and he has suffered no harm through using it in reliance upon its being as represented, he has suffered no loss and can recover nothing. The fact that he would have made a profit if the representation had been true does not entitle him to recover for his disappointment in not receiving the gain which he was led to expect. Thus where A induces B to purchase a parcel of farm land by falsely representing that it contains valuable mineral deposits, B is not entitled to recover anything if the land as farming land is worth as much as the price paid although had it contained the minerals represented it would have been worth much more. If the fraudulent misrepresentation is so made as to constitute a warranty, the person acting in reliance upon it may of course waive the fraud and bring an action on the warranty, in which case the measure of damages is that appropriate to a warranty, namely, the difference between the value of the article as it is and the value which it would have had had the fact warranted been true." * * *

Whatever may be the rule in other jurisdictions, it has long been settled in this state that, in tort actions for fraud inducing the sale or exchange of real property, the measure of damages is the difference between the value of the property parted with and the actual value of the property received. This court has never endeavored to treat a tort action as being equivalent to a breach of contract. It has adhered to the fundamental principles of tort. The party defrauded is entitled to be made whole—i.e., he is not to be out of pocket. * * *

Plaintiffs had their opportunity to introduce evidence relative to the market value of the land purchased, but they failed to do so. What they really sought was damages arising from breach of contract. The fallacy of such contention lies in the fact that the vendors did not contract to sell, nor did the plaintiffs agree to buy, 4000 cords of wood. Plaintiffs, under the terms of the contract, agreed to buy a 160-acre farm. Applying the "benefit of the bargain" rule to the facts in the instant case leads to absurdity for it amounts to the vendees' acquiring the land for practically nothing. * * *

What has been said thus far is on the assumption that the misrepresentations were made as alleged and that plaintiffs relied thereon, although it is difficult to understand how anyone, after inspection, could have been deceived about logged-off land. It would seem that the black stumps would speak for themselves. It is also difficult to understand why the Selmans continued to make payments after learning, in August 1933, of the shortage of wood and their alleged consequent damages. * * *

The equities of the case are not entirely with the plaintiffs. They have been in possession of 160 acres of land since August, 1933, and it has been their home, however humble it may be. They have paid $750, together with interest, on the purchase price. This farm or hill ranch had, according to Shirley, a rental value of $150 per year. It is utterly unreasonable to state that it is worth only $100. Yet that is what this court must say if we adhere to the decision on original hearing. Can it be that the testimony of all witnesses on market value is to be ignored? Mr. Dollarhide, a disinterested and fair witness, testified without contradiction that he offered Shirley $2,000 in cash for the ranch, but learned that it had just been sold to the plaintiffs. Dollarhide thereupon went out to see Mrs. Selman, "to see if she would sell it," but she would not do so. Dollarhide and three other witnesses testified that the market value of the 160-acre ranch was $2,000. Otherwise stated, that it was worth $12.50 per acre.

This farm is not all logged-off land, 40 acres are assessed as tillable land. It is a typical hill ranch, valuable mostly for pasturage purposes. Blakely, a witness friendly to plaintiffs, said that, at the time of inspecting the ranch, nothing was said about wood or timber. The plaintiffs, according to this witness, wanted a place off the main highway and out of traffic.

However, let it be understood that this opinion is bottomed on the legal proposition that the "benefit of the bargain" rule does not apply to the facts in this case. We have adverted to these features of the case only to refute the idea of a gross miscarriage of justice in the event the decree of the lower court is sustained. * * *

The decree of the lower court should, therefore, be affirmed.

Notes

1. The Restatement (Second) of Torts § 549 (1976), allows plaintiff to choose between the benefit of the bargain rule and the out of pocket rule.

In accord Turnbull v. LaRose, 702 P.2d 1331, 1336 (Alaska 1985): "A plaintiff should have the opportunity to use either measure, providing the measure selected accomplishes substantial justice."

2. In Hanson v. Ford Motor Co., 278 F.2d 586, 591 (8th Cir.1960), the court stated the elements of a fraud action for damages:

"1. There must be a representation;

2. That representation must be false;

3. It must have to do with a past or present fact;

4. That fact must be material;

5. It must be susceptible of knowledge;

6. The representer must know it to be false or in the alternative, must assert it as of his own knowledge without knowing whether it is true or false;

7. The representer must intend to have the other person induced to act, or justified in acting upon it;

8. That person must be so induced to act or so justified in acting;

9. That person's action must be in reliance upon the representation;

10. That person must suffer damage;

11. That damage must be attributable to the misrepresentation, that is, the statement must be the proximate cause of the injury.

These elements must be affirmatively proved; they are not to be presumed."

3. In *Hanson* a bankrupt auto dealer sued the Ford Motor Company. He claimed that he had entered into a franchise agreement to sell Lincoln and Mercury automobiles because of Ford employees' fraudulent misrepresentations that dealerships in neighboring cities, New Ulm, Mankato and Winona, were profitable. The dealer sought to recover the $37,000 he had invested in the defunct business. The court found sufficient evidence to support his fraud claim. Applicable state law followed the out of pocket damages rule. Judgment was entered for the dealer for his $37,000 business losses. Is this a proper application of out of pocket damages?

4. Plaintiff was induced to enter an agreement for a distributorship of welding products by defendants' fraudulent misrepresentations about the product and its profitability. Damages were based on anticipated lost profits. In reversing the judgment, the court of appeals in Magna Weld Sales Co. v. Magna Alloys & Research Pty., Ltd., 545 F.2d 668, 672 (9th Cir.1976), stated:

"First, damages for lost profits must be for profits actually lost, and these must be proven with reasonable certainty. Magna's false predictions cannot be used to measure the actual losses, if any, suffered by the Soderlings. Failure to obtain anticipated 'pie in the sky' is not a financial loss, however disappointing it may be.

"Second, even if such representations could be used to measure damages in some cases, Washington [state law] forbids awarding lost profits as damages for misrepresentation when the business is a new one with no established financial track record. Magna Sales was such a business.

"Third, to award the Soderlings lost profits for the entire time that they remained in business was error when, by H.L. Soderling's own admission, he became aware that Magna had misrepresented its products to him by March 15, 1970, less than half a year after the agreement was made. The agreement allowed him to terminate upon notice for cause, yet he continued to purchase Magna products for inventory. Once the Soderlings became aware of the falsity of representations, they were no longer entitled to rely on them, and they cannot recover losses incurred as a result of their choosing to remain in the business. In fact, it was Magna that finally terminated the agreement two years later, and surely, had it not done so, the Soderlings could not have continued to claim 'lost profits' indefinitely."

5. In 1968 Congress enacted comprehensive federal legislation to control irregular and deceptive practices in interstate sales of subdivision lands. Sales that fall within the definitional requirements must be registered with the Secretary of Housing and Urban Development. Interstate Land Sales Full Disclosure Act, 15 U.S.C.A. §§ 1701–1720 (1988).

This legislation borrows freely from the federal experience in regulating the sale of corporate securities. The civil liabilities section (15 U.S.C.A. § 1709) states the purchaser's measure of damages:

Damages Recoverable: (c) The suit authorized under * * * this section may be to recover such damages as shall represent the difference between the amount paid for the lot and the reasonable cost of any improvements thereto, and the lesser of (1) the value thereof as of the time such suit was brought, or (2) the price at which such lot shall have been disposed of in a bona fide market transaction before suit, or (3) the price at which such lot shall have been disposed of after suit in a bona fide market transaction but before judgment.

This measure of damages follows the pattern of the so-called federal out-of-pocket rule of Smith v. Bolles and Sigafus v. Porter. And it is essentially identical with that in the Securities Act of 1933 against persons responsible for false registration statements filed with the S.E.C. for *initial* issues of stock. 15 U.S.C.A. § 77k(e) (1988).

SHEPARD v. CAL–NINE FARMS

United States Court of Appeals, Ninth Circuit, 1958.
252 F.2d 884.

[Plaintiff's assignor contracted to buy a farm for $80,000. Defendant represented the output of a well for irrigation. A crop, planted in 1955, failed because of lack of water. In 1956, a new well was dug. Plaintiff sued for damages. The trial court awarded $35,106: two-thirds to drill an adequate well and the balance for crop damage. The court of appeals affirmed.]

POPE, CIRCUIT JUDGE. I concur. The only problem that appears difficult to me is whether the trial court in assessing the damages was in error in not applying literally the standard set forth in Lutfy v. R.D. Roper & Sons Motor Co., 57 Ariz. 495, 115 P.2d 161, 165. Instead of taking testimony as to the value of the ranch as it actually was, and the value it would have had had the representations been true, the trial court took a short cut by fixing this part of the damages as the cost of a new well.

It seems to me that the trial court was warranted in concluding that this would be the very minimum difference between the value of an irrigated ranch which the purchasers thought they were buying, and a dry ranch, or one nearly so, which the place turned out to be. I do not think that appellants have demonstrated any prejudice resulting to them from the court's method of calculation. * * *

Furthermore there is respectable authority which the Arizona courts would probably recognize that a person defrauded may recover as one of the proximate results of misrepresentation expenses to which he has been put.[1] A case holding proper the recovery of the expenses of repairing a building to make it rentable where the purchaser had bought the building falsely represented to be rentable but found not to be so, is Wood v. Niemeyer, 185 Cal. 526, 197 P. 795, 799 (1921). * * *

As for the loss of crop, it seems to me that this was plainly a proximate result of misrepresentations and that the award on account thereof was proper. [citation]

Notes

1. In Slack v. Sodal, 190 Colo. 411, 547 P.2d 923 (1976), a similar problem arose; the court allowed damages to be computed by the cost of acquiring water from the city. In Campbell v. Booth, 526 S.W.2d 167 (Tex.1975), the fraud consisted of concealing the effect of dog urine on carpets; the court proposed that damages be measured by the cost of replacing the carpets.

2. *Question:* P, the owner of stock, is induced by the fraudulent misrepresentations of D, a broker, not to sell his share holdings. The stock declines in value. P sues for deceit. What is the measure of damages? See Fottler v. Moseley, 179 Mass. 295, 60 N.E. 788 (1901).

3. *Question:* Suppose the vendor fraudulently misrepresents that a home has a sewer leading the vendee to pay an inflated price. May the vendee "waive" the tort and seek restitution? On what basis could a court grant restitution? See Addy v. Stewart, 69 Idaho 357, 207 P.2d 498 (1949).

WARD v. TAGGART

Supreme Court of California, 1959.
51 Cal.2d 736, 336 P.2d 534.

TRAYNOR, J. At plaintiff William R. Ward's request in February, 1955, LeRoy Thomsen, a real estate broker, undertook to look for properties that might be of interest to Ward for purchase. During a conversation about unrelated matters, defendant Marshall W. Taggart, a real estate broker, told Thomsen that as exclusive agent for Sunset Oil Company he had several acres of land in Los Angeles County for sale. Thomsen said that he had a client who might be interested in acquiring this property. When Thomsen mentioned to Taggart that another broker named Dawson had a "For Sale" sign on the property, Taggart replied that Sunset had taken the listing away from Dawson. With Ward's authorization Thomsen submitted an offer on his behalf to Taggart of $4,000 an acre. Taggart promised to take the offer to Sunset. Taggart later told Thomsen that Sunset had refused the offer and would not

1. [Footnote renumbered.] After discussing at length the various views as to the "benefit of the bargain" and the "out of pocket" rules, which he calls the "normal" measure of damages, Prosser states ("Law of Torts," 2nd Ed., p. 570): "In addition to such a normal measure of damages under whatever rule the court may adopt, the plaintiff may recover for consequential damages, such as personal injuries, damage to other property, or expenses to which he has been put, provided that they are regarded as 'proximate' results of the misrepresentation."

take less for the property than $5,000 an acre, one-half in cash. Thomsen conveyed this information to Ward, who directed Thomsen to make an offer on those terms. Thomsen did so in writing. * * *

Plaintiffs did not learn until after they had purchased the property that Taggart had never been given a listing by Sunset and that he had never presented to Sunset and never intended to present plaintiffs' offers of $4,000 and $5,000 per acre. Instead, he presented his own offer of $4,000 per acre, which Sunset accepted. He falsely represented to plaintiffs that the least Sunset would take for the property was $5,000 per acre, because he intended to purchase the property from Sunset himself and resell it to plaintiffs at a profit of $1,000 per acre. All the reasons he gave for the unusual handling of the sale were fabrications. He never disclosed Ward's offer to Sunset until after the escrow papers were signed. All of the money he used to pay Sunset the purchase price came from the Ward escrow.

Plaintiffs brought an action in tort charging fraud on the part of Taggart * * *. The case was tried without a jury, and the court entered judgment for $72,049.20 compensatory damages, and for $36,000 exemplary damages. * * *

Defendants contend that the judgment must be reversed on the ground that, there can be no recovery in a tort action for fraud without proof of the actual or "out-of-pocket" losses sustained by the plaintiff and that in the present case there was no evidence that the property was worth less than paid for it. Defendants invoke section 3343 of the Civil Code, which provides that one "defrauded in the purchase, sale or exchange of property is entitled to recover the difference between the actual value of that with which the defrauded person parted and the actual value of that which he received. * * *" Although, as defendants admit, the evidence is clearly sufficient to support the finding of fraud, the only evidence submitted on the issue of damages was that the property was worth at least $5,000 per acre, the price plaintiffs paid for it. Since there was no proof that plaintiffs suffered "out-of-pocket" loss, there can be no recovery in tort for fraud. (Bagdasarian v. Gragnon, 31 Cal.2d 744, 762–763 [192 P.2d 935]).

Plaintiffs contend, however, that their recovery is not limited to actual damages, on the ground that section 3343 does not apply to a tort action to recover secret profits. [citations] These cases all involved situations in which the defendant was the agent of the defrauded person or in which a confidential or fiduciary relationship existed between the parties. They rest on the theory that "the principal's right to recover does not depend upon any deceit of the agent, but is based upon the duties incident to the agency relationship and upon the fact that all profits resulting from that relationship belong to the principal." (Savage v. Mayer, 33 Cal.2d 548, 551, 203 P.2d 9, 11.) In the present case, however, there is no evidence of an agency or other fiduciary relationship between plaintiffs and defendant Taggart or defendant Jordan. Plaintiffs dealt at arm's length with Taggart through their agent Thomsen. * * * In the absence of a fiduciary relationship, recovery in a tort action for fraud is limited to the actual damages suffered by the plaintiff.

Even though Taggart was not plaintiff's agent, the public policy of this state does not permit one to "take advantage of his own wrong" (Civ.Code, § 3517), and the law provides a quasi-contractual remedy to prevent one from being unjustly enriched at the expense of another.[1] Section 2224 of the Civil Code provides that one "who gains a thing by fraud * * * or other wrongful act, is, unless he has some other and better right thereto, an involuntary trustee of the thing gained, for the benefit of the person who would otherwise have had it." As a real estate broker, Taggart had the duty to be honest and truthful in his dealings. * * * The evidence is clearly sufficient to support a finding that Taggart violated this duty. Through fraudulent misrepresentations he received money that plaintiffs would otherwise have had. Thus, Taggart is an involuntary trustee for the benefit of plaintiffs on the secret profit of $1,000 per acre that he made from his dealings with them.

* * * Although the facts pleaded and proved by plaintiffs do not sustain the judgment on the theory of tort, they are sufficient to uphold recovery under the quasi-contractual theory of unjust enrichment since that theory does not contemplate any factual situation different from that established by the evidence in the trial court. * * *

Accordingly, the judgment for $72,049.20, representing the $1,000 per acre secret profit, against defendant Taggart must be affirmed. The judgment against defendant Jordan, however, must be reversed. Although she permitted her name to be used in the dual escrows, she did not share in the illicit profit that Taggart obtained. One cannot be held to be a constructive trustee of something he has not acquired.

Taggart contends that if recovery is based on the theory of unjust enrichment the judgment for exemplary damages must be reversed. The argument runs that under this theory the law implies a promise to return the money wrongfully obtained, that the plaintiff waives the tort and sues in assumpsit on an implied contract, and that since such an action is "contractual" in nature, it does not admit of the exemplary damages allowed under section 3294 of the Civil Code. That section authorizes exemplary damages "in an action for the breach of an obligation not arising from contract, where the defendant has been guilty of oppression, fraud, or malice." The word "contract" is used in this section in its ordinary sense to mean an agreement between the parties, not an obligation imposed by law despite the absence of any such agreement. Taggart's obligation does not arise from any agreement between him and plaintiffs. It arises from his fraud and violation of statutory duties. His fraud is not waived, for it is the very foundation of the implied-in-law promise to disgorge. The promise is purely fictitious and unintentional, originally implied to circumvent rigid common law pleading. It was invoked not to deny a remedy, but to create one "for the purpose of bringing about justice without reference to the intention of the parties." * * * Since Taggart's obligation for his fraud does not arise from contract but is imposed by law, the judgment for exemplary damages clearly falls within section 3294. * * *

Courts award exemplary damages to discourage oppression, fraud, or malice by punishing the wrongdoer. Such damages are appropriate in cases like the present one, where restitution would have little or no deterrent effect, for wrongdoers would run no risk of liability to their victims beyond that of returning what they wrongfully obtained. * * *

1. [Footnote renumbered.] Section 3343 provides that "nothing herein contained shall be deemed to deny to any person having a cause of action for fraud or deceit any legal or equitable remedies to which such person may be entitled."

SCHAUER, J., concurring and dissenting. I concur in the judgment because it comes as close to affording justice to the wronged plaintiffs as appears possible under the presently established decisional law of this state as it interprets and applies section 3343 of the Civil Code. In fact this decision by its ingenious innovation and application of a constructive trust-unjust enrichment-quasicontractual theory to support an award of exemplary damages as against one of the defendants, avoids much of the evil effect of the majority holding in Bagdasarian v. Gragnon (1948), 31 Cal.2d 744, 759–763 [192 P.2d 935], and is therefore to that extent desirable.

But because the subject section as now interpreted and applied still constitutes more of a shield for, than a sword against fraud perpetrators, I deem it proper to once more direct attention to it in the hope that the Legislature—if not this court by forthright overruling of *Bagdasarian*—may provide a remedy.

Note

Question: In Haigler v. Donnelly, 18 Cal.2d 674, 680, 117 P.2d 331, 335 (1941), the court stated "there is a question" whether plaintiff may recover exemplary damages in an action for money had and received. Does Ward v. Taggart answer the question?

COLEMAN v. LADD FORD CO.

District Court of Appeal of California, Second District, 1963.
215 Cal.App.2d 90, 29 Cal.Rptr. 832.

BURKE, PRESIDING JUSTICE. * * * The case arises out of the fraud of defendant in inducing plaintiff to purchase a new automobile upon representations that defendant would dispose of another automobile owned by plaintiff. Damages were awarded on the basis of the "loss of bargain" rule involved in fraud sale cases, interpreted by Ward v. Taggart, instead of the "out-of-pocket" rule declared in Bagdasarian v. Gragnon, 31 Cal.2d 744, 192 P.2d 935. The decision of the Appellate Department of the Superior Court follows the reasoning of the *Ward* decision, and we transferred the case in order that it may be determined whether it qualifies as an exception to the *Bagdasarian* rule in order to avoid injustice in the particular case, or whether such "out-of-pocket" rule must be considered controlling as the uniform rule for all fraud sale cases.

At the time of plaintiff's purchase, she owned a used automobile on the purchase contract of which there remained a balance payable. Defendant's salesman represented to plaintiff that he had a buyer for her used car; that the balance due the finance company on the car would be paid off and she would have no further payments to make. Relying on these representations, plaintiff purchased the new car from defendant. The representations as to the old car were false and fraudulently made and the payments were never made. Later the finance company repossessed the used car, sold it, and the assignee of its claim obtained judgment against plaintiff for the balance of the purchase price and attorney's fees. Plaintiff did not elect to rescind her contract for the purchase of the new car, but brought suit for damages for fraud. * * *

Judgment was granted in her favor for the total amount of the deficiency, attorney's fees and interest represented in the finance company's judgment against her in the sum of $1,322.04 and, in addition, for attorney's fees and court costs to defend such action, of $214, aggregating $1,536.04.

Under the decision in Bagdasarian v. Gragnon, the plaintiff may recover only that which he is actually out-of-pocket, i.e., the difference, if any, between what the property is actually worth and the price he paid for it. * * * But the rigidity of this rule has been relaxed. In Ward v. Taggart, supra 51 Cal.2d 736, the Supreme Court opened the door for such further court interpretation of the section as may be necessary to do justice. * * *

The problems solved by Ward v. Taggart, conduce to a retention of the theory therein adopted—a theory neither pleaded nor raised by the parties, but evolved by the court to apply under the circumstances presented in the case in order to do justice which under the application of the exclusive test previously announced in *Bagdasarian* would have been impossible. The theory applied is that of a combination of constructive trust—unjust enrichment and quasi-contractual relationships which will support an award of exemplary damages in addition to permitting recovery under the "loss of bargain" rule. Its effect was not to overrule *Bagdasarian* but to interpret that ruling as being permissive of exceptions. Ward v. Taggart, affords justice to litigants who would be otherwise denied relief. It also preserves punitive damages as a strong deterrent to unacceptable conduct by defrauding parties. The decision indicates a proper base in law or equity for each aspect of the multiple theory adopted. * * *

Section 3343 of the Civil Code does not state that the out-of-pocket rule is the exclusive measure of damages for fraud. Accordingly this court upholds the decision of the trial court and the Appellate Department of the Superior Court in deciding that the rule announced in Ward v. Taggart reestablishes the right of recovery of damages other than upon the "out-of-pocket" rule in fraud sale cases; that such right is cumulative and alternative to that embraced by the rule in the *Bagdasarian* case; that the instant case is resolvable upon the theory presented in the Ward v. Taggart case.

The judgment of the municipal court is affirmed.

Notes

1. In 1971, the California Legislature amended § 3343 of the Civil Code. It is set out below with additions in italics. Would the statute as it reads now affect *Ward* or *Coleman?*

§ 3343. Fraud in Purchase, Sale or Exchange of Property; Additional Damages *(a)* One defrauded in the purchase, sale or exchange of property is entitled to recover the difference between the actual value of that with which the defrauded person parted and the actual value of that which he received, together with any additional damage arising from the particular transaction, *including any of the following:*

(1) Amounts actually and reasonably expended in reliance upon the fraud.

(2) An amount which would compensate the defrauded party for loss of use and enjoyment of the property to the extent that any such loss was proximately caused by the fraud.

(3) Where the defrauded party has been induced by reason of the fraud to sell or otherwise part with the property in question, an amount which will compensate him for profits or other gains which might reasonably have been earned by use of the property had he retained it.

(4) Where the defrauded party has been induced by reason of the fraud to purchase or otherwise acquire the property in question, an amount which will compensate him for any loss of profits or other gains which were reasonably

anticipated and would have been earned by him from the use or sale of the property had it possessed the characteristics fraudulently attributed to it by the party committing the fraud, provided that lost profits from the use or sale of the property shall be recoverable only if and only to the extent that all of the following apply:

(i) The defrauded party acquired the property for the purpose of using or reselling it for a profit.

(ii) The defrauded party reasonably relied on the fraud in entering into the transaction and in anticipating profits from the subsequent use or sale of the property.

(iii) Any loss of profits for which damages are sought under this paragraph have been proximately caused by the fraud and the defrauded party's reliance on it.

(b) Nothing in this section shall do either of the following:

(1) Permit the defrauded person to recover any amount measured by the difference between the value of property as represented and the actual value thereof.

(2) Deny to any person having a cause of action for fraud or deceit any legal or equitable remedies to which such person may be entitled.

California cases have held that amended § 3343 authorizes the recovery of both out of pocket damages and "lost profits." See Pat Rose Associates v. Coombe, 225 Cal.App.3d 9, 275 Cal.Rptr. 1 (1990).

2. In Stout v. Turney, 22 Cal.3d 718, 150 Cal.Rptr. 637, 586 P.2d 1228 (1978), the plaintiff purchased a mobile home park relying on the seller's misrepresentation about the capacity of the sewage disposal system. Because of the facts misrepresented, plaintiff anticipated that an additional eight mobile homes could be squeezed in. Plaintiff alleged: (a) loss of profits that would have been made from the eight spaces and (b) the cost of having to buy additional land on which to sprinkle the waste effluvients to meet requirements of the local Water Quality Control Board. Satisfactory evidence of lost profits was presented. No evidence of any out of pocket damages was presented, no doubt because there was none. The trial court awarded plaintiff $92,000 damages for lost profits and additional expenses under the California Civil Code section 3343 reprinted above.

On appeal the seller objected (a) that "consequential" or "additional" damages could not be assessed when plaintiff lacked out of pocket damages to add them to and (b) that the court was substituting the expressly forbidden "benefit of the bargain" damages for California's mandated out of pocket measure. The Supreme Court, however, affirmed the judgment: Plaintiff's failure to prove out of pocket damages did not preclude the "additional" or "consequential" ones. The court denied that a "benefit of the bargain" rule was adopted. Query: Is the result the same as if the "benefit of the bargain" rule were adopted?

3. As the decisions above illustrate, California lawyers have sought to create exceptions to the exclusive out of pocket damage rule or to avoid it altogether. Continental Airlines, Inc. v. McDonnell Douglas Corp., 216 Cal.App.3d 388, 264 Cal.Rptr. 779 (1989) took a large step in the direction away from out of pocket. The airline sued McDonnell Douglas alleging negligent misrepresentations about an airplane which contributed to the destruction of the aircraft when two tires blew out and caused it to crash. McDonnell Douglas argued that the out of pocket rule in § 3343 is the exclusive measure of damages. The court rejected this argument; it ruled that the Commercial Code controlled sales of goods and that § 2–714 governed damages for breach of warranty.

4. Should the rule of damages depend on whether defendant's misrepresentation was negligent as in *McDonnell Douglas* or intentional?

In Cunha v. Ward Foods, Inc., 804 F.2d 1418 (9th Cir.1986), rev'd, 878 F.2d 385 (9th Cir.1989), the court, interpreting Hawaii law, ruled that the Restatement of Torts rule in § 552B denying benefit of the bargain damages in negligence cases should be applied.

5. Should it matter whether the victim asserts fraud affirmatively or as a defense to the tortfeasor's claim? In Collins v. Burns, 103 Nev. 394, 741 P.2d 819 (1987), a vendor sued to recover on a note executed by the purchasers of a liquor store. The purchasers asserted fraud as a defense and filed a counterclaim for damages. The court ruled that benefit of the bargain damages were inappropriate in that situation; it awarded only out of pocket damages.

6. *Punitive Damages in Tort Actions for Fraud.* In Walker v. Sheldon, 10 N.Y.2d 401, 223 N.Y.S.2d 488, 490, 492, 179 N.E.2d 497, 498, 499–500 (1961), the New York Court of Appeals, in a four to three decision, ruled that punitive damages are permissible where proof established that defendants were engaged in a "virtually larcenous scheme to trap generally the unwary." In a strong dissenting opinion, Judge Van Voorhis argued that the New York rule "firmly established" that such damages are not allowed for fraud. The majority opinion supported exemplary damages where "a high degree of moral culpability" is found:

"Exemplary damages are more likely to serve their desired purpose of deterring similar conduct in a fraud case, such as that before us, than in any other area of tort. One who acts out of anger or hate, for instance, in committing assault or libel, is not likely to be deterred by the fear of punitive damages. On the other hand, those who deliberately and coolly engage in a far-flung fraudulent scheme, systematically conducted for profit, are very much more likely to pause and consider the consequences if they have to pay more than the actual loss suffered by an individual plaintiff. An occasional award of compensatory damages against such parties would have little deterrent effect. A judgment simply for compensatory damages would require the offender to do no more than return the money which he had taken from the plaintiff. In the calculation of his expected profits, the wrongdoer is likely to allow for a certain amount of money which will have to be returned to those victims who object too vigorously, and he will be perfectly content to bear the additional cost of litigation as the price for continuing his illicit business."

Following early disagreement about *Walker,* the New York courts have now established that a fraud victim may recover punitive damages where the fraud is gross, wanton or wilful regardless of whether it was directed at the public generally. Ostano Commerzanstalt v. Telewide Systems, Inc., 880 F.2d 642 (2d Cir.1989); Getty Petroleum Corp. v. Island Transportation Corp., 878 F.2d 650 (2d Cir.1989), cert. denied, 490 U.S. 1006 (1989); Whitney v. Citibank, N.A., 782 F.2d 1106 (2d Cir.1986).

May a fraud victim recover punitive damages without proving any compensatory damages? Nappe v. Anschelewitz, Barr, Ansell & Bonello, 97 N.J. 37, 50, 477 A.2d 1224, 1231 (1984). "Because of the fortuitous circumstance that an injured plaintiff failed to prove compensatory damages, the defendant should not be freed of responsibility for aggravated misconduct. People should not be able with impunity to trench wilfully upon a right. Moreover, it is especially fitting to allow punitive damage for actions such as legal fraud, since intent rather than mere negligence is the requisite state of mind.

"The punitive award is not required to have a fixed proportional relationship to the amount of compensatory damages."

7. A federal consumer protection statute prohibits altering odometers. 15 U.S.C.A. § 1901 et seq. It allows three times actual damages or $1,500 whichever is greater. The statute does not supersede state common law remedies. Edgar v. Fred Jones Lincoln–Mercury, Inc., 524 F.2d 162 (10th Cir.1975). Odometer tampering is considered a fraud; it not only disregards the rights of the individual buyer, but also the consuming public's. State common law may sanction heavy punitive damages, e.g. $12,500 against an auto dealer who took 7,000 miles off a demonstrator car. Boise Dodge, Inc. v. Clark, 92 Idaho 902, 453 P.2d 551 (1969).

8. *Mental Anguish Damages for Fraud?* Courts disagree about whether a fraud victim may recover for emotional distress damages. Merritt, Damages for Emotional Distress in Fraud Litigation: Dignitary Torts in a Commercial Society, 42 Vand.L.Rev. 1 (1989) argues that courts should award emotional distress damages for intentional fraud. See Anderson v. Knox, 297 F.2d 702 (9th Cir.1961), cert. denied, 370 U.S. 915 (1962) (loss of life insurance policies); Godfrey v. Steinpress, 128 Cal.App.3d 154, 180 Cal.Rptr. 95 (1982) (fraudulently concealing termites in a home).

UNITED STATES v. BOUND BROOK HOSPITAL, INC.

United States Court of Appeals, Third Circuit, 1958.
251 F.2d 12.

GOODRICH, CIRCUIT JUDGE. The sole question in this case is the correctness of the district court's measure of damages in a judgment rendered against the defendant, Dr. Louis S. Borow. The defendant purchased from the United States certain medical supplies pursuant to the Surplus Property Act of 1944. [Now 40 U.S.C.A. § 471 et seq.] Purporting to act on behalf of a nonprofit hospital corporation, Borow paid only five percent of the Government's valuation of the property. * * * Then in violation of the agreement that the hospital had made in its application for eligibility, all or nearly all of the supplies were immediately resold by the purchaser. It is now conceded that the defendant secured the supplies fraudulently and is liable for something. The only question is how much.

Section 26(b) of the Surplus Property Act provides three choices of consequences for fraud practiced on the United States under the provisions of the act. * * * We are concerned only with the first choice which was what the Government made in this case. The person liable "(1) Shall pay to the United States the sum of $2,000 for each such act, and double the amount of any damage which the United States may have sustained by reason thereof." [40 U.S.C. § 489(b)(1)]

At the trial the Government claimed damages to the extent of the unpaid portion of the inventory prices on which Borow was given his discount. The defendant admits liability for $2,000 but says that is all he owes. The district judge, however, found to the contrary and held that the defendant must pay not only the $2,000 but double what he got from the unlawful sale of these supplies less what he had already paid the Government therefor. * * *

What the defendant does argue, however, is that the United States has not proven that it sustained specific monetary damages in the amounts that were claimed by it at the trial or which were found by the trial court. As said above, responsibility for the statutory $2,000 is admitted.

* * * Nearly all of the prior cases which are reported arose out of the fraudulent use of a veteran's priority. Since the loss to the United States was

only a wrongful channeling of the property, proof of monetary damages would have been impossible. * * *

In the present case we have the added factor that the defendant's fraudulent scheme involved obtaining the material at an exceptionally favorable discount, notwithstanding what could have been received for it from the general public. It is obvious that this conduct did cause a potential loss of money to the United States. The real issue before us is whether the amount of that loss was properly determined by the district court.

We do not believe the question to be a difficult one. The defendant got property from the United States for about $2,000 which he resold for $34,000. The defendant is hardly in a position to urge that the property could not have been sold by the United States for as much as he got for it. It seems pretty clear, therefore, that the Government has suffered a pecuniary loss of at least as much as the difference between what it got from the defendant and what the defendant got from his purchaser. Under equitable principles of restitution the amount thus obtained by wrongful act could be recovered from the wrongdoer. See Restatement, Restitution § 151, com. f, 202, cl. a. (1937). We do not think the measure of damages is any less under the terms of this statute. The district court did determine the damages on this basis and then gave judgment pursuant to the statutory mandate for double the amount. The Government is content with this measure of damages and it is certainly not one of which the defendant can make complaint. Whether under other sets of facts a different method of ascertaining damages might be upheld we do not now decide.

The judgment of the district court will be affirmed.

JANIGAN v. TAYLOR

United States Court of Appeals, First Circuit, 1965.
344 F.2d 781.

ALDRICH, CHIEF JUDGE. This is a personal action brought by plaintiffs as a class in the district court for the district of Massachusetts in which they allege violations by the defendant of Rule 10b–5 (17 C.F.R. § 240, 10b–5) of the Securities and Exchange Commission promulgated pursuant to section 10 of the Securities Exchange Act of 1934 (15 U.S.C.A. § 78j). * * * The basic facts are simple. The plaintiffs are former stockholders, some of whom were also the controlling directors, of Boston Electro Steel Casting, Inc. (BESCO). For convenience they will be called stockholders, directors, or collectively, plaintiffs. The defendant was the president, general manager and a director of BESCO. In early 1956, following a directors' meeting on December 27, 1955, defendant purchased plaintiffs' stock (virtually all of the outstanding stock of the company) for approximately $40,000. In December 1957 he sold it for $700,000. Suit was brought in October 1958. Plaintiffs' action rests upon a statement by the defendant admittedly made at the December 27 meeting in response to a question by one of the directors. Asked whether he "knew of any material change in the affairs of the company or in the past months which could cause us to have any different opinion about the company," his answer was, "[T]here was none, it was about the same." For convenience we will call this the representation. Trial was had without jury. The district court found the representation consciously and materially false and, to the degree hereinafter set forth, that plaintiffs relied on it, and awarded as damages defendant's net profits. Defendant appeals. All events took place in Massachusetts and it is agreed that its law governs to the extent that federal law does not. * * *

We turn to the remedy. With respect to damages we draw a distinction between cases where, by fraud, one is caused to buy something that one would not have bought or would not have bought at that price, and where, by fraud one is induced to convey property to the fraudulent party. In the former case the damages are to be reckoned solely by "the difference between the real value of the property at the date of its sale to the plaintiffs and the price paid for it, with interest from that date, and, in addition, such outlays as were legitimately attributable to the defendant's conduct, but not damages 'covering' the expected fruits of an unrealized speculation." Sigafus v. Porter, 1900, 179 U.S. 116, 125 [citations]. On the other hand, if the property is not bought from, but sold to the fraudulent party, future accretions not foreseeable at the time of the transfer even on the true facts, and hence speculative, are subject to another factor, viz., that they accrued to the fraudulent party. It may, as in the case at bar, be entirely speculative whether, had plaintiffs not sold, the series of fortunate occurrences would have happened in the same way, and to their same profit. However, there can be no speculation but that the defendant actually made the profit and, once it is found that he acquired the property by fraud, that the profit was the proximate consequence of the fraud, whether foreseeable or not. It is more appropriate to give the defrauded party the benefit even of windfalls than to let the fraudulent party keep them. See Marcus v. Otis, 2 Cir., 1948, 168 F.2d 649, 660, 169 F.2d 148. We may accept defendant's position that there was no fiduciary relationship and that he was dealing at arm's length. Nonetheless, it is simple equity that a wrongdoer should disgorge his fraudulent enrichment. [citations]

There are, of course, limits to this principle. If an artist acquired paints by fraud and used them in producing a valuable portrait we would not suggest the defrauded party be entitled to the portrait, or to the proceeds of its sale. However, those limits are not reached in the case at bar. In answers to interrogatories defendant stated that following the acquisition he did nothing different, and worked no harder than he had before. In his pretrial memorandum he stated that the company's "turn-around" was due to price rises, increased efficiency, and an improvement in the business cycle particularly affecting BESCO's customers. Since defendant received his salary for his personal efforts, which would have been his regular duty, no extraordinary gains in the company's affairs attributable to himself fall within the principle suggested by our artist hypothetical. * * *

Judgment will be entered remanding the case to the District Court * * * affirming its judgment.

Notes

1. *Janigan followed:* Wilson v. Great American Industries, Inc., 855 F.2d 987 (2d Cir.1988). Plaintiffs claimed that they sold stock because of a materially false and misleading proxy statement. Unlike the insiders in *Janigan,* these defendants still owned the stock. Conceding that defendants' profits were somewhat speculative, the court nevertheless ruled that plaintiffs were entitled to the bargain that they would have struck if defendants had disclosed fully.

In Estate of Jones v. Kvamme, 449 N.W.2d 428 (Minn.1989), a constructive trust was imposed on the profits resulting from a fraudulent purchase. See also

SEC v. Thomas James Associates, 738 F.Supp. 88 (W.D.N.Y.1990) where the court decreed a "disgorgement" of the illegal profits.

2. *Janigan qualified:* In SEC v. MacDonald, 699 F.2d 47, 53–54, 57 (1st Cir.1983), Judge Aldrich, author of *Janigan,* wrote referring to *Janigan:* "We recognized that '[t]here are of course limits to this principle.' While not discussed there, one of the limits that has emerged in cases following *Janigan* is where the fraudulently obtained securities are publicly traded, and hence readily available, the defrauded sellers can recover only those accretions occurring up to a reasonable time after they discovered the truth [citations] * * *

"When a fraudulent buyer has reached the point of his full gain from the fraud, viz., the market price a reasonable time after undisclosed information has become public, any consequence of a subsequent decision, be it to sell or retain the stock, is res inter alios, not causally related to the fraud."

The dissent said: "[F]ull disgorgement leaves the wrongdoer in exactly the same financial position as rescission; if rescission is equitable, so is full disgorgement."

2. DAMAGES FOR INNOCENT MISREPRESENTATION AND NON-DISCLOSURE

CLEMENTS AUTO CO. v. SERVICE BUREAU CORP.

United States Court of Appeals, Eighth Circuit, 1971.
444 F.2d 169.

HEANEY, CIRCUIT JUDGE. The Service Bureau Corporation, a wholly-owned subsidiary of International Business Machines Corporation appeals from a judgment awarding SM Supply Company $480,811 in damages, the basis of the award being actionable misrepresentations made by SBC to SM in connection with the sale of data processing services. * * *

SBC is engaged in the business of electronic data processing, offering to the public its services in eighty-four branch offices throughout the United States. It sells data processing services in the following areas: payroll, personnel records, accounts receivable, billing, sales accounting, marketing studies, cost accounting, inventory record, budgets and general accounting.

SM operates wholesale supply houses at Mankato and Rochester, Minnesota, and at Eau Claire, Wisconsin. * * * The court denied recovery on all grounds other than misrepresentation,[1] but found that SBC had made one central actionable misrepresentation to SM, i.e., that the proposed data processing system would, when fully implemented, be capable of providing SM suffi-

1. [Editors' footnote.] The trial court's holding is at 298 F.Supp. 139: "In its multipronged effort to succeed in this case, SM Supply has proceeded on the theories of rescission, breach of implied warranty, reformation and breach of contract, in addition to the misrepresentation claim * * *. Since the latter claim constitutes an affirmation of the contract, rescission obviously is not available. [citation] Furthermore, rescission would not be an appropriate remedy in this case. [citation]

"The claim based on implied warranty cannot prevail because of the express negation of such warranties in the contracts: 'SBC makes no warranties, expressed or implied, other than the express warranties contained in this agreement.'

[citation]

"Reformation also is unavailable in this case * * * the fact that representations regarding this system were made by SBC does not, without more, establish that there was any prior valid agreement between SBC and SM Supply in accordance with which the written contracts should be reformed."

cient information in a form such that when properly utilized, it would constitute an effective and efficient tool to be used in inventory control.

[Other details as to the contract appear in the course of the opinion].

It is important to emphasize that, in Minnesota, the element of scienter, or intent to deceive, or even recklessness, is not necessary to actionable fraud. * * *

While accepting the above as a correct statement of Minnesota law, SBC raises two arguments in opposition to the trial court's finding of liability for fraud. It first argues that the trial court erred in applying the Minnesota law of fraud to the present situation. The argument is rooted in what SBC considers to be a legal inconsistency in the trial court's findings. It is developed by SBC as follows:

(1) The trial court found certain aforementioned representations made to SM to be actionable under the Minnesota law of fraud.

(2) The trial court found that these same representations did not give rise to an express warranty because there was no valid agreement by the parties incorporating these representations into the contract, and that a disclaimer in the various contracts effectively negated all implied warranties.

(3) Under the relevant law, innocent misrepresentations and warranties, either express or implied, are substantially similar in nature.

(4) The passage of the Uniform Commercial Code by the legislature evinced an intent to have that body of law control all commercial transactions.

The conclusion drawn is that:

> "In short, SBC does not believe that the law of innocent misrepresentations in Minnesota can or should be read as in conflict with commercial doctrine in that state, and believes it was error for the Trial Court to do so. The Trial Court treated the facts of this case as giving different results when viewed under Minnesota Tort Law than when viewed under Minnesota Contract Law. SBC does not believe the results can or should depend merely upon the label."

SBC candidly admits that this question has never been squarely faced by the Minnesota Supreme Court, but suggests that the governing policy of the U.C.C. compels its interpretation of the relationship between contract and tort law.

We cannot agree that this argument dictates a result other than that reached by the trial court. * * *

In Ganley Bros., Inc. v. Butler Bros. Building Co., 170 Minn. 373, 212 N.W. 602 (1927), two contractors had entered into an agreement involving subletting highway construction work. The subcontractor subsequently sued the prime contractor for damages alleging, inter alia, that the contract in question was induced by false and fraudulent misrepresentations. By way of defense, the prime contractor introduced a provision in the contract which stated:

> "The contractor has examined the said contracts of December 7, 1922, and the specifications and plans forming a part thereof, and is familiar with the location of said work and the conditions under which the same must be performed, and knows all the requirements, and is not relying upon any statement made by the company in respect thereto."

The trial court dismissed the fraud action on the grounds that this provision validly negated fraud. On appeal, the Supreme Court of Minnesota reversed, holding that:

> "The law should not, and does not, permit a covenant of immunity to be drawn that will protect a person against his own fraud. Such is not enforceable because of public policy."

In arriving at this decision, the court specifically considered the extent of freedom of contract and concluded that it did not extend to waiver of fraud either directly or indirectly.

SBC concedes that the teachings of *Ganley Bros.* are applicable where the fraud action is based on intentional conduct, but contends the rule must be different where innocent misrepresentations are the basis of the fraud action. * * *

A close reading of *Ganley Bros.* leaves us uncertain whether the fraud considered in that case included an element of bad intent. In any event, we do not believe that this gratuitous language sets out the controlling factor in determining the effect of an exculpatory contract provision on an action in fraud. * * *

It is worthwhile to note that a student article in the 1939 Minnesota Law Review would apparently agree with our conclusion as to the effect of a general disclaimer clause. Note, 23 Minn.L.Rev. 784 (1939). The article, entitled "Contractual Disclaimers of Warranties," is primarily concerned with various methods used by courts to nullify the effect of contract disclaimer provisions. After considering the orthodox approaches then used by courts, especially the Minnesota Supreme Court, in contract cases, the author suggests:

> "There is one other possible solution for the problem. If the buyer were to bring a suit in tort for deceit instead of in contract for breach of warranty, the action should not be defeated by a provision waiving warranties. Although in a majority of the American courts the purchaser undoubtedly would not be able to prevail if he could not prove scienter, a few states headed by Minnesota, do not make that requirement."

While the author concedes that this approach would not generally be effective where no affirmative representations had been made, it is undisputed that the present action is based on affirmative oral and written statements.

SBC's argument that the passage of the Uniform Commercial Code would lead the Minnesota Court to a contrary result is unpersuasive. * * *

The Uniform Commercial Code itself provides that:

> "Unless displaced by the particular provisions of this chapter, the principles of law and equity, including the law merchant and the law relative to * * * fraud, misrepresentation * * * or other validating or invalidating cause shall supplement its provisions."

1–103 (1966). * * *

In viewing earlier decisions, we believe it is relevant that the Minnesota Court has stated that:

> "The fact that one who has been defrauded has a remedy on the contract or on a guaranty or warranty is not any impediment or defense to an action for the fraud or deceit. * * *"

Osborn v. Will, 183 Minn. 205, 236 N.W. 197, 200 (1931). * * *

On other occasions, the Minnesota Court has reiterated the differences in the law governing breach of warranty and the law governing fraud. E.g., Hemming v. Ald, Inc., 279 Minn. 38, 155 N.W.2d 384, 386–387, n. 2 (1967) (time period in which rescission allowed); Lehman v. Hansord Pontiac Co., 246 Minn. 1, 74 N.W.2d 305, 311 (1955) (measure of damages). * * * In our view, we would distort the established body of Minnesota law were we to hold that under the U.C.C., an action for fraud, based on innocent misrepresentation, could not be maintained where the contract validly disclaimed all warranties. The Minnesota Supreme Court is free to make its own decision. All we decide is that, on the basis of the factors we can find, it would decide as we have. * * *

Lastly, SBC contends that even if SM was initially justified in their reliance on SBC's representations, SM discovered the falsity of the statements long before the relationship was terminated in January, 1967. The trial court found that while SM may have been aware of the problems with the system by the end of 1964, no duty to mitigate damages by terminating the contracts arose before September of 1966. It so held on the theory that SM was not aware of the exact cause of the problems and was so financially committed to the system that it was unreasonable for it to sever its contracts with SBC before that date.

Having carefully reviewed the applicable law and the lengthy record in this case, we conclude that the trial court erred in this finding.

The general rule in Minnesota is that "a party defrauded cannot, after discovery of the fraud, increase his damages by continuing to expend money on the property retained and recover for such expenditures." Perkins v. Meyerton, 190 Minn. 542, 251 N.W. 559, 560 (1934). As stated in L'Evesque v. Rognrud, 254 Minn. 55, 93 N.W.2d 672, 677 (1958):

> "[T]he measure of damages is the difference between the actual value of the property received and the price paid for it, and in addition thereto such other or special damages as were naturally and proximately caused by the fraud *prior to its discovery.*" (Emphasis added.)

* * * Following these principles, it is clear that a party to an executory contract, who prior to its performance discovers fraud, may not go forward with performance of the contract and subsequently sue for damages. * * * The exception to the above principle is that where the defrauded party discovers the fraud after substantial performance or where it would be economically unreasonable to terminate the relationship, he may affirm or continue the contract and then bring suit for his entire damages. * * *

In attempting to apply these legal principles, we must recognize two basic facts:

(1) The relationship involved here was based on a number of different contracts which were entered into over a period of approximately four years. Each of the basic contracts provided for continuing services and was terminable by either party upon thirty days' notice.

(2) The essential problems with the reports were apparent soon after they were provided to SM during 1963. While each of the three phases of the reports were progressively more sophisticated, the basic bulk and error-proneness of all the reports was a problem from the start.

Having considered the problem in light of the legal principles and factual relationship set out above, we conclude that as of April 30, 1965, SM was fully aware of the problems in the system and no longer had a basis for relying on the representations made by SBC. * * *

At this point, we do not believe continued reliance can be justified by economic compulsion or by the fact that SM may not have fully realized the technical cause of the system's flaws. SM's contracts with SBC were for services and were terminable on a month's notice. While SM had paid substantial sums to SBC at this point, these payments had not resulted in any equity which might be lost by termination. * * * Continuation of the contracts meant a continuation of the same monthly payments. The Minnesota Supreme Court has held that a party who discovers that he has been induced by fraud to enter into a 99–year lease shortly after the lease has begun to run cannot recover damages for the entire term of the contract. The court has so held on the basis that, in such a situation, the unperformed portion of the contract must be treated as a severable executory contract. O'Neil v. Davidson, 147 Minn. 240, 180 N.W. 102 (1920); * * * Here, it is even more apparent that the doctrine of substantial performance is inapplicable. SM's efforts and expense did justify some attempt to salvage the SBC system. However, we have already taken that factor into account in our conclusion. As Judge Blackmun stated in Hanson v. Ford Motor Company, supra, "the representer is not a guarantor."

The contracts between SBC and SM contained the following provision:

> "SBC's liability with respect to this agreement is limited to the total charge for the services provided herein and no special or consequential damages may be recovered."

SBC argues that this provision validly limits the damages which can be awarded here. Such contract provisions appear to be valid under New York law. Farris Engineering Corp. v. Service Bureau Corp., 406 F.2d 519 (3rd Cir.1969). There is also authority for the proposition that contract provisions may operate to limit liability in suits brought for breach of contract under Minnesota law. * * *

However, in our view, these cases do not resolve the issue we face here.[2] We think the issue is properly posed as follows: Where a cause of action for fraud has been established, would Minnesota law give effect to a contract provision limiting liability in awarding damages proven to result from the fraud? We believe that Minnesota law controls because in the final analysis the issue is controlled by the law of fraud.

In many ways, this question is substantially similar to SBC's earlier contention that a merger and warranty provision is effective to negate fraud. As it did there, SBC concedes that the contract provision is ineffective against intentional deceit, but argues it must be given effect where the fraud is based on "innocent misrepresentations." SBC again emphasizes the anomaly of obtaining different results in contract actions as opposed to fraud actions which do not include an element of bad faith.

However, we remain unconvinced that this difference in result would lead the Minnesota Court to give effect to the contract provision. In reaching this

2. [Footnote renumbered.] We are assuming, without deciding, the validity of this particular contract provision. If it were invalid, we would need to go no further. We have found no Minnesota case which has decided the validity of the precise provision in question here, either under the Uniform Commercial Code's unconscionability provision or under preexisting law.

decision, we have relied to a large extent on our earlier analysis of the Minnesota law of fraud vis-a-vis Minnesota contract law. Minnesota's strong policy of providing an effective remedy in fraud would be substantially undermined were we to give effect to this severe restriction on the amount of liability. Having previously held that Minnesota would not give effect to a contract provision which would negate the fact of liability, we believe it inconsistent to hold that the court would then give effect to a provision limiting the amount of liability.[3] * * *

The judgment of the lower court is affirmed in part. * * *

Notes

1. *Clements* emphasizes that Minnesota does not require scienter in a deceit action. This has long been regarded as the minority position. Rescission alone existed as a remedy for innocent misrepresentation in most jurisdictions. The effect of rescission, however, is basically the equivalent of the out of pocket measure of damages: the defrauded buyer in effect recoups the difference in value between what was paid for and what was received. The Restatement (Second) of Torts § 552C (1976) now allows damages for innocent misrepresentation in a sale, rental or exchange transaction, but expressly limits damages to the out of pocket measure.

2. See Hill, Breach of Contract as Tort, 74 Colum.L.Rev. 40 (1974); Hill, Damages for Innocent Misrepresentation, 73 Colum.L.Rev. 679 (1973).

3. Professor Grant Gilmore argued that contracts and torts were in the process of merging into a general law of obligations that he names "contorts." Death of Contract 87–94 (1974). Do the innocent misrepresentation decisions support or refute that argument?

4. For a contrary view of the effectiveness of a contractual limitation of liability for innocent misrepresentations see Wilkinson v. Carpenter, 276 Or. 311, 554 P.2d 512 (1976).

5. *Question:* A real estate broker has been held personally liable for passing on a seller's innocent misrepresentation, see Bevins v. Ballard, 655 P.2d 757 (Alaska 1982). What is the buyer's remedy?

LINGSCH v. SAVAGE

District Court of Appeal of California, First District, 1963.
213 Cal.App.2d 729, 29 Cal.Rptr. 201.

SULLIVAN, JUSTICE. In this action for damages for fraud brought against the sellers of certain real property and the real estate broker [Savage] representing them, plaintiffs appeal from a judgment for the defendant broker entered after the sustaining of his demurrer without leave to amend. * * *

It is alleged: that at the time of the sale, the "defendants and each of them specifically knew that the building was in a state of disrepair, and that units contained therein were illegal and that the building had been placed for

3. A recent case comment has reached the opposite conclusion. 54 Minn.L.Rev. 846 (1970). The article, however, is primarily a theoretical discussion of what the law ought to be, rather than an attempt to predict what the Minnesota Supreme Court would decide. Further, its analysis of the policy considerations in this area appears to deviate from the orthodox analyses of the Minnesota Court. Its reliance on our decision in Lack Industries, Incorporated v. Ralston Purina Company, 327 F.2d 266 (8th Cir. 1964), for the general proposition that "the degree of fault warrants a narrower liability for nonintentional than for intentional misrepresentation" is misplaced. *Lack Industries* stands only for the proposition that statements concerning future action will not, in the absence of intentional deceit, support an action in fraud.

condemnation by the proper officials" of San Francisco; that the plaintiffs did not know the foregoing matters and did not discover them until November 1961; that "the defendants and each of them willfully and fraudulently failed to reveal said information" to the plaintiffs; that the plaintiffs purchased the property "justifiably relying on said defendants' non-disclosure, as aforesaid, and in the belief that said property was in legal tenantable and properly repaired condition, as required by law"; that the defendants "knew that plaintiffs relied on their non-disclosure * * * and intended that they should so rely, and that said non-disclosure was in fact and law misrepresentation of a material fact"; and that the actual market value of the property was $5,000 less than what it would have been in the condition as represented. The complaint sought $5,000 general and $10,000 punitive damages.

The Exhibit 1 attached to the complaint is a printed form of "Uniform Agreement of Sale and Deposit Receipt" commonly available at local title companies. So far as is pertinent to the problem before us, the agreement acknowledges receipt from the plaintiffs of $1,000 on account of $21,000 the purchase price of the property in question "*in its present state and condition.*" (Emphasis added.) Among the terms and conditions of sale is the following provision: "No representations, guaranties or warranties of any kind or character have been made by any party hereto, or their representatives which are not herein expressed." The first part of the document then concludes with a statement that the "undersigned purchaser hereby agrees to purchase the herein described property for the price and *according to the conditions herein specified.*" (Emphasis added.)

Defendant George Savage filed a demurrer [1] asserting that the complaint failed to state facts sufficient to constitute a cause of action. * * *

The court below sustained the demurrer without leave to amend. * * *

An examination of the pleading under attack persuades us that the only kind of fraud or deceit which it purports to assert is one based on concealment or nondisclosure. We find no allegations which can reasonably be construed as asserting fraud predicated upon intentional and affirmative misrepresentations, negligent misrepresentations or false promises. * * * We should further point out that the concealment which is here the essence of the alleged deceit does not involve, in the light of the allegations before us, any affirmative acts on the part of the defendants in hiding, concealing or covering up the matters complained of. Nor do any allegations purport to set forth a confidential relationship subsisting between the plaintiffs on the one hand and all or any of the defendants on the other. We are therefore presented with an instance of mere nondisclosure, rather than active concealment, occurring between parties not in a confidential relationship.

* * * In order to fasten liability * * * on the person charged with the concealment or nondisclosure of certain facts, it is necessary to establish that he was under a legal duty to disclose them. * * * While such duty may arise from a fiduciary or other confidential relationship, no such relationship obtains in the case at bench and the duty of disclosure must therefore arise from other circumstances.

1. [Footnotes renumbered.] The demurrer is by Savage alone. The record does not disclose the status of the action in respect to the other defendants.

It is now settled in California that where the seller knows of facts materially affecting the value or desirability of the property which are known or accessible only to him and also knows that such facts are not known to, or within the reach of the diligent attention and observation of the buyer, the seller is under a duty to disclose them to the buyer.

* * * Failure of the seller to fulfill such duty of disclosure constitutes actual fraud. (Civ.Code, § 1572, subd. 3.)

The real estate agent or broker representing the seller is a party to the business transaction. In most instances he has a personal interest in it and derives a profit from it.[2] Where such agent or broker possesses, along with the seller, the requisite knowledge according to the foregoing decisions, whether he acquires it from, or independently of, his principal, he is under the same duty of disclosure. He is a party connected with the fraud and if no disclosure is made at all to the buyer by the other parties to the transaction, such agent or broker becomes jointly and severally liable with the seller for the full amount of the damages. * * * It is not necessary that there be a contractual relationship between the agent or broker and the buyer. * * * As this court said in Nathanson v. Murphy (1955), 132 Cal.App.2d 363, 368, 282 P.2d 174, 178 "[a]n action for deceit does not require privity of contract." No difficulty is encountered in imposing liability on an agent or broker for an affirmative and intentional misrepresentation on his part.

Similarly, no difficulty should be found in imposing liability on him for mere nondisclosure since his conduct in the transaction *amounts to a representation of the nonexistence of the facts which he has failed to disclose.* His fraud is of a different type; it is "negative" rather than "affirmative" (Barder v. McClung, 93 Cal.App.2d 692, 209 P.2d 808); but it is fraud nonetheless.

It should be pointed out that whether the matter not disclosed by the seller or his agent is of sufficient materiality to affect the value or desirability of the property, and thus make operative the rule announced by the foregoing authorities, depends on the facts of the particular case. Some idea can be obtained of the reach of the foregoing rule and of the vitiating character of the particular nondisclosure from the holding of some of the cases cited above. Thus nondisclosure of the fact that a lot was filled with debris thereafter covered over (Clauser v. Taylor, 44 Cal.App.2d 453, 112 P.2d 661) or that a lot contained filled ground to a substantial depth (Rothstein v. Janss Investment Corp., 45 Cal.App.2d 64, 113 P.2d 465) or that the house sold was constructed on filled land (Burkett v. J.A. Thompson & Son, 150 Cal.App.2d 523, 310 P.2d 56) or that improvements were added without a building permit and in violation of zoning regulations (Barder v. McClung, 93 Cal.App.2d 692, 209 P.2d 808) or in violation of building codes (Curran v. Heslop, 115 Cal.App.2d 476, 252 P.2d 378) has been held to be of sufficient substantiality to cause the duty of disclosure to arise.

Respondent cites a number of cases in support of the proposition that where parties deal at arm's length the rule of *caveat emptor* applies. We see no need of discussing the cases separately. As the court pointed out in Dyke v. Zaiser, 80 Cal.App.2d 639, 653, 182 P.2d 344, 353, undoubtedly there have been many cases "where it has been held that a man is not necessarily required to

2. The record shows that in the instant case the defendant Savage was to receive $1,000 from the sellers as his commission.

state everything he knows about the property involved. The present tendency, however, is to class concealment as actual fraud in those cases where the seller knows of facts which materially affect the desirability of the property which he knows are unknown to the buyer," citing *Clauser* and *Rothstein.* Respondent's contention that *caveat emptor* applies was made and rejected in Kallgren v. Steele, 131 Cal.App.2d 43, 46, 279 P.2d 1027, where the court held such rule inapplicable in a situation involving a seller's fraud. * * *

The elements of a cause of action for damages for fraud based on mere nondisclosure and involving no confidential relationship would therefore appear to be the following: (1) Nondisclosure by the defendant of facts materially affecting the value or desirability of the property; (2) Defendant's knowledge of such facts and of their being unknown to or beyond the reach of the plaintiff; (3) Defendant's intention to induce action by the plaintiff;[3] (4) Inducement of the plaintiff to act by reason of the nondisclosure; and (5) Resulting damages. (See 2 California Pleading, Chadbourn, Grossman, Van Alstyne, §§ 990 et seq., pp. 91 et seq.; 2 Witkin, Cal.Procedure, Pleading, § 348, pp. 1326–1327; § 352, pp. 1330–1331; § 356, p. 1334.)

While the complaint has not been carefully drawn, we feel that there is a reasonable possibility that its defects can be cured by amendment and that, unless other reasons for the trial court's action exist, the demurrer should not have been sustained without leave to amend. * * *

This brings us to the heart of the controversy. * * * Defendant's first contention is in essence that the complaint on its face precludes actionable fraud since under the contract incorporated therein the plaintiffs agreed to purchase the property "in its present state and condition." A provision in a contract of sale that the buyer takes the property in the condition in which it is, or "as is," does not necessarily confer on the seller a general immunity from liability for fraud. It is fairly well established in respect to sales of personal property that such a provision "does not prevent fraudulent representations relied on by the buyer from constituting fraud which invalidates the contract or is a ground for damages." (46 Am.Jur., Sales, § 319, p. 501) * * *.

The same rule has been applied where such a provision has been included in a contract for the sale of real property. (Smith v. Richards (1839), 38 U.S. (13 Pet.) 26; Wolford v. Freeman (1948), 150 Neb. 537, 35 N.W.2d 98; Cockburn v. Mercantile Petroleum, Inc. (Tex.Civ.App.1956), 296 S.W.2d 316.) In the early case of Smith v. Richards, rescission of a contract for the sale of a gold mine was upheld on the ground of the seller's fraudulent misrepresentations despite a provision in which the seller stated: "I, however, sell it for what it is, gold or snow-balls; and I leave it to you to decide, whether you will take it at my price, or not." In Wolford v. Freeman, the buyer sought rescission of a contract for the sale of a dwelling house for the fraud of the seller's agent in failing to disclose that the house had been constructed on filled ground. Repaired cracks in the walls and foundation were visible. There was testimony that the buyer asked the cause of the cracks and the agent said that he did not know. There was other evidence that the agent stated that he had been instructed by the seller to inform prospective purchasers that the damage had been corrected.

3. Chadbourn, Grossman and Van Alstyne, op. cit. p. 95 point out that in concealment cases this element is usually expressed in terms of "inducement" whereas in intentional misrepresentation cases, it is expressed in terms of reliance, citing Sanfran Co. v. Rees Blow Pipe Mfg. Co. (1959), 168 Cal.App.2d 191, 335 P.2d 995.

Included in the contract of sale was the following provision: "Purchaser acknowledges that he has been advised as to the settling of structure and is buying same as is." The Nebraska court held that the foregoing provision did not relieve the seller from fraud based on nondisclosure and upheld a decree of rescission on principles enunciating the seller's duty to disclose under such facts. Finally, in Cockburn v. Mercantile Petroleum, Inc., supra, the buyer of five gas wells "as is" recovered damages for the seller's fraud in misrepresenting that the wells were producing wells. The court's rationale was that the "as is" clause was based on the knowledge which the buyer had at the time "which knowledge was based on the false representation that there were five producing wells * * *." The "as is" agreement was executed in reliance upon such representations.

Under particular circumstances, the use of an "as is" provision seems to convey the implication that the property is in some way defective and that the buyer must take it at his own risk. * * * The parties hereto have not cited, nor have we found, a California case giving precise definition to such a provision when included in an agreement for the sale of real property. We are of the opinion that, generally speaking, such a provision means that the buyer takes the property in the condition visible to or observable by him. * * * Where the seller actively misrepresents the then condition of the property * * * or fails to disclose the true facts of its condition not within the buyer's reach and affecting the value or desirability of the property, an "as is" provision is ineffective to relieve the seller of either his "affirmative" or "negative" fraud. In either situation the seller's conduct has, as it were, infected the buyer's knowledge of the condition of the property. An "as is" provision may therefore be effective as to a dilapidated stairway but not as to a missing structural member, a subterranean creek in the backyard or an unexploded bomb buried in the basement, all being known to the seller. We feel that such a view of an "as is" provision not only makes good sense but equates sound law with good morals. To enlarge the meaning of such a provision so as to make it operative against all charges of fraud would be to permit the seller to contract against his own fraud contrary to existing law. (Civ.Code, § 1668.) * * *

It is also contended that the demurrer was properly sustained without leave to amend because of the inclusion of the following clause in the agreement at hand: "No representations, guaranties or warranties of any kind or character have been made by any party hereto, or their representatives which are not herein expressed."

It is well settled that where a principal is under a positive duty to make a disclosure, he cannot escape liability for his failure to do so by relying on a provision in the agreement of sale that there are no other representations except those therein expressed.

The present complaint is drawn on the theory that all defendants therein named were under a duty to make a disclosure. In essence, the foregoing statute and authorities prevent a party from contracting against his own fraud. If the sellers cannot escape liability, it is obvious that the defendant Savage, who is not even a party to the agreement, cannot do so. * * *

The judgment is reversed with directions to the trial court to grant the plaintiffs a reasonable time within which to prepare, serve and file a further complaint amended in such particulars as they may be advised.

Note

Compare Archuleta v. Kopp, 90 N.M. 273, 562 P.2d 834, cert. denied, 90 N.M. 636, 567 P.2d 485 (1977). Plaintiff, a blind person, bought a house "as is." It turned out to have a defective fireplace. The court held that plaintiff could affirm and recover damages from the seller for failure to disclose the defect.

3. CLASS ACTIONS FOR DAMAGES FOR DECEPTION

Consumer class actions for fraud have become increasingly common. As a practical remedy, this procedure may be affected by: (1) the proof of reliance and causation by each class member; (2) where the class includes members from several states, the rule in each jurisdiction governing liability for damages for other than deliberate and intentional deceit, e.g., damages for innocent misrepresentation as in Clements Auto Co. v. Service Bureau Corp., supra; (3) the general deceit damages measure in each jurisdiction, i.e., benefit of bargain or out of pocket; and (4) determination of damages for each individual. These problems exist apart from the procedural complexities of service, notice, and election of parties to join in the suit.

If a class action succeeds in establishing liability for damages for deceit, or simple overpayments, the further matter of distributing the award remains. Some of the options for distributing an antitrust settlement appear in State v. Levi Strauss & Co., 41 Cal.3d 460, 224 Cal.Rptr. 605, 715 P.2d 564 (1986). See also Daar v. Yellow Cab, 67 Cal.2d 695, 63 Cal.Rptr. 724, 433 P.2d 732 (1967); Wolfram, The Antibiotics Class Actions, 1967 A.B.A.F.Res.J. 253 (1976).

B. DISAFFIRMED TRANSACTIONS—SUBSTANTIVE ELEMENTS FOR RESCISSION AND RESTITUTION

1. MISREPRESENTATION—LIABILITY FOR NONDISCLOSURE

Moralists may argue about whether one person should consciously take economic advantage of another's ignorance. Our system of private enterprise rewards diligence and attention to business. Although legislatures increasingly require disclosure in certain types of transactions, we doubt that our economy could long survive a universal requirement that people disclose all relevant data to anyone else who could use such information. Data is costly and time consuming to accumulate. Professor Kronman says that: "One (seldom noticed) way in which the legal system can establish property rights in information is by permitting an informed party to enter—and enforce—contracts which his information suggests are profitable, without disclosing the information to the other party. Imposing a duty to disclose upon the knowledgeable party deprives him of a private advantage which the information would otherwise afford. A duty to disclose is tantamount to a requirement that the benefit of the information be publicly shared and is thus antithetical to the notion of a property right which—whatever else it may entail—always requires the legal protection of private appropriation." He suggests liability for failure to disclose information acquired casually, but none "where the information is the fruit of a deliberate search." Kronman, Mistake, Disclosure, Information and the Law of Contracts, 7 J.Legal Stud. 1, 15 (1978).

The common law has paused long before imposing damage liability for deceptive practices short of positive misrepresentation or active concealment.

Section 551 of the Restatement (Second) of Torts† indicates how limited is the tort penalty for silence in business transactions. It imposes upon a person a "duty to exercise reasonable care to disclose" only:

"(a) matters known to him that the other is entitled to know because of a fiduciary or other similar relation of trust and confidence between them; and

"(b) matters known to him that he knows to be necessary to prevent his partial or ambiguous statement of the facts from being misleading; and

"(c) subsequently acquired information that he knows will make untrue or misleading a previous representation that when made was true or believed to be so; and

"(d) the falsity of a representation not made with the expectation that it would be acted upon, if he subsequently learns that the other is about to act in reliance upon it in a transaction with him; and

"(e) facts basic to the transaction, if he knows that the other is about to enter into it under a mistake as to them, and that the other, because of the relationship between them, the customs of the trade or other objective circumstances, would reasonably expect a disclosure of those facts."

The last three instances of a "duty to disclose" are hardly impressive examples of tortious "silence" inasmuch as known actual misrepresentations are outstanding. Thus only fiduciaries or persons in a relation of trust and confidence are genuinely exposed to liability for silence.

Of course, continuing pressure exists to raise the ethical level of the marketplace or at least to keep a floor under it. Regulations and statutes to bring about truth in advertising, truth in security dealings, truth in proxy solicitations, truth in consumer credit financing, etc. now abound, bringing with them penalties discernible as damages for silence. Nor have the common law cases always confined themselves to the limited situations of the Restatement of Torts, as Lingsch v. Savage makes evident. Whether *Lingsch* becomes a widely accepted standard, the holding clearly reflects current attitudes toward real estate brokers who seek professional status without professional standards.

Laying aside Lingsch v. Savage, rescission of questionable bargains remains the principal judicial device for raising the ethical level of business practices. Equity hesitates to require full disclosure in arms length dealings; but it will deny the benefit of a bargain to one engaged in deceptive practices short of affirmative misrepresentations or active concealment.

Comment b to § 551 Restatement (Second) of Torts recognizes this in part:

"The conditions under which liability is imposed for nondisclosure in an action for deceit differ in one particular from those under which a similar nondisclosure may confer a right to rescind the transaction or to recover back money paid or the value of other benefits conferred. In the absence of a duty of disclosure, * * * one who is negotiating a business transaction is not liable in deceit because of his failure to disclose a fact that he knows his adversary would regard as material. On the other hand, as is stated in [Restatement (Second) of Contracts § 161 comment d (1981)] the other is entitled to rescind the transaction if the undisclosed fact is basic; and under Restatement of

Restitution, § 8, Comment e, and § 28, he would be entitled to recover back any money paid or benefit conferred in consummation of the transaction."

Under the Restatements the seller in Lingsch v. Savage, while not exposed to tort liability, would sustain a loss of the bargain since the facts there undisclosed were basic to the transaction. The broker, under the Restatement, would have incurred no loss other than a commission.

There are, in fact, other differences between the approach of § 551 of the Restatement of Torts and § 161 of the Restatement of Contracts than the one stated in comment b, § 551 above. The Torts Restatement requires that the promisor exercise reasonable care to disclose relevant facts. The Contracts Restatement requires *actual* disclosure; reasonable care is insufficient. Restatement of Contracts (Second) § 161 comment a (1981). The Contracts Restatement recognizes areas of contract considered by their very nature as requiring a highly moral approach, where special rules about nondisclosure govern. Examples are the contract of insurance, traditionally labelled as one "uberrima fides," or the contract of suretyship (see § 124 Restatement of Security.) Many policies have been avoided at the instigation of the insurer for want of disclosure by the insured, but policy holders rarely are sued in tort for failure to reveal information.

Perhaps the most important difference results from a more inclusive concept in the Contracts Restatement defining the type of relationship that will preclude bargaining without full disclosure. The Torts Restatement confines the relationship to that of fiduciary or similar relationship of trust and confidence. The Restatement of Contracts simply suggests that full disclosure is required to one who reasonably expects that the other party to the relationship will look after the former's interest. Thus if A writes to B asking B to be his agent to sell property and there is reasonable ground to expect that B might accept, B would be precluded from purchasing, directly or indirectly, the property without full disclosure.

These nuances of the rules of "nondisclosure," like those of "innocent misrepresentation," are microcosmic of the conceptual difficulties arising from the confluence of tort, contract and restitutionary substantive law. In one sense nondisclosure is indeed fraudulent. But it also resembles the passive reception of benefit from another's unilateral mistake, where the sense of tortious wrong is much muted.

In any event the rules of the game now restrict not only artificial lures, but, in some circumstances, require the fisherman to release the fish that leaps upon the bank.

2. SCIENTER—INNOCENT MISREPRESENTATION

Clements Auto Co. v. Service Bureau Corp., supra p. 805 and the notes following, particularly the reference to Restatement (Second) of Torts § 552C, show the trend to eliminate scienter in damage actions for deceit with limitations on the type of transaction and the measure of damages.

The extent that "strict liability" for innocent misrepresentation has been accepted in damage actions is covered in Prosser and Keeton, Torts § 107 (5th ed. 1984). Whether the rationale is found in a "duty to know," "imputed knowledge" or a tacit extension of the warranty notion beyond the sale of goods is of little practical moment, except that, as Professor Prosser observes, the warranty rationale would promptly encounter the parol evidence rule if the statement were not in writing. From the standpoint of Remedies, the departures from the "scienter" requirement enlarge the area in which damage for deceit is concurrent with rescission and restitution and allows consequential damages.

McCormick & Co., Inc. v. Childers, 468 F.2d 757, 766 (4th Cir.1972):

> "Misrepresentation as a basis for the jurisdiction of courts of equity evolved at a time when existing common law actions were inadequate to deal with a variety of injustices in cases which would not qualify as actions for deceit. Since the equity courts did not take jurisdiction for the purpose of awarding damages they were primarily concerned with the injustice of permitting a person who had made false representations, even innocently, to retain the fruits of a bargain induced by such representations. They therefore developed a remedy for innocent misrepresentation as well as for fraud and mistake. Often, however, an equity court declined to put a new label on the action but rather preferred to expand its definition of fraud and speak of an innocent misrepresentation as a form of fraud. [citations] While there is much apparent confusion in the cases resulting from the use of the word 'fraud' in several different senses, the same basic principles are applied in all three areas."

3. PECUNIARY DAMAGE

EARL v. SAKS & CO.

Supreme Court of California, 1951.
36 Cal.2d 602, 226 P.2d 340.

SCHAUER, J. A.K. Barbee appeals from judgments in consolidated actions hereinafter described, that respondent Mrs. Richard Earl is the owner of a certain mink coat and that Barbee owes respondent Saks and Company $3,981.25. He contends that an asserted sale of the coat to him by Saks, and an asserted gift of the coat by him to Mrs. Earl, were voidable, and were rescinded by him, because his consent thereto was induced by fraud of Mrs. Earl and Saks. We have concluded that these contentions are tenable.

On April 4, 1947, Barbee and Mrs. Earl went to the fur salon of Saks. A representative of Saks showed them a mink coat and told them its price was $5,000. Barbee told Saks that he would like to buy the coat for Mrs. Earl but that he would pay no more than $4,000 for it. Saks rejected repeated offers of Barbee to purchase the coat for $4,000. Unknown to Barbee, Mrs. Earl then asked Saks to pretend to sell the coat to him for $4,000, and stated that she would pay the difference between $4,000 and the price of the coat. Saks agreed to this. It told Barbee that it would sell the coat to him for $3,981.25, made out a sales slip for that amount, and Barbee signed it in the belief that that was the full price of the coat. Saks then delivered the coat to Barbee; he in turn delivered it to Mrs. Earl and said that he gave it to her. Mrs. Earl, wearing the coat, left the store with Barbee.

The next day, April 5, Mrs. Earl returned the coat to Saks to be monogrammed and paid Saks the balance of its price, $916.30. Later the same day Barbee told Saks that he had revoked the gift to Mrs. Earl, that he was the owner of the coat (which he thought he had purchased for $3,981.25), that he would pay the agreed price ($3,981.25) only if Saks would deliver the coat to him, and that it was not to deliver the coat to Mrs. Earl. Thereafter Mrs. Earl demanded that Saks deliver the coat to her; Saks refused and attempted to return her $918.30; but she refused to accept the money; Saks retained (and still retains) possession of the coat.

Mrs. Earl then sued Saks, alleging conversion of the coat. Saks answered, denying the conversion, and at the same time filed a pleading which it denominated "Cross–Complaint in Interpleader," which, however, not only named Mrs. Earl and Barbee as asserted interpleader cross-defendants but also implicitly and necessarily, in the light of the circumstances, required, if Saks was to prevail, the granting of affirmative adversary relief against Barbee or Mrs. Earl or both of them. Saks alleged that it sold the coat to Barbee for $3,981.25; that Mrs. Earl, "as additional consideration * * * to induce" Saks to make the sale to Barbee, agreed to pay Saks $916.30 and later paid Saks that sum; that Saks is indifferent between the claims of the cross-defendants and is willing to deliver the coat to either cross-defendant as the court may direct (but, it is implicit from Saks' several pleadings read together, only upon condition that it recover from Barbee or from Mrs. Earl or from both of them the full price of the coat); it asked that the cross-defendants be required to "litigate between themselves their claims to said mink coat"; it did not offer to relinquish its asserted claim for any part of the full price of approximately $4,900. Mrs. Earl's answer to the cross-complaint admitted that she paid Saks $916.30 and alleged that at that time title to the coat "was transferred to her as is more fully alleged in her complaint." The complaint, however, contains no allegations as to transfer of title. Barbee in answer to the cross-complaint admitted that he told Saks he would pay the price discussed between Saks and Barbee if and only if Saks "would sell and deliver the coat to him at and for [such] price," and alleged that Mrs. Earl's agreement to pay Saks $916.30 was fraudulently concealed from him by Saks and Mrs. Earl; that they represented to him that the full price of the coat was $3,981.25; and that if he had known of the secret agreement he would not have agreed to buy the coat. No pleadings joining issues between Barbee and Mrs. Earl were filed. Saks also brought a separate action against Barbee, alleging that he owed Saks $3,981.25 for goods sold and delivered. Barbee in answer made allegations of fraud substantially similar to those in his answer to Saks' cross-complaint. The two actions were consolidated for trial.

From what has been stated it appears that Saks, because of its duplicitous compact with Mrs. Earl, finds itself in this position: It knowingly and purposefully caused Barbee to believe that it was selling him—and him only—a certain fur coat for the full price of $3,981.25. It wants to collect the $3,981.25 from Barbee but it cannot (or will not) deliver the coat to him—fully paid, for $3,981.25 or otherwise—because, although it has possession of the coat, it has already collected $916.30 for the same coat from Mrs. Earl, and she claims to own the coat and refuses to release her claim to it (or for damages for its alleged conversion) as against either Saks or Barbee. Mrs. Earl further claims the coat as against both Saks and Barbee on the theory of an asserted gift from Barbee. But the gift is, necessarily, dependent upon Barbee's having purchased the coat from Saks and that purchase, it is obvious, was induced by the joint fraud of Mrs. Earl and Saks. Saks and Mrs. Earl—both guilty of express fraud—are seeking the aid of the court to recover that which they are entitled to, if at all, only because of their fraud.

While, as indicated above, the pleadings do not specifically allege, or suggest the theory of, the origin of Mrs. Earl's claim of title to the coat, the trial proceeded on the theory that the issues were whether there was a sale by Saks to Barbee and a gift by Barbee to Mrs. Earl, and whether the two transactions were voidable by Barbee because of the secret agreement and misrepresentation. Barbee testified that he would not have bought the coat if he had known that the price was more than $4,000. Every element of the transaction and all the circumstances shown appear to support this position; no evidence is inconsistent with it. At the trial Barbee's counsel restated the position which Barbee had announced to Saks before the actions were instituted: "we are perfectly willing to accept the coat and pay * * * the price that we agreed to pay for it [$3,981.25] * * * but we certainly are under the circumstances disclosed here already in this evidence [the secret agreement] * * * not willing to let this coat be handed over to this young lady." Counsel for Barbee also offered to prove that the gift was made in reliance on Mrs. Earl's representations that she would "reciprocate his affection and would give up running around with other men" and that Barbee rescinded the gift when he learned that those representations were false. The offered proof on the latter theory was properly rejected, for no such issue was raised by the pleadings.

The trial court gave judgment against Mrs. Earl on her complaint for conversion and in favor of Saks on its complaint against Barbee for goods sold and delivered. On Saks' "Cross–Complaint in Interpleader" it gave judgment that Mrs. Earl is the owner and entitled to possession of the coat. We are satisfied that the judgment in neither action is tenable insofar as it is adverse to the defendant and cross-defendant Barbee. * * *

Rescission of Gift. The trial court was not entitled to disbelieve Barbee's uncontradicted testimony (supported by the circumstances shown and by the undisputed evidence of all parties that he repeatedly insisted he would not pay more than $4,000) that he would not have bought the coat if he had known of the secret agreement between Saks and Mrs. Earl. Although Barbee did not expressly allege or testify that he would not have given the coat to Mrs. Earl if he had known of the secret agreement, it is apparent that the case was tried as if this were in issue and that in fact he would not have made the gift had he known of the secret agreement. Obviously Barbee's belief that the full price of the coat was $3,981.25 underlay and was a material element in, and inducing cause of, the gift as well as the immediately preceding purchase. As previously indicated, he could not have made the gift unless he made the purchase, and it is indisputably established that the purchase was induced by the express fraud of both Mrs. Earl and Saks. The facts that Barbee at the trial, by correctly rejected offers of proof, sought to show another fraudulent representation which also was an inducement to his making the gift, and that he announced rescission before he learned of the secret agreement, do not prevent him from now basing his defense on such secret agreement. "One may justify an asserted rescission by proving that at the time there was an adequate cause although it did not become known to him until later. One cannot waive or acquiesce in a wrong while ignorant thereof."

A gift can be rescinded if it was induced by fraud or material misrepresentation (whether of the donee or a third person) or by mistake as to a "basic fact." (Rest., Restitution, §§ 26, 39; see Murdock v. Murdock (1920), 49 Cal.App. 775, 783–785 [194 P. 762] [fraud of donee].

"A failure by the donee to reveal material facts when he knows that the donor is mistaken as to them is fraudulent nondisclosure." (Rest., Restitution, § 26, comment c.)

"A mistake which entails the substantial frustration of the donor's purpose entitles him to restitution. No more definite general statement can be made as to what constitutes a basic mistake in the making of a gift. The donor is entitled to restitution if he was mistaken as to the * * * identity or essential characteristics of the gift." (Rest., Restitution, § 26, comment c.)

Since Barbee was not merely mistaken but was actively misled as to a material element in the purchase and as to an essential characteristic of the gift—he believed that the coat was purchased entirely by him so that it could be given in its entirety as a gift—he was entitled to, as he did, rescind the gift.

Rescission of Contract. It appears from the findings of probative facts that Saks did more than merely fail to disclose its agreement with Mrs. Earl. In the circumstances, implicit in the finding that Barbee "was informed by Saks and Company's representatives that they would sell said mink coat to him for the sum of $3,981.25" is a finding that Saks actively misrepresented that the price had been reduced and that $3,981.25 was the full price. It is completely unreasonable to deny that a representation by a clerk in a reputable store that an article has a certain price, followed by the clerk's preparation and the customer's signing of a sales check showing purchase of the article for that price, amounts to a representation by the store that the *total* price and the *entire* sales transaction are as represented. This misrepresentation, it appears from the undisputed evidence, was made by Saks with knowledge that Barbee insisted on a reduction in price; from this it follows that such misrepresentation must have been made with intent to deceive Barbee and to induce him to buy the coat. * * *

Saks relies on California cases which say that "fraud which has produced and will produce no injury will not justify a rescission." [citations] It asserts that a person is not injured by being induced to buy a $5,000 coat for $4,000. But the coat was neither sold nor bought for $4,000. Saks was selling the coat for the full price, and a person other than seller Saks and buyer Barbee paid a substantial part—approximately one fifth—of the full price. Furthermore, this "no injury, no rescission" formula is not very helpful, because of disagreement in the authorities as to what is meant by "injury." In a sense, anyone who is fraudulently induced to enter into a contract is "injured"; his "interest in making a free choice and in exercising his own best judgment in making decisions with respect to economic transactions and enterprises has been interfered with." (See McCleary, Damage as a Requisite to Rescission for Misrepresentation, 36 Mich.L.Rev. 1, 227, 245.)

Also relied on by Saks is a definition of "injury" which has sometimes appeared in some California cases: "it may be conceded that it must be shown that [one who would rescind] * * * by reason of fraud, suffered an injury of a pecuniary nature, that is, an injury to his property rights, as distinguished from a mere injury to his feelings, but it will be sufficient if the facts alleged show that material injury will necessarily ensue from the fraud, although the amount of pecuniary loss is not stated." (Spreckels v. Gorrill (1907), supra, 152 Cal. 383, 388.) The "concession" or implication that in every case there must be "pecuniary loss" is incorrect. (See Hefferan v. Freebairn (1950), 34 Cal.2d 715, 721 [214 P.2d 386].) And the definition does not take account of the cases which allow rescission of a transaction induced by an agent's misrepresentation of his principal's identity, even though there was no economic reason for the unwillingness to deal with the principal.

The McCleary article suggests the following classification of the cases which have considered rescission for fraud:

1. The representee can rescind where he obtains the very thing that he expected but it is worth less than he was led reasonably to expect. In most cases where rescission is sought the representee has received something of less economic value than he expected.

2. The representee can rescind where he obtains something substantially different from that which he was led to expect. If one is induced to buy a certain lot of land by misrepresentation that it contains a vineyard, he need not keep it when he learns that it contains instead an apple orchard; even though the lot of land is the identical lot of land and although the orchard may be more valuable than the vineyard which he expected to get, it is obviously unfair to require him to keep what he did not bargain for and did not want. The undisputed evidence describing the present sale would put it in this class. The coat bargained for between Barbee and Saks, within the knowledge and belief of Barbee, as was known to Saks, was a coat fully paid for by Barbee, which Saks knew was to be used as a gift, but Saks intended to and did deliver something substantially different; i.e., a coat on which Barbee was charged only with a down payment and for which his intended donee had secretly agreed to pay in a substantial part. The seller was to receive approximately 25 per cent more for the coat than the buyer was paying and the element of a complete gift was being destroyed.

3. Where the representee obtains exactly that which he expects, although there was misrepresentation, the social interest in the stability of transactions may or may not outweigh the social interest in not having one intentionally take advantage of another. Saks attempts to describe the present sale so as to put it in this class. It says that Barbee bargained for and expected to get a certain coat for a cost to him of not more than $4,000, and this is what he got. In the present situation, however, where the motives of Barbee were clearly noneconomic, the general social interest in stability of transactions is overridden by the interest in not having a seller make intentional misrepresentations which mislead a would-be donor into the erroneous belief that he alone is purchasing and that his donee is to receive from him a fully paid for gift, when the seller is fully aware of the effect which the misrepresentations may have and intends that they should have that effect. Again, it is important, the element of a complete gift by donor to donee is being destroyed through the misrepresentation and concealment.

Saks contends that Barbee has not rescinded, and cannot rescind, the sale because he has stated that he was willing to carry out the objectively manifested bargain to purchase the coat for $3,981.25. But at no time since Barbee's announced willingness to stand on the transaction which he believed he had entered into with Saks, did Saks offer to comply with the transaction and give Barbee what he bargained for: a coat for which he was paying in full, without Mrs. Earl, a stranger to the Saks–Barbee transaction, paying a portion of the price. Indeed, Saks, at the time of the rescission and mentioned offer by Barbee, was apparently unable to sell Barbee the coat in question as a fully paid for coat for $3,981.25 because Mrs. Earl refused to take back the $916.30

which she paid for the coat and which Saks had previously accepted. Barbee's counsel, at the trial, made clear his position; after the secret agreement, misrepresentation and payment of $916.30 were in evidence he said, "under the circumstances of this case we shouldn't be required to pay Saks and company anything. * * * [He] would do anything that could be done to repudiate that transaction and say it never was a real transaction." We are satisfied that the contract of purchase and the gift were voidable and were properly rescinded.

For the reasons above stated, the judgments are reversed.

TRAYNOR, J. [dissenting]. Barbee received what he bargained for * * *. The mink coat that he examined and agreed to pay $3,981.25 for, was the one he received and gave to Mrs. Earl. He concedes that the fair value of the coat was $5,000. It was not unreasonable for the trial court to conclude that, since the coat Barbee received was actually worth more than he agreed to pay, he would not have rejected it because Mrs. Earl arranged to pay the difference. * * * It was under no compulsion to believe his statement that he would have rejected it. * * *

It was for the trial court to determine whether Barbee was a man of such temperament that he would have preferred having Mrs. Earl get along without the fur coat to accepting her contribution toward its purchase. He declared his love for her, expressing the sentiment several times that he wanted to give her a fur coat. She was "very much in love with the coat and wanted it badly." It was important to him that the woman he loved possess the coat; it was important to her to possess it. Her contribution enabled him to fulfill his wish and hers at a price he was willing to pay. Since they were both fur-coat-minded, it is a reasonable inference that he would not have risked disturbing the relationship between them by depriving her of the coat because she was willing to contribute toward its purchase.

Counsel at the trial made it clear that Barbee sought rescission of the sale because Mrs. Earl failed to live up to his expectations. This failure can in no way be attributed to Saks and Company. Its coat was of sound quality and came up to Mrs. Earl's expectations. The court properly rejected Barbee's offer of proof of his expectations and disappointment. Not only were they no concern of Saks and Company, but no issue was raised in the pleadings regarding his arrangements with Mrs. Earl. I would therefore affirm the judgments.

4. MATERIALITY

REED v. KING

Court of Appeal of California, Third District, 1983.
145 Cal.App.3d 261, 193 Cal.Rptr. 130.

BLEASE, ASSOCIATE JUSTICE. In the sale of a house, must the seller disclose it was the site of a multiple murder? Dorris Reed purchased a house from Robert King. Neither King nor his real estate agents (the other named defendants) told Reed that a woman and her four children were murdered there ten years earlier. However, it seems "truth will come to light; murder cannot be hid long." (Shakespeare, Merchant of Venice, Act II, Scene II.) Reed learned of the gruesome episode from a neighbor after the sale. She sues seeking rescission and damages. King and the real estate agent defendants successfully demurred to her first amended complaint for failure to state a cause of action. Reed appeals the ensuing judgment of dismissal. We will reverse the judgment.

We take all issuable facts pled in Reed's complaint as true. King and his real estate agent knew about the murders and knew the event materially affected the market value of the house when they listed it for sale. They represented to Reed the premises were in good condition and fit for an "elderly lady" living alone. They did not disclose the fact of the murders. At some point King asked a neighbor not to inform Reed of that event. Nonetheless, after Reed moved in neighbors informed her no one was interested in purchasing the house because of the stigma. Reed paid $76,000, but the house is only worth $65,000 because of its past. * * *

Does Reed's pleading state a cause of action? Concealed within this question is the nettlesome problem of the duty of disclosure of blemishes on real property which are not physical defects or legal impairments to use.

Reed seeks to state a cause of action sounding in contract, i.e. rescission, or in tort, i.e. deceit. In either event her allegations must reveal a fraud. * * *

The trial court perceived the defect in Reed's complaint to be a failure to allege concealment of a material fact. "Concealment" and "material" are legal conclusions concerning the effect of the issuable facts pled. As appears, the analytic pathways to these conclusions are intertwined.

Concealment is a term of art which includes mere non-disclosure when a party has a duty to disclose. See e.g. Lingsch v. Savage. Reed's complaint reveals only non-disclosure despite the allegation King asked a neighbor to hold his peace. There is no allegation the attempt at suppression was a cause in fact of Reed's ignorance.[1] (See Rest.2d Contracts, §§ 160, 162–164; Rest.2d Torts, § 550; Rest.Restitution, § 9.) Accordingly, the critical question is: does the seller have duty to disclose here? Resolution of this question depends on the materiality of the fact of the murders.

In general, a seller of real property has a duty to disclose: "where the seller knows of facts *materially* affecting the value or desirability of the property which are known or accessible only to him and also knows that such facts are not known to, or within the reach of the diligent attention and observation of the buyer, the seller is under a duty to disclose them to the buyer."[2] (Lingsch v. Savage, supra.)

Whether information "is of sufficient materiality to affect the value or desirability of the property * * * depends on the facts of the particular case." Materiality "is a question of law, and is part of the concept of right to rely or justifiable reliance." Accordingly, the term is essentially a label affixed to a normative conclusion.[3] Three considerations bear on this legal conclusion: the

1. [Footnotes renumbered.] Reed elsewhere in the complaint asserts defendants "actively concealed" the fact of the murders and this in part misled her. However, no connection is made or apparent between the legal conclusion of active concealment and any issuable fact pled by Reed. Accordingly, the assertion is insufficient. Similarly we do not view the statement the house was fit for Reed to inhabit as transmuting her case from one of non-disclosure to one of false representation. To view the representation as patently false is to find "elderly ladies" uniformly susceptible to squeamishness. We decline to indulge this stereotypical assumption. To view the representation as misleading because it conflicts with a duty to disclose is to beg that question.

2. The real estate agent or broker representing the seller is under the same duty of disclosure. (Lingsch v. Savage, supra.)

3. This often subsumes a policy analysis of the effect of permitting rescission on the stability of contracts. "In the case law of fraud, the word 'material' has become a sort of talisman. It is suggested that it has no meaning when

gravity of the harm inflicted by non-disclosure; the fairness of imposing a duty of discovery on the buyer as an alternative to compelling disclosure; and its impact on the stability of contracts if rescission is permitted.

Numerous cases have found non-disclosure of physical defects and legal impediments to use of real property are material. However, to our knowledge, no prior real estate sale case has faced an issue of non-disclosure of the kind presented here. (Compare Earl v. Saks & Co.) Should this variety of ill-repute be required to be disclosed? Is this a circumstance where "non-disclosure of the fact amounts to a failure to act in good faith and in accordance with reasonable standards of fair dealing [?]" (Rest.2d Contracts, § 161, subd. (b).)

The paramount argument against an affirmative conclusion is it permits the camel's nose of unrestrained irrationality admission to the tent. If such an "irrational" consideration is permitted as a basis of rescission the stability of all conveyances will be seriously undermined. Any fact that might disquiet the enjoyment of some segment of the buying public may be seized upon by a disgruntled purchaser to void a bargain. In our view, keeping this genie in the bottle is not as difficult a task as these arguments assume. We do not view a decision allowing Reed to survive a demurrer in these unusual circumstances as endorsing the materiality of facts predicating peripheral, insubstantial, or fancied harms.

The murder of innocents is highly unusual in its potential for so disturbing buyers they may be unable to reside in a home where it has occurred. This fact may foreseeably deprive a buyer of the intended use of the purchase. Murder is not such a common occurrence that *buyers* should be charged with anticipating and discovering this disquieting possibility. Accordingly, the fact is not one for which a duty of inquiry and discovery can sensibly be imposed upon the buyer.

Reed alleges the fact of the murders has a quantifiable effect on the market value of the premises. We cannot say this allegation is inherently wrong and, in the pleading posture of the case, we assume it to be true. If information known or accessible only to the seller has a significant and measureable effect on market value and, as is alleged here, the seller is aware of this effect, we see no principled basis for making the duty to disclose turn upon the character of the information. Physical usefulness is not and never has been the sole criterion of valuation. Stamp collections and gold speculation would be insane activities if utilitarian considerations were the sole measure of value.

Reputation and history can have a significant effect on the value of realty. "George Washington slept here" is worth something, however physically inconsequential that consideration may be. Ill-repute or "bad will" conversely may depress the value of property. Failure to disclose such a negative fact where it will have a foreseeably depressing effect on income expected to be generated by a business is tortious. (See Rest.2d Torts, § 551, illus. 11.) Some cases have held that *unreasonable* fears of the potential buying public that a gas or oil pipeline may rupture may depress the market value of land and entitle the

undefined other than to the user since the word actually means no more than that the fraud is the sort which will justify rescission or damages in deceit. However, courts continue to use materiality as a test without explanatory reference to the varying standards of reliance, damage, etc. they are following." (Note, Rescission: Fraud as Ground: Contracts (1951) 39 Cal.L. Rev. 309, 310–311, fn. 4.)

owner to incremental compensation in eminent domain. (See Annot., Eminent Domain: Elements and measure of compensation for oil or gas pipeline through private property (1954) 38 A.L.R.2d 788, 801–804.)

Whether Reed will be able to prove her allegation the decade-old multiple murder has a significant effect on market value we cannot determine. If she is able to do so by competent evidence she is entitled to a favorable ruling on the issues of materiality and duty to disclose.[4] Her demonstration of objective tangible harm would still the concern that permitting her to go forward will open the floodgates to rescission on subjective and idiosyncratic grounds.

A more troublesome question would arise if a buyer in similar circumstances were unable to plead or establish a significant and quantifiable effect on market value. However, this question is not presented in the posture of this case. Reed has not alleged the fact of the murders has rendered the premises useless to her as a residence. As currently pled, the gravamen of her case is pecuniary harm. We decline to speculate on the abstract alternative.

The judgment is reversed.

Note

Statutes to protect consumers and the environment expand the seller's duty to disclose. Most nondisclosure disputes involve zoning, termites, roofs, foundations, and the like. Other hazards which, if undisclosed, may trigger challenges include asbestos, radon, and mercury. Check pocket parts and advance sheets.

Should prospective buyers be told that the previous owner was a victim of acquired immune deficiency syndrome?

STUART v. LESTER

Supreme Court of New York, 1888.

49 Hun. 58, 1 N.Y.S. 699.

BARKER, P.J. An appeal from a judgment entered upon a verdict in the plaintiff's favor rendered at the Genesee circuit for the sum of $600 damages. The action is upon a written contract executed by both parties by which the plaintiff agreed to sell and convey to the defendant a farm of 120 acres situated in the town of Bethany, county of Genesee, for the consideration of $8,500 * * *. The damages for nonperformance were stipulated at $600, [in a liquidated damages clause]. * * * The defendant refused to accept the deed, and declined to perform any of the covenants on his part. * * * The defendant offered to prove that he was induced to enter into the contract by the false and fraudulent representations made by the plaintiff, at the time the contract was entered into; that the plaintiff had never offered the farm in question for a price less than $8,500, and that, on the contrary, he had offered it, on numerous occasions, in the market, for $6,000; that such representation was false and known by the plaintiff to be false at the time he made the same; that

4. The ruling of the trial court requiring the additional element of notoriety, i.e. widespread public knowledge, is unpersuasive. Lack of notoriety may facilitate resale to yet another unsuspecting buyer at the "market price" of a house with no ill-repute. However, it appears the buyer will learn of the possibly unsettling history of the house soon after moving in. Those who suffer no discomfort from the specter of residing in such quarters per se, will nonetheless be discomforted by the prospect they have bought a house that may be difficult to sell to less hardy souls. Non-disclosure must be evaluated as fair or unfair regardless of the ease with which a buyer may escape this discomfort by foisting it upon another.

the defendant relied upon such representation in making the contract, and would not have entered into the same but for such false representation; and, if he had known that the farm had been offered on the market for the sum of $6,000, he would not have entered into the contract; that the plaintiff made the representation in answer to a direct inquiry made by the plaintiff on the subject whether the farm had been offered for sale at a price less than $8,500. This evidence was objected to as immaterial, and was excluded by the court, and the defendant excepted. Thereupon the court directed a verdict in the plaintiff's favor for the sum of $600, to which the defendant then and there duly excepted. * * * It should be borne in mind that the defendant is not, in this action, claiming damages against the plaintiff, but is simply resisting the enforcement of a contract procured from him by fraud and deceit. It was not, therefore, necessary for the defendant to show, in order to defeat a recovery, that he had suffered a pecuniary loss in any particular sum by reason of the misrepresentation made by the plaintiff. The record does not disclose the reason given by the learned trial judge for holding that the evidence was immaterial, but the counsel for the plaintiff places his argument in support of the ruling upon the sole ground that, by the offers of proof, it did not appear that the defendant had suffered any loss by reason of the misrepresentation, as he had not offered to prove that the market value of the farm was less than he had agreed to pay.

* * * The real question in the case is, was the fraudulent statement a material one, in view of the nature and character of the contract, as the offer of proof embraced every other fact necessary to constitute a complete defense on the ground of fraud. The rule by which it is to be determined whether a statement is a material one or not has been frequently formulated by the courts in recent cases where the question was directly under consideration. In Smith v. Countryman, 30 N.Y. 679, Justice Davies in his opinion stated the rule to be that the representation which will vitiate a contract must be material; that it must relate distinctly and directly to the contract, and must affect its very essence and substance. Mr. Parsons, in his work on Contracts, gives the rule in this language: "If the fraud be such that, had it not been practiced, the contract would not have been made, or the transaction completed, then it is material to it." In an English case (Canham v. Barry, 15 C.B. 597,) the gauge by which the materiality of the statement is to be determined, is stated, in substance, as follows: A contract may be avoided by a false and fraudulent representation, though not relating directly to the nature and character of its subject-matter, if it is so closely connected with the contract as that the party sued upon it would not, but for the representation, have entered into it, and was induced to enter into it, to the knowledge of the other party, by such representation. * * * Valton v. Assurance Co., 20 N.Y. 32. Under the rule as stated in these cases, either party to a contract may make a collateral statement made by the other party, during the negotiations, as to the existence or nonexistence of a particular fact, a material one, in his own judgment; so if it turns out to be untrue, and was falsely and fraudulently made, it will vitiate the contract if he relied upon the same as true, and would not have entered into the contract but for the statement. This standard by which it is to be determined whether the fraud be material or not has been adopted and applied by the courts in this state in many adjudicated cases. In Valton v. Assurance Co., supra, it was held that a fraudulent misrepresentation made by the assured to the insurer upon his application for a policy, though not material to

the risk, yet material in the judgment of the insurer, and which induced him to take the risk, would avoid the policy; that the misrepresentation amounted to a fraud, not on the ground of the misrepresentation affecting the nature of the risk, but because it induced a confidence without which the party would not have acted. * * * The same state of facts which will enable a party to avoid a contract in a court of equity for fraud will constitute a proper defense at law in an action brought against the defrauded party to recover damages for non-performance. From the facts which the defendant offered to prove, the jury would have been justified in reaching the conclusion, as a fair and proper deduction therefrom, that the defendant, in his own judgment, regarded the statement as to the fact stated by the plaintiff, that the farm had not been offered by him for sale on the market at a sum less than $8,500, the price which he was to pay for the same, a material circumstance and that the plaintiff had reason to suppose that the defendant relied upon his answer as being true, and was induced thereby to conclude the agreement. The inquiry was a natural and pertinent one for a party to make who was negotiating for the purchase of property, either real or personal. It was one way of testing its market value. The circumstance that the farm had been offered by the plaintiff for sale on numerous occasions for the sum of $6,000 would have the effect, in a measure, to hinder and make it difficult for the owner to sell it for the price of $8,500, although its intrinsic value was the last-mentioned sum. A person negotiating for the purchase of property for the purpose of resale on the same market would ordinarily regard it as a material circumstance in determining his own judgment whether it would be a wise and proper investment to make, to purchase the same at a particular price, in the face of the fact that the owner had repeatedly offered it for sale at a much less amount. Suppose a person treating for the purchase of a span of horses for which the owner gave his price, and the proposed buyer should inquire whether they had been offered on that market at a less figure, and the answer should be that they had not, could the seller misapprehend the purpose of the inquiry, and doubt that the buyer was not influenced by his statement? * * * The rule invoked by the plaintiff, that fraud without damages resulting therefrom never gives a right to action in favor of the defrauded party, applies to those cases where the injured party is seeking to recover damages from the wrongdoer in an action on the case *ex delicto,* as an indemnity against the injury which he has sustained by reason of the fraud, and has no just application to a case like the one in hand, where the fraud is relied upon as a defense to the enforcement of an executory contract. If the false statement relates to a material fact, the law implies that the defrauded party has suffered an injury sufficient to defeat a recovery. Showing that the misstatement was a material one, relative to the subject-matter of the contract, is proof that damages in some degree have been sustained by the defrauded party; but he is not called upon to give direct proof of the nature and extent of his damages. Where a party is seeking affirmative relief upon the ground of fraud, whether it be legal or equitable, then he is called upon to prove that he has sustained damages in some tangible amount; and the rule, as stated in 1 Pom.Eq.Jur. § 598, is as follows: "Fraud without resulting pecuniary damage is not a ground for the exercise of remedial jurisdiction, equitable or legal. Courts of equity do not act as mere tribunals of conscience to enforce duties which are purely moral. If any pecuniary loss is shown to have resulted, the court will not inquire into the extent of the injury. It is sufficient if the party misled has been very slightly prejudiced, if the amount is at all appreciable."

Upon the case which the defendant offered to establish by competent proof, we think a court of equity would annul the contract upon the ground of fraud and deceit. The judgment should be reversed, and a new trial granted, with costs to abide the event.

Notes on Materiality

1. *"Materiality" As A Requirement For Tort Damages Compared To Restitution.*

Restatement (Second) of Torts†

§ 538. Materiality of Misrepresentation: (1) Reliance upon a fraudulent misrepresentation is not justifiable unless the matter misrepresented is material.

Comment c. The rule stated in this Section differs from the rules that determine the right to rescind a contract induced by fraudulent misrepresentation, [See Restatement (Second) of Contracts § 164 (1981)] and to obtain restitution for benefits procured by fraudulent misrepresentation. (See Restatement of Restitution, § 9, Comment b). In neither of these cases is it required that the misrepresentation, if fraudulent, be as to a matter that is material; materiality being important only when the misrepresentation is negligent and not fraudulent.

Restatement of Restitution††

§ 9. Causation and Materiality: (2) Where innocent misrepresentation or non-disclosure is the sole ground for restitution, restitution is granted only if the misrepresentation or non-disclosure was material.

Comment b. Fraud and innocent misrepresentation. Where a person causes another to enter into a transaction by a statement known to be untrue and intended to cause the other to act thereon, it is not essential that the misrepresentation be one that would be likely to affect the conduct of a reasonable man. It is sufficient that the misrepresentation in fact induces the other to act. On the other hand, if a person, without knowledge or suspicion of its untruth, makes a statement which is not material, that is, which would not be likely to affect the conduct of a reasonable man with reference to the transaction in question he is under no duty of restitution to the other party to the transaction even though the other party is induced to enter therein because of the misrepresentation.

Questions: If the principles laid down in the Restatement sections were applied in Stuart v. Lester, should the question of "materiality" even be relevant?

If the vendee in Stuart v. Lester had accepted the deed and sued for damages for deceit, would a cause of action exist?

2. *The Meaning Of "Materiality."* In Stuart v. Lester the expression "material fact" is used in one sentence, and the expression "the misstatement was a material one" in the next. Section 538 of the Restatement (Second) of Torts is entitled "Materiality of Misrepresentation," whereas § 162 of the Restatement (Second) of Contracts is titled in part, "When Misrepresentation is Material." The usage in § 9 of the Restatement of Restitution is that of "material misrepresentation." Comment c to § 162 of the Restatement (Second) of Contracts helpfully adds another dimension by saying: "Although a fraudulent misrepresentation need not be material in order to entitle the recipient to relief under the rule stated in § 164, a nonfraudulent misrepresentation will not entitle him to relief unless it is material." All of these usages of the adjective "Material" are in the context of the

deceptive practice. There is no apparent intention of conveying a change in meaning by a change in noun.

The ambiguity may be reduced by a two-step approach.

First we will restate the requirement of "Materiality" in full because the foregoing are but habitual condensations. The full expression is that there must be a "Material Misrepresentation of a Material Fact."

The second step is to perceive that the word "material" is used twice in the same clause with different meanings. This may be done most easily with antonyms. It can be said that no action for deception arises from an "immaterial misrepresentation of a material fact." It is readily apparent that "material" here is the equivalent of "non trivial." If the vendor in Stuart v. Lester had previously offered the property for $7980, the "de minimis" principle might merit dismissal as immaterial. (Query whether the same might not be said about the misrepresentation in Earl v. Saks.) Indeed, in a certain sense, trivial deviations from the truth overlap the obvious requirement that for deception there must be untruth.

Conversely, the expression "material misrepresentation of an immaterial fact" obviously connotes a major departure from the truth, but is of no consequence unless it concerns a "material fact." The critical element now appears to be isolated.

3. *The Tests For Determining The "Materiality" Of A Fact. (The "Reliance" Element Compared).*

a. Basis of the bargain. Stuart v. Lester quotes Justice Davies in a prior case: "the representation which will vitiate a contract must be material; that is it must relate distinctly and directly to the contract and must affect its very essence and substance." This test must be rejected as too strict. The Chapter on Mistake develops the distinction between a "basic fact" and a "material fact." The price at which property has been previously offered can hardly be said to be the essence and substance of the current transaction.

b. A subjective test. Stuart v. Lester also quotes Mr. Parson's work on Contracts: "If the fraud be such that, had it not been practiced, the contract would not have been made, or the transaction completed, it is material to it." The most that can be said for this criterion is that it has great hardihood. Without stopping for empirical demonstration, it can be safely asserted that the great bulk of cases continue to repeat it. The least that can be said about it is that it is a meaningless superfluity. It merely repeats the reliance requirement—i.e., that the deception has induced some conduct by the aggrieved party.

c. An objective test. The A.L.I.'s Restatements of the Law have consistently adhered to an objective standard, e.g.:

The matter is material if a reasonable man would attach importance to its existence or nonexistence in determining his choice of action in the transaction in question; Restatement (Second) of Torts § 538(2)(a) (1977).

A misrepresentation is material if it would be likely to induce a reasonable person to manifest his assent, or if the maker knows that it would be likely to induce the recipient to do so. Restatement (Second) of Contracts § 162(2) (1981).

See also Restatement of Restitution § 9 comment b, implicitly adopting the reasonable person standard.

The reported cases infrequently repeat this objective standard—with the notable exception of misrepresentations on insurance applications where the practice and usage of insurance companies is commonly a guide to the materiality of the facts misrepresented. The classic case is Pennsylvania Mutual Life Insurance Co.

v. Mechanics' Savings Bank & Trust Co., 72 Fed. 413 (6th Cir.1896), an opinion by William Howard Taft.

The objective model for determining "Materiality" at least separates it from reliance, although the circumstance that the fact misrepresented is material aids the determination of whether the particular plaintiff did rely upon it in entering the bargain.

This should be enough for our purposes, but a few loose ends remain. For example the Restatement (Second) of Torts § 538(2)(b) sees fit to add that a fact is material if "the maker of the representation knows or has reason to know that its recipient regards or is likely to regard the matter as important in determining his choice of action, although a reasonable man would not so regard it." The relevance of this remark to deceit is not apparent since no element of pecuniary damage could be present, else the reasonable person would be influenced. Absent the damage, the tort disappears for want of a substantive element. For restitution, however, the contract is avoidable because, as we have seen above, the damage element is eliminated.

We are left with one of the initial inquiries: whether a transaction is voidable for deliberate deception which would not influence a reasonable person. If the answer is yes, it may be because "materiality" is not required, or it may be more simple. In other words the complainant is asserting that he relied upon statements that a reasonable person would not rely upon. Ipso facto he is subnormal. Other grounds for restitution therefore exist.

Questions: a. Was the fact misrepresented in Earl v. Saks "material"?

b. A seller of realty states that Douglas Fairbanks, Sr. once lived in the house. The statement is knowingly false. Is the fact "material"? Suppose the statement was that an ancestor of the buyer once lived in the house. Material?

GRAY v. BAKER

Supreme Court of Mississippi, 1986.
485 So.2d 306,

ROBERTSON, JUSTICE. * * * On January 17, 1985, Morris L. Gray brought this action in the Chancery Court of Rankin County, Mississippi, seeking rescission of a conveyance he made to Faith Presbyterian Church and charging fraud in the procurement. Gray alleges that prior to June 22, 1983, he owned some 10.20 acres in Rankin County, that he was approached by Jerry E. Baker who held himself out as representing the church regarding the possible purchase of this land, that in fact Baker was acting at least in part for Hunter L. Roussel, Jr., one to whom Gray says he would not have sold any part of his land for any reason, that Baker wholly failed to disclose Roussel's involvement, that in fact on June 22, 1983, he (Gray) conveyed the property to the church whereupon one month later the church conveyed half of it to Roussel.

The matter came before the Chancery Court on the motion of all Defendants—Baker, Roussel and the church—to dismiss for failure to state a claim, Rule 12(b)(6), Miss.R.Civ.P., or, in the alternative, for summary judgment, Rule 56, Miss.R.Civ.P. On May 3, 1985, the Chancery Court entered its order granting each of these alternative motions and dismissing Gray's complaint with prejudice. Gray appeals. * * *

At its core, Gray's action charges that he was duped by Baker and Roussel, that the church—wittingly or unwittingly—lent itself to the deception. The record reflects that Gray lives in the area and had in years past sold some sixteen acres to Roussel upon which the latter has made his home. In later years a zoning dispute had led to less than amicable relations between the two. Gray maintains that he would not have sold any of his remaining property to Roussel under any circumstances and that he had no idea that Roussel had any connection with the sale he was negotiating with Baker. The fact appears that, one month after Gray sold the 10.20 acres, the church turned around and sold 5.10 acres to Roussel. Gray says this was according to a prearranged scheme.

Gray further charges that he reduced the sales price of the 10.20 acres out of consideration for the fact that the purchaser was a church. The record suggests that Gray originally placed a sales price of $150,000.00 on the property, that he subsequently offered the property for $125,000.00, but the sale was finally consummated at $110,000.00. Gray insists that he reduced the sales price to $110,000.00 solely because the purchaser was a church.

In his complaint Gray seeks various alternative forms of relief, his primary demand being that the conveyance to the church should be declared void. While it appears that we have no cases directly on the point, we recognize that transactions respecting interests in land may be voided when one party misrepresents a material fact and where the other relies to his detriment upon that material misrepresentation. [citations]

The identity of one's visible vendee is a material matter. Where a vendor would not have made a conveyance of land had he known of a prior agreement by the vendee to convey to another the vendor found objectionable, that vendor is entitled to a judicial rescission of the instrument of conveyance. It matters not that the advent of the obnoxious ultimate purchaser may cause the vendor no pecuniary loss. The vendor's rights in his property extend to the right to refuse to sell to such third party for good reason, for bad reason or for no reason at all—so long as he does not act for some legally impermissible reason (a caveat not applicable in today's factual setting).

On the other hand, and for purposes of clarification of the rule under which Gray proceeds, if a purchaser is acting in good faith at the time of sale—that is, if the ostensible purchaser has no deal with any third party that is not disclosed to the seller—that purchaser may the day after the closing himself sell to a third party. Absent deception practiced on the seller, one who by purchase acquires fee simple title to a parcel of real property has an unrestricted right in his next breath to convey to a third party. That such a third party may be offensive to the original seller, that the third party may be one the original seller would never have sold to in the first instance, in no way operates to vitiate the original sale. What may render that sale voidable is the original purchaser's act of deceit, his failure to disclose to the original seller plans that the property or part thereof will be ultimately conveyed to the obnoxious third party. * * *

What—and all—we hold this day is that Gray is entitled to trial on the merits of his claim. Nothing said here should be taken or construed as intimating any thought on our part that Gray may or ought prevail on the merits. The depositions in the record before us make it clear that Baker and Roussel and the church take great exception to Gray's perspective on the facts. Which side should prevail in the end is a matter which should be determined by reference to the proof offered at the trial on the merits on remand, wholly uninfluenced by any aspect of this opinion other than that summarizing the substantive rules of law under which Gray's action and the defense of Baker and the others proceed.

Reversed and Remanded.

Notes

1. Finley v. Dalton, 251 S.C. 586, 164 S.E.2d 763 (1968). An undisclosed acquisition agent for a power company's hydroelectric project lied to seller about the way the property would be used. The court: Seller did not allege a cause of action for rescission. No fiduciary relationship. No confidence reposed in vendee. No duty to disclose facts that increase value. Misrepresentation of intended use must be material.

2. A seller of land consciously misrepresents that he is the record owner of the land, and that the property to be conveyed is subject to an annual ground rent of $75. The land is held in the name of a corporation that is wholly owned by the vendor, and the ground rent is $78 per year. Is "materiality" a factor for purposes of either tort or restitution? Clark v. Kirsner, 196 Md. 52, 74 A.2d 830 (1950).

In Clark v. Kirsner, the court concluded that "the difference between a $75 ground rent and a $78 ground rent is obviously compensable by an abatement from the purchase price." Is this abatement a tort measure of damages or restitution for unjust enrichment?

3. *Materiality Compared To "Causation."* Not only has "materiality" been made to overlap the "reliance" element of fraud; it has also been analyzed in terms of the "causation." Lack Industries v. Ralston Purina Co., 327 F.2d 266, 276–277 (8th Cir.1964): "It is hornbook law, as well as long standing Minnesota case law, that in a fraud action recovery is dependent upon proof that the damage incurred be proximately caused by the alleged fraudulent misrepresentation. Hanson v. Ford Motor Co., supra; Edward Thompson Co. v. Peterson, 190 Minn. 566, 252 N.W. 438 (1933); Walsh v. Paine, 123 Minn. 185, 143 N.W. 718 (1913).

"In the Edward Thompson Co. v. Peterson case, an attorney was sued for default of payment by the vendor of certain lawbooks. The attorney contended unsuccessfully that his purchase was induced by misrepresentations of the vendor's agent when falsely told that two other leading local attorneys had acquired the same books. The Minnesota Supreme Court found:

" '(T)he misrepresentation of the agent was immaterial and * * * the value of the books to defendant was not in any way affected by the fact that the two lawyers in question had not purchased similar books.' Edward Thompson Co. v. Peterson, supra, 252 N.W. at 438.

"This causation element is often stated in terms of the 'materiality' of the fraud as pointed out in Kiefer v. Rogers, 19 Minn. 32, 42 (1872):

" 'It is true that a false representation in respect of an immaterial fact, as it can occasion no injury, is no ground for relief.' "

Question: Suppose the salesman in Edward Thompson Co. v. Peterson had falsely represented to the lawyer that no other lawyer in town had ordered the set of books. Material? See Edward Thompson Co. v. Schroeder, 131 Minn. 125, 154 N.W. 792 (1915).

4. *Statutory Remedies for Misrepresentation.* Someone injured by a fraudulent misrepresentation may supplement common law fraud with consumer protective legislation which may offer a more desirable and effective remedy. Variously called Consumers Legal Remedies Act (Cal.Civ.Code § 1750 et seq.) or Deceptive

Trade Practices–Consumer Protection Act (Tex.Bus. & Com.Code Ann. §§ 17.41–17.-63 (Vernon 1987)), these statutes let a fraud victim choose from a broad range of legal and equitable options. See David McDavid Pontiac, Inc. v. Nix, 681 S.W.2d 831 (Tex.App.1984). Administrative agency action also provides a variety of consumers' remedies. See Federal Trade Commission v. Kitco of Nevada, Inc., 612 F.Supp. 1282 (D.Minn.1985).

Chapter 11

REMEDIES FOR DURESS, UNDUE INFLUENCE, AND UNCONSCIONABILITY

A. DURESS

PROSSER AND KEETON, HANDBOOK OF THE LAW OF TORTS

5th ed. 1984, 121
[footnotes omitted]

Duress is an important defense in the criminal law, and will justify rescission of a contract or other transaction, with restitution, but there has been no discussion of its place in the law of torts. There are odd cases which have held that duress is a tort in itself; but much more commonly it is held merely to invalidate the consent given, and so permit any other tort action which would arise if there were no consent. As to false imprisonment or battery, it is clear that yielding to a threat of force, or the assertion of legal authority, must be treated as no consent at all, but submission against the plaintiff's will; and the same is undoubtedly true as to trespass or conversion. The same is probably true where the threat is directed against a member of the plaintiff's immediate family, or his valuable property. But if the threat is less direct, being merely one of future arrest, or of "economic" duress such as loss of employment, the courts have refused to say that the consent given, however reluctant it may be, is ineffective, so as to establish another tort. The distinction is of course one of degree. The growing tendency to recognize and extend the intentional infliction of mental suffering as an independent cause of action may perhaps afford a remedy for some of the more extreme cases. In the field of contracts, duress is more generally recognized as a ground for rescission, and it may in time receive more acceptance in the field of torts.

1. DURESS—LEGAL COMPULSION OR THREAT THEREOF

BANK OF TUCSON v. ADRIAN

United States District Court.
District of Minnesota, 1964.
245 F.Supp. 595.

NORDBYE, DISTRICT JUDGE. * * * The suit involves a promissory note in the sum of $24,214.30, together with interest and attorneys' fees. It is admitted that the note was executed and delivered to plaintiff by the defendants in the

City of Minneapolis, Minnesota, on May 29, 1963, and was due 90 days after the date of execution. Defendants Monica B. Bjornnes and John T. Bessesen, sometimes referred to hereafter as Monica and John, deny liability by reason of lack of consideration and duress. * * *

In May, 1963, defendant Henry A. Bessesen was a resident of Tucson, Arizona, and in business in that city. He had a bank account with the plaintiff entitled "Second Fund Tucson Inn," and the authorized signatures to the account were Henry A. Bessesen and his wife, who then used the names of Henry Adrian and B.A. Adrian. * * * Henry A. Bessesen, either under the name of "Second Fund Tucson Inn" or in trade names which he used, had bank accounts in several of the larger cities throughout the country, and during the period of May, 1963, and immediately prior thereto, began the practice of kiting checks with reference to deposits in the various bank accounts which he controlled, as the result of which the bank account of "Second Fund Tucson Inn" became depleted by his fraudulent practices to the extent of some $23,700. When this shortage was called to his attention, he readily admitted the amount due the plaintiff bank, and in that plaintiff feared that his practices had caused losses to other banks which would be pressing their claims, it attempted to obtain payment of its loss from Henry without any delay. It appears that the losses sustained by the plaintiff bank were being investigated by an official Bank Examiner or examiners, and that the Federal Bureau of Investigation had made some investigation with reference thereto. When Henry was interviewed by plaintiff's bank officials and its attorneys, he merely asked for a reasonable time to obtain funds to cover the loss and stated that it would take him about three weeks to get the money. The bank officials demurred to the time requested, and then Henry suggested that he had friends and relatives in Minneapolis from whom he could obtain the necessary funds. He suggested that he wanted to go alone to Minneapolis and that his sister there had securities which could be utilized for the payment of his shortage in plaintiff's bank within three weeks. The bank officials, lacking trust in the promises of Henry, insisted on accompanying him to Minneapolis and that the trip should be made forthwith. Thereupon, the President of the bank and its attorney arranged for the purchase of airplane tickets to Minneapolis for themselves and Henry and his wife. The tickets for the latter were paid for by the bank. The four arrived in Minneapolis on Tuesday, May 28, 1963. After their arrival the plaintiff's representatives found that the securities which Henry claimed to have access to were either non-existent or unavailable, and then they insisted that they would not extend the payments due the bank over ten days and would require a promissory note for the amount due signed by Henry and his wife, with cosigners acceptable to the bank. Henry was informed that, upon his failure to provide the bank with satisfactory security, felony charges against him would follow.

Henry immediately got in touch with his brother, John, and his brother-in-law, one Alfred O. Bjornnes, and a meeting was arranged with the bank representatives. At this meeting, John and Alfred O. Bjornnes were told by the bank representatives that Henry had committed a felony, and unless something was done about it immediately, both Henry and his wife would go to jail. They insisted that both John and Bjornnes should sign a note with Henry and his wife guaranteeing the amount due payable in ten days. Bjornnes refused to be a party to the transaction. John was asked by the bank representatives if he would put a second mortgage on his house as part of the guaranty which the bank insisted upon. When John indicated that he might consider doing so, he was informed later that that type of security would not be suitable, and that if the bank was not able to get the money from Henry, it would have to take a promissory note from him with joint makers approved by the bank. When Bjornnes refused to sign a note as a guarantor, the bank insisted on having Monica—Bjornnes's wife and Henry's sister—on the note. John apparently was agreeable to execute the note as a co-maker. Bjornnes, however, objected to the plan of having his wife interviewed, stating that she had undergone an illness and was in no position to be subjected to the mental distress which would undoubtedly follow in the event she was informed of Henry's predicament. However, the bank representatives insisted that Monica be told about Henry's trouble, and although there is a dispute in the testimony as to what Monica was to be told, the evidence fully supports a finding that John was told by the bank representatives that not only should Monica be informed of the seriousness of Henry's predicament, but that if she was not willing to sign as a guarantor or co-maker of the proposed promissory note the result would be that Henry would go to jail. Moreover, there can be no question in light of the evidence that John carried out the instructions of the plaintiff and informed Monica that she would either have to sign the note or Henry would go to jail. When Monica received that message from John, she became highly nervous and distraught, and although her husband, Bjornnes, advised his wife not to become a party to the note, she was convinced from the information she received from John that the bank's ultimatum was that either she should become a party to the note or her brother Henry would be jailed on felony charges.

It is clear from the evidence that she believed and relied upon the statements which the bank representatives made to John, and which John reiterated to her. The family relationship among these brothers and sisters was close, and it is evident from the testimony that both Monica and John dreaded the thought of Henry's going to jail, with the inevitable publicity which would follow and which would stain the family name. * * * The fact that Monica had no conversations with the bank representatives prior to signing the note seems immaterial; that is, it was the purpose and intent of plaintiff's agents that Monica should be informed by John of the consequences which would follow if she refused to become a signer to the note. John was delegated by them to carry the information, which he did relay. The note was prepared on May 29, 1963, the day after the bank officials arrived in Minneapolis and originally it was written to be due in ten days after date, but later the ten days was excised and changed to 90 days to comply with Henry's suggestion in that regard. Henry, his wife, and John signed the note on May 29th. On May 30, 1963, Monica signed the note. There is evidence that before she signed it, she went with Henry to see the latter's lawyer, but there is no showing that Monica sought the lawyer's advice, or that she attempted to discuss the factual situation with him. She testified, and there is no denial of her testimony, that the lawyer merely stated "Do you know what you are signing?" and she said, "I know it is a note." She further testified that "I asked him if I didn't sign it, if it meant my brother would go to jail, and he admitted that it did. I said, then I have to sign it." * * *

It is quite apparent that the Minnesota courts recognize that there may be duress where security or payment is furnished for one related by blood or marriage under threats that the person so related would be prosecuted for a crime unless the security or payment is made. * * *

As stated, it is evident that both Monica and John firmly believed that it was either a question of jail for Henry or the execution of the note in question by them. Monica was an emotional type of person who became so upset by the ultimatum delivered to her that she went ahead and became a co-maker of the note regardless of the fact that her husband strongly advised against it. She had had no experience in business, and it is entirely reasonable to find that the threats of jail for her brother entirely controlled her will when she was confronted with the ultimatum made by the bank.

Admittedly, the factual situation may not be so strong in John's behalf. He was in the advertising business and was forty-five years of age. He had a high school education and had been in the Army, where he attained the rank of Captain. At one time he formed an advertising company which had business throughout the entire United States. In 1962 he became connected with a company which was engaged in selling premium merchandise similar to that carried on by a trading stamp company. In May, 1963, he was connected with a concern known as Business Travelers Internationale, a company which employed about four employees. Consequently, it must be recognized that John was a man of varied business experience. However, he consulted no one as to the advisability of doing that which he did. As soon as he heard of the eventualities which would follow in absence of Henry's furnishing some security to satisfy the bank, he agreed to furnish a second mortgage on his home. Obviously, he did not owe the bank anything and it is quite evident that Henry had no available assets which he could utilize to satisfy the bank so as to avoid criminal prosecution. It seems clear, therefore, that as soon as John heard of Henry's predicament and the ultimatum of the plaintiff, he succumbed to their demands. If John's situation is to be considered a border-line case as to duress, the Court's view is that the scales fairly tip in his favor in establishing this defense. * * *

In addition to the foregoing, reference should be made to Section 613.65, Minn.Stat.Ann., which was in full force and effect in Minnesota in May, 1963, and which reads:

> "Every person who shall take money or other property, gratuity, or reward, or an engagement of promise therefor, upon any agreement or understanding, express or implied, to compound or conceal a crime or violation of a statute, or to abstain from, discontinue, or delay a prosecution therefor, or to withhold any evidence thereof, except in a case where a compromise is allowed by law, shall be guilty * * * of a felony."

Reference also should be made to the well-recognized principle of law enunciated in American Natl. Bank of Lake Crystal v. Helling, 161 Minn. 504, 510, 202 N.W. 20, 22:

> "The controlling rules of law are fairly well settled. A contract to reimburse the owner for property stolen or embezzled made under an agreement to protect the guilty person from criminal prosecution, or to conceal the crime, or to withhold or suppress evidence of it, is void as an attempt to obstruct the enforcement of the laws and the court 'will leave the parties where it finds them.' It will give no aid to either."

True, a well-informed person would immediately recognize that the bank could not control the activities of the Bank Examiners, the Federal Bureau of

Investigation, or other law enforcement agencies, if a felony had been committed by Henry, but that the bank would refrain from initiating any criminal complaint was the unquestioned agreement of the bank when the note was signed, and that there would be no criminal prosecution of any kind was the unquestioned implication in the negotiations when these two defendants understood that it was either jail for their brother or a fulfillment of the bank's demands. Common justice strongly supports a finding that there was an agreement to stifle criminal prosecution, and under such circumstances the law will leave this plaintiff without any relief against these two defendants. * * *

Plaintiff has made a motion in the above proceeding to amend the findings of this Court relative to the finding of duress as to the defendants Monica Bjornnes and John T. Bessesen, and as to the finding that plaintiff promised that criminal prosecution would not follow if the note in question was signed by these two defendants.

As to the question of the sufficiency of the evidence to establish duress, plaintiff relies primarily on American National Bank of Lake Crystal v. Helling. But clearly the facts in the *Helling* case are readily distinguishable from those in the instant proceeding. Here, these two defendants had no alternative but to sign the note or suffer the family disgrace of their brother going to jail. This was the ultimatum made by the plaintiff and to that ultimatum both of these defendants surrendered. These defendants, as distinguished from the *Helling* case, never made any proposition to plaintiff looking to a compromise so as to absolve their brother from being prosecuted criminally. Here, the ultimatum made by the plaintiff was that the defendants had to sign the note or "your brother goes to jail." These defendants never consulted any lawyer as to their rights or as to the course that they should pursue under the circumstances. * * *

After due consideration, the Court concludes that the plaintiff's motion must be in all things denied. It is so ordered.

Note

Question: If Monica and John had paid the note, would the court have ordered restitution of the payment? See Chapter 14 below, pp. 1246–47.

ADAMS v. CRATER WELL DRILLING, INC.

Supreme Court of Oregon, 1976.
276 Or. 789, 556 P.2d 679.

O'CONNELL, JUSTICE. In October of 1973 the parties agreed that defendant would drill a well for plaintiff at a rate of $4.00 per foot for soft rock and $8.00 per foot for hard rock. The well was drilled to a total depth of 500 feet. Defendant's charge of $3,878 for this service was based upon its claim that 437 of the 500 feet drilled was hard rock. Plaintiff disagreed with this assertion and paid only $2,000, the amount which would be due for drilling 500 feet in soft materials at the contract rate of $4.00 per foot. Defendant continued to assert that the balance of $1,878 was due.

Plaintiff and Wayne Chitwood, an agent of the defendant, met in February of 1974 to discuss the dispute. Chitwood was adamant in demanding the balance of the amount billed and advised plaintiff that unless the amount was paid the matter would be given to defendant's attorneys for collection. Shortly afterwards, plaintiff paid defendant $1,878 under protest in order to avoid litigation. Plaintiff sought to introduce evidence that he made the payment because he feared that the stress of litigation would harm his wife, who at the time was critically ill. The evidence was excluded on defendant's objection.

In March of 1975 plaintiff commenced this action against defendant. The complaint set forth the terms of the agreement, the amount billed, and the payment. Plaintiff further alleged that defendant falsely, knowingly and willfully represented that drilling took place in hard rock. Plaintiff prayed for the recovery of the overcharge and also punitive damages in the amount of $25,000. The jury returned a verdict for plaintiff in the amount of the overcharge and also punitive damages in the amount of $4,500. Defendant appeals claiming that the complaint failed to state a cause of action, that no fraud was proven, and that the award of punitive damages was improper.

The complaint apparently was framed on the theory of an action for fraud. * * * However, the facts show that payment was not made in reliance upon defendant's misrepresentation but, according to plaintiff's own testimony, to avoid the trauma his wife would feel if an action were brought. Therefore, plaintiff cannot recover on the theory of fraud and deceit.

The trial judge concluded that the complaint failed to state a cause of action for fraud, but expressed the view that a cause of action for money had and received was alleged. * * * The only question is whether plaintiff's payment was made under circumstances which would entitle him to restitution.

* * * The threat of a civil suit alone does not constitute duress or coercion sufficient to permit recovery of money paid to avoid the litigation.[1] However, if payment is made in response to a threat of civil proceedings and the threat is made "without probable cause and with no belief in the existence of the cause of action," recovery in an action for money had and received is permitted.[2]

In the present case, the jury in assessing punitive damages must have found defendant's conduct to be in bad faith. We may assume, then, that this also establishes that the jury found the defendant's threat to bring suit was "without probable cause and with no belief in the existence of the cause of action."

Defendant finally contends that because punitive damages are not allowed in a contract action, they are improper in a money had and received action which arises out of a contractual transaction between the parties. However, this contention does not take account of the fact that defendant, in threatening to sue knowing that he had no rightful claim, is a wrongdoer in a tortious sense. That being the case, the same reasons for allowing punitive damages in actions brought to recover damages for tortious conduct should apply when the

1. This is so not because such threats are not in one sense coercive, but because the coercion is not sufficient to override the strong policy of permitting free recourse to the courts. See Dawson, Duress Through Civil Litigation, 45 Mich.L.Rev. 571 (1947).

2. Restatement, Restitution § 71, p. 290 (1937). In Cram v. Powell, 100 Or. 708, 197 P. 280, 284 (1921) this court adopted the rule that, " 'It is the well-established general rule that it is not duress to institute or threaten to institute civil suits, or take proceedings in court, or for any person to declare that he intends to use the courts wherein to insist on *what he believes to be* his legal rights.' " (Emphasis added.) Similarly, in First Nat. Bank v. Multnomah Lbr. & Box Co., 125 Or. 598, 622, 268 P. 63, 71 (1928), the threat to use legal process to seize a debtor's goods was held not to be legal duress "as long as the creditor acts strictly within his legal rights."

action is to recover payment made as a result of essentially tortious conduct. This is the view taken by the court in Ward v. Taggart, 51 Cal.2d 736, 336 P.2d 534 (1959). In that case the California Supreme Court held that although recovery in an action for money had and received is based upon the theory of an implied promise to return money wrongfully obtained, the recovery does not arise from any agreement between the parties but arises from the wrongful conduct. We agree with the reasoning employed in Ward v. Taggart and hold, therefore, that the court properly submitted the issue of punitive damages to the jury.

Judgment affirmed.

Note

If duress alone is not an actionable tort, why did the court allow punitive damages? The plaintiff had an obvious defense to the civil proceedings initiated against him. Does the procedure adopted save litigation time?

WHITE LIGHTING CO. v. WOLFSON

Supreme Court of California, 1968.
68 Cal.2d 336, 66 Cal.Rptr. 697, 438 P.2d 345.

TOBRINER, J. * * * [White sued Wolfson for $850.] Wolfson added to his second amended cross-complaint a fifth count entitled "Abuse of Process." Wolfson alleged that White, in its action to recover $850 from Wolfson, procured issuance of process against Wolfson and that cross-defendants "maliciously, wilfully and with the intent solely to vex, harass and injure" used the process to attach both Wolfson's 5,000 White shares (allegedly worth $15,000) and his 1963 Porsche automobile (allegedly worth $4,500). Cross-defendants likewise attempted to attach Wolfson's bank account ($250). Cross-defendants threatened Wolfson that they would garnish his wages (allegedly in excess of $200 per week). Cross-defendants knew that the assets which they attached and attempted to attach bore no relation to the sum of White's claim against Wolfson; cross-defendants sought the above attachments to restrain Wolfson by extortion from bringing his cross-claims. As a result of the actual and attempted attachments, Wolfson lost the use of his car for one month with resulting loss of commissions, suffered impairment of his credit with his bank which accelerated a loan made to Wolfson, and incurred legal expenses in procuring the release of the attached assets.

The trial court erred in sustaining a general demurrer without leave to amend to this fifth count of the second amended cross-complaint on the asserted ground of the prematurity of the cause of action. A claim based on excessive attachment constitutes in essence a cause of action for abuse of process rather than a cause of action for malicious prosecution. "Consequently * * * it is unnecessary for [Wolfson] to prove that the proceeding [in which the attachment was issued] has terminated in his favor, or that the process was obtained without probable cause or in the course of a proceeding begun without probable cause." Spellens v. Spellens (1957) 49 Cal.2d 210, 232 [317 P.2d 613].) The claim may therefore be brought in the same action in which the attachment issued.

The case law on wrongful attachment presents a complicated and confused picture. Most of the California opinions have treated suits for wrongful attachment as actions for malicious prosecution rather than for abuse of process. Much of the confusion in the characterization of these actions for wrongful attachment results from the courts' failure to distinguish the following four different types of wrongful attachment: (1) levying attachment in an action prosecuted maliciously and without probable cause; (2) maliciously procuring attachment in a properly instituted action in which the creditor is not entitled to the writ; (3) attaching property which is exempt from attachment or possesses a value greatly in excess of the amount of the legitimate claim; (4) using regularly issued attachment for an improper purpose.

The courts generally and correctly treat the above-mentioned first type of wrongful attachment as constituting part of an action for malicious prosecution. * * * In those cases in which the courts have articulated the reasons for the alleged wrongfulness, they have in most instances properly treated the fourth type of wrongful attachment—wrongful use of properly procured attachment—as creating an action for abuse of process. * * * Thus the problem of proper characterization mainly arises in the second and third types of wrongful attachment cases: those cases in which the underlying action is proper but the creditor either is not entitled to a writ of attachment or attaches property which is exempt or possesses a value greatly in excess of the amount of the legitimate claim. * * *

We believe that in view of the reasons stated below excessive attachments should be treated as giving rise to a cause of action for abuse of process rather than for malicious prosecution. First, in the case of an excessive attachment action, two requirements of the malicious prosecution action may very well be lacking: absence of probable cause to institute the proceedings in which the attachment issued and termination of that action in favor of the attachment defendant. The attaching creditor typically prevails on his claim, but for a much smaller amount than the value of the property attached. Second, the wrongfulness in the excessive attachment lies, not in the institution of the suit or the procurement of the attachment, but in the illegitimate use of the attachment process to tie up more property than is reasonably necessary to secure the attaching creditor's claim. Third, the attachment defendant should not be forced to wait until final termination of the attaching creditor's action to sue for wrongful attachment: The attachment defendant should be able to assert the damages caused by the excessive attachment in the attaching creditor's primary action.

In cases such as the instant one in which the alleged wrongfulness of the attachment does not depend upon an alleged lack of probable cause and malice in instituting the action in which the attachment issued—i.e., in cases in which the alleged wrongful attachment falls under categories (2), (3), and (4)—a termination of that action in favor of the attachment defendant has no bearing upon the determination of whether the attachment writ was maliciously procured or improperly used. The attachment defendant should therefore not be forced to wait until the termination of the creditor's primary action to seek damages for the alleged wrongful attachment. "[I]t would, indeed, be extraordinary if the [attachment] defendant was denied the right in the same action, not only to defend against it, but to claim redress for the wrongs inflicted upon him by the [attachment] plaintiff. * * *" (Waugenheim v. Graham, 39 Cal. 169 at p. 178.)

Since cross-defendants' excessive attachment of Wolfson's property constituted the gravamen of the cause of action alleged in the fifth count of the second amended cross-complaint, the count sufficiently alleged a cause of action for abuse of process. It was not premature. The trial court erred in sustaining the general demurrer.

Note

See Moses v. MacFerlan, supra, p. 288. Would a tort action for malicious prosecution have been an alternative remedy? Would this remedy fail because it could not be asserted that MacFerlan v. Moses terminated in Moses's favor?

Munson v. Linnick, 255 Cal.App.2d 589, 593–96, 63 Cal.Rptr. 340, 343–44 (1967). A lawyer, in order to "bluff" payment of a nonexistent claim, sued on a contingency fee arrangement. He then reached a "tacit understanding" with the other attorney that no default would be taken without prior notice. However, he took a default without notice; and, after expiration of the period for a motion to set aside the judgment, he levied upon the other party's property. The victim thereupon sought a declaratory judgment that the default be set aside and for other relief. The trial court found in favor of the victim and entered judgment against the lawyer as a joint tortfeasor for general damages for "malicious prosecution" in the amount of the proceeds from the levy and execution, interest, attorney's fees and expenses in defense of the offending action, including that in setting aside the default plus punitive damages of $2500.

The lawyer argued that because the default was outstanding when the victim began the declaratory judgment suit, the "prior" judicial proceedings had not been terminated in plaintiff's favor and a cause of action for "malicious prosecution" had not been stated. The appellate court affirmed. The court noted that an action for declaratory relief is equitable in nature and that a "court of equity will make a complete determination of the controversy * * * in accord with the facts as they exist at the time of the decree." The court added that "no satisfactory reason supports the [argument] that the trial court should not have awarded damages under a malicious prosecution theory, as an incident to the declaratory relief sought, because a favorable termination of the [prior] action did not take place until the present suit commenced."

2. DURESS—BUSINESS COMPULSION

SELMER CO. v. BLAKESLEE–MIDWEST CO.

United States Court of Appeals, Seventh Circuit, 1983.
704 F.2d 924.

POSNER, CIRCUIT JUDGE. This appeal by the plaintiff from summary judgment for the defendants in a diversity case requires us to consider the meaning, under Wisconsin contract law, of "economic duress" as a defense to a settlement of a contract dispute.

On this appeal, we must take as true the following facts. The plaintiff, Selmer, agreed to act as a subcontractor on a construction project for which the defendant Blakeslee–Midwest Prestressed Concrete Company was the general contractor. Under the contract between Blakeslee–Midwest and Selmer, Selmer was to receive $210,000 for erecting prestressed concrete materials supplied to it by Blakeslee–Midwest. Blakeslee–Midwest failed to fulfill its contractual obligations; among other things, it was tardy in supplying Selmer with the prestressed concrete materials. Selmer could have terminated the contract without penalty but instead agreed orally with Blakeslee–Midwest to complete its work, provided Blakeslee–Midwest would pay Selmer for the extra costs of completion due to Blakeslee–Midwest's defaults. When the job was completed, Selmer demanded payment of $120,000. Blakeslee–Midwest offered $67,000 and refused to budge from this offer. Selmer, because it was in desperate financial straits, accepted the offer.

Two and a half years later Selmer brought this suit against Blakeslee–Midwest claiming that its extra costs had amounted to $150,000 ($120,000 being merely a settlement offer), and asking for that amount minus the $67,000 it had received, plus consequential and punitive damages. Although Selmer, presumably in order to be able to claim such damages, describes this as a tort rather than a contract action, it seems really to be a suit on Blakeslee–Midwest's alleged oral promise to reimburse Selmer in full for the extra costs of completing the original contract after Blakeslee–Midwest defaulted. But the characterization is unimportant. Selmer concedes that, whatever its suit is, it is barred by the settlement agreement if, as the district court held, that agreement is valid. The only question is whether there is a triable issue as to whether the settlement agreement is invalid because procured by "economic duress."

If you extract a promise by means of a threat, the promise is unenforceable. This is not, as so often stated, see, e.g., Totem Marine Tug & Barge, Inc. v. Alyeska Pipeline Serv. Co., 584 P.2d 15, 22 (Alaska 1978), because such a promise is involuntary, unless "involuntary" is a conclusion rather than the description of a mental state. If the threat is ferocious ("your money or your life") and believed, the victim may be desperately eager to fend it off with a promise. Such promises are made unenforceable in order to discourage threats by making them less profitable. The fundamental issue in a duress case is therefore not the victim's state of mind but whether the statement that induced the promise is the kind of offer to deal that we want to discourage, and hence that we call a "threat." Selmer argues that Blakeslee–Midwest said to it in effect, "give up $53,000 of your claim for extras [$120,000 minus $67,000], or you will get nothing." This has the verbal form of a threat but is easily recast as a promise innocuous on its face—"I promise to pay you $67,000 for a release of your claim." There is a practical argument against treating such a statement as a threat: it will make an inference of duress inescapable in any negotiation where one party makes an offer from which it refuses to budge, for the other party will always be able to argue that he settled only because there was a (figurative) gun at his head. It would not matter whether the party refusing to budge was the payor like Blakeslee–Midwest or the promisor like Selmer. If Selmer had refused to complete the job without being paid exorbitantly for the extras and Blakeslee–Midwest had complied with this demand because financial catastrophe would have loomed if Selmer had walked off the job, we would have the same case. A vast number of contract settlements would be subject to being ripped open upon an allegation of duress if Selmer's argument was accepted.

Sensitive—maybe oversensitive—to this danger, the older cases held that a threat not to honor a contract could not be considered duress. [citations] But the principle was not absolute, as is shown by Alaska Packers' Ass'n v. Domenico, 117 Fed. 99 (9th Cir.1902). Sailors and fishermen (the libelants) "agreed in writing, for a certain stated compensation, to render their services to the appellant in remote waters where the season for conducting fishing operations is extremely short, and in which enterprise the appellant had a large amount of money invested; and, after having entered upon the discharge of their contract, and at a time when it was impossible for the appellant to secure other men in their places, the libelants, without any valid cause, absolutely refused to continue the services they were under contract to perform unless the appellant would consent to pay them more money." The appellant agreed, but later reneged, and the libelants sued. They lost; the court refused to enforce the new agreement. Although the technical ground of decision was the absence of fresh consideration for the modified agreement, it seems apparent both from the quoted language and from a reference on the same page to coercion that the court's underlying concern was that the modified agreement had been procured by duress in the form of the threat to break the original contract.

Alaska Packers' Ass'n shows that because the legal remedies for breach of contract are not always adequate, a refusal to honor a contract may force the other party to the contract to surrender his rights—in *Alaska Packers' Ass'n,* the appellant's right to the libelants' labor at the agreed wage. It undermines the institution of contract to allow a contract party to use the threat of breach to get the contract modified in his favor not because anything has happened to require modification in the mutual interest of the parties but simply because the other party, unless he knuckles under to the threat, will incur costs for which he will have no adequate legal remedy. If contractual protections are illusory, people will be reluctant to make contracts. Allowing contract modifications to be avoided in circumstances such as those in *Alaska Packers' Ass'n* assures prospective contract parties that signing a contract is not stepping into a trap, and by thus encouraging people to make contracts promotes the efficient allocation of resources.

Capps v. Georgia Pac. Corp., 253 Or. 248, 453 P.2d 935 (1969), illustrates the principle of *Alaska Packers' Ass'n* in the context of settling contract disputes. The defendant promised to give the plaintiff, as a commission for finding a suitable lessee for a piece of real estate, 5 percent of the total rental plus one half of the first month's rent. The plaintiff found a suitable lessee and the lease was signed. Under the terms of the commission arrangement the defendant owed the plaintiff $157,000, but he paid only $5,000, and got a release from the plaintiff of the rest. The plaintiff later sued for the balance of the $157,000, alleging that when requesting payment of the agreed-upon commission he had "informed Defendant that due to Plaintiff's adverse financial condition, he was in danger of immediately losing other personal property through repossession and foreclosure unless funds from Defendant were immediately made available for the purpose of paying these creditors."

But "Defendant, through its agent * * * advised Plaintiff that though he was entitled to the sums demanded in Plaintiff's Complaint, unless he signed the purported release set forth in Defendant's Answer, Plaintiff would receive no part thereof, inasmuch as Defendant had extensive resources and powerful and brilliant attorneys who would and could prevent Plaintiff in any subsequent legal proceeding from obtaining payment of all or any portion of said sums." We can disregard the reference to the defendant's "powerful and brilliant attorneys" yet agree with the Oregon Supreme Court that the confluence of the plaintiff's necessitous financial condition, the defendant's acknowledged indebtedness for the full $157,000, and the settlement of the indebtedness for less than 3 cents on the dollar—with no suggestion that the defendant did not have the money to pay the debt in full—showed duress. The case did not involve the settlement of a genuine dispute, but, as in *Alaska Packers'*

Ass'n, an attempt to exploit the contract promisee's lack of an adequate legal remedy.

Although *Capps* is not a Wisconsin case, we have no reason to think that Wisconsin courts would reach a different result. But the only feature that the present case shares with *Capps* is that the plaintiff was in financial difficulties. Since Blakeslee–Midwest did not acknowledge that it owed Selmer $120,000, and since the settlement exceeded 50 percent of Selmer's demand, the terms of the settlement are not unreasonable on their face, as in *Capps.* Thus the question is starkly posed whether financial difficulty can by itself justify setting aside a settlement on grounds of duress. It cannot. "The mere stress of business conditions will not constitute duress where the defendant was not responsible for the conditions." Johnson, Drake & Piper, Inc. v. United States, 531 F.2d 1037, 1042 (Ct.Cl.1976) (per curiam). The adverse effect on the finality of settlements and hence on the willingness of parties to settle their contract disputes without litigation would be great if the cash needs of one party were alone enough to entitle him to a trial on the validity of the settlement. In particular, people who desperately wanted to settle for cash—who simply could not afford to litigate—would be unable to settle, because they could not enter into a *binding* settlement; being desperate, they could always get it set aside later on grounds of duress. It is a detriment, not a benefit, to one's long-run interests not to be able to make a binding commitment.

Matters stand differently when the complaining party's financial distress is due to the other party's conduct. Although Selmer claims that it was the extra expense caused by Blakeslee–Midwest's breaches of the original contract that put it in a financial vise, it could have walked away from the contract without loss or penalty when Blakeslee–Midwest broke the contract. Selmer was not forced by its contract to remain on the job, and was not prevented by circumstances from walking away from the contract, as the appellant in *Alaska Packers' Ass'n* had been; it stayed on the job for extra pay. We do not know why Selmer was unable to weather the crisis that arose when Blakeslee–Midwest refused to pay $120,000 for Selmer's extra expenses—whether Selmer was under-capitalized or overborrowed or what—but Blakeslee–Midwest cannot be held responsible for whatever it was that made Selmer so necessitous, when, as we have said, Selmer need not have embarked on the extended contract. * * *

Affirmed.

Notes

1. See Robison, Enforcing Extorted Contract Modifications, 68 Iowa L.Rev. 699 (1983).

2. Rich & Whillock v. Ashton Development, 157 Cal.App.3d 1154, 1158–59, 204 Cal.Rptr. 86, 89 (1984): "California courts have recognized the economic duress doctrine in private sector cases for at least 50 years. The doctrine is equitably based and represents 'but an expansion by courts of equity of the old common-law doctrine of duress.' As it has evolved to the present day, the economic duress doctrine is not limited by early statutory and judicial expressions requiring an unlawful act in the nature of a tort or a crime. Instead, the doctrine now may come into play upon the doing of a wrongful act which is sufficiently coercive to cause a reasonably prudent person faced with no reasonable alternative to succumb to the perpetrator's pressure. The assertion of a claim known to be false or a bad faith threat to breach a contract or to withhold a payment may constitute a wrongful act for purposes of the economic duress doctrine. [citations]."

3. *Mechanics of rescission for economic duress.* Gruver v. Midas International Corp., 925 F.2d 280, 283 n. 1 (9th Cir.1991). The court rejected the Gruvers' claim that they had signed a franchise termination agreement under economic duress, but added this footnote: "Midas' argument that [Gruvers] may not rely on economic duress because they have not promptly disaffirmed their termination agreements and returned all the benefits they received from these agreements lacks merit. While the law is clear that a court will not rescind a contract unless the party seeking rescission promptly disaffirms the contract, [citations] no Oregon court has applied this to invalidate a claim of economic duress in signing an agreement containing a release of claims. The whole point of an economic duress claim is that plaintiff had no reasonable choice but to enter into the contract. * * * [W]hen a plaintiff has no reasonable choice but to enter into a contract, the plaintiff cannot reasonably be expected immediately to return the benefit. * * * It would thus, be at odds with the purpose of the economic duress rule to bar claims of economic duress for failure to disaffirm the transaction. [citations] Traditional set-off rules, reducing a successful plaintiff's damages by the value of any benefit he has already received are sufficient to protect a defendant's interest."

FIZZELL v. MEEKER

United States District Court.
Western District of Missouri, 1970.
339 F.Supp. 624.

WILLIAM H. BECKER, CHIEF JUDGE. This is a diversity action under the Federal Declaratory Judgment Act, to determine the rights of plaintiffs and defendant in a deposit of $13,750 (called an "escrow fund") being held by the Home State Bank of Kansas City, Kansas, and for actual and punitive damages.

Plaintiffs state that they had negotiated for the sale of a corporation to Glenn D. and Colleen Z. Ferguson; that the Fergusons, pursuant to a contract entered into with plaintiffs for that purpose, sought and obtained an agreement of the Home State Bank to loan them $125,000, the balance of the original agreed purchase price of $135,000; that on August 5, 1969, defendant telegraphed the bank to assert a claim against the Fergusons for consultant services in the amount of $13,750; that, as a result thereof, plaintiffs were required by the bank to agree to the retention in escrow of $13,750 of the purchase price pending the determination of defendant's claim before the remaining proceeds of the loan would be paid out to plaintiffs; and that defendant later refused to withdraw his claim to the $13,750, though requested to do so by plaintiffs.

Thus the complaint of plaintiffs included: (1) a claim for damages, actual and punitive, for tortious interference with contractual relations in which the issues are ordinarily triable by a jury; and (2) an action for a declaratory judgment that the contract among plaintiffs, the Fergusons and Home State Bank to retain the fund of $13,750 in an "escrow fund" was made as a result of allegedly wrongful acts of defendant (determined to be economic coercion or duress) and therefore voidable. The issues of wrongful compulsion in the declaratory judgment action are equitable and triable to the Court without a jury. * * *

For convenience and to avoid multiple trials the equitable claim for a declaratory judgment and the legal claim for damages were heard simultaneously by the Court and by the jury. * * *

Defendant, the evidence shows, had been retained by the Fergusons to consult with them on the advisability of purchasing a Missouri corporation, Monatco Manufacturing Corporation ("Monatco of Missouri" hereinafter), from plaintiffs, and finally to assist them in procuring a loan of the purchase price of the corporation. Defendant rendered to the Fergusons advice and service as a consultant, but failed to procure a bank loan or to consummate the purchase.

Sometime before August 5, 1969, the Fergusons independently negotiated an agreement with plaintiffs and the Home State Bank to close the purchase of Monatco of Missouri on August 6, 1969. To finance the purchase the Fergusons paid $10,000 down and secured a commitment from Home State Bank to lend to them $125,000 to be secured by the assets of Monatco of Missouri (on their transfer to a receptacle of title, a Kansas corporation of the same name at the time of closing of the loan). By this means the total purchase price of $135,000 (with minor adjustments) would be paid to plaintiffs, the sellers. * * *

Defendant Meeker learned of the proposed transaction on or before August 5, 1969. He had not been paid by the Fergusons for his services and had reason to believe that the Fergusons had made no immediate plans to pay him when the transaction was to be closed on August 6, 1969. He consulted his counsel, who drafted for him a telegram which he sent to the Home State Bank on August 5, 1969, and which was received by the bank the same day. The telegram read as follows:

> "Please take note that I claim the amount of $13,750 for professional services against Glenn D. Ferguson and Monatco Manufacturing Corp. a Kansas corporation. The peckbrmances (sic) of said services and their value has been acknowledged (sic) by Glenn D. Ferguson and Monatco Manufacturing Corp. The extension of any credit by you to either of said parties is subject to this notice."
>
> "William D. Meeker
> *6020 Walnut*
> *Kansas City, Mo*"

The clear intent of the telegram was to expose the bank to risk of financial loss and thereby to require payment to defendant of the sum of $13,750 (unilaterally fixed by defendant as his compensation) as a condition of closing the sale by plaintiffs to the Fergusons or at least to require immediate negotiation of an acceptable sum and payment thereof to defendant. The telegram nearly had the desired effect. As expected the bank conservatively demurred at closing the loan. But counsel for the bank and the buyers and sellers agreed in the closing statement to secure the bank against risk by leaving $13,750 in escrow with the bank as a deposit to secure claims of the defendant. The Fergusons further agreed to indemnify the bank from liability, costs and expenses incurred by reason of defendant's claims.

The plaintiffs and the Fergusons and Monatco of Kansas reluctantly entered into these agreements only because of their anxiety to consummate the loan and sale transaction. In the closing statement the Fergusons and Monatco of Kansas denied in writing the claimed indebtedness to the defendant.

Thereafter, though frequently requested informally and formally to release his claim to the deposit, defendant, encouraged by his counsel, persisted, and still persists, in asserting the claim of a "security interest" in the $13,750 deposit. It did not seem to matter to defendant and his counsel that the

$13,750 was not the property of the alleged debtors, the Fergusons, nor that it was produced and secured by a lien on assets furnished by plaintiffs. Finally the defendant filed a suit in the District Court of Wyandotte County, Kansas, against the bank, the plaintiffs and the Fergusons as a further means to compel payment of defendant's demands. This suit was still pending against all but the bank when the trial of this case took place. The bank had secured a dismissal of the claim against it. * * *

[P]laintiffs are the innocent and injured parties and have no adequate remedy at law to protect themselves against the continued and repeated assertion that they created a security interest for the benefit of defendant Meeker unless this voidable contract is in equity cancelled and annulled and for naught held by a declaratory judgment of this Court.

Plaintiffs are clearly entitled to such a judgment. The modern doctrine of "business compulsion" is recognized both generally and in the law of Kansas, whose law is applicable to this case.

The Restatement of the Law of Contracts deals expressly with duress in the sense of economic coercion or business compulsion. In Section 492 is contained the following definition thereof:

"Duress in the Restatement of this subject means

(a) any wrongful act of one person that compels a manifestation of apparent assent by another to a transaction without his volition, or

(b) any wrongful threat of one person by words or other conduct that induces another to enter a transaction under the influence of such fear as precludes him from exercising free will and judgment, if the threat was intended or should reasonably have been expected to operate as an inducement." [1]

Criterion Holding Co., Inc. v. Cerussi, 140 Misc. 855, 250 N.Y.S. 735, is a case almost precisely in point. In that case, a realty company was alleged in a counterclaim to have been employed by Cerussi to procure a loan for a corporation in dire financial straits, and, knowing of the dire financial situation of the corporation, the realty corporation "threatened to use its influence

1. [Footnotes renumbered.] In § 493 of the Restatement, illustrations under clause (d) of Paragraph 5, read as follows:

"5. A pawnbroker has a pledge of a valuable heirloom belonging to B. B offers to redeem the pledge, but A refuses to surrender it unless B signs a note in satisfaction of another claim the validity of which is in dispute. A may avoid the note."

"8. A, the owner of a livery stable, has in his possession horses of B, who is engaged in a business which requires the constant use of these horses. A refuses to let B take the horses from the stable unless he gives a mortgage for a debt due A for which A has no lien on the horses. Fearing that otherwise his business would be ruined, B gives the mortgage. There is duress though legal remedies are available for the recovery of the horses, and though the debt due A is undisputed."

"12. A threatens B that unless B pays $100 that A claims for an injury caused by B to A's automobile, A will sue B and attach B's stock in hand for $5,000. Such an attachment would be ruinous to B's business and induced by fear he makes the payment. Although A has a genuine claim and $100 is not a grossly excessive estimate of A's damages, there is duress because the size of the threatened attachment makes it an abuse of process."

"13. A has a valid cause of action for unliquidated damages against B, and threatens B that unless B contracts to transfer B's motor car to A in satisfaction of the claim, A will attach a shipment of perishable goods belonging to B. Other nonperishable goods of B are available for attachment. An attachment of the perishable goods would be highly injurious to B, and induced by fear of consequences he enters into the contract. It is made under duress."

Section 493(d) states that duress may be exercised by "threats of wrongfully destroying, injuring, seizing or withholding land or other things."

with the title company [from whom the loan was sought] to cause the loan to be refused, unless the defendant corporation would enter into the transaction referred to in the complaint." It was held that the counterclaim thereby stated a claim of "business compulsion."

Defendant relies on a defense of advice of counsel. This defense is without merit. No one can be immunized from the consequences of duress and coercion by the advice of counsel. Coercion and duress which interfere with the rights of others is wrong and actionable whether accompanied by malice or other conduct warranting allowance of punitive damages. "The courts will hold that there is duress vitiating the contract, regardless of the intent with which the pressure was applied." C.J.S. Contracts § 168, p. 944. In this case the defense of advice of counsel was submitted to the jury on claim for punitive damages. In equity it is clear that the nature of the legal advice and the circumstances under which it was given, received and employed disqualify it from meeting minimal standards.

Defendant repeatedly and persistently insists that in sending the telegram and aggressively pursuing his claim to the $13,750 he was doing only what he had a legal right to do. This contention shows an obstinate refusal to recognize his obligation as a retained consultant to assist in securing a loan and in making a purchase. * * * He concededly had no lien under Kansas law, but attempted to secure payment as if he did. This was the act of an unfaithful agent of the Fergusons, and a tortious interference with the performance of a contract with respect to plaintiffs and perhaps others.

It is therefore evident that in equity plaintiffs are entitled to a declaratory judgment that the agreement of the closing statement insofar as it provides for the withholding by the bank of the deposit of $13,750 to secure defendant's claim is void and that plaintiffs' rights to the fund are superior to defendant's, and for other declaratory relief.

The plaintiffs are entitled to a declaratory judgment that the defendant is obligated to pay to the plaintiffs all costs, attorneys' fees and expenses and actual damages directly resulting from the original telegram of August 5, 1969, and the persistent continuing claims to a "security interest" in the deposit of $13,750, including the expenses and attorneys' fees reasonably expended in securing this declaratory judgment, agreed to be $3,500. The plaintiffs are further entitled to a declaratory judgment that defendant is obligated to pay to plaintiffs the post trial expenses, costs and attorneys' fees reasonably expended in defending this judgment.

* * * The remaining issues at law were liability for actual damages and for punitive damages.

Since the same conduct of defendant which constitutes "business compulsion" also constitutes tortious interference with the contractual relations of plaintiffs, a verdict for plaintiffs was directed on this claim, assessing actual damages for such interference at $3,500, in accordance with the declaratory judgment and the agreement on reasonableness. The remaining legal issue, namely, of the liability for punitive damages which should be awarded to plaintiffs, was submitted to the jury and by the jury fixed at $1.00. * * *

Ordered, adjudged and declared that defendant is under an obligation not to interfere with the payment of this deposit to the plaintiffs and is obligated if necessary or desirable to give a formal release to the bank of any interest he has therein claimed to be superior to those of plaintiffs. It is further

Ordered, adjudged and declared that defendant is under an obligation based on the void agreement to discontinue his suit for damages and other relief against the plaintiffs in the District Court of Wyandotte County, Kansas. It is further * * *

Ordered, adjudged and declared that jurisdiction is retained to grant conventional relief if future circumstances warrant it.

Notes

1. In disaffirming and seeking restitution the plaintiff must ordinarily act promptly after discovering the grounds for rescission. In duress, however, the plaintiff is only too well aware of the restitutionary claim. The "promptness" of plaintiffs' action must therefore be tested by their reactions after the duress is removed. See Leeper v. Beltrami, 53 Cal.2d 195, 1 Cal.Rptr. 12, 347 P.2d 12 (1959).

2. Wolf v. Marlton Corp., 57 N.J.Super. 278, 288, 154 A.2d 625, 630 (1959). Buyers of house in a subdivision threatened to resell to an "undesirable" purchaser unless subdivider cancelled the contract and refunded most of the deposit. Held: "The sale * * * to an 'undesirable purchaser' is, of course, a perfectly legal act regardless of any adverse effect it may have on the fortunes of the developer's enterprise. But where a party for purely malicious and unconscionable motives threatens to resell such a home to a purchaser, specially selected because he would be undesirable for the sole purpose of injuring the builder's business, fundamental fairness requires the conclusion that his conduct in making the threat be deemed 'wrongful' as the term is used in the law of duress."

B. UNDUE INFLUENCE

ODORIZZI v. BLOOMFIELD SCHOOL DISTRICT

District Court of Appeal of California, Second District, 1966.
246 Cal.App.2d 123, 54 Cal.Rptr. 533.

FLEMING, JUSTICE. Plaintiff Donald Odorizzi was employed during 1964 as an elementary school teacher by defendant Bloomfield School District and was under contract with the District to continue to teach school the following year as a permanent employee. On June 10 he was arrested on criminal charge of homosexual activity, and on June 11 he signed and delivered to his superiors his written resignation as a teacher, a resignation which the District accepted on June 13. In July the criminal charges against Odorizzi were dismissed under Penal Code, section 995, and in September he sought to resume his employment with the District. On the District's refusal to reinstate him he filed suit for declaratory and other relief.

Odorizzi's amended complaint asserts his resignation was invalid because obtained through duress, fraud, mistake, and undue influence and given at a time when he lacked capacity to make a valid contract. Specifically, Odorizzi declares he was under such severe mental and emotional strain at the time he signed his resignation, having just completed the process of arrest, questioning by the police, booking, and release on bail, and having gone for forty hours without sleep, that he was incapable of rational thought or action. While he was in this condition and unable to think clearly, the superintendent of the District and the principal of his school came to his apartment. They said they were trying to help him and had his best interests at heart, that he should take their advice and immediately resign his position with the District, that there was no time to consult an attorney, that if he did not resign immediately the District would suspend and dismiss him from his position and publicize the proceedings, his "aforedescribed arrest" and cause him "to suffer extreme embarrassment and humiliation"; but that if he resigned at once the incident would not be publicized and would not jeopardize his chances of securing employment as a teacher elsewhere. Odorizzi pleads that because of his faith and confidence in their representations they were able to substitute their will and judgment in place of his own and thus obtain his signature to his purported resignation. A demurrer to his amended complaint was sustained without leave to amend.

By his complaint plaintiff in effect seeks to rescind his resignation pursuant to Civil Code, section 1689, on the ground that his consent had not been real or free within the meaning of Civil Code, section 1567, but had been obtained through duress, menace, fraud, undue influence, or mistake. A pleading under these sections is sufficient if, stripped of its conclusions, it sets forth sufficient facts to justify legal relief. * * * In our view the facts in the amended complaint are insufficient to state a cause of action for duress, menace, fraud, or mistake, but they do set out sufficient elements to justify rescission of a consent because of undue influence. We summarize our conclusions on each of these points.

1. No duress or menace has been pleaded. Duress consists in unlawful confinement of another's person, or relatives or property, which causes him to consent to a transaction through fear. * * * Duress is often used interchangeably with menace [citation] but in California menace is technically a threat of duress or a threat of injury to the person, property, or character of another. (Civ.Code, § 1570.) We agree with respondent's contention that neither duress nor menace was involved in this case, because the action or threat in duress or menace must be unlawful, and a threat to take legal action is not unlawful unless the party making the threat knows the falsity of his claim. * * * The amended complaint shows in substance that the school representatives announced their intention to initiate suspension and dismissal proceedings under Education Code, sections 13403, 13408 et seq. at a time when the filing of such proceedings was not only their legal right but their positive duty as school officials. Although the filing of such proceedings might be extremely damaging to plaintiff's reputation, the injury would remain incidental so long as the school officials acted in good faith in the performance of their duties. * * * Neither duress nor menace was present as a ground for rescission.

2. Nor do we find a cause of action for fraud, either actual or constructive. (Civ.Code, §§ 1571 to 1574.) Actual fraud involves conscious misrepresentation, or concealment, or non-disclosure of a material fact which induces the innocent party to enter the contract. * * * A complaint for fraud must plead misrepresentation, knowledge of falsity, intent to induce reliance, justifiable reliance, and resulting damage. * * * While the amended complaint charged misrepresentation, it failed to assert the elements of knowledge of falsity, intent to induce reliance, and justifiable reliance. A cause of action for actual fraud was therefore not stated. * * * Constructive fraud arises on a breach of duty by one in a confidential or fiduciary relationship to another which induces justifiable reliance by the latter to his prejudice. (Civ.Code, § 1573.) Plaintiff has attempted to bring himself within this category, for the

amended complaint asserts the existence of a confidential relationship between the school superintendent and principal as agents of the defendant, and the plaintiff. Such a confidential relationship may exist whenever a person with justification places trust and confidence in the integrity and fidelity of another. * * * Plaintiff, however, sets forth no facts to support his conclusion of a confidential relationship between the representatives of the school district and himself, other than that the parties bore the relationship of employer and employee to each other. Under prevailing judicial opinion no presumption of a confidential relationship arises from the bare fact that parties to a contract are employer and employee; rather, additional ties must be brought out in order to create the presumption of a confidential relationship between the two. The absence of a confidential relationship between employer and employee is especially apparent where, as here, the parties were negotiating to bring about a termination of their relationship. In such a situation each party is expected to look after his own interests, and a lack of confidentiality is implicit in the subject matter of their dealings. We think the allegations of constructive fraud were inadequate.

3. As to mistake, the amended complaint fails to disclose any facts which would suggest that consent had been obtained through a mistake of fact or of law. The material facts of the transaction were known to both parties. Neither party was laboring under any misapprehension of law of which the other took advantage. * * *

4. However, the pleading does set out a claim that plaintiff's consent to the transaction had been obtained through the use of undue influence.

Undue influence, in the sense we are concerned with here, is a shorthand legal phrase used to describe persuasion which tends to be coercive in nature, persuasion which overcomes the will without convincing the judgment. The hallmark of such persuasion is high pressure, a pressure which works on mental, moral, or emotional weakness to such an extent that it approaches the boundaries of coercion. In this sense, undue influence has been called overpersuasion. [citation] Misrepresentations of law or fact are not essential to the charge, for a person's will may be overborne without misrepresentation. By statutory definition undue influence includes "taking an unfair advantage of another's weakness of mind; or * * * taking a grossly oppressive and unfair advantage of another's necessities or distress." (Civ.Code § 1575.) While most reported cases of undue influence involve persons who bear a confidential relationship to one another, a confidential or authoritative relationship between the parties need not be present when the undue influence involves unfair advantage taken of another's weakness or distress. [citations] * * *

In essence undue influence involves the use of excessive pressure to persuade one vulnerable to such pressure, pressure applied by a dominant subject to a servient object. In combination, the elements of undue susceptibility in the servient person and excessive pressure by the dominating person make the latter's influence undue, for it results in the apparent will of the servient person being in fact the will of the dominant person.

Undue susceptibility may consist of total weakness of mind which leaves a person entirely without understanding (Civ.Code § 38); or, a lesser weakness which destroys the capacity of a person to make a contract even though he is not totally incapacitated. (Civ.Code, § 39); * * * or, the first element in our equation, a still lesser weakness which provides sufficient grounds to rescind a contract for undue influence. (Civ.Code, § 1575).

Such lesser weakness need not be longlasting nor wholly incapacitating, but may be merely a lack of full vigor due to age * * * physical condition * * * emotional anguish * * * or a combination of such factors. The reported cases have usually involved elderly, sick, senile persons alleged to have executed wills or deeds under pressure. (Malone v. Malone, 155 Cal.App.2d 161, 317 P.2d 65 [constant importuning of a senile husband]; Stewart v. Marvin, 139 Cal.App.2d 769, 294 P.2d 114 [persistent nagging of elderly spouse].) In some of its aspects this lesser weakness could perhaps be called weakness of spirit. But whatever name we give it, this first element of undue influence resolves itself into a lessened capacity of the object to make a free contract.

In the present case plaintiff has pleaded that such weakness at the time he signed his resignation prevented him from freely and competently applying his judgment to the problem before him. Plaintiff declares he was under severe mental and emotional strain at the time because he had just completed the process of arrest, questioning, booking, and release on bail and had been without sleep for forty hours. It is possible that exhaustion and emotional turmoil may wholly incapacitate a person from exercising his judgment. As an abstract question of pleading, plaintiff has pleaded that possibility and sufficient allegations to state a case for rescission.

Undue influence in its second aspect involves an application of excessive strength by a dominant subject against a servient object. Judicial consideration of this second element in undue influence has been relatively rare, for there are few cases denying persons who persuade but do not misrepresent the benefit of their bargain. Yet logically, the same legal consequences should apply to the results of excessive strength as to the results of undue weakness. Whether from weakness on one side, or strength on the other, or a combination of the two, undue influence occurs whenever there results "that kind of influence or supremacy of one mind over another by which that other is prevented from acting according to his own wish or judgment." Undue influence involves a type of mismatch which our statute calls unfair advantage. (Civ.Code, § 1575.) Whether a person of subnormal capacities has been subjected to ordinary force or a person of normal capacities subjected to extraordinary force, the match is equally out of balance. If will has been overcome against judgment, consent may be rescinded.

The difficulty, of course, lies in determining when the forces of persuasion have overflowed their normal banks and become oppressive flood waters. There are second thoughts to every bargain, and hindsight is still better than foresight. Undue influence cannot be used as a pretext to avoid bad bargains or escape from bargains which refuse to come up to expectations. A woman who buys a dress on impulse, which on critical inspection by her best friend turns out to be less fashionable than she had thought, is not legally entitled to set aside the sale on the ground that the saleswoman used all her wiles to close the sale. A man who buys a tract of desert land in the expectation that it is in the immediate path of the city's growth and will become another Palm Springs, an expectation cultivated in glowing terms by the seller, cannot rescind his bargain when things turn out differently. If we are temporarily persuaded against our better judgment to do something about which we later have second thoughts, we must abide the consequences of the risks inherent in managing our own affairs. * * *

However, overpersuasion is generally accompanied by certain characteristics which tend to create a pattern. The pattern usually involves several of the following elements: (1) discussion of the transaction at an unusual or inappropriate time, (2) consummation of the transaction in an unusual place, (3) insistent demand that the business be finished at once, (4) extreme emphasis on untoward consequences of delay, (5) the use of multiple persuaders by the dominant side against a single servient party, (6) absence of third-party advisers to the servient party, (7) statements that there is no time to consult financial advisers or attorneys. If a number of these elements are simultaneously present, the persuasion may be characterized as excessive. * * *

The difference between legitimate persuasion and excessive pressure, like the difference between seduction and rape, rests to a considerable extent in the manner in which the parties go about their business. For example, if a day or two after Odorizzi's release on bail the superintendent of the school district had called him into his office during business hours and directed his attention to those provisions of the Education Code compelling his leave of absence and authorizing his suspension, on the filing of written charges, had told him that the District contemplated filing written charges against him, had pointed out the alternative of resignation available to him, had informed him he was free to consult counsel or any adviser he wished and to consider the matter overnight and return with his decision the next day, it is extremely unlikely that any complaint about the use of excessive pressure could ever have been made against the school district. * * *

But, according to the allegations of the complaint, this is not the way it happened, and if it had happened that way, plaintiff would never have resigned. * * *

Plaintiff has thus pleaded both subjective and objective elements entering the undue influence equation and stated sufficient facts to put in issue the question whether his free will had been overborne by defendant's agents at a time when he was unable to function in a normal manner. * * * The question cannot be resolved by an analysis of pleading but requires a finding of fact.

We express no opinion on the merits of plaintiff's case * * *.

The judgment is reversed.

Notes

1. Undue influence originated in equity and developed parallel to the law's concept of duress. The elements are (a) one party is under some pre-existing influence of another, and (b) an undue use of that influence to the gain of the person holding it and detriment to the other. The "position of influence" is the position of trust and confidence that equity has been so astute to regulate. See Eisenberg, The Bargain Principle and Its Limits, 95 Harv.L.Rev. 741, 773–78 (1982).

We have referred to the present scope of the relationship of "trust and confidence" and particularly emphasized the obligation of the person holding the position to disclose. While the failure to disclose fully may be one of the means of exercising undue influence, the concept is more extensive and may exist even though all facts are revealed. Undue influence has also been called "fraud" (as has duress); but this seems to further dilute the meaning of a word that cannot stand much more dilution. Unlike fraud, undue influence does not necessarily require tampering with the complainant's comprehension of the facts: tampering with judgment is enough. Unlike duress, undue influence does not involve overcoming the complainant's will but in misguiding it.

So much for the inescapable definition of undue influence. Unfortunately the definition has apparently unraveled anyhow—largely with the assistance of the Field Code [1] and its relatives. Thus undue influence is said to include the taking of unfair advantage of another's weakness of mind. This negates the necessity of any relationship of "trust and confidence" between the parties except in the general sense that the great legion of the unhinged are the wards of society as a whole. Nor is any actual "influence" exercised by the defendant necessarily required—for the mentally weak complainant may have initiated the whole transaction. The "weakness of mind" we refer to is a vaporous sort lacking precise definition. It must be a mental deficiency that is insufficient to warrant the complainant's commitment, since that transaction would be void, not voidable. Equity's solicitude for the weak is well grounded. The avoidance of unequal bargains between persons of unequal mental qualities is thoroughly justifiable. Only the characterization of the wrong as "undue influence" may be questioned.

Undue influence has also been said to include taking a grossly oppressive and unfair advantage of another's necessities and distress.[2] The same questions exist. Here again a relationship of trust or confidence is not required. Nor need the party benefitted be the one responsible for the complainant's necessity or distress—he may even have been importuned to make the bargain. The term "influence" seems an inept description where the parties are in markedly unequal economic bargaining positions, although their dealings are otherwise to be considered at arms' length. These include the wide range of bargains properly denounced as "unconscionable," "grossly inequitable," "the result of sharp practice," etc., as well as the "grossly oppressive" phrase that has found its way into the statutes.

The restitutionary consequences of "undue influence" are affected by its equitable origin. Strictly speaking the rescission of a bargain because of undue influence would require a suit for that purpose—as contrasted to the possible avoidance in pais for common law duress. The issue of undue influence should be determined without a jury—again in contrast to duress. Perhaps a sound reason for this exists, particularly on such issues as mental weakness, where the nuances of medical psychology should not be entrusted to jury interpretation.

2. *Effect of Equitable Undue Influence on "Business Compulsion."* If undue influence *does* include "taking advantage of another's necessity and distress" and if (as must be conceded) undue influence is a ground for rescinding an executed bargain, then the effect on business transactions could be marked. Actually, for obvious reasons, the doctrine has been cautiously applied here. Rarely does the "unfair taking advantage of another's necessities or distress" stand alone as the ground for avoiding a particular transaction. But the extension that has recently occurred in so-called "business compulsion" must be attributed to these equitable notions as well as to the recent prominence given to the equitable doctrine of "unconscionability" in commercial transactions.

C. UNCONSCIONABILITY

The "Chancellor's Conscience" has been the benchmark of equitable jurisdiction. The standard of good conscience is the standard of equitable relief.

1. See Redford v. Weller, 27 S.D. 334, 131 N.W. 296 (1911), for an account of the relationship of the South Dakota provision to the original Field Code.

2. Redford v. Weller, supra note 1.

"Unconscionability" is thus an avatar of inequity itself—descriptive rather than definitive. The word exists at a level of abstraction that had best be left alone. By definition (if the expression can now be excused) unconscionability is felt rather than reasoned.

Remedial analysis need not await enlightenment from deep thought. Subcategories have been developed to facilitate the determination of appropriate remedies. Professor Arthur Leff, Unconscionability and the Code—The Emperor's New Clause, 115 U.Pa.L.Rev. 485 (1967), suggested the categories of "procedural unconscionability" and "substantive unconscionability." Texts and decisions accept these characterizations.[1] Basically the distinction is between unconscionable conduct extrinsic to, but inducing, the contract ("procedural") and a contract itself unconscionable, either because of intrinsic unfairness or internally unfair terms ("substantive").

Professor Dobbs, Remedies § 10.7 (1973), discerns a third category which he terms "administrative unconscionability." He cites the Uniform Consumer Credit Code § 6.111(1)(c), which provides for the injunctive remedy against "fraudulent or unconscionable conduct in the collection of debts arising from consumer credit sales."

To sort out appropriate remedial alternatives, the foregoing categories are modified to accommodate the emphasis of this course. With deference, we relabel Professor Dobbs's classification of "administrative unconscionability" as "remedial unconscionability" and expand the category.

Procedural Unconscionability

Procedural unconscionability consists of practices like deceit, misrepresentation, non-disclosure, duress, undue influence, sharp practice, fiduciary breaches, contract breaches, etc. The complainant is induced, pressured, or duped into a transaction (commercial or otherwise). Since remedies for "unconscionable" conduct are elaborated upon throughout this book, the subject is dropped here.

Substantive Unconscionability

This notion has been presented by the authorities as including both (1) intrinsically bad bargains and (2) harshly unfair contract clauses like confessions of judgment, restrictions on remedies for breach of warranty, forfeiture and acceleration clauses upon default, and many others not yet invented. Since these clauses are invocable only upon default, the second subcategory may be more conveniently reclassified under the heading of "Remedial Unconscionability."

This leaves as "substantive unconscionability" only the very bad bargain, untainted by dubious conduct or by dramatically one-sided penalty provisions. Established learning, briefly stated, is that a contract supported by consideration is legal and that damages will lie for its breach. Equity, on the other hand, declines remedies on an *executory* contract substantially deficient in consideration. Modern practice may uniformly refuse any remedy on that

1. See D. Dobbs, Remedies § 10.7 (1973); J. White & R. Summers, Handbook of the Law under the Uniform Commercial Code §§ 4–1 to –9 (3d ed. 1988); and Johnson v. Mobil Oil Corp., 415 F.Supp. 264 (E.D.Mich.1976). Professor Eisenberg states, however, that the distinctions fail to "provide much help." The Bargain Principle and Its Limits, 95 Harv.L.Rev. 741, 800 (1982).

contract—a result apparently sanctioned under the U.C.C. For a *fully* executed contract, the claim of substantive unconscionability rings hollow.

Remedial Unconscionability

If the bargain itself is essentially fair, the court should let it stand. Judges may delete clauses imposing unnecessarily harsh consequences for default or unfair remedial advantages by reformation or selective enforcement.[2]

Where remedial unconscionability takes the form of tricky or harassive collection practices, the appropriate remedies need not involve the integrity of the bargain, but may be found in injunctions or proceedings for abuse of process.

VOCKNER v. ERICKSON

Supreme Court of Alaska, 1986.
712 P.2d 379.

RABINOWITZ, CHIEF JUSTICE. * * * In the spring of 1975, Erickson, then seventy-three years of age, ran an advertisement offering a twelve-person boarding house for sale. Bernd Vockner, a real estate agent, answered the advertisement and arranged to meet with Erickson. When Vockner arrived at the boarding house on the evening of April 30, 1975, Erickson informed him that the boarding house was not for sale, but that she desired to sell her twelve-unit apartment house located on East 13th Avenue in Anchorage.

After discussing the possible purchase of the apartment house, Vockner took Erickson with him to inspect the building. Upon returning to the boarding house, Vockner prepared an earnest money agreement with forms he had brought with him, detailing the terms of the sale.

Although Erickson initially asked for $265,000, they settled on a sale price of $250,000. Vockner agreed to assume Erickson's existing deed of trust to the Small Business Administration for approximately $90,000, and to make a down payment of $10,000. Additionally, Vockner promised to execute a second deed of trust in favor of Erickson for $153,365.46 with 8½ interest, payable at the rate of $500 per month commencing on August 13, 1976. The earnest money agreement also provided for a balloon payment in the amount of $15,000 on August 13, 1976. The parties signed the earnest money agreement that evening, and Vockner delivered to Erickson an earnest money check for $1,000.

Subsequently, Erickson became dissatisfied with the agreement for two reasons: another purchaser had offered her $265,000, and she realized that the $500 a month payment would not even cover the interest as it accrued on the note. She expressed her dissatisfaction with the purchase price in a letter to Vockner on May 23, 1975, and returned the $1,000 earnest money. Vockner responded, informing Erickson that he expected performance. Erickson contin-

2. Although this Chapter focuses on unconscionable bargains, unrelated forms of remedial unconscionability have been identified.

Others have applied the expression "remedial unconscionability" to excessive damages verdicts or judgments. In other words, the oppressor oppressed. The only relief for excessive tort judgments is through appellate review or legislative caps on noneconomic damages. See Chapters 2 and 7.

If excessive contract damages, though "foreseeable," far exceed the consideration the breaching party received, the opponent may characterize them as "remedially unconscionable." If the epithet sticks, the court may limit plaintiff's recovery to reliance expenses. Kiffin, A Newly Identified Contract Unconscionability: Unconscionability of Remedy, 63 Notre Dame L.Rev. 247 (1988), discusses § 351(3), Restatement (Second) of Contracts (1981).

ued to resist complying with the earnest money agreement. Consequently, Vockner filed a complaint for specific performance and in the alternative for damages. Erickson believed that she had to comply because an attorney had informally advised her that Vockner would win and because of her husband's ill health, so she filed a *pro per* answer stating that she was ready to perform the earnest money agreement.

The earnest money agreement was then forwarded to Alaska Title Guarantee for preparation of the closing documents. Paul Nangle, the attorney retained to prepare the closing documents, discovered that the earnest money agreement did not contain a payoff date. Nangle called Vockner's attorney, who suggested that Nangle insert a thirty-year term. The superior court found that Erickson was never asked whether she agreed to the thirty-year term.

Vockner and Erickson then proceeded to close the sale. The promissory note provided in part for a thirty-year term with a $311,000 balloon payment at the end. The closing agent specifically remembered explaining all of the terms of the contract to Erickson. Four-and-a-half years later, Erickson filed a *pro per* complaint seeking reformation and payment of accrued interest, or return of the property. This complaint, later amended, also named as a defendant the then owner of the apartment house, as Vockner had sold the property within three or four months of purchase.

The case proceeded to trial with the thirty-year term as one of the primary issues. Vockner testified that he discussed the thirty-year term with Erickson before drawing up the agreement. Erickson testified that she did not know about the thirty-year term until she signed the documents at the closing. The superior court found that Erickson was never asked if she agreed to the term, but that she was informed about it before signing the closing papers.

The superior court held that Erickson was not under duress sufficient to invalidate the transaction. In so deciding, the court concluded that Erickson had viable alternatives to bowing under to any duress that the filing of the specific performance action might have generated.

The superior court rejected the contention that Vockner or his attorney had committed an intentional misrepresentation. * * *

Overall, however, the superior court ruled that under the standards of § 208 of the Restatement (Second) of Contracts the contract was "clearly unconscionable." * * *

Finally, the superior court held that laches did not bar Erickson's action. Erickson filed her case four-and-a-half years after selling the apartment building to Vockner. The court reasoned that if this were a legal cause of action rather than an equitable cause of action, the applicable statute of limitations would be six years. The superior court further concluded that the passage of the four-and-a-half years had not prejudiced Vockner in any manner.

Based upon the foregoing rulings the superior court reformed the parties' agreement and entered judgment against Vockner for the principal amount of $52,559.72, an amount sufficient to amortize the principal and interest from June 1975 to June 1983, and $126,894.54, with 8.5% interest, due in monthly installments of $1,075.36, an amount that would amortize the principal and interest over the term of the thirty-year note.

Lastly, the superior court ordered Vockner to execute a deed of trust in favor of Erickson, encumbering other real property in an amount at least 10%

greater than the total amount of judgment. In return for this second deed of trust, the court ordered Erickson to convey her interest in the deed of trust and promissory note of June 30, 1975 to Vockner.

In ruling that the contract was unconscionable, the superior court relied in part on § 208 of the Restatement (Second) of Contracts. Section 208 provides that:

> "If a contract or term thereof is unconscionable at the time the contract is made a court may refuse to enforce the contract, or may enforce the remainder of the contract without the unconscionable term, or may so limit the application of any unconscionable term as to avoid any unconscionable result." [1]

The Restatement does not provide an explicit definition of unconscionability. It does identify factors, however, that support a finding of unconscionability. Additionally, it contains the following significant comment:

> "Theoretically it is possible for a contract to be oppressive taken as a whole, even though there is no weakness in the bargaining process and no single term which is in itself unconscionable. Ordinarily, however, an unconscionable contract involves other factors as well as an overall imbalance."

Concerning these "other factors," in comment b the Restatement quotes § 2–302 of the UCC, comment 1, which states: "[t]he principle is one of the prevention of oppression and unfair surprise and not of disturbance of allocation of risks because of superior bargaining power." (citation) [2]

[T]he superior court articulated numerous factors relating to the parties' respective circumstances and to the terms of the agreement that led it to the conclusion that the contract was unconscionable. The court considered determinative that: Erickson is elderly and would be 103 years old when the large balloon payment was due; the balloon payment at the end of thirty years would have been $311,000; and the value of the security would decrease over the course of this thirty-year term.[3] In addition the superior court also considered several indicia of unconscionability, which it termed "quasi-coercion." These were that Vockner filed suit for specific performance and damages; that Vockner hired counsel while Erickson was unrepresented in that suit; and that

1. [Footnotes renumbered.] Restatement (Second) of Contracts § 208 at 107 (1981). Comment a indicates the scope of this provision:

> "[T]he policy against unconscionable contracts or terms applies to a wide variety of types of conduct. The determination that a contract * * * is or is not unconscionable is made in light of its setting, purpose, and effect. Relevant factors include weakness in the contracting process like those involved in more specific rules as to contractual capacity, fraud, and other invalidating causes."

2. In Morrow v. New Moon Homes, Inc., 548 P.2d 279, 292 n. 43 (Alaska 1976) we said that "unconscionability":

> "has generally been recognized to include an absence of meaningful choice on the part of one of the parties together with contract terms which are unreasonably favorable to the other party."

Section 208, comment c to the Restatement states, "Inadequacy of consideration does not of itself invalidate a bargain, but gross disparity in the values exchanged may be an important factor in a determination that a contract is unconscionable."

Section 208, comment d to the Restatement states:

> "A bargain is not unconscionable merely because the parties to it are unequal in bargaining position, nor even because the inequality results in an allocation of risks to the weaker party. But gross inequality of bargaining power, together with terms unreasonably favorable to the stronger party, may confirm indications that the transaction involved elements of deception or compulsion, or may show that the weaker party had no meaningful choice."

3. In regard to the deteriorating security factor, the superior court further observed that it was "[c]ertainly a situation approaching that of near insanity for anyone to enter into a deal like this."

Vockner had an advantage over Erickson due to his real estate training. The superior court observed that, "They did not approach this transaction on an equal level of knowledge[;] [t]he cards were stacked in favor of Vockner with respect to making the particular bargain." [4]

Based upon our review of the record and in part for the reasons articulated by the superior court, we hold that the superior court's determination of unconscionability under section 208 of the Restatement (Second) of Contracts should be affirmed.[5] Additionally, we affirm because Vockner rather than Erickson retained the interest on the $6,000 annual interest that was due but not payable under the terms of the promissory note. Erickson should be the party earning interest on the interest. By depriving her of this interest, she would have lost approximately $600,000 over the thirty years, assuming 8% interest compounded monthly. Given the fact that $600,000 in thirty years is worth approximately $55,000, the promissory note had an actual fair market value of only $98,000.[6] This fact, in addition to those factors relied upon by the superior court, persuades us that the superior court's determination of unconscionability should be sustained.[7]

4. See Campbell Soup Co. v. Wentz, 172 F.2d 80, 84 (3d Cir.1948) where the court held that although the contract in question was legal, the contract taken as a whole drove too harsh a bargain for a court of conscience to assist. One commentator, in discussing § 2–302 of the UCC stated that:

> "Comment 1 goes to some lengths to establish a climate in which courts will feel emboldened to strike directly at contracts * * * which appear too heavily weighted in favor of one of the parties; that is to act, in some measures at least, as a tribunal of constitutional review applying 'bill-of-rights' prescriptions to the parties' private legislation."

M.P. Ellinghaus, In Defense of Unconscionability, 78 Yale L.J. 757, 773 (1969).

5. A determination of unconscionability is made as a matter of law. Restatement (Second) Contracts § 208 comment f at 111 (1981).

6. Erickson argues in part, on appeal, that were interest to accrue and be compounded annually, the balloon payment due in the year 2005 would be $568,498.

Erickson further persuasively argues that:

> If the note is construed so as not to require compounding of interest—i.e., payment of interest in year 29 on the accrued unpaid interest of years 1 through 28—then the balloon would "only" be $311,000 in 2005. While this "mitigates" the problem concerning the diminishing collateral, it creates an additional shocking abuse. Without compounding of interest, the *actual* present value of the note Mrs. Erickson received, even assuming the 8.5 interest rate is and was fair market, was some $50,000 less than its face value of $153,000. (The present value of $311,000 to be received in 30 years is some $24,000, rather than the $75,000 or so that the balloon should be worth at present value if the $153,000 note were to represent $153,000 in present value.) Thus, Mrs. Erickson lost 1/3 of her equity the instant she "accepted" the 30-year note at closing.
>
> If the note does not require compounding the interest accrued, the actual effective rate of interest declines each year. That is, while the $12,000 annual interest (paid or accrued) is 8.5% of the balance in year 1, it is something less than 4% in year 29 ($12,000 interest paid on accrued balance of $300,000+). Not only is Erickson thereby deprived of the interest rate for which she bargained, but the decreasing interest rate works as a powerful disincentive for future owners to refinance the property; refinancing was, effectively, the only hope that Erickson had of actually securing in her lifetime the benefits of the bargain she thought she was making—present and future payments with a present value of $250,000.

7. Inherent in this holding is our rejection of Vockner's argument that the superior court erred in finding unconscionability where there is no procedural unconscionability in the contract. In support of this contention Vockner argues that the trial court must find both procedural and substantive abuses before decreeing a contract unconscionable. [citations]

However, not all commentators agree that the court must find both procedural and substantive unconscionability. [citations] Even Williston, who adheres to the concept, states:

> Essentially a sliding scale is invoked which disregards the regularity of the procedural process of the contract formation, that creates the terms, in proportion to the greater harshness or unreasonableness of the substantive terms themselves.

15 S. Williston, Law of Contracts § 1763A at 226–27 (Jaeger Ed.1972).

Adopting Williston's analysis we think the superior court's conclusions that both procedur-

As noted at the outset, the superior court reformed the contract to provide that Vockner was to pay $1,075.36 in monthly installments, the amount that would amortize the principal and interest over the duration of the thirty-year note. Vockner contends that the superior court erred in reforming the agreement, based upon its finding of unconscionability, because "there was no finding of fraud, mistake, or overreaching, and because the contract represented the true intentions of the parties." [8] We hold that the superior court did not err in its judgment that partially reformed the contract between Vockner and Erickson.

Courts have reformed contracts to avoid unconscionable results. [citation] Professor Dobbs states that "[t]he unconscionable contract may be reformed to limit the unconscionable clause and then enforced as reformed." D. Dobbs, Law of Remedies § 10.1 at 654 (1973). Professor Dobbs further observes that "[I]f it is understood that this does not mean reformation to a true agreement, but reformation to minimum legal standards, then remedy seems entirely suitable." * * *

The superior court's actions, in our view, comport with Professor Dobbs' analysis that the aim of reformation in these circumstances is to bring the contract in conformity with minimal standards of conscionability.[9]

Vockner's final contention is that the superior court erred in rejecting his defense of laches. Vockner maintains that Erickson's four-and-a-half year delay in seeking reformation was unreasonable and prejudicial. The superior court rejected Vockner's laches defense on the grounds that Vockner did not suffer substantial prejudice, and that although late, Erickson instituted the action within the time limitations of the analogous statute of limitations. * * * We have also noted that where there is a long delay, a lesser degree of prejudice need be shown. Pavlik v. State, 637 P.2d 1045, 1048 (Alaska 1981). Here the record fails to show that Vockner has been unduly prejudiced. As the superior court pointed out, the delay did not prejudice Vockner in his conduct of the trial. Additionally, Vockner's contention that the delay in Erickson's bringing this action prejudiced him because he subsequently sold the property is meritless. Vockner sold the property within three or four months of purchasing it from Erickson. To successfully advance a claim of prejudice now, Vockner would have to establish that Erickson unreasonably delayed in not filing her suit within the three to four month period before he resold the property. This he has not done. Although Erickson did delay for four-and-one-half years in filing her suit, "[s]ufficient material prejudice will not be inferred * * * from mere lapse of a substantial period of time." Young v. Williams, 583 P.2d 201, 204 (Alaska 1978).

Since we do not entertain a definite and firm conviction that the superior court was mistaken in its laches ruling we affirm the superior court's exercise of its discretion in rejecting Vockner's laches defense.[10]

Affirmed.

al and substantive unconscionability were proven, if indeed both are required, are not erroneous on the facts of this record.

8. In the usual situation unconscionability is raised as an affirmative defense. The normal remedy when the court finds unconscionability is for the court to refuse specific performance. [citations]

9. Within a few months of his purchase of the property from Erickson, Vockner resold the property for $290,000. Thus Vockner is not losing the benefit of what he bargained for and the nonpunitive nature of the remedy, is served.

10. The superior court held that from the point of the subsequent sale it would have been impossible to undo the transaction.

Notes

1. *Unconscionability's Equity Origins: Right to Jury Trial.* County Asphalt, Inc. v. Lewis Welding and Engineering Corp., 444 F.2d 372, 378–79 (2d Cir.1971). Defendant contracted to erect two asphalt plants for the plaintiff for $460,000 cash and two old plants as trade-ins. Plaintiff sued for damages for breach of contract, breach of warranties, etc. Defendant counterclaimed for the unpaid price and other damages. A collateral issue arose. Plaintiff asserted that a provision in the contract limiting defendant's liability for consequential damages was unconscionable:

"On the basis of a provision in the contract agreements that the defendant 'shall in no event have any liability for loss of profits, losses caused by shutdowns or delays or other similar or dissimilar consequential damages,' its counsel moved in advance of trial that all claims of County Asphalt for consequential damages be dismissed and asked the court to make a preliminary determination of the issue. The judge denied the application for a preliminary determination but reserved decision on the motion. After a large part of County Asphalt's case had been presented, including the negotiations leading up to the execution of the contracts, the court, in the absence of the jury, ruled that the claims for consequential damages should be dismissed. We agree.

"Plaintiff's contention that it was entitled to a jury determination of the issue of unconscionability is completely without merit. Section 2–719(3) of the UCC specifically provides that:

" 'Consequential damages may be limited or excluded unless the limitation or exclusion is unconscionable. Limitation of consequential damages for injury to the person in the case of consumer goods is prima facie unconscionable but limitation of damages where the loss is commercial is not.'

"Whether such a limitation of damages is unconscionable in a particular contract is expressly made a question of law for determination by the court. This is provided for by Section 2–302 of the UCC: * * *

" '(2) When it is claimed or appears *to the court* that the contract or any clause thereof may be unconscionable the parties shall be afforded a reasonable opportunity to present evidence as to its commercial setting, purpose and effect *to aid the court in making the determination.*' (Emphasis added.)

"The official comments of the draftsmen of this section read in pertinent part as follows:

" 'The present section is addressed to the court, and the decision is to be made by it. The commercial evidence referred to in subsection (2) is for the court's consideration, not the jury's. Only the agreement which results from the court's action on these matters is to be submitted to the general triers of the facts.' (UCC § 2–302, Comment 3.)

"It is the intent of the Code to give the court the power to police explicitly against the contracts or clauses which they find to be unconscionable. UCC § 2–302, Comment 1. * * * Although a hearing at which the parties 'shall be afforded a reasonable opportunity to present evidence,' § 2–302(2), may be held at any time after the pleadings disclose the possibility that the limitation of damages may be unconscionable, it has been suggested 'that the hearing should not be postponed until the time of trial, and if the objection of unconscionability is raised at the time of trial the evidence thereon should not be heard by the jury, because of the possibility that it might tend to confuse or prejudice the jury. In any event, the fact that a hearing is held does not, regardless of when it is held, alter the status of the question of conscionability as one of law rather than one of fact.' Anderson, Uniform Commercial Code, Vol. 1 at 407 (2d ed. 1970).

"Plaintiff's argument that its right to a jury trial on the issue of unconscionability is guaranteed by the seventh amendment of the Constitution hardly merits consideration. In 1791, when the amendment was adopted, the discretionary power to grant equitable relief according to the 'conscience' of the chancellor was so unmistakably a matter for the equity side rather than the law side of the court no further discussion of the constitutional ground is warranted."

2. *Remedies for Unconscionability Under the U.C.C.* Section 2–302(1) provides: "If the court as a matter of law finds the contract or any clause of the contract to have been unconscionable at the time it was made the court may refuse to enforce the contract, or it may enforce the remainder of the contract without the unconscionable clause, or it may so limit the application of any unconscionable clause as to avoid any unconscionable result."

This is expansive authority, but it leaves detailed remedial solutions to the actual event. Always-cited Williams v. Walker-Thomas Furniture Co., 350 F.2d 445 (D.C.Cir.1965), frames the problem. A furniture store with a low-income clientele developed an installment merchandising scheme for its customers to buy on credit subject to an extraordinarily severe security provision. The contracts were drafted as leases with the store retaining title until the customer paid for the item; moreover all installment payments were prorated over all items the customer had purchased rather than being applied to any individual item. Consequently, as long as the customer owed something on the whole account, no single item was ever paid for. In addition, the store still owned everything. Williams had purchased many household items between 1957 and 1962; she had paid about $1400 during the period. The opinion recites what happened:

"[P]rior to the last purchase [Williams] had reduced the balance in her account to $164. The last purchase, a stereo set, raised the balance due to $678. Significantly, at the time of this and the preceding purchases, [the store] was aware of [her] financial position. The reverse side of the stereo contract listed the name of [her] social worker and her $218 monthly stipend from the government. Nevertheless, with full knowledge that [she] had to feed, clothe and support both herself and seven children on this amount, [the store] sold her a $514 stereo set." Williams v. Walker-Thomas Furniture Co., 350 F.2d 445, 448 (D.C.Cir.1965).

Inevitably Williams defaulted. In 1962 the store sought to replevy everything she had purchased since 1957. The Court of Appeals referred to the U.C.C. which had not yet been adopted in the District, reversed two lower court decisions, and held that the arrangement could be held unconscionable and the contract unenforceable. It remanded, but left the remedy dangling.

The problem, therefore is: bearing in mind that there is no indication that any of the merchandise, including the stereo, was overpriced, what should the appropriate remedy be? (a) rescission and restitution; (b) an injunction against the enforcement of the offensive security provision; (c) an "equitable" limitation upon the seller's claim; (d) total denial of recovery of the purchase price; or (e) some other "equitable" remedy?

3. Jones v. Star Credit Corp., 59 Misc.2d 189, 193, 298 N.Y.S.2d 264, 267 (Sup.Ct.1969). The plaintiff had paid $619.88 on a total contract price for a freezer of $1,234.80 (including time charges, tax and insurance). The maximum value of the freezer was found to be $300. Held: "[I]t is apparent that defendant has already been amply compensated. In accordance with [U.C.C. § 2–302(1)], the application of the payment provision should be limited to amounts already paid by

the plaintiffs and the contract be reformed and amended by changing the payment called for therein to equal the amount of payments actually so paid by plaintiffs."

4. Statutes such as U.C.C. §§ 3–303 and 3–304 now apply to the *Williams* situation. In addition, consumer protection acts that vest regulatory and punitive powers in state agencies now provide more efficient and effective remedies than individual private actions by retail customers.

5. Professor Richard Epstein comments: "One of the major conceptual tools used by courts in their assault upon private agreements has been the doctrine of unconscionability. That doctrine has a place in contract law, but it is not the one usually assigned it by its advocates. The doctrine should not, in my view, allow courts to act as roving commissions to set aside those agreements whose substantive terms they find objectionable. Instead, it should be used only to allow courts to police the process whereby private agreements are formed, and in that connection, only to facilitate the setting aside of agreements that are as a matter of probabilities likely to be vitiated by the classical defenses of duress, fraud, or incompetence. * * *.

"Ideally, the unconscionability doctrine protects against fraud, duress and incompetence, without demanding specific proof of any of them. Instead of looking to a writing requirement to control against these abuses, it looks both to the subject matter of the agreements and to the social positions of the persons who enter into them. The difficult question with unconscionability is not whether it works towards a legitimate end, but whether its application comes at too great a price. * * *

"One of the major risks to the seller of personal property is that the goods sold will lose value, be it through use or abuse, more rapidly than the purchase price is paid off. The buyer can, and quite often does, have a 'negative' equity in the goods. The seller, therefore, who takes back a security interest only in the goods sold, runs the real risk that repossession of the single item sold will still leave him with a loss on the transaction as a whole, taking into account the costs of interest and collection. One way to handle this problem is to require the purchaser of the goods to make a larger cash down payment, but that, of course, is something which many buyers, particularly those of limited means, do not want to do. Another alternative is for the buyer to provide the seller with additional collateral; yet here the best collateral is doubtless in goods sold by the seller to the buyer. Other goods already in the possession of the buyer may be of uncertain value, and they may well be subject to prior liens. Again, they may be of a sort that the seller cannot conveniently resell in the ordinary course of his business. Even if the goods are suitable collateral for the loan, it could take a good deal of time and effort for the seller to determine that fact. The 'add-on' clause allows both parties to benefit from the reduction in costs in the setting up of a security arrangement. * * *

"The sense of these clauses, regardless of the particular form which they take, is demonstrated anew, moreover, once we realize that they operate within one very strong constraint, often imposed by statute, which restricts the creditor in a secured transaction to the recovery of principal, interest and costs in cases of default by the buyer. Within the framework of these limitations, the add-on clause can do no harm at all, for it only makes it more certain that the seller will be able to collect that to which on any view he is entitled."

Epstein, Unconscionability: A Critical Reappraisal, 18 J. Law & Econ. 293, 294–95, 302–03, 307–08 (1975) © 1975, University of Chicago.

Professor Eisenberg analyzes *Williams* differently. "[I]f a provision changes the rights that a buyer would otherwise have on nonperformance in a manner the seller knows or should know many buyers would probably not knowingly agree to, it is unconscionable to word the provision in language the seller knows or should know many buyers lack capacity to understand." Eisenberg, The Bargain Principle and Its Limits, 95 Harv.L.Rev. 741, 771 (1982).

BEST v. UNITED STATES NATIONAL BANK OF OREGON

Court of Appeals of Oregon, 1986.

78 Or.App. 1, 714 P.2d 1049.

RICHARDSON, PRESIDING JUDGE. This is a class action challenging the validity of defendant bank's service charge for processing checks drawn against nonsufficient funds (NSF charge). * * *

The common gravamen of plaintiffs' claims is that the bank's NSF charges were unreasonably high. Plaintiffs introduced evidence, for example, that in 1979, although the bank's cost of processing an NSF check was $1.08, its charge was $5.00. * * *

[Plaintiffs] allege that the NSF charge was unconscionable, because it greatly exceeded the bank's cost of processing NSF checks. They sought restitution of the NSF charges they had paid. The trial court ruled that, under Rosboro Lumber Co. v. EBI, 65 Or.App. 679, 672 P.2d 1336 (1983), rev'd on other grounds, 297 Or. 81, 680 P.2d 386 (1984), the doctrine of unconscionability is not a basis for affirmative relief.

Plaintiffs cite Uniform Commercial Code § 2–302 and Restatement (Second) Contracts, § 208 (1979), as the bases of their claim.[1] They contend that the result will be the same whether their claim is analyzed under the UCC or the Restatement. Whether or not that is true, UCC § 2–302 does not apply in this case, because UCC Article 2 is limited to transactions in goods. However, because the Restatement follows UCC § 2–302, see Reporter's Note to § 208, and UCC § 2–302 has been influential in nonsales cases, see Comment *a* to § 208, cases decided under that section are helpful in analyzing plaintiffs' claim.

In *Rosboro Lumber,* the plaintiff sought restitution of workers' compensation insurance premiums it had paid to the defendant, on the basis, *inter alia,* that the defendant had engaged in unconscionable conduct. We analyzed that claim under the Restatement and held that, "although unconscionability may be a defense to the enforceability of a contract, it is not a basis for affirmative relief." We affirmed the dismissal of the plaintiff's unconscionability claim.

Rosboro Lumber is clearly on point and adverse to plaintiffs' claim. They offer a number of suggestions to avoid its holding. First, they point out that the emphasized portion of the following passage from Dobbs on Remedies 707 (1973), which we quoted in *Rosboro Lumber,* supports their claim for restitution:

> "[T]he remedy [for unconscionability] remains essentially defensive, for the plaintiff does not recover damages; he will only be relieved of the contractual

1. [Footnote renumbered.] Restatement (Second) Contracts, § 208 (1979), provides:

"If a contract or term thereof is unconscionable at the time the contract is made a court may refuse to enforce the contract, or may enforce the remainder of the contract without the unconscionable term, or may so limit the application of any unconscionable term as to avoid any unconscionable result."

obligation, *or, possibly, if he has already paid an unconscionable sum, will be allowed restitution to the limits of conscionability.*" (Emphasis supplied.)

Dobbs, however, cites no authority for that assertion and, as discussed below, we have found none. Furthermore, the *holding* of *Rosboro Lumber* is that the doctrine of unconscionability is not a basis for restitution. * * *

Finally, plaintiffs urge us to overrule *Rosboro Lumber.* We decline to do that. We have found no authority anywhere that the doctrine of unconscionability is a basis for restitutionary relief. In W.L. May Co. v. Philco–Ford Corp., 273 Or. 701, 707, 543 P.2d 283 (1975), decided under UCC § 2–302, the court noted that "[n]ormally, the doctrine [of unconscionability] is asserted as an affirmative defense, and it does not appear that it was originally intended as a basis for damage recovery." However, the court expressly left unanswered the question of whether UCC § 2–302 could be used offensively. Cases from other jurisdictions uniformly hold that UCC § 2–302 is not a basis for an award of damages. [citations]

At least one other court has specifically denied restitution in a non-UCC case. In Bennett v. Behring Corp., 466 F.Supp. 689 (S.D.Fla.1979), appeal dismissed, 629 F.2d 393 (5th Cir.1980), property owners brought an action against a developer and others alleging, *inter alia,* that a provision in their deeds requiring them to lease certain recreational facilities was unconscionable. They sought the return of the amounts they had paid under that provision. The court held that the provision was not unconscionable, but it also stated that unconscionability is not a basis for affirmative relief:

> "Plaintiffs [sic] attempt to obtain a judgment for money damages for sums previously collected by [the defendant] under the recreation leases must fail in any event, regardless of a finding of unconscionability. While plaintiffs may be able to recover monetary damages for fraud and/or intentional misrepresentations, as alleged in Counts I and VI, the equitable theory of unconscionability has never been utilized to allow for the affirmative recovery of money damages. * * *
>
> "The Court finds that neither the common law of Florida, nor that of any other state, empowers a court addressing allegations of unconscionability to do more than refuse *enforcement* of the unconscionable section or sections of the contract so as to avoid an unconscionable result." (Emphasis in original; citations omitted.)

Because the doctrine of unconscionability is not a basis for affirmative relief, the trial court was correct in granting the bank's motion for summary judgment against the unconscionability claim. * * *

THOMAS v. JONES

District Court of Appeal of Florida, Fifth District, 1988.
524 So.2d 693.

PER CURIAM. * * * Appellees, approximately one hundred resident mobile home owners in Friendly Adult Estates Mobile Home Park (residents), brought a class action alleging that appellant mobile home park owners had unconscionably raised their lot rental rates. The trial court determined that the residents' claim of unconscionability was maintainable as a class action pursuant to Florida Rule of Civil Procedure 1.220. After a bench trial, the court found the rent increase to have been unconscionable and entered a final judgment in favor of the residents, including an award of attorney's fees. The park owners appeal. We reverse.

A threshold issue in this case is whether a claim of unconscionability can be asserted in a class action. Under the current legal analysis, substantive and procedural unconscionability must both be established to prevail in an unconscionability action. *Substantive* unconscionability generally can be established by alleging and proving that the terms of a contract are onerous, unreasonable, or unfair. It has been held that substantive unconscionability can be asserted in a class action. [citation]

By contrast, *procedural* unconscionability "speaks to the individualized circumstances surrounding each contracting party at the time the contract was entered into." The manner in which a particular contracting party's age, education, intelligence, financial position, business experience, etc. affects that party's bargaining position, and whether such factors permit the party to have a "meaningful choice," vary from individual to individual.

The residents urge on appeal that because of the unique problems facing many similarly situated mobile home residents, a class action is appropriate to assert both substantive and procedural unconscionability. As in this case, many residents own their mobile homes but rent lots from park owners. In contrast to other living arrangements (such as most apartment rentals), if lot rents are raised, mobile home residents lack the option of simply refusing to renew their lease and moving out. Instead, residents must either accept the rent increases, sell their mobile homes, or attempt to move the mobile homes to other sites. The residents in this case conclude that this situation leaves each of them with an "absence of meaningful choice" which is sufficiently similar that the trial court correctly permitted them to assert procedural unconscionability in their class action.

We reject the residents' contentions. It may be true that each resident was faced with similar lot rental increases and left with similar choices. However, procedural unconscionability involves not external factors faced by an individual, such as an onerous contract term or increased rent, but rather the particular *effect* each external factor has on each individual and how the individual *reacts* to such factors. We find, therefore, that because of the basic differences between people, the requirements for procedural unconscionability are too personal, individualized, and subjective to be properly asserted in a class action. The trial court erred in permitting the residents to do so in this case.

This conclusion is supported by this court's opinion in K.D. Lewis Enterprises Corp. v. Smith, 445 So.2d 1032 (Fla. 5th DCA 1984). In that case, tenants brought a counterclaim alleging their landlord did not maintain their apartments and unfairly increased the amount of their rent. This court held that the trial court correctly refused to permit the tenants to appear as representatives of a class of all the tenants in the apartment complex. We reasoned that "[w]hile each tenant may have been affected by the omissions or non-compliance of the landlord, the extent, nature, and effect of such omissions and non-compliance would unquestionably vary from apartment to apartment and from tenant to tenant." * * *

In conclusion, we hold that, as a matter of law, procedural unconscionability can not be asserted in a class action. * * *

Reversed and Remanded.

SHARP, CHIEF JUDGE dissenting. In the context of a claim by tenants in a mobile home park that the park owner is seeking to charge unconscionably high rents through a rent increase, I do not think the class action suit should fail because of a lack of proof of "procedural unconscionability" on the part of the individual tenants. Procedural unconscionability is a technical, and not clearly defined requirement for the common law cause of action relating to relief from onerous contract terms. See discussion in Kohl v. Bay Colony Club Condominium, Inc., 398 So.2d 865 (Fla. 4th DCA); review denied, 408 So.2d 1094 (Fla.1981). As the court stated in *Kohl,* that doctrine does not necessarily apply to statutory causes of action, like this one.

Furthermore, procedural unconscionability may be established in a class action context, where the circumstances of each member of the class demonstrate "the absence of meaningful choice" on the part of each member. I do not think it necessary to delve into the individualized circumstances of each member of the class where the meaningfulness of the choice is negated by a gross inequality of bargaining power. In this case it was established that the plaintiffs were mobile home lot renters who when faced with an outrageous demand for increased rent, have no "meaningful choice" due to their common circumstances. They cannot freely move out of the park because their mobile homes are not truly "mobile." To avoid the enormous expense and disruption of moving, they are forced to pay unconscionable rents.

Notes

1. State Unfair Trade Practice Acts and Consumer Protection Acts usually allow the Attorney General to bring a class action on behalf of all aggrieved consumers. Some "victims" may have been misled, others not; some may be content with their purchases, though not unwilling to accept a rebate. The latter would not, in the absence of the Attorney General's lawsuit, consider themselves to have been treated unconscionably. These class actions, if more than state wide, may be affected by differing measures of fraud damages; and injunctions may encounter jurisdictional problems. See for example Kugler v. Romain, 58 N.J. 522, 279 A.2d 640 (1971).

2. *Statutory Right to Rescind or Cancel Without Cause: "Cooling Off" Period.* One technique to protect consumers from high pressure sales techniques without the onus of establishing the usual substantive elements for a tort damage action or for rescission is to create by statute a "cooling off" period within which the customer may choose to back out. The prototype of such statutes applies to door-to-door home sales usually but not invariably the installment type. Under New York law, the buyer has three business days to cancel a "home solicitation sale." The seller must furnish the buyer with a form clearly stating the buyer's right to cancel within that period. N.Y.Pers.Prop.Law §§ 427, 428, 429 (McKinney 1989).

Cal.Bus. & Prof.Code § 11028, provides that purchase contracts in rural tract subdivisions (as elsewhere defined in the Code) may be rescinded without cause by sending written notice to the subdivider within 14 calendar days of execution.

Chapter 12

REMEDIES FOR MISTAKES

A. MISTAKE IN BARGAINING TRANSACTIONS

1. MISTAKE IN PERFORMANCE

TERRA NOVA INSURANCE CO. v. ASSOCIATES COMMERCIAL CORP.

United States District Court, Eastern District of Wisconsin, 1988.
697 F.Supp. 1048.

TERENCE T. EVANS, DISTRICT JUDGE. It all began in February, 1982. Brian Scharbarth's truck started tormenting him with mechanical troubles on a run from Wisconsin to California. Lesser truckers might have gotten their vehicles repaired, but Scharbarth arranged to have his stolen. Right there at a truck stop in Sparks, Nevada. Sierra Sid's, to be exact. He did it for the insurance money. And before you could say "chop shop," the truck was in one in Albuquerque, New Mexico, where it was quickly stripped and dismantled. Scharbarth, just as quickly, made a claim for his "loss" with his insurers, the plaintiffs in this suit.

Suspecting fraud, the insurers put a gumshoe on the case. Investigator Heinz A. Rost came back with a blunt report. "My feeling about this claim," he told his superiors, "is about the same as someone trying to make me swallow a 3 lb. fish. First of all, I dislike fish, second, I surely wouldn't try to swallow it whole, especially when it offends my sense of smell the way this claim does."

That was April 1982. But the next month, the insurance companies coughed up anyway. They sent a check for $62,210 to Scharbarth and the payee on his policy, Associates Commercial Corporation, which held a security interest in the truck. The companies paid up because they were worried about their duty to act in good faith in their dealings with Scharbarth. In counsel's words, they "did not want to unduly delay the settlement of his claim." Call the payment lunkheaded, or call it bright. I call it a business decision.

Associates knew nothing about Scharbarth's fraud. It kept the amount that Scharbarth owed on the truck, $49,647.51, and it conveyed its interest in the vehicle to the plaintiffs. Another $11,500 went for a replacement tractor unit. Scharbarth personally netted only $1,057.49 of the $62,210, reminding us, yet again, that crime doesn't pay.[1]

1. [Footnotes renumbered.] The remaining five dollars are not important to this story, or so it seems.

Enter the G-men. Like Rost (no ichthyophagist he), the FBI had also been sniffing into the incident at Sierra Sid's. The Bureau's legwork eventually paid off: In October 1985, a grand jury indicted Scharbarth for mail fraud. He pleaded guilty, and I sentenced him to two years in the big house on February 10, 1986.

On April 16, 1986, the plaintiffs' lawyer wrote to Associates looking for the return of $62,210. Until it received that letter, Associates had remained in the dark regarding Scharbarth's ugly machinations. Even after learning the dark truth, though, Associates wouldn't part with a dime. So the plaintiffs sued in October 1987. Where lesser litigants might have settled, Associates and the plaintiffs have now moved for summary judgment.

In the circumstances of this dispute—where an innocent party received payment from insurers on a claim that the insurers strongly suspected was fraudulent four years earlier—I will grant summary judgment in favor of Associates. At the same time, however, I will grant the plaintiffs summary judgment against Scharbarth, who admitted his fraud in his answer to the complaint. My reasons follow. * * *

According to the plaintiffs' lawyer, "Only after he was convicted in February 1986 did the plaintiffs have the proof that Mr. Scharbarth was involved in the alleged theft and, therefore, that there was no coverage for the loss of the truck." But this statement is somewhat misleading. Only after the conviction did the plaintiffs have proof *beyond a reasonable doubt* that Scharbarth had defrauded them in February 1982. Weeks before they paid his claim, however, they strongly suspected that Scharbarth had arranged for the theft.

The plaintiffs' affairs in this matter were handled by Casualty Underwriters, Inc., which in turn delegated responsibility to Floyd Johnson of Commercial Equipment Adjustors, Inc. Mr. Johnson testified at a deposition that his firm checked out Scharbarth's claim and that he hired three outside investigators as well—Gar Riddle, Don Kluxdal, and Mr. Rost. Mr. Riddle reported to Mr. Johnson that "[w]hile this may be a legitimate theft report, there are several discrepancies [in Scharbarth's story] which stand out." Mr. Riddle found it suspicious, for example, that Scharbarth never told any employee at Sierra Sid's about the theft.

Mr. Kluxdal's initial report did not contain any smoking guns, though he did see fit to interview Scharbarth's passenger and ask him whether the two of them had anything to do with the theft. (The answer was "no.") In a later report to Mr. Johnson, Mr. Kluxdal wrote, "I guess I probably will never feel satisfied your insured wasn't involved, simply because he is not accustomed to telling the truth." Mr. Kluxdal's recommendation was this:

> "To sum it all up if we were to deny the claim on what information we have, we wouldn't win. We can't prove anything beyond a reasonable doubt that your insured was involved. Since this can't be done and after considerable length of time, we can see no alternative but to settle."

Mr. Rost's report raised a red flag, as suggested by the colorful quotation at the beginning of this opinion. "All verifiable evidence indicates the insured is not telling the truth," Mr. Rost also said. He recommended to Mr. Johnson that "this claim not be paid without clarification by the insured to the satisfaction of Mr. F.A. Johnson and this investigator." Mr. Johnson discussed the findings of his investigators with Casualty Underwriters.

The claim was paid on May 4, 1982. A single check was made out to Scharbarth and Associates. In settlement of the claim, Scharbarth and Associates gave the plaintiffs all rights to the truck.

On May 28, 1982, the indefatigable Mr. Rost contacted Mr. Johnson to say that an informer had linked Scharbarth to the theft. However, the plaintiffs did not attempt to recover their money at that time and never notified Associates about the problem until April 1986.

Two final facts may be important: First, the plaintiffs attempt to pay theft claims within sixty days, but they waited almost ninety days to pay Scharbarth and Associates. Second, neither Scharbarth nor Associates had threatened or initiated legal action against the plaintiffs to receive payment on the claim, although Scharbarth expressed a desire to receive a prompt payment.

The facts that I have related are not disputed. Instead, the plaintiffs and Associates disagree as to what legal theory ought to govern the case. The plaintiffs argue that Associates should make restitution under a theory of unjust enrichment. Associates counters that the plaintiffs are really asserting a claim that payment was made under a mistake of fact, *i.e.* that the plaintiffs assumed the "loss" was bona fide but later learned otherwise. Associates says the law of mistake of fact does not sustain the plaintiffs' claim (because the plaintiffs were conscious of the possibility that the claim may have been fraudulent). In addition, Associates asserts that the plaintiffs' claim is estopped and barred by laches (because Associates abandoned any effort to mitigate its loss in reliance on the plaintiffs' check). These issues are legal questions appropriate for summary judgment.

Rather than deciding which theory is *the* right one, I will analyze this dispute with general principles in mind. At the outset, it is indisputable that neither Associates nor Scharbarth was entitled to payment by the plaintiffs in the first instance. Once payment was made, however, Associates may have obtained some rights to the money.

A leading treatise says the following under the heading "Right of Insurer to Recover Payments:"

> "As a general rule, if the insurer pays a loss, being induced so to do by fraud, or by mistake as to facts which, if it had had knowledge thereof, would have been a sufficient defense in an action by the insured upon the policy, the money so paid may be recovered. * * *
>
> "An insurer is not entitled to recover a payment made by it under a mistake of law. * * *
>
> "The insurer is not entitled to recover an improper payment unless it can show that it was not aware of the true facts at the time of paying the loss, and could not have learned of them by reasonable diligence."

18 Couch, Anderson & Rhodes, Couch on Insurance 2d (Rev. ed.) §§ 74:191–205 (1983).

As for the theory of restitution,

> "if an obligation procured by fraud is paid voluntarily with a full knowledge of the facts, the amount so paid cannot be recovered. * * *

> "[W]here one who makes a payment upon a controverted claim or demand is conscious of a want of knowledge of the material facts, or is uncertain, doubtful, or speculative concerning them, particularly where they have been in dispute and their status is specially brought to his attention, such payment is not made under a mistake of fact justifying recovery thereof."

66 Am.Jur.2d §§ 116 & 122 (Restitution and Implied Contracts) (1973).

Applying these principles to the case at hand, one conclusion is immediately apparent. The plaintiffs are not entitled to get their money back just because they paid the claim to avoid charges of bad faith. That was a mistake of law, and restitution is inappropriate.[2]

Mistake of fact is a tougher call. The Couch formulation would seem to favor the plaintiffs, who exercised "reasonable diligence" in attempting to ascertain the true facts, or who should at least be afforded a trial on that question. The *American Jurisprudence* rule, on the other hand, would seem to favor Associates because the plaintiffs knew they were not sure of Scharbarth's veracity. Fortunately, an old Wisconsin case has clarified the approach taken in this state. It is closer to the *American Jurisprudence* rule.

In Meeme Mutual Home Protective Fire Insurance Co. v. Lorfeld, the Wisconsin Supreme Court refused to order restitution to an insurance company that paid a loss payee for fire damages even though the insured later confessed to having torched the insured property. 194 Wis. 322, 216 N.W. 507 (1927). The trial court had found that the insurance company *and* the third-party payee "had suspicions on that subject but lacked proof." The state Supreme Court held:

> "[W]here one waives an investigation after his attention has been called to the possibility of the existence of the fact, he is not acting under a mistake of fact in the legal sense. Here the attention of the plaintiff was called to the fact that the fire might be of incendiary origin. It had the benefit of investigation by the state fire marshal as well as such investigation as it had made or could make on its own account; and with full knowledge of all the facts, conscious of the fact that the fire might be of incendiary origin, it nevertheless paid. Under such circumstances, it cannot be said that the plaintiff acted under a mistake of fact in the legal sense."

In the instant case, the plaintiffs did not waive an investigation. To the contrary, they set three investigators on Scharbarth's trail. Still, the plaintiffs were conscious of the fact that Scharbarth's claim might have been fraudulent, and they nevertheless paid him and an innocent mortgagee. This is what I meant when I called the plaintiffs' payment a business decision. They made a calculated choice that payment of a dubious claim was a better risk than defending against a suit by Scharbarth and/or Associates. See Grand Trunk Western Railroad Co. v. Lahiff, 218 Wis. 457, 463, 261 N.W. 11 (1935) (insurance company in *Meeme* "must be taken to have elected to discount the possibilities of an incendiary fire"). Under Wisconsin law, then, the plaintiffs cannot recover from Associates for what turns out to have been their mistake of fact in the factual but not legal sense.

2. The plaintiffs probably would have incurred no extra liability if they had withheld payment pending further investigation or pending the outcome of the FBI inquiry, of which they were aware. This is so because anyone suing the insurers would have had to show the absence of a reasonable basis for their denial of benefits. [citation] But these insurers had a reasonable basis for delay, even if they did not have proof of Scharbarth's fraud beyond a reasonable doubt.

I think, too, that the plaintiffs are barred from recouping their money from Associates under restitutionary principles which Associates labels as estoppel. In reliance on the insurance settlement, Associates changed its position to its detriment, and restitution is therefore inappropriate. Myers v. Fidelity & Casualty Company of New York, 759 F.2d 1542, 1548 (11th Cir.1985) (insurer could not recover payment from innocent mortgagee under principles of restitution) (quoting 13 S. Williston & W. Jaeger, A Treatise on the Law of Contracts, § 1595 (1970)). Although Associates could not have recovered the truck itself—because the truck was quickly chopped into parts by the thieves—Associates gave up any effort to make up its loss in other ways. For example, it might have pursued Scharbarth (before he went to prison) or his coconspirators (when they could have been located) to return what was left of the truck.

The equities do not fall the same way when it comes to the plaintiffs' case against Scharbarth. He has been unjustly enriched. More fundamentally, he willfully defrauded the plaintiffs. The plaintiffs are entitled to summary judgment against him. The only question is, How much may the plaintiffs recover?

In his answer to the complaint, Scharbarth, appearing *pro se,* stated that the plaintiffs failed to mitigate their damages. In addition, he contended that if the plaintiffs were entitled to recover, his own liability would be limited to the amount he personally netted in the fraud—$1,057.49. These are weak arguments, but I will give Scharbarth an opportunity to flesh them out if he so desires. Accordingly, if Scharbarth wants to limit his liability, he will have thirty days from the date of this order to submit reasons why he should not be held responsible for the entire $62,210 plus prejudgment interest at the rate of 5 percent. He should label his response a "Brief on Award of Damages." * * *

If Scharbarth does not file such a document, I will enter judgment against him for the entire amount paid by the plaintiffs plus interest and court costs.

Notes

1. Even though two assertions in the opinion turn out to be extraneous, we will not let them pass without comment. First that the parties disagree about the governing "legal theory": one side argues it is a claim for restitution and the other that it is to recover money paid under a mistake of fact. Is there any difference?

Second is the curt comment that plaintiff cannot get its money back because it paid under a mistake of law. More about mistake of law later. But this insurer did not pay because it mistakenly believed that a rule of law required it pay; it paid to avoid being hit with a bad faith law suit. This enduring risk in the insurance business is unrelated to any illusions about what the law is.

2. "Mistake means a state of mind not in accord with the facts." Restatement of Restitution § 6 (1937). A little doubt is therefore a dangerous thing. If the insurer pays a claim upon demand and without investigation, unhampered by any doubts an inquiry might raise, it may recover that payment, as made under mistake. If the insurer investigates thoroughly and resolves latent doubts because nothing amiss is discovered, the payment is also under mistake. But if insurer pays despite unresolved doubts created by investigation, no recovery. What is the practical lesson?

3. *Problem:* An insured under a disability policy suffered an eye injury that caused total loss of sight which an ophthalmologist declared to be "irrecoverable."

Based on this opinion, the insurer paid the lump sum the policy provided for loss of eyes. Three years later the insured, as though by miracle, recovered his sight. Was the payment made under a mistake of fact and recoverable? See Metropolitan Life Insurance Co. v. Kase, 718 F.2d 306 (9th Cir.1983).

McDONALD'S CORP. v. MOORE

United States District Court, Western District of South Carolina, 1965.
237 F.Supp. 874.

WYCHE, DISTRICT JUDGE. Plaintiff in this action seeks the recovery of rental overpayments made to the defendant.

Plaintiff is an Illinois corporation with its principal office in Chicago, and the defendant and landowner is a citizen of South Carolina.

On January 10, 1961, the plaintiff, then known as Franchise Realty Corporation, as lessee, and defendant, as lessor, entered into a thirty-year written lease for a lot in the City of Spartanburg, South Carolina. The first ten years of the lease provided a monthly rental of Three Hundred, Seventy Five ($375.00) Dollars, the second ten years provided a monthly rental of Four Hundred, Twenty Five ($425.00) Dollars, and the last ten years provided a monthly rental of Four Hundred, Fifty ($450.00) Dollars. * * *

Due to a delay in obtaining a mortgage loan commitment, two months' rent had accrued at the time the plaintiff at its option, put the lease into effect. Therefore, the first rental check plaintiff sent defendant under the lease was for the months of February and March, 1961, and was paid by the plaintiff in one check for $750.00. * * * In this instance, the employee saw that on March 23, 1961, a check had been written for $750.00 for the rent, and in April, 1961, when she wrote the check for rent for the month of April, she wrote a check for $750, the amount she had previously written, * * * believing she was paying the rent for one month. After the checks were prepared they were signed either by the Secretary–Treasurer or the Comptroller–Vice–President of the company, believing that the check had been correctly prepared for one month's rent. At the same time each month it was the duty of this same employee to write about one hundred, seventy five checks, as well as the payroll checks, totaling at least two hundred checks, which she did under pressure because of the time element involved.

Each month after March, 1961, plaintiff through an honest mistake mailed to the defendant a check for $750, and continued to do so until March, 1964, when an accounting firm who [sic] was making an annual certified audit of plaintiff's records, discovered the mistake and the overpayments totaling $13,-125.00, and plaintiff thereupon demanded of the defendant a return of the overpayments of rent but defendant refused to make restitution.

* * * When defendant received the overpayments, in spite of the express terms of the lease, he decided to keep the money. When asked about the April check, the defendant testified, "Q Now, Mr. Moore, each month since May, 1961, until February, 1964, did you receive from McDonald's Corporation a check for $750? A That's right, sir. Q And how did you credit the excessive payment included in each of those checks? A As I have stated, I would apply $375 to the last month's—THE COURT: Have you got a record of that? THE WITNESS: Well, sir, I have a record, yes. THE COURT: I mean, have you got a record where you applied it? THE WITNESS: I don't have a record of that

but I have the checks. THE COURT: There's nothing in writing that you did apply it to it? THE WITNESS: No, sir." When the attorney for the plaintiff telephoned the defendant, long-distance, informing him that the records of the plaintiff indicated that there had been rental overpayments to him, the defendant stated "that he was aware that overpayments had been made, and further stated he was wondering when we would wake up in Chicago." * * * When asked why he did not write the plaintiff, he replied, "Well, I don't have a typewriter and I don't have a secretary and I don't write very well." * * *

When defendant was asked why he credited the overpayments to the last ten years of the lease, he replied, "Well, I had an idea that was customary." * * *

It seems to me that I should follow the principle laid down in the recent case of Town of Bennettsville v. Bledsoe, 226 S.C. 214, 84 S.E.2d 554, where the Supreme Court of South Carolina said:

> "The action is at law for money had and received but it is well-settled that equitable principles govern. There is in this case no equity alleged or apparent which offsets the unjust enrichment of appellant at respondent's expense, which would result if he were allowed to retain the overpayment. He is not entitled to it in equity and good conscience, which is the usual test in such cases."

The facts in the *Bennettsville* case are apposite with the exception that the mistake in that case as to payments was mutual, whereas in the case before me there is no mutuality of mistake, but only a mistake on the part of the payor.

South Carolina observes that even the negligence of one paying money under a mistake of fact should not, in all cases, preclude the recovery. [citation] Also, in the *Town of Bennettsville* case the South Carolina Supreme Court points out in a similar situation of an overpayment, "negligence is no moment because the change of position" by the party to whom the overpayment had been made was "of no consequence." In the case at bar, there is no change of position by the defendant, alleged or claimed, as the result of the overpayment which would make restitution inequitable.

In his answer defendant alleges that the overpayments have been applied by him to the rent for the last years of the thirty-year lease, and asserts that where a debtor at the time of making a payment does not direct the creditor as to which account it should be applied, the creditor is entitled to make the application. This position is not sound for the reason that the rent for the last years of the lease had not accrued and was not due. In the absence of any present debt owed by the plaintiff, the defendant was without any authority or right to retain the overpayments, under the pretense of crediting them against an obligation that would not become due for nearly thirty years.

In addition to recovery of the overpayments, plaintiff seeks interest from the dates of the respective overpayments.

The general rule is that in suits for the payment of quasi-contractual obligations arising from payments of money by mistake, interest is not allowed as a matter of right but depends upon consideration of practical justice and fairness.

* * *

It seems proper and just to allow interest on the overpayments from the time of the demand for return and I fix the time for the running of interest as April 1, 1964 [at 6% per annum].

Note

The Mistaken Payee—Equity to the Rescue. The constructive trust fiction remains useful to solve novel problems equitably and to unravel the consequences of a mistaken payout of money. Consider: Knight Newspapers, a personal holding company, is both a common stockholder and creditor of the Miami Herald Publishing Co. The publishing company mistakenly declared dividends on its common stock in violation of the rights of its preferred shareholders. The dividend was credited to Knight Newspaper's claim against the payor thereby subjecting Knight to a personal holding company surtax for failing to distribute accumulated income. When the preferred shareholders of the publishing company complained, the payor cancelled the dividend and the credit. The Commissioner and the Tax Court nevertheless held the tax due. But the sixth circuit, invoking a constructive trust based on a mistake of fact, held the holding company to be merely a mistaken payee, therefore a "trustee." It follows that the holding company never received a dividend because it merely held the money "in trust" for the payor. Knight Newspapers, Inc. v. Commissioner, 143 F.2d 1007 (6th Cir.1944). Net tax savings? = $121,086.87. Is that enough to create respect for fiction?

LYONS v. KEITH

Court of Civil Appeals of Texas, 1958.
316 S.W.2d 785.

HIGHTOWER, JUSTICE. * * * By written contract of January 5, 1951, appellee Keith and John C. White, as Independent Executors and Trustees of the Estate of Seawillow Caswell Keith, agreed to sell, and appellants agreed to purchase, the tract of land in controversy, describing the same therein as follows:

Lying and situated in the County of Jefferson, State of Texas, 164.325 acres out of the W.B. Dyches Survey, described as follows: (Here follows a description of the property by field notes, minerals reserved to the seller).

The purchase price was therein stated to be $9,859.50. No reference was had of the price to be paid per acre. By deed of January 17, 1951, appellee and John C. White, in the same capacities, conveyed the property by the same description as set out in the contract to the appellants for the recited consideration of $10 and other considerations. The full purchase price stated in the contract was thereafter paid. * * * By deed of April 9, 1953, appellants sold the tract of land to Federal Land Corporation for $85,000. This deed contained no designation of acreage, but described the tract only by metes and bounds. About this time appellee Keith learned that the tract contained an acreage greatly in excess of 164.325. He subsequently, August 24, 1954, instituted suit against the appellants to recover the value of the excess acreage, and alleged as grounds therefor a mutual mistake of fact of the parties concerning the true acreage of the tract. He alleged the purchase price agreed upon between the parties to be $60 per acre and sought recovery of the excess on such basis. The case was tried to the court without a jury and judgment in favor of appellee against the appellants, jointly and severally, was rendered and entered in the sum of $8,355.90, [139.265 excess acres at $60 per acre.]

* * * The court found the true acreage of the tract to be 303.950 instead of 164.325 for an excess acreage of 139.265, and such finding is not here in dispute. The substance of the findings of fact which are in dispute and with which we are first concerned are: (1) the sale was on a per acre basis; (2) the recital in the deed was a mutual mistake of the parties, all of whom believed the tract to contain only 164.325 acres of land. [The appellate court sustained both of these findings of fact as well as the further finding that the agreed purchase price was $60 per acre.]

[T]he appellants contend that it was error to render judgment for the excess upon the contract price of $60 per acre. They submit that the correct measure of recovery would be the actual value of the excess. In this connection, they call attention to the undisputed evidence that only 103 acres of the tract is above flood state; that much of the remainder is flooded several times a year and fit only for pasturage, and is, therefore, of much less value. The point is without merit. As hereinbefore observed, all of the parties to this transaction had for several years theretofore been intimately familiar with the tract in controversy. They had each been upon it, observed it and discussed it. All the evidence supports the conclusion that they agreed among themselves that each acre as a part of the undivided whole of the tract was of the value of $60. In these circumstances we refer to the Supreme Court's holding in Denman v. Stuart, 42 Tex. 129, 176 S.W.2d 730, 732, for the correctness of the trial court's judgment. The Court stated in that case, which was one involving a mutual mistake in the exchange of lands, as follows:

> "Surely there can be no fairer, more equitable valuation placed on acreage which the parties to an exchange believe, in good faith, that one of them is getting but which, because of mutual mistake, he does not get, than that which they themselves fix in negotiating and consummating the trade. * * * We are content to adopt the appraisement which the parties made when they entered into the contract, as they thereafter construed and reaffirmed it in making the adjustment on the shortage in the Tarrant County land. It is a matter of contract, as to which they must be held to have bound themselves. Certainly neither Stuart nor Denman can now say that their own yard-stick, once already used by them, is not both exact and dependable. We approve the measure of damages applied by the trial court."

Note

Denman v. Stuart, 142 Tex. 129, 176 S.W.2d 730 (1944), is discussed in the principal decision. A purchaser in a sale by acreage overpaid. Is the analogy apt? Are the issues really comparable?

FINDLAY v. STATE

Supreme Court of Texas, 1923.
113 Tex. 30, 250 S.W. 651.

PIERSON, J. We quote the following from the opinion of the Court of Civil Appeals:

> "The state of Texas brought suit in the district court against George Findlay, Francis C. Farwell, and Hobart C. Chatfield-Taylor, to recover an alleged excess in a great number of surveys in a number of counties in the Panhandle of Texas, which were patented to Abner Taylor, in payment for the building of the present state capitol. The allegation in this regard is that by

mutual mistake excesses were included in said surveys aggregating 55,116 acres, and that the state is the owner of an undivided interest in the entire tract to the extent of said excess, and entitled to possession of same; that Taylor and his assignees have conveyed a large portion of said land, but that the said Findlay, Farwell, and Chatfield–Taylor still hold the legal title to about 600,000 acres of same as trustees, out of which the state seeks to have the portion to which it is entitled set apart to it." [From a judgment in favor of the State, certain defendants bring error.]

In support of their claim of right to keep the excess, plaintiffs in error assert that the state contracted to give Abner Taylor, for building the capitol building, all the leagues of land surveyed, as a "whole tract," and that, therefore, he became entitled to all the acres contained therein; and they assert, further, that if the contract was limited to 3,000,000 acres, and they are not entitled to retain the excess as a matter of right, then, and in that event, they are entitled to keep the excess contained in all the leagues, the whole tract, by paying for it at the value per acre at the date of the contract. The facts and the contract itself dispose of these contentions against plaintiffs in error.

There was other unappropriated land besides these leagues—much more vacant state land. It is not that the state had a tract of land thought to contain 3,000,000 acres * * *. The state merely undertook to measure off from the general body of its land 3,000,000 acres. Three million acres was the subject of contract between the parties for building the state house. In measuring the 3,000,000 acres, mistakes aggregating 59,281 acres were made; * * * The state showed a readiness to make good a deficiency of acreage to the amount of 16,000 acres, due to mistake of the surveyor in running over into New Mexico, and did make good the shortage, out of excess discovered in some of the leagues, and the parties to the contract reiterated their intention that 3,000,000 acres should be conveyed, and by supplemental contract stipulated that it was intended that no more than 3,000,000 acres should be conveyed. Findlay v. State, supra (Tex.Civ.App.) 238 S.W. 961. Thus the parties themselves construed the contract. The conveyance was for 3,000,000 acres, and now, an excess being developed, the state is entitled to recover same through partition.

Plaintiffs in error insist that Abner Taylor and the Capitol Company acquired under the contract "*complete and perfect title*" to the *first* 3,000,000 acres patented down to what they term the 3,000,000 line, beginning, according to the contract, with league No. 1; that the state, upon delivering patents to Taylor to leagues and to land up to 3,000,000 acres, *including* excess, thereby ceased to have any interest in such lands whatsoever, the title being absolute under the contract, and therefore the state cannot maintain its suit for any excess land so included; that, if it has any remedy at all, it must be applied to those lands and leagues patented to Taylor after said 3,000,000 mark including excess, had been reached. * * *

This is a severely strained theory at best. It is true that Abner Taylor under the contract was to receive title to the land as the work progressed, beginning with league No. 1 on the north border of the state, and that they should be taken in numerical order. But this selfsame contract contemplated that all the leagues, containing 3,000,000 acres, should be so taken when earned. * * * The mistake of acreage applied to all the leagues, and the excess was scattered through them all.

* * * The issuing of the patent to the last league was just as much a performance of the contract as was the issuance of the patent to the first one, and yet he received too much land. The mistake in the acreage of the first league patented was as much a part of the total excess as that in the last league. We must view the performance of the contract as a whole; but this does not alter the fact that the contract was limited to 3,000,000. * * *

The Capitol Company having received the excess, and as it still has it through its representatives, plaintiffs in error, it violated no principle of equity, but is in accord with the principles of right and justice, for the state to have partition against it for the excess out of land still in its hands, and not disturb those parties to whom it has sold parts of the land.

* * * If Abner Taylor and the plaintiffs in error acquired the right to have the state convey to them all the leagues (nearly 700) of land as an entirety, regardless of acreage, for building the capitol, though 3,000,000 acres was the stipulated consideration, then, if a substantial excess was developed, the plaintiffs in error would be entitled to retain same by paying for it at its value as controlled by the contract, as contended by plaintiffs in error. But, this is not supported in the findings of fact, nor in the proper construction of the contract.

There was no stipulated price per acre, but a specified number of acres was given for building the capitol. Since there was no contractual obligation, and there being no stipulated price per acre, and its value being undetermined, the sale being for the specific acreage, and plaintiffs in error having received 59,281 acres more than was contracted for, they neither have the right to hold same, nor to retain it by paying for it, and partition was properly applied.

The judgment of the Court of Civil Appeals is affirmed.

Notes

1. The magnitude of mistakes in Texas is impressive, as are the corrective measures. Consider the following which appears near the end of the above opinion.

"[W]e will make mention of a fortunate circumstance that at first was apparently embarrassing to the contractor, Mr. Taylor, but redounded at last to the satisfaction of all. It was discovered that the white limestone out of which the capitol building was to have been built under the original contract was not to be found in quantities sufficient for the great structure. After much negotiation, the contract was changed, and Texas red granite, from Burnet county, was substituted for the white limestone. This entailed a large additional cost to the builder, but was partly compensated for by the state in three different ways: (1) The state agreed to furnish Mr. Taylor 500 state convicts for a period of two years, to be used in building 15 miles of railroad from Burnet to Roseville the granite quarries, and in working the granite quarries and the limestone quarries; (2) it agreed to give Mr. Taylor immediate possession of all the 3,000,000 acres of land without charge; (3) changes were made in the plans and specifications which reduced the cost of construction."

2. The Texas Supreme Court did not touch on the issue of materiality. The Court of Appeals said:

"Is the excess material? We think so. Equity will grant relief, even where the sale is in gross, if the excess is large. A much less excess will afford ground for relief where the sale is by the acre.

"It is true that the excess in the instant case is only 1.8 per cent. over the 3,000,000 acres intended to be granted, but it is nevertheless 55,089 acres, and we do not think so great an excess can be regarded as immaterial, whatever be the number of acres intended to be granted. When it was discovered that by reason of the conflict with New Mexico there was a shortage of 16,000 acres, Taylor did not consider this immaterial, although it was only about one-half of 1 per cent. of the 3,000,000 acres he was to receive under his contract. On the contrary, he demanded that this deficiency be made good. The state, the other party to the contract, recognized the justness of this demand, and complied with the same.

" 'It has long since been settled, that the *relative extent* [italics ours] of the surplus or deficit cannot furnish, per se, an infallible criterion in each case for its determination, but that each case must be considered with reference not only to that, but its other peculiar circumstances.' O'Connell v. Duke, 29 Tex. 310, 311.

"There is another circumstance which we think is entitled to some weight in determining what was the intention of the parties. In this connection, it should be remembered that the Capitol Commissioners who represented the state was composed of the Governor, the Attorney General, the Comptroller, the Treasurer, and the Commissioner of the Land Office; that they had no authority in the premises, except that which was conferred upon them by the Legislature; and that the Legislature had limited them to the use of 3,000,000 acres of land in procuring the erection of the capitol. It is not to be presumed that these honorable gentlemen did not know the limitation of their authority, or that they knowingly exceeded the same. Did they contemplate that the surveys as made might contain an excess of more than 55,000 acres, and, if so, that the contractor should have the same? One of these tests, as stated in O'Connell v. Duke is: Would 'such excess, if known, * * * have materially influenced the' parties? As private individuals they might have been willing to 'throw in' such excess, in a deal of this magnitude, should a subsequent survey reveal the existence of the same, but we cannot conceive that they contemplated any such possible unauthorized disposition of the public domain." Findlay v. State, 238 S.W. 956, 662 (Tex.App. 1921).

3. *Question:* The Capitol Company seemed willing, as a last resort, to reconvey the *last* 55,089 acres it received. The State and the court adamantly opposed this solution. Why?

NEW YORK LIFE INSURANCE CO. v. GILBERT

Court of Appeals of Missouri, 1923.
215 Mo.App. 201, 256 S.W. 148.

BLAND, J. This is a suit to reform or cancel on the ground of mutual mistake an indorsement upon a policy of insurance written upon the life of defendant Charles E. Gilbert and in favor of his wife, Myra M. Gilbert, as beneficiary. The judgment was for the defendants. The policy is on the 15 year payment plan and was issued on April 3, 1899, in the sum of $2,500. It provided for an annual premium of $117.08, the first premium being acknowledged. The other premiums were to be paid on the 2d day of January in each year thereafter until 15 full yearly premiums should have been paid, at which time the policy would be fully paid up. * * *

The policy contained a provision that cash loans might be obtained on it at any time after the policy had been in force for two full years if the premium had been duly paid to the anniversary of the insurance next succeeding the time when the loan was made. On April 11, 1913, defendant made a written application to plaintiff for a cash loan of $1,412 representing the full loan value of the policy at that time according to its terms. The loan was made. The policy provided that—

> "If any premium or interest is not duly paid, and if there is any indebtedness to the company, this policy will be indorsed for such amount of paid-up insurance as any excess of the reserve held by the company over such indebtedness will purchase according to the company's present published table of single premiums, upon written request therefore within six months from the date to which premiums were duly paid." * * *

Nothing further occurred material to this controversy until December 4, 1920, when the insured wrote the plaintiff as follows:

> "I believe I have a loan with you on policy 936346 which is paid up. I wish you would please let me know how much paid-up insurance I can get on this by your first canceling the loan and giving me this paid-up insurance on the residue.
>
> "I hope you will kindly figure this as fully and clearly as you can so that I may be able to understand it thoroughly."

On December 11, 1920, plaintiff's actuary wrote the insured that if the interest on the loan due on January 2, 1921, should not be paid, the paid-up insurance available after canceling the loan would be $768. Thereupon insured wrote:

> "Replying to yours of Dec. 11th in regard to above policy will say that since I have a loan, the policy is in your possession and I accept your terms of $768.00 paid-up insurance and cancellation of the outstanding loan."

The interest due on January 2, 1921, on the loan was not paid. Upon receipt of insured's letter accepting the $768 paid-up insurance, plaintiff wrote the insured that the interest not having been paid on January 2, 1921, the indebtedness had been canceled and the policy indorsed for paid-up insurance amounting to $768 as provided in the contract, and remitted to the insured the policy with an indorsement thereon to that effect. It is this indorsement that plaintiff attempts to correct by showing that the amount of paid-up insurance was incorrectly figured in plaintiff's actuarial office, and instead of the paid-up insurance being for $768 it should have been for $296.

The policy bearing the erroneous indorsement was sent to the insured on January 12, 1921. On February 2, 1921, plaintiff discovered that a mistake had been made in the calculation and caused its agent at Kansas City, Mo., to write the insured at Nevada, Mo., of the mistake, offering to give the insured paid-up insurance in the sum of $308. The difference between $296, the actual paid-up value of the policy as the undisputed evidence shows, and the amount offered, to wit, $308, was caused by plaintiff's employee's overlooking the fact that the insured was born in 1861 instead of in 1862. However, the insured refused to accept this amount of paid-up insurance "for the reason that the transaction is closed so far as I am concerned"; that he had accepted plaintiff's offer, "and if you had written me then that you would only allow me $308 paid-up insurance, I would not have allowed you to cancel the loan, and I would not have accepted the $308 paid-up insurance."

The petition seeks to reform the indorsement on the policy so as to substitute the figures $296 for $768, if defendants so desired, or that the court cancel the indorsement entirely and restore the policy to its status at the time the indorsement was made thereon, and that the court order any one of the final settlement options provided by the terms of the policy and loan agreement. * * *

It is quite apparent from all the facts that the agreement between plaintiff and the insured was that the settlement was to be made in accordance with the terms of an existing contract or policy; that it was not to be a new contract wholly outside the terms of the old one, or, in other words, a substitution of a new contract for the old one; but that it was to be merely a continuation of the old contract under an option in favor of insured that was provided for in it. * * *

The question then remains as to whether the mistake made by plaintiff's employee was a mutual one and not a unilateral one, or one confined to the plaintiff. A similar situation arose in the case of Hemphill v. N.Y. Life Ins. Co., 195 Ky. 783, 243 S.W. 1040. * * * The court found that the mistake was a mutual one. The contention of the insured was similar to the one made by the insured in the case at bar. Upon this authority, as well as the authority of the Missouri cases, we hold that the mistake in the case at bar was a mutual one, in fact that the insured mistakenly supposed that the amount indorsed on the policy was properly calculated as to what he was entitled to under the policy whereas it was not.

We have examined the cases cited by the defendants and find none of them at all similar to the case at bar, except possibly the case of New York Life Ins. Co. v. Kimball, 93 Vt. 147, 106 Atl. 676. There was a strong dissenting opinion in that case. However, we think the facts in the *Kimball* Case are clearly distinguishable from the facts in the case at bar. In that case the insured failed to pay his premium when due and failed to apply for paid-up insurance. Under the circumstances, the company, in compliance with the terms of the policy, indorsed it as continued at a reduced amount for a term of 3 years and 274 days. In making the calculation the company gave the policy credit for an unpaid dividend which should not have been allowed and the policy was continued in force for a longer period than it should have been. The insured died, but his death occurred outside of the time that should have been indorsed on the policy if the calculation had been made correctly. The company did not discover the mistake until after the death of insured and thereupon filed a bill in equity to reform and cancel the indorsement. The majority of the court held that the mistake was not mutual. This holding seems to have been based on the fact that the insured at no time during his life knew, or had reason to know, that any mistake had been made. The court held that the indorsement was not a contract; that it was a mistake of the company and in no way participated in by the insured. Quite different from the facts in this case. Here the insured applied for paid-up insurance and intended to get the amount of paid-up insurance that he was entitled to under the policy. * * *

The judgment therefore is reversed, and the cause remanded, with directions to the lower court to cancel the indorsement on the policy of $768 paid-up insurance and to fix a reasonable time within which plaintiff shall submit all of its options to defendants and a reasonable time thereafter in which defendants may exercise their right of option under the policy and loan agreement, and when such option shall have been exercised, the court will enter a decree in accordance therewith and as indicated in this opinion.

2. MISTAKEN PERFORMANCE IN THE BELIEF THAT A CONTRACT EXISTS

See these decisions in Chapter 4: Campbell v. Tennessee Valley Authority, p. 295, Farash v. Sykes Datatronics, p. 303, and Earhart v. William Low Co., p. 306.

3. MISTAKE IN BASIC ASSUMPTIONS

Preliminary Note

The material that follows emphasizes the substantive law of restitution for mistake—the quality of the mistake that justifies the avoidance of executed transactions. The restitutionary remedies resemble those utilized when the transaction is avoided for other reasons.

a. *Mutual Mistake*

RELIANCE FINANCE CORP. v. MILLER

United States Court of Appeals, Ninth Circuit, 1977.
557 F.2d 674.

[Reliance sought to rescind its purchase of a collection agency (Romer) on a number of theories, including mistake. The trial judge found for the seller. On appeal, the judgment was affirmed. Only the parts of the opinion that relate to mistake are reproduced below.]

FERGUSON, DISTRICT JUDGE. Reliance also sought rescission on the theory that neither buyer nor seller was aware that financial statements, relied upon during the parties' negotiations, significantly understated the liabilities due Romer's clients. Although this issue has repeatedly been tagged as a "trust account" problem, it is important to note that the difficulty did not arise in connection with the trust *bank account,* but rather with Romer's *accounting procedures.* It is undisputed that Romer's trust account properly reflected monies received from debtors and that no defalcation of funds had occurred. Rather, by retracing disbursements later made to clients, appellants attempted to show that the accounting entry which purported to represent the sums due clients out of trust account funds was in error and should have been significantly higher. This understatement of liabilities vis-a-vis funds received, they argue, led Reliance to assume that Romer had a higher profit margin than was in fact the case and to anticipate that a substantial sum could be safely diverted from the trust account to be used as working capital in the business.

* * * Rather than leaving the matter solely to common law development, California has codified the requirements for rescission on the basis of mistake as part of the Civil Code. Section 1689(b) provides in pertinent part that "A party to a contract may rescind the contract in the following cases: (1) If the consent of the party rescinding * * * was given by mistake." Section 1577 defines mistake of fact, insofar as is relevant here, as "a mistake, not caused by the neglect of a legal duty on the part of the person making the mistake, and consisting in: 1. An unconscious ignorance or forgetfulness of a fact past or present, material to the contract." Section 1568 is also relevant: "Consent is deemed to have been obtained through [mistake] only when it would not have been given had such [mistake] not existed."

California case law suggests that there is more to the law of mistake than might be apparent from the simple language of these statutes. While California courts appear never to have adopted the traditional requirement that rescission may be obtained only where mistake goes to the identity of the matter bargained for [citations] they require that, in addition to being material, the mistake must pertain to the essence of the contract [citations].[1] It has likewise been said by California courts that it must be other than incidental, and that it must involve more than a collateral matter [citations]. Only if the difference between the real and supposed quality or characteristic of the item sold is of such magnitude as to make it virtually a different thing will relief be granted.

Although articulating this idea in a number of different ways, it is evident that the courts have rather universally hesitated to undermine the stability of commercial transactions without serious provocation.

While we recognize that some California cases have failed to apply any more stringent standard than that of materiality in determining whether rescission may be granted, we here follow the more prevalent California rule which requires that the mistake go to the essence of the contract. But because rescission is also available in California on the basis of innocent misrepresentation, it is all too easy to confuse these two distinct doctrines and to assume that a simple materiality test applies to both. Proof of innocent misrepresentation is more complex than might appear to superficial analysis. Traditionally, rescission may be granted on this theory where the misrepresentation is material (i.e., nontrivial), where it concerns a material fact (i.e., one that would be taken into account by a reasonable person in deciding whether to enter into the transaction) (Restatement of Restitution § 9, comment (b) (1937) and where the rescinding party has both actually and reasonably relied on the representation in entering the contract to his detriment (Restatement of Restitution § 8, comment (e) (1937)). The prerequisites for relief based on mutual mistake, that the mistake be material (i.e., nontrivial) and that it go to the essence of the contract, may really encompass the same facts and concerns, although articulated in different terms. Despite this apparent overall equilibrium, care must be taken not to introduce an erroneous equation and one-to-one correspondence between individual elements of proof. Material, in any of its several connotations, is not the same as basic or essential, and "there is a greater requirement of materiality when rescission is asked on the grounds of mistake than when the theory is 'fraud' [including innocent misrepresentation]." Note, 12 Hastings L.J. 458, 465 (1961). We therefore, also decline to treat the California innocent misrepresentation cases cited by appellants as controlling California law on the issue of mutual mistake. * * *

The availability of working capital is undoubtedly a collateral matter which, although it might be material to a potential purchaser, cannot be said to relate to the *very essence* of the bargain. Nor can an erroneous calculation of expected profits based on the figures provided by Miller justify rescission. While the expectation of profit was undoubtedly also an inducement to the contract, it does not lie so close to the heart of the bargain as to qualify as basic mistake.

1. [Footnotes renumbered.] The rule included in the Restatement of Restitution § 9 reflects this idea as well. To warrant rescission, mistake must be "basic," i.e., be an error "as to a fact or rule of law constituting the assumed basis upon which the transaction rests." Restatement of Restitution § 9, comment (c) (1937).

Note

Simonson v. Fendell, 101 Wash.2d 88, 675 P.2d 1218, 1221–22 (1984). Simonson (S) and Teeter each owned one-half of a business; Fendell was the general manager. S became disenchanted with the business and offered to sell his interest to Teeter and Fendell for his investment. A financial statement prepared by the company accountant showed a net profit for the preceding accounting period and a book value of over $37,000. The buyers asked S if he really wanted to sell in the light of its profitable nature. He replied that he didn't care about the profit, he just wanted his money back; and if they didn't want to buy, he would liquidate the business. A later accounting revealed a mutual mistake although neither party was at fault. There had been a loss instead of a profit; the business was insolvent. The court allowed the buyers to rescind: "The parties agreed to buy and sell a business operating at a profit. The mistaken fact * * * was the underlying basis of the entire bargain * * * [Buyer] is entitled to rescission" even though S would have entered into the contract regardless of the mistake.

YORK, MISUNDERSTANDING MISTAKE: OR A QUASI REVIEW OF A QUASI-CONTRACTUAL BOOK

11 U.C.L.A. L.Rev. 653, 656–61 (1964), (reviewing G. Palmer, Mistake and Unjust Enrichment (1962)).

A diagram may be useful at this point to illustrate the considerations involved in setting aside bargains because of mistake.

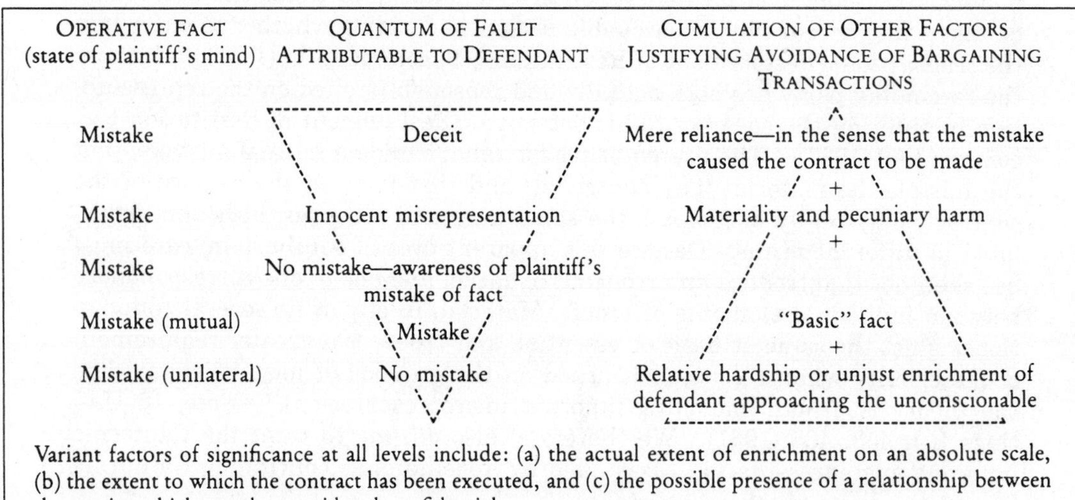

Only general principles are indicated by this schematic device. Precision is not pretended and the details are arguable.

It will be noted that "mistake," i.e., the plaintiff's erroneous state of mind, remains constant as the prime operative factor. As the causal connection between the plaintiff's mistake and the defendant's own conduct diminishes there is a natural, just, and progressive increase in the equitable elements required to justify setting aside the transaction. Whether the defendant's conduct is tortious in the sense of giving rise to an action for damages is of no concern in restitution, save on the collateral determination of whether his enrichment is unjust.

In sequence we note that if the plaintiff's mistaken state of mind is caused by defendant's deliberate misrepresentation the contract is voidable without more than a demonstration that the plaintiff relied upon the misrepresentation in the sense that he would not have entered into the bargain otherwise. There is doubt that the fact misrepresented need even be a material one in this instance, but that is a digression from the point. (Professor Palmer, incidentally, did not see fit in his book to pursue this particular digression of materiality either—it alone would be worth another volume).

In any event, if the misleading representation is innocently made, the plaintiff's burden increases. Beside establishing the subjective point that his mistaken frame of mind led him into the agreement, he must unquestionably here prove materiality (against an objective standard), and must also show some pecuniary damage. The same is true in all instances where plaintiff is unable to blame the defendant for his error although it is plain that the defendant was happily aware of it and profited by it.

At the next level, that of mutual mistake, the element of wrongful conduct or of fault by the defendant disappears. The transposition from tort to matters purely consensual has gradually been made; yet the operative factor of restitution remains constant. At the same time the law quite justifiably imposes stricter requirements for setting aside bargains fairly (apparently) arrived at. Subjective causality, objective materiality, pecuniary injury are insufficient to warrant unsettling commerce.

Something more is required and what that something is has taxed the vocabulary of judges and text writers. In addition to being material, the fact as to which the parties are mistaken must, we are variously told, "concern the nature or identity of the subject matter" (as distinguished from value), be "intrinsic" (as distinguished from extrinsic), "go to the root of the transaction," "be the basis on which the transaction was entered into," etc. All these are but expressions of the same fundamental idea.

Professor Palmer covers this topic very well in the first and second chapters of his book, discussing the more familiar cases and contributing helpful observations. Only one serious point of disagreement will be made. The author (after presenting Sherwood v. Walker [1]) states:

> "If both parties thought the cow was barren, the gain of the buyer as a consequence of its unexpected fertility was one that neither party contemplated as a product of the bargain. Avoidance of the contract does far less violence to the policies supporting adherence to bargains than would be the case if it deprived a party of an anticipated benefit." [2]

The last sentence is debatable. So much prose and poetry has been devoted to that poor damned cow in Sherwood v. Walker that one hesitates to add more. The cow was sold for the price of beef ($80) on the assumption she was barren. The buyer got much the better of the bargain because she was with calf (value between $750 and $1,000). The seller was aggrieved and refused to deliver claiming the right to rescind for mistake. The buyer brought replevin and lost. There is much by-play in the case as to whether the mistake "went to the whole substance of the agreement" or "went to the very nature of the thing," i.e., whether it was as to a basic fact. The point is debatable, the

1. [Footnotes renumbered.] 66 Mich. 568, 33 N.W. 919 (1887).

2. Palmer, Mistake and Unjust Enrichment 16 (1962).

debate is prolonged, and the case becomes classic. All this is beside the mark here. Professor Palmer's proposition is that avoidance of this sale by the seller does "less violence to the policies supporting adherence to bargains" than would be the reverse.

Very well, let us reverse the situation and see. If Professor Palmer is correct we would expect even more serious resistance to avoidance. Stated now, the sale is of a cow assumed to be with calf for its assumed value of $1,000. The cow is in fact barren and worth $80. The buyer is aggrieved. I am doubtful if such a case would have made the Rose II of Aberlone very famous. The buyer is "deprived of an anticipated benefit," in Professor Palmer's words, but avoiding the transaction hardly does violence to the sanctity of contracts. That is, unless the concept of implied warranties in the sale of goods is unjust and unjustifiable.

In point of fact, Sherwood v. Walker goes against the grain, if not the bold face statement of the law. This is always true where the seller, instead of the buyer, seeks to avoid for a mutual mistake. The buyer's position is instinctively favored.[3] The doctrine of implied warranties, as has been intimated, was evolved for his benefit (and actually disposes of virtually all cases in which mutual mistake exists in the sale of chattels to the buyer's disappointment). His hardship is severe, since he has paid out hard earned savings for little or nothing. Subjectively—although this should presumably not sway us, and factually it may not be so—we tend to visualize the seller as having a bit of the advantage in the situation—the superior sagacity, etc. of the merchant and all that.

Reverse again the roles (bringing us back to Sherwood v. Walker) and we find no warranties arrayed in favor of the seller. He gets exactly what he bargained for. His hardship does not consist of giving up something for nothing (although he later may be persuaded that such was the case) but of the loss of an unanticipated benefit. The old case of Wood v. Boynton [4] is typical. *S* sells a stone for one dollar to *B*. It is thought to be a topaz. In fact it is an uncut diamond worth $700. Restitution was denied to *S*. The Restatement of Contracts and the Restatement of Restitution both tinker slightly with these facts and pose a contrary result.[5] I suspect nevertheless that we buyers of a dingy old picture to cover the bad spot in the wallpaper will approve of Wood v. Boynton when the purchase turns out to be a lost masterpiece.

[For Professor Palmer's later article on the same topic, see The Effect of Misunderstanding on Contract Formation and Reformation Under the Restatement of Contracts Second, 65 Mich.L.Rev. 33 (1966).]

3. See parenthetical comment to note 5 infra.

4. 64 Wis. 265, 25 N.W. 42 (1885). (Discussed by Professor Palmer at p. 40.)

5. 2 Restatement, Contracts § 503, illustration 3 (1932); Restatement, Restitution § 16, illustrations 1, 9 (1937). (The observation was made in the preceding paragraph that the buyer is instinctively favored. This instinct was plainly possessed by the drafters of the Restatement of Restitution who chose to reverse the facts in Wood v. Boynton and make it still another illustration to § 16, i.e., illustration 1, where the buyer pays a large sum for a worthless pebble and is allowed recovery. The drafters of the Restatement are on psychologically sounder grounds in reversing the facts of Wood v. Boynton than they are in reversing the holding.)

DADOURIAN EXPORT CORP. v. UNITED STATES

United States Court of Appeals, Second Circuit, 1961.
291 F.2d 178.

MEDINA, CIRCUIT JUDGE. On December 14, 1956, the United States through the New Cumberland General Depot of the United States Army, at New Cumberland, Pennsylvania, circulated, together with forms for bidding and General Sale Terms and Conditions, an invitation for bids upon 91 items of government surplus property. Among the items listed for sale were items 65 through 73, which were described in the bid forms in the following manner:

Item No.	Description and Location of Property
65 to 73	Nets, Cargo, 20′ × 40′, Manila rope meshes 8″ square frame 3¾ circ mesh rope, 3″ circ with lanyards Paulsen Weber or equal loose

On the invitation there appeared in large capital letters the statement "It has been determined that this property is no longer needed by the federal government." Moreover, on both the invitation and on each bid form were the words "Caution: inspect the property," in italicized capitals. The invitation urged bidders to read the accompanying General Sale Terms and Conditions. These provided in pertinent part as follows:

> "1. Inspection.—Bidders are invited and urged to inspect the property to be sold prior to submitting bids. Property will be available for inspection at the places and times specified in the invitation. The Government will not be obliged to furnish any labor for such purpose. In no case will failure to inspect constitute grounds for a claim or for the withdrawal of a bid after opening.
>
> "2. Condition of Property.—All property listed herein is offered for sale 'as is' and 'where is,' and without recourse against the Government. * * * The description is based on the best available information, but the Government makes no guaranty, warranty, or representation, expressed or implied, as to quantity, kind, character, quality, weight, size, or description of any of the property, or its fitness for any use or purpose, and no claim will be considered for allowance or adjustment or for rescission of the sale based upon failure of the property to correspond with the standard expected; this is not a sale by sample."

Early in January, 1957 plaintiff, a corporation which had dealings in "military surplus goods," according to its letterhead, submitted bids on several items, including items 65 through 73. Bids were opened on January 8, 1957, and on January 16 plaintiff's bid of $30,893 on items 65 through 73, accompanied by a $7,000 deposit, was accepted. At no time before it submitted its bid did plaintiff inspect the nets although the nets were available for inspection, having been segregated and laid out on wooden pallets. * * *

After its bid was accepted plaintiff sold the nets to a third party. When this third party went down to New Cumberland to take delivery, he discovered that at least some of the nets tendered were not made of Manila rope. * * * Moreover, the nets were not cargo nets but saveall nets. According to the Armed Services Board of Contract Appeals which rendered a decision relating to the dispute now before us, a cargo net is a net used to move cargo, while a saveall net is a net which is strung between ship and pier to prevent cargo which is being loaded or unloaded from dropping into the water.

Plaintiff refused to pay the balance of $23,893 due on the contract, stated that it would take delivery only of those nets made of Manila rope and requested an adjustment of the total contract price on that basis. * * * The upshot was that the request for a price adjustment was denied. * * * [A]lmost a year after the nets were reclaimed by the government, the nets were resold to the highest bidders for $7,830.87. On the resale the nets were not described as made of Manila rope.

Having lost its appeal to the Armed Services Board of Contract Appeals, this action was brought by plaintiff under the Tucker Act, 28 U.S.C.A. § 1346(a)(2), for rescission and the return of its deposit, the government counterclaimed for damages for breach of contract in the amount of $17,152.81 with interest, and, on cross-motions for summary judgment the complaint was dismissed and judgment rendered in favor of the government for the full amount of its claim, including the expenses of the resale. Plaintiff appeals.

* * * The main ground on which appellant asserts its right to rescind and to have its deposit returned is that there was a mutual mistake of fact going to the existence or the identity of the subject matter of the contract. The argument runs that both appellant and the government intended to buy and sell cargo nets made of Manila rope and what was tendered were saveall nets at least some of which were not made of Manila rope. Insofar as the nets were saveall nets rather than cargo nets we are not impressed, because we do not believe that this went to the essence of the bargain between appellant and the government. While appellant here and in the District Court has made much of the fact that the nets were saveall nets rather than cargo nets, it objected to delivery only because some of the nets were not Manila, and this objection in turn was based on the alleged fact that the nets had been resold and represented as Manila nets. Nor do we think the fact that not all of the nets were Manila goes to the identity or the existence of the subject matter of the contract. We believe the subject matter of the contract was nets or nets used in shipping. The word Manila was merely descriptive. Appellant had no right to rely on such descriptive language, because Article 2 of the General Sale Terms and Conditions expressly disclaimed any "guaranty, warranty, or representation, express or implied, as to quantity, kind, character, quality, weight, size or description." What the case comes down to is that appellant disregarded repeated warnings to the Invitation and bid forms to inspect the property and has only itself to blame for the predicament in which it finds itself.

Appellant's theory of lack of identity apparently stems from a comment by the court below in United States v. Silverton, 1 Cir., 1952, 200 F.2d 824, to the effect that even if the bidder failed to inspect the goods he could prevail against the government if the government had offered to sell apples and delivered oranges. And in his opinion in that case Chief Judge Magruder did say that if the government in that case had offered to deliver "scrap webbing mixed" as a subhead under "Textile, Cotton," and instead delivered a shipment consisting "wholly of scrap metal," "it might be that the bidder, even though he had failed to make an inspection before submitting his bid, could have rejected the shipment as not conforming to the contract." The whole rationale of *Silverton,* however, is opposed to any recovery by appellant here. The invitation to bid, under the heading "Textile, Cotton," included 40,000 pounds of "Webbing, scrap, mixed." Silverton's bid of $2.51 per pound was accepted. When the shipment arrived it contained a miscellaneous assortment of army equipment, such as canteen covers, leggings, cartridge belts, gas masks and haversacks, mostly with pieces of metal attached. Silverton's claim was that "Webbing, scrap, mixed" had a definite meaning in the trade to the effect that the webbing is free of metal components, that he had purchased the material for resale for the purpose of conversion into fiber for paper-making and that the presence of the metal parts made the material useless for paper-making. The lower court agreed with this, cited by way of analogy a sale of apples and delivery of oranges, and ruled in favor of the bidder. On appeal the First Circuit reversed, held any trade meaning of the descriptive phrase "Webbing, scrap, mixed" and the presence of the metal to be immaterial. The reasoning of the First Circuit, with which we agree, follows:

> "The invitation to bid was evidently framed to spare the government the necessity of attending to the niceties of detail in describing the goods offered, for example, to make the description conform to any possible trade usages of which the salvage officers might not even be aware. Under the terms of the sale, with inspection invited prior to the submission of bids, *caveat emptor* was certainly intended to be applied to the furthest limit that contract stipulations could accomplish it." * * *

The judgment appealed from is affirmed, except that the case is remanded for a trial of the issue of damages arising out of the government's counterclaim.

FRIENDLY, CIRCUIT JUDGE (dissenting). In my view plaintiff's motion for summary judgment should have been granted and the Government's denied.

It is plain beyond peradventure that, had this been an ordinary sale, plaintiff would have been entitled not merely to rescind but to recover damages when it discovered that a portion of the nets were not "Manila rope," which the Government's trial attorney before the Board of Contract Appeals conceded to be worth "a vast deal more than fiber rope." Uniform Commercial Code, § 2–313. Here plaintiff properly makes no claim for damages; it insists only that it not be held to a bargain it never made.

If plaintiff is to be so held, this must be because of paragraphs 1 or 2 of the General Sale Terms and Conditions. Paragraph 1, entitled "Inspection," is not adequate to that office. It says only that "failure to inspect" will not "constitute grounds for a claim or for the withdrawal of a bid after opening." Although this ineptly worded clause may have the effect of excluding any liability under an implied warranty of quality, it surely does not go so far as to say that because the prospective buyer does not inspect before bidding, the seller may require him to accept goods not conforming to the description, see Uniform Commercial Code, § 2–316(3)(b) and comment 8.

The argument that paragraph 2 supports the Government's position is that, in a sale of specified goods, the buyer's right to reject for failure of the goods to conform to the description rests on the seller's breach of warranty that the goods will so conform, hence, since paragraph 2 negates any warranty "as to quantity, kind, character, quality, weight, size or description of any of the property, or its fitness for any use or purpose," the buyer has no right to reject or rescind.

The first answer to this is that courts properly decline to give so literal an effect to a disclaimer of a warranty of description, as is clearly shown by Chief Judge Magruder's opinion in United States v. Silverton, 1 Cir., 1952, 200 F.2d 824, 826 and this Court's in American Elastics, Inc. v. United States, 2 Cir., 1951, 187 F.2d 109, 113. My brother Medina's opinion makes it plain that he would not follow the logic of the Government's argument so as to hold the plaintiff if Items 65–73 had turned out to be canvas sheets rather than cargo nets; I doubt he would if the nets had proved to be made of cotton. Hence the question becomes one of degree. In my brother Medina's view "Manila rope" did not go to the essence; to my mind, the sharp differentiation among the three descriptions and the Government's concession that Manila rope was worth "a vast deal more" than fiber rope, make the case analogous to Chief Judge Magruder's example in United States v. Silverton, not, indeed, of apples and oranges, but of "Webbing, scrap, mixed" which turned out to be entirely scrap.

Finally—and I pose this as a question rather than a conclusion—does not a buyer's rights to reject goods not conforming to the description rest on a concept even more basic than breach of warranty? Clearly that is so when the goods are unspecified at the time of the sale. But even when the goods are specified, is there not a failure of the minds to meet, bringing into play a principle akin to that of Raffles v. Wichelhaus, [1864] 2 H. & C. 906, or the rule whereby courts of the British Commonwealth allow rescission after acceptance in such cases on the ground of a breach of condition despite the general English doctrine that the buyer's only remedy after acceptance is a suit for breach of warranty, 34 Halsbury, Laws of England (1960), pp. 48, 50? The Government intended to sell the advertised lots, whether Manila rope or not; plaintiff intended to buy only if they were Manila. When the error is discovered before the goods are delivered, and the transaction can be rescinded without cost to the Government other than readvertising the goods as what they really were, what reason is there to hold the buyer, even on a sale of surplus? *Per contra,* what reason would there be to force the Government to deliver surplus goods advertised as glass if these turned out to be rock crystals or industrial diamonds? Of course, parties can use language that gets them into precisely these predicaments, but it ought be very clear they have done so before they are held. * * *

Notes

1. Does a Stradivarius or a Guarnarius differ in nature or identity from a fiddle? Smith v. Zimbalist, 2 Cal.App.2d 324, 38 P.2d 170 (1934). Interesting, of course, but a buyer of an instrument described as a Stradivarius could, without deeper analysis, revoke acceptance under the U.C.C. for breach of a descriptive warranty.

2. *Problem:* Suppose a professional sports franchise desires to get rid of its coach after a losing season. It offers to buy up the remaining three years of his five-year contract. The offer is accepted and the money paid. Unknown to either party grounds exist to terminate the contract without payment. Can the money be recovered? Is a "voidable" employment contract (the subject matter of the purchase) different in nature or identity from a "valid" contract? Cf. Bell v. Lever Brothers Ltd., [1932] A.C. 161.

EWING v. BISSELL

Supreme Court of Nevada, 1989.
105 Nev. 488, 777 P.2d 1320.

ROSE, JUSTICE. The appellants (Ewings) purchased a parcel of real estate from respondents * * * (sellers) for $22,000. The sellers represented, and the Offer and Acceptance indicated, that the parcel contained approximately 1.34 acres. * * * Subsequent to the sale, the assessor informed the Ewings that their parcel contained only .83 acres.

The Ewings, alleging alternate theories of fraud, negligent misrepresentation and mutual mistake of fact, brought suit for an abatement of the purchase price to reflect the reduced acreage they received. After a non-jury trial, the district court determined that the Ewings had not established a right to an abatement under any theory, that the sale of the lot was a sale in gross, and that the respondents were entitled to attorney fees of $41,011. Because the record establishes substantial evidence of a mutual mistake of fact as to the acreage in the parcel sold, and because this was not a sale of real estate in gross, abatement of the purchase price was appropriate and the district court erred in not granting Ewings this relief.

Respondent Dennis Jaeger (Jaeger), a real estate agent, had conversations with one of the owners of the property in question and ascertained that they wanted to sell it. In his conversations, he discovered that the plat map listed two noncontiguous lots each as parcel No. 10, and on the larger parcel, the one ultimately purchased by the Ewings, was written 1.34 acres. * * *

The property was listed for sale and a Wayne Miller originally indicated that he would purchase the property for $22,000. Jaeger prepared an Offer and Acceptance which described the property as containing approximately 1.34 acres and it was signed by the sellers and Miller.

Wayne Miller was unable to consummate the purchase of the property and the Ewings considered assuming Miller's right to purchase as set forth in the Offer and Acceptance. When the Ewings called Jaeger, Jaeger read the Offer and Acceptance verbatim.

Ewings met briefly with Jaeger and told him that they wanted to build two homes on the lot to be fed by one community well. Local zoning required a minimum of one-half acre to construct a house, and Jaeger advised the Ewings that they would be able to build one home per one-half acre. The Ewings placed a $500 deposit on the property, thereby succeeding to Miller's interest as stated in the Offer and Acceptance.

A lot near the one in question was being purchased by a friend of the Ewings, Herb Roman. Roman was the person who informed the Ewings of the opportunity to purchase this lot and that it contained approximately 1.34 acres. * * * Jaeger told the sellers that they could get a survey of the property, but neither party requested a survey. In February, 1982, the escrow for the sale of the parcel to the Ewings closed simultaneously with the sale of the lot from the same sellers to Herb Roman. Roman purchased .92 acres for $18,000. The Ewings believed they were purchasing 1.34 acres for $22,000, but actually were purchasing only .83 acres.

At the close of escrow, the Ewings received a tax bill for 1.34 acres and paid the taxes on that acreage. In December, 1982, the Clark County Assessor's office informed the Ewings that they received only .83 acres in the transaction. At that time it was discovered that the 1.34 acre notation on the parcel purchased by the Ewings, as shown on the plat map, actually was the total amount of acreage contained in the two noncontiguous parcels marked No. 10.

Two weeks after the Ewings purchased the property in question, Jaeger's mother-in-law who lived with him purchased the smaller parcel of property, which contained .51 acres and also was labeled as Parcel 10, for $750. Jaeger's mother-in-law subsequently sold this parcel within the year to a third party for $7,000.

The first issue we must decide is whether to affirm the district court's decision that the evidence did not support the Ewings' assertion that relief was warranted on the theory of mutual mistake of fact. * * *

Testimony established that everyone connected with this sale believed the lot contained 1.34 acres: the sellers; the sellers' agent, Jaeger; the initial purchaser, Wayne Miller; the ultimate purchasers, the Ewings; and the neighbor who recommended the purchase, Herb Roman. * * *

We conclude that the Ewings established that there was a mutual mistake of fact and that there is no substantial evidence to hold otherwise.

Even if there is a significant mutual mistake of fact as to the acreage contained in a real estate parcel, the purchaser is usually not entitled to relief if the sale was of acreage in gross. Seyden v. Frade, 88 Nev. 174, 177, 494 P.2d 1281, 1283. Therefore, the second question we must answer is whether the district court correctly held that this was a sale of property in gross. In making this determination, the *Seyden* case again gives us guidance.

> "Whether a sale of land is a sale in gross or a sale by the acre depends primarily upon the intention of the parties, which is to be determined from a variety of factors such as the negotiations of the parties, the mode of stating the purchase price, the manner of describing the land and the language of the contract."

In that case, the purchasers were buying a ranch that was comprised of approximately 320 acres in Mason Valley and approximately 2,300 acres of range land located from Wabuska to Adrian Valley. Even though the range land was approximately 140 acres less than estimated, and the sellers were without title to convey an additional 40 acres, we reversed the district court and held that a substantial variance from the approximated acreage would not affect the sale when the sale was deemed to be one of acreage in gross.

Most sales that are held to be transfers in gross contain large amounts of acreage and rightly so because the specific acreage is less important than the general description of the large parcel being purchased. In the case at bar, however, we are dealing with a small amount of acreage and the purchasers were concerned about having at least one acre upon which to construct two homes. The Ewings received less than an acre and 38% less land than they bargained for.

When purchasing a residential lot, the price is usually set by two basic considerations: the location and the size of the parcel. In reviewing the limited evidence of comparable sales, it is shown that $22,000 was a fair price for 1.34 acres, but not for .83 acres. Herb Roman purchased less than an acre for $18,000 and Jaeger's mother-in-law sold her half acre parcel for $7,000. This leads to the inescapable conclusion that the Ewings would not have paid $22,000 for the lot if they realized it contained only .83 acres and the Ewings so testified. We conclude therefore that this was a sale by the acre and not one in gross as the district court found.

Courts have held that a purchaser is entitled to the equitable remedy of an abatement of the purchase price where the property is sold by the acre and there is a material difference between the actual and estimated quantity of land represented by the seller. [citation] The amount of the abatement is to be determined by multiplying the quantity of the deficiency by the price per acre. [citation] Accordingly, the Ewings are entitled to an abatement of $8,373.13, reflecting a reduction in the purchase price conforming to the quantity of land actually received.

Having held that there was a mistake of fact and that this was not a sale of acreage in gross, it is not necessary to consider the Ewings' additional claims of error. Since the Ewings are the prevailing parties and will receive a judgment in excess of the $5,000 purported offer of judgment, no attorney's fees or costs shall be assessed against them. This case is remanded to the lower court for entry of judgment conforming with this decision.

MOWBRAY, JUDGE, concurring in part and dissenting in part. Respectfully, I dissent from that part of the majority opinion declaring that the Ewings are entitled to an abatement. In this case, there is substantial evidence in the record to support the district court's decision that this was a sale in gross rather than a sale per acre. The parties negotiated for the purchase and sale of a residential lot, described as approximately 1.34 acres for a price of $22,000. The Ewings were interested in the specific lot because of its location next to their friend Herb Roman. The price expressed was for the lot in gross not per acre or square foot. Moreover, the Ewings expressed their desire to keep the lot and not rescind the contract. Therefore, I would affirm the district court's decision that the Ewings were not entitled to an abatement.

Note

The method of calculating the abatement might be appropriate for a large parcel of undeveloped land. But is it appropriate here?

If Ewing decided that he did not want to go through with the deal, could the sellers have sued for specific performance with abatement? Mutuality of remedy? See Chapter 13.

DLUG v. WOOLDRIDGE

Supreme Court of Colorado, 1975.

189 Colo. 164, 538 P.2d 883.

KELLEY, JUSTICE. * * * On September 8, 1969, the petitioners, Leon Jr. and Patricia L. Dlug (purchasers), and the respondent, Charles O. Wooldridge (seller), entered into a written contract for the purchase and sale of unimproved mountain property for the sum of $14,500. The subject property was described in the contract as "[t]hat portion of land in the NW¼ of the NW¼ of Section 20, T. 6 S., R. 70 W. of the 6th P.M. consisting of 26.5 acres, more or less * * *."

On October 2, 1969, the respondent conveyed the subject property to the petitioners by a warranty deed. The warranty deed's description of the property (identical to the contract) was based on the Oehlmann Park map, but omitted the reference to the quantity of the acreage being conveyed. A subsequent survey determined that instead of 26.5 acres, the subject property contained 16.5 acres. This discrepancy resulted from the fact that in platting Oehlmann Park in 1923, the NW¼ corner of section 20 had been mistakenly moved approximately 300 feet west of the point it had been located in the original United States survey of 1873.

The petitioners commenced this action seeking an abatement of the purchase price for the shortage of approximately ten acres. Trial was to the court. The court found, as a matter of fact, that the parties had been mutually mistaken as to the quantity of acreage contained in the subject property, both believing that the property contained 26.5 acres. The court also found that the property had been purchased on a *per-acre* basis of $547.19 per acre, rather than "in gross," and that under the equitable doctrine of unjust enrichment, the petitioners were entitled to an abatement of the purchase price in the amount of $5,471.90.

One further fact is material to the equities involved in this case. The abatement ordered by the trial court resulted in the respondent losing in excess of $3,000, he having purchased the tract as containing 26.5 acres for $12,500 two years previously.

On appeal, the Court of Appeals, in a two to one decision, concluded that where "a contract for the sale of land [is] based upon a substantial mutual mistake as to the number of acres involved, and where it * * * appears that the parties did not reach mutual agreement as to a specified price per acre for the sale, the [trial] court may not award an abatement of the purchase price. The proper remedy is to return the parties to the status quo." The Court of Appeals concluded that rescission was the proper remedy under the circumstances of the case. However, the Court of Appeals went on to hold that

> "since [the] buyers object to granting rescission in connection with this appeal, the judgment is reversed and the cause remanded with directions to the trial court to dismiss the buyers' complaint."

This holding had the effect of recognizing the inequity of the contract to both parties, but leaving the petitioners with a bargain they would not have made in the first instance had they known of the sellers' inability to deliver the quantity of land stated in the various preliminary documents.

We agree, under the circumstances appearing here, that rescission is the proper remedy, but we do not concur in the Court of Appeals' direction to the trial court to dismiss the petitioners' complaint. On appeal, the petitioners, not surprisingly, argued for the affirmance of the judgment of the trial court. The mere assertion of the correctness of "abatement" as the proper remedy was not tantamount to demanding abatement or nothing. The petitioners did not lose their entitlement to rescission by insisting on the correctness of the trial court judgment. * * *

Although the Court of Appeals recognized that rescission was the proper remedy, the petitioners were denied the right to their bargain even though it may now be more appropriate than rescission. In our opinion, the petitioners should have been provided the opportunity to choose between the alternatives of (1) rescission or (2) retention of the original contract.

The respective decisions of both the trial and appellate courts were the result of their resolution of the question whether the parties' contract was one for the sale of land "in gross" or "by the acre." While we recognize the utility of this dichotomy, it is axiomatic that in the realm of equity, no formulation is absolute and no rule is without exception.

This court, in Barth v. Deuel, 11 Colo. 494, 19 P. 471 (1888), announced the general rule applicable in this type of situation, stating:

> "Equitable relief will be granted in cases of mistake when the fact concerning which the mistake is made is material to the transaction, affecting its substance and not merely its incidents, and the mistake itself is so important that it determines the conduct of the mistaken parties." * * *

Here the parties were mutually mistaken as to the amount of land which was the subject of their contract. In view of the substantial variance involved, this mutual mistake must be considered material to the contract. The petitioners both stated that they would not have entered into the contract had they known the true size of the tract.

On the other hand, the respondent was not eager to enter into this contract and was interested in merely recouping his original investment. In no sense was the respondent unjustly enriched. To allow a reduction of the purchase price under these circumstances would be to render the consideration much less than the actual value of the land. For that reason rescission is a proper remedy. However, as stated above, this should not be the petitioner's sole avenue of recourse. * * *

The judgment of the Court of Appeals is reversed and the cause remanded for the entry of a judgment directing the trial court to enter judgment, giving the petitioners the choice of rescission or retaining their bargain pursuant to this opinion.

Notes

1. *Land Sale Contracts. Mistakes About Extent of Vendor's Title Discovered While Contract Is Executory.* Mistakes about the extent of the "owner's" interest are sufficiently similar to mistakes about quantity of land that they may be analyzed in the same terms. Ordinarily title is "basic." A mistaken assumption about the extent of title permits the buyer to avoid the transaction while executory. Minor deficiencies, like encumbrances easily removed, may be equated to minor shortages in area and remedied by abatement in the price.

In executory land contracts, the inability of the vendor to produce the agreed title (or for that matter, the agreed acreage) breaches the contract. The vendor may be honestly mistaken, but unfortunately he is also in default. And the vendee's option to claim rescission for mistake may be less productive than a claim for damages or rescission for breach of contract.

2. *Executed Conveyance by Warranty or Grant Deeds.* Remedies for mistakes about title depend on local practice. The consequence of breach of express or implied warranties, covenants of seisin, covenants to defend title, etc., are best left to courses on Real Property or Conveyances. In general, the grantee is restricted to claims for breach of warranty. See Coates v. Niven, 517 S.W.2d 744 (Ky.App. 1974); D. Dobbs, Remedies § 12.9 (1973).

3. *Executed Conveyances by Quitclaim or other Informal Transfer—Mistakes of Title.* A grantee who fails to protect himself by exacting a suitable covenant in his deed is generally held to lack a remedy for failure of the grantor's title. See Comment, Grantor and Grantee: Recovery by the Grantee of Money Paid Under Mistake as to Vendor's Title, 15 Cal.L.Rev. 53 (1926); Note, Equity—Cancellation and Rescission—Conveyance Without Warranty—Recovery of Purchase Money, 14 Tex.L.Rev. 227 (1936). This applies the assumption of risk defense to restitution for mistake. If the parties, aware of uncertainties in the grantor's title and desiring to clear title, choose the quitclaim, the compromise precludes a claim of mistake. Even quitclaim deeds, however, like releases and other settlements, may be avoided because of *basic* mistakes about facts *outside* the area of compromise.

LENAWEE COUNTY BOARD OF HEALTH v. MESSERLY

Supreme Court of Michigan, 1982.
417 Mich. 17, 331 N.W.2d 203.

RYAN, JUSTICE. The facts of the case are not seriously in dispute. In 1971, the Messerlys acquired approximately one acre plus 600 square feet of land. A three-unit apartment building was situated upon the 600–square–foot portion. The trial court found that, prior to this transfer, the Messerlys' predecessor in title, Mr. Bloom, had installed a septic tank on the property without a permit and in violation of the applicable health code. The Messerlys used the building as an income investment property until 1973 when they sold it, upon land contract, to James Barnes who likewise used it primarily as an income-producing investment.

Mr. and Mrs. Barnes, with the permission of the Messerlys, sold approximately one acre of the property in 1976, and the remaining 600 square feet and building were offered for sale soon thereafter when Mr. and Mrs. Barnes defaulted on their land contract. Mr. and Mrs. Pickles evidenced an interest in the property, but were dissatisfied with the terms of the Barnes–Messerly land contract. Consequently, to accommodate the Pickleses' preference to enter into a land contract directly with the Messerlys, Mr. and Mrs. Barnes executed a quit-claim deed which conveyed their interest in the property back to the Messerlys. After inspecting the property, Mr. and Mrs. Pickles executed a new land contract with the Messerlys on March 21, 1977. It provided for a purchase price of $25,500. A clause was added to the end of the land contract form which provides:

> "17. Purchaser has examined this property and agrees to accept same in its present condition. There are no other or additional written or oral understandings."

Five or six days later, when the Pickleses went to introduce themselves to the tenants, they discovered raw sewage seeping out of the ground. * * * The Lenawee County Board of Health subsequently condemned the property and initiated this lawsuit in the Lenawee Circuit Court * * * to obtain a permanent injunction proscribing human habitation of the premises until the property was brought into conformance with the Lenawee County sanitation code. The injunction was granted, and the Lenawee County Board of Health was permitted to withdraw from the lawsuit by stipulation of the parties.

When no payments were made on the land contract, the Messerlys filed a cross-complaint against the Pickleses seeking foreclosure, sale of the property, and a deficiency judgment. Mr. and Mrs. Pickles then counterclaimed for rescission. * * *

After a bench trial, the court concluded that the Pickleses had no cause of action * * *

Mr. and Mrs. Pickles appealed from the adverse judgment. The Court of Appeals * * * in a two-to-one decision, reversed the finding of no cause of action on the Pickleses' claims against the Messerlys. It concluded that the mutual mistake between the Messerlys and the Pickleses went to a basic, as opposed to a collateral, element of the contract, and that the parties intended to transfer income-producing rental property but, in actuality, the vendees paid

$25,500 for an asset without value.[1]

We granted the Messerlys' application for leave to appeal. * * *

An examination of the record reveals that the septic system was defective prior to the date on which the land contract was executed. The Messerly's grantor installed a nonconforming septic system without a permit prior to the transfer of the property to the Messerlys in 1971. Moreover, virtually undisputed testimony indicates that, assuming ideal soil conditions, 2,500 square feet of property is necessary to support a sewage system adequate to serve a three-family dwelling. Likewise, 750 square feet is mandated for a one-family home. Thus, the division of the parcel and sale of one acre of the property by Mr. and Mrs. Barnes in 1976 made it impossible to remedy the already illegal septic system within the confines of the 600–square–foot parcel. * * *

Appellants argue that the parties' mistake relates only to the quality or value of the real estate transferred, and that such mistakes are collateral to the agreement and do not justify rescission, citing A & M Land Development Co. v. Miller, 354 Mich. 681, 94 N.W.2d 197 (1959).

In that case, the plaintiff was the purchaser of 91 lots of real property. It sought partial rescission of the land contract when it was frustrated in its attempts to develop 42 of the lots because it could not obtain permits from the county health department to install septic tanks on these lots. This Court refused to allow rescission because the mistake, whether mutual or unilateral, related only to the value of the property. * * *

Appellees contend, on the other hand, that in this case the parties were mistaken as to the very nature of the character of the consideration and claim that the pervasive and essential quality of this mistake renders rescission appropriate. They cite in support of that view Sherwood v. Walker, 66 Mich. 568, 33 N.W. 919 (1887), the famous "barren cow" case. In that case, the parties agreed to the sale and purchase of a cow which was thought to be barren, but which was, in reality, with calf. When the seller discovered the fertile condition of his cow, he refused to deliver her. * * *

As the parties suggest, the foregoing precedent arguably distinguishes mistakes affecting the essence of the consideration from those which go to its quality or value, affording relief on a per se basis for the former but not the latter.

However, the distinctions which may be drawn from *Sherwood* and *A & M Land Development Co.* do not provide a satisfactory analysis of the nature of a mistake sufficient to invalidate a contract. Often, a mistake relates to an underlying factual assumption which, when discovered, directly affects value, but simultaneously and materially affects the essence of the contractual consideration. It is disingenuous to label such a mistake collateral.

Appellant and appellee both mistakenly believed that the property which was the subject of their land contract would generate income as rental property. The fact that it could not be used for human habitation deprived the

1. [Footnotes renumbered.] The trial court found that the only way that the property could be put to residential use would be to pump and haul the sewage, a method which is economically unfeasible, as the cost of such a disposal system amounts to double the income generated by the property. There was speculation by the trial court that the adjoining land might be utilized to make the property suitable for residential use, but, in the absence of testimony directed at the point, the court refused to draw any conclusions. The trial court and the Court of Appeals both found that the property was valueless, or had a negative value.

property of its income-earning potential and rendered it less valuable. However, this mistake, while directly and dramatically affecting the property's value, cannot accurately be characterized as collateral because it also affects the very essence of the consideration. "The thing sold and bought [income generating rental property] had in fact no existence." Sherwood v. Walker.

We find that the inexact and confusing distinction between contractual mistakes running to value and those touching the substance of the consideration serves only as an impediment to a clear and helpful analysis for the equitable resolution of cases in which mistake is alleged and proven. Accordingly, the holdings of *A & M Land Development Co.* and *Sherwood* with respect to the material or collateral nature of a mistake are limited to the facts of those cases.

Instead, we think the better-reasoned approach is a case-by-case analysis whereby rescission is indicated when the mistaken belief relates to a basic assumption of the parties upon which the contract is made, and which materially affects the agreed performances of the parties. Restatement Contracts, 2d, § 152, pp. 385–386.[2] Rescission is not available, however, to relieve a party who has assumed the risk of loss in connection with the mistake. Restatement Contracts, 2d, §§ 152, 154, pp. 385–386, 402–406.[3]

All of the parties to this contract erroneously assumed that the property transferred by the vendors to the vendees was suitable for human habitation and could be utilized to generate rental income. The fundamental nature of these assumptions is indicated by the fact that their invalidity changed the character of the property transferred, thereby frustrating, indeed precluding, Mr. and Mrs. Pickles' intended use of the real estate. Although the Pickleses are disadvantaged by enforcement of the contract, performance is advantageous to the Messerlys, as the property at issue is less valuable absent its income-earning potential. Nothing short of rescission can remedy the mistake. Thus, the parties' mistake as to a basic assumption materially affects the agreed performances of the parties.

Despite the significance of the mistake made by the parties, we reverse the Court of Appeals * * *

In cases of mistake by two equally innocent parties, we are required, in the exercise of our equitable powers, to determine which blameless party should assume the loss resulting from the misapprehension they shared.[4] * * *

2. Section 152 delineates the legal significance of a mistake.

"§ 152. When Mistake of Both Parties Makes a Contract Voidable

"(1) Where a mistake of both parties at the time a contract was made as to a basic assumption on which the contract was made has a material effect on the agreed exchange of performances, the contract is voidable by the adversely affected party unless he bears the risk of the mistake under the rule stated in § 154.

"(2) In determining whether the mistake has a material effect on the agreed exchange of performances, account is taken of any relief by way of reformation, restitution, or otherwise."

3. "§ 154. When a Party Bears the Risk of a Mistake

"A party bears the risk of a mistake when

"(a) the risk is allocated to him by agreement of the parties, or

"(b) he is aware, at the time the contract is made, that he has only limited knowledge with respect to the facts to which the mistake relates but treats his limited knowledge as sufficient, or

"(c) the risk is allocated to him by the court on the ground that it is reasonable in the circumstances to do so."

4. This risk-of-loss analysis is absent in both *A & M Land Development Co.* and *Sherwood,* and this omission helps to explain, in part, the disparate treatment in the two cases. Had such an inquiry been undertaken in *Sherwood,* we believe that the result might have been differ-

Equity suggests that, in this case, the risk should be allocated to the purchasers. We are guided to that conclusion, in part, by the standards announced in § 154 of the Restatement of Contracts 2d, for determining when a party bears the risk of mistake. Section 154(a) suggests that the court should look first to whether the parties have agreed to the allocation of the risk between themselves. While there is no express assumption in the contract by either party of the risk of the property becoming uninhabitable, there was indeed some agreed allocation of the risk to the vendees by the incorporation of an "as is" clause into the contract which, we repeat, provided:

> "Purchaser has examined this property and agrees to accept same in its present condition. There are no other or additional written or oral understandings."

That is a persuasive indication that the parties considered that, as between them, such risk as related to the "present condition" of the property should lie with the purchaser. If the "as is" clause is to have any meaning at all, it must be interpreted to refer to those defects which were unknown at the time that the contract was executed.[5] Thus, the parties themselves assigned the risk of loss to Mr. and Mrs. Pickles.[6]

We conclude that Mr. and Mrs. Pickles are not entitled to the equitable remedy of rescission and, accordingly, reverse the decision of the Court of Appeals.

WILLIAMS v. GLASH

Supreme Court of Texas 1990.
789 S.W.2d 261.

DOGGETT, JUSTICE. The question presented is whether execution of the release for personal injuries in this cause bars a subsequent suit for an injury unknown at the time of signing. The trial court granted summary judgment against Petitioners Margaret and David Williams based on execution of a release. The court of appeals affirmed. We reverse the judgment of the court of appeals and remand this cause to the trial court for further proceedings.

Margaret Williams ("Williams") was a passenger in her family car when it was struck from behind by a car driven by the respondent Stephen Glash. While damage to the Petitioners' car was apparent at the time of the accident, there were no observable injuries. Williams immediately contacted State Farm Mutual Automobile Insurance Company, Glash's insurer, who advised Williams to bring the car to its local office for an appraisal of the property damage claims. State Farm estimated the cost of repairs at $889.46 and provided Williams a check payable for that precise amount.

ent. Moreover, a determination as to which party assumed the risk in *A & M Land Development Co.* would have alleviated the need to characterize the mistake as collateral so as to justify the result denying rescission. Despite the absence of any inquiry as to the assumption of risk in those two leading cases, we find that there exists sufficient precedent to warrant such an analysis in future cases of mistake.

5. An "as is" clause waives those implied warranties which accompany the sale of a new home. [citation] or the sale of goods. [citation] Since implied warranties protect against latent defects, an "as is" clause will impose upon the purchaser the assumption of the risk of latent defects, such as an inadequate sanitation system, even when there are no implied warranties.

6. An "as is" clause does not preclude a purchaser from alleging fraud or misrepresentation as a basis for rescission. However, Mr. and Mrs. Pickles did not appeal the trial court's finding that there was no fraud or misrepresentation, so we are bound thereby.

At the State Farm office, Williams was asked to complete a claim form containing a question as to whether anyone had been injured by the accident. She checked "No" in response. There was no negotiating or bargaining for release of a personal injury claim; only property damage to the car was discussed. Nonetheless, the back of the check contained language purporting to release personal injury claims, providing that:

> "The undersigned payee accepts the amount of this payment in full settlement of all claims for damages to property and for bodily injury whether known or unknown which payee claims against any insured under the policy shown on the face hereof, or their respective successors in interest, arising out of an accident which occurred on or about the date shown. This release reserves all rights of the parties released to pursue their legal remedies, if any, against such payee."

This release language was never explained to nor discussed with Williams or her husband. The face of the check contained a State Farm code, "200–1," denoting the settlement of a property claim, rather than a separate code used by the insurer for personal injury claims. Petitioners subsequently endorsed the check over to the garage that repaired their car.

Williams was later diagnosed as having temporomandibular joint syndrome ("TMJ"), causing head and neck pain, as a result of the accident. Both the trial court and the court of appeals found that suit for this injury was barred by execution of the release.

Petitioners seek to avoid the effect of the release, imploring this court to follow the "modern trend" of setting aside releases when the injury later sued for was unknown at the time of signing. [citation] It is true that a majority of our sister states would, under a variety of theories, permit invalidation of the release under the circumstances presented in this case. [citations] The most common basis for invalidation is the doctrine of mutual mistake, which mandates that a contract be avoided "[w]here a mistake of both parties at the time the contract was made as to a basic assumption on which the contract was made has a material effect on the agreed exchange of performances." Restatement (Second) of Contracts § 152 (1981). Following the modern trend, the Restatement expressly recognizes avoidance of personal injury releases when, in view of the parties' knowledge and negotiations, the release language "flies in the face of what would otherwise be regarded as a basic assumption of the parties."

Under Texas law, a release is a contract and is subject to avoidance, on grounds such as fraud or mistake, just like any other contract. [citation] Pursuant to the doctrine of mutual mistake, when parties to an agreement have contracted under a misconception or ignorance of a material fact, the agreement will be avoided. [citations] The law of mutual mistake does not, of course, preclude a person from intentionally assuming the risk of unknown injuries in a valid release.

However, whether the parties to a release intended to cover an unknown injury cannot always be determined exclusively by reference to the language of the release itself. It may require consideration of the conduct of the parties and the information available to them at the time of signing. In a subsequent suit for an unknown injury, once the affirmative defense of release has been pleaded and proved, the burden of proof is on the party seeking to avoid the release to establish mutual mistake. The question of mutual mistake is determined not by self-serving subjective statements of the parties' intent, which would necessitate trial to a jury in all such cases, but rather solely by objective circumstances surrounding execution of the release, such as the knowledge of the parties at the time of signing concerning the injury, the amount of consideration paid, the extent of negotiations and discussions as to personal injuries, and the haste or lack thereof in obtaining the release. See Restatement (Second) of Torts § 152 comment f (1981).

We then turn to an application of the mutual mistake factors in this case. As this is a summary judgment case, the issue on appeal is whether State Farm met its burden of establishing that there exists no genuine issue of material fact, thereby entitling it to judgment as a matter of law. [citation] All doubts as to the existence of a genuine issue of material fact are resolved against the movant, and we must view the evidence in the light most favorable to the Petitioners. [citation] Summary judgment evidence manifesting Williams' objective intent shows that she had no knowledge of the TMJ injury at the time of signing the release. She neither discussed nor bargained for settlement of a personal injury claim, and the amount of consideration received was the exact amount of the property damage to her car. State Farm similarly had no knowledge of the TMJ injury and, in fact, used a code on the check indicating the settlement of property damage claims only. The only evidence that these parties intended to release a claim for unknown personal injuries is the language of the release itself. This summary judgment evidence is sufficient to establish the existence of a genuine issue of fact as to whether the parties intended the release to cover the injury for which suit was later brought.

The one case cited by State Farm as controlling precedent misapplies the Texas law of mutual mistake and is, therefore, unpersuasive. McClellan v. Boehmer, 700 S.W.2d 687 (Tex.App.—Corpus Christi 1985, no writ). In *McClellan* and in Houston & T.C.R. Co. v. McCarty, 94 Tex. 298, 60 S.W. 429 (1901), the courts were willing to look to the intent of the parties for the purpose of interpreting and applying the release but not to alter the unambiguous language of the contract. When mutual mistake is alleged, the task of the court is not to interpret the language contained in the release, but to determine whether or not the release itself is valid. We overrule *McCarty* and disapprove *McClellan* to the extent that they give controlling weight to the language of the release to defeat a claim of mutual mistake.

We do not today, as the dissent claims, release an injured tort victim from an unfair bargain. Rather, we hold only that the law of mutual mistake applies to personal injury releases the same as to other contracts. If it can be established that a release sets out a *bargain that was never made,* it will be invalidated. If the objective manifestation of the parties' intent—i.e., their conduct—indicates that no release of unknown personal injuries was contemplated, the courts cannot provide intent for them. The dissent is willing to hold the parties to a written agreement that is contrary to their intent and understanding and to ignore the law of mutual mistake, granting as a result a windfall to the insurer by releasing it from claims that it is contractually obligated to pay. A majority of our sister states have refused to follow such a harsh rule; and today we join them.[1]

1. [Footnotes renumbered.] While condemning the use in this opinion of a string-cite of cases from other states, the dissent nonetheless relies on a string-cite of its own to support deviation from the majority rule avoiding releases for unknown injuries. While in each of

The doctrine of mutual mistake must not routinely be available to avoid the results of an unhappy bargain. Parties should be able to rely on the finality of freely bargained agreements. However, in narrow circumstances a party may raise a fact issue for the trier of fact to set aside a release under the doctrine of mutual mistake. Because there is some evidence of such circumstances here, we reverse the judgment of the court of appeals and remand this cause to the trial court for further proceedings consistent with this opinion.

SPEARS, JUSTICE, dissenting. What the court has really decided today is that an injured tort victim should not be held to his bargain if the bargain later appears unfair. In order to reach this result, the court relies on the doctrine of mutual mistake and a long string citation. Yet, the reality is that the cases from other jurisdictions present a jumbled mish-mash of reasonings and results. The "mutual mistake" rationale does not adequately explain their holdings. See Casey v. Proctor, 59 Cal.2d 97, 28 Cal.Rptr. 307, 378 P.2d 579, 587 (1963). Therefore, rather than trying to resolve this case by simple string citation, the court ought to engage in a straight-forward analysis of the issue. *Cf.* Holmes, The Path of the Law, 10 Harv.L.Rev. 457, 466–67 (1897) (encouraging the candid articulation of judicial reasoning).

Two competing interests are involved. On the one hand, the law favors the peaceful settlement of disputes and the orderly resolution of claims. On the other hand, the law favors the just compensation of accident victims. Our dilemma is to resolve these competing interests, and we ought to do so openly rather than hiding behind the facade of mutual mistake.

Because I believe the law, in general, is better served by encouraging settlements, I would uphold the release and affirm the summary judgment in favor of Glash. In its effort to afford equitable relief, the court renders useless most releases. How is one to buy peace and settle a claim? If the release here can be avoided, then no release buys peace until the statute of limitations has run. "Consideration of the conduct of the parties and the information available to them at the time" will present a fact question so as to require a trial in every instance. Bad facts make bad law and that is what has happened here.

Insurers are now faced with a Hobson's choice. If they settle claims promptly, they are not protected from the later assertion of unknown claims. If they refuse to settle until all injuries are known, then they face potential liability under a bad faith claim. [citation] Their only alternative is to settle known damages only and this defeats their reason for settling. What the insurer wants is to buy peace and put an end to any further claims; this is the very essence of its position. Any mistake as to the nature of injuries is strictly unilateral, not mutual.

Courts cannot legitimately cast themselves in the role of saving people from bad bargains. This sort of benevolent paternalism oversteps the boundaries of our proper role in society. In the short run, it may make life easier for one injured party, but in the long run it distorts the law and creates more problems than it solves. The Maryland court expressed a similar view when it stated:

these cases the release scrutinized was upheld, it is far from clear that those courts would uphold the release before the court today. See, e.g., Maltais v. National Grange Ins. Co., 118 N.H. 318, 386 A.2d 1264, 1269 (1978) (release upheld because no evidence that "accident caused an injury more severe than originally thought or aggravated a preexisting condition of which the parties were originally unaware").

"We are convinced that our society will be best served by adherence to the traditional methodology for interpreting contracts. * * * In our view, the bastardization of the well-founded principles concerning mutual mistake of fact is entirely too high a price to pay for the obtention of an unprincipled, if temporarily desirable, result."

Bernstein v. Kapneck, 290 Md. 452, 430 A.2d 602, 606–608 (1981). And numerous other sister states have also refused to go along with the so-called "modern trend." [1] [citations]

Moreover, in some of the cases that have allowed releases to be avoided, the courts have at least moderated their decisions by imposing a higher burden of proof on the plaintiff. They have required clear and convincing proof that a mutual mistake was made or that the release was not fairly and knowingly made. [citations] By refusing to impose any higher burden, this court steps beyond even these more moderate decisions in other jurisdictions.

Finally, almost as an afterthought, the court looks to Texas precedent. In order to allow for the invalidation of this release, the court must overrule Houston & T.C.R. Co. v. McCarty, 94 Tex. 298, 60 S.W. 429 (1901) and must disapprove [citations]. In all of these cases, Texas courts upheld the validity of personal injury releases, and the *Ulschmid* case even involved the same "200–1" notation as exists in this case. This is a lot of Texas precedent for the court to address it in such a summary fashion.

I can understand the desire to do equity,[2] but the court's decision today is too one-sided to fall under the rubric of equity. If the court is determined to reach this result, it ought to at least be candid about its reasons. I respectfully dissent. I would affirm the judgment of the court of appeals.

b. *Unilateral Mistake*

MONARCH MARKING SYSTEM CO. v. REED'S PHOTO MART, INC.

Supreme Court of Texas, 1972.

485 S.W.2d 905.

POPE, JUSTICE. The Monarch Marking System Company (Monarch) sued Reed's Photo Mart, Inc., (Reed's) to recover the price of four million adhesive pricing labels which Monarch furnished Reed's pursuant to a written purchase order. Reed's defenses were that it mistakenly ordered four million instead of four thousand labels. * * *

On the morning of February 22, 1968, Alan Tromer, vice-president of Reed's, began filling out a purchase order for five different kinds of labels which Reed's desired to buy from Monarch. In handwriting he filled in the blank spaces for four different types of labels and in the quantity column he noted opposite each of the four orders "2M." At that point he was interrupted

1. I dislike the use of string-cites, but it was the majority's choice to rely on this mode of analysis. I would be happy to delete *all* citation to other states and rely solely on Texas authority for this decision.

2. I would prefer that Texas address this problem by legislation rather than by judicial fiat. For example, in Idaho, a personal injury release executed within fifteen days after the occurrence may be disavowed at anytime within one year after the occurrence. Idaho Code § 29–113 (1961). For other similar statutes, see also Md.Ann.Code art. 79, § 11 (1957); Utah Code Ann. § 78–27–3 (1953); N.C.Cent.Code § 9–08–08 (1987); Cal.Civ.Code § 1542 (West 1982); Me.Rev.Stat.Ann. tit. 17, § 3964 (1964); Conn.Gen.Stat. § 52–572a (1958).

by a customer and it was not until later in the afternoon that he finished filling in the order. He described the fifth label as "Label as Attached," attached the copy of the desired label, and in the quantity column wrote "4MM." It was this last item which forms the basis of this suit. The purchase order required delivery "At Once." * * *

On April 10, 1968, the four million labels were delivered to Reed's via motor freight. Alan Tromer refused the shipment and immediately called Cornelius, claiming that "a terrible mistake had been made." * * *

Most of the problems in this case are resolved by the jury findings that the term "MM" by custom and usage in the trade means one million; * * * the reasonable value of the labels shipped to Reed's was $2,680, and reasonable attorney fees for representing Monarch were $750. The jury refused to find that Monarch knew that the order for "4MM" labels was a mistake. The court of civil appeals reversed the judgment of the trial court and remanded the cause for trial by reason of that court's refusal to submit an issue which inquired whether Monarch should have known of Reed's error in preparing the purchase order. Monarch urges that this holding of the court of civil appeals is immaterial because Monarch cannot now be placed in status quo * * *.

The mistake was a unilateral one; it was made by Reed's and Monarch fully performed its part of the contract. The Texas rule has long been that relief from a unilateral mistake depends upon the ability of the party mistaken to put the other party into the same situation as he was prior to the transaction in question. * * * We reaffirmed that principle in James T. Taylor and Son, Inc. v. Arlington I.S.D., [160 Tex. 617, 335 S.W.2d 371 (1960)], wherein we said that one of the usual prerequisites to the granting of relief for a unilateral mistake was "the parties can be placed in status quo in the equity sense, i.e., rescission must not result in prejudice to the other party except for the loss of his bargain." The importance of the ability to restore the status quo was emphasized * * * by our comments about Clem Lumber Co. v. Marty, 26 S.W.2d 319 (Tex.Civ.App.1930, writ ref'd). Clem Lumber Company was not entitled to the equitable relief of rescission of its bid to furnish materials because the offeree had already used some of the materials, had purchased a lot and had entered into a contract to build a building. * * *

We have in this case a fully executed contract on the part of Monarch and the record is devoid of proof of any effort on the part of Reed's to restore Monarch to the status quo even to the extent that circumstances would permit. Accordingly, the judgment of the court of civil appeals is reversed and the judgment of the trial court is affirmed.

Notes

1. In Hall v. United States, 19 Cl.Ct. 558 (1990), a fuel control worth $167,553 that should have been sent to a repair facility was instead sold at a government surplus auction for $15. The government offered to settle for $15,000; the buyer refused; and the U.S. declined to deliver. Held: Sale voidable for unilateral mistake, plus unconscionability.

2. Plaintiff, a golfer participating in a club tournament, arrives at the 9th tee to find a new car with a sign "HOLE–IN–ONE" wins this car, "courtesy of [a local dealer]." Plaintiff aces the hole and demands the car. The dealer backs out. The sign was a promotion for a charitable tournament the previous day. Someone else had won. The car and signs should have been removed that afternoon. Assuming

a unilateral contract under conventional contracts lore, can the dealer rescind it for unilateral mistake plus unconscionability? Cf. Cobaugh v. Klick–Lewis, Inc., 385 Pa.Super. 587, 561 A.2d 1248 (1989).

3. NEWS ITEM (1972): "When this gets back to that lady, she's going to die * * *.

"She was going to just throw the photographs away and keep the pretty brass frames for pictures of her family, but she was mercenary enough to want to get anything she could, so I paid her $18 for the photos."

Thus did Michael Kessler warmly recount Wednesday how he retrieved from history's dustbin the seven oldest-known photographs of Washington, D.C. And turned a neat $12,000 profit.

It was last April, pursuing his hobby through San Francisco's antique shops and flea markets, that he spotted six daguerreotypes of Washington scenes.

He quietly paid the woman's asking price and took the deguerreotypes off to confer with another collector, who recognized one of the photos as the original from a series of lithographic copies.

The photos were identified as 1846 views taken by John Plumbe Jr., a U.S. photography pioneer.

Kessler then contacted the Library of Congress for information about the photos, he said, "and they were on the phone to me the next day."

After a little research into the value of old photographs, Kessler asked—and quickly got—$12,000 from the library for the six photographs.

The photograph sale is not the only killing Kessler has made on an investment of mere peanuts.

"Once in an antique store I found a daguerreotype camera that the dealer paid only $2 for. He sold it to me for $10 and thought he had done well. But the camera is really worth about $2,500. It dates from 1851."

4. Professor Kronman approves the courts' reluctance to excuse unilateral mistake on the ground that "the distinction between material and unilateral mistake makes sense from an economic point of view. * * *

"If we assume that courts can easily discriminate between those who have acquired information casually and those who have acquired it deliberately, plausible economic considerations might well justify imposing a duty to disclose on a case-by-case basis (imposing it where the information has been casually acquired, refusing to impose it where the information is the fruit of a deliberate search). A party who has casually acquired information is, at the time of the transaction, likely to be a better (cheaper) mistake-preventer than the mistaken party with whom he deals—regardless of the fact that both parties initially had equal access to the information in question. One who had deliberately acquired information is also in a position to prevent the other party's error. But in determining the cost to the knowledgeable party of preventing the mistake (by disclosure), we must include whatever investment he has made in acquiring the information in the first place. This investment will represent a loss to him if the other party can avoid the contract on the grounds that the party with the information owes him a duty of disclosure."

Kronman, Mistake, Disclosure, Information, and the Law of Contracts, 7 J. Legal Stud. 1, 5, 16 (1978).

Birmingham, The Duty to Disclose and the Prisoner's Dilemma: Laidlaw v. Organ, 29 Wm. & Mary L.Rev. 249 (1988).

5. *Unilateral Mistake in Accepting Offer.* Goodrich v. Lathrop, 94 Cal. 56, 29 P. 329 (1892): "Plaintiff, knowing that defendant had a certain lot for sale, went to examine the same, with a view to purchase, but by mistake looked at a different lot from the one defendant had for sale. She did not see defendant's lot, but the one she viewed being satisfactory, and believing it to be the lot defendant had for sale, she entered into a written contract of purchase with defendant, the description in said contract being for defendant's lot. Later, upon ascertaining her mistake, she gave notice of rescission and brought this action thereunder." *Held*: an "ample ground" for rescission presented unless defeated by the defense of negligence, a fact question to be determined at a new trial.

See Patterson, Equitable Relief for Unilateral Mistake, 28 Colum.L.Rev. 859, 890 (1928), where *Goodrich* is said to rest "upon a code provision."

Suppose the value of the lot had declined prior to the trial? Should the decree be unconditional? Cf. Cal.Civ.Code § 1692, par. 4.

PRESIDENT AND COUNCIL OF MOUNT ST. MARY'S COLLEGE v. AETNA CASUALTY & SURETY CO.

United States District Court.
District of Maryland, 1965.
233 F.Supp. 787, affirmed, 344 F.2d 331 (4th Cir.1965).

THOMSEN, CHIEF JUDGE. This is an action against a surety on a bid bond to recover the penalty thereof, wherein the low bidder, W. Harley Miller, Inc. (Miller, Inc.), the intervening defendant, seeks relief on the ground of mistake from any obligation created by its bid, cancellation of its bid, and return of the bid bond. The mistake consisted in the failure of Miller, Inc., to include in its Base Proposals certain Separate Price Quotes for kitchen and snack bar equipment, built-in furniture, etc. * * *

In 1961 plaintiff (the College) acting through its architects, May and Ruppert (the Architects), issued an invitation for bids to construct a student union building and a dormitory building on its campus at Emmitsburg, Maryland. The project was financed by the Federal Housing and Home Finance Agency (HHFA), which had agreed to purchase $1,400,000 of bonds of the College secured by a deed of trust, based upon the Architects' estimate of costs. The original loan agreement required the College to deposit in the construction account $360,000 over and above the loan from HHFA. Under the loan agreement the College was obligated to contract for the work upon free, open and competitive bidding, and to award each contract after approval by HHFA to the lowest responsible bidder as soon as practicable.

The bidding documents, which contained the usual general provisions, provided for three Base Proposals: (A) Combined bid for the construction of the Student Union Building and the Dormitory Building; (B) Student Union Building only; and (C) Dormitory Building only. The College reserved the right to reject any or all bids, and if the lowest bid submitted by a responsible bidder exceeded the amount of funds available to finance the contract, to reject all bids or award the contract on the base bid modified by certain deductible alternates. The Instructions to Bidders provided that any bid might be withdrawn prior to the scheduled time for the opening of bids, but that no bidder might withdraw a bid within thirty days after the date of the opening.

Each bidder was required to post a bid security bond in the amount of 10% of its bid. * * * [1]

The Form of Proposal for the submission of bids, prepared by the Architects, after providing Base Proposals for the construction of the buildings, contained the following provisions requiring the bidders to furnish prices for certain Separate Price Quotes * * *:

"Deductible (Include these prices in the base bid)

"Separate Price Quotes:

"1. *Kitchen and Snack Bar Equipment, Refrigerators & Refrigeration.* * * *

"(a) Furnish and install new kitchen and snack bar equipment, etc., as specified. * * *

"(b) *Install* the kitchen and snack bar equipment as specified. * * *

"2. Built-in-Furniture-Dormitory. * * *

"(a) Furnish and install built-in furniture (Student bedroom units and Perfect bedroom Units) as specified. * * * "

Upon the opening of the sealed bids at the office of the President of the College in Emmitsburg at 2 p.m. on August 8, the bid of Miller, Inc., was found to be the low bid for the combined construction of the Student Union and Dormitory Buildings, namely, $1,389,450; its separate bid ($734,450) for the Student Union Building only was also low; as was its separate bid ($659,450) for the Dormitory Building only. The other bids were as follows:

	Combined Bid	Student Union	Dormitory
Frederick Construction Co.	$1,478,064	$815,064	$700,064
Lawrence Construction Co.	1,483,987	783,428	703,871
Henry A. Knott, Inc.	1,490,000	765,000	782,000
Altimont Brothers, Inc.	1,498,000	788,400	788,400
Joseph F. Nebel Co.	1,567,000	No Bid	No Bid

In filling out the Form of Proposal and submitting its bids, Miller, Inc.—

"quoted $84,000 as the cost of Separate Price Quote 1(a), for kitchen and snack bar equipment for the Student Union Building;

"quoted $1,000 as the cost of Separate Price Quote 1(b), as the cost of capping off and revamping of plumbing and finishing; and

"quoted $85,000 as the cost of Separate Price Quote 2(a), for built-in furniture for the Dormitory Building."

1. [Footnotes renumbered.] Paragraph 1B–7 of the Instructions to Bidders reads as follows:

"LIQUIDATED DAMAGES FOR FAILURE TO ENTER INTO CONTRACT:

"(a) The successful bidder, upon his failure or refusal to execute and deliver the contract and bonds required within 10 days after he has received notice of the acceptance of his bid, shall forfeit to the Owner, as liquidated damages for such failure or refusal, the security deposited with his bid."

The Form of Bid provided on the last page before the signature of the bidders is as follows:

"Upon receipt of written notice of the acceptance of this bid, Bidder will execute the formal contract attached within 10 days and deliver a Surety Bond or Bonds as required by paragraph 29 of the General Conditions.

"The bid security attached in the sum of ______ ______ ($______) is to become the property of the Owner in the event the contract and bond are not executed within the time above set forth, as liquidated damages for the delay and additional expense to the Owner caused thereby."

Since the Specifications were prepared by the Architects for the College, any ambiguity must be resolved against the College; * * *.

Both W. Harley Miller (Miller), president and principal stockholder of Miller, Inc., and Jenkins, its estimator, interpreted and construed the Form of Proposal as not calling for the inclusion of the Separate Price Quotes in the Base Proposals, and Miller, Inc., did not include any of these Separate Price Quotes in its Base Proposals for the construction of the buildings.

The Architects and the College intended the form of Bid Proposal and the Specifications to mean that the kitchen equipment and the built-in furniture, for which Separate Price Quotes were requested, should be included in the Base Bids for the Student Union Building and for the Dormitory Building, respectively, and in the Combined Base Bid for both buildings. All of the bidders except Miller, Inc., so interpreted the bidding documents and considered that these special equipment items were included in their Base Bids; all of their bids were prepared and submitted on that basis.

* * * The Form of Proposal prepared by the Architects was confusing, but it was not uncertain or ambiguous in the sense that it was subject to more than one reasonable meaning. The only reasonable meaning was the one intended by the Architects and the College and recognized by all of the other bidders, namely, that the special equipment items for which Separate Price Quotes were requested, should be included in the Base Price.

[However], Miller and Jenkins were so certain that Separate Price Quotes were generally treated as entirely separate and not deductible items that they did not give much thought to the matter until the bids were opened.

In omitting the special equipment items from its Base Bids, Miller, Inc. did not make a clerical, mechanical or mathematical error. The bids which it submitted were made deliberately, intentionally and not inadvertently. The omission was an honest mistake or misunderstanding, made in good faith. * * *

The mistake was substantial and material. The omission amounted to $169,000 if based upon the Separate Price Quotes of Miller, Inc. for these items, $160,555 if based upon the lowest quotations which Miller, Inc. received from suppliers. The omission was more than the $140,000 which Miller, Inc. had included in its Base Proposal for overhead, bond expense and profit.[2]

Miller, Inc. was a responsible bidder. It was an experienced contractor and was then engaged in four or five construction jobs. It was financially able to perform its contract with the College, although, if it had done so, it would have suffered a loss.

To a person experienced in the building industry, such as the other bidders or the Architects, it was or should have been apparent that Miller's bid was probably the result of some error or mistake; it was $89,000 lower than the next lowest bid, and the next four were within a spread of $20,000.

On the other hand, the representatives of the College other than the Architects did not realize that there was a material error in the bid.[3]

2. Miller, Inc. had included a figure of $25,000 for profit. It was faced with a loss if it were required to construct the two buildings, including the kitchen and snack bar equipment and built-in furniture, for the sum of $1,389,450.

3. The College had received a written estimate from its Architects that the cost of the buildings would be $1,350,000, aside from Architects' fees and other items not included in the bidding documents. The bid of Miller, Inc. for the construction of both buildings was $88,614 (or 6%) less than the next lowest bid. Its bid

Byers, the representative of Miller, Inc. at the opening of the bids, telephoned Jenkins an hour or so later, and gave him all bid figures.

The governing body of the College met later that afternoon, August 8, and adopted resolutions to accept Miller, Inc.'s Base Proposal A to construct both buildings for $1,389,450. Ruppert, one of the Architects, was instructed to notify Miller, Inc. promptly of the acceptance of its bid, in order that the construction contract might be signed on Friday, August 11. The reason for the hurry was to avoid a labor cost increase effective at midnight August 11, applicable to any contract entered into after that date. Ruppert reached Miller by telephone the next morning, August 9, and told him that his combined bid for both buildings was low and had been accepted by the College, and that the College wanted the construction contract to be signed on August 11. Miller said that he thought Ferguson was the low bidder on the dormitory, but Ruppert pointed out that the Ferguson bid was not low, because it required the addition of the built-in furniture. Miller then said that he had left the built-in furniture out of his Base Bid and that he could not then agree to sign the proposed contract. Ruppert replied that Miller should come to the College on Friday prepared to sign the construction contract and, if he was not willing to do so, he should bring his attorney with him. The College never gave Miller written notice of the acceptance of its bid, although the bid bond required written notice.

Miller thereupon called his surety's agent, who advised him to withdraw the bid. The next day, August 10, on the advice of his lawyer, Miller, Inc., sent a telegram to the Architects, stating that it was giving formal notice of the withdrawal of its Bid Proposal and that a letter would follow. * * *

On August 11, Miller attended a meeting with the Architects and representatives of the College who demanded that Miller, Inc. sign that day a contract to construct both buildings for the sum of $1,389,450, including the equipment referred to in the Separate Price Quotes. This Miller refused to do. The College refused to allow Miller any further time to study the matter, in spite of the fact that Miller requested such opportunity and the Form of Bid required Miller to sign a contract within ten days after written notice of the acceptance of its bid. The Architects and the College demanded that Miller sign the contract that day, August 11, so that if he refused to sign they might award the contract to the next lowest bidder or bidders without readvertising, which would have been necessary because of the increase in labor rates if the contracts had not been signed on that day.

After Miller refused to sign the contract, the College awarded contracts to the next lowest bidders—Henry A. Knott & Co., on its bid of $765,000 for the construction of the Student Union Building, and Frederick Construction Co., Inc., on its bid of $700,064 for the construction of the Dormitory Building. HHFA required the College to increase its financial participation from $420,000 to $490,000.

No case precisely in point decided by the Court of Appeals of Maryland, or by any other court, has been cited or found. But the general principles which must control this case are set out and discussed in Baltimore v. DeLuca-Davis Construction Co., 210 Md. 518, 124 A.2d 557 (1956).

for the Student Union Building only was $734,450, as compared with the next lowest bid, $765,000, by Henry A. Knott & Co. The bid of Miller, Inc. for the dormitory Building was $659,450 as compared with the next lowest bid, $700,064, by Frederick Construction Co., Inc.

In that case DeLuca–Davis had submitted to the City a bid of $1,796,064.25, which by reason of a clerical, material, and palpable error, made in good faith, was at least $589,880 less than it was intended to be and some $700,000 less than the engineer's estimate and the next lowest bid. Before the bid was accepted by the City, DeLuca–Davis filed a bill in equity (a) to reform or (b) to rescind its bid. The Court of Appeals refused reformation, but held that DeLuca–Davis was entitled to cancellation of its bid and the return of its deposit.

The unanimous opinion of the Court, written by Judge Hammond, analyzed a great many decisions from Maryland and other states and the views expressed in Williston, Corbin, Black, and the Restatement, Contracts, and stated:

> "Although reformation requires that the mistake be mutual, rescission may be granted whether the mistake be that of one or both of the parties."

Most importantly for the purposes of the instant case the Court said:

> "The general rule as to the conditions precedent to rescission for unilateral mistakes may be summarized thus: 1, the mistake must be of such grave consequences that to enforce the contract as made or offered would be unconscionable; 2, the mistake must relate to a material feature of the contract; 3, the mistake must not have come about because of the violation of a positive legal duty or from culpable negligence; 4, the other party must be put in statu quo to the extent that he suffers no serious prejudice except the loss of his bargain."

In support of that rule the Court cited a number of Maryland cases, including Kappelman v. Bowie, 201 Md. 86, 93 A.2d 266 (1952).[4] The Court further noted:

> "There are numerous cases in many states that have granted contractors cancellation of bids based on clerical, material, palpable, bona fide mistakes. Where, as in the case at bar, the mistake has been brought to the attention of the contracting authority before the acceptance of the bid, the courts have been almost unanimous in granting relief. * * * Some courts have decided against the contractor on the facts, such as the lack of materiality of the mistake or the gross or culpable negligence of the bidder, but where the essential factual prerequisites have been found to be present, there is no substantial authority denying rescission for unilateral mistake except in Massachusetts. * * * In

4. Kappelman v. Bowie, 201 Md. 86, 93 A.2d 266 (1952), was a suit in equity for specific performance of a real estate contract repudiated by the vendors on the ground of mistake and inadequacy of price. Speaking through Judge Henderson, the court of Appeals said:

"It has long been established in Maryland that a unilateral mistake as to the terms of a contract of sale may be a defense to a suit for specific performance. These cases seem to be in accord with the law as laid down in other states. [citations] The defense has been sustained, despite the fact that there was more or less negligence in the party setting it up. It is true that in some cases, relief has been denied where the evidence did not show a bona fide or material mistake.

"The appellant contends, however, that even if the appellees made a mistake induced by a misrepresentation of their own agent, it would not be a defense if not induced by the opposite party. The contention overlooks the true basis for the rule, which is rooted in the proposition that equity may refuse the extraordinary remedy of specific performance where to do so would enforce a hard bargain, at least where the mistaken party was not grossly negligent and the opposite party would not be prejudiced except to the extent of losing a windfall. It may be that this recognition of a unilateral mistake as a defense is inconsistent with the objective theory of contracts, to the extent that it permits the rescission of an executory contract on equitable grounds. Whether it would be a good defense in an action at law under a plea on equitable grounds, is a question we need not now consider."

most of the cases cited below the contractor was found not to have violated a positive legal duty or to have been guilty of culpable negligence because the mistake was made in the haste and pressure of preparing the bid or was natural in the conduct of the business. The application of this standard of negligence has been recognized by this Court."

The Court refused to follow Baltimore v. J.L. Robinson Construction Co., 123 Md. 660, 91 A. 682 (1914). In that case the City had awarded a contract to a bidder who had advised it before the bid was opened and again before it was accepted that it was $11,000 less than was intended because an error had been made in putting down one item at $952.13 when it should have been $11,952.13.
* * *

The bidder refused to execute the contract, the City readvertised and forfeited the $500 deposit, and the bidder sued at law to recover the amount of the deposit. The Court of Appeals held that the bidder could not prevail, principally because of a provision in the City Charter which warned the bidder that his bid was irrevocable. The Court also noted that the action was at law and that all of the cases relied on by the bidder were cases in equity, and that in most of them no statute was involved.

In the *DeLuca–Davis* opinion, the Court distinguished the *Robinson* decision on the ground that in *Robinson* the bidder had the capacity to perform, whereas DeLuca–Davis did not, but placed the greatest emphasis on the fact that *Robinson* was an action at law, whereas *DeLuca–Davis* was a suit in equity. Judge Hammond said: "The *Robinson* opinion shows clearly that the form of the action, the circumstances that it was at law, was important, if not decisive in the result." And again: "The Court in the *Robinson* opinion gave definite indication that if equitable relief had been sought, the rules of decision might well have been different. It said: 'If the contract were made by the bid and acceptance the bidder then would be compelled to carry it out or be responsible for it, unless a *court of equity,* for sufficient cause, should relieve him, by rescinding the contract.' " (Emphasis supplied by Judge Hammond.) Rule 1, F.R.Civ.P., unified law and equity procedures in the Federal Courts.

The opinion in *DeLuca–Davis* concluded the discussion as follows:

> "If it be conceded that in the posture of the case as it came to the Court, the Robinson decision was sound in holding that a bidder could not withdraw his bid at will and was bound by his obligation as long as it was legally unrevoked, we agree with the views of the Court in the *McGraw* case, from which we have quoted above, that the proper effects of the charter requirements are to assure the municipality that a bidder will be relieved of his obligation only when it is legally justifiable, and that it is legally justifiable when a court of equity is satisfied by clear, cogent and convincing proof that an honest, clerical or mechanical error, not the result of gross or culpable negligence, made the bid that of the bidder in form only but in actual intent or substance, and the gain of the other party would be unconscionable if advantages were taken of the mistake and the loss would only be that of the bargain if the mistake was nullified. In such circumstances, the blundering bidder may be relieved in equity of his obligation created at law by his bid and deposit, and this is true even though the bid was submitted to a public body under a statute declaring the bid to be irrevocable and providing for the forfeiture of the deposit."

The *McGraw* case referred to by Judge Hammond was State of Connecticut v. F.H. McGraw & Co., D.Conn., 41 F.Supp. 369 (1941). In that case, Circuit

Judge Clark, sitting as District Judge, after noting that "McGraw's bid purported to conform to the specifications," said: "The issue therefore really involves contrary interpretations of the specifications, rather than an offer differing from that called for." The bidder's mistake was bona fide and was known to the state officials before they accepted the bid. Judge Clark followed the rule of Geremia v. Boyarsky, 107 Conn. 387, 140 A. 749, when the Court had said:

> "The mistake of the defendants was of so fundamental a character that the minds of the parties did not meet. It was not, under the circumstances, the result of such culpable negligence as to bar the defendants of redress, and the plaintiff, before the contract was signed, had good reason to believe that a substantial error had been made, and, while the contract was still executory, and he had been in no way prejudiced, refused to permit the correction of the error, and attempted to take an unconscionable advantage of it. The defendants were clearly entitled to a decree canceling the contract." [5]

After discussing Moffett, Hodgkins & Clarke Co. v. Rochester, 178 U.S. 373 (1900), Judge Clark said:

> "The only other distinction offered is that in the *Geremia* and *Rochester* cases the error was arithmetical, whereas here it is based on an incorrect reading of specifications in the light of the state engineer's requirements. The distinction seems artificial. In either event the bidder errs; in either event he is to a degree negligent. But in both, the offeree is aware of the error, and presses his advantage unfairly if he insists on the work at an inadequate price.
>
> "Of course, it is obvious, as the State contends, that the system of public bidding, developed by experience and usual in public contracts, should not be broken down by lightly permitting bidders to withdraw because of change of mind. Such a course would be unfair to other straight-forward bidders, as well as disruptive of public business. But it can hardly be a substantial impairment of such system to grant the relief—which would clearly be given as between private citizens—in a case where a bona fide mistake is proven and was known to the State before acceptance or any loss to it."

The *McGraw* case, cited with approval by the Maryland Court in *DeLuca-Davis,* answers the College's argument that rescission should be denied in the instant case because the mistake was not a clerical, mechanical mistake, but a mistake in the interpretation of the specification. The College contends that the mistake was a "mistake of judgment," and therefore not such a mistake as would justify relief, citing M.F. Kemper Constr. Co. v. Los Angeles, 37 Cal.2d 696, 235 P.2d 7 (1951). The *Kemper* case, which was cited in *DeLuca-Davis* on another point, said that there is a difference between a mistake in tabulating and transcribing figures and "errors of judgment as, for example, underestimating the cost of labor or materials." The mistake in the instant case was not such an "error of judgment."

The College argues that *Kappelman, DeLuca-Davis* and *McGraw* are distinguishable from the instant case because in each of those cases the mistake was palpable, and because in the instant case Miller, Inc. was negli-

5. Judge Clark added:

"It is objected that the rule should be different where, as here, there is a proviso forbidding the withdrawal of bids. To be sure, this puts a bidder on notice that there is a certain finality about bidding for a government contract. But this by no means should enable a governmental agency to take an unconscionable advantage of its special status as a government body. 'It is axiomatic that the Government must be held to the same general principles of equity and fair play in dealing with those who contract with it as are the contractors themselves.' Kemp v. United States, D.C.Md., 38 F.Supp. 568, 570. * * * "

gent in failing to clarify its confusion or uncertainty with respect to the specifications by asking the Architects for an authoritative interpretation.

Taking the latter point first, the Court finds that Miller, Inc. was negligent in failing to take the matter up with the Architects, and in relying on Miller's construction of the confusing though not ambiguous specifications; but the Court finds that Miller, Inc. was not guilty of gross or culpable negligence. Relief should not be denied because there was "more or less negligence," *Kappelman,* supra, nor because Miller was "to a degree negligent," *McGraw,* supra, since the mistake was not the result of "culpable negligence," *DeLuca–Davis,* supra.

On the question whether the mistake was palpable, the Court has found as a fact that the mistake was obvious, i.e. legally palpable, to the contractors present, when the bids were opened, and was or should have been obvious to the Architects, though not to the other representatives of the College. The Court doubts whether palpability is an essential element of relief in such a case as this; if it is, the College is charged with the knowledge of its Architects.

More importantly, the College knew of the mistake when Miller, Inc. sought to withdraw its bid, before the College had accepted the bid in writing, as it was required to do by the terms of the bid bond before it could hold Miller, Inc. or its surety liable thereunder. It is not necessary to decide whether the withdrawal of the bid was such a breach as excused the failure of the College to give written notice of acceptance, in view of the continued insistence of the College that Miller, Inc. sign the contract on Friday, August 11, a week before it was required to sign by the Instructions to Bidders, the Form of Bid and other relevant documents. The College knew of the mistake in time to be able to sign contracts with the next highest bidders, without loss of the favorable wage scale, for the amounts of their respective bids. The College lost nothing except the bargain which it would have obtained as a result of Miller's bona fide mistake.

The fact that the loss to Miller, Inc. would probably not have been so great as to put it out of business is an element to be considered, but it is not controlling. The mistake was substantial and material.

This Court is aware of the importance of preserving the integrity of the system of competitive bidding. * * * But, as Judge Clark concluded in *McGraw,* to grant relief in this type of case will not result in any substantial impairment of the system. * * *

Judgment will be entered in favor of the defendants, with costs.

Notes

1. Professor Kronman approves of allowing bidders to withdraw bids that contain apparent but unilateral errors or miscalculations: In mistaken bid cases, "the special knowledge of the non-mistaken party (his knowledge of the other party's error) is unlikely to be the fruit of a deliberate search. Put differently, a rule requiring him to disclose what he knows will not cause him to alter his behavior in such a way that the production of information of this sort will be reduced.

"A contractor receiving a mistaken bid, for example, usually becomes aware of the mistake (if he does at all) by comparing the mistaken bid with others that have been submitted, or by noting an error which is evident on the face of the bid itself. In either case, his knowledge of the mistake arises in the course of a routine examination of the bids which he would undertake in any event. The party receiving the bid has an independent incentive to scrutinize carefully each of the bids which are submitted to him: the profitability of his own enterprise requires that he do so. It is of course true that the recipient's expertise may make it easier for him to identify certain sorts of errors in bids that have been submitted. But the detection of clerical mistakes and errors in calculation is not likely to be one of the principal reasons for his becoming an expert in the first place. A rule requiring the disclosure of mistakes of this kind is almost certain not to discourage investment in developing the sort of general expertise which facilitates the detection of such mistakes." Kronman, Mistake, Disclosure, Information, and the Law of Contracts, 7 J. Legal Stud. 1, 32 (1978).

2. *Comments on Remedies—if any—Releasing a Construction Contractor from "Clerical" Errors in Bidding Offers.* Decisions may typify the maxim that "the remedy chosen determines the substantive law theory." The numerous opinions are characterized by unusually voluminous citation of cases, treatises on Contracts, Restatement sections, A.L.R. annotations, and analytical law review articles on a subject that seems to attract learned analysis. Also noteworthy are numerous allusions to substantive contract law concepts and principles. One reads at length of "misunderstandings," "lack of meeting of the minds," "palpable error," "impalpable error," "revocation of offers before acceptance," "snapping up," "irrevocable offers," "reasonable expectations," "objective manifestations of consent," "integrity of the bidding system," "sanctity of contracts," "non-negligence," "material," "essence of the bargain," and (sparing further belaboring of the obvious) the inevitable "unconscionability." All of this indicates the predetermined remedy in search of supportive doctrine.

The facts are reducible to a fairly standard format. A bid form is an offer intended for future incorporation in a construction contract and embodies penalty clauses (a possible genesis of remedial unconscionability). It is prepared and submitted along with others. Bids are opened revealing the offeror as the lowest by a certain dollar amount. This provides the essential calculation for ordinary breach of contract expectancy damages, which, if sufficiently high, serves as the ground for hinting at substantive unconscionability. The bidder claims a unilateral, usually arithmetical, error and declines to proceed. From this failure proceeds various possible out-of-pocket expenses of the other party, resulting from delay in construction, thereby affording a basis for damages.

It seems harsh to hold the bidder for penalty or expectancy damages because of a misplaced decimal point on a contract that has not progressed beyond opening the bid envelopes; but the position of the bidding contractor is not entirely a sympathetic one. The injury caused by the unintentional but nonetheless reproachable conduct goes beyond the immediate parties. The other bidders are affected as are subcontractors, working crews and the like; in the principal case, perhaps the prospective student residents will be adversely affected. These persons have no redress save from a policy strongly discouraging errors in making offers. Moreover assertion of error rests on the subjective state of mind of the adversely affected bidder; it will be proved by work sheets prepared by and under the control of that party. This assertion is not one likely to escape suspicion.

Against this background it is wholly unlikely that a lawyer for either party, or any trial judge, would initially focus on anything but the desired remedial outcome. The attorney for the aggrieved party would list the hoped for recovery in something like the following order, using the figures in *Mt. St. Mary's.* For the bidder and his lawyer the list would of course be inverted.

a. the security bond, i.e., 10% of the bid or $138,945 according to the liquidated damages provision.

b. the benefit of the bargain expectancy damages;—i.e., difference between bid and next lowest one or $88,614 plus possible special damages.

c. at least reliance damages or compensation for out-of-pocket losses proximately caused.

d. no recovery at all.

Having determined the desired outcome the task of preparing briefs embodying the theoretical support begins.

A test: You are a clerk for the trial judge who has indicated her decision on any of the four results. Quickly outline the substantive law theory or theories that will reach that outcome and indicate which of the various expressions noted above would individually be appropriate. For example: the decision in the principal case was to relieve the contractor entirely from liability. Two theoretical routes would lead to that result: (a) no contract or (b) an avoidable contract (including the elimination of the penalty provision). Which is easiest to support?

3. Statutes may provide a remedy for contractors submitting mistaken bids. In California, the statutory scheme is exclusive where the mistaken bid is submitted to a *public entity.* The contractor, upon satisfying certain prerequisites, recovers the amount forfeited (without interest). See Cal.Pub.Con.Code §§ 5100–5108; Balliet Brothers Construction Co. v. Regents of the University of California, 80 Cal.App.3d 321, 145 Cal.Rptr. 498 (1978); A & A Electric, Inc. v. City of King, 54 Cal.App.3d 457, 126 Cal.Rptr. 585 (1976).

4. Assume the lowest bidder clearly can prove a clerical mistake in the bid which, if corrected, would still leave it the lowest bidder. Any remedy? See Dick Corp. v. Associated Electric Cooperative Inc., 475 F.Supp. 15 (W.D.Mo.1979).

B. MISTAKE IN NON-BARGAINING SITUATIONS

DESKOVICK v. PORZIO

Superior Court of New Jersey, 1963.
78 N.J.Super. 82, 187 A.2d 610.

CONFORD, S.J.A.D. The issue here is one of asserted liability of the defendant executor for reimbursement of plaintiffs, sons of the decedent, for payments by them of medical and hospital expenses arising out of the father's last illness. * * *

Plaintiff Michael Deskovick gave the following testimony. He and his co-plaintiff were two, apparently the eldest, of ten children of the decedent. The latter and his wife, a stepmother of plaintiffs, lived in a house on a tract of land which was also the site of Michael's home and business office. The father, Michael and Peter went into business together in 1934, but the sons bought out the father's interest in 1945, partly in cash and partly in deferred installments, which were still being paid at the rate of $100 per month as of the time of decedent's death, August 2, 1959.

Decedent became seriously ill and was hospitalized for two months in 1958. He returned to the hospital in the spring of 1959 and remained there until his death of cancer. Plaintiffs began to pay hospital and medical bills in August, 1958, and paid some after decedent's death, as late as December 7, 1959. "Somebody" put the bills on Michael's desk from time to time "and [he] assumed them and paid them." He did not discuss the bills with his father "because [his] father was on his back. He was in a condition so that he couldn't talk." * * *

Over objection by defendant, Michael testified:

"Q. Did you intend to have your father repay you for these bills at a future date? A. I intended to do so somehow and in some way."

In the event of the father's death, Michael's intention, when he paid the bills, "was to get the estate to pay" them. He submitted the vouchers "in some hope that I would get that."

After reservation by the court on a motion for dismissal, the defense read Michael's pretrial depositions to the jury. Therein he testified, on examination by his own counsel:

"*Question:* You say you did have conversations with your father prior to this date—prior to the time he became ill—whereby he indicated to you that he was in a financially embarrassed position or didn't have the money? *Answer:* He always cried the blues that he was up against it, you know. That is nothing new. That went on and on all the time. We never dreamed he had this kind of money laying there. I mean, that is something we didn't expect, so we just paid the tabs and as they came in we picked it up and would take care of it. Nobody else would ever pick up a tab. They just brought them down and gave them to me."

On renewal of the motion for judgment of dismissal the court granted it, stating:

"It seems to me, based upon the deposition read into the record, that there was intended at the time of the payment by Mr. Deskovick no repayment. He was then under the impression that his father didn't have any money, so he could not have intended to get repayment."

If the question whether plaintiffs intended to be repaid at the time they advanced the moneys in question were the sole material issue, we would conclude the trial court erred in taking the case out of the jury's hands. While the weight of the credible evidence accorded with the judge's stated view, we cannot say that the proofs *contra* were of such insignificance as to have made the issue one of law. However, insofar as the theory of plaintiff's case was based on implied contract, their intention to be repaid was immaterial in the factual situation presented, for the following reasons.

It is elementary that the assertion of a contract implied in fact calls for the establishment of a consensual understanding as to compensation or reimbursement inferable from the circumstances under which one furnishes services or property and another accepts such advances. * * * Here an essential for such a mutual understanding was absent in that the decedent, on behalf of whom these advances were being made, was totally ignorant of the fact. Whatever plaintiff's subjective intent to be repaid, it could not supply the missing knowledge on the part of the beneficiary of the advances, required to sustain the inferential intent on his part to repay which would round out the postulated contract implied in fact.

It is elementary that one who pays the debt of another as a volunteer, having no obligation or liability to pay nor any interest menaced by the continued existence of the debt, cannot recover therefor from the beneficiary. * * * Nor can such a volunteer claim the benefit of the law of subrogation.

* * * If plaintiffs were mere volunteers, therefore, they would not, within these principles, be entitled to be subrogated to the creditor position of the hospitals and physicians whose bills they paid.

Notwithstanding the foregoing principles, however, we perceive in the evidence adduced at the trial, particularly in the version of the facts reflected in the deposition of Michael adduced by defendant a quasi-contractual basis of recovery which in our judgment ought to be submitted to a jury at a retrial of the case in the interest of substantial justice.

* * * The Restatement of Restitution (1937) undertakes to formulate a number of rules growing out of recognized principles of *quasi*-contract. Section 26, entitled "Mistake in Making Gifts," reads:

> "(1) A person is entitled to restitution from another to whom gratuitously and induced thereto by a mistake of fact he has given money if the mistake (a) was caused by fraud or material misrepresentation."

An innocent misrepresentation by the donee is within the rule. A "mistaken belief in the existence of facts which would create a moral obligation upon the donor to make a gift would ordinarily be a basic error" justifying restitution.

In the case of In re Marine Trust Co., 156 Misc. 297, 281 N.Y.S. 553 (Sup.Ct.1935), the Roman Catholic Archdiocese of Philadelphia was held entitled to restitution from the estate of a deceased priest of sums of money it had advanced for his support during his lifetime when incompetent and apparently impoverished. A surviving brother had during the same period defrayed the remaining expenses of maintaining the decedent out of the latter's own substantial funds of which the brother had been acting as trustee. The Archdiocese did not know of the trust fund until after the incompetent's death. Recovery was expressly allowed on the theory of unjust enrichment of the decedent's estate at the expense of the Archdiocese.

We think the foregoing authorities would apply in favor of sons, who, during the father's mortal illness, believing him without means of meeting medical and hospital bills as a result of what he had previously told them, and wishing to spare him the discomfort of concern over such expenses at such a time, themselves assumed and paid the obligations. The leaving by the father of an estate far more than sufficient to have met the expenditures would, in such circumstances, and absent others affecting the basic equitable situation presented, properly invoke the concept of a *quasi*-contractual obligation of reimbursement of the sons by the estate. * * * Such circumstances would take the payors out of the category of voluntary intermeddlers as to whom the policy of the law is to deny restitution or reimbursement.

Reversed and remanded for a new trial.

Notes

1. *Problem:* Extract from a letter from an insurance agency:

In our work, we see the problems that develop when the possibility of accidental death is not considered in a client's estate plan.

A man we'll call Monroe Walters was a widower. He had three children, all in the twenties. After his wife died, Monroe made each child the beneficiary of one of three $100,000 policies on Monroe's life. Two of them were individual policies but one was a group life certificate through Monroe's employer.

Monroe died in an automobile accident. His executor happened to be a client of ours so he asked us to help settle the death claim. When he brought in the policies, the executor told us each child would get the same amount.

After we examined the policies, one of us asked the executor, "Bill, did Monroe Walters intend to favor one child over the other two?"

"Of course not," he replied. "What are you getting at?"

"One of the policies," he was told, "contains a double indemnity clause so that child is entitled to receive $200,000, while each of the other two children will get only $100,000 plus any post mortem dividends and premium refunds."

"That's terrible!" Bill exclaimed. Then he realized what he had said and corrected himself. "I understand how the error must have happened," he mused, "I am sure I can explain Monroe's intentions to them and see if the boy who is entitled to the extra $100,000 will split it with his brother and sister."

We don't know how the story ended. We will have to ask Bill next time we see him. No matter what the child decided, he'll always wonder if his father didn't intend for him to have the larger share.

2. *Donee's Remedies For Donor's Mistakes.* The donor may readily reclaim an unintended "overperformance" of a gift; but the donee is not treated similarly when the donor, in error, has failed to complete the gift in whole or in part. A major factor is whether the donor is alive. A may wish to give Blackacre consisting in two acres to B. The deed describes only one acre of the tract. A dies. In Zabolotny v. Fedorenko, 315 N.W.2d 668 (N.D.1982) the court said:

"Generally, a court of equity will not reform a voluntary deed, conveying property without consideration, in favor of the grantee or those holding under him. I.e., Dunn v. Dunn, 242 N.C. 234, 239–40, 87 S.E.2d 308, 311–12 (1955). The basis for this rule of equity is well stated in *Dunn,* supra: * * * 'ordinarily equity will not reform a purely voluntary conveyance, the general rule with us being that equity will not assume jurisdiction to reform a deed unless it be shown that the transaction was based on a valuable or meritorious consideration. This rule is based on the proposition that in respect to a voluntary conveyance the grantee has no claim on the grantor, and that any mistake or defect is a mere failure in a bounty which the grantor was not bound to make and hence is not required to perfect. Thus, a volunteer must take the gift as he finds it. In short, one who accepts another's bounty ordinarily will not be heard to say something else should have been given.' * * *

"Some jurisdictions follow the rule that a voluntary deed cannot be reformed in favor of the grantee against the grantor's heirs. Other courts have held that a court of equity is not precluded from reforming a voluntary conveyance on behalf of the grantee against the grantor's heirs providing that the grantor, if living, would not have objected to the reformation requested by the grantee. We believe the latter is the better reasoned rule, and we choose to follow it. * * *

"In this case there is no evidence to demonstrate that Stephen, if living, would have objected to reforming the quit claim deed to include the Southeast Quarter. Rather, there is substantial evidence to support the district court's finding that Stephen intended to convey all of his inherited share of Katie's property to Anton and that he thought he had done so by signing the quit claim deed. Consequently, to uphold the reformation of the deed it is unnecessary to determine whether or not Anton gave consideration for the conveyance."

Question: In *Zabolotny* the donor's intent was clearly established by correspondence with his attorney. The donee had farmed the entire tract during the donor's lifetime without objection. But suppose, on the same evidence of intent, no deed at all had been executed and the donee had not entered into possession. Would the donee have any equitable remedy against the donor's heirs?

WALTON v. BANK OF CALIFORNIA

District Court of Appeal of California.
First District, 1963.
218 Cal.App.2d 527, 32 Cal.Rptr. 856.

SULLIVAN, J. [Plaintiff appeals from an adverse judgment in her action to rescind an irrevocable *inter vivos* trust.]

The law is clear that where no consideration is received by the trustor for the creation of an *inter vivos* trust, it can be rescinded or reformed for mistake to the same extent that an outright gift can be rescinded or reformed. (Rest.2d Trusts, § 333, see com. *a;* 3 Scott on Trusts (2d ed.) § 333, p. 2424; § 333.4, pp. 2427–2428.) As Scott states: "[W]here the settlor receives no consideration for the creation of the trust, as is usually the case, a unilateral mistake is ordinarily a sufficient ground for rescission, as it is in the case of an outright gift. It is immaterial that the beneficiaries of the trust did not induce the mistake or know of it or share it. It is immaterial whether the mistake was a mistake of fact or a mistake of law. The mistake may be such as to justify reformation rather than rescission of the trust."

The evidence in the record shows that Mrs. Walton had no misunderstanding about the irrevocability of the trust. * * * This feature was explained to her on May 14 at her home and carefully reviewed by her attorney when the trust was signed. She herself had indicated that she wanted her property put beyond her reach for her own protection. Before June 1, she told Mrs. Dilla, her nurse, that she was having a trust drawn up so that no one, including herself, could touch her property. After the signing of the agreement she told Mr. Charles, her attorney, that she was happy with the arrangement because she was free from the pressure of making gifts. After she returned to Twin Pines, she again mentioned the trust to Mrs. Dilla, remarking that she had the worry off her mind and that not even she, herself, could touch the property. * * *

As the court said in Reid v. Landon, 166 Cal.App.2d 476, 483, 333 P.2d 432, 437: "Whether the mistake of fact here is one consisting of 'an unconscious ignorance or forgetfulness of a fact present' or a 'belief in the present existence of a thing which does not exist' (Civ.Code, § 1577), it must be one material to the contract. *The mistake must be such that it animated and controlled the conduct of the party; go to the essence of the object in view and not be merely incidental.* The court must be satisfied that but for the mistake the complainant would not have assumed the obligation from which he seeks to be relieved [citation]." (Italics added.) Plaintiff was motivated to create the trust not for tax purposes but to free herself from the demands of her children. There is nothing in the evidence leading to the conclusion that plaintiff's decision to create the trust was predicated on a definite commitment to her and understanding by her that the tax liability would not exceed the $75,000 estimate. * * * It is apparent from the record that the estimated tax liability was something incidental to her main purpose and did not, to quote *Reid,* "go to the essence of the object in view."

Plaintiff relies on the following cases dealing with the effect of a mistake as to the tax consequences of the creation of a trust: Stone v. Stone (1947) 319 Mich. 194 [29 N.W.2d 271]; Miller v. National Bank of Detroit (1949) 325 Mich. 395 [38 N.W.2d 863]; Irish v. Irish (1949) 361 Pa. 410 [65 A.2d 345]; Hardy v. Bankers Trust Co. (1945) 137 N.J.Eq. 352 [44 A.2d 839]. She argues that in the above cases rescission or reformation of the trust was permitted because the mistake as to tax liability was material. We note that three of the cases, *Miller, Irish* and *Hardy,* involve the *modification or reformation* of the particular trust, a matter not here in issue. Moreover, in *Miller,* the sole purpose of the trust was to minimize taxes and reformation was allowed because the trustors were mistaken as to their rights to do so. In *Irish,* reformation was permitted to include a provision essential to certain tax laws which had been intended but omitted by inadvertence or mistake; in *Hardy,* modification was permitted to meet an unforeseen change in a tax law. Although the opinions in the last two cases do not expressly so state, there is an indication that the trusts there involved were established for tax reasons or that taxes were a substantial consideration in their creation. In the *Stone* case, the court allowed rescission of a trust created solely for tax purposes where its creation was induced by mistake of law. (Cf. *Miller,* supra.) On the other hand, as Scott points out (3 Scott on Trusts, pp. 2428–2429) in Lowry v. Kavanagh, Collector (1948) 322 Mich. 532 [34 N.W.2d 60], *rescission* of a gift of corporate stock was denied by the court where it appeared that the principal purpose in making the gift was not to minimize taxes.

In our view, the foregoing authorities are consistent with the rationale of Reid v. Landon. Where the trust is created solely or principally for a tax purpose, the mistake as to the tax consequence is a material one. In the instant case, however, there is no evidence that the trust was created to minimize taxes or that it was motivated by a tax purpose. We are therefore not persuaded that in the light of the evidence plaintiff created the trust on the rigid basis of a $75,000 gift tax liability and that she would not have done so if she had been informed of a liability of $92,500. * * *

[Affirmed.]

C. DEFENSES

Introductory Note

Defenses to the plaintiff's claim of "Mistake" tend to overlap and are frequently presented in shotgun fashion. They fall into two broad categories—first, general defenses to the effect that either there was no mistake or there should not have been; and second, special defenses that concede the mistake, but assert particular reasons why the other party should bear the loss. These particular defenses include the claim that the mistake was actually one of law or that the defendant has changed his position or has parted with value for the benefit he received in ignorance of the facts.

The general defenses are diffused throughout litigation involving mistake and are best absorbed in a distributive fashion. Apart from the blanket claim that the plaintiff could not, under the circumstances, have possibly possessed a state of mind not in accordance with the facts, the general defenses are usually located under the headings of negligence or compromise.

1. *Negligence of the plaintiff.* See President and Council of Mount St. Mary's College v. Aetna Casualty & Surety; and McDonald's Corp. v. Moore, reprinted, supra, this chapter, and Webb v. Webb, below. The careful person is less prone to error, but the haphazardly organized individual does not lose his possessions solely because he could have done better. The Restatement of Restitution § 59 (1937) makes this clear. Anno., 81 A.L.R.2d 7 (1962) collects cases about the effect of the common failure of the plaintiff to read the document that he later seeks to reform.

This defense of plaintiff's carelessness is usually make-weight; the plaintiff is denied restitution for other reasons and his carelessness is mentioned to rebuke. Or sometimes the defense disguises the true reason for denying recovery: the court is not convinced that the plaintiff was genuinely laboring under a misapprehension.

2. *Compromise. Settlement. Assumption of the Risk.* Terra Nova Insurance Co. v. Associates Commercial Corp. and Dadourian Export Co. v. United States, reprinted above in this chapter, and Restatement of Restitution § 1 (1937). This defense is another way of saying that there was really no mistake, but a conscious disposition of a dispute based on what is known. Even compromises can be set aside for mistakes outside the area of settlement.

The cases that follow show the special defenses to the claim of mistake, beginning with the defense that the error concerned a matter of "law." Mistakes of law are oft-times put under a separate heading—and well they may. Treated here as a special defense, a benefit conferred under a "mistake of law" is likely to be one conferred to end a legal dispute about the respective rights and liabilities of the parties. It is simply a variety of the defense of compromise, settlement, or assumption of the risk, which has just been labeled a general defense. But as we said, the defenses tend to overlap.

1. MISTAKE OF LAW

WEBB v. WEBB

Supreme Court of Appeals of West Virginia, 1983.
301 S.E.2d 570.

McGRAW, CHIEF JUSTICE. On March 24, 1979, Chester G. Webb died intestate, survived by his widow, Lillian Webb, and one adopted son, appellant Chester David Webb. The decedent's estate included a one-half undivided interest in the marital abode of the decedent and Lillian Webb. Under the laws of descent and distribution, title to this interest passed to the appellant, as the only surviving child of the decedent, subject to the dower interest of Lillian Webb.

Shortly after the funeral, the appellant and his mother consulted John Rist, a Beckley attorney. Believing that his father had desired Lillian Webb to have fee title to the real property, the appellant sought Rist's legal advice on the best method of effecting the decedent's wishes. Upon Rist's inquiry as to his marital status, the appellant stated that he was single and had been living in his own home in Florida for the past ten years. It appears from the record that prior to his father's death the appellant had twice been married and divorced, and that one of these marriages had produced a child, an infant daughter, who lived with her mother, Carol Webb. The appellant did not reveal this information to the attorney. Rist, who had no knowledge of the appellant's marriages and divorces, did not pursue the inquiry into the existence of any progeny. Rist advised the appellant that he could release his statutory share of the estate by means of a disclaimer of property interests passed by the law of intestate succession. Rist prepared the disclaimer, which was executed on April 3, 1979 and recorded on April 17, 1979.

Rist learned of the appellant's previous marriages and of the existence of the appellant's daughter in September 1979, when he was asked to represent the appellant in a nonsupport action brought by the child's mother in magistrate court in Beckley. Rist advised the appellant that, in these circumstances, the statutory effect of the disclaimer was to vest title to the appellant's share of the estate in his daughter rather than in his mother. The appellant instituted a declaratory judgment action in the circuit court to have the disclaimer declared void and set aside on the ground of mistake, naming Lillian Webb, Carol Webb and the infant child as parties defendant.

A hearing was held on April 10, 1981, at which the appellant testified that at the time of the discussion with Rist he was aware of the existence of the child, but that he did not think that fact was important and therefore made no mention of it. Rist's testimony indicates that he took the appellant's statement that he was single to mean that the appellant had never been married and had no children. Rist testified that had he known of the existence of the child, he would have advised the appellant to execute a deed conveying his interest in the estate to his mother, instead of the disclaimer. Although some testimony was elicited indicating that Rist, the appellant and Lillian Webb had discussed the tax advantages of executing a disclaimer, it is apparent from the record that the appellant's motivation in executing the disclaimer was to pass full title to the real estate to his mother, Lillian Webb, in accordance with his perception of his father's wishes.

From this evidence, the circuit court concluded that the mistake of the appellant in executing the disclaimer was a mistake of law rather than a mistake of fact, and denied relief on that ground. * * * [T]he appellant now prosecutes this appeal.

* * * [A]n individual should not be permitted to avoid obligations he undertook while laboring under a mistake of law. Harner v. Price, 17 W.Va. 523 (1880). The rationale underlying this rule was explained in Harner v. Price:

> "The ground of this distinction between ignorance of law and ignorance of fact seems to be, as every man of reasonable understanding is presumed to know the law, and to act upon the rights, which it confers or supports, when he knows all the facts, it is culpable negligence in him to do an act, or make a contract, and then to set up his ignorance of law as a defence. The general maxim here is, as in other cases, that the law aids them, who are vigilant, and not those who slumber over their rights. And this reason is recognized as the foundation of the distinction, as well in the civil law as in the common law. But no person can be presumed to be acquainted with all matters of fact; neither is it possible by any degree of diligence in all cases to acquire that knowledge; and therefore an ignorance of fact does not import culpable negligence."

The distinction between mistake of fact and mistake of law is easily stated. A mistake of fact consists of an unconscious ignorance or forgetfulness of a material fact, past or present, or of a mistaken belief in the past or present existence of a material fact which did not or does not actually exist. A mistake of law, on the other hand, consists of a mistaken opinion or inference arising from an imperfect or incorrect exercise of judgment upon the facts as they really are and occurs when a person, having full knowledge of the facts, is ignorant of or comes to an erroneous conclusion as to the legal effect of his acts.

Application of this distinction to individual cases has proven more difficult than the statement of it. Often mistakes of material fact have legal consequences, making it possible to argue persuasively that the mistake is one of law. In addition, courts have formulated numerous exceptions to the general rule that a transaction or act of a party will not be set aside on the ground of mistake of law, in some cases equating the mistake of law with one of fact.[1] * * *

We are of the opinion that the circuit court correctly categorized the mistake in this case as a mistake of law. The appellant's error here was not occasioned by his ignorance or forgetfulness of the fact that he had a child living at the time he executed the disclaimer. If that had been the case, we think the error could clearly be called a mistake of material fact which might afford grounds for rescission of the disclaimer. However, the appellant admits that when he executed the disclaimer he was fully aware of the existence of his daughter. His failure to advise counsel of her existence was the result of an active assumption that this fact was not relevant to the result he sought to accomplish by executing the disclaimer. The appellant's error is the result of his ignorance or misunderstanding of the legal consequences of his actions. Such an error may properly be classified as a mistake of law.

The appellant contends, however, that even if the circuit court correctly concluded that the error was a mistake of law, he is nevertheless entitled to have the disclaimer set aside on the ground that, as a long-term resident of Florida, he cannot be charged with knowledge of the laws of West Virginia. The appellant alleges that by seeking and following the advice of local counsel as to the laws of this state, he acted in a diligent manner. He argues that the mistake was, if anything, a mistake of fact on the part of counsel who, without knowledge of all of the facts, advised the appellant and prepared the disclaimer for execution. The appellant asserts that he should not be held accountable for counsel's failure to make further inquiries into the matter.

A mistake as to the laws of a country or state other than that in which the mistaken party is domiciled is generally treated as a mistake of fact which may be relieved by cancellation or rescission. Although one is presumed, as a matter of public policy, to know the laws of the state in which he resides, it would be unreasonable in most circumstances to presume that an individual is familiar with the laws of all other jurisdictions. Consequently, familiarity with the laws of a foreign jurisdiction is ordinarily treated as a matter of fact.

1. [Footnotes renumbered.] For example, it is generally recognized that a mistake as to the legal effect of a contract, though a mistake of law, will be treated as a mistake of material fact where the mistake is mutual, or common to all parties to the transaction, and results in a written instrument which does not embody the "bargained-for" agreement of the parties. [citations]

It is also well-settled in the Virginias that where a person is ignorant or mistaken with respect to his own antecedent and existing private legal rights, such as a mistake as to his title or interest in real property, and enters into a transaction, the legal scope and operation of which he correctly understands, for the purpose of affecting his assumed rights, equity will grant relief, treating the mistake as analogous to, if not identical with, a mistake of law. [citations]

We are of the opinion, however, that the appellant is not entitled to the benefit of this rule in the case at bar for two reasons. First, it is recognized that a party may not avoid the legal consequences on the ground of mistake, even a mistake of fact, where such mistake is the result of the negligence of the complaining party. We believe the appellant was negligent in his failure to reveal to counsel the existence of his infant daughter. The appellant's awareness that his daughter may have had some rights of inheritance should have been piqued, if only by virtue of the fact that he received his interest in the estate by virtue of the intestacy of his father. * * * We think it reasonable to assume that in similar circumstances a person of ordinary intelligence would be aware that children have some inheritance rights under the laws of all jurisdictions within the United States. Consequently, we conclude that if there was a mistake in this case, it was attributable to the negligence of the appellant.

Secondly, * * * where a nonresident acts upon the advice of local counsel, whose knowledge of the local law is presumed as a matter of public policy and as a natural inference resulting from counsel's legal training and his license to practice law, such nonresident cannot avoid the legal consequences of his actions on the ground of ignorance of the local law.

Nor do we think the appellant is entitled to relief on the ground that counsel committed a mistake of fact. Certainly under our general definition, counsel's advice to the appellant and his preparation of the disclaimer for execution without full knowledge of the facts would appear to be the result of a mistake of fact. We are of the opinion that counsel's mistake, like that of the appellant, arises from a lack of diligence. We believe that, in the circumstances presented, counsel had a duty to inquire of the appellant whether he had any children before advising him to execute the disclaimer.

We do not think, however, that counsel's failure to ascertain the true state of the appellant's familial relationships forms a basis for invalidating the disclaimer. In this case the appellant committed a mistake of law and counsel committed a mistake of fact. In both instances the mistake was the result of an omission on the part of the one who committed it. * * * In view of the lack of diligence on the part of both the appellant and counsel, we cannot say that the mistakes in this case, taken separately or together, are such that would justify invalidating the disclaimer. * * *

Affirmed.

GUTHRIE v. TIMES–MIRROR CO.

Court of Appeal of California, Fourth District, 1975.
51 Cal.App.3d 879, 124 Cal.Rptr. 577.

TAMURA, ASSOCIATE JUSTICE. This action arises out of the sale of The Sun Company of San Bernardino (Sun), a newspaper publishing company, to The Times–Mirror Company (Times). Plaintiffs (former Sun shareholders) in their own behalf and on behalf of other former Sun shareholders, seek to recover the profits and gains allegedly realized by the Times by virtue of its acquisition and subsequent resale of the Sun. The trial court sustained, without leave to amend, a general demurrer to the third amended complaint. Plaintiffs appeal from the ensuing judgment of dismissal.

In June 1964, plaintiffs and other Sun shareholders sold all of the capital stock in Sun to the Times for $15,000,000 cash. Shortly after the sale, the

United States brought an antitrust suit against the Times. In October 1967, the United States District Court rendered its judgment decreeing that the Times' control of the Sun properties through stock ownership violated section 7 of the Clayton Act. The judgment was affirmed by the United States Supreme Court and became final in June 1968. In January 1969, pursuant to the final judgment and with approval of the United States District Court, the Times sold the Sun to the Gannett Corporation for $17,700,000. The Times retained for itself other property and assets of the Sun worth $1,800,000.

Plaintiffs alleged that at the time the contract was entered into "all parties to said contract believed and were under the apprehension that the contract was not in violation of Federal antitrust laws." * * *

Plaintiffs alleged that before the sale the Sun had always shown a profit and had paid its shareholders annual dividends of $100 per share; that plaintiffs no longer receive these dividends; and that they have lost the benefit of the enhancement in the market value of their shares. The prayer was for rescission and for recovery of the sum of four and a half million dollars (the $2,700,000 alleged profit on the resale of the newspaper plus $1,800,000 as the value of the Sun's assets retained by the Times). * * *

The principal theory on which plaintiffs predicate their right to rescind and to have the Times adjudged to be an involuntary trustee of the alleged profits and gains from the resale of the Sun is mutual mistake of law. The substance of the allegations upon which they rely is that both parties contracted under the mistaken belief that the contract was not in violation of the federal antitrust laws when, in fact, unbeknownst to them it was.

In California a mutual mistake, whether of fact or law, which affects an essential element of the contract and is harmful to one of the parties is subject to rescission by the party harmed.

The Times urges that (1) the alleged mistake is not the kind of mistake which the law recognizes as a ground for rescission and (2) plaintiffs have failed to show that they were harmed by the mistake. From the analysis which follows, we have concluded that although the complaint purports to allege a mutual mistake of law as defined in Civil Code section 1578,[1] it is fatally defective because it fails to show that plaintiffs were injured by the alleged mistake.

Mistake is said to fall generally into two categories: (1) A person may know the specific facts upon which his rights depend but be ignorant of the rules of law the courts will apply to those facts,[2] or (2) a person may know the

1. [Footnotes renumbered.] Civil Code section 1578 provides:

"Mistake of law constitutes a mistake, within the meaning of this Article, only when it arises from:

"1. A misapprehension of the law by all parties, all supposing that they knew and understood it, and all making substantially the same mistake as to the law; or,

"2. A misapprehension of the law by one party, of which the others are aware at the time of contracting, but which they do not rectify."

2. The cases cited by plaintiffs are examples of situations where the parties, though aware of the facts, contracted in ignorance of the applicable rules of law. (Hannah v. Steinman, 159 Cal. 142, 112 P. 1094 [ignorance of the existence of a city ordinance prohibiting wooden structures on the leased premises]; Adams v. Heinsch, 89 Cal.App.2d 300, 200 P.2d 796 [mistaken belief that OPA regulations were not applicable to a lease of the premises in question]; Hartwig v. Clark, 138 Cal. 668, 72 P. 149 [ignorance by the parties of the statute of limitations barring recovery on a debt secured by a mortgage]; Spear v. Farwell, 5 Cal.App.2d 111, 42 P.2d 391 [mistaken belief by husband and wife that bank signature card executed by wife permitted husband to draw on the wife's account only after

applicable legal rules but be mistaken as to the specific facts to which the rules are to be applied. [citation] The instant case does not fit neatly into either category. The mistake is not alleged to have arisen out of a mistake concerning the existence of any specific operative facts or out of an ignorance of the pertinent legal rules. * * * The Times urges, in substance, that it must be inferred that the parties contracted, not in ignorance of the applicable legal rules or as to the existence of any operative facts, but rather on the basis of a mistaken judgment as to how a court would apply the legal rules to the facts. It is urged that ordinarily an error in judgment concerning an uncertain future occurrence is not a basis for avoiding a contract for mistake.

The Times further contends that the complaint reveals that at the time they contracted the parties were aware that the Times' acquisition and control of the Sun presented a possible or potential federal antitrust problem and that they therefore assumed the risk that their counsel's prophecy as to what a court would do might be wrong.

Where parties are aware at the time the contract is entered into that a doubt exists in regard to a certain matter and contract on that assumption, the risk of the existence of the doubtful matter is assumed as an element of the bargain. Otherwise stated, the kind of mistake which renders a contract voidable does not include "mistakes as to matters which the contracting parties had in mind as possibilities and as to the existence of which they took the risk." Williston, Contracts (3d ed.) § 1543.

It would be inappropriate, however, at the demurrer stage to determine the validity of the Times' contention that the kind of mistake alleged does not render the contract voidable. It cannot be said as an abstract legal proposition that a mistaken judgment, with knowledge of the law and the facts, concerning the legal effect a court will give to a transaction cannot form the basis for rescission for mutual mistake of law. To predict what a court will do in a complicated field such as antitrust may be a risky venture even for the most astute lawyer having knowledge of all the pertinent facts, applicable legal rules and apposite judicial precedents, but unless we know the nature of the legal advice on which the parties relied and their state of mind at the time they contracted, we cannot infer solely from the facts alleged that the parties doubted the validity of the transaction and therefore assumed the risk that the contract might be found to be violative of the federal antitrust laws. Although, as the Times suggests, it may be inferred that the parties sought and obtained legal advice *before they contracted* because they were concerned about the potential antitrust implications of the transactions, any doubts the parties may have had may have been laid to rest after their consultation with legal counsel.

We therefore conclude that construing the complaint liberally, as we must, it pleaded a mistake of law sufficient to survive a general demurrer.

The complaint, however, is fatally defective because it fails to set forth facts showing that plaintiffs were harmed or injured as a result of the claimed mistake. A contract is voidable for mistake only if enforcement would be materially harmful or more onerous to the party seeking avoidance than it would have been had the law or the facts been as believed. This is a necessary

her death instead of creating a joint tenancy]; Stock v. Meek, 35 Cal.2d 809, 221 P.2d 15 [ignorance of a city building and fire regulation precluding purchaser of space in apartment building from exercising exclusive occupancy of the space]; Benson v. Bunting, 127 Cal. 532, 59 P. 991 [ignorance of the applicable period of redemption following a mortgage foreclosure].)

corollary of the principle that the mistake, whether of law or fact, must materially affect an essential element of the contract. [citation] A party seeking to rescind a contract must show that he has suffered material injury or prejudice although he need not show pecuniary loss.

Had the "law" been as the parties supposed, plaintiffs would have been no better off. The alleged mistake did not affect the consideration for which plaintiffs contracted; they received the $15,000,000 cash for which they agreed to sell the Sun. * * * In short, the alleged mistake concerning the legal consequences which flowed from the Times' control of the Sun through stock acquisition had no effect upon the intrinsic merits of the contract insofar as plaintiffs were concerned. * * *

Plaintiff's reliance upon Earl v. Saks & Co., 36 Cal.2d 602, 226 P.2d 340 [Traynor, J. & Edmonds, J. dissenting] is misplaced. *Saks* involved rescission for *actual fraud.* Plaintiff was induced by fraudulent representations of his girl friend and of the department store to buy a fur coat priced at $5,000 for $4,000. He paid $4,000 for the coat on the representation that was the full price when in fact his girl friend, with the connivance of the store, paid an additional $1,000. Although plaintiff got what he expected, to wit, the fur coat, he was permitted to rescind. The court reasoned that since plaintiff's motive in buying the coat was to make a fully paid gift, the social interest in "not having one *intentionally take advantage of another*" outweighed society's interest in maintaining the stability of contracts. In the case at bench, plaintiffs disavow any suggestion of actual fraud on the part of the Times.

It is unnecessary to discuss other cases cited by the parties. As Professor Corbin has cautioned, because of the number and variety of factors to be considered, cases involving mistake are difficult to classify and it is perilous to construct a rule of law from them unless it be so circumscribed as to be applicable to a particular combination of many factors. Suffice it to say that in the case at bench lack of harm or injury to plaintiffs precludes rescission for the alleged mistake of law. * * *

Judgment of dismissal affirmed.

ALLEN v. ALLEN

Supreme Court of California, 1892.

95 Cal. 184, 30 P. 213.

PATERSON, J. It is claimed that at the time the contract was entered into, it was the established rule in this state that a conveyance absolute in form, but intended merely as security, did not pass the legal title to the grantee. It is true, there had been decisions to that effect; but in the year following it was held [citations] that a deed absolute in form, intended as a mortgage, did convey the legal title. These decisions did not change the law; they simply declared what was the law. Every one is conclusively presumed to know the law, although the ablest courts in the land often find great difficulty and labor in finally determining what the law is. The courts cannot make or repeal a law. "They can say what a law means; and if afterwards they see that they have made a mistake, they can correct their error by an overruling of a former decision, the consequence of which overruling is that the blunder is thenceforward deemed never to have been law." (Bishop on Contracts, sec. 569.)

It has been held here, that although it appears the parties have entered into a contract relying upon a previous decision of the supreme court, they would not be relieved from the obligations thereof because of a subsequent decision by the same court, overruling the former one, and declaring a different rule upon the same subject. (Kenyon v. Welty, 20 Cal. 637.) There are some cases in which the supreme court of the United States has held that the construction given to a statute by the highest tribunal in the state, whether sound or not, must be taken as correct, so far as contracts made under the act are concerned, and no subsequent decision altering the construction can impair their validity. The construction becomes a part of the statute,—as much so as if it were an amendment made by the legislature. [citations]

Notes

1. Courts consistently apply the general rule denying restitution of money paid to satisfy an honest claim asserted in reliance on precedents subsequently overruled. See Reporters' Notes, Restatement of Restitution, § 45 (1937). In view of the vast number of claims settled daily in lawyers' offices, is any other rule practicable?

2. Assume that overruling precedents creates new law rather than corrects a "blunder." Can we analyze the rights to payments made under the prior authority as "mistakes of law?"

2. CHANGE OF POSITION AND DISCHARGE FOR VALUE

News Item, 1977: St. Paul, Minn. (AP): Joseph G. Pearson had quite a party at the state's expense, but now Minnesota wants back the more than $25,000 it mistakenly sent him over 18 months. A computer error caused the state to mail the money in four separate checks starting in 1975 to the disabled construction worker, instead of to a school district that was supposed to receive it.

But Pearson thought he was entitled to the money and spent it.

"I did everything with the money I would have if I had been working," said Pearson, who now manages apartments. "I partied. I vacationed. I bought clothes and things that my wife and daughter didn't have during hard times.

"I bought baseball tickets and football tickets, stuff like that. And I'd go into a bar and set it up for $50 or maybe $100. It was things like that I spent the money on."

Pearson, 52, said he thought the money was his as part of a state rehabilitation program that he entered two years after injuring his back on a construction job in 1969.

"I saw 'Education Department' on the checks so I assumed they were from the division of vocational rehabilitation," Pearson said. "I didn't question them."

Now that the state has found out the whole thing was a mistake, Pearson says he "feels a moral obligation to repay it," but he is not sure how he can.

The money was actually intended for the Chandler, Minn., school district, and the mixup was uncovered when Supt. William Frietag noticed his district had not received its entire share of state aid.

HILLIARD v. FOX

United States District Court, Western District of Virginia, 1990.
735 F.Supp. 674.

GLEN M. WILLIAMS, SENIOR DISTRICT JUDGE. * * * The plaintiff, J.J.B. Hilliard, W.L. Lyons, Inc. ("Hilliard") is a stockbrokerage firm. T. Bryant Terry, Jr. ("Terry"), an employee of Hilliard, contacted defendant Gary Fox in either late January or early February of 1987 in order to discuss Gary and Catherine Fox's investments.

During their discussion, Terry mistakenly informed Mr. Fox that the market value of the 2,000 shares of Gibson Cryogenics, Inc. common stock which the Foxes owned was over ten dollars a share. Terry had quoted the market value of a share of Gibson C.R. Company common stock; the actual market value of the Foxes' shares was less than one dollar a share. Based on the erroneous valuation of the shares given by Terry, Mr. Fox directed that the 2,000 shares be sold.

Terry executed a sale of 2,000 shares of Gibson C.R. Company common stock at a price of $10.25 per share for 1,500 shares and $10.50 per share for the remaining 500 shares. He then remitted the proceeds of the sale, $20,625, less a commission of $421.80, to the Foxes on February 10, 1987. The Foxes delivered the certificates of their 2,000 shares of Gibson Cryogenics, Inc. common stock to Hilliard.

In early April of the same year, Hilliard discovered its mistake and requested that the Foxes return the amount paid them. [In October] Hilliard filed the complaint in the instant case seeking a money judgment against the Foxes in the amount of the $19,877.20, plus interest and court costs. Hilliard has tendered to the court the stock certificates of the 2,000 shares of Gibson Cryogenics, Inc. common stock. * * *

Hilliard paid the money in question to the Foxes because of the erroneous belief that he was performing the contract he had with Mr. Fox to remit to him the proceeds of the sale of the Gibson Cryogenics common stock. Therefore, Hilliard has a right to restitution of the money, even if the payment was made because of its negligence. * * *

The Foxes claim that, prior to the demand of Hilliard that they return the money, they "disbursed" the money remitted to them, investing most of it in Virginia Oil & Refinery Company, Inc., which is now a defunct corporation. They assert that their change in position, resulting from the investment and its loss in value, terminates any right of restitution that Hilliard may have against them. Hilliard, on the other hand, asserts that this change in position should not terminate its right to restitution because the investment was not "caused" by the receipt of the money and that no evidence has been submitted showing that the investment would not have been made anyway.

The Supreme Court of Appeals of Virginia, in Central Nat. Bank of Richmond v. First & Merchants Nat. Bank of Richmond, 171 Va. 289, 312–13, 198 S.E. 883, 893 (1938), quoted with approval section 69 of the Restatement of Restitution as follows: "The right of a person to restitution from another because of a benefit received is terminated or diminished if, after the receipt of the benefit, circumstances have so changed that it would be inequitable to require the other to make full restitution."

The issue to be addressed is whether the investment of money mistakenly received and the investment's subsequent decline in value constitute such a change in position as to terminate or diminish the plaintiff's right to restitution. That issue is directly answered by neither the Restatement nor any reported Virginia cases. Furthermore, the court has failed to find any American cases directly addressing the issue. Thus, the issue appears to be one of first impression.

Although not directly addressed by the Restatement, the commentary contained in the Restatement provides helpful guidance. It provides that "[a]ny change of circumstances which would cause * * * the recipient entire or partial loss if the claimant were to obtain full restitution, is such a change as prevents full restitution." Restatement of Restitution § 142 comment b. Thus, the primary rule is that if repayment will cause the recipient loss, restitution is barred to the extent that such loss would occur.

The commentary notes two situations where restitution would not cause a loss. The first is where the money was used for the payment of debts incurred prior to its receipt. The second, to which there is a limited exception, is where the money was used for payment of living expenses, business expenses,[1] or gifts. These situations are alike in that the money received was used to confer a net benefit on the recipient; thus, repayment will not normally cause the recipient any net loss—he will merely be returned to *status quo ante.* Conversely, where the recipient has received no net benefit from the payment, there is no duty of restitution. *Cf.* (in discussing a situation involving a principal and his agent, the commentary asserts that because the principal "received no net benefit from the payment," there was no duty of restitution).

The investing of money does not confer an immediate benefit upon the investor. Rather, one invests in the hope of receiving benefits in the future. Likewise, a decline in the value of an investment does not reflect consumption by or a benefit conferred upon the investor. Therefore, the investing of money received and the subsequent decline in value of the investment appear to be a change of circumstances which would diminish the right to restitution by the amount of the decline.[2]

The plaintiff raises the issue of "cause:" whether the receipt of the money caused or induced the defendants to make the investment. It asserts that if the defendants would have made the investment anyway using other sources for the necessary funds, then the investment does not constitute a change of circumstances justifying the termination or diminution of the right to restitution.

In most situations where the change of circumstances doctrine has been applied to terminate the right to restitution, the making of the payment had

1. [Footnotes renumbered.] The exception for the payment of business expenses has no application in the instant case even though the business venture may have ultimately used the proceeds invested in it for the payment of business expenses. From the Foxes' perspective, the investment in the business venture was a capital asset and not the payment of business expenses. The following example further clarifies this point. An investor purchasing stock from an issuing corporation is purchasing a capital asset even though the corporation uses the proceeds from that stock sale to pay its expenses.

2. An example of the application of this principle is the following. One is mistakenly paid $5000 through no fault of his own and has no notice that he is not entitled to the money. He uses all of the money to purchase publicly traded common stock. At the time that he becomes aware of the mistake, the market value of the stock which he has purchased has declined to $3,000. Any right of restitution that the payor has is limited to $3,000.

caused or, more precisely, induced the change in position; however, it is significant that the Restatement has avoided any reference to "cause." Annotation, Restitution—Payment Under Mistake, 40 A.L.R.2d 997, 1003 (1955). This lack of a "cause" requirement allows the change of circumstances doctrine to apply when specific chattels have been mistakenly received and subsequently lost or stolen even though their loss or theft is not "caused" by their previous receipt. Restatement of Restitution § 142 comment b. At least one commentator has concluded that the change of circumstances doctrine should apply also to money which is mistakenly received and subsequently lost or stolen. G. Costigan, Change of Position as a Defense in Quasi-Contracts, 20 Harv.L.Rev. 205, 212 (1912).

The annotation cited above, in discussing the issue, appears to find a common theme in the loss or theft of the money mistakenly received, its deposit in a bank that later fails, its investment in bonds or stock of enterprises which later become insolvent, and its investment in a house which is subsequently destroyed by fire, storm, or the public enemy. The common theme is that the recipient no longer has the money, has received no benefit from it, and through no fault of his own, cannot get it. The annotation concludes that "[i]f the true basis of the action for money had and received is that the defendant has money which belongs to the plaintiff, in equity and good conscience," then the presence of any of the situations noted above should constitute an adequate defense to that action.

The court concurs in the annotation's conclusion and further concludes that it follows from that principle that the loss in value of an investment in a business venture,[3] which investment was made with the money mistakenly received, also constitutes a change of circumstances diminishing the right to restitution by the amount of the loss.[4] Therefore, the plaintiff's motion for summary judgment is denied.

The defendants also seek summary judgment on the basis that the change of circumstances bars any recovery by the plaintiff. Once a claimant has proved that the recipient has received money from him under circumstances which would create a right to restitution, then the recipient has the burden of proving a sufficient change of circumstances that would make it inequitable for that right to be exercised. Restatement of Restitution § 142 comment g. Thus, the assertion by the recipient of a change of circumstances is an affirmative defense, of which the recipient has both the burden of coming forward with the evidence and the risk of non-persuasion.

The court concludes that whether the money received by the defendants was ultimately invested is to be determined by the common law rules of tracing. Thus, the defendants have the burden of proving by common law rules of tracing that the money mistakenly received from the plaintiff was invested in the business venture. * * *

3. If the recipient received the money without fault, then the recipient is under no duty of care with regard to the money until he has knowledge that he is not entitled to retain the money. Cf. Restatement of Restitution § 142 comment b (no such duty of care with regard to chattels). There is no allegation that the Foxes were at fault for the mistaken payment. Thus, the riskiness or prudence of the investment in the business venture is irrelevant in regard to the application of the change of circumstances doctrine.

4. The court limits its conclusion to the loss of value which occurred prior to the recipient receiving notice of the mistake. It does not need to address at this time the consequences of a loss of value occurring after notice has occurred.

The defendants have not submitted evidence sufficient to prove by common law tracing rules the amount of the money mistakenly received from Hilliard which was ultimately invested in the business venture. Furthermore; they have not shown that the change of circumstances defense should apply to a loss of value occurring after they received notice of the mistake and they also have not shown what portion of the loss of value took place prior to notice. * * * Therefore, the court denies the defendant's motion for summary judgment.

Notes

1. Examples of changes of position from instructions given to social security administrators: 20 C.F.R. § 404.509 (1982)

Example. A widow having been awarded benefits for herself and daughter, entered her daughter in college because the monthly benefits made this possible. After the widow and her daughter received payments for almost a year, the deceased worker was found to be not insured and all payments to the widow and child were incorrect. The widow has no other funds with which to pay the daughter's college expenses. Having entered the daughter in college and thus incurred a financial obligation toward which the benefits had been applied, she was in a worse position financially than if she and her daughter had never been entitled to benefits. In this situation, the recovery of the incorrect payments would be inequitable.

Example. X died without leaving an estate. Z, a friend, paid the burial expenses of $150 and filed a claim for a lump-sum death payment on X's earnings record. After receiving the lump-sum death payment of $150, Z used the payment to purchase a marker for the deceased's grave. Thereafter, it was discovered that X lacked the required insured status and thus the lump sum was paid in error. Recovery of the $150 from Z is considered to be against equity and good conscience because in reliance on the payment he changed his position for the worse. Solely by reason of the lump-sum death payment, he made a purchase which he otherwise would not have made.

2. Unger v. Travel Arrangements, Inc., 25 A.D.2d 40, 46–47, 266 N.Y.S.2d 715, 721–22 (1966). Defendant, a travel agency, booked plaintiff's passage from New York to the West Indies and received payment of $704.55. The cruise was cancelled, and the steamship company, defendant's principal, became insolvent. Plaintiff sued the agency for money had and received. The court said: " 'The fact that the agent credits the principal with the amount received does not release the agent from his obligation to make restitution so long as he continues to hold the money on behalf of the principal, Rest. Restitution § 143(b) * * *; but when the agent parts with the money in accordance with the agency, he is released from liability.'

"Applying the above * * *, the defendant having admitted that it retained as commissions $69 of plaintiff's payment, it is only fair and equitable that it return that sum to the plaintiff. Assuming that it [paid the balance over to its principal] without knowledge that plaintiff's trip would be cancelled, the defendant so changed its position * * * that it should be exonerated."

OAKLEY BUILDING & LOAN CO. v. MURPHY

Court of Appeals of Ohio, 1948.
84 Ohio App. 539, 84 N.E.2d 749.

MATTHEWS, PRESIDING JUDGE. This is an appeal on questions of law from a judgment rendered in an action for a declaratory judgment. The plaintiff is a corporation organized under the laws of Ohio relating to building and loan associations, and as such authorized to receive money on deposit. * * *

The defendant, Daniel F. Murphy, deposited [various amounts which, with dividends, amounted on December 18, 1947 to $3200.32] with the plaintiff.

On December 21, 1941, Murphy went to the plaintiff's place of business and delivered two envelopes, each containing $1000 through the receiving teller's window to the cashier, with whom he had had similar transactions and the cashier gave him a deposit slip showing $2000 had been deposited in his account with the plaintiff. The account was identified by its number, the cashier wrote on it "Dup." and signed his name thereunder and signed Murphy's name at the bottom under the printed words "Depositor's name." On one of the envelopes, Murphy had written his name and under his name was written "To be called for" * * * After the envelope was delivered to the cashier he endorsed thereon "A receipt given" and thereunder placed his initials.

There is evidence that there was a limitation at the time upon the amount of deposit the plaintiff could take from a single depositor, and that this money was left for safe keeping against the time when it could be accepted on an interest or dividend drawing basis. There is also evidence from which the inference can be drawn that the only purpose was to leave it for safe keeping, and returned to Murphy upon his demand. There is no evidence that the $2000 was received for immediate credit in the pass book. Murphy always considered it a different kind of deposit. * * *

About six months after this transaction, it was discovered that the cashier had embezzled some of the plaintiff's funds and had concealed the fact for awhile by using $1000 of this money to satisfy the demands of depositors. In other words, he had taken $1000 of this money and paid it to the plaintiff, leaving $1000 in the envelope in his personal box in the plaintiff's vault at the time of the exposure. The trial court found as a matter of law that as the plaintiff had received the benefit of this $1000, it would be inequitable for it to retain it.

During the trial, the $1000 which remained in the envelope was paid to the Clerk of Courts to abide the order of the court.

On these findings, the Court entered judgment against the plaintiff for $2000, with interest on $1000 at 6% per annum from July 18, 1942. A few days after the judgment was rendered, the Court ordered the Clerk of Courts to pay to Murphy the $1000 which had been paid to him to abide the action of the Court. * * *

As already noted, the trial court found two principles of law, both of which when applied to the facts found, imposed a liability upon the plaintiff to reimburse the defendant Murphy for the $1000 used by its cashier to replace the money embezzled by him: (1) Unjust enrichment by the plaintiff at Murphy's expense, and (2) the duty of a principal to answer for the acts of its agent in the course of his employment. While we have concluded that the second principle is sufficient, we shall briefly discuss the first to indicate our reasons for placing our affirmance on the second.

It will be observed that the purpose of the cashier in using Murphy's money was to satisfy his (the cashier's) hidden obligation to the plaintiff and that the net result of the double embezzlement was to place the plaintiff in the same position it would have occupied had there been no embezzlement at all. The question is, whether under such circumstances it is inequitable to permit the status quo to stand. Would it result in the unjust enrichment of plaintiff?

On this subject we find section 142, Restatement of Law, Restitution, in which it is stated that: "Change of circumstances is a defense [to an action for restitution] if the conduct of the recipient is not tortious."

And in the "Comment" on this section it is said:

> "Likewise although the money so obtained has been used for the payment of the principal's debts, if thereby the agent is enabled to steal other money from the principal, the fact that the principal has received no net benefit from the payment would prevent the existence of a duty of restitution."

And under "Illustration" this example is stated:

> "A without authority, but having power to bind B thereby, borrows $1000 from C purporting to be acting for B. A retains this for his own purposes. To prevent discovery, he borrows $1000 from D, purporting to act for B, but this time without power to bind him. With this he pays C and averts discovery in the meantime embezzling larger sums from B. B is under no duty of restitution to D."

Referring to the general rule, permitting a right of recovery from a principal who, with knowledge of the facts has received money through the unauthorized act of his agent on the theory that the retention of the money is a ratification of the agent's act, it is stated in 2 Am.Jur., 183:

> "But the principal cannot be said to have received the benefit of an unauthorized loan where the sum borrowed does not increase his money in hand or the amount he is entitled to receive from his agent, or where the money is not used to extinguish outstanding liabilities against him, and, accordingly, the general rule is held not to apply where the agent, being in default to his principal, borrows money in the principal's name and uses it to make good his defalcation."

The opposite conclusion was reached in Duffy v. Scott, 235 Wis. 142, 292 N.W. 273, 129 A.L.R. 487. The cases on this subject are collected in an annotation to this case from which it appears that the weight of authority is against the right of recovery.

We have been referred to no Ohio case on this subject. In view of that fact, our inclination would be to hold in accord with the Restatement and the weight of authority that such circumstances do not show an unjust enrichment, therefore, no cause of action arises.

However, if the act of receiving this money for safekeeping was within the apparent authority of the cashier, recourse to the principle of unjust enrichment was not necessary to impose a liability. We think the trial court was justified in so finding.

[Discussion of this proposition is omitted.]

For these reasons, the judgment is affirmed.

Notes

1. *Discharge for Value. Restitution in the Fast Lane—Mistakes by the Millisecond.* S, an Australian firm, owed B.W. a French bank $2,000,000 on a loan. S telexed SPIB, an American bank in New York where S then had $70,000 on deposit

to wire transfer $2,000,000 to B.W.; S indicated that funds to cover were on the way. Within the hour S sent a second telex directing SPIB to disregard the first telex and instead wire transfer $2,000,000 to a bank in Australia. When the funds from S arrived, SPIB wire transferred $2,000,000 to B.W. but within seconds wired B.W. that the transfer was a mistake. At the same time SPIB wire transferred $2,000,000 to the Australian bank in compliance with S's revised instructions—apparently believing that someone would reimburse it. In fact on that same day S filed for bankruptcy in Australia. B.W. now refuses to return the transfer, quoting § 14 of the Restatement of Restitution, the Discharge for Value defense. Could B.W. have possibly changed its position? Does it make any difference?

The facts are changed a bit but based on Banque Worms v. Bank America International, 726 F.Supp. 940 (S.D.N.Y.1989), aff'd 928 F.2d 538 (2d Cir.1991).

2. A embezzles money from B. B demands payment. By misrepresentation A causes C to make a check payable to B, which B accepts in discharge of A's debt. May C obtain restitution from B? Variations of this theme may be found in Jones v. Waring and Gillow, Ltd. [1926] A.C. 670; Douglass v. Wones, 120 Ill.App.3d 36, 458 N.E.2d 514 (1983); Federal Insurance Co. v. Banco de Ponce, 582 F.Supp. 1388 (D.P.R.1984). Cf. U.C.C. § 3–302(2): "A payee may be a holder in due course."

3. Rather than simply a "change of circumstance" it might be more enlightening to recognize Oakley Building & Loan as the more specialized form of "discharge for value." Suppose an agent owes the principal $1000 and steals $1000 cash from X and pays the debt. Absent special knowledge, the principal has accepted money in satisfaction of a pre-existing obligation—a discharge for value.

The agent in *Oakley Building & Loan* owes the employer $1000 because of embezzlement unknown to the principal. If the agent had stolen the money from X and covered the shortage, the court would have considered the principal to have "received" the money in satisfaction of a pre-existing indebtedness.

Can one discharge an "indebtedness" unknown to exist—particularly one arising out of a tort? The point is a variation of the one in Associates Discount Corp. v. Clements, infra, p. 939.

CONCORD COAL CO. v. FERRIN

Supreme Court of New Hampshire, 1901.

71 N.H. 33, 51 A. 283.

One Bean, being indebted to the defendants for labor upon a model of an appliance invented by him, and having been requested to make payment, informed the defendants that one of the plaintiffs, Day, was backing him, and that he would get the plaintiff company to furnish a ton of coal for application as payment upon his indebtedness; and the defendants agreed to accept a ton of coal in part payment. Bean thereupon informed the plaintiffs that the defendants wanted a ton of coal, without saying anything about the arrangement he had made with them. The coal was delivered to the defendants and used by them in their business. The plaintiffs charged the coal to the defendants. Demand for payment was made upon the defendants by the plaintiffs by letter within six months after the coal was delivered, and again after about a year.

* * * The defendants credited the coal to Bean's account. Day was not in fact backing Bean, and had given him no authority to bind him in any way. The defendants knew that the coal came from the Concord Coal Company, and that the plaintiffs were a firm composed of Day and one Emmons. Both parties

acted in entire good faith, but were deceived by Bean. The court found a verdict for the defendants, and the plaintiffs excepted.

PARSONS, J. Both parties understood that upon the delivery of the coal the title passed to the defendants. Their misunderstanding related solely to the mode of payment. The plaintiffs understood the defendants were to pay them the customary price, and charged the coal to them. The defendants understood the coal was delivered as a payment upon Bean's indebtedness to them, and credited it upon his account. The plaintiffs understood their delivery was of coal to be paid for in cash in the ordinary course of business. The defendants understood their acceptance was of coal for which they had already paid. To this branch of a contract of sale the parties did not agree in fact, either in terms or by inference. Hence there was no contract in fact, express or tacit * * * because of the mutual mistake as to payment. As there was no contract of sale, in the absence of any estoppel, upon discovery of the mistake the plaintiffs might have retaken their coal if it remained distinguishable from other coal of the defendants, or the defendants might have required the plaintiffs to remove it. As the plaintiffs had no right of action by virtue of the mistaken acceptance of the coal, they cannot now recover except by virtue of some further facts. The additional facts stated are that the defendants used the coal in their business, and the plaintiffs, within six months and subsequently, made sundry demands for payment. It does not appear that the plaintiffs ever demanded the return of the coal; but, on the contrary, they appear to have uniformly insisted upon the contract as they understood it. In the original transaction both parties acted in entire good faith, but were deceived by Bean. Upon these facts the trial court found a verdict for the defendants. * * *

The plaintiffs' claim is that the defendants by their use of the coal charged themselves with the legal duty of paying for it in accordance with the plaintiffs' understanding of the contract, rather than their own, or at least of paying anew in money the usual price or value of the coal. The question is, how ought the coal to be paid for,—in accord with the understanding of the plaintiffs, or with that of the defendants? It is manifest that if the plaintiffs had accompanied the delivery of the coal with an invoice charging the defendants with the price, or had informed them it was delivered on their credit, or if before delivery the plaintiffs had inquired of the defendants as to Bean's authority, or if the defendants, before accepting the coal, had informed the plaintiffs that they accepted it only for application on Bean's debt, the controversy would have been avoided. * * *

The facts disclose no contract in fact, express, tacit, by estoppel, or implied in fact; and the sole remaining question is whether the facts establish a contract implied in law, or a contract of legal duty, sometimes called a quasi contract. A promise to pay what it is one's legal duty to pay is implied by law. * * * In this case the legal duty is wanting, unless it can be predicated upon the mere possession and use of property. The mere fact of benefit received is insufficient to establish the legal duty of payment. Clark v. Sanborn [68 N.H. 411, 36 A. 14] is precisely in point. There the plaintiff was unable to recover for services valuable to the defendants, rendered under the expectation that they would be paid for, for the reason that the defendants did not accept the services with the understanding that they were to make payment. In the absence of privity of contract, the mere possession and use of property will not imply a promise to pay for it. * * * It is contended that the plaintiffs can recover because otherwise the defendants would be unjustly enriched at the plaintiffs' expense. But that fact is not found. Both parties trusted and were deceived by Bean. If the plaintiffs cannot recover of the defendants for the coal, they have a claim against Bean for its value; while, if the defendants were obliged to pay for the coal, they would also have a claim against Bean for the same amount. It may be assumed that Bean is worthless. But there is no equitable reason why the plaintiffs rather than the defendants should be released from the consequences of their trust in Bean. In view of the inference of freedom from fault which the general verdict finds for the defendants, the defendants' equity is at least equal with that of the plaintiffs.

Notes

1. Is the result in Concord Coal v. Ferrin simply the absence of enrichment? Is it an unexpressed application of the defense of discharge for value?

2. If Bean had paid Ferrin's bill with stolen coal, Ferrin would have been an innocent converter. The defense of discharge for value would not be available. Bean actually acquired the coal through fraudulent misrepresentations. What if he had acquired the coal through false personation—a crime and a tort—and then used the coal to pay his debt? Here U.C.C. § 2–403(1)(d) provides specially for the defendant.

3. Suppose A defrauds the plaintiff into executing a conveyance of land to the mistaken defendant who accepts it in satisfaction of A's indebtedness to the defendant. Could plaintiff compel a reconveyance? Is a "pre-existing" debt "value" for purposes of determining whether the grantee is a bona fide purchaser for value?

ASSOCIATES DISCOUNT CORP. v. CLEMENTS

Supreme Court of Oklahoma, 1958.
321 P.2d 673.

WILLIAMS, JUSTICE. This action was brought by Earl Clements, hereinafter referred to as plaintiff, against Associates Discount Corporation, a Corporation, and Associates Investment & Loan Company, a Corporation, hereinafter referred to as defendants, for money had and received. Plaintiff was a used car dealer in Oklahoma City, and defendants were affiliated corporations engaged in the automobile finance and loan business. On February 11, 1952, defendants made a loan in the amount of $1,871 to one Walker, taking a note secured by a mortgage on a 1951 Pontiac automobile. Walker was in possession of the automobile with an Oklahoma title certificate and represented himself to the defendant as being the owner. The loan was made in complete good faith. Thereafter, on March 24, Walker sold the automobile to plaintiff for the sum of $2,325, again representing himself to be the owner. Of the purchase price, $1,767.77 was used to pay off the mortgage debt to defendants, a check being made payable to Associates Discount Corporation and immediately endorsed to the Associates Investment & Loan Company, and the mortgage and note were marked "paid" and surrendered to Walker. The balance of the purchase price was paid to Walker. Plaintiff also acted in complete good faith. Thereafter it developed that the automobile in question had been stolen, probably by Walker, some time prior to Walker's obtaining the loan from defendants. Plaintiff then brought this action seeking to recover from defendants that part of the purchase price, $1,767.77, used to discharge the mortgage debt to defendants. Judgment was for the plaintiff, and defendants bring this appeal. * * *

Defendants' first proposition is: "An innocent purchaser of a stolen automobile cannot recover that portion of the purchase price paid to satisfy a mortgage given to secure a note executed by the thief for a prior bona fide loan by the mortgagee made in equal good faith, the debt secured being actual and enforceable and discharged so that the payment was not without consideration or made by mistake, nor paid under such circumstances as to require the mortgagee to repay that portion of the purchase price of the purchaser." Defendants' second proposition is that: "The purchaser of a stolen automobile and the holder of a mortgage thereon securing a prior loan to the thief, both being equally innocent of knowledge that the automobile was stolen and a portion of the purchase price being used to pay off the mortgage debt which was discounted and released and the note and mortgage surrendered, there is no mistake of fact in contemplation of law whereby the purchaser may recover from the mortgagee the money received by it to satisfy the mortgage debt, the mortgagee having changed its position by the release of the debt."

* * * [W]here money is paid to another under the influence of a mistake, that is on the mistaken supposition of the existence of a specific fact that would entitle the other to the money, and the money would not have been paid had it been known to the payor that the fact was otherwise, it can be recovered back. The ground upon which such rule rests is that money paid through misapprehension of fact in equity and good conscience belongs to the party paying it, and there is no controversy as to the correctness of such rule, the difficulty arising in the application of the same. The question which is presented to this court for the first time is, whether the principle or rule above stated is applicable to the situation where one advances money to pay a debt held by another upon the mistaken assumption of the existence of facts under which an apparent lien in favor of the other and securing the indebtedness would be valid, the facts actually being such as to render the lien invalid. This general question has arisen in a number of cases from other jurisdictions. Most of such cases deal with one or the other, or some slight variation thereof, of the following factual situations: (1) A steals tangible personal property and executes a mortgage on it in favor of B, after which he sells the property to C, a part of the purchase price being applied to the payment of the supposed mortgage in favor of B; (2) A impersonates the owner of real property and obtains a loan from B, giving the latter as security a forged mortgage purporting to be executed by the owner of the land, whereupon A repeats the impersonation and secures a larger loan from C under a second forged mortgage, a part of the proceeds of this loan being paid to B for a release or discharge of the purported mortgage in his favor. The question in each case is, of course, the right of C, under the circumstances, to recover back the payments made to B. It will be noticed that situation (1) is identical with the situation presented by the case at bar, and the cases dealing with that situation would therefore be more pertinent and persuasive. In this category we find decisions from the appellate courts of California and Washington in the cases of Gaffner v. American Finance Company, 120 Wash. 76, 206 P. 916, 28 A.L.R. 624, decided in 1922, and Hilliard v. Bank of America National Trust & Savings Ass'n, 102 Cal.App.2d 730, 228 P.2d 327, decided in 1951. Both of these cases hold that C cannot recover from B. The same holding is found in American Law Institute Restatement: Restitution, sec. 14, Illus. 6, which is used to

illustrate the general principle that restitution will not be ordered against an innocent defendant who has given value for the benefit received. [citations] * * *

Plaintiff also cites and relies upon National Shawmut Bank of Boston v. Fidelity Mutual Life Ins. Co., 318 Mass. 142, 61 N.E.2d 18 [citations] all of which involved factual situations substantially identical with that set out in illustration (2) above, and hold that C is entitled to recover from B. These cases by no means represent the weight of authority on the question, however, as we find the same question presented in the cases of [citations] and in all of such cases it was held that C could not recover from B. We also find situation (2) presented in American Law Institute Restatement: Restitution, sec. 14, Illus. 7, and the answer there given is that C cannot recover from B.

We do not find it necessary, however, in the case at bar, to determine which of the situation (2) lines of cases to follow in this jurisdiction, because the cited situation (2) cases which hold that C is entitled to recover from B distinguish themselves from the situation (1) type of cases and therefore of necessity from the case at bar.

The distinction between the two types of cases was likewise noted in Hilliard v. Bank of America National Trust & Savings Ass'n, a situation (1) case, in which the court used the following language:

> "Appellant relies on National Shawmut Bank of Boston v. Fidelity Mutual Life Ins. Co., but the opinion therein itself differentiates that case from Gaffner v. American Finance Co. In the *Gaffner* case the court said: 'The situation is different than in those cases where both the note and mortgage were tainted with fraud. *Here there was no mistake as to the indebtedness which was paid.*' (Emphasis added.) In the *Shawmut Bank* case Schneierson, whose name had been forged as the maker of the notes and the assignor of the insurance policies, by Meissel, was never indebted to the defendant insurance company, which had received from the Shawmut Bank the money to pay off the supposed indebtedness. Here Cassaro had become the respondent bank's debtor in a routine banking transaction and had given it a genuine promissory note. The court in the *Shawmut Bank* case, after citing the *Gaffner* case (among others) says: 'The case at bar differs from the cases just discussed primarily in the fact that in this case the defendant had no valid claim against its supposed debtor, Schneierson, or against anyone, except its claim against Meissel for the forgery.' When the court thus distinguishes the *Gaffner* case it likewise distinguishes the instant case, since the facts in both are substantially the same."

There is still a third line of cases, which it appears to us are more nearly in point with the case at bar than the situation (2) cases above cited, although not quite so squarely in point from a factual point of view as the situation (1) cases above cited. These cases, of which there are a great number, hold that the rule as to recovery of payments made under a mistake of fact does not apply where, as a result of a mistake or fraud between the original parties, money is paid by one of them on account of the other to a third party, either directly or through the intervention of the other, who receives the same in good faith without knowledge of the mistake or fraud, in payment of a claim by him against the latter. In such case, by the overwhelming weight of authority, no recovery may be had against such third party. Typical examples of these cases are Union Central Life Insurance Co. v. Glasscock, 270 Ky. 750, 110 S.W.2d 681, and Merchants' Insurance Co. of Providence v. Abbott, 131 Mass. 397. In the

Union Central Life Ins. Co. case plaintiff purchased part of a tract of land on which there was a mortgage held by defendant, the purchase price being paid to defendant to procure a release of the land sold from the lien of the mortgage. It subsequently appeared that there was a prior mortgage on the land, which had been overlooked by the abstractor and accordingly did not appear on any of the abstracts referred to by the parties during their negotiations. The first mortgage was later foreclosed, rendering defendant's mortgage worthless. The court held that the plaintiff purchaser of the land, who had paid to defendant mortgagee, through the vendor, the amount of the mortgage, at the request of the vendor, under a mistake of fact that the property was otherwise unencumbered, whereas, as a matter of fact there was a prior outstanding mortgage against it, could not recover back from the mortgagee the amount paid, on the theory that payment was made as a result of mistake and that there was a failure of consideration, where the mortgagee was not aware of such mistake and received the payment in good faith in satisfaction of its mortgage claim against vendor. In the case of Merchants' Insurance Co. of Providence v. Abbott, after a loss by fire, caused by the fraud of the assured Abbott, which had been adjusted by the insurers, Abbott assigned his claim under the policy to a creditor of his to secure a debt, and the insurers, at the request of the assured Abbott, paid to the creditor the amount of the policy so adjusted, both the insurers and the creditor being ignorant of the fraud invalidating the assigned insurance claim, and the court held that the insurers might recover from the insured, Abbott, the sum so paid, but could not recover it back from the creditor. The court, in discussing the question presented of when the implied obligation to make restitution will be imposed to prevent the unjust enrichment of one at another's expense, said:

> "There can be no doubt of the liability of Abbott in this action. If the money had been paid by the plaintiffs to him, it could be recovered back as money paid under the influence of a mistake between them and him as to the existence of a state of facts that would entitle him to the money. * * * Although Abbott has not in fact received the money, the payment of the money by the plaintiffs at his request in discharge of his debt to the other defendants is equivalent to the receipt by Abbott of so much money, and is sufficient to enable the plaintiffs to maintain the action against him upon the special count, if not upon the general count for money had and received. * * *
>
> "As to the other defendants a different question is presented. If, before receiving the money from the plaintiffs, they had known the true state of facts, and had participated in Abbott's fraud, they would have been liable to refund the money. * * * But the report states that there was no evidence offered, nor was it contended at the trial, that they had any knowledge of the fraudulent conduct of Abbott, but it was conceded that they were wholly innocent parties.
>
> "* * * The only contract of the plaintiffs was with Abbott, and the only mistake was as between them and him. The money was voluntarily paid by the plaintiffs in discharge of Abbott's supposed claim upon them under their policy, and to these defendants as the persons designated by Abbott to receive it, and was in legal effect a payment by the plaintiffs to Abbott. * * * In other words, the money was paid by the plaintiffs to these defendants, not as a sum which the latter were entitled to recover from the plaintiffs, but as a sum which the plaintiffs admitted to be due to Abbott, under their own contract with him, and which at his request and in his behalf they paid to these defendants, who at the time of receiving it knew no facts tending to show that it had not in truth become due from the plaintiffs to Abbott. * * * As between

the plaintiffs and these defendants, there was no fraud, concealment or mistake. These defendants had the right to receive from Abbott the sum which was paid to them. * * * They hold the money honestly, for value, with the right to retain it as their own, under a title derived from Abbott, and independent of the fraud practiced by him upon the plaintiffs.

"The case stands just as if the money had been paid by the plaintiffs to Abbott, and by Abbott to these defendants, in which case there could be no doubt that, while the plaintiffs could recover back the amount from Abbott, neither Abbott nor the plaintiffs could recover the amount from these defendants. The fact that the money, instead of being paid by the plaintiffs to Abbott, and by Abbott to these defendants, was paid directly by the plaintiffs to these defendants, does not make any difference in the rights of the parties. The two forms do not differ in substance. In either case, Abbott alone is liable to the plaintiffs, and these defendants hold no money which ex aequo et bono they are bound to return either to Abbott or to the plaintiffs."

In Gaffner v. American Finance Co., the court said:

"The general rule is that an action for money had and received can be maintained whenever one has received money from another by mistake, and which the receiver ought not, in equity and good conscience, to retain. We are of the opinion, however, that the facts of this case do not come within that rule. The respondent had made a bona fide loan to Hughes, not upon a forged note, but upon that given by the borrower himself. Hughes actually became indebted to the respondent. It is true the mortgage given to secure the indebtedness was upon a stolen machine, and was consequently fraudulently made and probably invalid, but the mortgage was a mere incident of the loan. Though the mortgage was invalid and worthless, the debt it secured was actual and enforceable. The appellant tried to purchase Hughes' automobile, but wished it to be clear of the apparent incumbrance. The money which was paid to the respondent was to discharge a bona fide indebtedness; consequently, it cannot be said that there was no consideration for the payment, or that the respondent cannot, in good conscience, keep the money. The situation is different than in those cases where both the note and mortgage was tainted with fraud. Here there was no mistake as to the indebtedness which was paid. * * *

"If we look at this case from a purely equitable viewpoint, the result to which we must come will not be different than that above announced. Appellant made the payment to the respondent in the belief that he was paying a bona fide, valid, indebtedness due from Hughes, and in so supposing there was no mistake. As to the mortgage; if respondent was innocent, so was the appellant. The equities in favor of the respondent are not less great than those running with the appellant."

Judgment reversed and the cause remanded with instructions to enter judgment for defendants.

Note

Even the learned drafters of the Restatement of Restitution (1937) had trouble with the various "situations" the principal case describes. See the Reporters' Notes to sections 13 and 14 of the Restatement.

Professor Palmer's treatment is helpful. G. Palmer, The Law of Restitution §§ 16.5, 16.6 (1978).

D. MISTAKE IN INTEGRATION

MUTUAL OF OMAHA INSURANCE CO. v. RUSSELL

United States Court of Appeals, Tenth Circuit, 1968.
402 F.2d 339.

JOHN R. BROWN, CIRCUIT JUDGE. * * * Rev. and Mrs. Russell were residents of Kansas City, Kansas. On Thursday, January 24, 1963, upon receiving word that one of her brothers had died in Lubbock, Texas, Mrs. Russell decided to fly to Lubbock for the funeral. Reservations were made for a flight the next day, Friday, but the return flight was left open because the funeral date had not been set. On Friday Rev. and Mrs. Russell and their son went to the airport in Kansas City, Missouri, picked up their tickets at the Continental Airlines counter, and proceeded toward the awaiting plane.

As the Russells passed one of Insurer's vending machines for dispensing flight insurance, Rev. Russell decided that Mrs. Russell should have insurance to cover her during the trip. This machine dispensed Insurer's policy T–20. In many ways the T–20 affords severely limited coverage in that it provides protection only for accidents while aboard an airplane or in established limousines going to or coming from the airport. On the other hand, the T–20's coverage expressly remains in effect for the duration of the round trip or for twelve months, whichever occurs first. Similarly, since events and covered occurrences were more restrictive, the face amount of insurance per premium dollar was larger than other policies. Had a T–20 been machine-issued the Assured's death would have been covered. But no one had the proper change to operate the machine, so the Russells stepped just south of the machine to one of Insurer's staffed insurance booths. The booth had signs overhead reading "Flight Insurance" and was attended by a Miss Fletcher.

Rev. Russell asked either for flight insurance or insurance to cover his wife on her round trip to Lubbock. Miss Fletcher then asked "How much?", meaning what amount of insurance coverage. Mrs. Russell asked for the least amount and $20,000 was the amount agreed upon. Without then explaining various policies available, Miss Fletcher took out an application form and began to fill it out. She then asked either how long would Mrs. Russell be gone or when would she be returning. Mrs. Russell turned to her husband and asked "Three days?" Rev. Russell said she should allow herself more than that—at least four days. Miss Fletcher completed the form and turned it around for Mrs. Russell's signature. Mrs. Russell signed and paid the $2.25 premium. Miss Fletcher stapled the policy together and handed it to Rev. Russell.

The policy purchased was not, however, the T–20; rather it was the T–18, a significantly different policy. The T–18 is a general accident policy that covers almost all risks—whether air related or not—during the life of the policy. The term is stated in terms of twenty-four hour periods on a daily basis up to thirty-one days. The premium is higher on the T–18 for the same dollar amount of insurance and the T–18 is not sold in vending machines. As the Schedule signed by Mrs. Russell shows, the T–18 was issued for only four days, and expired at 11:00 a.m., Tuesday, January 29, 1963, about twelve hours prior to the Assured's death.

The District Court credited Rev. Russell's testimony that Miss Fletcher never mentioned any other available policies,[1] did not explain the T–18, and did not warn plaintiff that the policy would expire at 11:00 a.m. on Tuesday, January 29, 1963. The Judge also found that the Assured intended to buy insurance that would cover Mrs. Russell's round trip, which both she and her husband thought would occur within four days.

After buying the insurance, Mrs. Russell boarded her plane and arrived safely in Lubbock, Texas. There the funeral was delayed because a son of the deceased had not arrived from England. The funeral was finally held on Tuesday, January 29, and Mrs. Russell was fatally injured when her airplane crashed that night at 10:45 p.m. while attempting to land at the Kansas City, Missouri, airport. The insurance policy had expired by its own terms about twelve hours earlier. The Insurer denied liability.

* * * The District Judge held that the contract was clear and unambiguous and as written did not cover the accident. But now of direct importance he held that as a matter of equity the policy should be reformed to cover the accident. Judgment for $20,000 was entered for the Assured. Insurer appealed contending that it is not liable since the policy had expired and the company was not guilty of any inequitable conduct that would give rise to the remedy of reformation. The Assured cross-appealed contending that the judgment should have been for $90,000, the amount of straight flight insurance (T–20) that $2.25 would have bought, but the Assured did not appeal the decision that the policy could not be construed to cover the accident. * * * Neither party disagrees about the general principles of equity applicable here.[2] The rub comes in the proper application of those principles to the facts of this case. Reformation is an ancient remedy used to reframe written contracts to reflect accurately the real agreement between contracting parties when, either through mutual mistake or unilateral mistake coupled with actual or equitable fraud by the other party, the writing does not embody the contract as actually made.

But reformation is an extraordinary remedy, and courts exercise it with great caution. * * * Even in situations where obvious mistakes have been made, courts will not rewrite the contract between the parties, but will only enforce the legal obligations of the parties according to their original agreement. * * * Here, of course, the Assured does not contend that mutual mistake occurred and it is well that he does not do so for obviously the Insurer intended to sell the exact policy with the exact coverage that it did. Rather, the Assured's theory rests on another accepted reformation doctrine—mistake by one party coupled with constructive or equitable fraud by the other.

Thus the whole case boils down in reality to one question: Did Insurer have a duty to tell the Assured that several insurance policies were available and to explain fully the provisions and limitations of those policies? * * *

As in nearly all cases, an inquiry of this type involves consideration of the competing interests. On the one hand we have the right of the public to be free of fraud and oppression wrought by those in a superior bargaining position. But on the other hand we are confronted with the realities of doing business, the enforcement of contracts, and instability which flows from opening up written contracts to oral accretions.

1. [Footnotes renumbered.] Insurer sold eleven different types of insurance policies at its sales booth.

2. And neither party disagrees that this is a case of first impression.

The Assured urges, and the District Court declared, that an explanation was owing. By whom was it to be given? In what form was it to be offered? Orally or in writing? If orally, how would an insurer conscious of its duty of fair dealing toward a peripatetic public in a hurry assure that an adequate, reliable statement was made? The "explanation" would vary as work shifts changed and sales personnel rotated. They would be expansive or restrictive as the loquacious or taciturn quality of the employee predominated. If the insurer turned to a written statement, how or in what manner would it assure itself that the impatient prospect would pay any more heed to it than the terms of the policy contract? And what happens when, out of an abundance of good faith, an effort is made to explain (in non-legalese) what a legal document prescribes? And as to either method or a mixture of both, what are the significant distinctions to be pointed out? Which ones to emphasize? To minimize? To omit? How many policies need to be explained? Just the two most common—T–20 and T–18? Or all eleven? In the meantime what is happening to time—that precious irreplaceable which accounts for the traveler's pressure at the airport facing either dispensing machine or an attractive sales person who may well try harder but without benefit of a legal education? The flight would either be missed or the "offer" of flight insurance withdrawn for want of adequate time for equity's mandated "explanation." [3] Hardship, or what seems to be hardship, may sometimes occur if the law adheres to its long-held notions of the non-variability of written contracts. But a too-quick relaxation in the contrails of the jet age might well be worse, not better.[4]

We think that imposing a duty to offer such explanations under circumstances of this kind—requiring as it does an effort by lay persons to interpret the legal meaning of the proposed contract as well as others available—would be fraught with great danger to the stability of contracts. * * *

The printed contract controls. There it ends.

Reversed.

Notes

1. News Item, 1972: Raymond George collected $6,745 at Hollywood Park Saturday, cashing in $50 worth of win tickets he desperately tried to unload before the fifth race.

George asked for five $10 win tickets on No. 9, Astor Place. By mistake, he was sold tickets on No. 10, Partner's Hope. When the mutuel clerk failed to sell the "wrong" tickets before the race, George was stuck with them. Partner's Hope won and paid $269.80 for $2.

To say he was unhappy about the situation—Partner's Hope was a 99–1 shot on the toteboard—when the error occurred, is an understatement.

3. Of course, if in answer to an inquiry by a prospect or by an affirmative statement made by the insurer's agent to the prospect it was indicated that the policy would cover the round trip, then the insurer would certainly have to give some explanatory warning before issuing a T–18 policy which is for a fixed period of time, and not written in terms of round trip.

4. Consider, for example, the T–18 policy which Rev. Russell bought. Although it is a short-term policy, the coverage provisions are much broader and more inclusive than a straight flight insurance policy (the T–20). For example, if Mrs. Russell had been killed in a taxi smashup while riding to the Lubbock airport for her return flight or had she been killed in a hotel fire while there, she would have been covered under the T–18 but not under the T–20. Would the machine-sale of a T–20 be defective for want of a warning recording that at the nearby counter, better or different coverage was available?

"He was really hot about it," said E.G. Anderson, a track security officer. "He was demanding his money back, and I took him to the information window to have him fill out the proper forms. About then one of his friends came running up to tell him the horse had won."

Question: Did the racetrack have the remedy of reformation?

2. *Reformation or Rescission?* Subtle considerations may bear on whether to request reformation or rescission. Consider the late Seavers, co-owners of an airplane. Mr. Seaver took out a liability policy in his name; he represented that he was the sole and unconditional owner. If he had listed Mrs. Seaver properly as co-owner, she would have been excluded from coverage if her husband was negligent. The Seavers were killed when the plane crashed. When her estate sued his estate, the insurance company was tendered the defense. The insurer requested reformation and won. Under the reformed policy with Mrs. Seaver a co-owner, the policy remained in force (figuratively speaking); but, because of the exclusion, it did not cover the claim. Why not rescind for the misrepresentation? If so, the premiums should be returned. See Monarch Insurance Co. v. Lankard, 715 F.Supp. 304 (D.Kan.1989).

TRAVELERS INSURANCE CO. v. BAILEY

Supreme Court of Vermont, 1964.
124 Vt. 114, 197 A.2d 813.

BARNEY, JUSTICE. The plaintiff insurance company has come into equity asking for reformation of the annuity provisions of a life insurance policy on the basis of mistake. Thirty years after issuance of the original policy it tendered the defendant insured an amended policy which he refused. On trial, the chancellor found that the amended policy represented the true insuring agreement originally entered into by the parties and allowed reformation. The defendant appealed.

At the instance of his mother, the defendant, when nineteen, submitted an application to an agent of the plaintiff for a life insurance policy. The plan requested in the application was one insuring the defendant's life for five thousand dollars, with an annuity at age sixty-five for five hundred dollars a year for the balance of his life, ten years certain. When the application was accepted and the policy prepared in the home office of the plaintiff, the correct descriptive information was inserted on the wrong policy form. The printed portion of the form used yielded the correct life insurance contract, but produced an annuity obligation to pay five hundred dollars a month for life, one hundred months certain. The application was made a part of the policy, by its terms. In accordance with its usual practice, the plaintiff did not retain a copy of the policy itself but kept a record of the information permitting reproduction of the policy if the occasion demanded.

The premiums were regularly paid on the policy issued in 1931, and about the middle of 1961 the actual policy came into the possession of the defendant for the first time. The semi-annual premiums charged and paid were identical with the prescribed premium for five thousand dollars of life insurance with annuity at age sixty-five of five hundred dollars annually, with payment for ten years certain. This $40.90 semi-annual premium was applicable only to that policy plan, issued at the defendant's then age of nineteen, and no other. The plaintiff had no rate for and did not sell a policy for five thousand dollars life insurance with an annuity at age sixty-five of five hundred dollars monthly, payment for one hundred months certain.

After being told by a third party that his policy could not have the provisions he claimed for it, the defendant took the policy to the office of the defendant's agent that sold the policy and made inquiry. Shortly thereafter, in late 1961, the amended policy was tendered. There is no evidence that the defendant then knew that his original policy provided for an annuity payment larger than he was entitled to in view of the premium paid and the life insurance coverage purchased.

* * * [T]he defendant does not question any of the findings relating to the facts already recited. His principal attack on the decision relates to the chancellor's finding that the mistake in issuing the policy furnished the defendant came about through no fault of the defendant, but solely through the negligence and inattention of the plaintiff. This, says the defendant, is a finding of unilateral mistake, and therefore, is not grounds for reformation. * * *

Other courts have exercised the equitable power of reformation in similar cases. In New England Mutual Life Insurance Co. v. Jones, D.C., 1 F.Supp. 984, a clerical mistake in the policy was discovered after the death of the insured when a double indemnity benefit claim for accidental death was made. The policy provided for double indemnity on the basis of the face amount of the policy, but in the black space stating the obligation the figure $5000.00 had been entered. This considerably increased the double indemnity figure above that computed on the face amount of the policy. Premiums had been assessed and paid on the basis of the correct figure. Reformation was allowed. * * *

A leading and frequently cited case dealing with this problem is Columbian National Life Insurance Co. v. Black, 10 Cir., 35 F.2d 571. In that case the reverse side of the "ordinary life" form erroneously had the valuation schedules of an "endowment" policy printed on it. These schedules showed a value of $10,000.00 when at the same point of maturity the ordinary life policy value was $3040.00. The policy was sold and the premiums were paid on it as an ordinary life policy. The premiums necessary to produce the endowment values would have been about twice as much. The court held that the true contract was arrived at when the company accepted the insured's application for an ordinary life policy, and allowed reformation even though twenty years had elapsed since the issuance of the policy.

Each of these cases speak of the reformation as justified either because there was "mutuality" of mistake or because the policy holder knew or ought to have known that there was a variation between the policy described in the accepted application and the one handed the insured. To insist on enforcement of the contract once knowledge of the error is acquired by the insured is held to be unconscionable, and classified as then a unilateral mistake known to the other party, which supports reformation. If the mistake exists in the writing unknown to both parties, it is classified as "mutual" and reformation is allowed.

Since these cases support reformation irrespective of the insured's knowledge of the existence of the mistake conferring a benefit on him beyond the bargain, talk of "mutual" or "unilateral" mistake seems to be of little help in this kind of situation. Metropolitan Life Insurance Co. v. Henriksen, 6 Ill. App.2d 127, 126 N.E.2d 736, granted reformation for a clerical error increasing a life annuity payable after twenty years from $10.51 to $1,051.00. The error involved was not discovered until eighteen years after issuance of the policy, and it made no difference whether the insured knew of the error or not.

If, in this kind of case, talk of "mutuality" of mistake is unnecessary, much confusion can be avoided. Invariably, two mistakes are involved. There is a natural tendency to concentrate on the making of the clerical error in the writing as the critical mistake involved, when the true crucial error is mistaken belief of the parties about the correctness of the written instrument. When a test of "mutuality" is applied to the clerical error, the confusion is compounded, since the concern of the court should be with the belief or knowledge of the parties. The concept of "mutuality" adds nothing to the right to a remedy in this type of case. It is important as a concept in other, different, reformation situations. Applying to all the common linguistic label of "mutuality" gives to unlike situations an illusion of similarity. This invites the misapplication of principles, sound for one type of situation, to a different type, for which they are unsound.

Accordingly, we hold that where there has been established beyond a reasonable doubt a specific contractual agreement between parties, and a subsequent erroneous rendition of the terms of the agreement in a material particular, the party penalized by the error is entitled to reformation, if there has been no prejudicial change of position by the other party while ignorant of the mistake. If such change of position can equitably be taken into account and adjusted for in the decree, reformation may be possible even then. [citations] Mistakes generally occur through some carelessness, and failure to discover a mistake may be in some degree negligent, but unless some prejudice to the other party's rights under the true contract results, so as to make its enforcement inequitable, reformation will not be refused because of the presence of some negligence.

Change of position is raised as an issue by the defendant. It cannot be said that the defendant acted in reliance on the terms of the policy which, he testified, were not exactly known by him until he received the policy in 1961. But he argues that the mere passage of time, in this case thirty years, should overcome the chancellor's finding to the contrary and establish a change of position. But clearly this aging process was inevitable, and not a prejudicial act induced by the mistaken term in the policy. The defendant has not demonstrated that he was prejudiced by the existence of the error.

Reformation was properly granted.

Notes

1. John Hancock Mutual Life Insurance Co. v. Cohen, 254 F.2d 417, 423 (9th Cir.1958). The insurer was denied relief for its mistake. The insurance company, through a scrivener's error, issued a 15–year policy with a 20– rather than a 15–year family income provision. Upon the death of the insured, monthly payments were made according to the terms of the policy for 15 years. The company refused to make further payments, claiming that "the company would never have issued a 20–year family income rider on a 15–year endorsement policy." The beneficiary sought to recover on the contract; the company counterclaimed for reformation. In upholding the district judge's refusal to order reformation, the court reasoned:

"The fact is that the company *did* issue such a rider on such a policy; that payments in the amount fixed by the company, though erroneous for the coverage promised, were paid by the insured quarterly from August 24th, 1939 to the time of his death in June 1945. But of this error he had no knowledge during his lifetime. Thereafter and on July 26th, 1945 the insurance company, with that portion of the policy before it which it thought necessary to obtain or retain, agreed to pay family income monthly in accordance with the rider attached to the policy, i.e., until 'the first day of the policy month directly preceding the expiration of 20 years from the date of issuance,' or to and including February 1, 1959. * * *

"[I]t is clear that the court * * * believed and found unilateral mistake of defendant alone; that the insured 'neither knew or suspected nor reasonably could or should have known or suspected any mistake therein.' "

2. Hopper Furs, Inc. v. Emery Air Freight Corp., 749 F.2d 1261 (8th Cir.1984). A carrier's shipping form limited liability for loss of cargo to $10 per pound unless a higher valuation was written in a designated box on the form and a higher fee paid. A shipper of 215 pounds of furs intended to declare a higher valuation. He wrote the figure of 61,045 in the box on the form entitled "zip code" which was next to the "declared value" box. No extra fee was asked for or paid. The shipment was lost. The carrier offers $2150; the shipper seeks reformation and $61,045. What decree?

METZLER v. BOLEN

United States District Court, District of North Dakota, 1956.
137 F.Supp. 457.

Register, District Judge. * * * In September, 1950, plaintiff and defendant entered into a contract for deed whereby defendant agreed to sell, and plaintiff agreed to purchase, the northeast quarter of section 25 in township 155 north of range 95 west of the 5th principal meridian in Williams county, North Dakota. * * * It is in the usual form, except as to the following provision which was typed therein by E.C. Rudolph (attorney for plaintiff) prior to the execution thereof:

> "The second party herein shall have unto himself 6½% of 50% of oils, metals, minerals found in, under, or upon said land herein described, but he agrees to join with first party, on the same terms as he (1st party) accepts drilling rights given to any drilling Co., which first party selects."

The "second party" referred to therein is the plaintiff, Mr. Harold Metzler.

Prior to the preparation of this agreement by Mr. Rudolph, the parties hereto had communicated with each other, over a period of years, concerning the purchase or rental by the plaintiff of the land involved in this lawsuit. * * * Under date of August 18, 1950, plaintiff wrote a letter to defendant in which he requested permission to have the agreement prepared on a North Dakota form, and which letter contained the following statement:

> "Then I also note that you reserve all the mineral and oil rights, in the land. I feel that I should be entitled to at least some of the oil and mineral rights in the said land, and that we should have this understanding before I sign up the papers." * * *

In defendant's letter of September 9, 1950, to Mr. E.C. Rudolph appears the following:

> "Enclosed is an abstract showing title in the M & M Bank. My deed has been recorded from them. The taxes became delinquent and I purchased the

same thru tax title, but the abstractor wrote me that the County retained 1/2 of the mineral and oil rights. If this land is ever drilled for oil, my understanding is that fee owner must give up to the Co. drilling all but 12 1/2%. I'll give him 6 1/4%. That is 1/2 of what I will own if the land is drilled, i.e. 1/2 of the 12 1/2% int. You can easily check on the abstract, as the title rests largely on mortgages, and the Tax Title cut them all out of having an interest in the title."

This letter was in possession of Mr. Rudolph at the time he prepared the executed Contract for Deed and was the basis for the provisions therein which have hereinbefore been quoted.

Plaintiff in his Complaint and with reference to said quoted provision alleges in part as follows:

> "That said provision in said Contract for Deed did not express the true Agreement between the Plaintiff, Harold Metzler, and the Defendant, R.J. Bolen; that the agreement between the Plaintiff and the Defendant was that the Defendant would convey to the Plaintiff all surface rights and an undivided fifty percent (50%) interest in and to all the oil, gas, metals and other minerals that the Defendant owned in the land described in this Complaint and said Contract for Deed; that at the time said Agreement was entered into it was believed mistakenly by the party preparing the Contract for Deed to be the fact that Williams County owned 50% of the oil, gas, metals and other minerals in said land.", and
>
> "That said Contract for Deed through and by a mistake of fact does not express the true agreement between the parties to said Contract for Deed."

Plaintiff alleges payment in full of the consideration pursuant to said Contract, and prays for specific performance of the alleged agreement by the execution and delivery of a warranty deed conveying said premises, including 50% of all of the oil, gas, metals and other minerals therein, for damages, and, in the event specific performance is not granted, judgment in the sum of $30,800, together with costs and disbursements. * * *

Doubtless, at the time of the execution of the Contract for Deed, both parties believed that Williams County did own 50% of all of the oil, gas and minerals in and under said land. The North Dakota statutes, [citation] provided for such a reservation. However, on March 21, 1951, the Supreme Court of North Dakota decided that such reservation was void, and that the tax deed from the County to the purchaser conveyed all right, title and interest of the County to the premises involved. Therefore, defendant was actually the owner of all of the oil, gas and minerals in and under said premises.

The sole question involved herein is whether, because of such mistaken belief on the part of both parties to the Contract concerning the extent of defendant's interest in said oil, gas and minerals, plaintiff is entitled to the relief asked for. * * *

To justify reformation on the ground of mistake, the mistake must have been made in the drawing of the instrument and not in the making of the contract which it evidences. A mistake as to the existing situation, which leads either one or both of the parties to enter into a contract which they would not have entered into had they been apprised of the actual facts, will not justify reformation. It is not what the parties would have intended if they had known better, but what did they intend at the time, informed as they were. [citation]

Not only has the plaintiff failed to sustain his burden of proving mutual mistake by clear, satisfactory, specific and convincing evidence, but, in the opinion of this Court, the evidence is to the contrary. The specific provisions of the contract involved were typed into the contract by plaintiff's attorney, at the time of a conference with the plaintiff, and with plaintiff's full knowledge, understanding and approval. The provisions were definite, specific, unambiguous and in accordance with the specific offer of the defendant contained in the latter's letter. There was no mistake as to the language of the contract; nothing intended to be inserted was omitted by mistake. No mistake occurred in reducing to writing the contract upon which the parties had agreed. The mistake complained of related to the extent of defendant's interest in the oil, gas and minerals—a matter which entered into the minds of the parties in formulating their agreement. However, it is the opinion of this Court that the minds of the contracting parties did meet upon the proposition expressed in the writing, and that the actual contract was as expressed therein; that is, that the written contract itself expressed the true intention of the parties which existed at that time.

For the reasons hereinbefore stated, judgment will be for the defendant.

Notes

United States v. Fusco–Amatruda Co., 239 F.Supp. 990, 993 (D.Conn.1965). Plaintiff claimed compensation for spreading loam calculated on the basis of 75 cents per *square* yard as set forth in a written contract. Defendant insisted that the agreement was to pay 75 cents per *cubic* yard and sought reformation of the contract. In denying reformation, the court said:

"Under all the circumstances of the case it seems clear that there was no real 'meeting of the minds' between the parties as to the exact price formula for the spreading operations. Reformation of the contract would be inequitable to the plaintiff. The mistake substantially affected the methods employed by Spector to spread the loam and, further, influenced him to perform substantial extra work to prepare the site for loam and spreading operations which was the responsibility of another subcontractor on the project. He cannot be put in status quo. Justice requires a rescission of the contract with compensation to the plaintiff in quantum meruit for the value rendered to the defendant by way of restitution."

PRINTING INDUSTRIES ASSOCIATION OF NORTHERN OHIO, INC. v. GRAPHIC ARTS INTERNATIONAL UNION, LOCAL NO. 546, et al.,

United States District Court, Northern District of Ohio, 1985.
628 F.Supp. 1103.

BATTISTI, CHIEF JUDGE. * * * On January 7, 1983, plaintiffs Printing Industries Association of Northern Ohio, Inc. ("PIANO") filed complaints in the above-captioned actions against four unions representing printing industry employees in the Greater Cleveland area. Plaintiffs are a multi-employer bargaining association and the individual member employers who comprise that association. Plaintiffs sought declaratory judgment and reformation of contract. Specifically, plaintiffs sought reformation of a cost-of-living allowance ("COLA") provision that appeared in two separate collective bargaining agreements entered into between PIANO and defendant Unions. * * * The gravamen of plaintiffs' Complaint is that the COLA provision in the collective bargaining agreements should be reformed such that the wage adjustment would be based on the *national* consumer price index ("CPI") rather than on the *Cleveland* consumer price index, the latter being the one provided for in the agreements. * * *

Part XXVIII of the contract provided for semi-annual wage adjustments based upon corresponding changes in the Consumer Price Index Revised for Urban Wage Earners and Clerical Workers, 1967–100, new series *for Cleveland, Ohio.* Similar wage adjustment provisions to compensate workers for inflation were included in contracts between the parties since 1972 and have been based upon the Cleveland CPI–W.

Plaintiffs contend that computation by the Bureau of Labor Statistics of its indices results in a "distortion" since "the Cleveland CPI–W is based upon a smaller sample, and hence is more prone to statistical distortion." * * * Plaintiffs are most concerned by the fact that since June 1982 the Cleveland CPI–W has exceeded the National CPI–W. For example, the Cleveland CPI–W exceeded the National CPI–W by 17.9 points in August 1982 and 20.5 points in October 1982. * * * Plaintiffs attribute this "substantial and unprecedented deviation" to Cleveland's depressed housing market and smaller sampling. Plaintiffs also extend the depressed economic conditions theory to explain distortions in the other components upon which the CPI–W are calculated. Plaintiffs assert that a disproportionate weight is placed upon the housing component of the index and the false assumption that home ownership costs in the Greater Cleveland area have increased dramatically compared to home ownership costs nationally.

Plaintiffs argue that the contract should be reformed since a "mutual mistake of the parties" occurred. Plaintiffs contend that the parties "believed that the Cleveland CPI–W was specifically reflective of the increases or decreases in the cost of living in the Greater Cleveland area due to inflation." This unprecedented distortion in October 1982, however, would result in a 56-cent-per-hour increase for employees covered by the collective bargaining agreement, or 36 cents more per hour than they would be entitled to under the National CPI–W. The plaintiffs contend that if the employees receive this "windfall," the individual member employers will sustain "severe financial hardship," including the inability to be competitive with shops not required to pay Cleveland COLA's, the impairment of operations, and substantial layoffs. In Count II of their Complaint, plaintiffs allege that payment of COLA's at the Cleveland CPI–W would frustrate the purpose of the collective bargaining agreement. The Complaint states that "neither party assumed the risk that the Cleveland CPI–W would not, at some point, accurately reflect changes in the cost of living in the Greater Cleveland area due to inflation." * * *

[I]n order to obtain reformation of the contract, plaintiff must show by clear and convincing evidence that a mutual mistake was made by the parties, specifically that "both PIANO and the Unions *definitely intended* that the major purpose of including a COLA provision in their contracts was to keep employees' wages even with inflation and that the parties formed the assumption that the Cleveland CPI–W would parallel and competently reflect the changes in the cost-of-living in the Cleveland area." Concomitantly, PIANO must show that it was not deemed to have assumed the risk for variances in the Cleveland CPI–W in order to obtain reformation. If only one party was mistaken or if the parties' intentions were conflicting, then the Court may not order reformation. * * * Mr. George Bockman, president of Local 546, testified that he was the chief negotiator and spokesman for the Union in arriving at the collective bargaining agreement that became effective May 1, 1982. * * *

When asked why the Cleveland CPI–W was used instead of the National CPI–W, he stated:

> "The only way I can answer that, being so long ago, is we were all new to the cost of living, both sides, and so when we finally agreed that they were going to put a cost of living in, I'm just guessing because I'm not sure, and I don't know who asked or why it was asked for, if it was asked even, that which index are we going to use, and our International Vice President was in at that time, and he did most of the talking, because he knew more about cost of living than we did and his expertise was far superior to ours.
>
> "All I can remember, very vaguely, is Neil Johnson, Carl's [Carl Zellers, president of PIANO] predecessor, and he said they wanted the Cleveland index, and that was it. Just the company wanted the Cleveland index. So there was no argument on that, as I recall anyway. We wanted the cost of living no matter what, and that was it, as I can remember."

He [also] responded that it was his "estimated guess," although unsubstantiated, that the parties thought the Cleveland index would more accurately reflect the cost-of-living in Cleveland than the National CPI–W. He continued that PIANO presented the language of the cost-of-living clause, that "it was presented to us by them," and that he didn't understand the language of the provision, "even to this day." Still, neither side questioned the reliability or accuracy of the Cleveland CPI–W prior to October 1982. * * *

This Court concludes that, in the strictest sense, a mutual mistake occurred. The language concerning the Cleveland CPI–W was proposed by PIANO and agreed to by the Unions. The Unions' intent, understandably, was to protect their members against loss in their real wages due to inflation. When PIANO refused the COLA provisions offered by the Unions, the Unions accepted PIANO's CPI–W. Similiarly, both parties accepted the use of the Cleveland CPI–W, as proposed by PIANO, on the assumption that it would most accurately measure the inflation rate in the Cleveland area. * * * Indeed, it appears that neither party had in 1973 or at any time prior to October 1982 considered divergence between these indices. While a Court always hesitates to draw conclusions about intent based on faulty or incomplete memories of events occurring years in the past, it is probable that the Union relied on the Cleveland CPI–W.

Having found a mutual mistake, the Court must decide whether the mistake here compels reformation of the contract. The Court has struggled between those cases in which mutual mistake as to a variable rate forces reformation, the so-called *ALCOA* line of cases (referring to Alcoa v. Essex Group, Inc., 499 F.Supp. 53 (W.D.Pa.1980)), and those cases in which courts have found that the parties necessarily assumed the risk of fluctuations in a variable rate. See, e.g., Wabash, Inc. v. Avnet, Inc., 516 F.Supp. 995 (N.D.Ill. 1981).

At this time, the Court holds that the variance between the Cleveland CPI–W and the National CPI–W was a risk assumed by the parties. In the instant case, the fluctuation is unfavorable to plaintiff-employers, but it could have redounded as well to the detriment of the Unions. This Court will not order the reformation of a contract simply because subsequent information has revealed that an index upon which both parties relied and which had been accurate over a period of years suddenly changed. The finality of contract and the certainty of the parties would be subject to the variability of fluctuations and "whose ox was gored." One can only speculate whether PIANO and the employers would call for reformation as a contract principle in the instant case if the divergence had resulted in the Cleveland CPI–W being lower than the National CPI–W.

Accordingly, this Court refuses to grant reformation of the relevant COLA provisions in the collective bargaining agreements based on mutual mistake; plaintiffs' request for reformation is denied.

[The court also refused reformation on the basis of Frustration–Impossibility. P. 1200, infra].

To the extent that plaintiffs seek reformation of the collective bargaining agreements based on frustration of purpose, however, plaintiffs must establish that (1) the divergence did in fact occur and "the non-occurrence of the frustrating event [was] a basic assumption on which the contract was made;" (2) the purpose frustrated was a "principal purpose" of that contract; and (3) the frustration must be "substantial." See Restatement (Second) of Contracts § 265.

Noting that the inquiry as to elements 1 and 2 of the above test have largely been addressed in the preceding section on mutual mistake, the Court will examine whether the divergence alleged did in fact occur and whether it is substantial.

Plaintiffs have resubmitted for the purposes of final adjudication the expert report of Dr. John F. Burke, Jr. which was originally considered in the motion for summary judgment. Dr. Burke, an associate professor of economics at Cleveland State University, states in his Report that in the short-run the National and Cleveland CPI–W indices can diverge and that "the two indexes can take obviously different routes in getting to similar ends." Dr. Burke concludes, "however, that any, even "seemingly minor" or "abnormal" deviations of the relevant metropolitan CPI index from the national all-city average will have a significant impact on wage adjustments." Finally, Dr. Burke contends that "changes in wages compound over time," such that minor adjustments would be incorporated into subsequent wage increases. The ultimate result, concludes the professor, is that as these printing firms are forced to increase their labor costs, they will become less competitive within their industry.

Dr. Burke identifies the divergence between the indices not only to the smaller sampling field of the Cleveland CPI–W but to one specific component, housing. The housing component consists of three subcomponents: fuel, household furnishings, and shelter. The shelter subcomponent is further divided into rent, other rent, and home ownership. According to Dr. Burke, between April and August 1982, the average price of a house increased in the Cleveland area while the average price of a house declined nationally during the same period; thus, the home ownership subcomponent of the Cleveland CPI–W index rose while the same component in the National CPI–W declined. He states, however, that the actual price of a home in Cleveland did not increase, but that "a sampling error resulting from insufficient home sales in the Greater Cleveland area" occurred. "When there are not sufficient home sales to justify computing an index for the home ownership item of the shelter subcomponent, the sample is expanded to other regions and the traditional geographic boundaries of the Cleveland CPI–W are disregarded in order to obtain the requisite number of home sales thereby producing a complete sample." As a result, argues Dr. Burke, BLS considered sales prices higher than the normal sample, which produces a higher homeownership subcomponent, which in turn increases the entire CPI–W. Plaintiffs indicate that in January 1983, BLS issued a news release which recognized and warned of the sampling errors in local CPI indices and urged use of the national CPI.

Defendant has offered the testimony of Professor Andrew Gross. The Court, however, is unable to assess the credibility of the proferred testimony, since defendant has not presented the professional credentials of the professor. The report of Professor Gross was filed with the Court on May 17, 1985 and was, therefore, not originally considered in the Summary Judgment Opinion. The Court will consider Professor Gross' testimony not for the truth of the matter asserted (since its credibility cannot be determined) but for the importance of the issues asserted as they bear on the question of the divergence in the indices in this matter.

Professor Gross recognizes the larger sampling variability of the Cleveland CPI–W but states that "[t]he CPI–W for Cleveland is still the best measure of the Cleveland area situation." Furthermore, Gross states that the BLS's practice of expanding the sampling area to surrounding regions when the original sample is too small is "valid." He states that these " 'imputed' or 'collapsed' models are used widely. * * *" He contends that whatever distortions are caused by examining a large area do not invalidate the Cleveland CPI–W, since "the surrounding area tends to move in a similar fashion to the Cleveland metropolitan area." Professor Gross also contends that the sources presented by Dr. Burke are "anecdotal" and are "statistically insufficient" to lead to the conclusion that the CPI–W housing component was distorted.

Above all, Gross concludes that "there is no consistent or persistent 'distortion' between the Cleveland CPI–W and the National CPI–W. He notes that the Cleveland CPI–W has been above and rising more rapidly than the National CPI–W for years, but that examinations of the divergence both on a month-to-month and year-to-year basis reveal "no meaningful distortion or discrepancy" between the indices. Gross found that the 1984 CPI–W was only 1.9% above the 1983 CPI–W whereas the 1984 National CPI–W was 3.4% over the 1983 index. Hence, he concludes that "the Cleveland index is only *very slightly* above the U.S.A. figure and furthermore, the annual percent increase for Cleveland was *significantly less* (1.9% v. 3.4% increase). (emphasis in original).

The Court is not equipped to determine whose statistical or economic analysis is correct and will therefore not do so. To quote the aphorism and invert it somewhat, "There are truths, half-truths and then statistics." It is clear, however, that to be substantial, the change in profit or loss must be great. The detriment to the complaining party must not simply be one of hardship but near commercial impracticability. The Court reiterates that while there is an 18% increase in the Cleveland CPI–W when compared to the National CPI–W for April 1982 through October 1982, and that the Cleveland CPI–W has been approximately 20 points above the National CPI–W for that period, the actual effect on wages is not as substantial as plaintiff contends.

[T]he wage adjustments using the Cleveland CPI–W rather than the National CPI–W are from 36 to 75 cents per hour (depending on the contract involved). "These differences, expressed as a percentage of the base wage rate, vary from 2.6% to 5.9%." The Court does not regard such increases to be sufficient to meet the showing of substantial frustration. The threat of the employers of PIANO becoming non-competitive within their industry is speculative, and the Court declines to reform these contracts based on such speculation. Furthermore, to the degree that the contracts at issue in this litigation have expired, the parties may enter subsequent collective bargaining negotiations wiser and may be more willing to obtain contract provisions which not only protect the wage-earners' interests but those of the PIANO employers and the printing industry. It appears certain that the parties are at least now aware of the validity of the Cleveland CPI–W and, based on the BLS's January 1983 warning, will draw future contracts appropriately. This Court does not believe, however, that the hardship exacted on plaintiffs by virtue of the fluctuations in a government index are substantial enough to warrant *post-hoc* reformulation of contracts.

For the reasons stated above, the Court denies plaintiffs' prayer for reformation of contract based on mutual mistake. As to Count II of the Amended Complaint, the Court denies plaintiffs' prayer for reformation of contract based on frustration of purpose. Hence, the COLA provisions in Part XXVIII of the Collective Bargaining Agreement dated October 1, 1981 will remain intact in their reference to the Cleveland CPI–W. To effect this finding, the funds placed in escrow accounts pursuant to the Order of April 25, 1983 representing the difference between wage adjustments paid using the National CPI–W and the Cleveland CPI–W will be released and distributed to defendants pursuant to the terms of the original collective bargaining agreements.

Judgment shall be entered for defendant.

It Is so Ordered.

STUBBS v. STANDARD LIFE ASSOCIATION

Supreme Court of Colorado, 1952.
125 Colo. 278, 242 P.2d 819.

STONE, JUSTICE. This is an action for reformation of mortgage and of sheriff's deed issued on foreclosure thereof. J.E. Stubbs and W.R. Stubbs were formerly owners of a tract of farm land consisting of 1006 acres in Crowley County, and made application for and procured a loan of $24,000 to be secured by mortgage thereon. The legal description of the property was long and complicated, and in drafting the loan and mortgage documents there was omitted one parcel of the farm property comprising about 290 acres. * * *

Thereafter the mortgage was sold and assigned to defendant in error, Standard Life Association, which foreclosed and bid the property in a foreclosure sale for the total amount due and received sheriff's deed. Throughout the foreclosure proceedings, and in the sheriff's deed, the property was described as in the mortgage. The foreclosing mortgagee was let into possession of the entire farm, including the parcel omitted from the description, prior to the issuance of the sheriff's deed, and continued in such possession for a period of more than ten years without objection or apparent knowledge by anyone that the entire farm was not included in the mortgage and sheriff's deed. In 1945, some nine years after acquiring sheriff's deed, the mortgagee leased the property for a long term, with option to purchase for the full price of $20,000, upon which it was agreed that there should be credited the rental paid under the lease above taxes and cost of upkeep and interest. Thereafter the mortgagee purchaser had a survey made of the property, whereby the omission was discovered, and this action was begun for reformation of the mortgage deed, the foreclosure proceedings and the sheriff's deed to show inclusion of the omitted parcel. Plaintiff had favorable judgment in the trial court. J.E. Stubbs and W.R. Stubbs are deceased and the defendant here appearing as plaintiff in error is the widow of W.R. Stubbs and the assignee of the other heirs of the mortgagors. * * *

The proof is ample to support the finding of the trial court that the parcel was omitted by mutual mistake. * * *

The one serious question with which we are here concerned is the right of reformation of a mortgage, as sought in this case, after foreclosure and issuance of sheriff's deed to the mortgagee. In some cases, such right has been denied. Trachtenberg v. Glen Alden Coal Co., 354 Pa. 521, 47 A.2d 820; in others, reformation both of mortgage and subsequent sheriff's deed has been decreed without resale; in others, while the mortgage has been reformed, reformation of the sheriff's deed has been held improper without resale of the mortgaged premises; and in still others, it has been held that the mortgage may properly be reformed in a proceeding therefor and that the requirement of new sale or foreclosure is a matter of judicial discretion. * * *

In Quivey v. Baker, 37 Cal. 465, one of the leading cases on the question before us, the court said, "It is said there was no mistake, either in the decree or Sheriff's deed, which followed the description in the mortgage, and could not have done otherwise; and consequently there is no mistake to reform in either of them. As well might it be claimed that if there be a mistake in the first of a series of conveyances, which was carried out through all the subsequent conveyances, that the Court could only correct the mistake in the first deed; and that, in fact, there was no mistake in the subsequent deeds, which were correctly copied from the first, as they were intended to be. But a Court of equity does not administer justice on these narrow principles. It will not only go back to the original error and reform it, but will administer complete justice, by correcting all subsequent mistakes which grew out of and were superinduced by the first."

In such cases no hard and fast rule can be laid down to govern courts of equity. Where it is established by adequate proof that by mutual mistake property has been omitted which was intended to be included in the security of a mortgage deed, and the rights of innocent parties have not intervened, we think justice should be accorded and that the method of effecting that end lies in the discretion of the court. It may be that if the foreclosure sale were very recent and the bids might have been affected by erroneous description, the sale should be set aside and new sale had under foreclosure. It may be that under some circumstances, without setting aside a foreclosure sale, equity would require resale of the premises under direction of the court in the interests of justice. However, in the case before us, the mortgagee took foreclosure decree, after waiting almost seven years from maturity of the mortgage and permitting five years of defaulted interest. It was given possession of the entire farm prior to the date of its sheriff's deed, and held such possession, paid taxes and maintained the property, without protest or objection or knowledge of the defect for sixteen years prior to the bringing of this action. It entered into lease with option to purchase at a price much less than the amount for which the mortgage was foreclosed in 1945, since which time the court may take notice that there has been generally a great increase in the market value of farm lands. The owners of the property who executed the mortgage have long since died. There is no evidence that the bidding at foreclosure was affected by the error in description. The trial court could hardly determine otherwise than that it would be inequitable to require a resale of the premises under the circumstances. * * *

Accordingly, the judgment is affirmed.

Notes

1. See in accord, First Federal Savings and Loan Association v. Racquet Club Condominiums, 801 P.2d 1360 (Nev.1990), 805 P.2d 601 (1991).

2. Suppose an insurance company issued an automobile liability policy to X that, by mistake, omitted a particular vehicle from coverage. X, while driving that vehicle, negligently injures Y. Can Y sue the company to reform the policy so that the proceeds will be available to pay for her injuries? See Wilhide v. Keystone Insurance Co., 195 F.Supp. 659 (M.D.Pa.1961).

BRECHMAN v. ADAMAR OF NEW JERSEY, INC.

Superior Court of New Jersey, Chancery Division, 1981.
182 N.J.Super. 259, 440 A.2d 480.

GIBSON, J.S.C. This action seeks specific performance of an alleged commercial lease. Defendant denies the existence of the lease and moves to have the complaint dismissed. The agreement relied on to sustain plaintiff's claim is in writing and signed by the parties, but it is silent with respect to the duration of the tenancy. On the other hand, it is alleged that there was a contemporaneous oral agreement that the lease would run for five years. The primary question thus raised by this motion is whether the agreement, as written, is enforceable within the requirements of the statute of frauds, N.J.S.A. 25:1–1 et seq.; and if not, may the missing term be supplied by parol evidence? For the reasons to be stated below, it is the opinion of the court that both questions must be answered in the negative.

The factual setting within which these issues are framed may be summarized as follows: Defendant is a subsidiary of Ramada Inns, Inc. and is the developer of a proposed hotel casino in Atlantic City known as the Tropicana. In October 1980, when the proposed casino was still under construction, representatives of defendant entered into negotiations with one Robert Mitchell, plaintiff's assignor, concerning a lease of commercial space within the hotel. A verbal agreement was reached and on October 23, 1980 a representative of defendant directed a letter to Mitchell entitled "Potential Lease of Retail Shop at the Proposed Tropicana Hotel/Casino." The letter recited the fact that, upon the receipt of a deposit of $2,000, defendant would hold open 1,900 square feet of space for a period of 60 days, the space to be used as an ice cream parlor. Lessee was to make all necessary interior and exterior improvements, subject to the approval of the lessor "in its sole discretion." Sketches and lay-outs were to be submitted with 60 days. A rental figure of $45 a square foot was stipulated and the terms of the agreement required the approval of the Casino Control Commission. In the event that the schedules outlined were not met, defendant reserved the right to retain the deposit as liquidated damages and to terminate the agreement. There was no mention concerning the duration of the lease, although plaintiff claims that it was orally agreed that it was to be for five years with an option for an additional five-year period. There was also no provision regarding a commencement date.

The letter was signed by the parties and Mitchell made a deposit of $2,000. Requests were thereafter made to defendant to provide architectural drawings of the site. Plaintiff claims that these were needed by its own architect in order to prepare the plans and sketches required by the terms of the agreement. No plans were provided by defendant, however, and the time limits contained in the letter were never met. On January 21, 1981 defendant addressed a letter to Mitchell rescinding the agreement, "since none of the terms or conditions [had] * * * been met." On February 25, 1981, despite the attempted rescission, Mitchell purported to assign his rights in the alleged lease to plaintiff Alan J. Brechman. Defendant had no knowledge of the assignment and did not consent to it. On June 9, 1981 plaintiff instituted this suit seeking specific performance. Defendant attempted to return the deposit on June 25, 1981, but it was refused.

An assessment of the enforceability of the October 23, 1980 agreement requires the examination of a combination of legal and equitable principles. For example, since the complaint seeks specific performance, equity requires that the contract be clear, definite and precise before such relief may be granted. [citation] There are, in addition, certain legal standards which must be met, the most significant of which appears to be the statute of frauds, N.J.S.A. 25:1–1 et seq.

* * * This provision has been held to include leases of real estate exceeding three years. Given plaintiff's claim that the agreement here was for at least five years, the statute clearly applies. The initial question thus becomes whether the letter of October 23, 1980 meets the requirements of the statute.

It is the general rule in New Jersey that a writing, in order to comply with the statute of frauds,

> "must contain all the essential terms of the bargain, expressed with such certainty that they may be ascertained from the writing itself, without the aid of oral evidence. Nothing can be added or supplied by parol proof, for the introduction of evidence of that kind would let in, at once, all the evils which the statute was designed to suppress." [Schenck v. Spring Lake Beach Improvement Co., 47 N.J.Eq. 44, 49, 19 A. 881 (Ch.1890).]

* * * Most courts agree that the essential terms include an adequate description of the property, a definite term (including the commencement date), the agreed rental and the manner of payment. [citations]

* * * The duration of the lease is therefore an essential term and its absence precludes the enforceability of the agreement. The same conclusion may be drawn from the absence of a commencement date. * * *

Plaintiff next urges that, since there was an oral agreement dealing with a five-year term, this court should permit the admission of that evidence to sustain enforcement. This argument raises another issue, and that is, whether parol evidence may be introduced to satisfy terms obviously absent from the writing. The question is significant because of the conclusion which follows from this court's ruling that the writing is lacking in essential terms and is thus incomplete on its face. Generally, a writing incomplete on its face may be modified by parol evidence. [citations] This principle recognizes that many agreements are not initially reduced to writing but there is nevertheless some written evidence of the parties' intent. Such a writing may take the form of a memorandum or a letter, but since it is clear from the document that it contemplates a more formal writing, the admission of oral testimony concerning terms unexpressed does no violence to the intent of the parties.

Despite the rule, the question remains as to whether this approach may be permitted when dealing with contracts controlled by the statute of frauds. Such agreements, it must be remembered, are required to contain "all the essential terms * * * without the aid of oral evidence." Schenck v. Spring Lake Beach Improvement Co., supra. Given this standard, oral testimony is presumably not permitted whether or not the writing is complete on its face. Although such a result may seem harsh, the Legislature has obviously elected to place certain types of agreements in a class which is beyond the rules of construction that might otherwise apply. Whether one agrees with that choice may be the subject of dispute, but the rule nevertheless remains. * * *

This same conclusion has been reached in other jurisdictions, where the precise issue was raised. Fosburgh v. Sando, 24 Wash.2d 586, 166 P.2d 850, 851 (Sup.Ct.1946); [citations] In Fosburgh v. Sando, the court made the following observation:

> "We are not unmindful of the rule that where a contract upon its face is incomplete resort may be had to parol evidence to supply the omitted stipulation. That rule applies only in cases unaffected by the statute of frauds."

* * * Accordingly, defendant's motion to dismiss the complaint insofar as it seeks equitable relief is hereby granted.

Notes

1. Friedman & Co. v. Newman, 255 N.Y. 340, 347, 174 N.E. 703, 706 (1931): "Equity has at times power to reform an instrument which conclusively embodies the intent of the parties; it has no power to reconstitute an evidentiary writing."

2. In Calhoun v. Downs, 211 Cal. 766, 297 P. 548 (1931), the written agreement to sell real property contained the sentence "I [meaning the seller] agree to pay a commission of $______ to ______." It had been orally agreed that the seller would pay a $500 commission to the broker, Calhoun. The broker sued for reformation to include his name and the sum of $500. Held: Reformation granted. Is this the same problem as in *Brechman?*

3. A small minority holds that the Statute of Frauds bars reformation of a deed to *increase* the amount of land conveyed. See Palmer, Reformation and the Statute of Frauds, 65 Mich.L.Rev. 421 (1967). Cf. Metzler v. Bolen, supra p. 950. Probably the real objection to enlarging a conveyance is that plaintiff has not actually paid for it.

Chapter 13

REMEDIES FOR BREACH OF CONTRACT

A. CONTRACTS FOR SALE OF AN INTEREST IN LAND

Introductory Note

A valid contract to transfer an interest in real property creates legal and equitable interests in the property. The following cases and notes review the nature and remedial consequences of these interests.

"Executory" land sale contracts fall into two general categories with distinguishable functions and purposes. The first category contemplates a "cash" transaction or sale. These contracts remain executory only for the time needed to close the deal when the seller will convey a deed to the property and thereupon become a grantor, and receive in return the agreed consideration in cash, secured notes or whatever.

The purpose of the other category is basically different. These transactions are called "installment land contracts." The buyer agrees to pay the purchase price in installments over a period, perhaps a long period, of time; and the seller retains the legal title as security. More and more courts are treating installment contracts as the essential equivalent of mortgages or trust deeds. Nevertheless, the special identity of "installment land sale" contracts has not been entirely suppressed; remedial problems continue to arise. See Nelson and Whitman, Installment Land Contracts—The National Scene Revisited, 1985 B.Y.U.L.Rev. 1.

1. DAMAGES

a. Vendor in Default

HORTON v. O'ROURKE

Florida District Court of Appeal, 1975.
321 So.2d 612.

McNulty, Chief Judge. * * * The operative facts are simply stated. Between March 3, 1972 and May 3, 1972, the four appellee families executed written contracts with H & H Construction Company to purchase homes being constructed on land owned by appellee Overlord Investments, Inc. Upon completion of the homes in the summer of 1972, the families took possession without closing, under rental agreements ranging from $90 to $135 per month. Closing was conditioned upon clearance of all outstanding title defects.

Upon taking possession, the purchasers-lessees received a notice of the existence of a Federal Tax Lien encumbering the property in excess of $94,000.

After receiving several assurances that the lien would soon be removed, they made improvements and continued the rental agreement for 22 months. But on March 15, 1974, appellant notified the purchasers in writing that clearance of the defect was impossible. Appellant offered either to return the earnest money deposits or enter into new rental agreements at a higher rate.

Thereafter, on April 15, 1974, appellee Overlord Investments, Inc., record title holder of the land, brought suit to oust each purchaser. After answering, the purchasers-appellees filed individual suits for specific performance against both Overlord Investments and appellant, alleging a principal-agent relationship, which resulted in this appeal.

Following a non-jury trial on the four consolidated cases, a final judgment was rendered denying specific performance, exonerating Overlord from any obligation to purchasers-appellees and awarding the purchasers pecuniary damages against appellant. In arriving at the amount of such damages, the court applied the standard measure of contract damages whereby a purchaser ordinarily receives the benefit of his bargain, measured by the court in this case by the difference between the value of the land when it should have been conveyed less the contract price as yet unpaid.

In the one meritorious point on appeal, appellant contends that application of this standard measure of damages giving purchasers *in a land sale contract* the benefit of their bargain is error in the absence of a showing of bad faith. We agree.

In Florida and many other jurisdictions the courts follow the English rule announced in Flureau v. Thornhill whereby in the absence of bad faith the damages recoverable for breach by the vendor of an executory contract to convey title to real estate are the purchase money paid by the purchaser together with interest and expenses of investigating title. Lest there be unjust enrichment, under the facts in this case, we would add to that here the cost of improvements made by purchasers in contemplation of the conveyance, with the express or implied approval of the vendor, which inure to the benefit of the vendor.

Appellees' reliance on A.J. Richey Corp. v. Garvey as authority to the contrary is misplaced in that, in that case, there was clearly a lack of good faith. Here, there is no suggestion of bad faith on appellant's part. Indeed, the record reveals that he dealt above board, made every effort and went to considerable expense to clear the title defect and to consummate ultimately the contract to convey. * * *

Accordingly, the judgment appealed from should be, and it is hereby, reversed.

Notes

Here we return to where we left off in Chapter 1 and pick up remedial goals in contract, with a gloss of economics. The substantial literature that applies economic analysis to legal problems includes the problem of contract remedies. Although expressed in graphs and stated in inaccessible jargon, economic analysis of contract remedies has an uncanny affinity for the outcomes that courts have reached through traditional legal analysis (or maybe vice-versa).

Contract law in a market economy structures the process of exchange. Each resource should be used by the person who values it the most to assure that society uses available resources in the most productive fashion. Economic theory assumes that people seek to maximize their utility through exchanges. People use contracts to exchange goods with others. Each party expects to improve his position from performance because each values the consideration he receives more highly than the consideration he surrenders. If the contract moves both exchanged assets to more highly valued uses, both parties benefit.

Future events may mar the happy scene. One of the functions of a contract is to allocate risk during the time the contract is executory. A party may conclude that performance will be unprofitable: that party may be tempted to withdraw. The economic function of contract remedies is to provide nonbreaching parties with some equivalent to performance when the other party to an executory contract breaches. The existence of a remedy will encourage parties to perform most unprofitable contracts.

Courts often refuse to order breaching parties to perform contracts and limit the nonbreaching party to recovering money damages. The way courts measure the money damages may determine whether and when parties tempted to breach will breach. Contract damage doctrine is intended to place the nonbreaching party in a financial position that compares favorably to performance. That normally calls for expectation damages: where the seller reneges, the buyer should receive the difference between the value of the asset the seller promised to deliver and the contract price.

Expectancy damages, properly measured, are economically efficient because that measure encourages parties to complete performance unless performance would consume resources inefficiently. Where performance would be inefficient, the expectancy measure allows a party to breach, pay damages, and allows the nonbreaching buyer to minimize loss by cover or otherwise. But courts should not award the nonbreaching party less than the expected profit; awarding the expectancy will encourage parties to perform contracts that increase social utility by moving assets from people who value them less to those who value them more.

The Florida court applies the rule of Flureau v. Thornhill, refuses to award the nonbreaching buyers their expected "profit," and remits them to a recovery measured by restitution and reliance. Restitution prevents a breaching seller from being unjustly enriched at the nonbreaching buyer's expense. Allowing the buyers to recover reliance expense discourages sellers from carelessly encouraging people to think that contracts exist and spending money in reliance. Nevertheless the *Flureau* rule is a puzzling anomaly because the way to assure that parties will breach only to promote efficiency is to award the nonbreaching party his lost profit. Generally also, measuring the nonbreaching party's loss by expectancy approximates the cost of breach to society better than the reliance measure. This occurs because the reliance measure excludes from recovery the nonbreaching party's shrewdness, luck, skill and opportunity costs.

Students who seek to pursue economic analysis of expectancy damages farther than this limited Note allows may consult a vast literature that includes the following sources: R. Posner, Economic Analysis of Law § 4.8 (3d ed. 1988); Birmingham, Legal and Moral Duty in Game Theory: Common Law Contracts and Chinese Analogies, 18 Buffalo L.Rev. 99 (1969); Barton, The Economic Basis of Damages for Breach of Contract, 1 J. Legal Stud. 277 (1972).

M. Horwitz, The Transformation of American Law 160–210 (1977), approaches *Flureau* and expectancy damages historically and from a different perspective. D. Dobbs, Remedies § 12.8 (1973), and 5 A. Corbin, Contracts §§ 1097–98 (1964), discuss the competing rules.

What explains the persistence of the anomalous *Flureau* rule? The Florida court admits the usual exception, long adopted in England, that *Flureau* does not apply when the seller lacked good faith. Corbin states another exception: "If the seller knows that he has not the title and expects to get it in time to keep his promise to convey, he must pay damages on his failure; and it makes no difference how reasonable may have been his expectation that he could procure title in himself." 5 A. Corbin, Contracts § 1098 (1964).

DONOVAN v. BACHSTADT

Supreme Court of New Jersey, 1982.
91 N.J. 434, 453 A.2d 160.

SCHREIBER, J. The central legal issue in this case concerns the damages to which a buyer of realty is entitled upon the breach of the executory agreement by the seller. * * *

The contract recited that the purchase price was $58,900. A deposit of $5,890 was paid to and held by the broker. At the closing scheduled for May 1, 1980, the Donovans were to pay an additional $9,010 in cash and the balance was to consist of a purchase money bond or note and mortgage in the principal amount of $44,000, for 30 years, at an [effective] interest rate of [10.5]%. * * * The contract also stated that title "shall be marketable and insurable * * * by any reputable title insurance company." There was no liquidated damage provision.

When defendant could not obtain marketable title, the Donovans commenced this suit for compensatory and punitive damages. * * * It was indisputable that the defendant had breached the agreement. The only issue was damages. The trial court held that plaintiffs were entitled under N.J.S.A. 2A:29–1 to recovery of their costs for the title search and survey. Plaintiffs had apparently in the interim purchased a home in Middlesex County and obtained a mortgage loan bearing interest at the rate of 13¼% per annum. Plaintiffs sought the difference between 10½% and 13¼% as compensatory damages, representing their loss of the benefit of the bargain. The trial court denied recovery because the contract was for the sale of the property and the financing "was only incidental to the basic concept." * * *

The initial inquiry is whether plaintiffs are entitled to compensatory damages. We had occasion recently to discuss the measure of damages available when a seller breaches an executory contract for the sale of real property. St. Pius X House of Retreats v. Diocese of Camden, 83 N.J. 571, 582–87, 443 A.2d 1052 (1982). We noted that New Jersey follows the English rule, which generally limits a buyer's recovery to the return of his deposit unless the seller wilfully refuses to convey or is guilty of fraud or deceit. The traditional formulation of the English rule has been expressed by T. Cyprian Williams, an English barrister, as follows:

> "Where the breach of contract is occasioned by the vendor's inability, without his own fault, to show a good title, the purchaser is entitled to recover as damages his deposit, if any, with interest, and his expenses incurred in connection with the agreement, but not more than nominal damages for the loss of his bargain." [T.C. Williams, The Contract of Sale of Land 128 (1930)]

We are satisfied that the American rule is preferable. The English principle developed because of the uncertainties of title due to the complexity of the rules governing title to land during the eighteenth and nineteenth centuries. At that time the only evidence of title was contained in deeds which were in a phrase attributed to Lord Westbury, "difficult to read, disgusting to touch, and impossible to understand." The reason for the English principle that creates an exception to the law governing damages for breaches of executory contracts for the sale of property is no longer valid, and the exception should be eliminated.

There is no sound basis why benefit of the bargain damages should not be awarded whether the subject matter of the contract is realty or personalty. Serious losses should not be borne by the vendee of real estate to the benefit of the defaulting vendor. This is particularly so when an installment purchase contract is involved that extends over a period of years during which the vendee makes substantial payments upon the principal, as well as extensive improvements to the property.

The innocent purchaser should be permitted to recover benefit of the bargain damages irrespective of the good or bad faith of the seller. Contract culpability depends on the breach of the contractual promise. Where, as here, the seller agreed that title would be marketable, the seller's liability should depend upon his breach of that promise.

The English rule is consistent with the limitation on recovery in suits on a covenant for breach of warranty. The damages for a buyer, who has taken title and is ousted because the title is defective, are limited to the consideration paid and interest thereon. There appears to be no real difference between that situation and one where the vendor who does not have good title refuses to convey. In both cases the buyer loses the property because of a defect in the title. The fact that one sues for breach of a warranty covenant does not justify depriving a buyer of compensatory damages to which he is justly entitled when the seller breaches the contract of sale. Professor Corbin has suggested that any inconsistency in this respect should be resolved by awarding full compensatory damages when the action is for breach of warranty. 5 A. Corbin, § 1098, at 533 (1951). Moreover, an anomaly already exists, for our courts have acknowledged that a buyer may recover such damages upon a showing of the seller's bad faith. See Ganger v. Moffett, 8 N.J. 73, 83 A.2d 769 (1951).

We are satisfied that a buyer should be permitted to recover benefit of the bargain damages when the seller breaches an executory contract to convey real property. Here the defendant agreed to convey marketable title. He made that bargained-for promise and breached it and is responsible to the plaintiff for the damages occasioned thereby. The next question is how to compute those compensatory damages.

Judicial remedies upon breach of contract fall into three general categories: restitution, compensatory damages and performance. Separate concepts undergird each of these remedial provisions. The rationale for restitution is to return the innocent party to his status before the contract was executed. Compensatory damages are intended to recompense the injured claimant for losses due to the breach, that is, give the innocent party the benefit of the bargain. Performance is to effect a result, essentially other than in terms of monetary reparation, so that the innocent party is placed in the position of having had the contract performed. We have now adopted the American rule providing for compensatory damages upon the seller's breach of an executory contract to sell realty and we must examine the appropriate elements that should properly be included in an award.

The specific elements to be applied in any given case of a seller's breach of an executory agreement to sell realty may vary in order to achieve the broad purposes of reparations; some items, however, will almost invariably exist. Thus the purchaser will usually be entitled to the return of the amount paid on the purchase price with interest thereon. Costs and expenses incurred in connection with the proposed acquisition, such as for the title search and survey, would fall in the same category. The traditional test is the difference between the market price of the property at the time of the breach and the contract price. * * *

The difference between market and contract price may not be suitable in all situations. Thus where a buyer had in turn contracted to sell the realty, it is reasonable to measure his damages in terms of the actual lost profit. See Bonhard v. Gindin, 104 N.J.L. 599, 142 A. 52 (E. & A.1928) (awarding the consideration paid, search fees, taxes and assessments paid, and lost profits from a sale to a third person). What the proper elements of damage are depend upon the particular circumstances surrounding the transaction, especially the terms, conditions and nature of the agreement.

The plaintiffs here assert that their damages are equivalent to the difference in interest costs incurred by them in purchasing a different home at another location. This claim assumes that the financial provision of the contract concerning the purchase money mortgage that the defendant agreed to accept was independent and divisible from the purchase of the land and house. The defendant contends that he did not agree to loan these funds in connection with the purchase of some other property, but that this provision was incidental to the sale of the house. Neither position is entirely sound. This financing was an integral part of the transaction. It can be neither ignored nor viewed as an isolated element.

The relationship of the financing to the purchase of a home has changed in recent years. * * * The seller's acceptance of a purchase money mortgage became an important factor in effecting a sale. In evaluating a contract such a financial arrangement could play an important part in determining price. * * * Favorable vendor financing could lead to increased market value. Only then might a buyer be able to purchase. * * *

In some circumstances interest rate differentials are an appropriate measure of damages. Where the buyer has obtained specific performance, but because of the delay has incurred higher mortgage rates, then his loss clearly should include the higher financing cost. Godwin v. Lindbert, 101 Mich.App. 754, 300 N.W.2d 514 (1981), is illustrative. The buyers lost their commitment for a mortgage with an interest rate of 8⅜% when the seller refused to convey. The buyers succeeded in obtaining specific performance but were compelled to borrow funds at 11½%. They were awarded the difference reduced to present value. See also Reis v. Sparks, 547 F.2d 236 (4th Cir.1976). * * *

This is not such a situation. The defendant's motive was to sell a house and not to lend money. In measuring the plaintiffs' loss there should be a determination of the fair market value of the property and house that could be acquired with a purchase money mortgage in the principal amount of $44,000 at an interest rate of 10½% for a 30-year term. The valuation should be at the time the defendant failed to [perform]. The plaintiffs would be entitled to the difference between $58,900 and that fair market value. If the fair market value was not more than the contract price, the plaintiffs would not have established any damage ascribable to the loss of the bargain. They are also entitled to their expenditures for the survey, search, and counsel fees for services rendered in preparation of the aborted closing. The plaintiffs have hitherto received the return of the deposit.

The judgment of the Appellate Division is modified and, as so modified, remanded to the trial court for further proceedings consistent with this opinion.

O'HERN, J., dissenting. If any modifications of existing law were to be made under the circumstances of this case, I would recommend that the Court follow the recommendations of the Commissioners on Uniform State Laws. They suggest the adoption of a rule that better conforms with prevailing American decisional law and reflects a "just method of determining damages." Zeliff v. Sabatino, 15 N.J. at 74, 104 A.2d 54. That rule is stated as follows:

Section 2–510 [Buyer's Damages for Seller's Failure to Convey]

(a) Except as provided in subsection (b); the measure of damages for a seller's repudiation or wrongful failure to convey is the difference between the fair market value at the time for conveyance and the contract price and any incidental and consequential damages (Section 2–514), less expenses avoided because of the seller's breach.

(b) Unless the title defect is an encumbrance securing an obligation to pay money which could be discharged by application of all or a portion of the purchase price, if a seller is unable to convey because of a title defect of which the seller had no knowledge at the time of entering into the contract, the buyer is entitled only to restitution of any amounts paid on the contract price and incidental damages (Section 2–514). [Unif. Land Transactions Act § 2–510, 13 U.L.A. 638 (1980)].

Note

In Burgess v. Arita, 5 Haw. App. 581, 590, 704 P.2d 930, 937 (1985), the court adopted the American damage rule because it is more "equitable." The court observed that, under the English rule, a seller is strongly tempted to avoid the contract when inflation causes the price of real estate to rise.

California, which had followed the English rule for fifty years, changed its code to permit benefit of the bargain damages. Cal.Civ.Code § 3306.

WOLF v. COHEN

United States Court of Appeals, District of Columbia Circuit, 1967.
379 F.2d 477.

BASTIAN, SENIOR CIRCUIT JUDGE. On August 31, 1962, Parkwood, Inc., the owner of a parcel of land in the District of Columbia, entered into a contract to sell the property to one Butler for $1,000,000. Thereafter, Parkwood, Inc., conveyed the property to the Cohens, subject to Butler's rights under his contract of purchase. Butler, in turn, assigned his rights under the contract to one Lovitz. It is clear that Lovitz was the straw party for the real parties in interest, Messrs. Wolf, Wolf, and Dreyfuss. * * *

On December 4, 1962, the date for the settlement of the contract, the Cohens and Parkwood, Inc. defaulted. Cross motions were filed in the District

Court and, on December 13, 1963, judgment was entered holding that there had been no anticipatory breach of the contract of August 31, 1962, and decreeing specific performance against the Cohens and Parkwood, Inc. Appeal was taken from this judgment and, on December 14, 1964, we affirmed the judgment of the District Court, with costs.

On January 25, 1965, an amendment of the original judgment of the District Court was entered by that court, directing the specific performance of the written agreement of purchase and providing that all rents, taxes, water, rent, insurance, interest on existing encumbrances, operating charges and other apportionable items should be adjusted to the date of the actual transfer of the property. The case was set for trial for determination of the damages, if any, to which Messrs. Wolf, Wolf, and Dreyfuss, et al., were entitled under the counterclaim as a result of the breach of contract by the Cohens and Parkwood, Inc. On February 5, 1965, the property was, pursuant to the decree of the District Court, conveyed to Messrs. Wolf, Wolf, and Dreyfuss.

From now on herein Messrs. Wolf, Wolf, and Dreyfuss, et al., will be denominated plaintiffs or appellants, and the Cohens and Parkwood, Inc., defendants or appellees.

After the filing of affidavits the case came on for hearing on the issue of damages on cross motions for summary judgment. It was claimed by plaintiffs that they were entitled to damages in the amount of $355,000, based on the following:

Under the contract of sale, the purchase price of the property was $1,000,000. Plaintiffs claimed that, prior to the original settlement date, they contracted to resell the property for $1,800,000 but, because of delay of performance, the prospective purchaser had withdrawn, as he had a right to do under his contract. Thus, plaintiffs claimed, they were deprived of a profit of $800,000. It appears without contradiction that the market value of the property was $1,000,000 on the date the contract of August 31, 1962, should have been settled, and that the market value on February 5, 1965, when the sale was finally completed, was $1,445,000. Thus plaintiffs claimed that the difference between this latter amount and $1,800,000, the price at which they claimed they could have sold the property on the originally scheduled date of conveyance, left them damaged in the sum of $355,000. Interest thereon from December 4, 1962, was claimed and they also sought reimbursement for counsel fees.

The District Court, after argument on the cross motions for summary judgment, filed its opinion on June 9, 1966, holding that plaintiffs were not entitled to receive damages for the delay in settlement and were not entitled to counsel fees. On June 30 formal judgment was entered and this appeal followed.

When the contract was breached, the case went forward as to the vendees' right to performance, and the claim for damages was severed. Thereafter the vendees filed their statement of undisputed material facts pursuant to the District Court's Rule 9(h). They specifically alleged: "The fair market value of the real estate on the actual date of settlement, February 5, 1965 was $1,445,000."

Despite the value as thus represented, in amount of $445,000 greater than the original price, the vendees contend that the District Court erred in denying their additional claim for what they alleged they might have received had there been timely settlement in the first place.

We do not agree. No matter what the rule in other jurisdictions may be, it has long been settled in this jurisdiction that the measure of damages for breach of a contract of sale is the difference between the contract price and the fair market value of the property. Here, as appears above, the *undisputed* evidence is that the value of the property was $1,000,000 at the time of the original settlement date, and that the value of the property as of February 5, 1965, the date the property was actually conveyed to appellants, was $1,445,-000.

In Quick v. Pointer, 88 U.S.App.D.C. 47, 186 F.2d 355 (1950), we had before us an appeal from a judgment of the District Court for breach of a contract to sell real estate. The contract price was $16,000. Some ten days after the contract was made, and before the settlement date, the purchaser made a contract for re-sale at $19,500. Because the original vendor did not have proper title, he was unable to conclude the sale and the vendee filed suit for damages. The District Court gave judgment for $3,500, the difference between the prices in the two contracts. In reversing, we held that the measure of damages for such a breach is the difference between the contract price and the fair market value of the property and, as there was before the court no evidence of the fair market value of the property, we reversed. * * *

In connection with its consideration of *Quick,* the District Court, in the judgment appealed from and in its opinion, used this language: "No reason appears discernible for applying a different principle where damages are sought in addition to specific performance than where action is brought solely to recover damages."

Nor do we see any such discernible reason. If appellants had sued for damages they would not, under *Quick,* have been entitled to damages as the evidence is that the sale price was exactly the same as the value put on the property by the expert who testified and whose testimony is accepted by both sides. *Quick* would have been on all fours with the present case. The fact that appellants elected to take the property is to our minds *a fortiori.*

Accordingly, we deny plaintiffs' claim for damages for the delay in settlement. * * *

Affirmed.

Notes

1. Where buyer plans to resell, should the court deny specific performance because damages are an adequate remedy? See Note 2, p. 1009 below.

2. In Gilmore v. Cohen, 95 Ariz. 34, 386 P.2d 81 (1963), the buyer was denied lost profit for lack of proof of reasonable certainty. The resale contract may establish the buyer's lost profit. But should the court invoke Hadley v. Baxendale to deny recovery of lost resale profit? E. Yorio, Contract Enforcement: Specific Performance and Injunctions §§ 9.6.6.5, 10.2.2.1, 10.2.2.2 (1989).

3. If the court uses the market-contract damage formula, should the date for calculating market value be the date of breach or the date of judgment? E. Yorio, Contract Enforcement: Specific Performance and Injunctions § 10.2.7 (1989).

4. Estate of Younge v. Huysmans, 127 N.H. 461, 466–68, 506 A.2d 282, 285–86 (1985). The court found that the Bank had breached a contract to sell a lot to the

Huysmanses. Specific performance was denied because of laches. The court discussed damages:

"The Bank appeals the master's award of $15,000 in damages to the Huysmanses for aggravation and harassment sustained by them as a consequence of the Bank's conduct. We reverse and remand.

"The master's award does not provide us with an explanation of the way in which the master computed it. Although we do not require mathematical certainty in the computation of damage awards, here no evidence exists to support the amount of damages awarded by the master.

"Damages for aggravation and harassment are damages for emotional distress. '[R]ecovery of damages for mental suffering and emotional distress is not generally permitted in actions arising out of breach of contract.' Crowley v. Global Realty, Inc., 124 N.H. 814, 817, 474 A.2d 1056, 1057 (1984). [citation]. Liberal compensatory damages, which include damages for mental suffering, will be awarded in tort actions, however, when the acts complained of were wanton, malicious, or oppressive. In *Crowley,* this court held that damages for family distress are permissible in a claim of intentional misrepresentation of fact in connection with the sale of a family home. The Huysmanses, however, did not bring an action in tort or allege and prove any wanton or malicious conduct in the Bank's breach of the contract, and are not entitled to damages for emotional distress.

"The Huysmanses nevertheless may be entitled to damages based upon the lost benefit of the bargain. 'In breach of contract cases, the purpose of awarding damages is not merely to restore the plaintiff to his former position, but to give him the benefit of his bargain—to put him in the position he would have been in if the contract had been fulfilled.' M.W. Goodell Construction Co. v. Monadnock Skating Club, Inc., 121 N.H. 320, 322, 429 A.2d 329, 330 (1981). A liquidated damages clause was not a part of the contract between the Huysmanses and the Bank and, therefore, the master could have properly calculated a damage award based upon the benefit of the bargain."

REIS v. SPARKS

United States Court of Appeals, Fourth Circuit, 1976.
547 F.2d 236.

WIDENER, CIRCUIT JUDGE. This diversity case is an appeal and cross-appeal of summary judgment under Maryland law ordering specific preformance and damages against the sellers of certain lands in Frederick County.

* * * The district court found that the option had been exercised properly. It awarded the buyers specific performance of the remaining acreage of the sellers' farm and the amount of $3,950.63, a figure representing increased closing and mortgage costs resulting because sellers had refused to convey the lands. We affirm. * * *

The sellers, a Mr. and Mrs. Reis, gave to a local real estate agent, Potter, two listing agreements which together authorized the sale of the entire Reis farm with a commission of 10 percent to the agent. The listed purchase prices were $78,500 for 60 acres and all the buildings, and $125,000 for the entire 125 acres of the farm and all the buildings.

The buyers, George and Elizabeth Sparks, offered, in writing, to purchase the buildings and 70 acres of the land for $78,000, with a 5-year option to purchase the remaining acres of the farm for an additional consideration. The sellers made a counter offer which changed the purchase price for the 70 acres from $78,500 to $83,500, and the option price for the balance of the land from $31,500 to $45,000. The sellers' counter offer also changed the term of the option to run for two years from settlement on the first tract, followed by a three-year right of the first refusal. Buyers accepted the counter offer, and settlement of the 70 acre tract and buildings was held on July 9, 1971. At that time, the parties executed a second contract under which the option to purchase the remaining acres was to survive the July 9 settlement and which also included the refusal for an additional three years.

Less than two years after settlement on the 70–acre tract, the buyers sent a letter dated April 23, (1973) [exercising the option]. * * *

Sellers did not respond to this letter. On June 29, 1973, the settlement attorney for buyers' lending institution, Dumler, notified the sellers' broker, Potter, by telephone that he was ready to schedule the settlement. * * *

Dumler held an ex parte settlement on July 6, 1973, at which time he collected the proceeds due the sellers. On July 23, Dumler sent a letter to the sellers saying he had held settlement on the remaining acreage and asking them to return the executed deed so that he could send them the check he was holding. Although his letter requested a response, the sellers never responded, as they had not to the earlier letter from the Sparks. Instead, they instituted this suit in September, 1973 asking for declaratory judgment to establish the rights of the parties under the May 8 and July 9, 1971 contracts. The buyers counterclaimed requesting specific performance. The district court ordered specific performance and awarded ancillary compensation to the buyers for the extra expenses they incurred because the sellers refused to convey the property on July 6. * * *

The sum awarded in the district court was $3,950.63. It found this amount to be a fair accounting of the buyers' increased expenses in that they would be required to hold another settlement on the 55 acre tract and to obtain another mortgage after the delay of two years. At their first attempt to settle, on July 6, 1973, buyers had caused all the title work to be done and had acquired a mortgage loan commitment in the amount of $33,000 for 20 years at 7½ percent interest. The loan was to be secured by a first mortgage on the additional 55 acres and a second mortgage on the 70 acres and buildings previously purchased from the Reises. But, by the time the case came before the district court, an intervening change in the Maryland usury law made a mortgage unavailable at the same interest. The district judge granted the buyers additional interest charges, fixing them at an amount "calculated on a $33,000 mortgage with an increase in interest from 7½ percent to 9½ percent for a period of 20 years, discounted at a rate of 5 percent to get the current value." The parties stipulated to additional settlement charges of $175.

Sellers base their argument against the award on the English rule of Hadley v. Baxendale, 9 Exch. 341 (1854).

The sellers take the position that they could not have known that a refusal to convey would result in increased mortgage costs to the buyers because the contract did not indicate that the 55–acre tract was to be financed. And it is true that, although the contract provided for financing the 70–acre tract, it was silent about financing the 55–acre tract. So, the sellers argue, the extra expense of financing was not foreseeable at the time the contract was entered into and is not a proper item of damages under the rule of Hadley v. Baxendale.

But we think that rule is inapposite here. This case is not one for breach of the contract, but for specific performance of it. In Bernardini v. Stefanowicz, 29 Md.App. 508, 349 A.2d 287 (1976), the Maryland Court of Special Appeals, in upholding an award of compensation ancillary to specific performance, explained that such is not the same as an award of legal damages for breach of contract. Instead, the contract remains in force and the court attempts to require its performance as nearly as possible in accordance with its terms:

> "One of the terms is the date fixed by it for completion, and since that date is past, the court, in order to relate the performance back to it, gives the complainant credit for any losses occasioned by the delay and permits the defendant to offset such amounts as may be appropriate. *The result is more like an accounting between the parties than like an assessment of damages.*"

Thus, the Hadley v. Baxendale rule should not be applied when the standard as here, is not for computing legal damages, but is for making the injured party whole.

Apparently, no Maryland case holds specifically that increase in mortgage interest is a proper item for compensating the injured party for the delay in conveying property. But, in view of the fact that the sellers were advised of the buyers' plans to finance the purchase, and the fact that the sellers adamantly refused to make the conveyance after having such knowledge, we do not believe the Maryland courts would consider such an award to be an abuse of discretion as defined in Maryland. * * *

Finally, sellers argue they are entitled to interest on the purchase price from the date of attempted settlement, because the money was not paid into court but was held by the settlement attorney. Such request, if raised in the district court, was within the discretion of that court to award or to deny. In any event, we do not find error in its denial because sellers remained in possession of the property and could have had the purchase money at any time by fulfilling their legal obligation to convey the property. "* * * [T]hey have no one to blame but themselves for not getting the purchase money sooner." Brewer v. Sowers, 118 Md. 681, 684, 86 A. 228, 231 (1912).

Affirmed.

Notes

1. Was the increased interest: (a) compensation for buyer's loss from the breach; or (b) restitution of seller's gain between the breached contract and the judgment? Is it simpler and more correct to hold that increased interest was within the contemplation of the parties? E. Yorio, Contract Enforcement: Specific Performance and Injunctions § 9.6.6.1 nn. 30, 31 (1989).

2. See Stratton v. Tejani, 139 Cal.App.3d 204, 212, 187 Cal.Rptr. 231, 236 (1982):

"First, when a buyer is deprived of possession of the property pending resolution of the dispute and the seller receives rents and profits, the buyer is entitled to a credit against the purchase price for the rents and profits from the time the property should have been conveyed to him. 'The concept of this monetary award to the buyer is not to give the buyer *damages* for the seller's breach of contract. Rather, it is designed to relate the performance back to the contract date of performance and to adjust the equities between the parties because of the delayed performance by the seller.' (Miller & Starr, Current Law of California Real Estate (1982 supp.) vol. 1, pt. 2, § 5:18, p. 52, italics in original.) Second, a seller also must be treated as if he had performed in a timely fashion and is entitled to receive the value of his lost use of the purchase money during the period performance was delayed."

3. Numerous decisions hold that compensation as an incident to specific performance is more like an accounting between the parties than an assessment of damages. In making the award, the court attempts to place the parties in the position they would have been in had the contract been performed at the agreed time. Bissonnette v. Hanton City Realty Corp., 529 A.2d 139 (R.I.1987); III Lounge, Inc. v. Gaines, 227 Neb. 585, 419 N.W.2d 143 (1988); Sandusky Properties v. Aveni, 15 Ohio St.3d 273, 473 N.E.2d 798 (1984).

This suggests that punitive damages would be entirely inappropriate. Mortgage Finance, Inc. v. Podleski, 742 P.2d 900 (Colo.1986). But see Pederson v. Cole, 501 A.2d 23 (Me.1985).

4. See also, North v. Newlin, 435 N.E.2d 314, 319 (Ind.App.1982): "A variety of courts in other jurisdictions have recognized the confusion which results when courts and parties commenting on orders for specific performance have referred to the award of lost rental income (which is offset against payment of the purchase price and interest thereon) as 'damages.' "

b. Vendee in Default

ABRAMS v. MOTTER

Court of Appeal of California, Second District, 1970.
3 Cal.App.3d 828, 83 Cal.Rptr. 855.

Reppy, Associate Justice. In a nonjury trial of an action brought by plaintiff and respondent Abrams as intended seller of a luxury residence, fully furnished, located on Angelo Drive in the City of Los Angeles (hereinafter "Angelo residence"), for breach of contract by defendant and appellant Motter as intended buyer, the trial court, on April 27, 1967, rendered judgment in favor of Abrams for his loss of bargain damages, for interest on the full purchase price (less existing encumbrance) from date of breach to date of resale, for interest on the loss of bargain damages from date of resale to date of judgment, for expenses incurred in connection with the aborted sale, and for costs of maintenance, taxes, insurance, and interest on existing encumbrance paid with respect to the Angelo residence during the period from date of breach to date of resale. * * *

In October 1964, by means of a deposit receipt and escrow instructions, the parties entered into a contract for the sale and purchase of the Angelo residence. The purchase price for the house and lot was set at $205,000, of which $160,000 was to be cash to Abrams and $45,000 was to be included in a promissory note secured by a deed of trust second to the first deed of trust which would secure the sum expected to be borrowed by Motter to make up the major portion of the cash payment. * * * The contract contained the following mutually recognized condition precedent: "SUBJECT to Buyer obtaining at least a $100,000 first trust deed loan with interest not to exceed 6¾%, payable not more than $649.00 per month including interest, at Buyer's expense." The escrow was to close January 13, 1965. * * *

On January 6, 1965, the attorney for Motter advised Abrams that he was not going to buy the Angelo residence because he could not get financing.

In the meantime, relying on his anticipation that the purchase and sale agreement would be consummated, Abrams purchased another, somewhat less luxurious, residence on Thrasher Avenue (hereinafter "Thrasher residence").

Upon receipt of Motter's withdrawal communication, Abrams advised Motter that he would consider the escrow open until January 13, 1965. After that date Abrams relisted the Angelo residence with Coldwell, Banker [a realty firm] and filed suit against Motter with a first cause of action for specific performance and a second cause of action for damages. * * *

Abrams continued to live in the Angelo residence so as to maintain it in good condition to facilitate its resale and to guard its furnishings. By doing this he also, of course, enjoyed its accommodations. He incurred expenses in keeping up the house, the grounds and the pool, and he paid taxes, insurance and interest on the existing encumbrance. He kept the Thrasher residence unfurnished and vacant, not knowing when he might resell the Angelo residence.

On November 8, 1965, a sale of the Angelo residence with carpets and drapes for $165,000, * * * was consummated. * * * [Abrams] incurred a termite charge and presumably an escrow fee, and he paid Coldwell, Banker a commission on the sale. That firm had not charged a commission on the aborted first sale.

[Editors' note: The trial court held that Motter had breached an implied covenant to use due diligence to obtain financing. The evidence and the law relating to the point is omitted. The appellate court ordered a new trial, holding that the trial judge erred in not making an express finding of fact on whether Motter could have obtained financing even if he had exercised diligence.]

In order to preclude the possibility that at retrial errors might be made on the issue of damages (as some were in the trial under review), we discuss that phase of the case and set out some guideposts.

1. Loss of Bargain Damages

The trial court used the correct legal formula to measure the loss of bargain damages as to the real property, i.e., the excess of the contract price over the value of the real property to the seller at the date of breach. (Civ.Code, § 3307; Royer v. Carter, 37 Cal.2d 544, 233 P.2d 539.) However, an uncertainty is inherent in the fact criteria as presented which if resolved one way would create error. It is generally accepted that the equivalent of value to the seller is fair market value. Fair market value is reckoned "in terms of money." (Sacramento Southern R.R. Co. v. Heilbron, 156 Cal. 408, 409, 104 P. 979.) The court in *Heilbron* said that a jury instruction which referred to cash was correct. Appraisers do not always make this distinction, particularly when comparing sale prices of comparable property. We do not know if the appraisal evidence was given on this basis. Therefore, if the issue of loss of bargain damages is relitigated, the market value on the date of breach should be estimated on an all-cash-to-seller basis. To be fair to Motter, in measuring loss of bargain damages, equivalents should be compared. Since by legal definition the date of breach standard is one based on an all-cash concept, the equivalents should be cash to cash, and this requires converting the contract price from its part-term basis to a full cash one. What figure will be arrived at will depend on evidence at retrial relating to this feature. Generally (but probably not always) a discount of the promissory note involved is in order, based on various factors, including but not limited to the value of the real property securing the note, the amount of prior encumbrances, the terms of the note, risk of economic changes during the term of the note, risk of expense of foreclosure and risk of change in interest rates.

Motter argues that the appraiser's concept of economic obsolescence (depression of value due to dissemination of information about the broken contract) is invalid because it evolves from post breach circumstances. However, the viewpoint that this effect can be anticipated in advance is not unreasonable. The concept is recognized in Bouchard v. Orange, 177 Cal.App.2d 521, 525–526, 2 Cal.Rptr. 388.

2. Interest on Loss of Bargain Damages

The trial judge apparently considered that loss of bargain damages ($35,000) (although derived from the subtraction of the fair market value as of date of breach, rather than of the price obtained at later resale, from the contract price) eventuated at date of resale (November 8, 1965), and he awarded interest on that damage element from that date. This action was contrary to the damage concept of Civil Code, section 3307 as explained in Royer v. Carter. When a seller, in face of the buyer's refusal to purchase, ultimately seeks damages only, he relieves the buyer of his obligation, and the law substitutes for the seller's rights under the contract (1) the property free of the buyer's right to purchase, and (2) the loss of bargain damages. Therefore, if interest were to be allowed on loss of bargain damages, it should run from the date of breach. The question remains, however, whether such prejudgment interest on loss of bargain damages can be recovered at all in light of Civil Code, section 3287 and decisions interpreting it. Section 3287 reads in part as follows: "Every person who is entitled to recover damages * * * capable of being made certain by calculation, and the right to recover which is vested in him upon a particular day, is entitled also to recover interest thereon from that day."

The logical point of commencement for analysis of this provocative issue is the decision in Lineman v. Schmid, 32 Cal.2d 204, 195 P.2d 408, decided in 1948. It is obvious that in the course of preparing its opinion the Supreme Court examined all the preceding cases dealing with this issue. It reviews most of them, no doubt cites all of them, quotes section 337(a) of the Restatement of the Law of Contracts, and distills from them this general rule: "[I]nterest is not allowable when damages cannot be computed *except on conflicting evidence,* such as in the present case, *because of the absence of* established or *reasonably ascertainable market* prices or *values.*" (Italics added.) *Lineman* involved baking flour of a unique variety as to which the market quotations for common brands of flour provided no index of value. The Supreme Court's mention of "conflicting evidence, such as in the present case" had reference to testimony and documents which dealt with such factors as costs of production, carrying charges and profits from which the value of the unique product could be estimated.

The cases since *Lineman,* which apply its general principle to situations where the *value of real property* was a factor in reaching a damage figure on which the allowance of prejudgment interest was in dispute, are not in uniform array.

[A review of the conflicting decisions is omitted.]

When a reason is given for the certainty-by-calculation rule, it is "that where the person liable does not know what sum he owes, he cannot be in default for not paying" or "that where a defendant does not know what amount he owes and cannot ascertain it except by accord or judicial process, he cannot be in default for not paying it." West v. Holstrom, 261 Cal.App.2d 89, 96, 67 Cal.Rptr. 831, 836. * * * The omitted sequel is that if he is not in default for not paying he should not be subject to the penalty effect of interest. * * * We also note that in cases like ours the breaching buyer does not pay what is likely to be found to be the loss of bargain damages, not because he cannot make a reasonable calculation thereof, but because he believes he is justified in withdrawing from the deal and is not really breaching a contract.

* * * In *Lineman,* because of the unique nature of the baking flour involved, the prices listed for normal types of flour were not usable. In our case, although the appraiser-witness checked sales of comparable parcels of real property (and found the price trend was up) their part in his opinion-reaching process was insignificant (if not non-existent) because the so-called "economic obsolescence" feature was the all-pervading factor supportive of the appraiser's opinion. Thus, a unique circumstance about the property made reference to current market prices of properties, unaffected by such a feature, of little value. They could not be considered as reasonable guides to Motter had he been of a mind to concede liability and pay Abrams' loss of bargain damages. Consequently, assuming the proofs remain the same on retrial, no prejudgment interest on loss of bargain damages should be awarded.

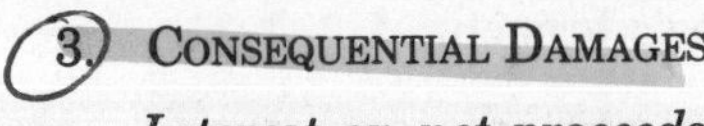

3. CONSEQUENTIAL DAMAGES

a. Interest on net proceeds.

The trial court awarded Abrams interest on the total net purchase price.

The trial court appears to have made such interest award on the theory that but for Motter's breach, Abrams would have had cash available for his use on January 13, 1965; that instead Abrams was forced to retain concededly non-income producing property until such time as he could effect a resale. Such an award necessarily would be based on the recognition that the property could not be resold immediately (assuming that the seller has shown that he still wants to sell it), that it is the buyer's breach that causes the delay in the conversion of the nonproductive real property into at least legal-interest-earning cash, and that the buyer should be held responsible for the loss of earning power of the seller's asset for the period involved. This would be particularly true where the breach itself created a stagnant market condition. Thus, Abrams' counsel argues that such an interest award should be includable within the category of consequential damages.

While Abrams' argument is provocative, we do not believe that the law of this state sanctions such an award.

It must be remembered that an equitable exchange takes place whenever a contract to purchase land is formed. At that moment the purchaser becomes the equitable owner of the land and the vendor's interest is in the unpaid purchase price. * * * When a material breach of such a contract occurs, the innocent party has his election between an action at law for damages, an equitable action for specific performance, and an action for recission on the contract. In the instant case, Abrams' complaint prayed in the alternative for specific performance or damages on the contract.

If the disappointed vendor chooses to remain at all times ready to perform and seeks specific performance of the contract, he foregoes his equitable ownership in, and right to possession of, the subject land and elects to retain his interest in the purchase price in accordance with the terms of the contract. A court sitting in such an equity suit, in addition to decreeing specific performance of the terms of the contract, may award damages in the form of interest for any delay in the vendee's performance of his obligation to pay. (Cf. Ellis v. Mihelis, 60 Cal.2d 206, 219, et seq., 32 Cal.Rptr. 415, 384 P.2d 7 [citations].) There would be no Civil Code, section 3287 problem because the sums would be certain.

However, in the instant case, Abrams did not proceed to judgment with the above described remedy. Rather, in due course, he sought damages based on the contract. In doing so, he gave up his interest in the unpaid purchase price and was awarded in turn, the equitable interest in the land plus damages equal to the difference between the value of the land to him at the date of breach and the contract price (Civ.Code, § 3307). The loss of bargain damages which section 3307 allows are, in their nature, a substitute for requiring the vendee to perform. * * * Thus, if the vendor is not entitled to receive the proceeds provided in the contract, but only a substitute therefor, he cannot be said to have been deprived of the use of those proceeds. It is the conception of the law that the vendor's reacquisition of access to the property, whether such property is productive or nonproductive, together with section 3307 damages, are full compensation for the vendee's breach. * * *

b. Resale expenses occasioned by breach.

If Abrams is successful in the retrial, he can be allowed as consequential damages expenses such as escrow fees and broker's commission based on a hypothetical resale at the $170,000 value-to-seller figure, but reduced by any sum saved by not having to pay all or any part of what would have been paid out as such expenses on the projected sale to Motter. [citations] With respect to brokers' commission, it appears that Coldwell, Banker did not make any claim for commission on the first sale so that Abrams did not have to pay Coldwell, Banker any portion of the $6,000 which would have been its part of the total projected commission on that sale. Presumably, the evidence will be the same on a retrial, in which event the hypothetical resale commission, as a damage item, would have to be reduced by this $6,000. * * *

There is considerable confusion in the record as to what payments were made for termite service in order to effect the first sale and in order to effect the second sale. The details can be cleared up at retrial. The proper measure will be what termite expenditures were necessary for the resale less anything which was to be, but was not, paid in connection with the Abrams–Motter sale and was, therefore, saved.

c. Other consequential damages.

One basic element of the trial court's damage award which remains to be discussed relates to the expenditures made in maintaining the Angelo property from the date of breach to the date of resale unreduced by the value of use to Abrams.

Before specifically dealing with this issue, some introductory comments are in order. The landmark case considering a vendee's breach of a land sale contract (Royer v. Carter) makes it clear that Civil Code section 3307 does *not* provide the exclusive measure of damages for the innocent vendor. The Supreme Court in *Royer* stated that: "the vendee's breach may make it necessary for the vendor to incur *additional expenses* to realize the benefit of his bargain [and] [w]hen such *additional expenses* are the natural consequence of the breach, they may be recovered in addition to those provided for in section 3307." (Italics added.) The *Royer* opinion deals specifically with the expenses which the innocent vendor would incur in a second sale. More recent cases have shed further light on the scope of "additional expenses" which *Royer* sanctioned.

In Allen v. Enomoto, 228 Cal.App.2d 798, 803–805, 39 Cal.Rptr. 815, the court allowed the vendor's out-of-pocket expenses for fire insurance, mortgage interest and real property taxes on the subject property. The award was premised on a finding that the vendor had continued diligently to attempt to resell the subject property and that the resale was made within the shortest period of time possible. The unspoken premise of such a holding is that the vendor (who still wishes to sell the property) actually has had to pay out-of-pocket expenses [1] proximately caused by the vendee's breach.

However, the vendor in *Allen* did not occupy the subject property after the vendee's breach and did not enjoy its use. Under circumstances such as found in *Allen* an award of out-of-pocket expenses may be in order. In the instant case Abrams continued to live in the Angelo residence for a dual purpose: (1) To enjoy its use; and (2) to keep it in presentable condition for prospective purchasers and to protect its valuable exterior and interior appointments. This was Abrams' choice. After the breach he sought a damage remedy, regained his equitable interest in the subject property and could utilize it in any way he saw fit. He cannot charge the expenses of normal occupation to the breaching vendee. If, however, at the trial of this matter, Abrams can isolate certain expenses that were unnecessary to such use but were reasonably related to the process of effecting a resale, these may be charged to Motter.[2]

In the instant case Abrams purchased the Thrasher residence before he knew positively that Motter had secured the financing which was a condition precedent to the deal between them. In certain instances expenses directly made in contemplation of and necessarily related to the carrying through of a contract have been allowed as consequential damages. (See, e.g., McKinley v. Lagae, 207 Cal.App.2d 284, 295, 24 Cal.Rptr. 454, [innocent vendor terminated lease with present tenant when he sold property; tenant removed; vendee breached; vendor awarded rental value from lost lease until resale]; McCul-

1. [Footnotes renumbered.] Some cases have gone so far as to sanction as "additional expenses" under the *Royer* formulation the vendor's loss of profits or deprivation of use resulting from the breach. These "additional expenses" were not required to have been "out of pocket." (Honey v. Henry's Franchise Leasing Corp., 64 Cal.2d 801, 805, 52 Cal.Rptr. 18, 415 P.2d 833; Luz v. Lopes, 55 Cal.2d 54, 61, 10 Cal.Rptr. 161, 358 P.2d 289; McKinley v. Lagae, 207 Cal.App.2d 284, 295, 24 Cal.Rptr. 454.)

[Editors' note: Of the three cases just cited, the first involves a vendee-plaintiff in default seeking restitution; the second was brought by a vendor-plaintiff seeking to quiet title *and* damages; the third involved a vendor-plaintiff seeking damages. Thus in the latter two cases "foreseeability" of the damages is present. Query whether it is a factor in the first case (*Honey*). This point will be raised later with the remedies of a vendee in default.]

2. See, e.g., discussion on termite expenses, ante.

loch v. Liguori, 88 Cal.App.2d 366, 375, 199 P.2d 25, [innocent lessee ordered equipment for manufacturing use in leased premises; lessor failed to deliver up premises; cost of storing such equipment in an alternative location allowed].) So upon retrial of this matter, the trier of fact must decide the questions whether Abrams' purchase of Thrasher property was foreseeable[3] and reasonable.[4] If the answers are both affirmative, the expenses connected with the Thrasher residence between the time of the breach and the resale of the Angelo residence would be allowable on a showing, * * * that such resale was made in the shortest period of time possible.

The judgment is reversed.

Notes

1. Smith v. Mady, 146 Cal.App.3d 129, 194 Cal.Rptr. 42 (1983). Defendant-buyer breached a contract to buy the plaintiff's home for $205,000. Within a few days after the breach, plaintiff entered into a new contract to sell the property for $215,000. Various expenses to maintain the property were incurred during the two months preceding the conveyance to the new buyer. Plaintiff sought to recover expenditures of $2648 as damages for buyer's breach. Ruling that the seller should not be permitted a windfall, the court held that the buyer may credit the higher price of the rapid resale against the damages.

2. Despite the rule that damages are measured by comparing the cash value of the contract to the cash fair market value at the time of the breach, if the property increases in value before trial and the vendor resells the property at a price higher than the contract price, vendor no longer has any loss of bargain damages. As a corollary courts have insisted that the vendor mitigate damages by diligently and promptly seeking to resell the property. Spurgeon v. Drumheller, 174 Cal.App.3d 659, 220 Cal.Rptr. 195 (1985); Nielsen v. Farrington, 223 Cal.App.3d 1582, 273 Cal.Rptr. 312 (1990).

If the breaching purchaser files a lis pendens and renders the property unmarketable, fair market value is determined at the time of trial. An actual resale of the property is not required to trigger the offset rule. Askari v. R & R Land Co., 179 Cal.App.3d 1101, 225 Cal.Rptr. 285 (1986).

If vendor resells the property at a loss, the resale price is evidence of the market value at the time of the breach. Roesch v. Bray, 46 Ohio App.3d 49, 545 N.E.2d 1301 (1988); American Mechanical Corp. v. Union Mach. Co., 21 Mass. App.Ct. 97, 485 N.E.2d 680 (1985).

2. STIPULATED DAMAGES

LEEBER v. DELTONA CORPORATION, INC.

Supreme Judicial Court of Maine, 1988.
546 A.2d 452.

CLIFFORD, JUSTICE. * * * This case arises out of a dispute involving a Florida real estate transaction. Defendant Marco Surfside, Inc., a wholly owned subsidiary of defendant The Deltona Corporation, was the developer of a condominium real estate development on Marco Island in Florida. The plaintiffs, Portland area residents, decided to invest as a group in one of the

3. Is it natural to suppose that one who contemplates a completed sale of his current residence will arrange for suitable accommodations to use when he turns over the subject property to its new owner?

4. Did he purchase prematurely?

condominium units being constructed by Deltona. On May 14, 1980, the plaintiffs, dealing with defendant Maine–Florida Properties, the exclusive sales agent in Maine for Deltona, signed a Subscription and Purchase Agreement ("the Agreement") to buy a condominium unit in the Marco Island project, designated as unit 711. The price for the unit was $150,200, with 15% of this amount, $22,530, paid at the time the Agreement was signed and the balance due at the closing date, to be specified by Deltona within four years from the time of the Agreement. Under the express terms of the Agreement, the $22,530 was to be retained by Deltona as liquidated damages in the event of a breach by the plaintiffs.

Beginning in May 1982, Deltona notified the plaintiffs several times that they would be required to close on the condominium on certain dates or the liquidated damages deposit would be retained by Deltona. After each notice, the plaintiffs were able to obtain an extension from Deltona. Deltona sent the plaintiffs a final closing notice on July 8, 1982, which set a closing date of July 20, 1982. The July 8 letter advised the plaintiffs that the Agreement would be cancelled if they did not close on unit 711. The plaintiffs did not close on the July 20 date. On July 27, 1982, Deltona informed the plaintiffs in writing that the Agreement had been cancelled and the liquidated damages deposit would be retained by Deltona. Deltona then sold unit 711 to another party on July 31, 1982, for what the trial court found to be $167,500. That party paid a 15% deposit of $25,125.

Deltona refused to return the plaintiffs' deposit, and this suit was initiated in the Superior Court. Plaintiffs' complaint contained three counts: Count I, directed against Deltona and Marco Surfside, alleged that the liquidated damages provision was unenforceable. * * * As to Count I, the trial justice determined that the enforcement of the liquidated damages provision was unconscionable. The trial justice found that Deltona had proved it incurred actual damages consisting of some administrative costs and a $5,704 commission paid to Maine–Florida from the deposit and awarded plaintiffs $15,020—the balance of the deposit. * * *

The defendants contend that the liquidated damages provision in the Agreement was valid and enforceable under Florida law. The Agreement provided for the retention by Deltona of the 15% deposit in the event of a breach of the Agreement on the part of the plaintiffs. The validity of a liquidated damages clause is assessed in the following way under Florida law:

> "If the damages are ascertainable on the date of the contract, the clause is a penalty and unenforceable; if they are not so ascertainable, the clause is truly one for liquidated damages and enforceable; however, if subsequent circumstances demonstrate it would be unconscionable to allow the seller to retain the sum in question as liquidated damages, equity may relieve against the forfeiture."

Bruce Builders, Inc. v. Goodwin, 317 So.2d 868, 869–70 (Fla.Dist.Ct.App.1975).

The plaintiffs do not dispute that damages were not ascertainable at the time the Agreement was entered into. Thus, the issue placed before us in this case is whether the Superior Court erred in its determination that retention of money by the sellers under an otherwise valid liquidated damage provision was unconscionable under the standard set out in *Bruce Builders*.

A determination of unconscionability cannot be made unless the circumstances of the case truly "shock the conscience" of the court. [citations] The factual findings upon which the conclusion of unconscionability is based are reviewed on a clearly erroneous basis. [citations]

Under Florida law, if the liquidated damages provision is not a penalty, it is enforceable unless the plaintiff proves the existence of one or more of the following factors:

> (1) an intimation of fraud on the seller's part; (2) misfortune beyond his control accounting for the buyer's failure to fulfill the contract; (3) a mutual rescission of the contract; or (4) a benefit to the seller "the retention of which [when compared to the total contract price would be] shocking to the conscience of the court."

Here, there was no showing of fraud on Deltona's part, nor evidence that plaintiffs' failure to buy was caused by misfortune beyond their control, nor evidence of mutual rescission. Only Deltona's retention of $22,530, 15% of the purchase price, examined under a "shocking to the conscience" standard, is properly considered by the court.

Liquidated damages are favored under Florida law [citation] and Florida courts have uniformly viewed liquidated damage sums in the range of 15% as reasonable. Wortzel, 517 So.2d at 43 (18.2% not unconscionable); Dade Nat'l Dev. Corp. v. Southeast Invs. of Palm Beach County, Inc., 471 So.2d 113, 116 (Fla.Dist.Ct.App.1985) (18%); Hooper v. Breneman, 417 So.2d 315, 318 (Fla. Dist.Ct.App.1982) (13.3%); O'Neill, 112 So.2d at 281–83 ($1500 deposit on $10,440 contract).

The Superior Court, despite its recitation that it found defendants' retention of the liquidated damages to be unconscionable, did not apply a true "shock the conscience" standard in overriding the liquidated damage provision in this case. The court considered the fact of the resale of the condominium unit by Deltona several days after the default but several months after the originally designated closing date, and allowed the plaintiff buyers to recover from Deltona all of the previously paid deposit except what Deltona convinced the court were its actual out of pocket losses resulting from plaintiffs' breach. Such an approach nullified the effect of the liquidated damages provision and made this case indistinguishable from one of ordinary breach of contract. This result undercut the traditional role of liquidated damages provisions, which have always served as an economical alternative to the costly and lengthy litigation involved in a conventional breach of contract action. [citations]

Efforts by contracting parties to avoid litigation and to equitably resolve potential conflicts through the mechanism of liquidated damages should be encouraged. Prompt resale of real estate units by sellers upon breach of contract by buyers likewise should be encouraged. However, the Superior Court ruling in this case, if allowed to stand, would have the opposite effect.

Florida law provides that, under a real estate contract containing a liquidated damages clause similar in language to the instant contract, sellers are denied the remedy of specific performance. [citation] Moreover, their damage recovery is limited to the liquidated damage amount. [citations] Buyers breaching such contracts, not being subject to specific performance nor to liability for excess damages should the sellers' losses exceed the amount of liquidated damages, would have nothing to lose in challenging the amount of liquidated damages retained or sought to be recovered by the sellers in every case where the buyers suspected the actual losses of the sellers to be less than the liquidated damage amount.

Under Florida law, the determination of the unconscionability of allowing a seller to retain liquidated damages under an otherwise valid liquidated damage provision should be based on the circumstances existent "at the time of breach." [1] [citation] A case of liquidated damages, when the liquidated damage amount is not unreasonable on its face, is not converted as a matter of course to one of ordinary breach of contract by the seller's fortuitous resale of the contract real estate subsequent to the buyer's breach. Sellers are inescapably bound by the liquidated damage provisions in such contracts. Buyers should be bound as well unless the plaintiff proves that the circumstances are so extraordinary that the sellers' retention of the liquidated damage amount would truly shock the conscience of the court.

It is undisputed that this liquidated damage amount of $22,530, 15% of the total contract price of the Florida real estate, was reasonable on its face and not a penalty. The retention of that sum by the sellers in this case, when plaintiff buyers delayed closing on the project for several months before breaching the contract, and sellers subsequently were able to resell the real estate through their own efforts and in doing so reduced their actual losses flowing from plaintiffs' breach, is not so extraordinary or unfair as to shock the conscience of the court. The plaintiffs having failed to demonstrate circumstances sufficiently extraordinary to meet the shock the conscience test of *Beatty,* defendants must be allowed to retain the liquidated damage amount.
* * *

Judgment vacated as to Count I.

Notes

1. A liquidated damage clause in a land sale contract does not in itself prevent specific performance. Specific performance will be precluded only where the contract clearly states that the parties intended to provide for an alternative performance through liquidated damages. North American Consolidated, Inc. v. Kopka, 644 F.Supp. 191 (D.Mass.1986); Miller v. United States Naval Institute, 47 Md.App. 426, 423 A.2d 283 (1980).

2. Siegel v. Levy Organization Development Co., 182 Ill.App.3d 859, 861, 538 N.E.2d 715, 716 (1989). Vendor counterclaimed for breach of a land sale contract that contained a valid liquidated damages clause. The court held that while the nondefaulting party could reject the clause "he does not have the right to seek a greater measure of damages than the amount bargained for."

3. Cal.Civ.Code § 1675 states in part that if the amount actually paid pursuant to a liquidated damages provision does not exceed 3% of the purchase price, the provision is valid unless the buyer proves the amount unreasonable. If over 3%, the provision is invalid unless the seller proves it is reasonable.

In Linster v. Regan, 108 Ill.App.2d 459, 462, 248 N.E.2d 751, 752 (1969), the seller was permitted to retain a down payment of $500 although the seller's actual loss was only $100. The court contended that this was not a penalty for nonperformance but rather was "an added incentive to perform."

1. [Footnotes renumbered.] Some states, including Maine, measure the soundness of a liquidated damage provision as of the time the contract is made and not at the time of the breach. [citations]

4. *Economic Analysis of Agreed Damages.* Assume, that Owner retains Cleaner to restore an oil portrait of Owner's late lamented cat Puff. The portrait may be worth about $5 on the open market, but Owner thinks it is priceless. Owner seeks a stipulated damage clause of $10,000 to assure that Cleaner restores and returns the portrait. Cleaner agrees and raises the regular $25 fee to $50. Will the clause encourage Cleaner to be careful and to perform as promised?

If Cleaner fails to perform, the stipulated damage clause advances the compensation goal by covering Owner's unprovable, impalpable, and otherwise unforeseeable damages even though Owner's loss is idiosyncratic and subjective. If the risk of paying $10,000 to Owner bothers Cleaner, she can use the extra $25 consideration to buy insurance. Cleaner is probably a more efficient insurer than Owner because Cleaner can assess the probability of loss and take steps to avoid loss at less cost than Owner.

Striking down such clauses means that the idiosyncratic values of Owner are not protected. It induces people like Owner to insure even though it is cheaper and more efficient for Cleaner to insure. And it increases litigation costs since present doctrine means that every clause is subject to attack on the ground that it may be a penalty. Goetz and Scott, Liquidated Damages, Penalties and the Just Compensation Principle, 77 Colum.L.Rev. 544 (1977), argue that the penalty rule is "anachronistic."

3. EQUITABLE REMEDIES

a. Equitable Conversion

(1) Nature of the Vendor's and Vendee's Interest

LACH v. DESERET BANK

Court of Appeals of Utah, 1987.
746 P.2d 802.

BILLINGS, JUDGE. * * * Lach brought this action seeking a declaratory judgment pursuant to Utah Code Ann. § 78–33–1 (1987) that Deseret Bank ("the Bank"), a judgment creditor, had no judgment lien against property conveyed to Lach by judgment debtors Thomas and Alice Dewsnup (the "Dewsnups").

The matter came before the trial judge on cross motions for summary judgment. Lach appeals from a grant of the Bank's cross motion for summary judgment and a denial of Lach's motion for summary judgment. We reverse.

The following facts are properly before this court. Beginning in October 1980, Lach entered into negotiations with the Dewsnups for the purchase of the Pink Cliffs Village property (the "property"). An earnest money receipt and offer to purchase agreement ("Earnest Money Agreement") was signed on November 28, 1980 by the Dewsnups as sellers and David Lach on behalf of the partnership as buyer.

On the same day the Earnest Money Agreement was signed, the Dewsnups executed and delivered to Lach an assignment of contract and quitclaim deed in favor of Foothill Properties, a name under which David Lach conducts business.

Sometime after January 1981, Lach received notice of an unsatisfied judgment in the amount of $49,000 plus interest and attorney's fees against the

Dewsnups in favor of the Bank, docketed in the Garfield County Clerk's office on December 12, 1980.

On January 6, 1981, the transaction for the sale of the property closed with the execution of a real estate contract between Lach as purchaser and the Dewsnups as sellers.

Lach claims the trial court erred in granting the Bank's cross motion for summary judgment because the Bank did not dispute Lach's statement of uncontroverted facts and those facts compelled summary judgment as a matter of law in favor of Lach. Specifically, Lach claims there was nothing before the judge to support his finding that in this case, the "practice of giving * * * a deed on each Earnest Money Agreement could be used to commit fraud on sellers creditors." Lach contends the court's ruling for the Bank was based upon speculation about facts not before the court and contrary to law.

The controlling statutory provision on judgment liens is Utah Code Ann. § 78–22–1 (1987):

> "*From the time the judgment* of the district court or circuit court *is docketed* and filed in the office of the clerk of the district court of the county *it becomes a lien upon all the real property of the judgment debtor,* not exempt from execution, in the county in which the judgment is entered, *owned by him at the time or by him thereafter acquired during the existence of said lien.*"

(emphasis added). * * *

Utah law is clear. A judgment creditor cannot place a lien against the property of a judgment debtor's grantee. In the present case, under the undisputed facts sworn to in Lach's affidavit, the Dewsnups (judgment debtors) quitclaimed the property to Lach on November 28, 1980. The Bank did not docket its judgment against the Dewsnups until December 12, 1980. Therefore, the Bank did not effect a lien on the property and the trial court improperly denied summary judgment to Lach.

Because the trial judge was concerned by the unique procedure of the execution of a quitclaim deed on the same day the earnest money agreement was signed, we further consider the doctrine of equitable conversion, as it applies to the earnest money agreement. However, we emphasize that there were simply no facts in the record to support the trial judge's speculation that the execution of a deed on the same date as the earnest money agreement was intended to, or operated as, a fraud on the Bank.

Under the previously recited facts, the Dewsnups, as judgment debtors, had no real property interest in the property to which any judgment lien could attach. The doctrine of equitable conversion provides that "an enforceable executory contract of sale [upon which an action for specific performance could be brought] has the effect of converting the interest of the vendor of real property to personalty." Willson v. State Tax Commission, 28 Utah 2d 197, 499 P.2d 1298, 1300 (1972) (quoting Allred v. Allred, 15 Utah 2d 396, 393 P.2d 791, 792 (1964)). The purchaser acquires the equitable interest in the property at the moment the contract is created and is thereafter treated as the owner of the land.

An earnest money agreement is a legally binding executory contract for the sale of real property. [citations] Consequently, no judgment lien can be created by a judgment docketed against a seller after the seller executes a binding earnest money contract. * * *

The Bank further relies on the fact that the full purchase price was not paid prior to when the judgment was docketed. However, whether the buyer pays the full purchase price before the judgment is docketed is immaterial under the doctrine of equitable conversion. In *Allred v. Allred,* the Utah Supreme Court relied on equitable conversion in declaring that a purchaser under an executory contract for the purchase of realty has an equitable interest in the property while the seller's interest is "converted to the *right to receive the proceeds* under the contract of sale." *Allred* (emphasis added).

Nor is it material whether the vendor retains possession of the property subject to conveyance at a later date [citation].

In the case at bar, Lach executed a binding earnest money agreement on November 28, 1980. Regardless of the effect of executing the deed on the same day, the Earnest Money Agreement precludes the attachment of the Bank's judgment lien. When this agreement was executed, Lach became the equitable owner of the property and the judgment debtors, the Dewsnups, held only a personalty interest in the property. The Bank's docketing of a judgment against the Dewsnups on December 12, 1980 did not create a judgment lien against the property because the Dewsnups did not then have a real property interest to which the lien could attach. Under the uncontroverted facts, and as a matter of law, Lach owns the property free from any judgment lien in favor of the Bank and the trial court improperly denied Lach's motion for summary judgment.

The judgment of the trial court is reversed and this case is remanded for the entry of judgment in favor of the Lachs.

Notes

1. In accord Bank of Santa Fe v. Garcia, 102 N.M. 588, 698 P.2d 458 (App.1985); Hannah v. Martinson, 232 Mont. 469, 758 P.2d 276 (1988). But compare Security Bank v. Chiapuzio, 304 Or. 438, 747 P.2d 335 (1987), where the court held that equitable conversion cannot be applied to negate a claim by a creditor on the vendor's continued interest in real property.

2. Butler v. Wilkinson, 740 P.2d 1244, 1254–56 (Utah 1987):

"Under an installment land sale contract, the vendor retains legal title as security for the purchase price of the property. [citations] Nevertheless, as a general proposition, the vendee is treated as the owner of the land. [citations] Thus, a vendee may mortgage his or her equity in the land, [citations] assign it to a third party as security for a loan [citations] or sell the interest by way of an assignment. [citation]

"By retaining the legal title, the vendor retains an important right in the land. The doctrine of equitable conversion characterizes the seller's interest as an interest in personalty and not as one in realty, whereas the vendee's interest under the executory contract is deemed an interest in realty. The doctrine gives a vendee the right to obtain a decree of specific performance from a court of equity. But the characterization of the vendee as 'owner' of the land and of the vendor as having no interest in the land is not wholly accurate. The vendor's retention of the legal title is usually coupled with a contract right to forfeit the vendee's interest and to take back the vendee's interests if the vendee defaults. [citation] The vendor also has an interest that he can sell or mortgage that is measured by the amount the vendee owes under the contract. * * *

"Thus, a vendor's security interest, like the interest of a purchase money mortgagee, protects the vendor's or owner's property rights from being appropriated by creditors of a vendee or by buyers or mortgagees of the vendee's interest. In short, the vendor's security interest or lien provides the critical security to a seller that is essential for an installment land sale contract to be a commercially reasonable way of selling real estate."

3. The purchaser's interest in a land sale contract is assignable; the assignee may enforce it against the vendor. Provisions prohibiting or restricting the right to assign protect the vendor; they are not enforceable against an assignee who is prepared to perform the contract. See Paperchase Partnership v. Bruckner, 102 N.M. 221, 693 P.2d 587 (1985); Panwitz v. Miller Farm–Home Oil Service, Inc., 228 Neb. 220, 422 N.W.2d 63 (1988); Obermeier v. Bennett, 230 Neb. 184, 430 N.W.2d 524 (1988).

When the parties are reversed and the vendor wishes to enforce the contract against the assignee of the purchaser, courts face the disputed question of whether the assignment imposes obligations as well as grants rights. Courts and commentators have reached conflicting answers to the question. Some decisions may be explained by the particular wording of the contract. See Pelz v. Streator National Bank, 145 Ill.App.3d 946, 496 N.E.2d 315 (1986).

4. May the interest of the vendor in a land sale contract be transferred? Distinguish between the vendor's interest in the land (legal title) and her contractual right to the payment. The latter right is assignable, but courts have held it to be a security interest governed by Article 9 of the Uniform Commercial Code. See Citicorp Person-to-Person Financial Center, Inc. v. Fremont National Bank, 738 P.2d 29 (Colo.App.1987); Security Bank v. Chiapuzio, 304 Or. 438, 747 P.2d 335 (1987).

An assignment of the debt, the right to the price, traditionally carried with it the security, the vendor's lien. As holder of the legal title, the vendor may also convey that title to a grantee; but, except for bona fide purchasers without notice, the grantee's title would be encumbered by the purchaser's equity. To avoid possible complication from different persons holding these rights, California adopted a statute stating explicitly that title cannot be transferred without an assignment of the contract and that the contract cannot be assigned without a transfer of title. Cal.Civ.Code § 2985.1. Some courts have reached a similar result by ruling that a transfer of the legal title operates as an assignment of the contract. See Kramer v. Davis, 371 Mich. 464, 124 N.W.2d 292 (1963).

(2) Devolution on Death

IN RE ESTATE OF SWEET

District Court of Appeal of Florida, 1971.
254 So.2d 562.

LILES, JUDGE. Mary Merwin Sweet agreed to sell her condominium apartment for cash. She and the buyer executed a customary contract and the buyer deposited earnest money with the broker. The contract was enforceable by either party. A week or two before the scheduled closing date, she was killed in an automobile accident. The buyer insisted that the contract be performed, and Mrs. Sweet's executor, with probate court approval, consummated the sale. The question is who gets the sale proceeds.

Mary Merwin Sweet died testate. She had executed her will before she made the contract to sell. At the time of her death she owned real property apart from the particular property now in question. She devised to her son "all of the real property of which I may die seized or possessed or to which I may be entitled at the time of my death." In her will, she identified no specific real property. Her residuary bequest was to a testamentary trustee. The trust is for the benefit of her son and grandchildren, with a remainder gift to a college as to part of the trust assets.

Appellant points out that his mother still held legal title to and possession of the property when she died, and therefore he asserts that the property, though subject to the sale contract, came under the devise, and he as devisee is entitled to the sale proceeds. The probate court thought otherwise, and the son appeals. We affirm.

Appellant denies applicability of the doctrine of ademption. Under this doctrine, if a testator by his will purports to give a specific object or right, which is not found in the testator's estate at the time of his death, the legatee receives nothing. Appellant asserts inapplicability on the ground that the doctrine applies only to specific legacies or devises and that the devise to him was not specific—i.e., an object or right distinct from all others—but was general—i.e., part of a class of completely interchangeable items, designed by quantity or amount, and payable from general assets of the estate.

We find it unnecessary to classify the devise as specific or general or to determine whether the doctrine of ademption applies.

If the devise was specific, then the testator's sale of the property worked an ademption, even though the testator died before conveying the legal title and receiving all of the purchase money, at least in the absence of a showing that the testator intended otherwise, a showing not made here. Some states have by statute changed this result with respect to property specifically devised or bequeathed, but Florida has not yet done so, and we do not feel at liberty to do so judicially.

If the devise was not specific, as appellant contends, he still cannot claim the property unless the particular property was all or part of the testator's real property at the time of her death. But the equitable conversion doctrine is well established in Florida; when an owner makes a specifically enforceable contract to sell his real property, the vendee becomes the beneficial owner and the vendor retains only naked legal title in trust for the vendee and as security for the vendee's performance. * * * Under this doctrine the vendor's interest is considered personalty and passes accordingly upon the vendor's death, at least in the absence of a showing of a contrary intent.

The testator contracted to sell the property before her death, and the contract was enforceable against her and binding upon her heirs, devisees, and personal representatives. Upon consummation of the sale, she may have increased her son's testamentary gifts or may have conferred other benefits upon him; we have little ground for speculation. One thing is clear: she intended to convert a particular item of her real property into money, and she expressed no intention that her son should have any money outright. Had she managed to close the sale and collect the purchase money the day before she died, the devise to her son would not have carried with it the sale proceeds. In the absence of a controlling statute, we find no substantial reason why it should do so when the closing was interrupted by her accidental death and her contract obligation had to be discharged by her personal representative.

Affirmed.

Note

Sweet was superseded by statute. Dobson v. Lawson, 370 So.2d 1238 (Fla.App. 1979).

See In re Krotzsch's Estate, 60 Ill.2d 342, 326 N.E.2d 758 (1975). The court held that the devise was adeemed by the contract. This rule has been changed (but not retroactively) by statute in Illinois, S.H.A. ch. 3, ¶ 46a, and in some other jurisdictions. See, e.g., Cal.Prob.Code § 77. In *Krotzsch,* the court noted that if the testator made the contract before executing the will, the testator is assumed to have intended to give the purchase money to the devisee.

BAUSERMAN v. DIGIULIAN

Supreme Court of Virginia, 1982.
224 Va. 414, 297 S.E.2d 671.

POFF, JUSTICE. The issue framed on this appeal is whether an executory land sales contract, conditioned upon the happening of an uncertain event, adeemed by extinction a specific devise of the property.

John P. DiGiulian and William C. Bauknight, executors of the estate of Inez A. DiGuilian, deceased, filed a petition for construction of Inez's will. * * *

By will executed March 10, 1966, Inez devised a fractional fee simple interest in two parcels of land to the devisees and bequeathed her personal property to the residuary legatees. On July 8, 1977, Inez entered into two conditional contracts to convey the land to strangers for a total price of $590,820. The relevant provisions of the two documents are essentially identical, and for purposes of this opinion, we treat them as a unit. The contract recites that the purchasers had paid $1,000 as a deposit which was to be credited against the purchase price if the sale was consummated. Paragraph (4) provides that "[t]his contract is subject and contingent upon the subject property being rezoned" but that "[t]he forfeiture provisions of paragraph (11) hereof shall apply regardless of the status of the rezoning." * * *

Inez died on November 16, 1977, and her will was admitted to probate. The property was rezoned on June 19, 1978. On December 15, 1978, the executors delivered deeds to the purchasers, and the purchasers paid the contract purchase price. A question arose whether the proceeds of sale should be distributed to the devisees or to the residuary legatees, and the executors sought the guidance of the court. The chancellor ruled in favor of the residuary legatees, and the devisees appealed.

To begin our analysis, we construe the provisions of the contract. The rights and duties of the seller and the purchasers were geared to the happening of an uncertain event. If rezoning occurred, Inez was obligated to sell upon demand. * * * Even if the rezoning condition was satisfied, the purchasers had the right to choose whether to buy or to refuse to buy, subject to forfeiture as liquidated damages a sum less than one-half of one percent of the purchase price. Thus, the duty to sell and the duty to buy were not reciprocal obligations, and we construe the contract as a contract of sale upon the purchasers' option.

If the purchasers had exercised their option before Inez's death, the prior devise would have been adeemed by extinction. [citation] In fact, the purchasers did not exercise their option until after her death. Nevertheless, the chancellor ruled that the devise "was adeemed by the sale of the property which was the subject thereto prior to [Inez's] death and that the proceeds of such sale passed to the [residuary legatees]." Necessarily inherent in that ruling was a holding that the sale by the executors converted the realty into personalty; that the conversion was retroactive the moment the contract was executed; and, hence, that the conversion "adeemed" the earlier devise.

In effect, the chancellor applied what may be loosely termed the doctrine of retroactive equitable conversion. That doctrine had its genesis in the early English case of Lawes v. Bennett, 1 Cox Ch.Cas. 167, 29 Eng.Rep. 1111 (1785). There, a landowner granted a stranger an option to purchase. Later, he executed his will devising the land to another. The testator died, his will was probated, the stranger exercised his option, and a dispute developed concerning distribution of the proceeds of sale. In a bill for an accounting, one of the legatees argued that exercise of the option related back to the date it was granted and had the effect of converting the realty into personalty at the testator's death. Upholding the legatee's claim, Lord Kenyon, Master of Rolls, held that "when the party who has the power of making the election has elected, the whole is to be referred back to the original agreement, and the only difference is, that the real estate is converted into personal [sic] at a future period."

While English courts, in reluctant deference to the eminence of Lord Kenyon, have generally applied or discreetly distinguished the rule in *Lawes* and a few courts in this country have done so, most have not. Based upon an exhaustive analysis of the relevant cases, the court in Durepo v. May, 73 R.I. 71, 54 A.2d 15 (1947), concluded:

> "The great weight of American authority is against applying the rule of the *Lawes* case in the same or similar circumstances. The decided trend of the decisions in this county is that the exercise of an option to purchase real property after the death of the owner does not relate back to the time of the option agreement so as to affect, under the doctrine of equitable conversion, the rights of the owner's heirs or devisees."

It is important to understand the reasons for the conflict between the American and English views. The doctrine of equitable conversion, unknown to common law, is a creature of courts of chancery. Yet, as applied in controversies over distribution of a decedent's estate, the differences in the equitable doctrine stem from differences in rules of law. When *Lawes* was decided, English laws of inheritance, rooted in feudal property concepts, favored the heir at law, the eldest son, and English courts construing wills tended to limit the donor's power of testamentary disposition to others. [citation] In America, the law does not favor intestacy; rather it favors the right of a donor to dispose of his property at death as he chooses, even if at the expense of his heirs at law. Where the testamentary intent of the donor is clear, the doctrine of equitable conversion will not be applied to defeat a testamentary gift of land.

One of the first American opinions repudiating the rule in *Lawes* is found in Rockland-Rockport Lime Co. v. Leary, 203 N.Y. 469, 97 N.E. 43 (1911). There, a lessee with an option to purchase attempted to exercise the option after the lessor's death. In a suit for specific performance, the lessee claimed that his election worked an equitable conversion retroactive to the date of the lease. Rejecting the claim the court reasoned:

> "The doctrine of equitable conversion rests on the presumed intention of the owner of the property and on the maxim that equity regards as done what ought to be done. * * * As [the lessor] intended no conversion unless the contingent event happened, he is presumed to have intended none until that event happened, for that would be the natural date to have it take effect in order to avoid confusion if not disaster. * * * We hold that conversion was effected only from the date when conveyance became a duty and that it did not relate back to the date of the lease."

Invoking a similar rationale, the Supreme Court of Wisconsin has held that equitable conversion does not occur on the date of an option contract because such a contract is not subject to specific performance on that date. * * * Estate of Bisbee, 177 Wis. 77, 80–81, 187 N.W. 653, 655 (1922).

We are persuaded that logic supports the majority American view * * *. Applying the rule in this case, we hold that the devise was not adeemed, and, hence, that the right to the proceeds of the sale devolved upon the devisees. * * *

Reversed and remanded.

Note

Where the only act remaining when seller dies is to pay the purchase price, the seller's right is personalty and passes as part of his personal estate. See In re Hill's Estate, 222 Kan. 231, 564 P.2d 462 (1977).

SHAFFER v. FLICK

Superior Court of Pennsylvania, 1987.
360 Pa.Super. 192, 520 A.2d 50.

WIEAND, JUDGE. * * * On or about May 1, 1980, Glenn and Violet Shaffer, husband and wife, decided to retire from farming and leased their farm property, consisting of 250 acres and including three residences, three barns, three silos, a shop and a milkhouse, to their son, Craig Newman Shaffer, and their son-in-law, William E. Carll. The lease agreement, in paragraph 13, granted the tenants an option to buy the farm for $140,000.00. On May 31, 1985, a tornado struck Forest County, killing Glenn and Violet Shaffer and destroying most of the improvements on the farmland. The tenants, pursuant to the terms of the lease agreement, had purchased fire insurance and extended coverage on the farm improvements, naming as insureds themselves and Glenn and Violet Shaffer as the interests of the insureds might appear. As a result, insurance proceeds became payable in the total amount of $147,000.00. Letters testamentary were issued to Eileen R. Flick, and the insurance proceeds were paid to and received by her in her representative capacity. On September 11, 1985 and again on October 23, 1985, Shaffer and Carll gave notice to Flick in writing that they intended to exercise their option to buy the farm and that they wished to apply the insurance proceeds on account of the purchase price. Flick refused to release the insurance proceeds and also refused to execute and deliver a deed for the farm property.

Shaffer and Carll thereupon filed an action for declaratory judgment. * * * Flick also filed a separate action to have the insurance proceeds declared assets of her parents' estates. All proceedings were consolidated for hearing, after which the trial court determined that Shaffer and Carll had validly exercised the option to purchase the farm and that they were entitled to have the proceeds of the insurance policy applied against the purchase price of the farm.

"The courts of this Commonwealth recognize the concept that when an option to purchase real estate is exercised, the optionee is considered as having had the equitable title to the property from the date of the option and not from the date that it is exercised." Hennebont Co. v. Kroger Co., 221 Pa.Super. 65, 72–73, 289 A.2d 229, 233 (1972). Thus, "when the option is exercised, the optionee's ownership reverts to the granting of the option." In re Powell's Appeal, 385 Pa. 467, 474, 123 A.2d 650, 654, citing Peoples Street Ry. Co. v. Spencer, 156 Pa. 85, 27 A. 113 (1893). In Peoples Street Ry. Co. v. Spencer, supra, the lessee had caused the buildings on the demised property to be insured for the protection of lessor and lessee as their interests might appear. After the buildings had been burned by fire, the lessee exercised its option. A dispute arose as to who was entitled to the insurance proceeds. The Supreme Court held that upon exercise of the option, the equitable title of the lessee-optionee reverted back to the date of the original agreement, and the lessee-optionee became the owner as of that date, or of the insurance money which stood *pro tanto* in its place.

Thus, the law pertaining to options is similar to that applicable to contracts of sale. Real estate law holds that although a vendor of real estate retains legal title, he is regarded as a trustee of the land for the purchaser, who has equitable title and who may recover the insurance proceeds if a loss occurs. Appellant contends, however, that an option agreement should be treated differently than a contract of sale. In the case of a contract for the purchase of real estate, appellant argues, the buyer is obligated to buy; whereas, in the case of an option, the optionee is not obligated to buy. Therefore, according to this argument, the optionee does not have equitable title to the land but merely a right to elect to buy. As such, appellant contends that the decision of the Supreme Court in *Peoples Street Ry. Co. v. Spencer, supra,* should be overruled. Inasmuch as there was no real risk of loss to the optionee, she contends, the insurance proceeds should become the absolute property of the optionor without duty to account therefor to the optionee. In support of this argument, appellant cites a decision by the Supreme Court of Oregon in Strong v. Moore, 105 Or. 12, 207 P. 179 (1922), which reached a result contrary to and was critical of the Pennsylvania rule. The answers to appellant's argument are several. In the first place, even though the *Peoples Street Railway* case was decided before the turn of the century, it was a decision by the Supreme Court of this Commonwealth which is binding upon and not subject to being overruled by an intermediate appellate court. Secondly and in any event, the facts of the instant case do not recommend the result for which appellant contends. Because of the circumstances of the instant case and notwithstanding the fact that the option was not exercised until after the loss occurred, it is necessary to relate the transfer of equitable title back to the date of the option contract in order to do equity between the parties. * * *

When we ascribe to the lease agreement in this case the most "reasonable, probable and natural" intent of the parties, "bearing in mind the objects manifestly to be accomplished," it seems clear that the parties did not intend to subvert the substantive law with respect to "extended coverage" risks while adhering to it solely with respect to "fire" losses. Rather, the parties contemplated fire insurance with extended coverage and intended that if the lessees exercised the option after destruction of the improvements, the lessees were to be entitled to a credit on account of the price to the extent that the lessors had been paid the proceeds of insurance purchased by appellees. The parents wished to retire from farming, and they wanted their son and son-in-law to continue farming the land. Therefore, they negotiated an agreement which would enable their wishes to be achieved while, at the same time, providing for their own security. The lessors did not intend to acquire a windfall at the lessees' expense. This intention became apparent to the trial judge who heard the testimony and saw the witnesses. We perceive no valid reason for disagreeing with the result which he achieved.

Affirmed.

Note

Compare In re Marriage of Joaquin, 193 Cal.App.3d 1529, 239 Cal.Rptr. 175 (1987). An option given prior to marriage was exercised during the marriage relation. The court ruled that the optionee acquired title when the option was given. The property was separate rather than community property.

KEIRSEY v. HIRSCH

Supreme Court of New Mexico, 1953.
58 N.M. 18, 265 P.2d 346.

SEYMOUR, J. Plaintiff below, C.L. Keirsey, appellee, brought suit seeking specific performance of an alleged contract to purchase from the defendant and appellant, Viola R. Hirsch, 600 acres of land located in Harding County, New Mexico. Also parties defendant to the original suit and appellants in this Court are J.T. Skinner and Bernice Clavel, administratrix, to whom the defendant, Viola R. Hirsch, deeded the property involved subsequent to her alleged contract with the plaintiff Keirsey. In addition to specific performance, the plaintiff prays for the cancellation of the deeds from the defendant Hirsch to the defendants Skinner and Clavel, and further seeks an abatement of the purchase price based upon the seller's failure to convey mineral rights under one 160-acre tract, together with damages for the loss of the use of the premises. * * *

The trial court in its decree held that there was a valid contract between the plaintiff Keirsey and the defendant Hirsch; that plaintiff, the administratrix of the estate of C.L. Keirsey, deceased, was entitled to a diminution of the agreed purchase price in the amount of $80 for the missing mineral interest and in the amount of $1,950 damages for loss of possession; that the Citizens State Bank, a nominal party defendant, deliver to plaintiff a warranty deed, the original warranty deed from defendant Hirsch to C.L. Keirsey; that the deeds from Hirsch to Skinner and Clavel be cancelled; and that Skinner and Clavel turn possession of the lands over to the plaintiff administratrix, all conditioned, of course, upon the payment by plaintiff of the balance of the agreed purchase price. * * *

The defendants Skinner and Clavel have raised a serious question in their contention that the trial court was without jurisdiction because the heirs of the original plaintiff, C.L. Keirsey, were indispensable parties to this suit.

It is settled in New Mexico that real estate owned by a decedent descends upon his death to his heirs and not to his administrators; it is further settled that the purchaser under a real estate contract has acquired a property interest in land of such a character that it descends to his heirs and not to his administrators. * * *

The fact that the foregoing is true does not necessarily determine the question of indispensable parties; it does, however, clearly show the trial court to have been in error in having allowed to the plaintiff, the administratrix of the estate of C.L. Keirsey, $1,950 credit against the purchase price as damages for failure of possession. At the moment Keirsey died, assuming the Hirsch–Keirsey contract to be valid, this interest in land belonged to the heirs and they were entitled to possession. Any damages accruing by reason of the seller's refusal to turn over possession could only belong to the heirs who were entitled to possession. The same error is apparent in that portion of the trial court's decree directing that Skinner and Clavel turn possession of the land itself over to the administratrix. Further, if the trial court's judgment in this regard were allowed to stand, the defendant Hirsch would be subject to second independent action for damages by the heirs.

There is no question that the heirs of the deceased Keirsey are "necessary" parties as distinguished from "indispensable" parties. These heirs have interests heavily involved and for the purpose of finally determining the rights of all the parties, should be included in this suit. However, the only question of which we can take cognizance is whether or not they are indispensable parties, a jurisdictional question which can be raised at any time. * * *

It is our judgment that the heirs of the original plaintiff Keirsey were indispensable parties in this action. The determination of the basic issue involved in this suit, namely, the specific enforcement of a contract which will vest in those heirs legal title to the property involved clearly and inevitably affects the interests of the heirs. In this respect and in the respects mentioned above in connection with damages, the rights of the heirs of Keirsey are so closely involved that an adjudication seeking the specific performance of this contract without the heirs before the court makes the trial court's decree one which is beyond its jurisdiction. While the question is not presently before us, it is our opinion that the administratrix is also an indispensable party to this litigation by reason of her obligation to pay the purchase price. * * *

Defendant Skinner and Clavel have raised one further point based primarily upon the decree of the trial court providing for payment by plaintiff into escrow for the benefit of Viola R. Hirsch of the remainder of the purchase price. Since Skinner and Clavel have already paid the defendant Hirsch once for the land, it is apparent that she is not entitled to receive payment a second time. The payment, if any is made, must be, necessarily, in trust for the defendants Skinner and Clavel.

In view of the foregoing, the judgment is reversed, the cause remanded to the district court with directions to set aside its judgment, and for further proceedings in conformity with the views herein expressed.

Note

Statutes frequently confer power on the administrator or executor of the deceased vendor to execute a deed in performance of a binding land sale contract. See Atkinson, Wills § 120 (2d ed. 1953). This avoids compelling a conveyance by all the heirs or devisees, who may be widely scattered.

Question: The testator as vendee during his lifetime would have the option, upon the vendor's default, of suing for specific performance, damages or restitution. Does his executrix have the same option after his death? Assuming that she does, and elects to sue for damages under the circumstances in the principal case, who should receive the proceeds—the devisee or the legatee?

(3) Risk of Loss

SKELLY OIL CO. v. ASHMORE

Supreme Court of Missouri, En Banc, 1963.
365 S.W.2d 582.

HYDE, JUDGE. * * * This is a suit by the purchaser, Skelly Oil Company, a corporation, against the vendors, Tom A. Ashmore and Madelyn Ashmore, husband and wife, in two counts. Count One is for the specific performance of a contract to sell the north half of a certain * * * lot.

* * * Count Two seeks an abatement in the purchase price of $10,000, being the proceeds received by the vendors under an insurance policy on a building on the property, which building was destroyed by fire in the interim between the execution of the contract of sale and the time for closing of said sale by the exchange of the $20,000 consideration for the deed to the property. * * * The trial court found the issues in favor of the purchaser, decreed specific performance, and applied the $10,000 insurance proceeds on the $20,000 purchase price. The vendors have appealed.

The vendors acquired this property about 1953, and operated a grocery store in the concrete block building, with fixtures and furniture, and a one story frame "smoke house" thereon. Deeds of trust on the property, securing notes of the vendors to the Bank of Neosho were of record. At all times here material and up to September 30, 1961, the property was leased to Don Jones at a rental of $150 a month. The vendors had a fire insurance policy, with a standard mortgage clause in favor of the Bank of Neosho attached, on the buildings and fixtures, issued February 8, 1958, for a term of one year.

Joe Busby, of the Kansas City office of the Skelly Oil Company real estate department, and Mr. Ashmore conducted the negotiations resulting in the contract of sale * * * and they agreed to meet in Joplin on April 16, 1958, to close the transaction.

The concrete block building, furniture and fixtures were destroyed by fire on April 7, 1958, without fault of either party.

Skelly's Kansas City headquarters advised Busby, who was in St. Joseph on April 7 of the fire. The next day Busby telephoned Ashmore from Kansas City. In this conversation Ashmore said he had insurance on the building and fixtures, naming the company in Kansas City carrying it. Asked on cross-examination whether he told Ashmore the fire would have no effect on the deal, Busby answered: "I told him absolutely not, we would go through with our deal. Q. Just like it was? A. Sure, just like this contract, sir, we're obligated, we can't get out of it." Busby called the insurance company and was informed there was $10,000 insurance on the building. * * * He reported this to the purchaser's legal department. Then, after research, the legal department concluded that Skelly was entitled to have the insurance on the building applied on the purchase price. The closing papers were prepared accordingly.

The closing of the transaction was considered by the parties on April 15, 16 and 17. Busby and Ashmore met on the evening of the 15th. Mr. Winbigler of Skelly's legal department arrived on the 16th. They informed Ashmore they were there to close the purchase of the property; that Skelly thought it was entitled to the insurance proceeds on the building and would like an assignment of the insurance proceeds. When Ashmore disagreed, they informed him Skelly would close the deal and pay him the contract price but would not waive its rights to the insurance proceeds in so doing. Ashmore would not agree to this [and later sent a letter purporting to "rescind" the agreement].

A month or so later the Phoenix Insurance Company, under the standard mortgage clause, paid the Bank of Neosho the balance due on the vendors' notes, $7,242.46, and $2,757.54, the balance of the $10,000 insurance on the building to the vendors. * * *

[The court found an enforceable contract. It continued:]

The contract of sale here involved contained no provision as to who assumed the risk of loss occasioned by a destruction of the building, or for protecting the building by insurance or for allocating any insurance proceeds received therefor. When the parties met to close the sale on April 16, the purchaser's counsel informed vendors and their attorney he was relying on Standard Oil Co. v. Dye, 223 Mo.App. 926, 20 S.W.2d 946, for purchaser's claim to the $10,000 insurance proceeds on the building. * * * It is stated in 3 American Law of Property, § 11.30, p. 90, that in the circumstances here presented at least five different views have been advanced for allocating the burden of fortuitous loss between vendor and purchaser of real estate. We summarize those mentioned: (1) The view first enunciated in Paine v. Meller (Ch. 1801, 6 Ves.Jr. 349, 31 Eng.Reprint 1088, 1089) is said to be the most widely accepted, holding that from the time of the contract of sale of real estate the burden of fortuitous loss was on the purchaser even though the vendor retained possession. (2) The loss is on the vendor until legal title is conveyed, although the purchaser is in possession, stated to be a strong minority. (3) The burden of loss should be on the vendor until the time agreed upon for conveying the legal title, and thereafter on the purchaser unless the vendor be in such default as to preclude specific performance, not recognized in the decisions. (4) The burden of the loss should be on the party in possession, whether vendor or purchaser, so considered by some courts. (5) The burden of loss should be on the vendor unless there is something in the contract or in the relation of the parties from which the court can infer a different intention, stating "this rather vague test" has not received any avowed judicial acceptance, although it is not inconsistent with jurisdictions holding the loss is on the vendor until conveyance or jurisdictions adopting the possession test.

We do not agree that we should adopt the arbitrary rule of Paine v. Meller, supra, and Standard Oil Co. v. Dye, supra, that there is equitable conversion from the time of making a contract for sale and a purchase of land and that the risk of loss from destruction of buildings or other substantial part of the property is from that moment on the purchaser. Criticisms of this rule by eminent authorities have been set out in the dissenting opinion of Storckman, J., herein and will not be repeated here.

We take the view stated in an article on Equitable Conversion by Contract, 13 Columbia Law Review 369, 386, Dean Harlan F. Stone, later Chief Justice Stone, in which he points out that the only reason why a contract for the sale of land by the owner to another operates to effect conversion is that a court of equity will compel him specifically to perform his contract. He further states: * * *

"Whether a plaintiff, in breach of his contract by a default which goes to the essence, as in the case of the destruction of a substantial part of the subject matter of the contract, should be entitled to specific performance, is a question which is answered in the negative in every case except that of destruction of the subject matter of the contract. To give a plaintiff specific performance of the contract when he is unable to perform the contract on his own part, violates the fundamental rule of equity that * * * *equity will not compel a defendant to perform when it is unable to so frame its decree as to compel the plaintiff to give in return substantially what he has undertaken to give* or to do for the defendant.

"The rule of casting the 'burden of loss' on the vendee by specific performance if justifiable at all can only be explained and justified upon one of two theories: first, that since equity has for most purposes treated the vendee as the equitable owner, it should do so for all purposes, although *this ignores the fact that in all other cases the vendee is so treated only because the contract is either being performed or in equity ought to be performed;* or, second, which is substantially the same proposition in a different form, the specific performance which casts the burden on the vendee is an incident to and a consequence of an equitable conversion, whereas in all other equity relations growing out of the contract, the equitable conversion, if it exists, is an incident to and consequence of, a specific performance. Certainly nothing could be more illogical than this process of reasoning." (Emphasis ours.)

For these reasons, we do not agree with the rule that arbitrarily places the risk of loss on the vendee from the time the contract is made. Instead we believe the Massachusetts rule is the proper rule. It is thus stated in Libman v. Levenson, 236 Mass. 221, 128 N.E. 13: When

"the conveyance is to be made of the whole estate, including both land and buildings, for an entire price, and the value of the buildings constitutes a large part of the total value of the estate, and the terms of the agreement show that they constituted an important part of the subject matter of the contract * * * the contract is to be construed as subject to the implied condition that it no longer shall be binding if, before the time for the conveyance to be made, the buildings are destroyed by fire. The loss by the fire falls upon the vendor, the owner; and if he has not protected himself by insurance, he can have no reimbursement of this loss; but the contract is no longer binding upon either party. If the purchaser has advanced any part of the price, he can recover it back. If the change in the value of the estate is not so great, or if it appears that the buildings did not constitute so material a part of the estate to be conveyed as to result in an annulling of the contract, specific performance may be decreed, *with compensation for any breach of agreement,* or relief may be given in damages." (Emphasis ours.)

However, the issue in this case is not whether the vendee can be compelled to take the property without the building but whether the vendee is entitled to

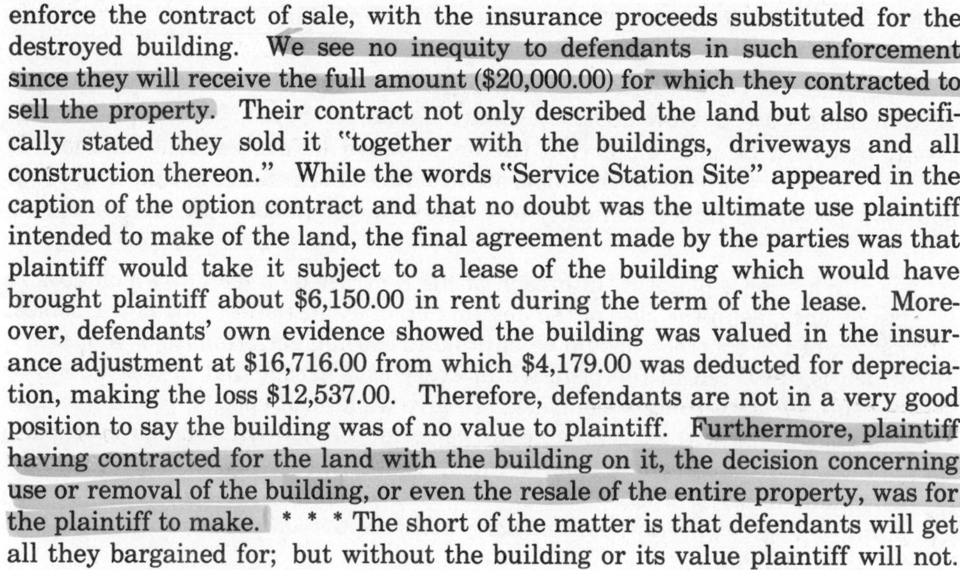

enforce the contract of sale, with the insurance proceeds substituted for the destroyed building. We see no inequity to defendants in such enforcement since they will receive the full amount ($20,000.00) for which they contracted to sell the property. Their contract not only described the land but also specifically stated they sold it "together with the buildings, driveways and all construction thereon." While the words "Service Station Site" appeared in the caption of the option contract and that no doubt was the ultimate use plaintiff intended to make of the land, the final agreement made by the parties was that plaintiff would take it subject to a lease of the building which would have brought plaintiff about $6,150.00 in rent during the term of the lease. Moreover, defendants' own evidence showed the building was valued in the insurance adjustment at $16,716.00 from which $4,179.00 was deducted for depreciation, making the loss $12,537.00. Therefore, defendants are not in a very good position to say the building was of no value to plaintiff. Furthermore, plaintiff having contracted for the land with the building on it, the decision concerning use or removal of the building, or even the resale of the entire property, was for the plaintiff to make. * * * The short of the matter is that defendants will get all they bargained for; but without the building or its value plaintiff will not.

We therefore affirm the judgment and decree of the trial court.

STORCKMAN, JUDGE (dissenting). I agree that the parties on March 7, 1958, entered into a valid contract for the transfer of the real estate, but in the circumstances I cannot assent to the holding that the plaintiff is entitled to specific performance on any terms other than those of the purchase contract without reduction in the contract price. * * *

The evidence is convincing that Skelly Oil Company was buying the lot as a site for a service station and that [it] intended to tear down and remove the building in question. * * *

Count 1 of the petition is for specific performance in accordance with the terms of the purchase contract; Count 2 seeks a declaration that the defendants hold the $10,000 insurance proceeds in trust for the benefit of the plaintiff and that the defendants be required to pay the proceeds to the plaintiff or that the amount thereof be applied in reduction of the purchase price of the property. Count 2 alleges that the concrete block, single-story building which was used as a grocery store was totally destroyed by fire, that the defendants collected the insurance thereon, and that "said building was a valuable appurtenance on said real estate worth more than $10,000.00 and that its destruction reduced the value of said real estate more than the sum of $10,000.00."

In spite of the issue made by Count 2 as to effect of the destruction of the building upon the value of the real estate, the trial court refused to permit cross-examination of plaintiff's witness to establish that the purpose and intent of Skelly was to remove the building from the premises when the lease was terminated, and the court rejected defendants' offer of proof to the same effect. In this equity action the testimony should have been received. It did not tend to vary or contradict the written contract but dealt with an issue made by plaintiff's petition based on a partial destruction of the subject matter subsequent to the acceptance of the option. Nevertheless, there was other evidence from which it could be reasonably inferred that the use of the real estate as a filling station site necessitated the removal of the building. Mr. Ashmore testified that he originally asked $27,000 for the property but reduced his price on Mr. Busby's representation that the improvements had no value to Skelly and that Skelly would be glad to have Mr. Ashmore remove them.

The plaintiff introduced no evidence of the market value of the property before or after the fire in support of the allegations in Count 2. The amount paid by the insurance company is of little or no benefit as evidence of the actual value of the building because of the valued policy law of Missouri which provides that in case of the total destruction of a building by fire, insurance companies shall not be permitted to deny that the property insured was worth at the time of issuing the policy or policies the full amount for which the property was insured. Sections 379.140 and 379.145, RSMo 1959, V.A.M.S. Defendants' evidence tended to prove that the real estate was worth more as a site for a service station after the fire than before and that the value of the real estate after the fire was in excess of $20,000.

The claim of neither party is particularly compelling insofar as specific performance in this case is concerned. The destruction of the building by fire, its insurance, and the disposition of the insurance proceeds were matters not contemplated by the parties and not provided for in the purchase contract documents. Skelly's representative did not know that Mr. Ashmore carried insurance on the building until after the fire, and he then told Mr. Ashmore that despite the fire the deal would be closed on the agreed date. Skelly's present claims are an afterthought inconsistent with its conduct throughout the negotiations and prior to the closing date.

In short, as to both Skelly and the Ashmores, the destruction of the insured building was a fortuitous circumstance supplying the opportunity to rid the property of a vexatious lease, to dispose of the building, and at the same time resulting in a windfall of $10,000. And the problem, in fact the only seriously contested issue between the parties, is which of them is to have the advantage of this piece of good fortune. * * *

In claiming the proceeds of the Ashmores' fire insurance policy, Skelly did not contend that the value of the real estate as a service station site had decreased. After learning of the fire and the existence of the insurance policy, Skelly's counsel did some research and, as he announced when the parties met in Joplin to close the deal, Skelly was relying on a case he had found, Standard Oil Company v. Dye, 223 Mo.App. 926, 20 S.W.2d 946. And in its basic facts the case, admittedly, is quite similar to this one although there were no attendant circumstances such as we have in the present case. As authority for its decision, the court in that case relied almost wholly on William Skinner & Sons' Shipbuilding & Dry–Dock Co. v. Houghton, 92 Md. 68, 48 A. 85. The doctrine of these two cases, laboriously evolved from Paine v. Meller, (1801) 6 Ves.Jr. 349, 31 Eng.Reprint 1088, is "that a contract to sell real property vests the equitable ownership of the property in the purchaser, with the corollary that any loss by destruction of the property through casualty during the pendency of the contract must be borne by the purchaser." The two fold rationale of this doctrine is a maxim that "equity regards as done that which should have been done," from which it is said the "vendor becomes a mere trustee, holding the legal title for the benefit of the purchaser or as security for the price." All of the experts and scholars seem to agree that this doctrine and its rationale is misplaced if not unsound. As to the maxim, Williston said, "Only the hoary age and frequent repetition of the maxim prevents a general recognition of its absurdity." 4 Williston, Contracts, § 929, p. 2607. As to the corollary, Williston points out that while the purchaser may have an interest in the property, it is equally clear that the vendor likewise has an interest, and as for the vendor's being a trustee for the purchaser observes, "However often the words may be repeated, it cannot be true that the vendor is trustee for the purchaser." 4 Williston, Contracts, § 936, p. 2622.

Nevertheless, adapting this doctrine and following a majority opinion in another English case, Rayner v. Preston, (1881) L.R. 81 Ch.Div. 1 (CA), the rule as stated in the *Dye* case has evolved: "Where the purchaser as equitable owner will bear the loss occasioned by a destruction of the property pending completion of the sale, the contract is silent as to insurance, the rule quite generally followed is that the proceeds of the vendor's insurance policies, even though the purchaser did not contribute to their maintenance, constitute a trust fund for the benefit of the purchaser to be credited on the purchase price of the destroyed property, the theory being that the vendor is a trustee of the property of the purchaser." Annotation, 64 A.L.R.2d 1402, 1406. Many jurisdictions have modified or do not follow this doctrine, some take the view that the vendor's insurance policy is personal to him, and Parliament has enacted a statute which entirely changes the English rule. The rule is not as general as the annotator indicated, and as with the rule upon which it is founded, all the experts agree that it is unsound, their only point of disagreement is as to what the rule should be. [citations] * * *

Automatic application of the doctrine that "equity regards that as done which ought to be done," in the circumstances of this case, begs the question of *what ought to be done.* Because the insurance proceeds may be a windfall to those legally entitled does not necessarily mean that justice will be accomplished by transferring them elsewhere. The substance of the purchase contract and the use to which the property is to be put must be considered. A resort to equity should involve a consideration of other equitable principles or maxims such as the equally important maxims that "equity follows the law" and "between equal equities the law will prevail."

A valid legal excuse is a sufficient reason for refusal of specific performance. * * * Destruction of a particular thing upon which the contract depends is generally regarded as a legal excuse for nonperformance. * * *

The plaintiff's petition alleges that the building destroyed by fire "was a valuable appurtenance on said real estate worth more than $10,000.00 and that its destruction reduced the value of said real estate more than the sum of $10,000.00." So far as Skelly's use of the property as a service station site is concerned, this allegation cannot be true if Skelly's intent was to tear down and remove the building. On the other hand, if the plaintiff retained the property or sold to an investor who proposed to rent the building for a store or a similar business purpose, then the loss would be substantial and the insurance proceeds would be necessary to restore a suitable building. The petition asserts that "as a matter of law" the defendant held "said $10,000.00 insurance proceeds in trust for the benefit of plaintiff as the vendee of the defendants." I know of no equitable or legal principle that justifies the award of the insurance proceeds automatically to the purchaser in the circumstances of this case. * * *

If plaintiff's contention is that there has been a substantial failure or impairment of the consideration of the contract by reason of the destruction of the building, then I do not think that the Ashmores should be entitled to specific performance, and because of the theory of mutuality it would seem that Skelly would not be entitled to specific performance unless it was willing to perform its legal obligations under the purchase contract as drawn. We would not be justified in making a new contract for the parties to cover the building insurance, and a court of equity will not decree specific performance of a contract that is incomplete, indefinite or uncertain. * * *

If the subject matter of the purchase contract was not as well or better suited to Skelly's purpose after the fire than it was before, then it appears from the authorities above discussed that Skelly could avoid the contract entirely or that it could clearly establish the amount and manner in which it was damaged. What would the situation be if the building had not been insured or for only a small amount? The fact that the building was insured and the amount thereof are hardly determinative of Skelly's alleged injury.

But Skelly did not after the fire or in this action elect to abandon the contract although the Ashmores gave it the opportunity to do so rather than to sell at the reduced price. It is quite evident that Skelly has received one windfall as the result of the fire in that the lease is terminated and the site can be cleared at less cost. It has not shown itself to be entitled to another, the one now legally vested in the Ashmores. Ideally the purchase contract should be set aside so that the parties could negotiate a new one based on the property in its present condition. But the plaintiff by its election to take title has foreclosed this possibility.

* * * This opinion, which will be referred to as the majority opinion, employs conflicting rules or theories. It purports to adopt one but applies another. It professes to repudiate the equitable conversion theory and to adopt unequivocally the Massachusetts rule, stating: "Instead we believe the Massachusetts rule is the proper rule." This rule as shown by the opinion's quotation from Libman v. Levenson, is that the sales contract will no longer be binding if the buildings are destroyed by fire and "the value of the buildings constitutes a large part of the total value of the estate, and the terms of the agreement show that they constituted an important part of the subject matter of the contract." In the same quotation from the *Libman* case, the circumstances and terms under which specific performance is granted are stated as follows: "If the change in the value of the estate is not so great, or if it appears that the buildings did not constitute so material a part of the estate to be conveyed as to result in an annulling of the contract, specific performance may be decreed, *with compensation for any breach of agreement, or relief may be given in damages.*" Emphasis added.

Obviously the majority opinion did not find that the value of the building constituted "a large part of the total value of the estate" or "an important part of the subject matter of the contract," else it would have declared the sales contract no longer binding under the Massachusetts rule. What it had to find was that the value of the building was not so great or such a material part of the estate to be conveyed as to interfere with the decree of specific performance.

But at this point the majority opinion abandons any pretense of following the Massachusetts rule and switches back to the equitable conversion theory and awards the insurance proceeds as such to the vendee without a determination of compensation for breach or relief to be given in damages. The value of the building for insurance purposes is not necessarily the proper measure of the compensation or damages to which the plaintiff is entitled. It might be considerably less than such a figure if Skelly intended to remove the building as soon as it had the legal right to do so. Obviously the Massachusetts rule is not tied in with insurance at all and that is as it should be. Logically the majority opinion should have remanded the case for a determination of the amount of actual damages suffered by Skelly or the compensation to which it is entitled if it still wants specific performance. This is undoubtedly what the Massachusetts rule contemplates. I would find no fault with such a procedure. * * *

The opinion simply awards the *proceeds* of the fire insurance policy. It does not, and could not on the evidence in the present record, ascertain the compensation or damages, if any, to which Skelly is entitled by reason of the destruction of the building. Evidence of this sort was excluded by the trial court. Count 2 of plaintiff's petition claims the insurance proceeds on the theory of a trust fund as a matter of law and that seems to be the basis of the majority opinions' award of the insurance fund to the purchaser. This is the antithesis of the Massachusetts rule which contemplates the ascertainment of the amount of compensation or damages that will assure the vendee receiving the value for which it contracted, and no more. * * *

On the present record the plaintiff has failed to show a superior equity in the insurance proceeds under the Massachusetts rule or otherwise, and on well-established equitable principles I would leave the legal title to that fund where it is. I would find against the plaintiff on Count 2 of its petition, but award it specific performance under Count 1 on the condition that it pay to the defendants the agreed purchase price of $20,000 less the amount of compensation or damages, if any, that it could establish against the defendants (not the insurance funds) at a plenary hearing of that issue in the trial court.

Notes

1. In two subsequent Missouri cases, the vendor was allowed to keep the proceeds of an insurance policy. In the first, Flath v. Bauman, 722 S.W.2d 125 (Mo.App.1986), the court found that the purchaser had abandoned the property and thus, unlike the *Skelly Oil* buyer, was precluded from seeking specific performance. In the second, Petrie v. Levan, 762 S.W.2d 103 (Mo.App.1988), the vendor collected insurance proceeds for a loss that occurred after the contract was signed but on the night before the property was deeded over to the purchaser. The purchaser claimed the proceeds on the ground that the vendor had breached a covenant to convey the property in good repair. Relief was denied since the court found no covenant. The court pointed out that in *Skelly Oil,* the purchaser had sought an equitable remedy; it suggested that the plaintiff would have better luck by asserting an equitable claim to the proceeds.

2. In Gilles v. Sprout, 293 Minn. 53, 196 N.W.2d 612 (1972), the risk of loss had shifted to the purchaser prior to the fire. The purchaser had taken possession of the premises pending the close of the escrow. Before that date, the dwelling was accidentally destroyed by fire. The seller, the only party insured, collected the proceeds of the policy. The purchaser sued for specific performance. The court held that so much of the proceeds of the insurance policy should be applied to reduce the purchase price as represents the market value of the dwelling at the time of the loss, reduced by the cost of maintaining the insurance during the period the purchaser was in possession.

The Pennsylvania Supreme Court explained this result in terms of unjust enrichment. Partrick & Wilkins Co. v. Reliance Insurance Co., 500 Pa. 399, 404, 456 A.2d 1348, 1351 (1983). Any proceeds of the policy in excess of the unpaid balance of the purchase price is "deemed to be held 'in trust' for the vendee."

3. Gilles v. Sprout is concerned with the disposition of the proceeds of the seller's insurance policy once collected. The decision represents the prevailing view that the buyer should benefit from the seller's policy. Suppose, however, that the insurance company refuses to pay. In Wolf v. Home Insurance Co., 100 N.J.Super. 27, 241 A.2d 28 (1968), the insurance company contended that the insured seller sustained no loss since the buyer had paid the full contract price subsequent to the fire. The seller sued the insurance carrier. The court, applying the "New York" rule, held that a loss covered by the terms of the policy had occurred and allowed recovery.

If the insurer indemnifies for the loss sustained by the seller in such cases, should the insurer be subrogated to the seller's rights against the buyer?

4. In Kindred v. Boalbey, 73 Ill.App.3d 37, 391 N.E.2d 236 (1979), the court held that the seller was entitled to receive the balance due on the installment contract from the proceeds of the buyer's fire insurance policy, with the remainder being retained by the buyer.

5. See Note, Risk of Loss in Executory Contracts for the Sale of Real Property, 14 Colum.J.L. & Soc.Probs. 453 (1979).

DIXON v. SALVATION ARMY

Court of Appeal of California, Fourth District, 1983.
142 Cal.App.3d 463, 191 Cal.Rptr. 111.

Cologne, Acting Presiding Justice. The Salvation Army appeals an order granting Albert D. Dixon's motion for summary judgment in Dixon's action for declaratory relief.

* * * Dixon and the Salvation Army entered a real estate purchase and sale agreement. The Salvation Army agreed to sell to Dixon two parcels, described herein as "8th & K property" and "8th & J property." Both parcels were improved with commercial structures. The 8th & K property included a two-story office building and warehouse building and the 8th and J property included a three-story brick warehouse. * * *

Before the escrow closed and before either title or possession passed from the Salvation Army to Dixon, one of the two buildings on the 8th & K property was destroyed by fire. The Salvation Army received $240,000 as fire insurance proceeds, but it became apparent during the negotiations following the fire that the destroyed building was significantly underinsured. The Salvation Army could not, of course, deliver the property in the "same general condition minus normal wear and tear as when inspected prior to opening of escrow" as the contract provided and the parties could not agree to a new price of the property as is. This litigation resulted.

Dixon sought and obtained a court declaration that "as a result of the destruction by fire of the improvements on the * * * '8th & K property,' the total purchase price to be paid * * * should be abated to reflect the loss—if any—of the proportionate value of the improvements on the 8th and K property to the total value of all of the property sold" under the agreement. The effect of this order was to authorize Dixon to seek specific enforcement of the contract at an abated price. This price was to be determined by the parties' negotiation or future litigation. The Salvation Army had requested a declaration that the contract should be rescinded or, alternatively, the contract could be enforced without an abatement of the sales price.

The Uniform Vendor and Purchaser Risk Act (Uniform Act) was adopted in California and codified as Civil Code section 1662. This statute provides:

> "Any contract hereafter made in this State for the purchase and sale of real property shall be interpreted as including an agreement that the parties shall have the following rights and duties, unless the contract expressly provides otherwise:
>
> "(a) If, when neither the legal title nor the possession of the subject matter of the contract has been transferred, all or a material part thereof is destroyed without fault of the purchaser or is taken by eminent domain, the vendor cannot enforce the contract, and the purchaser is entitled to recover any portion of the price that he has paid;
>
> "(b) If, when either the legal title or the possession of the subject matter of the contract has been transferred, all or any part thereof is destroyed without fault of the vendor or is taken by eminent domain, the purchaser is not thereby relieved from a duty to pay the price, nor is he entitled to recover any portion thereof that he has paid." * * *

Since neither title nor possession had passed to Dixon, the provisions of subdivision (a) apply and the Salvation Army had the risk of loss. This rule prohibits the Salvation Army from enforcing the contract and permits Dixon to rescind and recover any consideration. The statute is silent, however, on whether Dixon can specifically enforce the contract with or without an abatement in price.

Of the other jurisdictions which have enacted the Uniform Act, New York appears to be the only one which has previously resolved whether the vendee may obtain specific enforcement of the contract at an abated purchase price.

In Rizzo v. Landmark Realty Corp. (1950) 277 App.Div. 1094, 101 N.Y.S.2d 151, the court held the Uniform Act precludes a vendor from specifically enforcing a real estate sales contract when a material part of the subject property has been destroyed, but it does not destroy any common law rights of the purchaser to specific performance with abatement.

In Lucenti v. Cayuga Apartments, Inc. (1977) 59 App.Div.2d 438, 400 N.Y.S.2d 194, the court discussed the New York modified version of the Uniform Act. Section 5–1311 of New York's General Obligations Law is in essence the Uniform Act but with the added provision that "if an immaterial part thereof is destroyed without fault of the purchaser or is taken by eminent domain, neither the vendor nor the purchaser is thereby deprived of the right to enforce the contract, but there shall be, to the extent of the destruction or taking, an abatement of the purchase price."

Thus, the New York Legislature has expressly provided for the situation where the vendor has the risk of loss and an immaterial part of the property is destroyed. In *Lucenti,* the court considered a similar situation except found the destruction to the subject property was material. Finding "no logical basis for distinguishing between a loss to a 'material' and an 'immaterial' portion of the premises," the court allowed the vendee to specifically enforce the contract at an abated price. It is clear the court was also applying the common law rule of New York (which permitted the vendee to enforce a contract at an abated purchase price), thus providing no assistance in interpreting the California statute. In applying the common law rule, the New York court recognized, but chose not to follow, the recommendation of the New York Law Revision Commission Report of 1936 (the same year New York enacted the Uniform Act), which suggested rescission of the contract was the best remedy when a material part of the subject property was destroyed.

The long established rule in California, stemming from cases occurring after the San Francisco fire of 1906, differs from the common law of New York. * * *

[W]e thus hold where a material part of the subject property is destroyed without the fault of either party and neither title nor possession has passed to the purchaser, the vendor's performance is excused and the purchaser is entitled to the return of any consideration paid.

We believe the more equitable approach and one more compatible with the Uniform Act is to place the parties in their original position, free to make a new bargain. A rule that denies a vendor the ability to specifically enforce the sales agreement where the material part of the consideration is lost or destroyed calls out for the converse also to be applied. It would be grossly unfair to require either party to accept consideration less than the whole of what was bargained for under these circumstances. If it is unfair to force the purchaser to receive materially damaged property, it is equally unfair to compel the vendor to accept a price substantially below what he bargained for. Although a court in equity has broad powers, it should not use its jurisdiction to remake the contract for the parties, particularly on the critical term of the purchase price. This task is better left to the further negotiations of the parties, with neither compelled to strike an agreement. Specific performance with abatement of the purchase price is not an appropriate remedy for the purchaser.

Judgment reversed.

WORK, ASSOCIATE JUSTICE, dissenting. Under the majority analysis, buyer is denied his right to specifically enforce even those land contracts where adequate insurance coverage would give seller its entire contract price, or even more.

If we adhere to the concept that real property is unique and such sales may be specifically enforced, the destruction of one or all structures placed upon a piece of land should not prevent a buyer from electing to specifically enforce a sale even though the sale originally contemplated the land in its improved state. The policy reasons for denying a seller the right to force a materially different package upon an unwilling buyer are far different than those permitting an originally willing seller to refuse to specifically perform a contract to convey real property to the extent the property still exists when enforcement is requested. The majority does not quarrel with the harshness of the rule which forces a buyer * * * to pay full value for a leasehold interest which has been totally destroyed before possession was even turned over to him on a rule the risk of loss passed when paper title was transferred. Why it is so solicitous of concern for hardships which are only imaginary and which the statute, and common law, properly impose upon sellers retaining both title and legal possession when the risk is realized, is beyond me. If the agreement was to sell two parcels of unimproved property for a total of $1,000,000, and one parcel was condemned by the State before title or possession passed, what unfairness is there in permitting the buyer to specifically enforce that portion of the contract regarding the other parcel and, if the parties cannot agree on the proper abatement of the price, to have it determined judicially? (See Skelly Oil Co. v. Ashmore (Mo.) 365 S.W.2d 582, 589.) I find no substantive difference here.

Notes

1. Does the majority opinion simply apply Flureau v. Thornhill? See supra 962–65. As the court noted, the New York courts have permitted specific performance with abatement even after material destruction. In Burack v. Tollig, 10 N.Y.2d 879, 223 N.Y.S.2d 505, 179 N.E.2d 509 (1961), buyer contracted to buy a residence for $21,000. The house was destroyed by fire prior to the transfer of title or possession. The trial court found the value of the land and remaining improvements to be $15,000 and ordered specific performance upon the payment of that amount. The Appellate Division decided that the buyer was entitled to an abatement based on the actual value of the destroyed house which was found to be $13,500. The Court of Appeals unanimously approved. The buyer paid only $7,500 for the property. Which is the more equitable measure of abatement?

2. Arko Enterprises v. Wood, 185 So.2d 734, 738–39 (Fla.Dist.Ct.App.1966): "[I]t appears to be the law of this state that where land subject to a vendor's lien is appropriated under the power of eminent domain, the condemnation proceeding does not destroy the lien nor does it affect the right of the vendor to seek enforcement of his lien against the vendee for the full amount of the unpaid purchase price.

"The general rule governing the relationship of parties to an executory contract of purchase and sale involving land which is appropriated under the power of eminent domain before the contract is fully executed is stated by Nichols in his work on Eminent Domain [Vol. 2, § 5.21(1) (3rd ed. 1963)] as follows:

> 'Where the vendee of the land under an executory contract is in possession, and having made the payments agreed upon, is entitled to a deed, although he has not yet received one, it is generally held that he is the owner in respect to eminent domain proceedings.
>
> 'A more difficult question arises when a contract has been made for the sale of land at a certain price which is less than its fair market value as subsequently fixed, and the intending purchaser had made an initial payment but before the date fixed for conveyance the land is taken by eminent domain. The contract is, of course, rendered impossible of performance and the purchaser is not entitled to damages from the vendor for his failure to carry out his agreement. It would seem, however, that the purchaser is entitled to compensation from the condemnor for the taking of his equitable interest in the land, and, if the award is greater than the contract price, the vendor should receive the exact amount for which he had agreed to sell the property and the purchaser should be awarded the balance. The reasoning of the court is predicated upon the fact that such executory contract is considered, in effect, an assignment of the award to the purchaser who is considered the equitable owner.' "

See in accord, Hauben v. Harmon, 605 F.2d 920 (5th Cir.1979); Alhambra Redevelopment Agency v. Transamerica Financial Services, 212 Cal.App.3d 1370, 261 Cal.Rptr. 248 (1989).

b. *Specific Performance*

BD INNS v. POOLEY

Court of Appeal, Fourth District, 1990.
218 Cal.App.3d 289, 266 Cal.Rptr. 815.

SONENSHINE, ASSOCIATE JUSTICE. * * * Pooley agreed to buy an 840 unit motel being built by BD Inns. The $6,825,000 purchase price included: a cash down payment of $1,500,000, the assumption of a $4,400,000 first trust deed and a purchase money second trust deed of $925,000. * * * On May 22, Pooley, claiming the deal had been misrepresented, cancelled the sale.

BD Inns filed the underlying complaint seeking specific performance and damages for breach of contract. The court denied breach of contract relief but ordered Pooley, as an individual, to specifically perform the contract. If the purchase price plus interest was not paid within 30 days of the judgment, the property was to be sold and Pooley was to pay BD Inns the difference between the contract price, plus interest, and the ultimate sales price. BD Inns' request for incidental and consequential damages, due to Pooley's breach and delay in performance, was denied.

The major thrust of Pooley's argument is the trial court erred in granting specific performance. He alleges BD Inns failed to prove the essential elements because: * * * (3) there was an adequate remedy at law; and (4) Code of Civil Procedure section 580b bars specific performance. * * *

Former Civil Code section 3307 provides: "The detriment caused by the breach of an agreement to purchase an estate in real property, is deemed to be the excess, if any, of the amount which would have been due to the seller, under the contract, over the value of the property to him." The 1983 amendment expanded the definition of detriment to include consequential damages and interest.

Pooley contends, therefore, Civil Code section 3307 provides BD Inns with an adequate remedy at law. He maintains, at worst, he should have been responsible for the excess, if any, of the amount which would have been due to BD Inns under the contract over the value of the property, plus consequential damages and interest.

California Real Property Remedies and Practice (Cont.Ed.Bar Supp.1989) section 5:28, pages 44–45, notes: "Civil Code § 3307 now provides that on breach of an agreement to sell property a seller can recover consequential damages and interest as well as the excess (if any) of the amount that would have been due the seller under the contract over the value of the property. Consequently, there is some doubt whether a seller could obtain specific performance of a sales agreement if the fair market value of the property equaled [sic] the contract price, because under CC § 3307, the seller can now recover any consequential damages sustained, and thus has an adequate remedy at law." We cannot agree.

In reviewing the legislative history of Civil Code section 3307, it is apparent the Legislature intended to expand the damages available for the breach of a real property contract. It did not, however, intend to eliminate a seller's ability to seek, in the alternative, specific performance.

In Waratah Oil Co. v. Reward Oil Co. (1914) 23 Cal.App. 638, 139 P. 91, the court held a seller cannot be denied specific performance simply because the property could be sold.

BD Inns had more than one remedy available to it. "When [Pooley] repudiated the contract [BD Inns] had a choice of remedies which [it] might pursue. [It] might have sued for specific performance * * * [or it] might have treated the contract as breached and have sued the defendants for damages [it] suffered by reason of the breach." [citation]

Pooley argues Code of Civil Procedure section 580b prohibited the court from ordering specific performance. He maintains Goldsworthy v. Dobbins (1952) 110 Cal.App.2d 802, 243 P.2d 883, relied on by the trial judge, is distinguishable because, here, there is a purchase money second trust deed. *Goldsworthy* addressed a cash sale.

Pooley misunderstands both Code of Civil Procedure section 580b and *Goldsworthy.* "A 'deficiency judgment' is created whenever the seller recovers anything in addition to the property or the fair market value of the security. The purpose of the deficiency prohibition is to require the seller to look to the value of the security, first and foremost, as the actual security for the borrower-purchaser's monetary obligation, and thereby prevent land sales which are unsound because of over-valuation." (Real Estate Law, § 5:32, Part 2, p. 172, fn. omitted.) In other words, Code of Civil Procedure section 580b is inapt where the buyer cannot simultaneously lose the land and suffer personal liability. [citation]

"The land sale contract used as a security device should be distinguished from the land sale contract used as a marketing device. Section 580b applies only to land sale contracts where the *seller retains title to the property as security* for the payment of the purchase price and not to 'sales' in which there is contemplated a transfer of title. Therefore, where the seller transfers title to the buyer under a sale agreement and the buyer subsequently defaults in the payment of the purchase price according to the terms of the agreement, Section 580b would not be applicable to bar an action by the seller to collect the unpaid balance of the purchase price." (5 Augustine & Zarrow, Cal.Real Estate Law and Practice (1989) § 122.62, p. 122–42, fn. omitted, emphasis added.)

The trial judge was correct. If the property is to be sold, Pooley is responsible only for the difference between the sales price and the contract price. Section 580b does not apply because no security interest is to be created. No opportunity for a deficiency exists.

The trial court granted BD Inns' prayer for specific performance but found, as a matter of law, it was not entitled to compensation for operating losses and loss of income. * * *

[T]he injured seller has a choice of remedies. It can prove the contract to purchase has been breached and seek damages occasioned by that breach. In the alternative, a decree of specific performance can be sought. In that case, the goal is to put the parties back in the position they would have been had the contract been timely performed. "Confusion [insofar as what may be awarded in addition to specific performance] has existed because of the informal use of the term 'damages' in connection with such an award, but it is settled that such compensation neither constitutes damages as contemplated in an action for breach of contract, nor implies legal damages."

"In California the compensation which may be awarded incident to a decree of specific performance is not for breach of contract and is not legal damages. The complainant affirms the contract and asks that it be performed. Since the time for performance has passed, the court relates that performance back to that date, by treating the parties as if the change in ownership had taken place at that time. Thus the buyer is entitled to the rents and profits from the time the contract should have been performed, and the seller is entitled to an offset for the interest on the purchase money which he would have received had the contract been performed. The process is more like an accounting between the parties than an assessment of damages. [citations.]" (Hutton v. Gliksberg (1982) 128 Cal.App.3d 240, 248, 180 Cal.Rptr. 141.)

BD Inns seeks recompense for interest lost on the notes, extension fees, and operating losses. But having obtained a decree of specific performance, it is entitled only to be compensated for that to which it would have been entitled had the contract been performed: the net purchase price. Thus, the only accounting to be done here is a calculation of interest, which the trial court properly awarded.

Judgment affirmed.

Notes

1. The buyer's right to specific performance of a land sale contract is well established. The inadequacy of the remedy at law is generally accepted without discussion. California has a statutory presumption to this effect. Cal.Civ.Code § 3387.

2. Occasionally a seller argues that the remedy at law is adequate when the vendee has entered into a contract of resale. See Hazelton v. Miller, 25 App.D.C. 337 (1905), aff'd on other grounds, sub nom. Hazelton v. Sheckells, 202 U.S. 71 (1906). But most courts have rejected this contention. See Justus v. Clelland, 133 Ariz. 381, 651 P.2d 1206 (App.1982); Brenner, Specific Performance of Contracts for the Sale of Land Purchased for Resale or Investment, 24 McGill L.J. 513 (1978).

3. Traditionally, equity courts have ignored the technical categories of common law estates and have found the remedy at law inadequate for agreements to transfer lesser interests in land like leaseholds and easements.

A recent New York decision took a different approach. Van Wagner Advertising Corp. v. S & M Enterprises, 67 N.Y.2d 186, 501 N.Y.S.2d 628, 492 N.E.2d 756 (1986). A contract to lease advertising space on the exterior wall of a building was breached by the buyer of the lessor's interest. The lessee sought specific performance. Ruling that specific performance of real property leases is not granted as a matter of course and that mere physical uniqueness is insufficient to establish the inadequacy of the remedy at law, the court held that the proper test was whether damages were susceptible of calculation with reasonable certainty. It found that this could be done, and it denied specific performance.

4. Does the uniqueness test also falter when the agreement is to buy or sell a condominium unit in a large development project? Buyers have successfully resisted arguments that units are not unique and have specifically enforced contracts. Apparently courts see no reason to treat a condominium unit differently from other realty. See Pruitt v. Graziano, 215 N.J.Super. 330, 521 A.2d 1313 (1987); Giannini v. First National Bank, 136 Ill.App.3d 971, 483 N.E.2d 924 (1985).

Should the result differ where the vendor sues for specific performance? In Centex Homes Corp. v. Boag, 128 N.J.Super. 385, 320 A.2d 194 (1974), the court denied specific performance to the vendor; it ruled that vendor's damages are readily measurable and provided an adequate remedy. In accord, Lakshman v. Vecchione, 102 Ill.App.3d 629, 430 N.E.2d 199 (1981).

5. The seller's right to specific performance is also generally accepted, but the reasoning in support of that result is not entirely persuasive. Compare the rationale supporting the majority rule. Ayres v. Robins, 71 Va. (30 Grat) 105, 115 (1878):

"Now, an action at law by the vendor against the purchaser on an executory contract for sale to recover the purchase money due him, does fall short of what he is entitled to. It does not reach the whole mischief and secure the whole right of the vendor in a perfect manner. He may have his judgment in a court of law, and by execution pursue the personal property of the purchaser. He can go no further. He is entitled under his contract to more perfect relief. He has not only the right to a personal judgment against the purchaser and to subject his personal estate, which he may do in a court of law, but he has the right to subject the land for which the purchase money is owing. He has a *lien* upon it, which a court of law does not recognize and cannot enforce, and which is recognized and can be enforced only in a court of equity. In the latter forum he is entitled to a personal decree, and at the same time and in the same suit to a further decree for the sale of the land, if the personal decree be not satisfied. This is executing the contract fully, according to the agreement and intention of the parties, and this only is giving adequate relief, doing complete justice in the case."

See also Derwell Co. v. Apic, Inc., 278 A.2d 338 (Del.Ch.1971) (legal remedy of seller inadequate because "any award of money damages would be speculative at best and, in all probability, would not provide adequate compensation"); Shuptrine v. Quinn, 597 S.W.2d 728 (Tenn.1979) (specific performance granted to a seller who planned to use the cash realized from the sale of a residence to further his business interests). The Restatement (Second) of Contracts § 360 comment (e) (1981), retains the rule allowing specific performance to the nonbreaching seller.

6. With respect to the seller's right to foreclose a vendor's lien mentioned in *Ayres*, supra, the court in Hage v. Westgate Square Commercial, 598 S.W.2d 709, 713 (Tex.Civ.App.1980) said:

"A suit by the vendor of land for recovery of the purchase money and to foreclose the vendor's lien is not strictly a suit for specific performance. Nevertheless, it is settled that in a suit by the vendor for specific performance of a contract for the sale of land such relief may be granted in his favor, 'though the relief actually obtained by him is usually only a recovery of the purchase money, and differs from the suit to enforce a vendor's lien in the fact that the judgment is for the recovery of the money generally, and not out of the land itself as a special fund.' Because the decree of specific performance vests title in the vendee, the law implies an equitable lien on the land in favor of the vendor for the purchase money which he may foreclose."

The Virginia legislature abolished the implied vendor's lien. Va.Code § 55–53 (1986).

7. Professor Schwartz argues in favor of making specific performance more readily available. Schwartz, The Case for Specific Performance, 89 Yale L.J. 271 (1979).

On the other hand, Professor Yorio says, "[T]he case for giving the seller an automatic right to specific performance is weak. Since the seller has decided to part with the property in dispute, personal or subjective motives do not complicate the measurement of damages. Assuming that the property can be resold at the market price, an award of damages measured by the difference between the contract and market price fully compensates the seller for the loss caused by the breach. Specific performance may be proper in certain circumstances, such as when valuing or reselling the property in dispute is difficult or when the seller has an immediate need for liquidity, but none of these factors supports a universal rule entitling the seller to specific relief." E. Yorio, Contract Enforcement: Specific Performance and Injunctions § 10.3.1 (1989) (citations deleted).

8. May the parties agree to exclude specific performance as a remedy for breach of a land sale contract? In Greenstein v. Greenbrook, Ltd., 413 So.2d 842 (Fla.Dist.Ct.App.1982), the court upheld the restriction.

9. Petry v. Tanglwood Lakes, Inc., 514 Pa. 51, 60, 522 A.2d 1053, 1057 (1987). When plaintiff purchased her lot, it abutted unconstructed, but promised, Lake Briarwood. After the developer was reorganized in bankruptcy, a group of lot owners settled litigation with the developer, agreeing to substitute a recreational area for the lake.

Plaintiff sued the developer seeking damages, specific performance of the agreement to construct the lake, and an injunction forbidding performance of the settlement agreement. The Pennsylvania Supreme Court affirmed the trial judge's order transferring the case to law because damages were an adequate remedy.

"Those factors which outweigh Appellant's interest in the uniqueness or special value of having Lake Briarwood built include: the ability to calculate or ascertain Appellant's money damages; the fact that enforcing an affirmative covenant or contract imposes a supervisory burden on the trial court; the fact that purchasing in reliance on an affirmative undertaking involves greater risk than purchasing in reliance on a negative covenant or promise; and the fact that granting Appellant specific performance would adversely affect the rights of numerous other lot owners and the Community Association at large.

"This Court has repeatedly held that a decree of specific performance is a matter of grace and not of right, [citations] and that the exercise of the power to grant specific performance is discretionary [citation]. Based on a balancing of the equities set forth above, we find that no abuse of discretion occurred here in transferring this matter to the law side of the trial court based on the pleadings and oral argument."

Justice Larsen dissented: "This case is not about the value of a piece of property as it currently exists and the value of that same property if Briarwood Lake had been constructed. The questions raised here are much broader. They deal with life style values not cash values. The majority's acceptance of the theory that the failure to build the lake merely involves a diminution in the value of appellant's property fails to give due consideration to the very unique quality of the property as a lake front lot. Indeed, this unique feature is what attracts prospective owners and sells the lots." Petry v. Tanglwood Lakes, Inc., 514 Pa. 51, 61, 522 A.2d 1053, 1058 (1987).

c. *Prerequisites for Specific Performance*

In order to specifically enforce a land sale contract, the party seeking the remedy must tender to the other party whatever is required by the contract. The purchaser must tender the amount due and the vendor the appropriate instrument to transfer the interest agreed to be sold. If the contract contains a "time is of the essence" clause, a failure to tender on that date relieves the other party from contractual obligations. Wilson v. Klein, 715 S.W.2d 814 (Tex.App.1986).

Time of the Essence in Equity. As the court pointed out in Limpus v. Armstrong, 3 Mass.App.Ct. 19, 322 N.E.2d 187 (1975), however, time is not of the essence unless made so by express stipulation of the parties or is implied from the circumstances of a particular transaction. This represents the prevailing view in equity that mere delay in performance is not a substantial breach of the contract. In Cook v. Rezek, 89 S.D. 667, 237 N.W.2d 18 (1975), a seventeen-day delay by a buyer in making a $500 down payment was considered immaterial. On the other hand, the New York Court of Appeals held that the seller's failure to provide a recordable mortgage "estoppel certificate" on the closing date as required by the contract was a material breach that excused further performance by the buyer. Grace v. Nappa, 46 N.Y.2d 560, 415 N.Y.S.2d 793, 389 N.E.2d 107 (1979).

Compare the related problem of the optionee who fails to exercise the option within the agreed upon time. Time is usually regarded as of the essence; but where the delay is slight and defendant does not change position, specific performance may be granted where great harm to the optionee cannot otherwise be avoided. See Sosanie v. Pernetti Holding Corp., 115 N.J.Super. 409, 279 A.2d 904 (1971). Where the optionee does not seek to extend the time to exercise the option, but seeks instead to avoid forfeiture of the option for failure to tender an annual payment promptly, time is not regarded as of the essence and relief may be granted. See Holiday Inns of America, Inc. v. Knight, 70 Cal.2d 327, 74 Cal.Rptr. 722, 450 P.2d 42 (1969); Curley v. Mobil Oil Corp., 860 F.2d 1129 (1st Cir.1988).

HENDERSON v. FISHER

California Court of Appeals, First District, 1965.
236 Cal.App.2d 468, 46 Cal.Rptr. 173.

MOLINARI, JUSTICE. Plaintiffs appeal from a judgment entered after a trial by the court awarding them $381.85 on a quantum meruit basis but refusing to grant specific performance of a written contract entered into between plaintiffs and decedent, Marion D. Baker. The sole issue presented on appeal is whether plaintiffs are entitled to specific performance of the subject agreement. We have concluded that they are and that the trial court erred in refusing to grant plaintiffs relief in this form.

On August 11, 1959, plaintiffs and decedent entered into a written contract which provided as follows:

> "Whereas, the first party, Marion D. Baker, is 86 years of age and blind and is in need of constant care, the parties of the second part agree to move into the home of Mr. Baker at 717 College Street in the city of Healdsburg, state of California, and to furnish all food necessary or reasonably required by Mr. Baker; and to do all laundry work required by him and to keep the house clean and in good repair and to water the trees and shrubbery and to keep the premises in good conditions as long as Mr. Baker lives.
>
> "It is further agreed between the said parties that Mr. Baker shall pay the water and light bills and one-half of the gas bills, and that the second parties shall pay the telephone bills and the other half of the gas bills. It is also agreed that Mr. Baker shall pay for any new clothing that he may require, but that the second parties shall clean and repair said clothing when necessary.
>
> "It is further agreed that Mr. Baker shall execute and deliver a deed of his interest in the real property, including his home and furniture at 717 College

Street in Healdsburg, California, to the second parties, reserving to himself a life estate in the said property.

"It is further agreed between the parties hereto, that Mr. Baker shall pay for all taxes and insurance on the said property which may become due as long as he lives."

The factual background surrounding the making of this contract was as follows: For about 7 years prior to 1959 plaintiffs had been friends of decedent and his wife. They often referred to the Bakers as Grandma and Grandpa, and they had on numerous occasions helped the Bakers by performing various household chores for them. On July 24, 1959 Mrs. Baker died. About a week after her death and because Mr. Baker, who was blind and 86 years old, could not be left alone, plaintiffs moved into the Baker home. On August 11, 1959, at Baker's request, his attorney, Mr. Sayre, drew up the subject agreement. At this time Baker was in good health. However, 18 days after the execution of this agreement, Baker died. During this 18-day period plaintiffs performed the services set forth in the agreement. Baker did not, however, during this period execute the deed called for in the contract.

Based on these facts, plaintiffs on May 13, 1960 filed a creditor's claim in decedent's estate, demanding specific performance of the agreement or in the alternative $5,000, the reasonable value of the real and personal property which was the subject matter of the contract. This claim was rejected by defendant, the administratrix of decedent's estate. Plaintiffs then brought this action seeking specific performance or $5,000 as the value of the property in question, and alternatively $5,000 as the reasonable value of the services performed and the personal property supplied by them to decedent. The trial court in its findings of fact and conclusions of law determined that the subject agreement "is one not properly the subject of an action for specific performance against the estate of Marion D. Baker and is therefore not enforceable by plaintiffs," but that plaintiffs were entitled to $381.85 on a quantum meruit basis, this being the amount which it determined as the value of the services and supplies which plaintiffs furnished to decedent during his lifetime.

* * * In its opinion the trial court stressed the fact that because the agreement indicated that decedent was to convey to plaintiffs a remainder interest in the real and personal property, reserving a life estate for himself, it was apparent that the transfer was to be made during the lifetime of decedent; that as such, the agreement lacked "the mutuality, the certainty and the fairness and adequacy of consideration required to have permitted its specific performance during Baker's lifetime"; and that "so far as the attempt to enforce it specifically against his estate is concerned it is within the class of cases that afford an adequate remedy at law upon quantum meruit and are not specifically enforceable against the estate of the deceased promisor."

Beginning with some general principles concerning specific performance, we note that the type of action with which we are involved in the instant case is not truly one for specific performance since Baker, who is now deceased, cannot be compelled to execute the promised conveyance. However, if it is determined that plaintiffs are entitled to the property which Baker promised to convey to them, then the court may declare a constructive trust upon this property in the hands of those who have succeeded to the estate. This is, in effect, the equivalent of specific performance and is sometimes termed "quasi-specific performance."

Although the relief in a "quasi-specific performance" action differs from that in the traditional specific performance action the requisites for relief are identical. They are as follows: The plaintiff must show that his remedy at law is inadequate; the contract must be just and reasonable and must be supported by adequate consideration; there must be a mutuality of remedies, that is, the contract must be subject to specific performance by both of the contracting parties; the terms of the contract must be sufficiently definite for the court to know what to enforce; and the performance which the court is asked to compel must be substantially identical to that promised in the contract. (Civ.Code, §§ 3384, 3386, 3390, 3391.)

Proceeding to discuss each of these basic requirements as they specifically apply to the contract before us, we note, first, as to the inadequacy of plaintiffs' remedy at law, it is the general rule that in the case of a contract for the transfer of an interest in land it is presumed that damages would not adequately compensate for the breach. This presumption is based on the historic treatment of land as unique. * * *

Where, as in the instant action, only part of the subject matter of the contract consists of land, specific performance of the whole of the contract may be decreed even though compensation in money would be an adequate remedy for the promisor's failure to perform that part of the contract calling for the transfer of ordinary chattels.

As applied to the instant case, therefore, we conclude that the contract between plaintiffs and decedent being one involving the transfer of land, plaintiffs' remedy at law is inadequate. The trial court's statement in its opinion that this contract "is within the class of cases that afford an adequate remedy at law upon quantum meruit" is not a correct articulation of the principle involved. The question, in determining the adequacy of plaintiffs' remedy at law, is not whether they have some remedy at law apart from the contract, but whether their remedy at law upon the contract itself, that is, for damages, is sufficient. Accordingly, the fact that plaintiffs are entitled at law to reimbursement upon a quantum meruit theory for the services and supplies which they furnished decedent is not dispositive of the issue of whether their remedy at law upon the contract which they entered into with decedent is adequate.

The second requirement for the specific enforcement of a contract is that the consideration be adequate. (§ 3391, subd. 1.) The proper time for testing the adequacy of consideration is as of the formation of the contract. And the proper test to apply in determining adequacy of consideration in a contract involving the transfer of property is not whether the promisor received the highest price obtainable for his property, but whether the price he received is fair and reasonable under the circumstances. Moreover, in addition to the value of the property to be conveyed, the court may consider such factors as the relationship of the parties, their friendship, love, affection, and regard for each other, and the object to be obtained by the contract.

In the instant action, the trial court made no specific finding as to adequacy of consideration except insofar as it found that "the services and expenses laid out by plaintiffs for Marion D. Baker during his lifetime were not and are not worth the full value of the aforedescribed real property and personal property, nor any substantial part thereof." While the question of adequacy of consideration is generally considered as a question of fact, the determination of the trial court being final unless totally unsupported by the evidence, it appears in the instant case that the trial court erroneously determined this question as of the date of trial rather than as of the date of execution of the contract. Accordingly, we are not bound by such determination. We are satisfied, moreover, that the evidence adduced at the trial can support no other conclusion than that decedent's promise to convey his property to plaintiffs was amply supported by consideration. At the time the contract was entered into Baker was in good health and the duration of his life was uncertain. Moreover, he was in great need for plaintiffs' services as he did not want to go to an "old folks" home. Also the fact that decedent had a very warm and longstanding friendship with plaintiffs must be taken into consideration. And finally, we note that before entering into this contract with plaintiffs, Baker called a family conference and obtained the approval of his relatives regarding his proposed action. This being the state of the evidence on the issue of the adequacy of consideration when viewed at the time of formation of the contract, we are of the opinion that the subject contract was fair and reasonable as to Baker and that it was supported by adequate consideration. The fact that Baker died within a short time after entering into the contract so that plaintiffs' services were of short duration cannot alter this conclusion, since, as we have indicated, adequacy of consideration is determined as of the date of execution of the contract without regard to subsequent events. * * *

Adverting to the question of mutuality of remedies we first note the applicable rule as stated in section 3386 as follows: "Neither party to an obligation can be compelled specifically to perform it, unless the other party thereto has performed, or is compellable specifically to perform, everything to which the former is entitled under the same obligation, either completely or nearly so, together with full compensation for any want of entire performance." In contracts involving the performance of personal services by one of the contracting parties, it is clear that at the inception of the contract specific performance cannot be decreed against this party because of the rule of long standing that a person cannot be compelled to perform personal services. (§ 3390, Cooper v. Pena, 21 Cal. 403, 412.) Accordingly, such a contract, at its inception, lacks mutuality of remedies and is, therefore, not specifically enforceable against the other party. The prevailing rule, and that adopted in California in section 3386, is, however, that such contracts which lack mutuality in their inception may be specifically enforced after the want of mutuality is removed by the performance by one party of his obligation under the contract. * * *

It is clear from the foregoing cases that the appropriate time for determining whether the subject contract lacks mutuality is as of the time its enforcement is sought, and not as of its execution. In the present case, although the trial court made no specific finding or conclusion of law on the issue of mutuality, it may be implied from its other findings that it determined that there was no mutuality of remedy. This is apparent from the trial court's opinion wherein it is stated that the contract "is lacking in the mutuality * * * required to have permitted its specific performance during Baker's lifetime * * *." It is also apparent, however, that in making its determination as to mutuality the court did so on the basis of the mutuality of obligations which existed between plaintiffs and Baker while the latter was still alive. As we have indicated, the trial court should, instead, have considered the problem of mutuality as of the date at which plaintiffs sought enforcement of the contract, that is, after Baker's death. Had the court done so, it is clear that the defense of lack of mutuality would not have been valid since plaintiffs had at this time fully performed their obligation to take care of Baker during his lifetime.

With respect to the requirement for specific performance that the subject contract be certain in its terms, defendant contends that the contract which plaintiffs seek to enforce is uncertain for the reason that it does not indicate a time for performance by Baker. * * *

It is only where the uncertainty or incompleteness of a contract prevents the court from knowing what to enforce that the defense of uncertainty has rationality. No such doubt exists in the instant case where the court was asked to impress a constructive trust in favor of plaintiffs based on a contract which was to be performed at some time during the life of a person who is now deceased and obviously can no longer perform his promise.

The trial court's opinion indicates that the trial judge was persuaded in his decision by the fact that the promise which Baker made required him to execute a deed in favor of plaintiffs, reserving himself a life estate in the subject property. The trial court therein concluded that "The reservation of a life estate would be wholly inconsistent with any intent that his part of the contract would not be performable until on or after his death." While it is clearly the law that a court must adhere to the terms of the contract in decreeing specific performance, we are of the opinion that a decree of quasi-specific performance in the instant case is not violative of any equitable principles and is, in fact, proper in light of the willingness of courts to allow this result in analogous cases. We refer to the many cases * * * which have granted relief in the form of quasi-specific performance where the breached promise was one to convey certain property by will. Quite clearly in these cases the courts in granting equitable relief are deviating from the precise terms of the contract which invariably require the promisor-decedent to transform his promise into specific provisions of a will during his lifetime. However, although the promisor is obviously unable to perform the contract as it was made, the courts are not deterred by this fact and are willing in proper cases to grant relief, thereby securing to the injured party the performance which he would have received had the contract been performed by the promisor during his lifetime. Similarly, in those cases in which the decedent failed during his lifetime to perform his promise to adopt the promisee, courts of equity frequently allow the promisee to inherit from the promisor as though the latter had in fact performed his promise. In both types of cases the promise of which enforcement is sought is clearly one requiring the promisor to perform some act during his lifetime. Nonetheless, courts of equity will in proper circumstances grant relief in the form of quasi-specific performance, thereby deviating from the exact terms of the decedent's promise.

[Decree for plaintiff.]

Notes on Mutuality

1. In 1969 California Civil Code § 3386 was amended to read as follows:

§ 3386. Mutuality of Remedy

Notwithstanding that the agreed counter performance is not or would not have been specifically enforceable, specific performance may be compelled if:

(a) Specific performance would otherwise be an appropriate remedy; and

(b) The agreed counter performance has been substantially performed or its concurrent or future performance is assured or, if the court deems necessary, can be secured to the satisfaction of the court.

See Bleecher v. Conte, 29 Cal.3d 345, 173 Cal.Rptr. 278, 626 P.2d 1051 (1981).

2. *Mutuality of Remedy Applied.* Burger Chef Systems, Inc. v. Burger Chef of Florida, Inc., 317 So.2d 795, 796–98 (Fla.Dist.Ct.App.1975):

"This is an appeal by Burger Chef Systems (Franchisor) from an injunction preventing it from terminating its July 14th, 1966, franchise agreement with Burger Chef of Florida, Inc. (Franchisee). The injunction was entered upon a request by Franchisor for a declaratory judgment defining its right to terminate under the agreement. * * *

"We reverse this action of the trial court. The injunction, requiring as it does the continued performance of Franchisor, is essentially a grant of specific performance to Franchisee. * * *

"We are aware of the individual characteristics of a franchise; the personal efforts and commitment on the part of a Franchisee to market the Franchisor's products, the consideration given by Franchisee for the exclusive right to market Franchisor's product and the singular personal service performed by a Franchisee in establishing the product of a Franchisor. Nonetheless, the rules of specific performance must govern, and it is improper to—in effect—grant this Franchisee a decree of specific performance. Mutuality of obligation and remedy must exist for a specific performance suit to succeed. [citation] "Franchisee here is bound by the agreement to perform certain personal services to Franchisor. [Such as store visits and assistance, attendance at training programs, reporting, etc.] Personal services are not subject to a suit for specific performance. * * * As a result, the order granting, as it does, specific performance to Franchisee, is in error—as no like order could be had for Franchisor.

"Franchisee must seek his damages at law should Franchisor breach. We find that remedy of damages is adequate to compensate Franchisee, should Franchisor breach. The measure of damages would depend upon a jury evaluation of what would be a reasonable time for the contract duration."

The Florida courts have adhered to this position. See Florida Jai Alai, Inc. v. Southern Catering Services Inc., 388 So.2d 1076 (Fla.Dist.Ct.App.1980); Allington Towers North, Inc. v. Rubin, 400 So.2d 86 (Fla.Dist.Ct.App.1981).

3. *The Current "Mutuality" Rule.* Van v. Fox, 278 Or. 439, 440–42, 451–52, 564 P.2d 695, 696–97, 701–02 (1977):

"This is a suit for specific performance of an agreement to develop certain real property as a joint venture by the plaintiffs and the defendants. The trial court entered a decree granting specific performance. Defendants appeal from that decree and contend that the joint venture agreement [embodied in a letter of intent] should not be specifically enforced on the grounds that its terms are too uncertain, that there is a lack of mutuality of remedy, [and] that plaintiffs no longer have the financial ability to perform their part of the agreement * * *.

"Essentially, the letter of intent provides that plaintiffs and defendants were to form a joint venture for the purpose of developing approximately eight acres of riverfront property in the city of Eugene as a Planned Unit Development. This development project required both a zone change and approval of the specific P.U.D. plans before the actual development could begin. Under the terms of the agreement, plaintiffs Van and Safley were to secure the necessary zone change and approval of the P.U.D. plans. Defendants, in turn, put up $19,000 (substantially all of the down payment on the property involved), took legal title to the land, and agreed to make the necessary payments on the property until final approval of the P.U.D. plans. Plaintiff Irving contributed the remainder of the down payment by waiving his commission on the sale. The original purchase price of the property was approximately $83,000.

"The letter of intent was signed on July 26, 1974. At that time plaintiffs had already begun taking the necessary steps toward obtaining the zone change and eventual P.U.D. approval. Architects and engineers were employed, alternative designs were explored, preliminary plans were drawn up, consultations were had with the planning commission staff, and public hearings were held before both the planning commission and the city council. Plaintiffs also purchased two small adjacent parcels for $22,000 and added them to the project at the request of the planning commission. By December, a zone change had been granted, conditioned upon final approval of the P.U.D., and the initial stage of the approval process, pre-preliminary approval, had been successfully accomplished. As a result, the market value of the property had been greatly enhanced. * * *

"[W]e * * * hold that the doctrine of mutuality of remedy does not bar a decree of specific performance. In Paullus v. Yarbrough et ux., 219 Or. 611, 347 P.2d 620, we stated that the most workable doctrine of mutuality was that set forth in 5 Williston on Contracts 4022–023, § 1440 (rev. ed. 1937) (now 11 Williston on Contracts 936–37, § 1440 (3d ed. 1968)), and we quoted from that authority as follows:

> Where the contract is executory on both sides, the court may still give specific performance if it is satisfied that the person seeking relief will continue to perform. This may be shown by past conduct; or the person seeking specific performance may have such a strong economic interest in the carrying out of the contract by reason of extensive investment of his funds and labor that default on his part is highly improbable.'

"We feel that there was sufficient evidence in this case to afford reasonable assurance that plaintiffs will continue with the P.U.D. approval process and with the further performance of the joint venture agreement. Both the past conduct of plaintiffs under the agreement and their testimony at trial indicate that they stand ready, willing and able to continue with the joint venture. It is also clear that plaintiffs only hope to profit by this venture and to recoup their past efforts and expenses lies in their continued performance of the contract.

"Defendants also contend that plaintiffs' present financial difficulties may prevent them from obtaining sufficient financing to enable them to purchase the property from defendants and to proceed with further development and construction once the P.U.D. approval process is completed. However, the time for performance of these obligations has not yet arrived, and plaintiffs' testimony indicates that they will have sufficient personal assets and adequate borrowing power to finance their future obligations. It should also be noted that at this time plaintiffs are asking only that they be allowed to continue with their own efforts in performing the contract. This will not place any undue hardship on defendants, for if plaintiffs are eventually financially unable to complete their remaining obligations, the defendant will enjoy the benefits of plaintiffs' efforts during the interim."

In accord, Pallas v. Black, 226 Neb. 728, 414 N.W.2d 805 (1987); Rohlfing v. Tomorrow Realty & Auction Co., 528 So.2d 463 (Fla.Dist.Ct.App.1988).

4. The defense of lack of mutuality is frequently asserted where the contract for which specific enforcement is sought provides for termination by one party but

not the other. Such contracts are specifically enforced in favor of the party with power to cancel where the court is convinced for economic reasons that there is a high probability that performance of the contract will be completed. See Plastray Corp. v. Cole, 324 Mich. 433, 37 N.W.2d 162 (1949).

HOMART DEVELOPMENT CO. v. W.T. SIGMAN

United States Court of Appeals.
Eleventh Circuit, 1989.
868 F.2d 1556.

HILL, CIRCUIT JUDGE. * * * Homart, a Delaware corporation registered to do business in Georgia, purchases and develops land for shopping malls and office complexes. Mr. Sigman, a resident of Georgia, owns a parcel of approximately 75 acres of real property located in Rockdale County, Georgia. Several years ago, Homart decided to pursue the development of several regional shopping malls in the Atlanta market. Homart considered Mr. Sigman's property to be an ideal location for a regional mall in the eastern metropolitan area. On August 30, 1983, Homart and Mr. Sigman completed negotiations and entered into a conditional option contract wherein Mr. Sigman granted Homart an option to purchase his property for $1,125,000 until June 30, 1986.

In June, 1986, although negotiations for a one-year extension of the option failed, the parties agreed to extend the option through the next month. On July 28, 1986, Homart attempted to exercise its conditional option. Proper notice of the time, date, and place of closing was given to Mr. Sigman. Homart appeared at the closing with all necessary documentation and purchase proceeds, but neither Mr. Sigman nor his attorney attended to close the purchase.

Two months later, Homart filed this suit against Mr. Sigman. In four counts, Homart sought specific performance of the conditional option contract, actual and consequential damages for alleged breach of contract if specific performance were not granted, attorneys' fees, or, alternatively, recovery in *quantum meruit*. Mr. Sigman answered the complaint, counterclaimed, and filed a motion for judgment on the pleadings regarding plaintiff's claims. * * *

A federal magistrate considered the parties' various motions and recommended, in part, that defendant Sigman's motion for judgment on the pleadings be granted with respect to plaintiff's action for specific performance, actual and consequential damages, and attorneys' fees. After a *de novo* review, the district court, declaring that it was not persuaded by Homart's objections, entered an order approving and adopting the magistrate's report and recommendation. * * *

Initially, we shall review the district court's decision that the terms of the conditional option contract were not sufficiently definite to support either a claim for specific performance, or alternatively, a claim for actual and consequential damages for breach of contract.

As the district court correctly stated, the Supreme Court of Georgia has established the following rule requiring certainty of terms before a court will decree the specific performance of a contract:

> "A court of equity will not decree the specific performance of a contract for the sale of land unless there is a definite and specific statement of the terms of the contract. The requirement of certainty extends not only to the subject matter

and purpose of the contract, but also to the parties, consideration, and even the time and place of performance, where these are essential. Its terms must be such that neither party can reasonably misunderstand them. It would be inequitable to carry a contract into effect where the court is left to ascertain the intention of the parties by mere guess or conjecture, because it might be guilty of erroneously decreeing what the parties never intended or contemplated."

Green v. Zaring, 222 Ga. 195, 149 S.E.2d 115, 117–118 (1966); Williams v. Manchester Building Supply Co., 213 Ga. 99, 97 S.E.2d 129 (1957). The definite and specific statement of terms must be expressed by the writing itself or determined through use of a "key," a word or phrase in the writing referring to material that will make the terms definite. Beller & Gould v. Lisenby, 246 Ga. 15, 268 S.E.2d 611 (1980).

The district court decided that the terms of two of the "Additional Provisions" describing conditions to the option contract were not sufficiently definite to support a specific performance claim. The two provisions, paragraphs C.1 and C.2, read as follows:

"C.1. *Development Intent.* Purchaser agrees that it will not exercise the Option unless it has at the time of such exercise a reasonable intent to develop the Property.

"C.2. *Relocation of Residence.* After exercising the Option, Purchaser shall, at Purchaser's election either (i) move Seller's residence now located on the Property up to two miles and put it in the same operational and functional condition as it exists just prior to the time of the move, provided, however, that Seller's residence shall not be moved sooner than two (2) years after the Date of this Contract and not later than six months following beginning of construction, or, (ii) pay to the Seller the appraised value of the building (excluding land) at the time in question, provided, however, that if the appraised value is paid, Seller may within thirty (30) days after such payment remove all personal property, and appliances (which items shall not be included in appraised value)."

The district court was correct in its determination that the terms of paragraph C.1 are too indefinite, thereby precluding a decree of specific performance of the conditional option contract. As the district court recognized, there are several descriptive deficiencies in the terms of paragraph C.1. First, paragraph C.1 fails to describe the type or scope of development contemplated by the parties. In Green v. Zaring, the Supreme Court of Georgia found a contract too vague to enforce where the parties had agreed to form a corporation to develop the defendant's property "with apartment buildings and related structures." Nothing in the contract indicated what the parties intended regarding the number, size, design, or quality of the buildings and the court could not determine what the parties envisioned. In the present case, paragraph C.1 does not describe the development contemplated or furnish a key that leads to a certain description of the expected development. Appellant contends that the parties never intended that paragraph C.1 describe the type or scope of development to be pursued. Rather, the appellant maintains that the parties viewed paragraph C.1 as an anti-speculation clause insuring that Homart would not simply hold onto the land as an investment. This interpretation is not clearly stated in paragraph C.1 and no key exists that would lead to a certain illustration of this suggested meaning. In fact, appellant's urging that paragraph C.1 was meant as an anti-speculation clause only supports the conclusion that the paragraph is vague and indefinite. Second, C.1 leaves uncertain whether the corporate purchaser's state of mind, required to have a "reasonable intent" to develop, is to be objectively demonstrated, or whether subjective intent is sufficient. If the purchaser's intent is to be objectively demonstrated, paragraph C.1 fails to identify, either through its language or through a key, the legal entity that would determine whether or not Homart possesses the requisite intent to develop at the time of the exercise of the option. That is, it is unclear whether the decision is to be made by an expert real estate developer, an arbitration panel, a court of competent jurisdiction, or some other entity.

Appellant concedes that the terms of paragraph C.2 are not sufficiently certain to be enforced. Rather, it argues that C.2 is severable from the option contract. Because the unenforceability of paragraph C.1 alone provides sufficient grounds to preclude a decree that the contract be specifically performed, we need not discuss whether the terms of paragraph C.2 are sufficiently definite to be enforced or whether the paragraph is severable.

In Count II of its complaint, Homart alleged that it would suffer actual and consequential damages if specific performance were not granted. Georgia case law holds that a contract whose terms are too indefinite and unclear to state a cause of action for specific performance cannot support an alternative cause of action for damages. * * *

[Affirmed.]

Notes

1. Brownlee v. Ertzos, 289 Minn. 83, 182 N.W.2d 697 (1970). The court ruled against specific performance because of uncertainty about the times of payment and the nature of certain repairs the contract required; but it granted damages for the breach. Does it make sense to award damages for breach of a contract too uncertain to specifically enforce? Is the Georgia rule disallowing damages preferable?

2. In Ammerman v. City Stores Co., 394 F.2d 950 (D.C.Cir.1968), the court held that a contract could be specifically enforced even though some terms were subject to further negotiation. Of course a decree of specific performance may be facilitated if the court leans toward the defendant's interpretation of the intent of the "uncertain" language.

"The problems of any consequence which seemed to bother defendants at the time of trial were, in our opinion, resolved in favor of defendants by the decree of court." Howard v. Thomas, 270 Or. 6, 13, 526 P.2d 552, 555 (1974).

3. Reed v. Alvey, 610 P.2d 1374 (Utah 1980). The contract not only provided payment on "terms to be arranged," but also described the subject matter as "corner of Hillview and Ninth East." The court found sufficient detail to support specific performance. The general rule is that an offer by the buyer to pay the full purchase price in cash cures any formal defects in the written terms of payment. Cook v. Eilers, 586 S.W.2d 42 (Mo.App.1979).

Compare Living Christ Church, Inc. v. Jones, 734 S.W.2d 417 (Tex.App.1987). The contract referred to the subject matter as the "Broadmoor Garage" and the "Fernald Property." In denying specific performance, the court ruled that the terms were too uncertain in describing the location and ownership of the property.

4. The dissenting opinion in Genest v. John Glenn Corp., 298 Or. 723, 751–52, 696 P.2d 1058, 1075 (1985), explains the decisions: "The general theme that runs

through the cases and authorities is [that] a court cannot make a contract for the parties. The court cannot supply essential or material terms, but can fill in the gaps in a valid contract with subordinate or non-essential terms." Is this a helpful analysis of the problem?

Slip

MARKS v. GATES

United States Court of Appeals, Ninth Circuit, 1907.
154 F. 481.

[Plaintiff sought specific performance of a contract in which defendant had agreed to convey to plaintiff a twenty percent interest in all property defendant acquired in Alaska. The trial court dismissed plaintiff's complaint on the ground that the contract was inequitable.]

GILBERT, CIRCUIT JUDGE. * * * The contract in the present case had, at the time when it was made, no reference to any property then owned by the contracting parties, or even to property then in existence. It did not obligate the appellee, Gates, ever to go to Alaska or to acquire property there. It bound him during his lifetime to transfer to the appellant a one-fifth interest in all property of every description that he might acquire in Alaska by whatever means, whether by location, purchase, devise, gift, or inheritance—property of which neither party could know even approximately the value. It was a bargain made in the dark. The complaint is silent as to the means whereby the property therein described was obtained by Gates. It alleges that its value is more than $750,000. For aught that appears in the complaint to the contrary, the appellee, Gates, purchased this property and paid therefor its full value. The appellant, for the payment of $1,000 in cash and the cancellation of a debt of $11,225, which may or may not have been valid or collectible, now comes into a court of equity and asks the court to decree that the appellee, Gates, transfer to him property of the value of more than $150,000. If he now has the right to such relief, it follows that he may hereafter sustain suits to acquire a like interest in all property of every nature and description which Gates may at any time obtain in Alaska, and that such right will end only with the life of Gates. Courts of equity have often decreed specific performance where the consideration was inadequate, and it may be said in general that mere inadequacy of consideration is not of itself ground for withholding specific performance unless it is so gross as to render the contract unconscionable. But where the consideration is so grossly inadequate as it is in the present case, and the contract is made without any knowledge at the time of its making on the part of either of the parties thereto of the nature of the property to be affected thereby, or of its value, no equitable principle is violated if specific performance is denied, and the parties are left to their legal remedies, if any they have. In Day v. Newman, 10 Ves.Jr. 300, Lord Alvanley refused to enforce the specific performance of an agreement for the sale for £20,000 of an estate worth only £10,000. There was no actual fraud in the case, but the inadequacy was so great that the court would not enforce it. In Earl of Chesterfield v. Jansen, 2 Ves.Sr. 125, Lord Hardwicke declared unconscionable a contract whereby an expectant heir, in consideration of £5,000, obligated himself to pay £10,000 out of his grandmother's estate if he survived her, but was to pay nothing if she survived him. In Mississippi & Missouri R.R. Co. v. Cromwell, 91 U.S. 643, Mr. Justice Bradley said:

"He comes into court with a very bad grace when he asks to use its extraordinary power to put him possession of $30,000 worth of stock for which he paid only $50. The court is not bound to shut its eyes to the evident character of the transaction. It will never lend its aid to carry out an unconscionable bargain, but will leave the party to his remedy at law."

The facts presented in the complaint are not such as to entitle the court to retain the case for the assessment of such damages as the appellant may have sustained for breach of the contract. A court of equity will not grant pecuniary compensation in lieu of specific performance unless the case presented is one for equitable interposition such as would entitle the plaintiff to performance but for intervening facts, such as the destruction of the property, the conveyance of the same to an innocent third person, or the refusal of the vendor's wife to join in a conveyance. [citation]

The decree of the court below is affirmed.

Notes

1. Is *Marks* consistent with the principles of "adequacy of consideration" applied in Henderson v. Fisher, supra, p. 1012?

2. Assume, as was likely, that Marks v. Gates was a simple "grubstake" case and the pre-existing debts were advances to the prospector for ventures that yielded no gold. In Embola v. Tuppela, 127 Wash. 285, 220 P. 789 (1923), a similar plaintiff recovered damages for breach of contract. In Sigel v. McEvoy, 101 Nev. 623, 707 P.2d 1145 (1985), plaintiff had backed defendant in a poker series in return for twenty percent of any winnings. The court rejected the defense that would have barred a suit on an illegal gambling debt and allowed the suit to proceed on the theory that the business arrangement was lawful.

Is a life insurance policy for $1,000,000 issued on an initial premium of $2,000 inequitable when the insured is killed the next day?

3. Compare Peck v. Judd, 7 Utah 2d 420, 427–28, 326 P.2d 712, 717 (1958). In enforcing the forfeiture provisions of a real estate contract after buyer's breach the court said:

"Further than to determine if enforcement of the contract results in gross inequity, and unless and until the enforcement would be highly unconscionable, we should recognize and honor the right of persons to contract freely and to make real and genuine mistakes when the dealings are at arms' length. It will be conceded, we think, that where a seller seeks not only his pound of flesh but likewise a goodly supply of blood he should not be indulged.

"Nor should we fail to observe how many purchasers have made most advantageous bargains and when the contracts have run have secured property three times what the poor sellers received under their contracts. Should not equity, if we are going paternalistic, under the same tokens say to such a buyer, 'You can't do this to the poor seller—the property to which he still holds title is now worth two or three times what you are paying him and that is unconscionable; you will be required to pay more than the contract calls for in order that he be not required to give a deed to property worth three times what he is being paid.' "

4. The recent inflationary spiral made many agreed-upon prices so grossly inadequate that courts denied specific performance of the contracts. See Jensen v. Southwestern States Management Co., 6 Kan.App.2d 437, 629 P.2d 752 (1981). Inadequate consideration combined with undue influence, sharp practice or other forms of unconscionable conduct has always resulted in a denial of specific performance. See Wehringer v. Bullen, 120 N.H. 446, 417 A.2d 1 (1980), where an

attorney-friend of the widowed seller bought land worth $200 per acre for $30 per acre.

5. The significance of the unconscionable conduct emerges in a later New Hampshire decision. In Erin Foods Services, Inc. v. Derry Motel, Inc., 131 N.H. 353, 553 A.2d 304 (1988), the value of the property increased from the contract price of $500,000 to $2,850,000 at the time of trial. This was an arms' length transaction between parties experienced in the real estate business; there was no evidence of unconscionable conduct. The court ruled that the trial judge may not deny specific performance simply because the contract proved unexpectedly disadvantageous to one of the parties.

If adequacy of consideration is tested at the time the contract is formed, will the breaching party usually have to rely on something more potent than inflation to prevent specific performance?

BRANDOLINO v. LINDSAY

Court of Appeal of California, Second District, 1969.
269 Cal.App.2d 319, 75 Cal.Rptr. 56.

WOOD, PRESIDING JUSTICE. This is an action for specific performance or, in the alternative, for damages for the breach of an agreement whereby defendant Newton E. Lindsay, who owned an undivided one-half interest in forty acres of land, agreed to sell the forty acres to plaintiffs for $50,000. The court denied specific performance and awarded $25,000 damages to plaintiffs against defendant Lindsay for his breach of the agreement. He appeals from the judgment. * * *

On May 21, 1964, [three days after the escrow was set up] Lindsay notified the bank (escrow holder) to cancel the escrow. Ghiglia [the real estate broker] asked him why he wanted to cancel the escrow, and he said that he could "get twice as much." The bank advised the plaintiffs of Lindsay's notification to cancel the escrow, and they refused to cancel the escrow. Thereafter, the plaintiffs on several occasions requested that Lindsay "go through with" the escrow, but Lindsay refused the request.

Plaintiffs then filed this action and recorded a Notice of Lis Pendens which described the land.

The first cause of action of the first amended complaint (verified) is for specific performance of the agreement (escrow instructions) and includes allegations that the agreed sales price of the property was $50,000, and that plaintiffs are informed and believe and therefore allege that $50,000 was the fair and reasonable value of the property.

The second cause of action of that complaint is for damages for breach of the agreement, and it alleges, among other things, that by reason of the breach plaintiffs were damaged in the amount of $25,000, which is the difference between the agreed price, $50,000, of the property, and the value, $75,000, as of the date of the breach. The prayer is for specific performance of the agreement or, in the alternative, for $25,000.

The trial proceeded on plaintiffs' first amended complaint and the answers thereto. Several witnesses called by the plaintiffs testified as to the value of the property on May 21, 1964 (date when Lindsay repudiated agreement by cancelling escrow instructions). Mr. Snorgras, an appraiser, testified that the value was $76,000. Mr. Ghiglia, a real estate broker, testified that the value was $80,000 to $100,000. Mr. Lindsay (called as a witness under Evidence Code, § 776) and Dr. Brandolino testified that the value was $100,000. Plaintiff High testified that the value was $80,000 to $90,000. The judge stated that since plaintiffs' own witnesses testified that the value of the land exceeded the purchase price ($50,000), the purchase was not the fair and reasonable value of the property, and that specific performance would be denied. Plaintiffs' counsel said that plaintiffs would abandon the cause of action for specific performance.

[The trial court held that the fair market value of the property on the "date of the agreement" was $75,000.]

* * * Appellant contends that the court erred in awarding damages "in equity." He argues that although plaintiffs' complaint included a cause of action for specific performance and a cause of action for damages, the recordation by plaintiffs of the notice of *lis pendens* limited plaintiffs to their cause of action for specific performance and precluded their recovery of damages; and that since plaintiffs' evidence showed that the value of the land greatly exceeded the fair and reasonable value thereof as alleged in plaintiffs' verified (amended) complaint, "To permit them to falsify their own allegations to seek damages, under such circumstances, makes a mockery of equity," and that "The greater the discrepancy in the sworn allegation as to value, the greater would be their reward of damages." He asserts further that charging him with bad faith and loading him with heavy damages for refusing to perform the unfair agreement while he was prevented by the *lis pendens* notice from salvaging anything from the property rendered meaningless the equitable rule against enforcing performance of an unjust agreement.

A complaint may allege inconsistent theories of a cause of action in the alternative (2 Witkin, Cal.Procedure, Pleading, § 181, p. 1160), including theories seeking specific performance of an agreement, or in the alternative damages for the breach thereof [citation] and the court may award damages if plaintiffs are not entitled to specific performance. [citations] If specific performance of an agreement to convey real property cannot be decreed, and damages are awarded, then the measure of damages is the return of the principal paid and, in case of bad faith, the difference between the price agreed to be paid and the value of the property at the time of the breach. (Civ.Code, § 3306.) * * * There was evidence that the value at the time of the breach exceeded $75,000, and the court found that defendant acted in bad faith in repudiating the agreement and that plaintiffs were damaged in the amount of $25,000 (prayer of first amended complaint was for $25,000). The evidence supported the finding of bad faith. * * *

Appellant asserts, however, that plaintiffs, by recording the notice of *lis pendens,* were thereby limited to specific performance and were precluded from recovering damages; that by reason of the recordation of the *lis pendens* notice it cannot be concluded that plaintiffs intended the action to be "both" for specific performance and for damages; and that if it were so concluded, then plaintiffs came into equity with unclean hands. As previously stated plaintiffs properly could seek specific performance or, in the alternative, damages. Section 409 of the Code of Civil Procedure authorizes the recordation of a *lis pendens* notice in an action affecting the title or the right of possession of real property, and provides that the recordation is constructive notice to purchasers. "The purpose of a *lis pendens* is merely to furnish a means of notifying all

persons of the pendency of an action, and thereby to bind any person who may acquire an interest in property, subsequent to the institution of the action, by any judgment which may be secured in the action affecting the property." [citations] There is no merit to appellant's assertion that the recording of the *lis pendens* notice operated to preclude plaintiffs from recovering damages in the event specific performance could not be decreed. The court did not err in awarding damages to plaintiffs.

Appellant further contends that the court erred in applying the doctrine of election of remedies. He argues that plaintiffs were permitted to switch to the law side of the court only after they knew they had failed to win their case in equity.

In Tanforan v. Tanforan, 173 Cal. 270, 274, 159 P. 709, 711, it was said: "Since, then, inconsistent causes of action may be pleaded, it is not proper for the judge to force upon the plaintiff an election between those causes which he has a right to plead. Plaintiff is entitled to introduce his evidence upon each and all of these causes of action, and the election, or in other words the decision as to which of them is sustained, is, after the taking of all the evidence, a matter for the judge or the jury." In the present case, after the plaintiffs had called several witnesses who testified that the value of the land exceeded $75,000, the court stated that, in view of such testimony, the consideration ($50,000) for the purchase of the property was inadequate and specific performance would be denied. Counsel for plaintiffs then stated that they would abandon their cause of action for specific performance. The trial proceeded, and the court awarded plaintiffs damages for breach of the agreement. As above indicated the plaintiffs could seek specific performance or, in the alternative, damages; and, in the event specific performance could not have been decreed, the court could award damages. Furthermore, the record does not show that defendant raised the question regarding election of remedies, by motion, or otherwise, in the trial court prior to the time plaintiffs' counsel states that plaintiffs would abandon the cause of action for specific performance. * * *

The judgment is affirmed.

Notes

1. The major reason to distinguish law from equity is the right to a jury trial on legal issues. Before merger, equity developed the rule that if it obtained jurisdiction, it would decide both legal and equitable issues. This achieves economy of litigation and prevents statutes of limitations from expiring. See Ziebarth v. Kalenze, supra p. 241. But it may frustrate the right to a jury trial particularly where equity denies specific performance for reasons that do not prevent a legal remedy. The leading article is Levin, Equitable Clean-up and the Jury, 100 U.Pa.L.Rev. 320 (1951). See also Dairy Queen v. Wood, supra p. 235. Professor Dobbs says "under the federal system, the clean up doctrine seems to have little remaining significance" because legal issues will be "tried to the jury if one is properly demanded." D. Dobbs, Remedies § 84 (1973).

2. *Equitable Defenses.* Defenses that bar equitable relief but leave plaintiff free to pursue legal remedies include laches and unclean hands which were studied in Chapter 3. A judge may deny specific performance because of an equitable defense and nevertheless award damages. Estate of Younge v. Huysmans, 127 N.H. 461, 506 A.2d 282 (1985).

The equitable defenses we are now studying are unequal consideration, lack of mutuality of remedies, and uncertain or indefinite contract.

If, after an equitable defense succeeds, the "victorious" defendant is liable for damages, equitable success may be pyrrhic. Opposed to this double standard of morality is Dawson, Specific Performance in France and Germany, 57 Mich.L.Rev. 495, 535–36 (1959).

Are separate defenses to equitable remedies a good idea? Do you agree with equity's "ethical system that recognized a class of tainted agreements not so impure as to be voidable yet not so pure as to merit specific performance"? Levin, Equitable Clean-up and the Jury: A Suggested Orientation, 100 U.Pa.L.Rev. 320, 339 (1951).

If you disagree, should the equitable defenses be abolished or should they be extended to bar legal claims as well? See Homart Development v. W.T. Sigman, p. 1019.

Arguing that the equitable defense of inadequate consideration should be scuttled because it is anti-competitive and leads to confusion and unpredictability is Schwartz, The Case for Specific Performance, 89 Yale L.J. 271, 298–303 (1979).

Apparently arguing that equitable defenses should also defeat legal relief is Levin, quoted above and in Note 2 after the next principal case.

E. Yorio, Contract Enforcement: Specific Performance and Injunctions § 4.5.2 (1989): "Equitable defenses mirror a real world in which the facts often do not support an either/or result, but something in between. They can be responsive to a weakness in the plaintiff's case, to the harshness of specific performance on the defendant, or to a combination of factors that justify denying equitable relief, but no one of which is sufficient to entitle the promisor to rescission. They enable courts to avoid sharp discontinuities in result caused by the need to fit the facts into a procrustean bed of either granting specific performance or rescinding the contract. Matters would be clearer and simpler in a world without separate equitable defenses. But the legal system would lose tools that provide considerable flexibility in achieving justice in particular cases." [citations omitted]

3. Because both Marks v. Gates and Brandolino v. Lindsay involve valid contracts based on "inadequate" consideration, plaintiff has available a remedy at law. Do the decisions differ on whether the court of equity may "clean up" the lawsuit by deciding the remedy at law? Does the difference result from each court's initial reason for refusing specific performance?

4. Is *Marks* more faithful to the right to a jury trial than *Brandolino?* Does it follow from the right to plead inconsistent remedies that if the equitable remedy fails, the judge should decide the factual issues in the damage remedy?

GABRIELSON v. HOGAN

Skip

United States Court of Appeals, Eighth Circuit, 1924.
298 F. 722.

LEWIS, CIRCUIT JUDGE. M.L. Hogan and son, both residents of Iowa, went to Miner County, South Dakota, in August, 1920, with a view to buying a farm. They spent about two weeks driving through the country, making inquiries about prices of land and looking over farms reported to be for sale. In company with a Mr. Goff they went over and examined appellant's farm of 160 acres, and on August 28 entered into a contract to buy it. M.J. Quinn, son-in-law of the elder Hogan, signed the contract with them as purchaser.

The Hogans and Quinn agreed to purchase the farm on a basis of $29,000. It was incumbered with a mortgage lien for $16,000, which they agreed to assume. For the remaining $13,000 they were to give a second mortgage of $5,000 and pay $8,000 in cash installments, all to be completed and closed on February 1, 1921. They paid $3,450 of the $8,000 and then failed to make further payments. The $5,000 mortgage was not given. * * *

[Gabrielson, the vendor, sued for specific performance.]

Clearly, the appellant had a right to bring his suit as he did, in a court of equity for specific performance. He tendered a deed, performance on his part, and asked that defendants be required to pay the agreed consideration. A vendor is as much entitled to the equitable remedy as the vendee. * * *

The principal question here is whether the court was right in withholding from Gabrielson the equitable relief which he sought. We do not doubt the validity of the contract. Hogans and Quinn are clearly bound by it. Their defense of fraud was not made out. They present no facts that would sustain a decree relieving them. But the fact that they are bound and liable to Gabrielson for the breach does not determine the character of relief that he may have, whether equitable or legal. It has ever been held that specific performance is not an absolute right, but that it rests in sound judicial discretion, controlled by established principles of equity, to be exercised by the chancellor upon consideration of all the circumstances of each particular case.

* * * According to the court's finding, the contract price was a third more than the value of the farm. The pertinency of that fact to the question under consideration is clearly stated in Cathcart v. Robinson, 5 Pet. 264, 271 thus:

> "At any rate, this excess of price over value, if the contract be free from imposition, is not, in itself, sufficient to prevent a decree for a specific performance. But, though it will not, standing alone, prevent a court of chancery from enforcing a contract, it is an ingredient which, associated with others, will contribute to prevent the interference of a court of equity." † * * *

It is assigned as error that the dismissal of appellants' bill turned him out of court and denied him any relief, and that on the facts that should not have been done. Equity jurisdiction was at no time challenged, as already pointed out. The subject-matter, the facts stated, and the parties brought the controversy within equitable cognizance. That appellant was held to be not entitled to the equitable relief which he sought, was not a sufficient reason to deny to him any other relief to which he might be entitled. He prayed for such other relief as the court might find on the facts he ought to have. The whole controversy was submitted to the court by both parties; and having appropriately obtained jurisdiction over the entire matter we think it was the duty of the court to make final disposition, and that it was error not to do so. When the case brought is clearly one in equity, when both parties submit the case to equity jurisdiction, it is then the duty of the court to finally dispose of the whole controversy, and the relief to which the parties may be entitled on the facts should be granted, though that relief be legal and not equitable in character.

† [Editors' footnote. The additional ingredient was the defendants' reliance on the statements of Goff, a neighboring farmer who had previously owned the farm. While not an agent of Gabrielson, Goff testified that "he expected Gabrielson to pay him" if the sale to defendants was consummated.]

* * * When the Hogans and Quinn breached the contract Gabrielson was thereby damaged to the extent of the difference between the contract price and the value of the land * * *; and according to the finding of the court that difference amounted to $7,400. But Gabrielson received from appellees $3,450. We see no escape from the conclusion that he was entitled to a judgment for $3,950, the remainder of the amount to which he had been damaged; unless it be that either of the parties claims that the market value of the farm at the time of the breach had changed from what it was at the time the contact was made, and desires to and represents to the court that he can adduce evidence on that issue to his advantage.

The action of the court in denying specific performance is affirmed, its action in dismissing appellant's complaint is reversed. The cause will be remanded with directions to reinstate the complaint and adjudge the amount of damage sustained by Gabrielson either on the record already made, or after taking additional evidence on that issue. The court after hearing counsel will be advised as to further procedure in protection of the rights of the parties.

Notes

1. Assume a contemporary lawsuit wherein plaintiff seeks specific performance and, in the alternative, expectancy damages. Defendant denies that a contract was formed and demands a jury trial. Which of the following is more consistent with the right to a jury trial? (a) Try the action without a jury; if plaintiff's claim for specific performance fails for any reason, decide the damages claim under the cleanup doctrine. (b) Empanel a jury to hear common issues and enter equitable relief consistent with the jury's findings of fact. (c) Empanel a jury and allow both the judge and the jury to find facts. If the judge decides to grant specific performance, he will ignore the jury. If the judge rejects specific performance, the jury decides the contract and damage questions. F. James & G. Hazard, Civil Procedure § 8.7 (3d ed. 1985).

2. "To follow the [*Gabrielson*] court's decision in this type of factual situation would be to grant plaintiff damages directly proportioned to the hardship inherent in his original contract. Patently, the greater the hardship on defendant because he had agreed to too high a sales figure, the greater the plaintiff's measure of damages. The result borders on the absurd." Levin, Equitable Clean-up and the Jury, 100 U.Pa.L.Rev. 320, 340 (1951).

3. Should the courts in *Marks, Brandolino,* and *Gabrielson* limit each plaintiff's recovery to restitution?

4. Gordon v. Bauer, 177 Ill.App.3d 1073, 532 N.E.2d 855 (1988), cert. denied, 125 Ill.2d 564, 537 N.E.2d 809 (1989). The buyer sought specific performance and damages for seller's breach of a farm sale contract. Because of a dramatic drop in the value of the farm, the buyer dismissed the claim for specific performance prior to trial. At trial buyer did establish damages from the seller's breach. The trial court, sitting without a jury, awarded buyer damages. The seller appealed claiming the court lacked jurisdiction to grant damages after the specific performance claim was dismissed. In affirming the judgment for the buyer, the appellate court ruled that the dismissal of buyer's claim for specific performance did not alter the character of the damages award. That award was simply a part of the equitable relief buyer sought; and since the relief was equitable, there was no right to jury trial.

Can this denial of jury trial be justified as a proper application of the "in lieu" or cleanup doctrine? Can it be justified on any other basis?

5. Assume a suit by the buyer in a land sale contract for specific performance, or in the alternative, for damages. The court declines to give the equitable remedy because:

a. plaintiff has an adequate legal remedy,

b. the seller's spouse refuses to join in the conveyance,

c. the plaintiff has been guilty of unclean hands,

d. the plaintiff has been guilty of laches,

e. the seller never owned the property,

f. the contract is too uncertain to enforce specifically,

g. specific performance is too difficult to supervise, or

h. the consideration for the land is inadequate.

In which cases, if any, should the court dismiss the suit; award legal damages before a jury if requested; enter an equitable money decree in lieu of specific performance?

d. Specific Performance Plus Damages or Abatement

FLYGARE v. BRUNDAGE

Supreme Court of Wyoming, 1956.
76 Wyo. 350, 302 P.2d 759.

BLUME, CHIEF JUSTICE. This is an action for specific performance of a contract brought by the plaintiff Ralph W. Flygare against the defendant Wallace M. Brundage on April 15, 1954. The parties will be referred to herein as in the court below.

The action [for specific performance] involves a triangular piece of land * * * fronting highways 89 and 187. The land was sold for $15,000 as though containing 13 acres of land, but actually contained only 7.93 acres as discovered after the abstract of title was delivered. Plaintiff sued to have defendant fulfill his contract as near as possible. * * * The case was tried to the court without a jury. Judgment was entered for plaintiff. * * *

There were improvements on the land at the time of the sale of the property, but the court failed to make any finding regarding these improvements, so we shall briefly set out the testimony in that connection. The witness Ick testified that the living quarters with bath were worth $4,000; a service station, $4,500; a little cabin, $500; pipes and cistern, $1,700; a total of $10,700. The witness Kranenberg did not testify as to the value of the pipes or cistern but testified that the value of the house and bath was from $4,500 to $5,000; the store building (service station), $4,000; the little cabin $500; a total of $8,500 to $9,000. Testimony of the plaintiff in this connection was as follows:

> "There are three log cabin buildings there, which were there in the beginning. As far as I could tell, in putting in new subfloors, I think we found newspapers in the buildings that date back 35 years, but the outward appearances were good and I consider the buildings good and valuable for a purpose. There is no purpose for me on that property and I would be glad to make it a matter of record in this Court that anybody that wants those buildings may come and have them, including Mr. Brundage or anybody else, for a payment of less than half of whatever the price given in this testimony yesterday of the

buildings. So far as the pipe line from the spring to the reservoir, I consider it of no value whatsoever and when that pipe line is replaced that pipe will be discarded on the spot and anybody may have it for carrying it away." * * *

There is no justification in the contention of counsel for plaintiff herein that the sale was for so much per acre. It was a sale of a tract of land with certain boundaries. In other words, it was, as is commonly said, a sale in gross. There was, however, a representation on the part of the vendor that the tract contained at least 13 acres of land. The evidence indicates there was no intentional fraud, for a map in the office of the county clerk indicated the acreage to be 12.8 acres. However, the quantity was actually misrepresented and the tract contained only 7.93 acres, a difference of something like 35 to 40 percent. The rule applicable in such a case is considered in C.J.S., Vendor & Purchaser, § 266, p. 136, where it is stated:

> "As a general rule, where the sale is in gross or of a tract or parcel as a whole without regard to its specific quantity, the purchaser, unless there is an express provision for a deduction or unless the vendor has guaranteed the number of acres, if there has been no fraud or mistake, is not entitled to an abatement in the purchase price because the quantity of the land is less than thought or estimated by the parties at the time of the sale. The reason usually assigned for this rule is that the purchaser, in such cases, is considered as getting the specific land that he contracted for, and must be deemed to have assumed the risk of a deficiency in quantity."

But there is apparently a great diversity of opinion on the subject, although it may be that there would be more or less harmony under a certain state of facts. In C.J.S., Vendor & Purchaser, § 266, p. 137, it is stated:

> "Ordinarily, the size of the deficiency does not vary the application of the rule denying a right of abatement where the sale is in gross, unless, according to some authorities, the variation or deficiency from a quantity stated by way of description is so great as to cause the court to conclude that it was not within the probable contemplation of the parties, and to treat the case as one of fraud or mistake * * *. In at least one jurisdiction a deficiency in excess of ten per cent of the total amount of land sold is usually considered sufficiently large to justify an abatement on the ground of fraud or mistake, while an abatement will generally not be granted for a deficiency which is less than ten per cent."

* * * In the case at bar the difference is so great that we must conclude the vendee in this case is entitled to an abatement of the price.

What then is the measure of the abatement? The court allowed the plaintiff the proportion that 7.93 bears to 13. It figured the amount of abatement to be allowed should be approximately 5/13 of the total amount of $15,000 payable under the contract, as though the sale had been for so much per acre, and made no allowance whatever for any improvements, although the testimony for the defendant indicates the value of these improvements amounted to $10,700, and even the plaintiff's testimony indicates the value thereof was substantial. Counsel for defendant contends the court erred in this connection, and we think the contention is well taken. It may be these improvements do not exactly suit the purposes for which the plaintiff wants to use the property, but these purposes were not communicated to the defendant, so the value should be estimated as in any other case. If the tract had contained 13 acres, the plaintiff would have a greater frontage on the highway, but at the same time the property lying back of the highway, and of less value than the property fronting the highway, would have been greater.

In C.J.S., Vendor & Purchaser, § 266, p. 138, it is stated:

> "As a general rule the amount of the abatement or deduction, where the purchaser is entitled to an abatement because of a deficiency in quantity, is the value of the deficient land at the time of the sale. Usually this value is ascertained by taking the price fixed in the contract or conveyance. * * *
>
> "While it has been held that if improvements on the land form only a small portion of the value of the entire tract sold, they should not be taken into consideration to cause a departure from the general rule that the abatement is to be according to the average price per acre of the whole land, ordinarily, where the title to the land carries with it valuable appurtenant privileges, or where the land contains valuable improvements, or the land is sold with shares of stock, of which the purchaser receives the full benefit, the abatement should be according to the average value per acre after deducting the value of the privileges, improvements, or stock. For this purpose the value of the improvements should be fixed as of the date of the sale in their condition at that time."

The case of Doctor v. Hellberg, 65 Wis. 415, 27 N.W. 176, 179, 180, involved a sale of 49 acres of land, with improvements, for the sum of $23,000. It appeared that the acreage was in fact $16\frac{1}{2}$ acres less than represented. That was substantially a difference of one-third. The purchaser claimed the purchase price should be reduced in the same proportion. The claim was then exactly the same as was allowed by the trial court in this case. The supreme court of Wisconsin held that the claim of the purchaser was not well founded, and stated in part:

> "This court has held that in the absence of fraud, 'where the title fails to only a part of the land conveyed, the grantee may recover in an action on the covenants of seizin and right to convey, or upon an agreement to convey such fractional part of the whole consideration paid as the value at the time of the purchase of the piece to which the title fails bears to the whole purchase price and interest thereon during the time he had been deprived of the use of such fractional part, but not exceeding six years.' [citations]
>
> "Assuming the plaintiffs' right to specific performance and abatement of price on account of deficiency, as claimed, still they would not be entitled to any more favorable rule than the one just indicated; that is, an abatement of such fractional part of the whole consideration to be paid as the value at the time of the purchase of the piece to which the title failed bears to the whole purchase price. It stands confessed that the buildings and improvements are all on the land owned by the defendant, and it would be unfair to presume, in the absence of any allegation of proportionate values, that the portion of the land not improved is of equal value per acre with that which is improved."

To illustrate, taking for convenience 8 acres instead of 7.93: If the improvements were worth $8,000, the amount of abatement would be $\frac{5}{13}$ of $7,000 (the difference between $15,000, the purchase price, and $8,000) or approximately $2,700; if the improvements were worth $6,000, then the amount of the abatement would be $\frac{5}{13}$ of $9,000 (the difference between $15,000, the purchase price and $6,000) or approximately $3,460. The sums already paid would, of course, be added.

The trial court did not decide the case pursuant to this rule. It did not find the value of the improvements. So the case must be partially reversed and sent back to the trial court so that it may determine the value of the improvements on the property at the time of the purchase and then deduct from the purchase price of $15,000 an amount in abatement according to the foregoing rule. In other respects the judgment of the trial court is affirmed.

Notes

1. If buyer sues for specific performance with the purchase price reduced, the Restatement (Second) of Contracts § 358 comment c (1981), allows her a remedy for the seller's partial breach. What is the buyer's remedial theory? Damages or restitution.

McClintock suggests that buyer receives an abatement of the price rather than damages. McClintock, Equity § 66, at 177 (2d ed. 1948). Walsh would deny specific performance for radical discrepancies when the seller has a right to rescind. But when the contract is enforceable at law, he finds it "entirely clear" that in buyer's suit for specific performance, the contract price should be reduced pro rata. Apparently he assumes that the reduction is equivalent to money damages. W. Walsh, Equity 389 (1930). Williston, on the other hand, would permit specific performance with abatement even where the deficiency is extreme. He reasons that the equity court is "merely disposing in one suit of the two rights of the purchaser." 11 Williston on Contracts § 1436, at 904 (W. Jaeger 3d ed. 1968). Williston computes damages more cautiously than Walsh. Only in jurisdictions that restrict buyers' damages to a recovery of the purchase money is buyer's recovery measured by a proportional part of the purchase price. He does not comment on the measure of abatement in jurisdictions that apply the more generous expectancy rule of damages.

The remedial standards these writers suggest seem over-simplified. Prorating the purchase price works best where seller's breach is a deficiency in quantity; but where the deficiency relates to quality, like an inchoate dower right discussed below in Note 3, a proportional measure presents problems. Moreover, even if quantity is deficient, it does not follow that awarding the buyer a proportion of the purchase price is the equivalent of money damages for breach of contract. Prorating does not yield the same result as money damages where the expectancy rule governs seller's breach. Moreover there is certainly no equivalence to where buyer lacks a remedy at law because of the seller's right to rescind.

The distinction between damages and abatement is largely ignored, but it was recognized in Works v. Wyche, 344 S.W.2d 193 (Tex.Civ.App.1961). The seller contracted to sell two parcels of land for $93,000; the first tract contained 15.96 acres and the second 15 acres. The seller claimed that title to the second tract was in his deceased son and refused to perform. The trial court found bad faith in the seller's "dealings" and that the market value of the land was $5000 per acre; but it denied relief on grounds not relevant here.

The appellate court entered judgment for the buyer; it ordered specific performance for the first tract and damages of $30,000 for failure to convey the second tract. Since Texas law gave the buyer expectancy damages, buyer's damages were measured by the difference between the market value of the land ($5000 per acre) and the contract price ($3000 per acre). This is considerably more favorable to the buyer than simply apportioning the purchase price.

The Oregon Supreme Court, on the other hand, ruled that abatement was not a question of damages but of "equitable compensation" for incomplete performance. Such compensation "is not synonymous with damages at law for breach of contract; it is given ancillary to specific performance." Wittick v. Miles, 274 Or. 1, 545 P.2d 121 (1976).

In D–K Investment Corp. v. Sutter, 19 Cal.App.3d 537, 96 Cal.Rptr. 830 (1971), the California court took a different approach to abatement. The vendor sold a portion of the property to an innocent third person for $70,000. The third party improved the property; when plaintiff exercised his option to buy, it had a market value of $95,300. Plaintiff sought specific performance with an abatement in the purchase price measured by the market value of this property at the time the option was exercised. The court, relying on the flexible rule enunciated by the Restatement of Contracts § 365, limited the abatement to $70,000, the property's value unimproved.

Compare the analysis of the problem in Reis v. Sparks, supra p. 971.

2. In *Flygare* why isn't the defense of negative mutuality available to the vendor? Compare Security Land Co. v. Touliatos, 716 S.W.2d 918, modified, 721 S.W.2d 250 (Tenn.1986) with Miller v. Dyer, 20 Cal.2d 526, 127 P.2d 901 (1942).

3. A seller's spouse, not bound by the sales contract, who refuses to release dower rights creates a perplexing abatement problem. The allowance of an abatement adds coercive pressure on the non-signing spouse to release dower. The calculation of the present value of the inchoate interest for purposes of abatement involves such questions as: What is the anticipated life span of the selling spouse? Which spouse will die first? How long will the non-signing spouse survive?

Confronted with these variables, many, perhaps most, courts permit the buyer to choose specific performance of the selling spouse's interest but without abatement. A recent decision refused abatement where there was an inchoate curtesy interest. God v. Hurt, 218 Va. 909, 241 S.E.2d 800 (1978), on reh'g, 219 Va. 160, 247 S.E.2d 351 (1978). See also Bass v. Smith, 234 Va. 1, 360 S.E.2d 162 (1987).

An alternative solution is to decree specific performance while allowing the buyer a lien for indemnity or even to retain part of the purchase price against the contingency of a dower claim. See Box v. Dudeck, 265 Ark. 165, 578 S.W.2d 567 (1979); Horack, Specific Performance and Dower Rights, 11 Iowa L.Rev. 97 (1926); Note, 29 Minn.L.Rev. 280 (1945).

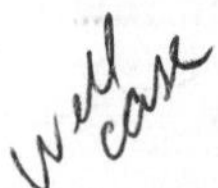

IDE v. JOE MILLER & COMPANY

Colorado Court of Appeals, 1984.
703 P.2d 590.

STERNBERG, JUDGE. John and Dora Ide, buyers, brought an action against Joe Miller and Co., seller, for specific performance and abatement of the purchase price of a farm. The dispute arose when a well on the property was determined to have the capacity to pump 115 gallons per minute instead of 350 gallons as specified in the contract of sale. The trial court ordered an abatement in the purchase price of $92,000 to approximately $55,000 based on testimony that the value of the increment of additional water—235 gallons per minute—was $37,000. However, the buyers' own appraiser testified that the property was worth $95,000 with the well "as is," and $135,000 if the well were capable of supplying 350 gallons per minute. The seller appeals, contending that the trial court erred in finding that the provision concerning the capacity of the well was a covenant rather than a condition, and in ordering specific performance and abatement. The seller argues that the provision in question was a condition, and thus upon its breach the buyers had the option between rescinding the contract and obtaining the return of their earnest money, or waiving the defect and accepting the farm at the contract price. We agree with the seller, and therefore reverse. * * *

The buyers contend that this case comes under the general rule that a purchaser of real estate may insist upon performance by the seller, to the extent that the seller is able to perform, with an abatement in the purchase price equal to the value of the deficiency or defect. [citations] However, specific performance is not a matter of right; whether it should be afforded depends upon the circumstances of the particular case. [citation] The court must fashion a remedy that does justice under the particular circumstances with which it is confronted. Dlug v. Wooldridge, 189 Colo. 164, 538 P.2d 883 (1975). Where, as here, the abatement ordered is 38% of the contract price, and the contract price is already below the actual value of the land and the abatement would make the purchase price much less than the actual value of the land, specific performance with abatement does not do justice to the parties, and is therefore an inappropriate remedy. *See* Dlug v. Wooldridge.

The remaining issue is the proper remedy for the seller's breach. The contract provides that upon failure of any of the conditions, the party not in default can opt for either termination of the contract with refund of monies paid, or may seek specific performance and damages. Specific performance and damages is inappropriate in this case; however, since the buyers should be allowed to take the benefit of their bargain, Dlug v. Wooldridge, they should be allowed to choose between purchasing the property as is, at the contract price, or terminating the contract.

The judgment is reversed and the cause is remanded for further proceedings consistent with this opinion.

SMITH and KELLY, JJ., concur.

FRIEDE v. POOL

(Supreme Court of Minnesota, 1944.
217 Minn. 332, 14 N.W.2d 454.)

STREISSGUTH, JUSTICE. Default having occurred in the payment of the last installment due under a contract for deed, plaintiff, as vendor, brought this suit in equity demanding judgment "adjudging the amount due plaintiff from defendants under said contract, and fixing a day at or before which defendants shall pay the same, and in default of such payment that said contract be forfeited and cancelled, and the plaintiff have restitution of said premises." The defense was that the plaintiff was unable to perform because of the fact that a narrow strip of land on the north line of the premises involved was in the adverse possession of a third party. * * *

According to the government survey, the tracts described in the contract contained 80 acres each. The plaintiff, however, was unable to deliver a good title to the entire 160 acres because of the fact that an adjoining owner, Vernon Towne, claimed title to a strip of land 1.8 acres in area on the north line of the premises conveyed. This strip varied in width from 19¾ feet at the northwest corner of the land to be conveyed to 34 feet at its northeast corner. The trial court found that the occupation and adverse claim of ownership of this small tract by Towne constituted "an encroachment upon the lands to be conveyed to the defendant by the plaintiff, but that the said tract * * * is composed of rough land cut up by a creek or riverbed, so the encroachment is of a minor degree and can be compensated for by the reduction of the amount to be paid by the defendant."

The court allowed $150 as compensation to defendant for the inability of plaintiff to deliver good title to the strip of 1.8 acres and found that the balance due plaintiff from defendant was $3,450. It accordingly ordered judgment that, upon payment by defendant of the sum of $3,450, with interest, plaintiff deliver to defendant a receiver's deed of said real estate free and clear of all encumbrances. * * *

Defendant failed to make any further payments on the contract, and, after the expiration of 60 days from the court's order, plaintiff made a motion for a further order directing the entry of final judgment cancelling the contract and adjudging that plaintiff was the owner and entitled to possession of the lands described in the contract. The motion having been granted, final judgment was entered.

Plaintiff admits his inability to give good and marketable title to the 1.8 acres of land in the adverse possession of Towne, but asserts that the deficiency in acreage is a minor and immaterial one within the rule of Restatement, Contracts, § 375, as follows: "Specific enforcement may properly be decreed, in spite of a minor breach or innocent misrepresentation by the plaintiff, involving no substantial failure of the exchange for the performance to be compelled."

* * * Specific performance will accordingly be granted to a vendor, with abatement in the purchase price or other adequate compensation to the purchaser, if there is only a slight and unsubstantial deficiency in quantity of the land to be conveyed or the land is subject to a slight or trivial encroachment which does not materially affect the value or enjoyment of that which can be conveyed. * * *

This is a proper case for the application of these rules unless a distinction must be made because of the special circumstances called to our attention by the defendant.

* * * [D]efendant, admitting that the 1.8 acres in the disputed strip is of little or no value as farming land, insists that the conveyance thereof to him is most important because without it he has no access to the north line of section three or to any highway established on that line. This presents a new aspect affecting plaintiff's right to specific performance with compensation, to-wit: the importance of the 1.8–acre strip to the enjoyment and use of the remainder of the farm, irrespective of the size of the strip or its value for farming purposes. * * *

By requiring defendant to accept compensation for the inability of plaintiff to deliver good title to the disputed strip, the trial court deprived him of more than the use and ownership of 1.8 acres of comparatively worthless land; it took from him all legal access to any four-rod road which theretofore had been or thereafter might be established or constructed on the section line. If defendant had accepted the conditions imposed by the judgment, he would have been without legal means of ingress to or egress from the land he purchased. * * *

In the early chancery practice, the courts were quite liberal in waiving strict compliance with his contract by a vendor seeking specific performance against a reluctant purchaser. Fry, Specific Performance, § 1217. Of recent years, however, the trend has definitely been to the contrary, especially in cases involving more than mere shortage in area. As said by a recent commentator:

"Equity grows increasingly hesitant to grant relief the further the nature of the defect departs from absence of a quantum of the subject matter. This distinction between quantity and other types of defect seems to bear out what has been said above: in cases involving quantity, more than anywhere else, the court regards itself as ordering the defendant to render part performance, rather than forcing him to give something different in partial substitution. When the defect consists in something other than quantity or quality of the res, the hesitancy hardens into refusal."

40 Harv.L.Rev. 478. * * *

There is always difficulty in applying the doctrine of compensation to a reluctant purchaser. There can be no uniform standard by which to ascertain what is essential to him. As pointed out in Knatchbull v. Grueber, 6 Eng.R.C. 676: "What is desirable to one is not so to another. One wants a wood for game, another desires it only as a beautiful object; one looks only to agriculture, another dislikes tithes; it therefore seems a little arbitrary to insist on a party taking compensation. Why am I bound to take what I did not mean to buy? You say you will give me compensation; but who is to judge of the compensation? Can you be sure it is a compensation?"

* * * [T]he duty to test the validity of the adverse claim of Towne should rest upon plaintiff and should not be cast upon defendant. Because of the importance to him of having title to the disputed strip, he should not be compelled to accept title to the balance of the land purchased, even though he be compensated liberally on the basis of the naked value of the strip for farm purposes only. We conclude that this is not a proper case for application of the rule of compensation.

Reversed.

Notes

1. *Question:* If the vendee had paid the full purchase price and received a conveyance, could he have rescinded?

2. Halcro v. Moon, 226 Mont. 121, 733 P.2d 1305 (1987). Specific performance was granted to a seller who had failed to keep his promise to repair a water leak before the buyer's family arrived at the house. The court ruled that seller's breach was immaterial and ordered the buyer to perform the contract.

e. Remedies for Breach of an Installment Land Sales Contract

(1) Non-statutory Remedies

SKENDZEL v. MARSHALL

Supreme Court of Indiana, 1973.
261 Ind. 226, 301 N.E.2d 641.

HUNTER, JUSTICE. In December of 1958, Mary Burkowski, as vendor, entered into a land sale contract with Charles P. Marshall and Agnes P. Marshall, as vendees. The contract provided for the sale of certain real estate for the sum of $36,000.00, payable as follows:

"$500.00, at the signing, execution and delivery of this contract, the receipt whereof is hereby acknowledged; $500.00 or more on or before the 25th day of December, 1958, and $2500.00 or more on or before the 15th day of January, 1960, and $2,500.00 or more on or before the 15th day of January of each and every year thereafter until the balance of the contract has been fully paid, all without interest and all without relief from valuation and appraisement laws and with attorney fees." * * *

The vendor, Mary Burkowski, died in 1963. The plaintiffs in this action are the assignees (under the vendor's will) of the decedent's interests in the contract. They received their assignment from the executrix of the estate of the vendor on June 27, 1968. One year after this assignment, several of the assignees filed their complaint in this action alleging that the defendants had defaulted through non-payment.

The schedule of payments made under this contract was shown by the evidence to be as follows:

"Date	Amount Paid	Total of Paid Principal
12/1/1958	$ 500.00	$ 500.00
12/25/1958	500.00	1,000.00
3/26/1959	5,000.00	6,000.00
4/5/1960	2,500.00	8,500.00
5/23/1961	2,500.00	11,000.00
4/6/1962	2,500.00	13,500.00
1/15/1963	2,500.00	16,000.00
6/30/1964	2,500.00	18,500.00
2/15/1965	2,500.00	21,000.00"

No payments have been made since the last one indicated above—$15,000.00 remains to be paid on the original contract price. * * *

Paragraph 17 of the contract provides that all prior payments "become forfeited and be taken and retained by the Vendor as liquidated damages." * * * Under the facts of this case, a $21,000 forfeiture is clearly excessive.

Under a typical conditional land contract, the vendor retains legal title until the total contract price is paid by the vendee. Payments are generally made in periodic installments. *Legal* title does not vest in the vendee until the contract terms are satisfied, but equitable title vests in the vendee at the time the contract is consummated. When the parties enter into the contract, all incidents of ownership accrue to the vendee. [citation] The vendee assumes the risk of loss and is the recipient of all appreciation in value. The vendee, as equitable owner, is responsible for taxes. [citation] The vendee has a sufficient interest in land so that upon sale of that interest, he holds a vendor's lien.

This Court has held, consistent with the above notions of equitable ownership, that a land contract, once consummated constitutes a present sale and purchase. The vendor " 'has, in effect, exchanged his property for the unconditional obligation of the vendee, the performance of which is secured by the retention of the legal title.' " Stark v. Kreyling, (1934) 207 Ind. 128, 135, 188 N.E. 680, 682. The Court, in effect, views a conditional land contract as a sale with a security interest in the form of legal title reserved by the vendor. Conceptually, therefore, the retention of the title by the vendor is the same as reserving a lien or mortgage. Realistically, vendor-vendee should be viewed as mortgagee-mortgagor. * * *

It is also interesting to note that the drafters of the Uniform Commercial Code abandoned the distinction between a conditional sale and a security interest. Section 1–201 of the UCC defines "security interest" as "an interest in personal property or fixtures which secures payment or performance of an obligation * * * retention or reservation of title by a seller of goods notwithstanding shipment or delivery to the buyer is limited in effect to a reservation of 'security interest.'" We can conceive of no rational reason why conditional sales of real estate should be treated any differently.[1]

A conditional land contract in effect creates a vendor's lien in the property to secure the unpaid balance owed under the contract. * * * Such a lien "[has] all the incidents of a mortgage" (D.S.B. Johnston Land Co. v. Whipple, 234 N.W. at 61), one of which is the right to foreclose.

There is a multitude of cases upholding the vendor's right to foreclose. The remedy is most often referred to as a foreclosure of an executory contract. (A land contract is "executory" until legal title is actually transferred to the vendee.) A 1924 New York case best describes this remedy:

> "Out of the nature of the relationship created by a land contract, where the vendee is in possession, there have developed certain equitable remedies, among which is the right of the vendor in a proper case to sell out the interest of the vendee for the purpose of satisfying his lien under the contract, in case of default, and while it seems a misnomer, for convenience this remedy is spoken of as foreclosure, and the action as one to foreclose the contract." Conners v. Winans (1924), 122 Misc. 824, 204 N.Y.S. 142, 145.

The foreclosure of a land sale contract is undeniably comprehended by our Trial Rules.

* * * We believe there to be great wisdom in requiring judicial foreclosure of land contracts pursuant to the mortgage statute. Perhaps the most attractive aspect of judicial foreclosure is the period of redemption, during which time the vendee may redeem his interest, possibly through refinancing.

Forfeiture is closely akin to strict foreclosure—a remedy developed by the English courts which did not contemplate the equity of redemption. American jurisdictions, including Indiana, have, for the most part, rejected strict foreclosure in favor of foreclosure by judicial sale. * * *

Guided by the above principles we are compelled to conclude that judicial foreclosure of a land sale contract is in consonance with the notions of equity developed in American jurisprudence. A forfeiture—like a strict foreclosure at common law—is often offensive to our concepts of justice and inimical to the principles of equity. This is not to suggest that a forfeiture is an inappropriate remedy for the breach of all land contracts. In the case of an abandoning, absconding vendee, forfeiture is a logical and equitable remedy. Forfeiture would also be appropriate where the vendee has paid a minimal amount on the contract at the time of default and seeks to retain possession while the vendor is paying taxes, insurance, and other upkeep in order to preserve the premises. Of course, in this latter situation, the vendee will have acquired very little, if any, equity in the property. However, a court of equity must always approach

1. [Footnote renumbered.] In fact, the Commissioners on Uniform State Laws have recognized the transparency of any such distinctions. Section 3–102 of the Uniform Land Transactions Code (working draft of first tentative draft) reads as follows:

> "This Article applies to security interests created by contract, including mortgage * * * land sales contract * * * and any other lien or title retention contract intended as security."

We believe this position is entirely consistent with the evolving case law in the area.

forfeitures with great caution, being forever aware of the possibility of inequitable dispossession of property and exorbitant monetary loss. * * *

Turning our attention to the case at hand, we find that the vendor-assignees were seeking forfeiture, including $21,000 already paid on said contract as liquidated damages and immediate possession. They were, in fact, asking for strict application of the contract terms at law which we believe would have led to unconscionable results requiring the intervention of equity. On the facts of this case, we are of the opinion that the trial court correctly refused the remedy sought by the vendor-assignees, but in so refusing it denied all remedial relief to the plaintiffs. * * * [T]his Court has the undeniable authority to remand with guidelines which will give substantial relief to plaintiffs under their secured interests and will prevent the sacrifice of the vendees' equitable lien in the property.

For all of the foregoing reasons, transfer is granted and the cause is reversed and remanded with instructions to enter a judgment of foreclosure on the vendor's lien, * * *. Said judgment shall include an order for the payment of the unpaid principal balance due on said contract, together with interest at 8% per annum from the date of judgment. The order may also embrace any and all other proper and equitable relief that the court deems to be just, including the discretion to issue a stay of the judicial sale of the property, * * *

PRENTICE, JUSTICE (concurring). I have some concern that our opinion herein might be viewed by some as indicating an attitude of indifference towards the rights of contract vendors. Such a view would not be a true reflection.

Because the installment sales contract, with forfeiture provisions, is a widely employed and generally accepted method of commerce in real estate in this state, it is appropriate that a vendee seeking to avoid the forfeiture, to which he agreed, be required to make a clear showing of the inequity of enforcement. In any given transaction anything short of enforcing the forfeiture provision may be a denial of equity to the vendor. It has been set forth in the majority opinion that if the vendee has little or no real equity in the premises, the court should have no hesitancy in declaring a forfeiture. It follows that if the vendee has indicated his willingness to forego his equity, if any, whether by mere abandonment of the premises, by release or deed or by a failure to make a timely assertion of his claim, he should be barred from thereafter claiming an equity.

If the court finds that forfeiture, although provided for by the terms of the contract, would be unjust, it should nevertheless grant the vendor the maximum relief consistent with equity against a defaulting vendee. In so doing, it should consider that, had the parties known that the forfeiture provision would not be enforceable, other provisions for the protection of the vendor doubtlessly would have been incorporated into the agreement. Generally, this would require that the transaction be treated as a note and mortgage with such provisions as are generally included in such documents customarily employed in the community by prudent investors. Terms customarily included in such notes and mortgages but frequently omitted from contracts include provisions for increased interest during periods of default, provision for the acceleration of the due date of the entire unpaid principal and interest upon a default continuing beyond a reasonable grace period, provisions for attorneys' fees and other expenses incidental to foreclosure, for the waiver of relief from valuation and appraisement laws and for receivers.

Notes

1. Following *Skendzel* the Indiana courts have reaffirmed their opposition to forfeiture of a land sale contract except in the unusual situations the court pointed out. In Morris v. Weigle, 270 Ind. 121, 383 N.E.2d 341 (1978), the court ruled that the buyer had a vendee's lien on the proceeds of the foreclosure sale in excess of the balance owed on the contract. The court further stated that a damages award in excess of the foreclosure is not "appropriate" unless the vendee was guilty of acts of waste. In later decisions, Indiana courts have insisted on foreclosure rather than ejectment. Ebersold v. Wise, 412 N.E.2d 802 (Ind.App.1980) forfeiture, Looney v. Farmers Home Administration, 794 F.2d 310 (7th Cir.1986), or rescission, S.B.D., Inc. v. Sai Mahen, Inc., 560 N.E.2d 86 (Ind.App.1990).

Compare the humorous opinion of the Judge Buttler in Braunstein v. Trottier, 54 Or.App. 687, 635 P.2d 1379 (1981), upholding a declaration of forfeiture followed by an action of ejectment. The Kentucky supreme court accepted *Skendzel's* view that a judicial sale is the appropriate remedy for a buyer's breach in Sebastian v. Floyd, 585 S.W.2d 381 (Ky.1979). On the other hand, the Alaska supreme court, in upholding a forfeiture of a buyer's interest, noted that in "some extreme cases the purchaser's history of performance is so inauspicious that equity not only allows a forfeiture, it demands a forfeiture." Curry v. Tucker, 616 P.2d 8, 13 (Alaska 1980).

In Nebraska, the vendor upon vendee's default may treat the contract as an ordinary real estate mortgage and foreclose it. Jones v. Burr, 223 Neb. 291, 389 N.W.2d 289 (1986). Where, however, the amount due on the contract is greater than the value of the property and a sale would not produce a surplus over the amount due, a decree of strict foreclosure is an appropriate remedy. Ryan v. Kolterman, 215 Neb. 355, 338 N.W.2d 747 (1983), where a final balloon payment of $196,832 on a $280,650 purchase price could not possibly be met.

2. *Vendor's Lien.* Grace Development Co. v. Houston, 306 Minn. 334, 335–36, 237 N.W.2d 73, 75 (1975):

"The basis for the vendor's lien is the broad equitable principle that a person having obtained the estate of another should not be allowed to keep it without paying the purchase price.

"The extent of a vendor's lien depends entirely on the amount of the unpaid purchase price. If there is no purchase price owing, then there is no vendor's lien. The fact that a purchaser of real property may owe a vendor money does not by itself establish a vendor's lien." The vendor's lien is the vendor's equitable right to resort to the property if the vendee fails to pay.

Creditors must use supplemental proceedings or other versions of the creditor's bill in equity to realize on it. Somers v. Clearwater Power Co., 684 P.2d 1006 (Idaho 1984).

3. *Grantor's Lien.* Sewer v. Martin, 511 F.2d 1134, 1136–37 (3d Cir.1975). Plaintiff executed a deed conveying property to defendant for $12,000 and "other valuable consideration." On default, plaintiff foreclosed on the property to collect the consideration. The foreclosure of the lien was challenged by defendant on appeal. The court, in affirming the judgment of foreclosure, stated:

"A grantor's or vendor's lien [1] of the nature recognized by the district court in this case was early established in England and is recognized in the majority of

1. "We will use the term 'grantor's lien' throughout our discussion since it is clear that plaintiff had conveyed full legal title plus possession to defendant and does not occupy the

American jurisdictions. The lien is the equitable right which a grantor who takes no other security retains to subject the land conveyed to the payment of the purchase price. So long as a portion of the purchase price remains unpaid, the law presumes the existence of a lien unless the terms of the agreement or attending circumstances demonstrate that the parties intended no lien to be present."

The grantor's lien is personal and not transferable. Cal.Civ.Code § 3047.

See also Whelan v. Midland Mortgage Co., 591 P.2d 287, 288 (Okl.1978). The lien "came into existence and attached to the realty the minute [seller] conveyed and surrendered possession."

4. *Vendor's Remedies.* Miller v. Radtke, 230 Neb. 561, 432 N.W.2d 542 (1988). The court summarized the vendor's remedies to effectuate a security interest in an executory land sale contract. "[I]n order of increasing severity toward the vendee in such a contract, as (1) foreclosure, where the land is sold as in other foreclosures, and the vendor is reimbursed out of the proceeds; (2) strict foreclosure, where the vendee is required to pay the balance due within a specified time or be disbarred of all interest in the land; and (3) ejectment, where the vendee is eliminated from the title, and the vendor acquires title and possession without giving the vendee an opportunity to redeem and without returning payments already made to the vendor. It is readily apparent that in enforcing a vendor's rights in a land contract, ejectment is a more severe disposition than is the remedy of strict foreclosure."

a. *Foreclosure of the Vendor's or Grantor's Lien By Sale.* This is contract enforcing procedure, compatible with the suit for specific performance, and frequently used as ancillary. The court controls the sale and the application of the proceeds, in the absence of statutory qualifications. Some jurisdictions authorize the trial court to fix an upset price for the foreclosure sale, thereby limiting the deficiency judgment against the buyer. See e.g., Kramer v. Davis, 371 Mich. 464, 124 N.W.2d 292 (1963).

b. *Strict Foreclosure.* Kallenbach v. Lake Publications, Inc., 30 Wis.2d 647, 142 N.W.2d 212 (1966). A vendor sought strict foreclosure of a land sale contract for failure of the vendee to pay installments. There was no provision in the contract accelerating the entire debt for a default. The trial judge ruled that in the absence of an acceleration clause, the vendee could redeem from the foreclosure by paying only the delinquent installments.

In reversing, the supreme court noted that a vendor has a choice of remedies upon purchaser's default. The vendor may sue for the price, seek specific performance and have a judicial sale of the property, quiet title and foreclose the vendee's equity, recover possession by ejectment, or seek a decree of strict foreclosure. The court held that the vendor, in electing strict foreclosure, relinquishes his claim for the price and seeks only recovery of the land. Under such circumstances, equity allows the vendee one more chance to redeem; but it conditions redemption after strict foreclosure on payment of the full purchase price.

If the contract is executory and the vendee has paid nothing, strict foreclosure is indistinguishable from a bill to cancel or to remove a cloud on title. If the vendee has paid a portion of the price, an unconditional decree of strict foreclosure may result in a forfeiture. Courts have responded to criticism: "[i]f this produces a harsh or unwanted result, it is for the legislature to remedy and not the job of the

status of a vendor who holds legal title subject to a duty to convey. Many cases, however, use the terms 'grantor's lien' and 'vendor's lien' interchangeably. [citation]."

court to change the plain meaning of the contract." Burgess v. Shiplet, 230 Mont. 387, 390, 750 P.2d 460, 462 (1988).

The court could make the decree of strict foreclosure conditional upon the return of the payments, however. This solution resembles framing the vendor's remedy in formal terms of "rescission." See Beitelspacher v. Winther, 447 N.W.2d 347 (S.D.1989). A problem remains: to determine whether the payments the vendor retains are a. an unconscionable forfeiture, or b. compensation for damages vendor sustained because of the purchaser's breach. Compare Clampitt v. A.M.R. Corp., 109 Idaho 145, 706 P.2d 34 (1985) (retention was not a forfeiture) with Safari, Inc. v. Verdoorn, 446 N.W.2d 44 (S.D.1989) (retention constitutes an unenforceable penalty). This issue will be reconsidered below.

As both *Kallenbach* and *Radtke* reveal, no matter how courts resolve the forfeiture issue, they usually extend the buyer an opportunity to redeem the foreclosed property by paying the balance of the unpaid purchase price. See Heisel v. Cunningham, 94 Idaho 461, 491 P.2d 178 (1971); Kincaid v. Fitzwater, 257 Or. 170, 474 P.2d 742 (1970); John R. Hansen, Inc. v. Pacific International Corp., 76 Wash.2d 220, 455 P.2d 946 (1969) (Buyer given a six month period of grace to "cash-out" seller's net equity). In some cases, buyer may merely pay past due installments. Moore v. Bunch, 29 Mich.App. 498, 185 N.W.2d 565 (1971). The supposition, however unfounded, that a strict foreclosure must permit possible forfeiture, abhorred by equity, has led some jurisdictions to deny that the remedy is permissible, at least *eo nomine*.

Despite the kinship of strict foreclosure to cancellation and rescission, jurisdictions where it is permitted have frequently maintained an ambivalence about its nature.

For example Nygaard v. Anderson, 229 Or. 323, 330–31, 366 P.2d 899, 903 (1961): "Vendors remedies upon default by the purchaser fall into either one of two classes: (1) remedies consistent only with the affirmance of the contract, or (2) remedies consistent only with the repudiation of the contract. If the vendor seeks to recover the installments due on the contract or brings suit for specific performance or brings suit for strict foreclosure [See footnote below] he has elected to affirm and enforce the contract. On the other hand, if he brings an action of ejectment or takes possession of the premises under circumstances indicating an intent to deprive the purchaser of possession under the forfeiture and right of entry provision of the contract, the vendor has elected to regard the contract as no longer continuing." [1]

Similar confusion sometimes appears in connection with the vendor's equitable remedy of "quiet title" which obviously performs the same function as "strict foreclosure" and is contract terminating. Yet the Supreme Court of California stated: "By seeking to quiet title, the defendant (vendor) has not elected to rescind the contract. Honey v. Henry's Franchise Leasing Corp., 64 Cal.2d 801, 803, 52 Cal.Rptr. 18, 20, 415 P.2d 833, 835 (1966).

1. "[Footnote renumbered.] It has been said that the vendor's suit to foreclose is of a hybrid nature and that "it cannot be placed entirely in either the affirmance or disaffirmance of contract category." New York Law Revision Commission Reports, p. 359 (1937). It is clear from our cases, however, that until the decree of foreclosure is entered the contract is regarded as subsisting. "A suit for strict foreclosure recognizes that the contract is presently in effect and seeks to enforce it. It is an affirmance of the contract." Morrison et al. v. Kandler et ux., 215 Or. 489, 500, 334 P.2d 459, 464 (1959)."

(2) Statutory Limitations

VENABLE v. HARMON

Court of Appeal of California, Second District, 1965.
233 Cal.App.2d 297, 43 Cal.Rptr. 490.

FOURT, JUSTICE. This is an appeal, from a judgment rendered in favor of the plaintiffs—sellers in an action with reference to a contract for the purchase and sale of real property.

The facts are stipulated in writing by the parties.

"According to the terms of said agreement, defendants were to pay total monthly payments of $575.00, commencing December 1, 1959, and were to pay plaintiffs the additional sums of $5,000.00 on June 1, 1960, and $3,260.00 on December 1, 1960. That of said payments of $575.00 per month, $145.00 per month was, according to the terms of said agreement, to apply upon the principal of $10,000.00, and, under the terms of said agreement, when defendants had paid a total of $10,000.00 on account of principal, the parties agreed to enter into an escrow whereby plaintiffs would execute and deliver to defendants a good and sufficient deed conveying said realty, and furnish defendants with a Policy of Title Insurance, of Title Insurance and Trust Company, showing title to said property vested in defendants, and defendants would assume the responsibility for and payment of that certain promissory note secured by a first deed of trust on said realty and were to execute and deliver to plaintiffs a promissory note secured by a second deed of trust on said realty in the amount of the difference between said $10,000.00 principal payment and the total sales price of $55,000.00 less the amount due on the promissory note secured by the first deed of trust on said property. * * *

"After the execution of said agreement above referred to, defendants entered into possession of said real property, but prior to the filing of the Complaint herein, defendants abandoned said property, but plaintiffs refused to and still refuse to accept a tender of said property in consideration of the release of all defendants' obligations under the terms of said agreement. * * *

"After the execution of the agreement above referred to, plaintiffs and defendants agreed that defendants were to continue to pay the sum of $575.00 on or before the first day of each month in consideration of which the plaintiffs agreed to defer the other payments on principal above referred to, and that of said payments of $575.00 per month, the sum of $145.00 per month would apply upon the principal payment of $10,000.00. * * *

"Defendants paid the monthly payments of $575.00 each month to and including the payment of $575.00 which was due and payable, according to the terms of the agreement on February 1, 1961, and since said date of February 1, 1961, defendants have not paid any sum of any kind or nature to plaintiffs. * * * That defendants have failed to pay the monthly installments of $575.00 each from March 1, 1961 to and including the installment which will become due on February 1, 1963, or a total of twenty-four (24) monthly payments, being in the aggregate the sum of $13,800.00." * * *

On September 7, 1961, plaintiffs filed a complaint for breach of contract seeking as damages the monthly payments past due and to become due up to the time of trial. The defendants based their defense solely upon section 580b of the Code of Civil Procedure. The cause was tried and the court made its findings of fact and conclusions of law, the significant portion of which state that "The plaintiffs' action herein and right of recovery thereon is not barred by the provisions of Section 580b of the Code of Civil Procedure of the State of California." The court found that the defendants were obligated to pay the monthly installments up to the day of trial and a judgment was entered awarding the plaintiffs the sum of $13,800. It is from this judgment the defendants appeal. The appellants contend that the contract, admittedly not a purchase money mortgage, is of the same character as purchase money paper and the judgment entered herein is in the nature of a deficiency judgment and should be barred by section 580b of the Code of Civil Procedure.

Section 580b of the Code of Civil Procedure (in effect at the time of this action) provided, in part, that "No deficiency judgment shall lie in any event after any sale of real property for failure of the purchaser to complete his contract of sale, or under a deed of trust or mortgage; given to the vendor to secure payment of the balance of the purchase price of real property. * * *"

It is to be noted that section 580b was amended in 1935 to extend the scope of the anti-deficiency statute to include contracts of sale. It is stated in California Land Security & Development (Continuing Education of the Bar) at page 402 that "This expansion of C.C.P. § 580b to include land contracts in addition to purchase-money mortgages and deeds of trust was dictated by the appreciation that land contracts which provide for deferred payment or payments of the purchase price, and which postpone the duty to convey until a part or the whole of the purchase price has been paid, in effect transform the vendor's title into a security interest for purchase money. Hence it appeared only fair and equitable to place all purchase-money security on an equal footing."

The single question for this court to decide is whether a judgment for past installment payments under an agreement for sale of real estate as herein set forth is within the scope of a deficiency decree and thus barred by section 580b, Code of Civil Procedure.

If the section is to apply to the instant case, it must appear that the agreement in question is a security device and not just a preliminary contract to sell the land. In the strictest sense of the word, the ordinary land sales contract is not a security device. The vendor, in most instances, is not loaning money to the vendee and receiving a lien on the property as security, as is ordinarily the case with a trust deed or mortgage. However, it does appear to be well settled that

> "a contract for the sale of land in return for installment payments, title to be retained by the vendor until all or a large part of the purchase price is paid, *serves the function of a security device,* similar to a mortgage. *The transaction is so similar to a purchase money mortgage that the consequences attributed to such a deal are substantially identical with those characteristic of a mortgage relation.*" (3 Powell, Real Property, § 450, p. 586 (1952).) (Emphasis added.)

Although there seems to be no clear cut test for determining when an earnest money contract becomes a security device, the test should be one of intent, which may be evidenced by such factors as the length of time the contract is to run, change in possession of the property, the number of installments to be made under the contract, the per cent payable under the contract contrasted to other financing methods which may be involved.

Upon the execution of the contract in question, the vendees were to take possession of the property and monthly payments of $575 were to be made by the vendees to the vendors. $145 of this monthly payment was to be applied to a principal amount of $10,000 and when $10,000 had been accumulated, the parties would enter into an escrow and complete the sale. Thus, it appears the parties intended in fact that this instrument would operate as a security device. * * *

The specific purposes underlying section 580b have been set forth in Roseleaf Corp. v. Chierighino, 59 Cal.2d 35, 27 Cal.Rptr. 873, 378 P.2d 97. They were summarized in Bargioni v. Hill, 59 Cal.2d 121, where the court said: "The purposes are to discourage land sales that are unsound because the land is overvalued and, in the event of a depression in land values, to prevent the aggravation of the downturn that would result if defaulting purchasers lost the land and were burdened with personal liability." * * *

Thus, when the vendor under a security-type contract for the sale of land receives a personal money judgment against the vendee for breach of this contract without first going against the security, he is, in effect, receiving a deficiency judgment. * * * It should also be noted that to allow the vendor to recover this judgment places him in a better position than under a trust deed or mortgage. It would allow him to recover a personal judgment and retain title to the land. * * *

Thus this court is forced to hold that where a contract for the sale of land is used as a security device, a defaulting vendee is not subject to any personal liability which would be in the nature of a deficiency judgment.

The strong policy of protecting the public is further evidenced by the fact that the provisions of this section may not be waived in advance by the debtor and any such waiver will be of no force and effect.

The respondent has relied upon Goldsworthy v. Dobbins, 110 Cal.App.2d 802, 243 P.2d 883 in support of the trial court's judgment. This case is not in point. The court in the Goldsworthy case found that the transaction was one for *cash and not a credit type sale.* The plaintiff, Goldsworthy, was the vendor, but was not receiving any security under the terms of the contract. There were existing trust deeds which defendant, vendee, agreed to assume. No such finding of a cash sale was made by the court in the case at bar.

Under the circumstances, as above set forth the judgment is reversed.

Notes

1. A vendor foreclosing a land sale contract is entitled to a deficiency judgment if the proceeds of the sale are insufficient to pay the price. Aveco Properties, Inc. v. Nicholson, 229 Mont. 417, 747 P.2d 1358 (1987); Wolken v. Bunn, 422 N.W.2d 417 (S.D.1988). As in *Venable,* however, statutory provisions may modify this right. See Larwood v. Profozich, 613 F.Supp. 1195 (W.D.Pa.1985), limiting damages under Pennsylvania law. The California anti-deficiency statutory protection for purchaser does not apply where the vendor's claim is fraud.

2. Absent a statutory prohibition, a seller may recover either past due installments or the purchase price by an action at law for damages or by a suit for specific performance. See Glacier Campground v. Wild Rivers, Inc., 182 Mont. 389, 597 P.2d 689 (1978). If the seller opts for forfeiture, however, the right to claim unpaid amounts due under the installment contract is lost. Hepperly v. Bosch, 172 Ill.App.3d 1017, 527 N.E.2d 533 (1988). In Keesee v. Fetzek, 111 Idaho 360, 723 P.2d 904 (1986), the seller was estopped from shifting to damages after filing a claim for forfeiture.

f. Restitutionary Remedies

(1) Vendee v. Vendor

BROWN v. YACHT CLUB OF COEUR D'ALENE, LTD.

Court of Appeals of Idaho, 1986.
111 Idaho 195, 722 P.2d 1062.

BURNETT, JUDGE. This appeal presents two questions. First, are buyers of real estate entitled to rescind the sale agreement when third-party communications reveal a cloud on the sellers' title? Second, if rescission is appropriate, may the buyers recover (a) profits they expected to realize from developing the property, (b) benefits allegedly bestowed upon the sellers before rescission, or (c) out-of-pocket expenses incurred while preparing to develop the land, in reliance on the sale agreement? The district court decided that rescission was proper but that the buyers were not entitled to recover in any of the categories indicated. Both sides have appealed. For reasons explained below, we affirm the district court's ruling on rescission, but we vacate that part of the judgment which precludes recovery of the buyers' out-of-pocket expenses.

These issues are framed by complex facts. Those essential to our opinion are summarized here. In late 1978, Baxter and Linda Lee Brown became interested in buying development property near Coeur d'Alene. Their attention was drawn to "Blackwell Island," a parcel on the Spokane River. The land was owned in part by the Yacht Club of Coeur d'Alene, Ltd., a partnership, and in part by the Yacht Club of Coeur d'Alene, Inc., a corporation. The Browns negotiated the purchase with J.E. Hall, president and principal stockholder of the Yacht Club corporation. Mr. Hall negotiated for the Yacht Club partnership as well, its partners consisting of Hall's children and a close business associate.

In 1980 the Browns agreed to purchase the property owned by the corporation and the partnership for a total price of three million dollars. Two virtually identical earnest money agreements were signed, one by the corporation and one by the partnership. Each agreement provided as follows:

> "The closing of this transaction shall be thirty (30) days after final zoning approval as a PUD [planned unit development] for the use of the property in accordance with the developmental plans of Purchaser has been obtained. Purchaser agrees to pursue in the most expeditious manner possible in a continuous and uninterrupted manner all steps, including various governmental agency approvals, necessary to obtain such zoning. The closing agent for this transaction will be the title company who furnishes title insurance on the property. Purchaser shall pay the closing costs and escrow fees.
>
> "Executed concurrently herewith is a Promissory Note * * * payable to Forrest Brown Realtors, Inc., to be transferred by the realty to the closing agent upon closing of this transaction. Should Purchaser fail to comply with the terms of this agreement and the attached Real Estate Contract, then the earnest money will be forfeited and retained by Seller. Purchaser will pay any real estate commissions involved in this transaction.

The promissory note accompanying the corporation's agreement was for $1,000; the note accompanying the partnership's agreement was for $9,000. The sale was contingent upon issuance of the necessary development permits by government agencies.

The buyers then hired consultants, prepared a development scheme comprised of commercial and residential uses, and sought approval from the pertinent government agencies. The buyers secured necessary zoning changes and tentative approval of the proposed PUD, subject to obtaining a permit for dredging operations contemplated by the development plan. The dredging permit was withheld, pending an engineering study of possible damage to Lake Coeur d'Alene and the underlying aquifer. Before the study could be completed and the dredging permit obtained, controversy erupted over an apparent cloud upon title to the property.

The earnest money agreements obligated the corporation and the partnership to convey "marketable" and "insurable" title. When the agreements were executed in 1980, the buyers were aware that Mr. Hall might have outstanding tax liabilities. In response to an inquiry from the buyers, Hall replied, "Don't go poking around on these tax problems, or we will just call the whole deal off." Nevertheless, the buyers proceeded with the transaction because Hall personally was not a record owner of "Blackwell Island" and because a preliminary title report disclosed no tax liens.

However, in late 1980, judgments were entered by a federal district court against J.E. Hall and James Emery Hall Contractors, Inc., for tax deficiencies totaling approximately two million dollars. Soon thereafter an article appeared in the Coeur d'Alene newspaper discussing the sale and development of "Blackwell Island." A local agent of the Internal Revenue Service saw the article and contacted Mr. Brown. The agent claimed that "Blackwell Island" was "pledged" to the IRS. Brown then spoke with an attorney at the U.S. Department of Justice. The attorney reiterated that a "pledge" existed, asserted that Hall had dealt with corporate and partnership assets as though they belonged to him personally, and advised Brown to proceed cautiously.

An updated title search failed to disclose the "pledge," but a title officer told Brown that IRS encumbrances were not always recorded. The IRS declined to furnish a copy of the "pledge" instrument. When asked, Hall refused as well. Hall insisted that the "pledge" did not affect "Blackwell Island." When the PUD proposal received tentative approval, Hall requested an early closing of the transaction, despite the lack of a dredging permit. When Brown inquired as to the reason for this request, Hall replied simply, "It is [to] your and my benefit to close early." The Browns then sued for rescission.

Following a bench trial, the district court found the facts recited above. The court concluded that the sellers had committed an anticipatory breach of the earnest money agreements by requesting that the transaction be closed when marketable and insurable title apparently could not be provided. The district judge characterized the breach as "substantial and fundamental." He allowed the buyers to rescind and he ordered cancellation of the promissory notes that had accompanied the earnest money agreements. No further relief was granted. These appeals followed.

We first consider the propriety of granting rescission for the asserted cloud on title. The evidence at trial disclosed that the mysterious "pledge" did in fact exist. It was an instrument that "irrevocably assigned, transferred and pledged" to the IRS all shares owned in the Yacht Club. * * *

* * *

Here, we agree with the judge's conclusion that title was not marketable. In light of the "pledge," which Hall barred Brown from examining at times critical to this case, and in light of the warning issued by the attorney at the Department of Justice, we believe that no reasonable and prudent business person would have closed the transaction and accepted title. The threat of litigation was imminent. [A] buyer is not required to purchase a lawsuit. We further believe that reasonable doubt concerning the title pervaded the entire transaction, not merely that portion of it relating to the corporation's land. * * *

We now turn to the question whether the buyers were entitled to compensation in addition to rescission. As noted, the district court held that the buyers were entitled to nothing more than cancellation of the promissory notes. However, in general, when a contract has been breached, the aggrieved party may seek compensation for infringement upon any of three separate interests embodied in the contract.

> "Judicial remedies * * * serve to protect one or more of the following interests of [one who has been promised performance under a contract]:
>
> "(a) his 'expectation interest,' which is his interest in having the benefit of his bargain by being put in as good a position as he would have been in had the contract been performed,
>
> "(b) his 'reliance interest,' which is his interest in being reimbursed for loss caused by reliance on the contract by being put in as good a position as he would have been in had the contract not been made, or
>
> "(c) his 'restitution interest,' which is his interest in having restored to him any benefit that he has conferred on the other party."

Restatement (Second) of Contracts § 344 (1979) (herein cited as the Second Restatement). We will consider each of these interests, as applied to the instant case. * * *

In our view, the claim of an expectancy interest in full performance of a contract is fundamentally inconsistent with a claim, made by the buyers here, for rescission of the contract. "Rescission is an equitable remedy that totally abrogates the contract and seeks to restore the parties to their original positions. * * * [One who seeks rescission] no longer treat[s] the contract as in existence." Blinzler v. Andrews, 94 Idaho 215, 218, 485 P.2d 957, 960 (1971), disapproved on other grounds, Bernard & Son, Inc. v. Akins, 109 Idaho 466, 708 P.2d 871 (1985). Consequently, we concur with the district court that compensation for the expectancy interest would have been inappropriate in this case.

The remaining interests—"reliance" and "restitutionary"—present a terminology problem. In some cases and texts, the term "restitution" is broadly used to denote compensation for both of these interests. It may refer to restoring the pre-contract status quo or to recovering the value of benefits bestowed upon the other party.

Nevertheless, we will consider each interest separately. The restitution interest, as envisioned by the Second Restatement, seeks recovery of the value of benefits bestowed, and which it would be unjust for the other party to retain. This form of recovery is available for breach of a contract. As noted in McEnroe v. Morgan, 106 Idaho 326, 678 P.2d 595 (Ct.App.1984), an aggrieved purchaser may "elect to rescind a land sale contract and seek restitution of the benefits he has conferred on the seller if the seller has materially breached the contract." However, the benefits must be real, not speculative; and they must actually have been conferred upon the breaching party. Second Restatement § 370. If it is determined that benefits actually were bestowed, other elements of the unjust enrichment doctrine must be satisfied. The value of the benefits must be realized by the breaching party under circumstances where it would be inequitable to avoid payment. [citation] Moreover, recovery for unjust enrichment is unavailable if the benefits are created incidentally by a party pursuing his own advantage. [citation]

In this case, the district court found that the alleged benefits—the procurement of governmental permits and the preparation of a development scheme—were merely of speculative value to the sellers. There was no cogent showing that the sellers would or could avail themselves of such benefits. The court further found that the monetary value of such benefits was not adequately established. In this regard, the district court evidently discounted the testimony of an expert witness who purported to place a dollar figure upon the increased value of the land due to the acquisition of permits. It is the province of the trier of fact to determine the weight to be ascribed to expert testimony. The court's findings that the supposed benefits were not actually bestowed or realized by the sellers, and that the pecuniary value of any benefits had not been satisfactorily established, are not clearly erroneous and will not be set aside.

Finally, we consider the "reliance" interest—the claim for recovery of out-of-pocket expenses incurred in anticipation of mutual performance of the contract. Compensation of this interest customarily is available when a contract has been breached, even if the aggrieved party elects to rescind the contract. [citations]

Here, the buyers presented undisputed evidence that they had expended some $303,000. Whether the entire amount is compensable may be doubtful, but the district court wholly rejected any compensation for the reliance interest. The court said that the buyers' obtaining of permits, preparation of the development plan, etc., were not "in furtherance" of the contract but were in furtherance of the buyers' own objectives. We believe this reasoning reflects an unduly narrow reading of the case law allowing recovery for the "reliance" interest. Such recovery is available for all expenses reasonably related to the purposes of the contract, which would not have been incurred but for the contract's existence. The district court, by focusing on the beneficiary of such services, may have confused the restitutionary interest—which is unavailable for services that primarily benefit the aggrieved party—with the "reliance" interest, which turns not upon the benefits but upon the relationship between the expenses and the purposes of the contract. In any event, we deem it clear that at least some of the expenses incurred by the purchasers were for the mutual benefit of both parties because they shared a common interest in seeing the contract eventually performed.

We conclude that the district court erred by wholly rejecting the buyers' claim of compensation for their "reliance" interest in the contract. On remand, the district court should reexamine the evidence. The court should determine which expenses have been proven; of those, which would not have been incurred but for the existence of the contract; and of those, which were reasonably necessary to effectuate the purposes of the contract.

Accordingly, the judgment of the district court is affirmed as to the declaration of rescission. It is vacated with respect to the issue of monetary recovery. The case is remanded for further proceedings regarding compensation of the "reliance" interest, consistent with this opinion.

WALTERS, C.J., and SWANSTROM, J., concur.

Notes

1. Should the right to recover reliance damages depend upon the basis for granting rescission? In Renner v. Kehl, 150 Ariz. 94, 99, 722 P.2d 262, 267 (1986), supra p. 776, the court ruled that where rescission was based on mutual mistake rather than fraud, the rescinding buyer's recovery is limited to "that amount of money which represents the enhanced value of the land due to the [buyer's] development efforts."

2. A rescinding buyer is entitled to a lien on the property to secure the repayment of the purchase price. Generally this lien includes buyer's expenditures for insurance, taxes, and maintenance. Does the lien extend to the buyer's attorney's fees and litigation costs.

In Warner v. Peterson, 234 Mont. 319, 762 P.2d 872 (1988), the court decreed a lien to the plaintiff to establish priority over defendant's attorney's mortgage that secured the payment of his fees.

3. *Vendor v. Vendee.* Where a land purchaser defaults by failing to make the required payments, a vendor may treat the breach as material, rescind the contract, and seek restitution of the property. Rescission and restitution is conditioned upon vendor returning the purchaser's payments plus interest less the rental value of the property. Vendors may seek rescission for buyer's fraud; but rescission is uncommon where the buyer's only breach is failure to make the required installment payments. Here the vendor's usual remedy is either to foreclose the vendor's lien or to forfeit the buyer's equity in the property. Where forfeiture is conditioned on restitution of the purchaser's payments in excess of the vendor's actual damages, strict foreclosure is the functional equivalent of rescission.

(2) Grantor v. Grantee

SUBURBAN PROPERTIES, INC. v. HANSON

Supreme Court of Oregon, 1963.
234 Or. 356, 382 P.2d 90.

LUSK, JUSTICE. This is a suit in equity to cancel a deed of conveyance of real property. The circuit court entered findings of fact, conclusions of law, and a decree for the plaintiff and the defendants have appealed.

During the pertinent times, the plaintiff was the owner of real property in Washington county, Oregon, which it was engaged in developing for residence purposes. The defendants are Howard Hanson, a builder and contractor, and his wife.

The dispute arose out of a sale in November, 1960, by the plaintiff to the defendant of two parcels of land referred to in the record as lot A and lot B in a subdivision known as "Harvest Hill." The agreed purchase price of each lot was $2,300 and, as to each lot, the defendant gave to the plaintiff two promissory notes, one for $1,000 payable on demand, the other for $1,300, payable six months after date. Defendant further agreed to build a house on each lot and that as to each lot the $1,000 note should be paid out of the first moneys received by the defendant from a building loan to be obtained by him and that the $1,300 note should be paid when the house built on such lot should be sold. The reason why the notes were split up in this manner was that the lots were part of a tract which plaintiff was buying on contract, which provided that upon each $1,000 payment, a lot would be released from such contract. To clear the title to the lots here involved and thus enable the defendant to get his building loan, plaintiff made payment of $2,000 on its contract of purchase. Payment of the $1,000 notes by the defendant would reimburse plaintiff for this outlay.

Deeds to both lots were delivered by the plaintiff to the defendant. No mortgage or other security was given by the defendant. The present controversy relates only to lot B and arises out of the failure of the defendant to build a house on that lot. * * *

The question is whether, under established rules in this class of cases, the plaintiff is entitled to the remedy of cancellation, or whether it must resort to its remedy at law in an action on the notes and for damages if any have been suffered.

This is a case in which there was a fully executed sale of land by the plaintiff to the defendant accompanied by a covenant on the part of the defendant to build a house on the land and pay the plaintiff two promissory notes given for the purchase price, one out of a building loan to be obtained by the defendant, the other when the house should be sold. The parties did not agree, however, that the loan and the proceeds of the sale of the contemplated house were to be the exclusive source of payment of the notes. Were that the case, we would have a different lawsuit. On the contrary, the defendant was legally bound to pay the principal and interest of these notes, one on demand, the other in six months, whether or not a loan was obtained or a house built and sold. Doubtless, one purpose of the agreement was to enable the defendant to make a profit out of the sale of the projected houses and another was to provide the defendant with the means of securing the funds for payment of the notes to the plaintiff, but neither of these facts in any way alters the unconditional character of the defendant's obligation.

If the house had been built as agreed, it would have been, together with the ground upon which it was built, the property of the defendant. All that plaintiff would have been entitled to in that case was payment of the notes. The question here is whether the different and drastic relief of cancellation of the deed is available to the plaintiff because of defendant's failure to build the house in accordance with his agreement. * * *

As authority for the claimed right, plaintiff cites Krebs Hop Co. v. Livesley, 51 Or. 527, 92 P. 1084, where the court enunciated the rule regarding the right of one party to an *executory* contract to rescind for some failure on the part of the other party. "To justify such a course of procedure" it was said "there must be a failure in some substantial particular, which goes to the essence of the contract, and renders the defaulting party incapable of performance, or makes it impossible for him to carry out the contract as intended." That case involved a contract for the sale of hops extending over a period of five years. The ground of the suit was that the plaintiff (the seller) had assigned the contract to a bank. The court said: "In order, therefore, to justify defendants' attempted abandonment or rescission of the contract between them and plaintiff, it is incumbent upon them to show that plaintiff has rendered itself incapable of performance." As the proof of the defendants did not meet this test the remedy of rescission was held to be not available.

The distinction of first importance between this and the *Krebs* case is that the contract in the latter was wholly executory, while here it is fully executed except for defendant's agreement to construct a building on lot B. * * *

The distinction in this regard between an executory and an executed contract was pointed out in McMillan v. American Suburban Corp., 136 Tenn. 53, 59, 188 S.W. 615, 617, in this language:

> "As has been well said, the power of a court of equity to decree the rescission of an executed contract and order its surrender for cancellation is one of the most delicate powers it is ever called upon to exercise. The equitable remedy of rescission is not one enforceable as a matter of right, and the court should not award it in [a] case where some such element as actual fraud, accident, mistake or insolvency does not appear to justify it. This is true even though the circumstances are such that were the contract still executory, the court would grant that relief. The vendee is left to resort to his legal remedy for damages for the breach."

In that case a vendee in possession under an executed contract who sued for rescission because of breach of the vendor's agreement to lay water pipe lines to the property was held to be limited to his legal remedy, there being no claim of fraud or mistake or that the vendor was insolvent. The court indicated, however, that had the contract been executory, there would have been a different decision.

A similar case was Emigrant Co. v. County of Adams, 100 U.S. 61, 60–71, where the court said:

> "The allegations of the bill to the effect that the Emigrant Company has not fulfilled its engagements with respect to the drainage and settlement of the land, rest in covenant merely, and afford no ground for avoiding the contract. Where covenants are mutual and dependent, the failure of one party to perform absolves the other, and authorizes him to rescind the contract. But here the contract was largely carried into execution soon after its inception. The engagements of the appellants to introduce settlers and the like were to be performed in the future; and their performance was not made a condition, but, as before stated, rested in covenant. In case of a breach, they would lay the foundation of an action, but nothing more."

It has not been suggested by the plaintiff, and it could not be successfully maintained, that the defendant's undertaking to build the two houses was a condition subsequent upon the breach of which restoration of the status quo could be decreed. The law with respect to the subject is thus stated in 5 Pomeroy's Equity Jurisprudence (2d ed.) 4755, § 2108:

> "It is, of course, the general rule that the mere failure by a grantee to perform a promise, which formed the whole or part of the consideration inducing an executed conveyance, gives rise to no right of rescission in the grantor, either at law or in equity, unless such promise amounts to a condition; and it is a rule of construction that, in case the language of intention is doubtful, 'the promise or obligation of the grantee will be construed to be a covenant, limiting the grantor to an action thereon, and not a condition subsequent, with the right to defeat the conveyance.'"

There was, of course, no express agreement making defendant's promise a condition and there is nothing in the evidence pertaining to this loose oral arrangement which would justify a court in so construing it. There is no evidence that plaintiff has sustained any damages by reason of defendant's breach that are not capable of reasonable ascertainment or, for that matter, that it has been damaged at all. If it should be said that plaintiff has suffered because of delay it could be answered that defendant must compensate for this delay by the payment of interest. So far as this record reveals, plaintiff has an adequate remedy at law by an action on the notes. * * *

The decree is reversed and the suit dismissed.

Note

State, by Pai v. Thom, 58 Haw. 8, 18, 563 P.2d 982, 989 (1977): "To hold that a vendor [grantor] of real property could upon vendee's [grantee's] failure to pay the purchase price, repudiate his deed and recover the property, would render real estate titles dangerously uncertain with ensuing unfortunate consequences."

DIETZ v. DIETZ

Supreme Court of Minnesota, 1955.
244 Minn. 330, 70 N.W.2d 281.

DELL, CHIEF JUSTICE. Action for an accounting and to recover real estate conveyed to plaintiff and defendant Donald Dietz in joint tenancy in consideration for an oral agreement to support. Said defendant appeals from an order denying his motion for a new trial.

Plaintiff, 69 years old at the time of trial is the mother of the defendant Donald Dietz (hereinafter referred to as the defendant). The trial court found, among others, the following facts: After the death of plaintiff's husband in 1942, the defendant, who had considerable business experience, took charge of plaintiff's assets and acted as her financial advisor. In May 1944 the defendant, who was then unmarried, entered into an oral agreement with the plaintiff to the effect that he would support her for the remainder of her life if she would purchase a certain duplex and have title conveyed to him and plaintiff as joint tenants. In reliance upon this promise, the plaintiff purchased the property and caused it to be conveyed to herself and the defendant as joint tenants. Plaintiff paid $5,200 for the property from her own funds, the balance of the purchase price consisting of a mortgage in the amount of $4,800.

The defendant categorically denied making an oral promise to support the plaintiff and testified that the money used to purchase the property in question was his. Plaintiff and defendant occupied the lower duplex of this property until his marriage to the defendant Virginia Dietz in March 1946. After the marriage the defendant and Virginia made their home with the plaintiff in the lower duplex. A strained relationship developed between plaintiff and Virginia and, according to plaintiff, on one occasion Virginia attempted to strike her with a scrub cloth. The disharmony between the parties was evidenced by several other incidents, including periods of time when plaintiff and Virginia did not speak to each other. Finally plaintiff testified that in March 1950 she asked defendant whether she might have her breakfast and was told that she could not have anything to eat in the house "now or at any time" and further that there was no need for her to stay there to protect her rights and that defendant wanted her to get out. * * * Plaintiff left the house that day and went to live with her sister. Neither the defendant nor his wife made any attempt to stop her nor thereafter made any inquiries as to her welfare or provisions for her support.

On the basis of the above evidence the court found that the defendant had breached his oral promise to support the plaintiff. An accounting of the equities of the parties, which is not disputed here, was made taking into consideration, among other things, the rents collected by the defendants, the reasonable value of his use of the premises, expenditures incurred by him, and the reasonable value of his services. Judgment was ordered in favor of the plaintiff for $1,651.48 with interest and awarding her possession and title of the premises free of any claim or interest by the defendants. * * *

The remainder of defendant's arguments are to the general effect that plaintiff is not entitled to recover since parol evidence cannot be used to establish an express trust, create a condition subsequent or otherwise vary the terms of a deed. It is clear, as defendant suggests, that, under the provisions of our statute, a purchase-money resulting trust could not arise in favor of the plaintiff. It is equally well settled that, as a general rule, an express trust in land must be in writing in order to be enforceable. The plaintiff, however, does not contend that she is entitled to relief on either of these theories. Nor is the plaintiff attempting to vary the terms of the deed by creating a condition subsequent. A condition subsequent, as opposed to a conditional limitation or a mere covenant is sometimes found to have been created where a deed, given in consideration for a promise to support, contains language evidencing the obligation. There is no such language in the deed here. A few courts notably those of Wisconsin, have treated the agreement to support, whether oral or in writing, as an "equitable condition subsequent," and have implied the condition in the conveyance even though the deed is absolute in form. [citations] In such a case the grantor may, upon breach of the condition, exercise his right of reentry or rescind and have the conveyance cancelled as if the condition had been incorporated in the deed. In Bruer v. Bruer, 109 Minn. 260, 123 N.W. 813, we approved of the general result reached by the Wisconsin court but held that in the absence of express language in the deed, a condition subsequent could not be implied.[1]

The plaintiff's right of recovery, however, is not dependent upon an implied condition subsequent. As the trial court indicated in its memorandum, recovery was allowed on the theory of an "implied or constructive trust." Apparently defendant has misconceived the nature and character of a constructive trust. It is an equitable remedy imposed to prevent unjust enrichment and is completely dissimilar to an express or resulting trust. Because it arises by operation of law rather than being dependent upon the intention of the parties, it is expressly exempted from the statute of fraud.

* * * We have held that a constructive trust may be imposed where the plaintiff shows "the existence of a fiduciary relation and the abuse by defendant of confidence and trust bestowed under it to plaintiff's harm." It is clear, however, that a fiduciary relationship in a strict sense is not a prerequisite, and any relationship giving rise to justifiable reliance or confidence is sufficient.

1. [Footnotes renumbered.] The Wisconsin theory has not generally been followed elsewhere. [citations] Since right of re-entry for breach of condition subsequent can be reserved only to the grantor, Fraser, Future Interests, Uses and Trusts in Minnesota, 28 M.S.A. pp. 53, 58, the question arises whether even under the broad Wisconsin view the plaintiff, as a grantee, could assert the fiction of a constructive condition subsequent and thereby affect the quality of the estate conveyed.

Not only were the parties here parent and child but the evidence amply supports the conclusion that plaintiff relied upon her son for business advice and counsel. We have previously held that such a relationship is of a confidential nature and fiduciary character. It is equally clear that the defendant was unjustly enriched as a result of his abuse of this confidential relationship.

[Discussion of the Statute of Frauds issue is omitted.]

It is well settled in this state that rescission and cancellation may be decreed in actions brought by the grantor where the grantee fails to furnish the support as agreed in consideration for the conveyance. The instant case, however, appears to be novel in this state in that the relief sought is not by a grantor but by a grantee who supplied the purchase money and caused the property to be placed in joint tenancy. * * * The equities of the instant case are * * * apparent. Under the circumstances the trial court was amply justified in restoring the property to the plaintiff and awarding her judgment for the amount due her under the accounting.

Affirmed.

g. Remedies in Favor of Defaulting Vendee

VINES v. ORCHARD HILLS, INC.

Supreme Court of Connecticut, 1980.
181 Conn. 501, 435 A.2d 1022.

PETERS, ASSOCIATE JUSTICE. This case concerns the right of purchasers of real property, after their own default, to recover moneys paid at the time of execution of a valid contract of sale. The plaintiffs, Euel D. Vines and his wife Etta Vines contracted, on July 11, 1973, to buy Unit No. 10, Orchard Hills Condominium. New Canaan, Connecticut from the defendant Orchard Hills, Inc. for $78,800. On or before that date, they had paid the defendant $7880 as a down payment toward the purchase. Alleging that the sale of the property was never consummated, the plaintiffs sought to recover their down payment. The trial court overruled the defendant's demurrer to the plaintiffs' amended complaint; subsequently, after a hearing, the trial court rendered judgment for the plaintiffs for $7880 plus interest. The defendant's appeal maintains that its demurrer should have been sustained, that its liquidated damages clause should have been enforced, and that evidence of the value of the property at the time of the trial should have been excluded.

The facts underlying this litigation are straightforward and undisputed. When the purchasers contracted to buy their condominium in July, 1973, they paid $7880, a sum which the contract of sale designated as liquidated damages.[1] The purchasers decided not to take title to the condominium because Euel D. Vines was transferred by his employer to New Jersey; the Vines so informed the seller by a letter dated January 4, 1974. There has never been any claim that the seller has failed, in any respect, to conform to his obligations under the contract, nor does the complaint allege that the purchasers are legally

1. [Footnote renumbered.] Paragraph 9 of the contract of sale provided: "DEFAULT: In the event Purchaser fails to perform any of the obligations herein imposed on the Purchaser, the Seller performing all obligations herein imposed on the Seller, the Seller shall retain all sums of money paid under this Contract, as liquidated damages, and all rights and liabilities of the parties hereto shall be at an end."

excused from their performance under the contract. In short, it is the purchasers and not the seller whose breach precipitated the present cause of action.

In the proceedings below, the purchasers established that the value of the condominium that they had agreed to buy for $78,800 in 1973 had, by the time of the trial in 1979, a fair market value of $160,000. The trial court relied on this figure to conclude that, because the seller had gained what it characterized as a windfall of approximately $80,000, the purchasers were entitled to recover their down payment of $7880. Neither the purchasers nor the seller proffered any evidence at the trial to show the market value of the condominium at the time of the purchasers' breach of their contract or the damages sustained by the seller as a result of that breach.

The seller's principal argument on this appeal is that the trial court improperly disregarded the parties' valid liquidated damages clause. That claim is pursued * * * by an argument on the merits of the evidence presented at the trial. * * * The trial court was in error in its conclusion that the evidence before it was sufficient to sustain a judgment in favor of the purchasers.

The ultimate issue on this appeal is the enforceability of a liquidated damages clause as a defense to a claim of restitution by purchasers in default on a land sale contract. Although the parties, both in the trial court and here, have focused on the liquidated damages clause per se, we must first consider when, if ever, purchasers who are themselves in breach of a valid contract of sale may affirmatively invoke the assistance of judicial process to recover back moneys paid to, and withheld by, their seller.

The right of a contracting party, despite his default, to seek restitution for benefits conferred and allegedly unjustly retained has been much disputed in the legal literature and in the case law. See 5A Corbin, Contracts §§ 1122–1135 (1964); Dobbs, Remedies § 12.14 (1973); 1 Palmer, Restitution, c. 5 (1978); 12 Williston, Contracts §§ 1473 through 1478 (3d Ed.1970); 5 Williston, Contracts § 791 (3d Ed.1961); [citations] Although earlier cases often refused to permit a party to bring an action that could be said to be based on his own breach; [citations] many of the more recent cases support restitution in order to prevent unjust enrichment and to avoid forfeiture. See, e.g., Hook v. Bomar, 320 F.2d 536, 541 (5th Cir.1963); Amtorg Trading Corporation v. Miehle Printing Press & Mfg. Co., 206 F.2d 103, 108 (2d Cir.1953); Honey v. Henry's Franchise Leasing Corporation, 64 Cal.2d 801, 803, 52 Cal.Rptr. 18, 415 P.2d 833 (1966); [citations]

A variety of considerations, some practical and some theoretical, underlie this shift in attitude toward the plaintiff in breach. As Professor Corbin pointed out in his seminal article, "The Right of a Defaulting Vendee to the Restitution of Installments Paid," 40 Yale L.J. 1013 (1931), the anomalous result of denying any remedy to the plaintiff in breach is to punish more severely the person who has partially performed, often in good faith, than the person who has entirely disregarded his contractual obligations from the outset. Only partial performance triggers a claim for restitution, and partial performance will not, in the ordinary course of events, have been more injurious to the innocent party than total nonperformance. Recognition of a claim in restitution is, furthermore, consistent with the economic functions that the law of contracts is designed to serve. The principal purpose of remedies for the breach of contract is to provide compensation for loss and therefore a party injured by breach of contract is entitled to retain nothing in excess of that sum which compensates him for the loss of his bargain. Indeed, there are those who argue that repudiation of contractual obligations is socially desirable, and should be encouraged, whenever gain to the party in breach exceeds loss to the party injured by breach. Birmingham, "Breach of Contract, Damage Measures, and Economic Efficiency," 24 Rut.L.Rev. 273, 284, (1970); Posner, Economic Analysis of Law § 4.9, pp. 89–90 (2d Ed.1977). To assign such primacy to inferences drawn from economic models requires great confidence that the person injured by breach will encounter no substantial difficulties in establishing the losses for which he is entitled to be compensated. It is not necessary to push the principle of compensatory damages that far, or to disregard entirely the desirability of maintaining some incentives for the performance of promises. A claim in restitution, although legal in form, is equitable in nature, and permits a trial court to balance the equities, to take into account a variety of competing principles to determine whether the defendant has been unjustly enriched. "Even though we adhere to the rule that only compensatory damages are to be awarded, there are other important questions of policy to be considered. One is whether aid is to be given to one who breaches his contract, particularly when the breach is deliberate and without moral justification. Another is whether restitution can be administered without leaving the innocent party with uncompensated damages." 1 Palmer, Restitution § 5.1, p. 574 (1978).

Recognition that there are circumstances under which a defaulting purchaser may be entitled to restitution for benefits conferred upon the innocent seller of land is consistent with parallel developments elsewhere in the law of contracts. Judicial resistance to enforcement of forfeitures has of course long been commonplace, particularly with regard to contract clauses purporting to liquidate damages. * * *

We therefore conclude that a purchaser whose breach is not willful has a restitutionary claim to recover moneys paid that unjustly enrich his seller. In this case, no one has alleged that the purchasers' breach, arising out of a transfer to a more distant place of employment, should be deemed to have been willful. The trial court was therefore not in error in initially overruling the seller's demurrer and entertaining the purchasers' cause of action.

The purchaser's right to recover in restitution requires the purchaser to establish that the seller has been unjustly enriched. The purchaser must show more than that the contract has come to an end and that the seller retains moneys paid pursuant to the contract. To prove unjust enrichment, in the ordinary case, the purchaser, because he is the party in breach, must prove that the damages suffered by his seller are less than the moneys received from the purchaser. It may not be easy for the purchaser to prove the extent of the seller's damages, it may even be strategically advantageous for the seller to come forward with relevant evidence of the losses he has incurred and may expect to incur on account of the buyer's breach. Nonetheless, only if the breaching party satisfies his burden of proof that the innocent party has sustained a net gain may a claim for unjust enrichment be sustained. Dobbs, Remedies § 12.14 (1973); 1 Palmer, Restitution § 5.4 (1978).

In the case before us, the parties themselves stipulated in the contract of sale that the purchasers' down payment of 10 percent of the purchase price represents the damages that would be likely to flow from the purchasers' breach. The question then becomes whether the purchasers have demonstrated the seller's unjust enrichment in the face of the liquidated damages clause to which they agreed. * * *

Most of the litigation concerning liquidated damages clauses arise in the context of an affirmative action by the party injured by breach to enforce the clause in order to recover the amount therein stipulated. In such cases, the burden of persuasion about the enforceability of the clause naturally rests with its proponent. [citations] In the case before us, by contrast, where the plaintiffs are themselves in default, the plaintiffs bear the burden of showing that the clause is invalid and unenforceable. [citations] It is not unreasonable in these circumstances to presume that a liquidated damages clause that is appropriately limited in amount bears a reasonable relationship to the damages that the seller has actually suffered. [citations] The seller's damages, as Professor Palmer points out, include not only his expectation damages suffered through loss of his bargain, and his incidental damages such as broker's commissions, but also less quantifiable costs arising out of retention of real property beyond the time of the originally contemplated sale. 1 Palmer, Restitution §§ 5.4, 5.8 (1978). [citations] A liquidated damages clause allowing the seller to retain 10 percent of the contract price as earnest money is presumptively a reasonable allocation of the risks associated with default.

The presumption of validity that attaches to a clause liquidating the seller's damages at 10 percent of the contract price in the event of the purchaser's unexcused nonperformance is, like most of the presumptions, rebuttable. The purchaser, despite his default, is free to prove that the contract, or any part thereof, was the product of fraud or mistake or unconscionability. In the alternative, the purchaser is free to offer evidence that this breach in fact caused the seller no damages or damages substantially less than the amount stipulated as liquidated damages.

The trial court concluded that the plaintiff purchasers had successfully invoked the principle of Norwalk Door Closer Co. v. Eagle Lock & Screw Co., 153 Conn. 689, 220 A.2d 263 (1966) by presenting evidence of increase in the value of the real property between the date of the contract of sale and the date of the trial. That conclusion was in error. The relevant time at which to measure the seller's damages is the time of breach. [citations] Benefits to the seller that are attributable to a rising market subsequent to breach rightfully accrue to the seller. There was no evidence before the court to demonstrate that the seller was not injured at the time of the purchasers' breach by their failure then to consummate the contract. Neither the seller's status as a developer of a condominium project nor the absence of willfulness on the part of the purchasers furnishes a justification for disregarding the liquidated damages clause, although these factors may play some role in the ultimate determination of whether the seller was in fact unjustly enriched by the down payment he retained.

Because the availability of, and the limits on, restitutionary claims by a plaintiff in default have not previously been clearly spelled out in our cases, it is appropriate to afford to the purchasers herein another opportunity to proffer evidence to substantiate their claim. What showing the purchasers must make cannot be spelled out with specificity in view of the sparsity of the present record. The purchasers may be able to demonstrate that the condominium could, at the time of their breach, have been resold at a price sufficiently higher than their contract price to obviate any loss of profits and to compensate the seller for any incidental and consequential damages. Alternatively, the purchasers may be able to present evidence of unconscionability or of excuse, to avoid the applicability of the liquidated damages clause altogether. The plaintiffs' burden of proof is not an easy one to sustain, but they are entitled to their day in court. There is error, the judgment is set aside, and the case is remanded for further proceedings in conformity with this opinion.

Notes

1. The principal case is the first one in this book about the restitution granted affirmatively in *favor* of a contract breaker. There are advantages in presenting this remedial concept in a unitary fashion as the Restatement (Second) of Contracts § 374 attempts; but the editors have chosen to deal with this remedy with particular types of contracts. We outline the recurring issues.

In Vines:

a. The buyers have partly performed the contract. They paid part of the purchase price and defaulted.

b. If sellers sued buyers for damages, the seller as plaintiff would have the burden of proving damages in accordance with established rules.

c. The seller, however, has not sued, but has kept the buyers' part performance. The defaulting buyers appear as plaintiff—a role only recently afforded. The question is whether they have any remedy at all. As plaintiffs seeking restitution, they have the burden of proving that *overall* they have enriched the innocent seller.

Assuming the remedy is recognized and the seller does not seek specific performance:

a. Everyone would agree that the buyer-plaintiff should recover no more than: part performance (payment) minus the seller's legal damages that the buyer would have to pay if sued.

b. But some will insist that the formula for restitution should be: part performance (payment) minus seller's detriment actually incurred whether provable as legal damages or not.

The burden should remain on the buyer to prove the seller's unjust enrichment—not upon the innocent seller to prove damages by way of offset.

Which approach is most fair? See Sutter v. Madrin, 269 Cal.App.2d 161, 74 Cal.Rptr. 627 (1969); Askari v. R & R Land Co., 179 Cal.App.3d 1101, 225 Cal.Rptr. 285 (1986); Knedlik v. Department of Commerce & Economic Development, 803 P.2d 400 (Alaska 1990).

The problem appears again in sales contracts, see pp. 1099–1100; construction contracts, Valentine v. Patrick–Warren Construction Co. and p. 1134; and service contracts, pp. 1165–68.

2. Since 1881, New York has adhered to the rule that a purchaser who defaults on a real estate contract without lawful excuse cannot recover her down payment. The Court of Appeals recently reaffirmed the precedents and observed that the legislature had failed to adopt proposals to change the rule. Maxton Builders, Inc. v. Lo Galbo, 68 N.Y.2d 373, 509 N.Y.S.2d 507, 502 N.E.2d 184 (1986).

See also Schweigert v. Fowler, 240 Mont. 424, 432, 784 P.2d 405, 411 (1990). The court, in refusing relief, stated: "Restitution is normally denied to a defaulting purchaser."

MacFADDEN v. WALKER

Supreme Court of California, 1971.

5 Cal.3d 809, 97 Cal.Rptr. 537, 488 P.2d 1353.

WRIGHT, CHIEF JUSTICE. In this case we are called upon to determine whether a vendee who would otherwise be entitled to specific performance of an installment land sale contract in which time is declared to be of the essence forfeits the right to that remedy because of her wilful failure to make installment payments when due after there has been substantial part performance of the contract. We conclude that the policy against forfeitures precludes denying the right to specific performance under such circumstances.

Sometime before 1950 defendant and cross-complainant Claudia Walker, who lived in Oakland, became interested in buying 80 acres of unimproved property. The property was located in Placer County near Auburn and was owned by plaintiff and cross-defendant Ellsworth MacFadden, who lived in Auburn. Early in 1950 the parties orally agreed that Mrs. Walker would buy the property for $2,500. She paid MacFadden $10, and he agreed to fix the road to the campsite on the property and move in some small buildings for $150. This work was done, and Mrs. Walker took possession, moved a caretaker onto the property, and undertook the payment of taxes. It does not appear that she paid the $150 but sometime before April 1953 a third party removed timber from the property for which MacFadden received $600.

In April 1953 the parties entered into a written contract for the sale of the property for $2,484.50. Pursuant to its terms Mrs. Walker paid $20 on the purchase price and $25 to MacFadden's attorney for preparing the contract. She agreed to pay $20 per month, which included 6 percent interest on the unpaid balance, and all taxes. The contract also provided that no timber could be removed without the consent of MacFadden; that Mrs. Walker had the right to pay all or any part of the unpaid principal at any time; that time was of the essence; and that on any default of Mrs. Walker, MacFadden could terminate all of her rights under the contract and retain all payments theretofore made as the reasonable value for the use of the property.

After the written contract was entered into, Mrs. Walker paid all of the installments due through November 1, 1963, a total of $2,500. She also paid the taxes, bought lumber and made improvements, kept a caretaker on the property, and paid for the installation of electricity. In late 1963, however, she discovered that timber had been cut and taken from the property and she therefore stopped making payments. There was no evidence as to who cut and took the timber.

In May 1964 MacFadden mailed a notice to Mrs. Walker that he was terminating her rights under the contract because of her default, but she testified that she did not receive this notice. In May 1966 MacFadden filed this action against Mrs. Walker to quiet title to the property. After she was served with summons Mrs. Walker offered to pay the entire principal balance of $1,174.70 with compound interest, but MacFadden rejected her offer. Thereafter she filed an answer and cross-complaint seeking specific performance and deposited the principal balance plus compound interest with the court. [She] further acknowledged an obligation to pay MacFadden an additional sum of $71.12 for taxes he paid for the year 1964 and $50 interest on the amount deposited in court. She paid the $50 into court and the $71.12 to MacFadden's attorney.

At the conclusion of the trial the court found that the property was reasonably worth the agreed price and that therefore the contract was "fair, just, and reasonable as between the parties and the consideration inuring to * * * [MacFadden] was adequate." (See Civ.Code, § 3391, subds. 1 and 2.) It also found that in December 1963 a dispute arose between the parties with respect to a credit of $600 because of the removal of timber, and that, although Mrs. Walker was mistaken with respect to her right to a credit, she acted in good faith and her cessation of monthly payments "did not constitute a grossly negligent, willful, or fraudulent act, or breach of duty." (See Civ.Code, § 3275.) Accordingly, it entered judgment awarding Mrs. Walker specific performance against MacFadden. Since the contract provided for the payment of attorney's fees and since Mrs. Walker's mistake with respect to her right to a credit precipitated the litigation, however, the court awarded MacFadden judgment for attorney's fees of $200 and costs incurred in bringing the action. MacFadden appeals.

* * * We agree with MacFadden's contention, * * * that the evidence does not support the finding that Mrs. Walker's breach was not wilful. She testified that she stopped payments "Because there was a lot of timber cut off the place," but she did not state that MacFadden was in any way responsible therefor or any facts that would suggest a good faith belief that he was. It appears from its memorandum opinion that the trial court considered Mrs. Walker's advanced age (she was 84 at the time of trial) in evaluating her testimony and in concluding that she had difficulty with her memory. Nevertheless, to qualify for relief from default under section 3275 of the Civil Code,[1] the burden was upon her to establish that her breach was not wilful, and a failure of memory on her part, if any, is not substantial evidence that fills the lacuna in her proof. Accordingly, the question presented is whether failure to qualify for relief from forfeiture under section 3275 precludes the right to specific performance.

In Barkis v. Scott, (1949), 34 Cal.2d 116, 208 P.2d 367, we reevaluated the long line of precedents dealing with the question of when the vendee's interest may be forfeited because of his default in the performance of a land sale contract in which time is declared to be of the essence. We concluded that when a forfeiture would otherwise result, the vendee can be relieved therefrom if he proves facts justifying relief under section 3275 of the Civil Code, and we held that the defaulting vendees in that case had established their right to keep their installment contract in force. Since it appeared as a matter of law that the vendees' breach in *Barkis* was neither grossly negligent, wilful, nor fraudulent, but was at most the result of simple negligence in the management of their checking account, we had no occasion to consider whether section 3275

1. [Footnote renumbered.] Section 3275 provides: "Whenever, by the terms of an obligation, a party thereto incurs a forfeiture, or a loss in the nature of a forfeiture, by reason of his failure to comply with its provisions, he may be relieved therefrom, upon making full compensation to the other party, except in case of a grossly negligent, willful, or fraudulent breach of duty."

was the exclusive source of their right to be relieved from forfeiture by keeping their contract in force.

Thereafter in Freedman v. The Rector (1951) 37 Cal.2d 16, 230 P.2d 629, we held that section 3275 is not the exclusive source of the right to relief from forfeiture. We concluded that the prohibition of punitive damages for breach of contract (Civ.Code, § 3294), the strict limitations on the right to provide for liquidated damages (Civ.Code, §§ 1670, 1671), and the provision that "Neither specific nor preventive relief can be granted to enforce a penalty or forfeiture in any case." (Civ.Code, § 3369) together established a policy that precludes any forfeiture having no reasonable relation to the damage caused by the vendee's breach even when that breach is wilful. Since in the *Freedman* case, however, the vendor had sold the property to a third party in reliance on the vendee's repudiation of the contract, specific performance was not an available remedy, and relief from forfeiture was necessarily limited to awarding the defaulting vendee restitution in the amount of the excess of his part payment over the damages caused by his breach.

We believe that the anti-forfeiture policy recognized in the *Freedman* case also justifies awarding even wilfully defaulting vendees specific performance in proper cases. As we pointed out in the *Barkis* case, allowing the defaulting vendee to cure his default and perform the contract may often be the fairest solution, for the unjust enrichment of the vendor that is precluded by restitution of the excess of part payments over the damages caused by the breach may bear little or no relation to the forfeiture imposed on the vendee if his right to perform the contract is terminated.

> "A vendee in default who is seeking to keep the contract alive, however, is in a better position to secure relief than one who is seeking to recover back the excess of what he has paid over the amount necessary to give the vendor the benefit of his bargain after performance under the contract has terminated. In the latter situation it may be so difficult to compute the vendor's damages that the vendee will be unable to prove that the vendor will be unjustly enriched by allowing him to keep all the money that has been paid. [citations.] On the other hand, when the default has not been serious and the vendee is willing and able to continue with his performance of the contract, the vendor suffers no damage by allowing the vendee to do so. In this situation, if there has been substantial part performance or if the vendee has made substantial improvements in reliance on his contract, permitting the vendor to terminate the vendee's rights under the contract and keep the installments that have been paid can result only in the harshest sort of forfeitures."

MacFadden contends, however, that the decision in Honey v. Henry's Franchise Leasing Corp. (1966) 64 Cal.2d 801, 52 Cal.Rptr. 18, 415 P.2d 833, establishes that restitution of the excess of the part payments over the damages caused by the breach is the exclusive remedy available to a wilfully defaulting vendee. He invokes the following language:

> "When a vendee has materially breached his contract, the vendor has an election to rescind or to enforce the contract. [citations] The defaulting vendee, however, has no such election. Otherwise, the contract of sale would in effect be a lease with an option to purchase. The vendee would receive the benefit of any increase in the value of the property, and the vendor would bear the entire risk of any decrease in its value. Such protection to a defaulting vendee would go beyond that provided by anti-deficiency legislation, which places the risk of depreciation in value on the vendor only to the extent that

the value of the property may decrease below the amount still owing on the contract."

In the *Honey* case, however, neither party sought specific performance, and our discussion of election of remedies was directed solely to the alternative measures of restitution that might be invoked following the vendee's breach. It was in that context that we stated that it was only the vendor who, on the vendee's breach, had the election to rescind the contract by retaining rental value damages or to enforce the contract by retaining benefit of the bargain damages. Accordingly, there is nothing in the *Honey* case that precludes granting specific performance to a wilful but repentant defaulting vendee.

It bears emphasis, of course, that we are here dealing with an equitable remedy that is carefully hedged around with protections to the person against whom it is invoked. The contract must be just and reasonable, and the consideration adequate (Civ.Code, § 3391), the vendor must be assured that he too will receive the benefit of his bargain (Civ.Code, § 3386), and the defenses of laches and unclean hands are available to preclude a defaulting vendee from seeking an unfair advantage over an innocent vendor. In the present case, however, we find no basis for upsetting the trial court's judgment awarding specific performance. The contract was just and reasonable and the consideration was adequate. MacFadden is assured and will receive the full benefit of his bargain. Mrs. Walker had paid over half of the price before she defaulted, and the value of the land adequately secured her obligation to pay the remainder. Although she failed to prove that her default was not wilful, it appears at worst to have been the petulant reaction of an elderly lady to an apparent theft of timber from her property. It is true that the default lasted for over two years, but such delay may be considered as much the responsibility of MacFadden as Mrs. Walker. A vendor can always bring an appropriate action immediately after the default if he deems it desirable to get, promptly, either his property back or the balance of the contract price. For ought that appears, however, it may have been in MacFadden's best interest to await further developments in the market for such property even though no installment payments were being made during the interim. Indeed, that apparently was the arrangement which was satisfactory to both parties during the three years between the 1950 oral contract and the 1953 written contract.

Finally, we note again, as we also did in the *Honey* case, Professor Hetland's persuasive arguments that installment land sale contracts should be treated as security devices substantially on a par with mortgages and deeds of trust, and that therefore "the law governing those security devices should be adopted with appropriate modifications in determining the remedies for breaches of installment contracts." That law affords even the wilfully defaulting debtor an opportunity to cure his default before losing his interest in the security. Since we have concluded, however, that Mrs. Walker is entitled to the remedy of specific performance, we need not decide whether she might also be entitled to some other remedy under the law governing security transactions.

The judgment is affirmed.

Notes

1. For a contrary view, see Barker v. Johnson, 591 P.2d 886, 889 (Wyo.1979). The court, emphasizing the terms of the contract agreed upon by the parties, stated

"that the tender of the full purchase price after default does not qualify as an equitable reason to ignore the default and order specific performance of the contract." See also Ellis v. Butterfield, 98 Idaho 644, 570 P.2d 1334 (1977), where, over a strong dissent, the court refused to grant specific performance to a defaulting buyer.

PETERSEN v. HARTELL

Supreme Court of California, In Banc, 1985.
40 Cal.3d 102, 219 Cal.Rptr. 170, 707 P.2d 232.

REYNOSO, JUSTICE. This appeal by plaintiff vendees who wilfully defaulted in making payments under an installment land sale contract requires us to reconsider such vendees' right to completion of performance. Though we upheld specific performance in MacFadden v. Walker, the trial court below concluded that the granting of such relief is only discretionary and dependent upon a weighing of the equities. Accordingly, it denied specific performance, adjudged that plaintiffs had no interest in the property, and awarded plaintiffs only restitution of the installments they had paid, with interest. * * *

Defendant is administratrix of the estate of Juanita Gaspar who, upon the death of her first husband in 1946, succeeded to sole ownership of a 160–acre tract of unimproved land southeast of Fort Bragg in Mendocino County. In the late 1960's she entered into agreements with three of her grandchildren to sell small portions of the land at $1,500 per acre, with no down payment and monthly installments of $50 or less. The agreement now relied on by plaintiffs was embodied in a written contract, executed in November 1967, providing for the sale to granddaughter Kathy Petersen and her husband, Richard Petersen, of slightly more than six acres for a total purchase price of $9,162, payable at $50 per month. The buyers were given the right to pay the entire balance of the purchase price at any time. There was no provision making time of the essence or specifying remedies in the event of default.

The Petersens missed occasional payments in 1968, 1969, 1971, and 1972. Of the 65 payments due from November 1967 through March 1973, they made 58 payments totaling $2,900. In April 1973 the couple separated and their payments ceased. * * *

In September 1975 Kathy Petersen sent Mrs. Gaspar a check for $250 as "back payments." Mrs. Gaspar's attorney then wrote the Petersens, stating that Mrs. Gaspar elected to terminate the contract. In February 1976 Mrs. Gaspar wrote to Kathy Petersen, returning the latter's check and explaining that she considered the contract broken. In September 1976 Richard Petersen wrote to the attorney requesting reinstatement of the contract and a statement of the amounts due, and enclosing a $250 money order, which the attorney promptly returned on instructions from Mrs. Gaspar. * * * By their amended complaint against Mrs. Gaspar's administratrix, plaintiffs seek specific performance, declaratory relief, damages, and the quieting of title to an easement of necessity to connect the property with a public road. They further tender the entire balance due under the contract on condition that defendant deliver a good and sufficient deed.

After a nonjury trial, the trial court denied plaintiffs' prayer for specific performance. It concluded that (1) plaintiffs' breach of the contract was grossly negligent and wilful, (2) plaintiffs failed to tender full performance until April 1, 1977, when the action was commenced, (3) defendant is entitled to restitution of the property, and (4) plaintiffs are entitled to restitution of $2,900 plus interest from April 1, 1977. Judgment was entered accordingly with costs to defendant. * * *

Unlike the trial court in *MacFadden,* the trial court below denied plaintiff vendees specific performance. Since that remedy is discretionary, we must consider whether the denial was an abuse of discretion and, if not, whether plaintiffs are entitled to relief on some other ground. * * *

The memorandum of intended decision recites seven factual differences between the present case and MacFadden v. Walker. One of the stated differences is that the vendee in *MacFadden* had taken possession of and made improvements on the property. Another is that the *MacFadden* vendee had paid a larger proportion of the purchase price. We consider both of those differences immaterial. Here the land was unimproved and unoccupied, and the contract was silent on the right to possession. Under those circumstances, the Petersens' payment of $2,900 out of a purchase price of $9,162 constituted sufficient part performance to qualify them for equitable relief regardless of possession.

The other five distinctions from *MacFadden* listed by the trial court deal with differences in the nature and extent of, and the circumstances surrounding, the defaults of the *MacFadden* vendee as contrasted with those of the Petersens as described in the findings. The materiality of those differences in the eyes of the trial court is not made explicit. It may be thought to relate to the court's express conclusion that the decedent seller "had no assurance that she would receive the benefit of the bargain." The Petersens' conduct in connection with defaults might well have a bearing on the seller's assurance of future performance if plaintiffs were seeking *reinstatement* of the contract, tendering only delinquent payments rather than the full balance of the purchase price. But where, as here, the relief sought is contingent upon plaintiffs' paying all amounts due or to become due under the contract, the judgment granting that relief will make the seller whole. (See § 3302 (detriment for breach of obligation to pay money is the amount due with interest thereon).)

The more likely connection between the findings of the Petersens' derelictions as to payments and the denial of specific performance is that the trial court weighed the seriousness of plaintiffs' defaults against them in a balancing of equities. That that was the court's theory seems likely from its citation of Kosloff v. Castle (1981) 115 Cal.App.3d 369, 171 Cal.Rptr. 308, where the Court of Appeal declared that whereas the wilfully defaulting vendee's right to restitution of installment payments made in excess of the seller's damages is unqualified, such vendee's right to specific performance is discretionary and dependent on a balancing of equities that include the seriousness of the vendee's defaults.

If that theory were correct, there would be ample basis in the evidence and findings to support the denial of specific performance. The Petersens' monthly payments were erratic and delinquent almost from the beginning even though the seller made clear her need of the payments for her support. By April 1973 the Petersens had made only 58 out of the 65 payments then due, and their first attempt to reinstate the contract was not until 29 months later, when they tendered only $250 out of the $1,800 that was by then overdue and unpaid.

The issue, therefore, is whether plaintiffs, despite their wilful defaults in payments, now have an absolute right to a conveyance of the property in exchange for payment of the entire balance of the purchase price (together with interest and any other damages) in light of their substantial part performance and the seller's notice of election to terminate the contract on account of such defaults. * * *

We think that as a matter both of stare decisis and of sound public policy, a vendee who has made substantial payments on a land installment sale contract or substantial improvements on the property, and whose defaults, albeit wilful, consist solely of failure to pay further amounts due, has an unconditional right to a reasonable opportunity to complete the purchase by paying the entire remaining balance plus damages before the seller is allowed to quiet title. * * * To that statement we add that the seller may be entitled to damages in addition to interest. Whatever the amounts due, their payment in full makes the seller whole regardless of the nature of the vendee's defaults in payments. * * *

Finally, we think that to retain specific performance under MacFadden v. Walker, as the utmost remedy available in a suit initiated by a wilfully defaulting vendee unduly burdens courts and litigants with time-consuming and expensive legal proceedings. The present case is illustrative. To settle a dispute over land sold for a total price of only $9,162 required two days of nonjury trial in which eight witnesses (only two of whom were parties) testified to circumstances bearing on whether the vendees' defaults were sufficiently egregious to bar them from specific performance under *MacFadden.* Yet, as already explained, if defendant seller had sued to quiet title, plaintiffs would have been entitled as a matter of right to a conveyance of title in exchange for payment of the balance of the purchase price with interest and damages. Such redemption by plaintiff would give defendant the entire benefit bargained for, free of any dependence on further performance by plaintiff vendees. The outcome will be no less fair to both parties if, as we hold, the vendees under a real property sales contract, as defined in section 2985, are entitled to judicial enforcement of the same absolute right of redemption in response to the seller's notice of election to terminate the contract for default in payments. The complaint initiating the vendee's action for that purpose, rather than being designated as one for specific performance, is more appropriately referred to as one to redeem the vendee's interest in real property.

Accordingly, we conclude that plaintiffs are entitled to a conveyance of title to the property in exchange for payment of the entire remaining balance due under the contract together with interest and any consequential damages as determined by the court. Should plaintiffs fail to make such payments within a reasonable time fixed by the court, the adjudication that plaintiffs have no further interest in the property should become effective only upon defendant's payment of the sums due to plaintiffs as restitution. * * *

The judgment is reversed.

* * *

MOSK, JUSTICE, dissenting. I dissent. The majority misread precedent and rely on questionable "policy" to reach a result that flouts what is undeniably equitable. Our long history of cases holds that when a vendee in an installment land sale contract wilfully defaults, it is in the trial court's discretion to weigh the equities and discern whether redemption is warranted. The trial court reacted properly to the overwhelming evidence and exercised its discretion to deny specific performance to vendees who have been wilfully untrustworthy and derelict in the performance of contract duties. * * *

As between the deliberately defaulting vendees and the elderly vendor who desperately needed the modest payments on the contract for her very survival, the equities clearly favor the latter. I am mystified at how the majority can conclude the ends of justice compel their callous result and rejection of the trial court's rational exercise of discretion. There being no reason to overturn our prior cases and ignore the policies clearly articulated therein, I would affirm the judgment denying the vendees specific performance.

B. CONTRACTS FOR THE SALE OF CHATTELS

1. BUYER v. SELLER

a. Damages

WILSON v. HAYS

Court of Civil Appeals of Texas, 1976.
544 S.W.2d 833.

JAMES, JUSTICE. This is a suit by the buyer against the seller for breach of an oral contract to sell and deliver used bricks. Trial was had to a jury, which rendered a verdict favorable to the Plaintiff buyer, pursuant to which verdict the trial court entered judgment. We affirm in part and reverse and render in part.

Plaintiff–Appellee W.D. Hays was in the business of buying and selling used building materials. Defendant–Appellant Bobby Wilson doing business as Wilson Salvage Co. was in the business of wrecking or demolishing buildings. * * * Hays and Wilson entered into an oral agreement whereby Wilson agreed to sell and deliver 600,000 used uncleaned bricks to Hays at a price of one cent per brick, and Hays agreed to buy said bricks at said price. Hays paid Wilson $6,000.00 in advance. Wilson delivered the uncleaned brick to a designated area where Hays had people hired to clean and stack the brick. Wilson delivered a lesser number of brick than 600,000, thereby precipitating this suit.

Plaintiff–Appellee Hays brought this suit for the return of the proportionate part of the purchase price paid for the bricks he did not get, plus damages. In answer to special issues the jury found: * * *

(6) That Bobby Wilson did not deliver 600,000 uncleaned bricks to Hays (but)

(6A) delivered only 400,000 bricks to Hays;

(7) The market value of used bricks in Midland, Texas in April 1972, was five cents per brick;

(8) Hays suffered lost profits in the amount of $6250.00 by virtue of the failure of Bobby Wilson to deliver to Hays at least 600,000 bricks;

(9) That Hays saved $2605.00 in expenses in consequence of the failure of Bobby Wilson to deliver to him (Hays) at least 600,000 bricks.

Pursuant to the jury verdict, the trial court entered judgment in favor of Plaintiff Hays against Defendant Bobby Wilson in the amount of $13,645.00, plus accrued interest. * * * From this judgment, Defendant Wilson appeals. * * *

By Appellant's remaining three points, he challenges the $13,645.00 judgment upon the ground, among other things, that there is no evidence to support the jury's findings in answer to Special Issues No. 8 (lost profits) and No. 9 (expenses). We sustain these points of error insofar as they assert no evidence to support the jury's findings concerning lost profits less expenses, and in all other respects we overrule such points.

Plaintiff–Appellee Hays's remedies and measures of damages as a buyer of goods in the case at bar are governed by Sections 2.711, 2.712, 2.713, and 2.715 of the Texas Business and Commerce Code. We herewith quote the portions of said sections that bear upon the case at bar:

"Section 2.711. Buyer's Remedies in General; * * *

(a) Where the seller fails to make delivery or repudiates * * * the buyer may cancel and whether or not he has done so may in addition to recovering so much of the price as has been paid

(1) 'cover' and have damages under the next section as to all the goods affected whether or not they have been identified to the contract; or

(2) recover damages for non-delivery as provided in this chapter (Section 2.713)." * * *

"Section 2.712. 'Cover' Buyer's Procurement of Substitute Goods

"(a) After a breach within the preceding section the buyer may 'cover' by making in good faith and without unreasonable delay any reasonable purchase of or contract to purchase goods in substitution for those due from the seller.

"(b) The buyer may recover from the seller as damages the difference between the cost of cover and the contract price together with any incidental or consequential damages as hereinafter defined (Section 2.715), but less expenses saved in consequence of the seller's breach.

"(c) Failure of the buyer to effect cover within the section does not bar him from any other remedy."

"Section 2.713. Buyer's Damages for Non–Delivery or Repudiation

"(a) * * * the measure of damages for non-delivery or repudiation by the seller is the difference between the market price at the time when the buyer learned of the breach and the contract price together with any incidental and consequential damages provided in this chapter (Sec. 2.715), but less expenses saved in consequence of the seller's breach." * * *

"Section 2.715. Buyer's Incidental and Consequential Damages

(b) Consequential damages resulting from the seller's breach include

(1) any loss resulting from general or particular requirements and needs of which the seller at the time of contracting had reason to know and which could not reasonably be prevented by cover or otherwise; * * *."

Let us analyze the verdict and judgment in the light of the foregoing statutory provisions. In the first place, it is established that Plaintiff Hays paid $6000.00 for 600,000 used brick at the rate of one cent per brick, whereas he received only 400,000. Therefore he paid $2000 for 200,000 brick that he never got, and he is thereby entitled to recover $2000.00 under Section 2.711 for "recovering so much of the price as has been paid."

Next, under Section 2.713, he is entitled to damages for "non-delivery or repudiation," and here his measure of damages is the difference between the market price and the contract price. The contract price of the 200,000 brick not delivered is established at $2000.00. The market price at the appropriate time and place of the undelivered brick was five cents per brick or $10,000.00. This jury finding of market value (five cents per brick) although challenged by Appellant for legal and factual insufficiency, is amply supported by the evidence and is well within the range of probative testimony. Therefore under Section 2.713 and appropriate jury findings, Plaintiff is entitled to $8000.00 damages (or $10,000.00 market price less $2000.00 contract price) for non-delivery.

Now we come to the problem of "consequential damages * * * less expenses saved in consequence of the seller's breach" as mentioned in Sec. 2.713 and which damages are provided for in Sec. 2.715. * * * There is no evidence in the record whatever that Plaintiff Hays at any time made any effort to cover or in any other manner attempt to prevent or mitigate a loss resulting from the Defendant Wilson's non-delivery of the 200,000 brick in question. In the absence of such a showing these consequential damages are unauthorized under Section 2.715. * * * This being so, we are of the opinion that there is no evidence to support these jury findings concerning consequential damages, and that the trial court's judgment insofar as it awarded Plaintiff Hays $3645.00 lost profits is improper and this amount should be deleted from said judgment.

As stated before, the judgment is proper and should be affirmed for the amount of $10,000.00, same being composed of $2000.00 paid by Plaintiff for which he received no bricks plus $8000.00 damages for non-delivery.

H-W-H CATTLE COMPANY, INC. v. SCHROEDER

United States Court of Appeals, Eighth Circuit, 1985.
767 F.2d 437.

HEANEY, CIRCUIT JUDGE. This is a breach of contract action before the Court on diversity jurisdiction. H-W-H Cattle Co. (HWH) appeals from the district court's judgment, contending that it erred in failing to award HWH greater damages. For the reasons set forth below, we affirm.

HWH was an order-buying cattle company which purchased cattle on commission for feedlots. As an order-buyer, HWH did not own any feedlots itself. HWH is owned by the Hitch family, which owns various cattle businesses, including several feedlots. On September 13, 1978, HWH entered into a contract with Clayton Schroeder to purchase 2,000 steers for $67.00 per hundredweight ($0.67 per pound). The contract specified that the cattle would be delivered between March 1, and May 31, 1979, in Artesia, New Mexico. HWH gave Schroeder a $50,000 downpayment for the cattle. HWH in turn had a contract with its customer, Western Trio Cattle Co. (Western Trio), to sell it 2,000 head of cattle of the same description for $67.35 per hundredweight. Western Trio had given HWH a $50,000 downpayment which it had used to pay Schroeder.

Schroeder was only able to deliver 1,397 cattle to HWH, leaving it 603 head short of fulfilling its contract. As a result, HWH filed an action for breach of contract against Schroeder in federal district court for the Northern

District of Iowa. The matter came to trial before the district court without a jury on April 15–16, 1982. The district court found that Schroeder breached its contract with HWH by failing to deliver 603 head of cattle. The court awarded to HWH $15,075, the remaining amount of HWH's downpayment which Schroeder had retained, and $1,371.83 in damages for HWH's lost commission on the 603 cattle not delivered. HWH now brings this appeal.

The parties agree that the dispute is governed by the Uniform Commercial Code as adopted in Iowa, and that the only issue before the Court is the proper measure of damages. Section 2711(1) provides that a buyer has two options when the seller fails to deliver; the buyer may:

> "(a) 'cover' and have damages under the next section [§ 2712] as to all the goods affected whether or not they have been identified to the contract; or
>
> "(b) recover damages for nondelivery as provided in this Article (§ 2713)."

Schroeder contends in his brief that HWH exercised the first option by purchasing replacement cattle in June, 1979. Section 2712 provides:

> "(1) After a breach within the preceding section the buyer may 'cover' by making in good faith and without unreasonable delay any reasonable purchase of or contract to purchase goods in substitution for those due from the seller.
>
> "(2) The buyer may recover from the seller as damages the difference between the cost of cover and the contract price together with any incidental or consequential damages as hereinafter defined (§ 2715), but less expenses saved in consequence of the seller's breach.
>
> "(3) Failure of the buyer to effect cover within this section does not bar him from any other remedy."

Although the district court did not make any findings concerning whether or not HWH effected cover, it is clear from the record that HWH did not do so. HWH's buyer, Gene McGlaun, testified at trial that he was in Dodge City, Kansas in June, 1979, and that he telephoned C.A. Heldridge, Schroeder's agent, to let him know that substitute cattle were available which could be purchased to fulfill the contract with a freight adjustment of roughly $0.50 per hundredweight over the contract price. According to McGlaun, Heldridge responded that such an offer sounded like a good deal and that he would call him back with a reply; Heldridge never called back. McGlaun further testified that he bought 120–130 head of cattle in Dodge City on that day, but it is clear that these 120 cattle were not to cover for the 603 cattle which were not delivered under the contract with Schroeder. McGlaun stated that his purchases were for other customers, and that "each set of cattle stood on their own to fill individual customers' needs." Schroeder introduced no evidence to contradict this testimony.

We conclude from this testimony and from other testimony by McGlaun concerning the nature of HWH's order-buying operation that any cattle McGlaun purchased in Dodge City were not substitute cattle to fulfill the contract with Schroeder. We thus reject Schroeder's contention that HWH elected to cover and thereby limit its damages under § 2712.

HWH contends that it is entitled to damages under the second option, § 2713, which provides:

"(1) Subject to the provisions of this Article with respect to proof of market price (§ 2723), the measure of damages for nondelivery or repudiation by the seller is the difference between the market price at the time when the buyer learned of the breach and the contract price together with any incidental and consequential damages provided in this Article (§ 2715), but less expenses saved in consequence of the seller's breach.

"(2) Market price is to be determined as of the place for tender or, in cases of rejection after arrival or revocation of acceptance, as of the place of arrival."

HWH contended before the district court, as it does here, that it is entitled to damages based upon the market price of cattle meeting the contract description in Artesia, New Mexico on June 1, 1979, the day after the last day of delivery under the contract. The district court rejected this argument because it concluded that it would result in an undeserved windfall to HWH, as HWH had already voluntarily limited its "market price" by agreeing to sell these cattle to Western Trio for $0.35 per hundredweight more than it paid for the cattle. The district court also found that the parties modified the time for delivery, in that HWH indicated it would have accepted delivery through the summer of 1979. During this time, the price of cattle fell back to around $67.00 per hundredweight.

We conclude that the district court did not err in so holding. To adopt HWH's position in this case would result in granting it a windfall, and thus violate the general principle concerning remedies underlying Article Two of the Uniform Commercial Code in Iowa Code Ann. § 1106, which provides:

"(1) The remedies provided by this Chapter shall be liberally administered to the end that *the aggrieved party may be put in as good a position as if the other party had fully performed* but neither consequential nor special nor penal damages may be had except as specifically provided in this Chapter or by other rule of law." (Emphasis added.)

We read this admonition from the Code to suggest that a court should look through the form of a transaction to its substance when necessary to fulfill the parties' expectations expressed in the contract. This is precisely what the district court did in this case, by limiting the damage award to HWH to its expectancy interest and thereby avoiding a windfall of some $62,000.

It is clear from McGlaun's testimony that HWH only purchased cattle to meet a specific customer's needs. As an order-buyer, it thus never expected to receive more than its $0.35 commission on any transaction, including its order purchase for Western Trio. HWH argues that it should receive market-price damages because it is liable to Western Trio for its failure to deliver the 603 cattle, and that Western Trio's damages would be measured by the difference between the market price on June 1, 1979, and the contract price. The district court properly rejected this contention, noting that Western Trio had made no demand on HWH to fulfill the remainder of the contract. The evidence at trial indicated that Western Trio would have, at best, only broken even on the resale of cattle delivered under the contract due to the fallen cattle market in the autumn of 1979. Moreover, McGlaun testified that Western Trio is managed by the Hitch family, which also owns HWH. We thus view Western Trio's failure to sue HWH as an equitable consideration in support of the district court's judgment.

HWH also contends that the district court's decision is contrary to Cargill, Inc. v. Fickbohm, 252 N.W.2d 739 (Iowa 1977). In *Cargill*, the seller failed to deliver 10,000 bushels of corn to the plaintiff. The contract price was $1.26 per bushel; the Iowa Supreme Court concluded that it was permissible for the plaintiff to receive damages based on the market price on the date it learned of the breach of $2.45 per bushel even though the plaintiff had hedged its purchase by selling 10,000 bushels on the futures exchange at $1.39 per bushel. The instant case is distinguishable from *Cargill* in that Cargill had made the independent decision to hedge its purchase on the futures exchange, thereby contracting with a party unrelated to the transaction with the defendant seller. Here HWH entered into a contract with Schroeder solely to meet the needs of Western Trio, a related company, and as an order-buyer, it never stood to gain more than its $0.35 commission. * * *

Affirmed.

Note

See generally, Anderson, An Overview of Buyer's Damages Remedies, 21 U.C.C.L.J. 28 (1988).

White and Summers summarize § 1–106(1); they add after the part the court italicizes "but no better." J. White & R. Summers, Uniform Commercial Code § 7–7 at 310 (3d ed. 1988).

OLOFFSON v. COOMER

Appellate Court of Illinois, Third District, 1973.

11 Ill.App.3d 918, 296 N.E.2d 871.

ALLOY, PRESIDING JUSTICE. * * * Oloffson was a grain dealer. Coomer was a farmer. Oloffson was in the business of merchandising grain. Consequently, he was a "merchant" within the meaning of section 2–104 of the Uniform Commercial Code. Coomer, however, was simply in the business of growing rather than merchandising grain. He, therefore, was not a "merchant" with respect to the merchandising of grain.

On April 16, 1970, Coomer agreed to sell to Oloffson, for delivery in October and December of 1970, 40,000 bushels of corn. Oloffson testified at the trial that the entire agreement was embodied in two separate contracts, each covering 20,000 bushels and that the first 20,000 bushels were to be delivered on or before October 30 at a price of $1.12¾ per bushel and the second 20,000 bushels were to be delivered on or before December 15, at a price of $1.12¼ per bushel. Coomer, in his testimony, agreed that the 40,000 bushels were to be delivered but stated that he was to deliver all he could by October 30 and the balance by December 15.

On June 3, 1970, Coomer informed Oloffson that he was not going to plant corn because the season had been too wet. He told Oloffson to arrange elsewhere to obtain the corn if Oloffson had obligated himself to deliver to any third party. The price for a bushel of corn on June 3, 1970, for future delivery, was $1.16. In September of 1970, Oloffson asked Coomer about delivery of the corn and Coomer repeated that he would not be able to deliver. Oloffson, however, persisted. He mailed Coomer confirmations of the April 16 agreement. Coomer ignored these. Oloffson's attorney then requested that Coomer perform. Coomer ignored this request likewise. The scheduled delivery dates referred to passed with no corn delivered. Oloffson then covered his obligation to his own vendee by purchasing 20,000 bushels at $1.35 per bushel and 20,000 bushels at $1.49 per bushel. The judgment from which Oloffson appeals awarded Oloffson as damages, the difference between the contract and the market prices on June 3, 1970, the day upon which Coomer first advised Oloffson he would not deliver.

Oloffson argues on this appeal that the proper measure of his damages was the difference between the contract price and the market price on the dates the corn should have been delivered in accordance with the April 16 agreement. Plaintiff does not seek any other damages. The trial court prior to entry of judgment, in an opinion finding the facts and reviewing the law, found that plaintiff was entitled to recover judgment only for the sum of $1,500 plus costs as we have indicated which is equal to the amount of the difference between the minimum contract price and the price on June 3, 1970, of $1.16 per bushel (taking the greatest differential from $1.12¼ per bushel multiplied by 40,000 bushels). We believe the findings and the judgment of the trial court were proper and should be affirmed.

It is clear that on June 3, 1970, Coomer repudiated the contract "with respect to performance not yet due." Under the terms of the Uniform Commercial Code the loss would impair the value of the contract to the remaining party in the amount as indicated. As a consequence on June 3, 1970, Oloffson, as the "aggrieved party," could then:

> "(a) for a commercially reasonable time await performance by the repudiating party; or
>
> "(b) resort to any remedy for breach (Section 2–703 or Section 2–711), even though he has notified the repudiating party that he would await the latter's performance and has urged retraction;"

If Oloffson chose to proceed under subparagraph (a) referred to, he could have awaited Coomer's performance for a "commercially reasonable time." As we indicate in the course of this opinion, that "commercially reasonable time" expired on June 3, 1970. The Uniform Commercial Code made a change in existing Illinois law in this respect, in that, prior to the adoption of the Code, a buyer in a position as Oloffson was privileged to await a seller's performance until the date that, according to the agreement, such performance was scheduled. To the extent that a "commercially reasonable time" is less than such date of performance, the Code now conditions the buyer's right to await performance.

If, alternatively, Oloffson had proceeded under subparagraph (b) by treating the repudiation as a breach, the remedies to which he would have been entitled were set forth in section 2–711 which is the only applicable section to which section 2–610(b) refers, according to the relevant portion of 2–711:

> "(1) Where the seller fails to make delivery or repudiates or the buyer rightfully rejects or justifiably revokes acceptance then with respect to any goods involved, and with respect to the whole if the breach goes to the whole contract (Section 2–612), the buyer may cancel and whether or not he has done so may in addition to recovering so much of the price as has been paid
>
> "(a) 'cover' and have damages under the next section as to all the goods affected whether or not they have been identified to the contract; or

"(b) recover damages from non-delivery as provided in this Article (Section 2-713)."

Plaintiff, therefore, was privileged under section 2-610 of the Uniform Commercial Code to proceed either under subparagraph (a) or under subparagraph (b). At the expiration of the "commercially reasonable time" specified in subparagraph (a), he in effect would have a duty to proceed under subparagraph (b) since subparagraph (b) directs reference to remedies generally available to a buyer upon a seller's breach.

Oloffson's right to await Coomer's performance under section 2-610(a) was conditioned upon his:

(i) waiting no longer than a "commercially reasonable time"; and

(ii) dealing with Coomer in good faith.

Since Coomer's statement to Oloffson on June 3, 1970, was unequivocal and since "cover" easily and immediately was available to Oloffson in the well-organized and easily accessible market for purchases of grain to be delivered in the future, it would be unreasonable for Oloffson on June 3, 1970, to have awaited Coomer's performance rather than to have proceeded under section 2-610(b) and, thereunder, to elect then to treat the repudiation as a breach. Therefore, if Oloffson were relying on this right to effect cover under section 2-711(1)(a), June 3, 1970, might for the foregoing reason alone have been the day on which he acquired cover.

Additionally, however, the record and the finding of the trial court indicates that Oloffson adhered to a usage of trade that permitted his customers to cancel the contract for a future delivery of grain by making known to him a desire to cancel and paying to him the difference between the contract and market price on the day of cancellation. There is no indication whatever that Coomer was aware of this usage of trade. The trial court specifically found, as a fact, that, in the context in which Oloffson's failure to disclose this information occurred, Oloffson failed to act in good faith. According to Oloffson, he didn't ask for this information: "I'm no information sender. If he had asked I would have told him exactly what to do. * * * I didn't feel my responsibility. I thought it his to ask, in which case I would tell him exactly what to do." We feel that the words "for a commercially reasonable time" as set forth in section 2-610(a) must be read relatively to the obligation of good faith that is defined in Section 2-103(1)(b) and imposed expressly in Section 1-203.

The Uniform Commercial Code imposes upon the parties the obligation to deal with each other in good faith regardless of whether they are merchants. The Sales Article of the Code specifically defines good faith, "in the case of a merchant * * * [as] honesty in fact and the observance of reasonable commercial standards of fair dealing in the trade." For the foregoing reasons and likewise because Oloffson's failure to disclose in good faith might itself have been responsible for Coomer's failure to comply with the usage of trade which we must assume was known only to Oloffson, we conclude that a commercially reasonable time under the facts before us expired on June 3, 1970.

Imputing to Oloffson the consequences of Coomer's having acted upon the information that Oloffson in good faith should have transmitted to him, Oloffson knew or should have known on June 3, 1970, the limit of damages he probably could recover. If he were obligated to deliver grain to a third party, he knew or should have known that unless he covered on June 3, 1970, his own capital would be at risk with respect to his obligation to his own vendee. Therefore, on June 3, 1970, Oloffson, in effect, had a duty to proceed under subparagraph (b) of section 2–610 and under subparagraphs (a) and (b) of subparagraph 1 of section 2–711. If Oloffson had so proceeded under subparagraph (a) of section 2–711, he should have effected cover and would have been entitled to recover damages all as provided in section 2–712, which requires that he would have had to cover in good faith without unreasonable delay. Since he would have had to effect cover on June 3, 1970, according to section 2–712(2), he would have been entitled to exactly the damages which the trial court awarded him in this cause.

Assuming that Oloffson had proceeded under subparagraph (b) of section 2–711, he would have been entitled to recover from Coomer under section 2–713 and section 2–723 of the Commercial Code, the difference between the contract price and the market price on June 3, 1970, which is the date upon which he learned of the breach. This would produce precisely the same amount of damages which the trial court awarded him. * * *

Affirmed.

Notes

1. Was the court correct to conclude that the grain buyer must cover on the same day the seller repudiates? Did trade usage limit the damage provisions of the contract and Article 2? Compare Cargill, Inc. v. Stafford, 553 F.2d 1222 (10th Cir.1977). See generally Jackson, "Anticipatory Repudiation" and the Temporal Element of Contract Law: An Economic Inquiry into Contract Damages in Cases of Prospective Nonperformance, 31 Stan.L.Rev. 69 (1978); Leibson, Anticipatory Repudiation and Buyer's Damages—A Look Into How the UCC Has Changed the Common Law, 7 U.C.C.L.J. 272 (1975).

2. Assume the grain dealer did what the court said he should have: covered by buying corn on June 3. Assume also that he covered at $1.12½, the price in the breached contract. Could the dealer then recover from the breaching farmer the difference between the market price, $1.16, and the contract price, $1.12½? See J. White & R. Summers, Uniform Commercial Code § 6.4, at 262–63 (3d ed. 1988).

3. Under *Oloffson,* could the farmer behave as follows: in May, sell his fall crop to the grain dealer for $1.13; conclude in June that the market was rising, breach the $1.13 contract, and pay the grain dealer $1500; and sell his harvested crop to someone else for $1.50 in December?

4. Should the court allow a nonbreaching buyer a specific performance remedy against the seller who repudiates before time to deliver?

In Duval & Co. v. Malcom, 233 Ga. 784, 214 S.E.2d 356 (1975), a buyer of cotton argued that a dramatic price rise made the cotton unique; but the court denied specific performance. Does the denial of specific performance allow sellers to breach, pay damages as of the date of breach, and resell for higher profits?

5. The questions in Notes 3 and 4 raise variations on the problem of efficient breach. The argument for efficient breach starts with Holmes's famous passage from The Path of the Law, 10 Harv.L.Rev. 457, 462 (1897): "The duty to keep a contract at common law means a prediction that you must pay damages if you do not keep it,—and nothing else. If you commit a tort, you are liable to pay a compensatory sum. If you commit a contract, you are liable to pay a compensatory sum unless the promised event comes to pass, and that is all the difference."

Judge Posner picks up the thread:

"But in some cases a party would be tempted to break the contract simply because his profit from breach would exceed his expected profit from completion of the contract. If his profit from breach would also exceed the expected profit to the other party from completion of the contract, and if damages are limited to the loss of that expected profit, there will be an incentive to commit a breach. But there should be, as an example will show. I sign a contract to deliver 100,000 custom-ground widgets at 10¢ apiece to A, for use in his boiler factory. After I have delivered 10,000, B comes to me, explains that he desperately needs 25,000 custom-ground widgets at once since otherwise he will be forced to close his pianola factory at great cost, and offers me 15¢ apiece for 25,000 widgets. I sell him the widgets and as a result do not complete timely delivery to A, causing him to lose $1,000 in profits. Having obtained an additional profit of $1,250 on the sale to B, I am better off even after reimbursing A for his loss, and B is no worse off. The breach is Pareto superior, assuming that A is fully compensated and no one else is hurt by the breach. True, if I had refused to sell to B, he could have gone to A and negotiated an assignment to him of part of A's contract with me. But this would have introduced an additional step, with additional transaction costs."

R. Posner, Economic Analysis of Law 107 (1986).

Opponents of efficient breach have argued that contract damages for the nonbreaching party are insufficient because they omit the cost of recovering the damages such as attorney fees and they fail to compensate subjective and idiosyncratic values. Farber, Reassessing the Economic Efficiency of Compensatory Damages for Breach of Contract, 66 Va.L.Rev. 1443 (1980). Another forceful argument asserts that people ought to keep their promises. Accordingly promisors who breach intending to take advantage of another opportunity should pay enhanced damages. Marschall, Willfulness: A Crucial Factor in Choosing Remedies for Breach of Contract, 24 Ariz.L.Rev. 733 (1982).

Consider how the position you take on efficient breach affects your view of whether to approve liquidated damage clauses, specific performance, punitive damages for breach of contract, and a tort of bad faith breach.

AM/PM FRANCHISE ASSOCIATION v. ATLANTIC RICHFIELD COMPANY

Supreme Court of Pennsylvania, 1990.

584 A.2d 915.

CAPPY, JUSTICE. * * * The Plaintiffs claim to represent a class of over 150 franchisees of ARCO that operated AM/PM Mini Markets in Pennsylvania and New York during a three and one-half year period.

ARCO entered into franchise agreements with the plaintiffs which were comprised of a premises lease, a lessee dealer gasoline agreement, and an AM/PM mini-market agreement. The products agreement mandated that the franchisees sell only ARCO petroleum products.

The complaint sets forth the following facts: ARCO began experimenting with its formula for unleaded gasoline and provided its franchisees with an unleaded gasoline blended with oxinol, * * * from early 1982 through September 30, 1985.

During this three and a half year period, the franchisees were required to sell the oxinol blend to their clients who desired unleaded gasoline. The franchisees were given no opportunity to buy regular unleaded gasoline from ARCO during that period.

Plaintiffs claim that numerous purchasers of the oxinol blend gasoline experienced poor engine performance and physical damage to fuel system components. Specifically, plaintiffs claim that the oxinol gasoline permitted an excess accumulation of alcohol and/or water which interfered with the efficiency of gasoline engines. * * * The plaintiffs claim that the gasoline did not conform to ARCO's warranties about the product.

As the problems with the oxinol blend became known, the plaintiffs claim to have suffered a precipitous drop in the volume of their business and an attendant loss of profits. Specifically, plaintiffs point to the rise in sales from 1973 until 1982, when sales began to fall dramatically; allegedly due to defective oxinol blend gasoline.

In their complaint, plaintiffs allege three counts of Breach of Warranty, Breach of Implied Duty, Misrepresentation, and Exemplary Damages. They request damages for "lost profits, consequential and incidental damages." [The trial court dismissed plaintiffs' action and they appealed.]

The point at which we start our inquiry is the Uniform Commercial Code Section 2714, entitled "Damages of buyer for breach in regard to accepted goods" is one of the governing provisions in the case before us,[1] and provides, in pertinent part:

> "(b) Measure of damages for breach of warranty.—The measure of damages for breach of warranty is the difference at the time and place of acceptance between the value of the goods accepted and the value they would have had if they had been as warranted, unless special circumstances show proximate damages of a different amount.
>
> "(c) Incidental and consequential damages.—In a proper case any incidental and consequential damages under section 2715 (relating to incidental and consequential damages of buyer) may also be recovered."

Section 2715 is entitled "Incidental and Consequential Damages of Buyer" and provides, in pertinent part:

> "(a) Incidental damages.—Incidental damages resulting from the breach of the seller include:
>
> > (3) any other reasonable expenses incident to the delay or other breach.[2]
>
> "(b) Consequential damages.—Consequential damages resulting from the breach of the seller include:
>
> > (1) any loss resulting from general or particular requirements and needs of which the seller at the time of contracting had reason to know and which could not reasonably be prevented by cover or otherwise."

Pursuant to the provisions of the U.C.C., plaintiffs are entitled to seek "general" damages, so-called, under section 2714(b), and consequential damages as provided by section 2714(c).

1. [Footnotes renumbered.] The plaintiffs claim they have accepted gasoline which allegedly does not conform to the warranty. Thus, we believe § 2714 is one of the governing provisions.

2. The incidental damage provision is aimed at reimbursing the buyer for expenses incurred in rightfully rejecting goods, or in connection with effecting cover. We have not quoted all the sections included in the subtitle of Incidental Damages. The courts below have not addressed the claim for incidental damages, nor have the parties to the litigation.

There has been substantial confusion in the courts and among litigants about what consequential damages actually are and what types of consequential damages are available in a breach of warranty case. Where a buyer in the business of reselling goods can prove that a breach by the seller has caused him to lose profitable resales, the buyer's lost profits constitute a form of consequential damages. We now hold that in addition to general damages, there are three types of lost profit recoverable as consequential damages that may flow from a breach of warranty: (1) loss of primary profits; (2) loss of secondary profits; and (3) a loss of good will damages (or prospective damages, as they are sometimes termed).

In order to alleviate the confusion that has developed concerning the various damages, we use an example to help illustrate the different types.

General damages in the case of accepted goods (such as occurred here) are the actual difference in value between the goods as promised and the goods as received. Thus, suppose a buyer bought five hundred tires from a wholesaler that were to be delivered in good condition, and in that condition would be worth $2,500. The tires were delivered with holes in them which rendered them worthless. The buyer would be entitled to $2,500 from the seller—the difference between the value of the tires as warranted and the value of the tires as received; those would be the general damages.

Consequential damages are generally understood to be other damages which naturally and proximately flow from the breach and include three types of lost profit damages: (1) lost primary profits; (2) lost secondary profits; and (3) loss of prospective profits, also commonly referred to as good will damages.

Lost primary profits are the difference between what the buyer would have earned from reselling the goods in question had there been no breach and what was earned after the breach occurred. Thus, if the buyer of the tires proved that he would have resold the tires for $5,000, he would be able to claim an additional $2,500 for loss of tire profits; the difference between what he would have earned from the sale of the tires and what he actually did earn from the sale (or lack of sales) from the tires.

If the buyer of the tires also sold, for example, hubcaps with every set of tires, he would also suffer a loss of hubcap profits. These types of damages are what we term "loss of secondary profits."

If the buyer's regular customers were so disgruntled about the defective tires that they no longer frequented the buyer's business and began to patronize a competitor's business, the buyer would have suffered a "loss of good will" beyond the direct loss of profits from the nonconforming goods; his future business would be adversely affected as a result of the defective tires. Thus, good will damages refer to profits lost on future sales rather than on sales of the defective goods themselves.

While this example provides a simple framework to understand the different types of possible damages in a breach of warranty case, it does not encompass the myriad of circumstances in which a claim for damages can arise, nor does it specify which of these different damages have been allowed in Pennsylvania.

In addition to recognizing general damages under § 2714 of the Code, Pennsylvania allows consequential damages in the form of lost profits to be recovered. [citations]

Pennsylvania has, however, disallowed good will damages; finding them to be too speculative to permit recovery. In the cases disallowing good will damages, part of the reason we found them too speculative is that the damages were not contemplated by the parties at the time the contract was made.

In 1977, this court had occasion to re-examine sections 2714 and 2715 of the Uniform Commercial Code in the case of *R.I. Lampus Co. v. Neville Cement Products Corp.*, 474 Pa. 199, 378 A.2d 288 (1977). Before the *Lampus* case, we required the party seeking consequential damages in the form of lost profits to show that there were "special circumstances" indicating that such damages were actually contemplated by the parties at the time they entered into the agreement. This rule, termed the "tacit-agreement" test, "permit[ted] the plaintiff to recover damages arising from special circumstances only if 'the defendant fairly may be supposed to have assumed consciously, or to have warranted the plaintiff reasonably to suppose that it assumed, [such liability] when the contract was made.' "

In *Lampus,* we overruled the restrictive "tacit-agreement" test and replaced it with the "reason to know" test; which requires that "[i]f a seller knows of a buyer's general or particular requirements and needs, that seller is liable for *the resulting consequential damages* whether or not that seller contemplated or agreed to such damages." (emphasis supplied). Thus, in order to obtain consequential damages, the plaintiff need only prove that the damages were reasonably foreseeable at the time the agreement was entered into.

Turning to the case at hand, we must determine whether the plaintiffs have alleged sufficient facts to permit them to proceed with a claim for consequential damages. * * *

The first claim the plaintiff makes for damages is for the profits lost from the sales of gasoline. The plaintiffs claim that the breach of warranty by the defendant concerning the gasoline caused the plaintiffs to lose sales during a three and one half year period while they received nonconforming gasoline from ARCO. In the case of *Kassab v. Central Soya,* 432 Pa. 217, 246 A.2d 848 (1968), we permitted lost profits for cattle sales when the plaintiff showed that the defective feed caused harm to their cattle, causing the public to stop buying their cattle. The allegation here is similar. When the gasoline buying public discovered that the gasoline was defective, many stopped purchasing ARCO gasoline.

Employing the reasoning of *Kassab* and taking it one step further, we believe that the plaintiffs here are entitled to show that the gasoline buying community did not buy their gasoline from 1982 through 1985 because of the reasonable belief that the gasoline was defective and would harm their engines. The lost gasoline sales are comparable to the lost cattle sales in *Kassab.* The distinction between the two cases is that the Kassabs had bought the feed all at one time and thus all their livestock was affected. The instant plaintiffs bought their gasoline in regular intervals and could only earn a profit on what they could sell per month. The defendant's argument—that the plaintiffs sold all the gasoline they bought—misses the point. While they may have sold every gallon, they sold significantly fewer gallons during the period that ARCO allegedly delivered nonconforming gasoline. Thus, during this period, the plaintiffs' lost sales were just as directly attributable to the defective gasoline as the lost profits were attributable to the defective tires in the example we used previously.[3]

Thus, if prior to the manufacture of defective gasoline the plaintiffs sold 100,000 gallons per month every month and then as a result of the defective gasoline, they sold only 60,000 gallons per month every month until ARCO discontinued that gasoline, then the plaintiffs have lost the profits they would have received on 40,000 gallons per month for the three year claimed period. Lost profits are, in fact, the difference between what the plaintiff actually earned and what they would have earned had the defendant not committed the breach. Because the gasoline was allegedly not in conformance with the warranties, the plaintiffs may be entitled to lost profits for the gasoline on a breach of warranty theory. The lost gasoline sales are what we have termed "loss of primary profits," and they are recoverable pursuant to § 2715 of the U.C.C. upon proper proof.

We note, furthermore, that the remedy of cover was unavailable to the plaintiffs. * * *

[T]hey were contractually required to purchase all their gasoline from ARCO. In effect, they had to accept the allegedly nonconforming gasoline and had no possible way to avoid the attendant loss of profits. Thus, since they could not cover, the only remedy that was available to them was to file suit. * * *

The plaintiffs allege that in addition to a loss of profits for sales of gasoline, they had a concomitant loss of sales for other items that they sold in their mini-marts during the period of time that ARCO supplied nonconforming gasoline. Their rationale is that when the number of customers buying gasoline decreased, so did the number of customers buying items at the mini-mart. In other words, related facets of their business suffered as a result of the defective gasoline. This type of injury is what we characterize as "loss of secondary profits"; meaning that the sales of other products suffered as a result of the breach of warranty. This court has not had an opportunity to address whether these types of damages are recoverable.

In the case before us, the essence of plaintiffs' allegations is that customers frequent the mini-marts because it is convenient to do so at the time they purchase gasoline. Customers of the mini-mart are foremost gasoline buying patrons; gasoline is their primary purchase and sundries are their incidental purchases. Here, the plaintiffs claim that the *primary product* sales so affected the incidental sales as to create a loss in other aspects of their business. It is reasonable to assume that if the gasoline sales dropped dramatically, there was a ripple effect on the mini-mart sales. Additionally, when a primary product does not conform to the warranty, we believe that it is foreseeable that there will be a loss of secondary profits. Thus, permitting these damages would correspond with the requirement of foreseeability as set forth in *Lampus,* and

3. The current case, unlike the tire example, involves a requirements contract rather than a fixed quantity agreement. In a requirement contract, profits lost during the period of time in which the seller supplies nonconforming goods constitute lost primary profits. The Code does not require that the buyer prove he would have purchased the same amount as usually required, for § 2715 permits the buyer to mitigate his damages by "cover or otherwise." Thus the buyer need not buy his usual amount of goods and then be unable to sell them before he can claim a loss of profits.

the Code. It is much less foreseeable to assume there will be a loss of secondary profits when the nonconforming products are not the primary ones. We believe that unless it is a primary product that does not conform to the warranty, the causal relationship between the breach and the loss is too attenuated to permit damages for the loss of secondary profits. * * *

We find that the present case presents compelling reasons for permitting damages for loss of secondary profits. Henceforth, in a breach of warranty case, when a primary product of the plaintiff is alleged to be nonconforming and the plaintiff is unable to cover by purchasing substitute goods, we hold that upon proper proof, the plaintiff should be entitled to sue for loss of secondary profits.[4]

Historically, Pennsylvania has disallowed recovery for loss of good will damages or prospective profits in breach of warranty cases. The cases generally relied upon for this proposition are Michelin Tire Co. v. Schulz, 295 Pa. 140, 145 A. 67 (1929); Harry Rubin & Sons, Inc. v. Consolidated Pipe Co. of America, 396 Pa. 506, 153 A.2d 472 (1959); and Kassab v. Central Soya, 432 Pa. 217, 246 A.2d 848 (1968).

The defendant and the lower courts rely on these cases for the proposition that the plaintiffs claims are for "good will damages" and thus too speculative as a matter of law to permit recovery. While this analysis is seductive in its simplicity, it ignores the nuances of each of these cases and the effect R.I. Lampus Co. v. Neville Cement Products Corp., has had on this area of law.

In fact, in the case of *Rubin & Sons,* the court remarked "[i]ndeed if such were the holding [permitting good will damages], damages which the parties never contemplated would seem to be involved in every contract of sale."

With the advent of the *Lampus* "reason-to-know" test—which is a test of foreseeability—the holdings under each of these cases have much less precedential effect, since the *Lampus* test is much less restrictive than the tacit-agreement test.

Although the plaintiffs do not style their claim as one for good will damages, the Superior Court, the trial court, and the defendant have all characterized the claim for lost profits in this case as good will damages. What actually constitutes good will damages has caused much consternation to the courts and litigants. We in fact have serious doubts that the plaintiffs are even seeking good will damages. However, in order to determine that issue in the case before us, we must first discuss what good will damages are and whether they are allowable.

As one commentator aptly noted, "[l]oss of good will is a mercurial concept and, as such, is difficult to define. In a broad sense, it refers to a loss of future profits."[5] Other jurisdictions have considered loss of good will to be a loss of profits and reputation among customers. [citation] Generally, good will refers to the reputation that businesses have built over the course of time that is reflected by the return of customers to purchase goods and the attendant

4. What constitutes a "primary product" will be dependent on the facts of each case. However, we would define a "primary product" as an item upon which the aggrieved party relies for a substantial amount of its revenue. The plaintiff must show that without that product, his business would be severely incapacitated.

5. Anderson, *Incidental and Consequential Damages,* 7 J.L. & Com. 327, 420 (1987).

profits that accompanies such sales. Thus the phrase "good will damages" is coextensive with prospective profits and loss of business reputation.

Secondly, we must decide when good will damages arise in a breach of warranty situation. Essentially, damage to good will in a case in which the seller supplies a quantity dictated by the buyer's requirements arises only *after* the seller has ceased providing nonconforming goods—or the buyer has purchased substitute goods. Damage to good will in this case would refer to the loss of business sales that occurred after the buyer was able to provide acceptable goods to his customers; it does not refer to the period of time during which he is forced to sell the nonconforming goods.

Thirdly, we must address whether good will damages are too speculative to permit recovery, as we held in *Michelin, Rubin & Sons,* and *Kassab.* Although we disallowed good will damages in those cases, they are not recent. They were written in a time when business was conducted on a more simple basis, where market studies and economic forecasting were unexplored sciences.

We are now in an era in which computers, economic forecasting, sophisticated marketing studies and demographic studies are widely used and accepted. As such, we believe that the rationale for precluding prospective profits under the rubric of "too speculative" ignores the realities of the marketplace and the science of modern economics. We believe that claims for prospective profits should not be barred *ab initio.* Rather, plaintiffs should be given an opportunity to set forth and attempt to prove their damages.

Twenty years ago, the Third Circuit Court of Appeals noted in a case disallowing claims for prospective profits that damages once considered speculative may not be in the future:

> "This is not to say we approve the Pennsylvania view or believe it will be the Pennsylvania position in the future [prohibiting good will damages]. Considering the advances made in techniques of market analysis and the use of highly sophisticated computers it may be that lost profits of this nature are no more speculative than lost profits from the destruction of a factory or hotel, and perhaps Pennsylvania will reconsider the reason for its rule in a future case."

Neville Chemical Co. v. Union Carbide Corp., 422 F.2d 1205, 1227 (1970).

We believe the time has come to reconsider that rule. In doing so, we find our position on recovery for good will damages (or prospective profits) to be out of step with modern day business practices and techniques, as well as the law of other jurisdictions. [citations] As noted by Professor Anderson in his well-crafted article on incidental and consequential damages,

> "[t]o date, only the Pennsylvania courts have categorically denied recovery for loss of goodwill under any circumstances, an issue which has been oft-litigated in Pennsylvania. If one removes the Pennsylvania cases from the court, a significant majority of the cases have allowed for the recovery of lost goodwill in proper circumstances."

Furthermore, our rule has been repeatedly criticized by other courts and commentators. [citations] In reviewing our case law on the issue of prospective profits, we have not had a significant case come before us since *Kassab* was decided in 1968. Since that time, astronauts have walked on the moon, engineers have developed computers capable of amazing feats and biomedical engineers and physicians have made enormous strides in organ transplantation and replacement. It is evident that the world of 1990 is not the same world as it was in 1929 when the *Michelin* case was decided, nor even the same world as it was in 1968 when *Kassab* was decided. While these rapid technological developments have not been without their concomitant problems, they have made possible many things that were not possible before; including the calculation of prospective profits. For these reasons, we overrule *Michelin, Rubin & Sons, Inc.,* and *Kassab,* to the extent they prohibit a plaintiff from alleging a claim for damage to good will as a matter of law. * * *

[W]e now hold that plaintiffs should be entitled to try to prove good will damages; provided they are able to introduce sufficient evidence (1) to establish that the such profits were causally related to a breach of warranty and (2) to provide the trier of fact with a reasonable basis from which to calculate damages.[6]

Turning to the facts of this case, we note that the plaintiffs have made no claim for good will damages, since none was incurred; ARCO having cured the breach by stopping the supply of the nonconforming gasoline. The damages claimed are only for the period of time that the plaintiffs were forced to purchase the gasoline with oxinol. Thus, we reverse the decision of the lower courts in holding that the plaintiffs' claim was for good will damages. * * *

We now hold that there are three types of lost profits recoverable as consequential damages available under § 2714 and § 2715 of the Uniform Commercial Code: (1) loss of primary profits; (2) loss of secondary profits; and (3) good will damages, defined as a loss of prospective profits or business reputation. While this categorization of damages represents a new direction for the court, we believe that it is the better direction.

As a final note, we do not find that this case should be decided on tort principles, but on warranty principles. The relationship between the parties is of a contractual nature and should be decided on contractual principles. For that reason, we uphold the decision of the court below dismissing the tort claims. Additionally, we do not believe that our case law or the Uniform Commercial Code authorizes a legitimate claim for exemplary damages and thus affirm the lower court's dismissal of such claim. * * *

It is so ordered.

Notes

1. Professor Danzig asked whether the U.C.C.'s version of Hadley v. Baxendale is economically efficient:

"Resting the seller's liability on whether the type of damages incurred was 'normal' (or, in the UCC's words, whether it was a type of damage of which the seller has 'reason to know'), seems undesirable because it lets an all-or-nothing decision ride on an indicator about which many sellers cannot, at the time of breach, speculate with confidence. Further, if the recoverability of a type of damages is established, a seller may often have no reasonable basis for determining

6. There are a number of different ways that damages may be removed from the realm of speculation and be submitted to the jury with a rational basis from which the amount can be inferred. As long as the method of proof provides the jury with "a reasonable basis" for calculating damages, the issue should be submitted to the trier of fact. This is the approach taken by most jurisdictions. [citations]

the magnitude of the damages involved. On this dimension—obviously critical to any calculus of the care warranted to avoid breach—the rule has nothing to say. Lastly, if the rule were truly finely geared to optimizing the allocation of resources, it would place its emphasis on the damage known to the seller at the time of breach, rather than at the time of contract, at least where the breach was voluntary. When the rule was framed stress had to be placed on communication at the time of the making of a contract because that was the only occasion on which information exchange could be coerced without fear of imposing enormous transaction costs. Now the telephone and vastly improved telegraphic facilities make it possible to mandate discussion at the time of breach. Would it be desirable to move the focus of the rule to this point? On this question, some empirical evidence would be desirable. Do the average transaction costs associated with information exchange at the time of the contract multiplied by the number of instances in which such information is exchanged exceed the average transaction costs of information exchange at the time of voluntary breach multiplied by the number of occasions when breach is seriously considered? If so, there is much to be said for a revision in the rule." Danzig, Hadley v. Baxendale: A Study in the Industrialization of the Law, 4 J. Legal Stud. 249, 282–283 (1975).

2. S.M. Wilson & Co. v. Reeves Red–E–Mix Concrete Inc., 39 Ill.App.3d 353, 357–58, 350 N.E.2d 321, 325 (1976). Defendant delivered concrete that did not meet contract specifications. Buyer spent $14,588.10 on tests to determine whether the concrete had to be replaced. It sought to set these costs off against the money it owed to seller for the concrete. Seller refused to deliver more concrete unless paid; buyer purchased the rest of its requirements elsewhere. Buyer sued seller to recover for the tests and the additional concrete. In affirming a judgment for buyer, the court said:

"The measure of damages under paragraph 2–714 is the 'loss resulting in the ordinary course of events' from the breach including incidental and consequential damages. Had plaintiff removed the slab defendant would have been liable for the cost of removal and replacement and for any loss incurred through the delay necessarily involved. Plaintiff chose to conduct tests approved in the industry to determine if the slab could be used. We believe the cost of these tests to be a reasonable incidental expense under paragraph 2–715. The cost of obtaining additional concrete after defendant's refusal to deliver the amount contracted for was a reasonable cost of 'cover' as it exceeded the contract price and is recoverable under paragraph 2–715, cover being the act of obtaining goods from another source to complete the project after the vendor refuses to supply the goods contracted for."

3. *Limitations of Damages by Disclaimers.* Remedies for breach of warranty are frequently affected by disclaimer and exclusionary clauses in the sales contract. See J. White & R. Summers, Uniform Commercial Code §§ 12.1–12.12 (3d ed. 1988). These clauses limit the seller's liability or restrict the available remedies. See, for example, Jones & McKnight Corp. v. Birdsboro Corp., 320 F.Supp. 39 (N.D.Ill.1970); Ford Motor Co. v. Moulton, 511 S.W.2d 690 (Tenn.1974) (disclaimer of implied warranties); Schroeder v. Fageol Motors, Inc., 86 Wash.2d 256, 544 P.2d 20 (1975) (disclaimer of liability for consequential damages); Clements Auto Co. v. Service Bureau Corp., supra p. 805. Problems, including remedial unconscionability, arising from these clauses are analyzed in Weintraub, Disclaimer of Warranties and Limitation of Damages for Breach of Warranty Under the UCC, 53 Tex.L.Rev. 60 (1974).

See also Samuels, The Unconscionability of Excluding Consequential Damages Under the Uniform Commercial Code When No Other Meaningful Remedy Is Available, 43 U.Pitt.L.Rev. 197 (1981). A & M Produce Co. v. FMC Corp., 135

Cal.App.3d 473, 186 Cal.Rptr. 114 (1982), held a disclaimer of warranty unconscionable despite technical compliance with the code. In Goddard v. General Motors Corp., 60 Ohio St.2d 41, 396 N.E.2d 761 (1979), a clause limiting a buyer's remedy to repair and replacement of defective parts was found to fail in its essential purpose when a new car was "riddled with defects."

Compare Rubin v. Telemet America, Inc., 698 F.Supp. 447 (S.D.N.Y.1988), where the court held the clause valid against an attack by a sophisticated investor. In Hydraform Products Corp. v. American Steel & Aluminum Corp., 127 N.H. 187, 498 A.2d 339 (1985), the court found a disclaimer valid against an assertion of unconscionability, but ruled it unenforceable because it failed in its essential purpose of providing a buyer with any effective remedy. See also Goddard v. General Motors Corp., 60 Ohio St.2d 41, 396 N.E.2d 761 (1979). For a review, see Foss, When to Apply the Doctrine of Failure of Essential Purpose to an Exclusion of Consequential Damages: An Objective Approach, 25 Duq.L.Rev. 551 (1987).

4. Consequential damages may be limited because of the failure of the buyer to take reasonable measures to mitigate the loss. In Carnation Co. v. Olivet Egg Ranch, 189 Cal.App.3d 809, 229 Cal.Rptr. 261 (1986), the court allocated to the buyer the burden of proving the loss, but placed on the seller the burden of proving the inadequacy of efforts to mitigate the consequential damages.

5. For those interested in the manufacture of a Rolls–Royce, see Zeff v. Rolls–Royce Motors, Inc., 694 F.Supp. 336 (E.D.Mich.1988). Buyer's claim for breach of warranty was lost when he failed to produce evidence of the allegedly defective vehicle's market value; he relied instead on his testimony of what the vehicle was worth to him personally.

6. Schiro, Prospecting for Lost Profits in the Uniform Commercial Code: The Buyer's Dilemmas, 52 S.Cal.L.Rev. 1727, 1773 (1979); Priest, Breach and Remedy for the Tender of Nonconforming Goods Under the Uniform Commercial Code: An Economic Approach, 91 Harv.L.Rev. 960 (1978).

b. Rescission and Restitution

JOHNSON v. GENERAL MOTORS CORP. CHEVROLET MOTOR DIVISION

Supreme Court of Kansas, 1983.

233 Kan. 1044, 668 P.2d 139.

LOCKETT, JUSTICE. This action involves revocation of acceptance pursuant to K.S.A. 2–608. The issues raised in this appeal focus on the appropriate measure of damages for a buyer's use of goods after revocation of acceptance.

John and Joan Johnson, the appellants, purchased a new 1981 Chevrolet Silverado half-ton diesel pickup truck from Ed Roberts Chevrolet in Bonner Springs, Kansas, on October 7, 1980. The Johnsons traded in a 1979 Chevrolet pickup and paid $4,202.10 in cash in exchange for the new pickup. The total cost of the new truck was $11,119.65. The Johnsons received a limited warranty for the truck from the General Motors Corporation (GMC).

Problems with the new truck appeared immediately. On the trip home from the dealership, the truck's accelerator stuck in a wide open position while the truck was in traffic. Also, a substantial amount of oil leaked from the truck. The pickup was brought to the dealer for repairs but the problems continued. * * * Repairs were attempted under GMC's warranty agreement but the Johnsons had lost confidence in the truck. On November 30, 1980, the

Johnsons, through their attorney, sought to revoke their acceptance of the truck and to return it for a refund of the purchase price. Their offer to return the truck was refused by GMC and the Johnsons continued to use the truck after a lawsuit was filed. Some repairs were performed under the warranty agreement during the time period after revocation and prior to trial.

On March 2, 1981, the Johnsons filed this action against GMC. The case was tried to the court April 2, 1982, and it was decided that the Johnsons' revocation was justified. GMC does not appeal this ruling. The court held a second hearing on June 18, 1982, to determine what setoff amount should be awarded to GMC because of the appellants' continued use of the truck after revocation. The trial court awarded a setoff of $4,702.94. The Johnsons would be refunded the remainder of the purchase price.

The principal issue is whether the trial court erred in allowing a setoff from the purchase price of the truck for the buyers' continued use of the truck after the buyers' revocation of acceptance. The buyers continued to drive the truck an additional 14,619 miles after notifying GMC of the revocation of acceptance. * * *

Under proper rejection or revocation of acceptance, the buyer is freed from his obligation to pay the purchase price. A buyer has a right to recover that portion of the purchase price already paid when rejection or revocation of acceptance is proper.

A buyer that has accepted a truck and sues for breach of warranty will recover only for the injury that resulted from defects in the truck at the time of the sale. A buyer that properly rejects or revokes after acceptance is first made whole from the injuries resulting from the seller's failure to perform his part of the agreement, escapes the bargain, and forces any loss resulting from depreciation of the goods back on the seller.

The basic policy for revocation of acceptance is contained in 2–608 which states in part:

> "(1) The buyer may revoke his acceptance of a lot or commercial unit whose nonconformity substantially impairs its value to him if he has accepted it. * * *
>
> "(*b*) without discovery of such nonconformity if his acceptance was reasonably induced either by the difficulty of discovery before acceptance or by the seller's assurances.
>
> "(2) Revocation of acceptance must occur within a reasonable time after the buyer discovers or should have discovered the ground for it and before any substantial change in condition of the goods which is not caused by their own defects. It is not effective until the buyer notifies the seller of it.
>
> "(3) A buyer who so revokes has the same rights and duties with regard to the goods involved as if he had rejected them."

The truck was purchased October 7, 1980. On November 30, 1980, through their attorney, the buyers notified the seller of their revocation of acceptance of the truck and requested a refund of the purchase price. GMC refused to accept the return of the truck but continued its offer to cure the defects under the warranty agreement given by GMC at the time of the sale. At the trial the court determined that the buyers' revocation of acceptance was proper and occurred within a reasonable time after buyers discovered the defects.

Since the buyers had taken possession of the goods, they had a security interest in the goods for the purchase price paid and any expenses reasonably incurred for the care and custody of the truck. Vesting the revoking buyer with a security interest for payments made and expenses incurred is pursuant to 2–711, which states in part:

> "(1) Where the seller fails to make delivery or repudiates or the buyer rightfully rejects or justifiably revokes acceptance then with respect to any goods involved, and with respect to the whole if the breach goes to the whole contract (section 2–612), the buyer may cancel and whether or not he has done so may in addition to recovering so much of the price as has been paid
>
> "(*a*) 'cover' * * * or
>
> "(*b*) recover damages * * *
>
> "(3) On rightful rejection or justifiable revocation of acceptance a buyer has a security interest in goods in his possession or control for any payments made on their price and any expenses reasonably incurred in their inspection, receipt, transportation, care and custody and may hold such goods and resell them in like manner as an aggrieved seller (section 2–706)."

A buyer who revokes has the same rights and duties with regard to the goods involved as if he had rejected them. 2–608(3). This places the revoking buyer in the same position with one who rejects prior to acceptance thus eliminating the need for different sets of standards for resolving commercial disputes. The manner and effect of rejection and revocation are contained in the UCC.

After notification of rejection or revocation to the seller, a merchant buyer is obligated to follow any reasonable instructions received from the seller. If no instructions are received from the seller, a merchant buyer or buyer may choose any of the options available to him under the UCC. The goods may be returned, stored for the seller, or sold for the seller's account with reimbursement to the buyer for reasonable expenses incurred caring for and expenses incurred in the sale of the goods. K.S.A. 2–603 and K.S.A. 2–604. A buyer is not permitted to retain such funds as he might believe adequate for his damages if he resells the goods. The proceeds are to be held by the selling buyer until his damages are properly determined.

Here buyers exercised none of the options available to them under the UCC. Instead, buyers, after revocation of acceptance, continued to use the truck. The UCC states after rejection any exercise of ownership by the buyer with respect to any commercial unit is wrongful as against the seller. K.S.A. 2–602(2)(*a*). A buyer's continued use of the goods after revocation of acceptance can constitute an acceptance of ownership and invalidate a cancellation of a sale. Here buyers were placed in a position where if they stored the truck or properly sold the truck, they would not have a vehicle for transportation until the trial of the issues or would be required to lease or purchase an additional vehicle. The buyers' continued use of the vehicle under these circumstances was not an act of continued use which constituted an acceptance of ownership after revocation. With little or no low-cost public transportation available to the public, private transportation has changed from a luxury to a necessity.

The buyers suggest that a revoking purchaser may use the goods after revocation without penalty or cost in limited circumstances where use of the goods is required even after notice of revocation of acceptance. This issue has not been settled by earlier Kansas decisions construing K.S.A. 2–608. * * * Precode decisions avoided the question altogether because the common law required purchasers to elect between "rescission" and recovery of damages. Prompt return of unsatisfactory goods was a condition precedent to an action for rescission. * * * The question of cancellation in the absence of immediate return of the goods did not arise until enactment of the Code.

There is much support for the proposition of awarding a setoff for continued use of goods after revocation of acceptance. Many courts have awarded setoffs in circumstances similar to the present case. [citations]

The Colorado Court of Appeals in Stroh v. Am.Rec., 35 Colo.App. at 201–03, 530 P.2d 989, used this reasoning to justify a setoff:

> "Having determined that plaintiffs' revocation of acceptance was effective, we must determine whether their acts thereafter entitled them to an award for the entire purchase price. A buyer who asserts a right to revoke acceptance has the same duties and obligations as a buyer who asserts a right to reject the goods before acceptance. C.R.S. 2–608(3). After rejection of goods, any exercise of dominion and ownership rights is considered wrongful as against the seller. C.R.S. 2–602(2)(a). The purpose of this requirement is to insure that the seller may regain possession of the goods in order to resell the goods or utilize them in order to minimize his loss. Accordingly, notice of revocation of acceptance is necessarily a recognition by the buyer that the property belongs to the seller. Here, after revocation of acceptance on October 15, 1970, plaintiffs retained only a security interest for return of their purchase price. C.R.S. 2–711(3). However, they continued to occupy the mobile home as their residence until they purchased a house in March of 1972 and thereupon vacated the mobile home. Even though defendants did not give instructions with respect to the home after they received notice of revocation of acceptance, plaintiffs' remedies under C.R.S. 2–711, do not include the right to beneficial use of the home. See C.R.S. 2–603. Therefore, we hold that plaintiffs' continued occupancy of the mobile home after the reasonable time at which plaintiffs should have acted under C.R.S. 2–604, was wrongful and defendants are entitled to an award of damages.
>
> "There is no specific provision in the Uniform Commercial Code for an offset award of damages for wrongful use by the buyer. However, C.R.S. 1–103, provides that:
>
> " 'Unless displaced by the particular provisions of this chapter, the principles of law and equity, including the law merchant and the law relative to capacity to contract, principal and agent, estoppel, fraud, misrepresentation, duress, coercion, mistake, bankruptcy, or other validating or invalidating cause shall supplement its provisions.'
>
> "We recognize that the general rule is that where a buyer is entitled to rescind the sale and elects to do so, the buyer shall thereafter be deemed to hold the goods as a bailee for the seller. [citations] Thus, if the buyer uses the goods while he holds them as a bailee, he becomes liable for the value of that use.
>
> "Since the evidence showed that plaintiffs used the mobile home for a considerable length of time after they should have acted under C.R.S. 2–604, it follows that this use reduced the value of the home. Accordingly, defendants are entitled to an offset of a fair and reasonable use value of the mobile home for this period." * * *

The weight of authority supports the granting of a setoff for use after revocation. We agree that a seller is entitled to a setoff for the buyers' continued use of the truck after their revocation of acceptance. * * *

The purpose of allowing revocation after acceptance is to restore the buyer to the economic position the buyer would have been in if the goods were never delivered. After revocation of acceptance any significant use by the buyer should allow the seller to recover from the buyers restitution for the fair value of any benefit obtained resulting from such use. The seller could avoid depreciation of the goods by accepting the buyers' revocation.

GMC contends the established rate of leased vehicle depreciation provides a simple and uniform method for calculating the value of the buyers' post-revocation use. The calculation would have been the same whether or not the buyer drove 10 or 14,619 miles after revocation of acceptance. The only variable is the cost per mile.

The buyers had attempted revocation of acceptance two months after purchase. It was GMC's failure to accept the vehicle's return by the buyers that necessitated a law suit. Sixteen plus months after the buyers' notice of revocation of acceptance the court tried the case and determined that the buyers' revocation was proper. GMC's pure depreciation method using the lease vehicle's monthly depreciation rate was not the proper method of determining the offset due to the buyers' use of the vehicle after revocation. This method allows the seller to recover a setoff based upon a period of time from the seller's refusal to accept back defective goods until there is a judicial determination that the seller was wrong not to accept the buyers' revocation of acceptance. The proper setoff is the value of use of the goods received by the buyer after his revocation of acceptance.

At the trial, over buyers' objection, GMC introduced into evidence the Federal Highway Administration booklet entitled "Cost of Owning and Operating Automobiles and Vans 1982." The booklet was authenticated by the government's resident administrator in compliance with K.S.A. 60–465. The trial court did not abuse its discretion when it overruled the buyers' objection to the introduction of the booklet into evidence. The Federal Highway Administration booklet stated the cost of owning and operating a similar vehicle to the truck purchased by the buyers is calculated at 33.2 cents per mile. After deduction of maintenance, gas and oil, parking and tolls, insurance and state and federal taxes, expenses the buyers have already paid, the booklet concluded the original vehicle cost to operate is 10.7 cents per mile. Since buyers drove the vehicle 14,619 miles at 10.7 cents per mile after revocation, the setoff would be $1,564.23. From the evidence presented in this case, GMC is entitled to the sum of $1,564.23 as a setoff for the buyers' use of the truck after revocation of acceptance.

The buyers claim the trial court erred in failing to award them prejudgment interest from the date of revocation of acceptance. K.S.A. 16–201 provides:

> "Creditors shall be allowed to receive interest at the rate of ten percent per annum, when no other rate of interest is agreed upon, for any money after it becomes due; for money lent or money due on settlement of account, from the day of liquidating the account and ascertaining the balance; for money received for the use of another and retained without the owner's knowledge of the receipt; for money due and withheld by an unreasonable and vexatious

delay of payment or settlement of accounts; for all other money due and to become due for the forbearance of payment whereof an express promise to pay interest has been made; and for money due from corporations and individuals to their daily or monthly employees, from and after the end of each month, unless paid within fifteen days thereafter." * * *

The price buyers paid for the truck is not disputed ($11,119.65). For prejudgment interest to be awarded, the amount owed must be a liquidated sum. A setoff or counterclaim does not alter the fact a liquidated sum is owed as of a certain date. However, the setoff is credited against the liquidated claim as of the date the claim was due. * * *

A party justifiably revoking acceptance pursuant to 2–608 is entitled to prejudgment interest from the date revocation is attempted. Any setoff due the seller because of a buyer's continued use of the goods after an attempt to revoke should be deducted from the total judgment which includes prejudgment interest. The setoff arises only after a seller refuses to accept return of the defective goods, and no setoff is due the seller on the revocation date.

Here there was no setoff at the date the claim was due. The setoff occurred after the due date because of seller's refusal to accept return of the defective vehicle. Prejudgment interest on the purchase price would commence to accumulate from November 30, 1980, until the date of judgment. * * *

The awarding of a setoff to GMC is affirmed, but from the evidence presented in this case, the setoff should be $1,564.23. The decision not to grant the plaintiffs prejudgment interest is reversed. The interest should be calculated upon the entire purchase price from the date revocation was attempted until the date of judgment at the rate of ten percent. The case is affirmed in part, reversed in part and remanded to enter judgment in accordance with this opinion.

Notes

1. A buyer who justifiably revokes an acceptance may recover any additional costs incurred in reliance on the contract plus restitution of benefits conferred on the seller. Thus in Aubrey's R.V. Center, Inc. v. Tandy Corp., 46 Wash.App. 595, 731 P.2d 1124 (1987), a buyer who revoked acceptance of a contract to purchase a computer was entitled to recover not only the price but also financing charges.

City National Bank v. Wells, ___ W.Va. ___, 384 S.E.2d 374 (1989). The buyer revoked a contract for breach of warranty. He claimed that a Toyota dealer's failure to repair a truck caused him to default on a note. The default impaired his credit rating. This in turn increased his costs of doing business. Buyer recovered these costs as consequential damages.

See Anderson, Monetary Recoveries for Reliance and in Restitution Under Article 2 of the U.C.C., 22 U.C.C.L.J. 248 (1990).

2. Whether continued use of a chattel defeats the right to revoke acceptance raises issues identical with those considered in Chapter 9 on affirmance of a contract. The applicable test appears to be whether the use is reasonable under the circumstances. CPC International, Inc. v. Techni–Chem, Inc., 660 F.Supp. 1509 (N.D.Ill.1987) (continued use may minimize economic waste); Aubrey's R.V. Center, Inc. v. Tandy Corp., 46 Wash.App. 595, 731 P.2d 1124 (1987). But where a buyer continued to use chattels for three years after discovery of the alleged defects, made no offer to return them, and rejected an offer to replace them, the attempted

revocation was ineffective. Sobiech v. International Staple & Machine Co., 867 F.2d 778 (2d Cir.1989).

3. As the *Johnson* court indicates, the buyer who revokes acceptance has a security interest in the chattel to secure return of the purchase price. Without this right, the buyer would be required to return the chattel and could end up with neither the price nor the chattel. See Ford Motor Credit Co. v. Caiazzo, 387 Pa.Super. 561, 564 A.2d 931 (1989).

The remedy permits the buyer to hold and resell rejected goods under U.C.C. § 2–706. Mobile Home Sales Management, Inc. v. Brown, 115 Ariz. 11, 562 P.2d 1378 (App.1977). See Clark v. Zaid, Inc., 263 Md. 127, 282 A.2d 483 (1971); Askco Engineering Corp. v. Mobil Chem. Corp., 535 S.W.2d 893 (Tex.Civ.App.1976).

Failure to conduct the sale as provided in § 2–706 constitutes an acceptance of the goods, leaving the buyer with only his damage action. Uganski v. Little Giant Crane & Shovel, Inc., 35 Mich.App. 88, 192 N.W.2d 580 (1971), held that a two-year delay in conducting the sale was not commercially reasonable and remanded the case to determine value at the time acceptance was revoked. A proper exercise of the right of resale, however, does not defeat or impair the buyer's action for damages for breach of contract. From the funds realized in the resale, the buyer may retain the amount necessary to reimburse prepayment and incidental expenses, accounting to the seller for any surplus. See Hawkland, A Transactional Guide to the Uniform Commercial Code § 1.45 (1964).

4. Ms. Consumer purchased a new Chariot automobile from Dealer. She thinks her Chariot is a lemon because Dealer is unable to keep it running. Dealer asserts that it can be fixed. What are the frustrated consumer's remedies?

Under the Commercial Code the buyer has two "goods oriented" remedies: she may reject nonconforming goods and she may revoke her acceptance of substantially nonconforming goods she has already "accepted." U.C.C. §§ 2–508, 2–608. These remedies are essentially rescission; buyer should be entitled to receive her consideration back. See Seekings v. Jimmy GMC of Tucson, Inc., 130 Ariz. 596, 638 P.2d 210 (1981); Johnson v. General Motors Corp., Chevrolet Motor Division, supra. As could be expected, automobile manufacturers and dealers have traditionally resisted this remedy when consumers wish to return "lemons." Despite repeated failures of dealers to repair a car, they assert that all cars can be fixed.

Where the buyer has accepted and retained defective goods, § 2–714(2) measures damages for breach of warranty as the value the goods should have had less the goods' actual value. In addition, §§ 2–714(3) and 2–715 allow the buyer to recover for reliance expenses, personal injury, and property damage.

Standard form contracts reduce sellers' liability for breach by disclaiming implied warranties and limiting buyers' remedies, U.C.C. §§ 2–316, 2–719, Congress responded by enacting the Magnuson–Moss Warranty Act. 15 U.S.C. §§ 2301–2312 (1976). That Act sets minimum standards for written warranties and makes it worthwhile for attorneys to sue dealers and manufacturers by allowing the consumer to recover attorney fees.

Magnuson–Moss applies to all consumer items and is used for a wide variety of products. State "lemon laws" apply only to automobiles. See Conn.Gen.Stat.Ann. § 42–179. That act forces manufacturers to refund the price or replace an automobile (minus "a reasonable allowance for use") if the car is out of service for more than 30 days in its first year or if a defect remains after four trips to the shop. It also provides for attorney fees. See Note, A Sour Note, A Look at the Minnesota Lemon Law, 68 Minn.L.Rev. 846 (1984).

Both Magnuson–Moss and state lemon laws provide for arbitration where the manufacturer has a procedure that meets Federal Trade Commission regulations. See 16 C.F.R. § 703 (1983). Arbitration binds the manufacturers, but if the consumer remains dissatisfied, she may file suit. The results of the arbitration are admissible in court.

Consumers may also pursue common law tort remedies for fraud and fraudulent misrepresentation. Jurors seem sympathetic to plaintiffs whose new Chariots give them nothing but grief. Fraud measures damages more generously and may lead to punitive damages. Consider also the special damages that Ms. Consumer may incur if, for example, the Chariot breaks down far from home on a business trip or vacation.

5. *Mechanical and Procedural Problems in Class Actions Based on Buyer's Disaffirmance.*

a. In Vasquez v. Superior Ct., 4 Cal.3d 800, 820, 94 Cal.Rptr. 796, 809, 484 P.2d 964, 977 (1971), 37 named plaintiffs sued in behalf of themselves and others similarly situated to rescind their installment purchases of freezers (one contract) and food (another contract) on grounds of misrepresentation. Joined as defendants were the finance companies who had purchased the contracts. Plaintiffs prayed for return of the amounts they paid on the contracts, less the value of the food they consumed, $1,300 or less for most plaintiffs and not more than $1,700 for any of them. They also sought damages for injury to their credit standing and for storing the "unused" freezers in their homes. These damages were alleged to be no more than $1,000 for any one plaintiff. In addition punitive damages of $5,000 each were sought.

The Supreme Court of California addressed the maintainability of the class action for misrepresentation in general (holding that it would lie); it did not approach the special problems created by casting it in the form of a suit for rescission. It merely appended a footnote:

"Defendants rely upon a statement in a 1938 annotation in American Law Reports that 'Class of representative suits to obtain the rescission of transactions based on similar frauds practiced by one defendant upon various and commonly numerous, persons, have so often been held not maintainable that one may well doubt whether under any circumstance such a suit will lie.' (114 A.L.R. 1015 at p. 1016). This 33-year-old categorical pronouncement is anachronistic in view of the numerous federal cases permitting class actions in securities fraud cases as well as other authorities."

Is the matter so easily disposed of? Freezers and food and finance companies present practical considerations somewhat different than stock certificates of little or no worth. It by no means appears that "other authorities" are rescission cases. Conceding that such matters as notice, proof of reliance, etc., are not insoluble objections, what difficulties remain in *Vasquez?* For example, is there a possessory lien for the storage costs of the freezers? Are there "election" issues?

b. Wade and Kamenshine, Restitution for Defrauded Consumers: Making the Remedy Effective Through Suit by Governmental Agency, 37 Geo.Wash.L.Rev. 1031 (1969):

"*Restitution at the State Level. Statutes Permitting Attorneys General to Obtain Court–Ordered Restitution.* In recent years, several states have adopted legislation permitting court-ordered restitution in cases where the state attorney general seeks injunctions prohibiting 'any deception, deceptive act or practice, fraud, false pretense, false promise, or misrepresentation * * * in connection with the sale or advertisement of any merchandise * * *.' The courts are empowered to make such orders, including appointment of a receiver, as may be necessary 'to restore to any person in interest any monies or property * * * real or personal' acquired by any of the practices declared unlawful. These statutes raise several questions concerning administration of restitution * * *.

"[One] question is whether these statutes contemplate that the consumer return purchased merchandise in order to obtain a refund, particularly where the item is of some value.[1] Considering the broad scope of the statute, it appears reasonable to require return or diminished recovery in at least some cases. If services (rather than a product) are involved, a similar allowance in the amount of recovery could be made, although the statutes (except Maryland's and the statute pending in Colorado) do not deal with recovery in connection with misrepresented services. Even where the character of the firm's conduct would seem to warrant the harshest treatment, the effect on the interests of the general creditors of not requiring return of the merchandise would have to be considered. However, if return is ordered, it would be reasonable to require the firm to pay any shipping costs involved, particularly where the consumer paid the initial cost of shipment. In addition, a requirement of return may impose new burdens on the customer. For example, where recovery is to be only partial, some estimate of the worth of the product or service would have to be made, so that additional problems of proof for the consumer may again be introduced.

"Another significant facet of the statutes is that certain practices are deemed unlawful 'whether or not any person has in fact been misled, deceived, or damaged thereby.' Conceivably, a consumer who had not been misled, but who, for example, was having difficulty meeting his monthly payments could seek to recover under one of these statutes. Unless his recovery were permitted merely to increase the detriment to the defendant firm, there would at first seem no reason to allow it. However, the statute's purpose of facilitating consumer redress must be considered. In all cases the consumer probably would have to show at least that his purchase was made at the time of the deceptive practice. And if his burden of proof were further increased by requiring him to present evidence of reliance, the result might be less effective implementation of the statute's goals. On balance, it is better for a court to keep the consumer's burden at a minimum, even though in rare cases some injustice to the defendant might result.

"*Other Possibilities for State–Obtained Restitution.* Almost half the states permit their attorneys general to seek injunctions against false, deceptive, or misleading advertising regardless of the product involved, and almost all states provide for such injunctions in cases concerning food, drugs or cosmetics. A state court, if asked to grant restitution based on such statutes, might be persuaded that it has jurisdiction to do so under the *DeMario* rationale.[2]

1. [Footnotes renumbered.] * * * Of course, if the state were always to recover and distribute only the profits from the deceptive practice the return issue would not arise. However, it has been recognized that this approach would present substantial, though not insoluble problems of proof. [citation]

2. The 1967 N.Y.Dept. of Law Ann.Rep. describes a case in which this appears to have been done. A manufacturer of an "electric insect destroyer" was enjoined from advertising falsely as to the device's effectiveness. A mail order advertisement had resulted in approximately 30,000 purchases nationwide. Augmenting the prohibition of further false advertising was an order requiring the defendant to make refunds when requested, either for nondelivery or upon return of the device.

It has been suggested that consumers have standing to obtain injunctive relief against deceptive practices under Section 3(a) of the Uniform Deceptive Practices Act and that such relief might be sought in a class action. While the Act (Section 3(c)) preserves concurrent common law remedies it contains no provisions for monetary recovery and thus would seem to preclude a class of consumers from taking advantage of its broad substantive standards (Section 2(a)) for this purpose. However, the *DeMario* rationale might be applied here so that restitution could be awarded.

"Moreover, one can argue that the new restitution statutes discussed in the preceding section serve only to make explicit the equitable jurisdiction which nevertheless would obtain under laws referring solely to injunctive relief. * * *

"Even absent legislation providing for injunctive relief, there may be some possibility of the state obtaining restitution. For example, it has been suggested that a state may sue to enjoin consumer fraud on the ground that it constitutes a public nuisance. However, this would represent some extension of the public nuisance concept, which traditionally has applied only to conduct having a fairly clear adverse impact on the general welfare over and above the adverse effect on any individuals specifically affected. Moreover, even if the courts accepted the nuisance theory as a basis for equitable relief (including restitution), its application in consumer fraud cases probably would be limited to serious, persistent and widespread types of deceptive conduct since such conduct would have the most substantial public aspect."

c. *Specific Performance*

COPYLEASE CORP. OF AMERICA v. MEMOREX CORP.

United States District Court, Southern District of New York, 1976.
408 F.Supp. 758.

LASKER, DISTRICT JUDGE. By Memorandum Opinion dated November 12, 1975, we determined that Memorex Corporation (Memorex) breached its contract with Copylease Corporation of America (Copylease) for the sale of toner and developer and directed the parties to submit proposed judgments with supporting documentation relating to the availability of injunctive relief, or, more precisely, specific performance. We have studied the submissions and conclude that further testimony is necessary to determine the propriety of such relief.

Memorex takes the position that under California law Copylease is not entitled to specific performance of this contract. Copylease argues that the remedy is available—if not under California law, then under our general federal equitable powers. * * *

[W]e are inclined to agree with Memorex that the law of California controls the issuance of the equitable relief sought here by Copylease.

We also agree with Memorex that the provision in the contract granting Copylease an exclusive territory, on which Copylease places primary reliance in its request for specific performance, is not in itself an adequate basis under California law for an award of such relief. Long Beach Drug Co. v. United Drug Co., 13 Cal.2d 158, 88 P.2d 698, 89 P.2d 386 (1939). California law does not consider a remedy at law inadequate merely because difficulties may exist as to precise calculation of damages. *Long Beach Drug* and *Thayer Plymouth* also demonstrate the more fundamental refusal of California courts to order specific performance of contracts which are not capable of immediate enforcement, but which require a "continuing series of acts" and "cooperation between the parties for the successful performance of those acts." Thayer Plymouth Center, Inc. v. Chrysler Motors Corp., 255 Cal.App.2d at 303, 63 Cal.Rptr. at 150. Absent some exception to this general rule, therefore, Copylease will be limited to recovery of damages for the contract breach.

An exception which may prove applicable to this case is found in U.C.C. § 2716(1). That statute provides that in an action for breach of contract a buyer may be entitled to specific performance "where the goods are unique or in other proper circumstances." In connection with its claim for interim damages for lost profits from the time of the breach Copylease argues strongly that it could not reasonably have covered by obtaining an alternative source of toner because the other brands of toner are distinctly inferior to the Memorex product. If the evidence at the hearing supports this claim, it may well be that Copylease faces the same difficulty in finding a permanent alternative supplier. If so, the Official Comment to § 2716 suggests that a grant of specific performance may be in order:

> "Specific performance is no longer limited to goods which are already specific or ascertained at the time of contracting. The test of uniqueness under this section must be made in terms of the total situation which characterizes the contract. Output and requirements contracts involving a particular or peculiarly available source or market present today the typical commercial specific performance situation. * * * However, uniqueness is not the sole basis of the remedy under this section for the relief may also be granted 'in other proper circumstances' and *inability to cover is strong evidence of 'other proper circumstances.'* " Comment 2 (emphasis added)

If Copylease has no adequate alternative source of toner the Memorex product might be considered "unique" for purposes of § 2716, or the situation might present an example of "other proper circumstances" in which specific performance would be appropriate.

If such a showing is made it will be necessary to reconcile California's policy against ordering specific performance of contracts which provide for continuing acts or an ongoing relationship with § 2716 of the Code. Although we recognize that the statute does not require specific performance, the quoted portion of the Official Comment seems clearly to suggest that where a contract calls for continuing sale of unique or "noncoverable" goods this provision should be considered an exception to the general proscription. Output and requirements contracts, explicitly cited as examples of situations in which specific performance may be appropriate, by their nature call for a series of continuing acts and an ongoing relationship. Thus, the drafters seem to have contemplated that at least in some circumstances specific performance will issue contrary to the historical reluctance to grant such relief in these situations. If, at the hearing, Copylease makes a showing that it meets the requirements of § 2716, the sensible approach would be to measure, with the particulars of this contract in mind, the uniqueness or degree of difficulty in covering against the difficulties of enforcement which have caused courts to refrain from granting specific performance. It would be premature to speculate on the outcome of such analysis in this case.

Notes

1. U.C.C. § 2–716 has been interpreted to permit specific performance where the goods cannot be replaced by alternate sources. See Laclede Gas Co. v. Amoco Oil Co., 522 F.2d 33 (8th Cir.1975) (contract to supply propane gas); Kaiser Trading Co. v. Associated Metals and Minerals Corp., 321 F.Supp. 923 (N.D.Cal.1970), appeal dismissed, 433 F.2d 1364 (9th Cir.1971); Tennessee Valley Authority v. Mason Coal, Inc., 384 F.Supp. 1107 (E.D.Tenn.1974) (coal supply contract); Eastern Air Lines, Inc. v. Gulf Oil Corp., 415 F.Supp. 429 (S.D.Fla.1975) (five year contract to supply aviation fuel); Ruddock v. First National Bank, 201 Ill.App.3d 907, 559 N.E.2d 483 (1990) (astronomical clock). The same reasoning supports specific performance of

contracts to sell stock in closely held corporations. Dominick v. Vassar, 235 Va. 295, 367 S.E.2d 487 (1988); Evangelista v. Holland, 27 Mass.App.Ct. 244, 537 N.E.2d 589 (1989).

Courts also regard contracts for the sale of a franchise to be specifically enforceable since baseball "[f]ranchises are by their very nature unique and exclusive * * *." Triple–A Baseball Club Associates v. Northeastern Baseball, Inc., 832 F.2d 214, 223 (1st Cir.1987), cert. denied, 485 U.S. 935 (1988).

Chattels found to be sufficiently unique to come within the rule include a Corvette, Sedmak v. Charlie's Chevrolet, Inc., 622 S.W.2d 694 (Mo.App.1981); a Mexican hot sauce, Madariaga v. Morris, 639 S.W.2d 709 (Tex.App.1982); and a horizontal boring machine, Stephan's Machine & Tool v. D & H Machinery Consultants, Inc., 65 Ohio App.2d 197, 417 N.E.2d 579 (1979). See generally, Greenberg, Specific Performance Under Section 2–716 of the Uniform Commercial Code: "A More Liberal Attitude" in the "Grand Style," 17 New Eng.L.Rev. 321 (1982).

2. For a more restrictive interpretation of § 2–716, see Klein v. PepsiCo, Inc., 845 F.2d 76, 80 (4th Cir.1988), aff'd, 875 F.2d 315 (1989). The contract was to buy a Gulfstream G–II corporate jet. In denying specific performance, the court ruled that the U.C.C. "does not abrogate the maxim that specific performance is inappropriate where damages are recoverable and adequate."

3. Northern Indiana Public Service Co. v. Carbon County Coal Co., 799 F.2d 265, 279–80 (7th Cir.1986).

NIPSCO agreed in 1978 to buy about 1.5 million tons of coal each year from Carbon County for $24 per ton, subject to escalation which had driven the price up to $44. When the price of coal fell to the point where the contract was onerous for NIPSCO, it sued to be released from its obligations arguing that the contract was illegal and that the force majeure clause and the doctrines of frustration-impossibility discharged the contract. After Carbon County won a jury verdict of $181 million, it sought specific performance requiring NIPSCO to comply with the contract.

After declining to upset the contract as illegal or to release NIPSCO on grounds of frustration-impossibility, Judge Posner turned to Carbon County's request for specific performance instead of damages:

"[W]e turn to Carbon County's cross-appeal, which seeks specific performance in lieu of the damages it got. Carbon County's counsel virtually abandoned the cross-appeal at oral argument, noting that the mine was closed and could not be reopened immediately—so that if specific performance (i.e., NIPSCO's resuming taking the coal) was ordered, Carbon County would not be able to resume its obligations under the contract without some grace period. In any event the request for specific performance has no merit. Like other equitable remedies, specific performance is available only if damages are not an adequate remedy, and there is no reason to suppose them inadequate here. The loss to Carbon County from the breach of contract is simply the difference between (1) the contract price (as escalated over the life of the contract in accordance with the contract's escalator provisions) times quantity, and (2) the cost of mining the coal over the life of the contract. Carbon County does not even argue that $181 million is not a reasonable estimate of the present value of the difference. Its complaint is that although the money will make the owners of Carbon County whole it will do nothing for the miners who have lost their jobs because the mine is closed and the satellite businesses that have closed for the same reason. Only specific performance will help them.

"But since they are not parties to the contract their losses are irrelevant. Indeed, specific performance would be improper as well as unnecessary here, because it would force the continuation of production that has become uneconomical. No one wants coal from Carbon County's mine. With the collapse of oil prices, which has depressed the price of substitute fuels as well, this coal costs far more to get out of the ground than it is worth in the market. Continuing to produce it, under compulsion of an order for specific performance, would impose costs on society greater than the benefits. NIPSCO's breach, though it gave Carbon County a right to damages, was an efficient breach in the sense that it brought to a halt a production process that was no longer cost-justified. [citations] The reason why NIPSCO must pay Carbon County's loss is not that it should have continued buying coal it didn't need but that the contract assigned to NIPSCO the risk of market changes that made continued deliveries uneconomical. The judgment for damages is the method by which that risk is being fixed on NIPSCO in accordance with its undertakings.

"With continued production uneconomical, it is unlikely that an order of specific performance, if made, would ever actually be implemented. If, as a finding that the breach was efficient implies, the cost of a substitute supply (whether of coal, or of electricity) to NIPSCO is less than the cost of producing coal from Carbon County's mine, NIPSCO and Carbon County can both be made better off by negotiating a cancellation of the contract and with it a dissolution of the order of specific performance. Suppose, by way of example, that Carbon County's coal costs $20 a ton to produce, that the contract price is $40, and that NIPSCO can buy coal elsewhere for $10. Then Carbon County would be making a profit of only $20 on each ton it sold to NIPSCO ($40–$20), while NIPSCO would be losing $30 on each ton it bought from Carbon County ($40–$10). Hence by offering Carbon County more than contract damages (i.e., more than Carbon County's lost profits), NIPSCO could induce Carbon County to discharge the contract and release NIPSCO to buy cheaper coal. For example, at $25, both parties would be better off than under specific performance, where Carbon County gains only $20 but NIPSCO loses $30. Probably, therefore, Carbon County is seeking specific performance in order to have bargaining leverage with NIPSCO, and we can think of no reason why the law should give it such leverage. We add that if Carbon County obtained and enforced an order for specific performance this would mean that society was spending $20 (in our hypothetical example) to produce coal that could be gotten elsewhere for $10—a waste of scarce resources.

"As for possible hardships to workers and merchants in Hanna, Wyoming, where Carbon County's coal mine is located, we point out that none of these people were parties to the contract with NIPSCO or third-party beneficiaries. They have no legal interest in the contract. [citations] Of course the consequences to third parties of granting an injunctive remedy, such as specific performance, must be considered, and in some cases may require that the remedy be withheld. [citations] The frequent references to 'public interest' as a factor in the grant or denial of a preliminary injunction invariably are references to third-party effects. [citation] But even though the formal statement of the judicial obligation to consider such effects extends to orders denying as well as granting injunctive relief, [citation] the actuality is somewhat different: when the question is whether third parties would be injured by an order denying an injunction, always they are persons having a legally recognized interest in the lawsuit, so that the issue really is the adequacy of relief if the injunction is denied. * * * Carbon County does not stand in a representative relation to the workers and businesses of Hanna, Wyoming. Treating them as real parties in interest would evade the limitations on the concept of a third-party beneficiary and would place the promisor under obligations potentially far heavier than it had thought it was accepting when it signed the contract. Indeed, if we are right that an order of specific performance would probably not be carried out—that instead NIPSCO would pay an additional sum of money to Carbon County for an agreement not to enforce the order—it becomes transparent that granting specific performance would make NIPSCO liable in money damages for harms to nonparties to the contract, and it did not assume such liability by signing the contract.

"Moreover, the workers and merchants in Hanna assumed the risk that the coal mine would have to close down if it turned out to be uneconomical. The contract with NIPSCO did not guarantee that the mine would operate throughout the life of the contract but only protected the owners of Carbon County against the financial consequences to them of a breach. As Carbon County itself emphasizes in its brief, the contract was a product of the international oil cartel, which by forcing up the price of substitute fuels such as coal made costly coal-mining operations economically attractive. The OPEC cartel is not a source of vested rights to produce substitute fuels at inflated prices."

4. *Academic Ferment.* Scholars continue to argue about whether specific performance is superior to money damages. Professor Laycock rejects the idea of a hierarchy of remedies with money damages preferred unless claimant shows them inadequate. "[T]he real ground for specific performance is irreplaceability, and * * * uniqueness is not the only cause of irreplaceability. Damages are inadequate unless they can be used to replace the specific thing that was lost, however ordinary that thing is." Laycock, The Death of the Irreparable Injury Rule, 103 Harv.L.Rev. 687, 707 (1990). Also favoring broadened access to specific performance: Linzer, On the Amorality of Contract Remedies—Efficiency, Equity and the Second Restatement, 81 Colum.L.Rev. 111 (1981); Schwartz, The Case for Specific Performance, 89 Yale L.J. 271 (1979).

Professor Yorio's view "is that the existing rules governing specific performance are more efficient on balance than a regime in which specific performance became the routine remedy for breach of contract." E. Yorio, Contract Enforcement: Specific Performance and Injunctions § 1.4 (1989). Concurring at least in the result are Kronman, Specific Performance, 45 U.Chi.L.Rev. 351 (1978); and Muris, The Costs of Freely Granting Specific Performance, 1982 Duke L.J. 1053.

5. *Buyer in Default as Plaintiff.*

A defaulting buyer who seeks restitution of payments made to the seller presents a problem previously discussed. See supra, pp. 1037–47, 1056–67. In sales of goods, the restitutionary rights of the defaulting buyer are governed by the U.C.C. § 2–718.

Procter & Gamble Distributing Co. v. Lawrence American Field Warehousing Corp., 16 N.Y.2d 344, 354, 266 N.Y.S.2d 785, 792–3, 213 N.E.2d 873, 878 (1965). This litigation grew out of the notorious oil fraud of Allied Crude Vegetable Oil Refining Corp. The court stated the law applicable to a buyer in default:

"It was firmly settled in New York [citation] and in New Jersey [citation] that one who has failed to perform his part of an executory contract of sale may not recover the purchase money he has paid thereon. It was so held also in most of the rest of the United States. This has been changed by the Uniform Commercial Code 2–718, subd. [2], par. [b]. These sections destroy the old rule that the buyer forfeits his down payment by breaching the contract, by providing that where the seller justifiably withholds delivery of goods because of the buyer's breach, the buyer is entitled to restitution of any amount by which the sum of his payments exceeds reasonable liquidated damages specified in the agreement, or 'in the absence of such terms, twenty per cent of the value of the total performance for which the buyer is obligated under the contract or $500, whichever is smaller.' "

In Stanturf v. Quality Dodge, Inc., 3 Kan.App.2d 485, 596 P.2d 1247 (1979), a buyer breached a contract to buy a van. He had traded in a vehicle valued at $1000 and paid $500 down. The court held that the buyer was entitled to restitution of $500 unless the seller proved special damages.

2. SELLER v. BUYER

a. *Damages*

JAGGER BROTHERS v. TECHNICAL TEXTILE CO.

Superior Court of Pennsylvania, 1964.
202 Pa.Super. 639, 198 A.2d 888.

MONTGOMERY, JUDGE. This appeal concerns the measure of damages in an action of assumpsit based on a written contract under which appellant agreed to purchase, at $2.15 per pound, 20,000 pounds of yarn to be manufactured by appellee. Appellee manufactured 3,723 pounds of the yarn and delivered it to appellant, who accepted and paid for it. The remaining 16,277 pounds were never manufactured because appellant advised appellee by letter, dated August 12, 1960, that it repudiated the contract and would refuse any future delivery of yarn.

Appellee was awarded $4,069.25 in a nonjury trial, which award was based on testimony offered by appellee that the market price of the yarn was $1.90 per pound on August 12, 1960. The award represents 16,277 times the difference between the contract price and the market price ($.25 per pound). No evidence was offered as to the cost of manufacturing the yarn.

Appellant contends that the proper measure of damages in such cases is the difference between the cost of manufacturing and the contract price; and, therefore, since appellee did not prove its cost of manufacture, it is entitled only to nominal damages.

Appellee contends that it has properly proved its damages under section 2–708 of the Uniform Commercial Code, which reads as follows:

> "Seller's Damages for Non-Acceptance or Repudiation—(1) Subject to subsection (2) and to the provisions of this Article with respect to proof of market price (Section 2–723) the measure of damages for non-acceptance or repudiation by the buyer is the difference between the market price at the time and place for tender and the unpaid contract price together with any incidental damage provided in this Article (Section 2–710), but less expenses saved in consequence of the buyer's breach."

Prior to the Uniform Commercial Code the law was the same [citation]. [F]or a breach of contract for the sale of personal chattels, yet to be manufactured, the vendor is entitled to recover the difference between the selling price and the market value at the time and place of delivery. * * *

Judgment affirmed.

Note

U.C.C. § 2–723: Proof of Market Price: Time and Place

(1) If an action based on anticipatory repudiation comes to trial before the time for performance with respect to some or all of the goods, any damages based on

market price (Section 2–708 or Section 2–713) shall be determined according to the price of such goods prevailing at the time when the aggrieved party learned of the repudiation.

(2) If evidence of a price prevailing at the times or places described in this Article is not readily available the price prevailing within any reasonable time before or after the time described or at any other place which in commercial judgment or under usage of trade would serve as a reasonable substitute for the one described may be used, making any proper allowance for the cost of transporting the goods to or from such other place.

R.R. WAITES CO. v. E.H. THRIFT AIR CONDITIONING, INC.

Missouri Court of Appeals, 1974.
510 S.W.2d 759.

SHANGLER, JUDGE. This action for the contract price of air cabinets made to order by plaintiff and delivered to defendant was initiated in the magistrate court. Plaintiff had judgment and defendant appealed to the circuit court. The cause was submitted de novo to a jury which returned a verdict for plaintiff. Defendant appeals to this court.

The defendant was engaged as subcontractor for the installation of air ducts at a Ramada Inn project. Plaintiff corporation is a manufacturer's representative for air products and on October 13, 1967, submitted to defendant a quotation to furnish air cabinets for the construction project. In June of 1968, at the request of the defendant, plaintiff sent defendant submittal drawings of the air cabinets conforming exactly to the plans and specifications of the architect. At the same time, plaintiff alerted the factory of the possible order with instructions to hold the air cabinets [made to order by the factory] until released by the purchaser. It was plaintiff's evidence [but denied by Thrift, president of the defendant corporation] that in November of 1968, Thrift requested plaintiff to release the equipment—which, in the industry, means an order to the supplier for shipment. On that same day, plaintiff instructed the factory to ship the air cabinets and in December of 1968 the merchandise was received by defendant.

Thrift testified that he informed plaintiff's salesman by telephone in December of 1968 that he could not use the air cabinets; there had been an error in the construction plans which rendered their use unfeasible. Thrift asked to return them; plaintiff refused to take them back but offered to find an outlet for the cabinets. * * * On May 14, 1969, without authority of plaintiff, defendant shipped the cabinets back to plaintiff. No payment has been made for the goods by defendant. * * *

The defendant contends error in that the instruction, which submits action for the price, fails to require [in the terms of § 2–709] that the goods were accepted or that plaintiff was unable after reasonable effort to resell the goods or that the circumstances reasonably indicated that such effort would be unavailing. The relevant portions of that statute provide:

"2–709 Action for the price

(1) When the buyer fails to pay the price as it becomes due the seller may recover, together with any incidental damages under section 2–710, the price

(a) of goods accepted * * *; and

(b) of goods identified to the contract if the seller is unable after reasonable effort to resell them at a reasonable price or the circumstances reasonably indicate that such effort will be unavailing."

Accordingly, under subsection (a), an action for the price accrues to the seller when the goods have been accepted by the buyer, in which event, the requirements of subsection (b) that the seller make an effort to resell the goods—which relate to goods that have been neither delivered, tendered, nor otherwise accepted—do not become operative. See U.C.C. Comment (2) to § 2–709. There can be no doubt that defendant accepted the goods. The only evidence on that issue was given by Thrift, the defendant's president. He acknowledged that the cabinets had been delivered to him and that, although they were of no use because of architectural error, they conformed in all respects to the contract. * * * When, as here, the goods conform to the contract, the buyer has a positive duty to accept and the legal obligation to pay according to the contract terms as established. [U.C.C. Comment (1) to § 2–606; U.C.C. Code Comment (3) to § 2–602; § 2–301.]

Nor may defendant's return of the air cabinets be construed as a rightful rejection of goods under § 2–602. A delivery or tender by the seller of goods which in all respects conform to the contract gives rise to a positive duty on the buyer to accept and his failure to do so constitutes a wrongful rejection which gives the seller immediate remedies for breach. [U.C.C. Comment (3) to § 2–602.] * * *

The judgment is affirmed.

Notes

1. Even though goods have not been delivered, the seller may still recover the price by meeting the requirements of § 2–709(1)(b).

2. U.C.C. § 2–709(2). Action for the Price.

Where the seller sues for the price he must hold for the buyer any goods which have been identified to the contract and are still in his control except that if resale becomes possible he may resell them at any time prior to the collection of the judgment. The net proceeds of any such resale must be credited to the buyer and payment of the judgment entitles him to any goods not resold.

3. If you represented the buyer in *Waites,* would you tell your client to pay the judgment? Does § 2–709(2) advance the policies of § 2–709(1)?

McMILLAN v. MEUSER MATERIAL AND EQUIPMENT CO.

Supreme Court of Arkansas, 1976.
260 Ark. 422, 541 S.W.2d 911.

HOLT, JUSTICE. The trial court, sitting as a jury, found appellant McMillan breached a contract to buy a bulldozer from appellee Meuser and assessed $2,700 as appellee's damages ($2,595 actual and $105 incidental). From that judgment comes this appeal.

On December 13, 1973, the parties entered into their agreement. The purchase price, including a bellhousing, was $9,825, f.o.b. Springdale. Meuser arranged transportation of the bulldozer to Greeley, Colorado, the residence of appellant. On December 24, 1973, McMillan stopped payment on his check asserting that since the agreed delivery date was December 21, the delivery was past due. Appellee's version is that the delivery date was January 1, 1974. After unsuccessful negotiations between the parties or about two months after the appellant purchaser stopped payment on his check, appellee brought this action. On March 5, 1975, or about fourteen months following the alleged breach of the purchase contract, appellee sold the bulldozer for $7,230 at a private sale. During this fourteen month interval, the equipment remained unsheltered, although regularly serviced, on an Arkansas farm, which was its situs when the sale contract was made. * * *

We turn now to appellant's contention that the resale by appellee Meuser was not in accordance with the requirements of § 2–706. The statute provides in pertinent part:

> "(1) Under the conditions stated in Section 2–703 on seller's remedies, the seller may resell the goods concerned [f]or the undelivered balance thereof. Where the resale is made in good faith and in a commercially reasonable manner the seller may recover the difference between the resale price and the contract price together with any incidental damages allowed under the provisions of this Article (section 2–710) but less expenses saved in consequence of the buyer's breach.
>
> "(2) Except as otherwise provided in subsection (3) or unless otherwise agreed resale may be at public or private sale including sale by way of one or more contracts to sell or of identification to an existing contract of the seller. Sale may be as a unit or in parcels and at any time and place and on any terms but every aspect of the sale including the method, manner, time, place, and terms must be commercially reasonable." * * *

The purpose of the resale provisions is discussed in Anderson, Uniform Commercial Code 2d, § 2–706:19, at p. 385, where it is stated:

> "the object of the resale is simply to determine exactly the seller's damages. These damages are the difference between the contract price and the market price at the time and place when performance should have been made by the buyer. The object of the resale in such a case is to determine what the market price in fact was. Unless the resale is made at about the time when performance was due it will be of slight probative value, especially if the goods are of a kind which fluctuate rapidly in value, to show what the market price actually was at the only time which is legally important."

In Comment 5 following § 2–706, the writers make it clear that "what is such a reasonable time depends upon the nature of the goods, the conditions of the market and the other circumstances of the case."

In Bache & Co., Inc. v. International Controls Corp., D.C., 339 F.Supp. 341 (1972), it was held, at least as to the sale of securities, that the resale must be as soon as practicable following notice of the buyer's refusal to accept tender of the goods. There a delay in excess of a month before resale was held unreasonable. In Uganski v. Little Giant Crane & Shovel, Inc., 35 Mich.App. 88, 192 N.W.2d 580 (1971), Uganski, the buyer, after his revocation of acceptance, resold heavy equipment, a crane, some two years and two months from the date of his notice of revocation of acceptance. There the court held his two year delay in reselling the crane was commercially unreasonable.

Here, even though we accord a liberal interpretation to the U.C.C., § 1–106, which mandates that remedies be so administered, we are of the view that the resale of the bulldozer, in excess of fourteen months after the alleged breach, will be of "slight probative value" as an indication of the market price at the time of the breach. Appellee Meuser is in the construction business and "deal[s] in bulldozers." Meuser himself testified that he was "aware of the state of the economy in the bulldozer market" and since the time of the alleged breach in December, 1973, the market for bulldozers had declined due to a recession in the construction industry and high fuel prices. As indicated, he testified he made no effort to resell the goods for in excess of a year. * * *

The court's award of $105 for incidental expenses incurred by appellee in servicing the bulldozer during the fourteen months from appellant's breach of the contract until appellee sold the equipment is supported by substantial evidence. In fact, appellee's testimony as to the necessity and the beneficial results of the servicing and maintenance of the equipment appears undisputed. As to the resale of the bulldozer, the appellee, admittedly, is in the construction business, sells bulldozer and was aware of the declining market. As previously indicated, as a matter of law, the long delay in the resale of the bulldozer by the appellee is commercially unreasonable. Consequently, the judgment is affirmed upon the condition that the award of $2,595 for actual damages is offered as a remittitur within the next seventeen days. Otherwise, the judgment is reversed and remanded.

Affirmed upon condition of remittitur.

Notes

1. In Coos Lumber Co. v. Builders Lumber & Supply Co., 104 N.H. 404, 406, 188 A.2d 330, 332 (1963), the court states the rationale for the resale remedy: "This rule is based on the principle of avoidable consequences. The defaulting buyer should be credited with the price actually obtained or obtainable for these goods by a new sale. The rule properly applies, however, only when a new sale can be made to a customer that the seller could not have supplied but for the buyer's repudiation."

2. Compare Carnes Construction Co. v. Richards & Conover Steel & Supply Co., 10 U.C.C.Rep.Serv. 797, ___ (1972). The seller sought to recover the price of goods found to have been wrongfully rejected by the buyer. In reversing, the court stated:

"However, we do agree with the buyer's contention that the evidence did not justify verdict and judgment against the buyer for the full purchase price of the goods. Except in the instances of lost or damaged goods where the risk of loss is on the buyer, or of accepted goods (not here relevant), a seller may recover the purchase price of goods from a defaulting buyer under the Uniform Commercial Code only '* * * if the seller is unable after reasonable effort to resell them at a reasonable price or the circumstances reasonably indicate that such effort will be unavailing.' § 2–709(1)(b). Otherwise, he must be content merely with the difference between the market price and the contract prices. § 2–708."

3. If the seller had conducted a "commercially reasonable" sale and sold to X for $12,000, could he recover from Buyer the $105 he spent to service the bulldozer? See D. Dobbs, Remedies § 12.19, at 888 (1973).

4. Assume the seller resold for $9,000. May he recover contract (10) less market value (8) instead of contract (10) less resale (9)? See J. White and R. Summers, Uniform Commercial Code § 7–7, at 310 (3d ed. 1988).

SPRAGUE v. SUMITOMO FORESTRY COMPANY, LIMITED

Supreme Court of Washington, En Banc, 1985.
104 Wash.2d 751, 709 P.2d 1200.

DORE, JUSTICE. [Sprague, a logger, entered into a contract with Sumitomo for the sale of logs. Because of difficulties with its sawmill, Sumitomo cancelled the contract.]

Subsequent to receiving Sumitomo's unequivocal cancellation of the log purchase contract, Sprague promptly filed a complaint against Sumitomo for breach of contract. Sumitomo served its answer alleging that Sprague had an affirmative duty to mitigate damages.

After receiving Sumitomo's answer, Sprague mitigated his damages by reselling the timber to five different purchasers at private sales.

At trial Sprague sought to recover the difference between the contract price and resale price of the timber, together with incidental damages arising from Sumitomo's unequivocal cancellation. Sumitomo claimed mutual rescission and asserted affirmative defenses, including that Sprague "failed to proceed as required by 2–702 et seq." * * *

Via a special verdict form, the jury found * * * that the contract price was $197,204 and the resale price was $144,924 with net contractual damages of $52,280; (4) that Sprague sustained incidental damages of $216,498 for the following items: (a) cost of refinancing, $39,674; (b) extra transportation cost, $5,612; (c) loss of revenue on Flip Blowdown not covered by contract, $9,121; (d) loss of logging time, 11 weeks, $171,200; and (e) cost of moving tower, $2,115.

The major thrust of Sumitomo's appellate argument here is that Sprague did not give the requisite notice of intention to resell the canceled goods as required by 2–706(3) and, therefore, Sprague is not entitled to recover the difference between the contract price and the resale price.

The catalogue of a seller's remedies in a breach of contract case governed by the sale of goods provisions of the Uniform Commercial Code is found in 2–703. In the present case, the catalogue of available remedies can quickly be reduced to two; these are:

(1) resale and recovery under 2–706, or

(2) recovery of the difference between the contract price and the market price under 2–708(1).

At trial Sprague apparently proceeded, pursuant to 2–706, to recover as damages the difference between the resale price and contract price. 2–706(1) provides that if the seller acts in good faith and in a commercially reasonable manner, he may recover the difference between the resale price and the contract price, together with any incidental damages allowed under 2–710, less expenses saved.

Section 2–706(2) goes on to permit resale at public or private sale. Of critical importance here is the requirement of 2–706(3) which provides that where an aggrieved seller resells goods which are the subject of a breach at a private sale, he must give the buyer "reasonable notification of his intention to resell."

In response to his failure to give specific notice of intention to resell, and in support of his judgment, Sprague argues: that the lack of notice was an affirmative defense which the buyer failed to plead, or that the buyer, from all the surrounding facts and circumstances, knew or should have known that the seller was going to resell the logs. * * *

To recover under 2–706, Sprague was required to give notice of intent to resell. This is an element of the seller's right to invoke the remedies of 2–706. Therefore, the buyer need not plead as an affirmative defense those elements which seller must prove.

Next, can the notice requirement be satisfied by the fact that the buyer knew or should have known that the seller intended to resell? From the plain language of 2–706, the giving by the seller of notice of intention to resell is a specific requirement to entitle seller to claim as damages the difference between resale price and the contract price. The words of subsection (3) are precise: "the seller *must* give the buyer reasonable notification of his intention to resell." (Italics ours.) 2–706(3). * * *

It is a general rule of appellate practice that the judgment of the trial court will not be reversed when it can be sustained on any theory, although different from that indicated in the decision of the trial judge. Although the jury verdict cannot be upheld under the resale method of determining damages, we find that the record supports the verdict under the alternate method of establishing damages, computed by measuring the difference between the market price and the contract price as provided in 2–708. * * *

It is fundamental under 2–703 and the sections that follow that an aggrieved seller is not required to elect between damages under 2–706 and 2–708. 2–703 cumulatively sets forth the remedies available to a seller upon the buyer's breach. The pertinent commentary thereto indicates specifically that the remedies provided are cumulative and not exclusive and that as a fundamental policy Article 2 of the U.C.C. rejects any doctrine of election of remedy.

The seller has the burden of proof with respect to market price or market value. A seller cannot avail himself of the benefit of 2–708 when he has not presented evidence of market price or market value. However, the resale price of goods may be considered as appropriate evidence of the market value at the time of tender in determining damages pursuant to 2–708.

While, admittedly, Sprague's resale came after the time for tender, it can still be utilized as a market price. 2–723(2) states:

> "(2) If evidence of a price prevailing at the times or places described in this Article is not readily available the price prevailing within any reasonable time before *or after* the time described or at any other place which in commercial judgment or under usage of trade would serve as a reasonable substitute for the one described may be used, * * * "

(Italics ours.)

The court is granted a "reasonable leeway" (Official Comments to 2–723) in measuring market price. During the trial of this action, not only was there testimony to the effect that in an effort to mitigate damages, respondent Sprague sold the Flip Blowdown logs to five purchasers at private sales in 1981 and 1982, there was also testimony that the market price remained at the same level as at the time and place of tender in late 1980.

The net contractual damages of $52,280 ($197,204 contract price—$144,924 resale price) which was awarded respondent under the jury verdict thus equaled the measure of damages available under 2–708(1). We affirm this award.

Sprague is entitled also to incidental damages. 2–708 provides that the seller is entitled to the difference between the market price and contract price "together with any incidental damages provided in this Article (2–710), but less expenses saved in consequence of the buyer's breach." Incidental damages are defined in 2–710 as follows:

> "Incidental damages to an aggrieved seller include any commercially reasonable charges, expenses or commissions incurred in stopping delivery, in the transportation, care and custody of goods after the buyer's breach, in connection with return or resale of the goods or otherwise resulting from the breach."

At trial, the jury found that respondent sustained incidental damages of $216,498 for the following items: (a) cost of refinancing, $39,674; (b) extra transportation cost, $5,612; (c) loss of revenue on Flip Blowdown not covered by contract, $9,121; (d) loss of logging time, 11 weeks, $171,200; and (e) cost of moving tower, $2,115.

Sumitomo contends that some of these items are not incidental damages but more properly classified as consequential. Consequential damages are *not* allowed except as specifically provided in RCW Title 62A or by other rule of law. 1–106. Washington Comment to section 2–710 indicates that consequential damages are denied to sellers under the Uniform Commercial Code. 2–710.

The distinction between consequential and incidental damages was made in Petroleo Brasileiro, S.A. Petrobras v. Ameropan Oil Corp. 372 F.Supp. 503, 508 (E.D.N.Y.1974).

> "While the distinction between the two is not an obvious one, the Code makes plain that incidental damages are normally incurred when a buyer (or seller) repudiates the contract or wrongfully rejects the goods, causing the other to incur such expenses as transporting, storing, or reselling the goods. On the other hand, *consequential damages* do not arise within the scope of the immediate buyer-seller transaction, but rather *stem from losses incurred by the non-breaching party in its dealings, often with third parties,* which were a proximate result of the breach, and which were reasonably foreseeable by the breaching party at the time of contracting."

(Citations omitted. Italics ours.)

We find that the loss of logging time is an inappropriate item of incidental damages. Sprague's damage claim for loss of logging time is essentially a claim for lost profits on a contract with Mt. Baker Plywood. In *Petroleo Brasileiro,* the court stated that "consequential damages do not arise within the scope of the immediate buyer-seller transaction [as do incidental damages], but rather stem from losses incurred by the non-breaching party in its dealings, often with third parties." *Petroleo Brasileiro.* Applying this test to Sprague's claim for loss of logging time, Sprague's loss clearly did not arise within the scope of his contract with Sumitomo; instead, Sprague incurred this loss as a consequence of his delay in performing his contract with Mt. Baker Plywood, a third party. The fact that Sumitomo's conduct proximately caused Sprague's loss is irrelevant to this analysis. The focus is upon losses arising within the scope of the immediate contract. Accordingly, Sprague's loss can only be characterized as consequential. Therefore, the judgment awarded Sprague is reduced by $171,200.

The remaining costs are not seriously contested by appellant and appear to be appropriate items of incidental damages. * * *

The judgment is reduced by $171,200 to eliminate an improper element of damages. As modified, the judgment is affirmed.

ANCHORAGE CENTENNIAL DEVELOPMENT CO. v. VAN WORMER & RODRIGUES, INC.

Supreme Court of Alaska, 1968.
443 P.2d 596.

Rabinowitz, Justice. In conjunction with the statewide celebration of the one hundredth anniversary of the purchase of Alaska from Russia, the Anchorage Centennial Commission contracted with Van Wormer & Rodrigues, Inc. to buy 50,000 gold-colored metal coins. After Van Wormer had partially completed the order, the commission notified Van Wormer that it was terminating the contract. Thereafter, Van Wormer sued the commission and, in the main, prevailed after trial to the court.

In its cross-appeal Van Wormer contends the trial court erred by virtue of its disallowance of anticipated profits. The trial court correctly found that at the time the commission purported to cancel its order for 50,000 coins, 29,000 coins had already been manufactured. Using the 29,000 figure at the agreed cost of 15 cents per coin, Van Wormer was awarded judgment in the amount of $4,350.[1]

Examination of the record in this cause fails to reveal any basis for the trial court's conclusion that Van Wormer was not entitled to recover its loss of profits in regard to the 21,000 coins which had been ordered by the commission, but had not been manufactured at the time of the commission's repudiation of the contract. In Green v. Koslosky [2] we said:

> "In awarding damages for breach of contract an effort is made to put the injured party in as good a position as he would have been had the contract been fully performed."

In the case at bar we are in accord with Van Wormer's argument to the effect that since there is no market for these made-to-order coins the proper measure of damages is governed by [2–708(2)] which provides:

> "If the measure of damages provided in (a) [difference between market price and contract price] of this section is inadequate to put the seller in as good a position as performance would have done, then the measure of damages is the profit (including reasonable overhead) which the seller would have made from full performance by the buyer, together with any incidental damages * * *, due allowance for costs reasonably incurred, and due credit for payments or proceeds of resale."

We, therefore, conclude that the judgment entered below should be modified to include an award to Van Wormer for its loss of profits on the remaining

1. [Footnotes renumbered.] In addition to the $4,350, the July 7, 1967, judgment awarded Van Wormer $26.85 for freight charges incurred, $626.91 for interest on $4,376.85 from February 26, 1965, $1,105.64 in attorney's fees, and $239.20 in court costs.

2. 384 P.2d 951, 952 (Alaska 1963).

21,000 coins under the contract.[3]

Notes

Other cases allow recovery of lost profits under § 2–708(2). See Unique Systems, Inc. v. Zotos International, Inc., 622 F.2d 373 (8th Cir.1980) (15,000 hair spray systems where there was no market price); Uchitel Co. v. Telephone Co., 646 P.2d 229 (Alaska 1982) (specially designed office telephone system not otherwise marketable); Cesco Manufacturing Corp. v. Norcross, Inc., 7 Mass.App.Ct. 837, 391 N.E.2d 270 (1979) (customized display racks for which seller had no reasonably accessible market); Detroit Power Screwdriver Co. v. Ladney, 25 Mich.App. 478, 181 N.W.2d 828 (1970); Copymate Marketing, Ltd. v. Modern Merchandising, Inc., 34 Wash.App. 300, 660 P.2d 332 (1983) (photocopies for which there was no reasonably accessible market); and Anno., 42 A.L.R.3d 182 (1972).

2. See Anderson, Damages For Sellers Under the Code's Profit Formula, 40 Sw.L.J. 1021 (1986); Anderson, "A Roadmap For Sellers' Damage Remedies Under the Uniform Commercial Code and Some Thoughts About Pleading and Proving Special Damages, 19 Rutgers L.J. 245 (1988).

R.E. DAVIS CHEMICAL CORP. v. DIASONICS, INC.

United States Court of Appeals, Seventh Circuit, 1987.
826 F.2d 678.

CUDAHY, CIRCUIT JUDGE. Diasonics is a California corporation engaged in the business of manufacturing and selling medical diagnostic equipment. Davis is an Illinois corporation that contracted to purchase a piece of medical diagnostic equipment from Diasonics. On or about February 23, 1984, Davis and Diasonics entered into a written contract under which Davis agreed to purchase the equipment. Pursuant to this agreement, Davis paid Diasonics a $300,000 deposit on February 29, 1984. * * * Davis then breached its contract with Diasonics; it refused to take delivery of the equipment or to pay the balance due under the agreement. Diasonics later resold the equipment to a third party for the same price at which it was to be sold to Davis.

Davis sued Diasonics, asking for restitution of its $300,000 down payment under section 2–718(2) of the Uniform Commercial Code (the "UCC" or the "Code").[1] Diasonics counterclaimed. Diasonics did not deny that Davis was entitled to recover its $300,000 deposit less $500 as provided in section 2–718(2)(b). However, Diasonics claimed that it was entitled to an offset under section 2–718(3). Diasonics alleged that it was a "lost volume seller," and, as

3. The undisputed evidence established that Van Wormer's profit would have been three cents per coin.

1. [Footnotes renumbered.] The pertinent portion of section 2–718 provides: § 2–718. Liquidation or Limitation of Damages; Deposits * * *

(2) Where the seller justifiably withholds delivery of goods because of the buyer's breach, the buyer is entitled to restitution of any amount by which the sum of his payments exceeds

(a) the amount to which the seller is entitled by virtue of terms liquidating the seller's damages in accordance with subsection (1), or

(b) in the absence of such terms, 20% of the value of the total performance for which the buyer is obligated under the contract or $500, whichever is smaller.

(3) The buyer's right to restitution under subsection (2) is subject to offset to the extent that the seller establishes

(a) a right to recover damages under the provisions of this Article other than subsection (1), and

(b) the amount or value of any benefits received by the buyer directly or indirectly by reason of the contract.

such, it lost the profit from one sale when Davis breached its contract. Diasonics' position was that, in order to be put in as good a position as it would have been in had Davis performed, it was entitled to recover its lost profit on its contract with Davis under section 2–708(2) of the UCC. Section 2–708 provides:

> § 2–708. Seller's Damages for Non-acceptance or Repudiation
>
> "(1) Subject to subsection (2) and to the provisions of this Article with respect to proof of market price (Section 2–723), the measure of damages for non-acceptance or repudiation by the buyer is the difference between the market price at the time and place for tender and the unpaid contract price together with any incidental damages provided in this Article (Section 2–710), but less expenses saved in consequence of the buyer's breach.
>
> "(2) If the measure of damages provided in subsection (1) is inadequate to put the seller in as good a position as performance would have done then the measure of damages is the profit (including reasonable overhead) which the seller would have made from full performance by the buyer, together with any incidental damages provided in this Article (Section 2–710), due allowance for costs reasonably incurred and due credit for payments or proceeds of resale."
> * * *

The [district] court entered summary judgment for Davis. The court held that lost volume sellers were not entitled to recover damages under 2–708(2) but rather were limited to recovering the difference between the resale price and the contract price along with incidental damages under section 2–706(1). Section 2–706(1) provides:

> § 2–706. Seller's Resale Including Contract for Resale
>
> "(1) Under the conditions stated in Section 2–703 on seller's remedies, the seller may resell the goods concerned or the undelivered balance thereof. Where the resale is made in good faith and in a commercially reasonable manner the seller may recover the difference between the resale price and the contract price together with any incidental damages allowed under the provisions of this Article (Section 2–710), but less expenses saved in consequence of the buyer's breach."

Davis was awarded $322,656, which represented Davis' down payment plus prejudgment interest less Diasonics' incidental damages. Diasonics appeals the district court's decision respecting its measure of damages * * *.

We consider first Diasonics' claim that the district court erred in holding that Diasonics was limited to the measure of damages provided in 2–706 and could not recover lost profits as a lost volume seller under 2–708(2). * * * Courts applying the laws of other states have unanimously adopted the position that a lost volume seller can recover its lost profits under 2–708(2). [citations] Contrary to the result reached by the district court, we conclude that the Illinois Supreme Court would follow these other cases and would allow a lost volume seller to recover its lost profit under 2–708(2).

We begin our analysis with 2–718(2) and (3). Under 2–718(2)(b), Davis is entitled to the return of its down payment less $500. Davis' right to restitution, however, is qualified under 2–718(3)(a) to the extent that Diasonics can establish a right to recover damages under any other provision of Article 2 of the UCC. Article 2 contains four provisions that concern the recovery of a seller's general damages (as opposed to its incidental or consequential damages): 2–706 (contract price less resale price); 2–708(1) (contract price less market price); 2–708(2) (profit); and 2–709 (price). The problem we face here is determining whether Diasonics' damages should be measured under 2–706 or 2–708(2).[2] To answer this question, we need to engage in a detailed look at the language and structure of these various damage provisions.

The Code does not provide a great deal of guidance as to when a particular damage remedy is appropriate. The damage remedies provided under the Code are catalogued in section 2–703, but this section does not indicate that there is any hierarchy among the remedies.[3] One method of approaching the damage sections is to conclude that 2–708 is relegated to a role inferior to that of 2–706 and 2–709 and that one can turn to 2–708 only after one has concluded that neither 2–706 nor 2–709 is applicable.[4] Under this interpretation of the relationship between 2–706 and 2–708, if the goods have been resold, the seller can sue to recover damages measured by the difference between the contract price and the resale price under 2–706. The seller can turn to 2–708 only if it resells in a commercially unreasonable manner or if it cannot resell but an action for the price is inappropriate under 2–709. The district court adopted this reading of the Code's damage remedies and, accordingly, limited Diasonics to the measure of damages provided in 2–706 because it resold the equipment in a commercially reasonable manner.

The district court's interpretation of 2–706 and 2–708, however, creates its own problems of statutory construction. There is some suggestion in the Code that the "fact that plaintiff resold the goods [in a commercially reasonable manner] does *not* compel him to use the resale remedy of § 2–706 rather than the damage remedy of § 2–708." Harris, A Radical Restatement of the Law of Seller's Damages: Sales Act and Commercial Code Results Compared, 18 Stan.L.Rev. 66, 101 n. 174 (1965) (emphasis in original). Official comment 1 to 2–703, which catalogues the remedies available to a seller, states that these

2. An action for the price, provided for under 2–709, is not an option in this case because Diasonics resold the equipment that it had intended to sell to Davis.

3. Section 2–703 provides: § 2–703. Seller's Remedies in General. Where the buyer wrongfully rejects or revokes acceptance of goods or fails to make a payment due on or before delivery or repudiates with respect to a part or the whole, then with respect to any goods directly affected and, if the breach is of the whole contract (Section 2–612), then also with respect to the whole undelivered balance, the aggrieved seller may

(a) withhold delivery of such goods;

(b) stop delivery by any bailee as hereafter provided (Section 2–705);

(c) proceed under the next section respecting goods still unidentified to the contract;

(d) resell and recover damages as hereafter provided (Section 2–706);

(e) recover damages for non-acceptance (Section 2–708) or in a proper case the price (Section 2–709);

(f) cancel.

4. Evidence to support this approach can be found in the language of the various damage sections and of the official comments to the UCC. See § 2–709(3) ("a seller who is held not entitled to the price under this Section shall nevertheless be awarded damages for non-acceptance under the preceding section [§ 2–708]"); UCC comment 7 to § 2–709 ("[i]f the action for the price fails, the seller may nonetheless have proved a case entitling him to damages for non-acceptance [under § 2–708]"); UCC comment 2 to § 2–706 ("[f]ailure to act properly under this section deprives the seller of the measure of damages here provided and relegates him to that provided in Section 2–708"); UCC comment 1 to § 2–704 (describes § 2–706 as the "primary remedy" available to a seller upon breach by the buyer).

As one commentator has noted, 2–706

> "is the Code section drafted specifically to define the damage rights of aggrieved reselling sellers, and there is no suggestion within it that the profit formula of section 2–708(2) is in any way intended to qualify or be superior to it."

Shanker, The Case for a Literal Reading of UCC Section 2–708(2) (One Profit for the Reseller), 24 Case W.Res. 697, 699 (1973).

"remedies are essentially cumulative in nature" and that "[w]hether the pursuit of one remedy bars another depends entirely on the facts of the individual case." [5]

Those courts that found that a lost volume seller can recover its lost profits under 2–708(2) implicitly rejected the position adopted by the district court; those courts started with the assumption that 2–708 applied to a lost volume seller without considering whether the seller was limited to the remedy provided under 2–706. None of those courts even suggested that a seller who resold goods in a commercially reasonable manner was limited to the damage formula provided under 2–706. We conclude that the Illinois Supreme Court, if presented with this question, would adopt the position of these other jurisdictions and would conclude that a reselling seller, such as Diasonics, is free to reject the damage formula prescribed in 2–706 and choose to proceed under 2–708.

Concluding that Diasonics is entitled to seek damages under 2–708, however, does not automatically result in Diasonics being awarded its lost profit. Two different measures of damages are provided in 2–708. Subsection 2–708(1) provides for a measure of damages calculated by subtracting the market price at the time and place for tender from the contract price.[6] The profit measure of damages, for which Diasonics is asking, is contained in 2–708(2). However, one applies 2–708(2) only if "the measure of damages provided in subsection (1) is inadequate to put the seller in as good a position as performance would have done." Diasonics claims that 2–708(1) does not provide an adequate measure of damages when the seller is a lost volume seller.[7] To understand Diasonics' argument, we need to define the concept of the lost volume seller. Those cases that have addressed this issue have defined a lost volume seller as one that has a predictable and finite number of customers and that has the capacity either to sell to all new buyers [citations] or to make the one additional sale represented by the resale after the breach. [citations] According to a number of courts and commentators, if the seller would have made the sale represented by the resale whether or not the breach occurred, damages measured by the difference between the contract price and market price cannot put the lost

5. UCC comment 2 to 2–708(2) also suggests that 2–708 has broader applicability than suggested by the district court. UCC comment 2 provides:

> "This section permits the recovery of lost profits in all appropriate cases, which would include all standard priced goods. The normal measure there would be list price less cost to the dealer or list price less manufacturing cost to the manufacturer."

The district court's restrictive interpretation of 2–708(2) was based in part on UCC comment 1 to 2–704 which describes 2–706 as the aggrieved seller's primary remedy. The district court concluded that, if a lost volume seller could recover its lost profit under 2–708(2), every seller would attempt to recover damages under 2–708(2) and 2–706 would become the aggrieved seller's residuary remedy. This argument ignores the fact that to recover under 2–708(2), a seller must first establish its status as a lost volume seller.

The district court also concluded that a lost volume seller cannot recover its lost profit under 2–708(2) because such a result would negate a seller's duty to mitigate damages. This position fails to recognize the fact that, by definition, a lost volume seller cannot mitigate damages through resale. Resale does not reduce a lost volume seller's damages because the breach has still resulted in its losing one sale and a corresponding profit.

6. There is some debate in the commentaries about whether a seller who has resold the goods may ignore the measure of damages provided in 2–706 and elect to proceed under 2–708(1). Under some circumstances the contract-market price differential will result in overcompensating such a seller. [citation] We need not struggle with this question here because Diasonics has not sought to recover damages under 2–708(1).

7. This is also the position adopted by those courts that have held that a lost volume seller can recover its lost profits under 2–708(2).

volume seller in as good a position as it would have been in had the buyer performed.[8] The breach effectively cost the seller a "profit," and the seller can only be made whole by awarding it damages in the amount of its "lost profit" under 2–708(2).

We agree with Diasonics' position that, under some circumstances, the measure of damages provided under 2–708(1) will not put a reselling seller in as good a position as it would have been in had the buyer performed because the breach resulted in the seller losing sales volume. However, we disagree with the definition of "lost volume seller" adopted by other courts. Courts awarding lost profits to a lost volume seller have focused on whether the seller had the capacity to supply the breached units in addition to what it actually sold. In reality, however, the relevant questions include, not only whether the seller could have produced the breached units in addition to its actual volume, but also whether it would have been profitable for the seller to produce both units. As one commentator has noted, under

> "the economic law of diminishing returns or increasing marginal costs[,] * * * as a seller's volume increases, then a point will inevitably be reached where the cost of selling each additional item diminishes the incremental return to the seller and eventually makes it entirely unprofitable to conclude the next sale."

Shanker, at 705. Thus, under some conditions, awarding a lost volume seller its presumed lost profit will result in overcompensating the seller, and 2–708(2) would not take effect because the damage formula provided in 2–708(1) does place the seller in as good a position as if the buyer had performed. Therefore, on remand, Diasonics must establish, not only that it had the capacity to produce the breached unit in addition to the unit resold, but also that it would have been profitable for it to have produced and sold both. Diasonics carries the burden of establishing these facts because the burden of proof is generally on the party claiming injury to establish the amount of its damages; especially in a case such as this, the plaintiff has easiest access to the relevant data. [citations]

One final problem with awarding a lost volume seller its lost profits was raised by the district court. This problem stems from the formulation of the measure of damages provided under 2–708(2) which is "the profit (including reasonable overhead) which the seller would have made from full performance by the buyer, together with any incidental damages provided in this Article (Section 2–710), due allowance for costs reasonably incurred and due credit for payments or *proceeds of resale.*" The literal language of 2–708(2) requires that the proceeds from resale be credited against the amount of damages awarded which, in most cases, would result in the seller recovering nominal damages. In those cases in which the lost volume seller was awarded its lost profit as damages, the courts have circumvented this problem by concluding that this language only applies to proceeds realized from the resale of uncompleted goods for scrap. [citations]; see also J. White & R. Summers, Handbook of the Law under the Uniform Commercial Code § 7–13 ("courts should simply ignore the 'due credit' language in lost volume cases") (footnote omitted). Although neither the text of 2–708(2) nor the official comments limit its application to

8. According to one commentator,

> "Resale results in loss of volume only if three conditions are met: (1) the person who bought the resold entity would have been solicited by plaintiff had there been no breach and resale; (2) the solicitation would have been successful; and (3) the plaintiff could have performed that additional contract."

Harris, (footnotes omitted).

resale of goods for scrap, there is evidence that the drafters of 2–708 seemed to have had this more limited application in mind when they proposed amending 2–708 to include the phrase "due credit for payments or proceeds of resale." [citations] We conclude that the Illinois Supreme Court would adopt this more restrictive interpretation of this phrase rendering it inapplicable to this case.

We therefore reverse the grant of summary judgment in favor of Davis and remand with instructions that the district court calculate Diasonics' damages under 2–708(2) if Diasonics can establish, not only that it had the capacity to make the sale to Davis as well as the sale to the resale buyer, but also that it would have been profitable for it to make both sales. Of course, Diasonics, in addition, must show that it probably would have made the second sale absent the breach.

Notes

1. What does Seller have to prove to establish lost volume status? A Notewriter commenting on the principal decision suggests only two questions to confine lost volume status to the needs that gave rise to the theory. (a) Whether the seller has capacity to make both sales. (b) Whether the sales are wholly independent events so that the second sale would have occurred without the breach. Note, Finding the "Lost Volume Seller": Two Independent Sales Deserve Two Profits Under Illinois Law, 22 John Marshall L.Rev. 363 (1988).

In Islamic Republic of Iran v. Boeing Co., 771 F.2d 1279 (9th Cir.1985), the court held that, where supply exceeds demand, the seller need not prove a market to recover "lost volume" profits. In a later appeal of the principal case, the court rejected the defendant's argument that seller "must precisely identify the resale buyer" to qualify for lost volume status. R.E. Davis Chemical Corp. v. Diasonics, Inc., 924 F.2d 709, 711 (7th Cir.1991). But the court remanded to the trial judge for additional "fact-intensive inquiry" on the amount of damages.

2. For a different view of the problem, see Scott, The Case for Market Damages: Revisiting the Lost Profit Puzzle, 57 U.Chi.L.Rev. 1155 (1990).

b. *Restitution*

WELLSTON COAL CO. v. FRANKLIN PAPER CO.

Supreme Court of Ohio, 1897.
57 Ohio St. 182, 48 N.E. 888.

MINSHALL, J. * * * On August 7, 1890, plaintiff and defendant made a written contract, by which defendant, for the term of one year, agreed to take its entire supply of coal from plaintiff at the rate of $1.90 per ton of 2,000 pounds, on the cars at Franklin, Ohio, which, after deducting freight, would net the plaintiff $1 per ton. The demand for such coal was greater during the late fall and winter months of each year, when plaintiff's business would be active, and less during the spring and summer months, at which times its business would be dull. The sum of $1 per ton for the coal was the market price, outside of freight charges, for coal of the kind mentioned in the contract, during the summer of 1890, and at the time the contract was made. Plaintiff and defendant were familiar with the ups and downs of the coal trade, and knew that the market price of such coal would be higher during the fall and winter months; and they both understood that defendant would require, for its manufacturing operations during the entire period covered by the contract, a large amount of such coal, which, taken by defendant during all the year covered by the contract, would give plaintiff an assured sale for this amount of coal during the dull season. Such contracts for the year's supply of coal were usually made by manufacturers with coal shippers during the summer, and were advantageous to both parties.

These facts were known to both plaintiff and defendant, who contracted with reference to them; and plaintiff would not have made the contract whereby it agreed to supply coal during the fall and winter months at the contract price, which would be less than the then market prices, except for the fact that it would supply the defendant coal at the same price for the balance of the year, when the price would be about the same as the contract price, and, the demand then being small, it would not otherwise be able to sell the coal. During the month of September, 1890, the market price of this coal, outside of freight charges, was $1.05 per ton; and from October 1, 1890, to February 1, 1891, such market price was $1.15 per ton. After February, during the rest of the year covered by the contract, the market price was the same as the contract price. During the period of time from August 1, 1890, to May 13, 1891, when the contract was broken by the defendant, plaintiff furnished defendant, during September and October, 1890, in all, 2,562½ tons of coal, for which it was paid the contract price; while, if the same coal had been sold at the market prices when delivered, plaintiff would have received $333 more for it. About May 13, 1891, defendant wrongfully broke the contract, and refused to take any more coal from plaintiff. The contract did not bind the defendant to take any specified quantity of coal per month, but the average number of tons per month taken before the contract was broken, was 434¼ tons; and, if it had continued to take coal under the contract at the same average number of tons for the balance of May and the months June and July, the plaintiff would have made a total profit for that time, under the contract, of $304.22.

The question is as to the measure of damages to which the plaintiff is entitled in a case like this. It, as before stated, is not on the contract, but for the value of the coal delivered at the market price, before the contract was wrongfully terminated by the defendant, less what had been paid therefor; i.e., the contract price. The plaintiff requested the court to charge the jury that it was entitled to recover, for the coal delivered prior to the repudiation of the contract by the defendant, its market value when the deliveries were made, and is not limited to the price specified in the contract. This the court refused to do, and directed the jury to find a verdict for the plaintiff for nominal damages only. The general rule is that, when full performance of a contract has been prevented by the wrongful act of the defendant, the plaintiff has the right either to sue for damages, or he may disregard the contract, and sue as upon a quantum meruit for what he has performed. The plaintiff has pursued the latter course; and it seems well settled, both in reason and authority, that he had the right to do so. * * *

But it is claimed, on the authority of Doolittle v. McCullough, 12 Ohio St. 360, that the contract price must still be the measure of the plaintiff's recovery. There are many expressions in the opinion in that case that seem to support this view, and much of the reasoning is to the same effect. But all that is there said must be taken as said with reference to the facts of that case. The rule there stated may be regarded as a proper one in a case where, as in that case, it appears from the claim of the plaintiff that the breach of the contract by the defendant worked no loss, but a benefit to him, on the ground, as appears that, had he been required to complete the work, he would have suffered a much greater loss; for, if the least inexpensive part of the work could not have been done without loss, it follows that the doing of the remaining part, under the contract, would have resulted in a still greater loss. The action upon a quantum meruit is of equitable origin, and is still governed by considerations of natural justice. Hence, when one has performed labor or furnished material under a contract that is wrongfully terminated by the other party before completion, the question arises whether the party not in fault should be confined to the contract for what he did, or to a quantum meruit; and this must depend upon whether the act of the other party in terminating the contract works a loss or not to him, regard being had to the contract. If it works no loss, but is in fact a benefit, as in the case of Doolittle v. McCullough, there are no considerations of justice requiring that he should be compensated in a greater sum for what he did than is stipulated in the contract. These considerations exercised a controlling influence in the case just referred to. The plaintiff had a contract with the defendant for the making of certain excavations in the construction of a railroad. He was to receive for the entire work 11 cents per cubic yard. He had performed the least inexpensive part of the work when the contract was wrongfully terminated by the defendant; and on this part, by his own showing, he had suffered a loss. The proof showed that the performance of the remainder, being hardpan, would have cost him a great deal more. It was then evident, as the court observed, that he had sustained no loss, but a benefit, from the termination of the contract by the defendant. But in the case before us the facts are very different. They are in fact just the reverse. The contract was for the delivery of coal at a price generally received during the dullest season of the whole year. The defendant received the coal during the season when the market was above the contract price. He had the benefit of the difference between the market and the contract price; but when the dull season arrived, and the advantages of the contract would accrue to the plaintiff, the defendant repudiated it. The difference between the two cases is thus apparent. In the case before us, justice and fair dealing require that the defendant, having repudiated the contract, should pay the market price for the coal at the time it was delivered. In the former case, as the repudiation of the contract by the defendant did not enrich him to the loss of the plaintiff, there were no considerations of justice on which the plaintiff could claim more than the contract price for what he had done under the contract. The object in allowing a recovery of this kind is not to better the condition of the plaintiff under the contract, were it performed, but to save him from a loss resulting from its wrongful termination by the defendant, or, in more general words, to prevent the defendant from enriching himself at the expense of the plaintiff by his own wrongful act. The real test in all cases of a plaintiff's right to recover as upon a quantum meruit for part performance of a contract, wrongfully terminated by the defendant, depends upon the consideration whether the defendant is thereby enriched at the loss and expense of the plaintiff. If so, then the law adds a legal to the moral obligation, and enforces it. And, while the action is not on the contract itself, yet it is so far kept in view as to preclude a recovery by the plaintiff where he would necessarily have lost more by performing the contract, for the consideration agreed upon, than he did by being prevented from doing so. In this view, the case of Doolittle v. McCullough was rightly decided, and, when limited to its facts, may well stand as authority in all similar cases. Judgment of the circuit court and that of the common pleas reversed, and cause remanded for a new trial.

Notes

1. *Restitution under the Uniform Commercial Code.* See Mather, Restitution as a Remedy for Breach of Contract: The Case of the Partially Performing Seller, 92 Yale L.J. 14 (1982); Nordstrom, Restitution on Default and Article Two of the Uniform Commercial Code, 19 Vand.L.Rev. 1143, 1164–66 (1966); D. Dobbs, Remedies § 12.20 (1973); G. Palmer, The Law of Restitution § 4.16 (1978).

2. Restitution is not available to a seller who has delivered the goods if the buyer's only breach is failure to pay the price. See Restatement (Second) of Contracts § 373(a) (1981); Woodward, Quasi Contracts § 262, at 412–416 (1913).

IN RE FLAGSTAFF FOODSERVICE CORP.

United States Bankruptcy Court, Southern District of New York, 1981.
14 B.R. 462.

BABITT, BANKRUPTCY JUDGE. Flagstaff, a distributor of food to institutional customers, filed its petition in this court on July 21, 1981 for the relief afforded by Chapter 11 of the 1978 Code. Upon learning of this filing, McCain, a seller on credit of $11,610 worth of frozen french fried potatoes, made a timely demand to reclaim these foodstuffs in accordance with Section 2–702(2) of New York's Uniform Commercial Code (U.C.C.). As this demand proved fruitless, McCain sought judicial aid in recovering the property sold to Flagstaff. * * *

Flagstaff's main defense was bottomed on the premise that McCain could reclaim only those potatoes in the debtor's possession * * * and that, in any event, McCain could not receive payment for the value of such goods but would have to settle for priority status as an administrative expense creditor. * * *

At common law, the right of a seller to reclaim his goods was governed by the law of contracts which permitted rescission by a seller who was induced to enter into a sales contract by a fraudulent or innocent misrepresentation. * * *

But the reach of the remedies flowing from rescission from the standpoint of the seller's ability to retrieve the property sold on application of common law principles yielded a melange of state court rulings. These turned on identification of the goods, their fungibility, commingling and the like where reclamation was not possible under applicable law because of problems of identification, the tracing of funds specifically allocable to the seller's goods yielded some solace in some places. * * *

Section 2–702(2) of the U.C.C. is as follows:

> "(2) Where the seller discovers that the buyer has received goods on credit while insolvent he may reclaim the goods upon demand made within ten days after the receipt, but if misrepresentation of solvency has been made to the particular seller in writing within three months before delivery the ten day limitation does not apply. Except as provided in this subsection the seller may not base a right to reclaim goods on the buyer's fraudulent or innocent misrepresentation of solvency or of intent to pay."

As the Official Uniform Comment discloses, Section 2–702(2):

> "takes as its base line the proposition that any receipt of goods on credit by an insolvent buyer amounts to a tacit business misrepresentation of solvency and therefore is fraudulent as against the particular seller. This Article makes discovery of the buyer's insolvency and demand within a ten day period a

condition of the right to reclaim goods on this ground. The ten day limitation period operates from the time of receipt of the goods."

And as to the goods involved in the seller's Section 2–702(2) quest, the rights there given bar all other remedies.

What emerges plainly from the section is that its predicate is the existence of the goods in the seller's possession and therefore able to be reclaimed. These must not have left the seller's possession as is clear from Section 2–702(3) making the rights of the seller seeking to recover subject to the rights of the purchasers there described.

Given the limitations on the seller's right to recover the goods and the problems inherent in tracing specific fungibles among others from the standpoints of the time of delivery of a given lot, it came as no surprise that the proceeds of a seller's identifiable goods would become the object of a seller's Section 2–702(2) claim. That such a remedy going beyond Section 2–702(2) would cause problems is nowhere made more clear than in the several opinions coming from the Fifth Circuit Court of Appeals in *Matter of Samuels & Co., Inc.* There, * * * the Court of Appeals divided in a dispute between a trustee in bankruptcy and a seller of cattle seeking to reclaim that which he could not get as the cattle had been slaughtered and butchered or, alternatively, seeking the proceeds attributable to the sale of the meat. Although the presence of a secured creditor loomed large, the majority opinion recognized that the cash seller's right to reclaim should not rest on the identity of the cattle as sold. In short, reclamation on the facts there, was found to be "a futile gesture" contrary to "reason or logic." Circuit Judge Godbold dissented. Among other chidings, Judge Godbold took Section 2–702 of the Texas version of the U.C.C. to confer a right to reclaim and not a "right to go after proceeds." Rehearing *en banc* was granted and the Court of Appeals, dividing 9–5, reversed the panel decision and adopted "as its opinion the dissenting opinion of Judge Godbold * * *." 526 F.2d 1238, 1240 (1976).

It would seem to follow, therefore, just from the tenor of the disparate views in the *Samuels* case itself and in others which need not be cited that the remedy of reclamation to a seller bringing himself within the plain language of U.C.C. Section 2–702(2) is secure as to the identifiable goods in the possession of the purchaser but much less so as to the proceeds yielded by the sale of those goods, for the tracing of specific funds attributable to specific sales is a formidable obstacle at best.

[The court found that Bankruptcy Act § 546(c) validated the seller's remedy under UCC § 2–702; but it limited the seller's priority to the goods in the debtor's possession on the date the petition in bankruptcy was filed.]

Notes

1. United States v. Westside Bank, 732 F.2d 1258 (5th Cir.1984), extended a seller's priority to proceeds that are traceable to the goods. But cf. In re Coast Trading Co., 744 F.2d 686 (9th Cir.1984).

2. Bankruptcy Code § 546(c):

(c) The rights and powers of the trustee * * * are subject to any statutory right or common-law right of a seller, in the ordinary course of such seller's business, of goods to the debtor to reclaim such goods if the debtor has received such goods while insolvent, but—

(1) such a seller may not reclaim any such goods unless such seller demands in writing reclamation of such goods before ten days after receipt of such goods by the debtor; and

(2) the court may deny reclamation to a seller with such a right of reclamation that has made such a demand only if court—

(A) grants the claim of such a seller priority as an administrative expense; or

(B) secures such claim by a lien.

C. CONSTRUCTION CONTRACTS

1. DAMAGES/RESTITUTION

PETROPOULOS v. LUBIENSKI

Court of Appeals of Maryland, 1959.
220 Md. 293, 152 A.2d 801.

HORNEY, JUDGE. * * * On April 15, 1955, the owners and builder entered into a written contract whereby the builder agreed to build a house for the owners in accordance with attached plans and specifications for $43,000, less an allowance of $350.

When the owners became dissatisfied with the builder's work in September of 1955 because requested changes had not been made and certain items of work were not in accordance with the contract, the builder submitted a bill for the "extras" he claimed. * * * [T]he owners refused to pay the bill as rendered.

When the parties were unable to adjust their differences, the owners notified the builder that they wished to have the controversy submitted to arbitration in accordance with the terms of the contract. After considerable bickering, each party chose his respective arbitrator and the two chose an umpire or referee as the third member of the panel. * * * The report allowed the builder $3,475 for extras—subsequently reduced to $2,475 by the court when it declined to allow $1,000 for certain plans—which the owners would not pay. When the owners refused to accept the award for extras, the builder countered by refusing to complete the house. The owners thereupon made other arrangements to have the house finished at a cost of $14,150 plus $1,250 for completion plans.

The builder filed suit for breach of contract on July 18, 1956. * * * There were four claims in the declaration: (1) a claim for the whole contract price; (2) a claim for the extras; (3) a claim for the arbitration award; and (4) a claim for moneys payable under the common counts. The owners counterclaimed for the cost of completing the house, damages for delay in completion and the cost of correcting defective work.

At the trial the parties were able to agree and it was stipulated that the builder had expended at least $25,359.75 for materials furnished and work done in the construction of the house. In addition to this sum, the builder offered proof that he had also expended $12,624.86 for other materials, work and "administrative costs or overhead," but the trial court allowed only $10,925.11 for these additional charges. The stipulated sum, plus the additional charges allowed, totaled $36,284.86.

The trial court, in arriving at the amount of its judgment *nisi* apparently proceeded on the theory that, the owners having refused to perform their part of the contract, the builder was entitled to rescind the contract and sue on quantum meruit, i.e., for as much as he deserved. But, in addition to finding that the builder had expended $36,284.86 for materials furnished and work done and for administrative costs and overhead, the court added a 10% profit, or $3,628.48.

* * * The owners further contend that the court did not apply the correct measure of damages. We agree that the trial court did err in several respects, all of which can be rectified without a remand. * * *

The builder, as he had a right to do under the provisions of Rule 313a, joined in one suit, as independent and alternate claims, the actions he had against the owners. * * * [I]t appears that under the rule permitting joinder of causes of actions it is not even necessary to put a builder to an election at the close of all the evidence when the court is the trier of the facts [but we expressly do not decide this point since it was not raised here]. In any event, the builder did not make an election and the trial court did not require him to elect between his action for damages for breach of the contract and his action of quantum meruit under the common counts for the value of the services performed and the outlays for materials furnished and work done. We see no reason, therefore, why the court could not under the circumstances select the measure of damages to be applied in order to arrive at a judgment *nisi* according to the evidence so long as only one measure of damages is used. While it is not entirely clear which measure of damages the trial judge intended to apply—indeed at first blush it appears she may have contemplated using parts of several measures of damages—nevertheless, when the apposite rules of law are applied to the evidence produced, it is apparent—with one exception hereinafter alluded to—that the trial court intended to and did arrive at its judgment *nisi* by applying the law applicable when the action is on quantum meruit.

The three measures of damages [herein referred to as measures (i), (ii) and (iii)] generally applied in suits on building contracts in this State are described in 5 Corbin, Contracts, § 1094, thus:

> "Full performance of the construction contract by both parties would have left the building contractor in possession of the full contract price, less the entire cost of construction required of him by the contract. To put him in as good a position as this, in case of a breach by the defendant, it is necessary to let the building contractor get judgment for the full amount of the contract price promised, diminished by the amount that is saved to the building contractor by reason of his not having to complete the construction. [Measure (i)]. The amount thus saved by reason of the defendant's breach is the cost of completion by the building contractor *himself* under the circumstances that existed at the time of the breach. * * *[1,2] (Emphasis added.)

1. [Footnotes renumbered.] Measure (i) is the formula commonly used when the builder can prove a profit, thus: Let BD = builder's damage; C = contract price; Y = remaining cost to complete contract. BD = C – Y.

2. Measure (i) in the circumstances stated is the simplest and best measure of damages and is generally applied where the builder can prove with reasonable certainty the cost of completing the work. See also Shapiro Engineering Corp. v. Francis O. Day Co., 1958, 215 Md. 373, 137 A.2d 695, which also applied the standard formula [BD = C – Y] as modified by payments on account [or A] and the cost of the extra work added by subsequent oral or written contract [or

"[Measure (ii)]. The rule for determining the damages recoverable by a building contractor is often stated in another form. It is said that he can recover damages measured by his actual expenditure to the date of breach, less the value of his materials on hand [if they are to be removed], plus the amount of the profit that he can prove with reasonable certainty would have been realized in case of full performance of the contract.[3] If correctly applied, this rule will attain exactly the same result as the rule previously stated. * * *

"[Measure (iii)]. A contractor who has been wrongfully prevented by the owner from rendering substantial performance, and thus creating a right to the contract price, has, in addition to his remedy in damages as above stated, an alternative restitutionary remedy. This is quantum meruit—a judgment for the reasonable value of the work, labor, and materials actually rendered and used in performance of the contract before the defendant's repudiation or other vital breach."[4]

From what has been said it is clear that the trial court could not and did not apply measure (i) since there was no proof of what it would cost the builder to complete the house. Likewise, it is certain that the court could not and did not apply measure (ii) because, although there was proof of the builder's expenditures to the date of breach, there was no proof of the value of the materials on hand, if there were any, nor was there any proof with reasonable certainty of the profit the builder would have realized if there had been full performance of the contract. Thus, it is apparent that the trial court applied measure (iii) since there was sufficient proof to justify a recovery on quantum meruit, which allows the value of services actually performed, when and if proved, and the outlays for materials furnished and work done. There was ample proof of the outlays, and, while there was no substantial testimony of the value of the builder's services, there was an allowance for administrative costs or overhead. If the builder failed or overlooked to prove with certainty the value of his services, we cannot say the trial court was clearly wrong in disallowing a claim therefor. Nor is the builder entitled to a remand for the purpose of supplying the proof omitted. Moreover, even if it was the intention of the trial court, in allowing a profit of 10% on the administrative costs, overhead and outlays made, to permit recovery for services performed, the court erred when it included a *positive* profit in the judgment *nisi.*

In summary we think that the judgment appealed from erroneously included an allowance for positive profit in the amount of $3,628.48. * * * Since the correct amount for which judgment should have been entered can be determined from the record, we shall reverse the judgment in part and enter judgment for the correct amount. * * *

Notes

1. Despite its disclaimer in Measure (iii), does the court by basing quantum meruit on "reasonable value" actually allow plaintiff to recover profits? Or is

E] with the result that BD = (C + E) – (A + Y).

3. Measure (ii), symbolically stated, would be: Let BP = Builder's profit on full performance; Z = cost of full performance; C = contract price. BP = C – Z. If Z, the cost of full performance, is split then X = net expenditures to date of breach; Y = cost to complete remainder, BD = [C – (X + Y)] + X. If the formula is cleared by subtraction, the result is the standard BD = C – Y.

4. Stated symbolically, measure (iii) would simply be: Let QM = quantum meruit; S = value of services performed; O = outlays for materials furnished and work done. QM = S + O. It should be noted that no profit is included in this formula.

quantum meruit here merely reliance damages? Compare City of Portland ex rel. Donohue & Fleskes Corp. v. Hoffman Construction Co., 286 Or. 789, 802, 596 P.2d 1305, 1311–13 (1979):

"The case was submitted to the jury under instructions that if Hoffman wrongfully terminated the contract, Donohue was entitled to recovery in quantum meruit. * * * We agree with the following authorities that the proper measure of recovery in quantum meruit for wrongful termination is the reasonable value of the contractor's performance rather than the value of the benefit conferred: [citations]

"Under circumstances where the proper measure of restitution is the reasonable value of the performance rendered by the plaintiff (as opposed to the value of the benefit received by the defendant), the reasonable value means the amount for which the services and materials furnished by plaintiff 'could have been purchased from one in plaintiff's position at the time they were rendered.' This is a market value measure rather than a measure directed at reimbursement for actual costs. A measure of recovery based on market value contemplates, we believe, a price that would enable the average subcontractor in plaintiff's position at the time the services and materials were furnished to make a reasonable profit. Profitability to the average seller is inherent in the concept of market value. So is an allowance for overhead.

"Evidence of the plaintiff's actual costs and the ordinary industry allowance for overhead and profit is relevant to the jury's determination of the reasonable value of the services and materials which were furnished."

Cf. C. Norman Peterson Co. v. Container Corp. of America, 172 Cal.App.3d 628, 218 Cal.Rptr. 592 (1985). The contractor established reasonable value of its services by showing its total actual costs.

2. Tull v. Gundersons, Inc., 709 P.2d 940 (Colo.1985), illustrates measure (i). The contractor established lost profits by proving itemized costs of completing a golf course. The court also ruled that evidence of the contractor's past profits on similar projects was admissible to prove lost profits on this contract.

3. Suppose that the owners breached in a way that delayed the construction project. The contractor asks for damages to compensate for the additional costs incurred because of the delay. Initially, the contractor has the burden of establishing that the delay did in fact cause losses, for example that alternative work was not available or that it was impractical to cut back on personnel. If the contractor shows the causal element, then the court calculates the contractor's damages in various ways. The "total cost" method, subtracting the estimated cost of the project from the actual costs incurred by the contractor, is used only where no other means of determining damages is available and the contractor can produce credible evidence of the various costs incurred. Glasgow, Inc. v. Commonwealth, Department of Transportation, 108 Pa.Cmwlth. 48, 529 A.2d 576 (1987). Another method used when the contractor seeks home office overhead costs incurred during the delay is the "Eichleay" formula. As explained in George Hyman Construction Co. v. Washington Metropolitan Transit Authority, 816 F.2d 753, 757 (D.C.Cir.1987), the calculation is: "The total home office overhead for the contract performance period is multiplied by the ratio of contract billings to total company billings; this calculation results in the amount of home office overhead allocable to the contract. That amount is then divided by the number of days of contract performance; the result is the daily home office overhead rate allocable to the contract. That rate is then multiplied by the number of days of delay; the result is the amount of recovery."

See also Nebraska Public Power District v. Austin Power, Inc., 773 F.2d 960 (8th Cir.1985); Golf Landscaping, Inc. v. Century Construction Co., a Division of Orvco, Inc., 39 Wash.App. 895, 696 P.2d 590 (1984).

4. In Indiana & Michigan Electric Co. v. Terre Haute Industries, Inc., 507 N.E.2d 588 (Ind.App.1987), appeal denied, 525 N.E.2d 1247 (Ind.1988), the owner breached the contract by discharging the contractor prior to the completion of the project. The court upheld an award of profits lost on that contract, but it refused to allow the contractor to recover for loss of future profits allegedly resulting from damage to its business reputation.

5. Suppose that a contractor seeks compensation for extra work or work done outside the terms of the contract. What is the legal basis of these claims? Professor Galligan, in a comprehensive review, suggests that courts rely on implied contract and restitution doctrines but employ them in a new way to resolve the problem of risks unanticipated at the time the contract was executed. See Galligan, Extra Work in Construction Cases: Restitution, Relationship, and Revision, 63 Tul.L.Rev. 799 (1989).

6. *Contractors' Damages and Pre-judgment Interest.* The judgment included prejudgment interest from the time the action was filed. Can we say, under the various possible formulae for damages, that the damages are liquidated or unliquidated or are capable of ascertainment before judgment? See Anno., 60 A.L.R.3d 487 (1974).

UNITED STATES v. ALGERNON BLAIR, INC.

United States Court of Appeals, Fourth Circuit, 1973.
479 F.2d 638.

CRAVEN, CIRCUIT JUDGE. May a subcontractor, who justifiably ceases work under a contract because of the prime contractor's breach, recover in quantum meruit the value of labor and equipment already furnished pursuant to the contract irrespective of whether he would have been entitled to recover in a suit on the contract? We think so * * *.

The subcontractor, Coastal Steel Erectors, Inc., brought this action under the provisions of the Miller Act, 40 U.S.C.A. § 270a et seq., in the name of the United States against Algernon Blair, Inc., and its surety, United States Fidelity and Guaranty Company. Blair had entered a contract with the United States for the construction of a naval hospital in Charleston County, South Carolina. Blair had then contracted with Coastal to perform certain steel erection and supply certain equipment in conjunction with Blair's contract with the United States. Coastal commenced performance of its obligations, supplying its own cranes for handling and placing steel. Blair refused to pay for crane rental, maintaining that it was not obligated to do so under the subcontract. Because of Blair's failure to make payments for crane rental, and after completion of approximately 28 percent of the subcontract, Coastal terminated its performance. Blair then proceeded to complete the job with a new subcontractor. Coastal brought this action to recover for labor and equipment furnished.

The district court found that the subcontract required Blair to pay for crane use and that Blair's refusal to do so was such a material breach as to justify Coastal's terminating performance. This finding is not questioned on appeal. The court then found that under the contract the amount due Coastal, less what had already been paid, totaled approximately $37,000. Additionally, the court found Coastal would have lost more than $37,000 if it had completed performance. Holding that any amount due Coastal must be reduced by any loss it would have incurred by complete performance of the contract, the court denied recovery to Coastal. While the district court correctly stated the " 'normal' rule of contract damages,"[1] we think Coastal is entitled to recover in quantum meruit.

In United States for Use of Susi Contracting Co. v. Zara Contracting Co., 146 F.2d 606 (2d Cir.1944), a Miller Act action, the court was faced with a situation similar to that involved here—the prime contractor had unjustifiably breached a subcontract after partial performance by the subcontractor. The court stated:

> For it is an accepted principle of contract law, often applied in the case of construction contracts, that the promisee upon breach has the option to forego any suit on the contract and claim only the reasonable value of his performance.

The Tenth Circuit has also stated that the right to seek recovery under quantum meruit in a Miller Act case is clear. Quantum meruit recovery is not limited to an action against the prime contractor but may also be brought against the Miller Act surety, as in this case. Further, that the complaint is not clear in regard to the theory of a plaintiff's recovery does not preclude recovery under quantum meruit. [citation] A plaintiff may join a claim for quantum meruit with a claim for damages from breach of contract.

In the present case, Coastal has, at its own expense, provided Blair with labor and the use of equipment. Blair, who breached the subcontract, has retained these benefits without having fully paid for them. On these facts, Coastal is entitled to restitution in quantum meruit.

> "The 'restitution interest,' involving a combination of unjust impoverishment with unjust gain, presents the strongest case for relief. If, following Aristotle, we regard the purpose of justice as the maintenance of an equilibrium of goods among members of society, the restitution interest presents twice as strong a claim to judicial intervention as the reliance interest, since if A not only causes B to lose one unit but appropriates that unit to himself, the resulting discrepancy between A and B is not one unit but two."

Fuller & Perdue, The Reliance Interest in Contract Damages, 46 Yale L.J. 52, 56 (1936).[2]

The impact of quantum meruit is to allow a promisee to recover the value of services he gave to the defendant irrespective of whether he would have lost money on the contract and been unable to recover in a suit on the contract. [citation] The measure of recovery for quantum meruit is the reasonable value of the performance; and recovery is undiminished by any loss which would have been incurred by complete performance. [citation] While the contract price may be evidence of reasonable value of the services, it does not measure the value of the performance or limit recovery.[3] Rather, the standard for

1. [Footnotes renumbered.] Fuller & Perdue, The Reliance Interest in Contract Damages, 46 Yale L.J. 52 (1936).

2. This case also comes within the requirements of the Restatements for recovery in quantum meruit. Restatement of Restitution § 107 (1937).

3. [citations] "It should be noted, however, that in suits for restitution there are many cases permitting the plaintiff to recover the value of benefits conferred on the defendant even though this value exceeds that of the return performance promised by the defendant. In these cases it is no doubt felt that the defen-

measuring the reasonable value of the services rendered is the amount for which such services could have been purchased from one in the plaintiff's position at the time and place the services were rendered.

Since the district court has not yet accurately determined the reasonable value of the labor and equipment use furnished by Coastal to Blair, the case must be remanded for those findings. * * *

Reversed and remanded with instructions.

Notes

1. The leading case adopting the contrary rule is Kehoe v. Rutherford, 56 N.J.L. 221, 27 A. 912 (1893). For an excellent analysis see Palmer, The Contract Price as a Limit on Restitution for Defendant's Breach, 20 Ohio St.L.J. 264 (1959).

2. *Blair* held that a contractor may recover more than the total contract price from a defaulting defendant. Would it be proper to extend the holding to a seller of goods such as *Wellston?* In other words, if the value of coal Wellston delivered in partial performance exceeded the total contract price for full delivery, should the defaulting customer pay more than it would have had to pay if all the coal had been delivered?

3. In ACME Process Equipment Co. v. United States, 347 F.2d 509, 528–29 (Ct.Cl.1965), plaintiff sought recovery from the United States under the Tucker Act for wrongful cancellation of a contract to manufacture rifles. After deciding that the cancellation was wrongful, the court addressed the measure of recovery:

"Plaintiff's main argument is that it is entitled to restitution as an alternative remedy. Under that standard of relief, a party whose contract has been repudiated or otherwise breached may, if he meets certain conditions, recover the reasonable value of his services, measured as of the time of performance. The purpose is to restore the injured party to the pre-contract status quo, not to put him in his post-contract position. Restitution has long been recognized by the commentators as one of three possible remedies for the substantial breach of an express contract, the others being damages and specific performance. * * *

"Although the Court of Claims has permitted quantum meruit recovery for contracts implied in fact [citation], no past contractor has successfully sought restitutionary relief for breach of an express contract. But unless this form of recovery is precluded by our general jurisdictional statute, 28 U.S.C.A. § 1491, we must be guided by the principle that, 'When the United States, with constitutional authority, makes contracts, it has rights and incurs responsibilities similar to those of individuals who are parties to such instruments.' Perry v. United States, 294 U.S. 330, 352 (1935). * * * Since contracts with the United States are to be governed by the same principles as 'those between man and man * * *,' we are obliged to award restitution to a petitioner meeting the prescribed qualifications, unless there is some jurisdictional impediment.

"The Tucker Act empowers this court 'to render judgment upon any claim against the United States founded * * * upon any express or implied contract with the United States * * *.' 28 U.S.C.A. § 1491. Although this precludes recovery on the basis of a contract merely implied in law [citation], the plaintiff seeks restitution for breach of an *express* contract, which clearly comes within the ambit of the Act."

dant's breach should work a forfeiture of his right to retain the benefits of an advantageous bargain." Fuller & Perdue.

4. Do you now agree that "quantum meruit" is an extraordinarily protean remedy?

HOURIHAN v. GROSSMAN HOLDINGS LTD.

District Court of Appeal of Florida, Third District, 1981.
396 So.2d 753.

NESBITT, JUDGE. * * * Appellants entered into a sale contract to purchase a house to be built by appellees on a particular lot. The contract provided that appellees would construct a dwelling on the lot "which is substantially the same as either the plans and specifications therefor on file at Seller's office, or, if constructed, the model therefor located in Seller's model area * * *." Prior to the commencement of the construction, the buyers learned of and remonstrated against the contractors' plan to build the house as a "mirror image" of the plans and model shown to the buyers when they entered into the contract. Their desire that the house be constructed in accordance with the plans was so that they could obtain the optimal benefit of the prevailing winds which would minimize the need for air conditioning as well as for esthetic reasons.[1] Nonetheless, the contractors erected a mirror image of the dwelling. The buyers then commenced this action for breach of contract. At the conclusion of the bench trial, the trial court found the builders had breached their contract by building the mirror image but denied all money damages to the buyers on the ground that the award of money damages under the circumstances would constitute economic waste and because the value of the house as constructed had enhanced substantially over the contract price.

We agree with the appellants' contention that the trial court applied the wrong measure of damages.

In Edgar v. Hosea, 210 So.2d 233 (Fla. 3d DCA 1968), this court aligned itself with what is now complained of as being the minority view as follows:

> "[D]amages for a contractor's breach of a contract to construct a dwelling, where it is not constructed in accordance with the plans and specifications, are the amount required to reconstruct it to make it conform to such plans and specifications, rather than the difference in loan or market value on the finished dwelling, since unlike a commercial structure, a dwelling has an esthetic value and must be constructed as the owner wants it, even though the finished dwelling may be just as good."

The appellees insist that: (a) application of the foregoing rule violates the fundamental concept that compensatory damages are not awardable where to do so would constitute economic waste; and (b) the application of Edgar v. Hosea, supra, would require a whole or partial dismantling or reassembling of a useable building. In this case, the rule against economic waste has no application for at least two reasons. First, as is made plain by Section 346 of the Restatement of Contracts, the rule is applicable only to instances for "*unavoidable* harm that the builder had reason to foresee * * *." [emphasis supplied] Secondly, it is clear that the rule for economic waste is applicable to commercial buildings rather than residential dwellings.

1. [Footnote renumbered.] Buyers were shown plans whereby the master bedroom, the "Great" room, and the living room would have a southeastern exposure thereby enabling them to take advantage of the tradewinds. The mirror image faced north and allegedly blocked off the winds. Additionally, the buyers would have had a view of the residential area. Instead, they now could view the "scenic" traffic of a major artery.

Moreover, in this case it is clear that the appellees/contractors may not proclaim that they substantially complied with the contract, because there was a willful and intentional failure to perform in accordance with the plans and specifications over the buyers' protests.

The rule in Edgar v. Hosea, to which we re-adhere, has not had the pernicious effect complained of by the building industry. We take judicial notice of the burgeoning construction of residences, notwithstanding that holding pronounced over twelve years ago. Indeed, it is our view that any other rule would be contrary to the pride of ownership that average homeowners expect when entering into what probably is the largest investment they will ever undertake—one which they may live with the greater portion of their lives.

The appellees also contend that the buyers were not damaged because the house had increased in value so as to offset the damages resulting from the breach. Whether the increase is illusory, because it is purely a result of inflation, or real, because of a general increase in the value of the home, this argument cannot aid the appellees. Upon entering into the contract to purchase the home, any increase in value (or decrease, for that matter) rightfully belongs to the buyers. Had the appellees constructed the house as contracted for, the buyers would have reaped the benefit of the increase in value of that home. Likewise, had the value of the home decreased, due to market conditions, the buyers would suffer the loss. Surely, the appellees do not suggest the buyers' damages would be increased due to a drop in value. Consequently, the trial court improperly applied the increase in the value of the home to offset the damages. * * *

[T]he final judgment in favor of the appellants is affirmed as to the breach of the contract. The judgment with respect to the issue of damages is reversed and remanded for a new trial.

GROSSMAN HOLDINGS, LTD. v. HOURIHAN

Supreme Court of Florida, 1982.

414 So.2d 1037.

McDonald, Justice. We have for review Hourihan v. Grossman Holdings Ltd., 396 So.2d 753 (Fla. 3d DCA 1981), which conflicts with Bayshore Development Co. v. Bonfoey, 75 Fla. 455, 78 So. 507 (1918), and Oven Development Corp. v. Molisky, 278 So.2d 299 (Fla. 1st DCA 1973), regarding the proper measure of damages for breach of a construction contract. We * * * disapprove the measure of damages applied by the third district in the instant case.

* * * [T]he third district held that the unreasonable economic waste doctrine does not apply to residential construction. It further found that Grossman's willful and intentional failure to perform according to the plans and specifications nullified its claim of substantial compliance with the contract. The court found the proper damages to be that amount necessary to reconstruct the dwelling to make it conform to the plans and specifications and remanded for a new trial on damages.

Grossman contends that *Bayshore Development* and *Oven Development* state the proper rule for determining the measure of damages for improperly constructed residences. These cases hold that the proper measure of damages is the difference in value between the building as constructed and as it should have been constructed. Grossman claims that subsection 346(1)(a) of the Restatement (First) of Contracts (1932) supports the diminution of value theory and urges this Court to adopt the Restatement as this state's law regarding damages for breach of a construction contract.

Subsection 346(1)(a) [1] of the Restatement provides as follows:

> "(1) For a breach by one who has contracted to construct a specified product, the other party can get judgment for compensatory damages for all unavoidable harm that the builder had reason to foresee when the contract was made, less such part of the contract price as has not been paid and is not still payable, determined as follows:
>
> (a) For defective or unfinished construction he can get judgment for either
>
> (i) the reasonable cost of construction and completion in accordance with the contract, if this is possible and does not involve unreasonable economic waste; or
>
> (ii) the difference between the value that the product contracted for would have had and the value of the performance that has been received by the plaintiff, if construction and completion in accordance with the contract would involve unreasonable economic waste."

The comment on subsection 346(1)(a) states:

> "The purpose of money damages is to put the injured party in as good a position as that in which full performance would have put him; but this does not mean that he is to be put in the same specific physical position. Satisfaction for his harm is made either by giving him a sum of money sufficient to produce the physical product contracted for or by giving him the exchange value that that product would have had if it had been constructed. In very many cases it makes little difference whether the measure of recovery is based upon the value of the promised product as a whole or upon the cost of procuring and constructing it piecemeal. There are numerous cases, however, in which the value of the finished product is much less than the cost of producing it after the breach has occurred. Sometimes defects in a complete structure cannot be physically remedied without tearing down and rebuilding, at a cost that would be imprudent and unreasonable. The law does not require damages to be measured by a method requiring such economic waste. If no such waste is involved, the cost of remedying the defect is the amount awarded as compensation for failure to render the promised performance."

Subsection 346(1)(a), therefore, is designed to restore the injured party to the condition he would have been in if the contract had been performed. This aim corresponds with general Florida law. [citations] We adopt subsection 346(1)(a) as the law in Florida regarding breaches of construction contracts.

Applying subsection 346(1)(a) to the instant case, we find that the district court reached an incorrect conclusion. The subsection itself makes no distinction between residential and nonresidential construction. Indeed, the illustrations contained in the Restatement deal with both types of buildings. We disagree with the district court's conclusion that the rule as enunciated in subsection 346(1)(a)(ii) is applicable only to commercial buildings.

Grossman also complains that the district court's ruling awards damages that are punitive in nature. Punitive damages are not recoverable for breach

1. [Footnote renumbered.] Similar provisions are contained in Restatement (Second) of Contracts § 348(2) (1981), but we prefer the language in Restatement (First).

of contract, but where the acts constituting the breach also amount to a cause of action in tort, punitive damages may be recovered. [citations] The Hourihans, however, presented only the breach of contract issue to the district court. The amount of compensatory damages flowing from a breach of contract is not affected by the manner of the breach.

Turning to the trial court's judgment, we agree in part and disagree in part with its findings. The record supports the trial court's finding that reconstructing the house would result in economic waste, and we will not disturb this finding. On the other hand, we find the trial court's refusal to consider awarding damages because of the then-current value of the house to be incorrect.

Damages for a breach of contract should be measured as of the date of the breach. [citations] Fluctuations in value after the breach do not affect the nonbreaching party's recovery. Here, it may be possible to demonstrate a difference in value as of the date of delivery between the house the Hourihans contracted for and the house that Grossman built. If such difference exists, the Hourihans should have the opportunity to prove it on remand and recover that amount as damages.

We therefore disapprove the measure of damages applied by the district court, but we agree that the case should be remanded for a new trial on damages.

Notes

1. In 1982, the Hourihans' house was worth $85,000, $35,000 more than when it was built; but they were living in Miami and renting it to tenants. They still preferred to charge the builder with the cost of tearing the house down and building it right. National Law Journal, May 10, 1982.

2. May the Hourihans recover for the increased expense of air conditioning the house? What about the loss of the view of the golf course? May the plaintiffs pocket the damages and sell the house for $85,000?

How can the judge be sure that the buyers' claim of aesthetic loss is not a late-blooming desire to exploit a small deviation to secure a windfall or cheaper house? Who should bear the burden of persuasion on the issue of aesthetic or subjective loss? Should the court ask whether the buyers are consumers purchasing a home to occupy?

Could the builder anticipate that the breach would cause a subjective loss? Can the factfinder measure the extent of the buyers' subjective loss? Should the court consider whether the cost to complete grossly exceeds the buyers' subjective loss?

If the court awards specific performance or a cost of rebuilding that exceeds the buyers' subjective loss, will bargaining between the buyer and the seller result in a settlement somewhere between cost and subjective value?

Consider the court's remarks in Advanced, Inc. v. Wilks, 711 P.2d 524, 527 (Alaska 1985). The owner was awarded the cost of repair of a home even though that exceeded the original contract price:

"It is true that in a case where the cost of repair exceeds the damages under the value formula, an award under the cost of repair measure may place the owner in a better economic position than if the contract had been fully performed, since he could pocket the award and then sell the defective structure. On the other hand, it is possible that the owner will use the damage award for its intended purpose and turn the structure into the one originally envisioned. He may do this for a number of reasons, including personal esthetics or a hope for increased value in the future. If he does this his economic position will equal the one he would have been in had the contractor fully performed. The fact finder is the one in the best position to determine whether the owner will actually complete performance, or whether he is only interested in obtaining the best immediate economic position he can. In some cases, such as where the property is held solely for investment, the court may conclude as a matter of law that the damage award cannot exceed the diminution in value. Where, however, the property has special significance to the owner and repair seems likely, the cost of repair may be appropriate even if it exceeds the diminution in value."

Other decisions wrestle with this problem. Gilbert v. Tony Russell Construction, 115 Idaho 1035, 772 P.2d 242 (App.1989); Shaw v. Bridges–Gallagher, Inc., 174 Ill.App.3d 680, 528 N.E.2d 1349 (1988). See Annotation, Modern Status of Rule as to Whether Cost of Correction or Difference in Value of Structures is Proper Measure of Damages for Breach of Construction Contract, 41 A.L.R.4th 131 (1985).

3. How can the buyers protect their interest in cooling breezes and a pleasant view?

a. Insert a liquidated damages provision into the binder contract?

b. Sue for specific performance?

c. Seek damages measured by cost of conforming the property to the contract?

4. *Variation:* Suppose the builder breached its contract in a way that saved it money but built a structure that was equal in value to the structure promised. May the owner recover the expense the builder saved by breach? Would that measure lead to a windfall for the owner? Discourage parties from breaching uneconomical contracts?

Remember the famous decision in Groves v. John Wunder Co., 205 Minn. 163, 286 N.W. 235 (1939), where the court awarded the $60,000 cost of performance even though performance would have only added $12,000 value. The majority of courts, however, award only diminished value. See Jones, The Recovery of Benefits Gained From a Breach of Contract, 99 Law Q.Rev. 443 (1983).

5. Professor Marschall suggests the following solution (citations deleted):

"In choosing the measure of damages, the willfulness factor should be considered first and should be deemed crucial. If willfulness is found, the court should automatically choose cost of repair damages because this higher measure tends to deter breach and more fully compensates the plaintiff's lost expectations. If the defendant's breach was inadvertent, and therefore unknowing, or if it was intended to benefit the plaintiff, the breach would be labeled nonwillful. Since deterrence of an unknowing breach cannot be achieved by automatically awarding the higher cost damages, the court should decide which of the two measures, cost or value, is the more reasonable under the circumstances of the particular case. To do this, the court should adopt an open-ended balancing approach in which the remaining factors are assigned weights and balanced against each other. Aesthetic preferences of the owner which are expressed through contract terms or specifications should be weighed more heavily than the economic factors of waste and disproportionality because remedies for breach of contract should focus most heavily on giving the plaintiff his precise expectations created at the time of the bargain. These expectations include not only any expected increase in the market value of plaintiff's house or land, but other more personal economic and noneconomic benefits as well.

"Assuming that a defendant has been found to be a nonwillful breacher, and the open-ended balancing approach is being used to determine which measure of damages is more reasonable, it has been suggested that any relevant factors should be considered. However, some factors should not be deemed relevant. One irrelevant factor is how the plaintiff may spend his damage award. The court's job is to determine a reasonable monetary substitute for what plaintiff bargained for but did not get due to the defendant's breach. Once this is done, the plaintiff is free to spend that award as he wishes. If the court awards cost of repair damages and the plaintiff then takes a trip to Europe instead of replacing his defective roof or leveling his land, the court should wish him bon voyage without any second thought about the propriety of the award."

Marschall, Willfulness: A Crucial Factor in Choosing Remedies for Breach of Contract, 24 Ariz.L.Rev. 733, 757–758 (1982). See also Muris, Cost of Completion or Diminution in Market Value: The Relevance of Subjective Value, 12 J.Legal Stud. 379 (1983).

6. As an alternative to benefit of the bargain damages represented by the two measures above, a buyer may opt instead to recover out of pocket expenditures made in reliance on the contract. In Herbert W. Jaeger & Associates v. Slovak American Charitable Association, 156 Ill.App.3d 106, 507 N.E.2d 863 (1987), the owner sought to recover payments made to the contractor and subcontractors plus the cost of demolishing the structure. The court ruled that this was an acceptable alternative measure of damages where the usual method was too speculative.

2. SPECIFIC PERFORMANCE

FRAN REALTY, INC. v. THOMAS

Court of Appeals of Maryland, 1976.
30 Md.App. 362, 354 A.2d 196.

MENCHINE, JUDGE. In early 1972 developers [defendants] entered into separate contracts for the sale of two separate specific lots within a recorded subdivision [in Anne Arundel County, Md.] One such contract was with Edward Thomas and Angela Thomas (Thomases); the second was with William Sipple and Geraldine Sipple (Sipples). * * *

In each instance developers agreed for a stated sum to construct a dwelling upon the respective lots for the Thomases and the Sipples. The contracts provided that the dwellings were "to be built in accordance with plans and specifications on file with Anne Arundel County and in the offices of Crown Realty Development, and similar to sample house, the Crown Jamaican—"Type A," located at 7947 Elvaton Road, Glen Burnie." Settlement dates in September, 1972, were set in the contracts, but time was not of the essence and extensions without a fixed time limitation had been agreed upon among the parties. In July, 1973, however, developers declined to go forward with construction and tendered the return of the down payments made by appellees. Developers' basis for declining to go forward was that "the sub-surface conditions of the lot[s] render it impossible to construct any dwelling in accordance with the plans and specifications agreed upon." Home buyers rejected the tender and filed separate bills for specific performance of their contracts. The actions were consolidated and tried together. The chancellor denied specific performance because he found that it was "likely that a decree of specific performance would require such extended supervision and continuing resolution of disputes as to outweigh the benefits to be gained." The chancellor decided to award monetary damages to the home buyers as alternative relief. A decree was passed entering judgment in favor of the Thomases for $11,350.00 and in favor of the Sipples for $10,600.00. * * * Developers seek reversal and dismissal of the bills of complaint. * * *

Developers thus state the questions presented by their appeal:

1. Did the chancellor have any right to decree specific performance or to award monetary damages? (Equity Jurisdiction)

[Editors: The other questions presented are omitted.]

Developers argue that there was no equitable jurisdiction because: (a) a building contract will not be specifically enforced; [and] (b) when the court denied specific performance, general equity jurisdiction was otherwise lacking * * *.

(a) Enforcement of a building contract

The general rule and an exception are thus stated in Pomeroy's Specific Performance of Contracts (3d Ed.1926) § 23 at 61, et seq.:

> "The general rule is now well settled that, on account of the great difficulty and often impossibility attending a judicial superintendence and execution of the performance, contracts for the erection or repair of buildings, the construction of works, and the conduct of operations requiring time, special knowledge, skill, and personal oversight, will not be specifically enforced. Notwithstanding this general rule and the cogent reason which supports it, there are certain exceptions; and contracts for building or for the construction of works, and the like, falling within them may be specifically enforced. 1. It has been said that if an agreement for erecting a building is in its nature defined, there is no difficulty in entertaining a suit for its specific performance. But a contract to build a house of a certain value merely, does not come within this description of an agreement sufficiently defined, and will not be enforced. 2. Whether or not the opinion of Ld. Rosslyn is to be regarded as a correct statement of the law, it is settled by the recent English decisions, that where the defendant has contracted to construct some work which is defined on his own land, and where the plaintiff has a material interest in the execution thereof, which is not susceptible of adequate compensation in damages, a specific performance of the undertaking will be compelled."

It is quite plain that Maryland recognizes the general rule and the cited exception.

The growth and the extent of the rule and the exception were discussed in Edison Realty Co. v. Bauernschub, where it was said, 191 Md. at 458, 62 A.2d at 357:

> "[W]e hold in this State that where complainants have purchased land improved by an unfinished house and the vendor has installed an insufficient heating apparatus, or has failed to do certain work which he agreed to do, the court of equity has power to decree specific performance, where the work which has not been performed is clearly defined."

In City Stores Company v. Ammerman, 266 F.Supp. 766, at 776–77 (U.S. D.C. for D.C.1967), affd. 129 U.S.App.D.C. 325, 394 F.2d 950 (1968), it was said:

> "Some jurisdictions in the United States have opposed granting specific performance of contracts for construction of buildings and other contracts requiring extensive supervision of the court, but the better view, and the one which increasingly is being followed in this country, is that such contracts should be

specifically enforced unless the difficulties of supervision outweigh the importance of specific performance to the plaintiff. This is particularly true where the construction is to be done on land controlled by the defendant, because in that circumstance the plaintiff cannot employ another contractor to do the construction for him at defendant's expense. In the case at bar, the fact that more than mere construction of a building is involved reinforces the need for specific enforcement of the defendants' duty to perform their entire contractual obligation to the plaintiff."

In the subject case, title to the land upon which the two houses were to be built was held by the developers. Early on, the Court of Appeals adopted the observation of Story that: "Where, indeed, a contract respecting real property is in its nature and circumstances unobjectionable, it is as much a matter of course for Courts of Equity to decree a specific performance of it, as it is for the Court of Law to give damages for a breach of it." Smoot v. Rea, 19 Md. 398 (1863). * * *

In the subject case the land was titled in the developers. The home buyers had a material interest in seeking to obtain the home of their choice at the place of their choice. The nature of the performance to be required of the developers was clearly defined—well within the certainty required by the decided cases.

An adequate basis for equitable jurisdiction was shown.

(b) Damages in lieu of specific performance

We regard the case of Charles County Broadcasting Co. v. Meares, to be dispositive of the question. In *Meares* it was said, 270 Md. at 325, 311 A.2d at 30–31:

"*It has long been established that if the remedy of specific performance is possible when the vendee brings suit, but while the action is pending a vendor disables himself from performing his contract, damages may be awarded in lieu of specific performance.*

"If a complainant files a bill for specific performance at a time when he knows specific performance is impossible, and the sole remaining prayer for relief is for damages, his bill will be dismissed. Although specific performance cannot be decreed once performance has become impossible, damages may be awarded in the same equitable proceeding, provided that at the time the action was commenced in equity, specific performance was in fact obtainable, [citations]."

Here, specific performance was not impossible when suit was brought. Indeed, the chancellor, in refusing specific performance, pointed out "that the model home which would serve as a standard for comparative purposes during construction, has been sold and is occupied by a family who is not a party to the suit. * * * The Court knows of no compulsory process to compel that family to submit to frequent interruptions for the purpose of checking ongoing construction." Significantly, that sample house was sold by the developers more than six months *after* the bills for specific performance were filed.

The equity court had jurisdiction to grant damages in lieu of specific performance. * * *

[Decree affirmed.]

Notes

1. The court held that the "in lieu" damages should be calculated as the difference between the contract price for the land and buildings and the value at the *time of breach* without consideration of any consequential damages. *Query:* When damages are in lieu of specific performance should the measure be the difference between the contract price and the value at the time set for *performance?* The court considered this point but rejected it. Why?

2. As the principal case illustrates, courts have granted specific performance of contracts to build on defendant's own land. The court can count on defendant's own self interest to perform the construction properly. Moreover, courts only grant specific performance where plaintiff minimizes the court's supervisory burden by showing that the building plans are relatively definite and certain. See Ammerman v. City Stores Co., 394 F.2d 950 (D.C.Cir.1968); Becker v. Sunrise at Elkridge, 226 N.J.Super. 119, 543 A.2d 977, cert. denied, 113 N.J. 356, 550 A.2d 465 (1988).

Where the contractor's obligations are uncertain or where the court believes that supervision would be difficult, specific performance is denied. Abrams v. Rapoport, 163 Ill.App.3d 748, 516 N.E.2d 943 (1987), cert. denied, 119 Ill.2d 553, 522 N.E.2d 1240 (1988) (contract to repair); Petry v. Tanglwood Lakes, Inc., 514 Pa. 51, 522 A.2d 1053 (1987) (contract to build a lake); Northern Delaware Industrial Development Corp. v. E.W. Bliss Co., 245 A.2d 431 (Del.Ch.1968) (court refused to order the employment of 300 additional workmen for a night shift on a construction project, citing the difficulty of effective enforcement).

3. PLAINTIFF IN DEFAULT

VALENTINE v. PATRICK WARREN CONSTRUCTION CO.

Supreme Court of Wisconsin, 1953.
263 Wis. 143, 56 N.W.2d 860.

CURRIE, JUSTICE WARREN [general contractor on an assembly building for Ford Motor Co. near St. Louis] had to meet a deadline of October 1, 1947, for the completion of the building, as Ford was then to bring in specially trained mechanics from Detroit to set up the assembly line machinery. Because of this October 1, 1947, deadline, Warren was very much worried that the painting by Capital [subcontractor] of the interior of the assembly building would not be completed by that date, and that is the reason it was continually pressing Capital to put on more painters. * * *

Because of Capital's defaults in the respects mentioned above, Warren, under date of July 22, 1947, rescinded the subcontract with Capital by registered letter mailed on that date to Capital at its Madison office. * * *

After this letter of July 22, 1947, Warren put the painters on its own payroll and hired additional painters and proceeded in this way to do the painting until August 19, 1947, when it subcontracted the balance of the painting with Busch & Latta, the largest painting contractors in the area, and Busch & Latta completed the painting work. Before engaging Busch & Latta, Warren solicited bids for the remainder of the painting work and two other reliable painting contractors beside Busch & Latta submitted bids, and the latter's bid was approximately $25,000 higher than the lowest bid. The reason Busch & Latta were awarded the job, even though its bid was high, was because of their large size, as Warren wanted to be sure that the work was completed in the time required by Ford.

Capital commenced action against Warren for damages for breach of contract, the complaint being verified on date of January 31, 1949. Warren counterclaimed, such counterclaim being for the total amount it had expended for the painting work on the Ford contract over and above the amount which would have been due under the subcontract with Capital.

* * * Having determined that Capital breached its contract to the extent that it entitled Warren to rescind the same the next question which arises is whether Capital is entitled to recover anything from Warren over and above the payments which it had received under the contract prior to recission. The applicable rule is to be found in Restatement, Contracts, sec. 357(1), which section is entitled "Restitution in Favor of Plaintiff who was himself in Default," as follows:

> "Where the defendant fails or refuses to perform his contract and is justified therein by the plaintiff's own breach of duty or non-performance of a condition, but the plaintiff has rendered a part performance under the contract that is a net benefit to the defendant, the plaintiff can get judgment * * * for the amount of such benefit in excess of the harm that he has caused to the defendant by his own breach, in no case exceeding a ratable proportion of the agreed compensation."

Comment g, appearing under such section of Contracts, Restatement, further states:

> "The plaintiff's right to restitution is merely to the excess of benefit received over the harm suffered. It is necessary for the plaintiff to show with a reasonable degree of certainty that there is such an excess and its amount, in order to get judgment. In no case will the benefit received by the defendant be reckoned at more than a proportionate part of the agreed price of full performance."

Illustration 3, appearing under Restatement, Contracts, 357(1), elucidates the above rule, and we quote such illustration as follows:

> "A contracts to erect a building for B, who promises to pay $10,000 on completion. After spending $8,000 on the work, A becomes insolvent and cannot complete it. The uncompleted building is worth $7,000 as an addition to B's property. It costs B $4,000 to complete the building, and he loses $500 in rent because of delay. A can get judgment against B for $5,500—this being the value of the part performance less the harm caused by the breach."

Williston on Contracts (Rev.Ed.), V. 5, secs. 1482, 1483, explains that this rule, which permits a party who has breached a contract to recover under certain circumstances for work already performed on the contract, is based upon the theory of quasi contract that it would be unjust to permit the defendant to be enriched at the expense of plaintiff. The author states:

> "The true measure of quasi contractual recovery where the performance is incomplete but readily remediable, is 'the unpaid contract price less the cost of completion and other additional harm to [the defendant] except that it must never exceed the benefit actually received by [him].' This is the net benefit by which the defendant is enriched."

Exhibit 108 is a computation disclosing that Warren sustained a net loss of $9,902.39 as a result of Capital's breach of its contract and Warren having to take over the completion of the painting on the Ford project. * * * It will also be noted that an adjustment of $25,263.91 was deducted in the above computation to cover the amount which was stipulated by counsel for both parties should be deducted because of Warren having let the subcontract to Busch & Latta when it could have let the same to other reliable painting contractors at a saving in cost of approximately $25,000.

Under the rule of damages set forth in Restatement, Contracts, and Williston on Contracts, hereinbefore quoted, Capital would be entitled to recover nothing further from Warren beyond the $30,891.60 already paid to it by Warren on the basis of the above loss sustained by Warren of $9,902.39, for the work performed by Capital.

Notes

The most important problem here is the measure of recovery. Various formulae have been proposed. The effect is demonstrated by referring to Illustration 3, § 357 of the Restatement (First) of Contracts, cited by the court in *Valentine.*

1. *The contract price less damages.* For a cessation of work, general damages are the cost of completion plus consequential damages. If the contract price is $10,000 and $4,000 is required to complete the contract, the quantum meruit recovery is $6,000 even though the contractor has expended $8,000 and no other builder would have performed the work to date for less. This is the usual measure of recovery; it was applied in *Valentine* and Miles Homes, Inc. v. Starrett, 23 Wis.2d 356, 127 N.W.2d 243 (1964).

2. *A fraction of the purchase price determined by the relation that the value of the part performance bears to the value of the full performance.* This formula was advocated by Woodward, Quasi Contracts § 178, at 284–85 (1913), without citation of case authority. It might be applied to the case above as follows: the value of the part performance is $8,000. Since $4,000 is required to complete, the value of the full performance is presumably $12,000. $\frac{8}{12} \times$ $10,000 (the contract price) = $6,666.67, the measure of recovery. In applying the formula, however, there may be a lingering doubt about how to determine the "value" of full performance. From the standpoint of accuracy, is there a better criterion than the next lowest bid on the *entire* job?

3. *The enhancement of the value of the premises because of the part performance less special damages.* This formula (with an overriding limitation) was suggested in the Massachusetts case of Gillis v. Cobe, 177 Mass. 584, 59 N.E. 455 (1901). It seeks to confine restitution to the defendant's actual pecuniary benefit, without reference to extrinsic standards as in (2) above. The dissenting opinion objected that a considerable amount of expensive work, labor and materials may be put into premises without enhancing their value, not because of the breach but because of the type of structure. Thus if B, an eccentric, contracts with A to put up a purple monstrosity that depreciate the land's value, A could recover under Gillis v. Cobe only for substantial performance.

4. *The Restatement (First) formula applied to a construction contract.* Section 357 of the Restatement partially quoted in *Valentine,* measures restitution to a defaulting plaintiff: (a) for a nonwilful breach, the enrichment of the defendant, or (b) for a wilful breach followed by defendant's "acceptance" of the benefit with knowledge of the breach, the price fixed or otherwise a ratable proportion of the total contract price.

The contract price is $10,000; the amount the contractor expended is $8,000; the cost to complete is $4,000. The structure, as is, enhances the value of the premises by $7,000. The contractor became insolvent (for obvious reasons) and so the breach must be regarded as nonwilful. The defendant's benefit is the amount he has been enriched. According to the illustration this will be the unpaid contract price less cost of completion—i.e. $6,000 here; *but* the defendant is never liable for more than the benefit to him, stipulated to be $7,000. If the enhanced value of the premises as a result of the contractor's expenditure of $8,000 is only $4,000, this would be the recovery.

This method is an alternative to (1) and (3) above, whichever is less. It is open to the criticism of Gillis v. Cobe previously advanced: that the enhancement of the premises' value by the potential construction largely depends on an extraneous fortuity, the type of structure. The illustration plainly poses this possibility. If plaintiff's expenditure of $8,000 increases the value of defendant's property by only $4,000, the builder is either woefully incompetent or the projected structure lacks much attraction in the real estate market. Even a contract breaker should not be made to bear this limiting factor, since it is unrelated to its conduct.

The Restatement formulation also suggests further difficulties. The breach in the illustration arose from the contractor's insolvency and must be considered nonwilful. If the breach were wilful and there is acceptance, recovery in quasi-contract is prescribed at the contract rate or ratable portion of the contract price. This intimates a return to Woodward's formula in (2) above. Having expended $8,000 with $4,000 to go, it must again be assumed that the plaintiff has done ⅔ of the work and a ratable portion of the contract price is $6,666.67. This leads to the uncomfortable conclusion, manifestly unintended, that the wilful defaulter would recover more than the nonwilful defaulter.

The Restatement's formulation, illustration, and discussion lack specific provision for the measure of recovery when the breach is a material deviation from the blueprints, the structure being otherwise complete and in use.

5. *The Restatement (Second) Formula and Illustration.* Former § 357 has been replaced by § 374 Restatement (Second) of Contracts. In part it states: "the party in breach is entitled to restitution for any benefit that he has conferred by way of part performance or reliance in excess of the loss that he has caused by his own breach."

Illustration 2 to § 374: A contracts to make repairs to B's building in return for B's promise to pay $10,000 on completion of the work. After spending $8,000 on the job, A fails to complete it because of insolvency. B has the work completed by another builder for $4,000, increasing the value of the building to him by a total of $9,000, but he loses $500 in rent because of the delay. A can recover $5,000 from B in restitution less $500 in damages for the loss caused by the breach, or $4,500.

The new illustration tracks the one examined above except (a) repair rather than new construction is involved, (b) the value of B's fully repaired building is increased by $9,000 rather than $7,000 as is, and (c) the defaulting contractor recovers $4,500 instead of $5,500. Obviously, something has happened here. Which formula above does the Restatement Second use?

Another similar innocuous change in § 374 is the substitution of the word "loss" for the word "harm" in the clause, "in excess of the *loss* that he has caused, etc." Refer back to the note following Vines v. Orchard Hills supra, pp. 1060–61. Should the owner be entitled to claim as "losses caused" items that may not be legal damages in most jurisdictions like annoyance and inconvenience occasioned by the breach?

Elementary principles of unjust enrichment require that the defaulting contractor should never recover more than its actual expenses. To do otherwise would allow a contract breaker expectancy damages in an action based on its own wrong.

6. *The Interplay of the "Substantial Performance" Rule and Quasi-Contractual Recovery by the Defaulting Contractor.*

If a contractor has *substantially* performed, it may bring a *contract* action for the agreed price less damages. Tolstoy Construction Co. v. Minter, 78 Cal.App.3d 665, 143 Cal.Rptr. 570 (1978). Where performance is adjudged less than substantial compliance with the contract, the contractor may actually recover nothing. DiMario v. Heeks, 116 R.I. 44, 351 A.2d 837 (1976).

The Restatement (Second) of Contracts § 374 permits quasi-contractual recovery by the defaulting contractor (a) if his breach is nonwilful; or (b) if wilful, the owner has *accepted* the work. As may be expected, people differ about what constitutes acceptance. The owner may have little choice except to grumble and make do with a bad situation; this may be taken as acceptance.

A sterner view has been expressed. Feeney v. Bardsley, 66 N.J.L. 239, 49 A. 443 (1901): "In determining the question of acceptance, it is not sufficient to find that the owner was occupying it. It is a house built upon his land and, unless he tears it down, he must make some use of it, so that the jury must find some positive act on his part showing an intention to accept it."

Professor Thurston, Cases on Restitution 160 (1940), comments that courts adopting this attitude tend to be more liberal in finding substantial performance. And see DiMario v. Heeks, supra, where the appellate court seemed extraordinarily reluctant to accept the trial court's holding that the plaintiff-contractor's performance was less than substantial.

D. EMPLOYMENT AND SERVICE CONTRACTS

1. DAMAGES

ROTH v. SPECK

Municipal Court of Appeals, District of Columbia, 1956.
126 A.2d 153.

QUINN, ASSOC. J. This suit was brought by plaintiff (employer) against defendant (employee) for breach of a written contract of employment. Trial by the court resulted in a finding and judgment for plaintiff for one dollar. Plaintiff appeals.

Plaintiff testified that he was the owner of a beauty salon in Silver Spring, Maryland; that his business was seasonal; and that on April 15, 1955, by a written contract he agreed to employ defendant as a hairdresser for one year. Defendant's salary was to be $75 a week or a commission of fifty percent on the gross receipts from his work, whichever sum was greater. Defendant remained in his employ for approximately six and one-half months and then left. Plaintiff testified that from the beginning defendant earned his salary, needed no special training, and soon built up and maintained a following because of his exceptional skill and talent.

Plaintiff also testified that his net profit was seven percent of the gross receipts per hairdresser. To substantiate this he introduced defendant's statement of earnings, which reflected gross receipts and salary paid to him. Plaintiff testified that in an effort to mitigate his damages he employed another person "to whom he paid $350, which was a complete loss and he had to let this employee go." He then hired still another operator who even at the date of trial was not earning his salary, and was thus employed at a loss to plaintiff. A witness for plaintiff testified that he had been the owner of a beauty salon for many years; that defendant had been in his employ since

November 1, 1955, at a weekly salary of $100; and that defendant was a very good operator.

Defendant testified that he left because conditions in plaintiff's shop were unbearable; that he complained to plaintiff on numerous occasions; that he had asked for more money but that salary was not the main reason for his leaving; and that he was presently earning $100 per week.

The sole question presented is what damages plaintiff was entitled to under these circumstances. Plaintiff argues that the trial court did not consider the value of defendant's services or the profits lost by plaintiff and therefore erroneously limited the award to nominal damages. It is established law that where a plaintiff proves a breach of a contractual duty he is entitled to damages; however, when he offers no proof of actual damages or the proof is vague and speculative, he is entitled to no more than nominal damages. While the facts warrant application of this principle to plaintiff's claim concerning lost profits, we think there was proof of actual damage and that the evidence with regard to the value of defendant's services provided an accurate measure of such damage.

The measure of damages for breach of an employment contract by an employee is the cost of obtaining other service equivalent to that promised and not performed. Compensation for additional consequential injury may be recovered if at the time the contract was made the employee had reason to foresee that such injury would result from his breach. However, we need not concern ourselves with the foreseeability of lost profits resulting from defendant's breach since plaintiff's proof on this point was at most conjectural and speculative. * * * It can be seen that defendant's gross receipts, and hence plaintiff's seven percent profit, depended on a number of contingencies—the seasonal fluctuations of business, defendant's skill and industry, and the judgment of the employee who assigned the operators. There was no criterion by which the trial court could have estimated plaintiff's profits with the degree of certainty necessary to allow their recovery; therefore they were not within the range of recoverable damages.

There remains the question as to the value of defendant's services. Defendant was evidently a hairdresser of exceptional talent. This is demonstrated not only by the fact that he experienced no difficulty in securing and retaining another position at a higher salary, but also by plaintiff's own testimony that he was unable to hire a satisfactory substitute. Defendant did not claim that he was required to render services other than those in his original contract with plaintiff in order to obtain a higher salary from his new employer, nor did plaintiff prove by expert testimony how much such services would bring in the market. But plaintiff did prove the amount defendant actually received. Under such circumstances, there was some evidence of the value of defendant's services and therefore of the cost of replacement. As was said in Triangle Waist Co. v. Todd, 223 N.Y. 27, 119 N.E. 85, 86:

> "If one agrees to sell something to another, and then, the next day, sells it to someone else at an advance, the new transaction is not to be ignored in estimating the buyer's loss. * * * The rule is not different when one sells one's labor. The price received upon a genuine sale either of property or of service is some evidence of value."

Twenty-four weeks yet remained when defendant abandoned his contract and obtained employment elsewhere at a higher salary. Until this new compensation is disproved as the value of his services, it may be presumed to be the fair value. That it was the fair value of defendant's services was partially supported by plaintiff's unsuccessful efforts to obtain a comparable replacement. Seemingly, plaintiff would have had to pay $100 a week in order to obtain an equally talented hairdresser, if one could have been found. If this be so, plaintiff having contracted for defendant's services at a guaranteed wage of $75 per week, would be entitled to the difference between the two salaries for the remainder of the contract period. The fact that defendant was entitled to a fifty-percent commission on his gross receipts—if such receipts were more than his salary—should not be a deterrent to the application of this measure of damages. It was defendant's duty to prove facts in mitigation of the damage he caused by his breach. If he believed his damages would be lessened by proving that if he had stayed for the remainder of his contract the fifty-percent commission on his gross receipts would have been higher than his guaranteed salary, it was his burden to offer such proof. Though such facts may be difficult to prove, one who breaches his contract " 'cannot wholly escape on account of the difficulty which his own wrong has produced of devising a perfect measure of,' or method of proving, damages." [1]

The judgment will be reversed with instructions to grant a new trial, limited to the issue of damages.

Reversed with instructions.

Note

Eckles v. Sharman, 548 F.2d 905 (10th Cir.1977). A professional basketball team sued a former coach and his new team for damages for breach of contract. In reversing a judgment for the plaintiff and ordering a new trial, the court stated:

"The potential of a new trial impels us to discuss one matter in which the parties are in disagreement. The problem is the measure of damages and the instructions relating thereto. The defendants say that they are not liable for lost profits and that the measure of damages is either the increased replacement expense or, if the employee is unique or irreplaceable, the increased remuneration which the employee would receive in the open market. Defendants point out that Sharman's replacements were obtained at lower salaries than that paid Sharman and that the Los Angeles Lakers paid Sharman basically what he received from the Utah Stars.

"Lost profits may be recovered in an employee breach of contract case if the employer can show that the parties had reason to believe that losses would result from the breach. We are aware of only one California case which addresses the issue. Steelduct Co. v. Henger–Seltzer Co., 26 Cal.2d 634, 160 P.2d 804, 812 (1945) says:

> '[T]he elements of the plaintiff's [employer's] damages are two: the reasonably necessary expense to which plaintiff was put in procuring a new agent, and the loss of profits (if any profits were lost) caused by defendants' breach.'

"Consequential damages such as lost profits may be recovered in an appropriate case for breach of an employment contract. In the case here, they can be justified only on a finding that Sharman, as a coach, was unique or irreplaceable. The evidence in this regard was conflicting. The jury should have been told that

1. [Footnote renumbered.] Steelduct Co. v. Henger–Seltzer Co., supra, 160 P.2d 804, 814 (1945).

the plaintiff could not recover damages for lost profits or diminished franchise value without a finding that Sharman was irreplaceable as a coach."

DIXIE GLASS CO. v. POLLAK

Court of Civil Appeals of Texas, 1960.
341 S.W.2d 530.

BELL, CH. J. The appellee was employed by written contract of January 1, 1953 as comptroller of appellant for a period of five years and was given an option to renew the contract for three additional five-year terms, the option to be exercised six months prior to the end of each term. The contract provided for a weekly salary of $200 and an annual bonus of 10% of the net profits before deduction for income taxes. The contract was authorized by the unanimous vote of all officers, directors and stockholders in a joint meeting held January 2, 1953. On October 19, 1955, the appellant discharged appellee.

Appellee sued appellant for breach of this contract, contending his discharge was without good cause, and sought recovery of his damages, alleging them to be the value if paid now of the amounts, salary and bonus, that he would have earned under the contract for the full term including the terms for which he was given an option, less any amounts that he should be able to earn during said term from other employment or business which he should be able to obtain by the exercise of reasonable diligence.

Trial was to a jury, which found the discharge was without good cause. The jury found the damages up to the time of trial to be $20,277. It also found appellee would earn $156,000 as salary under the contract up to its termination from the time of trial. It allowed no bonus after the time of trial. It also found appellee's earnings in the future, above all necessary expenses, should be $78,000. The court rendered judgment for appellee for $3,116.24, which was the bonus stipulated to be due appellee as of the date of his discharge on October 19, 1955, together with interest from February 1, 1956, and for $98,277, the amount found by the jury, together with interest from the date of judgment. Execution was stayed as to the $78,000 found to be appellee's damages from the date of trial to the end of the contract.

* * * The trial court submitted damage issues in a manner so as to separate damages up to the time of trial from damages beyond the date of trial. Appellant takes the position there can be no recovery beyond the date of the trial because it cannot be known with reasonable certainty whether the appellee will be damaged and if so how much. * * *

We find there is a conflict in the authorities in the United States. The majority rule is that recovery of damages may be had for the full term, regardless of when the trial occurs. The minority view is that anticipatory damages may not be recovered but recovery is limited to damages suffered to the date of trial. [citations]

We are of the view there is no Texas case authoritatively deciding the question. * * *

We, therefore, hold that where an employer wrongfully breaches a contract of employment prior to the time it has been completely performed, a cause of action for damages for breach of contract immediately arises in favor of the employee and he is entitled, if he elects, to recover his damages for the full term for which he was employed and he is not limited to damages proven only to the date of trial where trial is before the expiration of the term of employment.

Of course his suit is not for wages but is for damages. The measure of damages is the present cash value of the contract to him, if it had not been breached, less any amounts that he should in the exercise of reasonable diligence be able to earn through other employment. The duty is on the employee to use reasonable diligence to obtain other employment and thus minimize his damage. The maximum recovery would be the present value of the contract if it should be fully performed and in the exercise of reasonable diligence the employee could not obtain other employment. * * *

In the case of Granow v. Adler, 24 Ariz. 53, 206 P. 590, 592, the Supreme Court of Arizona held damages recoverable for the full term of the contract though trial occurred prior to the end of the term. The court said:

> "To limit recovery to the damages accrued to the term of trial, the contractual term not having elapsed, and then to hold the employee barred by such an award from any further recovery, seems to us to be at war with the general principle which imposes liability upon the party who breaches a contract, to respond to the other party for all damages which arise naturally from the breach, or such as may reasonably be supposed to have been within the contemplation of the parties at the time of making the contract, as a probable result of the breach. If the employee would have all his damages assessed and thereby realize the fruits of his contract, he is, under [this approach], offered the alternative of deferring the bringing of his suit or the trial of the cause until after the expiration of the term of employment. In many cases—more especially in the event of a long term contract—the acceptance of this alternative might deprive the employee of all redress for his injury. The uncertainty involved in the computation of the damages to accrue after trial is not introduced by the act of the employee, but arises from the fault and wrong of the employer, and it appears to us constitutes no just reason for depriving the employee of his right to recover all the damages he has sustained, if he makes the best proof of which the case is susceptible." * * *

The Texas cases hold that on breach of the contract, only one cause of action for damages for breach of contract arises. The employee may not split his cause of action. If, as in many cases he has, an employee sues for damages for less than the full contract period, he waives the balance of his damages. * * * Too, the cause of action arises immediately on breach so that the statute of limitation commences to run so that, at least as to damages that have accrued beyond the particular period of limitation before the filing of suit, recovery is barred. * * *

The result of adopting the minority rule would certainly in the case of a long term contract effectively deprive an employee of the fruits of his contract. He must sue within the period of limitation or lose the part of his damages barred by limitation. If he sues within the period of limitation and is required by the trial court to try the case before the end of the term, he must lose a part of his damages. Even if he is allowed to wait until the end of the term before going to trial he loses in the interim the enjoyment of the fruits of a valid contract that he has been willing to perform but which the employer has wrongfully breached.

We see no more uncertainty in allowing recovery of anticipatory damages in a breach of employment contract case than there is in the case of allowing recovery for diminished earning capacity in a personal injury case.

* * * Many factors, just as in a personal injury case, will have to be considered. Some factors are: age, probable life expectancy, education, experience, past earning capacity, and probable span of employability.

In the case before us there can be little doubt that appellee suffered and will suffer damage. He was at the time of the breach of the contract 58 years of age and he had a contract paying him $10,400 per year. Can there be any reasonable doubt that in the light of human experience appellee will in probability not be able to get any such remunerative employment during the balance of his life? It is a matter of common knowledge that a person of this age cannot well compete in the labor mart. Of course, it cannot be determined with mathematical exactness what his earnings will be. Mathematical exactness is not required. The evidence shows that between discharge and trial, a period of some two years, appellee had tried diligently to obtain work and had obtained some work which paid very little. We mention the facts of this case to demonstrate that in some cases of breach of employment contracts the evidence will show, with probability, resulting damage and the extent of damage. This demonstrates that the minority rule, which says that since it is a breach of employment contract you cannot recover anticipatory damages because they are too uncertain, is not sound. * * *

The contract here was for a term of five years. It provided that appellee could, at his option, renew the contract for three additional five-year terms by exercising his option six months before the termination of each five year period. Appellant says that at most appellee could recover for damages for the first five-year term because he had never exercised the options contained in the contract.

We overrule this contention. A substantial provision of the contract breached by appellant was the option of appellee to extend it. When the contract was breached time had not arrived for the exercise of the option. When appellant repudiated the contract, he deprived appellee of this contract right. Too, since appellant had repudiated the contract and discharged appellee, it would be useless for appellee to exercise the option. The law does not require a useless act. We think the fact there were options in the contract in favor of appellee is one element to be considered by the jury in determining damages, that is, the jury could consider the probability of the exercise of the options in determining the length of the term. * * *

In view of another trial it should be noted that on retrial the trial court should discount any future amounts recovered as salary to their present worth. Here the jury found appellee would have earned under his contract $156,000 and could earn from other employment $78,000. Judgment was given for $78,000. This should have been discounted to its present worth, based on the unexpired term of the contract at the date of judgment at the rate of 6% per annum. * * *

Notes

1. Taylor v. Tulsa Tribune Co., 136 F.2d 981, 983 (10th Cir.1943). Plaintiff entered into a written contract of employment, commencing work on February 1, 1933. Employment was wrongfully terminated; no services were rendered after

March 20, 1933. Plaintiff sued for damages in November, 1938. The trial court sustained the defense of a five year statute of limitations and dismissed the action. Affirming, the court stated:

"On the breach of the contract, the remedy in respect of the unpaid weekly amounts which had accrued was an action to recover for them as salary or compensation under the contract. But in respect of the weekly payments for the balance of the period and in respect of the increase in earnings for publication of display advertising, the sole remedy was an action for damages for the injury suffered as the result of the breach of the contract. * * *

"The cause of action for the weekly salary or compensation due prior to the breach of the contract accrued from week to week as the amounts became due. The cause of action for damages for the injury suffered as the result of the breach accrued at the time of the breach—on or before May 31, 1933. * * * And an action could have been instituted upon it immediately. * * * The action having been instituted more than five years after the cause of action pleaded in the complaint accrued, the statute of limitations raised its bar to recovery."

2. Lewis v. Loyola University of Chicago, 149 Ill.App.3d 88, 94, 500 N.E.2d 47, 51 (1986). "In Illinois, however, the damages awarded upon breach of an employment contract are limited to such damages as plaintiff may have accrued up to the date of trial, and damages beyond that date are disallowed due to their speculative and uncertain nature."

H. Specter & M. Finkin, Individual Employment Law and Litigation § 15.04 (1989): "Comment: The rationale behind decisions which limit or disallow damages beyond the date of trial conflicts with and seems to disregard the rule in tort actions for personal injury and wrongful death damages, where future lost earnings and impairment of earning capacity are determined routinely. Although such damages may not be susceptible of precise determination, they can be ascertained with reasonable specificity. There is no reason to reward the wrongdoer or contract breaker, due to the inability to calculate damages with precision, once the wrong has been established."

3. Loss of fringe benefits are also compensable damages. A university football coach enjoys many valuable perquisites as well as outside sources of income that are available only so long as the job lasts. Which "fringe" items represent compensation that the University might foresee that a coach would lose because of a wrongful firing? Check your list with Rodgers v. Georgia Tech Athletic Association, 166 Ga.App. 156, 303 S.E.2d 467 (1983):

"A. Benefits and Perquisites Received by Rodgers Directly from the Georgia Tech Athletic Association.

(1) gas, oil, maintenance, repairs, other automobile expenses;

(2) automobile liability and collision insurance;

(3) general expense money;

(4) meals available at the Georgia Tech training table;

(5) eight season tickets to Georgia Tech home football games during fall of 1980 and 1981;

(6) two reserved booths, consisting of approximately 40 seats at Georgia Tech home football games during fall of 1980 and 1981;

(7) six season tickets to Georgia Tech home basketball games for 1980 and 1981;

(8) four season tickets to Atlanta Falcon home football games for 1980 and 1981;

(9) four game tickets to each out-of-town Georgia Tech football game during fall of 1980 and 1981;

(10) pocket money at each home football game during fall 1980 and 1981;

(11) pocket money at each out-of-town Georgia Tech football game during fall of 1980 and 1981;

(12) parking privileges at all Georgia Tech home sporting events;

(13) the services of a secretary;

(14) the services of an administrative assistant;

(15) the cost of admission to Georgia Tech home baseball games during spring of 1980 and 1981;

(16) the cost of trips to football coaches' conventions, clinics, and meetings and to observe football practice sessions of professional and college football teams;

(17) initiation fee, dues, monthly bills, and cost of membership at the Capital City Club;

B. Benefits and Perquisites Received by Rodgers from Sources Other Than the Georgia Tech Athletic Association by Virtue of Being Head Coach of Football.

(1) profits from Rodgers' television football show, 'The Pepper Rodgers Show,' on Station WSB–TV in Atlanta for the fall of 1980 and 1981;

(2) profits from Rodgers' radio football show on Station WGST in Atlanta for the fall of 1980 and 1981;

(3) use of a new Cadillac automobile during 1980 and 1981;

(4) profits from Rodgers' summer football camp, known as the 'Pepper Rodgers Football School,' for June 1980 and June 1981;

(5) financial gifts from alumni and supporters of Georgia Tech for 1980 and 1981;

(6) lodging at any of the Holiday Inns owned by Topeka Inn Management, Inc. of Topeka, Kansas, for the time period from December 18, 1979 through December 31, 1981;

(7) the cost of membership in Terminus International Tennis Club in Atlanta for 1980 and 1981;

(8) individual game tickets to Hawks basketball and Braves baseball games during 1980 and 1981 seasons;

(9) housing for Rodgers and his family in Atlanta for the period from December 18, 1979 through December 31, 1981;

(10) the cost of premiums of a $400,000.00 policy on the life of Rodgers for the time period from December 18, 1979 through December 31, 1981."

4. *Consequential damages.* May a wrongfully discharged employee recover consequential damages for harm to her professional reputation caused by the discharge? In Redgrave v. Boston Symphony Orchestra, Inc., 855 F.2d 888 (1st Cir.1988), cert. denied, 488 U.S. 1043 (1989), Vanessa Redgrave claimed that she lost professional opportunities because the orchestra wrongfully cancelled her contract. The court first noted that contract claims for damage to reputation were frequently disallowed either because the loss was speculative or because the damages were not within the contemplation of the parties when the contract was executed. Plaintiff proved that certain specific job offers were cancelled because of

the discharge; these losses could be found to have been within the contemplation of the parties. An award of consequential damages was justified.

PARKER v. TWENTIETH CENTURY-FOX FILM CORP.

Supreme Court of California, 1970.
3 Cal.3d 176, 89 Cal.Rptr. 737, 474 P.2d 689.

BURKE, JUSTICE. * * * Plaintiff is well known as an actress, and in the contract between plaintiff and defendant is sometimes referred to as the "Artist." Under the contract, dated August 6, 1965, plaintiff was to play the female lead in defendant's contemplated production of a motion picture entitled "Bloomer Girl." The contract provided that defendant would pay plaintiff a minimum "guaranteed compensation" of $53,571.42 per week for 14 weeks commencing May 23, 1966, for a total of $750,000. Prior to May 1966 defendant decided not to produce the picture and by a letter dated April 4, 1966, it notified plaintiff of that decision and that it would not "comply with our obligations to you under" the written contract.

By the same letter and with the professed purpose "to avoid any damage to you," defendant instead offered to employ plaintiff as the leading actress in another film tentatively entitled "Big Country, Big Man" (hereinafter, "Big Country"). The compensation offered was identical, as were 31 of the 34 numbered provisions or articles of the original contract. Unlike "Bloomer Girl," however, which was to have been a musical production, "Big Country" was a dramatic "western type" movie. "Bloomer Girl" was to have been filmed in California; "Big Country" was to be produced in Australia. Also, certain terms in the proffered contract varied from those of the original. Plaintiff was given one week within which to accept; she did not and the offer lapsed. Plaintiff then commenced this action seeking recovery of the agreed guaranteed compensation. * * * [S]ummary judgment for $750,000 plus interest was entered in plaintiff's favor. This appeal by defendant followed. * * *

The general rule is that the measure of recovery by a wrongfully discharged employee is the amount of salary agreed upon for the period of service, less the amount which the employer affirmatively proves the employee has earned or with reasonable effort might have earned from other employment. * * * However, before projected earnings from other employment opportunities not sought or accepted by the discharged employee can be applied in mitigation, the employer must show that the other employment was comparable, or substantially similar, to that of which the employee has been deprived; the employee's rejection of or failure to seek other available employment of a different or inferior kind may not be resorted to in order to mitigate damages. * * *

In the present case defendant has raised no issue of *reasonableness of efforts* by plaintiff to obtain other employment; the sole issue is whether plaintiff's refusal of defendant's substitute offer of "Big Country" may be used in mitigation. Nor, if the "Big Country" offer was of employment different or inferior when compared with the original "Bloomer Girl" employment, is there an issue as to whether or not plaintiff acted reasonably in refusing the substitute offer. Despite defendant's arguments to the contrary, no case cited or which our research has discovered holds or suggests that reasonableness is an element of a wrongfully discharged employee's option to reject, or fail to seek, different or inferior employment lest the possible earnings therefrom be charged against him in mitigation of damages.[1]

Applying the foregoing rules to the record in the present case, with all intendments in favor of the party opposing the summary judgment motion—here, defendant—it is clear that the trial court correctly ruled that plaintiff's failure to accept defendant's tendered substitute employment could not be applied in mitigation of damages because the offer of the "Big Country" lead was of employment both different and inferior, and that no factual dispute was presented on that issue. The mere circumstance that "Bloomer Girl" was to be a musical review calling upon plaintiff's talents as a dancer as well as an actress, and was to be produced in the City of Los Angeles, where "Big Country" was a straight dramatic role in a "western type" story taking place in an opal mine in Australia, demonstrates the difference in kind between the two employments; the female lead as a dramatic actress in a western style motion picture can by no stretch of imagination be considered the equivalent of or substantially similar to the lead in a song-and-dance production.

Additionally, the substitute "Big Country" offer proposed to eliminate or impair the director and screenplay approvals accorded to plaintiff under the original "Bloomer Girl" contract, and thus constituted an offer of inferior employment. No expertise or judicial notice is required in order to hold that the deprivation or infringement of an employee's rights held under an original employment contract converts the available "other employment" relied upon by the employer to mitigate damages, into inferior employment which the employee need not seek or accept. * * *

[Affirmed]

SULLIVAN, ACTING CHIEF JUSTICE (dissenting). The familiar rule requiring a plaintiff in a tort or contract action to mitigate damages embodies notions of fairness and socially responsible behavior which are fundamental to our jurisprudence. Most broadly stated, it precludes the recovery of damages which, through the exercise of due diligence, could have been avoided. Thus, in essence, it is a rule requiring reasonable conduct in commercial affairs. This general principle governs the obligations of an employee after his employer has wrongfully repudiated or terminated the employment contract. Rather than permitting the employee simply to remain idle during the balance of the contract period, the law requires him to make a reasonable effort to secure

1. [Footnotes renumbered.] Instead, in each case the reasonableness referred to was that of the *efforts* of the employee to obtain other employment that was not different or inferior; his right to reject the latter was declared as an unqualified rule of law. Thus, Gonzales v. Internat. Assn. of Machinists, 213 Cal.App.2d 817, 823–824, 29 Cal.Rptr. 190, 194, holds that the trial court correctly instructed the jury that plaintiff union member, a machinist, was required to make "such efforts as the average [member of his union] desiring employment would make at that particular time and place" (italics added); but, further, that the court *properly rejected* defendant's *offer of proof of the availability of other kinds of employment* at the same or higher pay than plaintiff usually received and all outside the jurisdiction of his union, as plaintiff could not be required to accept different employment or a nonunion job.

In Harris v. Nat. Union of Marine Cooks and Stewards, 116 Cal.App.2d 759, 761, 254 P.2d 673, 676, the issues were stated to be, inter alia, whether comparable employment was open to each plaintiff employee, and if so whether each plaintiff made a *reasonable effort* to secure such employment. It was held that the trial court *properly sustained an objection to an offer to prove a custom of accepting a job in a lower rank* when work in the higher rank was not available, as "The duty of mitigation of damages * * * does not require the plaintiff 'to seek or to accept other employment of a different or inferior kind.' " * * *

other employment.[1] He is not obliged, however, to seek or accept any and all types of work which may be available. Only work which is in the same field and which is of the same quality need be accepted.

Over the years the courts have employed various phrases to define the type of employment which the employee, upon his wrongful discharge, is under an obligation to accept. Thus in California alone it has been held that he must accept employment which is "substantially similar" * * *; "comparable employment" * * *; employment "in the same general line of the first employment" * * *; "equivalent to his prior position" * * *; "employment in a similar capacity" * * *; employment which is "not * * * of a different or inferior kind." [citations]

For reasons which are unexplained, the majority cite several of these cases yet select from among the various judicial formulations which contain one particular phrase, "Not of a different or inferior kind," with which to analyze this case. I have discovered no historical or theoretical reason to adopt this phrase, which is simply a negative restatement of the affirmative standards set out in the above cases, as the exclusive standard. Indeed, its emergence is an example of the dubious phenomenon of the law responding not to rational judicial choice or changing social conditions, but to unrecognized changes in the language of opinions or legal treatises. However, the phrase is a serviceable one and my concern is not with its use as the standard but rather with what I consider its distortion. * * * It has never been the law that the mere existence of *differences between two jobs in the same field* is sufficient, as a matter of law, to excuse an employee wrongfully discharged from one from accepting the other in order to mitigate damages. Such an approach would effectively eliminate any obligation of an employee to attempt to minimize damage arising from a wrongful discharge. The only alternative job offer an employee would be required to accept would be an offer of his former job by his former employer.

I believe that the approach taken by the majority (a superficial listing of differences with no attempt to assess their significance) may subvert a valuable legal doctrine.[2] The inquiry in cases such as this should not be whether differences between the two jobs exist (there will always be differences) but whether the differences which are present are substantial enough to constitute differences in the *kind* of employment or, alternatively, whether they render the substitute work employment of an *inferior kind.*

* * * This necessitates a weighing of the evidence, and it is precisely this undertaking which is forbidden on summary judgment.

1. [Footnotes renumbered.] The issue is generally discussed in terms of a duty on the part of the employee to minimize loss. The practice is long-established and there is little reason to change despite Judge Cardozo's observation of its subtle inaccuracy. "The servant is free to accept employment or reject it according to his uncensored pleasure. What is meant by the supposed duty is merely this: That if he unreasonably reject, he will not be heard to say that the loss of wages from then on shall be deemed the jural consequence of the earlier discharge. He has broken the chain of causation, and loss resulting to him thereafter is suffered through his own act." (McClelland v. Climax Hosiery Mills (1930) 252 N.Y. 347, 359, 169 N.E. 605, 609, concurring opinion.)

2. The values of the doctrine of mitigation of damages in this context are that it minimizes the unnecessary personal and social (e.g., nonproductive use of labor, litigation) costs of contractual failure. If a wrongfully discharged employee can, through his own actions and without suffering financial or psychological loss in the process, reduce the damages accruing from the breach of contract, the most sensible policy is to require him to do so. I fear the majority opinion will encourage precisely opposite conduct.

Notes

1. The common law rules define substitute employment narrowly and do not allow the wrongfully discharged employee to retain income earned in nonsubstitute employment. Do these rules produce a "leisure windfall"? Is a risk-aversive discharged employee more likely to accept nonsubstitute employment?

Should courts expand the scope of the employee's duty to minimize damages by broadening the way they define substitute employment? Should courts give the employee a reasonable time to find comparable employment, then insist that the employee find other employment she is "fitted" for? How long should it take for the employee to lower her sights? Does this approach shift too many risks to the nonbreaching party and encourage employers to breach?

Do the common law rules discourage employers from terminating inefficient and uneconomical employment contracts? Can courts value an employee's expectancy at less than the full contract rate?

Professor Harrison suggests a "compensated duty rule" that will encourage a discharged worker to compare the value society places on her productive skills with the value she places on leisure and to limit her price for the contract rights to her expectancy.

"The compensated duty rule is designed to expand the scope of the duty to minimize, allow the employee to retain all income from nonsubstitute positions and reduce the size of any leisure windfall.

"An example will illustrate the approach. Suppose A, [a] wrongfully discharged aircraft designer, was earning $1,000 per month and had several months remaining on his contract when he was wrongfully discharged. If no reasonable substitutes were available, A could remain idle and collect damages equal to the contract wage. Suppose [an] ice cream sundae position were available at $500 per month. Under the expanded duty rule, after a reasonable time A's duty to minimize would extend to the job of making sundaes, and available earnings, whether obtained or not, would be credited to his former employer, B. Under the human capital approach the sundae job would not be within the scope of A's minimization duty, but if he did take the position he would be able to retain an amount equal to the newly acquired human capital component of the new position. If the components were allocated evenly, he would retain $250 and B would be credited with $250. A would receive the equivalent of $1,250 per month and he would, therefore, increase his income by $250 by accepting the position.

"The compensated duty rule reflects the view that there is little justification for allowing A to retain a fortuitous leisure windfall when reasonable substitutes are not available. In addition, B should be credited with the effort share of the income that A could have obtained by going beyond the common law duty to minimize, even if A declined to do so. Thus, under the rule, A's options would be either to accept the nonsubstitute employment and receive total income and damages of $1,250 per month or to decline the employment and receive damages equal to $750.[1]

"This approach is attractive for a number of reasons. First, the worker would make the re-entry decision on the basis of the full amount of potential income. Unlike the human capital strategy, in which the discharged worker would compare work disutility with a portion of income, here the worker would be more likely to

1. [Footnotes renumbered.] A would be indifferent to working for $1,000 and not working and receiving $750. Since the effort components of all positions are the same, $250 is the portion of the $1,000 that compensated *A* for foregoing leisure. Thus, either work and a $1,000 income or leisure and a $750 income gives *A* his expectancy.

make his decision independent of the breach. There is, however, an important difference between the re-entry decision and the original decision to contract. For example, although A would compare the ice cream sundae job with $500 income, he would be doing so while being assured of some income regardless of his decision. If the utility to A of additional income diminishes as his income increases, the assured income would influence his decision.[2] The decision would still be superior to that made under the common law because the worker would compare the value of his leisure to the value society attributes to his productivity.

"An additional advantage of this proposal is that it modifies the all-or-nothing nature of the common law rule. Under the common law rule, if the worker declines what is, in fact, a reasonable substitute, his recovery is reduced by the full amount that he could have earned. On the other hand, if the worker does accept employment[3] that is not a reasonable substitute, all of the income is credited to the former employer. Under the compensated duty approach, the risk involved in deciding to decline employment would be essentially the same as under the common law rule. The decision to accept employment would, however, be less risky than under the common law. If the new position were a reasonable substitute, the worker would receive the contracted-for compensation and suffer the contract disutility.[4] If it were not a reasonable substitute, he would still have improved his income position through the minimization efforts." Harrison, Wrongful Discharge: Toward a More Efficient Remedy, 56 Ind.L.J. 207, 232–233 (1981).

How would this rule have affected prebreach decisions and negotiations in Parker? Would it have changed the result?

2. Suppose a city police officer who "moonlights" as a security guard in a nightclub is wrongfully discharged from the police force. If he continues to serve as a guard during the period of his suspension, is the City entitled to credit earnings from the secondary job on the back pay award? Should the answer be different if he were discharged from private employment? See People ex rel. Bourne v. Johnson, 32 Ill.2d 324, 205 N.E.2d 470 (1965).

3. Blanton v. Mobil Oil Corp., 721 F.2d 1207, 1217 (9th Cir.1983):

"After Blanton and Healy were terminated by Mobil, they operated with considerable success, a service station leased from another oil company * * * [They] concede that after the third year of the breached [eight-year] contract, their actual income exceeded the projected income from the breached contract with Mobil. * * * We agree with Mobil that the mitigating income over the full life of the contract must be used to offset damages from the breach. Having asked the jury to compute damages over an 8–year contract period, Blanton and Healy cannot ignore the mitigating income over the full period. [B and H] argue that the contract can be divided into discrete periods of 1 year and that mitigated damages for any one period is recoverable, even if there is no net injury over the life of the contract. We cannot accept this novel statement of the law."

4. *Collateral Source Rule.* Does the employer have a right to reduce a wrongfully discharged employee's damages by the unemployment compensation the ex-employee collected? Some courts argue that the compensation is not from a

2. If the marginal utility of income does not decline over this income range, or if it declines very slowly, the existence of an assured income would have little or no impact on the re-employment decision.

3. The likelihood of this would depend on the risk aversion of the discharged worker. A risk-averse worker would be more likely to accept employment not within the common law duty to minimize.

4. A reasonable substitute position is one having basically the same disutility as the original position. A difference between the contract wage and the new wage will be part of the damages associated with the discharge.

collateral source since the employer pays into the fund; they allow the employer a deduction. See Mers v. Dispatch Printing Co., 39 Ohio App.3d 99, 529 N.E.2d 958 (1988); Dehnart v. Waukesha Brewing Co., 21 Wis.2d 583, 124 N.W.2d 664 (1963). Other courts disallow a reduction, ruling that an employer should not benefit because an employee worked long enough to qualify for unemployment compensation. Hayes v. Trulock, 51 Wash.App. 795, 755 P.2d 830 (1988); Seibel v. Liberty Homes, Inc., 305 Or. 362, 752 P.2d 291 (1988) (social security benefits).

FOLEY v. INTERACTIVE DATA CORPORATION

Supreme Court of California, In Bank, 1988.
47 Cal.3d 654, 254 Cal.Rptr. 211, 765 P.2d 373.

LUCAS, CHIEF JUSTICE. After Interactive Data Corporation (defendant) fired plaintiff Daniel D. Foley, an executive employee, he filed this action seeking compensatory and punitive damages for wrongful discharge. In his second amended complaint, plaintiff asserted three distinct theories: (1) a tort cause of action alleging a discharge in violation of public policy (Tameny v. Atlantic Richfield Co. (1980) 27 Cal.3d 167, 164 Cal.Rptr. 839, 610 P.2d 1330), (2) a contract cause of action for breach of an implied-in-fact promise to discharge for good cause only (e.g., Pugh v. See's Candies, Inc. (1981) 116 Cal.App.3d 311, 171 Cal.Rptr. 917 [all references are to this case rather than the 1988 post-trial decision appearing at 203 Cal.App.3d 743, 250 Cal.Rptr. 195]), and (3) a cause of action alleging a tortious breach of the implied covenant of good faith and fair dealing (e.g., Cleary v. American Airlines, Inc. (1980) 111 Cal.App.3d 443, 168 Cal.Rptr. 722).

According to the complaint, plaintiff is a former employee of defendant, a wholly owned subsidiary of Chase Manhattan Bank that markets computer-based decision-support services. Defendant hired plaintiff in June 1976 as an assistant product manager at a starting salary of $18,500.

Over the next six years and nine months, plaintiff received a steady series of salary increases, promotions, bonuses, awards and superior performance evaluations. * * * He alleges defendant's officers made repeated oral assurances of job security so long as his performance remained adequate.

Plaintiff also alleged that during his employment, defendant maintained written "Termination Guidelines" that set forth express grounds for discharge and a mandatory seven-step pretermination procedure. Plaintiff understood that these guidelines applied not only to employees under plaintiff's supervision, but to him as well. On the basis of these representations, plaintiff alleged that he reasonably believed defendant would not discharge him except for good cause, and therefore he refrained from accepting or pursuing other job opportunities.

The event that led to plaintiff's discharge was a private conversation in January 1983 with his former supervisor, vice president Richard Earnest. During the previous year defendant had hired Robert Kuhne and subsequently named Kuhne to replace Earnest as plaintiff's immediate supervisor. Plaintiff learned that Kuhne was currently under investigation by the Federal Bureau of Investigation for embezzlement from his former employer, Bank of America. Plaintiff reported what he knew about Kuhne to Earnest, because he was "worried about working for Kuhne and having him in a supervisory position, * * * in view of Kuhne's suspected criminal conduct." Plaintiff asserted he "made this disclosure in the interest and for the benefit of his employer," allegedly because he believed that because defendant and its parent do business with the financial community on a confidential basis, the company would have a legitimate interest in knowing about a high executive's alleged prior criminal conduct.

In response, Earnest allegedly told plaintiff not to discuss "rumors" and to "forget what he heard" about Kuhne's past. In early March, Kuhne informed plaintiff that defendant had decided to replace him for "performance reasons" and that he could transfer to a position in another division in Waltham, Massachusetts. [Plaintiff was discharged shortly thereafter.]

Defendant demurred to all three causes of action. After plaintiff filed two amended pleadings, the trial court sustained defendant's demurrer without leave to amend and dismissed all three causes of action. The Court of Appeal affirmed the dismissal as to all three counts. We will explore each claim in turn.

We turn first to plaintiff's cause of action alleging he was discharged in violation of public policy. Labor Code section 2922 provides in relevant part, "An employment, having no specified term, may be terminated at the will of either party on notice to the other." This presumption may be superseded by a contract, express or implied, limiting the employer's right to discharge the employee. Absent any contract, however, the employment is "at will," and the employee can be fired with or without good cause. But the employer's right to discharge an "at will" employee is still subject to limits imposed by public policy, since otherwise the threat of discharge could be used to coerce employees into committing crimes, concealing wrongdoing, or taking other action harmful to the public weal.

* * * Tameny v. Atlantic Richfield Co., declared that a tort action for wrongful discharge may lie if the employer "condition[s] employment upon required participation in unlawful conduct by the employee." In *Tameny,* the plaintiff alleged he was fired for refusing to engage in price fixing in violation of the Cartwright Act and the Sherman Antitrust Act. We held the trial court erred in sustaining Atlantic Richfield's demurrer to plaintiff's tort action for wrongful discharge. Writing for the majority, Justice Tobriner concluded that "an employer's authority over its employee does not include the right to demand that the employee commit a criminal act to further its interests. * * * An employer engaging in such conduct violates a basic duty imposed by law upon all employers, and thus an employee who has suffered damages as a result of such discharge may maintain a tort action for wrongful discharge against the employer." As we explained, "an employer's obligation to refrain from discharging an employee who refuses to commit a criminal act does not depend upon any express or implied ' "promise[s] set forth in the [employment] contract" ' [citation], but rather reflects a duty imposed by law upon all employers in order to implement the fundamental public policies embodied in the state's penal statutes. As such, a wrongful discharge suit exhibits the classic elements of a tort cause of action."

In the present case, plaintiff alleges that defendant discharged him in "sharp derogation" of a substantial public policy that imposes a legal duty on employees to report relevant business information to management. An employee is an agent, and as such "is required to disclose to [his] principal all information he has relevant to the subject matter of the agency." Thus, plaintiff asserts, if he discovered information that might lead his employer to conclude that an employee was an embezzler, and should not be retained, plaintiff had a duty to communicate that information to his principal.

Whether or not there is a statutory duty requiring an employee to report information relevant to his employer's interest, we do not find a substantial public policy prohibiting an employer from discharging an employee for performing that duty. Past decisions recognizing a tort action for discharge in violation of public policy seek to protect the public, by protecting the employee who refuses to commit a crime. No equivalent public interest bars the discharge of the present plaintiff. When the duty of an employee to disclose information to his employer serves only the private interest of the employer, the rationale underlying the *Tameny* cause of action is not implicated.

We conclude that the Court of Appeal properly upheld the trial court's ruling sustaining the demurrer without leave to amend to plaintiff's first cause of action.

Plaintiff's second cause of action alleged that over the course of his nearly seven years of employment with defendant, the company's own conduct and personnel policies gave rise to an "oral contract" not to fire him without good cause. [The court ruled that the claim was not barred by the Statute of Frauds.]

Although plaintiff describes his cause of action as one for breach of an oral contract, he does not allege explicit words by which the parties agreed that he would not be terminated without good cause. Instead he alleges that a course of conduct, including various oral representations, created a reasonable expectation to that effect. Thus, his cause of action is more properly described as one for breach of an implied-in-fact contract.

Before this court, defendant urges that we disapprove precedent permitting a cause of action for wrongful discharge founded on an implied-in-fact contract and require instead an express contract provision requiring good cause for termination, supported by independent consideration. Alternatively, defendant requests that we distinguish *Pugh* and its progeny from the present case. We conclude, however, that *Pugh* correctly applied basic contract principles in the employment context, and that these principles are applicable to plaintiff's agreement with defendant.

The plaintiff in *Pugh* had been employed by the defendant for 32 years, during which time he worked his way up the corporate ladder from dishwasher to vice president. When hired, he had been assured that "if you are loyal * * * and do a good job, your future is secure." During his long employment, the plaintiff received numerous commendations and promotions, and no significant criticism of his work. Throughout this period the company maintained a practice of not terminating administrative personnel without good cause. On this evidence, the Court of Appeal concluded that the jury could determine the existence of an implied promise that the employer would not arbitrarily terminate the plaintiff's employment.

A review of other jurisdictions also reveals a strong trend in favor of recognizing implied contract terms that modify the power of an employer to discharge an employee at will. [citations]

We begin by acknowledging the fundamental principle of freedom of contract: employer and employee are free to agree to a contract terminable at will or subject to limitations. Their agreement will be enforced so long as it does not violate legal strictures external to the contract, such as laws affecting union membership and activity, prohibitions on indentured servitude, or the many other legal restrictions already described which place certain restraints on the employment arrangement. As we have discussed, Labor Code section 2922 establishes a presumption of at-will employment if the parties have made no express oral or written agreement specifying the length of employment or the grounds for termination. This presumption may, however, be overcome by evidence that despite the absence of a specified term, the parties agreed that the employer's power to terminate would be limited in some way, e.g., by a requirement that termination be based only on "good cause."

Defendant contends that courts should not enforce employment security agreements in the absence of evidence of independent consideration and an express manifestation of mutual assent. Although, as explained below, there may be some historical basis for imposing such limitations, any such basis has been eroded by the development of modern contract law and, accordingly, we conclude that defendant's suggested limitations are inappropriate in the modern employment context. We discern no basis for departing from otherwise applicable general contract principles.

The limitations on employment security terms on which defendant relies were developed during a period when courts were generally reluctant to look beyond explicit promises of the parties to a contract. "The court-imposed presumption that the employment contract is terminable at will relies upon the formalistic approach to contract interpretation predominant in late nineteenth century legal thought: manifestations of assent must be evidenced by definite, express terms if promises are to be enforceable." (Note, Protecting At Will Employees, 93 Harv.L.Rev. at p. 1825, fns. omitted.) In the intervening decades, however, courts increasingly demonstrated their willingness to examine the entire relationship of the parties to commercial contracts to ascertain their actual intent, and this trend has been reflected in the body of law guiding contract interpretation. (See, Goetz & Scott, The Limits of Expanded Choice: An Analysis of the Interactions Between Express and Implied Contract Terms (1985) 73 Cal.L.Rev. 261, 273–276.

Similarly, 20 years ago, Professor Blumrosen observed that during the decades preceding his analysis, courts had demonstrated an increasing willingness to "consider the entire relationship of the parties, and to find that facts and circumstances establish a contract which cannot be terminated by the employer without cause." (Blumrosen, Settlement of Disputes Concerning the Exercise of Employer Disciplinary Power: United States Report, 18 Rutgers L.Rev. at p. 432, fn. omitted.) "This approach has been recognized as consistent with customary interpretation techniques of commercial contracts permitting 'gap filling' by implication of reasonable terms." Miller & Estes, Recent Judicial Limitations on the Right to Discharge: A California Trilogy (1982) 16 U.C.Davis L.Rev. 65, 101, fn. omitted.

Finally, we do not agree with the Court of Appeal that employment security agreements are so inherently harmful or unfair to employers, who do not receive equivalent guarantees of continued service, as to merit treatment different from that accorded other contracts. On the contrary, employers may benefit from the increased loyalty and productivity that such agreements may inspire. Permitting proof of and reliance on implied-in-fact contract terms does not nullify the at-will rule, it merely treats such contracts in a manner in keeping with general contract law.

Defendant's remaining argument is that even if a promise to discharge "for good cause only" could be implied in fact, the evidentiary factors outlined in *Pugh,* and relied on by plaintiff, are inadequate as a matter of law. This contention fails on several grounds.

First, defendant overemphasizes the fact that plaintiff was employed for "only" six years and nine months. Length of employment is a relevant consideration but six years and nine months is sufficient time for conduct to occur on which a trier of fact could find the existence of an implied contract. Plaintiff here alleged repeated oral assurances of job security and consistent promotions, salary increases and bonuses during the term of his employment contributing to his reasonable expectation that he would not be discharged except for good cause.

Second, an allegation of breach of written "Termination Guidelines" implying self-imposed limitations on the employer's power to discharge at will may be sufficient to state a cause of action for breach of an employment contract. *Pugh* is not alone in holding that the trier of fact can infer an agreement to limit the grounds for termination based on the employee's reasonable reliance on the company's personnel manual or policies. [citations]

Finally, unlike the employee in *Pugh,* plaintiff alleges that he supplied the company valuable and separate consideration by signing an agreement whereby he promised not to compete or conceal any computer-related information from defendant for one year after termination. The noncompetition agreement and its attendant "Disclosure and Assignment of Proprietary Information, Inventions, etc." may be probative evidence that "it is more probable that the parties intended a continuing relationship, with limitations upon the employer's dismissal authority [because the] employee has provided some benefit to the employer, or suffers some detriment, beyond the usual rendition of service."

In sum, plaintiff has pleaded facts which, if proved, may be sufficient for a jury to find an implied-in-fact contract limiting defendant's right to discharge him arbitrarily—facts sufficient to overcome the presumption of Labor Code section 2922. On demurrer, we must assume these facts to be true. In other words, plaintiff has pleaded an implied-in-fact contract and its breach, and is entitled to his opportunity to prove those allegations.

We turn now to plaintiff's cause of action for tortious breach of the implied covenant of good faith and fair dealing.

The distinction between tort and contract is well grounded in common law, and divergent objectives underlie the remedies created in the two areas. Whereas contract actions are created to enforce the intentions of the parties to the agreement, tort law is primarily designed to vindicate "social policy." (Prosser, Law of Torts (4th ed. 1971) p. 613.) The covenant of good faith and fair dealing was developed in the contract arena and is aimed at making effective the agreement's promises. Plaintiff asks that we find that the breach of the implied covenant in employment contracts also gives rise to an action seeking an award of tort damages.

In this instance, where an extension of tort remedies is sought for a duty whose breach previously has been compensable by contractual remedies, it is helpful to consider certain principles relevant to contract law. First, predictability about the cost of contractual relationships plays an important role in our commercial system (Putz & Klippen, Commercial Bad Faith: Attorney Fees—Not Tort Liability—Is the Remedy for "Stonewalling" (1987) 21 U.S.F.L. Rev. 419, 432). Moreover, "Courts traditionally have awarded damages for breach of contract to compensate the aggrieved party rather than to punish the breaching party." Note, "Contort": Tortious Breach of the Implied Covenant of Good Faith and Fair Dealing in Noninsurance, Commercial Contracts—Its Existence and Desirability (1985) 60 Notre Dame L.Rev. 510, 526, & fn. 94. With these concepts in mind, we turn to analyze the role of the implied covenant of good faith and fair dealing and the propriety of the extension of remedies urged by plaintiff.

"Every contract imposes upon each party a duty of good faith and fair dealing in its performance and its enforcement." (Rest.2d Contracts, § 205.) This duty has been recognized in the majority of American jurisdictions, the Restatement, and the Uniform Commercial Code. (Burton, Breach of Contract and the Common Law Duty to Perform in Good Faith (1980) 94 Harv.L.Rev. 369.) Because the covenant is a contract term, however, compensation for its breach has almost always been limited to contract rather than tort remedies. * * * Initially, the concept of a duty of good faith developed in contract law as "a kind of 'safety valve' to which judges may turn to fill gaps and qualify or limit rights and duties otherwise arising under rules of law and specific contract language." (Summers, The General Duty of Good Faith—Its Recognition and Conceptualization (1982) 67 Cornell L.Rev. 810, 812.) As a contract concept, breach of the duty led to imposition of contract damages determined by the nature of the breach and standard contract principles.

An exception to this general rule has developed in the context of insurance contracts where, for a variety of policy reasons, courts have held that breach of the implied covenant will provide the basis for an action in tort. California has a well-developed judicial history addressing this exception. In Comunale v. Traders & General Ins. Co. (1958) 50 Cal.2d 654, 658, 328 P.2d 198, we stated, "There is an implied covenant of good faith and fair dealing in every contract that neither party will do anything which will injure the right of the other to receive the benefits of the agreement." Thereafter, in Crisci v. Security Ins. Co. (1967) 66 Cal.2d 425, 58 Cal.Rptr. 13, 426 P.2d 173, for the first time we permitted an insured to recover in tort for emotional damages caused by the insurer's breach of the implied covenant. * * *

The first California appellate case to permit tort recovery in the employment context was *Cleary*. To support its holding that tort as well as contract damages were appropriate to compensate for a breach of the implied covenant, the *Cleary* court relied on insurance cases without engaging in comparative analysis of insurance and employment relationships and without inquiring into whether the insurance cases' departure from established principles of contract law should generally be subject to expansion.

* * * When a court enforces the implied covenant it is in essence acting to protect "the interest in having promises performed" (Prosser, Law of Torts (4th ed. 1971) p. 613)—the traditional realm of a contract action—rather than to protect some general duty to society which the law places on an employer without regard to the substance of its contractual obligations to its employee. Thus, in *Tameny,* as we have explained, the court was careful to draw a

distinction between "ex delicto" and "ex contractu" obligations. An allegation of breach of the implied covenant of good faith and fair dealing is an allegation of breach of an "ex contractu" obligation, namely one arising out of the contract itself. The covenant of good faith is read into contracts in order to protect the express covenants or promises of the contract, not to protect some general public policy interest not directly tied to the contract's purposes. The insurance cases thus were a major departure from traditional principles of contract law. We must, therefore, consider with great care claims that extension of the exceptional approach taken in those cases is automatically appropriate if certain hallmarks and similarities can be adduced in another contract setting. With this emphasis on the historical purposes of the covenant of good faith and fair dealing in mind, we turn to consider the bases upon which extension of the insurance model to the employment sphere has been urged.

The "special relationship" test gleaned from the insurance context has been suggested as a model for determining the appropriateness of permitting tort remedies for breach of the implied covenant of the employment context. * * *

After review of the various commentators, and independent consideration of the similarities between the two areas, we are not convinced that a "special relationship" analogous to that between insurer and insured should be deemed to exist in the usual employment relationship which would warrant recognition of a tort action for breach of the implied covenant. Even if we were to assume that the special relationship model is an appropriate one to follow in determining whether to expand tort recovery, a breach in the employment context does not place the employee in the same economic dilemma that an insured faces when an insurer in bad faith refuses to pay a claim or to accept a settlement offer within policy limits. When an insurer takes such actions, the insured cannot turn to the marketplace to find another insurance company willing to pay for the loss already incurred. The wrongfully terminated employee, on the other hand, can (and must, in order to mitigate damages [see Parker v. Twentieth Century–Fox Film Corp.]) make reasonable efforts to seek alternative employment. Moreover, the role of the employer differs from that of the "quasi-public" insurance company with whom individuals contract specifically in order to obtain protection from potential specified economic harm. The employer does not similarly "sell" protection to its employees; it is not providing a public service. Nor do we find convincing the idea that the employee is necessarily seeking a different kind of financial security than those entering a typical commercial contract. If a small dealer contracts for goods from a large supplier, and those goods are vital to the small dealer's business, a breach by the supplier may have financial significance for individuals employed by the dealer or to the dealer himself. Permitting only contract damages in such a situation has ramifications no different from a similar limitation in the direct employer-employee relationship.

Finally, there is a fundamental difference between insurance and employment relationships. In the insurance relationship, the insurer's and insured's interest are financially at odds. If the insurer pays a claim, it diminishes its fiscal resources. The insured of course has paid for protection and expects to have its losses recompensed. When a claim is paid, money shifts from insurer to insured, or, if appropriate, to a third party claimant.

Putting aside already specifically barred improper motives for termination which may be based on both economic and noneconomic considerations, as a general rule it is to the employer's economic benefit to retain good employees. The interests of employer and employee are most frequently in alignment. If there is a job to be done, the employer must still pay someone to do it. This is not to say that there may never be a "bad motive" for discharge not otherwise covered by law. Nevertheless, in terms of abstract employment relationships as contrasted with abstract insurance relationships, there is less inherent relevant tension between the interests of employers and employees than exists between that of insurers and insureds. Thus the need to place disincentives on an employer's conduct in addition to those already imposed by law simply does not rise to the same level as that created by the conflicting interests at stake in the insurance context. Nor is this to say that the Legislature would have no basis for affording employees additional protections. It is, however, to say that the need to extend the special relationship model in the form of judicially created relief of the kind sought here is less compelling.

We therefore conclude that the employment relationship is not sufficiently similar to that of insurer and insured to warrant judicial extension of the proposed additional tort remedies in view of the countervailing concerns about economic policy and stability, the traditional separation of tort and contract law, and finally, the numerous protections against improper terminations already afforded employees.

Our inquiry, however, does not end here. The potential effects on an individual caused by termination of employment arguably justify additional remedies for certain improper discharges. * * *

The issue is how far courts can or should go in responding to these concerns regarding the sufficiency of compensation by departing from long established principles of contract law. Significant policy judgments affecting social policies and commercial relationships are implicated in the resolution of this question in the employment termination context. Such a determination, which has the potential to alter profoundly the nature of employment, the cost of products and services, and the availability of jobs, arguably is better suited for legislative decisionmaking.

It cannot be disputed that legislation at both the state and national level has profoundly affected the scope of at-will terminations. As noted, regulation of employment ranging from workers' compensation laws to antidiscrimination enactments, fair labor standards, minimum compensation, regulation of hours, etc., all have significantly impinged on the laissez-faire underpinnings of the at-will rule. Moreover, unionization of a portion of the domestic workforce has substantial implications for the judicial development of employment termination law because the rights of such workers when terminated are often governed exclusively by the terms of applicable collective bargaining agreements. The slate we write on thus is far from clean.

We are not unmindful of the legitimate concerns of employees who fear arbitrary and improper discharges that may have a devastating effect on their economic and social status. Nor are we unaware of or unsympathetic to claims that contract remedies for breaches of contract are insufficient because they do not fully compensate due to their failure to include attorney fees and their restrictions on foreseeable damages. These defects, however, exist generally in contract situations. As discussed above, the variety of possible courses to remedy the problem is well demonstrated in the literature and include increased contract damages, provision for award of attorney fees, establishment of arbitration or other speedier and less expensive dispute resolution, or the tort remedies (the scope of which is also subject to dispute) sought by plaintiff here.

The diversity of possible solutions demonstrates the confusion that occurs when we look outside the realm of contract law in attempting to fashion remedies for a breach of a contract provision. As noted, numerous legislative provisions have imposed obligations on parties to contracts which vindicate significant social policies extraneous to the contract itself. As Justice Kaus observed in his concurring and dissenting opinion in White v. Western Title Ins. Co. (1985) 40 Cal.3d 870, 901, 221 Cal.Rptr. 509, 710 P.2d 309, "our experience * * * surely tells us that there are real problems in applying the substitute remedy of a tort recovery—with or without punitive damages—outside the insurance area. In other words, I believe that under all the circumstances, the problem is one for the Legislature. * * *"

Plaintiff may proceed with his cause of action alleging a breach of an implied-in-fact contract promise to discharge him only for good cause; his claim is not barred by the statute of frauds. His cause of action for a breach of public policy pursuant to *Tameny* was properly dismissed because the facts alleged, even if proven, would not establish a discharge in violation of public policy. Finally, as to his cause of action for tortious breach of the implied covenant of good faith and fair dealing, we hold that tort remedies are not available for breach of the implied covenant in an employment contract to employees who allege they have been discharged in violation of the covenant.

BROUSSARD, JUSTICE, concurring and dissenting. I maintain that we should retain the well-recognized tort cause of action for bad faith discharge. To demonstrate the point, I propose to show (1) that a tort cause of action for bad faith discharge is an established feature of California common law; (2) that the analogy between the insurance cases, in which a tort cause of action has long been recognized, justifies tort recovery for bad faith discharge; (3) that the existence of a cause of action in contract for discharge in breach of contract does not exclude a tort action for bad faith; and (4) that it is fundamentally illogical to abolish a tort cause of action on the ground that radical change in existing remedies should be left to legislative action.

A tort action for bad faith discharge * * * requires that the discharge be wrongful—that is, in breach of contract. But once that prerequisite is satisfied, it focuses not upon the employee's right to enforce a particular contractual provision, but upon society's right to deter and demand redress for arbitrary or malicious conduct which inflicts harm upon one of its members. This is the proper and traditional function of tort law.

Notes

1. As *Foley* indicates, the courts have used several different substantive theories to undermine the "at will" doctrine:

a. Contracts implied in fact. As in *Foley,* courts have been resourceful in finding promises for continued employment from employee manuals or from supervisors' verbal assurances. Diggs v. Pepsi–Cola Metropolitan Bottling Co., 861 F.2d 914 (6th Cir.1988) (assurance that discharge would be for "just cause" only); Toussaint v. Blue Cross & Blue Shield, 408 Mich. 579, 613–615, 292 N.W.2d 880,

891–892 (1980); Weiner v. McGraw–Hill, Inc., 57 N.Y.2d 458, 457 N.Y.S.2d 193, 443 N.E.2d 441 (1982). These courts award the employee contract damages based on a breach of the implied promise.

b. If the employee's discharge violates public policy, the employee has a tort claim for damages. The court in *Foley* recognized this possibility, but it ruled that the plaintiff had failed to show breach of any public policy. Compare Vigil v. Arzola, 102 N.M. 682, 699 P.2d 613 (App.1983), rev'd, 101 N.M. 687, 687 P.2d 1038 (1984) (retaliatory discharge for disclosing the misapplication of state funds); Southwest Forest Industries, Inc. v. Sutton, 868 F.2d 352 (10th Cir.1989), cert. denied, 110 S.Ct. 1320 (1990) (retaliatory discharge for filing a workers' compensation claim); Niblo v. Parr Manufacturing, 445 N.W.2d 351 (Iowa 1989) (semble); Cloutier v. Great Atlantic & Pacific Tea Co., 121 N.H. 915, 436 A.2d 1140 (1981) (violation of a public policy against allowing a hazardous environment). Since the underlying theory of these claims is tort, plaintiff may recover damages for emotional distress and punitive damages. See *Niblo* and *Southwest Forest Industries* above and Wiskotoni v. Michigan National Bank–West, 716 F.2d 378 (6th Cir.1983) where the court awarded punitive damages in addition to compensatory damages for mental anguish that resulted from loss of status and an unsuccessful search for a new job. The New Mexico court in *Vigil,* however, rejected nonpecuniary damages because it feared a "chilling effect on the employer's freedom in hiring." Vigil v. Arzola, 102 N.M. 682, 690, 699 P.2d 613, 621 (App.1983), rev'd, 101 N.M. 687, 687 P.2d 1038 (1984).

c. Several courts have recognized a covenant of good faith and fair dealing in employment contracts. But, as in *Foley,* damages have apparently been limited to contract-type losses. See McKinney v. National Dairy Council, 491 F.Supp. 1108, 1122 (D.Mass.1980); Maddaloni v. Western Massachusetts Bus Lines, Inc., 386 Mass. 877, 438 N.E.2d 351 (1982); Fortune v. National Cash Register Co., 373 Mass. 96, 364 N.E.2d 1251 (1977). Some courts, however, have treated the breach of the covenant as tortious and have allowed punitive damages. See Flanigan v. Prudential Federal Savings & Loan Association, 221 Mont. 419, 720 P.2d 257, cert. dismissed, 479 U.S. 980 (1986); K Mart Corp. v. Ponsock, 103 Nev. 39, 732 P.2d 1364 (1987) (tenured employee).

Consider the following comment from H. Specter & M. Finkin, Individual Employment Law and Litigation, § 10.53 (Supp.1989): "Comment: * * * The covenant of good faith and fair dealing represents an effort by the courts to reestablish limits on the employer's ability to abuse its power in the employment relationship." So we have gone from status to contract and now back to status.

d. As the court stated in *Foley,* wrongfully discharged employees may have remedies provided by statute. Federal civil rights legislation is a common source of claims where the employee asserts that the discharge was the result of unlawful discrimination based on gender, race, age, or religion. Where the employee establishes a violation of Title VII of the Civil Rights Act or the Age Discrimination in Employment Act, an award may include back pay, front pay, reinstatement or other equitable or declaratory relief. Babcock v. Frank, 729 F.Supp. 279 (S.D.N.Y. 1990) (sexual harassment); Fite v. First Tennessee Production Credit Association, 861 F.2d 884 (6th Cir.1988) (age discrimination); Bonura v. Chase Manhattan Bank, N.A., 629 F.Supp. 353 (S.D.N.Y.1986) (age discrimination). Unlike Civil Rights claims under Section 1983, compensatory and punitive damages are not available under Title VII. See Babcock v. Frank, supra. For a further discussion of Section 1983 actions, see supra, Chapter 7.

2. H. Specter & M. Finkin, Individual Employment Law and Litigation § 15.11 (1989): "Comment: * * * It is appropriate to note the collateral role [of

punitive damages and damages for emotional distress] in enabling wronged employees to compensate somewhat for the often inherently disparate litigating power of the employer by securing counsel on a contingent fee basis. Unless the contingent fee is paid wholly or partially through the recovery of such damages, the employee may be unable to afford counsel, and any victory may be hollow indeed."

3. Most of the decisions have been based on pleadings, and in others the components of the remedy have not been well explained. Clearly tort, contract, restitution, and statute have merged in this legal revolution. Remedial questions will emerge. What statute of limitations governs? Has plaintiff a duty to seek comparable employment? Are damages limited to back pay? May the discharged employee be awarded a severance payment? Are special damages limited by Hadley v. Baxendale or proximate cause? May plaintiff recover for emotional distress, mental anguish or suffering, and pain and suffering? Are punitive damages available? May the judge order the employer to reinstate plaintiff? May plaintiff's spouse sue for lost consortium?

4. The employer's answer is to draft employment at will contracts to forestall litigation. Summary judgment has been granted in favor of Michigan employers on the basis of this contract language: "In consideration of my employment, I agree to conform to the rules and regulations of Sears, Roebuck and Co., and my employment and compensation can be terminated, with or without cause, and with or without notice, at any time, at the option of either the Company or myself. I understand that no store manager or representative of Sears, Roebuck and Co., other than the president or vice-president of the Company, has any authority to enter into any agreement for employment for any specified period of time, or to make any agreement contrary to the foregoing." Batchelor v. Sears, Roebuck & Co., 574 F.Supp. 1480, 1483 (E.D.Mich.1983).

2. RESTITUTION

CHAMBLISS, BAHNER & CRAWFORD v. LUTHER

Court of Appeals, Tennessee, 1975.
531 S.W.2d 108.

GODDARD, JUDGE. This is a suit by a firm of attorneys for collection of a fee for a previous lawsuit. Plaintiff–Appellant Chambliss, Bahner, and Crawford is a Chattanooga law firm whose senior partner, Jac Chambliss, represented Defendants–Appellees in a lawsuit against the Detrex Corporation in a stock securities matter.

The case arose in the following manner: Mr. Chambliss had been engaged as an attorney by Lutex, Inc. since the formation of the corporation, and owned a few shares of its stock. In 1968 Detrex, a large chemical firm, became interested in acquiring Lutex and as a result of the ensuing negotiations, Detrex absorbed the smaller concern. The absorption was accomplished by an exchange of stock, the stockholders of Lutex receiving Detrex stock in exchange for their interest in Lutex.

In the latter part of 1969, the former principal shareholders of Lutex became concerned that the stock they had received was not as valuable as they had been led to believe. They contacted Attorney Chambliss, who took the case and managed to secure a compromise settlement offer of $860,000 from Detrex. The former stockholders of Lutex were not satisfied with this offer and decided to bring suit against Detrex for a violation of securities regulations.

On June 5, 1971, Attorney Chambliss was retained to bring that suit upon a contingency fee basis. It was agreed that his fee would be 15 percent of the recovery above the compromise offer.

The stockholders became dissatisfied with his representation. About one year after the suit was filed, the stockholders suggested to Attorney Chambliss that another local attorney, John I. Foster, Jr., be associated in the case. Mr. Foster's association was with the approval of Mr. Chambliss. They agreed among themselves that the division of the 15 percent contingency fee would be 70 percent to Chambliss and 30 percent to Foster. Thereafter, Attorney Foster was made lead counsel for the litigation by the stockholders. Chambliss did not approve of this move and withdrew as counsel by letter dated May 15, 1972. * * *

On October 31, 1972, that suit was settled for the sum of $965,150, a betterment of $105,150 over the base offer. It was agreed that Attorney Chambliss did not take part in the negotiations which led to the final settlement, although as counsel of record he approved the order of settlement and, as a stockholder, raised no objection. He received for his stock some $46,000 on an investment of $2,000.

Under the contingency fee contract, Attorney Chambliss' 15 percent would have been $15,772.50. The Chancellor in the present action held that the contract of employment had been breached by the appointment of Attorney Foster as lead counsel, but that the damages to Attorney Chambliss should be limited to the contract price. Attorney Chambliss seeks recovery in quantum meruit, claiming that he and his brother have spent over 1,000 hours on this lawsuit over the period of two years and that he is entitled to reasonable compensation for these services apart from the contract. The testimony as to the reasonable value of his services ranged from $60,000 to $175,000.

Under Tennessee law—and it appears the rule is practically universal—a client is entitled to discharge his attorney with or without cause.

Plaintiff while recognizing this rule, insists that because Defendants breached the employment contract it is entitled to proceed on the basis of quantum meruit and its recovery is not limited by the amount of the original contract. * * *

Plaintiff cites Re Montgomery, which unquestionably stands for the proposition he propounds. In that case an attorney for an estate, who had a contract fee for a fixed amount, was discharged without cause. The Court allowed the attorney to recover a sum in excess of his contract fee on the basis of quantum meruit. In so doing, the Court of Appeals of New York reasoned:

> "In the case at bar the recovery allowed is upon the basis of quantum meruit without regard to the contract price, and the question for determination is whether the right of the attorney to recover is limited by the contract price of $5,000.
>
> "Thus far it has been decided that the discharge of the attorney canceled and annulled the contract and that the contract having been canceled, it could not limit the amount of the recovery although it might be considered in fixing the amount of the reasonable value of the services rendered; the theory being that the cancellation could not be a half way cancellation.
>
> "Under that theory, the contract price does not constitute a limitation on the amount of an attorney's recovery, although its effect may be to enhance the

amount the client may be compelled to pay and in a certain sense penalizes the client for exercising a privilege given by law to discharge an attorney at will regardless of cause." Re Montgomery, 272 N.Y. 323, 6 N.E.2d 40, 41 (1936). * * *

[A] California Supreme Court case, Fracasse v. Brent, 6 Cal.3d 784, 100 Cal.Rptr. 385, 494 P.2d 9 (1972), uses language which we think is instructive:

"We have concluded that a client should have both the power and the right at any time to discharge his attorney with or without cause. Such a discharge does not constitute a breach of contract for the reason that it is a basic term of the contract, implied by law into it by reason of the special relationship between the contracting parties, that the client may terminate that contract at will. It would be anomalous and unjust to hold the client liable in damages for exercising that basic implied right." * * *

The only case we can find directly in point which is supportive of defendants' position, is Moore v. Fellner, 50 Cal.2d 330, 325 P.2d 857 (1958), wherein the California Supreme Court said:

"As declared in Salopek v. Schoemann (1942), 20 Cal.2d 150, 153[1], 155[3], 124 P.2d 21, 'if an attorney is discharged for sufficient cause he is entitled to no more than the reasonable value of his missing services rendered prior to his discharge,' has 'no cause to complain and is fully protected by payment of the reasonable value,' and may not recover the full contract amount (at least if such amount exceeds the reasonable value of the services). On the other hand in a case in which the discharge appears to have been without cause, it has been held that where the contract amount is less than the reasonable value of the services, recovery is nevertheless limited to the fee fixed by the contract. [citation] In the present case plaintiff sought and was awarded judgment based on reasonable value. Under the rules above stated his recovery must not, of course, exceed the fee fixed by the employment contract, less expenses to which the client (defendant) was put by the change of counsel."

It seems to us that a necessary corollary to the rule that a client has the unqualified right to discharge an attorney, must be that the exercise of this legal right does not subject the client to additional penalties requiring him to pay an amount above the contract price.

Plaintiff's counsel persuasively argues that the rule should be as insisted by him, especially in contingent fee cases, for the reason that a highly skilled and competent attorney might be discharged by the client, who then entrusts the case to a less skillful one. The resulting loss of the suit would preclude the first attorney from receiving any fee. This argument is certainly appealing. However, in this case we are not called upon to make a decision in regard to these assumptions.

It would seem to us that the better rule is that because a client has the unqualified right to discharge his attorney, fees in such cases should be limited to the value of the services rendered or the contract price, whichever is less. * * *

[In this case we] simply hold that under the circumstances here shown, wherein there is no claim of fraud or overreaching as to the discharged attorney, and the settlement ultimately received is not assailed as inadequate or improper, recovery is limited to the contract price.

The decision of the Chancellor in this case preserved for Attorney Chambliss every penny to which he would have been entitled had he not been discharged. Because he is an officer of the court and a minister of justice, we do not believe he should insist upon more.

To adopt the rule advanced by Plaintiff would, in our view, encourage attorneys less keenly aware of their professional responsibilities than Attorney Chambliss, as shown in this record (unfortunately, events of the last year have shown there are such), to induce clients to lose confidence in them in cases where the reasonable value of their services has exceeded the original fee and thereby, upon being discharged, reap a greater benefit than that for which they had bargained. * * *

The assignment of error is overruled and the judgment of the Trial court affirmed. * * *

Notes

1. Courts following the rationale of Kehoe v. Rutherford, supra, p. 1125 also limit the restitution for breach of an employment contract to the contract price. See Kitchell v. Crossley, 90 N.J.L. 574, 101 A. 179 (1917).

2. Suppose that the discharged attorney was employed on a contingency fee contract. May the attorney commence an action to collect attorney's fees immediately after being discharged, or must she wait until the lawsuit ends? In re Estate of Callahan, 188 Ill.App.3d 323, 544 N.E.2d 112 (1989). The Illinois court ruled that the attorney may collect the reasonable value of the services rendered without waiting.

MAYTAG CO. v. ALWARD

Supreme Court of Iowa, 1962.
253 Iowa 455, 112 N.W.2d 654.

GARFIELD, CHIEF JUSTICE. This is an action in equity brought by The Maytag Company against George L. Alward, a key employee at the time he resigned on April 1, 1960, to accept employment with The Brunswick-Balke-Collender Co. in Muskegon, Michigan. Plaintiff seeks to rescind option agreements under which defendant acquired 600 shares of its corporate stock and claims 400 additional shares which plaintiff refused to deliver. Restitution and cancellation of the stock are also asked. * * *

The trial court rescinded the option agreements and decreed cancellation of all 1000 shares upon repayment by plaintiff of the amounts defendant paid in exercising the options, less the amount of a dividend he received on the 600 shares before this action was commenced. * * *

We think defendant's voluntary termination of his employment was a repudiation and breach of the option contracts and amounted to such failure of consideration for the sales of stock as entitled plaintiff to restitution of the stock upon repayment of the purchase price. This is the relief the trial court granted.

When defendant resigned five months remained of his agreed period of service under the first option agreement and his three-year period of service under the second option agreement had not been reached. In other words, defendant was obligated to serve plaintiff three years and five months after he voluntarily quit.

Consideration for each of the option agreements was defendant's obligation to serve plaintiff for three years. Like agreements on the part of 40 other key employees to whom options were awarded constituted plaintiff's principal motive for adopting its option plan and granting options thereunder. The agreement to serve was also consideration for each of the stock sales upon defendant's exercise of the options. It is true defendant paid plaintiff the price at which the stock was optioned. But this was much less than the price for which plaintiff could have sold it on the market—both sales were at a sacrifice price.

Not every breach of a contract affords a ground for rescission. It will not be granted for a mere breach not so substantial as to defeat the object of the parties in making the contract. * * * Here, however, defendant's voluntary quitting his job was such a repudiation and breach of the contracts as to practically defeat their whole purpose and object. It went to the essence of the contracts. * * *

Damages would not be an adequate remedy in the present case. The stock issued to defendant had not been issued previously. It was issued with the approval of the stockholders under plaintiff's stock option plan in return for agreements of the employees to serve the company. The stock should not be issued except in furtherance of the plan. It is unique and of special value to plaintiff. Further, it would be difficult to place a money value on defendant's services which plaintiff lost by defendant's repudiation of his obligations to serve. * * *

Affirmed.

3. RESTITUTION: PLAINTIFF IN DEFAULT

LYNN v. SEBY

Supreme Court of North Dakota, 1915.
29 N.D. 420, 151 N.W. 31.

GOSS, J. Plaintiff has recovered judgment against defendant for a small amount as a balance of a threshing bill. Judgment was granted upon the pleadings. In brief, plaintiff agreed to thresh all of defendant's grain. He threshed the wheat and oats, but refused to thresh the flax. Defendant was unable to procure threshing of his flax that fall, and defends and counterclaims for the amount of the resulting damage from the flax remaining unthreshed through the winter. The contract for threshing was the usual one, with no special provision whereby plaintiff agreed to be responsible in damages for more than ordinary liability. Therefore the counterclaim did not plead a cause of action for damages, under the holding in Hayes v. Cooley, 13 N.D. 204, 100 N.W. 250, for the reason that the loss of grain through resulting exposure to the elements is a remote and not a proximate consequence of the breach of contract and will not sustain a recovery, the measure of which is defined by section 7146, C.L.1913, merely declaratory of the common law. It cannot be said that such damages are those "which in the ordinary course of events would be likely to result" from the breach of the contract by plaintiff. Defendant concedes this to be the declared law of this state, but avers that the same should be either overruled, or there should be ingrafted thereon the further condition that if defendant cannot recover such damages plaintiff should not be allowed to breach his contract and also recover for the part performance by him. Or, in other words, that the parties should be left as they are found, and, if plaintiff sees fit to breach his contract, that he should go without pay for the portion performed and for which he would have received payment had he fully performed.

The question is an important one, and no doubt much can be said towards, and much authority cited sustaining, the contention of the defendant. The rule at common law was against plaintiff's recovery until the case of Britton v. Turner, 6 N.H. 481, was decided in 1834, in disregard of precedent. But the reasoning of that case is so cogent that it seems to have at least divided, if not changed, the current of authority. It first recognized the fact of the benefits of the part performance to the party who would keep such benefits, incapable of being returned, and still avoid paying anything for the benefits accrued where the contract is not fully performed. It may be remarked that, besides affecting parties similarly situated to those before us, this decision must also be a precedent upon the right of recovery of those in analogous positions, as, for instance, the farm laborer who hires for the summer and at the end of six months' labor performed quits his employment, and similar cases, where the contract is indivisible. An equitable rule has gradually developed permitting a recovery for the value of the services rendered, irrespective of the breach, giving to the other party to the contract a corresponding right of action in damages separately or in mitigation of the plaintiff's recovery, so that the rights of both may be equitably adjusted at law, notwithstanding the breach and nonperformance of the contract. This is true only where that which has been received by the employer under the partial performance has been beneficial to him.

In this case it must be admitted that the threshing done was of substantial benefit to defendant and a partial performance of this contract. While there is a division of authority, and the weight of authority, from the number of holdings alone, would deny a right of recovery, yet we prefer to follow the other line of authority. Either rule must, under certain circumstances work injustice. Otherwise there would be no division in authorities. We elect to follow that which we believe to be the trend of authority. It may be noted that cases of default under sales contracts, similar to Pfeiffer v. Norman, 22 N.D. 168, 133 N.W. 97, must not be taken as analogous to contracts for work and labor as involved in the instant case. The implications arising from the reception of benefits of part performance of employment contracts, where that which is so received cannot be returned, has no analogy to sale transactions where a portion of the price is paid and the party to pay the balance sees fit to default and attempts to recover back what he has paid in partial performance and before his default. Likewise a different equitable rule has developed under building contracts, the rule of substantial compliance and performance, and such authorities are not strictly applicable.

The judgment is affirmed.

Notes

1. As the court states, Britton v. Turner, 6 N.H. 481 (1834), is the leading decision. Plaintiff agreed to work for one year for $120 but abandoned the contract after performing for nine and one-half months. The court permitted the employee to recover the value of his work less the employer's damages. The precise problem presented in Britton v. Turner rarely occurs today because statutes require periodic payments to employees (usually every two weeks) and the payment of wages due upon termination of employment. See Corman, The Partial Performance Interest of the Defaulting Employee—Part II, 38 Marq.L.Rev. 139, 162–68 (1955); Holt,

Recovery by The Worker Who Quits: A Comparison of the Mainstream, Legal Realist, and Critical Legal Studies Approaches to a Problem of Nineteenth Century Contract Law, 1986 Wis.L.Rev. 677.

2. In denying recovery to a lawyer who breached his employment contract, the California District Court of Appeals in Moore v. Fellner, 318 P.2d 526, 531 (Cal.App.1957), rejected Britton v. Turner, stating:

"The question is whether an attorney who undertakes to render an entire service may quit when an important part of the work remains undone and deserve to be paid for partial performance. As well might a surgeon claim compensation when he had quit in the middle of an operation, or a barber when he had shaved half of a customer's face. The answer is that there is no concept of law or fair dealing that permits one contracting party to repudiate his obligation to render personal service and hold another party to his reciprocal obligations under the contract. If this were permitted one who had contracted to render an entire service for an agreed price could avoid loss under a bad bargain by merely stopping work at any stage and demanding compensation for partial performance. Contracts for personal services would be worthless.

"The judgment in favor of Moore cannot be sustained unless there is some special rule of the law of contracts that is applicable only to lawyers. But this could not be. The law is the same for lawyers as for anyone else who undertakes to render personal service."

The California Supreme Court reversed this decision. The plaintiff had handled the trial, but declined to handle the appeal. The contract for services was "divisible." The opinion permitted compensation for past services less the client's expenses from the change of counsel. 50 Cal.2d 330, 325 P.2d 857 (1958).

DANDENEAU v. SEYMOUR

Supreme Court of New Hampshire, 1977.

117 N.H. 455, 374 A.2d 934.

BOIS, JUSTICE. Action for recovery in quantum meruit involving a contract dispute wherein the plaintiffs agreed to construct a "breezeway" and garage addition to defendant's main house in return for the conveyance to them by the defendant of three acres of land and a so-called sap house situated thereon. The plaintiffs failed to render substantial performance of the contract. The defendant cancelled, evicted the plaintiffs and never conveyed the land. * * *

The court found that the partial construction of the breezeway and garage * * * had conferred a net benefit to the defendant. However, relying on Roundy v. Thatcher, 49 N.H. 526 (1870), the court denied quantum meruit relief. In *Roundy,* this court reasoned:

> "So if it be expressly agreed that nothing shall be paid until the contract is fully performed, then the law will not, against such express stipulation imply a promise to pay for a part. * * * Upon the same principle, it would seem, that if the contract was to pay in a particular way, as in certain stocks, in land, or other specific articles, the law would not imply a promise, in case of a part performance, to pay in money."

Quantum meruit is a restitutionary remedy intended for use by contracting parties who are in material breach and thus unable to sue 'on contract.'" Berke v. Griffin, 116 N.H. 760, ___, 367 A.2d 583, 586 (1976). The "reasons of justice" supporting quantum meruit recovery were enunciated in the early case of Britton v. Turner, 6 N.H. 481, 492 (1834): "[W]here the party receives value—takes and uses the materials, or has advantage from the labor, he is liable to pay the reasonable worth of what he has received.

While the principle of "unjust enrichment" has thus been invoked by this court from an early date, we are not inclined to depart from our holding in Roundy v. Thatcher. The readiness of the law to create a remedy in favor of a defaulting party must be so limited as not to prejudice the interests of the innocent, nondefaulting party. As Professor Williston has observed:

> "To permit a quantum meruit recovery in such a case [where the return promise is not for money but for land or chattels] would compel the injured party to pay money for services for which he had bargained to pay only in another medium, and would not only give the defaulter something he would not have been entitled to had he completed his performance but might even give him more than the value of what he had been promised for completed performance."

12 S. Williston, Law of Contracts (3d ed.) § 1477, at 259 (1970). In the circumstances of the instant case, the law will not imply a promise by the defendant that she pay in money the value of plaintiffs' services under the contract.

4. INJUNCTIVE RELIEF—NEGATIVE COVENANTS

BEVERLY GLEN MUSIC, INC. v. WARNER COMMUNICATIONS, INC.

California Court of Appeal, Second District, 1986.
178 Cal.App.3d 1142, 224 Cal.Rptr. 260.

KINGSLEY, ACTING PRESIDING JUSTICE. The plaintiff appeals from an order denying a preliminary injunction against the defendant, Warner Communications, Inc. We affirm.

In 1982, plaintiff Beverly Glen Music, Inc. signed to a contract a then-unknown singer, Anita Baker. Ms. Baker recorded an album for Beverly Glen which was moderately successful, grossing over one million dollars. In 1984, however, Ms. Baker was offered a considerably better deal by defendant Warner Communications. As she was having some difficulties with Beverly Glen, she accepted Warner's offer and notified plaintiff that she was no longer willing to perform under the contract. Beverly Glen then sued Ms. Baker and sought to have her enjoined from performing for any other recording studio. The injunction was denied, however, as, under Civil Code section 3423, subdivision Fifth, California courts will not enjoin the breach of a personal service contract unless the service is unique in nature and the performer is guaranteed annual compensation of at least $6,000, which Ms. Baker was not.

Following this ruling, the plaintiff voluntarily dismissed the action against Ms. Baker. Plaintiff, however, then sued Warner Communications for inducing Ms. Baker to breach her contract and moved the court for an injunction against Warner to prevent it from employing her. This injunction, too, was denied, the trial court reasoning that what one was forbidden by statute to do directly, one could not accomplish through the back door. It is from this ruling that the plaintiff appeals.

From what we can tell, this is a case of first impression in California. While there are numerous cases on the general inability of an employer to enjoin his former employee from performing services somewhere else, apparently no one has previously thought of enjoining the new employer from accepting the services of the breaching employee. While we commend the plaintiff for its resourcefulness in this regard, we concur in the trial court's interpretation of the maneuver.

"It is a familiar rule that a contract to render personal services cannot be specifically enforced." [citation] An unwilling employee cannot be compelled to continue to provide services to his employer either by ordering specific performance of his contract, or by injunction. To do so runs afoul of the Thirteenth Amendment's prohibition against involuntary servitude. [citation] However, beginning with the English case of Lumley v. Wagner (1852) 42 Eng.Rep. 687, courts have recognized that, while they cannot directly enforce an affirmative promise (in the *Lumley* case, Miss Wagner's promise to perform at the plaintiff's opera house), they can enforce the negative promise implied therein (that the defendant would not perform for someone else that evening). Thus, while it is not possible to compel a defendant to perform his duties under a personal service contract, it is possible to prevent him from employing his talents anywhere else. The net effect is to pressure the defendant to return voluntarily to his employer by denying him the means of earning a living. Indeed, this is its only purpose, for, unless the defendant relents and honors the contract, the plaintiff gains nothing from having brought the injunction.

The California Legislature, however, did not adopt this principle when in 1872 it enacted Civil Code section 3423, subdivision Fifth, and Code of Civil Procedure section 526, subdivision 5. These sections both provided that an injunction could not be granted: "To prevent the breach of a contract the performance of which would not be specifically enforced." In 1919, however, these sections were amended, creating an exception for: "a contract in writing for the rendition or furnishing of personal services from one to another where the minimum compensation for such service is at the rate of not less than six thousand dollars per annum and where the promised service is of a special, unique, unusual, extraordinary or intellectual character."

The plaintiff has already unsuccessfully argued before the trial court that Ms. Baker falls within this exception. It has chosen not to appeal that judgment, and is therefore barred from questioning that determination now. The sole issue before us then is whether plaintiff—although prohibited from enjoining Ms. Baker from performing herself—can seek to enjoin all those who might employ her and prevent them from doing so, thus achieving the same effect.

We rule that plaintiff cannot. Whether plaintiff proceeds against Ms. Baker directly or against those who might employ her, the intent is the same: to deprive Ms. Baker of her livelihood and thereby pressure her to return to plaintiff's employ. Plaintiff contends that this is not an action against Ms. Baker but merely an equitable claim against Warner to deprive it of the wrongful benefits it gained when it "stole" Ms. Baker away. Thus, plaintiff contends, the equities lie not between the plaintiff and Ms. Baker, but between plaintiff and the predatory Warner Communications Company. Yet if Warner's behavior has actually been predatory, plaintiff has an adequate remedy by way of damages. An injunction adds nothing to plaintiff's recovery from Warner except to coerce Ms. Baker to honor her contract. Denying someone his livelihood is a harsh remedy. The Legislature has forbidden it but for one exception. To expand this remedy so that it could be used in virtually all breaches of a personal service contract is to ignore over one hundred years of common law on this issue. We therefore decline to reverse the order.

The order is affirmed.

McCLOSKY and ARGUELLES, JJ., concur.

Notes

1. The rule that personal service contracts will not be affirmatively enforced is codified in Cal.Civ.Code § 3390. See also § 367 of the Restatement (Second) of Contracts. Comment (a) to § 367 explains the basis for this rule:

"The refusal is based in part upon the undesirability of compelling the continuance of personal association after disputes have arisen and confidence and loyalty are gone and, in some instances, of imposing what might seem like involuntary servitude."

2. *Query*: Is the "injunction against breach" permitted by Cal.Civ.Code § 3423 a decree specifically enforcing the affirmative portion of the employment contract?

3. The employer's equitable remedies include enforcing a negative covenant. The employee promises (a) to work for the employer, and (b) not to work for others, not to compete with the employer. Courts sometimes enjoin the breaching employee to enforce (b), the negative covenant. So the court may enjoin the employee with unique talents from working for another employer during the contract's exclusive term. The court may also enjoin the other employer from encouraging the employee to breach under an inducing breach of contract theory. Central New York Basketball, Inc. v. Barnett, 19 Ohio Op.2d 130, 181 N.E.2d 506 (1961). Does the *Barnett* court ignore the factors that led the court in the principal case to deny an injunction?

4. York, Remedies, Cal.Law (1970), at 85:

"According to the case of Lemat Corp. v. Barry, 275 Cal.App.2d 671, 80 Cal.Rptr. 240 (1969), Rick Barry was employed by the San Francisco Warriors under a one-year professional basketball contract with a unilateral option for another year if the player failed to sign a renewal contract. At the end of the term, Barry failed to renew his contract with the Warriors and signed with a rival team, the Oakland Oaks. He was enjoined from playing for the Oaks for the year during which the reserve clause operated in the Warriors' favor. He did not play out the option with the Warriors but sat out the season pursuant to the injunction. In *Lemat* the Warriors contended that under the Labor Code,[1] an injunction for up to seven years should be granted. The trial court blew the whistle on this attempted double dribble. Although it found that the Warriors lost $356,000 in gate receipts by reason of Barry's absence (it would have been even greater had Barry actually played for the cross-bay rivals), it declined to award damages, while at the same time limiting the final injunction to the contract term.

"The appellate court agreed as to the injunction. The Labor Code section was held to embody a limitation upon enforcing these contracts of adhesion, rather than permitting enforcement beyond the termination of the contract period. On the

1. [Footnote renumbered.] Cal.Lab.Code § 2855 (1971): "A contract to render personal service, may not be enforced against the employee beyond seven years from the commencement of service under it. Any contract, otherwise valid, to perform or render service of a special, unique, unusual, extraordinary, or intellectual character, which gives it peculiar value and the loss of which can not be reasonably or adequately compensated in damages in an action at law, may nevertheless be enforced against the person contracting to render such service, for a term not to exceed seven years from the commencement of service under it. If the employee voluntarily continues his service under it beyond that time, the contract may be referred to as affording a presumptive measure of the compensation."

issue of damages, the appellate opinion said that a detailed discussion was not required, because it was clear that the request for relief was in the alternative and that damages would be of significance only if the equitable relief (as limited) had been denied. Having disposed of the issue in the case at bar, the opinion proceeded to include some questionable dicta. Describing plaintiff's contention as 'unique,' the court, citing California cases, recited a general rule limiting a plaintiff to an injunction against future injuries and damages for past injuries. Such a rule, however, overlooks the dual aspects of these *Lumley–Wagner* type cases. Whereas an injunction ordinarily precludes future damage, this is not so in the case here presented. Barry was enjoined (the negative aspect) from playing for Oakland for the final year of the contract. But the equity decree did not accomplish the affirmative aspect of performance; Barry did not play for the Warriors. Such damage is not prevented by an injunction. The so-called general rule does not apply. On the contrary, the more relevant maxim that equity will not do justice by halves, or the principle that equity having taken jurisdiction will proceed to give full relief, should be invoked to sanction both an injunction and damages.

"Commenting that 'damages' in a situation of this kind are speculative and uncertain and practically impossible to ascertain, the appellate court questioned, in passing, the evidentiary and logical basis for the trial court's finding that the Warriors had incurred a gate loss of $356,000 by reason of Barry's absence. This argument is fast losing persuasiveness in the modern era of professional athletics and electronic entertainment. Speculation as to amount remains, but the fact of damage is apparent to everyone. Enormously remunerative contracts are negotiated in hard-nosed business sessions between lawyers and agents, the gate-draw potential of a high draft choice being a dominant factor. Patronizing solicitude for the businessman-athlete seems curiously out of place. Conceding the necessity of some 'speculation,' it seems that modern courts are lagging behind the times in failing to deal adequately and realistically with prime business considerations in what are, with increasing frequency, million dollar transactions."

Question: Should at least liquidated damages be provided for?

5. When the employer breaches an employment contract, courts normally refuse to order specific performance to enforce the contract. Redgrave v. Boston Symphony Orchestra, Inc., 557 F.Supp. 230, 234–35 (D.Mass.1983) apparent final appeal, 855 F.2d 888 (1st Cir.1988), cert. denied, 488 U.S. 1043 (1989); Barndt v. County of Los Angeles, 211 Cal.App.3d 397, 404, 259 Cal.Rptr. 372, 377 (1989). The court refused to enforce specifically a settlement agreement that entitled plaintiff to reinstatement in a hospital's cardiology section; it noted that the position required "a marked degree of cooperation and goodwill among the parties which an equitable decree simply cannot regulate."

On the other hand when plaintiff's discharge violates a statute or the constitution, courts often reinstate the wrongfully discharged employee. Allen v. Autauga County Board of Education, 685 F.2d 1302 (11th Cir.1982) (first amendment violated); Ellis v. Glover & Gardner Construction Co., 562 F.Supp. 1054 (M.D.Tenn.1983) (C.C.P.A. prohibition on discharge for garnishment violated); Jeffreys v. My Friend's Place, Inc., 719 F.Supp. 639 (M.D.Tenn.1989) (employee discharged for reporting for jury duty).

In Brown v. Trustees of Boston University, 891 F.2d 337, 358, 361 (1st Cir.1989), the court reinstated a professor and ordered tenure. "[O]nce a university has been found to have impermissibly discriminated [on the basis of sex] in making a tenure decision, as here, the University's prerogative to make tenure decisions must be subordinated to the goals embodied in Title VII."

What overcomes the contract policies that prevent specific performance of employment contracts? See Hopkins v. Price Waterhouse, 920 F.2d 967, 980 (D.C.Cir.1990), where the court found that defendant had denied plaintiff partnership because of sexual stereotyping and ordered plaintiff reinstated as a partner.

For some of the complexities that may result when reinstatement is ordered, see Thompson v. Cleland, 782 F.2d 719 (7th Cir.1986).

HILL v. MOBILE AUTO TRIM, INC.

Supreme Court of Texas, 1987.
725 S.W.2d 168.

KILGARLIN, JUSTICE. Based on a covenant not to compete in a franchise agreement, Mobile Auto Trim, Inc. sought to enjoin Joel Hill, a former franchisee, from competing with it in a seven-county area. The trial court granted the temporary injunction. The court of appeals, with one justice dissenting, affirmed the temporary injunction. * * * In a single point of error, Hill complains that the non-competition agreement is a restraint on trade and is unreasonable. We agree and therefore reverse the judgment of the court of appeals, dissolve the temporary injunction, and hold the restrictive covenant in the franchise agreement void in all respects.

Mobile Auto Trim sells car trim franchises in which equipped vans are driven to car dealerships to make repairs at the premises. In August 1982, Mobile sold a franchise to Joel Hill for approximately $42,000 plus five percent of his gross revenues. Hill's franchise covered a large part of Dallas County and all of Denton County. The franchise agreement contained this covenant not to compete:

> "Franchisee (Hill) agrees that upon termination of this Franchise Agreement, for whatever reason, Franchisee shall not directly or indirectly, as an officer, director, shareholder, proprietor, partner, consultant, employee or in any other individual or representative capacity, engage, participate or become involved in any business that is in competition in any manner whatsoever with the business of the Company or its franchisees. Furthermore it is understood between the parties that substantial goodwill will exist between the Company and the managers of the various car dealerships serviced by the Company and the Company's franchisees. Because said managers are transient and frequently change employment among car dealerships, Franchisee further agrees that upon termination of this Franchise Agreement, for whatever reason, Franchisee will not directly or indirectly in any manner whatsoever, in any capacity whatsoever, contact said managers (irrespective of the car dealerships that employ them) regarding business in competition with the Company. This covenant shall extend for a period of three (3) years following the termination of this Franchise Agreement or any renewal hereof. Further, this covenant shall cover the following geographic area during said period: The following Texas Counties: Dallas, Tarrant, Ellis, Denton, Rockwall, Kaufman, and Collin."

For two and a half years, as Mobile's franchisee, Hill contacted car dealerships and made car trim repairs in his two-county area. In April 1985, after Hill had not paid his franchise fees for several months, Mobile Auto Trim picked up his van and terminated the franchise agreement. That day, after the franchise agreement had been terminated, Hill contacted a prior customer, a car dealership manager in Dallas County. Thereafter, Mobile Auto Trim sought a temporary injunction to enjoin Hill from competing with it or contacting car dealership managers in the seven counties listed in the covenant not to compete.

Courts in Texas encounter two general varieties of covenants not to compete: covenants specifying that the seller of a business will not compete with the buyer, and covenants specifying that an employee, upon discharge, will not compete with the former employer. These covenants commonly set forth temporal and geographical restraints on the promisor's ability to compete with the promisee, which restraints must be reasonable.

Under the common law of contracts, a covenant not to compete is in restraint of trade and its terms are enforceable only if, and to the extent that, they are, in other respects, also reasonable.[1] Whether a covenant not to compete is reasonable is a question of law for the court. A covenant is unreasonable "if it is greater than is required for the protection of the person for whose benefit the restraint is imposed or imposes undue hardship upon the person restricted."

A covenant must meet four criteria in order to be deemed reasonable. First, the covenant must be necessary for the protection of the promisee. That is to say, the promisee must have a legitimate interest in protecting business goodwill or trade secrets. Second, the covenant must not be oppressive to the promisor, as courts are hesitant to validate employee covenants when the employee has nothing but his labor to sell. In this respect, the limitations as to time, territory, and activity in the covenant not to compete must be reasonable. [citations] Third, the covenant must not be injurious to the public, since courts are reluctant to enforce covenants which prevent competition and deprive the community of needed goods. [citations]

Finally, as with any contract, the non-competitive agreement should be enforced only if the promisee gives consideration for something of value. [citation] This doctrine promotes economic efficiency. In the case of covenants not to compete incident to the sale of a business, the seller's promise not to compete with the buyer increases the value of the business to the buyer. Without such a covenant the value of the business would be reduced, lessening the likelihood that businesses would be purchased. In employee covenants, the special training or knowledge acquired by the employee through his employer is valuable consideration and often enhances the value of the employee to other firms. To allow employees to use or sell this valuable training or knowledge upon leaving a firm would create a disincentive for employers to train or educate employees. [citation]

But, the covenant before us today cannot be clearly categorized as either a covenant incident to the sale of a business or a post-employment covenant to prevent utilizing special training or knowledge. Hill obtained his skills as an auto trim repairman prior to his franchise agreement with Mobile Auto Trim.

1. Some states prohibit all or most forms of restrictive covenants by statute. State statutes prohibiting or limiting such post-employment restraints include: Alabama: Ala.Code § 8–1–1 (1975); California: Cal.Bus. & Prof.Code § 16600 (West 1964); Colorado: Colo.Rev.Stat. § 8–2–113 (1973) (however, the statute permits employee noncompete agreements where the employer wishes to recover the costs of *education or training* an employee or when the employee is an executive or staff member of an executive); Louisiana: La.Rev.Stat.Ann. § 23.921 (West 1964) (a maximum two-year restriction is permitted, however, if the employer has *trained* or *advertised* for the employee); Michigan: Mich.Comp.Laws § 445.761 (1967); North Dakota: N.D.Cent.Code § 9–08–06 (1960); Oklahoma: Okla.Stat. tit. 15 § 217 (1966); South Dakota: S.D.Codified Laws Ann. § 53–9–8 (1980).

Hill bought a franchise from Mobile for approximately $42,000 plus 5% of his gross revenues. In effect, Hill paid for the use of Mobile's name and accompanying goodwill.

This restrictive covenant is plagued by a lack of reasonableness. Initially, there is an apparent absence of consideration. What value did Mobile give in exchange for Hill's promise not to compete? It was not specialized training or knowledge, for that was acquired by Hill prior to his franchise agreement, nor was it Mobile's promise not to compete with Hill after their business relation terminated. And, although Mobile Auto Trim alleges that its trim services are trade secrets, they do not provide any substantiation, did not bring suit to stop the use of their trade secrets, and are willing to let Hill use their techniques anywhere except the Dallas–Fort Worth metroplex.

More importantly, we find no legitimate business interest of Mobile which the covenant is necessary to protect. The contract alleges, and the record indicates, that the purpose of this covenant not to compete was to prevent Hill from exploiting the contacts and "the substantial goodwill [that] exist[s] between the Company and the managers of the various car dealerships." However, there exists not only business goodwill but also franchisee goodwill. When people leave a business to work for another or to open a firm of their own, many are capable of taking with them a sizeable number of the clients whom they had served at their previous place of employment. If they were not in possession of some type of personal magnetism or personal goodwill, they would be incapable of retaining those clients or customers. Shrewd employers and franchisors know this and seek to deprive the employee/franchisee of the fruits of his goodwill by requiring that he enter into an agreement containing a restrictive covenant. The covenant is generally unfair to the employee/franchisee, for when that person is placed in the position of being unable to compete with the former employer/franchisor, his personal goodwill is effectively neutralized.

In the past this court has modified restrictive covenants in order to make the time, area and scope of the covenant reasonable. [citations] But, there has never been a presumption that so long as the restriction does not encumber the former franchisee's ability to compete for a long time or over a wide radius, the covenant is otherwise deemed fair. To presume such would be to ignore the fact that the franchisor ordinarily has no right to prohibit fair competition. If fair competition is injurious to the franchisor, then so be it: it is but a normal effect of a free market economy.

Finally, the covenant is oppressive to the promisor, Hill. Not only has he lost his franchise and investment therein, he is now prevented from using his previously acquired skills and talent to support him and his family in the county of their residence. We recognize that a man's talents are his own. Absent clear and convincing proof to the contrary, there must be a presumption that he has not bargained away the future use of those talents. Professor Williston referred to this concept in his authoritative work on contract law, and it is a fitting summary of the nearly forgotten notion:

> "A man's aptitudes, his skill, his dexterity, his manual or mental ability—all those things which in sound philosophical language are not objective, but subjective—they may and they ought not to be relinquished by a servant; they are not his master's property; they are his own property; they are himself. There is no public interest which compels the rendering of those things

dormant or sterile or unavailing; on the contrary, the right to use and to expand his powers is advantageous to every citizen, and may be highly so for the country at large."

S. Williston, A Treatise on the Law of Contracts § 1646 (rev. ed. 1937) (citing Morris v. Saxelby, 1 A.C. 688, 714 [H.L.1916]).

Today, we are presented with an individual who is skilled in auto trim repair and are asked to prohibit him from engaging in a common calling. We refuse to do so. The longevity of the reasonableness approach has been its flexibility. "The changing conditions of life modify from time to time the reasons for determining whether the public interest requires that a restrictive stipulation shall be deemed void as against public policy." Samuel Stores, Inc. v. Abrams, 94 Conn. 248, 252, 108 A. 541, 543 (1919). In 1982, the Utah Supreme Court refused to enforce a hearing aid distributor's non-competition agreement against a former salesman, setting forth the standard which we adopt today: "[c]ovenants not to compete which are primarily designed to limit competition or restrain the right to engage in a common calling are not enforceable." Robbins v. Finlay, 645 P.2d 623, 627 (Utah 1982).

The issue before us is whether Mobile Auto Trim is entitled to have the restrictive covenant enforced pending trial on the merits. [citation] Mobile must show a probable right of recovery and a probable injury in order to justify the issuance of a temporary injunction. [citation] For the foregoing reasons, we hold there is no probable right of recovery. Therefore, we reverse the judgment of the court of appeals, dissolve the temporary injunction, and hold the restrictive covenant in the franchise agreement void in all respects.

GONZALEZ, J., files a dissenting opinion in which HILL, C.J., and CAMPBELL, J., concur.

Notes

1. In Bess v. Bothman, 257 N.W.2d 791, 794 (Minn.1977), the court considered partial enforcement of a covenant unreasonably restraining trade. The seller of a small trucking company had made an unlimited covenant not to compete. The court rewrote it to apply only within the city for five years. Rejecting the view that unlimited covenants are completely void, the court accepted the minority version of the "blue pencil" doctrine, stating: "Although the 'blue pencil' doctrine, requiring that the reasonable and unreasonable restraints be severable, still commands a slight majority of jurisdictions, a substantial minority of courts modify unreasonable restraints of trade, whether formally divisible or not, and enforce them to the extent reasonable in the circumstances."

The partial enforcement doctrine applied in Bess v. Bothman, is generally available only where the employer was not guilty of bad faith or overreaching. Durapin, Inc. v. American Products, Inc., 559 A.2d 1051 (R.I.1989); Ellis v. James V. Hurson Associates, 565 A.2d 615 (D.C.App.1989). Where the restrictive covenant evidences a deliberate intent by the employer to place unreasonable and oppressive restraints on the employee, the covenant will not be modified but will be struck down as void, regardless of whether the clauses are severable. Dryvit System, Inc. v. Rushing, 132 Ill.App.3d 9, 477 N.E.2d 35 (1985); Holloway v. Faw, Casson & Co., 78 Md.App. 205, 552 A.2d 1311 (1989), aff'd in part, rev'd in part, 319 Md. 324, 572 A.2d 510 (App.1990).

2. The usual remedy for a violation of a valid covenant is an injunction prohibiting the offending conduct and an accounting of profits. Presto–X–Company v. Ewing, 442 N.W.2d 85 (Iowa 1989); Robert S. Weiss & Associates v. Wiederlight,

208 Conn. 525, 546 A.2d 216 (1988). Where the agreement provides for liquidated damages, that clause will be enforced where the penal amount is reasonable compensation for the anticipated loss. Holloway v. Faw, Casson & Co., supra.

3. *Hill* distinguishes between a business seller's covenant not to compete with the buyer and an employee's covenant not to compete with a former employer after employment terminates. Courts generally view employees' covenants with disfavor since they may deprive the employee of her livelihood by prohibiting the use of skill and knowledge acquired during the employment period. Alexander & Alexander, Inc. v. Danahy, 21 Mass.App.Ct. 488, 488 N.E.2d 22 (1986); Family Affairs Haircutters, Inc. v. Detling, 110 A.D.2d 745, 488 N.Y.S.2d 204 (1985).

4. Infants are permitted to disaffirm contracts, see infra pp. 1215–19. But should an infant be permitted to disaffirm a contract containing a negative covenant, like a covenant not to compete? Holding the infant bound, the court in Career Placement of White Plains v. Vaus, 77 Misc.2d 788, 354 N.Y.S.2d 764 (1974) observed that otherwise infants would never be employed in business having trade secrets. "The rule is a salutary one." The court granted a preliminary injunction against the precocious entrepreneur.

LONG BEACH DRUG CO. v. UNITED DRUG CO.

Supreme Court of California, 1939.

13 Cal.2d 158, 88 P.2d 698.

SHENK, J. The questions presented upon this appeal concern the validity and scope of a written agreement, and the right of plaintiff to permanently enjoin its violation by defendant, or to procure other relief. * * *

By the written agreement plaintiff was appointed the special and exclusive agent in Long Beach for the sale of defendant's Rexall remedies and other drug products. The contract was made on April 16, 1909, and was performed by the parties until the fall of 1936, when defendant gave notice that it would no longer be bound. In October, 1936, defendant started, without plaintiff's consent, to sell to other drug stores in Long Beach, and on May 10, 1937, it refused to make further sales to plaintiff. Plaintiff then brought this action and, upon trial of the cause, was awarded the relief for which it prayed, to wit: a decree which (1) permanently enjoined defendant from directly or indirectly selling Rexall products to any dealer in Long Beach other than plaintiff and certain sub-agents; (2) ordered an accounting to ascertain all damage suffered by plaintiff from sales made in violation of the contract; and (3) ordered judgment for plaintiff for all sums found to be due it on the accounting, together with costs. Defendant appealed from this decree. * * *

A primary question is that of the validity of this agreement. Is it void for uncertainty? If not, then is it capable of enforcement by a court of equity? "That a greater degree or amount of certainty is required in the terms of an agreement which is to be specifically executed in equity than is necessary in a contract which is the basis of an action at law for damages" has often been declared. * * *

It is the general rule that a contract is not fatally defective merely because it does not specify a time presently definite for its termination. While the agreement here does not state a definite term, it is not wholly silent with respect to its duration. It provides that the exclusive selling right of plaintiff is to endure so long as plaintiff "shall perform the terms of this agreement"; that is, so long as plaintiff shall * * * "uphold all of the products" of defendant to the full list retail prices, confining the sale thereof to its "own retail store and to consumers only." Provisions such as this for the duration of an agreement are sufficiently certain and have frequently been declared valid. * * *

The undisputed facts of the present case leave no doubt as to the manner in which the parties construed the contract. They performed under it for a period of twenty-seven years without complaint of its lack of definiteness or intimation that it was void for uncertainty. At all times plaintiff carried a stock of defendant's products and sold them at full list price in its retail store. Defendant, on its part, filled plaintiff's orders and expressed no dissatisfaction with the representation it was receiving. * * *

From the year 1909 until 1923, the record shows there was a substantial yearly increase in the sales by plaintiff of defendant's products, whereas from 1923 until defendant's repudiation of the contract in 1936, there was a gradual decline. As against $1639 for the year 1909, the 1923 sales totaled $19,927.07. Sales for the year 1934 declined to the low mark of $2,829.44. Between 1910 and 1920, according to the official census, the population of Long Beach rose from 18,809 to 55,593. Outside communities were included within the city area, and by 1930 there was an estimated population of 142,032. This rapid growth of the city, combined with the declining sales by plaintiff after the year 1923, made the agency contract increasingly disadvantageous to defendant. When defendant later acquired or became affiliated with the Owl Drug company, and desired to use the four Owl Drug stores in Long Beach as outlets for its products, it simply notified plaintiff that it would no longer recognize the 1909 agreement. Between October, 1936, and December, 1937, it sold $10,604.70 worth of its products to the four Owl stores. It continued to sell to them and to some of the other stores until the date of judgment herein.

This recital of undisputed facts shows that the construction of the agreement as lawful and operative accords with the recognition which was given to it by the parties themselves for some twenty-seven years. The further fact that during the latter portion of that period the obligation became burdensome to defendant does not alter the purport and effect of the writing. We hold that the contract is valid.

The next question is whether plaintiff is entitled, under this valid contract, to the equitable remedy of prohibitory injunction. Plaintiff, by its complaint herein, did not ask the court for a direct decree compelling defendant to specifically perform the contract, but sought such relief indirectly by means of the injunction, the assumption being that if defendant were permanently restrained from selling to other dealers in Long Beach, it would continue to sell to plaintiff rather than abandon so lucrative a territory.

Defendant contends that the prohibitory injunction will not lie, citing section 3423, subdivision 5 of the Civil Code, and section 526, subdivision 5, of the Code of Civil Procedure, both of which provide that "an injunction cannot be granted * * * to prevent the breach of a contract * * * the performance of which would not be specifically enforced." In Anderson v. Neal Institutes Co., 37 Cal.App. 174 [173 Pac. 779], this provision was construed and the doctrine was declared that where a contract contains both affirmative and negative stipulations, equity will not interfere to prevent a breach of the negative covenant when the affirmative covenant is of such a nature that it cannot be specifically enforced by a judicial decree. * * *

Seeking to distinguish the present case and to avoid application of the doctrine, plaintiff asserts that the instrument here contains only negative covenants. We cannot so view it. Clearly the contract is not wholly negative in character. In addition to the negative covenant of defendant to refrain from selling to dealers other than plaintiff, there are express and implied material affirmative covenants, notably an implied affirmative covenant on the part of defendant to sell to plaintiff as its special agent, and on the part of plaintiff an implied affirmative covenant to purchase from defendant and have available for resale a sufficient supply of its drug products to meet the demands of the retail trade, with the express covenant to "uphold all of the products * * * to the full list retail prices" set by defendant.

Unless these affirmative covenants are of such a nature that they could be specifically enforced by a judicial decree, the trial court erred in granting the prohibitory injunction. That specific enforcement would not be allowed has already been intimated in the foregoing discussion, and it becomes evident upon a consideration of the nature of the stipulations. It is, as stated in Poultry Producers, etc., v. Barlow, [189 Cal. 278, 208 P. 93] (189 Cal., at p. 289), "the cognate rule is that courts of equity will not decree the specific performance of contracts which by their terms stipulate for a succession of acts whose performance cannot be consummated by one transaction, but will be continuous and require protracted supervision and direction. * * * 'Courts of equity,' says the court in Pacific etc. Ry. Co. v. Campbell–Johnston, 153 Cal. 117 [94 Pac. 623, 628], 'only decree specific performance where the subject-matter of the decree is capable of being embraced in one order and is immediately enforceable. It will not decree specific performance when the duty to be performed is a continuous one extending possibly over a long period of time, and which, in order that the performance may be made effectual, will necessarily require constant personal supervision and oversight of it by the court.'" * * *

So, in the present case, to undertake to compel defendant to sell to plaintiff, and plaintiff to purchase from defendant and to uphold all products to the full list retail price set by defendant, over an indefinite term, would impose upon the court a duty well nigh impossible of performance. For this reason, if no other, the court would be constrained to deny equitable relief and to leave the parties to assert their legal rights under the contract. * * *

A petition for a rehearing was denied on April 19, 1939, and the following opinion then rendered thereon:

THE COURT. * * * Although the equitable remedy is not available to plaintiff, nevertheless the contract sued upon is valid and sufficiently certain to warrant the trial court in entertaining a plea for the recovery of damages.

Notes

1. *Remedies in franchising.* The principal case presents a simple example of the remedial difficulties of a franchisee who is being shaken off by a franchisor. This mode of merchandising has had phenomenal growth in recent years; the relationship is covered by complex and frequently one-sided contracts. Much attention has been paid to protecting the franchisee through statutory proposals. See, e.g., Brown, Franchising—a Fiduciary Relationship (or Franchising and Equity), 49 Tex.L.Rev. 650 (1971). The article suggests that the franchising relationship be treated as a fiduciary one—with you-know-who as the fiduciary. This might lead to the equitable jurisdiction that was denied in the main case.

In denying specific performance of a franchising agreement, the court in North American Financial Group v. S.M.R. Enterprises, 583 F.Supp. 691, 699 (N.D.Ill. 1984) said, "If specific performance were granted, the court would be placed in the untenable situation of a long-term supervision, judging the quality of training. * * * For that reason, it is hornbook law that a contract for personal services will not be specifically enforced as contrary to public policy."

Professors Goetz and Scott analyze franchising and similar long-term contracts from an economic perspective in Principles of Relational Contracts, 67 Va.L.Rev. 1089 (1981).

3. A number of states regulate the franchise relationship by statute. See Anno., 67 A.L.R.3d 1301 (1975).

Schultz v. Onan Corp., 737 F.2d 339 (3d Cir.1984), discusses the Minnesota Franchise Act and the Minnesota doctrine that imputes into a franchise contract, otherwise terminable at franchisor's option, a duration equal to the time reasonably necessary for a franchisee to recoup the investment and close up. If the franchise is terminated before this time, the franchisee may recover her lost investment as damages.

4. *Contracts to Pay over Money.* Aside from decrees against vendees of land, decrees to enforce obligations of trustees and other fiduciaries, and alimony and support decrees, courts seldom invoke equitable jurisdiction to enforce a mere agreement to pay over money. Trustees of Columbia University v. Mortgagee Investors Corp., 196 Misc. 92, 89 N.Y.S.2d 324 (1949); Jamison Coal & Coke Co. v. Goltra, 143 F.2d 889 (8th Cir.1944) (suit by seller of mortgage bonds).

On occasion, however, equitable jurisdiction has been upheld as in the case of agreements to make construction loans in installments, Southampton Wholesale Food Terminal, Inc. v. Providence Warehouse Co., 129 F.Supp. 663 (D.Mass.1955), or to finance a shopping center, First National State Bank v. Commonwealth Federal Savings, 455 F.Supp. 464 (D.N.J.1978). A contract by a surety to furnish an indemnity bond on behalf of the plaintiff contractor was specifically enforced in Milwaukie Construction Co. v. Glens Falls Insurance Co., 367 F.2d 964 (9th Cir.1966). The rationale is in terms of the equity *bill quia timet.* The court in American Bancshares Mortgage Co. v. Empire Home Loans, Inc., 568 F.2d 1124 (5th Cir.1978), refused to order specific performance of a contract to purchase a construction mortgage. See Groot, Specific Performance of Contracts To Provide Permanent Financing, 60 Cornell L.Rev. 718 (1975).

When lenders breach, the legal remedy, including special damages, deters borrowers from recourse to equitable remedies. United California Bank v. Prudential Insurance Co., 140 Ariz. 238, 681 P.2d 390 (App.1984), involved financing for the Hyatt Regency Hotel in Phoenix, Arizona: $10,494,000 plus $863,250 attorneys fees. K.M.C. Co. v. Irving Trust Co., 757 F.2d 752 (6th Cir.1985). A bankrupt wholesale grocery company was awarded a $7,500,000 judgment for breach of a financing agreement.

Contracts to insure, even where a loss has occurred so that money is presently payable, have been specifically enforced. E.g., Phoenix Insurance Co. v. Ryland, 69 Md. 437, 16 A. 109 (1888).

In Frank LeRoux, Inc. v. Burns, 4 Wash.App. 165, 480 P.2d 213 (1971), the court, in permitting the seller to recover a delinquent payment, stated that U.C.C. § 2–719(1) authorized the parties to contract for the remedy of specific performance.

Chapter 14

REMEDIES FOR NOMINALLY UNENFORCEABLE TRANSACTIONS

A. TRANSACTIONS UNENFORCEABLE FOR LACK OF A WRITING

1. RESTITUTION

SCHWEITER v. HALSEY

Supreme Court of Washington, 1961.
57 Wash.2d 707, 359 P.2d 821.

DONWORTH, JUDGE. Halsey and wife (appellants) owned a large farm in Asotin county (partly tillable land and partly pasture land) subject to a mortgage. They listed this land for sale with Mason & Teague (brokers) of Lewiston, Idaho.

These brokers showed the property to Schweiter brothers (respondents), who were desirous of purchasing the tillable land only. Appellants were agreeable to selling that portion of the land but had no legal description thereof.

Respondents needed not less than fifty thousand dollars to finance the deal. The mortgagee was willing to increase the amount of the mortgage to fifty thousand dollars at six percent interest. Respondents were so advised by the brokers, who also suggested that a loan might be obtained from a life insurance company at a lower rate.

On October 23, 1956, the parties executed an earnest-money receipt. Although the earnest-money receipt indicated that the legal description of the property to be sold was attached, there was, in fact, no legal description attached at the time the receipt was executed. The brokers had a legal description of the entire property, and respondents instructed them to retain respondents' copy of the receipt. Several weeks later, upon completion of a survey, the legal description of the tillable land was attached thereto by the brokers, and respondents were notified of this fact.

On December 1, 1956, respondents, together with one of the brokers, went to Spokane with a legal description of all the land to be covered by the mortgage and made a formal application for a loan. Ten days later, the brokers were notified by the insurance company that the loan had been approved. They promptly notified respondents of this fact. Respondents asked that the closing of the transaction be delayed until after January first for tax reasons.

Meanwhile, the insurance company asked for a preliminary title report and a copy of the proposed deed from appellants to respondents. These were furnished, and later a proposed note and mortgage to be signed by respondents were furnished by the insurance company.

Appellants executed the deed and the brokers requested respondents to execute the note and mortgage. Respondent J.E. Schweiter went to the brokers' office and stated that his wife had refused to sign the papers. On January 11, 1957, respondents gave notice of rescission of the transaction and appellants promptly tendered performance, which was refused by respondents.

On April 26, 1957, respondents instituted this action for the purpose of obtaining a declaration of the rights and duties of the parties under the earnest-money agreement. Shortly thereafter, appellants sold the tillable land to a third party for seven thousand dollars less than respondents had agreed to pay for it.

Appellants filed an answer containing a cross-complaint in which they sought to recover the seven-thousand-dollar loss on the sale, plus other special damages.

The trial court rendered a memorandum decision holding that the earnest-money agreement was void because it contained no legal description of the real estate involved in the transaction. * * *

Appellants assign error to the entry of conclusions of law Nos. 1 and 2, reading as follows:

> "I. That the earnest money [sic] executed by plaintiffs on October 23, 1956 * * * is void as being in violation of the Statute of Frauds;
>
> "II. That plaintiffs shall have judgment against defendants in the sum of $5,000.00";

We shall dispose of the assignments in the order in which they are raised.

Conclusion of Law No. 1 is in accord with the law of this state. We have consistently held that an earnest-money agreement containing an inadequate legal description of the property to be conveyed is void as being in violation of the statute of frauds. * * *

Conclusion of Law No. 2 does not follow from Conclusion of Law No. 1 and is, therefore, erroneous. Although the earnest-money agreement was unenforcible and could not be made the subject of reformation, this does not entitle respondents to a return of their earnest money. At no time did appellants repudiate the contract. On the contrary, they tendered performance and did not otherwise dispose of the property until after respondents commenced this action. Under these facts, the case falls directly within the rule of Dubke v. Kassa, 1947, 29 Wash.2d 486, 187 P.2d 611, wherein we said:

> "The applicable rule is that a vendee under an agreement for the sale and purchase of property which does not satisfy the statute of frauds, * * * cannot recover payments made upon the purchase price if the vendor has not repudiated the contract but is ready, willing, and able to perform in accordance therewith, even though the contract is not enforcible against the vendee either at law or in equity. [citations]
>
> Further in the opinion we also said:

"It does not seem to be, nor can it be, seriously urged that appellants sacrificed their right to retain the payment received, because they sold the property to a third person after the respondent had commenced this action."

Unfortunately, neither party called the trial court's attention to the *Dubke* case.

Thus it appears that this court, in accord with the great weight of authority, has consistently denied recovery of earnest money paid under a void or unenforcible agreement to convey real estate where the buyer has defaulted and the seller was at all times ready, able and willing to consummate the transaction. * * *

The judgment of the trial court, in so far as it awards the return of the five thousand dollars earnest money to respondents, is reversed with directions to dismiss the action. In all other respects, the judgment is affirmed.

FINLEY, CHIEF JUSTICE (dissenting). Frankly, I question the validity of the *Dubke ratio decidendi* and the assumption underlying the majority opinion. If the purported contract in the instant case is absolutely void—rather than being voidable or simply creative of a right as to which no remedy is available for enforcement—then there is simply and absolutely no consideration to support the payment made by the vendee, and he ought to recover it. Reedy v. Ebsen, 1932, 60 S.D. 1, 242 N.W. 592. Actually, it seems to me incongruous and a bit on the ridiculous side to say the writing is void or even unenforcible (which is the equivalent of saying that it created no legal relations between the parties), and then to say that for some unarticulated, vague or mysterious reason, the legal or other relationships of the parties were altered sufficiently to be judicially cognizable and to give the vendor a legal right to keep the vendees' down payment.

Our statute of frauds, RCW 64.04.010, provides:

"Every conveyance of real estate, or any interest therein, and every contract creating or evidencing any encumbrance upon real estate, shall be by deed:"

By way of comparison, note:

(1) RCW 19.36.010: "In the following cases, specified in this section, any agreement, contract and promise *shall be void,* unless such agreement, contract or promise, or some note or memorandum thereof, be in writing, and signed by the party to be charged there-with, or by some person thereunto by him lawfully authorized, that is to say: [Specified situations omitted.]" (Emphasis supplied.)

(2) English Statute of Frauds: " * * * no action shall be brought upon any contract or sale of lands, tenements or hereditaments, or any interest in or concerning them" unless in writing.

RCW 19.36.010 is clearly illustrative of the type of statute under which an attempt to contract, failing to meet the statutory requisites, is absolutely void. The English statute, on the other hand, lends itself readily to the construction that an oral contract for the sale of land is valid, but there is simply no remedy available for its enforcement. RCW 64.04.010, governing contracts for the sale of land in Washington does not fall neatly into either category. As is noted in the majority opinion, we have from time to time spoken of contracts not meeting the requirements of this statute, rather loosely, as being both void and unenforcible. In most cases it makes little difference. In the instant case, however, it makes a great deal of difference. The words *void* and *unenforcible* are terms of art and are mutually exclusive. Before this case can be decided, we must determine which of those terms is made appropriate by RCW 64.04.-010. As a matter of legal logic, it cannot be both.

In Reedy v. Ebsen, the South Dakota court set forth the following quotation from Brandies v. Neustadtl, 1860, 13 Wis. 142, 158, explaining the difference as follows:

> "The parol contract, being void, furnished no consideration for the payment. A consideration, to be sufficient, must be either a benefit to one party or a damage to the other. The purchaser can derive no benefit from the supposed contract. Nothing passes to him by virtue of it; he obtains no interest in the land, and no promise or agreement on the part of the seller to convey him any; and he can never derive any advantage from what has transpired, except it be as a matter of favor on the seller's part. * * * The reason given for not allowing the purchaser under the English statute, and those like it, to repudiate the agreement and recover back what he has paid, so long as the seller is in no default, is very obvious. But it cannot be given here. It is that the agreement is not void but voidable, or, to speak more correctly, not actionable. * * * The repeal of the statute in such case would at once enable the purchaser to maintain his action upon the agreement. With us it is otherwise. Its repeal would leave him in no better situation than formerly. There is in that case a valid living contract between the parties, and though the remedy be suspended, it binds the conscience, and, until it has been broken, constitutes a sufficient consideration for the payment of the money. There being thus a good consideration, if the purchaser chooses to rely upon the honor of the seller for the performance of his contract, instead of putting it in such form that the courts can enforce it, it is no injustice to say to him that he shall not ignore it, at least until that honor has been violated. * * * Under our statute there is no contract; nothing which can be the foundation of any legal or equitable obligation; and how can the court create one? * * * *It finds one party in the unexplained possession of the money of another, which he knowingly received without any legal equivalent, and not as a gift, and which he has no legal or equitable right to retain; and why should he not refund?* * * * *'" (Emphasis supplied.) [60 S.D. 1, 242 N.W. 594.]

[A]ssuming again that the legal description is defective, it seems to me that the language of RCW 64.04.010 most strongly supports a conclusion that the earnest-money agreement in the instant case is not merely unenforcible, but is void. Thus, I cannot agree with the reasoning of the majority.

Note

Question: Assume the purchaser has now changed his mind and desires to reform the earnest money receipt to insert an accurate legal description. What legal argument could be raised against this remedy?

In accord, Hayes v. Hartelius, 215 Mont. 391, 697 P.2d 1349 (1985).

BENNETT LEASING CO. v. ELLISON

Supreme Court of Utah, 1963.
15 Utah 2d 72, 387 P.2d 246.

CROCKETT, JUSTICE. Plaintiff's complaint contained two counts: In the first it sought to recover upon an express contract leasing the car for 24 months at the rate of $79.49 per month, alleging use for 22 months; and also for $173.35 for repairs, $33.48 for "late" charges, and $130.00 for adjustment for the time remaining when the car was repossessed, all as provided under the terms of the contract; and on its second count, for the reasonable value of the use of the car.

[The trial court held that plaintiff could not recover on the express contract because of the Statute of Frauds; but it allowed plaintiff to recover under the quantum meruit count. However, the sum it allowed, except for a minute mathematical error, was precisely the contract rate less the amount defendant had already paid: $1,144.52.]

The court did not allow the plaintiff to recover for the other items of damages claimed under the express lease.

* * * It is defendant's position that such contract having been stricken down, it could not properly be considered for any purpose; and that consequently there is no evidence of rental value upon which to base the court's finding.

The answer to this contention is * * * that even though the proposed agreement between the parties was not signed and was therefore barred from enforcement by the statute of frauds, that does not prevent the trial court from considering the proof concerning the proposed agreement between the parties as at least some evidence of the rental value.[1] The fact that this was an odd amount of $79.49 per month does not necessarily preclude the court from adopting that figure, if it believed, as it is apparent that it did, that such was the reasonable charge for the use of the car.

Nor do we find merit in the contention that inasmuch as the proposed written contract to rent the car was determined to be unenforceable, the plaintiff therefore cannot recover on the quantum meruit count. For the purpose of ascertaining whether the plaintiff is entitled to some relief, the proposed express contract can be bypassed just as the trial court did. The fact that the parties attempted but failed to complete a written contract does not foreclose the possibility that other contractual obligations could arise between them. Regardless of the abortive express contract, the fact cannot be escaped that the trial court found that the defendant Ellison had used the plaintiff's car for 22 months. The contract had thus been performed to that extent; and Ellison had to that extent used the plaintiff's car. In equity and good conscience he should not be permitted to accept this benefit, then invoke the statute of frauds with the result of cheating the plaintiff out of payment for the car it furnished him.

We are in accord with authorities which indicate that where one party has furnished and the other has accepted and used goods or services, even though pursuant to a contract which may be barred from enforcement by raising the statute of frauds, the former may nevertheless recover from the latter for the reasonable value of such goods or services. [citations] Accordingly, in the instant case the trial court very properly charged the defendant for the use of the car, less credit for the amounts which had been paid on the account.

Judgment affirmed.

1. [Footnote renumbered.] That evidence of an unenforceable oral contract fixing prices for services may be considered as some evidence of the value of the services, see McGilchrist v. F.W. Woolworth Co., 138 Or. 679, 7 P.2d 982.

HENRIOD, CHIEF JUSTICE (dissenting). * * * To this writer this conclusion completely ignores the profit factor that Bennett must have had in mind in letting his rental unit out for use by others. This of itself reveals the fallacy of this whole case. * * * The main opinion overlooks the fundamental principle that the *plaintiff* is the one upon whom the burden is placed to prove the market value in a quantum meruit case,—and there is not a syllable of evidence produced by plaintiff except an allegation in a pleading that was abandoned, based on a void contract, to support any such conclusion. It would be unthinkable, even to a layman, to assert that under a drive-it-yourself car rental contract that is void, the rental stated therein, being itself void, could be used as any evidence of market value or benefit conferred. The market value could be 50% below an agreed rental value in a particular case, especially where the contract, as here, was void, and for the main opinion to suggest that a defendant must bring evidence to discount an unproven judgment as to value, when the plaintiff has not sustained his burden of proving such value, is a novel departure from fundamental principles of pleading and proof. No evidence having been offered by plaintiff as to value or benefit to defendant, his complaint should have been dismissed,—irrespective of statute of frauds problems.

The main opinion seems to imply that because the court found that there were periodic payments totalling $604.24, defendant must have paid it, thus implying that such part performance took the contract out of the statute of frauds. If that be the implication, the judgment should have been based *on the contract,*—not on a quantum meruit basis. * * * [F]urthermore, if that be the implication, it cannot be sustained under the authorities, which generally hold that where personalty and not land is involved, part performance does not cut under the statute of frauds, and since the void contract is in no way involved here, part performance is no factor or issue.

Notes

1. Fabian v. Wasatch Orchard Co., 41 Utah 404, ___, 125 P. 860, 862 (1912). The court defines the meaning of benefit in a quantum meruit action. The plaintiff entered into an oral contract of employment to sell canned fruit and vegetables on commission. He solicited orders aggregating $30,000; but defendant because of its limited capacity, could only complete sales amounting to $16,000. The contract was unenforceable because not performable within one year. To defend against plaintiff's quantum meruit claim defendant asserted that it received no benefit because the orders were filled at a price less than defendant's manufacturing cost. In rejecting this contention, the court ruled that where one "rendered services for the adversary party, who, with knowledge or acquiescence, accepted them and received the benefit of them and repudiated the contract, he may recover on a quantum meruit the reasonable value thereof—not the profit or gain resulting to the adversary party by reason of the transaction, not the loss suffered or sustained by the other, but compensation for the reasonable value of the services rendered by the one and accepted and received by the other."

McGilchrist v. F.W. Woolworth Co., 138 Or. 679, ___, 7 P.2d 982, 985 (1932). Plaintiff orally agreed to work for the defendant at $18 to $25 per week for a three-year apprenticeship, after which he was promised a managerial position at a minimum salary of $25,000 per year. Plaintiff fully performed, but defendant repudiated its promise to appoint plaintiff a store manager. Since the contract was unenforceable, plaintiff sued for the reasonable value of his services, alleged to be $50 per week, and obtained a verdict for $2,899.80. On appeal, defendant argued that the contract price conclusively established the value of the services. In affirming judgment for plaintiff, the Oregon Supreme Court refused to follow that rule: The "better reasoned cases" state "that the contract may be received in evidence relative to the question of the value of the services, but that it is not conclusive, and the jury may consider it for what it may deem it to be worth."

2. A person who confers a benefit by performing an oral contract within the Statute of Frauds may be denied any relief because recovery would substantially defeat the purpose of the statute. The usual illustration is an oral real estate agency contract in states that prohibit enforcement of oral contracts. The agent who performs the contract has no remedy for the value of the services. Anno., 41 A.L.R.2d 905–20 (1955). See also Restatement of Restitution § 62(b) (1937).

Efforts to escape the rigor of this rule by claiming an equitable estoppel or by recharacterizing an agreement as one for a "finder's fee" have been unsuccessful. See Phillippe v. Shapell Industries, 43 Cal.3d 1247, 241 Cal.Rptr. 22, 743 P.2d 1279 (1987), cert. denied, 486 U.S. 1011 (1988); Buckingham v. Stille, 379 N.W.2d 30 (Iowa App.1985).

The rule applies only to licensed real estate brokers. A person who is not a broker may claim an estoppel to prevent the defendant from asserting the statute of frauds to bar recovery of a finder's fee. See Tenzer v. Superscope, Inc., 39 Cal.3d 18, 216 Cal.Rptr. 130, 702 P.2d 212 (1985).

The practice of denying relief to real estate agents has been applied to other types of regulatory statutes. For example a garage was denied recovery for repairing an automobile because it failed to provide a written estimate as required by statute. Osteen v. Morris, 481 So.2d 1287 (Fla.Dist.Ct.App.1986). And a building contractor was denied quantum meruit because it failed to comply with the writing requirement of the Home Improvement Act. Barrett Builders v. Miller, 215 Conn. 316, 576 A.2d 455 (1990).

FARASH v. SYKES DATATRONICS, INC.

Court of Appeals of New York, 1983.

59 N.Y.2d 500, 465 N.Y.S.2d 917, 452 N.E.2d 1245.

Supra p. 303.

2. ENFORCEMENT OF THE CONTRACT

a. Part Performance

WALKER v. IRETON

Supreme Court of Kansas, 1977.

211 Kan. 314, 559 P.2d 340.

PRAGER, JUSTICE. This is an action for the specific performance of an oral contract for the sale of farm land. The defendants answered asserting the defense of the statute of frauds. * * *

Sometime during the month of July 1973 Walker and Bernard Ireton commenced negotiations for the purchase of the Ireton farm which consisted of 160 acres in Saline county. Prior to this time Walker had only a speaking acquaintance with Bernard Ireton and did not know Mrs. Ireton. In response to a call from Ireton, Walker went to the Ireton farm where he was told that Ireton would sell the farm for $30,000. About a week later Walker advised Ireton that he would accept the proposal for sale at a price of $30,000. Ireton was to farm the crop land on shares and was to pay the real estate taxes through the year 1973. Agreements were made in regard to preparing and seeding the ground for alfalfa and for the cutting and storage of the prairie hay in the pasture. Walker was to be permitted to spray the trees in the pasture to kill them. It was agreed that Walker was to receive full possession of the farm in January 1974. The preparation of a written contract was discussed and it was agreed that one was to be executed. Ireton stated that he wanted to wait until he could see his tax man to find out how to take the money before preparing a written agreement. A week or so later Ireton stated to Walker that he had sold the farm too cheap but was not going to back out of the agreement. Ireton asked for another $500 on the purchase price to compensate him for alfalfa and because he intended to leave the air conditioner, drapes, and carpet in the house. Walker agreed to an increased sale price of $30,500. The purchase price was to be paid as follows: $50 on July 30, 1973; $7,612.50 on or before September 30, 1973; and $22,837.50 on or before January 1, 1974. * * * Walker also agreed to buy the range in the house for $25. On July 30, 1974, Walker delivered his $50 check to Ireton. This check was never endorsed or cashed. On at least four subsequent occasions thereafter Walker attempted to convince Ireton that a written contract was needed to complete the agreement. * * * On each occasion Ireton said that a written contract was not needed since he was honest. A written contract was never executed.

In August of 1973 Walker obtained the abstract of title to the property from Mrs. Ireton. Walker had it brought up to date and examined by his attorney at a cost of $36 for extension of the abstract and a $75 attorney fee for its examination. These sums were apparently paid by Walker. In September 1973 Walker took a hay rake to the property and left it in the pasture. Thereafter further differences began to occur. Ireton told Walker that their new home then being constructed would not be completed by January 1, 1974. Walker agreed that the Iretons should remain in possession until a later date after the house was completed. In late August 1973 Ireton offered Walker $200 to cancel the agreement. Walker declined the offer saying that at that time he had no other place to go. It should be noted that Walker planned to utilize the property as a home and place to breed and train thoroughbred horses. Prior to negotiating with Ireton, Walker had purchased another farm on contract but the Iretons' farm was larger and better situated for Walker's purposes. After making the oral contract with the Iretons, Walker sold the other farm because he could not afford two farms.

* * * Walker sent a man out to plant some alfalfa and Ireton sent the man away saying that he, Ireton, did not then have time to plant it and he would call him when he had time. On September 28, 1973, Walker tendered Ireton a check for $7,612.50, that sum being the second installment under the oral contract. At this time Ireton refused the payment and said that he was backing out of the oral agreement. Ireton said that he supposed Walker would have him in court. Ireton offered Walker the $50 check which had been received in July and Walker refused to take the check back. After this Walker offered the check to Mrs. Ireton which she refused but said she would pay the abstract expense and damages. Subsequently Walker was evicted from premises which he had leased for breeding and training his horses. In September 1974 Walker filed this action for specific performance. * * *

The trial court concluded that there was not sufficient equities in the case to justify the court in taking the case out of the statute of frauds. The trial court found that this was a classic case of an oral contract for the sale of land, and because of the statute of frauds the oral contract was not enforceable. * * * Walker appealed to this court.

Counsel for Walker takes the position that the statute of frauds should be held to be inapplicable as a matter of law on alternative theories of fraud, estoppel, acquiescence, waiver, ratification, inconsistency in conduct, or partial performance. In his brief counsel for Walker has cited a number of Kansas decisions which have approached this statute of frauds question from these various angles, using different terminology in particular cases.

In determining this case it would be helpful to consider some of the basic principles of law which have been applied in our cases involving oral contracts for sale of land where the statute of frauds was asserted as a defense. Literally applied K.S.A. 33–106 bars any action on an oral contract for the sale of land. Shortly after the original statute of frauds was enacted in England, courts of equity refused to apply the statute in certain cases where the purchaser under the contract in reliance upon the oral agreement performed acts required by the contract to such an extent as to make it grossly unjust and inequitable for a court of equity to refuse to enforce the oral agreement. Throughout our judicial history the courts of Kansas have enforced oral contracts for the sale of land because of equitable considerations in many cases. In 1872 in Edwards v. Fry, 9 Kan. 417, Justice Brewer upheld the specific performance of an oral contract for the sale of land where a vendee in possession of the land paid a portion of the purchase price and made valuable and lasting improvements on the land. In the course of the opinion Justice Brewer relied in part on the rule that a party who has permitted another to perform acts on the faith of an agreement, shall not insist that the agreement is bad, and that he is entitled to treat those acts as if it had never existed. From the beginning the basis for removal of a case from application of the statute of frauds has been the reliance by one of the parties to the oral contract to his detriment under circumstances where gross injustice would result unless the oral contract was enforced. In Baldridge v. Centgraf, 82 Kan. 240, 108 P. 83 this court again emphasized reliance as the basis for relief from a strict application of the statute of frauds in the following language:

> "The ground upon which a court, notwithstanding the statute of frauds, may compel the complete performance of an oral contract for the sale of real estate, which has been partly performed, is that such a decree may be necessary in order to avoid injustice toward one who in reliance upon the agreement has so altered his position that he can not otherwise be afforded adequate relief."

In other cases [citations] this court in dealing with oral contracts within the statute of frauds has applied the following principles of law:

> "(1) The statute of frauds does not render the oral contract void. It is valid for all purposes except that of suit.
>
> "(2) Since the contract is one which cannot be enforced, no action for damages will lie for its breach.
>
> "(3) The statute of frauds was enacted to prevent fraud and injustice, not to foster or encourage it, and courts will, so far as possible, refuse to allow it to be used as a shield to protect fraud and as a means to enable one to take advantage of his own wrong.

"(4) Where it is sought to enforce an oral contract for the sale of an interest in real estate on the grounds that it has been performed by the party seeking to enforce it, it must appear that a failure to enforce would amount to a fraud against the party.

"(5) Absent compelling equitable considerations an oral contract within the statute of frauds will not be specifically enforced.

"(6) Part performance of an oral contract will not take the case out of the statute where the performing party can be compensated in money.

"(7) Payment of the purchase price alone is not sufficient part performance to take a case out of the statute of frauds. Since the money can be recovered back by action, no fraud will be accomplished if the oral contract is not enforced.

"(8) Delivery of possession of the land alone without the making of improvements is not sufficient to take a case out of the application of the statute of frauds."

In dealing with statute of frauds cases courts throughout the country have often shifted their approach to the problem from a theory of part performance, to one of fraud, or one of estoppel. Because of this confusion in the cases the American Law Institute in 1973 adopted a tentative draft to the Restatement 2d, Contracts, to clarify the legal principle and to make it more understandable. Specifically, we note §§ 197 and 217A of the Restatement 2d, Contracts (Tentative draft 1973), which provide as follows:

"§ 197. Action in Reliance; Specific Performance.

"A contract for the transfer of an interest in land may be specifically enforced notwithstanding failure to comply with the Statute of Frauds if it is established that the party seeking enforcement, in reasonable reliance on the contract and on the continuing assent of the party against whom enforcement is sought, has so changed his position that injustice can be avoided only by specific enforcement.

"§ 217A. Enforcement by Virtue of Action in Reliance.

"(1) A promise which the promisor should reasonably expect to induce action or forbearance on the part of the promisee or a third person and which does induce the action or forbearance is enforceable notwithstanding the Statute of Frauds if injustice can be avoided only by enforcement of the promise. The remedy granted for breach is to be limited as justice requires.

"(2) In determining whether injustice can be avoided only by enforcement of the promise, the following circumstances are influential:

"(a) the availability and adequacy of other remedies, particularly cancellation and restitution;

"(b) the definite and substantial character of the action or forbearance in relation to the remedy sought;

"(c) the extent to which the action or forbearance corroborates evidence of the making and terms of the promise, or the making and terms are otherwise established by clear and convincing evidence;

"(d) the reasonableness of the action or forbearance and the misleading character of the promise."

We have not specifically mentioned or approved §§ 197 and 217A in our prior decisions. We have, however, recognized and applied in other cases a similar provision found in § 90 in the Restatement, Contracts, which sets forth the doctrine of "promissory estoppel." In our judgment sections 197 and 217A of Restatement 2d, Contracts (Tentative draft 1973), are clear and direct statements of the principles of law to be applied in determining whether or not an oral contract should be removed from the application of the statute of frauds and enforced by a court on equitable principles. They are based upon the equitable doctrine of reliance which is the fundamental theory upon which all of our prior cases are founded.

In determining the result in this case we will apply these sections to the factual situation in the record now before us. We have concluded that under all the facts and circumstances equity does not require the statute of frauds to be removed as a defense to this action for specific performance of the oral contract. Here there is no claim that there was any relationship of trust or confidence between the parties. There are no allegations or evidence of false misrepresentation of existing facts. The worst which can be said is that Ireton repeatedly promised that he would perform the oral contract and that he would enter into a written contract to evidence the same. It was stipulated that the parties understood a written contract was to be prepared. Ireton simply refused to sign a written contract on four or five different occasions. Although Walker made a $50 down payment he never took possession of the land involved and made no improvements thereon. Walker placed a hay rake on one of the pastures of the farm but this could not be considered a delivery of possession of the land.

The acts of reliance which Walker has asserted are limited by the record to delivery of the $50 check as an installment on the purchase price, payment of a $36 abstract expense and a $75 attorney fee for an abstract examination, the placing of a side-delivery hay rake on a pasture in September 1973, and the fact that Walker sold a farm near Hedville which he had recently purchased in reliance on Ireton's promise to sell his farm. * * * We have concluded that taken together they are not sufficient to justify specific performance of the oral contract. The fact that Walker sold another farm in expectation that the Iretons would sell their farm to him does not justify specific performance under the circumstances of this case. As a general rule an act which is purely collateral to an oral contract, although done in reliance on such contract is not such a part performance as to authorize the enforcement of the contract by a court of equity. [citations] An exception is recognized, however, where the agreement was made to induce the collateral act or where the collateral act was contemplated by the parties as a part of the entire transaction. [citation]

In the present case the plaintiff Walker does not contend that he advised the Iretons of his intention to sell the Hedville farm in advance of the sale or that the Iretons had any knowledge concerning the sale of the Hedville farm until after it had already been sold. Furthermore Walker does not contend at any place in the record that he lost money on the resale of the Hedville farm to others. We consider the resale of the Hedville farm by Walker to others as a matter wholly collateral to the Ireton contract and not within the contemplation of the parties nor within the scope of any understanding between Ireton and Walker. In support of this position is Dunn v. Winans, 106 Kan. 80, 186 P. 748. There plaintiff vendee brought an action for specific performance of an oral agreement to sell certain land. The petition alleged the making of some improvements on the property and further alleged that plaintiff was damaged in the amount of $300 for the sale of his home for the purpose of carrying out the contract with the defendant. This court denied specific performance holding that there had not been sufficient part performance to take the case out of the statute of frauds. The court further held that although specific performance was denied, the vendee was entitled to recover the expenses which were incurred by him for the improvements he made on the property. He was not, however, permitted to recover damages on account of the sale of his former home. Walker is entitled to the return of his $50 check and the cost of bringing Iretons' abstract up to date on the basis of quantum meruit or unjust enrichment. These expenditures were of benefit to the Iretons and Walker is entitled to restitution for these items. Walker is not, however, entitled to be reimbursed for his $75 attorney fee in obtaining a legal opinion. The Iretons received no benefit from this expenditure.

Where a vendee is denied specific performance under an oral contract for the sale of land his right to restitution is restricted to expenditures or services which benefitted the vendor on the basis of quantum meruit. * * *

Comment b under 217A states that the reliance of the promisee must be foreseeable by the promisor and enforcement must be necessary to avoid injustice. In this case equity and justice do not require specific enforcement of the oral contract, nor do they require reimbursement to Walker for the sale of the Hedville farm.

The judgment of the district court is affirmed.

Notes

1. Bank of Alton v. Tanaka, 247 Kan. 443, 799 P.2d 1029 (1990).

2. Partial or full payment of the price does not constitute sufficient part performance to take the case out of the statute of frauds. Chomicky v. Buttolph, 147 Vt. 128, 513 A.2d 1174 (1986); Gibson v. Hrysikos, 293 S.C. 8, 358 S.E.2d 173 (1987). On the other hand, taking possession of the property and substantially improving it are generally sufficient to provide a basis for specific relief. Hostetter v. Hoover, 378 Pa.Super. 1, 547 A.2d 1247 (1988); Gibson v. Hrysikos, supra.

3. *Oral promises to make a gift of land.* Oral promises to make a gift of land have been specifically enforced where the evidence establishing the gift is clear and unambiguous and the donee has taken possession of the property and made improvements in reliance on the promise. See Fuisz v. Fuisz, 386 Pa.Super. 591, 563 A.2d 540 (1989); Montoya v. New Mexico Human Services Department, Income Support Division, 108 N.M. 263, 771 P.2d 196 (App.1989).

4. *Oral promises to devise property.* Where a promise is made to devise property in exchange for consideration, usually services, the promise will be specifically enforced where injustice would otherwise result. Shepherd v. Mazzetti, 545 A.2d 621 (Del.1988). Where the value of the services can be readily evaluated and monetary compensation appears adequate, however, the promisee is restricted to quantum meruit recovery. Kennedy v. Bank of America, 237 Cal.App.2d 637, 47 Cal.Rptr. 154 (1965).

5. *Oral promises to a cohabitant.* Where a promise to convey property is made in exchange for services performed as a cohabitant and the agreement is not explicitly and inseparably based on sexual services, several courts grant recovery. Crowe v. De Gioia, 203 N.J.Super. 22, 495 A.2d 889 (1985), aff'd, 102 N.J. 50, 505 A.2d 591 (1986). The court may decline to award specific performance where the acts constituting the part performance do not unequivocally refer to a contract, Unitas v. Temple, 314 Md. 689, 552 A.2d 1285 (1989), or where a monetary award

provides an adequate remedy. In re Estate of Spaulding, 187 Ill.App.3d 1031, 543 N.E.2d 980 (1989).

6. Wisconsin has sought to solve this problem by enacting Wis.Stat. § 706–04:

706.04 *Equitable relief.* A transaction which does not satisfy one or more of the requirements of s. 706.02 [the Statute of Frauds] may be enforceable in whole or in part under doctrines of equity, provided all of the elements of the transaction are clearly and satisfactorily proved and, in addition:

(1) The deficiency of the conveyance may be supplied by reformation in equity; or

(2) The party against whom enforcement is sought would be unjustly enriched if enforcement of the transaction were denied; or

(3) The party against whom enforcement is sought is equitably estopped from asserting the deficiency. A party may be so estopped whenever, pursuant to the transaction and in good faith reliance thereon, the party claiming estoppel has changed his position to his substantial detriment under circumstances such that the detriment so incurred may not be effectively recovered otherwise than by enforcement of the transaction, and either:

(a) The grantee has been admitted into substantial possession or use of the premises or has been permitted to retain such possession or use after termination of a prior right thereto; or

(b) The detriment so incurred was incurred with the prior knowing consent or approval of the party sought to be estopped.

For judicial interpretations, see Spensley Feeds, Inc. v. Livingston Feed & Lumber, Inc., 128 Wis.2d 279, 381 N.W.2d 601 (App.1985); Krauza v. Mauritz, 78 Wis.2d 276, 254 N.W.2d 251 (1977); In re Estate of Lade, 82 Wis.2d 80, 260 N.W.2d 665 (1978).

b. *Estoppel to Assert the Statute*

OXLEY v. RALSTON PURINA CO.

United States Court of Appeals, Sixth Circuit, 1965.

349 F.2d 328.

WEINMAN, DISTRICT JUDGE. * * * Plaintiff, a successful business man who desired to own a farm and go into farming, terminated his employment and his business interests and in January of 1957 purchased a 160–acre farm near Byron, Michigan. He spent substantial sums on the house located on the farm to make it suitable for year-around living for his family. He began utilizing the farm for the production of corn and related cash crops. As he proceeded with this operation, he came into contact with Eugene King, the operator of the elevator at Byron and the local Ralston Purina dealer. During their visits together, there were discussions of plaintiff's undeveloped plans of going into a farming operation other than the simple cash crop program to which his farm was then devoted. Among various plans considered was a hog-fattening program. * * *

In February of 1959, plaintiff attended a meeting with [representatives of] Ralston Purina. These men felt that plaintiff was a good prospect for the Ralston hog-leasing program as he had the forty or fifty thousand dollars needed to launch such a program. Mr. Hamilton made certain projections of what could be done under such a program, relying in the main on quotations

ferred to the law side and plaintiff was given an opportunity to seek relief on a quantum meruit theory of benefit conferred upon defendant because of assets transferred to him and utilized by him to his benefit.

In each of the foregoing cases, and in numerous others which this Court has examined where the transfer of real property was not involved, the Michigan Supreme Court has repeatedly stated that an oral contract which cannot be performed in one year from the making thereof is void and partial or substantial performance does not take the contract out of the statute of frauds. However, none of the Michigan cases which we have read has stated the applicability of the doctrine of equitable estoppel to the problem.

We must note at this point that though the doctrine of part performance has its basis in an estoppel, part performance and equitable estoppel are not the same. The doctrine of part performance has historically been applied only to contracts involving the sale of land, whereas the doctrine of equitable estoppel is more encompassing. Under that doctrine, the principle is that

> "he who by his language or conduct leads another to do, upon the faith of an oral agreement, what he would not otherwise have done, and changes his position to his prejudice, will not be allowed to subject such person to loss or injury, or to avail himself of that change to the prejudice of such other party."

The Trial Judge, citing Brummel v. Brummel [363 Mich. 447, 109 N.W.2d 782 (1961)], a case involving an oral contract to convey real property, held that Michigan, like other jurisdictions, applies the doctrine of equitable estoppel in those cases where its application is called for by the facts. The language quoted by the Judge from that case is:

> " 'If one party to an oral contract, in reliance upon the contract, has performed his obligation thereunder so that it would be a fraud upon him to allow the other party to repudiate the contract, by interposing the statute, equity will regard the contract as removed from the operation of the statute.' "

In M.H. Metal Products Corporation v. April [251 N.Y. 146, 167 N.E. 201 (1929)], defendant guaranteed in writing payment of twenty thousand sets of jacks at 80 cents each "if manufactured and delivered * * * in accordance with the terms and conditions of the said contract." The sockets were somewhat weak and needed strengthening and plaintiff agreed to make the change at defendant's request. It was agreed that the change would cost 20 cents for each jack, making the agreed cost for each jack one dollar instead of eighty cents as provided in the original contract. The defendant, acting for the purchaser, and in the presence of the representative of plaintiff, ordered a new die, to be used in making the jacks as altered, at an agreed price to be paid to the man who was to make the die for the purchaser. However, defendant refused to guarantee the additional 20 cents, but orally agreed to remain bound by his original guaranty. Subsequently, plaintiff sued defendant on the original guaranty. Defendant raised the defense of the statute of frauds on the grounds that the original contract had been altered and his guaranty no longer applied. The Court held that defendant was estopped to raise that defense.

* * * [W]e do not believe that the application of the doctrine of equitable estoppel in such cases is incongruous with the holding that contracts void under the statute of frauds are "void for all purposes." The reason for this is that when the doctrine of equitable estoppel is invoked, defendant is precluded from asserting the statute and therefore the oral contract does not become "void for all purposes." Stated another way, the oral contracts which we are

considering become void because of the application of the statute of frauds and if defendant is denied the right to assert the statute, the oral contracts exist as if there were no such statute. * * *

The defendant has also urged that there was no fraud alleged or proved by plaintiff and therefore there can be no estoppel in this type of case. However, fraud in the usual sense is not required, as stated by Williston: [§ 533A]

> "Actual intent or design to mislead is not, however, essential. There need not be a corrupt motive or evil design; it is sufficient if the circumstances are such as to render it unconscionable to deny facts which the party by his silence or representation has caused the other party to believe in and act upon, and the denial of which must operate as a fraud upon him."

We pass now to the question of damages, which defendant alleges are excessive. The Trial Judge found that "expenses charged to the operation" were established in the amount claimed by plaintiff, being $56,567.20. The Court further stated that it "does not find a specific guarantee nor can the projections which were used (and achieved by the plaintiff, so far as his operations are concerned) respecting the projected cash income from the 'leasing farms' furnish a base for the award of damages, as they would be conjectural and speculative."

The Court listed as the damages warranted: "$56,567.20 net loss from the program; $75,900.00 value of herd after 3 and ½ years; $10,368.00 value of growing pigs; making a total of $142,735.20."

The amounts of $75,900.00 and $10,368.00 were, we assume, derived from the adoption of the figures testified to by plaintiff's witness, Mr. Hamilton, that after three and one-half years there would have been 1012 mature hogs in the program, valued at $75.00 each (equalling $75,900.00) and 576 growing pigs on plaintiff's farm, valued at $18.00 each (equalling $10,368.00). We note that the $75.00 and $18.00 respectively, are market values without subtracting the cost of raising the pigs. No law has been cited to us to sustain the awarding of gross profits as damages and we find it to be error in making such an award. We also note that the Trial Judge did not state the basis of his award of "expenses charged to the operations." (The Trial Judge did not find that defendant guaranteed that if the program failed defendant would reimburse plaintiff for his expenses. Were these damages which arose because of defendant's refusal to take and dispose of plaintiff's surplus stock?) Nor did he state how he arrived at the figure of three and one-half years as the length of time of the program for the purpose of determining the loss.

We are not holding that the awarding of the expenses or that the use of three and one-half years as the multiple were improper as a matter of law, we are holding that there are not sufficient facts stated in the opinion to sustain the foregoing as being proper. The Trial Judge shall, upon remand, make such additional findings as are necessary to form the basis of any damages which he may award. Of course, as to loss of profits as damages, they may be awarded only if they can be determined with a reasonable degree of certainty.

* * * Defendant argues that the award of $56,567.20 should be reduced * * * by $7,527.95 because of a tax saving to plaintiff because he had outside income against which he could apply his loss from the farm operations.

* * * Defendant cites no cases in support of the proposition which he urges and we reject the same.

[Remanded.]

Notes

1. Palandjian v. Pahlavi, 614 F.Supp. 1569, 1581 (D.Mass.1985), cert. denied, 481 U.S. 1037 (1987). The court summarized the factors that create an estoppel: (a) "A representation or conduct amounting to a representation intended to induce a course of conduct on the part of the person to whom the representation was made." (b) "An act or omission resulting from the representation, whether actual or by conduct, by the person to whom the representation is made." (c) "Detriment to such person as a consequence of the act or omission."

2. *The U.C.C. Statute of Frauds.* U.C.C. § 2–201 is a statute of frauds for sales of goods that exceed $500. Most states have recognized that estoppel applies under § 2–201. See Hoffmann v. Boone, 708 F.Supp. 78 (S.D.N.Y.1989); Allied Grape Growers v. Bronco Wine Co., 203 Cal.App.3d 432, 249 Cal.Rptr. 872 (1988).

3. One consequence of labeling promissory estoppel equitable is that there is no right to jury trial. See Nimrod Marketing (Overseas) Ltd. v. Texas Energy Investment Corp., 769 F.2d 1076 (5th Cir.1985), cert. denied, 475 U.S. 1047, 476 U.S. 1104 (1986) and C & K Engineering Contractors v. Amber Steel Co., 25 Cal.3d 1, 151 Cal.Rptr. 323, 587 P.2d 1136 (1978), supra, p. 237.

4. *Problem: The Statute of Frauds and Wholly Negative Oral Covenants:* A chiropractor makes an unwritten agreement to have an associate for an unspecified term. The associate agrees not to compete with the employer for five years after leaving employment. The association lasts for a year, whereupon the "associate" sets up a competing shop next door. His competition is fierce but not unfair enough to be a tort.

The statute of frauds applies to contracts not performable within one year. Can the unwritten noncompete covenant be enforced by using concepts like "full performance," "part performance" or "estoppel" to bar assertion of the statute? See Frantz v. Parke, 111 Idaho 1005, 729 P.2d 1068 (App.1986).

c. *The Special Case of Promissory Estoppel*

Introductory Note

Separate lines of doctrine converge under the heading of Promissory Estoppel—a variation of the broad and remedially useful equitable estoppel. *Walker* demonstrates the equitable "part performance" doctrine; the doctrine was originally invoked in land sales to remove or at least lower the Statute of Frauds barrier. But it can also evolve into a general principle of equitable estoppel. Only a short further step need be taken. Estoppel by conduct becomes promissory estoppel whenever the conduct itself is a promise.

The foregoing cases concern unenforceable contracts; equitable estoppel simply makes them enforceable and opens the way for legal damages as well. Another line of cases deals with promises, but no contract at all. In Chapter 4 we saw common law restitutionary remedies develop to recover the "benefit" conferred in reliance upon contractless promises. When the benefit consists of services in misreliance upon nonexistent contracts, courts tend to value the services according to the available market rather than their actual worth to the defendant. The consequence, as has been repeatedly observed, is damages disguised as restitution.

Another short step was taken in Earhart v. William Low Co. The court recognized that promissory estoppel can be applied and an alternative damage remedy be available through equitable intermediation. But the damages are equitable rather than legal.

EARHART v. WILLIAM LOW CO.

Supreme Court of California, 1979.
Cal.3d 503, 158 Cal.Rptr. 887, 600 P.2d 1344.

Supra, p. 306.

WALTERS v. MARATHON OIL CO.

United States Court of Appeals.
Seventh Circuit, 1981.
642 F.2d 1098.

SPEARS, DISTRICT JUDGE. This action arose as a result of the Iranian revolution and the uncertainty of oil supplies. Marathon Oil Company, the appellant, is engaged in the business of reselling and distributing petroleum products. The appellee, Dennis E. Walters, contacted appellant in late December, 1978, about the possibility of locating a combination foodstore and service station on a vacant gasoline service station site in Indianapolis. Appellees (husband and wife) purchased the service station in February, 1979, and continued to make improvements upon it, based upon promises made, and the continuing negotiations with representatives from appellant. Paper work apparently proceeded normally, and appellees' proposal was delivered to appellant along with a three-party agreement, signed by appellees and Time Oil Company, the previous supplier to the service station site appellees had purchased. Before appellees' proposal was accepted by appellant, but after it was received at the office, appellant placed a moratorium on the consideration of new applications for dealerships and seller arrangements, and refused to sign the three-party agreement.

After a bench trial, the court found for appellees and against appellant on the theory of promissory estoppel. This finding has not been challenged. * * *

The appellant argues that the trial court's computation of damages is clearly erroneous and contrary to the law. The trial court found that appellees lost anticipated profits of six cents per gallon for the 370,000 gallons they were entitled to receive under their allocation for the first year's gasoline sales, totalling $22,200.00, and awarded this amount in damages. The appellant insists that since appellees succeeded at trial solely on a promissory estoppel theory, and the district court so found, loss of profits is not a proper measure of damages. It contends that appellees' damages should have been the amount of their expenditures in reliance on the promise, measured by the difference between their expenditures and the present value of the property. Using this measure of damages, appellees would have received no award, for the present value of the real estate and its improvements is slightly more than the amount expended by appellees in reliance upon the promise. As a consequence, the appellant says that because appellees can recoup all they spent in reliance on appellant's promise, they would be in the same position they would have been in had the promise not been made.

However, in reliance upon appellant's promise to supply gasoline supplies to them, appellees purchased the station, and invested their funds and their time. It is unreasonable to assume that they did not anticipate a return of profits from this investment of time and funds, but, in reliance upon appellant's promise, they had foregone the opportunity to make the investment elsewhere. As indicated, the record reflects that had appellant performed according to its promise, appellees would have received the anticipated net profit of $22,200.00. The findings of the trial court in this regard were fully supported by the evidence. For example, it was shown that the 1977/78 base period for this particular station was 375,450 gallons. The appellant's own exhibit reflected the same amount. The testimony of the previous owner showed that the location pumped 620,000 gallons in 1972, and that he pumped 375,450 gallons in 1978. Furthermore, an expert witness testified that the site would pump 360,000 gallons a year. Appellant's own witness testified that all of its dealers received 100% of their base period allocation for the time in question. * * *

An equity court possesses some discretionary power to award damages in order to do complete justice. * * *

Since promissory estoppel is an equitable matter, the trial court has broad power in its choice of a remedy, and it is significant that the ancient maxim that "equity will not suffer a wrong to be without a remedy" has long been the law in the State of Indiana. [citations]

In this case the promissory estoppel finding of the district court is not challenged. Moreover, it is apparent that the appellees suffered a loss of profits as a direct result of their reliance upon the promise made by appellant, and the amount of the lost profits was ascertained with reasonable certainty.[1] * * * [A]n award of damages based upon lost profits was appropriate in order to do complete justice. * * *

Affirmed.

Notes

1. Signal Hill Aviation Co. v. Stroppe, 96 Cal.App.3d 627, 640–41, 158 Cal. Rptr. 178, 185–86 (1979): "Defendant contends that the trial court erred in awarding plaintiff 'loss of profits' damages, because there is authoritative support for the position that promissory estoppel damages should be limited to those sums actually incurred by the promisee in reliance on the promise.

"In Swinerton & Walberg Co. v. City of Inglewood–L.A. County Civic Center Authority (1974) 40 Cal.App.3d 98, 105, 114 Cal.Rptr. 834, the plaintiff was the low bidder on a public construction project, but the bid was awarded by defendants to another. *Swinerton* held that plaintiff had a cause of action based upon promissory estoppel, but declared that the damages which could be awarded 'might well be limited to those it sustained directly by reason of its justifiable reliance upon the Authority's promise—in other words, to the expenses it incurred in its fruitless participation in the competitive bidding process. * * *' No other California case law is cited in support of this limitation on recovery pursuant to the doctrine of promissory estoppel, but *Swinerton* does suggest that the unsuccessful bidder would

1. In Goodman v. Dicker, 169 F.2d 684 (D.C. Cir.1948), relied upon by appellant, the court held that the true measure of damages in that equitable estoppel case was the loss in the sum of $1150 sustained by expenditures made in reliance on assurances given to the injured parties, and that the trial court had erred in *adding* the item of $350 for lost profits. No reasons were assigned or authorities cited by the court for the action it took, and there was no suggestion that in an appropriate case loss of profits could not be a true measure of damages. In any event, it is apparent that the award of double damages was rejected and the higher figure of $1150 was chosen in order to do complete justice. * * *

not be able to claim the profit which would have been realized if the bid had been accepted and the work performed. *Swinerton* did recognize a divergence of opinion on this issue; it stated that '[o]n the other hand, the opinions of the commentators regarding the justice of limited as opposed to complete contractual recovery in promissory estoppel is divided.'

"Conceptually, promissory estoppel is distinct from contract in that the promisee's justifiable and detrimental reliance on the promise is regarded as a substitute for the consideration required as an element of an enforceable contract. There appears to be no rational basis for distinguishing the two situations in terms of the *damages* that may be recovered; both may involve the problem of ascertaining a future loss of profits, actually a problem of presenting adequate proof. Complete contractual recovery may include, under some circumstances, loss of profits when the loss is definite rather than speculative.

"We thus decline to limit plaintiff's recovery herein to only actual expenditures made in reliance on defendant's promise. We determine that the net profits derived by defendant were also appropriately awarded to plaintiff on equitable grounds, as the result of both promissory estoppel and constructive trust theories. The monetary award made below was 'more like an accounting between the parties than like an assessment of damages.' Ellis v. Mihelis, 60 Cal.2d 206, 220, 32 Cal.Rptr. 415, 423, 384 P.2d 7, 15 (1963)."

2. *Limiting recovery based on an estoppel to reliance damages.* R. Renaissance, Inc. v. Rohm and Haas Co., 674 F.Supp. 591 (S.D. Ohio 1987); Green v. Interstate United Management Services Corp., 748 F.2d 827 (3d Cir.1984). In Bower v. AT & T Technologies, Inc., 852 F.2d 361 (8th Cir.1988), a plaintiff who relied on the breach of an oral promise to employ him at will was allowed to recover all expenditures in reliance on the promise. See generally, Becker, Promissory Estoppel Damages, 16 Hofstra L.Rev. 131 (1987).

3. The cumulative impact of "promissory estoppel" on Remedies is striking. Despite the attention given the doctrine in Contracts, no legal "contract" is involved. Equity, unconcerned with legal niceties, has long compelled performance of promises that ought to be performed. The sum is that for breach of a non-contract, "equitable damages" not constrained by legal rules, but amounting to an accounting between the parties, are recoverable in a nonjury suit.

B. AGREEMENTS UNENFORCEABLE BECAUSE OF IMPOSSIBILITY

BUTTERFIELD v. BYRON

Supreme Judicial Court of Massachusetts, 1891.
153 Mass. 517, 27 N.E. 667.

[Plaintiff and defendant agreed to build a house on plaintiff's land. The details of the somewhat unusual arrangement are in the opinion. Briefly stated, the defendant contracted with the plaintiff to contribute labor and materials and to receive progress payments according to the amount of labor performed and material supplied. Defendant worked on the project and had received some of the agreed payments when fire destroyed the structure. The plaintiff (perhaps wishing to resolve matters in some fashion at a time before Declaratory Judgment statutes) sued for breach of contract.]

KNOWLTON, J. It is well established law that where one contracts to furnish labor and materials, and construct a chattel, or build a house, on land of another, he will not ordinarily be excused from performance of his contract by the destruction of the chattel or building without his fault before the time fixed for the delivery of it. * * * It is equally well settled that where work is to be done under a contract on a chattel or building which is not wholly the property of the contractor, or for which he is not solely accountable, as where repairs are to be made on the property of another, the agreement on both sides is upon the implied condition that the chattel or building shall continue in existence, and the destruction of it without the fault of either of the parties will excuse performance of the contract, and leave no right of recovery of damages in favor of either against the other. * * * In such cases, from the very nature of the agreements as applied to the subject-matter, it is manifest that, while nothing is expressly said about it, the parties contemplated the continued existence of that to which the contract relates. The implied condition is a part of the contract as if it were written into it, and by its terms the contract is not to be performed if the subject-matter of it is destroyed, without the fault of either of the parties, before the time for complete performance has arrived.

The fundamental question in the present case is, what is the true interpretation of the contract? Was the house, while in the process of erection, to be in the control and at the sole risk of the defendant, or was the plaintiff to have a like interest as the builder of a part of it? Was the defendant's undertaking to go on and build and deliver such a house as the contract called for, even if he should be obliged repeatedly to begin anew on account of the destruction again and again of a partly completed building by inevitable accident, or did his contract relate to one building only, so that it would be at an end if the building, when nearly completed, should perish without his fault? It is to be noticed that his agreement was not to build a house, furnishing all the labor and materials therefor. His contract was of a very different kind. The specifications are incorporated into it, and it appears that it was an agreement to contribute certain labor and materials towards the erection of a house on land of the plaintiff, towards the erection of which the plaintiff was to contribute other labor and materials, which contributions would together make a completed house. The grading, excavating, stone-work, brickwork, painting, and plumbing were to be done by the plaintiff. Immediately before the fire, when the house was nearly completed, the defendant's contract, so far as it remained unperformed, was to finish a house on the plaintiff's land, which had been constructed from materials and by labor furnished in part by the plaintiff and in part by himself. He was no more responsible that the house should continue in existence than the plaintiff was. Looking at the situation of the parties at that time, it was like a contract to make repairs on the house of another. His undertaking and duty to go on and finish the work was upon an implied condition that the house, the product of their joint contributions, should remain in existence. The destruction of it by fire discharged him from his contract. * * *

What are the rights of the parties in regard to what has been done in part performance of a contract in which there is an implied condition that the subject to which the contract relates shall continue in existence, and where the contemplated work cannot be completed by reason of the destruction of the property without fault of either of the parties, is in dispute, upon the authorities. The decisions in England differ from those of Massachusetts and of most of the other states of this country. There the general rule, stated broadly, seems to be that the loss must remain where it first falls, and that neither of the parties can recover of the other for anything done under the contract. In England, on authority, and upon original grounds not very satisfactory to the judges of recent times, it is held that freight advanced for the transportation of goods subsequently lost by the perils of the sea cannot be recovered back. [citations] In the United States and in continental Europe the rule is different. [citations] In England it is held that one who has partly performed a contract on property of another, which is destroyed without the fault of either party, can recover nothing; and, on the other hand, that one who has advanced payments on account of labor and materials furnished under such circumstances cannot recover back the money. [citations] One who has advanced money for the instruction of his son in a trade cannot recover it back if he who received it dies without giving the instruction. [citation] But where one dies, and leaves unperformed a contract which is entire, his administrator may recover any installments which were due on it before his death. [citation] In this country, where one is to make repairs on the house of another under a special contract, or is to furnish a part of the work and materials used in the erection of a house, and his contract becomes impossible of performance on account of the destruction of the house, the rule is uniform, so far as the authorities have come to our attention, that he may recover for what he has done or furnished. In Cleary v. Sohier, 120 Mass. 210, the plaintiff made a contract to lath and plaster a certain building for 40 cents per square yard. The building was destroyed by a fire which was an unavoidable casualty. The plaintiff had lathed the building, and put on the first coat of plaster, and would have put on the second coat, according to his contract, if the building had not been burned. He sued on an implied *assumpsit* for work done and materials found. It was agreed that, if he was entitled to recover anything, the judgment should be for the price charged. It was held that he could recover. * * * If the owner, in such a case, has paid in advance, he may recover back his money, or so much of it as was an overpayment. The principle seems to be that when, under an implied condition of the contract, the parties are to be excused from performance if a certain event happens, and by reason of the happening of the event it becomes impossible to do that which was contemplated by the contract, there is an implied *assumpsit* for what has properly been done by either of them; the law dealing with it as done at the request of the other, and creating a liability to pay for it its value, to be determined by the price stipulated in the contract, or in some other way if the contract price cannot be made applicable. Where there is a bilateral contract for an entire consideration moving from each party, and the contract cannot be performed, it may be held that the consideration on each side is the performance of the contract by the other, and that a failure completely to perform it is a failure of the entire consideration, leaving each party, if there has been no breach nor fault on either side, to his implied *assumpsit* for what he has done.

* * * The defendant is entitled to be compensated at the contract price for all he did before the fire. The plaintiff is to be allowed for all his payments.

Notes

1. The English position has been reversed. See Fibrosa Spolka Akcyjna v. Fairbairn Lawson Combe Barbour, Ltd., [1942] All E.R. 122; Frustrated Contract Act, 6 & 7 George VI, c. 40 [1943].

2. Posner & Rosenfield, Impossibility and Related Doctrines in Contract Law: An Economic Analysis, 6 J.Legal Stud. 83, 290–92 (1977): †

"From the standpoint of economics—and disregarding, but only momentarily, administrative costs—discharge should be allowed where the promisee is the superior risk bearer; if the promisor is the superior risk bearer, nonperformance should be treated as a breach of contract. * * *

"A party can be a superior risk bearer for one of two reasons. First, he may be in a better position to prevent the risk from materializing. This resembles the economic criterion for assigning liability in tort cases. It is an important criterion in many contract settings, too, but not in this one. Discharge would be inefficient in any case where the promisor could prevent the risk from materializing at a lower cost than the expected cost of the risky event. In such a case efficiency would require that the promisor bear the loss resulting from the occurrence of the event, and hence that occurrence should be treated as precipitating a breach of contract.

"But the converse is not necessarily true. It does not necessarily follow from the fact that the promisor could not at any reasonable cost have prevented the risk from materializing that he should be discharged from his contractual obligations. Prevention is only one way of dealing with risk; the other is insurance. The promisor may be the superior insurer. If so, his inability to prevent the risk from materializing should not operate to discharge him from the contract, any more than an insurance company's inability to prevent a fire on the premises of the insured should excuse it from its liability to make good the damage caused by the fire. * * *

"An easy case for discharge would be one where (1) the promisor asking to be discharged could not reasonably have prevented the event rendering his performance uneconomical, and (2) the promisee could have insured against the occurrence of the event at lower cost than the promisor because the promisee (a) was in a better position to estimate both (i) the probability of the event's occurrence and (ii) the magnitude of the loss if it did occur, and (b) could have self-insured, whereas the promisor would have had to buy more costly market insurance. As we shall see, not all cases are this easy."

M. AHERN CO. v. JOHN BOWEN CO.

Supreme Judicial Court of Massachusetts, 1956.
334 Mass. 36, 133 N.E.2d 484.

WHITTEMORE, JUSTICE. This is an action of contract to recover for labor and materials furnished by the plaintiff as a subcontractor, to the defendant as general contractor, in connection with the construction in Boston, by the Commonwealth, of the Chronic Disease Hospital and Nurses' Home. * * *

The essential facts are not in dispute. The labor and materials had been furnished under a partially performed contract, the further performance of which had become impossible because of the decision of this court in Gifford v. Commissioner of Public Health, 328 Mass. 608, 105 N.E.2d 476, declaring void the underlying general contract between the defendant and the Commonwealth. The amount claimed due, apart from interest, was the difference between the value of the materials and labor furnished and the sums paid by the defendant to the plaintiff under the terms of the contract prior to the *Gifford* decision. * * *

It is plain that the defendant does not owe the plaintiff any sum under the contract. * * * But the absence of an express provision in the contract to cover the unexpected contingency has not deterred this court or other American courts from giving recovery in cases of excusable impossibility for such performance as has been received. Butterfield v. Byron, [supra, p. 1200].

These decisions are not, as the defendant argues, based in the ultimate analysis on the principle of unjust enrichment which underlies restitution cases wherein recovery is limited to benefits received. Our decisions have spoken of "an implication that what was furnished was to be paid for," Vickery v. Ritchie, 202 Mass. 247, 250–251, 88 N.E. 835, 836, or have indulged the fiction of an implied contract that the subject matter will continue to exist so that even though the defendant is without fault in fact he is to be regarded as in default and hence liable to pay. Young v. Chicopee, 186 Mass. 518, 72 N.E. 63. In commenting upon the "benefit" theory Williston (Contracts [Rev.Ed.] § 1977, pages 5553–5554) says,

> "It is sometimes said that the defendant is liable for the benefit which he has received, but unless the word 'benefit' is given a meaning wider than is natural, the statement is inadequate. In the first place, the word 'benefit' suggests that the matter is to be examined as it exists after the impossibility has supervened; but * * * the American law seems clear that where the defendant has received part performance regarded as valuable under the contract between the parties, the fact that this value has been destroyed by the very circumstances which make full performance of the contract impossible will not preclude recovery. A second reason for discarding the use of the word 'benefit,' in this connection, is because it suggests that what has been received by the defendant must be of pecuniary advantage to him. This seems unnecessary. * * * Accordingly, it is well settled that a recovery on a quantum meruit or quantum valebat should prima facie be such a proportion of the price as the work which the plaintiff has done bears to the full amount of the work for which the contract provided."

Restatement: Contracts, § 468(3), gives "benefit" an appropriately limited meaning in saying, "The value of performance within the meaning of Subsections (1, 2) is the benefit derived from the performance in advancing the object of the contract, not exceeding, however, a ratable portion of the contract price."

[Judgment for plaintiff affirmed]

Notes

1. Transatlantic Finance Corp. v. United States, 363 F.2d 312 (D.C.Cir.1966). The United States chartered a ship to transport wheat to Iran. The Suez Canal was closed in 1956 which prevented the ship from taking the normal route through the Mediterranean. Instead it proceeded around the Cape of Good Hope. The operator sued the U.S. for additional compensation. The court rejected the contention that performance of the contract was legally impossible, but added this dicta:

"Even if we agreed with appellant, its theory of relief seems untenable. When performance of a contract is deemed impossible it is a nullity. In the case of a charter party involving carriage of goods, the carrier may return to an appropriate port and unload its cargo, [citation] subject of course to required steps to minimize damages. If the performance rendered has value, recovery in quantum meruit for the entire performance is proper. But here Transatlantic has collected its contract price, and now seeks quantum meruit relief for the additional expense of the trip around the Cape. If the contract is a nullity, Transatlantic's theory of relief should have been quantum meruit for the entire trip, rather than only for the extra expense. Transatlantic attempts to take its profit on the contract, and then force the Government to absorb the cost of the additional voyage. When impracticability without fault occurs, the law seeks an equitable solution, [citation] and quantum meruit is one of its potent devices to achieve this end. There is no interest in casting the entire burden of commercial disaster on one party in order to preserve the other's profit. Apparently the contract price in this case was advantageous enough to deter appellant from taking a stance on damages consistent with its theory of liability. In any event, there is no basis for relief."

2. Posner and Rosenfield argue that *Transatlantic Financing* "makes the decision on whether to discharge the contract turn on an examination of the key economic parameters that we have identified. The shipowner is the superior risk bearer because he is better able to estimate the magnitude of the loss (a function of delay, and of the value and nature of the cargo, which are also known to the shipowner) and the probability of the unexpected event. Furthermore shipowners who own several ships and are engaged in shipping along several different routes can spread the risks of delay on any particular route without purchasing market insurance or forcing their shareholders to diversify their common-stock portfolios. And the shipping company could, if it desired, purchase in a single transaction market insurance covering multiple voyages. Of course, the shipper in the particular case—the United States Government—was well diversified too, but decision should (and here did) turn on the characteristics of shippers as a class, if an unduly particularistic analysis is to be avoided."

Posner & Rosenfield, Impossibility and Related Doctrines in Contract Law: An Economic Analysis, 6 J.Legal Stud. 83, 104 (1977).

ALBRE MARBLE AND TILE CO. v. JOHN BOWEN CO.

Supreme Judicial Court of Massachusetts, 1959.
338 Mass. 394, 155 N.E.2d 437.

[Action by subcontractor against prime contractor arising out of the debacle involving the Chronic Disease Hospital and Nurses' Home in Boston. See M. Ahern Co. v. John Bowen Co., supra, p. 1203.]

SPALDING, JUSTICE. We turn now to counts 3 and 4 by which the plaintiff seeks a recovery for the fair value of work and labor furnished to the defendant prior to the termination of the general contract. The plaintiff seeks recovery in count 3 for "preparation of samples, shop drawings, tests and affidavits" in connection with the tile work; in count 4 recovery for similar work in connection with the marble contract is sought.

The defendant in its affidavit maintains that the tile and marble work to be furnished by the plaintiff could not have been done until late in the construction process; that no tile or marble was actually installed in the building; and that the expenses incurred by the plaintiff prior to the time the general contract was declared invalid consisted solely of expenditures in preparation for performance. Relying on the decision in Young v. Chicopee, 186 Mass. 518, 72 N.E. 63, the defendant maintains that where a building contract has been rendered impossible of performance a plaintiff may not recover for expenses incurred in preparation for performance, but may recover only for the labor and materials "wrought into" the structure. Therefore, the defendant says, the plaintiff should take nothing here.

The problem of allocating losses where a building contract has been rendered impossible of performance by a supervening act not chargeable to either party is a vexed one. In situations where the part performance of one party measurably exceeds that of the other the tendency has been to allow recovery for the fair value for work done in the actual performance of the contract and to deny recovery for expenditures made in reliance upon the contract or in preparing to perform. This principle has sometimes been expressed in terms of "benefit" or "lack of benefit." In other words, recovery may be had only for those expenditures which, but for the supervening act, would have enured to the benefit of the defendant as contemplated by the contract. The "wrought-in" principle applied in building contract cases is merely a variant of this principle. It has long been recognized that this theory is unworkable if the concept of benefit is applied literally. * * *

Although the matter of denial of reliance expenditures in impossibility situations seems to have been discussed but little in judicial opinions, it has, however, been the subject of critical comment by scholars. See Fuller and Perdue, The Reliance Interest in Contract Damages, 46 Yale L.J. 52, 373, 379–383. In England the recent frustrated contracts legislation provides that the court may grant recovery for expenditures in reliance on the contract or in preparation to perform it where it appears *"just to do so having regard to all the circumstances of the case"* (emphasis supplied). 6 & 7 George VI, c. 40. [1943]

We are of opinion that the plaintiff here may recover for those expenditures made pursuant to the specific request of the defendant as set forth in the contract clause quoted above. A combination of factors peculiar to this case justifies such a holding without laying down the broader principle that in every case recovery may be had for payments made or obligations reasonably incurred in preparation for performance of a contract where further performance is rendered impossible without fault by either party. * * *

The factors which determine the holding here are these: First, this is not a case of mere impossibility by reason of a supervening act. The opinion of this court in M. Ahern Co. v. John Bowen Co. Inc., 334 Mass. 36, 133 N.E.2d 484, points out that the defendant's involvement in creating the impossibility was greater than that of its subcontractors.

* * * Although the defendant's conduct was not so culpable as to render it liable for breach of contract, * * * nevertheless it was a contributing factor to a loss sustained by the plaintiff which as between the plaintiff and the defendant the latter ought to bear to the extent herein permitted.

We attach significance to the clause in the contract, which was prepared by the defendant specifically requesting the plaintiff to submit samples, shop drawings, tests, affidavits, etc., to the defendant. This is not a case in which all efforts in preparation for performance were solely within the discretion and control of the subcontractor. We are mindful that in Young v. Chicopee, 186 Mass. 518, 72 N.E. 63, recovery of the value of materials brought to the construction site at the specific request of the defendant therein was denied. But in that case the supervening act rendering further performance impossible was a fire not shown to have been caused by the fault of either party. We are not disposed to extend that holding to a situation in which the defendant's fault is greater than the plaintiff's.

Moreover, the acts requested here by their very nature could not be "wrought into" the structure. In Angus v. Scully, 176 Mass. 357, 57 N.E. 674 recovery for the value of services rendered by house movers was allowed although the house was destroyed midway in the moving. The present case comes nearer to the rationale of the *Angus* case than to that of the *Young* case. * * *

We hold that the damages to be assessed are limited solely to the fair value of those acts done in conformity with the specific request of the defendant as contained in the contract. Expenses incurred prior to the execution of the contract, such as those arising out of preparing the plaintiff's bid, are not to be considered.

Note

1. Professor Harrison argues that the parties should share the loss:

"The usual approach to reliance losses associated with excused performance is to assign the entire loss to one party. This remedy promotes efficiency or wealth maximization, and efficiency has been proposed as a guide for normative decisions. Legal scholars as well as the courts, however, frequently are dissatisfied with the all-or-nothing 'solution.' * * *

"An analysis of the all-or-nothing, or efficient, approach shows it is objectionable for two reasons. First, it miscasts contract as an adversarial relationship, when in fact contractual relationships are joint utility-creating endeavours involving the division of contributions and gains. When performance is excused, the traditional approach ignores the relationship as defined by the parties and forces them into a precontractual adversarial stance.

"Second, the all-or-nothing approach endangers the personal autonomy of the parties by ignoring the fact that neither consented to bear the entire loss. Although it can be argued that there is consent via *ex ante* compensation, *ex ante* compensation is an unreliable indicator of the type of consent that would justify burdening one party with the entire loss. The parties to a contract, in a context of sharing contributions and gains, have not consented in any meaningful way to an all-or-nothing assignment of losses.

"This Article suggests that loss sharing has a firm legal as well as moral basis. The legal basis is founded in the partnership-like quality of all contracts. Loss sharing has a moral basis in that it represents the solution the parties would be likely to consent to if they were forced to apportion the loss before knowing which share, as individuals, they would be assigned. This is demonstrated through the use of a partial ignorance construct, which forces the parties to contemplate a loss but shields them from knowledge that would assist them in estimating the probability that they would avoid the entire loss through litigation. Under these conditions, if the parties are minimally risk averse, they would regard an equal division of the loss as a just outcome." Harrison, A Case for Loss Sharing, 56 S.Cal.L.Rev. 573, 601 (1983).

Professors Posner and Rosenfield argue that courts should deny the contractor expectancy and reliance losses and award restitution for the value of actual benefits conferred: "The proposals to change the remedial outcome to one where reliance losses are shared result from a misplaced emphasis on ex post loss distribution rather than ex ante risk bearing. Viewed from the risk-bearing perspective the refusal to apportion reliance losses is well founded; it creates an incentive for the one efficient risk bearer to adopt cost-justified risk-avoidance or risk-minimization techniques (diversification, market insurance, or whatever)." Posner & Rosenfield, Impossibility and Related Doctrines in Contract Law: An Economic Analysis, 6 J.Legal Stud. 83, 113 (1977).

S. ANDERSON & SON v. SHATTUCK

Supreme Court of New Hampshire, 1911.
76 N.H. 240, 81 A. 781.

WALKER, J. * * * It is found in the case that the cost of the work and materials actually furnished and appropriated in the building is $10,764.58. If $2,500, the cost of finishing the building, is added to that sum, the entire cost of the completed structure would appear to be $13,264.58. By a simple process of division (10,764.58/13,264.58), it would further appear that the plaintiffs at the time of the fire had furnished to the defendant 81⅙ per cent. approximately of the work and materials he had agreed to furnish. Consequently he should receive 81⅙ per cent. of the whole contract price ($11,258.55), or $9,138.19. This may not be the only way of ascertaining what part of the work had been done at the time of the fire, but upon the facts reported it seems to be a reasonably convenient and accurate method. By any correct method the same result would follow.

* * * Under their bill in equity, the plaintiffs claim that they are entitled to recover the full value of the labor done and materials furnished by them out of the proceeds of the policies of insurance. * * * In the building contract the defendant agreed to keep the building insured during the progress of the work against loss or damage by fire, the "policies to cover all work incorporated in the building and of materials for the same, in or about the premises, and to be made payable to the parties * * * as their interest may appear." The defendant took out policies covering the property mentioned in the contract, in the joint names of himself and the plaintiffs, to the amount of $7,500, and also policies in his own name for $14,000. These amounts have been paid or deposited by the companies, subject to the order of the court as to the rights of the plaintiffs therein. The plaintiffs' contention rests upon the construction to be put upon the phrase in the contract, "as their interest may appear." Is the plaintiffs' interest to be measured by the cost of the labor and materials actually furnished by them, or by the price agreed upon in the contract? The answer to this question depends upon the intention of the parties as evidenced by the contract. The parties understood that from day to day as the work progressed the materials incorporated in the building, together with the attendant labor, constituted material additions to the defendant's real estate. The plaintiffs were not the owners of the materials after they were attached to the defendant's building, and, of course, they had no interest in it as owners. Their claim to the insurance money, therefore, cannot be sustained upon that ground. Upon a reasonable construction of the contract, it is clear that the parties had in mind the plaintiffs' lien on the building for work and materials furnished by them, and the value of this lien would vary according to the amount of work done and the payments the defendant might make on account. If at the time of the fire the defendant had paid the plaintiffs all that it is now found they were then entitled to, they would have had no insurable interest in the property and would have been entitled to no part of the insurance money. Their lien would have been discharged, as a mortgagee's lien is discharged by the payment of the mortgage debt. As the parties merely intended by means of the insurance to protect the plaintiffs against loss by the destruction of the building by fire, in which their only legal interest was that of a lienor, the value of their insurable interest at the time of the fire must be determined by

the contract price, which is the measure of the protection afforded by the lien. * * * The plaintiffs are not entitled to receive from the insurance fund an amount equal to the cost of their work and materials incorporated into the building, but only so much as is due them therefor under the contract from the defendant, which has already been determined in the action at law.

The court ruled, subject to the plaintiffs' exception, that they were not entitled to be reimbursed from the insurance money for the value of some lumber which they had brought to the premises to be used in the construction of the building and which was burned at the time of the fire. The agreement provided for insurance upon materials "in or about the premises." The lumber was about the premises, was owned by the plaintiffs, and was intended for, but had not been used in or attached to, the building. The lumber seems to fall within the description of the property to be insured; and, as the plaintiffs' interest in it appears to be that of an owner no reason is apparent why under the contract for insurance they are not entitled to receive from the insurance fund the fair value of it. The ruling of the court upon this point cannot be sustained.

Upon a revision of the findings in accordance with the views herein expressed, there will be judgment for the plaintiffs.

Notes

1. Calculate plaintiffs' loss on the contract if the building had not been destroyed. Compare the loss as a result of this decision. The plaintiff was losing a fractional claim on the insurance proceeds for each board taken from the lumber pile and nailed to the building. Should contractors who underbid be allowed to smoke on the job?

2. Plaintiff had also built four mantels of special dimensions, but these were not on the job site and were not destroyed. No recovery was allowed for them because they had not been attached to the building. An insurance claim under the form of policies here would be dubious. Cf. North River Insurance Co. v. Clark, 80 F.2d 202 (9th Cir.1935).

3. In Carroll v. Bowersock, 100 Kan. 270, 164 P. 143 (1917), the contract called for re-flooring a concrete floor. The old floor had been torn out and wooden forms with reinforcing rods standing to receive concrete for pilings were installed when fire destroyed the structure. Recovery was allowed for removing the floor but not for the temporary forms which were not incorporated in the structure. Nor was recovery allowed for the reinforcing rods or their installation. If the analysis is under the law of "fixtures," the contractor's recovery obviously is subject to further obstacles.

4. Usually the structure under repair or remodeling will continue in existence, and its destruction will excuse performance, see Butterfield v. Byron. Some courts have implied an inconsistent condition: the owner is under an implied contract to keep the building in existence. Carried to its logical conclusion, this implied condition would favor the contractor, allowing recovery of ordinary breach of contract damages. There is little evidence of the implication being carried this far. It has, however, led to restitutionary recovery for items, such as pews made to order, which were destroyed on the job site but not incorporated in the structure. Haynes, Spencer & Co. v. Second Baptist Church, 88 Mo. 285 (1885).

F.M. Gabler, Inc. v. Evans Laboratories, Inc., 129 Misc. 911, 223 N.Y.S. 408 (1927), reviews New York's retreat from Niblo v. Binsse, 40 N.Y. 476 (1864), where the implied condition that the owner would keep the premises in existence was at one time propounded. Gabler did permit the contractor to recover the value of destroyed lumber which had been merely stacked at the job site.

5. See Anno., 28 A.L.R.3d 788 (1969). Bell v. Carver, 245 Ark. 31, 431 S.W.2d 452 (1968), the basis for the annotation, allowed quantum meruit recovery, and reinforced it with a mechanic's lien.

BELL v. KANAWHA TRACTION & ELECTRIC CO.

Supreme Court of Appeals of West Virginia, 1913.
83 W.Va. 640, 98 S.E. 885.

RITZ, J. In the year 1901 the defendant secured from the plaintiff a right of way for its car track through a certain tract of land owned by him in the county of Wood; the sole consideration therefor being that the defendant, when its road was constructed, would furnish to the plaintiff free transportation thereover for himself and his family. In accordance with the agreement, such free transportation was furnished until the year 1906, when the Congress of the United States, by the passage of the Hepburn Act * * *, made it impossible for the defendant to comply with its contract. The agreement was, however, modified at that time so as to provide for the furnishing of such transportation only within the state of West Virginia, and as modified was performed by the defendant until the year 1913, when the Legislature of West Virginia, * * * made it unlawful for the defendant to further perform the contract even to that extent. This suit was thereafter brought to recover the value of the consideration given by the plaintiff for such free transportation to the extent that the same had not already been furnished.

* * * It is very well settled that, where the further performance of a contract, legal at the time it was made, is rendered unlawful by a subsequent act of Congress or of the Legislature of the state, the parties will be excused from further performance. * * * For this reason specific performance of the contract cannot be compelled, and, * * * rescission cannot be had, for the very obvious reasons that the railway company has partially performed the same, and, further, the right of way thus secured has been dedicated to the public use, and cannot be withdrawn therefrom in the interest of a private individual.

It is also very well settled that no action will lie to recover any consequential damages which may result from the failure to perform a contract the performance of which is forbidden by law, or prevented by some uncontrollable supervening cause. Butterfield v. Byron, [supra, p. 1200] and many authorities there cited. But these conclusions do not answer the question involved here. The plaintiff does not seek specific performance, but, on the contrary, admits that he cannot have it. He does not seek the cancellation or rescission of the contract, nor does he seek to recover any consequential damages for its nonperformance. The whole theory upon which the case proceeds is the recovery of that part of the consideration received by the defendant for which it has not made compensation. * * *

The exact question presented here seems not to have been passed upon by the courts of last resort of many of the American states. It was before the Supreme Court of the state of Kentucky in the case of Louisville & Nashville Railroad Co. v. Crowe, 156 Ky. 27, 160 S.W. 759. Crowe had granted to the railroad company a strip of land for a right of way in consideration that the railroad company would issue to him free transportation over its lines during his life. The railroad company refused to issue the transportation for the reason that it was forbidden to do so by the provisions of the Hepburn Act. It was then sued to recover compensation for the consideration given it, just as was done in this case, and it was contended by the railroad company that not only was it excused from the further performance of its contract, but that it had a right to keep the consideration without making any compensation therefor. This contention, however, was denied by the court, and the railroad company held liable for the value of the consideration received by it to the extent that it had not already made compensation therefor. In the case of Cowley v. Northern Pacific Railroad Co., 68 Wash. 558, 123 Pac. 998, exactly the same question was involved, and the Supreme Court of the state of Washington reached a contrary conclusion, holding that the railroad company was entitled to keep the land conveyed to it for a right of way without paying for it; that it was not only excused from performing its contract, but might keep the full consideration received by it without making compensation.

* * * [I]n the case of Jones–Gray Construction Co. v. Stephens, [infra] it is held that a party who has received in advance payment for work to be performed by him upon the barn of another, which is destroyed before performance of the contract by an accident for which neither is responsible, is liable to the party having made the payment for the repayment of the unearned consideration. In Jones & Jones v. Judd, 4 N.Y. 411, it was held that, where by the terms of a contract for work and labor the full price is * * * not to be paid until the work is completed, and complete performance becomes impossible by act of the law, the contractor may recover for the work actually done at the full price agreed on. It is a little difficult for us to understand why a party who has furnished only part of the consideration would be allowed to recover to the extent that he has furnished it when further performance is prevented by the law, but would not be allowed to recover when he has furnished the whole consideration for the contract to the extent that he has not received compensation. * * * We are of the opinion that the declaration states a cause of action, and that the plaintiff in this case is entitled to recover the value of the consideration delivered by him to the defendant to the extent that he has not received compensation by the performance of this contract on the part of the defendant.

Note

Pinkham v. Libbey, 93 Me. 575, 45 A. 823 (1900). Plaintiff agreed to pay $75 to defendants for their stallion to service plaintiff's mare, "with a privilege of return for the season." Plaintiff paid $75 at the time of the service. The service proved ineffective; but the stallion died before the privilege of return could be exercised. Held, plaintiff may not recover the money. The court said that Butterfield v. Byron was not controlling. Why?

JONES–GRAY CONSTRUCTION CO. v. STEPHENS

Court of Appeals of Kentucky, 1916.
167 Ky. 765, 181 S.W. 659.

[Stephens (plaintiff and appellee) leased land for one year to the Construction Co. (defendant and appellant). In payment the Construction Co. gave Stephens $100 and agreed to move a barn for him. The barn burned before it was moved.]

CLARKE, J. Under the contract the value of the use of appellee's land by appellant was fixed by the parties at $100.00 and what it would have cost appellant to have moved the barn. Having received the consideration for moving the barn, appellant cannot retain that consideration for the performance of the service it did not do, even though prevented by an unavoidable accident.

* * * [W]e think that portion of the instruction, which is as follows, was prejudicial: "You will find for plaintiff from the evidence what it would reasonably cost to move said barn."

This authorized the jury to find for appellee what it would cost a person not situated as was appellant, to have moved the barn. Appellant was on the ground with every appliance at hand necessary to do the work and could have done it for much less than one not so prepared. What it would have cost appellant is all appellee is entitled to recover. Evidence was introduced to prove what it would have cost others than appellant to have done the work, and the finding of the jury is in accord with these estimates.

Upon a retrial of the case the court will limit the evidence and appellee's recovery to what it would have reasonably cost appellant to have moved the barn under its contract.

Note

Irvine v. Postal Telegraph Cable Co., 37 Cal.App. 60, ___, 173 P. 487, 488 (1918). The plaintiff conveyed a right of way of the reasonable value of $1500 to the defendant "which said amount * * * shall be taken in the use of the telegraph privileges at the usual and ordinary rates." The plaintiff used telegraph privileges at such rates in the amount of $500.26 prior to a supervening impossibility, an Act of Congress that made telegraph franks for other than cash illegal. Plaintiff sued in quantum meruit for $999.74. An order sustaining a demurrer to the complaint was reversed on appeal.

MODEL VENDING INC. v. STANISCI

Superior Court of New Jersey, 1962.
74 N.J.Super. 12, 180 A.2d 393.

RIZZI, J.D.C. (temporarily assigned). This is an action for breach of contract by the defendant in which plaintiff seeks damages for loss of profits under a written contract entered into between the parties under date of August 15, 1958. Plaintiff is in the business of leasing various types of merchandise machines, and on the above date the parties entered into a written agreement whereby machines were to be placed by plaintiff into defendant's bowling alley premises for a period of five years. This contract gave plaintiff the exclusive privilege of placing its machines for the purpose of selling the merchandise described therein at defendant's location during the existence of the contract. The case was tried by the court without a jury and, after the trial was completed, the court pronounced its findings of fact and conclusions of law which included, *inter alia,* that defendant had breached the contract on or about July 28, 1959 by having closed down plaintiff's machines and having commenced the sale of various items of merchandise through other methods on the premises in question. There was also the finding of fact that defendant's bowling alley premises had been completely destroyed by fire on March 24, 1961 and had never been reconstructed thereafter. Plaintiff claimed damages for loss of profits that he would have enjoyed during the five-year period commencing on August 15, 1958 and continuing until August 15, 1963.

The issues remaining to be decided were whether the contract became impossible of performance by the fire of March 24, 1961, and if so, whether such impossibility, in the face of the prior breach of the said contract, would disentitle plaintiff to damages for the full five-year period or until August 15, 1963, or whether such damages would be limited to the time before the fire.

It is defendant's contention that the destruction of the premises on which the contract was to be performed thereby made the contract impossible of performance as of that date, and that plaintiff is only entitled to collect damages for loss of profits from the date of the contract to the date of the fire. Plaintiff contends that at the time of the fire defendant had already breached the contract, and therefore defendant's liability would continue during the full life of the contract, namely, until August 15, 1963, notwithstanding the destruction of the premises aforesaid. It has been conceded by the parties that if plaintiff is entitled to recover damages for the full five-year period, he will obtain a judgment for the sum of $7,924.21; but if plaintiff is limited in damages to the date of the fire aforesaid, he will be entitled to a judgment in the amount of $2,507.27.

* * * The diligent research of counsel has failed to produce any precedent by the courts of the State of New Jersey that deal directly with the factual situation herein described. The case of Von Waldheim v. Englewood Heights Estates, 115 N.J.L. 220, 179 A. 19 (E. & A. 1935), touches upon the problem. That case involved an installment contract for the sale of real estate, in which the buyer had been in default of payments at various times. After the contract had been entered into by the parties, the property was condemned by the State of New Jersey, the entire award having been paid over to the seller, who still held the legal title at the time of condemnation. The buyer started a suit against the seller for the return of the moneys that he had paid on the contract up to the time of condemnation. In allowing recovery to the plaintiff for the return of the moneys that he had paid, the court stated that:

> "It is apparent that the contract between the parties became an impossible one to perform so far as the seller was concerned because of the condemnation. Under these circumstances, the plaintiffs are entitled to recover what they paid out under a contract, which the seller could not perform. It would be an unconscionable thing, since the seller could not perform, to permit retention of the consideration that had been paid. No damage is suffered by the defendants by the plaintiffs' previous breach of the contract. As a matter of fact, each and every past breach was waived. The lands in question were taken by another buyer, the state, under the Eminent Domain Act. This visits no damage whatever upon the defendants that we can ascertain. If one party to a contract, at the time when further performance becomes impossible, has had, as here, a total failure of consideration for moneys paid, he may, in the absence of an express provision assuming the risk of the supervening impossibility, recover what he has paid or what has been disproportionately paid."

A reasonable analogy to the problem of supervening impossibility is found in the law of contracts concerning illegality as a defense, and particularly in situations where a contract was legal when made and an anticipatory repudiation of the contract followed by the promisor and thereafter the performance of the acts contracted for had become illegal. This type of a situation is treated in

6 Williston, Contracts (rev. ed. 1938), § 1759, p. 4996, wherein the author states the following to be the law:

> "Where there has been an anticipatory repudiation of the contract and subsequently, but before the date when the promised performance becomes due, that performance is made illegal, a practical defect in the doctrine of anticipatory breach is illustrated. The difficulty is not peculiar to cases of supervening illegality, but is involved in every other case where, after anticipatory breach, supervening impossibility occurs which would in any event prevent and excuse performance of the contract. The situation differs, also, in only a slight particular, hereafter referred to, from one where it appears after the anticipatory breach that though there were no legal excuse the return performance could not or would not have been rendered to the repudiator. In each of these cases, if all the facts could have been known or foreseen at the time of the repudiation, no cause of action on the contract would have arisen. It is a practical disadvantage of the doctrine of anticipatory breach that an action may be brought and perhaps judgment obtained before the facts occur which prove that there should have been no recovery. Fortunately in most cases this evidence, though not available at the time of the repudiation, becomes available before judgment can be obtained.
>
> "It seems clear that if the evidence thus becomes available the plaintiff can recover no substantial damages, and in the case of supervening illegality which is not due to the defendant's fault, there seems no reason to allow even nominal damages. The loss should rest where chance has placed it; and the same should be true in case of any supervening excusable impossibility."

Concerning the effect of impossibility occurring after a breach of contract, Professor Williston had this to say as being the general law on the subject:

> "Impossibility of performing his promise, of a kind that would have excused a contractual promisor if it had occurred before breach, may occur after he has already broken his contract. In considering the possible effects of this a distinction must be made between several situations:
>
> (1) It may be supposed not only that the breach is total but that the time for the entire performance of the undertaking by the promisor has elapsed before the impossibility occurs.
>
> (2) It may be supposed that the breach is total but that there has been actual failure to perform only part of the promisor's undertaking before the impossibility occurs.
>
> (3) It may be supposed that the breach is anticipatory and that there has been no actual failure to perform any part of the promisor's undertaking when the impossibility occurs.
>
> (4) It may be supposed that the breach is partial."

The case here would seem to fall squarely within the situation which Professor Williston describes in paragraph 2 above and as to which he summarized the law to be:

> "In the second situation supposed the amount of recovery should be limited if it can be shown that the remaining performance due from the defendant after the breach would have been excused by impossibility. Thus, in an action on a contract of employment, broken by the wrongful discharge of the servant, evidence should be admitted of the employer's death after the breach but during the term of the promised services."

Restatement, Contracts, § 457 (1932), discusses the effect of supervening impossibility in the following language:

> "Except as stated in § 455, where, after the formation of a contract facts that a promisor had no reason to anticipate, and for the occurrence of which he is not in contributing fault, render performance of the promise impossible, the duty of the promisor is discharged, unless a contrary intention has been manifested, even though he has already committed a breach by anticipatory repudiation; but where such facts occur after the time when performance of a promise is due, they do not discharge a duty to make compensation for a breach of contract."

Following the above statement of law, various comments appear. Comment (d) appears to be particularly appropriate to the issue here involved and is stated as follows:

> "Impossibility on the part of a promisor occurring after he has committed a breach does not ordinarily discharge him, but it will do so if the breach consists merely of an anticipatory repudiation. After a breach of any other kind impossibility supervening before the time for full performance has elapsed will limit the damages recoverable if the impossibility would have occurred had there been no breach. Thus, if an employer or employee who breaks his contract becomes so ill shortly afterwards that the contract could not have been performed, recovery will be limited." * * *

The weight of authority leads the court to the view that upon breach of contract by a promisor, supervening impossibility occurring through destruction of the subject matter without the fault of the promisor will limit the damages recoverable to the time before the impossibility has taken place. * * *

Judgment will be entered for the plaintiff in the sum of $2,507.27 and costs.

C. AGREEMENTS UNENFORCEABLE FOR WANT OF CAPACITY TO CONTRACT

HALBMAN v. LEMKE

Supreme Court of Wisconsin, 1980.
99 Wis.2d 241, 298 N.W.2d 562.

CALLOW, JUSTICE. * * * On or about July 13, 1973, James Halbman, Jr. (Halbman), a minor, entered into an agreement with Michael Lemke (Lemke) whereby Lemke agreed to sell Halbman a 1968 Oldsmobile for the sum of $1,250. Lemke was the manager of L & M Standard Station in Greenfield, Wisconsin, and Halbman was an employee at L & M. At the time the agreement was made Halbman paid Lemke $1,000 cash and took possession of the car. Arrangements were made for Halbman to pay $25 per week until the balance was paid, at which time title would be transferred. About five weeks after the purchase agreement, and after Halbman had paid a total of $1,100 of the purchase price, a connecting rod on the vehicle's engine broke. Lemke, while denying any obligation, offered to assist Halbman in installing a used engine in the vehicle if Halbman, at his expense, could secure one. Halbman declined the offer and in September took the vehicle to a garage where it was repaired at a cost of $637.40. Halbman did not pay the repair bill.

In October of 1973 Lemke endorsed the vehicle's title over to Halbman, although the full purchase price had not been paid by Halbman, in an effort to avoid any liability for the operation, maintenance, or use of the vehicle. On October 15, 1973, Halbman returned the title to Lemke by letter which disaffirmed the purchase contract and demanded the return of all money theretofore paid by Halbman. Lemke did not return the money paid by Halbman.

The repair bill remained unpaid, and the vehicle remained in the garage where the repairs had been made. In the spring of 1974, in satisfaction of a garageman's lien for the outstanding amount, the garage elected to remove the vehicle's engine and transmission and then towed the vehicle to the residence of James Halbman, Sr., the father of the plaintiff minor. Lemke was asked several times to remove the vehicle from the senior Halbman's home, but he declined to do so, claiming he was under no legal obligation to remove it. During the period when the vehicle was at the garage and then subsequently at the home of the plaintiff's father, it was subjected to vandalism, making it unsalvageable.

Halbman initiated this action seeking the return of the $1,100 he had paid toward the purchase of the vehicle, and Lemke counterclaimed for $150, the amount still owing on the contract. Based upon the uncontroverted facts, the trial court granted judgment in favor of Halbman, concluding that when a minor disaffirms a contract for the purchase of an item, he need only offer to return the property remaining in his hands without making restitution for any use or depreciation.

[Lemke appeals.]

Neither party challenges the absolute right of a minor to disaffirm a contract for the purchase of items which are not necessities. That right, variously known as the doctrine of incapacity or the "infancy doctrine," is one of the oldest and most venerable of our common law traditions. * * * Thus it is settled law in this state that a contract of a minor for items which are not necessities is void or voidable at the minor's option. [citations]

Once there has been a disaffirmance, however, as in this case between a minor vendee and an adult vendor, unresolved problems arise regarding the rights and responsibilities of the parties relative to the disposition of the consideration exchanged on the contract. As a general rule a minor who disaffirms a contract is entitled to recover all consideration he has conferred incident to the transaction. In return the minor is expected to restore as much of the consideration as, at the time of disaffirmance, remains in the minor's possession. [citations] The minor's right to disaffirm is not contingent upon the return of the property, however, as disaffirmance is permitted even where such return cannot be made. Olson v. Veum, 197 Wis. 342, 345, 222 N.W. 233 (1928). [citations]

The return of property remaining in the hands of the minor is not the issue presented here. In this case we have a situation where the property cannot be returned to the vendor in its entirety because it has been damaged and therefore diminished in value, and the vendor seeks to recover the depreciation. * * *

The law regarding the rights and responsibilities of the parties relative to the consideration exchanged on a disaffirmed contract is characterized by confusion, inconsistency, and a general lack of uniformity as jurisdictions attempt to reach a fair application of the infancy doctrine in today's market-place. [citations] That both parties rely on this court's decision in Olson v. Veum is symptomatic of the problem.

In *Olson* a minor, with his brother, an adult, purchased farm implements and materials, paying by signing notes payable at a future date. Prior to the maturity of the first note, the brothers ceased their joint farming business, and the minor abandoned his interest in the material purchased by leaving it with his brother. The vendor initiated an action against the minor to recover on the note, and the minor (who had by then reached majority) disaffirmed. The trial court ordered judgment for the plaintiff on the note, finding there had been insufficient disaffirmance to sustain the plea of infancy. This court reversed, holding that the contract of a minor for the purchase of items which are not necessities may be disaffirmed even when the minor cannot make restitution. Lemke calls our attention to the following language in that decision:

> "To sustain the judgment below is to overlook the substantial distinction between a mere denial by an infant of contract liability where the other party is seeking to enforce it and those cases where he who was the minor not only disaffirms such contract but seeks the aid of the court to restore to him that with which he has parted at the making of the contract. In the one case he is using his infancy merely as a shield, in the other also as a sword."

From this Lemke infers that when a minor, as a plaintiff, seeks to disaffirm a contract and recover his consideration, different rules should apply than if the minor is defending against an action on the contract by the other party. This theory is not without some support among scholars. See: Calamari and Perillo, The Law of Contracts, sec. 126, 207–09 (Hornbook Series 1970), treating separately the obligations of the infant as a plaintiff and the infant as a defendant.

Additionally, Lemke advances the thesis in the dissenting opinion by court of appeals Judge Cannon, arguing that a disaffirming minor's obligation to make restitution turns upon his ability to do so. For this proposition, the following language in Olson v. Veum is cited: "The authorities are clear that when it is shown, as it is here, that the infant cannot make restitution, then his absolute right to disaffirm is not to be questioned."

In this case Lemke argues that the *Olson* language excuses the minor only when restitution is not possible. Here Lemke holds Halbman's $1,100, and accordingly there is no question as to Halbman's ability to make restitution.

Halbman argues in response that, while the "sword—shield" dichotomy may apply where the minor has misrepresented his age to induce the contract, that did not occur here and he may avoid the contract without making restitution notwithstanding his ability to do so.

The principal problem is the use of the word "restitution" in *Olson.* A minor, as we have stated, is under an enforceable duty to return to the vendor, upon disaffirmance, as much of the consideration as remains in his possession. When the contract is disaffirmed, title to that part of the purchased property which is retained by the minor revests in the vendor; it no longer belongs to the minor. [citation] The rationale for the rule is plain: a minor who disaffirms a purchase and recovers his purchase price should not also be permitted to profit by retaining the property purchased. The infancy doctrine is designed to protect the minor, sometimes at the expense of an innocent vendor, but it is not to be used to bilk merchants out of property as well as proceeds of the sale. Consequently, it is clear that, when the minor no longer possesses the property which was the subject matter of the contract, the rule requiring the return of property does not apply.[1] The minor will not be required to give up what he does not have. We conclude that *Olson* does no more than set forth the foregoing rationale and that the word "restitution" as it is used in that opinion is limited to the return of the property to the vendor. We do not agree with Lemke and the court of appeals' dissent that *Olson* requires a minor to make restitution for loss or damage to the property if he is capable of doing so.

Here Lemke seeks restitution of the value of the depreciation by virtue of the damage to the vehicle prior to disaffirmance. Such a recovery would require Halbman to return more than that remaining in his possession. It seeks compensatory value for that which he cannot return. Where there is misrepresentation by a minor or willful destruction of property, the vendor may be able to recover damages in tort. [citations] But absent these factors, as in the present case, we believe that to require a disaffirming minor to make restitution for diminished value is, in effect, to bind the minor to a part of the obligation which by law he is privileged to avoid. [citations]

The cases upon which the petitioner relies for the proposition that a disaffirming minor must make restitution for loss and depreciation serve to illustrate some of the ways other jurisdictions have approached this problem of balancing the needs of minors against the rights of innocent merchants. In Barber v. Gross, 74 S.D. 254, 51 N.W.2d 696 (1952), the South Dakota Supreme Court held that a minor could disaffirm a contract as a defense to an action by the merchant to enforce the contract but that the minor was obligated by a South Dakota statute, upon sufficient proof of loss by the plaintiff, to make restitution for depreciation. Cain v. Coleman, 396 S.W.2d 251 (Tex.Civ.App. 1965), involved a minor seeking to disaffirm a contract for the purchase of a used car where the dealer claimed the minor had misrepresented his age. In reversing summary judgment granted in favor of the minor, the court recognized the minor's obligation to make restitution for the depreciation of the vehicle. The Texas court has also ruled, in a case where there was no issue of misrepresentation, that upon disaffirmance and tender by a minor the vendor is obligated to take the property "as is," Rutherford v. Hughes, 228 S.W.2d 909, 912 (Tex.Civ.App.1950). Scalone v. Talley Motors, Inc., 158 N.Y.S.2d 615, 3 App.Div.2d 674 (1957), and Rose v. Sheehan Buick, Inc., 204 So.2d 903 (Fla.App. 1967), represent the proposition that a disaffirming minor must do equity in the form of restitution for loss or depreciation of the property returned. Because these cases would at some point force the minor to bear the cost of the

1. Although we are not presented with the question here, we recognize there is considerable disagreement among the authorities on whether a minor who disposes of the property should be made to restore the vendor with something in its stead. The general rule appears to limit the minor's responsibility for restoration to specie only. [citation] But see: Boyce v. Doyle, 113 N.J.Super. 240, 273 A.2d 408 (1971), adopting a "status quo" theory which requires the minor to restore the precontract status quo, even if it means returning proceeds or other value. Fisher v. Taylor Motor Co., 249 N.C. 617, 107 S.E.2d 94 (1959), requiring the minor to restore only the property remaining in the hands of the minor, " 'or account for so much of its value as may have been invested in other property which he has in hand or owns and controls.' " Finally, some attention is given to the "New Hampshire Rule" or benefits theory which requires the disaffirming minor to pay for the contract to the extent he benefited from it. [citation]

very improvidence from which the infancy doctrine is supposed to protect him, we cannot follow them.

As we noted in *Kiefer,* modifications of the rules governing the capacity of infants to contract are best left to the legislature. Until such changes are forthcoming, however, we hold that, absent misrepresentation or tortious damage to the property, a minor who disaffirms a contract for the purchase of an item which is not a necessity may recover his purchase price without liability for use, depreciation, damage, or other diminution in value.

The decision of the court of appeals is affirmed.

Notes

1. The courts are divided about whether estoppel can be invoked against an infant when he misrepresents his age. See Anno., 29 A.L.R.3d 1270 (1970). In general, estoppel may be raised more readily if the infant seeks affirmative relief, particularly in equity. Inasmuch as an infant is reputedly liable for his torts, consider a tort action for deceit. What would be the measure of recovery?

From a practical aspect, a merchant dealing with a possible infant would be well advised to extract a written affirmation of his age.

Anno., Infant's Liability for Use or Depreciation of Subject Matter, In Action to Recover the Purchase Price Upon His Disaffirmance of Contract to Purchase Goods, 12 A.L.R.3d 1174 (1967).

2. Are house improvements "necessaries" that can be charged to a twelve-year-old girl? See Dalton v. Bundy, 666 S.W.2d 443 (Mo.App.1984).

NOEL v. COLE

Supreme Court of Washington, 1982.
98 Wash.2d 375, 655 P.2d 245.

UTTER, JUSTICE. The Commissioner of Public Lands and the Department of Natural Resources (DNR) entered into a contract with Alpine Excavating, Inc. (Alpine) by which DNR granted Alpine the right to cut timber from a tract of land on Whidbey Island. Local citizens brought an action seeking to enjoin the sale (*Noel* action) and Alpine thereupon filed a cross claim against DNR for breach of contract. The trial court held for the plaintiffs in the *Noel* action, enjoined all logging and found DNR liable for breach, awarding Alpine $1,043,413.61 in damages. From this judgment, DNR appeals. We reverse, holding that DNR's contract with Alpine was ultra vires and therefore unenforceable.

In 1977, DNR and the University of Washington, for whom DNR holds the tract in question in trust, decided to sell the logging rights by sealed bid. On May 23, 1977, bids were opened and Alpine was declared the apparent high bidder, at which time it paid a 10 percent deposit of $157,874.54. By letter of June 3, the Commissioner mailed a bill of sale to Alpine and on July 21, after Alpine put up a performance guaranty of $100,000, the parties executed a formal contract.

In reliance upon certain regulations exempting most timber sales from the State Environmental Policy Act of 1971 (SEPA), DNR did not prepare an Environmental Impact Statement (EIS). Alpine was unaware of this fact at the time of the auction and remained so until June 6 when it was served as a codefendant in the *Noel* action. At that time, it expressed concern to DNR about the validity of the sale, but DNR assured Alpine that the *Noel* action was frivolous and that logging could begin soon. DNR also contended that the contract could be enforced against Alpine if Alpine sought to avoid it. In light of these assertions and the fact that it had already made a deposit, Alpine treated the contract as valid and began construction of a logging road in August.

On August 12, 1977, however, the plaintiffs in the *Noel* action obtained a temporary restraining order against construction of the road and on October 5 obtained a preliminary injunction. On January 3, 1979, the trial court permanently enjoined further logging absent preparation of an EIS. It held that the regulations relied upon by DNR were invalid and found that the sale to Alpine was a major action which would have a significant effect on the quality of the environment. The parties agree that this permanent injunction terminated their contract.

Alpine's cross claim against DNR was bifurcated from the *Noel* action and tried separately in June 1981. The trial court found DNR liable for breach of contract and awarded Alpine over a million dollars in damages.

Historically, the unauthorized contracts of * * * governmental entities, which by their nature represent the interests of groups of individuals, have been rendered void and unenforceable under the ultra vires doctrine. [citations] The rationale for the rule is the protection of those unsuspecting individuals whom the entity represents. * * *

The doctrine applies to governmental action to "protect the citizens and taxpayers from unjust, ill-considered, or extortionate contracts, or those showing favoritism." 10 E. McQuillin, Municipal Corporations § 29.02, at 200 (3d rev. ed. 1981). * * *

In actions against governmental entities, * * * the doctrine retains its vitality. See Edwards v. Renton, 67 Wash.2d 598, 602, 409 P.2d 153 (1965). * * * A citizen and taxpayer has only one government in which to "invest" and may not withdraw except by death or expatriation. In addition, private parties dealing with a government agency are charged with knowledge of the agency's authority. [citation] * * * For both of these reasons, the ultra vires doctrine is properly applied to government contracts.

An agency may lack authority to make a contract for a multitude of reasons. It may simply lack *any* power to contract in the government's name. More commonly, an agency steps outside its authority by failure to comply with statutorily mandated procedures. One such set of procedures is that provided by SEPA. It *requires* an EIS prior to any major action significantly affecting the environment. [citation] Thus, an agency has no authority to undertake such an action until it has prepared an EIS.

While the vast majority of governmental ultra vires cases have dealt with government purchases in violation of spending guidelines [citation], the doctrine is equally applicable where authority is lacking due to failure to comply with SEPA. One of the central purposes of SEPA is to "insure that presently unquantified environmental amenities and values will be given appropriate consideration in decision making." It is intended to prevent action which is "ill-considered" from an environmental perspective. The ultra vires doctrine is just as necessary to prevent ill-considered environmental action as it is to prevent ill-considered financial action.

In the instant case, there is no question that DNR has general authority to sell timber on land held in trust for educational purposes and that such sales may be by sealed bid (see RCW 79.01.200). DNR did, however, fail to prepare a required EIS. * * * Since it did not do so, the contract of sale to Alpine was ultra vires and Alpine cannot recover for any alleged breach.

There remains, however, a question of whether Alpine is entitled to some recovery to compensate it for the losses it has suffered on this project. While the ultra vires doctrine prevents a governmental agency from favoring a private entity at the expense of the public interest, it does not leave the unsuspecting private party entirely at the mercy of governmental misfeasance. Under certain conditions, a private party acting in good faith is entitled to some recovery. First, the agency must have had the power it sought to exercise but merely have exercised it in an irregular manner or by unauthorized procedural means.[1] Finch v. Matthews, 74 Wash.2d 161, 172, 443 P.2d 833 (1968). Second, the action must not be malum in se, malum prohibitum, or manifestly against public policy. [citations] If these two conditions are satisfied, a private party acting in good faith may recover to the extent necessary to prevent "manifest injustice" or unjust enrichment. [citations]

* * * As noted above, DNR did not lack substantive authority to make this sale, but merely carried it out in an unauthorized procedural manner by failing to comply with statutory prerequisites.

Neither can we say that DNR's action was malum in se, malum prohibitum or manifestly against public policy. While SEPA mandates important policy goals, DNR's failure to prepare an EIS was excusable in light of the regulations it relied upon.[2]

Finally, there is no evidence here of bad faith on the part of Alpine. Indeed, it was not even aware of the absence of an EIS until it had already paid a 10 percent deposit. Even after the *Noel* action was filed, DNR continued to assure Alpine that the contract was valid and that Alpine would soon be logging. In addition, it indicated it would attempt to enforce the contract if Alpine did not perform. Under these circumstances, we cannot say that Alpine acted in bad faith.[3]

In sum, Alpine is entitled to recover under a theory of unjust enrichment. The proper measure of its recovery is the reasonable value of its improvement to the tract in question, namely its partial road construction, less any profits from the timber removed. Where, as here, the party seeking recovery is not at fault, reasonable value is measured by the amount which the benefit conferred would have cost the defendant had it obtained the benefit from some other person in the plaintiff's position. [citation] This amount is to be distinguished from cost and might be either more or less,[4] though cost is some evidence of value.

1. [Footnotes renumbered.] The distinction between procedural irregularity and a substantive lack of authority is justified by the fact that in the latter case, the agency lacks the power to do the act in any manner. Where authority is so completely lacking it seems fair to presume bad faith on the part of the private party.

2. In addition to the fact that the regulations on their face exempted almost all timber sales, DNR had relied upon the regulations in making numerous past sales, none of which had been challenged.

3. Had it done so, even recovery for unjust enrichment might be denied, as we have suggested in the past. See Edwards v. Renton.

4. In general, a court should not limit maximum recovery to cost as was directed in *Edwards*. That limitation was justified there because the statute violated was a bidding statute intended to bind contractors to their bids. [cita-

In the instant case, therefore, remand is necessary so that Alpine may prove the reasonable value of its road construction. Because the amount of this recovery for unjust enrichment is not liquidated interest on it may not be had until final judgment. Edwards v. Renton. Alpine may, however, recover interest at the legal rate for the time during which DNR held its deposit and performance guaranty. Since the contract was void at its purported inception, Alpine was entitled to immediate restitution of these amounts and, since they were liquidated, interest began to run on them immediately upon the accrual of Alpine's right to the funds. [citation]

The judgment is reversed. The cause is remanded to the trial court for the introduction of such further evidence as necessary and computation of damages as set forth above.

Note

Shea–Kaiser–Lockheed–Healy v. Department of Water & Power, 70 Cal.App.3d 1, 138 Cal.Rptr. 743 (1977). Plaintiff brought action to recover the reasonable market value of excess aggregate delivered to the Los Angeles Department of Water and Power under a contract (called "contract 709"). Plaintiff was the low bidder on the contract which, according to plaintiff, called for a maximum obligation to deliver 604,000 tons of aggregate at a price of $1.80 per ton. The defendant argued that the contract was a variety of a "requirements" contract, allowing the buyer the option of purchasing additional quantities of aggregate "during the contract period" up to its "maximum requirements." The defendant insisted upon the delivery of 191,957 tons over 604,000. The plaintiff reluctantly performed "under protest" and claimed breach of contract. The parties agreed that the fair market value of the "excess" aggregate was $2.90 per ton.

"Section 386(b) of the [City] charter provides that '*The City of Los Angeles shall not be, and is not bound by any contract involving the expenditure of more than twenty thousand dollars ($20,000.00) unless the officer, board, or employee authorized to contract shall first have complied with the procedure for competitive bidding established by this section.*'

"The law is well established that failure to comply with charter provisions relating to the making of purchases renders such purchases void. Where the power is thus limited liability cannot arise by estoppel or ratification. The mode of entering into contracts as prescribed by the city's charter is the measure of the *power* of the city to contract and a contract not made in conformity with the prescribed mode is void and unenforceable.

"Contracts which are beyond the *power* of the municipality or which its officers have no authority to make or which are not made in the manner required by its charter, are void and the city is not bound by such contracts, even on the theory of an implied undertaking to pay the reasonable value.

"California Constitution, article XI, section 10, subdivision (a) (adopted in 1970), reads in part as follows: 'A local government body may not grant extra compensation or extra allowance to a * * * contractor after service has been rendered or a contract has been entered into and performed in whole or in part, or pay a claim under an agreement made without authority of law.'

"We see no escape from the conclusion that either: (1) the excess aggregate was supplied under contract 709 at the contract price of $1.80 per ton which had been

tion] Other cases applying the rule described in *Edwards* in the face of different statutory violations have set no such limit. [citation] arrived at by competitive bidding in compliance with the city charter; or (2) the excess aggregate was not supplied under contract 709, in which event it was not supplied under a contract let by competitive bidding as required by City Charter section 386. An award of money based upon the court's calculation of the reasonable value of the excess aggregate on the theory of a quasi- or an implied contract or on the theory of damages for breach of contract is in direct contravention of section 386 of the Charter of the City of Los Angeles which provides that the city shall not be bound by any contract which is not executed in accordance with charter provisions for competitive bidding and also in direct contravention of California Constitution, article XI, section 10, which prohibits DWP from granting an extra allowance to a contractor after a contract has been entered into and performed in whole or in part.

"There is one further and unavoidable consideration. If DWP did not have the right under contract 709 to demand delivery of aggregate in excess of 604,000 tons (as the trial court found), then DWP did not have the *power* to pay for what it demanded without contractual authority. If this were true, DWP would be required to sue to recover the $1.80 per ton which it paid for the 191,957 tons of aggregate which it did not have the right to purchase or the power to pay for, since such purchase and payment for excess tonnage would be an illegal expenditure of public money and an ultra vires act. Upon the failure of DWP to collect such contractually unauthorized payment, a taxpayer could institute such an action on behalf of DWP. Such a result would clearly not be in the interest of SKLH."

The appellate court eventually concluded that the "excess" aggregate was properly includable under the terms of the original contract: plaintiff was allowed the solace of recovery at the $1.80 per ton contract rate.

S.T. GRAND, INC. v. CITY OF NEW YORK

Court of Appeals of New York, 1973.
32 N.Y.2d 300, 344 N.Y.S.2d 938, 298 N.E.2d 105.

JASEN, JUDGE. In November, 1966, plaintiff-appellant, S.T. Grand, Inc., entered into a contract with the defendant-respondent, City of New York, for the cleaning of the Jerome Park Reservoir. No bidding was required, since James Marcus, the city's Commissioner of Water Supply, Gas and Electricity, let the contract pursuant to the "public emergency" exception to the general bidding requirements for municipal contracts. (General Municipal Law, § 103, subd. 4.) The entire cleaning has been performed.

Subsequently, the appellant and its president were convicted in Federal court of conspiracy to use interstate facilities with intent to violate the New York State bribery laws. The conviction was based upon a series of events which culminated in an agreement by the appellant to pay a "kickback" to Marcus, in return for Marcus' award of the cleaning contract to the appellant.

When the appellant sued the city for the unpaid balance of $148,735 due on the cleaning contract, the city claimed, as a defense, that the contract was illegal by reason of the bribery of Marcus, and asserted a counterclaim for the $689,500 which it had previously paid under the contract. * * *

Special Term denied the city's motion for summary judgment, not on the ground that it found triable issues of fact, but because the court was of the opinion that the case of Gerzof v. Sweeney, 22 N.Y.2d 297, 292 N.Y.S.2d 640, 239 N.E.2d 521 "furnishes compelling authority for holding plaintiff not completely foreclosed from recovery or retaining the amount paid by [the city]."

The Appellate Divisions modified and directed judgment for the city upon both its counterclaim and appellant's claim for the unpaid balance. * * *

Turning to the question of remedy, the rule is that where work is done pursuant to an illegal municipal contract, no recovery may be had by the vendor, either on the contract or in quantum meruit. [citations] We have also declared that the municipality can recover from the vendor all amounts paid under the illegal contract.

The reason for this harsh rule, which works a complete forfeiture of the vendor's interest, is to deter violation of the bidding statutes. As we said in *Jered:* "The continuing growth of our cities and the expansion of governmental services on all levels has necessitated, over the years, the letting of greater numbers of public contracts. While the amount of money involved in these contracts was relatively small a few decades ago, today the amount is astronomical. It is, therefore, a matter of grave public concern that there be absolute honesty in the procuring of a public contract. If we are to effectively deter the unscrupulous practice of fraudulent and collusive bidding on public contracts, we cannot look alone to existing penal sanctions. The nature of the wrong is such that it is not easily discovered but, when it is, we make it quite clear that courts of this State will decline to lend their aid to the fraudulent bidder who seeks recovery."

However, in *Gerzof* we created an exception to the general rule, based upon the unusual circumstances of that case. There, the Village of Freeport, having decided to increase the capacity of its power plant, advertised for bids on a contract for the purchase and installation of a new electrical generator. Two bids were received, one from Enterprise for $615,685, and one from Nordberg for $673,840. The Village Water and Light Commission recommended that the Village Board of Trustees accept the Enterprise bid. Before the board of trustees could act, a new Mayor and two new trustees were elected, and upon the request of the former, the matter was deferred. When the reconstituted board of trustees met, it summarily dismissed the members of the Water and Light Commission, accepted Nordberg's higher bid and awarded the contract to Nordberg. Enterprise brought suit and succeeded in having the award set aside. Despite the court's direction to "award the contract as provided by law," the board of trustees, over the objection of the majority of Water and Light Commission, whose members had been reinstated by court order, had new specifications drawn up for a larger generator. These specifications were prepared with the active assistance of a representative of Nordberg and were so slanted as to make it impossible for anyone but Nordberg to bid on them. Accordingly, Nordberg was the only bidder, and its bid of $757,625 was accepted. After the generator had been installed and the contract price paid, a taxpayer's action was brought to annul the contract.

Our Court concluded that the contract was illegal and void and directed Nordberg to return $178,636 of the contract price of $757,625 to the village. This figure represented the damage which the village suffered by having to take Nordberg's larger and more expensive generator. The damage figure was arrived at by adding to the difference between the contract price and Enterprise's original low bid ($141,940), the increased cost of installation of the larger generator ($36,696). In short, the village was put in the position it would have been in had the original Enterprise low bid been accepted.

The equitable remedy which we fashioned for Nordberg in *Gerzof* is not available to the appellant. In *Gerzof,* we had a fair idea of the damage which the village had suffered because of Nordberg's machinations, since the village had already determined that it needed a new generator and there had been one round of legitimate bidding, from which there developed a responsible low bid. In the case before us, there was neither an untainted determination that the Jerome Park Reservoir needed to be cleaned, nor a round of competitive bidding from which the damages to the city could be computed. Moreover, in *Gerzof,* the vendor's illegality [1] infected only the final stages of the municipal contracting process, while in the instant case, the illegality goes to the origins of that process.

Thus, we conclude that the general rule of complete forfeiture should be applied here, rather than the equitable exception of *Gerzof.* The result may be harsh, but it is necessary in cases where the bribery of municipal officials is confirmed. As we recognized in *Gerzof,* "the application of the law to particular cases may not, of course, vary with the sums involved." If we would decree a complete forfeiture of an $8,000 contract, then justice demands that there be a complete forfeiture of an $800,000 contract.

Accordingly, we affirm the order of the Appellate Division.

D. AGREEMENTS UNENFORCEABLE BECAUSE OF ILLEGALITY

1. IN GENERAL

Introductory Note

The rule itself is simply stated: the illegality of a transaction is a defense to the claim of *any* remedy based on that transaction. See, S.T. Grand, Inc. v. City of New York, supra. The exclusions and exceptions that remove the remedial bar are the topic of this section.

One major exclusion is that if the illegality is "trivial," the remedies will not be barred. No attempt will be made to define the limits of this exclusion. Above the level of trivial, the graduations of illegality are infinite. While the degree of illegality has a direct bearing upon many of the exceptions, no serious attempt will be made to sort out the nuances suggested by such expressions as "malum in se" or "malum prohibitum" favored by tradition; "turpitude", "moral turpitude," "serious moral turpitude" favored by the Restatement [First] of Contracts §§ 600, 604, 605; "misconduct" or "serious misconduct" favored by the Restatement (Second) of Contracts §§ 198, 199; "very serious crime" or "minor offense" favored by the Restatement (Second) of Agency § 412; "grossly immoral" or "heinous" when other words fail. The sprinkling of these epithets throughout the opinions that follow will remain where they have dropped.

Changing lifestyles may remove the stigma of illegality. At one time, a plaintiff who had improved an adulterous cohabitant's property would have been barred from claiming post-breakup restitution. But this is no longer true. See Collins v. Davis, 68 N.C.App. 588, 315 S.E.2d 759 (1984), Mason v. Rostad,

1. [Footnote renumbered.] It should also be noted that there was no conviction or finding in the *Gerzof* case of any bribery of municipal officials.

476 A.2d 662 (D.C.1984). Improvements must not be gratuitous or made specifically in consideration of sexual favors because this would be prostitution.

The excellent article by Dean John Wade, Restitution of Benefits Acquired Through Illegal Transactions, 95 U.Pa.L.Rev. 261 (1947), is a text on most of the matters in this section.

BERNER v. DIAMOND

Court of Appeals of Ohio, 1947.
48 Ohio L.Abs. 505, 74 N.E.2d 568.

MORGAN, JUDGE. This was an action by Esther Berner against Leo Diamond to cancel a mortgage. Later Max Diamond filed a cross-petition for a judgment on the note and a foreclosure of the mortgage. The trial judge granted plaintiff a decree, cancelled the mortgage and dismissed Max Diamond's answer and cross-petition. * * *

The plaintiff testified that she and her husband owned a vicious dog named "Bozo" which had bitten a number of people and that after they had been compelled to pay a judgment of $2000 as a result of a law suit filed by a small child who had been bitten they conferred with Berner's partner, Max Diamond, who referred them to his lawyer. This lawyer suggested that a "convenient" mortgage be placed on the property in the name of some person whom the Berners could trust. Accordingly such a "convenient" mortgage for $8000 running to Max Diamond was placed on the home but for the purpose stated and for no other reasons.

As to plaintiff's right to have the mortgage cancelled, it is elementary that when the plaintiff mortgaged her property to accomplish such an illegal purpose as above described a court of equity will not aid the plaintiff to free the property from the mortgage. * * *

This disposes of plaintiff's claim for cancellation of the mortgage.

The stories told by Esther Berner and Harry Berner on the one hand, and Max Diamond on the other, are diametrically opposite. The trial judge evidently believed in the truth of the version given by Esther Berner and Harry Berner. Clearly, if their story is believed, Max Diamond has no right to recover on the note and mortgage. * * *

In a case such as is disclosed here a court of equity can do nothing better than to leave the parties where it finds them.

Accordingly, judgment will be rendered for the defendants on plaintiff's petition and for the plaintiff and Harry Berner on the cross-petition of the defendant Max Diamond.

Notes

1. *Failure of Intended Illegal Purpose.* Hanscom v. Hanscom, 186 Or. 541, 567–68, 208 P.2d 330, 341 (1949):

"The defendants contend that since Hanscom's purpose in conveying the land to Inez was to place it beyond the reach of a creditor, the transaction was binding between the parties, and the grantor has no standing to seek the aid of a court of equity to compel a reconveyance. There is no evidence that the plaintiff was indebted to anyone, either in 1930 or 1935, or that any creditor was hindered, delayed or defrauded as a result of the transfer. In that situation the decisions are not harmonious as to whether a conveyance can or cannot be deemed fraudulent to defeat creditors. We are of the opinion that the sounder rule is that where there are no actual creditors to be defrauded, and there is only a mental purpose to hinder imaginary creditors, equity will relieve against a transfer of property in circumstances such as those here present. In this view the plaintiff's motive for the conveyance will not prevent a court of equity from granting relief."

See in accord, Bailey v. Banther, 173 W.Va. 220, 314 S.E.2d 176 (1983).

2. The Restatement (Second) of Trusts § 422 (1957), would analyze the restitution in this type of case in terms of a "resulting" rather than a "constructive" trust. Does it make a difference?

3. Courts have allowed restitution where the property transferred in purported fraud on creditors is exempt from creditors' claims. Wantulok v. Wantulok, 67 Wyo. 22, 45, 214 P.2d 477, 223 P.2d 1030, 21 A.L.R.2d 572 (1950). Additional factors favoring restitution in *Wantulok* were that the court considered the basic debt merely a moral one, the intent was to delay rather than defraud the creditors, apparently the plaintiff paid the debt eventually because no creditors ever complained, and the real sufferers would be the plaintiff's innocent family.

4. The A.L.R.2d annotation on *Wantulok* distinguishes between cases where the creditors were not defrauded because their claims were paid and those where it was not established that there were creditors to defraud. Assuming the transferors' evil intent, is the classification fundamental?

5. A payor may not recover a bribe paid to a public official who nevertheless does his duty although in a certain sense the ultimate illegal purpose of the payment has failed. In Janzen v. Crum, 50 N.D. 544, 197 N.W. 138 (1924), $700 was paid the attorney general who promised that the payor would not go to the penitentiary for embezzlement. The plaintiff, who sued for money had and received, was the assignee of the payor who was in jail. Suppose the payor was legally innocent of any crime. Could any illegal purpose be ultimately effected? The point will be considered again, when the element of duress is introduced along with the illegal payment to suppress prosecution.

For the general rule denying restitution of monies paid to bribe a public official, see Anno., 60 A.L.R.2d 1273 (1958).

BOVARD v. AMERICAN HORSE ENTERPRISES, INC.

California Court of Appeal, Third District, 1988.
201 Cal.App.3d 832, 247 Cal.Rptr. 340.

PUGLIA, PRESIDING JUSTICE. * * * [P]laintiff Bovard separately sued defendants Ralph and American Horse Enterprises, Inc. a corporation, * * * to recover on promissory notes executed by defendants in connection with Ralph's purchase of the corporation in 1978 [from Bovard]. * * *

On the third day of trial, Bovard testified as to the nature of the business conducted by American Horse Enterprises, Inc., at the time the corporation was sold to Ralph. Bovard explained the corporation made jewelry and drug paraphernalia, which consisted of "roach clips" and "bongs" used to smoke marijuana and tobacco. At that point the trial court excused the jury and asked counsel to prepare arguments on the question whether the contract for sale of the corporation was illegal and void.

The following day, after considering the arguments of counsel, the trial court dismissed the * * * complaint. The court found that the corporation predominantly produced paraphernalia used to smoke marijuana and was not engaged significantly in jewelry production, and that Bovard had recovered the corporate machinery through self-help. The parties do not challenge these findings. The court acknowledged that the manufacture of drug paraphernalia was not itself illegal in 1978 when Bovard and Ralph contracted for the sale of American Horse Enterprises, Inc. However, the court concluded a public policy against the manufacture of drug paraphernalia was implicit in the statute making the possession, use and transfer of marijuana unlawful.[1] The trial court held the consideration for the contract was contrary to the policy of express law, and the contract was therefore illegal and void. Finally, the court found the parties were in pari delicto and thus with respect to their contractual dispute should be left as the court found them.

"The consideration of a contract must be lawful within the meaning of section sixteen hundred and sixty-seven." (Civ.Code, § 1607.) "That is not lawful which is: 1. Contrary to an express provision of law; 2. Contrary to the policy of express law, though not expressly prohibited; or, 3. Otherwise contrary to good morals." (Civ.Code, § 1667.) "If any part of a single consideration for one or more objects, or of several considerations for a single object, is unlawful, the entire contract is void." (Civ.Code, § 1608.)

The trial court concluded the consideration for the contract was contrary to the policy of the law as expressed in the statute prohibiting the possession, use and transfer of marijuana. Whether a contract is contrary to public policy is a question of law to be determined from the circumstances of the particular case. [citations] Here, the critical facts are not in dispute. Whenever a court becomes aware that a contract is illegal, it has a duty to refrain from entertaining an action to enforce the contract. [citations] Furthermore the court will not permit the parties to maintain an action to settle or compromise a claim based on an illegal contract. [citations]

The question whether a contract violates public policy necessarily involves a degree of subjectivity. Therefore, "* * * courts have been cautious in blithely applying public policy reasons to nullify otherwise enforceable contracts. This concern has been graphically articulated by the California Supreme Court as follows: 'It has been well said that public policy is an unruly horse, astride of which you are carried into unknown and uncertain paths, * * * While contracts opposed to morality or law should not be allowed to show themselves in courts of justice, yet public policy requires and encourages the making of contracts by competent parties upon all valid and lawful considerations, and courts so recognizing have allowed parties the widest latitude in this regard; and, unless it is entirely plain that a contract is violative of sound public policy, a court will never so declare. "The power of the courts to declare a contract void for being in contravention of sound public policy is a very delicate and undefined power, and, like the power to declare a statute unconstitutional, should be exercised only in cases free from doubt." [citation] * * * "No court ought to refuse its aid to enforce a contract on doubtful and uncertain grounds. The burden is on the defendant to show that its enforcement would be in violation of the settled public policy of this state, or injurious to the morals of its people. [citation]" Moran v. Harris (1982) 131

1. [Footnotes renumbered.] The manufacture of drug paraphernalia, including bongs and roach clips, was made criminal effective January 1, 1983.

Cal.App.3d 913, 919–920, 182 Cal.Rptr. 519, quoting Stephens v. Southern Pacific Co. (1895) 109 Cal. 86, 89–90, 41 P. 783.)

Bovard places great reliance on Moran v. Harris, supra, to support his argument the trial court erred in finding the contract violative of public policy. In *Moran,* two lawyers entered into a fee splitting agreement relative to a case referred by one to the other. The agreement was made in 1972, ten months before the adoption of a rule of professional conduct prohibiting such agreements. In 1975, the attorney to whom the case had been referred settled the case, but then refused to split the attorney's fees with the referring attorney. The trial court held the fee splitting contract violated public policy. The appellate court reversed, noting the rule of professional conduct had been amended effective January 1, 1979, to permit fee splitting agreements; thus there was no statute or rule prohibiting fee splitting agreements either at the time the attorneys' contract was formed or after January 1, 1979, during the pendency of the action to enforce the fee splitting contract. Therefore, the court held there was no basis for a finding that the contract violated public policy.

Here, in contrast to *Moran,* there is positive law on which to premise a finding of public policy, although the trial court did not find the manufacture of marijuana paraphernalia against public policy on the basis of the later enacted ordinance or statute prohibiting such manufacture. Rather, the court's finding was based on a statute prohibiting the possession, use and transfer of marijuana which long antedated the parties' contract.[2]

Moran suggests factors to consider in analyzing whether a contract violates public policy: "Before labeling a contract as being contrary to public policy, courts must carefully inquire into the nature of the conduct, the extent of public harm which may be involved, and the moral quality of the conduct of the parties in light of the prevailing standards of the community. [citations]"

These factors are more comprehensively set out in the Restatement Second of Contracts section 178:

"(1) A promise or other term of an agreement is unenforceable on grounds of public policy if legislation provides that it is unenforceable or the interest in its enforcement is clearly outweighed in the circumstances by a public policy against the enforcement of such terms.

"(2) In weighing the interest in the enforcement of a term, account is taken of

"(a) the parties' justified expectations,

"(b) any forfeiture that would result if enforcement were denied, and

"(c) any special public interest in the enforcement of the particular term.

"(3) In weighing a public policy against enforcement of a term, account is taken of

"(a) the strength of that policy as manifested by legislation or judicial decisions,

"(b) the likelihood that a refusal to enforce the term will further that policy,

2. "In determining whether the subject of a given contract violates public policy, courts must rely on the state of the law as it existed at the time the contract was made. [citations]" (Moran v. Harris.)

"(c) the seriousness of any misconduct involved and the extent to which it was deliberate, and

"(d) the directness of the connection between that misconduct and the term."

Applying the Restatement test to the present circumstances, we conclude the interest in enforcing this contract is very tenuous. Neither party was reasonably justified in expecting the government would not eventually act to geld American Horse Enterprises, a business harnessed to the production of paraphernalia used to facilitate the use of an illegal drug. Moreover, although voidance of the contract imposed a forfeiture on Bovard, he did recover the corporate machinery, the only assets of the business which could be used for lawful purposes, i.e., to manufacture jewelry. Thus, the forfeiture was significantly mitigated if not negligible. Finally, there is no special public interest in the enforcement of this contract, only the general interest in preventing a party to a contract from avoiding a debt.

On the other hand, the Restatement factors favoring a public policy against enforcement of this contract are very strong. As we have explained, the public policy against manufacturing paraphernalia to facilitate the use of marijuana is strongly implied in the statutory prohibition against the possession, use, etc., of marijuana, a prohibition which dates back at least to 1929. Obviously, refusal to enforce the instant contract will further that public policy not only in the present circumstances but by serving notice on manufacturers of drug paraphernalia that they may not resort to the judicial system to protect or advance their business interests. Moreover, it is immaterial that the business conducted by American Horse Enterprises was not expressly prohibited by law when Bovard and Ralph made their agreement since both parties knew that the corporation's products would be used primarily for purposes which were expressly illegal. We conclude the trial court correctly declared the contract contrary to the policy of express law and therefore illegal and void. * * *

Following entry of judgment dismissing the complaint, Ralph filed a memorandum seeking $26,356.06 in costs and attorney's fees. * * * Ralph contends he is entitled to costs and attorney's fees as a matter of right. Ralph is wrong.

The promissory notes, given as consideration for the sale of the corporation, contain provisions for the award of attorney's fees, but not for costs. Thus, the decision whether to award costs rested firmly in the trial court's discretion. * * *

Ordinarily, in an action on a contract which provides for an award of attorney's fees, the prevailing party in the action is entitled to attorney's fees. (Civ.Code, § 1717, subd. (a).) This is so even when the party prevails on grounds the contract is inapplicable, invalid, unenforceable or nonexistent, if the other party would have been entitled to attorney's fees had it prevailed. [citations] The rationale for this rule is that an award of attorney's fees pursuant to Civil Code section 1717 is governed by equitable principles, and it would be inequitable to deny attorney's fees to a party who successfully defends an action based on a contract simply because the party initiating the case filed a frivolous lawsuit. [citation]

However, a different rule applies where a contract is held unenforceable because of illegality. Geffen v. Moss (1975) 53 Cal.App.3d 215, 125 Cal.Rptr. 687 is directly on point. In that case, the court held a party may not recover attorney's fees when it successfully defends an action on a contract on the ground the contract violated public policy. In *Geffen*, the contract was declared void as violative of public policy. The court refused to award attorney's fees, explaining, "Civil Code section 1717 renders the obligation to pay attorney's fees mutual. However, since we have decided that the obligation to [perform under the contract] is contrary to public policy and unenforceable the right to attorney's fees created by this provision never matured."

A party to a contract who successfully argues its illegality stands on different ground than a party who prevails in an action on a contract by convincing the court the contract is inapplicable, invalid, nonexistent or unenforceable for reasons other than illegality. "The effect of the *Geffen* decision is that where neither party can enforce the agreement there is no need for a mutual right to attorney's fees." [citations]

Consistent with our decision that the contract is illegal and void, we affirm the trial court's order denying Ralph's claim for attorney's fees.

[Affirmed.]

McCONNELL v. COMMONWEALTH PICTURES CORP.

Court of Appeals of New York, 1960.
7 N.Y.2d 465, 199 N.Y.S.2d 483, 166 N.E.2d 494.

DESMOND, CHIEF JUDGE. Plaintiff sues for an accounting. Defendant had agreed in writing that, if plaintiff should succeed in negotiating a contract with a motion-picture producer whereby defendant would get the distribution rights for certain motion pictures, defendant would pay plaintiff $10,000 on execution of the contract between defendant and the producer, and would thereafter pay plaintiff a stated percentage of defendant's gross receipts from distribution of the pictures. Plaintiff negotiated the distribution rights for defendant and defendant paid plaintiff the promised $10,000 but later refused to pay him the commissions or to give him an accounting of profits.

Defendant's answer contains * * * two affirmative defenses the sufficiency of which we must decide. In these defenses it is asserted that plaintiff, without the knowledge of defendant or of the producer, procured the distribution rights by bribing a representative of the producer and that plaintiff agreed to pay and did pay to that representative as a bribe the $10,000 which defendant paid plaintiff. The courts below (despite a strong dissent in the Appellate Division) held that the defenses were insufficient to defeat plaintiff's suit. Special Term's opinion said that, since the agreement sued upon—between plaintiff and defendant—was not in itself illegal, plaintiff's right to be paid for performing it could not be defeated by a showing that he had misconducted himself in carrying it out. The court found a substantial difference between this and the performance of an illegal contract. We take a different view. Proper and consistent application of a prime and long-settled public policy closes the doors of our courts to those who sue to collect the reward of corruption.

* * * It is true that some of the leading decisions Oscanyan v. Arms Co., 103 U.S. 261, Stone v. Freeman, 298 N.Y. 268, 82 N.E.2d 571, were in suits on intrinsically illegal contracts but the rule fails of its purpose unless it covers a

case like the one at bar. Here, as in Stone v. Freeman * * * the money sued for was (assuming the truth of the defenses) "the fruit of an admitted crime." To allow this plaintiff to collect his commissions would be to let him "profit by his own fraud, or to take advantage of his own wrong, or to found [a] claim upon his own iniquity, or to acquire property by his own crime" (Riggs v. Palmer, 115 N.Y. 506, 511, 22 N.E. 188, 190). The issue is not whether the acts alleged in the defenses would constitute the crime of commercial bribery under section 439 of the Penal Law, Consol.Laws, c. 40, although it appears that they would. "A seller cannot recover the price of goods sold where he has paid a commission to an agent of the purchaser (Sirkin v. Fourteenth Street Store, 124 App.Div. 384, 108 N.Y.S. 830); neither could the agent recover the commission, even at common law and before the enactment of section 384–r of the Penal Law (now section 439)." (Judge Crane in Renier v. North American Newspaper Alliance, 259 N.Y. 250, 261, 181 N.E. 561, 565).

We are not working here with narrow questions of technical law. We are applying fundamental concepts of morality and fair dealing not to be weakened by exceptions. So far as precedent is necessary, we can rely on Sirkin v. Fourteenth Street Store, * * * and Reiner v. North American Newspaper Alliance. * * * *Sirkin* is the case closet to ours and shows that, whatever be the law in other jurisdictions, we in New York deny awards for the corrupt performance of contracts even though in essence the contracts are not illegal. *Sirkin* had sued for the price of goods sold and delivered to defendant. Held to be good was a defense which charged that plaintiff seller had paid a secret commission to an agent of defendant purchaser. There cannot be any difference in principle between that situation and the present one where plaintiff (it is alleged) contracted to buy motion-picture rights for defendant but performed his covenant only by bribing the seller's agent. In the *Reiner* case (supra), likewise, the plaintiff had fully performed the services required by his agreement with the defendant but was denied a recovery because his performance had involved and included "fraud and deception" practiced not on defendant but on a third party. It is beside the point that the present plaintiff on the trial might be able to prove a prima facie case without the bribery being exposed. On the whole case (again assuming that the defenses speak the truth) the disclosed situation would be within the rule of our precedents forbidding court assistance to bribers.

It is argued that a reversal here means that the doing of any small illegality in the performance of an otherwise lawful contract will deprive the doer of all rights, with the result that the other party will get a windfall and there will be great injustice. Our ruling does not go as far as that. It is not every minor wrongdoing in the course of contract performance that will insulate the other party from liability for work done or goods furnished. There must at least be a direct connection between the illegal transaction and the obligation sued upon. Connection is a matter of degree. Some illegalities are merely incidental to the contract sued on.

Perhaps this application of the principle represents a distinct step beyond *Sirkin* and *Reiner* in the sense that we are here barring recovery under a contract which in itself is entirely legal. But if this be an extension public policy supports it. We point out that our holding is limited to cases in which the illegal performance of a contract originally valid takes the form of commercial bribery or similar conduct and in which the illegality is central to or a dominant part of the plaintiff's whole course of conduct in performance of the contract. * * *

The order appealed from should be reversed.

FROESSEL, JUDGE (dissenting). It is to be noted that defendant does not charge that its own agent was bribed or that its contract with plaintiff contemplates any illegal act. Moreover, neither the answer nor the affidavit in opposition suggests that Universal or United has in anywise questioned the distribution contract or that defendant has not enjoyed the full fruits thereof.

The narrow question before us as framed by Special Term is "whether the unlawful acts imputed to the plaintiff in performance are fatal to recovery under a lawful contract." We agree with the courts below "that recovery for services under a valid agreement may be had, notwithstanding that the plaintiff has in the course of their rendition committed illegal acts." This was implicit in our holding in Chesebrough v. Conover, 140 N.Y. 382, 35 N.E. 633 and it was so squarely held in Dunham v. Hastings Pavement Co., 56 A.D. 244, at 251, 252, 67 N.Y.S. 632, where the court correctly stated the applicable rule of law as follows: "If the contract contemplated legal service, and that alone, we do not think that it would be rendered illegal by the fact that the plaintiff did illegal acts in its performance. The question is and continues, was the contract in fact for the performance of illegal service? If it was not, then it is valid and can be enforced."

This is not a case where the contract *sued upon* is intrinsically illegal [citations]; or was *procured* by the commission of a crime [citation]; or where a beneficiary under a will murdered his ancestor in order to obtain the speedy enjoyment of his property [citation]. In the *Sirkin* case, so heavily relied upon by the majority, the plaintiff obtained the very contract he was seeking to enforce by paying secret commissions to defendant's own purchasing agent. In Merchants' Line v. Baltimore & Ohio R. Co., 222 N.Y. 344, 347, 118 N.E. 788, we pointed out that in *Sirkin* "the plaintiff reached and bribed the man who made *the contract under which he was seeking to recover*" (emphasis supplied). * * *

This court is now adopting a rule that a party may retain the benefits of, but escape his obligations under, a wholly lawful contract if the other party commits some illegal act not contemplated nor necessary under the contract. By way of a single illustration, an owner may thus avoid paying his contractor for the cost of erecting a building because the contractor gave an inspector a sum of money to expedite an inspection.

The majority opinion seeks to distinguish between "major" and "minor" illegality and "direct" and "peripheral" corruption. It decides this case on the ground that the manner in which plaintiff performed his admittedly valid contract with defendant was "gravely immoral and illegal." Such distinctions are neither workable nor sanctioned by authority. If a contract was lawfully made, and did not contemplate wrongdoing, it is enforceable; if, on the other hand, it was *procured* by the commission of a crime, or was in fact for the performance of illegal services, it is not enforceable. These are the criteria distinguishing enforceable from unenforceable contracts—not "nice" distinctions between degrees of illegality and immorality in the performance of lawful contracts, or whether the illegal act of performance was "directly" or "peripherally" related to the main contract.

Moreover, a reversal here would be contrary to the spirit, if not the letter, of our holding in Southwestern Shipping Corp. v. National City Bank, 6 N.Y.2d 454, 190 N.Y.S.2d 352. The broad proposition for which that case stands is that a party unconnected with an illegal agreement should not be permitted to reap a windfall by pleading the illegality of that agreement, to which he was a stranger. There, the contract between the plaintiff and the bank was entirely lawful, and the bank attempted to avoid the consequence of its breach of contract and negligence by asserting the illegality of a different contract between plaintiff and a third party. Here, the contract between plaintiff and defendant was perfectly legal, and defendant is seeking to avoid its obligations under the contract—of which it has reaped the benefits for some 12 years—by asserting the illegality of a *different* and subsequent agreement between plaintiff and a third party. This it should not be permitted to do.

Note

Can a person who has sold or furnished goods to another knowing that they will be used for an illegal purpose recover the agreed consideration? In Carroll v. Beardon, 142 Mont. 40, 381 P.2d 295 (1963), the court allowed a seller to foreclose a purchase money mortgage on a house of prostitution. The court relied on Fuchs v. Goe, 62 Wyo. 134, 163 P.2d 783 (1945), which held that the lessor of a night club with gambling equipment could recover the rent. Knowledge of the defendant's illegal purpose is not enough. Defendant must show that the plaintiff participated in the wrong in some degree and intended that the property be so used.

The most famous case to the contrary is Pearce v. Brooks, 1 L.R.–Ex. 213, 6 Eng.Pub.Cas. 326 (1866). The owner of a carriage who let it to a prostitute knowing that she would use it to pursue her trade was denied recovery of the rent.

STOLZ–WICKS, INC. v. COMMERCIAL TELEVISION SERVICE CO.

United States Court of Appeals, Seventh Circuit, 1959.
271 F.2d 586.

HASTINGS, CHIEF JUDGE. This was an action for a declaratory judgment in which plaintiff sought construction of the terms of a "drawing" leading to the award by it of an Edsel automobile in a business promotion campaign and further sought a judgment returning the automobile to it or in the alternative a recovery of its actual cash value for its conversion.

Plaintiff (appellee), Stolz–Wicks, Inc., is an Illinois corporation engaged in business as a wholesaler of radio and television parts to repairmen in a multi-state operation. In the instant case, plaintiff sold and shipped directly in interstate commerce to defendants, two of its customers, who are citizens of Indiana. Defendants are Commercial T.V., a corporation (appellant), four of its officers, and Ray L. Norris d/b/a Hobby Craft T.V. Jurisdiction is asserted because of diversity of citizenship.

The district court found the facts and stated its conclusions of law on which it rendered judgment for $3,017.96 for plaintiff against defendant, Commercial T.V., from which judgment it is the sole appellant. There was a judgment in favor of the remaining defendants.

From the facts as found by the trial court the following transaction occurred: In an effort to stimulate sales, plaintiff conducted an advertising campaign which was to end in a drawing at which a 1958 Edsel automobile was to be presented to the *customer* holding the winning certificate. Plaintiff's customers were given a coupon with each fifty dollars worth of purchases from it and were entitled to receive one certificate for every ten coupons surrendered to plaintiff. Plaintiff held a dance in Chicago, Illinois, on February 1, 1958, for its customers and their guests; and as the customers entered the dance hall, they deposited their certificates in a box provided for that purpose. The rules of the drawing, as printed on the certificates, required that the holder of the certificate be present at the drawing to be eligible to win. At this time Norris was the holder of one such certificate (No. B 382), and Commercial T.V. had six of them.

Both Norris and Commercial T.V. conducted their businesses in Gary, Indiana. On the day of the drawing, February 1, 1958, Norris was in the shop of Commercial T.V. and asked its president, Cordinas, whether anyone from Commercial T.V. was planning to attend the dance and drawing that night. Cordinas answered in the affirmative. Norris then requested that some one from Commercial T.V. take his certificate and act as his representative at the drawing.

Norris had been told by one of plaintiff's salesmen, Chandler, that it would be within the contest rules for him to be represented by Commercial T.V.

Norris's certificate No. B 382 was deposited in the box from which the drawing was made by Casbon, the treasurer of Commercial T.V., along with Commercial's six certificates. Casbon was advised by Chandler to do this. Subjada, plaintiff's sales manager, acted as master of ceremonies and conducted the drawing. Certificate No. B 382 belonging to Norris was drawn from the box. No complaint is made here as to the manner of the drawing. Norris was not present.

Casbon presented the stub from the winning certificate to Subjada and in response to an inquiry from him said that he was from Hobby Craft T.V. Subjada then gave Casbon the certificate of title to the Edsel, assigned in blank by plaintiff, together with the keys to the car, and Casbon drove the car to Gary. The next day (Sunday) Norris was informed by Cordinas that Hobby Craft T.V. had won the Edsel and told him to come to Commercial T.V. the following day (Monday) to "settle things up." Norris went to Commercial T.V. on Monday but was refused possession of the Edsel. Later, Commercial refused to purchase Norris's equity in the automobile and refused further repeated demands to surrender the car to Norris. About two weeks before trial, Commercial T.V. sold the Edsel for approximately $2,000 and intends to retain the money obtained from the sale.

Appellant contends that the transaction in question was a lottery, illegal in character, and unenforceable in the federal courts. Assuming, *arguendo,* that plaintiff's campaign to stimulate sales did have some of the elements of a lottery, such a defense is not available to appellant in this case. Commercial T.V. was not a party to the lottery agreement between plaintiff and Norris. It had no legal or equitable right to the automobile or its value, but it is seeking the unjust enrichment of itself by attempting to assert the defense of illegality to benefit by its own wrongdoing.

In the absence of any express holding in Indiana or Illinois, "[t]he rule that the law will not enforce an illegal contract has application only between the immediate parties to the contract," as stated in Matta v. Katsoulas, 1927, 192 Wis. 212, 212 N.W. 261, 262, is sound and applicable. Hence, it follows that one in possession of the fruits of an illegal transaction to which he was not a party cannot invoke the defense of illegality.

We hold that on this issue plaintiff was entitled to recover from Commercial T.V. the cost to it of the automobile in question. * * *

The judgment of the district court is

Affirmed.

Notes

1. What is Norris's posture? If Stolz–Wicks declines to deliver the Edsel to him, does he have a remedy?

2. Assume that Norris had sued Commercial T.V., presumably in the state court. What result? See Lundstrom v. De Santos, infra p. 1260.

APPLICATION OF KAMERMAN

United States Court of Appeals, Second Circuit, 1960.
278 F.2d 411.

HERLANDS, DISTRICT JUDGE. The dispositive question upon this appeal is whether the appellant, an attorney, may have an attorney's lien for his professional services computed on the basis of quantum meruit despite the fact *arguendo* that his written retainer agreement with the respondent, pursuant to which he rendered the services (filing a tax refund action) was champertous. * * *

The District Judge held *sua sponte* that the retainer agreement was champertous and that the petitioner's "action in entering into this champertous contract precludes his seeking equitable relief from this court" but that "this does not bar recovery on a quantum meruit basis". The view thus expressed may be taken to intimate that the petitioner's only remedy was to sue at law in a plenary action, inasmuch as he was disentitled to any equitable relief in the District Court incidental to the tax refund case.

At this time, it is not necessary to decide whether the retainer agreement was champertous. If it be assumed *arguendo* that the agreement was champertous, in the particular circumstances of this case the petitioner would have a lien for the reasonable value of his services.

While the authorities are divided, the more widely supported view is that an attorney may recover upon the basis of quantum meruit for professional services rendered by him under a champertous retainer agreement.[1]

1. [Footnotes renumbered.] Corbin on Contracts, Vol. 6, section 1426 (1951) suggests that this variation among jurisdictions may be due to "differences in the specific conduct of the attorneys seeking compensation."

Williston on Contracts, Vol. VI, section 1713, p. 4842, note 3 (1938) comments that the decisions allowing quantum meruit recovery by an attorney who has rendered services under a champertous bargain "certainly indicate a very lenient attitude towards champerty." Mixed motivations and conflicting policies require accommodation. * * *

A.L.I. Restatement, Contracts, section 545, accords with the stricter view which denies the attorney the right to recover "either the agreed compensation for his services or their value."

In Matter of Snyder, 1907, 190 N.Y. 66, 69, 74–75, 82 N.E. 742, the court granted quantum meruit recovery to the attorney despite the fact that the retainer was held void as against public policy because it contained a provision precluding the client from settling the case without the attorney's consent.

In Watkins v. Sedberry, 1922, 261 U.S. 571, 577, the Court said, with respect to a champertous retainer:

"The making of the contract was not *malum in se*. The attorney's right to fair and reason-

The next proposition—that the attorney has a lien for an amount computed on a quantum meruit basis, notwithstanding the champertous retainer agreement—was squarely adopted in McCoy v. Gas Engine & Power Co., 2d Dept. 1912, 152 A.D. 642, 137 N.Y.S. 591, affirmed unanimously without opinion 1913, 208 N.Y. 631, 102 N.E. 1106. In *McCoy,* the attorney had been retained under a written agreement providing *inter alia* for the attorney to pay all expenses of every kind involved in the litigation, including fees of expert witnesses. The attorney succeeded in obtaining an award from the New York City Board of Assessors. The corporate client joined one of its stockholders in an equity action to rescind and annul the retainer on the ground that the retainer violated the champerty prohibition of section 74 of the then Code of Civil Procedure.[2] The retainer was set aside but the attorney was awarded $30,000 "as the reasonable value of the services performed by him" and "the sum so fixed" was "to be a lien upon the award."

* * * Reversed and the case remanded to the district court for a determination of the amount, if any, of petitioner's lien on the basis of quantum meruit.

Note

Agran v. Shapiro, 127 Cal.App.2d Supp. 807, 273 P.2d 619 (1954). A C.P.A. secured a tax refund for his client: "[A]s soon as his testimony disclosed that certain of the services for which he sought recovery constituted the practice of law, it became the imperative duty of the court to deny any recovery therefor."

Is the sometime favorable treatment of attorneys engaged in champerty as compared to C.P.A.s engaged in the unauthorized practice of law (or for that matter unlicensed plumbers) based upon the triviality of the illegality? If so, why isn't the express contract enforceable? If because it is not "malum in se," then why is champerty a misdemeanor?

COMET THEATRE ENTERPRISES v. CARTWRIGHT

United States Court of Appeals, Ninth Circuit, 1952.
195 F.2d 80.

DENMAN, CHIEF JUDGE. This is an appeal from a judgment against Comet Theatre Enterprises, Inc., hereafter Comet, a California corporation, plaintiff in an action against appellees, citizens of Utah, on a common count for money had and received. Recovery was sought by Comet of money voluntarily paid to the defendants for their full performance of a contract for services of a supervisory nature rendered by the defendants to Comet in connection with the construction of the latter's drive-in theatre. Comet contends that it is entitled to judgment because, as admitted, the defendants were not licensed under California Business and Professions Code, Sections 7025–7031.

able compensation is not forfeited. [Citing cases.]"

2. Section 74 of the Code of Civil Procedure (Bliss New York Annotated Code, Fifth Edition, Vol. 1) provided:

"§ 74. *Attorney must not pay to procure claims for suit.*

"§ 75. *Penalty for violation of last two sections.*

"An attorney or counsellor who violates either of the last two sections is guilty of a misdemeanor; and, on conviction thereof, shall be punished accordingly and must be removed from office by the supreme court."

Section 136 of the then New York Penal Code (L.1881, ch. 676) also made the same acts a misdemeanor. The foregoing provisions of the Code of Civil Procedure and the Penal Code have been consolidated in present section 274 of the New York Penal Law.

* * * That Code requires contractors to procure a license from a board created by the Act. The effect of the defendants' failure to get a license is stated in Loving & Evans v. Blick, 33 Cal.2d 603, 204 P.2d 23 where the California court held a contract made by an unlicensed contractor is illegal and void. The only provisions of the Act imposing sanctions on unlicensed persons are Section 7030 making failure to get a license a misdemeanor and Section 7031 providing that they cannot sue to recover compensation for services and goods furnished to another person.

There is no provision in the Act that when the unlicensed persons have completely performed a contract for agreed services and the person so benefited voluntarily has paid the agreed consideration he may recover back the money so paid. * * *

Comet voluntarily paid the consideration for what it received, acting under a mistake of its legal rights under § 7031 which provides: "No person engaged in the business or acting in the capacity of a contractor, may bring or maintain any action in any court of this State for the collection of compensation for the performance of any act or contract for which a license is required by this chapter without alleging and proving that he was a duly licensed contractor at all times during the performance of such act or contract." Had Comet when it paid appellees for their services known of its legal power under § 7031 to refuse payment and to set up that section as a perfect defense to any action brought by defendants, it then would have refused. Here is a clear case of a consummated illegal transaction where Comet acted under a mistake of law, much like the case of Harralson v. Barrett, 99 Cal. 607, 34 P. 342. There a mortgagor had agreed with his mortgagee to pay a mortgage tax prohibited by the California constitution. Payment was made under this invalid agreement and the court refused to allow the mortgagor a credit for this payment on the ground that if he voluntarily fulfills his promise to pay interest, it is through a mistake of law and he is bound by his own act. * * *

The appellant has strongly contended that the statute was passed for its benefit and that rescission and restitution are necessary to protect its rights. On this the Restatement of Contracts § 601 provides for such relief only where its refusal will harm the parties for whose benefit the statute making the contract illegal exists. We cannot perceive how such refusal in this case would harm the plaintiff since there is no proof that the services which were rendered to him were defective or that he in any other way did not receive value for the money which he paid. There is no equitable reason for invoking restitution when the plaintiff gets the exchange which he expected.

The judgment is affirmed.

Note

Unlicensed Professionals—Recovery for Value of Services. The expected ambivalence of holdings occurs where competent work is performed at the request of a client, who then refuses to pay because the other party lacked a license. The stringent attitude is exemplified in cases such as Bauman and Vogel, C.P.A. v. Del Vecchio, 423 F.Supp. 1041 (E.D.Pa.1976). A C.P.A. firm licensed in New Jersey was verbally requested by an M.D. in Pennsylvania to do accounting work on his various corporate ventures. The accountants did not procure the requisite public accounting certificate from the Pennsylvania State Board before performing the work. The doctor refused to pay a bill for $100,000. The accounting firm sued for the reasonable value of the services, and alleged fraud in that the doctor promised to pay without intent to perform. Recovery was denied.

See also Design Development, Inc. v. Brignole, 20 Conn.App. 685, 570 A.2d 221 (1990). Architectural firm denied any recovery for services, though client was aware that the firm was unlicensed.

On the other hand in Town Planning and Engineering Associates v. Amesbury Specialty Co., 369 Mass. 737, 744–47, 342 N.E.2d 706, 711–12 (1976), defendant claimed that the person in charge of the practice of engineering for the plaintiff, a contracting firm, did not hold a "certificate of registration" as required. A violation of the applicable statute was a misdemeanor. The firm prepared plans and related matters on a construction job for the defendant. The actual work was done by independently registered engineers. The defendant terminated plaintiff's contract, alleging its illegality, but apparently proceeded with the work as laid out by the plaintiff firm. Recovery was allowed. The Court said:

"Our cases warn against the sentimental fallacy of piling on sanctions unthinkingly once an illegality is found. As was said in Nussenbaum v. Chambers & Chambers, Inc., 322 Mass. 419, 422, 77 N.E.2d 780, 782 (1948): 'Courts do not go out of their way to discover some illegal element in a contract or to impose hardship upon the parties beyond that which is necessary to uphold the policy of the law.' Again the court said in Buccella v. Schuster, 340 Mass. 323, 326, 164 N.E.2d 141, 143 (1960), where the plaintiff was allowed to recover his compensation for blasting a ledge on the defendant's property although he had not given bond or secured a blasting permit as required by law: 'We do not reach the conclusion that blasting without complying with the requirements * * * is so repugnant to public policy that the defendant should receive a gift of the plaintiff's services.' Professor Corbin adds: 'The statute may be clearly for protection against fraud and incompetence; but in very many cases the statute breaker is neither fraudulent nor incompetent. He may have rendered excellent service or delivered goods of the highest quality, his non-compliance with the statute seems nearly harmless, and the real defrauder seems to be the defendant who is enriching himself at the plaintiff's expense. Although many courts yearn for a mechanically applicable rule, they have not made one in the present instance. Justice requires that the penalty should fit the crime; and justice and sound policy do not always require the enforcement of licensing statutes by large forfeitures going not to the state but to repudiating defendants.' "

For a similarly relaxed attitude see Asdourian v. Araj, 38 Cal.3d 276, 211 Cal.Rptr. 703, 696 P.2d 95 (1985), which allows "substantial" compliance to offset technical violations.

2. IN PARI DELICTO

DAVIS v. SLADE

District of Columbia Court of Appeals, 1970.
271 A.2d 412.

Fickling, Associate Judge. Appellants appeal from a summary judgment awarding appellee, a former tenant, $690 which represented rent paid under a lease which had been declared void in a prior landlord and tenant action.

The undisputed facts are that appellants, knowing that substantial housing violations existed, rented certain premises to appellee. For 6 months appellee paid rent totaling $690 and then defaulted. The appellants then brought an action to recover possession of the premises for nonpayment of rent. Their cause failed, however, since the lease was admittedly void under our decision in Brown v. Southall Realty Co., D.C.App., 237 A.2d 834 (1968). Appellee brought this action to recover $690 rent paid under the void lease and voluntarily moved from the premises during the pendency of her claim.

The basic question raised on this appeal is what, if any, compensation a landlord is entitled to receive from his tenant for the use and occupancy of the premises where the lease is void and illegal. The appellants contend that they are entitled to keep the rent received under this illegal lease since not all contracts which violate a regulation are unenforceable. The appellee contends that the landlord should not be allowed to benefit from his illegal bargain and, therefore, is not entitled to any compensation. We hold that the landlord is entitled to some compensation as hereinafter stated. * * *

It is argued that, since the tenant is *in pari delicto,* the court should leave the parties to this illegal bargain where it finds them. We cannot resolve this case by simply stating that the lease is void and the landlord cannot enforce the collection of the rent since no one is now trying to enforce this lease. What we have, instead, is a tenant seeking the return of consideration paid under an illegal bargain. This request is made in the face of the general rule of the law that "[a] party to an illegal bargain can neither recover damages for breach thereof nor, by rescinding the bargain, recover the performance that he has rendered." [Restatement of Contracts § 598 (1932)]

Though it is true that courts generally leave the parties to an illegal contract where they find them, there are exceptions. One such exception applies when one of the parties is not *in pari delicto.* That party will then be allowed to rescind the contract and recover any performance he has rendered.

There is no mechanical rule to determine whether a party is *in pari delicto;* yet, a party will be held *in pari delicto* and denied restitution if, judging from prevailing mores, by participating in the illegal transaction he is guilty of moral turpitude. The Housing Regulations state: "No owner, licensee, or tenant shall occupy or permit the occupancy of any habitation in violation of these regulations." This indicates that the tenant is also guilty of violating the regulations. That fact alone, however, does not require that we hold the appellee *in pari delicto.*

Courts in the District of Columbia have taken judicial notice of the housing shortage. The parties to this present action have stipulated to the existence of the shortage and have recognized that it is most acute for large families such as the appellee's. We must also consider the economic pressure on low income tenants [1] and the great disparity in bargaining position between landlords and such a tenant. In reality, a tenant is often unable to bargain at all and may be forced to accept a house that violates the regulations or sleep in the street.

Even if we were to hold that the appellee was *in pari delicto,* we would still refuse to apply the general rule denying restitution. Professor Williston has stated:

> "Occasionally, there may be cases where, in spite of both parties sharing in the illegality of an executed transaction, public policy will be best served by rescission, even though the result is to permit recovery by a guilty plaintiff." [2]

1. [Footnotes renumbered.] Mrs. Slade and her six children were receiving public assistance benefits.

In Rubin v. Douglas, D.C.Mun.App., 59 A.2d 690 (1948), this court recognized and accepted this theory, stating

> "even though a party be considered technically *in pari delicto* he may be permitted to recover if the law in question was passed for his protection and it appears that the purposes of the law will be better effectuated by granting relief than by denying it."

It is clearly appropriate to apply this rule to the present case. * * *

We must still consider whether a landlord can set off any amount under a quasi-contractual theory. It appears that as a general rule, such a theory is not available. * * *

In Diamond Housing Corp. v. Robinson, D.C.App., 257 A.2d 492 (1969), we held that a person occupying premises under a *Brown* lease is a tenant at sufferance. Since the lease is void *ab initio,* he becomes such a tenant from the time he first takes possession. In effect the law has ordered the landlord to award the tenant such a status. This tenancy, unlike the tenancy attempted by the lease, is legal. For this reason we feel that the normal rule denying quasi-contractual recovery should not be followed. Although the landlord is entitled to nothing for what he gave the tenant under the lease, he is entitled to the reasonable value of the premises in its condition as it was when occupied.

Reversed and remanded for proceedings not inconsistent with this opinion.

Notes

1. "Not in pari delicto" is an exception to the rule that disallows remedies under illegal bargains. There are two interchangeable ways of putting it. (a) The parties *are not* in pari delicto because a statute makes one less guilty or because the other is more guilty owing to his duress, his fraud, his special knowledge of facts, or what have you. (b) The parties *are* in pari delicto, but, because of the factors just enumerated, the plaintiff will be allowed restitution anyway. The only advantage of (a) is that it gives the appearance of a single exception rather than a plethora of exceptions as does (b).

2. The "not in pari delicto" exception is usually invoked to allow restitution, not contract damages or specific performance. However, this is not always true. Witness the unlicensed contractor who performs badly. To deny damages to the owner would impose a hardship upon the person for whose protection the statute was passed. See Cohen v. Mayflower Corp., 196 Va. 1153, 86 S.E.2d 860 (1955).

3. *Ignorance of the Law.* What if one party is not in pari delicto because he is ignorant of facts that make his participation in the bargain illegal. The "not in pari delicto" exception may permit restitution and damages. In Stevens v. Berger, 255 Wis. 55, 37 N.W.2d 841 (1949), plaintiff, a non-veteran, leased premises remodeled under regulations that required the premises to be offered first to veterans. Plaintiff was justifiably ignorant of the fact that the landlord had failed to comply with the regulation and that his lease was illegal. Damages were awarded.

2. Williston, Contracts § 1787 at 5081 (1938). This theory has also been accepted by the Restatement of Contracts at § 601.

JOHNSON v. JOHNSON

California Court of Appeal, Second District, 1987.
192 Cal.App.3d 551, 237 Cal.Rptr. 644.

EPSTEIN, ASSOCIATE JUSTICE. * * * The plaintiff, Zella Johnson, is the mother of defendant, Houston O. Johnson. In 1976, she lived with her elderly and ailing husband on their ranch in Lucerne Valley. Defendant urged them to move closer to his home so he could be more accessible to them. * * * After a time, they found a suitable property in the Tujunga area. It was to become the subject of the instant litigation.

Defendant's parents were fully able to purchase the home through conventional financing; they had $7,500 available for that purpose. Defendant, a veteran, was eligible for GI loan financing. He urged his parents to let him use that method to purchase the property. Since only he, and not his parents, was eligible for the GI loan, title was taken in defendant's name. But it was fully understood by defendant and his parents that the latter would be the actual and beneficial owners of the property.

The Johnsons paid into escrow the entire amount necessary to close the transaction, some $1,850. * * *

Plaintiff and her husband moved onto the property in February 1977. Shortly thereafter, defendant borrowed from his parents the $7,500 that they had planned to use as the down payment to purchase the property. He used the money, an interest-free loan, for real estate investments.

Payments on the GI loan amounted to $200 a month. The Johnsons sent monthly checks in that amount to defendant, who made the actual payments to the lending institution. This arrangement continued until shortly after Mr. Johnson's death, in March 1979.

After that, plaintiff's sole income was from Social Security. She agreed with defendant that she would credit him with $200 a month toward his personal loan, and that he would continue to make the monthly payments on the GI loan.

From the beginning, both parents and, later, plaintiff alone, paid all of the costs associated with maintenance of the home, with a single exception: defendant paid $165 to implant a lawn on the property. And almost from the beginning, they pressed defendant to transfer title to them. He responded that he could not do so until six months after the purchase. He did not transfer title then, or at any time thereafter, despite his mother's repeated entreaties.

In May 1979, plaintiff discussed with defendant her plans to remodel the garage of the home into an apartment, which she could rent in order to increase her income. Defendant told her that the property was her home, and she could do with it as she wished. Plaintiff then spent $5,500 of her funds to convert the garage into an apartment.

In 1981, defendant separated from his wife and moved into the property, paying no rent. In doing so, he gave no indication that he considered himself to be the owner of the property.

Some three years later, in 1984, defendant told his mother that he was going to sell the house and that she would have to move. She declined to do so, and again asked defendant to transfer title over to her. He refused, and plaintiff brought this suit for declaration of a resulting trust and for ancillary relief.

Defendant raises two issues on appeal:

1. Whether illegality of the underlying GI loan bars the decree of a resulting trust.

2. Whether the court erred in the extent of the resulting trust that it decreed.

Civil Code section 853[1] provides: "When a transfer of real property is made to one person, and the consideration therefor is paid by or for another, a trust is presumed to result in favor of the person by or for whom such payment is made." The trust that is "presumed to result" from this situation is termed a "resulting trust." * * *

[Defendant] now argues there can be no resulting trust because the underlying GI loan transaction was illegal. * * *

Section 1804, subdivision (c) of 38 U.S.C. provides that no loan may be made under the Act for the purchase or construction of residential property unless the veteran applicant certifies that he or she intends to occupy the property as a residence. It is settled law that transactions in which other persons use a veteran as a "straw" in order to obtain the benefits of the Act are against public policy. [citations]

These cases arise out of factual contexts in which the purported beneficial owner appears to have taken a far more active part in arranging GI loan financing than did defendant's parents in this case. Nevertheless, it is clear that it was improper to use the Act to finance the purchase of a home under facts as found by the trial court. We therefore will assume that the underlying loan contravened public policy, and was therefore illegal.

It does not follow that the arrangement between the parties cannot be enforced. In what was to become the leading California opinion on this point, Justice Peters stated the rule on enforcement of illegal contracts in these terms: "The rule that the courts will not lend their aid to the enforcement of an illegal agreement or one against public policy is fundamentally sound. The rule was conceived for the purposes of protecting the public and the courts from imposition. It is a rule predicated upon sound public policy. But the courts should not be so enamored with the Latin phrase *'in pari delicto'* that they blindly extend the rule to every case where illegality appears somewhere in the transaction. The fundamental purpose of the rule must always be kept in mind, and the realities of the situation must be considered. Where, by applying the rule, the public cannot be protected because the transaction has been completed, where no serious moral turpitude is involved, where the defendant is the one guilty of the greatest moral fault, and where to apply the rule will be to permit the defendant to be unjustly enriched at the expense of the plaintiff, the rule should not be applied. * * * (Norwood v. Judd (1949) 93 Cal.App.2d 276, 288–289, 209 P.2d 24).

In this case, each of the *Norwood* criteria is satisfied. The transaction is completed, not executory, so application of the rule cannot protect the public except by example. No serious moral turpitude is involved on the part of plaintiff. Instead, the "one guilty of the greatest moral fault" clearly is

1. [Editors' Note: This section has disappeared in a comprehensive revision of the code.]

defendant. He instigated the arrangement and then took advantage of it by making an interest-free loan of the money his parents had intended to use as a down payment for their home. Finally, application of the *in pari delicto* rule in this case would unjustly enrich defendant by allowing him to reap the full benefits of any appreciation in the value of the house, notwithstanding his role in the transaction and his subsequent conduct.

Defendant suggests that his mother's equities may be recognized by allowing an equitable lien in her favor equivalent to her cash investment in the house. That was the remedy provided in Hainey v. Narigon, 247 Cal.App.2d 528, 531, 55 Cal.Rptr. 638. But the plaintiff in *Hainey* was not importuned to enter into the transaction by the defendant veteran, as were plaintiff and her husband in this case. To the contrary, it did not appear that the principal defendant in *Hainey* did anything beyond telling the plaintiff (his brother-in-law) that he could use his GI loan entitlement, and making a single monthly payment.

Having decreed a resulting trust in plaintiff's favor, the trial court directed defendant to convey the property to her. Defendant argues that this remedy goes too far. * * *

Defendant's argument is that only a *pro tanto* resulting trust should be decreed because he "lent his credit" to the loan transaction.

Federal law provides protection to the veteran against the possibility of a deficiency on default of a GI loan. (38 U.S.C. § 1817.) We do not know what efforts, if any, defendant has made to assure himself of the benefits of this statute. Beyond the possibility of a deficiency, defendant's real "contribution" to the transaction was in arranging for the GI loan. We are not provided with any argument or authority as to how a *pro tanto* decision might be made in these circumstances. Even if such a formula could be derived, it would hardly be just, given the facts of this case, to allow defendant to retain any share of the title in recognition of his being the lender of record.

Nevertheless, two problems remain: the technical possibility of a default, and the mechanics involved in handling the remaining payments on the loan. These matters may easily be accommodated by the retention of jurisdiction in the trial court to issue such further orders as are necessary to fairly carry out its decree. We will modify the judgment to make that retention explicit.

The judgment is modified to provide that the trial court retains jurisdiction to make such orders as are appropriate to safeguard defendant against the contingency of liability on account of any default in payments on the loan by plaintiff or her successors. So modified, the judgment is affirmed.

NIZAMUDDOWLAH v. BENGAL CABARET, INC.

New York Supreme Court, Queens County, 1977.
92 Misc.2d 220, 399 N.Y.S.2d 854.

JOSEPH S. CALABRETTA, JUSTICE. * * * We have before us the plaintiff, a citizen of Bangladesh, and now a resident alien in the United States, seeking to recover from the defendants for working here, based upon an agreement made by both with the obvious intention of circumventing and disobeying the United States Immigration Law. The plaintiff claims ignorance of such law, and the defendants contend that the plaintiff did not work, and even if he did, such work contract was illegal, and therefore, he has no right to recover.

* * * Plaintiff had met defendant Shamsher Wadud (the principal owner of the Nirvana Restaurant) in August of 1972 in Bangladesh, at which time and place, the defendant offered to employ plaintiff at his restaurant in New York City. The agreement called for plaintiff to serve an apprentice period of about three months without salary, at the end of which time he would receive a waiter's salary, and eventually, become the manager of the restaurant. It is conceded by both sides that defendant Wadud did make all visa and travel arrangements.

Plaintiff came to this country at the expense of defendant Shamsher Wadud, arriving on September 17, 1972, and thereafter, resided at defendant Wadud's home for at least two to three months, and slept and ate at the defendant's restaurant for an additional two months.

During this time and continuing through May of 1974, plaintiff worked as a waiter in the restaurant, and after so working for a few months, made several demands for payment of wages, but all to no avail. The plaintiff had also made frequent inquiry of defendant regarding his resident visa (commonly called a "green card"), which defendant had promised to obtain for him through his attorney. But, defendant persistently stalled him through devious tactics, until finally, the plaintiff managed to obtain his resident visa at his own time and expense.

The court must now come to grips with the crucial issue in this case, and that is, whether or not an alien possessing a visitor's visa may recover wages under a contract of employment. It is well-settled law that:

> "Generally, a party to an illegal contract cannot recover damages for its breach. But as in the case of many such simplifications, the exceptions and qualifications to the general rule are numerous and complex." (Gates v. Rivers Construction Co., Inc., Alaska, 515 P.2d 1020, 1021.)

At bar, the dilemma is compounded by conflicting public policies and equitable doctrines. Plaintiff does not come into court with "clean hands" as he clearly violated the Immigration Laws by working after his arrival until the date he was issued his "green card"; and, although he acted out of a strong desire to emigrate to the United States, he willingly fell in with defendant, thus making him in effect a coconspirator. This type of conduct poses serious economic problems for our citizenry.

> "Employment of illegal aliens in times of high unemployment deprives citizens and legally admitted aliens of jobs; acceptance by illegal aliens of jobs on substandard terms as to wages and working conditions can seriously depress wage scales and working conditions of citizens and legally admitted aliens; and employment of illegal aliens under such conditions can diminish the effectiveness of labor unions." (De Canas v. Bica, 424 U.S. 351, 356–357.)

Additionally, the court cannot give credence to plaintiff's claim of ignorance.

However, the court finds that it is the defendant who is the main perpetrator, intent on evading and taking advantage of the Immigration Laws. It appears that the plaintiff was not the first "friend" that the defendant has manipulated into working for his restaurant with grandiose promises but without remuneration, and, unless this court takes action to prevent its continuance, will not be the last.

[T]he only equitable alternative available to this court is to allow the employee to recover based on the theory of unjust enrichment. Defendant was well aware that a party to an illegal contract cannot ask the court to help him carry out his illegal objective, and being quite knowledgeable about the Immigration Laws, has managed to run his enterprise without fairly compensating his employees.

This court holds that plaintiff's violation is overshadowed by defendant's entire course of deceptive conduct and, therefore, plaintiff is entitled to payment under the New York State Labor Law of the minimum wage then in effect for the period from January 1, 1973 to May 13, 1974, amounting to $6,629.60 (the initial 15 weeks constituting the period of plaintiff's apprenticeship), plus liquidated damages of $1,657.40, equal to 25%, totalling $8,287. In addition, defendant shall pay the sum of $1,500 as and for reasonable attorney's fees.

However, in arriving at any monies due to the plaintiff, credit must be given to the defendant for (a) the fair and reasonable value for room and board provided by the defendant in the sum of $2,400; (b) the payment of $450; and (c) air fare to New York in the sum of $688.

BANK OF TUCSON v. ADRIAN

United States District Court, District of Minnesota, 1965.
245 F.Supp. 595.

Supra, at p. 835.

Notes

1. In Union Exchange National Bank v. Joseph, 231 N.Y. 250, 253–55, 231 N.E. 905, 906 (1921), the plaintiff sued on a note made to prevent criminal prosecution of the defendant's brother-in-law. The defendant counterclaimed for payments already made, claiming duress. Justice Cardozo stated the counter-arguments:

"We think the defendant, if a victim of duress, was at the same time a wrongdoer when he stifled the charge of a crime. * * *

"We are urged in apportioning the blame to allot a heavier weight of guilt to the plaintiff who exacted than to the defendant who complied. The same argument was pressed in Haynes v. Rudd, 102 N.Y. 372, 7 N.E. 287. We found no inequality sufficient to set the law in motion at the suit of knowing wrongdoers to undo a known wrong. * * * They had chosen to put private welfare above duty to the state. The state would not concern itself with readjustments of their burdens unless for some better reason than the fact that indifference to duty had followed hard on temptation. Excuse would seldom fail if temptation could supply it. * * *

"In following Haynes v. Rudd, * * * we do not exclude the possibility that variant degrees of mitigation may permit variant conclusions. A different question would be put here, for illustration, if the charge of crime had been put forward in bad faith without reasonable foundation or genuine belief. Innocence maintaining its good repute against mere malice and oppression might move us to view with charity its methods of defense."

Does Justice Cardozo suggest that if the charge of crime is made maliciously, the duress outweighs the illegality? That no illegality would ultimately result?

2. A similar question arises where the accused payor is in fact innocent although the charge is made in apparent good faith. In short, can a nonexistent offense be compounded? Justice Cardozo said in Union Exchange National Bank v. Joseph:

"The contract is not helped by the suggestion that, for all that appears Block may have been innocent. That issue beyond doubt would be irrelevant if prosecution had begun. We are asked to hold otherwise when prosecution is merely threatened. Some cases do, indeed, give effect to that distinction. The prosecution once initiated, they say, must be left to take its course; the prosecution merely threatened, may be bought off, if directed against innocence. Cowen, J., so held in 1843 upon a trial in the Supreme Court. Steuben County Bank v. Mathewson. His decision has been followed in some jurisdictions * * * and rejected elsewhere. * * * We think that it has not been law in this state since the ruling in Haynes v. Rudd. There the plaintiff gave his note under duress to stifle a prosecution threatened but not begun. We approved a charge that 'an agreement to suppress the evidence of a crime alleged to have been committed' was as illegal as one 'to suppress the evidence or refrain from prosecuting a crime which had in fact been committed.' 131 N.E. at 906, 231 N.Y. at 253."

3. May a creditor use duress by threat of a criminal prosecution to collect a valid debt? See Clifford v. Great Falls Gas Co., 68 Mont. 300, 216 P. 1114 (1923).

4. A lawyer's intemperate dunning letters may jeopardize his client's case. See Gillikin v. Whitley, 66 N.C.App. 694, 311 S.E.2d 677 (1984).

5. A related query is whether the victim of a usurious contract can recover all interest paid or only that above the legal maximum. See Dennis v. Bradbury, 236 F.Supp. 683 (D.Colo.1964), aff'd, 368 F.2d 905 (10th Cir.1966).

GRIM v. CHEATWOOD

Supreme Court of Oklahoma, 1953.
208 Okl. 570, 257 P.2d 1049.

HALLEY, CH. J. Plaintiffs in their amended petition allege that * * * on or about the 12th day of August, 1945, defendant Vernie Cheatwood connived, enticed and induced plaintiff Orval Grim to become engaged in a poker game and with the collusion and collaboration of two of his cohorts, with the use of marked cards, defrauded said plaintiff out of checks totaling the sum of $1,000. That plaintiff Orval Grim, believing that the poker game was honest and on the square, executed and delivered to defendant Vernie Cheatwood certain mineral deeds in return for such checks.

Plaintiff Gladys Grim [a co-tenant] did not sign either deed. On or about the first day of November, 1949, plaintiff Orval Grim discovered that the poker game referred to was instituted through connivance, collusion, and a fraudulent plan of defendant Vernie Cheatwood and his cohorts for the purpose of defrauding him out of his money.

Upon discovery of the fraud plaintiffs brought this action to set aside and cancel the mineral deeds, and pray that such deeds be set aside and cancelled and title quieted in them in and to the minerals.

Defendants Cheatwood demurred to the amended petition on the ground that it did not state facts sufficient to constitute a cause of action. The trial court sustained the demurrer as to plaintiff Orval Grim but overruled it as to plaintiff Gladys Grim. * * *

It is the contention of defendants that plaintiffs' cause of action is based on a gambling transaction, a transaction forbidden by law and made a crime by statute, and that in such case neither a court of law nor one of equity will grant relief to either party to enforce any rights growing out of such transaction but will leave the parties where it found them. * * *

Plaintiffs concede the general rule to be as contended by defendants. It is their contention, however, that there is a well-established exception to the rule to the effect that where fraud is practiced by the winner in order to obtain his winnings (as is pleaded by them in their petition) equity will not permit such a party to benefit by his fraud and will grant relief to the one less guilty. * * *

In Lockman v. Cobb, 77 Ark. 279, 91 S.W. 546, the Supreme Court of Arkansas said:

> "Where plaintiff was induced to put up large sums of money as a bet on a foot race, it being represented to him that one of the racers was certain to win, but in fact there was no bona fide race, but in a pretended race the other party won, the plaintiff was entitled to recover the amount lost."

In that case the court said:

> "In what wrong or crime were the plaintiff and the defendants in pari delicto? If any, it was a conspiracy by the defendants to defraud the plaintiff and to steal his money; to obtain by deceit and falsehood the money of plaintiff by inducing him to believe that a foot race was to be run and that they were actually wagering their money, one against the other, upon it; and to induce him to believe he was betting upon a foot race. * * * But the race was never run. Two men ran, but according to a previous understanding the one upon whom he staked his money fell down, and the other passed out ahead and was declared the winner. * * * By fraud and deceit they caused him to make a pretended wager and robbed him of his money, pretending that he had lost it * * * and he was not in pari delicto with the defendants." * * *

Plaintiff Orval Grim, under the allegations in plaintiffs' petition did not voluntarily enter into a real and honest poker game with defendant Vernie Cheatwood and his confederates and lose his money in such a game. He was induced to enter into a fixed and pretended poker game for the purpose of cheating and robbing him of his money by the use of marked cards. Plaintiff had no knowledge of said conspiracy and fraud at the time he entered the game. Upon discovery of the fraud plaintiffs brought this action to set aside the deeds. Under such state of facts he was not in pari delicto with defendant Vernie Cheatwood and his confederates.

Plaintiffs' action is not an action to recover losses sustained in a gambling game. Their action is one in equity to cancel and set aside mineral deeds because of fraud in their procurement and lack of consideration for their execution, and since under the pleadings the parties were not in pari delicto, plaintiffs may maintain this action although it will be necessary for them to plead and prove the gambling transaction in order to establish fraud and lack of consideration.

Where the parties are not in pari delicto, equity will intervene in the protection of one less guilty, notwithstanding his unclean hands. [citations]

While there are some authorities to the contrary we think the better rule and weight of authority support the conclusion reached.

Plaintiffs' petition stated a cause of action, and the trial court erred in sustaining the demurrer thereto as against plaintiff Orval Grim. * * *

Reversed, with directions to overrule the demurrer. * * *

Notes

1. *Stock Frauds and "In Pari Delicto."* Rule 10b–5 of the Securities and Exchange Commission declares it unlawful to employ schemes and artifices to defraud, or to make untrue statements in connection with the purchase or sale of stock. S.E.C. v. Texas Gulf Sulphur Co., 446 F.2d 1301 (2d Cir.), cert. denied, 404 U.S. 1005 (1971), and later decisions established that persons with "inside information" concerning a corporation, who trade in the stock of that corporation before the information is made public violate the rule. Such persons include "tippees" who knowingly receive selective disclosure of inside information.

Suppose an individual receives hush-hush information ("not to be repeated to anyone") from a corporate insider that a merger is in the offing. She eagerly takes a plunge in the market which turns into a bath when the "inside information" proves to have been false. When the "tippee" sues the "tipper" for making untrue statements which induced her to purchase stock, may the "tipper" defend on the ground that his accuser was guilty of an unlawful act in purchasing the stock that led to her losses, and is therefore "in pari delicto"?

The United States Supreme Court in Bateman Eichler, Hill Richards, Inc. v. Berner, 472 U.S. 299, 315–316 (1985) resolved a conflict:

"Although a number of lower courts have reasoned that a broad rule of *caveat tippee* would better serve this goal [of a high standard of business ethics], we believe the contrary position adopted by other courts represents the better view * * *. The *in pari delicto* defense, by denying any incentive to a defrauded tippee to bring suit against his defrauding tipper, would significantly undermine this important goal * * * [to expose guilty parties] and render them more easily subject to appropriate civil, administrative and criminal penalties."

Stella v. Dean Witter Reynolds, Inc., 241 N.J.Super. 55, 74, 574 A.2d 468, 477–78 (1990). An account executive induced an investor to buy into a "Special Situations Fund" supposedly consisting of stock purchased at a discount by the brokerage firm and available only to "preferred" customers. There was no fund; if one had existed, it would have violated state securities regulation. Restitution was allowed: "[T]he victim of fraud is not in pari delicto with his victimizer, not even if the victim was deceived into thinking he was defrauding a third party. In the present case, it would be a perversion of public policy to hold, as Dean Witter urges us to do, that Sykes' gullibility and cupidity relieved [the account executive] or his employer from their obligation to repay the losses resulting from his fraud." The court relied on "Buckfoot Gang" cases as authority, including Lockman v. Cobb, 77 Ark. 279, 91 S.W. 546 (1905), which is quoted in the principal decision.

2. *Pari Delicto Between Lawyer and Client—A Tort Defense?* Client, expecting to file bankruptcy, conferred with Lawyer. She indicated that she had $10,000 in cash that she wished to protect. Lawyer advised Client to say that she had given the money to her mother and not to worry; no one would care and it would not be a matter of contention anyway. Client followed this advice and lied under oath at her first meeting of creditors. The bankruptcy trustee investigated. Client's bankruptcy petition has been dismissed, and she faces perjury charges.

Client sues Lawyer for malpractice. She claims damages for emotional distress and cost of hiring counsel to defend against perjury charges. Lawyer moves to dismiss her complaint arguing that her allegations placed the parties in pari delicto. What decision? Suppose Client had also alleged payment of Lawyer's fee and sought restitution. What decision? See Evans v. Cameron, 121 Wis.2d 421, 360 N.W.2d 25 (1985).

3. LOCUS POENITENTIAE

GREENBERG v. EVENING POST ASSOCIATION

Supreme Court of Errors of Connecticut, 1917.
91 Conn. 371, 99 A. 1037.

The defendant was engaged in publishing a daily newspaper commonly known as the "Hartford Post," and to increase its circulation employed one Fitch to conduct a so-called prize contest under which prizes were to be given to those who obtained the most votes. The contest was advertised as a "strictly competitive proposition," and every contestant was promised a "square deal." The plaintiff, after entering the contest, was informed by Fitch that a certain Jackson automobile of the alleged value of $2,500, which was offered as one of the prizes, could be won only by a person who was willing to put money into the contest and that, if the plaintiff would pay $300, he would win the automobile. Plaintiff paid the money, and about two weeks later Fitch demanded another $100, whereupon the plaintiff sought legal advice and was informed that he had become a party to a fraudulent scheme and that he should repudiate the whole transaction and demand back his money. Before the contest was closed or prizes awarded, plaintiff repudiated the bargain and demanded back his money. * * *

BEACH, J. [after stating the facts as above.] This action was brought to recover back money paid to Fitch as the agent of the defendant, and defendant appeals from a refusal to set aside a plaintiff's verdict. * * * No doubt the proposed transaction as the plaintiff testifies to it would, if carried out, have been a gross fraud upon the other competitors; and this is so evident that the plaintiff was bound to know it and cannot succeed in his attempt to pose as an inexperienced person innocently led into taking part in a fraudulent scheme. At the time when he paid the money, he was in pari delicto with Fitch, and, if this action were brought on the original corrupt bargain, he could not prevail. Ex turpi non oritur actio. But the plaintiff is not suing Fitch or the defendant to compel performance of the bargain, or to recover damages for the breach of it. His action is founded, not on the bargain, but on his repudiation of it, before the contest was closed, or the prizes awarded, or the rights of other competitors impaired.

The question is whether it is not quite as consistent with sound public policy to encourage the prompt repudiation of illegal and immoral contracts by permitting, under such circumstances, the recovery of money paid upon an illegal or immoral consideration, as to declare the money forfeited the moment it is paid, and thus discourage repentance in such cases. The defendant practically concedes that the weight of authority authorizes the recovery of money paid for a purpose which is merely illegal, in case the bargain is repudiated promptly and before it is performed by the other party; but it insists that the rule is otherwise where the money is paid under an arrangement involving moral turpitude. We fail to see the propriety of such a distinction. In either case the recovery is not allowed out of tenderness for the plaintiff, but in some cases on the ground that the maxim ex turpi non oritur actio does not apply, because the action is not brought on the corrupt bargain; in other cases on the same ground supplemented by the consideration that the law ought to favor the prompt repudiation of corrupt bargains. In all these cases the reasoning of the decisions would apply regardless of the degree of corruption involved in the original arrangement. It is true that in some cases when the original transaction involved only malum prohibitum it has been suggested that no recovery would have been allowed had the original transaction involved moral turpitude. Thus in Spring Co. v. Knowlton, 103 U.S. 49, it is said in the headnote that a party to a contract the making of which, "although prohibited by law, is not malum in se," may while it remains executory rescind and recover back money advanced thereon to the other party who had not performed any part of the contract. In the body of the opinion it is pointed out that the making of the contract in question was malum prohibitum and not malum in se, but the suggestion in the headnote that no recovery would have been allowed had the contract involved actual fraud is not to be found in the opinion itself. But in Tyler v. Carlisle, 79 Me. 210, 9 A. 356, the court in permitting the recovery of money paid for an alleged purpose which was never carried out does say that the doctrine applies only to minor offenses and not to infamous crimes.

On the other hand, recoveries have been permitted in several cases where the repudiated transaction contemplated the performance of an actual fraud. In Taylor v. Bowen, 1 Q.B.D. 291, quoted with approval in Spring Co. v. Knowlton and in Bowes v. Foster, 2 H. & N. 779, the plaintiffs were allowed to recover back property which had been conveyed away with the design of defrauding creditors. In Falkenberg v. Allen, 18 Okl. 210, 90 Pac. 415, and in other cases, money wagered on a foot race, the result of which was believed by the plaintiffs to have been agreed on in advance, was allowed to be recovered. Wassermann v. Sloss, 117 Cal. 425, 49 Pac. 566, was a case of shares of stock deposited for the purpose of corruptly influencing public officials to favor the execution of a government lease. And Swift illustrates the rule by citing a case in which money paid to procure a place in the customs was allowed to be recovered because the contract remained executory. 1 Swift's Dig. 219.

We think the court correctly charged the jury that, in an action to recover back money paid for the purpose of carrying out a proposed illegal or immoral design, the plaintiff may recover upon proof that he seasonably repented of his bargain, and evidenced such repentance by repudiating the arrangement with reasonable promptness and before the other party had so far acted in performance of it as to carry any part of the illegal or immoral design into effect. * * *

There is no error.

Notes

1. The Restatement (Second) of Contracts allows restitution if the claimant "withdraws from the transaction before the improper purpose has been achieved, or allowance of the claim would put an end to a continuing situation that is contrary to the public interest." Restatement (Second) of Contracts § 199 (1981). However, according to section 199, the claimant must not be guilty of any "serious misconduct." The principal case consciously declines to distinguish the degree of "turpitude" or "misconduct." If the purpose of the "locus poenitentiae" exception is to prevent injury to society, is the limitation to minor illegality sensible?

2. "Suppose a payment of 100£ by A to B on a contract that the latter shall murder C and D. He has murdered C but not D. Can the money be recovered back? In my opinion it cannot be." Kearly v. Thompson, 24 Q.B.D. 742 (1890).

3. News Item: Doctor Seeks Refund of $1000 Paid to "Hit Man": An Upland doctor who tried to hire someone to kill his wife is going to court in an effort to recover a $1000 down payment he made to an undercover police officer.

Dr. John Werner, 37, a radiologist, filed suit in Superior Court to get back the money he paid officer Dave Adkins last March to murder his wife, Carmelita, 38, and make it look like an accident.

The payment was to have been one-third of the contract murder price. The doctor gave Adkins photographs of his wife and told the officer he would arrange for her to be at a certain place at a specified time.

Werner pleaded no contest Aug. 31 to a charge of solicitation to commit murder, a felony, which Superior Judge Harold Haberkorn reduced to a misdemeanor on the basis of a probation department report.

The report said Werner and his wife were having marital difficulties when the doctor hired Adkins and at the time of the August hearing they were living together again.

Haberkorn fined Werner $2000 and placed him on probation for three years.

The doctor's attorney, John W. Kennedy, has contended that the state Penal Code directs that evidence in a criminal case should be returned to its owner after the case is concluded.

The chief trial deputy of San Bernardino County sheriff's office, Don Feld, disagreed.

"I just think, as a matter of policy, if a guy pays money to kill somebody, he shouldn't get the money back," Feld said. "It's a tax on crime, I guess."

If Werner is unsuccessful in recovering the $1000 in a hearing Oct. 14, the money will go to the general funds of the city of San Bernardino.

MARTIN v. FRANCIS

Court of Appeals of Kentucky, 1917.
173 Ky. 529, 191 S.W. 259.

[Sturgill had $500 which he entrusted to Smith who loaned it to Martin, et al. in exchange for a promissory note for $500 (or $600). Smith assigned the note to Cody who assigned it to Francis who brought this action thereon. At this juncture Richie, the unduly elected Democratic jailer of Knott County, Ky., asked to be made a party and filed a cross petition. He alleged that the $500 had been placed by him with Sturgill pursuant to an illegal agreement which he now repudiates and that the makers of the note had knowledge of the facts. He claims the money. A demurrer to the cross complaint was overruled. Other facts appear in the opinion.]

CARROLL, J. * * * It will be seen from the cross-petition that in consideration of the agreement of Richie to appoint Cody his deputy jailer and give him the fees of the office for one-half of his term, or two years, and in further consideration of the fact that he deposited with Sturgill $500 to insure the fulfillment of the contract with Cody, which money Cody was to have in the event Richie failed to comply with his agreement, Cody, who was the regular nominee of the Republican party for the office of jailer of Knott County, withdraw as a candidate for this office a few days before the regular election, and when it was too late for the Republican party to nominate another candidate for the office of jailer in place of Cody.

We may further assume, as a reasonable inference from the averments of the pleading and the failure of Cody to complain, that Richie was elected jailer at the November election, 1913, and performed his contract with Cody by appointing him deputy jailer and giving him the fees of the office as stipulated in the contract. * * *

Richie, of course, occupies no better place in this transaction than Cody. He was an active, participating party in the transaction, guilty of the same immoral, illegal, and corrupt conduct of which Cody was guilty. The public reasons that would forbid Cody to sell his nomination would forbid Richie to buy it. One of them was a bribe taker and the other a bribe giver, and in a court of justice neither of them, in any matter growing out of this transaction, should be entitled to any consideration. If Richie had failed to fulfill his corrupt bargain with Cody, plainly a suit by Cody, seeking performance of the contract or any part of it, would be promptly dismissed, and likewise, if Richie had performed this contract and in any way or manner Cody had secured possession of the $500 deposited by Richie to secure its performance, Richie, if he brought a suit to recover it from Cody, would be turned out of court. The courts would have nothing to do with either of them. * * *

But, conceding the illegality of the contract between Richie and Cody, and further conceding that a suit by either of them to obtain any relief arising out of this transaction would be dismissed, the argument is made on behalf of Richie that this money was delivered by Sturgill, the stakeholder, to Martin without the consent of Richie, and therefore Martin should be treated as holding it in the same manner that Sturgill held it, as he had knowledge of the arrangement under which the money was placed in the hands of Sturgill. And so it is said that, as Richie would have the right to recover the money from Sturgill while it was in his hands, so he has the right to recover it from Martin, who voluntarily and with knowledge of the facts took the place of Sturgill in the transaction.

In order to give Richie the full benefit of this argument we will assume that Martin occupies the place of Sturgill as stakeholder and consider the question as if it were a suit by Richie against Sturgill to recover from him the money. Looking at the matter from this standpoint is putting as favorable a view on the transaction as Richie could ask, and yet we are quite sure that Richie cannot have the relief he seeks. The arrangement between Richie and Cody was, as we have pointed out, corrupt and illegal, and the vicious qualities of the contract between them taint every aspect of the transaction to such an extent that neither of them should be afforded any redress in a court of justice on account of anything growing out of this business. * * *

[I]t is a general and well-settled principle of law that money deposited with a stakeholder on account of a wager or bet of any kind may be recovered from the stakeholder, while it is in his hands, by the person making the deposit. [citations] But in all of these cases that we have had opportunity to examine the stakeholder was holding the money pending the settlement of a wager or bet or the outcome of some kind of a gambling venture, and, so holding it, he was held to be acting as the agent of the depositor, with the right in the depositor to revoke the agency and demand the return of the deposit before it had been paid over. * * *

Ordinarily wagers or bets or gambling contracts do not affect the public generally, but only the individuals directly concerned in the transaction. * * *

But the question we have goes far beyond the scope of an ordinary gambling contract or an ordinary violation of a statute. Its evil consequences were not confined to the persons immediately concerned in the transaction, and we are not disposed to extend to the facts appearing in this case the rule that money on deposit with a mere stakeholder, awaiting the outcome of some wager or bet or the result of some gambling contract, may be recovered by the depositor.

Numerous cases can be found illustrating the disposition of the courts to put contracts that have a tendency to injure the public service, or to interfere with or corrupt the free exercise of the elective franchise, or that affect public offices in a class distinct from mere gambling contracts, or contracts involving the violation of a statute. * * *

Contracts such as the one entered into between Richie and Cody, and every branch of such contracts, and everything arising out of them, deserve the severest condemnation, and no party to such a contract should be allowed to come into a court and obtain relief on account of anything connected with or arising on such a contract, unless it affirmatively appears that the party asking relief had in good faith rescinded or repudiated, or attempted in good faith to rescind or repudiate, the contract before any material thing looking to its accomplishment had been done by any person connected with it. If the person asking relief from anything growing out of such a contract can affirmatively show that after entering into the contract he changed his mind and in good faith abandoned the contract and everything connected with it before it was consummated, he should have such relief as he would be entitled to in cases not affected by any vice or infirmity in the contract, but not otherwise.

And so in this case, if Richie had repented of his illegal purpose and demanded the return of this money before the withdrawal of Cody, we would say that he might recover it; but he did not do this. He did not seek to recover this money until long after Cody had withdrawn as a candidate, or until long after the corrupt bargain had been consummated and everything that was contemplated by the parties to it had been accomplished.

For the reasons set forth in the opinion, the judgment is reversed.

Notes

1. The "locus" of the poenitentiae is circumscribed. The Restatement [First] of Contracts § 605 confined it to the period when "the illegal part of the bargain is wholly unexecuted." The Restatement (Second) of Contracts § 199 moves it to where the purpose of the transaction is achieved. This introduces technical problems about the execution of contracts and the separability of legal from illegal portions of a bargain. In Eastern Expanded Metal Co. v. Webb Granite & Construction Co., 195 Mass. 356, 81 N.E. 251 (1907), the plaintiff contractor agreed to construct a building exceeding the statutory height limits. He quit work before the height limit was exceeded and successfully sought quantum meruit. One of the stated reasons was the "locus poenitentiae" exception: the plaintiff had acted while "the contract remains entirely executory in that part which is illegal." Yet all the construction executed an illegal or "malum prohibitum" contract if ever there was one; it was not divisible in the usual sense. Perhaps the Second Restatement evades the technicality by defining the "locus" as the period before the attainment of the illegal purpose for which the bargain was made.

2. In the stakeholder situation, may the loser recover his stake *after* the event has been determined? Held, yes, Lewy v. Crawford, 5 Tex.Civ.App. 293, 23 S.W.

1041 (1893); McAllister v. Hoffman, 16 Serg. & Rawle 146 (Pa.1827). In Cox v. Lee, 530 S.W.2d 273 (Mo.App.1975), the court agreed with the principal case that the "loser" who repudiated the bet before the event could recover on common law principles, but that once the event occurred the loser's only remedy was pursuant to an applicable Missouri statute.

3. Where stakeholding itself is a crime, there is no locus poenitentiae, because an illegal act is complete. Matthews v. Lopus, 24 Cal.App. 63, 140 P. 306 (1914).

4. AGENTS, PARTNERS, AND FIDUCIARIES

RIDDEL, A LEGAL SCANDAL TWO HUNDRED YEARS AGO

By Hon. William Renwick Riddell, Justice of Appeal, Ontario.
[16 ABA Journal 422 (1930)]

Every student-at-law has read of the famous Bill in Equity, filed by one Highwayman against another, his partner, for an account of the profits made in that occupation: many have wondered how any solicitor could be found to draw such a Bill, and what was his later career.

The actual existence of such a suit was for long doubted, although there are several references to it in legal literature. * * *

The plaintiff was John Everet, the defendant, Joseph Williams; White and William Wreathock being the plaintiff's solicitors. According to the note in Evans' Pothier, (Pothier on the Law of Obligations or Contracts, 1808, Vol. II at p. 3) the Bill alleged that

> "the plaintiff was skilled in dealing in several commodities, such as plate, rings, watches, &c.; that the defendant applied to him to become a partner; and that they entered into partnership, and it was agreed that they should equally provide all sorts of necessaries, such as horses, saddles, bridles, and equally bear all expenses on the roads and at inns, taverns, alehouses, markets and fairs; that the plaintiff and the defendant proceeded jointly in the said business with good success on Hounslow Heath, where they dealt with a Gentleman for a gold watch; and afterwards the defendant told the Plaintiff that Finchley, in the County of Middlesex, was a good and convenient place to deal in, and that commodities were very plenty at Finchley, and it would be almost clear gain to them; that they went accordingly, and dealt with several gentlemen for divers watches, rings, swords, canes, hats, cloacks, horses, bridles, saddles and other things; that about a month afterwards the defendant informed the plaintiff that there was a Gentleman at Blackheath who had a good horse, saddle bridle, watch, sword cane, and other things to dispose of, which he believed might be had for little or no money; that they accordingly went and met with the said Gentleman, and after some small discourse they dealt for the said horse, &c.; that the plaintiff and the defendant continued their joint dealings together until Michaelmas, and dealt together at several places, viz. at Bagshot, Salisbury, Hampstead and elsewhere, to the amount of £2000 and upwards."

The note proceeds: "The rest of the Bill was in the ordinary form for a partnership account. The Bill is said to have been dismissed, with costs, to be paid by the Counsel who signed it; and the Solicitors for the Plaintiff were attached and fined £50 apiece. The Plaintiff and the Defendant were, it is said, both hanged and one of the Solicitors for the Plaintiff was afterwards transported."

Another account is that the Solicitor was ordered to be led around Westminster Hall, when the Courts were sitting, with the obnoxious Bill cut in strings and hung around his neck.

The plaintiff John Everet (or someone of the same name) was hanged at Tyburn in February, 1780 (N.S.), and the defendant suffered the same punishment at Maidstone in 1776. Of White, one of the offending solicitors, I do not find any further account: But Wreathock himself became a Highwayman and in December, 1735, was convicted of robbery committed on Dr. Lancaster and was sentenced to death. However, his sentence was commuted, and he was transported to America.

MORELLI v. EHSAN

Supreme Court of Washington, En Banc, 1988.
110 Wash.2d 555, 756 P.2d 129.

DOLLIVER, JUSTICE. * * * The Court of Appeals in its opinion has recounted the facts.

In November 1980, Tito Morelli [and] Dr. Mike Ehsan, entered into a limited partnership agreement to establish and operate the Sunrise Emergency and Family Care Clinic in Everett, Washington. * * * The clinic was to provide minor emergency treatment and health care to the general public on an out-patient basis. Morelli told Ehsan that he had consulted his lawyers and had been assured it was legal for a physician and a non-physician to operate a medical clinic as partners.

Under the agreement, Morelli and Ehsan became co-general partners, sharing equally in profits and losses. The agreement provided that, in addition to their share of profits, Morelli and Ehsan could receive a salary for services rendered as employees of the partnership. The agreement also provided that, as general partners, Morelli and Ehsan would have equal rights in the management of the partnership business, and further defined Morelli's areas of responsibility as "Director of Operations" and those of Ehsan as the "Medical Director" of the clinic. The clinic also employed a medical staff, including licensed physicians, who were paid on an hourly basis.

For most of the next 3 years, the clinic operated at a loss, finally showing a small profit in 1984. The partners were obliged to advance additional funds to keep the business going during that time. Morelli's additional contributions to the clinic, totaling $75,000, were later characterized as loans and evidenced by a series of promissory notes, signed by Morelli and Ehsan as comakers.

During the latter part of 1983, the partners began to have a falling out, and in January 1985, Morelli petitioned the court for a dissolution of the partnership and an accounting. Ehsan moved to dismiss Morelli's complaint, arguing that the partnership agreement was illegal and void.

The trial court granted summary judgment for Ehsan, holding that Morelli's participation in the partnership constituted the unlicensed practice of medicine in violation of former RCW 18.71.020, and as a result, he had no legally cognizable interest in the assets, profits or management of the clinic. The court permanently enjoined Morelli from interfering in any way in the operation of the clinic. Ehsan was ordered to assume all the assets and liabilities of the business, but was held not to be liable for any of the funds contributed by Morelli to the partnership.

Tito and Diana Morelli (Morelli) appealed to the Court of Appeals, which held the partnership agreement was illegal, but remanded the case to the trial court for an accounting and distribution of the partnership assets on an equitable basis. We affirm in part and reverse in part. * * *

In challenging Ehsan's motion for summary judgment, Morelli contends the partnership was legal because his responsibilities and duties were limited strictly to business aspects while Ehsan's authority was limited to the clinic's medical affairs. Morelli recites facts which he claims support this view. However, the legality of a partnership to practice medicine is not a matter of fact. It is a question of law, which is addressed by both the statutory and common law of Washington.

At the time of the partnership formation, former RCW 18.71.020 provided:

> "Any person who shall practice or attempt to practice or hold himself out as practicing medicine * * * without * * * a valid * * * license * * * shall be guilty of a gross misdemeanor."

Under The Professional Service Corporation Act, RCW 18.100, lawyers, doctors, dentists, optometrists, and other professional specialists are authorized to form a corporate entity within their respective practices. However, the corporation must be organized by "[a]n individual or group of individuals duly licensed * * * to render the same professional services." Additionally, under RCW 18.100.080, "[n]o professional service corporation * * * shall engage in any business other than the rendering of the professional services for which it was incorporated" * * *

Both Morelli and Ehsan were violating statutes governing the practice of their respective professions by operating a medical clinic without both being licensed as physicians. The partnership agreement was illegal as a matter of law.

Having found the partnership agreement illegal, we next address whether the trial court properly precluded Morelli from an equitable distribution of the assets.

If the business of a partnership is illegal, we will not entertain an action for an accounting and distribution of the assets, Brower v. Johnson, 56 Wash.2d 321, 325, 352 P.2d 814 (1960), especially when the unlawful agreement is contrary to public policy. [citation] This is consistent with the general rule that illegal agreements are void, and courts will not enforce them. [citations] The parties are left where the court finds them regardless of whether the situation is unequal as to the parties. [citations] If the parties are not in pari delicto, however, the less culpable party may maintain an action based on an illegal contract. [citations]

In the present case, undisputed evidence indicated neither party entered into the transaction with any knowledge the partnership agreement was illegal. Furthermore, neither party had an illegal intent to form or conduct an illegal business partnership. Nevertheless, the partnership was illegal; good faith intentions do not excuse either party from knowing the law. [citations]

In remanding for an accounting, the Court of Appeals fashioned a "good faith" exception, a new and unprecedented exception to the general rule that the courts will not enforce an illegal agreement where both parties are equally at fault, but will leave the parties where it found them. This exception, apparently effective when both parties believe they were acting within the law, completely undermines the purpose of the rule—deterrence. There is no deterrence from violating a law if parties may claim both were ignorant of the law. * * *

By denying Morelli an accounting, the trial court followed the law in this jurisdiction and others leaving the parties where it found them. If the court had granted Morelli affirmative relief, as ordered by the Court of Appeals on remand, the parties would be using the court to enforce their illegal partnership agreement. Instead, after finding the agreement illegal, the trial court enjoined Morelli from entering the clinic to prevent his continued participation in the practice of medicine. The court further ordered Ehsan, as the only person authorized to practice medicine, to assume sole liability for all past, present, and contingent liabilities of the clinic. Whether Ehsan continued to practice medicine in the clinic building or go elsewhere, he was still responsible for all liabilities associated with the illegal partnership practice. Ehsan has not appealed from this order. While the order relieved Morelli of any liabilities, it also denied Morelli any recovery from his investment in the illegal partnership.

The trial court found the agreement illegal and issued orders to that effect. Had the trial court simply found the partnership illegal without issuing orders from the finding, both Morelli and Ehsan could then attempt to use the courts to resolve the very points addressed by the court's orders. Not only would this be an inefficient use of judicial resources, it would force another court to make a finding upon the result of their illegal agreement. By enjoining Morelli, the court was assured of no further participation by Morelli in the clinic or possible breach of the peace as Ehsan tried to restrain Morelli from interfering with his practice of medicine. The trial court's orders correctly followed the law by leaving the parties where it found them.

Finally, Morelli contends that even if an accounting is denied, the court should enforce the promissory notes because they were separate advances to the partnership after its formation. Because the promissory notes were advanced by Morelli, a general partner, in the operation and furtherance of the illegal partnership, allowing Morelli to enforce them would, in effect, sanction the illegal partnership and allow the enforcement of an illegal agreement. See Baugh v. Dunstan & Dunstan, Inc., 67 Wash.2d 710, 409 P.2d 658 (1966) (promissory note furnished direct connection with illegal transaction). The trial court correctly denied Morelli any contribution from Ehsan for the promissory notes. * * *

The Court of Appeals is partly affirmed and partly reversed, and the judgment of the trial court is reinstated.

Note

Accounting Between Partners Operating a Business Without a Required License. Where a license or permit is required for a partnership or the individual partners, a failure to comply with the law will be grounds for a court to refuse an equitable accounting. This is particularly true of partnerships for the sale of liquor. Nahas v. George, 156 Ohio St. 52, 99 N.E.2d 898 (1951). The rule has been applied to unlicensed real estate brokerage partnerships, Moslowski v. Bitter, 7 Wis.2d 167, 96 N.W.2d 349 (1959), and even an unlicensed partner in an undertaking business, Searles v. Haynes, 126 Ind.App. 626, 129 N.E.2d 362 (1955).

Whether exceptions will occur seems to depend on the way the court evaluates at least three variables. (a) The purpose of the licensing statute. (b) Whether the business has an innocuous character. (c) Whether denial of relief will lead to unjust enrichment of a fiduciary. In Norwood v. Judd, 93 Cal.App.2d 276, 282–06, 209 P.2d 24, 28–30 (1949), a contracting business was carried on by a partnership, but all partners were not licensed as required. The partner who was personally licensed carried on the actual construction. The other partner was unlicensed but only handled the bookkeeping. Most of the profit had been put back into the business. The unlicensed partner wanted to get out and was promised his share. After he received partial payment he sued for dissolution and an accounting. The court opined:

"It should be noted that this is not a case where the parties engaged in a business prohibited by statute or public policy, or where a license would not have been issued had application been made. * * * The principle that participants to an illegal contract who are *in pari delicto* can secure no relief based on such contract, is an ancient and most salutary one. * * *

"But there is a well-recognized exception to that rule which appears to be founded on good morals and sound judgment. When a business, which has been illegally conducted for lack of license, as distinguished from an unlawful and forbidden enterprise, has been completely terminated and one of the parties subsequently expressly agrees to divide in a specified manner the assets in his possession, courts will entertain suits for accounting, in assumpsit, or based on an implied trust, to recover the property belonging to the claimant. The reason assigned for the application of the foregoing exception to the general rule is * * * that:

" 'When the illegal transaction has been consummated, when no court has been called upon to give aid to it, when the proceeds of the sale have been actually received, and received in that which the law recognizes as having had value, and when they have been carried to the credit of the plaintiffs, the case is different. The court is there not asked to enforce an illegal contract. The plaintiffs do not require the aid of any illegal transaction to establish their case. It is enough that the defendants have in hand a thing of value that belongs to them. Some of the authorities show that, though an illegal contract will not be executed, yet, when it has been executed by the parties themselves, and the illegal object of it has been accomplished, the money or thing which was the price of it may be a legal consideration between the parties for a promise, express or implied, and the court will not unravel the transaction to discover its origin.' [Denning v. Taber, 70 Cal.App.2d 253, 160 P.2d 900 (1945).]

"If that distinction controls an executed agreement which was illegally designed by the parties, it should apply with greater justice and force to a division of assets expressly agreed upon by the parties after the termination of the business by mutual consent which was merely conducted without a license contrary to law. * * *

"It must be remembered that these licensing statutes are passed primarily for the protection and safety of the public. They are not passed for the benefit of a greedy partner who seeks to keep for himself all of the fruits of the partnership enterprise to the exclusion of another partner entitled to share therein. Where the illegal transaction has been terminated, public policy is not protected or served by denying one partner relief against the other."

Question: What if the partner seeking an accounting lacked a license because his previous one had been revoked?

LUNDSTROM v. DE SANTOS

City Court of New York, Trial Term, 1954.
205 Misc. 260, 127 N.Y.S.2d 610.

WOLFF, REFEREE. This is an action for the conversion of monies. * * * The plaintiff is a bartender in a Long Island roadside restaurant. The defendant was a frequent customer, as he had been for years. On an evening in May, 1951, a little before dinner time, the defendant entered the restaurant with ten or twelve Irish sweepstake tickets in his hand. These he offered to sell to various persons about the bar. None would buy, and in the end the defendant bestowed a ticket upon the plaintiff, even allowing the latter to make his own selection. This was a sportsmanlike gesture which at the time may have seemed to the defendant to have small importance. But soon afterward the ticket won a little over $5,000. When the defendant learned through a list of winning numbers published in the New York Journal–American that the gift which he had made to the plaintiff had acquired this unexpected value, he hurried over to the restaurant and got the plaintiff, who is a little young for his trade, to hand back the ticket. The defendant said at the time that as his name was on the stub he was the only person who could collect the winnings, for which purpose he proposed to journey to Ireland, and to take his wife along. He agreed with the plaintiff that the latter should have the first thousand dollars and that the remaining monies to be collected should be divided equally between them, the plaintiff to get half and the defendant to keep the other half to cover his wife's and his own traveling expenses. * * *

The defendant told an unlikely story. He denied altogether that he had made a gift of the ticket but testified that he had left it with the plaintiff to "hold" after the latter had refused to buy, because he wanted to prove that this would be the winning ticket. If the defendant is to be believed he allowed the plaintiff to hold the ticket temporarily merely to convince the latter that this particular ticket would be the "winner," perhaps in this way to make manifest his own prescience or perhaps so that the plaintiff might come to feel sorry that he had not availed himself of the opportunity to buy.

I find that the defendant arranged with the plaintiff to go to Ireland in order to collect the winnings in the plaintiff's behalf, and to deliver to the plaintiff the first thousand dollars and one-half of everything above that amount.

The important question to consider is whether the arrangement between plaintiff and defendant was illegal or contrary to public policy.

I think the case is distinguishable from Goodrich v. Houghton, 134 N.Y. 115, 31 N.E. 516, for there the plaintiff and the defendant were partners or joint adventurers. Together they bought the lottery ticket and agreed to share the winnings with each other. The point of the *Goodrich* case is that a court will not meddle in a gambling transaction. It will not help one partner against the other for the same reasons that it will not allow a recovery by the winner against the person who has conducted the lottery. In such a situation, the parties are held to be in pari delicto. I know of no New York case other than Goodrich v. Houghton, which directly involved an agreement to share in the winnings of a lottery. * * * However, there are cases in other jurisdictions which are factually much like the case in hand and in which a recovery was permitted by a principal against the agent whom he had appointed to collect the winnings but who instead converted them. [citations]

The law is well settled in New York and elsewhere that it is no defense to an agent who has converted monies belonging to his principal that such monies were the fruit of an illegal transaction. [citations]

When the plaintiff arranged with the defendant to collect the winnings in Ireland, the lottery was over and the ticket and the winnings were the plaintiff's property. There was no executory agreement between the plaintiff and the defendant to participate in an illegal transaction. The defendant has converted the monies which he induced the plaintiff to appoint him agent to collect. It need hardly be said that it is undesirable to exclude the property of any person from the protection of the law merely because of its origin, and that a judgment producing such a result should be, whenever possible, avoided. * * *

Judgment may be entered in favor of the plaintiff and against the defendant in the sum of $3,000 with interest as demanded in the complaint.

Notes

1. In Smith v. Williams, 698 F.2d 611 (3d Cir.1983), A bought chances on a raffle from B, not knowing that B did not have a permit to hold a raffle which was therefore illegal. The prize in the raffle was, in turn, tickets in the legal Virgin Islands lottery. A won the raffle, but found that the $100,000 winning lottery ticket had been abstracted by B. Who should get what?

2. If the person asserting the illegality owes an agency, fiduciary or confidential duty, this adds a factor of indeterminable weight on the side of restitution. The illegal aspects of a partnership enterprise—e.g., carrying on an unlicensed business—will be viewed more tolerantly in the partnership itself than if the same partnership and the general public is involved. Thus, despite reluctance to adjudicate the division of spoils between miscreants, an equally strong policy exists to hold fiduciaries to consciously assumed obligations. The Restatement (Second) of Agency § 412, reporter's note (1958), recognizes the conflicting considerations and the inevitable confusion:

"The cases dealing with the effect of illegality upon the agent's duty to account are in much confusion. Neither the text writers nor the courts have been in agreement as to the extent of the agents' liability. Some writers stress the importance of requiring the utmost fidelity on the agent's part and urge that the agent should be subject to a duty to account in all cases. See Wigmore, Summary of Quasi–Contract, 25 American Law Review [695], 1891, note k. Other writers believe that the courts have not been sufficiently severe in denying the plaintiff a right to an accounting where some illegality is present. See Williston, Contracts, Revised Edition, 1785, 1786, 1938. See also Woodward, Quasi Contracts, Sec. 148, 1913."

3. As the main case indicates, the agency element, when applied to the holding of stakes or the possession of proceeds of an illegal scheme, fits neatly with and reinforces the general exclusionary rule that third parties cannot assert illegality as a defense. See also Cal–Neva Lodge, Inc. v. Marx, 178 Cal.App.2d 186, 2 Cal.Rptr. 889 (1960).

4. The same is true of the locus poenitentiae exception where the principal has entrusted the agent with money or goods for an illegal purpose, but where the purpose for one reason or another was never accomplished. Wasserman v. Sloss, 117 Cal. 425, 49 P. 566 (1897), involved 400 shares of stock deposited with the

defendant to bribe U.S. and Russian officials to renew leases useful in the sealing industry. Defendant himself converted the stock. The court, allowing recovery strongly emphasized the agent's duties, particularly when the agent solicited the transfer. Bribery is serious business despite the court's assertion: "The good or bad morals of this undertaking is immaterial."

Restatement (Second) of Agency § 412, reporter's note (1958), cautions: "A hundred years ago the courts seemed inclined to enforce an accounting by an agent in almost all cases. The present tendency of the courts is less favorable to the principal where his transactions are tainted with an illegal element: there is to be noted, however, an increasing inclination to draw distinctions based on the seriousness or triviality of the criminal element."

Evidence of this tendency is to be found in McConnell v. Commonwealth Picture Corp., supra. 1231, and Sinnar v. Le Roy, 44 Wash.2d 728, 270 P.2d 800 (1954), where the plaintiff gave defendant, a customer, a neighbor and a "friend," $450 upon latter's promise to get a state license to sell beer, or return the money. The license was not granted. Restitution of the money was denied, since there was no evidence that it was intended for professional services and both parties knew some third party was to be involved.

5. Occasionally the fiduciary factor is added to overcome a pari delicto defense as where a person is importuned by a lawyer to make a fraudulent conveyance to the latter (or his family) and the case is otherwise a close one, e.g. Prickett v. Prickett, 379 Ill. 181, 39 N.E.2d 984 (1942).

6. *Cohabitants.* Watts v. Watts, 137 Wis.2d 506, 511, 405 N.W.2d 303, 306 (1987): "Nonmarital cohabitation does not render every agreement between the cohabiting parties illegal and does not automatically preclude one of the parties from seeking judicial relief, such as statutory or common law partition, damages for breach of express or implied contract, constructive trust and quantum meruit where the party alleges, and later proves, facts supporting the legal theory."

See Shold v. Goro, 449 N.W.2d 372 (Iowa 1989) (recovery awarded for unjust enrichment); Aehegma v. Aehegma, 8 Haw.App. 215, 797 P.2d 74 (1990) (unjust enrichment).

7. Finally, however, we are left with the well known anomaly that an agent who possesses the proceeds of his principal's illegal transaction must account lest he be unjustly enriched; yet, if the agent participated in bringing the underlying illegal transaction to fruition, his liability to the principal ends. Thus the law is that the agent's best defense is not impeccable honesty but rather active criminality.

Perhaps this is as appropriate a note as any upon which to end a book on Remedies.

Index

References are to Pages